LIFT

TAKE YOUR STUDYING
TO THE NEXT LEVEL.

This book comes with 1-year digital access to the
Examples & Explanations for this course.

Step 1: Go to www.**CasebookConnect.com/LIFT** and redeem your access code to get started.

Access Code:

STXT24036910784

Step 2: Go to your BOOKSHELF and select your online *Examples & Explanations* to start reading, highlighting, and taking notes in the margins of your e-book.

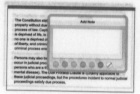

Step 3: Select the STUDY tab in your toolbar to access the questions from your book in interactive format, designed to give you extra practice and help you master the course material.

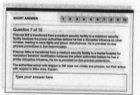

Is this a used casebook? Access code already scratched off?

You can purchase the online *Examples & Explanations* and still access all of the powerful tools listed above. Please visit CasebookConnect.com/Catalog to learn more about Connected Study Aids.

PLEASE NOTE: Each access code provides 12 month access and can only be used once. This code will also expire one year after the discontinuation of the corresponding print title and must be redeemed before then. CCH reserves the right to discontinue this program at any time for any business reason. For further details, please see the Casebook Connect End User Agreement.

PIN: 9111149628

04942

Employment Law

ASPEN CASEBOOK SERIES

Employment Law

Private Ordering and Its Limitations

Third Edition

Timothy P. Glynn
Professor of Law
Seton Hall Law School

Charles A. Sullivan
Professor of Law
Seton Hall Law School

Rachel S. Arnow-Richman
Professor of Law
University of Denver Sturm College of Law

Wolters Kluwer

Published by Wolters Kluwer in New York.

Wolters Kluwer serves customers worldwide with CCH, Aspen Publishers, and Kluwer Law International products. (www.wolterskluwerlb.com)

To contact Customer Service, e-mail customer.service@wolterskluwer.com, call 1-800-234-1660, fax 1-800-901-9075, or mail correspondence to:

>   Wolters Kluwer
>   Attn: Order Department
>   PO Box 990
>   Frederick, MD 21705

Printed in the United States of America.

2 3 4 5 6 7 8 9 0

ISBN 978-1-4548-5799-0

Library of Congress Cataloging-in-Publication Data

Glynn, Timothy P., 1967- author.
  Employment law : private ordering and its limitations / Timothy P. Glynn, Professor of Law, Seton Hall Law School; Rachel S. Arnow-Richman, Associate Professor of Law, University of Denver, Sturm College of Law; Charles A. Sullivan, Professor of Law, Seton Hall Law School. — Third Edition.
    pages cm
  Includes bibliographical references and index.
  ISBN 978-1-4548-5799-0 (alk. paper)
1. Labor laws and legislation — United States. 2. Labor laws and legislation — United States — Cases.
I. Arnow-Richman, Rachel, 1970- author. II. Sullivan, Charles A., author. III. Title.

  KF3455.G59 2015
  344.7301–dc23

                                                                    2014048353

About Wolters Kluwer Law & Business

Wolters Kluwer Law & Business is a leading global provider of intelligent information and digital solutions for legal and business professionals in key specialty areas, and respected educational resources for professors and law students. Wolters Kluwer Law & Business connects legal and business professionals as well as those in the education market with timely, specialized authoritative content and information-enabled solutions to support success through productivity, accuracy and mobility.

Serving customers worldwide, Wolters Kluwer Law & Business products include those under the Aspen Publishers, CCH, Kluwer Law International, Loislaw, ftwilliam.com and MediRegs family of products.

CCH products have been a trusted resource since 1913, and are highly regarded resources for legal, securities, antitrust and trade regulation, government contracting, banking, pension, payroll, employment and labor, and healthcare reimbursement and compliance professionals.

Aspen Publishers products provide essential information to attorneys, business professionals and law students. Written by preeminent authorities, the product line offers analytical and practical information in a range of specialty practice areas from securities law and intellectual property to mergers and acquisitions and pension/benefits. Aspen's trusted legal education resources provide professors and students with high-quality, up-to-date and effective resources for successful instruction and study in all areas of the law.

Kluwer Law International products provide the global business community with reliable international legal information in English. Legal practitioners, corporate counsel and business executives around the world rely on Kluwer Law journals, looseleafs, books, and electronic products for comprehensive information in many areas of international legal practice.

Loislaw is a comprehensive online legal research product providing legal content to law firm practitioners of various specializations. Loislaw provides attorneys with the ability to quickly and efficiently find the necessary legal information they need, when and where they need it, by facilitating access to primary law as well as state-specific law, records, forms and treatises.

ftwilliam.com offers employee benefits professionals the highest quality plan documents (retirement, welfare and non-qualified) and government forms (5500/PBGC, 1099 and IRS) software at highly competitive prices.

MediRegs products provide integrated health care compliance content and software solutions for professionals in healthcare, higher education and life sciences, including professionals in accounting, law and consulting.

Wolters Kluwer Law & Business, a division of Wolters Kluwer, is headquartered in New York. Wolters Kluwer is a market-leading global information services company focused on professionals.

Summary of Contents

Contents

PART SIX STATUTORY PROTECTIONS FOR EMPLOYEES

9 *Antidiscrimination*

Preface

Few institutions receive greater attention in Americans' private lives and in public policy debates than employment. Employment is everywhere: It is the means by which most Americans make their living; it is, for many, where they spend the majority of their waking hours and develop most of their interpersonal relationships; and it provides the primary economic input ("human capital") firms and government agencies rely on to produce their goods and services.

Because of its pervasiveness and importance, employment-related issues, such as outsourcing to foreign countries or whether to raise the minimum wage, receive significant public attention. More profoundly, many of the fundamental policy disputes of the day — immigration, health care, civil rights, environmental regulation, information privacy, globalization, social security, and tax policy — are either inherently entangled with employment or heavily influenced by employment-related considerations.

Thus, the institution of employment is paramount not just for individual workers and employing firms and government agencies, but also for society as a whole. Correspondingly, then, the legal rules governing the employment relationship have profound implications beyond the two parties to that relationship. This book will introduce you to the core aspects of this body of law and its implications.

As you work your way through the book, you will discover that the structure of employment law is complex and varied. It derives from multiple sources, including contract, tort, agency law, state and federal statutes, and, at least for government workers, federal and state constitutions. In addition, its application varies greatly depending upon a number of factors, including type of worker (e.g., employee v. nonemployee, unionized v. nonunionized, white collar v. blue collar, disabled v. nondisabled); type of employer (large v. small, public v. private); type of industry; and jurisdiction (state v. state). Moreover, because American employment law leaves fundamental aspects of the relationship largely for the parties to determine, the "law" governing the American workplace is subject to immense individual variation. Indeed, for many workers, the most important terms of their relationship — including wage levels, benefits, hours, job security, and privacy considerations — are far more likely to be determined by market forces than by externally imposed legal mandates. Finally, like the structure of the workplace itself, the law of employment is ever changing.

Given its intricate and dynamic nature, employment law is challenging to understand and apply. This is what makes your study of it so critical. Workers and firms must rely heavily on counsel for advice on how to (1) structure working relationships to protect their interests and minimize their risks and (2) advocate on behalf of these interests when disputes arise. Similarly, employment policy makers need a solid understanding of the legal doctrines that govern employment, their implications and limitations, and how the varied aspects of the law interact with one another. This need for employment law expertise extends well beyond those engaged in employment-related work since employment and its legal rules have implications for a wide range of other areas and disciplines.

This text provides an accessible and comprehensive introduction into the study of employment law. Following the Introduction, the book contains seven parts with thirteen chapters exploring various employment law topics. You will be introduced immediately to our unifying theme of private ordering and its limitations — that is, the core tension in the law between the terms the parties themselves establish and publicly imposed mandates. In pursuing this theme through the various subtopics that make up our discipline, not only will you master (sometimes abstruse) doctrine but you will also be asked repeatedly to consider the law from transactional, counseling, litigation, and policy-making perspectives.

We have included standard cases to provide you with a solid background in each topic area. These are supplemented with more recent decisions addressing cutting-edge issues in the twenty-first century, including the growth of outsourcing and contingent (semi- or nonpermanent) work arrangements, the role of new whistleblower protections such as those in the Sarbanes-Oxley and Dodd-Frank laws, privacy in the workplace, the enforcement of noncompetition agreements, new issues in antidiscrimination law, the law's role in facilitating the work/family balance, and the growth in various risk-management techniques by employers. We also provide extensive notes and commentary that offer further background and probe deeper into the compelling and difficult employment developments of the day. Finally, each chapter contains problems designed to expose you to the real-world challenges employment counsel face as both planners and litigators. If you want to sample even more recent developments in employment law, visit the casebook's website at http://law.shu.edu/private_ordering.

We believe this text offers a cohesive, thorough, and fascinating first look at employment-law theory and practice. We hope you enjoy it.

A Note on Editing

In cases and law review excerpts, all omissions are indicated by ellipses or brackets, except for footnotes and citations, many of which have been deleted or shortened to enhance readability. The footnotes that remain retain their original numbers.

Timothy P. Glynn
Charles A. Sullivan
Rachel S. Arnow-Richman

December 2014

Acknowledgments

Like all casebooks, Employment Law: Private Ordering and Its Limitations builds on the experiences of its authors in wrestling with the problems of employment law with their law students at Seton Hall and the University of Denver. At each of these law schools, colleagues provided important insights in the formation of our pedagogic approaches. In a more focused way, we are indebted to Mike Zimmer of Loyola Chicago (emeritus at Seton Hall) and Rebecca Hanner White, Dean of Georgia, for their generosity in allowing us to abridge portions of Cases and Materials on Employment Discrimination (Aspen, 7th ed. 2008) and to Mike Zimmer and to Deborah Calloway of the University of Connecticut for permitting us to draw on a precursor to the present book, Cases and Materials on Employment Law (Aspen, 1993). Despite these deep intellectual debts, Private Ordering is a radical departure from earlier efforts, offering a new understanding of employment law as both a scholarly discipline and a vibrant field of practice.

This casebook would not have been possible without the support of Aspen's Barbara Roth, Carol McGeehan, Richard Mixter, Troy Froebe, Kathy Langone, and Sylvia Rebert. Moreover, we all want to thank Mike Zimmer and Judd Sneirson who were brave enough to teach out of the first edition as it was being written and provided us with invaluable feedback. Professor Arnow-Richman particularly acknowledges the support of Melissa Hart, Martin Katz, Nantiya Ruan, and Catherine Smith. We are also grateful to the unidentified professors who Aspen retained to review chapters as they emerged from the three authors. While we do not know who these reviewers are, they will see our responses to their critiques throughout this work.

Then there are the individuals who helped us turn this project into reality. They include Silvia Cardoso, Beth Krauzlis, and Latisha Porter, Professors Sullivan's and Glynn's administrative assistants at Seton Hall, and the following Seton Hall research assistants for both Professors Sullivan and Glynn: John Dumnich and Angela Raleigh, Seton Hall class of 2016; Michael Amalfe, Kelly Bradshaw, Mark Heftler, Temenouga R. Kolarova, Renee Levine, Steven Morris, and Caitlin Petry, class of 2012; Alison Andolena, class of 2011; Michele Austin, Christina Bae, Joseph Fanning, Robert Flanagan, Angela Kopolovich, Gregory Reid, and Allison Scaduto, class of '08; Lauren DeWitt, Rawan Hmoud, and Mohamed Shiliwala, class of '07; Julie Yoo, class of '06; and Monica Perrette, Shulamit Shvartsman, and Lauren Walter, class of '05. Professor Arnow-Richman would like to thank Melissa Brand, Lindsay Burleson, Keenan Jones, Crystal Littrell-Miller,

Lindsay Noyce, Marlys Hartley Roehm, and Cristel Shepherd from the University of Denver; James Boyer and Ralph Powell from Temple Law School; and her fall 2005 Law of the Workplace students.

As the copious citations to scholarship indicate, we have benefited greatly from the many scholars who have focused their research on employment issues. We have collected the citations in a Table of Selected Secondary Authorities at page 1069, but we acknowledge more directly the following for permission to reprint parts of their work:

Price Fishback & Shawn Kantor, *The Adoption of Worker's Compensation in the United States, 1900–30*, 41 J.L. & Econ. 305, 315-19 (1998). Reprinted with permission.

Ethan Lipsig et al., Planning and Implementing Reductions in Force, C922 ALI-ABA 1165, 1231-36 (1994). Reprinted with permission.

Introduction

Private Ordering and Its Limitations

For most of its history, employment law in the United States has been a constant struggle between private ordering and government mandates. The term "private ordering" refers to the rules the parties themselves establish to govern their relationship. Such ordering may occur by the parties' express agreement, such as in a collective bargaining agreement or an individual employment contract. Absent formal agreement, such terms may be implied from the circumstances. In addition, private ordering may occur in absence of any express or implied agreement through a "default rule" establishing terms unless the parties "opt out" by an agreement to the contrary. As you will explore in later chapters, the most prominent default rule in American employment law is the notion that the relationship is "at will" — that is, that it may be terminated by either party at any time for any reason.

In contrast to a pure private-ordering regime, public mandates are government-imposed limitations that directly set terms and conditions of employment or affect such terms and conditions indirectly. Mandates range from flat commands — such as the requirement that employers pay a minimum wage, grant leave for certain family and medical needs, or provide compensation for workplace injuries — to rules creating procedural mechanisms to govern the workplace. Unionization and collective bargaining are the prime examples of the latter. Mandates are often negative: Employers must not discriminate on the basis of race, sex, or religion. But sometimes they are positive: Employers must reasonably accommodate disabilities if doing so would not cause an undue hardship. Mandates are often distinctive to employment law — such as the requirement that mass layoffs be conducted only with sufficient advance warning. However, they also come from more general sources of law; for instance, the U.S. Constitution provides federal and state government workers some protections that their private sector counterparts lack. A critical aspect of true mandates is the inability of workers to waive the substantive rights provided.

From the 30,000-foot level, the law governing the employment relationship has moved away from purely private ordering and toward greater government regulation. During much of the nineteenth century, laissez faire and "freedom of contract" prevailed in employment — with the striking exception of the law being largely constitutive of the subordination of African Americans and women (indeed, often removing both groups from "employment").

Thus, in the post–Civil War era, the law tended to view employers and employees as equals, whose participation in "market transactions" would result in employment contracts — often "at will" — that the courts would then neutrally enforce. The reality of this view was always dubious. Many scholars have pointed out that cases such as *Bradwell v. Illinois*, 83 U.S. 130 (1873) (upholding a state statute barring women from the practice of law), and the use of antitrust laws to repress unions showed that the law was far from a neutral arbiter and often placed a heavy thumb on the side of the scale favoring employers and the interests of capital. Nevertheless, the prevailing ideology during the nineteenth century and well into the twentieth was one of the supremacy of private ordering, reflected most dramatically by "*Lochner* Era" court decisions that struck down public mandates regulating work in the name of freedom of contract. *See, e.g.*, *Lochner v. New York*, 198 U.S. 45 (1905) (regulation of bakers' working hours); *Coppage v. Kansas*, 235 U.S. 1 (1915) (prohibition on agreements barring employees from joining unions); *Adkins v. Children's Hospital*, 261 U.S. 525 (1923) (minimum wage mandate for female workers).

Even as *Lochner* was decided, however, change was in the air. In the next two decades, workers' compensation regimes would supplant the minimal protections tort law accorded to workers injured on the job. Perhaps critically, this statutory inroad for workers involved a trade-off of more certain liability for lower recoveries and therefore was also in the interests of employers who avoided the risks of a developing tort regime. In any event, as the twentieth century proceeded, workers' rights became increasingly recognized in the law. The Great Depression brought the New Deal, and the New Deal brought, among other initiatives, the National Labor Relations Act ("NLRA"), 29 U.S.C. §§ 151-69 (2014), protecting the right to unionize and bargain collectively, and the Fair Labor Standards Act ("FLSA"), 29 U.S.C. §§ 201-19 (2014), establishing a federal minimum wage and regulating overtime and child labor practices. The demise of *Lochner* in the wake of President Roosevelt's court-packing proposal, *see West Coast Hotel Co. v. Parrish*, 300 U.S. 379 (1937), signaled for many the beginning of the end of private ordering.

Fast-forward 30 years, private ordering suffered another assault, beginning with a legislative response to the Civil Rights movement. Title VII of the Civil Rights Act of 1964, 42 U.S.C. § 2000e-2000e-17 (2014), ushered in, for the first time on a national level, federal regulation effectively limiting employers' ability to hire and fire at will, by prohibiting discrimination on the basis of race, sex, national origin, and religion. That statute was followed within three years by the Age Discrimination in Employment Act ("ADEA"), 29 U.S.C. §§ 621-634 (2014), and, after two more decades, by the Americans with Disabilities Act ("ADA") of 1990, 42 U.S.C.A. §§ 12101-12213 (2014). As a result of these three laws, most employers no longer have free rein in their hiring and firing decisions, and states, even in what had been the Deep South, added their own legislation prohibiting discriminatory employment practices to reach many employers too small to be covered by the federal antidiscrimination laws.

The 1970s saw two further federal inroads on private ordering in employment, the Employee Retirement Income Security Act ("ERISA"), 29 U.S.C. §§ 1001-1381 (2014), and the Occupational Safety and Health Act ("OSHA"), 29 U.S.C. §§ 651-78 (2014). ERISA was a response to horror stories of employers firing workers to avoid paying their pensions or otherwise reneging on promises of long-term benefits. The statute was designed to provide both carrots and sticks to ensure an equitable private retirement system. OSHA, more directly command-and-control, was intended to be proactive in protecting worker safety. While the workers' compensation regimes enacted decades earlier ensured payment for injuries suffered, OSHA was designed to prevent injuries in the first place through a series of explicit administrative regulations and corresponding agency enforcement.

On top of these statutory assaults on private ordering, state courts were busy cutting back on what they viewed as the excesses of the at-will rule. This movement produced two major strands — one contractual, the other tort-based. First, drawing on general contract principles, the courts in most states expanded protections for job security beyond formal, written employment contracts to include oral agreements and terms implied from the circumstances. They also began to enforce job security provisions in personnel manuals and read individual agreements or circumstances to provide something more than at-will status. Second, drawing in part on the statutes that proscribe certain reasons as illegitimate bases for employment decisions, the courts began to formulate a tort-based "public policy" exception to the at-will doctrine. That is, while employers remained generally free to fire an employee for most reasons, there were certain reasons that the courts declared to be impermissible. Unlike earlier efforts in this direction that condemned specific reasons for termination (e.g., antiunion animus, race), the newer decisions were more open-ended. An actionable termination was one which offended "public policy," a term whose meaning depends upon judicial interpretation. While employers still did not need a good reason to fire someone, they could not act from bad reasons, and the list of bad reasons was no longer confined to statutory prohibitions like the antidiscrimination laws.

Thus, by the mid-1980s, public mandates appeared to be winning the day, and private ordering correspondingly seemed in eclipse. But this view was accurate, if at all, only at the 30,000-foot level. Closer to the ground, the picture was significantly different. The NLRA, for example, legalized unions and put the power of the federal government behind collective bargaining. But statutory amendments and court and National Labor Relations Board decisions limited the economic power of unions. In part as a result of these subsequent legal developments, union representation of the private-sector workforce has experienced a steady and dramatic decline over the past half century. Similarly, the FLSA provides for a minimum wage and overtime protection, but it has always contained significant exemptions, and the failure of Congress to increase minimum wage levels to keep pace with inflation means that the federal floor provides very limited, and arguably inadequate, protection. In the antidiscrimination arena, legislative expansion has been countered by judicial contraction, with judicially crafted doctrines and proof problems blunting the thrust of the antidiscrimination laws. This was particularly true of the ADA whose definition of "disability" was subject to such narrow interpretations by the Supreme Court that Congress reacted with the Americans with Disabilities Act Amendments Act of 2008 ("ADAAA"), Pub. L. 110-325, 122 Stat. 3553, to try to provide rights to workers with a broader range of physical and mental impairments. Finally, both OSHA and ERISA have been harshly criticized as ineffective. Indeed, ERISA has come to be seen as a barrier to workers' rights. An example is the 2006 decision striking down a Maryland law requiring very large employers, such as Wal-Mart, to provide health insurance for their workers. The court held that the law was preempted by ERISA, which regulates, but does not require, employers to provide any benefits to its workforce. *Retail Indus. Leaders Ass'n v. Fielder*, 435 F. Supp. 2d 481 (D. Md. 2006), *aff'd*, 475 F.3d 180 (4th Cir. 2007). In reality then, despite substantial federal regulation, many aspects of the most important terms of the employment relationship — job security, wages, and benefits — are left to private ordering between employers and employees.

In addition, in recent decades there has been a retreat from mandates and a corresponding increased commitment to private ordering at the state level. While the public policy tort for wrongful discharge has survived, its reach has been narrowed in many states.

Further, progressive state contract-law decisions on employee handbooks have been largely negated by judicial approval of employer-drafted disclaimers of contractual liability. In the privacy area, state common-law protections that had emerged in the 1970s have largely disappeared as a practical matter, except where embodied in a few state statutes. Meaningful federal protections are scarce as well, contained only in a few discrete statutes like the Employee Polygraph Protection Act, 29 U.S.C. §§ 2001-2009 (2014), and the newly enacted Genetic Information Nondiscrimination Act of 2008 ("GINA"), Pub. L. 110-233, 122 Stat. 881 (May 21, 2008) (codified in various sections of 26, 29, and 42 U.S.C.).

Other recent developments in employment-law mandates have been mixed as well. For example, in enacting the Family and Medical Leave Act ("FMLA") in 1993, 29 U.S.C. §§ 2601-54 (2014), Congress finally responded to the calls for protection for employees who want to balance work and family demands. Yet the protection provided is limited both in substance (eligible workers receive only unpaid leave) and scope (only larger employers are covered). Similarly, there has been a substantial growth in statutory whistleblower protections at the state and federal levels, the most prominent examples being the Sarbanes-Oxley Act of 2002 ("SOX"), Pub. L. No. 107-204, 116 Stat. 745, the health care reform law, Pub. L. 111-148, 124 Stat. 119, and the Dodd-Frank financial reform statute, Pub. L. 111-203, 124 Stat. 1376. All of these statutes provide whistleblower protections for employees who report behavior by their employers that violates the substantive provisions of those laws. But these protections, too, tend to be fairly narrowly drawn, leaving workers with perhaps less protection in reality than they might think.

Finally, employers are becoming increasingly creative in augmenting their baseline rights through contract. This can be seen in the widespread reliance on noncompetition clauses and other restrictive covenants. In addition, employers are developing new forms of private ordering, including various liability and forum management provisions (e.g., arbitration clauses, severance agreements, and forum-selection provisions) that, despite meaningful limitations, fundamentally alter the law's control over private ordering, leaving employers freer to protect their interests and minimize their liability risks.

In short, employment law is a story of private ordering and its limitations. But today, more than ever, it is a complex story, and one in which neither private ordering nor mandates has achieved unqualified primacy. Importantly, the tension between these competing conceptions generally plays out not at the 30,000-foot level but on the ground in particular employment law practices and disputes. Because the practice of law is largely done from a close-up perspective, it is important to understand what is left to private ordering and what is not and to recognize that today's sphere of free enterprise may be tomorrow's field of government regulation (or vice versa).

The Importance and Elusiveness of Employment Law

This struggle between private ordering and public mandates within American employment law occurs in the context of a universally important relationship. Almost every adult in the United States is or has been an employee. The employment relationship is not only the vehicle though which most Americans make their living but the workplace is also the place where they spend most of their waking hours and develop many of their interpersonal relationships. For many, personal identity is bound up not only with what they do but with where they do it. Professor Paul Weiler summarized this reality:

The job rather than the state has become the source of most of the social safety net on which people must rely when they are not employed — that is, when they are sick, disabled, or retired. And the plants and offices in which we work are the places where we spend much of our adult lives, where we develop important aspects of our personalities and our relationships, and where we may be exposed to a variety of physical and psychological traumas.

PAUL WEILER, GOVERNING THE WORKPLACE: THE FUTURE OF LABOR AND EMPLOYMENT LAW. 3 (1990). The stakes today are perhaps even higher. The development of communications and other technologies has tended to push the "workplace" further into what was previously personal time and space, and aspects of the employment safety net have eroded, making access to "quality" employment (in terms of stability, flexibility, accommodations, wages, benefits, and prospects for intra- or inter-firm mobility, etc.) even more important to workers.

From the employer's perspective, the employment relationship is the means by which firms produce most of their value and government agencies provide most of their services. Indeed, in the modern economy, employers' success often depends more on the quality of their workers — their creativity, cooperation, adaptability, and productivity — than on other assets: "However rich its natural resources, however costly and sophisticated the capital technology, a firm or an economy which does not have a skilled or committed work force will not be able to transform those physical assets into efficient and productive enterprises." *Id.*

Thus, the institution of employment matters a great deal to individual workers, employing firms, government agencies, and society as a whole. Naturally then, the legal rules that govern this relationship have profound, wide-ranging implications.

Yet despite the overview laid out above, employment law is not easy to define or summarize. Even the threshold question of what constitutes "employment" — as opposed to one of several different kinds of relationships in which human beings work with and for others — is uncertain. Unlike other disciplines such as constitutional law, the law of employment does not flow from a single source, nor does it derive from a single doctrinal regime like contracts or torts. Rather, because employment law governs a relationship that is both pervasive and variable, it draws from many sources, for example, contract, tort, agency law, constitutional law, and federal and state statutes.

Just as the sources of employment law vary, so too do its rules. Different legal doctrines apply depending on the state in which an employee works, whether the workplace is unionized, and whether the employer is a public or private entity. Even federal statutes do not provide complete uniformity, but rather govern some employment relationships and not others. This is due to limitations on coverage (small employers are typically exempted, with "small" being defined differently in different statutes) and various codified exemptions (certain "professional" employees, for instance, are excluded from the maximum hours provisions of the FLSA and many agricultural and transportation workers are excluded from coverage completely). The governing law therefore depends on factors such as the type of occupation and the size of the employer. In application, it may also depend on more nebulous factors such as the autonomy and economic vulnerability of the worker, key considerations in determining whether a worker is an employee protected by federal employment statutes.

In addition, as suggested above, many of the terms governing a particular relationship may be established by, and therefore are unique to, the parties in that relationship.

The "law" in the American workplace, as it is currently constituted, leaves ample — some would say, too much — room for individual variation in its most important terms, including wage levels, benefits, hours, job security, and privacy protections. All of these critical terms and conditions of employment are far more likely to be determined by the parties' reactions to market forces than by legal constraints. Again, for example, the federally mandated minimum wage is too low to have a direct effect on most workers' negotiating for compensation because both employers and workers start compensation discussions at a point far in excess of that wage. In light of its patchwork nature, understanding when and how the law constrains or promotes these terms, either directly or indirectly, is a formidable challenge.

Finally, the law of employment is dynamic because the workplace is ever-evolving; indeed, the pace of technological, organizational, and market-based changes that affect work and workers is accelerating. Tomorrow's workplace will be very different than today's, and so will tomorrow's law — a law you will help shape after you graduate. At best, then, we can say that employment law embodies the legal rules and standards that govern the employment relationship, but those legal rules and standards vary enormously in kind, substance, and application.

The breadth and variability of employment law poses significant challenges to workers and firms trying to understand their rights and obligations. There is in fact much misunderstanding regarding both, especially among workers. One particularly important example is that most workers believe that the law provides them with greater job security than it actually does, as you will explore in Chapter 2. This misperception can affect worker behavior, for instance, lulling them into thinking they need not seek greater protections, whether through unions, individual contracts, or otherwise. In addition, uncertainty in the law can inflict real costs on employers, not only ex post (litigation expenses and unexpected liabilities) but also ex ante (in terms of risk aversion and investments in planning and compliance).

The maze of employment-law doctrines also creates enormous difficulties for counsel seeking to advise parties on how to comply with the law, protect their interests, and avoid liability and other risks attendant to employment relationships. Given the increasing importance of human capital in our information- and technology-driven economy, a basic understanding of the law of the workplace and its implications is essential even for lawyers practicing in other areas. For example, employment law needs to be understood by attorneys in the corporate and intellectual property fields. Indeed, surveys of corporate general counsel often show that, of the legal risks faced by their firms, labor and employment litigation ranks at or near the top. *See e.g.,* Adele Nicholas, *GCs Reveal Their Litigation Fears and Headaches,* CORP. LEGAL TIMES 72 (October 2004) (indicating that 62 percent of survey respondents ranked labor and employment litigation as their number one potential exposure). This concern is especially legitimate in tough economic times, like the Great Recession, when employers are more likely to layoff workers and terminated workers are less able to find replacement employment. The year 2010 saw the largest number of filings on record at the EEOC — nearly 100,000 — although a variety of other factors besides the economy may explain this surge. *See* Nathan Koppel, *Claims Alleging Job Bias Rise With Layoffs,* WALL STREET JOURNAL, Sept. 24, 2010, at A6.

The nature and scope of employment law mean that a single course cannot cover every legal issue and doctrine that may govern or affect the workplace. Largely for this reason, most law schools offer other courses addressing areas of employment law, including courses in Employment Discrimination, Labor Law, Workers' Compensation, Employee Benefits, and even more particularized disciplines, such as Disability Discrimination and

Labor and Employment Arbitration. In addition, some of these areas, most notably Labor Law (which governs unionization and collective bargaining), are sufficiently distinct doctrinally that they are best left to separate study, except to the extent they provide context for broader inquiries.

Private Ordering and Its Limitations as a Framework

So how should one approach learning employment law? Despite employment law's disparate sources and wide variability, there is, as we suggested at the outset, a theme common to the law of the workplace. Employment law is, at its core, a course about *private ordering and its limitations*. This description not only captures the core historical conflict over employment regulation but also provides a framework for analyzing the key pressure points in the various aspects of what we call "employment law" today. It is the lens through which we can not only begin to discuss what the law is and what it ought to be in a multitude of contexts but also explore various legal risks and incentives of the parties and the extent to which these may be altered by planning.

This tension between public ordering and private mandates is scarcely unique to employment law. Yet, because the employment relationship is consensual, pervasive, and of profound importance to individual stakeholders and society, this relationship is one of the primary contexts — both qualitatively and quantitatively — in which the law seeks to balance contractual freedoms and market forces with countervailing social interests. Indeed, this tension runs through each doctrinal area in employment, from formation (i.e., whether worker and firm have an "employment" relationship or some other kind of legal status or relationship defined purely by contract) to job security to issues of worker autonomy (e.g., privacy) to discrimination to accommodations for workers' personal needs to employment compensation to how and where employment disputes are resolved.

How to resolve this conflict is therefore a paramount issue in employment law. Unsurprisingly, it is the source of ongoing political, judicial, and scholarly controversy. Whether or not you have seen the term "private ordering" before, you undoubtedly have seen or heard of the conflict between private ordering and its limitations playing out in public policy debates. It is a central theme in the cyclical debates over whether to increase the minimum wage. It also appears frequently in discussions of the "hot" employment issues of the day, including whether to mandate certain types of employer health care coverage, whether to require employers to provide paid parental leave, the extent to which employees ought to be protected from intrusive employer monitoring or oversight, whether to expand whistleblower and other related protections for employees, and whether employers should be able to compel private arbitration of employment disputes.

Many scholars have argued that the various terms of employment should be almost exclusively the product of private ordering. They claim that leaving the terms of employment to individual bargaining ultimately will produce socially optimal arrangements, and that various market forces (such as workers' supposed ability to freely reject or abandon employment) will generally prevent abuse. Indeed, perhaps most famously (or infamously, depending on one's perspective), Professor Richard Epstein has urged that we ought to abandon antidiscrimination laws because market forces ultimately will do a better job of correcting the effects of status-based discrimination. *See generally* RICHARD A. EPSTEIN, FORBIDDEN GROUNDS: THE CASE AGAINST EMPLOYMENT DISCRIMINATION LAWS (1992).

Of course, the scholarly responses to these types of arguments have been legion. Private ordering raises two different sets of concerns. First, scholars have identified a number of "market failures" in labor markets, which they argue justify greater mandated protections for workers. Many have pointed out that individual workers, often due to economic and social vulnerabilities, lack the power and resources to bargain effectively on their own behalf. Other scholars have contended that, even when workers are not economically powerless to protect themselves, they may suffer from informational disadvantages and cognitive constraints in assessing proposed terms of employment. Still others argue for public mandates because, in their view, employer preferences often are based on factors or biases that are not rational in an economic sense, leading to inefficient, discriminatory, or otherwise problematic decisions about who to hire, retain, or promote, and under what terms and conditions. Some of these critiques of private ordering have marshaled empirical evidence to support their claims.

In addition, there is the question of the extent to which private ordering must be constrained because of the negative impact the parties' actions may have on third parties or society as a whole. Few would question whether the public has an interest in protecting itself from employee/employer conduct that inflicts direct and substantial social harm. Indeed, the NLRA was in large part a response to the economic (and sometimes physical) warfare between unions and management that impeded the flow of goods and services to the public. The current debate centers on when such harm exists, when it is sufficient to justify public intervention, how the law ought to intervene, and which decision makers ought to resolve these issues. Indeed, as you work your way through this book, you will see the potential tensions between the interests of worker, firm, and the public, as well as the differing views on when and how to address these competing interests, play out again and again.

This casebook will help you identify the role of private ordering and its limitations in each area and demonstrate how the law currently strikes a balance between them. You will be challenged to think critically about that balance and its effects on workplace incentives and risks from a policy perspective. At the same time, the focus on private ordering means that this casebook is designed to assist you in learning how to be an employment-law practitioner — someone whose decisions help create and structure, that is "order," work relationships. Of course, the lawyer's role includes understanding how to develop persuasive legal arguments in litigation and other employment disputes on behalf of both employees and employers. But, at least as importantly, it also includes assessing and managing risk. The defining aspect of private ordering is the ability of employees and employers to structure their work relationships to protect their interests and reduce legal risks — transactional skills that are becoming more and more dominant in the practice of employment law.

Employment Law at the Beginning of the Twenty-first Century

Now that you have been introduced to the challenges of learning and practicing employment law and the core tension that binds aspects of this discipline together, it is worth taking a moment to appreciate where the law is today. What we now think of as "employment law" in the United States reflects a relatively new development having its roots in the Industrial Revolution. Before that, "employment" in this country took a variety of forms, including indentured servitude, slavery, self-employment, personal service, and family work (primarily on farms). Employment as we know it, was not the primary means of earning a living.

After the Civil War, the United States rapidly industrialized and agriculture became increasingly less important. The population of employees grew, including for the first time large numbers of women working outside the home/farm and domestic service. By the dawn of the twentieth century, industry became the rule rather than the exception, and employment typically became not merely another option but the only choice. As a result, workers become increasingly dependent on their ability to obtain and retain positions working for others in order to survive. While "contract" theoretically ordered the relationship between these workers and their employers, the increasing economic dependency of employees severely diminished their bargaining power, thus tending to erode their rights.

Although some workers obtained greater protection by virtue of individual employment contracts specifying the terms and conditions of their work, most employers refused to enter into such arrangements with most workers. Employers preferred to be free to hire and fire as they wished, and the common law accommodated this desire by characterizing employment relationships as "at will" unless the parties were especially specific in providing otherwise.

While facially neutral, the at-will rule generally favored employers since they could easily replace an employee who quit; in contrast, a fired employee's options in a period of limited geographic mobility were typically very limited and often very unpalatable. The unrestrained power of employers sometimes manifested itself in starvation wages, unsanitary and dangerous working conditions, long hours, child labor, and little or no job security for many employees.

As sketched above, these conditions led to attempts to deal with the problem of unrestricted industrial power in sweeping ways. In addition to federal approaches to curbing abuse of industrial power, such as antitrust laws, state legislatures made some early attempts to deal directly with the exercise of such power as it affected employment, such as laws regulating maximum hours of work. Again, prior to the New Deal, *Lochner* Era courts repeatedly found such regulation unconstitutional. Still, there were some early reform successes, most notably the widespread creation and adoption of workers' compensation regimes during the Progressive Era.

Also during this period, the American union movement began to make some headway in securing rights for employees despite organized employer resistance and government hostility. The rallying cry of unions was the plight of the workers who were subjected to the unbridled power of employers. The "union solution" was to create countervailing power through the aggregation of workers in the hope that the resultant conflict would produce a balance in the interests of both workers and employers. *See generally* JOHN KENNETH GALBRAITH, AMERICAN CAPITALISM: THE CONCEPT OF COUNTERVAILING POWER (1952).

Unions were concerned with compensation, hours, job safety, and job security. Job security served unions not only by protecting individual members but also as a means to other ends (e.g., eliminating competition between union members to avoid weakening unity and protecting against employer retaliation). As a result, unions typically tried to negotiate contracts with employers limiting the power to discharge individual workers to situations involving "just cause" and specifying how employees should be treated in economic reductions in force, typically by requiring that workers be selected for layoff in reverse order of seniority.

Other initiatives also worked to strengthen job security, albeit among particular subgroups of workers. One was the civil service movement in government employment, which preserved employment "during good behavior" for those who qualified. While civil service protections originated in the nineteenth century, the growth of government during the twentieth century resulted in these systems covering significantly more employees. In addition, advocates of academic tenure (and the job security it provides) were also likewise successful not only for the college and university professors for whom tenure was originally devised, but also for teachers in public elementary and secondary schools. From an economic perspective, both civil service and academic tenure were originally viewed as a tradeoff between lower compensation, on the one hand, and less pressure combined with greater job security on the other.

The Great Depression ushered in leaders more interested in expanding government power and addressing the plight of the common worker. The revised view of government power brought on by the Depression enabled federal and state legislation according employees' basic rights to survive constitutional attack. New Deal legislation was in two forms: first, statutes protecting and supporting employees' efforts to bargain collectively with their employers, and, second, legislation providing the first effective national regulation of some terms and conditions of employment.

Regarding the first category, the NLRA granted workers the right to engage in "concerted action" by protecting such action from employer retaliation. The statute also established a structure for the recognition of unions as "exclusive bargaining representatives" for workers and imposed on employers a duty to bargain with them. This federal labor legislation (and subsequent state efforts aimed at the public sector) did not impose any particular terms and conditions on employers. Rather, it dealt with workplace problems indirectly by establishing a procedure whereby such problems could be resolved by bargaining between the parties. Where unions were strongest, the result was collective bargaining agreements that provided detailed regulation not only of wages and hours, but of many other aspects of employment, including job safety and job security. In its most developed form, this regulation is implemented by a quasi-judicial system of arbitration of disputes between labor and management.

In the short run, unionization became a dominant mode of regulating the employment relationship. Prior to the NLRA, the unionized percentage of the American workforce was less than 15 percent. By the mid 1950s, the number had increased to nearly 40 percent. But, over the next several decades, especially in the 1980s, the union movement faltered. Unions now represent a smaller percentage of American workers — 11.9 percent overall and less than 7 percent in the private sector — than before the NLRA was passed. The causes of the decline of the union movement are contested, although, as described previously, less favorable statutory, judicial, and agency treatment has certainly played a role. The merits of unions and collective bargaining remain disputed, but the decline in unionization is undeniable. Thus, for better or worse, although most employees enjoy protections for concerted actions under the NLRA, the vast majority are not employed under or governed by a collective bargaining regime.

The second form of regulation that emerged during the New Deal and thereafter directly regulated the terms and conditions of private employment. The FLSA, setting a minimum hourly wage, is one example. During this period, the federal government also regulated the terms and conditions of "unemployment" by fostering unemployment compensation.

Perhaps in part due to the notion that collective bargaining would address most problems, there was little new direct regulation of terms and conditions of employment for almost 40 years. The 1970s saw Congress enact both OSHA and ERISA: again, despite their differences — OSHA was designed to protect worker safety through a traditional New Deal–style command-and-control approach while ERISA embodied a carrot-and-stick approach to promoting and then protecting employee benefit plans — both regimes remain the subject of significant controversy and criticism. It is worth noting that ERISA was primarily intended to ensure pension benefits for workers, but it also addresses welfare benefits including employer-provided health insurance. It has been expanded over the years by some important amendments, and it now guarantees continuation of health coverage in most terminations of employment — assuming the temporary employee had health benefits to begin with and assuming she is able to bear the group-rate costs of the insurance. However, as discussed previously, this has come at a price since ERISA's preemptive effect has served as a barrier to state-level benefits reforms, most notably in the health care context.

None of these statutory regimes deals primarily or directly with job security; rather, they regulate various aspects of employment. Nevertheless, job security is implicated in most of these laws, at least to the extent that they contain provisions barring employers from retaliating against employees who exercise their statutory rights. A different approach to regulating employer abuses emerged most dramatically in the 1960s — beginning with Title VII and thereafter supplemented by the ADEA, the ADA, and other statutes. The centerpiece of these laws was not direct regulation of terms and conditions of employment; rather, they ruled out certain reasons for employer actions (race, sex, age, disability). Employers, at least in theory, remained free to hire and fire and structure their workplaces for any reason — good or bad — so long as these defined reasons did not influence their decisions. The states were also active during this period, enacting antidiscrimination laws that sometimes went beyond the protections provided by the federal government. One notable example is the numerous state laws prohibiting discrimination based on sexual orientation, which is not yet explicitly prohibited under Title VII or any other federal statute.

In sum, by the 1970s, a variety of different legal regimes addressed different aspects of the employment relationship. With respect to job security, individual employees with sufficient bargaining power could negotiate contractual protection. In addition, there were statutes encouraging "procedural" solutions for all workers (such as regulating unionism and the collective bargaining process) and statutes directly providing job security for civil servants and academics. Finally, there were statutes providing some degree of job security by prohibiting certain reasons for firing employees. With respect to terms and conditions of employment, workers were protected by the same set of laws, supplemented by additional statutes directly regulating certain matters (e.g., minimum wages, maximum hours) for private and public, unionized and nonunionized employees.

Although some may have thought this collection of protections adequate, others perceived more exceptions than rules. Certainly, the average worker (employed by a nonunionized, private, nonacademic employer) had relatively narrow protections. Such a person was unlikely to have a personal employment contract and thus was an "at will" employee. Beyond the floor protections provided by minimum wage laws, workers' compensation, OSHA, and prohibitions on status discrimination, a worker would have very little in the way of legal protections.

This reality triggered state common-law efforts to limit employer power and expand employee rights by carving away at the at-will principle through a more expansive view of contract protections and through the public policy tort. While some of these decisions have become a permanent part of the employment landscape, there has also been significant judicial retrenchment in these areas. Similarly, while new state statutory whistleblower and related protections have codified and even expanded the common law developments of the 1970s and 1980s, major new legislation seemed stalled until, in response to examples of corporate misfeasance, SOX provided employee protections, although admittedly not as an end in themselves but rather as a means to ensure an honest securities market. In the wake of the Great Recession, there has been a new spate of whistleblower protections on the federal level as part of the stimulus package and the comprehensive legislation dealing with health care and financial institution regulation. Like SOX, the goal of these provisions is not to protect employees per se but to encourage employees to report violations of the laws' substantive provisions.

Compounding the ferment in the law was a radical restructuring of the economy. As the twentieth century was coming to a close, changes in the nature of the American economy, the workforce, and the structure of the workplace brought new issues to the fore and, correspondingly, presaged new legal developments. For example, consistent with the growing number of households in which all employable adults work, there has been a growing awareness of the need for accommodation of workers' familial and personal needs. Legislative reforms along these lines have been modest, but they include the FMLA, which provides limited protections for employees' life needs in the form of mandated unpaid leave due to a personal medical condition or that of a family member. A very few states provide paid leave or more generous unpaid leave. Similarly, the ADA requires "reasonable accommodation" of disabled individuals in many circumstances and the enactment of the ADAAA promises to revive the significance of this requirement.

Moreover, as discussed previously, as the American economy has transformed into one dominated by services, information, and technology, the value of certain employees has increased. In significant sectors, firms are becoming more dependent on employee creativity, information, and innovation, resulting in a heightened concern among *employers* about protecting themselves. Some find it more than a little telling that a pure at-will regime is now being challenged not merely by advocates of employee interests but also by employers who find themselves increasingly at risk. There has been a rise in litigated conflicts between employers and (often former) employees in such areas as trade secrets, copyrights, and ownership of employee inventions, and claims to business good will, customer lists, and various types of confidential information. Because the default protections for employer interests — employee fiduciary duties and employer intellectual property and trade secrets protections — are limited and often difficult to enforce, there has been dramatic growth in the use of restrictive covenants in recent years. These covenants — including noncompetition, nondisclosure, nonsolicitation, and holdover agreements — are becoming more common, as are questions about the limits the law ought to place on them. Because the stakes on both sides are higher than in past decades, the validity and extent of such agreements are much more frequently litigated.

The governing employment law regime itself, market forces, and other factors have also wrought dramatic changes in the structure of the American workplace. Among the most important is the growth in the outsourcing — both domestic and foreign — of various aspects of production to independent firms or suppliers of labor and the rise of nontraditional working relationships, including growth in independent contracting and part-time work. Undoubtedly, firms take advantage of such nontraditional work structures to avoid some of the legal requirements of "employment" and reduce risks associated with having "employees." By avoiding "employment" relationships and opting instead for independent contractors or other work structures, firms can avoid most statutory protections — which apply only to "employees" and "employers" — along with other legal consequences of an employment relationship, including such things as respondeat superior liability and obligations under immigration laws. The corresponding rise in what some have called the "contingent workforce" may have significant social consequences because these workers, on average, are more likely to be both on the economic margins and less likely — for both legal and practical reasons — to be able to enforce whatever work-related rights they may have.

Yet another change in the workplace is the shift from a fairly hierarchical structure to less formal, more team-oriented workplaces. While hierarchy remains alive and well in many settings, the past decades have seen a flattening of hierarchies as tiers of management are replaced with more collaborative working arrangements. The result is, in one sense, fewer bosses and, in another, more bosses. Such structural changes pose a variety of challenges for the law, especially in areas like sexual harassment.

Finally, sweeping technological innovations are changing the workplace and, correspondingly, creating new legal issues and challenges. The rise of social media, for example, not only has altered the way workers and firms interact with one another, but also has raised new concerns about employer intrusions into worker interests in privacy and free expression. In addition, the availability of new tools for utilizing data (including so-called "big data") will assist enterprises in operating more efficiently, but methods of collection and utilization by managers and human resources professionals raise a host of potential legal concerns, from worker privacy to discrimination to fair wage and hour treatment.

All of these trends are being affected, in one way or another, by the Great Recession from which the country is slowly emerging Unemployment has dropped to 5.8% but wage growth has remained largely static. Although it is still too early to say precisely how economic conditions will affect employment going forward, one does not need a crystal ball to predict that a large number of qualified unemployed or underemployed workers hanging over the market would have dramatic effects on employment practices.

In short, the law continues to struggle to address these fundamental changes, both as a matter of doctrine and of on-the-ground enforcement. Despite the growth of regulation, the law leaves many decisions regulated only in skeletal ways. Nevertheless, the intersection of various legislative regimes and common-law doctrines means that few employment-related decisions are entirely immune from legal challenge. This reality has produced one final, burgeoning area of employment law, counseling, and litigation. Recent years have seen the rise of "second-level" risk management techniques, usually used by employers, to control or minimize the risks of downstream employment-related conflicts or liabilities. These techniques include internal compliance practices such as the implementation of sexual harassment policies and internal investigations, mandatory pre-dispute arbitration agreements, a rise in substantial severance pay in exchange for releases of claims upon termination, and the inclusion of choice-of-law and choice-of-forum clauses in employment contracts. The substantive law governing these various approaches to risk management differs, as does their success in shifting risk from employers to employees. However, as long as the law of the employment relationship remains uncertain, risk management techniques and the legal rules that constrain them will continue to play a central role in the life of the employment lawyer.

As you can see from this short tour of employment law, the American legal approach to employment in the twenty-first century is a crazy quilt of regulation and laissez faire. For many employees and employers, this means market forces remain far more important than "law" in determining the most important terms of their relationship, including whether "employment" exists at all and how long such a relationship lasts. But there are some significant legal constraints that frame the parties' choices. Understanding this patchwork of laws governing workplace relationships — a combination of contract-law principles operating against a backdrop of tort law rules and general and employment-specific statutes and regulations — presents serious challenges for workers, firms, policy makers, legal counsel, and, of course, law students.

The Organization of This Book

This casebook is organized in seven parts containing 13 chapters. Part I addresses issues of formation of an employment relationship, that is, whether there is an "employment" relationship at all — as opposed to some other type of relationship — and the consequences that flow from that determination. The two chapters in Part II then address how employment terms are set or limited by contract, particularly terms related to job security. They explore the contours of the at-will rule and its exceptions and the interpretation and enforcement of express agreements that vary from this rule and set other important terms of employment, such as compensation.

Part III then turns to tort-based protections for employees: Chapter 4 explores the public policy exception, state statutory antiretaliation and whistleblower provisions modeled on the public policy decisions, and federal approaches, focusing on Sarbanes-Oxley. Chapter 5 covers traditional workplace torts, including intentional interference with the employment relationship, defamation, intentional infliction of emotional distress, and fraud. The two chapters in Part IV then shift the focus to worker autonomy interests, that is, privacy and speech. In both of these contexts, the disparate sources of potential protection are considered (in both the public and the private employer settings) as well as the balance the law strikes between legitimate employer interests and the autonomy interests of workers.

Part V turns to workplace property rights and related interests of employers. Chapter 8 explores various legal safeguards for these interests, including those flowing from fiduciary duty, trade secrets, and intellectual property protections. It also addresses employers' attempts to supplement these legal protections through contract — for example, restrictive covenants such as noncompetition, nonsolicitation, and holdover agreements — and the limits the law places on the scope and enforcement of such provisions.

Part VI contains four chapters addressing the principal statutory regimes that govern directly or indirectly various terms and conditions of employment: Chapter 9 explores antidiscrimination mandates; Chapter 10 examines required accommodations for aspects of workers lives, including workers' disabilities, health, pregnancy, and family caregiving needs. Chapter 11 discusses regulation of employee wages and benefits; and Chapter 12 reviews legal regimes addressing workplace safety and health. These chapters cover not only the primary federal statutes addressing these matters — such as, Title VII, the ADEA, the ADA, the FMLA, the FLSA, ERISA, and OSHA — but also state workers' compensation regimes (Chapter 12) and state efforts to supplement federal antidiscrimination, accommodation, wage, and benefit protections and enforcement.

Finally, Part VII offers a fitting conclusion to the study of employment law by exploring various methods of managing the risks and costs of potential liabilities of employment — liabilities arising from the contractual, common-law, and statutory aspects of employment law you will have explored in earlier chapters. In other words, Chapter 13 addresses the second-level private ordering techniques that employers commonly utilize to control the risks and costs of employment disputes by minimizing liability exposure or choosing the forum within which such disputes are resolved. They include policies for preventing and correcting discriminatory harassment, internal investigations of misconduct, release and severance agreements, arbitration agreements, liquidated damages provisions, liability insurance, and bankruptcy protection. Of course, this survey discusses not only the content of these practices and contractual provisions but also the limitations the law imposes them.

Part One

THE BENEFITS AND BURDENS OF EMPLOYMENT

1

The Stakes of "Employment"

A useful starting point in the study of employment law is this fundamental question: Why does the existence of an "employment" relationship matter? Organizations, both governmental and private, structure their activities in a wide variety of ways, and the individuals who perform work or provide services for these institutions may have various kinds of legal relationships with them and with one another. For example, a person who works on a firm's behalf may be its sole proprietor, a partner, an employee, or an independent contractor. In addition, firms engage other firms to perform some of their productive activities, leaving to the second firm the task of engaging workers to perform these tasks. For instance, growing attention has focused on outsourcing various services across international borders and, in the domestic context, utilizing "contingent" — that is, temporary or nonpermanent — workers.

Distinguishing between employment and other types of relationships is important because each offers its own mix of risks and benefits, both legal and nonlegal — what we call the stakes of employment. For example, many well-known legal protections for workers apply only to "employees." Firms owe duties to employees that they do not owe to other workers, although they may also benefit from employer status in various ways. The nature of the work relationship also has important consequences for third parties, who are far more likely to be able to hold firms or government entities liable for injuries caused by their employees than by independent contractors.

To understand the stakes of employment, you must have a basic grasp of the potential rights and obligations arising from the employment relationship and how they differ from those arising from other relationships. Thus, in this chapter we explore not only the definitions of "employee" and "employer" and the distinctions between employment and other types of legal relationships but also the consequences of employment for employees, employers, and third parties. Workers may prefer to be employees for some reasons and in some circumstances but not others; similarly, firms and government agencies may seek to avoid being employers for certain purposes but may benefit from employer status in other ways. And third parties and the public may have an independent interest in treating some workers as employees but not others.

As you work your way through these preferences and interests, think about the role private ordering should play — that is, the extent to which worker and firm ought

3

to be able to define the nature of their relationship though contract. Should such agreements be enforceable and dispositive, or should the law limit parties' ability to decide whether theirs is an "employment" relationship?

Before reading the cases and notes in this chapter, take a moment to consider the following problem:

PROBLEM

1-1. Compliance Boom. Worldwide Compliance Education, LLC ("WCE"), is a small company that provides training and continuing education to compliance professionals in the financial services industry. WCE's founders and owners, Faith and Ethan Morales, historically have provided onsite, live training programs for compliance professionals within large enterprises, often tailored specifically to that client's needs. Through their efforts, WCE has become very successful and is known as an industry leader in compliance training. WCE now employees eight people (in addition to Faith and Ethan), including assistant trainers and support staff.

As a result of the strength of WCE's brand and the continuing increase in compliance risks, both domestically and abroad, Faith and Ethan have decided to expand the business. After consulting with their principal clients and a business adviser, and securing outside financing, they have decided to begin producing compliance and ethics training videos for sales, brokerage, and other noncompliance personnel working for financial services firms. In Phase I of the expansion, they plan to produce and market both client-specific training modules (tailored to a firm's particular compliance needs) and standard, off-the-shelf modules any company in the finance and insurance industries can purchase. Because they intend to deliver the videos through the web, as well as maintain assessment and interactive components, they will need to develop the web and human resources infrastructure for delivering and hosting the trainings. In Phase II, they intend to develop more advanced modules as well as modules focusing on new developments.

Until now, Faith and Ethan have overseen directly all aspects of WCE. With the new expansion, they will no longer be able to do so. They will have to devote significant time to developing the content of the videos, as well as continuing to serve their clients' live training needs. In addition, the video training venture will require IT, production, and marketing expertise they do not have. WCE will also be moving into a larger office space in a new building it just purchased.

Going forward, Faith and Ethan will continue to manage the entire operation, but they will need to utilize the services of the following people:

- An office manager
- A part-time accounting assistant to handle billing and accounts receivables
- A software engineer and/or information technology expert who will design the web-based system, and—whether the same person or not—an IT professional to maintain and expand the system once it is in operation

- A marketing expert to develop and implement a marketing plan for the videos
- A salesperson who will engage in customer relations and eventually take responsibility for most of WCE's video marketing and sales
- At least two production specialists to create the training videos in Phase I, and then, on the basis of need, a specialist to create and update videos in Phase II and beyond
- On a short-term or "need" basis, various other workers to assist in video production, including script writers, script readers, graphic designers, and editors
- One or more workers to provide maintenance and janitorial services for the new building

Consider this hypothetical from the following perspectives. First, why might WCE decide to treat these workers as employees or independent contractors, or, alternatively, to hire an independent firm to supply the labor or perform particular tasks? Second, why might some of the workers prefer employment with WCE while others may prefer a different relationship? Finally, might the public or third parties have a preference, and, if so, when should their interests override the interests of the parties? And, relatedly, to what extent should WCE's or a worker's expectations, or an agreement between WCE and a worker, determine the nature of the relationship? Continue to consider these questions as you read the material in this chapter.

A. DISTINGUISHING "EMPLOYEE" FROM "INDEPENDENT CONTRACTOR"

By far the most commonly litigated issue in defining the employment relationship is whether a worker is an employee or an independent contractor. This is true for three reasons. First, as explored below, a host of legal consequences that flow from the workers' status often make this issue worth litigating. Second, most workers—that is, participants in the production of firm goods and services—are either employees or independent contractors (as opposed to, inter alia, sole proprietors, corporate directors, or partners or some other type of co-owner). Finally, distinguishing between employees and independent contractors is often both difficult and highly fact-intensive.

Somewhat surprisingly, most statutes regulating employment do not attempt to define the term, other than by borrowing the definition of "employee" from the common law. Thus, the test that courts apply for determining whether a worker is an independent contractor or an employee typically derives from the definition of employee or "servant" found in the common law of agency. As summarized in the Restatement (Second) of Agency, a "master" or employer is "a principal who employs an agent to perform service in his affairs and who controls or has the right to control the physical conduct of the other in the performance of the service." RESTATEMENT (SECOND) OF AGENCY, §2(1) (1958). Correspondingly, a servant or employee is "an agent employed by a master to perform service in his affairs whose physical conduct in the performance of the service is controlled or is subject to the right to control by the master." *Id.* § 2(2). In contrast, an independent contractor is one "who contracts with another to do something for him but who is not controlled by the other nor subject to the other's right to control with respect to his physical conduct in the performance of the undertaking." *Id.* § 2(3). The Restatement goes on to provide a more detailed definition of "servant," a term that has since been displaced by "employee," containing a nonexclusive list of factors for determining servant/employee status:

§ 220. Definition of Servant

(1) A servant is a person employed to perform services in the affairs of another and who with respect to the physical conduct in the performance of the services is subject to the other's control or right to control.

(2) In determining whether one acting for another is a servant or an independent contractor, the following matters of fact, among others, are considered:

(a) the extent of control which, by the agreement, the master may exercise over the details of the work;

(b) whether or not the one employed is engaged in a distinct occupation or business;

(c) the kind of occupation, with reference to whether, in the locality, the work is usually done under the direction of the employer or by a specialist without supervision;

(d) the skill required in the particular occupation;

(e) whether the employer or the workman supplies the instrumentalities, tools, and the place of work for the person doing the work;

(f) the length of time for which the person is employed;

(g) the method of payment, whether by the time or by the job;

(h) whether or not the work is a part of the regular business of the employer;

(i) whether or not the parties believe they are creating the relation of master and servant; and

(j) whether the principal is or is not in business.

The Restatement (Third) of Agency contains a similar definition, although the wording varies slightly, including abandonment of "servant" in favor of "employee." *See* RESTATEMENT (THIRD) OF AGENCY § 7.07 (3)(a) (2006) ("an employee is an agent whose principal controls or has the right to control the manner and means of the agent's performance of work").

In contrast, the most recent draft of the new Restatement of Employment Law frames the inquiry somewhat differently. It provides that an employment relationship exists whenever a worker acts, at least in part, to serve the interests of the employer; the employer consents to receive the services of the worker; and the worker is not rendering services as an independent business, which means that the worker does not exercise entrepreneurial control over the manner and means of the work. *See* RESTATEMENT (THIRD) OF EMPLOYMENT LAW (Proposed Final Draft, April 18, 2014) § 1.01. Although control over the manner and means of the work remains central in this formulation, the test is framed in the negative, namely, that a worker is an employee *unless he or she exerts entrepreneurial control*. The section goes on to define entrepreneurial control as "control over important business decisions, including whether to hire and where to assign assistants, whether to purchase and where to deploy equipment, and whether and when to service other customers." *Id.*

Keep in mind that the ultimate impact of this new Restatement will remain unknown for some time. Although the final draft has been approved by the membership of the American Law Institute ("ALI"), no jurisdiction has yet adopted it. Moreover, from its outset, the very notion of such a Restatement of Employment Law has been criticized as being misconceived, in large part because the field is still evolving and many feel that it is too early to try to "freeze" the law into its present pattern. *See, e.g.*, Kenneth G. Dau-Schmidt, *A Conference on the American Law Institute's Proposed Restatement of Employment Law*, 13 EMP. RTS. & EMP. POL'Y J. 1 (2009); Michael J. Zimmer, *The Restatement of Employment Law Is the Wrong Project*, 13 EMP. RTS. & EMP. POL'Y J. 205 (2009). This could affect the extent to which state courts choose to rely on it. Nevertheless, as you read this chapter, consider whether such a formulation might change the outcome in any of the cases and, if so, whether it is better or worse than existing approaches.

McCary v. Wade
861 So. 2d 358 (Miss. Ct. App. 2003)

LEE, J.

. . . On August 2, 1999, appellants Jettie McCary and Lillie Fulwiley were riding in a van on their way home from work and were traveling north on Highway 25. The van was being driven by John Isonhood who was employed by Choctaw Maid Farms, the appellants' employer, to transport the workers from the facility to their homes. As Isonhood approached the intersection of Highway 25 and County Road, Grace Mills pulled out from County Road onto Highway 25 traveling south. However, Mills pulled out in front of another driver, Dexter Myrick, who was driving a logging truck. Myrick was forced to hit his breaks [sic] to avoid a collision with Mills, and this forced him into the opposite lane of traffic where he collided with the appellants' northbound van.

McCary incurred approximately $110,000 in related medical expenses and approximately $45,000 in past and future lost wages as a result of her injuries from the collision. She is totally disabled and has significant disfigurement to her lower body. Fulwiley incurred approximately $20,000 in related medical expenses, an estimated $20,000 in future medical expenses and approximately $100,000 in past and future lost wages.

McCary and Fulwiley filed suit against Myrick, Georgia Pacific Corporation, . . . Mills, John Isonhood, Choctaw Maid Farms, Inc., which provided the van transportation, Chris Wade who had contracted with Georgia Pacific for sale of timber, and Wade Land Management which was Chris Wade's company.

A question arose concerning whether or not Myrick was acting as an employee of Wade at the time of the accident and, if so, whether Wade could be held vicariously liable for Myrick's actions. Details of the employment relationship are addressed in more depth in the following discussion.

Discussion . . .

In their motion for summary judgment, Chris Wade and Wade Land Management ("WLM") argued that Myrick was an independent hauler for WLM and, therefore, WLM was not liable to the plaintiffs/appellants via *respondeat superior* for Myrick's negligence in causing the accident.

The general rule is that the employer of an independent contractor has no vicarious liability for the torts of the independent contractor or for the torts of the independent contractor's employees in the performance of the contract. In determining whether a[n] employer-employee or independent contractor relationship existed, especially where third parties are affected, courts are not confined to the terms of the contract, but may look as well to the conduct of the parties. In addition to the general rule . . . we have recognized many "tests" or aspects of a relationship to examine in determining whether a person is an employee or an independent contractor:

> [W]hether the principal master has the power to terminate the contract at will; whether he has the power to fix the price in payment for the work, or vitally controls the manner and time of payment; whether he furnishes the means and appliances for the work; whether he has control of the premises; whether he furnishes the materials upon which the work is done and receives the output thereof, the contractor dealing with no other person in respect to the output; whether he has the right to prescribe and furnish the details of the kind and character of work to be done; whether he has the right to supervise and inspect the working during the course of the employment; whether he has the right to direct the details of the manner in which the work is to be done; whether he has the right to employ and discharge the sub employees and to fix their compensation; and whether he is obliged to pay the wages of said employees.

Miller v. Shell Oil Co., 783 So. 2d 724 (¶ 11) (Miss. Ct. App. 2000). We look to the facts of this case *de novo* . . . to determine whether Myrick was an independent contractor or an employee of WLM, such that summary judgment was or was not proper in this case.

WLM purchases timber and sells it to wood yards. In 1996, WLM contracted with Georgia Pacific to provide timber, and WLM in turn hired haulers to move the timber, one of whom was Myrick. Myrick and WLM entered into a contract in 1996 whereby Myrick would cut and haul lumber to Georgia Pacific for WLM. Myrick was not subject to any quotas set by WLM concerning delivery amounts, and Georgia Pacific would accept any amount of the specified lumber that Myrick chose to deliver.

In his deposition, which is included in the record, Chris Wade explained that Myrick bought his own timber, cut it, and hauled it all himself, and Wade never knew where or when Myrick was producing any wood until Myrick called him alerting that he had a load of logs to sell. Wade affirmed that "he didn't have to pay a cent" for Myrick's cutting operation and that he only used independent contractors because otherwise he would have to pay for the haulers' trucks and operation costs. Wade explained that to his knowledge Myrick had other contracts with companies to deliver wood, just the same as he had a contract with WLM.

Myrick testified in his deposition that he decided his own work hours, which days he would work, and where he would work. He exclusively made decisions concerning harvest, sorting, loading and transportation of the timber. Myrick stated that he owned all of the equipment needed for his operation, including his two-ton truck which he and his brother exclusively purchased, repaired and maintained, and he had never gotten a loan for his logging business. Myrick testified that on the day of the accident he had left Georgia Pacific and was en route to his home at the time of the collision. Under the previously described test for determining independent contractor status, we find Myrick's relationship with WLM to be that of an independent contractor and not employee/employer. Having so found, we next direct our attention to *Richardson v. APAC-Mississippi, Inc.*, 631 So. 2d 143 (Miss. 1994), which the appellants cite in support of their argument. . . . The appellants direct our attention to *Richardson*'s addition of a public policy test to determine liability. The supreme court defined this new test as follows:

> When a contract is made between two parties that as between themselves creates an independent contractor relationship and involves employment generally performed under a simple master/servant or employer/employee relationship, it will be upheld as between the parties. When, however, third parties are adversely affected, this Court will carefully scrutinize the contract to see if public policy should permit the transformation of an ordinarily employer/employee relationship into that of an independent contractor. A necessary condition precedent for the application of this factor, however, is that the party challenging the claimed relationship will be adversely affected, and denied an adequate legal remedy. In the absence of this, the right of parties to contract as they please is a constitutionally-protected right. Conversely, neither of the parties should be permitted to dispute a contractually-created independent contractor relationship between them when to do so adversely affects an injured third party.

Id. (citations omitted). . . . In the present case, Myrick was shown to be bankrupt and without insurance coverage. Thus, the appellants claim that since Myrick was not insured and had no money to compensate them for their injuries, WLM should be made to pay in the interests of public policy.

The Fifth Circuit addressed the *Richardson* case in *McKee v. Brimmer*, 39 F.3d 94 (5th Cir. 1994), . . . and surmised the following:

> The public policy factor from *Richardson* becomes an issue when the relationship between the alleged employer and the alleged employee would "ordinarily" be characterized as that of an employer/employee, but they have a contract which defines their relationship as that of independent contractors. In that case, the court will scrutinize the contract to see if the parties should be allowed to transform an employer/employee relationship into that of an independent contractor. In essence, an employer will not be allowed to escape liability by drafting a contract which labels its employee an independent contractor, but retains employer-like control over him.

Id. (citations omitted). . . . [S]ince the evidence presented shows Myrick was an independent contractor and there is no evidence of any attempt by WLM to control Myrick through written contracts or otherwise, the appellants' public policy argument fails.

In the present case, the *Richardson* public policy test is not applicable because Myrick undeniably was an independent contractor in his work with WLM. . . . We find no confusion as to Myrick's role as working independently of WLM as employer. . . .

Fitzgerald v. Mobil Oil Corporation
827 F. Supp. 1301 (E.D. Mich. 1993)

FEIKENS, District Judge.

Plaintiff [Fitzgerald], a tractor-trailer driver, was injured on the job when he fell from the top of the tanker trailer he used to deliver oil. The trailer was owned by defendant Montgomery Tank Lines, Inc., and leased to Mobil Oil. The tractor was owned by a third party, Jerry Rieger, and also leased to Mobil Oil. Plaintiff was hired to deliver loads of oil from Mobil Oil's Woodhaven Lube Plant and Terminal in Woodhaven, Michigan to various Mobil Oil customers. Plaintiff's Complaint alleges that both defendants negligently provided plaintiff with an unsafe and defective tanker, and that the tanker was not equipped with adequate safety devices.

Mobil Oil's defense is based on the "exclusive remedy provision" of Michigan's Worker's Disability Compensation Act. M.S.A. § 17.237(131). It provides that "[t]he right to the recovery of benefits as provided in this act shall be the employee's exclusive remedy against the employer." Consequently, Mobil Oil's motion turns on whether or not it can be considered plaintiff's employer. Plaintiff denies that Mobil Oil was his employer. . . . Although plaintiff's employment situation was complex and confusing,[1] the facts, when interpreted in light of Michigan precedent, are susceptible of only one inference — Mobil Oil was plaintiff's employer.

Plaintiff was initially hired by Jerry Rieger, the owner and lessor of the tractor plaintiff used to haul loads. But before Rieger would agree to hire him, plaintiff had to pass a road test administered by Mobil Oil at a Mobil Oil facility in Pennsylvania. At the time, plaintiff knew that he was being considered for work involving Mobil Oil, and that if he failed the road test he would not have a job.

Plaintiff telephoned a Mobil dispatcher at least once a day for work assignments. The dispatcher told him where to deliver oil and how much to deliver. Plaintiff also contacted Jerry Rieger on a daily basis; and submitted his paperwork — travel logs, unloading records, fuel and other expense receipts — to Rieger on a weekly basis. Determination of his wages depended on these records. But plaintiff's paycheck was issued by yet another company, TLI, Inc. TLI had a contract with Mobil Oil to provide tractor-trailer drivers for Mobil Oil's use. Mobil reimbursed the company for driver wages and other expenses, including worker's compensation insurance premiums. However, the contract specifically disclaims the existence of an employer/employee relationship between Mobil Oil and TLI-supplied drivers. After his injury, plaintiff received worker's compensation benefits from TLI.

Mobil Oil argues that both TLI and Mobil Oil were plaintiff's employers for purposes of the worker's compensation laws. *Renfroe v. Higgins Rack Coating & Manufacturing Co.*, 169 N.W.2d 326 (Mich. Ct. App. 1969), recognized the "triangular relationship" that exists between a worker, a supplier of temporary workers (or labor broker) and a user of those workers. *Renfroe* concluded that both the labor broker and the end-user are employers of the worker, and therefore protected by the exclusive remedy provision. Plaintiff's situation involves a fourth player, Jerry Rieger. However, Rieger and TLI, in combination, fill the labor broker role. . . .

---

1. In his deposition plaintiff states: "I was totally confused the whole time I was there about who I was working for or who I was getting paid by."

The relationship between TLI and Mobil Oil does not match this description in all respects. Plaintiff was on long-term assignment to Mobil Oil, and, because of the nature of his job, was not closely supervised by Mobil Oil personnel. As a truck driver, plaintiff was unlikely to be subjected to the same close supervision often associated with factory and office work. This fact arguably decreases the closeness of the relationship between plaintiff and Mobil Oil. On the other hand, the fact that plaintiff was on long-term assignment to Mobil Oil strengthens their relationship. On balance the differences are not enough to alter the outcome.

Economic Realities Test

Michigan courts rely on the economic realities test to establish the existence of an employer/employee relationship. . . . The language of a written agreement, such as the one between TLI and Mobil Oil, is not controlling. Furthermore, the same test is used whether asserted by the plaintiff as a sword or by the defendant as a shield.

The economic realities test includes four elements: "(1) control of a worker's duties, (2) the payment of wages, (3) the right to hire and fire and the right to discipline, and (4) the performance of the duties as an integral part of the employer's business towards the accomplishment of a common goal." *Askew v. Macomber*, 247 N.W.2d 288 (Mich. 1976). No single element is controlling; the totality of the circumstances must be considered.

Control. Plaintiff's deposition indicates that he contacted a Mobil Oil dispatcher by phone on a daily basis to obtain work assignments. Those assignments involved hauling oil from Mobil Oil's Woodhaven processing plant and delivering it to Mobil Oil customers. The oil was generally loaded into plaintiff's tanker by Mobil Oil employees and unloaded by plaintiff. Plaintiff kept his truck at Mobil Oil's Woodhaven facility when it was not in use, and hauled exclusively for Mobil Oil. Plaintiff also contacted Mobil Oil when the tanker needed to be washed, to complain about the tanker, and to complain about other Mobil Oil employees.

On the other hand, plaintiff was trained by an individual who appeared to be an employee of Jerry Rieger. He invariably telephoned Rieger after receiving an assignment from Mobil Oil to obtain Rieger's approval. And on at least one occasion plaintiff refused an assignment after Rieger told him not to accept it. Plaintiff delivered his travel logs and other paperwork to Rieger. He contacted Rieger when his tractor needed servicing, and Rieger arranged for repairs.

These facts indicate that plaintiff's job duties were controlled, at least in significant part, by Mobil Oil. . . .

Payment of Wages. Mobil Oil clearly satisfies this element of the economic realities test. [The lease agreement between TLI and Mobil Oil provided that Mobil Oil was liable to TLI for reimbursement of various driver expenses, all wages and benefit payments that TLI made to drivers for services rendered, and Mobil Oil's share of the Social Security taxes, workers' compensation, and federal and state unemployment and liability premiums.] Payment of wages in this indirect fashion was enough to establish the wages element in several Michigan cases.

Right to Hire, Fire, and Discipline. Under the terms of Mobil Oil's contract with TLI it had the right to refuse plaintiff's services. Plaintiff argues that TLI had other customers, and that if Mobil Oil refused his services, he could have worked for another customer. According to plaintiff, only TLI or Jerry Rieger had the power to completely take away his livelihood.

However, the fact remains that plaintiff was hired for a specific job. If Mobil Oil had terminated his services he would have been without an assignment, at least temporarily. The power to stop plaintiff from engaging in the daily tasks he relied on for wages is enough to satisfy the test.

Moreover, approval by Mobil Oil was a condition precedent to plaintiff's hiring. Plaintiff was required to pass a road test administered by Mobil at a Mobil Oil facility in Pennsylvania before Rieger agreed to hire him. Without Mobil's approval plaintiff would have never been employed by Rieger or TLI.

Performance of Duties as an Integral Part of Employer's Business. As a deliverer of Mobil Oil's product, plaintiff's work constituted an integral part of the company's business. Delivery is an ongoing and necessary function, not a short term or irregular project. Furthermore, although truck drivers are often independent contractors, this is not necessarily the usual or normal arrangement. Mobil Oil satisfies this element of the test as well.

In conclusion, the economic realities of the situation are that Mobil Oil was plaintiff's employer. All of the relevant factors lean heavily in Mobil Oil's favor. Taken as a whole, there can be no doubt that Mobil Oil satisfies the test. As a consequence, Mobil Oil is protected from suit by the exclusive remedy provision of the Worker's Disability Compensation Act. . . .

Plaintiff argues with some force that Mobil Oil has effectively insulated itself from all responsibility for workers. By using a labor broker, Mobil Oil is relieved of direct responsibility for worker's compensation insurance premiums and payment of benefits. Presumably, Mobil Oil obtains other advantages from denying the existence of an employer/employee relationship as well. On the other hand, Mobil Oil escapes the potential tort liability non-employers normally face. Justice Ryan of the Michigan Supreme Court recognized this imbalance of rights in his dissenting opinion in *Farrell v. Dearborn Manufacturing Co.*, 330 N.W.2d 397:

> My colleague's approach suggests that if two companies can divide the attributes of employment equally enough, *both* will be entitled to the "exclusive remedy" bar of the statute, even though only one set of workers' compensation insurance premiums must be paid. In short, my colleague's opinion advertises "two bars for the price of one."

Moreover, from a purely policy perspective, the Court's decision enables a company to insulate itself from the economic consequences of an unsafe workplace. It seems clear that the Legislature contemplated that either total liability or higher workers' compensation insurance rates would provide an economic incentive for every company to care about worker safety. It now appears that the labor broker scheme may be an expedient method of avoiding either type of liability.

However, this was not the prevailing opinion. As a federal judge, I am not in a position to change the law, especially state law. Only the Michigan Legislature can address this inequity. [The court therefore granted Mobil Oil's motion for summary judgment, dismissing it from the case.]

NOTES

1. *Tests for Determining Employee/Independent Contractor Status.* Each court articulates a test for determining whether the worker at issue was an employee or independent contractor. How much do these tests differ from one another? Is there a particular element or consideration that appears predominant in both? Which case more closely tracks the common-law approach as reflected in the Restatement of Agency? Why might that be? *Hint:* Consider *why* the common-law test distinguishes between employees and independent contractors and what is at stake in each case. Now briefly consider whether application of the test set forth in the draft Restatement of Employment Law might alter the outcome in one or both of these cases. If so, would that be a better result in either case?

2. *Disparate Stakes and Outcomes.* In each of these cases, the worker was a truck driver, a firm for whom the worker was performing services was sued as the result of an accident relating to the operation of the vehicle, and the underlying issue the court had to resolve was whether the worker was an employee or an independent contractor of the defendant firm. Yet one employer — WLM — argued that its driver was an independent contractor while the other — Mobil Oil — contended its driver was an employee. Why? In answering this question, consider a key factual difference: The plaintiff in *McCary* was a third party while the plaintiff in *Fitzgerald* was a worker. Interestingly, *both* defendants prevailed, despite both courts' acknowledging counter-vailing public policy concerns. Based on the facts and public policy, did the two courts reach the right results? Would you reach the same conclusion if the facts were identical but the claims were reversed? That is, suppose Myrick had sued WLM in tort for injuries he suffered in the accident and a third-party tort victim had sued Mobil Oil for Fitzgerald's negligence in operating the truck. What would WLM and Mobil Oil have argued in these lawsuits regarding the status of the two workers?

3. *The Role of Private Ordering.* The *Fitzgerald* court found that Fitzgerald was an employee of Mobil Oil although Mobil's contract with TLI specifically disclaimed the existence of an employer/employee relationship between it and TLI-supplied drivers. What role should express contract terms play in determining whether the worker is an employee? In some circumstances, the intent or expectations of the firm and worker are different than the terms stated in the governing contract. If so, which should control? Does it matter who is relying on or disavowing the agreement (i.e., the firm, worker, or third party)? Ironically, the *Fitzgerald* court's willingness to look beyond the contract provision facilitated Mobil's victory in this case, but one might question whether this result really serves the firm's larger interests. Presumably, Mobil structured its arrangements as it did for good reasons, and the economic realities approach in *Fitzgerald* that resulted in the court finding Mobil to be an employer in this case could backfire when Mobil's status arises in another context.

4. *Respondeat Superior.* The doctrine of respondeat superior at issue in *McCary* may be the most important risk allocation doctrine in tort law. It provides that an employer is vicariously (hence strictly) liable for torts committed by its employees within the scope of their employment. *See, e.g.,* RESTATEMENT (SECOND) OF AGENCY § 219(1). As suggested in *McCary*, the doctrine is premised on protecting third parties and the public by extending accountability for workers' tortuous acts to those who exercise significant control over their conduct. By contrast, the tortious conduct of independent contractors generally does not give rise to vicarious liability for the principal. There are some important exceptions to the general rule that principals are not liable for the torts of their independent contractors, such as where the principal intended the violations, the principal was under a special duty to protect others from harm, or the principal's duty was, for one of various reasons, nondelegable to third parties. *See, e.g., id.* §212, §214, §219(2), §250, and §251; *see also* RESTATEMENT (THIRD) OF AGENCY §7.06 (2006) ("A principal required by contract or otherwise by law to protect another cannot avoid liability by delegating performance of the duty, whether or not the delegate is an agent."); *American Telephone & Telegraph Company v. Winback & Conserve Program*, 42 F.3d 1421, 1435 (3d Cir. 1994) (stating a principal is liable if she authorized or directed the agent's injurious act or intended the result); *Wiggs v. City of Phoenix*, 10 P.3d 625, 628 (Ariz. 2000) (finding a principal cannot avoid liability by delegating performance of a "special duty" to an independent contractor). Nevertheless, because employees generate tort liability risks under the doctrine of respondeat superior while independent contractors usually do not, the doctrine provides a strong incentive for businesses to outsource to independent firms or individuals, particularly those activities that pose a high risk to the public. *See, e.g.*, Eric W. Orts, *Shirking and Sharking: A Legal Theory of the Firm*, 16 YALE L. & POL'Y REV. 265, 305 (1998); Deanne M. Mosley & William C. Walter, *The Significance of the Classification of Employment Relationships in Determining Exposure to Liability*, 67 MISS. L. J. 613, 613-15 (1998). *But cf.* Richard R.W. Brooks, *Liability and Organizational Choice*, 45 J.L. & ECON. 91 (2002) (arguing that keeping some risky activities within the firm may be economically advantageous).

   5. *Workers' Compensation.* Unlike respondeat superior liability, workers' compensation law creates potentially conflicting incentives for firms with regard to employee/independent contractor status. As discussed in Chapter 5, workers' compensation regimes are premised on the trade-off of greater coverage but lower benefits: Employers pay premiums into a disability fund or insurance program from which employees injured on the job — regardless of fault — receive a defined amount of compensation for medical expenses and for lost wages while they are disabled and unable to work; in exchange, the workers' compensation program is the employees' exclusive remedial scheme for workplace injuries, thereby shielding the employer from potentially more costly tort liability. LEX K. LARSON, WORKERS' COMPENSATION LAW §§1.01, 100.01 (Matthew Bender & Co., Inc., Rev. Ed. 2014). Thus, when a worker is injured on the job, firms generally have an incentive to claim that the worker is an employee to preclude the possibility of tort liability. On the other hand, because workers' compensation coverage is no-fault and otherwise broader than tort liability, firms occasionally claim that a worker is an independent contractor and not entitled to coverage, particularly when the employee would have a weak tort claim against the firm. *See, e.g., Chouteau v. Netco Const.*, 132 S.W.3d 328 (Mo. Ct. App. 2004); *Roads West, Inc. v. Austin*, 91 P.3d 81 (Okla. Civ. App. 2003); Dean J. Haas, *Falling Down on the Job: Workers' Compensation Shifts from a No-Fault to a Worker-Fault Paradigm*, 79 N.D. L. REV. 203, 234 (2003). In addition, by classifying workers as independent contractors, the firm may avoid paying compensation insurance premiums for those individuals during their employment. How does this information shed light on Mobil's intentions in setting up its relationship with Fitzgerald?

6. *Legal Advantages of Common-Law "Employee" Status for Workers. Fitzgerald* provides one example of a worker's status as an employee under a statutory regime — workers' compensation — harming the worker's interests. Yet, in many other circumstances, workers have significant legal incentives to be classified as employees rather than independent contractors. For example, most of the federal statutory protections for workers studied in this course cover only "employees." These include federal labor, wage, hour, and benefit protections, *see, e.g.*, Labor Management Relations Act of 1947, 29 U.S.C. § 152(2)-(3) (2014); National Labor Relations Act, 29 U.S.C. § 158(b)(4)(i) (2014); Employee Retirement and Income Security Act, 29 U.S.C. § 1002 (5)-(6) (2014) ("ERISA"); Fair Labor Standards Act of 1938, 29 U.S.C. § 201(2) (2014); Family Medical Leave Act of 1993, 29 U.S.C. § 2611(3) (2014), as well as most federal prohibitions on status discrimination, *see, e.g.*, Age Discrimination in Employment Act of 1967, 29 U.S.C. § 630(f) (2014); Civil Rights Act of 1964, Title VII, 42 U.S.C. § 2000e(f) (2014); Americans with Disabilities Act of 1990, 42 U.S.C. § 12111(4) (2014). One notable exception is 42 U.S.C. § 1981, which prohibits race and alienage discrimination in most contractual relations. *See Runyon v. McCrary*, 427 U.S. 160 (1976).

7. *Defining "Employee" for Statutory Purposes.* In virtually all of the foregoing statutes, however, Congress failed to define meaningfully "employee" or "employer," offering only the unhelpful and circular statement that an "employee" is "an individual employed by an employer." Thus, in determining the meaning of "employee" and "employer" in these regimes, the Supreme Court has often held that Congress intended to describe the master-servant relationship as understood by common-law agency doctrine. *See, e.g.*, *Nationwide Mut. Ins. Co. v. Darden*, 503 U.S. 318, 322-23 (1992) (ERISA); *Cmty. for Creative Non-Violence v. Reid*, 490 U.S. 730, 739-40 (1989) (Copyright Act). Regulatory definitions of "employee" from other areas, such as tax law, likewise offer variations on the common law definition.

Some courts seeking to determine worker status for purposes of social welfare legislation such as the Fair Labor Standards Act ("FLSA") — which provides wage and hour protections by specifying a minimum wage and requirements for overtime pay — and some state workers' compensation laws, have taken a somewhat more inclusive approach. These courts suggest that the definition of employee and employer serve the broad remedial purposes of the statute and therefore expand the common-law definition by, among other things, focusing on worker dependence. This inquiry is sometimes referred to as the "economic realities test" — the term used by the *Fitzgerald* court. *See, e.g.*, *Bartels v. Birmingham*, 332 U.S. 126, 130 (1947); *Robincheaux v. Radcliff Material, Inc.*, 697 F.2d 662 (5th Cir. 1983); *Real v. Driscoll Strawberry Assoc., Inc.*, 603 F.2d 748 (9th Cir. 1979). Of course, *Fitzgerald* is somewhat ironic, since the court utilizes this expanded test designed to benefit workers to deny Fitzgerald's claim. However, the multifactored tests that the courts adopt, including those that seek to determine status based on so-called "economic reality," tend to use factors that, like the common law, emphasize employer control along with other considerations. *See Bartels*, 332 U.S. at 130 ("[P]ermanency of the relation, the skill required, the investment in the facilities for work and opportunities for profit or loss from the activities were also factors that should enter into judicial determination as to the coverage of the Social Security Act."); *Secretary of Labor v. Lauritzen*, 835 F.2d 1529, 1534 (7th Cir. 1987); RESTATEMENT (THIRD) OF EMPLOYMENT LAW (Proposed Final Draft, April 18, 2014) § 1.01 cmt. a (suggesting that courts that have relied on the common-law and economic realities approaches have tended to utilize the same factors and reach the same results); *see also Oestman v. National Farmers Union Ins. Co.*, 958 F.2d 303, 305 (10th Cir. 1992) (suggesting a "hybrid" approach that considers both control and dependence). Indeed, some courts deny any substantive difference between the tests. *See, e.g., Murray v. Principal Fin. Group, Inc.*, 613 F.3d 943, 945 (9th Cir. 2010) (clarifying that "there is no functional difference" between the tests of common-law control, economic realities, and a so-called hybrid of the two).

In sum, the common-law approach and related multifactored inquiries to distinguish employees from other types of workers continue to dominate. This is true despite the significant growth in employment statutes over the last half century. Thus, in most circumstances, to enjoy statutory labor and employment protections, workers must be common-law "employees."

8. *Legal Advantages of Employment Relationships for Firms.* The doctrine of respondeat superior and the legal protections for employees discussed in Note 6 may provide strong incentives for firms to contract with third parties for services and avoid direct employment relationships. As *Fitzgerald* suggests, workers' compensation laws may offer a countervailing incentive to hire workers as employees rather than independent contractors, at least in some circumstances.

In addition, firms may prefer employment over other statuses because employees may owe the firm more demanding fiduciary duties. As will be discussed in Chapter 8, the reach and content of such duties are controversial. Nevertheless, they may be particularly important from the firm's perspective when it is vulnerable to worker attempts to usurp its opportunities or good will or otherwise compete with it for business. *See, e.g., Midwest Ink Co. v. Graphic Ink Systems*, No. 98 C 7822 2003 WL 360089 (N.D. Ill. Feb. 18, 2003) (holding that whether a company's former salesman owed the firm a duty not to compete during his tenure on the sales force depended on his status an employee or independent contractor).The next case offers another example of a circumstance in which a firm has a strong incentive to have workers treated as employees, at least for certain purposes. Still, as you read, also consider why the firm did not structure the relationship differently at the outset to increase the probability of a favorable outcome on this issue. Consider also how a firm with a strong incentive to have workers treated as employees for certain purposes might protect its interests even without assurance of a judicial finding of an employment relationship.

═══ *Natkin v. Winfrey*
═══ *111 F. Supp. 2d 1003 (N.D. Ill. 2000)*

CASTILLO, District Judge.

This case is about eleven photographs of Oprah Winfrey taken by Plaintiffs Paul Natkin and Stephen Green on the set of her (rather) well-known television show. The photographs were subsequently published in Winfrey's book *Make the Connection*, co-authored with Bob Greene and published in 1996 by Buena Vista Books under the name Hyperion, without [Natkin's or Green's] permission. That publication resulted in this copyright infringement action and various other causes of action under the Lanham Act and Illinois state law. The defendants counterclaim seeking a declaration of rights.

. . . At base, we must decide whether either side has definitively established ownership of the copyrights to the photographs: To succeed on their motion, Natkin and

Green must show that they own the copyrights to the exclusion of the defendants. . . . For the reasons that follow, we conclude that there is no genuine issue that the defendants authored the photographs, either solely or jointly, but that a triable issue exists as to whether the defendants used the pictures pursuant to a valid license. . . .

Background

Natkin and Green are both professional "live event" photographers. Natkin owns (and owned during the relevant times) a private photography studio, Photo Reserve, Inc., and throughout the relevant time period he photographed concerts, live television broadcasts, movie sets, rock video productions, and album/CD covers. Green, since 1982, has been employed by the Chicago Cubs baseball organization, but also engages in freelance photography for others, such as the organizers of the World Series and NBA playoff games.

Natkin photographed *The Oprah Winfrey Show* between 1986 and 1993; Green worked on the show from 1989 to 1996. The photos at issue here were taken between 1988 and 1995. Natkin and Green primarily shot pictures of the show while it was being taped live in the Chicago studio. On occasion, however, when the show was broadcast from another location, they traveled with the show to take pictures. Additionally, Natkin and Green took posed photographs of Winfrey, usually with her more famous guests, either at the show's studio or their own studios. Both men used their own camera equipment and lenses, brought additional equipment (such as lights and backdrops) when taking posed shots, chose the appropriate film, and usually processed the film themselves. The record contains conflicting evidence about who arranged to process the film when Natkin and Green did not perform that task, which company processed the film, and in all cases who stored the negatives.

When photographing the live show, Natkin and Green had no control over the position or appearance of their subjects (i.e., Winfrey and her guests, the audience, etc.), the layout and design of the sets, or even the lighting of the set — Harpo [Winfrey's production firm and one of the defendants in the case] prohibited Natkin and Green from using flash bulbs or any other light source not provided by the studio. Additionally, during live taping of the show, Natkin and Green were restricted to certain locations — they were allowed to move freely about the set only during commercial breaks. But, as to creating the photographs, Natkin and Green had complete discretion over the technical aspects of the shoot: They chose which cameras, lenses, and film to use; the appropriate shutter speed, aperture settings, and timing for the shots; and how to frame the images.

During the relevant times, neither Natkin nor Green worked pursuant to a written agreement. Both men billed Harpo Productions a flat fee for each show they photographed and for any related expenses, including such items as parking and film. Harpo never withheld federal income taxes, FICA, or state income taxes from their payments to Natkin and Green and reported those payments to the IRS on 1099 forms (rather than W-2 forms) as "nonemployee compensation." Additionally, Harpo did not provide health or life insurance, pension benefits, or paid vacation to either Natkin or Green, and both men purchased the insurance for their equipment. Neither photographer was ever given a copy of the Harpo employee manual, but both received paid parking, access to the company cafeteria, Harpo security, and invitations to Harpo staff functions.

Additionally, both were referred to, and referred to themselves as, staff photographers for the show. When Natkin or Green was unable to photograph a show due to other commitments, they hired the substitute photographer and billed Harpo.

Green's invoices each contained the following provision: "*Terms/Conditions:* One time, non-exclusive reproduction rights to the photographs listed above, solely for the uses and specifications indicated. . . . Acceptance of this submission constitutes acceptance of these terms." . . . Natkin's invoices explicitly reserved his copyright to the invoiced photos: "All photos remain the property of, and copyrights remain with, Photo Reserve Inc." Natkin and Green contend that they were freelance photographers that were hired by Harpo and Winfrey as independent contractors to take pictures for publicity purposes only. They claim they are the sole authors of the photographs and, having never transferred their copyrights, are the sole owners of the rights to the pictures. Additionally, Natkin and Green maintain that the only possible license Harpo or Winfrey could have obtained was an oral, non-exclusive license to use the photos for publicity purposes. Thus, according to Natkin and Green, publication of the photos in *Make the Connection* infringed their copyrights.

The defendants, on the other hand, contend that Harpo and Winfrey are the authors of the pictures and thus own the copyrights to them. The defendants assert that Natkin and Green were employees of Harpo and that the pictures were taken within the scope of their employment. Alternatively, they argue that Harpo and Winfrey are joint authors of the photographs because they controlled the vast majority of the picture elements. Finally, as to the infringement claim, the defendants allege that their publication of the pictures in the book was pursuant to a valid license. . . .

I. Copyright Infringement Claims

To establish copyright infringement, Natkin and Green must demonstrate that they own the copyrights to the photographs. Under the Copyright Act, ownership of a copyright "vests initially in the author or authors of the work." Usually, the author of a work is "the person who translates an idea into a fixed, tangible expression entitled to copyright protection." *Community for Creative Non-Violence v. Reid*, 490 U.S. 730, 737 (1989). Under normal circumstances, a photographer is the author of his or her photographs. But, as with any general rule, exceptions exist. Two specific exceptions are relevant to this case: the "work made for hire" and "joint work" exceptions.

A. *Works Made for Hire*

Works made for hire are "authored" by the hiring party, and the "initial owner of the copyright is not the creator of the work but the employer or the party that commissioned the work." A work made for hire is "(1) a work prepared by an employee within the scope of his or her employment; or (2) a work specially ordered or commissioned . . . if the parties expressly agree in a written instrument signed by them that the work shall be considered a work made for hire." 17 U.S.C. § 101. The defendants concede that they do not have a written "work made for hire" agreement with either Natkin or Green covering the eleven photographs. Instead, they argue that Natkin and Green were Harpo employees, as opposed to independent contractors, when they took the pictures.

The Supreme Court has set forth a nonexhaustive, thirteen-factor test for determining whether a creator is an employee within the meaning of the Copyright Act's work made for hire provision. The *Reid* factors are

> the hiring party's right to control the manner and means by which the product is accomplished[;] . . . the skill required; the source of the instrumentalities and tools; the location of the work; the duration of the relationship between the parties; whether the hiring party has the right to assign additional projects to the hired party; the extent of the hired party's discretion over when and how long to work; the method of payments; the hired party's role in hiring and paying assistants; whether the work is part of the regular business of the hiring party; whether the hiring party is in business; the provision of employee benefits; and the tax treatment of the hired party.

Additionally, *Reid* instructs courts to use general common law agency principles to analyze whether the author of a work for hire is an independent contractor or an employee.

Applying the *Reid* factors to our circumstances demonstrates that Natkin and Green were not Harpo employees. Both men were highly skilled professionals specializing in live-action photography; both used (and insured) their own equipment; and both exercised discretion in hiring substitute photographers when they themselves were unavailable and paid those substitutes. Most importantly, neither photographer was ever treated like an employee in terms of compensation, benefits, and taxes: Natkin and Green, via their companies, billed Harpo for their services and expenses, they did not receive regular paychecks or salary; they received none of the employee benefits traditionally associated with employee status, such as health insurance, life insurance, and paid vacation;[5] and Harpo never withheld any payroll taxes on behalf of the photographers.

Further, Harpo's IRS reports describe the payments to Green and Natkin as "nonemployee compensation." We believe this factor alone would outweigh those few factors, discussed below, that favor the defendants' position. Harpo may not obtain the benefits associated with hiring an independent contractor and, at the same time, enjoy the advantages of treating that person as an employee; it must choose. Here, as to Natkin and Green, Harpo chose the independent contractor route and cannot now change its position to reap a different benefit it probably had not considered when making its choice (i.e., ownership of the photographs).

The only factors clearly favoring the defendants are that the defendants are engaged in business and the duration of the parties' relationship. That Harpo is a business and that Green and Natkin worked for Harpo over an extended period of time (seven years each) doesn't come close to overriding the impact of the factors favoring the photographers' status as independent contractors. Moreover, that Natkin and Green were referred to as "staff photographers" carries very little weight.

The remaining factors are either inconclusive or add insignificant weight in favor of either party's position. For example, all of the parties exercised control over the manner and means of production to some extent: Harpo controlled the appearance of Winfrey and her guests, the sets, and the lighting, while Natkin and Green controlled

---

5. The defendants' argument that staff parking, security on the set, and invitations to Harpo staff functions are employee benefits provided to Natkin and Green that weigh in favor of their employee status is unavailing, particularly in the face of the utter lack of any employee benefit normally associated with one's status as an employee.

the technical aspects of taking the photographs (i.e., lenses, film speed, etc.) and, ultimately, the image on the photographs. However, because the task was to create photographs, this factor weighs slightly in favor of independent contractor status. In any event, Harpo's control of the product here resembles the defendants' control over the statue at issue in *Reid*, where the Supreme Court concluded the artist was an independent contractor. . . .

Finally, the parties vigorously contest whether "the work is part of [Harpo's] regular business." Natkin and Green contend that the defendants are in the business of producing a television show, not taking pictures of the show, whereas the defendants maintain that they are in the business of promoting Oprah Winfrey, which includes taking photographs of her on the show. Even assuming this factor weighs in favor of the defendants' position, Harpo's treatment of Natkin and Green as independent contractors in terms of pay, taxes, and benefits; the photographers' use of their own equipment, judgment, and expertise; and that the relationship was technically between Harpo and the photographers' companies definitively establishes that Natkin and Green were independent contractors.

On the basis of the record before us, we conclude there is no genuine issue that Natkin and Green were ever Harpo employees. They were not. Harpo hired Natkin and Green as independent contractors, and they continued in that capacity during their tenures with the show. Thus, Harpo must produce a written work made for hire agreement signed by both sides to successfully claim exclusive ownership of the copyrights to these photographs. Harpo does not have such a document. Consequently, we grant Natkin and Green's motion for partial summary judgment on the work made for hire issue.

[The court went on to grant summary judgment denying defendants' claim that the photographs were a "joint work" of them and Natkin and Green, but denied summary judgment on defendants' claim that they had a license to publish the photographs.]

NOTES

1. *Conflicting Legal Incentives and Trying to Have It Both Ways.* You will learn more about the growing implications of employment on intellectual property rights (including copyrights) and other workplace intangibles in Chapter 8. Nevertheless, by now you have seen some of the considerations that influence a firm's decision to hire employees versus independent contractors, as well as the benefits and disadvantages of these two relationships for workers. These incentives may conflict depending on the context, and such a conflict is apparent in *Fitzgerald* and *Natkin*. Of course, decisions about the structure of a relationship are typically made at the point of hire, before the circumstances that might give rise to a dispute are known. Does this give firms a reason to be intentionally vague about the status of their workforce? *Natkin* suggests that one must take the bitter with the sweet: "Harpo may not obtain the benefits associated with hiring an independent contractor and, at the same time, enjoy the advantages of treating that person as an employee; it must choose." On the other hand, the *Fitzgerald* court was willing to look beyond Mobil Oil's express disclaimer of an employer/employee relationship.

And at least some workers have similarly conflicting incentives. In a famous case litigated in the 1990s, workers originally hired by Microsoft Corporation to perform various technical services — including editing, proofreading, and testing — claimed that they were employees entitled to take advantage (retroactively) of the firm's lucrative profit sharing plans, even though they had signed agreements expressly stating that they were "independent contractors" not entitled to participate. *See Vizcaino v. Microsoft Corporation*, 120 F.3d 1006 (9th Cir. 1997) (en banc). Of course, Microsoft had various incentives to classify the workers originally as independent contractors, including avoiding a number of tax obligations. But the workers also arguably benefited from this arrangement since they did not have taxes and other amounts withheld from their paychecks. Indeed, the workers did not complain about their status or their exclusion from the plans until after the Internal Revenue Service ("IRS") determined, applying its own variation of the common-law test in a separate dispute with Microsoft, that they were employees for tax purposes. After a long series of twists and turns, the workers achieved a partial victory, and Microsoft agreed to pay the class $97 million. *See Employee Benefits — Contingent Workforce: Microsoft to Pay $97 Million to Settle Temporary Workers' Class Action Lawsuits*, 69 U.S.L.W. 2363 (Dec. 19, 2000).

The parties in *Microsoft* wanted to have it both ways: Microsoft wanted to exercise fairly exacting control over workers, but wanted them treated as independent contractors for various reasons; the workers seemingly benefited in some ways from this arrangement, but later wanted to be treated as employees for other purposes. Despite this, the parties had not left the relationship ambiguous. On the contrary, they had expressly agreed up front that the workers were independent contractors. Should the workers have been held to the terms to which they initially agreed, just as Harpo Productions was in *Natkin*? What might justify the different outcome? Note that, whether the terms to which the parties had initially agreed were enforced or not, the prevailing party in *Microsoft* was going to have succeeded in having it both ways, at least to some extent.

Still, some types of alleged benefits workers receive from initial misclassification might constitute a setoff against damages in some circumstances. For example, this has been an issue in the recent wave of wage and hour litigation involving the employment status of exotic dancers, who frequently sign contracts with clubs stating that they are independent contractors but will retain a substantial portion of the performance fees they receive from customers. Courts have differed on whether and when these fees can constitute an offset against unpaid wages (under an unjust enrichment theory or otherwise) if the dancers are found to be employees. *Compare Doe v. Cin-Lan, Inc.*, No. 08-cv-12719, 2010 WL 726710 (E.D. Mich. Feb. 24, 2010) (refusing to dismiss breach of contract and unjust enrichment counterclaims brought by a strip club for return of dance fees as an offset in an exotic dancer's wage and hour suit brought under the FLSA and Michigan law; the club alleged that it had offered the dancer the opportunity to perform as an employee or an independent contractor, and, in a written contract, the dancer had opted for the latter, thereby retaining a substantial portion of the dance fees after paying portion to the club in the form of rent) *with Hart v. Rick's Cabaret Intern., Inc.*, 967 F. Supp. 2d 901 (S.D.N.Y. 2014) (refusing to recognize the club's unjust enrichment theory because the fees were not mandatory and because, in the face of law determining dancers elsewhere are employees, the club took the risk by misclassifying its dancers, and therefore, the court could not, in "equity and good conscience" allow the club to use an unjust enrichment theory to offset unpaid wages).

2. *Contracting to Have It Both Ways.* The last question addresses again the core issue of what role contract or party intent or expectations should play in defining the nature of the relationship between worker and firm. Now take this inquiry one step further. Suppose that, rather than leaving aspects of the relationship vague, an agreement provides unambiguously that a worker is an employee for purposes of workers' compensation and intellectual property laws, but an independent contractor for all other purposes. Should a court enforce the agreement, or are there reasons the law ought not to permit the parties to define their relationship in this way? To what extent do the stakes—that is, what and whose interest(s) the underlying legal doctrine is designed to protect—matter, if at all?

3. *Protecting Interests Despite Employee/Independent Contractor Status.* Although there are limits on firms' ability to disclaim employment status, parties can contract in some circumstances to avoid the default consequences of that relationship. For example, assuming the workers in *Natkin* were independent contractors, how might the firm have still protected its interests? If Harpo Productions could have protected its rights in the photographs, then is this case simply an example of poor planning?

In fact, not all consequences of relationship status may be altered or eliminated by contract. For example, an independent contractor cannot bargain for protection under federal antidiscrimination laws. The worker may bargain for some similar protections, for example, a just-cause term that explicitly or implicitly prohibits termination based on age, race, or sex, but that would not enable her to sue under the federal statutes. Likewise, once a firm is found to be a covered employer, it cannot bargain its way out of federal prohibitions on status discrimination. *See* Chapters 9 and 10. Nor can employers or employees waive the wage and hour requirements of the FLSA, via contract or otherwise. *See* Chapter 11. And, obviously, many third parties (including tort victims) will have no opportunity to contract around the legal implications of a worker's employment status. Thus, although private ordering can virtually eliminate the legal consequences of employment status in some contexts and ameliorate them in others, the status of the relationship still has enormous implications.

4. *Worker Status and Socioeconomic Considerations.* Distinctions that reflect the socioeconomic class of workers—skilled and unskilled, managerial and nonmanagerial, white collar and blue collar, permanent and temporary—pervade employment law and policy discussions. Consider the differences between the workers in *McCary* and *Fitzgerald* as compared to *Natkin*, and how the benefits and costs of employment status align with the workers' socioeconomic status in those cases. On balance, most workers, and particularly lower-skilled workers, probably would choose employee status over being an independent contractor or a worker hired through an independent supplier of labor. This is not simply because of the legal protections described above but also because regular employees tend to have greater job, hour, and wage stability, and better benefits. On the other hand, workers with skills or knowledge in high demand may benefit (personally, professionally, and economically) from the greater control and flexibility independent contractor status may afford. Indeed, workers with creative skills like the photographers in *Natkin* and those with established customer relationships, such as sales people or those providing direct professional services directly to customers, may have incentives to retain as much independence as possible. The workers in *Microsoft* might fall somewhere in the middle, since they have technical skills but not highly valuable talents or customer connections.

Given the differing market value, bargaining power, and vulnerabilities of such workers, should the role of contract in determining worker status also vary by workers' socioeconomic class? In which circumstances would a firm's "having it both ways" be more troublesome? Do the courts agree?

   5. *Other Costs of Employment for Potential Employers.* As we have seen, a firm often has strong employment-law-related reasons to avoid hiring "employees." Yet other regulatory regimes create further incentives to hire independent contractors or outsource labor to independent subcontracting firms. As the *Microsoft* case suggests, one is the avoidance of employment-related tax withholding and payment requirements, including income, FICA, and unemployment taxes. Indeed, firm avoidance of such obligations through "misclassification" of workers as independent contractors costs federal and state governments billions of dollars in tax revenue each year, and recently has led to enhanced enforcement efforts as well as some high-profile disputes. *See, e.g.,* LINDA H. DONAHUE ET AL., THE COST OF WORKER MISCLASSIFICATION IN NEW YORK STATE (Feb. 2007), *available at* http://digitalcommons.ilr.cornell.edu/cgi/viewcontent.cgi?article=1009&context=reports (finding that misclassification of workers as independent contractors in New York has a significant adverse impact on state and federal tax revenues); Steven Greenhouse, *U.S. Cracks Down on "Contractors" as a Tax Dodge,* N.Y. TIMES, Feb. 17, 2010, at A1; Greg Morcroft, *IRS Orders FedEx to Pay $319 Mln,* MARKETWATCH (December 22, 2007), *available at* http://www.marketwatch.com/news/story/irs-orders-fedex-pay319/story.aspx?-guid=%7B4270B177-25A2-4939-8535-A3C3749F7AEB%7D. California is one of the states that have become more aggressive in seeking to prevent misclassification. In 2011, it enacted legislation imposing significant penalties ($5,000 to $25,000 per violation) on employers that willfully misclassify workers as independent contractors. *See* CAL. LAB. CODE § 226.8 (West 2013). Other states recently have teamed with the Department of Labor to enhance enforcement and reduce misclassification. *See* Department of Labor, News Release, *US Labor Department Signs Agreements with NY Labor Department and NY Attorney General's Office to Reduce Misclassification of Employees* (November 18, 2013), http:// http://www.dol.gov/opa/media/press/whd/WHD20132180.htm.

   Another such regime is the Immigration Reform and Control Act of 1986 ("IRCA"), 8 U.S.C. §§ 1324a et seq. (2014). The Act prohibits employers from knowingly hiring or retaining workers who are "unauthorized aliens." It also requires employers to examine specific documents that establish worker identity and authorization to work in the United States. Hired workers, in turn, must provide the documentation required and also attest in writing (on Form I-9) that they are a U.S. citizen, an alien lawfully admitted to permanent residence, or an alien otherwise authorized to work. The employer must retain the Form I-9 and make it available for inspection by the Immigration and Naturalization Service.

   By outsourcing to a labor contractor, a firm can reduce the risk of violating IRCA (it remains liable only if it knows a worker is unauthorized), avoid compliance costs, and, often at the same time, reduce labor costs. Unlike the legal protections for employees described above, at least some workers — those that are in the country illegally or at least not authorized to work here — have strong incentives to participate in this arrangement when, as is often the case in certain industries, the subcontracting firm is less likely to demand or scrutinize documentation. *See, e.g.,* John A. Pearce II, *The Dangerous Intersection of Independent Contractor Law and the Immigration Reform and Control Act: The Impact of the Wal-Mart Settlement,* 10 LEWIS & CLARK L. REV. 597 (2006); Steven Greenhouse, *Wal-Mart Raids by U.S. Aimed at Illegal Aliens,* N.Y. TIMES, Oct. 24, 2003, at A1. As discussed below, however, the downside for these workers is that such subcontracting firms may also be less likely to comply with other legal mandates, including wage and hour laws, and, as undocumented workers, they may be functionally unable to vindicate these rights. *See* Steven Greenhouse, *Among Janitors, Labor Violations Go with the Job*, N.Y. Times, July 13, 2005, at A1.

6. *Why Are There Still So Many Employees?* Despite the many forgoing disincentives, firms and government agencies may have nonlegal incentives to hire workers as employees. Among these are worker preferences for employment, which matter in competitive markets for labor; economies of scale and other efficiencies; the productivity-enhancing or synergistic effects of intra-firm interaction; greater retention of sensitive or valuable information or techniques; and worker morale and a heightened sense of ownership over firm objectives.

But perhaps the most important overarching reason for choosing to employ workers rather than outsource or contract with independents is to exercise greater control over worker activities. Control over the enterprise — over the various aspects of the creation, production, marketing, sale, and/or distribution of the goods, services, and information the firm or agency provides — has enormous value. When control over work details or daily affairs is less valuable, for example, where work activities require few skills or no particularized training or where sufficient quality can be maintained without close supervision, outsourcing to independent workers or firms may be an attractive option (particularly when such outsourcing reduces costs). Yet when the exercise of more exacting control is perceived as necessary to maintain quality or content, preserve confidentiality, retain good will, ensure coordination between components of the enterprise, or reduce business or legal risks, hiring workers as employees may be preferable.

7. *Control and the Limits of Planning.* The centrality of control in the stakes of employment should now be apparent. Recall the cases we have seen so far: Although each articulates a slightly different test or standard for determining whether one is an employee or independent contractor, *all focus on the level of firm control over the activities of the worker.* Each test includes one or more factors that mention control explicitly, and most other factors address aspects of control, including supervisory authority, the power to terminate, and dominion over tools, tasks, the workspace, etc. This means that party expectations regarding the nature of the relationship, whether embodied in an agreement or not, often will not be dispositive in the face of countervailing facts about who exercises control over the worker's performance. Again, the *Microsoft* case provides an example. Microsoft and the workers expressly agreed that the workers were independent contractors, yet, in practice, Microsoft treated them much like its ordinary employees — that is, it integrated them into its regular workforce and exercised significant control over their work. This resulted in the IRS's determination and Microsoft's later concession in the litigation with the workers that they were in fact "employees" for legal purposes. *See Vizcaino*, 120 F.3d, at 1008-10. Thus, although there are strong legal incentives for firms to avoid employer status, the need for control is a key incentive for employing workers rather than outsourcing. As the cases suggest, this tension between firm incentives to exercise control and incentives to avoid the legal consequences of employment creates difficult planning challenges. It also accounts for many of the thousands of cases addressing independent contractor/employee status.

8. *The Common-Law Approach Critiqued.* The common-law approach to determining employment status across areas of employment regulation is problematic for a number of reasons. First, as the cases above illustrate, the test and its derivatives are highly fact-intensive and therefore often create uncertainties regarding the relationship. These uncertainties may impose real costs on both workers and firms: They increase ex ante planning and risk management costs and ex post costs, including the costs of litigation. Indeed, this lack of predictability may be particularly problematic for workers who have legitimate expectations — e.g., of workers' compensation coverage for workplace injuries — which ultimately are defeated ex post.

However, one should consider the counterargument: While bright-line rules offer greater predictability, there may be no bright line to draw, and thus, any such rule may suffer from over- or underinclusiveness. Having reviewed the material, isn't it clear that there is no phenomenon we can label "employment," but rather that the law pastes the term on situations in which it wants particular results to follow (or denies that label in situations in which other results are more desirable)? In addition, unless it is well calibrated to serve the remedial or other purposes of the underlying employment doctrine, a clearer but less fact-intensive rule may defeat these purposes; for example, if employment status were determined by the parties' agreement or firm-worker intent alone, firms often would be able to avoid altogether the strictures of wage and hour, and antidiscrimination laws.

A second, frequent criticism of the common-law test is that it was originally intended to draw a distinction between employees and independent contractors only for determining whether the worker's principal is liable under the doctrine of respondeat superior to a third party harmed by the workers' tortious conduct. Indeed, this is why the level of control is so central in the analysis: Tort and agency law seek to link legal accountability with control. Yet other forms of employment regulation serve different ends. Because the regimes discussed in this book — e.g., wage and hour protections, antidiscrimination laws, and whistleblower protections — advance social policies separate and distinct from the ends that respondeat superior was designed to serve, the common-law definition is ill-suited to determine who is subject to such regulation. *See, e.g.,* Steven F. Befort, *Revisiting the Black Hole of Workplace Regulation: A Historical and Comparative Perspective of Contingent Work*, 24 BERKELEY J. EMP. & LAB. L. 153, 168 (2003); Dennis R. Nolan et al., *Working Group on Chapter 1 of the Proposed Restatement of Employment Law: Existence of Employment Relationship*, 13 EMP. RTS. & EMP. POL'Y 43 (2009); Lewis L. Maltby & David C. Yamada, *Beyond "Economic Realities": The Case for Amending Federal Employment Discrimination Laws to Include Independent Contractors*, 38 B.C. L. REV. 239, 241 (1997).

In his concurrence in a case in which the Seventh Circuit held that migrant agriculture workers hired to pick cucumbers were "employees" under the FLSA and, hence, entitled to minimum wage protection, Judge Easterbrook offers such a critique:

> [The independent contractor doctrine] is a branch of tort law, designed to identify who is answerable for a wrong (and therefore, indirectly, to determine who must take care to prevent injuries). To say "X is an independent contractor" is to say that the chain of vicarious liability runs from X's employees to X but stops there. . . . All the details of the common law independent contractor doctrine having to do with the right to control the work are addressed to identifying the best monitor and precaution-taker. . . . The reasons for blocking vicarious liability at a particular point have nothing to do with the functions of the FLSA.

Secretary of Labor v. Lauritzen, 835 F.2d 1529, 1544-45 (7th Cir. 1987) (Easterbrook, J., concurring). What then should be the test for employee status under the

FLSA? Judge Easterbrook suggests that the inquiry ought to reflect the purposes of the FLSA and that, thus, the statute should cover all workers (common-law "employees" or not) with few or no skills — those "who possess *only* dedication, honesty, and good health." *Id*. at 145. Is this approach more appropriate than the common law or related economic reality approach? Are there other problems to his approach? And, should the definition of employee and employer under the FLSA be different from other federal employee protections?

All of this leads to a further question: When, if ever, should the statutory purpose trump the Supreme Court's repeated insistence that Congress's use of "employee" without meaningful gloss effectively incorporates the common law by reference? Consider, for example, whether the court correctly determined in *Lerohl v. Friends of Minnesota Sinfonia*, 322 F.3d 486 (8th Cir. 2003), that two female musicians were independent contractors of the symphony for which they performed regularly (until they were terminated) and therefore were unable to claim sex and disability discrimination under Title VII and the ADA. In analyzing the workers' status, the court purported to apply the factors set forth in § 220(2) of the RESTATEMENT (SECOND) OF AGENCY. In so doing, it recognized that the symphony's conductor exercised significant, almost exclusive, control over the work itself, namely, the production of music in rehearsals and concerts. Yet because the musicians were highly skilled professionals, required no on-the-job training, retained the discretion to play for others, could reject playing in particular performances (upon adequate notice), and were not treated as employees for tax and benefit purposes, the court found that they were not employees as a matter of law. Outcomes in other cases involving the employment status of musicians and performance artists are mixed. *Compare Alberty-Velez v. Corporacion de P.R. para la Difusion Publica*, 361 F.3d 1 (1st Cir. 2004) (holding that the host and producer of a local television show was an independent contractor and thus could not sue the station for discrimination under Title VII), *with Jackson v. Gaylord Entertainment Co*, 2007 U.S. Dist. LEXIS 92514 (M.D. Tenn. Dec. 14, 2007) (finding sufficient facts to support the contention that a performer at the Grand Old Opry was an employee for statutory purposes and distinguishing *Lerohl* because of the terms of the written agreement in this case suggesting employment) and *Lancaster Symphony Orchestra*, 357 NLRB No. 152 (2011) (in finding that members of the orchestra were employees for federal labor law purposes, the National Labor Relations Board distinguished the facts in *Lerohl* as well as noted that *Lerohl* was decided under a different statutory regime).

Whether the outcome in *Lerohl* was correct even under the common-law approach is debatable. *See* Jeff Clement, Lerohl v. Friends of Minnesota Sinfonia: *An Out of Tune Definition of "Employee" Keeps Freelance Musicians from Being Covered by Title VII*, 3 DEPAUL BUS. & COM. L.J. 489 (2005). Nevertheless, in the status discrimination context, it is not readily apparent why protection ought to hinge on such a balance of control and worker independence. *See generally* Lewis L. Maltby & David C. Yamada, *Beyond Economic Realities: The Case for Amending Federal Employment Discrimination Laws to Include Independent Contractors*, 38 B.C. L. REV. 239, 241-42 (1997). Should workers who are somewhat less controlled by those for whom they work or are less economically dependent because of their skills be unprotected from, say, sex discrimination? Or should these protections not hinge on such distinctions? There is some effort in this direction with regard to protecting student interns. *See* page 28. Is there a more appropriate way to determine who ought to be free from discrimination in paid work?

9. *"Covered Employees."* Not all employees fall within the coverage of every employment regulation. Limitations on the "protected class" in certain antidiscrimination statutes provide an obvious example. *See, e.g.*, ADEA, 29 U.S.C. § 631(a) (2014) (defining "age" to include only those 40 years of age or older); ADA, 42 U.S.C. § 12112(b)(5) (2014) (stating that the duty to reasonably accommodate under the ADA is owed to one who is a "qualified individual with a disability"). In addition, the FMLA excludes new employees and part-time workers, *see* Chapter 10, and the FLSA exempts many professional employees from its minimum wage and overtime protections, *see* Chapter 11.

Note on the Rise of Work at (or Beyond) the Edges of Employment

Among the most debated topics in employment law is whether and how to address the precipitous growth of work relationships that do not fit the traditional conception of employment. Although this discussion focuses on what we characterize as the edges of employment, it should not be viewed as unimportant since it implicates tens of millions of workers and tens of thousands of workplaces.

The Contingent Workforce

Much of the conversation centers on so-called contingent workers. This term encompasses a range of workers in different industries who, for one reason or another, have a less permanent relationship with the firm or government agency for which they work than the "typical" employee. It is, therefore, merely descriptive, having no uniform definition, and one's status as a contingent worker has no independent legal significance. These workers may be short-term employees or independent contractors of the primary firm, or may work (again, as employees or independent contractors) for another firm — a temporary help agency, labor subcontractor, or some other kind of intermediary — that performs services for the primary firm. Indeed, each of the workers at issue in the three cases in the last section (Myrick, Fitzgerald, Natkin, and Green) could be viewed as a "contingent worker."

Although the parameters of contingent work are far from clear, the growth and plight of contingent workers as a class has been the subject of intense scholarly interest. *See, e.g.*, DAVID WEIL, THE FISSURED WORKPLACE 271-74 (2014); Steven F. Befort, *Revisiting the Black Hole of Workplace Regulation: A Historical and Comparative Perspective of Contingent Work*, 1 BERKELEY J. EMP. & LAB. L. 153 (2003); Kenneth G. Dau-Schmidt, *The Labor Market Transformed: Adapting Labor and Employment Law to the Rise of the Contingent Work Force*, 52 WASH & LEE L. REV. 879 (1995); *see also* Matthew Bidwell, *Do Peripheral Workers Do Peripheral Work?: Comparing the Use of Highly Skilled Contractors and Regular Employees*, 62 INDUS. & LAB. REL. REV. 200 (2009). However defined, the contingent workforce has grown faster than the overall workforce in the last several decades, and it now accounts for over 30 percent of American workers. *See, e.g.*, Government Accountability Office, *Employment Arrangements: Improved Outreach Could Help Ensure Proper Worker Classification* 3 (July 2006) (discussing the size and nature of the contingent workforce); WEIL, *supra*, at 271-73 (same); Gideon Kunda et al., *Why Do Contractors Contract? The Experience of Highly Skilled Technical Professionals in a Contingent Labor Market*, 55 INDUS. & LAB. REL. REV. 234, 235 (2002) (discussing the dramatic growth in the contingent labor force in the late twentieth century). Moreover, the economic uncertainty and other conditions that have prevailed since the downturn of 2008 may have further accelerated the trend toward contingent work relationships. *See, e.g.*, Michael Luo, *Recession Adds to Appeal of Short-Term Jobs*, N.Y. TIMES, Apr. 19, 2010, at A14; *see also* Michael Grabell, *The Expendables: How the Temps Who Power Corporate Giants Are Getting Crushed*, PROPUBLICA (June 27, 2013), *available at* http://www.propublica.org/article/the-expendables-how-the-temps-who-power-corporate-giants-are-getting-crushe (documenting the tremendous growth of temporary workers in recent years and the legal and other consequences of this trend).

For the same reasons that firms may prefer contingent workers, many workers' interests may be harmed by such relationships. For example, on average, contingent workers receive lower wages and fewer benefits — vacation, disability insurance, medical coverage, etc. — than ordinary employees, and have less wage stability than their counterparts in more traditional employment relationships. *See, e.g.*, Eileen Silverstein & Peter Goselin, *Intentionally Impermanent Employment and the Paradox of Productivity*, 26 STETSON L. REV. 1, 5-10 (1996). *See also* Arindrajit Dube & Ethan Kaplan, *Does Outsourcing Reduce Wages in the Low-Wage Service Occupations? Evidence from Janitors and Guards*, 63 INDUS. & LAB. REL. REV. 287 (2010) (finding that outsourcing has the effect of reducing wages and benefits for janitors and security guards). Given all of this and the fact that members of this group tend to have lower skills, they are more likely to be on the economic margins. They are also disproportionately female and African American. *See, e.g.*, Befort, *supra*, at 164; *see also* Michelle A. Travis, *Telecommuting: The Escher Stairway of Work/Family Conflict*, 55 ME. L. REV. 261 (2003) (discussing how one form of contingent work — telecommuting — is producing greater gender inequalities).

An example of how temporary or occasional workers are denied the benefits to which "regular" employees are entitled is contained in Connecticut's recently enacted paid sick leave mandate. *See* 2011 Conn. Acts 11-52. (Reg. Sess.), *available at* http://www.cga.ct.gov/2011/ACT/PA/2011PA-00052-R00SB-00913-PA.htm. Although this mandate provides groundbreaking protection for many employees working for large firms, it explicitly excludes "day and temporary workers" from its coverage. While the law does not treat these workers as either a single or distinct group, recent litigation in a few areas of employment law addresses issues facing many contingent working relationships. One involves the wage and overtime protections of the Fair Labor Standards Act — *Ansoumana v. Gristede's Operating Corp.*, 255 F. Supp. 2d 184 (S.D.N.Y. 2003), reproduced at page 34, is a good example. But the vexing question is whether and how employment law ought to be reformed to confront more holistically the policy issues raised by the tremendous growth of these kinds of work arrangements. *See, e.g.*, Katherine V. W. Stone, *The New Psychological Contract: Implications of the Changing Workplace for Labor and Employment Law*, 48 U.C.L.A. L. REV. 519, 572-76 (2001) (discussing some of the implications of the changing nature of the workforce for existing workplace regulation).

The Treatment of Volunteers and Students

A related phenomenon that has received much recent attention is the employment status of workers who are not paid wages for the services they provide, including volunteers, student interns, and scholarship athletes. To begin with, although when volunteers can qualify as "employees" is not a new issue, it has produced some recent litigation. For example, with regard to antidiscrimination laws, remuneration is at least a factor (and in some jurisdictions a dispositive one) courts consider in determining whether a worker is an employee, although volunteers that receive no wage or salary can still be employees if they receive other types of benefits — e.g., workers' compensation, insurance or pension benefits, or certification. *See, e.g., Bryson v. Middlefield Volunteer Fire Dept., Inc.*, 656 F.3d 348 (6th Cir. 2011) (remanding to the district court the issue of whether volunteer firefighters count as employees for determining whether a volunteer fire department that is a nonprofit organization has enough employees to be covered by Title VII). *But see Juino v. Livingston Parish Fire Dist. No. 5*, 717 F.3d 431 (5th Cir. 2013) (remuneration is not merely a factor to be considered in deciding whether an individual is an employee but rather a threshold requirement). The new Restatement of Employment Law takes the position that an individual is a volunteer and *not* an employee "if the individual renders uncoerced services without being offered a material inducement." RESTATEMENT (THIRD) OF EMPLOYMENT LAW (Proposed Final Draft, April 18, 2014) § 1.02. The tension in this formulation is scope of "uncoerced services" and what constitutes an offer of a material inducement. For a discussion of the status of volunteers under various employment laws, *see* Mitchell H. Rubinstein, *Our Nation's Forgotten Workers: The Unprotected Volunteers*, 9 U. PA. J. LAB. & EMP. L. 147 (2006).

Another particularly hot topic is the extent to which unpaid internships, purportedly for educational purposes, violate wage and hour laws. Controversy over such internships in for-profit firms for domestic college students and graduates, as well as foreign students, has received growing media attention in recent years. *See, e.g., Steven Greenhouse, Jobs Few, Grads Flock to Unpaid Internships*, NY TIMES, May 5, 2012, at A1, *available at* http://www.nytimes.com/2012/05/06/business/unpaid-internships-dont-always-deliver.html?pagewanted=2&_r=0. And some have called for a re-examination of internships in nonprofits and government agencies as well. *See, e.g.*, Anthony J. Tucci, Note, *Worthy Exemption? Examining How the DOL Should Apply the FLSA to Unpaid Interns at Nonprofits and Public Agencies*, 97 IOWA L. REV. 1363 (2012).

In 2010, the Department of Labor issued new guidance on when unpaid internships in the for-profit private sector constitute an exception to the Fair Labor Standards Act's wage and hour requirements — that is, whether interns are covered employees under the act. *See* DOL, Wage and Hour Division, *Fact Sheet #71, Internship Programs Under the Fair Labor Standards Act* (April 2010), *available at* http://www.dol.gov/whd/regs/compliance/whdfs71.htm. The guidance provides a six-factor test, focused largely on whether the internship is genuinely educational in nature and whether the intern, as opposed to the firm, is the primary beneficiary. If the internship displaces work otherwise performed by employees in the firm's operations or is used as a trial period for employment with the firm, it is unlikely to survive scrutiny. The DOL emphasized that, because unpaid internships are an exception to the FLSA's mandates, their scope should be construed narrowly; thus, a firm can demonstrate it is not an employer of an intern only if all of the factors listed are met. *See id.* In contrast, however, the Department of Labor recently sent a letter to the ABA approving internships in law firms so long as the students worked on pro bono matters and some safeguards were in place. http://www.americanbar.org/content/dam/aba/images/news/PDF/ MPS_Letter_reFLSA_091213.pdf. Moreover, at least one circuit court recently refused to adopt this kind of onerous test in the context of determining whether a student was an employee or "trainee" of a boarding school he attended (which had mandated he perform various work tasks), opting instead for a more flexible "primary beneficiary" analysis that focuses on whether the student or the entity is the primary beneficiary of the internship. *See Solis v. Laurelbrook Sanitarium & Sch., Inc.*, 642 F.3d 518, 524 (6th Cir. 2011).

Nevertheless, a growing number of current and former interns are filing lawsuits alleging employee status and seeking unpaid wages for work performed during the internship. A well-publicized example in the entertainment industry — which is among the industries known for having large numbers of unpaid interns — involves claims brought by interns who worked on production and post-production of the movie *Black Swan*. In *Glatt v. Fox Searchlight Pictures Inc.*, 293 F.R.D. 516 (S.D.N.Y. 2013), the district court granted plaintiffs' motions for summary judgment on the question of whether they were employees of the production companies. After a detailed review of the facts in the case, utilizing the DOL guidance mentioned above and relying on the analysis in *Walling v. Portland Terminal Co.*, 330 U.S. 148 (1947) (which carved out the narrow "trainee exception" on which the guidance is premised), the court concluded as follows:

> Considering the totality of the circumstances, [the interns] were classified improperly as unpaid interns and are "employees" covered by the FLSA and NYLL. They worked as paid employees work, providing an immediate advantage to their employer and performing low-level tasks not requiring specialized training. The benefits they may have received — such as knowledge of how a production or accounting office functions or references for future jobs — are the results of simply having worked as any other employee works, not of internships designed to be uniquely educational to the interns and of little utility to the employer. They received nothing approximating the education they would receive in an academic setting or vocational school. . . . [The interns] do not fall within the narrow "trainee" exception to the FLSA's broad coverage.

Glatt, 293 F.R.D. at 534. The court also conditionally granted another intern's motion for certification of a class of unpaid interns who worked on the production during the same period. *See id.* at 538. At the time this book went to press, the *Glatt* decision was on appeal.

At the same time we observe growing litigation over the employment status of unpaid interns, states have begun to enact laws providing nonemployee interns with some employee-like protections. While these statutes obviously do not mandate wages or wage levels, they do provide employment-like antidiscrimination and antiretaliation protections. *See, e.g.*, 2014 N.Y. Sess. Laws Ch. 97 (McKinney); OR. REV. STAT. §659A.350 (2014). *But see Masri v. State of Wisconsin Lab. and Indus. Rev. Comm'n*, 850 N.W.2d 298 (2014) (holding that an unpaid intern cannot state a claim under a Wisconsin whistleblower statute because she received no compensation or tangible benefits and therefore was not an employee).

A further area of recent controversy is the employment status of scholarship college athletes, particularly in revenue-generating sports (usually football and basketball). Of course, unlike volunteers and unpaid interns, such athletes receive a financial benefit for their participation in the form of scholarship grants. Nevertheless, the issue remains whether such participation constitutes employment. This question made front-page headlines when, in response to a petition by the College Athletes Players Association (CAPA), the National Labor Relations Board's regional director in

Chicago held that students who were on athletic scholarships to play football for Northwestern University were employees within the meaning of the Act. Northwestern University, Case 13–RC–121359, 2014 WL 1246914 (N.L.R.B.) (March 26, 2014). In reaching this conclusion, the director noted that these players received significant sums for playing and the university received a substantial economic benefit from their services — tens of millions of dollars over the prior decade. In addition, the players devoted a considerable amount of time to their athletic training and performance, at times much more than they devoted to their academic work. Moreover, the players were subject to strict and extensive control by the coaching staff, who also wielded the authority to terminate their scholarships. At the same time, the director found distinguishable *Brown University*, 342 N.L.R.B. 483 (2004), an earlier NLRB precedent finding graduate assistants are not employees under the National Labor Relations Act because their teaching was an integral part of their educational program.

Following the decision, the players voted on whether to unionize, although the ballots were sequestered pending Northwestern's appeal to the full Board. As this book went to press, the matter is still before the Board, which invited briefing on a number of issues, including whether it should adhere to or overrule *Brown University*. If the Board were to affirm, the decision may have implications well beyond Northwestern and the right to unionize. For example, an obvious further question is whether, given the level of control the coaches exercised over the players' athletic and other activities, the players are also employees for wage and hour regulations and other purposes. For a discussion of the case and its potential ripple effects, *see* Steven Willborn, *College Athletes as Employees: An Overflowing Quiver*, 69 U. Miami L. Rev. ___ (forthcoming Fall 2014).

Prison Work

Generally speaking, prisoners who are required to do work in a correctional facility for purposes of punishment or rehabilitation are viewed as not being in an employment relationship with the facility. Thus, absent performance of services beyond those legitimately related to punishment or rehabilitation, prisoners are not treated as employees of the correctional institution, despite the exercise of control by the facility. Work for third parties as part of work release or other related programs, as well as work in other custodial contexts is more likely to be treated as employment. *See, e.g.*, Restatement of Employment Law, *supra*, § 1.02 cmt. c. For a history and critique of the treatment of prisoners' employee status, *see* Noah D. Zatz, *Working at the Boundaries of Markets: Prison Labor and the Economic Dimension of Employment Relationships*, 61 Vand. L. Rev. 857 (2008).

PROBLEM

1-2. Suppose you have been retained as employment counsel by Microsoft. The firm plans to launch a number of new software products over the next several years. As in earlier years, it will need a large number of code and text reviewers — proofreaders, testers, and editors — to assist in final stages of production. If possible, the firm would prefer to hire these workers as independent contractors for various reasons, including flexibility in an uncertain, post-recession economy; the fact that the workers' services will be needed only for discrete projects; its belief that many skilled reviewers might prefer such an arrangement; and the avoidance of various legal obligations to them. The firm does not know how long it might retain these workers — that will depend on how well the software products perform and how robust sales are. It concedes that it will need to maintain quality control, which will require monitoring and reviewing the workers' performance, although it does not need to oversee their work on a daily basis.

Microsoft asks you to offer your advice as to how to structure the relationships to reduce the probability that the workers might be found to be its "employees" for one or more regulatory purposes. Obviously, the firm's earlier problems with the IRS and the benefits litigation that followed loom large, and the firm wants to avoid any similar problems in the future. With that in mind, here are some additional facts — "hints" — from that case. The Ninth Circuit described the circumstances regarding the workers' tenure at Microsoft as follows:

> At various times before 1990, Microsoft hired the Workers to perform services for it. They did perform those services over a continuous period, often exceeding two years. They were hired to work on specific projects and performed a number of different functions, such as production editing, proofreading, formatting, indexing, and testing. "Microsoft fully integrated [the Workers] into its workforce: They often worked on teams along with regular employees, sharing the same supervisors, performing identical functions, and working the same core hours. Because Microsoft required that they work on site, they received admittance card keys, office equipment and supplies from the company."
>
> Microsoft did not withhold income or Federal Insurance Contribution Act taxes from the Workers' wages, and did not pay the employer's share of the FICA taxes. Moreover, Microsoft did not allow the Workers to participate in the [firm's profit sharing benefit plans]. The Workers did not complain about those arrangements at that time.

Vizcaino v. Microsoft Corporation, 120 F.3d 1006, 1008 (9th Cir. 1997) (en banc). However, the workers were treated differently in other ways:

> They had different color employee badges, different e-mail addresses, and were not invited to company parties and functions. Instead of receiving a regular paycheck from Microsoft's Payroll department (like Microsoft's regular employees), [these workers] submitted invoices for their services to the Accounts Payable department.

Id. at 1019 (O'Scannlain, concurring in part and dissenting in part). In addition, the workers signed contracts that provided, among other things, the following terms:

> CONTRACTOR is an independent contractor for [Microsoft]. Nothing in this Agreement shall be construed as creating an employer-employee relationship, or as a guarantee of a future offer of employment. CONTRACTOR further agrees to be responsible for all federal and state taxes, withholding, social security, insurance and other benefits. . . .

[A]s an Independent Contractor to Microsoft, you are self-employed and are responsible to pay all your own insurance and benefits.

Id.

What would you recommend the firm do if, in fact, it is serious about hiring "real" independent contractors to do software editing and testing? Specifically, what language and provisions should it include in its contracts with the workers, and how should it structure its interactions (e.g., pay, training, oversight, allocation of risk, and provision of office space and resources) with the workers? How confident would you be in your advice — that is, in your ability to ensure that the firm avoids its earlier fate?

B. THE FLIP SIDE: WHO IS AN "EMPLOYER"?

The prior section introduced you to the realities of the modern business enterprise. For example, fewer and fewer workers and firms are engaged in what was traditionally thought of as the standard employment relationship — that is, a (long-term) relationship in which the managers of a single firm exert exclusive control over their workers' day-to-day activities in the production of the firm's goods or services. These changes have created challenges for parties, regulators, and courts as more and more workers and entities fit less neatly into the traditional categories of independent contractor, employee, and employer. Indeed, whether they were correctly decided or not, none of the principal cases in the last section (*McCary*, *Fitzgerald*, and *Natkin*) involved what an observer from the middle of the last century would view as a typical employee-employer relationship.

While that section focused primarily on the distinction between employees and independent contractors, this section explores the obviously related questions of who is an "employer" and how to distinguish employers both from nonemployer firms and from "employees." Given the structure of the modern business enterprises, two commonly litigated issues surrounding the definition of employer are (1) to whom to extend employer status and (2) the status of firm owners — manager-owners and parent corporations.

1. "Employer" Status and Accountability for Violations in Disaggregated Enterprises

Business enterprises are now frequently splintered into smaller, independent parts. The arrangements in *McCary* and *Fitzgerald* are examples of this phenomenon — in each case, a large, end-user firm had contracted with smaller, independent firms to perform certain tasks within the enterprise, and these smaller firms then retained workers (employees or independent contractors) to provide labor. Although there are other reasons for end-user firms to outsource services and production, as you are now aware, limitations on liability for work-law violations invite these arrangements. Once limited to the margins, these kinds of structures now are present in most large enterprises, capturing many millions of workers.

Such disaggregation may create significant enforcement obstacles for workers' vindicating their work-related rights, particularly at the low end of the labor market. Smaller operations are less visible, so detection of violations by regulators and others who might offer assistance to vulnerable workers is more difficult. Moreover, workers may be left to seek remedies against an undercapitalized labor supplier, which is likely to lead to unpaid judgments, heavily discounted settlements, or unprosecuted claims. Outsourcing therefore may do more than shift legal responsibility from one firm to others: It may allow end-user firms to avoid noncompliance risks while benefitting from labor at a price discounted by the low probability of enforcement of employment-law mandates. For a detailed exploration of the disaggregation phenomenon in many sectors of the economy, as well as its legal, economic, and social consequences, *see generally* DAVID WEIL, THE FISSURED WORKPLACE (2014).

A frequently litigated question then is whether and when "employer" status — that is, legal responsibility for employment law violations — can be extended beyond the third-party labor supplier that retained the workers. As foreshadowed in the note about contingent workers, this issue now often arises in FLSA litigation (as well as suits under state wage and hour laws).

The FLSA is a Depression-era statute that requires employers to pay employees a minimum wage, as well as overtime pay for hours worked beyond a 40-hour work week. *See* 29 U.S.C.A. §§ 206(a)-(b), 207(a)(1) (2010). It also bans sex discrimination in pay for equal work, *see id.* § 206(d), and child labor, *see id.* § 212(c). Most of the planning, litigation, and public policy issues relate to the wage and hour requirements. The FLSA requires nonexempt "employees" to be paid a minimum hourly wage and receive overtime compensation at one and one half their "regular rate of pay" for hours worked in excess of 40 hours per week. The minimum wage, set by Congress, currently is $7.25 per hour, although, as discussed in Chapter 11, some states and municipalities have their own laws that set a higher minimum wage.

In most circumstances, the substantive requirements of the FLSA are straightforward; in other words, when they apply, the FLSA's wage and hour requirements are mandatory and fairly simple. Thus, FLSA litigation often focuses on the statute's coverage, including whether workers are employees or independent contractors in the first instance — as discussed in the last section — and whether employees are exempt or nonexempt, which is taken up in Chapter 11. The next case addresses who — that is, *which* firms and firm managers — are potentially accountable as "employers" or "joint employers" for unpaid wages.

Ansoumana v. Gristede's Operating Corp.
255 F. Supp. 2d 184 (S.D.N.Y. 2003)

HELLERSTEIN, District Judge.

Plaintiffs Faty Ansoumana et al., and the class they represent, were delivery workers for supermarkets and drugstore chains, including stores owned and operated by Duane Reade, Inc., a defendant. The delivery workers were hired by the Hudson/Chelsea group of defendants[1] and assigned to Duane Reade stores to make deliveries to customers and to provide general in-store services, as directed by the store supervisors. I am asked to decide, on these cross-motions for summary judgment, whether, as to the Hudson/Chelsea defendants, the plaintiffs were independent contractors or employees entitled to be paid a minimum wage and time-and-a-half for overtime and, if plaintiffs were employees, whether Duane Reade was a "joint employer," jointly obligated with the Hudson/Chelsea defendants to pay minimum wages and overtime. I will be applying, in determining the issues put to me, the Fair Labor Standards Act ("FLSA"), 29 U.S.C. §§ 201-219 (2002), and the New York Minimum Wage Act, N.Y. Lab. Law §§ 650-665 (2002).

The defendant, Duane Reade, Inc. is a large retail drugstore chain in the New York metropolitan area. Duane Reade outsourced its requirements for delivery workers by engaging the Hudson/Chelsea defendants to provide delivery workers to the Duane Reade stores, at the rate of $250 to $300 per week, per worker. The Hudson/Chelsea defendants, in turn, paid the delivery workers whom they assigned $20-$30 per day, characterizing them as independent contractors in order to avoid the minimum wage and overtime provisions of federal and New York law.

I hold in this decision that those delivery workers who were assigned to work in Duane Reade stores and made deliveries on foot were not independent contractors, that the Hudson/Chelsea defendants are liable to them for violations of the FLSA and the New York Labor law, and that Duane Reade and the Hudson/Chelsea defendants were joint employers within the meaning of those laws and were jointly and severally obligated to pay minimum wages and overtime to the delivery workers. . . .

I. Background

Plaintiffs filed this action on January 13, 2000 against three large chains of New York supermarkets and drugstores, and several companies and individuals who hired employees to work as deliverymen in such chains. Plaintiffs alleged that the defendants were operating in violation of the FLSA and the New York Minimum Wage Law. They claimed that the defendants, who had hired the delivery workers, and the chains to which they were assigned and in which they worked were jointly and severally liable to them. In May 2001, I certified a class of delivery workers and dispatchers who had worked for defendants between January 13, 1994 and May 24, 2001 and who had not been paid the minimum wage or overtime required under New York law. More than 500 delivery workers have filed consents and are participating in this lawsuit pursuant to the collective action provisions of the FLSA.

The delivery workers involved in the motion before me were hired by the Hudson/Chelsea defendants and were assigned to and worked for Duane Reade stores in Manhattan. The workers are mainly unskilled immigrants, mostly from West Africa. They provided services in the stores and made deliveries from the stores, and, despite

---

1. The group is made up of Scott Weinstein, Steven Pilavin, Hudson Delivery Service, Inc., and Chelsea Trucking, Inc. Hudson Delivery Service, Inc. is owned and operated by Weinstein, and Chelsea Trucking, Inc. is owned and operated by Pilavin, Weinstein's brother-in-law. The opinion will refer to these defendants as "the Hudson/Chelsea defendants."

working eight to eleven hours a day, six days a week, were paid a flat rate of between $20-$30 per day, well below minimum wage requirements.

The record developed in discovery shows that the Hudson/Chelsea defendants hired the delivery workers for 45 to 60 of the 200 Duane Reade stores located in Manhattan and the boroughs. By oral agreement between Duane Reade and the Hudson/Chelsea defendants, Duane Reade has depended on the Hudson/Chelsea defendants exclusively, since 1994, to supply its stores with delivery workers and has been paying the Hudson/Chelsea defendants a flat weekly rate of $250-$300 per worker. The Hudson/Chelsea defendants hired their workers essentially without advertising, from recommendations by one worker to another, and provided them with uniforms and delivery carts. Since 1989, the Hudson/Chelsea defendants have regarded their delivery workers as independent contractors, not employees, and have required some of the workers to sign statements so acknowledging. The Hudson/Chelsea defendants have not withheld federal, state, or local taxes, nor made FICA or other statutory required withholdings from the payments to the workers, and have given them IRS Forms 1099 rather than W-2s to reflect their compensation. The Hudson/Chelsea defendants did not maintain a system for tracking the delivery workers' hours or pay and did not keep records of any tips the delivery workers received.

In March 2000, the Hudson/Chelsea defendants entered into a collective bargaining agreement with those of its delivery workers who had joined Local 338, Retail, Wholesale and Department Store Workers Union, AFL-CIO. That agreement required that all employees hired by the Hudson/Chelsea defendants earn at least $5.15 an hour and time and a half for overtime. Employees assigned to drug stores are allowed $1.65 of the wage to be credited as tip allowance. Since the agreement was signed, the Hudson/Chelsea defendants have been issuing IRS Forms W-2 to their delivery workers.

The delivery workers assigned to Duane Reade stores reported to the Duane Reade store to which they had been assigned and received directions from Duane Reade personnel in that store. Generally, they were assigned to the pharmacy departments and made deliveries of pharmaceutical items to customers. Duane Reade personnel provided the pharmaceutical stickers, issued the delivery instructions and, if payment was to be collected, instructed the delivery workers how much money to bring back from the customer. The Duane Reade stores maintained logs at the stores, and the delivery workers signed in and out of the logs upon each delivery, recording deliveries and receipts. In their spare time, the delivery workers were often asked to help customers with heavy items, provided bagging services at check-out registers, helped with security, stocked shelves, and moved products from one Duane Reade store to another. If a delivery worker was unsatisfactory, the Duane Reade manager asked Hudson/Chelsea to reassign the worker and provide another to replace him. Thus, the delivery worker, although not hired or paid by Duane Reade, was directed by Duane Reade managers and supervisors and provided services essentially similar to other Duane Reade employees.

II.   Legal Framework

A.   *The Fair Labor Standards Act*

The Fair Labor Standards Act mandates that "employees" receive a minimum wage and overtime pay of time and a half of the workers' regular hourly rate for each hour worked in excess of forty hours per workweek.[2] 29 U.S.C. §§ 206(a)(1), 207(a)(1) (2002). The FLSA defines an "employee," with certain exceptions not relevant here, as "any individual employed by an employer." *Id.* § 203(e)(1). The statute in turn defines "employ" as "to suffer or permit to work," *id.* § 203(g), and "employer" to include "any person acting directly or indirectly in the interest of an employer." *Id.* § 203(d). The terms are to be expansively defined, with "striking breadth," in such a way as to "stretch . . . the meaning of 'employee' to cover some parties who might not qualify as such under a strict application of traditional agency law principles." *Nationwide Mut. Ins. Co. v. Darden*, 503 U.S. 318, 326 (1992). As the Second Circuit has ruled, the FLSA, in accordance with its remedial purpose, has been written in the "broadest possible terms," *Carter v. Dutchess Cmty. Coll.*, 735 F.2d 8, 12 (2d Cir. 1984), and is to be construed broadly, for it would run "counter to the breadth of the statute and to the Congressional intent to impose a qualification which permits an employer who exercises substantial control over a worker . . . to escape compliance with the Act."

The regulations implementing the FLSA contemplate that an employee may have more than one employer. 29 C.F.R. § 791.2(a) ("a single individual may stand in the relation of an employee to two or more employers at the same time" under the FLSA). Such "joint employment" arises when the employee "performs work which simultaneously benefits two or more employers" and "one employer is acting directly or indirectly in the interest of the other employer (or employers) in relation to the employee." 29 C.F.R. § 791.2(b). This question of joint employment of plaintiffs, by Duane Reade and by the Hudson/Chelsea defendants, is a central issue in these cross motions.

[The New York Minimum Wage Act largely tracks the FLSA, although at times it has required a higher wage than did the federal statute.]

III. Plaintiffs Are Employees of the Hudson/Chelsea Defendants

There is no dispute that the plaintiffs were hired by one or the other of Scott Weinstein, Hudson Delivery Service, Inc., Steven Pilavin, and Chelsea Trucking, Inc. (also known as Hudson York) — the defendants to whom I have been referring as "the Hudson/Chelsea defendants." These defendants also do not dispute that they may be treated interchangeably. Thus, if one corporate entity is held liable, that finding may extend to the others. There is also no dispute that the Hudson/Chelsea defendants regarded the plaintiffs as independent contractors, not employees, and until the collective bargaining agreement with Local 338, which became effective March 26, 2000, the Hudson/Chelsea defendants did not keep the records mandated for employees by the FLSA and the New York Minimum Wage Act, did not pay minimum wages or overtime, did not withhold taxes or FICA from payroll, and issued IRS Forms 1099, rather than W-2s.

An employer's characterization of an employee is not controlling, however, for otherwise there could be no enforcement of any minimum wage or overtime law.

---

2. During the class period, January 13, 1994 to May 24, 2001, the minimum wage was $4.25 until September 30, 1996, $4.75 between October 1, 1996 and August 31, 1997, and $5.15 thereafter.

There would be nothing to prevent old-fashioned labor contractors from rounding up workers willing to sell their labor cheaply, and assigning them to perform outsourced work, without complying with minimum wage requirements. Thus, not the characterization of a hiring hall, but the test of "economic reality," governs how a relationship of employment is to be characterized in relation to the FLSA.

In *Brock v. Superior Care, Inc.*, 840 F.2d 1054, 1059 (2d Cir. 1988), the Court set out an "economic reality" test to distinguish between employees and independent contractors. The test considers five factors: (1) the degree of control exercised by the employer over the workers; (2) the workers' opportunity for profit or loss and their investment in the business; (3) the degree of skill and independent initiative required to perform the work; (4) the permanence or duration of the working relationship; and (5) the extent to which the work is an integral part of the employer's business. *Brock; United States v. Silk*, 331 U.S. 704 (1947). No one factor is dispositive; the "ultimate concern" is "whether, as a matter of economic reality, the workers depend upon someone else's business for the opportunity to render service or are in business for themselves." *Brock.*

Normally, the existence and degree of each factor is a question of fact, and the legal conclusion to be drawn from those facts is a question of law. *Id.* Here, however, as the discussion below makes clear, there is no genuine issue of material fact as to plaintiffs' proper status as employees.

The Hudson/Chelsea defendants argue that they merely "placed" workers with the Duane Reade stores, and it was the store managers and supervisors, not the Hudson/Chelsea defendants, who exercised control. However, the Hudson/Chelsea defendants were more than a placement agency. Hudson/Chelsea, not Duane Reade, paid the delivery workers, and controlled their hiring, firing, transfer and pay. If a worker assigned to a Duane Reade store met with disfavor, the store manager asked the Hudson/Chelsea defendants to transfer him out and assign someone else. Moreover, the Hudson/Chelsea defendants never offered proof of any license as an employment agency, and did not function, vis-à-vis Duane Reade, in the manner of an employment agency, receiving a commission based on several weeks or months of earnings.

The Hudson/Chelsea defendants' relationship with plaintiffs satisfies the first of the *Brock* considerations, showing a substantial degree of control over the workers. As *Brock* made clear, "[a]n employer does not need to look over his workers' shoulders every day in order to exercise control." . . . The fact that the Hudson/Chelsea defendants hired, fired, transferred and paid the delivery workers weighs substantially in favor of finding an employment relationship between the Hudson/Chelsea defendants and plaintiffs.

The second consideration of *Brock* — opportunity for investment, and profit or loss — also weighs heavily in favor of an employment relationship. As defendants conceded, plaintiffs' investment in the business was negligible. Plaintiffs are not asked to invest in Duane Reade, Hudson/Chelsea, or their own jobs. Hudson/Chelsea provided the delivery workers with delivery carts that they could rent and uniforms that they could purchase; the workers did not have to make an up-front investment in such things in order to be hired or assigned to a Duane Reade store.

Hudson/Chelsea argues that delivery services require plaintiffs to exercise "skill and independent initiative," the third consideration of *Brock*, but clearly this is not so in any objective sense. The Duane Reade stores are located throughout Manhattan and the boroughs, and customers typically reside within a neighborhood of a few blocks.

Little "skill" or "initiative" is needed to find one's way from a Duane Reade store to a customer's residence.

The fourth consideration, the permanence and duration of the plaintiffs' working relationship with the Hudson/Chelsea defendants, is disputed. Plaintiffs claim that most delivery workers have been working for the Hudson/Chelsea defendants for years, but offer testimony of only four deliverymen, of approximately 500 delivery workers who opted into the lawsuit, to support their claim, and even these four had only a three-year working relationship with the Hudson/Chelsea defendants. Nevertheless, the transience of the work force here says less about the status of the worker than about the nature of the job. Many delivery workers do not endure for long periods of time in this line of work due to the long hours, the low pay, the dangers of the streets, and the vagaries of the weather inherent in delivery work. Any transience of the work force therefore reflects "the nature of [the] profession and not [the workers'] success in marketing their skills independently." *Brock.*

The fifth consideration looks at the extent to which the work is integral to the business, and it also weighs heavily in favor of an employment relationship. The Hudson/Chelsea defendants concede that they are engaged primarily in the business of providing delivery services to retail establishments and that plaintiffs perform the actual delivery work. Thus, plaintiffs' services constitute an integral part of the Hudson/Chelsea defendants' business.

It is clear, from the "economic reality" and the totality of circumstances, that the delivery workers depend upon the Hudson/Chelsea defendants for the opportunity to sell their labor and are not in any real sense in business for themselves. . . . The delivery workers, as a matter of law, are employees, not independent contractors, and are entitled to summary judgment against the Hudson/Chelsea defendants. . . .

IV. Defendants Weinstein and Pilavin Are Individually Liable as Employers

Plaintiffs argue that, along with their companies Hudson Delivery Service, Inc. and Chelsea Trucking, Inc., Scott Weinstein and Steven Pilavin are "employers," and are therefore individually liable under the FLSA for underpayments of minimum wages and overtime. Plaintiffs are correct.

Officers and owners of corporations may be deemed employers under the FLSA where "the individual has overall operational control of the corporation, possesses an ownership interest in it, controls significant functions of the business, or determines the employees' salaries and makes hiring decisions." *Lopez v. Silverman*, 14 F. Supp. 2d 405, 412 (S.D.N.Y. 1998). In *Herman v. RSR Security Services, Ltd.*, 172 F.3d 132 (2d Cir. 1999), the Second Circuit found that a shareholder and member of the board was an "employer" under the FLSA where he had the authority to hire managerial staff, occasionally supervised and controlled employee work schedules, and had the authority to sign payroll checks. The Court emphasized that "the overarching concern is whether the alleged employer possessed the power to control the workers in question," and looked at the "totality of the circumstances" in determining whether defendant had "operational control." Thus, it did not matter that the putative employer did not directly hire workers, but only managerial staff, and that he did not have direct control over the workers in question; instead, the Court looked at whether he had "operational control" over the business.

Weinstein and Pilavin argue that they should not be held individually liable for underpayments because they did not directly control the delivery workers. Clearly, however, Weinstein and Pilavin exercised operational management of Hudson Delivery and Chelsea Trucking, and that is sufficient under the law to satisfy the broad statutory definition of "employer." *See* 29 U.S.C. § 203(d). Weinstein and Pilavin are the founders, owners, and sole shareholders of Hudson Delivery Service and Chelsea Trucking, and together they personally oversee and operate the companies and their agents on a daily basis. Thus, under *Herman*, each is an "employer" under the FLSA, and can be held individually liable for failure to pay minimum wages to their employees.

Weinstein and Pilavin argue that they could not be said to exercise control over the delivery workers if Duane Reade exercised such control. This argument misses the point; as I discuss below, the FLSA recognizes joint employment, meaning that more than one employer can be responsible for FLSA obligations. Because Weinstein and Pilavin had operational control over Hudson Delivery Service and Chelsea Trucking, they are individually liable under the FLSA for any underpayments in plaintiffs' salaries. Thus, plaintiffs are entitled to summary judgment against Weinstein and Pilavin, as well as against Hudson Delivery Services, Inc. and Chelsea Trucking, Inc.

V. Duane Reade Is a Joint Employer

The FLSA contemplates that more than one employer may be responsible for underpayments of minimum wages and overtime. 29 C.F.R. § 791.2(a)-(b). Duane Reade may be liable to plaintiffs for such underpayments, jointly and severally with the Hudson/Chelsea defendants, if Duane Reade was also their "employer" under the FLSA. The issue is determined by an "economic reality" test, which takes into account the real economic relationship between the employer who uses and benefits from the services of workers and the party that hires or assigns the workers to that employer.

In *Rutherford Food Corporation v. McComb*, 331 U.S. 722 (1947), meat boners who worked on the premises of a slaughterhouse were hired by another employer under contract with the slaughterhouse, much as the delivery workers for Duane Reade were hired to work there by the Hudson/Chelsea defendants. The issue in *Rutherford* was whether the slaughterhouse should be considered the employer of the meat boners when there already was an employer, the head boner who had hired the workers, and also managed and paid them.

The Supreme Court held that the slaughterhouse was a joint employer with the head meat boner for the purpose of minimum wage obligations under the FLSA. The Supreme Court considered that the boners' work was "part of the integrated unit of production," and that the workers did a "specialty" job on the production line, integral to the entire operation of the line. It was the boners themselves, not their company, functioning like piece-workers on a production line, who used the premises and equipment of the slaughterhouse to do their work, rather than shifting from one slaughterhouse to another as "an enterprise that actually depended for success upon the initiative, judgment or foresight of the typical independent contractor."

In *Carter v. Dutchess Community College*, 735 F.2d 8, 12 (2d Cir. 1984), the Second Circuit considered a work-release program of the New York State Department of Correctional Services ("DOCS"), which assigned inmates to work at sites of private employers. The plaintiff was a prison inmate and, under a DOCS program for college graduates, was assigned to work as a teaching assistant at Dutchess County Community College ("DCC"). DOCS paid plaintiff a stipulated allotment, less than the minimum wage, and plaintiff sued under the FLSA for back wages, punitive damages, and an injunction requiring defendants to pay all tutors, including inmate tutors, the same compensation.

The Second Circuit set out a four-part set of criteria to help determine whether DOCS, or DCC, or both, were "employers" required to pay minimum wages, examining who hired and fired the workers; who supervised and controlled their work schedules and conditions of employment; who determined the rate and method of payment; and who was to maintain employment records. Applying the criteria, the Court of Appeals found that it was DCC that had initially proposed to employ prisoners and suggested the wage to pay them; that DCC had established the standards to decide who would be eligible to be a teaching assistant and had identified several inmates whom it proposed to accept; that DCC reserved the right to refuse those inmates whom it did not want; and that DCC had decided for how many sessions and for how long an inmate would be permitted to tutor. On this record, the Court of Appeals held that there were questions of fact whether DCC had exercised sufficient control over the prison inmates to make DCC an "employer" required to pay minimum wages and overtime under the FLSA. Nevertheless, even taking into account the plaintiff's status as a prisoner, the Court did not rule out the possibility that he had FLSA claims against DCC as an employer, stating that the record, while not perhaps reflecting "the full panoply of an employer's prerogatives," may be sufficient to warrant FLSA coverage.

In *Torres-Lopez v. May*, 111 F.3d 633, 642-44 (9th Cir. 1997), farm laborers were procured through a labor agent, who hired them and assigned them to a farm. The Ninth Circuit Court of Appeals found that because these laborers constituted an integral part of the farm's business and because the farm exercised indirect control over them by supervising them and controlling the harvest schedule and the number of workers it needed for harvesting, the farm was a joint employer, along with the labor agent who hired them.

Like the meat boners in *Rutherford*, [and] the farm workers in *Torres-Lopez* . . . , the delivery workers assigned to Duane Reade performed an integral service for the stores in which they worked, enabling Duane Reade to compete more effectively with mail order fulfillment companies and other drug stores by offering drug deliveries to its customers. The delivery workers worked from the premises of the Duane Reade stores, and assisted other workers in those stores with bagging items at check-out counters, stocking shelves, providing security, and making inter-store deliveries.

Duane Reade offers an analogy to Federal Express, United Parcel, and other delivery services, but the analogy is misplaced. Duane Reade's delivery workers worked out of the Duane Reade stores, and not from a central depot; deliveries were made directly from the pharmacy counters to customers' homes, and not via a central facility; and control was exercised throughout by Duane Reade, and not by some independent service. Duane Reade used the delivery workers to extend its shelves and counters to the homes of customers, allowing them the convenience of shopping from home instead of having to come physically into a store. Duane Reade managers and supervisors directed the delivery workers in their tasks, instructing them what to pick up, where to make deliveries, how to log their deliveries, and how much to receive in payment. The delivery workers worked as individuals, and not as a group shifting from store to store according to seasonal and hourly needs. Indeed, it was not until they were organized by Local 338, in March 2000, that they even had a bargaining representative to negotiate for them as a collective. Clearly, the economic reality of the relationship between Duane Reade and the delivery workers reveals that Duane Reade was an employer of the delivery workers, responsible for assuring that they were paid the wages required by the FLSA and the New York Minimum Wage Act as a condition of their employment.

Additionally, the relationship between Duane Reade and the Hudson/Chelsea defendants establishes joint employment. That relationship was "so extensive and regular as to approach exclusive agency." The Hudson/Chelsea defendants acted directly in the interest of Duane Reade in relation to the delivery workers, 29 C.F.R. §791.2, and Duane Reade used the Hudson/Chelsea defendants' services almost exclusively, for a lengthy period of years, since 1994, showing consistent dependence on them for delivery services.

I therefore hold, looking at the "circumstances of the whole activity," that plaintiffs were economically dependent on both the Hudson/Chelsea defendants and Duane Reade, and that both were their "employers" under the FLSA and the New York Minimum Wage Act. . . .

VII. Conclusion

Duane Reade had the right to "outsource" its requirement for delivery services to an independent contractor, here the Hudson/Chelsea defendants, and seek, by such outsourcing, an extra measure of efficiency and economy in providing an important and competitive service. But it did not have the right to use the practice as a way to evade its obligations under the FLSA and the New York Minimum Wage Act. Both Duane Reade and the Hudson/Chelsea defendants were the "employers" of the plaintiffs under these laws, jointly and severally obligated for underpayments of minimum wage and overtime during the period between January 13, 1994 and March 26, 2000. . . .

NOTES

1. *The FLSA and Contingent Workers.* Duane Reade's use of independent suppliers of laborers reflects the common practice of contracting out low-skilled work by large corporations and other end-user firms. *See, e.g.,* Cynthia Estlund, *Who Mops the Floors at the Fortune 500? Corporate Self-Regulation and the Low-Wage Workplace,* 12 LEWIS & CLARK L. REV. 671, 685 (2008). Avoidance of the FLSA's requirements (and corresponding liability risks) is among the most cited and controversial reasons for outsourcing. *See, e.g.,* Stephen F. Befort, *Labor and Employment Law at the Millennium: A Historical Review and Critical Assessment,* 43 B.C. L. REV. 351, 367-71 (2002); Richard R. Carlson, *Why the Law Still Can't Tell an Employee When It Sees One and How It Ought to Stop Trying,* 22 BERKELEY J. EMP. & LAB. L. 295, 360 (2001); Katherine V.W. Stone, *Legal Protections for Atypical Employees: Employment Law for Workers Without Workplaces and Employees Without Employers,* 27 BERKELEY J. EMP.

& LAB. L. 251 (2006); Alan Hyde, *Who Speaks for the Working Poor?: A Preliminary Look at the Emerging Tetralogy of Representation of Low-Wage Service Workers,* 13 CORNELL J. L. & PUB. POL'Y 599 (2004).

Although many violations go unchallenged, this phenomenon has resulted in a significant number of FLSA and state-law wage and hour suits. As exemplified by *Ansoumana,* these disputes implicate the employee/independent contractor distinction, the definition of employer and joint employer, or both. Most of these challenges have arisen in areas commonly known to be rife with wage and other employment-law violations, including delivery services, garment work, light manufacturing, janitorial services, light construction, and landscaping. Some have led to high-profile wage and hour litigation, including the claims by janitorial workers against Wal-Mart, *see e.g.,* *Zavala v. Wal-Mart Stores, Inc.,* 393 F. Supp. 2d 295 (D.N.J. 2005), and the numerous suits by drivers against FedEx, *see, e.g., In re FedEx Ground Package Sys., Inc. Employment Practices Litig.,* 2010 U.S. Dist. LEXIS 53733 (N.D. Ind. May 28, 2010) (holding that FedEx misclassified plaintiff driver as an independent contractor instead of an employee and noting that there were over 60 pending wage-related lawsuits pending against FedEx in other jurisdictions); Todd D. Saveland, *FedEx's New "Employees": Their Disgruntled Independent Contractors,* 36 TRANSP. L. J. 95 (2009). Note, however, that wage and hour claims also have emerged in unexpected contexts, such as the recent wave of claims brought by exotic dancers mentioned previously. *See also* Anna Kwidzinski, *More Exotic Dancers' Misclassification Suits Dispute Clubs' Business Model, Lawyers Say,* BLOOMBERG BNA DAILY LABOR REPORT (August 11, 2014), http://www.bna.com/exotic-dancers-misclassification-n17179893648/.

2. *Individual Liability.* The *Ansoumana* court found that Defendants Weinstein and Pilavin were "employers" under the FLSA, along with the entities they owned, because they had direct managerial control over the firms. Note that operational control, not mere ownership, is the touchstone, which means that, even in smaller or closely held entities, holding owners liable will depend on the extent and depth of such control. *Compare Gray v. Powers,* 673 F.3d 352 (5th Cir. 2012) (holding an owner/member of a limited liability company was not an "employer" potentially liable under the FLSA for wage violations because, although he had an ownership interest in the employing firm, he did not exercise operational or active control over the employees) *with Irizarry v. Catsimatidis,* 722 F.3d 99 (2d Cir. 2013) (finding that the owner of a chain of supermarkets, Catsimatidis, was an "employer" despite the fact that he was not personally responsible for the FLSA violations and the business entity was larger than others in the cases that have considered this question, because of "Catsimatidis's actions and responsibilities — particularly as demonstrated by his active exercise of overall control over the company, his ultimate responsibility for the plaintiffs' wages, his supervision of managerial employees, and his actions in individual stores").

There are a few other contexts in which individual owners and supervisors may be held individually liable for employment-law violations. Employees may have personal liability to a discrimination victim under § 1981. *See, e.g., Smith v. Bray,* 681 F.3d 888 (7th Cir. 2012); *Jemmott v. Coughlin,* 85 F.3d 61 (2d Cir. 1996). Likewise, those who engage or assist in violations of the FMLA may be subject to aiding and abetting liability or FLSA-like supervisory liability. *See* Chapter 10; *see also* 29 C.F.R. § 825.104(d) ("As under the FLSA, individuals such as corporate officers 'acting in the interest of an employer' are individually liable for any violations of the requirements of FMLA."). Individual officers and directors also are potentially liable for violations of Sarbanes-Oxley's whistleblower protections (discussed in Chapter 4). *See* 18 U.S.C. § 1514A(a) (2014). Moreover, individual employees may be liable as tortfeasors for the commonly litigated workplace torts not involving personal injury — intentional interference with contract/business advantage, defamation, intentional infliction of emotional distress, and fraud (discussed in Chapter 5). Finally, a few states have enacted narrow "veil piercing" statutes providing that certain shareholders can be held personally liable for unpaid wages. *See* N.Y. Bus. Corp. Law § 103 (McKinney 2014); Wis. Stat. Ann. § 180.0622 (West 2013).

However, under most common law and statutory schemes, only the entity (whether a partnership, limited liability company, corporation, or government agency) is the "employer." Thus, manager-owners, supervisors, and other employees within the entity generally are not subject to liability. For example, federal circuit courts are in agreement that supervisory or controlling persons are not subject to liability as employers under Title VII, the ADEA, or the ADA. *See, e.g., Butler v. City of Prairie Village*, 172 F.3d 736 (10th Cir. 1999) (ADA); *Miller v. Maxwell's Int'l, Inc.*, 991 F.2d 583 (9th Cir. 1993) (Title VII and ADEA); *see also Indest v. Freeman Decorating, Inc.*, 164 F.3d 258, 267 (5th Cir. 1999); *Hiller v. Brown*, 177 F.3d 542, 545-46 (6th Cir. 1999); *Gastineau v. Fleet Mortgage Corp.*, 137 F.3d 490, 494 (7th Cir. 1998).

What purposes does individual liability serve in circumstances like *Ansoumana*? Are such purposes unique to the FLSA and small number of other regimes that provide for individual liability? Or are there similar reasons to hold firm managers and controlling personnel liable for other firm torts and statutory violations? Consider how the risk of individual liability might alter firm incentives and affect choices regarding how to structure firm activities and manage liability risk. *See generally* Timothy P. Glynn, *Beyond "Unlimiting" Shareholder Liability: Vicarious Tort Liability for Corporate Officers*, 57 Vand. L. Rev. 329 (2004).

3. *"Joint Employer" Liability.* The court also held that Duane Reade is subject to FLSA liability as a "joint employer" because of Duane Reade's direct supervision of the plaintiffs, plaintiffs' economic dependence on it, and Duane Reade's relationship with the Hudson/Chelsea defendants. The joint employer doctrine is recognized in other contexts as well. *See, e.g.,* EEOC Compliance Manual, Section 2: Threshold Issues, No. 915.003, section 2-III.B.1.a.iii.b (discussing application of the joint employer doctrine under antidiscrimination laws); *see also* Restatement (Third) of Employment Law (Proposed Final Draft, April 18, 2014) § 1.04 (recognizing that workers can be employees of two more employers at the same time). *Compare Service Employees Intern. Union v. N.L.R.B.*, 647 F.3d 435 (2nd Cir. 2011) (applying the joint employer doctrine under the National Labor Relations Act, but affirming the National Labor Relations Board's finding that the secondary firm in this case did not exercise sufficient control over how the workers performed their work to constitute a joint employer).

In a sense, *Ansoumana* was an "easy" — or at least conventional — joint employer case, since the plaintiffs interacted directly with (and were directly supervised by) Duane Reade personnel at Duane Reade stores. But enforcement agencies and private plaintiffs have also sought to extend accountability for employment law violations in other types of enterprise arrangements in which significant control by a second entity is alleged, but there is not this kind of direct interaction with the workers. One high-profile example is the recent enforcement activity against McDonald's Corporation for underlying labor violations at its franchised stores. McDonald's owns a very small percentage of its restaurants; the vast bulk are owned independently by franchisees, and McDonald's does not directly supervise the workers at those locations. Yet, through its franchise agreements and monitoring, McDonald's protects its brand by imposing strict requirements on franchisees with regard to food, equipment, cleanliness, some employment practices, and various other matters. Indeed, the National Labor Relations Board's general counsel recently announced that he would be pursuing unfair labor practices against McDonald's for alleged labor violations occurring at some of its franchises, and the Board itself has called for briefing on the scope of the joint employer doctrine in another matter. *See* Press Release, NLRB Office of Public Affairs, *NLRB Office of the General Counsel Authorizes Complaints Against McDonald's Franchisees and Determines McDonald's, USA, LLC Is a Joint Employer* (June 29, 2014); NLRB, Notice and Invitation to File Briefs, *Browning-Ferris Indus.*, 32-RC-109684 (May 12, 2014); *see also* Stephen Greenhouse, *Ruling Says McDonald's Is Liable for Workers*, NY TIMES, July 29, 2014, at B1 (discussing the matter and its potential implications). Moreover, McDonald's has been named as a defendant in a number of wage and hour suits brought by employees working at franchised McDonald's restaurants, *see* Stephen Greenhouse, *McDonald's Workers File Wage Suits in 3 States*, NY TIMES, May 14, 2014, at B8. Although, to date, most claims against restaurant franchisors have failed for various reasons, the potential franchisor liability for unpaid wages has been recognized in a handful of other recent decisions, *see, e.g.*, *Cano v. DPNY, Inc.*, 287 F.R.D. 251, 258-59 (S.D.N.Y. 2012) (refusing to dismiss allegations of franchisor's joint employment status); *Orozco v. Plackis*, No. A11–CV–703, 2012 WL 2577522, at *8 (W.D. Tex. July 3, 2012) (same).

Is the joint employer doctrine socially beneficial, and, if so, how far should it extend? On the positive side, how might it enhance compliance? Note that one study found that wage and hour violations are much more likely to occur at franchised restaurants than those owned and operated by the branded company, suggesting that the franchise enterprise structure itself may induce noncompliance for a host of reasons — financial, reputational, and otherwise. *See* Min Woong Ji and David Weil, *Does Ownership Structure Influence Regulatory Behavior? The Impact of Franchising on Labor Standards Compliance* (2010), *available at* http://fortunedotcom.files.wordpress.com/2014/05/ franchising_and_compliance_20100716_ji_weil.pdf. On the other hand, might this kind of enterprise liability also create incentives for firms to change their operations in ways that actually harm the interests of at least some kinds of contingent workers? Relatedly, how might firms such as Duane Reade and McDonald's seek to avoid "joint employer" status?

4. *Beyond "Employer" and "Joint Employer" Liability.* Despite the significant amount of litigation discussed in Note 1 and the FLSA's reach in terms of potentially accountable "employers" and "joint employers," enforcement of wage and hour laws at the low end of the labor market remains rare and is, according to many commentators and employee rights advocates, inadequate. There are many reasons for this, including the socioeconomic vulnerability of low-wage workers; regulatory agencies' limited enforcement resources; often insufficient economic incentives for plaintiffs' attorneys to bring suit; and, as suggested above, the fact that down-enterprise labor suppliers often operate below the radar and are judgment-proof. *See generally* WEIL, *supra*, at 15-20, 215-22; Cynthia Estlund, *Rebuilding the Law of the Workplace in an Era of Self-Regulation*, 105 COLUM. L. REV. 319 (2005); Craig Becker & Paul Strauss, *Representing Low-Wage Workers in the Absence of a Class: The Peculiar Case of Section 16 of the Fair Labor Standards Act and the Underenforcement of Minimum Labor Standards*, 92 MINN. L. REV. 1317 (2006); Nanitya Ruan, *Same Law, Different Day: A Survey of the*

Last Thirty Years of Wage Litigation and Its Impact on Low-Wage Workers, 30 HOFSTRA
LAB. & EMP. L.J. 355 (2013); Noah Zatz, *Working Beyond the Reach or Grasp of
Employment Law*, in THE GLOVES-OFF ECONOMY: WORKPLACE STANDARDS AT THE BOT-
TOM OF AMERICA'S LABOR MARKET 31 (Annette Bernhardt et al. eds., Cornell University
Press 2008). But another reason is that the reach of employer and joint employer
liability, although arguably more expansive under the FLSA than elsewhere, remains
limited to firms exercising fairly detailed control over the work. *See, e.g.*, *Martinez v.
Combs*, 231 P.3d 259 (Cal. 2010) (finding produce merchants did not exercise enough
control over seasonal agricultural workers hired by an insolvent farmer to constitute
"employers" liable for unpaid wage violations under California law, despite some financial and operational integration between the merchants and the farmer).

While these concerns have resulted in various calls for regulatory and doctrinal
reform, one potentially promising approach involves expanding liability beyond controlling persons and firms — that is, beyond those who exercise sufficient control to be
deemed "employers" or "joint employers." The central idea is to counteract the powerful incentives for end-user (or top-of-the-enterprise) firms to undercut the market by
purchasing labor services over which they need not exercise exacting control from
labor suppliers that maintain low prices by violating wage laws. Although such reform
has not emerged at the federal level, a number of states have enacted provisions that
extend liability for wage violations beyond its traditional limits. *See* CAL. LAB. CODE
§ 2810(a) (Deering 2010) (holding firms in certain low-skill industries responsible for
labor violations committed by subcontractors where such violations were reasonably
foreseeable from the terms of the contract); 820 ILL. COMP. STATS. § 175(85) (2010)
(extending responsibility for staffing agency violations in certain industries to firms
purchasing such agencies' services). In addition, commentators have proposed extending liability beyond firms and persons with direct control over workers. *See generally*
WEIL, *supra*, at 184-214 (discussing various strategies for extending legal responsibility in "fissured" enterprises); Timothy P. Glynn, *Taking the Employer Out of Employment Law? Accountability for Wage and Hour Violations in an Age of Enterprise
Disaggregation*, 15 EMP. RTS. & EMP. POL'Y J. 201 (2011) (arguing that commercial
actors should be held strictly liable for wage and hour violations in the production of
any goods and services they purchase, sell, or distribute, whether directly or through
intermediaries); Brishen Rogers, *Toward Third-Party Liability for Wage Theft*, 11
BERKELEY J. EMPL. & LAB. L. 1 (2010) (proposing a third-party negligence regime
under which firms would be held to a duty of reasonable care to prevent wage and hour
violations within their domestic supply chains); Zatz, *supra*, at 31-32, 50-56 (offering
a number of proposals to expand responsibility beyond employers). *See also* Matthew
T. Bodie, *Participation as a Theory of Employment*, 89 NOTRE DAME L. REV. 661
(2014); Jeffrey M. Hirsch, *Employee or Entrepreneur?*, 68 WASH. & LEE L. REV. 353
(2011); Mitchell H. Rubinstein, *Employees, Employers, and Quasi-Employers: An Analysis of Employees and Employers Who Operate in the Borderland Between an Employer-
and-Employee Relationship*, 14 U. PA. J. BUS. L. 605 (2012).

5. *Immigration, Wages, and Wage Protections*. As the court noted, many of the
plaintiffs in *Ansoumana* were immigrants. Although the plaintiffs' immigrant status
was not central to this case, immigration and wage protection issues often are closely
linked. For example, a recurring issue in the contemporary immigration reform debate
is the effect of both documented and undocumented immigration on wages, given
that immigration has provided a steady supply of low-skilled workers, and whether that
effect (combined with other benefits and costs of immigration) is good or bad for the

country. *See, e.g.*, Harry J. Holzer, *Economic Impacts of Immigration, Testimony of Harry J. Holzer to the Committee on Education and the Workforce, U.S. House of Representatives*, Nov. 16, 2006, *available at* http://www.urban.org/url.cfm?ID=900908 (indicating that immigration depresses wages modestly, but also considering other benefits and costs of immigration); Arian Campo-Flores, *Why Americans Think (Wrongly) That Illegal Immigrants Hurt the Economy*, NEWSWEEK, May 14, 2010, at A1 (arguing that the negative effects such as straining public services and moderately depressing wages are outweighed by other positive economic and social effects).

Another concern is the plight of immigrant workers, since undocumented workers in particular are highly vulnerable to work and wage abuses. As a group, immigrants (both documented and undocumented) constitute a significant portion of the workforce at compensation levels at or near the minimum wage. *See id.* at 2-3; Randolph Capps et al., *A Profile of the Low-Wage Immigrant Workforce, in* "Immigrant Families and Workers: Facts and Perspectives": Brief No. 4, Oct. 27, 2003, *available at* http://www.urban.org/url.cfm?ID=310880 (discussing that although immigrants represent only 11 percent of all U.S. residents, they constitute 20 percent of low-wage workers). Thus, in *Ansoumana* and many similar FLSA minimum wage cases—and particularly those also involving the outsourcing of low-skilled work to subcontracting firms (which is also motivated by the IRCA, *see* page 23)—the plaintiff workers are immigrants. *See, e.g.*, Scott L. Cummings, *Hemmed In: Legal Mobilization in the Los Angeles Anti-Sweatshop Movement*, 30 BERKELEY J. EMP. & LAB. L. 1 (2009); Shirley Lung, *Exploiting the Joint Employer Doctrine: Providing a Break for Sweatshop Garment Workers*, 34 LOY. U. CHI. L.J. 291 (2003).

Whether and when undocumented workers may take advantage of federal labor and employment protections remains unresolved. For example, in *Hoffman Plastic Compounds, Inc. v. NLRB*, 535 U.S. 137 (2002), the Court held that federal immigration policy, as expressed by Congress in the Immigration Reform and Control Act of 1986, foreclosed the National Labor Relations Board from awarding back pay to an undocumented alien after the employer terminated the worker for engaging in union organizing activities. However, *Hoffman* and its reasoning may not extend to other contexts. Most notably, recent decisions have generally held that undocumented workers are entitled to full FLSA protections. *See, e.g.*, *Zavala v. Wal-Mart Stores, Inc.*, 393 F. Supp. 2d 295 (D.N.J. 2005) (holding that undocumented immigrants employed through maintenance contractors who performed janitorial services for Wal-Mart Stores were not precluded from seeking relief under FLSA on unpaid minimum wage and overtime claims). Yet even though such workers have wage protections in theory, they often cannot take advantage of them. Immigrants present or working in the country illegally face various risks, including deportation, if they seek enforcement of these protections. *See, e.g.*, Tyche Hendricks, *Worker Wins Her Rights but Loses Hope: Someone Told Feds She's Here Illegally*, S.F. CHRON., May 11, 2006. As a practical matter then, these workers often have little recourse against employer abuses.

Although there may be other reasons for hiring undocumented workers, avoiding wage and hour mandates is one obvious and problematic incentive. *See, e.g.*, Holzer, *supra*, at 3; Hendricks, *supra*. This moral hazard raises important policy and enforcement questions in both the employment and immigration areas. For further discussion of the intersection between employment law and immigration law, *see, e.g.*, Robert I. Correales, *Did* Hoffman Plastic Compounds, Inc., *Produce Disposable Workers?*, 14 LA

RAZA L.J. 103 (2003); Lori A. Nessel, *Undocumented Immigrants in the Workplace: The Fallacy of Labor Protection and the Need for Reform*, 36 HARV. C.R.-C.L. L. REV. 345 (2001); Leticia M. Saucedo, *A New "U": Organizing Victims and Protecting Immigrant Workers*, 42 U. RICH. L. REV. 891 (2008); Rebecca Smith & Catherine Ruckelshaus, *Solutions, Not Scapegoats: Abating Sweatshop Conditions for All Low-Wage Workers as a Centerpiece of Immigration Reform*, 10 N.Y.U. J. LEGIS. & PUB. POL'Y 555 (2007); Note, *Developments in the Law — Jobs and Borders: Legal Protections for Illegal Workers*, 118 HARV. L. REV. 2224 (2005).

In recent years, numbers of states have enacted legislation seeking to address undocumented workers through employment-based enforcement measures. These controversial mandates have produced a significant amount of litigation over the limits of state authority regarding immigration matters, culminating in two Supreme Court decisions. First, in *Chamber of Commerce v. Whiting*, 131 S. Ct. 1968 (2011), the Court upheld an Arizona law imposing sanctions on employers who knowingly hire undocumented workers or fail to confirm workers' status. The Court's conclusion that the Arizona mandate is not preempted by the IRCA — because it falls within that statute's preemption savings clause allowing for enforcement through licensing laws — was seen as potentially opening the door to a broad range of state-level employment-based approaches to addressing unlawful immigration. *See, e.g.*, Marisa S. Cianciarulo, *The "Arizonification" of Immigration Law: Implications of* Chamber of Commerce v. Whiting *for State and Local Immigration Legislation*, 15 HARV. LATINO L. REV. 85 (2012); Lauren Gilbert, *Immigrant Laws, Obstacle Preemption and the Lost Legacy of* McCulloch, 33 BERK. J. EMP. & L. LAW 153 (2012). The following term, however, the Court held in *Arizona v. United States*, 132 S. Ct. 2492 (2012), that federal law preempts three other provisions of Arizona law, including one that criminalized the conduct of undocumented employees (thereby going far beyond the civil sanctions for undocumented workers under the IRCA). The Arizona decision thus limits the potential reach of state immigration-related employment regulation, at least to the extent such regulation seeks to impose sanctions on undocumented workers beyond those contained in the IRCA. How *Arizona* and *Whiting* might be interpreted and applied to future workplace laws remains uncertain. For a discussion of the two decisions and their implications, *see* Stella Burch Elias, *The New Immigration Federalism*, 74 OHIO ST. L. REV. 703 (2013); Note, *Developments in the Law — State and Local Regulation of Unauthorized Immigrant Employment*, 126 HARV. L. REV. 1608 (2013).

6. *FLSA Enforcement and the Role of Unions.* The workers in *Ansoumana* got exceedingly lucky. First, although it is not mentioned in the opinion, they had the support of the National Employment Law Project and state authorities. The local retail union also successfully organized these workers into a union before the resolution of the case, although, according to one commentator, the union was unhelpful in the litigation. *See* Hyde, *supra*, at 607-08. Nevertheless, in the future, union representation might help these workers obtain and maintain greater protections.

Unionization of such workers is rare since there are practical and statutory impediments to organizing contingent workers (which you will study if you take Labor Law). And without such unionization and the rights and resources that result, this segment of the workforce has little protection at all — no statutory regulation, no access to the courts, and no collective bargaining.

7. *"Professional" Workers as Contingent Laborers.* The discussion in this section has focused primarily on low-skilled workers. Recall, however, that higher-skilled workers — such as the photographers in *Natkin* and the technical workers in *Microsoft* — also can be described as contingent laborers. There are obvious differences between such workers and those at issue in *Ansoumana* as well as differences between what was at stake in the underlying cases. Such high-skilled workers may benefit from their contingent status. Indeed, in his dissent in the *Microsoft* case, Judge O'Scannlain speculated that the plaintiffs may have enjoyed higher wages as independent contractors than they would have if they had been hired as standard employees. *See Vizcaino*, 120 F.3d at 1021. Moreover, these workers may not fit within the category of "involuntary, impermanent" contingent workers for whom commentators express the most concern.

On the other hand, just because a worker is skilled does not ensure that he or she will be treated fairly or will have the power or sophistication to bargain for alternative protections. What is to prevent an employer who saves money by hiring contract workers or through temporary staffing agencies from pocketing the difference rather than passing along a portion of that benefit to its workers in the form of higher pay? Moreover, as discussed previously, many firms have responded to hard economic times by converting employee positions to independent contractor positions, often with loss of benefits. Should differences in the professional status of workers matter in determining who is an employee or how far to extend accountability of employment-law violations?

8. *Is Enterprise Disaggregation and Contingent Work Too Socially Costly?* In light of what you have learned thus far in this chapter, consider some of the bigger questions arising from increasing enterprise disaggregation and the growth of contingent work arrangements. These phenomena are likely to have various social effects — perhaps both good and bad. Think about possible effects both within and outside the firm. Might increased reliance on contingent or third-party supplied labor harm firms' long-term productivity? Consider the court's observation in *Microsoft* that the benefits associated with employment status "guarantee a competent and happy workforce." As for the interests of the public, we have already discussed how worker misclassification may reduce tax revenues and how disaggregation may lead to greater noncompliance with employment law standards in certain sectors. Does a firm's ability to externalize certain costs by outsourcing or engaging independent contractors harm society in other ways? Consider, for instance, how our society manages the costs of a nonnegligent personal injury sustained on the job by a worker not covered by workers' compensation or the company health plan. While we might expect firms to strike the optimal balance on contingent/permanent labor with respect to their productivity and morale, they have little incentive to take account of costs borne by society, as in the personal injury example. Do such costs justify legal reform? If so, what kind?

2. Determining the Status of Firm Owners

As *Ansoumana* demonstrates, high-ranking supervisory personnel, including owner-managers, may be liable as "employers" under the FLSA and in a few other contexts, and independently chartered firms exercising sufficient control over workers employed by another entity, may be liable as "joint employers." Elsewhere, however, firm owners rarely are considered "employers" for liability purposes.

Nevertheless, unresolved questions regarding the status of firm owners remain. The most frequently litigated issue relates to individual owners: Since they usually are not employers for liability purposes, when, if ever, are owner-managers considered "employees"? The next two cases address this issue. A note at the end of this section addresses a second question: When, if ever, may an employee of a subsidiary "pierce the corporate veil" to hold a parent corporation liable as an "employer" for the subsidiary's employment law violations?

As originally conceived, the common-law test was designed to distinguish employees from independent contractors. It does not purport to distinguish employees from others who perform services for a firm but are more akin to firm owners than employees (e.g., partners, stakeholders in professional corporations, members of limited liability companies, and shareholders in closely held corporations). Determining the status of such workers has been the subject of intense litigation in the federal employment discrimination area. Whether owners are treated as employees rather than employers (or vice versa) matters for two reasons. First, the number of statutory employees often determines whether a particular firm meets the threshold for coverage under the various employment statutes that might be invoked in a suit by an employee. Workers who are deemed to be employers are not counted for these purposes. Second, if the worker is considered an employer, rather than employee, then, like independent contractors, he or she will not be protected by applicable employment statutes.

Clackamas Gastroenterology Associates v. Wells
538 U.S. 440 (2003)

STEVENS, J.

The Americans with Disabilities Act of 1990 ("ADA" or "Act"), 42 U.S.C. §12101 *et seq.*, like other federal antidiscrimination legislation,[1] is inapplicable to very small businesses. Under the ADA an "employer" is not covered unless its workforce includes "15 or more employees for each working day in each of 20 or more calendar weeks in the current or preceding calendar year." §12111(5). The question in this case is whether four physicians actively engaged in medical practice as shareholders and directors of a professional corporation should be counted as "employees."

I

Petitioner, Clackamas Gastroenterology Associates, P.C., is a medical clinic in Oregon. It employed respondent, Deborah Anne Wells, as a bookkeeper from 1986 until 1997. After her termination, she brought this action against the clinic alleging unlawful discrimination on the basis of disability under Title I of the ADA. Petitioner denied that it was covered by the Act and moved for summary judgment, asserting that it did not have 15 or more employees for the 20 weeks required by the

---

1. *See, e.g.,* 29 U.S.C. §630(b) (setting forth a 20-employee threshold for coverage under the Age Discrimination in Employment Act of 1967 (ADEA)); 42 U.S.C. §2000e(b) (establishing a 15-employee threshold for coverage under Title VII of the Civil Rights Act of 1964).

statute. It is undisputed that the accuracy of that assertion depends on whether the four physician-shareholders who own the professional corporation and constitute its board of directors are counted as employees.

[The district court relied on an economic realities test and concluded that the four doctors were "more analogous to partners in a partnership than to shareholders in a general corporation" and therefore were "not employees for purposes of the federal antidiscrimination laws." The Ninth Circuit reversed. It saw "no reason to permit a professional corporation to secure the 'best of both possible worlds' by allowing it both to assert its corporate status in order to reap the tax and civil liability advantages and to argue that it is like a partnership in order to avoid liability for unlawful employment discrimination."]

II

"We have often been asked to construe the meaning of 'employee' where the statute containing the term does not helpfully define it." *Nationwide Mut. Ins. Co. v. Darden*, 503 U.S. 318, 322 (1992). The definition of the term in the ADA simply states that an "employee" is "an individual employed by an employer." 42 U.S.C. § 12111(4). That surely qualifies as a mere "nominal definition" that is "completely circular and explains nothing." *Darden*. As we explained in *Darden*, our cases construing similar language give us guidance on how best to fill the gap in the statutory text.

In *Darden* we were faced with the question whether an insurance salesman was an independent contractor or an "employee" covered by the Employee Retirement Income Security Act of 1974 (ERISA). Because ERISA's definition of "employee" was "completely circular," we followed the same general approach that we had previously used in deciding whether a sculptor was an "employee" within the meaning of the Copyright Act of 1976, *see Community for Creative Non-Violence v. Reid*, 490 U.S. 730 (1989), and we adopted a common-law test for determining who qualifies as an "employee" under ERISA. Quoting *Reid*, we explained that "when Congress has used the term 'employee' without defining it, we have concluded that Congress intended to describe the conventional master-servant relationship as understood by common law agency doctrine."

Rather than looking to the common law, petitioner argues that courts should determine whether a shareholder-director of a professional corporation is an "employee" by asking whether the shareholder-director is, in reality, a "partner." The question whether a shareholder-director is an employee, however, cannot be answered by asking whether the shareholder-director appears to be the functional equivalent of a partner. Today there are partnerships that include hundreds of members, some of whom may well qualify as "employees" because control is concentrated in a small number of managing partners. Thus, asking whether shareholder-directors are partners — rather than asking whether they are employees — simply begs the question.

Nor does the approach adopted by the Court of Appeals in this case fare any better. The majority's approach, which paid particular attention to "the broad purpose of the ADA," is consistent with the statutory purpose of ridding the Nation of the evil of discrimination. *See* 42 U.S.C. § 12101(b).[6] Nevertheless, two countervailing considerations must be weighed in the balance. First, . . . the congressional decision to limit the coverage of the legislation to firms with 15 or more employees has its own justification that must be respected—namely, easing entry into the market and preserving the competitive position of smaller firms. Second, as *Darden* reminds us, congressional silence often reflects an expectation that courts will look to the common law to fill gaps in statutory text, particularly when an undefined term has a settled meaning at common law. . . .

Perhaps the Court of Appeals' and the parties' failure to look to the common law for guidance in this case stems from the fact that we are dealing with a new type of business entity that has no exact precedent in the common law. State statutes now permit incorporation for the purpose of practicing a profession, but in the past "the so-called learned professions were not permitted to organize as corporate entities." 1A W. Fletcher, Cyclopedia of the Law of Private Corporations § 112.10 (rev. ed. 1997-2002). Thus, professional corporations are relatively young participants in the market, and their features vary from State to State.

Nonetheless, the common law's definition of the master-servant relationship does provide helpful guidance. At common law the relevant factors defining the master-servant relationship focus on the master's control over the servant. The general definition of the term "servant" in the Restatement (Second) of Agency § 2(2) (1958), for example, refers to a person whose work is "controlled or is subject to the right to control by the master." *See also id.* § 220(1). In addition, the Restatement's more specific definition of the term "servant" lists factors to be considered when distinguishing between servants and independent contractors, the first of which is "the extent of control" that one may exercise over the details of the work of the other. *Id.* § 220(2)(a). We think that the common-law element of control is the principal guide-post that should be followed in this case.

This is the position that is advocated by the Equal Employment Opportunity Commission (EEOC), the agency that has special enforcement responsibilities under the ADA and other federal statutes containing similar threshold issues for determining coverage. It argues that a court should examine "whether shareholder-directors operate independently and manage the business or instead are subject to the firm's control." . . .

We are persuaded by the EEOC's focus on the common law touchstone of control . . . and specifically by its submission that each of the following six factors is relevant to the inquiry whether a shareholder-director is an employee:

> Whether the organization can hire or fire the individual or set the rules and regulations of the individual's work
>
> Whether and, if so, to what extent the organization supervises the individual's work
>
> Whether the individual reports to someone higher in the organization

---

6. The meaning of the term "employee" comes into play when determining whether an individual is an "employee" who may invoke the ADA's protections against discrimination in "hiring, advancement, or discharge," 42 U.S.C. § 12112(a), as well as when determining whether an individual is an "employee" for purposes of the 15-employee threshold. *See* § 12111(5)(A). Consequently, a broad reading of the term "employee" would—consistent with the statutory purpose of ridding the Nation of discrimination—tend to expand the coverage of the ADA by enlarging the number of employees entitled to protection and by reducing the number of firms entitled to exemption.

Whether and, if so, to what extent the individual is able to influence the organization

Whether the parties intended that the individual be an employee, as expressed in written agreements or contracts

Whether the individual shares in the profits, losses, and liabilities of the organization.[7]

As the EEOC's standard reflects, an employer is the person, or group of persons, who owns and manages the enterprise. The employer can hire and fire employees, can assign tasks to employees and supervise their performance, and can decide how the profits and losses of the business are to be distributed. The mere fact that a person has a particular title — such as partner, director, or vice president — should not necessarily be used to determine whether he or she is an employee or a proprietor. *See ibid.* ("An individual's title . . . does not determine whether the individual is a partner, officer, member of a board of directors, or major shareholder, as opposed to an employee"). Nor should the mere existence of a document styled "employment agreement" lead inexorably to the conclusion that either party is an employee. *See ibid.* (looking to whether "the parties intended that the individual be an employee, as expressed in written agreements or contracts"). Rather, as was true in applying common law rules to the independent-contractor-versus-employee issue confronted in *Darden*, the answer to whether a shareholder-director is an employee depends on "'all of the incidents of the relationship . . . with no one factor being decisive.'"

III

Some of the District Court's findings — when considered in light of the EEOC's standard — appear to weigh in favor of a conclusion that the four director-shareholder physicians in this case are not employees of the clinic. For example, they apparently control the operation of their clinic, they share the profits, and they are personally liable for malpractice claims. There may, however, be evidence in the record that would contradict those findings or support a contrary conclusion under the EEOC's standard that we endorse today. Accordingly, as we did in *Darden*, we reverse the judgment of the Court of Appeals and remand the case to that court for further proceedings consistent with this opinion. . . .

GINSBURG, J., with whom BREYER, J. joins, dissenting.

"There is nothing inherently inconsistent between the coexistence of a proprietary and an employment relationship." *Goldberg v. Whitaker House Cooperative, Inc.*, 366 U.S. 28, 32 (1961). As doctors performing the everyday work of petitioner Clackamas Gastroenterology Associates, P.C., the physician-shareholders function in several respects as common-law employees, a designation they embrace for various purposes under federal and state law. Classifying as employees all doctors daily engaged as caregivers on Clackamas' premises, moreover, serves

---

7. The EEOC asserts that these six factors need not necessarily be treated as "exhaustive." We agree. . . .

the animating purpose of the [ADA]. Seeing no cause to shelter Clackamas from the governance of the ADA, I would affirm the judgment of the Court of Appeals.

An "employee," the ADA provides, is "an individual employed by an employer." 42 U.S.C. § 12111(4). Where, as here, a federal statute uses the word "employee" without explaining the term's intended scope, we ordinarily presume "Congress intended to describe the conventional master-servant relationship as understood by common-law agency doctrine." *Nationwide Mut. Ins. Co. v. Darden*. The Court today selects one of the common-law indicia of a master-servant relationship—control over the work of others engaged in the business of the enterprise—and accords that factor overriding significance. I would not so shrink the inquiry.

Are the physician-shareholders "servants" of Clackamas for the purpose relevant here? The Restatement defines "servant" to mean "an agent employed by a master to perform service in his affairs whose physical conduct in the performance of the service is controlled or is subject to the right to control by the master." RESTATEMENT (SECOND) OF AGENCY § 2(2) (1958) (hereinafter Restatement). When acting as clinic doctors, the physician-shareholders appear to fit the Restatement definition. The doctors provide services on behalf of the corporation, in whose name the practice is conducted. . . . The doctors have employment contracts with Clackamas, under which they receive salaries and yearly bonuses, and they work at facilities owned or leased by the corporation. In performing their duties, the doctors must "compl[y] with . . . standards [the organization has] established."

The physician-shareholders, it bears emphasis, invite the designation "employee" for various purposes under federal and state law. The Employee Retirement Income Security Act of 1974 (ERISA), much like the ADA, defines "employee" as "any individual employed by an employer." 29 U.S.C. § 1002(6). Clackamas readily acknowledges that the physician-shareholders are "employees" for ERISA purposes. Indeed, gaining qualification as "employees" under ERISA was the prime reason the physician-shareholders chose the corporate form instead of a partnership. Further, Clackamas agrees, the physician-shareholders are covered by Oregon's workers' compensation law. . . . Finally, by electing to organize their practice as a corporation, the physician-shareholders created an entity separate and distinct from themselves, one that would afford them limited liability for the debts of the enterprise. I see no reason to allow the doctors to escape from their choice of corporate form when the question becomes whether they are employees for purposes of federal antidiscrimination statutes.

Nothing in or about the ADA counsels otherwise. As the Court observes, the reason for exempting businesses with fewer than 15 employees from the Act, was "to spare very small firms from the potentially crushing expense of mastering the intricacies of the antidiscrimination laws, establishing procedures to assure compliance, and defending against suits when efforts at compliance fail." The inquiry the Court endorses to determine the physician-shareholders' qualification as employees asks whether they "ac[t] independently and participat[e] in managing the organization, or . . . [are] subject to the organization's control." Under the Court's approach, a firm's coverage by the ADA might sometimes turn on variations in ownership structure unrelated to the magnitude of the company's business or its capacity for complying with federal prescriptions.

This case is illustrative. In 1996, Clackamas had 4 physician-shareholders and at least 14 other employees for 28 full weeks; in 1997, it had 4 physician-shareholders and at least 14 other employees for 37 full weeks. Beyond question, the corporation would have been covered by the ADA had one of the physician-shareholders sold his stake in the business and become a "mere" employee. Yet such a change in ownership arrangements would not alter the magnitude of Clackamas' operation: In both circumstances, the corporation would have had at least 18 people on site doing the everyday work of the clinic for the requisite number of weeks.

The Equal Employment Opportunity Commission's approach, which the Court endorses, it is true, "excludes from protection those who are most able to control the firm's practices and who, as a consequence, are least vulnerable to the discriminatory treatment prohibited by the Act." As this dispute demonstrates, however, the determination whether the physician-shareholders are employees of Clackamas affects not only whether they may sue under the ADA, but also—and of far greater practical import—whether employees like bookkeeper Deborah Anne Wells are covered by the Act. Because the character of the relationship between Clackamas and the doctors supplies no justification for withholding from clerical worker Wells federal protection against discrimination in the workplace, I would affirm the judgment of the Court of Appeals.

NOTES

1. *Employer vs. Employee Muddle?* The issue in *Clackamas* is *not* the plaintiff's employment status, but that of her bosses. Only if the physicians are counted as employees can the defendant be a covered employer meeting the 15-employee threshold. Given this very different question, why is the common-law test—originally fashioned to distinguish employees from independent contractors for purposes of respondeat superior liability—given such prominence in the *Clackamas* analysis? The dissent argues that, given the remedial purposes of the ADA, its coverage should be interpreted broadly in terms of who is an employee and, therefore, who is a covered employer.

Should "employee" mean different things even within the same statute depending on what issue the court is seeking to address? For example, should "employee" mean one thing when, as here, the issue is whether the firm is large enough to be covered, but something else when the issue is whether the alleged victim(s) of unlawful discrimination are employees, as would be the case had one of the four doctors sued? A well-known case in which "owners" alleged unlawful discrimination against the firm is *EEOC v. Sidley Austin Brown & Wood*, 315 F.3d 696 (7th Cir. 2002). The underlying claim in *Sidley* was that a law firm mandatory retirement policy resulting in the demotion of 32 partners violated the ADEA. The parties disputed whether the partners affected by the policy were "employees" in light of the firm's management and control structure. The court did not resolve the issue, and the case ultimately settled, with the firm's agreeing to pay $27.5 million to the partners. Judge Posner's majority opinion and Judge Easterbrook's concurrence provide a useful survey of the difficult issues raised in this context and the considerable differences—within and between courts prior to

Clackamas—in analyzing the proper status given to workers with ownership interests. *See also* Leonard Bierman & Rafael Gely, *So, You Want to Be a Partner at Sidley & Austin?*, 40 Hous. L. Rev. 969, 990 (2003); Tiffani N. Darden, *The Law Firm Caste System: Constructing a Bridge Between Workplace Equity Theory and the Institutional Analyses of Bias in Corporate Law Firms*, 30 Berkeley J. Emp. & Lab. L. 85 (2009); Donald J. Labriola, *But I'm Denny Crane! Age Discrimination in the Legal Profession After* Sidley, 72 Alb. L. Rev. 367, 368 (2009); Ann C. McGinley, *Functionality or Formalism? Partners and Shareholders as "Employees" Under the Anti-Discrimination Laws*, 57 S.M.U. L. Rev. 3 (2004).

Despite the lingering disputes over the proper analytical framework for determining the employment status of workers who have an ownership interest, the new Restatement of Employment Law essentially adopts the *Clackamas* formulation, albeit offering a bit more guidance through its underlying illustrations and making clear that minority ownership interests generating little or no effective control are insufficient to support "employer" status. *See* Restatement (Third) of Employment Law (Proposed Final Draft, April 18, 2014) § 1.03 (and corresponding illustrations). It is also worth noting that, although it remains unresolved whether *Clackamas* might be extended to sweep in other managerial personnel who are not owners, the one circuit court that has addressed the issue in detail held that high placed workers lacking an ownership interest (or director status) are employees under federal antidiscrimination laws. *See Smith v. Castaways Family Diner*, 453 F.3d 971 (7th Cir. 2006).

2. *Significance of the Corporate Form.* The majority in *Clackamas* downplayed the significance of the physicians' choice to organize their practice as a professional corporation, indicating that it would look beyond mere formalities and titles and focus instead on the substantive question of whether the physicians exercised employer-like control over the enterprise. The Court did so in part because it seemed to assume that individuals who are "employers" or, at least, exercise employer-like control, cannot also be "employees." Is this a correct assumption? Aren't firm owners also frequently employed by the corporations, LLCs, and partnerships for which they work? *See generally* Frank Menetrez, *Employee Status and the Concept of Control in Federal Employment Discrimination Law*, 63 SMU L. Rev. 137 (2010) (arguing that applying the common law control test should often, perhaps usually, result in owners of the enterprise also being employees).

Indeed, why did the physicians organize their practice as a corporation in the first place? Recall that the physicians had classified themselves as shareholders, directors, *and* supervisory employees. As the dissent mentioned, it seems that the physicians incorporated in order to gain employee status for ERISA and workers' compensation purposes. It also appears likely that the corporate form was used to take advantage of the legal fiction that the corporation itself, and not its physician-owners, is the employer. That would limit individual exposure of each physician to malpractice (and other third-party liability) for the acts of the other physicians. Indeed, it seems ironic that the majority suggested that the physicians may be akin to employers under the common-law test, given that the original purpose of that test was to determine when a controlling party is liable under the doctrine of respondeat superior, and the physicians incorporated their practice to *avoid* such liability (and other forms of liability) by shifting employer status to the corporation. Undoubtedly, if the practice had been slightly larger — 15 undisputed employees — and plaintiff's discrimination claim therefore had been viable, the physicians would have argued that, despite their control of the enterprise, the corporation is the only "employer" subject to potential liability in this case. And, as discussed in Note 1 following *Ansoumana*, page 43, *supra*, they almost certainly would have won this argument.

3. *Different Inquiry, Same Problems and Policy Issues?* Recall some of the recurring themes in the previous cases in the chapter: (1) private ordering's role in determining employment status, (2) whether a firm or worker "can have it both ways" in terms of such status, (3) the importance of the case's posture and the underlying interests at stake, and (4) the central role that control plays when determining if an employment relationship exists. How do these themes play out in *Clackamas?* Should the questions raised be answered differently when the court is not assessing the status of the plaintiff herself but rather the status of others on whom her right to relief depends?

In addition, how successful is the opinion in avoiding or addressing the other two concerns discussed throughout this chapter, namely, the costs of uncertainty and the disconnect between the test for determining employee/employer status and the aims of the underlying employment doctrine? In thinking about this question, put yourself in the shoes of corporate counsel. In light of the Court's analysis, how might you structure a small business to minimize the likelihood of being subject to the ADA's obligations? How confident are you that such structuring would achieve its purposes?

4. *"Covered Employers."* Like the ADA, many other federal employment statutes limit the definition of employer based on the number of employees. Title VII, for example, has a 15-employee floor, *see* 42 U.S.C. §2000e(b) (2014), and the ADEA applies only to employers with twenty or more employees, *see* 29 U.S.C. §630(b) (2014). The Family and Medical Leave Act ("FMLA") applies only to employers with 50 or more employees, and only to employees employed at a worksite where the employer employs at least 50 employees within a 75-mile radius. *See* 29 U.S.C. §2611(2)(B)(ii), (4)(A)(i) (2014). Federal employment statutes also contain other exceptions to employer status; for example, religious entities are exempted from Title VII's prohibition of discrimination on the basis of religion. *See* 42 U.S.C. §2000e-1(a). Thus, the issue presented in *Clackamas* will be relevant any time a small business is sued by an employee raising claims under any number of employment protection statutes.

Whether an employer is public or private also affects statutory coverage or remedies. Some federal labor statutes, including the Labor Management Relations Act and National Labor Relations Act, do not apply to public employers, *see* 29 U.S.C. §152(2) (2014), although the federal government has its own regime for federal employees and states frequently have their own statutes governing state and local public sector labor relations. On the other hand, federal constitutional protections — including constitutional rights to speech, association, religious freedom, and due process — apply only in public workplaces. Moreover, federal, state, and local government employees often enjoy substantive protections pursuant to civil service codes that are unavailable in the private sector.

Yates v. Hendon
541 U.S. 1 (2004)

GINSBURG, J.

This case presents a question on which federal courts have divided: Does the working owner of a business (here, the sole shareholder and president of a professional corporation) qualify as a "participant" in a pension plan covered by the Employee Retirement Income Security Act of 1974 (ERISA or Act), 29 U.S.C. § 1001 *et seq.* The answer, we hold, is yes: If the plan covers one or more employees other than the business owner and his or her spouse, the working owner may participate on equal terms with other plan participants. Such a working owner, in common with other employees, qualifies for the protections ERISA affords plan participants and is governed by the rights and remedies ERISA specifies. In so ruling, we reject the position, taken by the lower courts in this case, that a business owner may rank only as an "employer" and not also as an "employee" for purposes of ERISA-sheltered plan participation.

I

A

[ERISA's four titles regulate covered employee pension plans in a variety of ways. One of the benefits of an ERISA plan is favorable tax treatment.]

B

Dr. Raymond B. Yates was the sole shareholder and president of Raymond B. Yates, M.D., P.C., a professional corporation. The corporation maintained the Raymond B. Yates, M.D., P.C. Profit Sharing Plan (Profit Sharing Plan or Plan), for which Yates was the administrator and trustee. From the Profit Sharing Plan's inception, at least one person other than Yates or his wife was a participant. The Profit Sharing Plan qualified for favorable tax treatment under § 401 of the Internal Revenue Code (IRC). As required by both the IRC and Title I of ERISA, the Plan contained an anti-alienation provision. That provision, entitled "Spendthrift Clause," stated in relevant part: "Except for . . . loans to Participants as [expressly provided for in the Plan], no benefit or interest available hereunder will be subject to assignment or alienation, either voluntarily or involuntarily."

In December 1989, Yates borrowed $20,000 at 11 percent interest from the Raymond B. Yates, M.D., P.C. Money Purchase Pension Plan (Money Purchase Pension Plan), which later merged into the Profit Sharing Plan. The terms of the loan agreement required Yates to make monthly payments of $433.85 over the five-year period of the loan. Yates failed to make any monthly payment. In June 1992, coinciding with the Money Purchase Pension Plan-Profit Sharing Plan merger, Yates renewed the loan for five years. Again, he made no monthly payments. In fact, Yates repaid nothing until November 1996. That month, he used the proceeds from the sale of his house to make two payments totaling $50,467.46, which paid off in full the principal and interest due on the loan. Yates maintained that, after the repayment, his interest in the Profit Sharing Plan amounted to about $87,000.

[Three weeks after Yates repaid the loan to the Profit Sharing Plan, Yates's personal creditors filed an involuntary petition against him under Chapter 7 of the Bankruptcy Code. The Bankruptcy Trustee (overseeing the bankruptcy estate for the benefit of Yates' creditors) asked the Bankruptcy Court to avoid the $50,467.46 payments to the Profit Sharing Plan and to order Yates to pay over that amount plus interest to them. The Bankruptcy Court ruled in favor of the Trustee. In its ruling, the court found that the Profit Sharing Plan and Yates could not rely on the Plan's anti-alienation provision — which protects the Plan's assets from transfer or attachment — to prevent the Bankruptcy Trustee from recovering the loan repayment because, as "a self-employed owner of the professional corporation that sponsor[ed] the pension plan," Yates could not "participate as an employee under ERISA." Since Yates could not participate in the Plan as an employee, he could not rely on ERISA's provisions to avoid transferring the payments to the Trustee.

The District Court agreed. Since Dr. Yates was not qualified to participate in an ERISA-protected plan, none of his contributions to the Plan as an "employee" were protected, including the $50,467.46 he returned to the Plan." The Sixth Circuit affirmed.]

We granted certiorari in view of the division of opinion among the Circuits on the question whether a working owner may qualify as a participant in an employee benefit plan covered by ERISA.

II

A

ERISA's definitions of "employee," and, in turn, "participant," are uninformative.[*] We therefore look to other provisions of the Act for instruction. ERISA's text contains multiple indications that Congress intended working owners to qualify as plan participants. Because these indications combine to provide "specific guidance," there is no cause in this case to resort to common law.[3]

Congress enacted ERISA against a backdrop of IRC provisions that permitted corporate shareholders, partners, and sole proprietors to participate in tax-qualified pension plans. Working shareholders have been eligible to participate in such plans since 1942. Two decades later, still prior to ERISA's adoption, Congress permitted partners and sole proprietors to establish tax-favored pension plans, commonly known as "H. R. 10" or "Keogh" plans. Thus, by 1962, working owners of all kinds could contribute to tax-qualified retirement plans.

---

*[ERISA defines the term "participant" as "any employee or former employee of an employer" who is eligible to receive benefits under an employee pension plan. *See* 29 U.S.C. § 1002(7). "Employee," means "any individual employed by an employer," *id.* § 1002(6), and "employer" includes "any person acting directly as an employer, or indirectly in the interest of an employer, in relation to an employee benefit plan," *id.* § 1002(5). — Eds.]

3. *Cf. Nationwide Mut. Ins. Co. v. Darden*, 503 U.S. 318 (1992), and *Clackamas Gastroenterology Assocs., P.C. v. Wells*, [reproduced at page 50], (finding textual clues absent, Court looked to common law for guidance).

ERISA's enactment in 1974 did not change that situation. Rather, Congress' objective was to harmonize ERISA with longstanding tax provisions. Title I of ERISA and related IRC provisions expressly contemplate the participation of working owners in covered benefit plans. Most notably, several Title I provisions partially exempt certain plans in which working owners likely participate from otherwise mandatory ERISA provisions. Exemptions of this order would be unnecessary if working owners could not qualify as participants in ERISA-protected plans in the first place.

To illustrate, Title I frees the following plans from the Act's fiduciary responsibility requirements:

(1) a plan which is unfunded and is maintained by an employer primarily for the purpose of providing deferred compensation for a select group of management or highly compensated employees; or

(2) any agreement described in section 736 of [the IRC], which provides payments to a retired partner or deceased partner or a deceased partner's successor in interest.

The IRC defines the term "highly compensated employee" to include "any employee who . . . was a 5-percent owner at any time during the year or the preceding year." A "5-percent owner," the IRC further specifies, is "any person who owns . . . more than 5 percent of the outstanding stock of the corporation or stock possessing more than 5 percent of the total combined voting power of all stock of the corporation" if the employer is a corporation, or "any person who owns more than 5 percent of the capital or profits interest in the employer" if the employer is not a corporation. Under these definitions, some working owners would fit the description "highly compensated employees." Similarly, agreements that make payments to retired partners, or to deceased partners' successors in interest, surely involve plans in which working partners participate. . . .

Particularly instructive, Title IV and the IRC, as amended by Title II, clarify a key point missed by several lower courts: Under ERISA, a working owner may have dual status, *i.e.*, he can be an employee entitled to participate in a plan and, at the same time, the employer (or owner or member of the employer) who established the plan. Both Title IV and the IRC describe the "employer" of a sole proprietor or partner. *See* 29 U.S.C. § 1301(b)(1) ("An individual who owns the entire interest in an unincorporated trade or business is treated as his own employer, and a partnership is treated as the employer of each partner who is an employee within the meaning of section 401(c)(1) of [the IRC]."); 26 U.S.C. § 401(c)(4) ("An individual who owns the entire interest in an unincorporated trade or business shall be treated as his own employer. A partnership shall be treated as the employer of each partner who is an employee within the meaning of [§ 401(c)(1)]."). These descriptions expressly anticipate that a working owner can wear two hats, as an employer and employee. *Cf. Clackamas Gastroenterology Assocs., P.C. v. Wells* (Ginsburg, J., dissenting) ("Clackamas readily acknowledges that the physician-shareholders are 'employees' for ERISA purposes.").

In sum, because the statute's text is adequately informative, we need not look outside ERISA itself to conclude with security that Congress intended working owners to qualify as plan participants.

Congress' aim is advanced by our reading of the text. The working employer's opportunity personally to participate and gain ERISA coverage serves as an incentive to the creation of plans that will benefit employer and nonowner employees alike.

Treating working owners as participants not only furthers ERISA's purpose to promote and facilitate employee benefit plans. Recognizing the working owner as an ERISA-sheltered plan participant also avoids the anomaly that the same plan will be controlled by discrete regimes: federal-law governance for the nonowner employees; state-law governance for the working owner. ERISA's goal, this Court has emphasized, is "uniform national treatment of pension benefits." *Patterson v. Shumate*, 504 U.S. 753, 765 (1992). Excepting working owners from the federal Act's coverage would generate administrative difficulties and is hardly consistent with a national uniformity goal. . . .

NOTES

1. *A Different Approach. Yates* offers an initial taste of how technical — perhaps painfully technical — ERISA interpretation and litigation is, something you can explore in detail in an Employee Benefits class. More pertinent for our purposes here, however, is the stark contrast between the Court's analytic approach in this case and that in *Clackamas*. The *Yates* majority explicitly avoided analyzing Yates' employment status under the common-law framework that dominated the *Clackamas* decision, opting instead to focus only on the language of ERISA and its predecessors, and the purposes behind the statutory scheme. It was also far more willing, in this case, to take into account formalistic distinctions relating to a working owner's status and role. Why are the approaches in these two decisions, which the Court handed down in successive terms, so different? Does the answer lie in the differences between the statutory schemes at issue, or is there a more fundamental difference?

2. *The Bitter with the Sweet. Yates* seems to resolve definitively the question raised in *Clackamas* whether an owner can "have it both ways" in terms of employment status, at least for ERISA purposes. This makes sense, doesn't it? After all, it would frustrate the purposes of Statute *A* if someone it was designed to protect was denied those protections simply because she was not covered by Statute *B*. But does this make you reconsider the conclusions you reached in connection, for example, with *Natkin*, reproduced at page 16? On this point, however, recall Justice Ginsberg's opinion in *Clackamas*, which suggested that one needs to take the bitter with the sweet: "Finally, by electing to organize their practice as a corporation, the physician-shareholders created an entity separate and distinct from themselves, one that would afford them limited liability for the debts of the enterprise. I see no reason to allow the doctors to escape from their choice of corporate form when the question becomes whether they are employees for purposes of federal antidiscrimination statutes." What reason does she see in *Yates* to allow the doctor there to escape from his choice of the corporate form?

Note on Parent Corporation Liability for Employment-law Violations

Clackamas and *Yates* introduced you to the role of the corporate form — limiting owners' liability for the debts and other obligations of the enterprise. Indeed, limited liability is the *primary reason* why business owners incorporate or charter an alternative limited liability entity, such as an LLC or limited partnership. Keep in mind, however, that business entities also are owners (e.g., shareholders) of other entities — that is, their subsidiaries. Although there are a number of reasons why firm managers might separately assign aspects of their enterprise's operations into parent and subsidiary firms, avoiding liability exposure for the larger enterprise (from the obligations of one or more of its subdivisions) is central among them. Akin to the rise of outsourcing, the splintering of enterprises into separately chartered entities has proliferated in recent years.

Such formal intra-enterprise distinctions may matter a great deal in the employment context. As an initial matter, at least in some circumstances, corporate formalities themselves may define the limits of employment-related protections. For example, until the Dodd-Frank Wall Street Reform and Financial Protection Act extended coverage, *see* 111 Pub. L. 203, §922, 124 Stat. 1376, §922, amending 18 U.S.C.A. §1514A (2010), employees of privately held subsidiaries of publicly traded firms who reported possible securities violations were found to be outside of the scope of the Sarbanes-Oxley's whistleblower protections, *see* Richard E. Moberly, *Unfulfilled Expectations: An Empirical Analysis of Why Sarbanes-Oxley Whistleblowers Rarely Win*, 49 WM. & MARY L. REV. 65, 71, 109, 134 (2007).

More broadly, where this kind of structure exists, a question of growing importance in the employment context is whether and when an employee of a subsidiary entity can hold the parent liable for employment-law violations. Given what you already have learned, you can deduce what might be at stake. It may be that, like the fly-by-night labor contractors discussed in the FLSA context, a subsidiary lacks the capital or insurance to cover its employment-related legal obligations or liabilities. Or it may be that, similar to the circumstances in *Clackamas*, a subsidiary alone has too few employees to be a covered employer under various statutory protections, even though it is part of a large enterprise. In addition, the ability of the plaintiff to reach the parent may affect other matters, such as the extent to which evidence of practices and violations elsewhere in the enterprise might be relevant and discoverable.

If the subsidiary's corporate veil could never be pierced to hold the parent accountable for the subsidiary's employment-law violations, one can imagine the compliance-avoidance techniques that firms might implement. While parent corporations do not enjoy such absolute protection, the law on when parents are accountable for subsidiaries' employment-law violations is far from clear. This is not surprising, since the more generalized "veil piercing" and "enterprise-entity liability" doctrines governing the liability of corporate parents in other contexts are in conceptual disarray. *See generally* Timothy P. Glynn, *Beyond "Unlimiting" Shareholder Liability: Vicarious Tort Liability for Corporate Officers*, 57 VAND. L. REV. 329 (2004); Stephen M. Bainbridge, *Abolishing Veil Piercing*, 43 CORP. PRAC. COMMENTATOR 517 (2001). Under these theories, a plaintiff typically must show, at the very least, significant control by the parent over the subsidiary's activities and some failure to maintain formal distinctions between the two entities, but application varies wildly. *See* Glynn, *supra*, at 353-56. This kind of traditional veil-piercing analysis may also apply to employment-law claims brought against parent corporations. *See, e.g., Corrigan v. U.S. Steel Corp.*, 478 F.3d 718 (6th Cir. 2007) (applying a traditional piercing framework and granting summary judgment on state-law claims brought against a parent by a subsidiary's employees because plaintiffs failed to show that the parent exercised "complete control" over the subsidiary such that the firms were fundamentally indistinguishable).

In addition, the Supreme Court has adopted a framework for determining whether two or more related but formally distinct (e.g., separately chartered) entities constitute a "single employer" under the National Labor Relations Act. *See Radio & Television Broadcast Technicians Local Union 1264 v. Broadcast Service of Mobile, Inc.*, 380 U.S. 255, 256 (1965) (per curiam). This four-part test examines the "interrelation of operations, common management, centralized control of labor relations and common ownership." *Id.* This issue continues to arise with some frequency in labor disputes before the National Labor Relations Board and reviewing courts, and outcomes vary in light of the contextual nature of the four factors. For a recent example, *see Carnival Carting, Inc. v. NLRB*, 455 F. App'x 20 (2d Cir. 2012) (upholding the NLRB's determination that two commonly owned and managed corporate entities constitute a "single employer" under this framework).

Although there is no broadly applicable statutory treatment of this question under federal or state employment laws, in a 1984 amendment to the ADEA and the 1991 Civil Rights Act (abrogating *EEOC v. Arabian American Oil Co.*, 499 U.S. 244 (1991)), Congress addressed a related issue when it extended the reach of antidiscrimination laws to American employees working in foreign countries for U.S. employers or their subsidiaries. *See* 29 U.S.C. § 623(h) (2014) (ADEA); 42 U.S.C. § 2000e-1(c) (2014) (Title VII); 42 U.S.C. § 12112(c)(2) (2014) (ADA). Title VII and the ADA now provide that if "an employer controls a corporation whose place of incorporation is a foreign country, any [violation] . . . engaged in by such corporation shall be presumed to be engaged in by such employer." The determination of whether an employer controls a corporation is based on the following factors:

- The interrelation of operations
- The common management
- The centralized control of labor relations
- The common ownership or financial control of the employer and the corporation

See 42 U.S.C. § 2000e-1(c) (2014); 42 U.S.C. § 12112(c)(2)(2014).

Outside the context of application abroad, increasing numbers of lower courts appear to be confronting the issue of holding parents accountable for employment-law violations by subsidiaries, and a number of circuit courts have now addressed the question in the antidiscrimination context. There are similarities in the courts' approaches; for example, each of the circuit courts and the EEOC has adopted a framework focused on the level of parent-corporation control and operational entanglement that is similar to or mirroring the four-factor test Congress adopted in the foreign entity context. *See Sandoval v. American Bldg. Maintenance Indus., Inc.*, 578 F.3d 787 (8th Cir. 2009); *Frank v. U.S. West, Inc.*, 3 F.3d 1357 (10th Cir.1993); *Johnson v. Flowers Indus., Inc.*, 814 F.2d 978 (4th Cir. 1987); EEOC COMPLIANCE MANUAL, Section 2: Threshold Issues, No. 915.003, section 2-III.B.1.a.iii.a (addressing "integrated enterprises" in the context of determining whether an employer has a sufficient number of employees to be subject to antidiscrimination laws).

But there are also important differences. Contrary to Congress's approach to the treatment of foreign entities, most of the circuit courts have stated that, in light of the doctrine of limited liability, there is a "strong presumption" against finding a parent corporation liable to subsidiary's employees. *See Johnson*, 814 F.2d at 980-81; *Frank*, 3 F.3d at 1362 (suggesting that such an extension of accountability beyond the employing subsidiary should occur only in extraordinary circumstances). However, the Eighth Circuit recently adopted — consistent with EEOC guidance — an approach less hostile to finding that a parent and subsidiary form an integrated enterprise. *Sandavol*, 578 F.3d at 792-96; EEOC COMPLIANCE MANUAL, *supra* (focusing on control and articulating no presumption against a finding of sufficient integration).

Like the common-law and related approaches to determining "employee" status, as well as the "joint employer" doctrine and the test adopted in *Clackamas*, such a fact-specific, multifactored test focused on control is destined to produce variations in outcomes over time, unless a "strong presumption" against extension of liability to the parent corporation sets the bar prohibitively high. It also raises the kinds of planning, litigation, and policy challenges we have discussed throughout the chapter. How should we balance the benefits (and, arguably, legislative preference) for shareholder limited liability against the moral hazard — the incentive to utilize corporate formalities to slice up the enterprise into undercapitalized or otherwise unaccountable subparts — that may result from adhering to strictly the formal distinctions between parents and subsidiaries? How might a rule be crafted to reflect this balance?

PROBLEM

1-3. A Second Look at "Compliance Boom." Building on what you have learned in this chapter, return again to the Compliance Boom hypothetical on page 4.

Assume first that you represent WCE. In light of what you have now learned about the stakes of employment and the scope of the employment relationship, what legal advice would you give regarding how WCE ought to structure its relationships with the various types of workers? What arrangements — contract provisions, management structures, corporate formalities, use of third-party labor suppliers, provision of resources (tools, equipment, vehicles) — might assist in achieving the desired outcome? And think about the types of additional information you would need or want from Faith and Ethan before offering such advice. For example, with regard to both the video production and office maintenance tasks, how might the need for detailed oversight matter? How might your advice regarding software/IT workers be affected by the fact that the video training platform to be developed would be so firm-specific that it likely would be of limited use to others in the industry? With regard to the assistants and salesperson, would it make a difference if there were significant barriers to entry into the compliance training market, such as high start-up costs, special equipment needs, and a limited number of potential clients? Would your advice with regard to one or more categories of workers depend on how close to having 15 workers the firm is (or will become)? Finally, how confident are you that, once you are satisfied that you have all of the client information you need, your advice will produce optimal results for your client?

Now assume you represent each of the workers. What expectations do you believe each worker may have regarding his or her employment status? How likely is it that each worker will be able to bargain for protections that meet these expectations? If a worker is in a position to bargain, what kind of relationship and additional protections should he or she seek? What kinds of contractual provisions are most likely to achieve these ends? How confident are you that the result of the bargaining would be accepted by a court?

Finally, consider whether and when the public has an interest in determining the type of relationship that exists between WCE and each of its workers. When, if ever, should the public interest or the interests of third parties trump the interests of the firm and worker? And, relatedly, when and to what extent should WCE's or a worker's intent, or an agreement between the two, determine the nature of the relationship?

Part Two

PRIVATE ORDERING AND DEFAULT TERMS

2

The "At-Will" Default Rule and Its Limits

What rights does an employee have to job security under our legal system? In contrast to most European countries, employment in the United States is "at will," meaning that both the employer and the employee may terminate the relationship at any time and for any reason in the absence of a special exception. The rule is considered a "default" rule because it may be varied by the parties. The employer and employee may agree, for instance, that their relationship will endure for a certain number of years, or until the employer has just cause to terminate the worker. Barring such a contract, however, the law deems the relationship to be terminable at will.

Most employees implicitly understand part of this equation. They know that they can quit their job any time they want without providing an explanation. Indeed, popular culture is replete with images of workers who, fed up with the daily grind, spontaneously decide to walk off the job, usually following a final snide remark to the boss.

What many employees do not appreciate is that at will is a two-way street. The default rules of the workplace allow employers to terminate workers at any time, with or without reason. If asked the right question, employees may acknowledge that they are at will. But with surprising illogic, empirical studies of employee perceptions of workplace law reveal that most workers simultaneously, and mistakenly, believe that they can be fired only for cause, and they believe, again wrongly, that they are entitled to advance notice of termination.

What accounts for this disconnect? It may be due in part to the fact that employer practices tend to be in accord more with employee expectations of how employers should act than with what the law allows employers to do. Most employers do not terminate employees unless there is a business-related reason, such as poor performance or economic necessity. After all, employers benefit from a consistent, high-quality workforce. They also benefit from good workforce morale, which job security occasions. That said, most employers do not promise their employees job security. That is, they rarely contractually bind themselves to terminate only for cause, except in the instances of agreements with individual high-level employees or collectively bargained agreements. They prefer to give more than the law requires without changing the rules of the game. Indeed, employers often go to great lengths to try to ensure that the at-will rule remains the default position for their employees.

69

This raises several questions. What is the function of the at-will default rule in the modern employment regime in light of basic managerial practices? How does this legal principle intersect with nonlegal (or, at least, "unlawyered") aspects of the employment relationship? Should the expectations of employees or the implicit commitments they make to their jobs have any bearing on their legal entitlements? Should the actions of the employer — its past practices, its procedures for discipline and termination, and its promises to its workers — affect at-will status? In short, when, if ever, should courts imply job security absent an explicit negotiated agreement between the parties? And what type of job protection, if any, should apply?

This chapter explores such questions. It begins with a description of employment at will and the historical approach to deviations from the default principle. It then considers the erosion of the traditional at-will approach through contract and related common law doctrines that courts have adopted in responding to inequitable terminations.

A. JOB SECURITY AND THE PRINCIPLE OF AT-WILL EMPLOYMENT

Hanson v. Central Show Printing Co., Inc.
130 N.W.2d 654 (Iowa 1964)

THOMPSON, J.

. . . The case as made by the plaintiff's evidence is that he was a skilled pressman, and had been in the employ of the defendant corporation at Mason City for many years prior to 1959. In the autumn of that year he had an opportunity to obtain a steady job with the Stoyles Printing Company, also of Mason City. He knew that the defendant's business was often slack in the winter, and contacted G. C. Venz, the president of defendant, to learn whether he would have steady work with it. This resulted, after some negotiations, in an arrangement expressed in a letter from Venz to the plaintiff, which is set out:

Oct. 21, 1959
Mr. Harry Hanson,

Starting today Oct. 21, I will guarantee you 40 hours work per week thru out the entire year each year until you retire of your own choosing.

/s/ G. C. Venz, Pres.

The plaintiff thereupon elected to remain in the employ of the defendant, and did so until October 21, 1961, when he was discharged, without cause. His hourly rate of pay was $2.77 1/2. He asks "damages in the past and in the future at the rate of $2.77 1/2 per hour for 40 hours per week throughout the entire year for each year and until he retires, all according to the terms of the employment contract," and for costs. At the close of his evidence the trial court granted the defendant's motion for a directed verdict. . . .

The question before us is essentially a simple one, and has been before the courts of the various jurisdictions many times. The rule which has been generally followed is thus set forth:

> [I]n the absence of additional express or implied stipulation as to the duration of the employment or of a good consideration additional to the services contracted to be rendered, a contract for permanent employment, for life employment, for as long as the employee chooses, or for other terms purporting permanent employment, is no more than an indefinite general hiring terminable at the will of either party.

This rule fits the situation before us, where the employment was to be "until you retire of your own choosing." . . .

The defendant urges here lack of mutuality; that is, it contends the plaintiff was not bound to any specific or enforceable term of employment. This is true; but lack of mutuality is not always proof of want of consideration. We have said: "If the lack of mutuality amounts to a lack of consideration, then the contract is invalid. But mere lack of mutuality in and of itself does not render a contract invalid. Though consideration is essential to the validity of a contract, it is not essential that such consideration consist of a mutual promise." *Standard Oil Co. v. Veland*, 224 N.W. 467, 469 [(Iowa 1929)].

So the lack of mutuality in itself is not fatal to plaintiff's case, if there is other consideration. He contends that he gave up the opportunity to take other employment; that this was a detriment to him, and so furnished consideration for the agreement. But it has been repeatedly held that this is not sufficient in contracts for permanent employment, or, as the plaintiff contends here, until he should "retire of your own choosing."

. . . The question was extensively considered in *Skagerberg v. Blandin Paper Co.*, 266 N.W. 872 (Minn. 1936). The plaintiff's case showed that he was a consulting engineer, specializing in the field of heating, ventilating, and air conditioning. While he was employed by the defendant, he received an offer from Purdue University for employment at a yearly salary, which would leave him free for three months to continue his practice; and while performing his duties at the university he would be permitted to carry on his private work so far as time permitted. He communicated this offer to the defendant, which promised, if he would refuse the Purdue offer, it would give him permanent employment. . . .

With reference to plaintiff's contention that consideration passed from him to the defendant, the court said: [The plaintiff] "merely abandoned other activities and interests to enter into the service of defendant — a thing almost every desirable servant does upon entering a new service, but which, of course, cannot be regarded as constituting any additional consideration to the master."

. . . In *Faulkner v. Des Moines Drug Co.*, 90 N.W. 585 (Iowa 1902), . . . the plaintiff claimed a contract for employment "until mutually agreed void." Much of [this Court's] discussion pertained to the indefiniteness of the contract, as to amount of prospective earnings, and the length of time the damages should be computed. We said: . . . "if it be said that the profits earned before the breach of the contract furnish a basis for estimating future returns, then for what length of time shall they be computed? Shall it be for one month, one year, ten years, or for the entire period of the plaintiff's expectancy of life? Who can place any reasonable estimate upon the period which would probably elapse before the parties 'mutually agree' that the contract between them shall be considered 'void'?" If we substitute for the "mutually agree" the words "until you retire of your own choosing," an equally uncertain happening, we have the identical case. . . . How would the trier of the facts have any guide as to how many years it might be "until he chose to retire"; or how much his loss might be mitigated by other employment which he might secure? . . .

There is a class of cases in which sufficient consideration to uphold a contract for permanent, or life, employment, or employment so long as the employee chooses, has been found. These are cases in which the servant has been found to have paid something for the promise of the employment, in addition to his agreement to render services. A majority of them are cases in which the employer, faced with a claim for damages, agreed to give the claimant permanent employment in consideration of the release of his claim. A case involving a different but also valid consideration is *Carning v. Carr*, 46 N.E. 117 (Mass. 1897), [in which the] plaintiff had been engaged in a competing business with the defendant, and had accepted permanent employment which involved the abandonment of his own enterprise. The defendant thereby received the benefit of removal of competition. . . .

We think the real basis for the majority rule is that there is in fact no binding contract for life employment when the employee has not agreed to it; that is, when he is free to abandon it at any time. So in the instant case, the plaintiff was bound only so long as he chose to work. It does not help to say that a contract for life employment, or permanent employment, may be binding if it is fully agreed upon, even though the only consideration furnished by the employee is his agreement to serve. The fact is he has not agreed to serve for life, or permanently; but only so long as he does not elect to "retire of his own choosing." What the rule might be if he had bound himself to work for life, or so long as he was able, we have no occasion to determine. These observations go to the lack of mutuality and would not be important if there was other consideration. Many difficulties would arise even if such a contract had been made and upheld, in the way of determining the damages because of uncertainty of type of employment, or rate of pay, or how much his loss might be mitigated, in the event of wrongful discharge, by other employment which he might find. But we have no occasion to go further into those questions here. . . .

NOTES

1. *The "Additional Consideration" Requirement.* The *Hanson* court articulates the traditional rule that, absent an express term of employment or "additional" consideration to the employer, a contract of employment is deemed terminable at will. What does the court mean by "additional" consideration? Additional to what?

2. *The Express Term Exception.* Is the additional consideration requirement even relevant here? The court says that additional consideration is necessary where the parties do not agree to a fixed term of employment. Look at the employer's letter. It promises Hanson 40 hours per week each week of every year until his retirement. Isn't that an express provision as to the duration of employment? Surprisingly, no: courts generally treat indefinite time periods like this — as well as promises of "lifetime employment," "permanent employment," or "long-term employment" — as expressing nothing more than an ordinary at-will relationship. *See, e.g., Turner v. Newsom,* 3 So. 3d 913, 915 (Ala. App. 2008); *Henkel v. Educ. Research Council,* 344 N.E.2d 118, 121-22 (Ohio 1976); *Forrer v. Sears, Roebuck & Co.,* 153 N.W.2d 587, 589-90 (Wis. 1967). Why? Don't these phrases suggest intent to provide job security, albeit for an indefinite term?

3. *Proof of Additional Consideration.* What would Hanson have had to prove in order to show additional consideration? Why isn't it sufficient that Hanson turned down a "steady job" at another printing company? In *Skagerberg v. Blandin Paper Co.,* 266 N.W. 872 (Minn. 1936), described in *Hanson,* the Minnesota Supreme Court rejected the plaintiff's argument that he had supplied sufficient additional consideration upon accepting the defendant's offer of "permanent" employment by foregoing a faculty position at Purdue University. Compare these facts (and the facts in *Hanson* itself) to the two precedents cited in the opinion in which the courts found proof of additional consideration. Those cases involved the settlement of a claim against the employer and the surrender of a competitive business. Do you see the distinction between these cases and *Hanson*? Can you think of other factual scenarios in which a plaintiff might be able to establish additional consideration as understood by these courts? *See, e.g., Kabe's Rest. v. Kinter,* 538 N.W.2d 281, 284 (Iowa 1995) (finding fact that employee personally invested in employer's business and was a motivating force in its creation to be evidence of additional consideration sufficient to submit breach of contract claim to a jury). Are there any circumstances under which simply rejecting alternative employment should constitute additional consideration? Does it matter whether the plaintiff is a new employee choosing between competing offers (as in *Skagerberg*) or an existing employee who is contemplating leaving (as in *Hanson*)?

4. *The Uncertain Damages Rationale.* The court talks about the difficulty of calculating damages where the duration of employment is uncertain. Do you find this a convincing rationale for the additional consideration requirement? Consider that courts routinely calculate lost earnings as damages in commercial cases involving a going concern in which it is uncertain how long the business would have endured. They also calculate lost wages in cases involving breach of a fixed-term contract (as where the employer promises continued employment for a set number of years), although the employee could have departed before the expiration of the term. Suppose that Hanson is 50 years old at the time of the letter agreement. Can you think of a fair way to calculate his damages had the court found an enforceable contract for job security? What proof would you expect each side to submit on this issue?

5. *A Historical View of at Will.* The wide adoption of the at-will presumption by American jurisdictions is generally attributed to an 1877 treatise on "master and servant" law by attorney Horace Gray Wood. In it, Wood famously stated that, unlike the British system,

> [w]ith us the rule is inflexible, that a general or indefinite hiring is *prima facie* a hiring at will, and if the servant seeks to make it out a yearly hiring, the burden is upon him to establish it by proof. . . . [I]t is an indefinite hiring and is determinable at the will of either party.

HORACE G. WOOD, MASTER AND SERVANT § 134 (1877).

Some modern scholars have cast doubt on the accuracy of Wood's statement as a reflection of the law of his time. *See, e.g.,* Jay Feinman, *The Development of the Employment at Will Rule,* 20 AM. J. LEGAL HIST. 118, 126-27 (1976) (noting that the cases cited by Wood did not support his conclusion and that he incorrectly stated that no American court had adopted the British rule that an indefinite hiring is presumed to endure one year). Nonetheless, "Wood's rule" has not only become black letter doctrine, it is arguably the centerpiece of all of American employment law.

What accounts for the vast appeal of the at-will presumption? Professor Feinman has suggested that the rule reflected the development of American capitalism in the late nineteenth century. He explains:

> [T]hrough the first half of the nineteenth century owners and managers of smaller businesses comprised the bulk of the commercial middle class. Enterprises were not usually impersonal; the managers were frequently the owners of the businesses. . . . As the century progressed and the scale of production increased, however, enterprises became larger and more impersonal and many workers became farther removed from ownership. . . . Salaried employees with little control of their employment situation became a larger proportion of the work force and an important segment of the economy. Thus the many suits brought [by mid-level managers] to establish interests in their jobs were an attempt by a newly important group in the economy to apply a traditional doctrine to their new situation, but the courts rejected the attempt and instead announced the new principle of employment at will. The reasons for this lie in the class division fundamental to the capitalist system: the distinction between owners and non-owners of capital. . . .
>
> Employment at will is the ultimate guarantee of the capitalist's authority over the worker. The rule transformed long-term and semi-permanent relationships into non-binding terminable at will. If employees could be dismissed on a moment's notice, obviously they could not claim a voice in the determination of the conditions of work or the use of the product of their labor. Indeed, such a fleeting relationship is hardly a contract at all. . . .

Id. at 132.

6. *Other Bases for the At-Will Rule?* If you are not convinced by the rationales put forth by the *Hanson* court in support of the historical presumption of at-will employment, can you think of other justifications for the rule? Consider the arguments put forth in the next case, decided some 20 years later.

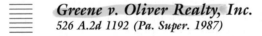

Greene v. Oliver Realty, Inc.
526 A.2d 1192 (Pa. Super. 1987)

CIRILLO, President Judge.

. . . Appellant, William Greene[,] began working for Grant Building, Inc. in 1959. Greene allegedly agreed to work at a pay rate below union scale in exchange for a promise that Grant would employ him "for life." In 1975, appellee Oliver Realty, Inc. took over management of Grant Building but Oliver's president assured former Grant employees that existing employment contracts would be honored. During that same year Greene explained the terms of his agreement to an Oliver Realty supervisor. The supervisor stated that he would look into the matter but never got back to Greene. . . . In 1983, Greene was laid off and he brought this action for breach of contract. The trial court ruled that under Pennsylvania law a contract "for life" is a contract at will. The court also held that a contract at will may become a contract for a reasonable time if it is supported by sufficient additional consideration other than the employee's services. The court stated that there was no such consideration in this case. . . . [T]he court granted Oliver's motion for summary judgment. . . .

Contemporary contract law generally provides that a contract is enforceable when the parties reach mutual agreement, exchange consideration and have outlined the terms of their bargain with sufficient clarity. An agreement is sufficiently definite if the parties intended to make a contract and there is a reasonably certain basis upon which a court can provide an appropriate remedy. . . .

However, there is one area of contract law which is strikingly idiosyncratic. That is the law of employment contracts. It has developed contrary to all of the standard, modern contract principles discussed above. If the parties to an employment contract do not specify the duration of the contract, a court will not imply a reasonable duration. The contract is considered terminable at will. If the parties contract for "lifetime" employment, many courts will refuse to enforce their bargain even if their intentions are clear. Even if the agreement is oral, courts refuse to consider the surrounding circumstances. Though mutuality of obligation is a discredited notion, it is often required in the employment context, even when the employment agreement is a unilateral contract. Also, courts routinely refuse to enforce employment contracts if they entail a single promise made in exchange for several promises. In reaching these results, courts rely on anachronistic theories which they would never apply in other fields of contract law. The strong resistance of employment law to modern contract doctrine is a testament to the influence of a uniquely American legal tradition: the at-will presumption. . . .

[T]here are five policies underlying the presumption: (1) The policy of freedom of contract; (2) the need for mutuality of obligation; (3) common experience that it usually effectuates the intent of the parties; (4) as a procedural protection against meritless but vexatious lawsuits; and (5) fairness and equity. . . .

[F]reedom of contract implies that the parties are free to determine the terms of their relationship. The at-will presumption was supposedly based upon this principle. Yet, courts [have] formalistically enforced the rule, allowing it to become a substantive limitation upon the parties' freedom to contract. . . . If two parties desire to contract "for life," courts should be encouraged to enforce their agreement. Of course, the at-will presumption may still be a sound legal rule. It is only when it is allowed to conclusively foreclose proof of the parties['] intent that it becomes an obstacle to freedom of contract. . . .

One rationale for the rule which is illogical and undeserving of perpetuation is that of mutuality of obligation. Courts have often held that mutuality of obligation is lacking in the employment context, particularly in regard to contracts for permanent employment. . . .

However, consideration may be any bargained for benefit or detriment. An employer is free to promise lifetime employment to someone in exchange for that person coming to work for the employer. Once that person accepts and starts work, the employer has received exactly what he bargained for. The employee has performed the desired act. That act is the consideration for the employer's promise and their agreement is a unilateral contract. It is irrelevant that the employee's services are also consideration for his salary. Modern contract law recognizes that consideration may be a single act exchanged for several promises. *See* RESTATEMENT CONTRACTS (SECOND) § 79. Therefore, an employee is free to sell his services in exchange for wages *and* a promise of lifetime employment.

Once the employee begins work, the employer may be the only party obligated, but that is standard in situations involving a unilateral contract. The promisor has requested a performance as the price of his promise. Once he receives that performance, it would defy all notions of equity to allow him to avoid his obligation by claiming that the promisee is no longer obligated. He is no longer obligated because he has already performed the agreed upon acts. . . .

The at-will presumption, like most other legal presumptions, is also based upon common experience. In the vast majority of employer-employee relationships, both sides are silent about the expected duration of the employment agreement. The employee usually feels free to leave and take another job if it presents a more desirable opportunity. Similarly, the employer generally feels free to discharge the employee if he no longer wants his services. The at-will presumption is simply a legal recognition of the parties' normal expectations. . . . It is a waste of time and resources to require parties to re-prove time and again that which experience shows is normally true. It is much more efficient . . . [to] require the parties to demonstrate if exceptional circumstances are present. . . .

The at-will presumption also provides another important procedural protection. If there were no such rule, any dismissed employee could file suit based on an alleged oral contract. The ensuing lawsuit would then hinge solely on credibility. We note that a jury is much more likely to be composed of employees as opposed to employers. We hope that it does not exhibit too cynical a view of humanity for us to be concerned that this might affect more than an occasional verdict. The law is replete with procedural rules designed to guard against the danger of prejudicial jury verdicts. The at-will presumption . . . can be rebutted by clear evidence that the parties intended a contrary result. This is a sufficient safeguard. It balances the need to protect against prejudicial verdicts with the legal system's obligation to enforce the individual parties['] expectations. . . . A contract for life is a heavy burden to impose upon an employer. Courts should be careful that when such a burden is imposed it is because that is what was contracted for. . . . The parties may have used the words "permanently" or "for life" in an off-hand manner. These words are much too ambiguous to provide the sole basis for a jury's imposition of such a tremendous obligation. Courts must look to the surrounding circumstances to determine the parties['] intent. . . .

Another policy supporting continued recognition of the at-will presumption is that of simple fairness. . . .

[W]here the employer and employee both agree that the employment relation is to last for a definite period[, b]oth parties are then bound for that period. If the employer fires the employee, he can sue his former boss and recover damages. However, if the employee quits before the agreed upon period of time has expired, what recourse is available to the employer? If he sues the employee, he will have difficulty proving damages. He will need to show that the loss of this one employee caused his business to lose money. Even if the employer wins a judgment he would then have to enforce it. The old adage that you cannot get blood from a stone is particularly apt in this situation. Most individuals do not have the resources to satisfy anything but the most meager judgment. Therefore, an aggrieved employee will probably have a legal remedy, but an aggrieved employer will not. . . .

The at-will presumption is a partial response to this quandary. . . . The presumption may make it slightly more difficult for the employee to recover if he brings an action. But this merely serves as a partial redress of the unfair situation which would otherwise occur. . . .

Therefore, our review of the applicable policies demonstrates that the at-will presumption remains a sound legal rule. It provides a sensible balance of the relevant concerns. . . . But, courts must remain flexible and not allow the presumption to foreclose proof of the parties' intent. . . .

[I]n cases involving lifetime employment contracts, many courts ignore the parties' desires. In some jurisdictions, lifetime employment contracts are terminable at will unless the[r]e is proof of "sufficient additional consideration." . . . In these jurisdictions, the presumption will not be rebutted even by strong, independent evidence that the parties intended the contract to last for life. . . .

However, other courts utilize a more flexible approach. These courts view the presence of such consideration as proof that the parties intended the employment relation to be more binding than the standard terminable at will agreement. These courts view additional consideration as a factor to consider in determining the parties intent but not as a rigid requirement. . . .

If the parties exchanged "extra" consideration, it is logical that they expected their relationship to be more lasting than the usual employment agreement. However, it is very possible that the parties so intended but did not exchange additional consideration. The surrounding circumstances and the parties' own expressions may still provide clear evidence of that intent. . . .

We agree with [this] reasoning. The at-will presumption may only be rebutted by clear evidence that the parties contracted for a definite period. . . . A promise of permanent or lifetime employment may be nothing more than a casual aside. Or, it may be purely aspirational. The employer may be expressing his hope that a valued employee will stay with him forever. However, he may not have intended to create a binding agreement. These dangers are sufficiently real that courts must look to the circumstances surrounding the parties' agreement. . . . The presence of additional consideration is only a single factor, albeit an important one, which a court must consider to ascertain that intent. When the court is certain of the parties' intent, it must enforce that intent, irrespective of whether additional consideration is present. . . .

In the instant case, Oliver Realty impliedly adopted Grant Building's promise to Greene of lifetime employment. In exchange for that promise, Greene alleges that he worked for twenty-four years at a pay rate below union scale. . . . The [trial] court concluded that Greene worked at sub-union rates in exchange for a promise that he would not be laid off and not in exchange for a lifetime contract. This is an inappropriate conclusion. . . . Greene's belief that he had been promised lifetime employment was sufficiently strong that he explained his position to a supervisor after Oliver took over Grant Building. The court must allow the jury to consider Greene's alleged "additional consideration" as well as all the circumstances surrounding the agreement. A jury might reasonably . . . conclude that Greene has clearly rebutted the at-will presumption. . . .

NOTES

1. *Policy Support for at Will? Greene* provides a more considered analysis of the validity of the at-will presumption than *Hanson*. The court rejects the doctrinal arguments grounded in notions of mutuality and criticizes precedents invoking the additional consideration requirement. Yet the court ultimately comes out in favor of the at-will presumption based largely on pragmatic concerns. Articulate these concerns and the policy arguments the court advances in favor of the at-will rule. Are they convincing?

2. *Employer and Employee Expectations.* The *Greene* court suggests that treating at will as a presumption is administratively efficient because it accords with what most parties want. If at will is in fact a "legal recognition of the parties' normal expectations," then using the presumption reduces costs that litigating this issue would entail. Do you agree with the premise of this argument? Do most "parties" desire an at-will relationship? Some commentators say yes, citing the prevalence of at-will relationships. Given that parties can contract out of at will, the fact that they generally do not, attests to their preference for at-will relationships. *See, e.g.*, Richard A. Epstein, *In Defense of the Contract at Will*, 51 U. CHI. L. REV. 947, 951-52 (1984); J. Hoult Verkerke, *An Empirical Perspective on Indefinite Term Employment Contracts: Resolving the Just Cause Debate*, 1995 WIS. L. REV. 837. Other commentators see the predominance of at-will relationships as a reflection of employee vulnerability and suggest that a rule favoring continued employment more closely approximates employee expectations and preferences. *See, e.g.*, Lawrence E. Blades, *Employment at Will vs. Individual Freedom: On Limiting the Abusive Exercise of Employer Power*, 67 COLUM. L. REV. 1404, 1404-05 (1967); Clyde W. Summers, *The Contract of Employment and the Rights of Individual Employees: Fair Representation and Employment at Will*, 52 FORDHAM L. REV. 1082, 1105-06 (1984). Which position do you find more persuasive?

Do employees even think in terms of negotiating for job security? In her studies of workers' perceptions of employment rights, Professor Pauline Kim found that a majority of respondents erroneously believed that the law protected them from certain types of arbitrary discharge. *See* Pauline T. Kim, *Bargaining with Imperfect Information: A Study of Worker Perceptions of Legal Protection in an At-Will World*, 83 COR-NELL L. REV. 105, 133-36 (1997); *see also* Larry A. Dimatteo, Robert C. Bird, & Jason A. Colquitt, Justice, *Employment, and the Psychological Contract*, 90 OR. L. REV. 449, 513 (2011) (empirical study showing that "scenarios involving procedural or substantive unfairness were positively correlated with increased propensities [of employees] to retaliate and litigate").

Stories about seemingly frivolous or unjustified terminations occasionally spark headlines. One prominent example was the firing of car salesman John Stone for wearing a Green Bay Packers tie to work at a Chicago car dealership — and then refusing to remove it — the day after the Packers defeated the Chicago Bears in the 2011 NFC Championship Game. Stone claimed he wore the tie to support the team and to honor his late grandmother, a life-long Packers fan who passed away before the big victory. Stone's manager fired him after repeatedly telling Stone to remove the tie. The manager admitted firing Stone for failure to remove necktie, contending that it was inconsistent with the dealership's promotions associated with the Bears and might be off-putting to customers. For a discussion of this incident, *see* posting of Jeffery M. Hirsch to Workplace Prof Blog, *Apparently Someone Isn't a Packers Fan* (Jan. 26, 2011); *see also* http://sports.yahoo.com/nfl/blog/shutdown_corner/post/Chi-cago-man-wears-Packers-tie-to-work-is-prompt?urn=nfl-311976. Does the outrage or criticism that usually follows such an arbitrary termination tell us something about worker expectations regarding the legality of such discharges? Or does it simply reflect moral disapproval of how the employer "conducts business," unconnected to presumed legal protections?

If most employees do not fully understand the at-will regime, is it possible to draw conclusions about their contractual preferences? Does the prevalence of misinformation and the risk of employer overreaching suggest a need to rethink at will as a default rule? *See* Cynthia Estlund, *How Wrong Are Employees About Their Rights?*, 77 N.Y.U. L. Rev. 21-27 (2002) (suggesting that erroneous beliefs held by employers that they are overly vulnerable to litigation and those of employees — that they can only be fired for just cause — justify a need for a law requiring an explicit waiver of just cause protection). For additional scholarship supporting employment at will reform on various grounds, *see* Rachel Arnow-Richman, *Mainstreaming Employment Contract Law: The Common Law Case for Reasonable Notice of Termination*, 66 Fla. L. Rev. 1513 (2014); Jeffrey M. Hirsch, *The Law of Termination: Doing More with Less*, 68 Md. L. Rev. 89 (2008); Nicole B. Porter, *The Perfect Compromise: Bridging the Gap Between At-Will Employment and Just Cause*, 87 Neb. L. Rev. 62, 84 (2008); Ann C. McGinley, *Rethinking Civil Rights and Employment at Will: Toward a Coherent National Discharge Policy*, 57 Ohio St. L. J. 1443 (1996); Theodore J. St. Antoine, *A Seed Germinates: Unjust Discharge Reform Heads Toward Full Flower*, 67 Neb. L. Rev. 56 (1988).

3. *Who Is the Employer?* What does it mean to talk about the interests of the "employer"? Since the employer is usually an entity, not a person, actions or decisions of its individual representatives — its managers, supervisors, and executives — may not be consistent. Note that in *Greene* the employer that made the alleged lifetime employment commitment was Grant Building; the defendant in the case was Oliver Realty, a successor company. Unionized employees generally have provisions in their collective bargaining agreements dealing with the possibility of a change of control, but unrepresented workers without written contracts may be at the mercy of the new employer. Similar problems can arise in the context of ordinary managerial turnover. What one supervisor tells a subordinate may not be acceptable to his or her replacement in subsequent years, or even to that supervisor's own immediate supervisor who may be unaware of the assurances being made. Does the risk of managerial turnover or changes in corporate philosophy suggest the need for greater job security for the workers? Or does it underscore the need for the flexibility that the at-will presumption protects?

4. *The Role of the Jury.* What do you make of the court's concern about jury sympathies? Does this reflect an elitist view of the intellectual capabilities and emotional susceptibility of ordinary people? Or do you think there are legitimate reasons to distrust juries in employment cases? Is this kind of dispute different from other cases involving a single individual suing a business or commercial entity?

5. *Mutuality of Obligation.* Both *Hanson* and *Greene* allude to "mutuality of obligation," a notion historically invoked by courts as a justification for the additional consideration requirement. Mutuality is the idea that, where there is an exchange of promises, both parties must be bound for the court to recognize a contract. Mutuality does not, however, require equivalency of obligation. So viewed, it is just another term for consideration. *See Avion Syst. v. Thompson*, 666 S.E.2d 464, (Ga. App. 2008) ("[Where] the employer offers employment and agrees to pay definite compensation, this consideration is adequate to sustain the contract, and '[t]he fact that the employee agrees to further restrictions and warranties not placed upon the employer does not divest the contract of mutuality.'"); *Worley v. Wyoming Bottling Co.*, 1 P.3d 615, 623 (Wyo. 2000) ("The demand for mutuality of obligation, although appealing in its symmetry, is simply a species of the forbidden inquiry into the adequacy of consideration."). The *Hanson* court seems to acknowledge this, noting that "lack of mutuality in itself is not fatal to the plaintiff's case" if the consideration requirement is satisfied. But the court ultimately finds against the plaintiff, concluding "that there is in fact no binding contract for life employment when the employee has not agreed to it; that is, when he is free to abandon it at any time." Similarly, although *Greene* disclaims the relevance of mutuality of obligation, it expresses concern that the employer and employee do not have equal ability to enforce their contractual rights. That is, in a situation where the employer and employee both agree to be bound for a set period of time, it can be difficult for the employer to obtain relief if the employee breaches the agreement. Don't such statements cast doubt on the courts' assertions that mutuality, in the sense of equivalency of obligation, is a dead letter? Are the concerns raised by *Greene*, with respect to remedies, relevant in a case where no one is alleging a fixed commitment by the employee? Or is the court just bringing mutuality of obligation in through the back door?

6. *Employment and Unilateral Contract Theory.* A further criticism of the mutuality rationale draws on the distinction between unilateral and bilateral contracts. Recall your first-year contracts class. Bilateral contracts involve two promises, made in exchange for each other, which each party is obligated to perform. The presence of a promise on each side creates mutuality. Unilateral contracts involve a single promise made in exchange for a performance, which obligates the promisor only if the offeree renders the requested performance. *See generally Cook v. Johnson*, 221 P.2d 525, 527 (Wash. 1950). In a unilateral contract there is no mutuality, nor is mutuality required, because the contract is formed following performance, at which point only the promisor is bound. Historically, employment has been viewed as unilateral: The employer promises to pay wages if the employee performs the job. However, the employee is not obligated to work; he or she may quit at any point. Do you agree with this characterization of the relationship? Does the employee make any return promises to the employer? If so, do they make the relationship bilateral? If the relationship is unilateral, as courts suggest, mutuality should not pose an obstacle to claims for job security. On the other hand, there may be reasons why treating the relationship as bilateral can benefit employees, for instance, in cases involving implied contracts for job security based on employer policies, which will be discussed later in this chapter.

7. *Understanding the Significance of a Presumption.* What is the status of the at-will presumption in Pennsylvania following *Greene*? What factors are relevant in determining whether a contract for job security exists? Does *Greene*'s refinement of the additional consideration requirement alter the traditional at-will presumption articulated in Wood's treatise? Or does it represent a return to the true meaning of presumption as a vehicle for determining intent? Consider Professor Clyde Summers's view of the additional consideration requirement as traditionally applied by courts:

> [One] spurious contractual doctrine, sometimes used [by courts] . . . was that to overcome the presumption that employment for an indefinite term was employment at will the employee must give some additional consideration. . . . An employee must give something more. Why something more than faithful service was required was never clearly explained. There seems to be an assumption that because wages for work performed had been paid, the work could not be consideration for a promise of continued employment. As any first semester law student knows, however, one performance can be consideration to support two or even twenty promises. The work performed could be consideration for both the wages paid and the promise of future employment. The requirement of additional consideration was but a device for converting [the at-will] presumption into a substantive rule so that even an express promise of permanent employment would not bind the employer.

Clyde W. Summers, *The Contract of Employment and the Rights of Individual Employees: Fair Representation and Employment At Will*, 52 FORDHAM L. REV. 1082, 1098 (1984).

Compare the following defense of the historical rule:

> The Wood formulation has been characterized as unduly rigid, in that it "force[s]" courts to ignore facts and circumstances indicative of the intention of the parties. But there is nothing "rigid" or inflexible about Wood's formulation. Wood does not suggest that it should be impermissible or even difficult for a plaintiff to prove that the parties intended that the employment relationship would last for a certain length of time. All it says is that plaintiff has the burden of proving that a contract of employment with no express duration was nevertheless intended by the parties to continue for a fixed duration. Nothing in the rule forecloses a jury from considering all the facts and circumstances from which inferences might be drawn concerning what the contract had been. Of course, that is the role of a presumption: to decide issues where facts are skimpy or absent; presumptions are not supposed to keep facts from being introduced into evidence, nor are they supposed to decide what "surrounding circumstances" may count as a fact.

Mayer G. Freed & Daniel D. Polsby, *The Doubtful Provenance of "Wood's Rule" Revisited*, 22 ARIZ. ST. L.J. 551, 553 (1990); *see also* Arnow-Richman, *supra* (arguing that the ability of at-will parties to terminate the relationship without notice "is neither historically supported nor legally correct"; instead, "reasonable notice" should be required).

8. *A Phoenix from the Ashes?* In *Scott v. Extracorporeal*, 545 A.2d 334 (Pa. Super. Ct. 1988), decided by the same court one year after *Greene*, the plaintiff alleged breach of a contract for job security on the basis of a combination of circumstances, including her manager's promise of "permanent" employment, references to permanent employment status and to "for cause" bases for discipline and termination in the employer's personnel manual, and the employee's execution of an agreement assigning any inventions derived during employment to the employer. The court disregarded the references to "permanent" employment as "too broad to be enforced" and found nothing in the personnel manual suggesting that discharge could only be for cause. *Id.* at 337. The court also held that the assignment of inventions agreement did not constitute additional consideration. It explained:

> [T]here is no indication that appellant brought any abilities to the job, aside from the services for which she was compensated, which were beneficial to her employer or that she sacrificed anything tangible pursuant to the agreement beyond that for which she was paid. The at-will presumption is not overcome every time a worker sacrifices theoretical rights and privileges. . . . We have no indication that she did conceive anything of value during her employment, or that at the time she was hired it was reasonably likely she would. The privileges and rights which appellant sacrificed were so minimal that in no sense can we say the agreement rose to the level of "additional consideration" as our courts have defined it.
>
>   . . . We do not read *Greene [v. Oliver Realty]* to stand for the proposition that any time a discharged employee talismanically recites that he was promised "permanent" employment, the case must automatically proceed to trial.

Id. at 339-40. Does this excerpt change your understanding of the significance of *Greene?*

While the strength of the employment at will presumption may vary in particular cases, it is important to bear in mind that some modern courts continue to hold fast to the historical version of the rule set out in *Hanson*. *See, e.g., Edwards v. Geisinger Clinic*, 459 F. App'x 125 (3d Cir. 2012) (holding that the parties did not enter into an express employment contract for a definite term when the clinic agreed to sponsor the physician's three-year H-1B visa or by virtue of the Clinic's statements to the American Board of Radiology that the plaintiff was participating in four-year certification program); *Turner v. Newsome*, 3 So. 3d 913, 922 (Ala. App. 2008) (concluding that the written promise to employ plaintiff "until the retirement of the President" was an indefinite contract and employee accepting additional responsibilities and work hours, putting educational opportunities on hold, and not revealing employer's "immoral conduct" were not sufficient consideration to support an "extraordinary" contract for lifetime employment).

9. *Just Cause and Legislative Reform.* One U.S. jurisdiction has statutorily rejected the employment at will presumption. The Montana Wrongful Discharge from Employment Act of 1987 ("WDEA") alters the at-will presumption by creating a statutory cause of action for employees terminated without "good cause" subsequent to their completion of the employer's designated probationary period. *See* MONT. CODE ANN. § 39-2-904(2) (2013). Similarly, under the proposed Model Employment Termination Act of 1991 ("META"), an employer could not terminate without good cause unless the parties mutually agree to waive the good cause requirement in a written agreement. *See* META §§ 3(a), 4(c). These approaches essentially reverse the at-will presumption, making job security the default rule. In exchange for this benefit, they place certain limits on damages that protect employers. *See, e.g.*, MONT. CODE ANN. § 39-2-905 (2013) (capping damages at four years of wages and disallowing other forms of compensatory damages). Although comparable legislation has been introduced in other jurisdictions, to date no state has adopted META or followed Montana's lead. Why do you think that is?

History suggests a possible answer. The movement to adopt unjust dismissal legislation came about in the 1980s following the issuance of a number of pro-plaintiff decisions, several of which you will read in the subsequent sections. Many perceived these decisions as heralding judicial adoption of a broad rule requiring just cause for termination. In such an environment, employers were willing to support unjust dismissal legislation that offered increased predictability over common law expansion of employee rights and created an opportunity for employer interest groups to exact some pro-business concessions in the legislative drafting process. Indeed, both the WDEA and META were widely viewed as compromise proposals, and employers played a significant role in securing adoption of the Montana law. *See* Alan B. Krueger, *The Evolution of Unjust-Dismissal Legislation in the United States*, 44 INDUS. & LAB. REV. 644 (1990-91); Daniel J. Libenson, *Leasing Human Capital: Toward A New Foundation for Employment Termination Law*, 27 BERKELEY J. EMP. & LAB. L. 111 (2006); Theodore J. St. Antoine, *The Making of the Model Employment Termination Act*, 69 WASH. L. REV. 361 (1994).

As the previous note suggests, however, fears of a full-scale retreat from employment at will proved unfounded. In fact, contemporary developments have led some to speculate that the law is moving in the opposite direction, toward a refortified presumption of employment at will. *See e.g.*, Rachel Arnow-Richman, *Employment as Transaction*, 39 SETON HALL L. REV. 447 (2009); Jonathan Fineman, *The Inevitable Demise of the Implied Employment Contract*, 29 BERKELEY J. EMP. & LAB. L. 345 (2008); *cf.* Matthew Finkin, *Shoring Up the Citadel (At-Will Employment)*, 24

HOFSTRA LAB. & EMP. L.J. 1, 27 (2006) (arguing that the draft Restatement of Employment Law chapter on termination "manhandles doctrine to achieve a specific end — to permit employers to free themselves of what they might conceive in hindsight to be an undesirable commitment to job security"). If such assertions are true, it is perhaps unsurprising that employer support for legal reform (and consequently the ability to pass unjust dismissal legislation) ultimately dwindled.

PROBLEM

2-1. Suppose that William Greene hires you to serve as his trial attorney on remand following the Superior Court's decision. What litigation strategy would you pursue? Would you try to demonstrate additional consideration? Can you? What other evidence, if any, can Greene use to establish the parties' intention to create a lifetime employment contract? Who would you rather have as a client given the rules articulated by the Superior Court — Greene or Hanson?

B. ORAL AND IMPLIED CONTRACT RIGHTS TO JOB SECURITY

As you can see from *Greene*, despite the entrenched idea of employment at will, modern courts have questioned the justifications for the rule and the inflexible manner in which it has traditionally been applied. Indeed, in the last several decades, courts have recognized a variety of exceptions grounded in contract and related common law principles that have significantly weakened the at-will presumption. No one reason explains this trend. Depending on the case and the court, judicial resistance to the at-will presumption may reflect disenchantment with the rule on policy grounds, doctrinal objections to its application as a presumption, sympathy for individual plaintiffs in particular cases, or a desire to make the law conform more closely to the real expectations of parties in a complex relationship.

As you read, keep these possible explanations in mind. In each case, consider whether courts are correctly applying contract doctrine, whether the result they reach is fair under the particular facts, and what policy implications flow from the decision, both in terms of how the result will influence employers in running their businesses and the ultimate social consequences to employees. Is it fair to say that the contract rules surrounding at-will employment are in disarray, as some commentators have suggested, or can you see any unifying themes in the exceptions?

1. Reliance on Offers of Employment

The ability to terminate employment at will can have harsh effects on neophyte employees who may quit an existing job, relocate, or turn down other job offers in order to accept a new position. Should the law provide any recourse for at-will employees terminated shortly after accepting work?

≡≡≡ *Goff-Hamel v. Obstetricians & Gynecologists*
588 N.W.2d 798 (Neb. 1999)

WRIGHT, J.

[Julie] Goff-Hamel worked for Hastings Family Planning for 11 years. Prior to leaving Hastings Family Planning, Goff-Hamel was earning $24,000 plus [benefits].

In July 1993, Goff-Hamel met with representatives of Obstetricians regarding the possibility of employment. Present at the meeting were [Dr. George Adam, a part owner of Obstetricians] and Larry Draper, a consultant of Obstetricians involved in personnel decisions. Adam had approached Goff-Hamel in June 1993 about working for him as a patient relations and outreach coordinator. [She initially declined the offer.] Adam spoke to her one month later, asking her to reconsider and whether she was ready to "jump ship and come work for him." Goff-Hamel told Adam she would be interested in hearing some details, and an interview was set for July 27 at Adam's office.

At the meeting, Adam represented to Goff-Hamel that the position would be full time and would start at a salary of $10 per hour and that she would be provided 2 weeks' paid vacation, three or four paid holidays, uniforms, and an educational stipend. A retirement plan would start after the end of the second year, retroactive to the end of the first year. The job would not provide health insurance.

Goff-Hamel was offered a job with Obstetricians during the July 27, 1993, meeting, and she accepted the job offer at that time. . . . [I]t was agreed that she would start her employment on October 4. Goff-Hamel gave notice to Hastings Family Planning in August. . . .

Subsequently, Goff-Hamel was provided with uniforms for her job. She was given a copy of her schedule for the first week of work. . . .

On October 3, 1993, Goff-Hamel was told by Draper that she should not report to work the next morning as had been planned. Draper told her that Janel Foote, the wife of a part owner of Obstetricians, Dr. Terry Foote, opposed the hiring of Goff-Hamel.

. . . Goff-Hamel sought replacement employment, but was unable to obtain employment until April 1995, when she was employed part time at the rate of $11 per hour.

The trial court concluded that since Goff-Hamel was to be employed at will, her employment could be terminated at any time, including before she began working. The court concluded that under either contract law or promissory estoppel, Obstetricians was entitled to a judgment as a matter of law. . . .

We have consistently held that when employment is not for a definite term and there are no contractual, statutory, or constitutional restrictions upon the right of discharge, an employer may lawfully discharge an employee whenever and for whatever cause it chooses. Therefore, the trial court correctly determined as a matter of law that Goff-Hamel could not bring a claim for breach of an employment contract.

Goff-Hamel's second cause of action was based upon promissory estoppel. "[T]he development of the law of promissory estoppel 'is an attempt by the courts to keep remedies abreast of increased moral consciousness of honesty and fair representations in all business dealings.'" *Rosnick v. Dinsmore*, 457 N.W.2d 793, 801 (Neb. 1990).

Promissory estoppel provides for damages as justice requires and does not attempt to provide the plaintiff damages based upon the benefit of the bargain. It requires only that reliance be reasonable and foreseeable. It does not impose the requirement that the promise giving rise to the cause of action must be so comprehensive in scope as to meet the requirements of an offer that would ripen into a contract if accepted by the promisee.

We have not specifically addressed whether promissory estoppel may be asserted as the basis for a cause of action for detrimental reliance upon a promise of at-will employment. . . .

Other jurisdictions which have addressed the question of whether a cause of action for promissory estoppel can be stated in the context of a prospective at-will employee are split on the issue. Some have held that an employee can recover damages incurred as a result of resigning from the former at-will employment in reliance on a promise of other at-will employment. They have determined that when a prospective employer knows or should know that a promise of employment will induce an employee to leave his or her current job, such employer shall be liable for the reliant's damages. Recognizing that both the prospective new employer and the prior employer could have fired the employee without cause at any time, they have concluded that the employee would have continued to work in his or her prior employment if it were not for the offer by the prospective employer. Although damages have not been allowed for wages lost from the prospective at-will employment, damages have been allowed based upon wages from the prior employment and other damages incurred in reliance on the job offer.

In contrast, other jurisdictions have held as a matter of law that a prospective employee cannot recover damages incurred in reliance on an unfulfilled promise of at-will employment, concluding that reliance on a promise consisting solely of at-will employment is unreasonable as a matter of law because the employee should know that the promised employment could be terminated by the employer at any time for any reason without liability. These courts have stated that an anomalous result occurs when recovery is allowed for an employee who has not begun work, when the same employee's job could be terminated without liability 1 day after beginning work. . . .

In *Grouse v. Group Health Plan, Inc.*, 306 N.W.2d 114 (Minn. 1981), a pharmacist working at a drugstore desired employment with a hospital or clinic. He accepted employment with a clinic and gave 2 weeks' notice to the drugstore. During this period, he declined a job with a hospital because he had accepted employment with the clinic. Upon reporting to work, he was told that someone else had been hired because the pharmacist did not satisfy certain hiring requirements of the clinic. He had difficulty obtaining other full-time employment and suffered wage loss as a result.

. . . The court stated:

> [A]ppellant had a right to assume he would be given a good faith opportunity to perform his duties to the satisfaction of respondent once he was on the job. He was not only denied that opportunity but resigned the position he already held in reliance on the firm offer which respondent tendered him.

Id. at 116.

The court also recognized that under appropriate circumstances, promissory estoppel could apply even if the employee was fired after he had commenced employment, thus concluding that its ruling would not necessarily create an anomalous result.

[The court went on to summarize additional cases from other jurisdictions.]

Having reviewed and considered decisions from other jurisdictions, we conclude under the facts of this case that promissory estoppel can be asserted in connection with the offer for at-will employment and that the trial court erred in granting Obstetricians summary judgment. A cause of action for promissory estoppel is based upon a promise which the promisor should reasonably expect to induce action or forbearance on the part of the promisee which does in fact induce such an action or forbearance. Here, promissory estoppel is appropriate where Goff-Hamel acted to her detriment in order to avail herself of the promised employment. . . .

STEPHAN, J., dissenting.

I respectfully dissent. In my opinion, the district court correctly determined as a matter of law that Goff-Hamel could not proceed under either a breach of contract or a promissory estoppel theory of recovery. I cannot reconcile the result reached by the majority or its rationale with our firmly established legal principles governing at-will employment. As succinctly and, in my view, correctly stated by the district court: "Since plaintiff could have been terminated after one day's employment without the defendant incurring liability, logic dictates she could also be terminated before the employment started."

The majority relies in part on *Grouse v. Group Health Plan, Inc.*, which concluded that the principles of promissory estoppel set forth in the RESTATEMENT OF CONTRACTS § 90 (1932) could apply to a termination of at-will employment which occurred before the employee actually started working because "under appropriate circumstances we believe [Restatement of Contracts] section 90 would apply even after employment has begun." However, we held in *Merrick v. Thomas*, 522 N.W.2d 402 (Neb. 1994), that an at-will employee who was discharged a short time after she began working could not, as a matter of law, assert a promissory estoppel claim for damages resulting from resignation of her previous employment. Thus, this essential premise of the holding in *Grouse* is directly contrary to our law. Another basis for the decision in *Grouse*, as quoted in the majority opinion, is that one who is offered employment has "a right to assume he would be given a good faith opportunity to perform his duties to the satisfaction" of the employer. This concept is foreign to our law and entirely inconsistent with the established principle, acknowledged by the majority, that in the absence of contractual, statutory, or constitutional restrictions, an employer may discharge an at-will employee "whenever and for whatever cause it chooses." *Myers v. Nebraska Equal Opp. Comm.*, 582 N.W.2d 362 (Neb. 1998). Thus, whether an at-will employee performs in a satisfactory manner is immaterial to the employer's right to discharge, and there is no basis under our law for an assumption that satisfactory performance by such an employee would create an entitlement to continued employment. . . .

The conflict between the court's decision today and the law of at-will employment is further demonstrated by the manner in which the majority addresses the issue of damages. Goff-Hamel's damage claim is based entirely upon her allegation that after learning on October 3, 1993, that appellee had withdrawn its offer of employment, she was unable to find "comparable" full-time employment until May 15, 1995. The majority acknowledges that under the theory of recovery which it recognizes in this case, damages cannot be "based upon the wages the employee would have earned in the prospective employment because the employment was terminable at will." Following the same logic, damages based upon wage loss during any *interval* between withdrawal of a promise of at-will employment and the securing of "comparable" employment would not be recoverable, because the promised employment could have been terminated by either party at any time after it had begun. Thus, the record reflects no factual basis upon which damages claimed by Goff-Hamel could be awarded under the remedy which the majority recognizes.

I would follow what I consider to be the better reasoned view, that promissory estoppel may not be utilized to remedy an unfulfilled promise of at-will employment. I acknowledge that this reasoning would produce a seemingly harsh result from the perspective of Goff-Hamel under the facts of this case, but to some degree, this is inherent in the concept of at-will employment. For example, in *Hamersky v. Nicholson Supply Co.*, 517 N.W.2d 382, 385 (Neb. 1994), a 22-year employee was discharged "without any notification, cause or reason," and although this action may seem harsh, we held that it was permissible where there was no contractual provision for employment of specific duration. Similarly, an employer which has made a significant expenditure in training an at-will employee may feel harshly treated if, upon completing the training, the employee immediately utilizes his or her newly acquired skills to secure more remunerative employment with a competitor. If the law of at-will employment were regularly bent to circumvent what some may consider a harsh result in a particular case, its path would soon become hopelessly circuitous and impossible to follow.

Employment for a specific duration imposes certain benefits and burdens upon each party to the relationship. Under our established law, parties wishing to create such a relationship must do so by contract. Where, as in this case, the parties have not chosen to impose contractual obligations upon themselves, it is my view that a court should not utilize the principle of promissory estoppel to impose the subjective expectations of either party upon the other. I agree with the view that in the context of an employment relationship, promissory estoppel "should be construed 'in such a way that it compl[e]ments, rather than undermines, traditional contract principles.'"

NOTES

1. *Promissory Estoppel, Employment at Will, and Newly Hired Employees.* In recognizing the plaintiff's promissory estoppel claim, *Goff-Hamel* cites *Grouse v. Group Health Plan* for the proposition that an employee is entitled to a good faith opportunity to perform to the employer's satisfaction. The dissent criticizes this premise as "directly contrary" to employment at will. Which opinion do you find more convincing? In practice, many employers designate starting employees as "probationary," reinforcing the idea that the employee has no job security during the first few months of employment. Does this point to a logical flaw in the courts' analyses in *Goff-Hamel* and *Grouse*? Or is it still possible to reconcile promissory estoppel protection with the at-will presumption?

2. *The One-Day Worker.* A Minnesota court directly addressed the *Goff-Hamel* and *Grouse* scenario of the one-day-hired, one-day-fired employee. In *Gorham v. Benson Optical*, 539 N.W.2d 798 (Minn. Ct. App. 1995), Gorham accepted a job offer as a regional manager with the defendant. After confirming the position he gave notice to his current employer, who tried to entice him to stay by offering him a raise, which he declined. Prior to starting his new job, however, the company officer who had hired

Gorham left, and Gorham was terminated on his first day at work. In addressing his subsequent promissory estoppel claim, the court opined:

> We see no relevant difference between Gorham, who reported to the national sales meeting on his first day of employment, and Grouse, who was denied even one day on the job. Both men relied to their detriment on the promise of a new job, only to discover that the opportunity had disintegrated before they ever actually started working. Neither man had a "good faith opportunity to perform his duties."

Id. at 801. Gorham was fired the very day he showed up for work. How much more time would have constituted a "good faith opportunity" to perform his duties? Two weeks? A month? A 90-day "probationary" period?

3. *Reasonableness of Reliance.* Courts rejecting the applicability of promissory estoppel often do so on the grounds that, while the worker does in fact rely, the reliance is not reasonable if the offer is for at-will employment. *See, e.g., White v. Roche Biomedical Labs., Inc.,* 807 F. Supp. 1212, 1219-20 (D.S.C. 1992) (concluding that "reliance on a promise consisting solely of at-will employment is unreasonable as a matter of law since such a promise creates no enforceable rights in favor of the employee other than the right to collect wages accrued for work performed"); *cf. Petitte v. DSL,* 925 A.2d 457, 463 (Conn. App. 2007) (noting in rejecting plaintiff's breach of contract claim based on revoked offer of employment that "this clarification of the law serves to put employees on notice of the risk they take when leaving existing employment for another one"). Pushed to its logical conclusion, this argument would seem to foreclose promissory estoppel liability entirely since, by definition, there is no promise of continued employment and any reliance to the contrary would be ipso facto unreasonable.

Do you agree? Can it be reasonable (as a practical matter) for an employee to rely on a job offer even if there is no legal commitment to continued employment? If you said yes, does your answer change if the employer is more explicit about the plaintiff's at-will status? In an episode that made at least the academic headlines, the University of Illinois rescinded an offer of employment to a professor who had apparently quit his prior tenured position and moved to Champaign-Urbana to begin teaching there. Although the facts are as yet unclear and much of the debate has focused on First Amendment and academic freedom issues, there is an interesting contract overlay. Reportedly, the "offer" was subject to the approval of the University's Board of Trustees and therefore (despite the fact that such approval may have been routine), there was no offer at all. Even if that were true, does it follow that promissory estoppel would not apply because it would be unreasonable to rely on a nonoffer? Or is that the exact gap in contract law that promissory estoppel is supposed to fill? The contrasting views are on full display at http://www.concurringopinions.com/archives/2014/08/steven-salaitas-promissory-estoppel-claim-is-weak.html. For a discussion as to whether the "offer" was an offer after all (and thus there might have been an enforceable contract), *see* http://www.concurringopinions.com/archives/2014/08/does-salaita-have-a-contract-claim.html#more-90272.

4. *Remedy.* The majority in *Goff-Hamel* is careful to point out the limited nature of the promissory estoppel remedy. Understand the difference between the amount of damages permitted under these opinions and what would have been available had the plaintiffs been able to establish breach of a contract for job security. Suppose, for instance, that Goff-Hamel earned $1,500 per month in her old job and was promised

$1,600 per month by the defendant. After being terminated, she searches unsuccessfully for alternate employment for two months before accepting a position at $1,400 per month. How should the court calculate her damages, assuming she prevails on remand? Now suppose instead that following her termination Goff-Hamel's former employer happily takes her back at the same salary she had earned prior to giving notice. Is she entitled to anything?

Damages in promissory estoppel cases are often calculated based on the plaintiff's *prior* employment — the loss of that is his "reliance" interest. But what if that position was itself at will? Should that limit recovery or should the plaintiff be able to recover his "expectation" interest — the amount he would have earned in the new position? And even as to the reliance interest, there is no guarantee that the plaintiff would have remained in the prior job. The employer in *Toscano v. Greene Music*, 21 Cal. Rptr. 3d 732 (Ct. App. 2004), made such an argument in seeking to limit the plaintiff's damages to wages lost between resigning his prior employment and the anticipated start date of the promised job. The court rejected the limitation, holding that lost future wages with a prior employer are recoverable under a promissory estoppel theory, provided they are not "speculative, remote, contingent or merely possible." *Id.* at 738. It went on, however, to hold that the trial court's award of lost wages until plaintiff's retirement was improper under this standard because it was based solely on the fact that Toscano had a history of remaining with his current employer until offered new employment.

Do results like this diminish the significance to employees of courts' recognition of the promissory estoppel cause of action? Or do such limitations strike an appropriate balance in light of the presumption of employment at will? Given the result in *Toscano*, how would you go about helping a future plaintiff overcome such hurdles to establishing damages? *Cf. Helmer v. Bingham Toyota Isuzu*, 29 Cal. Rptr. 3d 136 (Ct. App. 2005) (affirming award of damages of lost future wages with prior employer from time of resignation through retirement on plaintiff's promissory fraud claim where prior supervisor testified that plaintiff was a reliable employee and would have been rehired but for a strict no-rehire policy).

5. *Proof of Reliance.* What constitutes detrimental reliance for purposes of promissory estoppel? The most convincing cases are those involving employees who relocate or incur significant expense in preparing for their new job. *See, e.g., Sheppard v. Morgan Keegan & Co.*, 266 Cal. Rptr. 784, 787 (Ct. App. 1990) ("[A]n employer cannot expect a new employee to sever his former employment and move across the country only to be terminated before the ink dries on his new lease[.]"). *Goff-Hamel* suggests giving up one's current job alone is sufficient to state a promissory estoppel claim. In *Grouse*, the employee gave up his job and turned down a second offer. What if the employee simply refrains from applying for other jobs based on the assurances of his or her current employer? *See Hanly v. Riverside Methodist Hosps.*, 603 N.E.2d 1126, 1131 (Ohio Ct. App. 1991) (no promissory estoppel claim where plaintiff neither looked for nor turned down other employment nor was expressly dissuaded by employer from seeking outside opportunities). If an employee truly refrains from seeking alternative work because of a promise of job security, isn't that still reliance? In such a situation, what evidence could there be other than the employee's "bare assertion" of foregoing a job search? Perhaps the issue is not whether the employee actually relied on the promise in not looking for work, but rather, whether that reliance was detrimental. *See Fregara v. Jet Aviation Business Jets*, 764 F. Supp. 940, 949 (D.N.J. 1991) (no promissory estoppel claim where plaintiff was unemployed at time of job offer and therefore did not forgo anything of value in accepting position). If so, would it be enough to show that more lucrative alternative positions were available?

6. *Promises, Offers, and Representations.* Difficulties in proving reliance are not the only potential pitfalls for plaintiffs pursuing promissory estoppel claims. The way in which courts interpret and apply other elements often makes establishing promissory estoppel difficult. An example is found in *Schoff v. Combined Insurance Company of America*, 604 N.W.2d 43 (Iowa 1999). Plaintiff Ronald Schoff interviewed with Michael Hageman, a district manager for Defendant Combined Insurance Co. During the interview, Schoff completed an application that stated that bonding by Combined's bonding company was a condition of employment and asked about Schoff's criminal history. Schoff answered "no" to the question of whether he had ever been convicted of a felony although he had been convicted of serious misdemeanors, a fact that he disclosed to Hageman. Hageman never asked whether Schoff had ever been charged with a felony, and Schoff did not volunteer that the original charges resulting in his misdemeanor convictions were felony charges. In light of his belief that only felony convictions were pertinent to bonding, Hageman assured Schoff that "as long as [you] have no felony convictions, [your] criminal record [will] be no problem." *Id.* at 46. Prior to accepting Combined's offer to hire him as a sales representative, Schoff asked Hageman whether his criminal record would have any impact on his employment. Hageman again assured Schoff that it would not. When Schoff applied for fidelity bond coverage. Hageman completed an enrollment form for him, placing an "N/A" after a question about whether the applicant had ever been convicted, sentenced, or imprisoned. After three months on the job, Schoff was terminated when the bonding company denied coverage because Schoff had been charged with two felonies and had failed to disclose the information about his conviction history on the enrollment form. *See id.*

Although Hageman told Schoff that his criminal record would not affect his employment and that only felony convictions were relevant to employment and bonding decisions, the court rejected Schoff's claim that these statements provide a basis to estop Combined from firing him. The court reasoned as follows:

> Initially, we conclude that any statements made by Hageman that only felony convictions were important do not constitute an assertion that Combined would forbear a certain specific act, namely, discharging Schoff because of his felony charges and/or his failure to be bonded. These statements by Hageman more clearly fall within the common definition of a representation: "a statement . . . made to convey a particular view or impression of something with the intention of influencing opinion or action." Statements that only felony convictions are relevant to employment and bonding decisions are not the equivalent of a declaration that Combined would not fire Schoff because of his felony record. Hageman's statements merely conveyed his *impression* or *understanding* of a certain fact — that only felony convictions were relevant; as a matter of law, these statements do not constitute a promise.
>
> . . . . [W]e will not imply a promise from representations made by an employer, but will require strict proof that the defendant promised to do or not to do a specific act, and did not simply state the employer's view or impression of something.

Id. 51. As to the second statement made by Hageman — that Schoff's criminal record would not be a problem, even if the statement constituted a promise, it was not clear and definite:

[A]ny statement that Schoff's "criminal record" would not affect his employment is subject to some ambiguity in that the parties did not have the same knowledge with respect to the nature and extent of Schoff's criminal record. This ambiguity is crucial because Schoff was not fired because of his criminal record in general; he was fired because he could not be bonded. Similarly, he was not denied a bond due to his criminal record in general; rather he was not bonded because he had been charged with felonies and/or had not revealed his criminal record on his bond application. As a matter of law, any "promises" that Schoff's criminal record would not be a problem simply do not clearly and definitely encompass a promise that Schoff's felony charges would not be a problem or that his failure to be bonded would not be a problem. . . .

Id.

Note that the court goes to some length to distinguish between the "representations" made by Hageman and the type of definitive promise required for promissory estoppel. Do you understand the distinction the court is drawing? Do you agree with its characterization of the issue? Consider that in promissory estoppel claims outside of the employment context courts have held that the plaintiff need not demonstrate a definite offer to contract in order to show the defendant made a promise justifying reliance. *See, e.g., Hoffman v. Red Owl Stores, Inc.,* 133 N.W.2d 267, 276 (Wis. 1965) (noting in suit over promise to provide a franchise that §90 "does not impose the requirement that the promise . . . be so comprehensive in scope as to meet the requirements of an offer that would ripen into a contract if accepted"). Yet the court in *Schoff,* as well as courts in other employment cases, often construe the elements of a promissory estoppel claim more strictly. *See, e.g., Dumas v. Infinity Broadcasting Corp,* 416 F.3d 671, 677 (7th Cir. 2005) (suggesting that disc jockey who gave up previous job based on negotiations for employment that failed to come to fruition could not sustain a claim for promissory estoppel unless capable of establishing all of the elements of a valid contract other than consideration); *Ruud v. Great Plains Supply, Inc.,* 526 N.W.2d 369, 372 (Minn. 1995) (finding statements that "good employees would be taken care of" and plaintiff would be offered a "similar" position if things did not work out after he accepted relocation to management position at unprofitable store insufficiently definite to give rise to promissory estoppel claim). Does the employment context require a different interpretation of the doctrine than in other failed contract scenarios?

7. *Promissory Estoppel in the Real World.* As *Schoff* suggests, although many courts have recognized promissory estoppel claims in at-will relationships, they often establish high thresholds for proving the elements of the claim, making it difficult for employees to prevail. In a study of all reported promissory estoppel cases decided on the merits during a two-year period in the mid-1990s, Professor Robert Hillman found that employees were successful only 4.23 percent of the time. *See* Robert A. Hillman, *The Unfulfilled Promise of Promissory Estoppel in the Employment Setting,* 31 RUTGERS L.J. 1, 2 (1999), less than one-third the success rate in non-employment contexts. *Id.*

2. Assurances Made During Employment

The last section involved promises made to newly hired employees, some of whom had not even begun working for the employer. This section addresses the extent to which employees who have been working for some length of time for the employer are protected when relying on assurances of obtaining a certain position or of continued employment. The discussion begins where it left off above, with promissory estoppel. It then turns to various contract theories.

Cocchiara v. Lithia Motors, Inc.
297 P.3d 1277 (Ore. 2013)

BALMER, C.J.

In this employment case we must determine whether a prospective employee may bring a promissory estoppel claim or a fraudulent misrepresentation claim based on an employer's representations regarding a job that is terminable at will. Plaintiff worked as a salesperson for defendant for nearly eight years before he had a heart attack that required him to seek a less stressful job. In reliance on his manager's promise that plaintiff had been given a new "corporate" job with defendant that would meet his health needs, plaintiff turned down a job with a different employer. Ultimately, defendant did not hire plaintiff for the corporate job, and plaintiff subsequently had to take jobs that paid less than the corporate job with defendant or less than the position that he had turned down. Plaintiff brought this action against defendant claiming [*inter alia* promissory estoppel and fraudulent misrepresentation].

Facts

We state the facts in the light most favorable to plaintiff because the trial court granted defendant's motion for partial summary judgment. Plaintiff worked as a salesperson at a Lithia Dodge dealership from 1997 to October 2005. Following a major heart attack in 2004, plaintiff's doctors recommended that he find a less stressful job that would allow him to work shorter hours and avoid working on the weekends. Plaintiff discussed those needs with Summers, his General Sales Manager at the dealership, but he also pursued other employment because his sales job could not meet his health needs.

Plaintiff received an offer to be a sales representative for the Medford Mail Tribune, a position that satisfied his health requirements. Plaintiff went to Summers to tell him that he planned to take the Medford Mail Tribune job, and he told Summers that that job would be less stressful and would provide compensation that was comparable to his current position. Summers responded that plaintiff should not accept the Medford Mail Tribune position because he was "too valuable" to defendant. Summers then told plaintiff that there was a new "corporate" job available with defendant that would meet his health needs.

After placing a call to defendant's corporate offices, Summers advised plaintiff that he had been given the corporate position and that he would be contacted the next day to come in to finalize the paperwork. Plaintiff then asked Summers to confirm that the offer was definite, given plaintiff's outstanding offer from the Medford Mail Tribune. Summers confirmed that plaintiff had been given the job and that the meeting the next day was a "mere formality." Plaintiff acknowledges that there was no discussion as to whether or not the corporate job would be terminable at will. After his discussion with Summers, plaintiff told the Medford Mail Tribune that he had decided not to accept its offer because he had received another job with defendant.

When plaintiff met with one of defendant's representatives the next day, the representative told plaintiff that he had not been hired for the corporate job. Instead, the representative was meeting with plaintiff to interview him as one possible candidate for the corporate job. Ultimately, defendant did not hire plaintiff for that job. When plaintiff then tried to accept the Medford Mail Tribune's prior job offer, that job had been filled. Plaintiff later accepted a different sales representative job with the Medford Mail Tribune, but the job paid less than the previously offered job at the Medford Mail Tribune. Plaintiff subsequently accepted yet another job that paid less than the promised corporate job with defendant.

. . . As part of his claim for damages, plaintiff sought economic damages for the income that he would have earned in the corporate job with defendant. Defendant filed a motion for partial summary judgment, arguing that, because the corporate job was an at-will position that defendant could have fired plaintiff from at any time, plaintiff had no reasonable basis to rely on the corporate job offer, as required for both the promissory estoppel and fraudulent misrepresentation claims. Moreover, defendant argued, it would be illogical to hold defendant liable for damages that plaintiff would have been unable to recover had he been terminated on his first day. The trial court granted summary judgment on the promissory estoppel and fraudulent misrepresentation claims, noting that, even if plaintiff had relied on all the statements that Summers allegedly had made, plaintiff would lose

> [b]ecause they didn't tell him you got a job for the rest of your life here. * * * He didn't rely on having a job for more tha[n] a day because * * * nobody said to him, and you're going to have this job for X amount of days, months, or years. * * * [H]e couldn't rely on something that was never said to him.

[The Court of Appeals affirmed, relying on its prior decision in *Slate v. Saxon, Marquoit, Bertoni & Todd,* 999 P.2d 1152 (2000), which had held that a law clerk at the defendant law firm had no cause of action when the firm reneged on its offer of an associate attorney position. Given the nature of at-will employment, there was no reasonable basis for reliance since "the plaintiff could not *reasonably* have understood that the promised employment would last for any particular length of time"; further, "the plaintiff would have experienced the same losses if the defendants had hired him, but had 'discharged [him] immediately after he came to work rather than before.'" The Oregon Supreme Court had affirmed *Slate.*

Plaintiff argued that *Slate* was incorrectly decided "because it ignored the reality that prospective employees often rely on offers of at-will employment and that employers expect prospective employees to rely on those offers." Defendant responded that recognition of such a rule would essentially render the at-will rule meaningless. Holding that a prospective employee could recover for reasonable reliance on an offer of at-will employment "would create an unworkable rule regarding how long an employer would have to employ new hires."]

At-Will Employment Doctrine

Both parties agree that, in Oregon, "the general rule is that an employer may discharge an employee at any time and for any reason, absent a contractual, statutory, or constitutional requirement to the contrary." . . .

Perhaps because the at-will employment doctrine focuses on termination, courts have disagreed regarding the significance of the at-will nature of employment before employment begins. In particular, courts have disagreed whether it is reasonable to rely on an offer of at-will employment, which in turn affects whether an employer's termination of an at-will employment agreement before the employee begins working is actionable under a theory of promissory estoppel or fraudulent misrepresentation.

Promissory Estoppel

[Oregon has adopted §90 of the Restatement (Second) of Contracts] and [n]othing in our case law or the RESTATEMENT (SECOND) suggests that a promisee's reliance is *per se* unreasonable if the underlying promise is for a contract that is terminable at will. . . . Far from foreclosing such a claim, the RESTATEMENT (SECOND) provides the following illustration in the section on promissory estoppel:

> A applies to B, a distributor of radios manufactured by C, for a "dealer franchise" to sell C's products. Such franchises are revocable at will. B erroneously informs A that C has accepted the application and will soon award the franchise, that A can proceed to employ salesmen and solicit orders, and that A will receive an initial delivery of at least 30 radios. A expends $1,150 in preparing to do business, but does not receive the franchise or any radios. B is liable to A for the $1,150 but not for the lost profit on 30 radios.

RESTATEMENT (SECOND) § 90 comment d, illustration 8. Similarly to that illustration, in this case, Summers erroneously informed plaintiff that he had been given a job (that was terminable at will) and told him that he should turn down the position with the Medford Mail Tribune. The RESTATEMENT (SECOND) illustration indicates that the at-will nature of an underlying promise of employment does not bar a claim based on promissory estoppel, even if it might limit the nature of the damages available in some cases.

The RESTATEMENT (SECOND) approach is sound. An employer's legal right to fire an employee at any time and for any reason absent contrary contractual, statutory, or constitutional requirements does not carry with it a conclusive presumption that the employer will exercise that right. *See Tadsen v. Praegitzer Industries, Inc.,* 928 P.2d 980 (Ore. 1996) (rejecting the premise in a wrongful discharge case that "an employer should enjoy a conclusive presumption that, had it not discharged the employee illegally, it would have discharged him or her lawfully at any time after it in fact did so unlawfully"). Absent that presumption, it may be reasonable for an employee to rely on a promise of employment, because the employee may have reason to believe that the employer's right to terminate at will not be exercised before the employee begins work. Particularly where, as here, the employee has had a lengthy employment relationship with his employer, and the employer asserts the employee's value to the company, it may be reasonable for the employee to rely on the promise of employment, even though the job is terminable at will. We caution, however, that reasonableness is an issue for the jury, considering all the relevant circumstances. *See Schafer* (noting that issue of reliance in promissory estoppel claim "presented a question for the jury").

[The court rejected the argument in *Slate* that no injustice would be avoided by allowing a party to recover for revocation of a promise of employment when the same party would not be entitled to recover for the "termination of the consummated contract."] Although an employer has a right to fire an at-will employee — though not for an unlawful reason — without liability, the fact that the employer has that right does not mean that a prospective employee can never reasonably rely on a promise of at-will employment. And if a prospective employee does reasonably rely on such a promise, a remedy may be necessary to avoid injustice.

[As for whether the plaintiff can recover damages for failure to be awarded the corporate job, the court stressed that defendant did not argue] that, in general, damages associated with the corporate job could not be recovered in an action for promissory estoppel (or fraudulent misrepresentation). Instead, both defendant and the Court of Appeals relied on *Slate* for the proposition that the at-will nature of the corporate job precluded plaintiff from recovering lost wages for that job. However, this court has rejected a similar proposition in a wrongful discharge case. In *Tadsen* a jury awarded front pay to an at-will employee who had alleged unlawful employment practices, including wrongful discharge, and this court affirmed the trial court's denial of a motion to strike the claim for front pay. In that case, the employer had argued that an at-will employee cannot recover front pay because the employee has no "'right' to, or assurance of" future employment. *Tadsen.* This court rejected that argument:

> We decline to hold that an at-will employee never can prove the requisite facts for an award of front pay. The fact that at-will employment may be terminated for any nondiscriminatory purpose does not necessarily mean that the likely duration of that employment is incapable of proof to the required degree of certainty. At-will employment may be a factor that bears on whether the proof is sufficient in a particular case, but *the right to terminate someone's employment does not establish as a matter of law that an employee cannot prove the existence of front pay damages.*

(emphasis added).

Similarly, in this case, the fact that the corporate job was terminable at will, standing alone, does not create a conclusive presumption that plaintiff cannot prove damages related to the loss of that job. Instead, as in *Tadsen,* plaintiff may seek to prove what he would have earned in the corporate job and how long he likely would have remained in that job had he been hired as promised and allowed to start work. Although it may be easier for a plaintiff to prove the likely duration of employment in a wrongful discharge case, where the employee has a history of employment with the employer, a plaintiff is entitled to attempt to make such a showing outside the wrongful discharge context. Of course, if an employer lawfully fires an employee after the employee has started work, which could include firing the employee for no reason at all under the at-will employment doctrine, the employee will not be able to show that the job would have continued beyond that point. In this case, however, plaintiff was not allowed to start the corporate job; indeed, the employer told him that he had never actually been hired for that job, making it difficult for the employer to argue that plaintiff was lawfully fired. Thus, the general principle from *Tadsen* applies in this case: The at-will nature of the employment does not foreclose plaintiff from attempting to prove the likely duration of employment had he been hired as promised and allowed to start work, although "[a]t-will employment may be a factor that bears on whether the proof is sufficient in a particular case [.]" *Id.* Whether plaintiff is ultimately entitled to recover damages associated with not being hired for the corporate job, and in what amount, is not before this court. Nonetheless, defendant is not entitled to judgment as a matter of law solely because the corporate job was terminable at will.

We recognize that allowing a prospective employee to bring a promissory estoppel claim raises practical concerns that the Court of Appeals articulated in *Slate:* "It would serve the interests of no one — least of all new professional persons in search of work — to discourage putative employers from discharging them earlier rather than later, under circumstances where there is no possibility that an actual employment relationship will ever exist." On the other hand, as the Eighth Circuit has recognized:

> [I]f damages sustained in reasonable reliance on an employer promise were not available, the effect of such a rule would be to allow the employer to take advantage of whatever benefits might accrue to him by his inducing a potential employee to leave behind home and/or steady employment while at the same time being completely free of any obligation to keep his word.

Bower v. AT & T, Technologies, Inc., 852 F.2d 361, 364 (8th Cir.1988). Moreover, a rule barring a promissory estoppel (or fraudulent misrepresentation) claim would allow an employer to abuse its ability to induce the reliance of prospective employees. For example, an employer could promise an at-will job to multiple people to keep them available while the employer continued to vet them or to prevent them from accepting a position with a competitor. Acknowledging the possibility of reasonable reliance "encourages employers [and employees] to take [their] promises seriously," *id.,* and, more importantly, is consistent with the law of promissory estoppel. . . .

[The portion of the opinion dealing with plaintiff's fraud claim is reproduced at page 310]

NOTES

1. *Comparing and Contrasting New Hire and Mid-Term Employee Promissory Estoppel Claims.* Note that the same conceptual issues that courts struggle with in the new hire context regarding promissory estoppel animate the discussion of the viability of the theory in a mid-term employment case like *Cocchiara.* In both contexts, courts continue to disagree on the extent to which promissory estoppel is simply inconsistent with at-will employment; whether a worker can reasonably rely on promises of employment in an at-will relationship; how definite the assurances must be; and whether damages exist and how they can be calculated. But are there distinctions between the two contexts that might make a difference, legally or factually? For example, is reliance on assurances by a current employee of a better position or continued employment more likely to be found reasonable than an assurance of continued employment to one being hired, when the employment itself is at will?

2. *Why Not Breach of Contract?* Cocchiara either did not plead breach of contract or abandoned the claim by the time the case was appealed. Why? After all, assuming Summer's promise was sufficiently definite, wasn't it in exchange for valuable consideration — namely, Cocchiara's turning down his other (existing) job offer — and, hence, a unilateral contract? Furthermore, wouldn't the forbearance of an existing job offer elsewhere be enough to show "additional consideration," and, thus, satisfy any evidentiary burden required to overcome the at-will or other presumption?

One answer might be concern about the statute of frauds. In cases based on oral promises, employees frequently face challenges based on the statute of frauds, a rule of contract law that requires particular classes of contracts to be evidenced by a written instrument. In most jurisdictions, the requirements of the statute of frauds apply to contracts "not capable of performance within a year from the time of their formation." RESTATEMENT (SECOND) OF CONTRACTS § 178(1) (1981). This rule may provide employers with a valid defense, at least in cases involving oral promises guaranteeing a fixed term of employment, such as employment for three years.

Employers sometimes argue that "lifetime" or "permanent" employment contracts similarly cannot be completed within a year and therefore must be established through written evidence. A majority of courts have rejected this argument, however, noting that such contracts *could* be fully performed within one year, for example, where the employee dies or quits or the employer has cause to terminate the employee within a year of his or her hiring. *See, e.g., Foley v. Interactive Data Corp.*, 765 P.2d 373 (Cal. 1988); *see also Kalmus v. Oliver*, 390 S.W.3d 586, 593 (Tex. App. 2012) ("The evidence in this case shows only an oral at-will employment agreement with an indefinite duration, and such agreements do not fall within the statute of frauds' one-year provision."). While some judges have criticized such legal gymnastics, the rejection of the statute-of-frauds defense in cases involving oral employment contracts is consistent with the general contract law trend limiting the application of the statute of frauds to situations where completion within one year is truly foreclosed. *See generally* Daniel P. O'Gorman, *The Statute of Frauds and Oral Promises of Job Security: The Tenuous Distinction Between Performance and Excusable Nonperformance*, 40 SETON HALL L. REV. 1023, 1026-27 (2010).

A more likely explanation is that courts are reluctant to find that oral assurances create any kind of binding job security terms — lifetime employment, employment for a definite term, or otherwise — when the promise is only for employment itself (in the new hire cases) or only for a better position within the company (such as in *Cocchiara*). Put another way, in oral promise cases involving assurances making no reference to job security or length of term, courts resist finding that the relationship is anything other than at will, and hence, that the assurance produced some other kind of binding contract. In such cases then, promissory estoppel is the worker's only potential recourse. *Cf. Peters v. Gilead*, 533 F.3d 594 (7th Cir. 2008) (after the employer confirmed in writing that an employee was entitled to leave to undergo surgery pursuant to terms in the employer's handbook, the court found that the employer's failure to abide by these assurances, while not necessarily establishing that a binding contract had been created, gave rise to a valid promissory estoppel claim).

3. *Assurances of Continued Employment Enforceable in Contract.* In contrast, when oral assurances provide something more, courts may find them to be promises enforceable in contract. For example, in *Shebar v. Sanyo Business Systems Corp.*, 544 A.2d 377 (N.J. 1988), as in *Cocchiara*, the plaintiff (Shebar) turned down a position at another company after his current employer (Sanyo) made oral assurances. The assurances in *Shebar*, however, included references to job security and the long-term nature of the relationship. The court described the circumstances as follows:

> The critical events allegedly occurred on October 1, 1984, when plaintiff accepted the Sony offer and tendered his written resignation to Sanyo. According to Shebar's certification, Sanyo's president, Mr. Yamazaki, called him into his office after he received plaintiff's letter of resignation. When plaintiff went into Mr. Yamazaki's office, Mr. Yamashita, executive vice president of Sanyo, was also present. According to plaintiff, Mr. Yamashita told him that he was personally insulted by his resignation, that his performance was exceptionally good, that plaintiff should have brought any problems or dissatisfaction

to his attention, and that the company did not want plaintiff to resign, but rather wanted to eliminate any problems that existed. Yamazaki apparently agreed with Yamashita. Yamazaki held the resignation letter, ripped it to shreds, and said "I will not accept your resignation. We will solve your problems."

Plaintiff claims that Yamazaki and Yamashita expressly stated to him that Sanyo does not fire its managers. They told him, plaintiff contends, that he had a job for the rest of his life, and that Sanyo had never fired, and never intended to fire, a corporate employee whose rank was manager or above. Plaintiff acknowledges that they did not discuss money at this meeting, but maintains that they assured him that he would receive a substantial raise in March 1985.

As a result of this meeting and in reliance on the assurances made to him there, plaintiff revoked his acceptance of Sony's offer. Thereafter, he informed Mr. Yamashita that he had rejected the Sony offer. According to plaintiff, Yamashita congratulated him on a wise decision, and again assured him that he was "married" to Sanyo and no divorce was allowed.

Id. at 379-30.

When Sanyo terminated Shebar four months later, Shebar sued, alleging breach of oral contract. The court held that Shebar had produced sufficient evidence to go to trial on whether a contract existed between him and Sanyo, and whether it had been breached. Interestingly, the court characterized the potential contract not as one guaranteeing lifetime employment, but rather as for an indefinite term terminable only for cause. The court did so in part to distinguish earlier precedent that had rejected mere oral assurances as sufficient to support a claim of lifetime employment because "such contracts for lifetime employment [are] extraordinary, and would be enforced only in the face of clear and convincing proof of a precise agreement setting forth all of the terms of the employment relationship, including the duties and responsibilities of both the employer and the employee." *Id.* at 382. However, according to the *Shebar* court, "a lifetime contract that protects an employee from any termination is distinguishable from a promise to discharge only for cause. The latter protects the employee only from arbitrary termination." *Id.* The court then went on to describe why Shebar's evidence could establish the elements of such a contract claim:

> We find that plaintiff has presented a material issue of fact concerning whether his employer orally promised to discharge him only for cause. Plaintiff's superiors specifically represented to him that he would have continued employment at the company. Those representations were obviously intended to induce plaintiff to remain with Sanyo as Sanyo's computer sales manager and revoke his acceptance of Sony's employment offer. Plaintiff acted in reliance on the alleged promise by forgoing the job opportunity he had secured at Sony. . . . Furthermore, we hold that a factfinder could conclude that plaintiff gave valuable consideration for Sanyo's promise of continued employment with termination only for cause. The essential requirement of consideration is a bargained-for exchange of promises or performance that may consist of an act, a forbearance, or the creation, modification, or destruction of a legal relation. . . .
>
> Taking plaintiff's allegations as true, he agreed to relinquish his new position at Sony in exchange for job security at Sanyo. Sanyo, in turn, agreed to relinquish its right to terminate plaintiff's employment at will in exchange for the retention of a valued employee. Such bargained-for and exchanged promises furnish ample consideration for an enforceable contract. . . .
>
> Additionally, in order to be enforceable the terms of such a contract must be sufficiently clear and capable of judicial interpretation. We find that as a matter of law, the purported contract at issue is not so vague and indefinite that it cannot be enforced. . . .

Id. at 383-84.

4. *The Nature of the Promise.* The precedent the *Shebar* court distinguished was *Savarese v. Pyrene Manufacturing Co.*, 89 A.2d 237 (N.J. 1952), which had articulated the traditional rule that "permanent" employment is considered at will absent additional consideration. In *Savarese*, an employee's supervisors induced him to play on the company baseball team, despite his fear of being injured, by allegedly stating that "If you get hurt I will take care of you. You will have a foreman's job the rest of your life." Plaintiff alleges that the supervisor specified the job as "'the one I had, the one I earned.'" The plaintiff in fact sustained an injury while playing baseball, but returned to the company and continued to work there for 21 years, at which point the company terminated his employment. Afterwards, Savarese sued, contending that the company breached his contract of lifetime employment. Recall that the *Shebar* court distinguishes between promises of "lifetime" employment and promises to terminate only for cause, characterizing Sanyo's promise as the latter. Do you see a meaningful factual difference between the promises in the two cases? If not, one might argue that the court should have simply overruled *Savarese*.

Still, the distinction the *Shebar* court draws is potentially significant. First, as the opinion itself suggests (as well as the cases that follow), reconceptualization of the nature of the assurance(s) is important because courts remain reluctant — sometimes deeply reluctant — to recognize lifetime employment contracts. Indeed, former University of Iowa football coach Hayden Fry may have been on point when he said: "I thought I had a lifetime contract. Then I found out the other day that if I have a losing season, they're going to declare me legally dead." Ray Yasser, *A Comprehensive Blueprint for the Reform of Intercollegiate Athletics*, 3 MARQ. SPORTS L.J. 123, 148 (1993).

Second, what constitutes "cause" to terminate an employee may vary by type of employment contract. For example, because lifetime and definite term contracts purport to protect the employment from uncertainties such as changing circumstances, courts often find that economic downtown does not constitute cause to terminate under such contracts. Cause protections in indefinite term contracts may be less robust. *See, e.g.*, RESTATEMENT (THIRD) OF EMPLOYMENT LAW (Proposed Final Draft, April 18, 2014) § 2.04 (distinguishing between definite and indefinite term contracts, and stating that significant changes in the employer's economic circumstances constitute cause only with regard to the latter type of contract). You will see an example of this in the next case and confront such distinctions again in Chapter 3.

5. *Proof on Remand.* One historical justification for the statute of frauds was that evidence of oral contracts is likely to be factually unreliable, yet highly persuasive to juries. An interested plaintiff has a strong incentive to testify untruthfully about past promises or, absent bad faith, to misremember the defendant's precise statements. How will Cocchiara and Shebar prove their claims on remand? Absent corroboration of some kind (e.g., something in writing or third-party testimony regarding what was said), is it just their word against that of their respective employers? Is this a good reason to insist on a writing in cases like *Shebar*?

6. *"Married" to the Company.* Assuming Shebar's rendition of his employer's statements is true, long-term employment among high-level employees was the norm at Sanyo. As anyone who has worked more than one job knows, organizations differ widely in their treatment and expectations of their workers. These differences may result from a combination of factors, including the employer's corporate philosophy, the management styles of key personnel, the nature of the work itself, industry standards, and the personality of the company's clientele and workforce. The organizational culture of a particular workplace can create shared understandings about the way work relationships will progress and under what circumstances they may be terminated. Thus, employees may feel deeply wronged when denied regular raises and promotions, long-term employment absent poor performance, and other benefits and rewards commonly bestowed within the organization. Such shared understandings are sometimes referred to as "psychological" or "implicit" contracts of employment. *See, e.g.*, Katherine V. W. Stone, *The New Psychological Contract: Implications of the Changing Workplace for Labor and Employment Law*, 48 UCLA L. REV. 519, 549-50 (2001). To what extent should employer practices, mid-term worker expectations, and organizational culture affect the existence of legally recognized job security rights? Consider the case that follows.

Pugh v. See's Candies, Inc.
171 Cal. Rptr. 917 (Ct. App. 1981)

GRODIN, J.

After 32 years of employment with See's Candies, Inc., in which he worked his way up the corporate ladder from dishwasher to vice president in charge of production and member of the board of directors, Wayne Pugh was fired. [Asserting that he had been fired in breach of contract, he sued his former employer for wrongful termination. The trial court granted defendants' motions for nonsuit, and this appeal followed.]

Pugh began working for See's at its Bay Area plant (then in San Francisco) in January 1941 washing pots and pans. From there he was promoted to candy maker, and held that position until the early part of 1942, when he entered the Air Corps. Upon his discharge in 1946 he returned to See's and his former position. After a year he was promoted to the position of production manager in charge of personnel, ordering raw materials, and supervising the production of candy. When, in 1950, See's moved into a larger plant in San Francisco, Pugh had responsibility for laying out the design of the plant, taking bids, and assisting in the construction. While working at this plant, Pugh sought to increase his value to the company by taking three years of night classes in plant layout, economics, and business law. When See's moved its San Francisco plant to its present location in South San Francisco in 1957, Pugh was given responsibilities for the new location similar to those which he undertook in 1950. By this time See's business and its number of production employees had increased substantially, and a new position of assistant production manager was created under Pugh's supervision.

In 1971 Pugh was again promoted, this time as vice president in charge of production and was placed upon the board of directors of See's northern California subsidiary, "in recognition of his accomplishments." In 1972 he received a gold watch from See's "in appreciation of 31 years of loyal service."

In May 1973 Pugh traveled with Charles Huggins, then president of See's, and their respective families to Europe on a business trip to visit candy manufacturers and to inspect new equipment. Mr. Huggins returned in early June to attend a board of director's meeting while Pugh and his family remained in Europe on a planned vacation.

Upon Pugh's return from Europe on Sunday, June 25, 1973, he received a message directing him to fly to Los Angeles the next day and meet with Mr. Huggins.

Pugh went to Los Angeles expecting to be told of another promotion. The preceding Christmas season had been the most successful in See's history, the Valentine's Day holiday of 1973 set a new sales record for See's, and the March 1973 edition of See's Newsletter, containing two pictures of Pugh, carried congratulations on the increased production.

Instead, upon Pugh's arrival at Mr. Huggins' office, the latter said, "Wayne, come in and sit down. We might as well get right to the point. I have decided your services are no longer required by See's Candies. Read this and sign it." Huggins handed him a letter confirming his termination and directing him to remove that day "only personal papers and possessions from your office," but "absolutely no records, formulas or other material"; and to turn in and account for "all keys, credit cards, et cetera." The letter advised that Pugh would receive unpaid salary, bonuses and accrued vacation through that date, and the full amount of his profit sharing account, but "No severance pay will be granted." Finally, Pugh was directed "not to visit or contact Production Department employees while they are on the job."

The letter contained no reason for Pugh's termination. When Pugh asked Huggins for a reason, he was told only that he should "look deep within [him]self" to find the answer, that "Things were said by people in the trade that have come back to us." Pugh's termination was subsequently announced to the industry in a letter which, again, stated no reasons.

When Pugh first went to work for See's, Ed Peck, then president and general manager, frequently told him: "if you are loyal to [See's] and do a good job, your future is secure." Laurance See, who became president of the company in 1951 and served in that capacity until his death in 1969, had a practice of not terminating administrative personnel except for good cause, and this practice was carried on by his brother, Charles B. See, who succeeded Laurance as president.

During the entire period of his employment, there had been no formal or written criticism of Pugh's work.[1] No complaints were ever raised at the annual meetings which preceded each holiday season, and he was never denied a raise or bonus. He received no notice that there was a problem which needed correction, nor any warning that any disciplinary action was being contemplated.

Pugh's theory as to why he was terminated relates to a contract which See's at that time had with the defendant union. . . .

In 1968 [See's supplemental union contract] contained a new rate classification which permitted See's to pay its seasonal employees at a lower rate. At a company meeting prior to the 1968 negotiations, Pugh had objected to the proposed new seasonal classification on the grounds that it might make it more difficult to recruit seasonal workers, and create unrest among See's regular seasonal workers who had worked previously for other manufacturers at higher rates. Huggins overruled Pugh's

---

1. Huggins testified that in 1953 there was some personality conflict between Pugh and Huggins' assistant, a Mr. Forrest, on account of which Huggins recommended to Laurance See that Pugh be terminated, but See declined. Huggins again recommended Pugh's termination in 1968, under circumstances to be described in this opinion, and again See declined. It does not appear that Huggins' actions in this regard, or the criticism of Pugh which they implied, were made known to Pugh.

objection and (unknown to Pugh) recommended his termination for "lack of cooperation" as to which Pugh's objection formed "part of the reason." His recommendation was not accepted. . . .

In April of that year, Huggins asked Pugh to be part of the negotiating team for the new union contract. Pugh responded that he would like to, but he was bothered by the possibility that See's had a "sweetheart contract" with the union. In response, someone banged on the table and said, "You don't know what the hell you are talking about." Pugh said, "Well, I think I know what I am talking about. I don't know whether you have a sweetheart contract, but I am telling you if you do, I don't want to be involved because they are immoral, illegal and not in the best interests of my employees." At the trial, Pugh explained that to him a "sweetheart contract" was "a contract whereby one employer would get an unfair competitive advantage over a competitor by getting a lower wage rate, would be one version of it." He also felt, he testified, that "if they in fact had a sweetheart contract that it wouldn't be fair to my female employees to be getting less money than someone would get working in the same industry under the same manager." . . .

The presumption that an employment contract is intended to be terminable at will is subject, like any presumption, to contrary evidence. This may take the form of an agreement, express or implied, that the relationship will continue for some fixed period of time. Or, and of greater relevance here, it may take the form of an agreement that the employment relationship will continue indefinitely, pending the occurrence of some event such as the employer's dissatisfaction with the employee's services or the existence of some "cause" for termination. Sometimes this latter type of agreement is characterized as a contract for "permanent" employment, but that characterization may be misleading. In one of the earliest California cases on this subject, the Supreme Court interpreted a contract for permanent employment as meaning "that plaintiffs' employment . . . was to continue indefinitely, and until one or the other of the parties wish, *for some good reason*, to sever the relation."

A contract which limits the power of the employer with respect to the reasons for termination is no less enforceable because it places no equivalent limits upon the power of the employee to quit his employment. "If the requirement of consideration is met, there is no additional requirement of . . . equivalence in the values exchanged, or 'mutuality of obligation.'" Rest. 2d Contracts § 81.

Moreover, while it has sometimes been said that a promise for continued employment subject to limitation upon the employer's power of termination must be supported by some "independent consideration," i.e., consideration other than the services to be rendered, such a rule is contrary to the general contract principle that courts should not inquire into the adequacy of consideration. "A single and undivided consideration may be bargained for and given as the agreed equivalent of one promise or of two promises or of many promises." 1 Corbin on Contracts § 125 (1963). Thus there is no analytical reason why an employee's promise to render services, or his actual rendition of services over time, may not support an employer's promise both to pay a particular wage (for example) and to refrain from arbitrary dismissal.

The most likely explanation for the "independent consideration" requirement is that it serves an evidentiary function: it is more probable that the parties intended a continuing relationship, with limitations upon the employer's dismissal authority, when the employee has provided some benefit to the employer, or suffers some detriment, beyond the usual rendition of service. . . .

In determining whether there exists an implied-in-fact promise for some form of continued employment courts have considered a variety of factors in addition to the existence of independent consideration. These have included, for example, the personnel policies or practices of the employer, the employee's longevity of service, actions or communications by the employer reflecting assurances of continued employment, and the practices of the industry in which the employee is engaged. . . .

[In this case] there were facts in evidence from which the jury could determine the existence of such an implied promise: the duration of appellant's employment, the commendations and promotions he received, the apparent lack of any direct criticism of his work, the assurances he was given, and the employer's acknowledged policies. While oblique language will not, standing alone, be sufficient to establish agreement, it is appropriate to consider the totality of the parties' relationship: Agreement may be "'shown by the acts and conduct of the parties, interpreted in the light of the subject matter and of the surrounding circumstances.'" We therefore conclude that it was error to grant respondents' motions for nonsuit as to See's.

Since this litigation may proceed toward yet uncharted waters, we consider it appropriate to provide some guidance as to the questions which the trial court may confront on remand. We have held that appellant has demonstrated a prima facie case of wrongful termination in violation of his contract of employment. The burden of coming forward with evidence as to the reason for appellant's termination now shifts to the employer. Appellant may attack the employer's offered explanation either on the ground that it is pretextual (and that the real reason is one prohibited by contract or public policy), or on the ground that it is insufficient to meet the employer's obligations under contract or applicable legal principles. Appellant bears, however, the ultimate burden of proving that he was terminated wrongfully. *Cf. McDonnell Douglas Corp. v. Green* (1973) 411 U.S. 792.

By what standard that burden is to be measured will depend, in part, upon what conclusions the jury draws as to the nature of the contract between the parties. The terms "just cause" and "good cause," "as used in a variety of contexts . . . have been found to be difficult to define with precision and to be largely relative in their connotation, depending upon the particular circumstances of each case." Essentially, they connote "a fair and honest cause or reason, regulated by good faith on the part of the party exercising the power." Care must be taken, however, not to interfere with the legitimate exercise of managerial discretion. "Good cause" in this context is quite different from the standard applicable in determining the propriety of an employee's termination under a contract for a specified term. And where, as here, the employee occupies a sensitive managerial or confidential position, the employer must of necessity be allowed substantial scope for the exercise of subjective judgment. . . .

NOTES

1. *Cause on Remand.* At the end of the opinion, the court sets out the procedural steps for determining whether See's had cause to terminate Pugh's employment. When employees allege implied contracts for job security, demonstrating the existence of such a contract is only half the battle; the plaintiff must then show that the employer is in breach. As *Pugh* cautions, in determining whether a termination was justified, courts must not interfere with subjective managerial decision making. The burden of

proof, coupled with this deference to management, can make it difficult for an employee to ultimately prevail. Indeed, Pugh himself did not succeed. On retrial, the jury returned a verdict for the defendant, crediting Huggins's testimony that Pugh was "rude, argumentative, belligerent, and uncooperative" on their trip to Europe and testimony of other See's employees that Pugh was "disrespectful to his superiors and subordinates, disloyal to the company, and uncooperative with other administrative staff." *See Pugh v. See's Candies, Inc.* (*Pugh II*), 250 Cal. Rptr. 195, 214 (Ct. App. 1988) (affirming judgment for defendant).

2. *Terminations That Offend Public Policy.* Pugh believed he was terminated for objecting to corruption in his employer's negotiations with union representatives. In an omitted portion of the opinion, he alleged that he had been tortiously discharged in violation of public policy, in addition to claiming breach of an implied contract. Pugh's tort argument was rejected. In Chapter 4, you will take up public policy torts. When you do, try to figure out why Pugh lost on this count.

3. *Additional Consideration Revisited. Pugh* invokes the traditional rule that additional consideration is required to support a promise of job security. How does its treatment of this doctrine compare to the *Hanson* and *Greene* decisions you read earlier? What does the court in *Pugh* mean by the "evidentiary function" of additional consideration?

4. *Implied-in-Fact Theory.* In answering the last question, consider the contractual theory that the court espouses. An implied-in-fact contract is one in which an agreement to be legally bound is implied from the circumstances, albeit without any clear oral or written communication between the parties. A classic example of an implied-in-fact contract is getting a haircut or styling. When you sit down, you agree to pay the posted charge (or perhaps a reasonable charge in the absence of a pricelist) and the stylist agrees to cut your hair, although none of this is stated. How does this theory of liability compare to the others you have seen so far — oral contract and promissory estoppel? Does the idea of an implied-in-fact contract better reflect the realities of workplace relationships? Or does it seem a contrived (or result-oriented) way of doing justice under the circumstances?

5. *Hard Facts? There* is an adage that hard facts make bad law. *Pugh* is a rags-to-riches tale in which the employer seemingly takes advantage of the industry and dedication of a long-term employee. From the first sentence of the opinion it is clear which way the court will hold. Was the court unduly influenced by sympathy for the employee, or is there a broader justification for the decision?

Dean Stewart Schwab suggests there is. Under the "efficiency-wage" theory of long-term employment relationships, employers set wages to rise steadily over the course of employment in order to motivate employees throughout the relationship. *See* Stewart J. Schwab, *Life-Cycle Justice: Accommodating Just Cause and Employment at Will*, 92 MICH. L. REV. 8, 39 (1993). As a result, new employees may be underpaid relative to the value they produce while senior employees may actually earn more than their marginal work product (because wages continue to rise when productivity reaches its zenith). *Id.* at 16-17. While the difference balances out if the employment relationship is allowed to run its full course, senior employees may be at risk of "opportunistic" firings, at which point the employer has already reaped the benefits of the arrangement. As Dean Schwab explains:

[E]mployees invest heavily as they pursue a career with a single employer. First, they obtain training that is more useful for their own employer than it would be elsewhere — what economists term job-specific human capital. Second, they join the company's career path [which] ties pay, promotions, and benefits to seniority and generally forbids lateral entry. A major cost of pursuing a career with one firm is that one forgoes other ladders and must start over at the bottom if one leaves the firm. Additionally, as they plan for a lifetime with an employer, workers put down roots, establish networks of friends in the workplace and the community, buy homes within commuting distance of the job, and build emotional ties to the community. . . .

[T]hese investments, roots, and ties are sunk costs that trap the worker in his current firm, inhibiting him from departing voluntarily. Even if the career does not proceed as anticipated, the employee is reluctant to quit because the job remains preferable to alternative jobs. Such trapped workers are vulnerable to opportunism. The employer might pay them less than the implicit contract requires or work them harder, knowing they cannot easily quit. . . .

Court scrutiny of opportunistic firings may offer [one] method of policing long-term contracts. . . . The danger, of course, is that court intervention will diminish the employer's flexibility in firing [shirkers]. The question is whether court intervention can be limited to opportunistic firings, rather than to a broader supervision against unfair firings in general.

Id. at 24-28. As the excerpt suggests, while judicial intervention may be appropriate in some instances, the risk of opportunistic firings does not necessarily justify a general rule requiring just cause for all terminations. Can courts craft an administrable rule that will identify only opportunistic firings? Does the multi-factored test articulated in *Pugh* succeed?

Guz v. Bechtel National, Inc.
8 P.3d 1089 (Cal. 2000)

BAXTER, J.

This case presents questions about the law governing claims of wrongful discharge from employment as it applies to an employer's motion for summary judgment. Plaintiff John Guz, a longtime employee of Bechtel National, Inc. (BNI), was released [when his work unit was eliminated and its tasks transferred to another office]. Guz sued BNI and its parent [(collectively Bechtel) alleging] breach of an implied contract to be terminated only for good cause and breach of the implied covenant of good faith and fair dealing. The trial court granted Bechtel's motion for summary judgment. [T]he Court of Appeal reversed. . . .

In 1971, Bechtel hired Guz as an administrative assistant at a salary of $750 per month. Throughout his Bechtel career, Guz worked in "management information," performing, at various times, duties on both the "awarded" and "overhead" sides of this specialty. He received steady raises and promotions. His performance reviews were generally favorable. . . .

BNI, a division of Bechtel Corporation, is an engineering, construction, and environmental remediation company that focuses on federal government programs, principally for the Departments of Energy and Defense. . . .

Guz had worked for BNI-MI, [BNI's six staff member Management Information Group] since 1986. In 1992, at age 49, he was employed as a financial reports supervisor. . . .

During this time, Bechtel maintained Personnel Policy 1101, dated June 1991, on the subject of termination of employment (Policy 1101). Policy 1101 stated that

"Bechtel employees have no employment agreements guaranteeing continuous service and may resign at their option or be terminated at the option of Bechtel."

Policy 1101 also described several "Categories of Termination," including "Layoff" and "Unsatisfactory Performance." With respect to Unsatisfactory Performance, the policy stated that "[e]mployees who fail to perform their jobs in a satisfactory manner may be terminated, provided the employees have been advised of the specific shortcomings and given an opportunity to improve their performance." A layoff was defined as "a Bechtel-initiated termination [ ] of employees caused by a reduction in workload, reorganizations, changes in job requirements, or other circumstances. . . ." Under the Layoff policy, employees subject to termination for this reason "may be placed on 'holding status' if there is a possible Bechtel assignment within the following 3-month period." Guz understood that Policy 1101 applied to him.

[In 1992, Robert Johnstone became president of BNI and soon became unhappy with the size, cost, and performance of BNI-MI. In April 1992, he advised BNI's manager of government services, Edward Dewey, Guz's manager, Ronald Goldstein, and Guz that BNI-MI's work could be done by three people.] . . .

On December 9, 1992, Goldstein informed Guz that BNI-MI was being disbanded, that its work would be done by another unit of Bechtel, SFRO-MI (San Francisco Regional Office Management Information Group), and that Guz was being laid off. Goldstein told Guz the reason he had been selected for layoff was to reduce costs. . . .

[Two members of BNI-MI, were transferred to SFRO-MI, while all the remaining BNI-MI employees, like Guz, were laid off. During early 1993, while Guz was on holding status, three other positions became available in SFRO-MI, partly because of that unit's expanded responsibilities for BNI-MI. Two of these positions were filled by SFRO-MI employees and one was filled by a newcomer.]

Guz sought to furnish evidence that the cost reduction and workload downturn reasons given him for the elimination of BNI-MI, and his own consequent layoff, were arbitrary, false, and pretextual. To rebut the implication that a general business slowdown required BNI to lay off workers, Guz submitted an excerpt from Bechtel Corporation's 1992 Annual Report. There, Bechtel Corporation's president stated that the "Bechtel team had an exceptional year," and that the company as a whole had achieved healthy gains in both revenue from current projects and new work booked. In his own declaration, Goldstein stated that BNI-MI's 1992 and projected 1993 workload was high, . . . [and that] the net savings from elimination of BNI-MI were only a small fraction of its budget.

Guz also submitted . . . Bechtel's 1989 Reduction-in-Force Guidelines (RIF Guidelines) and Bechtel's Personnel Policy 302 (Policy 302).

Policy 302 described a system of employee ranking . . . based on the fair, objective, and consistent evaluation of employees' comparative job-relevant skills and performance. . . .

The RIF Guidelines specified that when choosing among employees to be retained and released during a reduction in force, the formal ranking system set forth in Policy 302 was to be employed. . . .

The RIF Guidelines also explained the term "holding status" and its benefits [which included] "[t]ransfer and [p]lacement [a]ssistance." . . . In his deposition, BNI president Johnstone agreed that Bechtel's practice was to place an employee on holding status prior to termination, to attempt to reassign the employee during this period, and to "continue to look for positions even after the employee has been laid off."

In their declarations, Goldstein and Guz insisted Guz was qualified for each of the several vacant positions in SFRO-MI, as well as for several other positions that became available within Bechtel. . . .

The trial court granted summary judgment. The court reasoned that "[Guz] was an at-will employee and has not introduced any evidence that he was ever told at any time that he had permanent employment or that he would be retained as long as he was doing a good job. [The Court of Appeal reversed, reasoning that, under *Foley v. Interactive Data*, 765 P.2d 373 (Cal. 1988)], Guz's longevity, promotions, raises, and favorable performance reviews, together with Bechtel's written progressive discipline policy and Bechtel officials' statements of company practices, raised a triable issue that Guz had an implied-in-fact contract to be dismissed only for good cause. There was evidence that Bechtel breached this term by eliminating BNI-MI, on the false ground that workload was declining, as a pretext to weed out poor performers without applying the company's progressive discipline procedures.

II. Implied contract claim . . .

While the statutory presumption of at-will employment is strong, it is subject to several limitations. . . .

One example of a contractual departure from at-will status is an agreement that the employee will be terminated only for "good cause." . . .

The contractual understanding need not be express, but may be implied in fact, arising from the parties' conduct evidencing their actual mutual intent to create such enforceable limitations. In *Foley* we identified several factors, apart from express terms, that may bear upon "the existence and content of an . . . [implied-in-fact] agreement" placing limits on the employer's right to discharge an employee. These factors might include "'the personnel policies or practices of the employer, the employee's longevity of service, actions or communications by the employer reflecting assurances of continued employment, and the practices of the industry in which the employee is engaged.'" *Id.* (quoting *Pugh* . . .).

Foley asserted that "the totality of the circumstances" must be examined to determine whether the parties' conduct, considered in the context of surrounding circumstances, gave rise to an implied-in-fact contract limiting the employer's termination rights. We did not suggest, however, that every vague combination of *Foley* factors, shaken together in a bag, necessarily allows a finding that the employee had a right to be discharged only for good cause, as determined in court.

On the contrary, "courts seek to enforce the actual understanding" of the parties to an employment agreement. Whether that understanding arises from express mutual words of agreement, or from the parties' conduct evidencing a similar meeting of minds, the exact terms to which the parties have assented deserve equally precise scrutiny. . . .

Every case thus turns on its own facts. Where there is no express agreement, the issue is whether other evidence of the parties' conduct has a "tendency in reason" to demonstrate the existence of an actual mutual understanding on particular terms and conditions of employment. . . .

Guz alleges he had an agreement with Bechtel that he would be employed so long as he was performing satisfactorily and would be discharged only for good cause. Guz claims no express understanding to this effect. However, he asserts that such an agreement can be inferred by combining evidence of several *Foley* factors, including (1) his long service; (2) assurances of continued employment in the form of raises, promotions, and good performance reviews; (3) Bechtel's written personnel policies, which suggested that termination for poor performance would be preceded by progressive discipline, that layoffs during a work force reduction would be based on objective criteria, including formal ranking, and that persons laid off would receive placement and reassignment assistance; and (4) testimony by a Bechtel executive that company practice was to terminate employees for a good reason and to reassign, if possible, a laid-off employee who was performing satisfactorily.

Guz further urges there is evidence his termination was without good cause in two respects. First, he insists, the evidence suggests Bechtel had no good cause to eliminate BNI-MI, because the cost reduction and workload downturn reasons Bechtel gave for that decision (1) were not justified by the facts, and (2) were a pretext to terminate him and other individual BNI-MI employees for poor performance without following the company's progressive discipline rules. Second, Guz asserts, even if there was good cause to eliminate his work unit, his termination nonetheless lacked good cause because Bechtel failed to accord him fair layoff rights set forth in its written personnel rules, including (1) use of objective force ranking to determine which unit members deserved retention, and (2) fair consideration for other available positions while he was in holding status.

As we shall explain, we find triable evidence that Bechtel's written personnel documents set forth implied contractual limits on the circumstances under which Guz, and other Bechtel workers, would be terminated. On the other hand, we see no triable evidence of an implied agreement between Guz and Bechtel on additional, different, or broader terms of employment security. . . .

At the outset, Bechtel insists that the existence of implied contractual limitations on its termination rights is negated because Bechtel expressly disclaimed all such agreements. Bechtel suggests the at-will presumption was conclusively reinforced by language Bechtel inserted in Policy 1101, which specified that the company's employees "have no . . . agreements guaranteeing continuous service and may be terminated at [Bechtel's] option." . . .

[N]either the disclaimer nor the statutory presumption necessarily foreclosed Guz from proving the existence and breach of [an agreement limiting Bechtel's termination rights]. Cases in California and elsewhere have held that at-will provisions in personnel handbooks, manuals, or memoranda do not bar, or necessarily overcome, other evidence of the employer's contrary intent. [But even if a handbook disclaimer is not controlling, such language must be taken into account, along with all other pertinent evidence, in ascertaining the terms on which a worker was employed.]

At the outset, it is undisputed that Guz received no individual promises or representations that Bechtel would retain him except for good cause, or upon other specified circumstances. Nor does Guz seriously claim that the practice in Bechtel's industry was to provide secure employment. Indeed, the undisputed evidence suggested that because Bechtel, like other members of its industry, operated by competitive bidding from project to project, its work force fluctuated widely and, in terms of raw numbers, was in general decline.

However, Guz insists his own undisputed long and successful service at Bechtel constitutes strong evidence of an implied contract for permanent employment except upon good cause. . . .

A number of post-*Foley* California decisions have suggested that long duration of service, regular promotions, favorable performance reviews, praise from supervisors, and salary increases do not, without more, imply an employer's contractual intent to relinquish its at-will rights. These decisions reason that such events are but natural consequences of a well-functioning employment relationship. . . .

We agree that an employee's mere passage of time in the employer's service, even where marked with tangible indicia that the employer approves the employee's work, cannot alone form an implied-in-fact contract that the employee is no longer at will. Absent other evidence of the employer's intent, longevity, raises and promotions are their own rewards for the employee's continuing valued service. . . .

On the other hand, long and successful service is not necessarily irrelevant to the existence of such a contract. Over the period of an employee's tenure, the employer can certainly communicate, by its written and unwritten policies and practices, or by informal assurances, that seniority and longevity do create rights against termination at will. The issue is whether the employer's words or conduct, on which an employee reasonably relied, gave rise to that specific understanding. . . .

Insofar as *Foley* applied the long service factor to its own facts, it did so consistent with the principles of implied-in-fact contracts. In *Foley*, the employer claimed the employee's six years and nine months of service was too short a period to evidence an implied agreement not to discharge at will. We answered that "[l]ength of employment [was] a relevant consideration" and the plaintiff's length of service was "sufficient time for conduct to occur on which a trier of fact could find the existence of an implied contract." Prominent among the conduct alleged by the *Foley* plaintiff was "repeated oral assurances of job security."

. . . Guz claims no particular "'actions or communications by [Bechtel]'" and no industry customs, practices, or policies which suggest that by virtue of his successful longevity in Bechtel's employ, he had earned a contractual right against future termination at will.

If anything, Bechtel had communicated otherwise. The company's Policy 1101 stated that Bechtel employees had no contracts guaranteeing their continuous employment and could be terminated at Bechtel's option. Nothing in this language suggested any exception for senior workers, or for those who had received regular raises and promotions. While occasional references to seniority appear in other sections of Bechtel's personnel documents, the narrow context of these references undermines an inference that Bechtel additionally intended, or employees had reason to expect, special immunities from termination based on their extended or successful service.

Finally, Guz asserts there is evidence that, industry custom and written company personnel policies aside, Bechtel had an unwritten "polic[y] or practice[ ]" to release its employees only for cause. As the sole evidence of this policy, Guz points to the deposition testimony of Johnstone, BNI's president, who stated his understanding that Bechtel terminated workers only with "good reason" or for "lack of [available] work." But there is no evidence that Bechtel employees were aware of such an unwritten policy, and it flies in the face of Bechtel's general disclaimer. This brief and vague statement, by a single Bechtel official, that Bechtel sought to avoid arbitrary firings is insufficient as a matter of law to permit a finding that the company, by an unwritten practice or policy on which employees reasonably relied, had contracted away its right to discharge Guz at will.

In sum, if there is any significant evidence that Guz had an implied contract against termination at will, that evidence flows exclusively from Bechtel's written personnel documents. . . .

The parties do not dispute that certain of these provisions, expressly denominated "Policies" . . . were disseminated to employees and were intended by Bechtel to inform workers of rules applicable to their employment. There seems little doubt, and we conclude, a triable issue exists that the specific provisions of these Policies did become an implicit part of the employment contracts of the Bechtel employees they covered, including Guz.

As Bechtel stresses, Policy 1101 itself purported to disclaim any employment security rights. However, Bechtel had inserted other language, not only in Policy 1101 itself, but in other written personnel documents, which described detailed rules and procedures for the termination of employees under particular circumstances. Moreover, the specific language of Bechtel's disclaimer, stating that employees had no contracts "guaranteeing . . . continuous service" (italics added) and were terminable at Bechtel's "option," did not foreclose an understanding between Bechtel and all its workers that Bechtel would make its termination decisions within the limits of its written personnel rules. Given these ambiguities, a fact finder could rationally determine that despite its general disclaimer, Bechtel had bound itself to the specific provisions of these documents. . . .

The Court of Appeal did not address Guz's second theory, i.e., that Bechtel also breached its implied contract by failing, during and after the reorganization, to provide him personally with the fair layoff protections, including force ranking and reassignment help, which are set forth in its Policies and RIF Guidelines. This theory raises difficult questions, including what the proper remedy, if any, should be if Guz ultimately shows that Bechtel breached a contractual obligation to follow certain procedural policies in the termination process. . . . On remand, the Court of Appeal should confront this issue and should determine whether Guz has raised a triable issue on this theory.

III. Implied covenant claim . . .

Guz urges that even if his contract was for employment at will, the implied covenant of good faith and fair dealing precluded Bechtel from "unfairly" denying him the contract's benefits by failing to follow its own termination policies.

Thus, Guz argues, in effect, that the implied covenant can impose substantive terms and conditions beyond those to which the contract parties actually agreed. [However, the] covenant of good faith and fair dealing, implied by law in every contract, exists merely to prevent one contracting party from unfairly frustrating the other party's right to receive the benefits of the agreement actually made. . . . It cannot impose substantive duties or limits on the contracting parties beyond those incorporated in the specific terms of their agreement.

[The presumption is] that an employer may terminate its employees at will, for any or no reason. A fortiori, the employer may act peremptorily, arbitrarily, or inconsistently, without providing specific protections such as prior warning, fair procedures, objective evaluation, or preferential reassignment. Because the employment relationship is "fundamentally contractual," limitations on these employer prerogatives are a matter of the parties' specific agreement, express or implied in fact. The mere existence of an employment relationship affords no expectation, protectible by law, that employment will continue, or will end only on certain conditions, unless the parties have actually adopted such terms. Thus if the employer's termination decisions, however arbitrary, do not breach such a substantive contract provision, they are not precluded by the covenant.

This logic led us to emphasize in *Foley* that "breach of the implied covenant cannot logically be based on a claim that [the] discharge [of an at-will employee] was made without good cause." As we noted [in *Foley*], "[b]ecause the implied covenant protects only the parties' right to receive the benefit of their agreement, and, in an at-will relationship there is no agreement to terminate only for good cause, the implied covenant standing alone cannot be read to impose such a duty."

The same reasoning applies to any case where an employee argues that even if his employment was at will, his arbitrary dismissal frustrated his contract benefits and thus violated the implied covenant of good faith and fair dealing. Precisely because employment at will allows the employer freedom to terminate the relationship as it chooses, the employer does not frustrate the employee's contractual rights merely by doing so. . . .

Similarly at odds with *Foley* are suggestions that independent recovery for breach of the implied covenant may be available if the employer terminated the employee in "bad faith" or "without probable cause," i.e., without determining "honestly and in good faith that good cause for discharge existed." Where the employment contract itself allows the employer to terminate at will, its motive and lack of care in doing so are, in most cases at least, irrelevant.

Of course, as we have indicated above, the employer's personnel policies and practices may become implied-in-fact terms of the contract between employer and employee. If that has occurred, the employer's failure to follow such policies when terminating an employee is a breach of the contract itself.

A breach of the contract may also constitute a breach of the implied covenant of good faith and fair dealing. But insofar as the employer's acts are directly actionable as a breach of an implied-in-fact contract term, a claim that merely realleges that breach as a violation of the covenant is superfluous. This is because, as we explained at length in *Foley*, the remedy for breach of an employment agreement, including the covenant of good faith and fair dealing implied by law therein, is solely contractual. In the employment context, an implied covenant theory affords no separate measure of recovery, such as tort damages. Allegations that the breach was wrongful, in bad faith, arbitrary, and unfair are unavailing; there is no tort of "bad faith breach" of an employment contract.

We adhere to these principles here. To the extent Guz's implied covenant cause of action seeks to impose limits on Bechtel's termination rights beyond those to which the parties actually agreed, the claim is invalid. To the extent the implied covenant claim seeks simply to invoke terms to which the parties did agree, it is superfluous. Guz's remedy, if any, for Bechtel's alleged violation of its personnel policies depends on proof that they were contract terms to which the parties actually agreed. The trial court thus properly dismissed the implied covenant cause of action.

NOTES

1. Pugh *Claims Post-*Pugh. What does *Guz* suggest about the significance of *Pugh* in the twenty-first century? Seven years after *Pugh*, the California Supreme Court reaffirmed its holding in *Foley v. Interactive Data Corp.*, 765 P.2d 373 (Cal. 1988), discussed at length in *Guz*. Foley worked for six years as a product manager, during which time he received steady salary increases, promotions, bonuses and positive performance evaluations, before being terminated, allegedly for reporting that his supervisor was under FBI investigation for embezzlement. Like Pugh, Foley alleged he received repeated assurances that his job was secure so long as his performance remained adequate. In allowing the claim to go forward, the court declined the defendant's invitation to distinguish *Pugh* based on the fact that Foley had worked for the defendant only six years. *See id.* at 387-88. It also explicitly disagreed that employment security agreements are "inherently harmful or unfair to employers," finding that "[o]n the contrary, employers may benefit from the increased loyalty and productivity that such agreements may inspire." *Id.* at 387.

However, the California Supreme Court's subsequent decision in *Guz* offers a much narrower view of the kinds of employer conduct that will give rise to an implied-in-fact promise. In light of *Guz*, can you articulate the type of evidence that would create a prima facie case of breach of an implied contract in California? Can you identify the type of evidence that might preclude such a claim? How concerned do contemporary employers need to be about the costs associated with implied-in-fact rights? Professor Jonathan Fineman argues that companies have little to fear as long as they keep their house in order. *See The Inevitable Demise of the Implied Employment Contract*, 29 Berkeley J. Emp. & Lab. L. 345 (2008). He explains:

> [Following judicial recognition of implied-in-fact contract claims, e]mployers began restructuring their employment documents, policies and practices to avoid liability [and] eventually were able to find a way to immunize themselves against implied contract claims. With careful drafting of personnel documents, employers today have little fear of implied contract lawsuits. As a result, many employees are arguably now worse off than they were in the 1970s.
>
> [T]his failure of implied contract doctrine law to provide enduring job protections was inevitable. Although courts seeking to enforce implied employment contracts have some flexibility to interpret contract principles to reach a "fair" result, [w]hen faced with a clear expression of employer intent that the employment relationship be at-will, there is only so much a court can do. In this respect, the implied contract remedy is fundamentally different from other "exceptions" to the at-will rule. Unlike antidiscrimination statutes that impose upon the parties certain unavoidable obligations based on public policy, implied contract doctrine does not import external values into the employment relationship.
>
> Conceptualizing the employment relationship as one of private contract, the terms of which as a practical matter are established by employers, means that we will always end up with employment contracts that benefit employers. As long as individual employers are able to define the scope of their own obligations, efforts to instill more structured, effective and binding workplace norms through the doctrine of implied contracts will be unsuccessful.

Id. at 349-50. Do you agree with this critique, or is Professor Fineman overly pessimistic about the viability of employee claims? If you represented an employer, would you feel confident that with careful planning you could fully eliminate the risk of a successful employee claim in a situation where your client did not intend to provide job security?

2. *The Decline of Long-Term Employment. Pugh* and *Guz* together suggest that longevity and consistent advancement may be necessary although not sufficient facts from which a court can discern an implied-in-fact contract. How typical is it for workers to have 20- to 30-year employment records like the plaintiffs in those cases? In the contemporary economy, long-term employment with a single company is in decline, as are clear promotional hierarchies within individual firms. Instead, many employees have what Professor Katherine Stone describes as "boundaryless careers." She explains:

> A boundaryless career is a career that does not depend upon traditional notions of advancement within a single hierarchical organization. It includes an employee who moves frequently across the borders of different employers, such as a Silicon Valley technician, or one whose career draws its validation and marketability from sources outside the present employer, such as professional and extraorganizational networks. It also refers to changes within organizations, in which individuals are expected to move laterally, without constraint from traditional hierarchical career lattices. . . .
>
> The concept of a boundaryless career, like that of the new psychological contract, reflects the shift in job structures away from [early twentieth century] internal labor markets. Instead of job ladders along which employees advance within stable, long-term employment settings, there are possibilities for lateral mobility between and within firms, with no set path, no established expectations, and no tacit promises of job security. As [writer Peter] Drucker says, "there is no such thing as 'lifetime employment' anymore. . . ."

Katherine V. W. Stone, *The New Psychological Contract: Implications of the Changing Workplace for Labor and Employment Law*, 48 UCLA L. Rev. 519, 554-55 (2001). As a result, Professor Stone suggests that parties no longer share an implicit expectation of long-term employment. Rather, employers reward loyal work by enhancing their employees' marketability, by providing skills training, networking opportunities, and externally competitive pay. *Id.* at 568-72. Does this trend suggest that the utility of implied-in-fact contract theory is diminishing? Or might implied-in-fact theory be adapted to redress other types of opportunistic employer behavior that violate what Professor Stone calls the "new psychological contract" of employment?

Professor Arnow-Richman has suggested as much. She argues that rather than implying job security rights, the law should enforce the contemporary psychological contract by imposing an obligation on employers to provide advance notice (or its equivalent in pay) to terminated workers. *Just Notice: Re-Reforming Employment At-Will*, 58 UCLA L. Rev. 1 (2010). She explains:

> [T]he distinguishing feature of the new social contract of employment is the increased expectation of possible job loss. If employers no longer implicitly offer workers long-term job security, and employees no longer expect to remain in the same job for their lifetime, the guiding theory of worker protection should focus on enabling continued labor market participation rather than on preserving particular jobs.
>
> [This] could take the form of a legislative "pay-or-play" obligation upon termination. Under such a system, employers would be obligated to provide workers advance notice of termination or, at the employer's election, continued pay and benefits for the duration of the notice period. This system would allow employees a degree of income continuity,

enabling them to search for new employment or, in the event the employer elects severance pay, to invest in training.

Just cause reform, with its focus on the reason for termination and its goal of job preservation, would do [little to help workers in the contemporary economy]. In contrast, pay-or-play reform would advance an entirely different set of goals and expectations. [W]hereas just cause would foster job retention, pay-or-play would ease employment transitions, . . . giving legal force to employers' implicit promise of long-term employ*ability*. . . . Whereas just cause protection would oblige employers to justify termination, in effect to defend their deviation from the norm of continued employment, a pay-or-play system would translate the implicit promise of marketability into a legal obligation to directly underwrite the costs of re-employment.

Id. at 38-41. Recall the discussion in Note 9, page 82 of the history of unjust dismissal in Montana or elsewhere. How viable is Professor Arnow-Richman's alternative reform strategy? Would "pay or play" reform be appealing only to employees or might employers support it as well? What are the limitations of such an approach? Does a system that allows employers the right to terminate arbitrarily (for the right price) overlook workers' dignity (if not their property) interest in their jobs?

3. *Policies as Contracts. Pugh* identified the "policies and practices" of the employer as an important factor in determining the existence of an implied contract. It involved an employer that allegedly made a *practice* of retaining workers long term. In contrast, *Guz* involves employer *policies*, written materials that set forth the formal rules and procedures of the company. Such documents are increasingly common in large companies, and, as *Guz* describes, they offer advantages to both employers and employees. A frequent source of employer policies is the company's personnel manual or handbook, a collection of materials usually provided to employees upon hire. Courts can treat polices and handbooks in at least two ways: as evidence of an implied-in-fact contract or as a contract in and of themselves (generally analyzed as a unilateral contract). How does *Guz* use Bechtel's policies in determining the plaintiff's rights? Does the existence of the policies help Guz's case? Hurt it? Both? The role of personnel manuals, and in particular language in such documents that disclaim employee rights, will be explored in greater detail in the next section.

4. *The Implied Duty of Good Faith.* In addition to his implied contract claim, Guz proceeded under the theory that the employer had breached an implied duty of good faith. As you may recall from your first year, every contract contains an implicit promise that the parties will do nothing to interfere with the other's ability to reap the fruits of the agreement. *See* RESTATEMENT (SECOND) OF CONTRACTS § 205. An important limitation on the implied duty, however, is that it may not be used to alter express terms of the parties' agreement. For this reason, at-will employees have generally fared poorly in using the good faith duty to challenge the reason for their termination. *See, e.g., Murphy v. American Home Prod. Corp.* 448 N.E.2d 86 (N.Y. 1983) (rejecting breach of implied duty of good faith claim by at-will accountant, allegedly terminated for revealing internal financial irregularities, noting that "parties may by express agreement limit or restrict the employer's right of discharge, but to imply such a limitation from the existence of an unrestricted right would be internally inconsistent"). There are two exceptions, however. Some early cases allowed breach of the implied duty of good faith claims in situations where the plaintiff's termination violated public policy. In *Monge v. Beebe Rubber Co.*, 316 A.2d 549, 552 (N.H. 1974), for instance, the court sanctioned the good faith claim of a woman who was terminated for refusing to date her foreman. Today such cases would be pursued on statutory grounds (for instance, as sex discrimination) or as claims of wrongful discharge violating public policy, topics that will be explored in later chapters. The other situation in which plaintiffs have succeeded is where the termination resulted in the plaintiff losing vested compensation or benefits. *See, e.g., Fortune v. National Cash Register*, 364 N.E.2d 1251 (Mass. 1977) (recognizing limited cause of action for lost commission where plaintiff was terminated after consummation of large sale but prior to merchandise delivery date upon which final installment of earned commissions were to be paid). We will pick up this theory in Chapter 3 when we turn to compensation.

PROBLEMS

2-2.   James Pert worked for 15 years at Thistletown Race Track, a family-run horse track in Ohio. He started his employment as a stable boy and worked his way up to being a track manager and judge. Pert had no written contract of employment. Throughout his employment he received positive evaluations and consistent salary increases. At one point during Pert's tenure, the track fell on hard times and Pert asked the president of the race track, Edward DeBart, if he should consider looking for other work. DeBart responded, "There's no need. You have been one of our best employees. Whatever happens, your future is secure."

Recently, Pert's wife received a desirable job offer in Florida. The couple had always wanted to live in a warmer climate, but they knew they could not afford to move without Pert's salary. The national market for track judges tends to be tight because there are relatively few jobs and limited turnover in the position. Pert met with DeBart and asked him if it would be possible for him to keep his job working part-time from Florida and flying back to Ohio at his own expense for the four races per year that the track sponsored. DeBart agreed to this proposal. "We are more than willing to accommodate you," he said, "and if things don't work out in Florida, your job is always open here."

Pert and DeBart shook hands to seal the long-distance arrangement, but they did not draft any written document. Pert and his wife sold their house, bought a house in Florida, and moved their belongings. One year later, Ed DeBart passed away and his daughter, Donna York, assumed responsibility for the track. Several months later, DeBart received a notice of termination from York, stating that the company had decided to eliminate the "part-time manager position." Pert subsequently learned that he had been replaced by a full-time manager on location in Ohio.

Suppose that you are hired to represent Pert in an action against Thistletown. Do you think Pert can establish an implied-in-fact contract? Are any other theories of recovery that you have studied in this chapter relevant to his situation? What further information would you need to know to answer these questions? *See generally Pertz v. Edward J. DeBartolo Corp.*, 188 F.3d 508 (6th Cir. 1999).

2-3.   Christine Montell had been working as a student loan account representative for the Huntington Corporation for ten years, when she received a competing offer for a position with the Student Loan Fund ("SLF"). SLF offered her an annual salary of $50,000, a 5 percent increase above her current salary with Huntington, an annual 3 to 6 percent bonus based on performance, and moving expenses. Montell needed the extra cash, but was reluctant to leave her current employment because she had a good relationship with her boss, Keith Berner, had always received good feedback and training, and was reluctant to relocate. Before responding to the offer, she e-mailed Berner and asked whether Huntington would be able to match SLS's offer.

(a) Suppose that prior to answering Montell's e-mail, Berner contacts his own boss, Janis Goodman, who has the foresight to contact you, the company's legal counsel. Goodman would like to do everything possible to retain Montell, including matching SLF's salary and offering Montell a promotion, but does not want to put the company at risk of long-term liability. What do you recommend she do? Is there anything in particular that Goodman or Berner should avoid saying or doing in responding to Montell's e-mail?

(b) Suppose instead that Montell does not send an e-mail, but rather meets with Berner over lunch to discuss her competing offer. Upon hearing the offer, Berner immediately promises to meet SLF's salary. Berner also tells Montell, "You are a valuable member of our team, and the only one with the technical expertise to run student loans. Losing you would really hurt the company. If you stay, I promise Huntington will take care of you for the long run." As in-house counsel, you learn about this exchange only after you come across the paperwork altering Montell's title and pay, and contact Berner to inquire about it. What concerns might you have at this point about the statements Berner made to Montell? Is there anything you recommend doing now that could reduce the risk of any long-term obligation on the part of the company?

3. Written Employment Manuals and Employee Contract Rights

As you saw in *Guz*, the written documents prepared by an employer and distributed in the workplace can in some cases be a source of employee rights. Depending on what the documents say, they can also be a means by which employers constrict rights or reinforce the idea that employment is at will. Thus, from the lawyer's perspective, reviewing employment documents is a critical component of assessing the viability of an employee claim or, on the employer's side, in preventing claims and avoiding liability. This section looks at two recurring situations in which a plaintiff's success in challenging termination turns on the documentation provided by the employer—situations in which employer documentation seeks to disclaim the existence of contractual rights and situations in which employers try to alter existing employment policies.

In both situations, the analysis begins with what today is a relatively uncontroversial principle—that employment manuals and other written policies can be contractually binding. That idea was first established in two influential 1980s decisions, *Woolley v. Hoffmann-LaRoche, Inc.* 491 A.2d 1257 (N.J. 1985), and *Toussaint v. Blue Cross & Blue Shield*, 292 N.W.2d 880 (Mich. 1980). In *Woolley*, the employer distributed a "Personnel Policy Manual" to all its employees, including the plaintiff, who received it shortly after he began employment. The self-described purpose of the manual was to offer "a practical operating tool in the equitable and efficient administration of our employee relations program." The New Jersey Supreme Court summarized the provisions related to termination:

> [The manual] defines "the types of termination" as "layoff," "discharge due to performance," "discharge, disciplinary," "retirement" and "resignation." As one might expect, layoff is a termination caused by lack of work, retirement a termination caused by age, resignation a termination on the initiative of the employee, and discharge due to performance and discharge, disciplinary, are both terminations for cause. There is no category set forth for discharge without cause. The termination section includes "Guidelines for discharge due to performance," consisting of a fairly detailed procedure to be used before an employee may be fired for cause. Preceding these definitions of the five categories of termination is a section on "Policy," the first sentence of which provides: "It is the policy of Hoffmann-La Roche to retain to the extent consistent with company requirements, the services of all employees who perform their duties efficiently and effectively."

491 A.2d at 1258. Rejecting the defendant's contention that the manual was "simply an expression of the company's 'philosophy,'" the court found a jury question as to whether it contained an enforceable implied promise that termination would occur only for cause. The court concluded first that the manual could constitute a contractual offer:

> In determining the manual's meaning and effect, we must consider the probable context in which it was disseminated and the environment surrounding its continued existence. The manual, though apparently not distributed to all employees, [covers all of them. It] represents the most reliable statement of the terms of their employment. At oral argument counsel conceded that it is rare for any employee [to have an individual contract]. Having been employed, like hundreds of his co-employees, without any individual employment contract, by an employer whose good reputation made it so attractive, the employee is given this one document that purports to set forth the terms and conditions of his employment, a document obviously carefully prepared by the company with all of the appearances of corporate legitimacy that one could imagine. If there were any doubt about it (and there would be none in the mind of most employees), the name of the manual dispels it, for it is nothing short of the official policy of the company, it is the Personnel Policy Manual. As every employee knows, when superiors tell you "it's company policy," they mean business.
>
> The [Manual's] changeability—the uncontroverted ability of management to change its terms—is argued as supporting its non-binding quality, but one might as easily conclude that, given its importance, the employer wanted to keep it up to date, especially to make certain, given this employer's good reputation in labor relations, that the benefits conferred were sufficiently competitive with those available from other employers, including benefits found in collective bargaining agreements. The record suggests that the changes actually made almost always favored the employees.
>
> Given that background, then, unless the language contained in the manual were such that no one could reasonably have thought it was intended to create legally binding obligations, the termination provisions of the policy manual would have to be regarded

as an obligation undertaken by the employer. It will not do now for the company to say it did not mean the things it said in its manual to be binding . . . no matter how sincere its belief that they are not enforceable.

Job security is the assurance that one's livelihood, one's family's future, will not be destroyed arbitrarily; it can be cut off only "for good cause," fairly determined. Hoffmann-La Roche's commitment here was to what working men and women regard as their most basic advance. It was a commitment that gave workers protection against arbitrary termination.

Many of these workers undoubtedly know little about contracts, and many probably would be unable to analyze the language and terms of the manual. Whatever Hoffmann-La Roche may have intended, that which was read by its employees was a promise not to fire them except for cause.

Id. at 1265-66.

The court went on to consider whether this offer had been accepted by Hoffmann-La Roche's employees:

> In most of the cases involving an employer's personnel policy manual, the document is prepared without any negotiations and is voluntarily distributed to the workforce by the employer. It seeks no return promise from the employees. It is reasonable to interpret it as seeking continued work from the employees, who, in most cases, are free to quit since they are almost always employees at will, not simply in the sense that the employer can fire them without cause, but in the sense that they can quit without breaching any obligation. Thus analyzed, the manual is an offer that seeks the formation of a unilateral contract — the employees' bargained-for action needed to make the offer binding being their continued work when they have no obligation to continue.

Id. at 1267. The court noted that its analysis was "perfectly adequate for that employee who was aware of the manual and who continued to work intending that continuation to be the action in exchange for the employer's promise; it is even more helpful in support of that conclusion if, but for the employer's policy manual, the employee would have quit." *Id.* Absent such evidence, however, the court suggested that reliance on the manual should be presumed. It drew on *Toussaint*, in which the Michigan court analyzed the legal effect of a personnel manual containing similar statements. In discussing workers' reliance on the manual, *Toussaint* noted:

> While an employer need not establish personnel policies or practices, where an employer chooses to establish such policies and practices and makes them known to its employees, the employment relationship is presumably enhanced. The employer secures an orderly, cooperative and loyal work force, and the employee the peace of mind associated with job security and the conviction that he will be treated fairly. No pre-employment negotiations need take place and the parties' minds need not meet on the subject; nor does it matter that the employee knows nothing of the particulars of the employer's policies and practices or that the employer may change them unilaterally. It is enough that the employer chooses, presumably in its own interest, to create an environment in which the employee believes that, whatever, the personnel policies and practices, they are established and official at any given time, purport to be fair, and are applied consistently and uniformly to each employee. The employer has then created a situation "instinct with an obligation."

Toussaint, 292 N.W.2d at 892.

Woolley went on the address possible concerns of employers. Seemingly undermining its plaintiff-friendly holding, the final paragraphs of the decision offer employers a way to avoid contractual liability for the promises made in their manuals:

> Our opinion need not make employers reluctant to prepare and distribute company policy manuals. Such manuals can be very helpful tools in labor relations, helpful both to employer and employees, and we would regret it if the consequence of this decision were that the constructive aspects of these manuals were in any way diminished. We do not believe that they will, or at least we certainly do not believe that that constructive aspect should be diminished as a result of this opinion.
>
> All that this opinion requires of an employer is that it be fair. It would be unfair to allow an employer to distribute a policy manual that makes the workforce believe that certain promises have been made and then to allow the employer to renege on those promises. What is sought here is basic honesty: If the employer, for whatever reason, does not want the manual to be capable of being construed by the court as a binding contract, there are simple ways to attain that goal. All that need be done is the inclusion in a very prominent position of an appropriate statement that there is no promise of any kind by the employer contained in the manual; that regardless of what the manual says or provides, the employer promises nothing and remains free to change wages and all other working conditions without having to consult anyone and without anyone's agreement; and that the employer continues to have the absolute power to fire anyone with or without good cause.

491 A.2d at 1271.

Woolley is important for several reasons. Like *Pugh* and *Guz*, it stands for the proposition that in the workplace contractual rights are determined by an examination of factual circumstances, including the reasonable expectations of employees inculcated by management policy and practice. This line of decisions is distinguishable from traditional contracts jurisprudence, which tends to draw a clearer line between what are sometimes called "relational" norms and enforceable obligations. *See generally* Melvin A. Eisenberg, *Why There Is No Law of Relational Contracts*, 94 Nw. U. L. Rev. 805 (2000) (distinguishing classical contract doctrine and relational contract theory).

Woolley is also notable for its use of unilateral contract principles in assessing the legal enforceability of Hoffmann-La Roche's manual. For better or worse, this approach has been espoused by most courts dealing with disputes over manuals and written policies. How convincing do you find *Woolley*'s analysis of offer and acceptance? Consider one commentator's view:

> [U]nilateral contract analysis fits uneasily into the handbook context. Except for the communication prerequisite, all of [the] unilateral contract elements are implied by the court rather than intended by the parties. [M]ost employers have no intention of extending a contractual offer when issuing an employee handbook. Similarly, the court infers the employee's acceptance and consideration from conduct that, in reality, could occur regardless of the handbook's existence.
>
> The notion of a bargained-for exchange in this setting is a fiction, but the fiction is convenient and understandable. These advantages have induced courts to stretch unilateral contract theory in order to achieve a desirable policy result: the enforcement of handbook promises that benefit employers by creating legitimate expectations among the work force.

Stephen F. Befort, *Employee Handbooks and the Legal Effect of Disclaimers*, 13 Indus. Rel. L. J. 326, 342-43 (1991/1992). In the cases that follow, consider whether unilateral contract theory offers an accurate description of the parties' relationship. Consider also the degree to which this theory allows courts to achieve particular policy goals.

Finally, *Woolley* is important because of its particular facts and its concluding dicta, which together create uncertainty about the extent to which any particular manual will be held enforceable. A critical fact in the case is the strength of the assurances in the company's manual. Does it surprise you that Hoffmann-La Roche was willing to make such an explicit commitment to job security? How common is it for modern employers to make such statements, let alone in writing? *Cf. Green v. Vermont Country Store*, 191 F. Supp. 2d 476, 481 (D. Vt. 2002) ("value statement" in employer handbook espousing equal treatment contained only general statements of policy and did not constitute a definitive promise for a specific course of treatment). An even more important limitation is the final paragraph permitting employers to disclaim the contractual significance of their handbooks. What drafting techniques would you expect management attorneys to adopt in light of the court's opinion? As you will see, this final paragraph is the source of a great deal of case law limiting the enforceability of written manuals and polices in the contemporary workplace.

≣≣≣ *Conner v. City of Forest Acres*
≣≣≣ *560 S.E.2d 606 (S.C. 2002)*

WALLER, Justice.

. . . Respondent Evelyn Conner worked for the City of Forest Acres ("the City") as a police dispatcher. She was hired in July 1984 and was terminated in October 1993. At the time of her termination, J.C. Rowe was the Chief of Police, and Corporal Lewis Langley was her immediate supervisor. Beginning in November 1992, Conner received numerous reprimands for such things as violating the dress code, tardiness, performing poor work, leaving work without permission, and using abusive language. In July 1993, Conner was evaluated as unsatisfactory and placed on a 90-day probation. She was reprimanded twice in August 1993, and her October 1993 evaluation showed only slight improvement; therefore, the City terminated her on October 7, 1993.

Conner filed a grievance, and at the hearing before the grievance committee, she disputed many of the reprimands. The grievance committee voted 2-1 to reinstate Conner. The City Council, however, rejected the grievance committee's decision and voted to uphold Conner's termination.

During her employment, Conner received two employee handbooks. After receiving each one, Conner signed an acknowledgment form. The 1993 acknowledgment stated as follows:

> I acknowledge that I have received a copy of the City of Forest Acres Personnel Policy and Procedures Manual (Adopted July 1, 1993). I understand that I am responsible for reading, understanding, and abiding by the contents of these policies and procedures. I further understand that all the policies contained herein are subject to change as the need arises. I further understand that nothing in these policies and procedures creates a contract of employment for any term, that I am an employee at-will and nothing herein limits the City of Forest Acres's rights for dismissal.

On page 1 of the handbook, entitled INTRODUCTION, there is the following language:

Important Notice

MANY OF THE POLICIES CONTAINED IN THIS HANDBOOK ARE BASED ON LEGAL PROVISIONS, INTERPRETATIONS OF LAW, AND EMPLOYEE RELATIONS PRINCIPLES, ALL OF WHICH ARE SUBJECT TO CHANGE. FOR THIS REASON, THIS HANDBOOK IS CONSIDERED TO BE A GUIDELINE AND IS SUBJECT TO CHANGE WITH LITTLE NOTICE. THE HANDBOOK DOES NOT CONSTITUTE A CONTRACT OF EMPLOYMENT FOR ANY TERM. NOTHING IN THIS HANDBOOK SHALL BE CONSTRUED TO CONSTITUTE A CONTRACT. THE CITY HAS THE RIGHT, AT ITS DISCRETION, TO MODIFY THIS HANDBOOK AT ANY TIME. NOTHING HEREIN LIMITS THE CITY'S RIGHTS TO TERMINATE EMPLOYMENT. ALL EMPLOYEES OF THE CITY ARE AT-WILL EMPLOYEES. NO ONE EXCEPT THE CITY ADMINISTRATOR HAS THE AUTHORITY TO WAIVE ANY OF THE PROVISIONS OF THIS HANDBOOK, OR MAKE REPRESENTATIONS CONTRARY TO THE PROVISIONS OF THIS HANDBOOK.

This same language appears on the last page of the handbook.

The handbook contained a section entitled "Code of Conduct." In this section, the handbook states that conduct "reflecting unfavorably upon the reputation of the City, the Department, or the employee will not be tolerated." Furthermore, this section advises that:

This code of conduct is designed to guide all employees in their relationship with the City.

The following is a non-exclusive list of acts which are considered a violation of the Code of Conduct expected of a City employee, and such conduct will be disciplined in accords with its seriousness, recurrence, and circumstances. Degrees of discipline are given under the section entitled "Discipline" in this manual.

The list enumerates 23 different acts.

The Disciplinary Procedures section of the handbook states that it is the "duty of all employees to comply with, and to assist in carrying into effect [t]he provisions of the personnel policy and procedures." Additionally, the handbook states the following:

Ordinarily, discipline shall be of an increasingly progressive nature, the step of progression being (1) oral or written reprimand, (2) suspension, and (3) dismissal. Discipline should correspond to the offense and therefore NO REQUIREMENT EXISTS FOR DISCIPLINE TO BE PROGRESSIVE. FIRST VIOLATIONS CAN RESULT IN IMMEDIATE DISMISSAL WITHOUT REPRIMAND OR SUSPENSION.

Furthermore, this section states that violations of the code of conduct "*are declared*" to be grounds for discipline and that discipline "*will be used* to enforce the City's Code of Conduct." (Emphasis added.) Finally, the grievance procedure is outlined in detail. In this section, the handbook states "[i]t is the policy of the City of Forest Acres that all employees shall be treated fairly and consistently in all matters related to their employment."

[Conner brought suit against the City alleging breach of contract. The trial court granted the defendants' motions for summary judgment, but the Court of Appeals reversed.]

The City argues there was no contract created by the handbook because: (1) the procedures in the employee handbook did not alter Conner's at-will status, (2) the disclaimers in the handbook were conspicuous and therefore effective, and (3) Conner signed acknowledgments of her at-will status. Additionally, the City contends that even if the handbook did create a contract, it did not breach the contract because it followed the prescribed procedures.

The general rule is that termination of an at-will employee normally does not give rise to a cause of action for breach of contract. However, where the at-will status of the employee is altered by the terms of an employee handbook, an employer's discharge of an employee may give rise to a cause of action for wrongful discharge. Because an employee handbook may create a contract, the issue of the existence of an employment contract is proper for a jury when its existence is questioned and the evidence is either conflicting or admits of more than one inference.

The Court in *Small* [*v. Springs*, 357 S.E.2d 452, 455 (S.C. 1987)] stated that "[i]t is patently unjust to allow an employer to couch a handbook, bulletin, or other similar material in mandatory terms and then allow him to ignore these very policies as 'a gratuitous, nonbinding statement of general policy' whenever it works to his disadvantage." The *Small* Court instructed that if an employer wishes to issue written policies, but intends to continue at-will employment, the employer must insert a conspicuous disclaimer into the handbook. However, in *Fleming v. Borden*, 450 S.E.2d 589 (S.C. 1994), the Court indicated that whether the disclaimer is conspicuous is generally a question for the jury. Specifically, the *Fleming* Court stated that "[i]n most instances, summary judgment is inappropriate when the handbook contains both a disclaimer and promises."

Relying primarily on *Fleming*, the Court of Appeals in the instant case found that summary judgment was inappropriate. We agree. While the City argues that its handbook contained disclaimers which were effective as a matter of law and that Conner signed acknowledgments of her at-will status, the fact remains that the handbook outlines numerous procedures concerning progressive discipline, discharge, and subsequent grievance. The language in the handbook is mandatory in nature[4] and therefore a genuine issue of material fact exists as to whether Conner's at-will status was modified by the policies in the handbook.

The City also argues that if a contract exists, then as a matter of law, it did not breach the contract because it followed the procedures outlined in the handbook. The Court of Appeals found that because "Conner disputes the City's version of the events resulting in her reprimands and subsequent termination," summary judgment was not proper "on the issue of whether Conner was fired for cause."

Although this is a closer question, we agree with the Court of Appeals that there is a genuine issue of material fact as to whether Conner was wrongfully terminated. The appropriate test on the issue of breach is as follows: "If the fact finder finds a contract to terminate only for cause, he must determine whether the employer had *a reasonable good*

---

4. For example, the handbook states that: (1) violations of the Code of Conduct *will be* disciplined," (2) "discipline *shall be* of an increasingly progressive nature," and (3) "all employees *shall be* treated fairly and consistently in all matters related to their employment." (Emphasis added.)

faith belief that sufficient cause existed for termination."[5] We note that the fact finder must not focus on whether the employee actually committed misconduct; instead, the focus must be on whether the employer reasonably determined it had cause to terminate.

Conner's basic argument is there was no just cause for her termination. Although it appears that the City followed its handbook procedures in effectuating Conner's termination, the grievance committee voted to reinstate Conner; i.e., the committee found no just cause for Conner's firing. Subsequently, the City Council overturned the committee's decision. While the committee and City Council both could have reached their respective conclusions reasonably and in good faith, it nonetheless appears that reasonable minds can differ as to whether just cause existed to support Conner's termination. Thus, there remains the ultimate question of whether the City had a reasonable good faith belief that sufficient cause existed for termination. This is a question that generally should not be resolved on summary judgment, and therefore, the Court of Appeals correctly reversed the trial court's grant of summary judgment in favor of the City. . . .

NOTES

1. *Putting* Woolley *and* Conner *Together.* Why did the city of Forest Acres lose this case? Didn't its manual contain the requisite *Woolley* disclaimers in abundance? What exactly is the outstanding factual issue on the enforceability of the manual that requires a remand?

2. *Clarity and Conspicuousness.* One reason that plaintiffs sometimes prevail despite the presence of at-will language in a handbook or other document is because the clause is not clear or conspicuous. *See Evenson v. Colorado Farm Bureau Mut. Ins. Co.*, 879 P.2d 402, 409 (Colo. Ct. App. 1993) (jury question presented on whether handbook formed contract where language disclaiming contractual significance was clear, but not "emphasized"); *Nicosia v. Wakefern Food Corp.*, 643 A.2d 554, 560 (N.J. 1994) (disclaimer ineffective under *Woolley* because it contained "legalese" such as "not contractual," "consideration," and "subject to . . . interpretation"); *Sanchez v. Life Care Ctrs. of Amer., Inc.*, 855 P.2d 1256, 1259 (Wyo. 1993) (reversing summary judgment for employer where disclaimer language was "not bold lettered," was "buried in introductory paragraphs," was "not designed to attract attention," and was "stated in language that does not tell the employee what he needs to know"). *See also Becker v. Fred Meyer Stores, Inc.*, 335 P.3d 1110 (Alaska 2014) (given the sheer level of detail, and disclaiming language would have to be very prominent to be effective). From what you can tell, was the disclaimer in *Conner* prominently placed? Was the text emphasized in any way? Assuming it was noted and read, was it understandable to an employee?

3. *Judicial Deference to Employer Disclaimer Language. Connor* represents one extreme in judicial treatment of employer disclaimers. Not all courts parse so closely the language of the manual or recognize possible inconsistencies of the type that led to a plaintiff victory in *Connor*. Recall *Guz*, for instance, in which the California Supreme Court rejected the employee's claim, based in part on the at-will provision of the employer's manual, notwithstanding other provisions and policies that made promises

---

5. The Court in *Small* noted that where the jury found that a handbook created an employment contract, it was for the jury to decide whether the employer "reasonably could have determined that Small's actions" warranted immediate discharge as a "serious offense." Therefore, it is generally a jury question as to whether the employer acted reasonably pursuant to the employment contract.

about the method by which workers would be selected for termination. In contrast to *Connor*, many courts treat disclaimer language as dispositive of employee contract rights, routinely awarding summary judgment to employers in such cases. *See, e.g., Finch v. Farmers Co-op Oil Co. of Sheridan*, 109 P.3d 537, 541-42 (Wyo. 2005); *Grossman v. Computer Curriculum Corp.*, 131 F. Supp. 2d 299, 305-06 (D. Conn. 2000); *Rowe v. Montgomery Ward & Co.*, 473 N.W.2d 268, 271 (Mich. 1991). Some scholars have speculated that judicial tendency to "rubberstamp" employer disclaimer language may be on the rise. *See* Arnow-Richman, *Employment as Transaction, supra*, at 468-71 (linking judicial treatment of disclaimers to larger trend of increasing deference to private ordering in employment relationships); Fineman, *The Inevitable Demise, supra*, at 365-77 (tracing increasing judicial deference to disclaimer language in California as employers refined their drafting techniques to avoid liability).

4. *Disclaimers and Oral Assurances.* The effectiveness of written disclaimers is a recurring theme in all types of employment contract disputes, not just those centered on manuals. In part as a result of cases like *Woolley*, employers frequently place recitals of at-will status in a variety of personnel materials, including employment applications, offer letters, and reimbursement forms. Often these are standardized documents that are distributed as a matter of course to all personnel. The effect of these statements in the face of other evidence suggesting a contract for job security depends both on the facts and the court. The contrary evidence may be treated as inadmissible parol statements, evidence of a modification, or simply additional evidence to be submitted to a fact finder who will determine the contractual status of the employee under the circumstances. Not surprisingly, the outcomes of such cases tend to be highly fact-dependent. For example, oral assurance-based contract claims sometimes prevail, despite the presence of clear written disclaimers. *See, e.g., Worley v. Wyoming Bottling Co.*, 1 P.3d 615 (Wyo. 2000) (holding plaintiff may proceed with breach of contract and promissory estoppel claims based on express assurances of job security by supervisor despite at-will disclaimers contained in job application, noncompete and employee handbook). In many other cases, however, courts reject claims that express, written waivers can be overcome by oral assurances or other surrounding circumstances. *See, e.g., Edwards v. Geisinger Clinic*, 459 F. App'x 125 (3d Cir. 2012) (holding physician who signed a practice agreement acknowledging that his employment with the clinic was "at will" had no breach of contract claim when his employment was terminated earlier despite recruitment discussions and an offer letter proposing a four-to-six-year relationship); *Scott v. Merck & Co., Inc.*, 497 F. App'x 331, 335-36 (4th Cir. 2012) (concluding that a statement in plaintiff's employment application acknowledging that Merck had the right to terminate at will, together with Manager's Policies to the same effect, barred any suit based on subsequent assurance of nonretaliation for reporting objectionable business practices); *see also Carroll v. Stryker Corp.*, 658 F.3d 675, 682-684 (7th Cir. 2011) (holding plaintiff could not recover under unjust enrichment theory because, although an at-will employee, he had an express contract regarding the terms of compensation, his continuing to work after receiving this document indicated his consent even if he never signed it, and the contract was not illusory merely because the employer reserved the right to change the terms of payment).

5. *Turnabout Is Fair Play.* Most cases turning on the significance of disclaimer language involve suits by employees who, like Connor, claim their employer breached a promise of job security. However, employers occasionally have found themselves in the uncomfortable position of having to circumvent their own language in trying to enforce promises made by employees. Such cases can arise when the employer has placed an arbitration policy or a prohibition on post-employment competition in its handbook. When an employee subsequently engages in prohibited behavior — for instance, filing suit against the employer in court — the company is at pains to explain why the employee's commitment should be enforced when the handbook in which it was found expressly disclaims its contractual significance. *See, e.g., Heurtebise v. Reliable Bus. Computers*, 550 N.W.2d 243, 247 (Mich. 1996) (policy in handbook did not constitute enforceable arbitration agreement where handbook's opening statement disclaiming contractual significance of manual "demonstrate[d] that employer did not intend to be bound to any provision [it] contained"); *Snow v. BE & K Const. Co.*, 126 F. Supp. 2d 5 (D. Maine 2001) (refusing to enforce arbitration clause because employer was "trying to have it both ways" by including disclaiming language in handbook to avoid being bound while, at the same time, seeking to enforce its terms against employees); *Gibson v. Neighborhood Health Clinics, Inc.*, 121 F.3d 1126, 1132-33 (7th Cir. 1997) (Cucahy, J., concurring) ("[W]hatever 'promise' is contained in the Associate Policy Manual is illusory because it is subject to the sweeping disclaimer language contained in the opening two paragraphs of the Manual."); Unfortunately, for employees, such victories are short-lived. Employers are able to correct the problem easily by removing such commitments from the general personnel handbook and placing them in formal contract documents separately signed by the employee. *See, e.g., Currier, McCabe & Assocs. v. Maher*, 906 N.Y.S.2d 129, 131 (N.Y. App. 2010) (defendant-employee bound by handbook's tuition repayment policy despite disclaimer where employee's separately executed employment agreement provided the he had "read the EMPLOYEE HANDBOOK and agrees to [its] terms and conditions"). If you find yourself representing management, you would do well to remember these examples.

PROBLEM

2-4. Imagine that, following *Woolley*, the Human Resources director at Hoffmann-La Roche contacts you about revising the company's personnel manual. The HR director feels that the manual is good for employee morale and would like to continue using it, but hopes to alter the language so as to protect the company from future contractual liability. Look at footnote 2 of *Woolley*, which contains the key language that gave rise to Woolley's claim. How would you redraft this? What might you add? Will the revision you create satisfy the company's goals?

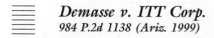
Demasse v. ITT Corp.
984 P.2d 1138 (Ariz. 1999)

FELDMAN, Justice.

The United States Court of Appeals for the Ninth Circuit certified to us [the following question] of Arizona law. . . .

1. Once a policy that an employee will not be laid off ahead of less senior employees becomes part of the employment contract . . . as a result of the employee's

legitimate expectations and reliance on the employer's handbook, may the employer thereafter unilaterally change the handbook policy so as to permit the employer to layoff employees without regard to seniority? . . .

ITT hired Roger Demasse, Maria A. Garcia, Billy W. Jones, Viola Munguia, Greg Palmer, and Socorro Soza (collectively "Demasse employees") as hourly workers at various times between 1960 and 1979. Although it is unclear when ITT first issued an employee handbook, evidently there have been five editions, the most recent in 1989. . . .

The issues presented focus on the 1989 handbook, which included two new provisions. First, a disclaimer added to the first page "Welcome" statement provided that "nothing contained herein shall be construed as a guarantee of continued employment. . . . ITT Cannon does not guarantee continued employment to employees and retains the right to terminate or layoff employees." Second, this Welcome statement included a new modification provision, which read:

> Within the limits allowed by law, ITT Cannon reserves the right to amend, modify or cancel this handbook, as well as any or all of the various policies, rules, procedures and programs outlined in it. Any amendment or modification will be communicated to affected employees, and while the handbook provisions are in effect, will be consistently applied.

. . . When the 1989 handbook was distributed, ITT employees signed an acknowledgment that they had received, understood, and would comply with the revised handbook.

Four years passed before ITT notified its hourly employees that effective April 19, 1993, its layoff guidelines for hourly employees would not be based on seniority but on each employee's "abilities and documentation of performance." Demasse, Soza, and Palmer were laid off ten days after the new policy went into effect, Munguia five days later, and Jones and Garcia almost nine months later. All were laid off before less senior employees but in accordance with the 1993 policy modification.

The Demasse employees brought an action in federal district court alleging they were laid off in breach of an implied-in-fact contract created by the pre-1989 handbook provisions requiring that ITT lay off its employees according to seniority. [The court granted summary judgment for the employer finding that the employer had validly modified its layoff policy in the 1993 handbook.]

A. The Implied-in-Fact Contract . . .

At-will employment contracts are unilateral and typically start with an employer's offer of a wage in exchange for work performed; subsequent performance by the employee provides consideration to create the contract. Thus, before performance is rendered, the offer can be modified by the employer's unilateral withdrawal of the old offer and substitution of a new one: The employer makes a new offer with different terms and the employee again accepts the new offer by performance (such as continued employment). Thus a new unilateral contract is formed — a day's work for a day's wages. . . .

While employment contracts without express terms are presumptively at will, an employee can overcome this presumption by establishing a contract term that is either expressed or inferred from the words or conduct of the parties. . . .

When employment circumstances offer a term of job security to an employee who might otherwise be dischargeable at will and the employee acts in response to that promise, the employment relationship is *no longer at will* but is instead governed by the terms of the contract. . . .

This, of course, does not mean that all handbook terms create contractual promises. A statement is contractual only if it discloses "a promissory intent or [is] one that the employee could reasonably conclude constituted a commitment by the employer. If the statement is merely a description of the employer's present policies . . . it is neither a promise nor a statement that could reasonably be relied upon as a commitment." *Soderlun v. Public Serv. Co.*, 944 P.2d 616, 620 (Colo. App. 1997). An implied-in-fact contract term is formed when "a reasonable person could conclude that both parties intended that the employer's (or the employee's) right to terminate the employment relationship at-will had been limited." *Metcalf v. Intermountain Gas Co.*, 778 P.2d 744, 746 (Idaho 1989).

When an employer chooses to include a handbook statement "that the employer should reasonably have expected the employee to consider as a commitment from the employer," that term becomes an offer to form an implied-in-fact contract and is accepted by the employee's acceptance of employment. . . .

B. Modification

ITT argues that it had the legal power to unilaterally modify the contract by simply publishing a new handbook. But as with other contracts, an implied-in-fact contract term cannot be modified unilaterally. . . .[3]

[T]o effectively modify a contract, whether implied-in-fact or express, there must be: (1) an offer to modify the contract, (2) assent to or acceptance of that offer, and (3) consideration.

The 1989 handbook, published with terms that purportedly modified or permitted modification of pre-existing contractual provisions, was therefore no more than an offer to modify the existing contract. Even if the 1989 handbook constituted a valid offer, questions remain whether the Demasse employees accepted that offer and whether there was consideration for the changes ITT sought to effect.

1. Continued Employment Alone Does Not Constitute Consideration for Modification

. . . Consideration will be found when an employer and its employees have made a "bargained for exchange to support [the employees'] . . . relinquishment of the protections they are entitled to under the existing contract."

The cases ITT cites hold that continued work alone both manifested the Demasse employees' assent to the modification and constituted consideration for it.

---

3. In the unilateral or at-will context, once the offer is accepted by commencement of performance, the terms cannot be changed. RESTATEMENT (SECOND) OF CONTRACTS § 45. Thus, if an employer offers a day's pay for a day's work, the employer cannot, after employee performance, reduce the offer of pay that induced the performance.

We disagree with both contentions and the cases that support them. Separate consideration, beyond continued employment, is necessary to effect a modification.

. . . Any other result brings us to an absurdity: The employer's threat to breach its promise of job security provides consideration for its rescission of that promise.

2. Acceptance

Continued employment after issuance of a new handbook does not constitute acceptance, otherwise the "illusion (and the irony) is apparent: To preserve their right under the [existing contract] . . . plaintiffs would be forced to quit." *Doyle* [*v. Holy Cross*, 708 N.E.2d 1140 (Ill. 1999)]. It is "too much to require an employee to preserve his or her rights under the original employment contract by quitting working." *Brodie* [*v. General Chem. Corp.*, 934 P.2d 1263, 1268 (Wyo. 1997)]. Thus, the employee does not manifest consent to an offer modifying an existing contract without taking affirmative steps, beyond continued performance, to accept. . . . If passive silence constituted acceptance, the employee "could not remain silent and continue to work. Instead [he] would have to give specific notice of rejection to the employer to avoid having his actions construed as acceptance. Requiring an offeree to take affirmative steps to reject an offer . . . is inconsistent with general contract law." The burden is on the employer to show that the employee assented with knowledge of the attempted modification and understanding of its impact on the underlying contract.

To manifest consent, the employee must first have legally adequate notice of the modification. Legally adequate notice is more than the employee's awareness of or receipt of the newest handbook. An employee must be informed of any new term, aware of its impact on the pre-existing contract, and affirmatively consent to it to accept the offered modification.

When ITT distributed the 1989 handbook containing the provisions permitting unilateral modification or cancellation, it did not bargain with those pre-1989 employees who had seniority rights under the old handbooks, did not ask for or obtain their assent, and did not provide consideration other than continued employment. The employees signed a receipt for the "1989 handbook stating that they had received the handbook[,] understood that it was their responsibility to read it, comply with its contents, and contact Personnel if they had any questions concerning the contents." The Demasse employees were not informed that continued employment—showing up for work the next day—would manifest assent, constitute consideration, and permit cancellation of any employment rights to which they were contractually entitled. Thus, even if we were to agree that continued employment could provide consideration for rescission of the job security term, that consideration would not have been bargained for and would not support modification. . . .

C . . .

If a contractual job security provision can be eliminated by unilateral modification, an employer can essentially terminate the employee at any time, thus abrogating any protection provided the employee. For example, an employer could terminate an employee who has a job security provision simply by saying, "I revoke that term and, as of today, you're dismissed" — no different from the full at-will scenario in which the employer only need say, "You're fired." This, of course, makes the original promise illusory. . . .

To those who believe our conclusion will destroy an employer's ability to update and modernize its handbook, we can only reply that the great majority of handbook terms are certainly non-contractual and can be revised, that the existence of contractual terms can be disclaimed in the handbook in effect at the time of hiring and, if not, permission to modify can always be obtained by mutual agreement and for consideration. In all other instances, the contract rule is and has always been that one should keep one's promises.

JONES, Vice Chief Judge, concurring in part and dissenting in part:

I respectfully dissent. . . . The [majority's] response undermines legitimate employer expectations in a remarkable departure from traditional at-will employment principles. It transforms the conventional employer-employee contract from one that is *unilateral* (performance of an act in exchange for a promise to pay) to one that is *bilateral* (a promise for a promise). The decision is unsupported by Arizona precedent and unwarranted as a matter of law.

The majority exacts from the certified question the premise that the employment relationship between the Demasse plaintiffs and ITT is "no longer at-will." I disagree. A single contract term in a policy manual may, while it exists, become an enforceable condition of employment, but it does not alter the essential character of the relationship. In my view, ITT, as the party unilaterally responsible for inserting it into the manual may, on reasonable notice, exercise an equal right to remove it.

For purposes of this discussion, it is assumed the reverse-seniority layoff provision became part of the "employment contract" years earlier when ITT initially placed it into the policy manual and that it remained a part of the "contract" as long as it remained a part of the manual. The simple question put to us is whether ITT may unilaterally bring about its removal and thereafter be free of any prospective reverse-seniority obligation in the event of a layoff. That question does not catapult the case beyond the reach of at-will employment principles.

. . . ITT added a contract disclaimer to its 1989 handbook: "[N]othing contained herein shall be construed as a guarantee of continued employment." In the same handbook, ITT expressly reserved "the right to amend, modify, or cancel this handbook, as well as any or all of the various policies, rules, procedures, and programs outlined within it." Each of the Demasse plaintiffs signed a certification acknowledging that the new policy had been received and reviewed.

The "at-will" status of the Demasse-ITT contract both before and after the 1989 amendments is confirmed by at least two factors: (1) the contract was always one of indefinite duration, and (2) the Demasse employees had the absolute right to quit at any time. . . .

The right to quit in opposition to changed policies, despite the majority's view, is properly characterized as a right. It is an inherent feature of at-will employment. . . .

When ITT modified its policy manual in 1989 by adding the contract disclaimer and the power to amend, and offered continuing employment to employees having received notice and having signed the acknowledgment, the employees effectively gave their acceptance to the amendment by continuing to work. Moreover, in 1993, when ITT revised its layoff policy, the employees had known for four years that such change could occur.

The majority overlooks another point. Just as at-will employees are unilaterally free to quit at any time, employers may be unilaterally forced by economic circumstance to curtail or shut down an operation, something employers have the absolute right to do.

When the employer chooses in good faith, in pursuit of legitimate business objectives, to eliminate an employee policy as an alternative to curtailment or total shutdown, there has been forbearance by the employer. Such forbearance constitutes a benefit to the employee in the form of an offer of continuing employment. The employer who provides continuing employment, albeit under newly modified contract terms, also provides consideration to support the amended policy manual. . . .

The majority imposes a bilateral principle on the at-will relationship by holding that in order for ITT to eliminate the reverse-seniority layoff policy, some form of new consideration, in addition to an offer of continuing employment, is necessary to support each individual employee's assent to the amended manual. The majority's approach effectively mandates that ITT, in order to free itself of future reverse-seniority obligations, would be required to give a wage increase, a one-time bonus, or some other new benefit to the employees with the explicit understanding that such benefit was given in exchange for the amendment to the policy manual. This becomes artificial because it is foreign to the unilateral at-will relationship and, as a practical matter, it leaves the employer unable, at least in part, to manage its business. I disagree with the proposition that "new" consideration is necessary.

The majority further asserts that ITT's exercise of the unilateral right to amend the handbook renders the employer's original reverse-seniority promise illusory. Once again, I disagree. An illusory promise is one which by its own terms makes performance optional with the promisor whatever may happen, or whatever course of conduct he may pursue. The reverse-seniority promise was not illusory because it was not optional with ITT as long as it remained a part of ITT's handbook policy. During the years of its existence, it was fully enforceable. . . .

The majority opinion produces the net result that the reverse-seniority layoff policy, as a permanent term of the "employment contract" with respect to any employee who at any time worked under it, gains parity with a negotiated collective bargaining agreement having a definite term, usually three years. In fact, the ITT policy would have force and effect even greater than a collective agreement because its existence, as to the Demasse plaintiffs and others similarly situated, becomes perpetual. This result grants preferential treatment to every employee who worked under the policy but denies such treatment to employees hired after its removal. A collective bargaining agreement is bilateral, and to impose a bilateral relationship on simple at-will employment is, in my view, an attempt to place a square peg in a round hole. Inevitably, this will impair essential managerial flexibility in the workplace. It will also cause undue deterioration of traditional at-will principles. . . .

Principles of equity and pragmatic reason have also governed the employer's unilateral right to change an implied-in-fact term in a handbook. The federal district court, applying Arizona law in *Bedow* [*v. Valley National Bank*, 5 BNA IER CAS 1678 (D. Ariz. 1988)], correctly asserted that the last-distributed handbook controls employment conditions and trumps prior inconsistent handbook terms:

> *Any other conclusion would create chaos for employers who would have different contracts of employment for different employees depending upon the particular personnel manual in force when the employee was hired.* Such a result would effectively discourage employers from either issuing employment manuals or subsequently upgrading or modifying personnel policies.

(emphasis added) . . .

The majority's answer to the certified question will frustrate the legitimate expectations of both employers and employees. The notion that one term in an employee handbook — a reverse-seniority layoff term — can be perpetually binding as to some but not all employees will effectively undermine [cases] on which employers have relied for years. The opinion unduly punishes ITT and other employers similarly situated. We said [previously] that employers should place contract disclaimer language in their handbooks to preserve the at-will relationship. ITT responded by inserting such language. We should leave it at that.

NOTES

1. *"Separate" Consideration.* The majority rejects the idea that continued employment can be consideration for the change in ITT's layoff policy, insisting on "separate" consideration for the modification. What is "separate" consideration? Is it any different from the discredited notion of "additional" consideration used by courts to defeat plaintiffs' claims to "permanent" or "lifetime" employment? Recall from your first-year contracts class the general common law rule that contract modifications require consideration to be binding. A corollary to this rule is that a "pre-existing legal duty" does not constitute consideration. *See* RESTATEMENT (SECOND) OF CONTRACTS § 370 (1981). Does the pre-existing legal duty concept help you distinguish between the "permanent" employment and handbook modification scenarios? Or is *Demasse* simply co-opting the additional consideration doctrine in order to turn the tables on employers?

2. *The Fiction of Assent.* The majority suggests that even if continued employment constituted consideration it could not suffice as an acceptance because it was not given knowingly. If tacit acceptance worked in *Woolley* to establish contractual rights based on a handbook, why doesn't it work here? Are *Demasse* and *Woolley* inconsistent? Which court's treatment of assent is more in keeping with basic contract law? Must parties actually negotiate terms in order to be contractually bound? Must they at least know what the terms are? Know they are contracting?

3. *Advising the Employer.* The law of personnel manual modification is currently evolving; not every jurisdiction has addressed the issue, nor has there been agreement among those that have. *Compare Torosyan v. Boehringer Ingelheim Pharmaceuticals, Inc.*, 662 A.2d 89, 98-99 (Conn. 1995) (employee continuing work does not constitute acceptance of a modified handbook that "substantially interferes with [the] employee's legitimate expectations") *with Asmus v. Pac. Bell*, 999 P.2d 71, 78 (Cal. 2000) (unilaterally conferred contract rights may be reduced or eliminated unilaterally); *see generally Fleming v. Borden, Inc.*, 450 S.E.2d 589, 594-95 (S.C. 1994) (summarizing various court approaches to enforceability of employer's unilateral modification of handbook to include disclaimer). This uncertainty can pose difficulties for employers. Assuming the law in your jurisdiction is undecided, how would you advise an employer seeking to modify the terms of a pre-existing handbook? Would you recommend trying to comply with the majority opinion in *Demasse*? If yes, by what means would you recommend obtaining employee assent? Would it be enough to amend the signature receipts to include an explanation of the modifications? Now consider what you might provide as "separate" consideration. Would a one-time bonus of $1000 suffice? How about a one-time bonus of $10? Does the employer have to provide something that is distinct from the usual adjustments made regularly to employee salaries? For instance, what about making the modification coincident with an annual cost-of-living adjustment? Might these examples offer ways to avoid the "chaos" envisioned by the dissent of different manuals applying to different employees depending on their date of hire?

4. *Square Peg in a Round Hole?* Consider the various objections raised by the dissent. Chief among them is a disagreement with the majority's premise that, upon the employer's adoption of the original personnel manual, the parties' relationship changed from a unilateral at-will relationship to a bilateral relationship with job security. Who is right? In commercial settings, it is not uncommon for parties to have long-term sales or service contracts that are terminable at will but which bind both parties to a variety of terms during the life of the agreement. Generally such contracts provide that a designated amount of notice must be given prior to termination. Does the commercial context offer a viable analogy for handbook modifications?

The draft Restatement of Employment Law adopts a comparable approach. It rejects efforts to apply contract principles to employer handbooks as "analytically unsatisfying" and permits the employer to "modify or revoke an obligation established pursuant to a unilateral statement" by providing "reasonable notice" of the change. *See* RESTATEMENT (THIRD) OF EMPLOYMENT LAW (Proposed Final Draft, April 18, 2014) § 2.05. If notice is the touchstone for enforceable unilateral modifications, how much time is reasonable? In *Demasse*, four years passed between ITT's change in policy and the lay-offs in question. Would four months suffice? Four days? *See, e.g., Asmus v. Pac. Bell*, 999 P.2d at 78 (sanctioning unilateral modification made two years after notice to employees that job security program might be eliminated); *Bankey v. Storer Broad. Co.*, 443 N.W.2d 112, 117-20 (Mich. 1989) (denying breach of contract claim by employee discharged two months after unilateral modification of employer's policy digest in recognition of employer's need for managerial flexibility). What is the point of notice — to allow employees who are unhappy to seek another job? If so, does that help determine the proper length of notice?

PROBLEM

2-5. During the mid-1990s, Pacific Telecom was facing competitive pressure from the burgeoning technology industry in California and lost several key employees to startup ventures offering stock option deals. In response, the company disseminated a new "Management Employment Security Policy" to all management personnel. The document provided, "It will be our policy to offer all management employees who continue to meet our changing business expectations employment security through reassignment to and retraining for other management positions, even if their present jobs are eliminated."

Five years later, following a crash in the tech sector, Pacific Bell realized it could not afford to maintain its employment security policy and needed to institute a reduction in force. It announced to all management personnel that the Employment Security Policy had been terminated and was being replaced with a new Management Force Reduction Program under which designated employees would be offered enhanced pension and severance benefits in exchange for their voluntary resignations. Craig Astor was a technical manager at Pacific Telecom who received both documents. He declined to resign under Pacific's Reduction Program. Six months later he was involuntarily terminated.

    (a) Suppose Astor sues for breach of an implied contract for job security under the original Security Policy. Is he likely to succeed? Are there any other legal theories he might be able to pursue?

    (b) How would it affect your analysis if Pacific Telecom had sent a notice to all managers one year prior to announcing its Management Force Reduction Program, alerting them to the fact that it would shortly be altering its Security Policy?

    (c) What if the original Security Policy contained the following additional sentence: "This Policy will remain in effect unless and until changing market conditions necessitate its revocation"?

3

Written Contracts and Expressly Negotiated Terms of Employment

As discussed in the previous chapter, the at-will presumption is merely a default rule; the words, actions, and practices of the employer can confer greater contractual rights to job security. This chapter continues our discussion of how parties alter the default rules of their relationship. While Chapter 2 dealt primarily with oral and implied promises, this chapter looks at situations where the employer and an individual employee explicitly discussed particular terms of employment—issues such as job duration, bases for termination, and methods of compensation—and then took the time to reduce those terms to writing, sometimes with the help of a lawyer.

Employers and employees who opt for a written contract do so for the same reasons that parties choose written contracts in other contexts. They hope to memorialize their understanding in a fixed form so that it will not be forgotten or challenged in the future by competing understandings. For employers, written contracts might also be desirable given the uncertainty of implied contract theory. An employer may use a writing to make clear that the employment relationship is at will in order to avoid subsequent claims to job security based on oral assurances or workplace practices like those explored in the last chapter. In contrast, employees will desire written contracts mostly to lock in employment and its benefits.

Employers are increasingly using narrowly focused agreements, like an acknowledgment of at-will status or arbitration agreements, even with rank and file employees. As a result written agreements providing for any kind of job security remain the exception, not the rule, in the American workplace. Drafting such an agreement requires time, advanced planning, and, particularly when a lawyer is involved, expense. From the perspective of the employer, the party who generally controls whether a written contract will be executed, the default rule already adequately protects its interest in being able to terminate at will. As a result, written contracts guaranteeing some variety of job security are found primarily in those situations in which the employee has sufficient bargaining power to insist that the employer commit to more generous terms. These include the collective bargaining context where unionized employees (through their union representatives) negotiate a written "collective bargaining agreement," a process generally studied in a separate course on Labor Law. These "CBAs" govern all workers in the relevant "bargaining unit" and are often very detailed, covering various terms and conditions of employment including job security. Individual written contracts, by contrast, are used most frequently with high-level employees, such as executives and upper-level managers, who command significant pay and hold critical positions that enable them to insist on generous terms and justify a written instrument. Individual written contracts are also used with some regularity among sales employees and other workers whose compensation fluctuates based on performance. In those instances, the writing rarely guarantees any length of employment; instead, it usually serves the employer's practical need to document a complex commission or bonus structure.

While written contracts will resolve some uncertainties, they can create others. Planning and drafting are imperfect processes that can result in a document that is ambiguous, vague, or simply incomplete. Although such difficulties plague all types of contracts, they are especially likely in the employment context where the parties' expectations change, sometimes dramatically, over the course of the relationship. Think how hard it would be to capture every obligation of the employer and employee in a particular work relationship in a single written document. Even if you could do it, circumstances and expectations are almost certain to change over time, especially in the high-powered situations where such contracts are typically used. As a result, when employment disputes arise, parties often find that their written contracts are silent as to a particular issue or even inconsistent with the way the relationship has developed.

This chapter explores written contracts in the context of a dynamic employment relationship. Section A begins by looking at situations where the written contract is ambiguous as to job security, either because of the language itself or the circumstances surrounding the agreement. Section B turns to how written provisions conferring job security apply in the context of termination, as where an employee's performance is substandard or an employer fails to comply with specific obligations. Finally, Section C tackles problems related to special compensation arrangements such as commissions and profit sharing. Note throughout how context and other circumstances extraneous to the written instrument affect both the parties' perception of their obligations to one another and the court's interpretation of their contract. Consider whether and how parties might have avoided litigation by drafting their agreement differently and what the resulting decisions say about the value and efficacy of written employment contracts.

A. JOB SECURITY TERMS

1. Identifying and Interpreting Job Security Provisions

≡≡≡ *Tropicana Hotel Corporation v. Speer*
≡≡≡ 692 P.2d 499 (Nev. 1985)

GUNDERSON, Justice.

This appeal arises out of the brief association of Donald Speer with Tropicana Hotel. In July 1975 Mitzi Stauffer Briggs acquired a controlling interest in the Tropicana Hotel Corporation . . . [and] looked for a competent general manager who could restore the hotel to its former prosperity. She offered the position to Donald Speer, general manager at the Desert Inn.

Speer indicated that he would accept the position only if, in addition to a generous salary, he could have equity in the Tropicana Hotel Corporation. After some preliminary discussions, Briggs invited Speer, his counsel and her counsel to her home in Atherton, California, in the hope of concluding an agreement. It is undisputed that agreement was reached on the terms of the employment contract; the parties could not agree, however, on how the stock should be transferred.

After Speer returned to Las Vegas, he left his position at the Desert Inn and began working as general manager at the Tropicana Hotel. Two months later Briggs signed an employment agreement prepared by her attorneys according to drafts of the Atherton discussions, and forwarded it to Speer. Speer never signed the agreement. He testified at trial that his counsel advised him not to sign it until a satisfactory stock option agreement was prepared and signed by Briggs.

In March 1976 a culinary strike forced the hotel to close. Disagreements over hotel management developed between Speer and Briggs, and after two of Speer's trusted subordinates were fired by the executive committee, Speer left the hotel. The parties disagreed at trial over whether Speer had resigned or whether he had been terminated. Speer filed suit [alleging breach of an oral employment contract reached at Atherton by his termination without cause and] breach of an oral stock option agreement. The district court, sitting without a jury, found that binding oral agreements existed, and that Tropicana had breached the employment contract. . . . [H]owever, it found that the statute of frauds rendered the stock option agreement unenforceable.

We turn first to the stock option transfer. . . . We need not decide here whether [the statute of frauds] applies to stock option agreements executed in connection with employment contracts, because our examination of the record compels us to conclude that no agreement on the transfer of stock was ever reached.

The record shows that at Atherton the parties merely agreed that Speer would receive $100,000 worth of points, or approximately 3.2% of Briggs's holding. The parties could not agree on the precise form of the transfer, because Speer wished to be left with $100,000 after the payment of his capital gains tax, and counsel could not work out the tax consequences to their satisfaction. Even after the meeting at Atherton, numerous drafts of proposed agreements circulated between counsel but were never satisfactory to both parties. When important terms remain unresolved, a binding agreement cannot exist.

We next turn to Speer['s claim of] breach of his oral employment contract. . . .

The record shows that during their negotiations the parties contemplated that any agreement concerning Speer's employment would become effective only when reduced to writing and signed by the parties.[3] At trial Speer as well as Briggs admitted that the terms of the proposed written agreement corresponded to the terms agreed on

---

3. This is shown by the testimony of Speer himself.

Counsel for Tropicana: Mr. Speer, when you left the Atherton meeting, was it your understanding that a written contract embodying the terms of your employment contract as well as the points would be drawn up and signed by the parties?

Speer: I did.

Counsel for Tropicana: Mr. Speer, it was always your intention, was it not, both pre-Atherton, at Atherton and post-Atherton that you would have a written contract or that you would be protected as far as your position as general manager at the Tropicana Hotel; is that true?

Speer: That's true.

at Atherton. Nevertheless, on advice of counsel Speer decided not to sign the draft until Briggs signed a satisfactory stock option agreement. Clearly, Speer withheld his signature to pressure Briggs to consummate the stock option transfer, and his conduct is inconsistent with his assertion that the oral agreement reached at Atherton was intended to be immediately binding. Had the proposed written agreement been merely a memorialization of a binding oral contract, Speer's signature would not have been of sufficient legal significance to exert any influence on Briggs. We have previously stated that since some measure of agreement must usually be reached before a written draft is prepared, the evidence that the parties intended to be presently bound must be convincing and subject to no other reasonable interpretation. . . .

A similar situation confronted us in *Loma Linda Univ. v. Eckenweiler,* 469 P.2d 54 (Nev. 1970). Negotiations regarding plaintiff's employment contract continued during his employment by the University. A written agreement was prepared but rejected by the plaintiff. Neither party signed the agreement. After plaintiff's employment was terminated, he attempted to enforce an alleged oral agreement regarding severance pay. We held that even accepting the district court's view that the parties had reached a meeting of the minds on the issue of severance pay, judgment for plaintiff had to be reversed. The proposed written agreement was an offer by the University which plaintiff had declined to accept. Important terms remained unresolved and the oral agreement was incomplete; moreover, the parties had contemplated consummation by written agreement and plaintiff himself had rejected the written contract. Similarly, since Speer refused to sign the written draft and clearly demonstrated his intent not to be immediately bound, no contract arose between the parties.

Speer contends that the fact that he commenced his employment at the Tropicana Hotel before a written contract was even prepared shows that he regarded the oral employment agreement as binding. Generally, performance by a party after agreement has been reached but before a writing has been prepared is regarded as some evidence that the writing was only a memorial of a binding agreement. However, where the evidence clearly shows that the party performing did not consider the agreement to be binding, the fact that he began performance does not compel a contrary conclusion.

Moreover, even assuming *arguendo* that a binding agreement existed, Speer has not demonstrated that it was breached. The district court determined that the termination of two of Speer's trusted associates by Briggs and the executive committee so undermined Speer's ability to perform his duties that it amounted to a constructive discharge. We do not find this theory persuasive. In spite of protracted negotiations, the continued employment of members of Speer's "team" was never suggested as a term of any proposed agreement. In the absence of such an understanding, the termination of the two men over Speer's objections cannot be regarded as an invasion of Speer's authority sufficient to amount to a constructive discharge. . . .

We affirm [the denial of damages] for breach of an alleged stock option agreement . . . [and] reverse judgment for Speer on the alleged employment agreement. . . .

NOTES

1. *Significance of an Unsigned Writing.* Understand the difference between drafting a written contract and memorializing an oral one. When parties draft a written document, they generally expect their execution of that document (i.e., their

signatures on the page) to consummate the deal. Their discussions, including oral commitments, that led up to that point are viewed as part of the negotiation process. It is this assumption that undergirds core contracts principles, such as the parol evidence rule, which (you may be disappointed to learn) we will be revisiting shortly.

However, *Speer* suggests that it is possible in some instances that parties will intend to reach an agreement orally and use a subsequent writing merely to capture after the fact what they have already committed to. In these situations, there is the intent to be bound requisite to contract enforcement from the moment of the oral agreement. Which of these two scenarios describes what happened in *Speer*? How does the court know?

2. *Intent of the Parties.* Consider the role of party intent in your response to the preceding note. Based in part on the testimony set out in footnote 3, the court concludes that Speer and Tropicana "contemplated that any agreement concerning Speer's employment would become effective only when reduced to writing and signed by the parties." Does it necessarily follow that there was no binding contract? Even if, at that point in time, no contract existed, Speer started working and continued in his position for roughly a year, so he had to be subject to some employment agreement. Might the parties have impliedly agreed to those terms by their conduct? What does the court think the terms of the parties' oral or implied contract were if not those agreed to in the writing? *Cf. Hendricks v. Smartvideo Techs. Inc.*, 511 F. Supp. 2d 1219, 1228 (M.D. Fla. 2007) (finding question of fact as to whether parties entered into contract notwithstanding plaintiff's failure to sign written agreement where "Hendricks reported for work and remained employed for several months [and] Smartvideo also partially performed, paying Hendricks a salary pursuant to the alleged agreement").

3. *The Stock Option Agreement.* It appears that the only written term on which the parties could not agree was the stock option provision. Would it have been a better litigation strategy for Speer to concede he had no stock rights and seek to enforce only the other terms of employment? The court suggests that Speer withheld his signature from the final written document in order to pressure Tropicana into conceding to his stock demands. If so, the court arguably should not allow Speer to have his cake and eat it too — that is, to have the benefit of terms he deliberately chose to reject in order to secure a bargaining advantage. If that is what happened, perhaps Speer got his just deserts. On the other hand, is this view of the facts consistent with Speer accepting employment absent an executed agreement? What bargaining advantage could he gain at that point by refusing the written document? The opinion does not indicate how Speer was compensated during his one year of employment. Suppose, however, that he was being paid the exact salary that the parties had agreed to in the unsigned contract. How would this affect your understanding of what happened?

4. *Restitution.* Another way to conceptualize this arrangement is as a failed contract — the parties never agreed to final terms of employment but began performance nonetheless. If so, should Speer be entitled to the reasonable value of his services under a restitution theory? *See generally* RESTATEMENT (SECOND) OF CONTRACTS § 370 (1981). The employer would be credited for whatever wages it paid Speer, but that does not necessarily compensate him for the reasonable value of his services. Since the parties contemplated additional compensation in the form of stock options, restitution seems to offer an alternative approach to compensating Speer.

5. *Constructive Discharge.* Understand the significance of the penultimate paragraph in the opinion. Speer does not contend that Tropicana formally terminated him, but rather that it "constructively discharged" him by breaching its contractual obligations. The concept of constructive discharge is important in many areas of employment law. Although employees often resign voluntarily, *but see O'Neil v. Clinically Home, LLC,* 2014 Tenn. App. LEXIS 416 (Tenn. Ct. App. July 16, 2014) (ultimatum threatening resignation did not constitute actual resignation), employees sometimes claim that their quitting was in some sense coerced, thus constituting a constructive discharge. Absent such a doctrine, employers would be able to avoid liability for unlawful termination by creating working conditions so intolerable as to force the employee to resign. In the context of status discrimination, constructive discharge analysis can be used, for example, to hold employers liable for damages that result when an employee reasonably quits in response to workplace harassment based on a protected characteristic such as race or gender. *See* Chapter 9. The challenge with any allegation of constructive discharge is figuring out whether the employer's conduct was sufficiently severe to justify the employee's resignation. Otherwise, the law deems the employee's departure voluntary. Indeed, such a departure can be a breach of contract by the employee if she is bound by the contract to a longer term.

Under discrimination law, adverse employment actions amounting to a constructive discharge include "a humiliating demotion, extreme cut in pay, or transfer to a position [involving] unbearable working conditions." *Pa. State Police v. Suders,* 542 U.S. 129, 134 (2004). Claims of constructive discharge in cases involving a contract for job security have had mixed success. *Compare Guiliano v. Cleo, Inc.,* 995 S.W.2d 88 (Tenn. 1999) (finding constructive discharge where vice president of marketing was stripped of responsibilities, reassigned to his home, and told to await future assignments, which never came), *with Rubin v. Household Comm. Fin. Servs., Inc.,* 746 N.E.2d 1018, 1028 (Mass. App. Ct. 2001) (no constructive discharge of plaintiff-CEO where temporary management team brought in to turn around company circumvented plaintiff on some financial issues but plaintiff retained title and position and management team continued to rely on plaintiff's expertise on customers and production). Often the determination turns on whether the employer's behavior was itself in breach of the parties' employment agreement. In what way does Speer claim Tropicana breached its contract? How critical is the fact that there were no specific terms in the proposed written agreement dealing with Speer's staff?

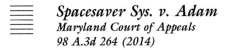

Tropicana, of course, was a case in which no document was finally executed. But legal problems can arise even when the parties have signed what purports to be an employment agreement. The next case dramatically illustrates the point while at the same time introducing us to a variety of employment contracts.

Spacesaver Sys. v. Adam
Maryland Court of Appeals
98 A.3d 264 (2014)

ADKINS, J.

Oil and water naturally resist each other. No matter how much one tries, the two cannot be mixed together successfully. As this case demonstrates, the same is often true of family and business. Following a dispute between sibling business partners, we are asked to re-examine the contours of the firmly established doctrine of at-will employment. We do so in order to determine if a written contract containing a for-cause provision, but no definite term of employment, exists as an at-will contract, a lifetime contract, or something else.

Facts and Legal Proceedings

Petitioner, Spacesaver Systems, Inc. ("SSI"), was incorporated in the District of Columbia in 1973 by Jack and Alyce Schmidt. SSI sells and installs mobile storage equipment, including tracked shelving systems, to businesses and governmental organizations with large storage needs. In the 1990's, the Schmidts began transferring ownership of the business to their three children: Carla Adam ("Respondent"), Amy Hamilton ("Hamilton"), and David Craig ("Craig"). As the Schmidts eased out of the business and moved to Florida, the three siblings assumed greater responsibility in the company.

In 2006, Adam and Hamilton became concerned that Craig was stealing from SSI. Hamilton, Respondent, Albert Ellentuck (SSI's corporate attorney), and Erik Kloster (SSI's corporate accountant) met to discuss Craig's affiliation with SSI. As a result of this meeting, Ellentuck revised the siblings' employment agreements, which subsequently contained a provision for termination for cause. This provision appeared as follows:

> 4.2 Termination by the Company For Cause. The Company may, at any time and without notice, terminate the Employee for "cause." Termination by the Company of the Employee for "cause" shall include but not be limited to termination based on any of the following grounds: (a) insubordination or refusal to perform duties of employee's position as directed by the President of Company and affirmed by a majority vote of the Directors; (b) fraud, misappropriation, embezzlement or acts of similar dishonesty; (c) conviction of a felony involving moral turpitude; (d) illegal use of drugs or excessive use of alcohol in the workplace; (e) intentional and willful misconduct that may subject the Company to criminal or civil liability; (f) breach of the Employee's duty of loyalty, including the diversion or usurpation of corporate opportunities properly belonging to the Company; (g) willful disregard of Company policies and procedures; (h) material breach of any of the terms herein; and (i) material nonperformance or negligence in Employee's performance of her duties.

Adam's Executive Employment Agreement (the "Employment Agreement") references a "term of this Employment Agreement," but the parties failed to define this term.

Along with the revised employment agreements, Ellentuck drafted a Stock Purchase Agreement so that if an employee were terminated from SSI, she could be compelled to sell her stock to the other shareholders. Articles 3 and 5 of the Stock Purchase Agreement provide that SSI will redeem the stock in the event of disability or death of a shareholder. Article 4 provides that shareholders can be forced to sell their shares if they engage in "Prohibited Acts." These "Prohibited Acts" generally mirror the for-cause provisions listed in the Employment Agreement.

On October 19, 2006, Adam, Craig, and Hamilton each signed the individual executive employment agreements and stock purchase agreements drafted by Ellentuck. Shortly after the employment agreements were executed, Craig resigned as President and Director of SSI. Pursuant to Adam's Stock Purchase Agreement, Craig's stock was sold equally to Adam and Hamilton, who consequently each held a 50% interest in SSI.

Despite Craig's departure, sibling harmony did not last long, as Hamilton and Adam began to have disputes about their respective job responsibilities and compensation. According to Hamilton, Adam's sales performance was "not very good." Consequently, Adam was removed from the sales force.

On May 28, 2009, Hamilton wrote Adam expressing her intent to acquire Adam's SSI stock, and concluding that Adam's employment was terminated.

The conflict reached its apex when, on January 28, 2010, SSI sent Adam a letter terminating her employment. In response, Adam filed a Complaint on April 9, 2010 against SSI and Hamilton in the Circuit Court for Montgomery County. On July 30, 2010, Adam filed an Amended Complaint, which alleged that she was terminated without cause in violation of her Employment Agreement.

Adam filed a Motion for Partial Summary Judgment, contending that the Employment Agreement established that she could only be terminated for cause. SSI filed an Opposition to Motion for Partial Summary Judgment and Cross-Motion for Summary Judgment, denying that the Employment Agreement guaranteed Adam lifetime employment and asserting that even if the Employment Agreement were so construed, Adam had failed to give "additional consideration" for a lifetime contract.

Following a hearing, the motions court denied both motions for summary judgment on August 19, 2011. The hearing judge found the contract ambiguous, ruling that "extraneous evidence of what the parties intended may be admitted to assist the court in determining the agreement of the parties." After three days of testimony, the trial court ultimately concluded that the Employment Agreement transformed what had previously been an "at-will relationship" to a "lifetime contract," such that Adam could only be terminated for cause, death, or disability. Crucial to the trial court's analysis was that the for-cause provision would be rendered superfluous if the Employment Agreement were construed as at-will. The trial judge rhetorically asked, "why in the world would you have to worry about [cause] if you had an at-will contract?" The trial judge found a breach of the Employment Agreement, and awarded Adam $255,868.20, representing lost salary and commission.

SSI appealed to the Court of Special Appeals [which affirmed in part and reversed in part, and this court granted certiorari] to answer the following questions:

1. Is there any difference between lifetime and "continuous for-cause" contracts?
2. Did the Court of Special Appeals err in applying dicta from *Towson University v. Conte*, 862 A.2d 941 (2004), which suggests that a "just cause" provision transforms at-will employment into lifetime employment terminable only for cause?
3. Does the presence of a for-cause provision, which does not state employment is terminable only for cause, transform at-will employment to lifetime employment terminable only for cause?

As to the second question, we affirm the judgment of the Court of Special Appeals. The first and third questions we shall answer in the course of explaining why this written employment contract is distinct from the alleged "lifetime employment contracts" that we have historically held to be unenforceable.

Standard of Review

"The interpretation of a contract, including the determination of whether a contract is ambiguous, is a question of law, subject to *de novo* review." *Conte.* Maryland law dictates the objective interpretation of contracts, which provides for the following:

> [A court is to] determine from the language of the agreement itself what a reasonable person in the position of the parties would have meant at the time it was effectuated.

In addition, when the language of the contract is plain and unambiguous there is no room for construction, and a court must presume that the parties meant what they expressed. In these circumstances, the true test of what is meant is not what the parties to the contract intended it to mean, but what a reasonable person in the position of the parties would have thought it meant. Consequently, the clear and unambiguous language of an agreement will not give away [sic] to what the parties thought that the agreement meant or intended it to mean. In determining whether a contract is ambiguous, a court may consider "the character of the contract, its purpose, and the facts and circumstances of the parties at the time of execution[.]"

Discussion

Petitioner attacks the opinion of the Court of Special Appeals on several grounds. First, Petitioner maintains that when the Employment Agreement is read in conjunction with SSI's Employee Handbook, it is clear that the contract could be terminated with or without cause. SSI highlights that the Employment Agreement's for-cause provision says that SSI "may" terminate for cause. The provision did not say that Adam can "only" be terminated for cause. Petitioner contends that if the for-cause provision were meant to carry so much weight, it would have authorized termination "only" for cause, which the Employment Agreement did not do.

Petitioner's most significant argument concerns the distinction that the intermediate appellate court drew between "continuous for-cause" and lifetime contracts. In Petitioner's view, there is no distinction between the two. SSI contends that both are terminable by the employer only for cause and terminable by the employee without cause. SSI alleges that the Court of Special Appeals described Adam's employment with the novel moniker of "continuous for-cause" to escape the requirements to establish a lifetime employment contract.

Expanding on this theme, Petitioner leans on the major presumption under Maryland law that an employment relationship is presumptively at-will unless the parties clearly and expressly set forth their agreement that the contract is to last for a specific period of time. In SSI's view, the lower court failed to apply the heightened standard applicable to lifetime contracts, making no finding that SSI's intent to provide lifetime employment was specific, definite, and unequivocal. Moreover, Petitioner argues that Adam failed to provide the "special consideration" required to support such a contract. In sum, Petitioner contends that, instead of addressing the various issues surrounding lifetime employment contracts, the Court of Specials Appeals simply created an "evil twin" and said "it is a for-cause contract that is of continuous duration, but it is not a lifetime contract."

Finally, and in a similar vein, Petitioner argues that the Court of Special Appeals ignored a strong precept of Maryland law that the at-will doctrine invariably applies when an employment contract is of an indefinite duration. Specifically, SSI posits that the intermediate appellate court has wrongly elevated dicta to law by holding that under *Conte*, the inclusion of a for-cause provision transforms an at-will contract to a for-cause contract. In SSI's view, this directly contravenes our previous holding in *Suburban Hospital, Inc. v. Dwiggins*, 596 A.2d 1069 (Md. 1991), that an employment contract of indefinite duration is employment at-will, even if it states some bases giving the employer cause for termination. In this respect, SSI contends that this holding erodes the doctrine of lifetime employment.

In reply, Respondent urges us to affirm the Court of Special Appeals. Rather than responding directly to each of Petitioner's arguments, Respondent lays out a number of propositions that, in her view, compel the affirmance of the Court of Special Appeals. First, Respondent alleges that the Employment Agreement is not an unambiguous at-will contract. She underscores that two lower courts have rejected the contract as unambiguously at-will based on the rationale that a for-cause provision is inconsistent with an at-will contract. In her view, the very terms of the Employment Agreement establish that it is not an at-will agreement. Similarly, Respondent rejects any applicability of the SSI Employee Handbook, observing that the Employment Agreement itself explicitly states that it will trump the provisions of the Handbook.

Respondent similarly rejects the relevance of "special consideration." Respondent states that no Maryland authority supports the position that "special consideration" is necessary to establish a contract such as this one. Adam avers that, although some jurisdictions require that lifetime contracts be supported by "special consideration," we are dealing with a "continuous for-cause" contract, not a lifetime contract.

Finally, moving to a policy perspective, Adam maintains that affirming the judgment below will not have adverse repercussions for employers generally. She argues that any decision on this case will be limited to the facts of this case — one involving a closely held corporation and an employment agreement for high-level corporate officers. Moreover, Respondent contends that employers can easily avoid the burdens of for-cause employment by drafting employment contracts explicitly to say "at-will" when they are meant to be at will.

Presumption of At-Will Employment

We begin by laying out the fundamentals of Maryland employment law. Our starting place is one of our most venerated common law precepts, the employment at-will doctrine. . . . [The court traced the at-will rule in Maryland precedents, stressing that it "reflects the courts' concern with promoting freedom of contract and fundamental fairness." It quoted Samuel Williston & Richard A. Lord, A Treatise on the Law of Contracts, § 54:39 (4th ed. 2001):]

> [T]he courts have shown a marked reluctance to enforce contracts for life employment. In large part, this stems from the realization that such contracts frequently are, in practical effect, unilateral undertakings by the employer to provide a job for so long as the employee wishes to continue in it but impose no corresponding obligation upon the employee. When this is the case, the burden of performance is unequal, as the employer appears to be bound to the terms of the contract, while the employee is free to terminate it at will. Accordingly, it has been said:
>
> > An employee is never presumed to engage his services permanently, thereby cutting himself off from all chances of improving his condition; indeed, in this land of opportunity it would be against public policy and the spirit of our institutions that any man should thus handicap himself; and the law will presume . . . that he did not so intend. And if the contract of employment be not binding on the employee for the whole term of such employment, then it cannot be binding upon the employer; there would be lack of "mutuality"

Yet we observe that presumptions can only act as an aid to interpreting a contract, not as a substantive limit on parties' ability to contract. . . .

Indeed the presumption of at-will employment can be defeated through the inclusion of a just-cause requirement, or by specifying a duration of employment:

> While the language of the contract itself may express a just cause requirement, a contractual delineation of the length of the employment period will also create a just cause employment relationship because by specifying the length or term of employment, the employer usually is considered to have surrendered its ability to terminate the employee at its discretion.

Conte.

One type of for-cause employment is lifetime employment. We discussed lifetime employment at length in *Chesapeake & Potomac Telephone Co. of Baltimore City v. Murray,* 84 A.2d 870 (1951). "[A] contract for permanent or life employment is valid and continues to operate as long as the employer remains in the business and has work for the employee and the employee is able and willing to do his work satisfactorily and does not give good cause for his discharge." We declared, however, that those claiming a lifetime employment contract faced an uphill climb.

First, the law protects stockholders' ability to alter a corporation's management by electing boards of directors. Recognizing that the directors' authority would be hollow if corporate officers were able to grant "persons of their selection employment for life," we stated that one hurdle to lifetime contacts is "proof that there was definite authority, by by-law, action by the board of directors, or otherwise, to make such a contract."

Second, a lifetime employment contract must be supported by consideration beyond that incident to accepting the position. *See id; see also Page v. Carolina Coach Co.,* 667 F.2d 1156, 1158 (4th Cir. 1982) (holding that relinquishing a job and benefits to assume a new position was not sufficient consideration for lifetime employment).

Third, a lifetime employment contract must clearly stipulate the "terms as to work and salary" in order to be enforceable. *Murray, see also Balt. & Ohio R. Co. v. King,* 176 A. 626, 628 (Md. 1935) (holding that lifetime contracts "at least should be specific and definite, with little or no room for misunderstanding, even if they are not required to be in writing"); *Yost v. Early,* 589 A.2d 1291, 1300-01 (Md. App. 1991) (reaffirming that an alleged oral lifetime employment contract was only employment at-will because there was no showing that it clearly expressed the specific terms of the agreement, including duties, wages, and performance guidelines).

Before evaluating the Employment Agreement, we observe that our primary inquiry concerns whether the contract created at-will or for-cause employment. For our purposes here, employment contracts can be broken into three categories, those with: (i) specific temporal duration, terminable before the expiration only for cause; (ii) no specified temporal duration, but containing a clear for-cause termination provision; and (iii) no temporal duration, and no for-cause termination provision, which are terminable at will. Placing the Employment Agreement in one of these three categories will determine the resolution of this controversy, as Adam has no cause of action sounding in breach of her employment contract if she fits in the third category, at-will employment.

Nature of the Employment Agreement

"Our analysis begins, as it should, with the language of the employment contract at issue." *Conte.* Under the objective interpretation of contracts, we focus upon whether a reasonable person, in the parties' position, would have thought that the contract provided any measure of job security. "Under the objective view, a written contract is ambiguous if, when read by a reasonably prudent person, it is susceptible of more than one meaning." *Calomiris* [*v. Woods*, 727 A.2d 358, 363 (Md. 1999)] (citation omitted). Moreover, this Court has been clear in observing that:

> [a] recognized rule of construction in ascertaining the true meaning of a contract is that the contract must be construed in its entirety and, if reasonably possible, effect must be given to each clause so that a court will not find an interpretation which casts out or disregards a meaningful part of the language of the writing unless no other course can be sensibly and reasonably followed.

Cochran v. Norkunas, 919 A.2d 700, 710 (Md. 2007).

Although the Employment Agreement is silent as to its duration, which can signify at-will employment, it also contains a for-cause provision, which negates an at-will employment contract. *Conte* is instructive on this point. After evaluating Dr. Conte's employment contract, which had a for-cause provision similar to Adam's and a definite durational term, we held that the contract "makes clear that Dr. Conte was not an 'at-will' employee." *Conte.* We also held that the university could not avail itself of the protections afforded employers who terminate at-will employees. *Id.*

Of special import here, the *Conte* Court also opined that either a for-cause provision or "a contractual delineation of the length of the employment period" will *independently* establish that an employee was not at-will. *Id.* Petitioner characterizes this pronouncement as dicta that is at odds with *Dwiggins.* We agree that it was dicta, but feel secure in embracing it here. Indeed, *Conte* finds support from a number of other jurisdictions that have adopted a similar rule. *See Bell v. Ivory*, 966 F. Supp. 23, 29 (D.D.C. 1997) ("The presumption of 'at will' employment can be overcome by the creation of a contract of employment for a fixed term *or an indefinite contract that allows termination only for cause.*") (emphasis added); *Gladden v. Ark. Children's Hosp.*, 728 S.W.2d 501, 505 (Ark. 1987) ("[W]e reject as outmoded and untenable [the view] that the at will rule applies even where the employment agreement contains a provision that the employee will not be discharged except for cause, unless it is for a definite term."); *Dillman v. N.H. College*, 838 A.2d 1274, 1276 (N.H. 2003) ("Where, however, an employment agreement specifies a definite term, it is generally implied that the employee can be discharged only for cause.").

We disagree with Petitioner's claim that the rule from *Conte* that we embrace here is in any way contradicted by *Dwiggins.* In *Dwiggins*, an employee was suspended for violating rules set by his employer. He was reinstated but placed on probation and required to sign a document with very specific performance conditions. After violating the terms of this probation, he was terminated, but then brought suit claiming that he was no longer an at-will employee. The Court held that the reinstatement agreement that the parties signed to resolve the employee's disciplinary action and govern his probationary status would not convert an at-will employment agreement into a for-cause agreement. Thus, *Dwiggins* involved performance conditions with which an employee must comply to maintain satisfactory probationary status under a *reinstatement agreement*. This is fundamentally distinct from an employee who, free from probationary status, contracts the terms under which her employer will have cause to terminate her employment in an *employment agreement*. Thus, we find no reason to hesitate in relying on the dictum in *Conte* to support our conclusion that the for-cause termination clause in the Employment Agreement removed it from the category of at-will employment.

This conclusion is consonant with the position of the parties at the time that the contract was executed. We emphasize that each of the three siblings owned one-third of SSI and also served as a high-level executive. Moreover, they each signed a Stock Purchase Agreement allowing the corporation to acquire their shares at a reduced value if their employment were terminated. A reasonable person in that position could only have thought that the language of the for-cause provision would be operative and provide for the job security stated by its terms. Thus, the only legitimate interpretation of the plain language of the Employment Agreement is that the parties reasonably expected and mutually assented to some degree of job security. This is in contrast to other situations in which the employee has no reasonable expectation of job security.

Yet the conclusion that Adam's Employment Agreement was for-cause, on its own, would leave one key issue unaddressed. As described above, Adam's Employment Agreement did not provide a specific term of employment. Significantly, Section 2.1 of the Employment Agreement referenced an "Exhibit A" that would set forth Adam's salary "for years beyond the first year" of employment, but this exhibit was never created. In other words, SSI had the option of setting a definite term for Adam's employment but chose not to. Thus, the Court is presented with a for-cause contract with an indefinite durational term. Petitioner argues that such a contract must be characterized as providing for lifetime employment and, consequently, tested against the three requirements for a lifetime contract. We move to this contention now.

"Continuous For-Cause" v. Lifetime Contracts . . .

The Court of Special Appeals then described these contracts as "essentially continuous for-cause contracts that remain in effect until the employee is removed for cause, or until the employee is no longer 'competent to discharge the duties of the office or efficient in the performance of them.'" *Spacesaver*. In this sense, the intermediate appellate court held "continuous for-cause" contracts to be distinct from at-will, satisfaction,[10] and lifetime employment contracts. . . .

As both a legal and terminological matter, "continuous for-cause" better describes the nature of Adam's Employment Agreement than the term, "lifetime

---

10. A "satisfaction contract" is one "in which the employer, notwithstanding the inclusion of a durational term of employment, expressly reserves the right to terminate if it deems the employee's performance unsatisfactory." *Conte*. As we explained in *Ferris v. Polansky*:

> In a contract where the employer agrees to employ another as long as the services are satisfactory, the employer has the right to terminate the contract and discharge the employee, whenever he, the employer, acting in good faith is actually dissatisfied with the employee's work. This applies, even though the parties to the employment contract have stipulated that the contract shall be operative during a definite term, if it provides that the services are to be performed to the satisfaction of the employer.

59 A.2d 749, 752 (Md. 1948). We agree with the Court of Special Appeals' observation that a satisfaction contract without a durational term of employment is distinct from a lifetime employment contract terminable for cause. In our view, the intermediate appellate court properly stated that under Maryland law, a trial court will evaluate an employer's objective motivation for termination of a lifetime contract, whereas under a satisfaction contract, the jury must focus on the employer's subjective motivation for termination.

contract." This Court has previously expressed its assumption that even a so-called "lifetime contract" only "continues to operate as long as the employer remains in the business and has work for the employee and the employee is able and willing to do his work satisfactorily and does not give good cause for his discharge." *Murray.* The same is true of Adam's contract. Surely, Adam's continued employment depended on, in addition to her compliance with the for-cause provisions listed in the Employment Agreement, the continued success of SSI's current business and its resulting need for Adam's services.[11] We see that, to some extent, the so-called "lifetime contract" and "continuous for-cause" contract are similar, and do overlap.

Yet in significant respects, Adam's Employment Agreement is distinct from the alleged "lifetime employment" that was generally rejected by this Court.[12] The cases in which this Court has wrestled with alleged lifetime employment have arisen from lower-level employees' allegations that someone higher up in a company had given an oral representation that they would have a job "for life." *See, e.g., Pullman Co. v. Ray*, 94 A.2d 266, 267 (Md. 1953) (alleged oral promise of lifetime employment in exchange for forbearance from suit); *Murray* (alleged oral promise of lifetime employment in exchange for refraining from selling to previous customers for commissions). These cases support the proposition that alleged oral contracts for continued employment stand on weaker ground than written contracts. Indeed, although a Maryland appellate case has expressly contemplated the potential that oral representations could support a "lifetime contract," we have found no Maryland cases actually upholding such alleged oral contracts. . . .

Our intermediate appellate court embraced the same wisdom when it observed that

> [a] promise of permanent or lifetime employment may be nothing more than a casual aside. Or, it may be purely aspirational. The employer may be expressing his hope that a valued employee will stay with him forever. However, he may not have intended to create a binding agreement.

Spacesaver (alteration in original) (quoting *Greene v. Oliver Realty, Inc.*, 526 A.2d 1192, 1202 (Pa. Super. Ct. 1987)). Based on the above considerations, we have held allegations of lifetime employment subject to a requirement of definiteness.

But unlike those cases involving alleged lifetime agreements, in which the lack of definiteness and "verifiability" inherent in oral representations justified a court's skepticism, Adam's Employment Agreement contained an express for-cause provision *in writing*. This provision, in concert with SSI's failure to specify a term of employment on "Exhibit A," cannot but be read to imply a continued period of employment. The Agreement's operative terms are expressed — or in the case of the employment's durational term, omitted — definitively. Therefore, the concerns over its accuracy, probability, and provenance are not present. The contract is clear, as is the fact that the

---

11. Surely SSI could change the nature of its business in a way that rendered Adam's services superfluous, and therefore her employment would end. This would have to be done in good faith, for a legitimate business reason, and not with the motivating intent to rid the company of her services.

12. Testimony at the trial court indicated that at least two of the siblings envisioned a lifetime tenure when they signed the Employment Agreement. Under the objective interpretation of contracts, the court will only look at extrinsic evidence if the contract is found to be ambiguous, a finding that, as we discuss *infra*, we disclaim here. *See Sy-Lene of Wash., Inc. v. Starwood Urban Retail II, LLC*, 829 A.2d 540, 544 (Md. 2003).

parties assented to it. In this context, we refrain from imposing the additional require-ment of special consideration, which evolved from a line of lifetime employment cases, to contracts of a "continuous for-cause" nature.[15]

In drawing a distinction between lifetime and "continuous for-cause" contracts, we follow a path laid by other courts. . . . In so holding, we signal no retreat from our recognition and veneration of the employment at-will doctrine. This judgment in no way erodes that doctrine, as the presumption for at-will employment persists and is only defeated when the parties explicitly negotiate and provide for a definite term of employment or a clear for-cause provision. We emphasize that in this case, SSI's cor-porate attorney could easily have kept Adam's employment at-will by inserting an at-will provision in the Employment Agreement, or making sure that no for-cause provision made its way into the contract.

We also reject any contention that the Employee Handbook should change our decision. The Employment Agreement states that SSI's Employee Handbook governs "to the extent not described in this Employment Agreement[.]" It further states that "[i]n the event of a conflict between this Employment Agreement and the employees' handbook or existing practices, the terms of this agreement shall govern." We reject any argument that the two documents, read together, make clear that the contract could be terminated *either* with or without cause.[16] It would defy the plain language of the Employment Agreement to hold otherwise.

The same can be said for Petitioner's argument that if the for-cause provision were meant to carry so much weight, the Employment Agreement would have authorized termination "only" for cause. The parties do not cite, and the Court has not found, any case holding that the inclusion of "may" in a for-cause provision defeats the purpose of that provision. This argument logically fails, and the trial court was right to reject it.

Conclusion

For the reasons stated above, we agree with the Court of Special Appeals that the Employment Agreement should not be interpreted as at-will employment. We distin-guish this Employment Agreement from those alleged oral lifetime employment con-tracts that were consistently rejected by Maryland courts. It was a formal written employment contract executed by each of the three shareholders and did not lack

---

15. We recognize that the concerns over corporate authority to execute a "continuous for-cause" contract and shareholders' ability to change the management of the corporation could potentially arise in another case. That concern is not present here because the Employment Agreement was identical to the ones signed by the other two shareholders, and all shareholders and directors, including the corporate counsel who was a non-shareholder director, consented to the terms thereof.

16. Even if for-cause language in an employee handbook could support a "continuous for-cause" employment agreement, we would carefully examine the handbook to see if other language therein was inconsistent with such conclusion. For example, if the handbook also stated that employment was at-will or expressly provided that the handbook was not a contract, we would consider that language as negating any claim that the handbook created "continuous for-cause" or lifetime employment. *See Dell v. Montgomery Ward and Co.*, 811 F.2d 970, 972-73 (1987) (holding that at-will language in employee handbook stating that "[e]mployment . . . is for no definite period and may . . . be terminated at any time by the company or by an employee, *with or without cause, and without any previous notice*" prevailed over due process procedures provided in the same handbook) (emphasis in original); *Castiglione v. Johns Hopkins Hosp.*, 517 A.2d 786, 787 (Md. 1986) (holding that at-will language in employee handbook stating "this handbook does not constitute an express or implied contract" prevailed over annual performance appraisals provided in the same handbook).

for clarity in terms. We consider the best moniker for this type of contract to be "continuous for-cause" employment. We affirm the judgment of the Court of Special Appeals.

NOTES

1. *At-Will and Satisfaction Contracts.* The *Spacesaver* court identifies and discusses a bewildering number of potential employment contracts. Least protective of employees is the at-will arrangement, which we've met before. But, at the risk of repetition, note that these are not just one kind of employment contract: They are *the* presumptive agreement unless sufficiently clear language creates something stronger.

Somewhat more employee protective are "satisfaction" agreements. Courts vary in their interpretation of such agreements, but they are generally understood to provide less job security than a just-cause agreement. *See, e.g., Silvestri v. Optus Software, Inc.*, 814 A.2d 602, 607-08 (N.J. 2003) (subjective assessment of employer satisfaction applies where contract preserved right to terminate). According to footnote 10, in Maryland at least, an agreement providing for job security as long as the employer is "satisfied" with the employee's performance allows for review of "the employer's *subjective* motivation" for termination" rather than the objective basis. However, unlike the *Spacesaver* court's focus on subjective motivation, some contracts speak of "reasonable satisfaction." *See, e.g., McKnight v. Simpson's Beauty Supply, Inc.*, 358 S.E.2d 107 (N.C. Ct. App. 1987) (contract requiring plaintiff to perform "to the reasonable satisfaction of employer" did not mean plaintiff was subject to dismissal for failing to satisfy unreasonable or capricious demands, but only for not carrying out his duties in a reasonably diligent and effective manner).

2. *Durational or Term Contracts.* From the employee's perspective, a satisfaction contract is better than at-will, but maybe not by much. If you represented an employee, what's the next stage of protection? That's not so clear. You could try to negotiate what *Spacesaver* calls a durational contract, sometimes called a contract for a term. That provides great protection but only for the specified duration since, as the court suggests, it is generally understood that an employee with a fixed-term contract can only be terminated for "just cause." *See, e.g., Sarvis v. Vermont State Colleges,* 772 A.2d 494, 497 (Vt. 2001). This is consistent with the contract principle of material breach: If an individual does not perform at all or performs so poorly that he is in material breach of his or her duties as an employee, then the employer is excused from performing its end of the bargain and may terminate the agreement. In the next section, we will take up the question what constitutes "just cause" or performance sufficient to constitute material breach. For now, it is important to know that even a fixed-term contract is not an absolute guarantee of employment, but the protection it provides during the term is fairly robust.

3. *How Long a Duration?* Employees have strong protection during the term of a durational contract, but the length of the term is obviously critical. So a ten-year contract is very protective; a ten-week one not so much. This reality gives rise to an oddity to the uninitiated: contracts that describe themselves as, say, five-year employment contracts but which provide either party the right to terminate on, say, a month's notice. In any meaningful sense, these are one-month durational contracts. *See Cave*

Hill Corporation v. Hiers, 570 S.E.2d 790 (Va. 2002). That is, contracts with notice provisions are generally treated as definite-term agreements for the duration of the notice period as of the date notice is given. The remedy for an employer's failure to give notice is damages equal to the compensation that would have been paid during the notice period. *See, e.g., Shivers v. John H. Harland Co.,* 423 S.E.2d 105, 107 (S.C. 1992).

4. *Rate-of-Pay Recitals.* A recurring question is whether the inclusion of a compensation period, such as an annual salary term, in an offer letter or other document indicates an intention that employment will endure for at least the length of the pay period. According to the traditional British rule, a hiring at a stated price per week, month, or year is presumed to be a hiring for the named time period. Under the modern American rule, however, a stated term of compensation does not in itself defeat the presumption that employment is at will. *See, e.g., Thomas v. Ballou-Latimer Drug Co.,* 442 P.2d 747, 751 (Idaho 1968) (adopting "the American rule . . . that a [rate of pay] term, standing by itself, fixes the rate of compensation and not the period of employment"). *But see* GA. CODE ANN. § 34-7-1 (2006) ("If a contract of employment provides that wages are payable at a stipulated period, the presumption shall arise that the hiring is for such period."). Of course, that presumption, like the at-will presumption itself, can always be rebutted. *See, e.g., Carriker v. Am. Postal Workers Union,* No. 13900, 1993 WL 385807 (Ohio Ct. App. Sept. 30, 1993) (finding that, while contract containing annual pay rate is presumed to be at will, such a term coupled with a provision providing for periodic pay increases over three years created sufficient ambiguity as to duration of contract to justify admission of additional evidence regarding parties' intent).

5. *Just Cause and Lifetime Contracts.* Even more protective than durational contracts are contracts guaranteeing a position unless there is just cause to discharge (and the contract might define just cause very narrowly to maximize protection). Look at the language in Spacesaver's Employment Agreement. The qualifying conduct is pretty extreme. Does that mean that an employee has a right to lifetime employment (absent just cause)? *Spacesaver* says no: Continuous for-cause contracts are not contracts for lifetime employment, terminable for cause." But that's not because an employer's business might not change "in a way that rendered Adam's services superfluous." *See* footnote 11. That might happen, and be a legitimate reason for termination — but that would be true under either a lifetime contract or a "continuous for-cause" contract. And while Ms. Adam has a continuous for-cause agreement, she doesn't have a lifetime contract. Why isn't that the same thing? The answer for the court seems to lie in the unreliability of most alleged agreements for lifetime employment. The *Spacesaver* court worries about the informality of the usual claim and thus requires definiteness and, maybe, addition consideration. Recall that we ran into the additional consideration question before. *See* Chapter 2 at page 72.

By the way, continuous for-cause" contracts, like the one found in *Spacesaver,* are not as uncommon as you might think. Academic tenure in private educational institutions can be viewed as exactly that. Such arrangements, though sometimes described as such, are not promises of lifetime employment, because the teacher can typically be discharged not only for performance problems but also for programmatic reasons. Tenure in public schools and public colleges and universities is more often a creature of statute but tends to adopt the same type of approach.

6. *The Parol Evidence Rule.* There was a trial in *Spacesaver* because the contract was ambiguous as to whether it simply set out the terms and conditions of at-will

employment or created a continuous for-cause relationship. That seems questionable. As the trial judge said, "Why in the world would you have to worry about [cause] if you had an at-will contract?" But the finding of ambiguity created the necessity for a trial to determine the meaning of the agreement: If the contract is susceptible of only one meaning, the court should so interpret it. When a contract is ambiguous, however, a court can look to "extrinsic evidence" to decide the correct interpretation. That's exactly what happened here, with extensive testimony as to what the parties thought the contract meant. But consideration of such evidence for interpretive purposes is permissible *only* when the contract is ambiguous. *See also Cruz v. Visual Perceptions, LLC*, 84 A.3d 828, 835 (Conn. 2014) (since letter agreement "reasonably may be interpreted as evincing either an intent to create a definite term of employment or an intent to set the terms and conditions of an at-will employment contract," parol evidence should be admitted at trial to resolve the ambiguity). *Cf. Dore v. Arnold Worldwide*, 139 P.3d 56, 58 (Cal. 2006) (provision that "your employment with Arnold Communications, Inc. is at will. This simply means that Arnold Communications has the right to terminate your employment at any time . . ." was not ambiguous, despite separate clause speaking of a 90-day assessment period).

In another case, *Cave Hill Corporation v. Hiers*, 570 S.E.2d 790 (Va. 2002), the plaintiff claimed that a one-page contract, stating "EFFECTIVE DATES: August 14, 1998 –August 1, 2003," was for that definite term and, after hearing the plaintiff's testimony of his understanding of the relationship, the jury so found. The Virginia Supreme Court reversed. While the document did state it was effective for the designated time, it also expressly provided that either party could terminate it upon 30-days' notice. "This notice provision trumped the effect of the designated time period." *Id.* at 793. In the court's view, then, the contract was clear and unambiguous and the case should not have been submitted to the jury. The court may have gotten this wrong, but once it found no ambiguity, its application of the parol evidence rule was consistent with what you learned in your first-year contracts class: Evidence of prior or contemporaneous oral negotiations is inadmissible to alter, contradict, or explain the terms of a written instrument provided the document is complete, unambiguous, and unconditional. *Id.* at 794.

One of the subtler aspects of parol evidence is that courts must determine whether a written agreement is fully or partially "integrated" (that is, final) before deciding what, if any, parol evidence can be admitted. If an agreement is "completely integrated," no parol evidence may be admitted other than for interpretation; but if the agreement is only "partially integrated," evidence may be admitted to supplement the agreement. In no case, however, may parol evidence be used to contradict the written terms. *See generally* RESTATEMENT (SECOND) OF CONTRACTS § 213 (1981). We will explore the contours of the parol evidence rule again in the next case.

6. *Individual Contracts and Employee Handbooks.* We met employee handbooks as possible contracts in Chapter 2. As you might guess, whatever contractual rights such handbooks might or might not create tend to be trumped by individual contracts, and that was true in *Spacesaver*. Note particularly its Employee Handbook, which indicates that employment with Spacesaver is at will, has no effect. In the case itself that is because the handbook had a disclaimer of contractual effects. And note the court's skepticism about such sources of rights to begin with. *See* footnote 16. But even if it were framed to contractually make all employees at will, wouldn't it be trumped by a subsequent individual contract? But what if such a disclaimer were signed *after* the individual contract? In thinking about these questions, recall again from your

Contracts class that parol evidence is admissible to establish a later modification of a contractual relationship, even if the original agreement was fully integrated at the time at which it was entered.

Hinkel v. Sataria Distrib. & Packaging, Inc.
920 N.E.2d 766 (Ind. Ct. App. 2010)

VAIDIK, J:

The appellant, Mark Hinkel, was hired to work for the appellee, Sataria Distribution and Packaging, Inc. ("Sataria"). Hinkel was allegedly promised a year's worth of salary and insurance coverage if he were ever terminated involuntarily, but his written employment contract did not provide for severance pay or post-employment benefits. Hinkel was soon terminated, and he did not receive the severance package he says he was promised. Hinkel sued for breach of contract and/or promissory estoppel. The trial court entered summary judgment in favor of Sataria. We hold that (1) Hinkel's written employment contract is a completely integrated agreement which precludes consideration of any prior or contemporaneous oral promises, (2) to the extent the severance agreements were made after the execution of the written contract, they were not supported by additional consideration, and (3) Hinkel is unable to sustain his claim of promissory estoppel. We affirm.

Facts and Procedural History

Hinkel was employed by Refractory Engineers, Inc. and Ceramic Technology, Inc. John Jacobs was the owner of Sataria. In late August or September 2005, Hinkel and Jacobs met to discuss working together. Jacobs offered Hinkel a job at Sataria. Hinkel had reservations. Jacobs told him, "Mark, are you worried that I'll f*** you? If so, and things don't work, I'll pay you one (1) year's salary and cover your insurance for the one (1) year as well. But let me make it clear, should you decide this is not for you, and you terminate your own employment, then the agreement is off." Jacobs later sent Hinkel the following written job offer:

Dear Mark,
This is written as an offer of employment. The terms are as described below:

1. Annual Compensation:	$120,000
2. Work Location:	Belmont Facility
3. Initial Position:	Supervisor Receiving Team
4. Start Date:	08/19/2005
5. Paid Vacation:	To be determined
6. Health Insurance:	Coverage begins 09/01/2005 pending proper Enrollment submission

Please sign and return.

Hinkel signed the offer and resigned from his other employers. He began working at Sataria in September 2005. According to Hinkel, Jacobs reiterated the severance promise again in November 2005 and December 2005.

Sataria terminated Hinkel's employment involuntarily on January 23, 2006. Sataria paid Hinkel six weeks of severance thereafter. Hinkel brought this action for breach of contract and/or promissory estoppel against Sataria. He claimed that Sataria owed him the severance package that Jacobs promised. Sataria moved for summary judgment. The trial court granted Sataria's motion. Hinkel now appeals. . . .

I. Breach of Contract Claim

According to Hinkel, Jacobs orally promised him a year's salary and insurance coverage if he were ever involuntarily terminated. Sataria argues that any alleged oral promises are barred from consideration by the parol evidence rule.

The parol evidence rule provides that "[w]hen two parties have made a contract and have expressed it in a writing to which they have both assented as the complete and accurate integration of that contract, evidence . . . of antecedent understandings and negotiations will not be admitted for the purpose of varying or contradicting the writing." *Dicen v. New Sesco, Inc.*, 839 N.E.2d 684, 688 (Ind. 2005) (quoting 6 Arthur Linton Corbin, Corbin on Contracts § 573 (2002 reprint)) (emphasis removed). This rule "effectuates a presumption that a subsequent written contract is of a higher nature than earlier statements, negotiations, or oral agreements by deeming those earlier expressions to be merged in to or superseded by the written document." 11 Richard A. Lord, Williston on Contracts § 33:1 (4th ed. 1999) (footnote omitted).

The first step when applying the parol evidence rule is determining whether the parties' written contract represents a complete or partial integration of their agreement. *See* Restatement (Second) of Contracts §§ 209, 210 (1981). If the contract is completely integrated, constituting a final and complete expression of all the parties' agreements, then evidence of prior or contemporaneous written or oral statements and negotiations cannot operate to either add to or contradict the written contract. *Franklin v. White*, 493 N.E.2d 161, 167 (Ind. 1986). The preliminary question of integration, either complete or partial, requires the court to hear all relevant evidence, parol or written. *Id.* "Whether a writing has been adopted as an integrated agreement is a question of fact to be determined in accordance with all relevant evidence." Restatement (Second) of Contracts §§ 209 cmt. c. Nevertheless, what is ordinarily a question of fact may become a question of law "where the facts are undisputed and only a single inference can be drawn from those facts." *Jones v. Ind. Bell Tel. Co.*, 864 N.E.2d 1125, 1127 (Ind. Ct. App. 2007) (breach of duty). "[T]he absence of an integration clause is not conclusive as to whether parties intend a writing to be completely integrated." *Sees v. Bank One, Ind., N.A.*, 839 N.E.2d 154, 163 n.7 (Ind. 2005) (Boehm, J., concurring and dissenting) (citing Restatement (Second) of Contracts § 209 cmt. b).

In addition,

> The test of [parol evidence] admissibility is much affected by the inherent likelihood that parties who contract under the circumstances in question would simultaneously make both the agreement in writing which is before the court, and also the alleged parol agreement. The point is not merely whether the court is convinced that the parties before it did in fact do this, but whether reasonable parties so situated naturally would or might obviously or normally do so. . . . The vast majority of courts assessing the admissibility of parol evidence at common law apply this test. . . .

11 *Williston on Contracts* § 33:25 (footnotes omitted).

Here, Jacobs and Hinkel negotiated the terms of Hinkel's employment before completing their written contract. Jacobs allegedly promised Hinkel that he would receive one year of salary and benefits if he were ever terminated involuntarily. The parties then executed their written agreement. The written employment offer specified Hinkel's compensation, work location, title, start date, and the date on which his insurance coverage would begin. It did not provide that Hinkel would receive severance pay or benefits following termination. Hinkel signed the letter and began working at Sataria. In light of all the relevant evidence, we find as a matter of law that Hinkel's contract represented a complete integration of the parties' employment agreement. Jacobs allegedly promised Hinkel a severance package, but the written contract enumerates both compensation and insurance coverage while saying nothing of post-employment salary and/or benefits. The offer leaves one term to be decided — paid vacation — but the contract imports on its face to be a complete expression with respect to salary and insurance. And since a lucrative severance provision would "naturally and normally" be included in an employment contract, its glaring omission here further supports the conclusion that Hinkel's written contract superseded any alleged prior oral promises. We hold that the written contract constituted a final representation of the parties' agreement, and any contemporaneous oral agreements that the parties made as to severance are not subject to interpretation.

To the extent Jacobs may have promised Hinkel a severance package after their written contract was executed, an additional question is whether Jacobs's promise could have constituted a valid contract modification. "The modification of a contract, since it is also a contract, requires all the requisite elements of a contract." *Hamlin v. Steward*, 622 N.E.2d 535, 539 (Ind. Ct. App. 1993). "A written agreement may be changed by a subsequent one orally made, upon a sufficient consideration." *Id.* . . .

Here, if Jacobs promised Hinkel a severance package after the written employment contract was executed, there is no evidence that Hinkel provided additional consideration in exchange for the promise. Hinkel argues that he had to agree "to continue working for Sataria" and "to not *voluntarily* resign his employment." But Hinkel had assumed those duties and employment obligations as consideration for the original agreement. *See Buschman v. ADS Corp.*, 782 N.E.2d 423, 430 (Ind. Ct. App. 2003) ("Buschman's work at ADS was the consideration for ADS's offer embodied in the Second Offer Letter and is not new consideration."). Any subsequent promise by Jacobs respecting severance was not supported by an independent, bargained-for exchange. Accordingly, Jacobs's alleged oral promises could not have constituted valid modifications of Hinkel's employment contract. . . .

II. Promissory Estoppel Claim

[The court rejected any promissory estoppel claim because, even if Hinkel gave up his prior employment, he "was provided with a period of employment at Sataria, a substantial salary, and six weeks of severance. Hinkel has not shown an injury so independent and severe that injustice could only be avoided by enforcement of Jacobs's alleged promise."]

RILEY, J., concurs.

CRONE, Judge, dissenting.

I respectfully dissent because I disagree with the majority's conclusion that Jacobs's oral promise to Hinkel regarding a severance package is "barred from consideration by the parol evidence rule." I do so for two reasons. First, I believe that a genuine issue of material fact exists regarding whether the parties intended for Jacobs's written job offer to Hinkel to be completely integrated, i.e., a "final and complete expression of *all* the parties' agreements[.]" (emphasis added).[1] Although not conclusive, the offer — a one-page document with six bullet points for a position paying $120,000 per year — does not contain an integration clause. More persuasive is its statement that Hinkel's vacation terms were yet to be determined, which indicates to me that the parties had not yet reached agreement on that issue. Based on the foregoing, a factfinder reasonably could conclude that the offer is more akin to a memorandum of understanding and represents only a partial integration of the parties' agreements, and that therefore the parol evidence rule would not apply to bar consideration of Jacobs's oral promise regarding the severance package.

Second, the terms of the severance package do not vary from or contradict the terms of the written offer, but merely cover that which was not covered in the offer. As such, even assuming that the offer is completely integrated, the terms of the severance package would not be barred by the parol evidence rule. *See Malo v. Gilman*, 379 N.E.2d 554, 557 and note 5 (Ind. App. 1978) ("[P]arol evidence may be admitted to supply an omission in the terms of the contract. . . . Using parol evidence to supply an omission will not modify the written agreement, but merely adds to it."). Therefore, I would reverse the trial court's grant of summary judgment in favor of Sataria and remand for further proceedings.

NOTES

1. *Complete vs. Partial Integration.* Students are often confused as to what it means for a term (or a contract) to be "integrated." The answer is almost tautological: It means that the parties have agreed that the writing reflects their final agreement — on that term (if partial) or the entire contract (if complete). The *Hinkel* court is certainly correct that, if the contract is a complete integration, no parol evidence can be admitted to add to it. If it is a partial integration, parol evidence may supplement but not contradict the writing; in other words, the alleged agreement must be "consistent" with the writing. As we have seen, in either case parol evidence may be introduced to clarify an ambiguity — once the court determines that the writing is ambiguous.

The trick, of course, is how to figure out whether a writing is integrated. Does it make any sense to think that the document in *Hinkel* is completely integrated? Aren't there a hundred things the parties might have agreed to that are not reflected in the sketchy offer? For example, work hours, work week, office, expense account, 401(k)?

---

1. The majority concedes that the offer "leaves one term to be decided" but paradoxically concludes that it "constituted a final representation of the parties' agreement[.]" I fail to see how a contract can be completely integrated if it expressly defers agreement on a particular issue.

Some courts have been much more sympathetic to claims that contracts are at most partially integrated. In *Esbensen v. Userware International, Inc.,* 14 Cal. Rptr. 2d 93 (Ct. App. 1992), the court found the written document to be only a partial integration even though the contract was more formal than that in *Hinkel* and even though the plaintiff was arguing for an oral agreement that his one-year contract would be renewed "perpetually" if he continued to perform — essentially claiming a continuous for-cause contract. Two factors led to this result: the absence of a merger or integration clause (as in *Hinkel*) and the absence of any provision for termination. "It is hardly unnatural to think that small business entrepreneurs and a computer programmer, unsophisticated in legal matters and unadvised by lawyers, might have discussed those uncertainties and resolved them orally." *Esbensen* at 97.

2. *Consistent Collateral Agreement.* Having decided that the contract was a complete integration, the *Hinkel* majority's work was basically done: No parol evidence was admissible even to supplement the writing. In *Esbensen,* by contrast, having found the agreement was not completely integrated, the court had to go on to decide whether the oral agreement was consistent with the partial integration. Again, that is because an oral agreement that contradicts even a partially integrated writing is not admissible, and the defendant argued that a promise of renewal was inconsistent with the provision for a one-year term. The court wrote:

> We agree with Userware that the one-year term provision of the contract must have some meaning. We disagree, however, that the only possible reason for including this provision was to allow for Esbensen's termination at the end of the year for any reason. As Esbensen points out, the contract specifically provided that his salary would be reviewed on an annual basis. If the written contract was supplemented by an oral understanding that the one-year agreements would be renewed absent good cause not to do so, it might be that the one-year contract term merely reflected the interval between salary reviews. Under such circumstances, "good cause" for nonrenewal would necessarily include the parties' failure to agree on the terms for renewal. In effect, the parties would be obligated to negotiate in good faith at the end of each year toward the goal of renewal on mutually acceptable terms.
>
> . . . It could be argued that the failure to specify grounds [for termination] necessarily implies that *any* reason was acceptable. As we have explained, however, the fact that something is presumed or implied in the absence of an express statement to the contrary does not preclude a party to an incomplete written contract from attempting to demonstrate an express oral agreement contrary to the term which would otherwise be presumed or implied.

14 Cal. Rptr. 2d at 98. Do you agree? Or is this stretching to avoid finding an inconsistency?

3. *The "Naturally Excluded" Test.* Viewed together *Hinkel* and *Esbensen* suggest that finding the relevant document to be a complete integration often will be outcome determinative. And both opinions (and most, but not all, other courts) use the same test, asking whether the oral understanding sought to be admitted might "naturally" have been excluded from the written contract. This approach, sometimes referred to as the "modern" or "California" approach to parol evidence, tends to favor the admission of extrinsic evidence that stricter approaches would exclude. It is to be contrasted with the "four corners" test, under which a court looks to see if the writing *appears* to be complete. *See Kay v. Prolix Packaging, Inc.,* 993 N.E.2d 39, 52 (Ill. App. 2013) ("Looking at the four corners of the instrument reveals whether or not it is fully integrated."). As *Hinkel* makes clear, however, even the more liberal test is not a slam dunk for the party seeking to have the court consider parol evidence.

4. *An Integration Clause to the Rescue?* The more detailed the contract, the more likely that an omitted term will be found to be inconsistent with one or more provisions. But asking that every employment contract reduce almost everything to writing may be asking too much. An obvious safeguard is for the parties to include an integration clause (sometimes called a merger clause) to the effect that the written document supersedes all other understandings. While such clauses do not necessarily preclude parol evidence, they are usually effective in doing so. *See Migliore v. Nu Flow Holdings*, 2014 Cal. App. Unpub. LEXIS 1089, 30 (Cal. App. Feb. 14, 2014) ("By signing the document, Migliore agreed to both the at-will termination clause and the integration provision, and that document superseded all other agreements on the grounds for his termination.").

5. *Prior or Contemporaneous Evidence.* An important limitation on the parol evidence rule is that it bars evidence only of agreements or actions prior to or contemporaneous with the execution of the written contract. It has no application to subsequent agreements, which are admissible to show the parties modified their written agreement. That's why the *Hinkel* court had to consider the significance of promises supposedly made after the contract had been signed. As that decision indicates, however, while subsequent statements are not barred by the parol evidence rule, employees face a separate set of obstacles when trying to prove that such a statement modified a written contract. For instance, as in *Hinkel,* contract formation rules generally require that modifications be supported by consideration. Further, the statue of frauds may apply to modified agreements not capable of being performed within one year.

6. *Backfiring Integration Clauses.* As discussed in Chapter 2, employers often place disclaimers of contractual rights or recitals of employees' at-will status in the personnel documents they use in the workplace. Such documents are frequently effective to foreclose suits based on prior oral assurances about job security or other terms of employment. This is a pretty straightforward operation of the parol evidence rule.

But such disclaimers can have disadvantages — obvious ones for the employee, who will lose the benefit of any bargain struck orally. However, such documents typically have merger clauses providing that they incorporate the entire agreement of the parties and that any prior agreements are superseded and not enforceable (pretty standard language), and such provisions have sometimes backfired on employers. For example, employers often require applicants for employment to agree to arbitration should a dispute arise. While that agreement might be perfectly enforceable when signed, a later agreement that doesn't mention arbitration and has an integration clause may well negate it. *See Grey v. American Management Services*, 139 Cal. Rptr. 3d 210, 214 (Cal. App. 2012) ("Thus, the employment contract supersedes the IRA [an application packet containing an arbitration agreement]. AMS cannot use the IRA as extrinsic evidence that the parties did not intend the employment contract to be the sole agreement because it contradicts the plain terms of the contract's integration clause."); *see also MAPEI Corp. v. Prosser,* 761 S.E.2d 500 (Ga. Ct. App. 2014) (a second agreement omitting a non-compete clause superceded an agreement containing such a clause signed only a week earlier when it had a merger clause so providing). *But see Pelletier v. Yellow Transportation, Inc.,* 549 F.3d 578 (1st Cir. 2008) (finding an arbitration agreement signed at the same time as an employment application with a merger clause reaching "contemporaneous agreements" to nevertheless be consistent). *See generally* Charles A. Sullivan, *Man Bites Dog: The Parol Evidence Rule as the Employee's Friend?*, http://lawprofessors.typepad.com/labor-prof_blog/2009/02/sullivan-on-the.html (arguing that integration clauses sometimes undercut employer efforts to achieve their contractual objectives).

7. *The Value of an Imperfect Writing.* Many employment agreements are pretty sketchy (maybe in both senses of the term!). Perhaps most often, this reflects the absence of an attorney. But even where the contract has been "lawyered," there are often gaps. These can, of course, result from failure to anticipate issues or carelessness in drafting. Other times, particularly in heavily negotiated contracts, gaps mean that the parties were unable to come to agreement on those points. Contract drafters sometimes "punt" on hard issues, using indefinite terms to paper over their disagreement. An integration clause can preclude parol evidence to fill such gaps — but the court will still have to interpret the written terms of the contract to resolve the problem.

PROBLEMS

3-1. Paula Adams, a travel agent, is employed by Evan's Vacation, Inc. under a written contract which sets out Adams's salary and benefits and contains a noncompete agreement. The contract includes the following language:

> 5. **Term.** The "Term of Employment," as used herein, shall mean a period commencing January 1, 2012, and ending on the third anniversary of such date (the "Ending Date"); provided, however, that the occurrence of any of the following prior to the Ending Date shall result in the immediate termination of the Term of Employment, but shall not result in the termination of this Agreement:
>
> > i. the termination by the Employer of the Term of Employment for any reason, including, but not limited to, the commission by the Employee of any act constituting a dishonest or other act of material breach or a fraudulent act or a felony under the laws of any state or of the United States to which the Employer or Employee is subject; or
> > ii. the death of the Employee; or
> > iii. the failure of the Employee to perform her duties hereunder.

Suppose that in January 2014, Evan's Vacation decides to reduce its staff due to a downturn in business and selects Adams for layoff. Prior to informing Adams, the company consults you. What would you advise the company about its legal obligations under this agreement? Can you make a plausible argument that would support the employer's decision if it goes through with the termination? Would it matter if the contract contained the following additional language?

> Employee shall be on a probationary employment period ("Probationary Period") of ninety (90) days during which Employer has the sole right to terminate Employee without cause.

What would your ultimate recommendation be with respect to whether the employer should terminate Adams under each of these scenarios? Is there any other information you would like to know before deciding? Regardless of your ultimate conclusion, can you think of a better way for the company to draft this agreement in the future? *See generally Evan's World Travel, Inc. v. Adams*, 978 S.W.2d 225 (Tex. App. 1998).

3-2. Irving Sliff was hired as general counsel of Condec Corp. At the time, Sliff was 55 years old and had been employed for 20 years as general counsel at Shell Corp., where he was fully vested in his employer's pension plan. During his negotiations with the president of Condec, Sliff made clear that he was not interested in the new position unless he was guaranteed employment until such time as he would fully vest in Condec's pension plan, which would require a minimum employment term of 10 years. The president orally assured him that this would be the case, and Sliff accepted the position. Several years later, as a result of changes in the management, Sliff became concerned that he had nothing in writing to confirm his oral understanding with the company. He prepared the following memo for execution by the president:

> This will confirm our discussions, both prior and subsequent to my employment, relating to my completion of sufficient years of service during my employment as General Counsel of Condec Corporation to qualify for 100% vesting in each of the employee benefit plans currently offered, as they now exist or may be modified or amended in the future, and any such plans which may hereafter be adopted. It is agreed that I shall be employed by Condec Corporation at a competitive and adequate compensation for at least such period of years as is required to accomplish 100% vesting in the employee benefit plans referred to above, unless discharged for due cause, i.e., dishonesty, or criminal conduct injurious to Condec.

Suppose that the president refuses to sign the memo asserting that it is "too specific." One year later, Sliff is terminated for unsatisfactory performance. When asked for an explanation, he is told by the president that he "hasn't grown with the job."

Does Sliff have a viable claim for breach of contract? Of what significance, if any, is the unsigned memo? If Sliff has a contract for a fixed term equaling the number of years until he is 100% vested in the company pension plans, can he be fired prior to that time nonetheless? On what grounds? *See generally Slifkin v. Condec Corp.*, 538 A.2d 231 (Conn. App. Ct. 1988).

2. Defining "Just Cause" to Terminate

In assessing whether a terminated worker has a legitimate breach of contract claim, analyzing whether the contract contemplates a fixed term of employment or contains some other type of job security term is just the beginning of the inquiry. Assuming a contractual right to job security exists, either based on clear language in the contract or through the resolution of ambiguous circumstances in favor of the employee, the court must then determine whether the employee's right has been violated. In other words, did the employer breach the job security provision of the contract in terminating the employee?

This question raises a number of related legal issues. As we saw in *Hinkel*, this often means asking whether the employer had "just cause" to terminate the employee.

Some employment contracts expressly define that term, some do not. If the contract defines cause, the question becomes one of interpretation: Does the conduct at issue meet the definition the parties adopted in their agreement? But what happens if the employee commits misconduct that does not fall within the contractual definition? Is the employer still liable to the employee, or can it argue that the employee materially breached his or her duties to the employer? On the other hand, what happens if the contract fails to define cause? As a practical matter, this is frequently the case even in expressly negotiated written instruments. What standard should be used to determine if the termination was justified in such a case? And who gets to decide whether that standard was satisfied — the judge or the jury?

A variety of factual issues also are implicated in breach of contract inquiries. For obvious reasons, employees generally do not admit to engaging in misconduct. Suppose the employer argues that it terminated an employee for embezzling funds from the company. The employee will no doubt deny the charge, creating a factual issue as to whether the embezzlement occurred. Who bears the burden of proof on this issue, the employer or the employee? Is it necessary even to establish that the misconduct occurred, or is it enough that the employer believed it occurred? If the latter, must that belief be objectively reasonable, reached in good faith, or both? *See Sanders v. Kettering Univ.*, 411 F. App'x 771, 778 (6th Cir. 2010) ("Although there is no genuine issue of material fact that Kettering held an honest belief that Sanders' actions constituted 'just cause' under their employment contract, justifying his termination, a jury hearing Sanders' evidence may reach an honest belief opposite that of Kettering."). Remember *Hinkel's* discussion of the difference between "satisfaction" contracts and cause? Finally, regardless of whether the misconduct actually occurred, to what extent should courts inquire into the honesty of the employer's asserted reason for termination? It is entirely possible for an employer to fire an employee for a reason prohibited under the contract, but justify its decision based on a reason permitted under the contract. How should breach of contract be resolved where the employer's motive is in doubt?

These questions have yet to be fully resolved by courts. Indeed, most breach of employment contract cases will raise only a small subset of these issues, and it is not always clear which ones are implicated or what standards courts are using to address them.

Benson v. AJR, Inc.
599 S.E.2d 747 (W. Va. 2004)

PER CURIAM:

Danny L. Benson appeals from [a grant of summary judgment to AJR, Inc. in connection with his claim of breach of employment contract]. [W]e determine that there is a genuine issue of material fact concerning the basis for [defendant's] decision to terminate Mr. Benson's employment with AJR. Accordingly, the grant of summary judgment was improper. . . .

I. Factual and Procedural Background

AJR is a small heavy manufacturing business engaged in the manufacture and welding of truck beds. At the time when Appellant was first employed by AJR as a general welder in 1990, the company was owned by three individuals: Jackie L. Benson; Robert W. Benson; and Patricia Benson. Appellant is the son of Jackie Benson. On May 1, 1997, Appellant was promoted to supervisor and was assigned primary responsibility over three aspects of the company's operations, one of which was safety. In his supervisory position, Appellant was charged with the responsibility for directing and leading the company's safety programs and ensuring that AJR's safety rules were both observed and enforced.

During the summer of 1997, the three AJR shareholders decided to sell the company to an employee, Appellee John M. Rhodes. As part of the sales transaction, Mr. Rhodes agreed to enter into an employment agreement with Appellant whereby Mr. Benson would be guaranteed employment for a period of eight years beginning on August 29, 1997.[2] While AJR had the right to terminate appellant with only one day's written notice under this agreement, it was required to continue paying Mr. Benson his salary for the balance of the eight-year term of employment in the absence of three specified conditions. Those conditions were: (a) dishonesty; (b) conviction of a felony; and (c) voluntary termination of the agreement by Appellant.[3]

Within less than a month after the execution of the employment agreement, Appellant acknowledged in writing his receipt of an employee manual which specified certain acts that were grounds for termination. Those grounds included the sale, possession, or use of controlled substances while on the job, during working hours, or while on company business. At the end of September 1997, concurrent with his receipt of the employee manual, Appellant signed a consent form permitting his employer to conduct random controlled substance tests.

On March 2, 1998, a drug test was administered to the employees of AJR. The results of the drug testing revealed that Appellant had more than three times the limit utilized by the United States Department of Transportation ("DOT") to establish drug use and impairment. Between the time when the drug test was administered and the results were made available, Mr. Rhodes conducted meetings with various AJR personnel during which he inquired of those in attendance whether anyone was aware of an employee who was using illegal drugs or who was arriving at work with illegal drugs or alcohol in their system. Appellant attended one of those meetings and admits that he did not respond to this question despite personal knowledge that his drug test would come back positive.

Along with eleven other employees who also tested positive for drug use, Appellant was terminated from the employ of AJR on March 6, 1998. AJR prepared two different termination forms in connection with Appellant's dismissal from the company. The first of the two forms indicated that Mr. Benson had resigned from

---

2. In explanation of why this agreement was entered into, the document states that "it is in the best interests of the Company that key management employees, including the Employee [Mr. Benson], continue to be employed by the Company upon" the sale of AJR.

3. This Court *sua sponte* recognized an issue regarding the contract's interpretation based on the words chosen to draft the agreement. Because the contract was written in terms of permitting AJR to terminate Appellant "without cause," and because the subsequent salary payment obligations arise in reference to a termination "without cause," we initially questioned whether the payment obligations would be invoked in a case, such as this, where the employee was undeniably dismissed for cause. We determine, however, that the contract should be read in the fashion undertaken by the parties and the court below predominantly because the three contractual conditions that excuse AJR's requirement to pay Appellant his salary (two of which are clearly "for cause" type of dismissals) would be rendered meaningless if the payment provisions could only be invoked in a non-cause dismissal situation.

his employment.[7] The second of the two termination forms lists a different reason for termination — "controlled substance testing" and "tested positive for cocaine." . . .

Discussion

A. Breach of Employment Contract

At the center of this dispute is whether AJR is required to comply with the salary payment obligation contained in the employment agreement. Under the terms of the agreement, in the event AJR decided to terminate Mr. Benson, the company was required to pay Appellant the salary that was in effect on August 29, 1997, absent a dismissal that was based on dishonesty, conviction of a felony, or if Mr. Benson voluntarily terminated the employment agreement. Appellant contends that the lower court erred in its determination that the basis for AJR's termination of Mr. Benson was dishonesty. . . .

To resolve the critical question of whether Appellant's positive drug test fell within the parameters of "dishonest" conduct, the trial court defined the term "dishonesty" by referring to entries in Webster's Dictionary and Black's Law Dictionary.[9] Relying on these generalized definitions, the lower court concluded that Appellant's "actions in failing a drug test and arriving at work with drugs in his system demonstrates a lack of integrity, probity, or adherence to a code of moral values." Rather than limiting its analysis to just the definition of "dishonesty," however, the circuit court included a listing of various definitions of "integrity" and found that "[a]ctions which lack integrity are, by definition, dishonest." After weighing these two definitions in essentially *pari materia,* the trial court ruled that "[p]laintiff's positive drug test, in light of all the facts and circumstances of the case, demonstrates dishonesty and a lack of integrity."[10]

In marked contrast to the trial court's willingness to define the term "dishonesty" within the meaning of the employment contract at issue, we recognize the futility of attempting to fashion a "one size fits all" definition for such term. Dishonesty, like any term that has significance in a given contract, must be defined based on the subject matter of the contract and the intent of the document's drafters. We note, however, that it has been observed that "[d]ishonesty, unlike embezzlement or larceny, is not a term of art." More often than not, the issue of whether conduct qualifies as dishonest is determined to be a question best resolved by a jury.

In this case, the record evidences Mr. Benson's admission that he was dishonest in connection with his failure to truthfully answer the question posed by Mr. Rhodes with regard to his awareness of drug use by any AJR employees. Given Appellant's clear

---

7. While Appellant was given the opportunity to resign from AJR, he did not choose to resign his employment.

9. The trial court cited a definition in Webster's, which described dishonesty as "a lack of honesty or integrity; a disposition to defraud or deceive." As defined by the legal dictionary, dishonesty included a "[d]isposition to lie, cheat, deceive, or defraud; untrustworthiness; lack of integrity."

10. One of the circumstances relied upon by the trial court was Mr. Benson's admission that he had been dishonest in failing to answer Mr. Rhodes' question regarding knowledge of drug use in the work place when he "knew to an absolute certainty that he had used illegal drugs and had them in his system when asked the question." Additional evidence cited by the trial court to support its conclusion regarding Appellant's dishonesty was the fact that "[p]laintiff admitted that he used cocaine and does not challenge the drug test."

admission of dishonesty, we proceed to determine what impact, if any, this admission of dishonesty has on the case at hand.

The lower court appears to have assumed that upon finding conduct that qualified as dishonest, this case could be resolved solely on legal grounds without requiring the assistance of a jury. The trial court reasoned that "[n]o reasonable jury could find that Plaintiff's failing of the drug test, under all the circumstances present herein, was not dishonest behavior." Critically, however, a factual issue that must be determined for purposes of ascertaining whether AJR was required under the terms of the contract to pay Appellant his salary for the remainder of the eight-year contractual period is the *reason* upon which AJR relied in terminating Mr. Benson's employment. Under the employment contract at issue, the determining factor that controls the issue of continued salary payment is whether the basis for the termination was "dishonesty" or "conviction of a felony," or, alternatively, whether there was a "voluntary termination of . . . [the] agreement."

The record in this case is unclear as to whether AJR dismissed Mr. Benson from its employ for drug use or for dishonesty. As Appellant emphasizes in his argument, nowhere on either of the two termination forms that were introduced below is there any indication that he was dismissed for dishonesty. We are unwilling to make the leap that the trial court did to broadly encompass testing positive for drug use within the meaning of the term "dishonesty." Consequently, we conclude that Appellant is entitled to have a jury determine the basis for AJR's decision to terminate Mr. Benson from its employ. If the jury determines that drug use, rather than dishonesty, was the basis for the dismissal, then the provisions of the employment contract with regard to continued payment of Appellant's salary for the duration of the contractual term are applicable. If, however, the jury determines that Mr. Benson was in fact terminated for being dishonest, then AJR is not required to pay his salary under the terms of the employment contract. . . .

MAYNARD, C.J., concurring, in part, and dissenting, in part.

What a terrible message this case sends to small West Virginia employers and businesses! This Court tells this company that it should not have fired an employee who:

1. admitted that he used cocaine;
2. reported to work with cocaine in his system;
3. failed a drug test in which he tested positive for cocaine;
4. misrepresented his drug use by failing to truthfully answer management's inquiries about drug use;
5. worked in a plant where steel fabrication involving constant welding occurs;
6. continually worked around large quantities of explosives and highly volatile gases and liquids including acetylene, oxygen tanks, thinner paint, and other explosive substances; and, here is the icing on the cake;
7. was the SAFETY DIRECTOR of the company!! Appalling!

This Court now says that AJR was wrong to fire a deceitful, coke-head safety director in a plant where tanks of acetylene, oxygen, and other explosives are everywhere! The irony is that if there had been some explosion or other accident which killed or seriously injured another employee, the victim of that accident could have successfully sued under our workers' compensation deliberate intent statute and obtained a large verdict. This Court doubtless would have upheld the large verdict based on the fact that the company allowed a cocaine user to be its safety director.

In distinguishing between dishonesty and drug use under the specific facts of this case, the majority opinion does one of the finest jobs of legalistic hairsplitting in the history of American jurisprudence. The undisputed facts show that if Appellant was terminated for dishonesty, AJR was not obligated to pay Appellant his salary for the balance of the employment agreement. Appellant was responsible for safety at AJR's facility including enforcing AJR's drug-free workplace policy. Appellant received a copy of AJR's employee manual which states, in part, that employees may be terminated for the sale, possession, or use of controlled substances while on the job, during work hours, or while on company business. After Appellant failed a drug test, he admitted that he used cocaine the Saturday immediately prior to the Monday drug test. Finally, he also admitted that he was dishonest with management when he failed to answer management's questions regarding possible drug use in the workplace because he knew to an absolute certainty that he had used illegal drugs and had them in his system when asked the question.

Given these facts, I must disagree with the majority that a jury could determine that drug use rather than dishonesty was the basis for Appellant's dismissal. This is a distinction without a difference. Appellant's drug use, established by the positive drug test, demonstrates dishonesty. Specifically, Appellant, who was responsible for enforcing a drug-free workplace, knowingly violated his employer's drug-free workplace policy by coming to work with cocaine in his system. This is dishonest conduct. Actually testing positive for the drug use is evidence of this dishonest conduct. Therefore, it is irrelevant whether the official reason for Appellant's dismissal was dishonesty or drug use.

Finally, troubling also is the majority opinion's failure to address AJR's argument that Appellant's decision to appear for work under the influence of cocaine was tantamount to a willful quit; substantial public policy against rewarding a person for his or her dishonesty; and the impact of Appellant's admission of dishonesty. The plain fact is that any of these matters would have been sufficient for this Court to affirm the summary judgment on behalf of AJR. . . .

STARCHER, J., concurring.

I write separately to emphasize what the majority's opinion really says, and what it does not say.

This case is all about the power of a contract. The defendant-employer, AJR, Inc., entered into a written contract in 1997 with plaintiff-employee Danny L. Benson that guaranteed Mr. Benson employment until August 2005. Nobody disputes the clarity of this part of the agreement.

However, nowhere does the contract say that Mr. Benson cannot be fired. The contract did allow the defendant-employer to show Mr. Benson the door with pink slip in hand any time it chose to do so. But the contract also contained a clear, black-and-white penalty clause which said that if the defendant-employer let Mr. Benson go, then the defendant-employer would still be required to pay Mr. Benson his remaining wages through August 2005. Again, none of the parties disputes the clarity of this penalty clause built into the agreement.

The fuzzy area in this case is a loophole for the defendant-employer that was built into the contract which allowed the defendant-employer to escape the penalty clause if Mr. Benson was fired because of "dishonesty." The contract does not define "dishonesty." So, when Mr. Benson's drug use was discovered, and the defendant-employer fired him, the question was raised whether Mr. Benson's firing was motivated by Mr. Benson's dishonesty, or for some other reason.

The defendant-employer vigorously asserts that it fired Mr. Benson because the owner of the company conducted meetings with company employees that included Mr. Benson, at which time the owner asked if anyone was aware of an employee who was using illegal drugs or was arriving for work with illegal drugs in his or her system; Mr. Benson said nothing when asked the question. The defendant-employer now asserts that Mr. Benson was fired when the cocaine test results were returned because his dishonesty — in the form of not responding to the question — was revealed. The defendant-employer therefore asserts that it does not have to pay Mr. Benson his remaining wages in compliance with the penalty clause.

The problem with the employer's argument is the written documentation surrounding Mr. Benson's firing. When Mr. Benson was fired, the employer completed a form indicating he was fired in accordance with the employees' manual (which mandated automatic termination for drug usage) for "controlled substance testing" and "tested positive for cocaine." This position was reiterated in writing several times by the company's owner and the company's counsel. The contractual "dishonesty" loophole was not raised by the employer until sometime later, when Mr. Benson asserted his contractual right to his remaining years of wages.

The competing positions taken by the employer raise, beyond a doubt, is a question of fact for jury resolution as to the true motivating factor behind Mr. Benson's termination. The circuit court was wrong to substitute its judgment on this factual question for that of the jury. A jury should hear the witnesses to Mr. Benson's firing testify, should review the documentation surrounding that firing, and should decide for themselves if Mr. Benson's firing was motivated by (a) dishonesty or (b) drug use. If the jury's answer is the former, Mr. Benson gets nothing; if the jury's answer is the latter, the defendant-employer must comply with the written employment contract and pay Mr. Benson his wages under the contract's penalty clause.

That said, let's get straight what this case is *not* about. This case is not — as my dissenting colleague suggests — a case that says a small employer cannot fire an employee who uses drugs. The employer in this case was fully within its rights to fire Mr. Benson — but it had to be willing to pay the price if that firing breached the employment contract. A contract is a promise, and a breach of that promise carries consequences. I disagree with my dissenting colleague's implicit suggestion that because of bad facts, this Court should make bad law, throw hundreds of years of contract law to the wind, and find that because Mr. Benson's actions are less-than-palatable, the contract should be ignored.

If anything, this case says that small employers should not give their employees open-ended contracts guaranteeing them employment. The defendant-employer in this case could have easily put in the contract a clause allowing Mr. Benson to be fired, without penalty to the defendant-employer, for using illicit substances on the job. Luckily, the majority opinion makes clear that the defendant-employer might still be able to hang its hat on the vague term "dishonesty," and prevail before a jury by showing that a lack of veracity on Mr. Benson's part was the motivating factor behind his termination.

NOTES

1. *Clarifying the Issue.* The various opinions in this case express very different views about what is at stake. What is the majority trying to accomplish by remanding, given that Benson has admitted to both drug use and dishonesty? Do you see, as the majority does, a meaningful distinction between the possible grounds for termination under these facts? Or, to use the dissent's term, is this just "legalistic hairsplitting"? If you do see a difference, do you think it will ultimately affect the outcome? In other words, how do you think the jury will receive Benson's argument? (Stay tuned for the answer to this question.)

2. *The Meaning of Dishonesty. Benson* takes the lower court to task for using a dictionary definition of "honesty" rather than attempting to elucidate what the parties meant by this term. Consider why this might have mattered had the issue not been moot as a result of Benson's admission. Benson's purported "dishonesty" consists of the failure to own up to his drug use and his appearance at work with drugs in his system. Does this seem like dishonesty to you? If you answered no, or if you are unsure, then perhaps Benson made a tactical error in conceding this point. Certainly the employer appears to have made an error in carving out a "dishonesty" exception without defining that term. Or might there be a reason why it chose to leave "dishonesty" vague?

3. *Pretext Analysis.* As the majority suggests, the key factual issue that must be determined in this case is the employer's motive for terminating Benson. How does a party prove motive, and who bears the burden of proof on this issue? Motive issues arise with great frequency in the context of status discrimination where the employee alleges that the employer based its decision to terminate on a protected characteristic such as gender or race. The employer typically responds by asserting a legitimate personnel-based reason for its decision. In discrimination cases, the plaintiff bears the ultimate burden of proving that discrimination was at least a motivating factor in the employer's decision. *See* Chapter 9. By contrast, in the typical express contract case, once the employee has established a contractual right to job security, the employer typically has the burden of proving that cause to terminate existed (e.g., was the employee late, insubordinate, a poor performer). As we will see in *Uintah Basin Med. Ctr. v. Hardy*, page 173, courts apply several different standards in determining the first issue. But this is a different inquiry from that in *Benson,* where factual cause has already been established. It is unclear how the burden of proof should be allocated on the remaining question, whether a particular cause actually motivated the decision to terminate. Given the doctrine laid out above, what arguments might each party make with respect to the proper allocation of proof on remand in *Benson*? Are there any policy arguments that can be made in support of allocation to one party over the other? Is the allocation of proof likely to have an impact on the outcome in this case?

4. *Contractual Definitions of Cause. Benson* makes clear that the meaning of cause depends on the terms of the agreement. For this reason, attention to drafting is extremely important when hiring an employee whose termination rights will turn on the presence or absence of cause. Recall the maxim of contract interpretation "construe a contract against its drafter." *Benson* is just one example of cases where employers lost due to the narrowness of their own clauses. A dramatic example of this is a case in which a panel of arbitrators found that the CEO of Massachusetts Mutual Life Insurance was not properly fired for cause despite the fact that he had affairs with two female employees, made millions in profits by trading using the previous day's closing price, and misused the company's aircraft. None of this conduct, the panel concluded, constituted "willful gross misconduct" resulting in "material harm" to the company, as required under the executive's contract. Julie Creswell, *Firing Chief Was Wrong, Panel Says*, N.Y. TIMES, Oct. 21, 2006, at C1.

In response to this problem, drafters have taken different approaches, some insisting on significant detail and formality and others opting for more general language. Compare, for instance, the handwritten "Termination Agreement" of the plaintiff-vice president in *Chard v. Iowa Machinery & Supply Co.*, 446 N.W.2d 81, 83 (Iowa Ct. App. 1989), which defined cause as "no performance, violation of company policy, insubordination, etc.," to the following language in the contract of an executive assistant in *Ten Cate Enbi, Inc. v. Metz*, 802 N.E.2d 977, 979 (Ind. Ct. App. 2004):

> Cause shall mean (i) a reasonable certainty exists establishing that [Metz] has engaged in embezzlement, theft, misappropriation or conversion of any assets of [Enbi]; (ii) a material breach by [Metz] of a provision of this agreement or the Basic Business Regulations unless cured by [Metz] within ten days after [Enbi] gives [Metz] written notice thereof excepting that no notice need be given by [Enbi] in the event of a second material breach by [Metz] of the same provision, and (iii) [Metz's] failure or refusal to follow standard policies of [Enbi] or the reasonable directions of and guidelines established by the Board of Directors unless cured by [Metz] within ten days after [Enbi] gives [Metz] written notice thereof excepting that no notice need be given by [Enbi] in the event of a second material failure or refusal by [Metz] of the same policy, direction or guideline.

Which contract provision would you prefer as an employer? If you were the employee?

5. *Managing Risk upon Termination.* Another lesson from *Benson* is that employers should carefully review an employee's contract before making a personnel decision. Note the critical piece of evidence that, according to the concurrence, allows Benson to survive summary judgment: The reason for termination contained in his separation notice (drug use) differed from the reason the employer advanced in the litigation (dishonesty). A similar inconsistency resulted in a jury verdict for the employee in *Ainsworth v. Franklin County Cheese Corp.*, 592 A.2d 871 (Vt. 1991). There the plaintiff was a plant manager whose contract provided for severance upon termination without cause. In August 1986, the employer requested the plaintiff's resignation, providing no explanation for its decision. The plaintiff acquiesced and went about training a replacement and winding down his work. At one point he inquired when his severance benefits would commence, to which the company president responded that he "hadn't gotten that far yet." One month later, the plaintiff received a letter stating that he had been terminated for cause for "failure to follow [the president's] directions . . . and the Company Operations Manual" and that he was not entitled to severance. The employee prevailed before a jury on his breach of contract claim, and the Vermont Supreme Court affirmed. It held that, even assuming cause for termination existed, the jury could reasonably have concluded that the employer terminated the plaintiff pursuant to the no cause provision of his contract and was therefore obligated to pay severance. From the employer's perspective, both *Ainsworth* and *Benson* illustrate the risks of poorly planned terminations. Had the employers examined the contracts at issue and consulted with counsel before acting, liability might have been avoided. The employee likewise can benefit from a better understanding of his or her agreement. In *Benson*, wouldn't it have been better for the plaintiff to have admitted his drug use when asked since the contract permitted discharge for dishonesty, but not for drug use? Of course, there are obvious downsides to admitting addictions, and perhaps he was not in a condition to make such decisions.

6. *Forms of Job Security in Written Contracts.* Durational contracts are perhaps the most common agreements providing employees with some kind of job security. But such contracts are not a guarantee of employment so much as a guarantee of pay. Of course, either party to any contract can decide that it is in its best interest to breach the agreement and pay damages rather than perform. Since an employee cannot be ordered to specifically perform, it would be a rare case in which an employer were required, as a matter of contract law, to either reinstate the employee or pay damages in excess of the agreed compensation. In the employment context, many agreements providing job security are expressly structured to ensure this result, using entitlement to severance pay as a means of discouraging arbitrary or opportunistic firings while at the same time limiting employer liability to the compensation specified. A typical executive employee contract, for instance, will provide for both termination for cause and termination without cause, granting the employee different rights depending on which provision of the agreement the employer invokes. Under the "for cause" provision, the terminated executive will get little or no compensation or benefits, compared to what is generally a very lucrative payout under the "no cause" provision. *See generally* Stewart Schwab & Randall Thomas, *An Empirical Analysis of CEO Employment Contracts: What Do Top Executives Bargain For?* 63 Wash. & Lee L. Rev. 231 (2006).

That said, as *Hinkel* indicates, the universe of possible job security provisions is broad, and, indeed, the case does not embrace all the possibilities. For important positions, contracts may be extremely complex and highly idiosyncratic. Consider the following provision in the 2005 "offer letter" provided by Microsoft to its chief operating officer, Kevin Turner. Recognizing the loss of "accumulated equity compensation" when he left his current employer, Microsoft promised an "on-hire payment of $7,000,000" but also required Turner to repay it all in "the unlikely event that you leave the company of your own volition or due to termination for cause by the company prior to completing 12 months of employment"; progressively lesser amounts had to be repaid if Turner left between one year and three years. The letter also promised a Stock Award over a several-year vesting schedule, all designed to provide Turner incentives to remain with the company. Finally the letter carefully defined "for cause," (requiring only "a good faith determination" by the company of nonperformance or misconduct) but also allowed Microsoft to discharge him without cause, although in that case Turner got to keep his $7 million. In short, and in contrast to *Benson*, the Microsoft offer calls for a return of money to the company in the event of a "for cause" termination or voluntary departure, rather than a payout in the event of a termination without cause. Why might parties prefer this arrangement instead of a structure based on severance? Does the prospect of the employee paying the company, rather than the reverse, change parties' incentives? Are there other interests in play here besides concerns about permissible bases for an employer-initiated termination?

7. *Severance as Liquidated Damages.* Along these lines, can severance be thought of as a type of liquidated damages clause specifying the amount to be paid to the employee in the event that the employer terminates the relationship in breach of contract? It is generally difficult to predict to what extent an employee will be injured by an unlawful termination, as damages will depend on various factors outside the parties' control, such as the future market for the employee's services. This makes job

security contracts good candidates for a liquidated damage provision. Note, however, that while liquidated damages clauses are presumptively valid under contract law, they will not be enforced if they provide for damages that are disproportionate to actual or foreseeable loss. *See* RESTATEMENT (SECOND) OF CONTRACTS § 356 (1981). Can an employer avoid its obligation to pay an employee upon termination by arguing that the amount of pay provided for in the contract is excessive? *See Guiliano v. Cleo, Inc.*, 995 S.W.2d 88, 101 (Tenn. 1999) (upholding contractual severance in excess of $90,000 for terminated employee who found immediate reemployment at higher salary because, at the time of contract formation, "[i]t was within the fair contemplation of the parties that [plaintiff] might not be able to find a similar professional position . . . and might suffer damages that would be difficult to prove, including loss of professional status, prestige, and advancement opportunities."). We will discuss liquidated damages again in Chapter 8, but notice that often the duty to pay is not framed as damages for breach in the first place, but rather as simply what is owed to the employee upon termination.

8. *The Right to Fire?* The concurring justice in *Benson* emphasizes that the court's decision does not constrain the employer's ability to fire at will but merely enforces the continuation of the salary provision the parties adopted in their agreement. The dissent, in contrast, believes the court's decision saddles the employer with an irresponsible and potentially dangerous worker who is effectively immune from termination. Which justice gets it right?

Consider that Benson's contract ran from 1997 to 2005. Isn't there some truth to the assertion that a small, family-run business like the defendant is unlikely to be able to shoulder the expense of paying a terminated employee for that length of time while employing someone else to do his job? Does this observation incline you toward the dissent's conclusion? Or does it just mean, as the concurrence points out, that small employers should be more prudent in entering into job security agreements with their workers? Which approach is ultimately better for future employees, most of whom are unlikely to engage in similarly egregious behavior?

9. *Choosing Between Cause and No Cause.* In *Benson*, AJR could have fired Benson for any reason and paid his salary, or fired him for an enumerated reason (dishonesty) and avoided further liability. While it may seem like an obvious choice, employers often elect to fire high-level employees under no-cause provisions despite the financial disincentives to doing so. Sometimes this choice simply reflects a desire to avoid conflict or publicity. It may also reflect an unwillingness to risk legal exposure. In cases involving more obscure or less serious performance deficiencies than *Benson*, it can be difficult for the employer to establish poor performance or that the employee's behavior constituted cause within the contractual definition of the term. Perhaps most critically, terminating without cause allows the executive and the company to part amicably, preserving key relationships in the small world of big business.

Yet there are disadvantages to the strategy as well. By making sizeable and seemingly unwarranted payouts to departing executives, firm directors may put themselves at risk of shareholder derivative suits and, in some circumstances, intense public criticism that may be even more damaging than legal action. In a highly publicized example, shareholders of the Walt Disney Company sued the company's board of directors for breach of fiduciary duty based on its 1996 decision to terminate former CEO Michael Ovitz without cause. Ovitz left his position with Disney after a turbulent 14 months of employment, with a severance package estimated at $140 million. Employers' decisions as to whether and on what grounds to terminate an executive are usually insulated by the business judgment rule, and the Disney plaintiffs ultimately lost on the merits following a bench trial. *Brehm v. Eisner*, 906 A.2d 27 (Del. 2006). The fact that the class was successful in getting to trial, however, was widely seen as a cautionary tale in the business community about the growing reluctance of the public (and the judiciary) to give companies free rein on rewarding their own. *See Brehm v. Eisner*, 746 A.2d 244, 249 (Del. 2000) (noting that "the sheer size of the payout to Ovitz . . . pushes the envelope of judicial respect for the business judgment of directors in making compensation decisions").

10. *Material Breach Analysis.* An employer's argument that it had "just cause" to terminate is sometimes framed in terms of the employee committing a "material breach" of the employment agreement that relieves the employer of its contractual obligations. In *Prozinski v. Northeast Real Estate Services, Inc.*, 797 N.E.2d 415 (Mass. App. 2003), the employee was the chief operating and financial officer of a newly formed firm. His contract provided: "During the first 24 months of employment if your employment is terminated by the Company then the Company will pay you the equivalent of 1 full year's pay including benefits." It said nothing about just cause and contained no termination clause. Less than a year later, the firm terminated Prozinski for misconduct and withheld severance. In Prozinski's subsequent suit, the court viewed the agreement as a 24-month, fixed-term contract but held that genuine issues of fact precluded an award of summary judgment in favor of the employee. Specifically, the court held that the alleged behavior giving rise to Prozinski's termination — financial misconduct and sexual harassment — might have excused the employer's duty to pay. It explained:

> The record in this case reflects a genuine issue of material fact on the question whether Prozinski's conduct amounted to a material breach of his contract with Northeast and not simply . . . "boorish conduct" and "sloppy record keeping." As COO-CFO, Prozinski owed Northeast the duties of loyalty, utmost good faith, and of protecting Northeast's interests.
>
> . . . First, Northeast alleged, with some support, that Prozinski knowingly submitted false expense reports. Second, for his own purposes, Prozinski fostered an environment within the workplace that was hostile to its female employees. . . .
>
> Prozinski's placement of his own interests above those of the company he served could be found by a fact finder to constitute an act of disloyalty. One claim of sexual harassment or discrimination can be sufficient to establish a hostile work environment and subject the company to liability. "Under Massachusetts law, officers and directors owe a fiduciary duty to protect the interests of the corporation they serve" Prozinski's conduct put Northeast at risk of litigation.
>
> A fact finder could also conclude that any such breach of Prozinski's fiduciary duty to Northeast amounted to a material breach of his contract, i.e., a "substantial breach going to the root of the contract." *See generally* RESTATEMENT (SECOND) OF CONTRACTS § 241. Such a conclusion would terminate Northeast's obligation to fulfill the contractual promises it had made, for "it is well established that a material breach by one party excuses the other party from further performance under the contract." *See* RESTATEMENT (SECOND) OF CONTRACTS § 237.

Id. at 423-24

Does this result make sense? If the parties agree that severance will be paid and do not provide for any contingencies in their contract, why shouldn't the courts enforce that provision? Is the breach of a "fiduciary duty" the problem? *See* Chapter 8, page 480.

That aside, suppose an employer and an employee drafted an agreement containing the following language: "If Employer terminates employee for any reason, including a material breach of this agreement by Employee, Employer shall pay Employee's salary for the balance of the contract period." Would the *Prozinski* court enforce this clause? Should it? *See also Fields v. Thompson Printing Co.*, 363 F.3d 259, 269 (3d Cir. 2004) (finding in favor of employee denied benefits and pay upon termination for sexual harassment because "[the contract] requires [the employer] to pay certain sums if they terminated Fields, ostensibly for any reason, including improper and offensive conduct. Had [the employer] intended to avoid this result, [it] could have bargained for a limiting provision."). *But see Bennett v. Sage Payment Solutions, Inc.*, 710 S.E.2d 736 (Va. 2011) (holding that an employee's threat, four months into his year-long contract, to leave the company unless his pay was increased justified a jury finding that he had repudiated his obligation, permitting the employer to treat it as a material breach, even though the employee continued to work).

11. *Material vs. Immaterial Performance Deficiencies.* In your first-year contracts course, you probably learned that a material breach is one that goes to the essence of the contract. Engaging in sexual harassment and stealing from the company undoubtedly provide good support for an employer's argument that an employee materially breached his or her employment agreement, but what about less egregious conduct? *See, e.g., Shah v. Cover-It, Inc.*, 859 A.2d 959, 963 (Conn. 2004) (manager materially breached employment contract where he overstayed vacation, did not report to work for weeks upon return, and spent long time periods at work visiting Internet Web sites unrelated to his job); *Central Alaska Broadcasting, Inc. v. Bracale*, 637 P.2d 711, 712 (Alaska 1981) (finding employee's refusal to obey order of board of directors to terminate subordinate a material breach where employee's contract granted him "management authority and right over . . . personnel . . . subject to the supervision and control of the Board").

What about drug use like that at issue in *Benson?* In the ordinary case the answer depends on the severity of the employee's conduct. Off-duty behavior that does not affect on the job performance will rarely if ever constitute a material breach. Thus the analysis would turn on such things as whether Benson actually showed up to work impaired, how often, and whether, if there were only isolated instances of impairment, special circumstances (like access to or use of hazardous materials or equipment) justified a finding of material breach.

If Benson's drug use did rise to this level, the question would be whether the material breach could excuse the employer's payment obligation given the termination provision in the contract. Indeed, this question brought Benson's case back before the West Virginia Supreme Court six years after the remand ordered in the opinion you just read. *See Benson v. AJR*, 698 S.E.2d 638 (W. Va. 2010) (*Benson II*). At trial, AJR argued both that dishonesty (not drug use) motivated its termination decision and that Benson's drug use was a material breach relieving it of contractual liability. The jury returned a general verdict stating that plaintiff had materially breached and, on special interrogatories also submitted to the jury, answered that drug use, not dishonesty, had motivated the employer's decision. The judge awarded Benson his lost wages. AJR appealed, and the West Virginia Supreme Court affirmed:

> Mr. Benson's material breach of the Employment Agreement is not an enumerated reason that would relieve AJR of the duty to pay him his salary under the remainder of the contract period. Thus, while the [jury found] that Mr. Benson had materially breached

his employment contract, such a judgment did not finally resolve the central issue of whether AJR remained obligated to pay Mr. Benson contractual damages when it terminated his employment. [W]hether Mr. Benson may recover damages from AJR is governed solely by the parties' Employment Agreement. . . . AJR is not relieved of its obligation to pay damages to Mr. Benson thereunder. Given the plain language of the Employment Agreement, the circuit court was bound to enforce its terms.

Id. at 649. In light of this result (and the mixed verdict), do you think AJR's material breach argument helped or hurt its case? Do you think the jury might have reached a different conclusion had it been given only a general verdict asking whether the plaintiff or the defendant had breached the contract?

It would appear from *Benson II* that a contractual definition of cause will in some situations preclude a generic material breach argument. Given the availability of material breach analysis under ordinary contract law, why would an employer ever choose to enumerate causes for termination in an employment agreement? A concurring justice in *Benson II* concluded that the parties' "amazingly narrow" agreement indicated that "[F]rom a business sense, the eight years of employment was . . . factored into the purchase price of AJR." *Id.* at *15. Does this description shed some light on the question?

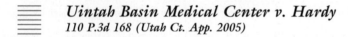

Uintah Basin Medical Center v. Hardy
110 P.3d 168 (Utah Ct. App. 2005)

JACKSON, J.:

. . . Background

Dr. Hardy is a board-certified pathologist. On November 29, 1994, he executed an employment agreement [to provide pathology services for Uintah Basin Medical Center.] Under the Agreement, which consists of only two pages taken almost verbatim from that of Dr. Hardy's predecessor, UBMC was to refer certain types of laboratory work to Dr. Hardy and pay a $400 monthly laboratory director's fee. In return, Dr. Hardy would work as the director of UBMC's laboratory and provide related services, which included weekly visits to the hospital. The Agreement does not include a fixed termination date; rather, it would "continue to bind parties . . . until terminated after ninety (90) days written notice for just cause of termination by either party or by mutual consent of the parties to a shorter notice period." The Agreement does not define "just cause" or otherwise clarify what grounds would justify termination.

On July 29, 1996, UBMC sent Dr. Hardy notice of termination and later hired Dr. Thomas Allred in his place. [UBMC brought a suit for declaratory judgment to establish that its termination of the Agreement with Dr. Hardy was for "just cause," and Dr. Hardy counterclaimed for breach of contract. The trial court granted UBMC summary judgment, finding the Agreement unreasonable in duration based on Dr. Hardy's deposition testimony that he understood the agreement to be terminable only upon his death or incapacity, or the hospital's discontinuance of pathology services.]

Analysis

I. *Interpretation of the Just Cause Provision*

The key question in this case is what the "just cause" provision in the Agreement means. Once this question is answered, we may gauge . . . whether UBMC had just cause to terminate Dr. Hardy.

To interpret the "just cause" provision, the trial court relied primarily on extrinsic evidence, namely Dr. Hardy's deposition testimony regarding his understanding of the term. . . .

Although both parties here have ascribed different meanings to the "just cause" provision, we cannot conclude that the term is ambiguous. UBMC has taken the position that it has "just cause" to terminate Dr. Hardy's employment when the business exigencies of the hospital and the interests of the patients warrant a change in personnel. In contrast, Dr. Hardy testified in his post-remand affidavit that he understood the "just cause" provision to allow UBMC to terminate the Agreement only under specific circumstances:

> In essence, UBMC would have just cause to terminate my Agreement if I failed to perform or something substantial changed as to the need of UBMC for pathology services (e.g., hospital closure) which may be caused by financial concerns. Those financial concerns, however, could not include merely getting a lower price for the pathology services or histology lab supervision.

Hardy also asserts that he understood "just cause" to imply that

> [i]f UBMC perceived a need for changes in scope or manner of the provided pathology services, I expected them to approach me regarding such a need, and if jointly agreed upon, I would have adjusted accordingly. If I could not accommodate these changes, then UBMC would be free to terminate the Agreement.

Dr. Hardy's interpretation is ultimately untenable for two reasons. First, the evidence on record does not indicate that the parties understood the "just cause" provision to have a unique meaning particular to the Agreement, much less the detailed meaning understood by Dr. Hardy. The parties have stipulated that the Agreement is, for all practical purposes, identical to that of Dr. Hardy's predecessor, Dr. Joseph Sannella. The "just cause" termination provision was copied from the Sannella contract and included in the Agreement without any substantial negotiation. The parties did not incorporate other documents, such as the UBMC bylaws, to define when either party would have cause to terminate the Agreement. Thus, we must conclude that any particular meaning of "just cause" as understood or intended by Dr. Hardy is unique to himself and is, as he concedes in his brief, irrelevant to its interpretation.

Second, Dr. Hardy's interpretation of "just cause" is at odds with the ordinary meaning of the term. Unlike an at-will employment agreement, which allows an employer to discharge an employee for any, or no, reason, termination for just cause is widely understood to permit discharge only for "a fair and honest cause or reason, regulated by good faith . . . as opposed to one that is trivial, capricious, unrelated to business needs or goals, or pretextual." *Guz v. Bechtel Nat'l, Inc.*, 8 P.3d 1089,

1100 (Cal. 2000) This broad definition of just cause allows an employer to discharge an employee not only for misconduct or poor performance but also for other legitimate economic reasons.[4] Courts have recognized that "'[i]n deciding whether [just] cause exists, there must be a balance between the employer's interest in operating its business efficiently and profitably and the employee's interest in continued employment. . . . Care must be exercised so as not to interfere with the employer's legitimate exercise of managerial discretion.'" *Cotran v. Rollins Hudig Hall Int'l, Inc.*, 948 P.2d 412, 417 (Cal. 1998).

In sum, absent evidence that the parties intended a meaning of "just cause" unique to this particular agreement, we must conclude that the parties intended the term to have its ordinary meaning. Accordingly, we hold that the "just cause" provision is unambiguous and is ordinarily understood to provide employers with power to terminate an employee for legitimate business reasons and in the interest of improving client services as long as the justification is not a mere pretext for a capricious, bad faith, or illegal termination. . . .

III. UBMC's Just Cause to Terminate

The only remaining issue is whether the Board discharged Dr. Hardy for just cause. Because the trial court did not reach this issue in its summary judgment ruling, we remand for the trial court to determine whether the Board terminated Dr. Hardy for legitimate business reasons or whether the termination was capricious, in bad faith, or illegal.

However, we address here the question of what an employer must show to prove it terminated an employee for just cause, a matter of first impression for Utah courts. There appear to be three different approaches to this question. Some courts seem to give deference to the justifications stated by the employer. *See e.g., Gaudio v. Griffin Health Servs. Corp.*, 733 A.2d 197, 208 (Conn. 1999) ("[A]n employer who wishes to terminate an employee for cause must do nothing more rigorous than 'proffer a proper reason for dismissal.'"). A few other courts have taken the opposite approach and required the employer to prove that the conditions necessitating termination actually existed. *See, e.g., Toussaint v. Blue Cross & Blue Shield of Mich.*, 292 N.W.2d 880, 895 (Mich. 1980) ("[W]here an employer has agreed to discharge an employee for cause only, its declaration that the employee was discharged for unsatisfactory work is subject to judicial review. The jury as trier of fact decides whether the employee was, in fact, discharged for unsatisfactory work.").

A far greater number of states have adopted a more balanced approach that requires an employer to justify termination with an objective good faith reason supported by facts reasonably believed to be true by the employer. *See, e.g., Towson Univ. v. Conte*, 862 A.2d 941, 950-51, 954 (Md. App. 2004) ("[I]n the just cause employment context, a jury's role is to determine the objective reasonableness of the employer's decision to discharge, which means that the employer act in objective good

---

4. *See also Zoerb v. Chugach Elec. Ass'n*, 798 P.2d 1258, 1262-63 (Alaska 1990) ("A reduction in work force compelled by legitimate and sufficient business reasons may constitute 'good cause' to terminate an employee."); *Havill v. Woodstock Soapstone Co.*, 783 A.2d 423, 428 (Vt. 2001) ("Economic circumstances that necessitate employer layoffs constitute good cause for termination." (quotations, citation, and alteration omitted)).

faith and base its decision on a reasoned conclusion and facts reasonably believed to be true by the employer.") These courts recognize that an employer's justification for discharging an employee should not be taken at face value but also recognize that a judge or jury should not be called upon to second-guess an employer's business decisions.

We agree with the majority of courts and adopt the objective reasonableness approach. Accordingly, in order to establish just cause on remand, UBMC need not prove that the Board's assumptions in terminating Dr. Hardy were true or that the benefits it expected were actually realized. Rather, UBMC need only show that the Board acted in good faith by adequately considering the facts it reasonably believed to be true at the time it made the decision.

NOTES

1. *Cause in the Absence of a Contractual Definition.* UBMC deals with the problem of determining whether termination of a contractually protected employee was based on "cause" where the parties' agreement fails to define the term. In answering that question, a court has essentially two choices: Either it can apply a general definition or standard of cause, or it can try to ascertain the parties' intended definition of cause in the particular agreement. In *UBMC*, the court opts for the former approach, concluding that "cause" is an unambiguous term subject to a generally understood meaning.

The choice of approach, however, will vary depending on the court, the contract, and the circumstances. In *Joy v. Hay Group, Inc.*, 403 F.3d 875 (7th Cir. 2005), a case arising under Illinois law, Joy was hired as an executive compensation consultant under a contract providing for one year's salary in the event of termination "for reasons other than cause." She was subsequently fired for failing to meet her billing quota and denied severance. In her suit for breach of contract, Joy argued that upon receiving the contract she asked what cause meant and was told it meant "serious wrongdoing." The employer asserted that cause unambiguously meant unsatisfactory performance in the opinion of the employer. In an opinion by Judge Posner, the court reversed summary judgment for the employer, permitting Joy to present her understanding of the agreement to a jury:

> [T]here may be a difference between "cause" for discharge and "cause" for denial of severance pay. Business firms almost always reserve the right to fire an employee . . . if the firm decides that the employee's performance is unsatisfactory. But it is precisely because of the insecurity of such employment — the determination that Joy's performance was unsatisfactory was based on a criterion selected by the firm after she went to work for it, rather than being specified in her employment contract — that employment contracts often provide for severance pay. Joy was leaving a good job to go to work for HGI and in doing so may have been taking a risk . . . especially since she was going to be working in what was a new line of business for HGI. If she lost her job she would need money to tide her over while she looked for a new job. Hence the severance-pay provision in her employment contract with HGI.

Id. at 877. Do you agree with Posner's distinction between severance and termination? Does it help explain the approach taken by the court in *UBMC*? Are there other factual differences that might justify the decision to treat "cause" as having a generally understood meaning in *UBMC* but permit the plaintiff to demonstrate a unique meaning in *Joy*?

2. *Cause Not Attributable to Performance.* If there is a generally understood definition of cause, as *UBMC* suggests, what does it encompass? In *UBMC*, the employer offered an economic reason for its decision to terminate Dr. Hardy: By hiring a replacement, it could obtain pathology services more cost-effectively. In finding in favor of the employer, the court asserts that a business reason of this sort fits within the "widely understood" meaning of cause, despite the fact that it is unrelated to the employee's performance. Does this statement of the legal definition of cause surprise you? Is it consistent with your own understanding of what constitutes just cause for termination?

Collective bargaining agreements almost always distinguish between terminations (which can only be for just cause related to performance) and "layoffs," which can be for economic reasons and are usually done on the basis of seniority — last in, first out. *See* Roger I. Abrams & Dennis R. Nolan, *Toward a Theory of "Just Cause" in Employee Discipline Cases*, 1985 DUKE L.J. 594-95 ("Virtually every collective bargaining agreement contains [limitations on employer's power to discipline or discharge workers] by far the most common of which is the requirement that there be 'just cause' for discipline. This requirement is so well accepted that often it is found to be implicit in the collective agreement, even when there is no stated limitation on the employer's power to discipline."). A similar distinction exists in both academic tenure and civil service. In the latter situation, the source of just cause protection is frequently statutory rather than contractual, but the focus is on the conduct of the particular employee, and economic concerns are addressed under a different rubric. *See, e.g., Yoder v. Town of Middleton*, 876 A.2d 216, 218 (N.H. 2005) (cause for removal of police chief pursuant to state statute requires demonstration of unfitness or incapacity to perform job duties).

In cases like those we have been studying involving individual private sector employment contracts, whether economic bases for termination constitute cause is a question that often turns on the form and context of the parties' agreement. Consistent with *UMBC*, courts generally interpret cause as encompassing legitimate, non-performance-based reasons for termination in indefinite just-cause contracts like Dr. Hardy's, that is, contracts promising protection against arbitrary dismissal but guaranteeing no particular term of employment. On the other hand, under a contract providing for a fixed term of employment, courts usually treat cause as meaning a reason for termination related to the employee's conduct or performance. The RESTATEMENT (THIRD) OF EMPLOYMENT, (Proposed Final Draft, April 18, 2014), captures this by defining cause for termination of agreements "for a definite term" to require "misconduct, malfeasance, or other material breach" § 2.04(a), while adding an additional basis where the contract is for an indefinite term. In that situation, "cause" also includes "a significant change in the employer's economic circumstances [such that] the employer no longer has a business need" for the employee's services.

3. *Termination Based on Poor Results.* Once it is clear that an employee's contract requires a performance-based reason for termination (either by its express terms or as interpreted by a court), the question remains how serious the employee's performance problems must be to constitute cause. Must the employee engage in intentional misconduct, or is there sufficient cause when an employee performs in good faith but achieves poor results? The answer often turns on the specific facts of the case, including the circumstances of hire, performance expectations of the parties, and, of course, the terms of the contract. *See, e.g., Chard v. Iowa Machinery & Supply Co.*, 446 N.W.2d 81 (Iowa Ct. App. 1989) (finding vice president entitled to severance under "no cause" provision of contract where plaintiff was hired to turn around lagging division over the long term and was fired after only two months on the job, during which time state legislature was debating economic recovery legislation that had chilling effect on sales market); *Cole v. Valley Ice Garden, L.L.C.*, 113 P.3d 275, 280 (Mont. 2005) (firing ice hockey coach based on team's poor win-loss record constituted termination for cause despite his good faith efforts and the fact that contract did not contain performance goals).

4. *Actual Cause vs. Reasonable Decision Making.* A related factual question is whether the grounds asserted by the employer in support of termination are true. What happens, for instance, if an employer terminates a worker for embezzlement — something that everyone would agree constitutes cause — but the employer was mistaken about the employee's culpability? As previously discussed, courts generally agree that the employer bears the burden of proof where cause is disputed, at least with respect to express contracts, but they disagree about what exactly the employer needs to prove. The last part of *UMBC* describes a number of approaches that courts take, ranging from significant deference to the employer's proffered reason to requiring the employer to establish that cause in fact existed. Which approach discussed in *UBMC* makes the most sense as a policy matter? Consider the following rationale for applying a reasonable good faith test like that adopted in *UBMC*:

> The decision to terminate an employee for misconduct is one that not uncommonly implicates organizational judgment and may turn on intractable factual uncertainties, even where the grounds for dismissal are fact specific. If an employer is required to have in hand a signed confession or an eyewitness account of the alleged misconduct before it can act, the workplace will be transformed into an adjudicatory arena and effective decisionmaking will be thwarted. Although these features do not justify a rule permitting employees to be dismissed arbitrarily, they do mean that asking a civil jury to reexamine in all its factual detail the triggering cause of the decision to dismiss — including the retrospective accuracy of the employer's comprehension of that event — months or even years later, in a context distant from the imperatives of the workplace, is at odds with an axiom underlying the jurisprudence of wrongful termination. That axiom . . . is the need for a sensible latitude for managerial decisionmaking and its corollary, an optimum balance point between the employer's interest in organizational efficiency and the employee's interest in continuing employment.

Cotran v. Rollins Hudig Hall Int'l, Inc., 948 P.2d 412, 421 (Cal. 1998). From a management perspective, this is certainly understandable, but doesn't it amount to allowing some employers to get away with breach? After all, if there really was no cause, there was no contractually legitimate basis for the termination. In contrast, consider a typical commercial contract involving a sale of goods. Clearly a buyer could not reject a shipment under contract merely because he or she reasonably and in good faith, but mistakenly, thought the goods were defective. Is there a reason why a lower standard should govern employment?

One consideration may be the type of contract involved. *Cotran* was based on an implied just cause agreement rather than a written job security contract. Should the source of protection, express versus implied agreement, matter at all? *See Towson*

Univ. v. Conte, 862 A.2d 941 (Md. App. 2004) (no difference); *Khajavi v. Feather River Anesthesia Med. Group*, 100 Cal. Rptr. 2d 627 (Ct. App. 2000) (holding that, unlike wrongful discharge based on an implied contract, employment for a specified term may not be terminated prior to the term's expiration based upon employer's honest but mistaken belief of misconduct).

5. *Procedural Aspects of Just Cause.* In *UBMC*, Dr. Hardy argued not only that there was no cause for termination but also that the employer should have consulted with him first about its desire to reduce costs. Some courts incorporate a procedural component in the obligation to dismiss only for cause. *See Nadeau v. Imtec, Inc.*, 670 A.2d 841, 844 (Vt. 1995) ("To be upheld, a discharge for just cause must meet two criteria: first, that the employee's conduct was egregious enough that the discharge was reasonable, and second, that the employee had fair notice, express or implied, that such conduct could result in discharge."); *Cotran*, 948 P.2d at 422 (Good cause means "fair and honest reasons . . . supported by substantial evidence gathered through an adequate investigation that includes notice of the claimed misconduct and a chance for the employee to respond."). *But see New England Stone v. Conte*, 962 A.2d 30, 33 (R.I. 2009) (declining to impose any "due-process mandates" on the employer where a contract enumerated grounds for cause and provided "that cause 'shall be determined by the [c]ompany in good faith'"). Why should procedure matter, at least if the employer can ultimately prove cause? If a procedural component exists and is breached, what should the remedy be? What could a court award Dr. Hardy if his contract required the hospital to consult with him about costs?

6. *It Isn't Over 'Til It's Over.* Dr. Hardy lost this round of the litigation but subsequently defeated UBMC's motion for summary judgment on the issue of cause. On remand, UBMC filed for summary judgment arguing that there was no material factual issue in dispute as to the reason for termination, asserting various business-related reasons for replacing Dr. Hardy with Dr. Allred. The trial court granted the motion, but the Utah Supreme Court reversed, finding that the facts, read in the light most favorable to Dr. Hardy, could support the conclusion that the reasons proffered by UBMC were pretextual. *See UBMC v. Hardy (UBMC II)*, 179 P.3d 786 (Utah 2008). It explained:

> First, UBMC did not give Dr. Hardy any contemporaneous reason for the termination of his Agreement. UBMC simply thanked Dr. Hardy for his service and told him that he had been replaced. And UBMC's administrator, Brad LeBaron, admitted in his deposition that he told Dr. Hardy after the termination that he would need to look and see what kind of potential issues could be raised to defend UBMC's decision. In addition, even though UBMC now relies on its desire for an on-site pathologist as a justification for the termination decision, this desire was never expressed to Dr. Hardy before his Agreement was terminated, and Dr. Hardy was given no opportunity to cure or address any demonstrated need or desire of UBMC for an on-site pathologist. Indeed, UBMC undertook no investigation into the actual need or the financial impact of hiring an on-site pathologist before it terminated Dr. Hardy's Agreement. This lack of investigation before the termination suggests that UBMC's stated need for an on-site pathologist was merely pretextual. The facts also establish that UBMC failed to conduct a comprehensive investigation of Dr. Allred prior to hiring him. . . . Finally, UBMC did not terminate Dr. Hardy for poor performance, misconduct, breach of the Agreement, or failure to fulfill his obligations.

Id. at 790-91. Does this victory for the employee surprise you given the very deferential standard adopted by the court in *UBMC I*? Does it give you insight into the advantages of the litigation strategies that parties often pursue in termination cases? The result perhaps explains why employers often vehemently dispute the existence of contractual job security protection even when they have a plausible reason for terminating.

PROBLEM

3-3. Bonnie Blackwell was hired by the board of directors of a television merchandising company for the position of general manager. During Blackwell's employment there was significant conflict on the board of directors, involving accusations by the chair of the board and company president that two other board members were improperly documenting withdrawals of company funds. The Chair on several occasions asked Blackwell informally to look into this problem. Blackwell, reluctant to get involved in an internal matter between board members, repeatedly resisted this request explaining that it was outside her authority. One year into her employment, Blackwell submitted a request for a two-week unpaid leave of absence for health reasons, a benefit available to all employees per company policy. Upon receiving the request, the president called Blackwell to his office and informed her that it was "a very bad time to plan a vacation." He cited the recent loss of a cable affiliate and an upcoming meeting with a possible new affiliate and stated that it was a "critical time" for the company. Blackwell responded that her request was not for vacation and that the meeting could be handled by her subordinates. Blackwell did not appear at work for the next two weeks, although she conferenced into the meeting with the potential affiliate by telephone. When she returned to work, she was terminated, effective immediately, and given no severance pay. During her one year of employment, Blackwell received only one performance evaluation, which was positive, and the company met all of its sales and budgetary goals under her leadership.

Assess whether Blackwell has any claim against the company under each of the following scenarios:

A. Blackwell's contract provides: "This agreement shall run for two years from the date of hire unless terminated earlier on the basis of just cause. Just cause means gross misconduct, dishonesty, commission of a crime, or other conduct that seriously jeopardizes the company."

B. Blackwell's contract provides: "This agreement shall run for two years from the date of hire. In the event that the company terminates Blackwell prior to that date, Blackwell shall receive her full salary for the remainder of the contract term."

C. Blackwell's contract provides: "This agreement can only be terminated on the basis of just cause and upon one month's notice."

See generally Video Catalog Channel v. Blackwelder, No. 03A01-9705-CH-00155, 1997 Tenn. App. LEXIS 636 (Tenn. Ct. App. Sept. 19, 1997).

B. COMPENSATION TERMS

Job security and cause for discharge are not the only contractual issues fueling litigation in sophisticated employment relationships. The main reason job security is important to workers, after all, is that it ensures a steady flow of income. For high-level employees especially, compensation can mean much more than base wages. You have already seen that written contracts frequently promise exit pay or other separation benefits upon termination. High-level employees are often paid during the course of their relationship pursuant to complex compensation schemes that include incentive pay.

"Incentive pay" generally refers to compensation that is tied to performance, such as bonuses, stock options, profit sharing or other arrangements under which the amount of compensation varies depending on the success of the employee or the company as a whole. Where compensation structures are properly aligned with performance indicators and the health and success of the firm, they can be extremely beneficial to both parties. From the perspective of the employer, such arrangements not only encourage superior performance, they help retain good workers who might otherwise defect to competitors (the so-called golden handcuffs effect). For employees, incentive pay arrangements offer a degree of control over their earning capacity and create the potential for high payoffs. Indeed, for some employees, incentive pay greatly exceeds their base salary.

However, many believe that this is not the way incentive compensation works in practice. A wide body of literature has criticized the current system for rewarding executives for moderate or even poor firm performance. *See generally* Lucian Arye Bebchuk et al., *Managerial Power and Rent Extraction in the Design of Executive Compensation*, 69 U. CHI. L. REV. 751, 761-83 (2002) (describing and critiquing the "optimal contract approach" to executive compensation). It suggests that outsize pay packages result not from legitimate market forces but rather from cozy relationships between corporate managers and directors, and arrangements that encourage executives to place short-term management interests ahead of larger corporate goals. Professors Lucian Bebchuk and Jesse Fried explain some of these concerns:

> According to the "official" view of executive compensation, corporate boards setting pay arrangements are guided solely by shareholder interests and operate at arm's-length from the executives whose pay they set. [This] view serves as the practical basis for legal rules and public policy. . . .
>
> The official arm's-length story is neat, tractable, and reassuring. But it fails to account for the realities of executive compensation. . . .
>
> Directors have had and continue to have various economic incentives to support, or at least go along with, arrangements that favor the company's top executives. A variety of social and psychological factors — collegiality, team spirit, a natural desire to avoid conflict within the board, friendship and loyalty, and cognitive dissonance — exert additional pull in that direction. Although many directors own some stock in their companies, their ownership positions are too small to give them a financial incentive to take the personally costly, or at the very least unpleasant, route of resisting compensation arrangements sought by executives. In addition, limitations on time and resources have made it difficult for even well-intentioned directors to do their pay-setting job properly. Finally, the market constraints within which directors operate are far from tight and do not prevent deviations from arm's-length contracting outcomes in favor of executives. . . .

The same factors that limit the usefulness of the arm's-length model in explaining executive compensation suggest that executives have had substantial influence over their own pay. Compensation arrangements have often deviated from arm's-length contracting because directors have been influenced by management, insufficiently motivated to insist on shareholder-serving compensation, or simply ineffectual. Executives' influence over directors has enabled them to obtain "rents," benefits greater than those obtainable under true arm's-length contracting.

Pay Without Performance: Overview of the Issues, 30 J. Corp. L. 647, 653-59 (2005). The debate continues both in the law reviews and the mainstream media, often these days in terms of the corrosive effects of income inequality on the social fabric. *See, e.g.,* Paul Krugman, *Iron Men of Wall Street,* NY Times, Feb. 16, 2014.

It is important to remember, however, that not all recipients of incentive compensation are high-level executives able to secure lucrative pay packages and other favorable terms of employment. Many sales workers, for instance, are compensated primarily through commissions, a structure that can create hardships for workers struggling to generate revenue in difficult economic times. In addition, incentive compensation is often deferred, meaning that under the employer's policy a worker may not realize payment until a future date, possibly after the entitlement has "accrued." We have seen that high-level employees generally negotiate contractual protection against termination. For mainstream workers, however, the employer's unfettered ability to terminate can jeopardize the realization of incentive compensation. Thus the interplay between employment at will and contractual bonus and commission schemes is important in evaluating employee compensation rights.

For all of these reasons, alleged failures to pay earned compensation are a common source of employment litigation. These disputes raise issues similar to those that arise with respect to job security or any other contractual term of employment, such as whether the employer's promise is binding and whether it has been breached.

≡≡≡ ### Hess v. Kanoski & Assocs.
≡≡≡ *668 F.3d 446 (7th Cir. 2012)*

Wood, Circuit Judge.

This case involves a spat over attorneys' fees — in particular, the fees that the firm of Kanoski & Associates allegedly owes to its former associate, Lawrence Hess. After some five years at the firm, Hess was abruptly dismissed. Afterwards, the firm settled several of the cases on which Hess had been working and refused to pay Hess bonuses or fees based on those settlements. Hess believes that he is entitled to some of that money. . . .

I

Kanoski & Associates bills itself as the "largest personal injury law firm in central Illinois." Kanoski & Associates, http://www.kanoski.com/ (last visited Jan. 30, 2012). The firm hired Hess on May 9, 2001, to work primarily on medical malpractice cases. His employment was governed by an agreement that set out his salary and bonus pay. At first Hess apparently performed well for the firm and obtained several favorable settlements. But by 2007, things had gone south; on February 14 of that year, Ronald

Kanoski [the firm's president] fired Hess. In the wake of that action, the firm transferred several of Hess's cases to Kennith Blan, Jr., a lawyer working as an independent contractor for the firm. Over the course of the next year and a half, the firm — largely through Blan's efforts — settled many of these cases. For example, in June 2008, one case settled for $1.25 million.

Hess believed that Blan and the firm had pushed him out in order to settle his cases without sharing with him the generous compensation that accompanied the settlements. . . .

At its essence, this case boils down to a single question of contract interpretation: Was Hess entitled under his employment agreement to compensation arising out of any of the post-termination settlements? . . .

II

A

We begin with the two counts in Hess's complaint that rest most directly on his employment agreement: Count I, the claim under the [Illinois Wage Payment and Collection Act]; and Count IV, the claim for breach of contract. . . .

To succeed on his breach of contract claim, Hess must show "(1) the existence of a valid and enforceable contract; (2) performance by the plaintiff; (3) breach of contract by the defendant; and (4) resultant injury to the plaintiff." *Henderson-Smith & Assocs. v. Nahamani Family Serv. Ctr..*, 752 N.E.2d 33, 43 (Ill. App. Ct. 2001). To prevail on his IWPCA claim, Hess must first show that he had a valid contract or employment agreement. Illinois courts have explained that an agreement under the IWPCA is "broader than a contract." *Zabinsky v. Gelber Group, Inc.*, 807 N.E.2d 666, 671 (Ill. App. Ct. 2004) (the IWPCA "requires only a manifestation of mutual assent on the part of two or more persons; parties may enter into an 'agreement' without the formalities and accompanying legal protections of a contract"). The IWPCA requires an employer to pay an employee any final compensation due under that contract or agreement at the time of separation; it defines final compensation to include "wages, salaries, earned commissions, earned bonuses, . . . and any other compensation owed by the employer pursuant to an employment contract or agreement between the two parties." 820 ILCS 115/2 (2006).

The parties do not dispute that Hess had a valid contract with the firm (his "employment agreement," not to be confused with "agreement" as it is used by the IWPCA) and that, until his termination, he adequately performed as an employee under that contract. The dispute is solely over whether Hess's employment agreement entitled him to bonuses on settlements that were collected after he left the firm. The employment agreement originally provided that Hess would receive "15% of all fees generated over the base salary (or $5,000 per month) with a guarantee of One Hundred and Twenty Five Thousand ($125,000). Bonus shall increase to 25% of all fees received annually in excess of $750,000.00." The firm later modified Hess's compensation on June 21, 2002, increasing his base salary and changing the bonus structure to "40% of all fee revenue generated" (with some exceptions). (While the district court was apparently unsure whether the agreement included the terms found in a June 21 letter from the firm to Hess that Hess had never signed, we see no reason not to include that material. The critical signature is that of the party against whom the contract is being enforced, and that signature was present.)

No court has ever resolved the question whether this contract requires the firm to pay Hess bonuses from post-termination settlements. The language of the contract is not clear because the contract does not define when fees are "generated." Fees might be "generated" when work is performed on a case, because the work ultimately leads to the settlement. This does not seem odd if one considers the scenario in which an attorney works on a case until it is nearly ready for settlement, is fired, and then the next day the firm accepts a settlement without her. If, on the other hand, fees are "generated" only when received by the firm, Hess would not be entitled to the post-termination settlement earnings.

Under Illinois law, undefined terms are generally given their "plain, ordinary, and popular meaning" as found in dictionary definitions. *Outboard Marine Corp. v. Liberty Mut. Ins. Co.*, 607 N.E.2d 1204, 1215 (Ill. 1993). Resort to dictionary definitions often, however, does not settle the question; that is the case here. The infinitive "to generate" means (among other things) "to bring into existence" or "to be the cause of." Merriam-Webster Dictionary Online, http://www.merriam-webster.com/ dictionary/ generated (last visited Jan. 30, 2012); *see also* Oxford English Dictionary Online, http://www.oed.com/ viewdictionaryentry/Entry/77518 (defining "generated" as "[p]roduced, created; caused") (last visited Jan. 30, 2012). Work performed before a settlement is obtained in some sense produces or brings that settlement into existence. On the other hand, it is possible that the parties intended "generated" to be limited to the final act of bringing a fee into existence, i.e., actually obtaining the cash in hand. Where language in a contract appears to be "susceptible to more than one meaning," Illinois courts will "consider extrinsic evidence to determine the parties' intent." *Thompson v. Gordon*, 948 N.E.2d 39, 47 (Ill. 2011).

Even if the district court concludes that Hess's interpretation is too broad and thus the contract does not entitle Hess to bonuses on *all* of the post-termination settlements, Hess has a good argument that he is entitled at least to the fees related to settlements obtained within the 30-day period after he was fired. The contract required the firm to give Hess 30 days' notice before it ended his employment, but it did not do so. A 30-day provision is consistent with an at-will contract, *H. Vincent Allen & Associates, Inc. v. Weis*, 379 N.E.2d 765, 771-72 (Ill. App. Ct. 1978), but breach of the 30-day provision requires the firm to pay Hess whatever compensation he was due during that time. *See, e.g., Equity Ins. Managers of Ill., LLC v. McNichols*, 755 N.E.2d 75, 81 (Ill. App. Ct. 2001). At least one of the settlements Hess has identified — the Hoelscher settlement — was obtained within that 30-day period. He is entitled to press his argument that the contract gave him the right to bonuses in connection with that settlement, no matter what the parties meant by the term "generated." . . .

[The court remanded for the district court "to interpret the contract and consider the merits of Hess's theories under Counts I and IV."]

Weiss v. DHL Express, Inc.
718 F.3d 39 (1st Cir. 2013)

HOWARD, Circuit Judge.

Jeremy Weiss was a rising star at DHL Express, Inc. ("DHL") until his termination in September 2009, ostensibly for his failure to properly investigate, document, and ameliorate the misconduct of an employee under his supervision. The termination occurred just months before Weiss was to receive a $60,000 bonus. Weiss filed suit in Massachusetts state court to recover the bonus on the grounds that he was terminated without good cause, which under the terms of the bonus plan entitled him to a full payout. He asserted breach of the implied covenant of good faith and fair dealing, detrimental reliance, unjust enrichment, and violation of the Massachusetts Wage Act. DHL removed the case to federal court on diversity grounds. The court allowed a single cause of action to go to the jury—a "straightforward" breach-of-contract claim. The jury found for Weiss. DHL's main claim on appeal is that the court erroneously allowed the jury to independently determine whether good cause existed for Weiss's termination because the bonus plan reserved this determination for a committee of the company. In his cross-appeal, Weiss challenges the grant of summary judgment to DHL on his Wage Act claim and the denial of his attorney's fees. We reverse the jury verdict and affirm the summary judgment order.

I.

The relevant facts are undisputed. In 2004, DHL, an international express mail services company, acquired Airborne Express, a package delivery company operating in the United States. Weiss, who had been employed at Airborne Express since 1996, continued his employment at DHL as District Sales Manager for downtown Boston. He was promoted within a year to the post of Regional Sales Director in charge of overseeing a number of sales districts in the Northeast, including Brooklyn, New York. The following year, DHL named him "Regional Sales Director of the Year." Weiss was then elevated to the position of Director of National Accounts in August 2007. He remained in that position until his termination two years later.

A. *The Bonus Plan*

In December 2007, DHL informed Weiss that it had selected him to participate in the company's "Commitment to Success Bonus Plan" (the "Plan"). Under the Plan, Weiss became eligible for a $60,000 service-based bonus if he remained with the company through the end of 2009, and a $20,000 bonus if DHL met its performance objectives in 2009. The Employment Benefits Committee (the "Committee") of the company was given broad authority to administer the Plan:

> The Committee shall have full power and discretionary authority to interpret the Plan, make factual determinations, and to prescribe, amend and rescind any rules . . . and to make any other determinations and take such other actions as the Committee deems necessary or advisable in carrying out its duties under the Plan. Any action required of the Committee under the Plan shall be made in the Committee's sole discretion and not in a fiduciary capacity and need not be uniform as to similarly situated individuals. The Committee's administration of the Plan, including all such rules and regulations, interpretations, selections, determinations, approvals, decisions, delegations, amendments, terminations and other actions, shall be final, conclusive and binding on the Company, the Participant, and any other persons having or claiming an interest hereunder.

> The Committee could delegate its functions to a subcommittee or to one or more individuals. It also reserved the right to amend or terminate the Plan.

In October 2008, Weiss received notice that "some adjustments to the Plan" were made "in order to better reflect our changing work environment." Under the amended Plan, Weiss was still eligible to receive $80,000, but no portion of it was tied to the company's performance. Instead, the entire bonus was now contingent on continued employment through the end of 2009, with Weiss's performance remaining "in good standing." The first installation of $20,000 was payable in January 2009 and the remaining $60,000 in January 2010. In the event that DHL terminated him "without cause" and eliminated his position, Weiss would receive the full payout upon termination. If he voluntarily left DHL or if terminated for "good cause" prior to the payment dates, he would be ineligible for the bonus.

DHL paid Weiss the first installment of the bonus in January 2009. When he was terminated in September 2009, DHL refused to pay the remaining $60,000 on the basis that his termination was for good cause.

B. *The Termination*

In 2007, while Weiss was still Regional Sales Director, DHL shifted the Brooklyn district to another Regional Sales Director, Christopher Cadigan. Following the organizational change, Cadigan informed Weiss that Sergio Garcia, a sales representative in Brooklyn, had incorrectly set up rates on a customer account. Weiss and Cadigan discussed the billing issue with their boss, Vice President of Sales David Katz, and Garcia's supervisor, District Sales Manager Michael Gargiles. They agreed that Cadigan would work with Garcia to fix the issue. Although he no longer had oversight over Garcia, Weiss was in the Brooklyn area on other business and offered to speak to him.

At that meeting, which Gargiles also attended, Weiss warned Garcia that his conduct could result in disciplinary action, including termination. He also instructed Garcia to work with the pricing team to correct the billing issue. Weiss followed up with Katz and Cadigan, informing them of his warning to Garcia. Although the company handbook for managers provided that verbal warnings must be documented, Weiss was unaware of the policy. Neither he nor Gargiles documented the warning to Garcia, nor did they inform the human resources department of the warning.

Several months later, Cadigan received a customer complaint regarding one of its competitors receiving "shockingly low" DHL rates. Cadigan conducted an investigation and found that several sales representatives in Brooklyn had extended unauthorized rates to certain customers by circumventing company procedures. He reported this to Vice President of Sales Jonathan Routledge (apparently Katz's successor). Routledge and Cadigan interviewed a group of six representatives, including Garcia, about using so-called "rogue" rates. Three representatives resigned rather than face disciplinary action. As there was no concrete evidence linking Garcia to the dishonest activities, he only received a three-day suspension (which the human resources department apparently rescinded as unauthorized) and then was transferred to the sales district in Long Island. Weiss, who at this time was Director of National Accounts, was involved neither in Cadigan's investigation nor in the decision to discipline Garcia.

The unauthorized practice of selling "rogue" rates continued in the New York area. In October 2008, the company's loss prevention department launched an investigation into the matter and discovered that the scheme had resulted in a multimillion-dollar loss to DHL in 2008 alone. During the course of the investigation, Fraud Manager Scott Kamlet interviewed Cadigan and Routledge and learned about their 2007 investigation of the very same issue. He then gathered information implicating Garcia in the unauthorized practice and attempted to interview him. After Garcia refused to cooperate, Kamlet recommended that he be terminated. In his recommendation, Kamlet stated that Garcia had received a verbal warning from Weiss in 2007 for similar unauthorized actions and that it was Kamlet's belief that Garcia's supervisors did not know the extent of Garcia's misconduct at the time of this warning.

Kamlet's recommendation apparently was not enough for Garcia to lose his job. In April 2009, Weiss received a customer complaint alleging that Garcia was asking customers to pay kickbacks in exchange for receiving preferential shipping rates. The customer threatened to go public with the information. Weiss immediately forwarded the complaint to his superiors. A few days later, Garcia resigned.

DHL responded to the allegation by retaining attorney Kenneth Thompson to conduct an investigation. In addition to confirming the kickbacks allegation, Thompson also found that Garcia and several other representatives in Brooklyn had engaged in various improper sales practices during the preceding years, including while Weiss was in charge of the district. Specifically, Thompson reported that the billing issue that precipitated Weiss's verbal warning to Garcia involved an unauthorized shipping rate extension. Thompson informed DHL of Weiss's "management failures" relating to his oversight of Garcia, including his failure to properly discipline Garcia in 2007, to document the 2007 verbal warning, to consult the human resources and security departments about the verbal warning, and to further investigate Garcia's conduct to determine of the scope of the misconduct.

At the conclusion of the investigation, Michael Berger, Weiss's supervisor at the time, informed Weiss that DHL was terminating his employment. The termination letter stated that Weiss was terminated for "just cause" because the results of the Thompson investigation "present[ed] a picture of significant management failures" while Weiss was Regional Sales Director in charge of the Brooklyn district "and thereafter." Berger was unaware of those failures until the Thompson investigation. When Weiss asked who made the decision to fire him, Berger told him, "it's above me."

Upon termination, Weiss did not receive the $60,000 bonus that he was set to receive in four months. DHL's General Counsel John Olin, who was the head of the Committee in charge of administering the Plan, testified that this was because Weiss was terminated for "good cause," which under the terms of the Plan made him ineligible for the bonus.

C. The Court Proceedings

Weiss sued DHL over the unpaid bonus, alleging that he was entitled to payment because his termination was without good cause. He asserted four claims for relief: (1) non-payment of wages in violation of the Massachusetts Wage Act, *see* Mass. Gen. Laws ch. 149, § 148; (2) violation of the implied covenant of good faith and fair dealing; (3) detrimental reliance; and (4) unjust enrichment. The district court granted DHL's motion for summary judgment on the Wage Act claim, ruling that the bonus was not "wages" within the meaning of the Act.

After Weiss presented his evidence at trial, the court announced that only a "straightforward" breach-of-contract claim would go to the jury. The court then directed a verdict in favor of DHL on the remaining claims. Weiss did not object to the recasting of his contract claim or the directed verdict, and he does not challenge either that action or the directed verdict on appeal.

The court instructed the jury that the key issue was whether Weiss was terminated without "good cause" because, if so, DHL breached the Plan by not paying him the bonus. DHL objected on the ground that the Plan reserved the good cause determination for the Committee. The court acknowledged that the Plan "has the language in it" reserving for the Committee decisions "about performance and the like." But because the Plan uses the words "good cause," the court explained, it was for the jury to decide whether the termination was without good cause, regardless of the Committee's nomenclature. So instructed, the jury found for Weiss. After the court denied DHL's motion for judgment as a matter of law without comment, DHL filed this timely appeal.

II.

A. The Breach-of-Contract Claim

DHL maintains that the Plan gives the Committee the sole and exclusive authority to determine whether good cause existed for a participant's termination, and that in this instance the Committee so determined. Accordingly, DHL argues, it is entitled to judgment as a matter of law because there could be no breach of contract under the undisputed facts. Weiss retorts that it was for the jury to decide whether Weiss's termination was for good cause because the Plan is ambiguous as to whether the Committee retained such authority. . . .

We begin by reviewing long-standing principles of contract law Interpretation of a contract is ordinarily a question of law for the court. *Seaco Ins. Co. v. Barbosa*, 761 N.E.2d 946, 951 (Mass. 2002). "[W]hen several writings evidence a single contract or comprise constituent parts of a single transaction, they will be read together." *FDIC v. Singh*, 977 F.2d 18, 21 (1st Cir. 1992). Absent an ambiguity, the court interprets a contract "according to its plain terms," *Den Norske Bank AS v. First Nat'l Bank of Bos.*, 75 F.3d 49, 52 (1st Cir. 1996), in a manner that gives reasonable effect to each of its provisions, *J.A. Sullivan Corp. v. Commonwealth*, 494 N.E.2d 374, 378 (Mass. 1986).

"A contract is not ambiguous simply because litigants disagree about its proper interpretation." *Singh.* Ambiguity arises only if the language "is susceptible of more than one meaning and reasonably intelligent persons would differ as to which meaning is the proper one." *S. Union Co. v. Dep't of Pub. Utils.*, 941 N.E.2d 633, 640 (Mass. 2011) (internal quotation marks omitted). There is no ambiguity in the instant contract.

The plain language of the Plan designates the Committee as the sole arbiter of whether a Plan participant is terminated for good cause. The original Plan document makes clear that it is for the Committee to determine bonus eligibility and to construe the Plan's terms. The Plan specifies that the Committee "shall have full power and discretionary authority" to make determinations under the Plan and that its decisions regarding "rules and regulations, interpretations, selections, determinations, approvals, decisions, delegations, amendments, terminations and other actions, shall be final, conclusive and binding." In short, as the Plan administrator, the Committee was given broad discretionary authority to determine all matters pertaining to the Plan, including whether a participant qualified for payment.

The amendment to the Plan neither trumps the Committee's sweeping authority nor creates an ambiguity in this regard. By its express terms, the amendment only made "some adjustments" to the Plan, namely to provide that the bonus was no longer tied to the company's performance but only to continued service and to permit a participant terminated without good cause to receive the payout. The amendment did not purport to modify the Committee's role in any way . . . Interpreting the original Plan document and the amendment as a single agreement, as we must, it becomes plain that the contract is susceptible only to one plausible construction: whether Weiss was terminated without good cause and thus remained eligible for the bonus was a decision within the ambit of the Committee's sole and final decision-making authority.

Weiss argues that the Plan is ambiguous because the amendment provides for the good cause determination but is silent about who decides, whereas the original Plan document addresses the Committee's decision-making authority but not the good cause protection. According to Weiss, this "tension" between the two documents could plausibly suggest that the employer and not the Committee is to determine whether a participant is terminated for good cause, in which case the jury could review the employer's decision. We disagree. The provision designating the Committee as the sole and final authority on decisions of this type is broad enough to encompass the good cause determination. And nothing in the amendment suggests that someone other than the Committee would make such decisions. Hence, the two documents are not incongruous. The only plausible construction of the Plan as a whole that gives reasonable effect to the provisions in both writings is that the Committee's decision-making authority extends to this eligibility determination.

Simply put, under the Plan, the Committee was free to deny Weiss the bonus if, in its sole judgment, his employment was terminated for good cause. *Cf. Nolan v. CN8*, 656 F.3d 71, 82 (1st Cir. 2011) (Selya, J., concurring) (where the employment agreement designated the employer as "the sole arbiter of whether the plaintiff's actions reflected unfavorably on [the employer's] interests or reputation (and, thus, warranted termination)," the plaintiff's contractual right to continued employment was extinguished when the employer exercised its prerogative). Neither we nor the district court can rewrite the contract to take away the Committee's discretion and empower the jury to decide whether Weiss was terminated for good cause.

The only relevant question regarding Weiss's breach-of-contract claim, then, is whether the Committee determined that Weiss was terminated for good cause. There is no room to doubt that it did so. Olin, the head of the Committee, testified unrebutted that, as permitted under the Plan, the Committee delegated to DHL's management its authority to determine whether good cause existed for a Plan participant's termination. DHL's executives testified, again unrebutted, that they decided to terminate Weiss because of his management failures in overseeing Garcia.

That effectively ends the matter. The Committee's determination that Weiss was terminated for good cause made him ineligible for the bonus, precluding his breach-of-contract claim. Accordingly, we reverse the judgment against DHL.

This outcome is not unfair, as Weiss urges. Weiss was a handsomely compensated employee in a significant position at DHL. He accepted the terms of the Plan that gave the Committee unfettered discretion in matters such as the eligibility decision at issue here. The preclusion of his breach-of-contract claim, moreover, does not mean that Weiss had no recourse but to bow his head and accept the Committee's decision. As Weiss recognized early in the game, Massachusetts law implies in every contract a covenant of good faith and fair dealing. *Ayash v. Dana-Farber Cancer Inst.*, 822 N.E.2d 667, 683 (Mass. 2005). A party may breach the covenant without breaching any express term of the contract. *See Fortune v. Nat'l Cash Register Co.*, 364 N.E.2d 1251, 1255-56 (Mass. 1977). In his complaint, Weiss asserted a claim for breach of the covenant. We pass no judgment on the viability of the claim, however, because it is not before us. When the district court discarded the good faith and fair dealing claim, leaving only a "straightforward" breach-of-contract claim, Weiss did not object. And he does not argue on appeal that the covenant claim remains. We therefore have no choice but to conclude that Weiss has abandoned the claim. *See United States v. Zannino*, 895 F.2d 1, 17 (1st Cir. 1990).

[The court also rejected Weiss's claim under the Massachusetts Wage Act, Mass. Gen. Laws ch. 149, § 148, which generally "requires prompt payment of 'wages earned' on pain of civil and criminal penalties, treble damages, and attorney's fees." That Act did not reach Weiss's bonus because, given his termination and the defendant's determination of "good cause," it was never "earned."]

NOTES

1. *A Bird's Eye View.* The two principal cases are a study in contrasts, not least because the employee prevails on appeal in *Hess* and loses in *Weiss*, although on remand in Hess, the employee also lost. *Hess v. Kanoski & Assocs.*, 2014 U.S. Dist. LEXIS 42584 (C.D. Ill. Mar. 28, 2014). Beyond that, however, each involves a different kind of incentive pay: Hess reflects an arrangement structured to encourage performance. In contrast, all Weiss had to do was stick around (and not give DHL good cause to fire him): This latter kind of arrangement is frequently described as a "retention bonus," and is often used when a firm is being acquired in order to help ensure that the target firm's employees remain in place. *See Uphoff v. Wachovia Securities*, 2009 U.S. Dist. LEXIS 116679, *2 (S.D. Fla. 2009) ("It is a standard practice in the brokerage/ securities business to pay retention bonuses to current brokers and financial advisors when institutional sales and mergers are announced in order to reduce the attrition of established brokers and financial advisors who would otherwise be lured by bonus and compensation promises of competitors."). But the two categories are not mutually exclusive: Incentive bonuses often get paid at the end of the calendar year, which provides an incentive for employees contemplating departure to remain employed until after the bonus is paid. *See, e.g., Pick v. Norfolk Anesthesia*, 755 N.W.2d 382, 387-88 (Neb. 2008) (distinguishing between retention bonuses and those designed to improve productivity in holding that nurses who left employment prior to the end of December were not entitled to profit-based bonus awarded annually at firm holiday party).

Yet another distinction between the two cases is that the DHL bonus plan is heavily "lawyered" while the arrangement in *Hess*—despite being between a law firm and one of its attorneys—has a "back of the envelope" feel to it. It's probably not an accident that the employee prevailed in the latter case—at least on the first round—and lost in the former.

2. *Legal Entitlement or Something Less?* A threshold issue in any dispute over incentive pay is whether the employee has a legal entitlement as opposed to a contingent right or a mere expectation of compensation based on employer practices. Where a bonus system gives the employer discretion in determining whether to compensate and how much, courts generally treat the bonuses as gratuities. *See, e.g., Jensen v. International Business Machines Corp.,* 454 F.3d 382, 388 (4th Cir. 2006); *Arby's, Inc. v. Cooper,* 454 S.E.2d 488 (Ga. 1995). In *Weiss,* the employer seemed to go further and actually promise a particular amount. However, the "good cause" provision, especially because it reserved the absolute power to determine good cause, renders that promise illusory. Do you think that Weiss understood that his retention bonus was dependent on the whim of DHL? Or is that too strong a statement for the court's result? *Cf. Schaffart v. ONEOK, Inc.,* 686 F.3d 461 (8th Cir. 2012) (employees had right to *pro rata* recovery under a stock incentive plan when they retired; the decision that certain conditions were not met was not entitled to deference when not made by the designated agent for the plan); *Arbeeny v. Kennedy Exec. Search, Inc.,* 893 N.Y.S.2d 39 (App. Div. 2010) ("Although generally an at-will employee is not entitled to post-termination commissions, the parties are certainly free to provide otherwise in a written agreement.").

3. *More Employee Victories. Hess* is not the only case finding an employer potentially liable for a bonus. In a remarkably similar scenario, *Guggenheimer v. Bernstein Litowitz & Grossman, L.L.P.,* 810 N.Y.S.2d 880 (Sup. Ct. 2006), plaintiff, an associate at a law firm specializing in class action litigation, was told upon hire that she would be eligible for bonuses for bringing successful cases to the firm. There was no written bonus policy, but it was commonly understood that the associate could receive up to 10 percent of the legal fees awarded to the firm. The plaintiff subsequently brought in and developed several high-profile cases. While they were pending, she wrote a memo to a supervising partner detailing her work and was orally assured that she would receive her bonus. The partner later circulated an e-mail message, titled "Special Bonuses for Business Referrals," stating that fees awarded to associates would be capped at $250,000. Following this message, the partner e-mailed Guggenheimer that the cap would not apply to cases referred to the firm prior to the institution of the new policy.

Ultimately the firm received fees of $1.35 million and $900,000 in two of her cases. When it balked at giving her 10 percent, she sued. The firm moved to dismiss on the ground that it retained discretion not to award bonus compensation. The court denied that motion because, whether the disputed amount was a discretionary "bonus" or "earned wages" was an issue of fact

> Defendant's assertion that the law firm's policy made payment of a bonus totally discretionary, contradicts plaintiff's conflicting contention that the company entered into an explicit oral employment agreement, reaffirmed by the statements of two of its partners that plaintiff was assured of receiving a bonus as part of her compensation. Thus, although the bonus plan, as conceived by the firm, may have been discretionary, there is a question of fact as to whether there was an oral contract agreeing to exercise that discretion in plaintiff's favor. . . .
>
> The fact that the precise amount of the bonus to be awarded was not specified does not make the contract unenforceable. Employment contracts that contain open additional compensation clauses are nonetheless binding contracts. . . . A determination of whether there exist sufficiently definite guidelines to enable a court to supply a bonus figure is a factual issue and survives a motion to dismiss. . . .

Id. at 885-86. There have been a number of other recent cases where plaintiffs successfully sought recovery of bonuses. *See Ryan v Kellogg Partners Institutional Servs.*, 967 N.E.2d 947 (N.Y. 2012) (plaintiff entitled to a guaranteed, nondiscretionary bonus of $175,000 orally promised by the managing partner; since the bonus constituted "wages" within the meaning of the Labor Law, failure to pay it entitled the employee to an award of attorney's fees); *Fishoff v. Coty Inc.*, 634 F.3d 647 (2d Cir. 2011) (once the CFO optionee validly exercised his rights, the employer was obligated to pay him the fair market value of the optioned shares and could not arbitrarily and retroactively revalue those shares); *Lewitton v. ITA Software, Inc.*, 585 F.3d 377, 381 (7th Cir. 2009) (rejecting the argument that a stock option incentive system resulted in a windfall to plaintiff above and beyond the value of his contributions to the company; the contract had mechanisms to strip the employee of vested shares, but the employer did not rely on any of them during plaintiff's employment).

4. *Was There Good Cause to Terminate Weiss?* The jury found for Weiss, although that verdict was overturned on appeal. Had it been appropriate to review the employer's decision, was the jury correct? Garcia seems to have been a real bad apple, but Weiss's sin might boil down to simple failure to record in writing a verbal warning of what at the time seemed a pretty mild offense. Weiss claimed not to have known that DHL policy was to make such a record. Considering that it was a "verbal" warning to begin with, is that so surprising or so egregious? Further, the Garcia saga, both at the time of Weiss's interactions with him and thereafter, involved a number of high-level officials who also failed to discipline Garcia. There is no indication that disciplinary action was taken against them. On the other hand, perhaps had Weiss been more proactive, Garcia's misconduct would have come to light earlier.

5. *Promissory Estoppel and Incentive Pay.* In *Uphoff v. Wachovia Securities,* 2009 U.S. Dist. LEXIS 116679 (S.D. Fla. 2009), the plaintiffs alleged that Wachovia orally promised to pay retention bonuses to their approximately 14,600 financial advisors and brokers in order to retain their services and client base in the wake of an October 2008 announcement that it would be purchased by Wells Fargo. While no exact amount was promised, the plaintiffs cited an industry custom that justified each broker reasonably anticipating a minimum of $100,000. The court rejected the contract claim because there was no allegation of either an amount actually promised or a method for determining that amount. "Custom in a particular industry . . . cannot change the requirement of contract law that the parties mutually agree on the essential term of price." *Id.* at 8.

However, the plaintiffs also asserted a promissory estoppel claim and alleged that class members had chosen not to pursue alternative employment on the basis of Wachovia's promise. On that claim, the court found the promise of a bonus sufficiently clear to support suit — although the question of whether it was reasonable to rely on that promise in the circumstances of the financial industry at the time would have to be resolved at trial. Why did the court reject the brokers' contract claim but permit their promissory estoppel claim to proceed? Is it because the remedy — compensating the plaintiffs' reliance interest — seems fairer? How likely was it that the plaintiffs could have found other jobs in the midst of a financial meltdown? In any event, promissory estoppel is no panacea. *See Geras v. IBM*, 638 F.3d 1311 (10th Cir. 2011) (although the employer's records reflected an accrued commission of $156,072 for plaintiff, the employer owed him neither that sum nor separation pay since its plan did not constitute an enforceable promise because it disclaimed any contractual obligation and therefore could not be reasonably relied on by an employee).

6. *Bonuses and Public Outrage.* History tells us why Wachovia retracted the promised bonuses: The decision came in the midst of the economic crisis of 2008 and shortly after billions of dollars in federal bailout funds were handed over to private financial firms through the Troubled Asset Relief Program (TARP). Public controversy over the federal bailout program grew to a fever pitch in 2009 when several TARP recipients announced millions of dollars in bonuses to employees. Wells Fargo, which bought Wachovia, was a TARP fund recipient. Yielding to public pressure, Wachovia rescinded the bonuses.

In contrast to Wachovia, insurance giant AIG, which received $170 billion in bailout funds, went forward with paying $165 million in promised bonuses one month after Wachovia opted to forego them. The company was skewered by Congress and the media for the payments. *See* Liam Pleven et al., *AIG Faces Growing Wrath Over Payouts*, WALL ST. J., March 19, 2009, at A1. AIG defended its decision to pay out, stating that their lawyers had concluded that the bonuses were "legal, binding obligations" of the company. *See id.*

While the public outcry was driven mostly by the perception that the bonuses were rewards for financial failure, another sore point for many was the belief that, in the middle of a financial crisis, none of the firms had to pay retention bonuses in order to keep their workforces in place. Given the massive blow to Wall Street, there were probably very few opportunities for reemployment even for the best workers. Whichever view you find more persuasive, consider the position of the AIG employees who had been promised the pay. Some of them received death threats upon the announcement of the bonuses; some voluntarily paid their bonuses back. *See* Randall Smith, *Some Will Pay Back AIG Bonuses*, WALL ST. J., March 19, 2009, at A1.

7. *Reforming Executive Pay.* Calls to end outlandish pay for corporate executives are nothing new, but the recession of 2008 heightened interest in reform. Whereas past calls had focused on the need to protect shareholders, the events of 2008 and 2009 exposed how poorly structured compensation could incent unduly risky behavior with detrimental consequences to the economy as a whole. As a condition of receiving federal bailout funds, firms were obligated to comply with Treasury Department "guidelines" that set limits on executive compensation but did not address bonuses. Subsequently, Congress imposed executive pay requirements on all publicly traded companies in its financial overhaul legislation, the Dodd-Frank Wall Street Reform and Consumer Protection Act of 2010. While the law does not put any substantive limits on the amounts companies may pay, it requires that pay packages, including "golden parachute" compensation, be put to a shareholder vote, and that executive compensation committee members, as well as their advisors, be independent decision makers. *See* 15 U.S.C.A. §§ 78n-1, 78j-3 (2014). In addition, the law creates new disclosure rules and requires companies to develop a mechanism to "clawback" erroneously awarded compensation. *See* 15 U.S.C.A. § 78j-4 (2014); 17 C.F.R. 229.402 (2014). *See generally* Jesse Fried & Nitzan Shilon, *Excess-Pay Clawbacks*, 36 IOWA J. CORP. L. 721 (2011).

8. *Wage Payment Laws.* The plaintiff in *Weiss* also asserted a claim under the state's Wage Act, although it was unsuccessful. Such laws are common in the United States, generally prohibiting the willful failure to pay earned wages and enhancing the remedies that would otherwise be available. *See, e.g.,* N.Y. LAB. LAW § 198(1-a) (McKinney 2014) (providing for 25 percent penalty on wages wrongfully withheld and attorney's fees). However, the viability of such claims in incentive compensation scenarios rests on the plaintiff's ability to show that the bonus is in fact an "earned" wage. As a result, such statutes serve principally to enhance damages for workers who can demonstrate the existence of a vested benefit and would consequently have succeeded under common law. They generally are unavailing for plaintiffs alleging entitlement to discretionary or non-performance-based bonuses, such as those based on retention or firm performance. *See Ziotas v. Reardon Law Firm*, 997 A.2d 453 (Conn. 2010) (rejecting law firm associate's claim to double damages under Connecticut Wage Act where bonus was to be determined annually by board of directors based on assessment of multiple subjective factors including productivity, performance quality, and firm loyalty).

* * *

You may have noticed that Weiss asserted a claim that his employer violated the duty of good faith and fair dealing implied in every contract, although the court did not address that issue. After you've read the next principal case, ask yourself whether Weiss had a good claim under that theory.

Phillips v. U.S. Bank, N.A.
781 N.W.2d 540 (Wis. App.),
aff'd by an equally divided court, 791 N.W.2d 190 (Wis. 2010)

FINE, J.

Deanne Phillips appeals the circuit court's final order granting summary judgment to U.S. Bank, N.A., dismissing her claims against U.S. Bank. We reverse because: (1) contrary to the circuit court's ruling, an at-will employee does not forfeit benefits that have accrued during his or her employment even though the agreement governing those benefits conditions their receipt on the employee's continued employment *if* the employer fires the employee solely to prevent the employee from getting the accrued benefits; and (2) there are genuine issues of material fact whether the reasons U.S. Bank gave for firing Phillips were pretextual.

I.

Phillips worked for U.S. Bank from January of 1998, in various financial-planning positions, until she was fired in October of 2007. During the latter part of that time, she worked with another U.S. Bank employee, James Janikowski. As a U.S. Bank employee, Phillips participated in a benefit plan that is at issue here. The Plan was governed by two documents: the 2007 U.S. Bank Line-of-Business Incentive Plan and the Private Asset Management Portfolio Manager Sales Incentive Plan. The Line-of-Business Incentive Plan made employment a condition of eligibility to receive payment:

> In order to encourage employee retention, participants whose employment with the company is terminated, voluntarily or involuntarily for reasons other than position elimination, prior to the date of actual payment are ineligible for an award, except as required by state law or specifically provided in the Performance Measures document.

The Private Asset Management Portfolio Manager Sales Incentive Plan makes being an employee in good standing a condition of eligibility:

> In order to participate in this plan, *there must be no outstanding performance related issues* in the following areas [compliance with regulatory matters not at issue here] and U.S. Bank policies and procedures[.] In addition, the participant must be in good standing. Good standing includes no violations of law or Company policies, any current disciplinary action and satisfactory job performance.

(emphasis in original.) U.S. Bank does not dispute that Phillips's benefits under the Plan fully accrued.

U.S. Bank contends that it fired Phillips because she knew about Janikowski's plans to go with a competitor and not only did not tell the pertinent U.S. Bank supervisors but also lied when asked about it. The fulcrum of U.S. Bank's contention is set out in an affidavit submitted to the circuit court by Dave Isaacson, who oversaw the group in which Phillips worked until she was fired. His affidavit asserts that he had heard about the alleged Phillips/Janikowski matter from other U.S. Bank employees and that he confronted Phillips about it at an October 16, 2007 meeting with her. According to Isaacson's affidavit, "[t]he purpose of that meeting was to provide Phillips with an opportunity to come forward with what she knew about Janikowski's plans to leave the Bank and solicit its clients, as well as to ascertain whether she intended to leave the Bank." His affidavit continues:

> At the meeting, I explicitly asked Phillips whether she had any knowledge of Janikowski's plans to leave the Bank and take Bank clients with him. She responded, "No."

> I then asked Phillips whether she herself intended to leave the Bank. She responded, "No."

> I did not believe her response to my first question, in light of what I had heard from [a co-employee] the day before. [Phillips's immediate supervisor] did not believe her either.

> I had two more conversations over the course of October 19 with Phillips in the same vein. Each time, Phillips denied having any knowledge of Janikowski's plans.

Isaacson's affidavit asserts that after the "conversations" he had with Phillips on October 19, he "decided I could no longer trust Phillips. I also decided that she had violated the U.S. Bank Code of Ethics by failing [to] be forthright with me when I gave her several opportunities to do so." Isaacson and others in the bank's chain of command then decided to fire Phillips. U.S. Bank fired her on October 26, 2007.

As we have seen, Phillips claims that the excuse recounted in the Isaacson affidavit was a pretext to fire her so the bank would not have to pay her what had accrued but not yet been paid under the benefit Plan. Insofar as this contention is concerned, the following excerpts from Phillips's deposition about the October 19 meeting are key:

Q: Did he [Isaacson] ask you whether you knew that Jim [Janikowski] was planning to leave, or something to that effect?
A: No.
Q: Did he ask you whether you had any knowledge of Jim's intention to take clients away from the bank?
A: No.

If Isaacson testified at trial consistent with his affidavit, and Phillips testified at trial consistent with her deposition, a reasonable jury could assess their credibility and find that at least one of them was lying. U.S. Bank admitted as much during oral argument. U.S. Bank contends, however, and the circuit court agreed, that because Phillips was an employee at will and could be fired for any reason or no reason, and because the Plan requires that Plan participants be employed when payment under the Plan is due, Phillips was not entitled to be paid under the Plan because the bank fired her before payment was due. Thus, the circuit court opined:

> Because . . . her termination alone precludes her entitlement to the bonus whether or not there's a factual dispute as to whether or not she violated the ethics code [that] is something the Court doesn't have to address at this time even though the parties themselves have set forth responses in the depositions as to whether or not she, more or less, as the defense said, lied or misrepresented to the employer her knowledge of Janikowski's participation and in leaving the bank.

As explained below, on our *de novo* review, we disagree.

II.

The parties agree that an at-will employee like Phillips can be fired for any reason as long as the reason does not implicate a status protected by law. *See Repetti v. Sysco Corp.*, 2007 730 N.W.2d 189, 192 (Wis. 2007). That does not mean, however, that an at-will employee may be deprived of benefits that accrued before he or she was let go if the firing was to prevent payment of those benefits. Although there is no Wisconsin decision on this precise issue, the law applicable to the principal/agent relationship is directly analogous and applies here. Thus, we have previously recognized the rule as formulated by Restatement (Second) of Agency § 454 (1958):

> An agent to whom the principal has made a revocable offer of compensation if he accomplishes a specified result is entitled to the promised amount if the principal, in order to avoid payment of it, revokes the offer and thereafter the result is accomplished as the result of the agent's prior efforts.

Leen v. Butter Co., 501 N.W.2d 847, 848 (Wis. App. 1993) ("[W]hen the agent accomplishes the result for which he or she was retained a principal cannot avoid paying commissions by merely terminating the agency.").[2] Although "[t]his general rule does not apply, however, when the agency agreement specifically limits the recovery of commissions following termination," *id.*, the termination must not be in bad faith; that is, it must not be done in order to avoid paying what would otherwise be

---

2. The parties debate whether the benefits under the Plan were a "commission" or a "bonus." In our view, the argument concerns a distinction that is immaterial here and is an attempt by U.S. Bank to limit *Leen v. Butter Co.*, to "commissions" because that is what was specifically at issue there. The principle recognized by *Leen*, which we have discussed in the main body of this opinion, is applicable to the Plan benefits here irrespective of how they may be characterized — the Plan promised to pay employees money calculated on past performance unless those employees were no longer employed when the payments were due. The Plan payments could, therefore, be characterized with equal accuracy as a "bonus" for a job well done, or as a "commission" for work well fulfilled. Here at least, this is a difference between twilight and dusk.

due, *id. See also Compton v. Shopko Stores, Inc.*, 287 N.W.2d 720, 726 (Wis. 1980) ("Executive Bonus Plan" was "a binding unilateral contract" when the employee fulfilled the duties called for by the plan); *Fortune v. National Cash Register Co.*, 364 N.E.2d 1251, 1255-1256 (Mass. 1977) (An at-will employment agreement is subject to the requirement that the parties act in good faith when termination of employment cuts off an employee's entitlement to a "bonus commission.").

While it is true, as U.S. Bank argues, that in the at-will-employee context there is no "duty to *terminate* in good faith," *Brockmeyer v. Dun & Bradstreet*, 335 N.W.2d 834, 836, 838 (Wis. 1983) (at-will employee) (emphasis added), the requirement that parties act in "good faith" inheres in every contract and, therefore, an employer must comply in good faith with its "contractual obligations," *Hale v. Stoughton Hosp. Ass'n, Inc.*, 376 N.W.2d 89, 93 (Wis. App. 1985) ("*Brockmeyer* does not relieve an employer of contractual obligations it has undertaken."). Here, U.S. Bank contracted to pay employees benefits under the Plan so long as the employees fulfilled the Plan's prerequisites and were employed when payment of those benefits were due. As we have seen, U.S. Bank does not contest that Phillips fulfilled the Plan requirements. Under *Leen*, U.S. Bank cannot avoid paying Phillips benefits that accrued under the Plan if it fired her in order to not pay her. *See also Compton; Fortune.* Since, as we have seen, there is a genuine issue of material fact whether the excuse recounted in Isaacson's affidavit was a pretext, we reverse the circuit court's order granting summary judgment.[3] . . .

NOTES

1. *The Duty of Good Faith — Again.* Recall the discussion of the implied duty in *Guz v. Bechtel* in Chapter 2. There the court rejected the employee's claim that by terminating him unfairly the employer breached the duty of good faith, concluding that such an interpretation ran counter to employment at will, which specifically allows arbitrary and unfair terminations. However, plaintiffs have often been successful in using the implied duty to challenge refusals to pay earned wages or benefits as opposed to challenging the termination itself. The seminal case is *Fortune v. National Cash Register*, 364 N.E.2d 1251 (Mass. 1977), where the employer had a policy provided that employees would receive some commissions on sales only on delivery of the goods to customer. Fortune was terminated a few days after closing on a record-breaking sale but prior to delivery on that order. On his suit for those commissions, the Supreme Court of Massachusetts held that, while there was no breach under the express terms of the contract, it was reasonable for the jury to find bad faith in breach of the implied duty. It explained:

> Fortune argues that, in spite of the literal wording of the contract, he is entitled to a jury determination on NCR's motives in terminating his services under the contract and in finally discharging him. We agree. . . .

3. The parties discuss many other matters, including whether Phillips violated the bank's code of ethics. Those matters are, however, incapable of resolution on summary judgment. . . . Insofar as U.S. Bank's contention that the Plan imposed only a discretionary duty on it is concerned, the bank has conceded that Phillips fulfilled all her obligations under the Plan. Thus, the bank could not exercise whatever discretion it reserved in the Plan to revoke benefits that had already accrued. *See Compton* ("Executive Bonus Plan" was "a binding unilateral contract" when the employee fulfilled the duties called-for by the plan); *see also Leen* (may not terminate agency in bad faith merely to avoid paying what is owed).

We do not question the general principles that an employer is entitled to be motivated by and to serve its own legitimate business interests; that an employer must have wide latitude in deciding whom it will employ in the face of the uncertainties of the business world. . . . However, we believe that where, as here, commissions are to be paid for work performed by the employee, the employer's decision to terminate its at will employee should be made in good faith. . . .

In so holding we are merely recognizing the general requirement in this Commonwealth that parties to contracts and commercial transactions must act in good faith toward one another. Good faith and fair dealing between parties are pervasive requirements in our law; it can be said fairly, that parties to contracts or commercial transactions are bound by this standard.

Id. at 1256-58.

2. *The Meaning of the Duty.* Are *Phillips* and *Fortune* consistent with the court's rejection of the implied duty claim in *Guz?* The latter case focused on whether an employer's right to fire an at-will employee was limited by good faith, holding no. Neither *Phillips* nor *Fortune* infringe this employer right directly — they merely refuse to allow an employer to use the expedient of discharge to deny benefits that would have earned but for the discharge. In other words, an employee suing on the covenant can't recover damages for being discharged; she can merely recover the otherwise earned benefits. *See also Kmak v. Am. Century Cos.*, 754 F.3d 513 (8th Cir. 2014) (looking to Missouri's public policy to find that retaliation for testifying in an arbitration proceeding, Kmak breached the implied covenant : American Century may have had the right to call Kmak's shares "at any time," but it did not have the right to call those shares for any reason, if doing so would violate public policy).

This distinction now appears to be good law in Wisconsin. In *Phillips*, the Wisconsin Supreme Court affirmed only because a majority couldn't be mustered for a ruling, but in *Beidel v. Sideline Software, Inc.*, 811 N.W.2d 856 (Wis. 2013), the court recognized a former employee's — and shareholder's — action for specific performance of stock repurchase agreement for violation of duty of good faith and fair dealing when he alleged that he was discharged without cause in order to limit his recovery to a lesser appraised value of shares.

While not all jurisdictions recognize the doctrine's limit on employer power, *see, e.g., Cramer v. Fairfield Med. Ctr.*, 914 N.E.2d 447, 455 (Ohio App. 2009) ("Ohio law does not recognize a good faith and fair dealing requirement in employment-at-will relationships."), the draft RESTATEMENT OF EMPLOYMENT LAW (Council Draft No. 10, Sept. 30, 2013), does recognize a contractual "non-waivable duty of good faith and fair dealing" between employer and employee, "which includes an agreement by each not to hinder the other's performance under, or deprive the other of the benefit of, the contract," § 2.07(a). Tracking the distinction between *Phillips/Fortune* and *Guz*, it cautions that that duty "must be read consistently with the nature of the relationship such that it cannot be read to require cause for termination" of at-will employment. § 2.07(a). More specifically, the section goes on to provide that the implied covenant "includes the duty not to terminate . . . the employment relationship for the purpose of . . . preventing the vesting or accrual of an employee right or benefit." § 2.07(c)(1). Illustration 1 is essentially *Fortune*.

Perhaps more radically, the proposed Restatement also invokes the duty to bar an employer from "retaliating against the employee for performing the employee's obligations under the employment contract or law." § 2.07(c)(2). Illustration 2 hypothesizes an accounting manager under a contractual duty to certify his employer's financial statements as consistent with applicable professional standards. According to the Illustration "termination of E for performing this contractual obligation violates the duty of good faith and fair dealing." The Reporters' Notes state that the Illustration is "based on the facts, while rejecting the holding" of *Sabetay v. Sterling Drug Co.,* 514 N.Y.S.2d 209 (N.Y. 1983).

3. *Proving Bad Faith.* Presumably, any violation of the duty of good faith is dependent on proof that the termination was intended to prevent the payment of the earned benefit. How does a plaintiff convince the factfinder that his or her employer had the requisite intent? Not surprisingly, employers are unlikely to admit it, and the employee often must rely on circumstantial evidence, such as the timing of the termination relative to the anticipated payment and the length and history of the employment relationship. *Fortune* is the poster boy for this kind of proof. *See also Maddaloni v. Western Mass. Bus Lines, Inc.,* 438 N.E.2d 351, 354-55 (Mass. 1982). At least one case has seemingly loosened the intent requirement, finding it sufficient that a termination without cause deprived an employee of anticipated commissions. In *Gram v. Liberty Mutual Insurance Co.,* 429 N.E.2d 21 (Mass. 1981), an insurance salesman, the most productive seller in his office, was terminated after a disagreement over a letter sent to clients. As a result, he lost out on potential commissions from policy renewals. The court determined that the termination was without cause, but that the evidence did not support a finding that the employer had considered Gram's accrual of commissions in making its decision. It nonetheless allowed Gram's claim of breach of an implied duty of good faith. Although recognizing what later became the generally accepted rule that discharge of an at-will employee without cause is not per se a violation of good faith, the court explained:

> There is in this case, however, an element of Gram's compensation that requires special consideration. Although there is no evidence warranting an inference that Liberty discharged Gram for the purpose of appropriating his renewal commissions, the fact remains that Gram lost reasonably ascertainable future compensation based on his past services. Gram had a reasonable expectancy of some renewal commissions. . . . We think that the obligation of good faith and fair dealing imposed on an employer requires that the employer be liable for the loss of compensation that is so clearly related to an employee's past service, when the employee is discharged without good cause.

Id. at 28-29. The dissent accused the court of "restructur[ing] an at-will employment agreement to reflect an imposed condition never heretofore recognized by this court and one of doubtful legitimacy." *Id.* at 30. Re-read the proposed Restatement rule. Isn't it clear from the "purpose" language that *Gram* goes further than the American Law Institute?

4. *Vested Benefits Versus Anticipated Earnings.* In both *Phillips* and *Fortune,* the parties limited their damages claim to the value of the lost commissions and salary that had vested or accrued prior to termination. In some cases, the tie between the employee's past performance and the benefits sought is less certain. In *Gram,* described above, the court permitted the plaintiff to seek recovery for commissions that would have accrued upon renewal of policies he serviced. 429 N.E.2d at 29. The dissent called this "ordering the trier of fact to engage in extravagant speculation." *Id.* at 30; *see also Coll v. PB Diagnostic Sys. Inc.,* 50 F.3d 1115, 1125 (1st Cir. 1995) (rejecting CEO's claim for loss of incentive payments as a result of termination due to corporate

restructuring where at least two of the four specified performance goals on which payment contingent could not have been met). Although courts differ on the degree of certainty required to permit recovery for anticipated benefits under a good faith theory, it is generally agreed that plaintiffs cannot recover future wages, as would be available under breach of an implied or express contract for job security. Nor are punitive damages available, despite the cause of action's close relationship to tort. *See Foley v. Interactive Data Corp.*, 765 P.2d 373 (Cal. 1988). These restrictions place a critical limitation on the cause of action as a vehicle for challenging at-will terminations.

5. *"Earned," "Accrued," and Non-Waivable.* The theory of good faith and fair dealing is said by the draft Restatement to be "non-waivable," which is consistent with the general approach to that duty in the law of contracts. But the duty is also generally recognized to be a gap-filler, which means that it cannot trump an explicit provision of the contract. In cases like *Phillips* and *Fortune,* the governing contract required continued employment in order for the benefit to be paid, but it did not expressly allow the employer to fire the employees in order to forestall the compensation. That created a "gap" that the duty of good faith and fair dealing could then fill: the employer was allowed to fire the employee but not for the purpose of preventing the accrual of the benefit.

You won't be surprised to learn that employers are now drafting their contracts to close the gap: While the duty of good faith remains unwaivable, it has no role absent a gap in the express agreement of the parties. To see this, suppose the agreements in *Phillips* and *Fortune* provided something like: "Employee must remain with the company in order to receive the designated compensation, and employer reserves the right to discharge her in order to prevent her from receiving said compensation"? *See Gans & Pugh Assocs. v. Technical Communications Corp.*, 1993 U.S. App. LEXIS 32005, 4-6 (4th Cir. Dec. 9, 1993) ("[T]he holding in *Fortune* does not apply to the facts of this case. The contract in *Fortune* did not have an express provision applicable to the manner in which commissions would be paid on orders accepted before termination. Instead, the contract governed the salesperson's right to commissions independently of termination.").

6. *Back to* Weiss. In light of what you've learned, what do you think of Weiss's claim of breach of the duty of good faith and fair dealing? Given the facts alleged, is it a good claim? Is there something else he would have to assert to make it viable?

PROBLEMS

3-4. Roseland Property Company, a real estate development firm, entered into an agreement with Carol Naderny to serve as the main developer in its new Boston office. The relevant parts of her contract provided:

4. your title will be that of "Partner," although your relationship to Roseland, and your interests in projects, will be established and governed by the provisions of this agreement. . . .

8. you will be entitled to a participation interest in all new projects which originate out of Roseland's Boston office during the period of your employment. Your participation interest in each applicable project will

be equal to 15 percent of the cash distributed to the Roseland Entity after the Roseland Entity has received cash distributions equal to the Roseland Entity's capital contributions plus an 8 percent return on such contributions for such project. Your interest in such new projects will vest at the same time that the Roseland Entity's interests vest. Your participation percentage is subject to review each year.

14. Roseland will have and retain sole ownership and control of all new business developed by you while at Roseland and all Roseland business will remain with Roseland following termination of our relationship for any reason.

15. the relationship between you and Roseland is and at all times will be strictly an "at will" relationship, and either you or Roseland may terminate your employment and this relationship at any time with or without cause, for any reason or no reason, and with or without notice.

Three years later, Roseland and Naderny amicably parted ways as a result of differences in their business philosophy. During her employment, Naderny had initiated four projects but none had closed or begun construction as of the date of her departure. As a result, Roseland did not pay her a "participation interest." One year later, however, Roseland succeeded in closing on one of Naderny's projects and received a sizeable sum. Naderny has since sent Roseland a demand letter requesting my "15 percent interest now that the project has vested."

(a) Suppose you represent Roseland. How would you respond to Naderny's letter?

(b) Suppose you had represented Roseland during the negotiation of Naderny's contract. How would you have drafted it to prevent future liabilities to terminated employees?

(c) Suppose you represented Naderny during the negotiation of her contract. How would you have drafted it to ensure that she received her cut on all projects she initiated?

(d) Returning to part (a), suppose that as a result of your efforts on behalf of Roseland, the parties reach a settlement, resolve their differences, and decide they want to work together again. In order to avoid any possible future disputes, they would like to enter into a revised contract that clarifies any points of ambiguity. Consider the competing versions of the contract you have created in response to parts (b) and (c). Can you think of ways in which the parties might compromise their positions to achieve an agreement? What would it look like in writing?

3-5. Don Broadbent was employed by Westport Inc. as a Senior Vice President in charge of operations. He was hired under a five-year written contract containing the following provisions related to termination:

Termination without cause. If the Executive is involuntarily terminated without cause, the Executive will receive severance equaling two years' salary and 25,000 shares of common stock.

Termination for cause. If the Executive is involuntarily terminated for cause, the Executive forfeits rights to further payment and all obligations of the Company under this contract will cease.

Termination following a change in control. If the Executive is involuntarily terminated within six months of a sale of substantially all of the Company's assets, or a merger in which the Company is not the surviving entity, the Executive will receive severance equal to one year's salary and 25,000 shares of the common stock of the purchasing or surviving entity.

Three years after hiring Broadbent, Westport experiences legitimate and sustained financial difficulties. It begins discussions with Motoport Co., a successful competitor, about the possibility of Motoport buying the company. In order to make itself more marketable, Westport undertakes a corporate restructuring and lays off a significant percentage of its workforce, including Broadbent, who is paid pursuant to the "termination without cause" provision of his contract. Five months later, Motoport purchases Westport, and Motoport's stock rises significantly as a result of the acquisition.

Broadbent subsequently reads about Motoport's purchase and stock rise in the newspaper. He pulls out a copy of his contract, does the math, and realizes that, due to the dramatic increase in stock price, he would have come out with a lot more money had he been terminated under the "change in control" provision of his contract despite the lesser amount of severance he would have received. Might he have a viable breach of contract claim?

Part Three

TORT-BASED
PROTECTIONS
FOR WORKERS

4

The Public Policy Exception to the At-Will Rule

When is the firing of an employee tortious under the common law? Prior to the 1970s, the conventional answer to this question would have been never. Actions taken *in connection with* a discharge could be tortious, even if the discharge itself were not. For example, an employee who was coercively interrogated in connection with employer investigation of a theft might have a cause of action for false imprisonment, or one who was publicly slandered in connection with his discharge could have sued in defamation. While such torts continue to constrain employer conduct, *see* Chapter 5, it was not until the late 1970s that some discharges themselves became tortious and employees were no longer limited to claims based on contract or statutory law.

Currently, many jurisdictions recognize the termination of an employee as actionable in tort in a number of circumstances. This new law encompasses several theories; some are expansive of older theories and others are true innovations. Perhaps the most developed approach is "the public policy exception" to the at-will rule, often referred to as "wrongful discharge." Although some courts view the doctrine as partially contractual, the more widely held view is that discharging an employee for a reason that offends public policy constitutes a tort. It is this tort that will be the subject of section A of this chapter.

A natural outgrowth of the common-law public policy exception was legislation codifying protection for employees who engage in conduct required or permitted by public policy. Thus, a number of statutes provide protection that may be viewed as ancillary to the main thrust of the law itself. For example, Title VII of the Civil Rights Act of 1964 bars discrimination on account of race, sex, religion, and national origin, but it also bars retaliation for employees who file charges of discrimination or otherwise oppose unlawful employment practices under the statute. *See* Chapter 9. As this example indicates, a wide range of federal and state laws have statute-specific provisions aimed at protecting employees from reprisal for engaging in particular activities. But increasingly there are also more general statutes, often described as "whistleblower" laws, which create protection for employees who engage in a wide range of activities furthering public policy. This topic is the subject of Section B.

A. THE COMMON LAW PUBLIC POLICY EXCEPTION

The emergence of a public policy exception to the at-will rule has been one of the most important developments in employment law. Not only has it provided employees with an important new source of rights but it has also led employers to reconsider their entire approach to termination. While relatively few discharges, in the final analysis, implicate public policy, employers are well advised to ensure that all terminations are reviewed carefully. Research shows that even public *allegations* of corporate financial misdeeds can have significant adverse effects on a firm. Robert M. Bowen, Andrew C. Call, & Shivaram Rajgopal, *Whistle-Blowing: Target Firm Characteristics and Economic Consequences*, 85 ACCOUNTING REV. 1239 (2010) (finding, inter alia, that "whistle-blowing announcements were associated with a negative 2.8% market-adjusted five day stock price reaction, and this reaction was especially negative for allegations involving earnings management (7.3%)").

The paradigm public policy case arises when an employee claims that she has been discharged for engaging in conduct that has been mandated, or at least encouraged, by some public policy not directly connected with employment. For example, an employee may claim that she has been fired because she testified truthfully before a legislative body or court. When such testimony adversely affects the employer, it is easy to see the motivation for discharge. Originally, the common law recognized no legal bar to discharging an at-will employee in these circumstances, however reprehensible it might seem and however perverse from a societal perspective. But courts have moved away from that position. An early case recognizing a cause of action in such circumstances was *Petermann v. International Brotherhood of Teamsters*, 344 P.2d 25 (Cal. App. 1959), which upheld an employee's suit when he was fired for refusing to perjure himself before the California legislature. This tort was at first very limited — *Petermann* stressed that the employee had been fired for refusing to commit a felonious act — but it gradually expanded. By 1975, for example, a court recognized that discharge of an employee for serving on a jury was actionable, even though at the time there was no state statute according protection against adverse employment actions on that ground. *See Nees v. Hocks*, 536 P.2d 512 (Or. 1975).

As cases accumulated where courts encountered actions by employers that tended to frustrate matters of public concern, the downside of pure private ordering became apparent. Even if it was appropriate to leave to private ordering questions that affected the employer and its employees alone, a different set of considerations developed when the relationship between the two affected third parties — such as legislative investigation in *Petermann* or the availability of qualified jurors in *Nees*. Thus, there gradually developed what came to be called the wrongful discharge or public policy tort: Where public policy is sufficiently implicated, a discharge in contravention of that policy is actionable as a tort. Understanding this tort requires considering a number of related questions. The initial one — whether the courts (as opposed to the legislature) recognize such a cause of action — has been generally resolved in favor of court action although some jurisdictions have rejected the tort entirely. *See Murphy v. Am. Home Prods. Corp.*, 448 N.E.2d 86, 89 (N.Y. 1983) ("Plaintiff would have this court adopt this emerging view. We decline his invitation, being of the opinion that such a significant change in our law is best left to the Legislature.").

Others have applied the tort sparingly as a kind of gap filler where the state had announced a policy in a statute but did not legislate directly with respect to the employment setting. For example, some state legislation creating workers' compensation schemes failed to explicitly provide a cause of action for employees discharged for filing a claim. In such instances, it was common for states to vindicate the public policy underlying workers' compensation by protecting those who filed claims. *See, e.g., Freas v. Archer Servs., Inc.*, 716 A.2d 998 (D.C. 1998) (recognizing public policy tort for discharge for seeking unemployment compensation). The view of tort as a gap filler is reinforced by those courts that have refused to apply the tort when predicate legislation provides its own remedial scheme. For example, most courts have been unwilling to find a public policy tort based on sex discrimination. While there is obviously a strong public policy against such conduct, it is expressed in statutes that provide their own enforcement schemes, and these courts have held that there is therefore no need to recognize a separate tort. *See, e.g., Makovi v. Sherwin-Williams Co.*, 561 A.2d 179 (Md. 1989) (sex discrimination); *Sands Regent v. Valgardson*, 777 P.2d 898 (Nev. 1989) (age discrimination); *but see Hill v. Ky. Lottery Corp.*, 327 S.W.3d 412 (Ky. 2010) ("Because the statutes that declare the unlawful act of perjury are not the same statutes that declare and remedy civil rights violations, the Hills' claims under KRS Chapter 344 does not preempt the Hills' common law claims for wrongful discharge based on the public policy against perjured testimony."). *See generally* Jarod Spencer González, *State Anti-Discrimination Statutes and Implied Preemption of Common Law Torts: Valuing the Common Law*, 59 S. Car. L. Rev. 115 (2007).

When a court accepts the premise of the public policy tort, what should count as "public policy"? In its narrowest formulation, the tort might bar employers only from discharging employees for doing what the law requires or for not doing what the law forbids. For instance, in *Petermann*, a state statute required truthful testimony in response to a subpoena, and permitting an employer to discharge someone for providing such testimony would discourage this conduct. At the other extreme, the public policy tort could bar employers from terminating workers for activities that the judiciary views as "socially useful." For instance, education is generally viewed as a social good, but is it appropriate to bar employers from terminating someone for enrolling in law school? *See Scroghan v. Kraftco Corp.*, 551 S.W.2d 811 (Ky. App. 1977) (no). As might be expected, the cases are strung along this spectrum, with conflicting views of the scope of the tort competing for attention.

One recent attempt to bring coherence to the cases is the American Law Institute's ("ALI") proposed Restatement (Third) of Employment Law (Proposed Final Draft, April 18, 2014) provides:

§ 5.02 Employer Discipline in Violation of Public Policy: Protected Activities

An employer is subject to liability in tort under § 5.01 for discharging an employee because the employee, acting in a reasonable manner,

(a) refuses to commit an act that the employee reasonably and in good faith believes violates a law or other well-established public policy, such as a code of professional conduct or an occupational code protective of the public interest;

(b) performs a public duty or obligation that the employee reasonably and in good faith believes is imposed by law;

(c) files a charge or claims a benefit in good faith under the procedures of an employment statute or law (irrespective of whether the charge or claim is meritorious);

(d) refuses to waive a nonnegotiable or nonwaivable right where the employer's insistence on the waiver as a condition of employment or the court's enforcement of the waiver would violate well-established public policy;

(e) reports or inquires about conduct that the employee reasonably and in good faith believes violates a law or established principle of professional conduct or an occupational code protective of the public interest; or

(f) engages in other activity directly furthering a well-established public policy.

As you work through this chapter, consider whether this proposal is an accurate "restatement" of the law as it has evolved or as it should be formulated in the future.

But before you begin this study, note what is *not* protected by this formulation of the public policy tort: an employee's conscientious performance of his duties to his employer. The seminal case for this proposition is *Foley v. Interactive Data Corp.*, 765 P.2d 373, 380 (Cal. 1988), where plaintiff claimed he had been discharged for reporting internally that a supervisor was being investigated for embezzlement from another company. The court rejected the public policy tort:

> Whether or not there is a statutory duty requiring an employee to report [to his own employer] information relevant to his employer's interest, we do not find a substantial public policy prohibiting an employer from discharging an employee for performing that duty. Past decisions recognizing a tort action for discharge in violation of public policy seek to protect the public, by protecting the employee who refuses to commit a crime . . . or who discloses other illegal, unethical, or unsafe practices. . . . No equivalent public interest bars the discharge of the present plaintiff. When the duty of an employee to disclose information to his employer serves only the private interest of the employer, the rationale underlying the [public policy] cause of action is not implicated.

Id. This limitation is consistent with the idea that a public policy must concern the public interest, not just a private matter between a worker and employer. In an extreme example of this, one court rejected a public policy claim when a female employee was fired because of an incident in which she was the victim of an assault and rape. *Green v. Bryant*, 887 F. Supp. 798 (E.D. Pa. 1995).

While some legal commentators and many would-be plaintiffs are not happy with the result, it reflects the law's line-drawing between private ordering and its limitations. The employer is free to structure its internal operations and reward (or punish) those who serve its private interests. When, however, actions taken against employees have effects on third parties, it is appropriate to constrain the employer's freedom of action.

Fitzgerald v. Salsbury Chemical, Inc.
613 N.W.2d 275 (Iowa 2000)

CADY, Justice.

Tom Fitzgerald was employed by Salsbury Chemical, Inc. at its production plant in Charles City. Salsbury manufactures chemicals and pharmaceutical bulk actives. Fitzgerald was employed as a production foreman at the plant.

Fitzgerald was terminated from his employment with Salsbury on September 19, 1995. The termination followed an incident on August 30, 1995, involving a production worker named Richard Koresh. Koresh failed to properly monitor the temperature and pressure of a tank used to mix a chemical compound. His conduct created a potentially dangerous condition.

Koresh was suspended from his employment on September 4, 1995, after Salsbury conducted a preliminary investigation into the incident. He was ultimately terminated on September 19, 1995, a few hours prior to the time Fitzgerald was terminated. Fitzgerald was responsible for supervising Koresh on the date of the incident.

Salsbury asserted Fitzgerald was terminated for failing to properly supervise Koresh and to prevent the potentially dangerous incident. Fitzgerald, however, believed he was discharged because he did not support Salsbury's decision to discharge Koresh and Salsbury officials feared he would provide testimony in support of Koresh in the course of threatened legal action by Koresh.

The events supporting this claim extend back to August 15, 1995, when Koresh gave deposition testimony in a wrongful discharge action against Salsbury by a former employee named John Kelly. Kelly was terminated several years earlier, one day prior to his scheduled deposition in a wrongful death action against Salsbury by the estate of a former employee. The former employee died after a chemical compound he was mixing at the plant overheated and exploded. Salsbury claimed Kelly was terminated because his unsafe conduct caused the explosion. Kelly claimed he was terminated by Salsbury in an effort to cover up its culpability in the incident. During the deposition on August 15, 1995, Koresh contradicted earlier deposition testimony by two Salsbury management officials concerning the internal investigation of the work practices of Kelly. Koresh also testified he believed Kelly was a safe operator. Following the deposition, Koresh felt shunned by Salsbury management. He was also told by a foreman the company was going to find a way to fire him. After Koresh was suspended on September 4, 1995, he told a Salsbury official that he had hired an attorney and was "not going to be another John Kelly."

Fitzgerald engaged in a conversation with the plant operations manager on September 19, 1995, a few hours prior to the time he was told of his termination. The manager asked Fitzgerald what discipline he believed should result to Koresh because of the incident on August 30. Fitzgerald responded he did not believe it was fair to fire Koresh over a single mistake. Fitzgerald also indicated he did not believe Koresh should be fired in light of his long years of service to the company. The manager then informed Fitzgerald he needed to begin to think like a foreman if he was going to be one, and he needed to find out which side he was on. Fitzgerald was also informed the matter may result in a lawsuit. Fitzgerald does not claim he responded to the statements.

Fitzgerald instituted this wrongful discharge action against Salsbury. He alleged his termination violated a public policy of this state to protect workers who oppose the unlawful termination of a co-worker. Additionally, he claimed he was terminated because he intended to provide testimony in Koresh's future wrongful termination lawsuit that would be unfavorable to Salsbury and the company wanted to discredit his potential testimony as a disgruntled former employee. Fitzgerald claims Salsbury's motivation to terminate him violated the public policy of this state to provide truthful testimony in court proceedings.

The trial court dismissed the action following a hearing on the motion for summary judgment. It found no public policy of this state was implicated by the two factual claims urged by Fitzgerald. Although the trial court found the criminal statutes against committing and suborning perjury established a public policy prohibiting such conduct, it found no facts to show the criminal statutes had been violated by Salsbury. . . .

III. The Employer-Employee Relationship . . .

B. *The Public Policy Exception*

We have identified the elements of an action to recover damages for discharge in violation of public policy to require the employee to establish (1) engagement in a protected activity; (2) discharge; and (3) a causal connection between the conduct and the discharge. *Teachout v. Forest City Community Sch. Dist.*, 584 N.W.2d 296 (Iowa 1998). These elements properly identify the tort of wrongful discharge when a protected activity has been recognized through the existence of an underlying public policy which is undermined when an employee is discharged from employment for engaging in the activity. However, when we have not previously identified a particular public policy to support an action, the employee must first identify a clear public policy which would be adversely impacted if dismissal resulted from the conduct engaged in by the employee.[2] *See Yockey v. State*, 540 N.W.2d 418 (Iowa 1995) (the public policy in favor of permitting employees to seek workers' compensation benefits not jeopardized by termination from employment for missing work following injury); *Borschel v. City of Perry,* 512 N.W.2d 565 (Iowa 1994) (no public policy in favor of presumption of innocence in work place to give rise to an action for wrongful discharge for conduct which resulted in criminal charges).

1. Determining Public Policy

In first recognizing the public policy exception to the at-will employment doctrine, we were careful to limit the tort action for wrongful discharge to cases involving only a well-recognized and clear public policy. This requirement has been incorporated

---

2. Some courts are beginning to articulate the elements of a cause of action for wrongful discharge as:

1. The existence of a clear public policy (the clarity element).
2. Dismissal of employee under circumstances alleged in the case would jeopardize public policy (the jeopardy element).
3. The plaintiff engaged in public policy conduct and this conduct was the reason for the dismissal (the causation element).
4. Employer lacked an overriding business justification for the dismissal (the absence of justification element).

Gardner v. Loomis Armored, Inc., 913 P.2d 377 (Wash. 1996); *Collins v. Rizkana*, 652 N.E.2d 653 (Ohio 1995).

This approach is derived from the methodology proposed by Dean and Law Professor Henry H. Perritt, Jr. *See generally* Henry H. Perritt, Jr., *The Future of Wrongful Dismissal Claims: Where Does Employer Self-Interest Lie?*, 58 U. Cin. L. Rev. 397 (1989). This four part structure of proof is now detailed in Professor Perrit's multi-volume treatise on the subject. Employee Dismissal Law and Practice [now in its 5th edition, 2006]. . . .

in our subsequent cases. This important element sets the foundation for the tort and it is necessary to overcome the employer's interest in operating its business in the manner it sees fit. It also helps ensure that employers have notice that their dismissal decisions will give rise to liability.

In determining whether a clear, well-recognized public policy exists for purposes of a cause of action, we have primarily looked to our statutes but have also indicated our Constitution to be an additional source. We have not been asked to extend our sources of public policy beyond our statutes and Constitution, but recognize other states have used additional sources such as judicial decisions and administrative rules.

Some statutes articulate public policy by specifically prohibiting employers from discharging employees for engaging in certain conduct or other circumstances.[3] Yet, we do not limit the public policy exception to specific statutes which mandate protection for employees. *Teachout.* Instead, we look to other statutes which not only define clear public policy but imply a prohibition against termination from employment to avoid undermining that policy. *See Borschel.*

Our insistence on using only clear and well-recognized public policy to serve as the basis for the wrongful discharge tort emphasizes our continuing general adherence to the at-will employment doctrine and the need to carefully balance the competing interests of the employee, employer, and society. An employer's right to terminate an employee at any time only gives way under the wrongful discharge tort when the reason for the discharge offends clear public policy.

The need for clarity in public policy is similarly recognized in our reluctance to search too far beyond our legislative pronouncements and constitution to find public policy to support an action. Thus, we must proceed cautiously when asked to declare public policy to support an exception to the at-will doctrine, and only utilize those policies that are well recognized and clearly defined. Any effort to evaluate the public policy exception with generalized concepts of fairness and justice will result in an elimination of the at-will doctrine itself. Moreover, it could unwittingly transform the public policy exception into a "good faith and fair dealing" exception, a standard we have repeatedly rejected.

2. Determining Jeopardy to Public Policy

Once a clear public policy is identified, the employee must further show the dismissal for engaging in the conduct jeopardizes or undermines the public policy. Thus, this element requires the employee to show the conduct engaged in not only furthered the public policy, but dismissal would have a chilling effect on the public policy by discouraging the conduct. In *Lara* [*v. Thomas*, 512 N.W.2d 777 (Iowa 1994)], we said

---

3. *See* Iowa Code §§ 29A.43 (2005) (absences for membership in military reserves protected); 49.109-.110 (absence for voting protected); 70A.2 (employee may take medical leave of absence upon recommendation of physician without retaliation); 70A.28 (no retaliation for whistleblower reporting of mismanagement of funds); 85.18 (workers' compensation rights protected); . . . (actions for wage and hour disputes are protected); 598.22 (employee cannot be terminated based upon child support withholdings) . . . 607A.45 (absence for jury duty is protected); 642.21 (garnishments for consumer credit transactions); 730.2-.4 (employee may not be blacklisted for terminating relationship, employer may not mislead former employee's potential employer with false statement, nor require successful polygraph test); 731.2 (employment may not be denied to employee based upon membership in labor union).

Employers cannot be permitted to intimidate employees into foregoing the benefits to which they are entitled in order to keep their jobs. To hold otherwise in this context would create a chilling effect by permitting an employer to indirectly force an employee to give up certain statutory rights.

Thus, when the conduct of the employee furthers public policy or the threat of dismissal discourages the conduct, public policy is implicated. On the other hand, if a public policy exists, but is not jeopardized by the discharge, the cause of action must fail. *See Yockey, French* [*v. Foods, Inc.*, 495 N.W.2d 768 (Iowa 1993)] (public policy against suborning perjury not implicated if employer terminates the employee after using coercive and high-handed tactics to obtain confession). This element guarantees an employer's personnel management decisions will not be challenged unless the public policy is genuinely threatened.

3. Claim of Public Policy to Oppose Wrongful Termination of Co-Employee

Fitzgerald first claims there is a public policy in this state which protects an employee from discharge by an employer for opposing the wrongful termination of a co-employee. He claims this public policy in favor of opposing the unlawful termination of a co-employee is derived from [state and federal antidiscrimination statutes]. While those laws prohibit retaliation only where the employee is opposing a discriminatory practice as defined by the legislation, plaintiff argues that such statutes "reveal a broad public policy for employees to oppose all unlawful employment practices including the termination of a co-employee which is contrary to public policy."[4] Fitzgerald claims the termination of Koresh was contrary to public policy of this state to provide truthful testimony and he should be afforded the same protection as the law provides Koresh.

We are reluctant to infer a broad public policy from a statute which is limited in its scope to specific discriminatory practices. Instead, we continue to adhere to our guiding principle to only declare public policy which is clearly articulated by a statute or other appropriate source. The statutes identified by Fitzgerald clearly do not expressly protect his conduct. . . .

We also observe Fitzgerald has failed to show how any public policy in favor of opposing the claimed unlawful termination of a co-employee would be jeopardized by his dismissal. Fitzgerald offered no evidence that he expressed opposition to the discharge of a co-worker because it was unlawful. Instead, Fitzgerald admits the only objection he voiced to his employer over the termination of Koresh was the length of his employment service and the lack of prior infractions. He offered no evidence he objected to the termination of Koresh for providing truthful deposition testimony. The conduct of Fitzgerald, therefore, did not promote the claimed public policy, and

---

4. It is not necessary for us to specifically decide if the public policy to support the tort of wrongful discharge in Iowa can be derived from a federal statute. There is a split of authority among the states. *See, e.g., Faulkner v. United Techs. Corp.*, 693 A.2d 293, 297-98 (Conn. 1997) (a federal law can be a source of public policy); *Griffin v. Mullinix*, 947 P.2d 177 (Okla. 1997) (federal statute cannot serve as a basis for state public policy); *see also* Perritt § 7.13, at 31-32. The issue gives rise to a host of considerations, including potential federal preemption issues. *See* 1 HENRY H. PERRITT, JR., EMPLOYEE DISMISSAL LAW AND PRACTICE §§ 2.39-.46, at 168-91 (4th ed. 1998).

his actions were not necessary to enforce any public policy. Fitzgerald failed to tie his conduct with his claim of public policy.

4. Claim of Public Policy to Provide Truthful Testimony in a Legal Proceeding

We next address the claim by Fitzgerald that he was terminated because he intended to provide truthful testimony, adverse to his employer, in a threatened future lawsuit of a co-employee against Salsbury. Our first task is to decide whether a public policy exists in this state against discharge of an employee for giving or intending to give truthful testimony in a legal proceeding.

Before considering our statutes, we observe other jurisdictions have recognized a public policy against firing an employee for giving testimony in court proceedings. [Here the court cited *Petermann*, an early case that first recognized a cause of action for wrongful discharge when an employee was terminated for refusing to perjure himself at his employer's request.]

This same reasoning has appealed to other courts when faced with actions by employees who were discharged either for refusing to perjure themselves or for testifying truthfully against their employers. Similarly, we find ample statutory support for a public policy in Iowa in favor of refusing to commit perjury. Our statutes make it a crime to commit perjury, suborn perjury, or tamper with a witness. Moreover, this public policy is not simply confined to the refusal to commit perjury but clearly embraces a broader public policy to provide truthful testimony in legal proceedings. *Page v. Columbia Natural Resources, Inc.*, 480 S.E.2d 817 (W. Va. 1996). A policy in favor of refusing to commit perjury necessarily implies an inverse corresponding public policy to provide truthful testimony. Additionally, the integrity of the judicial system, its fundamental ability to dispense justice, depends upon truthful testimony. This principle forms the basis for our perjury and related statutes. Furthermore, a reasonable employer should be aware that attempts to interfere with the process of obtaining truthful testimony, whether through intimidation or retaliation, is a violation of this public policy. Thus, we conclude the public policy derived from our statutes against perjury and suborning perjury also supports a public policy to provide truthful testimony. We next consider whether this public policy is undermined when an employee is discharged from employment for engaging in the conduct claimed by Fitzgerald.

[Defendant argued that this public policy was inapplicable because "Fitzgerald never testified in a legal proceeding, was never requested to testify in a legal proceeding, and never expressed an intent to testify."]

We agree a dismissed employee must engage in conduct related to public policy before the discharge can undermine that public policy. However, we view the good faith intent to engage in a protected activity the same as performing the protected activity. This is because employees would be discouraged from engaging in the public policy if they were discharged for their intent to engage in the public policy the same as if they actually engaged in the conduct. Thus, Fitzgerald must only show he had a good faith intent to truthfully testify.

An essential element of proof to establish the discharge undermines or jeopardizes the public policy necessarily involves a showing the dismissed employee engaged in conduct covered by the public policy. Although proof the employee engaged in the conduct is also a part of the causation element of the tort, we must review Fitzgerald's conduct in this case to determine if it sufficiently matched the public policy of providing truthful testimony.[5]

Fitzgerald did not directly express an intention to testify truthfully in the lawsuit threatened by Koresh. Furthermore, he never told any company officials he possessed any particular damaging information about the threatened lawsuit. These facts suggest Fitzgerald did not contemplate testifying in a threatened lawsuit by Koresh prior to his discharge. Thus, we must review the summary judgment record to determine if a reasonable inference can be drawn that Fitzgerald maintained a good faith intent to testify truthfully in a lawsuit action prior to the discharge. . . .

The conduct engaged in by Fitzgerald prior to his discharge amounted to internal opposition to the termination of a co-employee. Generally, mere internal opposition by an employee to the employer's decision to discharge a co-employee would not suggest an inference the employee intended to give truthful testimony in future litigation brought by the discharged co-employee. The internal expression of support for a co-employee under these circumstances is far removed from the external concepts of perjury and truthful testimony in court proceedings. However, there are additional facts which must be considered in our analysis at this stage of the proceedings.

This case is not simply about Fitzgerald expressing support for Koresh. Salsbury not only admonished Fitzgerald for failing to support his employer, but warned him that the matter could result in litigation and he must decide which side he would support. Thus, Salsbury placed Fitzgerald's support for Koresh in the context of litigation and transformed the conversation into choosing sides in a lawsuit. There was no evidence to suggest Fitzgerald backed down from his support for Koresh after the conversation turned to litigation. These facts permit a reasonable inference to be drawn that Fitzgerald, prior to his discharge, developed an intent to testify in threatened future litigation against his employer.

There are, of course, other inferences that could be drawn from the evidence. However, at this stage we are required to draw those reasonable inferences in favor of Fitzgerald as the nonmoving party to the summary judgment proceedings. In light of these inferences, we conclude that there is evidence to support the claim Fitzgerald engaged in policy-based conduct.

Nevertheless, Salsbury argues the jeopardy element of the tort cannot be satisfied as a matter of law because it never requested Fitzgerald to testify inconsistent with the public policy. . . .

Some jurisdictions require the employer to actually make a request to the employee to commit perjury before finding the public policy against perjury is implicated. *Bushko v. Miller Brewing Co.*, 396 N.W.2d 167 (Wis. 1986). Thus, a discharge based on an employer's concern that the employee will testify truthfully if asked to testify or that the employee intends to testify contrary to the interests of the employer is insufficient to support a cause of action under the public policy exception. *See Daniel v. Carolina Sunrock Corp.*, 436 S.E.2d 835 (N.C. 1993) (statement by employer reminding employee for whom she worked and to say as little as possible prior to providing testimony was insufficient to implicate the public policy against the perjury).

_____

5. No jeopardy can be shown if the plaintiff fails to match the conduct with the public policy. Causation, however, also involves proof of conduct. With this element, the plaintiff must show the dismissal resulted from the protected conduct, and not for some other reason.

We believe the dismissal of an employee can jeopardize public policy when the employee has engaged in conduct consistent with public policy without a request by the employer to violate public policy just as it can when the employee refuses to engage in conduct which is inconsistent with public policy when requested by the employer. The focus is on the adverse actions of the employer in response to the protected actions of the employee, not the actions of the employer which may give rise to the protected actions of the employee. Furthermore, in considering whether the dismissal undermines public policy, we not only look to the impact of the discharge on the dismissed employee, but the impact of the dismissal on other employees as well. Public policy applies to all employees. If the dismissal of one employee for engaging in public policy conduct will discourage other employees from engaging in the public policy conduct, public policy is undermined.

In this case, if Salsbury was motivated to dismiss Fitzgerald because he intended to testify truthfully in a future lawsuit, a dismissal would have a chilling effect on other employees by discouraging them from engaging in similar conduct. Thus, it makes no difference that a dismissal in this particular case may give the employee an enhanced incentive to testify after a dismissal. The action by the employer could inhibit other employees from truthfully testifying in the future out of fear of dismissal.

Salsbury further argues that interpreting the tort to include conduct alleged by Fitzgerald will open the flood gates to litigation for wrongful discharge on public policy grounds whenever an employee internally expresses reservations over the termination of a co-employee and then is later dismissed for some valid reason unrelated to the prior termination of the co-employee. This argument, however, can be made to practically every public policy claim which serves as the basis for a wrongful discharge action. We simply recognize a tort for discharge in violation of a public policy to provide truthful testimony, and leave it to the jury to determine if the facts support the claim. The action in this case is based in part upon an internal complaint by the employee, but is enough to withstand summary judgment because the context of the internal complaint justifies an inference of an intent to testify against the employer which may have caused the employer to dismiss the employee.

5. Causation Element

We next consider if the evidence is sufficient to support a casual connection between the conduct engaged in by Fitzgerald and the discharge. The protected conduct must be the determinative factor in the decision to terminate the employee. Of course, if the employer has no knowledge the employee engaged in the protected activity, causation cannot be established. Similarly, the existence of other legal reasons or motives for the termination are relevant in considering causation.

The causation standard is high, and requires us to determine if a reasonable fact finder would conclude Fitzgerald's intent to testify truthfully was the determinative factor in the decision to discharge him. Generally, causation presents a question of fact. Thus, if there is a dispute over the conduct or the reasonable inferences to be drawn from the conduct, the jury must resolve the dispute. Additionally, any dispute over the employer's knowledge of the conduct is generally for the jury, as well as the existence of other justifiable reasons for the termination. . . .

In this case, the different inferences to be drawn from the evidence precludes [sic] summary judgment. After a recommendation was made to Salsbury to terminate

Koresh, Salsbury wanted to know if Fitzgerald supported Koresh. Moreover, Salsbury gathered this information in the context of a potential lawsuit threatened by Koresh. In light of these inferences, summary judgment was improper. . . .

NOTES

1. *Recognition of the Public Policy Tort.* As reflected in the *Fitzgerald* decision, Iowa is one of the vast majority of jurisdictions that recognize some version of what is now generally called the public policy tort. There are, however, states where the tort is still not recognized. For example, New York has continued to adhere to a strict version of the at-will rule: No matter the degree to which public policy may be implicated, a firing is not actionable unless there is a statute expressly according such a right to an employee. *See Murphy v. Am. Home Prods. Corp.*, 448 N.E.2d 86, 87 (N.Y. 1983). In that case, plaintiff asserted that he was fired in retaliation for reporting to his employer's officers and directors that "he had uncovered at least $50 million in illegal account manipulations of secret pension reserves which improperly inflated the company's growth in income and allowed high-ranking officers to reap unwarranted bonuses from a management incentive plan." Although this conduct might currently be actionable for a publicly traded company under the Sarbanes-Oxley Act, *see* page 248, there was no New York or federal statute providing a cause of action for an employee at that time.

For the New York Court of Appeals, this was a sufficient basis to deny plaintiff's claim since "such a significant change in our law is best left to the Legislature," which was better equipped to answer not only the fundamental question of whether such liability should be recognized but also to craft the appropriate solution:

> The Legislature has infinitely greater resources and procedural means to discern the public will, to examine the variety of pertinent considerations, to elicit the views of the various segments of the community that would be directly affected and in any event critically interested, and to investigate and anticipate the impact of imposition of such liability. Standards should doubtless be established applicable to the multifarious types of employment and the various circumstances of discharge. If the rule of nonliability for termination of at-will employment is to be tempered, it should be accomplished through a principled statutory scheme, adopted after opportunity for public ventilation, rather than in consequence of judicial resolution of the partisan arguments of individual adversarial litigants.

Id. at 79-80. Does this make sense to you, given that the at-will rule is a judicial innovation to begin with? Or is the point less separation of powers than institutional competence? In other words, that common law development over a wide variety of settings may be seen as an inefficient method of furthering the public interest.

Most states follow some version of Iowa's approach, not New York's. *See generally* Restatement (Third) of Employment Law § 5.01, Reporters Notes, cmt. a (Proposed Final Draft, April 18, 2014) (listing seven states rejecting the public policy tort). This is true even in states with statutes providing protection in varying situations. Such focused legislative interventions have not generally been viewed as a reason for the courts to refuse to recognize the broader tort. Indeed, Iowa seems to have a grab bag of statutes that protect employees in a variety of settings, but *Fitzgerald* did not view that as a reason to stay the judicial hand. Nevertheless, the diversity of rules emerging in the jurisdictions adopting the tort suggests that there is something to be said for a statutory solution. Indeed, we will see that several states have enacted comprehensive laws, sometimes called whistleblowing statutes, to address the problem. In New York itself, there has been an outpouring of special-purpose statutes focusing on what *Murphy* called "the various circumstances of discharge." Nevertheless, New York remains largely true to *Murphy*. *See Sullivan v. Harnisch*, 969 N.E.2d 758, 761 (N.Y. 2012) (denying public policy protection to a hedge fund's compliance officer: While compliance with federal regulations is an integral part of the securities business, the existence of such "furnishes no reason to make state common law governing the employer-employee relationship more intrusive."). *But see Wieder v. Skala*, 609 N.E.2d 105 (N.Y. 1992), discussed in Note on Attorneys and the Public Policy Tort, page 221.

2. *Specificity of the Public Policy.* Some courts have been hesitant to limit employer freedom when the predicate public policy is too generalized. *Fitzgerald* is obviously not one of those cases since it allows a very generic policy (truthful testimony) to be the predicate for the tort. Can you imagine public policies that are so diffuse as to not justify a restriction on the employer's right to discharge a worker? *See Turner v. Mem'l Med. Ctr.*, 911 N.E.2d 369 (Ill. 2009) (discharge for a respiratory therapist reporting his hospital's deviation from an electronic patient-charting accreditation standard not actionable; although providing good medical care is in the public interest, the court required a more focused public policy). *See also* RESTATEMENT § 5.03 cmt. d ("Broad, vague, and highly abstract language in judicial decisions, however, does not provide a sufficiently defined source of public policy upon which the wrongful discharge tort may be based.") (Proposed Final Draft, April 18, 2014). *But see Feliciano v. 7-Eleven, Inc.*, 559 S.E.2d 713 (W. Va. 2001) (discharge because of exercise of right of self-defense in response to lethal imminent danger may violate state's public policy).

3. *The Jeopardy Element.* The principal case notes that an employee must not only identify a clear public policy but "must further show the dismissal for engaging in the conduct jeopardizes or undermines the public policy," which requires "the employee to show the conduct engaged in not only furthered the public policy, but dismissal would have a chilling effect on the public policy by discouraging the conduct." The Washington Supreme Court addressed the jeopardy question in *Cudney v. ALSCO, Inc.*, 259 P.3d 244 (Wash. 2011) (en banc), giving a decidedly unplaintiff-friendly answer. A former employee challenged his discharge for reporting violations of drunk driving laws by other workers at the company. The court, however, found the "jeopardy" element not satisfied because, to state a public policy claim, "a tort of wrongful discharge in violation of public policy should be precluded unless the public policy is inadequately promoted through other means and thereby maintaining only a narrow exception to the underlying doctrine of at-will employment." *Id.* at 247. One of the predicate statutes at issue was the state's drunk driving law, and the court concluded that, for plaintiff to sue "the criminal laws, enforcement mechanism, and penalties all have to be inadequate to protect the public from drunk driving. . . . Police and state troopers patrol our roads and highways looking for signs of driving under the influence. There is a huge legal and police machinery around our state designed to address this very problem. It is very hard to believe that the 'only available adequate means' to protect the public from drunk driving was for Cudney to tell his manager about Bartich's drunk driving." *Id.* at 250. *See also Weiss v. Lonnquist*, 293 P.3d 1264, 1271 (Wash. App. 2013) (jury verdict for attorney reversed when she was discharged for refusing to engage in unethical conduct because the disciplinary rules of the state bar offered an adequate means of protecting that public policy at issue by her reporting to the authorities; the inability of the state bar to offer redress to plaintiff was irrelevant). *But see Becker v. Cmty. Health Sys., Inc.*, 332 P.3d 1085, 1087 (Wash. Ct. App. 2014) (refusing to dismiss a wrongful discharge complaint despite "a myriad of statutes and regulations adequately promote the public policy of honesty in corporate financial reporting, rendering a private common law tort remedy superfluous.").

4. *The Predicate Policy Must Protect the "Public." Fitzgerald* suggests that opposition to unwise or unfair employment decisions or policies (as opposed to illegal ones) is not a basis for tort protection. As we have seen, this is consistent with allowing private ordering full rein except when the conduct in question affects the public interest. Recall *Foley v. Interactive Data Corp.*, 765 P.2d 373 (Cal. 1988), where plaintiff claimed that he was discharged after he informed management that his new supervisor was under criminal investigation for embezzlement. California had previously recognized a public policy tort, but the court cautioned:

> [W]e must still inquire whether the discharge is against public policy and affects a duty which inures to the benefit of the public at large rather than to a particular employer or employee. For example, many statutes simply regulate conduct between private individuals, or impose requirements whose fulfillment does not implicate fundamental public policy concerns. . . . Whether or not there is a statutory duty requiring an employee to report information relevant to his employer's interest, we do not find a substantial public policy prohibiting an employer from discharging an employee for performing that duty.

Id. at 379-80. Justice Mosk's dissent in *Foley* stressed the intolerable choice facing the plaintiff: remaining silent, and abandoning his duty to his employer or speaking up and risking discharge. But isn't that the essence of the at-will rule — good reason, bad reason, or no reason?

Many courts agree with the *Foley* point, that the thrust of the tort is to protect third parties and society as a whole, *see* RESTATEMENT § 5.01, cmt. a (Proposed Final Draft, April 18, 2014), but the distinction between public and private has shifted over time. Recall *Murphy*, in which the plaintiff claimed that his employer fired him for opposing its accounting improprieties. The New York court rejected limiting the at-will rule, essentially because it viewed the matter as affecting only the rights of employer and employee. Where only two parties are concerned, private ordering is normally appropriate.

But were the facts of *Murphy* to arise today, the dispute would be viewed very differently: After the enactment of Sarbanes-Oxley ("SOX"), which is discussed in more detail at page 248, this scenario might be seen as implicating a public interest precisely because "third parties" — shareholders and the securities market generally — would now be seen as affected. American Home Products was publicly traded, and Murphy raised serious questions about financial mismanagement or worse. Of course, since *Murphy* rejects a public policy tort entirely, a New York employee's only resort might be SOX itself. *See Sullivan v. Harnisch*, 969 N.E.2d 758, 761 (2012) (refusing to recognize claim by hedge fund compliance officer, despite acknowledging importance of compliance with federal securities law, but noting that, after events at issue, Congress passed Dodd–Frank to reach some kinds of securities whistleblowing).

But could you imagine other states taking a broader view of conduct harming third parties in the wake of SOX and the Great Recession, whose causes included much conduct that years ago would have been viewed as purely private? In any event, the critical point is that courts must see some adverse consequences on some person *outside* the employment relationship in order for the public policy tort to have traction. Thus, even today, after SOX, *Foley* itself would still be within the private sphere because the plaintiff was questioning the wisdom of employing an embezzler, not claiming that he was embezzling. And, of course, even a claim of embezzlement from the employer would not trigger federal protection if the employer were a closely held, rather than a publicly traded, company. In short, the public/private distinction remains operative, even if the borders are in flux.

5. *Wrongful Discipline?* The public policy tort arose in the context of discharges, and most cases have considered employees who are challenging terminations. As with employment discrimination, however, the public policy tort has been applied to constructive discharge cases, *e.g., Colores v. Bd. of Trustees,* 130 Cal. Rptr. 2d 347 (App. 2003), and even adverse employment actions that fall short of either actual or constructive discharge. *See, e.g., Trosper v. Bag'N Save,* 734 N.W.2d 704 (Neb. 2007) (recognizing cause of action for retaliatory demotion); *Brigham v. Dillon Cos.,* 935 P.2d 1054 (Kan. 1997) (wrongful demotion). *But see Touchstone Television Productions v. Superior Court,* 145 Cal. Rptr. 766 (Cal. App. 2012) (no public policy claim when the only adverse action was failure to renew a contract after it expired, which is not actionable in tort); *Mintz v. Bell Atl. Leasing Sys. Int'l,* 909 P.2d 559 (Ariz. App. 1995) (no cause of action for wrongful failure to promote). The proposed RESTATEMENT OF EMPLOYMENT LAW originally reached action that significantly affected terms and conditions of employment or would be "reasonably likely to deter a similarly situated employee from engaging in protected activity." §4.01(b) (Proposed Final Draft, April 18, 2014). The final version will take no position on the issue Would allowing employers to punish workers so long as they don't (constructively) discharge them be consistent with the rationale for the tort in the first place?

6. *Judge and Jury Functions.* Who decides what is public policy? In an omitted portion of its opinion, the *Fitzgerald* court wrote: "It is generally recognized that the existence of a public policy, as well as the issue whether that policy is undermined by a discharge from employment, presents questions of law for the court to resolve. . . . On the other hand, the elements of causation and motive are factual in nature and generally more suitable for resolution by the finder of fact." 613 N.W.2d at 282. This is the general approach. *See, e.g., Turner v. Mem'l Med. Ctr.,* 911 N.E.2d 369 (Ill. 2009). If the question is protecting the public interest, shouldn't the jury be allowed to decide whether a public policy qualifies for the tort?

7. *Tort or Contract? Fitzgerald* takes the majority view that the public policy cause of action sounds only in tort, and some jurisdictions carry this principle so far as to impose individual liability on those supervisors who participate in the wrongful conduct. *VanBuren v. Grubb,* 733 S.E.2d 919, 920 (Va. 2012); *Jasper v. H. Nizam, Inc.,* 764 N.W.2d 751 (Iowa 2009). *Contra Farrow v. St. Francis Med. Ctr.,* 407 S.W.3d 579, 595 (Mo. 2013). However, a few jurisdictions define it as contract-based and not tortious, generally looking to the implied duty of good faith. *See, e.g., Knight v. Am. Guard & Alert, Inc.,* 714 P.2d 788 (Alaska 1986); *Brockmeyer v. Dun & Bradstreet,* 335 N.W.2d 834 (Wis. 1983). Viewing the cause of action as contractual limits plaintiff's recovery to economic damages and would seem to foreclose individual liability, while tort law permits recovery for mental distress, *see, e.g., Wendeln v. Beatrice Manor, Inc.,* 712 N.W.2d 226 (Neb. 2006), and only in torts may punitive damages be awarded. However, statutes of limitations are typically longer for contracts than torts, so a time-barred tort suit might be "cured" by a timely contract action.

8. *Reasonable or Right?* Should protection depend on the employee being correct or just reasonable in the perception that he or she is acting in the public interest? Suppose the employee believes, for example, that the company's actions violate the law? Would an employee be protected if she "blew the whistle" to state agencies even if her charges were incorrect, as long as she reasonably and/or in good faith believed the company was violating a criminal statute? Revisit § 5.02 of the draft Restatement on page 207. Several of the categories of protection require the employee to act "reasonably and in good faith," which seems to require both subjective and objective reasonableness. But other categories in § 5.02 require only good faith or have no intent requirement. Do you see why? There is, however, a kicker in the section: The employee must not only have the requisite basis for acting but also must be "acting in a reasonable manner" to be protected. In any event, the notion that the employee has to be reasonable in both what she is protesting and how she goes about doing it generally reflects what the courts are doing with the public policy tort and parallels the general rule with respect to retaliation for opposing discrimination. *See* Chapter 9, page 713. That means that, no matter how clear the public policy, the plaintiff may not recover unless he is reasonable in believing that the employer is contravening it. *See Fine v. Ryan Int'l Airlines*, 305 F.3d 746 (7th Cir. 2002) (in determining whether employer is acting unlawfully, a reasonable employee might rely on what she learns from co-workers). Further, no matter how clear the public policy and the employee's reasonableness in believing it to be jeopardized, an employee may not be protected if the manner of his protest is viewed as unreasonable.

9. *Advising the Employee.* Suppose an employee comes to you for advice in Mr. Fitzgerald's situation. That is, she has previously been in hot water for backing another employee suit, and she now believes that her supervisor is sending signals that she had better "cooperate" with respect to the discharge of another worker. *Fitzgerald* states the law, but isn't the real problem proof? Do you advise your client to elicit less ambiguous orders that she commit perjury? Do you advise her to secretly tape record any conversations in order to have proof later? How would she do this and what are the risks?

Of course, before you consider the latter course, you should ascertain whether secret taping is criminal in the jurisdiction. In most jurisdictions, the secret taping of a conversation by one of the parties (as opposed to a third party) is *not* criminal. A few states declare such conduct criminal; for example, California criminalizes taping a "confidential" conversation without the consent of all parties. *Cal. Penal Code* § 632 (2014). There is also a private cause of action for any person injured as a result of such a taping. *See Coulter v. Bank of Am.*, 33 Cal. Rptr.2d 766 (1994) (upholding counterclaims in sexual harassment suit for plaintiff's taping of conversations with her supervisor and coworkers). Even absent criminal repercussions, there have been ethical concerns for attorneys when tape recording or advising clients to tape record conversations, although those concerns seem less now in light of the American Bar Association's Formal Opinion 01-422, which concludes that undisclosed taping is not necessarily prohibited. If it is not unethical for you to tape or advise your client to tape, are there still reasons to be wary of it?

10. *Advising the Employer.* Suppose you represent an employer in a public policy-saturated setting — say, a pharmaceutical company whose manufacturing is subject to detailed regulation by the Food and Drug Administration. Maybe virtually everything you do has public policy implications. Management is ready to fire a compliance officer because, although he is very good at his job, he is a perfectionist whose demands make it impossible to work with the team. What advice do you have for your client?

Note on Attorneys and the Public Policy Tort

In footnote 2, the *Fitzgerald* court suggested that an element for a public policy case is that "[e]mployer lacked an overriding business justification for the dismissal (the absence of justification element)." Since it is hard to imagine a justification for perjury, *Fitzgerald* itself never pursued that element. But justifications for some dismissals implicating public policy are possible, typically those in which there is a countervailing public policy. One such scenario is when an attorney blows the whistle on his client. Client confidentiality requirements generally bar such disclosure, although there are situations in which it is permitted or even required. *See* MODEL RULES OF PROF'L CONDUCT R. 1.6 (2003). Isn't it clear that a law firm can discharge an attorney who reports a client's violation to public authorities, at least where the reporting violates state ethics rules? In that case, one public policy (confidentiality) cancels out the other. *See* Alex Long, *Whistleblowing Attorneys and Ethical Infrastructures,* 68 MD. L. REV. 786 (2009); Alex Long, *Retaliatory Discharge and the Ethical Rules Governing Attorneys,* 79 U. COLO. L. REV. 1043 (2008).

Suppose instead that the attorney is discharged for refusing to perform an illegal act. Is the public policy tort available now? Even New York, which is generally hostile to the public policy tort, has recognized something akin to that tort in this situation. *Wieder v. Skala,* 609 N.E.2d 105 (N.Y. 1992), involved an associate in a law firm who claimed to have been discharged because he insisted that the firm report another associate's misconduct to the Disciplinary Committee, as required by the state's Code of Professional Responsibility. While reaffirming that New York did not recognize a general public policy tort, the Court of Appeals found a cause of action in contract stated. Wieder's role in providing legal services to the firm's clients as a member of the Bar "was at the very core and, indeed, the only purpose of his association" with the law firm and his "responsibilities as a lawyer and as an associate of the firm" are "incapable of separation." *Id.* at 635. Further, the ethical rule at issue was indispensable to attorney self-regulation, and Wieder's failure to comply with it would have put him at risk of serious discipline. The unique characteristics of the legal profession made the relation of an associate to a law firm employer "intrinsically different" from such relationships as financial manager to corporate employers as in *Murphy.* The court also stressed that both Wieder and the firm were bound to follow the ethical rule in question. MODEL CODE OF PROF'L RESPONSIBILITY DR 1-103 (A). But New York has been resolute in refusing to extend common law public policy protection beyond attorneys. *Sullivan v. Harnisch,* 969 N.E.2d 758 (2012) (refusing to extend *Wieder* to a hedge fund compliance officer).

Other courts have found that the special role that lawyers play in our society makes the public policy tort inappropriate precisely because lawyers are governed by the rules of ethics. For example, in *Herbster v. North American Co. for Life & Health Ins.,* 501 N.E.2d 343 (Ill. App. 1986), the court held that an in-house attorney discharged for refusing to destroy information sought in discovery had no cause of action. The court stressed the right of a client to end the relationship at will. *See also Tartaglia v. UBS PaineWebber, Inc.,* 961 A.2d 1167 (N.J. 2008) (holding that, in order to prevail on a common law public policy tort claim, plaintiff must "demonstrate that the employer's behavior about which she complained actually violated [the Rules of Professional Conduct]. Any lesser standard of proof . . . would inappropriately intrude on the role of our disciplinary authorities."); *Balla v. Gambro Inc.*, 584 N.E.2d 104 (Ill. 1991) (no cause of action because attorneys already have a duty to abide by rules of professional ethics); This is true even when there is a state whistleblower law that does not contain an explicit exception for attorneys. *See Kidwell v. Sybaritic*, Inc., 784 N.W.2d 220 (Minn. 2010) (an attorney would be protected under the state whistle-blower law if he was acting to expose illegal conduct rather than simply seeking to bring his client into compliance with legal requirements).

Rackley v. Fairview Care Centers, Inc.
23 P.3d 1022 (Utah 2001)

HOWE, J. . . .

[In] 1993, plaintiff Cathleen L. Rackley began working as an at-will employee for defendant Fairview Care Centers, Inc., as the administrator of a nursing home known as Fairview West.

Sometime in February 1994, Karleen Merkley, the manager responsible for resident funds at Fairview West, informed most of the members of the staff that a check for $720 from the Veteran's Administration was expected to arrive for resident Ms. Mellen, and that Ms. Mellen was not to be notified when it came. Plaintiff was not informed of that prohibition. Sharon Mellen, Ms. Mellen's daughter-in-law who had been aiding Ms. Mellen in managing her financial affairs for many years, had requested that Ms. Mellen not be told about the money because she feared Ms. Mellen would try to use it to move out of Fairview West and attempt to live on her own. Sharon wanted to inform Ms. Mellen of the check's arrival personally and to convince her to use the money to purchase a new wheelchair.

In the latter part of February, upon notification that the check had arrived, Sharon went to Fairview West, signed an authorization form in the presence of a witness, and took the check and deposited it in Ms. Mellen's personal bank account. Soon there-after, plaintiff became aware that the check had arrived and had been picked up by Sharon. She notified Ms. Mellen of that fact. Ms. Mellen was upset that she had not been informed of the check's arrival or subsequent deposit and consequently requested that plaintiff contact Sharon on her behalf.

There is some dispute about the content of the phone call to Sharon. Plaintiff contends that she simply told Sharon she had notified Ms. Mellen of the arrival of the check and expressed concern about the impropriety of keeping the information from Ms. Mellen. Plaintiff asserts that Sharon "screamed" at her for telling Ms. Mellen about the money because "she was promised that nobody would find out about the money, that Karleen had talked to her and nobody should find out about it." Sharon contends that plaintiff called her at her place of work, yelled at her over the phone, and accused her of dishonesty and improper conduct. She stated, "all she did was kept telling me, you're stealing Ms. Mellen's money, you can't do that, you need to turn it — return the money to Fairview West. . . . She was very unprofessional. She had me in tears." Plaintiff did not then notify Joseph Peterson, owner and general manager of Fairview, of what had transpired or request investigation by any outside authority.

[However, Sharon later contacted Peterson and told him her version of what had happened. Peterson ultimately reprimanded Merkley, and Sallie Maroney, the manager of Fairview East, for failing to tell Ms. Mellen about the check. A new policy was promulgated requiring that residents be informed of their incoming funds. Plaintiff, however, was reprimanded for calling Sharon at work and later terminated.]

The parties dispute the precise issue before us. Fairview contends that the key issue is whether notification to care center residents of the arrival of their personal funds is a clear and substantial public policy. . . . We agree with plaintiff that if we were to require the law to be so specifically tailored, the public policy exception would be meaningless. Thus, we hold that the proper issue before us is whether a care facility resident's right to manage her own funds constitutes a clear and substantial public policy.

[To succeed on a public policy wrongful discharge claim], plaintiff must satisfy a four-pronged test. Plaintiff must prove that (1) her employment was terminated; (2) a clear and substantial public policy existed; (3) the plaintiff's conduct implicated that clear and substantial public policy; and (4) the termination and conduct in furtherance of the public policy are causally connected. Because Fairview concedes for purposes of this case that plaintiff was terminated, we move directly to the second prong.

I. Clear and Substantial Public Policy

The public policy exception to the employment at-will presumption is much narrower than traditional notions of public policy. Only "clear and substantial public policies will support a claim of wrongful discharge in violation of public policy." . . .

We have stated that a public policy is "clear" if it is plainly defined by one of three sources: (1) legislative enactments; (2) constitutional standards; or (3) judicial decisions. *See Dixon v. Pro Image Inc.*, 987 P.2d 48 (Utah 1999). For example, we have held that the enforcement of a state's criminal code that reflects Utah policy constitutes a clear and substantial public policy. *See Peterson* [*v. Browning*, 832 P.2d 1280 (Utah 1992)] (holding that employer who fired employee for refusing to feloniously provide false information on tax forms could be held liable for wrongful termination).

We have also held that a public policy is "substantial" if it is of "overreaching importance to the public, as opposed to the parties only." *Ryan* [*v. Dan's Food Stores, Inc.*, 972 P.2d 395 (Utah 1998)]. "We must . . . inquire whether the discharge is against public policy and affects a duty which inures to the benefit of the public at large rather than to a particular employer or employee." *Foley v. Interactive Data Corp.*, 765 P.2d 373 (Cal. 1988); *see, e.g., Fox* [*v. MCI Commun. Corp.*, 931 P.2d 857 (Utah 1997)] (holding that retaliatory termination for reporting possible criminal conduct of co-workers to employer does not give rise to a violation of substantial public policy). Statutes that simply regulate conduct between private individuals or impose requirements whose fulfillment does not implicate fundamental public policy concerns are not sufficient to require an exception to the at-will presumption. . . .

[The court stressed that "not every employment termination that has the effect of violating some public policy is actionable." Rather, the scope of the public policy exception must be kept narrow "to avoid unreasonably eliminating employer discretion in discharging employees."]

Plaintiff first asserts that two provisions in the Utah Constitution form the basis of a clear public policy. Article I, section 1 of the Utah Constitution provides in pertinent part that "all men have the inherent and inalienable right to . . . acquire, possess and protect property. . . ." Article I, section 27 provides that "frequent recurrence to fundamental principles is essential to the security of individual rights and the perpetuity of free government." While these two provisions do protect the right to acquire, possess, and protect property, they do not enunciate the narrow type of policy envisioned by our case law creating the public policy exception. The right of a care facility resident to manage her own funds is not "plainly defined by . . . [these] constitutional standards." . . .

Next, plaintiff contends that 42 U.S.C. §§ 3058g(a)(3) and (5), and sections 62A-3-201 to 208 of the Utah Code also plainly define such a public policy.[5] Plaintiff specifically points to subsections (a)(3) and (a)(5) in support of her position. However, subsections (a)(3) and (a)(5) are devoid of any language relating to a resident's right to manage her funds. While these provisions broadly discuss the duty of the ombudsman to monitor and protect the rights of care facility residents, they in no way state a narrow and clear public policy necessary for an exception to the at-will rule. This statute governs the duties and functions of the office of the ombudsman and its representatives and entities, and in no way enunciates rights of care facility residents.

Similarly, we find sections 62A-3-201 and -202 of the Utah Code unavailing. The stated purpose of these provisions "is to establish within the division [of Aging and Adult Services] the [Utah] long-term care ombudsman program for the aging . . . and identify duties and responsibilities of that program . . . in order to address problems relating to long-term care." In pertinent part, the ombudsman is to address the difficulties of the aging citizens of the state by assisting in asserting their civil and human rights as residents of care facilities through legal means. We similarly find this language too broad to constitute a clear and substantial specific public policy. . . .

[As for 42 U.S.C. § 1396r(c)(6),] which governs the requirements care facilities must meet to obtain grants for medical assistance programs, provides that "the nursing facility . . . may not require residents to deposit their personal funds with the facility." Subsection (c)(6) includes guidelines for how care facilities are to manage resident funds when management of such funds has been authorized by the resident. Although not clearly stated, this section could imply that care facility residents have the right to manage their own financial affairs. In the past we have held that we may look beyond the provision in question to determine whether the motivating policy behind it constitutes a clear and substantial public policy. However, we conclude that a mere hint to such an underlying policy, as is the case here, is insufficient to constitute the type of clear and substantial policy necessary to establish an exception to the employment-at-will doctrine. Thus, we hold that 42 U.S.C. § 1396r(c)(6) does not rise to the level of a clear public policy.

Rule 432-150-4.400 of the Utah Administrative Code provides that "the resident has the right to maintain his financial affairs and the facility may not require a resident to deposit his personal funds with the facility." Both of these sections plainly state that care facility residents have the right to manage their own finances.

Additionally, 42 C.F.R. § 483.10, governing resident rights that must be recognized by long-term care facilities, provides the most detailed and applicable provision. It states:

> The resident has a right to a dignified existence, self-determination, and communication with and access to persons and services inside and outside the facility. A facility must

---

5. In general, 42 U.S.C. § 3058g provides that in order to receive federal funding for state long-term care ombudsman programs, states must meet certain requirements, including appointing an ombudsman and establishing an official office of the ombudsman. *See* 42 U.S.C. § 3058g(a)(1), (2).

protect and promote the rights of each resident, including . . . the right to manage his or her financial affairs, and the facility may not require residents to deposit their personal funds with the facility.

This regulation explicitly states that care facility residents have the right to manage their own funds.

However, we have earlier pointed out that a clear public policy must be found in our statutes or constitutions, or judicial decisions. The provision in 42 C.F.R. § 483.10 is an executive agency regulation that governs practice and procedure before federal administrative agencies. Similarly, R432-150-4.400 is a provision in the Utah Administrative Code.

Administrative regulations by their very nature are not "substantial" under our case law. The character of the public policy exception is that it furthers policies that "protect the public or promote public interest." Agency regulations are created by the agencies themselves and are tailored to govern specific agency needs. The public policy exception must be "narrow enough in its scope and application to be no threat to employers who operate within the mandates of the law and clearly established public policy as set out in the duly adopted laws." Thus, we hold that while 42 C.F.R. § 483.10 and R432-150-4.400 of the Utah Administrative Code expressly state that care facility residents have the right to manage their own funds, our case law does not allow for administrative regulations alone to constitute expressions of clear public policy.[8]

In so holding, we recognize that care facility residents are often at the mercy of the facilities in which they reside. Residents face many challenges as their mobility decreases and their ability to take care of themselves physically, mentally, and emotionally deteriorates. However, while we agree with plaintiff that "the rights of nursing home residents, especially with the increasing longevity of Utah residents and the growth of Utah's population, are a matter of most significant public concern," we also recognize the reality that many residents, while remaining in control of their funds, voluntarily seek the assistance of family members or friends with their banking and spending decisions. That appears to have been the situation in the instant case. Such efforts by honest and helpful advisors should be encouraged and not discouraged by rigid, government-imposed requirements. . . .

DURHAM, Justice, dissenting:

I respectfully dissent. There is, I believe, abundant support for the proposition that a long-term care facility resident's right to manage her own funds is a matter of clear and substantial public policy. We are dealing here with one of our system's most fundamental and well-understood rights: the right of a legally competent person to control her property and manage her financial affairs. . . .

This court is now faced with the question of whether to recognize a public policy exception protecting the right of a legally competent long-term care facility resident to manage her own financial affairs. I believe that the majority's view of the legitimacy of the public policy in question is mistaken. We can, and should, recognize administrative regulations as a valid source of Utah public policy for exceptions to the at-will employment doctrine; the regulatory process occurs through legislative delegation and under

---

8. We do not hold that an administrative regulation may not provide support to a legislatively or judicially created public policy.

legislative oversight. It is undertaken by persons and entities with considerable expertise and knowledge regarding legislative intent. Furthermore, there is clear and substantial public policy supporting a long-term care facility resident's right to manage her funds in related federal regulations identical to those adopted by this state, in the Utah Probate and Criminal Code, in Utah case law, and in the Utah Constitution. . . .

[The dissent, in reviewing other sources of public policy, cited *In re Guardianship of Valentine*, 294 P.2d 696 (Utah 1956), a case involving the appointment of a guardian for the property of an alleged incompetent; *Valentine* held that "the right of every individual to handle his own affairs even at the expense of dissipating his fortune is a right jealous[l]y guarded and one which will not be taken away except in extreme cases." It interpreted Sharon Mellen's request to Ms. Merkeley, the Fairview employee in charge of residents' funds, not to inform Ms. Mellen of the arrival of a check as an effort to manage Ms. Mellen's affairs for her. As stated in *Valentine*] the right of every individual to manage his or her own financial affairs is jealously guarded. It is impossible for one to manage one's financial affairs if one is purposefully deprived of the knowledge of relevant information, such as the arrival or deposit of a personal check. . . .

It is important to note that Ms. Merkeley and Ms. Maroney received written reprimands from Fairview for failing to tell Ms. Mellen about her check. In fact, a new policy was instituted by Fairview after this incident requiring that residents be informed of all their incoming funds, regardless of who assists them with their financial affairs. This change was, I submit, an acknowledgment by Fairview of what the laws and public policy of Utah require. . . .

NOTES

1. *Sources of Public Policy.* In states recognizing the public policy tort, the first question is what policies count, that is, what sources may a court look to? *Fitzgerald* and *Rackley* both deal with the sources of public policy that will support a tort suit. *Fitzgerald* writes that the state constitution and state statutes will suffice, but it does not decide whether administrative regulations will do so. What about *Rackley?* Is the court too grudging in its analysis of applicable public policies? Even assuming that the Utah constitutional provisions relating to owning property are too generalized, don't the federal and state laws requiring an ombudsmen to protect residents of nursing homes nevertheless indicate a strong public interest in maintaining the integrity and autonomy of such persons? If there is any doubt about this, isn't it resolved by the federal and state laws related to safeguarding the property of nursing home residents?

Other states have gone further and recognized judicially created public policies, *see Feliciano v. 7-Eleven, Inc.* 559 S.E.2d 713 (W. Va. 2001) (judicially recognized policy favoring self-defense could trump the at-will rule where store employee violated company policy to disarm a robber). Perhaps the most far-reaching decision in terms of sources of public policy is *Pierce v. Ortho Pharm. Corp.*, 417 A.2d 505 (N.J. 1980), which holds that even a professional code of ethics might be a source of public policy. The draft Restatement adopts this view. § 5.02(a), (e). *See also* Note on Attorneys and the Public Policy Tort, page 221. Under this view, might Ms. Rackley have prevailed? Where would you look for codes of conduct that bear on her situation?

2. *Administrative Regulations.* The *Rackley* court recognizes that administrative regulations directly address a patient's right to manage her own financial affairs. But it

refuses to accord "public policy" status to such regulations. Are you persuaded by the court's analysis? Isn't it true, at least on the federal level, that courts view (valid) administrative regulations as an exercise of congressional law-making authority delegated to the agency? *See Chevron U.S.A. Inc. v. Nat. Resources Def. Council, Inc.*, 467 U.S. 837 (1984); *United States v. Mead Corp.*, 533 U.S. 218 (2001). Why should such laws be insufficient predicates for the public policy tort? Is it because regulations may be too detailed and technical? Even so, aren't regulated industries expected to obey governing regulations? Why should they be free to fire employees whose actions further the regulatory regime? The dissent in *Rackley* stressed that other states recognized regulations as an appropriate source of public policy. *See also Jasper v. H. Nizam, Inc.*, 764 N.W.2d 751, 764-65 (Iowa 2009) (While an administrative regulation can be a source of public policy to support the tort of wrongful discharge, to do so it "must state a clear and well-defined public policy that protects an activity in the same way as a statute must state a clear and well-defined public policy to support the tort."). In one sense, *Rackley* may seem divorced from much of employment law because it involves a set of statutes and administrative regulations focused on one particular setting — the nursing home. But it is common in our highly regulated society for particular segments of the economy to be subject to detailed administrative controls. *Rackley* involved only one aspect of the highly regulated health care industry where public policy concerns are pervasive. Other highly regulated industries include transportation and energy. An attorney advising employees or employers in these settings must be alert to the potential of the public policy tort limiting the employer's discretion to terminate, a matter that would otherwise be left to private ordering.

Notice the Catch-22[*] that *Rackley* creates for employees. Constitutional and statutory provisions are likely to be too general to address a particular question. Precisely for that reason, Congress and state legislatures authorize agencies to provide more specific rules through regulations. However, the very regulations that are specific enough to satisfy the court in this respect are not of sufficient authority to state public policy. Reread footnote 8. Is the court suggesting that in some cases regulations may make general policy statements sufficiently concrete to support the tort? If so, why was this not true in *Rackley* itself?

3. *Federal Law Supporting State Public Policy Torts.* In a system with an enormous amount of federal regulation, the relationship between the state public policy tort and federal law is critical. In a footnote, *Fitzgerald* avoided deciding whether federal law could have provided the underlying public policy for a tort action in Iowa. Other cases have looked to federal law as a source of state public policy. As *Fitzgerald's* footnote 4 indicates, this has raised the question whether the federal statute preempts even consistent state law, perhaps by occupying the field. While a few decisions have found preemption by particular federal laws, *see, e.g., Fasano v. FRB*, 457 F.3d 274 (3d Cir. 2006) (federal reserve banks not subject to state employment laws); *Chrisman v. Philips Indus., Inc.*, 751 P.2d 140 (Kan. 1988) (state tort action for discharge for refusing to approve defective nuclear products preempted by federal energy law), most have not. *See, e.g., Sargent v. Cent. Natl. Bank & Trust Co.*, 809 P.2d 1298

---

[*]"There was only one catch and that was Catch-22, which specified that a concern for one's own safety in the face of dangers that there were real and immediate was the process of a rational mind. Orr was crazy and could be grounded. All he had to do was ask; and as soon as he did, he would no longer be crazy and would have to fly more missions. . . . If he flew them he was crazy and didn't have to; but if he didn't want to he was sane and had to. . . ."
JOSEPH HELLER, CATCH-22, 46 (1961).

(Okla. 1991) (no National Bank Act preemption); *Fragassi v. Neiburger*, 646 N.E.2d 315 (Ill. App. 1995) (no OSHA preemption). *See generally* Nancy Modesitt, *Wrongful Discharge: The Use of Federal Law as a Source of Public Policy*, 8 U. PA. J. LAB. & EMP. L. 623 (2006).

4. *Plaintiff's Conduct.* Suppose the dissent had prevailed as to the requisite public policies. Did plaintiff's call to Sharon further those policies? Even if it did, would Fairview have been within its rights to discharge Ms. Rackley for the *manner* in which she made the call — calling Sharon at work and screaming at her? Of course, plaintiff denied she screamed, but would that matter if Fairview thought (reasonably?) that she had? *See Curlee v. Kootenai County Fire & Rescue*, 224 P.3d 458 (Idaho 2008) (an employee terminated for documenting her co-workers' time-wasting activities had a triable claim under the Idaho whistleblowing statute, which protects one who "communicates in good faith the existence of any waste of public funds, property or manpower").

Reviewing the Public Policy Exception

We saw earlier that § 5.02 of the proposed Restatement (Third) of Employment Law identifies six categories under the public policy exception. There is considerable debate both as to whether these categories are too restrictive and whether the formulation of the categories accurately captures the decisions in the area, but understanding the various possible headings for the tort is important.

Refusing to Commit an Illegal Act. Perhaps the most obviously justifiable instance of protection is where the employee is discharged for refusing to perform an illegal act, or violate a code of professional conduct or other occupational code. The employee must only reasonably and in good faith believe the conduct to be illegal or a violation. *See McGarrity v. Berlin Metals Inc.*, 774 N.E.2d 71 (Ind. App. 2002) (refusal to be a party to an illegal tax underreporting scheme for the purpose of defrauding the state and creditors). The principle has been applied to protect employees who testified against their employer's wishes in legal proceedings. *Reust v. Alaska Petroleum Contrs., Inc.*, 127 P.3d 807 (Alaska 2005) (retaliation against employees who testify in legal proceedings actionable, in part because the tort "reduces the temptation for employees, fearing adverse responses from their employers, to provide false testimony or disobey a subpoena"). *But see Harney v. Meadowbrook Nursing Ctr.*, 784 S.W.2d 921 (Tenn. 1990) (termination of nurse who testified at a co-worker's compensation hearing did not implicate public policy tort if the employer had a good faith belief that her testimony was perjured).

Whistleblowing. The proposed Restatement also protects an employee who "reports or inquires about employer conduct that the employee reasonably and in good faith believes violates a law or established principle of professional conduct or an occupational code protective of the public interest." § 5.02(e). Many believe that, after protecting employees for refusing to violate the law, the next most compelling case for protection is when the employee reports a serious violation of law. Unlike instances where employees testify under court process, citizens generally do not have any affirmative duty to make such reports. It, therefore, cannot be said that the employer who discharges a worker for reporting a violation forces her to choose between retaining her job and violating the law; an employee who did not volunteer information would be acting perfectly legally. *See* WAYNE R. LAFAVE, CRIMINAL LAW, § 13.6(c) (5th ed. 2010). Nevertheless, it is certainly in the public interest for individuals to report violations; indeed, statutes such as the federal False Claims Act, *see* note on page 262, essentially offer bounties for pursuing fraud where federal funds are involved. And, as *Fitzgerald* indicated, all states bar interference with witnesses. Accordingly, a great number of cases have recognized a public policy suit where the employee alleges that she was discharged for reporting violations to appropriate public authorities. *See, e.g., Kanagy v. Fiesta Salons, Inc.*, 541 S.E.2d 616 (W. Va. 2000) (cause of action stated for discharge in retaliation for reporting violations to the state Board of Barbers and Cosmetologists); *Prince v. Rescorp Realty*, 940 F.2d 1104 (7th Cir. 1991) (reporting faulty fire safety equipment to town).

But many courts sharply distinguish between reports to public authorities and internal reports, with only the latter being protected — presumably because of the absence of effects beyond the two parties to the employment relationship. *See, e.g., Bielser v. Prof'l Sys. Corp.*, 177 F. App'x 655 (9th Cir. 2006). Note that whether external reporting is required is distinct from whether the public interest is implicated: The plaintiff in *Bielser* claimed that her employer was defrauding a customer. That clearly violated public policy, and, had she reported it to the authorities, she would have been protected. While an external reporting requirement limits the tort in terms of what conduct is protected, isn't it a perverse rule even from an employer's perspective insofar as it tends to require employees to wash their company's dirty laundry in public rather than seek to remedy problems internally? The draft Restatement protects reports made internally. *See* 5.02, Ill. 18.

Performing a Public Duty. As framed by the proposed Restatement, employees are also protected when "perform[ing] a public duty or obligation that the employee reasonably and in good faith believes is imposed by law." The cases dealing with refusals to commit perjury could be so described. The other major "public duty" category is jury service. *Nees v. Hock*, 536 P.2d 512 (Or. 1975). The draft Restatement views this as a very narrow category: The obligation must be a public one, "not merely a personal, familial, or moral obligation." § 5.02, cmt. c.

But the line between the two is not always so bright. Illustration 10 of § 5.02 would protect an employee who is late to work because the police "require" him to fill out a witness report about an accident he observed, but suppose the employee is late because the police *request* him to comfort an injured family member until the EMTs arrive? *See Gaspar v. Peshastin Hi-Up Growers*, 128 P.3d 627 (Wash. Ct. App. 2006) (recognizing a public policy encouraging cooperation with police and prosecutors in criminal investigations). *But see Brennan v. Cephalon, Inc.*, 298 F. App'x 147 (3d Cir. 2008) (a "statutorily imposed duty" claim failed because the statutes in question, while requiring the disclosure of certain "compliance indicators," did not impose an affirmative duty on the employee to report his audit findings to the Food and Drug Administration).

Claiming a Benefit. Still another category of protection under the draft Restatement is "fil[ing] a charge or claim[ing] a benefit in good faith" under "an employment statute or law (irrespective of whether the charge or claim is meritorious)." § 5.02(c). Some of the court cases spoke in terms of "the exercise of a public right," with the prototype being decisions recognizing a cause of action for filing a workers' compensation claim. *See, e.g., Springer v. Weeks & Leo Co.*, 429 N.W.2d 558 (Iowa 1988). But even the public right cases take a more limited view of the rights that are protected than might first appear. For example, a number of cases rejected claims by employees who were fired for doing what, in normal speech, we would say they had a right to do. *See, e.g., Beam v. IPCO*, 838 F.2d 242 (7th Cir. 1988) (hiring an attorney not protected); *Scroghan v. Kraftco Corp.*, 551 S.W.2d 811 (Ky. Ct. App. 1977) (discharge of an employee for attending law school permitted). *See also Hoven v. Walgreen Co.*, 751 F.3d 778 (6th Cir.. 2014) (finding no public policy basis for wrongful discharge by a pharmacist fired by his employer for shooting at armed robbers since self-defense statutes applied only to criminal laws). The Restatement shifts the focus from "right" in the abstract to rights accorded by "an employment statute or law." It would, however, protect workers who act in "good faith," cmt. d, thus avoiding any objective reasonableness requirement for those claiming a benefit.

Waiving a Nonwaivable Right. The Restatement also recognizes a public policy tort for an employee who) "refuses to waive a nonnegotiable or nonwaivable right where the employer's insistence on the waiver as a condition of employment or the court's enforcement of the waiver would violate well-established public policy." § 5.02(d) (Proposed Final Draft, April 18, 2014). It relies on *Edwards v. Arthur Andersen LLP*, 189 P.3d 285, 289 (Cal. 2008), where the court recognized that firing an employee for refusing to waive his statutory rights to compete with, and to be indemnified by, his employer would be actionable. That court, however, tempered the decision by reading the indemnity waiver not to violate this principle. The waiver was framed in terms of "any and all" claims, including "claims that in any way arise from or out of, are based upon or relate to Employee's employment by, association with or compensation from" the employer. Nevertheless, the court found this not specific enough to include the nonwaivable right of indemnification.

The Catchall? Although hotly debated, the Restatement retains a catchall category, inserted because of concerns that limiting the public policy tort to the other categories would tend to freeze the law and not permit appropriate judicial responses to situations that might arise in the future. Accordingly, § 5.02(f) protects an employee from discipline for "engag[ing] in other activity directly furthering a well-established public policy." Illustration 24, based on *Gardner v. Loomis Armored Inc.*, 913 P.2d 377 (Wash. 1996), involves an armored car driver who, in violation of company policy, left his vehicle to rescue a hostage during a bank robbery. Is *Danny v. Laidlaw Transit Services, Inc.*, 193 P.3d 128, 138 (Wash. 2008), another example? There, the court recognized "a clear public policy of protecting domestic violence survivors and their children and holding domestic violence perpetrators accountable." The result would be to preclude the employer from firing the plaintiff for absences due to her dealing with domestic violence, at least if such absences were unavoidable.

* * *

The public policy exception necessarily means that the right of an employee to blow the whistle trumps any employer expectation that the employee's duty of loyalty forbids such disclosure. *See* Chapter 8. *See generally* Orly Lobel, *Lawyering Loyalties: Speech Rights and Duties Within Twenty-First Century New Governance*, 77 FORDHAM L. REV. 1245 (2010). But the relationship between the two conflicting obligations is ill defined. The problem may be illustrated by the employee who is approached by the FBI investigating the employer — say, in a False Claims Act case. *See* page 262.

The employee doesn't believe the employer has done anything wrong, so she doesn't fit within § 5.02(e). The law does not require her to cooperate with the FBI, so it's not a "public duty or obligation," which raises questions about § 5.02(b) (although maybe she would "reasonably believe" that the law required her to respond). There might be a "public right" to cooperate with a criminal government investigation, but the Restatement is limited to claiming benefits connected to employment. Is the catchall provision the solution? Cooperating with the government has to be protected, doesn't it? And it can't violate the duty of loyalty, can it?

Note on Free Speech and the Public Policy Tort

Many of the public policies we have examined implicate speech rights, but the First Amendment articulates a policy only against *state* repression of speech. Under that view, public policy concerns do not reach beyond state action. *See Grinzi v. San Diego Hospice Corp.*, 14 Cal. Rptr. 3d 893 (Ct. App. 2004) (First Amendment free speech not a basis for a public policy claim against a private employer); *Edmondson v. Shearer Lumber Products*, 75 P.3d 733 (Idaho 2003) (free speech is not a sufficiently strong public policy to sustain a wrongful discharge cause of action). A few courts, however, have found private coercion of political activity to be actionable even if restrictions on free speech, as such, are not. *See Chavez v. Manville Products. Corp.*, 777 P.2d 371 (N.M. 1989) (dismissal for refusal to participate in company's lobbying efforts actionable). Even in the public sector, which is treated in more detail in Chapter 7, much employee speech is unprotected: (1) The matter must be one of "public concern," (2) the matter must not be part of the employee's official duties, and (3) the employee's speech must not be too disruptive. *See Garcetti v. Ceballos*, 547 U.S. 410 (2006), reproduced at page 420.

One state generally protects speech against private interference. Connecticut's Free Speech Act, CONN. GEN. STAT. § 31-51q (2006), bars adverse action against an employee "on account of the exercise of rights under the first amendment of the United States Constitution" or under the corollary provisions of the Connecticut constitution. This prohibition is subject to the condition that the employee's "activity does not substantially or materially interfere with the employee's bona fide performance or the working relationship between the employee and the employer. . . ." A few other states have limited laws prohibiting discrimination on the basis of political affiliation or have statutes guaranteeing the right to run for office or to vote. *See* CAL. LABOR L. § 1101 (2014).

Would a public employee who spoke out as Fitzgerald or Rackley did be protected from discharge by the First Amendment? Did either of them speak on matters of public concern? What about under the Connecticut statute?

PROBLEMS

4-1. Lauren Lopez was a fifth-year associate at one of the top defense firms in Gotham. In the course of representing Dr. Sidley in a medical malpractice case, Lopez became suspicious that her client used cocaine. Sidley was a surgeon, and the case involved a claim by a woman who was left paralyzed after back surgery.

The basis for Lopez's suspicions of Sidley's drug use included a constantly irritated nose, occasional "high" states, and extreme mood swings during the course of the two-year representation. As the case neared trial, Lopez became increasingly convinced that Sidley had a drug addiction problem. She received what she believed to be confirmation of this when she interviewed one of the prospective witnesses, an operating room nurse, who told her, "off the record," that Sidley "had had a cocaine problem, but was really working on it."

Lopez took her concerns to the partner supervising her section, L. L. Cohen. He downplayed her worries, telling her she was no expert on symptoms of drug abuse, and she shouldn't believe the nurse's "hearsay." He concluded, "Just forget about it." She was still worried about the matter a week later when Cohen called her into his office on another case and, as she was leaving, said, "Oh, by the way, we've settled that claim against Sidley." Lopez was surprised, since she would normally have been involved in the settlement negotiations. When she asked what the settlement was, Cohen named a figure that was several hundred thousand dollars higher than what Cohen had previously said Sidley's malpractice carrier would be willing to pay.

Rather than lay her concerns to rest, this settlement actually increased Lopez's distress. After wrestling with her conscience, Lopez decided that she had to report her concerns to the state licensing authorities. She wrote a letter to them, copying both Sidley and Cohen and setting forth the bases for her concern.

A day after the letter was sent, Cohen came into Lopez's office and said, "I got your letter. You know I don't agree with you, but I guess we all have to do what we all have to do." He never mentioned the matter again.

You are managing partner of the firm. Both Cohen and Lopez separately speak with you about these events. Lopez is scheduled to be considered for partnership next year. The general sentiment before this episode was that she was unlikely to make partner, although no formal action has been taken. What, if anything, should you do?

4-2. Now imagine you represent Lopez, who is concerned about these events and her consideration for partnership. What advice would you give her? Would it be a good idea to contact the firm before the partnership decision? If so, what would you say or write? If you decide to do nothing, and she is turned down for partnership, what course of action would you advise?

B. STATUTES CREATING PUBLIC POLICY CAUSES OF ACTION

The early public policy cases looked to preexisting statutes for the public policy they discerned. But as the courts began to expand the public policy tort, some legislatures responded by enacting laws designed to protect employees. Such statutes create their own causes of action. The materials that follow explore these statutes and their relationship to the public policy tort created by the courts.

Of course, these general "whistleblower" laws had precursors; it was common for statutes providing substantive protections to employees to also bar employers from retaliating against workers for initiating or participating in enforcement proceedings. For example, the Fair Labor Standards Act bars retaliation for seeking enforcement of that statute's minimum wage and maximum hour provisions. 29 U.S.C.S. §215(a)(3) (2014). Another example is the retaliation provisions of the antidiscrimination laws, which we will encounter in Chapter 9. Less directly related to employment are whistleblowing provisions in federal statutes regulating such areas as nuclear energy, *see* Energy Reorganization Act of 1974, 42 U.S.C. §5851(a) (2014); transportation, *see* Surface Transport Assistance Act, 49 U.S.C. §2305(a) (2014); and heath care, *see* Patient Protection and Affordable Care Act, Pub. L. No. 111-148, 124 Stat. 119, §1150B(d) (2014) (penalizing long-term care facilities for retaliation against an employee who engaged in lawful acts).

While these and similar state laws could be viewed as whistleblowing statutes, that term is often reserved for more open-ended enactments that create civil remedies for employees who are discharged or otherwise adversely treated by their employees because they disclose violations of the law or engage in other conduct in which there is a legitimate public concern. Prior to 1980 there were no general statutes, at either the state or federal level, that broadly protected private whistleblowers. Indeed, it was the absence of such statutes that led so many courts to recognize a public policy suit for discharges of employees who reported violations of the law to relevant authorities. In the wake of such decisions, however, several states enacted whistleblower statutes—that is, laws providing a measure of protection to employees, whether in the public or private sector, for conduct the legislature deemed to be worthy of protection. At the federal level, there is still no comprehensive statute, but a new wave of protection has taken hold this century, starting with the Sarbanes-Oxley Act. *See* page 248.

1. State Approaches

State statutes have varying substantive provisions, but an appreciation of the problems faced in drafting and applying these laws may be gained by comparing two state statutes in detail.

≡ **Conscientious Employee Protection Act ("CEPA")**
≡ *N.J. Stat. Ann. §34:19-1 (2014)*

§34:19-3. Retaliatory action prohibited

An employer shall not take any retaliatory action against an employee because the employee does any of the following:

a. Discloses, or threatens to disclose to a supervisor or to a public body an activity, policy or practice of the employer, or another employer, with whom there is a business relationship, that the employee reasonably believes:
(1) is in violation of a law, or a rule or regulation promulgated pursuant to law, including any violation involving deception of, or misrepresentation to any shareholder, investor, client, patient, customer, employer, former employee,

retiree or pensioner of the employer or any governmental entity, or, in the case of an employee who is a licensed or certified health care professional, reasonably believes constitutes improper quality of patient care; or

(2) is fraudulent or criminal, including any activity, policy or practice of deception or misrepresentation which the employee reasonably believes may defraud any shareholder, investor, client, patient, customer, employee, former employee, retiree or pensioner of the employer or any governmental entity;

b. Provides information to, or testifies before, any public body conducting an investigation, hearing or inquiry into any violation of law, or a rule or regulation promulgated pursuant to law by the employer, or another employer, with whom there is a business relationship, including any violation involving deception of, or misrepresentation to, any shareholder, investor, client, patient, customer, employee, former employee, retiree or pensioner of the employer or any governmental entity, or, in the case of an employee who is a licensed or certified health care professional, provides information to, or testifies before, any public body conducting an investigation, hearing or inquiry into the quality of patient care; or

c. Objects to, or refuses to participate in any activity, policy or practice which the employee reasonably believes:

(1) is in violation of a law, or a rule or regulation promulgated pursuant to law, including any violation involving deception of, or misrepresentation to, any shareholder, investor, client, patient, customer, employee, former employee, retiree or pensioner of the employer or any governmental entity, or, if the employee is a licensed or certified health care professional, constitutes improper quality of patient care;

(2) is fraudulent or criminal, including any activity, policy or practice of deception or misrepresentation which the employee reasonably believes may defraud any shareholder, investor, client, patient, customer, employee, former employee, retiree or pensioner of the employer or any governmental entity; or

(3) is incompatible with a clear mandate of public policy concerning the public health, safety or welfare or protection of the environment.

CEPA goes on to provide for a one-year statute of limitations and a jury trial. § 34:19-5. Remedies include legal or equitable relief, including punitive damages, attorneys' fees, and a civil fine, although punitive damages can be awarded only if "upper management" is implicated and the violation is "especially egregious." *Longo v. Pleasure Prods., Inc.*, 71 A.3d 775 (2013). In an unusual provision, § 34:19-6 allows the reasonable attorneys' fees and court costs to the *employer* "if the court determines that an action brought by an employee under this act was without basis in law or in fact."

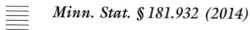

Minn. Stat. § 181.932 (2014)

Disclosure of Information by Employees

1. Prohibited action.

An employer shall not discharge, discipline, threaten, otherwise discriminate against, or penalize an employee regarding the employee's compensation, terms, conditions, location, or privileges of employment because:

(1) the employee, or a person acting on behalf of an employee, in good faith, reports a violation, suspected violation, or planned violation of any federal

or state law or common law or rule adopted pursuant to law to an employer or to any governmental body or law enforcement official;

(2) the employee is requested by a public body or office to participate in an investigation, hearing, inquiry;

(3) the employee refuses an employer's order to perform an action that the employee has an objective basis in fact to believe violates any state or federal law or rule or regulation adopted pursuant to law, and the employee informs the employer that the order is being refused for that reason;

(4) the employee, in good faith, reports a situation in which the quality of health care services provided by a health care facility, organization, or health care provider violates a standard established by federal or state law or a professionally recognized national clinical or ethical standard and potentially places the public at risk of harm;

(5) a public employee communicates the findings of a scientific or technical study that the employee, in good faith, believes to be truthful and accurate, including reports to a governmental body or law enforcement official; or

(6) an employee in the classified service of state government communicates information that the employee, in good faith, believes to be truthful and accurate, and that relates to state services, including the financing of state services, to:

(i) a legislator or the legislative auditor; or

(ii) a constitutional officer.

The disclosures protected pursuant to this section do not authorize the disclosure of data otherwise protected by law.

The Minnesota statute bars not only discharge but also "penalizing" employees for protected conduct, with that term being defined to mean "conduct that might dissuade a reasonable employee from making or supporting a report." § 181.931. The statute authorizes a civil suit for "all damages recoverable at law" in addition to reasonable attorney's fees, and appropriate equitable relief. It explicitly authorizes "reinstatement, back pay, restoration of lost service credit, if appropriate, compensatory damages, and the expungement of any adverse records of an employee who was the subject of the alleged acts of misconduct." § 181.935. The two-year state statute of limitations for intentional torts applies. *Larson v. New Richland Care Ctr.*, 538 N.W.2d 915 (Minn. Ct. App. 1995) *abrogated on other grounds by Gordon v. Microsoft Corp.*, 645 N.W.2d 393 (Minn. 2002).

NOTES

1. *Applying the Statutes.* Suppose CEPA had been in effect in Utah. Would Rackley have fared better? Section 3 protects disclosures, inter alia, to "supervisors" of "an activity, policy or practice of the employer that the employee reasonably believes is in violation of a law. . . ." Did Rackley satisfy this standard? What about Iowa — would it have affected Fitzgerald's suit? Fitzgerald won under the Iowa common law. Would he have won under CEPA? Read § 3 carefully. Now apply the Minnesota analysis to the facts of the two cases. Rackley's conduct might or might not be protected, depending in part on whether it relates to the quality of health care the home provided.

2. *"Exhaustion."* CEPA's § 4 requires the employee to have brought the problem "to the attention of [her] supervisor . . . *by written notice*" (emphasis added) before

the employee makes disclosure to a public body. This departs from the common-law cases, which have not generally imposed any duty of "exhaustion of internal remedies," much less required a writing. Indeed, to the extent that many states do not extend public policy tort protection to internal complaints, it is a radical departure. The Minnesota statute requires notice (but does not require it be in writing) in only one circumstance, when the employee "refuses an employer's order to perform an action that the employee has an objective basis in fact to believe violates any state or federal law or rule or regulation adopted pursuant to law." In such cases, protection depends on the employee's informing the employer that the order is being refused for that reason. § 181.932(1)(c). If your jurisdiction were considering a statute along the lines of the CEPA or the Minnesota law, would you recommend any requirement of resort to internal remedies? If so, when?

3. *Reasonable Belief.* How certain must an employee be that his employer is violating public policy in order to receive statutory protection? Neither state requires the employee to be correct. CEPA speaks in terms of the employee's "reasonable belief," but the Minnesota statute is even more protective. It protects "good faith" reports of violations, § 181.932(1)(c), and the statute essentially defines good faith to mean not knowing or reckless falsehoods. § 181.931(4). However, when the employee refuses to perform what he views as an illegal act, he must have an "objective basis in fact" for believing that the performance would violate the law. § 181.932(1)(c). An "objective basis in fact" appears to be something akin to a "reasonable belief." Why do you suppose the Minnesota legislature decided to include different standards in subparts (a) and (c)?

In contrast to the expansive approaches of Minnesota and New Jersey, a few other states take more restrictive views. For example, Michigan refused to protect a worker who was nonrenewed since the state whistleblower law reached only "employees" and a worker whose contract was not renewed was more akin to an applicant). *Wurtz v. Beecher Metro. Dist.*, 848 N.W.2d 121 (Mich. 2014). More common are states that take an "at the employee's peril" approach to protection. For example, *Pooler v. Maine Coal Products*, 532 A.2d 1026 (Me. 1987), applied that state's narrow law protecting employees who refuse to follow an employer order that violates a law and would put anyone's health and safety at risk. It held that an employee who refused to drive an allegedly unsafe truck must prove an actual safety violation. Which of these three approaches is preferable? *See also Webb-Weber v. Community Action for Human Servs., Inc.*, 15 N.E.3d 1172 (N.Y. 2014) (while Labor Law § 740(2) prohibits employers from retaliation against employee for disclosing employer practices violating laws related to public health or healthcare fraud, it requires plaintiff to prove an actual violation that creates a substantial and specific danger to the public health or safety); *Koch Foods, Inc. v. Sec'y, U.S. Dep't of Labor*, 712 F.3d 476, 484 (11th Cir. 2013) (Surface Transportation Assistance Act requires an employee to be correct about the existence of a violation before he can refuse to work).

Suppose the employee has a reasonable belief in a public policy violation but is motivated by self-interest, not public spiritedness? *Whitman v. City of Burton*, 831 N.W.2d 223, 225-26 (Mich. 2013), applying the Michigan Whistleblower Protection Act, held it immaterial that the plaintiff "acted to advance own financial interests, not to inform public on matter of public concern," since the state statute did not require a public-minded "primary motivation." The federal Whistleblower Protection Act was amended to make irrelevant "the employee's or applicant's motive for making [a protected] disclosure." 5 U.S.C. § 2302(f)(1)(C).

4. *Complaint Box or 1-800 Number?* Section 7 of CEPA requires an employer to designate "the persons . . . to receive written notifications pursuant to section 4 of this act." Would you consider retaining individuals who are required to keep the name of the notifying employee confidential from others within the company? Such an approach, if effective, would tend to immunize complainers from retaliation and thereby tend to protect you from suit. How could you make the confidentiality provision credible? Name an ombudsman? Choose an outside professional such as an attorney? Ironically, in *Estate of Roach v. TRW, Inc.*, 754 A.2d 544 (N.J. 2000), the employer set up a hotline staffed by its attorneys, but the plaintiff's call "fell through the cracks."

5. *Scope of Public Policy.* CEPA and the Minnesota statute seem to be both broader and narrower than the common law. For example, neither protects an employee from reprisal for "claiming a benefit arising from employment." On the other hand, CEPA's catch-all language — protecting an employee who refuses to participate in an activity she reasonably believes to be "incompatible with a clear mandate of public policy concerning the public health, safety, or welfare or protection of the environment," 3(c)(3) — seems to go far beyond a refusal to participate in activities that are "illegal." And Minnesota protects communicating "the findings of a scientific or technical study," which does not require any nexus to public policy. Again, imagine you are drafting a statute for your jurisdiction. How would you frame the substantive protections in terms of the scope of public policy?

6. *Limitations on Whistleblowing. Fitzgerald* recognized that an employer's retaliation might be justified if the employee's whistleblowing were somehow inappropriate, and we saw in the Note on Attorneys and the Public Policy Tort on page 221 that professional ethics might bar disclosure of client confidences and therefore, justify actions against an attorney who violated those confidences. CEPA contains no explicit exceptions to its protection, but the Minnesota statute expressly excludes from its general protection (1) most disclosures of "the identity of any employee making a report to a governmental body or law enforcement official"; (2) false disclosures — that is, "statements or disclosures [made by an employee] knowing that they are false or that they are in reckless disregard of the truth"; and (3) and disclosure of "confidential information" — that is, "disclosures that would violate federal or state law or diminish or impair the rights of any person to the continued protection of confidentiality of communications provided by common law." § 181.932 (2), (3), (5). If you were drafting a statute, would you include any exceptions? If so, do the Minnesota ones make sense? Do you understand what the last one is driving at?

7. *A Job Duties Exception?* When we reach Chapter 7, we will discover that First Amendment protection does not extend to public employees whose actions fall within their job duties. Does such an exception operate under the Minnesota or New Jersey laws? In *Kidwell v. Sybaritic, Inc.*, 784 N.W.2d 220 (Minn. 2010), Minnesota rejected such an exception under that state's statute, largely because it was inconsistent with the broad statutory language. However, "we do not go so far as to hold that an employee's job duties are irrelevant in determining whether an employee has engaged in protected conduct." The court was concerned that a protected employee be motivated by a desire to "expos[e] an illegality," and when action was within an employee's job duties, it might not have been taken for this purpose. In the case before it, *Kidwell* found that the plaintiff, in-house general counsel for the defendant, had not adduced sufficient evidence to allow a jury to find that his opinion concerning the legality of his client's withholding discovery was offered in order to expose illegality. New Jersey seems similarly conflicted, with Appellate Division decisions cutting both ways. *Compare*

Lippman v. Ethicon, Inc., 432 N.J. Super. 378, 381-82 (App. Div. 2013) (an employee's job title or employment responsibilities not outcome determinative in deciding whether the employee has presented a cognizable cause of action under CEPA) *with Massarano v. New Jersey Transit*, 400 N.J. Super. 474, 491 (App. Div. 2008) ("[P]laintiff was merely doing her job as the security operations manager by reporting her findings and her opinion.").

In contrast, the federal Whistleblower Protection Act, 5 U.S.C. § 2302(b)(8) (2014), was originally interpreted restrictively to include a "job duties" exception. However, the statute was amended in 2012 to broaden its protection. Thus, it now provides that conduct is protected from reprisal even if "made during the normal course of duties" of an employee. § 2302(f)(2). In addition, the amendments explicitly ruled out a number of other limitations on protected conduct, including that the disclosure was made to a participant in the challenged activity, the information had been previously disclosed, the disclosure was not made in writing, and the disclosure was made while the employee was off duty. *See generally* Nancy Modesitt, *The* Garcetti *Virus,* 80 U. CIN. L. REV. 137 (2011).

PROBLEMS

4-3. Review Problem 4-1. How would you resolve it under the New Jersey and Minnesota statutes?

4-4. Review Problem 4-2. How would you resolve it under the New Jersey and Minnesota statutes?

≡ *Maimone v. City of Atlantic City*
≡ 903 A.2d 1055 (N.J. 2006)

SKILLMAN, J.

This appeal involves a claim under the [CEPA] by a police officer who alleges he was transferred from detective to patrolman in retaliation for his objections to the Chief of Police's decision to terminate enforcement of provisions of the Code of Criminal Justice prohibiting promotion of prostitution and restricting the location of sexually-oriented businesses.

I.

Plaintiff Angelo Maimone has been a member of the Atlantic City Police Department since 1988. He was transferred in 1991 from a patrolman position to detective in the Special Investigations Unit. As a result, plaintiff became contractually entitled after one year to receive an additional 3% of his base salary. Beginning in 1993, plaintiff was assigned to conduct investigations of prostitution and other sexually-related offenses, which he continued to do until early 2001.

In May 2000, defendant Arthur C. Snellbaker was appointed Chief of the Atlantic City Police Department. According to plaintiff, around eight months after Snellbaker's appointment, Captain William Glass told him at a staff meeting that he could not initiate any new promotion of prostitution investigations unless they "directly impacted the citizens of Atlantic City." Shortly thereafter, plaintiff's immediate supervisor, Sergeant Glenn Abrams, directed him to terminate all pending investigations into the promotion of prostitution and to conduct only narcotics investigations. Plaintiff alleges that Abrams told him that "they," referring to prostitution investigations, "don't exist." Plaintiff, who at that point was the only detective still actively involved in promotion of prostitution investigations, understood this directive to apply not only to him but also to all other officers in the Special Investigations Unit.

Around the same time Abrams gave plaintiff this directive, the files plaintiff had maintained regarding persons involved in the promotion of prostitution were removed from a filing cabinet under his control, and thereafter, plaintiff's access to those files was restricted. When plaintiff complained to Abrams about his loss of access to these files, Abrams allegedly told him: "You're never going to see the files again."

[In April 2001, plaintiff sent a memorandum to Sergeant Abrams complaining about his inability to access those files. It noted that he routinely updated files "on Escort and Massage services working in Atlantic City," and referred to "at least seven new services operating this month alone." The memorandum complained about the absence of file space for new files and the absence of any means of cross-referencing these files against current files. It asked for Chief Snellbaker's response.]

According to plaintiff, after Abrams read this memorandum, he shook his head and said to plaintiff: "You're asking for it."

In 2001, Maimone also complained about Atlantic City's failure to enforce *N.J.S.A.* 2C:34-7, which makes it a fourth-degree offense for a sexually-oriented business to operate within 1,000 feet of a church or school. After the county prosecutor decided that *N.J.S.A.* 2C:34-7 should be enforced by the revocation of the mercantile licenses of offenders rather than by criminal prosecution, plaintiff wrote letters to the municipal solicitor requesting the initiation of proceedings to revoke the licenses of sexually-oriented businesses that were operating in violation of this prohibition. When the city solicitor failed to take any action, plaintiff sent a memorandum to Abrams, dated May 26, 2001, which stated in part:

> I am respectfully asking, that this Office request that the mercantile license of AC News and Video be revoked, due to the fact that this location is clearly in violation of 2C:34-7. This location is clearly a detriment to the neighborhood. There is a Covenant House for juveniles on the same block as well as an elementary school and Synagogue being nearby. As you are aware, it has been and continues to be the practice of the Atlantic County Prosecutor's Office, not to prosecute this statute. It is their contention that civil remedies (IE: Removal of Mercantile license) would be sufficient and thus relieving the Prosecutors Office from utilizing their limited resources in prosecution.
>
> If the city chooses not to enforce this statute in this matter, all future prosecutions will be jeopardized.

Within days after he sent this memorandum, Captain Glass said to plaintiff: "You're out of here, you're going to patrol." Effective June 10, 2001, plaintiff was transferred from his detective position in the Special Investigations Unit to patrol officer. Plaintiff was told that the reason for his transfer was an April 17, 2001 newspaper story that disclosed he had attended the wedding of a daughter of a suspected organized crime figure.

II.

[The trial court granted summary judgment to the defendants because plaintiff could not create a genuine issue of material fact that he reasonably believed Atlantic City's decision to cease enforcing the provisions of the Code relating to promotion of prostitution and restricting the location of sexually oriented businesses "violat[ed] . . . a clear mandate of public policy." The Appellate Division reversed, and Supreme Court granted defendants' petition for certification.]

III.

Plaintiff's CEPA claim is based on *N.J.S.A.* 34:19-3c, which provides:

> An employer shall not take any retaliatory action against an employee because the employee does any of the following. . . .
> c. Objects to, or refuses to participate in any activity, policy or practice which the employee reasonably believes:

[T]he Court held in *Dzwonar* [*v. McDevitt*, 828 A.2d 893 (N.J. 2003)] that a plaintiff who brings an action under this section must demonstrate that:

> (1) he or she reasonably believed that his or her employer's conduct was violating either a law, rule, or regulation promulgated pursuant to law, or a clear mandate of public policy; (2) he or she performed a "whistle-blowing" activity described in *N.J.S.A.* 34:19-3c; (3) an adverse employment action was taken against him or her; and (4) a causal connection exists between the whistle-blowing activity and the adverse employment action.

These requirements must be liberally construed to effectuate CEPA's important social goals.

Defendants do not dispute that plaintiffs' objections to Atlantic City's alleged policy decision to cease enforcement of the provisions of the Code that prohibit promotion of prostitution and restrict the location of sexually-oriented businesses constituted a "whistle-blowing" activity, thus satisfying the second requirement of a claim under *N.J.S.A.* 34:19-3c identified in *Dzwonar*. However, defendants argue that the evidence plaintiff presented in opposition to their motion for summary judgment was insufficient to establish the other three requirements of a claim under this section. We address those requirements in the order set forth in *Dzwonar*.

A.

Plaintiff rests his claim solely on subsection (3) of *N.J.S.A.* 34:19-3c. At the outset, it is appropriate to compare the elements of a claim under this subsection with a claim under c(1). While an employee who proceeds under c(1) must show that he or she reasonably believed that the employer's activity, policy or practice "violat[ed]" a law, rule, or regulation, an employee who proceeds under c(3) is only required to show that the employer's activity, policy, or practice is "incompatible" with a clear mandate of public policy. To "violate" a law, a person must commit "[a]n infraction or breach of the law," BLACK'S LAW DICTIONARY 1564 (7th ed.1999), but a person's conduct may be found "incompatible" with a law based solely on a showing that the conduct is "irreconcilable" with that law, *id.* at 768. Moreover, since the recognized sources of public policy within the intent of c(3) include state laws, rules and regulations, *Mehlman v. Mobil Oil Corp.*, 707 A.2d 1000 (N.J. 1998), a plaintiff who pursues a CEPA claim under this subsection may rely upon the same laws, rules and regulations that may be the subject of a claim under c(1).). Consequently, it is easier for an employee who proceeds under c(3) to prove that he or she reasonably believed the employer's conduct was "incompatible" with a clear mandate of public policy expressed in a law, rule or regulation than to show, as required by c(1), a reasonable belief that the employer's conduct "violated" a law, rule or regulation.

However, an employee who proceeds under c(3) must establish an additional element that is not required to prove a claim under c(1). Although an employee may pursue an action under c(1) based on objections to employer conduct that he or she reasonably believes violated any law, rule or regulation, an employee who proceeds under c(3) must make the additional showing that the "clear mandate of public policy" he or she reasonably believes the employer's policy to be incompatible with is one that "concern[s] the public health, safety or welfare or protection of the environment." *See Estate of Roach v. TRW, Inc.*, 754 A.2d 544 (N.J. 2000). This requirement is "unique" to c(3). *Id.*

The significance of this additional element of a claim under c(3) is illustrated by *Maw v. Advanced Clinical Commc'ns*, 846 A.2d 604 (N.J. 2004), in which an employee brought a CEPA claim challenging her termination for refusing to execute an employment agreement containing what the employee believed to be an overly expansive do-not-compete clause. This Court concluded that case law which allows a no-compete provision only if it is reasonable does not constitute "a clear mandate of public policy" within the intent of c(3) because an employer's attempt to impose an unreasonable no-competition agreement impacts solely upon the individual employee and does not "implicate the public interest." *Maw.*

Unlike in *Maw* the provisions of the Code of Criminal Justice that prohibit promotion of prostitution and restrict the location of sexually-oriented businesses constitute "a clear mandate of public policy concerning the public health, safety or welfare[.]" The Code makes promotion of prostitution either a third or fourth-degree offense, depending on the circumstances, *see N.J.S.A.* 2C:34-1b(2) and *N.J.S.A.* 2C:34-1c(3), and it makes the operation of a sexually-oriented business within 1,000 feet of a school or church a fourth-degree offense, *N.J.S.A.* 2C:34-7. These provisions reflect a legislative recognition that the promotion of prostitution and other commercial sexual activities are a source of "venereal disease, . . . profit and power for criminal groups who commonly combine it with illicit trade in drugs and liquor, illegal gambling and even robbery and extortion[,] . . . [and] corrupt influence on government and law enforcement machinery." II *The New Jersey Penal Code, Final Report of the N.J. Criminal Law Revision Commission*, 301-2-cmt. 1 on NJSA §2C:34-2 (1971).

To prevail on a CEPA claim under c(3), plaintiff is not required to show that defendants' alleged policy decision to cease enforcement of the provisions of the Code prohibiting the promotion of prostitution and restricting the location of sexually-oriented businesses actually violated or was incompatible with a statute, rule or other clear mandate of public policy. *See Dzwonar.* Plaintiff only has to show that he had an "objectively reasonable belief" in the existence of such a violation or incompatibility. Plaintiff may carry this burden by demonstrating that "there is a substantial nexus between the complained-of conduct" — the cessation of investigations of promotion of prostitution and failure to enforce laws relating to the location of sexually-oriented businesses — and "[the] law or public policy identified by . . . plaintiff" — in this case the provisions of the Code proscribing such criminal conduct.

We conclude that plaintiff's proofs met this burden. Viewing the evidence in the light most favorable to plaintiff, as required on a motion for summary judgment, it could support a finding that he had an objectively reasonable belief that defendants made a policy decision to cease all investigation and enforcement of the Code provisions prohibiting the promotion of prostitution and restricting the location of sexually-oriented businesses. Plaintiff testified that Captain Glass told him at a staff meeting in January 2001 not to initiate any new prostitution investigations unless they directly impacted the citizens of Atlantic City, and shortly thereafter, Sergeant Abrams issued a directive to terminate all pending promotion of prostitution investigations. Around the same time Sergeant Abrams issued this directive, the files plaintiff had maintained regarding persons involved in the promotion of prostitution were removed from a filing cabinet under his control, and thereafter, his access to those files was severely restricted. Since plaintiff was the only detective still actively involved in promotion of prostitution investigations at that time, he could reasonably have believed that the intent of Sergeant Abrams' directive and the removal of his investigation files was to terminate all such investigations in Atlantic City.

In addition, when plaintiff sent a memorandum requesting his superiors' assistance in persuading the municipal solicitor to initiate proceedings to revoke the mercantile licenses of sexually-oriented businesses operating in violation of *N.J.S.A.* 2C:34-7, the only response he received was Captain Glass' comment: "You're out of here, you're going to patrol." Plaintiff further testified that the City never took any action to revoke the licenses of sexually-oriented businesses that were operating in violation of *N.J.S.A.* 2C:34-7. Therefore, a trier of fact could find that plaintiff had an objectively reasonable belief that Atlantic City had made a policy decision not to enforce this statutory prohibition.

[Unlike an earlier case in which plaintiff had alleged that his employer had failed to follow his recommendations regarding two petitions of exclusion from casinos, Maimone's] claim is not simply that defendants decided to assign a "lower degree of priority" to investigations of violations of the Code provisions prohibiting promotion of prostitution and restricting the location of sexually-oriented businesses, but rather that they made a policy decision to terminate all enforcement of these criminal laws. Plaintiff was not told, and had no other reason to believe, that this alleged policy decision was due to budgetary constraints or an administrative determination that there was a need to assign additional officers to the investigation of more serious crimes. Therefore, a trier of fact could find that plaintiff had an objectively reasonable belief that defendants made a policy decision that was incompatible with a clear mandate of public policy concerning the public health, safety and welfare.

B.

We next consider defendants' argument that plaintiff failed to present sufficient evidence to support a jury finding that "an adverse employment action" was taken against him.

CEPA prohibits an employer from taking "retaliatory action" against an employee for protected conduct. *N.J.S.A.* 34:19-3. "Retaliatory action" is defined by CEPA to mean "the discharge, suspension or demotion of an employee, or *other adverse employment action* taken against an employee *in the terms and conditions of employment.*" *N.J.S.A.* 34:19-2(e) (emphasis added). Under this definition, any reduction in an employee's compensation is considered to be an "adverse . . . action . . . in the terms and conditions of employment." Moreover, even without any reduction in compensation, a withdrawal of benefits formerly provided to an employee may be found in some circumstances to constitute an adverse employment action.

Plaintiff presented sufficient evidence that his transfer from a detective position to patrol duty resulted in both a reduction in his compensation and a loss of other benefits to satisfy this element of a cause of action under *N.J.S.A.* 34:19-3. Although plaintiff's transfer to patrol duty was not considered a demotion in rank, it resulted in a 3% reduction in his compensation. . . . In addition, plaintiff testified that detectives have an opportunity to earn substantially more overtime than officers assigned to patrol duty, that the 3% salary differential is reflected in the calculation of a retiring police officer's pension, and that detectives are assigned unmarked police cars that they can use to commute back and forth to work. We conclude that this alleged reduction in compensation and loss of other benefits as a result of plaintiff's transfer from his detective position to patrol duty could support a finding that he suffered an "adverse employment action."

C.

The requirement that an employee who brings a CEPA claim under *N.J.S.A.* 34:19-3 must show "a causal connection exists between the whistle-blowing activity and the adverse employment action[,]" *Dzwonar,* can be satisfied by inferences that the trier of fact may reasonably draw based on circumstances surrounding the employment action, *Roach v. TRW, Inc.* The temporal proximity of employee conduct protected by CEPA and an adverse employment action is one circumstance that may support an inference of a causal connection. . . .

Furthermore, there is evidence that would support a finding that the reason defendants gave for plaintiff's transfer to patrol was pretextual. On April 17, 2001, during the period plaintiff was complaining to Sergeant Abrams about the City's alleged non-enforcement of the laws relating to the promotion of prostitution, Chief Snellbaker requested the Internal Affairs Bureau to conduct an investigation into plaintiff's attendance at the 1998 wedding of the daughter of a suspected organized crime figure. On May 25, 2001, the Internal Affairs Bureau issued a report that concluded plaintiff's superiors had authorized his attendance at the wedding for the purpose of "gathering intelligence information," and that plaintiff had submitted an intelligence report after the wedding describing what he had observed and heard. Consequently, the Internal Affairs Bureau concluded plaintiff's attendance at the wedding was "justified, legal and proper." Although the Internal Affairs Bureau exonerated plaintiff of any wrongdoing in connection with his attendance at the wedding, plaintiff was told that this was the reason for his transfer to patrol duty. The implausibility of this explanation for plaintiff's transfer is an additional circumstance that could support a finding that the real reason for this adverse employment action was plaintiff's complaints about defendants' alleged failure to enforce the laws relating to promotion of prostitution and the location of sexually-oriented businesses. . . .

IV.

The dissent charges that our opinion "appears to graft a new limitation on the discretionary governance prerogatives of an employer[.]" However, there is nothing novel in the proposition that a statute — in this instance the Code of Criminal Justice — constitutes a "clear mandate of public policy" within the intent of CEPA. Plaintiff does not seek, as the dissent asserts, "to determine law enforcement policy for [the] entire [Atlantic City Police Department]." He only seeks to avail himself of the judicial remedies provided by CEPA for the adverse employment action taken against him for objecting to the police department's alleged policy decision to cease enforcement of the Code provisions prohibiting promotion of prostitution and restricting the location of sexually-oriented businesses. Plaintiff's claim does not rest simply on his personal disagreement with this policy decision, but on an objectively reasonable belief that it "is incompatible with a clear mandate of public policy concerning the public health, safety or welfare[.]" *N.J.S.A.* 34:19-3c(3). Therefore, our recognition of plaintiff's right to pursue this claim before a jury is mandated by the State legislative policy expressed in CEPA to protect employee whistle-blowing activity. . . .

RIVERA-SOTO, Justice, dissenting. . . .

I.

In this case, a police officer alleges that his reassignment was precipitated by his complaints that the Atlantic City Police Department was not enforcing the laws against prostitution and related offenses to a degree that was personally satisfactory to that police officer. . . . Highlighting the patent absurdity that results from allowing a rank-and-file police officer to determine law enforcement policy for an entire department, the trial court narrowed the inquiry to the decision-making discretion vested in the police officer on patrol and made the common sense observation that "[i]t is self-evident that no police officer can, without prioritizing, effectively prosecute every violation of the law that comes to his or her attention." The trial court further noted that "[o]ne may reasonably conclude that a police officer should have the discretion to determine that there are legitimate priorities that would preclude the investment of the same level of resources in the enforcement of every provision of law."

[The trial court's decision was correct in viewing plaintiff's claim as "an unsupportable extension" of CEPA "to afford to every police officer the ability, under the authority of a CEPA claim, to hold his or her department accountable to the officer for any discretionary determinations of resource allocation and law enforcement priorities solely because those determinations differed from the officer's views." Further, "[i]t would be manifestly inappropriate to substitute, for the City's judgment, [plaintiff's] view or that of a court or jury with regard to the appropriate priorities for applying the law enforcement resources available to the City."]

II.

There is a further notion in the majority's reasoning that is particularly troublesome. . . .

Under the majority's view, a municipality now must be governed by its lowest common denominator or risk the imposition of liability. Stripped to its essence, the majority rules that plaintiff's claim survives summary judgment not because of any wrongful municipal action, but because "[p]laintiff was not told, and had no other reason to believe, that this alleged policy decision [to limit the resources assigned to combat the promotion of prostitution or sexually oriented businesses] was due to budgetary constraints or an administrative determination that there was a need to assign additional officers to the investigation of more serious crimes." That turns the basis of the employer/employee relationship on its head, requiring that, in order to avoid a potential CEPA lawsuit, an employer must explain every discretionary decision to the satisfaction of every line employee. That was never CEPA's purpose or intendment. . . .

NOTES

1. *"Whistleblowing Activity."* New Jersey has made clear that, to invoke paragraph (c), the plaintiff must "identify a statute, regulation, rule, or public policy that closely relates to the complained-of conduct." *Dzwonar v. McDevitt*, 177 N.J. 451, 463 (2003). Assuming he can do that, what does the plaintiff have to do to trigger CEPA protections? The *Maimone* court described him as engaged in a "whistleblowing activity," but the plaintiff did not, even metaphorically, blow a whistle — he just stood up to his bosses. Paragraph (c), however, reaches "objecting to" employer conduct, and Maimone's actions were apparently enough to count as "objecting." The Supreme Court has similarly broadly construed Title VII's antiretaliation provision, which in part protects individuals who "oppose" unlawful employment practices. *Crawford v. Metropolitan Government of Nashville & Davidson County*, 129 S. Ct. 846, 851 (2009).

Whatever the reach of paragraph (c), paragraphs (a) and (b) describe yet additional kinds of protected conduct, some of which are more intuitively whistleblowing. But *Maimone* quickly determines that (a) does not apply — to be protected under that prong, the employee must reasonably believe that the "activity, policy, or practice" being disclosed "is in violation of a law." Accordingly to the court, there was no way a police officer could reasonably believe a shift in law enforcement priorities was illegal. What if plaintiff believed that the new policy was the result of a payoff to Snellbaker? That would be in violation of law, but, absent more information, would Maimone have had a basis to "reasonably believe" (as opposed to suspect) that that was the explanation?

Thus, as interpreted by the court, (c) is broader than (a). The employee must, again, reasonably believe that what he objects to occurs, but the policy or practice does not have to violate any law or regulation. *See also Estate of Frank L. Roach v. TRW, Inc.*, 754 A.2d. 544, 551 (N.J. 2000) (Paragraph (c)(3) "evidences a legislative recognition that certain forms of conduct might be harmful to the public although technically not a violation of a specific statute or regulation."). Doesn't the structure of (3) clearly justify this conclusion? After all, if an employee objects to what she reasonably believes is a violation of law, she is already protected by paragraph (c)(1). But the result is a sweeping statute that cuts the statutory protection loose from any particular statute. Can you identify why, exactly, the court felt Maimone's conduct was protected?

2. *Patent Absurdity?* The dissent speaks of the majority "allowing a rank-and-file police officer to determine law enforcement policy for an entire department." Surely, that's an overstatement. The question isn't whether the department must follow Maimone's views of proper enforcement priorities; rather, it's whether the department can retaliate against Maimone for objecting to the new priorities. But note that paragraph (c)(1) protects employees not only for objecting to activities but also for "refusing to participate" in them. Might the dissent have been concerned that, had Maimone continued to pursue sex-based violations, he couldn't have been demoted for insubordination?

3. *Reasonable Belief.* The *Maimone* decision stresses that plaintiff need not be correct about the activity in question violating a law or a clear mandate of public policy; he or she need only be reasonable. This is a consistent theme in the New Jersey cases. *See Mehlman v. Mobil Oil Corp*, 707 A.2d 1000, 1015-16 (N.J. 1998) ("The object of CEPA is not to make lawyers out of conscientious employees but rather to prevent retaliation against those employees who object to . . . conduct that they reasonably believe to be unlawful or indisputably dangerous to the public health, safety or welfare."). But the court has suggested some limitations. In *Estate of Roach v. TRW, Inc.*, 754 A.2d 544, 552 (N.J. 2000), for example, plaintiff claimed to have been terminated because he reported two of his co-workers for conflicts of interest and for false expense reports and time cards. It wrote:

> Although the term "reasonably believes" in sections 3c.(1) and 3c.(2) provides ample justification to sustain the jury's verdict in the present case, we caution that in future cases that language may prove fatal to an employee's claim. For instance, if an employee were to complain about a co-employee who takes an extended lunch break or makes a personal telephone call to a spouse or friend, we would be hard pressed to conclude that the complaining employee could have "reasonably believed" that such minor infractions represented unlawful conduct as contemplated by CEPA. CEPA is intended to protect those employees whose disclosures fall sensibly within the statute; it is not intended to spawn litigation concerning the most trivial or benign employee complaints.

See also Battaglia v. United Parcel Serv., Inc., 70 A.3d 602 (N.J. 2013) (vague comments about inappropriate use of credit cards and employees going out for liquid lunches did not suggest fraudulent activity protected under CEPA). In *McMillin v. Ted Russell Ford, Inc.*, 2014 Tenn. App. LEXIS 450 (Tenn. Ct. App. July 31, 2014), the court found no significant public concern implicated by plaintiff's refusal to take potential buyers on test drives in cars without dealer plates or proof of insurance.

4. *Adverse Employment Action.* In most of the cases we have seen so far, the claim is for "wrongful dismissal," but plaintiff in *Maimone* wasn't discharged — he was demoted with relatively minor economic consequences. The court, nevertheless, found that the requisite adversity for a violation of CEPA. *See also Donelson v. DuPont Chambers Works*, 20 A.3d 384 (N.J. 2011) (not necessary to show constructive discharge in order to recover lost wages under CEPA). This is an important point of distinction between statutory claims and common-law claims. While some courts have applied the common-law tort to less severe actions than dismissal, *see* Note 5, page 219, whistleblower statutes tend to be framed to reach at least any actions with economic consequences. This is generally true even under the more restrictive federal decisions requiring an "adverse employment action" in the discrimination context. *See* Chapter 9.

5. *Notifying the Employer.* CEPA protects employees for actions directed at their employer. Thus, paragraph (a) reaches disclosures to a supervisor and paragraph (c) protects the kind of objection Maimone made. But CEPA also protects disclosure to a public body, paragraph (a), as well as participating in a public hearing or investigation. Paragraph (b). However, in the latter case, CEPA requires the employee to bring the matter "to the attention of a supervisor of the employee by written notice." § 34:19-4. Had Maimone later taken his concerns to the state attorney general, his memorandum presumably would have satisfied this requirement. The written notice requirement is not applicable where the employee "is reasonably certain that the activity, policy, or practice is known to one or more supervisors." *Id.* Isn't this likely to almost always be true? The notice requirement is also inapplicable "where the employee reasonably fears physical harm as a result of the disclosure." *Id.*

6. *Relationship of CEPA to the Public Policy Tort and Other Causes of Action.* The question of the relationship of a whistleblower statute to whatever other claims might exist is an important one. Section 34:19-8 preserves an employee's rights under other laws, including any "federal or State law or regulation or under any collective bargaining agreement or employment contract," but simultaneously provides that the institution of a CEPA action "shall be deemed a waiver of the rights and remedies available under any other contract, collective bargaining agreement, state law, rule or regulation, or under the common law." This is evidently intended to preserve claims of employment discrimination as well as breach of just cause provisions in individual contracts and collective bargaining agreements. But it also seems to require the employee to elect between pursuing CEPA claims and the other causes of action. *Young v. Schering Corp.*, 660 A.2d 1153 (N.J. 1995), held that this provision does not require dismissal of tort and contract claims because they are sufficiently distinct from the CEPA claim. Rejecting a literal reading, the court wrote, "we are thoroughly convinced the Legislature did not intend to penalize former employees by forcing them to choose between a CEPA claim and other legitimate claims that are substantially, if not totally, independent of the retaliatory discharge claim." *Id.* at 25. Prior to CEPA, however, New Jersey had recognized a common-law public policy tort. *Pierce v. Ortho Pharm. Corp.*, 417 A.2d 505 (N.J. 1980). Presumably, such tort claims would not be "independent of the retaliatory discharge claim" and an employee would have to elect between them and the statute. In making that decision, consider that CEPA has the advantage of a possible award of attorneys' fees, but the CEPA statute of limitations is only one year while tort suits in New Jersey are normally subject to a two-year limitation. *See McGrogan v. Till*, 771 A.2d 1187 (N.J. 2001).

2. Federal Whistleblower Protection

While statutory protection is increasingly common in the states, the federal government has long had statutes providing protection for specific disclosures. Generally speaking, however, these were intended to bulwark particular regulatory regimes, such as nuclear energy or transportation or the antidiscrimination laws. As a result of Enron and other corporate meltdowns, Congress enacted the most sweeping federal statute providing whistleblower protections in the form of the Sarbanes-Oxley Act ("SOX") of 2002, Pub. L. 107-204, 116 Stat. 745. While SOX is not a true general whistleblower statute, in the sense that it does not provide protection for conduct furthering a wide range of public policies, it is the first wide-angle federal enactment that broadly reaches the private sector. Further, it turned out to be the prototype for more aggressive uses of whistleblower protections in federal legislation. As we will see, the Obama administration's stimulus package, health care reform legislation, and financial reform law all have whistleblowing provisions, all of which are variations on the SOX theme.

Professor Miriam Cherry summarized the origins of SOX:

> As the accounting scandals surrounding Enron and WorldCom dominated the headlines and business ethics became increasingly suspect, two whistleblowers became symbols of integrity to the American public. Indeed, Sherron Watkins and Cynthia Cooper were among "The Whistleblowers" named as Time magazine's "Persons of the Year" for 2002. At significant risk to their careers, financial well-being, and mental health, Cooper and Watkins alerted high-level executives at their respective companies to accounting fraud. Unfortunately, most whistleblowers take all these risks when they report illegal activities occurring within their organizations. The magnitude of these recent frauds is startling and, unfortunately, appears to be indicative of a widespread problem. . . . In response to the corporate scandals of 2002, Congress enacted the Sarbanes-Oxley Act (the Act) to prevent future corporate corruption and securities fraud. The Act contains a provision, § 806, that aims to protect whistleblowers such as Cooper and Watkins who report accounting fraud. [The Act covers] all workers at publicly traded companies who "blow the whistle" on suspect accounting practices, whether that whistleblowing is done within the organization, to government agencies, or as part of a shareholder lawsuit. . . .

Miriam A. Cherry, *Whistling in the Dark? Corporate Fraud, Whistleblowers, and the Implications of the Sarbanes-Oxley Act for Employment Law*, 79 WASH. L. REV. 1029, 1031-33, 1063-64 (2004). *See also* Elizabeth C. Tippett, *The Promise of Compelled Whistleblowing: What the Corporate Governance Provisions of Sarbanes-Oxley Mean for Employment Law*, 11 EMPL. RTS. & EMPLOY. POL'Y J. 1 (2007).

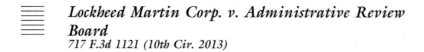

Lockheed Martin Corp. v. Administrative Review Board
717 F.3d 1121 (10th Cir. 2013)

MURPHY, Circuit Judge.

I. Introduction

[Lockheed sued to set aside a decision of the Administrative Review Board of the Department of Labor concluding that it had violated Section 806 of the

Sarbanes–Oxley Act of 2002, 18 U.S.C. §1514A(a). The Board had affirmed an administrative law judge's decision that Lockheed violated the Act by constructively discharging employee Andrea Brown after she had engaged in protected activity. The Tenth Circuit affirmed.]

II. Background

Brown worked as Communications Director for Lockheed from June 2000 to February 2008. In 2003, she became the Director of Communications in Colorado Springs, Colorado. In that position, she reported to Wendy Owen, Vice President of Communications, and Ken Asbury, President of Lockheed Martin Technical Operations. In May 2006, Brown began having difficulty getting responses from Owen on work-related matters. She discussed the problem with Asbury as well as Tina Colditz, a coworker and personal friend. Colditz was a longtime Lockheed employee who reported directly to Owen. Colditz also ran a pen pals program for the company, through which Lockheed employees could correspond with members of the U.S. military deployed in Iraq. Colditz told Brown that Owen had developed sexual relationships with several of the soldiers in the program, had purchased a laptop computer for one soldier, sent inappropriate emails and sex toys to soldiers stationed in Iraq, and traveled to welcome-home ceremonies for soldiers on the pretext of business while actually taking soldiers to expensive hotels in limousines for intimate relations. Colditz told Brown she was concerned Owen was using company funds for these activities, and Brown understood that most employee expenses incurred were passed on to Lockheed's customers, in this case the government. Brown thus became concerned Owen's actions were fraudulent and illegal and that there could be media exposure which could lead to government audits and affect the company's future contracts and stock price.

Brown brought her concerns to Jan Moncallo, Lockheed's Vice President of Human Resources. Moncallo told Brown she would submit an anonymous ethics complaint on Brown's behalf, and that she would be protected from retaliation because no one would know her identity. On May 25, 2006, Moncallo sent an email to Jean Pleasant, the office Ethics Director, for an investigation. The email detailed Brown's allegations, including, *inter alia,* the purchase of a laptop with company funds, the use of company funds to rent limos to transport soldiers, the use of company funds for lodging with soldiers, the use of company funds to purchase gifts for soldiers, communications with staff stating she was meeting with generals when in fact she was meeting with soldiers, not responding to calls from staff due to non-business related meetings with soldiers, having affairs with soldiers, sending pornographic material to soldiers, using her position to influence staff to cover for her, and tarnishing Lockheed's image. The email identified Brown as an individual who should have some knowledge about the allegations.

Lockheed investigated Owen from May 2006 to August 2006. Within a few days of Brown's anonymous complaint, the pen pal program was discontinued. Owen later changed positions but remained a vice president. Apparently believing Colditz to have reported her, Owen began to treat Colditz unfairly. Brown recalled an email from Colditz indicating Owen had told Colditz she would soon be out of work. In the fall of 2006, Brown revealed to Asbury and Colditz that it was she who made the complaint. On December 19, 2006, Owen called Brown to try to find out who had reported her.

According to Brown, Owen told her she had lost her annual bonus due to the complaint. Brown revealed to Owen that Brown had told Moncallo "a few things," but stated she was not sure if her comments had resulted in the complaint. Brown reported the phone call with Owen to Asbury and Moncallo. Prior to 2006, Brown received a "high contributor" or "exceptional contributor" rating in her performance evaluations. In late 2006, and thereafter, however, Brown received a lower rating of "successful contributor."

On February 22, 2007, Lockheed announced to all employees it was undergoing a corporate-structure reorganization. On March 1, 2007, Lockheed's Communications Department announced that further reorganizations would be made. Brown began reporting to Judy Gan, the Senior Vice President of Communications. Owen became Gan's assistant, but retained her title as Vice President. According to Brown, Gan's attitude toward her was negative from the beginning of their professional relationship. For example, Gan told Brown she was not the right person for her current position and indicated there would be a reduction in staff. On June 12, 2007, Brown received a phone call from Owen who announced that Brown's job had been posted on the internet and that she should get her resume together. Distraught, Brown told Asbury and Gan about the phone call in an email.

At this point, Brown first began discussing with Moncallo the possibility of leaving the company. However, she instead decided to apply for the new Director of Communications position. [Gan "lambasted her for applying" and told her she was not qualified for the position. Brown withdrew her application.]

In September 2007, Lockheed hired David Jewell as the new Director of Communications. Owen had a good relationship with Jewell prior to his hiring and had told him to apply for the position. Owen was also a member of the selection committee which considered Jewell. Jewell sought Owen's advice regarding his position and his employees, and was told that Brown had received less-than-perfect evaluations in the past. Shortly after Jewell assumed his new position, Brown was asked to vacate her office and either work from home or use the visitor's office. The visitor's office doubled as a storage room for office supplies, files, and canned food donations that were being collected for a food drive. Brown also lost her title and her supervisory responsibilities over four employees. Further, Gan told Brown she could not attend an annual communications conference, which she had always attended previously, even though she was to receive an award at the conference. Around this time, Brown repeatedly requested information as to the nature of her position and future with Lockheed, but received no answer. Jewell informed her that either she or a Lockheed employee in Houston would be laid off, but would not provide her with any additional information. On January 3, 2008, Brown came into the office at Jewell's request and found someone else working in the visitor's office. When she asked Jewell what she should do, he told her he was looking for a cubicle for her. Brown protested that, as a Level 5 employee with a leadership position (L–Code), she was entitled to an office. Jewell responded that he was in the process of removing her L–Code. Brown then had an emotional breakdown, fell into a deep depression, and took medical leave.

Brown brought a complaint with the Occupational Safety and Health Administration (OSHA)[2] on January 25, 2008, alleging violations of Sarbanes–Oxley.

---

2. An employee alleging wrongful discharge under Sarbanes Oxley may file a complaint with the Secretary of Labor. 49 U.S.C. §42121(b)(1). The Secretary must then "conduct an investigation and

On February 4, 2008, with the assistance of counsel, Brown provided Lockheed with a notice of forced termination. On February 6, 2008, Brown amended her OSHA complaint to allege constructive discharge. OSHA denied Brown's complaint on May 27, 2008.

Brown subsequently requested a hearing before the Office of Administrative Law Judges. A two-day hearing was held [with the ALJ holding in Brown's favor and awarding "reinstatement, back pay, medical expenses, and non-economic compensatory damages in the amount of $75,000." The Administrative Review Board of the Department of Labor affirmed.]

III. Discussion

A. Standard of Review

[The Administrative Procedure Act (APA), 5 U.S.C. § 706, standard of review governs, which means "the Board's legal determinations are reviewed de novo, giving deference to its construction of the Act if reasonable" and factual determinations may be set aside only if they are unsupported by "substantial evidence." Where, as here, the Board's agrees with and is based in part on the ALJ's credibility determinations, "it is entitled to great deference."]

B. Statutory Framework

Section 806, the anti-retaliation provision of Sarbanes–Oxley, provides, in relevant part:

> **Whistleblower protection for employees of publicly traded companies.** —
> No [publicly traded] company . . . , or any officer [or] employee . . . of such company . . . may discharge, demote, suspend, threaten, harass, or in any other manner discriminate against an employee in the terms and conditions of employment because of any lawful act done by the employee —
> (1) to provide information, cause information to be provided, or otherwise assist in an investigation regarding any conduct which the employee reasonably believes constitutes a violation of . . . [18 U.S.C. §§] 1341, 1343, 1344, or 1348, any rule or regulation of the Securities and Exchange Commission, or any provision of Federal law relating to fraud against shareholders, when the information or assistance is provided to or the investigation is conducted by —
> . . . .
> (C) a person with supervisory authority over the employee. . . .

determine whether there is reasonable cause to believe that the complaint has merit." *Id.* § 42121(b)(2)(A). After the Secretary has notified the parties of his findings, either party may request a hearing on the record. *Id.* The Secretary of Labor has delegated his investigative responsibilities under the Act to OSHA. *See* Secretary's Order No. 4–2010, 75 Fed. Reg. 55,355, 55,355–56 (Sept. 10, 2010); 29 C.F.R.1980.104(a). Objections and requests for hearings must be filed with the Chief Administrative Law Judge of the Department of Labor. 29 C.F.R. § 1980.106. Either party may seek review of an ALJ's decision by the Board. *See id.* § 1980.110.

18 U.S.C. §1514A. The regulations implementing Section 806, as well as the decisions of numerous circuit courts, establish the elements of a prima facie claim for violation of §1514A. A claimant must show: (1) she engaged in protected activity or conduct; (2) the employer knew of her protected activity; (3) she suffered an unfavorable personnel action; and (4) her protected activity was a contributing factor in the unfavorable personnel action. *See* 18 U.S.C. §1514A(b)(2)(C); 49 U.S.C. §42121(b); 29 C.F.R. §1980.104(b)(1) (2007); *Harp v. Charter Commc'ns, Inc.*, 558 F.3d 722, 723 (7th Cir. 2009) (collecting cases). . . . [3]

C. Protected Activity

The ALJ concluded Brown established by a preponderance of the evidence that she (1) reasonably believed Owen had committed mail or wire fraud; and (2) communicated that belief "definitely and specifically" to Lockheed. The ALJ also concluded, however, that Brown "fail[ed] to establish protected activity under a general shareholder fraud theory on the basis of loss of shareholder value." . . .

1. Scope of 18 U.S.C. §1514A(a)

Lockheed argues the ALJ's uncontested finding that Brown's complaint did not relate to shareholder fraud is fatal to her retaliation claim because Section 806's protection of employees who report conduct reasonably believed to constitute mail or wire fraud applies only if such conduct "relat[es] to fraud against shareholders." 18 U.S.C. §1514A(a)(1). Thus, under Lockheed's reading of Section 806, the phrase "relating to fraud against shareholders" modifies not only the clause which immediately precedes it, "any provision of Federal law," but also the other enumerated protected activities. Lockheed thus reads the statute as prohibiting a covered employer from retaliating against an employee who provides information regarding violations of 18 U.S.C. §§1341, 1343, 1344, and 1348; rules or regulations of the Securities and Exchange Commission; or any provision of federal law, only if such alleged violations relate to fraud against shareholders. This interpretation of the statute is incorrect.

The plain, unambiguous text of §1514A(a)(1) establishes six categories of employer conduct against which an employee is protected from retaliation for reporting: violations of 18 U.S.C. §1341 (mail fraud), §1343 (wire fraud), §1344 (bank fraud), §1348 (securities fraud), any rule or regulation of the SEC, or any provision of Federal law relating to fraud against shareholders. Because 18 U.S.C. §§1341, 1343, 1344, and 1348 are all clearly provisions of federal law, Lockheed's reading of the statute would render their enumeration in §1514A(a)(1) wholly superfluous. It is a rudimentary canon of statutory construction that such superfluities are to be avoided. *See, e.g., Hibbs v. Winn*, 542 U.S. 88, 101 (2004). Congress could have accomplished the more limited purpose attributed to it by Lockheed by limiting whistleblower

---

3. An employer may still avoid liability notwithstanding an employee's prima facie showing under Section 806 by proving, through clear and convincing evidence, it would have taken the same unfavorable personnel action in the absence of the protected activity. 49 U.S.C. §42121(b)(2)(B); *Harp v. Charter Commc'ns, Inc.*, 558 F.3d 722, 723 (7th Cir. 2009). Because Lockheed did not attempt to make such a showing below, Brown prevails if she meets her prima facie burden.

protection under Sarbanes–Oxley only to an employee who reports conduct "the employee reasonably believes constitutes a violation of any provision of Federal law relating to fraud against shareholders." Because Congress did not so phrase the statute, the proper interpretation of § 1514A(a) gives each phrase distinct meaning and holds a claimant who reports violations of 18 U.S.C. §§ 1341, 1343, 1344, or 1348 need not also establish such violations relate to fraud against shareholders to be protected from retaliation under the Act.

[Even if the language of § 1514A(a) were ambiguous, Lockheed's interpretation of the statute is inconsistent with the interpretation of the agency charged with its enforcement under *Chevron U.S.A., Inc. v. Natural Resources Defense Council, Inc.,* 467 U.S. 837, 844 (1984), and its progeny. The Board's construction of § 1514A(a) is "indisputably permissible," thus requiring the court to defer to it.]

2. Reasonable Belief

Section 806 requires that, to be protected from retaliation, an employee must "reasonably believe" the conduct she reports violates one of the enumerated federal statutes or regulations. 18 U.S.C. § 1514A(a)(1). Further, the ALJ required Brown to prove she "definitively and specifically" communicated her belief Owen had engaged in illegal activity to her supervisor. The Board has defined "reasonable belief" to include both a subjective and an objective component; an employee must actually believe in the unlawfulness of the employer's actions and that belief must be objectively reasonable. The decisions of multiple Circuit Courts of Appeals are in accord. *See Harp* (collecting cases). "Objective reasonableness is evaluated based on the knowledge available to a reasonable person in the same factual circumstances with the same training and experience as the aggrieved employee." *Id.* (quotation omitted).

The conclusion of the ALJ and Board that Brown met these requirements is supported by substantial evidence. Brown testified that, based on her experience as a Lockheed employee, costs incurred by Lockheed employees were billed back to the customer, often the government. She further testified she reported these concerns to Asbury, who could not recall speaking to her, and Moncallo, who could. The ALJ found Moncallo's testimony to be "essential." Moncallo agreed employee travel expenses and purchases of equipment are generally billed to the government. Further, while Moncallo testified Brown did not use the words "fraud" or "illegal," Moncallo recognized that some of the actions Brown complained of could be considered fraudulent and illegal. Additionally, although Asbury and Moncallo testified that Brown did not specifically use the words "fraud" and "illegal" in her reports to them, the ALJ found this disagreement to tarnish Brown's testimony only somewhat since the ALJ considered Brown's testimony to be credible. Thus, the ALJ found Brown communicated a reasonable belief that Owen was fraudulently and illegally diverting company funds for her personal use, and that she was using the company's pen pal program to perpetuate the scheme. This finding was heavily and explicitly based on a credibility determination, i.e., the ALJ chose to place more weight on Brown's testimony that she used the terms "fraud" and "illegal" than on the contrary testimony of Asbury and Moncallo. Lockheed makes no sufficiently persuasive argument for this court to take the extraordinary step of disturbing that credibility determination,

Lockheed also argues any belief Owen's activities amounted to fraud is objectively unreasonable as a matter of law due to a lack of evidence Owen acted with specific intent to defraud. *See United States v. Washington*, 634 F.3d 1180, 1183 (10th Cir. 2011) (listing intent to defraud as an element of 18 U.S.C. § 1341). Specifically, Lockheed argues Owen's lack of attempts to conceal her involvement with the pen pal program negate any inference she acted with the requisite intent. While attempted concealment is one method of proving specific intent in a fraud case, *see United States v. Prows*, 118 F.3d 686, 692 (10th Cir. 1997), it is not essential. For example, this court has also recognized intent can be inferred from whether a defendant "profited or converted money to his own use." *Id*. (quotation omitted). Brown's allegations clearly amounted to a claim that Owen had converted company money to her own use. There was thus substantial evidence supporting the ALJ and Board's findings that Brown reasonably believed Owen had committed fraud and that she definitely and specifically communicated that belief to her superiors.

D. Constructive Discharge

In *Strickland v. United Parcel Service, Inc.*, this court set forth the requirements for establishing constructive discharge:

> Constructive discharge occurs when an employer unlawfully creates working conditions so intolerable that a reasonable person in the employee's position would feel forced to resign. The plaintiff's burden is substantial. The standard is objective: the employer's subjective intent and the employee's subjective views on the situation are irrelevant. Whether a constructive discharge occurred is a question of fact.

555 F.3d 1224, 1228 (10th Cir. 2009) (quotation and citations omitted). . . .

[T]he ALJ recited the correct legal standard for a claim of constructive discharge and concluded, after reciting the litany of adverse circumstances Brown faced following her ethics complaint, "a reasonable person such as Complainant would see resignation as her only option under these circumstances." While portions of the ALJ's opinion also analyze whether Lockheed's actions were "materially adverse" to Brown, that is, "harmful to the point that they could well dissuade a reasonable worker from making or supporting a charge of discrimination," *Burlington N. & Santa Fe Ry. Co. v. White*, 548 U.S. 53, 57 (2006), that analysis does not conflict with the ALJ's ultimate conclusion that Brown's working conditions became objectively intolerable so as to constitute a constructive discharge. . . .

As to Lockheed's second argument, numerous facts cited by the ALJ and Board are indicative of constructive discharge. Prior to making an ethics complaint, Brown held a leadership position, had her own office, and received consistently high performance ratings. After her complaint, Brown received lower performance ratings. A position with an identical job description to the job Brown had been performing for the previous five years was posted on Lockheed's website. When Brown indicated she would apply for the new position, Gan strongly discouraged her from doing so and told her she was not qualified. When Jewell was selected for the new position, Brown lost her title, office, supervisory responsibilities, and L-code. Brown was made to work from home or out of the visitor's office, which doubled as a storage room. She was also denied permission to attend an annual communications conference which she had attended in the past and where she was scheduled to be recognized with an award. Most importantly, Brown was told she would be one of two employees considered for a layoff and kept in a constant state of uncertainty as to whether she would continue to have a job and, if so, what her job would be. That uncertainty continued when, after taking medical leave due to the stress and uncertainty regarding her job situation, she received no response to her inquiries as to whether she was laid off.

A reasonable person would deem this evidence adequate to support the Board's ultimate conclusion that Brown's working conditions were so intolerable she would have viewed quitting as her only option. The circumstances Brown faced at the time she tendered her resignation are analogous to those faced by employees in multiple instances in which this court has found constructive discharge. . . .

Lockheed's attempts to undercut the Board's findings are unavailing. Lockheed argues Brown had alternatives to quitting, and left prematurely before the details of those alternatives were revealed to her. *See Exum v. U.S. Olympic Comm.,* 389 F.3d 1130, 1136 (10th Cir. 2004) (rejecting claim of constructive discharge and noting that "even after Plaintiff submitted his resignation, the [employer] provided him with alternatives to quitting and offered to investigate his complaints"); *Garrett v. Hewlett–Packard Co.,* 305 F.3d 1210, 1222 (10th Cir. 2002) (concluding employee allegations failed to raise inference of constructive discharge when employee "resigned before he had complete details as to the position into which [the employer] was in the process of transferring him"). Unlike the employers in *Exum* and *Garrett,* however, Lockheed points to no evidence in the record that Brown was ever made aware of any purported alternatives. . . .

Lockheed further argues Brown herself had repeatedly given notice that she intended to resign and that her final resignation notice, which was prepared with the assistance of counsel, indicates she was in control of the circumstances of her resignation. Even assuming Lockheed's account of the record is correct, Brown's attempts to stay at Lockheed are irrelevant to the question of whether conditions were so intolerable that she had no alternative but to quit. . . .

E. Contributing Factor

To establish a prima facie case under Section 806, a complainant must show her protected activity was a contributing factor in the unfavorable personnel action. 18 U.S.C. § 1514A(b)(2)(C); 49 U.S.C. § 42121(b)(2)(B)(I); 29 C.F.R. § 1980.109(a); *Harp.* This element is broad and forgiving: the Board has defined a "contributing factor" as "any factor, which alone or in combination with other factors, tends to affect *in any way* the outcome of the decision." *Klopfenstein v. PCC Flow Techs. Holdings, Inc.,* No. 04–149, 2006 WL 3246904, at *13 (Admin. Rev. Bd. May 31, 2006) (emphasis added) (quotation omitted). "[T]he contributing factor standard was 'intended to overrule existing case law, which requires a whistleblower to prove that his protected conduct was a "significant," "motivating," "substantial," or "predominant" factor in a personnel action in order to overturn that action.'" *Klopfenstein* (quoting *Marano v. Dep't of Justice,* 2 F.3d 1137, 1140 (Fed. Cir. 1993)). Temporal proximity between the protected activity and adverse employment action may alone be sufficient to satisfy the contributing factor test. *Van Asdale v. Int'l Game Tech.,* 577 F.3d 989, 1003 (9th Cir. 2009).

The conclusion that Brown's protected activity was a contributing factor in her eventual constructive discharge was supported by the Board's finding that the adverse employment actions Brown experienced began shortly after the conclusion of the investigation against Owen. This finding is supported by substantial evidence. The investigation into Brown's allegations against Owen concluded with the preparation of a formal written report on August 21, 2006. In December 2006 Owen called Brown several times, attempting to determine who had reported her. Eventually, Brown revealed to Owen that she may have shared some information with Moncallo regarding Owen's activities. Shortly thereafter, the cascade of difficulties which culminated in Brown's constructive termination — her lower performance ratings, Gan's harsh treatment of her, and the loss of her privileges and responsibilities as Director of Communications — began.

Lockheed seeks to discredit this conclusion by arguing a significant amount of time passed between Brown's report of Owen's activities and her ultimate constructive discharge. Specifically, Lockheed argues more than twenty months passed between Brown's ethics complaint in May 2006 and her departure from the company in January 2008. Even if the time is calculated from December 2006, when Owen became aware it was Brown who made the ethics complaint against her, Lockheed argues the adverse action and the protected activity are still separated by a full calendar year. [The court distinguished a Title VII case requiring a closer temporal proximity because, under that statute, plaintiff "was required to make a prima facie showing of causation, whereas Brown was required only to show her protected activity was a contributing factor in her discharge."] More importantly, when evaluating temporal proximity for purposes of determining whether Brown's protected activity was a contributing factor in her constructive discharge, the relevant time frame is not when the constructive discharge occurred, but when the conduct leading up to the discharge began. Moreover, . . . Brown's showing that her protected activity was a contributing factor in her constructive discharge was not based solely on temporal proximity.

The Board also concluded that, although neither Gan nor Jewell knew of Brown's ethics complaint against Owen, both were poisoned against Brown by Owen's biased reports regarding Brown's professional competence. This court has applied the subordinate bias, or "cat's paw" theory of liability in other employment discrimination contexts. The Supreme Court recently endorsed the theory in the context of an action under the Uniformed Services Employment and Reemployment Rights Act (USERRA). *Staub v. Proctor Hosp.*, 131 S. Ct. 1186, 1191–92 (2011). Importantly, however, the required showing to establish causation for a claimant under Section 806 is less onerous than the showing required under Title VII, the ADEA, or USERRA. We thus must determine whether the ALJ's finding that Owen "poisoned" Gan and Jewell's opinion of Brown is supported by substantial evidence, keeping in mind that Brown satisfies the causation element of her Section 806 claim by demonstrating merely that her ethics complaint contributed to the adverse employment actions taken against her.

We conclude it is. The ALJ accepted as credible Brown's testimony that Gan was inexplicably hostile to her from their first encounter following the reorganization of the company in early 2007. Further, the ALJ accepted as credible Brown's account of Owen placing a phone call to Brown in which she mockingly advised her that her job had been posted on the company website and she needed to get her resume together. The ALJ also relied upon Moncallo's testimony that it was normal for new supervisors to consult with old supervisors regarding employee performance. Moncallo further testified that she did not discuss with Gan whether she knew about the ethics complaint or advise Gan she should not be seeking Owen's input into Brown's performance. The ALJ also relied on Gan's deposition testimony that she had a high opinion of Owen and relied on her for input into personnel matters. Jewell's deposition testimony was similar. He testified that he discussed the employees under his supervision in his new position with Owen, who told him Brown "had received a less-than-perfect performance appraisal."

Undoubtedly, the inference the ALJ drew from this testimony, that Owen biased Gan and Jewell against Brown, is not the only possible inference which could have been drawn. The ALJ could have chosen, as Lockheed urges, to place more weight on Gan's testimony that Owen was merely a peer with whom she did not maintain a personal relationship, or on Jewell's testimony that Owen was careful not to divulge too much information about Brown and "wanted [him] to evaluate the situation for [him]self." The possibility of drawing different inferences from the administrative record, however, is a grossly insufficient basis to disturb an agency's findings on appeal. . . .

NOTES

1. *Protected Conduct Under SOX.* As *Lockheed* suggests, the conduct at issue must be of a certain nature to come within SOX protection. First, the employee must "provide information or otherwise assist in an investigation." Brown clearly did that, but not all "whistleblowing" qualifies. *See Tides v. Boeing Co.*, 644 F.3d 809 (9th Cir. 2011) (finding SOX did not protect internal auditors who reported problems with compliance to a newspaper since the law protected only employees' disclosures to federal regulatory and law enforcement agencies, Congress, and employee supervisors). *See also Asadi v. G.E. Energy (USA), L.L.C.*, 720 F.3d 620, 625 (5th Cir. 2013) ("Under Dodd–Frank's plain language and structure, there is only one category of whistleblowers: individuals who provide information relating to a securities law violation to the SEC. [Other categories in the statute] represent the protected activity in a whistleblower-protection claim. They do not, however, define which individuals qualify as whistleblowers.").

Second, SOX reaches only "a publicly traded company," thus exempting other employers from potential liability. However, the Supreme Court has held that statute's language reaching "any officer, employee, contractor, subcontractor, or agent" of a company reaches retaliation by contractors against their own employees (not merely against employees of the public company itself). *Lawson v. FMR LLC*, 114 S. Ct. 1158 (2014). Since the publicly traded defendant in that case, a mutual fund, was structured (like all mutual funds) to have no employees, the decision essentially prevented SOX from being entirely inapplicable in that part of the financial sector. Further, "gatekeeper" firms, such as law firms and accounting firms, were effectively swept within SOX's protection throughout the financial industry.

Third, the employee's action must be taken with respect to "conduct which the employee reasonably believes" constitutes a violation of six identified federal statutes. These include mail fraud, 18 U.S.C. § 1341, wire fraud, § 1343, bank fraud, § 1344, or securities fraud, § 1348, or "any [SEC] rule or regulation . . . or any provision of Federal law relating to fraud against shareholders, when the information or assistance is provided to . . . a person with supervisory authority over the employee . . ." 18 U.S.C. § 1514A(a)(1). *Lockheed* rejected a frontal assault on the statute, concluding that it was not limited to violations resulting in loss of shareholder value. However, the requisite nexus to other federal laws raises issues of the scope of those statutes. *See, e.g., Flake v. United States DOL*, 248 F. App'x 287 (2007) (alternative holding that ARB decision not clearly erroneous in finding that SOX did not apply when there were fewer than 300 holders of the employer's securities, and the employer therefore had no duty to file certain reports).

2. *Objectively and Subjectively Reasonable.* As *Lockheed* states, the employee's belief must be both objectively and subjectively reasonable, it follows that plaintiffs must identify a predicate law and establish the relationship between that law and their allegedly protected conduct. *See Nielsen v. AECOM Tech. Corp.*, 762 F.3d 214 (2d Cir. 2014)("[R]elief pursuant to § 1514A turns on the reasonableness of the employee's belief that the conduct violated one of the enumerated provisions. . . . The objective prong of the reasonable belief test focuses on the 'basis of knowledge available to a reasonable person in the circumstances with the employee's training and experience.'"); *Wiest v. Lynch*, 710 F.3d 121, 135 (3d Cir. 2013) (upholding ARB's revised standard for "reasonable belief," that the employee "have a subjective belief that the employer's conduct violates one of the listed laws and that the belief is objectively reasonable"; plaintiff sufficiently plead such a belief when he foresaw a potentially fraudulent tax deduction and misstatement of accounting records when the employer was reporting as "advertising expenses" costs that were more appropriately characterized as employee income); *see also Harp v. Charter Communs., Inc.*, 558 F.3d 722, 725 (7th Cir. 2009) ("If the specific conduct reported was violative of federal law, the report would be sufficient to trigger Sarbanes-Oxley protection even if the employee did not identify the appropriate federal law by name.").

A number of plaintiffs have had their claims dismissed because they could not reasonably believe the laws they identified had in fact been violated. *See, e.g., Day v. Staples, Inc.*, 555 F.3d 42 (1st Cir. 2009) (inefficient business practices, even if they might lead to a short-term reduction in profits, could not support an objectively reasonable belief that they were "shareholder fraud"); *Livingston v. Wyeth, Inc.*, 520 F.3d 344, 355 (4th Cir. 2008) ("even if Wyeth had made the false statements to compliance auditors and the FDA that Livingston supposed could be made, none would amount to a material statement as necessary to violate § 10(b) of the Securities Exchange Act and Rule 10b-5.").

3. *Adverse Employment Action.* SOX bars covered employers from taking certain actions — to "discharge, demote, suspend, threaten, harass, or in any other manner discriminate" — against an employee for engaging in protected conduct. Brown was not formally discharged but she convinced the court she was constructive discharged. As is clear from *Lockheed*, that's a pretty high standard. In an omitted footnote, the court stressed that Brown did not seek to impose liability "for other, lesser adverse employment actions such as demotions, threats, or harassment." Note 8. Suppose Lockheed's actions fell short of constructive discharge. Would they have nevertheless been sufficiently egregious to warrant relief? Note the court's citation to *Burlington N. & Santa Fe Ry. Co. v. White*, 548 U.S. 53, 57 (2006), which used a lower standard for Title VII retaliation cases. *See* page 720. Might a better test be whether the retaliatory actions were of the kind that would dissuade a reasonable employee from reporting violations? *See Halliburton, Inc. v. Admin. Review Bd.*, No. 13-60323, 2014 WL 5861790, at *6 (5th Cir. Nov. 12, 2014) (applying *Burlington* standard to hold it not reversible error for the ARB to conclude that the employer's disclosure of plaintiff's identity as the whistleblower was a "materially adverse" action given the "the undesirable consequences, from a whistleblower's perspective, of the whistleblower's supervisor telling the whistleblower's colleagues that he reported them to authorities for what are allegedly fraudulent practices.")

4. *Proof of a Contributing Factor.* Unlike other regimes, SOX does not require the complaining party to prove that her protected conduct actually resulted in her discharge — sometimes called "but for" causation or "determinative factor" causation. Rather, she must show only that the protected conduct was a "contributing factor" to the challenged employment action. 49 U.S.C. §42121 (2014) (incorporated by reference in 18 U.S.C. §1514A). If the plaintiff does so, it is the employer's burden to prove that it would have made the same decision in any event. *See also Bechtel v. Admin. Review Bd., U.S. Dep't of Labor*, 710 F.3d 443, 448-49 (2d Cir. 2013) ("Bechtel's sole burden was to prove, by a preponderance of the evidence, that his protected activity contributed to the adverse employment action. If he had successfully made such a showing, the burden would then have shifted to CTI to prove, by clear and convincing evidence, that it would have taken the same action absent Bechtel's protected activity."); *Taylor v. Admin. Review Bd.*, 288 F. App'x 929 (5th Cir. 2008) (upholding an agency finding that defendant's clear and convincing evidence of plaintiff's insubordinate conduct, which included belligerence and even screaming at her supervisor, would have caused her dismissal regardless of whether SOX-protected conduct was a motivating factor).

Of course, to prove even a contributing factor, the plaintiff must establish that the employer knew of the protected conduct, *see Vander Boegh v. EnergySolutions, Inc.*, 536 F. App'x 522 (6th Cir. 2013) (while an employer's knowledge of an employee's protected conduct is necessary for a retaliation claim, a reasonable jury could infer such knowledge of environmental complaints either through the DOE's website or through other channels), but what else will suffice? *See Feldman v. Law Enforcement Assocs. Corp.*, 752 F.3d 339, 350 (4th Cir. 2014) (While the contributing factor standard "is indeed meant to be quite broad and forgiving," it did not reach long-past activities given a "lengthy history of antagonism and the intervening events" that caused the plaintiff to be viewed as insubordinate.). What does it mean to be a "contributing factor" when, by definition, the protected conduct doesn't have to cause the adverse employment action.

While the issue is explored in more detail in Chapter 9, antidiscrimination law originally used but-for causation, requiring a showing that discriminatory intent was a "determinative factor" for the decision in question. That standard still operates under the Age Discrimination in Employment Act, *Gross v. FBL Fin. Servs.*, 129 S. Ct. 2343 (2009), and for retaliation cases under Title VII, *Univ. of Texas Sw. Med. Ctr. v. Nassar*, 133 S. Ct. 2517 (2013), and probably in a large swath of other intent-oriented employment laws. Where applicable, it means that the plaintiff can prevail only if he can show that, but for the intent to discriminate, the adverse employment action would not have occurred. However, a lower standard applies under Title VII since the 1991 Amendments reduced the level of causation required to "motivating factor." As a result, discriminatory intent can be a "motivating factor" and therefore violate Title VII, even if the trier of fact ultimately concludes that the employer would have made the "same decision" even had it not been motivated by the prohibited consideration. *See generally* Martin J. Katz, *The Fundamental Incoherence of Title VII: Making Sense of Causation in Disparate Treatment Law*, 94 Geo. L. J. 489 (2006).

"Motivating factor" as used in Title VII is scarcely self-explanatory in the confused world of causation. Further, Congress's use of "contributing factor" in Sarbanes-Oxley suggests the same or perhaps even a lower level of causation. Presumably, it is the slightest degree that can still be said to "play a role" in the termination decision. That must be true since the defendant can still prevail by proving that it would have made the same decision even had the plaintiff not engaged in protected conduct. This necessarily means that the plaintiff's proof can be less than but-for causation since the defendant's affirmative defense of "same decision anyway" amounts to establishing the absence of "but for" causation. While the plaintiff's proof of "contributing factor" must be something less than "but for," how much less is not clear. Note also that the field is not level. The plaintiff must prove a "contributing factor" only by a preponderance of the evidence, while defendant must establish that it "would have taken the same unfavorable personnel action in the absence of [the protected] behavior" by "clear and convincing evidence."

This proof structure makes the question of what suffices for proof of a contributing factor critical. "Temporal proximity" can help, but *Lockheed* establishes that the protected conduct and the adverse action do not have to be very close in time in order for plaintiff to prevail. What kind of evidence enabled Brown to show this level of "minimal causation"?

5. *Administrative Procedure for SOX Claims.* As *Lockheed's* procedural history suggests, Sarbanes-Oxley has a somewhat complicated enforcement procedure. In this it borrows from AIR 21 (the Wendell H. Ford Aviation Investment and Reform Act for the 21st Century), now codified at 49 U.S.C. §42121 (2014), which requires resort to the Department of Labor's Occupational Safety and Health Administration ("OSHA") within 180 days of the violation, although there are often questions about when a SOX cause of action accrues. *See Coppinger-Martin v. Solis*, 627 F.3d 745 (9th Cir. 2010) (refusing to equitably toll then-applicable 90-day filing period where cause of action accrued when she was discharged and she had sufficient information on that date to make out prima facie case). OSHA, in turn, processes the complaint in a quasi-judicial setting, which involves a hearing before an administrative law judge, an administrative appeal, and judicial review in the appropriate circuit court, as in *Lockheed*.

There is, however, an alternative procedure. To guard against agency delay, the statute provides, "if the Secretary has not issued a final decision within 180 days of the filing of the complaint and there is no showing that such delay is due to the bad faith of the claimant," the claimant may bring suit in federal district court. 18 U.S.C.A. §1514A(b). However, the regulations also provide that a plaintiff must file a notice of her intent to file a complaint in federal court 15 days in advance of doing so. 29 C.F.R. §1980.114(b). Filing this notice of intent to sue presumably gives the agency a last chance to complete its proceedings. Where the agency fails to do so, suit may be brought in federal court, *see Collins v. Beazer Homes USA, Inc.*, 334 F. Supp. 2d 1365 (N.D. Ga. 2004), where the action is heard de novo. That means that, even if the agency later rules on the complaint, its decision is not in any way preclusive, although it is possible that such a decision may be introduced in evidence in the civil suit. *See Chandler v. Roudebush*, 425 U.S. 840, 864 (1976) ("Prior administrative findings made with respect to an employment discrimination claim may, of course, be admitted as evidence at a federal-sector trial de novo. *See* Fed. Rule Evid. 803(8)(c).").

Lockheed, however, reflects the more typical circuit court review of agency actions, and the decision is most striking for its great deference to the agency findings. For Brown, that was a good thing since it resulted in the employer's being essentially unable to challenge any fact findings, which is typical in these cases. However, what is good for the goose is good for the gander, and deference to agency decisions can cut both ways. There is considerable reason to believe that OSHA decisions are mostly adverse to employees. Richard Moberly, *Unfulfilled Expectations: An Empirical Analysis of Why Sarbanes-Oxley Whistleblowers Rarely Win*, 49 Wm. & Mary L. Rev. 65 (2007) (during its first three years, only 3.6 percent of SOX whistleblowers won relief through the initial administrative process that adjudicates such claims, and only 6.5 percent of whistleblowers won appeals through the process); *see also* Terry Morehead

Dworkin, *SOX and Whistleblowing*, 105 MICH. L. REV. 1757, 1764 (2007) ("Despite the intended promotion and use of whistleblowing to help enforce Sarbanes-Oxley and deter wrongdoing in the securities market, the statutory scheme gives the illusion of protection without truly meaningful opportunities or remedies for achieving it."); Nancy M. Modesitt, *Why Whistleblowers Lose: An Empirical and Qualitative Analysis of State Court Cases*, 62 U. KAN. L. REV. 165, 194 (2013) (limited study finding that plaintiffs in state court whistleblowing cases prevail at a rate well below that of torts plaintiffs and more akin to the whistleblower plaintiffs in SOX cases at the administrative level; the biggest single reason is failure to prove causation). *But see* Richard Moberly, *Sarbanes-Oxley's Whistleblower Provisions: Ten Years Later*, 64 S.C. L. REV. 1 (2012) (concluding that lessons have been learned from the early experiences with SOX by regulators and legislators who have implemented new strategies that may encourage more effective whistleblowing); Richard E. Moberly, *Sarbanes-Oxley's Structural Model to Encourage Corporate Whistleblowers*, 2006 BYU. L. REV. 1107, 1109 (arguing that SOX's structural model is an improvement over prior efforts in providing a structure that encourages whistleblowers).

6. *State Claims.* Suppose that this case arose in New Jersey or Minnesota. Would Ms. Brown have a cause of action under those state statutes? If so, would such an action arise only because of the public policy evinced in SOX itself, or would the claim have been actionable even before that federal statute was passed as a means of vindicating the federal policy in favor of accurate disclosures of financial information by publicly traded companies? If you conclude that an adverse employment action would have been actionable under either or both state laws only because SOX created a right to be free of reprisal for engaging in this conduct, do you think there is any problem with the states creating a cause of action that duplicates the federal one? Would the federal claim be prejudiced by the state cause of action? Before you answer no too quickly, wouldn't a state claim allow an employee to end-run the requirement of filing with OSHA? Sarbanes-Oxley provides that "[n]othing in this section shall be deemed to diminish the rights, privileges, or remedies of any employee under any Federal or State law, or under any collective bargaining agreement." 18 U.S.C. § 1514A. But if a state were to predicate a public policy tort on SOX itself, would this language apply?

7. *Employer Reaction.* It will not always be clear whether an employee's actions are within the umbrella of SOX protections. Ironically, some of the defendant's reactions to the plaintiff's allegations will lead a court to conclude that the conduct is protected. *See Collins v. Beazer Homes USA, Inc.*, 334 F. Supp. 2d 1365 (N.D. Ga. 2004). In that case, although the plaintiff also complained about inefficient business practices, her supervisor's description of the plaintiff's complaint as a "serious allegation," and the supervisor's recognition that "there was something that may be criminal, against the law or against company policy, including violations of the company's Standards of Corporate Conduct" were factors in the court's finding the plaintiff's conduct protected.

8. *Remedies.* SOX provides for "all relief necessary to make the employee whole," including "reinstatement with the same seniority status" and "back pay, with interest," 18 U.S.C. § 1514A. Punitive damages are not available but "compensation for any special damages sustained as a result of the discrimination, including litigation costs, expert witness fees, and reasonable attorney fees" is to be awarded. *Id.* The Dodd-Frank Wall Street Reform and Financial Protection Act amended SOX to make clear that, when court suit is brought, there is a right to a jury trial. 18 U.S.C.A. § 1514A(b)(2)(e). That statute also amended SOX to bar mandatory arbitration.

18 U.S.C.A. § 1514(e). The parties can still agree to arbitrate, but only after a dispute has arisen.

9. *A New Wave of Federal Protection.* SOX was just the first in a new wave of federal laws containing antiretaliation provisions that may help workers. This includes the American Recovery and Reinvestment Act of 2009, 111 P.L. 5, 123 Stat. 115, and the Patient Protection and Affordable Care Act of 2010, 111 P.L. 148, 124 Stat. 119, better known as the health care reform act, and the Food Safety Modernization Act, 111-353. But perhaps most importantly, the Dodd-Frank Wall Street Reform and Consumer Protection Act, better know as financial reform act, Pub. L. 111-203, §922, 124 Stat. 2129, created three new whistleblower protections related to the Commodities Futures Trading Commission ("CFTC"), Securities and Exchange Commission ("SEC"), and newly established Consumer Financial Protection Bureau ("CFPB"). With respect to both the CFTC and SEC, the statute creates both a bounty system and an antiretaliation provision. This antiretaliation protection is enforced through court suit, not an administrative procedure, and double back-pay is one of the remedies provided. *See, e.g.,* http://www.sec.gov/whistleblower. As for protection of disclosures related to the new CFPB, the coverage reaches a broad array of entities dealing with financial products. This protection, however, is enforced through an administrative filing although, like SOX, de novo suit may be brought if the Department of Labor does not act quickly enough. 12 U.S.C. § 1558 (2014). Like SOX, the burden-shifting provisions are plaintiff-friendly. All three provisions generally bar predispute arbitration agreements or other waivers of rights and remedies.

The False Claims Act

The False Claims Act ("FCA"), 31 U.S.C. § 3730(b) (2014), is not merely a "whistleblower" act, but rather, it functions as a very powerful source of employee rights in a wide range of situations. Its general thrust is to empower any citizen to bring a claim, often referred to as a qui tam suit, in the name of the United States against any entity that submits "a false or fraudulent claim for payment" to the federal government. Because of the federal government's huge expenditures on Medicare and Medicaid reimbursement, much FCA litigation has centered on the health care industry, but claims may arise against any corporation that does business with the government. 18 U.S.C.A. § 1514A.

Although the FCA traces its origins back to the Civil War, a series of recent amendments designed to make it more effective show Congress's continued commitment to using a bounty system to protect the federal fisc. *See* Anthony J. Casey & Anthony Niblett, *Noise Reduction: The Screening Value of Qui Tam,* 91 WASH. L. REV. 1169 (2014) (arguing that qui tam actions are superior to straight bounty programs because the plaintiff's need to invest resources in bringing suit ensures that such claims are likely to be higher value than mere reports of supposed violations by bounty hunters). *See also* Jarod González, *A Pot of Gold at the End of the Rainbow: An Economic Incentives-Based Approach to OSHA Whistleblowing,* 14 EMPL. RTS & EMPL. POL'Y J. 325 (2010) (recommending a similar bounty approach for OSHA violations). Further, the statute now prohibits retaliation for "lawful acts done by an employee . . . in furtherance of an action under this section or other efforts to stop" FCA violations.

False Claims actions are often very attractive from the plaintiff's perspective since the statute authorizes award of from 15 to 30 percent of any recovery to the private plaintiff. 31 U.S.C. § 3730(d). *See generally* Marsha J. Ferziger & Daniel G. Currell, *Snitching for Dollars: The Economics and Public Policy of Federal Civil Bounty Programs*, 1999 U. ILL. L. REV. 1141 (1999). Fraud, especially health care fraud is big business, and the government often recovers billions of dollars, with significant recoveries by "relators." *See* Katie Thomas & Michael S. Schmidt, *Glaxo Agrees to Pay $3 Billion in Fraud Settlement*, N.Y. TIMES, July 2, 2012, A1. Beyond the health care industry, both military procurement and disaster relief offer large opportunities for employees who believe their employer is seeking compensation from the federal government to which it is not entitled.

Since employees are typically in the best position to know when a company may be submitting false claims for reimbursement, the FCA is often invoked in what otherwise seems a garden-variety dispute about employment. *See ex rel. Mikes v. Straus*, 274 F.3d 687 (2d Cir. 2001) (plaintiff doctor sued her former employer not only for damages caused by wrongful discharge but also sought the bounty provided by recovery on a qui tam basis for false Medicare reimbursement claims). In addition, the statute has a section explicitly providing any employee "discharged, demoted, suspended, threatened, harassed, or in any other manner discriminated against in the terms and conditions of employment" for furthering of False Claim Act actions is "entitled to all relief necessary to make the employee whole," including "2 times the amount of back pay" due. 31 U.S.C. § 3730(h). As a result, when an employee can plausibly claim that her discharge was due to a dispute about incorrectly billing the government, the potential recoveries include not only normal remedies but also double back pay and the statutory bounty. *See Thompson v. Quorum Health Res., LLC*, 485 F. App'x 783 (6th Cir. 2012) (jury reasonably could have found that the employer's proffered reason for terminating the employee was pretextual because it did not terminate him when it learned of his violations of the code of conduct but suspended him a month after learning of his FCA suit). *But see United States ex rel. Parks v. Alpharma, Inc.*, 493 F. App'x 380 (4th Cir. 2012) (FCA retaliation suit failed when employee could not establish that anyone at the employer would have reasonably believed that she was contemplating or acting in furtherance of an FCA action).

The False Claims Act has somewhat unusual procedures. As described by David Freeman Engstrom,

> While the FCA empowers the United States to bring enforcement actions, the far more common mode of enforcement is private lawsuits initiated under the FCA's qui tam provisions. These provisions authorize private persons, dubbed "relators," to sue private parties alleging fraud against the United States and earn a cash bounty equal to a portion — ranging from 15% to 30% — of any recovery. . . .
>
> Not anyone can initiate a qui tam suit. The FCA contains several provisions designed to minimize wasteful private enforcement efforts, including: (i) a "first-to-file" provision precluding claims that mirror a previously filed qui tam suit; (ii) a bar on claims related to an already existing government enforcement proceeding; and (iii) a bar on claims that were previously "publicly disclosed" except where the relator is an "original source" — that is, has direct, firsthand knowledge — of the information underlying the fraud claim. Together, these provisions are designed, as the Supreme Court has noted, to achieve "the golden mean between adequate incentives for whistle-blowing insiders . . . and discouragement of opportunistic plaintiffs who have no significant information to contribute of their own."

A final set of FCA provisions vests the Attorney General . . . with substantial authority to oversee and control qui tam litigation. For instance, DOJ may dismiss or settle a qui tam case out from under a private relator, subject only to a basic fairness hearing, or veto private dismissals or settlements. This latter power is critically important: because a relator stands in the shoes of the United States and sues on its behalf, any judgment will have preclusive effect on the government's later assertion of transactionally related claims, creating incentives for relators and defendants to trade an unduly wide release of liability for a larger settlement pot. . . .

Perhaps the most significant form of oversight authority is DOJ's ability to intervene in qui tam suits. By statute, a qui tam relator files her complaint with the court under seal, serving it only on the government. A statutory sixty-day period (often subject to extensions follows, during which DOJ investigates the allegations and decides whether to terminate or settle the case out from under the relator, intervene and take "primary responsibility" for the litigation of the case, or decline to intervene and allow the relator to proceed alone. Importantly, the amount of the bounty paid to a successful relator turns, at least in part, on DOJ's case-election decision: where DOJ declines intervention, a successful relator earns 25% to 30% of any recovery; if DOJ intervenes, a relator keeps only 15% to 25%. During legislative debates leading up to the FCA's 1986 revival, this tiered system of payoffs was seen as essential to incentivize relators to go it alone where a politicized bureaucracy refused to enforce.

Public Regulation of Private Enforcement: Empirical Analysis of DOJ Oversight of Qui Tam Litigation Under the False Claims Act, 107 Nw. U. L. Rev. 1689 (2013); *see also* David Freeman Engstrom, *Harnessing the Private Attorney General: Evidence from Qui Tam Litigation*, 112 Colum. L. Rev. 1244 (2012).

In such a suit, the plaintiff must establish that the defendant submitted a false claim within the meaning of the statute. As the extract suggests, the FCA contains what the Supreme Court has described as "three categories of jurisdiction-stripping disclosures," *Graham County Soil & Water Conservation Dist. v. United States ex rel. Wilson*, 559 U.S. 280, 285 (2010), although they seem to be more properly viewed as exceptions to the statute. These are based on "public disclosure" in (1) criminal, civil, or administrative hearings; (2) a congressional, or administrative reports or investigations; or (3) the news media, "unless . . . the person bringing the action is an original source of the information." § 3730(e)(4)(A). *See Schindler Elevator Corp. v. U.S. ex rel. Kirk*, 131 S. Ct. 1885 (2011) (government Freedom of Information Act (FOIA) responses were "reports" subject to FCA's public disclosure bar); *Graham County* (state or local government reports satisfied the public disclosure bar).

As with other whistleblower causes of action, FCA claims pose special problems for attorneys.

United States Ex Rel. Fair Laboratory Practices Associates v. Quest Diagnostics, Inc.
734 F.3d 154 (2d Cir. 2013)

José A. Cabranes, C. J.:

[Plaintiff appeals from dismissal of this qui tam action and disqualification] of plaintiff, its individual members — including a former general counsel to defendant — and its outside counsel from bringing a subsequent qui tam action on the basis that the suit was brought in violation of the general counsel's ethical obligations under the New York Rules of Professional Conduct (the "N.Y. Rules"). The issues on appeal arise out of the tension between an attorney's ethical duty of confidentiality and the federal interest in encouraging "whistleblowers" to disclose unlawful conduct harmful to the government. . . .

We agree [with the district court] that the attorney in question, through his conduct in this qui tam action, violated N.Y. Rule 1.9(c) which, in relevant part, prohibits lawyers from "us[ing] confidential information of [a] former client protected by Rule 1.6 to the disadvantage of the former client," N.Y. Rule 1.9(c), except "to the extent that the lawyer reasonably believes necessary . . . to prevent the client from committing a crime," *id.* 1.6(b)(2).

In addition, we hold that the District Court did not err by dismissing the complaint as to all defendants, and disqualifying plaintiff, its individual relators, and its outside counsel on the basis that such measures were necessary to avoid prejudicing defendants in any subsequent litigation on these facts.

Accordingly, we affirm. . . .

Background

Plaintiff-appellant Fair Laboratory Practices Associates ("FLPA" or "plaintiff") brought this qui tam action pursuant to the federal False Claims Act ("FCA"), 31 U.S.C. §§ 3729–3733, against defendants-appellees Quest Diagnostics Incorporated ("Quest") and Unilab Corporation ("Unilab") for alleged violations of the federal Anti–Kickback Statute, 42 U.S.C. § 1320a–7b ("AKS"). One of FLPA's general partners, Mark Bibi, was formerly General Counsel to defendant Unilab. . . .

A. The Parties . . .

FLPA, the "relator" in this qui tam action, is a Delaware general partnership formed in 2005 by three former Unilab executives, Andrew Baker ("Baker"), Richard Michaelson ("Michaelson"), and Mark Bibi ("Bibi" and jointly, the "individual relators") for the purpose of bringing this qui tam action. The individual relators worked for Unilab prior to its acquisition by Quest in 2003. . . .

Bibi's role as Unilab's General Counsel is central to the issues presented on appeal. Bibi, who has been practicing law in New York since 1985, was Unilab's sole "in-house" lawyer from 1993–2000. In that capacity, he was responsible for all of Unilab's legal and compliance affairs, such as advising Unilab on matters relating to its MCO [managed care organizations] contracts and managing all litigation against the company.

B. The Alleged Scheme

FLPA alleges that "[f]rom at least 1996 through at least 2005, Unilab and Quest violated the AKS by operating a 'pull-through' scheme by which they charged MCOs and IPAs [independent practice associations of doctors] commercially unreasonable discounted prices [on non-federal business] to induce referrals of Medicare and Medicaid business and then billed the Medicare and Medicaid business to the Government at dramatically higher prices than those charged to the MCOs and IPAs [on the nonfederal business]." Specifically, FLPA argues that the "commercially unreasonable discounted prices" constituted "kickback[s], bribe[s] or rebate[s]" insofar as they were designed to induce referrals of Medicare and Medicaid business.

Between 1993 and 1996, the individual relators began to question whether Unilab's pricing structure violated the AKS. For example, as Chief Financial Officer, Michaelson allegedly knew that Unilab often charged its MCO clients prices that were sometimes less than 50% of Unilab's actual testing costs. And Bibi allegedly advised Baker that Unilab's pricing structure, as it was then formulated, potentially facilitated "kickbacks."

In response to these concerns about Unilab's pricing structure, "Unilab, under its then-CEO [Baker], established a new pricing policy . . . that included negotiated increases to the rates under its existing contracts." Specifically, in 1996 Unilab delivered a letter to its MCO and physician-association customers "stating that it was reserving its contractual right to terminate its contract with that customer and would, in thirty days, cease providing laboratory services to any customer that did not agree to a price increase." Following Unilab's notice that it was raising its prices, some of Unilab's "customers began to slowly slip away to [its] competitors."

FLPA asserts that Baker's tenure as CEO ended in 1997 as a result of the falling profits caused by this increase in Unilab's prices. When Baker left, Unilab's shares were selling for less than $3 per share. In 1999, Kelso & Co. completed a leveraged buy-out of Unilab for $5.85 per share and installed a new management team, including Robert Whalen as CEO. Whalen reversed course from Baker's pricing policy, informing other executives that "Baker's increased pricing had been a mistake, and that Unilab needed to (i) accept commercially unreasonable contracts with MCOs and physician associations and (ii) implement a strategy that required physicians to refer, and the MCOs to arrange for or recommend that physicians refer, fee-for-service business, including Medicare and Medicaid-reimbursable business, to Unilab."

In December 1999, the U.S. Department of Health and Human Services Office of Inspector General ("OIG") published Advisory Opinion ("AO") 99–13, which addressed the pricing practices of clinical pathologists. In particular, AO 99–13 indicated that if the prices offered to MCOs on non-federal business were below "actual cost," such an arrangement "might" violate the AKS because the OIG would infer that such discounts were offered for the purpose of inducing physicians to refer their Medicare and Medicaid business.

The month after AO 99–13 was published, Bibi had a meeting with Whalen during which Bibi stated his "personal opinion," that AO 99–13 created an inference of illegality with respect to Unilab's existing pricing structure. Whalen allegedly instructed Bibi to work with outside counsel to "find a way around" AO 99–13. In response Bibi obtained an opinion letter from an outside law firm, Winston & Strawn, on this issue. Bibi never reported his concerns to the Unilab Board.

FLPA alleges that Bibi was subsequently "frozen out" by Unilab's management as a result of his concerns related to Unilab's pricing structure and was no longer asked for advice on compliance matters. By March 2000, Bibi had been replaced as General Counsel.

After the individual relators left Unilab, the company allegedly "continued its illegal pull-through strategy and as a result significantly improved its profitability." In 2003, Quest acquired Unilab at a price of $26.50 per share. . . . .

C. Procedural History

Baker initiated the filing of this qui tam action and invited Michaelson and Bibi to join him as individual relators; in particular, he believed Bibi's status as a lawyer "would improve our credibility with the government." Recognizing the potential ethical implications of a former general counsel bringing a qui tam lawsuit against his former company and client, Bibi consulted the N.Y. Rules and the American Bar Association's Model Rules of Professional Conduct to determine whether he could participate. Bibi concluded that certain exceptions to the attorney-client confidentiality rules permitted his participation, and "did not feel it was necessary" to verify his understanding with the New York state bar.

On January 1, 2005, FLPA was formed for the purpose of acting as a relator in one or more qui tam actions against defendants for alleged violations of the AKS. Pursuant to the FLPA partnership agreement, Bibi stands to collect 29% of any qui tam recovery, while Baker and Michaelson would receive 57% and 14%, respectively. [FLPA then filed this qui tam action.]

[Defendants argued, first, that Bibi violated N.Y. Rule 1.9(a), known as the "side-switching" rule, which bars a lawyer who has formerly represented a client in a matter from representing another person in the same or a substantially related matter, N.Y. Rule 1.9(a), and, second, that Bibi violated the N.Y. Rules by making use of Unilab's confidential information for this litigation. Rule 1.9(c). The court found Bibi's conduct to violate the confidentiality rule and therefore did not address the side-switching rule. As it existed at the time, Rule 1.9(c) provided

> [a] lawyer who has formerly represented a client in a matter or whose present or former firm has formerly represented a client in a matter shall not thereafter . . . (1) use confidential information of the former client protected by Rule 1.6 to the disadvantage of the former client, except as these Rules would permit or require with respect to a current client or when the information has become generally known; or (2) reveal confidential information of the former client protected by Rule 1.6 except as these Rules would permit or require with respect to a current client.]

FLPA, in turn, relied upon the exception in N.Y. Rule 1.6(b), which permits a lawyer to "reveal or use confidential information to the extent that the lawyer reasonably believes necessary . . . to prevent the client from committing a crime. . . ." N.Y. Rule 1.6(b)(2). . . .

Discussion

On appeal, FLPA argues principally that (1) the District Court erred in holding that Bibi violated his ethical duties under the N.Y. Rules; and (2) the District Court erred in granting an overly broad remedy in favor of the defendants. We consider each argument in turn.

A. Bibi Violated N.Y. Rule 1.9(c) by Disclosing Unilab's Confidential Information

1. The FCA Does Not Preempt State Ethical Rules

As a general matter, the "salutary provisions [of New York's ethical rules] have consistently been relied upon by the courts of this district and circuit in evaluating the ethical conduct of attorneys." *Hull v. Celanese Corp.*, 513 F.2d 568, 571 n.12 (2d Cir.1975). Nothing in the False Claims Act evinces a clear legislative intent to preempt state statutes and rules that regulate an attorney's disclosure of client confidences. . . .

At the same time, we are mindful that the central purpose of the N.Y. Rules — to protect client confidences — can be "inconsistent with or antithetical to federal interests," *Grievance Comm. for S.D.N.Y. v. Simels*, 48 F.3d 640, 646 (2d Cir.1995), which under the FCA, are to "'encourage private individuals who are aware of fraud being perpetrated against the [g]overnment to bring such information forward,'" *U.S. ex rel. Dick v. Long Island Lighting Co.*, 912 F.2d 13, 18 (2d Cir. 1990) (quoting H.R. Rep. No. 660, 99th Cong., 2d Sess. 22 (1986)). In such instances courts must interpret and apply the N.Y. Rules in a manner that "balances the varying federal interests at stake." *Simels*. We conduct the following analysis with these principles in mind.

2. Bibi Violated Rule 1.9(c) by Disclosing Confidential Information Beyond What Was "Necessary" Within the Meaning of N.Y. Rule 1.6(b).

[Given that Rule 1.6 creates an exception to the command of Rule 1.9's command of confidentiality] review of the District Court's determination that Bibi's participation in the qui tam action violated Rule 1.9(c) requires us to decide whether Bibi reasonably believed that (1) the defendants intended to commit a crime when FLPA filed this action in 2005, and (2) the disclosures were necessary to prevent the defendants from committing a crime.

A.

We agree with the District Court that "Bibi could have reasonably believed in 2005 that [d]efendants had the intention to commit a crime." . . .

B.

The second question is whether Bibi reasonably believed that his disclosures were necessary to prevent defendants from committing a crime. FLPA asserts that it was "necessary" — within the meaning of N.Y. Rule 1.6(b) — for Bibi to reveal the confidential information disclosed in this lawsuit because the terms of the FCA required Bibi to make "'written disclosure of substantially all material evidence and information the person possesses'" to the government. 31 U.S.C. § 3730(b)(2)). Thus, FLPA argues, "[u]nder elementary principles of the supremacy of federal law, the

FCA preempts application of Rule 1.6. . . ." We disagree, in light of the balancing principles set forth in Part A.1.

Rule 1.6(b)(2) implicitly accounts for the federal interests at stake in the FCA by permitting disclosure of information "necessary" to prevent the ongoing commission of a crime. As illustrated by this very case, Rule 1.6's prohibition on Bibi's disclosures could not have undermined the qui tam action in light of the alternative means, discussed below, of exposing the alleged kickback scheme. Because Rule 1.6 itself balances the interests at stake, it need not give way to section 3730(b)(2)'s requirement of full disclosure of material evidence.

Alternatively, FLPA contends that even if Rule 1.6(b) does not give way to section 3730, Bibi complied with its requirements by "tempering his disclosures" until his deposition, when he finally testified as to the details of his conversations with Whalen and revealed the existence of the Winston & Strawn opinion letter upon solicitation by Unilab. FLPA argues further that the ongoing nature of the alleged crime necessitated the broad disclosures.

The District Court concluded that "[e]vidence of the continuing crime in 2005 could be shown by evidence of Quest's pricing agreements with MCOs and IPAs in effect in 2005 and not, for example, through Bibi's disclosures [of confidential information]." Thus, the Court reasoned, the confidential information divulged by Bibi, dating back to 1996, went beyond what was reasonably necessary to prevent any alleged ongoing crime in 2005, when the suit was filed.

We agree with the District Court that the confidential information Bibi revealed was greater than reasonably necessary to prevent any alleged ongoing fraudulent scheme in 2005. By FLPA's own admission, it was unnecessary for Bibi to participate in this qui tam action at all, much less to broadly disclose Unilab's confidential information. FLPA could have brought the qui tam action based on the information that Baker and Michaelson possessed as former executives of Unilab, or, if necessary, Bibi could have made limited disclosures. Instead, Bibi chose to participate in the action and disclose protected client confidences, in violation of N.Y. Rule 1.9(c). . . .

B. *The District Court Did Not Err or "Abuse Its Discretion" in Dismissing the Complaint and Disqualifying FLPA and Its Counsel*

[Applying an abuse of discretion standard, the court affirmed the District Court's dismissal of the complaint and disqualification of FLPA, FLPA's counsel, and the individual relators from bringing this action or any subsequent action based on the same facts. It did so even while noting that it was "conscious that, notwithstanding any salutary effect on attorney ethics or the appearance of fairness, dismissal or disqualification for violations of ethical rules may impede the pursuit of meritorious litigation to the detriment of the justice system," and therefore it needed to "balance these competing concerns by limiting remedies for ethical violations to those necessary to avoid 'taint[ing] the underlying trial.'"

In striking this balance, the court stressed "FLPA's unusual posture in this litigation by virtue of its status as relator," which meant that "it acts neither as the real party in interest nor in a representative capacity." The decision to dismiss and disqualify the relators did not foreclose either the government or different relators from bringing suit, thus the district court's actions did "not significantly impair the federal interests embodied in the FCA." As for disqualification of FLPA's counsel, even though the firm did not engage in any ethical violations, that action was necessary to protect the defendants from the use of their confidential information against them.]

NOTES

1. *FCA and AKS.* Do you understand the basic claim? Qui tam actions under the False Claims Act must be predicated on the defendant submitting a false claim to the government (or keeping funds that should be remitted to the government). Thus, any FCA claim must also allege that the defendant violated a federal statute or at least breached a contract with the government. In *Quest* itself, the allegation was that the defendants violated the Anti-Kickback Statute by charging providers below-cost discounts in order to induce them to refer more lucrative federally funded business.

2. *Ethical Rules.* The court applied the New York ethical rules governing at the time of the events in question, rather than the version now in effect. However, it viewed the two sets of rules as substantively the same. Most states tend to follow the ABA Model Rules of Professional Conduct, which have increasingly recognized exceptions to the duty of confidentiality; nevertheless, these exceptions are prefaced by "to the extent the lawyer reasonably believes necessary," § 1.6, which was the point upon which Bibi's disclosures foundered.

3. *Lawyers Are Different.* This is not the first instance we've seen where whistle-blower protections are dramatically reduced when attorneys are involved. *See* Note on Attorneys and the Public Policy Tort, page 221. One difference, however, between *Quest* and the previous other cases is that *Quest* involved a federal statute, and there was at least an argument that state rules of professional responsibility were trumped by the FCA. The court gave short shrift to that contention. *See generally* Kathleen M. Boozang, *The New Relators: In-House Counsel and Compliance Officers*, 6 J. HEALTH & LIFE SCIENCES L. 16 (2010). The court's decision on Bibi's revelation of confidential information is very problematic for attorneys, but had the court gone further and found that Bibi had "switched sides," presumably all suits by former counsel would presumably been barred.

4. *How Necessary Is Necessary?* Key to the court's decision was that the plaintiffs could have prosecuted their False Claims Act suit without Bibi's disclosure of confidential information. And, indeed, the court focused on an opinion letter that was doubtless confidential. But it also quoted in an omitted footnote the New York rule on confidential information that is extraordinarily broad, including anything "embarrassing or detrimental" to the client or any "information that the client has requested be kept confidential." Does that mean that a general counsel like Bibi will rarely be able to make any disclosure unless that disclosure is truly critical to the case? Would Bibi have been able to make his disclosures if he hadn't allied with the other two former Unilab workers? In other words, did their presence and ability to provide non-confidential information render Bibi's contribution unnecessary? *See* Posting of Charles A. Sullivan to Workplace Prof Blog, *Balancing Away Qui Tam Actions*, Nov. 25, 2013, http://lawprofessors.typepad.com/laborprof_blog/2013/11/balancing-away-qui-tam-actions.html.

5. *Public Disclosure.* The court stresses that other relators can bring qui tam actions even if these plaintiffs and their attorneys could not. Would you file a suit against Quest on the basis of the information in the court's docket and pay off that law school debt with the bounty? Unfortunately, the "public disclosure" exception to the FCA, mentioned above, bars relator suits based on disclosures, *inter alia,* in civil litigation in which the government is a party unless the relator is the "original source." Was the government a party to this suit brought in its name? If so, and despite the court's statement that other qui tam suits could be brought, it seems unlikely that anyone else would be able to state a claim.

6. *Pleading a FCA Violation.* Although the *Quest* court doesn't mention it, a number of relators have fallen afoul of pleading requirements. Because such claims necessarily involve fraud, the heightened pleading requirements of Rule 9 of the Federal Rules of Civil Procedure apply. Given the enhanced scrutiny of even "normal" Rule 8 pleading under the "*Twiqbal*" regime, *Bell Atlantic Corp. v. Twombly,* 550 U.S. 544 (2007); *Ashcroft v. Iqbal,* 556 U.S. 662 (2009), requiring fraud to be plead "with particularity" has proved a serious barrier. *See, e.g., U.S. ex rel. Ge v. Takeda Pharm. Co. Ltd.,* 737 F.3d 116, 124 (1st Cir. 2013) (even assuming the adequacy of plaintiff's allegations of fraud on the FDA, the relator "alleged next to no facts in support of the proposition that Takeda's alleged misconduct resulted in the submission of false claims or false statements material to false claims for government payment."). *But see Foglia, ex rel. U.S. v. Renal Ventures Management, LLC,* 754 F.3d 153 (3d Cir. 2014) (adopting the "nuanced" approach of several circuits to pleading False Claims Act complaints rather than the approach of several others that require a plaintiff to plead representative samples of the alleged fraudulent conduct, including the time, place, and content of the acts and the identity of the actors) And, of course, a plaintiff must survive a Rule 12(b)(6) motion to dismiss in order to obtain the discovery that might be necessary to prove his FCA claim. It may be that disclosures in some cases would reasonably be believed to be necessary to survive dismissal for failure to state a claim. In *Quest* itself, however, Bibi "tempered his disclosures" until his deposition, and, of course, the court believed them not necessary at all because of the information provided by the other ex-employees.

5

Traditional Torts in the Employment Relationship

The history of tort law's approach to the employment relationship starts with the struggle during the latter part of the nineteenth century over injuries sustained in the workplace. At the time, tort law theoretically offered redress for workplace injuries. In fact, however, employees seeking compensation for negligence were often frustrated by three doctrines — contributory negligence, assumption of risk, and the fellow servant rule — that together rendered it difficult or impossible for employees to recover from their employers. In large measure, then, tort law left workplace safety to private ordering. Rather than abolishing these restrictive doctrines while operating within the traditional tort system, populist reformers advanced workers' compensation laws as the means of reform. The system, which won universal acceptance, was a compromise between full compensation for employees and the hit-or-miss cause of action for negligence. Workers' compensation laws replaced the common law tort of negligence with an administrative system of strict liability for work-related injuries and diseases, providing more certain recovery but restricting the amounts recovered. *See generally* LEX K. LARSON, LARSON'S WORKERS' COMPENSATION LAW (Matthew Bender and Co., Inc. Rev. Ed. 2014); Price Fishback & Shawn Everett Kantor, *The Adoption of Workers' Compensation in the United States*, 1900-1930, 41 J.L. & ECON. 305 (1998). The trade-off of lower amounts for more certain recovery required that workers' compensation be the exclusive remedy against the employer for physical injuries to employees in accidents arising out of their employment. Thus, tort law as a means to redress employee injuries largely disappeared during the twentieth century.

We will explore the parameters of workers' compensation exclusivity and the system as a whole at the end of this chapter. For now it is enough to know that workers' compensation systems typically left intentional torts actionable. Employee suits for intentional torts against their employers or individual supervisors or co-workers are therefore possible, but they remain problematic and more the exception than the rule in employment law. A few torts play an occasional role. For example, employees sometimes claim assault and battery for physical altercations, *Kelly v.*

County of Monmouth, 883 A.2d 411 (N.J. App. Div. 2005) (suit against co-worker who grabbed plaintiff's genitals when hand-shaking contest escalated into a "testosterone type thing"), and occasionally allege false imprisonment, most often in the context of too-enthusiastic interrogation during employer investigations of employee dishonesty. *Levin v. Canon Bus. Solutions, Inc.*, 2010 WL 731645 (Cal. Ct. App. Mar. 4, 2010) (false imprisonment verdict upheld when employer investigators required plaintiff to ride in their car to his home under threat of criminal charges); *Foley v. Polaroid Corp.*, 413 N.E.2d 711 (Mass. 1987) (jury question as to whether employee was physically restrained, but the threat of discharge if employee left the office during interrogation could not constitute imprisonment for tort purposes). Malicious prosecution claims are also sometimes brought against employers who report suspected theft to the police without an adequate basis. *See Bennett v. R & L Carriers Shared Servs.*, LLC, 492 F. App'x 315 (4th Cir. 2012) (upholding jury verdict for malicious prosecution stemming from a "brief and ham-handed" internal investigation); *Lochridge v. Pioneer Health Servs.*, 86 So. 3d 942 (Miss. Ct. App. 2012) (a reasonable jury could find malicious prosecution when plaintiff's former employer caused her to be indicted for burglary when she entered its facility to retrieve her personal property). These kinds of intentional torts are also commonly deployed as ancillary causes of action to other claims. For example, in the sexual harassment context, the tort of assault may allow suit against the individual harasser, who might otherwise not be personally liable since discrimination statutes typically apply only to the corporate employer. *See* Chapter 9. Even here, however, some courts have found tort suits for sexual assault to be barred by workers' compensation exclusivity. *See* Chapter 12.

Of somewhat more general application are four other intentional torts that are treated in this chapter, and privacy torts, which are treated in Chapter 6. Of these, only one — intentional interference with contract or prospective advantage — is primarily used to seek compensation for lost employment per se. For that reason intentional interference is treated first in Section A. The other three torts focus more on terms and conditions of employment than on job security and are only incidentally concerned with discharge. They are treated here in declining order of their importance in the employment law landscape. Defamation, taken up in Section B, and intentional infliction of emotional distress, treated in Section C, both focus on the employee's right to be treated with dignity. Although both may be implicated in terminations, that is not their primary focus, and both offer relatively weak protection in this context. Finally, fraud or misrepresentation is typically raised in the context of inducement to enter employment or with respect to compensation or other benefits, but it may also be raised in connection with termination. Discussed in Section D, it is a very powerful tool when applicable, but is so narrowly confined as to be rarely useful for employees.

This chapter concludes with Section E, which considers two important limitations on the use of tort doctrines. First, there is some question as to the extent to which the exclusivity provisions of state workers' compensation laws we have noted bar tort suit. Second, the increased recognition of tort actions for employee termination under state law has led to questions about whether such state causes of action are preempted by federal law.

A. INTENTIONAL INTERFERENCE WITH THE EMPLOYMENT RELATIONSHIP

Tort law has long protected parties to a contract from third parties intentionally interfering with their relationship. In the employment field, this tort has traditionally been asserted by employers seeking to prevent other employers from "pirating" their workers or seeking compensation for the loss of key employees. *See* Chapter 8. But employees can use this tort too. The employment relationship between company and worker may be viewed as the contract (or at least the "prospective advantage") interfered with, and, if so, the question becomes whether a third party has unjustifiably interfered with that relationship. *See generally* Alex Long, *Tortious Interference with Business Relations: "The Other White Meat" of Employment Law*, 84 MINN. L. REV. 863 (2000).

The RESTATEMENT (THIRD) OF EMPLOYMENT LAW states the general rule:

> An employer wrongfully interferes with an employee's employment or prospective employment with another employer when the employer by improper means or without a legitimate business justification intentionally causes another employer (i) to terminate the employment; or (ii) not to enter into an employment relationship with the employee.

§ 6.03(a) (Proposed Final Draft (April 18, 2014)). This tort is, however, subject to a qualified privilege, *see* § 6.02, which permits the publication of statements to, inter alia, other employers, unless the statement is "false and defamatory" and made "without a reasonable intent to serve a legitimate interest of the employer or of the recipient." *See, e.g., Reeves v. Hanlon*, 95 P.3d 513 (Cal. 2004) (immigration law firm could recover damages for intentional interference against former employees who had persuaded other employees to quit and join their newly established firm).

A threshold question is whether the tort applies to at-will employment. While there is clearly a cause of action when there is the requisite interference with a contract for a specified term, the tenuous nature of at-will employment has generated questions about the applicability of the tort to this relationship. Nevertheless, as the Restatement reflects, most courts have found at-will contracts still to be contracts and so within the tort, and, in any event, the intentional interference tort reaches not only contracts but also interference with "prospective advantage." *See, e.g., Reeves v. Hanlon, supra*; *Stanek v. Greco*, 323 F.3d 476, 480 (6th Cir. 2003); *Hensen v. Truman Med. Ctr., Inc.*, 62 S.W.3d 549, 553 (Mo. Ct. App. 2001). There is, however, some contrary authority. *See, e.g., Stanton v. Tulane Univ.*, 777 So. 2d 1242 (La. Ct. App. 2001) (at-will employee could not assert the tort); *McManus v. MCI Comm. Corp.*, 748 A.2d 949 (D.C. 2000) (same); *see generally* Alex Long, *The Disconnect Between At-Will Employment and Tortious Interference with Business Relations: Rethinking Tortious Interference Claims in the Employment Context*, 33 ARIZ. ST. L.J. 491 (2001). However, the scope of the privilege to interfere is broader when the employment is at will. *See CRST Van Expedited, Inc. v. Werner Enters.*, 479 F.3d 1099, 1106-07 (9th Cir. 2007) ("If CRST's employment contract provided for 'at-will' employment of [workers when Werner] induced them to leave their posts, there would be an additional requirement that CRST allege an *independently wrongful act* by Werner.") (emphasis in original).

A more difficult problem arises when the interference is by someone who is, in some sense, the employer itself. The EMPLOYMENT RESTATEMENT speaks in terms of liability when an employer "causes *another employer* not to enter into or to discontinue an employment relationship" (emphasis added). This means that the employer cannot be liable for the tort when it terminates its own employee. The RESTATEMENT OF TORTS likewise imposes liability only for interference "with the performance of a contract . . . between another and a third person by inducing or otherwise causing the third person not to perform the contract." §766. In *Cambio Health Solutions, L.L.C. v. Reardon*, 234 F. App'x. 331 (6th Cir. 2007), the question was whether three corporations with majority ownership in the employer could be sued for interference. The court found the defendants liable for intentional interference with the plaintiff's employment contract after concluding that a company with less than 100 percent interest in a subsidiary did not enjoy a qualified privilege to interfere with the contractual relations of the subsidiary.

Can an officer or director of an employer be liable for causing the employer to fire someone? How about a co-worker? Jurisdictions have taken inconsistent approaches to whether such a defendant is a third party with respect to the plaintiff's contract or business relationship with the employer. One view is that a supervisor is not a "third party" since the supervisor has an absolute privilege to interfere with the employment relationship. *See, e.g., Halvorsen v. Aramark Unif. Servs., Inc.*, 77 Cal. Rptr. 2d 383, 390 (Ct. App. 1998). Under this approach, a co-worker may be liable since his interference will not normally be within the scope of his employment, but a supervisor will not be.

In most jurisdictions, the answer turns on whether the defendant is acting within the scope of his or her employment. *E.g., Gruhlke v. Sioux Empire Fed. Credit Union, Inc.*, 756 N.W.2d 399, 408 (S.D. 2008) ("In sum, when corporate officers act within the scope of employment, even if those actions are only partially motivated to serve their employer's interests, the officers are not third parties to a contract between the corporate employer and another in compliance with the requirements for the tort of intentional interference with contractual relations); *Trail v. Boys & Girls Clubs of Northwest Ind.*, 845 N.E.2d 130, 138 (Ind. 2006) ("[W]hen officers or directors act in their official capacity as agents of the corporation, they act not as individuals but as the corporation itself. In doing so, they are not acting as a third party, but rather as a party to the contract and cannot be personally liable for tortious interference with the contract."); *Porter v. Oba, Inc.*, 42 P.3d 931, 935 (Or. Ct. App. 2002) ("A corporate agent who induces a corporation to breach a contract with another party cannot be liable for intentional interference with that contract if the agent acted in the scope of the agent's employment. In that situation, the agent is the corporation.").

However, according to §228 of the RESTATEMENT (SECOND) OF AGENCY (1957), acting within the scope of employment requires that the supervisor be motivated, at least in part, by a desire to serve the principal. Thus, a supervisor will be liable only when his actions are intended to further only "some individual or private purpose not related to the interests of the employer." *Huff v. Swartz*, 606 N.W.2d 461, 467 (Neb. 2000). As one court framed it, "While a party to a contract may breach it, it is logically impossible for a party to interfere tortiously with its own contract. However, if the agent's sole purpose is one that is *not* for the benefit of the corporation, the agent is not acting within the scope of employment and may be liable." *Kaelon v. USF Reddaway, Inc.*, 42 P.3d 344 (Ore. Ct. App. 2002); *Reed v. Michigan Metro Girl Scout Council*, 506 N.W.2d 231, 233 (Mich. Ct. App. 1993) ("It is now settled law that corporate agents are not liable for tortious interference with the corporation's contracts unless they acted solely for their own benefit with no benefit to the corporation.").

Think about the desirability of these various approaches as you consider the next case.

Kumpf v. Steinhaus
779 F.2d 1323 (7th Cir. 1985)

EASTERBROOK, Circuit Judge.

From 1973 until August 1983 William A. Kumpf was the president and chief executive officer of Lincoln National Sales Corp. of Wisconsin (Lincoln Wisconsin). He owned 20% of Lincoln Wisconsin's stock. Lincoln National Sales Corp. (Lincoln Sales) owned the other 80% of the stock, and two of the three members of Lincoln Wisconsin's board of directors were employees of Lincoln Sales. Lincoln Sales is in turn a subsidiary of Lincoln National Life Insurance Co. (Lincoln Life). Lincoln Sales is the marketing arm of Lincoln Life; Lincoln Wisconsin was the Wisconsin agency of Lincoln Sales.

In April 1981 Orin A. Steinhaus became an executive vice-president of Lincoln Life, leaving a post as head of Lincoln's sales agency in Columbus, Ohio. The president of Lincoln Life gave Steinhaus and other employees the task of revising the firm's sales structure, which was losing money. Lincoln Life closed 25 sales agencies and decided to consolidate others. In August 1983 Steinhaus decided to consolidate five Midwestern sales agencies into a single agency. (Doubtless other officers of Lincoln Life concurred in these decisions, but for simplicity we write as if Steinhaus made all decisions himself.) He instructed Lincoln Sales's directors on the board of Lincoln Wisconsin to approve a merger of Lincoln Wisconsin into Lincoln Chicago Corp. (Lincoln Chicago); Lincoln Wisconsin's board approved the merger by a vote of two to one, over Kumpf's dissent. Lincoln Wisconsin disappeared, and so did Kumpf's job. This litigation is the residue.

The district court dismissed most of Kumpf's claims for relief but sent to the jury a claim that Steinhaus and the Lincoln corporations tortiously interfered with the employment contract between Kumpf and Lincoln Wisconsin. Kumpf was an employee at will, but even at-will employment is contractual and therefore potentially the basis of a tort action. *Mendelson v. Blatz Brewing Co.*, 101 N.W.2d 805 (Wis. 1960). Kumpf was fired by Lincoln Wisconsin, and Lincoln Wisconsin cannot "interfere" with its own employment relations. But because Lincoln Sales owned only 80% of Lincoln Wisconsin's stock, Kumpf argued that other participants in the Lincoln family of firms could not intervene.

The defendants maintain that their interference with Kumpf's contract was privileged because it took place in the course of business. Kumpf replied that it was not privileged because it was done with an improper motive. After the reorganization, Steinhaus became president of Lincoln Chicago. In the insurance business the head of an agency receives a percentage of the agency's revenue. Income that used to go to Kumpf now went to Steinhaus, and the reorganization increased Steinhaus's total income. Kumpf argued that Steinhaus engineered the reorganization to advance his personal interests, and that this defeats the claim of privilege.

Kumpf asked the judge to instruct the jury that if the defendants' acts were "based — even in part — upon personal considerations, malice or ill will" then their acts were not privileged. Kumpf later proposed an instruction that would make privilege turn on "predominant" motivation. The district court, however, told the jury that "if you find that the actions of the defendants were motivated solely by a desire for revenge, ill will or malice, or in the case of the defendant Orin Steinhaus, solely by personal considerations, then you may find their actions improper." The jury returned a verdict for the defendants, and Kumpf attacks the "sole motive" instruction. . . .

Malice, ill will, and the like mean, in Wisconsin, an intent to act without justification. *Mendelson.* So the initial question is whether Kumpf has identified an unsupportable consideration that led to his dismissal. The only one Kumpf presses on us is Steinhaus's self-interest (Kumpf calls it "greed"). . . .

The basis of the privilege in question is the economic relations among the Lincoln family of corporations. The managers of the firm at the apex of the structure have an obligation to manage the whole structure in the interests of investors. Kumpf and Lincoln Wisconsin knew that when they started — when Kumpf took the risks associated with owning 20% of the stock, and holding one of three seats on the board, in a subsidiary of Lincoln Life. The superior managers in such a structure try to serve the interests of investors and other participants as a whole, and these interests will not always be congruent with the interests of managers of subsidiaries. Corporate reorganizations may reduce the costs of operation and put the structure in the hands of better managers, though this may be costly to existing managers.

If Kumpf had directly challenged the wisdom of a business decision of the managers of Lincoln Life, he would have been rebuffed with a reference to the business judgment doctrine — a rule of law that insulates business decisions from most forms of review. Courts recognize that managers have both better information and better incentives than they. The press of market forces — managers at Lincoln Life must continually attract new employees and capital, which they cannot do if they exploit existing participants or perform poorly — will more effectively serve the interests of all participants than will an error-prone judicial process. *See* Daniel R. Fischel, *The Business Judgment Rule and the Trans-Union Case*, 40 Bus. Law. 1437, 1439-43 (1985).

The privilege to manage corporate affairs is reinforced by the rationale of employment at will. Kumpf had no tenure of office. The lack of job security gave him a keen motive to do well. Security of position may diminish that incentive. *See* Richard A. Epstein, *In Defense of the Contract at Will*, 51 U. Chi. L. Rev. 947 (1984). Employment at will, like the business judgment doctrine, also keeps debates about business matters out of the hands of courts. People who enter a contract without a fixed term know there is some prospect that their business partners may try to take advantage of them or simply make a blunder in deciding whether to continue the relationship. Yet people's concern for their reputation and their ability to make other advantageous contracts in the future leads them to try to avoid both mistakes and opportunistic conduct. Contracting parties may sensibly decide that it is better to tolerate the risk of error — to leave correction to private arrangements — than to create a contractual right to stay in office in the absence of a "good" reason. The reason for a business decision may be hard to prove, and the costs of proof plus the risk of mistaken findings of breach may reduce the productivity of the employment relation.

Many people have concluded otherwise; contracts terminable only for cause are common. But in Wisconsin, courts enforce whichever solution the parties select. A contract at will may be terminated for any reason (including bad faith) or no reason, without judicial review; the only exception is a termination that violates "a fundamental and well-defined public policy as evidenced by existing law." *Brockmeyer v. Dun & Bradstreet*, 335 N.W.2d 834 (Wis. 1983). Greed — the motive

Kumpf attributes to Steinhaus — does not violate a "fundamental and well-defined public policy" of Wisconsin. Greed is the foundation of much economic activity, and Adam Smith told us that each person's pursuit of his own interests drives the economic system to produce more and better goods and services for all. "It is not from the benevolence of the butcher, the brewer, or the baker, that we expect our dinner, but from their regard to their own interest. We address ourselves, not to their humanity but to their self-love, and never talk to them of our own necessities but of their advantages." THE WEALTH OF NATIONS 14 (1776; Modern Library ed.).

The reasons that led Wisconsin to hold in *Brockmeyer* that it is "unnecessary and unwarranted for the courts to become arbiters of any termination that may have a tinge of bad faith attached" also establish that greed is not the sort of prohibited motive that will support Kumpf's tort action. In *Mendelson* the court stated that majority shareholders possess a privilege "to take whatever action they deem[ ] advisable to further the interests of the corporation." The court then quoted with approval from a text stating that a person enjoys no privilege "if his object is to put pressure upon the plaintiff and coerce him into complying with the defendant's wishes in some collateral matter."

If Steinhaus got rid of Kumpf because Kumpf would not marry Steinhaus's daughter, that would have been pressure in a "collateral matter." It is quite another thing to say that a jury must determine whether Steinhaus installed himself as head of Lincoln Chicago "predominantly" because he thought that would be good for Lincoln Life or "predominantly" because Steinhaus would enjoy the extra income. The decision to consolidate agencies and change managers is not "collateral" to the business of Lincoln Life, and the rationale of the business judgment rule interdicts any attempt to look behind the decision to determine whether Steinhaus is an astute manager.

Often corporations choose to align the interests of investors and managers by giving the managers a share of the firm's revenue or profits. Commissions, the ownership of stock or options, and bonuses all make managers and investors do well or poorly together. Lincoln Life chose to give managers a financial stake in each agency's revenues. Steinhaus was privileged to act with that incentive in mind. Suppose a major auto manufacturer decides to pay its chief executive officer $1 per year plus a percentage of the firm's profit. The officer then closes an unprofitable subsidiary (owned 80% by the firm), discharging its employees. Under Kumpf's theory any of the employees would be entitled to recover from the executive if the jury should estimate that in the executive's mind making money for himself predominated over making money for the firm. Yet since the two are the same thing, that would be a bootless investigation, and one with great potential to stifle the executive's vigorous pursuit of the firm's best interests. We do not think this is the law in Wisconsin or anywhere else.

Kumpf presents one last argument. He asked the judge to charge the jury that it should consider "recognized ethical codes or standards for a particular area of business activity" and "concepts of fair play" in deciding whether the defendants' acts were privileged. This "business ethics" instruction, Kumpf contends, would have allowed the jury to supplement the rules of tort and contract with "the rules of the game" in business. Although language of this sort appears in the RESTATEMENT (SECOND) OF TORTS § 767 comment j (1979), it was not designed to be given to a jury. It would leave the jury at sea, free to impose a brand of ethics for which people may not have bargained. No case in Wisconsin has required an instruction even remotely like this one.

The "rules of the game" are important in deciding what sorts of acts are privileged. If Lincoln Life had assured Kumpf that his agency would not be obliterated without his being given an opportunity to take a new job within the firm, that might cast a different light on his claim for interference with contract. But Kumpf does not say that he received such assurance or that any other understood "rule" has been breached. He therefore had to be content with the rules reflected in the definition of privileged acts.

The contention that businesses should be more considerate of their officers should be addressed to the businesses and to legislatures. Some firms will develop reputations for kind treatment of executives, some will be ruthless. Some will seek to treat executives well but find that the exigencies of competition frustrate their plans. The rule of this game is that Kumpf was an employee at will and had no right to stay on if his board wanted him gone. His board was dominated by people who answered to Lincoln Sales, which answered to Lincoln Life. Kumpf did not bargain for legal rights against Lincoln Life, and the judge properly declined to allow the jury to convert moral and ethical claims into legal duties.

NOTES

1. *Proper and Improper Motives.* In the movie *Wall Street* (1987) (the original, not the much later sequel, *Wall Street: Money Never Sleeps* (2010)), Gordon Gekko, played by Michael Douglas, celebrates the virtues of greed:

> The point is, ladies and gentlemen, that greed, for lack of a better word, is good; greed is right; greed works; greed clarifies, cuts through and captures the essence of the evolutionary spirit; greed in all its forms: greed for life, for money, for love, knowledge, has marked the upward surge of mankind, and greed — you mark my words — will not only save Teldar Paper but that other malfunctioning corporation called the U.S.A.

(20th Century Fox 1987); *see also* M. Todd Henderson & James C. Spindler, *Corporate Heroin: A Defense of Perks, Executive Loans, and Conspicuous Consumption*, 93 GEO. L. J. 1835 (2005). *But see* Eric A. Posner, *The Jurisprudence of Greed*, 151 U. PA. L. REV. 1097 (2003). Is this the point of Judge Easterbrook's defense of Steinhaus's conduct? Because *Kumpf* finds that greed is not an improper motive, it need not address whether liability would be appropriate if the termination decision was based only in part on that motive. Had greed counted as an improper motive, how should the mixed-motive question have been decided? We encountered this question in Chapter 4 in connection with Sarbanes-Oxley liability for whistleblowers and we will meet it again in Chapter 9 in connection with the antidiscrimination laws, but it is not clear that these statutory questions will influence the common law on issues such as intentional interference.

2. *A Detour into Judgecraft.* Judge Easterbrook is associated with the Chicago School of economic analysis of the law. One of the chief thrusts of the Chicago School is that "economic efficiency" ought to inform legal rules, frequently displacing (or at least modifying) notions of ethics and morals, and Easterbrook gives short shrift to the plaintiff's "business ethics" argument. Further, as Easterbrook's citation indicates, Professor Epstein is a strong defender of the economic efficiency of the at-will rule. As a federal judge deciding a diversity case like *Kumpf*, Easterbrook is supposed to be applying Wisconsin law, not the theories of the Chicago School. *See Erie R.R. v. Tompkins,* 304 U.S. 64 (1938). Do you think that he is faithful to *Erie?*

3. *More on Motives.* Kumpf argued that pursuit of self-interest by Steinhaus, as distinct from pursuit of corporate interests, suffices to make the interference actionable. What's wrong with that argument, aside from the mixed-motive question? Judge Easterbrook appeals to the business-judgment analogy, which ordinarily insulates corporate directors from liability for their decisions. But business-judgment protection may be lost if one or more directors are interested in the transaction. *See* R. CLARK, CORPORATE LAW § 3.4 (1986).

In addition, reading Easterbrook's opinion, one might forget that the business judgment rule applies to protect decisions of *directors* of a corporation, acting in their capacity as board members, not all of its "managers." Indeed, Easterbrook's language elides this distinction and effectively extends the business judgment rule to "managers" without benefit of any citation: "Courts recognize that managers have both better information and better incentives than they. The press of market forces — managers at Lincoln Life must continually attract new employees and capital, which they cannot do if they exploit existing participants or perform poorly — will more effectively serve the interests of all participants than will an error-prone judicial process." But is he right on what the law should be? Does Easterbrook's auto manufacturer hypothetical help you? He may be correct that the CEO should not be subject to suit by ex-employees if he closes an unprofitable subsidiary. But suppose the CEO's only motive was to increase his personal profits, regardless of whether his corporation lost or made money. Should this be actionable under the intentional interference tort?

One way to avoid this entire problem would be doctrinal — holding that Steinhaus is absolutely privileged to take the actions he did. While some states take this approach, Wisconsin is not one of those jurisdictions, leaving Judge Easterbrook to struggle with the question of what motives taint a decision. If greed does not count as an improper motive in Wisconsin, what motives will? Easterbrook suggests that Kumpf would have had a good claim if Steinhaus had persuaded his firm to fire Kumpf because Kumpf refused to marry Steinhaus's daughter. But in a subsequent Seventh Circuit case, Judge Posner rejected an interference claim based on the defendant having fired him to advance his lover:

> But unless courts are to be overwhelmed by suits by disgruntled former employees against corporate officers, more is required than that a discharge be tainted by some private motive, such as greed, personal dislike, or, in this case perhaps, a personal attachment to a competing employee. Few are the employees whose actions are motivated solely by a selfless devotion to the employer's interests. The plaintiff must prove both that the employer did not benefit from the defendant's act and that the act was independently tortious, for example as fraud or defamation.

Preston v. Wis. Health Fund, 397 F.3d 539, 543-44 (7th Cir. 2005). This goes further than Easterbrook because it would appear to take the court out of the business of deciding motives at all and leave only "independent" torts as actionable and even then, only if there was no benefit at all to the employer.

4. *Personal Enough?* In *Kaelon v. USF Reddaway, Inc.,* 42 P.3d 344 (Ore. Ct. App. 2002), the plaintiff claimed that an executive had "openly carried on a romantic affair with another female employee and gave preferential employment treatment to

this employee," and that he believed (incorrectly) that the plaintiff had gossiped about the affair. She claimed that, in retaliation, he had denied her promotion and belittled and humiliated her to force her to leave her employment. Contrary to *Preston*, the court found such conduct would be actionable:

> [A] reasonable juror could find that defendant, in humiliating plaintiff in the workplace, in denying her promotions, and in causing her to leave her employment, was retaliating against plaintiff for complaining about his romantic relationship with Hiepler. Under several of our prior cases, such a finding by the jury would support the further finding that defendant acted solely for his own benefit, and not at all for the benefit of Reddaway.

Id. at 348. While the defendant would not be liable unless the jury found that his actions were taken purely out of personal motives, summary judgment could not be granted against defendant where plaintiff produced sufficient evidence to establish the personal motive. In short, the dispute would be whether the defendant acted solely from that motive or instead (or also) from a desire to advance his employer's interests. *See also Stanek v. Greco*, 323 F.3d 476 (6th Cir. 2003) (discharge by president because plaintiff had reported his misuse of funds actionable); *Sides v. Duke Hospital*, 328 S.E.2d 818 (N.C. App. 1985) (doctors who induced a hospital to discharge plaintiff, a nurse, because her deposition in a malpractice suit was damaging to them were acting for improper or strictly personal motives).

   5. *Terminology.* The threshold question of whether the defendant is a "third party" tends to merge with the question of justification for his conduct or privilege, although note that the defendant need only be motivated "partially" by an intent to serve the employer. Thus, some courts recognize that the supervisor is not the employer but nevertheless is privileged to cause the employer to breach its contract. As we have seen, some jurisdictions see the privilege as absolute, *Halvorsen v. Aramark Unif. Servs., Inc.*, 77 Cal. Rptr. 2d 383 (Ct. App. 1998) (recognizing an absolute "manager's privilege" to interfere), but most courts view it as qualified. *See, e.g., Luketich v. Goedecke*, 835 S.W.2d 504, 508 (Mo. Ct. App. 1992) ("defendant-employer was justified in attempting to enforce its rights under the non-compete agreement with its former employee as long as the former employer had a reasonable, good faith belief in the validity of the agreement"); *Nordling v. N. States Power Co.*, 478 N.W.2d 498, 506 (Minn. 1991) ("A company officer, agent or employee is privileged to interfere with or cause a breach of another employee's employment contract with the company, if that person acts in good faith, whether competently or not, believing that his actions are in furtherance of the company's business. This privilege may be lost, however, if malice and bad faith predominantly motivate the defendant's actions, that is, by personal ill-will, spite, hostility, or a deliberate intent to harm the plaintiff employee.").

   6. *Reputational Constraints.* The court in *Steinhaus* suggests that the law need not provide a remedy to deter harms like the one inflicted on the plaintiff because the market is generally self-correcting: "[P]eople's concern for their reputation and their ability to make other advantageous contracts in the future leads them to try to avoid both mistakes and opportunistic conduct." Obviously, such a "remedy" provides little solace for individual plaintiffs, but are you convinced that reputational consequences sufficiently reduce mistakes and opportunism? Summarizing the literature, Professor Sam Estreicher describes reputation as "a late-appearing deus ex machina explaining why opportunistic behavior by employers . . . is likely to be relatively unimportant,"

and questions whether it is likely to have this effect in employment markets. *Employer Reputation at Work*, 27 HOFSTRA LAB. & EMP. L. J. 1 (2009); *see also* Seth D. Harris, *Re-Thinking the Economics of Discrimination:* U.S. Airways v. Barnett, *the ADA, and the Application of Internal Labor Market Theory*, 89 IOWA L. REV. 123 (2003) (questioning the significance of reputational effects for ADA accommodation); Gillian Lester, *Restrictive Covenants, Employee Training, and the Limits of Transaction-Cost Analysis*, 76 IND. L. J. 49, 64 (2001) (explaining why there is ample room for opportunism with respect to restrictive covenants despite potential reputational consequences).

PROBLEM

5-1. Marco Ramirez, the president of Free Market Enterprises, Inc., called Ashley Appleton into his office at salary review time near the end of the year. He congratulated her on a superlative job that year and told her that she would receive a 15 percent raise. Appleton was very happy until, at the end of the meeting, Ramirez told her that he was sure she would "show her gratitude with a small gift, say of 5 percent of her salary, in cash — small bills only, please."

Appleton comes to you for help. She had heard rumors from co-workers of required kickbacks, but this is the first time that she has been asked for money. Free Market Enterprises is a publicly held company, although your client believes that Ramirez, its founder, holds about 20 percent of the stock and is generally thought to have a controlling interest. Next, suppose Appleton does not make a gift and the following year, Ramirez selects her for termination in a company-wide layoff. Advise her.

B. DEFAMATION

Defamation originated as a common law tort designed to protect an individual's reputation against false and harmful words. A cause of action for defamation arises when statements made in writing (libel) or orally (slander) "harm the reputation of another so as to lower him in the estimation of the community or to deter third persons from association or dealing with him." RESTATEMENT (SECOND) OF TORTS § 558 (1977). The Restatement establishes four elements of the tort: "(a) a false and defamatory statement concerning another; (b) an unprivileged publication to a third party; (c) fault amounting at least to negligence on the part of the publisher; and (d) either actionability of the statement irrespective of special harm or the existence of special harm caused by the publication." *See generally* RESTATEMENT (THIRD) OF EMPLOYMENT LAW § 6.01 (Proposed Final Draft (April 18, 2014)) ("An employer is subject to liability for harm caused by the employer's publication of a false and defamatory statement concerning the employee."). When judges enforce the law of defamation, however, they impose restrictions on speech, restrictions that may interfere with the constitutional free speech interests of defamation defendants. Much of the modern law of defamation, therefore, focuses on balancing the conflicting interests of reputation and freedom of speech inherent in every defamation case. The weight accorded to speech interests varies, however, with the identity of the parties to the suit. When public officials or public figures sue the media for defamation, the media's free speech interests predominate and constitutional standards play a large role in the case. *New York Times v. Sullivan*, 376 U.S. 254 (1964). At the other extreme, when a private individual sues a nonmedia defendant, the individual's interest in reputation predominates and the constitution plays a far lesser role in limiting the common law of defamation. *Dun and Bradstreet v. Greenmoss Builders*, 472 U.S. 749 (1985). Because defamation in the context of employment almost always involves the latter situation, this section will concentrate on traditional common law issues that dominate employment-related defamation law, including the meaning of "publication," when a statement can be characterized as defamatory, and when defamation is privileged. We will also consider the fault element of defamation in the employment context.

Cockram v. Genesco, Inc.
680 F.3d 1046 (8th Cir. 2012)

GRUENDER, Circuit Judge.

Jessica Cockram sued her former employer, Genesco, Inc., after the company made public statements about Cockram's involvement in an incident in which a pernicious racial slur appeared on a return receipt that Cockram handed to a customer. The district court dismissed Cockram's claim for false light invasion of privacy and granted summary judgment in favor of Genesco on her defamation claim. Cockram now appeals, and we affirm the dismissal of the false light claim and reverse and remand the defamation claim.

I. Background

On October 17, 2008, in the course of her duties at a Journeys retail store owned by Genesco, Cockram assisted Keith Slater, an African-American, with a merchandise return. For efficiency in processing the return, Cockram entered a generic phone number, (913) 555-5555, into the store register. Unbeknownst to Cockram, Richard Hamill, a former employee whom Journeys had fired prior to this incident, had inserted into a store-level database a racial slur as one of the names associated with the phone number Cockram entered. Cockram unwittingly selected the entry with the racial slur from the list of names associated with the phone number. She then printed a return receipt that included the racial slur, signed it without reading it, and handed it to Slater.

The next day, Slater, accompanied by members of his family, returned to Journeys with the return receipt. Slater's sister demanded Cockram's name, and Cockram complied. Slater and his family were outraged about the incident and told people in and near Journeys about what had happened, resulting in what Cockram described as a "riot."

On October 20, Genesco fired Cockram. In response to inquiries about the incident, Genesco provided a statement ("first statement") on October 21, 2008, reading:

> While we are continuing to investigate this incident, it now appears that an employee in one of our stores entered highly inappropriate statements in a form used to process a

merchandise return. Needless to say, such an act was not authorized by Journeys, and will not be tolerated. This employee has been terminated.

At Journeys, we pride ourselves on valuing and respecting every customer. We are shocked and sickened that a former associate could be responsible for an act so out of keeping with our culture and our values. We profoundly regret this incident.

Multiple news stories regarding the incident quoted the first statement, and some people posting comments to the online versions of those stories labeled as racist the involved employee. Additionally, after Genesco released the statement, Cockram received numerous messages and calls from people who called her a racist, blamed her for the racial slur, and threatened her. These accusations and threats made Cockram fearful, and she moved out of her apartment and temporarily placed her young child with her parents.

On October 22, 2008, Genesco learned that a different former employee, later identified as Hamill, may have been involved with the return-receipt incident. Genesco determined that the substance of the first statement was valid, but it also issued the following clarifying statement ("clarification"):

> The inappropriate references were entered by employees in the Overland Park store in a store-level customer database. No preprogrammed transaction codes were involved.
>
> We are currently working to develop mechanisms that allow us to monitor the store-level customer databases more closely than has been possible in the past, in an effort to ensure that nothing like this ever happens again.

Cockram sued Genesco for defamation and false light invasion of privacy based on the content of the first statement and the clarification . . .

II. Discussion

Our jurisdiction in this case is based on diversity of citizenship, and the parties agree that Missouri law governs. . . .

A. Defamation

In a defamation action, a plaintiff must establish: "1) publication, 2) of a defamatory statement, 3) that identifies the plaintiff, 4) that is false, 5) that is published with the requisite degree of fault, and 6) damages the plaintiff's reputation." *Missouri ex rel. BP Prods. N. Am. Inc. v. Ross,* 163 S.W.3d 922, 929 (Mo. 2005). In seeking summary judgment, Genesco argued that Cockram could not establish that the statements were false, that Genesco published them with the requisite degree of fault, and that Cockram's reputation was damaged. . . .

1. Falsity of the Statements

We must determine whether the "gist" or "sting" of the statements was false. *See Turnbull v. Herald Co.,* 459 S.W.2d 516, 519 (Mo. Ct. App. 1970). Under

Missouri law, a statement is not considered "false" for purposes of defamation simply because it contains an erroneous fact. *Thurston v. Ballinger*, 884 S.W.2d 22, 26 (Mo. Ct. App. 1994) ("A person is not bound to exact accuracy in his statements about another, if the statements are essentially true."). Rather, if a statement is essentially true, such that its divergence from the truth "would have no different effect on the reader's mind than that produced by the literal truth," the statement is not actionable in defamation. *See id.*

As a preliminary matter, we note that counsel for Genesco conceded at oral argument that the first statement could be read as referring to Cockram and that Genesco knew prior to issuing the first statement that Cockram's name had appeared in news reports. Moreover, Roger Sisson, an officer at Genesco, agreed during his deposition that the words "[t]his employee has been terminated" in the first statement referred to Cockram. Thus, there is no real dispute that the reference to an "employee" in the first statement could be interpreted as referring to Cockram.

Genesco argues that the first statement was truthful as a matter of law because (1) Cockram did enter a racial slur into a form by selecting it from a list of names, and (2) her action was not authorized because she used a generic phone number, rather than entering Slater's actual information into the register as required by Genesco policy. We are not persuaded. When the entirety of the first statement is considered in the light most favorable to Cockram, it can be read as asserting that Cockram intentionally directed a racial slur at Slater, not just that she violated company policy requiring the entry of a customer's actual phone number to generate a return receipt. In other words, the first statement did not necessarily assert that Cockram was terminated merely because she violated company policy by entering a generic phone number into the register and generating a return receipt containing a racial slur without being conscious of the offensive output. It is not "[n]eedless to say" that Genesco would not authorize entering a generic phone number and blindly selecting a name entry in order to expedite a customer's return. And a reasonable jury may not consider such a practice by itself to be so out of line with Genesco's culture and values as to make Genesco "shocked and sickened." Instead, the use of these phrases in Genesco's statement reasonably could be read to imply that Cockram intentionally communicated the racial slur. Because Cockram denies that she intentionally produced a return receipt with a racial slur, and produced evidence supporting this assertion, a genuine issue of material fact exists as to whether the gist of the first statement was true. Thus, the district court erred by determining as a matter of law that the first statement was substantially true.

Regarding the clarification, Genesco disputes whether that statement referred to Cockram. To the contrary, the first statement reasonably could be read as saying that Cockram entered the racial slur into a form, and the clarification does nothing to indicate that Cockram was not one of the "employees" who entered the racial slur into the database. Furthermore, the clarification used the plural term "employees," and Genesco has never contended that anyone other than Hamill and Cockram was involved in the return-receipt incident. Therefore, we conclude that a reasonable jury could find that the word "employees" in the clarification included Cockram. A jury also could view as false the clarification's statement that Cockram entered the racial slur into a "database." Even if we were to accept as true that Cockram entered the racial slur into a "form," as stated in the first statement, her selection of the racial slur from a list of names previously stored in a database does not equate to entering the racial slur into the database in the first place. Indeed, Genesco's investigation revealed that Hamill entered the racial slur into the database. Thus, the district court erroneously found as a matter of law that the clarification was substantially true.[3]

2. Requisite Degree of Fault

Genesco argues that Cockram did not present sufficient evidence that Genesco published the relevant statements with actual malice, "that is, with knowledge that the statements were false, or with a reckless disregard as to whether they were true or false," which is the applicable standard if Cockram was a limited-purpose public figure. *See Warner v. Kan. City Star Co., 726 S.W.2d 384, 385 (Mo. Ct. App. 1987)*. However, if Cockram was simply a private figure, she only needs to show negligence on the part of Genesco, even if Genesco's statement is considered to relate to an issue of "public concern or interest." *See Englezos v. Newspress & Gazette Co., 980 S.W.2d 25, 30–31 (Mo. Ct. App. 1998)*. Thus, we must decide whether Cockram was a limited-purpose public figure or, as Cockram contends, a private figure.

In explaining the rationale for the differing burdens borne by public figures and private figures in defamation suits, the Supreme Court noted that public figures are more likely to have access to the media to minimize a defamatory statement's "adverse impact on reputation," and, more importantly, public figures typically "thrust themselves to the forefront of particular public controversies in order to influence the resolution of the issues involved," thus "invit[ing] attention and comment." *Gertz v. Robert Welch, Inc., 418 U.S. 323, 344–45 (1974)*. The Court did state, however, that, "[h]ypothetically, it may be possible for someone to become a public figure through no purposeful action of his own, but the instances of truly involuntary public figures must be exceedingly rare." A limited-purpose public figure "is defined as one who 'voluntarily injects himself or is drawn into a particular public controversy and thereby becomes a public figure for a limited range of issues.'" *Stepnes v. Ritschel, 663 F.3d 952, 963 (8th Cir. 2011)* (quoting *Gertz*). An examination of "the 'nature and extent of an individual's participation in the particular controversy giving rise to the defamation' . . . [allows for a determination of] whether the individual has voluntarily and purposefully injected himself into that controversy in an attempt to influence the resolution of the controversy." *Lundell Mfg. Co. v. Am. Broad. Cos., 98 F.3d 351, 362 (8th Cir. 1996)* (quoting *Gertz*).

Here, Cockram entered a generic phone number into the register that resulted in a racial slur appearing on a return receipt and found herself in the middle of a public controversy. She did not "voluntarily inject" herself into a preexisting controversy, nor did she knowingly produce the racial slur that initiated the controversy. It was only after the controversy arose and Genesco blamed Cockram for the racial slur by issuing the first statement that Cockram responded to media inquiries in an attempt to salvage her reputation. *See Hutchinson v. Proxmire, 443 U.S. 111, 134–35 (1979)* (stating that the defendant's argument that the plaintiff was a limited-purpose public figure based on the plaintiff's access to the media was

---

3. Because of our conclusion that there is a genuine issue of material fact as to whether Genesco's statements were false, we do not address "whether 'truth' is an affirmative defense to be proved by defendant, or 'falsity' is an element of the cause of action to be proved by plaintiff." *See Kenney v. Wal–Mart Stores, Inc., 100 S.W.3d 809, 814 n.2 (Mo. 2003)*.

unavailing where, *inter alia,* the plaintiff's access to the media occurred after the alleged libel). When Cockram ultimately did agree to be interviewed, she insisted that her name not be used, thus indicating an intent to defend her reputation among those who knew that she was the subject of the reports while avoiding any additional exposure among those unaware of her involvement in the incident. And, even though Cockram succeeded in gaining some access to the media, the more important point is that she did not voluntarily place herself at the center of controversy, but merely found herself there. Thus, we conclude that Cockram was a private figure, not a limited purpose public figure. Because private figures need only show negligence to recover for defamation, and Genesco does not argue that Cockram failed to produce sufficient evidence of negligence, Genesco's argument for affirmance based on the "requisite degree of fault" element fails.

3. Damages to Cockram's reputation

Under Missouri law, "proof of actual reputational harm is an absolute prerequisite in a defamation action." *Kenney v. Wal–Mart Stores, Inc.,* 100 S.W.3d 809, 817 (Mo. 2003). Because "rules of *per se* and *per quod*" defamation do not apply in Missouri, a plaintiff must always prove actual damages. *Id.* "To demonstrate actual damages [in Missouri], plaintiffs must show that defamatory statements caused a quantifiable professional or personal injury, such as interference with job performance, psychological or emotional distress, or depression." *Arthaud v. Mut. of Omaha Ins. Co.,* 170 F.3d 860, 862 (8th Cir.1999). "[T]he question of whether a plaintiff's damages were caused by the defamatory statement is for the jury to decide," *Topper v. Midwest Div., Inc.,* 306 S.W.3d 117, 130 (Mo. Ct. App. 2010). . . .

Genesco argues that it is entitled to summary judgment because Cockram "failed to present any evidence that Genesco's statements caused her reputational damage and cannot differentiate between damages that she allegedly sustained as a result of Genesco's statements and damages resulting from the media's coverage of the receipt incident before Genesco published any statements." When the facts are viewed in the light most favorable to Cockram and all reasonable inferences are made in her favor, the evidence is sufficient to allow a reasonable jury to find actual reputational harm flowing from Genesco's statements.

Cockram argues that there are multiple pieces of evidence indicating that her reputation was harmed by Genesco's statements. She stated that "[p]eople posting comments to media stories carrying Genesco's statement would call me racist." For example, one person writing a comment in response to an online article containing Genesco's first statement said that a "racist teenager entered the words on their [sic] own" and was "rightfully fired." Cockram also received numerous messages containing threats and accusations of racism after Genesco released the first statement. Cockram claims that these "accusations and threats made [her] afraid and [she] moved out of [her] apartment and placed [her] child with [her] parents temporarily." Cockram's father confirmed that Cockram was so concerned about the threats that she asked him to allow her daughter to live with him for a period. Furthermore, Cockram's father stated that his family's friends and acquaintances contacted him and questioned whether Cockram was racist after the stories with Genesco's statements appeared.

Thus, we cannot say as a matter of law that Cockram cannot show actual reputational harm.[4] . . .

[As for the argument that Cockram cannot differentiate the reputational harm caused by her employer as compared to other news source] comments to online news stories containing portions of Genesco's first statement provide evidence that some readers viewed Cockram as a racist after reading Genesco's statement. Additionally, . . . Cockram did not suggest that Genesco's statements placing blame on her inflicted the "same kind of injury" as the generic news stories covering the incident. Indeed, a news story that includes Genesco's statement placing blame on Cockram is likely to cause a greater degree of harm to reputation than one simply providing general information about the incident. Finally, Cockram's receipt of personal threats and messages accusing her of racism *after* Genesco released its statements (where Genesco points to no instances in the record of Cockram receiving such personal messages before Genesco's first statement despite three prior days of news coverage) also supports her causation argument. Under these circumstances, a reasonable jury could conclude that at least some of the reputational harm Cockram suffered resulted from Genesco's statements blaming her for using the racial slur as opposed to news stories that did not mention Genesco's statements. *See Topper* (determining that a "jury may well have inferred" that false statistics "played a role in the removal" of the plaintiff from his position when the statistics were published prior to his termination and made his management "look very bad," even though other negative statements were made about the plaintiff that could have contributed to the loss of his job). Accordingly, we cannot say that a properly instructed jury will be unable to address reasonably the question of causation. Therefore, we decline to affirm on this ground.

In sum, Cockram is a private figure and a reasonable jury could conclude that Genesco's statements were false, that they harmed Cockram's reputation, and that this harm was distinguishable from any harm flowing from the generic news stories. Hence, the district court erred by granting summary judgment to Genesco on Cockram's defamation claim.

NOTES

1. *The Meaning of "Defamatory."* The court has little problem with finding the "gist" or "sting" of the defendant's statements to be that plaintiff was a racist and that such an accusation would be defamatory. But not every negative false statement concerning an individual gives rise to a defamation claim. "Defamation" requires something more serious. Statements accusing the plaintiff of a crime are obviously defamatory. *See Forster v. W. Dakota Veterinary Clinic, Inc.*, 689 N.W.2d 366 (N.D. 2004). But what of other derogatory statements? In the employment context, much less damning comments may also be actionable. *See Government Micro Resources, Inc. v. Jackson*, 624 S.E.2d 63 (Va. 2006) (holding that statements suggesting that plaintiff's incompetence had caused his employer to lose millions of dollars was defamatory).

---

4. Although we do not assume damages, one certainly can suffer severe reputational harm if accused of a racist act.

Even vaguer statements challenging an employee's competence have been found to be defamatory. In *Falls v. Sporting News Publishing Co.*, 834 F.2d 611, 613-15 (6th Cir. 1987), plaintiff was a columnist for a newspaper. He successfully established defamation based on his editor's comment, made in response to a reader's inquiry about the discontinuance of plaintiff's column: "I know Joe brightened a lot of hearts with his column through the years but we felt it was time to make a change, with more energetic columnists who attend more events and are closer to today's sports scene." Similarly defamatory was a statement by another Sporting News official, "Those who seem to have reached maturity and are on the downswing are giving way to up-and-coming young writers who we think deserve a chance."

The test of whether a statement is defamatory, according to section 559A of the RESTATEMENT (SECOND) OF TORTS, is whether it "tends so to harm the reputation of another as to lower him in the estimation of the community or to deter third persons from associating or dealing with him." The "community" includes any "substantial and respectable minority of members of the community." It is not enough, however, if the statement "offends some individual or individuals with views sufficiently peculiar to regard as derogatory what the vast majority of persons regard as innocent." § 559 cmt. e. Who was the "community" in *Falls*? In the employment context, would not any statement explaining a former employee's deficiencies in the job risk being sufficiently defamatory to be actionable? *See Hogan v. Winder*, 762 F.3d 1096 (10th Cir. 2014) (no reasonable reader would take a vague reference to "performance issues" at face value because the context makes clear that the reason for plaintiff's termination was "the subject of an ongoing, obviously nasty, employment dispute," and the characterization "is simply too nonspecific to sustain a defamatory meaning.").

2. *Fact versus Opinion.* Whether the statement is "fact" or "opinion" will determine whether a defamatory statement is actionable. As the RESTATEMENT OF EMPLOYMENT LAW says, "[a]n opinion or prediction alone cannot be actionable. Neither is subject to verification at the time that it is made." § 6.01 cmt. e (Proposed Final Draft, April 18, 2014). How, then, did the *Falls* court find the at-issue statements actionable? Consistent with the Employment Restatement, which says that "[a]n employer's opinion . . . may be actionable if it implies a factual basis that is not disclosed," *id.* *Falls* explained:

> [Looking at the phrase "reached maturity and on the downswing,"] whether "a person has 'reached maturity' may be a statement of fact, and insofar as plaintiff is concerned [57 years old], it could not be false." It also might be viewed as a derogatory opinion, a mild form of ridicule, but it reasonably could not be regarded as defamatory. *See* RESTATEMENT (SECOND) OF TORTS § 559 (1977). However, the statement that plaintiff was "on the downswing" is capable of bearing a defamatory meaning since a jury could reasonably find that it implied that Waters knew undisclosed facts that would justify such an opinion — for example, that plaintiff's writing and reasoning abilities had deteriorated, or that the quality of his work had declined to the point that others had to rewrite or cover for him. . . .
>
> Similarly, Barnidge's [the editor] letter can be construed, by negative implication, as an expression of opinion that plaintiff was inferior to his replacements because he was less energetic than other columnists, attended fewer events, and was not as close as they to the current sports scene. This comment creates a reasonable inference that it is justified by the existence of undisclosed facts, such as, for example, that plaintiff did not work hard or he was prevented by his physical condition from exerting himself; that he did not frequently attend sports events to obtain first-hand knowledge of the events reported in his

sports columns; and that he was out-of-touch with current sports personalities, an outsider who lacked good "sources." Obviously, these kinds of undisclosed facts could be defamatory. In the alternative, the letter can be viewed as expressing a derogatory opinion of plaintiff—that he was inferior to his replacements—based on Barnidge's own statement as fact that the new writers were more energetic, attended more events, and were closer to the sports scene. If these stated facts were found to be false and defamatory, Barnidge would be subject to liability for the factual statements but not for the expression of opinion.

834 F.2d at 616. Courts have had great difficulty formulating standards for distinguishing fact from opinion. Are you satisfied with the *Falls* resolution? *See also Thomas v. United Steelworkers Local 1938*, 743 F.3d 1134, 1142-43 (8th Cir. 2014) (holding that while statement such as "Thomas is a prick," merely expressed the speaker's subjective view or opinion and therefore weren't by themselves actionable, other statements about the number of complaints supposedly received about plaintiff's harassing behavior were capable of being proven false even if they included adjectives and characteristics rather than specific acts). *See generally* John Bruce Lewis & Gregory V. Mersol, *Opinion and Rhetorical Hyperbole in Workplace Defamation Actions: The Continuing Quest for Meaningful Standards*, 52 DePaul L. Rev. 19 (2002).

   3. *Truth as a Defense.* Defamation is sometimes confused with falsehood. The Restatement of Employment Law speaks in terms of actionable statements "being false and defamatory." §6.01. In other words, a statement can be both defamatory and true, although there can be no liability for true statements. A plaintiff was traditionally not required to prove that a defamatory statement was false, but merely to allege falsity, in order to make out a prima facie case of defamation. The burden was on the defendant to establish the truth of the statement. While many states continue to allocate the burden on truth in this fashion, Supreme Court decisions raise questions about the constitutionality of this approach. The argument is that the First Amendment requires, as a prerequisite to liability, proof that the defendant is at fault with respect to the falsity of a communication. *See Philadelphia Newspapers, Inc. v. Hepps*, 475 U.S. 767, 776 (1986); *BE&K Construction Co. v. NLRB*, 536 U.S. 516 (2002). *See generally* Restatement (Second) of Torts §581A cmts. a, b (1977). Note the *Cockram* court's dodging this issue in footnote 3.

   Cockram also makes clear that what might be called "technical truth" will not necessarily avoid liability. Although the statements made by the defendant may have been technically true, the message they conveyed—that plaintiff was intentionally printed out a racist receipt—were not. Illustration 10 of the proposed Restatement makes the point by positing a statement that a worker was discharged for "gross insubordination." It explains: "The truth of E being charged with 'gross insubordination' is not a defense to a claim that the charge of gross insubordination damaged E's reputation by falsely portraying him as an uncooperative worker."

   4. *Publication and Self-Publication.* "Publication" is a term of art in defamation. It consists merely of "communication [of defamatory matter] intentionally or by a negligent act to one other than the person defamed." Restatement (Second) of Torts §577 (1977). In *Cockram* there was no dispute about publication. In *Falls*, some of the defamation was published in the more intuitive meaning of the word: It had been printed in a newspaper.

   Suppose, however, that someone in Genesco had made similar statements about Cockram to another Genesco employee, perhaps the director of Human Resources.

Comment i of Restatement § 577 states that "[t]he communication within the scope of his employment by one agent to another agent of the same principal" is a publication. Thus, intracorporate communications will constitute publication under the RESTATEMENT OF TORTS. *See also* RESTATEMENT (THIRD) OF EMPLOYMENT LAW § 6.01(2)(b) (Proposed Final Draft, April 18, 2014) (liability for publication "internally within the employer's organization"); *Trail v. Boys & Girls Clubs of Northwest Ind.*, 845 N.E.2d 130, 136 (Ind. 2006) (employee evaluations communicated intracompany to management personnel are published for purposes of defamation); *Taggart v. Drake Univ.*, 549 N.W.2d 796 (Iowa 1996) (communications between corporate supervisors concerning a corporate employee may be subject to a qualified privilege, but they are published). *But see Halsell v. Kimberly-Clark Corp.*, 683 F.2d 285, 288-89 (8th Cir. 1982) ("Until the defamatory statement is communicated outside the corporate sphere or internal organization, it has not been published.").

A few courts have even found the defendant responsible when the plaintiff himself republishes the defamation under the "compulsory self-publication" doctrine. *See, e.g., Lewis v. Equitable Life Assurance Soc'y*, 389 N.W.2d 876 (Minn. 1986). *But see Emery v. Northeast Ill. Reg'l Commuter R.R. Corp.*, 880 N.E.2d 1002, 1011-12 (Ill. App. Ct. 2007) (rejecting the compulsory self-publication doctrine as a minority rule in only four states). Where this doctrine exists, an employee's revealing the reasons for his former employer's adverse action against him in order, say, to obtain a new position, will satisfy the publication requirement. *See generally* Markita D. Cooper, *Between a Rock and a Hard Case: Time for a New Doctrine of Compelled Self-Publication*, 72 NOTRE DAME L. REV. 373 (1997). The RESTATEMENT OF EMPLOYMENT LAW would recognize a modified version of the doctrine, which would apply only if the employer tells the worker that it "intends to communicate in substance the same message to third parties" or, despite the employee's request refuse [sic] to promise that it will not be so communicated." § 6.01. cmt. d (Proposed Final Draft, April 18, 2014).

5. *Actions as Statements.* A number of cases have considered whether actions can be treated as statements for defamation purposes, which is especially important in the employment context. For example, *Krolikowski v. University of Massachusetts Memorial Medical Center*, 2002 U.S. Dist. LEXIS 8984 (D. Mass. May 16, 2002), upheld a cause of action by a doctor who claimed she was defamed when the Chair of the Radiology Department barred her from reading mammograms; she argued that this sent a signal to her colleagues that she had serious performance problems. While there was a fact question as to whether a "supervisory privilege" was exceeded, the defendant's conduct was actionable. Similarly, in *Tyler v. Macks Stores of N.C. Inc.*, 272 S.E.2d 633 (S.C. 1980), an employee was required to take a polygraph and soon afterward was discharged. He argued that this led other employees and others to believe that his discharge was based on some wrongful activity and that "this insinuation and inference of wrongdoing can amount to the publication of defamatory matter." The court agreed. Defamation may be "by actions or conduct as well as by word" and "need not be accomplished in a direct manner. To render the defamatory statement actionable, it is not necessary that the false charge be made in a direct, open and positive manner. A mere insinuation is as actionable as a positive assertion if it is false and malicious and the meaning is plain." *Id.* at 634. However, mere silence has been held not actionable even when it was alleged that the natural inference was defamatory. *See Trail v. Boys & Girls Clubs of Northwest Ind.*, 845 N.E.2d 130, 137 (Ind. 2006) (where an allegation refers only to a speculative effect of "non-actionable silence" on plaintiff's reputation, "[i]t would be an odd use of the defamation doctrine

to hold that silence constitutes actionable speech."). *See also Schmitt v. MeritCare Health Sys., Dakota Clinic, Ltd.*, 834 N.W.2d 627, 634 (N.D. 2013) (delay in responding to a credentialing questionnaire could not reasonably be interpreted as a false assertion related to plaintiff's medical incompetence).

If defamation may be accomplished through actions as well as through words, is the act of sending security guards to escort a fired employee from the building defamatory? Does it matter whether this is standard practice in cases of suspension or discharge? *See Phelan v. May Dep't Stores Co.* 819 N.E.2d 550 (Mass. 2004) (employer's conduct during investigation of potential theft too ambiguous to be actionable by employee). The RESTATEMENT concludes that "employer implementation of a policy to protect the security of property, such as the guard-escorted removal or discharged employees or reasonable searches to discover stolen goods, cannot be reasonably interpreted as communicative." §6.01, cmt. f.

6. *Employer Fault.* The *Cockram* court makes clear that there are varying degrees of fault necessary for actionable defamation. The lowest standard is for "private figures," who need prove only negligence. Public figures, even "limited purpose public figures," have to prove the defendant published the defamation with "knowledge that the statements were false, or with a reckless disregard as to whether they were true or false." In the principal case, the court concluded that Cockram was a private figure, which was probably crucial to her success. Note that, as we will discuss below, overcoming one of the various "qualified privilege" protections ordinarily will require plaintiffs who are private figures to prove some kind of fault greater than negligence. In other words, these privilege protections heighten the fault standard.

7. *Counseling the Employer.* What can an employer do to protect against defamation actions? Obviously, care should be taken to ensure that discharges are based on proven violations. Truth will avoid liability. Even after careful investigation, however, erroneous judgments will sometimes be made. Would you advise an employer not to tell employees the reason they are being discharged? Informing only the employee would not usually be actionable because of the publication requirement — but recall the compelled self-publication doctrine. One commentator recommends regularly scheduled, objective evaluations, accessible only by those with a need to see them, and investigation of possible employee misconduct, preferably by a designated person to ensure consistency. When discharge is necessary:

> Handle terminations sensitively. Make sure termination is done only after a proper and thorough investigation. Release information about the discharged employee to only those in the organization who need to know. Take action to prevent and/or stop false rumors that might begin circulating. . . . To the extent possible, assist the employee in locating new employment. Remember that lawsuits of this nature are brought by disgruntled employees who believe they were not treated fairly by the employer. . . . Consider asking for a signed release from the employee which authorizes you to release information to prospective employers who may inquire.
>
> Respond carefully to reference inquiries. Direct inquiries to a centralized office such as personnel or human resources offices. Verify the identity of the person seeking the information to confirm that they have a legitimate need for the information. Insist that inquiries be made in writing. Disclose only dates of employment, positions held, and wage/salary information, or keep discussions with prospective employers limited to other verifiable and objective facts. Avoid giving subjective or emotional evaluations.
>
> Correct mistakes. Take prompt action to correct any inaccuracies in information provided about the employee.

> Train supervisory personnel in the proper methods of employee evaluation, investigation and termination. . . .

Thomas A. Jacobson, *Avoiding Claims of Defamation in the Workplace*, 72 N. DAK. L. REV. 247, 264-65 (1996). What do you think of this advice? How will implementing the suggested practices help employers avoid defamation liability? Might adopting these practices create other legal risks or costs for the employer?

8. *Mishandling Matters.* For a good example of how *not* to handle a reference request, consider *Matthews v. Wis. Energy Corp.*, 534 F.3d 547, 553-54 (7th Cir. 2008), which is all the more striking because a lawyer caused the problem. The case arose from settlement of a discrimination suit. The employer's in-house attorney, English, recited the terms regarding references in open court, which required the company to follow its policy of limited disclosure, "what you call name, rank, and serial number." That is, the company would "confirm people worked there, the dates of employment, and their position or at least their last position." Later, Matthews hired Schwartz to help find employment, and Schwartz ended up talking to English on the phone. In that conversation, she discussed far more than name, rank, and serial number, and, according to Schwartz, displayed an "obvious sense of distrust" of Matthews. The Seventh Circuit found the attorney's comments actionable:

> As represented by Wisconsin Energy, its policy entailed verifying only the dates of employment, final salary, and the title of the last position held. Neither participant in the conversation denies that English told Schwartz of Matthews's litigation history. This information went well beyond the objective information concerning Matthews's dates of employment, final salary, and final position held. A jury could believe Schwartz's version of the conversation, which included what would be unfavorable information regarding Matthews. And it could likewise conclude that the parties agreed that Wisconsin Energy would provide only the objective information set out in its "policy." If so, this would show that Wisconsin Energy breached the settlement agreement.

Note that this is not defamation per se, but rather breach of a settlement agreement. Note also that for the same reason, the plaintiff would be limited to contract damages rather than the lucrative damages available under tort law.

9. *Overly Positive Recommendations.* Another reason for an employer to adopt a policy limiting the information that will be provided about present or former employees is to limit liability to third parties when an employment reference is too favorable. This can arise when an employer provides a reference while withholding negative information about a former employee from a prospective employer, perhaps for fear of a defamation suit, and the employee subsequently engages in misconduct or causes injury upon being hired by the new employer. While liability in such situations is rare, it is not unknown and is most common in cases involving affirmative misrepresentations, rather than mere nondisclosure. *See, e.g., Kadlec Med. Ctr. v. Lakeview Anesthesia Assocs.*, 527 F.3d 412 (5th Cir. 2008) (no duty for a hospital to disclose doctor's narcotic addiction to another hospital when its letter merely confirmed dates of work; however, glowing letters from a practice group to second hospital were actionable because they were misleading); *Randi W. v. Muroc Joint Unified School Dist.*, 929 P.2d 582 (Cal. 1997) (although "ordinarily a recommending employer should not be held accountable to third persons for failing to disclose negative information regarding a former employee, nonetheless liability may be imposed" if the recommendation letter amounts to an affirmative misrepresentation presenting a foreseeable and substantial risk of physical harm to a third person). *See also Thomas v. Dep't of Hous. & Urban Dev.*, 124 F.3d 1439, 1442 (Fed. Cir. 1997) (criticizing settlement agreement "requiring the whitewashing of an employee's disciplinary record," which results in "some agency officials [being] willing to palm off their problems on others, including sister agencies," and suggesting that perhaps "as a matter of sound governmental administration such agency agreements should be prohibited.").

10. *Libel and Slander.* To this point, we have spoken of "defamation" without distinguishing the old common-law categories of libel and slander. For most purposes, these categories are no longer important, but in some jurisdictions they retain some vitality. Libel is a defamation embodied in a permanent form such as a letter or a newspaper article, or on the Internet. According to the RESTATEMENT (SECOND) OF TORTS § 568A, libel in the modern world also includes "[b]roadcasting of defamatory matter by means of radio or television . . . whether or not it is read from a manuscript." The "downswing" statement in *Falls* was libel. Slander is characterized by impermanence and includes, therefore, unrecorded spoken words as well as gestures. The significance of the distinction lies in whether the plaintiff must prove "special damages" — actual provable damages such as loss of employment — in order to sustain an action. *See* RESTATEMENT (SECOND) OF TORTS § 75 cmt. b (1977). Libel, because its permanence rendered it more dangerous, was traditionally actionable without such proof. However, certain kinds of slander (slander "per se") could also be established without showing special damages. And such per se slander included that relating to a person's trade or profession. *See Wilcox v. Newark Val. Cent. School Dist.*, 904 N.Y.S.2d 523, 527 (3d Dep't 2010) As a result, the distinction between libel and slander will not often be significant in defamation cases in the employment setting, even if it retains some significance in other contexts in a particular jurisdiction.

11. *Reconsidering Perverse Incentives.* Potential liability for defamation discourages providing references to prospective employers. As the extract in Note 7 suggests, many employers have adopted policies regarding employment references, under which supervisors and Human Resources officers are told to provide minimal information. Such policies often limit the information to be given to confirming the fact of employment, the position, and the dates. In some cases, the policy allows confirming last salary. Adherence to such policies will, obviously, limit defamation exposure and the possibility of liability for overly positive recommendations. Of course, it also limits the extent to which any potential employer can be sure about the work history and habits of an applicant. In extreme cases, the failure to provide information may result in the hiring of a sexual predator or a thief. For that reason, there have been repeated calls for statutory immunity for employment references. As of 2009, 39 states had enacted job reference immunity statutes, *see* MATTHEW FINKIN, PRIVACY IN EMPLOYMENT LAW 911-38 (4th ed. 2013 and 2014 Supp.), but the provisions vary widely, and scholars do not believe that such laws have meaningfully changed employer unwillingness to provide references. *See generally* Matthew W. Finkin & Kenneth G. Dau-Schmidt, *Solving the Employee Reference Problem: Lessons from the German Experience*, 57 AM. J. COMP. L. 387 (2009); Markita D. Cooper, *Job Reference Immunity Statutes: Prevalent But Irrelevant*, 11 CORNELL J.L. & PUB. POL'Y 1 (2001); *cf.* J. Hoult Verkerke, *Legal Regulation of Employment Reference Practices*, 65 U. CHI. L. REV. 115, 199 (1998) (finding that the "existing combination of defamation liability for falsely negative references and the conditional common interest privilege applicable to supplying reference information strikes an appropriate balance between quantity and quality concerns," but recommending modest reforms such as "adopting targeted reporting and disclosure systems for certain high-risk occupations."). Reconsider the need for such statutes after you have read the next principal case, which explores the concept of privilege. Recently, firms have been using technology to avoid the problems posed by the refusals of most employers to provide references. Using a service called "Reference Search" on LinkedIn (available only to premium account holders) to identify former co-workers, the employers have been contacting such persons to obtain information about applicants. Natasha Singer, *Funny, They Don't Look Like My References*, N.Y. TIMES, NOV. 9, 2014, p. BU4. This has generated a class-action suit by plaintiffs who claim it is a violation of the Fair Credit Reporting Act, discussed at page 357.

12. *Consenting to Being Defamed.* Employers seem to be increasingly asking applicants for consent to inquire of former employees and presumably using such consent to obtain information that might not otherwise be provided. The extent to which consent may operate to absolve a speaker of liability is unclear. *See* Alex B. Long, *The Forgotten Role of Consent in Defamation and Employment Reference Cases*, 66 FLA. L. REV. 719 (2014) (noting that employers are increasingly asking prospective employees for consent to inquire of past employers and exploring the extent to which any resulting consent will bar defamation suits).

13. *And Then There's False Light.* The *Cockram* court rejected the plaintiff's "false light" claim, reading the Missouri cases as not recognizing such a tort where the essence of the allegation was defamation. It therefore did not have to reach the question of whether Missouri would permit false light suits in other situations. As this suggests, there is an overlap between defamation and false light liability, but, in theory at least, the two torts protect different interests: Defamation protects reputation while false light protects privacy. *See* RESTATEMENT (SECOND) OF TORTS, § 652E ("One who gives publicity to a matter concerning another that places the other before the public in a false light is subject to liability to the other for invasion of his privacy, if (a) the false light in which the other was placed would be highly offensive to a reasonable person, and (b) the actor had knowledge of or acted in reckless disregard as to the falsity of the publicized matter and the false light in which the other would be placed."). The viability of this tort is questionable. Andrew Osorio, Note, *Twilight: The Fading of False Light Invasion of Privacy*, 66 N.Y.U. ANN. SURV. AM. L. 173 (2010).

═══ *Shannon v. Taylor AMC/Jeep, Inc.*
═══ *425 N.W.2d 165 (Mich. Ct. App. 1988)*

MCDONALD, J.

. . . Plaintiff worked for Taylor for approximately twelve years, the last eight years as parts manager. Plaintiff's employment was terminated in June, 1982, for his alleged involvement with stolen parts.

During his employment as parts manager, one of the employees under plaintiff's supervision was Laurie Cherup. Around the beginning of 1982, plaintiff had to discipline Cherup and eventually fire her. Rick Howard, the AMC branch manager responsible for Taylor AMC, reinstated Cherup and told plaintiff to leave her alone. Howard and Cherup were involved in a physical relationship in late 1981 or early 1982. Following plaintiff's termination, Cherup became the new parts manager. Cherup was overheard on several occasions telling customers over the phone that plaintiff was no longer parts manager because plaintiff had "gotten caught stealing," and that plaintiff was fired "for being involved in theft of parts."

Plaintiff testified that he was not involved with stolen parts for profit or personal gain, but was working with Taylor Police Officer James Black in an attempt to set up persons attempting to sell stolen parts to Taylor. On June 15, 1982, plaintiff was contacted on the phone and asked if he wanted to buy a Jeep hardtop. The phone call made plaintiff suspicious that the hardtop was stolen, so plaintiff called Black, a personal friend, for advice. Black advised plaintiff that the police would need "hard evidence" such as names and driver's license numbers of the suspects. Plaintiff purchased two hardtops which he suspected to be stolen, and placed them in the back of the parts department. When another Taylor employee indicated that a customer was interested in purchasing one of the hardtops, plaintiff responded that they were not for sale as he had reason to believe the hardtops were stolen. Plaintiff was fired the same day Black was allegedly going to write up a report on the stolen goods. . . .

[This appeal questions the propriety of the verdict of no cause of action on the slander claim. The court held that the trial judge erred in instructing the jury on qualified privilege and actual malice.]

A communication is defamatory if it tends to lower an individual's reputation in the community or deter third persons from associating or dealing with him. *Swenson-Davis v. Martel*, 354 N.W.2d 288 (Mich. App. 1984). Slander per se is found where the words spoken are false and malicious and are injurious to a person in his or her profession or employment. *Swenson-Davis.*

Here, the trial court found that Cherup's statements about plaintiff to defendant's customers were protected from action by a qualified privilege. The initial determination of whether a privilege exists is one of law for the court. *Lawrence v. Fox*, 97 N.W.2d 719 (Mich. 1959). In general, a qualified privilege extends to "all communications made bona fide upon any subject matter in which the party communicating has an interest, or in reference to which he has a duty, to a person having a corresponding interest or duty. . . ."

Thus, in order to have a qualified privilege, the communication must be: (1) bona fide; (2) made by a party who has an interest, or a duty to communicate the subject matter; and (3) made to a party who has a corresponding interest or duty.

Although in the instant case neither party addresses the first prerequisite, the "bona fide" nature of the communication, we question whether Cherup's statements were bona fide. Not only had plaintiff previously fired Cherup, but there was testimony indicating that another employee overheard a conversation between Cherup, Howard and two others regarding possible ways in which to "get rid of" plaintiff, and wherein Howard allegedly suggested that they "link" plaintiff with some stolen parts.

Nonetheless, even if the statements were bona fide, we find that they do not meet the remaining two requirements. The problem with determining if a qualified privilege applies is that privilege varies with the situation; it is not a constant. Defendant Taylor contends that the particular facts of this situation call for the application of qualified privilege, arguing that it had a duty to inform customers that the parts manager (plaintiff) had been fired for purchasing stolen parts. Taylor asserts that if the customers were not presently told and found out years later that stolen parts were purchased from Taylor, they would cease to do business with the dealership. In Taylor's opinion, the potential detrimental effect on customer relations justifies the application of qualified privilege to the statements. We disagree.

For defendant's argument to have merit, and before defendant could acquire an interest in telling customers why plaintiff was fired, a determination should have been made as to whether stolen goods were actually sold to customers. Taylor knew that plaintiff had possession of the Jeep hardtops. There was no reason to believe that any stolen goods ended up in customers' hands. Therefore, there was no qualified privilege to tell customers that plaintiff was fired because he dealt with stolen parts. Thus, absent evidence that stolen parts had been passed along to customers, plaintiff's good name should have been protected by not allowing an employee to tell customers why plaintiff was fired. When dealing with a duty/interest privilege, the Michigan Supreme Court has said "the occasion determines the question of privilege." *Bacon v. The Michigan C.R. Co.*, 33 N.W. 181 (Mich. 1887). The instant occasion did not give the employer a qualified privilege to defame plaintiff.

Furthermore, we find no corresponding interest or duty to hear the communication on the part of the customers. In *Merritt v. Detroit Memorial Hospital*, 265 N.W.2d 124 (Mich. App. 1978), this Court stated that an employer has a qualified privilege to tell those of its employees responsible for hiring and firing of accusations of employee misconduct. However, an employer cannot tell all employees why someone was fired in order to quiet rumors or restore morale. *Sias v. General Motors Corp.*, 127 N.W.2d 357 (Mich. 1964). In the instant case Taylor does not allege or offer proof that any customer received stolen goods purchased from plaintiff. If Taylor had a good faith belief that stolen auto parts had been sold to a particular customer, the customer may have had an interest, but that is not the situation in the instant case. Here, the customer's interest is like the employees' interest in *Sias*: just a general interest or curiosity in finding out why a former employee was fired.

The trial court erred in instructing the jury that a qualified privilege existed. Absent the existence of a qualified privilege, plaintiff would not have been required to prove actual malice. We cannot say that the instructional error was harmless beyond a reasonable doubt and therefore reverse for a new trial.

NOTES

1. *Underpinnings of the Privilege.* As *Shannon* indicates, defamatory information communicated in the ordinary course of the employment relationship frequently will be subject to a qualified privilege. The law recognizes a public policy interest in frank and open communication when the speaker has a duty to speak or an interest in speaking. In the employment context, this includes employment references and communications between employers and employees, employees complaining to supervisors, supervisors evaluating and reviewing employees' work product, and employers informing employees of the reason for disciplinary action. It may also include customers of the business. *See* RESTATEMENT (SECOND) OF TORTS §§ 594-96 (1977).

In *Shannon*, the court found that no privilege existed to inform customers: The customers had no interest in the matter because there was no claim plaintiff had been selling stolen goods to them. In contrast, *Grice v. FedEx Ground Package Sys.*, 925 So. 2d 907, 912 (Miss. Ct. App. 2006), dealt with statements to co-workers and contractors that plaintiff had tuberculosis. These were qualifiedly privileged because the individuals informed "had a genuine interest in knowing whether a co-worker with whom they were in frequent contact had a highly contagious disease." Even if there were no privilege to tell customers in *Shannon*, there may have been a privilege as to internal communications. This suggests the highly contextual nature of conditional privileges.

2. *Qualified vs. Absolute Privileges.* Privileges may be absolute or qualified. An absolute privilege confers immunity from liability regardless of motive. For example, while communication of a reason for discharge to courts or agencies, such as an unemployment compensation board, clearly constitutes publication, that communication serves the needs of a judicial or quasi-judicial process and therefore is absolutely privileged. In *Fulghum v. United Parcel Service, Inc.*, 378 N.W.2d 472 (Mich. 1985), the court held that accusations of dishonesty made during the course of the grievance procedure under a collective bargaining agreement are accorded an absolute privilege. According to the court, actions for defamation based on statements made about an employee during a proceeding about the discharge of that employee would "directly and severely impair the functioning of the agreed-upon grievance procedure. . . ." *See also Rosenberg v. Metlife, Inc.*, 866 N.E.2d 439 (N.Y. 2007) (statements made in brokerage's U-5 filing with NASD were absolutely privileged). *But see Galarneau v. Merrill Lynch, Pierce, Fenner & Smith Inc.*, 504 F.3d 189 (1st Cir. 2007) (U-5 filings were only conditionally privileged).

Most privileges, however, are not absolute, but rather are qualified in that false statements made with actual malice are not privileged even if made in what ordinarily would be a privileged context. A qualified privilege obviously reflects a lower public interest in free communication. The burden lies with the defendant to establish that the defamation is subject to a qualified privilege, but such a privilege may be lost (i.e., exceeded) in a variety of ways. For example, § 6.02(1) of the RESTATEMENT OF EMPLOYMENT LAW provides:

> Absent abuse, an employer has a privilege to publish statements concerning an employee
> (a) to prospective employers and employment agencies,
> (b) to public or private regulatory or licensing authorities, and
> (c) to the employer's own employees and agents.

(Proposed Final Draft, April 18, 2014). "Abuse" takes the employer out from under the protection of the privilege when the statement is made "without a reasonable intent to serve a legitimate interest of the employer or of the recipient." § 6.01(2). This occurs "when (a) the employer knows the statement to be false or acts with reckless disregard of its truth or falsity; or (b) knows or should know that the recipient and the employer have no legitimate interest in the recipient receiving the particular information." *Id.*

3. *Malice and the Privilege.* The first prong of abuse of privilege requires showing that the employer made the defamatory statements with knowledge of their falsity or without regard to whether they were true. This is sometimes referred to as "actual malice." *See Sherman v. Rinchem Co.*, 687 F.3d 996 (8th Cir. 2012) (defamatory statement to employee to explain his termination was protected by a qualified privilege since it was based on reasonable grounds and the employee failed to prove actual malice). Recall that, as in *Cochram*, defamation may ordinarily be established by demonstrating mere negligence. Actual malice requires something more: The court must find that the defendant knew the statement to be false or made the statement recklessly without regard to its truth or falsity. Some courts also find malice when the speaker was actuated by improper motives, regardless of whether she believed her statements to be true. Is that what the *Shannon* court had in mind when it questioned whether Cherup's statements were "bona fide"? What else could it have meant? *See Gambardella v. Apple Health Care, Inc.*, 969 A.2d 736 (Conn. 2009) (any qualified privilege was lost for two reasons: "'actual malice,' namely, the publication of a false statement with actual knowledge of its falsity or reckless disregard for its truth, [and] 'malice in fact,' namely, the publication of a false statement with bad faith or improper motive"). In general, the privilege seeks to balance the defendant's legitimate need to speak and the listener's legitimate need to hear against the possible damage to the plaintiff's reputation. These competing interests are reconciled by permitting the defendant to speak if she honestly and reasonably believes the information is true, but not if she knows the information is false or is reckless as to the possibility that it is false.

In *Soto-Lebron v. Fed. Express Corp.*, 538 F.3d 45 (1st Cir. 2008), the court found that circulation of written statements within the corporation to the effect that plaintiff had shipped cocaine were actionable. The statements were published, although only circulated internally, and the conditional privilege was properly found to have been exceeded: "[O]nce FedEx was on notice that the drug allegations were questionable, it was obligated to either stop repeating them or adequately investigate them. It did neither. As a result, the jury was entitled to conclude that FedEx had 'improper motives' and thereby lost the benefit of the conditional privilege because it acted with reckless disregard for the truth." 538 F.3d at 64; *cf. Dugan v. Mittal Steel USA, Inc.*, 929 N.E.2d 184, 189 (Ind. 2010) (the common interest qualified privilege for intracompany communications about theft of company property does not apply only to statements made on personal knowledge; reporting information received from others may be privileged).

4. *Exceeding the Privilege.* The other way to "abuse" the privilege is for the employer to make the defamatory statements to a wider audience than necessary. In other words, the protection of the privilege can be exceeded by providing the information to those who do not have a legitimate interest in the information or by providing more information than necessary.

How these doctrines interact can be seen by revisiting *Cockram*. As made, the statements would not have been subject to the Restatement's formulation of a qualified privilege because they were made to the broader community, not merely to coworkers. But had similar statements been made to Genesco's own employees, a qualified privilege would attach. At that point the plaintiff would have to show that the defendant abused the privilege. It could have done so by showing knowing falsity or reckless disregard (not just the negligence proved in the case itself). Failing that, the plaintiff could have prevailed only by showing that some or all of the employees to whom it was made had no legitimate interest in the information. *See also Thomas v. United Steelworkers Local 1938*, 743 F.3d 1134, 1144 (8th Cir. 2014) (no qualified privilege where the statements, although made in connection with an employer investigation of an incident went far beyond the incident in question and, in any event, the speaker's failure to investigate any of the supposed complaints "prevents such statements from being based upon reasonable or probable cause").

5. *Damages.* Prevailing plaintiffs in defamation actions are entitled to compensatory damages, damages for emotional distress, and potentially punitive damages. The latter forms of damages are important because it may be difficult for an at-will employee to prove compensatory damages. In both *Falls* and *Shannon*, for example, the loss of the plaintiffs' jobs was separate from the defamation — and therefore lost salary and benefits were not caused by the defamation. In *Soto-Lebron*, the court affirmed a finding of liability but vacated the damages award because the jury might have been improperly influenced by plaintiff's testimony as to his emotional distress and his inability to get other jobs. There was no showing that either was linked to the libelous statements, as opposed to the fact that he was terminated. 538 F.3d at 67.

As for punitive damages, they are available when "the defendants' conduct is shown to be motivated by evil motive or intent, or when it involves reckless or callous indifference to the federally protected rights of others." *Smith v. Wade*, 461 U.S. 30, 56 (1983) Some courts will not award punitive damages unless there have been actual damages as well, while others require a showing of actual malice as a prerequisite to recovery in defamation actions. *See Senna v. Florimont*, 958 A.2d 427 (N.J. 2008). In some states, tort reform has affected punitive awards. An extreme example is Massachusetts, which denies plaintiffs any such recovery in defamation actions. *See* Mass. Gen. Laws ch. 231, §93 (2010) ("In no action of slander or libel shall exemplary or punitive damages be allowed, whether because of actual malice or want of good faith or for any other reason.").

PROBLEMS

5-2. Tina Kim is a carpenter. Until recently, she worked for Cozy Cabinets, a small company producing custom-built furniture. Tina was responsible for completing the finish work on some of the more elaborate designs. Last week, Mr. Gregory, the vice president in charge of production at Cozy Cabinets, discharged Tina. Gregory told Tina that she was fired. His explanation was that Jim Mineta, Tina's supervisor, had evaluated her finish work as "just not up to Cozy's standards." Tina has come to you for advice. She is afraid to apply for any carpentry jobs because she doesn't know what Cozy will say about her discharge, and she is certain that she won't get another job if she explains why Cozy let her go. She tells you that she thinks Mineta "had it in for her" because a few weeks ago, she complained to Gregory that Mineta had failed to provide her with adequate supplies to complete a job on time. Tina worked for Cozy for two years and all of her previous evaluations were good. She is an at-will employee. Tina is terribly upset because she is afraid that she will never get another carpentry job. She wants to know if there is any way to get her job back or if she has any other remedies.

5-3. Suppose you represent Cozy Cabinets. Gregory received a voice mail from an old friend in the industry who is considering hiring Kim but wants to know "the scoop" on her. Gregory would like to be honest because the two exchange favors all the time. Should he return the call? If so, what should he say?

C. INTENTIONAL INFLICTION OF EMOTIONAL DISTRESS

≡ *Subbe-Hirt v. Baccigalupi*
≡ 94 F.3d 111 (3d Cir. 1996)

Nygaard, Circuit Judge.
. . . [Elaine Subbe-Hirt was a salesperson for Prudential Insurance Company, and brought suit against Prudential, her former employer] and Robert Baccigalupi, her former supervisor at Prudential, presenting several claims arising out of her

employment with Prudential. The district court granted summary judgment in favor of the defendants on Subbe-Hirt's claim for intentional infliction of emotional distress. It held alternatively that her claim was barred by the exclusive remedy provided by the New Jersey Worker's Compensation Act and that, in any event, the claim would fail on its merits because defendants' conduct was not sufficiently outrageous under New Jersey law. Subbe-Hirt appeals from that ruling. [Subbe-Hirt did *not* appeal from the adverse resolution of her other claims, including discrimination claims under New Jersey law. The appeals court first reversed the district court finding that workers' compensation exclusivity barred plaintiff's tort suit and then turned to the tort claim.]

III

Subbe-Hirt contends that the district court also committed legal error by basing its summary judgment on a conclusion that defendants' conduct was not sufficiently outrageous to support a claim for intentional infliction of emotional distress. On this allegation of error we have but two issues to decide: 1) whether Robert Baccigalupi intended to inflict emotional distress upon Elaine Subbe-Hirt; and 2) whether the evidence supports appellant's contention that Baccigalupi succeeded in inflicting that distress. We answer both questions in the affirmative and hold that the record in this case exceeds a threshold showing of outrageous behavior sufficient to preclude summary judgment.

A

The present record, when viewed in the light most favorable to Subbe-Hirt, shows that Robert Baccigalupi unquestionably intended to inflict emotional distress upon Elaine Subbe-Hirt. According to sales manager Mark Parisi, Baccigalupi "would berate [Subbe-Hirt] or talk about getting her." Indeed, Baccigalupi stated, "I'm going to get her."

Moreover, according to the deposition testimony of Parisi and sales manager Robert LaNicca, Baccigalupi stated, in the presence of other managers and on more than one occasion, that he "was going to trim her bush";[1] a blatantly sexist metaphor to brag of how Baccigalupi would handle females in general and Subbe-Hirt in particular. According to sales manager David Meyer, "when it was brought to R. Baccigalupi's attention that [Subbe-Hirt] was soon going to be returning from disability, R. Baccigalupi quickly remarked, 'Well, don't worry about her. I'm going to trim her bush.'" When asked by counsel to explain what he understood Baccigalupi's remark to mean, Meyer testified, "I understood it that he was going to lay into her quite hard and put her in her place." LaNicca said that on another occasion Baccigalupi stated, "Let's bring Elaine in here on Friday and we'll trim her bush." Parisi understood that phrase to mean:

> That he was going to come down on her, whatever his particular style was, forcing her to either go out on disability or leave the company or to cease the union activity. . . . [This]

1. I.e., pubic hair. Sales manager David Meyer testified, "Well, he wasn't going to go out and trim her azalea bush at home. It was a sexist remark."

is, unfortunately with Prudential, is an avenue that agents take when they can't take the — you know, when management pressure goes up, and that's what [Baccigalupi] might use that for.

Likewise, Robert King, a district agent, said:

> There came a point in time where it was almost embarrassing for many of us to watch a woman being — . . . it was pretty much obvious that Elaine wouldn't and couldn't bear up under the general atmosphere . . . — her time was expiring. . . . We talked amongst ourselves that, you know, this was a critical stage. . . . There was a persecution going of myself and Elaine, and Elaine in particular. . . . [Baccigalupi said] more or less than [sic] she was history and that if I intended to continue that I would — I should leave things go as they are going.

Baccigalupi's intent to inflict emotional distress can be further seen in his total lack of any vestige of compassion for any woman in the office. On one occasion Meyer told Baccigalupi that he "couldn't continue performing 'root canal'[2] on women agents on his staff because they broke down in tears." At that point, Baccigalupi simply selected a woman agent to abuse as a demonstration, saying "Well, don't worry. I'll show you how to handle it." Appellant describes this contrived encounter as follows:

> He then called one of the women agents in for a review, and started the "root canal" and the intimidation on her until she broke down and started crying. R. Baccigalupi kept tearing and pressing into her and when it was over and she had left the office, he was holding out his suspender straps as if to say, "this is how you handle it; don't let their emotions get in your way."

Indeed, Baccigalupi admitted his intent when he said to Subbe-Hirt, "do you know who Joan of Arc is, read between the lines, do you know why I'm looking at your work so closely, do you think I do this to everyone?"

We have no difficulty in concluding that a reasonable jury could find from this evidence that Baccigalupi intended that his conduct subject Elaine Subbe-Hirt to emotional distress, and will turn next to whether Baccigalupi's conduct had its intended effect, and whether that effect was sufficient as a matter of law to state a claim of intentional infliction.

B

1

The district court erred when it held that Subbe-Hirt did not allege, nor did the record on summary judgment show, conduct sufficiently outrageous to state a claim that Baccigalupi had intentionally inflicted emotional distress upon her. In *Buckley v. Trenton Sav. Fund Soc'y*, 544 A.2d 857 (N.J. 1988) the New Jersey Supreme Court applied the view of the RESTATEMENT (SECOND) OF TORTS § 46 to the tort of intentional infliction. The district court was therefore correct that, under New Jersey law,

---

2. "Root canal" is a term coined by Baccigalupi to describe intense and emotionally painful sessions in which he would berate and demean disfavored agents with the purpose of forcing them out of the company.

intentional infliction of emotional distress comprehends conduct "so outrageous in character, and so extreme in degree, as to go beyond all possible bounds of decency, and to be regarded as atrocious, and utterly intolerable in a civilized community." RESTATEMENT (SECOND) OF TORTS § 46 comment d. We disagree, however, with the district court's conclusion that Baccigalupi's conduct was not sufficiently outrageous, and are led inexorably to the conclusion that summary judgment should have been denied.

2 . . .

Baccigalupi created a predatory tactic he descriptively termed "root canal," which he used to control older agents such as Subbe-Hirt. Baccigalupi instructed his sales managers how to perform this verbal attack "operation." According to sales manager Meyer, Baccigalupi "came up with the concept of root canal as a way to intimidate and basically destroy these people to the point of submission or of just getting the hell out of the business." Meyer related at his deposition that Baccigalupi picked the term "root canal" specifically because it was made to be a very uncomfortable, pain-producing, anxiety-producing procedure that you would keep going deeper and deeper until you struck a nerve, which would either end up in the agent submitting, or reaching the point of anxiety where they just couldn't stand any job any longer.

According to Meyer, at Thursday management meetings, sales managers would role play with each other how to deal with "problem agents:"

> . . . Bob LaNicca had brought up that he was having problems dealing with [Subbe-Hirt]. And then [Baccigalupi] would role play with Bob LaNicca how to perform root canal on Elaine to harass, intimidate her into submitting to management's requests.

LaNicca's deposition indicates that Subbe-Hirt was "brought in more often than others for performance reviews," which was Baccigalupi's opportunity for using his root canal procedure on her. According to Subbe-Hirt, Baccigalupi "held [her] in the office twice as long as anyone else."

Baccigalupi was relentless in his contumely against Subbe-Hirt. To begin with, according to Meyer and Parisi, Baccigalupi replaced females' given names, and other polite nouns such as "lady" and "woman," with the term "cunt," to depersonalize and deride the women in the office. He would also taunt Subbe-Hirt by asking if she "knew the word heretic" and threaten her "by asking if she knew who Joan of Arc was." Moreover, he would ask Subbe-Hirt for her resignation almost every time she was in the office. Baccigalupi even went so far as to have an unsigned resignation on his desk; we would then ask Subbe-Hirt "why don't you sign it; if you don't want to sign it, go on disability."

In his meetings with Subbe-Hirt, Baccigalupi would "grill" her on work she submitted, asking "why did you do this, what did you do here, what was said here?" If he was not "satisfied" with her answer, he would call Subbe-Hirt's clients in front of her and say "Elaine says this; what do you say?"

Baccigalupi's conduct had a devastating consequence. After one meeting with Baccigalupi, Subbe-Hirt "literally blacked out behind the wheel and hit a tractor trailer just from stress and emotion[,]" suffering severe injuries that required eight days of hospitalization. This incident forced Subbe-Hirt to take temporary disability leave;

indeed, her treating psychiatrist has opined that she remains totally disabled with post traumatic stress disorder triggered by Baccigalupi's badgering and intimidation.

Baccigalupi was on notice that such an incident was a distinct possibility. Before the collision, Subbe-Hirt had consulted with her family doctor because of stress. The doctor wrote a letter which Subbe-Hirt showed to Baccigalupi before the incident, asking that it be placed in her personnel file. It stated:

> Elaine Subbe[-Hirt] is currently under my care for tension syndrome. It is my opinion, that she is capable of working a regular forty hour week at her present position. However, she should not be subject [sic] to any undue stress or work load at this time.

When Subbe-Hirt requested that the letter be placed in her personnel file, Baccigalupi refused, his exact words being: "I'll decide what goes in your personnel file." According to the evidence, "Mr. Baccigalupi handed it back to [her] and said he didn't see that letter, and he never wanted to see it again and he wouldn't put it in [her] file." From this evidence, a jury could well conclude that, in his attempt to drive Subbe-Hirt out of Prudential, Baccigalupi targeted her now-documented weakness, of which he was fully cognizant. Such specific targeting of an individual's weak point is itself a classic form of "outrageous" conduct under Restatement § 46, comment f, which provides:

> The extreme and outrageous character of the conduct may arise from the actor's knowledge that the other is peculiarly susceptible to emotional distress, by reason of some physical and mental condition or peculiarity. The conduct may be heartless, flagrant, and outrageous when the actor proceeds in the face of such knowledge, where it would not be so if he did not know.

We conclude that the record is sufficient to support a finding that Baccigalupi essentially set out to put Subbe-Hirt under unnecessary stress to force her out of the company, all the while knowing that her physician had stated specifically that her condition required her to avoid such stress. We hold that the evidence described above is more than sufficient to withstand defendants' motion for summary judgment. . . .

COWEN, Circuit Judge, dissenting.

[The dissent thought that the district court should be upheld both on grounds of workers' compensation exclusivity and because] the facts of the case as alleged by the plaintiff fall short of the New Jersey cause of action of intentional infliction of emotional distress. The New Jersey Supreme Court has defined this tort as requiring conduct "so outrageous in character and so extreme in degree as to go beyond all possible bounds of decency, and to be regarded as atrocious and utterly intolerable in a civilized community." *Buckley.* The conduct of the perpetrator of such a tort must be by its nature "so severe that no reasonable man could be expected to endure it."

Conduct which the New Jersey courts have found to meet this extremely high level of uncivilized conduct are such matters as a doctor knowingly and untruthfully advising parents that their child had cancer, *Hume v. Bayer*, 428 A.2d 966 (Law Div. 1981); a hospital unable to locate the body of a dead baby for three weeks, *Muniz v. United Hospitals Medical Center*, 379 A.2d 57 (App. Div. 1977). [Indeed, the district court in New Jersey frequently] recognized the extreme difficulty of establishing such a claim in a mere employment relationship when the conduct alleged does not exceed the employer/employee relationship.

The New Jersey Supreme Court has made it abundantly clear in *Buckley*, that when a claim is made for intentional infliction of emotional distress, the trial court must clearly exercise a gatekeeping rule: "the court decides whether as a matter of law such emotional distress can be found" and the jury decides whether it has in fact been proved. It is the obligation of the trial court to determine in the first instance whether the plaintiff has set forth conduct which is sufficiently extreme such that a jury could reasonably conclude that outrageous conduct permits it to award damages. . . .

The district court correctly performed its function by determining that under New Jersey law the facts alleged as a matter of law failed to reach the elevated and high standard required for the cause of action of intentional infliction of emotional distress. The district court recognized that Baccigalupi's statements, if credited, were "inexcusable" and "offensive," but did not rise to the level of outrageous and unacceptable in a civilized society. Plaintiff's claims boil down to an assertion that her supervisor's choice of words required her to put up with "more than the normal pressure of a job." Being subject to "more than normal pressure" at work is a long distance from conduct that is "so outrageous in character and so extreme in degree as to go beyond all possible bounds of decency, and to be regarded as atrocious, and utterly intolerable in a civilized community." Even plaintiff had a difficult time labeling Baccigalupi's actions as anything beyond harmless threats, intimidation, and ridicule. Admittedly, the words allegedly spoken by Baccigalupi were strong and even harsh at times, but they were merely words. There is no proof, nor even an allegation, that Baccigalupi even touched her or that he set in motion any physical or other instrumentality to bring about an injury or illness.

III

The majority is to be lauded in its desire to upgrade the repartee of the workplace and to be offended by language which it deems inappropriate. But the workplace is not the dance of a minuet and employers are not nursemaids. As judges we will rue the day we sat in judgment of the propriety of speech which should transpire in the workplace between an employer and his employee. I respectfully dissent.

NOTES

1. *Outrageous or Merely Offensive?* The majority and dissent seem to basically agree on the legal standard for an intentional infliction of emotional distress claim — also known as the tort of "outrage." Their agreement is not surprising since New Jersey, like most jurisdictions, looks to the Restatement's definition of the elements of the tort. Section 46(1) of the RESTATEMENT (SECOND) OF TORTS provides that "One who by extreme and outrageous conduct intentionally or recklessly causes severe emotional distress to another is subject to liability for such emotional distress. . . ." To limit the tort from reaching garden-variety emotional harms, "[l]iability has been found only where the conduct has been so outrageous in character, and so extreme in degree, as to go beyond all possible bounds of decency, and to be regarded as atrocious, and

utterly intolerable in a civilized community." §46 cmt. d. An important factor in judging outrageousness is whether the defendant is abusing a position of power over the plaintiff. *Id.* at cmt. e. But, as a counterbalance, the "actor is never liable . . . where he has done no more than to insist upon his legal rights in a permissible way, even though he is well aware that such insistence is certain to cause emotional distress." *Id.* at cmt. g.

The problem, of course, is that the tort turns on whether the conduct challenged is "outrageous." This is less a standard than an epithet, and it is not surprising that some, like the majority, will be outraged and others, like the dissent, merely offended. But the dissent would uphold the district court judgment because reasonable minds could *not* differ over whether this was too extreme. Is that possible? You might be surprised to learn that the dissent is more typical of intentional infliction cases than is the majority. Indeed, the situations in which courts have found egregious conduct not sufficiently outrageous to be actionable are legion. *See, e.g., Tomlinson v. NCR Corp.,* 296 P.3d 760, 769 (Utah Ct. App. 2013) *cert. granted,* 304 P.3d 469 (Utah 2013) (allegations of false reports to police of plaintiff's embezzlement fail to state a claim for intentional infliction of emotional distress.); *Island v. Buena Vista Resort,* 103 S.W.3d 671, 681 (Ark. 2003) (an employer's sexual advances not sufficiently outrageous because "[w]hile it is clear that the allegations of [the employer's] behavior are egregious, it appears that appellant has failed to offer proof that she suffered damages or emotional distress so severe that no reasonable person could be expected to endure it" since she endured the advancements for several years without protesting).

Baccigalupi, however, indicates that the theory may sometimes be fruitful, and there are some other successful claims in the employment setting. *See, e.g., Durham v. McDonald's Restaurants of Oklahoma, Inc.,* 256 P.3d 64, 66 (Okla. 2011) (manager's denial of three requests by 16-year-old plaintiff to take prescription anti-seizure medication and calling plaintiff a "f***ing retard" in denying the last request created a triable issue of outrage); *Craig v. M&O Agencies, Inc.,* 496 F.3d 1047 (9th Cir. 2007) (individual supervisor liable: "Despite society's 'rough edges,' Craig should not be required to become 'hardened to' her supervisor repeatedly propositioning inside and outside of the office, following her into the bathroom, standing outside the toilet stall and then grabbing her and sticking his tongue in her mouth. While this conduct is deplorable in any setting, a reasonable observer or trier of fact could find it to be 'outrageous' and 'extreme,' particularly in an employment context."); *Archer v. Farmer Bros. Co.,* 70 P.3d 495 (Colo. App. 2002) (worker fired by his supervisors who came to his home to do so while he was in bed recovering from a heart attack).

2. *How Is the Workplace Different?* One might take the view that employees are particularly vulnerable to abuse and therefore entitled to heightened protection against infliction of emotional distress. The paucity of successful claims, however, suggests to the contrary that most judges believe the demands of many workplaces require managerial practices that would be unacceptable in other settings. Judge Cowen's dissent stresses "the extreme difficulty of establishing such a claim in a mere employment relationship when the conduct alleged does not exceed the employer/ employee relationship." The argument is essentially that employers are justified in pressuring and disciplining employees in ways that are perhaps inappropriate elsewhere. Further, victims can always quit if they want to avoid further abuse. Look at the last paragraph of the dissent. Is Judge Cowen asserting a free speech claim or privilege for verbal abuse? Is his position equivalent to saying that emotional abuse is "standard operating procedure," at least in some workplaces?

3. *That's Life.* Several years before Judge Cowen wrote his opinion, Professor Regina Austin critiqued such an approach:

> It is generally assumed that employers and employees alike agree that some amount of such abuse is a perfectly natural, necessary, and defensible prerogative of superior rank. It assures obedience to command. Bosses do occasionally overstep the bounds of what is considered reasonable supervision, but, apart from contractually based understandings and statutory entitlements to protection from harassment, there are few objective standards of "civility" by which to judge a superior's treatment of a subordinate. Workers for their part are expected to respond to psychologically painful supervision with passivity, not insubordination and resistance. They must and do develop stamina and resilience. If the supervision is intolerable, they should quit and move on to another job.
>
> In sum, there is little reason for workers to take undue umbrage at the treatment they receive at work. The pain, insults, and indignities they suffer at the hands of employers and supervisors should be met with acquiescence and endurance. That's life. Who believes this?

Regina Austin, *Employer Abuse, Worker Resistance, and the Tort of Intentional Infliction of Emotional Distress*, 41 STAN. L. REV. 1 (1988). *See also* Dennis P. Duffy, *Intentional Infliction of Emotional Distress and Employment at Will: The Case Against "Tortification" of Labor and Employment Law*, 74 B.U. L. REV. 382 (1994).

4. *Workplace Bullying.* The limitations of the intentional infliction tort have led some commentators to conclude that it is ineffective in dealing with the phenomenon of workplace bullying, and they have urged legislation to deal with serious emotional and psychological abuse of workers that may, nevertheless, not be sufficiently "outrageous" to be actionable under current tort law. *See, e.g.*, David C. Yamada, *Crafting a Legislative Response to Workplace Bullying*, 8 EMPL. RTS. & EMPLOY. POL'Y J. 475 (2004); David C. Yamada, *The Phenomenon of "Workplace Bullying" and the Need for Status-Blind Hostile Work Environment Protection*, 88 GEO. L. J. 475 (2000). While legislative efforts addressing bullying have been successful in the school context, no workplace antibullying legislation has yet been passed in this country.

5. *Other Claims.* Because the plaintiff in *Baccigalupi* did not or was unable to raise her other claims on appeal, the Third Circuit did not consider them. One that jumps out is sex discrimination, particularly sexual or gender harassment. This topic is discussed in Chapter 9. *See generally* Kerri Lynn Stone, *From Queen Bees and Wannabes to Worker Bees: Why Gender Considerations Should Inform the Emerging Law of Workplace Bullying*, 65 N.Y.U. ANN. SURV. AM. L. 35 (2009). Is it clear that Baccigalupi was discriminating against plaintiff because she was a woman? In other words, might he have been an "equal opportunity harasser" who abused both men and women alike? The "root canal" strategy was not gender-specific, and a male co-worker, Robert King, also claimed to be a target of such abuse. However, Baccigalupi's crude anatomical references certainly suggest a discrimination claim, and the opinion seems to imply he was targeting plaintiff for especially severe abuse because she was a woman. Claims of racial or ethnic slurs have also been held actionable under the outrage tort, *see, e.g.*, *Woods v. Graphic Communs.*, 925 F.2d 1195 (9th Cir. 1991), either as the sole cause of action or as supplementary to a racial discrimination claim. *See also Pollard v. E.I. DuPont de Nemours, Inc.*, 412 F.3d 657, 664-65 (6th Cir. 2005) (applying Tennessee law as the sole cause of action); *Wal-Mart, Inc. v. Stewart*, 990 P.2d 626, 634-36 (Alaska 1999) (race discrimination).

While Title VII expressly allows for supplementary tort claims, 42 U.S.C. § 2000e-7 (2014), state civil rights statutes vary widely in both their express terms and their judicial construction, with some preempting tort claims and others permitting overlap. The outrage tort may function as a "gap filler" or "reinforcement" to civil rights protection where not preempted. For example, some courts hold that intentional infliction of emotional distress cannot be brought where "the gravamen of the complaint is really another tort." *Hoffman-La Roche, Inc. v. Zeltwanger*, 144 S.W.3d 438, 447-48 (Tex. 2004); *see also Haubry v. Snow*, 31 P.3d 1186, 1193 (Wash. Ct. App. 2001) ("employee may recover damages of emotional distress . . . but only if the factual basis for the claim is distinct from the factual basis for the discrimination claim"). *See also* RESTATEMENT (SECOND) OF TORTS § 47 cmt. a (1965) (outrage tort inapplicable when actor "intends to invade some other legally protected interest"). *See generally* Martha Chamallas, *Discrimination and Outrage: The Migration from Civil Rights to Tort Law*, 48 WM. & MARY L. REV. 2115, 2115-16 (2007) ("The dominant approach views tort claims as mere "gap fillers" that should come into play only in rare cases that do not fit comfortably under other recognized theories of redress"). Even where a discrimination claim is viable, a tort cause of action may be helpful in fixing liability on the individual tortfeasor or in end-running statutory caps on discrimination remedies. *See* Chapter 9 at pages 769-771.

PROBLEM

5-4. Wilma is a vegan who had no on-the-job problems with her dietary practices until a new manager was hired. Once he learned that Wilma was a vegan, he continually made negative comments about her eating. They have occurred two or three times a week for the past year, usually when she is leaving for lunch. During the past few weeks, the comments have gotten more extreme. At two recent company social events, the manager sat down next to Wilma, ordered a hamburger ("extra rare, I want to see the blood"), and offered Wilma a bite. Wilma believes that this pattern of abuse is undercutting her ability to interact with co-workers, who are beginning to avoid her. The manager has taken to calling Wilma "Veg." She has experienced stress, nervousness, and difficulty sleeping as a result of the name calling and other comments. The supervisor also "picks on" other co-workers for a variety of personal traits. Wilma does not view her veganism as "religious." Does she have a case under tort law?

D. FRAUD AND OTHER MISREPRESENTATION

In the law, "fraud" is often used broadly to encompass intentional misrepresentation, negligent misrepresentation, and even failure to disclose when there is a duty to do so. It is easiest to establish when used as a shield — that is, when used as a defense to a contract claim, that is, to "avoid" a contract. For example, an employee under a contract for a term of years might seek to escape liability for breach by arguing misrepresentation or failure to disclosure material facts. To void a contract, a misrepresentation must be either "fraudulent" or "material." RESTATEMENT (SECOND) OF CONTRACTS § 164 (1981). Voiding a contract for nondisclosure is more difficult but is possible in a variety of circumstances that may arise in entering an employment relation. *Id.* at § 161.

As a sword, however — that is, as a tort cause of action for damages suffered in reliance on false statements — fraud is most often used when an employee is discharged after being recently hired and typically after being recruited from another position and/or relocating to the new job. The employee then claims that, although she was admittedly employed at will, statements made in the hiring process were false and led her to accept the position. A variation on this scenario occurs when an employer makes false statements in order to retain an employee who is considering a competing offer. What if the employer promises job security to the employee but has no intent to provide such security? An employee who is a victim of such misrepresentation and who subsequently is discharged may have a remedy in tort.

Section 525 of the RESTATEMENT (SECOND) OF TORTS sets forth the elements of the cause of action:

> One who [1] fraudulently makes [2] a misrepresentation of fact, opinion, intention or law [3] for the purpose of inducing another to act or to refrain from action in reliance upon it, is subject to liability to the other in deceit for pecuniary loss caused to him by his [4] justifiable reliance upon the misrepresentation.

See also RESTATEMENT (THIRD) OF EMPLOYMENT LAW § 6.05 (Proposed Final Draft, April 18, 2014) ("An employer is subject to liability for intentionally inducing an employee or prospective employee through knowingly false representation of fact, opinion, current intention, or law, (1) to enter into, to maintain, or to leave an employment relationship with the employer or (2) to refrain from entering into or maintaining an employment relationship with the employer or with another employer.").

In the employment setting, the following case is a classic application of the doctrine.

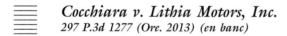

Cocchiara v. Lithia Motors, Inc.
297 P.3d 1277 (Ore. 2013) (en banc)

BALMER, C.J.

[The facts of this case are reproduced in Chapter 2, at page 96. In the portion of the opinion there, the Supreme Court dealt with the promissory estoppel claim; in this section, the court deals with the plaintiff's claim of fraud.]

Fraudulent Misrepresentation

This court has previously articulated the elements of a common law fraud claim, also known as an action in deceit, in more than one way, which is not surprising because "fraud" is "'a term so vague that it requires definition in nearly every case.'" *Riley Hill General Contractor v. Tandy Corp.*, 737 P.2d 595 (1987) (quoting W. PAGE KEETON, ET AL., PROSSER AND KEETON ON THE LAW OF TORTS § 105, 727 (W. Page Keeton ed., 5th ed. 1984)). For purposes of this case, two elements that are consistently required for a fraud claim are relevant: justifiable reliance and damages. *See Riley Hill General Contractor* (listing five elements of action in deceit, including "'[j]ustifiable reliance upon the representation'" and "'[d]amage to the plaintiff, resulting from such reliance'" (quoting KEETON, PROSSER AND KEETON ON THE LAW OF TORTS § 105 at 728)); *U.S. National Bank v. Fought,* 630 P.2d 337 (1981) (listing nine elements of an action in deceit, including "'reliance on [the misrepresentation's] truth,'" a "'right to rely thereon,'" and "'consequent and proximate injury'").

[W]e disagree with the Court of Appeals that, for purposes of his fraud claim, plaintiff could not reasonably rely on defendant's statement that plaintiff had definitely been given the corporate job. In a fraud claim, "[t]he principal argument in support of some such requirement as justifiability of reliance would seem to be that of providing some objective corroboration to plaintiff's claim that he did rely. . . . [T]he foolish nature of the plaintiff's conduct if he did rely is relevant primarily because of the likelihood that he did not rely." KEETON, PROSSER AND KEETON ON THE LAW OF TORTS § 108 at 749–50. In this case, a jury could find that plaintiff reasonably relied on defendant's promise, because a jury could find that he was planning to accept the job with the Medford Mail Tribune — as evidenced by plaintiff notifying Summers that he planned to take that job — until defendant offered him the corporate job.

Moreover, the standard for reasonable or justifiable reliance in the context of fraud is both subjective and objective:

> If he is a person of normal intelligence, experience and education, he may not put faith in representations which any such normal person would recognize at once as preposterous . . . or which are shown by facts within his observation to be so patently and obviously false that he must have closed his eyes to avoid discovery of the truth, and still compel the defendant to be responsible for his loss. . . .
>
> [T]he matter seems to turn upon an individual standard of the plaintiff's own capacity and the knowledge which he has, or which may fairly be charged against him from the facts within his observation in the light of his individual case[.]

KEETON, PROSSER AND KEETON ON THE LAW OF TORTS § 108 at 750–51 (footnote omitted). "Normal" people rely on offers of at-will employment every day, or at least a jury would be entitled to so find, based on the facts in a particular case. Here, a jury could find that plaintiff's reliance was not "preposterous" or based on plaintiff ignoring an obviously false statement, particularly given Summers' assertion about plaintiff's value to the company and his recommendation that plaintiff turn down the Medford Mail Tribune job.

In addition, allowing fraud claims in the context of at-will employment serves the purpose behind allowing fraud claims: "The type of interest protected by the law of deceit is the interest in formulating business judgments without being misled by others — in short, in not being cheated." *Riley Hill General Contractor.* If employers could make misleading statements to prospective at-will employees without liability, business judgments regarding employment would not be protected from deceit. Business judgments regarding at-will employment inherently involve some risk, and a prospective employee (or employer) should be able to evaluate that risk without the interference of fraud.

Although a prospective employee can bring a fraudulent misrepresentation claim in the context of at-will employment, we emphasize that there are limitations on those claims. Most notably, a plaintiff will have to prove damages to bring a successful claim. *See, e.g., Riley Hill General Contractor* (listing damage to the plaintiff as an element of a fraud claim). Nonetheless, plaintiff's decision to plead only damages associated with the loss of the corporate job — rather than damages associated with turning down the Medford Mail Tribune job — does not defeat his fraud claim, as the Court of Appeals suggested. As noted, the at-will nature of employment does not create a conclusive presumption barring a plaintiff from recovering future lost pay where the employee has been unlawfully terminated from the job, *Tadsen [v. Praegitzer Industries, Inc.*, 928 P.2d 980 (Ore, 1996)], or, as in this case, where plaintiff was never hired as promised or allowed to start work. Because this case was decided on a motion for summary judgment, however, whether plaintiff can sufficiently prove his damages associated with not being hired for the corporate job is not now before this court.

For those reasons, the Court of Appeals erred in determining that, as a matter of law, plaintiff could not reasonably rely on defendant's representations and could not recover future lost wages solely because of the at-will nature of the corporate job. We emphasize that our holding goes no further, and we express no view as to whether plaintiff's reliance was in fact reasonable, whether plaintiff can satisfy the other elements of his promissory estoppel and fraudulent misrepresentation claims, or whether plaintiff is entitled to recover his claimed damages. . . .

NOTES

1. *Fraud versus Contract.* In Chapter 2, we saw that Lithia Motors's alleged promises stated a cause of action in promissory estoppel. In this extract, we see that the same promise was also the basis for a fraud claim, but there was, of course, a twist. A mere failure to perform a promise can be actionable in contract but not in tort. For such a failure to be tortious, the defendant must have intended at the time it made the promise not to perform. The theory behind this requirement is that a promisor who makes a promise by that very act implies that he intends to perform that promise when the time for performance arrives. If the promisor lacks that intent, he has made a misrepresentation of fact (his state of mind), which satisfies one element of fraud. *See, e.g., Clement-Rowe v. Michigan Health Care Corp.*, 538 N.W.2d 20, 23 (Mich. Ct. App. 1995) (evidence suggests that the employer knew that the statement about funding for the position "was untrue or made it without any knowledge of its truth" in order to "allay plaintiff's hesitancy to accept the job because of concern about the financial health of the company"); *Neco, Inc. v. Larry Price & Assocs., Inc.*, 597 N.W.2d 602, 607 (Neb. 1999) (while "fraud cannot be based on predictions or expressions of mere possibilities in reference to future events . . . , fraud may be predicated on the representation that an event, which is in control of the maker, will or will not take place in the future, if the representation as to the future event is known to be false when made or is made in reckless disregard as to its truthfulness or falsity and the other elements of fraud are present."). *See generally* RESTATEMENT (SECOND) OF TORTS § 536 (1977); Frank J. Cavico, *Fraudulent, Negligent, and Innocent Misrepresentation in the Employment Context: The Deceitful, Careless, and Thoughtless Employer*, 20 CAMPBELL L. REV. 1 (2007); Richard P. Perna, *Deceitful Employers: Intentional Misrepresentation in Hiring and the Employment-at-Will Doctrine*, 54 KAN. L. REV. 587 (2006).

An earlier, similar case arose out of New Jersey, with the claim being that, in order to retain a current employee, the employer promised him a job for life. *Shebar v. Sanyo Business Systems Corp.*, 544 A.2d 377 (N.J. 1988). Like *Cocchiara*, the plaintiff in *Shebar* asserted both contract and fraud claims. The fraud claim was predicated on evidence that, at the time Sanyo promised to continue plaintiff's employment, it did not intend to perform. The court thought that a jury could find that to be true in the very extreme circumstances at bar — the executive recruiter who had arranged the Sony offer informed plaintiff that Sanyo was searching for his replacement. Further, when Shebar confronted his supervisor with this information, he denied it. Since Sanyo was in fact seeking a replacement after just having promised plaintiff lifetime employment, and lied about whether it was doing so, a jury could find that the promise of lifetime employment was itself fraudulent when made in that Sanyo did not intend to perform it at that time.

Proving fraudulent misrepresentation, however, is often difficult. If the plaintiff did not have evidence of intent to breach at the time the promise was made, the plaintiff would have had only a breach of contract or promissory estoppel claim. The *Cocchiara* court does not delve into the evidence that Lithia Motors made the promise of a "corporate job" without an intent to perform. In *Sanyo*, there was evidence both that the employer was angry at the plaintiff's disloyalty and wanted to retain his services until his replacement could be hired. Does that seem likely here?

2. *A Different View.* Not every court allows claims such as Cocchiara's. *Smalley v. Dreyfus Corp.*, 882 N.E.2d 882 (N.Y. 2008), rejected this approach entirely in the at-will context. Several employees had accepted positions with the defendant in reliance on its promise that there were no merger talks that would eliminate those positions. Although the Court of Appeals did not seem to question that the elements of fraud were alleged, the court found any misrepresentation not actionable precisely because it occurred in the context of at-will employment:

> The core of plaintiffs' claim is that they reasonably relied on no-merger promises in accepting and continuing employment with Dreyfus, and in eschewing other job opportunities. Thus, . . . plaintiffs alleged no injury separate and distinct from termination of their at-will employment. In that the length of employment is not a material term of at-will employment, a party cannot be injured merely by the termination of the contract — neither party can be said to have reasonably relied upon the other's promise not to terminate the contract. Absent injury independent of termination, plaintiffs cannot recover damages for what is at bottom an alleged breach of contract in the guise of a tort.

882 N.E.2d at 884-85. Presumably, *Smalley* would have rejected *Cocchiara's* claim because he was an at-will employee. *See also Sawyer v. E. I. du Pont de Nemours & Co.*, 430 S.W.3d 396 (Tex. 2014) (plaintiff cannot sue an employer for fraud when the fraudulent representation related to prospective employment since such a promise would be illusory in any event); *Mackenzie v. Miller Brewing Co.*, 623 N.W.2d 739 (Wis. 2001) (no cause of action for intentional misrepresentation to induce continued employment.). As we have seen, the Restatement of Employment Law opts for liability in such situations.

3. *Negligent Misrepresentation.* Some jurisdictions recognize a tort of negligent misrepresentation, in which case it is, of course, unnecessary to prove intent to deceive. In *D'Ulisse-Cupo v. Board of Directors of Notre Dame H.S.*, 520 A.2d 217 (Conn. 1987), for instance, the court held that statements made by the high school principal assuring her that "there would be no problem" with plaintiff teaching the following year and that "everything looked fine for rehire" may have negligently led her to reasonably believe she would be employed for the next year. *See also Sevigny v. DG FastChannel, Inc.*, CV 11-9197-CAS JEMX, 2013 WL 753489 (C.D. Cal. Feb. 25, 2013) (denying summary judgment on negligent misrepresentation claim that defendants' agents assured that defendant would provide a defense should she be sued by her former employer for violation of a noncompete agreement since plaintiff could prove that the agents should have been aware that they lacked the authority to make such a representation); *Berger v. Security Pac. Info. Sys.*, 795 P.2d 1380 (Colo. Ct. App. 1990) (statements about the company's glowing prospects to a prospective employee created a duty to disclose serious problems); *see generally* RESTATEMENT (SECOND) OF TORTS § 552 (1977). Note that the RESTATEMENT OF EMPLOYMENT LAW requires more than negligence.

4. *Reliance.* In addition to a misrepresentation and the requisite fault, a plaintiff claiming fraud must show detrimental reliance. *See Coffel v. Stryker Corp.*, 284 F.3d 625, 637 (5th Cir. 2002) (jury could find that plaintiff, in giving up his rights under a prior bonus plan, relied on Stryker's representations that a new bonus plan would adequately compensate him and that this reliance was justified because of Stryker's past practice and assurances). This element may be hard to establish, especially in cases involving current employees who were hired before the allegedly fraudulent statement and who likely cannot show that they abandoned other opportunities because of it. Further, any reliance that the employee can establish must also be reasonable. *See Shelby v. Zayre Corp.*, 474 So. 2d 1069 (Ala. 1985) (reliance on promise of permanent employment unreasonable in face of signed application form that employment was at will).

5. *The Specificity of the Representation.* Some employees have tried to predicate tort claims on more amorphous employer statements than the ones we have seen to this point. In Chapter 2 we considered when an employer's failure to follow its policies might be actionable as a breach of contract under some version of the employee handbook doctrine. But occasionally an employee also asserts a tort claim in that situation. For example, *Daley v. Aetna Life & Casualty Company*, 734 A.2d 112 (Conn. 1999), involved a plaintiff who was repeatedly denied requested accommodations when she became a mother. When she was finally discharged, she claimed, among other things, negligent misrepresentation by Aetna because of numerous statements it had made indicating that it was family-friendly. The court upheld a jury verdict against her:

> In its instructions, the trial court explained the nature of Daley's claim to be that "Aetna negligently represented to [her] that it was committed to helping its employees balance the demands of work and family and that it would support its employees in balancing their commitments by means of work and family programs including work-at-home options, part-time hours and flextime." In connection with its instructions on the burden of demonstrating that these representations were false, the trial court stated: "In other words, [Daley bears] the burden of establishing that Aetna was *not* committed to help its employees balance the demands of work and family and that it would *not* support its employees in balancing their commitment by means of work and family programs, including work-at-home options, part-time options, and flextime." (Emphasis added.)
>
> Daley contends that the trial court's charge imposed an impossible burden of proof by making it appear that she could not prevail if the jury found that Aetna had any

commitment whatsoever to its work and family programs. According to Daley, because Aetna likely had *some* level of commitment to its programs, the charge prevented the jury from determining whether Aetna had been negligent in representing those programs. Daley argues that, in accordance with its proposed instructions, the trial court should have charged the jury that she could prevail upon a showing that Aetna was "'not as committed'" to helping its employees "'to the extent [that] it represented.'" Aetna, on the other hand, argues that the trial court's instructions adequately presented the case to the jury because, notwithstanding its flexible scheduling options, Aetna never represented to Daley that a work-at-home arrangement was an entitlement, nor that an employee who relentlessly pursued such an arrangement would not be discharged. In addition, Aetna argues that Daley's proposed instructions would have misled the jury to find Aetna liable without proving an actual misrepresentation. We agree with Aetna. . . .

Id. at 127-28. Thus, *Daley* strongly suggests that general policies will rarely support a claim for negligent misrepresentation and, of course, it would be even harder to pitch an intentional misrepresentation claim on such policies. We will revisit the accommodation issue in Chapter 10, but you might note that the court also upheld a directed verdict for Aetna on Daley's public policy tort claim: There was no "important public policy that requires employers to provide flexible work schedules for working parents, and that prohibits employers from discriminating against individuals who pursue such arrangements." *Id*. at 130.

6. *A Statutory Solution?* Indeed, one state has a statute directed at exactly this kind of conduct. MINN. STAT. § 181.64 (2014). *See Vaidyanathan v. Seagate US LLC*, 691 F.3d 972 (8th Cir. 2012) (holding that a statute making actionable "knowingly false representations" to induce, any person to relocate was satisfied only when statements were actually known to be false; it was not satisfied by statements that suggested knowledge that the speaker did not at that time possess).

E. LIMITATIONS ON TORT ACTIONS

There are two potentially important limitations on tort suits against employers. Although we have previously touched on both workers' compensation and preemption, a more detailed consideration of both follows.

1. Workers' Compensation

As described earlier in the chapter, workers' compensation statutes embody a fairly explicit trade-off: Employers are strictly liable for on-the-job injuries, but the amount of recovery for employees is much more limited than under traditional tort law. "A predicate of workers' compensation laws is that the compensation system is the exclusive remedy" for covered injuries. For example, the New Jersey statute provides, "If an injury or death is compensable under this article, a person shall not be liable to anyone at common law or otherwise on account of such injury or death for any act or omission occurring while such person was in the same employ as the person injured or killed, except for intentional wrong." N.J. STAT. ANN. § 34:15-8 (West 2000). This clearly precludes tort suits in what was the paradigmatic situation for which workers' compensation was designed: negligently caused personal injury on the job. Ironically, employees originally preferred to be within workers' compensation regimes because of the hostility of the tort system. But, a century later, employees often seek higher damages by claiming that their injuries are not covered by workers' compensation. Concomitantly, employers now frequently seek to defeat tort suits by arguing workers' compensation exclusivity.

The dispute typically centers on the meaning of "except for intentional wrong" or similar language in other states' workers' compensation laws. This may not be as obvious an exclusion as one might think. Recall that in *Subbe-Hirt v. Baccigalupi*, page 301, the majority and dissent disagreed not only on whether the conduct was sufficiently outrageous to be actionable but also as to whether plaintiff's tort claim was barred by the New Jersey workers' compensation exclusivity provisions. There was no doubt that plaintiff had pled an "intentional tort" but some question as to what that meant. Although that portion of the opinions is not reproduced, the majority reasoned that the conduct was actionable if "a plaintiff show[s] *deliberate intention* to avoid the exclusive remedy provided by the Compensation Act," *Baccigalupi*, 94 F.3d at 112-13 (emphasis in original), while the dissent read state workers compensation law as making such conduct actionable in tort only if it was substantially certain to cause the harm plead. *Id.* at 116.

Another example of the uncertain line separating torts that are actionable and those that are preempted by workers' compensation is *Ford v. Revlon, Inc.*, 734 P.2d 580 (Ariz. 1987), in which an employee charged that her supervisor, Karl Braun, sexually harassed her. His conduct included demanding sex from her, threatening reprisals when she rejected him, and physical molestation. Ford tried to get Revlon management to address her complaints for an extended period of time without success. During this period, Braun continued to threaten her and Ford developed "high blood pressure, a nervous tic in her left eye, chest pains, rapid breathing, and other symptoms of emotional stress." Ultimately, she attempted suicide. The suit charged both Braun and Revlon with assault and battery and intentional infliction of emotional distress. One of Revlon's defenses was the exclusivity of Arizona's workers' compensation law, which covered employees "injured by accident arising out of and in the course of employment." ARIZ. REV. STAT. ANN. § 23-1021(B). Further, § 23-1043.01(B) specifically provided that "mental injury" was not "a personal injury by accident" unless "unexpected, unusual or extraordinary stress . . . or some physical injury . . . was a substantial contributing cause."

The Arizona Supreme Court stressed that Ford's severe emotional distress was neither caused by an "accident" nor was it "unexpected." Since the injury was not within the workers' compensation scheme, plaintiff's tort suit remained viable. Judge Feldman concurred with the result, but disagreed with the majority's analysis. He argued that under Arizona law, Ford's injuries were the result of "accident because an 'accident' is any work-connected injury between the extremes of a 'purposely self-inflicted' injury and one inflicted by the employer acting 'knowingly and purposely with the direct object of injuring' the employee." *Id.* at 589 (citations omitted). However, he concluded that the plaintiff may nevertheless recover in tort because the challenged conduct was "one of those torts outside the purpose and intent of the workers' compensation scheme." *Id.* at 588. The concurrence explained:

Regardless of the label placed on the action, it is outside the workers' compensation scheme only if the wrong is one not ordinarily resulting from an inherent risk or danger of the employment and if the essence of the tort action ordinarily is non-physical with physical injury only incidental to emotional, mental, or other injury. Among these types of torts and actions, . . . are defamation, invasion of privacy, false imprisonment, sexual, religious or racial discrimination, wrongful termination, constitutional torts, and similar matters.

. . . The essence of the wrong was sexual harassment. Revlon failed to react to Ford's complaints, in reckless disregard of the consequences, thus making itself liable for outrageous conduct. While the form of the action — intentional infliction of emotional distress — is not always outside workers' compensation, the essence of the tort in the case before us involves a violation of rights protected by law and policy. By law, exposure to sexual harassment is not an inherent or necessary risk of employment, even though it may be or may have been endemic. The cost of such conduct ought not to be included in the cost of the product and passed to the consumer. If my employer invades my right to privacy by tapping my telephone, it is my employer who should pay the piper for such a wrong, not his compensation carrier.

Id. at 590-91. *Revlon* poses sharply the central issue, but the split between majority and concurrence illustrates the kind of problems that arise in this area. The question is complicated because statutory and constitutional provisions differ from state to state. Further, the answer could conceivably differ based on the tort alleged or the particular facts.

The *Revlon* majority's distinction between an "accident" and "intent" is a common approach to the problem. This distinction finds support in the language of many workers' compensation statutes, which define compensable injuries in terms of "accidents" and frequently have an express exclusion for "intentional" harm. *See Grover C. Dils Med. Ctr. v. Menditto*, 112 P.3d 1093, 1102 (Nev. 2005) (per curium) (ruling that the claimant could not recover under Nevada's workers' compensation statutes for a work-related car accident because exacerbation of preexisting symptoms did not constitute "sudden or unforeseen injuries"); *Lichtman v. Knouf*, 445 S.E.2d 114 (Va. 1994) (sexual harassment action not barred by workers' compensation because injury was not an "injury by accident" since it was gradually incurred and not the result of an identifiable incident). Nevertheless, the concurrence's alternative approach, which looks to the purposes of the workers' compensation statute, also has support. *See Cole v. Chandler*, 752 A.2d 1189, 1195 (Me. 2000) ("We have refused to carve out an exception [to worker's compensation exclusivity] for intentional torts" since doing so would counteract the purpose of the workers' compensation exclusivity provision and since the legislature would have provided an exception for intentional torts if they had intended to do so.).

Is the argument persuasive that sexual harassment is not the kind of injury intended to be within the statute? *See Cox v. Chino Mines/Phelps Dodge*, 850 P.2d 1038 (1993) (workers' compensation does not provide an adequate remedy for sexually harassed workers; such claims are better pursued under other causes of action). *Contra Doe v. Purity Supreme*, 664 N.E.2d 815 (Mass. 1996) (exclusivity provision of workers' compensation precludes an action against an employer for intentional infliction of emotional distress arising out of sexual harassment and even for injuries resulting from a rape or other sexual assault). Isn't association with co-workers an inherent risk of being employed? In a "post-industrial" economy, isn't bureaucratic incompetence a more likely cause of injury than "machinery breaking, objects falling, explosives exploding, tractors tipping, fingers getting caught in gears, excavations caving in," *Ford*, 734 P.2d at 590, which the concurrence cited as the original focus of workers' compensation laws? Is Judge Feldman persuasive when he says that sexual harassment, though "endemic," is not an inherent risk because it is illegal? If a worker's injury were caused by a condition that was illegal under a state fire code, could the employee sue in tort? *See generally* Jane Byeff Korn, *The Fungible Woman and Other Myths of Sexual Harassment*, 67 TUL. L. REV. 1363, 1384-89 (1993); Ruth C. Vance, *Workers' Compensation and Sexual Harassment in the Workplace: A Remedy for Employees, or a Shield for Employers?* 11 HOFSTRA LAB. L.J. 141 (1993).

Even if sexual harassment is outside workers' compensation under this view, what about some of the other types of claims we have examined, such as intentional infliction of emotional distress? *See Gantt v. Sec., USA, Inc.*, 356 F.3d 547 (4th Cir. 2004) (intentional infliction claims not actionable under Maryland law, unless the employer had a deliberate intent to injure); *Driscoll v. General Nutrition Corp.*, 752 A.2d 1069, 1076 (Conn. 2000) (although plaintiff limited her tort action to recovery only for emotional distress and emotional injury, the workers' compensation law could not be "unbundled" for pleading purposes simply to escape the exclusivity provision). *Contra Coates v. Wal-Mart Stores, Inc.*, 976 P.2d 999 (N.M. 1999) (outrage claim not barred).

How about an interference case? *Vacanti v. State Comp. Ins. Fund*, 14 P.3d 234, 243-44 (Cal. 2001) (tortious interference claim not barred). What about defamation? *Nassa v. Hook-SupeRx, Inc.*, 790 A.2d 368 (R.I. 2002) ("The prevalent view throughout the nation, however, is that the exclusive-remedy provisions of workers' compensation laws do not bar employment-related defamation claims.").

The leading treatise, LEX K. LARSON, LARSON'S WORKERS' COMPENSATION LAW (Matthew Bender, 2014), would limit workers' compensation to physical injuries, and remit nonphysical harm — such as emotional harm or the reputational damage caused by defamation — to the tort system. § 68.30, at 13-40. *See Hart v. Webster*, 894 N.E.2d 1038 (Ind. 2008) (defamation); *Nassa v. Hook Superx, Inc.* 790 A.2d 368 (R.I. 2002) (slander); *Le v. Federated Dept. Stores*, 595 A.2d 1067 (Md. 1991) (false imprisonment and intentional infliction of emotional distress actionable in tort). *But see Shoemaker v. Myers*, 801 P.2d 1054 (Cal. 1990) (disabling injuries, whether physical or mental, stemming from employment termination are subject to workers' compensation exclusivity, except where a particular statutory right, such as a whistleblower law, suggests otherwise). *See generally* John T. Burnett, *The Enigma of Workers' Compensation Immunity: A Call to the Legislature for a Statutorily Defined Intentional Tort Exception*, 28 FLA. ST. U. L. REV. 491 (2001).

2. Federal Preemption

The law we have studied in this chapter is largely state law and, as such, is vulnerable to being overridden by federal enactments. Indeed, the checkered pattern of federal and state regulation of employment has resulted in frequent preemption issues. For example, in *Ingersoll-Rand Co. v. McLendon*, 498 U.S. 133 (1990), the Court held that a Texas decision recognizing a public policy cause of action for discharge to avoid employer contributions to a pension plan was preempted by the Employee Retirement Income Security Act ("ERISA"), a federal statute regulating pensions and other benefit plans, such as health insurance. ERISA is more fully explained in Chapter 11.

See also Aetna Health Inc. v. Davila, 542 U.S. 200, 209 (2004) ("[A]ny state-law cause of action that duplicates, supplements, or supplants the ERISA civil enforcement remedy conflicts with the clear congressional intent to make the ERISA remedy exclusive and is therefore pre-empted" since the ERISA has "extraordinary pre-emptive power."). On the other hand, *English v. General Elec.,* 496 U.S. 72 (1990), found that the Energy Reorganization Act did not preempt a state-law claim for intentional infliction of distress in retaliation for nuclear safety complaints. *See also Schweiss v. Chrysler Motors,* 922 F.2d 473 (8th Cir. 1990) (Occupational Safety and Health Administration ["OSHA"] does not preempt public policy tort for worker terminated for reporting alleged employer violations to OSHA); *Parten v. Consolidated Freightways,* 923 F.2d 580 (8th Cir. 1991) (Surface Transportation Act did not preempt state public policy tort); *But see Andrews v. Alaska Operating Engineers-Employers Training Trust Fund,* 871 P.2d 1142, 1147 (Alaska 1994) (claim for wrongful discharge in contravention of Alaska public policy is preempted by ERISA).

Preemption arises in two varieties, conflict preemption and field preemption. Where there is a conflict between federal and state law, the Supremacy Clause dictates that state law must yield. Thus, any potential conflict between federal and state law will raise a preemption issue. In such a case, a court must decide whether the putative conflict is real. A broader approach is "field preemption," which describes situations where it can be claimed that Congress has "occupied" an entire field such that any state law, even one that seems consistent with federal mandates, is preempted. Even with field preemption, courts must mark out the precise field that Congress has occupied. For example, the defendant in *English v. General Electric* claimed that the Energy Reorganization Act preempted the entire field of nuclear safety. It therefore argued that a state tort claim for retaliation for nuclear safety complaints was barred. The Court, however, defined the field of exclusive federal authority very narrowly— radiological safety—and even there federal law preempted only those state laws that had a "direct and substantial effect" on such safety.

While preemption can arise in a variety of contexts, one of the most important areas for employment law purposes is just-cause discharge under collective bargaining agreements. On its face § 301 of the National Labor Relations Act, codified at 29 U.S.C. § 185(a) (2006), merely provides a cause of action and federal court jurisdiction over suits for violation of collective bargaining agreements. Nevertheless, it has been interpreted to broadly preempt state law. *See, e.g., Local 174, Teamsters, Chauffeurs, Warehousemen & Helpers of Am. v. Lucas Flour Co.,* 369 U.S. 95 (1962). While § 301 and other labor law preemption doctrines do not apply outside the collective bargaining arena, employers have frequently resisted suits by unionized employees on the basis that federal labor law preempts state remedies. While it will not be explored in detail here, § 301 has been the basis for a very elaborate jurisprudence on the respective roles of state and federal law in the employment arena predicated on a few relatively straightforward principles. First, the law to be applied by both state and federal courts is federal law, a common law to be developed setting uniform standards for the entire country. Second, the touchstone for § 301 preemption is whether the state law in question requires interpreting a collective bargaining agreement.

For example, *Allis-Chalmers Corp. v. Lueck,* 471 U.S. 202 (1985), involved a suit by an employee against both his employer and the insurance company for a nonoccupational back injury. Plaintiff claimed that the defendants "intentionally, contemptuously, and repeatedly failed" to make disability payments under a company-provided disability plan, in breach of their duty "to act in good faith and deal fairly with his disability claims." *Id.* at 206. The Supreme Court found his state law claim preempted because the Wisconsin tort action for breach of the duty of good faith was "inextricably intertwined" with the terms of the labor contract. Since any attempt to assess liability would inevitably involve contract interpretation, the Court held that the claim must either be treated as a § 301 claim or dismissed as preempted by federal labor-contract law.

In contrast to *Lueck*, the Court in *Lingle v. Norge Division of Magic Chef, Inc.*, 486 U.S. 399 (1988), found no preemption. Plaintiff had been fired for allegedly filing a false workers' compensation claim. Although she was protected by a union and in fact filed a grievance under the governing collective bargaining agreement, her tort suit alleged she had been discharged in retaliation for exercising her rights under Illinois's workers' compensation laws. A retaliatory discharge claim did not require interpretation of the collective-bargaining agreement, nor did the defense of such a suit turn on the meaning of the agreement. Since the state-law remedy was "independent" of the collective-bargaining agreement, there was no § 301 preemption. *Id.* at 407. *See also Hawaiian Airlines v. Norris*, 512 U.S. 246, 263 (1994) (holding that claims for discharge in violation of public policy and the Hawaii Whistleblower Protection Act are not preempted by the Railway Labor Act).

In short, the Court has held that an application of state law is preempted by § 301 of the Labor Management Relations Act of 1947 only if such application requires the interpretation of a collective-bargaining agreement. However, the question of whether an interpretation is necessary is more complicated than would appear on its face. This is reflected in varying results in the lower courts as to preemption of various state law tort claims. *See generally* William R. Corbett, *The Narrowing of the National Labor Relations Act: Maintaining Workplace Decorum and Avoiding Liability*, 27 BERKELEY J. EMP. & LAB. L. 23 (2006); Rebecca Hanner White, *Section 301's Preemption of State Law Claims: A Model for Analysis*, 41 ALA. L. REV. 377 (1990); Richard A. Bales, *The Discord Between Collective Bargaining and Individual Employment Rights: Theoretical Origins and a Proposed Reconciliation*, 77 B.U. L. REV. 687 (1997); Jane Byeff Korn, *Collective Rights and Individual Remedies: Rebalancing the Balance After* Lingle v. Norge Div., 41 HASTINGS L.J. 1149 (1990).

Part Four

PROTECTING WORKER AUTONOMY

6

Workplace Privacy Protections

The protection of privacy in the workplace is but one aspect of a much larger, burgeoning inquiry into the public policy implications of the recognition and protection of privacy interests. *See, e.g.*, DANIEL J. SOLOVE & PAUL M. SCHWARTZ, INFORMATION PRIVACY LAW (4th ed. 2012). This broader debate is reflected in the controversy surrounding both the federal government's mass surveillance programs — most notably those revealed in recent years by Edward Snowden — and the collection and utilization of consumer and other information by private entities. But these issues also pervade the workplace: Although employers have always used a variety of means to keep tabs on their workers, employee privacy interests have become increasingly salient due to technological advances in testing, monitoring, data collection, and record keeping, which allow for far more effective control than previously. *See, e.g.*, Steve Lohr, *Unblinking Eyes Track Employees*, N.Y. TIMES, June 21, 2014, at A1 (discussing employers' increasingly sophisticated and detailed methods of data collection and monitoring of employees at work).

In addition, with the rise of smartphones, social media, and other forms of electronic communications, how employees interact and communicate has undergone tremendous transformation in recent years. These profound changes have blurred the lines between work and nonwork. They also coincide with increasing employer concerns about what used to be viewed as the "private lives" of employees, in part because of growing stakes involving everything from seeking to hire the best employees to protecting employer property to avoiding legal and reputational risks. Indeed, recent studies have found that most major employers in the United States monitor employee communications and activities. Some employers also test some or all employees for drugs. Still others require physical exams or engage in other potentially intrusive activities upon hiring workers.

Privacy law in the employment context involves interests that are strongly contested. Not only is the workplace considerably more public than some protected areas, such as the home, but there also are strong countervailing considerations to personal privacy. After all, while at work, employees are not simply pursuing their own goals but are primarily engaged in furthering their employers' ends. Some commentators go so far as to suggest the law should have close to no role in protecting employee privacy in

323

the workplace. For example, Professor Michael Selmi argues that, as a policy matter, we ought to concede that the workplace is the employers' domain, although he advocates that the law limit strictly employer encroachments into workers' lives outside of work. Michael Selmi, *Privacy for the Working Class: Public Work and Private Lives*, 66 LA. L. REV. 1035, 1042-49 (2006). Even among those arguing for greater privacy protections, there is little agreement on the scope of the right.

Ultimately, an employee's interest in privacy must be balanced against the employer's legitimate business and risk-management reasons for intruding. It is therefore not surprising that this area of law is far from settled, offering significant challenges for employees, firms, policy makers, and, of course, counsel. And recent statutory developments, particularly at the state level, suggest continued changes in the law going forward. For a review of various aspects of the law of workplace privacy, related doctrinal problems, and proposed solutions, *see* Symposium, *Examining Privacy in the Workplace*, 66 LA. L. REV. 923 (2006) (articles by Anita Bernstein, Matthew Finkin, Steven Willborn, Pauline Kim, Charles Craver, Rafael Gely and Leonard Bierman, and Catherine Fisk); *cf.* Jessica Fink, *In Defense of Snooping Employers*, 16 U. PA. J. BUS. LAW 101 (2013) (identifying various employer interests for monitoring, surveillance, and other practices that potentially implicate employee privacy concerns).

Workplace privacy issues arise in a variety of circumstances. As an initial matter, "privacy" involves several related but distinct employee interests. The new RESTATE-MENT OF EMPLOYMENT LAW, for example, identifies three: the interest in the employee's person and in the employer-provided physical and electronic work locations in which the employee has a reasonable expectation of privacy; the interest in the employee's private information of a personal nature; and the interest in the employee's private information disclosed in confidence to the employer. RESTATEMENT (THIRD) OF EMPLOYMENT LAW (Proposed Final Draft, April 18, 2014) §§ 7.02-7.05. Further, the Restatement recognizes additional employee "autonomy" interests, including engaging in lawful conduct away from work, adhering to religious and other beliefs, and participating in lawful associations. *See id.* at §7.08. These interests implicate many different laws and legal theories. For a discussion of these laws and theories, *see generally* MATTHEW W. FINKIN, PRIVACY IN EMPLOYMENT LAW 3 (4th ed. 2013 and 2014 Supp.)

Nevertheless, despite the seemingly endless array of workplace privacy disputes, the vast majority of the litigated cases in this area fall into one of the following, sometimes overlapping, categories:

1. *Physical and Psychological Testing.* Many employers subject job applicants or employees to intrusive tests. Among these, the most commonly litigated is drug and alcohol testing. *National Treasury Employees Union v. Von Raab*, 489 U.S. 656 (1989), reproduced at page 367, and *Borse v. Piece Goods Shop, Inc.*, 963 F.2d 611 (3d Cir. 1992), reproduced at page 344, address such testing disputes, the former involving a public employer and the latter a private one. Recently, however, other kinds of testing, including physical examinations, psychological examinations, "honesty" testing, polygraphs, and genetic testing, have received growing judicial and legislative attention. Although some employers contend such tests provide important information relevant to applicant and employee qualifications and future job performance (including skills, potential safety concerns, health risks, and compatibility), workers often consider these procedures to be highly intrusive, intimidating, and overreaching. Indeed, as discussed below, privacy concerns have resulted in legislation specifically limiting the use of polygraph, physical examinations, and genetic testing by employers.

2. *Investigatory Interrogations and Searches of Persons and Spaces.* After receiving reports of misconduct in the workplace, employers sometimes interrogate workers and search their possessions and work spaces, with or without what might be called reasonable suspicion. Interrogations, which may include polygraph examinations, sometimes delve into personal issues or otherwise implicate worker privacy interests. Investigatory searches frequently include electronic and cyber searches of worker computer files, e-mail, and Internet activities. *Stengart v. Loving Care Agency, Inc.*, 990 A.2d 650 (N.J. 2010), reproduced at page 399, involves such an electronic search.

3. *Monitoring and Surveillance.* Employers engage in various forms of monitoring and surveillance to promote productivity, provide security, and prevent, discover, and remedy worker misconduct. Such monitoring historically had been limited to oversight of supervisors and other personnel and standard audits of activity in the workplace, such as the review of employee timesheets and telephone records. However, recent advances in communications and surveillance technology have dramatically increased the opportunities, effectiveness, and sometimes incentives for greater employee monitoring. The use of video and other surveillance technologies in the workplace and the monitoring of employee computer use, electronic communications, and Internet activities have received much attention in recent years. Thus, it is no surprise that there has been significant litigation in this area recently. A prominent example is the first case in this chapter, *City of Ontario v. Quon*, 560 U.S. 746 (2010).

4. *Inquiries into or Prohibitions of Off-site Conduct.* Another sphere of employee activity with privacy implications is an employee's off-site or after-hours conduct and associations. Employees and applicants typically view their activities away from work as beyond their employer's legitimate concern, unless such activity has some kind of direct impact on workplace performance. Workers may view some of these activities—including the pursuit of personal interests, intimate relationships, password-protected Internet communications, and religious and political preferences—as very private matters. Beyond "privacy" in the sense of protection from disclosure of private activities, employees often view other more "public" activities as "private" in the autonomy sense—they are simply none of the employer's business. Nevertheless, employers sometimes have legitimate reasons (e.g., protecting good will, avoiding public relations problems, ensuring loyalty, and preserving morale) to inquire into employees' or applicants' activities away from work and either regulate or take disciplinary action for such conduct. *Rulon-Miller v. International Business Machines Corp.*, 208 Cal. Rptr. 524 (Ct. App. 1984), reproduced at page 360, explores this tension.

5. *Revelations of Private Matters.* A final type of employer conduct implicating employee privacy interests involves challenges to employer-compelled revelations by employees of private matters or employer publication of employee confidential information. The employer may define as a job requirement (or a supervisor may demand that an employee reveal) something the employee considers very personal. Sometimes these obligations involve physical revelations, such as commands that an employee undress or perform some otherwise-revealing physical act. Such demands or requirements have been challenged occasionally, including in *Feminist Women's Health Center v. Superior Court*, 61 Cal. Rptr. 2d 187 (Ct. App. 1997), reproduced at page 391. Other times, employees have challenged required revelations about information, involving intimate thoughts or beliefs, embarrassing facts, or matters of personal history the employee prefers not to share. In still other situations, an employee challenges not the employer's initial mandate to disclose or reveal information to it, but, rather, the employer's publication or sharing of this information with others.

This chapter is structured around three themes that dominate the inquiry regardless of the circumstances — the five situations discussed above — in which employee privacy interests are implicated. These are (1) the search for sources of protection, (2) the balance between worker and employer interests, and (3) private ordering and the limits of employee consent. To begin thinking about these themes and the various issues they raise, consider the following problem.

PROBLEM

6-1. Data Enterprises, Inc. ("DEI") provides each of its office employees with desktop computers that are linked to DEI's network, access to DEI's e-mail system, and access to the Internet. DEI has included in its employee guidelines a "Computer Use and Electronic Communications Policy," which provides as follows:

> Employees may use office computers to engage in electronic communications for authorized purposes only. As a general matter, an authorized purpose includes work-related activities and communications. However, authorized use also includes limited personal use by employees during non-work time *provided* such use does not interfere with or disrupt DEI's business in any way, involves minimal additional expense, and does not otherwise harm DEI's interests.
>
> To ensure compliance with this policy and to protect DEI from harm and disruption, DEI may at any time audit, inspect, and/or monitor employee's electronic communications and review, audit, and inspect employee computers and information stored therein.

Amy Smith is an at-will employee working in DEI's main office. She frequently accesses the Internet from her desktop computer during her lunch hour, and, among other things, checks messages and sends e-mails to friends through her personal Gmail account. One evening after Smith left the office, her supervisor, with whom she has had some personality conflicts, decided to review her computer and Internet activities. He, along with an IT staff member, noticed Smith's frequent visits to her Gmail internet page and, after guessing her password (her birthday), accessed her account. The two discovered a number of e-mails sent by Smith to friends who are not co-workers in which she criticizes the supervisor and makes derogatory comments about him and several other employees. All of these messages were sent by Smith on days she was at work and from her work computer, but always during her lunch break. When Smith arrived at the office the next morning, the supervisor terminated her.

As you read the materials in this chapter, consider the following. First, think about whether and in what circumstances Smith might have a cognizable privacy-based claim against DEI. Second, if there is any risk of such liability to DEI, consider how DEI, through better planning, might have reduced this risk. Finally, think like a policy maker and consider whether electronic communications like the e-mails at issue in this situation ought to receive additional protection and, if so, to what extent.

A. SOURCES OF PRIVACY PROTECTION

1. Constitutional Protections

City of Ontario v. Quon
560 U.S. 746 (2010)

KENNEDY, Justice, delivered the opinion of the Court.

This case involves the assertion by a government employer of the right, in circumstances to be described, to read text messages sent and received on a pager the employer owned and issued to an employee. The employee contends that the privacy of the messages is protected by the ban on "unreasonable searches and seizures" found in the Fourth Amendment to the United States Constitution, made applicable to the States by the Due Process Clause of the Fourteenth Amendment. *Mapp v. Ohio*, 367 U.S. 643 (1961). Though the case touches issues of far-reaching significance, the Court concludes it can be resolved by settled principles determining when a search is reasonable.

I

A

The City of Ontario (City) is a political subdivision of the State of California. The case arose out of incidents in 2001 and 2002 when respondent Jeff Quon was employed by the Ontario Police Department (OPD). He was a police sergeant and member of OPD's Special Weapons and Tactics (SWAT) Team. The City, OPD, and OPD's Chief, Lloyd Scharf, are petitioners here. In October 2001, the City acquired 20 alphanumeric pagers capable of sending and receiving text messages. Arch Wireless Operating Company provided wireless service for the pagers. Under the City's service contract with Arch Wireless, each pager was allotted a limited number of characters sent or received each month. Usage in excess of that amount would result in an additional fee. The City issued pagers to Quon and other SWAT Team members in order to help the SWAT Team mobilize and respond to emergency situations.

Before acquiring the pagers, the City announced a "Computer Usage, Internet and E-Mail Policy" (Computer Policy) that applied to all employees. Among other provisions, it specified that the City "reserves the right to monitor and log all network activity including e-mail and Internet use, with or without notice. Users should have no expectation of privacy or confidentiality when using these resources." In March 2000, Quon signed a statement acknowledging that he had read and understood the Computer Policy.

The Computer Policy did not apply, on its face, to text messaging. Text messages share similarities with e-mails, but the two differ in an important way. In this case, for instance, an e-mail sent on a City computer was transmitted through the City's own data servers, but a text message sent on one of the City's pagers was transmitted using wireless radio frequencies from an individual pager to a receiving station owned by Arch Wireless. It was routed through Arch Wireless' computer network, where it remained until the recipient's pager or cellular telephone was ready to receive the message, at which point Arch Wireless transmitted the message from the transmitting station nearest to the recipient. After delivery, Arch Wireless retained a copy on its computer servers. The message did not pass through computers owned by the City.

Although the Computer Policy did not cover text messages by its explicit terms, the City made clear to employees, including Quon, that the City would treat text messages the same way as it treated e-mails. At an April 18, 2002, staff meeting at which Quon was present, Lieutenant Steven Duke, the OPD officer responsible for the City's contract with Arch Wireless, told officers that messages sent on the pagers "are considered e-mail messages. This means that [text] messages would fall under the City's policy as public information and [would be] eligible for auditing." Duke's comments were put in writing in a memorandum sent on April 29, 2002, by Chief Scharf to Quon and other City personnel.

Within the first or second billing cycle after the pagers were distributed, Quon exceeded his monthly text message character allotment. Duke told Quon about the overage, and reminded him that messages sent on the pagers were "considered e-mail and could be audited." Duke said, however, that "it was not his intent to audit [an] employee's text messages to see if the overage [was] due to work related transmissions." Duke suggested that Quon could reimburse the City for the overage fee rather than have Duke audit the messages. Quon wrote a check to the City for the overage. Duke offered the same arrangement to other employees who incurred overage fees.

Over the next few months, Quon exceeded his character limit three or four times. Each time he reimbursed the City. Quon and another officer again incurred overage fees for their pager usage in August 2002. At a meeting in October, Duke told Scharf that he had become "'tired of being a bill collector.'" Scharf decided to determine whether the existing character limit was too low—that is, whether officers such as Quon were having to pay fees for sending work-related messages—or if the overages were for personal messages. Scharf told Duke to request transcripts of text messages sent in August and September by Quon and the other employee who had exceeded the character allowance.

[At Duke's request,] Arch Wireless provided the desired transcripts. Duke reviewed the transcripts and discovered that many of the messages sent and received on Quon's pager were not work related, and some were sexually explicit. Duke reported his findings to Scharf, who, along with Quon's immediate supervisor, reviewed the transcripts himself. After his review, Scharf referred the matter to OPD's internal affairs division for an investigation into whether Quon was violating OPD rules by pursuing personal matters while on duty.

The officer in charge of the internal affairs review was Sergeant Patrick McMahon. Before conducting a review, McMahon used Quon's work schedule to redact the transcripts in order to eliminate any messages Quon sent while off duty. He then reviewed the content of the messages Quon sent during work hours. McMahon's report noted that Quon sent or received 456 messages during work hours in the month of August 2002, of which no more than 57 were work related; he sent as many as 80 messages during a single day at work; and on an average workday, Quon sent or received 28 messages, of which only 3 were related to police business. The report concluded that Quon had violated OPD rules. Quon was allegedly disciplined.

B

[Quon filed suit in federal court claiming that, by obtaining and reviewing the transcript of Quon's pager messages, the City violated his Fourth Amendment rights, the Stored Communications Act (SCA), 18 U.S.C. § 2701 et seq., and California law. Quon was joined by the recipients of his text messages: Jerilyn Quon, Jeff Quon's then-wife, from whom he was separated; April Florio, an OPD employee with whom Jeff Quon was romantically involved; and Steve Trujillo, another member of the OPD SWAT Team. The complaint also named Arch Wireless as a defendant, alleging it violated the SCA by turning over the transcript to the City.

Both the district court and the Ninth Circuit held that Quon had a reasonable expectation of privacy in the content of his text messages. The district court would have made liability turn on whether the purpose of the audit was to determine whether Quon was wasting time (impermissible) or assessing the appropriateness of the existing character limits (permissible). The Ninth Circuit reversed in part, holding that even though the search was conducted for "a legitimate work-related rationale," it was not reasonable in scope. The court found that there was a "host of simple ways" for the OPD to achieve its legitimate goals that were less intrusive than the audit.] The Court of Appeals further concluded that Arch Wireless had violated the SCA by turning over the transcript to the City. . . .

II

The Fourth Amendment states: "The right of the people to be secure in their persons, houses, papers, and effects, against unreasonable searches and seizures, shall not be violated. . . ." It is well settled that the Fourth Amendment's protection extends beyond the sphere of criminal investigations. . . . The Fourth Amendment applies as well when the Government acts in its capacity as an employer. *Treasury Employees v. Von Raab,* 489 U.S. 656, 665 (1989).

The Court discussed this principle in [*O'Connor v. Ortega,* 480 U.S. 709 (1987)]. There a physician employed by a state hospital alleged that hospital officials investigating workplace misconduct had violated his Fourth Amendment rights by searching his office and seizing personal items from his desk and filing cabinet. All Members of the Court agreed with the general principle that "[i]ndividuals do not lose Fourth Amendment rights merely because they work for the government instead of a private employer." A majority of the Court further agreed that "'special needs, beyond the normal need for law enforcement,'" make the warrant and probable-cause requirement impracticable for government employers. (plurality opinion) (quoting *New Jersey v. T. L. O.,* 469 U.S. 325, 351 (1985) (Blackmun, J., concurring)); *O'Connor* (opinion of Scalia, J.) (quoting same).

The *O'Connor* Court did disagree on the proper analytical framework for Fourth Amendment claims against government employers. A four-Justice plurality concluded that the correct analysis has two steps. First, because "some government offices may be so open to fellow employees or the public that no expectation of privacy is reasonable," a court must consider "[t]he operational realities of the workplace" in order to determine whether an employee's Fourth Amendment rights are implicated. On this view, "the question whether an employee has a reasonable expectation of privacy must be addressed on a case-by-case basis." Next, where an employee has a legitimate privacy expectation, an employer's intrusion on that expectation "for non-investigatory, work-related purposes, as well as for investigations of work-related misconduct, should be judged by the standard of reasonableness under all the circumstances."

Justice Scalia, concurring in the judgment, outlined a different approach. His opinion would have dispensed with an inquiry into "operational realities" and would conclude "that the offices of government employees . . . are covered by Fourth Amendment protections as a general matter." But he would also have held "that government searches to retrieve work-related materials or to investigate violations of workplace rules — searches of the sort that are regarded as reasonable and normal in the private-employer context — do not violate the Fourth Amendment."

Later, in the *Von Raab* decision, the Court explained that "operational realities" could diminish an employee's privacy expectations, and that this diminution could be taken into consideration when assessing the reasonableness of a workplace search. In the two decades since *O'Connor*, however, the threshold test for determining the scope of an employee's Fourth Amendment rights has not been clarified further. Here, though they disagree on whether Quon had a reasonable expectation of privacy, both petitioners and respondents start from the premise that the *O'Connor* plurality controls. It is not necessary to resolve whether that premise is correct. The case can be decided by determining that the search was reasonable even assuming Quon had a reasonable expectation of privacy. The two *O'Connor* approaches — the plurality's and Justice Scalia's — therefore lead to the same result here.

III

A

Before turning to the reasonableness of the search, it is instructive to note the parties' disagreement over whether Quon had a reasonable expectation of privacy. The record does establish that OPD, at the outset, made it clear that pager messages were not considered private. The City's Computer Policy stated that "[u]sers should have no expectation of privacy or confidentiality when using" City computers. Chief Scharf's memo and Duke's statements made clear that this official policy extended to text messaging. The disagreement, at least as respondents see the case, is over whether Duke's later statements overrode the official policy. Respondents contend that because Duke told Quon that an audit would be unnecessary if Quon paid for the overage, Quon reasonably could expect that the contents of his messages would remain private.

At this point, were we to assume that inquiry into "operational realities" were called for, it would be necessary to ask whether Duke's statements could be taken as announcing a change in OPD policy, and if so, whether he had, in fact or appearance, the authority to make such a change and to guarantee the privacy of text messaging. It would also be necessary to consider whether a review of messages sent on police pagers, particularly those sent while officers are on duty, might be justified for other reasons, including performance evaluations, litigation concerning the lawfulness of police actions, and perhaps compliance with state open records laws. These matters would all bear on the legitimacy of an employee's privacy expectation.

The Court must proceed with care when considering the whole concept of privacy expectations in communications made on electronic equipment owned by a government employer. The judiciary risks error by elaborating too fully on the Fourth Amendment implications of emerging technology before its role in society has become clear. *See, e.g., Olmstead v. United States*, 277 U.S. 438 (1928), overruled by *Katz v. United States*, 389 U.S. 347, 353 (1967). In *Katz*, the Court relied on its own knowledge and experience to conclude that there is a reasonable expectation of privacy in a telephone booth. It is not so clear that courts at present are on so sure a ground. Prudence counsels caution before the facts in the instant case are used to establish far-reaching premises that define the existence, and extent, of privacy expectations enjoyed by employees when using employer-provided communication devices.

Rapid changes in the dynamics of communication and information transmission are evident not just in the technology itself but in what society accepts as proper behavior. As one *amici* brief notes, many employers expect or at least tolerate personal use of such equipment by employees because it often increases worker efficiency. Another *amicus* points out that the law is beginning to respond to these developments, as some States have recently passed statutes requiring employers to notify employees when monitoring their electronic communications [(citing DEL. CODE ANN., tit. 19, § 705 (2005)); CONN. GEN. STAT. ANN. § 31-48d (West 2003)]. At present, it is uncertain how workplace norms, and the law's treatment of them, will evolve.

Even if the Court were certain that the *O'Connor* plurality's approach were the right one, the Court would have difficulty predicting how employees' privacy expectations will be shaped by those changes or the degree to which society will be prepared to recognize those expectations as reasonable. Cell phone and text message communications are so pervasive that some persons may consider them to be essential means or necessary instruments for self-expression, even self-identification. That might strengthen the case for an expectation of privacy. On the other hand, the ubiquity of those devices has made them generally affordable, so one could counter that employees who need cell phones or similar devices for personal matters can purchase and pay for their own. And employer policies concerning communications will of course shape the reasonable expectations of their employees, especially to the extent that such policies are clearly communicated.

A broad holding concerning employees' privacy expectations vis-á-vis employer-provided technological equipment might have implications for future cases that cannot be predicted. It is preferable to dispose of this case on narrower grounds. For present purposes we assume several propositions *arguendo:* First, Quon had a reasonable expectation of privacy in the text messages sent on the pager provided to him by the City; second, petitioners' review of the transcript constituted a search within the meaning of the Fourth Amendment; and third, the principles applicable to a government employer's search of an employee's physical office apply with at least the same force when the employer intrudes on the employee's privacy in the electronic sphere.

B

Even if Quon had a reasonable expectation of privacy in his text messages, petitioners did not necessarily violate the Fourth Amendment by obtaining and reviewing the transcripts. Although as a general matter, warrantless searches "are *per se* unreasonable under the Fourth Amendment," there are "a few specifically established and well-delineated exceptions" to that general rule. *Katz*. The Court has held that the "'special needs'" of the workplace justify one such exception. *O'Connor*; *Von Raab*.

Under the approach of the *O'Connor* plurality, when conducted for a "noninvestigatory, work-related purpos[e]" or for the "investigatio[n] of work-related misconduct," a government employer's warrantless search is reasonable if it is "'justified at its inception'" and if "'the measures adopted are reasonably related to the objectives of the search and not excessively intrusive in light of'" the circumstances giving rise to the search. *O'Connor*. The search here satisfied the standard of the *O'Connor* plurality and was reasonable under that approach.

The search was justified at its inception because there were "reasonable grounds for suspecting that the search [was] necessary for a noninvestigatory work-related purpose." As a jury found, Chief Scharf ordered the search in order to determine whether the character limit on the City's contract with Arch Wireless was sufficient to meet the City's needs. This was, as the Ninth Circuit noted, a "legitimate work-related rationale." The City and OPD had a legitimate interest in ensuring that employees were not being forced to pay out of their own pockets for work-related expenses, or on the other hand that the City was not paying for extensive personal communications.

As for the scope of the search, reviewing the transcripts was reasonable because it was an efficient and expedient way to determine whether Quon's overages were the result of work-related messaging or personal use. The review was also not "'excessively intrusive.'" *O'Connor* (plurality opinion). Although Quon had gone over his monthly allotment a number of times, OPD requested transcripts for only the months of August and September 2002. While it may have been reasonable as well for OPD to review transcripts of all the months in which Quon exceeded his allowance, it was certainly reasonable for OPD to review messages for just two months in order to obtain a large enough sample to decide whether the character limits were efficacious. And it is worth noting that during his internal affairs investigation, McMahon redacted all messages Quon sent while off duty, a measure which reduced the intrusiveness of any further review of the transcripts.

Furthermore, and again on the assumption that Quon had a reasonable expectation of privacy in the contents of his messages, the extent of an expectation is relevant to assessing whether the search was too intrusive. *See Von Raab*. Even if he could assume some level of privacy would inhere in his messages, it would not have been reasonable for Quon to conclude that his messages were in all circumstances immune from scrutiny. Quon was told that his messages were subject to auditing. As a law enforcement officer, he would or should have known that his actions were likely to come under legal scrutiny, and that this might entail an analysis of his on-the-job communications. Under the circumstances, a reasonable employee would be aware that sound management principles might require the audit of messages to determine whether the pager was being appropriately used. Given that the City issued the pagers to Quon and other SWAT Team members in order to help them more quickly respond to crises — and given that Quon had received no assurances of privacy — Quon could have anticipated that it might be necessary for the City to audit pager messages to assess the SWAT Team's performance in particular emergency situations.

From OPD's perspective, the fact that Quon likely had only a limited privacy expectation, with boundaries that we need not here explore, lessened the risk that the review would intrude on highly private details of Quon's life. OPD's audit of messages on Quon's employer-provided pager was not nearly as intrusive as a search of his personal e-mail account or pager, or a wiretap on his home phone line, would have been. That the search did reveal intimate details of Quon's life does not make it unreasonable, for under the circumstances a reasonable employer would not expect that such a review would intrude on such matters. The search was permissible in its scope.

The Court of Appeals erred in finding the search unreasonable. It pointed to a "host of simple ways to verify the efficacy of the 25,000 character limit . . . without intruding on [respondents'] Fourth Amendment rights." The panel suggested that Scharf "could have warned Quon that for the month of September he was forbidden from using his pager for personal communications, and that the contents of all his messages would be reviewed to ensure the pager was used only for work-related purposes during that time frame. Alternatively, if [OPD] wanted to review past usage, it could have asked Quon to count the characters himself, or asked him to redact personal messages and grant permission to [OPD] to review the redacted transcript."

This approach was inconsistent with controlling precedents. This Court has "repeatedly refused to declare that only the 'least intrusive' search practicable can be reasonable under the Fourth Amendment." That rationale "could raise insuperable barriers to the exercise of virtually all search-and-seizure powers," because "judges engaged in *post hoc* evaluations of government conduct can almost always imagine some alternative means by which the objectives of the government might have been accomplished." The analytic errors of the Court of Appeals in this case illustrate the necessity of this principle. Even assuming there were ways that OPD could have performed the search that would have been less intrusive, it does not follow that the search as conducted was unreasonable.

Respondents argue that the search was *per se* unreasonable in light of the Court of Appeals' conclusion that Arch Wireless violated the SCA by giving the City the transcripts of Quon's text messages. The merits of the SCA claim are not before us. But even if the Court of Appeals was correct to conclude that the SCA forbade Arch Wireless from turning over the transcripts, it does not follow that petitioners' actions were unreasonable. Respondents point to no authority for the proposition that the existence of statutory protection renders a search *per se* unreasonable under the Fourth Amendment. And the precedents counsel otherwise. *See Virginia v. Moore*, 553 U.S. 164, 168 (2008) (search incident to an arrest that was illegal under state law was reasonable); *California v. Greenwood*, 486 U.S. 35, 43 (1988) (rejecting argument that if state law forbade police search of individual's garbage the search would violate the Fourth Amendment). Furthermore, respondents do not maintain that any OPD employee either violated the law him- or herself or knew or should have known that Arch Wireless, by turning over the transcript, would have violated the law. The otherwise reasonable search by OPD is not rendered unreasonable by the assumption that Arch Wireless violated the SCA by turning over the transcripts.

Because the search was motivated by a legitimate work-related purpose, and because it was not excessive in scope, the search was reasonable under the approach of the *O'Connor* plurality. For these same reasons — that the employer had a legitimate reason for the search, and that the search was not excessively intrusive in light of that justification — the Court also concludes that the search would be "regarded as reasonable and normal in the private-employer context" and would satisfy the approach of Justice Scalia's concurrence. The search was reasonable, and the Court of Appeals erred by holding to the contrary. Petitioners did not violate Quon's Fourth Amendment rights.

C

Finally, the Court must consider whether the search violated the Fourth Amendment rights of Jerilyn Quon, Florio, and Trujillo, the respondents who sent text messages to Jeff Quon. Petitioners and respondents disagree whether a sender of a text message can have a reasonable expectation of privacy in a message he knowingly sends to someone's employer-provided pager. It is not necessary to resolve this question in order to dispose of the case, however. Respondents argue that because "the search was unreasonable as to Sergeant Quon, it was also unreasonable as to his correspondents." They make no corollary argument that the search, if reasonable as to Quon, could nonetheless be unreasonable as to Quon's correspondents. In light of this litigating position and the Court's conclusion that the search was reasonable as to Jeff Quon, it necessarily follows that these other respondents cannot prevail.

[Justice Stephens concurred.] . . .

Scalia, Justice, concurring in part and concurring in the judgment.

I join the Court's opinion except for Part III-A. I continue to believe that the "operational realities" rubric for determining the Fourth Amendment's application to public employees invented by the plurality in *O'Connor v. Ortega* is standardless and unsupported. In this case, the proper threshold inquiry should be not whether the Fourth Amendment applies to messages on *public* employees' employer-issued pagers, but whether it applies *in general* to such messages on employer-issued pagers.

Here, however, there is no need to answer that threshold question. Even accepting at face value Quon's and his co-plaintiffs' claims that the Fourth Amendment applies to their messages, the city's search was reasonable, and thus did not violate the Amendment. Since it is unnecessary to decide whether the Fourth Amendment applies, it is unnecessary to resolve which approach in *O'Connor* controls: the plurality's or mine. That should end the matter.

The Court concedes as much, yet it inexplicably interrupts its analysis with a recitation of the parties' arguments concerning, and an excursus on the complexity and consequences of answering, that admittedly irrelevant threshold question. That discussion is unnecessary. (To whom do we owe an *additional* explanation for declining to decide an issue, once we have explained that it makes no difference?) It also seems to me exaggerated. Applying the Fourth Amendment to new technologies may sometimes be difficult, but when it is necessary to decide a case we have no choice. The Court's implication that where electronic privacy is concerned we should decide less than we otherwise would (that is, less than the principle of law necessary to resolve the case and guide private action) — or that we should hedge our bets by concocting case-specific standards or issuing opaque opinions — is in my view indefensible. The-times-they-are-a-changin' is a feeble excuse for disregard of duty.

Worse still, the digression is self-defeating. Despite the Court's insistence that it is agnostic about the proper test, lower courts will likely read the Court's self-described "instructive" expatiation on how the *O'Connor* plurality's approach would apply here (if it applied) as a heavy-handed hint about how *they* should proceed. Litigants will do likewise, using the threshold question whether the Fourth Amendment is even implicated as a basis for bombarding lower courts with arguments about employer policies, how they were communicated, and whether they were authorized, as well as the latest trends in employees' use of electronic media. In short, in saying why it is not saying more, the Court says much more than it should.

The Court's inadvertent boosting of the *O'Connor* plurality's standard is all the more ironic because, in fleshing out its fears that applying that test to new technologies will be too hard, the Court underscores the unworkability of that standard. Any rule that requires evaluating whether a given gadget is a "necessary instrumen[t] for self-expression, even self-identification," on top of assessing the degree to which "the law's treatment of [workplace norms has] evolve[d]," is (to put it mildly) unlikely to yield objective answers.

I concur in the Court's judgment.

NOTES

1. *The Fourth Amendment and the Basic Framework. Quon* is an important decision because the Court applies the Fourth Amendment to electronic communications on employer-provided equipment, a context rife with litigation and controversy. However, much of the legal doctrine in *Quon* simply reaffirms the analysis set forth in *O'Connor v. Ortega*, 480 U.S. 709 (1987). In that case, which involved the search of a public employee's office space and file drawers, the Court initially recognized that, pursuant to its prohibition on unreasonable searches and seizures, government workers enjoy some Fourth Amendment protection while at work. This recognition alone was significant: There are more than 23 million government (federal, state, and local) employees in the United States, and, at least as a default matter, they have some claim to privacy while at work.

The *Quon* decision goes on to apply the operative framework set forth in *O'Connor* for determining whether there has been a violation of a public employee's Fourth Amendment rights. It provides a two-step inquiry. First, in order to enjoy any Fourth Amendment protection, the employee must have had a "reasonable expectation of privacy" in the area or thing (physical or metaphorical) intruded upon or searched. Second, if the employee had such an expectation, then it must be determined whether the employer's intrusion into this area or thing was "reasonable." In *Quon*, the Court found it unnecessary to resolve the first inquiry, since it determined that the resulting search was reasonable at its inception. Nevertheless, the Court's arguably gratuitous discussion of the subject—as well as Justice Scalia's scolding response in his concurrence—offers some new guidance and plenty of fodder for debate.

2. *The First Prong: Reasonable Expectation of Privacy.* The Court assumes arguendo that Quon had a reasonable expectation of privacy in the content of the pager messages. Thus, it initially states that it need not resolve definitively which approach—the *O'Connor* plurality's "operational realities" standard or Justice Scalia's categorical approach—governs the determination of whether an employee had a reasonable expectation of privacy. Nevertheless, the majority goes on to discuss in some detail why it cannot and should not adopt a "broad holding concerning employees' privacy expectations vis-á-vis employer-provided technological equipment." Is Justice Scalia right that, in so doing, the majority is endorsing an operational realities approach?

To appreciate what is at stake, take a moment to consider the policy and practical implications that are at the heart of the dispute. The *O'Connor* plurality justified its case-by-case approach to determining the reasonableness of an employee's expectation of privacy (regarding physical spaces in the workplace) this way:

Individuals do not lose Fourth Amendment rights merely because they work for the government instead of a private employer. The operational realities of the workplace, however, may make *some* employees' expectations of privacy unreasonable when an intrusion is by a supervisor rather than a law enforcement official. Public employees' expectations of privacy in their offices, desks, and file cabinets, like similar expectations of employees in the private sector, may be reduced by virtue of actual office practices and procedures, or by legitimate regulation. . . . The employee's expectation of privacy must be assessed in the context of the employment relation. An office is seldom a private enclave free from entry by supervisors, other employees, and business and personal invitees. Instead, in many cases offices are continually entered by fellow employees and other visitors during the workday for conferences, consultations, and other work-related visits. Simply put, it is the nature of government offices that others — such as fellow employees, supervisors, consensual visitors, and the general public — may have frequent access to an individual's office. We agree with Justice Scalia that "[constitutional] protection against *unreasonable* searches by the government does not disappear merely because the government has the right to make reasonable intrusions in its capacity as employer," but some government offices may be so open to fellow employees or the public that no expectation of privacy is reasonable. Given the great variety of work environments in the public sector, the question whether an employee has a reasonable expectation of privacy must be addressed on a case-by-case basis.

O'Connor, 480 U.S. at 718.

Like the *O'Connor* plurality, Justice Scalia concluded in that case that Ortega had a reasonable expectation of privacy in his office spaces, desk, and office drawers. But, in arriving at this conclusion, he criticized the plurality's case-by-case methodology much as he does in *Quon*. As an initial matter, he expressed concern that the plurality's formulation would lead to uncertainty. *See* 480 U.S. at 729-30 (arguing that the plurality's standard is "so devoid of content that it produces rather than eliminates uncertainty").

He went on to argue that a categorical approach to determining whether the employee had a privacy interest in the space or area is also more consistent with existing Fourth Amendment jurisprudence:

> Whatever the plurality's standard means, however, it must be wrong if it leads to the conclusion on the present facts that if Hospital officials had extensive "work-related reasons to enter Dr. Ortega's office" no Fourth Amendment protection existed. It is privacy that is protected by the Fourth Amendment, not solitude. A man enjoys Fourth Amendment protection in his home, for example, even though his wife and children have the run of the place — and indeed, even though his landlord has the right to conduct unannounced inspections at any time. Similarly, in my view, one's personal office is constitutionally protected against warrantless intrusions by the police, even though employer and co-workers are not excluded. . . . Constitutional protection against *unreasonable* searches by the government does not disappear merely because the government has the right to make reasonable intrusions in its capacity as employer. . . .

> I would hold, therefore, that the offices of government employees, and *a fortiori* the drawers and files within those offices, are covered by Fourth Amendment protections as a general matter. (The qualifier is necessary to cover such unusual situations as that in which the office is subject to unrestricted public access, so that it is "[exposed] to the public" and therefore "not a subject of Fourth Amendment protection." *Katz v. United States*, 389 U.S. 347, 351 (1967).) . . .

Id. at 730-32. Which opinion do you find more convincing? Is one approach more likely to provide public employees with meaningful privacy protections than the other? Should that matter?

Turning back to *Quon*, do you see similar arguments and themes in the majority's discussion of the first prong and in Justice Scalia's response? Is your assessment of which side has the better argument affected at all by the nature of the privacy interest at stake — that is, text messages on an employer-provided communications device — rather than physical spaces in employer-provided offices?

Courts addressing employee Fourth Amendment claims after *O'Connor* (but before *Quon*) usually adopted the plurality's contextual approach although, as a practical matter, the application of this standard has been categorical with regard to certain types of searches or intrusions. For example, for searches and testing involving an employee's person or bodily fluids, including drug testing, the Supreme Court and other courts have virtually always assumed or found some reasonable expectation of privacy. *See, e.g., Nat'l Treasury Employees Union v. Von Raab*, 489 U.S. 656 (1989) (drug testing) (reproduced at page 367); *Skinner v. Railway Labor Executives' Ass'n*, 489 U.S. 602 (1989) (same). In cases involving intrusions into spheres in which employee privacy expectations are less obvious — for example, physical work spaces like those at issue in *Ortega* and, as more commonly litigated today, electronic files and communications like those at issue in *Quon* — the results are mixed, often hinging on the specific areas of alleged privacy involved and workplace practices and policies. Importantly, then, whether an employee enjoys any Fourth Amendment protection at all will depend on both the nature of the intrusion and the particulars of the workplace.

3. *An Invitation to Regulate Privacy out of Existence? Quon* assumes a reasonable expectation of privacy in the underlying communications, but did plaintiff have one? On a purely technical level, one might ask whether the oral assurance overrode the written policy, which might require an inquiry into agency law. Or is a "reasonable expectation" less a question of what documents say than what most employees in the situation might expect?

Those favoring privacy protections for workers might view *Quon* as a partial victory, given that the Ninth Circuit — applying the *O'Connor* plurality's approach — did find that Quon had a reasonable expectation of privacy in the content of his communications on equipment provided by the City, *see Quon v. Arch Wireless Operating Co., Inc.*, 554 F.3d 769, 772 (9th Cir. 2009) (Wardlaw, J. concurring in denial of *en banc* review), and the Supreme Court expressly left open the question. But because particular workplace practices and circumstances will affect whether such an expectation exists (at least under the contextual approach), the partial victory for the plaintiffs in this case likely was more a function of employer missteps than an expansion of employee privacy interests in electronic communications or otherwise. What are the lessons here for employers who want discretion to review the content of employee electronic communications? What mistakes did the Department make and what steps could an employer take to prevent them? In other words, can a public employer effectively negate any reasonable expectation of privacy by establishing and abiding by clear policies and procedures regarding employee communications and work spaces?

Courts analyzing constitutional and other kinds of workplace privacy claims often find that employees have no reasonable expectation of privacy in electronic communications or files on employer-provided devices where the employer has in place a sufficiently broad policy that clearly states that employee communications and files may be monitored. *See, e.g., Biby v. Bd. of Regents*, 419 F.3d 845 (8th Cir. 2005); *Muick v. Glenayre Elecs*, 280 F.3d 741 (7th Cir. 2002); *United States v. Angevine*, 281 F.3d 1130 (10th Cir. 2002); *United States v. Simons*, 206 F.3d 392 (4th Cir. 2000); *Holmes v. Petrovich Development Co.*, 119 Cal. Rptr. 3d 878 (Cal. Ct. App. 2011); *see also State v. M.A.*, 954 A.2d 503 (N.J. App. Div. 2008) (concluding employee lacked reasonable expectation of privacy in the personal information stored in his employer-provided computer where employee was advised that computers were company property and that the firm and co-workers had access to it). Indeed, the new RESTATEMENT OF EMPLOYMENT LAW's limitations on an employee's "reasonable expectation of privacy" for a physical or virtual location are consistent with this treatment of employer monitoring and use policies:

> (b) An employee has a reasonable expectation in the privacy of a physical or electronic work location provided by the employer if:
>   (1) the employer has provided express notice that the location or aspects of the location are private for employees; or
>   (2) the employer has acted in a manner that treats the location or aspects of the location as private for employees, the type of location is customarily treated as private for employees, and the employee has made reasonable efforts to keep the location private.

RESTATEMENT (THIRD) OF EMPLOYMENT LAW (Proposed Final Draft, April 18, 2014) §7.03

Still, the existence of such a policy is not necessarily enough; as the Restatement articulation suggests, employer treatment and practices are what matters. Thus, when employees are able to establish a reasonable expectation of privacy, it tends to be because the employer did not adhere to the policy (as in *Quon*) or the policy was, for one reason or another, insufficiently clear or broad to cover the particular communications or electronic files in question. *See United States v. Ziegler*, 474 F.3d 1184, 1189-90 (9th Cir. 2007) (holding that an employee possessed a reasonable expectation of privacy in a computer in a locked office despite a company policy that computer usage would be monitored); *Pure Power Boot Camp, Inc. v. Warrior Fitness Boot Camp, LLC*, 587 F. Supp. 2d 548, 560 (S.D.N.Y. 2008) (finding that an employee had a reasonable privacy expectation in personal Hotmail account that he accessed on his employer-provided work computer because the company's e-mail policy did not state that e-mails stored on third-party providers and not within the employer's e-mail system could be subject to inspection); *see also Stengart v. Loving Care Agency, Inc.*, 990 A.2d 650 (N.J. 2010), reproduced at page 399 (stating that an employer policy regarding access to employee e-mail could not trump the employee's attorney-client privilege). It might be that the seemingly idiosyncratic *Quon* facts are more typical than they appear. Employers usually have "appropriate use" policies on paper, but there are many reasons why workplace norms could vary significantly from written policies. Even before *Quon*, if an employer really wished to forestall any expectations of privacy, it was advisable to frequently monitor worker communications—and let them know that's being done. But can you see why employers, whatever documents their attorneys draft, might be reluctant to do so?

Nevertheless, if employer monitoring and review of employee electronic communications is or becomes the standard practice, doesn't this cut against the legitimacy of an expectation that such communications are private? Wouldn't these practices help to form the norms and societal expectations to which the majority refers? Would such expectation-reducing actions by employers have the same effect under Justice Scalia's categorical approach? If his view were to prevail, the reasonableness of an employee's expectation of privacy would not hinge on the particulars of given workplace practices or structures. But what is the likely treatment of the category — electronic communications on employer-provided devices — in a world in which employer monitoring and review are standard practice? In light of these lessons, *Quon* might lead many (most?) employers to act in ways that, as a practical matter, reduce the amount of privacy or autonomy employees enjoy at work or while using employer-provided communications devices. Or are there reasons to be more optimistic?

4. *The Second Prong: The Reasonableness of the Search or Intrusion.* *Quon*'s central holding was on the second prong of the inquiry: After assuming Quon had a reasonable expectation of privacy in the content of the text messages, the Court concluded that the department's review of the text message transcripts was "reasonable." In *O'Connor*, the Court had determined that the need to balance the legitimate interests of the government employer against the privacy interests of its employees justified exempting work-related searches from the usual Fourth Amendment requirement of obtaining a warrant:

> In our view, requiring an employer to obtain a warrant whenever the employer wished to enter an employee's office, desk, or file cabinets for a work-related purpose would seriously disrupt the routine conduct of business and would be unduly burdensome. Imposing unwieldy warrant procedures in such cases upon supervisors, who would otherwise have no reason to be familiar with such procedures, is simply unreasonable. In contrast to other circumstances in which we have required warrants, supervisors in offices such as at the Hospital are hardly in the business of investigating the violation of criminal laws. Rather, work-related searches are merely incident to the primary business of the agency. Under these circumstances, the imposition of a warrant requirement would conflict with "the common-sense realization that government offices could not function if every employment decision became a constitutional matter." *Connick* v. *Myers*, 461 U.S. 138, 143 (1983).

O'Connor, 480 U.S. at 721-22. The Court also rejected a warrantless "probable cause" standard as impracticable:

> The governmental interest justifying work-related intrusions by public employers is the efficient and proper operation of the workplace. Government agencies provide myriad services to the public, and the work of these agencies would suffer if employers were required to have probable cause before they entered an employee's desk for the purpose of finding a file or piece of office correspondence. Indeed, it is difficult to give the concept of probable cause, rooted as it is in the criminal investigatory context, much meaning when the purpose of a search is to retrieve a file for work-related reasons. Similarly, the concept of probable cause has little meaning for a routine inventory conducted by public employers for the purpose of securing state property. To ensure the efficient and proper operation of the agency, therefore, public employers must be given wide latitude to enter employee offices for work-related, noninvestigatory reasons.
>
> . . . Public employers have an interest in ensuring that their agencies operate in an effective and efficient manner, and the work of these agencies inevitably suffers from the inefficiency, incompetence, mismanagement, or other work-related misfeasance of its employees. Indeed, in many cases, public employees are entrusted with tremendous

responsibility, and the consequences of their misconduct or incompetence to both the agency and the public interest can be severe. In contrast to law enforcement officials, therefore, public employers are not enforcers of the criminal law; instead, public employers have a direct and overriding interest in ensuring that the work of the agency is conducted in a proper and efficient manner. In our view, therefore, a probable cause requirement for searches of the type at issue here would impose intolerable burdens on public employers. The delay in correcting the employee misconduct caused by the need for probable cause rather than reasonable suspicion will be translated into tangible and often irreparable damage to the agency's work, and ultimately to the public interest. . . . [Additionally, it] is simply unrealistic to expect supervisors in most government agencies to learn the subtleties of the probable cause standard. . . .

Id. at 723-24.

Instead, the *O'Connor* Court adopted a much less searching "reasonableness" standard for determining the validity of the intrusion. This inquiry addresses the reasonableness of both the inception and scope of the intrusion:

> Ordinarily, a search of an employee's office by a supervisor will be "justified at its inception" when there are reasonable grounds for suspecting that the search will turn up evidence that the employee is guilty of work-related misconduct, or that the search is necessary for a noninvestigatory work-related purpose such as to retrieve a needed file. . . .
>
> [A] search will be permissible in its scope when "the measures adopted are reasonably related to the objectives of the search and not excessively intrusive in light of . . . the nature of the [misconduct]."

Id. at 726.

Applying this standard, *Quon* held that the department's review of the text messages was justified at its inception by a legitimate, noninvestigatory work-related rationale and found the level of intrusiveness to be reasonable. Perhaps the most significant doctrinal takeaway from the Court's analysis was its rejection of the Ninth Circuit's finding that the search was unreasonable in scope because the department had less intrusive means at its disposal for achieving the same work-related end. Thus, to survive scrutiny with regard to the extensiveness of the intrusion, a government employer need not utilize the "least intrusive" search practicable. Do you agree with the Court's reasoning? It's hard to imagine a "reasonableness" test that doesn't consider alternatives. Is the Court saying that alternatives are irrelevant or only that the employer doesn't have to use the less intrusive one? If the latter, how unnecessarily intrusive can a search be and still be "reasonable"?

5. *Reasonableness, Deference, and Uncertainty.* As you may have noticed already, deference to government employers' interests plays a crucial role in the Fourth Amendment analysis. For example, as Justice Scalia's critique of the *O'Connor* plurality's approach to the first prong suggests, because actual workplace practices and structures are relevant to determining whether an employee's privacy expectation is reasonable, employers' decisions regarding the need to monitor and search the physical and virtual spaces in the workplace may profoundly affect that inquiry. As for the second prong, the need for some deference to government employers' decision making and practical constraints were central to the *O'Connor* Court's adoption of a reasonableness inquiry instead of imposing the traditional warrant and probable cause requirements. The perceived necessity to give employers some leeway also informed *Quon*'s rejection of a more onerous "least intrusive means" requirement.

Moreover, outcomes in individual cases may hinge on the level of deference courts accord government employers' justifications for their intrusions and the means they utilize to serve these ends. If, as Justice Scalia suggests, the *O'Connor* plurality's approach to the "expectation of privacy" inquiry may lead to uncertainty, the same undoubtedly can be said of the second prong's reasonableness standard as articulated in *O'Connor* and *Quon*. This standard is more deferential to the employer than a probable cause or strict scrutiny requirement would be, but how much deference is to be accorded to the government's articulated justification and chosen means remains unclear. For example, is an intrusion valid as long as an employer is able to articulate (truthfully) some workplace productivity, security, or efficiency justification and the intrusion is not greater than that needed to serve this end? The extent to which the level of scrutiny varies by circumstance or by the nature of intrusion likewise remains unresolved. The *Quon* majority states that "the extent of an expectation is relevant to assessing whether the search was too intrusive," but how this seemingly sliding scale is to be applied in other cases is unclear.

The critical role of deference is, of course, not unique to this area; indeed, it may be dispositive whenever a court is asked to scrutinize government activities. But the extent of deference may vary with the nature of the governmental activities and the countervailing interests at stake. How much deference should a court give a government employer in scrutinizing its justification for an intrusion into an employee's sphere of potential privacy? What are the social benefits of such deference and the countervailing costs? Does your answer depend on the type of intrusion at issue — for example, drug testing, office searches, locker searches, video surveillance of work spaces, and monitoring of computer and Internet use? Are your views influenced by your own work experiences and expectations, and the extent to which you may value your privacy in various contexts? We will revisit some of these issues at greater length in Section B.

6. *Due Process Protections for Public Sector Employees.* In addition to the protection accorded by the Fourth Amendment, public employees may enjoy other privacy protections. The Fifth and Fourteenth Amendments' due process clauses protect employees' "liberty interests," including privacy interests, and these interests may be enforceable under 42 U.S.C. § 1983 or directly against federal officials under *Bivens v. Six Unknown Named Agents*, 403 U.S. 388 (1971). For example, in *Whalen v. Roe*, 429 U.S. 589 (1977), the Supreme Court recognized constitutional privacy interests in "avoiding disclosure of personal matters" and in "independence in making certain kinds of important decisions." *See also Nixon v. Administrator of General Services*, 433 U.S. 425 (1977) ("[P]ublic officials, including the President, are not wholly without constitutionally protected privacy rights in matters of personal life unrelated to any acts done by them in their public capacity."). Although this right to "information privacy" is widely recognized in the circuits, its contours are not well defined.

In *National Aeronautics and Space Administration v. Nelson*, 562 U.S. 134 (2011), the Supreme Court had the opportunity to weigh in on this issue. The Court confronted privacy-based challenges to the National Aeronautics and Space Administration's (NASA) background checks for employees in nonsensitive or low-risk positions. Among other things, NASA required these employees to submit to in-depth background investigations and answer questions about private matters including "adverse information" about financial issues, alcohol and drug abuse, and mental and emotional stability. *See id.* at 752-53. However, as a number of scholars had predicted, the Court found no violation in this case while avoiding the constitutional question:

> We assume, without deciding, that the Constitution protects a privacy right of the sort mentioned in *Whalen* and *Nixon*. We hold, however, that the challenged portions of the Government's background check do not violate this right in the present case. The Government's interests as employer and proprietor in managing its internal operations, combined with the protections against public dissemination provided by the Privacy Act of 1974 satisfy any "interest in avoiding disclosure" that may "arguably ha[ve] its roots in the Constitution."

Id. at 751. Concurring, Justice Scalia (joined by Justice Thomas) would have found no such right exists. *See id.* at 764-69.

With regard to other types of claims based on "substantive due process" rights, protection depends largely on whether the privacy interest at stake has been identified as "fundamental." Where it has not, the government employer's action must simply be rational or nonarbitrary, and employees invariably lose such challenges. Where, however, the interest has been deemed fundamental — for example, involving marriage or other intimate relations, procreation, abortion, child rearing, or perhaps intimate personal information — the alleged infringement of these rights will be subjected to more searching scrutiny, and courts have found violations in various contexts. *See, e.g., Barrett v. Steubenville City Schs.*, 388 F.3d 967, 974 (6th Cir. 2004) (finding an employee stated a claim of violation of constitutional right to rear a child after school district denied her permanent position because she removed her child from the public schools); *Barrow v. Greenville Indep. Sch. Dist.*, 332 F.3d 844 (5th Cir. 2003) (recognizing the same right); *Thorne v. City of El Segundo*, 726 F.2d 459 (9th Cir. 1983) (holding that the rejection of a police officer candidate in part because a polygraph test revealed her sexual relationship with a married police officer violated the candidate's constitutional rights). However, courts have often rejected such claims, finding either no fundamental right and a legitimate employment-related justification for the action, or that the agency's survives strict scrutiny. *See, e.g., Seegmiller v. Laverkin City*, 528 F.3d 762 (10th Cir. 2008) (holding that a police officer did not have fundamental liberty interest to engage in private act of consensual sex, and that, under rational basis review, the city reasonably reprimanded officer under its code of ethics); *Sylvester v. Fogley*, 465 F.3d 851 (8th Cir. 2006) (holding that an investigation into whether a police officer had sexual relations with victim of crime he was investigating did not violate officer's right to privacy because the police investigation was narrowly tailored to serve a compelling interest).

7. *State Constitutions.* Many state constitutions also protect privacy rights of government workers. For example, the plaintiffs in *Quon* claimed violations of Article I, Section 1 of the California Constitution, which provides that all people have inalienable rights, including life, liberty, and "privacy." *See also* Ak. Const. art. I, § 22 ("The right of the people to privacy is recognized and shall not be infringed."); Wash. Const. art. I, § 7 ("No person shall be disturbed in his private affairs, or his home invaded, without authority of law.").

8. *Statutory Protections for Public Sector Employees.* While there is no comprehensive workplace privacy statute or statutory scheme protecting federal workers' privacy, federal employees have some additional protections from intrusions. For example, under the Civil Service Reform Act, 5 U.S.C. § 2302 (2014), civil service workers

are protected against termination for conduct that does not adversely affect their employment performance or the performance of others. Also, federal employees may enjoy protection against the government collecting, using, and disclosing some kinds of personal information under the Privacy Act of 1974, 5 U.S.C. § 552a (2014). State protections for public workers vary, but many have civil service regimes akin to the one under federal law. Many other state statutory protections apply to both public and private sectors.

9. *Spillovers Between the Public and Private Workplace.* Although *Quon* involves a public employer, two of plaintiffs' three primary legal theories — the Stored Communications Act, 18 U.S.C. §§ 2702-2711 (2014), discussed in more detail on page 356, and California constitutional claims — could also be available in the private employer context. Indeed, while most state constitutional protections, like their federal counterparts, are limited to government intrusions, California's privacy provision applies to private actors, including private employers. *See Hernandez v. Hillsides, Inc.*, 211 P.3d 1063 (Cal. 2009); *Soroka v. Dayton Hudson Corp.*, 1 Cal. Rptr. 2d 77 (Ct. App. 1991); *cf. Hennessey v. Coastal Eagle Point Oil Co.*, 609 A.2d 11 (N.J. 1992) (holding that the right to privacy in the New Jersey Constitution does not apply to private actors directly, but can form part of the basis for a clear mandate of public policy supporting a wrongful discharge claim). Nevertheless, since federal constitutional, most state constitutional, and other statutory protections (like those discussed in Note 8) are available only to government workers, the public/private sector distinction is a potentially dispositive one in the privacy context. *See, e.g.*, S. Elizabeth Wilborn, *Revisiting the Public/Private Distinction: Employee Monitoring in the Workplace*, 32 Ga. L. Rev. 825 (1998).

Still, there are a number of other ways in which privacy claims in public and private workplace converge. First, Justice Scalia's concurrence in *O'Connor* suggests that private sector norms and practices may be relevant to the reasonableness inquiry. *See O'Connor*, 480 U.S. at 732 (Scalia, concurring) (stating that "searches of the sort that are regarded as reasonable and normal in the private-employer context" do not violate the Fourth Amendment). Reliance on private sector norms and practices might seem odd, given that worker expectations about when the government can intrude upon certain spaces and communications may vary greatly (and legitimately) from their views of when private employers may intrude. Indeed, isn't it likely that the background constitutional and statutory constraints themselves shape public sector employees' expectations differently than those in the private sector? Nevertheless, Justice Scalia's view at least suggests the potential relevance of prevailing private sector practices in the constitutional analysis. For criticism of the suggestion in *Quon* that private sector norms might influence expectations of privacy for public sector workers, *see* Paul M. Secunda, *Privatizing Workplace Privacy*, 88 Notre Dame L. Rev. 277 (2012).

On the flip side, Fourth Amendment cases like *O'Connor* have proven highly influential beyond the public workplace as courts analyzing private sector claims borrow heavily from the legal framework developed in the Fourth Amendment cases. As we will see, the analytical framework set forth in *O'Connor* is similar to those adopted by courts addressing privacy claims based on statutory, state constitutional, and tort theories. For example, as the Ninth Circuit's panel decision in *Quon* stated, the analysis under the California Constitution tracks the Fourth Amendment. *See* 529 F.3d 892, 903 (9th Cir. 2008). Moreover, the new Restatement, which seeks to provide guidance on common law principles (recall the discussion in Chapter 1), expressly relies on the reasoning in the government sector cases because they have been influential in

shaping the analysis in the private sector context. *See* Restatement (Third) of Employment Law (Proposed Final Draft, April 18, 2014) § 7.01 cmt. g ("Although decisions
involving government workers generally do not apply to workers in private firms
because of the absence of constitutional and civil-service protections in the private
sector, principles developed in the course of elaborating such protections can help
shape common law rulings. Thus, for example, courts have utilized Fourth Amendment principles in deciding whether employees, generally, have a reasonable expectation of privacy in their offices regardless of whether they work for the government or
for a private company.").

2. Tort-based Protections

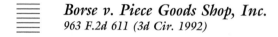

Borse v. Piece Goods Shop, Inc.
963 F.2d 611 (3d Cir. 1992)

Becker, Circuit Judge.

Plaintiff Sarah Borse brought suit against her former employer, Piece Goods
Shop, Inc. ("the Shop"), in the district court for the Eastern District of Pennsylvania.
She claimed that, by dismissing her when she refused to submit to urinalysis screening
and personal property searches (conducted by her employer at the workplace pursuant
to its drug and alcohol policy), the Shop violated a public policy that precludes employers from engaging in activities that violate their employees' rights to privacy and to
freedom from unreasonable searches. . . . This appeal requires us to decide whether an
at-will employee who is discharged for refusing to consent to urinalysis screening for
drug use and to searches of her personal property states a claim for wrongful discharge
under Pennsylvania law.

Because we predict that, under certain circumstances, discharging a private-
sector, at-will employee for refusal to consent to drug testing and to personal property
searches may violate the public policy embodied in the Pennsylvania cases recognizing
a cause of action for tortious invasion of privacy, and because the allegations of Borse's
complaint are not sufficient for us to determine whether the facts of this case support
such a claim, we will vacate the district court's [dismissal for failure to state a claim] and
remand with directions to grant leave to amend.

I. The Allegations of the Complaint . . .

Borse was employed as a sales clerk by the Piece Goods Shop for almost fifteen
years. In January 1990, the Shop adopted a drug and alcohol policy which required its
employees to sign a form giving their consent to urinalysis screening for drug use and
to searches of their personal property located on the Shop's premises.

Borse refused to sign the consent form. On more than one occasion, she asserted
that the drug and alcohol policy violated her right to privacy and her right to be free
from unreasonable searches and seizures as guaranteed by the United States Constitution. The Shop continued to insist that she sign the form and threatened to discharge her unless she did. On February 9, 1990, the Shop terminated Borse's
employment.

The complaint alleges that Borse was discharged in retaliation for her refusal to sign the consent form and for protesting the Shop's drug and alcohol policy. It asserts that her discharge violated a public policy, embodied in the First and Fourth Amendments to the United States Constitution, which precludes employers from engaging in activities that violate their employees' rights to privacy and to freedom from unreasonable searches of their persons and property. Plaintiff seeks compensatory damages for emotional distress, injury to reputation, loss of earnings, and diminished earning capacity. She also alleges that the discharge was willful and malicious and, accordingly, seeks punitive damages.

II. Overview of the Public Policy Exception to the Employment-at-Will Doctrine in Pennsylvania

[The Court recognized that, as a federal court sitting in diversity, it must apply Pennsylvania tort law in this case. In so doing, it was obliged to predict how the Pennsylvania Supreme Court would resolve the question of whether discharging an at-will employee who refuses to consent to urinalysis and to searches of his or her personal property located on the employer's premises violates public policy. After a detailed discussion of Pennsylvania Supreme Court and Superior Court cases addressing the public policy exception, and Third Circuit cases applying Pennsylvania law on the exception, the court concluded that Pennsylvania law continues to recognize a claim for wrongful discharge when dismissal of an at-will employee violates a clear mandate of public policy.]

III. Sources of Public Policy

In order to evaluate Borse's claim, we must attempt to "discern whether any public policy is threatened" by her discharge. As evidence of a public policy that precludes employers from discharging employees who refuse to consent to the practices at issue, Borse primarily relies upon the First and Fourth Amendments to the United States Constitution and the right to privacy included in the Pennsylvania Constitution. As will be seen, we reject her reliance on these constitutional provisions, concluding instead that, to the extent that her discharge implicates public policy, the source of that policy lies in Pennsylvania common law.

A. Constitutional Provisions

1. The United States Constitution

Although the Supreme Court has made clear that the Con[...] [...]cribes only the *government* from violating the individual's right to privacy, a[...] [...]n from unreasonable searches, *Skinner v. Railway Labor Executives Associ[...]* [...].S. 602 (1989) (Fourth Amendment does not apply to searches by private [...] [...]orse argues that our decision in *Novosel v. Nationwide Insurance Co.*, 721 F.2d [...] 3d Cir. 1983), permits us to consider the public policies embodied in the First and Fourth Amendments despite the lack of state action. In *Novosel,* defendant Nationwide instructed its employees to participate in its effort to lobby the Pennsylvania House of Representatives, which was then considering an insurance reform act. Specifically, Nationwide directed its employees to clip, copy, and obtain signatures on coupons bearing the insignia of the Pennsylvania Committee for No-Fault Reform. Novosel alleged that he was discharged for refusing to participate in the lobbying effort and for privately stating opposition to his employer's political stand.

In response to Novosel's claim, Nationwide argued that a wrongful discharge action depends upon the violation of a *statutorily* recognized public policy. We disagreed. . . . After noting that the public policy exception applies only in the absence of statutory remedies, we reasoned:

> Given that there are no statutory remedies available in the present case and taking into consideration the importance of the political and associational freedoms of the federal and state Constitutions, the absence of a statutory declaration of public policy would appear to be no bar to the existence of a cause of action. Accordingly, a cognizable expression of public policy may be derived in this case from either the First Amendment of the United States Constitution or Article I, Section 7 of the Pennsylvania Constitution.[5]

In deciding not to extend *Novosel* to Borse's claim, the district court remarked upon the Pennsylvania Superior Court's reluctance to rely upon constitutional provisions as sources of public policy. . . .

To the extent that the district court's opinion suggests that a constitutional provision may never serve as a source of public policy in Pennsylvania wrongful discharge actions, we disagree. . . .

Even though the district court may have overestimated the Superior Court's hostility to reliance upon constitutional provisions as sources of public policy, it correctly refused to extend *Novosel* to Borse's claim. As the district court observed, the Superior Court has refused to extend constitutional provisions designed to restrict governmental conduct in the absence of state action. . . .

The Pennsylvania Supreme Court has not considered the propriety of applying constitutional principles to wrongful discharge actions against private employers. Its most recent decisions regarding the cause of action admonish us, however, that the public policy exception applies "only in the most limited of circumstances," *Paul* [*v. Lankenau Hospital,* 569 A.2d 346, 348 Pa. (1990)]. . . .

Novosel's holding (i.e., that using the power of discharge to coerce employees' political activity violates public policy) is not at issue here and thus we need not decide whether the recent Pennsylvania cases constitute such "persuasive evidence of a change in Pennsylvania law" that we are free to disregard it. Instead, we need only decide whether to *extend* the approach taken in *Novosel.* In light of the narrowness of the public policy exception and of the Pennsylvania courts' continuing insistence upon the state action requirement, we predict that if faced with the issue, the Pennsylvania Supreme Court would not look to the First and Fourth Amendments

---

5. Article I, section 7 states in pertinent part:

The free communication of thoughts and opinions is one of the invaluable rights of man, and every citizen may freely speak, write and print on any subject, being responsible for the abuse of that liberty.

as sources of public policy when there is no state action. Accordingly, we decline to extend the approach taken in *Novosel* to this case.

2. The Pennsylvania Constitution

[The court predicted that the Pennsylvania Supreme Court would find that the state constitution does not encompass privacy invasions by private actors and would not look to that constitution's right to privacy as a source of public policy in a wrongful discharge action.]

B. *Pennsylvania Common Law*

Although we have rejected Borse's reliance upon constitutional provisions as evidence of a public policy allegedly violated by the Piece Goods Shop's drug and alcohol program, our review of Pennsylvania law reveals other evidence of a public policy that may, under certain circumstances, give rise to a wrongful discharge action related to urinalysis or to personal property searches. Specifically, we refer to the Pennsylvania common law regarding tortious invasion of privacy.

Pennsylvania recognizes a cause of action for tortious "intrusion upon seclusion." *Marks v. Bell Telephone Co.*, 331 A.2d 424, 430 (Pa. 1975). The Restatement defines the tort as follows:

> One who intentionally intrudes, physically or otherwise, upon the solitude or seclusion of another or his private affairs or concerns, is subject to liability to the other for invasion of his privacy, if the intrusion would be highly offensive to a reasonable person.

RESTATEMENT (SECOND) OF TORTS § 652B.[8]

Unlike the other forms of tortious invasion of privacy,[9] an action based on intrusion upon seclusion does not require publication as an element of the tort. *Harris by Harris v. Easton Publishing Co.*, 483 A.2d 1377, 1383 (1984). The tort may occur by (1) physical intrusion into a place where the plaintiff has secluded himself or herself; (2) use of the defendant's senses to oversee or overhear the plaintiff's private affairs; or (3) some other form of investigation or examination into plaintiff's private concerns. Liability attaches only when the intrusion is substantial and would be highly offensive to "the ordinary reasonable person."

We can envision at least two ways in which an employer's urinalysis program might intrude upon an employee's seclusion. First, the particular manner in which the program is conducted might constitute an intrusion upon seclusion as defined by

---

8. In *Vogel v. W.T. Grant Co.*, 327 A.2d 133 (Pa. 1974), the Pennsylvania Supreme Court adopted the definition of tortious invasion of privacy as stated in a tentative draft of the RESTATEMENT (SECOND) OF TORTS § 652 (Tent Draft Nov. 13, 1967). Although the Pennsylvania Supreme Court has not expressly adopted the final version of section 652, our analysis of Pennsylvania law in *O'Donnell v. United States*, 891 F.2d 1079 (3d Cir. 1989), led us to predict that it would do so if presented with the issue. *See also Vernars v. Young*, 539 F.2d 966 (3d Cir. 1976) (upholding invasion of privacy claim under Pennsylvania law when corporate officer opened and read personal mail addressed to fellow employee).

9. The action for invasion of privacy encompasses four analytically distinct torts. In addition to intrusion upon seclusion, the tort also includes: (1) appropriation of name or likeness; (2) publicity given to private life; and (3) publicity placing a person in a false light. *See Marks.*

Pennsylvania law. The process of collecting the urine sample to be tested clearly implicates "expectations of privacy that society has long recognized as reasonable," *Skinner v. Railway Labor Executives Association*, 489 U.S. 602, 617 (1989).[10] In addition, many urinalysis programs monitor the collection of the urine specimen to ensure that the employee does not adulterate it or substitute a sample from another person. . . . Monitoring collection of the urine sample appears to fall within the definition of an intrusion upon seclusion because it involves the use of one's senses to oversee the private activities of another. RESTATEMENT (SECOND) OF TORTS § 652B, comment b. *See also Harris*. . . .

Second, urinalysis "can reveal a host of private medical facts about an employee, including whether she is epileptic, pregnant, or diabetic." *Skinner*. A reasonable person might well conclude that submitting urine samples to tests designed to ascertain these types of information constitutes a substantial and highly offensive intrusion upon seclusion.

The same principles apply to an employer's search of an employee's personal property. If the search is not conducted in a discreet manner or if it is done in such a way as to reveal personal matters unrelated to the workplace, the search might well constitute a tortious invasion of the employee's privacy. *See, for example, K-Mart Corp. Store No. 7441 v. Trotti*, 677 S.W.2d 632 (Tex. App. 1984) (search of employee's locker). *See also Bodewig v. K-Mart, Inc.*, 635 P.2d 657 (1981) (subjecting cashier accused of stealing to strip search).

The Pennsylvania courts have not had occasion to consider whether a discharge related to an employer's tortious invasion of an employee's privacy violates public policy. . . .

[W]e believe that when an employee alleges that his or her discharge was related to an employer's invasion of his or her privacy, the Pennsylvania Supreme Court would examine the facts and circumstances surrounding the alleged invasion of privacy. If the court determined that the discharge was related to a substantial and highly offensive invasion of the employee's privacy, we believe that it would conclude that the discharge violated public policy.[11] Indeed, the following language in [*Geary v. United States Steel Corp.*, 319 A.2d 174 (Pa. 1974)] might well be considered to presage such an approach:

> It may be granted that there are areas of an employee's life in which his employer has no legitimate interest. An intrusion into one of these areas by virtue of the employer's power of discharge might plausibly give rise to a cause of action, particularly where some recognized facet of public policy is threatened. . . .

Only a handful of other jurisdictions have considered urinalysis programs implemented by private employers.[12] The majority of these decisions balance the employee's

---

10. [W]e caution against the wholesale application to private employers of the limitations imposed on public employers by the Fourth Amendment. We find the cases involving government employers helpful, however, in defining the individual privacy interest implicated by urinalysis.

11. The Sixth Circuit recently rejected an invasion of privacy claim challenging an employer's urinalysis program. *Baggs v. Eagle-Picher Industries, Inc.*, 957 F.2d 268 (6th Cir. 1992) (applying Michigan law). Michigan law permits an employer to use "intrusive and even objectionable means to obtain employment-related information about an employee." In contrast, Pennsylvania has not exempted employers from the principles ordinarily applied in actions for tortious invasion of privacy.

12. Several of these cases are inapposite because they involve state law that differs significantly from Pennsylvania's. For example, some state constitutions include a right of privacy that applies to private action.

privacy interest against the employer's interests in order to determine whether to uphold the programs. *See,* for example, *Luedtke v. Nabors Alaska Drilling, Inc.,* 768 P.2d 1123 (Alaska 1989). In *Luedtke,* two employees challenged their employer's urinalysis program, alleging violation of their state constitutional right of privacy, common-law invasion of privacy, wrongful discharge, and breach of the covenant of good faith and fair dealing. (Under Alaska law, the public policy exception to the employment-at-will doctrine is "largely encompassed within the implied covenant of good faith and fair dealing.") After determining that the relevant provision of the Alaska constitution did not apply to private action, the Alaska Supreme Court concluded that a public policy protecting an employee's right to withhold private information from his employer exists in Alaska and that violation of that policy "may rise to the level of a breach of the implied covenant of good faith and fair dealing."

As evidence of public policy, the court looked to the state's statutes,[13] Constitution,[14] and common law.[15] The court concluded:

> Thus, the citizens' rights to be protected against unwarranted intrusions into their private lives has been recognized in the law of Alaska. The constitution protects against governmental intrusion, statutes protect against employer intrusion, and the common law protects against intrusions by other private persons. As a result, there is sufficient evidence to support the conclusion that there exists a public policy protecting spheres of employee conduct into which employers may not intrude.

The court then turned to the question "whether employer monitoring of employee drug use outside the work place is such a prohibited intrusion." The Court reasoned that the boundaries of the employee's right of privacy "are determined by balancing [that right] against other public policies, such as 'the health, safety, rights and privileges of others.'" Because the *Luedtke* plaintiffs performed safety-sensitive jobs, the court concluded that the public policy supporting the protection of the health and safety of other workers justified their employer's urinalysis program.

[The West Virginia Supreme Court also applied a balancing test in *Twigg v. Hercules Corp.,* 406 S.E.2d 52 (W. Va. 1990), reasoning that its holding that requiring employees to submit to polygraph examinations violated public policy should be extended to requiring an employee to submit to drug testing. West Virginia, however, recognized two exceptions: when the urinalysis is based on "reasonable good faith objective suspicion" of an employee's drug use or when the employee's job involves public safety or the safety of others. Not all other jurisdictions have applied a balancing

---

Our discussion in the text focuses on selected cases typifying the various approaches taken in the remaining cases. We are unaware of any case considering whether the dismissal of an at-will employee who refuses to consent to personal property searches violates public policy.

13. The court observed that a statute prohibiting employers from requiring employees to take polygraph tests as a condition of employment supports "the policy that there are private sectors of employees' lives not subject to direct scrutiny by their employers." The court also noted that a statute prohibiting employment discrimination on the basis of, among other things, marital status, changes in marital status, pregnancy or parenthood, demonstrates "that in Alaska certain subjects are placed outside the consideration of employers in their relations with employees."

14. The court reasoned that although Alaska's constitutional right of privacy does not proscribe private action, the inclusion of a specific clause protecting the right "supports the contention that this right 'strike[s] as the heart of a citizen's social rights.'"

15. The court observed that the action for tortious intrusion upon seclusion evidences the existence of a common-law right of privacy.

As *Borse* indicates, the tort requires (1) an intentional intrusion (2) into an area of solitude or seclusion (3) that would be highly offensive to the reasonable person. Note the similarity between this articulation and the Fourth Amendment analysis in *O'Connor* and *Quon*. As in a Fourth Amendment case, much hinges on whether the intrusion was into an area (spatial or otherwise) in which the employee has a reasonable expectation of privacy. This is satisfied in the drug and medical testing and other bodily intrusion contexts since courts agree that one has a reasonable expectation of privacy in his or her person. But whether such an expectation exists with regard to employee work spaces or communications is a more difficult issue that depends on the particulars of the job and workplace. *Compare Fischer v. Mt. Olive Lutheran Church*, 207 F. Supp. 2d 914 (W.D. Wis. 2002) (finding that employee had reasonable expectation in the e-mails in his personal Hotmail account); *Hernandez v. Hillsides, Inc.*, 211 P.3d 1063 (Cal. 2009) (concluding that employees had reasonable expectation that office that could be locked would not be secretly videotaped); *Koeppel v. Speirs*, 808 N.W.2d 177 (Iowa 2011) (finding a genuine issue of material fact as to whether a security camera that the employer had surreptitiously installed in a workplace bathroom, though inoperable when discovered could have potentially transmitted images of the employee, thereby intentionally intruding into a matter in which the employee had a right to expect privacy) *with Holmes v. Petrovich Development Co.*, 119 Cal. Rptr. 3d 878 (Cal. Ct. App. 2011) (holding employee's belief that her emails were private was unreasonable because she was warned that the company would monitor email to ensure employees were complying with office policy and she was told that she had no expectation of privacy in any messages she sent from the company computer) and *Thygeson v. U.S. Bancorp*, 2004 U.S. Dist. LEXIS 18863 (D. Or. Sept. 15, 2004) (suggesting an employee has no reasonable expectation of privacy in e-mails on employer's e-mail system).

If there is such an intrusion by the employer, the next inquiry is whether it was objectively offensive. Oddly enough, whether the intrusion is offensive is not measured by how subjectively offensive it is to the employee but rather whether it is justified by a legitimate employer interest and appropriately tailored to serving that interest. Indeed, this is stated expressly in the new RESTATEMENT OF EMPLOYMENT LAW's version of the tort:

> § 7.06. Wrongful Employer Intrusions
> (a) An employer is subject to liability for a wrongful intrusion upon an employee's protected privacy interest (as described in §§ 7.03-7.05) if the intrusion would be highly offensive to a reasonable person under the circumstances.
> (b) An intrusion is highly offensive under subsection (a) if the nature, manner, and scope of the intrusion upon the employee's protected privacy interest are clearly unreasonable when judged against the employer's legitimate business interests or public interests in effecting the intrusion.

In short, a reasonable employee should not be offended by a justifiable intrusion. As in the Fourth Amendment context, resolution of this inquiry often depends on the leeway courts are willing to give employers in terms of their articulated ends and means for achieving them. *Compare Speer v. Ohio Dep't of Rehab. and Corr.*, 624 N.E.2d 251 (Ohio Ct. App. 1993) (finding that a supervisor's hiding in the ceiling of a staff rest room to monitor an employee suspected of misconduct was unreasonable) *with Saldana v. Kelsey-Hayes*, 443 N.W.2d 382 (Mich. Ct. App. 1989) (upholding an employer's surveillance of an employee's home because the employer had a legitimate right to investigate the employee's claim of workplace injury); *see generally* Daniel P. O'Gorman, *Looking Out for Your Employer: Employers' Surreptitious Physical Surveillance of Employees and the Tort of Invasion of Privacy*, 85 NEB. L. REV. 212 (2006).

4. *Other Privacy Torts.* Other privacy torts are litigated occasionally in the workplace context. For example, RESTATEMENT (SECOND) OF TORTS § 652D recognizes the tort of public disclosure of private facts, which creates a cause of action when one publicly discloses a private matter that is "highly offensive" to the reasonable person and as to which the public has no legitimate concern. Employers typically have access to private information about employees (e.g., disabilities or more general health information), and thus, their disclosure of such information to the public or third parties without justification may give rise to liability. *See, e.g., Miller v. Motorola, Inc.*, 560 N.E.2d 900 (Ill. App. Ct. 1990). However, the sharing of such information with workplace personnel may not give rise to liability, either because such a sharing is not sufficiently "public" to satisfy the public disclosure element, or because a legitimate business justification may render such disclosure "reasonable." *See, e.g., Bratt v. Int'l Bus. Machines*, 785 F.2d 352 (1st Cir. 1986) (finding no liability for the sharing of information about an employee's psychological condition with other managerial personnel); *see generally* Jonathan B. Mintz, *The Remains of Privacy's Disclosure Tort: An Exploration of the Private Domain*, 55 MD. L. REV. 425 (1996). Another theory that may provide protection in certain workplace contexts is the tort of false light, that is, where the employer discloses a matter about the employee that places the employee in a "false light" that is "highly offensive" to a reasonable person. *See* RESTATEMENT (SECOND) OF TORTS § 652C (1977).

Despite the theoretical applicability of these tort causes of action, the statutory protections discussed in the next subsection are more likely to provide meaningful protection for the workplace privacy interests implicated. However, other workplace tort theories that implicate privacy or related dignitary interests are more likely to be pursued, including defamation, discussed in Chapter 5, and intentional infliction of emotional distress, discussed below.

5. *Intentional Infliction of Emotional Distress.* The means by which an employer may seek to monitor employee activities or gain information from an employee may give rise to an intentional infliction of emotional distress claim. As discussed in this chapter, the Restatement (Second) of Torts provides that such a cause of action exists when "one who by extreme and outrageous conduct intentionally or recklessly causes severe emotional distress to another." In most cases, the key inquiry is whether the employers' conduct — in this context, intrusive actions — is sufficiently "extreme and outrageous" to justify liability. Courts occasionally have found that employers' methods reach this level; indeed, *Rulon-Miller v. Int'l Bus. Machines Corp.*, 208 Cal. Rptr. 524 (Ct. App. 1984), reproduced at page 360, is one example. *See also Bodewig v. K-Mart, Inc.*, 635 P.2d 657 (Or. Ct. App. 1981) (recognizing a claim for intentional infliction of emotional distress after the employer required an employee to disrobe in front of a customer who claimed the employee had taken her money).

6. *The Request for Consent "Catch-22."* Numerous courts have found consent (or, at least, fully informed consent) to an alleged privacy intrusion to be a near-absolute defense to common-law privacy claims. *See, e.g., Stewart v. Pantry, Inc.*, 715 F. Supp. 1361 (W.D. Ky. 1988) (holding consent is a complete defense to an intrusion claim involving polygraph tests); *Jennings v. Minco Tech. Labs, Inc.*, 765 S.W.2d 497 (Tex. Ct. App. 1989) (same in drug-testing context); *cf. Baggs v.*

Eagle-Picher Indus., Inc., 750 F. Supp. 264 (W.D. Mich. 1990) (finding no expectation of privacy because employees were on notice of possible drug testing); *TBG Ins. Services Corp. v. Superior Court*, 117 Cal. Rptr. 2d 155 (Cal. App. 2002) (finding, in the context of a discovery dispute, that employee had no reasonable expectation of privacy in files on an employer-provided home computer because he had agreed in writing to employer's policy that computer use would be monitored). Should an employee's agreement to be tested, searched, or monitored, in response to an employer's request (or insistence) be a defense to a public policy claim? Similarly, should such agreement preclude recovery under an intrusion upon seclusion theory, either because consent destroys any reasonable expectation of privacy or because consent makes the intrusion not objectively offensive? On the other hand, if the employee refuses to agree to the intrusion, and no intrusion thereby occurs (i.e., no drug test, no intrusive questioning, no requested search of spaces or communications), some courts have held that that there is no intrusion upon seclusion claim. *See, e.g., Rushing v. Hershey Chocolate-Memphis*, 2000 WL 1597849 (6th Cir. 2000); *Baggs, supra* (holding that those who did not participate in the drug-testing program cannot recover because there was no intrusion); *Luedtke v. Nabors Alaska Drilling, Inc.*, 768 P.2d 1123 (Alaska 1989) ("[N]o cause of action for invasion of privacy arises where the intrusion is prevented from taking place").

And here lies the catch-22: If the employee agrees to the test, search, or other intrusion, she has consented to it; if she refuses (and loses her job as a result), there is no intrusion. Either way, she has no claim. Under this framework then, an employer can shield itself from liability by always asking for the employee's agreement or waiver before any intrusion occurs because any response by the employee will bar the claim. Obviously, not all courts have taken this view, and some courts, including *Borse* and *Luedtke*, as well as §7.07 of the Restatement, have recognized that a public policy claim arising out of the employee's termination might exist even if an intrusion upon seclusion claim fails. Nevertheless, the potential waiver of rights and remedies when employers seek consent to otherwise actionable intrusions creates a further incentive for employers to make the demand for consent (to monitoring, surveillance, workplace searches, etc.) standard practice, and employees are then in a very difficult position when deciding how to respond.

3. Statutory Protections

a. Federal Law

While there is no comprehensive federal statutory scheme governing privacy rights or claims in the private workplace, there are a number of federal statutory regimes that protect privacy interests of private sector employees. Some protect such interests incidentally or as part of a larger scheme addressing other regulatory objectives. For example, antidiscrimination statutes provide indirect protection from certain forms of invasive employer activity or inquiries. While the Americans with Disabilities Act ("ADA") explicitly prohibits inquiry into its protected category, all antidiscrimination laws prohibit employers from altering the terms and conditions of employment based on an employee's protected status, which means that employers may steer clear of inquiries that may implicate such status — such as one's religion, age, or pregnancy status. *See, e.g., Norman-Bloodshaw v. Lawrence Berkeley Lab.*, 135 F.3d

1260 (9th Cir. 1998) (holding that challenges to employer's medical and genetic testing program raised cognizable discrimination claims because they revealed sex- and race-linked traits or conditions). In addition, offensive intrusions into private matters by supervisors or co-workers may contribute to a discriminatory harassment claim if the conduct is linked to the victim's protected status (e.g., sex or religion). Various employment screening procedures — testing, medical screening, questioning, and so forth — also may violate antidiscrimination statutes if they have a disparate impact on a protected class and cannot be justified by business necessity. *See* Chapter 9.

In the past several decades, however, there have been a number of statutory developments that focus directly on privacy interests. A high-profile recent example is the Genetic Information Nondiscrimination Act of 2008 ("GINA"), Pub. L. 110-233, 122 Stat. 881 (May 21, 2008), which is discussed at the end of this subsection. These statutory regimes offer meaningful protections, but, as you will see, they are sometimes qualified or limited in important respects.

Earlier federal enactments tended to focus on intrusive interrogation techniques and employee surveillance and monitoring. For example, the Employee Polygraph Protection Act of 1988 ("EPPA"), 29 U.S.C. §§ 2001-09 (2014), bans the use of a polygraph for pre-employment screening and delineates both the circumstances in which polygraphs may be used in employer investigations following a theft of property and the procedures for such use. The EPPA applies to most private employees; however, government employees and employees working in various defense and security contexts are exempted.

In addition, the federal wiretapping statute, now embodied in the Electronic Communications Privacy Act of 1986 ("ECPA"), 18 U.S.C. §§ 2510-22 (2014), protects against various kinds of electronic surveillance and interception of communications by public and private actors, including private employers. It declares unlawful the intentional interception of oral wire communications, other oral communications, and electronic communications (all non-oral wire communications). While this act may appear to provide robust protections for electronic communications, including e-mails and Internet activity, three exemptions from its prohibitions limit protection for employee communications: (1) the law does not protect against interceptions by a service provider (often the employer) to protect the rights or property of the provider, (2) the protections do not apply to interception by certain devices of communications made in the "ordinary course of business," and (3) the protections do not apply when one party to the communication consents to the interception. Moreover, courts have construed "interception" narrowly in various contexts. *See, e.g., Konop v. Hawaiian Airlines, Inc.*, 302 F.3d 868 (9th Cir. 2002) (construing "interception" to cover only communications acquired during transmission); *see also McCann v. Iroquois Mem'l Hosp.*, 622 F.3d. 745 (7th Cir. 2010) (granting summary judgment to individual hospital managers on ECPA claims for allegedly retaliating against two workers based on a conversation that had been recorded by another worker; there was no evidence the managers knew that the recording had been illegally made); Ariana Levinson, *Toward a Cohesive Interpretation of the Electronic Communications Privacy Act for the Electronic Monitoring of Employees*, 114 W. VA. L. REV. 461 (2012) (arguing that the ECPA's protections can and should be interpreted broadly to provide employees greater protection for their electronic communications). On the other hand, the exceptions also have been interpreted narrowly. *See, e.g., Deal v. Spears*, 980 F.2d 1153 (8th Cir. 1992) (ordinary course of business exception); *Burrow v. Sybaris Clubs International, Inc.*, 2013 WL 5967333 (N.D. Ill., Nov. 08, 2013) (refusing to find secret recordings of employees' personal and business telephone conversations on a separate computer protected by the ordinary course of business exception and also refusing to dismiss state statutory and intrusion upon seclusion claims). Nevertheless, these carve-outs — particularly the third — significantly limit protections for most workers.

The Stored Communications Act ("SCA"), 18 U.S.C. §§ 2702-11 (2014), provides similar protections against unauthorized access to stored electronic communications, although it too is subject to the limitations of the ECPA. Recall that in *Quon*, the SCA was one of theories underlying the claims brought against Arch Wireless by Quon and his co-workers. It therefore is a potential source of protection for employees against third parties; indeed, Quon's claims against Arch Wireless as a remote computing service for its unauthorized release of the transcripts of the text messages were successful. For a detailed discussion of the SCA claims in *Quon*, see the underlying panel opinion, *Quon v. Arch Wireless Operating Co., Inc.*, 529 F.3d 892 (9th Cir. 2008). In addition, despite the limited protections against employer monitoring of electronic communications in the workplace, the ECPA and SCA are potential sources of protection from unauthorized employer intrusions into employee communications and other electronic activities outside of work. *See, e.g., Pietrylo v. Hillstone Rest. Group*, No. 06-5754 (FSH), 2009 WL 3128420 (D.N.J. Sept. 25, 2009) (upholding a jury verdict finding that employees' managers violated the SCA by knowingly accessing a chat group on MySpace without authorization). With the rise of smart phones and other technologies, employees' secret recordings of conversations with co-workers and supervisors have become more common. Because the recording party consents to the communications being recorded, protection under federal and state law is limited. For a discussion of this phenomenon and potential legal and practical implications, *see* David Koeppel, *More People Are Using Smartphones to Secretly Record Office Conversations*, BUSINESS INSIDER (Jul. 28, 2011), http://www.businessinsider.com/smartphones-spying-devices-2011-7.

In recent years, Congress has increasingly focused on privacy interests involving health, medical, and personal financial information. For example, the ADA, 42 U.S.C. § 12112 (2014), prohibits employers from inquiring about or asking applicants whether such applicant is an individual with a disability. The ADA permits an employer to make pre-employment inquiries into the applicant's ability to perform job-related functions and to require all entering employees to undergo a medical examination *after* an initial offer of employment has been made. But the statute also prohibits employers from requiring current employees to undergo medical examinations unless they are job-related and "consistent with business necessity." *See* § 12112(d)(4) (prohibiting "inquiries of an employee as to whether [an] employee is an individual with a disability or as to the nature or severity of the disability, unless such examination or inquiry is shown to be job-related and consistent with business necessity"); *see also Karraker v. Rent-a-Center, Inc.*, 411 F.3d 831 (7th Cir. 2005) (finding that the administering of a psychological test to job applicants as part of a regime of exams violated the ADA because the test, as administered and applied, could be used to reveal a mental disorder); *Horgan v. Simmons* 704 F. Supp. 2d 814 (N.D. Ill. 2010) (upholding a claim under this section by HIV-positive employee who allegedly was compelled to respond to supervisor inquiries regarding his medical condition); *see also Kroll v. White Lake Ambulance Auth.*, 691 F.3d 809 (6th Cir. 2012) (psychological counseling required of employee was a medical examination because it was designed to reveal a mental health impairment). The ADA also requires employers to treat certain information confidentially, but not all health information an employer obtains from its workers is protected. *See EEOC v. Thrivent Fin. for Lutherans*, 700 F.3d 1044

(7th Cir. 2012) (holding that an inquiry into the reasons for an employee's absence was not a "medical inquiry" within the meaning of § 12112(d)(4)(B) and thus the employer had no need to treat the response, which revealed a history of migraine headaches, as a confidential medical record).

In addition, the Health Insurance Portability and Accountability Act ("HIPAA"), 42 U.S.C. § 300gg (2014), imposes certain conditions on the release of medical records by health care providers. Thus, an employer's requirement that an applicant release medical information often must conform to these requirements. Although HIPAA's medical records mandates may sound mundane, employers potentially have great access to this kind of employee information since they frequently provide health insurance. Thus, HIPAA's requirements have had a significant impact on medical record keeping and confidentiality practices. For a discussion of the ADA, HIPAA, and medical testing and records, *see* Sharona Hoffman, *Employing E-Health: The Impact of Electronic Health Records on the Workplace*, 19 KAN. J. L. & PUB. POL'Y 409 (2010); Sharona Hoffman, *Preplacement Examinations and Job-Relatedness: How to Enhance Privacy and Diminish Discrimination in the Workplace*, 49 KAN. L. REV. 517 (2001).

Another federal statute that provides procedural protections for personal information regarding employees and employment applicants is the Fair Credit Reporting Act, 15 U.S.C. §§ 1681-1681x (2014). It requires an employer to notify employees or applicants if it intends to obtain a consumer report on the individual prepared by a consumer reporting agency, obtain written authorization to review such a report, and notify the person promptly if information in the report may result in a negative employment decision (e.g., a decision not to hire or promote). In addition, the FCRA prohibits use or dissemination of the information for any purpose other than those listed in the act. *See Doe v. Saftig*, No. 09-C-1176, 2011 WL 1792967 (E.D. Wis. 2011) (holding that the plaintiff raised a triable issue of fact on the question of whether a co-worker and employer who had obtained financial information from the plaintiff as part of the application process had shared the information with co-workers for purposes not permitted under the FCRA).

Finally, Congress enacted GINA in 2008, after various versions of the law had been considered for more than a decade. GINA marked the first direct and comprehensive federal response to the discriminatory use of genetic information by insurers and employers.

At first blush, Congress's concern about this issue might seem puzzling, since few employers have actually engaged in this practice, and there have been only a handful of federal cases addressing it. Nevertheless, concerns about such testing had already produced significant regulatory and legislative responses. A majority of states had imposed some kind of restriction on genetic testing by employers, *see* http://www.ncsl.org/programs/health/genetics/ndiscrim.htm, and discrimination in federal employment based on genetic information has been prohibited by Executive Order. *See* Exec. Order No. 13145, 65 Fed. Reg. 6877 (Feb. 8, 2000). Commentators had also expressed grave concerns about the future of such testing, its potential discriminatory effects, and its implications for employee privacy. *See, e.g.*, Pauline T. Kim, *Genetic Discrimination, Genetic Privacy: Rethinking Employee Protections for a Brave New Workplace*, 96 NW. U. L. REV. 1497 (2002); Jennifer Krumm, *Why Congress Must Ban Genetic Testing in the Workplace*, 23 J. LEGAL MED. 491 (2002); Paul M. Schwartz, *Privacy and the Economics of Personal Health Care Information*, 76 TEX. L. REV. 1 (1997).

What is troubling to many about such testing is precisely what makes it potentially appealing to employers; that is, genetic testing could potentially provide them with otherwise hidden, but highly valuable information about employees or applicants—for example, employers and their insurers could discern which employees or applicants are likely to be more costly in terms of potential health problems or other risks. Thus, GINA addresses the widespread concern that genetic testing might be utilized to make preemptive insurance and employment decisions, including screening out those who are genetically predisposed to developing diseases or other medical conditions. It is also designed to ensure that patients are not deterred from genetic testing for medical purposes out of fear that the data might be utilized to their detriment by health insurers and employers. Interestingly, unlike most other kinds of testing addressed in this chapter, legal decision makers have almost uniformly favored the privacy or autonomy interests at stake over employers' interests in gathering useful information.

Title I of the Act addresses genetic discrimination in health insurance. Of particular note is §101, which amends ERISA to generally prohibit health plans from requesting or requiring an individual or family members of an individual to undergo genetic testing and requesting, requiring, or purchasing genetic information about an individual or family member. *See* 29 U.S.C.A. §§ 1132, 1182, 1191 (2014). It also prohibits use of genetic information to establish eligibility for health coverage. *See* 42 U.S.C.A. § 300gg-52. The term "genetic information" is defined as information about an individual's genetic tests, the genetic tests of family members of such individual, and the manifestation of a disease or disorder in family members of such individual. The term "genetic test" means "an analysis of human DNA, RNA, chromosomes, proteins, or metabolites that detects genotypes, mutations, or chromosomal changes." 26 U.S.C.A. § 9832; 42 U.S.C.A. § 2000ff.

Title II prohibits employment discrimination based on genetic information. Among other things, it provides that it is unlawful to discriminate against an employee (or applicant) in the terms and conditions of employment because of genetic information with respect to the employee or to limit or classify employees in any way that would deprive them of employment opportunities or adversely affect their status because of their genetic information. Employers are also prohibited from requesting, requiring, or purchasing genetic information with respect to an employee or a family member of the employee, except in certain specified circumstances. These include where the collection of such information is necessary to comply with other federal laws; is for certain law enforcement purposes; is pursuant to health or genetic services offered by the employer (with consent and pursuant to confidentiality measures and other limitations); or is to be used for genetic monitoring of the biological effects of toxic substances in the workplace, but only if various notice, disclosure, and other requirements are satisfied. *See* 42 U.S.C.A. § 2000ff.

Title II further requires employers possessing any genetic information about an employee to treat such information as a confidential medical record, and prohibits disclosure of genetic information except to the employee or in other narrowly defined circumstances. *See* 42 U.S.C.A. § 2000ff-5. In large part, the coverage, remedies, and procedures are applicable under Title VII. The statute does, however, expressly state that disparate impact on the basis of genetic information does not establish a cause of action. *See* 42 U.S.C.A. § 2000ff-7. Finally, GINA prohibits retaliation against anyone who has opposed any act or practice made unlawful under the act or because such individual made a charge, testified, assisted, or participated in any manner in an investigation or proceeding under the statute. *See* 42 U.S.C.A. § 2000ff-6.

The near-unanimous support for GINA in Congress is noteworthy in an age of bitter disagreements over the federal government's role in regulating the workplace.

It is possible that this support is explained by the near-total absence of evidence of genetic discrimination, which suggests that few constituencies utilized genetic information for employment or insurance purposes. But that explanation does not account for the long delay in passage of the Act, and, more generally, the strong resistance in recent years (in Congress and elsewhere) to enhancing federal employee protections. Why, do you suppose, is there now consensus on the need for a law prohibiting in most circumstances insurers and employers from collecting and using genetic information? Is it for the reasons discussed above, or is there something more intuitive going on?

Of course, strong support for such a prohibition may not translate into successful claims against employers alleged to have utilized genetic information improperly. Indeed, we will not know for years how GINA-based claims will fare in litigation. For an overview of the implications of GINA as well as some commentary critical of GINA's scope or other limitations, *see generally* Bradley A. Areheart, *GINA, Privacy, and Antisubordination*, 46 GA. L. REV. 705 (2012); Pauline T. Kim, *Regulating the Use of Genetic Information: Perspectives from the U.S. Experience*, 31 COMP. LAB. L. & POL'Y J. 693 (2010); Jessica L. Roberts, *Preempting Discrimination: Lessons from the Genetic Information Nondiscrimination Act*, 63 VAND. L. REV. 439 (2010); Jessica L. Roberts, *The Genetic Information Nondiscrimination Act as an Antidiscrimination Law*, 86 NOTRE DAME L. REV. 597 (2011).

b. State Law

No state has a statutory scheme that generally governs privacy in the workplace, but some states have enacted laws that provide specific protections for workers. These laws and the protections they provide vary greatly. As stated above, prior to the passage of GINA, most states had restricted employers from testing employees or prospective employees for genetic traits. Many states also have their own statutory protections for communications and surveillance, some of which extend beyond federal protections. *See, e.g.*, CONN. GEN. STAT. § 31-48B (2014) (prohibiting use of certain electronic surveillance devices). Some states also impose restrictions on other medical inquiries such as HIV testing, *see, e.g.*, WIS. STAT. § 103.15(2) (2013), and commitments to medical treatment facilities, *see, e.g.*, MASS. GEN. LAWS. ch. 151B § 4(9) (2014), or existing or past medical or psychological conditions, *see, e.g.*, MD. CODE ANN. LAB. & EMPL. § 3-701 (2014); *see also Doe v. Walgreens Co.*, 2010 WL 4823212 (Tenn. Ct. App. Nov. 24, 2010) (concluding employee and her husband stated a claim for relief under Tennessee statutes protecting confidential health records and in tort based on allegations that the employee's co-worker unlawfully accessed Walgreen's database and shared confidential information regarding her HIV status with other co-workers, causing the employee to resign due to humiliation).

A number of states have enacted statutes either limiting drug testing or regulating the means by which drug testing is implemented. *See, e.g.*, CONN. GEN. STAT. § 31-51x (2014) (requiring a safety-related interest in drug testing); MINN. STAT. § 181.951(4) (2014) (same). Some state statutes also prohibit employers from asking job applicants questions or making inquiries concerning certain other private matters. *See, e.g.*, NEB. REV. STAT. § 81-1932 (2014) (prohibiting inquiries into sexual practices or marital relationships); OR. REV. STAT. § 659A.885 (2014) (prohibiting inquiries into and use of employees' credit history for employment purposes except in narrowly defined circumstances). Finally, state antidiscrimination laws serve the same intrusion-deterrence function as federal antidiscrimination statutes, and thus protect workers against additional forms of discrimination that implicate private matters, such as discrimination based on sexual orientation, political affiliation, marital status, or physical or psychological conditions not covered under the ADA. The recent legislative activity involving protections for employee and applicant social media accounts and limiting inquiries into criminal and arrest histories are discussed in the next section.

4. Contractual Privacy Protections

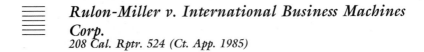

Rulon-Miller v. International Business Machines Corp.
208 Cal. Rptr. 524 (Ct. App. 1985)

RUSHING, Associate Justice.

International Business Machines (IBM) appeals from the judgment entered against it after a jury awarded $100,000 compensatory and $200,000 punitive damages to respondent (Virginia Rulon-Miller) on claims of wrongful discharge and intentional infliction of emotional distress. Rulon-Miller was a low-level marketing manager at IBM in its office products division in San Francisco. Her termination as a marketing manager at IBM came about as a result of an accusation made by her immediate supervisor, defendant Callahan, of a romantic relationship with the manager of a rival office products firm, QYX.

Factual Background

IBM is an international manufacturer of computers, office equipment and telecommunications systems. As well, it offers broad general services in the data processing field. . . . IBM is an employer traditionally thought to provide great security to its employees as well as an environment of openness and dignity. The company is organized into divisions, and each division is, to an extent, independent of others. The company prides itself on providing career opportunities to its employees, and respondent represents a good example of this. [Rulon-Miller started in 1967 as a receptionist in the Philadelphia Data Center, and was promoted through several levels and worked in several departments and locations before enrolling at the IBM sales school in Dallas.] After graduation, she was assigned to San Francisco.

[She was remarkably successful there, being continuously graded highest on the company's evaluation scale, becoming one of the most successful sales persons in the office, and receiving prizes and awards for her sales efforts. Her success was reflected in her being enrolled in the] "Accelerated Career Development Program" which was a way of rewarding certain persons who were seen by their superiors as having management potential. IBM's prediction of her future came true and in 1978 she was named a marketing manager in the office products branch.

IBM knew about respondent's relationship with Matt Blum well before her appointment as a manager. Respondent met Blum in 1976 when he was an account manager for IBM. That they were dating was widely known within the organization. In 1977 Blum left IBM to join QYX, an IBM competitor, and was transferred to Philadelphia. When Blum returned to San Francisco in the summer of 1978, IBM personnel were aware that he and respondent began dating again. This seemed to present no problems to respondent's superiors, as Callahan confirmed when she was promoted to manager. Respondent testified: "Somewhat in passing, Phil said: I heard the other day you were dating Matt Blum, and I said: Oh. And he said, I don't have any problem with that. You're my number one pick. I just want to assure you that you are my selection." The relationship with Blum was also known to Regional Manager Gary Nelson who agreed with Callahan. Neither Callahan nor Nelson raised any issue of conflict of interest because of the Blum relationship.

Respondent flourished in her management position, and the company, apparently grateful for her efforts, gave her a $4,000 merit raise in 1979 and told her that she was doing a good job. A week later, [Callahan] left a message that he wanted to see her.

When she walked into Callahan's office he confronted her with the question of whether she was *dating* Matt Blum. She wondered at the relevance of the inquiry and he said the dating constituted a "conflict of interest," and told her to stop dating Blum or lose her job and said she had a "couple of days to a week" to think about it.[2]

The next day Callahan called her in again, told her "he had made up her mind for her," and when she protested, dismissed her.[3] IBM and Callahan claim that he merely "transferred" respondent to another division.

---

2. Because of the importance of this testimony, we set it out verbatim. Respondent testified: "I walked into Phil's office and he asked me to sit down and he said: Are you dating Matt Blum?

"And I said, What? I was kind of surprised he would ask me and I said: Well, what difference does it make if I'm dating Matt Blum? . . .

"And he said, well, something to the effect: I think we have a conflict of interest, or the appearance of a conflict of interest here.

"And I said: Well, gee, Phil, you've, you've pointed out to me that there are no problems in the office because I am dating Matt Blum, and I don't really understand why that would have any, you know, pertinency to my job. You said I am doing an okay job. I just got a raise.

"And he said: Well, I think we have a conflict of interest. . . .

"He said: No and he said: I'll tell you what. He said: I will give you a couple of days to a week. Think this whole thing over.

"I said: Think what over?

"And he said: You either stop dating Matt Blum or I'm going to take you out of your management job.

"And I was just kind of overwhelmed."

3. Respondent stated the next day she was again summoned to his office where Callahan sat ominously behind a desk cleared of any paperwork, an unusual scenario for any IBM manager.

She further testified: "I walked into Phil's office, and he asked me to shut the door, and he said he was removing me from management effectively immediately. And I said: What?

"And he repeated it. And I was taken aback, I was a little startled, and I think I said: Well, gee, I thought I had a couple of days to a week to think over the situation that we discussed yesterday.

"And he said: I'm making the decision for you.

"And I said: Phil, you've told me that I'm doing a good job. You told me that we are not losing anybody to QYX because I am dating Matt Blum, that we are not losing any equipment to QYX. I just don't understand what bearing dating has to do with my job.

"And he said: We have a conflict of interest. . . .

"I said: Well, what kind of a job would it be?

"And he said: Well, I don't have it, but it will be non-management. You won't be a manager again.

"Pardon me? . . .

"And I think I was getting very upset so I think I said something because of that respect for the individual tenet of IBM's that I really believed in I didn't think that he was following what I thought IBM really did believe in. And he just said: You know, you are removed from management effective immediately.

"And I said: I think you are dismissing me.

"And he said: If you feel that way, give me your I.D. card and your key to the office. [¶] I want you to leave the premises immediately.

"And I was just about to burst into tears, and I didn't cry at work, so I basically fled his office.

"I felt he dismissed me."

Discussion . . .

The test for the court here is substantial evidence and without any question there was substantial evidence to support the jury verdict that the respondent was wrongfully discharged rather than routinely reassigned.

The initial discussion between Callahan and respondent of her relationship with Blum is important. We must accept the version of the facts most favorable to the respondent herein. When Callahan questioned her relationship with Blum, respondent invoked her right to privacy in her personal life relying on existing IBM policies. A threshold inquiry is thus presented whether respondent could reasonably rely on those policies for job protection. Any conflicting action by the company would be wrongful in that it would constitute a violation of her contract rights. [*See Pugh v. See's Candies, Inc.*, reproduced at page 100.]

Under the common law rule codified in Labor Code section 2922, an employment contract of indefinite duration is, in general, terminable at "the will" of either party. This common law rule has been considerably altered by the recognition of the Supreme Court of California that implicit in any such relationship or contract is an underlying principle that requires the parties to deal openly and fairly with one another. *Seaman's Direct Buying Service, Inc. v. Standard Oil Co.* (Cal. 1984) 686 P.2d 1158. This general requirement of fairness has been identified as the covenant of good faith and fair dealing. *Tameny v. Atlantic Richfield Co.* (Cal. 1980) 610 P.2d 1330. The covenant of good faith and fair dealing embraces a number of rights, obligations, and considerations implicit in contractual relations and certain other relationships. At least two of those considerations are relevant herein. The duty of fair dealing by an employer is, simply stated, a requirement that like cases be treated alike. Implied in this, of course, is that the company, if it has rules and regulations, apply those rules and regulations to its employees as well as affording its employees their protection.

As can be seen from an analysis of other cases, this is not in any substantial way a variation from general contract law in California, for if an employee has the right in an employment contract (as distinct from an implied covenant), the courts have routinely given her the benefit of that contract. Thus, the fair dealing portion of the covenant of good faith and fair dealing is at least the right of an employee to the benefit of rules and regulations adopted for his or her protection.

In this case, there is a close question of whether those rules or regulations permit IBM to inquire into the purely personal life of the employee. If so, an attendant question is whether such a policy was applied consistently, particularly as between men and women. The distinction is important because the right of privacy, a constitutional right in California could be implicated by the IBM inquiry. Much of the testimony below concerned what those policies were. The evidence was conflicting on the meaning of certain IBM policies. We observe ambiguity in the application but not in the intent. The "Watson Memo" (so called because it was signed by a former chairman of IBM) provided as follows:

TO ALL IBM MANAGERS:
The line that separates an individual's on-the-job business life from his other life as a private citizen is at times well-defined and at other times indistinct. But the line does exist, and you and I, as managers in IBM, must be able to recognize that line.

I have seen instances where managers took disciplinary measures against employees for actions or conduct that are not rightfully the company's concern. These managers usually justified their decisions by citing their personal code of ethics and morals or by quoting some fragment of company policy that seemed to support their position. Both arguments proved unjust on close examination. What we need, in every case, is balanced judgment which weighs the needs of the business and the rights of the individual.

Our primary objective as IBM managers is to further the business of this company by leading our people properly and measuring quantity and quality of work and effectiveness on the job against clearly set standards of responsibility and compensation. This is performance — and performance is, in the final analysis, the one thing that the company can insist on from everyone.

We have concern with an employee's off-the-job behavior only when it reduces his ability to perform regular job assignments, interferes with the job performance of other employees, or if his outside behavior affects the reputation of the company in a major way. When on-the-job performance is acceptable, I can think of few situations in which outside activities could result in disciplinary action or dismissal.

When such situations do come to your attention, you should seek the advice and counsel of the next appropriate level of management and the personnel department in determining what action — if any — is called for. Action should be taken only when a legitimate interest of the company is injured or jeopardized. Furthermore the damage must be clear beyond reasonable doubt and not based on hasty decisions about what one person might think is good for the company.

IBM's first basic belief is respect for the individual, and the essence of this belief is a strict regard for his right to personal privacy. This idea should never be compromised easily or quickly.

/s/ Tom Watson, Jr.

It is clear that this company policy insures to the employee both the right of privacy and the right to hold a job even though "off-the-job behavior" might not be approved of by the employee's manager.

IBM had adopted policies governing employee conduct. Some of those policies were collected in a document known as the "Performance and Recognition" (PAR) Manual. IBM relies on the following portion of the PAR Manual:

A conflict of interest can arise when an employee is involved in activity for personal gain, which for any reason is in conflict with IBM's business interests. Generally speaking, 'moonlighting' is defined as working at some activity for personal gain outside of your IBM job. If you do perform outside work, you have a special responsibility to avoid any conflict with IBM's business interests.

Obviously, you cannot solicit or perform in competition with IBM product or service offerings. Outside work cannot be performed on IBM time, including "personal" time off. You cannot use IBM equipment, materials, resources, or 'inside' information for outside work. Nor should you solicit business or clients or perform outside work on IBM premises.

Employees must be free of any significant investment or association of their own or of their immediate family's [sic], in competitors or suppliers, which might interfere or be thought to interfere with the independent exercise of their judgment in the best interests of IBM.

This policy of IBM is entitled "Gifts" and appears to be directed at "moonlighting" and soliciting outside business or clients on IBM premises. It prohibits "significant investment" in competitors or suppliers of IBM. It also prohibits "association" with such persons "which might interfere or be thought to interfere with the independent exercise of their judgment in the best interests of IBM."

Callahan based his action against respondent on a "conflict of interest." But the record shows that IBM did not interpret this policy to prohibit a romantic relationship. Callahan admitted that there was no company rule or policy requiring an employee to terminate friendships with fellow employees who leave and join competitors. Gary Nelson, Callahan's superior, also confirmed that IBM had no policy against employees socializing with competitors.

This issue was hotly contested with respondent claiming that the "conflict of interest" claim was a pretext for her unjust termination. Whether it was presented a fact question for the jury.

Do the policies reflected in this record give IBM a right to terminate an employee for a conflict of interest? The answer must be yes, but whether respondent's conduct constituted such was for the jury. We observe that while respondent was successful, her primary job did not give her access to sensitive information which could have been useful to competitors. She was, after all, a seller of typewriters and office equipment. Respondent's brief makes much of the concession by IBM that there was no evidence whatever that respondent had given any information or help to IBM's competitor QYX. It really is no concession at all; she did not have the information or help to give. Even so, the question is one of substantial evidence. The evidence is abundant that there was no conflict of interest by respondent.

It does seem clear that an overall policy established by IBM chairman Watson was one of no company interest in the outside activities of an employee so long as the activities did not interfere with the work of the employee. Moreover, in the last analysis, it may be simply a question for the jury to decide whether, in the application of these policies, the right was conferred on IBM to inquire into the personal or romantic relationships its managers had with others. This is an important question because IBM, in attempting to reargue the facts to us, casts this argument in other terms, namely: that it had a right to inquire even if there was no evidence that such a relationship interfered with the discharge of the employee's duties *because* it had the effect of diminishing the morale of the employees answering to the manager. This is the "Caesar's wife" argument; it is merely a recast of the principal argument and asks the same question in different terms.[5] The same answer holds in both cases: there being no evidence to support the more direct argument, there is no evidence to support the indirect argument.

Moreover, the record shows that the evidence of rumor was not a basis for any decline in the morale of the employees reporting to respondent. Employees Mary Hrize and Wayne Fyvie, who reported to respondent's manager that she was seen at a tea dance at the Hyatt Regency with Matt Blum and also that she was not living at her residence in Marin, did not believe that those rumors in any way impaired her abilities as a manager. In the initial confrontation between respondent and her superior the assertion of the right to be free of inquiries concerning her personal life was based on substantive direct contract rights she had flowing to her from IBM policies.

---

5. What we mean by that is that if you charge that an employee is passing confidential information to a competitor, the question remains whether the charge is true on the evidence available to the person deciding the issue, in this case, the respondent's managers at IBM. If you recast this argument in the form of the "Caesar's wife" argument attempted by IBM, it will be seen that exactly the same question arises, namely, "is it true?" Indeed, the import of the argument is that the rumor, or an unfounded allegation, could serve as a basis for the termination of the employee.

Further, there is no doubt that the jury could have so found and on this record we must assume that they did so find.

[The court went on to find that the jury instructions were proper and that the evidence supports the jury verdict in favor of the plaintiff.] . . .

NOTES

1. *Contractual Privacy Protection.* As with many other terms and conditions of employment, employees may bargain for specific privacy rights. These may come in the form of particular guarantees not to intrude or monitor, accommodations that may implicate privacy interests, or limits on the scope of employment or employer oversight authority that shield certain employee activities or spaces from employer scrutiny. Yet such express terms are rare in individual employment contracts for various reasons, among them limited bargaining power and the failure to foresee privacy-related "problems" at the outset of the relationship. In addition, there is an inevitable tension in a prospective employee demanding greater than normal privacy — the very demand might reveal information the employee would prefer to keep private. Moreover, some of the most common employer requirements that implicate privacy — various forms of testing, disclosures, and intrusive questioning — occur at the application stage, before an employee has a meaningful ability to bargain. And, ironically, some workers who have the incentives and are in a position to bargain for significant freedom from firm intrusions may end up attaining independent contractor rather than employee status. Indeed, as will be discussed below, express terms generally reduce rather than expand privacy protections: It is far more common for employers to demand that employees consent to various kinds of intrusions and monitoring as a condition of employment and for employees to agree to such conditions to secure the job.

Thus, contract-based protections for employees typically come in several other forms. The first is collective bargaining agreements. One high-profile example of addressing privacy interests through collective bargaining involves the limitations on the use of on steroid testing in Major League Baseball: In response to mounting public pressure, the players' union agreed to a strict testing regimen and stiff penalties after years of protecting the players' privacy interest in avoiding testing. *See, e.g.*, Jack Curry, *Baseball Backs Stiffer Penalties for Steroid Use*, N.Y. TIMES, Nov. 16, 2005. These kinds of terms and related procedures are often addressed in the bargaining process and in labor arbitration thereafter. *See generally* Ariana R. Levinson, *Industrial Justice: Privacy Protection for the Employed*: 18 CORNELL J. L. & PUB. POL'Y 609 (2009).

A second kind of contractual protection, albeit a less direct one, flows from the just-cause provisions contained in some employment contracts. Although a just-cause termination provision would not protect against employer intrusions directly, it would provide a remedy for unjustified adverse employment actions resulting from such intrusions. An employer could not, for instance, terminate an employee simply because it does not like the employee's off-site associations or activities. On the other hand, just-cause provisions may create an incentive for an employer to monitor its employees' activities more closely since, to take adverse actions against them, the employer would need evidence showing employee misconduct or some other legitimate business reason for so acting.

A further kind of contractual privacy protection is implied-in-fact, as recognized in *Rulon-Miller*. Indeed, the *Rulon-Miller* court finds a limited but nevertheless enforceable privacy right from various representations of IBM executives and other circumstances. Recall the discussion of implied-in-fact contract terms in Chapter 2. Is the analysis in *Rulon-Miller* consistent with the courts' approach to implied-in-fact terms in other contexts? In what way might the recognition of implied-in-fact right to privacy in the workplace require a different analysis? Do you agree with the court's reasoning and conclusion in this case?

2. *Tort Versus Contract.* Beyond the contract theory discussed in the *Rulon-Miller* decision, might there be a basis for tort liability? In a portion of the opinion not reproduced, the court upheld the jury finding of intentional infliction of emotional distress as well as the award of punitive damages. For reasons discussed in Chapter 5, whether other courts might extend the tort to this kind of circumstance is in doubt. For example, as troubling as Callahan's alleged misconduct may be, does it rise to the level of "utterly intolerable" in a civilized society? Alternatively, would the plaintiff have been able to succeed under the theory of intrusion upon seclusion? In light of that tort's elements, can you see why establishing liability in cases involving conduct or associations away from work that are not secret or protected (say, by a password or limited to secluded locations such as the home) might be very difficult? And, looking back at *Borse*, why might a public policy claim moored to constitutional notions of "freedom of association" or "fundamental rights" be unlikely to succeed?

As it turns out, there are no existing tort theories that easily fit this kind of circumstance. Notably, however, the new Restatement endorses such a theory. Section 7.08 recognizes protected employee autonomy interests in lawful conduct, adherence to religious and other personal beliefs, and belonging to or participating in associations, provided these activities and beliefs do not reference or involve the employer or its business. This section then goes on to provide:

> (b) Unless the employer and employee agree otherwise, an employer is subject to liability for intruding upon an employee's personal autonomy interests if the employer discharges the employee because of the employee's exercise of a personal autonomy interest under § 7.08(a).

> (c) The employer is not liable under § 7.08(b) if it can prove that it had a reasonable good-faith belief that the employee's exercise of her or his autonomy interest interfered with the employer's legitimate business interests, including its orderly operations and reputation in the marketplace.

See RESTATEMENT (THIRD) OF EMPLOYMENT LAW (Proposed Final Draft, April 18, 2014) § 7.08. Still, at least in work settings with heavily lawyered employment agreements, the "unless the employer and employee agree otherwise" caveat very well could be the contracted term that swallows the tort — something we will address again in Part C of this chapter. And notice that the Restatement does not require the employer to be correct that the employee's activities interfered with its legitimate interests, it merely needs to have a "reasonable good-faith belief" to that effect. Apply the Restatement to Rulon-Miller's case. Did she have an autonomy interest in whom she was dating? If so, did IBM have a reasonable, good-faith belief that such dating was a conflict of interest?

3. *Employer Incentives and Employer Policies and Practices After* Rulon-Miller. This case was a victory for the particular employee plaintiff, but the long-term effects may be far less favorable for employees generally. If you were counsel for an employer in the wake of this case, what would you advise your client to do to avoid liability? Would your advice be similar to the advice you would give to avoid the types of implied-in-fact contract claims discussed in Chapter 2 at page 100? What other practices would you advocate your clients adopt to avoid liability for implied-in-fact privacy claims? If employers were to follow such advice, would employees be better off? Do you see parallels between such potential unintended consequences and those that might flow from the Supreme Court's discussion of the reasonable expectation of privacy issue in *Quon*?

B. "BALANCING" EMPLOYEE AND EMPLOYER INTERESTS

If there is a potential source of protection — constitutional, statutory, tort, or contractual — available, and the employer has intruded upon or compromised an employee's privacy interest, the analysis usually focuses next on whether the employer's alleged intrusion and resulting actions were justified. Regardless of the theory, courts often describe this inquiry as one of "balancing" the employer's interests with the privacy interests of the employee. How is this concept recognized or applied in the cases discussed above? Now, consider how the Supreme Court engages in this inquiry in the following case.

National Treasury Employees Union v. Von Raab
489 U.S. 656 (1989)

KENNEDY, J., with REHNQUIST, C.J. and WHITE, BLACKMUN, and O'CONNOR, JJ. joined.

We granted certiorari to decide whether it violates the Fourth Amendment for the United States Customs Service to require a urinalysis test from employees who seek transfer or promotion to certain positions.

I

A

The United States Customs Service, a bureau of the Department of the Treasury, is the federal agency responsible for processing persons, carriers, cargo, and mail into the United States, collecting revenue from imports, and enforcing customs and related laws. An important responsibility of the Service is the interdiction and seizure of contraband, including illegal drugs. In 1987 alone, Customs agents seized drugs with a retail value of nearly $9 billion. In the routine discharge of their duties, many Customs employees have direct contact with those who traffic in drugs for profit. Drug import operations, often directed by sophisticated criminal syndicates, may be effected by violence or its threat. As a necessary response, many Customs operatives carry and use firearms in connection with their official duties.

In December 1985, respondent, the Commissioner of Customs, established a Drug Screening Task Force to explore the possibility of implementing a drug-screening program within the Service. After extensive research and consultation with experts in the field, the task force concluded that "drug screening through urinalysis is technologically reliable, valid and accurate." Citing this conclusion, the Commissioner announced his intention to require drug tests of employees who applied for, or occupied, certain positions within the Service. The Commissioner stated his belief that "Customs is largely drug-free," but noted also that "unfortunately no segment of society is immune from the threat of illegal drug use." Drug interdiction has become the agency's primary enforcement mission, and the Commissioner stressed that "there is no room in the Customs Service for those who break the laws prohibiting the possession and use of illegal drugs."

In May 1986, the Commissioner announced the implementation of the drug-testing program. Drug tests were made a condition of placement or employment for positions that meet one or more of three criteria. The first is direct involvement in drug interdiction or enforcement of related laws, an activity the Commissioner deemed fraught with obvious dangers to the mission of the agency and the lives of Customs agents. The second criterion is a requirement that the incumbent carry firearms, as the Commissioner concluded that "[p]ublic safety demands that employees who carry deadly arms and are prepared to make instant life or death decisions be drug free." The third criterion is a requirement for the incumbent to handle "classified" material, which the Commissioner determined might fall into the hands of smugglers if accessible to employees who, by reason of their own illegal drug use, are susceptible to bribery or blackmail.

After an employee qualifies for a position covered by the Customs testing program, the Service advises him by letter that his final selection is contingent upon successful completion of drug screening. An independent contractor contacts the employee to fix the time and place for collecting the sample. On reporting for the test, the employee must produce photographic identification and remove any outer garments, such as a coat or a jacket, and personal belongings. The employee may produce the sample behind a partition, or in the privacy of a bathroom stall if he so chooses. To ensure against adulteration of the specimen, or substitution of a sample from another person, a monitor of the same sex as the employee remains close at hand to listen for the normal sounds of urination. Dye is added to the toilet water to prevent the employee from using the water to adulterate the sample.

Upon receiving the specimen, the monitor inspects it to ensure its proper temperature and color, places a tamper-proof custody seal over the container, and affixes an identification label indicating the date and the individual's specimen number. The employee signs a chain-of-custody form, which is initialed by the monitor, and the urine sample is placed in a plastic bag, sealed, and submitted to a laboratory.

The laboratory tests the sample for the presence of marijuana, cocaine, opiates, amphetamines, and phencyclidine. Two tests are used. An initial screening test uses the enzyme-multiplied-immunoassay technique (EMIT). Any specimen that is identified as positive on this initial test must then be confirmed using gas chromatography/mass spectrometry (GC/MS). Confirmed positive results are reported to a "Medical Review Officer," "[a] licensed physician . . . who has knowledge of substance abuse disorders and has appropriate medical training to interpret and evaluate an individual's positive test result together with his or her medical history and any other relevant biomedical information." HHS Reg. § 1.2, 53 Fed. Reg. 11980 (1988); HHS Reg. § 2.4(g), 53

Fed. Reg. at 11983. After verifying the positive result, the Medical Review Officer transmits it to the agency.

Customs employees who test positive for drugs and who can offer no satisfactory explanation are subject to dismissal from the Service. Test results may not, however, be turned over to any other agency, including criminal prosecutors, without the employee's written consent.

B

[A union of federal employees and a union official filed suit on behalf of current Customs Service employees who sought covered positions claiming that the drug-testing program violated, inter alia, the Fourth Amendment. The District Court agreed and enjoined the drug-testing program. The Fifth Circuit, although holding that requiring an employee to produce a urine sample for chemical testing is a Fourth Amendment search, found the searches at issue to be reasonable under that Amendment. The Supreme Court first affirmed the Fifth Circuit to the extent it upheld the testing of employees directly involved in drug interdiction or required to carry firearms. However, it vacated the judgment to the extent it upheld the testing of applicants for positions requiring the incumbent to handle classified materials, and it remanded for further proceedings.]

II

In *Skinner v. Railway Labor Executives' Assn.*, 489 U.S. 602, decided today, we held that federal regulations requiring employees of private railroads to produce urine samples for chemical testing implicate the Fourth Amendment, as those tests invade reasonable expectations of privacy. Our earlier cases have settled that the Fourth Amendment protects individuals from unreasonable searches conducted by the Government, even when the Government acts as an employer, *O'Connor v. Ortega*, and, in view of our holding in *Railway Labor Executives* that urine tests are searches, it follows that the Customs Service's drug-testing program must meet the reasonableness requirement of the Fourth Amendment.

While we have often emphasized, and reiterate today, that a search must be supported, as a general matter, by a warrant issued upon probable cause, our decision in *Railway Labor Executives* reaffirms the longstanding principle that neither a warrant nor probable cause, nor, indeed, any measure of individualized suspicion, is an indispensable component of reasonableness in every circumstance. As we note in *Railway Labor Executives*, our cases establish that where a Fourth Amendment intrusion serves special governmental needs, beyond the normal need for law enforcement, it is necessary to balance the individual's privacy expectations against the Government's interests to determine whether it is impractical to require a warrant or some level of individualized suspicion in the particular context.

It is clear that the Customs Service's drug-testing program is not designed to serve the ordinary needs of law enforcement. Test results may not be used in a criminal prosecution of the employee without the employee's consent. The purposes of the program are to deter drug use among those eligible for promotion to sensitive positions within the Service and to prevent the promotion of drug users to those positions.

These substantial interests, no less than the Government's concern for safe rail transportation at issue in *Railway Labor Executives*, present a special need that may justify departure from the ordinary warrant and probable-cause requirements. . . .

B

Even where it is reasonable to dispense with the warrant requirement in the particular circumstances, a search ordinarily must be based on probable cause. Our cases teach, however, that the probable-cause standard "'is peculiarly related to criminal investigations.'" In particular, the traditional probable-cause standard may be unhelpful in analyzing the reasonableness of routine administrative functions, especially where the Government seeks to *prevent* the development of hazardous conditions or to detect violations that rarely generate articulable grounds for searching any particular place or person. Our precedents have settled that, in certain limited circumstances, the Government's need to discover such latent or hidden conditions, or to prevent their development, is sufficiently compelling to justify the intrusion on privacy entailed by conducting such searches without any measure of individualized suspicion. We think the Government's need to conduct the suspicionless searches required by the Customs program outweighs the privacy interests of employees engaged directly in drug interdiction, and of those who otherwise are required to carry firearms.

The Customs Service is our Nation's first line of defense against one of the greatest problems affecting the health and welfare of our population. . . .

Many of the Service's employees are often exposed to this criminal element and to the controlled substances it seeks to smuggle into the country. The physical safety of these employees may be threatened, and many may be tempted not only by bribes from the traffickers with whom they deal, but also by their own access to vast sources of valuable contraband seized and controlled by the Service. The Commissioner indicated below that "Customs [o]fficers have been shot, stabbed, run over, dragged by automobiles, and assaulted with blunt objects while performing their duties." At least nine officers have died in the line of duty since 1974. He also noted that Customs officers have been the targets of bribery by drug smugglers on numerous occasions, and several have been removed from the Service for accepting bribes and for other integrity violations.

It is readily apparent that the Government has a compelling interest in ensuring that front-line interdiction personnel are physically fit, and have unimpeachable integrity and judgment. Indeed, the Government's interest here is at least as important as its interest in searching travelers entering the country. . . . This national interest in self-protection could be irreparably damaged if those charged with safeguarding it were, because of their own drug use, unsympathetic to their mission of interdicting narcotics. A drug user's indifference to the Service's basic mission or, even worse, his active complicity with the malefactors, can facilitate importation of sizable drug shipments or block apprehension of dangerous criminals. The public interest demands effective measures to bar drug users from positions directly involving the interdiction of illegal drugs.

The public interest likewise demands effective measures to prevent the promotion of drug users to positions that require the incumbent to carry a firearm, even if the incumbent is not engaged directly in the interdiction of drugs. Customs employees who may use deadly force plainly "discharge duties fraught with such risks of injury to others that even a momentary lapse of attention can have disastrous consequences." We agree with the Government that the public should not bear the risk that employees who may suffer from impaired perception and judgment will be promoted to positions where they may need to employ deadly force. Indeed, ensuring against the creation of this dangerous risk will itself further Fourth Amendment values, as the use of deadly force may violate the Fourth Amendment in certain circumstances.

Against these valid public interests we must weigh the interference with individual liberty that results from requiring these classes of employees to undergo a urine test. The interference with individual privacy that results from the collection of a urine sample for subsequent chemical analysis could be substantial in some circumstances. We have recognized, however, that the "operational realities of the workplace" may render entirely reasonable certain work-related intrusions by supervisors and co-workers that might be viewed as unreasonable in other contexts. *See O'Connor v. Ortega.* While these operational realities will rarely affect an employee's expectations of privacy with respect to searches of his person, or of personal effects that the employee may bring to the workplace, it is plain that certain forms of public employment may diminish privacy expectations even with respect to such personal searches. Employees of the United States Mint, for example, should expect to be subject to certain routine personal searches when they leave the workplace every day. Similarly, those who join our military or intelligence services may not only be required to give what in other contexts might be viewed as extraordinary assurances of trustworthiness and probity, but also may expect intrusive inquiries into their physical fitness for those special positions.

We think Customs employees who are directly involved in the interdiction of illegal drugs or who are required to carry firearms in the line of duty likewise have a diminished expectation of privacy in respect to the intrusions occasioned by a urine test. Unlike most private citizens or government employees in general, employees involved in drug interdiction reasonably should expect effective inquiry into their fitness and probity. Much the same is true of employees who are required to carry firearms. Because successful performance of their duties depends uniquely on their judgment and dexterity, these employees cannot reasonably expect to keep from the Service personal information that bears directly on their fitness. While reasonable tests designed to elicit this information doubtless infringe some privacy expectations, we do not believe these expectations outweigh the Government's compelling interests in safety and in the integrity of our borders.[2]

2. The procedures prescribed by the Customs Service for the collection and analysis of the requisite samples do not carry the grave potential for "arbitrary and oppressive interference with the privacy and personal security of individuals," *United States v. Martinez-Fuerte,* 428 U.S. 543, 554 (1976), that the Fourth Amendment was designed to prevent. Indeed, these procedures significantly minimize the program's intrusion on privacy interests. Only employees who have been tentatively accepted for promotion or transfer to one of the three categories of covered positions are tested, and applicants know at the outset that a drug test is a requirement of those positions. Employees are also notified in advance of the scheduled sample collection, thus reducing to a minimum any "unsettling show of authority," *Delaware v. Prouse,* 440 U.S. 648, 657 (1979), that may be associated with unexpected intrusions on privacy. There is no direct observation of the act of urination, as the employee may provide a specimen in the privacy of a stall.

Further, urine samples may be examined only for the specified drugs. The use of samples to test for any other substances is prohibited. *See* HHS Reg. § 2.1(c), 53 Fed. Reg. 11980 (1988). And, as the Court of Appeals noted, the combination of EMIT and GC/MS tests required by the Service is highly accurate, assuming proper storage, handling, and measurement techniques. Finally, an employee need not disclose personal medical information to the Government unless his test result is positive, and even then any such information is reported to a licensed physician. Taken together, these procedures significantly minimize the intrusiveness of the Service's drug-screening program.

Without disparaging the importance of the governmental interests that support the suspicionless searches of these employees, petitioners nevertheless contend that the Service's drug-testing program is unreasonable in two particulars. First, petitioners argue that the program is unjustified because it is not based on a belief that testing will reveal any drug use by covered employees. In pressing this argument, petitioners point out that the Service's testing scheme was not implemented in response to any perceived drug problem among Customs employees, and that the program actually has not led to the discovery of a significant number of drug users. Counsel for petitioners informed us at oral argument that no more than 5 employees out of 3,600 have tested positive for drugs. Second, petitioners contend that the Service's scheme is not a "sufficiently productive mechanism to justify [its] intrusion upon Fourth Amendment interests" because illegal drug users can avoid detection with ease by temporary abstinence or by surreptitious adulteration of their urine specimens. These contentions are unpersuasive.

Petitioners' first contention evinces an unduly narrow view of the context in which the Service's testing program was implemented. Petitioners do not dispute, nor can there be doubt, that drug abuse is one of the most serious problems confronting our society today. There is little reason to believe that American workplaces are immune from this pervasive social problem, as is amply illustrated by our decision in *Railway Labor Executives*. Detecting drug impairment on the part of employees can be a difficult task, especially where, as here, it is not feasible to subject employees and their work product to the kind of day-to-day scrutiny that is the norm in more traditional office environments. Indeed, the almost unique mission of the Service gives the Government a compelling interest in ensuring that many of these covered employees do not use drugs even off duty, for such use creates risks of bribery and blackmail against which the Government is entitled to guard. In light of the extraordinary safety and national security hazards that would attend the promotion of drug users to positions that require the carrying of firearms or the interdiction of controlled substances, the Service's policy of deterring drug users from seeking such promotions cannot be deemed unreasonable.

The mere circumstance that all but a few of the employees tested are entirely innocent of wrongdoing does not impugn the program's validity. The same is likely to be true of householders who are required to submit to suspicionless housing code inspections, *see Camara v. Municipal Court of San Francisco*, 387 U.S. 523 (1967), and of motorists who are stopped at the checkpoints we approved in *United States v. Martinez-Fuerte*, 428 U.S. 543 (1976). The Service's program is designed to prevent the promotion of drug users to sensitive positions as much as it is designed to detect those employees who use drugs. Where, as here, the possible harm against which the Government seeks to guard is substantial, the need to prevent its occurrence furnishes an ample justification for reasonable searches calculated to advance the Government's goal.[3]

---

3. The point is well illustrated also by the Federal Government's practice of requiring the search of all passengers seeking to board commercial airliners, as well as the search of their carry-on luggage, without any basis for suspecting any particular passenger of an untoward motive. Applying our precedents dealing with administrative searches, *see, e.g., Camara v. Municipal Court of San Francisco*, 387 U.S. 523 (1967), the lower courts that have considered the question have consistently concluded that such searches are reasonable under the Fourth Amendment. . . . It is true, as counsel for petitioners pointed out at oral argument, that these air piracy precautions were adopted in response to an observable national and international hijacking crisis. Yet we would not suppose that, if the validity of these searches be conceded, the Government would be precluded from conducting them absent a demonstration of danger as to any particular airport or airline. It is

We think petitioners' second argument — that the Service's testing program is ineffective because employees may attempt to deceive the test by a brief abstention before the test date, or by adulterating their urine specimens — overstates the case. As the Court of Appeals noted, addicts may be unable to abstain even for a limited period of time, or may be unaware of the "fade-away effect" of certain drugs. More importantly, the avoidance techniques suggested by petitioners are fraught with uncertainty and risks for those employees who venture to attempt them. A particular employee's pattern of elimination for a given drug cannot be predicted with perfect accuracy, and, in any event, this information is not likely to be known or available to the employee. Petitioners' own expert indicated below that the time it takes for particular drugs to become undetectable in urine can vary widely depending on the individual, and may extend for as long as 22 days. Thus, contrary to petitioners' suggestion, no employee reasonably can expect to deceive the test by the simple expedient of abstaining after the test date is assigned. Nor can he expect attempts at adulteration to succeed, in view of the precautions taken by the sample collector to ensure the integrity of the sample. In all the circumstances, we are persuaded that the program bears a close and substantial relation to the Service's goal of deterring drug users from seeking promotion to sensitive positions.[4]

In sum, we believe the Government has demonstrated that its compelling interests in safeguarding our borders and the public safety outweigh the privacy expectations of employees who seek to be promoted to positions that directly involve the interdiction of illegal drugs or that require the incumbent to carry a firearm. We hold that the testing of these employees is reasonable under the Fourth Amendment.

C

We are unable, on the present record, to assess the reasonableness of the Government's testing program insofar as it covers employees who are required "to handle classified material." We readily agree that the Government has a compelling interest in protecting truly sensitive information from those who, "under compulsion of circumstances or for other reasons, . . . might compromise [such] information." We also agree that employees who seek promotions to positions where they would handle sensitive information can be required to submit to a urine test under the Service's screening program, especially if the positions covered under this category require

---

sufficient that the Government have a compelling interest in preventing an otherwise pervasive societal problem from spreading to the particular context.

Nor would we think, in view of the obvious deterrent purpose of these searches, that the validity of the Government's airport screening program necessarily turns on whether significant numbers of putative air pirates are actually discovered by the searches conducted under the program. . . . By far the overwhelming majority of those persons who have been searched, like Customs employees who have been tested under the Service's drug-screening scheme, have proved entirely innocent — only 42,000 firearms have been detected during the same period. When the Government's interest lies in deterring highly hazardous conduct, a low incidence of such conduct, far from impugning the validity of the scheme for implementing this interest, is more logically viewed as a hallmark of success.

4. Indeed, petitioners' objection is based on those features of the Service's program — the provision of advance notice and the failure of the sample collector to observe directly the act of urination — that contribute significantly to diminish the program's intrusion on privacy. Thus, under petitioners' view, "the testing program would be more likely to be constitutional if it were more pervasive and more invasive of privacy."

background investigations, medical examinations, or other intrusions that may be expected to diminish their expectations of privacy in respect of a urinalysis test. . . .

It is not clear, however, whether the category defined by the Service's testing directive encompasses only those Customs employees likely to gain access to sensitive information. Employees who are tested under the Service's scheme include those holding such diverse positions as "Accountant," "Accounting Technician," "Animal Caretaker," "Attorney (All)," "Baggage Clerk," "Co-op Student (All)," "Electric Equipment Repairer," "Mail Clerk/Assistant," and "Messenger." We assume these positions were selected for coverage under the Service's testing program by reason of the incumbent's access to "classified" information, as it is not clear that they would fall under either of the two categories we have already considered. Yet it is not evident that those occupying these positions are likely to gain access to sensitive information, and this apparent discrepancy raises in our minds the question whether the Service has defined this category of employees more broadly than is necessary to meet the purposes of the Commissioner's directive.

We cannot resolve this ambiguity on the basis of the record before us, and we think it is appropriate to remand the case. . . . [T]he Court of Appeals should examine the criteria used by the Service in determining what materials are classified and in deciding whom to test under this rubric. [T]he court should also consider pertinent information bearing upon the employees' privacy expectations, as well as the supervision to which these employees are already subject.

Justice SCALIA, with whom Justice STEVENS joins, dissenting.

The issue in this case is not whether Customs Service employees can constitutionally be denied promotion, or even dismissed, for a single instance of unlawful drug use, at home or at work. They assuredly can. The issue here is what steps can constitutionally be taken to *detect* such drug use. The Government asserts it can demand that employees perform "an excretory function traditionally shielded by great privacy," *Skinner v. Railway Labor Executives' Ass'n*, while "a monitor of the same sex . . . remains close at hand to listen for the normal sounds," and that the excretion thus produced be turned over to the Government for chemical analysis. The Court agrees that this constitutes a search for purposes of the Fourth Amendment — and I think it obvious that it is a type of search particularly destructive of privacy and offensive to personal dignity.

Until today this Court had upheld a bodily search separate from arrest and without individualized suspicion of wrongdoing only with respect to prison inmates, relying upon the uniquely dangerous nature of that environment. *See Bell v. Wolfish*, 441 U.S. 520, 558-60 (1979). Today, in *Skinner*, we allow a less intrusive bodily search of railroad employees involved in train accidents. I joined the Court's opinion there because the demonstrated frequency of drug and alcohol use by the targeted class of employees, and the demonstrated connection between such use and grave harm, rendered the search a reasonable means of protecting society. I decline to join the Court's opinion in the present case because neither frequency of use nor connection to harm is demonstrated or even likely. In my view the Customs Service rules are a kind of immolation of privacy and human dignity in symbolic opposition to drug use.

The Court's opinion in the present case . . . will be searched in vain for real evidence of a real problem that will be solved by urine testing of Customs Service employees. Instead, there are assurances that "[t]he Customs Service is our Nation's first line of defense against one of the greatest problems affecting the health and welfare of our population"; that "[m]any of the Service's employees are often exposed to [drug smugglers] and to the controlled substances [they seek] to smuggle into the country"; that "Customs officers have been the targets of bribery by drug smugglers on numerous occasions, and several have been removed from the Service for accepting bribes and other integrity violations"; that "the Government has a compelling interest in ensuring that front-line interdiction personnel are physically fit, and have unimpeachable integrity and judgment"; that the "national interest in self-protection could be irreparably damaged if those charged with safeguarding it were, because of their own drug use, unsympathetic to their mission of interdicting narcotics"; and that "the public should not bear the risk that employees who may suffer from impaired perception and judgment will be promoted to positions where they may need to employ deadly force." To paraphrase Churchill, all this contains much that is obviously true, and much that is relevant; unfortunately, what is obviously true is not relevant, and what is relevant is not obviously true. The only pertinent points, it seems to me, are supported by nothing but speculation, and not very plausible speculation at that. It is not apparent to me that a Customs Service employee who uses drugs is significantly more likely to be bribed by a drug smuggler, any more than a Customs Service employee who wears diamonds is significantly more likely to be bribed by a diamond smuggler — unless, perhaps, the addiction to drugs is so severe, and requires so much money to maintain, that it would be detectable even without benefit of a urine test. Nor is it apparent to me that Customs officers who use drugs will be appreciably less "sympathetic" to their drug-interdiction mission, any more than police officers who exceed the speed limit in their private cars are appreciably less sympathetic to their mission of enforcing the traffic laws. (The only difference is that the Customs officer's individual efforts, if they are irreplaceable, can theoretically affect the availability of his own drug supply — a prospect so remote as to be an absurd basis of motivation.) Nor, finally, is it apparent to me that urine tests will be even marginally more effective in preventing gun-carrying agents from risking "impaired perception and judgment" than is their current knowledge that, if impaired, they may be shot dead in unequal combat with unimpaired smugglers — unless, again, their addiction is so severe that no urine test is needed for detection.

What is absent in the Government's justifications — notably absent, revealingly absent, and as far as I am concerned dispositively absent — is the recitation of *even a single instance* in which any of the speculated horribles actually occurred: an instance, that is, in which the cause of bribe-taking, or of poor aim, or of unsympathetic law enforcement, or of compromise of classified information, was drug use. Although the Court points out that several employees have in the past been removed from the Service for accepting bribes and other integrity violations, and that at least nine officers have died in the line of duty since 1974, there is no indication whatever that these incidents were related to drug use by Service employees. Perhaps concrete evidence of the severity of a problem is unnecessary when it is so well known that courts can almost take judicial notice of it; but that is surely not the case here. The Commissioner of Customs himself has stated that he "believe[s] that Customs is largely drug-free," that "[t]he extent of illegal drug use by Customs employees was not the reason for establishing this program," and that he "hope[s] and expect[s] to receive reports of very few positive findings through drug screening." The test results have fulfilled those hopes and expectations. According to the Service's counsel, out of 3,600 employees tested, no more than 5 tested positive for drugs.

The Court's response to this lack of evidence is that "[t]here is little reason to believe that American workplaces are immune from [the] pervasive social problem" of drug abuse. Perhaps such a generalization would suffice if the workplace at issue could produce such catastrophic social harm that no risk whatever is tolerable — the secured areas of a nuclear power plant, for example, *see Rushton v. Nebraska Pub. Power District*, 844 F.2d 562 (CA8 1988). But if such a generalization suffices to justify demeaning bodily searches, without particularized suspicion, to guard against the bribing or blackmailing of a law enforcement agent, or the careless use of a firearm, then the Fourth Amendment has become frail protection indeed. In *Skinner, Bell, T.L.O.*, and *Martinez-Fuerte*, we took pains to establish the existence of special need for the search or seizure — a need based not upon the existence of a "pervasive social problem" combined with speculation as to the effect of that problem in the field at issue, but rather upon well-known or well-demonstrated evils *in that field*, with well-known or well-demonstrated consequences. . . .

[I]n extending approval of drug testing to that category consisting of employees who carry firearms, the Court exposes vast numbers of public employees to this needless indignity. Logically, of course, if those who carry guns can be treated in this fashion, so can all others whose work, if performed under the influence of drugs, may endanger others — automobile drivers, operators of other potentially dangerous equipment, construction workers, school crossing guards. A similarly broad scope attaches to the Court's approval of drug testing for those with access to "sensitive information." Since this category is not limited to Service employees with drug interdiction duties, nor to "sensitive information" specifically relating to drug traffic, today's holding apparently approves drug testing for all federal employees with security clearances — or, indeed, for all federal employees with valuable confidential information to impart. Since drug use is not a particular problem in the Customs Service, employees throughout the Government are no less likely to violate the public trust by taking bribes to feed their drug habit, or by yielding to blackmail. Moreover, there is no reason why this super-protection against harms arising from drug use must be limited to public employees; a law requiring similar testing of private citizens who use dangerous instruments such as guns or cars, or who have access to classified information, would also be constitutional.

There is only one apparent basis that sets the testing at issue here apart from all these other situations — but it is not a basis upon which the Court is willing to rely. I do not believe for a minute that the driving force behind these drug-testing rules was any of the feeble justifications put forward by counsel here and accepted by the Court. The only plausible explanation, in my view, is what the Commissioner himself offered in the concluding sentence of his memorandum to Customs Service employees announcing the program: "Implementation of the drug screening program would set an important example in our country's struggle with this most serious threat to our national health and security." Or as respondent's brief to this Court asserted: "[I]f a law enforcement agency and its employees do not take the law seriously, neither will the public on which the agency's effectiveness depends." What better way to show that the Government is serious about its "war on drugs" than to subject its employees on the front line of that war to this invasion of their privacy and affront to their dignity? To be sure, there is only a slight chance that it will prevent some serious public harm resulting from Service employee drug use, but it will show to the world that the Service is "clean," and — most important of all — will demonstrate the determination of the Government to eliminate this scourge of our society! I think it obvious that this justification is unacceptable; that the impairment of individual liberties cannot be the means of making a point; that symbolism, even symbolism for so worthy a cause as the abolition of unlawful drugs, cannot validate an otherwise unreasonable search. . . .

NOTES

1. *Sources of Protection.* Since *Von Raab* involves a public employer the Fourth Amendment provided the source of privacy protection. Again, however, as *Borse* and the notes that followed suggested, the public policy and intrusion upon seclusion torts provide possible theories of liability for drug testing. Statutory protections also exist in some states. And, as described elsewhere in this chapter, other invasive procedures and inquiries utilized in screening applicants or existing employees run afoul of statutory protections, including genetic testing, some medical testing, and polygraph examinations.

Still other intrusive screening procedures have resulted in liability. One that has been the subject of a large number of legal challenges in the last century is (paper and pencil) psychological testing. Although not physically invasive like drug or other types of physical testing, psychological testing arguably is intrusive because it tends to include questions about intimate matters, including religious beliefs and sexual desires and preferences. In *Soroka v. Dayton Hudson Corp.,* 1 Cal. Rptr. 2d 77 (Ct. App. 1991), the court found in favor of a group of applicants for security guard jobs at Target who challenged a testing program on state constitutional grounds and pursuant to state statutes protecting against discrimination based on religious beliefs and political affiliations. Although these bases for private-sector protection are California specific, a small number of other states directly restrict employer use of paper and pencil honesty testing, *see, e.g.,* MASS. GEN. LAWS ch. 149, § 19B (2014) and R.I. GEN. LAWS § 28-6.1-1 (2014). However, there may be other more indirect forms of protection; for example, referring back to the possible sources of privacy protection already discussed in this chapter, might claimants today have other potential theories of liability against Target in these circumstances? *See, e.g., Karraker v. Rent-a-Center, Inc.,* 411 F.3d 831 (7th Cir. 2005) (finding that the administering of a psychological test to job applicants as part of a regime of exams violated the ADA because the test, as administered and applied, could be used to reveal a mental disorder); *see generally* Scott P. Kramer, *Why Is the Company Asking About My Fear of Spiders? A New Look at Evaluating Whether an Employer-Provided Personality Test Constitutes a Medical Examination Under the ADA,* 2007 U. ILL. L. REV. 1279 (2007). David C. Yamada, *The Regulation of Pre-Employment Honesty Testing: Striking a Temporary(?) Balance Between Self-Regulation and Prohibition,* 39 WAYNE L. REV. 1549 (1993); *see also* Susan J. Stabile, *The Use of Personality Tests as a Hiring Tool: Is the Benefit Worth the Cost?,* 4 U. PA. J. LAB. & EMP. L. 279 (2002) (critiquing the use of personality tests as a screening tool).

2. *Comparing* Von Raab *with* O'Connor *and* Quon. The *Von Raab* court relies on *O'Connor* and finds that neither a warrant nor probable cause is needed for the government's drug-testing program. Yet *Von Raab*'s "reasonableness" inquiry may not be consistent with the standards *O'Connor* describes. While *O'Connor* suggested that the employer must merely demonstrate the reasonableness of its privacy intrusion in terms of ends and means, the *Von Raab* court uses language such as "compelling interest" in upholding most aspects of the drug-testing program and suggesting that

one portion of the program may be broader than "necessary." The Court's use of such language suggests that some more rigorous level of scrutiny is in play, although the Court never expressly says as much. Isn't this inconsistent with the deferential approach apparent in *Quon*, especially that Court's rejection of the "least intrusive means" inquiry?

One explanation, consistent with at least some of the language in *Quon* (*see* Note 5, page 340), is that the reasonableness inquiry itself involves a balancing of the interests at stake. In other words, whether the employer's actions are reasonable is determined by using a sliding scale: the more serious the intrusion into an employee's privacy, the more compelling the employer's justification must be. Thus, to be "reasonable," searches involving bodily fluids, including urine testing, must be justified by more substantial governmental interests than other, less serious intrusions. This may also explain why the *Von Raab* majority went out of its way to emphasize that the urine testing in this circumstance was a somewhat less serious intrusion (involving a "diminished" expectation of privacy) than such testing might be in other contexts. Is there a countervailing suggestion in *Quon* that the intrusion at issue there — the review of the text messages — was a less serious one? Would you rather have your bodily fluids tested or have your supervisor rummage through your employer-provided computer?

Of course, Justice Scalia might find all of this particularly ironic, since, in his view, the government failed to demonstrate *any* pressing need for such a testing program. His objections bring us back yet again to issues of deference; it may matter less what level of scrutiny is articulated than how willing the courts are to accept the government's proffered reasons for acting. In your view, was the *Von Raab* majority correct to accept the interests on which the government relied?

3. *Deference to the Employer's Interest.* What are the interests articulated by the government in *Von Raab*? As Scalia's dissent hints, perceived importance alone may be dispositive. In other words, even though courts may suggest that they are "balancing" the employer interest against the interest of the employee to be free from intrusions into his or her sphere of privacy, if the employer is able to *articulate* (not necessarily demonstrate with evidence) a sufficiently compelling justification, the court is likely to uphold all but the most severe intrusions. For example, drug-testing programs involving employees engaged in inherently dangerous work or work that puts third parties at risk of physical harm are almost always upheld, regardless of whether the policy arises in the public or private context and regardless of the nature of the underlying claim. *See, e.g., Von Raab*; *Skinner v. Ry. Labor Executives' Ass'n*, 489 U.S. 602 (1989) (upholding drug testing of railroad employees who had been involved in an accident after detailing just how intrusive urinalysis testing is); *Krieg v. Seybold*, 481 F.3d 512 (7th Cir. 2007) (upholding random drug testing of city sanitation worker who operated large vehicles and equipment); *Luedtke v. Nabors Alaska Drilling, Inc.*, 768 P.2d 1123 (Alaska 1989) (upholding drug testing for oil rig workers); *Kramer v. City of Jersey City*, 2010 U.S. Dist. LEXIS 56449 (D.N.J. 2010) (finding no constitutional or other violation for drug-testing regimen for steroid use among police officers); *Robinson v. City of Seattle*, 10 P.3d 452 (Wash. Ct. App. 2000) (holding that a government employer has a compelling interest in drug testing employees in positions that are truly safety sensitive but no such interest in testing other employees). Similarly, when the employer has well-founded, particularized suspicion that an employee has engaged in unlawful or otherwise harmful conduct, courts almost always uphold resulting searches and the monitoring of work spaces and communications. *See, e.g., United States v. Slanina*, 283 F.3d 670 (5th Cir. 2002) (upholding employer's and law enforcement's searches of employee's computers after employer discovered links to Web sites containing child pornography). And in many settings, the degree of deference the court gives to the employer's assertions regarding the importance of the interests to be served will be dispositive.

When courts perceive the articulated reasons as less compelling, they are more likely to scrutinize closely the employer's methods and show concern for the employee interests. The interests articulated in the *Soroka* case discussed above — a preference for hiring people with "good judgment and emotional stability" to be unarmed store security guards, 1 Cal. Rptr. 2d at 79 — and perhaps the one underlying the testing in *Borse* may be examples of this. Indeed, proffered employer justifications lie along a continuum. Such justifications may include, for example, protecting public health and safety, protecting worker health and safety, addressing known criminal conduct, preventing criminal conduct, protecting employer tangible and intangible property, preventing other types of employee misconduct or shirking, determining who is better qualified for a job or promotion, protecting the employer's public image, and improving workplace morale or efficiency. How would you order the interests in this listing to reflect a continuum from more to less compelling?

4. Negligent Hiring and Retention. Another interest employers sometimes advance is the avoidance of civil liability. In a variety of contexts, employers may be liable for failing to prevent employee conduct that causes harm to third parties or other employees. *See, e.g., Doe v. XYC Corp.*, 887 A.2d 1156 (N.J. App. Div. 2005) (holding an employer potentially liable to daughter of employee who posted nude photographs of her on the Internet after employer was placed on notice that employee was viewing graphic forms of pornography — although not necessarily child pornography — on his workplace computer; there was a triable claim that the employer failed to exercise reasonable care to report and/or take effective action to stop employee's Internet activities). Sometimes avoiding such harm may require greater monitoring of employee conduct or intrusions into private or intimate matters. *See generally* Niloofar Nejat-Bina, Comment, *Employers as Vigilant Chaperones Armed with Dating Waivers: The Intersection of Unwelcomeness and Employer Liability in Hostile Work Environment Sexual Harassment Law*, 20 Berkeley J. Emp. & Lab. L. 325 (1999) (discussing potential employer liability for sexual harassment when supervisors become romantically involved with subordinates and employer responses thereto).

Along these lines, in recent years there has been growth in the number of negligent hiring, supervision, and retention claims brought against employers by third parties (including co-workers) injured by the employer's workers. Although the elements of negligence theories vary, most are based on section 213 of the Restatement (Second) of Agency (1957), which provides that an employer is liable if it is negligent or reckless:

> (b) in the employment of improper persons or instrumentalities in work involving risk of harm to others;
> (c) in the supervision of the activity; or
> (d) in permitting, or failing to prevent, negligent or other tortious conduct by persons, whether or not his servants or agents, upon premises or with instrumentalities under his control.

See also Restatement (Second) of Torts § 317 (1965) (providing for a negligent supervision claim where the employer fails to exercise reasonable care to prevent an employee from intentionally harming others on the employer's premises or in other circumstances in which the employer can exercise control). Liability under these theories is often difficult to establish. For example, to prevail on a negligent hiring where a third party is harmed by an employee's criminal act, the plaintiff normally must establish not only that the employer failed to exercise ordinary care in selecting the employee — that is, failed to perform an adequate background check — but also that the exercise of such care would have made the type of crime the employee later committed reasonably foreseeable. *See, e.g., McCafferty v. Preiss Enterprises, Inc.,* 534 Fed. App'x 726 (10th Cir. 2013) (holding that plaintiff failed to establish a negligent supervision claim because, for activities such as sexual misconduct that fall outside the scope of his employment, the employer is liable only if the conduct occurs on its premises or through use of its chattels, which was not true here); *Monroe v. Universal Health Servs., Inc.,* 596 S.E.2d 604 (Ga. 2004) (finding that, although the mental health assistant who sexually assaulted plaintiff — a patient of employer — had provided incomplete or inaccurate information during his application process, employer did not breach its duty of care because the application and background investigation process had not revealed a risk of violent or criminal activity); *Saine v. Comcast Cablevision of Arkansas, Inc.,* 126 S.W.3d 339 (Ark. 2003) (finding no cognizable negligent hiring claim because employer had performed an adequate background check before hiring cable repair employee).

Nevertheless, these sources of potential liability create strong incentives for employers to engage in robust background screening and testing of applicants, establish intrusive techniques for monitoring current employees, and conduct very thorough investigations of employees alleged to have engaged in tortious or wrongful conduct. *See, e.g., Saine,* 126 S.W.3d at 343-45 (while adequate background check precluded negligent hiring claim, finding material issues of fact with regard to negligent supervision and retention claims because employer had notice of complaints of inappropriate conduct of employee toward another female cable customer prior to his rape and attempted murder of plaintiff).

5. *The Employee's Interest.* As discussed in each of the cases in this chapter, in order for an employee or applicant to have a cognizable breach of privacy claim (of any kind), he or she must have a legitimate or reasonable expectation of privacy in the sphere upon which the employer intruded. Without such an expectation, there is nothing to "balance" against the employer's interest. As discussed above, establishing the existence of such an expectation may often be the employee's most difficult hurdle.

Assuming the worker can establish such an expectation, however, the value the court places on the interest, and hence, the scrutiny the court will apply, may vary by the perceived intrusiveness of the employer's conduct. *See, e.g., Anchorage Police Dep't Empls. Ass'n v. Municipality of Anchorage,* 24 P.3d 547 (Alaska 2001) (upholding portions of drug-testing program linked to hiring, promotion, and investigating accidents but striking down random drug testing in part because it is more intrusive); *Robinson v. City of Seattle,* 10 P.3d 452 (Wash. Ct. App. 2000) (stating that government intrusions into certain personal information or confidentiality interests receive rational basis scrutiny while infringements of the right to autonomy warrant strict scrutiny). As *Von Raab* suggests, intrusions involving bodily functions or integrity — drug and medical testing, polygraph testing, strip searches, video surveillance of locker rooms or restrooms — may be subjected to the most rigorous scrutiny. *See, e.g., Carter v. County of Los Angeles,* 770 F. Supp. 2d 1042 (C.D. Cal. 2011) (holding public works department's covert video surveillance of its dispatch room —

locked and inaccessible to the public—violated employees' Fourth Amendment and California constitutional rights despite the fact that the department installed the camera in response to alleged employee misconduct).

Slightly less intrusive conduct, such as questioning applicants about intimate matters, monitoring personal communications at work, audio surveillance, and searches of personal work spaces and stored data, may receive somewhat less scrutiny. Still less intrusive practices, such as overt video surveillance of less personal work areas, periodically auditing work-related communications (as in *Quon*), and monitoring or searches of less personal spaces and data compilations, often receive the least scrutiny.

Even if there is general agreement about which employer activities are more or less intrusive, and thus, which should receive greater scrutiny, "balancing" such intrusions against employer interests remains elusive. Despite common references to that term, courts and other lawmakers avoid the unwieldy task of attempting to weigh and then balance these competing interests in particular contexts. For example, although genetic and polygraph tests could produce a number of efficiencies for employers, protect employees themselves from various risks, and even benefit the public in some circumstances, legislative enactments addressing these forms of testing often include outright prohibitions across categories of employment, rather than provide for any type of balancing of interests in particular cases.

6. *The "Nexus" Requirement.* Once it is determined that there are both legitimate employer and employee privacy interests at stake, courts—including the *Von Raab* and *Soroka* courts—often focus on the nexus between the articulated interest and the nature of the intrusion. While *Quon* used different terminology, it too acknowledged that reasonableness of the intrusion is measured not just by the work-related purpose of the search, but also by the relationship between that purpose and the means utilized (i.e., the scope of the search). Thus, under the analytical framework provided in each of these cases, intrusions justified for reasons of equal importance may not receive equal treatment by the courts because the means chosen in one context might be more closely tailored to serve the end than in the other context. However, some decisions diverge on how closely the means must be tied to the purpose. Recall that *Quon* rejected arguments that the employer must utilize the least intrusive means, holding that the review of the text messages was reasonable despite the availability of less intrusive alternatives. Contrast that analysis with *Soroka*, in which the court stated that the employer "must demonstrate a compelling interest and must establish that the test serves a job-related purpose" and then found that the employer had made no showing—nothing beyond generalized assertions—that the intrusive questions in the psychological test had any bearing on the emotional stability or on the ability of a security guard to fulfill the job's responsibilities. *See Soroka*, 1 Cal. Rptr. 2d at 86. Thus, *Soroka* suggested that intrusions may be held unlawful not only when they are clearly overbroad, or but also when they are unnecessarily broad—that is, when the same legitimate employer interest may be served as effectively by less intrusive means. Still, much may depend on the deference courts are willing to give employers when it comes to this nexus; that is, courts may vary in how demanding they may be in requiring narrow tailoring. Ultimately, how much deference should the employer's chosen means be given?

7. *The Limits on Drug Testing.* On the same day the Supreme Court decided *Von Raab*, it decided *Skinner v. Ry. Labor Executives' Ass'n*, 489 U.S. 602 (1989), which upheld as permissible under the Fourth Amendment mandatory blood and urine tests, for alcohol and drugs, of railroad employees who have been involved in railroad accidents. In both cases, the majority focused on the safety-sensitive or high-risk nature of the positions. Since these two cases were decided, lower courts have routinely upheld mandatory drug-testing programs (random or otherwise) in safety- or security-sensitive positions in public workplaces and pursuant to regulatory requirements in some private workplaces.

However, in *Chandler v. Miller*, 520 U.S. 305 (1997), the Supreme Court struck down a Georgia law that required candidates for some state offices to take a drug test to qualify for election. In so doing, the Court distinguished *Von Raab* and *Skinner*, noting that Georgia had presented no evidence that the state's elected officials performed the kinds of high-risk or safety-sensitive tasks that the employees in the previous cases performed. The Court then rejected the symbolic value — that is, commitment to the fight against drug abuse — of such a testing program as being sufficiently important to justify the intrusion. Recall Justice Scalia's opinion in *Von Raab*. *See also National Federation of Federal Employees v. Vilsack*, 681 F.3d 483 (D.C. Cir. 2012) (concluding that the secretary of agriculture had not shown a genuine safety concern or record of drug use that demonstrated the "special needs" necessary to justify random drug testing of all Forest Service Job Corps Center employees).

Courts recognizing breach of privacy claims for drug testing in the private employer context have likewise tended to focus on the nature of the employee's job and, hence, the importance of the testing program. *See, e.g., Luedtke*, 768 P.2d at 1123; *Hennessey v. Coastal Eagle Point Oil Co.*, 609 A.2d 11 (N.J. 1992).

Occasionally, however, the methods or procedures utilized in drug testing have been invalidated even in safety-sensitive contexts. *See, e.g., Anchorage Police Dep't Empls. Ass'n*, 24 P.3d at 557-60 (striking down only random portion of drug-testing program); *AFGE v. Sullivan*, 744 F. Supp. 294 (D.D.C. 1990) (enjoining testing regulations in part because government articulated insufficient reasons for requiring urine samples be provided under direct visual observation); *see generally* John Gilliom, Surveillance, Privacy and the Law: Employee Drug Testing and the Politics of Social Control (1994); Pauline T. Kim, *Collective and Individual Approaches to Protecting Employee Privacy: The Experience with Workplace Drug Testing*, 66 La. L. Rev. 1009 (2006); Lindsay J. Taylor, *Congressional Attempts to "Strike Out" Steroids: Constitutional Concerns About the Clean Sports Act*, 49 Ariz. L. Rev (2007); John B. Wefing, *Employer Drug Testing: Disparate Judicial and Legislative Responses*, 63 Alb. L. Rev. 799 (2000). In light of this backdrop, and assuming testing procedures themselves are reasonable, what classes of employees are unlikely to prevail in challenges against mandatory drug-testing requirements? Any employee with access to a firearm? Any employee working with hazardous materials or chemicals? Any employee who drives a motor vehicle? Any teacher?

8. *Applicant vs. Employee.* Some statutory and common-law privacy protections draw a distinction between applicants for employment and employees — protecting the latter to a greater extent than the former. *Soroka* recognizes, but ultimately rejects, the possible distinction between employees and applicants. Are there good reasons to protect employees to a greater extent than applicants? Are there ways in which employees are more vulnerable than the applicants? How about vice versa?

Even if breach of privacy claims are equally available to applicants, establishing such a breach may be more difficult for them. An applicant may not have the same expectation of privacy as current employees. Also, it is highly unlikely that an applicant could establish a contract-based privacy claim, since, at the application stage, no express or implied contract will have been formed. Moreover, the "catch-22" described in Note 6 on page 353 is even more pronounced for applicants than employees because applicants must consent even to be considered for the job but such consent may bar his or her claims.

Note on Off-site Activities Including Associational Preferences and Internet Use

A broad array of off-site activities or lifestyle choices — from political and religious affiliations, to intimate relationships, to hobbies and leisure activities, to consumption choices (food, alcohol, tobacco, etc.) might conflict with employer preferences and affect their hiring, retention, and promotion decisions. As discussed in the last section, public sector workers enjoy some, albeit limited, constitutional and statutory protections in this context. And there have been a few new developments that suggest their robustness. For example, utilizing monitoring devices to track employee activity away from work has garnered recent attention. Indeed, in the wake of *United States v. Jones*, 132 S. Ct. 945 (2012), in which the Supreme Court held that placing a global positioning (GPS) device on a vehicle constitutes a search for Fourth Amendment purposes, the New York Court of Appeals suppressed the evidence in a disciplinary hearing of a state employee because it was collected by placing such a device on the employee's automobile. *See Cunningham v. New York State Dept. of Labor*, 997 N.E.2d 468 (N.Y. 2013). Because the device tracked much activity with which the state had no legitimate concern, including the employee's activities on weekends and evenings, the court found that its attachment to the vehicle was excessively intrusive and, hence, an unreasonable search under the Fourth Amendment. *See id.* at 473-74.

Furthermore, in recent years, the Food and Drug Administration has come under heavy criticism in the media and in Congress for engaging in surveillance of several of its scientists' communications regarding certain medical devices, including the interception of thousands of e-mails and other documents. *See, e.g.*, Eric Lichtblau, *Vast F.D.A. Effort Tracked E-Mails of Its Scientists*, N.Y. TIMES, July 14, 2012, at A1; Eric Lichtblau, *Investigation Sought of Extensive F.D.A. Surveillance*, N.Y. TIMES, June 16, 2012, at A14. Along with Edward Snowden's revelations regarding the federal agencies' much broader domestic and international surveillance programs, the FDA controversy illustrates society's ambivalence towards mass electronic surveillance by government employers. *See, e.g.*, Jennifer Stisa Granick & Christopher Jon Sprigman, *The Criminal N.S.A.*, N.Y. TIMES, June 27, 2013, *available at* http://www .nytimes.com/2013/06/28/opinion/the-criminal-nsa.html?pagewanted=all (discussing the "twin revelations that telecom carriers have been secretly giving the National Security Agency information about Americans' phone calls, and that the N.S.A. has been capturing e-mail and other private communications from Internet companies as part of a secret program).

Although these Fourth Amendment decisions and background concerns regarding excessive government surveillance do not apply to the private sector workplace, as discussed earlier in the chapter, we have seen that the reasoning in Fourth Amendment cases may influence courts in determining whether private sector employees who have been monitored away from work in this or similar ways may have viable intrusion upon seclusion or public policy claims. Nevertheless, in private, at-will employment, employees historically have enjoyed few protections from employer retaliation for such activities, choices, or associations. *See, e.g., Brunner v. Al Attar*, 786 S.W.2d

784 (Tex. Ct. App. 1990) (dismissing an employee's claim alleging breach of privacy after employer terminated employee for volunteering for the AIDS Foundation). Many such off-site conduct and associational claims are unsuccessful, often because they do not fit neatly within statutory or common-law theories. *See, e.g., Curay-Cramer v. The Ursuline Acad. of Wilmington*, 450 F.3d 130 (3d Cir. 2006) (rejecting employee's Title VII retaliation theory in circumstances in which employee was terminated from her position as a teacher at a Catholic school after allowing her name to be included in a prochoice advertisement in the local newspaper and admitting her association with a prochoice organization); *Edmondson v. Shearer Lumber Prods.*, 75 P.3d 733 (Idaho 2003) (refusing to recognize a public policy claim for a worker terminated for participating in a local government task force). And, again, while the new Restatement recognizes potentially protectable autonomy interests in such activities, such protection is subject to waiver, which is likely to greatly reduce the protection in practice.

However, as *Rulon-Miller* and the *Soroka* decision discussed above suggest, there is some protection from employer interference with or repercussions from some such activities and choices. When available, such protection often hinges on whether the employer can articulate a sufficient business-related reason for its actions. For example, in both *Soroka* and *Rulon-Miller*, the employer was found to have breached worker privacy rights, at least in part because it inquired into such private matters outside the workplace and acted upon those inquiries without sufficient justification.

And the law in this area is changing, mostly, but not exclusively, as a result of state-level legislative reforms. For instance, a growing number of state legislatures are protecting workers against adverse employment actions caused by a worker's political and other affiliations, recreational activities, or other kinds of legal off-site conduct where employers do not have a sufficiently compelling reason for taking such action. *See, e.g.,* Cal. Lab. Code §§ 96(k), 98.6 (2014) (prohibiting adverse employment actions in response to lawful employee conduct occurring during nonworking hours away from the employer's premises); Col. Rev. Stat. § 24-34-402.5 (2014) (prohibiting employers from terminating employees for lawful off-site activities absent job relatedness); Minn. Stat. § 181.938 (2014) (prohibiting employers from taking adverse actions against employees or applicants because the applicant or employee uses or enjoys lawful consumable products—including food, alcohol, and tobacco products—if the use or enjoyment takes place off the employer's premises during nonworking hours, unless the employer can demonstrate a bona fide occupational requirement for doing so or to avoid a conflict of interest); N.Y. Lab. Law § 201-d (2010) (prohibiting employers in most circumstances from taken adverse actions against employees based on employee political affiliations, legal use of consumable products, recreational activities, or union membership); *see also* Eugene Volokh, *Private Employees' Speech and Political Activity: Statutory Protection Against Employer Retaliation*, 16 Tex. Rev. L. & Pol. 295 (2012) (providing a comprehensive survey of state statutes protecting various forms of speech and political activity). Of course, whether these statutes will provide meaningful protection for employees' offsite activities and associations depends on judicial interpretation. *See, e.g., McCavitt v. Swiss Reins. Am. Corp.* 237 F.3d 166 (2001) (finding "romantic dating" of a co-worker not to be a protected recreational activity under the New York statute). For further discussion of the burgeoning workplace conflicts over such activities and choices, and the range of legal issues raised regarding employer prohibitions or other responses, *see, e.g.,* Rafael Gely & Leonard Biermanm, *Workplace Blogs and Workers' Privacy*, 66 La. L.

Rev. 1079 (2006) (discussing blogging and its privacy implications); James A. Sonne, *Monitoring for Quality Assurance: Employer Regulation of Off-Duty Behavior*, 43 Ga. L. Rev. 133 (2008); Stephen D. Sugarman, *"Lifestyle" Discrimination in Employment*, 24 Berkeley J. Emp. & Lab. L. 377 (2003).

Another growing area of potential employer-employee conflict is Internet activities. As we have seen, employers may have significant interests in regulating employee Internet use at work or on employer time, networks, or equipment. As the discussion in Note 3 following *Quon* suggested, *see* page 377, employers often prevail in such Internet monitoring and computer search cases. *See also Thygeson v. U.S. Bancorp*, 2004 U.S. Dist. LEXIS 18863 (D. Or. Sept. 15, 2004) (rejecting breach of privacy claims after employer monitored website addresses employee accessed and searched e-mail files). *But see Fischer v. Mt. Olive Lutheran Church, Inc.*, 207 F. Supp. 2d 914 (W.D. Wis. 2002) (finding that employee had reasonable expectation of privacy in e-mails in his Web-based e-mail account, which employer searched after guessing employee's password, for intrusion upon seclusion claim). Of course, that does not mean employees like such monitoring; indeed, a number of federal judges themselves became quite irate when they discovered that their Internet activity was to be monitored under a newly enacted Judicial Conference policy. *See* Hardeep Kaur Josan & Sapna K. Shah, Note, *Internet Monitoring of Federal Judges: Striking a Balance Between Independence and Accountability*, 20 Hofstra Lab. & Emp. L. J. 153 (2002).

But what about employee Internet activities — including maintaining personal websites, social networking, participation in interactive websites or chat rooms, or basic surfing — that occur off-site, during nonwork hours, and without using employer equipment? Many employers have adopted "blogging" policies, warning workers about potential adverse consequences if employee blogging activities or other web-based activities harm the employer. And, unsurprisingly, employees are terminated for such activities with growing frequency, particularly when they make online statements critical of their employers. *See, e.g.*, Posting of Jeffrey M. Hirsh to Workplace Prof. Blog, http://lawprofessors.typepad.com/laborprof_blog/2009/08/the-dangers-of-facebook. html (Aug. 11, 2009); Posting of Richard Bales to Workplace Law Blog, http:// lawprofessors.typepad.com/laborprof_blog/2009/03/fired-for-faceb.html (Mar. 9, 2009). *But see* posting of Nathan Koppel to Wall Street Journal Law Blog, High School Principal Harshly Criticizes Teacher/Blogger Natalie Munroe (Aug. 3, 2011, 2:59 p.m. EDT), http://blogs.wsj.com/law/2011/08/03/high-school-principal-harshly-criti-cizes-teacherblogger-natalie-munroe/ (discussing the reinstatement of high school teacher Natalie Munroe after she was suspended for harshly criticizing her students in blog posts). Case law on the subject remains sparse, although litigation over such issues appears to be growing. *See, e.g., Pietrylo v. Hillstone Rest. Group*, No. 06-5754 (FSH), 2009 WL 3128420 (D.N.J. Sept. 25, 2009) (upholding a jury verdict finding that employees' managers violated the Stored Communications Act (SCA) by knowingly accessing a chat group on a social networking website without authorization); *see also Dible v. City of Chandler*, reproduced at page 445 (upholding summary judgment on police officer's speech, privacy, and other claims arising out of his termination by the City for maintaining sexually explicit website featuring him and his wife).

However, in recent years, there has been much attention focused on employer access to, and demands for access to, electronic communications on personal devices or in password-protected social media and other accounts, both at the application stage and during employment. As an initial matter, employers occasionally face trouble, legal or otherwise, for overly aggressive off-site surveillance or investigatory activities to flush out anonymous posters or leakers. One high-profile example is the scandal surrounding Hewlett-Packard's use of highly aggressive spying techniques and deceptive tactics to discover the identity of a leaker (who turned out to be on its board of directors). The controversy that followed resulted in a number of directors and officers in the company resigning. *See, e.g.*, Damon Darlin, *H.P., Red-Faced but Still Selling*, N.Y. TIMES, Oct. 1, 2006, at 31. Criminal charges against the chair of Hewlett-Packard's board of directors ultimately were dismissed, although one of its investigators did plead guilty to theft and conspiracy. *See* Matt Richtel, *Charges Dismissed in Hewlett-Packard Spying Case*, N.Y. TIMES, Mar. 15, 2007, *available at* http://www.nytimes .com/2007/03/15/technology/15dunn.html?_r=1&ref= patricia_c_dun. In addition, Hewlett-Packard ultimately agreed to pay $14.5 million to settle a civil suit brought by the California attorney general. *See* Damon Darlin, *H.P Will Pay $14.5 Million to Settle Suit*, N.Y. TIMES, Dec. 8, 2006, *available at* http://www .nytimes.com/2006/12/08/technology/08hewlett.html.

The Illinois Supreme Court recently upheld a jury verdict in favor of a former employee on her intrusion upon seclusion claim against her former employer for the "pretexting" activities of a third-party private investigator the employer had retained. *Lawlor v. North American Corp. of Illinois*, 983 N.E.2d 414 (Ill. 2012). The jury found that the investigator had engaged in pretexting to obtain the employee's phone records as part of the former employer's efforts to determine whether she had violated the terms of a noncompetition agreement or engaged in other conduct that violated her duties to the employer. The court did reduce the punitive damages award, however, in light of the finding below that the former employer's wrongful conduct — as opposed to that of the investigator — was relatively minor. *See id.* at 432-33; *see also Ehling v. Monmouth-Ocean Hosp. Service Corp.*, 872 F. Supp. 2d 369 (D.N.J. 2012) (finding an employee's allegations that her postings to a Facebook page accessible only by those invited by the employee sufficient to plead a reasonable expectation of privacy in her page, when the supervisor compelled another employee with access to the page to view it in front of the supervisor).

Furthermore, since 2012, there has been a burst of state legislation barring or restricting employers from demanding access to applicants' and employees' personal e-mail and social media passwords, which will quickly and profoundly alter hiring practices in certain contexts. *See, e.g.*, CAL. LAB. CODE §980 (2014); 820 ILL. COMP. STAT. 55/10 (2014); MD. CODE LAB. & EMPL. §3-712 (2014); N.J. STAT. 34:6B-6 (2014). Many other states have passed or are considering such legislation. The National Conference of State Legislatures tracks these developments at http://www.ncsl.org/ research/telecommunications-and-information-technology/employer-access-to-social-media-passwords-2013.aspx; *see also* Ariana R. Levinson, *Social Media, Privacy, and the Employment Relationship: The American Experience*, SPANISH LAB. L. AND EMPL. REL. J., Vol. 2, No. 1 (2013) (discussing statutory and common law developments).

But these prohibitions vary, and some expressly allow such requests in investigations involving existing employees. For example, New Jersey's statute, generally prohibits employers from retaliating or discriminating against employees for refusing to provide access to social media accounts, but also provides the following exclusion:

Nothing in this act shall prevent an employer from conducting an investigation:

(1) for the purpose of ensuring compliance with applicable laws, regulatory requirements or prohibitions against work-related employee misconduct based on

the receipt of specific information about activity on a personal account by an employee; or

(2) of an employee's actions based on the receipt of specific information about the unauthorized transfer of an employer's proprietary information, confidential information or financial data to a personal account by an employee.

N.J. Stat. 34:6B-6 (2014). Still, this investigation exception is quite narrow. There must be more than a generalized suspicion of wrongdoing or other "reasonable justification" for seeking access; the employer must have "specific information" to believe the suspected offense involved use of the particular account. These protections have other limitations as well; for example, some statutes, including New Jersey's, impose only minor administrative fines for violations and do not provide for a private right of action.

In addition, if workers utilize social networking or other electronic means to discuss work-related conditions with one another, their communications may be protected as "concerted activity" under the National Labor Relations Act. *See* 29 U.S.C. § 157 (2014); *see also* page 464, *infra* (discussing protection for concerted activity). Indeed, the National Labor Relations Board and its general counsel have addressed the issue of concerted activity and employer social media policies a number of times. The Board found, for example, that Facebook postings by two employees expressing concern about working late at night in an unsafe neighborhood were protected activity. *Design Technology Group, LLC,* 359 NLRB No. 96 (2013). To the extent such postings are protected concerted activity, employers are prohibited from disciplining employees for such postings and cannot promulgate social media policies that might have a chilling effect on such activity. *See* Operations Management Memorandum 1259 from Ann Purcell, Assoc. Gen. Counsel, to all Reg'l Dirs., Officers in Charge, and Resident Officers, "Report of the Acting General Counsel Concerning Social Media Cases" (May 30, 2012), available at http://www.nlrb.gov/reports-guidance/operations-management-memos?memo_number=OM%5C+12 (discussing employer social media policies and rules that violate Sections 7 and 8(a)(1)); *see also* Pauline T. Kim, *The Piper Lecture: Electronic Privacy and Employee Speech,* 87 Chi.-Kent L. Rev. 901 (2012) (discussing the interaction between employee privacy interests in electronic communications and protections for socially valuable speech, including concerted activity); Ann C. McGinley & Ryan P. McGinley-Stempel, *Beyond the Water Cooler: Speech and the Workplace in an Era of Social Media,* 30 Hofstra Lab. & Emp. L.J. 75 (2012) (discussing social media and speech in the private workplace context and the implications of the NLRB's recent concerted-activity decisions).

At this point, and despite some calls for legislative action by the blogger community and others, the potential sources of protection for publicly accessible Internet activities are limited. As will be discussed in the next chapter, public employee speech on the Internet enjoys qualified First Amendment protection, and may be protected if the topic of that speech is wholly unrelated to employment. *See, e.g., City of San Diego v. Roe,* 543 U.S. 77, 80 (2004); *United States v. Nat'l Treasury Employees,* 513 U.S. 454, 465 (1995). Also, in the private employment context, Internet activities that touch on other protected spheres, such as religious or political affiliations, may receive some protection under federal antidiscrimination law, state associational protections, or, conceivably, the public policy exception.

It is unlikely, however, that most intrusion upon seclusion or other breach of privacy claims relating to internet activity will succeed since rarely will one have a reasonable expectation of privacy in postings or other activities on the Internet. And, of course, unless protected as "concerted activity," the more closely the content of the Internet activity or speech relates to areas of employer concern—for example, complaints about the employer or co-workers, statements that may embarrass or otherwise harm the employer or co-workers, revelations of confidential or proprietary interests, and so forth—the less likely the conduct is to be protected. *See, e.g., Roe, supra* (finding no constitutional violation where city terminated employee after employee made clear references to his status as a police officer in sexually explicit videos he sold on an online auction site); *see also* Helen Norton, *Constraining Public Employee Speech: Government's Control of Its Workers' Speech to Protect Its Own Expression*, 59 Duke L.J. 1 (2009) (discussing how courts are increasingly concluding that off-duty/off-site conduct by government workers—including Internet activities—affect employer interests).

As a practical matter then, at-will employees and job applicants ought to assume that they have little protection against adverse employment actions resulting from things they say or see on non-password-protected areas of the Internet. Indeed, workers, and job applicants in particular, would be well advised to assume that anything they say or post in publicly accessible areas of the Internet will become known to potential employers since many employers now conduct Internet searches for information on prospective employees. *See, e.g.*, Microsoft Online Reputation Data Study, *Online Reputation in a Connected World* (Jan. 2010) *available at* http://www.microsoft .com/privacy/dpd/research.aspx (finding that 70 percent of employers in the United States have rejected employees because of information discovered online, and that nearly all employers believe it is appropriate to consider prospective employees' online reputation as appropriate). Although anonymous participation may provide greater protections, maintaining such anonymity forever may be both difficult and costly (in the sense that one cannot take credit for his or her postings), and examples of repercussions upon an employer's discovery of the true identity of a blogger or poster now abound. *See, e.g.*, Jonathan Miller, *He Fought the Law. They Both Won*, N.Y. Times, Jan. 22, 2006 (discussing the strange journey of David Lat, who, while serving as an Assistant United States Attorney, led a secret life as "Article III Groupie," a supposedly female blogger who maintained an irreverent, gossipy blog about the federal judiciary called "Underneath Their Robes," until he revealed his true identity and ultimately changed careers).

Finally, there is the related issue regarding the extent to which employers can inquire into employees' past or present unlawful conduct. Drug testing (including for illicit drug use) is addressed above, as are psychological test questions that may probe into such matters. But another concern is employer inquiries and searches regarding applicants' criminal backgrounds. A number of states have statutes prohibiting employers from considering an applicant's criminal and/or arrest records absent job-relatedness. *See, e.g.*, Haw. Rev. Stat. § 378-2.5(a) (2014) (an employer may inquire about and consider an applicant's criminal conviction record if it bears "a rational relationship to the duties and responsibilities of the position); Mass. Gen. Laws Ann. ch. 151B, § 4(9) (2014) (prohibiting employer or its agent from requesting information regarding, inter alia, "an arrest . . . in which no conviction resulted" or any conviction of a misdemeanor which occurred five years prior to date of employee's application); N.Y. Correct. Law § 752 (McKinney) (2014) (prohibiting denial of employment based on previous conviction of applicant unless there is "a direct relationship" between the offenses and the specific license or position or where accepting the applicant would involve "an unreasonable risk" to property or public safety). Other states impose such limitations only on public employers. *See, e.g.,* CONN. GEN. STAT. §46a-80 (2014). And the so-called Ban the Box movement—pressing cities and counties to stop screening out those with criminal records at the application stage—has had significant successes. *See, e.g.,* National Employment Law Project, *Ban the Box: Major U.S. Cities and Counties Adopt Fair Hiring Policies to Remove Unfair Barriers to Employment of People with Criminal Records* (July 2014), available at http://www .nelp.org/page/-/sclp/2011/cityandcountyhiringinitiatives.pdf?nocdn=1. Such laws, however, generally still permit an inquiry at an interview.

Laws prohibiting discrimination based on criminal history serve various social goals, ensuring fairness to the individual worker and helping to facilitate ex-convicts' reentry into the mainstream economy, a key factor in preventing recidivism. For their part, employers often legitimately fear damage or loss to their property or business as well as possible tort liability to other employees or third parties in the event that the worker commits another offense. For instance, where an employer knows (or should know) of a worker's criminal history and that individual subsequently injures or assaults a co-worker, the employer may be found to have engaged in a negligent hiring. Do the statutory examples provided above offer a way of striking a balance between employers' risk-management concerns and other societal interests? Should an employer faced with a negligent hiring claim be able to use such a statute as a defense to liability? Note too that, even if warranted, these kinds of laws are difficult to enforce: an ordinary Internet search can turn up information about criminal background, and it may be difficult to prove reliance on information from such a search in litigation in the unlikely event that one denied employment is willing to bring suit in the first instance.

Note on Employee Dress and Appearance

Choices about dress and grooming are also often an expression of individual autonomy and dignitary interests. For this reason, disputes over employee appearance in the workplace may be conceptualized as matters of worker privacy. Despite significant scholarly and public attention in recent years, there are few protections for worker preferences with regard to their appearance, and challenges to employer policies and practices in this area rarely succeed. Statutory protections that address dress and grooming choices directly are rare, and, where they exist, they may be subject to significant limitations. *See, e.g.* D.C. CODE §2-1402.11 (2014) (prohibiting discrimination based on "personal appearance" but expressly exempting various policies, including those that relate to cleanliness, health or safety, and uniform requirements that apply across a class of employees). In the absence of free speech or free exercise implications, public employees' challenges to dress and grooming policies on substantive due process grounds are unlikely to be successful since they are subject only to rational basis review. *See, e.g., Kelley v. Johnson,* 425 U.S. 238 (1976) (rejecting a challenge to hair-grooming standards for members of a police force).

Perhaps the most important sources of potential protection in this area are those that prohibit status-based discrimination, including antidiscrimination statutes and the First Amendment's Free Exercise Clause. Employees have had some success challenging some such policies as discriminatory. *See, e.g., Frank v. United Airlines,* 216 F.3d 845 (9th Cir. 2000) (striking down the airline's disparate weight standards for male and female flight attendants as facially discriminatory); *FOP Newark Lodge*

No. 12 v. City of Newark, 170 F.3d 359 (3d Cir. 1999) (holding the city's refusal to accommodate officers whose religion required them to wear beards violated the free exercise clause), However, other such challenges have failed, including claims addressing gender-specific differences in dress and grooming codes, and the disparate effects of such codes on women and religious and other minorities. *See, e.g.*, *Webb v. City of Philadelphia*, 562 F.3d 256 (3d Cir. 2009); *Jespersen v. Harrah's Operating Co.*, 444 F.3d 1104 (9th Cir. 2006) (en banc); *Harper v. Blockbuster Entm't Corp.*, 139 F.3d 1385 (11th Cir. 1998). Courts afford employers substantial deference in making decisions about the appearance of their workers even when the result is to reinforce gender-conformity norms. The limiting principle is that no particular protected group may be singled out or subjected to far greater burdens. There may also be legal restrictions on dress requirements that increase the risk that women will be subjected to sexual harassment from customers or co-workers. *But see* Elizabeth Dwoskin, *Is This Woman Too Hot to Be a Banker?*, VILLAGE VOICE (June 1, 2010) (discussing a sex-discrimination lawsuit filed by a former Citibank employee alleging that she was terminated because the male bosses found her attractive dress and appearance too distracting). Despite the limits of current law, many commentators have focused attention on the discriminatory effect of such policies and other sources of pressure to conform to "majority" expectations with regard to appearance, habits, and demeanor while at work. *See, e.g.*, Katharine T. Bartlett, *Only Girls Wear Barrettes: Dress and Appearance Standards, Community Norms and Workplace Equality*, 92 MICH. L. REV. 2541, 2543-46 (1994); Mary Anne C. Case, *Disaggregating Gender from Sex and Sexual Orientation: The Effeminate Man in the Law and Feminist Jurisprudence*, 105 YALE L. J. 1, 68-69 (1995); Catherine L. Fisk, *Privacy, Power, and Humiliation at Work: Re-Examining Appearance Regulation as an Invasion of Privacy*, 66 LA. L. REV. 1111 (2006); Roberto J. Gonzalez, *Cultural Rights and the Immutability Requirement in Disparate Impact Doctrine*, 55 STAN. L. REV. 2195, 2227 (2003); Tristin K. Green, *Work Culture and Discrimination*, 93 CAL. L. REV. 623 (2005); Karl E. Klare, *Power/Dressing: Regulation of Employee Appearance*, 26 NEW ENG. L. REV. 1395 (1992); Gowri Ramachandran, *Intersectionality as "Catch-22": Why Identity Performance Demands Are Neither Harmless nor Reasonable*, 69 ALB. L. REV. 299 (2005); Camille Gear Rich, *Performing Racial and Ethnic Identity: Discrimination by Proxy and the Future of Title VII*, 79 N.Y.U. L. REV. 1134 (2004); Kenji Yoshino, *Covering*, 111 YALE L. J. 769 (2002); *see generally* Symposium, *Makeup, Identity Performance & Discrimination*, 14 DUKE J. GENDER L. & POL'Y 1 (2007).

C. PRIVATE ORDERING: ARE THERE ANY LIMITS TO CONSENT?

The first part of this chapter discussed contract as a possible source of privacy rights. One might say, from the employee perspective, that the use of contract to create or expand the sphere of employee privacy protection is the "positive" side of private ordering. On the "negative" side is the use of contract, workplace guidelines and practices, and employee consent to eliminate or reduce the legally cognizable sphere of privacy that otherwise might exist.

In light of this, and employers' increasing use of employment "privacy" policies and waiver forms, whether otherwise cognizable privacy rights may be limited or eliminated through such private ordering may be the most important question in this area today. And it raises critical, ultimate questions: Are there and should there be any limitations on employers' ability to extract employee consent to intrusions or, more broadly, eliminate spheres of expected privacy? If so, what kinds? Consider these questions as you read the next case.

Feminist Women's Health Center v. Superior Court
61 Cal. Rptr. 2d 187 (Ct. App. 1997)

PUGLIA, P.J., with SPARKS, J., and NICHOLSON, J., concurring.

The issue presented by this petition is whether a female health center employee who agrees voluntarily to demonstrate a cervical self-examination to female clients and employees at the health center may sue the health center (and several of its supervisory employees) because the self-examination violates her constitutional right to privacy.

Respondent superior court granted summary adjudication of all of plaintiff Claudia Jenkins's claims except the one alleging she was wrongfully terminated from employment in violation of her right to privacy. The defendants — Feminist Women's Health Center ("Center") and several of its employees — filed the instant petition seeking a writ to compel the superior court to adjudicate this remaining claim in their favor. We shall order the writ to issue. . . . [1]

Plaintiff alleged: She was hired by defendants as a health worker pursuant to an oral contract entered in August 1993; defendants mandated that all female employees disrobe and display their vaginas to the employee defendants and various other employees; those who refused were advised that they either would be fired or would not receive promotions or raises; plaintiff refused to disrobe and was transferred to an intake clerk position before being terminated from employment on January 6, 1994; defendants' policy violated plaintiff's right to privacy and her right freely to maintain and practice religious and cultural beliefs as they pertained to the treatment and care of her body. . . .

Defendant Dido Hasper, executive director of the Center, declared that the Center was founded as a nonprofit corporation in Chico in 1974. The Center was created because unmarried women found it difficult to obtain abortion and midwifery services as well as information regarding birth control, adoption and reproduction. The Center was inspired by the existence of similar centers in Los Angeles and Oakland. The Chico Center began offering services in 1975, including abortion services, pregnancy screening, well-woman gynecology, family planning, and a speakers' bureau on women's health topics. The Center expanded and presently has four clinics, located in Chico, Sacramento, Santa Rosa, and Redding.

---

1. Plaintiff's first cause of action alleged a breach of the implied covenant of good faith and fair dealing. The second alleged intentional infliction of emotional distress. In the third cause of action, a violation of the California Fair Employment and Housing Act was alleged. In the fourth cause of action — which is the only one at issue herein — plaintiff alleged wrongful termination in violation of California public policy (violation of privacy). There also was a supernumerary "fourth cause of action," for a civil conspiracy.

Hasper's declaration discussed self-help groups at which cervical self-examination was demonstrated. Hasper defined a self-help group as a gathering of women who want to learn more about their bodies and reproductive health care. She declared: "The goal is to give women the opportunity to talk to each other, share experiences, learn from each other, and learn about their own bodies. A common realization of participants in self-help groups is that women's bodies and their normal reproductive functions have been medicalized and remain a mystery to them. The goal of self-help is to demystify and redefine the normal functions of a woman's body. Our unique and effective, although not strictly necessary tool to accomplish this is for women to visualize their own cervixes and vaginas, which are not usually seen with the naked eye without the use of a vaginal speculum. In many, but not necessarily all, self-help clinic sessions, women are given the opportunity to learn how to use a plastic speculum. . . . The Health Center offers self-help 'clinics' as a community education service to other women's groups, high school and college classes, and makes self-help group facilitators available for any appropriate gathering of interested women. . . . When self-examination occurs in a self-help group, two customs are observed. A woman does self-examination only if and when she feels comfortable doing so, and she looks at her own cervix first before any of the other participants in the self-help group."

Hasper declared that the position of "feminist health worker" (for which plaintiff was hired) was a unique one, requiring, at a minimum, "a great deal of empathy and training, strict absence of judgmentalism, a sophistication to react to a variety of clients' circumstances in a calm, respectful manner, and the ability to think on one's feet and appropriately respond to the needs of Health Center clients."

Hasper further declared that an element of the health worker's training process was an orientation to the self-help educational process. A senior health worker or director presides over the orientation, which includes a slide show about the history of the women's self-help movement and self-examination. Self-examination of the cervix thereafter is demonstrated for those attendees who express an interest. A plastic speculum is used to observe the cervix, and attendees are given the opportunity to take one home to examine themselves. Hasper concluded: "It is not the goal of self-help or of the Health Center, nor is it possible, to compel or require any woman to do self-examination of her own cervix. . . . Many senior health workers become facilitators for self-help clinics, although this too is not a job requirement. It has been the Center's experience that those health workers who are genuinely enthusiastic about the concept of self-help, if they possess the other qualities stated above, become outstanding staff members, embracing the goals of their organization. . . . A health worker cannot perform as a woman's advocate during the abortion process at the Health Center's standard if she has a strong aversion to the self-help concept."

Defendant Lisa Williams, the clinic manager for the Center's Sacramento office in August 1993, submitted a declaration detailing the circumstances of plaintiff's employment. Williams declared that plaintiff was hired as a health worker at the Center's Sacramento branch in August 1993. Williams interviewed plaintiff and explained the role of the health worker in the abortion clinic. She gave plaintiff a copy of the health worker job description, which plaintiff read and acknowledged reading. Williams detailed the training program for health workers. She explained the self-help philosophy of the clinic and that health workers, as part of their training, would be oriented to self-help and invited to participate in a self-help clinic.

In October 1993, several months after plaintiff had been hired, plaintiff applied for a vacant position of intake clerk. Williams explained to plaintiff that she would have to undergo a new interview process for the intake clerk position, since a different supervisor was involved. Williams declared that plaintiff never expressed dissatisfaction with self-help, even though she had many opportunities to do so at regularly scheduled staff meetings where dissent was encouraged. Williams declared that she did not participate in the decision to hire or fire plaintiff from the intake worker position.

Appended to Williams's declaration is a hiring interview form, signed by plaintiff, which states in part: "I have read and understand the job description for the position I am being hired. [sic] [¶] I have read and understand the Personnel Policies of the Feminist Women's Health Center."

The health worker job description which plaintiff reviewed also was appended. Under "qualifications" for the health worker position, two of the qualifications emphasize self-help:

1. Must attend Orientation and Self-Help demonstration
. . .
3. Must have an interest in women's healthcare and Self-Help

Under the heading "responsibilities and duties" in the health worker job description, participation in self-help clinics and the demonstration of the self-cervical exam at those clinics is explicitly stated:

1. *Attends and conducts self-help clinics as assigned.*
. . .
4. Is a Healthworker for drop-in pregnancy screening and pregnancy screening groups as scheduled:
   a. Facilitates pregnancy screening groups.
   b. *Demonstrates self cervical exam to pregnancy screening groups.*
   c. Counsels clients about pregnancy screening.
   d. Makes appropriate referrals for clients.
   e. Performs UCG pregnancy test or early urine pregnancy tests for clients.
   f. Acts as an advocate during exams by the medical professional as needed.

Defendants argued that their evidence establishes that plaintiff's wrongful termination cause of action lacks merit because plaintiff, as an at-will employee, was subject to reasonable conditions of employment, of which cervical self-examination was one.

In order to rebut defendants' showing that plaintiff understood and expressly agreed to demonstrate cervical self-examination, plaintiff's opposition papers explain the circumstances surrounding self-help and how she was pressured into demonstrating it. Plaintiff declared that during her employment interview "I was not told it was mandatory to disrobe and insert a speculum in my vagina in front of a group of health workers." At a September 1993 self-help session (one month after she was hired), plaintiff was instructed by defendant Eileen Schnitger to disrobe and insert a speculum in her vagina. Plaintiff refused. After further refusals, defendant Lisa Williams instructed plaintiff that she was required to participate in self-help. In October 1993, plaintiff applied for an intake clerk position because it was her understanding that it would not require participation in self-help, although she wasn't sure. Plaintiff became an intake worker on November 1, 1993, at the same rate of pay she had received as a health worker. Tensions were high at this time due to the self-help controversy. Plaintiff and fellow employee Kimya Lambert tried to defuse the problem by suggesting less personally intrusive methods such as using mannequins or privately inserting the speculum and then discussing results in the group sessions. Defendant Eileen Schnitger steadfastly refused these alternatives.

In December 1993, at the insistence of plaintiff and others, volunteer nurse Maggie Gunn wrote [an anonymous letter requesting that the Center "stop pressuring people to do the self-help"]. Gunn and another employee, Shirley Anderson, quit soon thereafter because of the self-help mandate. Plaintiff and Kimya Lambert were fired because of their work performance. Plaintiff's declaration concluded: "I believe and continue to believe 'self-help' in general has no relation to my position as a health worker because as a health worker I did not counsel clients about 'self-help.' I merely assisted in the abortion process. In fact, many of the movies we viewed at 'self-help' meetings featured issues such as how to climax and I know for certain I was not going to discuss this with any abortion client. I had a very difficult time sitting through these movies about climaxing but did so to preserve my job. I had to draw the line, although, at the request to disrobe in front of a group of people."

Shirley Anderson, employed as a nurse and health worker at the Center from May 1993 to January 1994, submitted a declaration in which she declared that she was not informed that she would have to disrobe in front of people as part of self-help. It was only after a few sessions that Eileen Schnitger clarified that self-examination was a job requirement. Lisa Williams told her she would receive no raises or promotions unless she participated in self-examination.

[The trial court granted summary judgment as to all claims except the one for wrongful termination in violation of public policy, and as to that, "limited [it] to the exception with regard to a contention of discharge in invasion of the right of privacy." After the court denied defendants' motion for reconsideration, the instant petition was filed.]

Defendants argue there can be no liability of the Center or its employees for terminating an employee who, having been hired as a health worker whose duties included the demonstration of cervical self-examination before groups of women, objected to and refused to perform that job duty. Defendants argue it was undisputed that the written job description for the health worker position for which plaintiff was hired expressly states that cervical self-examination is a job duty of the health worker. In defendants' view, the trial court ignored this express agreement and also failed to engage in the balancing analysis required in cases involving an alleged violation of the constitutional right to privacy. Defendants posit that the court's denial, pro tanto, of their summary adjudication motion cripples the Center's health education program and threatens the Center's existence by giving every health worker the right to sue for damages for violation of privacy rights.

Plaintiff responds that these arguments are specious as the superior court's order "does not prohibit or eliminate anything nor declare anything illegal." Plaintiff contends that summary adjudication was properly denied based on the existence of a number of disputed issues, namely: whether there was a self-help program in effect during plaintiff's employment; whether such a program included cervical self-examination; whether cervical self-examination was a vital part of the self-help program; whether the cervical self-examination required employees to disrobe in front of other females; whether an employee had the right to refuse to perform cervical self-examination; and whether the Center's interest outweighed plaintiff's right to privacy.

[After reviewing the relevant case law, the court concluded that California's constitutional right to privacy forms a sufficient touchstone of public policy to serve as a basis for plaintiff's wrongful termination claim. The defendants did not dispute the existence of such a cause of action, but argued instead that there is no material factual dispute that plaintiff's right to privacy was not violated.]

The principal case discussing the elements of a violation under California's constitutional privacy provision is *Hill v. National Collegiate Athletic Ass'n,* [865 P.2d 633 (Cal. 1994), involving university students' action against the National Collegiate Athletic Association ("NCAA") to enjoin the NCAA's drug testing program for student athletes. The Supreme Court held that] the drug testing program did not violate the California Constitution's right to privacy.

The court summarized the elements of a privacy claim and defenses thereto as follows:

> [W]e hold that a plaintiff alleging an invasion of privacy in violation of the state constitutional right to privacy must establish each of the following: (1) a legally protected privacy interest; (2) a reasonable expectation of privacy in the circumstances; and (3) conduct by defendant constituting a serious invasion of privacy.
>
> Whether a legally recognized privacy interest is present in a given case is a question of law to be decided by the court. Whether plaintiff has a reasonable expectation of privacy in the circumstances and whether defendant's conduct constitutes a serious invasion of privacy are mixed questions of law and fact. If the undisputed material facts show no reasonable expectation of privacy or an insubstantial impact on privacy interests, the question of invasion may be adjudicated as a matter of law.
>
> A defendant may prevail in a state constitutional privacy case by negating any of the three elements just discussed or by pleading and proving, as an affirmative defense, that the invasion of privacy is justified because it substantially furthers one or more countervailing interests. The plaintiff, in turn, may rebut a defendant's assertion of countervailing interests by showing there are feasible and effective alternatives to defendant's conduct which have a lesser impact on privacy interests. Of course, a defendant may also plead and prove other available defenses, e.g., consent, unclean hands, etc., that may be appropriate in view of the nature of the claim and the relief requested.
>
> The existence of a sufficient countervailing interest or an alternative course of conduct present threshold questions of law for the court. The relative strength of countervailing interests and the feasibility of alternatives present mixed questions of law and fact. Again, in cases where material facts are undisputed, adjudication as a matter of law may be appropriate.

In *Hill*, the court accepted as given that the NCAA's policy of observing athletes urinate into vials impinged on a legally protected privacy interest. The court further concluded, though, that student athletes had diminished expectations of privacy by reason of their participation in intercollegiate athletic activities and advance notice of the drug testing. Notwithstanding the diminished expectation of privacy resulting therefrom, the court evaluated the competing interests at stake due to the seriousness of the privacy invasion. The court ultimately concluded that "[t]he NCAA's information-gathering procedure (i.e., drug testing through urinalysis) is a method reasonably calculated to further its interests in enforcing a ban on the ingestion of specified substances in order to secure fair competition and the health and safety of athletes participating in its programs."

Applying the analytical framework of *Hill*, we agree with plaintiff that the observation of the insertion of a speculum into plaintiff's vagina by fellow employees and female clients of the Center infringes a legally protected privacy interest. This invasion is at least as serious as observing urination, and we do not question plaintiff's assertions that it was contrary to her religious and cultural beliefs.

The reasonableness of plaintiff's expectation of privacy is no greater than in the *Hill* case, however. In *Hill*, the student athletes had diminished expectations of privacy by reason of occasional communal undress and the sharing of information regarding physical fitness and bodily condition. Two elements of the NCAA's drug testing program further diminished the student athlete's reasonable expectation of privacy: advance notice and the opportunity to consent to testing. The court acknowledged that participation in athletic contests was conditioned on consent to testing, but that this did not render the consent involuntary, since the students did not have a right to participate in such competitions.

In the present case, the evidence established that plaintiff agreed to demonstrate cervical self-examination as a job requirement. She signed a form which manifested her understanding of and agreement to fulfill certain job duties. Those duties included participating in self-help and demonstrating cervical self-examinations to pregnancy screening groups.

Plaintiff did not dispute that she had agreed to these employment terms. Her dispute, rather, centered on the meaning of the phrase "demonstrates self-cervical exam to pregnancy screening groups." According to plaintiff's declaration, "I was not told it was mandatory to disrobe and insert a speculum in my vagina in front of a group of health workers." Assuming this statement to be true, it still fails to undermine her agreement to demonstrate cervical self-examinations. Disrobing and inserting a speculum in the vagina is a means by which cervical self-examination is demonstrated. Plaintiff's professed ignorance of the particulars of cervical self-examination does not vitiate her agreement to perform it.

The real issue is whether this type of cervical self-examination may reasonably be required of the Center's employees. In other words, the seriousness of the privacy invasion leads us to the third part of the *Hill* test: consideration of the Center's countervailing interests and the feasibility of the alternatives proposed by plaintiff.

Defendant Dido Hasper, the Center's executive director, stated the following reasons for use of cervical self-examination: "The goal is to give women the opportunity to talk to each other, share experiences, learn from each other, and learn about their own bodies. A common realization of participants in self-help groups is that women's bodies and their normal reproductive functions have been medicalized and remain a mystery to them. The goal of self-help is to demystify and redefine the normal functions of a woman's body. Our unique and effective, although not strictly necessary tool to accomplish this is for women to visualize their own cervixes and vaginas, which are not usually seen with the naked eye without the use of a vaginal speculum. In many, but not necessarily all, self-help clinic sessions, women are given the opportunity to learn how to use a plastic speculum."

It is true, as plaintiff notes, that Hasper's declaration reveals that the job requirement of cervical self-examination varies with the circumstances. These variations give rise to an inference that self-help is not an inflexible part of the Center's self-examination orientation sessions or demonstrations to interested groups.

But the declaration also makes clear that cervical self-examination is important in advancing the Center's fundamental goal of educating women about the function and health of their reproductive systems. Other parts of Hasper's declaration also show that the ability to demonstrate self-examination properly and without reservation identified employees who would be outstanding health care workers and potential group leaders. The declaration implied that the identification and retention of such employees was critical to the continued success of the Center. Considering the Center's expansion since its inception some 20 years ago, it was not unreasonable for Hasper to infer that new clients were drawn to the candid knowledge and intimacy imparted by the Center's unique methods, of which cervical self-examination was one.

The Center also could reasonably conclude that the alternative methods of self-examination proposed by plaintiff would have stifled such candor. These alternatives, such as the use of mannequins, or the private use of the speculum followed by discussion, are pale imitations of uninhibited group cervical self-examination.

It goes without saying that certain individuals would have an aversion to cervical self-examination or other aspects of self-help which were used to advance the Center's goal of shared experiences and learning. Plaintiff, for one, acknowledges that her religious and cultural background was not well suited to the practices of the Center.

In balancing these competing interests, we return to plaintiff's consent to demonstrate cervical self-examination as part of her employment agreement with the Center. The Center was not obligated to hire plaintiff, and consent remains a viable defense even in cases of serious privacy invasions. (*Hill.*) Therefore, we believe the facts as disclosed in the trial court give rise to the following inferences only: the requirement that health workers perform cervical self-examinations in front of other females is a reasonable condition of employment and does not violate the health worker's right to privacy where the plaintiff's written employment agreement evidences her knowledge of this condition and agreement to be bound by it. Where the employee thereafter refuses to abide by the agreement, the employee's wrongful termination claim based on a violation of the right to privacy is rendered infirm. Such is the case under the facts presented, and the superior court should have granted summary adjudication of this claim.

As plaintiff's wrongful discharge claims against the individual employees of the Center depend on her claim against the Center, they necessarily fail as well. . . .

NOTES

1. Quon *and* FWHC: *Disparate Facts, Common Themes.* In some ways, *Quon* and *Feminist Women's Health Center* ("*FWHC*") — are very different. First, the claims involve different types of employers, one public, one private, and therefore derive from different sources of law. In addition, *Quon* involves a fairly typical challenge to employer monitoring of electronic communications. *FWHC* addresses a unique set of circumstances, involving an employee challenge to a highly unusual job requirement — the cervical self-examination demonstration — allegedly tied to the employer's particular mission. Indeed, the controversy underlying *FWHC* and the resulting litigation over privacy rights seem ironic, given that a core component of the employer's mission is to further women's autonomy.

Yet consider what these cases have in common. As we have seen throughout this chapter, although the factual circumstances and articulations of the legal standards may differ, the courts tend to ask the same questions: whether the employee has a legitimate expectation of privacy, whether the employer has articulated a workplace-related interest to justify the alleged intrusion, the strength or importance of this employer interest, the nexus between the employer interest and the intrusion, and the extent to which the employee consented to or was on prior notice of the intrusion(s).

2. *The Role of Consent.* As a formal matter, there are two different ways in which explicit or implicit employee consent to particular intrusions defeat privacy claims. The employer electronic communications and computer use policy cases mentioned above provide an example of the first. These claims frequently fail because the employee's consent to monitoring and oversight eliminates any reasonable expectation of privacy in the underlying communications or files. Now consider why the *FWHC* analysis is different. Ask yourself, does plaintiff in *FWHC* have a reasonable expectation of privacy even though she consented? If yes, then how does consent operate to defeat her claim?

Given these potential effects of consent, and the growing sophistication of employers in crafting employment policies and waivers, the more courts accept private ordering in the workplace, the less privacy protection will exist for workers. The fact that *FWHC* is a California decision may be particularly troubling to workplace privacy advocates since California is one of the few jurisdictions that recognizes a state constitutional right to privacy in the private workplace and is considered among the *most* amenable to employee privacy claims. And recall that employees may fare no better even if they are in a position to challenge ex ante employer demands for consent because of the "Request for Consent Catch-22." Thus, the employer's request for consent itself may effectively preclude many privacy claims. Could plaintiff in *FWHC* have sued if she had been denied a job when she first applied because of the job description?

3. *The Limits of Consent.* Some of the particular statutory protections discussed in this chapter — for example, prohibitions on polygraph, genetic, and forms of medical testing as well as the new state laws protecting social media accounts — cannot be waived by employees, even by express consent. Also, in the public employer context, employees cannot be compelled to shed their constitutional rights at the workplace door, *see Pickering v. Board of Educ.*, 391 U.S. 563 (1968), although, as *Quon* and the *O'Connor* plurality's framework suggest, implicit consent to workplace monitoring, surveillance, testing, and other intrusive activities may limit or destroy an employee's legitimate expectation of privacy, and hence, any real hope of establishing a Fourth Amendment or due process violation.

Should there be other limits to the immunizing effect of consent? As we have seen in other contexts, one reason to curtail private ordering between worker and firm is to protect the public or third parties. Is the public interest implicated in the privacy context? If so, when, how, and to what extent? *Cf. Cramer v. Consol. Freightways, Inc.*, 255 F.3d 683 (9th Cir. 2001) (en banc) (holding that even if collective bargaining agreement expressly contemplated employer's video surveillance of employee restrooms, the term would be unenforceable because such surveillance violated a California criminal statute).

Should there be further substantive or procedural limitations? For example, in *Quon* the possibility that the employees had a reasonable expectation of privacy in the text messages despite the employers' fairly clear use policy suggests that inconsistent employer practices or representations can defeat apparent expectation-eliminating language in written policies or waivers. But, assuming no such inconsistency, how clear must a workplace policy or practice be before a court should find that it immunizes the employer from liability? In a case like *FWHC*, how explicit should the disclosure of the job requirement be in order to preclude the employee from later challenging the requirement? Should consent be limited at all by the importance of the employer interest to be served or the "nexus" between that interest and the particular intrusion to which the employee has consented? Should consent obtained at the start of employment be treated differently than consent obtained or notice provided after the employee has started work? For a discussion of the role of consent in the workplace privacy context and various potential limitations on it, *see generally* Steven L. Willborn, *Consenting Employees: Workplace Privacy and the Role of Consent*, 66 LA. L. REV. 975 (2006); *see also* James A. Sonne, *Monitoring for Quality Assurance: Employer Regulation of Off-Duty Behavior*, 43 GA. L. REV. 133, 166 (2008).

Are there other reasons for discounting even clear and unequivocal forms of express consent to employer intrusions? Consider the next case.

Stengart v. Loving Care Agency, Inc.
990 A.2d 650 (N.J. 2010)

CHIEF JUSTICE RABNER delivered the Opinion of the Court.

In the past twenty years, businesses and private citizens alike have embraced the use of computers, electronic communication devices, the Internet, and e-mail. As those and other forms of technology evolve, the line separating business from personal activities can easily blur.

In the modern workplace, for example, occasional, personal use of the Internet is commonplace. Yet that simple act can raise complex issues about an employer's monitoring of the workplace and an employee's reasonable expectation of privacy.

This case presents novel questions about the extent to which an employee can expect privacy and confidentiality in personal e-mails with her attorney, which she accessed on a computer belonging to her employer. Marina Stengart used her company-issued laptop to exchange e-mails with her lawyer through her personal, password-protected, web-based e-mail account. She later filed an employment discrimination lawsuit against her employer, Loving Care Agency, Inc. (Loving Care), and others.

In anticipation of discovery, Loving Care hired a computer forensic expert to recover all files stored on the laptop including the e-mails, which had been automatically saved on the hard drive. Loving Care's attorneys reviewed the e-mails and used information culled from them in the course of discovery. In response, Stengart's lawyer demanded that communications between him and Stengart, which he considered privileged, be identified and returned. Opposing counsel disclosed the documents but maintained that the company had the right to review them. Stengart then sought relief in court. . . .

We hold that, under the circumstances, Stengart could reasonably expect that e-mail communications with her lawyer through her personal account would remain private, and that sending and receiving them via a company laptop did not eliminate the attorney-client privilege that protected them. By reading e-mails that were at least arguably privileged and failing to notify Stengart promptly about them, Loving Care's counsel breached *RPC* 4.4(b). We therefore modify and affirm the judgment of the Appellate Division and remand to the trial court to determine what, if any, sanctions should be imposed on counsel for Loving Care.

I.

This appeal arises out of a lawsuit that plaintiff-respondent Marina Stengart filed against her former employer, defendant-appellant Loving Care, its owner, and certain board members and officers of the company. She alleges, among other things, constructive discharge because of a hostile work environment, retaliation, and harassment based on gender, religion, and national origin, in violation of the New Jersey Law Against Discrimination, *N.J.S.A.* 10:5–1 to–49. Loving Care denies the allegations and suggests they are an attempt to escape certain restrictive covenants that are the subject of a separate lawsuit.

Loving Care provides home-care nursing and health services. Stengart began working for Loving Care in 1994 and, over time, was promoted to Executive Director of Nursing. The company provided her with a laptop computer to conduct company business. From that laptop, Stengart could send e-mails using her company e-mail address; she could also access the Internet and visit websites through Loving Care's server. Unbeknownst to Stengart, certain browser software in place automatically made a copy of each web page she viewed, which was then saved on the computer's hard drive in a "cache" folder of temporary Internet files. Unless deleted and overwritten with new data, those temporary Internet files remained on the hard drive.

On several days in December 2007, Stengart used her laptop to access a personal, password-protected e-mail account on Yahoo's website, through which she communicated with her attorney about her situation at work. She never saved her Yahoo ID or password on the company laptop.

Not long after, Stengart left her employment with Loving Care and returned the laptop. On February 7, 2008, she filed the pending complaint.

In an effort to preserve electronic evidence for discovery, in or around April 2008, Loving Care hired experts to create a forensic image of the laptop's hard drive. Among the items retrieved were temporary Internet files containing the contents of seven or eight e-mails Stengart had exchanged with her lawyer via her Yahoo account.[1] Stengart's lawyers represented at oral argument that one e-mail was simply a communication he sent to her, to which she did not respond.

A legend appears at the bottom of the e-mails that Stengart's lawyer sent. It warns readers that

> THE INFORMATION CONTAINED IN THIS EMAIL COMMUNICATION IS INTENDED ONLY FOR THE PERSONAL AND CONFIDENTIAL USE OF THE DESIGNATED RECIPIENT NAMED ABOVE. This message may be an Attorney–Client communication, and as such is privileged and confidential. If the reader of this message is not the intended recipient, you are hereby notified that you have received this

---

1. The record does not specify how many of the e-mails were sent or received during work hours. Loving Care asserts that the e-mails in question were exchanged during work hours through the company's server. However, counsel for Stengart represented at oral argument that four of the e-mails were transmitted or accessed during non-work hours — three on a weekend and one on a holiday. It is unclear, and ultimately not relevant, whether Stengart was at the office when she sent or reviewed them.

communication in error, and that your review, dissemination, distribution, or copying of the message is strictly prohibited. If you have received this transmission in error, please destroy this transmission and notify us immediately by telephone and/or reply email.

At least two attorneys from the law firm representing Loving Care, Sills Cummis (the "Firm"), reviewed the e-mail communications between Stengart and her attorney. The Firm did not advise opposing counsel about the e-mails until months later. In its October 21, 2008, reply to Stengart's first set of interrogatories, the Firm stated that it had obtained certain information from "e-mail correspondence" — between Stengart and her lawyer — from Stengart's "office computer on December 12, 2007 at 2:25 p.m." In response, Stengart's attorney sent a letter demanding that the Firm identify and return all "attorney-client privileged communications" in its possession. The Firm identified and disclosed the e-mails but asserted that Stengart had no reasonable expectation of privacy in files on a company-owned computer in light of the company's policy on electronic communications.

Loving Care and its counsel relied on an Administrative and Office Staff Employee Handbook that they maintain contains the company's Electronic Communication policy (Policy). The record contains various versions of an electronic communications policy, and Stengart contends that none applied to her as a senior company official. Loving Care disagrees. We need not resolve that dispute and assume the Policy applies in addressing the issues on appeal.

The proffered Policy states, in relevant part:

> The company reserves and will exercise the right to review, audit, intercept, access, and disclose all matters on the company's media systems and services at any time, with or without notice. . . .
> E-mail and voice mail messages, internet use and communication and computer files are considered part of the company's business and client records. Such communications are not to be considered private or personal to any individual employee.
> The principal purpose of electronic mail (*e-mail*) is for company business communications. Occasional personal use is permitted; however, the system should not be used to solicit for outside business ventures, charitable organizations, or for any political or religious purpose, unless authorized by the Director of Human Resources.

The Policy also specifically prohibits "[c]ertain uses of the e-mail system" including sending inappropriate sexual, discriminatory, or harassing messages, chain letters, "[m]essages in violation of government laws," or messages relating to job searches, business activities unrelated to Loving Care, or political activities. The Policy concludes with the following warning: "Abuse of the electronic communications system may result in disciplinary action up to and including separation of employment."

Stengart's attorney applied for an order to show cause seeking return of the e-mails and other relief. . . . The trial court concluded that the Firm did not breach the attorney-client privilege because the company's Policy placed Stengart on sufficient notice that her e-mails would be considered company property. Stengart's request to disqualify the Firm was therefore denied.

The Appellate Division . . . reversed the trial court order and directed the Firm to turn over all copies of the e-mails and delete any record of them. Assuming that the Policy applied to Stengart, the panel found that "[a]n objective reader could reasonably conclude . . . that not all personal e-mails are necessarily company property."

In other words, an employee could "retain an expectation of privacy" in personal e-mails sent on a company computer given the language of the Policy. . . .

II.

Loving Care argues that its employees have no expectation of privacy in their use of company computers based on the company's Policy. In its briefs before this Court, the company also asserts that by accessing e-mails on a personal account through Loving Care's computer and server, Stengart either prevented any attorney-client privilege from attaching or waived the privilege by voluntarily subjecting her e-mails to company scrutiny. Finally, Loving Care maintains that its counsel did not violate *RPC* 4.4(b) because the e-mails were left behind on Stengart's company computer — not "inadvertently sent," as per the *Rule* — and the Firm acted in the good faith belief that any privilege had been waived.

Stengart argues that she intended the e-mails with her lawyer to be confidential and that the Policy, even if it applied to her, failed to provide adequate warning that Loving Care would save on a hard drive, or monitor the contents of, e-mails sent from a personal account. Stengart also maintains that the communications with her lawyer were privileged. When the Firm encountered the arguably protected e-mails, Stengart contends it should have immediately returned them or sought judicial review as to whether the attorney-client privilege applied. . . .

III.

Our analysis draws on two principal areas: the adequacy of the notice provided by the Policy and the important public policy concerns raised by the attorney-client privilege. Both inform the reasonableness of an employee's expectation of privacy in this matter. We address each area in turn.

A.

We start by examining the meaning and scope of the Policy itself. The Policy specifically reserves to Loving Care the right to review and access "all matters on the company's media systems and services at any time." In addition, e-mail messages are plainly "considered part of the company's business . . . records."

It is not clear from that language whether the use of personal, password-protected, web-based e-mail accounts via company equipment is covered. The Policy uses general language to refer to its "media systems and services" but does not define those terms. Elsewhere, the Policy prohibits certain uses of "the e-mail system," which appears to be a reference to company e-mail accounts. The Policy does not address personal accounts at all. In other words, employees do not have express notice that messages sent or received on a personal, web-based e-mail account are subject to monitoring if company equipment is used to access the account.

The Policy also does not warn employees that the contents of such e-mails are stored on a hard drive and can be forensically retrieved and read by Loving Care.

The Policy goes on to declare that e-mails "are not to be considered private or personal to any individual employee." In the very next point, the Policy acknowledges that "[o]ccasional personal use [of e-mail] is permitted." As written, the Policy creates ambiguity about whether personal e-mail use is company or private property.

The scope of the written Policy, therefore, is not entirely clear.

B.

[The policies underlying the attorney-client privilege further animate this discussion. The primary purpose of the privilege is to encourage free and full disclosure of information between client and attorney. E-mail exchanges are covered by the privilege.]

The e-mail communications between Stengart and her lawyers contain a standard warning that their contents are personal and confidential and may constitute attorney-client communications. The subject matter of those messages appears to relate to Stengart's working conditions and anticipated lawsuit against Loving Care.

IV.

Under the particular circumstances presented, how should a court evaluate whether Stengart had a reasonable expectation of privacy in the e-mails she exchanged with her attorney?

A.

Preliminarily, we note that the reasonable-expectation-of-privacy standard used by the parties derives from the common law and the Search and Seizure Clauses of both the Fourth Amendment and Article I, paragraph 7 of the New Jersey Constitution. The latter sources do not apply in this case, which involves conduct by private parties only.

The common law source is the tort of "intrusion on seclusion," which can be found in the RESTATEMENT (SECOND) OF TORTS § 652B (1977). That section provides that "[o]ne who intentionally intrudes, physically or otherwise, upon the solitude or seclusion of another or his private affairs or concerns, is subject to liability to the other for invasion of his privacy, if the intrusion would be highly offensive to a reasonable person." RESTATEMENT, *supra*, § 652B. A high threshold must be cleared to assert a cause of action based on that tort. A plaintiff must establish that the intrusion "would be highly offensive to the ordinary reasonable man, as the result of conduct to which the reasonable man would strongly object." RESTATEMENT, *supra*, § 652B cmt. d.

As is true in Fourth Amendment cases, the reasonableness of a claim for intrusion on seclusion has both a subjective and objective component. . . . Moreover, whether an employee has a reasonable expectation of privacy in her particular work setting "must be addressed on a case-by-case basis." *O'Connor v. Ortega*, 480 U.S. 709, 718 (1987) (plurality opinion) (reviewing public sector employment).

B.

A number of courts have tested an employee's claim of privacy in files stored on company computers by evaluating the reasonableness of the employee's expectation. No reported decisions in New Jersey offer direct guidance for the facts of this case. . . .

[Courts in other jurisdictions have recognized a lesser expectation of privacy when employees communicate with attorneys using a company e-mail system and have found the existence of a clear company policy banning personal e-mails to also diminish the reasonableness of an employee's claim to privacy in e-mail messages with his or her attorney. The location of the company's computer may also be relevant.]

V.

A.

Applying the above considerations to the facts before us, we find that Stengart had a reasonable expectation of privacy in the e-mails she exchanged with her attorney on Loving Care's laptop.

Stengart plainly took steps to protect the privacy of those e-mails and shield them from her employer. She used a personal, password-protected e-mail account instead of her company e-mail address and did not save the account's password on her computer. In other words, she had a subjective expectation of privacy in messages to and from her lawyer discussing the subject of a future lawsuit.

In light of the language of the Policy and the attorney-client nature of the communications, her expectation of privacy was also objectively reasonable. As noted earlier, the Policy does not address the use of personal, web-based e-mail accounts accessed through company equipment. It does not address personal accounts at all. Nor does it warn employees that the contents of e-mails sent via personal accounts can be forensically retrieved and read by the company. Indeed, in acknowledging that occasional personal use of e-mail is permitted, the Policy created doubt about whether those e-mails are company or private property.

Moreover, the e-mails are not illegal or inappropriate material stored on Loving Care's equipment, which might harm the company in some way. They are conversations between a lawyer and client about confidential legal matters, which are historically cloaked in privacy. Our system strives to keep private the very type of conversations that took place here in order to foster probing and honest exchanges.

In addition, the e-mails bear a standard hallmark of attorney-client messages. They warn the reader directly that the e-mails are personal, confidential, and may be attorney-client communications. . . .

Under all of the circumstances, we find that Stengart could reasonably expect that e-mails she exchanged with her attorney on her personal, password-protected, web-based e-mail account, accessed on a company laptop, would remain private.

It follows that the attorney-client privilege protects those e-mails. See [*In re Asia Global Crossing, Ltd.* 322 B.R. 247, 258-59 (Bankr. S.D.N.Y. 2005)] (noting "close correlation between the objectively reasonable expectation of privacy and the objective reasonableness of the intent that a communication between a lawyer and a client was given in confidence"). In reaching that conclusion, we necessarily reject Loving Care's claim that the attorney-client privilege either did not attach or was waived. In its reply brief and at oral argument, Loving Care argued that the manner in which the e-mails were sent prevented the privilege from attaching. Specifically, Loving Care contends that Stengart effectively brought a third person into the conversation from the start—watching over her shoulder—and thereby forfeited any claim to confidentiality in her communications. We disagree.

Stengart has the right to prevent disclosures by third persons who learn of her communications "in a manner not reasonably to be anticipated." *See* N.J.R.E. 504(1)(c)(ii). That is what occurred here. The Policy did not give Stengart, or a reasonable person in her position, cause to anticipate that Loving Care would be peering over her shoulder as she opened e-mails from her lawyer on her personal, password-protected Yahoo account. The language of the Policy, the method of transmittal that Stengart selected, and the warning on the e-mails themselves all support that conclusion.

Loving Care also argued in earlier submissions that Stengart waived the attorney-client privilege. For similar reasons, we again disagree.

A person waives the privilege if she, "without coercion and with knowledge of [her] right or privilege, made disclosure of any part of the privileged matter or consented to such a disclosure made by anyone." N.J.R.E. 530 (codifying N.J.S.A. 2A:84A–29). Because consent is not applicable here, we look to whether Stengart either knowingly disclosed the information contained in the e-mails or failed to "take reasonable steps to insure and maintain their confidentiality." [*Trilogy Communications, Inc. v. Excom Realty, Inc.* 652 A.2d 1273 (N.J. Super. 1994).]

As discussed previously, Stengart took reasonable steps to keep discussions with her attorney confidential: she elected not to use the company e-mail system and relied on a personal, password-protected, web-based account instead. She also did not save the password on her laptop or share it in some other way with Loving Care.

As to whether Stengart knowingly disclosed the e-mails, she certified that she is unsophisticated in the use of computers and did not know that Loving Care could read communications sent on her Yahoo account. Use of a company laptop alone does not establish that knowledge. Nor does the Policy fill in that gap. Under the circumstances, we do not find either a knowing or reckless waiver.

B.

Our conclusion that Stengart had an expectation of privacy in e-mails with her lawyer does not mean that employers cannot monitor or regulate the use of workplace computers. Companies can adopt lawful policies relating to computer use to protect the assets, reputation, and productivity of a business and to ensure compliance with legitimate corporate policies. And employers can enforce such policies. They may discipline employees and, when appropriate, terminate them, for violating proper workplace rules that are not inconsistent with a clear mandate of public policy. . . . For example, an employee who spends long stretches of the workday getting personal, confidential legal advice from a private lawyer may be disciplined for violating a policy permitting only occasional personal use of the Internet. But employers have no need or basis to read the specific *contents* of personal, privileged, attorney-client communications in order to enforce corporate policy. Because of the important public policy concerns underlying the attorney-client privilege, even a more clearly written company manual—that is, a policy that banned all personal computer use and provided unambiguous notice that an employer could retrieve and read an employee's attorney-client communications, if accessed on a personal, password-protected e-mail account using the company's computer system — would not be enforceable.

VI.

[The Court went on to hold the defendant's law firm's review and use of the privileged e-mails violated RPC 4.4(b), which provides that "[a] lawyer who receives a document and has reasonable cause to believe that the document was inadvertently sent shall not read the document or, if he or she has begun to do so, shall stop reading the document, promptly notify the sender, and return the document to the sender." Although the firm did not act in bad faith, the court found that its review fell within the rule and that the firm erred in] not setting aside the arguably privileged messages once it realized they were attorney-client communications, and failing either to notify its adversary or seek court permission before reading further. . . . [T]he Firm should have promptly notified opposing counsel when it discovered the nature of the e-mails.

[The Court then agreed with the Appellate Division's decision to remand to the trial court to determine the appropriate remedy, including what sanctions, if any, to impose.]

We leave to the trial court to decide whether disqualification of the Firm, screening of attorneys, the imposition of costs, or some other remedy is appropriate. . . .

NOTES

1. Stengart *and Electronic Communications.* With regard to whether Stengart had a reasonable expectation of privacy in e-mails to her attorney on the employer's computer, the court's holding boils down to two key (although arguably alternative) conclusions: (1) the employer's ambiguous company policy did not put an employee on notice that personal e-mail was company property and, hence, Stengart had a reasonable expectation of her privacy in those e-mails; and (2) because of the important public policy concerns underlying the attorney-client privilege, even a clearer policy — one that banned all use for personal reasons and provided unambiguous notice that an employer could retrieve and read an employee's attorney-client communications, if accessed on a personal, password-protected e-mail account using the company's computer system — would not be enforceable.

The court's first conclusion is not particularly novel, although its narrow reading of the policy (construing it against the drafter, the employer) might not be emulated by all courts. And, as the note materials following *Quon* emphasize, even a clearer policy may not immunize the employer, since underlying, inconsistent practices have been found to support a reasonable expectation of privacy. The court's second conclusion, however, is potentially much more groundbreaking. While at least one court has expressly rejected *Stengart*'s reasoning, *see Aventa Learning, Inc. v. K12, Inc.*, 830 F. Supp. 2d 1083 (W.D. Wash. 2011), it remains to be seen whether other courts will reach a similar conclusion, at least with regard to electronic files reflecting attorney-client privileged communications in an employee's personal e-mail account.

2. *Uncertain Implications.* A straightforward takeaway from *Stengart* is that, at least once identified as communications between an attorney and client, there is likely to be little justification or excuse for delving into the content. Note that this is true even though such communications are likely to be *highly relevant* (i.e., very helpful) to

the employer in an investigatory or litigation context. However, even in New Jersey, it is unclear how far *Stengart*'s reasoning and protection might extend. First, we do not know whether *Stengart*'s conclusion extends to attorney-client privileged communications contained in company e-mail. *Compare Holmes v. Petrovich Development Co.,* 119 Cal. Rptr. 3d 878 (Ct. App. 2011) (distinguishing *Stengart* because the attorney-client communications in this case were on the company's email system). Indeed, one could argue that such attorney-client communications are not even privileged in the first place, since the privilege requires reasonable efforts to maintain confidentiality, and communicating through someone else's e-mail system falls short. Second, because this was a case about attorney conduct and sanctions, not potential privacy-based liability brought by the employee, it is not clear whether the decision will be extended to support such a claim, although the court's public policy-based reasoning would seem to suggest as much. Finally, given the court's emphasis on the particular policies underlying the attorney-client privilege, e-mails containing highly confidential and personal, but not privileged, communications might or might not be protected. In other words, it is unclear whether even the New Jersey courts would extend *Stengart*'s reasoning to protect communications in personal e-mail accounts that might reveal, for example, familial interactions, medical or health-related information, sensitive financial issues, or other intimate or otherwise confidential matters.

3. *Risk Management Implications.* This discussion offers a number of lessons for employers, employees, and counsel. First, with regard to employer monitoring and accessing employee electronic communications, the employer's policies need to be both clear and sufficiently broad to cover all anticipated uses. And, as repeated throughout this chapter, employers should ensure that employees read these policies and that workplace norms do not stray from these written provisions. Forestalling any expectations of privacy may require frequently monitoring worker communications — and letting employees know that is being done. But you can imagine why employers and individual supervisors, regardless of whatever documents their attorneys' have drafted, might be reluctant to do that. So immunizing the workplace from potential privacy claims arising out of such communications is an ongoing and far more complex endeavor than it might first appear.

Second, at the auditing, investigation, or post-termination stages, *Stengart* counsels great care reviewing employee/former employee files. No one should assume that the content of files backing up electronic communications are the employer's property simply because the computer or other device is owned by the employer. Again, the state-level statutory developments with regard to protecting employee social media accounts press in the same direction. Those conducting the investigation or review therefore ought to know that there are potential pitfalls in reviewing the content of files apparently containing employees' personal communications on nonemployer provided e-mail systems or other media. Moreover, even employer-provided communication systems (such as the messaging system in *Quon*) might contain content that is prima facie protected, if, for example, the employers' policy or practices have not been airtight. All of this suggests that monitoring and audits should be overseen by counsel or others who are cognizant of the risks and aware of potential steps that may have to be taken with regard to certain types of information.

On the flip side, given the uncertain reach of *Stengart*'s reasoning, and the fact that it has not been adopted in other jurisdictions, attorneys representing employees should counsel them to avoid attorney-client communications not only through employer-provided e-mail, but also on work time and through employer-provided equipment—computers, smart-phones, etc. Indeed, warning employees away from such forms of communications ought to be standard practice, since employees themselves frequently will not understand the larger risks, much less the nuanced distinctions discussed here.

4. FWHC, Stengart, *and Consent Reconsidered.* Having read both *FWHC* and *Stengart*, do you think both were correctly decided? If so, why? Certainly, it cannot be that the privacy interest at stake was greater in *Stengart* than *FWHC*, at least not in an abstract sense. Maybe it is the lack of clarity of the policy in the former, although again, one could argue the job requirements as described at the outset in *FWHC* were not entirely unambiguous. Nor can it be said, at a level of generality, that the intrusion in *FWHC* was employment related while the one in *Stengart* was not—again, the employer had a powerful interest/incentive in reviewing the attorney-client communications, since it was preparing for anticipated litigation with the employee! So why else? Does it turn on close nexus considerations—that is, the *necessity* of the intrusion in *FWHC* and its absence in *Stengart*? If so, then the conversation circles back to whether the cervical self-examination was really necessary and how much deference courts should accord employer assertions of such need.

If you think *Stengart* was wrongly decided, why? If it is because workplace policies or consent ought to trump privacy interests (including the privilege), then, for all practical purposes, there is no privacy in the workplace. If so, are you comfortable with that result? Or is this an overstatement? If you think *FWHC* was wrongly decided, then how would you draw the line between appropriate and inappropriate job-related intrusions or commands?

All of this, of course, simply leads back to where to the discussion at the beginning of this chapter: Grappling with the contours of privacy in the workplace is challenging because the interests at stake and appropriate role of private ordering are contestable, and the workplace and technology are constantly changing. This assures that, at minimum, there will continue to be new legal developments in this area as well as ongoing debate.

PROBLEM

6-2. Return now to the facts in Problem 6-1 set forth at the outset of this chapter. If DEI is a private sector employer, what potential claims might be available to Smith, the terminated employee? Obviously, given the nature of the intrusion, the Stored Communications Act might provide a starting point, but what limitations discussed above might preclude recovery under this theory? Assuming there is no liability under the Act, what other theories might be available? What barriers might there be to recovery? What other kinds of information would you need to assess the possibilities? Would your answer change if DEI is a public sector employer?

Now turn to counseling the employer. To the extent DEI faces potential liability, what could it have done differently to prevent or reduce the risk of this liability? Again, what additional information would be useful in providing advice? As a general matter, how confident are you in your assessments?

Finally, think about these circumstances from a policy perspective. Should Smith's communications be protected? Why or why not?

7

Workplace Speech and Association Protections

Another area where employee and employer prerogatives and preferences often collide is employee expression, whether in the form of speech or association. The employee interests at stake in this area often differ from the interests underlying privacy claims. Speech rights protect one's ability to express or "share" through words (and sometimes conduct) one's views or beliefs and to associate with those who have common views. Privacy rights, on the other hand, usually shield one from having to share; that is, these rights allow the exclusion of others from one's "space" (literal or metaphorical).

Despite their differences, speech and privacy in the workplace have much in common. First, speech and privacy rights both protect aspects of autonomy, and, in fact, some autonomy interests could be characterized as implicating both spheres. For example, as discussed in Chapter 6, one could conceptualize various expressive activities at work—such as dress and grooming—and conduct away from work—including associational, leisure, and Internet activities—as either "speech" or "private" activities. *See* Chapter 6 at page 383. Accordingly, various protections for worker expressive activities and off-site conduct could be viewed as preserving either speech or privacy rights.

Moreover, because worker speech and privacy protections both involve a clash between worker autonomy and employer prerogatives, the themes dominating the public policy debates and legal inquiry are often similar. For instance, as with privacy, public employees enjoy qualified constitutional protections for speech and association, while employees in the private sector may lack a "source" of such protection. Indeed, in the speech context, the divide between public and private employment is even greater, with public employees enjoying at least limited protection for certain kinds of speech and association and private employees left largely unprotected. In addition, where there is a potential source of protection, the courts often focus on the balance between employee and employer interests, and, as in the privacy cases, the level of deference a court accords the employer's justification for its speech-related restriction or actions is often dispositive. Finally, private ordering may alter the rights and obligations of employee and employer. Workplace speech cases tend to fall into three broad categories. The first, exemplified by *Connick v. Myers*, 461 U.S. 138 (1983),

Garcetti v. Ceballos, 547 U.S. 410 (2006), and *Lane v. Franks*, 134 S. Ct. 2369 (2014), reproduced at pages 410, 420, and 434, respectively, involves disputes arising out of adverse employment actions resulting from public employee speech or expressive activity at or related to work. The second concerns employer regulation of, coercion of, or retaliation for an employee's political, religious, or other associational preferences or affiliations. *Edmondson v. Shearer Lumber Products*, 75 P.3d 733 (Idaho 2003), reproduced at page 464, is an example of such litigation in the private employer context. Finally, the third category, addressed in *Dible v. City of Chandler*, 515 F.3d 918 (2008), reproduced at page 445, includes disputes over employer attempts to control employee speech and expression outside of work.

Although these three types of claims raise distinct issues, the public/private employer divide is by far the most important in terms of assessing the potential scope of protection for employee speech or association. This chapter explores potential rights and claims in each of these settings. Most of this chapter is devoted to the public context for a simple reason: While public employees often enjoy less-than-robust protections for their speech and association, protections in the private context are even more limited.

A. THE PUBLIC WORKPLACE

Connick v. Myers
461 U.S. 138 (1983)

WHITE, J.

In *Pickering v. Board of Education*, 391 U.S. 563 (1968), we stated that a public employee does not relinquish First Amendment rights to comment on matters of public interest by virtue of government employment. We also recognized that the State's interests as an employer in regulating the speech of its employees "differ significantly from those it possesses in connection with regulation of the speech of the citizenry in general." The problem, we thought, was arriving "at a balance between the interests of the [employee], as a citizen, in commenting upon matters of public concern and the interest of the State, as an employer, in promoting the efficiency of the public services it performs through its employees." We return to this problem today and consider whether the First and Fourteenth Amendments prevent the discharge of a state employee for circulating a questionnaire concerning internal office affairs.

I

The respondent, Sheila Myers, was employed as an Assistant District Attorney in New Orleans for five and a half years. She served at the pleasure of petitioner Harry Connick, the District Attorney for Orleans Parish. During this period, Myers competently performed her responsibilities of trying criminal cases.

In the early part of October 1980, Myers was informed that she would be transferred to prosecute cases in a different section of the criminal court. Myers was strongly opposed to the proposed transfer[1] and expressed her view to several of her supervisors, including Connick. Despite her objections, on October 6, Myers was notified that she was being transferred. Myers again spoke with Dennis Waldron, one of the First Assistant District Attorneys, expressing her reluctance to accept the transfer. A number of other office matters were discussed and Myers later testified that, in response to Waldron's suggestion that her concerns were not shared by others in the office, she informed him that she would do some research on the matter.

That night Myers prepared a questionnaire soliciting the views of her fellow staff members concerning office transfer policy, office morale, the need for a grievance committee, the level of confidence in supervisors, and whether employees felt pressured to work in political campaigns. Early the following morning, Myers typed and copied the questionnaire. She also met with Connick who urged her to accept the transfer. She said she would "consider" it. Connick then left the office. Myers then distributed the questionnaire to 15 Assistant District Attorneys. Shortly after noon, Dennis Waldron learned that Myers was distributing the survey. He immediately phoned Connick and informed him that Myers was creating a "mini-insurrection" within the office. Connick returned to the office and told Myers that she was being terminated because of her refusal to accept the transfer. She was also told that her distribution of the questionnaire was considered an act of insubordination. Connick particularly objected to the question which inquired whether employees "had confidence in and would rely on the word" of various superiors in the office, and to a question concerning pressure to work in political campaigns which he felt would be damaging if discovered by the press. . . .

II

For at least 15 years, it has been settled that a State cannot condition public employment on a basis that infringes the employee's constitutionally protected interest in freedom of expression. Our task, as we defined it in *Pickering*, is to seek "a balance between the interests of the [employee], as a citizen, in commenting upon matters of public concern and the interest of the State, as an employer, in promoting the efficiency of the public services it performs through its employees." . . .

A

. . . Connick contends at the outset that no balancing of interests is required in this case because Myers' questionnaire concerned only internal office matters and that such speech is not upon a matter of "public concern," as the term was used in *Pickering*. Although we do not agree that Myers' communication in this case was wholly without First Amendment protection, there is much force to Connick's submission. The repeated emphasis in *Pickering* on the right of a public employee "as a citizen, in commenting upon matters of public concern," was not accidental. This language, reiterated in all of *Pickering*'s progeny, reflects both the historical evolvement of

---

1. Myers' opposition was at least partially attributable to her concern that a conflict of interest would have been created by the transfer because of her participation in a counseling program for convicted defendants released on probation in the section of the criminal court to which she was to be assigned.

the rights of public employees, and the common-sense realization that government offices could not function if every employment decision became a constitutional matter.

For most of this century, the unchallenged dogma was that a public employee had no right to object to conditions placed upon the terms of employment — including those which restricted the exercise of constitutional rights. The classic formulation of this position was that of Justice Holmes, who, when sitting on the Supreme Judicial Court of Massachusetts, observed: "[A policeman] may have a constitutional right to talk politics, but he has no constitutional right to be a policeman." *McAuliffe v. Mayor of New Bedford*, 29 N.E. 517, 517 (Mass. 1892). For many years, Holmes' epigram expressed this Court's law.

The Court cast new light on the matter in a series of cases arising from the widespread efforts in the 1950's and early 1960's to require public employees, particularly teachers, to swear oaths of loyalty to the State and reveal the groups with which they associated. In *Wiemann v. Updegraff*, 344 U.S. 183 (1952), the Court held that a State could not require its employees to establish their loyalty by extracting an oath denying past affiliation with Communists. In *Cafeteria Workers v. McElroy*, 367 U.S. 886 (1961), the Court recognized that the government could not deny employment because of previous membership in a particular party. . . .

In all of these cases, the precedents in which *Pickering* is rooted, the invalidated statutes and actions sought to suppress the rights of public employees to participate in public affairs. The issue was whether government employees could be prevented or "chilled" by the fear of discharge from joining political parties and other associations that certain public officials might find "subversive." The explanation for the Constitution's special concern with threats to the right of citizens to participate in political affairs is no mystery. The First Amendment "was fashioned to assure unfettered interchange of ideas for the bringing about of political and social changes desired by the people." *Roth v. United States*, 354 U.S. 476, 484 (1957); *New York Times Co. v. Sullivan*, 376 U.S. 254, 269 (1964). "[Speech] concerning public affairs is more than self-expression; it is the essence of self-government." *Garrison v. Louisiana*, 379 U.S. 64, 74-75 (1964). Accordingly, the Court has frequently reaffirmed that speech on public issues occupies the "'highest rung of the hierarchy of First Amendment values,'" and is entitled to special protection.

Pickering v. Board of Education followed from this understanding of the First Amendment. In *Pickering*, the Court held impermissible under the First Amendment the dismissal of a high school teacher for openly criticizing the Board of Education on its allocation of school funds between athletics and education and its methods of informing taxpayers about the need for additional revenue. Pickering's subject was "a matter of legitimate public concern" upon which "free and open debate is vital to informed decisionmaking by the electorate."

Our cases following *Pickering* also involved safeguarding speech on matters of public concern. . . . Most recently, in *Givhan v. Western Line Consolidated School District*, 439 U.S. 410 (1979), we held that First Amendment protection applies when a public employee arranges to communicate privately with his employer rather than to express his views publicly. . . .

Pickering, its antecedents, and its progeny lead us to conclude that if Myers' questionnaire cannot be fairly characterized as constituting speech on a matter of public concern, it is unnecessary for us to scrutinize the reasons for her discharge. When employee expression cannot be fairly considered as relating to any matter of political, social, or other concern to the community, government officials should enjoy wide latitude in managing their offices, without intrusive oversight by the judiciary in the name of the First Amendment. Perhaps the government employer's dismissal of the worker may not be fair, but ordinary dismissals from government service which violate no fixed tenure or applicable statute or regulation are not subject to judicial review even if the reasons for the dismissal are alleged to be mistaken or unreasonable. . . .

Whether an employee's speech addresses a matter of public concern must be determined by the content, form, and context of a given statement, as revealed by the whole record.[7] In this case, with but one exception, the questions posed by Myers to her co-workers do not fall under the rubric of matters of "public concern." We view the questions pertaining to the confidence and trust that Myers' co-workers possess in various supervisors, the level of office morale, and the need for a grievance committee as mere extensions of Myers' dispute over her transfer to another section of the criminal court. . . . [W]e do not believe these questions are of public import in evaluating the performance of the District Attorney as an elected official. Myers did not seek to inform the public that the District Attorney's Office was not discharging its governmental responsibilities in the investigation and prosecution of criminal cases. Nor did Myers seek to bring to light actual or potential wrongdoing or breach of public trust on the part of Connick and others. Indeed, the questionnaire, if released to the public, would convey no information at all other than the fact that a single employee is upset with the status quo. While discipline and morale in the workplace are related to an agency's efficient performance of its duties, the focus of Myers' questions is not to evaluate the performance of the office but rather to gather ammunition for another round of controversy with her superiors. These questions reflect one employee's dissatisfaction with a transfer and an attempt to turn that displeasure into a cause célèbre.[8]

To presume that all matters which transpire within a government office are of public concern would mean that virtually every remark — and certainly every criticism directed at a public official — would plant the seed of a constitutional case. While as a matter of good judgment, public officials should be receptive to constructive criticism offered by their employees, the First Amendment does not require a public office to be run as a roundtable for employee complaints over internal office affairs.

One question in Myers' questionnaire, however, does touch upon a matter of public concern. Question 11 inquires if assistant district attorneys "ever feel pressured to work in political campaigns on behalf of office supported candidates." We have recently noted that official pressure upon employees to work for political candidates not of the worker's own choice constitutes a coercion of belief in violation of fundamental constitutional rights. *Branti v. Finkel*, [445 U.S. 507, 515-16 (1980]; *Elrod v. Burns*, 427 U.S. 347 (1976). . . . [W]e believe it apparent that the issue of

---

7. The inquiry into the protected status of speech is one of law, not fact.

8. This is not a case like *Givhan*, where an employee speaks out as a citizen on a matter of general concern, not tied to a personal employment dispute, but arranges to do so privately. Mrs. Givhan's right to protest racial discrimination — a matter inherently of public concern — is not forfeited by her choice of a private forum. Here, however, a questionnaire not otherwise of public concern does not attain that status because its subject matter could, in different circumstances, have been the topic of a communication to the public that might be of general interest. The dissent's analysis of whether discussions of office morale and discipline could be matters of public concern is beside the point — it does not answer whether *this* questionnaire is such speech.

whether assistant district attorneys are pressured to work in political campaigns is a matter of interest to the community upon which it is essential that public employees be able to speak out freely without fear of retaliatory dismissal.

B

Because one of the questions in Myers' survey touched upon a matter of public concern and contributed to her discharge, we must determine whether Connick was justified in discharging Myers. Here the District Court again erred in imposing an unduly onerous burden on the State to justify Myers' discharge. The District Court viewed the issue of whether Myers' speech was upon a matter of "public concern" as a threshold inquiry, after which it became the government's burden to "clearly demonstrate" that the speech involved "substantially interfered" with official responsibilities. Yet *Pickering* unmistakably states . . . that the State's burden in justifying a particular discharge varies depending upon the nature of the employee's expression. Although such particularized balancing is difficult, the courts must reach the most appropriate possible balance of the competing interests.

C

The *Pickering* balance requires full consideration of the government's interest in the effective and efficient fulfillment of its responsibilities to the public. One hundred years ago, the Court noted the government's legitimate purpose in "[promoting] efficiency and integrity in the discharge of official duties, and [in] [maintaining] proper discipline in the public service." *Ex parte Curtis*, [106 U.S. 371, 373 (1882)]. As Justice Powell explained in his separate opinion in *Arnett v. Kennedy*, 416 U.S. 134, 168 (1974):

> To this end, the Government, as an employer, must have wide discretion and control over the management of its personnel and internal affairs. This includes the prerogative to remove employees whose conduct hinders efficient operation and to do so with dispatch. Prolonged retention of a disruptive or otherwise unsatisfactory employee can adversely affect discipline and morale in the work place, foster disharmony, and ultimately impair the efficiency of an office or agency.

We agree with the District Court that there is no demonstration here that the questionnaire impeded Myers' ability to perform her responsibilities. The District Court was also correct to recognize that "it is important to the efficient and successful operation of the District Attorney's office for Assistants to maintain close working relationships with their superiors." Connick's judgment, and apparently also that of his first assistant Dennis Waldron, who characterized Myers' actions as causing a "mini-insurrection," was that Myers' questionnaire was an act of insubordination which interfered with working relationships. When close working relationships are essential to fulfilling public responsibilities, a wide degree of deference to the employer's judgment is appropriate. Furthermore, we do not see the necessity for an employer to allow events to unfold to the extent that the disruption of the office and the destruction of working relationships is manifest before taking action. We caution that a stronger showing may be necessary if the employee's speech more substantially involved matters of public concern.

. . . Questions, no less than forcefully stated opinions and facts, carry messages and it requires no unusual insight to conclude that the purpose, if not the likely result, of the questionnaire is to seek to precipitate a vote of no confidence in Connick and his supervisors. Thus, Question 10, which asked whether or not the Assistants had confidence in and relied on the word of five named supervisors, is a statement that carries the clear potential for undermining office relations.

Also relevant is the manner, time, and place in which the questionnaire was distributed. . . . Here the questionnaire was prepared and distributed at the office; the manner of distribution required not only Myers to leave her work but others to do the same in order that the questionnaire be completed.[13] Although some latitude in when official work is performed is to be allowed when professional employees are involved, and Myers did not violate announced office policy, the fact that Myers, unlike Pickering, exercised her rights to speech at the office supports Connick's fears that the functioning of his office was endangered.

Finally, the context in which the dispute arose is also significant. This is not a case where an employee, out of purely academic interest, circulated a questionnaire so as to obtain useful research. Myers acknowledges that it is no coincidence that the questionnaire followed upon the heels of the transfer notice. When employee speech concerning office policy arises from an employment dispute concerning the very application of that policy to the speaker, additional weight must be given to the supervisor's view that the employee has threatened the authority of the employer to run the office. . . .

III

Myers' questionnaire touched upon matters of public concern in only a most limited sense; her survey, in our view, is most accurately characterized as an employee grievance concerning internal office policy. The limited First Amendment interest involved here does not require that Connick tolerate action which he reasonably believed would disrupt the office, undermine his authority, and destroy close working relationships. Myers' discharge therefore did not offend the First Amendment. We reiterate, however, the caveat we expressed in *Pickering:* "Because of the enormous variety of fact situations in which critical statements by . . . public employees may be thought by their superiors . . . to furnish grounds for dismissal, we do not deem it either appropriate or feasible to attempt to lay down a general standard against which all such statements may be judged."

Our holding today is grounded in our longstanding recognition that the First Amendment's primary aim is the full protection of speech upon issues of public concern, as well as the practical realities involved in the administration of a government office. Although today the balance is struck for the government, this is no defeat for the First Amendment. For it would indeed be a Pyrrhic victory for the great principles of free expression if the Amendment's safeguarding of a public employee's right, as a

---

13. The record indicates that some, though not all, of the copies of the questionnaire were distributed during lunch. Employee speech which transpires entirely on the employee's own time, and in nonwork areas of the office, bring different factors into the *Pickering* calculus, and might lead to a different conclusion.

citizen, to participate in discussions concerning public affairs were confused with the attempt to constitutionalize the employee grievance that we see presented here. The judgment of the Court of Appeals is *Reversed*.[*]

NOTES

1. *The* Pickering/Connick *Balancing Test.* In determining whether Myers' termination violated her First and Fourteenth Amendment speech rights, the Court applied an analytical framework that has come to be known as the "*Pickering/Connick* balancing test." For speech in or related to the workplace, the employee must establish that the expression addresses a matter of public concern. As *Connick* demonstrates, aspects of the employee's speech that do not address matters of public concern receive no First Amendment protection. If the speech or portions of it do address matters of public concern, the court then "balances" the employee's interest in speaking on matters of public concern with the employer's interest in promoting workplace efficiency. Finally, even if the employee's interest in free expression prevails in the balance, the employee must also demonstrate causation; that is, the employer disciplined or dismissed the employee because of the employee's speech. This issue was not reached in *Connick*, given the Court's conclusion on the application of the balancing test; had the dissenting opinion been the majority, a remand would likely have been necessary to determine whether the district attorney fired Myers because of her questionnaire or, as the district attorney's office alleged, because of her refusal to accept the transfer.

2. *"A Matter of Public Concern."* Why does the Court limit employee protection against speech-related adverse employment actions to matters of public concern? Obviously, the distinction is important: Indeed, whether Myers' speech addressed a matter of public concern was dispositive. Yet what is a matter of public concern? From *Connick*, we have guidance as to what is *not* a matter of public concern: "When employee expression cannot be fairly considered as relating to any matter of political, social, or other concern to the community." Moreover, the *Connick* majority views speech addressing the internal affairs of the agency and not rising above mere dissatisfaction or displeasure with one's supervisors as not implicating public concern. In other words, mere personal concerns or interests, as opposed to those of the employee as a citizen, are not matters of public concern. *See, e.g., Rodgers v. Banks*, 344 F.3d 587, 599 (6th Cir. 2003) (noting *Connick's* personal interest versus citizen dichotomy).

---

[*] *Editor's Note: Employment Law Trivia.* The defendant in *Connick v. Myers* was Harry Connick, Sr., district attorney for Orleans Parish. You may have heard of his son, musician Harry Connick, Jr. The father became district attorney by beating a famous (or infamous) predecessor in the post, Jim Garrison, who played a role in investigating the Kennedy assassination and, depending on who you believe, either (1) uncovered the true conspiracy only to be foiled by the FBI, (2) bungled a potentially effective investigation, or (3) went on a wild goose chase. Coincidentally, *Garrison v. Louisiana*, cited by the Supreme Court in *Connick* as one of the foundational free speech cases, involved Jim Garrison, who had been found guilty of "criminal defamation"—when he claimed that the large backlog of pending criminal cases was due to the laziness of the judges and that failures of law enforcement were due to their failure to authorize funds for the district attorney. 379 U.S. at 66. The Supreme Court reversed Garrison's conviction. Undoubtedly, Ms. Myers relied heavily on her boss's predecessor's claims of free-speech rights in pursuing her suit against Connick. In the aftermath, Connick, Sr. continued on as New Orleans District Attorney until 2002, Dennis Waldron became a judge in the Criminal Court, and Sheila Myers is a well-respected criminal defense attorney who litigates frequently against her former employer. Myers' biggest regret, though, is that the decision "is cited as the case against public employees." http://www.freedomforum.org/templates/.

On the flip side, *Connick* makes clear that employee expression need not be shared with the public to address a matter of public concern. In other words, it may be purely internal, although the fact that it is not shared with the public may affect the analysis of whether it implicates a public concern. *See also Rankin v. McPherson*, 483 U.S. 378 (1987) (finding one worker's statement to a co-worker, after finding out that President Reagan had been shot, that "[i]f they go after him again, I hope they get him" addressed a matter of public concern). In terms of content, speech relating to broad public policy issues and improprieties in the agency, as well as public statements questioning the effectiveness of the agency have been recognized as matters of public concern. *See, e.g., Pickering*, 391 U.S. at 571-73; *Rodgers*, 344 F.3d at 600-01 (finding a memo addressing patient care deficiencies occurring at a public nursing care facility addressed matters of public concern). In addition, statements about current political events or high-ranking public officials are matters of public concern. *See, e.g., Rankin*, 483 U.S. at 386-87; *Bland v. Roberts*, 730 F.3d 368 (4th Cir. 2013) (finding deputy sheriff's stated preferences about county sheriff candidates to be protected speech). Moreover, issues or information regarding the functioning, decisions, or initiatives of the department or agency have been found to be matters of public concern where the larger community has shown interest. *See, e.g., Kennedy v. Tangipahoa Parish Library Bd. of Control*, 224 F.3d 359, 373 (5th Cir. 2000) (asserting that "speech made against the backdrop of ongoing commentary and debate in the press involves the public concern"); *Burnham v. Ianni*, 119 F.3d 668 (8th Cir. 1997) (en banc) (holding a display in a public university's history department containing pictures of professors with props associated with their areas of expertise that sparked controversy was a matter of public concern because of the public interest in it). Speech related to the collective bargaining process and other union activities (beyond personal grievances) has been found to be a matter of public concern. *See, e.g., Davignon v. Hodgson*, 524 F.3d 91 (1st Cir. 2008). And, as the majority's citation of *Givhan* indicates, courts have usually found that allegations of discrimination raise matters of public concern. *See, e.g., Love-Lane v. Martin*, 355 F.3d 766 (4th Cir. 2004) (finding concerns regarding discriminatory practices in school system to be matter of public concern).

In *Snyder v. Phelps*, 131 S. Ct. 1207 (2011), the Supreme Court held that the First Amendment shielded the Westboro Baptist Church and its members from tort liability for picketing outside of the funeral of Matthew Snyder, a soldier killed in the line of duty in the Iraq War. Because the Court determined that First Amendment protection depended on whether the speech involved matters of public concern, it explored that concept in some detail. *Id.* at 1215-17. In so doing, it quoted liberally from the government employee speech decisions — *Pickering, Connick, Rankin*, and *San Diego v. Roe* (discussed in the notes below). *See id.* at 1216-17.

Although the Court did not provide significantly greater guidance on how to distinguish matters of public concern from those that are private in nature, it did confirm that the inquiry is contextual, requiring an examination of the "content, form, and context" of the speech as revealed by the whole record. *Id.* at 1211. Despite being deeply offensive to many, Westboro's signs plainly related to public matters — the political and moral conduct of the United States and its citizens, the fate of the nation, homosexuality in the military, and scandals involving the Catholic clergy — and were designed to reach a broad public audience even though some of the messages related to a particular individual. *Id.* at 1216. Additionally, while the picketing coincided with Snyder's funeral, it did not disrupt the ceremony because it occurred in a peaceful manner, 1,000 feet away in a public park, and Snyder's family was unaware of the context of the signs until they saw the display on the news later that evening. *Id.* at 1219-20. Thus, the Court concluded that the connection of the picketing with Snyder's funeral did not transform the nature of the speech, even though Westboro's selection of Snyder's funeral may have been particularly hurtful to his family. *Id.* at 1220.

Still, it remains unclear whether other matters of public interest not necessarily involving prevailing political issues, government policies, or government officials constitute matters of public concern. For example, although a resulting adverse action against a public employee may seem unlikely in this context, what about obnoxious statements regarding a celebrity, a sports team or famous athlete, or well-known entertainment event? Similarly, what about comments regarding popular but controversial movies — for example, *An Inconvenient Truth, The Passion of the Christ,* or *Brokeback Mountain* — that may anger or offend other employees? In other words, does "public concern" simply mean something that has captured the public's interest or imagination, or is something more required? *See generally* Randy J. Kozel, *Free Speech and Parity: A Theory of Public Employee Rights,* 53 WM. & MARY L. REV. 1985 (2012); Cynthia L. Estlund, *Speech on Matters of Public Concern: The Perils of an Emerging First Amendment Category,* 59 GEO. WASH. L. REV. 1 (1990); *see also* George Rutherglen, *Public Employee Speech in Remedial Perspective,* 24 J. L. & POLITICS 129, 130 (2008) (questioning whether the "public concern" test is appropriate in light of its uncertain application).

3. *"Balancing" the Interests.* In balancing the employee's interest against the employer's, the Supreme Court has likewise provided less-than-clear guidance. The Court was unwilling in either *Connick* or *Pickering* to lay down clear parameters for how to engage in the balancing inquiry. *See, e.g., Pickering,* 391 U.S. at 569. Rather than weighing the competing interests, both opinions focused on the employer's interest in efficiency, exploring whether the employee's statements might have actually disrupted the workplace. Indeed, in *Pickering,* the Court's balancing analysis consisted entirely of the following discussion, after which the Court found in favor of the employee:

> The [teacher's] statements are in no way directed towards any person with whom appellant would normally be in contact in the course of his daily work as a teacher. Thus no question of maintaining either discipline by immediate superiors or harmony among coworkers is presented here. Appellant's employment relationships with the Board and, to a somewhat lesser extent, with the superintendent are not the kind of close working relationships for which it can persuasively be claimed that personal loyalty and confidence are necessary to their proper functioning.

Id. at 569-70; *see also Rankin,* 483 U.S. at 388-89 (finding employee's interests outweighed employer's in the case involving a deputy constable's comments about attempted presidential assassination after rejecting the employer's claims of disruption, public relations problems, and loss in efficiency).

Thus, once the employee has made his or her threshold showing, so-called "balancing" in the speech-in-the-workplace context — as in the privacy-in-the-workplace context — tends instead to be an inquiry into the strength of the employer's proffered justification for taking action against the employee. Occasionally, however, courts have recognized that the importance of the content of the speech increases the burden on the government to show that efficiency concerns ought to prevail. *See, e.g., Love-Lane*, 355 F.3d at 785 (stating that because race discrimination in schools involves a substantial issue of public concern, the government's burden is heightened). Other efficiency interests offered by government employers and recognized by the courts include preserving confidentiality and protecting the public, and, where it is necessary, ensuring loyalty. *See, e.g., Sheppard v. Beerman*, 317 F.3d 351 (2d Cir. 2003) (finding no constitutional violation after the judge terminated a law clerk who directed an obscene epithet at him because of the potential disruptiveness of retaining a disloyal and disrespectful clerk in the extremely close and confidential work setting).

The Supreme Court has also indicated that the employer bears the burden of establishing the objective good faith of its proffered efficiency concerns. In other words, it is the employer's obligation to demonstrate that its action was in good faith (not pretextual) and based on a reasonable assessment of the circumstances in terms of whether the speech actually occurred and the extent to which it is likely to lead to disruption or harm efficiency. *See Waters v. Churchill*, 511 U.S. 661, 677-78 (1994).

4. Pickering/Connick *Applied.* Unsurprisingly, this framework has produced mixed results in the lower federal courts, although the defending government institution more often prevails. *Compare Nichols v. Dancer*, 657 F.3d 929 (9th Cir. 2011) (stating that the employer cannot prevail in *Pickering* balancing test merely because of speculation that the employee's show of support for her former boss at a school board meeting would cause some workplace disruption), *and Love-Lane*, 355 F.3d at 785 (indicating that "some disharmony" caused by employee's criticisms of allegedly discriminatory practices is not enough to justify adverse employment action), *with Vanderpuye v. Cohen*, 94 F. App'x 3 (2d Cir. 2004) (finding that, although city employee's speech regarding conflicts of interest was a matter of public concern, it was outweighed by potential for disruption in functioning of department), *and Sheppard*, 317 F.3d at 355 (upholding constitutionality of termination of judicial clerk after outbursts).

Public employers tend to prevail in cases in which the speech is offensive, threatening, or harassing to protected groups, including women and minorities, although courts are often unwilling to find that vague or indirect statements, even if hyperbolic, are threatening or harassing. *Compare Pappas v. Giuliani*, 290 F.3d 143 (2d Cir. 2002) (upholding municipality's right to terminate police officer after his anonymous dissemination of racist and anti-Semitic materials), *with Bauer v. Sampson*, 261 F.3d 775 (9th Cir. 2001) (rejecting defendant college's contention that professor's scathing and hyperbolic criticisms of new administrator were threatening or discriminatory and were sufficiently disruptive to warrant discipline). To the extent that the employee's speech might itself violate the law, such as constituting racial or sexual harassment of co-workers, *see* Chapter 9, the employer will obviously have a greater interest in acting. *See, e.g.,* J.M. Balkin, *Free Speech and Hostile Environments*, 99 COLUM. L. REV. 2295 (1999); Cynthia L. Estlund, *Freedom of Expression in the Workplace and the Problem of Discriminatory Harassment*, 75 TEX. L. REV. 687 (1997); Eugene Volokh, *What Speech Does "Hostile Work Environment" Harassment Law Restrict?*, 85 GEO. L. J. 627 (1997).

5. *The Petition Clause and Workplace Speech. Borough of Duryea v. Guarnieri*, 131 S. Ct. 2488 (2011), addressed a public employee's claims under the Petition

Clause of the First Amendment. After Charles Guarnieri was terminated as the police chief of Duryea, he filed a union grievance and was reinstated to his position. When the borough council later issued directives instructing Guarnieri how to perform his duties, he filed suit, alleging that the directives were issued in retaliation for the filing of his first grievance, violating his First Amendment right to petition the government for a redress. He later amended his complaint to allege that the council also violated the Petition Clause by denying his request for overtime pay in retaliation for his having filed the suit. *Id*. at 2492. The Court held that a government employer's retaliatory actions against an employee do not give rise to liability under the Petition Clause unless the employee's petition relates to a matter of public concern. The Court reasoned that, although the Speech and Petition Clauses should not be treated identically, petitions, like speech, can "interfere with the efficient and effective operation of government." *Id*. at 2495. Because public employers have a substantial interest in controlling petitions that can "bring the mission of the employer and professionalism of its officers into serious disrepute," employees should not be able to circumvent the limitations applicable to speech claims by simply labeling their grievance as a "petition." *Id*. at 2495-96.

Turning to the question of whether an employee's petition relates to a matter of public concern, resolution depends on "the content, form, and context" of the petition, as revealed by the whole record. *Id*. at 2501. The Court then noted, citing *Snyder, supra*, that the forum in which a petition is lodged will be relevant to determining whether the petition relates to a matter of public concern. It went on to state that "[a] petition filed with an employer using an internal grievance procedure in many cases will not seek to communicate to the public or to advance a political or social point of view beyond the employment context." *Id*.

In *Guarneiri*'s wake, it is unclear whether the Petition Clause affords public employees much meaningful protection. The Court's treatment of the public concern test suggests that statements made by employees in internal grievance procedures are unlikely to be protected. Yet the Court also emphasized that external petitions, such as lawsuits (although more likely to implicate matters of public concern), may be highly disruptive to the public employer, and, hence, may not survive *Pickering/Connick* balancing. *See id*. at 2496-97. Whether public employee Petition Clause claims can successfully travel this seemingly narrow path remains an open question.

6. *Speech and Employee Duties.* What if employee speech on a matter of public concern is not only in the workplace, but also in the context of the employee performing his or her particular job duties? The Court took up this issue in the next case.

═══ *Garcetti v. Ceballos*
═══ *547 U.S. 410 (2006)*

JUSTICE KENNEDY delivered the opinion of the Court.

It is well settled that "a State cannot condition public employment on a basis that infringes the employee's constitutionally protected interest in freedom of expression." *Connick v. Myers*. The question presented by the instant case is whether the First Amendment protects a government employee from discipline based on speech made pursuant to the employee's official duties.

I

Respondent Richard Ceballos has been employed since 1989 as a deputy district attorney for the Los Angeles County District Attorney's Office. During the period relevant to this case, Ceballos was a calendar deputy in the office's Pomona branch, and in this capacity he exercised certain supervisory responsibilities over other lawyers. In February 2000, a defense attorney contacted Ceballos about a pending criminal case. The defense attorney said there were inaccuracies in an affidavit used to obtain a critical search warrant. The attorney informed Ceballos that he had filed a motion to traverse, or challenge, the warrant, but he also wanted Ceballos to review the case. According to Ceballos, it was not unusual for defense attorneys to ask calendar deputies to investigate aspects of pending cases.

After examining the affidavit and visiting the location it described, Ceballos determined the affidavit contained serious misrepresentations. The affidavit called a long driveway what Ceballos thought should have been referred to as a separate roadway. Ceballos also questioned the affidavit's statement that tire tracks led from a stripped-down truck to the premises covered by the warrant. His doubts arose from his conclusion that the roadway's composition in some places made it difficult or impossible to leave visible tire tracks.

Ceballos spoke on the telephone to the warrant affiant, a deputy sheriff from the Los Angeles County Sheriff's Department, but he did not receive a satisfactory explanation for the perceived inaccuracies. He relayed his findings to his supervisors, petitioners Carol Najera and Frank Sundstedt, and followed up by preparing a disposition memorandum. The memo explained Ceballos' concerns and recommended dismissal of the case. On March 2, 2000, Ceballos submitted the memo to Sundstedt for his review. A few days later, Ceballos presented Sundstedt with another memo, this one describing a second telephone conversation between Ceballos and the warrant affiant.

Based on Ceballos' statements, a meeting was held to discuss the affidavit. Attendees included Ceballos, Sundstedt, and Najera, as well as the warrant affiant and other employees from the sheriff's department. The meeting allegedly became heated, with one lieutenant sharply criticizing Ceballos for his handling of the case.

Despite Ceballos' concerns, Sundstedt decided to proceed with the prosecution, pending disposition of the defense motion to traverse. The trial court held a hearing on the motion. Ceballos was called by the defense and recounted his observations about the affidavit, but the trial court rejected the challenge to the warrant.

[Ceballos sued, claiming that he was subjected to a series of retaliatory employment actions for his March 2 memo. The district court granted defendants summary judgment, but the Ninth Circuit reversed, holding that "Ceballos's allegations of wrongdoing in the memorandum constitute protected speech under the First Amendment."]

II

As the Court's decisions have noted, for many years "the unchallenged dogma was that a public employee had no right to object to conditions placed upon the terms of employment—including those which restricted the exercise of constitutional rights." *Connick*. That dogma has been qualified in important respects. *See id*. The Court has made clear that public employees do not surrender all their First

Amendment rights by reason of their employment. Rather, the First Amendment protects a public employee's right, in certain circumstances, to speak as a citizen addressing matters of public concern. *See, e.g.,* [*Pickering; Connick; Rankin v. McPherson*, 483 U.S. 378, 384 (1987); *United States v. Treasury Employees*, 513 U.S. 454, 466 (1995)]. . . .

[The Court outlined the *Pickering/Connick* balancing test.] A government entity has broader discretion to restrict speech when it acts in its role as employer, but the restrictions it imposes must be directed at speech that has some potential to affect the entity's operations.

To be sure, conducting these inquiries sometimes has proved difficult. . . .

When a citizen enters government service, the citizen by necessity must accept certain limitations on his or her freedom. Government employers, like private employers, need a significant degree of control over their employees' words and actions; without it, there would be little chance for the efficient provision of public services. *Cf. Connick* ("[G]overnment offices could not function if every employment decision became a constitutional matter"). Public employees, moreover, often occupy trusted positions in society. When they speak out, they can express views that contravene governmental policies or impair the proper performance of governmental functions.

At the same time, the Court has recognized that a citizen who works for the government is nonetheless a citizen. The First Amendment limits the ability of a public employer to leverage the employment relationship to restrict, incidentally or intentionally, the liberties employees enjoy in their capacities as private citizens. *See Perry v. Sindermann*, 408 U.S. 593, 597 (1972). So long as employees are speaking as citizens about matters of public concern, they must face only those speech restrictions that are necessary for their employers to operate efficiently and effectively. *See, e.g., Connick*.

The Court's employee-speech jurisprudence protects, of course, the constitutional rights of public employees. Yet the First Amendment interests at stake extend beyond the individual speaker. The Court has acknowledged the importance of promoting the public's interest in receiving the well-informed views of government employees engaging in civic discussion. *Pickering* again provides an instructive example. The Court characterized its holding as rejecting the attempt of school administrators to "limi[t] teachers' opportunities to contribute to public debate." It also noted that teachers are "the members of a community most likely to have informed and definite opinions" about school expenditures. The Court's approach acknowledged the necessity for informed, vibrant dialogue in a democratic society. It suggested, in addition, that widespread costs may arise when dialogue is repressed. The Court's more recent cases have expressed similar concerns. *See, e.g., San Diego v. Roe*, 543 U.S. 77, 82 (2004) *(per curiam)* ("Were [public employees] not able to speak on [the operation of their employers], the community would be deprived of informed opinions on important public issues. The interest at stake is as much the public's interest in receiving informed opinion as it is the employee's own right to disseminate it" (citation omitted)); *cf. Treasury Employees* ("The large-scale disincentive to Government employees' expression also imposes a significant burden on the public's right to read and hear what the employees would otherwise have written and said").

The Court's decisions, then, have sought both to promote the individual and societal interests that are served when employees speak as citizens on matters of public concern and to respect the needs of government employers attempting to perform their important public functions. Underlying our cases has been the premise that while the First Amendment invests public employees with certain rights, it does not empower them to "constitutionalize the employee grievance." *Connick.*

III

With these principles in mind we turn to the instant case. Respondent Ceballos believed the affidavit used to obtain a search warrant contained serious misrepresentations. He conveyed his opinion and recommendation in a memo to his supervisor. That Ceballos expressed his views inside his office, rather than publicly, is not dispositive. Employees in some cases may receive First Amendment protection for expressions made at work. *See, e.g., Givhan v. Western Line Consol. School Dist.*, 439 U.S. 410, 414 (1979). Many citizens do much of their talking inside their respective workplaces, and it would not serve the goal of treating public employees like "any member of the general public," *Pickering*, to hold that all speech within the office is automatically exposed to restriction.

The memo concerned the subject matter of Ceballos' employment, but this, too, is nondispositive. The First Amendment protects some expressions related to the speaker's job. As the Court noted in *Pickering:* "Teachers are, as a class, the members of a community most likely to have informed and definite opinions as to how funds allotted to the operation of the schools should be spent. Accordingly, it is essential that they be able to speak out freely on such questions without fear of retaliatory dismissal." The same is true of many other categories of public employees.

The controlling factor in Ceballos' case is that his expressions were made pursuant to his duties as a calendar deputy. That consideration — the fact that Ceballos spoke as a prosecutor fulfilling a responsibility to advise his supervisor about how best to proceed with a pending case — distinguishes Ceballos' case from those in which the First Amendment provides protection against discipline. We hold that when public employees make statements pursuant to their official duties, the employees are not speaking as citizens for First Amendment purposes, and the Constitution does not insulate their communications from employer discipline.

Ceballos wrote his disposition memo because that is part of what he, as a calendar deputy, was employed to do. It is immaterial whether he experienced some personal gratification from writing the memo; his First Amendment rights do not depend on his job satisfaction. The significant point is that the memo was written pursuant to Ceballos' official duties. Restricting speech that owes its existence to a public employee's professional responsibilities does not infringe any liberties the employee might have enjoyed as a private citizen. It simply reflects the exercise of employer control over what the employer itself has commissioned or created. *Cf. Rosenberger v. Rector and Visitors of Univ. of Va.*, 515 U.S. 819, 833 (1995) ("[W]hen the government appropriates public funds to promote a particular policy of its own it is entitled to say what it wishes"). Contrast, for example, the expressions made by the speaker in *Pickering*, whose letter to the newspaper had no official significance and bore similarities to letters submitted by numerous citizens every day.

Ceballos did not act as a citizen when he went about conducting his daily professional activities, such as supervising attorneys, investigating charges, and preparing filings. In the same way he did not speak as a citizen by writing a memo that addressed the proper disposition of a pending criminal case. When he went to work and performed the tasks he was paid to perform, Ceballos acted as a government employee. The fact that his duties sometimes required him to speak or write does not mean his supervisors were prohibited from evaluating his performance.

This result is consistent with our precedents' attention to the potential societal value of employee speech. Refusing to recognize First Amendment claims based on government employees' work product does not prevent them from participating in public debate. The employees retain the prospect of constitutional protection for their contributions to the civic discourse. This prospect of protection, however, does not invest them with a right to perform their jobs however they see fit.

Our holding likewise is supported by the emphasis of our precedents on affording government employers sufficient discretion to manage their operations. Employers have heightened interests in controlling speech made by an employee in his or her professional capacity. Official communications have official consequences, creating a need for substantive consistency and clarity. Supervisors must ensure that their employees' official communications are accurate, demonstrate sound judgment, and promote the employer's mission. Ceballos' memo is illustrative. It demanded the attention of his supervisors and led to a heated meeting with employees from the sheriff's department. If Ceballos' superiors thought his memo was inflammatory or misguided, they had the authority to take proper corrective action.

Ceballos' proposed contrary rule, adopted by the Court of Appeals, would commit state and federal courts to a new, permanent, and intrusive role, mandating judicial oversight of communications between and among government employees and their superiors in the course of official business. This displacement of managerial discretion by judicial supervision finds no support in our precedents. When an employee speaks as a citizen addressing a matter of public concern, the First Amendment requires a delicate balancing of the competing interests surrounding the speech and its consequences. When, however, the employee is simply performing his or her job duties, there is no warrant for a similar degree of scrutiny. To hold otherwise would be to demand permanent judicial intervention in the conduct of governmental operations to a degree inconsistent with sound principles of federalism and the separation of powers.

The Court of Appeals based its holding in part on what it perceived as a doctrinal anomaly. The court suggested it would be inconsistent to compel public employers to tolerate certain employee speech made publicly but not speech made pursuant to an employee's assigned duties. This objection misconceives the theoretical underpinnings of our decisions. Employees who make public statements outside the course of performing their official duties retain some possibility of First Amendment protection because that is the kind of activity engaged in by citizens who do not work for the government. The same goes for writing a letter to a local newspaper, see *Pickering*, or discussing politics with a co-worker, *see Rankin*. When a public employee speaks pursuant to employment responsibilities, however, there is no relevant analogue to speech by citizens who are not government employees.

The Court of Appeals' concern also is unfounded as a practical matter. The perceived anomaly, it should be noted, is limited in scope: It relates only to the expressions an employee makes pursuant to his or her official responsibilities, not to statements or complaints (such as those at issue in cases like *Pickering* and *Connick*) that are made outside the duties of employment. If, moreover, a government employer is troubled by the perceived anomaly, it has the means at hand to avoid it. A public employer that wishes to encourage its employees to voice concerns privately retains the option of instituting internal policies and procedures that are receptive to employee criticism.

Giving employees an internal forum for their speech will discourage them from concluding that the safest avenue of expression is to state their views in public.

Proper application of our precedents thus leads to the conclusion that the First Amendment does not prohibit managerial discipline based on an employee's expressions made pursuant to official responsibilities. Because Ceballos' memo falls into this category, his allegation of unconstitutional retaliation must fail.

Two final points warrant mentioning. First, as indicated above, the parties in this case do not dispute that Ceballos wrote his disposition memo pursuant to his employment duties. We thus have no occasion to articulate a comprehensive framework for defining the scope of an employee's duties in cases where there is room for serious debate. We reject, however, the suggestion that employers can restrict employees' rights by creating excessively broad job descriptions. The proper inquiry is a practical one. Formal job descriptions often bear little resemblance to the duties an employee actually is expected to perform, and the listing of a given task in an employee's written job description is neither necessary nor sufficient to demonstrate that conducting the task is within the scope of the employee's professional duties for First Amendment purposes.

Second, Justice Souter suggests today's decision may have important ramifications for academic freedom, at least as a constitutional value. There is some argument that expression related to academic scholarship or classroom instruction implicates additional constitutional interests that are not fully accounted for by this Court's customary employee-speech jurisprudence. We need not, and for that reason do not, decide whether the analysis we conduct today would apply in the same manner to a case involving speech related to scholarship or teaching. . . .

IV

Exposing governmental inefficiency and misconduct is a matter of considerable significance. As the Court noted in *Connick*, public employers should, "as a matter of good judgment," be "receptive to constructive criticism offered by their employees." The dictates of sound judgment are reinforced by the powerful network of legislative enactments — such as whistle-blower protection laws and labor codes — available to those who seek to expose wrongdoing. Cases involving government attorneys implicate additional safeguards in the form of, for example, rules of conduct and constitutional obligations apart from the First Amendment. *See, e.g.,* Cal. Rule Prof. Conduct 5-110 (2005) ("A member in government service shall not institute or cause to be instituted criminal charges when the member knows or should know that the charges are not supported by probable cause"); *Brady v. Maryland,* 373 U.S. 83 (1963). These imperatives, as well as obligations arising from any other applicable constitutional provisions and mandates of the criminal and civil laws, protect employees and provide checks on supervisors who would order unlawful or otherwise inappropriate actions.

We reject, however, the notion that the First Amendment shields from discipline the expressions employees make pursuant to their professional duties. Our precedents do not support the existence of a constitutional cause of action behind every statement a public employee makes in the course of doing his or her job. . . .

JUSTICE SOUTER, with whom JUSTICE STEVENS and JUSTICE GINSBURG join, dissenting.

. . . I agree with the majority that a government employer has substantial interests in effectuating its chosen policy and objectives, and in demanding competence, honesty, and judgment from employees who speak for it in doing their work. But I would hold that private and public interests in addressing official wrongdoing and threats to health and safety can outweigh the government's stake in the efficient implementation of policy, and when they do public employees who speak on these matters in the course of their duties should be eligible to claim First Amendment protection.

I

Open speech by a private citizen on a matter of public importance lies at the heart of expression subject to protection by the First Amendment. At the other extreme, a statement by a government employee complaining about nothing beyond treatment under personnel rules raises no greater claim to constitutional protection against retaliatory response than the remarks of a private employee. *See Connick v. Myers.* In between these points lies a public employee's speech unwelcome to the government but on a significant public issue. Such an employee speaking as a citizen, that is, with a citizen's interest, is protected from reprisal unless the statements are too damaging to the government's capacity to conduct public business to be justified by any individual or public benefit thought to flow from the statements. *Pickering.* Entitlement to protection is thus not absolute.

This significant, albeit qualified, protection of public employees who irritate the government is understood to flow from the First Amendment, in part, because a government paycheck does nothing to eliminate the value to an individual of speaking on public matters, and there is no good reason for categorically discounting a speaker's interest in commenting on a matter of public concern just because the government employs him. Still, the First Amendment safeguard rests on something more, being the value to the public of receiving the opinions and information that a public employee may disclose. "Government employees are often in the best position to know what ails the agencies for which they work." *Waters v. Churchill*, 511 U.S. 661, 674 (1994).

The reason that protection of employee speech is qualified is that it can distract co-workers and supervisors from their tasks at hand and thwart the implementation of legitimate policy, the risks of which grow greater the closer the employee's speech gets to commenting on his own workplace and responsibilities. It is one thing for an office clerk to say there is waste in government and quite another to charge that his own department pays full-time salaries to part-time workers. Even so, we have regarded eligibility for protection by *Pickering* balancing as the proper approach when an employee speaks critically about the administration of his own government employer. In *Givhan v. Western Line Consol. School Dist.* we followed *Pickering* when a teacher was fired for complaining to a superior about the racial composition of the school's administrative, cafeteria, and library staffs, and the same point was clear in *Madison Joint School Dist. No. 8 v. Wisconsin Employment Relations Comm'n*, 429 U.S. 167 (1976) . . . [holding] that a schoolteacher speaking out on behalf of himself and others at a public school board meeting could not be penalized for criticizing pending collective-bargaining negotiations affecting professional employment. . . . In each case, the Court realized that a public employee can wear a citizen's hat when speaking on subjects closely tied to the employee's own job, and *Givhan* stands for the same conclusion even when the speech is not addressed to the public at large.

The difference between a case like *Givhan* and this one is that the subject of Ceballos's speech fell within the scope of his job responsibilities, whereas choosing personnel was not what the teacher was hired to do. The effect of the majority's constitutional line between these two cases, then, is that a *Givhan* schoolteacher is protected when complaining to the principal about hiring policy, but a school personnel officer would not be if he protested that the principal disapproved of hiring minority job applicants. This is an odd place to draw a distinction,[1] and while necessary judicial line-drawing sometimes looks arbitrary, any distinction obliges a court to justify its choice. Here, there is no adequate justification for the majority's line categorically denying *Pickering* protection to any speech uttered "pursuant to . . . official duties."

As all agree, the qualified speech protection embodied in *Pickering* balancing resolves the tension between individual and public interests in the speech, on the one hand, and the government's interest in operating efficiently without distraction or embarrassment by talkative or headline-grabbing employees. The need for a balance hardly disappears when an employee speaks on matters his job requires him to address; rather, it seems obvious that the individual and public value of such speech is no less, and may well be greater, when the employee speaks pursuant to his duties in addressing a subject he knows intimately for the very reason that it falls within his duties.[2]

The majority's response, that the enquiry to determine duties is a "practical one," does not alleviate this concern. It sets out a standard that will not discourage government employers from setting duties expansively, but will engender litigation to decide which stated duties were actual and which were merely formal.

As for the importance of such speech to the individual, it stands to reason that a citizen may well place a very high value on a right to speak on the public issues he decides to make the subject of his work day after day. Would anyone doubt that a school principal evaluating the performance of teachers for promotion or pay adjustment retains a citizen's interest in addressing the quality of teaching in the schools? (Still, the majority indicates he could be fired without First Amendment recourse for fair but unfavorable comment when the teacher under review is the superintendent's daughter.) Would anyone deny that a prosecutor like Richard Ceballos may claim the interest of any citizen in speaking out against a rogue law enforcement officer, simply because his job requires him to express a judgment about the officer's performance? (But the majority says the First Amendment gives Ceballos no protection, even if his judgment in this case was sound and appropriately expressed.) . . .

Indeed, the very idea of categorically separating the citizen's interest from the employee's interest ignores the fact that the ranks of public service include those who

---

1. It seems strange still in light of the majority's concession of some First Amendment protection when a public employee repeats statements made pursuant to his duties but in a separate, public forum or in a letter to a newspaper.

2. I do not say the value of speech "pursuant to . . . duties" will always be greater, because I am pessimistic enough to expect that one response to the Court's holding will be moves by government employers to expand stated job descriptions to include more official duties and so exclude even some currently protectable speech from First Amendment purview. Now that the government can freely penalize the school personnel officer for criticizing the principal because speech on the subject falls within the personnel officer's job responsibilities, the government may well try to limit the English teacher's options by the simple expedient of defining teachers' job responsibilities expansively, investing them with a general obligation to ensure sound administration of the school. Hence today's rule presents the regrettable prospect that protection under *Pickering* may be diminished by expansive statements of employment duties.

share the poet's "object . . . to unite [m]y avocation and my vocation";[3] these citizen servants are the ones whose civic interest rises highest when they speak pursuant to their duties, and these are exactly the ones government employers most want to attract. . . .

Nor is there any reason to raise the counterintuitive question whether the public interest in hearing informed employees evaporates when they speak as required on some subject at the core of their jobs. Two terms ago, we recalled the public value that the *Pickering* Court perceived in the speech of public employees as a class: "Underlying the decision in *Pickering* is the recognition that public employees are often the members of the community who are likely to have informed opinions as to the operations of their public employers, operations which are of substantial concern to the public. Were they not able to speak on these matters, the community would be deprived of informed opinions on important public issues. The interest at stake is as much the public's interest in receiving informed opinion as it is the employee's own right to disseminate it." *San Diego v. Roe* (citation omitted). This is not a whit less true when an employee's job duties require him to speak about such things: when, for example, a public auditor speaks on his discovery of embezzlement of public funds, when a building inspector makes an obligatory report of an attempt to bribe him, or when a law enforcement officer expressly balks at a superior's order to violate constitutional rights he is sworn to protect. (The majority, however, places all these speakers beyond the reach of First Amendment protection against retaliation.)

Nothing, then, accountable on the individual and public side of the *Pickering* balance changes when an employee speaks "pursuant" to public duties. On the side of the government employer, however, something is different, and to this extent, I agree with the majority of the Court. The majority is rightly concerned that the employee who speaks out on matters subject to comment in doing his own work has the greater leverage to create office uproars and fracture the government's authority to set policy to be carried out coherently through the ranks. . . .

But why do the majority's concerns, which we all share, require categorical exclusion of First Amendment protection against any official retaliation for things said on the job? Is it not possible to respect the unchallenged individual and public interests in the speech through a *Pickering* balance without drawing the strange line I mentioned before[?] . . . It is thus no adequate justification for the suppression of potentially valuable information simply to recognize that the government has a huge interest in managing its employees and preventing the occasionally irresponsible one from turning his job into a bully pulpit. Even there, the lesson of *Pickering* (and the object of most constitutional adjudication) is still to the point: when constitutionally significant interests clash, resist the demand for winner-take-all; try to make adjustments that serve all of the values at stake.

Two reasons in particular make me think an adjustment using the basic *Pickering* balancing scheme is perfectly feasible here. First, the extent of the government's legitimate authority over subjects of speech required by a public job can be recognized in advance by setting in effect a minimum heft for comments with any claim to outweigh it. Thus, the risks to the government are great enough for us to hold from the outset that an employee commenting on subjects in the course of duties should not prevail on balance unless he speaks on a matter of unusual importance and satisfies high standards

---

3. R. FROST, TWO TRAMPS IN MUD TIME, COLLECTED POEMS, PROSE, & PLAYS 251, 252 (R. Poirier & M. Richardson eds., 1995).

of responsibility in the way he does it. The examples I have already given indicate the eligible subject matter, and it is fair to say that only comment on official dishonesty, deliberately unconstitutional action, other serious wrongdoing, or threats to health and safety can weigh out in an employee's favor. . . .

My second reason for adapting *Pickering* to the circumstances at hand is the experience in Circuits that have recognized claims like Ceballos's here. First Amendment protection less circumscribed than what I would recognize has been available in the Ninth Circuit for over 17 years, and neither there nor in other Circuits that accept claims like this one has there been a debilitating flood of litigation. . . .

For that matter, the majority's position comes with no guarantee against fact-bound litigation over whether a public employee's statements were made "pursuant to . . . official duties." In fact, the majority invites such litigation by describing the inquiry as a "practical one," apparently based on the totality of employment circumstances. *See* n.2. Are prosecutors' discretionary statements about cases addressed to the press on the courthouse steps made "pursuant to their official duties"? Are government nuclear scientists' complaints to their supervisors about a colleague's improper handling of radioactive materials made "pursuant" to duties?

II

The majority seeks support in two lines of argument extraneous to *Pickering* doctrine. The one turns on a fallacious reading of cases on government speech, the other on a mistaken assessment of protection available under whistle-blower statutes.

A

The majority accepts the fallacy propounded by the county petitioners and the Federal Government as *amicus* that any statement made within the scope of public employment is (or should be treated as) the government's own speech, and should thus be differentiated as a matter of law from the personal statements the First Amendment protects. . . . Some public employees are hired to "promote a particular policy" by broadcasting a particular message set by the government, but not everyone working for the government, after all, is hired to speak from a government manifesto. There is no claim or indication that Ceballos was hired to perform such a speaking assignment. . . .

It is not, of course, that the district attorney lacked interest of a high order in what Ceballos might say. If his speech undercut effective, lawful prosecution, there would have been every reason to rein him in or fire him; a statement that created needless tension among law enforcement agencies would be a fair subject of concern, and the same would be true of inaccurate statements or false ones made in the course of doing his work. But these interests on the government's part are entirely distinct from any claim that Ceballos's speech was government speech with a preset or proscribed content. . . .

This ostensible domain beyond the pale of the First Amendment is spacious enough to include even the teaching of a public university professor, and I have to hope that today's majority does not mean to imperil First Amendment protection of academic freedom in public colleges and universities, whose teachers necessarily speak and write "pursuant to official duties."

B

The majority's second argument for its disputed limitation of *Pickering* doctrine is that the First Amendment has little or no work to do here owing to an assertedly comprehensive complement of state and national statutes protecting government whistle-blowers from vindictive bosses. . . .

To begin with, speech addressing official wrongdoing may well fall outside protected whistle-blowing, defined in the classic sense of exposing an official's fault to a third party or to the public; the teacher in *Givhan*, for example, who raised the issue of unconstitutional hiring bias, would not have qualified as that sort of whistle-blower, for she was fired after a private conversation with the school principal. In any event, the combined variants of statutory whistle-blower definitions and protections add up to a patchwork, not a showing that worries may be remitted to legislatures for relief. Some state statutes protect all government workers, including the employees of municipalities and other subdivisions; others stop at state employees. Some limit protection to employees who tell their bosses before they speak out; others forbid bosses from imposing any requirement to warn. . . . My point is not to disparage particular statutes or speak here to the merits of interpretations by other federal courts, but merely to show the current understanding of statutory protection: individuals doing the same sorts of governmental jobs and saying the same sorts of things addressed to civic concerns will get different protection depending on the local, state, or federal jurisdictions that happened to employ them.

III

[The opinion recounted in some detail the plaintiff's claims of retaliation not only for his written reports but also for his spoken statements to his supervisors, testimony at the hearing in the pending criminal case, and his speech at a meeting of the Mexican-American Bar Association about misconduct of the Sheriff's Department in the criminal case and the failure of the District Attorney's Office to handle allegations of police misconduct.]

Upon remand, it will be open to the Court of Appeals to consider the application of *Pickering* to any retaliation shown for other statements; not all of those statements would have been made pursuant to official duties in any obvious sense, and the claim relating to truthful testimony in court must surely be analyzed independently to protect the integrity of the judicial process.

NOTES

1. *Almost Eroded Away? Connick* was viewed at the time as substantially chipping away at speech protections for employees in the workplace, both because of its narrower definition of "matters of public concern," and its deferential approach to management's prerogatives in the balancing analysis. Now, in the wake of *Garcetti*, how much genuine protection for public employee speech is left? Not only is there no protection for speech that does not address a matter of public concern, but *all* speech falling within the scope of an employee's official duties appeared to be unprotected, although we will see a limited retreat from such an absolutist position shortly. Moreover, even where workplace speech does address a matter of public concern and does not fall within the scope of an employee's official duties, it will still be subjected to a balancing of interests and, hence, may be unprotected if it is disruptive or otherwise threatens efficient operation of the agency. Perhaps employees can rest assured that truly nondisruptive speech—that is, speech within the workplace about matters of public concern unrelated to work or the employee's duties—is still safe, but employees engaging in other types of workplace speech or public speech about work must do so at their peril. If this statement is accurate, does the First Amendment afford much protection to government workers? Should it? *Connick* and both *Garcetti* opinions emphasize the important civic interests First Amendment speech protections are supposed to foster. Does the protection actually afforded in the wake of these decisions match this rhetoric?

2. *Deference, Balancing, and Categorical Rules.* As we saw in the privacy context, the focus of the "balancing" inquiry on the employer's interest means that the outcome of a case often hinges on the extent to which the Court is willing to defer to the employer's justification. Indeed, the level of deference was the primary dispute between the majority and the omitted dissent of Justice Brennan in *Connick*. Are the disagreements in *Garcetti* driven by much the same thing? Put another way, although the dispute between the majority and dissent in *Garcetti* involves whether there ought to be a categorical rule governing speech within the scope of an employee's official duties, isn't this disagreement largely about how much deference to the public employer is warranted or needed? Certainly, the majority's language goes further, indicating, for example, that one does not speak as a "citizen" when the speech is pursuant to job duties. But can you identify language in the opinion suggesting that the majority's concern about the practical implications of judicial interference with employer prerogatives makes *no* interference the only option? If so, the bar to judicial review in *Garcetti* may be akin to the various abstention or sovereign immunity doctrines in other areas of the law, which are designed to avoid the downstream disruption and other harmful effects judicial scrutiny may cause. What is the dissent's response to such concerns? Which approach strikes the right balance?

3. *Private Ordering. Connick* and *Garcetti* both state that employees do not waive their constitutional speech and association protections when accepting government work. Although, as discussed in Chapter 6, government employees also cannot be required to jettison prospectively their Fourth Amendment rights, one could contend, at least prior to *Garcetti*, that the Constitution provides more robust protection for speech than for privacy rights. That is because privacy rights may be diminished or eliminated by workplace structures and policies that curtail reasonable expectations of privacy. Speech rights are not "bounded" by any such reasonable expectation requirement.

Post-*Garcetti*, however, acceptance of a particular government position defined by various job duties may impose constraints resulting in the substantial narrowing of one's freedom of expression, at least at work. In fact, the *Garcetti* dissenters express concern that the majority's categorical approach may prompt government employers to manipulate job definitions and duties to capture as much employee speech as possible. *See* Elizabeth M. Ellis, Garcetti v. Ceballos: *Public Employees Left to Decide "Your Conscience or Your Job,"* 41 IND. L. REV. 187 (2008) (arguing that *Garcetti's* threshold "official duties" test should be applied narrowly to prevent employers from broadly defining job descriptions). Is this danger real, or, as the majority suggests, is it overstated?

Suppose a government agency decides to require all employees to "report to their supervisor or other appropriate agency official any acts or omissions by other government employees or officials the employee believes in good faith to be in violation of state or federal law or agency policy or regulations." Failure to do so "may result in suspension, termination, or other disciplinary action." Are all such reports now per se unprotected by the First Amendment? Is the majority's assurance that what matters is not formal policies but actual job practices a sufficient response? *Cf. D'Olimpio v. Crisafi*, 462 F. App'x 79 (2d Cir. 2012) (holding that a state employee's complaints to the inspector general regarding alleged official misconduct by his supervisor were made pursuant to and in furtherance of performance of employee's duties under New York law, and thus, any retaliation against employee for having made report to inspector general did not violate employee's free speech rights). If an employee reports misconduct elsewhere — outside the agency or to the public — the First Amendment may be implicated, but then the speech is more likely to be disruptive by straining office morale and working relationships. Also, there may be a need for confidentiality in some contexts, such as when one works with classified or other sensitive information or in an investigatory capacity. Moreover, some government positions may require a public appearance of "neutrality" or the avoidance of conflicts of interest; speech contrary to these demands is unlikely to be protected. Thus, when an employee chooses to "go public," the government's countervailing interest in this area is more likely to trump the worker's interest in expression.

4. *Whither the Whistleblower?* As the prior note suggests, a paramount concern surrounding *Garcetti* is the plight of government whistleblowers. Indeed, Ceballos was a whistleblower, and his claim is premised on alleged retaliation for both his internal report of illegal activity and for certain external steps he took — that's the point of the dissent's argument as to what should happen on remand. The dissent also argues that *Garcetti* will have a chilling effect on government employees coming forward to report perceived misconduct, while the majority downplays this concern. The dissent and majority further contest whether *Garcetti* will create a perverse incentive for employees to go public with their concerns (report them externally) rather than report them internally up the chain of command within the agency.

Moreover, the dissent suggests that independent whistleblower and antiretaliation protections are inadequate to protect employees attempting to further the public's interest in good government. Recall the discussion in Chapter 4 of whistleblowing and the public policy tort more generally. Isn't the dissent correct that such protections are a patchwork? Yet, even if your answer is yes, should this concern have affected the outcome in *Garcetti*? Put another way, how is this an argument for enhancing *constitutional* protections for employees?

Also note that many of the same themes that framed the public policy tort discussion in Chapter 4 are present in *Garcetti* — for example, separation of powers, the conflict between social benefits and employer prerogatives, calibrating employer and employee incentives, and floodgates and litigation cost concerns. Similarly, much of the discussion in Chapter 4 involved the balancing of employer, employee, and public interests. Naturally, one aspect of this discussion is how this balance might differ by type of employer — that is, public versus private. Does *Garcetti* shed any light on this? In other words, in the whistleblower context, are there reasons to strike the balance between the interests of employees, employers, and the public differently in the public employer context?

Whatever you think of *Garcetti*, it does not affect statutory or common-law antiretaliation or other public policy protections. Consider Justice Souter's discussion of Ceballos's claims on remand. Recalling the discussion in Chapter 4, might some of the activities Ceballos alleges led to retaliation give rise to state law public policy claims?

5. *The Aftermath.* Unsurprisingly, public employee free speech claims are now commonly defeated on the basis of *Garcetti*—many of which, like Ceballos's claim, might be characterized as involving whistleblowing. *See, e.g., Morris v. Philadelphia Housing Authority*, 487 F. App'x 37 (3d Cir. 2012) (holding that a city housing authority employee's statements resisting orders to engage in lobbying activities and to work for an affiliated nonprofit organization as well as his reports to his supervisors about co-workers' embezzlement were not protected by First Amendment, where employee's work duties included oversight of the non-profit organization and addressing authority financial problems, and the employee made statements to his superiors in the course of performance of his official duties); *Weintraub v. Bd. of Educ. of the City of New York*, 593 F.3d 196 (2d Cir. 2010) (holding that a public school teacher's filing of a grievance with the union after the school administrator had refused to discipline a student who had thrown books at him was pursuant to official duties); *Morales v. Jones*, 494 F.3d 590 (7th Cir. 2007) (dismissing a police officer's First Amendment claim after finding that his report to an assistant DA that the police chief was harboring a convicted felon falls within the scope of his official duties). Even when a claim overcomes the barriers *Garcetti* imposes, employee speech claims often fail for other reasons. *See, e.g., Bowers v. Scurry*, No. 07-1382, 2008 WL 1931263 (4th Cir. May 2, 2008) (holding that a state university's interest in providing effective services to the public strongly outweighed a human resources employee's interest in using her university e-mail to disseminate information regarding the potential impact on university employees of pending salary restructuring).

Scholarly criticisms of the majority opinion in *Garcetti*—as a matter of First Amendment doctrine and in terms of its practical implications for government whistleblowers and others—are legion. *See, e.g.*, Cynthia Estlund, *Free Speech Rights That Work at Work: From the First Amendment to Due Process*, 54 UCLA L. Rev. 1463 (2007); Orly Lobel, *Citizenship, Organizational Citizenship, and the Laws of Overlapping Obligations*, 97 Calif. L. Rev. 433 (2009); Scott A. Moss, *Students and Workers and Prisoners—Oh, My! A Cautionary Note About Excessive Institutional Tailoring of First Amendment Doctrine*, 54 UCLA L. Rev. 1635 (2007); Helen Norton, *Constraining Public Employee Speech: Government's Control of Its Workers' Speech to Protect Its Own Expression*, 59 Duke L.J. 1 (2009); Paul M. Secunda, Garcetti*'s Impact on the First Amendment Speech Rights of Federal Employees*, 7 First Amend. L. Rev. 117, 118 (2008); Paul M. Secunda, *The Solomon Amendment, Expressive Associations, and Public Employment*, 54 UCLA L. Rev. 1767 (2007); Adam Shinar, *Public Employee Speech and the Privatization of the First Amendment*, 46 Conn. L. Rev. 1 (2013); Terry Smith, *Speaking Against Norms: Public Discourse and the Economy of Racialization in the Workplace*, 57 Am. U. L. Rev. 523 (2008). *But see* Lawrence Rosenthal, *The Emerging First Amendment Law of Managerial Prerogative*, 77 Fordham L. Rev. 33 (2008) (defending *Garcetti* as consistent with First Amendment principles).

Nevertheless, there are some government employee speech claims that have survived post-*Garcetti*. *See, e.g., Westmoreland v. Sutherland*, 662 F.3d 714 (6th Cir. 2011) (upholding firefighter's First Amendment claim arising out of alleged retaliation after he appeared before and criticized the city council, and, in so doing, rejecting the argument that *Garcetti* barred the claim because, although "plaintiff identified himself as a public employee, he appeared off duty, out of uniform, and at a public meeting to address the Mayor and City Council during the public comment period"); *Charles v. Grief*, 522 F.3d 508 (5th Cir. 2008) (holding that state lottery commission employee stated viable First Amendment claim because the speech at issue — an e-mail to state legislators complaining about discrimination at the commission — was not directly related to employee's job and addressed a matter of public concern); *Marabel v. Nitchman*, 511 F.3d 924 (9th Cir. 2007) (concluding that plaintiff's complaints about superiors' corrupt overpayments were not related to his official job duties as a ferry engineer and, hence, entitled to First Amendment protection); *Lindsey v. City of Orrick*, 491 F.3d 892 (8th Cir. 2007) (finding that an employee's accusation that the city council violated Missouri's open meetings law was protected because there was no evidence that raising such matters with the council fell within the employee's official job duties even though he was required to attend council meetings and make reports on other matters); *Love v. Rehfus*, 946 N.E.2d 1 (Ind. 2011) (finding e-mail criticizing the fire department sent to the public was not an employee grievance, but a general grievance on a matter of public concern, warranting First Amendment protection).

The next case is the Supreme Court's most recent foray into this area and reflects a potentially significant limitation on the *Garcetti* rule.

≡ **Lane v. Franks**
≡ *134 S. Ct. 2369 (2014)*

Justice Sotomayor delivered the opinion of the Court.

. . . Today, we consider whether the First Amendment . . . protects a public employee who provided truthful sworn testimony, compelled by subpoena, outside the course of his ordinary job responsibilities. We hold that it does.

I

In 2006, Central Alabama Community College (CACC) hired petitioner Edward Lane to be the Director of Community Intensive Training for Youth (CITY), a statewide program for underprivileged youth. CACC hired Lane on a probationary basis. In his capacity as Director, Lane was responsible for overseeing CITY's day-to-day operations, hiring and firing employees, and making decisions with respect to the program's finances.

At the time of Lane's appointment, CITY faced significant financial difficulties. That prompted Lane to conduct a comprehensive audit of the program's expenses. The audit revealed that Suzanne Schmitz, an Alabama State Representative on CITY's payroll, had not been reporting to her CITY office. After unfruitful discussions with Schmitz, Lane shared his finding with CACC's president and its attorney. They warned him that firing Schmitz could have negative repercussions for him and CACC.

Lane nonetheless contacted Schmitz again and instructed her to show up to the Huntsville office to serve as a counselor. Schmitz refused; she responded that she wished to "continue to serve the CITY program in the same manner as [she had] in the past." Lane fired her shortly thereafter. Schmitz told another CITY employee, Charles Foley, that she intended to "get [Lane] back" for firing her. She also said that if Lane ever requested money from the state legislature for the program, she would tell him, "[y]ou're fired."

Schmitz' termination drew the attention of many, including agents of the Federal Bureau of Investigation, which initiated an investigation into Schmitz' employment with CITY. In November 2006, Lane testified before a federal grand jury about his reasons for firing Schmitz. In January 2008, the grand jury indicted Schmitz on four counts of mail fraud and four counts of theft concerning a program receiving federal funds. The indictment alleged that Schmitz had collected $177,251.82 in federal funds even though she performed "virtually no services," "generated virtually no work product," and "rarely even appeared for work at the CITY Program offices." It further alleged that Schmitz had submitted false statements concerning the hours she worked and the nature of the services she performed.

[Schmitz was tried and convicted of mail fraud and theft from a program receiving federal funds. She was sentenced to 30 months in prison and ordered to pay $177,251.82 in restitution and forfeiture. The proceedings garnered extensive press coverage.]

Meanwhile, CITY continued to experience considerable budget shortfalls. In November 2008, Lane began reporting to respondent Steve Franks, who had become president of CACC in January 2008. Lane recommended that Franks consider layoffs to address the financial difficulties. In January 2009, Franks decided to terminate 29 probationary CITY employees, including Lane. Shortly thereafter, however, Franks rescinded all but 2 of the 29 terminations — those of Lane and one other employee — because of an "ambiguity in [those other employees'] probationary service." Franks claims that he "did not rescind Lane's termination . . . because he believed that Lane was in a fundamentally different category than the other employees: he was the director of the entire CITY program, and not simply an employee." In September 2009, CACC eliminated the CITY program and terminated the program's remaining employees. Franks later retired, and respondent Susan Burrow, the current Acting President of CACC, replaced him while this case was pending before the Eleventh Circuit.

In January 2011, Lane sued Franks in his individual and official capacities under Rev. Stat. § 1979, 42 U.S.C. § 1983, alleging [*inter alia*] that Franks had violated the First Amendment by firing him in retaliation for his testimony against Schmitz. Lane sought damages from Franks in his individual capacity and sought equitable relief, including reinstatement, from Franks in his official capacity.[3]

[Relying on *Garcetti v. Ceballos* the district court granted Franks summary judgment, and the Eleventh Circuit affirmed. It reasoned] that Lane spoke as an employee and not as a citizen because he was acting pursuant to his official duties when he investigated Schmitz' employment, spoke with Schmitz and CACC officials regarding the issue, and terminated Schmitz. "That Lane testified about his official activities pursuant to a subpoena and in the litigation context," the court continued, "does not bring Lane's speech within the protection of the First Amendment." . . .

---

3. Because Burrow replaced Franks as President of CACC during the pendency of this lawsuit, the claims originally filed against Franks in his official capacity are now against Burrow.

II

. . . In *Pickering,* the Court held that a teacher's letter to the editor of a local newspaper concerning a school budget constituted speech on a matter of public concern. And in balancing the employee's interest in such speech against the government's efficiency interest, the Court held that the publication of the letter did not "imped[e] the teacher's proper performance of his daily duties in the classroom" or "interfer[e] with the regular operation of the schools generally." The Court therefore held that the teacher's speech could not serve as the basis for his dismissal.

In *Garcetti,* we described a two-step inquiry into whether a public employee's speech is entitled to protection:

> The first requires determining whether the employee spoke as a citizen on a matter of public concern. If the answer is no, the employee has no First Amendment cause of action based on his or her employer's reaction to the speech. If the answer is yes, then the possibility of a First Amendment claim arises. The question becomes whether the relevant government entity had an adequate justification for treating the employee differently from any other member of the general public.

(citations omitted).

In describing the first step in this inquiry, *Garcetti* distinguished between employee speech and citizen speech. Whereas speech as a citizen may trigger protection, the Court held that "when public employees make statements pursuant to their official duties, the employees are not speaking as citizens for First Amendment purposes, and the Constitution does not insulate their communications from employer discipline." Applying that rule to the facts before it, the Court found that an internal memorandum prepared by a prosecutor in the course of his ordinary job responsibilities constituted unprotected employee speech.

III

Against this backdrop, we turn to the question presented: whether the First Amendment protects a public employee who provides truthful sworn testimony, compelled by subpoena, outside the scope of his ordinary job responsibilities.[4] We hold that it does.

A

The first inquiry is whether the speech in question — Lane's testimony at Schmitz' trials — is speech as a citizen on a matter of public concern. It clearly is.

---

4. It is undisputed that Lane's ordinary job responsibilities did not include testifying in court proceedings. *See Lane v. Central Ala. Community College,* 523 Fed. App'x 709, 712 (C.A.11 2013). For that reason, Lane asked the Court to decide only whether truthful sworn testimony that is not a part of an employee's ordinary job responsibilities is citizen speech on a matter of public concern. We accordingly need not address in this case whether truthful sworn testimony would constitute citizen speech under *Garcetti* when given as part of a public employee's ordinary job duties, and express no opinion on the matter today.

1

Truthful testimony under oath by a public employee outside the scope of his ordinary job duties is speech as a citizen for First Amendment purposes. That is so even when the testimony relates to his public employment or concerns information learned during that employment.

In rejecting Lane's argument that his testimony was speech as a citizen, the Eleventh Circuit gave short shrift to the nature of sworn judicial statements and ignored the obligation borne by all witnesses testifying under oath. When the person testifying is a public employee, he may bear separate obligations to his employer — for example, an obligation not to show up to court dressed in an unprofessional manner. But any such obligations as an employee are distinct and independent from the obligation, as a citizen, to speak the truth. That independent obligation renders sworn testimony speech as a citizen and sets it apart from speech made purely in the capacity of an employee.

In holding that Lane did not speak as a citizen when he testified, the Eleventh Circuit read *Garcetti* far too broadly. It reasoned that, because Lane learned of the subject matter of his testimony in the course of his employment with CITY, *Garcetti* requires that his testimony be treated as the speech of an employee rather than that of a citizen. It does not.

The sworn testimony in this case is far removed from the speech at issue in *Garcetti* — an internal memorandum prepared by a deputy district attorney for his supervisors recommending dismissal of a particular prosecution. . . .

But *Garcetti* said nothing about speech that simply relates to public employment or concerns information learned in the course of public employment. The *Garcetti* Court made explicit that its holding did not turn on the fact that the memo at issue "concerned the subject matter of [the prosecutor's] employment," because "[t]he First Amendment protects some expressions related to the speaker's job." In other words, the mere fact that a citizen's speech concerns information acquired by virtue of his public employment does not transform that speech into employee — rather than citizen — speech. The critical question under *Garcetti* is whether the speech at issue is itself ordinarily within the scope of an employee's duties, not whether it merely concerns those duties.

It bears emphasis that our precedents dating back to *Pickering* have recognized that speech by public employees on subject matter related to their employment holds special value precisely because those employees gain knowledge of matters of public concern through their employment. . . .

The importance of public employee speech is especially evident in the context of this case: a public corruption scandal. The United States, for example, represents that because "[t]he more than 1,000 prosecutions for federal corruption offenses that are brought in a typical year . . . often depend on evidence about activities that government officials undertook while in office," those prosecutions often "require testimony from other government employees." Brief for United States as *Amicus Curiae* 20. It would be antithetical to our jurisprudence to conclude that the very kind of speech necessary to prosecute corruption by public officials — speech by public employees regarding information learned through their employment — may never form the basis for a First Amendment retaliation claim. Such a rule would place public employees who witness corruption in an impossible position, torn between the obligation to testify truthfully and the desire to avoid retaliation and keep their jobs.

Applying these principles, it is clear that Lane's sworn testimony is speech as a citizen.

2

Lane's testimony is also speech on a matter of public concern. Speech involves matters of public concern "when it can 'be fairly considered as relating to any matter of political, social, or other concern to the community,' or when it 'is a subject of legitimate news interest; that is, 'a subject of general interest and of value and concern to the public.'" (citation omitted). The inquiry turns on the "content, form, and context" of the speech. *Connick.*

The content of Lane's testimony — corruption in a public program and misuse of state funds — obviously involves a matter of significant public concern. . . .

B

This does not settle the matter, however. A public employee's sworn testimony is not categorically entitled to First Amendment protection simply because it is speech as a citizen on a matter of public concern. Under *Pickering*, if an employee speaks as a citizen on a matter of public concern, the next question is whether the government had "an adequate justification for treating the employee differently from any other member of the public" based on the government's needs as an employer. *Garcetti.*

As discussed previously, we have recognized that government employers often have legitimate "interest[s] in the effective and efficient fulfillment of [their] responsibilities to the public," including "'promot[ing] efficiency and integrity in the discharge of official duties,'" and "'maintain[ing] proper discipline in public service.'" *Connick.* We have also cautioned, however, that "a stronger showing [of government interests] may be necessary if the employee's speech more substantially involve[s] matters of public concern." *Id.*

Here, the employer's side of the *Pickering* scale is entirely empty: Respondents do not assert, and cannot demonstrate, any government interest that tips the balance in their favor. There is no evidence, for example, that Lane's testimony at Schmitz' trials was false or erroneous or that Lane unnecessarily disclosed any sensitive, confidential, or privileged information while testifying.[5] In these circumstances, we conclude that Lane's speech is entitled to protection under the First Amendment. The Eleventh Circuit erred in holding otherwise and dismissing Lane's claim of retaliation on that basis.

IV

[The Court then found that, even if Lane's testimony is protected under the First Amendment, the claims against him in his individual capacity should be dismissed on

---

5. Of course, quite apart from *Pickering* balancing, wrongdoing that an employee admits to while testifying may be a valid basis for termination or other discipline.

the basis of qualified immunity since Franks reasonably could have believed at the time he fired Lane that he could fire an employee on account of testimony the employee gave, under oath and outside the scope of his ordinary job responsibilities. The Court affirmed in part, reversed in part, and remanded for further proceedings.]

JUSTICE THOMAS, with whom JUSTICE SCALIA and JUSTICE ALITO join, concurring.

This case presents the discrete question whether a public employee speaks "as a citizen on a matter of public concern," , when the employee gives "[t]ruthful testimony under oath . . . outside the scope of his ordinary job duties." Answering that question requires little more than a straightforward application of *Garcetti*. . . .

We accordingly have no occasion to address the quite different question whether a public employee speaks "as a citizen" when he testifies in the course of his ordinary job responsibilities. *See* n.4. For some public employees—such as police officers, crime scene technicians, and laboratory analysts—testifying is a routine and critical part of their employment duties. Others may be called to testify in the context of particular litigation as the designated representatives of their employers. The Court properly leaves the constitutional questions raised by these scenarios for another day.

NOTES

1. *The Contours of "Ordinary Job Duties."* Lane demarcates an important limitation on *Garcetti*: A public employee's speech—in this case, truthful testimony— that "relates to his public employment or concerns information learned during that employment" does not necessarily fall within the employee's "ordinary" job duties. And the decisive way in which the Court unanimously said so, at least with regard to sworn testimony, may roll back some of the more aggressive approaches to extending the sweep of "ordinary job duties" we have seen in some lower courts.

Nevertheless, *Lane*'s effect on the ground itself may be limited. First, as stated in footnote 4 of Justice Sotomayor's opinion, and re-emphasized by Justice Thomas in his concurrence, the Court expressly avoided deciding whether a public employee's truthful sworn testimony would constitute citizen speech under *Garcetti* when given as part of the employee's job responsibilities. As the concurrence also notes, testifying is a routine part of job duties for the broad swath of public employees involved in investigatory and enforcement work, including police officers. Thus, whether testimony in such circumstances will receive First Amendment protection remains an open question.

Perhaps more importantly, however, the *Lane* Court did not need to address how "ordinary" job duties are determined because it was undisputed that Lane's testimony fell outside of his ordinary responsibilities. This means that the questions raised in Note 3 following *Garcetti* remain open; whether and in what circumstances public employers, through private ordering, will be able to sweep otherwise potentially protected speech into the sphere of ordinary job responsibilities. Indeed, what if, as part of Lane's job responsibilities, he had been required to report—to appropriate government authorities or *through testifying in court proceedings*—activities within the agency that he reasonably believed to be unlawful, fraudulent, corrupt, etc.? The point is that public employers still may be able to reduce substantially potential First Amendment protections by crafting job duties and practices to encompass additional types of workplace speech, including, testimony and cooperation with other government officials. *Cf. Hurst v. Lee County*, 764 F.3d 480 (5th Cir. 2014) (holding that, in contrast to the speech in *Lane*, a correction officer's statements to the media that allegedly led to his discharge were not protected under the First Amendment because department policy permitted officers to speak to media if granted permission by management, and the officer's failure to seek permission did not convert his comments into citizen speech — that is, to speech outside of his job duties).

And then there's the causation question. Suppose the defense claimed Lane was fired not for his testimony per se but for raising the issue of Schmitz's no-show job in the first place. A job duties defense? Finally, the *Lane* Court found the balancing prong of *Pickering* to be easy since the employer had failed to articulate any legitimate interest in efficiency to balance against Lane's interest in providing truthful testimony. But, as the court suggests, in other contexts, such as nonobligatory statements to officials in other government agencies and nontestimonial public statements, the balance might come out differently. Once again, how much deference courts will accord articulated governmental interests remains an open question.

2. *Freedom of Association.* Beyond the First Amendment's protection for speech is freedom of association. Public sector workers enjoy qualified protections with regard to their political preferences and affiliations, and the Supreme Court has struck down various government requirements that infringe upon such rights. *See, e.g., Rutan v. Republican Party*, 497 U.S. 62 (1990) (holding unconstitutional promotion, transfer, recall, and hiring decisions involving low-level public employees based on political party affiliation and support); *Elrod v. Burns*, 427 U.S. 367 (1976) (holding that a public-sector employee who is not a policy-level decision maker may not be denied employment based on political affiliation); *Cafeteria & Rest. Workers Union v. McElroy*, 367 U.S. 886 (1961) (recognizing that the government could not deny employment because of previous membership in a particular party); *Shelton v. Tucker*, 364 U.S. 479 (1960) (finding unconstitutional an Arkansas requirement that public school teachers file annually an affidavit listing each organization to which they have contributed for five preceding years). Although these employee association cases are 20 or more years old, more recent Supreme Court and circuit court decisions upholding the right to expressive association suggest they have continued vitality. *See, e.g., Boy Scouts of America v. Dale*, 530 U.S. 640 (2000); *Montone v. City of Jersey City*, 709 F.3d 181 (3d Cir. 2013) (finding the First Amendment would be violated if the political conduct of a more senior police officer in a local election was a motivating factor in the city's decision to not promote less senior officers); *Wagner v. Jones*, 664 F.3d 259 (8th Cir. 2011) (finding applicant for legal writing instructor position at the University of Iowa Law School offered sufficient evidence for a factfinder to infer that the dean's repeated decisions not to hire the applicant were in part motivated by her constitutionally protected First Amendment rights of political belief and association); *Morin v. Tormey*, 626 F.3d 40, 42 (2d Cir. 2010) (holding that various judges and other county employees were not entitled to qualified immunity from clerk's § 1983 action alleging her termination was in retaliation for her refusal to engage in political activity in violation of her First Amendment right to association); *see generally* Paul M. Secunda, *The Solomon Amendment, Expressive Associations, and Public Employment*, 54 UCLA L. Rev. 1767 (2007).

A few courts have also held that employees may not be dismissed because of other personal or familial associations. *See, e.g., Sowards v. Loundon County*, 203 F.3d 426 (6th Cir. 2000) (upholding law enforcement employee's right to political and intimate association in context in which she supported her husband's campaign for sheriff); *see also Roberts v. United States Jaycees*, 468 U.S. 609, 617-18 (1984) (stating that one type of protected freedom of association is the right to maintain certain intimate relationships because of the role such relationships have in safeguarding individual freedom). *But see Shahar v. Bowers*, 114 F.3d 1097 (11th Cir. 1997) (even assuming an attorney had a constitutionally protected right to participate in a marriage ceremony when same-sex marriages were not recognized as legal, Georgia's attorney general did not violate her right of association by withdrawing job offer because the employer's efficiency interests would be jeopardized given the policy-making nature of the position and working relationships within the department).

As in the speech context, employee association rights may be limited when there is a substantial governmental interest for doing so. In *Rutan*, 497 U.S. at 74, the Court struck down an Illinois executive order that established a *de facto* political patronage system ensuring that government agencies would promote and hire only Republican Party members. In so holding, the Court recognized the government's interest in ensuring employee effectiveness and efficiency but found that this interest could be served through the less drastic means of disciplining or discharging staff members whose work is inadequate. *See id.* However, the Court limited strong protection — that is, strict scrutiny — to the treatment of lower-level employees, reaffirming the prerogative of elected officials to fill policy-making positions with like-minded appointees. *See id.; see also Elrod*, 427 U.S. at 366-67.

3. *Worker Rank and Status.* In both the speech and association cases, the worker's rank and status often determine the outcome of the case. Indeed, in both contexts, lower-level employees appear to enjoy greater protection than higher-level workers. At the extreme, the president or a governor or mayor can choose members of his or her own party for his cabinet, and probably for most "policy making" positions. Beyond this, the greater protection for lower-level employees is a product not of their vulnerabilities, but rather, of the fact that the actions of higher-level employees are more likely to threaten the efficient functioning of the government employer, and thus more likely to justify employer intrusions or prohibitions. Do you think that an assistant district attorney's circulation of a survey on personnel issues (*Connick*) would be more disruptive to the workplace than a deputy's comments to her co-worker expressing a wish that the president had been killed (*Rankin*)? *See also Pickering*, 391 U.S. at 571-72 (noting that because the speaker was a teacher rather than a higher-ranking school district employee, incorrect assertions in his public statements could be easily corrected by the district and any harm done thereby alleviated). Also, consider whether the outcome in *Lane* might have been different if Lane had revealed his reasons for firing Schmitz to the media rather than recounting it in sworn testimony. Might the employer's interest in maintaining confidentiality with regard to personnel matters outweigh his interest in such revelations?

In addition to rank, the nature of the employee's work may affect the analysis. For example, as discussed below, courts seem to accord more deference to employer regulation of employee speech for certain types of workers, including law enforcement officials who interact with the public and teachers. In an omitted separate dissent, Justice Breyer found Ceballos's attorney status to be dispositive in his determination that the speech ought to protected:

> [T]he speech at issue is professional speech — the speech of a lawyer. Such speech is subject to independent regulation by canons of the profession. Those canons provide an obligation to speak in certain instances. And where that is so, the government's own interest in forbidding that speech is diminished. The objective specificity and public

availability of the profession's canons also help to diminish the risk that the courts will improperly interfere with the government's necessary authority to manage its work.

547 U.S. at 447. Recall the unique treatment of attorneys in the context of the public policy tort in Chapter 4. Are there similar strands of thought running through the *Garcetti* opinions?

Note on *Garcetti* and Academic Freedom

One group of workers who may be treated differently with respect to speech rights are academics. Both the majority and dissent in *Garcetti* acknowledge the potential implications for academic freedom, recognizing that speech — expressed through scholarship, commentary, and classroom instruction — is at the center of an academic's work. Previously, the Court had recognized that the preservation of academic freedom is an important First Amendment concern. *See, e.g., Keyishian v. Bd. of Regents*, 385 U.S. 589, 603 (1967) ("The vigilant protection of constitutional freedoms is nowhere more vital than in the community of American schools." (quoting *Shelton v. Tucker*, 364 U.S. 479, 487 (1960)); *see also Rodriguez v. Maricopa County Cmty. Coll. Dist.*, 605 F.3d 703 (9th Cir. 2009) (stating that a college is entitled to substantial deference in choosing not to discipline a professor whose racially charged e-mail offended some employees and expressing doubt that a professor's speech on a matter of public concern directed at the college community could ever form the basis of a hostile work environment claim under Title VII). Given the nature of their work and the social functions educational institutions serve, should academics employed by public colleges or universities receive special constitutional protection? What would be the rationale for such a distinction consistent with the text of the First Amendment? If you believe academic speech should not receive such heightened protection, how do you respond to the claim that, without such safeguards, academics will be chilled from engaging in socially useful but controversial or unpopular work, research, or commentary?

Despite the *Garcetti* Court's acknowledgment that academic freedom may raise unique First Amendment issues, some have expressed concern that its analysis may weaken protections for such speech. *See, e.g.*, Sheldon H. Nahmod, *Public Employee Speech, Categorical Balancing and § 1983: A Critique of* Garcetti v. Ceballos, 42 U. Rich. L. Rev. 561 (2008) (asserting that *Garcetti*'s modification of the prior "public concern" test significantly undermines the historical protection afforded to academic freedom). Issues surrounding academic freedom are taken up again in Note 9 at page 473. Moreover, the availability of a First Amendment claim does not always translate into meaningful protection for professors who make highly unpopular or controversial statements in the course of their work. Consider University of Colorado Professor Ward Churchill, whose controversial essay likening 9/11 victims to Nazis caused an uproar and sparked calls for reevaluating the tenure system. The university ultimately terminated Churchill, purportedly for unrelated research misconduct (plagiarism). Churchill then sued, claiming that the university violated his First Amendment rights. At trial, the jury found in Churchill's favor, concluding that the content of the essay was the university's real reason for terminating him. This victory was a hollow one, however, since the jury awarded only $1.00 in compensatory damages and the judge later determined that Churchill was not entitled to reinstatement. *See, e.g.*, Kirk

Johnson & Katherine Seelye, *Jury Says Professor Was Wrongly Fired*, N.Y. TIMES, Apr. 2, 2009; Tom McGhee, *No Job, No Money for Churchill*, DENVER POST, July 7, 2009; *see also* Archive of Postings to The Race to the Bottom Blog, http://www.theracetothe bottom.org/ward-churchill/ (containing archive of blog posts on the Churchill trial and its aftermath, and links to court documents and commentary).

Nevertheless, expression-based claims in the academic context have had mixed success since *Garcetti*. In what is perhaps the leading case, *Adams v. Trustees of the University of North Carolina-Wilmington*, 640 F.3d 550, 554 (4th Cir. 2011), the Fourth Circuit upheld such a claim. Michael Adams, an associate professor in criminology and prominent conservative commentator, filed suit against the university for failing to promote him to the rank of full professor. Adams alleged that UNCW did not promote him because of his speeches, articles, and books related to his outspoken Christian/conservative views. *Id*.

The district court relied on *Garcetti* in dismissing Adam's speech claim, holding that the speeches, articles, and books were sufficiently related to Adams' professional capacity (as a professor) to fall within his official duties. In reversing, the Fourth Circuit noted that *Garcetti* itself had reserved the question of its rule's application to academic teaching and writing, and further suggested that the scholarship and other speech upon which Adams based his claim extended well beyond the specific, baseline duties demanded by the university:

> There may be instances in which a public university faculty member's assigned duties include a specific role in declaring or administering university policy, as opposed to scholarship or teaching. In that circumstance, *Garcetti* may apply to the specific instances of the faculty member's speech carrying out those duties. However, that is clearly not the circumstance in the case at bar. Defendants agree Adams' speech involves scholarship and teaching; indeed, as we discuss below, that is one of the reasons they say *Garcetti* should apply — because UNCW paid Adams to be a scholar and a teacher regardless of the setting for his work. But the scholarship and teaching in this case, Adams' speech, was intended for and directed at a national or international audience on issues of public importance unrelated to any of Adams' assigned teaching duties at UNCW or any other terms of his employment found in the record. Defendants concede none of Adams' speech was undertaken at the direction of UNCW, paid for by UNCW, or had any direct application to his UNCW duties.
>
> Applying *Garcetti* to the academic work of a public university faculty member under the facts of this case could place beyond the reach of First Amendment protection many forms of public speech or service a professor engaged in during his employment. That would not appear to be what *Garcetti* intended, nor is it consistent with our long-standing recognition that no individual loses his ability to speak as a private citizen by virtue of public employment. In light of the above factors, we will not apply *Garcetti* to the circumstances of this case.
>
> The Defendants nonetheless contend that because Adams was employed as an associate professor, and his position required him to engage in scholarship, research, and service to the community, Adams' speech constituted "statements made pursuant to [his] official duties." *Cf., Garcetti*. In other words, the Defendants argue Adams was employed to undertake his speech. This argument underscores the problem recognized by both the majority and the dissent in *Garcetti*, that "implicates additional constitutional interests that are not fully accounted for" when it comes to "expression related to academic scholarship or classroom instruction.". . . . Put simply, Adams' speech was not tied to any more specific or direct employee duty than the general concept that professors will engage in writing, public appearances, and service within their respective

fields. For all the reasons discussed above, that thin thread is insufficient to render Adams' speech "pursuant to [his] official duties" as intended by *Garcetti*.

Id. at 563-64. Although *Adams* is protective of professor speech, it might simply mean that speech a professor engages in *outside* of his or her official duties as a professor is protected, meaning that there might not be protected "academic freedom" within such duties (however defined). *See, e.g.*, Scott R. Bauries, *Individual Academic Freedom: An Ordinary Concern of the First Amendment*, 83 Miss. L.J. 677 (2014); Mark P. Strasser, *The Onslaught on Academic Freedom*, 81 UMKC L. Rev. 657 (2013). Suppose Adams had expressed his views in the classroom? If so, would it make any difference whether those views were directly relevant to the subjects he taught?

Thus, while the *Adams* opinion does offer some insights into how courts might grapple with the *Garcetti* majority's seeming reluctance to extend an expansive official duties rule to the academic context, much remains uncertain. *See also Keating v. Univ. of South Dakota*, 569 Fed. App'x 469 (8th Cir. 2014) (finding university's civility policy, pursuant to which tenure-track professor was terminated, was not impermissibly vague under the Due Process Clause of the Fourteenth Amendment). It will be interesting, in light of the foregoing, to see how the University of Illinois's "unhiring" of Steven Salaita — the ongoing, high-profile contract- and academic freedom-based controversy discussed in Chapter 2, page 88 — will play out.

In any event, *Adams* and other court decisions in the wake of *Garcetti* also may signal that instructor and professor speech in the university setting will be treated differently than class or instruction-related speech in primary or secondary schools. *See* Strasser, *supra*, at 671-73 (reviewing cases); *see also Evans-Marshall v. Bd. of Educ. of Tipp City Exempted Vill. Sch. Dist.*, 624 F.3d 332 (6th Cir. 2010) (upholding the dismissal of a high school teacher's free speech claim premised on her curricular and pedagogical choices in the classroom because these choices were made pursuant to her official duties and therefore were unprotected speech under *Garcetti*).

* * *

The final broad category of speech claims involves speech or other forms of expression away from work and, unlike *Lane, not* primarily about work or directed at work-related issues. The key question in this context is often whether the government employer has a sufficiently substantial interest to justify regulating or prohibiting such off-site speech. In *United States v. National Treasury Employees Union*, 513 U.S. 454 (1995) ("*NTEU*"), the Supreme Court struck down a federal statute banning certain honoraria for expressive activities including published works and presentations by broad classes of federal employees, including activities that bore no direct relation to the nature of the employees' government work. In so doing, the Court found the government's interest in protecting integrity and ethics in government insufficient to support such a broad ban, stating that the "speculative benefits the honoraria ban may provide the Government are not sufficient to justify this crudely crafted burden on respondents' freedom to engage in expressive activities." *See id.* at 477.

The Supreme Court again addressed off-site expressive activity in *City of San Diego v. Roe*, 543 U.S. 77 (2004) (per curiam). In this case, the Court upheld the San Diego Policy Department's termination of an officer after discovering that he had sold a video in the adults-only section of eBay of himself stripping off a police uniform and performing a sex act, as well as selling police equipment and uniforms. *Id.* at 78. Relying on *NTEU*, the *Roe* Court stated that, first, it must be determined whether there is a relationship between the expression and the workplace, and then, if there is such a relationship, the *Pickering/Connick* analysis applies. Under this approach, the case was easy: Because Roe chose to tie his Internet activities to his status as a police officer and to his department, his expression related to the workplace; the Court thus applied the *Pickering/Connick* analysis, and the City prevailed because Roe's expressive conduct did not address a matter of public concern. *See Roe*, 543 U.S. at 80-82.

In reaching this conclusion, the Court was able to avoid a number of more difficult questions. For example, it did not address whether, in order to receive *any* protection, the off-site expressive conduct must address a matter of public concern. *NTEU* likewise had not addressed this because the Court had found that much of the prohibited expressive activity in that case *did* address matters of public concern. *See* 513 U.S. at 466. Also, the *Roe* Court did not clarify how close the nexus must be between the expressive activity and the person's employment to trigger the *Pickering/ Connick* analysis. Moreover, the Court never reached the question of what governmental interest would be sufficient to justify regulation of employees' expressive activities, the content of which is entirely unrelated to the workplace. *NTEU* had held that, where the prohibited expressive activity does not relate directly to the workplace, and involves speech beyond that of highly ranked officials, the government must make some kind of evidentiary showing that the activity actually has a disruptive effect on the workplace. *See* 513 U.S. at 468-74. Again, however, *NTEU* involved a sweeping prohibition on honoraria for entire classes of workers (including workers at lower levels); it had not addressed an adverse employment action with regard to an individual worker. Finally, in reaching its conclusion that the officer's expression in this case did not address a matter of public concern, the *Roe* Court offered another specific example of speech that fails the test while providing little useful guidance for other cases. Each of these issues emerges again in the next case.

Dible v. City of Chandler
515 F.3d 918 (9th Cir. 2008)

JUDGE FERNANDEZ delivered the opinion of the Court.

I

Ronald and Megan Dible appeal from the district court's grant of summary judgment against them in their action against the City of Chandler, Arizona, the Chandler Police Department, and the Chandler Police Chief Bobby Joe Harris (collectively "the City"). Principally, the Dibles assert that Ronald Dible was a police officer whose rights under the First Amendment to the United States Constitution were violated when he was terminated for participating in (performing in, recording and purveying) a sexually explicit website with his wife. We affirm.

II

In January of 2002, the Chandler Police Department learned that one of its officers, Ronald Dible, was running a website featuring sexually explicit photographs and videos of his wife. After initially placing Ronald Dible on administrative leave and conducting an internal investigation into his involvement with the website, the City terminated his employment as a police officer.

Ronald Dible and his wife Megan Dible began running the website in September of 2000, after Megan Dible signed a contract with CDM Networks, which operated the website. The Dibles then posted pictures of Megan Dible on the website, under the pseudonym "Katelynn." Those photographs portrayed Megan Dible in various sexual poses and activities with Ronald Dible, another woman, and inanimate objects. The Dibles also posted, among other things, a videotape of Megan Dible masturbating that had been filmed by Ronald Dible. The Dibles did not intend to express any kind of message or engage in social or political commentary through the material they posted on their website. They participated in those activities to make money; it was as simple as that.

. . . Any computer user with internet capability could access the website's home page without charge. The home page featured partially nude pictures of Megan Dible in order to entice customers. If the user wanted to view more pictures of Megan Dible, a fee was required, but before the pictures could be reviewed, the user had to enter into a purported contract with CDM Networks. Once the user accepted the terms of the contract and paid the fee, he was free to view the website's sexually explicit photographs and videos.

The Dibles also offered a CD-ROM for sale on the website. . . . Although the photographs on the website and the CD-ROM generally did not show Ronald Dible's face, one of the photographs did.

The Dibles also promoted their website by attending "barmeets." The purpose of the bar-meets was to have fans of the website meet Megan Dible, although Ronald Dible also attended. The bar-meets, which took place at local bars, were open to the public, and attendees were free to take photographs. They did, and sometimes posted those on their own websites. Although some attendees knew Megan Dible only as Katelynn, others knew her true identity. At those barmeets, both Megan Dible and Ronald Dible posed in sexually suggestive ways with each other and with other people, some of whom were partially nude. The Dibles' photographs from the bar-meets were compiled on a CD-ROM and were then sold through their website.

Ronald Dible believed, indeed most likely knew, that his position in the disreputable sexually explicit website business was not compatible with his position as a police officer and risked violating the City and Police Department rule against engaging "in conduct which might bring discredit to the City service." So he took steps to cover up his participation, and in so doing violated the rule that he could not engage in outside employment unless he first filled out and filed a request to engage in employment outside the department. He did not inform any Department officials about it.[1] He did, however, tell a few people about it, including a fellow police officer, whom he urged to start his own website. The officer eventually did.

Sometime in the later part of 2001, rumors about the Dibles' website began circulating among members of the department, and eventually the news of the website filtered up to department officials. Upon learning about it, the police chief on January 25, 2002, ordered Ronald Dible to cease all activity with the website and placed him on administrative leave. The chief then opened an investigation into

---

1. In fact, he lied about his participation when police department people asked.

Ronald Dible's involvement with the website. The investigators questioned Ronald Dible about it, and, in response, he provided several misleading answers. After establishing that he was, in fact, involved in the website, the investigators questioned him about, among other things, whether he and Megan Dible had earned money from the site, and asked to see the contract between Megan Dible and CDM Networks.

By January 25, 2002, the press had also learned about the website and began reporting on it in an unflattering manner. The press reported that the website was run by the Dibles and that he was employed as a city police officer. The record contains no evidence identifying the person who alerted the press to the website's existence or to the Dibles' involvement in it, but, of course, a lot of people already knew. The result of that publicity was disquieting to say the least. A police lieutenant assigned to look into the situation spoke to a large number of officers and others, found that it had severely impacted their working situation, and declared that police officer morale "really hit bottom."

In due course, Ronald Dible's supervisor recommended his dismissal. The supervisor found that Ronald Dible had violated the department's regulation prohibiting its officers from bringing discredit to the city service, and that Ronald Dible had provided false answers to district investigators in the course of their investigation. Chief Harris approved Ronald Dible's dismissal.

Ronald Dible then appealed that decision to the City's Merit Board, which conducted an evidentiary hearing. At the hearing, several officers testified that they had been questioned and ridiculed about the website. A female officer, Amy Hedges, testified that she was called a "porn whore" by an individual she was attempting to arrest. She further testified that she was subjected to derogatory remarks while responding to a bar fight. Specifically, when she arrived at the bar, a patron began gyrating, told her to take off her clothes, and harassed her about the website. Officer Hedges testified that the patron's comments added to the instability of an already fluid field situation and confrontation. Another officer testified to the disrespect that he was shown after the website became publicly known. An investigating officer, who had interviewed many other officers, as well as other people, also testified to the impact of the Dibles' activity on the department. In addition, potential police recruits questioned an officer about the website on each of the five separate recruitment trips that she had conducted after the existence of the site became widely known to members of the public. Assistant Chief Joseph Gaylord testified that he believed the scandal involving Ronald Dible's participation in the sexually explicit website would negatively impact the department's efforts to recruit female officers for years to come. Ultimately, on April 3, 2002, the Merits Board issued a recommendation affirming the decision to discharge Ronald Dible.

IV

The major issue before us [in reviewing the district court's grant of summary judgment] is whether Ronald Dible's First Amendment right to freedom of speech[3] was violated when he was terminated for maintaining and participating in a sexually

---

3. We recognize that the Dibles' conduct was more expression (nudity and sexual activity) than speech as such. That does not change the analysis.

explicit website with his wife, Megan Dible. In fact, for all practical purposes, the other issues in this case hinge on the decision of that issue. We will, therefore, consider it first and consider the other issues raised by the Dibles thereafter.

Freedom of Speech

[The court discussed *City of San Diego v. Roe*, 543 U.S. 77 (2004) as setting forth an analytical framework for consideration of First Amendment rights of governmental employees.] The Court first recognized that "[a] government employee does not relinquish all First Amendment rights otherwise enjoyed by citizens just by reason of his or her employment." That said, when a government employee's speech is under consideration, there are two paths of analysis, depending on whether the speech is related or unrelated to the person's employment. As the Court put it:

> [A] governmental employer may impose certain restraints on the speech of its employees, restraints that would be unconstitutional if applied to the general public. The Court has recognized the right of employees to speak on matters of public concern, typically matters concerning government policies that are of interest to the public at large, a subject on which public employees are uniquely qualified to comment. *See* [*Connick v. Myers; Pickering v. Bd. of Ed.*]. Outside of this category, the Court has held that when government employees speak or write on their own time on topics unrelated to their employment, the speech can have First Amendment protection, absent some governmental justification "far stronger than mere speculation" in regulating it. *United States v. Treasury Employees (NTEU)*. We have little difficulty in concluding that the City was not barred from terminating Roe under either line of cases.

The Court then went on to consider whether Roe's speech activities were related or unrelated to his position as a police officer with the city. It determined that Roe's indecent activity, indeed, related to his employment. In so doing, the Court observed that in *NTEU* the speech in question was not only unrelated but also "had no effect on the mission and purpose of the employer." The Court also emphasized that in *NTEU* "none of the speech at issue 'even arguably [had] any adverse impact' on the employer." It finally pointed out that the City of San Diego had conceded that Roe's activities were unrelated in the sense that they were not concerned with the "workings or functioning" of the police department, but, it concluded:

> It is quite a different question whether the speech was detrimental to the SDPD. On that score the City's consistent position has been that the speech is contrary to its regulations and harmful to the proper functioning of the police force. The present case falls outside the protection afforded in *NTEU*. The authorities that instead control, and which are considered below, are this Court's decisions in *Pickering*, *Connick*, and the decisions which follow them.

Of course, as the Court noted, Roe had gone out of his way to identify himself with police work. Perhaps that alone would have sufficed to make his activity related to his employment. If that were the case, it must be said that Ronald Dible did not do what Roe did. Ronald Dible took some pains to keep the police out of the pictures, but because of other clues and information, it became publicly known that he was involved and that he was a police officer. In any event, Ronald Dible's attempts to conceal his activity came to nought and do not distinguish the underlying situation in *Roe*. Many a rule breaker does so clandestinely in the hope that his violations will not come to light and have untoward consequences. When that hope is dashed, the results and consequences for him are the same as they would have been if he had broken the rules overtly. Roe overtly broke his employer's rules (outside employment and immoral conduct) and he properly suffered the consequences by losing his job. Ronald Dible's discovered clandestine activity also broke his employer's rules (outside employment and conduct that brought disrepute) and he properly suffered the consequences by losing his job. In addition, it can be seriously asked whether a police officer can ever disassociate himself from his powerful public position sufficiently to make his speech (and other activities) entirely unrelated to that position in the eyes of the public and his superiors. Whether overt or temporarily hidden, Ronald Dible's activity had the same practical effect — it "brought the mission of the employer and the professionalism of its officers into serious disrepute."

That said, the Court has never explicitly defined what is or is not related, and we need not do so here. As in *Roe*, the result would be the same "under either line of cases." The Dibles cannot prevail. We will explain.

(1) *Related Speech*. If we determined that Ronald Dible's activities were related to his public employment, we would necessarily approach his First Amendment claim as did the Supreme Court in *Roe*. It said:

> To reconcile the employee's right to engage in speech and the government employer's right to protect its own legitimate interests in performing its mission, the *Pickering* Court adopted a balancing test. It requires a court evaluating restraints on a public employee's speech to balance "the interests of the [employee], as a citizen, in commenting upon matters of public concern and the interest of the State, as an employer, in promoting the efficiency of the public services it performs through its employees."

As the Court explained, before an employee is even entitled to have the balancing test applied, the "speech must touch on a matter of 'public concern.'" The Court further pointed out: "*Connick* held that a public employee's speech is entitled to *Pickering* balancing only when the employee speaks 'as a citizen upon matters of public concern' rather than 'as an employee upon matters only of personal interest.'" And, while the borders of the territory of public concern are not entirely defined, they do encompass matters that are "of legitimate news interest; that is, a subject of general interest and of value and concern to the public at the time of publication," and even some private comments in the proper circumstances. So, for example, the Court has said that an employee's quiet statement to a fellow employee at a county constable's office, that she hoped that a future attempt at assassination of the President would succeed, touched on a matter of public concern. *See Rankin v. McPherson*.

No matter. Whatever a periplus of the outer limits of public concern might show, it was pellucid that Roe's vulgar behavior would be discovered to be outside of those borders. As the Court said, "there is no difficulty in concluding that Roe's expression does not qualify as a matter of public concern under any view of the public concern test. He fails the threshold test and *Pickering* balancing does not come into play." *Roe*.

The same is true of Ronald Dible's activities in this case. They did not give the public any information about the operations, mission or function of the police department, and were not even close to the kind of private remarks that the Court has countenanced. His activities were simply vulgar and indecent. They did not contribute speech on a matter of public concern. The Dibles could not prevail if Ronald Dible's speech is deemed to have been related to his employment.

(2) *Unrelated Speech.* If we determined that Ronald Dible's activities were unrelated to his public employment, we would also have to apply a balancing test. Interestingly enough, it is not entirely clear whether the public concern concept would be a necessary threshold to that balancing. In *Roe* the Supreme Court did not exactly say that the public concern concept must be considered, but it also did not expressly hold that the Court of Appeals' determination that public concern was part of the test was incorrect. And in *NTEU*, the Court pointed out that:

> Respondents' expressive activities in this case fall within the protected category of citizen comment on matters of public concern rather than employee comment on matters related to personal status in the workplace. The speeches and articles for which they received compensation in the past were addressed to a public audience, were made outside the workplace, and involved content largely unrelated to their government employment.

Moreover, in *Rankin*, the Court did indicate that a comment about the President was a matter of public concern, but *Rankin* dealt with an unrelated comment made at the workplace itself. We, however, need not resolve whether the public concern test must be satisfied in this instance. *See Locurto v. Giuliani*, 447 F.3d 159, 175 (2d Cir. 2006).

If a statement must be one of public concern when it consists of unrelated activity away from the workplace, Ronald Dible's conduct was no more protected than it would be if the activity were related, and the Dibles' claim would fail on that account. But, suppose passing the public concern test is not required when unrelated expressive activity takes place away from the work setting. What then? Again, we must balance the asserted First Amendment right against the government's justification. *See Roe.* The Dibles' First Amendment claim cannot survive that balance either.

We first note that a number of Supreme Court justices have expressed some dubiety about the strength of the protection offered to activities that can be said to be of the same ilk as those we deal with here, or, perhaps, of an even less indecent ilk. *See City of Erie v. Pap's A.M.*, 529 U.S. 277, 289, (2000) (plurality opinion) (stating that public nude dancing is "only within the outer ambit of the First Amendment protection"). . . . However, this court has said that plurality decisions of the Supreme Court do not make law and that "the degree of protection the first amendment affords speech does not vary with the social value ascribed to that speech by the courts." *Kev, Inc. v. Kitsap County*, 793 F.2d 1053, 1058 (9th Cir.1986). None of those cases is exactly like the one at hand. We are not dealing with the rights of an ordinary citizen vis-à-vis the government; we are dealing with the rights of a governmental employee (a police officer at that) vis-à-vis his employer. In this context, the reflections of the Justices about the weight of the right to engage in public indecent activity commend themselves to our consideration. As *Roe* suggests, it is a bit difficult to give that activity the same weight as the right to engage in political debate [as in *City of Erie*] or to lecture on religion and black history or to write articles about the environment [as in *NTEU*]. Especially is that true where, as here, the employee admits that he was not interested in conveying any message whatsoever and was engaged in the indecent public activity solely for profit.

In any event, the interest of the City in maintaining the effective and efficient operation of the police department is particularly strong. It would not seem to require an astute moral philosopher or a brilliant social scientist to discern the fact that Ronald Dible's activities, when known to the public, would be "detrimental to the mission and functions of the employer." *Roe.* And although the government's justification cannot be mere speculation, it is entitled to rely on "reasonable predictions of disruption." *Waters v. Churchill,* 511 U.S. 661 (1994) (plurality opinion).

Police departments, and those who work for them, are engaged in a dangerous calling and have significant powers. The public expects officers to behave with a high level of propriety, and, unsurprisingly, is outraged when they do not do so. The law and their own safety demands that they be given a degree of respect, and the sleazy activities of Ronald and Megan Dible could not help but undermine that respect. Nor is this mere speculation.

Almost as soon as Ronald Dible's indecent public activities became widely known, officers in the department began suffering denigration from members of the public, and potential recruits questioned officers about the Dibles' website. Moreover, the department feared that the recruiting of female officers would be affected because of what it seemed to say about the climate at the department. That is not rank speculation. In a similar case involving police officers' public sexual activities, the Eleventh Circuit Court of Appeals noted that this kind of activity by officers, once known, could not help but interfere with the functions and mission of the police department because "it reflected on [deputies'] fitness as deputies and undermined public confidence" in the department. *Thaeter v. Palm Beach County Sheriff's Office,* 449 F.3d 1342, 1356 (11th Cir. 2006). Just so.

We are not gallied by the Dibles' claim that Ronald Dible is being subjected to some kind of heckler's veto. Worries about a heckler's veto have generally dealt with the restriction of a citizen's speech based upon the anticipated disorderly reaction by members of an audience. *See Rosenbaum v. City and County of San Francisco,* 484 F.3d 1142, 1158-59 (9th Cir. 2007). Those worries do not directly relate to the wholly separate area of employee activities that affect the public's view of a governmental agency in a negative fashion, and, thereby, affect the agency's mission. The Dibles' argument ignores the fact that the public can form a negative view of a person due to his particular mode of expression — there is nothing unconstitutional about that. It also ignores the unique and sensitive position of a police department and its necessary and constant interactions with the public. . . .

As the Second Circuit Court of Appeals has pointed out, even where the unrelated expression is a matter of public concern — there a comment on race relations — police officers "are quintessentially public servants" and "part of their job is to safeguard the public's opinion of them." *Locurto.* Thus, said the court, the actions of the police department were not due to a heckler's veto, but rather an example of the government's accounting for the public's perception of the officers' actions when it considered the potential for disruption of the department's functions. *See also Rankin* (taking particular note of the fact that a clerical employee's comments were not made public and, therefore, did not discredit the constable's office).[7]

---

7. We have not overlooked *Flanagan v. Munger,* 890 F.2d 1557, 1566-67 (10th Cir. 1989) and *Berger v. Battaglia,* 779 F.2d 992, 1000-01 (4th Cir. 1985). However, to the extent that they minimize the potential for an actual effect on the efficiency and efficacy of police department functions arising from public perceptions of the inappropriate activities of police officers, they are severely undermined by *Roe,* and we decline to follow them.

In fine, whether Ronald Dible's activities were related to his employment or not, the City could discipline him for those activities without violating his First Amendment rights. Thus, the Dibles' claim to the contrary must be rejected.

[The court rejected the Dibles' claim that their First Amendment rights to privacy and freedom of association were violated by the City. It recognized that the First Amendment implicates a right of privacy, which includes a right to make personal decisions and a right to keep personal matters private, and contains a right to the freedom of intimate expression and to associate with others in activities otherwise protected by the First Amendment. Nevertheless, the court found that, because the City had not released any information that connected the Dibles to the website, it could not have violated their right to privacy and intimate association by giving them unwanted publicity. The court went on to reject the association claim for the same reasons that it had rejected the speech claim, stating that "a governmental employee cannot avoid the strictures of the balancing tests that we have heretofore described by attempting to resurrect fallen speech claims as privacy and associational claims." It also affirmed the district court's grant of summary judgment on the Dibles' state law right to privacy, intentional infliction of emotional distress, and wrongful termination claims.]

CANBY, Circuit Judge, concurring in the judgment:

I

With all due respect, I am unable to join the majority opinion because I disagree with its resolution of Dible's First Amendment speech claim. Under the facts of this case and the existing precedent, the police department could not discharge Dible for his website expression without violating the First Amendment.

I have no quarrel with some of the majority's analysis. I agree that, if Dible's expressive website activity were properly characterized as employment-related, then his First Amendment claim would fail because his expression, while protected, was not of public concern. The majority opinion correctly reasons that this point is established by [*City of San Diego v. Roe*].

Dible's website activity was not employment-related, however. As the majority opinion points out, Dible was careful not to identify himself or his website with the police department or with police status at all. That fact differentiates his case from *Roe*. Certainly nothing in the activity Dible portrayed suggested a connection with the police. I am unwilling to conclude, for reasons I will set forth below, that such unrelated expression becomes related to Dible's employment simply because people who disapprove of his expression find out that he is a policeman and make their disapproval or disdain known to the police department in ways that could affect its work.

As the majority opinion points out, the Supreme Court has not, in *Roe* or its antecedents, made perfectly clear whether a governmental employee's expression unrelated to the employment must be of public concern to be protected. In my view it makes little sense to impose the public concern requirement for the protection of unrelated speech. The requirement of public concern comes from *Pickering*. Its usefulness is in making an exception to the right of a public employer to control the expression of employees in matters relating to their employment. One way of limiting the rule to its context, which I would follow, is to hold that there is no requirement that an employee's speech that is unrelated to his employment be of public concern in order to merit First Amendment protection. The Tenth Circuit adopted that rule in *Flanagan v. Munger*, 890 F.2d 1557, 1562-64 (1989). Another way of reaching the same result is to hold, as we did in *Roe v. City of San Diego*, 356 F.3d 1108, 1119 (9th Cir.), *rev'd*, 543 U.S. 77 (2004), that *any* speech by a government employee that is not about his employer, that occurs outside the workplace, and is directed to a segment of the general public, qualifies *ipso facto* as a matter of public concern. As the majority opinion here recognizes, the Supreme Court did not say this approach was incorrect when it reversed *Roe*. Similarly, in *Berger v. Battaglia*, 779 F.2d 992, 998 (4th Cir. 1985), the Fourth Circuit held, in a case of unrelated expression, that *all* such expression was of public concern unless it constituted a private personnel grievance. Either way — whether the public concern requirement is simply dispensed with for expression unrelated to employment, as I prefer, or whether the public concern requirement for unrelated speech is broadened to include virtually the universe of unrelated speech — the outcome is the same. Public concern should not be a hurdle depriving employee speech of First Amendment protection when that speech is unrelated to the employment.

Now, I recognize that pornography, although apparently popular, is not a very respected subject of First Amendment protection in many quarters. The majority opinion here reflects that distaste, variously characterizing Dible's expressive activities as "vulgar," "indecent," "sleazy," and "disreputable." But vigorous enforcement of the free speech guarantee of the First Amendment often requires that we protect speech that many, even a majority, find offensive. Pornography, and sexual expression in general, is protected by the First Amendment when it does not constitute obscenity (and there is no showing that Dible's expression meets that extreme standard). We should accept that fact and accord Dible's expression the constitutional protection to which it is entitled. The majority opinion here falls short of the First Amendment standard in two major respects.

Because Dible's expressive activity was not employment-related, the police department must demonstrate that the alleged harm caused by his expression was "'real, not merely conjectural.'" *NTEU*. The evidence of harm in this case is so insubstantial that it can be characterized as "conjectural." An officer testified that he feared the effect on recruitment of female officers, but no such effect was demonstrated. At least three officers testified that they had been verbally harassed in a manner attributable to the website, but there was no testimony that this seriously interfered with the performance of their duties. In sum, the findings of interference with the mission of the police department are based on the conjecture that Dible's expressive activities might cause some persons to think less well of the police department and that this disfavor might in some ways lead to disruption of police activities. The evidence simply does not meet the *Treasury Employees* standard. It does not outweigh Dible's interest in expression, which is his "interest in engaging in free speech, not the value of the speech itself." *Flanagan*.[1]

---

1. I place no significance at all on Dible's statement that he did not intend to convey any message in his expressive activity. His website constituted expression, and he has raised a First Amendment defense to his termination because of his website activity. It is equally irrelevant to his First Amendment protection that he sought to make money from his expression, as many speakers or writers do. *See, e.g., Smith v. California*, 361 U.S. 147, 150 (1959).

A second flaw in the majority's analysis is that it enshrines the "heckler's veto" with respect to *all* conduct of a public employee, or at least of a police department employee. Nothing that Dible did or said in relation to his website activities in itself caused any disruption to police department functions. The alleged (and minimal) disruption was caused by other persons' disapproval of Dible's activities once it became known that he was an officer of the police department. The rule to be drawn from the majority's analysis, apparently, is that police officers may be fired for engaging in expressive activities, unrelated to their employment, when numbers of the public disapprove of the expression vigorously and possibly disruptively. That rule empowers the heckler to veto the speech, and is inconsistent with the First Amendment. *See Terminiello v. Chicago*, 337 U.S. 1, 4-5 (1949). In such a situation, it is the duty of the police department to prevent the disruption by those opposed to the speech, not to suppress or punish the speech. [*See Cohen v. California*, 403 U.S. 15, 23 (1971).]

The heckler's veto applied to sexually expressive activities has disturbing potential for expansive application. A measurable segment of the population, for example, is vigorously antagonistic to homosexual activity and expression; it could easily be encouraged to mobilize were a police officer discovered to have engaged, off duty and unidentified by his activity, in a Gay Pride parade, or expressive cross-dressing, or any number of other expressive activities that might fan the embers of antagonism smoldering in a part of the population. For this reason, it is far better to adopt a rule that protects off-duty speech unrelated to employment when the speech itself causes no *internal* problems, and the only disruption is in the external relations between the police department and the public unhappy with the police officer's expression. The Tenth Circuit adopted just such a rule. *See Flanagan*. The Fourth Circuit avoided adopting an inflexible rule, but held that a police department could not prohibit off-duty, unrelated speech by an officer under circumstances parallel to those in Dible's case: "[N]ot only was the perceived threat of disruption only to external operations and relationships, it was caused not by the speech itself but by threatened reaction to it by offended segments of the public." *Berger*. This public reaction in *Berger* was not inconsequential; it threatened to disrupt the tenuous relationship between the police department and the black community. Even so, "this sort of threatened disruption by others reacting to public employee speech simply may not be allowed to serve as justification for public employer disciplinary action directed at that speech."

The majority opinion states that to the extent that *Flanagan* and *Berger* "minimize the potential for an actual effect on the efficiency and efficacy of police department functions arising from public perceptions of the inappropriate activities of police officers, they are severely undermined by *Roe*." The rationale of *Flanagan* and *Berger*, however, was not that disruption was minimal, but that as part of the heckler's veto it could not support discipline of the employee. It is true that *Roe* permitted discipline of an officer because of public reaction to his expressive conduct, but that expressive conduct was purposely employment-related. The head of a governmental agency is entitled to control the speech of members of the agency with regard to agency-related matters, unless that speech is a matter of public concern. *Pickering*. But that rule is an exception to the general First Amendment protection of speech. *See NTEU*. To apply the same restriction to off-duty expression by a public employee, unrelated to his employment, is to reject the established principle that public employees may not be required to surrender their constitutional right of free speech as a condition of their employment. *Roe* did not extend to off-duty conduct unrelated to employment, and accordingly it did not undermine *Flanagan* and *Berger*. . . .

II

I concur in the judgment, however, because the record demonstrates that any rational trier of fact would find that Dible would have been discharged for making false statements to police department investigators, had he not been discharged for his website activity. *See Mt. Healthy City Sch. Dist. Bd. of Educ. v. Doyle*, 429 U.S. 274, 287 (1977). . . . Dible contends, however, that his false statements cannot be a ground for discharge because the entire investigation was instituted because of his First Amendment protected activity. [However, the] investigation by the police department in the present case was not illegitimate in its inception. The department was entitled to inquire into Dible's off-duty activity to see whether it was employment-related, which would bring it within the unprotected scope of *Roe*. In addition, the department had a policy requiring police officers to obtain prior approval before engaging in any outside employment, because certain jobs were deemed compromising. The department was entitled to inquire whether this policy had been violated. Nothing in the nature of the investigation entitled Dible to lie. . . .

NOTES

1. *Unresolved Issues Surrounding Off-Site Expression.* Recall the issues left unresolved in *NTEU* and *Roe*: (1) Must off-site expression be a matter of public concern to receive *any* protection? (2) How close must the nexus be between the expressive activity and the person's employment to trigger *Pickering/Connick* balancing? (3) What government interests are sufficient to justify regulation of employee expressive activity that is entirely unrelated to work? The *Dible* majority works hard to avoid answering the first two questions, but, in so doing, must answer the third — at least as necessary to support its alternative holding, which assumed the speech was unrelated to work. Look closely at how the majority reaches the conclusion that, regardless of whether Ronald Dible's activities were related to his employment, the City could discipline him for those activities. Under this kind of analysis, the first two unresolved questions often will not matter. Put another way, how likely is it that *any* expressive conduct by a police officer will be protected if it is an embarrassment to, or fosters criticism of, the department?

Now compare this to how the concurring judge would resolve these three matters and how each resolution would affect the analysis of whether the speech is protected. For Judge Canby, the relatedness inquiry becomes paramount. Under this alternative framework, how likely is it that off-site expression related to work will be protected? But how about unrelated expression, whether involving a "matter of public concern" or not? What must the department show in order to regulate such unrelated expression? In making the determination that the speech in this case, unlike that in *Roe*, was unrelated to work, Judge Canby does not provide much analysis, but his focus appears to be on the extent to which the police officer made some reference to police work, the department, or his status as an officer. Other matters, including the content of the speech (i.e., how repugnant or embarrassing it might be) and how disruptive it is, are left to the second part of the inquiry, namely whether the department can demonstrate that the speech caused "real" harm. This approach offers a nice, clean analytical framework, but does it serve to protect any speech if one accepts the view that, given the nature of their work, police officers are representatives of the department and city 24/7?

The vast differences between the approaches to analyzing off-site expression claims reflected in the majority and concurring opinions are not merely a matter of academic interest. As their competing citations to other circuits make clear, federal courts are split on these matters. For a host of reasons, defendant police departments and individual supervisors prevail more often than not in these cases, but the *Flanagan* and *Berger* decisions are important counterexamples. *See also Leverington v. City of Colorado Springs,* 643 F.3d 719 (10th Cir. 2011) (holding that off-site speech by a nurse at a public hospital must relate to a public concern to be protected, and hence, her statements to a police officer during a traffic stop suggesting that she hoped she never had him as a patient — which he reported to the hospital as a threat, leading to her termination — were unprotected speech); *see generally* Mary-Rose Papandrea, *The Free Speech Rights of Off-Duty Government Employees,* 2010 B.Y.U. L. Rev. 2117 (2010) (arguing that off-duty, non-work-related speech by government employees should be entitled to presumptive protection under the First Amendment because it is never entirely possible to separate the citizen from the employee).

2. *Even More Difficult Facts? Dible* was a more difficult case than *Roe* because Dible had made no reference to his position as a police officer or his police department on his website. Nevertheless, the majority did not find this difference to be dispositive. It emphasized that neither Ronald nor Megan Dible made much of an effort to disguise their identity on the website or keep these activities secret, and the connection between Ronald's Internet activities and his status as a police officer quickly emerged. He then compounded his problems by not telling the truth about his activities to department officials. Suppose he had taken more pains to hide his identity from the beginning (to avoid the public's drawing the connection with his police work) or to limit access to the site to a more selective group, but the public and his department ultimately found out anyway. Would the outcome on the First Amendment question have been different? Should it have been? If no, does that mean that a police department may prohibit *all otherwise legal*, sexually explicit expressive activity by its police officers? If yes, should a police officer's First Amendment right to expression depend on his or her ability or efforts to remain anonymous or unknown?

3. *Type of Speech.* In *Roe*, the Supreme Court had held that the sexually explicit video at issue in that case did not address a matter of public concern. The Court defined such a matter as "something that is a subject of legitimate news interest; that is, a subject of general interest and of value and concern to the public at the time of publication." 543 U.S. at 83-84. This standard may not provide much guidance for courts assessing very different kinds of speech (*see* the examples in Note 2 on page 416), thus requiring the periplus around its boundaries so feared by the *Dible* majority. But the speech at issue in *Roe* is similar enough to the expressive activity in *Dible* that the majority had no problem finding that Dible's Web site did not address a matter of public concern. Whether this conclusion is correct or not, are you gallied by the irony — that is, the sexually explicit expression at issue is deemed not a matter of public concern even though the principal reason the government employer wishes to regulate it is because it is a matter of significant concern to the public?

The *Dible* majority emphasized that certain forms of sexually explicit expression enjoy minimal First Amendment protection, Indeed, the majority went out of its way to make clear not only its distaste for such expression, but also the limited social value of sexually explicit materials distributed for profit. But, as the concurrence notes, much expression that may be deemed sexual in nature is still protected by the First Amendment. Can a police department's prohibition on "conduct which might bring discredit to the City service," "conduct unbecoming of an officer," and "immoral conduct" bar all such expression, consistent with the Constitution? How about the (legal) publication of semi-nude photos on an officer's Facebook page, for example, or sexual jokes or banter in off-site conversations, at a comedy club, or in an Internet chat room? Courts tend to side with police departments in off-site speech and association cases. *See, e.g., Piscottano v. Murphy*, 511 F.3d 247 (2d Cir. 2007) (holding that the Department of Corrections established that the conduct of several officers, expressing their approval of the nature and character of the Outlaws Motorcycle Club, had the potential to disrupt and reflect negatively on its operations, and that its interest in "maintaining the efficiency, security, and integrity of its operations outweighed the associational interests" of the officers). But should they?

4. *Beyond Law Enforcement Officers.* Whatever you might think of the deference courts tend to accord to law enforcement agencies, how free should other types of government employers be in determining what off-site conduct is unbecoming or immoral, or, for that matter, sufficiently embarrassing or scandalous to justify regulation? Certainly, attempts by a government agency to regulate off-site expressive conduct or associations that implicate fundamental rights — religious freedom, intimate relationships, etc. — will be subject to some scrutiny. *See, e.g., Cameron v. Grainger County*, 274 F. App'x 437 (6th Cir. 2008) (denying summary judgment because a reasonable jury could find that former deputy county clerk's decision to marry into a family that was politically opposed to reelection of her employer was a motivating factor in the employer's decision to fire her); *cf. Flaskamp v. Dearborn Pub. Schs.*, 385 F.3d 935 (6th Cir. 2004) (upholding a school board's decision to disallow tenure to a teacher who had an intimate relationship with a former student). But what about other expressive conduct? Would your answer depend on the type of public employee who engages in the conduct of, for example, teachers, attorneys, public health workers, regulatory inspectors, clerical staff, or janitors? Does the mission of the agency matter, or whether the particular employee is supposed to be a "role model"? Also, would your answer depend as well on the viewpoint or opinions expressed? *See, e.g., Wales v. Bd. of Educ.*, 120 F.3d 82, 85 (7th Cir. 1997) (asserting that "[a] school district is entitled to put in its classrooms teachers who share its educational philosophy"). Should the fact that the speech or association is highly offensive to the community the agency serves be enough to justify the employer's adverse employment action? *See Melzer v. Bd. of Educ.*, 336 F.3d 185 (2d Cir. 2003) (upholding the termination of a teacher after it became known that he was a member of the North American Man/Boy Love Association in part because teachers must respect the views of parents in the community). For a discussion of the complicated First Amendment issues arising out of school teachers' use of social media both when students and the school community are the intended audience and when they are not, *see* Mary-Rose Papandrea, *Social Networks and the Law: Social Media, Public School Teachers, and the First Amendment*, 90 N.C. L. REV. 1597 (2012).

5. *Hate Speech.* Should a government agency have greater discretion to regulate off-site, legal expression that might be characterized as "hate speech" — for example,

the publication of racist or sexist statements or jokes, anti-Semitic caricatures, or cartoon depictions deeply offensive to Muslims—than expressive conduct that is "merely" irreverent or offensive to some but not within the foregoing categories? *See, e.g., Pappas v. Giuliani*, 290 F.3d 143, 147 (2d Cir. 2002) (noting the importance of maintaining legitimacy in the community in upholding the termination of a police officer who disseminated racist and anti-Semitic writings). If yes, why? Note that much of this expression is more likely than that in *Roe* and *Dible* to address matters of public concern, *see* Note 2, page 416—although again, the extent to which this matters for off-site conduct unrelated to work is unresolved. Recall that the fact that the particular expression would be unacceptable or offensive to most people does not preclude constitutional protection, even if the expression is at work. *See Rankin*, 483 U.S. at 390. So why is "hate speech" and certain other forms of "highly offensive" speech distinguishable? Is greater deference to the employer justified because, at least in some contexts (e.g., employment discrimination) the speech itself might be illegal? If employers did not have broad discretion to regulate such speech might there be troublesome downstream consequences for them, at least in some contexts?

6. *Private Ordering and Deference.* As in Chapter 6, the overarching themes of private ordering and the appropriate level of deference to employer prerogatives are also central to the off-site conduct inquiry. While public employees cannot be required to "waive" prospectively their First Amendment rights, *Roe* and *Dible* demonstrate how a public employer's framing of job responsibilities and conditions, and, accordingly, a worker's decision to accept the position so defined, may limit the freedom the employee has in off-site expression and conduct. Indeed, law enforcement departments may apply the motto that "you are a police officer twenty-four hours a day, seven days a week" more or less aggressively, and this may ultimately determine the scope of the employee's speech rights. Moreover, as a practical matter, an employee begins litigation in a far weaker position if he or she must concede knowledge of an agreement to department guidelines and practices with regard to off-site and after-hours conduct, whether classified as "unbecoming," "immoral," offensive, or otherwise.

Deference also plays a role if, ultimately, the court seeks to balance the employee's interest in off-site expression against the employer's interest in avoiding harm to its mission or disruption of its operations. Note how the majority and concurring opinions in *Dible* differ on this question. How searching is the majority's review of the reasons given by the department for terminating *Dible*? How is level of scrutiny applied by Judge Canby different? What are the costs and benefits of each approach?

7. *Blogging and Other Web-based Activities.* This discussion brings us back to the high-profile issue of employee blogging and other Web-based activities, discussed more fully at page 383 in Chapter 6. Under the framework in *NTEU* and *Roe*, public employee Internet activity that has a nexus with the workplace—either occurs at work or has work-related content—may have First Amendment protection but will be subject to the *Pickering/Connick* analysis. Internet activity that bears no relationship to work may be more likely to receive protection, although much remains unclear and seemingly depends on the nature of the expression, the worker's position, the role or mission of the agency, and, again, the level of deference courts may be willing to accord the government's justification for its actions. *See generally* Paul M. Secunda, *Blogging While (Publicly) Employed: Some First Amendment Implications*, 47 U. Louisville L. Rev. 679 (2009).

8. *Other Protections for Public Employees.* Public employees may also enjoy certain additional protections for their speech or associational activities. Government

restrictions on employee speech and expressive activity may run afoul of the Free Exercise, Equal Protection, and Due Process clauses of the Constitution. Thus, as discussed in Chapter 6, a government employer could not discipline or discharge an employee because of the employee's bona fide religious associations, *see Shrum v. City of Coweta*, 449 F.3d 1132 (10th Cir. 2006), or off-site associations that implicate fundamental rights, including intimate associations, unless the action is the result of a generally applicable policy that is justified by some governmental interest. *See* Chapter 6, at page 342. Similarly, statutory prohibitions on discrimination will limit a government agency's ability to regulate or prohibit both workplace and off-site conduct. *See id.*

Also, civil service codes and other statutes governing the public workplace often contain prohibitions against termination absent just cause, "good behavior," and other terms that restrict public employers' discretion in—and limit the reasons for—disciplining or terminating their employees. For example, federal law limits employee dismissals for misconduct to situations in which the agency can demonstrate that the misconduct impairs the efficiency of the service it provides and, hence, that a dismissal would promote efficiency. *See* 5 U.S.C. §§ 1101-5 (2014); 5 U.S.C. § 7513(a) (2014). However, this greater substantive protection also has a procedural price: The Supreme Court has held that employees covered by the federal government's comprehensive civil service regime may seek remedies—even for constitutional violations—only within that scheme. *See Bush v. Lucas*, 462 U.S. 367 (1983). State civil service codes do not preclude federal constitutional claims brought under 42 U.S.C. § 1983, but employee remedies for constitutional violations may nevertheless be limited by qualified immunity and other employer defenses. *See generally* Paul M. Secunda, *Whither the* Pickering *Rights of Federal Employees?* 79 U. Colo. L. Rev. 1101 (2007).

In addition, collective bargaining agreements governing some government workers may carve out additional areas of protection and offer additional procedural constraints on agency discretion. Moreover, government agencies certainly may otherwise grant to their employees—unilaterally or by agreement—more protection than the First Amendment affords. *See, e.g., Waters v. Churchill*, 511 U.S. 661, 674 (1994) ("[T]he government may certainly choose to give additional protections to its employees beyond what is mandated by the First Amendment. . . .").

9. *Statutory Restrictions on Political Activity.* The Hatch Act, 5 U.S.C. §§ 7321-7326 (2014), and parallel state statutes, place restrictions on political activities by covered government employees, but also preserve certain freedoms. The Act and comparable state regimes were passed to prevent corruption and undue influence and, hence, impose significant restrictions on the partisan political activities of government workers. Many of these restrictions have been upheld in the face of First Amendment challenges. *See, e.g., United States Civil Serv. Comm'n v. Ass'n of Letter Carriers*, 413 U.S. 548 (1973); *Broadrick v. Oklahoma*, 413 U.S. 601 (1973) (upholding Oklahoma's version of the statute). However, amendments to the Hatch Act in 1993, *see* Pub. L. No. 103-94, 107 Stat. 1001 (1993), and exceptions in state statutes now provide limited rights for employees to take part in campaigns and other political activities while off-duty. Other activities are still banned, including the use of one's position for political influence, soliciting contributions from parties with business before the employee's agency, or engaging in political activities while on duty.

PROBLEMS

7-1. Michael Rasmusson is employed by the City Department of Health Services ("DHS") as a chemist's aide. In late May, DHS's Director of Workplace Diversity ("the Director") alerted all of its employees that June would be designated "Gay, Lesbian, Bisexual, and Transgender ("GLBT") Pride Month."

On June 2, another employee sent an e-mail to all co-workers, including Rasmusson, outlining the history of the gay and lesbian movement in the United States. Rasmusson e-mailed a reply to all recipients, which stated in part:

> I will not participate in gay celebrations because the Bible teaches that homosexuality is a horrible sin and those who practice it will not inherit the Kingdom of God. It is just as wrong for homosexuals to cause civil disorder today as it was in 1969 [the year the movement was founded], and they shouldn't have any more rights today than they did then.

The other employee then complained to the Director, as did other employees. The Director and a human resources officer then informed Rasmusson that sexual orientation is a protected status under state law and that it is unlawful to discriminate against individuals based on this status. He was further informed at the meeting that the DHS considered his e-mail messages to be in violation of this law.

On June 10, Rasmusson sent an e-mail message to one of DHS's high ranking officials, in which he objected to the display of homosexual literature in the lobby of DHS's building and stated that homosexuality is an unhealthy lifestyle that should not be promoted.

On June 17, Rasmusson received an e-mail from another employee inviting members of the department to a voluntary Ellen DeGeneres "coming out" party (at which they would watch together the famous 1997 television episode of *Ellen*, now on DVD). Rasmusson sent the following e-mail in response to this message:

> How could a program such as this where Ellen "comes out" and tells everyone she is a lesbian be humorous? This is nothing for her to be proud of and we should not encourage her in this. Should we also have a party when a man "comes out" and tells everyone he is a child molester?

DHS contends that the employee who sent the invitation, and hence, the recipient of Rasmusson's responsive e-mail, is a lesbian.

Shortly thereafter, Rasmusson was advised by his supervisor that he should not send out any further messages expressing his views on homosexuality. The supervisor further told Rasmusson that, although he is entitled to his personal views, his actions could constitute harassment as defined by DHS's harassment policy. In response, Rasmusson told the supervisor that he should be able to express his opinion on these matters like any other employee and that he intends to do so in response to any further DHS e-mails or activities endorsing homosexuality. At that point, the supervisor terminated Rasmusson.

Assume for purposes of this problem that the relevant state law prohibits employment discrimination based on sexual orientation. Also, assume that Rasmusson has no claim under the Free Exercise Clause or for religious discrimination.

Does Rasmusson have a free speech claim? What are Rasmusson's best arguments? How about DHS's? How likely is Rasmusson to prevail? What additional information, if any, would help you assess the likelihood of success? *See Brown v. Minnesota Dep't of Health*, Civ. No. 98-63 (JRT/RLE) (D. Minn. 1998).

If DHS asks for your advice on how it should structure or restructure GLBT Pride Month to reduce the risk of liability (to Rasmusson or others) in the future, what advice would you give? Does this kind of initiative create inherent liability risks, or can it be organized in a way that no speech-related liability is possible?

7-2.　Assume the same facts as in 7-1 except, instead of sending the messages described above, Rasmusson was terminated or disciplined by DHS after he responded to GLBT Pride Month in one of the following three ways:

a. Posting information about and criticisms of the event on a socially conservative blog.
b. Criticizing what he called the "perverse gay and lesbian lifestyle" on the blog, but never referring to his employer or the Pride Month event in his postings.
c. Publicly supporting a local campaign pursuing a ballot initiative to repeal the state statute prohibiting discrimination based on sexual orientation and posting campaign flyers in his work cubicle.

Would the change in the facts in each of these three scenarios affect your analysis? If so, how?

7-3.　In a well-publicized incident, Derek Fenton, a New Jersey Transit Authority employee, was fired from his job after he burned pages of the Koran on the ninth anniversary of the September 11 terrorist attacks on the United States to protest the proposed Islamic center near Ground Zero. The ACLU filed suit on behalf of Fenton against the Authority, alleging that his termination violated his First Amendment rights. Eventually, the case settled, and NJ Transit reinstated Fenton without requiring him to recant or disavow his actions. For further discussion of the facts of the case and its ultimate resolution, *see* http://www.npr.org/blogs/thetwo-way/2011/04/22/135635324/new-jersey-to-rehire-transit-worker-fired-for-burning-quran/;http://www.nj.com/news/index.ssf/2010/11/nj_aclu_to_sue_nj_transit_for.html

If this case had not settled, what would Fenton have had to prove? What defenses would have been available to the New Jersey Transit Authority? In light of the facts and the law as set forth in this chapter, how likely is it that Fenton would have prevailed? What other reasons might have led the Authority to settle the matter?

B. THE PRIVATE WORKPLACE

In the private workplace, where neither civil service codes nor constitutional protections for expressive activity protect workers from employer actions, the sources of protection for employee speech and associational preferences are very limited. *See* David C. Yamada, *Voices from the Cubicle: Protecting and Encouraging Private Employee Speech in the Post-Industrial Workplace*, 19 BERKELEY J. EMP. & LAB. L. 1 (1998). Indeed, unlike privacy, there are *no* traditional common-law torts that protect employee speech directly. The more recently developed public policy tort may provide some protection, but only in very narrow situations such as speech protected as whistleblowing. And, as discussed in Chapter 6, although the new RESTATEMENT OF EMPLOYMENT LAW would provide some limited protections for associational activities, it has yet to be considered by the courts. *See* Chapter 6 at page 366 (discussing § 7.08 of the RESTATEMENT). Thus, as a general matter, employees in the private sector are left with a limited number of statutory protections for speech. These protections tend to apply only to certain types or categories of speech or association.

First, various statutory protections discussed elsewhere in this text may protect employee speech and expression directly or indirectly. For example, as discussed in Chapter 4, employee statements may be protected due to their content under federal and state statutes that prohibit employer retaliation against whistleblowers and those who testify in judicial or administrative proceedings. Also, as discussed in Chapter 6, federal and state antidiscrimination laws may protect employees from adverse treatment for certain associations, including religious affiliations and interracial intimate relationships, and occasional expressive conduct associated with other protected classifications. *See* Chapter 6 at page 383. Moreover, some of the privacy protections discussed in that chapter, including the federal wiretapping statute, protect employees from highly intrusive or secret monitoring of their communications, which has the effect of protecting the content of these communications.

In addition, as also discussed in Chapter 6, a number of states have enacted statutes that protect both public- and private-sector employees from adverse employment actions resulting from legal, off-site conduct and personal and political associations. *See, e.g.*, CAL. LAB. CODE §§ 96(k), 98.6 (2014); COL. REV. STAT. § 24-34-402.5 (2014) (prohibiting employers from terminating employees for lawful off-site activities absent job relatedness); MINN. STAT. § 181.938 (2014) (same); N.Y. LAB. LAW § 201-d (McKinney 2014); WASH. REV. CODE § 42.17.680(2) (2014) ("No employer or labor organization may discriminate against an officer or employee in the terms or conditions of employment for (a) the failure to contribute to, (b) the failure in any way to support or oppose, or (c) in any way supporting or opposing a candidate, ballot proposition, political party, or political committee."). In a recent article, Professor Eugene Volokh provides the most comprehensive survey to date of state statutes protecting private employees' speech and political activities. He finds that about half of the states have statutes addressing these matters, although their protections vary widely. *See generally* Eugene Volokh, *Private Employees' Speech and Political Activity: Statutory Protection Against Employer Retaliation*, 16 TEX. REV. L. & POL. 295 (2012); *see also* RESTATEMENT (THIRD) OF EMPLOYMENT LAW (Proposed Final Draft, April 18, 2014) § 7.08, cmt. c (citing state statutes). Of course, none of these statutes provides absolute protections: Each allows, explicitly or implicitly, employers to defend their actions by showing that they are necessary to serve a legitimate business purpose.

On its face, the most sweeping state protection is a Connecticut statute that makes an employer liable for discharging or disciplining an employee on account of the employee's exercise of rights guaranteed in the First Amendment or parallel portions of the state constitution, provided that such exercise does not "materially interfere with the employee's bona fide job performance or the working relationship between the employee and employer." CONN. GEN. STAT. § 31-51q (2014). The Connecticut Supreme Court confirmed that the statute was intended to apply the free speech guarantees of the federal and state constitutions directly to private employers. *See Cotto v. United Technologies Corp.*, 738 A.2d 623 (Conn. 1999). The statute therefore provides potentially broad protection for public and private employee speech and association. However, given the qualifying language in the statute and, as you have now seen, the qualified nature of employee speech rights under the Constitution, it is not clear how meaningful the protection is. Indeed, in *Cotto* itself, the court found that an employee allegedly terminated for refusing to display at his workstation an American flag distributed by his employer did not state a claim under the statute. The court reasoned that no First Amendment–type interest was implicated because the employer's flag display directive did not require the employee to do or say anything related to his own political beliefs, did not compel him to "assume the risk that others might attribute to him any political beliefs about the flag that he did not share," and, hence, did not constitute coercion of expression or belief. *Id.* at 633-34. More recently, in *Shumann v. Dianon Systems, Inc.*, 43 A.3d 111 (Conn. 2012), the Connecticut Supreme Court rejected the argument that protections under the act are broader than those guaranteed under the Constitution, and therefore held that *Garcetti* official duties framework applies to claims under the statute. Thus, private employee speech falling with the scope of the employee's official duties is unprotected.

Federal labor law provides another potentially important, albeit limited protection for employee expressive activities regarding workplace terms and conditions, even in the nonunionized context. Section 8(a)(1) of the National Labor Relations Act ("NLRA"), 29 U.S.C. § 158(a)(1) (2014), protects an employee's expressive conduct in two important respects. First, it prohibits discharging an employee for organizing workers. Beyond this, however, it protects all workers in their right under § 7 of the NLRA to "concerted activities for the purpose of . . . mutual aid or protection," even apart from the formation of a union. *See* 29 U.S.C. § 157 (2014) ("Employees shall have the right to . . . engage in other concerted activities for the purpose of collective bargaining or other mutual aid or protection, and shall also have the right to refrain from any or all such activities. . . ."). In order to qualify for this protection, the employee activity must be "concerted" — that is, it must involve or be in preparation for group activity and involve a matter of potential common concern among employees, rather than merely activity by the worker solely on his or her own behalf. It must also involve "mutual aid and protection," which requires that it be reasonably work-related, addressing the conditions or terms of employment. Note that while other sources of speech and association rights tend to accord the greatest protection to off-site expressive activities unrelated to work, the "mutual aid and protection" requirement means that the protection under the NLRA applies *only* to work-related expression, whether it occurs on or off-site. For updates on the NLRB's Facebook-related actions, *see* Chapter 6, page 387. Finally, even if the conduct is concerted and has a work-related object, it is protected only if it constitutes "protected activity," a term of art in labor law. Activity is unprotected if it is unlawful, violent, or unduly disruptive to the workplace, but even peaceful but "disloyal" conduct can be unprotected. *See, e.g., NLRB v. Fansteel Metallurgical Corp.*, 306 U.S. 240 (1939) (finding prolonged sit-down strike resulting in seizure of employer's plant and destruction of some of its property to be concerted but unprotected activity).

Consider how this protection for concerted activity might protect employee speech in already familiar fact patterns. First, as discussed in Chapter 6 at page 387, the National Labor Relations Board ("NLRB") has now alleged, in a potentially groundbreaking case, that an employer violated this mandate by terminating an employee after she criticized her supervisor on her Facebook page. In addition, recall *Connick*. Although Myers would have had no concerted activity claim under the NLRA because the act does not apply to public employers; a number of state labor statutes — which may apply to some classes of state and municipal employees — provide parallel protections for such activities. *See, e.g.*, Note, *Free Speech, The Private Employee, and State Constitutions*, 91 YALE L. J. 522, 523-24 & n.12 (1982) (discussing state statutes). Suppose Myers had been working as a prosecutor in one of these states and was covered under the state's statute. If she had circulated a similar questionnaire in her office, might her speech have been entitled to protection? Or was it not "concerted"?

Beyond these provisions, the two other potential, albeit rarely available sources of protection for employees in the private sector are the public policy tort and contract.

≡ ### *Edmondson v. Shearer Lumber Products*
75 P.3d 733 (Idaho 2003)

WALTERS, Justice.

This is a wrongful termination of employment case. The employee appeals from the district court's dismissal of the action upon the employer's motion for summary judgment [and later motion to amend his complaint]. We affirm.

Facts

Michael Edmondson was employed by Shearer Lumber Products for twenty-two years at the company's Elk City mill. In 1999, he became a salaried employee and on his most recent performance review, he received a rating of "very good." However, on February 15, 2000, the plant manager, David Paisley, following directions from his superiors fired Edmondson, by reading a statement that informed Edmondson: "Because of your continued involvement in activities that are harmful to the long term interests of Shearer Lumber Products, we are terminating your employment immediately."

It was well known at Shearer Lumber that Edmondson was extensively involved in the community and regularly attended public meetings concerning matters of public interest and concern, such that he was recognized with the Idaho GEM Citizen Award by then Governor Batt. In January of 2000, Edmondson attended a public meeting of a group known as Save Elk City. One of the leaders of the group was the resource manager at Shearer Lumber, Dick Wilhite, who at the group meetings encouraged public support for the proposal that Save Elk City had submitted to the Federal Lands

Task Force Working Group for consideration as to how best to manage the Nez Perce National Forest. Edmondson attended the group meetings, but he made no comments on the group's proposal. Nor did he discuss his opinions regarding the Save Elk City proposal at work with other employees.

Shearer Lumber did not openly campaign for the Save Elk City proposal, but Edmondson later learned from Wilhite that the proposal submitted in the name of Save Elk City was the project of Shearer Lumber's owner, Dick Bennett. At that time, Wilhite and Edmondson discussed the various outstanding proposals that might be competing for the Task Force's recommendation to the State Land Board, but Edmondson did not declare a preference for any of the proposals.

Shearer Lumber obtained information that Edmondson had attended meetings of the Task Force, had contacted someone in the administration of the Task Force, and was opposed to the collaborative project that Shearer had sponsored and submitted on behalf of the Save Elk City group. Edmondson was twice called into meetings at Shearer Lumber, where he claimed he was subjected to intimidation and pressure from Wilhite, Paisley, and John Bennett, Shearer's general manager. It was made clear that Edmondson was *not* to form any opinions on or make any statements to the Federal Lands Task Force. In effect, Edmondson was warned that any opposition to the collaborative project that was contrary to Shearer's interest would lead to serious consequences. Edmondson was informed at the February 2, 2000, meeting that Shearer Lumber wanted all of its employees to support the projects the mill was involved in, if they wanted to avoid serious consequences that would result if the project was derailed or negatively impacted.

John Bennett testified in his deposition that the reason Edmondson was terminated was that Edmondson was opposing the project that Shearer Lumber Products supported, in direct conflict with the company's goals that could ultimately jeopardize a Task Force decision favorable to Shearer's interests. Bennett also attributed to Edmondson contact with the Task Force administration, although it was Edmondson's wife, Jamie, who had made inquiries to the Task Force. Edmondson speculated further as to the reason for his termination, which occurred the day after federal agents impounded some logs stored on the Shearer Mill site, as part of a U.S. Forest Service investigation in which Jamie Edmondson had also played a role. However, John Bennett testified that the logs belonged to a third party, and Shearer had no interest in how the logs were handled.

* * *

[Edmondson sued Shearer Lumber for wrongful termination of employment, but the lower court awarded summary judgment to Shearer because Edmondson's allegations did not fall within Idaho's limited public policy exception.]

Discussion

I . . .

A. The district court did not err in granting summary judgment on the claim of breach of public policy exception to the at-will doctrine.

In Idaho, the only general exception to the employment at-will doctrine is that an employer may be liable for wrongful discharge when the motivation for discharge contravenes public policy. *MacNeil v. Minidoka Memorial Hosp.*, [701 P.2d 208 (Idaho 1985)]; *Jackson v. Minidoka Irrigation Dist.*, 563 P.2d 54 (Idaho 1977); *Anderson v. Farm Bureau Mut. Ins. Co. of Idaho*, 732 P.2d 699, 707 (Idaho Ct. App. 1987). The purpose of the exception is to balance the competing interests of society, the employer, and the employee in light of modern business experience. *Crea v. FMC Corp.*, 16 P.3d 272. 275 (Idaho 2000). The public policy exception has been held to protect employees who refuse to commit unlawful acts, who perform important public obligations, or who exercise certain legal rights or privileges. *Sorensen v. Comm Tek, Inc.*, 799 P.2d 70, 74 (Idaho 1990). Public policy of the state is found in the constitution and statutes. *Boise-Payette Lumber Co. v. Challis Indep. Sch. Dist. No. 1*, 268 P. 26 (Idaho 1928). "In the absence of case law or statutory language . . . , the Court finds no basis for expanding the Idaho law that defines the public policy exception to the at-will doctrine." *Lord v. Swire Pacific Holdings, Inc.*, 203 F. Supp. 2d 1175, 1180 (D. Idaho 2002).

Courts have recognized that public policy expressed in the constitution and the statutes of the state may serve as a basis for finding an exception to the employment at-will doctrine. *See generally* 82 AM. JUR. 2d *Wrongful Discharge* § 19, at 692 (1992). The First Amendment prohibits the government from restraining or abridging freedom of speech and assembly. Article I, § 9 of the Idaho Constitution also guarantees the right of free speech: "Every person may freely speak, write and publish on all subjects, being responsible for the abuse of that liberty." Article I, § 10 of the Idaho Constitution guarantees the right of freedom of association: "The people shall have the right to assemble in a peaceful manner, to consult for their common good; to instruct their representatives, and to petition the legislature for the redress of grievances." The First Amendment and Article I, §§ 9 and 10 of the Idaho Constitution do not apply to alleged restrictions imposed by private parties, however. . . .

Edmondson maintains that he was wrongfully terminated because he exercised his constitutionally protected rights of free speech and association. He argues that the public policy at issue prohibits restrictions on free speech and association. [But the cases he relies on] all deal with governmental restrictions on free speech and associative rights of employees of public agencies, which are inapplicable in the private employment context in which Edmondson worked. The prevailing view among those courts addressing the issue in the private sector is that state or federal constitutional free speech cannot, in the absence of state action, be the basis of a public policy exception in wrongful discharge claims. *See Tiernan v. Charleston Area Med. Ctr., Inc.*, 506 S.E. 578, 589-90 (W. Va. 1998), and cases cited therein.

Edmondson argues that I.C. § 18-7901[1] expresses a public policy extending constitutional free speech protection to relationships between private employers and its employees. The district court did not make a finding specifically addressing I.C. § 18-7901, but even if it had, the facts alleged by Edmondson regarding his termination fall far short of describing conduct that was harassing, intimidating or threatening and based upon the descriptive list set forth in the statute.[2]

---

1. I.C. § 18-7901 provides as follows: The legislature finds and declares that it is the right of every person regardless of race, color, ancestry, religion or national origin, to be secure and protected from fear, intimidation, harassment, and physical harm caused by the activities of groups and individuals.

2. We do not suggest that the legislature's descriptive list should be deemed to exclude other well-recognized protected classes such as age, gender, or persons with mental or physical disabilities.

Finally, Edmondson urges that public policy is implicated wherever the power to hire and fire is utilized to dictate the terms of an employee's political activities and associations, relying on *Novosel v. Nationwide Ins. Co.*, 721 F.2d 894, 900 (3d Cir. 1983). There the court held that an important public policy was at stake and that Novosel's allegations that the employer coerced political activity stated a wrongful discharge claim. *Id.* However, the public policy adopted in *Novosel* has not been endorsed by any other court, not even the Pennsylvania state courts within the federal district of the Circuit that issued *Novosel.* We likewise decline to extend Idaho's public policy exception through the adoption of *Novosel.*

Accordingly, we hold that an employee does not have a cause of action against a private sector employer who terminates the employee because of the exercise of the employee's constitutional right of free speech. The district court's dismissal of the claim of breach of public policy exception to the at-will doctrine is affirmed. . . .

III.

The district court did not err in denying Edmondson's motion to amend.

Following the decision of the district court on summary judgment, Edmondson filed a motion to amend his complaint to assert a breach of contract claim and a breach of the covenant of good faith and fair dealing. The district court denied the motion after a hearing, holding that the record did not support a claim for breach of an implied-in-fact contract. The district court also held that the record failed to show that the at-will relationship was somehow modified or did not apply to Edmondson.

. . . A limitation of an at-will employment will be implied when, from all the circumstances surrounding the relationship, a reasonable person could conclude that both parties intended that either's party's right to terminate the relationship was limited by the implied-in-fact agreement. *Mitchell v. Zilog, Inc.*, 874 P.2d 520, 523 (Idaho 1994). A plaintiff's subjective understanding is insufficient to establish an express or implied agreement limiting at-will employment. *Arnold v. Diet Center, Inc.*, 746 P.2d 1040 (Idaho Ct. App. 1987). Edmondson's personal belief that the company would not terminate him for attending public meetings, which the company allowed him to attend, or, would not terminate him without good cause, does not create limitations on Shearer's right to terminate him at will.

Unless an employee is hired pursuant to a contract which specifies the duration of the employment or limits the reasons why an employee may be discharged, the employee is at-will and can be terminated for any reason or no reason at all. *Thomas v. Med. Ctr. Physicians, P.A.*, 61 P.3d 557 (Idaho 2002); *Jackson [supra].* Furthermore, as the district court ruled, the employee handbook expressly defined the relationship as at-will and negates Edmondson's claim of intent to restrict the grounds for discharge. *See Moser v. Coca-Cola Nw. Bottling Co.*, 931 P.2d 1227 (Idaho Ct. App. 1997). As a matter of law, therefore, the plaintiff failed to show that an implied contract changed the employee's at-will status. *Raedlein v. Boise Cascade Corp.*, 931 P.2d 621, 624 (Idaho 1996). The district court also held that the covenant of good faith and fair dealing does not prohibit an employer from terminating an employee at-will. We agree. *See Farnworth v. Femling*, 869 P.2d 1378, 1384

(Idaho 1994). We find no error in the district court's decision denying the Edmond-son's motion to amend. . . .

Justice KIDWELL, dissenting.

I wholeheartedly support the presumption that employment in Idaho is "at-will" unless otherwise provided. Unlike the majority, however, I would hold that there is a narrow, but important, public policy exception to the at-will presumption for certain exercises of one's first amendment rights. Therefore, I respectfully dissent. . . .

As the majority has stated, public policy may be imbedded in statutes. *See, e.g., Watson v. Idaho Falls Consol. Hosps., Inc.*, 720 P.2d 632 (Idaho 1986). I believe that statutes are not the only place in which one may find public policy. Indeed, one may find the most significant public policies in this state and our nation in the Idaho Constitution and the Constitution of the United States. Thus, I would hold that certain constitutional public policies deserve protection and vindication through the public policy exception to at-will employment even in the absence of a statutory enactment.

One such policy that deserves protection in the at-will employment context is the policy of encouraging participation and debate regarding issues of public concern. The Idaho Constitution makes clear that "[a]ll political power is inherent in the people. Government is instituted for their benefit, and they have the right to alter, reform, or abolish the same whenever they may deem it necessary. . . ." ID. CONST. Art. 1, § 2. In order to exercise the political power inherent in the people, the Idaho and United States constitutions endow individuals with the liberty to speak freely and participate in vigorous public debate. U.S. CONST. Amend. 1; ID. CONST. Art. 1, § 9. Allowing employers to terminate employment based on an individual's association and speech regarding public issues that may have little or nothing in connection with the employ-er's business, invites employers to squelch the association, speech, and debate so necessary to our system of government. This is particularly true in the context of the myriad of small Idaho communities with only one or two prominent employers. Thus, I would hold it against public policy to discharge an employee for constitutionally-protected political speech or activities regarding a matter of public concern, provided that such speech or activity does not interfere with the employee's job performance or the business of the employer.

The majority cites to *Tiernan v. Charleston Area Med. Ctr.*, for the proposition that absent a state action, the constitutional exercise of free speech is not a public policy exception to at will employment. It is my opinion that even absent a state action, a very narrowly drawn public policy exception to the employment at-will doctrine should apply. That narrowly drawn exception would require a two-step analysis. First, did the at-will employee's speech impact the employer's business in *any* manner? If so, was the employee terminated because of his or her speech? The free speech public policy exception would apply to at-will employment in the case where the employee's speech does not impact the employer's business and the employee was terminated for the speech. In *Tiernan* the plaintiff was fired because she wrote a letter to the editor criticizing her employer. Under this proposed public policy exception, the plaintiff's speech clearly impacted her employer and her termination was lawful.

In this case, the evidence in the record clearly creates genuine issues of material fact regarding whether Edmondson was terminated for political speech or activities regarding a matter of public concern. Further, the record shows genuine issues regarding whether Edmondson's speech and activities interfered with his job performance or the business of his employer. On these grounds, I would vacate summary judgment and remand this matter for further proceedings.

NOTES

1. *Freedom of Expression and the Public Policy Tort.* Work your way through Edmondson's public policy claim. Why does the majority reject this theory? Now consider Justice Kidwell's dissent. With which aspects of the majority's reasoning does he take issue, and what dangers does he identify that fail to sway his colleagues?

Both opinions cited *Novosel v. Nationwide Insurance Co.*, 721 F.2d 894 (3d Cir. 1983), undoubtedly the leading case in which a court has found that state and federal constitutional protections for political expression and association are important public policies that can form the basis of an employee's wrongful discharge claim. In that case, a federal circuit panel sitting in diversity held that Novosel stated a claim under Pennsylvania law where he alleged that he was discharged for refusing to participate in his employer's lobbying effort and privately expressing opposition to the company's political stand:

> Although Novosel is not a government employee, the public employee cases do not confine themselves to the narrow question of state action. Rather, these cases suggest that an important public policy is in fact implicated wherever the power to hire and fire is utilized to dictate the terms of employee political activities. In dealing with public employees, the cause of action arises directly from the Constitution rather than from common law developments. The protection of important political freedoms, however, goes well beyond the question whether the threat comes from state or private bodies. The inquiry before us is whether the concern for the rights of political expression and association which animated the public employee cases is sufficient to state a public policy under Pennsylvania law. While there are no Pennsylvania cases squarely on this point, we believe that the clear direction of the opinions promulgated by the state's courts suggests that this question be answered in the affirmative.
>
> Having concluded thereby that an important public policy is at stake, we now hold that Novosel's allegations state a claim [under Pennsylvania law] in that Novosel's complaint discloses no plausible and legitimate reason for terminating his employment, and his discharge violates a clear mandate of public policy.

Id. at 900. Compare this reasoning with that of the majority and dissent in *Edmondson*. Thinking back to the discussion of the public policy tort in Chapter 4, which approach is more consistent with the contours of the theory outlined in that chapter? Which approach is more convincing?

2. *State of the Law on Public Policy Speech Claims.* The *Novosel* decision has generated an enormous amount of attention, often negative. Indeed, Judge Becker of the Third Circuit dissented from the full Third Circuit's denial of an *en banc* rehearing of this decision because, in his view, the panel greatly overreached:

> First, the opinion ignores the state action requirement of first amendment jurisprudence, particularly by its repeated, and, in my view, inappropriate citation of public employee cases, and by its implicit assumption that a public policy against government interference with free speech may be readily extended to private actors in voluntary association with

another. Second, the opinion could be read to suggest that an explicit contractual provision authorizing an employer to dismiss a lobbyist for failure to undertake lobbying might be unenforceable or subject to a balancing test. Third, the opinion fails to consider other public policy interests, such as the economic interests of the public in efficient corporate performance, the first amendment interests of corporations, and the legitimate interests of a corporation in commanding the loyalty of its employees to pursue its economic well being.

721 F.2d at 903. There are a few other published cases in which courts have recognized speech or association-based claims under the public policy doctrine. *See, e.g., Chavez v. Manville Prods. Corp.*, 777 P.2d 371 (N.M. 1989). Yet, as *Edmondson* suggests, the courts that have rejected *Novosel*'s reasoning are legion, and, absent a statute, the vast majority of courts have refused to recognize a public policy claim for employee political, social, or associational choices in private workplaces. *See, e.g., Dixon v. Coburg Dairy, Inc.*, 330 F.3d 250 (4th Cir. 2003) (refusing to extend South Carolina's public policy doctrine to cover termination for the placement of Confederate flag stickers on a tool box); *Grinzi v. San Diego Hospice Corp.*, 14 Cal. Rptr. 3d 893 (Cal. App. 2004) (rejecting *Novosel*'s reasoning and citing to numerous decisions where other courts have done the same); *Tiernan v. Charleston Area Med. Ctr., Inc.*, 506 S.E.2d 578 (W. Va. 1998) (same); *Brunner v. Al Attar*, 786 S.W.2d 784 (Tex. App. 1990) (holding that the termination of an employee because she worked as a volunteer at the AIDS Foundation does not violate public policy).

3. *Comparison to* Borse. Interestingly, the Third Circuit decided both *Borse*, the public policy case involving drug testing set forth in Chapter 6 at page 344, and *Novosel*. And, in both cases, the court, sitting in diversity jurisdiction, attempted to anticipate and apply Pennsylvania law on the public policy doctrine. Broadly speaking, which decision is more consistent with the public policy doctrine cases set forth in Chapter 4? In answering this question, consider what or who the public policy tort is designed to protect. If your answer is that *Novosel* is more in line with the other public policy cases, note the irony, since a number of other courts have adopted the reasoning in *Borse*, while *Novosel* remains an outlier.

4. *Should There Be Stronger Protection for Private-Sector Employees?* Despite the criticism and widespread rejection of *Novosel*'s extension of the public policy doctrine, the power of the court's critique of the employer's conduct ensures its continuing relevance in the debate. Are the *Novosel* court and the dissent in *Edmondson* on to something when they suggest that coerced political activity by a private employer is potentially problematic? *See* Lisa B. Bingham, *Employee Free Speech in the Workplace: Using the First Amendment as Public Policy for Wrongful Discharge Actions*, 55 Ohio St. L. J. 341 (1994) (arguing in favor of a *Novosel*-like public policy claim).

Consider that *Novosel* was handed down more than 20 years ago. Are private enterprises today more or less powerful economically and politically? How about employees, individually or collectively? Given that most employees work in the private sector, are the dangers associated with employer conduct like that in *Novosel* and *Edmondson* significant? Indeed, the conduct in *Novosel* and *Edmondson* might be particularly troublesome since the employer in each of these cases sought not only to prohibit employee activities but also to coerce employees into affirmatively participating in political activity on its behalf. If employer-coerced political activity is widespread, did *Novosel* correctly identify a danger to the functioning and legitimacy of our political system? Even if such coercion does not become standard practice, doesn't the prospect of it as well as the chill of employer prohibitions sufficiently threaten aspects of autonomy we view as so fundamental in democratic society that we ought to recognize that such behavior violates public policy?

Justice Kidwell seems deeply troubled by this, noting that the lack of protection for employees "invites employers to squelch the association, speech, and debate so necessary to our system of government[,]" and expressing particular concern "in the context of the myriad of small Idaho communities with only one or two prominent employers." Might this be even more true now in the wake of *Citizens United v. Federal Election Commission*, 558 U.S. 310 (2010), in which the Supreme Court held that independent political expenditures by for-profit corporations are protected by the First Amendment and therefore cannot be prohibited? Put another way, now that firms — that is, private employers — have robust protections accompanying their significant resources to influence the political process, perhaps we should be even more concerned about their coercing their employees to support or at least not oppose their policy preferences.

If so, what is the response to Judge Becker's claim that the *Novosel* panel's approach might threaten an employer's ability to terminate a lobbyist? Would there be a workable way to limit such protection such that it would not inhibit, for example, a public relations firm's ability to terminate an employee who refused to speak out against state legislation harmful to the tobacco industry even though he was hired to improve the image and advocate on behalf of clients engaged in cigarette manufacturing?

5. *A Defense of or Threat to the Legislative Process?* As discussed in Chapter 4, a core objection to an expansive common-law public policy tort is that it violates separation of powers principles — that is, the legislature and not the courts ought to decide state public policy and, as importantly, which breaches of such policies should give rise to a private right of action. Even if one generally accepts this proposition, is the argument in favor of the legislative prerogative less strong here, where the concern is the distortion of the political process itself? In other words, should the protection at issue in *Novosel* and *Edmondson* be left to the political process when the public policy supporting the protection is to ensure the legitimacy of that process?

Nevertheless, if, as the *Edmondson* majority and most other courts have concluded, *Novosel* nevertheless went too far, perhaps the employer activity the opinion addresses and the dangers it identifies should be, at minimum, a call for legislative reform to protect both workers and the integrity of the political process. If you agree with this proposition, consider what kind of legislated protections would be appropriate and meaningful. As discussed above, a few states have enacted statutes that may protect employee political activities and associations, although, interestingly, under some of the statutory regimes, off-site political conduct would receive protection while compelled political participation at work, of the type at issue in *Novosel*, would not. Again, the Connecticut statute, as interpreted by the Connecticut Supreme Court in *Cotto, see* page 463, probably would protect employees from such employer demands because it applies constitutional associational protections against private employers, and thereby likely prohibits affirmative coercive measures such as compelled political patronage. Is the Connecticut approach the correct one, or does it also go too far?

6. *Nonpolitical Speech in and Outside the Workplace.* Both *Novosel* and *Edmondson* involve political speech and association. If you believe such activity ought to receive some protection in the private workplace, would you extend the protection to nonpolitical speech addressing a matter of public interest — for example, recent world events, community activities, or entertainment and sports news? Similarly, would you extend associational protections to nonpolitical activities, such as participation in social clubs, corporate boards, nondenominational charities, volunteer organizations, and self-help groups? If so, why? What public policies are served by protecting nonpolitical speech? Is the free exchange of ideas, or at least the exchange of ideas on matters of public concern or importance, a strong enough reason to support such far-reaching protection in the private workplace? Are there other ends to be served by protecting expressive interests in the private workplace? Finally, which of these ends, if any, are worth the costs—for example, litigation costs, counseling and administrative costs, hesitation to fire underperforming workers, the costs of uncertainty—additional restrictions invariably impose on employers?

7. *The Restatement Approach.* Chapter 5 of the new Restatement addresses the tort of wrongful discharge in violation of public policy. *See* RESTATEMENT (THIRD) OF EMPLOYMENT LAW (Proposed Final Draft, April 18, 2014) § 5.01-5.03. Advocates of employee speech rights will be disappointed to learn that this draft contains no *Novosel*-like protection for employee speech or association. The draft does contain a "catch-all" provision, *see* § 5.02(f) (protecting an employee who "engages in other activity directly furthering a substantial public policy"), but there is no suggestion that this would support a *Novosel*-like claim. Indeed, the Reporters Notes following this section recognize that courts generally have disfavored such claims. *See* § 5.02 Reporters Notes cmt. d. Moreover, the Illustration 12 following section 7.08 (which provides limited autonomy protections) adopts the reasoning in *Edmondson*. *See* § 7.08 Ill. 12 and cmt. h.

8. *Private Ordering and Employee Expression.* In addition to rejecting Edmondson's public policy claim, the court also rejected his contract theories, finding no express or implicit promise on the part of Shearer that Edmondson's employment was anything but at will. However, other courts have found that contract-based theories are available to employees terminated for speech and associational activities.

For instance, in *Rulon-Miller*, reproduced at page 360, the court upheld an implied-in-fact contract claim arising out of an employee's associational preferences—in that case, involving an employee's intimate association. *See also Novosel*, 721 F.2d *at* 902-03 (concluding that the allegation "that Nationwide's custom, practice or policy created either a contractual just cause requirement or contractual procedures by which defendant failed to abide is a factual matter that should survive a motion to dismiss"). Given the fairly wide acceptance of the theory of implied-in-fact contractual modifications to the at-will relationship, this is a potentially viable theory for employees claiming some right to expression.

Nevertheless, implied just-cause/good-cause terms (such as those alleged in *Edmondson* and *Novosel*) differ from the terms in *Rulon-Miller* in important respects. Recall that the terms enforced against the employer in *Rulon-Miller* addressed the employee's autonomy interests directly; that is, IBM had instituted a general policy of not interfering with its employees' off-site associations and activities. Implied just-cause/good-cause terms do not purport to protect associational rights in particular. In many speech and association cases, such a term may be of limited assistance to employees because it would be fairly easy for employers to articulate a legitimate business reason for terminating employees for their expression or associations. For example, assuming that the employer demands in *Novosel* and *Edmondson* violated no state law, didn't the employers in those cases have just cause/good cause to terminate the employees? Suppose, for instance, that the employer was lobbying for a government contract, which the employee opposed as not in the public interest. Wouldn't the employer be able to terminate the employee without breaching the contract? Recall that *Rulon-Miller* cautioned, "We have concern with an employee's off-the-job behavior only when it reduces his ability to perform regular job assignments, interferes with the job performance of other employees, or if his outside behavior affects the reputation of the company in a major way."

9. *Express Contractual Speech and Association Rights.* In addition to the implied-in-fact contract theory, a few common forms of express contractual provisions protect individual employee expression. Collective bargaining agreements, for example, may include not only just cause provisions, but also specific protections for employee unionizing activity, political activity, and other forms of expression. In addition, high-level workers or those who are in high-demand, including entertainers, sports figures, and executives, may negotiate for terms that give them significant expressive freedom. Such negotiated terms may include the ability to moonlight, the right to engage in philanthropic activities and social causes of one's choosing, and "for cause only" termination, defined so as to shield a great deal of expressive conduct from employer retaliation.

Consider those workers who are hired to express their opinions — for example, editorial writers, political commentators, cartoonists, certain performing artists, and, more and more frequently, bloggers. Obviously, these workers have incentives to negotiate for protections that provide them with sufficient "space" to express their opinions without fear of retribution. But given the many business and legal risks that might arise from such expression, what limitations are their employers likely to demand? These issues have garnered significant attention at different times, for example in the wake of National Public Radio's termination of news analyst Juan Williams (for his remarks regarding Muslims made on Fox News) and MSNBC's short suspension of host Keith Olbermann (for his failure to disclose political contributions as required by network policy).

The group of employees enjoying perhaps the most robust speech protections is tenured faculty members in academic institutions. The primary policy supporting tenure is academic freedom, although it is intended to serve other values as well, including economic security. *See, e.g.,* American Association of University Professors, *1940 Statement of Principles on Academic Freedom and Tenure,* in AAUP Policy Documents and Reports (1995), *available at* http://www.aaup.org/statements/Redbook/1940stat .pdf. Academic tenure provides protected faculty with guaranteed employment subject to termination only for cause, and, because the aim is to preserve academic freedom, cause generally does not include the views expressed by the faculty member. As discussed above, in the public education context, academic freedom has been recognized as a potentially important First Amendment concern. Academic tenure has generally held strong in both the public and private context. There are, however, economic and political pressures to the contrary, as well as the occasional "spike" in anti-tenure sentiment, *see supra* Note 3, page 88 (discussing the controversy over the University of Illinois's refusal to follow through on its appointment of Steven Salaita for tweets concerning Israel's attacks in Gaza); Note on Garcetti and Academic Freedom, page 442. (discussing the uproar that followed Ward Churchill's statements about 9/11 victims); *see also* James J. Fishman, *Tenure: Endangered or Evolutionary Species,* 38 AKRON L. REV. 771 (2005) (addressing some of the current challenges to tenure).

There are relatively few litigated cases regarding "de-tenuring" or the discharge of tenured employees. Indeed, dismissal of tenured university faculty is relatively rare. *See, e.g.*, James J. Fishman, *Tenure and Its Discontents: The Worst Form of Employment Relationship Save All of the Others*, 21 PACE L. REV. 159, 172-73 (2000). However, in a controversial recent decision, the Sixth Circuit held, under Michigan law, that a former law professor was due only the employment protection and process specified in her employment contract with the law school, despite references to "tenure" in the professor's contract and in school policies. *Branham v. Thomas M. Cooley Law School*, 689 F.3d 558 (6th Cir. 2012). The court concluded that such references, which did not define tenure as right to continuous employment, created no obligation of employment beyond the single year term to which the contract referred. *See id.* at 562-63. According to the court, the professor had tenure in the sense that she had academic freedom, but nothing in her contract or documents incorporated by reference therein provided for a term of employment greater than one year. *See id.* The ultimate impact of *Branham* outside of the Sixth Circuit (and, indeed, the facts of the case itself) remains unclear, but it calls into question the extent to which academic tenure provides robust job security in private educational institutions.

The most likely expression-related cause for dismissal of a tenured faculty member is sexual or other forms of harassment. *See* Fishman at 200-01 (stating that the other most frequent causes are other illegal activities, incompetence, and the institution's financial exigency). Another is plagiarism and related forms of research misconduct. Tenure, however, does not typically protect faculty members with regard to administrative positions they also hold, such as deanships and department chairs. *See, e.g., Jeffries v. Harleston*, 52 F.3d 9 (2d Cir. 1995) (holding right to academic freedom does not prevent removal of professor as chair of department). For further discussion of academic tenure, *see generally* Matthew W. Finkin, *"A Higher Order of Liberty in the Workplace": Academic Freedom and Tenure in the Vortex of Employment Practices and Law*, 53 LAW & CONTEMP. PROBS. 357 (1990).

Most other workers (i.e., nonunionized, non–high-level, non–civil service, and nontenured) have neither the bargaining power nor inclination at the outset of their employment to negotiate for terms that protect their speech and association prerogatives, and raising such issues at the formation stage may raise unwanted red flags. Such provisions, therefore, are rare and, as a result, the typical nonunionized worker enjoys no express contractual protection for expressive activities. This, combined with the limited availability of other common-law or statutory protections, means that most expressive and associational activity by private-sector employees has no legal protection.

10. *Contractual "Suppression" of Employee Speech.* For most employees, the far more likely kinds of contractual provisions are those designed to suppress or restrict employee speech. A typical example is an employee agreeing as a condition of employment, promotion, or severance not to disclose broad categories of confidential and other work- or employer-related information to third parties during and after his or her term of employment. The enforceability of such provisions—or at least those that purport to limit expression beyond trade secrets, privileged communications, and other traditionally recognized forms of proprietary information—is controversial. One high-profile example is the confidentiality agreement between Jeffrey Wigand and his former employer, Brown & Williamson Tobacco Company ("B & W"), which purported to prohibit Wigand from discussing anything about B & W's business, products, or practices that were not generally known during and after termination of his employment relationship. *See, e.g.*, Terry Morehead Dworkin & Elletta Sangrey Callahan, *Buying Silence*, 36 AM. BUS. L. J. 151, 191 (1998); Bryan Styker Weinstein,

In Defense of Jeffrey Wigand: A First Amendment Challenge to the Enforcement of Employee Confidentiality Agreements Against Whistleblowers, 49 S.C. L. REV. 129 (1997). B & W's attempts to enforce this agreement against Wigand and to prevent the CBS show *60 Minutes* from airing interviews with him received significant public attention and were ultimately the subject of the movie *The Insider*. For further discussion of such agreements and their social implications, *see generally* Alan E. Garfield, *Promises of Silence: Contract Law and Freedom of Speech*, 83 CORNELL L. REV. 261 (1998); *see also* Daniel J. Solove & Neil M. Richards, *Rethinking Free Speech and Civil Liability*, 109 COLUM. L. REV. 1650 (2009) (offering a detailed account and critique of how courts confront the clash between free speech and private ordering in the confidentiality agreement context and elsewhere).

11. *Should There Be a Qualified Right to Free Expression in the Private Workplace?* A number of commentators have argued that there ought to be protection for various kinds of employee expression and association in the private workplace. *See, e.g.*, Bruce Barry, SPEECHLESS: THE EROSION OF FREE EXPRESSION IN THE AMERICAN WORKPLACE (2007); Cynthia L. Estlund, *Free Speech and Due Process in the Workplace*, 71 IND. L.J. 101 (1995); Joseph R. Grodin, *Constitutional Values in the Private Sector Workplace*, 13 INDUS. REL. L.J. 1 (1991); Stephen D. Sugarman, *"Lifestyle" Discrimination in Employment*, 24 BERKELEY J. EMP. & LAB. L. 377 (2003); David C. Yamada, *Voices from the Cubicle: Protecting and Encouraging Private Employee Speech in the Post-Industrial Workplace*, 19 BERKELEY J. EMP. & LAB. L. 1 (1998). Now that you are familiar with the entire legal landscape (statutory, tort, and private ordering) and the practical realities for most workers, does the law treat employee expression appropriately? What reforms, if any, would you advocate?

PROBLEMS

7-4. Look back at Problems 7-1 and 7-2. This time, however, assume that the employer is not a city agency, but rather the health services department of a private, nonsectarian university, and that Rasmusson is a nontenured employee of the university. Assume all other facts and circumstances remain the same. What are the possible legal theories on which Rasmusson may pursue a claim against his employer for his termination under any of the scenarios described? How probable is it that he will prevail? If there is a risk of liability, how could the university reduce such risk in the future?

7-5. Patricia Patterson was employed by DollarSave Stores, Inc. ("DSI"), where she had been an accountant working at a large distribution facility for a dozen years. DSI is a large food wholesaler and retailer. Patterson had no written employment contract, although her superiors had always given her very positive work reviews and indicated to her that she had a bright future with DSI. Her job duties required no contact with the public.

After she experienced serious health problems several years ago, Patterson was diagnosed as highly allergic to certain synthetic hormones. These hormones are common in domestic nonorganic beef, poultry, and pork. They also are present in meat byproducts, including stocks, bullions, and lard. To avoid recurring health problems, Patterson's physicians imposed a no–nonorganic meat/meat byproduct dietary restriction on her. As a result, Patterson became a semi-observant vegetarian, read food labels carefully, and purchased organic foods whenever possible. She also became an avid reader of health and organic food journals and a frequent participant in various online discussion groups supporting vegetarianism and organic lifestyles.

Recently, a food-labeling bill began to work its way through the state legislature. This bill would mandate detailed disclosures of both the origins of meat products and byproducts and the hormones and antibiotics used in their production. DSI sells a substantial amount of domestic meat products and other foods containing meat-based ingredients and byproducts, none of which is organic. It therefore opposed further food labeling. DSI informed its workers about its lobbying efforts in a monthly newsletter for employees, but it never asked its own employees to take any action.

On the eve of a legislative hearing on the bill, Patterson was contacted by one of her friends and asked if she could give a statement supporting food labeling. She agreed. At the hearing, she described her health problems, the difficulty she had in determining which foods contained meat byproducts containing hormones, and the corresponding need for better labeling. She never mentioned in her statement that she was employed by DSI. To her surprise, when she arrived at work the next morning, her supervisor terminated her.

First, consider whether Patterson has a cause of action against DSI sounding in tort or contract. What theories may be available to her, and how likely would she be to succeed on such claims? Next, consider whether she would have a viable claim under state statutes like those described at page 462. What barriers to establishing liability might she face? Finally, in your view, should Patterson enjoy any legal protection in this context? Why or why not?

Part Five

WORKPLACE PROPERTY RIGHTS AND RELATED INTERESTS

8

Competition, Employee Loyalty, and the Allocation of Workplace Property Interests

By now you should have a good sense of the rights of employees upon termination. Most employment relationships are at will, and the burden is on the plaintiff-employee to establish additional contractual protection or an available tort or statutory remedy. The cases you read, while proposing different theories of liability, all involved an employee who was involuntarily terminated and sought to prove that the employer had breached a binding promise of job security or violated tort or statutory law. This chapter is different. It looks not at the rights of employees who have been fired, but rather the rights of employers to prevent harm to their business interests by current and former employees. Thus, in the cases that follow, it is typically the employer who is the plaintiff and the employee who is the defendant.

Usually an employer sues a former employee because it believes the employee threatens its business position through competitive behavior. The employee may have left to work for a rival company and may have enticed other employees to join the competitor. The employee's new position might make use of his past work experience in ways that create a competitive advantage for the rival. The employee may rely on knowledge of the former employer's product or business model, or she may solicit customers or clients previously serviced by the employer. In addition, employers may pursue litigation against a former employee for strategic reasons, for example, to deter other employees from leaving.

Whether the former employee's conduct is illegal is often a complicated question. One of the rationales for the at-will regime in the United States is that in theory it gives employees the freedom to move between jobs. That ability would be compromised if the employee could not meaningfully use her knowledge and skills, including industry-specific ones, upon departure. Moreover, society as a whole benefits from healthy competition between multiple providers of goods and services. On the other hand, many employers spend significant time and money developing their customer base, intellectual property, and other business assets. They may also invest in training their employees. In his seminal article on noncompete agreements, Professor Harlan Blake explained the competing policy considerations:

> From the point of view of the employer, postemployment restraints are regarded as perhaps the only effective method of preventing unscrupulous competitors or employees

from appropriating valuable trade information and customer relationships for their own benefit. Without the protection afforded by such covenants, it is argued, business[es] could not afford to stimulate research and improvement of business methods to a desirably high level, nor could they achieve the degree of freedom of communication within a company that is necessary for efficient operation.

The opposite view is that postemployment restraints reduce both the economic mobility of employees and their personal freedom to follow their own interests. These restraints also diminish competition by intimidating potential competitors and by slowing down the dissemination of ideas, processes, and methods. They unfairly weaken the individual employee's bargaining position vis-à-vis his employer and, from the social point of view, clog the market's channeling of [labor] to employments in which its productivity is greatest.

Harlan M. Blake, *Employee Agreements Not to Compete*, 73 HARV. L. REV. 625, 627 (1960).

Recognizing these conflicting impulses, the law accords the employer protection against worker competition during the course of the parties' relationship but only limited protection against competition upon termination. This chapter examines those rights and the legal tools available to an employer seeking to safeguard what it considers to be its business interests prior to and upon an employee's departure. It looks specifically at three areas: worker recruitment and training; trade secrets and confidential information; and access to customers, clients, and co-workers. As you read, be conscious of how both public law and private ordering play a role in allocating rights in each of these contexts. The rights and obligations of workers who wish to compete are governed by the tort duty of loyalty and statutory protection against the misappropriation of trade secrets, but employers often seek to expand these protections through contract. How do courts treat these different sources of legal protection? Should the source of legal protection make a difference in the outcome in a particular dispute? Does employers' use of written instruments, such as noncompete agreements, point out genuine deficiencies in public protection for employer property rights? Or is this an illustration of the employer unfairly reaching beyond what the law permits to the detriment of its employees?

Throughout the chapter, also keep in mind the inherent conflict between freedom of competition for the employee and protection of employer property interests and investments. How do these competing concerns influence court decisions? Do courts strike a fair balance between employer and employee rights? If not, how can the situation be improved? Do we need clearer rules? More private ordering? A legislative solution?

A. FIDUCIARY DUTIES OF CURRENT EMPLOYEES

≡ *Scanwell Freight Express STL, Inc. v. Chan*
≡ *162 S.W.3d 477 (Mo. 2005)*

LIMBAUGH, Jr., J.

Scanwell Freight Express STL, Inc., sued Stevie Chan for breach of fiduciary duty and Dimerco Express (U.S.A.) Corp. for conspiracy to breach fiduciary duty. Following a jury trial, Scanwell was awarded $54,000 in damages from Chan and $254,000 from Dimerco. . . . The judgment is reversed, and the case is remanded.

I

In brief, and in the light most favorable to the verdict . . . the facts are as follows:

Scanwell, a freight forwarding business, hired Chan in April 1996 to be the general manager of its St. Louis Office. Chan was an at-will employee, and she was not required to sign a noncompete agreement. While serving as Scanwell's general manager, Chan made arrangements with Dimerco, Scanwell's direct competitor, to open a Dimerco office in St. Louis. At Dimerco's request, Chan created a "business proposal" for this purpose. She also arranged for Dimerco to take over the lease of Scanwell's St. Louis office upon its expiration. Chan resigned from Scanwell effective March 1, 2001, and approximately one month later, Dimerco opened its St. Louis office with Chan as its general manager. Dimerco operated in the same premises that Scanwell previously occupied, employed most of the same employees as Scanwell, and for a while even used the same telephone number. Dimerco also acquired a number of Scanwell's customers.

Thereafter, Scanwell filed the suit against Chan and Dimerco that is the subject of this appeal.

II . . .

In the employer-employee relationship, this Court, drawing on the Restatement (2d) of Agency, has implicitly recognized a separate cause of action for breach of the duty of loyalty, *Nat'l Rejectors, Inc. v. Trieman*, 409 S.W.2d 1, 41 (Mo. 1966). . . .

Under Trieman, the seminal case on which both sides rely, . . . certain at-will employees were accused of misappropriating trade secrets from their employer in a scheme to compete with the employer. The factual context of the case is especially important because it involves the most common manifestation of the duty of loyalty, and the essence of Scanwell's claim here, which is that an employee has a duty not to compete with his or her employer concerning the subject matter of the employment. This Court described the duty of loyalty in the broad and general terms of section 387 of the Restatement (2d) of Agency, stating, "[an employee] must not, while employed, act contrary to the employer's interests." However, in addressing the corresponding duty not to compete, the Court held, nonetheless, that employees are allowed to "agree among themselves to compete with their then employer upon termination of their employment," and "[t]hey may plan and prepare for their competing enterprises while still employed." Admittedly, the mere decision to enter into competition is "contrary to the employer's interests," but the Court saw the need to balance the duty not to compete with the interest of promoting free competition. As some courts have put it, the law allows employees the privilege to plan and prepare for competition in recognition of the "competing interests of allowing an employee some latitude in switching jobs and at the same time preserving some degree of loyalty owed to the employer." *Cudahy Co. v. Am. Lab., Inc.*, 313 F. Supp. 1339, 1346 (D. Neb. 1970).

Although the *Trieman* Court did not elaborate on the conduct that would constitute a breach of the duty, it necessarily follows that a breach arises when the employee goes beyond the mere planning and preparation and actually engages in direct competition, which, by definition, is to gain advantage over a competitor. The Restatement (2d) of Agency, sec. 393, cmt. e, which this Court cited with favor in *Trieman*, plays on the same idea, further describing the kinds of activities that can constitute a breach of the duty of loyalty. That comment, in pertinent part, states:

> After termination of his agency, in the absence of a restrictive agreement, the agent can properly compete with his principal as to matters for which he has been employed. Even before the termination of the agency, he is entitled to make arrangements to compete, except that he cannot properly use confidential information peculiar to his employer's business and acquired therein. Thus, before the end of his employment, he can properly purchase a rival business and upon termination of employment immediately compete. He is not, however, entitled to solicit customers for such rival business before the end of his employment nor can he properly do other similar acts in direct competition with the employer's business.

III

Applying these standards, this Court concludes that Scanwell presented a submissible case that Chan breached her duty of loyalty. Chan's actions were clearly contrary to Scanwell's interests, and . . . went beyond mere planning and preparation to compete. . . .

First, Chan gave Dimerco confidential information about Scanwell's operations and customers. This included general information on Scanwell's customer base and detailed information on a few of Scanwell's customers. Most of the evidence centered on the fact that Chan gave Dimerco a customer profile of one of Scanwell's largest customers, which included contact information, special handling requirements, rate structure, billing instructions, and other information. At trial, Chan admitted that the customer profile was confidential "[to] some degree" and that it would be helpful to a competitor in soliciting the business of the customer. Dennis Choy, Scanwell's president, also testified that this information was confidential and that, in fact, customer profiles were "the most vital pieces of information for any company to keep within [itself]." Although Chan and Dimerco argue that some of the information in the profile was not confidential because it could be obtained from other sources such as the customers themselves, at least some of the information in the profile, such as Scanwell's air freight rates, was entirely unavailable. Regardless of the extent of the disclosure of confidential information, as other courts have aptly noted, even "slight assistance to a direct competitor can constitute a breach of the employee's duty of loyalty." *Cameco, Inc. v. Gedicke*, 724 A.2d 783, 521-22 (N.J.1999).

A second and more egregious activity was that Chan, while still employed by Scanwell, secured Scanwell's leased premises — Scanwell's business office — for Dimerco. The key testimony on the matter was uncontroverted. [Chan, as office manager, had signed the original and an amended, renewable lease for Scanwell. She forwarded these documents to headquarters, but as the December 1, 2000 renewal deadline approached,] Chan, who was by then preparing to leave Scanwell and open the Dimerco office, took no action to renew the lease for Scanwell and did not notify Scanwell's home office that the renewal deadline was approaching.

Then in early February 2001, while still employed by Scanwell and at a time the Scanwell's premises still could have been relet to Scanwell, Chan, with Dimerco's approval, negotiated and signed a lease of the same premises for Dimerco. Although Chan signed the lease on February 15, 2001, it was on February 20, 2001, that Chan first informed Scanwell that she planned to resign. That same day, she sent a letter to her supervisor at Scanwell, M.B. Hassan, stating, "[t]he new rental lease has been turned back to the landlor[d] and will not be renewed. You can contact [the landlord's agent] if you have [a] different arrangement. Otherwise the lease will end[] [in] March."

While Chan and Dimerco claim that there are no cases holding that an employee owes a "duty to remind" his employer of its legal rights and obligations, they miss the larger issue. Chan did not merely fail to remind Scanwell of the renewal deadline, she arranged for Scanwell's direct competitor to take over the premises, and, in doing so, prevented Scanwell from being able to re-lease the premises after the renewal deadline had passed. As a result of her actions, Scanwell lost its business office, and Scanwell customers who thereafter called or visited the office talked with Dimerco representatives.

IV

Despite this Court's conclusion, [an instructional error requires reversal].

The definitional instruction given in this case stated that "A fiduciary relationship is established when one reposes trust and confidence in another in the handling of certain business affairs." . . . [T]he instruction set out nothing more than the relationship that gives rise to a duty, but without identifying the duty. . . .

Where, as here, an allegation of breach of the duty of loyalty is presented in the context of an employee acting in competition with his or her employer, a proper definitional instruction of the duty of loyalty, consistent with the foregoing analysis, must set out the following elements: 1) In general, an employee must not, while employed, act contrary to the employer's interest; 2) however, an employee may agree with others to compete upon termination of the employment and may plan and prepare for their competing enterprise while still employed; and 3) but an employee may not, while still employed, go beyond mere planning and preparation and act in direct competition with the employer. *See Trieman*; Rest. (2d) Agency, sec. 393, cmt. e. In the absence of such a definitional instruction, the jury was unaware of the conduct that the law prohibits, and prejudice resulted because the jury was allowed to conclude that even mere planning and preparation for competition breached the duty.

This Court also concludes that [the following instruction requires reversal]:

> Your verdict must be for Plaintiff on its claim against Defendant Stevie Chan for breach of fiduciary duties if you believe:
>
> > First, Defendant Stevie Chan, the General Manager of Plaintiff, owed a duty of loyalty to Plaintiff, and
> > Second, during her employment with Plaintiff, Defendant Stevie Chan made arrangements to have defendant Dimerco take over Plaintiff's business operation including securing Plaintiff's business lease for Defendant Dimerco, disclosing confidential information of Plaintiff to Dimerco, and
> > Third, in so acting, Defendant Stevie Chan breached a duty of loyalty owed to Plaintiff, and
> > Fourth, as a direct result of Defendant Stevie Chan's conduct Plaintiff was harmed.

. . . Paragraph "Second" is fatally defective. By couching paragraph Second so that the ultimate allegation was that "Chan made arrangements for Dimerco to take over Scanwell's business operation," the verdict director made actionable the aggregate of all of Chan's conduct in making those arrangements, even those arrangements that involved mere "planning and preparation." The jury was not limited to the allegations relating to the lease and the dissemination of confidential information. . . .

NOTES

1. *The Scope of the Duty of Loyalty.* Cases in which employers pursue breach of loyalty claims against employees for pre-departure activities typically involve one of several recurring fact patterns: while still employed, the employee solicits customers and/or co-workers and opens a competitive business; the employee aids a competitor or discloses information to a competitor, usually planning to join the competitor down the road; or the employee usurps a corporate opportunity. *See* RESTATEMENT (THIRD) OF EMPLOYMENT LAW § 8.01(b) (Proposed Final Draft, April 18, 2014). There are, of course, some exceptions. The Restatement would allow "moonlighting" at a competitor in limited situations — mostly of low-level workers whose performance is more or less fungible. § 8.04(c) & cmt. b. And the *Scanwell* privilege to make preparations for departure is generally recognized and will sometimes insulate the employee from liability for this type of conduct. What particular facts make Chan's behavior egregious enough to submit to a jury? Can you find the lines that she crossed? How would you have advised her had she consulted you about how to transition to Dimerco without running afoul of the law?

2. *Fiduciary Duties of High-Level Employees.* The application and extent of any duty of loyalty is the threshold question and sometimes a difficult one. The Restatement provides that employees "in a position of trust and confidence" owe a fiduciary duty of loyalty and, further, that "[o]ther employees may depending on their position," owe a "contractual duty of loyalty." § 8.01(a). These duties normally expire at the end of the relationship, but the Restatement would extend the duty to preserve trade secrets beyond that point. § 8.01(b)(i), § 8.03.

It is unclear how fiduciary duties and the contractual duty of loyalty differ in reach although, as we will see, they differ radically in remedies. Some courts take the view that a fiduciary relationship "establishes a distinct and separate obligation than the duty of loyalty" owing to "the 'peculiar' trust between the employee-agent and his employer-principal." *Rash v. J.Y. Intermediate, Ltd.*, 498 F.3d 1201, 1211 (10th Cir. 2007). From this perspective, fiduciaries are held to a higher standard than ordinary employees and could in theory be found in breach for conduct that would be permissible if perpetrated by a nonfiduciary employee. *See, e.g., id.* (noting that, under Texas law, a fiduciary must show that she acted with the utmost good faith and most scrupulous honesty toward the principal, including placing the principal's interests before her own). Under this approach, the contours of the duty of loyalty will vary based on the employee's position, the relative status of the employee, and the vulnerability of the employer. Courts are likely to look harder at alleged breaches by high-level employees, including corporate executives, employees with long-term or exclusive relationships with customers, employees possessing highly specialized or unique skills or knowledge, and employees who have been entrusted with confidential information upon which their employer's business depends.

3. *Fiduciary Duties and Private Ordering.* Although the Restatement states that fiduciary duties cannot be disclaimed or modified, § 8.01 cmt. a, this is incorrect, at least in the sense that the parties can agree to actions that, absent agreement, would violate a fiduciary duty. For example, a corporate officer may not appropriate a corporate opportunity, but the parties are free to define some ventures as not corporate opportunities. *See, e.g.,* Del. Code Ann. tit. 8, § 122(17) (2014) ("Every corporation created under this chapter shall have power to . . . [r]enounce, in its certificate of incorporation or by action of its board of directors, any interest or expectancy of the corporation in, or in being offered an opportunity to participate in, specified business opportunities or specified classes or categories of business opportunities that are presented to the corporation or 1 or more of its officers, directors or stockholders."). Further, the types of employees and executives who are most likely to be held liable as fiduciaries are also those who are likely to be able to bargain for concessions from their companies, including the right to moonlight and provisions in separation agreements authorizing the taking of certain accounts, customers, and opportunities. In addition, when an employee wishes to pursue a business opportunity otherwise "owned" by his or her employer, the employee can do so consistent with her fiduciary obligations by fully disclosing the extent and nature of the opportunity and receiving advance permission to pursue it from the employer. As one court explained:

> [V]arious considerations affect determination of the breach of an employee's duty of loyalty and the appropriate remedy for a breach. . . . One consideration is the possible existence of contractual provisions. A provision might permit an employee to seek a second source of income, whether through a second job or an independent business. Conversely, a non-competition covenant might limit an employee's economic activities both during and after employment. A second consideration is whether the employer knew of or agreed to its employee's secondary profit-seeking activities. An employee's disclosure of an intention to pursue a second source of income alerts the employer to potential problems and protects the employee from a charge of disloyalty. The third consideration concerns the status of the employee and his or her relationship to the employer. An officer, director, or key executive, for example, has a higher duty than an employee working on a production line. Fourth, the nature of the employee's second source of income and its effect on the employer are relevant. . . . Employees should not engage in conduct that causes their employers to lose customers, sales, or potential sales. Nor should they take advantage of their employers by engaging in secret self-serving activities, such as accepting kickbacks from suppliers or usurping their employer's corporate opportunities.

Cameco v. Gedicke, 724 A.2d 783, 521-22 (N.J. 1999); *see also* ALI PRINCIPLES OF CORPORATE GOVERNANCE § 5.05 (1994) (addressing the appropriation of corporate opportunities by directors and senior executives).

4. *Solicitation.* A recurring issue in duty of loyalty cases is whether the departing employee solicited co-workers or clients before departure. In *Scanwell,* the competitor company hired most of Scanwell's employees and acquired many of its customers upon taking over its lease. Under the privilege to make preparations articulated in the case, what is an employee permitted to say to potential customers and employees prior to an anticipated departure?

The Colorado Supreme Court wrestled with this issue in *Jet Courier v. Mulei,* 771 P.2d 486 (Colo. 1989). Mulei was the head of the Denver office of an Ohio-based courier service when he decided to establish a competitive business. While still employed by Jet, Mulei met with several of Jet's Denver customers, told them he would be leaving, that he could "give them the same service," and that he "would be in a position, sometime later, to reduce cost." He also met with several of Jet's Denver employees and offered the Denver office staff better working conditions, insurance, and part ownership of his new endeavor if they joined him. In reversing a decision in favor of Mulei, the court held that "an employee may advise current customers of his employer that he will be leaving. However any pretermination solicitation of those customers for a new competing business violates an employee's duty of loyalty." With respect to co-worker solicitation, the court established a multifactored test for determining whether the employee breached the duty of loyalty:

> A court should consider the nature of the employment relationship, the impact or potential impact of the employee's actions on the employer's operations, and the extent of any benefits promised or inducements made to co-workers to obtain their services for the new competing enterprise. No single factor is dispositive[.]

Id. at 497. How easy is it to draw a line between "advising" and "soliciting"? What if the departing employee asks co-workers about their job satisfaction and desire to stay with their current employer but doesn't actually ask them to defect? *See Kopka, Landau & Pinkus v. Hansen*, 874 N.E.2d 1065 (Ind. Ct. App. 2007) (no breach of duty of loyalty where law firm associate talked to other associates about their salary requirements and willingness to quit but made no offers of employment). The Restatement would bar "recruiting" co-workers to leave "en masse" when that would "materially damage" the employer. § 8.04 cmt. c. But it would simultaneously permit a "group of employees" to agree among themselves to leave for a new business or a competitor so long as the departures did not leave the present employer's business "immediately crippled." Cmt. d. This creates serious counseling difficulties when an attorney is advising a group considering moving on.

    5. *Tortious Interference with Contract.* In addition to breach of the duty of loyalty, solicitation cases sometimes give rise to intentional interference with contract claims against the departing employee. *See* Chapter 5. However, a former employer may establish interference only in situations where the solicited individual was under an existing or, in some cases, imminent contract of which the departing employee was aware. *See Volt Services v. Adecco Employment Services*, 35 P.3d 329, 333 (Or. App. 2001) ("The elements of . . . intentional interference with economic relations[ ] are: (1) intentional interference with a proposed or existing economic relationship; (2) with an improper motive or by use of improper means; and (3) damage beyond the fact of interference itself."). Thus, a competitor or departing employee's solicitation of a co-worker employed at will generally does not give rise to an interference claim. On the other hand, a tortious interference claim can arise if the departing employee or the competitor solicits a worker employed under a contract containing restrictive covenants or a fixed term of employment or a customer with an existing or prospective service or supply contract. *See, e.g., Volt*, 35 P.3d at 337. The tort also lies if independently wrongful means are used. *Lewis-Gale Med. Ctr., LLC v. Alldredge*, 710 S.E.2d 716 (Va. 2011) (no showing of "improper methods," such as fraud or defamation). *See also Western Blue Print Co., LLC v. Roberts*, 367 S.W.3d 7 (Mo. 2012) (defendants were guilty of tortious interference with a valid business expectancy by virtue of using their specialized knowledge to compete successfully for a contract and by inducing other employees to leave their jobs with the plaintiff in a staggered fashion that impeded its ability to function effectively).

6. *Employer Remedies for the Conduct of "Faithless Servants."* What is the appropriate remedy in a case involving breach of loyalty? It is too late to enjoin the employee's competitive conduct, though it can be enjoined for the future. In cases where an employee usurps clients or a corporate opportunity, the employee may be required to pay for the losses sustained by the employer or to turn over profits gleaned from the competitive behavior. However, the losses or profits sought must be attributable to the disloyal behavior. *See Cameco v. Gedicke*, 724 A.2d 783, 521-22 (N.J. 1999).

Another possible remedy goes under the quaint name of the "faithless servant doctrine," which, where applicable, permits forfeiture (sometimes called disgorgement) of compensation paid during the period of breach. In addition to paying any damages due to the employer and being liable for any profits attributable to the disloyalty, the employee is obligated to return any salary or other compensation he received from the employer during his period of disloyalty. *See, e.g., Design Strategies, Inc. v. Davis*, 469 F.3d 284 (2nd Cir. 2006) (requiring former sales manager to pay damages equivalent to salary for two pay periods corresponding to time period in which he promoted competitor company to client interested in obtaining staffing contract). This approach has sometimes been used in situations where the breach of loyalty stems not from competitive behavior but from serious misconduct of the employee. *Astra USA, Inc. v. Bildman*, 914 N.E.2d 36 (Mass. 2009), for instance, involved a CEO who engaged in a pattern of sexual harassment, retaliation, and cover-up, as well as a variety of financial misdeeds over a period of years. Applying New York's faithless servant doctrine, the court held that the employee must "forfeit all of his salary and bonuses from Astra for the period of disloyalty" even if the faithless servant "otherwise performed valuable services for his principal." Perhaps most surprisingly, and unlike other situations where a party materially breaches a contract, the wrongdoer was not permitted to recover in restitution for the reasonable value of the other services he rendered during the period of his faithlessness. Does this strike you as an unusually harsh remedy? Although the defendant in *Astra* was a former CEO, the court suggested in dicta that the disgorgement remedy could apply to lower-level employees as well. *Id.* at 49. *See also Morgan Stanley v. Skowron*, 989 F. Supp. 2d 356 (S.D.N.Y. 2013) (insider trading in violation of firm's code of conduct, which also imposes an affirmative duty to report misconduct, constitutes faithlessness sufficient to allow former employer to recover $31 million of compensation paid to employee during the period of his faithlessness). *But see Rash v. J.Y. Intermediate, Ltd.*, 498 F.3d 1201 (10th Cir. 2007) (forfeiture applicable only to "'clear and serious' violations of fiduciary duty" considering such factors as the gravity, timing and willfulness of the breach, the harm caused by the breach, and the adequacy of other remedies). *See also* RESTATEMENT § 9.09. *See generally* Charles A. Sullivan, *Mastering the Faithless Servant?: Reconciling Employment Law, Contract Law, and Fiduciary Duty*, 2011 WIS. L. REV. 777.

7. *Liability of the New Employer.* As a practical matter, even if a court awards damages to the aggrieved employer, the company may face hurdles trying to recover the judgment. For this reason, employers commonly sue not only the breaching employee but also the company on whose behalf the employee acted. If the defecting employee agreed to a fixed term of employment with her former employer or signed a noncompete agreement, the new employer's actions could constitute tortious interference with contract. But that is not always the case. Chan was not under contract with Scanwell, and the claims against her were based entirely on tort law. In such instances, plaintiff-employers may proceed on the theory that the new employer "aided and abetted" or "conspired with" the employee to breach the duty of loyalty. In *Scanwell*, the lower court held Dimerco liable along with Chan under this theory. While it seems clear that Dimerco and Chan were working together to spin off Scanwell's business, in other cases the competitor's role is less obvious, creating questions as to whether the new employer had the requisite knowledge or intent to justify liability. *Compare Design Strategies*, 469 F.3d at 303-4 (defendant IT Web not liable to former employer despite knowing about co-defendant Davis's employment during time that he promoted IT Web's business to Microsoft where Davis had told IT Web that plaintiff was not interested in expanding into web solutions and IT Web had no reason to know Davis had not told his former employer about the Microsoft opportunity) *with Security Title Agency, Inc. v. Pope*, 200 P.3d 977 (Ariz. App. 2008) (defendant title insurance company liable for aiding and abetting defecting branch manager who brought 66 employees to new employer where new employer participated in recruiting sessions with employee, prepared written comparison of two companies' job benefits for distribution, agreed to title and compensation terms to offer solicited workers, and agreed to indemnify defendant employee against former employer). Aiding and abetting liability generally requires that the new employer provide assistance and encouragement with knowledge that the conduct encouraged will constitute a breach of loyalty. *See Security Title* 200 P.3d at 987. Thus, the tort includes a scienter requirement. If you represent a company recruiting an employee from a competitor or undertaking a business venture with an individual employed elsewhere, would you recommend that the client ask about the employee's duties to their current employer? What are the pros and cons of remaining ignorant? What are the ethical implications of this course of action?

8. *Whistleblowing.* It should be apparent that a broad duty of loyalty regarding confidential information is in considerable tension with the public policy tort and the federal and state statutes we explored in Chapter 4. Put simply, a duty of confidentiality would seem to often prevent an employee from doing exactly what those laws encourage. The solution of the Restatement of Employment Law is straightforward in theory, if perhaps not so easy to apply in practice: The duty of loyalty "must be interpreted in a manner consistent with the employee's rights and responsibilities" under those and other laws. § 8.01(c) (Proposed Final Draft, April 18, 2014); *see also* § 8.02 cmt. a ("Information regarding an employer's illegal activities is not a 'trade secret' . . . nor is such information protectable by means of restrictive covenant. . . .").

9. *Post-employment Contractual Restraints.* The most significant limitation on the duty of loyalty is that it applies only while the employment relationship exists. To extend protection beyond termination, the employer may obtain a contractual commitment from the employee. Perhaps the most common such agreement, and certainly the broadest, is a covenant not to compete, under which an employee promises not to engage in competition with the employer for a period of time following employment. Employers might also seek, either alone or in conjunction with a noncompete agreement, a commitment not to solicit the employer's clients or other employees (a nonsolicitation agreement) and a commitment not to disclose any confidential information learned during employment (a nondisclosure agreement). The enforceability of restrictive covenants generally and noncompetes in particular is the subject of the next section.

PROBLEM

8-1. Sam Miller was Vice President of H&R Metals, a company that processed scrap metal. He was employed at will with no written contract. On behalf of H&R, Miller investigated the purchase of a high-tech "shredder" from Newell Manufacturing that would increase H&R's operations. Miller negotiated preliminary terms for the purchase; however, H&R's board of directors subsequently voted not to go through with the deal, considering the investment in new technology premature. Dissatisfied with the direction of the business, Miller met with the President of H&R and told him he was planning to leave the company unless H&R made him an equity partner in the business. The President refused. Subsequently, and while still employed by H&R, Miller secured a small business loan from a local bank and contracted with Newell to purchase the shredder himself. He also filed the necessary paperwork to incorporate "Miller's Metals," obtained the state and local permits needed to run a shredding operation, and engaged an advertising company to prepare brochures and other informational materials that he planned to distribute once his business became operational.

One week before tendering his resignation, Miller had lunch with H&R Metals' Operations Manager Georgia Sidway. Miller told Sidway about his disagreement with the President and his plans to open a competitive venture. Sidway asked Miller if he was offering her a job. Miller responded, "Well, at the moment I'm still on company time. But there are options out there. Why don't we have lunch again next week." The following week, Miller quit H&R and Miller's Metals became operational. Due to his extensive advance planning, the business was able to secure its first contract and begin processing metal within a week. Miller met again with Georgia Sidway and offered her a job at a salary that he knew was far above what she had been paid at H&R. Together, Miller and Sidway met with several scrap metal suppliers who had previously provided metal to H&R. One of these suppliers, Packwell Parts, held a one-year contract to supply its scrap output to H&R on a monthly basis. As a result of the meetings, Packwell and three other suppliers decided to shift their business to Miller's Metals.

Suppose H&R learns of Miller's activities and files suit. What causes of action would you expect the former employer to pursue? What defenses would you raise if you were defending Miller? Who is likely to succeed? Regardless of your answer, is there anything you would have told Miller to do differently to avoid this lawsuit? *See generally Metzner v. Maryland Metals*, 382 A.2d 564 (Md. App. 1978).

B. POST-EMPLOYMENT RESTRAINTS ON COMPETITION

By far the most common means by which employers constrain post-employment competition is through contractual agreement. *See* Randall S. Thomas, et al.,

An Empirical Analysis of Non-Competition Clauses and Other Restrictive Post-Employment Covenants, http://papers.ssrn.com/sol3/papers.cfm?abstract_id=2401781 (A random sample drawn from S&P 1500 companies showed that 80% had noncompetes, usually from 1 to 2 years and often with a broad geographic scope; 76% had nonsoliciation agreements and 87% had nondisclosure agreements; the study noted a trend of more such clauses over time). To some extent, trade secret law offers employers a means of restricting the competitive behavior of departing employees absent private agreement. Unlike the duty of loyalty, trade secret protection continues after the employment relationship ends. However, except in very limited situations described in this section, trade secret law proscribes the use and disclosure of protected information, not competition per se.

Contractual protection — covenants not to compete, nonsolicitation clauses, and nondisclosure clauses — provide employers a more reliable route to protecting their interests following an employee departure, although, as we will see, the enforceability of such covenants in individual cases is far from certain.[*] The most controversial of these clauses — because it is the most restrictive — is the noncompetition agreement, under which an employee agrees not to work in a competitive endeavor for a designated period of time, often (though not always) within a designated geographical area. Depending on how broadly they are drafted, these agreements can have the effect of keeping an individual out of the work force (or tied to his or her current employer); they have therefore been subject to significant judicial scrutiny and scholarly debate. As we will see, there is some common ground among many jurisdictions on how to approach noncompete enforcement. However, there is a significant degree of variation in results owing to the fact-specific nature of most courts' approach. There are also outlier jurisdictions such as California, which prohibits enforcement of employee noncompete agreements in that economically important state. The first part of this section provides an overview of the competing doctrinal approaches and policy issues at stake in enforcing contractual restraints on competition. The next parts explore how those jurisdictions that enforce noncompetes negotiate these tensions in three commonly occurring factual scenarios: disputes over skills and training, disputes over trade secrets and information, and disputes over customers and clients.

1. Approaches to Noncompete Enforcement

Cal. Bus. & Prof. Code §§ 16600 et seq. (2014)

§ 16600. Void Contracts

[E]very contract by which anyone is restrained from engaging in a lawful profession, trade, or business of any kind is to that extent void.

---

[*] These kinds of agreements have traditionally been formally executed documents, but more recently there have been efforts to impose restraints on employees in less formal ways. *See Newell Rubbermaid, Inc. v. Storm,* 2014 Del. Ch. LEXIS 45, 23-25 (Del. Ch. Mar. 27, 2014) (upholding a TRO against plaintiff for violation of confidentiality and nonsolicitation agreement made by "clickwrap": "Newell's method of seeking Storm's agreement to the post-employment restrictive covenants, although certainly not the model of transparency and openness with its employees, was not an improper form of contract formation. Storm, to accept her RSUs, was directed to a screen which informed her in several places that she was agreeing to the 2013 Agreements.").

Restatement (Second) of Contracts

§ 188 Ancillary Restraints on Competition

(1) A promise to refrain from competition . . . is unreasonably in restraint of trade if

(a) the restraint is greater than is needed to protect the promisee's legitimate interest, or

(b) the promisee's need is outweighed by the hardship to the promisor and the likely injury to the public.

Outsource International, Inc. v. Barton
192 F.3d 662 (7th Cir. 1999)

[Defendant Barton was a staffing consultant for Plaintiff Outsource's predecessor company. He signed a noncompete, nonsolicitation and confidentiality agreement upon hire. Six years later, Outsource acquired Barton's employer and Barton resigned. He subsequently opened his own temporary staffing company within the geographic area proscribed by his employment agreement. The Seventh Circuit affirmed the district court's finding that Outsource had presented a prima facie case for a preliminary injunction against Barton under Illinois law.]

POSNER, Chief Judge, dissenting.

I regret my inability to agree with the court's disposition of the case, because it is the right disposition from the standpoint of substantive justice. Mr. Barton is an adult of sound mind who made an unequivocal promise, for which he was doubtless adequately compensated, not to compete with his employer within 25 miles for a year after he ceased being employed. He quit of his own volition — quit in fact to set up in competition with his employer. And all the customers whom he obtained for his new company, before the preliminary injunction which the court affirms today put him temporarily out of business, were customers of his former employer. So he broke his contract. But Illinois law, to which we must of course bow in this diversity suit, is hostile to covenants not to compete found in employment contracts. An Illinois court would not enforce this covenant.

There is no longer any good reason for such hostility, though it is nothing either new or limited to Illinois. The English common law called such covenants "restraints of trade" and refused to enforce them unless they were adjudged "reasonable" in time and geographical scope. *Mitchel v. Reynolds*, 24 Eng. Rep. 347 (K.B. 1711). The original rationale had nothing to do with restraint of trade in its modern, antitrust sense. It was paternalism in a culture of poverty, restricted employment, and an exiguous social safety net. The fear behind it was that workers would be tricked into agreeing to covenants that would, if enforced, propel them into destitution. This fear, though it continues to be cited, has no basis in current American conditions.

Later, however, the focus of concern shifted to whether a covenant not to compete might have anticompetitive consequences, since the covenant would eliminate the covenantor as a potential competitor of the covenantee within the area covered by, and during the term of, the covenant. This concern never had much basis, especially when the covenant was found in an employment contract. It would be unlikely for the vitality of competition to depend on the ability of a former employee to compete with his former employer. So unlikely that it would make little sense to place a cloud of suspicion over such covenants, rather than considering competitive effects on a case by case basis.

At the same time that the concerns behind judicial hostility to covenants not to compete have waned, recognition of their social value has grown. The clearest case for such a covenant is where the employee's work gives him access to the employer's trade secrets. The employer could include in the employment contract a clause forbidding the employee to take any of the employer's trade secrets with him when he left the employment, as in fact the employer did in this case. Such clauses are difficult to enforce, however, as it is often difficult to determine whether the former employee is using his former employer's trade secrets or using either ideas of his own invention or ideas that are in the public domain. A covenant not to compete is much easier to enforce, and to the extent enforced prevents the employee, during the time and within the geographical scope of the covenant, from using his former employer's trade secrets.

A related function of such a covenant is to protect the employer's investment in the employee's "human capital," or earning capacity. The employer may give the employee training that the employee could use to compete against the employer. If covenants not to compete are forbidden, the employer will pay a lower wage, in effect charging the employee for the training. There is no reason why the law should prefer this method of protecting the employer's investment to a covenant not to compete.

I can see no reason in today's America for judicial hostility to covenants not to compete. It is possible to imagine situations in which the device might be abused, but the doctrines of fraud, duress, and unconscionability are available to deal with such situations. A covenant's reasonableness in terms of duration and geographical scope is merely a consideration bearing on such defenses. . . . Had Barton signed a covenant in which he agreed that if he ever left the employ of Outsource he would never again work in the business of providing temporary industrial labor anywhere in the world, there would be at least a suspicion that he had been forced or tricked into signing the covenant and therefore that it should not be enforced. There is no suggestion of that here, and so if I were writing on a clean slate I would agree wholeheartedly with the district court's granting a preliminary injunction against Barton's violating the covenant.

But the Illinois courts approach covenants not to compete in a different way, not radically different perhaps but different enough to require a reversal in this case. Their view is that a covenant not to compete that is contained in an employment contract is enforceable in only two circumstances — either where the covenant protects a "near permanent" relationship between the former employer and his customers, or where it protects "confidential information" (that is, trade secrets) of the former employer. . . .

The Illinois courts appear to place the burden of proving that the covenant meets one of the two criteria of validity on the employer. In effect Illinois requires the employer to prove that the covenant not to compete serves a social purpose. Such a requirement is inconsistent with the idea of freedom of contract, which animates contract law and a corollary of which is that courts do not limit the enforcement of contracts to those the social point of which the court can see. They enforce a contract unless there is some reason to think it imposes heavy costs on third parties, offends the moral code, fails to comply with formal requirements (such as those imposed on some contracts by the statute of frauds), or doesn't embody an actual deal between competent consenting adults.

Still, we must take the Illinois law as we find it, and apply it as best we can to the facts of the case. Barton was employed by Outsource as a salesman, soliciting orders for temporary industrial workers that Outsource would supply. . . . Deciding to go out on his own, he quit Outsource and quickly obtained business from a dozen customers of Outsource with whom he had dealt. There is no question that he violated the covenant not to compete in his employment contract, which barred him for one year after his employment ended from competing with Outsource in the Chicago area. But there is no evidence that he stole any of Outsource's trade secrets. Outsource's customer list [was not secret.] The wages that Outsource pays its workers are not secret either. Barton did not take the list of workers on Outsource's roster, but obtained workers for his customers in the same way that Outsource does, by radio and newspaper advertisements. . . .

[With respect to customers, the] only users of temp labor who testified at the preliminary injunction hearing agreed that such users have no sense of loyalty to particular suppliers. Both witnesses used multiple agencies. It was feasible for Barton to use standard selling techniques, rather than any techniques that he had learned from Outsource or information that he took with him when he left Outsource, to get customers for his new business. . . .

[A]s far as this record shows, all he used in signing up customers for his new venture were the standard sales techniques used in this business.

Since the irreparable harm to Barton from the grant of a preliminary injunction to Outsource exceeds the irreparable harm that Outsource would experience from the denial of the injunction (as a start-up, Barton would find it difficult to prove damages from being frozen out of business for a year as a result of the enforcement of the covenant), Outsource must prove not just that it has a better case than Barton but that it has a much better case. It has a worse case. . . .

NOTES

1. *A Spectrum of Approaches.* The three excerpts—from the California state code, the Restatement (Second) of Contracts, and Judge Posner's dissenting decision in *Outsource v. Barton*—above offer a range of approaches to enforcing noncompetes signed by employees. Judge Posner's opinion offers a pure freedom of contract perspective: Noncompetes are contracts and should be enforced like any other legal agreement. However, Judge Posner acknowledges that this is not the law in Illinois, the state whose law he is charged with applying in the case before him. In fact, it is not the law in any jurisdiction, owing in part to the countervailing policy concerns Posner raises (albeit to dismiss them).

At the opposite extreme is California, which categorically prohibits noncompete agreements between employers and employees. California has repeatedly defended this position in various cases involving employer attempts to circumvent the rule. *See, e.g., Edwards v. Arthur Andersen*, 189 P.3d 285 (Cal. 2008) (defendant-employer's refusal to release former employee from noncompete agreement except on his waiver of claims against the company, resulting in employee not being hired by prospective employer, constituted an "independently wrongful act" that could support employee's claim against former employer for tortious interference with prospective economic advantage); *Silguero v. Cretguard, Inc.* 113 Cal. Rptr. 3d 653 (Cal. App. 2010) (finding employee stated claim for wrongful termination in violation of public policy where new employer fired her upon learning of her noncompete with former employer because of an "understanding" between the two despite acknowledging the agreement was unenforceable under California law); *VL Syst., Inc. v. Unisen, Inc.*, 61 Cal. Rptr. 3d 818, 824 (Cal. App. 2007) (refusing to enforce "no hire" agreement between two firms because "enforcement of th[e] clause would present many of the same problems as covenants not to compete and unfairly limit the mobility of an employee"). One other state, North Dakota, has a similarly restrictive statute. N.D. CENT. CODE § 9-08-06 (2013). *See also* Colo. Rev. Stat. 8-2-113(2) (barring such covenants subject to certain exceptions).

Most jurisdictions (like Illinois) follow some version of the Restatement approach, which enforces "reasonable" noncompetes necessary to protect employers' "legitimate interests," although the "near permanent" standard seems peculiar to that state. Illinois has, since *Outsource*, further refined its test to make it less hostile to noncompetes. *See Reliable Fire Equip. Co. v. Arredondo*, 965 N.E.2d 393, 403 (Ill. 2011) ("[W]hether a legitimate business interest exists is based on the totality of the facts and circumstances of the individual case. Factors to be considered in this analysis include, but are not limited to, the near-permanence of customer relationships, the employee's acquisition of confidential information through his employment, and time and place restrictions. No factor carries any more weight than any other, but rather its importance will depend on the specific facts and circumstances of the individual case.").

But this tripartite division of approaches to covenants not to compete might suggest a coherence that does not exist. Even within single jurisdiction,

> [p]ractitioners report that it is very difficult to predict how a trial court will respond to an employee non-compete case. One commentator has stated that "the courts have frequently vacillated on [non-compete] provisions — even when the employees' agreements and positions were essentially the same, and even at the same company." Another has stated that "different judges can look at the same set of facts and reach completely different conclusions." Another has stated that "the outcome of an emergency motion to enforce a non-compete agreement can be all but impossible to predict . . . [and] past performance is no guarantee of future results." Legal scholars agree, one stating that "despite the nettlesome policy issues that plague non-compete law, there is one thing everyone can agree on — the current law is in a state of near chaos. Years upon years of seemingly inconsistent enforcement decisions have provided little concrete guidance as to what constitutes an enforceable agreement."

Daniel P. O'Gorman, *Contract Theory and Some Realism About Employee Covenant Not to Compete Cases*, 65 SMU L. REV. 145, 147-48 (2012).

2. *Of Paternalism and Employee Bargaining Power.* Posner describes judicial disfavor of noncompetes as rooted in a fear of employee abuse that "has no basis in current American conditions." Do you agree? Certainly employees today are more mobile and have more flexibility than in the eighteenth century when noncompete law developed. Does that mean they are more autonomous? More able to refuse a noncompete agreement? *See* Charles A. Sullivan, *The Puzzling Persistence of Unenforceable Contract Terms*, 70 OHIO ST. L.J. 1127 (2009) (exploring why employers rationally choose to use noncompetition clauses that are too broad to be enforced as written); Rachel Arnow-Richman, *Cubewrap Contracts and Worker Mobility: The Dilution of Employee Bargaining Power via Standard Form Noncompetes*, 2006 MICH. ST. L. REV. 963 (asserting that employers frequently present noncompetes to workers in the form of standardized agreements to be signed as routine paperwork after hire when their ability to refuse employment on such terms is highly constrained); Katherine V.W. Stone, *The New Psychological Contract*, 48 UCLA L. REV. 519 (2001) (providing case law examples of employers' use of noncompete agreements with lower-level employees, including manicurists and deliverymen).

In assessing the enforceability of noncompetes, courts often seem more willing to find in favor of an employer if the departing employee participated in drafting the agreement or demonstrated bargaining ability in some other capacity. *See, e.g., Campbell Soup Co. v. Desatnik*, 58 F. Supp. 2d 477, 479-81 (D.N.J. 1999) (finding for employer where former senior executive negotiated terms of a prior contract of employment and successfully refused noncompete, but subsequently signed renewal agreement with noncompete without making significant effort to renegotiate); *Delli-Gatti v. Mansfield*, 477 S.E.2d 134 (Ga. Ct. App. 1996) (holding noncompete enforceable against physician who negotiated favorable changes in vacation time and partnership opportunities under employment contract she accepted). Should the current rules of reasonableness be replaced by a heightened examination of employee volition? Some commentators have suggested that such an approach could be useful. *See, e.g.*, Rachel Arnow-Richman, *Bargaining for Loyalty in the Information Age*, 80 OR. L. REV. 1163, 1235-36 (2001).

3. *What Can You Get for Giving Up Your Right to Compete?* In contrast to this view, some scholars, consistent with Judge Posner's analysis, believe that judicial refusal to enforce noncompetes deprives employees of the opportunity to freely negotiate the sale of their skills and human capital. *See* Stewart E. Sterk, *Restraints on the Alienation of Human Capital*, 79 VA. L. REV. 383 (1993). From this perspective, employees who sign noncompetes should realize some additional benefits — higher wages, better employment conditions, or enhanced opportunities for training and promotion — in compensation for their concession. However, empirical data suggest otherwise. Studies show that employees who sign noncompetes have lower executive compensation, are less likely to invest in human capital, and are more likely to take "occupational detours" that amount to a step back in their careers. *See* Orly Lobel, TALENT WANTS TO BE FREE (2013); *see generally* Viva R. Moffat, *The Wrong Tool for the Job: The IP Problem with Non-Competition Agreements*, 52 WILL. & MARY L. REV. 873, 895-98 (2010).

4. *The Complex Economics of Noncompete Agreements.* Whether individual workers are better or worse off is a different question from whether society as a whole benefits or suffers from noncompete enforcement. On this score, are you surprised to discover that Judge Posner, a pillar of the law and economics school, would advocate for the enforcement of agreements that interfere with interfirm competition? Noncompete agreements pit two core law and economics principles against one another: freedom of contract for the individual parties to the agreement and freedom of competition generally. Judge Posner expresses what has been the dominant economic view of these agreements — that their anticompetitive effects are minimal and they should be enforced like other contracts. *See* Michael J. Trebilcock, THE COMMON LAW OF RESTRAINTS OF TRADE (1986); Stewart E. Sterk, *Restraints on the Alienation of Human Capital*, 79 VA. L. REV. 383, 406-7 (1993).

Not everyone agrees. Professor Ronald Gilson has argued that California statutory law prohibiting noncompetes in employment contributed to the vast development of the high-tech industry in Silicon Valley during the late twentieth century by enabling healthy information "spillovers" between firms. He explains:

> From the outset, Silicon Valley developed a business structure that reflected non-linear career patterns and a special status for entrepreneurs. [Engineers and managers]

moved between companies, founded start-ups, supplied former employers, purchased from former employees, and in the course of their careers developed personal and professional relationships that cut across companies and competition. [The result] is a pattern of industrial organization in which firms are remarkably porous to outside influence. . . .

Thus, Silicon Valley's form of industrial organization institutionalized [knowledge spillovers.]

A postemployment covenant not to compete prevents knowledge spillover of an employer's proprietary knowledge . . . by blocking the mechanism by which the spillover occurs: employees leaving to take up employment with a competitor or to form a competing start-up. . . . Given the speed of innovation and the corresponding telescoping of product life cycles, knowledge more than a year or two old likely no longer has significant competitive value. The hiatus imposed by a covenant not to compete thus assures that . . . [t]he value of proprietary tacit knowledge embedded in the employee's human capital . . . will have dissipated over the covenant's term. Nothing of value is left to spill over to a new employer or start-up venture. . . .

Ronald J. Gilson, *The Legal Infrastructure of High Technology Industrial Districts: Silicon Valley, Route 128, and Covenants Not to Compete*, 74 N.Y.U. L. Rev. 575, 589-603 (1999); *see also* Charles A. Sullivan, *Revisiting the "Neglected Stepchild": Antitrust Treatment of Postemployment Restraints of Trade*, 1977 U. Ill. L. F. 621, 647-50 (suggesting need for more searching inquiry of anticompetitive effects of noncompetes that considers, among other things, the totality of restraints imposed by an employer or used within an industry). Yet another perspective suggests that noncompetes may be self-defeating in terms of employer interests by dampening employees' incentives to improve their skills. On Amir & Orly Lobel, *Driving Performance: A Growth Theory of Noncompete Law*, 16 Stan. Tech. L. Rev. 833 (2013) (reporting an experimental study supporting the proposition that postemployment restrictions "may discourage employees from investing in their own human capital and work performance, as well as restrict regional positive spillovers and endogenous growth over time").

As you read the next set of materials, keep in mind these different views of the costs and benefits of noncompetes, both to individuals and to society.

2. Disputes over Skills and Training

Rem Metals Corporation v. Logan
565 P. 2d 1080 (Or. 1977)

Tongue, Justice.

This is a suit in equity to enforce "noncompetition" provisions of two employment agreements between plaintiff and defendant, who had been employed by plaintiff as a welder of precision titanium castings. Defendant appeals from a decree enjoining him from engaging in such work for a period of six months in Oregon for Precision Castparts Corporation, a competitor of plaintiff. We reverse.

The primary question presented for decision in this case, according to plaintiff Rem, is whether, as an employer, it had a sufficient "protectable interest" in the skills and knowledge of defendant as a skilled craftsman engaged as a repair welder of precision titanium castings, so as to justify enforcement of such a "noncompetition" agreement as a "reasonable restraint" upon defendant.

The titanium castings on which defendant Logan worked as a repair welder were produced by his employer, the plaintiff, under contract with Pratt & Whitney Aircraft Division for use as bearing housings for jet aircraft engines under exceedingly strict specifications. Only three companies are engaged in the production of such castings for Pratt & Whitney. These include plaintiff, Precision Castparts (its principal competitor) and Misco of Michigan (a smaller company).

In the process of the production of such castings any defects are repaired by welding performed by skilled welders who are "certified" by Pratt & Whitney inspectors as being sufficiently skilled to be entrusted with this important work. There was also some evidence that titanium is a "rare" or "reactive" metal and is difficult to weld.

Defendant was one of two or three "certified" welders employed by plaintiff and was plaintiff's best welder, with a proficiency rating of 98.3 per cent. Other welders rated below 95 per cent. There was testimony, however, that three other welders had been able to become sufficiently qualified so as to be "certified" for Pratt & Whitney work after 20 hours of training and that during 1966 seven of plaintiff's welders (including defendant) were so "certified."

Defendant Logan had been previously employed by Wah Chang Corporation, where he learned to weld electrodes of titanium. He was employed by plaintiff in 1969 and subsequently signed two employment contracts, as did nearly all Rem employees, including provisions to the effect that for a period of one year after termination he would not engage in any business in competition with Rem within the United States, "whether as principal, agent, employer, consultant or otherwise."

In 1972 defendant was transferred to the welding department. He testified that he became "certified" in "less than two weeks," and that no one gave him "any instruction before he took the certification test" for the welding of titanium.

Plaintiff offered testimony describing its training program for welders. When asked whether Rem had any "trade secrets in the welding department that are not generally known in the industry," that witness answered that "Rem was able to do a better job," to ship ahead of its schedules, and with fewer "rejects" from Pratt & Whitney than its competitors, so that "there is something we must be doing that our competitors are not doing." Rem's president testified that defendant received job training at Rem and "extensive written procedures prepared by Rem" which enabled him to weld titanium castings. He also testified, however, that it was nevertheless not surprising that defendant Logan was able to become "certified" within "a matter of a few days," as testified by Logan. Rem's supervisor of welding testified that:

> I don't think it's a matter of disclosing inasmuch as it is its instructional nature. If a welder's in the tank doing the work, we're qualifying it and giving what instructions we are capable of.

There was also testimony by another former Rem titanium welder, since employed by Precision Castparts, that he observed no differences in the welding procedures and techniques at Rem and at PCP except that Rem uses a "vacuum tank," while PCP uses a "plastic bubble," both of which are standard techniques.

On September 18, 1976, defendant Logan, after being refused a wage increase of 50 cents per hour by Rem, went to work at that increased rate for Precision Castparts. Plaintiff offered evidence that, as a result, it was unable for a period of two weeks to ship castings worth approximately $25,000 to Pratt & Whitney and that it then had difficulty in maintaining its shipping schedules of such titanium castings because it did not have welders who were "able to complete the weld repair cycle in a satisfactory manner." It appears, however, that Rem was then able to train two welders who "shortly thereafter were able to pass the qualification test of Pratt & Whitney." Plaintiff's witnesses also testified to their concern over Rem's continued ability to compete with Precision Castparts, its principal competitor, which by then had 14 or 15 titanium welders, including defendant Logan.[2]

[On the subject of the enforcement of noncompetition provisions in employment contracts, the general rule is as follows:]

> Three things are essential to the validity of a contract in restraint of trade: (1) it must be partial or restricted in its operation in respect either to time or place; (2) it must be on some good consideration; and (3) it must be reasonable, that is, it should afford only a fair protection to the interests of the party in whose favor it is made, and must not be so large in its operation as to interfere with the interests of the public.

Eldridge v. Johnson, 245 P.2d 239, 250 (Or. 1952). As also stated in *North Pacific Lbr. v. Moore*, 551 P.2d 431, 434 (1976):

> To be entitled to the protection which a noncompetition covenant purports to provide, the employer must show that he has a legitimate interest entitled to protection.

At the outset, it is important to bear in mind that this is not a case involving an employee whose regular duties involved frequent dealings with customers of his employer and who had access to "customer lists" or other similar confidential information relating to customers. . . .

In our judgment, this case falls within the rule as stated in Blake, *Employee Agreements Not to Compete*, 73 Harv. L. Rev. 625, 652 (1960), as follows:

> . . . It has been uniformly held that general knowledge, skill, or facility acquired through training or experience while working for an employer appertain exclusively to the employee. The fact that they were acquired or developed during the employment does not, by itself, give the employee a sufficient interest to support a restraining covenant, even though the on-the-job training has been extensive and costly. In the absence, of special circumstances the risk of future competition form the employee falls upon the employer and cannot be shifted, even though the possible damages is greatly increased by experience gained in the course of the employment.

To the same effect, although under different facts, it was held in *McCombs v. McClelland*, 354 P.2d 311, 316 (1960) that:

> . . . The fact that defendant may have gained considerable experience while in plaintiff's employ is not grounds for injunctive relief. An employer cannot by contract prevent his employee upon termination of the employment from using skill and intelligence acquired or increased and improved through experience or through instruction received in the course of employment. . . .

---

2. It also appears that Precision Castparts is "underwriting" the cost of Mr. Logan's defense.

We recognize, however, as does Blake, that on any given set of facts it may be difficult to "draw a line" between "training in the general skills and knowledge of the trade, and training which imparts information pertaining especially to the employer's business" and that this is the "central problem" in such cases. In other words, as stated by Blake:

> Its objective is not to prevent the competitive use of the unique personal qualities of the employee — either during or after the employment but to prevent competitive use, for a time, of information or relationships which pertain peculiarly to the employer and which the employee acquired in the course of the employment. . . .[6]

In such a case, however, the burden of proof is upon the employer to establish the existence of "trade secrets," "information or relationships which pertain peculiarly to the employer," or other "special circumstances" sufficient to justify the enforcement of such a restrictive covenant.

Based upon our examination of this record, which we review de novo, and under the facts and circumstances of this case, we hold that this employer failed to sustain that burden of proof. Although defendant received training and experience while employed by plaintiff which developed his skill as a repair welder of titanium castings, plaintiff did not, in our judgment, establish by sufficient and credible evidence "special circumstances" of such a nature as to entitle Rem to demand the enforcement upon this defendant by injunction of this "noncompetition" clause as a "reasonable restraint."

NOTES

1. *The Threshold Issue. Rem Metals* introduces a critical threshold question in assessing the enforceability of noncompete agreements — does the employer have an underlying interest justifying protection? This inquiry is unique to the law of restrictive covenants in employment. In theory, it protects workers by limiting the situations in which they can be contractually constrained. One justification is simple fairness, but is Logan in need of judicial protection? Who is the more vulnerable party in *Rem Metals*, the employer or employee?

In answering that question, consider the following. First, it appears uncontradicted that Rem Metals lost $25,000 in the two weeks following Logan's departure before it was able to train replacements. But that damage flowed from Logan's departure, not from his competition. The employer would have suffered the same loss had Logan retired suddenly. Second, Logan was obviously an exceptionally good worker with a skill that is in demand. This may mean he was in a better position than some employees to protect himself in negotiating the terms of his employment, although his inability to secure a raise suggests otherwise. Finally, what would have happened had the employer prevailed? Would you expect Logan would be able to find equally lucrative employment opportunities if he were precluded from competing with Rem Metals for one year? Do your answers explain the court's application of the "protectable interest" requirement?

---

6. As stated in *Sarkes Tarzin, Inc. v. Audio Devices, Inc.*, 166 F. Supp. 250, 265 (S.D. Cal. 1958): ". . . Trade secrets must be 'the particular secrets of the employer as distinguished from the general secrets of the trade in which he is engaged.' . . ."

2. *Protecting General Training: A Law and Economics View. Rem Metals* articulates the majority rule that an employer may not enforce a noncompete to protect employer investments in general knowledge and training. Maybe the justification for the rule is not fairness per se but rather property-like notions.

Professor Gary Becker's well-known human capital theory distinguishes between specific training that is useful only to one employer and general training that is useful to many. He contends that employers have an incentive to invest in specific training of employees because it benefits their business and cannot be usurped by competitors. On the other hand, employers are unlikely to invest in general training, leaving it to the worker to finance this training herself, either by paying for outside schooling or, in the case of on-the-job training, accepting lower wages during the training period. This theory supports the general rule in *Rem Metals*: Since the employee pays for the training herself, the employer should not be permitted to use a noncompete to prevent use of that general training on behalf of a competitor. *See* Gary S. Becker, HUMAN CAPITAL: A THEORETICAL AND EMPIRICAL ANALYSIS 19-37 (2d ed. 1975); Edmund W. Kitch, *The Law and Economics of Rights in Valuable Information*, 9 J. LEGAL STUD. 683, 684 (1980) (summarizing Becker's theories).

Several commentators disagree that employees pay for their own general training. Professors Rubin and Shedd note that some forms of general training are too costly for an employee to finance out of her wages, as where an employer imparts to an employee an industry trade secret worth millions of dollars to competitors. In that situation, the employer would require a noncompetition agreement to prevent the employee from defecting to another firm willing to pay her a premium in light of her valuable knowledge. Of course, trade secrets are theoretically protectable without a noncompete, but, as Judge Posner suggested, misappropriation of trade secrets is sometimes hard to prove and a valid covenant not to compete solves that problem. Were such noncompetes unenforceable, firms would have lower incentive to invest in acquiring this type of highly valuable information or sharing it with its workforce. *See* Paul H. Rubin & Peter Shedd, *Human Capital and Covenants Not to Compete*, 10 J. LEGAL STUD. 93, 96-7 (1981).

Still, Professors Rubin and Shedd acknowledge that employers may overenforce noncompete agreements. A firm might pay a worker less than the value of her marginal product taking into account its investments, or a firm might seek to enforce the noncompete to preclude the employee's use of all training, including general training paid for in the form of reduced wages. For these reasons, Rubin and Shedd ultimately conclude that noncompetes should not be enforceable to protect general training unless the training includes trade secrets or confidential information. *Id.* at 109-10. This is the approach that most courts take. *See, e.g., Girtman & Assoc. v. St. Amour,* 2007 Tenn. App. LEXIS 271 (Tenn. Ct. App. 2007) (enforcement of noncompete against former door and hardware salesman not justified despite fact that employee had no prior experience and company paid for him to attend multiple training sessions leading to industry certification where training provided was not specific to employer and programs were open to anyone in industry); *Tom James Co. v. Mendrop,* 819 S.W.2d 251, 253 (Tex. App. 1991) (measuring methods and tools used in custom tailored men's clothing business were not specific enough to justify protection). *But see* FLA. STAT. ANN. § 542.335(1)(b)(5) (recognizing "extraordinary or specialized training" as a legitimate business interest justifying a noncompete). As we will see, employers sometimes try to circumvent this by requiring employees to sign training repayment agreements, an approach that has been sanctioned by at least some jurisdictions. *See, e.g.*, COLO. REV. STAT. 8-2-113(2) (recognizing exception to prohibition on noncompetes to allow enforcement of an agreement "providing for recovery of the expense of educating and training" against an employee who has worked less than two years). The RESTATEMENT OF EMPLOYMENT LAW takes this approach, stating that recoupment of training investments justifies repayment promises but not a noncompetition agreement. § 8.07, cmt. f.

Do these theories about employer and employee investments help explain the result in *Rem Metals*? Who "paid" for Logan's training? Is that a question that can be answered from the facts of the case?

3. *Training and Customer Goodwill.* In holding against the employer, *Rem Metals* distinguishes situations in which the employee has frequent dealings with customers. In some situations employers' asserted interests in training elide with a more particularized interest in preserving client contacts or customer goodwill. This might occur, for instance, where the employee is a salesperson who had no prior experience in the employer's industry and the on-the-job experience and "training" she receives allows her to develop relationships with customers that she may use to her competitive advantage upon departure. *See Roberson v. C.P. Allen Construction Co.*, 50 So. 3d 471, 476 (Ala. App. 2010) (enforcing concrete-cutting company's noncompete against salesman who prior to employment "knew nothing about that business" and through his employment "learned the trade" and was provided with "the means to entertain client contacts and to develop relationships with [the employer's] customers"). We will talk about the viability of noncompetes designed to protect this distinct interest beginning at page 528. For now, it is important to be aware that, even if the type of training provided to an employee does not support a noncompete, there may be other justifications for enforcement.

4. *Noncompetes as Alternatives to Fixed-Term Contracts.* If an employer's principal concern is worker retention — and in the case of an interest in employee skills and training, it often is — why use a noncompete? Why doesn't the employer simply obtain a fixed-term employment contract from the desirable employee? Indeed, if the employer forgoes such a contract, perhaps because it does not want to make an equivalent commitment to retaining the employee for a fixed term, why should it be permitted to use a noncompete to achieve the same result? One possible answer is that, because fixed-term contracts cannot be specifically enforced against employees, they do not adequately address employers' concerns about retention. It is also possible that employers are unable to predict in advance the precise length of employment needed to protect their interests, and noncompetes provide greater flexibility. On the other hand, does it trouble you that noncompetes give employers the discretion to seek enforcement based on their unilateral assessment of the circumstance at the time of departure? In part because of such concerns, some commentators have suggested that certain noncompetes should be enforced only if the employer promised the employee some degree of job security in exchange for the covenant. *See* Rachel Arnow-Richman, *Noncompetes, Human Capital, and Contract Formation: What Employment Law Can Learn from Family Law*, 10 TEX. WESLEYAN L. REV. 155 (2003); *cf.* Kate O'Neill, *Should I Stay or Should I Go? — Covenants Not to Compete in a Down Economy: A Proposal for Better Advocacy and Better Judicial Opinions*, 6 HASTINGS BUS. L. J. 83 (2010) (suggesting that a "diminution in the quality of employment," as where the former employer's business is deteriorating, should weigh against the failing firm in any subsequent efforts to enforce a noncompete against a worker who left for these reasons).

5. *The Departure Dispute as Morality Play.* Another way of understanding the result in *Rem Metals* is to consider general concepts of fairness. It is hard to feel sorry for an employer who refuses his star welder a $0.50 pay increase. Similarly, it is not surprising to see courts enforcing noncompetes against employees who affirmatively take or destroy documents or otherwise attempt to sabotage the employer's business upon departure. In this way, disputes about competition often turn on assessments of fairness and loyalty. *See* Alan Hyde, WORKING IN SILICON VALLEY: ECONOMIC AND LEGAL ANALYSIS OF A HIGH-VELOCITY LABOR MARKET 37 (2003) (describing the "moralistic" quality of trade secret litigation). Professor Catherine Fisk attributes courts' attention to such matters to the evolution of the law of employment competition in the "'moral economy' of the early nineteenth century, in which notions of honor, trust, and the moral value of work ('industry') loomed [large]." *See* Catherine Fisk, *Working Knowledge: Trade Secrets, Restrictive Covenants in Employment, and the Rise of Corporate Intellectual Property*, 1800-1920, 52 HASTINGS L. J. 441 (2001). As you read the cases in this chapter, pay attention to how courts' assessment of fault and loyalty correlate with its decisions in favor of or against enforcement of restraints against competition.

6. *The Costs of Litigation.* No matter who is right, disputes over competition can be costly, and that burden weighs more heavily on employees, who are usually less able to bear the expense of defending themselves against a company. Notice how Logan is financing this litigation. At least in reported cases, the new employer is often a co-defendant in litigation over employee competition and/or bearing the cost of defending the defecting employee. Indeed, in the case of a coveted employee, the new employer may well contemplate and plan for the possibility of future litigation in its recruiting and hiring process. *See, e.g., Saks Fifth Ave. v. James, Ltd.*, 630 S.E.2d 304, 307 (Va. 2006) (new employer obtained employees' noncompetes during interview process, referred them to its attorneys, and agreed in writing to defend employees in the event of legal challenge by former employer).

A high-profile example of the new employer's role in noncompetition litigation is the widely publicized 2005 dispute between Google and Microsoft over Google's hiring of former Microsoft Vice President, Kai-fu Lee. Google vigorously defended Mr. Lee against Microsoft's efforts to use its noncompete agreement to prevent him from starting work at Google. The litigation resulted in a ruling permitting Mr. Lee to join Google and begin recruiting for its China office but restricting him from working in the competitive area of search technology or from participating in budgetary or research and development decision making. *See* Kevin J. Delaney & Robert A. Guth, *Ruling Lets Lee Go to Work at Google*, WALL ST. J., Sept. 14, 2005, B2.

Of course, few employees are likely to be in such demand. How might the prospect of litigation influence an ordinary employee's decision whether to leave for a competitor?

7. *Legitimate Interests.* If general training is not a basis for enforcing a noncompete, what is? Can you discern from the court's treatment of Logan's agreement a possible set of facts under which Rem Metals would have had a protectable interest justifying an injunction? Would it have made a difference, for instance, if the certification Rem Metals provided took three months and cost $3,000 to administer? What if Rem Metals had trained Logan on equipment that he had not used in his previous employer? What if Logan had told Rem Metals' contractors that he was leaving Rem Metals and the contractors decided to bring their future business to Logan's new employer? We will explore the two most commonly recognized "legitimate interests" of employers in the next sections — employer-owned confidential information and employer customer relations—but note that other legitimate interests have been recognized. Thus, the RESTATEMENT OF EMPLOYMENT LAW also recognizes noncompetes to protect the employer's investment in the employee's reputation in the market or the purchase of an employee-owned business. § 8.07(b)(iii), (iv) (Proposed Final Draft April 18, 2014).

3. Disputes over Information

CTI, Inc. v. Software Artisans, Inc.
3 F.3d 730 (4th Cir. 1993)

WILLIAMS, Circuit Judge:

[Comprehensive Technologies International, Inc., "CTI," brought this action against several former employees and Software Artisans, Inc., "SA," asserting trade secret misappropriation and breach of contract in connection with the defendants' development of a computer program called "Transend." The district court entered judgment for the defendants. In 1988, the founder and CEO of CTI, Celestino Beltran, established a Software Product Group, headed by defendant Dean Hawkes, to expand the company in the area of electronic data interchange ("EDI"). EDI is the computer-to-computer transmission of business transactions in proprietary or standard formats. Hawkes was given responsibility for developing software that would enable clients to process and transmit data through EDI technology. Defendant Filippides was hired to market the software, and the other defendant employees wrote the code.]

Each of the Defendant employees except Hawkes signed CTI's standard Confidentiality and Proprietary Information Agreement. Under the Agreement, each employee agreed not to disclose or use, directly or indirectly, during his employment and for three years thereafter any confidential, proprietary, or software-related information belonging to CTI. The Agreement specifically identified the Claims Express and EDI Link projects as confidential. [Hawkes signed] an Employment Agreement that contained similar but more restrictive provisions. In addition to promising confidentiality, Hawkes agreed that during the term of his employment he would not compete with CTI, solicit CTI's customers, or employ CTI's current or former employees.

The Software Products Group undertook to develop two software packages for personal computers. The first, Claims Express, is an electronic medical billing system. Claims Express transmits information that conforms to two specific insurance claims forms [and] has been successfully marketed. CTI's second software package, EDI Link, is not specific to the health care industry. It is designed to permit users to create generic forms, enter data on the forms electronically, test that data for errors, and store both the forms and the data on a computer. Although CTI expended substantial effort on EDI Link, at the time of trial the program had not been completed and had never been sold or marketed. Trial testimony indicated that between 35 and 85 percent of the program had been completed.

In February 1991, all of the Defendant employees left CTI. . . .

In April 1991, the Defendants incorporated Software Artisans, Inc., located in Fairfax, Virginia. By July 1991, SA had developed and begun to market its own program called Transend. According to its User's Manual, Transend creates a "paper-less office environment" by enabling its users to process business forms on a computer. Transend is similar to Claims Express and EDI Link in that it is designed to prepare forms for transmission by EDI. Transend permits the user to input data, check the data for errors, and prepare the data for transmission by EDI.

... III

Trade Secrets

The district court . . . found that CTI did not prove that the Defendants misap-propriated a trade secret. Under Virginia law a "trade secret" is information, including but not limited to, a formula, pattern, compilation, program, device, method, tech-nique, or process, that:

1. Derives independent economic value, actual or potential, from not being gen-erally known to, and not being readily ascertainable by proper means by, other persons who can obtain economic value from its disclosure or use, and
2. Is the subject of efforts that are reasonable under the circumstances to main-tain its secrecy.

VA. CODE ANN. § 59.1-336. For purposes relevant to this case, "misappropriation" means the "use of a trade secret of another without express or implied consent by a person who . . . [a]t the time of . . . use, knew or had reason to know that his knowl-edge of the trade secret was . . . [a]cquired under circumstances giving rise to a duty to maintain its secrecy or limit its use." *Id.*

In denying CTI's claim for trade secret misappropriation, the district court found that CTI did not possess any trade secrets and that, even if CTI did possess trade secrets, the Defendants had not misappropriated them. The court found no evidence that CTI's purported trade secrets — the organization of Claims Express and EDI Link, the database access techniques of the two programs, and the unique iden-tifiers of the two programs — derived independent economic value from not being generally known or were not readily ascertainable by proper means. Consequently, the court concluded that CTI's purported trade secrets failed to satisfy all of the elements necessary to prove a trade secret. The district court also concluded that the Defendants did not "copy" any trade secrets, implying that Defendants did not "use" or otherwise misappropriate them.

CTI argues that in granting judgment for Defendants on its trade secrets claim, the district court misapplied the law. . . .

CTI reads the district court's opinion as ruling as a matter of law that the organization of its database, its database access techniques, and its unique identifiers could not constitute trade secrets because each of their composite elements was in the public domain. CTI argues vociferously (and correctly) that although a trade secret cannot subsist in information in the public domain, it can subsist in a combination of such information, as long as the combination is itself secret. *See Integrated Cash Management v. Digital Transactions*, 920 F.2d 174 (2d Cir. 1990). According to CTI, each of its alleged trade secrets is just such a combination of publicly available information.

In making this argument, CTI misreads the district court's opinion. The district court did not rule that unique combinations or arrangements of publicly available information cannot receive protection as trade secrets. Rather, the district court held that CTI failed to present any evidence that its database organization, its access techniques, and its identifiers were not themselves publicly available. The court specifically found that the arrangement and interaction of the functions of Claims Express and EDI Link were "common to all computer programs of this type." Information that is generally known cannot qualify as a trade secret. Consequently, the district court did not misapply the law; it simply found insufficient evidence to support CTI's claim. The district court correctly concluded that CTI failed to prove that the organization, database access techniques, and identifiers of CTI's software constituted trade secrets.

Even if CTI had demonstrated that these items constituted trade secrets, CTI has not convinced us that the district court clearly erred in finding that the Defendants did not misappropriate any of CTI's alleged trade secrets. CTI points to the short development time and the complete lack of design documentation for Transend as strong circumstantial evidence of misappropriation. Although this evidence does raise some suspicions, Defendants provided a colorable explanation for the absence of design documentation. First, Defendant's expert . . . testified that it was not atypical for small software companies to neglect to prepare extensive design documentation. Second, [Defendant] Sterba testified that he and the others disliked the amount of paperwork involved in documenting their designs, that they preferred to use a "whiteboard" for their design work, and that they placed much of the information that would ordinarily appear in design documentation in the code itself. In light of this testimony, CTI's circumstantial evidence is not enough to convince us that the district court clearly erred in finding that the Defendants did not copy (or "use") any of CTI's alleged trade secret information. . . .

IV

Covenant Not to Compete

CTI next argues that the district court should have enforced Dean Hawkes's covenant not to compete. In his Termination Agreement, Hawkes agreed that, for a period of twelve months following his departure from CTI, he would not engage directly or indirectly in any business within the United States (financially as an investor or lender or as an employee, director, officer, partner, independent contractor, consultant or owner or in any other capacity calling for the rendition of personal services or acts of management, operation or control) which is in competition with the business of CTI. For purposes of this Agreement, the "business of CTI" shall be defined as the design, development, marketing, and sales of CLAIMS EXPRESS and EDI LINK type PC-based software with the same functionality and methodology. . . .

Virginia has established a three-part test for assessing the reasonableness of restrictive employment covenants. Under the test, the court must ask the following questions:

1. Is the restraint, from the standpoint of the employer, reasonable in the sense that it is no greater than is necessary to protect the employer in some legitimate business interest?

2. From the standpoint of the employee, is the restraint reasonable in the sense that it is not unduly harsh and oppressive in curtailing his legitimate efforts to earn a livelihood?

3. Is the restraint reasonable from the standpoint of a sound public policy?

If a covenant not to compete meets each of these standards of reasonableness, it must be enforced. As a general rule, however, the Virginia courts do not look favorably upon covenants not to compete, and will strictly construe them against the employer. The employer bears the burden of demonstrating that the restraint is reasonable.

The district court refused to enforce the covenant not to compete because it concluded that the covenant was broader than necessary to protect CTI's legitimate business interests. First, the court held that the scope of the employment restrictions was too broad because the restrictions precluded Hawkes from working for a competitor in any capacity, even as a janitor. The court implied that CTI did not have a legitimate interest in preventing Hawkes from working for a competitor in a menial capacity. Second, the district court concluded that the geographic scope of the agreement was broader than necessary to protect CTI's interests. The court found that CTI had marketed Claims Express only in Virginia, Nebraska, and perhaps one other state, and therefore CTI did not have a legitimate interest in restricting Hawkes's employment throughout the United States.

Although the district court believed that the covenant was categorically overbroad because it precluded Hawkes from working for a competitor of CTI in any capacity, the Virginia Supreme Court has enforced similarly broad restrictions. . . .

Moreover, as Vice President of CTI's Software Products Group, Hawkes necessarily came in contact with confidential information concerning both CTI's products and its customers. Hawkes's access to such confidential information makes the covenant not to compete more reasonable. As the Virginia Supreme Court has noted,

> [t]he fact that the employment is of such a character as to inform the employee of business methods and trade secrets which, if brought to the knowledge of a competitor, would prejudice the interests of the employer, tends to give an element of reasonableness to a contract that the employee will not engage in a similar business for a limited time after the termination of his employment, and is always regarded as a strong reason for upholding the contract.

Stoneman [v. Wilson], 192 S.E. [816, 819 (Va. 1938)]. Similarly, in Roanoke Engineering [v. Rosenbaum, 290 S.E. 2d 882, 885 (Va. 1982)], an employee had access to confidential financial records, lists of customers and suppliers, and detailed knowledge of overhead factors, pricing policies, and bidding techniques. The Virginia Supreme Court held that this information enabled the employee to become a "formidable competitor" of his former employer, and concluded that a restriction barring the employee from working for competitors in any capacity was no greater than necessary to protect the employer's legitimate business interests.

Hawkes poses a similar danger to CTI's business. As the individual primarily responsible for the design, development, marketing and sale of CTI's software, Hawkes became intimately familiar with every aspect of CTI's operation, and necessarily acquired information that he could use to compete with CTI in the marketplace. When an employee has access to confidential and trade secret information crucial to the success of the employer's business, the employer has a strong interest in enforcing a covenant not to compete because other legal remedies often prove inadequate. It will often be difficult, if not impossible, to prove that a competing employee has misappropriated trade secret information belonging to his former employer. On the facts of this case, we conclude that the scope of the employment restrictions is no broader than necessary to protect CTI's legitimate business interests.

As a second ground for invalidating the covenant not to compete, the district court concluded that the geographic scope of the employment restrictions — "within the United States" — was greater than necessary to protect CTI's business. The district court merely noted that CTI had marketed Claims Express in only three states and therefore did not have a national market for its product.

The district court clearly erred in concluding that CTI did not have a national market for Claims Express. CTI licensed Claims Express in at least ten states. . . . CTI also identified for the district court specific customer prospects in [nineteen states] and the District of Columbia. CTI presented Claims Express and EDI Link (albeit in preliminary form) at national EDIA trade shows in both 1989 and 1990. Finally, CTI presented evidence that it faced direct [and potential] competition from companies located [throughout the country]. Given the breadth of the market for Claims Express, we cannot see how anything less than a nationwide prohibition could conceivably protect CTI's business interests. . . .

Having determined that the covenant not to compete is reasonable from CTI's point of view, we must next determine whether the covenant is reasonable from Hawkes's point of view, i.e., whether the curtailment on Hawkes's ability to earn a living is unduly harsh or oppressive. Although the agreement applies throughout the United States, it restricts Hawkes from engaging in only an extremely narrow category of business. Hawkes may not render personal services to, or perform acts of management, operation, or control for, any business in competition with "the business of CTI," which the agreement defines as "the design, development, marketing and sales of CLAIMS EXPRESSTM and EDI LINK™ type PC-based software with the same functionality and methodology." The agreement therefore permits Hawkes to design, develop, market and sell any software of a type different from Claims Express or EDI Link, any software of the same type having a different functionality or methodology, or any software of the same type having the same functionality and methodology that is not designed to run on personal computers. Hawkes is also free to compete with any other branch of CTI's business. Because Hawkes retains broad employability under the agreement, the agreement is not unduly harsh or oppressive.

In light of the foregoing, we conclude that the covenant not to compete is no greater than necessary to protect CTI's business and is not unduly harsh or oppressive. . . .

NOTES

1. *Trade Secret Defined.* CTI's primary cause of action against its former employees was misappropriation of a trade secret. Virginia, like a majority of states, has adopted the Uniform Trade Secrets Act ("UTSA"), which attempts to standardize the common-law definition of the term. It lists two requirements for a trade secret: The item in question must derive independent economic value from not being generally known and be subject to the employer's reasonable efforts to maintain its secrecy. *See* UTSA, 14 U.L.A. 437 (1990); *see also* Restatement of Employment Law § 8.02

(Proposed Final Draft, April 18, 2014) ("an employer's information is a trade secret . . . if it derives independent economic value from being kept secret and the employer has taken reasonable steps to keep it secret."). Older trade secret cases often involved disputes over particular manufacturing processes or the secret ingredients for a particular product. The recipe for Coca-Cola is often cited as the paradigmatic trade secret. Today, however, many employers seek trade secret protection for more general information, either technical information (as is the case in *CTI*) or confidential business information (financial documentation, marketing strategies, etc.). This poses new challenges in identifying what constitutes a trade secret. Although CTI may have made efforts to keep its project under wraps, according to the court the actual components of CTI's programs and their structure followed techniques and configurations that were in common use.

    2. *Independently Valuable Information.* Another question that arises in analyzing trade secrets in information is whether that information — even if not generally known — has independent economic value. While few cases discuss this requirement, Professor Arnow-Richman interprets it to mean that information sought to be protected must be useable to competitors outside of the employer's project or business environment. This often is not the case with secret information that is highly technical and company-specific. Rachel Arnow-Richman, *Bargaining for Loyalty in the Information Age: A Reconsideration of the Role of Substantive Fairness in Enforcing Employee Noncompetes*, 80 OR. L. REV. 1163, 1190 (2001); *see also* Catherine Fisk, *Working Knowledge: Trade Secrets, Restrictive Covenants in Employment, and the Rise of Corporate Intellectual Property*, 1800-1920, 52 HASTINGS L. J. 441, 503-4 (2001) (from 1890-1930, the "[f]ocus shifted from the drawings of a machine to the design innovations contained in them; from the list of the customers to the knowledge of their identities, locations, needs and their goodwill; and from the precise written formula for a substance to the general knowledge of the process and techniques for making it").

    Was this part of the problem in *CTI*? In other words, was the employer trying to protect the work its employees were doing rather than a particular programming technique? If so, is that a good reason for denying CTI trade secret protection, or should the definition of a trade secret be understood to include such interests? The Restatement explicitly rejects protection of information "acquired by employees through their general experience, knowledge, and skills during the ordinary course of employment. § 8.02(b)(iii).

    3. *Evidence of Misappropriation.* To succeed on its trade secret claim, CTI had to show not only that its software products were trade secrets but also that those secrets had been misappropriated. The UTSA offers an expansive definition of misappropriation. The portion most relevant in the competitive employment context defines the concept as

> disclosure or use of a trade secret of another without express or implied consent by a person who . . . at the time of disclosure or use knew or had reason to know that his knowledge of the trade secret was . . . acquired under circumstances giving rise to a duty to maintain its secrecy or limit its use.

14 U.L.A. 437; *see also* Restatement § 8.03 (disclosure or use of a trade secret breaches the duty of loyalty).

    As *CTI* illustrates, it can be difficult to prove misappropriation of trade secrets. However, the increasing sophistication of computer forensics has made it easier to track the downloading, copying, and e-mailing of files, allowing companies to demonstrate that particular documents were taken by departing employees. *See, e.g., Bimbo Bakeries USA Inc. v. Botticella*, 613 F.3d 102 (3d Cir. 2010) (employer's computer expert identified pattern of accessing multiple documents consistent with copying in the week leading up to former employee's departure and established that portable hard drives had been attached to the computer); *Rapid Temps, Inc. v. Lamon*, 192 P.2d 799 (N.M. App. 2008) (relying on evidence of files found on employee's computer and portable hard drive). But where alleged secrets are intangible and do not exist in written form, or where the employee resorts to less technical means of "copying," the employer must rely on circumstantial evidence of misappropriation. *See, e.g., San Jose Construction, Inc. v. S.B.C.C., Inc.*, 67 Cal. Rptr. 3d 54 (Cal. App. 2007) (similarities between project proposals submitted by plaintiff's former construction manager and those he submitted for same projects while in plaintiff's employ and speed with which they were produced created issue of fact on misappropriation of trade secret claim notwithstanding fact that former manager had returned all project files); *Sunbelt Rentals, Inc. v. Head & Engquist Equip.*, 620 S.E.2d 222, 229 (N.C. Ct. App. 2005) (treating as evidence of misappropriation fact that defendant's new company evolved from having no customers to converting several of plaintiff's customers and making extraordinarily high profit in first year of operation following mass defection of plaintiff's employees). If you were representing the employer, what other evidence of misappropriation would you look for and how would you go about obtaining it? If you were counseling an employee about to engage in competition with a former employer, what precautions would you recommend taking to help avoid or potentially defend against a misappropriation claim?

4. *The Role of Contract in Protecting Information.* To avoid the challenges facing employers in pursuing trade secret misappropriation claims, employers often seek contractual protection for information through a nondisclosure or noncompete clause. *See* Ronald J. Gilson, *The Legal Infrastructure of High Technology Industrial Districts: Silicon Valley, Route 128, and Covenants Not to Compete*, 74 N.Y.U. L. Rev. 575 (1999); Gillian Lester, *Restrictive Covenants, Employee Training, and the Limits of Transaction-Cost Analysis*, 76 Indiana L. J. 49, 53 (2001). Do you see the advantages of noncompete agreements reflected in *CTI*, in which the company pursued separate tort and contract theories against Hawkes? If contractual agreements are helpful to employers, why didn't CTI obtain broader restrictive covenants from the other employee-defendants?

A criticism of employers' use of noncompetes is that it circumvents the threshold requirements of trade secret law. Recall from *Rem Metals* that employers must make a threshold showing of a legitimate interest in order to enforce a noncompete. What is CTI's "legitimate" interest in enforcing a noncompete against Hawkes if there are no trade secrets to protect? Consider Professor Katherine Stone's perspective:

> The long-standing view has been that to be enforceable, a covenant not to compete must protect an employer's legitimate interest in a trade secret or confidential information. This view creates a paradox, however, because if a court requires a trade secret or confidential information in order to enforce a covenant, the existence of the covenant becomes, at least theoretically, irrelevant. Disclosure of trade secrets and confidential information can be restrained in the absence of such a covenant.
>
> If the law of noncompete covenants merely restates or incorporates the law of trade secrets and confidential relationships, then there is little independent role for the covenant.

Katherine V. W. Stone, *The New Psychological Contract*, 48 UCLA L. REV. 519, 583-84 (2001). Professor Stone attempts to explain this paradox, noting the possibility that a covenant makes it easier for an employer to obtain injunctive relief before the secret is disclosed.

In contrast to trade secret law, misappropriation is *not* a prerequisite to noncompete enforcement in most jurisdictions. *See Certainteed Corp. v. Williams*, 481 F.3d 528 (7th Cir. 2007) (noting in enforcing noncompete that "keeping a business executive with a wealth of information from taking an equivalent position with a rival is [a legitimate interest] when the executive's use of trade secrets would be hard to detect"). But noncompete law does require a threshold showing of the employer's interest in the information to be protected. As Stone puts it: "In theory, the standard of proof for finding a trade secret in the two cases should be no different, unless the court is sub rosa imposing a different test for finding a trade secret where there is a contractual obligation." She goes on:

> . . . A case in point is [*CTI*]. While the court did not find that the knowledge the employee possessed was a trade secret, it justified its decision on the ground that the employee had access to confidential information concerning both the products and customers of the former employer, so that "it will often be difficult . . . to prove that a competing employee has misappropriated trade secret information belonging to his former employer." This rationale suggests that the court acted to protect the trade secret, not to enforce the parties' agreement, but the existence of the covenant enabled it to sidestep the difficult trade secret issue.
>
> When a court requires that there be a trade secret or confidential information in order to enforce a noncompete covenant, employee consent plays only a minor role in the case. [T]he covenant permits the court to enlarge remedies for trade secret misappropriation; in the view of some courts, the covenant permits it to cut corners in its analysis of what constitutes a trade secret.

Id. at 585. The RESTATEMENT OF EMPLOYMENT LAW disagrees with Stone that the standard for trade secret and noncompete claims should be the same since a valid covenant can protect not only trade secrets but also "other protectable confidential information that does not meet the statutory definition of a trade secret." Do you see why a court might be more inclined to find for an employer on the basis of a noncompete than on a trade secret claim? Do you understand Professor Stone's concern about this practice? What does she mean by "consent plays a minor role" in such decisions?

Consider that a contractual expansion of employer rights beyond that conferred by trade secret law has implications not only for the worker but for society. One criticism of the use of noncompetes in this manner is that it upsets the balance struck by the background intellectual property regime, which is intentionally limited so as to preserve public access to information while still incentivizing creation. *See* Viva R. Moffat, *The Wrong Tool for the Job: The IP Problem with Non-Competition Agreements*, 52 WILL. & MARY L. REV. 873 (2010).

5. *Narrower Restraints as Alternatives.* Do contractual *nondisclosure* agreements pose similar problems to noncompetes? Or does the narrower scope of the prohibition reduce the concern? If the latter, what is the point of having a nondisclosure agreement? Where an employer succeeds in enforcing the broadest restraint in its employment agreement, in Hawkes's case the noncompete provision, such additional language is often irrelevant — an employee who is precluded from competing with his former employer is most likely precluded from disclosing information that will help the competitor compete. However, from a planning perspective, it may be important for the employer to include narrower restrictive covenants in an employment agreement. If the court ultimately refuses to enforce the noncompete agreement, it might still provide a degree of protection to the employer by ordering compliance with the other clauses or even providing damages to the employer based on breach of other clauses.

Some courts apply the same rule of reasonableness to lesser restraints like non-disclosure and nonsolicitation clauses. *See, e.g., Milliken & Co. v. Morin*, 731 S.E.2d 288 (S.C. 2012) (upholding confidentiality and invention assignment agreements as not in restraint of trade since such holdover provisions did not limit the employee's post-employment activities except with respect to the affected inventions). But such clauses are more likely to be found reasonable if only because they are more tailored to the interest to be protected and less onerous. A nondisclosure clause, for example, may prevent an employee from using certain knowledge but not bar her from working for a competitor. And a nonsolicitation clause might allow the former employee to work for a competitor as long as she did not contact, or perhaps deal with former customers. But such clauses can still pose a serious obstacle to a former employee's activity. *See Corporate Techs., Inc. v. Harnett*, 731 F.3d 6, 12 (1st Cir. 2013) (nonsolicitation clause can be violated even if former employee does not initiate any contact with former customers since who makes the initial contact "is just one factor among many that the trial court should consider in drawing the line between solicitation and acceptance in a given case"). *But see Vulcan Steel Structures, Inc. v. McCarty*, 2014 Ga. App. LEXIS 654 (Ga. Ct. App. Oct. 6, 2014) (approving agreement barring solicitation but invalidating clause to the extent it would prevent the employee from serving unsolicited clients). As a result even applying the same rule regarding validity to these lesser restraints may lead to a different assessment of the balance of hardships. Further, confidentiality agreements and nondisparagement clauses may have unforeseen consequences for attorneys. *See generally* Maura Irene Strassberg, *An Ethical Rabbit Hole: Model Rule 4.4, Intentional Interference with Former Employee Non-Disclosure Agreements and the Threat of Disqualification, Parts I & II*, 89 Neb. L. Rev. 923, 90 Neb. L. Rev. 141 (2011) (exploring the professional responsibility implications of attorneys interviewing potential witnesses subject to confidentiality agreements).

Beyond providing an alternative to trade secret protection, nondisclosure agreements frequently serve an important evidentiary role in trade secret litigation. Revisit the UTSA definition of a trade secret, quoted in *CTI*, and see if you can guess why.

6. *Reasonableness.* Even if an employer is using a noncompete agreement to protect a legitimate interest, the agreement is not enforceable unless it is "reasonable." *CTI* discusses two factors that courts consider in assessing whether a noncompete is reasonable — its geographic reach and the scope of competition prohibited. (A third factor, duration of the restraint, is taken up in the next case.) Note the relationship between the two factors the court considers. The court permits a very broad geographic reach (the whole country) in part because the definition of competition is extremely narrow (only companies developing PC software with the same functionality and methodology). In past decades, courts frequently struck down noncompetes precluding competition throughout the country as categorically overbroad, reflecting the view (and probably the reality in that era) that few businesses could be meaningfully competitive beyond the borders of their state or geographic region. In today's world, however, such geographic provisions are both more common and more commonly enforced, particularly if the scope of prohibited competition is narrowly drawn. Illustration 7 of the Restatement's §8.06 approves a "worldwide" ban on competition when reasonably tailored to protect the employer's interest. Indeed, courts have occasionally enforced worldwide restrictions on narrow forms of competitive behavior on behalf of companies operating in an international market. *See, e.g., Superior Consulting Co. v. Walling*, 851 F. Supp. 839, 847 (E.D. Mich. 1994) (finding absence of any geographic term acceptable where former employer did business in 43 states and with foreign nations and scope of competitive behavior could be reduced); *Farr Assocs., Inc. v. Baksin*, 530 S.E.2d 878, 882 (N.C. Ct. App. 2000) (rejecting argument that covenant was overly broad due to absence of defined territorial limit where covenant was limited to not servicing clients of former employer).

Note on Injunctive Relief and the Mechanics of Enforcement

When an important employee departs, employers are most interested in the remedies a court will order if the employee violates the law. If negotiations fail and the employer decides to sue the employee, it will typically seek preliminary injunctive relief from the court. That is, the employer will obtain an immediate, abbreviated hearing at which it will argue that the court should enjoin the employee from disclosing a trade secret and/or breaching his or her noncompete agreement, pending a full trial.

Although the tests vary somewhat among circuits, to obtain a preliminary injunction, an employer must show that there is a danger of irreparable harm, that it is likely to succeed on the merits at trial, that a balance of the equities favors issuing the injunction, and that an injunction will not violate the public interest. *See, e.g., SI Handling Systems, Inc. v. Heisley* 753 F.2d 1244, 1254 (3d Cir. 1985). During the preliminary injunction stage, the parties can take advantage of a compressed discovery schedule and will often mount a full-blown minitrial at the hearing. Speed is important not only because harm may transpire during any delay but also because some courts refuse to issue a preliminary injunction if a decision is not reached before the noncompetition period expires. *See EMC Corp. v. Arturi*, 655 F.3d 75, 76 (1st Cir. 2011) (affirming denial of a preliminary injunction against competition under Massachusetts law since, by the time the matter was decided, the year's restriction had expired). Other courts, however, will recognize "equitable extensions" to account for delays in the legal system. *Guy Carpenter & Co. v. Provenzale*, 334 F.3d 459, 464 (5th Cir. 2003). In any event, so much effort is put into obtaining or defeating a temporary order because the preliminary injunction proceeding is often the only step that matters in this kind of litigation. By the time the case goes to trial on the merits, months may have passed. From the employer's perspective, any damage to its interests will have already been done. Although an employer who succeeds at trial after losing at the preliminary injunction stage may obtain damages, monetary injury in such cases is often hard to prove and quantify, and damage awards can be difficult to collect from an individual employee.

For the employee, the issuance of a preliminary injunction means that he may be unemployed or underemployed, at least for the period until trial. Even if he ultimately succeeds on the merits, he may not be able to recoup wages lost during the preliminary injunction period, and often the competitive employment opportunity that he sought to pursue will have passed. *See, e.g., FLIR Syst. v. Parrish*, 95 Cal. Rptr. 3d 307 (Cal. App. 2009) (prospective business partner in former employees' new venture broke off discussions and rejected deal upon former employer's initiation of lawsuit). For some high-level employees, a competitor may be willing to wait for the employee to "sit out" the period of his noncompetition agreement. But for many ordinary employees, a preliminary injunction means lost career time, lost income, and lots of legal bills.

If an employer is successful in obtaining injunctive relief, what will the court order say? Where the employer successfully alleges breach of a noncompete, the court will enjoin the employee from competing. The scope of the injunction will reflect the terms of the contract, subject to any modifications the court may fashion to ensure that its effects are not unduly burdensome to the employee. In the case of a trade secret claim, the scope of the injunction is less clear. Trade secret law does not prohibit competition per se; rather, it prohibits misuse of certain information. Therefore, a preliminary injunction in a trade secret case might simply enjoin the employee from using or disclosing that information.

What if the former employer alleges the employee's new job is so closely related to his or her former position that the employee will inevitably use the employer's trade secrets? In *PepsiCo v. Redmond*, 54 F.3d 1262 (7th Cir. 1995), Pepsi sought to enjoin the former General Manager of its California Business Unit from taking a comparable position with rival drink manufacturer Quaker. It argued that Redmond had extensive knowledge of the company's annual operating plan, its pricing architecture, and its marketing and distribution strategies for the upcoming year. Redmond had signed a confidentiality agreement with Pepsi, but not a noncompete. Pepsi nonetheless sought an injunction against competition. The court granted it, finding that "unless Redmond possessed an uncanny ability to compartmentalize information, he would necessarily be making decisions about [Quaker's] Gatorade and Snapple by relying on his knowledge of [Pepsi's] trade secrets." *Id.* at 1269. The court explained:

> Admittedly, PepsiCo has not brought a traditional trade secret case, in which a former employee has knowledge of a special manufacturing process or customer list and can give a competitor an unfair advantage by transferring the technology or customers to that competitor. PepsiCo has not contended that Quaker has stolen the [Pepsi] All Sport formula or its list of distributors. Rather PepsiCo has asserted that Redmond cannot help but rely on PCNA trade secrets as he helps plot Gatorade and Snapple's new course, and that these secrets will enable Quaker to achieve a substantial advantage by knowing exactly how PCNA will price, distribute, and market its sports drinks and new age drinks and being able to respond strategically. . . .
>
> The defendants' arguments [that Quaker has not and does not intend to use Pepsi's confidential information, much of which would be useless to it anyway] fall somewhat short of the mark. Again, the danger of misappropriation in the present case is not that Quaker threatens to use PCNA's secrets to create distribution systems or co-opt PCNA's advertising and marketing ideas. Rather, PepsiCo believes that Quaker, unfairly armed with knowledge of PCNA's plans, will be able to anticipate its distribution, packaging, pricing, and marketing moves. . . . In other words, PepsiCo finds itself in the position of a coach, one of whose players has left, playbook in hand, to join the opposing team before the big game. Quaker and Redmond's protestations that their distribution systems and plans are entirely different from PCNA's are thus not really responsive.

Id. at 1269-70. Is *PepsiCo* consistent with what *CTI* teaches about the elements of a trade secret claim? Is it consistent with the distinction *Rem Metals* draws between protectable information and an employee's skills and experience? Note that both parties in *PepsiCo* agreed that Redmond had not taken any documents upon departure, nor was he likely to use directly any of the information he remembered. Does the risk to Pepsi that Redmond's decisions at Quaker would be informed by his awareness of Pepsi's strategies justify enjoining Redmond from starting his job? Consider Professor Alan Hyde's opinion of the case:

> PepsiCo never identified any specific piece of information that Redmond had and Quaker wanted. PepsiCo did not show that Redmond knew the recipe for All Sport, or new flavors being worked on secretly, or which athletes had been approached for endorsements, or anything of that sort.
>
> What *did* Redmond know? He was far from the key figure in All Sport. He was one of many regional general managers. He had access, said PepsiCo, to its "Strategic Plan" and "Annual Operating Plan" covering "financial goals, marketing plans, promotional event calendars, growth expectations, and operational changes." He knew which markets Pepsi would focus on, and some aspects of a new delivery system. In other words, he knew what any manager knows.
>
> The *PepsiCo* decision is unusually proplaintiff, [and therefore] not typical. It inhabits a world in which all managers on distribution lists for "strategic plans" and "annual operating plans" serve for life, and may have their departures to work in the area they know enjoined at the option of their employer. It seems not to relate at all to today's world of corporate downsizing and managerial layoffs. It does not rest on any economic analysis of the efficiency advantages of letting Redmond go as against letting PepsiCo enjoin him, even though the Court of Appeals for the Seventh Circuit is famous for its law and economic approach. Nor does it reinforce employment-at-will, to which, in other cases, that court has paid homage. Employees with other options, such as competent managers, may choose not to accept employment at will if, following involuntary termination, they will be unable to work in their area of expertise.

Alan Hyde, Working in Silicon Valley: Economic and Legal Analysis of a High-Velocity Labor Market 34-35 (2003). Is Professor Hyde suggesting that the PepsiCo decision is out of date? What characteristics of the modern labor market does he identify in his critique and how are they relevant to the legal protection of employer interests? Does the law need to better account for employee mobility in what Professor Hyde calls a "high-velocity labor market"? The inevitable disclosure doctrine has not fared well in the courts, *e.g.*, *Holton v. Physician Oncology Servs., LP*, 742 S.E.2d 702 (Ga. 2013) (no stand-alone inevitable disclosure doctrine in Georgia), although some continue to rely on it. *See Bimbo v. Botticella*, 613 F.3d 102, 118 (3d Cir. 2010) (the defendant subject to a confidentiality agreement was one of only seven people with the knowledge necessary to produce the "nooks and crannies" texture of plaintiff's popular Thomas' English Muffin product and was properly enjoined from competing when he posed a "substantial threat" of trade secret disclosure, in large part because of "suspicious conduct during his final weeks of employment.").

Professor Hyde's views substantially influenced the Restatement of Employment Law. After considerable debate, the final version of the Restatement of Employment Law narrows substantially the inevitable disclosure theory. § 8.05, cmt. b (Proposed Final Draft, April 18, 2014) (no injunction should issue absent "actual use or disclosure" or "a high likelihood, based on the employee's statements or conduct" that the employee will violate the restriction). It seems likely, therefore, that the focus of future suits will be on whether there was actual use, or some reason to suspect an intent to use, confidential information. However, if courts are less likely in the future to enjoin prophylactically disclosure of trade secrets, and if proof of actual disclosure is often difficult to establish, employers will have even more incentive to rely on noncompetition clauses to achieve their goals. To the extent that occurs, a lesser restraint will be replaced by a greater one.

Still, this does not mean that noncompetition terms moored to the former employer's interest in protecting disclosure of trade secrets are easily enforced. On the contrary, such clauses might fail for a host of reasons. Consider, for example, the court's refusal to enter an injunction based on a noncompetition agreement in *Earth-Web, Inc. v. Schlack*, 71 F. Supp. 2d 299 (S.D.N.Y. 1999). The court in that case first rejected the former employer's (EarthWeb) inevitable disclosure of trade secrets claim against its former employee (Schlack) who had left to take a job with an Internet startup (ITworld.com). The court then refused to enforce the noncompetition agreement Schlack had signed, concluding that ITworld was not a directly competitive business with Earthlink and that, in any event, the one-year restriction was too long "given the dynamic nature of this industry, its lack of geographical borders, and Schlack's former cutting-edge position with EarthWeb where his success depended on keeping abreast of daily changes in content on the Internet." *Id*. at 313. Even aside from these concerns, the court was not convinced an injunction was justified to protect the claimed secrets (the most salient of which was the claim that Schlack was intimately familiar with the "strategic thinking" behind the company's websites and its overall business plan):

> [A] serious question remains as to whether the "strategic thinking" behind EarthWeb's websites is necessarily revealed when those websites are launched on the Internet, and therefore not entitled to trade secret protection. Finally, even if Schlack knows where the "gaps or holes" remain in particular websites EarthWeb has not cited any case law for the proposition that a product's perceived deficiencies are trade secrets. . . .
>
> Based on these facts, the Court finds no imminent risk that Schlack will disclose or use EarthWeb's trade secrets in connection with his employment at ITworld.com. Consequently, EarthWeb has failed to demonstrate a likelihood of irreparable injury entitling it to judicial enforcement of the restrictive covenant, even if that covenant were applicable by its terms and otherwise reasonable in duration.

Id. at 315. As the final nail in the coffin, the court found that "enforcement of this provision would work a significant hardship on Schlack. When measured against the IT industry in the Internet environment, a one-year hiatus from the workforce is several generations, if not an eternity." *Id*. at 316.

Even if, unlike in *EarthWeb*, a noncompetition agreement premised on trade secrets protection is enforceable by injunction, remedies beyond such equitable relief can be problematic. Consider the next case.

═══ *Fishkin v. Susquehanna Partners, G.P.*
═══ *340 F. App'x 110 (3d Cir. 2009)*

VAN ANTWERPEN, Circuit Judge.

This appeal stems from a dispute between Appellant Susquehanna International Group, LLP ("SIG"), a securities trading firm, and two of its former employees, Cal Fishkin and Igor Chernomzav, who left SIG and formed a competing securities trading joint venture, TABFG, LLC ("TABFG"), in partnership with NT Prop Trading, LLC ("NT Prop"). . . .

I . . .

In the spring of 1999, Cal Fishkin and Igor Chernomzav began working for SIG as securities traders, and each executed an employment contract containing restrictive covenants. One such covenant, the "Non–Competition" clause, provided in part that,

> [f]or a period of nine (9) months following the later of the termination of [Employee's] employment or the third anniversary following Employee's entry into the training course, Employee shall not trade in any products in which he or she was trading for [SIG] at any time during the three (3) month period prior to the termination of Employee's employment.

The noncompetition clause also barred Fishkin and Chernomzav from disclosing confidential information about SIG's business and restricted them from associating with anyone employed at SIG during the nine months prior to their termination for a period of five years. The employment agreement provided SIG with alternative remedies in the event of a breach: (a) liquidated damages of $700,000 or $800,000, depending on when the breach occurred; or (b) injunctive relief and other remedies to which it was entitled at law.

In August 1999, SIG assigned Francis Wisniewski to trade Dow Futures, which are futures contracts in the Dow Jones Industrial Average ("DJIA"),[1] in the trading pit at the Chicago Board of Trade. Following about a month of unsuccessful trading, Wisniewski developed a formula for calculating the expected values of Dow Futures based on his observation that successful traders of Dow Futures monitored trading data for the S&P 500 Index. Because all of the individual stocks in the DJIA are also included in the S&P 500 Index, Dow Futures and S&P Futures tend to move in the same direction, with S&P Futures typically adjusting to market movements slightly before such adjustments are reflected in the price of Dow Futures. Accordingly, SIG's Dow Fair Value formula reflected the relationship between S&P Futures and Dow Futures. After developing this formula, Wisniewski created a spreadsheet to make the formula's calculations more quickly. After two months of trading Dow Futures, SIG reassigned Wisniewski. He saved the spreadsheet containing the Dow Fair Value formula.

In August 2001, SIG reassigned Wisniewski to the Dow Futures pit and, shortly thereafter, assigned Fishkin to trade Dow Futures (and engage in related hedging transactions) with Wisniewski. They used the Dow Fair Value formula that Wisniewski previously developed and traded the product until March 2003; for the year 2002, Wisniewski and Fishkin earned SIG net trading profits of approximately $30 million.

Fishkin grew dissatisfied with his compensation and, in June 2002, sought to negotiate a new employment contract with SIG. SIG did not immediately respond to his request. Later that year, Fishkin was approached by a non-SIG trader representing a group that later became NT Prop about whether he would be interested in forming a new company to trade Dow Futures. Fishkin indicated that he would be interested in participating in the new trading group as of March 2003, when his contract with SIG expired. Between December 2002 and April 2003, Fishkin met

---

1. A "future" is a derivative, which is a security that derives its value from an underlying security or asset. Specifically, a future is a contract to buy or sell a particular commodity at a specific price at a set time in the future. The futures at issue in this litigation were contracts to buy or sell stocks in the DJIA or Standard & Poor's ("S&P") 500 Index — Dow Futures and S&P Futures, respectively — at a set price on a set date.

with NT Prop representatives several times to discuss a trading venture; at one such meeting, NT Prop representatives asked Fishkin about SIG's profitability in trading Dow Futures. Fishkin told them that confidentiality provisions precluded him from revealing such information, but, when asked if he made more than $5 million at SIG, Fishkin replied by saying "you'll be pleased." In February 2003, Fishkin stopped trading for SIG and officially left the company in March 2003 (along with Chernomzav) to start a competing business, TABFG, LLC. On March 31, 2003, articles of incorporation were filed for TABFG. In late April 2003, TABFG and NT Prop entered into a joint venture to trade securities and financial products on the Chicago Board of Trade (as well as other exchanges). TABFG began trading on April 25, 2003; it traded for four and one-half months until September 16, 2003, when it was enjoined from doing so by the District Court.

On March 30, 2003, Fishkin and Chernomzav, along with Francis Wisniewski, filed suit in the Court of Common Pleas of Montgomery County, Pennsylvania, seeking declaratory and injunctive relief to the effect that the noncompetition agreements in their employment contracts with SIG were unenforceable. SIG filed a counterclaim seeking an injunction preventing Fishkin and Chernomzav from trading as well as damages for breach of contract, misappropriation of trade secrets, conversion, tortious interference with contract, and civil conspiracy. [TABFG and NT Prop were also joined and NT Prop removed the case to federal court.]

[SIG was granted a preliminary injunction to enforce Fishkin's and Chernomzav's noncompetition agreements by restraining them and TABFG from trading in violation of the former employees' promises; that injunction was ultimately made permanent. This appeal does not consider that ruling].

III.

A. *Damages for Contractual Breach*[8]

SIG appeals the District Court's ruling that, because SIG could not establish its lost profits resulting from Fishkin's and Chernomzav's breach of their employment contracts, it was entitled only to nominal damages on its breach of contract claim. SIG argues that the District Court erred in denying its motion for summary judgment and in barring it from recovering restitution damages measured by the net trading profits made by TABFG during the four and one half months of 2003 during which it actively traded at the Chicago Board of Trade.

Pennsylvania law recognizes three possible remedies for a breach of contract: expectation damages, reliance damages, and restitution damages. *Ferrer v. Trustees of Univ. of Pa.*, 825 A.2d 591, 609 (2002); *see also ATACS Corp. v. Trans World Commc'ns, Inc.*, 155 F.3d 659, 669 (3d Cir. 1998); *Trosky v. Civil Serv. Commc'n*, 652 A.2d 813, 817 (1995); RESTATEMENT (SECOND) OF CONTRACTS § 344 (1981). Although the preferred remedy for a contractual breach is the award of expectation damages, "measured by 'the losses caused and gains prevented by defendant's breach,'" *ATACS Corp.*), a party may also sue for reliance or restitution damages in limited instances.

---

8. The parties agree that the substantive contract law of Pennsylvania governs the issues raised in this dispute.

"This is especially so where an injured party is entitled to recover for breach of contract, but recovery based on traditional notions of expectation damages is clouded because of the uncertainty in measuring the loss in value to the aggrieved contracting party." *Id*.

Before the District Court, SIG conceded that it could not calculate its lost profits resulting from the breach, thereby rendering inappropriate the preferred remedy of expectation damages. Nevertheless, SIG argued that it was entitled to restitution damages, which require a breaching party to "disgorge the benefit he has received by returning it to the party that conferred it." *Trosky* (quoting RESTATEMENT (SECOND) OF CONTRACTS § 344). In particular, SIG asserts that it conferred benefits on Fishkin and Chernomzav, in the form of training and opportunities to learn the market and develop goodwill with other traders, and that the proper measure of restitution for those benefits would require the breaching parties to "disgorge" their net trading profits.

The District Court concluded that this Court's decision in *American Air Filter* barred SIG's claim for disgorgement of TABFG and NT Prop's profits. In that case, American Air Filter sued its former employee, McNichol, and his new employer for breach of a noncompetition agreement, seeking injunctive and monetary relief. . . . On appeal, American Air Filter sought to establish damages via (1) an accounting of profits made by McNichol's new employer, (2) McNichol's commissions earned with his new employer, and (3) its own decrease in profit in the territory served by the former employee after it left the company. This Court rejected American Air Filter's attempt to measure its damages by the profits of the breaching party's new employer, observing that "[t]he basic failing of the plaintiff's theory is that the defendant's profits are not necessarily equivalent to the plaintiff's losses. . . . To compel defendant to disgorge these profits could give plaintiff a windfall and penalize the defendant, neither of which serves the purpose of contract damages." *Id*. ("[A] defendant's profits are not the measure of a contract plaintiff's losses. . . .").

[*ATACS* recognized] the possible remedy of restitution damages as measured by "'the fair value of [the subcontractor's contribution]'" [which] corresponds to RESTATEMENT (SECOND) OF CONTRACTS § 344's characterization of a party's restitutionary interest as the "interest in having restored . . . any benefit that [it] has conferred on the other party." *See Trosky* (discussing § 344). Although SIG asserts that the benefits it conferred on Fishkin and Chernomzav "reasonably equate [ ] to the $3.5 million in profit they generated for themselves and their co-venturers," it has failed to demonstrate that the value of the benefit it conferred in the form of training and opportunities corresponds to the breaching parties' net trading profits. As the District Court noted, "the 'basic failing' of SIG's theory is that the counterclaim defendant's profits are not necessarily equivalent to SIG's losses, whether those losses are viewed as SIG's lost profits or SIG's restitution interest in the benefit of its training." Because SIG did not prove that the value of the benefit conferred equated to net trading profits earned by the breaching parties, the District Court's rejection of SIG's claim for restitution damages was proper.

We acknowledge that, in the securities trading industry, harm occasioned by the breach of a noncompetition covenant can be uniquely difficult to calculate. Nevertheless, securities trading firms are not without a means to protect themselves against this difficulty; they can include liquidated damages clauses in their employment agreements that provide for the disgorgement of profits by the breaching party. *See, e.g., Worldwide Auditing Servs., Inc. v. Richter*, 587 A.2d 772, 777–78 (1991) (holding that a liquidated damages provision that provided for disgorgement of profit attributable to breaching party's violation of contractual covenant was enforceable). The parties' contract did include a liquidated damages provision — drafted by SIG — that did not provide for disgorgement. Instead, the provision gave SIG the choice to (a) accept liquidated damages of $700,000 or $800,000, or (b) pursue an injunction and other available, legal remedies. SIG chose the latter.

Accordingly, we will affirm the District Court's denial of SIG's claim for restitution damages.

B. Trade Secret Misappropriation

SIG also appeals the District Court's [Order] denying trade secret protection for the knowledge that SIG's Dow Futures trading methodology was profitable.[11] In particular, SIG asserts that, during Fishkin's discussions with NT Prop representatives between December 2002 and April 2003, Fishkin was asked about the profitability of SIG's Dow Futures trading. Although Fishkin told NT Prop that confidentiality provisions precluded him from revealing profitability information, when asked whether he made more than $5 million trading for SIG, Fishkin responded by saying "[y]ou'll be pleased." SIG contends that Fishkin's disclosure contained an implied assertion that its Dow Futures trading method was profitable to some degree greater than $5 million and that the disclosure of the extent of SIG's profitability motivated NT Prop's representatives to form a joint venture with TABFG to trade Dow Futures with Fishkin and Chernomzav.

To prevail on a claim for trade secret protection in Pennsylvania,[12] the party seeking protection must demonstrate:

> (1) that the information constitutes a trade secret; (2) that it was of value to the employer and important in the conduct of his business; (3) that by reason of discovery or ownership the employer had the right to the use and enjoyment of the secret; and (4) that the secret was communicated to the defendant while employed in a position of trust and confidence under such circumstances as to make it inequitable and unjust for him to disclose it to others, or to make use of it himself, to the prejudice of his employer.

Doeblers' Pa. Hybrids, Inc. v. Doebler, 442 F.3d 812, 829 (3d Cir. 2006).

As the District Court noted, "[t]he threshold inquiry in a trade secret misappropriation claim under Pennsylvania law is whether the information is a trade secret." Pennsylvania courts have adopted the definition of a trade secret as set forth in RESTATEMENT OF TORTS § 757 cmt. b. *See Doebler.* This provision states that "[a] trade secret may consist of any formula, pattern, device or compilation of information which is used

---

11. The District Court also concluded that SIG's Dow Fair Value concept, formula, and spreadsheet did not warrant trade secret protection because, although SIG took steps to keep its method secret and the method was valuable for SIG, the Dow Fair Value trading approach was known and used by other traders, SIG did not invest a tremendous amount of time or money to develop the method, and other traders could duplicate SIG's approach fairly easily. *See also Doeblers' Pa. Hybrids, Inc. v. Doebler,* 442 F.3d 812, 829 (3d Cir. 2006) (setting forth six-factor test for whether a trade secret exists). On appeal, SIG abandons its claim that the trading strategy itself merited trade secret protection.

12. . . . Although Pennsylvania adopted the Uniform Trade Secrets Act, 12 Pa. Cons. Stat. Ann. § 5301 *et seq.,* effective April 19, 2004, the Act does not apply to misappropriation occurring before its effective date. Because the conduct at issue occurred before April 19, 2004, the Uniform Trade Secrets Act does not apply; instead, Pennsylvania's common law governing trade secrets applies.

in one's business, and which gives him an opportunity to obtain an advantage over competitors who do not know or use it." Information is not entitled to trade secret protection if it is generally known, or easily derived from available information, in the relevant business community.

This Court has enumerated several factors to consider when determining whether information constitutes a trade secret deserving of protection:

> (1) the extent to which the information is known outside of the owner's business; (2) the extent to which it is known by employees and others involved in the owner's business; (3) the extent of measures taken by the owner to guard the secrecy of the information; (4) the value of the information to the owner and to his competitors; (5) the amount of effort or money expended by the owner in developing the information; and (6) the ease or difficulty with which the information could be properly acquired or duplicated by others.

Doebler, accord RESTATEMENT OF TORTS § 757 cmt. b.

In some circumstances, courts have applied Pennsylvania law to permit trade secret protection of information concerning a company's profitability, such as that company's specific profit margins. *SI Handling Sys., Inc.*[*v. Heisley,* 753 F.2d 1244, 1260 (3d Cir. 1985)] (concluding that "range of data relating to materials, labor, overhead, and profit margin, among other things" qualified for trade secret protection to extent it was not "readily obtainable by anyone in the industry"); *see also Den–Tal–Ez, Inc. v. Siemens Capital Corp.,* 566 A.2d 1214, 1230 (1989) ("[I]nformation like . . . inventory data and projections, details unit costs and product-by-product profit margin data is protectable as trade secrets.").

Despite the recognition that some profitability information may warrant trade secret protection, the District Court properly rejected SIG's misappropriation claim. The information for which SIG sought protection was not its specific profit margins or its precise profitability; it was the fact of its profitability coupled with a limited suggestion of the extent of its profitability. In particular, Fishkin's statement that NT Prop representatives would be "pleased" with the profitability of SIG's Dow Futures trading method implied that SIG was profitable to some extent greater than $5 million.

As the District Court noted, the fact that Fishkin and Wisniewski were making money for SIG was already known to other traders. Under the circumstances, Fishkin's statement, while implying a certain threshold of profitability, did not sufficiently convey the extent of SIG's profitability to merit trade secret protection. Indeed, at the same time that Fishkin stated NT Prop would be pleased, he also declined to provide actual profitability information. A suggestion about the extent of a company's profitability, without more, is of limited value to the competitor and could easily be interpreted as mere puffery. Thus, Fishkin's statement is akin to the knowledge of the "hotness" of a product, which the Pennsylvania Supreme Court has rejected as a basis for trade secret protection. *See Van Products Co. [v. Gen. Welding & Fabricating Co.,* 213 A.2d 769 (Pa. 1965) (denying trade secret protection to a drying machine manufacturer when its former employee joined a competitor and disclosed fact that deliquescent desiccant air dryers were "hot product[s]"). Just as the Pennsylvania Supreme Court held that the "hotness" of a particular product was ascertainable to industry competitors in *Van Products,* other industry participants could observe and determine that SIG's trading in Dow Futures was profitable.

SIG points to more recent Pennsylvania case law in support of its claim for trade secret protection. Specifically, in *Air Products & Chemicals, Inc. v. Johnson,* 442 A.2d

1114 (1982), the Superior Court of Pennsylvania affirmed a trial court's issuance of an injunction preventing a former vice-president of Air Products from participating in certain employment practices at Liquid Air, a competitor of Air Products. The *Air Products* court found that "the identification of opportunities in the field as well as the extremely complex technological problems and commercial plans which must be made to exploit those opportunities" constituted information entitled to trade secret protection. While at Air Products, the employee had gained knowledge specific to the "on-site" business of industrial gas sales, including methods of delivery of on-site gas and an analysis of market opportunities; Liquid Air was not aware of this information. SIG contends that, like the information found protectable in *Air Products*, the knowledge that its trading business was profitable to an extent greater than $5 million was "extremely valuable to a competitor since it would cut the development risk involved in a similar project." Nevertheless, the justifications for protecting the information at issue in *Air Products*—specifically the "considerable expense" of Air Products' research and the "extremely complex technological problems" involved—are not implicated by SIG's claim for protection in the knowledge of the profitability of its Dow Futures trading method. Accordingly, the District Court's denial of SIG's claim of a trade secret in the fact and extent of the profitability of its Dow Fair Value trading method was proper. . . .

NOTES

1. *Enforcing the Noncompete.* The *Fishkin* case illustrates a number of complications at the intersection of noncompetition and trade secret law. First, SIG did "win" in the sense that it enforced its noncompete clause, with the apparent legitimate interest supporting that clause being preservation of confidential information. That may have caused real pain to the defendants, but it didn't put a dime in the plaintiffs' pocket.

With respect to its damages remedy, SIG failed to get any meaningful recovery for breach of the noncompete because, according to the court, it could not establish its damages resulting from the defendants' breach on any of the three bases that contracts law usually provides. This should not be so mysterious: The harm suffered by SIG did not flow from the defendants not working for SIG (since they did not have a contractual commitment to do so, their leaving was no violation). Instead, the expectation interest would be measured by the harm flowing from business lost to a competitor, and there was apparently no proof of that. *Cf. Southwest Stainless, LP v. Sappington*, 582 F.3d 1176 (10th Cir. 2009) (upholding damage award for lost profits employer suffered as a result of ex-employees' breach of noncompetition clause as measured by the loss of orders from two customers). As the court suggests, there are other measures of contract recovery (reliance and restitution) but neither did SIG any good: The court simply refused to equate what the defendants earned after their employment with the training it provided while they were employed—which seems consistent with *Rem Metals*. What SIG wanted—and failed to get—on its contract theory was the profits the defendants made by competing. This is standard contract analysis, although we have seen that where disloyalty is sufficiently implicated, *see* Note 6 on page 487, such profits may be disgorged. The court obviously did not think that principle was triggered on these facts. In an omitted footnote 9, the court noted that SIG had also sought restitution of the costs of its training program, which the district court had held inappropriate under Pennsylvania law.

2. *Liquidated Damages.* Difficulties of proof of damages are a classic reason for parties to include liquidated damages clauses in their noncompetition agreements. And, in fact, SIG had done just that — and pretty hefty ones. We will discuss the standards for valid liquidated damages clauses at the end of this chapter, but the important point for present purposes is that SIG forfeited its right to obtain up to $800,000 when it sought compensatory damages. Do you think the company (or its attorneys) should have been surer of their theory and their facts before they made that decision? Of course, hindsight is always 20/20, and maybe there were problems with the enforceability of the liquidated damages provision.

3. *Another Arrow.* But SIG had another arrow in its quiver — a claim for misappropriation of trade secrets. As the court's citation to the Restatement of Torts suggests, such a claim was traditionally viewed as a tort (in part because it reached those who "discovered the secret by improper means," §757(a)) although it had a contractual aspect (when "disclosure or use constitutes a breach of confidence," §757(b), with the entrusting typically arising by virtue of an employment relationship). While in a few states, trade secret law continues to be largely a common law creature, most jurisdictions, as happened in Pennsylvania, have now adopted the Uniform Trade Secrets Act. Where the UTSA has been enacted, it preempts common law claims. *See Ram Tool & Supply Co. v. HD Supply Constr. Supply, Ltd.*, 2014 Tenn. App. LEXIS 500 (Tenn. Ct. App. Aug. 19, 2014) (the UTSA preempted plaintiff's common law breach of fiduciary duty/loyalty claims insofar as they were based upon the misappropriation of trade secrets, but it did not preempt common law breach of fiduciary duty/loyalty claims for soliciting employees since they were not grounded in the misappropriation of trade secrets).

As you might guess, the remedy for misappropriation of a trade secret is more attractive than the remedy for a mere breach of contract. While the UTSA provides for both injunctive relief and damages measured by "the actual loss caused by misappropriation," it also permits recovery of "the unjust enrichment caused by misappropriation that is not taken into account in computing actual loss." § 3. This was exactly the measure SIG sought — and failed to get — for the contract breach.

4. *Qualifying as a Trade Secret.* Both the Restatement, §757, cmt. b, and Pennsylvania's six-factor test try to define "trade secret," but a more rigorous formulation is found in the Uniform Trade Secrets Act, a definition that has generally been adopted by the jurisdictions passing the uniform act:

> Information, including a formula, drawing, pattern, compilation including a customer list, program, device, method, technique or process that:
>
> (1) Derives independent economic value, actual or potential, from not being generally known to, and not being readily ascertainable by proper means by, other persons who can obtain economic value from its disclosure or use.
>
> (2) Is the subject of efforts that are reasonable under the circumstances to maintain its secrecy.

UTSA § 1. *See generally* Roger Milgrim and Eric E. Bensen on Trade Secrets (2013).

5. *Back to* SIG. The district court ruled against plaintiff as to the "Dow Fair Value concept, formula, and spreadsheet," because the approach was "known and used by other traders." More plausibly protected was the employer's profitability, but the problem for SIG was that Fishkin's disclosure "while implying a certain threshold of profitability, did not sufficiently convey the extent of SIG's profitability to merit trade secret protection."

6. *Disgorgement.* Trade secret law allows recovery of profits earned by the thief; disgorgement; contract law does not allow recovery of profits by the breaching party. But we saw that fiduciary law allows recovery both of compensation paid to a "faithless servant" and any profits that the employee may earn during his period of faithlessness. *See* page 487. But most, if not all, of the defendant's profits were earned after they ceased employment for the plaintiff—which meant they did not breach any duty of loyalty.

7. *Intersection of Noncompetition Law with Trade Secret Law.* As Professor Stone has suggested, *see* page 509, there is an interesting intersection of trade secret law and the law governing noncompetition agreements. From the employer's perspective, trade secret law is clearly superior in the remedies available, but, as *SIG* makes clear, that is true only when the employer can prove misappropriation of a trade secret. The decline of the inevitable disclosure doctrine has made it much less likely that trade secret law can bar an employer's competition where such proof is lacking.

A noncompete has the advantage of being prophylactic—it will prevent use of confidential information by barring the former employee from competing with her ex-employer. But a noncompete requires a legitimate employer interest, and one such interest is protecting trade secrets. Thus, an employer may have to be prepared to establish the existence of trade secrets to support an agreement not to compete In *SIG* itself, information as to plaintiff's profitability would probably have sufficed to support the noncompete—and the district court did enjoin the defendants—even though the court did not find an actual misappropriation.

But might a noncompetition clause be justified where no trade secret is concerned? The RESTATEMENT OF EMPLOYMENT LAW says yes: An employer has a legitimate interest in protecting "trade secrets . . . and other protectable confidential information that does not meet the statutory definition of a trade secret." § 8.07(b)(1) (Proposed Final Draft, April 18, 2014). The Restatement is singularly unhelpful in explaining what non-trade secret confidential information might be, and the justification for this broader approach—the employee "was put on notice of which information the employer considered confidential and proprietary"—seems dubious. The Restatement does caution that it does not include public domain information or "information that would be considered part of the general experience, knowledge, and skills that employee acquires" through her employment. Cmt. b. In any event, the Restatement is correct that some opinions would enforce a noncompete or a nondisclosure agreement in the absence of a trade secret. *E.g., Bernier v. Merrill Air Eng'rs*, 770 A.2d 97, 103 (Me. 2001) ("The confidential knowledge or information protected by a restrictive covenant need not be limited to information that is protected as a trade secret by the UTSA."); *Lamorte Burns & Co. v. Walters*, 770 A.2d 1158, 1166 (N.J. 2001) ("information need not rise to the level of a trade secret to be protected").

8. *"Negative Knowledge."* In some cases, the plaintiff seeks to protect what has been called "negative knowledge." In *EarthWeb*, excerpted above, for example, Earth-Web sought to protect the former employee's knowledge of the trial-and-error process EarthWeb had undertaken in implementing its products. The court discounted this information. Is it not valuable? Or is there simply no way to protect it in a way that does not unfairly disadvantage the employee? Courts take different approaches to this issue, with some reaching results contrary to *EarthWeb. See, e.g., Metallurgical Indus. Inc. v.*

Fourtek, Inc., 790 F.2d 1195, 1203 (5th Cir. 1986) (finding no distinction between "positive" and "negative" knowledge because "knowing what not to do often leads to knowing what to do"); *On-line Technologies, Inc. v. Perkin-Elmer Corp.*, 253 F. Supp. 2d 313, 323 (D. Conn. 2003) (finding "negative knowledge" to be a recognized form of "using" a trade secret proscribed under state law). The Restatement recognizes information that has "negative or 'dead end' value." § 8.02 cmt. b & Ill. 3.

9. *Reasonable Duration of a Noncompete in an Information Economy. EarthWeb* is also interesting because the court found a one-year duration in Schlack's contract to be unreasonably long. The same duration received implicit approval in *CTI*. Why? Is the difference due to the nature of the information being protected? The nature of the subsequent employment? The industry in question? Or is it just a difference in perspective between two courts deciding cases six years apart? In the last decade, courts have generally been stricter in deciding what constitutes a reasonable duration, recognizing that in many dynamic industries, knowledge does not remain secret or valuable for very long. *See, e.g., Estee Lauder Cos., Inc. v. Batra*, 430 F. Supp. 2d. 158 (S.D.N.Y. 2006) (reducing 12-month restraint with international scope to 5 months in recognition of limited long-term utility of marketing information). On the other hand, some courts are willing to enforce noncompetes of as much as three years or more, particularly where the industry in question is more stable or different interests, such as long-term client relationships, are at stake.

10. *Competition Defined.* The reach of any noncompetition agreement depends on the definition of "competition," which is why it is best drafting practice to define the term. But there are landmines in the process. Using a very general definition of competition can sometimes help employers avoid a court finding that the at-issue activity is not competition, but it also creates the risk of overbreadth. If an agreement does not set out a clear definition of competition, the court must reach its own conclusion based on the facts submitted about the nature of the two businesses. *See, e.g., Victoria's Secret Stores, Inc. v. May Dept. Stores Co.*, 157 S.W.3d 256, 261 (Mo. App. 2004) (finding that specialty lingerie store and department store that carried lingerie were not in "material competition" under terms of the noncompete).

PROBLEM

8-2. Julie Hanaco was a biomedical engineer. While in graduate school, she worked for a university-sponsored hospital outreach program as a technical liaison for wheelchair-bound patients. Her job consisted of assessing and translating the medical needs of patients into technical requirements for the production of customized wheelchairs. After graduating, she was hired by Invocare Corp. as a product manager in its sales and marketing department with responsibility for research and development of motorized wheelchairs. Upon hire, she signed a contract prohibiting her "for a period of three years from termination of employment with Invocare, from rendering services as an officer, director, partner or employee, or otherwise providing assistance to, any competitor in the production of custom wheelchairs or other custom medical equipment."

Hanaco worked for Invocare for three years, during which time she was a key employee in the research, testing, and production of Invocare's "Mark V" motorized wheelchair. Although she was not primarily responsible for marketing, she was copied on documents containing the marketing strategy for the Mark V and related financial documentation. One month prior to the public debut of the Mark V, Hanaco left Invocare and opened her own biomedical engineering consulting company. She was immediately approached by Suncare, an Invocare competitor in the end stages of a two-year development process for a new prototype chair. Suncare wants to hire Hanaco as a technical liaison to conduct field trials with potential users of its new chair.

How would you advise Hanaco? Can she take the job with Suncare? If she declines, is she still at risk of liability by running her consulting company? Would it make a difference to know that the typical lead time for developing and producing a new prototype wheelchair is two years? Or that once a new chair debuts, it is common in the industry for competitors to "reverse engineer" the product to discern its technical components?

Note on Employee Creative Works and Inventions

The preceding cases dealt with disputes over information — the employers alleged that the workers had a competitive advantage as a result of the knowledge they obtained or the confidences they received during the course of their employment. In some instances, however, particularly in creative or technically innovative fields, parties will dispute ownership of a particular project or invention that the employee wishes to use subsequent to employment, either herself or on behalf of a competitor. Questions of ownership in such situations can be avoided through private ordering — worker and firm agree in advance how to allocate such rights. When such agreement does not exist, however, intellectual property law, including copyright and patent protection, must dictate the result. We have seen one example of a dispute between workers and firms over ownership and future use of such work product and related works in *Natkin v. Winfrey* in Chapter 1, reproduced at page 16. In that case the plaintiffs were photographers, hired to shoot photos at the *Oprah Winfrey Show*, who claimed the show had violated their copyright rights by using their photos in publicity material. This note provides a brief overview of the legal framework governing claims to such property interests.

A.   Employee-Authored Creative Works

The Copyright Act of 1976 provides that copyright protection subsists "in original works of authorship fixed in any tangible medium of expression, now known or later developed, from which they can be perceived, reproduced, or otherwise communicated." 17 U.S.C. § 102. Works of authorship include literary works, artistic works, motion pictures, sound recordings, and other works including some forms of software code. The statute gives copyright owners the exclusive right to reproduce the copyrighted work; to prepare derivative works; to distribute, license, and sell the work; and, in certain circumstances, to display and perform the work. *See id.* Subject to various qualifications, a copyright owner has the sole prerogative to exercise these rights and to exclude others from doing so during the term of the copyright, which is the life of the author plus 70 years. *See* 17 U.S.C. § 302.

Copyright ownership "vests initially in the author or authors of the work." 17 U.S.C. § 201(a). Generally, the author is the party who actually creates the copyright-able work. The statute provides an important exception, however, for "works made for hire." *See id.* at § 201(b). If the work is for hire, "the employer or other person for whom the work was prepared is considered the author" and owns the copyright, unless there is a written agreement to the contrary. *Id.* A work is for hire if it was "prepared by an employee within the scope of his or her employment" or, in some circumstances, specially ordered or commissioned by written agreement. *See* 17 U.S.C. § 101.

Thus, the operative inquiry in most copyright disputes between firm and worker is whether the worker created the work as an employee acting within the scope of employment, rather than as an independent contractor. As *Natkin* indicated, the Supreme Court set forth a nonexhaustive, 13-factor test for determining employment status for such purposes in *Community for Creative Non-Violence v. Reid*, 490 U.S. 730 (1989). The *Reid* inquiry has resulted in significant litigation, and the contours of the employment relationship therefore may be important in the many areas of the economy in which creative activity is important to business operations, including the creative arts, publishing, advertising, music, media, technology, and communications sectors.

Of course, as the statutory scheme clearly contemplates, the difficulties in distinguishing employees from independent contractors usually may be avoided by contract. The "work for hire" rule is merely the default. The status of the underlying relationship does not matter if the parties have agreed in writing to share one or more rights to the work or allocate all rights to one party. This works both ways: An "employee" can contract to retain her copyright, or an independent contractor can contract to assign it. Again, *Natkin* provides a good example: The entire dispute between the photographers and the production company over employment status could have been avoided if the parties had negotiated and signed a commission or licensing agreement clearly allocating rights regarding the photographs.

The book you are reading was written by law professors as part of their scholarly duties, and with the support of their law schools. Neither of the law schools involved has a specific policy dealing with copyrights. Do Professors Glynn, Sullivan, and Arnow-Richman own the copyright, or do Seton Hall and Denver have a claim? Who else might have an ownership interest? Look at the copyright page to determine one party's (admittedly not disinterested) views on the matter. How do you think this entity (who is neither the employee nor the employer) obtained copyright ownership?

B. Employee Inventions

Under the existing patent regime, *see* 35 U.S.C. § 101 *et seq.*, whoever invents or discovers any new, useful, and nonobvious "process, machine, manufacture, or composition of matter, or any new and useful improvement thereof" may obtain a patent for such invention or discovery, subject to various conditions. When such an invention is made, the inventor often has a choice between trade secret protection and patent protection (although not every trade secret satisfies the requirements for patentability). The basic trade-off is between the time-limited but exclusive rights given by patent law and the theoretically perpetual (but less absolute) protection provided by trade secret law. As we have seen, a trade secret essentially evaporates once it becomes generally known.

In contrast, the patent holder has the right to exclude others from making, using, or selling the patented invention or discovery during the term of the patent, generally 20 years from the date of filing. *See* 35 U.S.C. § 271. Federal law provides that patent rights may be assigned only if the assignment is in writing, *see* 35 U.S.C. § 261, but the enforceability of assignments in the employment context is usually governed by state law. *See, e.g., University Patents, Inc. v. Kligman*, 762 F. Supp. 1212, 1219 (E.D. Pa. 1991); *see also United States v. Dubilier Condenser Corp.*, 289 U.S. 178, 187 (1933) ("The respective rights and obligations of employer and employee, touching an invention conceived by the latter, spring from the contract of employment.").

If a person invents or discovers something patentable during employment, he or she is the presumptive owner of the invention and of the resulting patent. RESTATEMENT OF EMPLOYMENT LAW § 8.09(a) (Proposed Final Draft, April 18, 2014). The operative default rule in the patent context is therefore opposite that in copyright, where, again, the employer presumptively owns employee-authored works. As with the copyright regime, however, patent law recognizes the primacy of private ordering through agreements allocating rights between worker and firm. *See Dubilier Condenser Corp.*, 289 U.S. at 187-88. Further, it shifts the default principle in one important way: Even absent an employee's outright assignment of the patent after it is obtained, the employer will own the patent if it hired the employee to invent or discover its subject. *See id.* at 187 ("One employed to make an invention, who succeeds, during his term of service, in accomplishing that task, is bound to assign to his employer any patent obtained."). *See* RESTATEMENT § 8.09(b). When the employment contract expressly so provides, the right of assignment and the default rule coincide. *See id.* In the absence of an express agreement, however, the employer may demonstrate from the circumstances of employment an implied agreement by the employee to invent on behalf of the employer. *See id.* at 187-88. Such an agreement may be inferred from employer instructions and employee duties, among other things, although courts sometimes express reluctance to recognize such implied terms. *See, e.g., id.* at 188; *Standard Parts Co. v. Peck*, 264 U.S. 52, 58-59 (1923); *see also Scott Sys., Inc. v. Scott*, 996 P.2d 775, 778 (Colo. Ct. App. 2000) ("If an employee's job duties include the responsibility for inventing or for solving a particular problem that requires invention, any invention created by that employee during the performance of those responsibilities belongs to the employer . . . and the courts will find an implied contract obligation to assign any rights to the employer.").

Obviously then, firms that foresee substantial, innovative activity have a strong incentive to include job descriptions and assignment clauses in employment agreements that clarify ownership rights and the employee's inventive duties. Workers seeking to retain the fruits of their activity have a countervailing incentive to bargain for ownership or co-ownership rights for their inventions or to include language that limits the scope of their duties to the employer. State law often places some restrictions on employee assignments of rights to inventions; for example, some state statutes preclude assignments of inventions unrelated to the employer's business, developed entirely on the employees' own time, or for which no employer equipment or resources were used. *See, e.g.,* CAL. LAB. CODE § 2870 (2014); MINN. STAT. ANN. § 181.78 (2014); N.C. GEN. STAT. § 66-57.1 (2013). Nevertheless, employee assignment clauses are standard among firms engaged in research and development, and such assignments are typically enforced if reasonably tied to the nature of the employee's position.

Some employers seek further protection by including so-called "holdover" or "trailer" clauses in their employment agreements. These clauses commonly require an employee to assign to the employer patent rights for inventions created within a defined period after termination of the employment relationship if the invention is related to or conceived as a result of the employee's work for the employer. In determining whether such clauses are enforceable, courts may engage in a "reasonableness" or "balancing" inquiry akin to those applied to restrictive covenants; that is, they assess the extent to which holdover provisions may protect legitimate employer interests, prevent a former employee from seeking other employment, and adversely affect the public interest. *See, e.g., Ingersoll-Rand Co. v. Ciavatta*, 542 A.2d 879, 888 (N.J. 1988).

Even if an employee retains ownership of a patent created during the course of employment, the employer may be entitled to a limited equitable use known as a "shop right." A shop right grants—or compels the employee to grant—the employer a nonexclusive right to practice or use the employee-owned invention when the employee conceived of and perfected the invention during the hours of employment, working with the employer's materials, tools, and other resources. *See Dubilier Condenser Corp.*, 289 U.S. at 187-88; *Francklyn v. Guilford Packing Co.*, 695 F.2d 1158, 1161 (9th Cir. 1983); RESTATEMENT OF EMPLOYMENT LAW § 8.10. Some courts have taken a broader view, suggesting that a shop right will exist when, after viewing the circumstances surrounding the development of the patented invention and the inventor's activities, "the facts of a particular case demand, under principles of equity and fairness, a finding that a 'shop right' exists." *McElmurry v. Arkansas Power and Light Co.*, 995 F.2d 1576, 1582-83 (Fed. Cir. 1993). The shop right extends throughout the term of the patent, but, generally, the shop right may not be assigned to third parties. *See, e.g., Wommack v. Durham*, 715 F.2d 962, 965 (5th Cir. 1983).

For further discussion of employee creative works and inventions, and the application of copyright and patent law within the workplace, *see* Dan L. Burk, *Intellectual Property and the Firm*, 71 U. CHI. L. REV. 3 (2004); Catherine L. Fisk, *Authors at Work: The Origins of the Work-for-Hire Doctrine*, 15 YALE J. L. & HUMAN. 1 (2003); Robert P. Merges, *The Law and Economics of Employee Inventions*, 13 HARV. J. L. & TECH. 1 (1999).

4. Disputes over Customers and Co-workers

Hopper v. All Pet Animal Clinic, Inc.
861 P.2d 531 (Wyo. 1993)

TAYLOR, Justice.

[This appeal tests the enforceability of a covenant not to compete in an employment contract. The district court found that the covenant was reasonable and enjoined a veterinarian from practicing small animal medicine for three years within a five-mile radius. The veterinarian appealed.]

We hold that the covenant's three year duration imposed an unreasonable restraint of trade permitting only partial enforcement of a portion of that term of the covenant. . . .

II. Facts

Following her graduation from Colorado State University, Dr. Glenna Hopper (Dr. Hopper) began working part-time as a veterinarian at the All Pet Animal Clinic, Inc. (All Pet) in July of 1988. All Pet specialized in the care of small animals; mostly domesticated dogs and cats, and those exotic animals maintained as household pets. Dr. Hopper practiced under the guidance and direction of the President of All Pet, Dr. Robert Bruce Johnson (Dr. Johnson).

Dr. Johnson, on behalf of All Pet, offered Dr. Hopper full-time employment in February of 1989. The oral offer included a specified salary and potential for bonus earnings as well as other terms of employment. According to Dr. Johnson, he conditioned the offer on Dr. Hopper's acceptance of a covenant not to compete, the specific details of which were not discussed at the time. Dr. Hopper commenced full-time employment with All Pet under the oral agreement in March of 1989 and relocated to Laramie, discontinuing her commute from her former residence in Colorado.

A written Employment Agreement incorporating the terms of the oral agreement was finally executed by the parties on December 11, 1989. Ancillary to the provisions for employment, the agreement detailed the terms of a covenant not to compete:

> 12. This agreement may be terminated by either party upon 30 days' notice to the other party. Upon termination, Dr. Hopper agrees that she will not practice small animal medicine for a period of three years from the date of termination within 5 miles of the corporate limits of the City of Laramie, Wyoming. Dr. Hopper agrees that the duration and geographic scope of that limitation is reasonable.

The agreement was antedated to be effective to March 3, 1989.

[The parties subsequently agreed to an Addendum in 1990 which raised Hopper's salary, eliminated the bonus, and added a newly acquired corporate entity, Alpine Animal Hospital, Inc. (Alpine), Laramie, to share Hopper's services. The modified agreement reaffirmed the covenant not to compete.]

One year later, reacting to a rumor that Dr. Hopper was investigating the purchase of a veterinary practice in Laramie, Dr. Johnson asked his attorney to prepare a letter which was presented to Dr. Hopper. The letter, dated June 17, 1991, stated:

> I have learned that you are considering leaving us to take over the small animal part of Dr. Meeboer's practice in Laramie.
>
> When we negotiated the terms of your employment, we agreed that you could leave upon 30 days' notice, but that you would not practice small animal medicine within five miles of Laramie for a three-year period. We do not have any non-competition agreement for large-animal medicine, which therefore does not enter into the picture.
>
> I am willing to release you from the non-competition agreement in return for a cash buy-out. I have worked back from the proportion of the income of All-Pet and Alpine which you contribute and have decided that a reasonable figure would be $40,000.00, to compensate the practice for the loss of business which will happen if you practice small-animal medicine elsewhere in Laramie.
>
> If you are willing to approach the problem in the way I suggest, please let me know and I will have the appropriate paperwork taken care of.

Sincerely,
[Signed]
R. Bruce Johnson,
D.V.M.

Dr. Hopper responded to the letter by denying that she was going to purchase Dr. Meeboer's practice. Dr. Hopper told Dr. Johnson that the Employment Agreement was not worth the paper it was written on and that she could do anything she wanted to do. Dr. Johnson terminated Dr. Hopper's employment and informed her to consider the 30-day notice as having been given. . . .

[Dr. Hopper subsequently purchased a small and large animal practice within the city of Laramie. The practice grew from 368 clients at the time of purchase to approximately 950 at the time of trial, including 187 clients who were also clients of All Pet or Alpine. Small animal work contributed from 51 to 52 percent of Dr. Hopper's gross income in the practice.]

IV.   Discussion. . . .

Two principles, the freedom to contract and the freedom to work, conflict when courts test the enforceability of covenants not to compete. There is general recognition that while an employer may seek protection from improper and unfair competition of a former employee, the employer is not entitled to protection against ordinary competition. . . .

A valid and enforceable covenant not to compete requires a showing that the covenant is: (1) in writing; (2) part of a contract of employment; (3) based on reasonable consideration; (4) reasonable in durational and geographical limitations; and (5) not against public policy. *A.E.P. Industries, Inc. v. McClure*, 302 S.E.2d 754, 760 (1983). Wyo. Stat. § 1-23-105 (1988). The reasonableness of a covenant not to compete is assessed based upon the facts of the particular case and a review of all of the circumstances. . . .

Wyoming has previously recognized that the legitimate interests of the employer, covenantee, which may be protected from competition include: (a) the employer's trade secrets which have been communicated to the employee during the course of employment; (b) confidential information communicated by the employer to the employee, but not involving trade secrets, such as information on a unique business method; and (c) special influence by the employee obtained during the course of employment over the employer's customers.

The enforceability of a covenant not to compete using the rule of reason analysis depends upon a determination, as a matter of law, that the promise not to compete is ancillary to the existence of an otherwise valid transaction or relationship. . . .

When Dr. Johnson made the oral promise of employment to Dr. Hopper, the specific terms of the covenant were not discussed. Dr. Johnson testified that no terms for a geographic radius or time restriction on competition were stated during formation of the oral contract of employment. Without terms and without a writing, a promise not to compete at this time failed as ancillary to the creation of the relationship.

The written Employment Agreement Dr. Hopper signed does contain a covenant not to compete which is ancillary to the previously agreed provisions for employment memorialized from the oral contract. RESTATEMENT (SECOND) OF CONTRACTS, *supra*, § 187 cmt. b recognizes that in an ongoing transaction or relationship, a promise not to compete may be made before the termination of the relationship and still be ancillary *as long as it is supported by consideration* and meets other requirements for enforceability. . . .

Wyoming has never determined whether a promise not to compete made during the employment relationship is supported merely by the consideration of continued employment or must be supported by separate contemporaneous consideration. This court's decision in *Ridley* [*v. Krout*, 180 P.2d 124 (Wyo. 1947)] offers useful insight. An employment relationship with a mechanic was formed prior to the execution of the written contract containing the employee's ancillary promise not to compete. *Ridley*. While we did not specifically address the sufficiency of the consideration, the written contract with the mechanic contained separate consideration. In addition to the promise to continue employment for a term of ten years, the employer agreed, as consideration for the promise not to compete, to teach the mechanic new skills as a locksmith and in business operation.

Authorities from other jurisdictions are not in agreement on whether continued employment provides sufficient consideration or whether separate consideration is required to create an ancillary covenant not to compete made during the existence of the relationship. *See* Howard A. Specter & Matthew W. Finkin, Individual Employment Law and Litigation § 8.02 (1989) (collecting cases). We believe strong public policy favors separate consideration.

> The better view, even in the at-will relationship, is to require additional consideration to support a restrictive covenant entered into during the term of the employment. This view recognizes the increasing criticism of the at-will relationship, the usually unequal bargaining power of the parties, and the reality that the employee rarely "bargains for" continued employment in exchange for a potentially onerous restraint on the ability to earn a living.

Id., § 8.02 at 450. The separate consideration necessary to support an ancillary promise not to compete made after creation of the employment relationship would include promotion, pay raise, special training, employment benefits or other advantages for the employee.

The written Employment Agreement Dr. Hopper signed contains no evidence of separate consideration, such as a pay raise or other benefit, in exchange for the covenant not to compete. Standing alone, the covenant not to compete contained in the Employment Agreement failed due to lack of separate consideration. However, on June 1, 1990, the parties executed the Addendum to Agreement. In that agreement, Dr. Hopper accepted a pay raise of $550.00 per month. This agreement restates, by incorporation, the terms of the covenant not to compete. We hold that the Addendum to Agreement, with its pay raise, represented sufficient separate consideration supporting the reaffirmation of the covenant not to compete. Therefore, the district court's findings that the covenant was ancillary to an employment contract and that consideration was received in exchange for the covenant are not clearly erroneous. . . .

Employers are entitled to protect their business from the detrimental impact of competition by employees who, but for their employment, would not have had the ability to gain a special influence over clients or customers. . . .

The special interests of All Pet and Alpine identified by the district court as findings of fact are not clearly erroneous. Dr. Hopper moved to Laramie upon completion of her degree prior to any significant professional contact with the community. Her introduction to All Pet's and Alpine's clients, client files, pricing policies, and practice development techniques provided information which exceeded the skills she brought to her employment. While she was a licensed and trained veterinarian when she accepted employment, the additional exposure to clients and knowledge of clinic operations her employers shared with her had a monetary value for which the employers are entitled to reasonable protection. . . .

Enforcement of the practice restrictions Dr. Hopper accepted as part of her covenant not to compete does not create an unreasonable restraint of trade. While the specific terms of the covenant failed to define the practice of small animal medicine, the parties' trade usage provided a conforming standard of domesticated dogs and cats along with exotic animals maintained as household pets. As a veterinarian licensed to practice in Wyoming, Dr. Hopper was therefore permitted to earn a living in her chosen profession without relocating by practicing large animal medicine, a significant area of practice in this state. The restriction on the type of activity contained in the covenant was sufficiently limited to avoid undue hardship to Dr. Hopper while protecting the special interests of All Pet and Alpine.

In addition, as a professional, Dr. Hopper certainly realized the implications of agreeing to the terms of the covenant. While she may have doubted either her employers' desires to enforce the terms or the legality of the covenant, her actions in establishing a small animal practice violated the promise she made. In equity, she comes before the court with unclean hands. If Dr. Hopper sought to challenge the enforceability of the covenant, her proper remedy was to seek a declaratory judgment.

The public will not suffer injury from enforcement of the covenant. . . . While Dr. Hopper provided competent care to All Pet's and Alpine's clients, her services there were neither unique nor uncommon. Furthermore, the services which Dr. Hopper provided in her new practice to small animal clients were available at several other veterinary clinics within Laramie. Evidence did not challenge the public's ability to receive complete and satisfactory service from these other sources. Dr. Hopper's short term unavailability resulting from enforcement of a reasonable restraint against unfair competition is unlikely, as a matter of law, to produce injury to the public. . . .

The geographical limit contained in the covenant not to compete restricts Dr. Hopper from practicing within a five mile radius of the corporate limits of Laramie. As a matter of law, this limit is reasonable in this circumstance. The evidence presented at trial indicated that the clients of All Pet and Alpine were located throughout the county. Despite Wyoming's rural character, the five mile restriction effectively limited unfair competition without presenting an undue hardship. Dr. Hopper could, for example, have opened a practice at other locations within the county.

A durational limitation should be reasonably related to the legitimate interest which the employer is seeking to protect.

> In determining whether a restraint extends for a longer period of time than necessary to protect the employer, the court must determine how much time is needed for the risk of injury to be reasonably moderated. When the restraint is for the purpose of protecting customer relationships, its duration is reasonable only if it is no longer than necessary for the employer to put a new [individual] on the job and for the new employee to have a reasonable opportunity to demonstrate his [or her] effectiveness to the customers. If a restraint on this ground is justifiable at all, it seems that a period of several months would

usually be reasonable. If the selling or servicing relationship is relatively complex, a longer period may be called for. Courts seldom criticize restraints of six months or a year on the grounds of duration as such, and even longer restraints are often enforced.

[Expert testimony at trial indicated that 70 percent of veterinary clients visit a clinic more than once per year. The remaining 30 percent of the clients use the clinic at least one time per year. In addition,] Dr. Johnson estimated that at All Pet and Alpine, the average client seeks veterinarian services one and one-half times a year. . . . Dr. Johnson admitted that influence over a client disappears in an unspecified "short period of time," but expressed a view that three years was "safe." He also agreed that the number of clients possibly transferring from All Pet or Alpine to Dr. Hopper would be greatest in the first year and diminish in the second year.

We are unable to find a reasonable relationship between the three year durational requirement and the protection of All Pet's and Alpine's special interests. . . . Based on figures of client visits, a replacement veterinarian at All Pet and Alpine would be able to effectively demonstrate his or her own professionalism to virtually all of the clinics' clients within a one year durational limit. . . .

Under the formulation of the rule of reason inquiry, [in] the first Restatement of Contracts, the unreasonableness of any non-divisible term of a covenant not to compete made the entire covenant unenforceable. . . .

The conceptual difficulty of the position taken in the former Restatement of Contracts, *supra*, § 518 leads to strong criticism by noted authors and the rejection of this so-called "blue pencil rule" by many courts. In very many cases the courts have held the whole contract to be illegal and void where the restraint imposed was in excess of what was reasonable and the terms to the agreement indicated no line of division that could be marked with a "blue pencil." In the best considered modern cases, however, the court has decreed enforcement as against the defendant whose breach has occurred within an area in which restriction would clearly be reasonable, even though the terms of the agreement imposed a larger and unreasonable restraint. Thus, the seller of a purely local business who promised not to open a competing store anywhere in America has been prevented by an injunction from running such a store with the same block as the one that he sold.

We believe the ability to narrow the term of a covenant not to compete and enforce a reasonable restraint permits public policy to be served in the most effective manner. Businesses function through the efforts of dedicated employees who provide the services and build the products desired by customers. Both the employer and the employee invest in success by expressing a commitment to one another in the form of a reasonable covenant not to compete. For the employer, this commitment may mean providing the employee with access to trade secrets, customer contacts or special training. These assets of the business are entitled to protection. For the employee, who covenants as part of a bargained for exchange, the covenant provides notice of the limits both parties have accepted in their relationship. The employee benefits during his tenure with the employer by his or her greater importance to the organization as a result of the exposure to the trade secrets, customer contacts or special training. When the employer-employee relationship terminates, a reasonable covenant not to compete then avoids unfair competition by the employee against the former employer and the specter, which no court would enforce, of specific performance of the employment agreement. When the parties agree to terms of a covenant, one of which is too broad, the court is permitted to enforce a narrower term which effectuates these public policy goals without arbitrarily invalidating the entire agreement between the parties and creating an uncertain business environment. In those instances where a truly unreasonable covenant operates as a restraint of trade, it will not be enforced.

. . . We, therefore, affirm the district court's conclusions of law that the type of activity and geographic limitations contained in the covenant not to compete were reasonable and enforceable as a matter of law. Because we hold that the covenant's three year durational term imposed a partially unreasonable restraint of trade, we remand for a modification of the judgment to enjoin Dr. Hopper from unfair competition for a duration of one year from the date of termination.

NOTES

1. *Consideration. All Pet* begins with a treatment of contract formalities. Generally, an offer of employment is treated as the requisite consideration for the employee's covenant not to compete. However, where the employee signs an agreement after employment commences, courts take different approaches. Some, probably most, hold that continued employment is sufficient consideration for the noncompete agreement where the worker is employed at will and could otherwise be terminated. *See, e.g., Summits 7, Inc. v. Kelly*, 886 A.2d 365, 372-73 (Vt. 2005) *Lake Land Emp. Group of Akron, LLC v. Columber*, 804 N.E.2d 27, 31-32 (Ohio 2004). Others, like *All Pet*, require further consideration to support the post-hire agreement. *See, e.g., McKasson v. Johnson*, 315 P.3d 1138 (Wash. App. 2013) (continued employment not sufficient consideration to support a noncompetition clause and supposed other consideration in the form of oral promises was not valid since the plain language of the written contract's integration clause expressly disclaimed the enforceability of any such agreements); *Fifield v. Premier Dealer Servs., Inc.*, 993 N.E.2d 938, 943-44 (Ill. App. Ct. 2013) ("Illinois courts have repeatedly held that there must be at least two years or more of continued employment to constitute adequate consideration in support of a restrictive covenant," even if the employee resigns instead of being terminated.). *See generally* Tracy L. Staidl, *Enforceability of Noncompetition Agreements When Employment Is At-Will: Reformulating the Analysis*, 2 EMPLOYEE RTS. & EMP. POL'Y J. 95 (1998) (summarizing approaches). Do you recognize this concept of "separate" consideration from courts' treatment of employer modifications of contractually binding handbooks? *See* Chapter 3.

In this case, Dr. Hopper received a pay raise upon re-executing her employment contract, which included the noncompete. How meaningful is that raise if her employment is at will and she can be fired at any time? What other types of consideration might support a post-hire noncompete? What if Dr. Johnson offered Hopper an All Pet Animal Clinic T-shirt and a free pass to a local movie theater in exchange for her signature? Would the noncompete be enforceable?

2. *Involuntarily Terminated Employees.* A related question is whether noncompetes are enforceable if the at-will employee is terminated involuntarily. Although Dr. Hopper may have been planning to leave, she was fired by Dr. Johnson. Some courts have concluded that an employer that terminates its employee forfeits the right to enforce that employee's noncompete agreement. *See, e.g., Insulation Corp. of Am. v. Brobston*, 667 A.2d 729, 735 (Pa. Super. Ct. 1995) ("The employer who fires an employee for failing to perform in a manner that promotes the employer's business interests deems the employee worthless. . . . [I]t is unreasonable as a matter of law to permit the employer to retain unfettered control over that which it has effectively discarded."). Other courts seem to disregard the manner of termination, focusing solely on the reasonableness of the restraint. *See, e.g., James & Penhall Co. Roberson v. C.P. Allen Const. Co., Inc.*, 50 So. 3d 471 (Ala. App. 2010); *Twenty Four Collection v. Keller*, 389 So. 2d 1062 (Fla. Dist. Ct. App. 1980). Yet a third approach relies on principles of good faith and fair dealing. In an omitted part of the decision, *All Pet* considered the good faith of Dr. Johnson's actions. Noting that the agreement permitted termination at will, subject to a notice requirement, the court stated:

> Without more, the terms present the potential for an unreasonable restraint of trade. For example, if an employer hired an employee at will, obtained a covenant not to compete, and then terminated the employee, without cause, to arbitrarily restrict competition, we believe such conduct would constitute bad faith. Simple justice requires that a termination by the employer of an at will employee be in good faith if a covenant not to compete is to be enforced.
>
> Under the present facts, we cannot say that the termination of Dr. Hopper occurred in bad faith. Trial testimony presented evidence of increasing tension prior to termination in the professional relationship between Dr. Johnson and Dr. Hopper. This tension, however, did not appear to result in the termination. The notice of termination was given after Dr. Hopper was confronted about her negotiations to purchase a competitive practice and after Dr. Hopper had termed the employment contract worthless. We cannot find in these facts a bad faith termination which would provide a reason to depart from the district court's finding that the contract of employment was valid.

Hopper, 861 P.2d. at 541-42; *see also Rao v. Rao*, 718 F.2d 219, 223 (7th Cir. 1983) (concluding that implied contractual covenant of good faith and fair dealing precludes employer enforcement of noncompete following unjustified termination of employee). The RESTATEMENT OF EMPLOYMENT LAW would make restrictive covenants generally unenforceable where the employer materially breaches the governing contract, § 8.06 cmt. g or, failing that, for employees terminated without cause or who quit "for cause attributable to the employer" § 8.06 cmt. f (Proposed Final Draft, April 18, 2014). *See also Figueroa v. Precision Surgical, Inc.*, 423 F. App'x 205 (3d Cir. 2011) (not error to deny preliminary injunctive relief for violations of nonsolicitation, noncompetition, and confidentiality covenants by an independent contractor when the principal likely breached its agreement, inter alia, by failing to pay commissions).

3. *Negotiating a Buy-out.* Prior to termination, the employer in *All Pet* offered to release Hopper from the noncompete agreement for $40,000. Private resolution of noncompete disputes, like other legal disputes, is common, and agreeing to a "buy out" is one way to settle. Would accepting this offer have been a better choice for Dr. Hopper? Her decision to reject her employer's offer was apparently based, at least in part, on her belief that the agreement was "not worth the paper it was written on." If that was her belief, and not just a bargaining ploy, what does this tell us about the limits of private ordering? On the one hand, private resolution of noncompete disputes might achieve efficient results, as the parties themselves may be in the best position to identify an amount that compensates the employer for the value of the restraint. On the other hand, it is unlikely that results will be efficient if employees are unaware of their background rights or their employer's. Hopper was a fairly sophisticated employee — a veterinarian and a business owner with several employment options.

If she did not appreciate the legal significance of her noncompete agreement, what does this mean for less educated employees?

4. *The Public Interest. All Pet* explicitly takes account of the effects of the employer's restraint on the public. As traditionally articulated, the common-law rule of reason requires the court to weigh the interest of the employer against "hardship to the promisor and the likely injury to the public." RESTATEMENT (SECOND) OF CONTRACTS § 188. However, in most cases, courts do not treat societal interest as a separate factor to be considered in the analysis; rather, the assumption is that a covenant that is reasonable in relation to a protectable interest is unlikely to be harmful to the public. Those instances where courts give societal interest distinct attention tend to involve highly specialized employees engaged in essential services. *See, e.g., Columbus Med. Serv. LLC v. Thomas*, 308 S.W.3d 368 (Tenn. Ct. App. 2009) (noncompete agreement between physical therapists and staffing company that placed therapists in residential facility for disabled was not enforceable despite employer's legitimate interests in training and goodwill where enforcement would interrupt continuity of care for vulnerable patient population); *cf. Merrill Lynch v. de Linier*, 572 F. Supp. 246, 249 (D. Ga. 1983) (noting in denying injunction to enforce noncompete that "[a] stock broker stands in a different relationship to his customers from that of other kinds of salesman [because] of the important role of the broker in protecting the financial welfare of his clients"). Other jurisdictions address public concerns by statutorily prohibiting noncompetes in certain fields, most notably medicine. *See, e.g.*, MASS. GEN. LAW ANN. 112 § 12X (2013) (declaring void any restriction on a physician's right to practice in an employment or professional agreement); 6 DEL. C. § 2707 (2014) (same). The Model Rules of Professional Conduct similarly prohibit noncompetes between lawyers. *See* MRPC 5.6. Is the protection of public choice as important of a concern with respect to lawyers as it is with respect to doctors? Or is the Model Rule simply an example of lawyers protecting themselves?

5. *Reasonableness Assessments from the Employee's Perspective.* While "fairness" rarely plays an independent role in contracts analysis, *cf. Williams v. Walker-Thomas*, 350 F.2d 445 (D.C. Cir. 1965) (unconscionability), many formulations of the test for reasonableness of a noncompetition agreement speak in terms of the restraint not being too great a hardship on the employee. *E.g.*, RESTATEMENT OF CONTRACTS § 188(1)(b). It is, however, a rare case where this consideration is more than a makeweight in the reasonableness inquiry.

6. *Reasonableness from the Employer's Perspective.* Most courts require the employer to demonstrate the reasonableness of its noncompete. *See, e.g., Omniplex World Services Corp. v. U.S. Investigations Services, Inc.*, 618 S.E.2d 340, 342 (Va. 2005). Consider the evidence presented as to the reasonableness of the *All Pet* restraint. Do you think allocation of burden of proof was significant in determining the result?

Regardless of the burden of proof, whether a restraint is reasonable with respect to each of the relevant considerations — duration, geography, and definition of competition — depends on an assessment of the value and scope of the particular interest the employer seeks to protect, in this case All Pet's customers. This is why the *All Pet* parties sought expert testimony about patient relationships in the veterinary industry. The analysis is often undertaken in relation to the nature and extent of the work the former employee performed since that ensures that the noncompete does not restrain the employee other than in relying on information or contacts he gained on the job. Thus, in the case of an employer's legitimate interest in customers, a restraint that prohibits the employee from competing only in the region where he had customer contact is more likely to be found reasonable than one based broadly, albeit accurately, on the geographic scope of the employer's business. *See, e.g., Home Paramount Pest Control Cos. v. Shaffer,* 718 S.E.2d 762 (Va. 2011) (noncompete provision in contract with employee of pest-control company was overbroad and unenforceable since it barred the employee from working in the pest control industry in any capacity or even being a passive stockholder of a publicly traded company in that business); *King v. Head Start Family Hair Salons,* 886 So. 2d 769 (Ala. 2004) (finding non-compete prohibiting hairdresser from working within two miles of any of employer's salons overbroad and modifying geographic scope to a two-mile radius of the location where employee worked). If customer relationships is the interest being protected, is it arguable that a noncompete is always overbroad to the extent it bars the former employee from dealing with others in the geographic area? *See* Employment Restatement § 8.07, cmt. c ("Because a covenant prohibiting former employees from soliciting customers with whom they dealt while employed will ordinarily fully protect this legitimate interest, a broader restriction barring all competition by former employees is ordinarily not enforceable.").

7. *Successorship.* What happens when a company having noncompetes with its employees merges with another company? Might the scope of the noncompete suddenly change radically because the employer is now operating in more markets? Reversing field after an initial decision to the contrary, the Supreme Court of Ohio held that an LLC could step into the shoes of the original contracting company in order to enforce noncompetition agreements. *Acordia of Ohio, L.L.C. v. Fishel,* 978 N.E.2d 823 (2012). However, it simultaneously suggested that employees could raise the question "whether the numerous mergers in this case created additional obligations or duties so that the agreements should not be enforced on their original terms." *Id.* at 826.

8. *Industry Standards of Reasonableness.* Might industry practices surrounding the use of noncompetes be relevant to the reasonableness inquiry? In *UZ Engineered Products v. Midwest Motor Supply,* 770 N.E.2d 1068 (Ohio. Ct. App. 2001), a sales-person for a metal parts manufacturer accepted employment at a competitor in violation of his two-year noncompetition and nondisclosure agreement. In support of its argument that the agreement was reasonable in duration, the former employer introduced a copy of the noncompete agreement used by the competitor with its own employees, which also contained a two-year restriction. *Id.* at 392-93. In the commercial context, courts routinely look at trade usages and other industry practices in interpreting contracts. *See* U.C.C. § 2-202 (2001) (providing that a final written agreement may be supplemented by usages of trade). Are there reasons to give similar consideration to noncompete practices common to a particular industry? Or could it cut the other way? That is, could the industry's pervasive use of noncompetes be a factor against enforcement because of the generalized effect on competition?

9. *Judicial Responses to Overbroad Agreements.* As *All Pet* illustrates, jurisdictions vary in their response to noncompetes that satisfy the protectable interest requirement but are overbroad in scope. As the First Circuit explains:

Courts presented with restrictive covenants containing unenforceable provisions have taken three approaches: (1) the "all or nothing" approach, which would void the restrictive covenant entirely if any part is unenforceable, (2) the "blue pencil" approach, which enables the court to enforce the reasonable terms provided the covenant remains grammatically coherent once its unreasonable provisions are excised, and (3) the "partial enforcement" approach, which reforms and enforces the restrictive covenant to the extent it is reasonable, unless the "circumstances indicate bad faith or deliberate overreaching" on the part of the employer.

Ferrofluidics Corp. v. Advanced Vacuum Components, 968 F.2d 1463 (1st Cir. 1992). Which approach does *All Pet* adopt? What are the relative advantages and disadvantages of each? Consider *Team Environmental Services v. Addison*, 2 F.3d 124, 127 (5th Cir. 1993), in which the court expressed concern over the *in terrorem* effects of overbroad agreements:

> An employee barred from plying his trade within 200 miles of his home would be far more hesitant to leave his job than if the proscription affected a substantially smaller area. This increased hesitancy obviously impacts the bargaining relationship with the current employer. Were courts to reform and enforce agreements like those at bar, employers would be free routinely to present employees with grossly overbroad covenants not to compete. While the employer presumptively would know that the agreement would be enforced only to the limit of the law, the employee likely would not.

Id. at 127. Scholars have raised similar concerns. *See, e.g.*, Charles A. Sullivan, *The Puzzling Persistence of Unenforceable Contract Terms*, 70 OHIO ST. L.J. 1127 (2009); Rachel Arnow-Richman, *Cubewrap Contracts and Worker Mobility: The Dilution of Employee Bargaining Power Via Standard Form Noncompetes*, 2006 MICH. ST. L. REV. 963. On the other hand, refusal to enforce any form of restraint in the face of an overbroad agreement penalizes those employers who draft their agreements in good faith, denying even their legitimate rights. As one court put it, "The man who wildly claims that he owns all the cherry trees in the country cannot be denied protection of the orchard in his backyard." *Sidco Paper Co. v. Aaron*, 351 A.2d 250 (Pa. 1976). The RESTATEMENT OF EMPLOYMENT LAW would allow deletion or modification of overbroad covenants if "the employer lacked a reasonable and good-faith basis for believing the covenant was enforceable," and "gross overbreadth alone" permits such finding. § 8.08 (Proposed Final Draft, April 18, 2014). Noncompetition agreements tend to be off-the-shelf documents applicable to all employees or at least to all employees at certain levels, which has led to some truly bizarre situations. Neil Irwin, *When the Guy Making Your Sandwich Has a Noncompete Clause*, http://www.nytimes.com/2014/10/15/upshot/when-the-guy-making-your-sandwich-has-a-noncompete-clause.html?_r=0&abt=0002&abg=1. Would that approach necessarily mean that a firm does not have a reasonable, good faith basis for enforcing any noncompete even for high level employees?

There are, however, ways to discourage overbroad agreements other than to refuse to blue pencil them. In *Sentinel Integrity Solutions, Inc. v. Mistras Grp., Inc.*, 414 S.W.3d 911 (Tex. App. 2013), the court, applying a provision of the Texas Business and Commerce Code, upheld an award of $750,000 in attorneys' fees to a defendant who successfully defended a suit for alleged breach of a noncompetition agreement. And, in a man-bites-dog case, *Guinn v. Applied Composites Eng'g, Inc.*, 994 N.E.2d 1256 (Ind. Ct. App. 2013), a court held that a former employee stated a claim of intentional interference with contract against his prior employer based on its threat of an interference suit against the plaintiff's new employer, which caused his discharge; the basis of the threat was alleged to be an overbroad and unenforceable noncompetition agreement. *See also Wells v. Daugherty Sys.*, 2014 U.S. Dist. LEXIS 127762 (N.D. Ga. Sept. 12, 2014) (enjoining employer from seeking to enforce a noncompete or informing third parties that it intends to enforce that agreement).

PROBLEMS

8-3.   Reexamine the noncompete agreement in Problem 8-2 in light of *All Pet*'s treatment of reasonableness. Assuming Julie Hanaco's former employer has a legitimate interest in protecting the technical and marketing information related to its new wheelchair, is its restraint reasonable in scope? In what respects — duration, geographic scope, and definition of competition — might Hanaco argue it is overbroad? If she were to prevail on such an argument, how would a court respond under each of the three approaches to overbroad agreements discussed above? How would you recommend the employer redraft its agreement to ensure that it is enforceable as written in the maximum number of jurisdictions?

8-4.   KFN is a national executive search firm that helps Fortune 500 companies recruit and hire key employees. KFN employs a large number of recruiters whose job it is to pair "prospects" and "talent," that is, to identify job opportunities at top companies and find suitably experienced job seekers to fill them. Recruiters spend significant time cultivating relationships with top personnel at the "prospect" companies, learning about the operations of the company and getting to know its work culture and hiring patterns in order to maintain that company's consistent business. Recruiters also spend time researching "talent," which includes getting to know candidates who have registered with KFN as well as cold-calling employed executives to see if they might be interested in a job change. Frequently, recruiters develop an area of specialty, such as placing executives with expertise in technology, or servicing companies seeking talent with experience in emerging markets. All of the information that KFN gleans about both its prospects and talent is kept in an extensive database that includes general information about the company or individual, a history of the services KFN has provided to the company or individual, and the recruiters' ideas and impressions about how to best market the individual or assist the company.

Up until now, KFN has never required its recruiters to sign any written agreement upon hire, largely because it feared such an agreement would impede its ability to hire experienced recruiters who bring prior contacts with them to the firm. However, it is revisiting the issue due to recent publicity about large-scale employee defections and data stealing in the job placement industry. Suppose KFN hires you. Would you advise the firm to use a contract containing restrictive covenants? What other practices and precautions would you recommend? If KFN asks you to draft a form contract for use with new recruiters, what would it look like?

C. NEW FRONTIERS IN NONCOMPETITION LITIGATION AND PRIVATE ORDERING

As the previous materials suggest, the laws surrounding competitive behavior of employees offer little certainty, even where the parties have planned for possible post-employment competition through contract. However conscientiously an employer may have drafted a noncompete agreement, it is often unclear whether a court will deem its underlying interests protectable and the terms of the restraint reasonable at the time enforcement is sought. How do parties (and lawyers) manage this type of uncertainty? For employers, one approach is to devise new drafting techniques, or even forge new types of contractual instruments, in an effort to address (or circumvent) judicial hostility to standard noncompetition covenants. Employees, on the other hand, may have limited ability to influence this process. Unless they are exceptionally skilled or highly sought after, employees will often have to accept the terms provided by employers. However, employees may be able to get a leg up in avoiding enforcement of such agreements by seeking to channel disputes into employee-friendly fora, resulting in some cases in a "race to the courthouse." This in turn has led employers to adopt second-order risk management techniques, such as the inclusion of choice-of-law and choice-of-forum clauses in their agreements. The variety of emerging strategies, in both the litigation and drafting contexts, are discussed in this section.

1. The Race to the Courthouse

≣ ***Advanced Bionics Corp. v. Medtronic, Inc.***
≣ *59 P. 3d 231 (Cal. 2002)*

CHIN, J. . . .
Medtronic, Inc. (Medtronic), a Minnesota corporation with headquarters in Fridley, Minnesota, manufactures implantable neurostimulation devices used to treat chronic pain. In 1995, Medtronic hired plaintiff Mark Stultz in Minnesota as a senior product specialist responsible for spinal cord stimulator lead wires. He was soon promoted to senior product manager in the "Neurostimulation-Pain Division," where he was responsible for managing Medtronic's neurostimulation products.

[Stultz signed the "Medtronic Employee Agreement," which contained a two-year covenant not to compete after employment termination. The Agreement also] included a choice-of-law provision: "The validity, enforceability, construction and interpretation of this Agreement shall be governed by the laws of the state in which the Employee was last employed by Medtronic." For the duration of his employment, Stultz worked for Medtronic's Minnesota office.

On June 7, 2000, Stultz resigned from Medtronic and went to California to work for Advanced Bionics Corporation (Advanced Bionics), a Delaware corporation with headquarters in Sylmar, California. The company, a competitor of Medtronic's, develops and manufactures implantable medical devices used to restore hearing to the profoundly deaf. It hired Stultz as a director of business development to market its own spinal cord stimulation device. On the same day, in Los Angeles County Superior Court, Stultz and Advanced Bionics sued Medtronic for declaratory relief, alleging that Medtronic's covenant not to compete and choice-of-law provisions violate California's law and public policy and are void under Business and Professions Code section 16600. Section 16600 provides in pertinent part that "every contract by which anyone is restrained from engaging in a lawful profession, trade, or business of any kind is to that extent void."

[On June 8, 2000, Stultz and Advanced Bionics notified Medtronic that they were applying for a temporary restraining order to enjoin Medtronic from "taking any action, other than in this court, to enforce its non-competition agreement." Medtronic immediately removed the action to federal court, thus avoiding the scheduled hearing on the TRO. The next day, June 9, it filed an action in Minnesota state court alleging claims for breach of contract against Stultz and tortious interference with contract against Advanced Bionics. Medtronic then obtained a TRO from the Minnesota court enjoining Advanced Bionics from hiring Stultz in any competitive role and barring them "[f]rom making any motion or taking any action or obtaining any order or direction from any court that [would] prevent or interfere in any way with [the Minnesota court's] determining whether it should determine all or any part of the claims alleged in [the Minnesota] lawsuit"

Within a week, the federal court remanded the California action to state court, finding that removal was improper because Medtronic, a Minnesota company, purported to rely on diversity jurisdiction, even though it knew Stultz was still a Minnesota resident. Once back in state court in California, Medtronic moved to dismiss or stay the California action because of the pending Minnesota case. The trial court denied the motion, thus leaving competing actions in both California and Minnesota.]

On August 3, 2000, the Minnesota court issued a preliminary injunction that was similar to its TRO, except it did not include the provision restraining Stultz and Advanced Bionics from pursuing other litigation; it simply restricted Stultz's activities as an Advanced Bionics employee. [Stultz and Advanced Bionics appealed in Minnesota.]

On August 8, 2000, Stultz and Advanced Bionics applied ex parte to the California court for a TRO and order to show cause re preliminary injunction to prohibit Medtronic from taking any further steps in the Minnesota action. The court granted the application, finding there was a "substantial chance" that Medtronic would "go to the Minnesota court [and] attempt to undercut the California court's jurisdiction." Medtronic was "restrained and enjoined from taking any action whatsoever, other than in this Court, to enforce [its covenant not to compete] against . . . Stultz or to otherwise restrain . . . Stultz from working for Advanced Bionics in California, including but not limited to making any appearance, filing any paper, participating in any proceeding, posting any bond, or taking any other action in the second-filed [Minnesota] lawsuit. . . ."

On August 16, 2000, the Minnesota court amended its August 3 preliminary injunction (purportedly nunc pro tunc), stating it had "failed to incorporate language enjoining [Stultz and Advanced Bionics] from obtaining relief in another court that would effectively stay or limit [the Minnesota] action." The court added a provision enjoining Stultz and Advanced Bionics "from seeking any interim or temporary relief from any other court that would effectively stay, limit or restrain [the Minnesota] action," and ordered them to "move to vacate and rescind the August 8, 2000

[TRO] obtained in the California action and refrain from seeking any relief in that action that stays or restrains [the Minnesota] action in any way."[4]

Stultz and Advanced Bionics informed the Los Angeles County Superior Court that the Minnesota court had directed them to seek vacation of the TRO. The superior court refused to vacate its order. . . .

[On appeal, the Second District Court of Appeal held that] (1) the trial court's TRO was necessary and proper to protect plaintiffs' interests pending final disposition of the action . . . (2) notwithstanding the choice-of-law provision in the Agreement, the case would be decided under California law; and (3) because California law would apply and the California action was filed first, California courts should decide the dispute. . . . This appeal followed.

. . . Antisuit TRO's Must Be Granted with Restraint

Although Medtronic acknowledges that, under certain circumstances, a California court has the power to issue a TRO prohibiting a party from taking action in a case pending in another jurisdiction that would interfere with the California court's proceedings, it asserts that the Court of Appeal here erred in concluding that the TRO entered in this action was proper. Medtronic claims that the Court of Appeal did not place sufficient emphasis on principles of judicial restraint and comity that strongly inform against issuance of the TRO in this case.

We recognize this is a case of first impression, but note that nearly 100 years ago, this court observed that "[t]he courts of this state have the same power to restrain persons within the state from prosecuting actions in either domestic or foreign jurisdictions which courts of equity have elsewhere." (*Spreckels v. Hawaiian Com. etc. Co.* (1897) [49 P. 35].)

. . . Although *Spreckels* recognized that a California court might have power to issue a TRO to prevent multiple proceedings, and implicitly recognized a forum court's power to restrain proceedings, the court never suggested, implicitly or otherwise, that a court may ignore additional proceedings that arise after the initial action commences. The significant principles of judicial restraint and comity inform that we should use that power sparingly.

Several sister state decisions guide our reasoning. These decisions hold that even if a sister state applies different substantive law than the forum state, that fact alone does not justify the issuance of a TRO enjoining proceedings in the sister state. . . .

. . . The possibility that one action may lead to a judgment first and then be applied as res judicata in another action "is a natural consequence of parallel proceedings in courts with concurrent jurisdiction, and not reason for an injunction." (*Auerbach v. Frank* (D.C. 1996) 685 A.2d 404, 407.) "[T]he possibility of an 'embarrassing race to judgment' or potentially inconsistent adjudications does not outweigh the respect and deference owed to independent foreign proceedings." (*Ibid.*)

---

4. [T]he Minnesota Court of Appeal affirmed the preliminary TRO, rejecting Stultz and Advanced Bionics contention that the trial court erred by failing to defer to the "first-filed" California action and observing that the "first-filed rule" is not intended to be applied in a rigid or inflexible manner. The court concluded that "Minnesota . . . has a strong interest in having contracts executed in this state enforced in accordance with the parties' expectations."

Stultz and Advanced Bionics . . . contend that although we should pay deference to foreign state proceedings, California's strong public policy against noncompetition agreements under section 16600 weighs against allowing the action to proceed in Minnesota and provides the exceptional circumstance that warrants our upholding the California court's TRO. As they observe, the law protects Californians, and ensures "that every citizen shall retain the right to pursue any lawful employment and enterprise of their choice." (*Metro Traffic Control, Inc. v. Shadow Traffic Network* (1994) 27 Cal. Rptr. 2d 573.) It protects "the important legal right of persons to engage in businesses and occupations of their choosing." (*Morlife, Inc. v. Perry* (1997) 66 Cal. Rptr. 2d 731.) We have even called noncompetition agreements illegal. (*See, e.g., Armendariz v. Foundation Health Psychcare Services, Inc.* (2000) [6 P.3d 669].) Therefore, according to Stultz and Advanced Bionics, because the noncompetition provision in the Agreement is broad in application and forbids Stultz from working for any competitor on a competitive product for two years after employment termination, it is likely that a California court would conclude the provision is void under section 16600.

We agree that California has a strong interest in protecting its employees from noncompetition agreements under section 16600. But even assuming a California court might reasonably conclude that the contractual provision at issue here is void in this state, this policy interest does not, under these facts, justify issuance of a TRO against the parties in the Minnesota court proceedings. A parallel action in a different state presents sovereignty concerns that compel California courts to use judicial restraint when determining whether they may properly issue a TRO against parties pursuing an action in a foreign jurisdiction.

The comity principle also supports our conclusion. Comity is based on the belief "'that the laws of a state have no force, *proprio vigore*, beyond its territorial limits, but the laws of one state are frequently permitted by the courtesy of another to operate in the latter for the promotion of justice, where neither that state nor its citizens will suffer any inconvenience from the application of the foreign law. This courtesy, or comity, is established, not only from motives of respect for the laws and institutions of the foreign countries, but from considerations of mutual utility and advantage.' . . . 'The mere fact that state action may have repercussions beyond state lines is of no judicial significance so long as the action is not within that domain which the Constitution forbids.'" (*Estate of Lund* (1945) 159 P.2d 643). The comity principle requires that we exercise our power to enjoin parties in a foreign court sparingly, in line with the policy of judicial restraint discussed above.

Notwithstanding comity principles, Advanced Bionics contends that the first-filed rule provides alternative support for the Court of Appeal's decision to uphold the TRO and to enjoin the litigants from proceeding in Minnesota. We disagree. [The first-filed rule in California applies only to two California courts; it] "was never meant to apply where the two courts involved are not courts of the same sovereignty. Restraining a party from pursuing an action in a court of foreign jurisdiction involves delicate questions of comity and therefore 'requires that such action be taken only with care and great restraint.'" (*Compagnie des Bauxites de Guinea v. Ins. Co. of N. Am.* (3d Cir. 1981) 651 F.2d 877, 887, fn. 10.)

We conclude, therefore, that the Court of Appeal erred in upholding the TRO issued against the parties in the Minnesota proceedings. California courts have the same power as other courts to issue orders that assist in protecting their jurisdiction. However, enjoining proceedings in another state requires an exceptional circumstance that outweighs the threat to judicial restraint and comity principles. As explained, the circumstances of this case do not provide sufficient justification to warrant our court's issuing injunctive orders against parties pursuing the Minnesota litigation. . . .

We hold that the trial court improperly issued the TRO enjoining Medtronic from proceeding in the Minnesota action. We also conclude, however, that the Minnesota action does not divest California of jurisdiction, and Advanced Bionics remains free to litigate the California action unless and until Medtronic demonstrates to the Los Angeles County Superior Court that any Minnesota judgment is binding on the parties. . . .

BROWN, J., concurring.

I agree with most of Justice Moreno's concurrence. . . . I do not, however, agree with the implication in Justice Moreno's opinion that a choice-of-law analysis is irrelevant to determining whether to enjoin parties from litigating a dispute in a foreign jurisdiction. If a careful choice-of-law analysis indicates that the foreign jurisdiction's law applies to the parties' dispute, I think that fact weighs heavily in favor of permitting the foreign proceeding to go forward unimpeded. . . .

This case involves a contract dispute between Medtronic, Inc. (Medtronic), a Minnesota corporation, and Mark Stultz, a former Medtronic employee who worked for Medtronic in Minnesota and, at that time, resided in Minnesota. The parties executed the employment contract in Minnesota, and the choice-of-law provision in the contract designates Minnesota law. Under the terms of the contract, Stultz agreed not to work for a competitor of Medtronic for two years after termination of his employment with Medtronic, and that provision is enforceable under Minnesota law, though not under California law. California had absolutely no interest in this matter until Stultz relocated to California, terminated his employment with Medtronic, and began employment with Advanced Bionics Corporation, a Delaware corporation with headquarters in California. Under these circumstances, where almost all the geographic points of contact in the dispute lie in Minnesota, California's concededly strong interest in promoting competition by encouraging the free movement of personnel laterally across an industry is not "'materially greater'" than Minnesota's countervailing interest in enforcing bargained-for restrictions on that free movement. (*Nedlloyd Lines B.V. v. Superior Court* (1992) 834 P.2d 1148.) Therefore, the contract's choice-of-law provision, designating Minnesota law, controls. Stultz, having enjoyed the benefits of his contract with Medtronic, should not be free to avoid his side of the agreement and thereby cancel some of the value for which Medtronic legitimately bargained. . . .

Relocating to California may be, for some people, a chance for a fresh start in life, but it is not a chance to walk away from valid contractual obligations, claiming California policy as a protective shield. We are not a political safe zone vis-à-vis our sister states, such that the mere act of setting foot on California soil somehow releases a person from the legal duties our sister states recognize. Rather, we give full faith and credit to the laws of our sister states, and in a case such as this one, I think doing so requires California courts to apply Minnesota law. Moreover, that conclusion is highly relevant to determining whether the trial court's antisuit injunction in this case was appropriate. I see no reason for a trial court to enjoin parties from litigating in a foreign jurisdiction when the foreign jurisdiction's law applies to the dispute and therefore the task of the California courts will ultimately be to discern how the enjoined proceeding would have come out.

MORENO, J., concurring. . . .

In determining which criteria courts of this state should apply when deciding whether to issue an antisuit injunction, I agree with the majority that considerations of comity and judicial restraint should be paramount. . . . I would therefore adopt the restrictive approach [, favored by some federal courts, under which] courts should only issue antisuit injunctions in two situations: if "necessary to protect the jurisdiction of the enjoining court, or to prevent the litigant's evasion of the important public policies of the forum." [N]either exception applies in this case.

[T]he parallel proceeding initiated by Medtronic in Minnesota does not threaten the jurisdiction of the California courts. At the time when the California court issued the TRO at issue here, enjoining Medtronic "from taking any action whatsoever, other than in this Court," the Minnesota court had issued a preliminary injunction restricting Stultz's activities as an Advanced Bionics Corporation employee but not restraining the parties from pursuing other litigation. After the California court issued the antisuit TRO, the Minnesota court revised its preliminary injunction. Notably, however, the Minnesota court did not enjoin the action from proceeding in a California court; instead, the Minnesota injunction was *defensive*; it enjoined the parties "from obtaining relief in another court that would effectively stay or limit [the Minnesota] action." [Unlike situations where the foreign proceedings are designed to rob the alternative court of its jurisdiction by carving out exclusive jurisdiction for the foreign court], the Minnesota injunction did not seek to terminate the litigation in California, but was instituted merely to protect the jurisdiction of the Minnesota court. Further, as courts applying the restrictive approach have held, the possibility that Medtronic may receive a more favorable ruling in a Minnesota court does not threaten the jurisdiction of a California court. . . .

[As for use of an antisuit injunction to protect an important public policy of the forum state, this] exception does not allow for an injunction merely because two states may apply different substantive laws. . . .

The crucial determination is whether the suit was filed in another state for the purpose of *evading* the important policies of the forum state. Such a purpose may be inferred, for example, if neither party has ties to the sister state in which a parallel suit has been initiated. Courts have found that a party's connection to the foreign jurisdiction minimizes the possibility that such a suit was filed for purposes of evading the forum state's law. . . .

In the present case, the issue is not simply whether California has a strong public policy against noncompetition agreements. Instead, the question is whether Medtronic initiated its action in Minnesota for the purpose of *evading* California's public policy. Based on the facts of this case, I conclude that Medtronic did not institute its suit in Minnesota to evade California law. Medtronic is a Minnesota corporation. Medtronic entered into an employment contract with Stultz, a Minnesota resident, in Minnesota. The contract contained a choice-of-law provision that stated: "The validity, enforceability, construction and interpretation of this Agreement shall be governed by the laws of the state in which the Employee was last employed by Medtronic." Stultz worked for Medtronic's Minnesota office for the duration of his employment. Based on these significant ties to a Minnesota forum, as well as the choice-of-law clause designating Minnesota as the chosen forum, I cannot conclude that Medtronic filed suit in Minnesota for the purpose of evading California public policy. . . .

NOTES

1. *Civil Procedure Dream or Nightmare?* Depending on your view of Civil Procedure, *Advanced Bionics* is either an enormous amount of fun or incredibly confusing. It has everything: parallel actions in two states, TROs, removal, interlocutory appeals, comity, choice of law, and so on. But driving all of this seems to be a simple concern of both parties — having the case decided on home turf. Why is it so important to Stuntz and Advanced Bionics that California decide the case? Why is Medtronic so determined to have a Minnesota court hear it?

2. *Choice-of-Forum Clauses.* If Medtronic cared so much about litigating its rights in Minnesota, why didn't it include in its contract a choice-of-forum clause specifying that claims could be pursued only in Minnesota, rather than merely a choice-of-law clause? You might have run into choice-of-forum clauses in Civil Procedure in *Carnival Cruise Lines v. Shute*, 499 U.S. 585 (1991), which upheld a Florida forum clause for a cruise line despite the difficulties litigating in that forum caused the plaintiffs, who were citizens of Washington. The Court found the clause valid under federal law even though plaintiffs had boarded the ship in California, the injury occurred in the waters off Mexico, and the clause was clearly adhesive (it was printed on the back of the cruise ticket).

Litigants' strategies with respect to both choice of law and choice of forum are inextricably intertwined. The Stultz/Advanced Bionics argument against enforcing the Minnesota choice-of-law clause was apparently that, if California public policy prohibited restraints of trade, employers should not be able to end run that prohibition by specifying that some other body of law governed. Obviously, however, a California court is more likely to be persuaded by that argument than is a court in another jurisdiction. This explains the race to the courthouse — while choice of law was what mattered, the validity of the choice-of-law clause likely depended on which forum heard the case.

Suppose the contract *had* contained a choice-of-forum clause limiting actions to Minnesota courts. Would this have solved Medtronic's problems? The enforceability of such clauses, like choice-of-law clauses, is a matter of state contract law. Couldn't Stultz and Advanced Bionics still have sued in California arguing that, under the circumstances, this clause also was invalid because, like the choice-of-law clause, it represented an attempt to frustrate California public policy? For more on the stakes and implications of such interjurisdictional disputes, *see* Timothy P. Glynn, *Interjurisdictional Competition in Enforcing Noncompetition Agreements: Regulatory Risk Management and the Race to the Bottom*, 65 Wash. & Lee L. Rev. 1381 (2008). *See also* David A. Linehan, *Due Process Denied: The Forgotten Constitutional Limits on Choice of Law in the Enforcement of Employee Covenants Not to Compete*, 2012 Utah L. Rev. 209, 268.

3. *Odd Planning.* The Medtronic choice-of-law clause provided that the contract "shall be governed by the laws of the state in which the Employee was last employed by Medtronic," which in this case was Minnesota. Is this a good way to draft a clause? It certainly does not guarantee any particular jurisdiction's law will apply. Even if, at the time of drafting, Medtronic had operations only in Minnesota, doesn't this clause create potential problems down the road should it expand to other states? Why do you think it chose this language?

4. *No Holds Barred in the Race to the Courthouse?* After the California case had been "unremoved" from federal court and was back in California state court, Medtronic moved to have it dismissed or stayed because of the pending Minnesota suit. But, of course, the California suit had been filed *before* the Minnesota suit, and any delay in California was due to Medtronic's failed attempt at removal to federal court for the "improper purpose" of avoiding a ruling on the pending TRO. As the lawyer for

Medtronic, would you have had the audacity to make a motion to dismiss on these grounds after the case returned to state court?

5. *What's Really Going On?* How important is the fact that Stultz/Advanced Bionics got to the courthouse first? That move may have given them certain procedural advantages in the injunction game, but isn't the real question which of the two jurisdictions has the stronger interest in the case? From Medtronic's perspective, the more "natural" jurisdiction is Minnesota, where the contracting parties were located at all relevant times — both at the time of contract formation and during the course of the employment relationship. Only by bringing a declaratory judgment action did Stultz/Advanced Bionics bring California into the picture. On the other hand, California is the jurisdiction where the alleged breach has occurred, and ultimately the effects of any judgment will be felt there. Maybe there is no "natural" forum.

Interjurisdictional tangles like this are especially likely where one state departs radically from the law operative in other states, as is the case with California's restrictive approach to noncompetition clauses. *Advanced Bionics* simply reflects the collision between the public policy of most states (here, Minnesota), which permit such clauses, and California, which does not. While one could argue that Minnesota has more of an interest in the underlying contract than California, giving effect to Minnesota's public policy means cutting off a California business — Advanced Bionics — from highly valued workers, and thus disadvantaging it in the interstate marketplace in which it seeks to compete.

6. *The Rose Bowl: California v. Minnesota.* The Minnesota court preliminarily enjoined Stultz from competing but did not, initially at least, enjoin Stultz and Advanced Bionics from pursuing their California action. Had this situation continued, the race would have become not a race to the courthouse but rather a race to judgment. That is, Stultz could not engage in competitive employment with Advanced Bionics pending a final judgment (on penalty of contempt), and the first judgment entered would, as a matter of full faith and credit, bind the second court. Thus, Minnesota is leading at this point in the game by virtue of issuing the preliminary injunction in favor of Medtronic; but California could still prevail by deciding the case first. For example, if the California court entered summary judgment for Stultz and Advanced Bionics (disposing of all issues), that judgment would be binding on Minnesota, which would in theory have to dissolve the injunction.

But no one seems content with this scenario. As the second half opens, Stultz and Advanced Bionics (1) appeal the preliminary injunction issued by the Minnesota court, and (2) obtain an order from the California court precluding Medtronic from proceeding in Minnesota, an order that is broad enough to preclude Medtronic from opposing the Minnesota appeal! At this point, California seems to be winning, but Minnesota responds with a razzle-dazzle play — amending its order *nunc pro tunc* to preclude Stultz and Advanced Bionics from getting the order that they had already gotten. At this point, not only are the two states tied, but all parties seem to be in contempt of some court. Not surprisingly, when informed of the Minnesota court order, the California court refused to budge.

One doesn't have to be a sophisticated lawyer to find this situation more than a little absurd. In fact, maybe only sophisticated attorneys wouldn't find this absurd. But, other than the requirement that states give full faith and credit to final judgments of other states, nothing in our federal system prevents situations like this from arising. In theory, antisuit injunctions, like the one issued by the California trial court, offer one "solution" to this problem, but the California Supreme Court is clearly unhappy with this approach. While it affirms the power of its courts to issue such injunctions, it finds that principles of comity sharply limit its ability to exercise that power. Even the risk of frustrating a strong California public policy — prohibiting restraints on employee competition — is not enough, and certainly the mere fact that a party filed first in California does not suffice. Do you agree? Do you think Minnesota would also agree as to its own power to issue antisuit injunction?

7. *Who Wins in Overtime?* Notice that the court's decision does not really resolve the underlying issues. Following *Advanced Bionics*, Medtronic's pursuit of its case in Minnesota is permissible, but the California court on remand might find the noncompetition clause to be invalid as against California public policy. So we seem to be back to the race to judgment situation — whoever gets a final judgment first wins.

Or maybe not. While the full faith and credit clause requires a court to respect a *judgment* entered by a sister state, state courts are rarely required to enforce *injunctions* entered by sister states. *See Baker by Thomas v. GMC*, 522 U.S. 222 (1998). *See generally* Polly J. Price, *Full Faith and Credit and the Equity Conflict*, 84 Va. L. Rev. 747 (1998). This might mean that a Minnesota injunction against Stultz and Advanced Bionics will not be enforced in California, suggesting that, as long as Stultz doesn't visit Minnesota again, the Minnesota judgment will be a nullity. Note that the Minnesota court could issue a money judgment that California would be compelled to enforce, but, as we saw in *SIG*, proving damages in cases such as this, not to mention getting them from an employee, is notoriously difficult. And the Minnesota judgment would be preclusive in California, so Stultz and Advanced Bionics could not recover against Medtronic.

If there is no way for Medtronic to win the war, even if it prevails in some important battles, perhaps it should rethink the way it manages the risk of employee competition by a geographically mobile worker. It might, for example, consider utilizing other risk management techniques such as including arbitration clauses in its employment contracts. Such clauses will be addressed in detail in Chapter 13. Nevertheless, it is worth noting that the utility of an arbitration provision might be limited in important respects. An arbitrator may not have the ability to craft the type of relief Medtronic is seeking, and, even if it could, Medtronic might face obstacles in attempting to enforce the arbitral ruling. Maybe it would make more sense to adopt a different type of contract all together. For instance, some employers use compensation — through stock options, deferred compensation, or pay-back agreements — to create incentives for employees to remain with the company rather than going to a competitor. Some examples of these approaches follow.

2. Innovations in Contract Drafting

≡ ### Heder v. City of Two Rivers
≡ *295 F.3d 777 (7th Cir. 2002)*

EASTERBROOK, Cir. J.

After the City of Two Rivers decided that all of its firefighters must be certified as paramedics, the City and the firefighters' union agreed [to compensate the firefighters at half of their regular hourly rate for time spent in paramedic training]. The deal between the City and the union included a 3% increase in the wages of firefighters who held certifications, plus an undertaking that any firefighter leaving the City's employ within the next three years would reimburse the City for the cost of the training, which would give each firefighter a portable credential. Two and a half years after beginning his training, Heder quit. Two Rivers withheld all of Heder's pay from his last two pay periods. Heder filed suit under the [Fair Labor Standards Act ("FLSA")], and the City counterclaimed for the remainder of the money that it believes Heder owes under its memorandum of agreement with the union.

[The court first addressed Heder's FLSA claim. The City] concedes that Heder was entitled to compensation that the FLSA specifies as a statutory floor below which no contract may go. That means, in particular, that Heder was entitled to at least the statutory minimum wage for his final two pay periods (leaving the City to collect any residue as an ordinary creditor) and that Heder is entitled to time and a half for any overtime hours for which the FLSA requires that premium. But the parties do not agree on what this means in practice, because the firefighters do not work an ordinary 40-hour week. [Based on the way the City calculated work time, the City was required to pay time and a half for all hours over 204 per 27-day period, even if some of those hours were devoted to training.]

Next we must decide whether the City has a good claim for reimbursement of at least some outlays.

Heder depicts a repayment obligation as a covenant not to compete that is invalid under WIS. STAT. § 103.465. The district judge adopted this characterization; we do not, because in Wisconsin (as in other states) a covenant not to compete must be linked to competition. An agreement to repay Two Rivers if a firefighter goes to work for a rival fire department would be treated as a covenant not to compete. But the agreement between Two Rivers and the firefighters' union does not restrict Heder's ability to compete against the City after leaving its employ. The obligation is unconditional: a firefighter departing before three years have expired must repay training costs even if he goes back to school, changes occupation, or retires. Competition has nothing to do with the matter.

According to Heder, Wisconsin would act as if this were a covenant not to compete, on the ground that repayment induces "involuntary servitude" that is more onerous than the agreements explicitly regulated under § 103.465. Yet this is not what the Supreme Court of Wisconsin said in [*Union Central Life Insurance Co. v. Balistrieri*, 120 N.W.2d 126 (1963)]): there it limited application of § 103.465 to agreements that condition repayment on going to work for the ex-employer's rival. True enough, as the district judge emphasized, Two Rivers' repayment obligation shares with genuine restrictive covenants the feature that it makes changing jobs costly. But that is not enough to throw a contract out the window. Employers offer their workers many incentives to stay, so that they can reap the benefit of training and other productivity enhancers that depend on employees' tenure with the firm. Pay that increases with longevity is one common device; an employee who leaves must start elsewhere at the bottom rung. Firm-specific training (the value of which is lost if the employee changes jobs) likewise penalizes departures. . . . Seniority systems that link duration of service to better assignments, protection against layoffs, and so on, have a similar effect; to quit is to give up accumulated seniority. Private employers give employees profit-sharing plans and stock options that vest later (if the person remains employed) and bonuses that accrue after extra years have been served. Defined-benefit pension systems usually are back-loaded, so that the last years of work before retirement add more to the monthly pension benefit than do earlier years. . . .

The common formula that starts with multiplying the final salary by the number of years served produces this effect automatically because salaries tend to rise with inflation and years of service. Yet no one believes that this powerful financial incentive to stick with one's employer until retirement is unlawful, even though it is much larger than the amount Heder must repay Two Rivers for paramedic training. The parties do not cite, and we could not find, any Wisconsin decision that characterizes the kind of incentives mentioned above as restrictive covenants regulated by Wis. Stat. § 103.465. Instead, Wisconsin applies WIS. STAT. § 103.465 only to the extent that a consequence is linked on working for a competitor. . . .

Nor can we see any reason why Wisconsin would want to extend its precedents to block reimbursement agreements such as the one Two Rivers made with its union. Employees received considerable benefits as a result: paramedic training that will be useful for years to come, a 3% increase in compensation starting in 1998 (rising to 3.5% in 1999) for those who are certified paramedics, and extra compensation (at overtime rates) for the training time. Residents of Two Rivers received the benefit of a fire department more likely to save lives. Cities fearing that employees would take their new skills elsewhere would be less likely to provide these benefits. Or they might use other ways to acquire a workforce with better skills. They could, for example, require the employees to undergo and underwrite their own training, with none of the time compensated. This is what law firms do when they limit hiring to persons who already have law degrees, what school systems do when hiring only teachers who hold state certificates. The employer must pay indirectly, through a higher salary, but no court would dream of calling this system (under which employees finance their own training) "involuntary servitude." If an employer may require employees to pay up front, why can't the employer bear the expense but require reimbursement if an early departure deprives the employer of the benefit of its bargain? A middle ground also would be feasible (and lawful): The employer could require the worker to pay for his own training but lend the worker the money and forgive repayment if he sticks around. . . . A worker who left before the loan had been forgiven would have to come up with the funds from his own sources, just as Heder must do. If that system is lawful, as it is, then the economically equivalent system that Two Rivers adopted must be lawful. The cost of training equates to the loan, repayment of which is forgiven after three years.

The district judge objected to the cliff in the repayment system: instead of a slow reduction (equivalent to amortization of a loan), the collective bargaining agreement calls for full repayment before three years and none after. The judge inferred from this that the useful life of paramedic training is three years; as Heder quit with only 1/6 of this time remaining his union could not legally bind him to repay more than 1/6 of these expenses. The inference is unsound: One could as easily infer from the fact that the 3% wage boost is perpetual that paramedic training lasts indefinitely. We know from the record that Heder spent 582 hours undergoing the initial round of training and eight hours to re-certify two years later. This implies that paramedic skills have a useful life that can be extended indefinitely with small recurring investment — and it also implies that the three-year period is generous to workers. Two Rivers could have made the period much longer (say, 10 years). Then even if the debt had been amortized, as the district judge preferred, many workers (all who stayed longer than 3 years but quit or retired before 10) would have been worse off. The actual structure cannot be set aside as onerous — even if Wisconsin had a rule, which it does not, that no onerous term in a collective bargaining agreement is enforceable. The day Heder quit, his paramedic skills were effectively as valuable as the day he received his certification. We do not think that the Supreme Court of Wisconsin is apt to require employers and employees to amortize training costs with precision, to factor in the time value of money (the agreement does not require Heder to pay interest, though it might have done so), or to craft an individual schedule based on the number of years each employee is expected to remain able to work. The collective bargaining agreement is valid under state law, so Heder must repay the full cost of his books and tuition, which came to about $1,400.

American Consulting Environmental Safety Services, Inc. v. Schuck
888 N.E.2d 874 (Ind. Ct. App. 2008)

Friedlander, J.

American Consulting Environmental Safety Services, Inc. (American Consulting) appeals from the trial court's judgment in favor of Lynette Schuck and against American Consulting on American Consulting's claim for damages. On appeal, American Consulting presents one issue: Did the trial court err in concluding that Section 12 of an employment contract between American Consulting and Schuck constituted an unenforceable penalty rather than a valid provision for liquidated damages?

We affirm.

American Consulting is an Indiana corporation that provides safety compliance services and materials to customers located within a 200-mile radius of South Bend, Indiana. To carry out its purpose, American Consulting evaluates the safety and accident prevention policies of businesses and offers programs and courses to bring them into compliance with regulatory agencies' requirements. On January 14, 2005, Schuck was hired by American Consulting as a safety instructor. Schuck signed an employment agreement setting forth the terms and conditions of her employment. Although Schuck had received training in occupational safety and health prior to coming to work for American Consulting, American Consulting required that Schuck undergo additional training. Specifically, Section 12 of the employment agreement provided:

> The Company requires its Employees to be properly trained in safety compliance and state and federal OSHA and EPA standards and the sales, marketing, and other functions of its business. Accordingly, the Company requires each Employee to undergo this training during the initial 180 day probationary period of employment for set [sic] Employee. This training shall cost the Employee the sum of $3,000.00. Set [sic] sum shall be initially due at the first session of training, or when training materials are provided to the Employee, whichever comes first.
>
> However, the Company agrees to pay the cost of this training on the Employees [sic] behalf, but subject to reimbursement by the Employee within the first 12 calendar months of employment. If the Employee remains employed by the Company for 12 continuous calendar months from the first date of hire, the Employee shall not be obligated to reimburse the Company for the cost of training. If, however, the Employee shall voluntarily terminate the employment or if the Employee is terminated by the Employer for good cause, the Employee shall reimburse the Company for the cost of training in accordance with [a schedule that required the employee to repay progressively smaller amounts as she worked longer, but $3,000 if her employment was terminated in less than 3 months.]

Schuck's training by American Consulting consisted of spending one day watching videos and taking several short quizzes. The videos were part of a video library American Consulting had accumulated over the course of several years. Additional training included Schuck shadowing another American Consulting employee during visits to existing customers. In total, Schuck completed twelve and one-half days of "shadow training". During the training period, Schuck was paid $9.00 per hour and was not paid overtime.

In June 2005, Schuck informed American Consulting that she had been experiencing medical problems and had found out that she was pregnant. After five months of productive employment, Schuck felt it necessary, due to her pregnancy, to resign from her position. . . .

[American Consulting sued Schuck seeking repayment of $1,500.00 under Section 12 of her employment contract. T]he trial court made the following findings pertinent to our review:

> 13. In considering the facts of this case, the only credible evidence submitted as to the actual loss of the plaintiff is the wages paid to defendant during her training. Defendant testified that her hourly wage was $9.00 per hour and that she had one day of training by watching video tapes [and 12 days of shadow training by following an experienced employee] while that employee was actually earning money for the plaintiff while training employees of customer corporations. Assuming 13 days at 8 hours per day at $9.00 per hour equals $72.00 per day times 13 days equals $936.00. However, the plaintiff's schedule as found in Paragraph 12, provided that because the defendant had already worked six [sic] months at the time of her pregnancy-related request to leave employment, only one-half of that sum would be due, under the intent of the parties. The maximum damages that plaintiff could recover under the actual evidence would be $468.00, assuming that this provision is enforceable. Four Hundred Sixty-Eight Dollars ($468.00) is approximately thirty-one (31%) percent of the amount claimed by the plaintiff.
>
> 15. The lack of reasonableness of the stipulation for repayment of training costs under the circumstances of this case weighs in favor of finding that this is a penalty clause and is unenforceable.

. . . The term "liquidated damages" applies to a specific sum of money that has been expressly stipulated by the parties to a contract as to the amount of damages to be recovered by either party in the event of a breach of the contract by the other. Liquidated damages provisions are useful and generally enforceable in situations where actual damages would be uncertain or difficult to ascertain. To be enforceable, the sum stipulated as liquidated damages must "fairly be allowed as compensation for the breach." Where the stipulated sum is grossly disproportionate to the loss that may result from a breach of contract, we should treat the sum as a penalty rather than as liquidated damages.

As our Supreme Court has noted with regard to the history of litigation of liquidated damage clauses, in cases where actual damages could be readily ascertained and the amount stipulated exceeded the actual damages, then the contract provision has been treated as a "penalty" and only actual damages awarded. "The distinction between a penalty provision and a liquidated damages provision is that a penalty is imposed to secure performance of the contract, and liquidated damages are to be paid in lieu of performance."

In determining whether a stipulated sum payable on a breach of contract constitutes liquidated damages or a penalty, we will consider the facts, the intention of the parties, and the reasonableness of the stipulation under the circumstances of the case. Where there is uncertainty as to the meaning of a liquidated damages provision, classification as a penalty is favored. . . .

Here, Schuck's training consisted of watching videos accumulated over the years by American Consulting. These videos were also used to train other employees. Schuck also shadowed an American Consulting employee for twelve days. American Consulting did not send Schuck for specialized off-site training, seminars, or the like, or bring in specialists to provide on-site training. American Consulting failed to explain how the training it did provide amounted to its stated cost of $3,000.00. American Consulting also failed to demonstrate a reasonable relationship between the reimbursement amounts listed in the Section 12 schedule and the amount of actual damages incurred by the termination of employment.

To be sure, the primary damages American Consulting suffered (if indeed any damages at all) would have been the wage paid to Schuck during her training. This is precisely what the trial court used to compute American Consulting's damages. The trial court calculated Schuck's wage for thirteen days of training at a rate of $9.00 per hour for an eight-hour day and concluded that, at most, American Consulting's loss was $468.00, or thirty-one percent of American Consulting's claimed amount. American Consulting's claimed damages of $1,500.00 is not commensurate with or reasonably related to its actual damages. Furthermore, upon reading the contract, the purpose of Section 12 appears to be to secure performance of the contract for at least a twelve-month period, an earmark of a penalty provision. Based on the foregoing, we can only conclude that Section 12 amounts to an unenforceable penalty.

NOTES

1. *Training Repayment Agreements as an Alternative to Noncompetes.* In what ways might training repayment agreements better serve employers' interests than noncompetes? In theory, such agreements circumvent the problem of courts' general disfavor of noncompetes and the particular reluctance to recognize training as a protectable interest. As *Heder* illustrates, at least some courts have taken that view, *see also Pembroke v. Hagin*, 391 S.E.2d 465 (Ga. Ct. App. 1990) (enforcing contract under which peace officer promised to repay city employer for basic training course should he voluntarily terminate employment within 12 months of graduating), as have some state legislatures. *See* COLO. REV. STAT. 8-2-113(2) (2013) (permitting enforcement of repayment agreements against employees who serve less than two years). There is also some reason to think that repayment agreements may be more efficient and less likely to overreach than noncompete agreements given that such agreements are tailored to a particular interest and usually apply only if the employee departs within a designated time period. *See* Gillian Lester, *Restrictive Covenants, Employee Training, and the Limits of Transaction-Cost Analysis*, 76 IND. L. J. 49, 75-76 (2001); Brandon S. Long, *Protecting Employer Investment in Training: Noncompetes vs. Repayment Agreements*, 54 DUKE L. J. 1295, 1318-19 (2005).

However, training repayment agreements are hardly a panacea for employers or employees. Where the repayment obligation is tied to post-employment competition, courts are likely to view the agreement as a noncompete and evaluate its reasonableness under comparable standards. *See, e.g., Brunner v. Hand Indus.*, 603 N.E.2d 157 (Ind.

Ct. App. 1992) (holding unenforceable agreement obligating former employee to repay costs of training if he joined competitor because employer had no protectable interest in general training and payments were unreasonable). In addition, as *Heder* and *American Consulting* indicate, repayment agreements that do not hinge on noncompetition can still run afoul of other laws and doctrines such as restrictions on liquidated damage clauses and state and federal wage payment laws. *See also Sands Appliance Serv. v. Wilson*, 615 N.W.2d 241 (Mich. 2000) (finding training repayment arrangement violated state anti-kickback law prohibiting employer from requiring any form of compensation in exchange for job). From the employee's perspective training repayment agreements might in some instances prove more onerous than noncompetes. Whereas an employee can comply with a noncompete by refraining from competition, a training repayment agreement requires that she have the funds to pay back the company. If the amount is high, it is easy to see how such an agreement can result in a total, if temporary, restraint on mobility.

2. *Liquidated Damages Analysis.* The two cases you read take very different analytical approaches to repayment agreements. *American Consulting* finds the repayment agreement to be an unenforceable penalty without regard to the law of restrictive covenants. *Heder*, on the other hand, concerns itself with whether the agreement is a noncompete, and upon concluding that it is not, enforces the repayment provision without regard to liquidated damages issues.

Although both liquidated damages provisions and restrictive covenants are matters of contract, the law treats the two types of clauses very differently. A liquidated damages provision that is part of a valid contract is presumptively enforceable, and the party seeking to avoid payment (the employee in repayment cases) bears the burden of overcoming that presumption by showing that the liquidated amount is disproportionate to probable or actual loss. *Cf. Sisters of Charity Health Sys. v. Farrago*, 21 A.3d 110 (Me. 2011) (a practice's patient base and goodwill were protectable business interests, which justified a liquidated damages clause that was a reasonable approximation of the damages that the employer would incur if a doctor left the practice to compete within a 25-mile radius). In contrast, we have seen that in most states, noncompetes are presumed void unless reasonable in relation to the employer's legitimate interests; it is the party seeking enforcement (the employer) who bears the burden of proof.

Why do the employees in *Heder* and *American Consulting* pursue such different legal theories? Is there any reason why the firefighters in *Heder* could not have availed themselves of the penalty argument that persuaded the court in *American Consulting*? Would a liquidated damages analysis lead to a different outcome in *Heder*? Or are competing results in the cases better explained by factual differences? If so, which facts?

Another question is whether a liquidated damages analysis is apt in either case. A typical liquidated damages provision is one that provides for a certain remedy in the event of a party's breach. For instance, an employer might include a repayment clause in a fixed-term contract under which an employee was bound to remain with the company for a set period, a technique you encountered in studying written contracts of high-level employees in Chapter 3. However, neither Heder nor Schuck had any contractual obligation to remain with their employers. *See Dresser-Rand Co. v. Bolick*, 14-12-00192-CV, 2013 WL 3770950 (Tex. App. July 18, 2013) (a repayment obligation for relocation expenses if an employee resigned within a year was not a liquidated damages provision when the defendant, as an at-will employee, had no obligation to work for the year and therefore did not breach to begin with).

Another situation in which employers might seek liquidated damages provisions is in settling claims. You will see an example of this in Chapter 13.

3. *"Garden Leave" Clauses.* Another way in which employers try to circumvent judicial disfavor of noncompetes is by adding clauses to their agreements promising to continue an employee's salary for the duration of the restraint. Offering pay — sometime referred to as "garden leave" — is a standard feature of noncompete contracts in the United Kingdom. *See generally* Greg T. Lembrich, Note, *Garden Leave: A Possible Solution to the Uncertain Enforceability of Restrictive Employment Covenants*, 102 Colum. L. Rev. 2291, 2292 (2002). A variation on this idea is to give the employee a choice between not competing and receiving some form of compensation or competing and sacrificing that benefit. *See, e.g., Lucente v. IBM*, 310 F.3d 243, 248 (2d Cir. 2002). Under such agreements, the employer essentially pays the worker to temporarily "sit out." *See, e.g., Kirby v. Frontier Medex, Inc.* 2013 U.S. Dist. LEXIS 155357 (D. Md. Oct. 30, 2013) Such clauses do not necessarily eliminate all of the harsh effects of noncompetes on employees — in fast-paced industries, skills can atrophy quickly and an employee kept from the field may lose touch with cutting-edge developments. Employers interested in hiring the defecting employee may not be willing to wait out the period of restraint, and the employee might miss out on key opportunities. However, compensating the employee makes the restraint significantly less onerous, which could make some courts more willing to enforce the agreement. *See, e.g., Nike v. McCarthy*, 379 F.3d 576, 587 (9th Cir. 2004) (finding fact that agreement obligated Nike to pay employee full salary during period of restriction a factor mitigating potential harm to the employee and supporting issuance of preliminary injunction). "Pay to sit out" clauses might increase the employer's chances of prevailing in other ways as well. Such clauses could support the employer's contention that it has a significant legitimate interest underlying the restraint. After all, it is unlikely that an employer would be willing to pay an employee *not* to work absent a significant economic reason to do so. *See* Cynthia L. Estlund, *Between Rights and Contract: Arbitration Agreements and Non-Compete Covenants as a Hybrid Form of Employment Law*, 155 U. Pa. L. Rev. 379, 425 (2006) (suggesting that mandatory garden leave could encourage employer self-policing in determining whether to seek noncompete enforcement). Alternatively, where the agreement is structured to allow the employee to compete or be paid, a court might be convinced that the special rules of noncompete enforcement do not apply. *See, e.g., Fraser v. Nationwide Mut. Ins. Co.*, 334 F. Supp. 2d 755, 760-61 (E.D. Pa. 2004) (describing clause under which insurance agent gave up deferred compensation if he chose to compete post-employment as more akin to incentive program than noncompete in finding contract enforceable without need for balancing of parties' interests). *But see Spiegel v. Thomas, Mann & Smith*, 811 S.W.2d 528, 530 (Tenn. 1991) (clause in law firm's stockholder's agreement under which lawyer who resigned but continued practice of law would forfeit deferred compensation was against public policy and unenforceable under state disciplinary rules prohibiting restriction of practice agreements between lawyers).

4. *No-Hire Agreements.* Still another option for employers is to bypass the employee altogether in favor of contracting directly with customers or competitors. Consulting and placement companies have long required clients to sign "no hire" agreements under which the client agrees that for a period of time it will not hire any employee leased to it by the consulting or placement company. *See, e.g., Blase Indus. v. Anorad Corp.*, 442 F.3d 235 (5th Cir. 2006). In some industries, competitors are adopting a similar technique, entering into mutual "no switching" agreements under which they agree not to "poach" one another's employees. In one sense, these contracts may be less problematic than noncompetes insofar as they are formed between companies possessing roughly equal bargaining power and eliminate only one possible employer for the individual worker. But in another sense, they are more troubling since there are serious antitrust concerns with such agreements, as indicated by litigation involving no poaching agreements by some of the biggest technology firms in Silicon Valley. The Department of Justice entered a consent decree with the defendants, and a class action was brought on behalf of the engineers whose compensation was presumably suppressed by the agreement. David Streitfeld, *Engineers Allege Hiring Collusion in Silicon Valley*, N.Y. TIMES, Mar. 1, 2014, A-1. At this writing, a $325 million settlement is under review. http://www.reuters.com/article/2014/06/19/us-apple-google-settlement-idUSKBN0EU2OP20140619. As these developments suggest, such agreements could easily be viewed as per se illegal market division (the market being the market for services). *See Palmer v. BRG of Georgia, Inc.*, 498 U.S. 46, 50 (1990) (horizontal market division per se illegal).

Further, where such agreements are widely used, or affect an industry that is dominated by a few large entities, no-switching agreements may have even harsher effects on employees than some noncompetes. *See, e.g., Heyde Companies, Inc. v. Dove Healthcare*, 654 N.W.2d 830, 833-34 (Wis. 2002) (finding no-hire agreement used by physical therapist supplier with multiple nursing homes it serviced to be an indirect noncompete that failed statutory reasonableness test). Indeed, such agreements are arguably more objectionable than ordinary noncompetes because the affected workers do not assent to or necessarily even know about them. *Id.* at 836. In addition, the anticompetitive effects of such agreements on society at large may be significant, particularly when made by large rival companies. *See generally* David Haase, *Agreements Between Employers Not to Hire Each Other's Employees: When Are They Enforceable?*, 21 LABOR LAWYER 277 (2006) (exploring enforceability issues under antitrust and state law).

5. *The Future of Private Ordering.* The legal significance of emerging contractual forms, like those described above, is as yet unknown. Both employers and companies must wait to see how courts and legislatures respond once such agreements start facing more consistent legal challenges. What is certain is that whatever way the law evolves in the area of employee competition, firms are likely to seek out newer and more creative ways of using private ordering to structure their relationships to maximum advantage.

Note on the Computer Fraud and Abuse Act

Although not limited to the scenario of competition by former employees, the Computer Fraud and Abuse Act ("CFAA"), 18 U.S.C. § 1030 (2014), has played an increasingly important role in such situations and is worth noting in its own right. The CFAA was enacted in 1986 with the primary purpose of combating computer "hacking," but it reaches not only access to computers "without authorization" (the paradigmatic anonymous hacker) but also actions "exceeding authorized access," which obviously could include employees taking confidential information with them when they depart. The CFAA creates criminal liability, but its use in the employment context is increasingly on the civil side with employers seeking compensatory damages or injunctive relief under the statute's authorization of suit by "[a]ny person who suffers damage or loss by reason of a violation." A typical civil case is an employer's suit against a former employee claiming misappropriation or destruction of its data.

A critical issue for CFAA litigation is whether an employee who violates the employer's restrictions on the use of information stored on a computer — for example, through an appropriate use policy — "exceeds authorized access." Some courts have been reluctant to read the statute this broadly, *e.g., WEC Carolina Energy Solutions LLC v. Miller*, 687 F.3d 199, 206 (4th Cir. 2012) *cert. dismissed*, 133 S. Ct. 831 (2013) ("[W]e adopt a narrow reading of the terms 'without authorization' and 'exceeds authorized access' and hold that they apply only when an individual accesses a computer without permission or obtains or alters information on a computer beyond that which he is authorized to access."); *United States v. Nosal*, 676 F.3d 854, 863 (9th Cir. 2012) (en banc) ("We need not decide today whether Congress *could* base criminal liability on violations of a company or website's computer use restrictions. Instead, we hold that the phrase 'exceeds authorized access' in the CFAA does not extend to violations of use restrictions. If Congress wants to incorporate misappropriation liability into the CFAA, it must speak more clearly."), but others have been more expansive. *E.g., Int'l Airport Centers, L.L.C. v. Citrin*, 440 F.3d 418 (7th Cir. 2006) (claim stated when an employee used a secure-erasure program to delete files on a laptop he had been assigned). Notice, of course, that a CFAA claim does not require a noncompetition clause nor does it require a finding that the information obtained is a trade secret or otherwise confidential. Rather, the gist of the claim is that the information was destroyed or taken without the necessary authority to do so. *See generally* Audra A. Dial & John M. Moye, *The Computer Fraud and Abuse Act and Disloyal Employees: How Far Should the Statute Go to Protect Employers from Trade Secret Theft?*, 64 HASTINGS L.J. 1447 (2013).

PROBLEM

8-5. Revisit the cases in this chapter in light of the developments in company contracting practices described above. Are there any cases in which it might have been prudent for the employer to use a "pay to sit out" clause, a training repayment agreement, or a "no-switching" contract? Are there other contract forms or clauses that you can think of that might have been appropriate? Choose one case and try your hand at drafting the alternative agreement.

Part Six

STATUTORY PROTECTIONS FOR EMPLOYEES

9

Antidiscrimination

A. THE POLICY BASES FOR ANTIDISCRIMINATION LAW

Federal laws bar discrimination by employers on a number of grounds: race, sex, religion, national origin, age, and disability. In addition, many state laws extend the list of prohibited grounds to marital status, political affiliation, and, increasingly, sexual orientation. What is so bad about discrimination? Employers "discriminate" all the time in the sense that they differentiate between employees for all sorts of reasons. But some bases of differentiation — race, sex, religion, national origin, age, disability — are impermissible, while other bases are perfectly legal. Still other bases, such as sexual orientation, are illegal in only a minority of states. Antidiscrimination laws generally prohibit employers from basing their employment decisions on protected group membership, rather than on an employee's qualifications or some other neutral factor. But reliance on neutral factors that disadvantage protected groups is also sometimes prohibited as discrimination unless the neutral factor is job-related.

The choice to prohibit discrimination emerges from two considerations. Most obviously, discrimination on the basis of certain characteristics, especially race and sex, is viewed as unfair since such characteristics are immutable and, therefore, beyond an individual's control. Because discrimination harms the victim for reasons he or she cannot control, it is also often viewed as immoral. This rationale, however, does not explain the prohibition against discrimination on the basis of religion or other characteristics over which the individual exercises some degree of choice. But discrimination based on religion or other mutable characteristics, such as political affiliation and marital status, is often viewed as wrongful because of deep-rooted concerns about human autonomy and the inalienability of fundamental rights. From this perspective, then, discrimination is wrongful because it damages the dignity of its victims.

Second, there is a socioeconomic agenda to antidiscrimination laws. This emerges most explicitly with respect to the Age Discrimination in Employment Act ("ADEA"), 29 U.S.C. §§ 621 et seq. (2014), and the Americans with Disabilities Act ("ADA"), 42 U.S.C.A. §§ 12101 et seq. (2014), where Congress stressed the waste of human resources caused by discrimination against older workers and workers with disabilities: Such action results not only in individual harm but also in the loss to society of the contributions of those whose abilities are not fully utilized. Although subordinate to dignity values, a concern for the potentially devastating economic consequences of discrimination was also prominent in the enactment of Title VII.

From this perspective, antidiscrimination statutes are united by two simple premises: First, the groups to be protected by the statute are disadvantaged economically; second, employers' discriminatory conduct causes, or at least contributes to, that disadvantage. Approached this way, the statutes seek to end discrimination in order to improve the economic condition of members of protected groups by allowing them to compete freely for jobs on the basis of their qualifications. Improving the economic condition of such groups can also redound to the benefit of society more generally.

Although equal employment opportunity has received almost unanimous support among all racial groups as an abstract principle, the antidiscrimination laws have often proved controversial in their application. The basic prohibition against express intentional racial discrimination is generally accepted, but a number of specific issues, including affirmative action, pregnancy discrimination, sexual harassment, disparate impact, and discrimination on the basis of sexual orientation, have generated intense national debate. Questions have also been raised about the effectiveness of antidiscrimination laws in raising the standard of living of protected groups.

To begin, not everyone agrees that discrimination should be legally prohibited. Some even question the basic prohibition against express intentional discrimination on account of race. From the beginning, some defended both the wisdom and morality of discrimination or at least questioned the morality of legislating nondiscrimination. While few still subscribe to such views, it has been argued more recently that discrimination may be rational and efficient. Still another view is that, even if discrimination is wrongful, antidiscrimination laws are unnecessary either because market forces will eliminate discrimination without government interference or because discrimination is no longer a significant social problem. An employer that discriminates, after all, must pay a price: Artificially contracting the supply of available labor tends to raise the price of the labor purchased. If many employers discriminate, the price (wages) of their workforce will climb. Competitors will be free to exploit the pool of excluded black (or female) workers at lower wages, thus gaining a competitive advantage. As more employers seek lower-cost black workers, their value will rise. Thus, the market will correct discrimination, without the need for legal intervention. *See* John J. Donohue III, *Advocacy Versus Analysis in Assessing Employment Discrimination Law*, 44 STAN. L. REV. 1583, 1591 (1992) (recounting such opposition to Title VII's enactment); Richard A. Epstein, FORBIDDEN GROUNDS: THE CASE AGAINST EMPLOYMENT DISCRIMINATION LAWS (1992) (adding to the economic argument a strong libertarian critique of government intervention to eliminate discrimination).

Despite these theoretic objections, a variety of statistical studies suggest the continued existence of discrimination in a number of settings, ranging from sports to bankruptcy. In sports, for example, studies of basketball fouls seem to document race bias by referees. *See* Joseph Price & Justin Wolfers, *Racial Discrimination Among NBA Referees*, 125 Q. J. ECON. 1859 (2010) ("[M]ore personal fouls are called against players when they are officiated by an opposite-race refereeing crew than when officiated by an own-race crew. These biases are sufficiently large that we find appreciable differences in whether predominantly black teams are more likely to win or lose, based on the racial composition of the refereeing crew."). In the bankruptcy arena, a study suggests that federal judges are more likely to allow white debtors to reorganize than black debtors, even after holding constant all relevant factors. Sumit Agarwal et al., *Dismissal with Prejudice? Race and Politics in Personal Bankruptcy* (Vanderbilt L. & Econs. Research Paper Aug. 25, 2010), *available at* http://papers.ssrn.com/sol3/papers.cfm?abstract_id=1633083 ("[W]hite judges are 21% more likely to dismiss the chapter 13 petition of an African American debtor relative to a white debtor."). Perhaps most dramatically, Laura Giuliana, David I. Levine, & Jonathon Leonard, *Manager Race and the Race of New Hires*, 27 J. Lab. Econ. 589 (Oct. 2009), use data from a large retailer with frequent employee turnover to conclude that nonblack managers hire more whites and fewer blacks than do African American managers; in areas with large Hispanic populations, Hispanic managers hire more Hispanics and fewer whites than white managers.

This kind of statistical analysis of the persistence of discrimination in the workplace is confirmed by a number of field experiments. For example, Marianne Bertrand & Sendhil Mullainathan, *Are Emily and Greg More Employable than Lakisha and Jamal? A Field Experiment on Labor Market Discrimina*tion, 94 Am. Econ. Rev. 991 (2004), report that, when identical fictitious resumes were sent to employers in Boston and Chicago, those receiving more favorable treatment were those containing non–African American sounding names. More recently, a study showed that legal memoranda supposedly written by black attorneys were rated much lower than the same workproduct supposedly written by white attorneys. Nextions, *Written in Black and White: Exploring Confirmation Bias in Racialized Perceptions of Writing Skills*, http://www.nextions.com/wp-content/files_mf/13972237592014040114Writtenin BlackandWhiteYPS.pdf.

With respect to sex, Claudia Goldin & Cecilia Rouse, *Orchestrating Impartiality: The Impact of "Blind" Auditions on Female Musicians*, 90 Am. Econ. Rev. 715 (2000), report that auditions held with the performer behind a screen substantially increased the likelihood that a female candidate would advance out of the preliminary round in an orchestra's selection process. And concerning age, Michael Winerip, *Three Men, Three Ages. Which Do You Like?*, N.Y. Times July 27, 2013, at B-1, reported a study in which three versions of the same person at three different ages were treated differently by a test group of Princeton undergraduates; the "assertive" version of the character was viewed more negatively than the younger versions even when saying the same thing. *See generally* Nilanjana Dasgupta, *Implicit Ingroup Favoritism, Outgroup Favoritism, and Their Behavioral Manifestations*, 17 Soc. Just. Res. 143 (2004) (collecting research showing biased behavior in employment situations).

Such findings are consistent with older studies showing that, when pairs of black and white "auditors" applied for jobs, the white applicant was able to advance farther through the hiring process than an equally qualified black counterpart in one of five audits. "In other words, the white was able to either submit an application, receive a formal interview, or the white was offered a job when the black was not. Overall, in one out of eight or 15 percent of the audits, the white was offered a job although his equally qualified black partner was not." Margery Austin Turner, Michael Fix, & Raymond J. Struyk, Opportunities Denied, Opportunities Diminished: Discrimination in Hiring 31-32 (1991).

In an attempt to explain the discrepancy between economic theory and the reality on the ground, Gary Becker in THE ECONOMICS OF DISCRIMINATION (2d ed. 1971), posited that employers have a "taste for discrimination," for which they are willing to pay. Professor David A. Strauss, in *The Law and Economics of Racial Discrimination in Employment: The Case for Numerical Standards*, 79 GEO. L. J. 1619 (1991), notes that the "taste" may be that of the employer itself or of someone whose preferences the employer has to consider — other employees or customers. A version of this argument appeared in Professor Epstein's book FORBIDDEN GROUNDS, in which he claimed that homogeneity in a workplace could be conducive to productivity: where "individual tastes are grouped by race, by sex, by age, by national origin — and to some extent they are — then there is a necessary conflict between the commands of any antidiscrimination law and the smooth operation of the firm." *Id*. at 66-67; *see also* Devon Carbado & Mitu Galati, *The Law and Economics of Critical Race Theory: Crossroads, Directions, and a New Critical Race Theory*, 112 YALE L. J. 1757, 1762 (2003) (while disagreeing with Professor Epstein's normative view, agreeing that "employers have incentives to screen prospective employees for homogeneity, and, in order to counter racial stereotypes, employees have incentives to demonstrate a willingness and capacity to assimilate."); Scott A. Moss, *Women Choosing Diverse Workplaces: A Rational Preference with Disturbing Implications for Both Occupational Segregation and Economic Analysis of Law*, 27 HARV. WOMEN'S L. J. 1 (2004) (women rationally use the level of diversity as a proxy for discrimination and therefore tend to prefer workplaces with more women).

A related argument that seeks to explain (but not justify) the persistence of discrimination is that some protected characteristics are correlated with ability or other desirable characteristics. For instance, men are statistically more likely than women to have longer job tenure and not terminate or cut back employment after becoming a parent. This theory is sometimes called "statistical discrimination." Strauss, *supra*, at 1622. The logic of statistical discrimination does not require that racial or gender differences be inherent — the correlation between race or gender and productivity could be the result of factors such as past societal discrimination. Further, "statistical discrimination" does not necessarily mean that the employer acts only on the basis of scientifically ascertained differences. Indeed, such discrimination will be more or less "rational" depending on the relationship between the stereotype used and statistical reality.

Is statistical discrimination objectionable even if it is accurate in group terms? Rational or not, relying on generalizations (perhaps better called stereotypes) excludes entire groups without any assessment of individual abilities. This is particularly problematic if the generalization is itself rooted in prior discrimination. *See* Mary Becker, *The Law and Economics of Racial Discrimination in Employment: Needed in the Nineties: Improved Individual and Structural Remedies for Racial and Sexual Disadvantages in Employment*, 79 GEO. L. J. 1659, 1664 (1991). Even if perceived productivity differences are real across groups, should employers be free to rely on them? Professor Samuel Issacharoff, in *Contractual Liberties in Discriminatory Markets*, 70 TEX. L. REV. 1219, 1222 (1992), criticizes Epstein's "fundamental assumption that each individual is delivered to the labor market as a more or less intact bundle of skills and abilities." This is "a shockingly static view" of what is, in fact, a dynamic process. Indeed, Issacharoff argues, it is the very "disincentives for optimal acquisition of human capital" brought about by discrimination that justify intervention in the market. Professor Nancy E. Dowd, in *Liberty vs. Equality: In Defense of*

Privileged White Males, 34 Wm. & Mary L. Rev. 429, 442 (1993), views Epstein as a relatively frank apologist for racism and sexism. Quoting Epstein that individual tastes are grouped to some extent by race and sex and that these tastes necessarily conflict with the smooth operation of at least some firms, she states, "These are outrageous statements, filled with stereotypes and race and gender essentialism reduced to implicit biological 'natural' preference, amounting to an outright justification for skin and gender privilege." *See also* Andrew Koppelman, *Feminism & Libertarianism: A Response to Richard Epstein*, 1999 U. Chi. Legal F. 115 (1999).

B. INDIVIDUAL DISPARATE TREATMENT DISCRIMINATION

1. Introduction

In order to address the pervasive problem of employment discrimination, Congress enacted a series of statutes dealing with various aspects of the phenomenon. These laws include Title VII of the Civil Rights Act of 1964; the Civil War Reconstruction statutes, especially 42 U.S.C. § 1981; the Age Discrimination in Employment Act of 1967 ("ADEA"); and the Americans with Disabilities Act of 1990 ("ADA"). The avenues of relief under the statutes differ from each other in important ways, but all are concerned with discrimination in employment. The concept of "discrimination," however, has been developed in ways that are not always intuitively obvious. Indeed, "discrimination" is a term of art that embraces several different definitions, each with its own distinctive theory and methods of proof.

Three of the statutes adopt a unitary definition of "disparate treatment" discrimination. The term originated in cases decided under Title VII and has been applied essentially unchanged in both ADEA cases and suits brought under § 1981. Disparate treatment, however, has developed in two distinct ways. Individual disparate treatment is the focus of this section, while systemic disparate treatment is taken up in section C. Individual disparate treatment dominates the cases, at least measured by number filed, in the federal courts.

Title VII, 42 U.S.C. §§ 2000e to 2000e-17 (2014), which embraces almost all employers of 15 or more employees, proscribes discrimination in employment on the basis of race, color, religion, sex, or national origin. Section 703(a), 42 U.S.C. § 2000e-2(a)(1), states the basic standard: It is an "unlawful employment practice" for an employer "to fail or refuse to hire or to discharge any individual, or otherwise to discriminate against any individual with respect to his compensation, terms, conditions, or privileges of employment, because of such individual's race, color, religion, sex, or national origin. . . ." The ADEA, 29 U.S.C. §§ 631-34 (2014), applies to employers with 20 or more workers. It tracks Title VII's language but ends each clause with "because of such individual's age." § 623(a). The ADEA, however, defines "age" to include only those at least 40 years of age. § 631(a).

Finally, in its present form, 42 U.S.C. § 1981 (2014), guarantees "all persons within the jurisdiction of the United States . . . the same right in every State and Territory to make and enforce contracts . . . as is enjoyed by white citizens. . . ."

Section 1981 originated in the Civil War Reconstruction era as one of several statutes intended to protect former slaves. While its success in promoting racial equality was limited for a century, doubts about whether it barred private discrimination ended in 1975 with *Johnson v. Railway Express Agency, Inc.*, 421 U.S. 454, 459-60 (1975), in which the Supreme Court wrote: "§ 1981 affords a federal remedy against discrimination in private employment on the basis of race."

Slack v. Havens
7 FEP 885 (S.D. Cal. 1973), aff'd as modified, 522 F.2d 1091 (9th Cir. 1975)

THOMPSON, J.

This action is brought by the plaintiffs, four black women, who allege they were discriminatorily discharged, due to their race, in violation of the Civil Rights Act of 1964, specifically 42 U.S.C. § 2000e-2(a)(1). . . .

4. On January 31, 1968, plaintiffs Berrel Matthews, Emily Hampton and Isabell Slack were working in the bonding and coating department of defendant Industries' plant, engaged in preparing and assembling certain tubing components for defendant's product. A white co-worker, Sharon Murphy, was also assigned to the bonding and coating department on that day and was performing the same general work as the three plaintiffs mentioned above. The fourth plaintiff, Kathleen Hale, was working in another department on January 31st.

Near the end of the working day, plaintiffs Matthews, Hampton and Slack were called together by their immediate supervisor, Ray Pohasky, and informed that the following morning, upon reporting to work, they would suspend regular production and engage in a general cleanup of the bonding and coating department. The cleanup was to consist of washing walls and windows whose sills were approximately 12 to 15 feet above the floor, cleaning light fixtures, and scraping the floor which was caked with deposits of hardened resin. Plaintiffs Matthews, Hampton and Slack protested the assigned work, arguing that it was not within their job description, which included only light cleanup in their immediate work areas, and that it was too hard and dangerous. Mr. Pohasky agreed that it was hard work and said that he would check to see if they had to do it.

5. On the following work day, February 1, 1968, plaintiffs Matthews, Hampton, and Slack reported to the bonding and coating department along with Sharon Murphy, their white co-worker. However, Mr. Pohasky excused Sharon Murphy to another department for the day, calling in plaintiff Kathleen Hale from the winding department where she had been on loan from the bonding and coating department for about a week. Mr. Pohasky then repeated his announcement that the heavy cleaning would have to be done. The four plaintiffs joined in protest against the heavy cleanup work. They pointed out that they had not been hired to do janitorial type work, and one of the plaintiffs inquired as to why Sharon Murphy had been excused from the cleanup detail even though she had very little seniority among the ladies in the bonding and coating department. In reply, they were told by Mr. Pohasky that they would do the work, "or else." There was uncontradicted testimony that at sometime during their conversation Pohasky injected the statement that "Colored people should stay in their places," or words to that effect. Some further discussion took place between plaintiffs and Pohasky and then with Gary Helming, plaintiffs' general supervisor, but eventually

each of the plaintiffs was taken to the office of Mr. Helming where she was given her final paycheck and fired. Plaintiff Matthews testified without contradiction that on the way to Mr. Helming's office Mr. Pohasky made the comment that "Colored folks are hired to clean because they clean better."

6. The general cleanup work was later performed by newly-hired male employees. Sharon Murphy was never asked to participate in this cleanup before or after the plaintiffs' termination.

7. The day following the plaintiffs' firing a conference was held between plaintiffs and defendant Glenn G. Havens, together with Mr. Helming, Mr. Pohasky and other company officials, but the dispute was not resolved as to the work plaintiffs were expected to do. Apparently, the plaintiffs were offered reinstatement if they would now agree to do the same cleanup work. They refused. . . .

8. Having concluded that defendant Industries is an "employer" under Title VII of the Civil Rights Act for the purposes of this action, we must next consider whether plaintiffs' termination amounted to unlawful discrimination against them because of their race. Defendants deny that the facts support such a conclusion, contending that plaintiffs' case amounts to nothing more than a dispute as to their job classification.

Admittedly, the majority of the discussion between plaintiffs and Industries' management on January 31 and February 1, 1968 centered around the nature of the duties which plaintiffs were ordered to perform. Plaintiffs pointed out that they had not been hired with the understanding that they would be expected to perform more than light cleanup work immediately adjacent to their work stations. They were met with an ultimatum that they do the work — or else. Additionally, no explanation was offered as to why Sharon Murphy, a white co-worker, had been transferred out of the bonding and coating department the morning that the heavy cleaning was to begin there, while plaintiff Hale was called back from the winding department, where she had been working, to the bonding and coating area, specifically for participation in the general cleanup. It is not disputed that Sharon Murphy had less seniority than all of the plaintiffs except plaintiff Hale (having been hired 8 days prior to plaintiff Hale) and no evidence of a bona fide business reason was ever educed by defendants as to why Sharon Murphy was excused from assisting the plaintiffs in the proposed cleaning project.

The only evidence that did surface at the trial regarding the motives for the decisions of the management of defendant Industries consisted of certain statements by supervisor Pohasky, who commented to plaintiff Matthews that "colored folks were hired to clean because they clean better," and "colored folks should stay in their place," or words to that effect. Defendants attempt to disown these statements with the argument that Pohasky's state of mind and arguably discriminatory conduct was immaterial and not causative of the plaintiffs' discharge.

But defendants cannot be allowed to divorce Mr. Pohasky's conduct from that of Industries so easily. First of all, 42 U.S.C. § 2000e(b) expressly includes "any agent" of an employer within the definition of "employer." Secondly, there was a definite causal relation between Pohasky's apparently discriminatory conduct and the firings. Had Pohasky not discriminated against the plaintiffs by demanding they perform work he would not require of a white female employee, they would not have been faced with the unreasonable choice of having to choose between obeying his discriminatory work order and the loss of their employment. Finally, by backing up Pohasky's ultimatum the top level management of Industries ratified his discriminatory conduct and must be held liable for the consequences thereof. . . .

From all the evidence before it, this Court is compelled to find that defendant Industries, through its managers and supervisor, Mr. Pohasky, meant to require the plaintiffs to perform the admittedly heavy and possibly dangerous work of cleaning the bonding and coating department, when they would not require the same work from plaintiffs' white fellow employee. Furthermore, it meant to enforce that decision by firing the plaintiffs when they refused to perform that work. The consequence of the above was racial discrimination whatever the motivation of the management of defendant Industries may have been. Therefore, the totality of Industries' conduct amounted, in the Court's opinion, to an unlawful employment practice prohibited by the Civil Rights Act, specifically, 42 U.S.C. § 2000e-2(a)(1).

NOTES

1. *Inroad into at Will.* As we have repeatedly seen, the traditional common law rule of employment contracts is that any contract not for a definite time is terminable at will by either party — for any reason or for no reason, for good reason or for bad reason. *Slack v. Havens* clearly changes this. How would you state the rule in cases to which Title VII and other antidiscrimination statutes apply?

2. *Proving Discrimination.* Would there be sufficient evidence of discrimination in the case without the statements of Pohasky — that "colored folks are hired to clean because they clean better" — to support a finding that the cleaning assignment was made to plaintiffs because they were African Americans? What other evidence supports the conclusion of race discrimination? Is there any evidence that the assignment was *not* made because of plaintiffs' race? Suppose you represented the defendant in *Slack*. What defenses might you consider when faced with this fact situation? What information would you look for with respect to Sharon Murphy?

3. *The Meaning of "Race."* While "race" seems an intuitive concept (and probably did to Pohasky), "race" as a legal concept is more complicated. In *Saint Francis College v. Al-Khazraji*, 481 U.S. 604 (1987), the Court considered a suit by a U.S. citizen who had been born in Iraq and claimed that he was denied tenure at the college based on his Arab ancestry. The district court rejected his § 1981 claim because Arabs are generally considered Caucasians. The Supreme Court disagreed. While today we tend to think in terms of broader racial groups, many biologists and anthropologists criticize racial classifications as arbitrary and of little use in understanding the variability of human beings. *See, e.g.*, Erik Lillquist & Charles A. Sullivan, *The Law and Genetics of Racial Profiling in Medicine*, 39 HARV. C.R.-C.L. L. REV. 391 (2004). Current scientific thinking on race, however, was ultimately irrelevant to the *Al-Khazraji* Court. Even if Arabs are now considered Caucasians, that was not the understanding in the nineteenth century when § 1981 was enacted. At that time, "race" was used to include distinct tribes and ethnic groups: "The 1863 version of the New American Cyclopaedia divided the Arabs into a number of subsidiary races; represented the Hebrews as of the Semitic race, and identified numerous other groups as constituting races, including Swedes, Norwegians, Germans, Greeks, Finns, Italians (referring to mixture of different races), Spanish, Mongolians, Russians, and the like." *See also Shaare Tefila Congregation v. Cobb*, 481 U.S. 615, 617 (1987) (holding that § 1982 suit by a synagogue for defacement of its walls with anti-Semitic slogans is permissible because, when § 1982 was adopted, "Jews and Arabs were among the people then considered to be distinct races and hence within the protection of the statute"). As a result, some "race" discrimination suits under § 1981 are probably better characterized as "national origin" suits under Title VII.

4. *Admissions of Discriminatory Intent.* Pohasky's statements suffice to show his intent to discriminate because they constitute admissions of the state of mind that motivated him to assign the plaintiffs to this job. Where such statements can be proven, they are very powerful indications of discriminatory intent on various grounds:

a. In a race discrimination case, a police officer testified that the chief of police "loudly stated in my presence that he would not allow 'Spics and Niggers' to run his department within very close earshot of me." *Perez v. N.J. Transit Corp.*, 341 F. App'x 757, 761 (3d Cir. 2009).

b. In a sex discrimination case, plaintiff's supervisor "referred to women buyers as 'PMS,' 'menstrual,' and 'dragon lady.' He also stated that most women probably just wanted to stay home." *Passantino v. Johnson & Johnson Consumer Prods.*, 212 F.3d 493 (9th Cir. 2000).

c. In a religious discrimination case, a letter demoting plaintiff because he was a member of a church whose creed was white supremacy (and therefore the employees he supervised would not have confidence in his objectivity) constituted direct evidence of discriminatory intent on the basis of religion. *Peterson v. Wilmur Communications, Inc.*, 205 F. Supp. 2d 1014 (E.D. Wis. 2002).

d. In ADEA age discrimination cases, referring to an older worker as "'an F'n dinosaur.'" *Loveless v. John's Ford, Inc.*, 232 F. App'x 229, 232 n.3 (4th Cir. 2007).

e. In a national origin hostile work environment case, referring to a Mexican-American employee as "'Wetback,' 'Spic,' and 'Mexican Mother F_____.'" *Miller v. Kenworth of Dothan Inc.*, 277 F.3d 1269, 1273-74 (11th Cir. 2002).

In our society, such statements are increasingly rare (whether or not the underlying belief systems have changed), but they continue to exist, as the national furor over the racist statements of Donald Sterling indicates. *See* John Branch, *NBA Bans Clippers Owner Donald Sterling for Life*, N.Y. TIMES, Apr. 30, 2014, at A-1.

5. *Animus or Intent?* In these examples, the statement indicates the employer's animus or hostility to the group in question. But Pohasky apparently assigned plaintiffs to the cleaning work in question because he believed them to be better cleaners. Is this pejorative? If so, is it pejorative because it suggests that blacks can do only menial jobs like cleaning? Perhaps it does not matter. While discrimination may be motivated by hate, fear, or revulsion, the statutes do not require such negative impulses. If Pohasky chose the plaintiffs because he thought they were better workers than whites, at cleaning as well as everything else, he would still have been discriminating within the meaning of the statute. He would be intending to assign jobs by race.

6. *Conscious and Unconscious Stereotyping.* Mr. Pohasky was, presumably, aware of the beliefs he had about African Americans. If they were "stereotypes," he thought of them as true generalizations. Many stereotypes are like this—we employ them deliberately because they conform to our view of reality (whether or not that view is correct). But, as we have suggested earlier, there is a different view of how stereotypes operate in today's society. Professor Linda Hamilton Krieger, in *The Content of Our Categories: A Cognitive Bias Approach to Discrimination and Equal Employment*

Opportunity, 47 STAN. L. REV. 1161 (1995), broke ground for a different view of intent to discriminate, one that has come to dominate the academic literature under rubrics such as "cognitive bias," "unreflective discrimination," "subtle bias," and "unconscious" (or "subconscious") "discrimination." *See generally* Marc R. Poirier, *Using Stereotyping and Cognitive Bias Evidence to Prove Gender Discrimination: Is Cognitive Bias at Work a Dangerous Condition on Land?*, 7 EMPLOYEE RTS. & EMP. POL'Y J. 459 (2003). As the diversity of labels indicates, the precise phenomena at issue are often contested, but Professor Krieger offers an excellent place to start. Using the insights provided by cognitive psychology, she concludes that stereotyping by race and gender is far more insidious than is often recognized because it is often an "unintended consequence" of the necessity for humans to categorize their sensory perceptions in order to make any sense of the world:

> [The] central premise of social cognition theory [is] that cognitive structures and processes involved in categorization and information processing can in and of themselves result in stereotyping and other forms of biased intergroup judgment previously attributed to motivational processes. The social cognition approach to discrimination comprises three claims relevant to our present inquiry. The first is that stereotyping . . . is nothing special. It is simply a form of categorization [of our sensory perceptions], similar in structure and function to the categorization of natural objects. According to this view, stereotypes, like other categorical structures, are cognitive mechanisms that all people, not just "prejudiced" ones, use to simplify the task of perceiving, processing, and retaining information about people in memory. They are central, and indeed essential to normal cognitive functioning.
>
> The second claim posited in social cognition theory is that, once in place, stereotypes bias intergroup judgment and decisionmaking. . . . [T]hey function as implicit theories, biasing in predictable ways the perception, interpretation, encoding, retention, and recall of information about other people. These biases are cognitive rather than motivational. They operate absent intent to favor or disfavor members of a particular social group. And, perhaps most significant for present purposes, they bias a decisionmaker's judgment long before the "moment of decision" [when the employment decision in question is made], as a decisionmaker attends to relevant data and interprets, encodes, stores, and retrieves it from memory. These biases "sneak up on" the decisionmaker, distorting bit by bit the data upon which his decision is eventually based.
>
> The third claim follows from the second. Stereotypes, when they function as implicit prototypes or schemas [by which we evaluate each other], operate beyond the reach of decisionmaker self-awareness. Empirical evidence indicates that people's access to their own cognitive processes is in fact poor. Accordingly, cognitive bias may well be both unintentional and unconscious.

Id. at 1187-88; *see also* Tristin K. Green, in *Discrimination in Workplace Dynamics: Toward a Structural Account of Disparate Treatment Theory*, 38 HARV. C.R.-C.L. L. REV. 91, 128 (2003); Tristin K. Green, *Targeting Workplace Context: Title VII as a Tool for Institutional Reform*, 72 FORDHAM L. REV. 659 (2003).

When stereotyping is unintentional and unconscious, should acting based on stereotypes constitute individual disparate treatment discrimination? It is treating people differently based on their race or gender, but is that what antidiscrimination law proscribes? Or does intentional discrimination require a conscious intent to discriminate? For example, Professor Amy Wax argues in *Discrimination as Accident*, 74 IND. L.J. 1129 (1999), that, when discrimination is not conscious, employer efforts to reduce it will likely be unavailing. She therefore opposes liability for this variety of discrimination. *See also* Patrick Shin, *Liability for Unconscious Discrimination?*

A Thought Experiment in the Theory of Employment Discrimination Law, 62 HASTINGS L. J, 67 (2010). But even Professor Wax agrees that, from a pure causation perspective, Title VII could be read to bar unconscious discrimination if it could be established as resulting in an adverse employment action. Amy L. Wax, *The Discriminating Mind: Define It, Prove It*, 40 CONN. L. REV. 979, 894 (2008). And others argue against limiting the antidiscrimination statutes to conscious actions. *See* Michael Selmi, *Discrimination as Accident: Old Whine, New Bottle*, 74 IND. L. J. 1234 (1999); Melissa Hart, *Subjective Decisionmaking and Unconscious Discrimination*, 56 ALA. L. REV. 741, 790-91 (2005) (the "judicially imposed requirement of employer dishonesty — with its attendant focus on the consciously intentional nature of prohibited discrimination — was never an element of Title VII, and it should be abandoned."); *see also* Tristin K. Green & Alexandra Kalev, *Discrimination-Reducing Measures at the Relational Level*, 59 HASTINGS L. J. 1435, 1435 (2008) (discrimination-reducing measures should be broadened to address the relational sources of discrimination — social interactions and relations at work that operate to reinforce stereotypes and bias). What do you think? Should disparate treatment discrimination require a conscious intent to discriminate, or is it enough to find that the plaintiff's protected class status caused the decision to occur? If a supervisor honestly believed he was acting for a nondiscriminatory reason, even if his unconscious biases in fact influenced his decision, should liability be imposed? If so, how would a plaintiff prove that, despite the supervisor's "honest belief," racial bias caused the decision?

7. *Are the Bad Old Days Still Around?* While most employment discrimination scholars agree that some variation of the cognitive bias theory explains an increasing percentage of cases in which women and minorities are disadvantaged relative to white males, others have warned against too quickly concluding that "old fashioned" discrimination is not a continuing and serious problem. *See* Michael L. Selmi, *Sex Discrimination in the Nineties, Seventies Style: Case Studies in the Preservation of Male Norms*, 9 EMPLOYEE RTS. & EMP. POL'Y J. 1 (2005) ("[T]here remains a significant amount of discrimination in the workplace that is not properly labeled as subtle but which involves the active and conscious exclusion of women from the workplace."). *See also* Ralph Richard Banks & Richard Thompson Ford, *(How) Does Unconscious Bias Matter?: Law, Politics, and Racial Inequality*, 58 EMORY L. J. 1053, 1059 (2009) ("The unconscious bias approach not only discounts the persistence of knowing discrimination, it elides the substantive inequalities that fuel conscious and unconscious bias alike. While we do not doubt the existence of unconscious bias, we do doubt that contemporary racial bias accounts for all, or even most, of the racial injustice that bedevils our society."). As Selmi documents, discrimination cases are frequently emotionally charged because members of traditionally excluded groups are often resented when they arrive in the workplace or seek to rise above their traditional roles. Discrimination may also be motivated by a desire to subordinate. Mary Becker, *The Law and Economics of Racial Discrimination in Employment: Needed in the Nineties: Improved Individual and Structural Remedies for Racial and Sexual Disadvantages in Employment*, 79 GEO. L. J. 1659, 1667 (1991). Certainly, the continued harassment litigation, challenging explicit sexual and racial harassment, suggests that not all discriminatory biases operate below the level of consciousness.

8. *Intent, Motive, and the Prohibited Trait.* To this point, we have spoken of discriminatory "intent," which is often the way the Supreme Court has framed the individual disparate treatment theory. But the Court also often spoke of discriminatory "motive." As we will see in more detail in *Staub v. Proctor Hospital*, 131 S. Ct. 1186 (2011), reproduced at page 620, there is a distinction between the two concepts,

although the Court often continues to speak of them as interchangeable. The distinction can be seen in *Hazen Paper Co. v. Biggins*, 507 U.S. 604 (1993), where a jury found violations under both the ADEA and ERISA when the 62-year-old plaintiff was fired as he approached a critical vesting date for his pension. The Supreme Court overturned the verdict, focusing on what has since come to be known as the "mixed motives" question: what the law should do when the employer acts because of two separate motives. While Hazen Paper obviously intended to fire the plaintiff, it might have been motivated to do so by his age, his pension status, a work-related reason, or all three. *Biggins* held that, when there were two or more potential motives, "a disparate treatment claim cannot succeed unless the employee's protected trait actually played a role in that process and had a determinative influence on the outcome." 507 U.S. at 610. This principle continues to operate under the Age Discrimination Act, *see Gross v. FBL Fin. Servs.*, 557 U.S. 167 (2009) (age must be the "but for" cause of adverse employment action), and for Title VII retaliation cases, *University of Texas Sw. Med. Ctr. v. Nassar*, 133 S. Ct. 2517 (2013), but we will see that it has been altered under Title VII for "status" discrimination. *See* page 597.

Biggins also focused more closely on the meaning of discriminatory motive. The Court held that firing someone to avoid his pension vesting, while a violation of ERISA, was not per se age discrimination.

> It is the very essence of age discrimination for an older employee to be fired because the employer believes that productivity and competence decline with old age. As we explained in *EEOC v. Wyoming*, 460 U.S. 226 (1983), Congress' promulgation of the ADEA was prompted by its concern that older workers were being deprived of employment on the basis of inaccurate and stigmatizing stereotypes.
>
> Although age discrimination rarely was based on the sort of animus motivating some other forms of discrimination, it was based in large part on stereotypes unsupported by objective fact. . . . Moreover, the available empirical evidence demonstrated that arbitrary age lines were in fact generally unfounded and that, as an overall matter, the performance of older workers was at least as good as that of younger workers. . . .
>
> When the employer's decision is wholly motivated by factors other than age, the problem of inaccurate and stigmatizing stereotypes disappears. This is true even if the motivating factor is correlated with age, as pension status typically is. Pension plans typically provide that an employee's accrued benefits will become nonforfeitable, or "vested," once the employee completes a certain number of years of service with the employer. On average, an older employee has had more years in the work force than a younger employee, and thus may well have accumulated more years of service with a particular employer. Yet an employee's age is analytically distinct from his years of service. An employee who is younger than 40, and therefore outside the class of older workers as defined by the ADEA, may have worked for a particular employer his entire career, while an older worker may have been newly hired. Because age and years of service are analytically distinct, an employer can take account of one while ignoring the other, and thus it is incorrect to say that a decision based on years of service is necessarily "age-based."

Id. at 610-11 (citation omitted). The Court did recognize that it would violate the ADEA were the employer to use "[p]ension status [as] a proxy for age, not in the sense that the ADEA makes the two factors equivalent, but in the sense that the employer may suppose a correlation between the two factors and act accordingly." *Id.* at 613 (citation omitted).

But does this approach make sense? Suppose an employer discriminated against workers because they had gray hair. That's pretty highly — but not perfectly — correlated with age. How about wrinkles, which are even more highly (but still not perfectly) correlated with age? And there are many traits that are correlated with, but scarcely essential to, sex and race. We will see that the disparate impact theory to a considerable extent protects against an employer's use of irrational but highly correlated factors, but isn't there something odd about saying that discrimination against gray-haired, wrinkled people isn't age discrimination?

9. *Employer Reaction to the Protected Trait. Biggins* focuses our attention on the employer's subjective reaction to the "protected class." In the case itself, of course, that class was older workers. While the Court viewed an employer's belief that "productivity and competence decline with old age" to be "the very essence of age discrimination," surely that cannot be the only impermissible kind of discriminatory intent within the statute: What if the jury found that Biggins was fired because the Hazens thought customers would not like working with older people? Older people are also often seen as "stuck in their ways," resistant to new ideas. If Hazen Paper viewed Biggins as not being sufficiently innovative, might that also indicate age stereotyping?

But *Biggins* can be generalized to other protected classes, most notably race, sex, national origin, or religion under Title VII. For liability to attach, the employer must have some aversion to the class in question. In *Slack*, that aversion was proven in part by Pohasky's remarks. While *Biggins* was remanded for further proceedings, this kind of "direct" evidence was lacking. Without such evidence, could Biggins prevail? How likely is it that the Hazens incorrectly believed Biggins' competence declined? Aren't employers more likely to act on "inaccurate and stigmatizing stereotypes" regarding competence in refusing to hire older workers than in firing them? The Hazens had the opportunity to watch plaintiff perform over almost a decade. If they fired him because they believed his competence was diminishing, how could that be the result of a stereotype? Or does Professor Krieger's article help explain this? To prevail, would Biggins have had to show (a) that they incorrectly evaluated his competence and (b) that they attributed his perceived loss of competence to his age? What if they correctly believed Biggins' performance was declining but also attributed it to his age?

10. *Looking Forward.* Neither *Slack* nor *Biggins* focuses on burdens of proof, but it has become clear that, under the disparate treatment theory, the plaintiff has the burden of establishing discriminatory intent. This raises two distinct problems. *Slack* primarily involved "direct" evidence of intent: Pohasky's statements indicating why he acted as he did. In contrast, *Biggins* primarily involved "circumstantial," or inferential, methods of proof. The next section considers the structure of an inferential case of individual disparate treatment.

2. Proving Discrimination: The Traditional Framework

a. The Plaintiff's Prima Facie Case

McDonnell Douglas Corp. v. Green
411 U.S. 792 (1973)

Justice POWELL delivered the opinion of the Court.

. . . Petitioner, McDonnell Douglas Corp., is an aerospace and aircraft manufacturer headquartered in St. Louis, Missouri, where it employs over 30,000 people.

Respondent, a black citizen of St. Louis, worked for petitioner as a mechanic and laboratory technician from 1956 until August 28, 1964 when he was laid off in the course of a general reduction in petitioner's work force.

Respondent, a long-time activist in the civil rights movement, protested vigorously that his discharge and the general hiring practices of petitioner were racially motivated. As part of this protest, respondent and other members of the Congress on Racial Equality illegally stalled their cars on the main roads leading to petitioner's plant for the purpose of blocking access to it at the time of the morning shift change. The District Judge described the plan for, and respondent's participation in, the "stall-in" as follows:

[F]ive teams, each consisting of four cars would "tie up" five main access roads into McDonnell at the time of the morning rush hour. The drivers of the cars were instructed to line up next to each other completely blocking the intersections or roads. The drivers were also instructed to stop their cars, turn off the engines, pull the emergency brake, raise all windows, lock the doors, and remain in their cars until the police arrived. The plan was to have the cars remain in position for one hour.

Acting under the "stall in" plan, plaintiff [respondent in the present action] drove his car onto Brown Road, a McDonnell access road, at approximately 7:00 a.m., at the start of the morning rush hour. Plaintiff was aware of the traffic problem that would result. He stopped his car with the intent to block traffic. The police arrived shortly and requested plaintiff to move his car. He refused to move his car voluntarily. Plaintiff's car was towed away by the police, and he was arrested for obstructing traffic. Plaintiff pleaded guilty to the charge of obstructing traffic and was fined.

[O]n July 25, 1965, petitioner publicly advertised for qualified mechanics, respondent's trade, and respondent promptly applied for re-employment. Petitioner turned down respondent, basing its rejection on respondent's participation in the "stall-in." . . .

II

The critical issue before us concerns the order and allocation of proof in a private, non-class action challenging employment discrimination. The language of Title VII makes plain the purpose of Congress to assure equality of employment opportunities and to eliminate those discriminatory practices and devices which have fostered racially stratified job environments to the disadvantage of minority citizens. *Griggs v. Duke Power Co.*, 401 U.S. 424, 429 (1971) [reproduced at page 592]. As noted in *Griggs*, "Congress did not intend by Title VII, however, to guarantee a job to every person regardless of qualifications. In short, the Act does not command that any person be hired simply because he was formerly the subject of discrimination, or because he is a member of a minority group. Discriminatory preference for any group, minority or majority, is precisely and only what Congress has proscribed. What is required by Congress is the removal of artificial, arbitrary, and unnecessary barriers to employment when the barriers operate invidiously to discriminate on the basis of racial or other impermissible classification."

There are societal as well as personal interests on both sides of this equation. The broad, overriding interest, shared by employer, employee, and consumer, is efficient and trustworthy workmanship assured through fair and racially neutral employment and personnel decisions. In the implementation of such decisions, it is abundantly clear that Title VII tolerates no racial discrimination, subtle or otherwise. In this case, respondent, the complainant below, charges that he was denied employment "because of his involvement in civil rights activities" and "because of his race and color." Petitioner denied discrimination of any kind, asserting that its failure to re-employ respondent was based upon and justified by his participation in the unlawful conduct against it. Thus, the issue at the trial on remand is framed by those opposing factual contentions. . . .

The complainant in a Title VII trial must carry the initial burden under the statute of establishing a prima facie case of racial discrimination. This may be done by showing (i) that he belongs to a racial minority; (ii) that he applied and was qualified for a job for which the employer was seeking applicants; (iii) that, despite his qualifications, he was rejected; and (iv) that, after his rejection, the position remained open and the employer continued to seek applicants from persons of complainant's qualifications.[13] In the instant case, we agree with the Court of Appeals that respondent proved a prima facie case. Petitioner sought mechanics, respondent's trade, and continued to do so after respondent's rejection. Petitioner, moreover, does not dispute respondent's qualifications[14] and acknowledges that his past work performance in petitioner's employ was "satisfactory."

The burden then must shift to the employer to articulate some legitimate, nondiscriminatory reason for the employee's rejection. We need not attempt in the instant case to detail every matter which fairly could be recognized as a reasonable basis for a refusal to hire. Here petitioner has assigned respondent's participation in unlawful conduct against it as the cause for his rejection. We think that this suffices to discharge petitioner's burden of proof at this stage and to meet respondent's prima facie case of discrimination.

. . . Respondent admittedly had taken part in a carefully planned "stall-in," designed to tie up access to and egress from petitioner's plant at a peak traffic hour.[16] Nothing in Title VII compels an employer to absolve and rehire one who has engaged in such deliberate, unlawful activity against it.[17] . . .

Petitioner's reason for rejection thus suffices to meet the prima facie case, but the inquiry must not end here. While Title VII does not, without more, compel rehiring of respondent, neither does it permit petitioner to use respondent's conduct as a pretext for the sort of discrimination prohibited by § 703(a)(1). On remand, respondent must, as the Court of Appeals recognized, be afforded a fair opportunity to show that petitioner's stated reason for respondent's rejection was in fact pretext. Especially relevant to such a showing would be evidence that white employees involved in acts against petitioner of comparable seriousness to the "stall-in" were nevertheless retained or

13. The facts necessarily will vary in Title VII cases, and the specification above of the prima facie proof required from respondent is not necessarily applicable in every respect to differing factual situations.

14. We note that the issue of what may properly be used to test qualifications for employment is not present in this case. Where employees have instituted employment tests and qualifications with an exclusionary effect on minority applicants, such requirements must be "shown to bear a demonstrable relationship to successful performance of the jobs" for which they were used, *Griggs v. Duke Power Co.*

16. The trial judge noted that no personal injury or property damage resulted from the "stall-in" due "solely to the fact that law enforcement officials had obtained notice in advance of plaintiff's . . . demonstration and were at the scene to remove plaintiff's car from the highway."

17. The unlawful activity in this case was directed specifically against petitioner. We need not consider or decide here whether, or under what circumstances, unlawful activity not directed against the particular employer may be a legitimate justification for refusing to hire.

rehired. Petitioner may justifiably refuse to rehire one who was engaged in unlawful, disruptive acts against it, but only if this criterion is applied alike to members of all races.

Other evidence that may be relevant to any showing of pretext includes facts as to the petitioner's treatment of respondent during his prior term of employment; petitioner's reaction, if any, to respondent's legitimate civil rights activities; and petitioner's general policy and practice with respect to minority employment. On the latter point, statistics as to petitioner's employment policy and practice may be helpful to a determination of whether petitioner's refusal to rehire respondent in this case conformed to a general pattern of discrimination against blacks. *Jones v. Lee Way Motor Freight, Inc.*, 431 F.2d 245 (C.A. 10 1970); Blumrosen, *Strangers in Paradise: Griggs v. Duke Power Co., and the Concept of Employment Discrimination*, 71 Mich. L. Rev. 59, 91-94 (1972).[19] In short, on the retrial respondent must be given a full and fair opportunity to demonstrate by competent evidence that the presumptively valid reasons for his rejection were in fact a coverup for a racially discriminatory decision.

NOTES

1. *Rationale for the Proof Structure. McDonnell Douglas* established the structure for litigating cases of individual disparate treatment based on what has been considered "circumstantial evidence" of discrimination, so much so that the case name has become a kind of mantra for analyzing the vast majority of Title VII cases. The first step, the prima facie case, was framed in terms of the four elements. It is obvious, however, that these elements do not fit every fact situation. Indeed, if you think about it, you will see that they describe very few cases: Most employment settings are competitive, which means that an employer hires B instead of A rather than leaving the job vacant. The employer's failure to rehire Green while still seeking other applicants was truly remarkable. How could such an anomalous fact situation become the gold standard in Title VII litigation? In *Teamsters v. United States*, 431 U.S. 324, 358 n.44 (1977), the Court described the rationale for the prima facie case:

> The *McDonnell Douglas* case involved an individual complainant seeking to prove one instance of unlawful discrimination. An employer's isolated decision to reject an applicant who belongs to a racial minority does not show that the rejection was racially based. Although the *McDonnell Douglas* formula does not require direct proof of discrimination, it does demand that the alleged discriminate demonstrate at least that his rejection did not result from the two most common legitimate reasons on which an employer might rely to reject a job applicant: an absolute or relative lack of qualifications or the absence of a vacancy in the job sought. Elimination of these reasons for the refusal to hire is sufficient, absent other explanation, to create an inference that the decision was a discriminatory one.

19. The District Court may, for example, determine after reasonable discovery that "the [racial] composition of defendant's labor force is itself reflective of restrictive or exclusionary practices." *See* Blumrosen, *supra*, at 92. We caution that such general determinations, while helpful, may not be in and of themselves controlling as to an individualized hiring decision, particularly in the presence of an otherwise justifiable reason for refusing to rehire. *See generally* Blumrosen, *supra*, n.19, at 93.

2. *Generalizing* McDonnell Douglas *to Different Contexts. McDonnell Douglas* is focused on the failure-to-rehire context. Suppose, however, that Green had never worked for the defendant. If you represented him, how would you prove the "qualification" aspect of element (ii)? What if Green had no prior experience in the industry and the employer required experience? Would Green not have a prima facie case? Similarly, what if the job Green sought had not remained open because the employer hired a white worker over Green? This would bar application of the fourth prong as *McDonnell Douglas* formulated it. How could Green then make out a prima facie case? By proving that the white was *less* qualified?

a. In the far more common situation where a plaintiff loses out to a competitor, the Supreme Court has not required plaintiff to prove that she was as well qualified as that competitor in order to make out a prima facie case. In *Patterson v. McLean Credit Union*, 491 U.S. 164, 186-87 (1989), a § 1981 suit in which a black bank employee had been repeatedly passed over for promotions that were given to whites, the Court applied the *McDonnell Douglas* proof structure: "The burden [of establishing a prima facie case] is not onerous. Here, petitioner need only prove by a preponderance of the evidence that she applied for and was qualified for an available position, that she was rejected, and that after she was rejected respondent either continued to seek applicants for the position, or, as is alleged here, filled the position with a white employee." (citations omitted). Thus, to carry her initial burden, plaintiff need only show that she met the minimum qualifications for the job. Of course, if the defendant asserts the successful competitor's superior qualifications as its non-discriminatory reason, plaintiff will have to challenge that claim at the pretext stage in order to prevail.

b. What are the elements of a prima facie case in a *discharge* case? Most discrimination cases involve discharges, and the lower courts have had to formulate the elements for this context. Indeed, two alternative formulations of *McDonnell Douglas* have emerged — one for individual discharges and the other for discharges in the course of reductions in force. In individual discharge cases, those involving a single employee, courts have tended to require him to show that he was doing "apparently satisfactory" work in order to carry his prima facie case burden. *E.g., Diaz v. Eagle Produce, Ltd.*, 521 F.3d 1201, 1207-8 (9th Cir. 2008); *Rivera v. City & County of Denver*, 365 F.3d 912, 920 (10th Cir. 2004). An alternative approach would allow the plaintiff to show that he was replaced by a person outside the protected class — say, a younger person in the ADEA context. *Wooler v. Citizens Bank*, 274 F. App'x 177, 179-80 (3d Cir. 2008).

c. In contrast, in reductions in force, that is, situations where a number of employees are terminated simultaneously, the "legitimate, nondiscriminatory reason" — the need to reduce expenses — is apparent on its face. Because *positions* are being eliminated, the power of proof that the plaintiff is doing an apparently satisfactory job diminishes. *See Schoonmaker v. Spartan Graphics Leasing, LLC*, 595 F.3d 261 (6th Cir. 2010). Courts have, therefore, tended to require a plaintiff to produce other evidence, such as identifying younger workers who were retained when she was discharged. *Geiger v. Tower Auto.*, 579 F.3d 614 (6th Cir. 2009); *Martino v. MCI Communs. Servs.*, 574 F.3d 447, 454 (7th Cir. 2009). *See generally* Parisis G. Filippatos & Sean Farhang, *The Rights of Employees Subjected to Reductions in Force: A Critical Evaluation*, 6 EMPLOYEE RTS. & EMP. POL'Y J. 263, 326-27 (2002).

d. Suppose a plaintiff is fired but replaced by a member of the same protected class? In *Kendrick v. Penske Transportation Services*, 220 F.3d 1220, 1226 (10th Cir. 2000), the court held that a discharged employee did not have to show that he was replaced by an employee outside of the protected group in order to establish a prima facie case of race discrimination. Indeed, most federal courts of appeals have held that, in a termination case, the plaintiff need not prove as part of the prima facie case that she was replaced by someone outside the relevant class. *E.g., Stella v. Mineta*, 284 F.3d 135, 146 (D.C. Cir. 2002) (holding that plaintiff in a discrimination case need not demonstrate that she was replaced by a person outside her protected class in order to carry her burden of establishing a prima facie case under *McDonnell Douglas*). Why? Even if this is correct for the prima facie case, the same-class replacement may make it extraordinarily difficult to prove pretext when defendant asserts a nondiscriminatory reason for its action. *See generally* Michael J. Zimmer, *A Chain of Inferences Proving Discrimination*, 79 U. COLO. L. REV. 1243, 1279-80 (2008).

3. *Consequences of the Prima Facie Case.* In *Texas Department of Community Affairs v. Burdine*, 450 U.S. 248 (1981), the Court described the consequences of proving a prima facie case:

> Establishment of the prima facie case in effect creates a presumption that the employer unlawfully discriminated against the employee. If the trier of fact believes the plaintiff's evidence, and if the employer is silent in the face of the presumption, the court must enter judgment for the plaintiff because no issue of fact remains in the case.

In accompanying footnote 7, *Burdine* said the use of the term "prima facie case" in *McDonnell Douglas* denoted "the establishment of a legally mandatory, rebuttable presumption"; it did *not* describe "the plaintiff's burden of producing enough evidence to permit the trier of fact to infer the fact at issue." The point of the distinction is that a plaintiff's proof of a prima facie case is not necessarily sufficient to create a jury question, but that plaintiff will nevertheless win if defendant fails to carry its burden of production. *Burdine* made clear, however, that when defendant did introduce into evidence a nondiscriminatory reason, plaintiff had the burden of persuasion as to pretext:

> The burden that shifts to the defendant, therefore, is to rebut the presumption of discrimination by producing evidence that the plaintiff was rejected, or someone else was preferred, for a legitimate, nondiscriminatory reason. The defendant need not persuade the court that it was actually motivated by the proffered reasons. It is sufficient if the defendant's evidence raises a genuine issue of fact as to whether it discriminated against the plaintiff. To accomplish this, the defendant must clearly set forth, through the introduction of admissible evidence, the reasons for the plaintiff's rejection. The explanation provided must be legally sufficient to justify a judgment for the defendant. If the defendant carries this burden of production, the presumption raised by the prima facie case is rebutted, and the factual inquiry proceeds to a new level of specificity. . . .
>
> The plaintiff retains the burden of persuasion. She now must have the opportunity to demonstrate that the proffered reason was not the true reason for the employment decision. This burden now merges with the ultimate burden of persuading the court

that she has been the victim of intentional discrimination. She may succeed in this either directly by persuading the court that a discriminatory reason more likely motivated the employer or indirectly by showing that the employer's proffered explanation is unworthy of credence.

450 U.S. at 256. We will see that later cases went further to impose another require-ment on the plaintiff: She must prove that the supposed legitimate nondiscriminatory reason was not only a pretext in the sense that it was untrue but that it was *a pretext for discrimination*, that is, that it hid a true discriminatory motive.

4. *The Role of Comparators.* "Disparate" treatment, as the phrase suggests, requires ultimately proving that the plaintiff was treated differently than a person of a different race or sex was (or would have been) treated. Thus, many disparate treat-ment cases turn on whether the plaintiff can identify "comparators" who are similarly situated to her except for her race, sex, and so forth, but were treated differently. The comparator may enter the analysis at the prima facie case stage or, more commonly, to show pretext by establishing that the defendant did not apply its supposed nondis-criminatory reason in, for example, a color- or sex-blind manner. *See generally* Charles A. Sullivan, *The Phoenix from the Ash: Proving Discrimination by Comparators*, 59 ALA. L. REV. 191 (2009). *But see* Suzanne B. Goldberg, *Discrimination by Comparison*, 120 YALE L.J. 728, 750 (2011). The significance of comparators turns on how much similarity courts will require before dissimilar treatment will give rise to an inference of discrimination. The Supreme Court's decision in *Ash v. Tyson Foods, Inc.*, 546 U.S. 454 (2006), rejected the most extreme circuit court approach in the context of comparative qualifications. The Eleventh Circuit had overturned a jury verdict for plaintiff and, in the course of its opinion had, apparently in all seriousness, stated that a plaintiff can use her asserted superior qualifications relative to a comparator to prove discrimination only when "the disparity in qualifications is so apparent as virtually to jump off the page and slap you in the face." *Id.* at 456-57. In reversing, the Supreme Court stressed that its prior decisions established that "qualifications evidence may suffice, at least in some circumstances, to show pretext," *id.* at 457 (quoting *Patterson v. McLean Credit Union*, 491 U.S. 164, 187-88 (1989)), and that plaintiff's proof that the employer "misjudged the qualifications" of the applicants "may be probative of whether the employer's reasons are pretexts for discrimina-tion[,]" *id.* (quoting *Texas Dep't of Community Affairs v. Burdine*, 450 U.S. 248, 259 (1981)).

Perhaps not surprisingly, the Court then wrote that "[t]he visual image of words jumping off the page to slap you (presumably a court) in the face is unhelpful and imprecise as an elaboration of the standard for inferring pretext from superior quali-fications." 456 U.S. at 457. While "slap in the face" was too restrictive, the Court did not endorse an particular alternative but did note other possible tests, and subsequent lower courts have tended to require plaintiff to show "that the disparities between the successful applicant's and her own qualifications were 'of such weight and significance that no reasonable person, in the exercise of impartial judgment, could have chosen the candidate selected over the plaintiff.'" *Brooks v. County Comm'n*, 446 F.3d 1160, 1163 (11th Cir. 2006) (citation omitted).

Ash dealt only with comparative *qualifications*, but comparisons can be drawn in other contexts. In *Holmes v. Trinity Health*, 729 F.3d 817, 823 (8th Cir. 2013), the plaintiff, a hospital COO, was unable to show sex discrimination when the comparator she chose, although at a comparable job level, did not engage in the same conduct she did — criticizing the CEO's management style. Another example is disparate discipline cases — that is, those in which plaintiff claims that, although he may have been guilty of misconduct, members of a different race or sex committed similar infractions with lesser or no discipline. In many circuits, the courts require a very close correspondence between the plaintiff and her putative comparator(s) before such proof is given much weight. *Gates v. Caterpillar, Inc.*, 513 F.3d 680 (7th Cir. 2008) (plaintiff, who was discharged for improper telephone and Internet use, was not similarly situated to three male employees who also misused employer's electronic equipment where they had a different supervisor, their conduct was limited to misuse of computers and did not involve telephone use, and they did not continue to engage in misconduct after being initially disciplined). *But see Jackson v. Fedex Corporate Servs.*, 518 F.3d 388, 397 (6th Cir. 2008) ("The district court's narrow definition of similarly situated effectively removed Jackson from the protective reach of the anti-discrimination laws. [Its] finding that Jackson had no comparables from the six other employees in the PowerPad project deprived Jackson of any remedy to which he may be entitled under the law.").

5. Legitimate Nondiscriminatory Reason. Defendant may rebut a prima facie case by "articulat[ing] some legitimate, nondiscriminatory reason" for its action. *McDonnell Douglas* established that disloyalty is such a reason. Suppose the court finds as a fact that Green was not rehired because he was a vegetarian. Is this a "legitimate, nondiscriminatory reason"? If so, what does "legitimate" mean? *Biggins* held that a firing to avoid a pension vesting, which would have been an ERISA violation, did not violate the ADEA; it was, therefore, "legitimate" under the latter statute. While the courts continue to speak of the employer's burden of producing a "legitimate nondiscriminatory reason," it seems clear that any reason is "legitimate" if it is "nondiscriminatory." This should not be so surprising in an at-will world.

6. Retaliation. *McDonnell Douglas* was framed as a discrimination case, that is, whether plaintiff was denied reemployment because of his race. You probably noticed that it might have been framed as what we would today call a public policy case — he was not reemployed because of his civil rights activities. The law we studied in Chapter 4 on the public policy tort was largely nonexistent when *McDonnell Douglas* was handed down, but Title VII has its own ban on retaliation. Percy Green raised this issue below, but the Supreme Court did not address it. Retaliation is considered beginning at page 712.

Note on "Adverse Employment Actions"

Refusals to hire (as in *McDonnell Douglas*) and discharges (as in *Slack* and *Biggins*) are obviously sufficient to justify relief if wrongfully motivated. But not all differences in treatment because of race, sex, religion, or age have been viewed as actionable. Some courts, often relying on the notion that the antidiscrimination statutes reach only "terms and conditions" of employment, hold that minor harms do not give rise to a claim. They require "material adverse effects" for a suit to go forward, but often differ on what is material. *Compare Alexander v. Casino Queen, Inc.*, 739 F.3d 972, 980 (7th Cir. 2014) (floor assignments on the basis of race could constitute an adverse employment action "because of the relative importance that tips had for these cocktail waitresses, given their compensation structure and the alleged frequency of these reassignments [which together] demonstrate a significant financial impact."); *with*

Kidd v. Mando Am. Corp., 731 F.3d 1196, 1204 (11th Cir. 2013) ("Kidd's demotion claim — grounded on a loss of supervisory responsibility of the accounts payable department, not a loss of salary or benefits — does not rise to" the level of an adverse employment actions); *see also Kuhn v. Washtenaw County*, 709 F.3d 612 (6th Cir. 2013) (investigation of a complaint of employee wrongdoing was not an adverse employment action when there was no disciplinary action, demotion, or change in job responsibilities).

Some courts seem far more receptive to holding actions with no direct economic consequences to be actionable. *E.g., Deleon v. Kalamazoo County Rd. Comm'n*, 739 F.3d 914, 919-920 (6th Cir. 2014) (adverse employment action could be found when a lateral transfer resulted in exposure to toxic and hazardous fumes on a daily basis, causing bronchitis and frequent sinus headaches); *Crawford v. Carroll*, 529 F.3d 961 (11th Cir. 2008) (denial of merit raise actionable if discriminatory, even if the denial was later reversed by the employer); *Holcomb v. Powell*, 433 F.3d 889, 903 (D.C. Cir. 2006) (finding that being put in "professional purgatory" by being assigned duties that were not only far below her grade level but below the level at which plaintiff had entered federal employment ten years earlier was an adverse employment action).

Professor Rebecca Hanner White, in *De Minimis Discrimination*, 47 EMORY L. J. 1121, 1148, 1151 (1998), criticized the more restrictive decisions, arguing that the term "adverse employment action" is not found in the statutory language. The statute's bar on discrimination in connection with hiring, firing, or the "compensation, terms, conditions, or privileges" of employment "is better read as making clear that an employer who discriminates against an employee in a non-job-related context would not run afoul of Title VII, rather than as sheltering employment discrimination that does not significantly disadvantage an employee." *Id.; see also* Tristin K. Green, *Discrimination in Workplace Dynamics: Toward a Structural Account of Disparate Treatment Theory*, 38 HARV. C.R.-C.L. L. REV. 93, 102 (2003).

Note on "Reverse" Discrimination

In *McDonald v. Santa Fe Trail Transportation Co.*, 427 U.S. 273 (1976), the Court held that both Title VII and § 1981 barred discrimination against whites. The plaintiffs, both white, were discharged for their involvement in misappropriating company property while an African American involved in the same incident was retained. The district court ruled that neither Title VII nor § 1981 protected white plaintiffs from racial discrimination. The Supreme Court disagreed. The Court focused on the legislative history and the language of Title VII, which prohibits the discharge of "any individual" because of "such individual's race." Turning to the interpretation of § 1981, the Court rejected the employer's assertion that the operation of the phrase "as is enjoyed by white citizens" in the statute precluded its use by whites. To the contrary, the statute explicitly applies to "all persons," including whites. Additionally, the Court acknowledged that the original purpose in enacting § 1981 was to provide protection for African Americans, but it was "routinely viewed, by its opponents and supporters alike, as applying to the civil rights of whites as well as nonwhites." Accordingly, the Court held Title VII and § 1981 protections are available to plaintiffs of all races.

Since *Santa Fe*, whites have been protected against race discrimination under both Title VII and § 1981. It is equally clear that men are protected against sex discrimination in employment under Title VII. Thus, all employees are protected, but they are protected only from discrimination on the prohibited ground. That is, the employer need not have a good reason to discharge as long as its reason is not a prohibited one (e.g., race, sex, or age). While this is the law, employers are well advised to have defensible reasons for firing their workers. In that sense, the enactment of antidiscrimination statutes tends toward a just-cause rule since all workers — African Americans, Caucasians, women, men, older workers, individuals with disabilities, etc. — are free to challenge adverse decisions as discriminatory. While most such challenges will fail, the costs of litigation can themselves be considerable, and defensible employment decisions conduce to good employee morale. *See* Ann C. McGinley, *Rethinking Civil Rights and Employment at Will*, 57 Ohio St. L.J. 1443 (1996).

Although *Santa Fe* makes clear that "reverse" discrimination is cognizable under both Title VII and § 1981, the question of the validity of an affirmative action plan, reserved in footnote 8 in *Santa Fe*, was later resolved in favor of the voluntary use of racial and gender preferences. *Johnson v. Transportation Agency of Santa Clara County*, 480 U.S. 616 (1987) (approving affirmative action plan benefiting women); *United Steelworkers v. Weber*, 440 U.S. 969 (1979) (approving affirmative action plan benefiting African Americans). We will discuss these cases at page 649. And, while not explicitly an "affirmative action" case, *Ricci v. DeStefano*, 457 U.S. 457 (2009), reproduced at page 668, may suggest a new approach to the question. After you have read that decision, you will be finally in a position to assess the current status of affirmative action under Title VII.

Putting the affirmative action question aside, how does, say, a white plaintiff prove racial discrimination? *Santa Fe* did not explain how a white or male plaintiff makes out a prima facie case, and the lower courts seem unclear. Suppose that the employer is Harlem Enterprises, Inc., a black-owned and -operated business. *See Lincoln v. Board of Regents*, 697 F.2d 928 (11th Cir. 1983) (affirming judgment against a predominantly black university in an action brought by a white faculty member). Might one also expect that employers will discriminate against males when they attempt to perform traditionally female jobs? In such cases, plaintiffs are "minorities" in the institution or occupation where they sought work. *McDonnell Douglas* applies with little adjustment. But when a predominantly white institution discharges a white worker, how will he establish a prima facie case? In *Santa Fe*, did the plaintiffs make out a prima facie case by showing that they were whites who were fired, while a black was not, although he engaged in the same conduct? Clearly, an African American plaintiff would make out a prima facie case by proving that similarly situated white workers were favored. Does that mean that whites can also?

A number of circuits have adopted some version of a "background circumstances" test — that is, to establish a prima facie case, a "reverse" discrimination, plaintiff must establish "background circumstances" that support an inference that the defendant employer is "that unusual employer who discriminates against the majority." *Parker v. Baltimore & Ohio R.R. Co.*, 652 F.2d 1012, 1017 (D.C. Cir. 1981). While the notion has been criticized as "irremediably vague and ill-defined," *Iadimarco v. Runyon*, 190 F.3d 151, 161 (3d Cir. 1999), it continues to be applied to require something more for a white plaintiff than would be required were the plaintiff a member of a minority group. *See also Coulton v. Univ. of Pa.*, 237 F. App'x 741 (3d Cir. 2007) (African American decision makers and a manager's predictions by a manager that a white would have problems working in a department with an overwhelming majority of African American did not suffice to prove discrimination where white plaintiff could not show that similarly situated African American employees were treated more favorably); *Stockwell v. City of Harvey*, 597 F.3d 895, 901 (7th Cir. 2010) (applying "background circumstances" test in reverse discrimination case). *See generally* Charles A. Sullivan, *Circling Back to the Obvious: The Convergence of Traditional and Reverse Discrimination in Title VII Proof*, 46 Wm. & Mary L. Rev. 1031 (2004).

b. Defendant's Rebuttal and Plaintiff's Proof of Pretext

Assuming that the plaintiff establishes her prima facie case, the next step is for the defendant to put into evidence its nondiscriminatory reason. Given that this is merely a burden of production, employers almost always satisfy it. The *McDonnell Douglas* analysis then proceeds to the third and final step, in which the plaintiff attempts to prove that that reason is a pretext for discrimination. The courts have been rigorous in resisting efforts to collapse the employer's rebuttal case with the plaintiff's prima facie case. For example, *Ruiz v. County of Rockland*, 609 F.3d 486, 493 (2d Cir. 2010), held that defendant's claim of serious misconduct by plaintiff does not bar plaintiff from making out a prima facie case when his performance evaluations showed satisfactory work: "[T]he step at which the court considers such evidence is important" because "no amount of evidence permits a plaintiff to overcome a failure to make out a prima facie case." *See also Lake v. Yellow Transp., Inc.*, 596 F.3d 871, 874 (8th Cir. 2010) (a plaintiff is not required to disprove the asserted reason for firing him at the prima facie stage of the analysis since to do so would collapse the defendant's burden of production into the prima facie case; thus, plaintiff carried its burden by showing that he met the employer's expectations "other than the tardiness and unavailability Yellow offers as its reasons for firing him."). *But see Zayas v. Rockford Mem. Hosp.*, 740 F.3d 1154, 1158 (7th Cir. 2014) (prior satisfactory performance evaluations did not establish that plaintiff was meeting the employer's legitimate job expectations at the time she was fired, given more recent disciplinary actions; in any event analysis of satisfactory performance is not limited to actual job performance but includes "factors such as insubordination and workplace camaraderie").

As a practical matter, the vast majority of individual disparate treatment cases are resolved at the pretext stage, typically on a motion for summary judgment when the court finds that the plaintiff has not adduced sufficient evidence for a jury to determine the defendant's nondiscriminatory reason is pretextual. This is true despite the Supreme Court's permissive approach to proving pretext. In *Patterson v. McLean Credit Union*, 491 U.S. 164 (1989), plaintiff brought a § 1981 suit challenging the defendant's repeated failures to promote her. On appeal, she questioned the district court's instructions to the jury that, in order to prevail, she had to show that she was better qualified than her successful white competitor. The Supreme Court agreed, finding this to be error. Applying the *McDonnell Douglas/Burdine* proof structure to claims of racial discrimination under § 1981, the Court agreed that plaintiff "retains the final burden of persuading the jury of intentional discrimination" by proving that a defendant's legitimate nondiscriminatory reason was a pretext:

> The evidence which petitioner can present in an attempt to establish that respondent's stated reasons are pretextual may take a variety of forms. Indeed, she might seek to demonstrate that respondent's claim to have promoted a better qualified applicant was pretextual by showing that she was in fact better qualified than the person chosen for the position. The District Court erred, however, in instructing the jury that in order to

succeed petitioner was required to make such a showing. There are certainly other ways in which petitioner could seek to prove that respondent's reasons were pretextual. Thus, for example, petitioner could seek to persuade the jury that respondent had not offered the true reason for its promotion decision by presenting evidence of respondent's past treatment of petitioner, including the instances of the racial harassment which she alleges and respondent's failure to train her for an accounting position. While we do not intend to say this evidence necessarily would be sufficient to carry the day, it cannot be denied that it is one of the various ways in which petitioner might seek to prove intentional discrimination on the part of respondent. She may not be forced to pursue any particular means of demonstrating that respondent's stated reasons are pretextual.

Id. at 188. Earlier in this chapter, we saw that when plaintiff is passed over in favor of another, she need not prove her qualifications were equal or superior to those of the successful competitor to make out a prima facie case; it is enough to show that she has the minimum qualifications for the position. This is clearly the logic of *Patterson:* Plaintiff may establish her prima facie case without showing she is equal or superior to the whites promoted. However, the defendant will typically claim that it promoted the better-qualified persons, who happened to be white. Simply putting into evidence its view that the successful applicant was superior to plaintiff in some respects will suffice to carry the defendant's burden of production. Plaintiff must then prove pretext and, while *Patterson* holds that she may do this in a variety of different ways, the most obvious path is for plaintiff to show that her qualifications were equal or superior to those of the successful competitor. *See generally* Anne Lawton, *The Meritocracy Myth and the Illusion of Equal Employment Opportunity*, 85 MINN. L. REV. 587, 645 (2000). That, of course, brings us back to the whole question of comparators. *See* Note 4, page 579.

But even this inquiry reveals the complexity of the concept of "pretext." Suppose the plaintiff shows that the defendant's reason is objectively false — for example, the plaintiff proves she has a college degree, while the defendant claims it did not promote her because she did not have a degree. This would seem to prove pretext, but maybe not: Although the reason is not objectively true, the employer may have believed it to be true and acted on it, rather than on the basis of the employee's protected class. This "honest belief" rule has doomed many claims. *See, e.g., Johnson v. AT&T Corp.*, 422 F.3d 756, 762 (8th Cir. 2005) ("[T]he proper inquiry is not whether AT&T was factually correct in determining that Johnson had made the bomb threats. Rather, the proper inquiry is whether AT&T honestly believed that Johnson had made the bomb threats."); *Ramirez Rodriguez v. Boehringer Ingelheim Pharms., Inc.*, 425 F.3d 67, 77 (1st Cir. 2005) (finding no hearsay problem with statements of physicians criticizing a discharged pharmaceutical representative because the evidence was not offered to prove the truth of the matter asserted "but rather to demonstrate that his superiors had reason, based on a thorough investigation, to believe that he had"). In such cases, the employer's asserted reason is not a "pretext" although it is factually incorrect. Of course, perhaps proof that the employer was objectively wrong is a reason for thinking that something more objectionable than an honest mistake explains the decision.

Alternatively, the defendant's reason might be true but fail to explain the decision. For example, if the employer claims the employee was discharged for tardiness, the female plaintiff might admit that she was frequently late, but claim that men who were also late were not fired. Again, we're discussing comparators: By proving that males were treated more favorably in regard to the asserted reason, the plaintiff undercuts the defendant's explanation. *See Ekokotu v. Fed. Express Corp.*, 408 F. App'x 331 (11th Cir. 2011) (if the plaintiff cannot show the asserted reason is false, she must establish that it was not applied to similarly situated individuals). To add a final layer of complication, a showing that others were guilty of the same act or omission as plaintiff does not necessarily prove that the adverse action taken against plaintiff was a pretext. Most obviously, the employer might have been unaware of the violations by others. *Mechnig v. Sears, Roebuck & Co.*, 864 F.2d 1359 (7th Cir. 1988).

Patterson allows plaintiff to challenge defendant's claimed reason indirectly, "by presenting evidence of respondent's past treatment of petitioner, including the instances of the racial harassment which she alleges and respondent's failure to train her for an accounting position." The partial dissent of Justices Brennan and Stevens argued that the jury instruction below was

> much too restrictive, cutting off other methods of proving pretext plainly recognized in our cases. We suggested in *McDonnell Douglas*, for example, that a black plaintiff might be able to prove pretext by showing that the employer has promoted white employees who lack the qualifications the employer relies upon, or by proving the employer's "general policy and practice with respect to minority employment." And, of particular relevance given petitioner's evidence of racial harassment and her allegation that respondent failed to train her for an accounting position because of her race, we suggested that evidence of the employer's past treatment of the plaintiff would be relevant to a showing that the employer's proffered legitimate reason was not its true reason.

Id. at 217. How is this proof relevant to the ultimate issue of whether the plaintiff was discriminated against?

1. Proving that the employer promoted whites without the asserted qualifications tends to show that the qualifications are unnecessary, even in the employer's own view.
2. Showing the employer's "general policy and practice with respect to minority employment" suggests that, if the employer generally discriminates, it is more likely it discriminated as to the particular plaintiff.
3. While harassment itself, if sufficiently severe, violates Title VII, *see* Section D, perhaps a company that condones racial harassment is more likely to be discriminatory in promotions.
4. Defendant's failure to train plaintiff, and its general past treatment of her may be probative of discrimination — unless the reason for adverse treatment was peculiar to plaintiff and unrelated to her race.

Will plaintiff at least get to the jury if she adduces evidence sufficient to raise a material issue of fact on one of these claims? *See Ridout v. JBS USA, LLC,* 716 F.3d 1079, 1084 (8th Cir. 2013) ("A strong showing that the plaintiff was meeting his employer's reasonable expectations at the time of termination may create a fact issue as to pretext when the employer claims that the employee was terminated for poor or declining performance."); *Hudson v. United Sys. of Ark.,* 709 F.3d 700 (8th Cir. 2013) (upholding jury verdict when there was evidence that defendant's supposed nondiscriminatory reason for plaintiff's discharge — her failure to call him on his cell phone when sick — was pretextual when plaintiff denied ever being informed of it and other executives testified that they never heard of this policy; in addition, there was evidence that the manager frequently belittled women, including plaintiff, whom he ordered "sit down, little girl."); *Kragor v. Takeda Pharms. Am., Inc.*, 702 F.3d 1304, 1307 (11th Cir. 2012) (a jury question as to discrimination when the decisionmaker, after terminating an employee for misconduct, said that the employee is exceptional, did nothing wrong, did everything right, and should not have been fired).

Suppose defendant puts into evidence more than one nondiscriminatory reason. Some lower courts have required the plaintiff to adduce proof of the pretextual nature of *all* the reasons, *see e.g., Kautz v. Met-Pro Corp.*, 412 F.3d 463 (3d Cir. 2005) (granting summary judgment against employee who could not show that all of employer's nondiscriminatory reasons were pretextual). Other courts believe that proof that any reason is pretextual will usually permit the jury to infer that the pretext conceals a discriminatory motive. *See generally* Lawrence D. Rosenthal, *Motions for Summary Judgment When Employers Offer Multiple Justifications for Adverse Employment Actions: Why the Exceptions Should Swallow the Rule*, 2002 UTAH L. REV. 335, 335-36 (2002). Of course, sometimes an employer's multiple reasons will conflict, or change over time, thus providing another basis to infer pretext. *See, e.g., Hitchcock v. Angel Corps, Inc.*, 718 F.3d 733 (7th Cir. 2013) (at least four potentially different explanations for plaintiff's discharge were "sufficiently inconsistent or otherwise suspect to create a reasonable inference that they do not reflect the real reason for Hitchcock's firing" and were a pretext for pregnancy discrimination); *Jones v. Nat'l Am. Univ.*, 608 F.3d 1039 (8th Cir. 2010) (a change in the employer's reasons for its action between those offered the [EEOC] and those adduced at trial can be evidence of pretext sufficient to uphold a jury verdict, at least in the context of other evidence of age bias).

Employers have also attempted to buttress their nondiscriminatory reason with what is sometimes called the "same actor defense." Courts have often declined to infer a discriminatory intent when the person who hired an older worker also discharged him within a relatively short period of time. The rationale is that, had the employer held stereotypical views, he would not have hired the plaintiff in the first place. *Brown v. CSC Logic, Inc.* 82 F.3d 651 (5th Cir. 1996); *Proud v. Stone*, 945 F.2d 796 (4th Cir. 1991). Several circuits have applied this inference to discrimination cases outside the ADEA. *See, e.g., Jaques v. Clean-Up Group, Inc.*, 96 F.3d 506 (1st Cir. 1996) (disability discrimination); *Jiminez v. Mary Washington College*, 57 F.3d 369 (4th Cir. 1995) (race and national origin discrimination). The conditions for the "same actor" defense are restrictive: Obviously, the same supervisor must make both decisions, and the decisions must be in tension with one another. For example, a person who hires an older worker or a woman for one position might be expected not to discriminate in discharging that person, but could easily hold stereotypic views about the limitations of such persons with respect to higher-level jobs. Further, the time between the hiring and firing decisions may make a substantial difference as to the strength of the inference. *See Potter v. Synerlink Corp.*, 562 F. App'x 665 (10th Cir. 2014) (inference did not apply where the decisionmaker hired the plaintiff three and a half years before he fired her). The strength of the inference will also vary depending on the circumstances. *See EEOC v. Boeing Co.*, 577 F.3d 1044, 1052 (9th Cir. 2009) ("Although a termination is rarely motivated by bias when it is initiated by the same actors who recently selected the same employee for the job or promotion in the first place, the logic differs when applied to less overtly 'positive' employment decisions, such as refraining from firing an employee at the earliest opportunity or giving an employee a lukewarm evaluation, rather than a poor one."); *see generally* Natasha T. Martin, *Immunity for Hire: How the Same-Actor Doctrine Sustains Discrimination in the Contemporary Workplace*, 40 CONN. L. REV. 1117 (2008).

Patterson was not the Supreme Court's last encounter with the question of pretext. *St. Mary's Honor Center v. Hicks*, 509 U.S. 502 (1993), involved a race discrimination claim. At the bench trial, the plaintiff established a prima facie case under *Burdine*, thus triggering the *McDonnell Douglas* presumption. Defendant, in turn, produced two alternative explanations to rebut the presumption, but both were rejected by the judge. Since he credited neither explanation, one might have thought that the judge would have necessarily found them to be "pretexts" for discrimination. However, that was not his conclusion. Rather, the trial judge believed that the action was taken on the basis of personal animosity by the supervisor toward the plaintiff, something the supervisor had denied on the stand. The court therefore determined that the plaintiff had not met his burden of persuasion that the adverse actions were based on race. The Court of Appeals reversed, reasoning that, since the judge disbelieved the proffered explanations, the defendants were in "no better position than if they had remained silent."

The Supreme Court disagreed. The *McDonnell Douglas* presumption shift did not shift the plaintiff's ultimate burden of persuasion. To this point, the opinion was consistent with *Burdine*. But the majority went further. Looking to statements in prior opinions that the plaintiff always carries the burden of persuading the trier of fact that the defendant intentionally discriminated against him because of his race, the majority held that mere disbelief of the defendant's asserted nondiscriminatory reason was not enough to find for plaintiff. Rather, the trier of fact had to find that the rejected reasons were not just a pretext for some hidden motivation but were a pretext for discrimination.

The dissent argued that the Court's decision would encourage employers to perjure themselves to defeat the *McDonnell Douglas* presumption. The Court responded by pointing out other procedural devices that gave the defendant an "advantage" even if ultimately proved to be false.

After *Hicks*, a prima facie case creates a mandatory presumption in favor of the plaintiff, but one that disappears as soon as the defendant carries its burden of production. But what is the effect of the proof that established the prima face case? In the wake of *Hicks*, there was considerable uncertainty as to whether plaintiff had to produce *additional* evidence of discrimination, that is, evidence beyond the prima facie case and any proof of pretext. This was called the "pretext plus" reading of *Hicks*. The alternative reading, the "pretext only" view, was that the trier of fact's disbelief of the purported nondiscriminatory reason permitted, although it did not require, a finding of discrimination. The Court resolved this dispute in the next case, which also casts light on the current approach to analyzing individual disparate treatment cases.

Reeves v. Sanderson Plumbing Products, Inc.
530 U.S. 133 (2000)

Justice O'CONNOR delivered the opinion of the Court.

This case concerns the kind and amount of evidence necessary to sustain a jury's verdict that an employer unlawfully discriminated on the basis of age. Specifically, we must resolve whether a defendant is entitled to judgment as a matter of law when the plaintiff's case consists exclusively of a prima facie case of discrimination and sufficient evidence for the trier of fact to disbelieve the defendant's legitimate, nondiscriminatory explanation for its action. We must also decide whether the employer was entitled to judgment as a matter of law under the particular circumstances presented here.

I

In October 1995, petitioner Roger Reeves was 57 years old and had spent 40 years in the employ of respondent, Sanderson Plumbing Products, Inc., a manufacturer of toilet seats and covers. Petitioner worked in a department known as the "Hinge Room," where he supervised the "regular line." Joe Oswalt, in his mid-thirties, supervised the Hinge Room's "special line," and Russell Caldwell, the manager of the Hinge Room and age 45, supervised both petitioner and Oswalt. Petitioner's responsibilities included recording the attendance and hours of those under his supervision, and reviewing a weekly report that listed the hours worked by each employee.

In the summer of 1995, Caldwell informed Powe Chesnut, the director of manufacturing and the husband of company president Sandra Sanderson, that "production was down" in the Hinge Room because employees were often absent and were "coming in late and leaving early." Because the monthly attendance reports did not indicate a problem, Chesnut ordered an audit of the Hinge Room's timesheets for July, August, and September of that year. According to Chesnut's testimony, that investigation revealed "numerous timekeeping errors and misrepresentations on the part of Caldwell, Reeves, and Oswalt." Following the audit, Chesnut, along with Dana Jester, vice president of human resources, and Tom Whitaker, vice president of operations, recommended to company president Sanderson that petitioner and Caldwell be fired. In October 1995, Sanderson followed the recommendation and discharged both petitioner and Caldwell.

At trial, respondent contended that it had fired petitioner due to his failure to maintain accurate attendance records, while petitioner attempted to demonstrate that respondent's explanation was pretext for age discrimination. Petitioner introduced evidence that he had accurately recorded the attendance and hours of the employees under his supervision, and that Chesnut, whom Oswalt described as wielding "absolute power" within the company had demonstrated age-based animus in his dealings with petitioner.

[The jury returned a verdict in favor of petitioner of $35,000 in compensatory damages, which the judge doubled as liquidated damages pursuant to the jury's finding that the employer's age discrimination was "willful." The judge also awarded plaintiff $28,490.80 in front pay for two years' lost income. The Fifth Circuit reversed], holding that petitioner had not introduced sufficient evidence to sustain the jury's finding of unlawful discrimination. After noting respondent's proffered justification for petitioner's discharge, the court acknowledged that petitioner "very well may" have offered sufficient evidence for "a reasonable jury [to] have found that [respondent's] explanation for its employment decision was pretextual." The court explained, however, that this was "not dispositive" of the ultimate issue — namely, "whether Reeves presented sufficient evidence that his age motivated [respondent's] employment decision." Addressing this question, the court weighed petitioner's additional evidence of discrimination against other circumstances surrounding his discharge. Specifically, the court noted that Chesnut's age-based comments "were not made in the direct context of Reeves's termination"; there was no allegation that the two other individuals who had recommended that petitioner be fired (Jester and Whitaker) were motivated by age; two of the decision makers involved in petitioner's discharge (Jester and Sanderson) were over the age of 50; all three of the Hinge Room supervisors were accused of inaccurate record keeping; and several of respondent's management positions were filled by persons over age 50 when petitioner was fired. On this basis, the court concluded that petitioner had not introduced sufficient evidence for a rational jury to conclude that he had been discharged because of his age. . . .

II

Under the ADEA, it is "unlawful for an employer . . . to fail or refuse to hire or to discharge any individual or otherwise discriminate against any individual with respect to his compensation, terms, conditions, or privileges of employment, because of such individual's age." When a plaintiff alleges disparate treatment, "liability depends on whether the protected trait (under the ADEA, age) actually motivated the employer's decision." *Hazen Paper Co. v. Biggins.* That is, the plaintiff's age must have "actually played a role in [the employer's decision making] process and had a determinative influence on the outcome." Recognizing that "the question facing triers of fact in discrimination cases is both sensitive and difficult," and that "there will seldom be 'eyewitness' testimony as to the employer's mental processes," *Postal Service Bd. of Governors v. Aikens,* the Courts of Appeals, including the Fifth Circuit in this case, have employed some variant of the framework articulated in *McDonnell Douglas* to analyze ADEA claims that are based principally on circumstantial evidence. . . . This Court has not squarely addressed whether the *McDonnell Douglas* framework, developed to assess claims brought under §703(a)(1) of Title VII of the Civil Rights Act of 1964, also applies to ADEA actions. Because the parties do not dispute the issue, we shall assume, arguendo, that the *McDonnell Douglas* framework is fully applicable here.

[Under this framework, petitioner established a prima facie case and respondent rebutted it.] Although intermediate evidentiary burdens shift back and forth under this framework, "the ultimate burden of persuading the trier of fact that the defendant intentionally discriminated against the plaintiff remains at all times with the plaintiff." And in attempting to satisfy this burden, the plaintiff—once the employer produces sufficient evidence to support a nondiscriminatory explanation for its decision—must be afforded the "opportunity to prove by a preponderance of the evidence that the legitimate reasons offered by the defendant were not its true reasons, but were a pretext for discrimination." That is, the plaintiff may attempt to establish that he was the victim of intentional discrimination "by showing that the employer's proffered explanation is unworthy of credence." Moreover, although the presumption of discrimination "drops out of the picture" once the defendant meets its burden of production, the trier of fact may still consider the evidence establishing the plaintiff's prima facie case "and inferences properly drawn therefrom . . . on the issue of whether the defendant's explanation is pretextual."

In this case, the evidence supporting respondent's explanation for petitioner's discharge consisted primarily of testimony by Chesnut and Sanderson and documentation of petitioner's alleged "shoddy record keeping." Chesnut testified that a 1993 audit of Hinge Room operations revealed "a very lax assembly line" where employees were not adhering to general work rules. As a result of that audit, petitioner was placed on 90 days' probation for unsatisfactory performance. In 1995, Chesnut ordered another investigation of the Hinge Room, which, according to his testimony, revealed that petitioner was not correctly recording the absences and hours of employees. Respondent introduced summaries of that investigation documenting several attendance violations by 12 employees under petitioner's supervision, and noting that each should have been disciplined in some manner. Chesnut testified that this failure to discipline absent and late employees is "extremely important when you are dealing with a union" because uneven enforcement across departments would keep the company "in grievance and arbitration cases, which are costly, all the time." He and Sanderson also stated that petitioner's errors, by failing to adjust for hours not worked, cost the company overpaid wages. Sanderson testified that she accepted the recommendation to discharge petitioner because he had "intentionally falsified company pay records."

Petitioner, however, made a substantial showing that respondent's explanation was false. First, petitioner offered evidence that he had properly maintained the attendance records. Most of the timekeeping errors cited by respondent involved employees who were not marked late but who were recorded as having arrived at the plant at 7 A.M. for the 7 A.M. shift. Respondent contended that employees arriving at 7 A.M. could not have been at their workstations by 7 A.M., and therefore must have been late. But both petitioner and Oswalt testified that the company's automated timeclock often failed to scan employees' timecards, so that the timesheets would not record any time of arrival. On these occasions, petitioner and Oswalt would visually check the workstations and record whether the employees were present at the start of the shift. They stated that if an employee arrived promptly but the timesheet contained no time of arrival, they would reconcile the two by marking "7 A.M." as the employee's arrival time, even if the employee actually arrived at the plant earlier. On cross-examination, Chesnut acknowledged that the timeclock sometimes malfunctioned, and that if "people were there at their work stations" at the start of the shift, the supervisor "would write in seven o'clock." Petitioner also testified that when employees arrived before or stayed after their shifts, he would assign them additional work so they would not be overpaid.

Petitioner similarly cast doubt on whether he was responsible for any failure to discipline late and absent employees. Petitioner testified that his job only included reviewing the daily and weekly attendance reports, and that disciplinary write-ups were based on the monthly reports, which were reviewed by Caldwell. Sanderson admitted that Caldwell, and not petitioner, was responsible for citing employees for violations of the company's attendance policy. Further, Chesnut conceded that there had never been a union grievance or employee complaint arising from petitioner's record keeping, and that the company had never calculated the amount of overpayments allegedly attributable to petitioner's errors. Petitioner also testified that, on the day he was fired, Chesnut said that his discharge was due to his failure to report as absent one employee, Gina Mae Coley, on two days in September 1995. But petitioner explained that he had spent those days in the hospital, and that Caldwell was therefore responsible for any overpayment of Coley. Finally, petitioner stated that on previous occasions that employees were paid for hours they had not worked, the company had simply adjusted those employees' next paychecks to correct the errors.

Based on this evidence, the Court of Appeals concluded that petitioner "very well may be correct" that "a reasonable jury could have found that [respondent's] explanation for its employment decision was pretextual." Nonetheless, the court held that this showing, standing alone, was insufficient to sustain the jury's finding of liability: "We must, as an essential final step, determine whether Reeves presented sufficient evidence that his age motivated [respondent's] employment decision." And in making this determination, the Court of Appeals ignored the evidence supporting petitioner's prima facie case and challenging respondent's explanation for its decision. The court confined its review of evidence favoring petitioner to that evidence showing that Chesnut had directed derogatory, age-based comments at petitioner, and that Chesnut had singled out petitioner for harsher treatment than younger employees. It is therefore apparent that the court believed that only this additional evidence of discrimination was relevant to whether the jury's verdict should stand. That is, the Court of Appeals proceeded from the assumption that a prima facie case of discrimination, combined with sufficient evidence for the trier of fact to disbelieve the defendant's legitimate, nondiscriminatory reason for its decision, is insufficient as a matter of law to sustain a jury's finding of intentional discrimination.

In so reasoning, the Court of Appeals misconceived the evidentiary burden borne by plaintiffs who attempt to prove intentional discrimination through indirect evidence. This much is evident from our decision in *St. Mary's Honor Center*. There we held that the factfinder's rejection of the employer's legitimate, nondiscriminatory reason for its action does not compel judgment for the plaintiff. The ultimate question is whether the employer intentionally discriminated, and proof that "the employer's proffered reason is unpersuasive, or even obviously contrived, does not necessarily establish that the plaintiff's proffered reason . . . is correct." In other words, "it is not enough . . . to disbelieve the employer; the factfinder must believe the plaintiff's explanation of intentional discrimination."

In reaching this conclusion, however, we reasoned that it is permissible for the trier of fact to infer the ultimate fact of discrimination from the falsity of the employer's explanation. Specifically, we stated:

> The factfinder's disbelief of the reasons put forward by the defendant (particularly if disbelief is accompanied by a suspicion of mendacity) may, together with the elements of the prima facie case, suffice to show intentional discrimination. Thus, rejection of the defendant's proffered reasons will permit the trier of fact to infer the ultimate fact of intentional discrimination.

Proof that the defendant's explanation is unworthy of credence is simply one form of circumstantial evidence that is probative of intentional discrimination, and it may be quite persuasive. [*St. Mary's Honor Center*.] ("Proving the employer's reason false becomes part of (and often considerably assists) the greater enterprise of proving that the real reason was intentional discrimination"). In appropriate circumstances, the trier of fact can reasonably infer from the falsity of the explanation that the employer is dissembling to cover up a discriminatory purpose. Such an inference is consistent with the general principle of evidence law that the factfinder is entitled to consider a party's dishonesty about a material fact as "affirmative evidence of guilt." *Wright v. West*, 505 U.S. 277 (1992); 2 J. WIGMORE, EVIDENCE §278(2), p. 133

(J. Chadbourn rev. ed. 1979). Moreover, once the employer's justification has been eliminated, discrimination may well be the most likely alternative explanation, especially since the employer is in the best position to put forth the actual reason for its decision. *Cf. Furnco Constr. Corp. v. Waters*, 438 U.S. 567, 577 (1978) ("When all legitimate reasons for rejecting an applicant have been eliminated as possible reasons for the employer's actions, it is more likely than not the employer, who we generally assume acts with some reason, based his decision on an impermissible consideration"). Thus, a plaintiff's prima facie case, combined with sufficient evidence to find that the employer's asserted justification is false, may permit the trier of fact to conclude that the employer unlawfully discriminated.

This is not to say that such a showing by the plaintiff will always be adequate to sustain a jury's finding of liability. Certainly there will be instances where, although the plaintiff has established a prima facie case and set forth sufficient evidence to reject the defendant's explanation, no rational factfinder could conclude that the action was discriminatory. For instance, an employer would be entitled to judgment as a matter of law if the record conclusively revealed some other, nondiscriminatory reason for the employer's decision, or if the plaintiff created only a weak issue of fact as to whether the employer's reason was untrue and there was abundant and uncontroverted independent evidence that no discrimination had occurred. *See Fisher v. Vassar College*, 114 F.3d 1332, 1338 (2d Cir. 1997) ("If the circumstances show that the defendant gave the false explanation to conceal something other than discrimination, the inference of discrimination will be weak or nonexistent"). To hold otherwise would be effectively to insulate an entire category of employment discrimination cases from review under Rule 50, and we have reiterated that trial courts should not "treat discrimination differently from other ultimate questions of fact." *St. Mary's Honor Center*.

Whether judgment as a matter of law is appropriate in any particular case will depend on a number of factors. Those include the strength of the plaintiff's prima facie case, the probative value of the proof that the employer's explanation is false, and any other evidence that supports the employer's case and that properly may be considered on a motion for judgment as a matter of law. For purposes of this case, we need not—and could not—resolve all of the circumstances in which such factors would entitle an employer to judgment as a matter of law. It suffices to say that, because a prima facie case and sufficient evidence to reject the employer's explanation may permit a finding of liability, the Court of Appeals erred in proceeding from the premise that a plaintiff must always introduce additional, independent evidence of discrimination.

III . . .

A

The remaining question is whether, despite the Court of Appeals' misconception of petitioner's evidentiary burden, respondent was nonetheless entitled to judgment as a matter of law. Under Rule 50, a court should render judgment as a matter of law when "a party has been fully heard on an issue and there is no legally sufficient evidentiary basis for a reasonable jury to find for that party on that issue." . . .

[In entertaining a motion for judgment as a matter of law, the court should review all of the evidence in the record.] In doing so, however, the court must draw all reasonable inferences in favor of the nonmoving party, and it may not make credibility determinations or weigh the evidence. *Lytle v. Household Mfg., Inc.*, 494 U.S. 545, 554-55 (1990). "Credibility determinations, the weighing of the evidence, and the drawing of legitimate inferences from the facts are jury functions, not those of a judge." *Anderson v. Liberty Lobby*, 477 U.S. 242 (1986). Thus, although the court should review the record as a whole, it must disregard all evidence favorable to the moving party that the jury is not required to believe. *See* Wright & Miller 299. That is, the court should give credence to the evidence favoring the nonmovant as well as that "evidence supporting the moving party that is uncontradicted and unimpeached, at least to the extent that that evidence comes from disinterested witnesses."

B

Applying this standard here, it is apparent that respondent was not entitled to judgment as a matter of law. In this case, in addition to establishing a prima facie case of discrimination and creating a jury issue as to the falsity of the employer's explanation, petitioner introduced additional evidence that Chesnut was motivated by age-based animus and was principally responsible for petitioner's firing. Petitioner testified that Chesnut had told him that he "was so old [he] must have come over on the May-flower" and, on one occasion when petitioner was having difficulty starting a machine, that he "was too damn old to do [his] job." According to petitioner, Chesnut would regularly "cuss at me and shake his finger in my face." Oswalt, roughly 24 years younger than petitioner, corroborated that there was an "obvious difference" in how Chesnut treated them. He stated that, although he and Chesnut "had [their] differences," "it was nothing compared to the way [Chesnut] treated Roger." Oswalt explained that Chesnut "tolerated quite a bit" from him even though he "defied" Chesnut "quite often," but that Chesnut treated petitioner "in a manner, as you would . . . treat . . . a child when . . . you're angry with [him]." Petitioner also demonstrated that, according to company records, he and Oswalt had nearly identical rates of productivity in 1993. Yet respondent conducted an efficiency study of only the regular line, supervised by petitioner, and placed only petitioner on probation. Chesnut conducted that efficiency study and, after having testified to the contrary on direct examination, acknowledged on cross-examination that he had recommended that petitioner be placed on probation following the study.

Further, petitioner introduced evidence that Chesnut was the actual decision-maker behind his firing. Chesnut was married to Sanderson, who made the formal decision to discharge petitioner. Although Sanderson testified that she fired petitioner because he had "intentionally falsified company pay records," respondent only introduced evidence concerning the inaccuracy of the records, not their falsification. A 1994 letter authored by Chesnut indicated that he berated other company directors, who were supposedly his co-equals, about how to do their jobs. Moreover, Oswalt testified that all of respondent's employees feared Chesnut, and that Chesnut had exercised "absolute power" within the company for "as long as [he] can remember."

In holding that the record contained insufficient evidence to sustain the jury's verdict, the Court of Appeals misapplied the standard of review dictated by Rule 50.

Again, the court disregarded critical evidence favorable to petitioner—namely, the evidence supporting petitioner's prima facie case and undermining respondent's non-discriminatory explanation. The court also failed to draw all reasonable inferences in favor of petitioner. For instance, while acknowledging "the potentially damning nature" of Chesnut's age-related comments, the court discounted them on the ground that they "were not made in the direct context of Reeves's termination." And the court discredited petitioner's evidence that Chesnut was the actual decision maker by giving weight to the fact that there was "no evidence to suggest that any of the other decision makers were motivated by age." Moreover, the other evidence on which the court relied—that Caldwell and Oswalt were also cited for poor record keeping, and that respondent employed many managers over age 50—although relevant, is certainly not dispositive. In concluding that these circumstances so overwhelmed the evidence favoring petitioner that no rational trier of fact could have found that petitioner was fired because of his age, the Court of Appeals impermissibly substituted its judgment concerning the weight of the evidence for the jury's.

The ultimate question in every employment discrimination case involving a claim of disparate treatment is whether the plaintiff was the victim of intentional discrimination. Given the evidence in the record supporting petitioner, we see no reason to subject the parties to an additional round of litigation before the Court of Appeals rather than to resolve the matter here. The District Court plainly informed the jury that petitioner was required to show "by a preponderance of the evidence that his age was a determining and motivating factor in the decision of [respondent] to terminate him." The court instructed the jury that, to show that respondent's explanation was a pretext for discrimination, petitioner had to demonstrate "1, that the stated reasons were not the real reasons for [petitioner's] discharge; and 2, that age discrimination was the real reason for [petitioner's] discharge." Given that petitioner established a prima facie case of discrimination, introduced enough evidence for the jury to reject respondent's explanation, and produced additional evidence of age-based animus, there was sufficient evidence for the jury to find that respondent had intentionally discriminated. The District Court was therefore correct to submit the case to the jury, and the Court of Appeals erred in overturning its verdict.

Justice GINSBURG, concurring.

The Court today holds that an employment discrimination plaintiff may survive judgment as a matter of law by submitting two categories of evidence: first, evidence establishing a "prima facie case," as that term is used in *McDonnell Douglas Corp. v. Green*, and second, evidence from which a rational factfinder could conclude that the employer's proffered explanation for its actions was false. Because the Court of Appeals in this case plainly, and erroneously, required the plaintiff to offer some evidence beyond those two categories, no broader holding is necessary to support reversal.

I write separately to note that it may be incumbent on the Court, in an appropriate case, to define more precisely the circumstances in which plaintiffs will be required to submit evidence beyond these two categories in order to survive a motion for judgment as a matter of law. I anticipate that such circumstances will be uncommon. As the Court notes, it is a principle of evidence law that the jury is entitled to treat a party's dishonesty about a material fact as evidence of culpability. Under this commonsense principle, evidence suggesting that a defendant accused of illegal discrimination has chosen to give a false explanation for its actions gives rise to a rational inference that the defendant could be masking its actual, illegal motivation. Whether the defendant was in fact motivated by discrimination is of course for the finder of fact to decide; that is the lesson of *St. Mary's Honor Center v. Hicks*. But the inference remains — unless it is conclusively demonstrated, by evidence the district court is required to credit on a motion for judgment as a matter of law, that discrimination could not have been the defendant's true motivation. If such conclusive demonstrations are (as I suspect) atypical, it follows that the ultimate question of liability ordinarily should not be taken from the jury once the plaintiff has introduced the two categories of evidence described above. Because the Court's opinion leaves room for such further elaboration in an appropriate case, I join it in full.

NOTES

1. *Beyond Pretext Plus.* Professor Michael Zimmer, *Slicing & Dicing of Individual Disparate Treatment Law*, 61 LA. L. REV. 577 (2001), views *Reeves* as broader than merely rejecting the lower court's "pretext-plus" rule. He argues that the Court rejected the underpinning for that rule, which was that the probative value of the evidence supporting plaintiff's prima facie case "drops out of the picture" once defendant introduces evidence of its nondiscriminatory reason for its action. *Id.* at 587-88. *Reeves* also made clear that all the evidence in the record needs to be reviewed in deciding motions for summary judgment or judgment as a matter of law: "That evidence includes evidence supporting the prima facie case, evidence tending to prove the defendant's proffered reason to be false, and all other circumstantial evidence such as age-related comments of decision makers that supports plaintiff's case. Slicing and dicing away plaintiff's evidence to leave only evidence supporting defendant's case is inconsistent with the true nature of the *McDonnell Douglas* method of analyzing individual disparate treatment cases." *Id.* at 591-92.

2. *"Unreasonable" Decision Versus Business Judgment.* Courts have often recognized that the more unusual and idiosyncratic a decision is — in terms of the way business is normally conducted — the more appropriate it is to infer discrimination. This principle is in obvious tension with what has sometimes been called the "business judgment" rule, which is that courts should not second-guess business decisions. One illustration of the conflict is *White v. Baxter Healthcare Corp.*, 533 F.3d 381, 393 (6th Cir. 2008), in which the majority reaffirmed that "the plaintiff may also demonstrate pretext by offering evidence which challenges the reasonableness of the employer's decision 'to the extent that such an inquiry sheds light on whether the employer's proffered reason for the employment action was its actual motivation'" (citation omitted). It went on:

> [O]ur Circuit has never adopted a "business-judgment rule" which requires us to defer to the employer's "reasonable business judgment" in Title VII cases. Indeed, in most Title VII cases the very issue in dispute is whether the employer's adverse employment decision resulted from an objectively unreasonable business judgment, i.e., a judgment that was based upon an impermissible consideration such as the adversely-affected employee's race, gender, religion, or national origin. In determining whether the plaintiff has produced enough evidence to cast doubt upon the employer's explanation for its decision, we cannot . . . unquestionably accept the employer's own self-serving claim that the decision resulted from an exercise of "reasonable business judgment." Nor can we decide "as a matter of law" that "an employer's proffered justification is reasonable." The question of

whether the employer's judgment was reasonable or was instead motivated by improper considerations is for the jury to consider. . . .

Id. at 394 n.6; *see also Latowski v. Northwoods Nursing Ctr.*, 549 f. App'x 478 (6th Cir. 2013) ("A reasonable jury could easily conclude that North Woods's business decision — to implement a policy terminating otherwise qualified workers whose doctors imposed any restrictions arising from nonworkplace injuries, even if those restrictions do not limit the employees' ability to competently perform their jobs — is so lacking in merit as to be a pretext for discrimination."). Nevertheless, scholars suggest that, even when a business reason seems implausible, courts are too willing to look to other factors — whether personal animosity or cronyism — to explain such decisions. *See* Ann C. McGinley, *The Emerging Cronyism Defense and Affirmative Action: A Critical Perspective on the Distinction Between Color-Blind and Race-Conscious Decision Making Under Title VII*, 39 ARIZ. L. REV. 1003 (1997); Chad Derum & Karen Engle, *The Rise of the Personal Animosity Presumption in Title VII and the Return to "No Cause" Employment*, 81 TEX. L. REV. 1177, 1182 (2003),

3. *"Me, Too" Proof of Pretext*. In *Sprint/United Management Co. v. Mendelsohn*, 552 U.S. 379 (2007), a reduction-in-force case, plaintiff wanted to call as witnesses five other older workers who claimed that they, too, were discriminated against because of their age in the downsizing. Defendant objected because none of these potential witnesses worked under the same supervisor as the plaintiff. The trial court excluded the testimony, but the court of appeals reversed because, as it saw it, the district court had relied on a per se rule of exclusion of all such so-called me too evidence.

The Supreme Court found "such evidence [to be] neither *per se* admissible nor *per se* inadmissible." *Id*. at 381. Emphasizing the broad discretion accorded trail courts' evidentiary rulings — reviewable under a deferential abuse of discretion standard — the trial court should make the admissibility determination: "With respect to evidentiary questions in general [including "relevance" under federal Rule of Evidence 401] and Rule 403 [as to "prejudice"] in particular, a district court virtually always is in the better position to assess the admissibility of the evidence in the context of the case before it." *Id*. at 387. Discrimination cases are well suited to this generally applicable approach since:

> [t]he question whether evidence of discrimination by other supervisors is relevant in an individual ADEA case is fact based and depends on many factors, including how closely related the evidence is to the plaintiff's circumstances and theory of the case. Applying Rule 403 to determine if evidence is prejudicial also requires a fact-intensive, context-specific inquiry.

Id. at 388. Indeed, discrimination cases may be especially fact sensitive. One scholar has argued that the focus on "insular individualism" of supervisors and managers is inconsistent with how workplaces operate in practice, with any particular decision being influenced by a web of other decisions and practices, sometimes influencing individual actors in ways they do not themselves understand. Tristin Green, *Insular Individualism: Employment Discrimination Law After* Ledbetter v. Goodyear, 43 HARV. C.R-C.L. L. REV. 353 (2008).

After *Mendelsohn* the determination in every case will be contextual, taking into account the requirements of FED. R. EVID. 401 and 403. As to Rule 401, Sprint claimed that any discrimination by other supervisors was simply irrelevant to the question at issue: Did plaintiff's supervisor pick her for discharge because of her age? If the intent of a single individual is the touchstone, isn't that right? Is that still true even if there is some umbrella policy that allowed each supervisor freedom to make such decisions? And what about the possibility that a supervisor would feel freer to discriminate if others were so acting, and then the actions of others would be admissible (at least if they happened before the challenged action and the supervisor knew about them)?

As for prejudice under Rule 403, "[a]lthough relevant, evidence may be excluded if its probative value is substantially outweighed by the danger of unfair prejudice, confusion of the issues, or misleading the jury, or by considerations of undue delay, waste of time, or needless presentation of cumulative evidence." Thus, a low level of relevance may not be sufficient to justify admission of evidence if it is likely to prejudice the jury. *See Mattenson v. Baxter Healthcare Corp.*, 438 F.3d 763, 770-71 (7th Cir. 2006) (in a division of 7,000 employees with hundreds of executives, the fact that some may dislike old workers and even fire old workers because of their age is weak evidence that a particular older employee was fired because of his age; absent proof of a pervasive culture of prejudice, such evidence may be excluded under Rule 403, although it not reversible error to admit it). Isn't there a real danger that a jury would punish Sprint for being a "bad employer" if all this evidence were admitted, even if the decision as to Mendelsohn herself was not discriminatory?

The significance of *Mendelsohn* will, of course, ultimately depend on how the district courts apply their discretion. As a practical matter, this means that "me too" evidence will largely disappear from the radar screen, becoming less a question of "law" than a question of how a particular district court views the evidence in the context of the case before it. Whatever the results in the district courts, the determinations will be reviewed only under the highly deferential abuse of discretion standard, which means that few questions of admissibility will be overturned. Commentary on *Mendelsohn* can be found by Professors Mitchell Rubenstein, Paul Secunda, and David Gregory, Sprint/United Management Co. v. Mendelsohn: *The Supreme Court Appears to Have Punted on the Admissibility of "Me Too" Evidence of Discrimination. But Did It?*, 102 Nw. U. L. Rev. Colloquy 264, 374, 382, 387 (2008).

3. Proving Discrimination: Mixed-Motive Analysis

Price Waterhouse v. Hopkins
490 U.S. 228 (1989)

Justice BRENNAN announced the judgment of the Court and delivered an opinion, in which Justice MARSHALL, Justice BLACKMUN, and Justice STEVENS join. . . .

. . . At Price Waterhouse, a nationwide professional accounting partnership, a senior manager becomes a candidate for partnership when the partners in her local office submit her name as a candidate. All of the other partners in the firm are then invited to submit written comments on each candidate — either on a "long" or a "short" form, depending on the partner's degree of exposure to the candidate. Not every partner in the firm submits comments on every candidate. After reviewing the comments and interviewing the partners who submitted them, the firm's Admissions

Committee makes a recommendation to the Policy Board. This recommendation will be either that the firm accept the candidate for partnership, put her application on "hold," or deny her the promotion outright. The Policy Board then decides whether to submit the candidate's name to the entire partnership for a vote, to "hold" her candidacy, or to reject her. The recommendation of the Admissions Committee, and the decision of the Policy Board, are not controlled by fixed guidelines: a certain number of positive comments from partners will not guarantee a candidate's admission to the partnership, nor will a specific quantity of negative comments necessarily defeat her application. Price Waterhouse places no limit on the number of persons whom it will admit to the partnership in any given year.

Ann Hopkins had worked at Price Waterhouse's Office of Government Services in Washington, D.C., for five years when the partners in that office proposed her as a candidate for partnership. Of the 662 partners at the firm at that time, 7 were women. Of the 88 persons proposed for partnership that year, only 1 — Hopkins — was a woman. Forty-seven of these candidates were admitted to the partnership, 21 were rejected, and 20 — including Hopkins — were "held" for reconsideration the following year. Thirteen of the 32 partners who had submitted comments on Hopkins supported her bid for partnership. Three partners recommended that her candidacy be placed on hold, eight stated that they did not have an informed opinion about her, and eight recommended that she be denied partnership.

In a jointly prepared statement supporting her candidacy, the partners in Hopkins' office showcased her successful 2-year effort to secure a $25 million contract with the Department of State, labeling it "an outstanding performance" and one that Hopkins carried out "virtually at the partner level." Despite Price Waterhouse's attempt at trial to minimize her contribution to this project, Judge Gesell specifically found that Hopkins had "played a key role in Price Waterhouse's successful effort to win a multimillion dollar contract with the Department of State." Indeed, he went on, "[n]one of the other partnership candidates at Price Waterhouse that year had a comparable record in terms of successfully securing major contracts for the partnership."

The partners in Hopkins' office praised her character as well as her accomplishments, describing her in their joint statement as "an outstanding professional" who had a "deft touch," a "strong character, independence and integrity." Clients appear to have agreed with these assessments. At trial, one official from the State Department described her as "extremely competent, intelligent," "strong and forthright, very productive, energetic and creative." Another high-ranking official praised Hopkins' decisiveness, broadmindedness, and "intellectual clarity"; she was, in his words, "a stimulating conversationalist." Evaluations such as these led Judge Gesell to conclude that Hopkins "had no difficulty dealing with clients and her clients appear to have been very pleased with her work" and that she "was generally viewed as a highly competent project leader who worked long hours, pushed vigorously to meet deadlines and demanded much from the multidisciplinary staffs with which she worked."

On too many occasions, however, Hopkins' aggressiveness apparently spilled over into abrasiveness. Staff members seem to have borne the brunt of Hopkins' brusqueness. Long before her bid for partnership, partners evaluating her work had counseled her to improve her relations with staff members. Although later evaluations indicate an improvement, Hopkins' perceived shortcomings in this important area eventually doomed her bid for partnership. Virtually all of the partners' negative remarks about Hopkins — even those of partners supporting her — had to do with her "interpersonal skills." Both "[s]upporters and opponents of her candidacy," stressed Judge

Gesell, "indicated that she was sometimes overly aggressive, unduly harsh, difficult to work with and impatient with staff."

There were clear signs, though, that some of the partners reacted negatively to Hopkins' personality because she was a woman. One partner described her as "macho"; another suggested that she "overcompensated for being a woman"; a third advised her to take "a course at charm school." Several partners criticized her use of profanity; in response, one partner suggested that those partners objected to her swearing only "because it['] a lady using foul language." Another supporter explained that Hopkins "ha[d] matured from a tough-talking somewhat masculine hard-nosed mgr to an authoritative, formidable, but much more appealing lady ptr candidate." But it was the man who, as Judge Gesell found, bore responsibility for explaining to Hopkins the reasons for the Policy Board's decision to place her candidacy on hold who delivered the coup de grace: in order to improve her chances for partnership, Thomas Beyer advised, Hopkins should "walk more femininely, talk more femininely, dress more femininely, wear make-up, have her hair styled, and wear jewelry."

Dr. Susan Fiske, a social psychologist and Associate Professor of Psychology at Carnegie-Mellon University, testified at trial that the partnership selection process at Price Waterhouse was likely influenced by sex stereotyping. Her testimony focused not only on the overtly sex-based comments of partners but also on gender-neutral remarks, made by partners who knew Hopkins only slightly, that were intensely critical of her. One partner, for example, baldly stated that Hopkins was "universally disliked" by staff, and another described her as "consistently annoying and irritating"; yet these were people who had had very little contact with Hopkins. According to Fiske, Hopkins' uniqueness (as the only woman in the pool of candidates) and the subjectivity of the evaluations made it likely that sharply critical remarks such as these were the product of sex stereotyping — although Fiske admitted that she could not say with certainty whether any particular comment was the result of stereotyping. Fiske based her opinion on a review of the submitted comments, explaining that it was commonly accepted practice for social psychologists to reach this kind of conclusion without having met any of the people involved in the decisionmaking process.

In previous years, other female candidates for partnership also had been evaluated in sex-based terms. As a general matter, Judge Gesell concluded, "[c]andidates were viewed favorably if partners believed they maintained their femin[in]ity while becoming effective professional managers"; in this environment, "[t]o be identified as a 'women's lib[b]er' was regarded as [a] negative comment." In fact, the judge found that in previous years "[o]ne partner repeatedly commented that he could not consider any woman seriously as a partnership candidate and believed that women were not even capable of functioning as senior managers — yet the firm took no action to discourage his comments and recorded his vote in the overall summary of the evaluations."

Judge Gesell found that Price Waterhouse legitimately emphasized interpersonal skills in its partnership decisions, and also found that the firm had not fabricated its complaints about Hopkins' interpersonal skills as a pretext for discrimination. Moreover, he concluded, the firm did not give decisive emphasis to such traits only because Hopkins was a woman; although there were male candidates who lacked these skills but who were admitted to partnership, the judge found that these candidates possessed other, positive traits that Hopkins lacked.

The judge went on to decide, however, that some of the partners' remarks about Hopkins stemmed from an impermissibly cabined view of the proper behavior of women, and that Price Waterhouse had done nothing to disavow reliance on such comments. He held that Price Waterhouse had unlawfully discriminated against Hopkins on the basis of sex by consciously giving credence and effect to partners' comments that resulted from sex stereotyping. Noting that Price Waterhouse could avoid equitable relief by proving by clear and convincing evidence that it would have placed Hopkins' candidacy on hold even absent this discrimination, the judge decided that the firm had not carried this heavy burden. . . .

II . . .

In passing Title VII, Congress made the simple but momentous announcement that sex, race, religion, and national origin are not relevant to the selection, evaluation, or compensation of employees. Yet, the statute does not purport to limit the other qualities and characteristics that employers may take into account in making employment decisions. The converse, therefore, of "for cause" legislation, Title VII eliminates certain bases for distinguishing among employees while otherwise preserving employers' freedom of choice. This balance between employee rights and employer prerogatives turns out to be decisive in the case before us.

Congress' intent to forbid employers to take gender into account in making employment decisions appears on the face of the statute. In now-familiar language, the statute forbids an employer to "[discriminate] *because of* such individual's . . . sex." (emphasis added). We take these words to mean that gender must be irrelevant to employment decisions. To construe the words "because of" as colloquial shorthand for "but-for causation," as does Price Waterhouse, is to misunderstand them.

But-for causation is a hypothetical construct. In determining whether a particular factor was a but-for cause of a given event, we begin by assuming that that factor was present at the time of the event, and then ask whether, even if that factor had been absent, the event nevertheless would have transpired in the same way. The present, active tense of the operative verbs of §703(a)(1) ("to fail or refuse"), in contrast, turns our attention to the actual moment of the event in question, the adverse employment decision. The critical inquiry, the one commanded by the words of §703(a)(1), is whether gender was a factor in the employment decision *at the moment it was made.* Moreover, since we know that the words "because of" do not mean "solely because of,"[8] we also know that Title VII meant to condemn even those decisions based on a mixture of legitimate and illegitimate considerations. When, therefore, an employer considers both gender and legitimate factors at the time of making a decision, that decision was "because of" sex and the other, legitimate considerations — even if we may say later, in the context of litigation, that the decision would have been the same if gender had not been taken into account.

To attribute this meaning to the words "because of" does not, as the dissent asserts, divest them of causal significance. A simple example illustrates the point. Suppose two physical forces act upon and move an object, and suppose that either force acting alone would have moved the object. As the dissent would have it, neither physical force was a "cause" of the motion unless we can show that but-for one or

---

8. Congress specifically rejected an amendment that would have placed the word "solely" in front of the words "because of." 110 Cong. Rec. 2728, 13837 (1964).

both of them, the object would not have moved; to use the dissent's terminology, both forces were simply "in the air" unless we can identify at least one of them as a but-for cause of the object's movement. Events that are causally overdetermined, in other words, may not have any "cause" at all. This cannot be so.

[Congress did not intend to require a plaintiff "to identify the precise causal role played by legitimate and illegitimate motivations"; it meant only to require her "to prove that the employer relied upon sex-based considerations" in its decision.]

To say that an employer may not take gender into account is not, however, the end of the matter, for that describes only one aspect of Title VII. The other important aspect of the statute is its preservation of an employer's remaining freedom of choice. We conclude that the preservation of this freedom means that an employer shall not be liable if it can prove that, even if it had not taken gender into account, it would have come to the same decision regarding a particular person. The statute's maintenance of employer prerogatives is evident from the statute itself and from its history, both in Congress and in this Court. . . .

The central point is this: while an employer may not take gender into account in making an employment decision . . . , it is free to decide against a woman for other reasons. We think these principles require that, once a plaintiff in a Title VII case shows that gender played a motivating part in an employment decision, the defendant may avoid a finding of liability only by proving that it would have made the same decision even if it had not allowed gender to play such a role. This balance of burdens is the direct result of Title VII's balance of rights.

Our holding casts no shadow on *Burdine*, in which we decided that, even after a plaintiff has made out a prima facie case of discrimination under Title VII, the burden of persuasion does not shift to the employer to show that its stated legitimate reason for the employment decision was the true reason. We stress, first, that neither court below shifted the burden of persuasion to Price Waterhouse on this question, and in fact, the District Court found that Hopkins had not shown that the firm's stated reason for its decision was pretextual. Moreover, since we hold that the plaintiff retains the burden of persuasion on the issue whether gender played a part in the employment decision, the situation before us is not the one of "shifting burdens" that we addressed in *Burdine*. Instead, the employer's burden is most appropriately deemed an affirmative defense: the plaintiff must persuade the factfinder on one point, and then the employer, if it wishes to prevail, must persuade it on another. *See NLRB v. Transportation Management Corp.*, 462 U.S. 393 (1983).[12]

Price Waterhouse's claim that the employer does not bear any burden of proof (if it bears one at all) until the plaintiff has shown "substantial evidence that Price Waterhouse's explanation for failing to promote Hopkins was not the 'true reason' for its action" merely restates its argument that the plaintiff in a mixed-motives case must squeeze her proof into *Burdine*'s framework. Where a decision was the product of a

---

12. [Contrary to the dissent, it is] perfectly consistent to say both that gender was a factor in a particular decision when it was made and that, when the situation is viewed hypothetically and after the fact, the same decision would have been made even in the absence of discrimination. . . . [W]here liability is imposed because an employer is unable to prove that it would have made the same decision even if it had not discriminated, this is not an imposition of liability "where sex made no difference to the outcome." In our adversary system, where a party has the burden of proving a particular assertion and where that party is unable to meet its burden, we assume that that assertion is inaccurate. Thus, where an employer is unable to prove its claim that it would have made the same decision in the absence of discrimination, we are entitled to conclude that gender did make a difference to the outcome.

mixture of legitimate and illegitimate motives, however, it simply makes no sense to ask whether the legitimate reason was "the 'true reason'" for the decision — which is the question asked by *Burdine.*[13] . . .

In saying that gender played a motivating part in an employment decision, we mean that, if we asked the employer at the moment of the decision what its reasons were and if we received a truthful response, one of those reasons would be that the applicant or employee was a woman. In the specific context of sex stereotyping, an employer who acts on the basis of a belief that a woman cannot be aggressive, or that she must not be, has acted on the basis of gender.

. . . As to the existence of sex stereotyping in this case, we are not inclined to quarrel with the District Court's conclusion that a number of the partners' comments showed sex stereotyping at work. As for the legal relevance of sex stereotyping, we are beyond the day when an employer could evaluate employees by assuming or insisting that they matched the stereotype associated with their group. . . . An employer who objects to aggressiveness in women but whose positions require this trait places women in an intolerable and impermissible Catch-22: out of a job if they behave aggressively and out of a job if they don't. Title VII lifts women out of this bind.

Remarks at work that are based on sex stereotypes do not inevitably prove that gender played a part in a particular employment decision. The plaintiff must show that the employer actually relied on her gender in making its decision. In making this showing, stereotyped remarks can certainly be evidence that gender played a part. In any event, the stereotyping in this case did not simply consist of stray remarks. On the contrary, Hopkins proved that Price Waterhouse invited partners to submit comments; that some of the comments stemmed from sex stereotypes; that an important part of the Policy Board's decision on Hopkins was an assessment of the submitted comments; and that Price Waterhouse in no way disclaimed reliance on the sex-linked evaluations. This is not, as Price Waterhouse suggests, "discrimination in the air"; rather, it is, as Hopkins puts it, "discrimination brought to ground and visited upon" an employee. By focusing on Hopkins' specific proof, however, we do not suggest a limitation on the possible ways of proving that stereotyping played a motivating role in an employment decision, and we refrain from deciding here which specific facts, "standing alone," would or would not establish a plaintiff's case, since such a decision is unnecessary in this case. *But see* [O'Connor, J., at page 604, concurring in the judgment].

As to the employer's proof, in most cases, the employer should be able to present some objective evidence as to its probable decision in the absence of an impermissible motive.[15] Moreover, proving "that the same decision would have been justified . . . is not the same as proving that the same decision would have been made." An employer may not, in other words, prevail in a mixed-motives case by offering a legitimate and sufficient reason for its decision if that reason did not motivate it at the time of the

13. [A case need not be labeled either a "pretext" case or a "mixed motives" case from the beginning; plaintiffs often will allege both. At some point, however, the district court must decide whether mixed motives are involved.] If the plaintiff fails to satisfy the factfinder that it is more likely than not that a forbidden characteristic played a part in the employment decision, then she may prevail only if she proves, following *Burdine,* that the employer's stated reason for its decision is pretextual. The dissent need not worry that this evidentiary scheme, if used during a jury trial, will be so impossibly confused and complex as it imagines. Juries long have decided cases in which defendants raise affirmative defenses. . . .

15. Justice White's suggestion that the employer's own testimony as to the probable decision in the absence of discrimination is due special credence where the court has, contrary to the employer's testimony, found that an illegitimate factor played a part in the decision, is baffling.

decision. Finally, an employer may not meet its burden in such a case by merely showing that at the time of the decision it was motivated only in part by a legitimate reason. The very premise of a mixed-motives case is that a legitimate reason was present, and indeed, in this case, Price Waterhouse already has made this showing by convincing Judge Gesell that Hopkins' interpersonal problems were a legitimate concern. The employer instead must show that its legitimate reason, standing alone, would have induced it to make the same decision.

III

The courts below held that an employer who has allowed a discriminatory impulse to play a motivating part in an employment decision must prove by clear and convincing evidence that it would have made the same decision in the absence of discrimination. We are persuaded that the better rule is that the employer must make this showing by a preponderance of the evidence. . . .

IV

[Price Waterhouse challenged as clearly erroneous the district court's findings both that stereotyping occurred and that it played any part in the decision to place Hopkins' candidacy on hold. The plurality disagreed.]

In finding that some of the partners' comments reflected sex stereotyping, the District Court relied in part on Dr. Fiske's expert testimony. Without directly impugning Dr. Fiske's credentials or qualifications, Price Waterhouse insinuates that a social psychologist is unable to identify sex stereotyping in evaluations without investigating whether those evaluations have a basis in reality. This argument comes too late. At trial, counsel for Price Waterhouse twice assured the court that he did not question Dr. Fiske's expertise and failed to challenge the legitimacy of her discipline. Without contradiction from Price Waterhouse, Fiske testified that she discerned sex stereotyping in the partners' evaluations of Hopkins and she further explained that it was part of her business to identify stereotyping in written documents. We are not inclined to accept petitioner's belated and unsubstantiated characterization of Dr. Fiske's testimony as "gossamer evidence" based only on "intuitive hunches" and of her detection of sex stereotyping as "intuitively divined." Nor are we disposed to adopt the dissent's dismissive attitude toward Dr. Fiske's field of study and toward her own professional integrity.

Indeed, we are tempted to say that Dr. Fiske's expert testimony was merely icing on Hopkins' cake. It takes no special training to discern sex stereotyping in a description of an aggressive female employee as requiring "a course at charm school." Nor, turning to Thomas Beyer's memorable advice to Hopkins, does it require expertise in psychology to know that, if an employee's flawed "interpersonal skills" can be corrected by a soft-hued suit or a new shade of lipstick, perhaps it is the employee's sex and not her interpersonal skills that has drawn the criticism.

Price Waterhouse also charges that Hopkins produced no evidence that sex stereotyping played a role in the decision to place her candidacy on hold. As we have stressed, however, Hopkins showed that the partnership solicited evaluations from all of the firm's partners; that it generally relied very heavily on such evaluations in making its decision; that some of the partners' comments were the product of stereotyping; and that the firm in no way disclaimed reliance on those particular comments, either in Hopkins' case or in the past. Certainly a plausible — and, one might say, inevitable — conclusion to draw from this set of circumstances is that the Policy Board in making its decision did in fact take into account all of the partners' comments, including the comments that were motivated by stereotypical notions about women's proper deportment. . . .

Nor is the finding that sex stereotyping played a part in the Policy Board's decision undermined by the fact that many of the suspect comments were made by supporters rather than detractors of Hopkins. A negative comment, even when made in the context of a generally favorable review, nevertheless may influence the decisionmaker to think less highly of the candidate. . . . The additional suggestion that the comments were made by "persons outside the decisionmaking chain" — and therefore could not have harmed Hopkins — simply ignores the critical role that partners' comments played in the Policy Board's partnership decisions.

Price Waterhouse appears to think that we cannot affirm the factual findings of the trial court without deciding that, instead of being overbearing and aggressive and curt, Hopkins is in fact kind and considerate and patient. If this is indeed its impression, petitioner misunderstands the theory on which Hopkins prevailed. The District Judge acknowledged that Hopkins' conduct justified complaints about her behavior as a senior manager. But he also concluded that the reactions of at least some of the partners were reactions to her as a woman manager. Where an evaluation is based on a subjective assessment of a person's strengths and weaknesses, it is simply not true that each evaluator will focus on, or even mention, the same weaknesses. Thus, even if we knew that Hopkins had "personality problems," this would not tell us that the partners who cast their evaluations of Hopkins in sex-based terms would have criticized her as sharply (or criticized her at all) if she had been a man. It is not our job to review the evidence and decide that the negative reactions to Hopkins were based on reality; our perception of Hopkins' character is irrelevant. We sit not to determine whether Ms. Hopkins is nice, but to decide whether the partners reacted negatively to her personality because she is a woman.

V

We hold that when a plaintiff in a Title VII case proves that her gender played a motivating part in an employment decision, the defendant may avoid a finding of liability only by proving by a preponderance of the evidence that it would have made the same decision even if it had not taken the plaintiff's gender into account. . . .

Justice O'CONNOR, concurring in the judgment.

I agree with the plurality that on the facts presented in this case, the burden of persuasion should shift to the employer to demonstrate by a preponderance of the evidence that it would have reached the same decision concerning Ann Hopkins' candidacy absent consideration of her gender. I further agree that this burden shift is properly part of the liability phase of the litigation. I thus concur in the judgment of the Court. My disagreement stems from the plurality's conclusions concerning the substantive requirement of causation under the statute and its broad statements regarding the applicability of the allocation of the burden of proof applied in this case. . . .

I

. . . The legislative history of Title VII bears out what its plain language suggests: a substantive violation of the statute only occurs when consideration of an illegitimate criterion is the "but-for" cause of an adverse employment action. The legislative history makes it clear that Congress was attempting to eradicate discriminatory actions in the employment setting, not mere discriminatory thoughts. Critics of the bill that became Title VII labeled it a "thought control bill," and argued that it created a "punishable crime that does not require an illegal external act as a basis for judgment." Senator Case . . . responded:

> The man must do or fail to do something in regard to employment. There must be some specific external act, more than a mental act. Only if he does the act because of the grounds stated in the bill would there be any legal consequences.

Thus, I disagree with the plurality's dictum that the words "because of" do not mean "but-for" causation; manifestly they do. We should not, and need not, deviate from that policy today. . . .

The evidence of congressional intent as to which party should bear the burden of proof on the issue of causation is considerably less clear. . . . [In the area of tort liability,] the law has long recognized that in certain "civil cases" leaving the burden of persuasion on the plaintiff to prove "but-for" causation would be both unfair and destructive of the deterrent purposes embodied in the concept of duty of care. Thus, in multiple causation cases, where a breach of duty has been established, the common law of torts has long shifted the burden of proof to multiple defendants to prove that their negligent actions were not the "but-for" cause of the plaintiff's injury. *See, e.g., Summers v. Tice*, 199 P.2d 1 (Cal. 1948). The same rule has been applied where the effect of a defendant's tortious conduct combines with a force of unknown or innocent origin to produce the harm to the plaintiff. *See Kingston v. Chicago & N.W.R. Co.*, 211 N.W. 913, 915 (Wis. 1927). . . . *See also* 2 J. Wigmore, SELECT CASES ON THE LAW OF TORTS, § 153, p. 865 (1912). . . .

[At times, however, the but-for] "test demands the impossible. It challenges the imagination of the trier to probe into a purely fanciful and unknowable state of affairs. He is invited to make an estimate concerning facts that concededly never existed. The very uncertainty as to what might have happened opens the door wide for conjecture. But when conjecture is demanded it can be given a direction that is consistent with the policy considerations that underlie the controversy."

. . . There is no doubt that Congress considered reliance on gender or race in making employment decisions an evil in itself. . . . Reliance on such factors is exactly what the threat of Title VII liability was meant to deter. While the main concern of the statute was with employment opportunity, Congress was certainly not blind to the stigmatic harm which comes from being evaluated by a process which treats one as an inferior by reason of one's race or sex. . . . At the same time, Congress clearly conditioned legal liability on a determination that the consideration of an illegitimate factor caused a tangible employment injury of some kind.

Where an individual disparate treatment plaintiff has shown by a preponderance of the evidence that an illegitimate criterion was a substantial factor in an adverse employment decision, the deterrent purpose of the statute has clearly been triggered. More importantly, as an evidentiary matter, a reasonable factfinder could conclude that absent further explanation, the employer's discriminatory motivation "caused" the employment decision. The employer has not yet been shown to be a violator, but neither is it entitled to the same presumption of good faith concerning its employment decisions which is accorded employers facing only circumstantial evidence of discrimination. Both the policies behind the statute, and the evidentiary principles developed in the analogous area of causation in the law of torts, suggest that at this point the employer may be required to convince the factfinder that, despite the smoke, there is no fire. . . .

[The plurality, however, goes too far by holding that the burden shifts when "a decisional process is 'tainted' by awareness of sex or race in any way."] In my view, in order to justify shifting the burden on the issue of causation to the defendant, a disparate treatment plaintiff must show by direct evidence that an illegitimate criterion was a substantial factor in the decision. . . .

NOTES

1. *The Holding of* Price Waterhouse. Understanding the significance of *Price Waterhouse* is complicated by the lack of a majority opinion for the Court. There was a four-judge plurality opinion written by Justice Brennan with separate concurrences by Justices O'Connor and White. In such circumstances, the holding of the Court is said to be the narrowest point on which five justices concurring in the judgment agree. *See Marks v. United States*, 430 U.S. 188 (1977). Although Justice White had also concurred, the narrowest holding was generally accepted by the lower courts to be found in the opinion of Justice O'Connor. In contrast, Justice Stevens's dissent in *Gross v. FBL Fin. Servs.*, 557 U.S. 167 (2009), argues that Justice White's opinion generated the controlling rule.

To put it simply, the trial judge had found that Price Waterhouse had relied on Hopkins's gender in putting her application for partnership on "hold," but it also found that legitimate objections to plaintiff's interpersonal skills were a factor in the decision. The plurality held that in a situation where a defendant's motives were mixed — that is, where legitimate and illegitimate considerations were both present — a plaintiff need only prove by a preponderance of the evidence that her race, gender, or other protected characteristic was "a motivating factor" for the challenged decision. Upon that showing, the burden of persuasion shifted to the defendant to avoid liability by proving as an affirmative defense that it would have made the same decision absent the discrimination.

If Justice O'Connor's concurrence controlled, it narrowed the plurality's rule in two ways: First, she raised the bar by requiring the plaintiff to show that the impermissible factor, such as plaintiff's sex, was a "substantial," not just a "motivating," factor. And, second, to trigger the *Price Waterhouse* shift in the burdens, she required plaintiff to introduce "direct" evidence of discrimination. Finding this concurrence to be the narrowest holding, the lower courts generally read *Price Waterhouse* to apply when the plaintiff had sufficient direct evidence to determine that discrimination was a "substantial" factor. If the trier of fact so found, plaintiff would prevail unless defendant carried the burden of persuasion that it would have made the same decision even if the prohibited trait was not a substantial factor.

2. *Direct Evidence.* What is "direct" evidence anyway? If the term means anything, it refers to evidence that, if believed, would establish a fact at issue without the need to draw any inferences. In disparate treatment cases, the fact at issue is whether the employer relied on a prohibited characteristic in making its decision. An evidence purist would say that there can be no direct evidence of the state of mind of a person because intent is internal and cannot be directly observed. *See generally* Charles A. Sullivan, *Accounting for* Price Waterhouse: *Proving Disparate Treatment Under Title VII*, 56 BROOK. L. REV. 1107 (1991).

As used by Justice O'Connor, "direct evidence" would seem to require a statement by the decision maker that showed he was motivated by illegitimate considerations with respect to the at-issue decision. Analytically, this raises at least two questions. First, what did the decision maker actually say? The decision maker may, of course, testify as to his reasons. But testimony of out-of-court statements will be allowed even if the party allegedly making the statement now denies that he did so. *EEOC v. Warfield-Rohr Casket Co.*, 364 F.3d 160, 163-64 (4th Cir. 2004) ("[T]here is no requirement that an employee's testimony be corroborated in order to apply the mixed-motive framework."). Second, does the comment reflect illegitimate considerations? Obviously some comments are explicitly racist or sexist, but less explicitly racist comments have also been held to be capable of being found to be racist. *Ash v. Tyson Foods, Inc.*, 546 U.S. 454 (2006), held that a manager's use of "boy" to refer to an African American man could reveal discriminatory intent: "The speaker's meaning may depend on various factors including context, inflection, tone of voice, local custom, and historical usage. Insofar as the Court of Appeals held that modifiers or qualifications are necessary in all instances to render the disputed term probative of bias, the court's decision is erroneous." *Id.* at 456; *see also McGinest v. GTE Serv. Corp.*, 360 F.3d 1103, 1116-17 (9th Cir. 2004) (the use of "code words" for race, like "drug dealer," can indicate discrimination). *But see Putman v. Unity Health Sys.*, 348 F.3d 732 (8th Cir. 2003) (comments about plaintiff not being "humble enough" and being "too prideful" not clearly linked to race). *See generally* Leora F. Eisenstadt, *The N-Word at Work: Contextualizing Language in the Workplace*, 33 BERKELEY J. EMP. & LAB. L. 299, 303 (2012) (arguing for "expert testimony from disciplines outside of the law that can inform courts about the way in which linguistic meaning is created in our culture and the contextually based meanings of specific terms.").

3. *Lower Court Confusion About "Direct" Evidence.* Some lower-court cases applied the direct evidence requirement for the *Price Waterhouse* case with little difficulty. *See Fuhr v. Sch. Dist. of Hazel Park*, 364 F.3d 753, 759 (6th Cir. 2004). But the circuits evolved a range of definitions of "direct evidence." Some courts read *Price Waterhouse* as applying only in cases involving "direct evidence," in the classic evidentiary sense of the term, that is, that the evidence proves the fact at issue without need to draw any inferences. *See, e.g., Fuller v. Phipps*, 67 F.3d 1137 (4th Cir. 1995). These cases demanded a very close connection between the evidence and the alleged discriminatory decision. A startling example is *Shorter v. ICG Holdings, Inc.*, 188 F.3d 1204 (10th Cir. 1999), which held that defendant's manager referring to plaintiff as an "incompetent nigger" within a day or two of having fired her was not direct evidence of discriminatory intent. The statement was merely a matter of personal opinion.

As we will see in the next principal case, "direct" evidence is no longer a meaningful category under Title VII, since the Supreme Court has held that the Civil Rights Act of 1991 overturned any requirement of direct evidence for what we have termed mixed-motive cases. And the Court's decision in *Gross v. FBL Fin. Servs.*, 557 U.S. 167

(2009), rejecting any "mixed-motive" burden-shifting under the ADEA altogether, rendered the concept of "direct" evidence inapplicable under that statute as a legal category. *See also Univ. of Texas Sw. Med. Ctr. v. Nassar*, 133 S. Ct. 2517 (2013) ("motivating factor" causation not applicable to Title VII retaliation suits brought under §704(a); thus, there is no burden shifting in such cases even if there is "direct evidence"). However, the "directness" of the evidence at issue, that is, how closely it was linked to the decision in question and how probative it is of discriminatory motivation, can be expected to continue to influence courts in deciding more "gestalt" questions — such as whether a reasonable jury could find discrimination on the available evidence.

4. *Causation.* Perhaps the most significant aspect of *Price Waterhouse* was the Court's conclusion that an employer could be liable even if the discriminatory intent *did not actually cause* an employment action. All that was necessary is that such intent be a motivating factor. Even Justice O'Connor would impose liability without proof of causation where discriminatory intent was a "substantial factor." But this description of causation may be somewhat deceptive — if the employer established it would have made the same decision in any event, the employer is not liable. Thus, the plaintiff need not show but-for causation to win a judgment, but plaintiff will lose if the defendant shows no such causation. In that sense, *Price Waterhouse* can still be said to be consistent with *Biggins'* requirement that discrimination be a "determinative influence." After *Price Waterhouse*, the question was not so much causation as who proves causation.

5. *No Harm, No Foul?* This requirement of causation, however, did not last long. Ironically, the one point on which all nine justices agreed in *Price Waterhouse* — that the discriminatory intent had to cause harm before Title VII liability attached — was legislatively rejected by the Civil Rights Act of 1991, which added a new §703(m), 42 U.S.C. §2000e-2(m). That section provides that "an unlawful employment practice is established when the complaining party demonstrates that race, color, religion, sex, or national origin was a motivating factor for any employment practice, even though other factors also motivated the practice." Thus, the "motivating factor" test of the *Price Waterhouse* plurality is accepted, as is the corollary of "mixed-motive" violations. Perhaps even more significant, the amendment also modifies *Price Waterhouse* by establishing that the plaintiff's proof of an illegitimate "motivating factor" does not merely shift the burden of proving no causation to the defendant, but actually establishes a violation, without regard to what the defendant can prove on rebuttal. "But-for" or "determinative factor" causation has been replaced by "motivating factor" causation. Precisely how strong a factor must be in order to count as motivating is unclear. *See* Martin J. Katz, *The Fundamental Incoherence of Title VII: Making Sense of Causation in Disparate Treatment Law*, 94 Geo. L.J. 489 (2006) (describing the concept as "minimal causation); Brian S. Clarke, *A Better Route Through the Swamp: Causal Coherence in Disparate Treatment Doctrine*, 65 Rutgers L. Rev. 723, 772-73 (2013) (arguing for application of the notion of "necessary element of a sufficient set" of factors causing a decision).

The new statute, however, offers an opportunity for defendants to limit plaintiff's remedies even if a violation has been established. A new paragraph was added to §706(g), 42 U.S.C. §2000e-5(g), which provides that, in §703(m) cases, if a respondent can "demonstrate" that it "would have taken the same action in the absence of the impermissible motivating factor," plaintiff's remedies are limited. Thus, a court

(i) may grant declaratory relief, injunctive relief (except as provided in clause (ii)), and attorney's fees and costs demonstrated to be directly attributable only to the pursuit of a claim under section 703(m); and (ii) shall not award damages or issue an order requiring any admission, reinstatement, hiring, promotion, or payment. . . .

In such a situation, then, the plaintiff is essentially limited to a declaration of defendant's liability plus attorney's fees. She is not entitled to any monetary damages. While this scheme continues to govern discrimination cases under Title VII, the Supreme Court rejected such analysis for the ADEA in *Gross v. FBL Fin. Servs.*, 557 U.S. 167 (2009), where plaintiff's burden is to prove that age was a determinative factor in all cases. Further, *University of Texas Southwestern Medical Center v. Nassar*, 133 S. Ct. 2517 (2013), held that "motivating factor" causation is not applicable to Title VII retaliation suits brought under § 704(a) since § 703(m) was limited to "status" discrimination claims under § 703; thus, there is no burden shifting even if there is "direct evidence"). These two cases suggest that but-for causation is likely to be the plaintiff's burden under statutes that do not explicitly require otherwise, such as the ADA, *e.g., Lewis v. Humboldt Acquisition Corp.*, 681 F.3d 312 (6th Cir. 2012) (ADA suit requires determinative factor proof); *Serwatka v. Rockwell Automation, Inc.*, 591 F.3d 957 (7th Cir. 2010) (same), even though some have argued that the ADA's incorporation by reference of VII procedures and remedies requires a different result under that statute. *See* Catherine T. Struve, *Shifting Burdens: Discrimination Law Through the Lens of Jury Instruction*, 51 B.C. L. Rev. 279 (2010); Melissa Hart, *Procedural Extremism: The Supreme Court's 2008-2009 Employment and Labor Cases*, 13 Emp. Rts. & Emp. Pol'y J. 253 (2010).

6. *No Blacks Need Apply.* Suppose an employer places a sign outside its personnel office, saying, "No blacks need apply." Is that a violation of § 703? Surprisingly, the plurality opinion in *Price Waterhouse* suggests that the answer is "not necessarily" because the sign might not be a causative factor in any particular decision. What is the law now that § 703(m) and (g) have been added? Wouldn't a plaintiff still need to prove that race was a motivating factor in denying her a job in order to establish a violation?

7. *Expert Testimony on Stereotyping and Cognitive Bias.* Can expert testimony be used to prove that ambiguous comments reflect bias? What were the various views in *Price Waterhouse* about Dr. Susan Fiske? In his dissent, Justice Kennedy wrote that "Fiske purported to discern stereotyping in comments that were gender neutral — e.g., 'overbearing and abrasive' — without any knowledge of the comments' basis in reality and without having met the speaker or subject." Is this criticism valid? May not certain statements be susceptible of varying meanings, with expert testimony helping the factfinder in deciding whether the statements are likely to reflect stereotyping? *See generally* Tristin K. Green, *"It's Not You, It's Me": Assessing an Emerging Relationship Between Law and Social Science*, 46 Conn. L. Rev. 287 (2013); Melissa Hart & Paul M. Secunda, *A Matter of Context: Social Framework Evidence in Employment Discrimination Class Actions*, 78 Fordham L. Rev. 37 (2009); David L. Faigman, Nilanjana Dasgupta, & Cecilia L. Ridgeway, *A Matter of Fit: The Law of Discrimination and the Science of Implicit Bias*, 59 Hastings L. J. 1389, 1426-27 (2008).

8. *Carrying the Employer's Burden of Proof.* How can an employer shoulder its burden to prove "same decision" under amended § 706(g)? The employer could try to extract from the pattern of its other decisions a kind of template of requirements for advancement. The employer might introduce expert testimony of the factors that

operated in its decision making and how they would have netted out in the plaintiff's case. Another method would be a "customs of the trade" approach, again employing expert testimony, but this time to establish how a "reasonable" employer would have evaluated the candidate. In the abstract, this evidence is less probative than proof of how the employer treated favored workers because the issue is what the defendant, not a hypothetical employer, would have done absent bias. After all, the defendant might be stricter or more liberal than others in the industry and is entitled to be so. But trade practice is nevertheless relevant because it seems appropriate to assume that a particular employer conforms to industry standards or general practice until it is shown otherwise.

* * *

The plurality in *Price Waterhouse* notes that at "some point in the proceedings . . . the District Court must decide whether a particular case involves mixed motives." At what point in the trial does this decision take place? How would you prepare jury instructions on *McDonnell Douglas/Burdine* and *Price Waterhouse*? If the instructions accurately stated the law, would jurors be likely to understand them? The next case might help.

≡≡≡ *Desert Palace, Inc. v. Costa*
≡≡≡ 539 U.S. 90 (2003)

Justice THOMAS delivered the opinion of the Court.

The question before us in this case is whether a plaintiff must present direct evidence of discrimination in order to obtain a mixed-motive instruction under Title VII of the Civil Rights Act of 1964, as amended by the Civil Rights Act of 1991. We hold that direct evidence is not required.

I

A

Since 1964, Title VII has made it an "unlawful employment practice for an employer . . . to discriminate against any individual . . . , *because of* such individual's race, color, religion, sex, or national origin." (emphasis added). In *Price Waterhouse v. Hopkins*, the Court considered whether an employment decision is made "because of" sex in a "mixed-motive" case, *i.e.*, where both legitimate and illegitimate reasons motivated the decision. The Court concluded that, under § 2000e-2(a)(1), an employer could "avoid a finding of liability . . . by proving that it would have made the same decision even if it had not allowed gender to play such a role." The Court was divided, however, over the predicate question of when the burden of proof may be shifted to an employer to prove the affirmative defense.

Justice Brennan, writing for a plurality of four Justices, would have held that "when a plaintiff . . . proves that her gender played a *motivating* part in an employment decision, the defendant may avoid a finding of liability only by proving by a preponderance of the evidence that it would have made the same decision even if it had not taken the plaintiff's gender into account." The plurality did not, however, "suggest a limitation on the possible ways of proving that [gender] stereotyping played a motivating role in an employment decision."

Justice White and Justice O'Connor both concurred in the judgment. Justice White would have held that the case was governed by *Mt. Healthy City Bd. of Ed. v. Doyle*, 429 U.S. 274 (1977), and would have shifted the burden to the employer only when a plaintiff "showed that the unlawful motive was a *substantial* factor in the adverse employment action." Justice O'Connor, like Justice White, would have required the plaintiff to show that an illegitimate consideration was a "substantial factor" in the employment decision. But, under Justice O'Connor's view, "the burden on the issue of causation" would shift to the employer only where "a disparate treatment plaintiff [could] show by *direct evidence* that an illegitimate criterion was a substantial factor in the decision."

Two years after *Price Waterhouse*, Congress passed the 1991 Act "in large part [as] a response to a series of decisions of this Court interpreting the Civil Rights Acts of 1866 and 1964." *Landgraf v. USI Film Products*, 511 U.S. 244 (1994). In particular, § 107 of the 1991 Act, which is at issue in this case, "responded" to *Price Waterhouse* by "setting forth standards applicable in 'mixed motive' cases" in two new statutory provisions.[1] The first establishes an alternative for proving that an "unlawful employment practice" has occurred:

> Except as otherwise provided in this subchapter, an unlawful employment practice is established when the complaining party demonstrates that race, color, religion, sex, or national origin was a motivating factor for any employment practice, even though other factors also motivated the practice.

42 U.S.C. § 2000e-2(m)

The second provides that, with respect to "'a claim in which an individual proves a violation under section 2000e-2(m),'" the employer has a limited affirmative defense that does not absolve it of liability, but restricts the remedies available to a plaintiff. The available remedies include only declaratory relief, certain types of injunctive relief, and attorney's fees and costs. In order to avail itself of the affirmative defense, the employer must "demonstrate that [it] would have taken the same action in the absence of the impermissible motivating factor."

Since the passage of the 1991 Act, the Courts of Appeals have divided over whether plaintiff must prove by direct evidence that an impermissible consideration was a "motivating factor" in an adverse employment action. Relying primarily on Justice O'Connor's concurrence in Price Waterhouse, a number of courts have held that direct evidence is required to establish liability under § 2000e-2(m). In the decision below, however, the Ninth Circuit concluded otherwise.

B

Petitioner Desert Palace, Inc., dba Caesar's Palace Hotel & Casino of Las Vegas, Nevada, employed respondent Catharina Costa as a warehouse worker and heavy

---

1. This case does not require us to decide when, if ever, § 107 applies outside of the mixed-motive context.

equipment operator. Respondent was the only woman in this job and in her local Teamsters bargaining unit.

Respondent experienced a number of problems with management and her co-workers that led to an escalating series of disciplinary sanctions, including informal rebukes, a denial of privileges, and suspension. Petitioner finally terminated respondent after she was involved in a physical altercation in a warehouse elevator with fellow Teamsters member Herbert Gerber. Petitioner disciplined both employees because the facts surrounding the incident were in dispute, but Gerber, who had a clean disciplinary record, received only a 5-day suspension.

. . . At trial, respondent presented evidence that (1) she was singled out for "intense 'stalking'" by one of her supervisors, (2) she received harsher discipline than men for the same conduct, (3) she was treated less favorably than men in the assignment of overtime, and (4) supervisors repeatedly "stacked" her disciplinary record and "frequently used or tolerated" sex-based slurs against her.

Based on this evidence, the District Court denied petitioner's motion for judgment as a matter of law, and submitted the case to the jury with instructions, two of which are relevant here. First, without objection from petitioner, the District Court instructed the jury that "the plaintiff has the burden of proving . . . by a preponderance of the evidence" that she "suffered adverse work conditions" and that her sex "was a motivating factor in any such work conditions imposed upon her."

Second, the District Court gave the jury the following mixed-motive instruction:

> You have heard evidence that the defendant's treatment of the plaintiff was motivated by the plaintiff's sex and also by other lawful reasons. If you find that the plaintiff's sex was a motivating factor in the defendant's treatment of the plaintiff, the plaintiff is entitled to your verdict, even if you find that the defendant's conduct was also motivated by a lawful reason.
>
> However, if you find that the defendant's treatment of the plaintiff was motivated by both gender and lawful reasons, you must decide whether the plaintiff is entitled to damages. The plaintiff is entitled to damages unless the defendant proves by a preponderance of the evidence that the defendant would have treated plaintiff similarly even if the plaintiff's gender had played no role in the employment decision.

Petitioner unsuccessfully objected to this instruction, claiming that respondent had failed to adduce "direct evidence" that sex was a motivating factor in her dismissal or in any of the other adverse employment actions taken against her. The jury rendered a verdict for respondent, awarding backpay, compensatory damages, and punitive damages. The District Court denied petitioner's renewed motion for judgment as a matter of law.

The Court of Appeals upheld the District Court's judgment after rehearing the case en banc. The en banc court saw no need to decide whether Justice O'Connor's concurrence in *Price Waterhouse* controlled because it concluded that Justice O'Connor's references to "direct evidence" had been "wholly abrogated" by the 1991 Act. And, turning "to the language" of § 2000e-2(m), the court observed that the statute "imposes no special [evidentiary] requirement and does not reference 'direct evidence.'" Accordingly, the court concluded that a "plaintiff . . . may establish a violation through a preponderance of evidence (whether direct or circumstantial) that a protected characteristic played 'a motivating factor.'" Based on that standard, the Court of Appeals held that respondent's evidence was sufficient to warrant a mixed-motive instruction and that a reasonable jury could have found that respondent's sex was a "motivating factor in her treatment."

II

This case provides us with the first opportunity to consider the effects of the 1991 Act on jury instructions in mixed-motive cases. Specifically, we must decide whether a plaintiff must present direct evidence of discrimination in order to obtain a mixed-motive instruction under 42 U.S.C. § 2000e-2(m). Petitioner's argument on this point proceeds in three steps: (1) Justice O'Connor's opinion is the holding of *Price Waterhouse*; (2) Justice O'Connor's *Price Waterhouse* opinion requires direct evidence of discrimination before a mixed-motive instruction can be given; and (3) the 1991 Act does nothing to abrogate that holding. Like the Court of Appeals, we see no need to address which of the opinions in *Price Waterhouse* is controlling: the third step of petitioner's argument is flawed, primarily because it is inconsistent with the text of § 2000e-2(m).

Our precedents make clear that the starting point for our analysis is the statutory text. And where, as here, the words of the statute are unambiguous, the "judicial inquiry is complete." Section 2000e-2(m) unambiguously states that a plaintiff need only "demonstrate" that an employer used a forbidden consideration with respect to "any employment practice." On its face, the statute does not mention, much less require, that a plaintiff make a heightened showing through direct evidence. Indeed, petitioner concedes as much.

Moreover, Congress explicitly defined the term "demonstrates" in the 1991 Act, leaving little doubt that no special evidentiary showing is required. Title VII defines the term "'demonstrates'" as to "meet the burdens of production and persuasion." § 2000e(m). If Congress intended the term "'demonstrates'" to require that the "burdens of production and persuasion" be met by direct evidence or some other heightened showing, it could have made that intent clear by including language to that effect in § 2000e(m). Its failure to do so is significant, for Congress has been unequivocal when imposing heightened proof requirements in other circumstances, including in other provisions of Title 42. . . . 42 U.S.C. § 5851(b)(3)(D) (providing that "relief may not be ordered" against an employer in retaliation cases involving whistleblowers under the Atomic Energy Act where the employer is able to "*demonstrate by clear and convincing evidence* that it would have taken the same unfavorable personnel action in the absence of such behavior") (emphasis added); cf. *Price Waterhouse* ("Only rarely have we required clear and convincing proof where the action defended against seeks only conventional relief.").

In addition, Title VII's silence with respect to the type of evidence required in mixed-motive cases also suggests that we should not depart from the "conventional rule of civil litigation [that] generally applies in Title VII cases." That rule requires a plaintiff to prove his case "by a preponderance of the evidence," using "direct or circumstantial evidence," *Postal Service Bd. of Governors v. Aikens*, 460 U.S. 711, 714, n.3 (1983). We have often acknowledged the utility of circumstantial evidence in discrimination cases. For instance, in *Reeves v. Sanderson Plumbing Products, Inc.* we recognized that evidence that a defendant's explanation for an employment practice is "unworthy of credence" is "one form of *circumstantial evidence* that is probative of intentional discrimination." (emphasis added). The reason for treating circumstantial and direct evidence alike is both clear and deep-rooted: "Circumstantial evidence is not only sufficient, but may also be more certain, satisfying and persuasive than direct evidence." *Rogers v. Missouri Pacific R. Co.*, 352 U.S. 500, 508, n.17 (1957).

The adequacy of circumstantial evidence also extends beyond civil cases; we have never questioned the sufficiency of circumstantial evidence in support of a criminal conviction, even though proof beyond a reasonable doubt is required. And juries are routinely instructed that "the law makes no distinction between the weight or value to be given to either direct or circumstantial evidence." 1A K. O'Malley, J. Grenig, & W. Lee, FEDERAL JURY PRACTICE AND INSTRUCTIONS, CRIMINAL § 12.04 (5th ed. 2000); *see also* 4 L. Sand, J. Siffert, W. Loughlin, S. Reiss, & N. Batterman, MODERN FEDERAL JURY INSTRUCTIONS P74.01 (2002) (model instruction 74-2). It is not surprising, therefore, that neither petitioner nor its *amici curiae* can point to any other circumstance in which we have restricted a litigant to the presentation of direct evidence absent some affirmative directive in a statute.

Finally, the use of the term "demonstrates" in other provisions of Title VII tends to show further that § 2000e-2(m) does not incorporate a direct evidence requirement. *See, e.g.*, 42 U.S.C. §§ 2000e-2(k)(1)(A)(i), 2000e-5(g)(2)(B). For instance, § 2000e-5(g)(2)(B) requires an employer to "demonstrate that [it] would have taken the same action in the absence of the impermissible motivating factor" in order to take advantage of the partial affirmative defense. Due to the similarity in structure between that provision and § 2000e-2(m), it would be logical to assume that the term "demonstrates" would carry the same meaning with respect to both provisions. But when pressed at oral argument about whether direct evidence is required before the partial affirmative defense can be invoked, petitioner did not "agree that . . . the defendant or the employer has any heightened standard" to satisfy.

Absent some congressional indication to the contrary, we decline to give the same term in the same Act a different meaning depending on whether the rights of the plaintiff or the defendant are at issue.

For the reasons stated above, we agree with the Court of Appeals that no heightened showing is required under § 2000e-2(m).

In order to obtain an instruction under § 2000e-2(m), a plaintiff need only present sufficient evidence for a reasonable jury to conclude, by a preponderance of the evidence, that "race, color, religion, sex, or national origin was a motivating factor for any employment practice." Because direct evidence of discrimination is not required in mixed-motive cases, the Court of Appeals correctly concluded that the District Court did not abuse its discretion in giving a mixed-motive instruction to the jury. Accordingly, the judgment of the Court of Appeals is affirmed. . . .

Justice O'CONNOR, concurring.

I join the Court's opinion. In my view, prior to the Civil Rights Act of 1991, the evidentiary rule we developed to shift the burden of persuasion in mixed-motive cases was appropriately applied only where a disparate treatment plaintiff "demonstrated by direct evidence that an illegitimate factor played a substantial role" in an adverse employment decision. *Price Waterhouse v. Hopkins* (O'Connor, J., concurring in judgment). This showing triggered "the deterrent purpose of the statute" and permitted a reasonable factfinder to conclude that "absent further explanation, the employer's discriminatory motivation 'caused' the employment decision." (O'Connor, J., concurring in judgment).

As the Court's opinion explains, in the Civil Rights Act of 1991, Congress codified a new evidentiary rule for mixed-motive cases arising under Title VII. I therefore agree with the Court that the District Court did not abuse its discretion in giving a mixed-motive instruction to the jury.

NOTES

1. *What Was the Fuss About?* If you were a newcomer to discrimination law and had not been steeped in the intricacies of *McDonnell Douglas* and *Price Waterhouse* proof structures, you might wonder what all the fuss was about in *Desert Palace* and why the Court was so focused on questions of proof more than 40 years after Title VII was enacted. After all, what is so remarkable about a case holding that "[i]n order to obtain an instruction under § 2000e-2(m), a plaintiff need only present sufficient evidence for a reasonable jury to conclude, by a preponderance of the evidence, that 'race, color, religion, sex, or national origin was a motivating factor for any employment practice.'"? This seems simple to the point of banality.

However, having struggled with the prior cases, you should understand that *Desert Palace* made a profound difference in at least one branch of the prior law. Congress had modified *Price Waterhouse* in the Civil Rights Act of 1991 by adopting Justice Brennan's "motivating factor" articulation of plaintiff's burden and, indeed, expanded on the plurality's holding by providing that plaintiff's proof of a motivating factor was sufficient for liability. While, as under *Price Waterhouse*, defendant could still carry its burden of persuasion that it would have made the same decision even absent the illegitimate consideration, that proof no longer negates liability; the 1991 amendments narrow the "same decision" defense to reducing plaintiff's remedies.

Congress, however, did not explicitly address Justice O'Connor's "direct" evidence threshold for applying this method of analysis, and we have seen that the lower courts generally continued to require some version of "direct evidence" in order to trigger *Price Waterhouse* burden-shifting. In this light, the significance of *Desert Palace* is to eliminate the direct evidence barrier to burden-shifting and avoid the complicated inquiry into whether evidence is sufficiently "direct." If a plaintiff can prove, by any kind of evidence, that a particular factor motivated the at-issue decision, the plaintiff prevails — although the defendant may limit the plaintiff's remedies if it establishes it would have made the same decision anyway.

2. *Have O'Connor's Worst Fears Been Realized?* In *Price Waterhouse*, Justice O'Connor expressed concern about not imposing liability on the employer, or even shifting a burden of persuasion, because of inconclusive indications of discrimination:

> Thus, stray remarks in the workplace . . . cannot justify requiring the employer to prove that its hiring or promotion decisions were based on legitimate criteria. Nor can statements by nondecisionmakers, or statements by decisionmakers unrelated to the decisional process itself suffice to satisfy the plaintiff's burden in this regard. In addition, in my view testimony such as Dr. Fiske's in this case, standing alone, would not justify shifting the burden of persuasion to the employer. Race and gender always "play a role" in an employment decision in the benign sense that these are human characteristics of which decisionmakers are aware and may comment on in a perfectly neutral and nondiscriminatory fashion. For example, in the context of this case, a mere reference to "a lady candidate" might show that gender "played a role" in the decision, but by no means could support a

rational factfinder's inference that the decision was made "because of" sex. What is required is what Ann Hopkins showed here: direct evidence that decisionmakers placed substantial negative reliance on an illegitimate criterion in reaching their decision.

In the wake of *Desert Palace*, can "stray remarks" be sufficient to get to the jury on a claim that sex or race was a motivating factor? *See generally* Michael J. Zimmer, *A Chain of Inferences Proving Discrimination*, 79 U. Colo. L. Rev. 4 (2008) ("Direct, direct-lite, or circumstantial evidence" (or any combination) can be used to prove individual disparate treatment discrimination; discriminatory motivation can be shown by unequal treatment, defendant's admissions that it discriminated, actions based on stereotypes, and the *McDonnell Douglas* approach); *see also* Kerri Lynn Stone, *Shortcuts in Employment Discrimination Law*, 56 St. Louis U. L.J. 111 (2011).

3. *Does* Desert Palace *Destroy* McDonnell Douglas? While there is no dispute that *Desert Palace* eliminates direct evidence as a precondition to what used to be called a *Price Waterhouse* case, is it even more radical in that it eliminates the whole *McDonnell Douglas* proof structure? *Desert Palace* can be read narrowly. For example, footnote 1 indicates that the Court was not deciding the impact of this decision "outside of the mixed-motive context." But prior to *Desert Palace*, one boundary between *Price Waterhouse* and *McDonnell Douglas* was "direct" evidence. With direct evidence gone, is there still a boundary between these two methods of proof or have the two been collapsed into one? Put another way, even though *Desert Palace* does not explicitly purport to do so, has it destroyed the *McDonnell Douglas* approach?

After *Price Waterhouse*, the distinction between the *Price Waterhouse* and *McDonnell Douglas* cases had been framed in two ways. First, *Price Waterhouse* governed "direct evidence" cases, while *McDonnell Douglas* applied to "circumstantial evidence" proof. Second, *Price Waterhouse* was viewed as involving "mixed motives," while *McDonnell Douglas* was viewed as involving a single motive. If circumstantial evidence can be used to prove liability using § 703(m)'s "motivating factor" standard of liability, *Price Waterhouse*—or, more accurately, § 703(m) cases—cannot be viewed as a "direct" evidence proof structure in contrast to *McDonnell Douglas's* "circumstantial" or "indirect" evidence structure.

The second way the two methods of proof have been distinguished is by viewing *McDonnell Douglas* as involving proof of a "single motive," while *Price Waterhouse* involves "mixed motives." Finding a "single motive" based on the process of elimination is the core of *McDonnell Douglas*—plaintiff proves that the most obvious nondiscriminatory reasons do not apply to her case, thereby establishing a prima facie case; defendant introduces evidence of a nondiscriminatory reason in rebuttal; plaintiff then introduces evidence that defendant's reason is not the true reason in order to establish that such a reason is a pretext for discrimination. This process leads to the factfinder thinking about the case as an either/or proposition: either the defendant's reason explains the decision or the plaintiff's claim of discrimination explains it. That makes the method seem to be about "single motives." However, *Price Waterhouse* also held that Congress did not establish a sole cause standard under Title VII. And, more generally, we have seen that, even under the most restrictive schemes, the plaintiff need only establish but-for or determinative factor causation, not that no other motive was involved. Thus, the plaintiff wins even if the factfinder finds that another reason is involved, as long as discrimination is the but-for reason. Is that possible in a traditional *McDonnell Douglas* case? Has the description of *McDonnell Douglas* as involving a "single motive" always been metaphorical?

St. Mary's Honor Center v. Hicks may shed some light here. As you will recall, in *Hicks*, the trial had determined that personal animosity, not discrimination, explained the adverse decision, even though the individual defendant denied such animosity. Thus, the court found a fact claimed by neither party. The narrow holding of *Hicks* is that disbelief of the supposed nondiscriminatory reason was not necessarily sufficient: The trier had to find not merely that the defendant's reason was pretextual but that it was a pretext for discrimination. But the broader holding of the case is that the trier of fact can make any determination justified by the record before it. This would seems to point toward letting the jury reach the motivating factor question even in a pure *McDonnell Douglas* setting if the factfinder so determined from the record. A jury could find that both impermissible and permissible reasons motivated a decision, even though the parties each claim only one motivation — plaintiff's claim of discrimination and defendant's claim of a nondiscriminatory reason. Thus, after *Desert Palace*, a jury could disbelieve both plaintiff's claim that discrimination entirely explained the challenged decision and defendant's claim that nondiscrimination entirely explained it.

Or does *McDonnell Douglas* survive *Desert Palace*? When faced with a motion for summary judgment, will plaintiffs still be able to rely on the process of elimination of nondiscriminatory reasons that then support the drawing of an inference that the reason for defendant's action was discrimination? If so, *McDonnell Douglas* appears to live, at least at that procedural level. Can plaintiff use this process of elimination argument before the jury?

After *Desert Palace*, the Seventh Circuit restructured its analysis in terms of the "indirect" and "direct methods of proof." The indirect method is *McDonnell Douglas*. The direct method is either "direct evidence," of discriminatory motivation, such as admissions by the employer, or a "'convincing mosaic' of circumstantial evidence" that would justify that inference without the employer's admission. *Coleman v. Donahoe*, 667 F.3d 835, 860, (7th Cir. 2012) (citations and internal quotations omitted). Does this make things any clearer?

4. *Splitting the Baby.* Is there a downside for plaintiffs if *Desert Palace* becomes the uniform method of analyzing individual disparate treatment cases? While § 703(m) provides the "motivating factor" standard for liability, it is subject to § 706(g)(2)(B)'s same decision defense. On the one hand, a jury finding that defendant discriminated may be unlikely to believe defendant's proof that it would have made the same decision even if it had not discriminated; on the other, a jury may be tempted to "split the baby," that is, accept both the plaintiff's proof that discrimination was a motivating factor *and* the defendant's proof that it would have made the same decision regardless. That would substantially limit the remedies plaintiff would get. Some have cautioned about the professional responsibility tensions this situation creates — the prospect of attorneys' fees for the plaintiff's lawyer and no recovery at all for the plaintiff. *Coe v. N. Pipe Prods., Inc.,* 589 F. Supp. 2d 1055, 1098 (N.D. Iowa 2008). Might *McDonnell Douglas* survive at least in cases where a risk-preferring plaintiff and a risk-preferring defendant both choose not to invoke *Desert Palace* by asking for the instruction approved in that case but rather place all their eggs in the *McDonnell Douglas* either/or basket? Should courts defer to parties' request of jury instructions based on *McDonnell Douglas* if they believe they mischaracterize the facts?

5. *Lower Courts and Commentators.* Will the lower courts continue to maintain the single-versus-mixed-motive distinction after *Desert Palace*? So far, they have been reluctant to inter so long standing and influential a doctrine as the *McDonnell Douglas* framework, although they have not persuasively justified its survival. One decision summarized the confusion:

> Since *Desert Palace*, the federal courts of appeals have, without much, if any, consideration of the issue, developed widely differing approaches to the question of how to analyze summary judgment challenges in Title VII mixed-motive cases. The Eighth Circuit has explicitly held that the *McDonnell Douglas/Burdine* burden-shifting framework applies to the summary judgment analysis of mixed-motive claims after *Desert Palace*. *See Griffith v. City of Des Moines*, 387 F.3d 733, 736 (8th Cir. 2004). The Eleventh Circuit seems to have joined the Eighth Circuit in this regard. *See Burstein v. Emtel, Inc.*, 137 F. App'x 205, 209 n.8 (11th Cir. 2005).
>
> The Fifth Circuit, in contrast, has adopted a "modified *McDonnell Douglas*" approach, under which a plaintiff in a mixed-motive case can rebut the defendant's legitimate non-discriminatory reason not only through evidence of pretext (the traditional *McDonnell Douglas/Burdine* burden), but also with evidence that the defendant's proffered reason is only one of the reasons for its conduct (the mixed-motive alternative). *See Machinchick v. PB Power, Inc.*, 398 F.3d 345, 352 (5th Cir. 2005).
>
> Adopting a sort of middle ground between these two positions are the Fourth and Ninth Circuits which permit a mixed-motive plaintiff to avoid a defendant's motion for summary judgment by proceeding either under the "pretext framework" of the traditional *McDonnell Douglas/Burdine* analysis or by "presenting direct or circumstantial evidence that raises a genuine issue of material fact as to whether an impermissible factor such as race motivated [, at least in part,] the adverse employment decision." *Diamond v. Colonial Life & Accident Ins. Co.*, 416 F.3d 310, 318 (4th Cir. 2005); *McGinest v. GTE Serv. Corp.*, 360 F.3d 1103, 1122 (9th Cir. 2004) The D.C. Circuit appears to have recently joined this middle ground approach. *See Fogg v. Gonzales*, 3 492 F.3d 447, 451 & n* (D.C. Cir. 2007).

White v. Baxter Healthcare Corp., 533 F.3d 381, 399-400 (6th Cir. 2008) (some citations and all parentheticals omitted). According to *Baxter*, the other circuits have either refused to decide the issue or it has not arisen. Turning to the appropriate rule, the Sixth Circuit wrote:

> [T]he *McDonnell Douglas/Burdine* burden-shifting framework does not apply to the summary judgment analysis of Title VII mixed-motive claims. We likewise hold that to survive a defendant's motion for summary judgment, a Title VII plaintiff asserting a mixed-motive claim need only produce evidence sufficient to convince a jury that: (1) the defendant took an adverse employment action against the plaintiff; and (2) "race, color, religion, sex, or national origin was a *motivating factor*" for the defendant's adverse employment action. 42 U.S.C. § 2000e-2(m) (emphasis added). This burden of producing some evidence in support of a mixed-motive claim is not onerous and should preclude sending the case to the jury only where the record is devoid of evidence that could reasonably be construed to support the plaintiff's claim. Moreover, as it is irrelevant, for purposes of a summary judgment determination, whether the plaintiff has presented direct or circumstantial evidence in support of the mixed-motive claim, *see Desert Palace*, we direct that this summary judgment analysis just described, rather than the *McDonnell Douglas/Burdine* burden-shifting framework, be applied in all Title VII mixed-motive cases regardless of the type of proof presented by the plaintiff.

Id. at 400 (citations omitted). But this apparent clarity was offset by a footnote:

> However, . . . the *McDonnell Douglas/Burdine* framework continues to guide our summary judgment analysis of single-motive discrimination claims brought pursuant only to

Title VII's general anti-discrimination provision, 42 U.S.C. §2000e-2(a)(1), and not pursuant to 42 U.S.C. §2000e-2(m). We decline to adopt the view, proposed by some courts and commentators, that the *McDonnell Douglas/Burdine* framework has ceased to exist entirely following *Desert Palace*. Indeed, post-*Desert Palace*, the Supreme Court has continued to apply the *McDonnell Douglas/Burdine* analysis to summary judgment challenges in single-motive Title VII cases. *See Raytheon Co. v. Hernandez*, 540 U.S. 44, 53-54, (2003).

Id. The court, however, did not notice that *Raytheon* was brought under the ADA, which does not have, explicitly at least, a parallel to 703(m). As suggested by the footnote, the commentators have generally read *Desert Palace* as destroying *McDonnell Douglas*, in effect if not in theory. *E.g.*, Michael J. Zimmer, *The New Discrimination Law:* Price Waterhouse *Is Dead, Whither* McDonnell Douglas?, 53 Emory L. J. 1887 (2004); Kenneth R. Davis, Price-*Fixing: Refining the* Price Waterhouse *Standard and Individual Disparate Treatment Law*, 31 Fla. St. U. L. Rev. 859, 861 (2004); William R. Corbett, McDonnell Douglas, *1973-2003: May You Rest in Peace?*, 6 U. Pa. J. Lab. & Emp. L. 199, 212-13 (2003); Henry L. Chambers, Jr., *The Effect of Eliminating Distinctions Among Title VII Disparate Treatment Cases*, 57 SMU L. Rev. 83, 102-3 (2004).

Even if the commentators are correct and *McDonnell Douglas* is doctrinally no longer required, the case law applying it will continue to have utility. Even if a court *need* no longer pursue the three-step ritual of that line of cases, it will still have to decide whether evidence of a motivating discriminatory reason is sufficient for a jury to find for plaintiff. This includes assessing whatever evidence the plaintiff adduces to exclude the nondiscriminatory reasons — whether those would have been the "most common" legitimate reasons that in the past were negated as part of plaintiff's prima facie case or the more specific reason articulated in defendant's case. While plaintiff will not need to exclude all potential nondiscriminatory reasons, she may have to cast sufficient doubt on innocent reasons to allow the jury to find in her favor by a preponderance of the evidence that an impermissible reason was a motivating factor. Some would say that this is *McDonnell Douglas* in substance if not form.

In practice, then, we might expect to see courts continue to use the *McDonnell Douglas/Reeves* structure as a way of implementing the more gestalt "sufficient evidence" approach of *Desert Palace*. But a court that wished to save itself time in granting summary judgment to defendant might summarize the evidence and conclude that it was not sufficient for a reasonable jury to find intent to discriminate motivating the challenged decision. Nevertheless, such a court would be well advised to find "sufficient evidence" in a case such as *Reeves*, where the Supreme Court has held that proof of a prima facie case plus proof of pretext will generally be sufficient at least to allow the trier of fact to decide that discrimination occurred.

6. *Multiple Decision Makers.* While disparate treatment is often discussed in terms of the intent of the "employer," employers typically are corporations or other business organizations. Where entities are concerned, the intent that matters is presumably that of the actual decision maker. But many decisions involve not a single decision maker, but multiple deciders, in a collegial or hierarchical structure, or some combination of the two. Multiple decision makers will be found where the decision is made collegially (as by a board or a committee) and where it is made by a hierarchical process (A recommends to B, who recommends to C, who "decides").

If the factfinder decides that one person in the process acted with intent to discriminate, does that establish that discrimination was a "motivating factor" under § 703(m), or must more be shown to establish liability?

≡ ### *Staub v. Proctor Hospital*
≡ 131 S. Ct. 1186 (2011)

Justice SCALIA delivered the opinion of the Court.

I

Petitioner Vincent Staub worked as an angiography technician for respondent Proctor Hospital until 2004, when he was fired. Staub and Proctor hotly dispute the facts surrounding the firing, but because a jury found for Staub in his claim of employment discrimination against Proctor, we describe the facts viewed in the light most favorable to him.

While employed by Proctor, Staub was a member of the United States Army Reserve, which required him to attend drill one weekend per month and to train full time for two to three weeks a year. Both Janice Mulally, Staub's immediate supervisor, and Michael Korenchuk, Mulally's supervisor, were hostile to Staub's military obligations. Mulally scheduled Staub for additional shifts without notice so that he would "pa[y] back the department for everyone else having to bend over backwards to cover [his] schedule for the Reserves." She also informed Staub's co-worker, Leslie Sweborg, that Staub's "military duty had been a strain on th[e] department," and asked Sweborg to help her "get rid of him." Korenchuk referred to Staub's military obligations as "a b[u]nch of smoking and joking and [a] waste of taxpayers['] money." He was also aware that Mulally was "out to get" Staub.

In January 2004, Mulally issued Staub a "Corrective Action" disciplinary warning for purportedly violating a company rule requiring him to stay in his work area whenever he was not working with a patient. The Corrective Action included a directive requiring Staub to report to Mulally or Korenchuk "when [he] ha[d] no patients and [the angio] cases [we]re complete[d]." According to Staub, Mulally's justification for the Corrective Action was false for two reasons: First, the company rule invoked by Mulally did not exist; and second, even if it did, Staub did not violate it.

On April 2, 2004, Angie Day, Staub's co-worker, complained to Linda Buck, Proctor's vice president of human resources, and Garrett McGowan, Proctor's chief operating officer, about Staub's frequent unavailability and abruptness. McGowan directed Korenchuk and Buck to create a plan that would solve Staub's "'availability' problems." But three weeks later, before they had time to do so, Korenchuk informed Buck that Staub had left his desk without informing a supervisor, in violation of the January Corrective Action. Staub now contends this accusation was false: he had left Korenchuk a voice-mail notification that he was leaving his desk. Buck relied on Korenchuk's accusation, however, and after reviewing Staub's personnel file, she decided to fire him. The termination notice stated that Staub had ignored the directive issued in the January 2004 Corrective Action.

Staub challenged his firing through Proctor's grievance process, claiming that Mulally had fabricated the allegation underlying the Corrective Action out of hostility toward his military obligations. Buck did not follow up with Mulally about this claim. After discussing the matter with another personnel officer, Buck adhered to her decision.

Staub sued Proctor under the Uniformed Services Employment and Reemployment Rights Act of 1994, 38 U.S.C. §4301 et seq., claiming that his discharge was motivated by hostility to his obligations as a military reservist. His contention was not that Buck had any such hostility but that Mulally and Korenchuk did, and that their actions influenced Buck's ultimate employment decision. A jury found that Staub's "military status was a motivating factor in [Proctor's] decision to discharge him" and awarded $ 57,640 in damages.

The Seventh Circuit reversed, holding that Proctor was entitled to judgment as a matter of law. The court observed that Staub had brought a "'cat's paw' case," meaning that he sought to hold his employer liable for the animus of a supervisor who was not charged with making the ultimate employment decision.[1] It explained that under Seventh Circuit precedent, a "cat's paw" case could not succeed unless the nondecisionmaker exercised such "singular influence" over the decisionmaker that the decision to terminate was the product of "blind reliance." [Buck looked beyond Mulally and Korenchuk's statements; although his investigation could have been more robust," they were not a "singular influence."].

II

[USERRA bars discrimination in employment on the basis of membership or an obligation to perform service in a uniformed service. §4311(a). It has a structure similar to Title VII's 703(m) in that an employer is considered to have violated the statute when uniformed service membership is "a motivating factor in the employer's action, unless the employer can prove that the action would have been taken in the absence of such membership." §4311(c).]

The central difficulty in this case is construing the phrase "motivating factor in the employer's action." When the company official who makes the decision to take an adverse employment action is personally acting out of hostility to the employee's membership in or obligation to a uniformed service, a motivating factor obviously exists. The problem we confront arises when that official has no discriminatory animus but is influenced by previous company action that is the product of a like animus in someone else.

In approaching this question, we start from the premise that when Congress creates a federal tort it adopts the background of general tort law. *See Burlington Industries, Inc. v. Ellerth* [reproduced at p. 720]. Intentional torts such as this, "as distinguished from negligent or reckless torts, . . . generally require that the actor intend 'the *consequences*' of an act, not simply 'the act itself.'" *Kawaauhau v. Geiger*, 523 U.S. 57 (1998).

---

1. The term "cat's paw" derives from a fable conceived by Aesop, put into verse by La Fontaine in 1679, and injected into United States employment discrimination law by Posner in 1990. *See Shager* v. *Upjohn Co.*, 913 F.2d 398, 405 (CA7). In the fable, a monkey induces a cat by flattery to extract roasting chestnuts from the fire. After the cat has done so, burning its paws in the process, the monkey makes off with the chestnuts and leaves the cat with nothing. A coda to the fable (relevant only marginally, if at all, to employment law) observes that the cat is similar to princes who, flattered by the king, perform services on the king's behalf and receive no reward.

Staub contends that the fact that an unfavorable entry on the plaintiff's personnel record was caused to be put there, with discriminatory animus, by Mulally and Korenchuk, suffices to establish the tort, even if Mulally and Korenchuk did not intend to cause his dismissal. But discrimination was no part of Buck's reason for the dismissal; and while Korenchuk and Mulally acted with discriminatory animus, the act they committed — the mere making of the reports — was not a denial of "initial employment, reemployment, retention in employment, promotion, or any benefit of employment," as liability under USERRA requires. If dismissal was not the object of Mulally's and Korenchuk's reports, it may have been their result, or even their foreseeable consequence, but that is not enough to render Mulally or Korenchuk responsible.

Here, however, Staub is seeking to hold liable not Mulally and Korenchuk, but their employer. Perhaps, therefore, the discriminatory motive of one of the employer's agents (Mulally or Korenchuk) can be aggregated with the act of another agent (Buck) to impose liability on Proctor. Again we consult general principles of law, agency law, which form the background against which federal tort laws are enacted. *See Burlington.* Here, however, the answer is not so clear. The RESTATEMENT OF AGENCY suggests that the malicious mental state of one agent cannot generally be combined with the harmful action of another agent to hold the principal liable for a tort that requires both. *See* RESTATEMENT (SECOND) AGENCY § 275, Illustration 4 (1958). Some of the cases involving federal torts apply that rule. But another case involving a federal tort, and one involving a federal crime, hold to the contrary. Ultimately, we think it unnecessary in this case to decide what the background rule of agency law may be, since the former line of authority is suggested by the governing text, which requires that discrimination be "a motivating factor" *in the adverse action.* When a decision to fire is made with no unlawful animus on the part of the firing agent, but partly on the basis of a report prompted (unbeknownst to that agent) by discrimination, discrimination might perhaps be called a "factor" or a "causal factor" in the decision; but it seems to us a considerable stretch to call it "a motivating factor."

Proctor, on the other hand, contends that the employer is not liable unless the *de facto* decisionmaker (the technical decisionmaker or the agent for whom he is the "cat's paw") is motivated by discriminatory animus. This avoids the aggregation of animus and adverse action, but it seems to us not the only application of general tort law that can do so. Animus and responsibility for the adverse action can both be attributed to the earlier agent (here, Staub's supervisors) if the adverse action is the intended consequence of that agent's discriminatory conduct. So long as the agent intends, for discriminatory reasons, that the adverse action occur, he has the scienter required to be liable under USERRA. And it is axiomatic under tort law that the exercise of judgment by the decisionmaker does not prevent the earlier agent's action (and hence the earlier agent's discriminatory animus) from being the proximate cause of the harm. Proximate cause requires only "some direct relation between the injury asserted and the injurious conduct alleged," and excludes only those "link[s] that are too remote, purely contingent, or indirect." *Hemi Group, LLC v. City of New York,* 559 U.S. 1 (2010) (internal quotation marks omitted).[2] We do not think that the

---

2. Under the traditional doctrine of proximate cause, a tortfeasor is sometimes, but not always, liable when he intends to cause an adverse action and a different adverse action results. *See* RESTATEMENT (SECOND) TORTS §§ 435, 435B and Comment *a* (1963 and 1964). That issue is not presented in this case since the record contains no evidence that Mulally or Korenchuk intended any particular adverse action other than Staub's termination.

ultimate decisionmaker's exercise of judgment automatically renders the link to the supervisor's bias "remote" or "purely contingent." The decisionmaker's exercise of judgment is also a proximate cause of the employment decision, but it is common for injuries to have multiple proximate causes. *See Sosa v. Alvarez-Machain*, 542 U.S. 692, 704 (2004). Nor can the ultimate decisionmaker's judgment be deemed a superseding cause of the harm. A cause can be thought "superseding" only if it is a "cause of independent origin that was not foreseeable." *Exxon Co., U.S.A. v. Sofec, Inc.*, 517 U.S. 830, 837 (1996) (internal quotation marks omitted).

Moreover, the approach urged upon us by Proctor gives an unlikely meaning to a provision designed to prevent employer discrimination. An employer's authority to reward, punish, or dismiss is often allocated among multiple agents. The one who makes the ultimate decision does so on the basis of performance assessments by other supervisors. Proctor's view would have the improbable consequence that if an employer isolates a personnel official from an employee's supervisors, vests the decision to take adverse employment actions in that official, and asks that official to review the employee's personnel file before taking the adverse action, then the employer will be effectively shielded from discriminatory acts and recommendations of supervisors that were *designed and intended* to produce the adverse action. That seems to us an implausible meaning of the text, and one that is not compelled by its words.

Proctor suggests that even if the decisionmaker's mere exercise of independent judgment does not suffice to negate the effect of the prior discrimination, at least the decisionmaker's independent investigation (and rejection) of the employee's allegations of discriminatory animus ought to do so. We decline to adopt such a hard-and-fast rule. As we have already acknowledged, the requirement that the biased supervisor's action be a causal factor of the ultimate employment action incorporates the traditional tort-law concept of proximate cause. *See, e.g., Anza v. Ideal Steel Supply Corp.*, 547 U.S. 451, 457-458, 126 (2006); *Sosa*. Thus, if the employer's investigation results in an adverse action for reasons unrelated to the supervisor's original biased action (by the terms of USERRA it is the employer's burden to establish that), then the employer will not be liable. But the supervisor's biased report may remain a causal factor if the independent investigation takes it into account without determining that the adverse action was, apart from the supervisor's recommendation, entirely justified. We are aware of no principle in tort or agency law under which an employer's mere conduct of an independent investigation has a claim-preclusive effect. Nor do we think the independent investigation somehow relieves the employer of "fault." The employer is at fault because one of its agents committed an action based on discriminatory animus that was intended to cause, and did in fact cause, an adverse employment decision.

Justice Alito claims that our failure to adopt a rule immunizing an employer who performs an independent investigation reflects a "stray[ing] from the statutory text." We do not understand this accusation. Since a supervisor is an agent of the employer, when he causes an adverse employment action the employer causes it; and when discrimination is a motivating factor in his doing so, it is a "motivating factor in the employer's action," precisely as the text requires. Justice Alito suggests that the employer should be held liable only when it "should be regarded as having delegated part of the decisionmaking power" to the biased supervisor. But if the independent investigation relies on facts provided by the biased supervisor — as is necessary in any case of cat's-paw liability — then the employer (either directly or through the ultimate decisionmaker) will have effectively delegated the factfinding portion of the investigation to the biased supervisor. Contrary to Justice Alito's suggestion, the biased supervisor is not analogous to a witness at a bench trial. The mere witness is not an actor in the events that are the subject of the trial. The biased supervisor and the ultimate decisionmaker, however, acted as agents of the entity that the plaintiff seeks to hold liable; each of them possessed supervisory authority delegated by their employer and exercised it in the interest of their employer. In sum, we do not see how "fidelity to the statutory text," requires the adoption of an independent-investigation defense that appears nowhere in the text. And we find both speculative and implausible Justice Alito's prediction that our Nation's employers will systematically disfavor members of the armed services in their hiring decisions to avoid the possibility of cat's-paw liability, a policy that would violate USERRA in any event.

We therefore hold that if a supervisor performs an act motivated by antimilitary animus that is *intended* by the supervisor to cause an adverse employment action,[3] and if that act is a proximate cause of the ultimate employment action, then the employer is liable under USERRA.[4]

III

[Applying the analysis to the present case, the Seventh Circuit's judgment must be reversed. Although there was evidence that (1) Mulally and Korenchuk were acting within the scope of their employment; (2) their actions "were motivated by hostility toward Staub's military obligations"; (3) they had the "specific intent to cause Staub to be terminated"; and (4) their actions "were causal factors underlying Buck's decision to fire Staub," the jury instructions "did not hew precisely to the rule we adopt today."]

Justice KAGAN took no part in the consideration or decision of this case.

Justice ALITO, with whom Justice THOMAS joins, concurring in the judgment.

I agree with the Court that the decision of the Court of Appeals must be reversed, but I would do so based on the statutory text, rather than principles of agency and tort law that do not speak directly to the question presented here.

. . . For present purposes, the key phrase [in the governing statute] is "a motivating factor in the employer's action." A "motivating factor" is a factor that "provide[s] . . . a motive." *See* Webster's Third New International Dictionary 1475 (1971) (defining "motivate"). A "motive," in turn, is "something within a person . . . that incites him to action." *Ibid.* Thus, in order for discrimination to be "a

---

3. Under traditional tort law, "'intent' . . . denote[s] that the actor desires to cause consequences of his act, or that he believes that the consequences are substantially certain to result from it." *Id.*, § 8A.

4. Needless to say, the employer would be liable only when the supervisor acts within the scope of his employment, or when the supervisor acts outside the scope of his employment and liability would be imputed to the employer under traditional agency principles. *See Burlington Industries, Inc. v. Ellerth,* 524 U.S. 742 (1998). We express no view as to whether the employer would be liable if a co-worker, rather than a supervisor, committed a discriminatory act that influenced the ultimate employment decision. We also observe that Staub took advantage of Proctor's grievance process, and we express no view as to whether Proctor would have an affirmative defense if he did not. *Cf. Pennsylvania State Police v. Suders,* 542 U.S. 129, 148-49 (2004).

motivating factor in [an] employer's action," discrimination must be present "within," *i.e.*, in the mind of, the person who makes the decision to take that action. And "the employer's action" here is the decision to fire petitioner. Thus, petitioner, in order to recover, was required to show that discrimination motivated that action.

The Court, however, strays from the statutory text by holding that it is enough for an employee to show that discrimination motivated *some other action* and that this latter action, in turn, caused the termination decision. That is simply not what the statute says.

The Court fears this interpretation of the statute would allow an employer to escape liability by assigning formal decisionmaking authority to an officer who may merely rubberstamp the recommendation of others who are motivated by antimilitary animus. But fidelity to the statutory text does not lead to this result. Where the officer with formal decisionmaking authority merely rubberstamps the recommendation of others, the employer, I would hold, has actually delegated the decisionmaking responsibility to those whose recommendation is rubberstamped. I would reach a similar conclusion where the officer with the formal decisionmaking authority is put on notice that adverse information about an employee may be based on antimilitary animus but does not undertake an independent investigation of the matter. In that situation, too, the employer should be regarded as having delegated part of the decisionmaking power to those who are responsible for memorializing and transmitting the adverse information that is accepted without examination. The same cannot be said, however, where the officer with formal decisionmaking responsibility, having been alerted to the possibility that adverse information may be tainted, undertakes a reasonable investigation and finds insufficient evidence to dispute the accuracy of that information.

Nor can the employer be said to have "effectively delegated" decisionmaking authority any time a decisionmaker "relies on facts provided by [a] biased supervisor." A decisionmaker who credits information provided by another person—for example, a judge who credits the testimony of a witness in a bench trial—does not thereby delegate a portion of the decisionmaking authority to the person who provides the information.

This interpretation of §4311(c)(1) heeds the statutory text and would provide fair treatment for both employers and employees who are members of the uniformed services. . . .

For these reasons, I cannot accept the Court's interpretation of §4311(c)(1), but I nevertheless agree that the decision below must be reversed. There was sufficient evidence to support a finding that at least Korenchuk was actually delegated part of the decisionmaking authority in this case. Korenchuk was the head of the unit in which Staub worked and it was Korenchuk who told Buck that Staub left his work area without informing his supervisors. There was evidence that Korenchuk's accusation formed the basis of Buck's decision to fire Staub, and that Buck simply accepted the accusation at face value. According to one version of events, Buck fired Staub immediately after Korenchuk informed her of Staub's alleged misconduct, and she cited only that misconduct in the termination notice provided to Staub. All of this is enough to show that Korenchuk was in effect delegated some of Buck's termination authority. There was also evidence from which it may be inferred that displeasure with Staub's Reserve responsibilities was a motivating factor in Korenchuk's actions.

NOTES

1. *Intent & Motive.* Prior to *Staub*, the Court used "intent" and "motive" interchangeably. *Staub* clearly changes that, requiring a plaintiff to prove both intent and motive.

As for "intent," Justice Scalia writes in footnote 3 that, under traditional tort law, "'intent' . . . denote[s] that the actor desires to cause consequences of his act, or that he believes that the consequences are substantially certain to result from it." For the Court a violation seems to require a supervisor, acting within the scope of his or her employment, having the intent, in this sense, to cause an adverse employment action. In other words, Mulally and Korenchuk must have either wanted Buck to fire Staub (what the Court calls "specific intent") or at least believe that such a result was "substantially certain" to follow from their actions. Note, however, that what they intended must amount to an adverse employment action. If, for example, they had merely intended him to be reprimanded (not an adverse action), no liability would attach from Buck's subsequent discharge.

As for "motive," this is where "hostility toward Staub's military obligations" enters the picture. As Justice Alito defines it, motive "is 'something within a person . . . that incites him to action.'" In the Title VII context, it is race or sex bias, although we have seen that such motives can be pretty complicated. Notice, however, that the Alito definition of motive doesn't distinguish between conscious actions and unconscious ones. A person may be incited to act by impulses of which he is not aware. This, of course, takes us back to the cognitive bias question we explored earlier.

2. *Proximate Cause.* After breaking out intent and motive into two separate concepts, *Staub* needed to link them together, and, for the first time in the discrimination context, imported the concept of proximate cause from its usual home in negligence law to create the necessary linkage. Why it chose proximate cause rather than but-for causation is a mystery. The way the Court defined intent and motive surely meant that any time the adverse employment action met both requirements the resultant causation was "proximate."

However, the only purpose of proximate cause anywhere in the law is to limit liability short of the full reach of but-for causation, which might suggest future deployment of the concept outside the cat's paw context. In other areas of federal statutory law, the Court has not only applied proximate cause to *intentional conduct* as in did in *Staub* (a notion largely foreign to tort law from which the Court is theoretically borrowing) but has also adopted a more rigorous view of what proximate cause requires. Rather than looking only to the foreseeability of the plaintiff or the harm, which is the majority approach in the negligence arena, the Court has articulated a policy-driven perspective that allows it to restrict liability in the name of applying traditional tort doctrine. *See generally* Charles A. Sullivan, *Tortifying Employment*, 92 B.U. L. REV. 1431 (2012); Sandra F. Sperino, *Discrimination Statutes, the Common Law, and Proximate Cause*, 2013 U. ILL. L. REV. 1 (2013); Sandra F. Sperino, *Statutory Proximate Cause*, 88 NOTRE DAME L. REV. 1199 (2013).

In any event, it is clear the Court has created a much more complicated liability structure for individual disparate treatment cases than existed before, although how much practical effect this will have on how most such cases are litigated remains to be seen. A number of subsequent cases have found *Staub* to support liability. *E.g.,* *EEOC v. DynMcdermott Petroleum Operations Co.*, 537 F. App'x 437 (5th Cir. 2013) (fact that one manager was the cat's paw of another could be inferred from the former's influence or leverage over the latter given his power over discipline and compensation); *Sharp v. Aker Plant Servs. Grp., Inc.*, 726 F.3d 789, 797 (6th Cir. 2013) (although a manager was not the ultimate decision maker, those who were relied solely on his forced rankings and recommendation of who could be fired without disrupting current projects; "[w]ithout considering information from an independent source, [the employer's] review could not have scrubbed [the manager's] alleged age bias from the forced rankings and recommendation"); *Haire v. Bd. of Sup'rs of Louisiana State Univ. Agric. & Mech. Coll.*, 719 F.3d 356, 366-67 (5th Cir. 2013) (University chancellor could be found to be cat's paw for biased campus police officer when the chancellor was new to the university and unfamiliar with its security policy and attributed plaintiff's supposed violation of those policies to misinformation provided him by the biased individual). *But see Lobato v. New Mexico Env't Dep't*, 733 F.3d 1283, 1294-95 (10th Cir. 2013) (a cat's paw case can be made out only if the decisionmaker relies on facts provided by a biased supervisor; "an employer is not liable under a subordinate bias theory if the employer did not rely on any facts from the biased subordinate in ultimately deciding to take an adverse employment action — even if the biased subordinate first alerted the employer to the plaintiff's misconduct.").

3. *Whose Intent/Motive?* The Court's holding is apparently straightforward: "We therefore hold that if a supervisor performs an act motivated by antimilitary animus that is *intended* by the supervisor to cause an adverse employment action, and if that act is a proximate cause of the ultimate employment action, then the employer is liable. . . ." (emphasis in original). The Court cautioned that not only must the act be performed by a "supervisor" but it must also be within the scope of the supervisor's employment. In footnote 4, the Court explicitly refused to decide whether liability could ever follow from the acts of a co-worker (and, presumably, those of a supervisor acting outside the scope of his employment.)

So who's a supervisor? In the harassment context, that was a live issue when *Staub* was decided, with two competing views in the circuits. In 2013, however, the Supreme Court decided *Vance v. Ball State University*, 133 S. Ct. 2434, 2439 (2013), holding that "an employee is a 'supervisor' for purposes of vicarious liability under Title VII if he or she is empowered by the employer to take tangible employment actions against the victim. . . ." The Court rejected the lower court cases taking "the more open-ended approach advocated by the EEOC's Enforcement Guidance, which ties supervisor status to the ability to exercise significant direction over another's daily work." *Id.* at 2443.

If the *Vance* approach applies to the *Staub* scenario, the *Staub* holding will shrink in significance. To appreciate this, consider that it is not so clear that Mulally and Korenchuk, the "supervisors" whose intent and motive were proximate causes of Staub's discharge by Buck, would qualify as supervisors under *Vance*. They certainly did not have the power to discharge Staub, which is why Buck was involved in the first place, although it's possible that they had power to take other "tangible employment actions" against him. By the way, if you're wondering what the difference is between an "adverse employment action" necessary for Title VII liability generally and a "tangible employment action" that is relevant to liability in the sexual harassment content, we'll explore this question at page 686.

Perhaps "supervisor" means two different things in the two contexts. Or maybe the Court will resolve the question it explicitly avoided and decide that "subordinate bias liability" can follow from the actions of "co-workers." Or maybe the "delegation" concept will turn nonsupervisors (in a formal sense) into supervisors (in a practical sense). Look at the Alito concurrence for this possibility. The lower courts have noted, but not grappled with, these questions. *E.g., Shazor v. Prof'l Transit Mgmt.*, 744 F.3d 948 (6th Cir. 2014).

* * *

Note on Age Discrimination Variations on the Individual Disparate Treatment Theme

To some extent, the law developed under Title VII, §1981, and the ADEA is similar. For example, in describing the core violation, *Hazen Paper Co v. Biggins*, 507 U.S. 604 (1993), drew heavily on Title VII precedents establishing the disparate treatment theory. After quoting from the *Teamsters v. United States*, 431 U.S. 324, 335 n.15 (1977), description of disparate treatment, the Court went on to state that "[t]he disparate treatment theory is of course available under the ADEA, as the language of that statute makes clear." *Id.* at 609. Implementing this perception, the Supreme Court has assumed the *McDonnell Douglas* framework applies to age discrimination claims, although it has inexplicably refused to so hold. *Reeves v. Sanderson Plumbing Prods., Inc.*, 530 U.S. 133, 142 (2000) ("This Court has not squarely addressed whether the *McDonnell Douglas* framework . . . also applies to ADEA actions. Because the parties do not dispute the issue, we shall assume, arguendo, that the *McDonnell Douglas* framework is fully applicable here.").

Although the Court has not explicitly revisited the *McDonnell Douglas* framework's applicability to cases under the ADEA, it has driven a wedge between the analysis of Title VII claims and ADEA claims in terms of causation. In *Gross v. FBL Fin. Serv.*, 557 U.S. 167 (2009), the Supreme Court not only rejected the application of Title VII's motivating factor analysis under §703(m) to cases under the ADEA, but also refused to apply *Price Waterhouse* analysis to ADEA cases, reaffirming that a plaintiff claiming age discrimination must prove that discrimination was a determinative factor in a challenged decision.

The majority adopted a three-step rationale. First, it held that the amendment of Title VII in the 1991 to add the "motivating factor" standard of liability in §703(m) did not apply to the ADEA. Thus, *Desert Palace* is limited to Title VII cases. Given *Smith v. City of Jackson*, 544 U.S. 228 (2005), which focused on differences between the ADEA's language and Title VII's as a result of the 1991 amendment to Title VII, this step was not surprising. The second step, however, was startling, which was to also hold that the burden-shifting approach established by the Court for Title VII in *Price Waterhouse* did not apply. Given the Court's stress on statutory language in *City of Jackson*, and the fact that *Price Waterhouse* interpreted identical language in the pre-1991 version of Title VII and the ADEA, the Court's analysis is inexplicable. The third step in rejecting applying *Price Waterhouse* to the ADEA was even more bizarre: *Gross* appeared to overrule *Price Waterhouse* even though it had just found it inapplicable to the ADEA, and, as to Title VII, it had already been superseded by the 1991 amendments to Title VII. If there is a point to this, it might be to foreclose the application of *Price Waterhouse* to other statutes, such as §1981. Indeed, the court recently applied but-for causation to Title VII retaliation cases, reasoning that §703(m)'s motivating factor analysis did not explicitly reach those claims, which are governed by a different statutory provision, §704(a). *University of Texas Sw. Med. Ctr. v. Nassar*, 133 S. Ct. 2517 (2013). *See generally* Catherine T. Struve, *Shifting Burdens: Discrimination Law Through the Lens of Jury Instruction*, 51 B.C. L. Rev. 279 (2010) (critiquing *Gross* for its unpersuasive effort to reject burden shifting under the ADEA in part because the majority failed to support its claim that jury confusion would result); Martin J. Katz, Gross *Disunity*, 114 Penn St. L. Rev. 857 (2010); Michael C. Harper, *The Causation Standard in Federal Employment Law: Gross v. FBL Financial Services, Inc., and the Unfulfilled Promise of the Civil Rights Act of 1991*, 58 Buffalo L. Rev. 69 (2010). The lower courts have generally applied *Gross* broadly to reach all statutes that lack language like §703(m). *E.g., Lewis v. Humboldt Acquisition Corp.*, 681 F.3d 312 (6th Cir. 2012) (ADA suit requires determinative factor proof); *Serwatka v. Rockwell Automation, Inc.*, 591 F.3d 957 (7th Cir. 2010) (same); *Palmquist v. Shinseki*, 689 F.3d 66, 73-74 (1st Cir. 2012) (same for Rehabilitation Act), and the *Nassar* opinion is likely to reinforce that trend.

However, the circuit courts have so far read *Gross* not to affect the application of *McDonnell Douglas* analysis in ADEA cases. *E.g., Sims v. MVM, Inc.*, 704 F.3d 1327, 1333 (11th Cir. 2013) ("Our continued application of the *McDonnell Douglas* framework in ADEA cases is also consistent with all of our sister circuits that have addressed the issue."). They have also continued to look to something like "direct evidence" — not as a burden-shifting device but rather as a reason to find that age was a determinative factor. *Mora v. Jackson Mem'l Found., Inc.*, 597 F.3d 1201 (11th Cir. 2010); *Baker v. Silver Oak Senior Living Mgmt. Co.*, 581 F.3d 684 (8th Cir. 2009).

While *Gross* creates a formal split between the analyses of cases under both statutes, the ADEA also differs in other respects from Title VII. For example, *Biggins* itself noted that "age discrimination rarely was based on the sort of animus motivating some other forms of discrimination," although the Court recognized that "it was based in large part on stereotypes unsupported by objective fact." *Id.* at 610-11 (quoting *EEOC v. Wyoming*, 460 U.S. 226, 231 (1983)). Some commentators have agreed that age discrimination is different but warn that it may actually be worse because of "opportunistic" conduct by employers. In Governing the Workplace: The Future of Labor and Employment Law 64–65 (1988), Professor Paul Weiler argued that workers tend to be paid less than they are worth when first hired and more than they are worth in the later stages of their careers. Compensation tends to be linked to seniority in the firm, and workers with greater seniority receive more than their increased productivity would justify. This structure tends to keep employees loyal to the firm throughout their working lives but also creates a potential for "opportunistic" employer behavior, that is, taking advantage of the situation by replacing senior employees with younger, lower-paid workers. Older discharged workers rarely will be able to command the same compensation from another employer because their skills tend to be firm-specific. By narrowly defining what it means to discriminate on account of age, *Biggins* freed employers to make productivity-based judgments and perhaps resurrected the problem of opportunistic behavior. When you study disparate impact discrimination, *see* page 654, consider whether the ADEA version of that theory offers a better way to challenge this phenomenon than disparate treatment.

Another dramatic difference between Title VII and the ADEA flows from the fact that, given the limitation of the ADEA to those 40 and older, age discrimination against individuals below the cutoff is legal. *Cf. Bergen Commer. Bank v. Sisler*, 723

A.2d 944 (N.J. 1999) (state antidiscrimination law protects young workers from discrimination on account of their youth). Further, the Supreme Court has held that, even within the protected class of those over 40, it is permissible to discriminate against younger workers in favor of older workers (although not vice versa). *General Dynamics Land Systems, Inc. v. Cline*, 540 U.S. 581, 586 (2004) (while the ADEA's language could be read as flatly barring all "age" discrimination, "Congress's interpretive clues speak almost unanimously to an understanding of discrimination as directed against workers who are older than the ones getting treated better.").

Still another difference between the ADEA and Title VII arises because, unlike race and sex, which tend to be viewed as discrete points, age is a continuum. Inferring age discrimination from differences in treatment, therefore, is more or less plausible depending on the size of the age disparity at issue. In *O'Connor v. Consolidated Coin Caterers Corp.*, 517 U.S. 308, 311-12 (1996), the lower court had found that a 56-year-old plaintiff had not made out a prima facie case of age discrimination under *McDonnell Douglas/Burdine* because he was replaced by a worker over age 40 and thus in the same protected group as plaintiff. The Supreme Court rejected this approach. The bar on discrimination "because of age," means that it is irrelevant "that one person in the protected class has lost out to another person in the protected class . . . so long as he has lost out because of his age. Or to put the point more concretely, there can be no greater inference of age discrimination (as opposed to '40 or over' discrimination) when a 40-year-old is replaced by a 39-year-old than when a 56-year-old is replaced by a 40-year-old." *Id.* *O'Connor* held that an inference of age discrimination "cannot be drawn from the replacement of one worker with another worker insignificantly younger. Because the ADEA prohibits discrimination on the basis of age and not class membership, the fact that a replacement is substantially younger than the plaintiff is a far more reliable indicator of age discrimination than is the fact that the plaintiff was replaced by someone outside the protected class." 517 U.S. at 313. How large an age discrepancy is necessary to infer age discrimination from a comparison? *See Emmett v. Kwik Lok Corp.*, 528 F. App'x 257, 260 n.2 (3d Cir. 2013) ("five-year difference between Emmett and the average age of the three individuals who took over his job duties — is very thin"); *Ramlet v. E.F. Johnson Co.*, 507 F.3d 1149 (8th Cir. 2007) (one year's and five years' age difference between plaintiff and comparators insufficient to establish a prima facie case). Obviously, this is highly contextual, depending on what other evidence is available.

Note on Pleading

In 2002, the Supreme Court reversed a Second Circuit decision that had required plaintiff to plead at least a *McDonnell Douglas* claim in order to survive a Rule 12(b)(6) motion to dismiss for failure to state a claim. *Swierkiewicz v. Sorema, N.A.*, 534 U.S. 506 (2002). The plaintiff had alleged that he had been first demoted and ultimately fired by his employer because of his national origin and age in violation of Title VII of the Civil Rights Act of 1964 and the ADEA. He did plead his age (49) and national origin (Hungarian) and the younger age (32) and different national origin (French) of the favored co-worker. He also alleged that he had 25 years' more experience than the co-worker. For the Second Circuit that was not enough — he had to at least plead a prima facie case under the *McDonnell Douglas* proof structure.

In a unanimous opinion written by Justice Thomas, the Supreme Court reversed, reaffirming the traditional view of notice pleading under the Federal Rules of Civil Procedure. Put simply, the plaintiff's complaint gave the defendant employer adequate notice of both the act being challenged — plaintiff's discharge — and of the legal bases upon which he was suing — national origin discrimination in violation of Title VII and age discrimination in violation of the ADEA. Since the employer knew what adverse actions were being charged, who the supposed favored employee was, and what statutory requirements were allegedly violated, it had all the information that notice pleading requires. As for the failure to plead a prima facie case under *McDonnell Douglas*, the Court noted that *McDonnell Douglas* provides "an evidentiary standard, not a pleading requirement"; therefore, "under a notice pleading system, it is not appropriate to require a plaintiff to plead facts establishing a prima facie case." 534 U.S. at 511. Whatever hurdles employment discrimination plaintiffs had to face in their quest for vindication, pleading problems appeared to be a thing of the past. For example, in *Bennett v. Schmidt*, 153 F.3d 516, 518 (7th Cir. 1998), the Seventh Circuit wrote "[b]ecause racial discrimination in employment is 'a claim upon which relief can be granted,' this complaint could not be dismissed under Rule 12(b)(6). 'I was turned down for a job because of my race' is all a complaint has to say."

In the past few years, however, this certainty has been severely shaken. In two remarkable cases, *Bell Atlantic Corp. v. Twombly*, 550 U.S. 544 (2007), and *Ashcroft v. Iqbal*, 556 U.S 662 (2009), the Court adopted a "plausible pleading" standard for Rule 12(b)(6) motions, a standard whose operational meaning remains unclear but that many believe has radically changed pleading requirements under the Federal Rules.

The *Iqbal* opinion essentially sets out an analytic structure that suggest that a court analyze a complaint under "[t]wo working principles." 556 U.S at 678. Drawing on *Twombly, Iqbal* requires a court deciding a Rule 12(b)(6) motion to identify the "factual" allegations as distinct from legal conclusions in a complaint. "Facts" plead must be taken as true, but allegations that do not state "facts" need not be credited: "[T]he tenet that a court must accept as true all of the allegations contained in a complaint is inapplicable to legal conclusions. Threadbare recitals of the elements of a cause of action, supported by mere conclusory statements, do not suffice." *Id*. Obviously, what counts as a "fact" as opposed to a legal conclusion is key to understanding this first prong of *Iqbal*. For purposes of this course, one critical question is whether a complaint alleging "discrimination" pleads a fact or a conclusion.

Once the facts alleged are identified, the second *Iqbal* step is to determine whether, accepting such allegations as true, the "complaint that states a plausible claim for relief." Quoting heavily from *Twombly*, the Court explained:

> To survive a motion to dismiss, a complaint must contain sufficient factual matter, accepted as true, to "state a claim to relief that is plausible on its face." A claim has facial plausibility when the plaintiff pleads factual content that allows the court to draw the reasonable inference that the defendant is liable for the misconduct alleged. The plausibility standard is not akin to a "probability requirement," but it asks for more than a sheer possibility that a defendant has acted unlawfully. Where a complaint pleads facts that are "merely consistent with" a defendant's liability, it "stops short of the line between possibility and plausibility of 'entitlement to relief.'"

Id. This is "a context-specific task that requires the reviewing court to draw on its judicial experience and common sense." *Id.* at 679. If a plaintiff's allegations of "discrimination" are only conclusions, the court must look to the rest of the complaint for "facts" that show that the claim of discrimination is plausible." *Iqbal* itself was a discrimination claim, albeit one arising under the Constitution, not Title VII, and the Court found implausible the plaintiff's claim that he was subjected to especially harsh conditions of incarceration because of his nationality and religion. While it might have been plausible that lower-level officials acted from such motives, it was not plausible that Attorney General Ashcroft and Federal Bureau of Investigation Director Mueller did so when other motives — such as a desire to protect national security by keeping "suspected terrorists in the most secure conditions available until the suspects could be cleared of terrorist activity" — were more apparent. *Id.* at 683.

The $64 question is whether *Swierkiewicz* survives the new regime. *Twombly* cited it with apparent approval, but *Iqbal* did not cite it at all. Some commentators argue that *Swierkiewicz* remains good law, and therefore that plausible pleading, properly understood, will have relatively little effect on employment discrimination claims. *E.g.*, Joseph A. Seiner, *After* Iqbal, 45 WAKE FOREST L. REV. 179, 194 (2010); Joseph A. Seiner, *Pleading Disability*, 51 B.C. L. REV. 95 (2010); Joseph A. Seiner, *The Trouble with* Twombly: *A Proposed Pleading Standard for Employment Discrimination Cases*, 2009 U. ILL. L. REV. 1011. This view is supported by numerous cases that continue to apply *Swierkiewicz*. Others are more skeptical. *E.g.*, Suzette M. Malveaux, *Front Loading and Heavy Lifting: How Pre-Dismissal Discovery Can Address the Detrimental Effect of* Iqbal *on Civil Rights Cases*, 14 LEWIS & CLARK L. REV. 65, 82 (2010); Suja A. Thomas, *The New Summary Judgment Motion: The Motion to Dismiss Under* Iqbal *and* Twombly, 14 LEWIS & CLARK L. REV. 15 (2010). This view is supported by the lower court authority viewing *Swierkiewicz* as overruled at least in part. *E.g.*, *Fowler v. UPMC Shadyside*, 578 F.3d 203, 211 (3d Cir. 2009) ("We have to conclude, therefore, that because *Conley* has been specifically repudiated by both *Twombly* and *Iqbal*, so too has *Swierkiewicz*, at least insofar as it concerns pleading requirements and relies on *Conley*."). And one commentator, looking at the worst-case scenario, offers suggestions for effectively pleading claims under the new pleading standard. Charles A. Sullivan, *Plausibly Pleading Employment Discrimination*, 52 WM. & MARY L. REV. 1613, 1622 (2011); *see also* Michael J. Zimmer, *Title VII's Last Hurrah: Can Discrimination Be Plausibly Pled?*, http://papers.ssrn.com/sol3/papers.cfm?abstract_id=2369479.

PROBLEM

9-1. In response to a help-wanted ad, Jane Armstrong, a 38-year-old woman, applies for a job as a cab driver at the Hacker Cab Company. She has a valid driver's license and has driven extensively, but not for pay, for 20 years. She is a vegetarian and a Capricorn. After a brief interview, at which all these facts emerge, she is rejected by "Tip" O'Neill, Hacker's president. Armstrong comes to you for legal counsel. You do some investigation. The first call you make is to O'Neill, who admits that the job is still open, but explains that he rejected Armstrong because "Capricorns make lousy drivers; besides she's too old to adjust to the rigors of cab driving, especially since she doesn't eat meat." When asked whether Armstrong's gender played a part in the decision,

O'Neill replied, "Hell no. Some of my best friends are women. I don't care if my brother marries one. Har, har." A "windshield survey" of the Hacker Cab Company at shift-changing times reveals an almost total absence of women drivers. It is common knowledge that there is a heavy turnover in the cab-driving business.

How would you analyze this case based on *Price Waterhouse, McDonnell Douglas*, and *Desert Palace*?

C. SYSTEMIC DISCRIMINATION

We have seen that individual challenges to adverse employment decisions require the courts to focus on how a particular plaintiff has been treated by a defendant. But employment policies that sweep more broadly can also be challenged — for example, an employer's policy to hire only men, to fire older workers, or to separate employees by race, gender, or age. Challenges might also be mounted against employer practices that are not consciously designed to exclude, but that have the effect of disproportionately disadvantaging employees with protected characteristics. Such policies and practices raise systemic issues that may be addressed through one of the two concepts of systemic discrimination presently governing Title VII actions: systemic disparate treatment and disparate impact.

1. Systemic Disparate Treatment

Systemic disparate treatment can be proven in two ways. First, the plaintiff may simply demonstrate that the employer has an announced, formal policy of discrimination. Second, the plaintiff who fails to prove a formal policy may nevertheless establish that the defendant's employment decisions reveal a "pattern or practice" of disparate treatment. In both cases, motive is critical, but it is obvious from the facial discrimination in a formal policy and inferable from the impact of the practices.

a. Formal Policies of Discrimination

Historically, formal systems excluding women and minority group members or segregating them into inferior jobs were common. While there were rarely "white only" signs outside workplaces in the same way such signs were posted near public restrooms and drinking fountains in the South, many employers, particularly in the South, formally segregated jobs by race, with blacks typically consigned to lower-paying, less-attractive jobs. For example, Duke Power in North Carolina limited African Americans to the "Labor Department," the lowest-level jobs in the company. *See Griggs v. Duke Power Co.*, 401 U.S. 424 (1971). Most employers also segregated many jobs by gender, again with lower-level jobs assigned to female workers. Before the 1964 Civil Rights Act, it was standard practice for newspaper classified employment advertisements to be separately listed under "help wanted male" and "help wanted female."

With the passage of Title VII in 1964, most formal discriminatory policies of race or sex discrimination ended. Similarly, prior to the passage of the ADEA, employers typically imposed mandatory retirement at age 65. Since the ADEA now generally bars age discrimination for those over 40, most such formal discriminatory policies have disappeared.

Nevertheless, not all formal policies were rescinded without court intervention. An example is *Trans World Airlines, Inc. v. Thurston*, 469 U.S. 111 (1985), in which the defendant airline permitted pilots disqualified from serving in that capacity for reasons other than age to transfer automatically to the position of flight engineer but barred those who were required by a federal regulation to stop flying as pilots at age 60 from doing so. The Court had no trouble finding the policy facially discriminatory. "Since [the policy] allows captains who become disqualified for any reason other than age to 'bump' less senior flight engineers, Trans World Airline's ("TWA") transfer policy is discriminatory on its face." *Id.* at 121. Because the policy drew an age line, it necessarily reflected an intent to discriminate on that basis. *But see Ky. Ret. Sys. v. EEOC*, 554 U.S. 125 (2008) (permitting a retirement plain to explicitly take age into account when there was no reason to believe it systematically disadvantaged older workers).

Today, most employers understand the requirements of the antidiscrimination laws and would not normally adopt a facially discriminatory plan unless the employer believed that the plan did not violate the statute, either because it was not technically discrimination or because it believed the policy to be permissible under a statutory exception. The first possibility is not as far-fetched as one might think. Sex distinctions in employer dress and grooming codes generally have been held not to constitute illegal sex discrimination under Title VII when they treat male and female employees separately but equally. *See* page 708. We will also encounter racial and gender preferences that are sometimes permissible under Title VII as part of valid affirmative action plans. *See* page 649. As for exceptions to the statute, police and fire departments continue to have age restrictions because of an exception written into the ADEA. And with respect to gender, age, and national origin, the bona fide occupational qualification ("BFOQ") defense permits classification on these bases in limited circumstances where the protected characteristic is strongly enough related to success on the job. In *Thurston*, the court rejected the airline's attempt to use this defense because many pilots over age 60 continued to work as flight engineers for TWA, thus undercutting the claim that being younger than 60 was a BFOQ.

b. Systemic Practices

Trans World Airlines v. Thurston involved a formal policy that facially treated older workers differently. There was no need, therefore, to search further for intent to discriminate. But the systemic disparate treatment theory goes beyond formal policies to reach pervasive practices rooted in intentional discrimination. Thus, the second type of systemic disparate treatment arises where no formal, announced policy of using race or gender can be established, but the plaintiff nevertheless shows a pattern of decisions explainable by the operation of bias in employment decisions.

In short, the plaintiff can establish a prima facie case of such treatment by showing that the employer's personnel practices reveal discrimination by decisionmakers. Whether described as a covert "policy" or simply the cumulative result of biased decision making, the result is the same. Such a showing is usually by statistical evidence of a gross and long-lasting disparity between, say, the racial or gender composition of the employer's workforce and the composition that would be expected, given the labor market from which the defendant picks its workers. The statistical evidence can be buttressed by anecdotal evidence supporting the inference that the employer had a policy of discriminating. For example, in *Teamsters v. United States*, 431 U.S. 324 (1977), the plaintiff showed that almost no black or Hispanic workers had been assigned to the "line driver" job despite their availability in the lower-status "city driver" jobs and in the general population from which the employer selected its employees. Buttressing this "inexorable zero" in minority representation in the line driver jobs was testimony by workers that supervisors had told them that the company was not ready for black and Hispanic line drivers. The Court undertook a similar analysis in *Hazelwood School District v. United States*, 433 U.S. 299 (1977), although there the question was whether a school district could be shown to have discriminated in hiring when the representation of minority teachers was compared to the racial composition of the relevant labor market for teachers.

Where plaintiff's case is based primarily on statistical evidence, as in *Teamsters*, determining whether there is disparate treatment often leads to a battle between the parties' statistical experts. The defendant may challenge the plaintiff's prima facie case by introducing evidence showing that plaintiff's statistical data or techniques are flawed. For instance, a common tactic is to challenge the labor pool on which the expectancy for female or minority work force representation was based.

Alternatively, the employer may admit the disparity but offer an explanation for the statistics that negates its intent to discriminate. Perhaps the most famous example of this defense is *EEOC v. Sears, Roebuck & Co.*, 839 F.2d 302 (7th Cir. 1988). Women constituted some 60 percent of the applicants for full-time sales jobs at Sears (both commissioned and noncommissioned) but only 27 percent of the newly hired commissioned salespeople. Median hourly wages were about twice as high for commissioned as for noncommissioned salespeople. The EEOC argued that, given the desirability of the commissioned jobs, this disparity could be explained only by an inference of intentional discrimination by Sears and that, even though the Commission had the burden of proving such intent, the statistics were a sufficient basis to carry that burden.

The employer, however, successfully blunted the EEOC's statistical showing by convincing the trial court that the large disparity between men and women in commission sales jobs was explained by women generally lacking interest in those jobs, in part because of the competitive nature of the work. To be more precise, the district court found that the EEOC had not sustained its burden because, in light of the lack of interest argument, it had not established that the disparity resulted from Sears' discrimination. Ironically, Sears based its defense on a school of feminist thinking that stresses the differences between men and women, reasoning that the divergent life experiences of men and women lead them to develop different perspectives and attitudes. Thus, Sears argued it was the women's lack of interest in commission sales jobs, not the employer's discrimination, that resulted in underrepresentation of women in those jobs. While *Sears* illustrates the upsides and downsides of even apparently strong statistical showings, it may be equally indicative of a major failure of trial strategy by the EEOC, which produced not a single female employee or applicant to testify as to having been denied a commissioned position. *See also EEOC v. Consolidated Service Systems*, 989 F.2d 233 (7th Cir. 1993) (while finding a statistically significant overrepresentation of Koreans at the employer, the court found that this resulted from the employer's reliance on word-of-mouth recruiting, not intent to prefer Koreans).

Sears was a major setback for the systemic disparate treatment, but perhaps a worse setback for the theory was *Dukes v. Wal-Mart Stores, Inc.*, 131 S. Ct. 2541 (2011), where the Supreme Court reversed the Ninth Circuit certification of a class action on behalf of a class of over a million current and former employees. Although that opinion focused on whether the "commonality" requirement for a class action was met (an inquiry that is not necessary when the EEOC sues, as in *Sears*), the opinion did not bode well for the robustness of systemic disparate treatment as a theory of liability. The plaintiffs relied largely on expert evidence, which included statistical evidence of the lower relative success of female workers as compared with men within Wal-Mart (as in *Sears*) as well as statistical evidence showing that female success at Wal-Mart was lower than at other big box retailers. Finally, the plaintiffs introduced "social framework" expert testimony that sought to link the statistics to company policies permitting the operation of bias in promotion and compensation decisions by delegating largely standardless and unreviewed decisions to lower-level managers.

The majority opinion, written by Justice Scalia, recognized that if the plaintiffs could establish that Wal-Mart operated under a *general policy* of discrimination that manifested itself in the pay and promotion practices of the company, then certification of the class would be justified. However, the Court found such proof lacking. Wal-Mart had no formal policy of discrimination; indeed, the majority emphasized that its policies emphasized equal opportunity. To avoid this problem, the plaintiffs relied heavily on "social framework" testimony from a Dr. Bielby that Wal-Mart's "strong corporate culture" makes it "vulnerable" to "gender bias." Even accepting this testimony, however, the expert could not go on to "determine with any specificity how regularly stereotypes play a meaningful role in employment decisions at Wal-Mart," which for the majority did "nothing to advance respondents' case. '[W]hether 0.5 percent or 95 percent of the employment decisions at Wal-Mart might be determined by stereotyped thinking' is the essential question on which respondents' theory of commonality depends. If Bielby admittedly has no answer to that question, we can safely disregard what he has to say. It is worlds away from 'significant proof' that Wal-Mart 'operated under a general policy of discrimination.'" *Id.* at 2552-54.

In fact, Wal-Mart's according discretion to local managers seemed, to the majority, to be the diametric opposite of a uniform employment discrimination practice: In a company the size of Wal-Mart, it is "quite unbelievable" that all managers would exercise their discretion in a common, much less commonly discriminatory way without a common direction. 131 S. Ct. at 2555. Even if the plaintiffs had established a pattern of gender-linked pay and promotion discrepancies in all of Wal-Mart's 3,400 stores, the Court continued, commonality would still not exist because there could be different explanations for the discrepancies in different stores and regions. Finally, although (unlike the EEOC in *Sears*), the plaintiffs had also submitted 120 declarations of female workers regarding discrimination they suffered, the Court deemed this anecdotal evidence too weak to raise an inference that all the stores' personnel decisions were discriminatory given the small number of declarations compared to the large size of the class.

Since the *Wal-Mart* decision was formally about commonality for class action purposes, it does not necessarily suggests a dilution of the systemic disparate treatment theory, which can be asserted either in a government enforcement action (as in *Teamsters* or *Hazelwood*) or in a private class action. While *Wal-Mart* makes it much harder to have a class action certified, it does not necessarily affect EEOC "pattern or practice" suits, such as *Sears*. Nevertheless, the opinion may portend greater problems for that theory in the future. *See* Noah D. Zatz, Tristin K. Green, Melissa Hart, Richard Ford, *Working Group on the Future of Systemic Disparate Treatment Law*, 32 BERKELEY J. EMP. & LAB. L. 387 *et seq.* (2011).

To the extent the theory remains robust, the establishment of a prima facie of systemic disparate treatment has been held to result in a *Price Waterhouse* — like shifting of the burden of persuasion. That is, when systemic disparate treatment toward the class is proven, and an individual plaintiff is shown to be a member of that class, discrimination as to the individual is established — subject to the defendant carrying a burden of proof that the individual was not harmed by the pattern of discrimination. *See Teamsters; Franks v. Bowman Transp. Co.*, 424 U.S. 747, 772 (U.S. 1976) ("petitioners here have carried their burden of demonstrating the existence of a discriminatory hiring pattern and practice by the respondents and, therefore, the burden will be upon respondents to prove that individuals who reapply were not in fact victims of previous hiring discrimination."). However, it seems clear that this burden shifting is available only in an EEOC suit or class action, not to an individual plaintiff. *E.g., Daniels v. UPS*, 701 F.3d 620 (10th Cir. 2012) (individual plaintiffs cannot bring pattern-or-practice claims — only the federal government or a certified class can do so); *Chin v. Port Auth. of N.Y. & N.J.*, 685 F.3d 135, 147 (2d Cir. 2012) (rejecting the pattern-or-practice method of proof in private suits outside the class action context).

c. Bona Fide Occupational Qualifications

Section 703(e) of Title VII provides:

> Notwithstanding any other provision of this title . . . it shall not be an unlawful employment practice for an employer to hire and employ employees . . . on the basis of religion, sex, or national origin in those certain instances where religion, sex, or national origin is a bona fide occupational qualification reasonably necessary to the normal operation of that particular business or enterprise.

The ADEA also provides a BFOQ defense that uses language identical to Title VII. This defense, while a potentially large loophole in the antidiscrimination statutes' prohibitions, has been read very narrowly as to sex, age, and national origin. The Title VII provision does not by its terms allow race discrimination to be a BFOQ. *See Chaney v. Plainfield Healthcare Ctr.*, 612 F.3d 908 (7th Cir. 2010) (holding that honoring a patient's request for white caregivers was not a justification for discrimination in job assignments, even if the employer had a good faith belief that it was required by state law to honor such requests). *See also Ferrill v. The Parker Group, Inc.*, 168 F.3d 468 (11th Cir. 1999) (rejecting, in a §1981 case, a BFOQ for racially segregating telemarketers aimed at getting out the vote for an election, with blacks calling blacks and whites calling whites).

The Supreme Court's first meaningful treatment of the BFOQ defense was in *Dothard v. Rawlinson*, 433 U.S. 321 (1977), in which the Court upheld a rule requiring prison guards in "contact" positions to be the same gender as the inmates they guarded. The majority stressed that Alabama's penitentiaries had been held unconstitutional because of their dangerous and inhumane conditions. Since inmates were not segregated according to dangerousness, the 20 percent of male prisoners who were sex offenders were scattered throughout the dormitories. While characterizing the BFOQ defense as "an extremely narrow exception to the general prohibition of discrimination on the basis of sex," the Court recognized that in an "environment of violence and disorganization, it would be an over-simplification to characterize [the rule against women] as an exercise in 'romantic paternalism.'" *Id.* at 334-35. Title VII normally allows individual women to decide whether jobs are too dangerous for them, but the Alabama prisons conditions made it likely that women could not perform the essence of the correctional counselor's job — to maintain security:

> A woman's relative ability to maintain order in a male, maximum-security, unclassified penitentiary of the type Alabama now runs could be directly reduced by her womanhood. There is a basis in fact for expecting that sex offenders who have criminally assaulted women in the past would be moved to do so again if access to women were established within the prison. There would also be a real risk that other inmates, deprived of a normal heterosexual environment, would assault women guards because they were women.

Id. at 336. Thus, an employee's "very womanhood" could undermine her ability to do the job. The dissent by Justice Marshall protested this analysis as justifying discrimination by the barbaric state of the prisons. Those conditions violate the Constitution and, therefore, cannot constitute "the normal operation of that particular business or enterprise" required by the BFOQ defense. Further, the notion that the employee's "very womanhood" makes assaults more likely

> regrettably perpetuates one of the most insidious of the old myths about women — that women, wittingly or not, are seductive sexual objects. The effect of the decision, made I am sure with the best of intentions, is to punish women because their very presence might provoke sexual assaults. It is women who are made to pay the price in lost job opportunities for the threat of depraved conduct by prison inmates. Once again, "[t]he pedestal upon which women have been placed has . . . , upon closer inspection, been revealed as a cage." It is particularly ironic that the cage is erected here in response to feared misbehavior by imprisoned criminals.

Id. at 345 (Marshall, J., dissenting).

The Supreme Court's next encounter with the BFOQ defense was in a suit under the ADEA. *Western Air Lines v. Criswell*, 472 U.S. 400 (1985), involved whether an airline could limit flight engineer positions to pilots no older than 60 under the BFOQ exception to the ADEA. Flight engineers monitored side-facing instrument panels in commercial aircraft of that era such as the Boeing 727. A Federal Aviation Administration ("FAA") regulation barred those over age 60 from the other two pilot jobs — captain and first officer — but did not set any standard for flight engineers.

Defendant's evidence focused on the possibility that flight engineers would suffer a heart attack, the risks of which generally increase with age. Plaintiff's evidence established that physiological deterioration was individualized and could be ascertained through physical examinations that the FAA required for all flight engineers. Further, other airlines allowed flight engineers over age 60 to continue to fly without any apparent safety problems.

The Court upheld a jury instruction that included a "two-part inquiry [, which] properly identifies the relevant considerations for resolving a BFOQ defense to an age-based qualification purportedly justified by considerations of safety." *Id.* at 416. That test was whether it was (1) highly impractical to make individualized determinations as to ability to perform the job safely; and (2) some persons over the defined age possess "traits of a physiological, psychological or other nature which preclude safe and efficient job performance that cannot be ascertained by means other than knowing their age." *Id.*

The Court later elaborated on this test and applied it in the sex discrimination context in *International Union, UAW v. Johnson Controls, Inc.*, 499 U.S. 187 (1991), which involved a "fetal protection policy" that broadly excluded women from jobs that exposed them to lead. Lower courts had reached conflicting results in deciding whether such policies even distinguished workers on the basis of sex, as opposed to a neutral characteristic, such as fetal safety. However, the Supreme Court had no difficulty with that question: "The bias in Johnson Controls' policy is obvious. Fertile men, but not fertile women, are given a choice as to whether they wish to risk their reproductive health for a particular job." *Id.* at 197. Further, "the absence of a malevolent motive does not convert a facially discriminatory policy into a neutral policy with a discriminatory effect." *Id.* at 199. While a discriminatory policy can nevertheless be justified as a bona fide occupational qualification, Johnson Controls' policy did not meet the strict requirements of this exception:

> The wording of the BFOQ defense contains several terms of restriction that indicate that the exception reaches only special situations. The statute thus limits the situations in which discrimination is permissible to "certain instances" where sex discrimination is "reasonably necessary" to the "normal operation" of the "particular" business. Each one of these terms — certain, normal, particular — prevents the use of general subjective standards and favors an objective, verifiable requirement. But the most telling term is "occupational"; this indicates that these objective, verifiable requirements must concern job-related skills and aptitudes.

Id. at 201. The majority rejected the argument that "occupational" merely meant "related to a job," holding, rather, that the term related to "qualifications that affect an employee's ability to do the job." *Id.* Since susceptibility of a fetus to lead poisoning was entirely unconnected to whether its mother could make batteries, this approach effectively foreclosed the BFOQ defense.

The Court recognized that the safety of third parties had been important in cases such as *Criswell* but drew a distinction, observing that in those cases

> safety concerns were not independent of the individual's ability to perform the assigned tasks, but rather involved the possibility that, because of age-connected debility, a flight engineer might not properly assist the pilot, and might thereby cause a safety emergency. Furthermore, although we considered the safety of third parties in *Dothard* and *Criswell*, those third parties were indispensable to the particular business at issue. In *Dothard*, the third parties were the inmates; in *Criswell*, the third parties were the passengers on the plane. We stressed that in order to qualify as a BFOQ, a job qualification must relate to the "essence," or to the "central mission of the employer's business."

Id. at 202-3. While the health of future children was a deep social concern, the BFOQ did not render it essential to battery making.

The *Johnson Controls* reasoning was reinforced by the Pregnancy Discrimination Act, which had amended Title VII in 1978 to declare that pregnancy discrimination was sex discrimination. The Court described the PDA as "contain[ing] a BFOQ standard of its own: Unless pregnant employees differ from others 'in their ability or inability to work,' they must be 'treated the same' as other employees 'for all employment-related purposes.'" *Id.* at 204. This meant that "women as capable of doing their jobs as their male counterparts may not be forced to choose between having a child and having a job." *Id.*

While the Court was not persuaded that tort liability to fetuses was a real danger, it did note that "[w]e, of course, are not presented with, nor do we decide, a case in which costs would be so prohibitive as to threaten the survival of the employer's business. We merely reiterate our prior holdings that the incremental cost of hiring women cannot justify discriminating against them." Finally, the majority specifically noted that its decision did not suggest that sex could not constitute a BFOQ when privacy interests are implicated.

In the wake of *Johnson Controls*, most BFOQ claims have arisen in the institutional context, most often prisons, as in the next principal case, but also in hospitals, *Slivka v. Camden-Clark Mem'l Hosp.*, 594 S.E.2d 616 (W. Va. 2004), and psychiatric facilities, *Healey v. Southwood Psychiatric Hospital*, 78 F.3d 128 (3d Cir. 1996). Can you guess why?

Breiner v. Nevada Department of Corrections
610 F.3d 1202 (9th Cir. 2010)

BERZON, Circuit Judge:

The Nevada Department of Corrections (NDOC) hires only female correctional lieutenants at a women's prison. The district court granted summary judgment upholding NDOC's discriminatory employment policy, concluding that the policy imposed only a "de minimis" restriction on male prison employees' promotional opportunities and, alternatively, that the policy falls within Title VII's exception permitting sex discrimination in jobs for which sex is a bona fide occupational qualification, 42 U.S.C. § 2000e-2(e)(1). We reverse as to both holdings.

Factual & Procedural Background

[While being operated by a private company, Corrections Corporation of America (CCA), problems at the Southern Nevada Women's Correctional Facility (SNWCF) prompted an investigation by the NDOC's inspector general. The inspector general concluded] that SNWCF had become "an uninhibited sexual environment." He noted "frequent instances of inappropriate staff/inmate interaction," "flirtatious activities between staff and inmates," and "widespread knowledge" of "long-term inmate/inmate sexual relationships." In exchange for sex, prison staff "routinely introduce[d] . . . contraband into the institution, including alcohol, narcotics, cosmetics, [and] jewelry." The inmates' sexual behavior—which they freely admitted was designed to "compromise staff and enhance inmate privileges" — was, in the Inspector General's view, "predictable." The Inspector General attributed the guards' misconduct to "a lack of effective supervisory management oversight and control. . . . There is no evidence that supervisors or managers recognize this risky behavior or do anything to stop it." To address this "leadership void," the Inspector General recommended that "line supervisors undergo leadership training" and that "subordinate staff undergo re-training with emphasis on inmate con games and ethical behavior."

In the wake of the Inspector General's report, which ignited "very high profile" media coverage, CCA announced that it was terminating its contract to operate SNWCF. NDOC resumed control of the facility and, according to Crawford, faced intense political pressure to "mitigate the number of newspaper articles" and to "assure the State of Nevada that we would not be embarrassed like this again." To achieve this goal, Crawford decided to restaff the facility so that seventy percent of the front line staff at SNWCF would be women.

Crawford also decided to hire only women in SNWCF's three correctional Lieutenant positions. The correctional lieutenants are shift supervisors and are the senior employees on duty seventy-five percent of the time. Correctional lieutenants report to wardens or deputy wardens and are responsible for supervising the prison's day-to-day operations, including directing the work of subordinate staff, inspecting the facility and reporting infractions, and monitoring inmates' activities and movement through the facility. There is one correctional lieutenant assigned to SWNCF per shift. Although the correctional lieutenant posting specified that "only female applicants will be accepted for these positions," several males applied for the positions, which were eventually filled by three women.

[Three male Nevada correctional officers brought suit although they had not applied for the lieutenant positions. They challenged only the gender limitation with respect to that position; the "seventy-percent-female restriction on front line guards" was, therefore, not at issue in this litigation. The district court granted NDOC's motion for summary judgment, holding, first, that the gender restriction "had a 'de minimis' impact on the plaintiffs' overall promotional opportunities," and, second, it in any event fell within Title VII's BFOQ exception. The Ninth Circuit first found that, despite not having applied for the positions at issue, at least one plaintiff had standing to bring suit because he was discouraged from applying by the employer's conduct and was otherwise qualified. It then reversed the district court on both grounds.]

A. The "De Minimis" Theory

NDOC asserts that the three SNWCF positions were the only correctional lieutenant promotions in the NDOC system as a whole restricted to women applicants and that twenty-nine out of thirty-seven correctional lieutenant positions filled over a four year period went to men. Relying on these statistics, NDOC maintains that the concededly discriminatory policy of excluding men from the SNWCF correctional lieutenant positions had only a "de minimis" impact on the plaintiffs and so did not violate Title VII with regard to them. This conclusion reflects a fundamental misunderstanding of the basic precepts of Title VII and is not supported by our case law.

[The court stressed the desirability of the positions at issue, and noted "[t]hat another opportunity may later arise for which the applicant is eligible does not negate the injury of being denied an earlier position on the basis of one's sex, with the resulting loss of pay for a period and delayed eligibility for another promotion." Further, positions are not fungible, and some may be more desirable for individuals than others, for example, because of location. Cases like *Robino v. Iranon*, 145 F.3d 1109 (9th Cir. 1998), were inapposite. That decision approved assigning only female guards to certain posts to protect female inmate privacy, but involved only assignments within the prison, not positions.] *Robino*'s premise, then, was necessarily that a minor impact on job assignments was too minimal to be actionable. This very limited concept has no application to NDOC's policy. An employer's "fail[ure] or refus[al] to hire" on the basis of sex is, without limitation, actionable under Title VII. 42 U.S.C. § 2000e-2(a)(1). NDOC's refusal to hire men in the correctional lieutenant positions therefore violates Title VII unless NDOC can demonstrate that gender is a BFOQ for the positions. NDOC cannot meet that burden, as we now explain.

B.   Gender as a Bona Fide Occupational Qualification . . .

NDOC has not explicitly articulated the "job qualification" for correctional lieutenants for which it claims sex is a legitimate proxy. We are left to try to adduce what that "qualification" might be from the declarations by NDOC officials on which the defendants rely in their briefs as justification for the facially discriminatory policy. . . .

From this panoply of explanations, it appears that NDOC administrators sought to "reduce the number of male correctional employees being compromised by female inmates," and that they believed the gender restriction on shift supervisors would accomplish this because (1) male correctional lieutenants are likely to condone sexual abuse by their male subordinates; (2) male correctional lieutenants are themselves likely to sexually abuse female inmates; and (3) female correctional lieutenants possess an "instinct" that renders them less susceptible to manipulation by inmates and therefore better equipped to fill the correctional lieutenant role.[5]

The first theory fails because NDOC has not shown that "all or nearly all" men would tolerate sexual abuse by male guards, or that it is "impossible or highly impractical" to assess applicants individually for this qualification. As to the second theory, there is no "basis in fact," *Dothard*, for believing that individuals in the correctional lieutenant role are particularly likely to sexually abuse inmates. The third theory — and, to a significant degree, the first two — relies on the kind of unproven and invidious stereotype that Congress sought to eliminate from employment decisions when it enacted Title VII.

---

5. NDOC also suggests that privacy and rehabilitation were among the "factors . . . considered important" in implementing the gender restriction. Neither in its briefs nor at oral argument, however, was NDOC able to direct the court to any evidence that Crawford or other administrators actually considered privacy or rehabilitation in developing the policy. This void is not surprising, as it is the guards who have direct daily contact with the inmates, not the correctional lieutenants. As noted, NDOC, in a separate policy not here challenged, restricts the number of front line guards in female prisons. As there is no evidence in this record to indicate that concern about privacy or rehabilitation was a basis for the decision to preclude men from serving in the supervisory positions, we do not consider those rationales in our BFOQ analysis.

[The court reviewed *Dothard*, concluding that its finding of a BFOQ] was premised on a level of violence among inmates atypical even among maximum security facilities. *See Gunther v. Iowa State Men's Reformatory*, 612 F.2d 1079, 1085 (8th Cir. 1980).

Appellate courts, including this court, have followed *Dothard* in requiring prison administrators to identify a concrete, logical basis for concluding that gender restrictions are "reasonably necessary." In *Everson v. Michigan Department of Corrections*, 391 F.3d 737 (6th Cir. 2004), the Sixth Circuit upheld a gender restriction imposed by the Michigan Department of Corrections (MDOC) to eradicate "rampant sexual abuse of female prisoners." MDOC had "pledged . . . to minimize access to secluded areas and one-on-one contact between male staff and female inmates" pursuant to settlement of two lawsuits, one brought by the United States Department of Justice, alleging that the failure to protect female inmates from ongoing sexual abuse violated their constitutional rights. To effectuate the settlement agreements, MDOC employed only female guards in the housing units of women's prisons. MDOC data showed that most allegations of sexual abuse, and all of the sustained allegations, involved male employees, and that sexual abuse occurred most frequently in the housing units. This data, the court held, "established that the exclusion of male [guards] will decrease the likelihood of sexual abuse."

In *Henry v. Milwaukee County*, 539 F.3d 573 (7th Cir. 2008), a juvenile detention center decided to staff each housing "pod" with at least one guard of the same sex as the juveniles housed on that pod, to achieve a "direct role model/mentoring form of supervision." During the day, one of the two guards on each male "pod" could be female, but the sole night shift slot on each pod had to be staffed by a man. The Seventh Circuit accepted the administrator's "professional judgment" that same-gender mentoring was "necessary to achieve the [facility's] mission of rehabilitation." Yet, the court found no factual support for the administrator's conclusion that the program's effectiveness required same-sex staff at all times, including on the night shift, when the juvenile inmates were sleeping.

In *Robino*, we held that even had the gender-based restriction on assignments been actionable under Title VII, it fell within the BFOQ exception. The prison, based on "a study conducted by a specially appointed task force in compliance with an EEOC settlement agreement," designated as female only those posts that "require[d] the [guard] on duty to observe the inmates in the showers and toilet areas . . . or provide[d] unsupervised access to the inmates." Because "a person's interest in not being viewed unclothed by members of the opposite sex survives incarceration," we held that protecting inmate privacy and preventing sexual misconduct warranted the restriction.

These cases illustrate that, even in the unique context of prison employment, administrators seeking to justify a BFOQ must show "a high correlation between sex and ability to perform job functions." *Johnson Controls.* Moreover, the particular staffing restriction at issue must match those "job functions" with a high degree of specificity to be found reasonably necessary. *See id.*; *Robino*. In *Henry*, for example, the application of the gender restriction on the night shift would not address privacy concerns, as "the vast majority of the time that the juveniles were unclothed occurred during [ ] daytime shifts" when women were permitted to staff the pods, and was not justified by the mentoring objective because "the opportunity . . . to interact with the juveniles on the [night] shift [wa]s very minimal."

Applying this "high correlation" requirement, NDOC's first rationale for restricting the supervisory correctional lieutenant positions to women cannot suffice. Crawford's testimony suggests that because the supervisors employed by CCA were male and had failed to prevent sexual abuse, NDOC was entitled to conclude that men as a class were incapable of adequately supervising front line staff in female prisons. While we must defer to the reasoned judgment of prison administrators, *see Robino*, CCA's acknowledged leadership failure falls far short of providing "a factual basis for believing that all or substantially all [men] would be unable to safely and effectively perform the duties of the job," or that it would be "impossible or highly impracticable to determine job fitness" — here, the ability to enforce workplace rules prohibiting sexual misconduct — "on an individualized basis." *Williams v. Hughes Helicopters, Inc.*, 806 F.2d 1387, 1391 (9th Cir. 1986) [ADEA]. The fundamental switch in operational responsibility to NDOC, moreover, made any inference from the experience under CCA's extremely poor management all the weaker.

NDOC's second rationale fares no better. There is no evidence indicating that any correctional lieutenant at SNWCF had sexual relationships with an inmate. In contrast, in *Everson*, copious data about the actual incidence of sexual abuse in Michigan's women's prisons supported the conclusion that the gender restriction on guards in the housing units would be effective. In *Robino*, prison administrators used "a study by a specially appointed task force" and "an extensive inventory of post duties" to limit the gender restriction to those posts that "provide[d] unsupervised access to the inmates." NDOC, however, offers neither data nor logical inferences about the opportunities for abuse inherent in the correctional lieutenant position to support the restriction.

In fact, the one substantiated case of sexual abuse Crawford mentioned was the front line guard who impregnated an inmate, yet NDOC continues to employ men in thirty percent of these positions. *See Everson*. When asked why the complete prohibition on the hiring of men was limited to correctional lieutenants, Crawford stated, "We did not want to go globally on this. We wanted to be specifically, what can we do to bring this thing under control . . . ? And it was the recommendation that we just look at . . . not the line level, but the supervisor level." This explanation falls short of the "reasoned decision-making process, based on available information and experience," *Robino*, that can support a BFOQ.

Even if there were a factual basis to believe that any correctional lieutenant sexually abused any inmate, there is no basis to presume that sexual abuse, by correctional lieutenants or by guards with their supervisors' tacit permission, would continue after the state resumed control over the prison. CCA's lax oversight provided male correctional lieutenants "the opportunity not to take action against male correctional subordinates that sexually abused female inmates." That opportunity cannot be presumed to exist after the wholesale change of SNWCF's leadership, designed precisely to cure wholesale management defects going well beyond the sexual abuse issue.

To hold otherwise would be to absolve NDOC from their fundamental responsibility to supervise their staff, from wardens to front-line guards. In *Dothard*, the inmates' violent behavior, which prison administrators could not directly control, rendered the gender restriction reasonably necessary. Neither *Dothard* nor any of the cases on which NDOC relies support finding a BFOQ based on the bald assertion that it would be "impossible . . . to ensure that any given male correctional lieutenant will take action to prevent and stop sexual misconduct." Where, as here, the problem is *employee* behavior, prison administrators have multiple resources, including background checks, prompt investigation of suspected misconduct, and severe discipline for infractions, to ensure compliance with institutional rules.

NDOC has not demonstrated that these alternative approaches—including the Inspector General's suggestion of enhanced training for both supervisors and front-line guards—are not viable. *See Henry; Forts v. Ward*, 621 F.2d 1210, 1216 (2d Cir. 1980) (upholding a district court order "prohibit[ing] the stationing of male guards at locations where inmates could be viewed . . . unclothed" but reversing a ban on male guards during the night shift because inmate privacy could be protected by means that did not infringe on employment rights); *Gunther* (holding that gender was not a BFOQ where administrative changes in job functions and procedures would adequately protect inmate privacy). [One witness's] conclusory assertion that "more training is not a cure for this serious issue" is, without more, wholly inadequate. Even the NIC report, on which NDOC purportedly relied, recommends "improving training programs to heighten staff awareness of [sexual abuse] and its consequences."

Disturbingly, in suggesting that all men are inherently apt to sexually abuse, or condone sexual abuse of, female inmates, NDOC relies on entirely specious gender stereotypes that have no place in a workplace governed by Title VII. NDOC's third theory, that women are "maternal," "patient," and understand other women, fails for the same reason. To credit NDOC's unsupported generalization that women "have an instinct and an innate ability to discern . . . what's real and what isn't" and so are immune to manipulation by female inmates would violate "the Congressional purpose to eliminate subjective assumptions and traditional stereotyped conceptions regarding the . . . ability of women to do particular work." *Rosenfeld v. S. Pac. Co.*, 444 F.2d 1219, 1225 (9th Cir. 1971). "The harmful effects of occupational cliches," *Gerdom v. Continental Airlines*, 692 F.2d 602, 607 (9th Cir. 1982), are felt no less strongly when invoked as a basis for one gender's unique suitability for a particular job than when relied on to exclude members of that sex from employment. Simply put, "we are beyond the day when an employer could . . . insist[ ] that [employees] matched the stereotype associated with their group." *Price Waterhouse v. Hopkins.*

A BFOQ can be established only by "objective, verifiable requirements [that] concern job-related skills and aptitudes." *Johnson Controls.* Though the professional judgment of prison administrators is entitled to deference, *see Robino*, "[t]he refusal to hire a [man] because of [his] sex based on assumptions of the comparative employment characteristics of [men] in general" will not support a BFOQ. 29 C.F.R. § 1604.2(a)(1).

In sum, NDOC has not met its burden of showing "a basis in fact," *Dothard*, for concluding that all male correctional lieutenants would tolerate sexual abuse by their subordinates; that all men in the correctional lieutenant role would themselves sexually abuse inmates; or that women, by virtue of their gender, can better understand the behavior of female inmates. Nor has it refuted the viability of alternatives that would achieve that goal without impeding male employees' promotional opportunities. . . .

NOTES

1. *Adverse Employment Action?* The court's rejection of the de minimis argument might suggest that any sex discrimination is impermissible unless justified by a BFOQ. But a closer reading suggests that this is not true. As we saw on page 580, a "de minimis" exception seems alive and well under Title VII, although it is framed in terms of whether the at-issue decision constitutes an "adverse employment action." For many courts, a "lateral transfer," that is, one that does not result in loss of pay or a demotion, is not actionable. In jurisdictions with stringent definitions of adverse employment action, an employer may be able to assign individuals by sex, age, or even race without having to establish a BFOQ. *See Tipler v. Douglas County*, 482 F.3d 1023, 1025 (8th Cir. 2007 ("a bona fide occupational qualification analysis is unnecessary if (1) the policy requiring female-only supervision of female inmates is reasonable, and (2) such a policy imposes only a 'minimal restriction' on the employee"). *But see Piercy v. Maketa*, 480 F.3d 1192 (10th Cir. 2007) (facial discrimination might be actionable when it was not clear that assignments were purely lateral). *See generally* Rebecca Hanner White, *De Minimis Discrimination*, 47 EMORY L. J. 1121, 1148, 1172-73 (1998) ("When there is direct evidence of a discriminatory act, or when a fact finder has concluded the discrimination was motivated by the protected characteristic, the 'de minimis' nature of the discrimination should not serve as a basis for dismissing the claim. That the discrimination may be viewed as 'trivial' or 'de minimis' goes merely to remedies and not to liability.").

2. *Avoiding Sexual Harassment and Exploitation.* Although it could be described in "privacy" terms, *Breiner* is about more than privacy in the sense of an interest in not being seen unclothed by members of the opposite sex. The scandal that gave rise to the policy at issue indicates the serious problems that can arise in custodial settings, which may explain why employers in such settings often resort to such policies. And, while the court struck down the sex-limitation for lieutenants, it made clear that the policy as to the sex of the front-line guards themselves was not at issue. In purely numerical terms, the number of positions reserved for female guards undoubtedly dwarfed the three supervisory slots at issue in the case. If a male guard sued the prison, would he win? It's safe to assume that avoiding harassment and exploitation of female inmates is an appropriate goal, but is a gender line reasonably necessary to achieve it? *See generally* Kim Shayo Buchanan, *Beyond Modesty: Privacy in Prison and the Risk of Sexual Abuse*, 88 MARQ. L. REV. 751 (2005) ("[T]he modesty critics' concern about stereotyping is misguided. [W]hen women prisoners are sexually exploited by guards, they are victims of sexual aggression; feminists do them no favor by pretending that they are not.").

3. *Rehabilitation.* The court finds that neither rehabilitation nor privacy concerns were proffered as justifications for the sex limitation. In some cases, however, courts have found rehabilitation to be a legitimate basis for a BFOQ. In *Healey v. Southwood Psychiatric Hospital*, 78 F.3d 128, 132-33 (3d Cir. 1996), plaintiff challenged a gender-specific rule for assigning childcare specialists at a hospital for emotionally disturbed children and adolescents, some of whom had been sexually abused. The court upheld summary judgment for the employer based on the BFOQ defense:

> The "essence" of Southwood's business is to treat emotionally disturbed and sexually abused adolescents and children. Southwood has presented expert testimony that staffing both males and females on all shifts is necessary to provide therapeutic care. "Role modeling," including parental role modeling, is an important element of the staff's job, and a male is better able to serve as a male role model than a female and vice versa. A balanced staff is also necessary because children who have been sexually abused will disclose their problems more easily to a member of a certain sex, depending on their sex and the sex of the abuser. If members of both sexes are not on a shift, Southwood's inability to provide basic therapeutic care would hinder the "normal operation" of its "particular business." Therefore, it is reasonably necessary to the normal operation of Southwood to have at least one member of each sex available to the patients at all times.

See also Torres v. Wisconsin Dep't of Health & Social Services, 859 F.2d 1523 (7th Cir. 1988) (rehabilitation in a prison context).

4. *Privacy.* The *Breiner* court cites *Rubino* for the proposition that an individual's interest in not being seen unclothed by a member of the opposite sex survives incarceration. A number of cases have concurred, but they have often stressed, as in *Robino* itself, that measures short of denying individuals jobs because of their sex can suffice. *E.g., Henry v. Milwaukee County,* 539 F.3d 573 (7th Cir. 2008). What about the privacy of patients and clients? The *Johnson Controls* majority denied that its opinion would do away with privacy protections, 99 U.S. 187, 206 n.4, and a few cases have upheld sex-specific rules on this basis. *See Wade v. Napolitano,* 2009 U.S. Dist. LEXIS 132628, 26 (M.D. Tenn. Mar. 24, 2009) (approving privacy-based BFOQ for TSA screeners).

5. *Deference.* Many BFOQ cases turn on the level of deference courts accord the professional judgment of employers. Particularly in the prison context, the cases tend to at least claim to be deferring to some extent. In *Breiner* itself, the prison officials' cavalier rationale for their own rule probably was largely responsible for the opinion's evident disdain. But the Ninth Circuit stated that some deference was due. How much? *See also Henry,* 539 F.3d 580-81 ("We agree that the administrators of juvenile detention facilities, like the administrators of female correctional facilities, are entitled to substantial deference when fashioning policies to further the goals of the facility. We do not agree, however, that the discretion accorded to these individuals in either context is effectively unlimited.").

6. *Essence of the Business.* Although not at issue in *Breiner* some BFOQ cases have turned not on whether one gender was better than another in some respect but rather whether such superiority went to the "'essence' of the business." This test originated in *Diaz v. Pan American Airways, Inc.,* 442 F.2d 385 (5th Cir. 1971), holding that sex was not a BFOQ for the job of flight attendant — despite the asserted superiority of women in being sexually attractive to male passengers and comforting to female passengers — because those characteristics are peripheral to the airline's essential concern with safe transportation. *Johnson Controls* confirms the importance of "essence" analysis in applying the BFOQ. However, the fact that a policy relates to an essential function, and even promotes it, is not sufficient to establish a BFOQ: "Title VII's standard is not satisfied simply because a policy promotes an essential function of an institution. Although sex-based assignments might be helpful in pursuing [the goals of rehabilitation, security, and privacy], in order to satisfy the antidiscrimination strictures of Title VII, [the employer] must show that the contested sex classifications are "'reasonably necessary.'" *Henry,* 539 F.3d 581. In *Henry,* the court held that "Although reducing the number of opposite-sex staff on the pods may *help* to promote security, efficient risk management and privacy, Milwaukee County has failed to establish that its policy was *reasonably necessary* for these goals." *Id.* at 581.

7. *Customer Preference.* Whatever the correct view of privacy, it would support relatively narrow inroads into Title VII's proscriptions. It does, however, tend to merge into a larger question: When, if ever, is "customer preference" a basis for a BFOQ? So framed, the courts have not been sympathetic. For example, the Ninth Circuit rejected a BFOQ claim in *Fernandez v. Wynn Oil Co.,* 653 F.2d 1273 (9th Cir. 1981), where the defendant argued that the plaintiff could not be made vice president of international operations because Latin American clients would react negatively to a woman in such a position. Although finding the defense not factually supported, the Ninth Circuit also held the defense inadequate as a matter of law because customer preference cannot justify gender discrimination. *Id. See also EEOC v. HI 40 Corp.*, 953 F. Supp. 301 (W.D. Mo. 1996) (being female was not a BFOQ for counselors at weight-loss centers, despite the centers' mostly female customers' preference for female counselors). *But see EEOC v. University of Texas Health Science Ctr.*, 710 F.2d 1091, 1095 (5th Cir. 1983) (upholding as a BFOQ an age-45 limitation on initial hiring of campus police in part because of testimony that "younger officers are better able to handle frequent confrontational episodes on campus because of their ability to relate to youthful offenders."). What does *Johnson Controls* suggest about this question? *See* Ernest F. Lidge III, *Law Firm Employment Discrimination in Case Assignments at the Client's Insistence: A Bona Fide Occupational Qualification?*, 38 CONN. L. REV. 159 (2005).

8. *Sex Appeal as a BFOQ.* Is selling sex appeal a BFOQ? In *Frank v. United Airlines*, 216 F.3d 845 (9th Cir. 2000), female flight attendants challenged the airlines' maximum weight requirements requiring women to meet a standard for medium body frames while the standard for men corresponded to standards for large body frames. Women were required to weigh 14 to 25 pounds less than male colleagues of the same height and age. The court found this to be a formal policy of sex discrimination and struck it down because the airline failed to justify it as a BFOQ:

> United made no showing that having disproportionately thinner female than male flight attendants bears a relation to flight attendants' ability to greet passengers, push carts, move luggage, and, perhaps most importantly, provide physical assistance in emergencies. . . . Far from being "reasonably necessary" to the "normal operation" of United's business, the evidence suggests that, if anything, United's discriminatory weight requirements may have inhibited the job performance of female flight attendants.

Id. at 855. Why would United adopt such a policy? Is it to satisfy customer preference for conventional views of attractiveness? *See also Wilson v. Southwest Airlines Co.*, 517 F. Supp. 292 (N.D. Tex. 1981) (being female was not a BFOQ for defendant who marketed itself as "love airline," using the female allure and sex appeal of its employees).

A current example is Hooters, a chain of restaurants that hires only women, who are clad in provocative outfits, to serve food to customers. In an investigation by the EEOC in the mid-1990s, the company defended its practice by arguing that "[a] lot of places serve good burgers. The Hooters' Girls, with their charm and All-American sex appeal, are what our customers come for." *Restaurant Chain to Resist Hiring Men*, N.Y. TIMES, Nov. 16, 1995, at A20, col. 5. The EEOC dropped its investigation against Hooters after the company's massive public relations campaign. A private action was then settled, under terms that allowed Hooters to continue to hire only women as waitpersons. The men who were discriminated against by this company policy did, however, receive monetary compensation. *Hooters to Pay $3.75 Million in Sex Suit*, USA TODAY, Oct. 1, 1997, at 1A; *see generally* Kimberly A. Yuracko, *Private Nurses and Playboy Bunnies: Explaining Permissible Sex Discrimination*, 92 CAL. L. REV. 147, 191 (2004) (differentiating approaches taken by courts to cases raising issues of patient privacy versus sexual titillation). *See also* Russell Robinson, *Casting and Caste-ing: Reconciling Artistic Freedom and Antidiscrimination Norms*, 95 CAL. L. REV. 1, 5 (2007) ("[W]hen it comes to casting, an entire industry effectively disregards Title VII.").

d. *Voluntary Affirmative Action*

As we have seen, Title VII and § 1981 bar race discrimination, not merely discrimination against African Americans and other racial minorities. Title VII also bars sex discrimination, not merely discrimination against women. Accordingly, discrimination against whites and males is as impermissible as discrimination against minorities and women, although we have also seen that "reverse" discrimination may be harder to prove. One kind of reverse discrimination that is subject to somewhat different rules are racial and gender preferences pursuant to a valid affirmative action plan.

The Supreme Court first encountered this problem in *United Steelworkers of America v. Weber*, 443 U.S. 193 (1979), where a five-to-two majority upheld an employer's use of a voluntary affirmative action plan benefiting unskilled black workers. Kaiser Aluminum had negotiated with the union representing its workers to create a training program for incumbent, unskilled workers to fill skilled job categories. Until this plan was adopted, craft positions were filled by people with craft experience, typically learned in craft unions that had historically excluded blacks from membership. In order to address the resultant lack of trained minorities, the plan reserved for black employees 50 percent of the openings in these newly created in-plant training programs until the percentage of skilled black craft workers approximated the percentage of blacks in the local labor force. While the plan provided as many training openings for whites as for blacks, African Americans with less seniority than whites were admitted to it because there were far fewer of them available.

After holding that Title VII's prohibition against racial discrimination does not condemn all private, voluntary, race-conscious affirmative action plans, the Court upheld the particular plan in the instant case and rejected the plaintiffs' discrimination claim.

> We need not today define in detail the line of demarcation between permissible and impermissible affirmative action plans. It suffices to hold that the challenged Kaiser-USWA affirmative action plan falls on the permissible side of the line. The purposes of the plan mirror those of the statute. Both were designed to break down old patterns of racial segregation and hierarchy. Both were structured to "open unemployment opportunities for Negroes in occupations which have been traditionally closed to them."
>
> At the same time, the plan does not unnecessarily trammel the interests of the white employees. The plan does not require the discharge of white workers and their replacement with new black hirees. . . . Nor does the plan create an absolute bar to the advancement of white employees; half of those trained in the program will be white. Moreover, the plan is a temporary measure; it is not intended to maintain racial balance, but simply to eliminate a manifest racial imbalance.

Id. at 208.

The Court reaffirmed *Weber* in *Johnson v. Transportation Agency, Santa Clara County, California*, 480 U.S. 616 (1987), and extended its application to affirmative action on behalf of women. The employer had promoted Diane Joyce to the position of road dispatcher, making her the first woman included among the 238 skilled craft worker jobs. A male, who had scored two points higher on an interview, sued, claiming reverse discrimination. Although Diane Joyce was qualified for the job, the district court found that the woman's sex was the determining factor in her selection.

When the case reached the Supreme Court, it used the opportunity to broadly approve affirmative action plans. As to the litigation structure of such cases, the Court held that, when a defendant claims it has acted in accordance with an affirmative action plan, the plaintiff has the burden of persuasion in establishing the invalidity of that affirmative action plan. Interestingly, the Court used the inferential method of proof established in *McDonnell Douglas Corp. v. Green*, even though the decision maker admitted that sex was a factor in the selection decision. But the employer's explanation that it had relied upon its affirmative action plan was viewed by the Court as a "legitimate, nondiscriminatory reason," leaving it up to the male plaintiff to prove the plan invalid. Thus, in a reverse discrimination case, the plaintiff bears the burden of persuasion to prove discrimination, either because the challenged action was not taken pursuant to an affirmative action plan, *see* page 572, or because it was taken pursuant to an invalid plan. As to the substantive standard, *Weber* and *Johnson* specify two requirements: the "manifest imbalance" requirement and the "not unduly trammel" requirement.

Manifest Imbalance. The plan's use of race or sex must be aimed at remedying a "manifest imbalance in a traditionally segregated job category." Such an imbalance brings the affirmative action plan into alignment with the purposes of Title VII, which include breaking down historic patterns of discrimination. Justice Blackmun's concurrence in *Weber* demonstrated how broad this first factor is: "[T]he Court considers a job category to be 'traditionally segregated' when there has been a societal history of purposeful exclusion of blacks from the job category, resulting in a persistent disparity between the proportion of blacks in the labor force and the proportion of blacks among those who hold jobs within the category." *Weber*, 443 U.S. at 212.

This approach is cast in terms of statistical disparity alone, without regard to the underlying cause of the disparity. *Weber* made clear that an employer may adopt an affirmative action plan in the absence of any prior discrimination on its own part; remedying the effects of societal discrimination will suffice. *See id.* at 214. As for determining whether a manifest imbalance in a traditionally segregated job category exists, the *Johnson* Court observed that the proper comparison is between the percentage of minorities or women in the job category in the employer's work force and the percentage of those workers in the *relevant labor pool. Johnson*, 480 U.S. at 632. A comparison with general population figures is appropriate only when the job involves no skills or skills easily acquired by the general population, as in *Weber. Id.* For skilled jobs, the appropriate comparison is to the skilled labor pool. *See Hazelwood Sch. Dist. v. United States*, 433 U.S. 299 (1977). Because *Johnson* involved skilled trade positions, the Court viewed the appropriate comparison to be that between the percentage of skilled craft workers in the employer's work force (zero) and the percentage of women in the relevant labor market having the requisite skills. *Johnson*, 480 U.S. at 632. Once the proper comparison is established, it is still necessary to determine whether the imbalance is great enough to justify the affirmative action remedy.

An important, and as yet unresolved, issue is whether a voluntary affirmative action plan must be "remedial"—in the sense of aimed at remedying a manifest imbalance—to be lawful under Title VII. The affirmative action plans in both *Weber* and *Johnson* were designed to ameliorate a traditionally segregated job category, and the Court's decisions in those cases addressed when such a remedial interest would support an affirmative action plan. But when no such manifest imbalance exists, may a voluntary affirmative action plan yet be permissible? *Taxman v. Board of Education of Township of Piscataway*, 91 F.3d 1547 (3d Cir. 1996) (en banc), involved a claim by a white school teacher who had been laid off while an equally qualified black teacher was retained. The Third Circuit rejected the school district's use of race under its affirmative action plan to choose between two equally qualified teachers when one needed to be laid off. Since there was no underrepresentation of blacks in the Piscataway school system, the board did not assert a remedial purpose for the plan but instead relied upon a diversity rationale, reasoning that students would benefit from a racially diverse teaching staff. The Third Circuit, however, held that a nonremedial interest would not support an affirmative action plan under Title VII. The Supreme Court granted certiorari, and many expected a decision affirming *Taxman* and thus narrowing the affirmative action exception under Title VII. In what was then a very unusual move, recounted in Michael J. Zimmer, Taxman: *Affirmative Action Dodges Five Bullets*, 1 U. PA. J. LAB. & EMP. L. 229 (1998), civil rights groups underwrote a settlement that resulted in dismissal of the writ as moot. In the wake of the Supreme Court's decision approving nonremedial affirmative action under the Equal Protection Clause in the context of higher education in *Grutter v. Bollinger*, 539 U.S. 306 (2003), the lower courts might be more open to such justifications in the context of Title VII, but the Court's decision in *Parents Involved in Community Schools v. Seattle School Dist. No. 1*, 551 U.S. 701 (2007), cuts the other way. *See generally* Kingsley R. Browne, *Title VII and Diversity*, 14 NEV. L.J. 806 (2014).

Not Unduly Trammel. The second prong for determining the legitimacy of an affirmative action plan under *Weber* and *Johnson* is that the plan must not "unduly trammel" the interests of majority group members. A common criticism of affirmative action by its opponents is that such programs disadvantage majority workers. In *Weber*, the Court described three possible concerns of white workers, but it thought none of these were at stake in the *Weber* plan:

> The plan does not require the discharge of white workers and their replacement with new black hires. . . . Nor does the plan create an absolute bar to the advancement of white employees; half of those trained in the program will be white. Moreover, the plan is a temporary measure; it is not intended to maintain racial balance, but simply to eliminate a manifest racial imbalance.

Weber, 443 U.S. at 209. Consequently, when a plan does not deprive an employee of a vested right, when it is not an absolute bar to majority workers' advancement, and when it is aimed at attaining, not maintaining, racial balance, it will satisfy this second prong.

Most affirmative action plans focus on hiring and promotion, making them more easily defensible under the second prong of the *Weber/Johnson* standard. *Weber* itself involved a training program to which no one had automatic entitlement. Similarly, in *Johnson*, the male plaintiff had no entitlement to the position but was one of several qualified applicants for the job. Moreover, the plan did not block plaintiff from being promoted in the future, and he in fact received a promotion when another opening arose. *Johnson*, 480 U.S. at 639, n.15. The Court emphasized that no rigid quotas had been set; instead, sex was only one factor out of several considered by the employer in deciding whom to promote. An affirmative action plan used to determine layoffs, as opposed to hiring or promotion, would likely find more difficulty satisfying this prong.

Again, the *Taxman* case provides a useful comparison. Using race as a tiebreaker to decide which teacher to lay off when seniority and qualifications were equal was viewed by the Third Circuit as unduly trammeling the interests of Taxman, who lost her job and was unemployed for some time. In *Weber* and *Johnson*, no one lost a job or any position to which they were otherwise entitled. Upholding a layoff for affirmative action purposes is particularly unlikely when the interest asserted for the plan is not a remedial one. Even if the Court were to approve adoption of voluntary affirmative action plans for nonremedial purposes, upholding the application of such plans in a layoff context seems unlikely.

Although the Supreme Court has not decided a Title VII affirmative action case since *Johnson*, *Ricci v. DeStefano*, 457 U.S. 457 (2009), reproduced at page 668, may have cast doubt on *Weber* and *Johnson*. *Ricci* arose from a promotion test administered by the fire department in New Haven, Connecticut, which yielded racially skewed results. The rate of white candidates who passed the test was significantly higher than the rate of minority candidates. When the city decided not to certify the test results because of potential disparate impact liability, white firefighters sued the city, alleging that the refusal to certify constituted disparate treatment based on race under Title VII. In a sharply divided opinion, the Supreme Court determined that the city's actions amounted to intentional disparate treatment discrimination against white fire-fighters and granted them summary judgment. The fact that the racial disparity in the test results created a prima facie case for disparate impact was not a defense to the disparate treatment claim unless the employer had a "strong basis in evidence" to believe that it would be liable for disparate impact discrimination. *Id.* at 563. In order to meet this requirement, an employer had to demonstrate a strong basis to believe that the test was not a business necessity or job-related or, if it were, that practices with less discriminatory impact on minorities were available. *Id.* at 587.

The meaning of *Ricci* for affirmative action is unclear. On the one hand, the majority never cited either *Johnson* or *Weber*, perhaps suggesting that there are simply two lines of authority governing two different situations. This is bulwarked by the fact that the city did not articulate the usual justifications for affirmative action but rather simply argued that its refusal to certify results was justified by its fear of disparate impact liability. On the other hand, *Ricci* takes a more stringent approach to practices designed to help minorities, and many suspect that the majority that decided *Ricci* would take a much more stringent approach to the issue of affirmative action under Title VII than prior cases. The Second Circuit has suggested that there are now two different lines of authority governing racial preferences. In *United States v. Brennan*, 650 F.3d 65, 72 (2d Cir. 2011), it held that

> *Johnson* and *Weber* do not apply to all race- or gender-conscious employer actions. In light of *Ricci*, the "manifest imbalance" and "no unnecessary trammeling" analysis of those cases extends, at most, to circumstances in which an employer has undertaken a race- or gender-conscious affirmative action plan designed to benefit all members of a racial or gender class in a forward-looking manner only. Where, as here, the employer instead provides individualized race- or gender-conscious benefits as a remedy for previous disparate impact, the employer must satisfy the requirements of *Ricci*, not *Johnson* and *Weber*, in order to avoid disparate-treatment liability.

Note on Voluntary Affirmative Action Plans of Public Employers

A public employer's affirmative action plan may be lawful under Title VII but still fall afoul of the Equal Protection Clause when a constitutional claim is brought. As you learned in Constitutional Law, all racial classifications by the state, local, or federal government are to be measured by strict scrutiny. Under this test, "such classifications are constitutional only if they are narrowly tailored measures that further compelling governmental interests." *Adarand Constr. v. Pena*, 515 U.S. 200 (1995); *Richmond v. J.A. Croson*, 488 U.S. 469 (1989). According to the Supreme Court, providing a remedy for the victims of proven discrimination is a sufficiently important governmental interest to withstand constitutional attack but remedying the effects of societal discrimination is not. *Wygant v. Jackson Bd. of Educ.*, 476 U.S. 262 (1986). Thus, one way to withstand a reverse equal protection claim is for an employer to have convincing evidence of its own prior discrimination before embarking on an affirmative action program.

Are there other compelling governmental interests justifying racial preferences? The Court's most definitive word on race-conscious decision making emerged in five-to-four decisions in two nonemployment cases, *Grutter v. Bollinger*, 539 U.S. 306 (2003), and *Gratz v. Bollinger*, 539 U.S. 244 (2003). In considering challenges by white students denied admission to the University of Michigan, the Supreme Court upheld diversity, at least for an educational institution, as a compelling governmental interest. Justice O'Connor, speaking for the Court in *Grutter*, implied that diversity may be a compelling governmental interest in areas beyond higher education by citing favorably the amici briefs of large corporations and the brief of military leaders arguing in favor of racially diverse workforces.

The Court disagreed, however, about whether the programs at issue were narrowly tailored to achieving that diversity interest. In *Grutter*, the Court upheld the law school admissions program as narrowly tailored to the diversity objective; however, in *Gratz*, dealing with undergraduate admissions, the Court struck down that program as not being tailored enough. The essential difference between the two programs was that the law school assessed the complete admissions file of each individual applicant, including membership in underrepresented minority groups, while the undergraduate program mechanically gave applicants who were members of underrepresented minority groups certain points. *See also Parents Involved in Community Schools v. Seattle School Dist. No. 1*, 551 U.S. 701 (2007) (striking down the use of race to achieve greater diversity in elementary and secondary schools).

The Court revisited diversity in college admissions in *Fisher v. University of Texas at Austin*, 133 S. Ct. 2411 (2013), a case that many believed would overturn *Grutter*. However, while it reversed the Fifth Circuit's approval of the university's admissions plan, the Court nevertheless did not disturb *Grutter's* core premise that diversity could be a sufficiently compelling state interest to survive strict scrutiny. Rather, the majority believed that the Fifth Circuit had been too deferential to the university's tailoring of its plan to the diversity interest claimed, looking only to its "good faith." Moreover,

> [o]nce the University has established that its goal of diversity is consistent with strict scrutiny, however, there must still be a further judicial determination that the admissions process meets strict scrutiny in its implementation. The University must prove that the means chosen by the University to attain diversity are narrowly tailored to that goal. On this point, the University receives no deference.

Id. at 2419-20. According to the Court, "[n]arrow tailoring also requires that the reviewing court verify that it is 'necessary' for a university to use race to achieve the educational benefits of diversity," *id.* at 2420, which requires "a careful judicial inquiry into whether a university could achieve sufficient diversity without using racial classifications." *Id.* That means "[t]he reviewing court must ultimately be satisfied that no workable race-neutral alternatives would produce the educational benefits of diversity." *Id.* The Court then remanded for an application of the correct standard to the litigation. On remand, the Fifth Circuit again upheld the admissions program. 758 F.3d 633 (5th Cir. 2014).

Prior to *Fisher* but after the Michigan cases, the Seventh Circuit considered the "diversity" question in the employment context. At issue was a challenge to the Chicago police department's practice of "standardizing" test scores racially to increase the number of African Americans and Hispanics promoted within the force. In rejecting a suit by white officers, the court held that "there is an even more compelling need for diversity in a large metropolitan police force charged with protecting a racially and ethnically divided major American city like Chicago. Under the *Grutter* standards, we hold, the City of Chicago has set out a compelling operational need for a diverse police department." *Petit v. Chicago*, 352 F.3d 1111, 1117-18 (7th Cir. 2003).

Despite *Petit*, the constitutionality of affirmative action in the employment context is uncertain. Two circuits, including the Seventh which decided *Petit*, have sustained challenges to race-conscious diversity programs on the basis of the Equal Protection Clause. *Alexander v. City of Milwaukee*, 474 F.3d 437, 446 (7th Cir. 2007) (*Petit* "never approved such a loose and indeed effectively standardless approach" as the one at issue); *Lomack v. City of Newark*, 463 F.3d 303, 310 (3d Cir. 2006) (unlike *Petit*, "the City does not argue that diversity within individual fire companies is in any other way necessary, or even beneficial, to the Fire Department's mission of fighting fires, *i.e.*, that the Department has an operational need for diverse fire companies"). *Adarand, Grutter/Gratz, Parents Involved,* and *Fisher* are all constitutional, not statutory, decisions, but public employers' affirmative action plans must fall within both constitutional and statutory limits. That the Court found diversity to be a compelling state interest in the context of university admissions in *Grutter* does not necessarily mean it will be viewed as a compelling state interest in the employment setting, were a constitutional challenge brought. It seems likely, however, that in at least some employment contexts, public employers will be able to contend successfully that a compelling state interest in diversity exists. A public elementary or high school, for example, may have a compelling state interest in employing a racially diverse faculty much as the University of Michigan had a compelling interest in a diverse student body. Thus it is possible that cases like *Taxman* might come out differently in the future.

Of course, in cases involving race-based decision making by governmental actors, courts apply the highest level of constitutional scrutiny, or strict scrutiny. Traditionally, sex-based classifications have been judged by a less demanding level of scrutiny under the Fourteenth Amendment, sometimes called "intermediate scrutiny." *United States v. Virginia*, 518 U.S. 515 (1996). It would thus seem that affirmative action in favor of women would be easier to constitutionally justify than affirmative action based on race.

2. Systemic Disparate Impact Discrimination

While disparate treatment discrimination is the purposeful exclusion of minorities or women from jobs, disparate impact discrimination exists when employment policies, regardless of intent, adversely affect one group more than another and cannot be justified. This section briefly outlines the structure of disparate impact analysis, the policies subject to disparate impact analysis, and defenses to a disparate impact case.

As we will see, the disparate impact theory clearly applies under Title VII of the Civil Rights Act of 1964 and under the ADA. It also operates under the ADEA, although in a very diluted form. *See Meacham v. Knolls Atomic Power Lab.*, 554 U.S. 84 (2008); *Smith v. City of Jackson*, 544 U.S. 228 (2005). *See page 685.* The Supreme Court has held that disparate impact is *not* available under 42 U.S.C. § 1981 (2014); *see Gen. Bldg. Contractors Ass'n v. Pennsylvania*, 458 U.S. 5 (2002), or under 42 U.S.C. § 1983 (2014) in suits enforcing the equal protection clause of the United States Constitution; *see, e.g., Personnel Admin. of Mass. v. Feeney*, 442 U.S. 256, 272 (1979).

Even under Title VII, where disparate impact originated as a theory of liability, recent developments have altered the landscape. The theory originated in 1971 in *Griggs v. Duke Power Co.*, 401 U.S. 424 (1971), and was elaborated on in a number of Supreme Court decisions until 1989. In that year, *Wards Cove Packing Co. v. Atonio*, 490 U.S. 642 (1989), radically reconceptualized the law. Congress, in turn, revived disparate impact analysis as the centerpiece (and most controversial part) of the Civil Rights Act of 1991. Most recently, the Supreme Court decided *Ricci v. DeStefano*, 457 U.S. 457 (2009), which at least limited the disparate impact theory and which some believe signals its end.

Griggs v. Duke Power Co.
401 U.S. 424 (1971)

Chief Justice BURGER delivered the opinion of the Court.

[Prior to the effective date of Title VII, Duke Power explicitly discriminated on the basis of race. "Negroes were employed only in the Labor Department where the highest paying jobs paid less than the lowest paying jobs in the other four 'operating' departments in which only whites were employed." With the enactment of Title VII, the Company abandoned its prior policy and allowed blacks to be hired into, or transfer to, any other department. However, Duke Power applied to these workers a high school diploma requirement that had applied for a decade to white workers seeking operating jobs. Further, on the effective date of Title VII, Duke Power for the first time required satisfactory scores on two professionally prepared tests for initial employment (although for current employees only the high school diploma was required for transfer). Shortly thereafter, Duke Power permitted incumbent employees who lacked a high school education to transfer by passing the two tests, the Wonderlic Personnel Test, which purports to measure general intelligence, and the Bennett Mechanical Comprehension Test. The district court found neither test directed or intended to measure the ability to learn to perform a particular job or category of jobs. The requisite scores used for both initial hiring and transfer approximated the national median for high school graduates. The test standards would thus screen out approximately half of all high school graduates.

Both the district court and the Fourth Circuit found that, despite the prior policy of overt racial discrimination, there was no showing of a racial purpose or invidious intent in the adoption of the high school diploma requirement or general intelligence test and that these standards had been applied fairly to whites and Negroes alike.]

The objective of Congress in the enactment of Title VII is plain from the language of the statute. It was to achieve equality of employment opportunities and remove barriers that have operated in the past to favor an identifiable group of white employees over other employees. Under the Act, practices, procedures, or tests neutral on their face, and even neutral in terms of intent, cannot be maintained if they operate to "freeze" the status quo of prior discriminatory employment practices.

The Court of Appeals' [judges] agreed that, on the record in the present case, "whites register far better on the Company's alternative requirements" than Negroes.[6] This consequence would appear to be directly traceable to race. Basic intelligence must have the means of articulation to manifest itself fairly in a testing process. Because they are Negroes, petitioners have long received inferior education in segregated schools and this Court expressly recognized these differences in Gaston County v. United States, 395 U.S. 285 (1969). There, because of the inferior education received by Negroes in North Carolina, this Court barred the institution of a literacy test for voter registration on the ground that the test would abridge the right to vote indirectly on account of race. Congress did not intend by Title VII, however, to guarantee a job to every person regardless of qualifications. In short, the Act does not command that any person be hired simply because he was formerly the subject of discrimination, or because he is a member of a minority group. Discriminatory preference for any group, minority or majority, is precisely and only what Congress has proscribed. What is required by Congress is the removal of artificial, arbitrary, and unnecessary barriers to employment when the barriers operate invidiously to discriminate on the basis of a racial or other impermissible classification.

Congress has now provided that tests or criteria for employment or promotion may not provide equality of opportunity merely in the sense of the fabled offer of milk to the stork and the fox. On the contrary, Congress has now required that the posture and condition of the job-seeker be taken into account. It has — to resort again to the fable — provided that the vessel in which the milk is proffered be one all seekers can use. The Act proscribes not only overt discrimination but also practices that are fair in form, but discriminatory in operation. The touchstone is business necessity. If an employment practice which operates to exclude Negroes cannot be shown to be related to job performance, the practice is prohibited.

On the record before us, neither the high school completion requirement nor the general intelligence test is shown to bear a demonstrable relationship to successful performance of the jobs for which it was used. Both were adopted, as the Court of Appeals noted, without meaningful study of their relationship to job-performance ability. Rather, a vice president of the Company testified, the requirements were instituted on the Company's judgment that they generally would improve the overall quality of the work force.

The evidence, however, shows that employees who have not completed high school or taken the tests have continued to perform satisfactorily and make progress in departments for which the high school and test criteria are now used. The promotion record of present employees who would not be able to meet the new criteria thus

---

6. In North Carolina, 1960 census statistics show that, while 34% of white males had completed high school, only 12% of Negro males had done so. U.S. Bureau of the Census, U.S. Census of Population: 1960, Vol. 1, Characteristics of the Population, pt. 35, Table 47.

Similarly, with respect to standardized tests, the EEOC in one case found that use of a battery of tests, including the Wonderlic and Bennett tests used by the Company in the instant case, resulted in 58% of whites passing the tests as compared with only 6% of the blacks. Decision of EEOC, CCH Empl. Prac. Guide, ¶ 17,304.53 (Dec. 2, 1966). *See also* Decision of EEOC 70-552, CCH Empl. Prac. Guide, ¶ 6139 (Feb. 19, 1970).

suggests the possibility that the requirements may not be needed even for the limited purpose of preserving the avowed policy of advancement within the Company. In the context of this case, it is unnecessary to reach the question whether testing requirements that take into account capability for the next succeeding position or related future promotion might be utilized upon a showing that such long-range requirements fulfill a genuine business need. In the present case the Company has made no such showing.

The Court of Appeals held that the Company had adopted the diploma and test requirements without any "intention to discriminate against Negro employees." We do not suggest that either the District Court or the Court of Appeals erred in examining the employer's intent; but good intent or absence of discriminatory intent does not redeem employment procedures or testing mechanisms that operate as "built-in headwinds" for minority groups and are unrelated to measuring job capability.

The Company's lack of discriminatory intent is suggested by special efforts to help the undereducated employees through Company financing of two-thirds the cost of tuition for high school training. But Congress directed the thrust of the Act to the *consequences* of employment practices, not simply the motivation. More than that, Congress has placed on the employer the burden of showing that any given requirement must have a manifest relationship to the employment in question.

The facts of this case demonstrate the inadequacy of broad and general testing devices as well as the infirmity of using diplomas or degrees as fixed measures of capability. History is filled with examples of men and women who rendered highly effective performance without the conventional badges of accomplishment in terms of certificates, diplomas, or degrees. Diplomas and tests are useful servants, but Congress has mandated the common sense proposition that they are not to become masters of reality.

[The Court also rejected the defendant's argument that §703(h), which authorizes the use of "any professionally developed ability test" that is not "designed, intended or used to discriminate because of race," justified the test requirements. Looking to EEOC guidelines and the legislative history of the statute, "the conclusion is inescapable that the EEOC's construction of §703(h) to require that employment tests be job related comports with congressional intent."]

Nothing in the Act precludes the use of testing or measuring procedures; obviously they are useful. What Congress has forbidden is giving these devices and mechanisms controlling force unless they are demonstrably a reasonable measure of job performance. Congress has not commanded that the less qualified be preferred over the better qualified simply because of minority origins. Far from disparaging job qualifications as such, Congress has made such qualifications the controlling factor, so that race, religion, nationality, and sex become irrelevant. What Congress has commanded is that any tests used must measure the person for the job and not the person in the abstract. . . .

NOTES

1. *Disparate Impact History in a Nutshell.* The disparate impact theory was refined by the Court in a number of decisions from 1971 until 1989, at which point the Supreme Court decided *Wards Cove Packing Co. v. Atonio*, 490 U.S. 642 (1989),

which most observers viewed as essentially gutting the theory. *Wards Cove* generated a national controversy about the disparate impact theory that was ultimately resolved by the enactment of the Civil Rights Act of 1991, whose centerpiece was a debate over "quotas," *Wards Cove*, and the appropriate structure of the disparate impact theory. During the debates, proponents argued that a strong impact theory was needed to open up job opportunities to minorities and women. Opponents vociferously claimed that disparate impact would result in quotas by encouraging employers to hire minorities and women, without regard to qualifications, merely to avoid potential liability. What do you think of the argument?

In any event, since 1991 disparate impact has largely been framed in terms of the meaning of the amendments made by the Civil Rights Act. As we will see, however, those amendments refer back to prior law, so that some of the history of disparate impact must be revisited to determine what the present statute prohibits and permits. And the Supreme Court's 2009 decision in *Ricci v. DeStefano* once again cast doubt on the viability of the theory.

2. *Rationales for Disparate Impact.* Why should a showing of adverse impact alone, without intent to discriminate, be sufficient to establish illegal discrimination? Is it because defendants may be acting with intent to discriminate, but proof of such intent is not available to plaintiff? Duke Power imposed the challenged rules just as Title VII became effective. Was the Supreme Court merely trying to get around the lower court's finding of no intent to discriminate? "It might be possible to defend the [disparate impact theory] by framing it as simply an evidentiary tool used to identify genuine, intentional discrimination — to 'smoke out,' as it were, disparate treatment. But arguably the disparate-impact provisions sweep too broadly to be fairly characterized in such a fashion — since they fail to provide an affirmative defense for good-faith (i.e., nonracially motivated) conduct, or perhaps even for good faith plus hiring standards that are entirely reasonable." *Ricci v. DeStefano*, 557 U.S. 557, 595 (2009) (Scalia, J., concurring) (citations omitted).

Or perhaps the North Carolina school system was responsible. *Griggs* dealt with an educational prerequisite as well as test results, which probably correlate highly with increased level and quality of education. These requirements were imposed in a state that segregated African Americans in underfunded and inferior school systems. Is it this de jure discrimination in education that caused blacks in North Carolina to be disproportionately affected by Duke Power's rule? If so, why should the employer be responsible? Ramona L. Paetzold & Steven L. Willborn, in *Deconstructing Disparate Impact: A View of the Model Through New Lenses,* 74 N.C. L. Rev. 325, 353-54 (1995), argue that the cause of impact is irrelevant to the disparate impact theory since "[t]he law treats the employer's criterion as the cause of a disparity, even though it may be only one of a wide array of factors necessary to produce the disparity." *See also* Kathryn Abrams, *Title VII and the Complex Female Subject,* 92 Mich. L. Rev. 2479, 2524 (1994).

Another rationale for employer liability in such cases is grounded in efficiency. Professor Paulette Caldwell believes that Title VII was designed to increase productive efficiency by allowing individuals to achieve their full economic potential. *See* Paulette Caldwell, *Reaffirming the Disproportionate Effects Standard of Liability in Title VII Litigation,* 46 U. Pitt. L. Rev. 555 (1985). Caldwell's point is that, in the long run, efficiency will be improved if the pool of potential workers is widened by adding persons whose full potential would never be developed if denied entry-level positions. Is this what Chief Justice Burger meant when he wrote in *Griggs* that "[h]istory is filled with examples of men and women who rendered highly effective performance without the conventional badges of accomplishment in terms of certificates, diplomas, and degrees?" If so, does it have much to do with "discrimination"?

At first blush, whatever the underlying justifications, disparate impact seems in tension with the basic premise of antidiscrimination legislation: because members of protected groups are indistinguishable from similarly situated members of the majority, they ought not be treated differently in the workplace. While group differences may exist, disparate treatment ignores those differences and focuses instead on members of the protected group who are similarly situated to other individuals. In contrast, impact analysis not only acknowledges, but also focuses on, differences between groups. Individuals will be entitled to a remedy precisely because they are members of a group that is different.

The impact approach, however, does not abandon the equality principle. The business necessity defense permits the employer to rely on differences between employees when those differences are relevant to the job. Employers are prohibited from considering only differences that are not related to job performance. Thus, for purposes of qualifying for work, the underlying premise remains true: Protected group members should be treated equally when their work qualifications are the same.

Disparate impact liability effectively creates a duty for employers to identify and eliminate employment practices that unnecessarily operate as "built-in headwinds" for protected groups that have not yet achieved economic parity with white males. Viewed in this light, disparate impact can be considered a form of liability for negligence — an employer who does not intend to discriminate may nonetheless be liable for failing to exercise its duty of care toward protected group members. *See* David Benjamin Oppenheimer, *Negligent Discrimination*, 141 U. PA. L. REV. 899 (1993).

3. *Proving Impact.* The Court's use of statistics in *Griggs* is unsophisticated — even naive — compared with later refinements. The impact statistics on high school diplomas and tests were not linked in any direct way to the defendant's practices. Nevertheless, *Griggs* is a landmark case because it validates a statistical approach to discrimination litigation. Further, the decision establishes another critical point: When data that relates directly to the practices of the defendant itself is not available, a plaintiff may make out a prima facie case with more general statistics, leaving the defendant to show the inapplicability of those statistics to its practices.

In contrast, in *Wards Cove Packing Co. v. Atonio*, 490 U.S. 642 (1989), the Supreme Court undertook a much more sophisticated view of statistical proof. At issue in that case was a remote, seasonal salmon-canning facility with two main classes of workers — cannery jobs (almost all Native Alaskan and Filipino) and noncannery jobs (almost all white). The comparison between the racial breakdown of those working in cannery jobs and those in unskilled noncannery jobs was more dramatic than the comparative pass rates in *Griggs*, and the plaintiffs in *Wards Cove* sought to prove the discriminatory impact of a number of neutral hiring practices, including "nepotism, a rehire preference, a lack of objective hiring criteria, separate hiring channels, [and] a practice of not promoting from within." *Id.* at 647. Consider how the plaintiffs could establish disparate impact based on the employer's use of the practices in hiring. If the unskilled noncannery workforce is predominantly white, nepotism and rehire preferences are likely to yield predominantly white hiring. But to what group should the workforce numbers be compared to determine whether the results are disparate?

Wards Cove held that the "proper comparison [is] between the racial composition of [the at-issue jobs] and the racial composition of the qualified . . . population in the relevant labor market." The concept of the relevant labor market is borrowed from systemic disparate treatment law. Is the relevant labor market concept as used in disparate treatment cases appropriate for disparate impact analysis? Consider two systemic disparate treatment cases discussed in the previous section. In *Teamsters v. United States* (*see* page 635), the relevant labor market was the general population, while in *Hazelwood*, it was persons certified to teach in the relevant geographic area. In *Teamsters*, there was no reason to believe that the subset of those interested in and otherwise qualified for truck-driving jobs varied much from the general population. That was obviously not true in *Hazelwood*, which involved school teachers. In both cases, however, the issue was whether the statistics supported an inference of discriminatory intent. The Court was seeking to identify the pool from which the employer drew its employees so it could compare that pool with the group selected in order to determine whether the difference between the two was significant enough to suggest intentional discrimination.

The question in a disparate impact case is not whether the statistics allow an inference of discriminatory intent but whether the employer's neutral employment practice has a disparate impact on a statutorily protected group. For purposes of this inquiry, what is the "relevant labor market"? Is it the applicant pool, the labor pool from which the employer recruited, the labor pool in the geographic area surrounding the workplace, or the general population—and, if the last, the general population where? Each of these options creates potential problems. The applicant pool is perhaps the most relevant comparison group because it is directly affected by the employer's practices. The applicant pool, however, might be distorted by the employer's choice of recruitment sources, or posted qualifications, or reputation for discrimination. Similarly, the employer's choice of labor pool may not be appropriate because that pool may be distorted by the employer's practices. The geographic area "around" the workplace may not be appropriate because the job in question may require a broader search. Is the best choice the labor pool from which a reasonable nondiscriminatory employer would draw its employees? But a reasonable employer who had no intention to discriminate might select a labor pool that is very homogenous just because it is convenient. Should that pool be compared with the most diverse pool of qualified applicants available in order to determine whether there is a disparate impact? Does impact analysis impose on employers a duty to seek out the most diverse labor pool?

4. *Who Can Use the Disparate Impact Theory?* The cases invoking disparate impact have almost all involved minorities or women. Can whites or males invoke the theory? *See* Charles A. Sullivan, *The World Turned Upside Down?: Disparate Impact Claims by White Males*, 98 Nw. U. L. Rev. 1505 (2004) (exploring possible uses of disparate impact by these groups and concluding that while as a matter of pure statutory interpretation, Title VII is better read not to permit such suits, it should be construed to permit them because of equal protection concerns).

5. *Roller Coaster.* As we have seen, disparate impact has gone through a kind of legal roller coaster, reaching a highpoint in *Griggs*, a nadir in *Wards Cove*, and some kind of intermediate position in the Civil Rights Act of 1991. And we'll soon see another plunge in *Ricci v. DeStefano*, reproduced at page 668. Students and practicing attorneys are understandably less interested in this history than in what the statute presently requires, but the 1991 Civil Rights Act itself incorporates by reference some pieces of that history. As a result, while the following discussion focuses on the statute as it now exists, *Wards Cove* and Supreme Court decisions between *Griggs* and *Wards Cove* are cited where relevant. At the end of this discussion, we'll examine *Ricci's* impact on disparate impact.

6. *Current Applications of the Impact Theory.* The most successful challenges under disparate impact have undoubtedly been to tests, often traditional pen-and-paper (or computer-administered examinations) but also often to physical fitness tests. *See* page 665. However, the cases' disparate impact analysis can be aimed at a wide variety of practices, including objective criteria such as height and weight requirements, and subjective ones such as unstructured interviews. Three current issues concern the possible disparate impact of policies against hiring those who are currently unemployed, *see* Jennifer Jolly-Ryan, *Have a Job to Get a Job: Disparate Treatment and Disparate Impact of the "Currently Employed" Requirement*, 18 MICH. J. RACE & L. 189 (2012); those with low credit scores (probably highly correlated with unemployment), *see* Lea Shepard, *Toward a Stronger Financial History Antidiscrimination Norm*, 53 B.C. L. REV. 1695 (2012); and those with arrest and conviction records, *see* Johnathan J. Smith, *Banning the Box but Keeping the Discrimination?: Disparate Impact and Employers' Overreliance on Criminal Background Checks*, 49 HARV. C.R.-C.L. L. REV. 197 (2014); Terence G. Connor & Kevin J. White, *The Consideration of Arrest and Conviction Records in Employment Decisions: A Critique of the EEOC Guidance*, 43 SETON HALL L. REV. 971 (2013). The EEOC is pursuing enforcement on all three fronts, although it is too early to know whether these efforts, or potential private suits, will be successful. In addition, some states and cities have addressed some of these questions without framing the issue as racial discrimination. For example, "ban the box" legislation limits the timing of inquiries about criminal history. Michael Pinard, *Criminal Records, Race and Redemption*, 16 N.Y.U. J. LEGIS. & PUB. POL'Y 963, 985-86 (2013) ("At present, ten states and over fifty cities and counties have removed the 'box' from their respective initial employment applications. As a result, all applicants for state or local jobs in these jurisdictions are evaluated equally at the outset solely on their respective qualifications. The inquiry into the existence of the applicant's criminal record comes later in the application process. . . .").

a. Plaintiff's Proof of a Prima Facie Case

Section 703(k)(1)(A)(i) states the general rule for a disparate impact case: Plaintiff carries the burden of persuasion that the employer "uses a particular employment practice that causes disparate impact on the basis of race, color, religion, sex, or national origin." This embraces two questions that arose before the 1991 Amendments: (1) Is every employment-related action of an employer a qualifying "employment practice"? (2) How does a plaintiff establish that a disparate impact resulted from a "particular" practice as opposed to a congeries of causes?

Both points can be illustrated by *Connecticut v. Teal*, 457 U.S. 440 (1982), which involved a two-part selection process: a written test and a more subjective assessment of the candidates who passed the written test. The employer attempted to avoid disparate impact analysis of its written test on the ground that the "bottom line" — the end product of the employer's total selection procedure — did not have a disparate racial impact, even though the test considered by itself had such an impact. The Supreme Court rejected that approach, focusing on the right of individual black applicants to be free from barriers in the employment process that impact blacks as a group.

While blacks were not disproportionately screened out of jobs in *Teal*, they were disproportionately screened out of the opportunity to compete for those jobs by the test. The 1991 Civil Rights Act, by requiring the plaintiff to prove "a particular employment practice that causes disparate impact," essentially codifies *Teal*.

Teal, however (like *Griggs*), involved a challenge to an objective, pass/fail requirement. The plaintiffs in *Griggs* challenged the employer's requirements for a high school diploma and a passing score on two standardized tests. The *Teal* plaintiffs also challenged a test. Thus, the practices being challenged in both cases, and in other Supreme Court disparate impact decisions, were objective requirements, and the impact of each could be readily measured. What would have happened if the test in *Teal* did not have a disparate impact but plaintiffs had been able to show that the subjective portion of the selection process resulted in the disproportionate exclusion of African Americans? Can subjective components comprise "a particular employment practice" under the amended statute? The answer seems clearly yes. In *Watson v. Fort Worth Bank & Trust*, 487 U.S. 977 (1988), the Court unanimously held that subjective employment practices could also be attacked under the disparate impact theory. *Id.* at 989. *Watson*'s employer relied upon supervisors' subjective assessments of employees in deciding who would receive promotions, a subjective evaluation process that allegedly had resulted in a disparate impact on black employees. Rejecting the employer's argument that subjective practices did not lend themselves to disparate impact analysis, the Court determined that its "decisions in *Griggs* and succeeding cases could largely be nullified if disparate impact analysis were applied only to standardized selection practices." *Id.* at 990. The Court was persuaded that "disparate impact analysis is in principle no less applicable to subjective employment criteria than to objective or standardized tests. In either case, a facially neutral practice, adopted without discriminatory intent, may have effects that are indistinguishable from intentionally discriminatory practices." *Id.* Accordingly, the Court held that disparate impact claims may be brought to attack either objective or subjective practices. In light of *Watson*, §703(k) will undoubtedly be read to include subjective practices that have an impact.

This suggests that the disparate impact theory will sweep very broadly, but there are some statutory and judicially crafted exceptions. Thus, §703(k)(3) exempts employer rules prohibiting the employment of an individual who currently, knowingly, and illegally uses or possesses a controlled substance. Additional limitations may be created by the courts. An example of a "volitional exception" is *Garcia v. Spun Steak Co.*, 998 F.2d 1480 (9th Cir. 1993), where the employer required its bilingual employees to speak only English while on the job. Although the impact of the rule fell more harshly on employees of Hispanic origin, the Ninth Circuit found the rule immune from impact attack: Bilingual employees could comply with the rule and thus could avoid discipline through choosing to follow the rule. The court, moreover, found that employees have no affirmative right to speak their language of choice or otherwise to express their cultural heritage at work. *See also Lanning v. SEPTA*, 308 F.3d 286, 293 (3d Cir. 2002) (suggesting that the ability of women to improve their performance on a physical fitness test by training for it was relevant to assessing the test's validity). *But see Maldonado v. Altus*, 433 F.3d 1294, 1304-5 (10th Cir. 2006) (holding that English-only rules can create or contribute to a hostile work environment under disparate treatment and disparate impact theories).

Another judge-made exception may be employer passivity: At least one circuit has held that, for a disparate impact claim, the practice being challenged must be affirmatively adopted by the employer. In *EEOC v. Chicago Miniature Lamp Works*, 947 F.2d 292, 305 (7th Cir. 1991), the employer relied upon a word-of-mouth recruiting method for hiring new employees. Although the EEOC contended this resulted in a disparate impact on blacks, the court refused to permit an impact claim to proceed, reasoning it was the employees' actions of referring their friends and relatives, not any employer policy, that had caused the impact. "Passive reliance" on employee action is not an employer policy for purposes of disparate impact analysis, said the court.

While these kinds of limitations on disparate impact may be significant, the most difficult problem for plaintiffs is likely to be identifying the "particular" employment practice that causes an impact. We have seen that in *Connecticut v. Teal*, the Supreme Court rejected the "bottom line" defense to disparate impact claims, reasoning that if a particular component of a selection process had a disparate impact, that component could be challenged even if the overall result of the selection process produced no impact. *Teal*, 457 U.S. 440. In *Wards Cove v. Atonio*, the Court confronted the flip side of *Teal*, and held that plaintiffs could *not* mount a disparate impact challenge to the bottom line results of the employer's hiring practices: "[A] Title VII plaintiff does not make out a case of disparate impact simply by showing that, 'at the bottom line' there is racial *imbalance* in the work force. As a general matter, a plaintiff must demonstrate that it is the application of a specific or particular employment practice that has created the disparate impact under attack." *Wards Cove*, 490 U.S. at 657; *see generally* Charles A. Sullivan, *Disparate Impact: Looking Past the* Desert Palace *Mirage*, 47 Wm. & Mary L. Rev. 911, 960-64 (2005).

In the 1991 Civil Rights Act, Congress essentially codified this aspect of *Wards Cove*. Section 703(k)(1)(A) provides that an unlawful employment practice based on disparate impact is established under this title only if "(i) a complaining party demonstrates that a respondent uses a particular employment practice that causes a disparate impact. . . ." Importantly, however, the statute provides an exception: Plaintiffs may attack the bottom line if they can show that the individual components of the whole process are not capable of separation. §703(k)(1)(B)(i).

Thus, if more than one employment practice is involved in a selection process (as in *Teal*), plaintiff must identify the component or components that are causing the disparate impact and must prove the impact of each. This is not a dramatic change in the law. *Griggs*, after all, involved a challenge to both standardized testing and to the high school diploma requirement. Evidence of the impact of each was presented to and relied upon by the Court. Discovery of employer records and testimony may produce evidence to support a showing of impact. If the plaintiff cannot prove the impact of each separate practice of the overall selection process, how can a plaintiff prove that the multiple components are not capable of separation for analysis? The answer should be a pragmatic one: Has the plaintiff taken all reasonable steps to establish the impact of the separate practices? If plaintiff shows she did her best and still could not separate out the impact of each practice, then the case should be analyzed by looking at the bottom line outcome of the total of the employer's selection procedures. *Compare Chin v. Port Auth. of N.Y. & N.J.*, 685 F.3d 135, 154-155 (2d Cir. 2012) (while a promotion process involved three steps, the recommendations in the first two steps could not be separated from the third for statistical analysis since both played an indeterminate role), *with Davis v. Cintas Corp.*, 717 F.3d 476 (6th Cir. 2013) (plaintiff neither identified a "particular employment practice" by including several distinct subjective elements of a multi-interview hiring system nor showed that the "many steps were so intertwined that they were not capable of separation for analysis").

Yet another question is how much disparity must the plaintiff show to establish disparate impact? In *Griggs*, for example, the disparate pass rates on the tests of whites and blacks were substantial. Even with respect to high school diplomas, the white graduation rate was three times that of the blacks. Might some practices have a real impact, but one that is not large enough to satisfy the statute? The answer is unclear. The EEOC uses a "four-fifths rule" as evidence of impact — that is, it regards "a selection rate for any race, sex, or ethnic group which is less than four-fifths (4/5) (or eighty percent) of the rate for the group with the highest rate" as sufficient and "a greater than four-fifths rate" as generally insufficient. The Supreme Court has neither adopted nor rejected the four-fifths rule, *see Connecticut v. Teal*, 457 U.S. 440, 453 n.12 (1982) (stressing that the rule was designed to allocate government enforcement resources, not to define liability). It has been cited by a number of courts, even when recognized only as a rule of thumb. *See EEOC v. Joint Apprenticeship Committee*, 186 F.3d 110 (2d Cir. 1998); *Bullington v. United Air Lines, Inc.*, 86 F.3d 1301 (10th Cir. 1999). *But see Bew v. City of Chicago*, 252 F.3d 891 (7th Cir. 2001) (upholding a finding of a prima facie case of disparate impact even though 98.24 percent of blacks and 99.96 percent of whites had passed a test because there was a statistical correlation between race and test failure).

Once the plaintiff has made such a showing, the statute further provides that:

> If the respondent demonstrates that a specific employment practice does not cause the disparate impact, the respondent shall not be required to demonstrate that such practice is required by business necessity.

Section 703(k)(B)(ii); 42 U.S.C. §2000e-2(k)(B)(ii). The new Act does not further define this "no cause" defense.

PROBLEM

9-2. The Naperville police department chief wants to replace the traditional police revolver used as standard equipment with the much more powerful Smith & Wesson Model 59 semi-automatic. The Model 59 is very powerful and is quite large, with a wide hand grip. National data show that over 50 percent of all women and about 10 percent of all men would be unable to handle the gun because of the size of the hand grip. Assume the police chief asks you if there would be any legal problem with the department adopting the Model 59. What additional facts would you like to know before you render an opinion? Could you recommend that the department take any steps before requiring that the Model 59 be used by all department officers that might help insulate the department from disparate impact liability?

---

b. *Defendant's Rebuttal*

There are several rebuttal possibilities available to the employer to respond to a prima facie case of disparate impact discrimination. The most obvious is simply for employers to try to undermine the plaintiff's showing of a prima facie case by introducing evidence that the data on which plaintiff relied were flawed. The second is for the employer to attempt to carry the burden of persuasion that the practice at issue is within the statutory business necessity/job-related defense. *Griggs* provides one example of a failed effort: The fact that the employer had legitimate, and even plausible, justifications for its policies was not sufficient absent some kind of empirical demonstration that its policies conduced to greater productivity. Other Supreme Court cases have taken a hard line toward what suffices where testing is concerned. *See Albemarle Paper Co. v. Moody*, 422 U.S. 405 (1975); *but see Washington v. Davis*, 426 U.S. 229 (1976). We will encounter a taste of the complications of testing validation and, indeed, of business necessity in *Ricci*, but a brief recounting of one case suggests some of the complications.

Lanning v. Southeastern Pennsylvania Transportation Authority, 181 F.3d 478 (3d Cir. 1999) (*Lanning I*), involved a physical fitness test instituted by SEPTA, to upgrade the quality of its transit police force. Designed by an expert exercise physiologist with extensive experience in designing physical fitness tests for various law enforcement agencies, the test required applicants to complete a 1.5 mile run within 12 minutes. This would require an aerobic capacity of 42.5 mL/kg/min, the aerobic capacity the expert determined would be necessary to perform the job of SEPTA transit officer. Implementation of the test had a strongly disparate impact on women: Between 6 and 12 percent of women applicants passed it as compared to 55 to 60 percent of male applicants. While SEPTA rigorously applied the test to new applicants, it did not impose similar requirements on incumbents, merely offering incentives for current officers to meet such aerobic levels. Most did, but many did not, and SEPTA never attempted to measure the performance of those who failed to keep fit. Indeed, some "unfit" incumbent officers were promoted and also given special recognition, commendations, and satisfactory performance evaluations.

Turning to the meaning of business necessity, *Lanning I* pursued a complex analysis that began by recognizing that the 1991 Act instructed the courts that in interpreting that language, "[n]o statements other than the interpretive memorandum . . . shall be considered legislative history of, or relied upon in any way as legislative history. . . ." Pub. L. 102-66, Sec. 105 (1991), 105 Stat. 1071, 1074. The interpretive memorandum, in turn, stated: "The terms 'business necessity' and 'job related' are intended to reflect the concepts enunciated by the Supreme Court in *Griggs*, and in the other Supreme Court decisions prior to *Wards Cove*. 137 Cong. Rec. 28, 680 (1991)." This meant, according to *Lanning I*, that Congress endorsed the business necessity standard enunciated in *Griggs* (and not *Wards Cove*'s watering down of that standard). It concluded:

> Taken together, *Griggs, Albemarle* and *Dothard* teach that in order to show the business necessity of a discriminatory cutoff score an employer must demonstrate that its cutoff measures the minimum qualifications necessary for successful performance of the job in question. Furthermore, because the Act instructs us to interpret its business necessity language in conformance with *Griggs* and its pre-*Wards Cove* progeny, we must conclude that the Act's business necessity language incorporates this standard.

Lanning I, 181 F.3d at 489. Thus, what you learned about business necessity from reading *Griggs* seems largely applicable.

But if the *Lanning I* approach to the proper standard is simply a return to *Griggs*, the application of that standard generated greater difficulties. The aerobic test at issue was "job related" in the sense that everyone who passed it will be fit, at least aerobically, for the job. It might not be "job related" if that term means that those who fail the test are not fit to be police officers. The majority in *Lanning I* believed that the aerobic test must measure only the *minimum* qualifications necessary for the job. What is wrong with the "more is better" approach? Is it that more may be *better* for business but not *necessary*? Since SEPTA did not require aerobic fitness of current employees, although it did encourage such fitness, how could the specified aerobic level be "necessary"?

Lanning I, thus, took a very stringent approach to business necessity and seemed to presage a victory for plaintiffs. However, the court remanded, and on remand the district court found that the test satisfied the Third Circuit's requirements. In *Lanning II*, 308 F.3d 286 (3d Cir. 2002), the court of appeals affirmed:

> SEPTA argued that the run test measures the "minimum qualifications necessary" because the relevant studies indicate that individuals who fail the test will be much less likely to successfully execute critical policing tasks. For example, the District Court credited a study that evaluated the correlation between a successful run time and performance on 12 job standards. The study found that individuals who passed the run test had a success rate on the job standards ranging from 70% to 90%. The success rate of the individuals who failed the run test ranged from 5% to 20%. The District Court found that such a low rate of success was unacceptable for employees who are regularly called upon to protect the public. In so doing, the District Court implicitly defined "minimum qualifications necessary" as meaning "likely to be able to do the job."
>
> Plaintiffs argued, however, that within the group that failed the run test, significant numbers of individuals would still be able to perform at least certain critical job tasks. They argued that as long as some of those failing the run test can do the job, the standard cannot be classified as a "minimum." In essence, plaintiffs proposed that the phrase "minimum qualifications necessary" means "some chance of being able to do the job." Under this logic, even if those failing the test had a 1% chance of successfully completing critical job tasks, the test would be too stringent.
>
> We are not saying, as our distinguished brother in dissent suggests we are saying, that "more is better." While, of course, a higher aerobic capacity will translate into better field performance — at least as to many job tasks which entail physical capability — to set an unnecessarily high cutoff score would contravene *Griggs*. It would clearly be unreasonable to require SEPTA applicants to score so highly on the run test that their predicted rate of success be 100%. It is perfectly reasonable, however, to demand a chance of success that is better than 5% to 20%. . . .
>
> [W]e reject without more the argument that applicants — male and female — should not be tested until they have graduated from the police academy, perhaps two and one-half years after they first applied to SEPTA; indeed, the dissent recognizes but relegates to a footnote the increase in SEPTA's costs and the uncertainty in planning and recruitment this would occasion. [And] all incumbents — male and female — are now required to take a physical fitness test every six months, another step toward improving the workforce. In this connection, it bears mention that SEPTA is unable to discipline incumbents who do not pass the test only because of the patrol officers' union's challenge, sustained by an arbitrator. With the union's blessing, however, SEPTA offers financial incentives to those officers who do pass.
>
> One final note. While it is undisputed that SEPTA's 1.5 mile run test has a disparate impact on women, it is also undisputed that, in addition to those women who could pass the test without training, nearly all the women who trained were able to pass after only a

moderate amount of training. It is not, we think, unreasonable to expect that women — and men — who wish to become SEPTA transit officers, and are committed to dealing with issues of public safety on a day-to-day basis, would take this necessary step.

Lanning II, 308 F.3d at 291-93. Are you convinced that it is a "business necessity" to require only recruits to be fit? Is the last paragraph the real basis for the result, that the impact could easily have been avoided by the female candidates? If so, how does that fit into the statutory analysis?

PROBLEM

9-3.   Rath Packing had a rule prohibiting the employment of spouses of current employees. The plaintiff has succeeded in establishing that the no-spouse rule has a disparate impact on the employment of women. Rath asserts that the rule is necessary to promote optimum production and employee performance because spousal relationships in the workplace create problems of efficiency, productivity, and ease of management. It says that its no-spouse rule resulted from past problems that occurred when married couples worked at Rath. These included dual absenteeism, vacation scheduling, supervision, and pressure to hire spouses. However, during a three-year period for which information on absenteeism is available, employees with spouses working at Rath exhibited a lower absentee rate than did those without spouses working there. Rath was able to point to one incident of habitual dual absenteeism, which was perceived by Rath management as having a significant disruptive effect on plant operations. *See EEOC v. Rath Packing Co.*, 787 F.2d 318 (8th Cir. 1986).

Is Rath's policy legal?

---

c.   Alternative Employment Practices

The Civil Rights Act of 1991 permits a plaintiff to prevail by showing a particular employment practice with a disparate impact if the employer fails to establish job relation and business necessity. But a disparate impact violation also exists when, despite the employer's successful proof of job relation and business necessity, the plaintiff shows that there exists an alternative employment practice "and the [employer] refuses to adopt such alternative employment practice." §703(k)(1)(A).

However, proving an "alternative employment practice" may not be easy and there is no case law holding an employer liable under this alternative path and little explaining it in any detail. *See IBEW v. Miss. Power & Light Co*, 442 F.3d 313 (5th Cir. 2006) (noting plaintiffs did not offer meaningful alternative); *Allen v. City of Chicago*, 351 F.3d 306 (7th Cir. 2003) (plaintiffs did not prove that merit promotions alone were an effective alternative).

Among unanswered questions is whether the alternative practice need be non-discriminatory or merely less discriminatory in effect. A second question is whether this path to liability exists when the alternative devices are effective, but not *equally* effective, or more costly. Under the statute, a successful alternative selection practice claim also requires that the employer "refuse" to adopt the alternative practice. Does the plaintiff have the burden of proving that the employer refused? "Refuse" seems to mean more than mere failure to use the alternative practice. Would proof that the employer knew of the existence of the practice and failed to adopt it suffice? What if an employee proposed an alternative practice by placing it in the employer's suggestion box? What if the alternative practice is offered during discovery or at trial and the employer fails or "refuses" to adopt it?

d. Another Defense

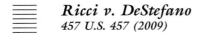

Ricci v. DeStefano
457 U.S. 457 (2009)

Justice KENNEDY delivered the opinion of the Court.

. . . In 2003, 118 New Haven firefighters took examinations to qualify for promotion to the rank of lieutenant or captain. Promotion examinations in New Haven (or City) were infrequent, so the stakes were high. The results would determine which firefighters would be considered for promotions during the next two years, and the order in which they would be considered. Many firefighters studied for months, at considerable personal and financial cost.

When the examination results showed that white candidates had outperformed minority candidates, the mayor and other local politicians opened a public debate that turned rancorous. Some firefighters argued the tests should be discarded because the results showed the tests to be discriminatory. They threatened a discrimination lawsuit if the City made promotions based on the tests. Other firefighters said the exams were neutral and fair. And they, in turn, threatened a discrimination lawsuit if the City, relying on the statistical racial disparity, ignored the test results and denied promotions to the candidates who had performed well. In the end the City took the side of those who protested the test results. It threw out the examinations.

Certain white and Hispanic firefighters who likely would have been promoted based on their good test performance sued the City and some of its officials. Theirs is the suit now before us. The suit alleges that, by discarding the test results, the City and the named officials discriminated against the plaintiffs based on their race, in violation of both Title VII and the Equal Protection Clause of the Fourteenth Amendment. The City and the officials defended their actions, arguing that if they had certified the results, they could have faced liability under Title VII for adopting a practice that had a disparate impact on the minority firefighters. The District Court granted summary judgment for the defendants, and the Court of Appeals affirmed.

We conclude that race-based action like the City's in this case is impermissible under Title VII unless the employer can demonstrate a strong basis in evidence that, had it not taken the action, it would have been liable under the disparate-impact statute. The respondents, we further determine, cannot meet that threshold standard. As a result, the City's action in discarding the tests was a violation of Title VII. In light of our ruling under the statutes, we need not reach the question whether respondents' actions may have violated the Equal Protection Clause.

I . . .

A . . .

[The City's promotion process was governed by its charter, which included a civil service merit system as determined by job-related tests, as well as by a collective bargaining agreement with the firefighters' union and state and federal law. The charter imposed a "rule of three" — whoever was promoted had to be among the top three scorers. The CBA with the union required that, for promotion eligibility, a written examination would account for 60% and an oral examination 40% of each applicant's total score.]

After reviewing bids from various consultants, the City hired Industrial/Organizational Solutions, Inc. (IOS) to develop and administer the examinations, at a cost to the City of $100,000. IOS is an Illinois company that specializes in designing entry-level and promotional examinations for fire and police departments. In order to fit the examinations to the New Haven Department, IOS began the test-design process by performing job analyses to identify the tasks, knowledge, skills, and abilities that are essential for the lieutenant and captain positions. IOS representatives interviewed incumbent captains and lieutenants and their supervisors. They rode with and observed other on-duty officers. Using information from those interviews and ride-alongs, IOS wrote job-analysis questionnaires and administered them to most of the incumbent battalion chiefs, captains, and lieutenants in the Department. At every stage of the job analyses, IOS, by deliberate choice, oversampled minority firefighters to ensure that the results — which IOS would use to develop the examinations — would not unintentionally favor white candidates.

With the job-analysis information in hand, IOS developed the written examinations to measure the candidates' job-related knowledge. For each test, IOS compiled a list of training manuals, Department procedures, and other materials to use as sources for the test questions. IOS presented the proposed sources to the New Haven fire chief and assistant fire chief for their approval. Then, using the approved sources, IOS drafted a multiple-choice test for each position. Each test had 100 questions, as required by CSB rules, and was written below a 10th-grade reading level. After IOS prepared the tests, the City opened a 3-month study period. It gave candidates a list that identified the source material for the questions, including the specific chapters from which the questions were taken.

IOS developed the oral examinations as well. These concentrated on job skills and abilities. Using the job-analysis information, IOS wrote hypothetical situations to test incident-command skills, firefighting tactics, interpersonal skills, leadership, and management ability, among other things. Candidates would be presented with these hypotheticals and asked to respond before a panel of three assessors.

IOS assembled a pool of 30 assessors who were superior in rank to the positions being tested. At the City's insistence (because of controversy surrounding previous examinations), all the assessors came from outside Connecticut. IOS submitted the assessors' resumes to City officials for approval. They were battalion chiefs, assistant chiefs, and chiefs from departments of similar sizes to New Haven's throughout the country. Sixty-six percent of the panelists were minorities, and each of the nine three-member assessment panels contained two minority members. IOS trained the panelists for several hours on the day before it administered the examinations, teaching them how to score the candidates' responses consistently using checklists of desired criteria.

Candidates took the examinations in November and December 2003. Seventy-seven candidates completed the lieutenant examination — 43 whites, 19 blacks, and 15 Hispanics. Of those, 34 candidates passed — 25 whites, 6 blacks, and 3 Hispanics. Eight lieutenant positions were vacant at the time of the examination. As the rule of three operated, this meant that the top 10 candidates were eligible for an immediate promotion to lieutenant. All 10 were white. Subsequent vacancies would have allowed at least 3 black candidates to be considered for promotion to lieutenant.

Forty-one candidates completed the captain examination — 25 whites, 8 blacks, and 8 Hispanics. Of those, 22 candidates passed — 16 whites, 3 blacks, and 3 Hispanics. Seven captain positions were vacant at the time of the examination. Under the rule of three, 9 candidates were eligible for an immediate promotion to captain — 7 whites and 2 Hispanics.

B

[Although the City's contract with IOS contemplated "a technical report" by IOS after the examinations, City officials, including its counsel, Thomas Ude, met in early 2004 with IOS Vice President Chad Legel, who had led the IOS team that developed and administered the tests. They] expressed concern that the tests had discriminated against minority candidates. Legel defended the examinations' validity, stating that any numerical disparity between white and minority candidates was likely due to various external factors and was in line with results of the Department's previous promotional examinations.

Several days after the meeting, Ude sent a letter to the CSB [New Haven Civil Service Board] purporting to outline its duties with respect to the examination results. Ude stated that under federal law, "a statistical demonstration of disparate impact," standing alone, "constitutes a sufficiently serious claim of racial discrimination to serve as a predicate for employer-initiated, voluntar[y] remedies-even . . . race-conscious remedies."

1

The CSB first met to consider certifying the results on January 22, 2004. Tina Burgett, director of the City's Department of Human Resources, opened the meeting by telling the CSB that "there is a significant disparate impact on these two exams." She distributed lists showing the candidates' races and scores (written, oral, and composite) but not their names. Ude also described the test results as reflecting "a very significant disparate impact," and he outlined possible grounds for the CSB's refusing to certify the results.

Although they did not know whether they had passed or failed, some firefighter-candidates spoke at the first CSB meeting in favor of certifying the test results. Michael Blatchley stated that "[e]very one" of the questions on the written examination "came from the [study] material. . . . [I]f you read the materials and you studied the material, you would have done well on the test." Frank Ricci stated that the test questions were based on the Department's own rules and procedures and on "nationally recognized" materials that represented the "accepted standard[s]" for firefighting. Ricci stated that he had "several learning disabilities," including dyslexia; that he had spent more than $1,000 to purchase the materials and pay his neighbor to read them on tape so he could "give it [his] best shot"; and that he had studied "8 to 13 hours a day to prepare" for the test. "I don't even know if I made it," Ricci told the CSB, "[b]ut the people who passed should be promoted. When your life's on the line, second best may not be good enough."

Other firefighters spoke against certifying the test results. They described the test questions as outdated or not relevant to firefighting practices in New Haven. Gary Tinney stated that source materials "came out of New York. . . . Their makeup of their city and everything is totally different than ours." And they criticized the test materials, a full set of which cost about $500, for being too expensive and too long.

[There was a second CSB meeting on February 5, at which both proponents and opponents of the test appeared. Some asked for a validation study to determine whether the tests were job-related, while others suggested that "the City could 'adjust' the test results to 'meet the criteria of having a certain amount of minorities get elevated to the rank of Lieutenant and Captain.'"]

3

At a third meeting, on February 11, Legel addressed the CSB on behalf of IOS. Legel stated that IOS had previously prepared entry-level firefighter examinations for the City but not a promotional examination. He explained that IOS had developed examinations for departments in communities with demographics similar to New Haven's, including Orange County, Florida; Lansing, Michigan; and San Jose, California.

Legel explained the exam-development process to the CSB. . . . Near the end of his remarks, Legel "implor[ed] anyone that had . . . concerns to review the content of the exam. In my professional opinion, it's facially neutral. There's nothing in those examinations . . . that should cause somebody to think that one group would perform differently than another group."

4

At the next meeting, on March 11, the CSB heard from three witnesses it had selected to "tell us a little bit about their views of the testing, the process, [and] the methodology." The first, Christopher Hornick, spoke to the CSB by telephone. Hornick is an industrial/organizational psychologist from Texas who operates a consulting business that "direct[ly]" competes with IOS. Hornick, who had not "stud[ied] the test at length or in detail" and had not "seen the job analysis data," told the CSB that the scores indicated a "relatively high adverse impact." He stated that "[n]ormally, whites outperform ethnic minorities on the majority of standardized testing procedures," but that he was "a little surprised" by the disparity in the candidates' scores — although "[s]ome of it is fairly typical of what we've seen in other areas of the countr[y] and other tests." Hornick stated that the "adverse impact on the written exam was somewhat higher but generally in the range that we've seen professionally."

When asked to explain the New Haven test results, Hornick opined in the telephone conversation that the collective-bargaining agreement's requirement of using written and oral examinations with a 60/40 composite score might account for the statistical disparity. He also stated that "[b]y not having anyone from within the [D]epartment review" the tests before they were administered—a limitation the City had imposed to protect the security of the exam questions—"you inevitably get things in there" that are based on the source materials but are not relevant to New Haven. Hornick suggested that testing candidates at an "assessment center" rather than using written and oral examinations "might serve [the City's] needs better." Hornick stated that assessment centers, where candidates face real-world situations and respond just as they would in the field, allow candidates "to demonstrate how they would address a particular problem as opposed to just verbally saying it or identifying the correct option on a written test."

Hornick made clear that he was "not suggesting that [IOS] somehow created a test that had adverse impacts that it should not have had." He described the IOS examinations as "reasonably good test[s]." He stated that the CSB's best option might be to "certify the list as it exists" and work to change the process for future tests, including by "[r]ewriting the Civil Service Rules." Hornick concluded his telephonic remarks by telling the CSB that "for the future," his company "certainly would like to help you if we can."

[The Court then described at length further proceedings, including (1) statements by a Homeland Security fire program specialist who viewed the questions as job-relevant, and (2) statements by a Boston College professor specializing in "race and culture as they influence performance on tests," who had not reviewed the tests themselves but viewed the racial impact as consistent with results across the country. The City's counsel argued against the tests, claiming that they "had one of the most severe adverse impacts that he had seen" and that "there are much better alternatives to identifying [firefighting] skills." He offered his "opinion that promotions . . . as a result of these tests would not be consistent with federal law." The mayor's representative took a similar tack. Ultimately, the CSB voted 2 to 2 on the use of the test results, which meant that the results would not be certified.]

II . . .

A . . .

As enacted in 1964, Title VII's principal nondiscrimination provision held employers liable only for disparate treatment. That section retains its original wording today. It makes it unlawful for an employer "to fail or refuse to hire or to discharge any individual, or otherwise to discriminate against any individual with respect to his compensation, terms, conditions, or privileges of employment, because of such individual's race, color, religion, sex, or national origin." §2000e-2(a)(1). Disparate-treatment cases present "the most easily understood type of discrimination," *Teamsters* v. *United States,* and occur where an employer has "treated [a] particular person less favorably than others because of" a protected trait. *Watson* v. *Fort Worth Bank & Trust.* A disparate-treatment plaintiff must establish "that the defendant had a discriminatory intent or motive" for taking a job-related action.

The Civil Rights Act of 1964 did not include an express prohibition on policies or practices that produce a disparate impact. But in *Griggs v. Duke Power Co.*, the Court interpreted the Act to prohibit, in some cases, employers' facially neutral practices that, in fact, are "discriminatory in operation." The *Griggs* Court stated that the "touchstone" for disparate-impact liability is the lack of "business necessity": "If an employment practice which operates to exclude [minorities] cannot be shown to be related to job performance, the practice is prohibited." Under [*Griggs* and its progeny], if an employer met its burden by showing that its practice was job-related, the plaintiff was required to show a legitimate alternative that would have resulted in less discrimination.

Twenty years after *Griggs*, the Civil Rights Act of 1991 was enacted. The Act included a provision codifying the prohibition on disparate-impact discrimination. That provision is now in force along with the disparate-treatment section already noted. Under the disparate-impact statute, a plaintiff establishes a prima facie violation by showing that an employer uses "a particular employment practice that causes a disparate impact on the basis of race, color, religion, sex, or national origin." An employer may defend against liability by demonstrating that the practice is "job related for the position in question and consistent with business necessity." Even if the employer meets that burden, however, a plaintiff may still succeed by showing that the employer refuses to adopt an available alternative employment practice that has less disparate impact and serves the employer's legitimate needs.

B

Petitioners allege that when the CSB refused to certify the captain and lieutenant exam results based on the race of the successful candidates, it discriminated against them in violation of Title VII's disparate-treatment provision. The City counters that its decision was permissible because the tests "appear[ed] to violate Title VII's disparate-impact provisions."

Our analysis begins with this premise: The City's actions would violate the disparate-treatment prohibition of Title VII absent some valid defense. All the evidence demonstrates that the City chose not to certify the examination results because of the statistical disparity based on race — *i.e.*, how minority candidates had performed when compared to white candidates. As the District Court put it, the City rejected the test results because "too many whites and not enough minorities would be promoted were the lists to be certified." Without some other justification, this express, race-based decisionmaking violates Title VII's command that employers cannot take adverse employment actions because of an individual's race.

The District Court did not adhere to this principle, however. It held that respondents' "motivation to avoid making promotions based on a test with a racially disparate impact . . . does not, as a matter of law, constitute discriminatory intent." And the Government makes a similar argument in this Court. It contends that the "structure of Title VII belies any claim that an employer's intent to comply with Title VII's disparate-impact provisions constitutes prohibited discrimination on the basis of race." But both of those statements turn upon the City's objective — avoiding disparate-impact liability — while ignoring the City's conduct in the name of reaching that objective. Whatever the City's ultimate aim — however well intentioned or benevolent it might have seemed — the City made its employment decision because of race. The City rejected the test results solely because the higher scoring candidates were white. The question is not whether that conduct was discriminatory but whether the City had a lawful justification for its race-based action.

We consider, therefore, whether the purpose to avoid disparate-impact liability excuses what otherwise would be prohibited disparate-treatment discrimination. Courts often confront cases in which statutes and principles point in different directions. Our task is to provide guidance to employers and courts for situations when these two prohibitions could be in conflict absent a rule to reconcile them. In providing this guidance our decision must be consistent with the important purpose of Title VII — that the workplace be an environment free of discrimination, where race is not a barrier to opportunity.

With these principles in mind, we turn to the parties' proposed means of reconciling the statutory provisions. . . . Petitioners would have us hold that, under Title VII, avoiding unintentional discrimination cannot justify intentional discrimination. That assertion, however, ignores the fact that, by codifying the disparate-impact provision in 1991, Congress has expressly prohibited both types of discrimination. We must interpret the statute to give effect to both provisions where possible. We cannot accept petitioners' broad and inflexible formulation.

Petitioners next suggest that an employer in fact must be in violation of the disparate-impact provision before it can use compliance as a defense in a disparate-treatment suit. Again, this is overly simplistic and too restrictive of Title VII's purpose. The rule petitioners offer would run counter to what we have recognized as Congress's intent that "voluntary compliance" be "the preferred means of achieving the objectives of Title VII." *Firefighters v. Cleveland*, 478 U. S. 501, 515 (1986); *see also Wygant v. Jackson Bd. of Ed.*, 476 U. S. 267, 290 (1986) (O'Connor, J., concurring in part and concurring in judgment). Forbidding employers to act unless they know, with certainty, that a practice violates the disparate-impact provision would bring compliance efforts to a near standstill. Even in the limited situations when this restricted standard could be met, employers likely would hesitate before taking voluntary action for fear of later being proven wrong in the course of litigation and then held to account for disparate treatment.

At the opposite end of the spectrum, respondents and the Government assert that an employer's good-faith belief that its actions are necessary to comply with Title VII's disparate-impact provision should be enough to justify race-conscious conduct. But the original, foundational prohibition of Title VII bars employers from taking adverse action "because of . . . race." §2000e-2(a)(1). And when Congress codified the disparate-impact provision in 1991, it made no exception to disparate-treatment liability for actions taken in a good-faith effort to comply with the new, disparate-impact provision in subsection (k). Allowing employers to violate the disparate-treatment prohibition based on a mere good-faith fear of disparate-impact liability would encourage race-based action at the slightest hint of disparate impact. A minimal standard could cause employers to discard the results of lawful and beneficial promotional examinations even where there is little if any evidence of disparate-impact discrimination. That would amount to a *de facto* quota system, in which a "focus on statistics . . . could put undue pressure on employers to adopt inappropriate prophylactic measures." *Watson*. Even worse, an employer could discard test results (or other employment practices) with the intent of obtaining the employer's preferred racial balance. That operational principle could not be justified, for Title VII is express in disclaiming any interpretation of its requirements as calling for outright racial balancing. § 2000e-2(j). The purpose of Title VII "is to promote hiring on the basis of job qualifications, rather than on the basis of race or color." *Griggs.*

In searching for a standard that strikes a more appropriate balance, we note that this Court has considered cases similar to this one, albeit in the context of the Equal Protection Clause of the Fourteenth Amendment. The Court has held that certain government actions to remedy past racial discrimination — actions that are themselves based on race — are constitutional only where there is a "'strong basis in evidence'" that the remedial actions were necessary. *Richmond v. J. A. Croson Co.*, 488 U.S. 469, 500 (1989). This suit does not call on us to consider whether the statutory constraints under Title VII must be parallel in all respects to those under the Constitution. That does not mean the constitutional authorities are irrelevant, however. Our cases discussing constitutional principles can provide helpful guidance in this statutory context. . . .

The same interests [as operated in *Wygant* and *Croson*] are at work in the interplay between the disparate-treatment and disparate-impact provisions of Title VII. Congress has imposed liability on employers for unintentional discrimination in order to rid the workplace of "practices that are fair in form, but discriminatory in operation." *Griggs.* But it has also prohibited employers from taking adverse employment actions "because of" race. Applying the strong-basis-in-evidence standard to Title VII gives effect to both the disparate-treatment and disparate-impact provisions, allowing violations of one in the name of compliance with the other only in certain, narrow circumstances. The standard leaves ample room for employers' voluntary compliance efforts, which are essential to the statutory scheme and to Congress's efforts to eradicate workplace discrimination. And the standard appropriately constrains employers' discretion in making race-based decisions: It limits that discretion to cases in which there is a strong basis in evidence of disparate-impact liability, but it is not so restrictive that it allows employers to act only when there is a provable, actual violation.

Resolving the statutory conflict in this way allows the disparate-impact prohibition to work in a manner that is consistent with other provisions of Title VII, including the prohibition on adjusting employment-related test scores on the basis of race. *See* § 2000e-2(*l*). Examinations like those administered by the City create legitimate expectations on the part of those who took the tests. As is the case with any promotion exam, some of the firefighters here invested substantial time, money, and personal commitment in preparing for the tests. Employment tests can be an important part of a neutral selection system that safeguards against the very racial animosities Title VII was intended to prevent. Here, however, the firefighters saw their efforts invalidated by the City in sole reliance upon race-based statistics.

If an employer cannot rescore a test based on the candidates' race, § 2000e-2(*l*), then it follows *a fortiori* that it may not take the greater step of discarding the test altogether to achieve a more desirable racial distribution of promotion-eligible candidates — absent a strong basis in evidence that the test was deficient and that discarding the results is necessary to avoid violating the disparate-impact provision. Restricting an employer's ability to discard test results (and thereby discriminate against qualified candidates on the basis of their race) also is in keeping with Title VII's express protection of bona fide promotional examinations. *See* § 2000e-2(h) ("[N]or shall it be an unlawful employment practice for an employer to give and to act upon the results of any professionally developed ability test provided that such test, its administration or action upon the results is not designed, intended or used to discriminate because of race"); *cf. AT&T Corp. v. Hulteen*, 556 U.S. 701 (2009).

For the foregoing reasons, we adopt the strong-basis-in-evidence standard as a matter of statutory construction to resolve any conflict between the disparate-treatment and disparate-impact provisions of Title VII.

Our statutory holding does not address the constitutionality of the measures taken here in purported compliance with Title VII. We also do not hold that meeting the strong-basis-in-evidence standard would satisfy the Equal Protection Clause in a future case. As we explain below, because respondents have not met their burden under Title VII, we need not decide whether a legitimate fear of disparate impact is ever sufficient to justify discriminatory treatment under the Constitution.

Nor do we question an employer's affirmative efforts to ensure that all groups have a fair opportunity to apply for promotions and to participate in the process by which promotions will be made. But once that process has been established and employers have made clear their selection criteria, they may not then invalidate the test results, thus upsetting an employee's legitimate expectation not to be judged on the basis of race. Doing so, absent a strong basis in evidence of an impermissible disparate impact, amounts to the sort of racial preference that Congress has disclaimed, § 2000e-2(j), and is antithetical to the notion of a workplace where individuals are guaranteed equal opportunity regardless of race.

Title VII does not prohibit an employer from considering, before administering a test or practice, how to design that test or practice in order to provide a fair opportunity for all individuals, regardless of their race. And when, during the test-design stage, an employer invites comments to ensure the test is fair, that process can provide a common ground for open discussions toward that end. We hold only that, under Title VII, before an employer can engage in intentional discrimination for the asserted purpose of avoiding or remedying an unintentional disparate impact, the employer must have a strong basis in evidence to believe it will be subject to disparate-impact liability if it fails to take the race-conscious, discriminatory action.

C

The City argues that, even under the strong-basis-in-evidence standard, its decision to discard the examination results was permissible under Title VII. That is incorrect. Even if respondents were motivated as a subjective matter by a desire to avoid committing disparate-impact discrimination, the record makes clear there is no support for the conclusion that respondents had an objective, strong basis in evidence to find the tests inadequate, with some consequent disparate-impact liability in violation of Title VII.

On this basis, we conclude that petitioners have met their obligation to demonstrate that there is "no genuine issue as to any material fact" and that they are "entitled to judgment as a matter of law." Fed. Rule Civ. Proc. 56(c). . . .

[The majority agreed with the City that the adverse racial impact here was significant, which required it "to take a hard look at the examinations to determine whether certifying the results would have had an impermissible disparate impact." But] a prima facie case of disparate-impact liability — essentially, a threshold showing of a significant statistical disparity, *Connecticut v. Teal*, and nothing more — is far from a strong basis in evidence that the City would have been liable under Title VII had it certified the results. That is because the City could be liable for disparate-impact discrimination only if the examinations were not job related and consistent with business necessity, or if there existed an equally valid, less-discriminatory alternative that served the City's needs but that the City refused to adopt. We conclude there is no strong basis in evidence to establish that the test was deficient in either of these respects. . . .

1

There is no genuine dispute that the examinations were job-related and consistent with business necessity. The City's assertions to the contrary are "blatantly contradicted by the record" [including the statements of Chad Legel and city officials outlining the detailed steps taken to develop and administer the examinations. The only outside witness who reviewed the examinations in any detail was the only one with any firefighting experience, and he stated that the "questions were relevant for both exams."].

2

Respondents also lacked a strong basis in evidence of an equally valid, less-discriminatory testing alternative that the City, by certifying the examination results, would necessarily have refused to adopt. Respondents raise three arguments to the contrary, but each argument fails. First, respondents refer to testimony before the CSB that a different composite-score calculation — weighting the written and oral examination scores 30/70 — would have allowed the City to consider two black candidates for then-open lieutenant positions and one black candidate for then-open captain positions. (The City used a 60/40 weighting as required by its contract with the New Haven firefighters' union.) But respondents have produced no evidence to show that the 60/40 weighting was indeed arbitrary. In fact, because that formula was the result of a union-negotiated collective-bargaining agreement, we presume the parties negotiated that weighting for a rational reason. Nor does the record contain any evidence that the 30/70 weighting would be an equally valid way to determine whether candidates possess the proper mix of job knowledge and situational skills to earn promotions. Changing the weighting formula, moreover, could well have violated Title VII's prohibition of altering test scores on the basis of race. *See* § 2000e-2(*l*). On this record, there is no basis to conclude that a 30/70 weighting was an equally valid alternative the City could have adopted.

Second, respondents argue that the City could have adopted a different interpretation of the "rule of three" [such as "banding, which is "rounding scores to the nearest whole number and considering all candidates with the same whole-number score as being of one rank." However, had] the City reviewed the exam results and then adopted banding to make the minority test scores appear higher, it would have violated Title VII's prohibition of adjusting test results on the basis of race. § 2000e-2(*l*); *see also Chicago Firefighters Local 2 v. Chicago*, 249 F. 3d 649, 656 (CA7 2001) (Posner, J.) ("We have no doubt that if banding were adopted in order to make lower black scores seem higher, it would indeed be . . . forbidden").

As a matter of law, banding was not an alternative available to the City when it was considering whether to certify the examination results.

Third, and finally, respondents refer to statements by Hornick in his telephone interview with the CSB regarding alternatives to the written examinations. Hornick stated his "belie[f]" that an "assessment center process," which would have evaluated candidates' behavior in typical job tasks, "would have demonstrated less adverse impact." But Hornick's brief mention of alternative testing methods, standing alone, does not raise a genuine issue of material fact that assessment centers were available to the City at the time of the examinations and that they would have produced less adverse impact. . . .

3

On the record before us, there is no genuine dispute that the City lacked a strong basis in evidence to believe it would face disparate-impact liability if it certified the examination results. In other words, there is no evidence — let alone the required strong basis in evidence — that the tests were flawed because they were not job-related or because other, equally valid and less discriminatory tests were available to the City. Fear of litigation alone cannot justify an employer's reliance on race to the detriment of individuals who passed the examinations and qualified for promotions. The City's discarding the test results was impermissible under Title VII, and summary judgment is appropriate for petitioners on their disparate-treatment claim.

* * *

The record in this litigation documents a process that, at the outset, had the potential to produce a testing procedure that was true to the promise of Title VII: No individual should face workplace discrimination based on race. Respondents thought about promotion qualifications and relevant experience in neutral ways. They were careful to ensure broad racial participation in the design of the test itself and its administration. As we have discussed at length, the process was open and fair.

The problem, of course, is that after the tests were completed, the raw racial results became the predominant rationale for the City's refusal to certify the results. The injury arises in part from the high, and justified, expectations of the candidates who had participated in the testing process on the terms the City had established for the promotional process. Many of the candidates had studied for months, at considerable personal and financial expense, and thus the injury caused by the City's reliance on raw racial statistics at the end of the process was all the more severe. Confronted with arguments both for and against certifying the test results — and threats of a lawsuit either way — the City was required to make a difficult inquiry. But its hearings produced no strong evidence of a disparate-impact violation, and the City was not entitled to disregard the tests based solely on the racial disparity in the results.

Our holding today clarifies how Title VII applies to resolve competing expectations under the disparate-treatment and disparate-impact provisions. If, after it certifies the test results, the City faces a disparate-impact suit, then in light of our holding today it should be clear that the City would avoid disparate-impact liability based on the strong basis in evidence that, had it not certified the results, it would have been subject to disparate-treatment liability. . . .

Justice SCALIA, concurring.

I join the Court's opinion in full, but write separately to observe that its resolution of this dispute merely postpones the evil day on which the Court will have to confront the question: Whether, or to what extent, are the disparate-impact provisions of Title VII of the Civil Rights Act of 1964 consistent with the Constitution's guarantee of equal protection? The question is not an easy one. *See generally* Primus, *Equal Protection and Disparate Impact: Round Three*, 117 HARV. L. REV. 493 (2003).

The difficulty is this: Whether or not Title VII's disparate-treatment provisions forbid "remedial" race-based actions when a disparate-impact violation would *not* otherwise result — the question resolved by the Court today — it is clear that Title VII not only permits but affirmatively *requires* such actions when a disparate-impact violation *would* otherwise result. But if the Federal Government is prohibited from discriminating on the basis of race, *Bolling v. Sharpe*, 347 U. S. 497, 500 (1954), then surely it is also prohibited from enacting laws mandating that third parties — *e.g.*, employers, whether private, State, or municipal — discriminate on the basis of race. As the facts of these cases illustrate, Title VII's disparate-impact provisions place a racial thumb on the scales, often requiring employers to evaluate the racial outcomes of their policies, and to make decisions based on (because of) those racial outcomes. That type of racial decisionmaking is, as the Court explains, discriminatory. . . .

The Court's resolution of these cases makes it unnecessary to resolve these matters today. But the war between disparate impact and equal protection will be waged sooner or later, and it behooves us to begin thinking about how — and on what terms — to make peace between them.

Justice ALITO, with whom Justice SCALIA and Justice THOMAS join, concurring.

[The concurrence "join[ed] the Court's opinion in full" but wrote separately to correct important omissions in Justice GINSBURG's dissent. The major thrust of the concurrence was that, even were the Court to accept the dissent's "good cause" standard, resolving the case required a trial as to whether the avoidance of disparate impact liability was a pretext because there was a genuine issue of material fact, even under that lower standard, whether "the City's real reason was illegitimate, namely, the desire to placate a politically important racial constituency."]

Justice GINSBURG, with whom Justice STEVENS, Justice SOUTER, and Justice BREYER join, dissenting.

[The dissent started with the observation that, when Title VII was applied to public employment in 1972 "municipal fire departments across the country, including New Haven's, pervasively discriminated against minorities." She noted that in the early 1970's, "African-Americans and Hispanics composed 30 percent of New Haven's population, but only 3.6 percent of the City's 502 firefighters. The racial disparity in the officer ranks was even more pronounced: '[O]f the 107 officers in the Department only one was black, and he held the lowest rank above private.'" While some progress had been made, "[b]y order of this Court, New Haven, a city in which African-Americans and Hispanics account for nearly 60 percent of the population, must today be served — as it was in the days of undisguised discrimination — by a fire department in which members of racial and ethnic minorities are rarely seen in command positions." . . .]

Neither Congress' enactments nor this Court's Title VII precedents (including the now-discredited decision in *Wards Cove*) offer even a hint of "conflict" between an employer's obligations under the statute's disparate-treatment and disparate-impact provisions. Standing on an equal footing, these twin pillars of Title VII advance the same objectives: ending workplace discrimination and promoting genuinely equal opportunity. *See McDonnell Douglas Corp. v. Green.*

Yet the Court today sets at odds the statute's core directives. When an employer changes an employment practice in an effort to comply with Title VII's disparate-impact provision, the Court reasons, it acts "because of race"—something Title VII's disparate-treatment provision generally forbids. This characterization of an employer's compliance-directed action shows little attention to Congress' design or to the *Griggs* line of cases Congress recognized as pathmarking. . . . [Because a court is bound to read the provisions of any statute as harmonious] Title VII's disparate-treatment and disparate-impact proscriptions must be read as complementary.

In codifying the *Griggs* and *Albemarle* instructions, Congress declared unambiguously that selection criteria operating to the disadvantage of minority group members can be retained only if justified by business necessity. In keeping with Congress' design, employers who reject such criteria due to reasonable doubts about their reliability can hardly be held to have engaged in discrimination "because of" race. A reasonable endeavor to comply with the law and to ensure that qualified candidates of all races have a fair opportunity to compete is simply not what Congress meant to interdict. I would therefore hold that an employer who jettisons a selection device when its disproportionate racial impact becomes apparent does not violate Title VII's disparate-treatment bar automatically or at all, subject to this key condition: The employer must have good cause to believe the device would not withstand examination for business necessity. *Cf. Faragher v. Boca Raton*, 524 U. S. 775, 806 (1998) (observing that it accords with "clear statutory policy" for employers "to prevent violations" and "make reasonable efforts to discharge their duty" under Title VII). . . .

This litigation does not involve affirmative action. But if the voluntary affirmative action at issue in *Johnson* [*v. Transportation Agency, Santa Clara Cty.*] does not discriminate within the meaning of Title VII, neither does an employer's reasonable effort to comply with Title VII's disparate-impact provision by refraining from action of doubtful consistency with business necessity. . . .

NOTES

1. *Putting It All Together or Tearing It All Apart?* If you want an opportunity to think about big concepts spread across this entire chapter, *Ricci* has it all: systemic disparate treatment, disparate impact, testing, and affirmative action from a statutory or constitutional perspective. What more could a professor (or student) ask for? The other perspective on *Ricci*, however, is that it tears apart quite a lot of what you've learned to this point. Indeed, there are those who think that it is the end of disparate impact liability. That may be an overstatement, but *Ricci* is at least a sea change that will reverberate in a variety of ways.

2. *The Holding.* The majority was clear: Defendants' decision to not use test results because their use would have meant no promotions for African Americans and only two for Hispanics, who together made up over half of the test takers, was intentional disparate treatment discrimination against the white test takers who would have been promoted had the test been certified. That the test results amounted to a prima facie case of disparate impact discrimination was not a defense to a disparate treatment case unless the employer also had a strong basis in evidence to believe that it would be liable for disparate impact discrimination, which means that it would have no business necessity/job relation defense and that there is no viable alternative employment practice.

What exactly is a "strong basis"? *United States v. Brennan*, 650 F.3d 65, 109-10 (2d Cir. 2011), tried to explain:

> [W]e hold that, under *Ricci*, a "strong basis in evidence" of non-job-relatedness or of a less discriminatory alternative requires more than speculation, more than a few scattered statements in the record, and more than a mere fear of litigation, but less than the preponderance of the evidence that would be necessary for actual liability. This is what it means when courts say that the employer must have an objectively reasonable fear of disparate-impact liability.

See generally Herman N. Johnson, Jr., *The Evolving Strong-Basis-In-Evidence Standard*, 32 BERKELEY J. EMP. & LAB. L. 347 (2011).

3. *Relation to Affirmative Action.* Only Justice Ginsburg in dissent puts *Ricci* in context with the Court's Title VII affirmative action decisions. Recall that under *Weber/Johnson, see* page 649, a prima facie case of disparate treatment is not required in order to justify an affirmative action plan; all that is necessary is a manifest imbalance in a traditionally segregated job category and no unnecessary trammeling of majority rights. In *Ricci*, however, even an uncontested prima facie case of disparate impact (a clear manifest imbalance in terms of the test itself) is not enough to permit the employer to take steps to reduce or eliminate the impact.

The parallels between affirmative action analysis under Title VII and *Ricci's* approach to the intersection of disparate treatment and disparate impact are obvious. In both, race may influence an employer's decision, but only under certain circumstances. For a valid affirmative action plan, there must be a manifest imbalance, and majority interests must not be unduly trammeled. In the case of tests with a disparate impact, the test may be thrown out precisely because of that impact, but only under a strong basis in evidence test. So both doctrines allow disparate treatment under more-or-less tight constraints.

Prior to *Ricci*, some wondered if the Roberts Court would overrule *Weber/Johnson's* approval of voluntary affirmative action. Does *Ricci* suggest that the answer is no because it allows some systemic disparate treatment? On the other hand, *Ricci* was not an affirmative action case, at least as that term is normally used. No one was preferred over anyone else, although white firefighters lost promotions they would otherwise have gotten. Since the majority condemned actions taken for racial reasons absent a strong basis in evidence for disparate impact liability, *Ricci* can be viewed as harsher than the affirmative action cases. And the "strong basis in evidence test" seems to require more in the way of proof than "manifest imbalance" does in the affirmative action context.

In *United States v. Brennan*, 650 F.3d 65 (2d Cir. 2011), the Second Circuit distinguished between the *Weber/Johnson* affirmative action analysis and *Ricci's* "strong basis in evidence" defense: The threshold determination is now "whether the race- and sex-conscious action constitutes an affirmative action plan at all." *Id*. at 97. In its view,

> when an employer, acting ex ante, although in the light of past discrimination, establishes hiring or promotion procedures designed to promote equal opportunity and eradicate future discrimination, that may constitute an affirmative action plan. But where an employer, already having established its procedures in a certain way — such as through a seniority system — throws out the results of those procedures ex post because of the racial or gender composition of those results, that constitutes an individualized grant of employment benefits which must be individually justified, and not affirmative action.

Id. at 99-100. Where only ex post benefits are at issue, therefore, "the employer may not invoke the 'affirmative action' defense of *Johnson* and *Weber*." *Id*. at 104.

4. *Does Knowledge Equal Intentional Discrimination?* The majority finds intent to discriminate against whites because the City acted to avoid disparate impact liability to blacks (absent the "strong evidence" defense). But does the fact that the City acted because it knew of a "statistical disparity based on race" necessarily lead to the conclusion that it rejected the test "solely because the higher scoring candidates were white"? Is there a difference between intending not to disadvantage African American and Hispanic candidates and intending to discriminate against the white candidates? Did New Haven invalidate the test in order to deprive whites of promotions? Or was that merely a foreseeable consequence? Or does it matter? *See generally* Michael J. Zimmer, *Ricci's Color-Blind Standard in a Race Conscious Society: A Case of Unintended Consequences?*, 2010 BYU L. REV. 1257; Cheryl I. Harris & Kimberly West-Faulcon, *Reading* Ricci: *White(ning) Discrimination, Race-ing Test Fairness*, 58 UCLA L. REV. 73 (2010); Kerri Stone, *The Unexpected Appearance of Transferred Intent in Title VII*, 55 LOY. L. REV. 752 (2010); Nancy L. Zisk, *Failing the Test: How* Ricci v. DeStefano *Failed to Clarify Disparate Impact and Disparate Treatment Law*, 34 HAMLINE L. REV. 27, 28-29 (2011); Helen Norton, *The Supreme Court's Post-Racial Turn Towards a Zero-Sum Understanding of Equality*, 52 WM. & MARY L. REV. 197 (2010); Charles A. Sullivan, Ricci v. DeStefano: *End of the Line or Just Another Turn on the Disparate Impact Road?*, 104 NW. U. L. REV. 411 (2010).

5. *A Hierarchy of Theories?* The majority thinks that disparate treatment is the main evil that Congress proscribed; disparate impact is a late addition to the statute and must be tailored to minimize any conflict with the disparate treatment bar. Justice Ginsburg takes an opposite view — *Griggs* made clear that disparate impact was implicit in Title VII from the beginning. This difference influences the approach of each side: Disparate treatment can be sacrificed to disparate impact, for the majority, only if the "strong basis in evidence" test is met, thus ensuring that disparate treatment is generally avoided. (You might also wonder, from a legislative intent perspective, why it matters to the majority that disparate impact was added only in the 1991 Civil Rights Act. Doesn't the application of the theory, no matter when, require trying to reconcile both in a nongrudging manner?).

But let's probe Justice Ginsburg's view a bit more. She sees no conflict between disparate treatment and disparate impact claims. Disparate treatment prohibits intentional discrimination but, even if the employer's practices were not intentionally discriminatory, there is a duty to not use practices with a disparate impact unless the practices were justified as job-related and consistent with business necessity. By enacting both theories, Congress thus intended to allow race consciousness to avoid an unjustified racial impact. To put it another way, such race consciousness could not be the kind of disparate treatment Title VII meant to proscribe. For the dissent, the *Ricci* Court's invalid equation of consciousness of race with intent to discriminate creates the tension that it then resolves with its new hierarchy of theories.

6. *What's the Disagreement on the Standard?* The various opinions disagree about a lot, especially the application of the appropriate standard to the facts of the case. But Supreme Court decisions are usually more about law than facts, and, on the law, is there much difference between the majority and the Ginsburg dissent? The majority articulates the "strong basis in evidence" standard. Justice Ginsburg found no violation if the employer has "good cause to believe the device would not withstand examination for business necessity." So the difference is "strong basis" versus "good cause." A tempest in a teapot?

At one point, Justice Ginsburg argues against the majority's standard because "[i]t is hard to see how these requirements differ from demanding that an employer establish 'a provable, actual violation' *against itself.*" (emphasis in original). In the affirmative action cases, some justices sought to avoid requiring an employer, in defending an affirmative action plan favoring minorities, having to adduce proof that would make it liable to minorities. This would, obviously, discourage the adoption of such plans. But how does this argument apply here? By definition, if there is such a "strong basis," the employer can scrub the test. There will then be no disparate impact liability because the test is never used, and there will be no disparate treatment liability because of the strong basis for disparate impact liability.

7. *Isn't There Strong Basis for Disparate Impact Liability?* The Court wrote "a prima facie case of disparate-impact liability — essentially a threshold showing of a significant statistical disparity and nothing more — is far from a strong basis in evidence that the City would have been liable under Title VII had it certified the results." Can that be true in light of § 703(k), which shifts the burden of persuasion to the defendant upon the showing of disparate impact? In other words, if black firefighters were to mount a disparate impact attack, they would win upon showing the fact of impact — unless the employer carried its burden of showing business necessity/job relation defense. *Ricci*, however, requires the employer seeking to avoid disparate impact liability in the first place to show that it has no business necessity, or at least show that it has a strong basis in evidence that it has no business necessity. *Wards Cove* shifted the burden of proving no business necessity to black plaintiffs. Is *Ricci* a very convoluted way of doing the same thing, with the employer acting as a kind of proxy for potential black plaintiffs?

8. *Was the Test Job-Related/Business Necessity as a Matter of Law?* Given (a) the majority's strong basis in evidence test, (b) its acknowledgment of the existence of a prima facie case, and (c) its grant of summary judgment to the white firefighters, it must follow that the test was valid as a matter of law. While we haven't explored test validation in detail, is it so clear that the test was valid? The mere fact that effort is put into test design isn't necessarily enough to validate it under governing principles. Indeed, the *Ricci* majority does not address the jurisprudence associated with the test exception in original § 703(h). Why?

9. *Alternative Employment Practices.* The Court agrees that even a valid test can't be used if there's an alternative employment practice that achieves the same purposes with lesser racial impact. The record before the CSB showed alternatives that were less discriminatory — simply altering the ratio of written to oral scores (as did Bridgeport, a city just down the interstate from New Haven), using "assessment centers," or altering

the "rule of three" to a banding approach — all were alternatives that may have had less impact and that may have equally served the employer's needs. So why not remand on this question?

10. *Suppose Minority Test Takers Claim Disparate Impact?* Pursuant to *Ricci* decision, the City certified the test results, and a black plaintiff brought suit challenging the promotions in the *Ricci* case. He wasn't a party to the *Ricci* litigation, which means that under normal principles of res judicata, he wasn't technically bound by the result, *Martin v. Wilks*, 490 U.S. 755 (1989), although admittedly a provision added to Title VII by the 1991 CRA, 42 U.S.C. §2000e-2(n) (2006) might foreclose his suit. Charles A. Sullivan, Ricci v. DeStefano: *End of the Line or Just Another Turn on the Disparate Impact Road?*, 104 Nw. U. L. Rev. 411, 424-25 (2010). But, civil procedure principles aside, Justice Kennedy concluded the opinion for the Court with a statement about a subsequent disparate impact suit:

> If, after it certifies the test results, the City faces a disparate-impact suit, then in light of our holding today it should be clear that the City would avoid disparate-impact liability based on the strong basis in evidence that, had it not certified the results, it would have been subject to disparate-treatment liability.

Relying heavily on this sentence, the district court dismissed the suit. *Briscoe v. City of New Haven*, 2010 U.S. Dist. LEXIS 69018, *22 (D. Conn. July 12, 2010), but the Second Circuit reversed:

> [W]e cannot reconcile all of the indications from the Supreme Court in *Ricci*. After a careful review of that decision and relevant nonparty preclusion and Title VII case law, we conclude that Briscoe's claim is neither precluded nor properly dismissed. *Ricci* did not substantially change Title VII disparate-impact litigation or preclusion principles in the single sentence of dicta targeted at the parties in this action.

Briscoe v. City of New Haven, 654 F.3d 200, 209 (2d Cir. 2011).

11. *The End of Disparate Impact?* Is the disparate impact theory of liability gone? In other words, while the *Ricci* majority *allows* an employer to take race into account when it has the requisite strong basis in fact, does Kennedy's sentence suggest that the employer can *choose* never to apply disparate impact because doing so will always be disparate treatment? Under this view, avoidance of disparate treatment is always a complete defense to disparate impact. Or does the sentence make sense only when the employer does not (as New Haven didn't) have a strong basis to believe that it was subject to disparate impact liability? Under this view, an employer *must* avoid a practice with a disparate impact, even if it results in disparate treatment, so long as it has the requisite strong basis in evidence. But hold it — that can't be right. Before *Ricci*, an employer could prevail in a suit by black firefighters only by proving that it had a business necessity for its practice, not by showing that it had a strong basis in evidence that it had a business necessity. *See generally* Joseph Seiner & Benjamin Gutman, *Does* Ricci *Herald a New Disparate Impact?* 90 B.U. L. Rev. 2181 (2010) (arguing that the sentence suggests the creation of yet another affirmative defense to disparate impact discrimination).

12. *Or Maybe It Matters When?* *Ricci* focuses on New Haven's decision whether to certify the test. At that point, the CSB had to favor either those who were successful or those who were not, with obvious racial consequences. As Kennedy wrote, "[t]he problem, of course, is that *after the tests were completed*, the raw racial results became the predominant rationale for the City's refusal to certify the results." (emphasis added). He went on to stress that "[t]he injury arises in part from the high, and justified, expectations of the candidates who had participated in the testing process on the terms the City had established for the promotional process." Elsewhere, he spoke of "competing expectations."

But the majority seems to recognize that, in deciding whether or what to test, and before the competing expectations crystallized, potential racial effects can be taken into account:

> Title VII does not prohibit an employer from considering, before administering a test or practice, how to design that test or practice in order to provide a fair opportunity for all individuals, regardless of their race. And when, during the test-design stage, an employer invites comments to ensure the test is fair, that process can provide a common ground for open discussions toward that end.

This strongly suggests that an employer need not be color-blind in its approach to test design.

13. *1989 Redux?* It has been 25 years, but has a new conservative majority in the Roberts Court been able to undermine Title VII just as the Rehnquist Court majority did in 1989? Is the fear that employers would have an incentive to use racial quotas what drives the *Ricci* decision, just as it drove the decision in *Wards Cove*? If Congress were to act to create a statutory defense less stringent than strong basis in evidence, would this new majority take the step suggested by Justice Scalia to embed *Ricci* in the Constitution by striking down disparate impact analysis as unconstitutional?

Note on Impact Analysis Under the ADEA

In *Smith v. City of Jackson*, 544 U.S. 228 (2005), the Supreme Court held that disparate impact is available under ADEA but in a considerably diluted form. *City of Jackson* involved a challenge by older police officers to raises that disparately favored younger workers. The Court reasoned that the ADEA should be interpreted identically to Title VII to the extent that both statutes were identical. However, two textual differences between the ADEA and Title VII combined to lead the Court to conclude that the scope of the disparate-impact theory is narrower under the ADEA. The first textual difference is ADEA §4(f)(1), 29 U.S.C. §623(f)(1), which lacks any Title VII analog. That section expressly permits differentiations "based on reasonable factors other than age." This indicated to the Court that Congress thought that factors correlated with age, albeit not age-based themselves, sometimes have relevance in employment decisions. *See* Judith J. Johnson, *Rehabilitate the Age Discrimination in Employment Act: Resuscitate the "Reasonable Factors Other Than Age" Defense and the Disparate Impact Theory*, 55 HASTINGS L. J. 1399 (2004).

Further developing the significance of the reasonable factor other than age ("RFOA") language, *Meacham v. Knolls Atomic Power Lab.*, 554 U.S. 84 (2008), held that the RFOA was an affirmative defense as to which the defendant bore the burden of persuasion. Further, *Meacham* ruled that the RFOA defense superseded the normal business necessity/job relation defense for disparate impact claims under Title VII: "[W]e are now satisfied that the business necessity test should have no place in

ADEA disparate-impact cases." *Id.* at 97. Rather, the only question is whether a non-age factor that produces an age impact is "reasonable," although what that means and how it might differ from normal business necessity/job relation analysis is not clear.

The second difference is the Civil Rights Act of 1991, which amended Title VII but not the ADEA with respect to refining disparate impact. In short, the 1991 CRA was widely seen as restoring disparate impact law to its state under *Griggs v. Duke Packing*, following the Court's more limiting decision in *Wards Cove Packing Co. v. Atonio.* Since that amendment did not apply to the ADEA, the Court concluded that the *Wards Cove* version of disparate impact applies in age discrimination cases.

Applying this standard to the case, the *City of Jackson* majority found that the plaintiffs had not sufficiently identified the challenged practice to satisfy *Wards Cove. See also Allen v. Highlands Hosp. Corp.*, 545 F.3d 387, 404 (6th Cir. 2008) ("the plaintiffs have at best alleged that HHC desired to reduce costs associated with its highly paid workforce, including those costs associated with employees with greater seniority. But the plaintiffs have not established that this corporate desire evolved into an identifiable practice that disproportionately harms workers who are at least 40 years old"). *City of Jackson* also stated that, in any event, the City's decision to grant raises based on seniority and positions was reasonable given the City's goal of raising employees' salaries to match those in surrounding communities.

D. SEXUAL AND OTHER DISCRIMINATORY HARASSMENT

In this section, we consider employees' rights to a workplace in which they are free from sexual and other discriminatory harassment. Under Title VII, the ADEA, and the ADA, employees have a cause of action for harassment when the harassment is on the basis of membership in a protected group. Harassment poses different challenges than the theories of discrimination discussed previously in this chapter. For example, much conduct underlying sexual harassment, unlike other discriminatory behavior, is unobjectionable, even desired, in contexts outside the workplace. Further, sexual harassment, like other kinds of discriminatory harassment, typically does not result in any adverse economic impact on the victim, even if the emotional distress is severe. The decision to find a violation of the discrimination laws under such circumstances is in sharp contrast to efforts by courts in other antidiscrimination contexts to limit suits to cases where there is an "adverse employment action." In addition, discriminatory harassment typically occurs in violation of, rather than in compliance with, company policy, and harassers often are satisfying their own personal interests, rather than seeking to further their employer's interests. This attribute of discriminatory harassment raises a new issue: What is the employer's liability for harassment by supervisors and co-workers in violation of company policy? Finally, because controlling discriminatory harassment in the workplace by disciplining harassing employees may relieve an employer of liability, discriminatory harassment raises questions about the rights of employees who perpetrate this form of discrimination.

Although the lower federal courts were originally dismissive of sexual harassment as a theory of liability under Title VII, the Supreme Court decision in *Meritor Savings Bank v. Vinson*, 477 U.S. 57 (1986), signaled a sea change in the acceptance of this theory. The facts in *Meritor* were extreme. Sidney Taylor, a vice president of Meritor and manager of one of its branch offices, hired Michelle Vinson and became her supervisor. Vinson started as a trainee but ultimately was promoted to assistant branch manager, working at the same branch until her discharge in 1978. While her advancement at the bank was based on merit, she alleged that she had been constantly harassed by Taylor during her four years of employment. According to Vinson's testimony, Taylor "invited her out to dinner and, during the course of the meal, suggested that they go to a motel to have sexual relations. At first she refused, but out of what she described as fear of losing her job she eventually agreed. . . . Taylor thereafter made repeated demands upon her for sexual favors, usually at the branch, both during and after business hours; she estimated that over the next several years she had intercourse with him some 40 or 50 times. In addition, Taylor fondled her in front of other employees, followed her into the women's restroom when she went there alone, exposed himself to her, and even forcibly raped her on several occasions." *Meritor*, 477 U.S. at 60.

The Supreme Court declared that: "Without question, when a supervisor sexually harasses a subordinate because of the subordinate's sex, that supervisor 'discriminate[s]' on the basis of sex." *Id.* at 64. As importantly, the Court rejected the argument that harassment was limited to economic losses. Looking in large part to EEOC Guidelines on Sexual Harassment, 29 C.F.R. § 1604.11, the Court held that "a plaintiff may establish a violation of Title VII by proving that discrimination based on sex has created a hostile or abusive work environment." *Meritor*, 477 U.S. at 66. It did caution, however, that "not all workplace conduct that may be described as 'harassment' affects a 'term, condition, or privilege' of employment within the meaning of Title VII. For sexual harassment to be actionable, it must be sufficiently severe or pervasive 'to alter the conditions of [the victim's] employment and create an abusive working environment.'" *Id.* at 67. The Court also made clear that "the fact that sex-related conduct was 'voluntary,' in the sense that the complainant was not forced to participate against her will, is not a defense to a sexual harassment suit brought under Title VII. The gravamen of any sexual harassment claim is that the alleged sexual advances were 'unwelcome.' 29 C.F.R. § 1604.11(a) (1985)." *Id.* at 68.

Meritor established what was essentially a new cause of action under Title VII, one that is in many ways very different than the kind of discrimination we have studied to this point. However, it left a myriad of questions to be answered. Two of the most important were when the offensive conduct was "because of sex" and what conduct is sufficiently "severe or pervasive" to be actionable.

≡ **Oncale v. Sundowner Offshore Services, Inc.**
≡ *523 U.S. 75 (1998)*

Justice SCALIA delivered the opinion of the Court.

This case presents the question whether workplace harassment can violate Title VII's prohibition against "discrimination . . . because of . . . sex," when the harasser and the harassed employee are of the same sex.

I

The District Court having granted summary judgment for respondent, we must assume the facts to be as alleged by petitioner Joseph Oncale. The precise details are irrelevant to the legal point we must decide, and in the interest of both brevity and dignity we shall describe them only generally. In late October 1991, Oncale was working for respondent Sundowner Offshore Services on a Chevron U.S.A., Inc. oil platform in the Gulf of Mexico. He was employed as a roustabout on an eight-man crew which included respondents John Lyons, Danny Pippen, and Brandon Johnson. Lyons, the crane operator, and Pippen, the driller, had supervisory authority. On several occasions, Oncale was forcibly subjected to sex-related, humiliating actions against him by Lyons, Pippen and Johnson in the presence of the rest of the crew. Pippen and Lyons also physically assaulted Oncale in a sexual manner, and Lyons threatened him with rape.

Oncale's complaints to supervisory personnel produced no remedial action; in fact, the company's Safety Compliance Clerk, Valent Hohen, told Oncale that Lyons and Pippen "picked [on] him all the time too," and called him a name suggesting homosexuality. Oncale eventually quit — asking that his pink slip reflect that he "voluntarily left due to sexual harassment and verbal abuse." When asked at his deposition why he left Sundowner, Oncale stated "I felt that if I didn't leave my job, that I would be raped or forced to have sex."

[The district court held that "Mr. Oncale, a male, has no cause of action under Title VII for harassment by male co-workers." The Fifth Circuit affirmed.]

II

Title VII's prohibition of discrimination "because of . . . sex" protects men as well as women, *Newport News* [*Shipbuilding & Dry Dock Co. v. EEOC*, 462 U.S. 669, 678 (1983)], and in the related context of racial discrimination in the workplace we have rejected any conclusive presumption that an employer will not discriminate against members of his own race. "Because of the many facets of human motivation, it would be unwise to presume as a matter of law that human beings of one definable group will not discriminate against other members of that group." *Castaneda v. Partida*, 430 U.S. 482 (1977). In *Johnson v. Transportation Agency*, Santa Clara County, 480 U.S. 616 (1987), a male employee claimed that his employer discriminated against him because of his sex when it preferred a female employee for promotion. Although we ultimately rejected the claim on other grounds, we did not consider it significant that the supervisor who made that decision was also a man. If our precedents leave any doubt on the question, we hold today that nothing in Title VII necessarily bars a claim of discrimination "because of . . . sex" merely because the plaintiff and the defendant (or the person charged with acting on behalf of the defendant) are of the same sex.

Courts have had little trouble with that principle in cases like *Johnson*, where an employee claims to have been passed over for a job or promotion. But when the issue arises in the context of a "hostile environment" sexual harassment claim, the state and federal courts have taken a bewildering variety of stances. Some, like the Fifth Circuit in this case, have held that same-sex sexual harassment claims are never cognizable under

Title VII. Other decisions say that such claims are actionable only if the plaintiff can prove that the harasser is homosexual (and thus presumably motivated by sexual desire). Still others suggest that workplace harassment that is sexual in content is always actionable, regardless of the harasser's sex, sexual orientation, or motivations.

We see no justification in the statutory language or our precedents for a categorical rule excluding same-sex harassment claims from the coverage of Title VII. As some courts have observed, male-on-male sexual harassment in the workplace was assuredly not the principal evil Congress was concerned with when it enacted Title VII. But statutory prohibitions often go beyond the principal evil to cover reasonably comparable evils, and it is ultimately the provisions of our laws rather than the principal concerns of our legislators by which we are governed. Title VII prohibits "discrimination . . . because of . . . sex" in the "terms" or "conditions" of employment. Our holding that this includes sexual harassment must extend to sexual harassment of any kind that meets the statutory requirements.

Respondents and their amici contend that recognizing liability for same-sex harassment will transform Title VII into a general civility code for the American workplace. But that risk is no greater for same-sex than for opposite-sex harassment, and is adequately met by careful attention to the requirements of the statute. Title VII does not prohibit all verbal or physical harassment in the workplace; it is directed only at "discrimination . . . because of . . . sex." We have never held that workplace harassment, even harassment between men and women, is automatically discrimination because of sex merely because the words used have sexual content or connotations. "The critical issue, Title VII's text indicates, is whether members of one sex are exposed to disadvantageous terms or conditions of employment to which members of the other sex are not exposed." *Harris* [*v. Forklift Systems, Inc.,* 510 U.S. 17 (1993)].

Courts and juries have found the inference of discrimination easy to draw in most male-female sexual harassment situations, because the challenged conduct typically involves explicit or implicit proposals of sexual activity; it is reasonable to assume those proposals would not have been made to someone of the same sex. The same chain of inference would be available to a plaintiff alleging same-sex harassment, if there were credible evidence that the harasser was homosexual. But harassing conduct need not be motivated by sexual desire to support an inference of discrimination on the basis of sex. A trier of fact might reasonably find such discrimination, for example, if a female victim is harassed in such sex-specific and derogatory terms by another woman as to make it clear that the harasser is motivated by general hostility to the presence of women in the workplace. A same-sex harassment plaintiff may also, of course, offer direct comparative evidence about how the alleged harasser treated members of both sexes in a mixed-sex workplace. Whatever evidentiary route the plaintiff chooses to follow, he or she must always prove that the conduct at issue was not merely tinged with offensive sexual connotations, but actually constituted "discrimination . . . because of . . . sex."

And there is another requirement that prevents Title VII from expanding into a general civility code: As we emphasized in *Meritor* and *Harris,* the statute does not reach genuine but innocuous differences in the ways men and women routinely interact with members of the same sex and of the opposite sex. The prohibition of harassment on the basis of sex requires neither asexuality nor androgyny in the workplace; it forbids only behavior so objectively offensive as to alter the "conditions" of the victim's employment. "Conduct that is not severe or pervasive enough to create an objectively hostile or abusive work environment—an environment that a reasonable person would find hostile or abusive—is beyond Title VII's purview." *Harris.* We have always regarded that requirement as crucial, and as sufficient to ensure that courts and juries do not mistake ordinary socializing in the workplace—such as male-on-male horseplay or intersexual flirtation—for discriminatory "conditions of employment."

We have emphasized, moreover, that the objective severity of harassment should be judged from the perspective of a reasonable person in the plaintiff's position, considering "all the circumstances." *Harris.* In same-sex (as in all) harassment cases, that inquiry requires careful consideration of the social context in which particular behavior occurs and is experienced by its target. A professional football player's working environment is not severely or pervasively abusive, for example, if the coach smacks him on the buttocks as he heads onto the field—even if the same behavior would reasonably be experienced as abusive by the coach's secretary (male or female) back at the office. The real social impact of workplace behavior often depends on a constellation of surrounding circumstances, expectations, and relationships which are not fully captured by a simple recitation of the words used or the physical acts performed. Common sense, and an appropriate sensitivity to social context, will enable courts and juries to distinguish between simple teasing or roughhousing among members of the same sex, and conduct which a reasonable person in the plaintiff's position would find severely hostile or abusive. . . .

NOTES

1. *Sex-as-Conduct versus Gender.* Oncale makes clear that, regardless of the gender of the harasser and victim, the central issue for purposes of establishing liability under Title VII is whether the terms and conditions of the victim's employment were altered because of "sex." This term has generated some confusion because "sex" is sometimes used to refer to sexual conduct and sometimes to refer to biological sex. Although *Oncale* establishes that same-sex harassment is actionable under Title VII, the question remains: When is harassment because of or on the basis of sex? The Court confirms prior opinions that the gender of the target must cause the harassment. Thus, an inference of sex-based discrimination was often drawn by the lower courts based on sexual advances made by a heterosexual toward a victim of the opposite sex. Consistent with this logic, the Court indicates that sexual advances by a homosexual toward an individual of the same sex also may give rise to the inference that such action is "because of sex." *See* Rebecca Hanner White, *There's Nothing Special About Sex: The Supreme Court Mainstreams Sexual Harassment*, 7 WM. & MARY BILL RTS. J. 725, 734 (1999) ("The fact that harassment is sexual in nature may (and often will) be powerful evidence that the victim is suffering harassment because of her sex. The defendant may, however, avoid liability if the fact finder is convinced that the victim was not a target of harassment because of her sex, whether or not the harassment was sexual in nature."); Steven Willborn, *Taking Discrimination Seriously:* Oncale *and the Fate of Exceptionalism in Sexual Harassment Law*, 7 WM. & MARY BILL RTS. J. 677 (1999). In contrast, David S. Schwartz, *When is Sex Because of Sex? The Causation Problem in Sexual Harassment Law*, 150 U. PA. L. REV. 1697 (2002), argues for a "sex per se" rule that would go beyond a presumption and find sexual conduct sufficient to satisfy the "because of sex" requirement.

Another approach finds harassment to be sexual when it is predicated on a plaintiff's failure to conform to gender norms. The paradigm example is an "effeminate" male or a "butch" woman. The cases have recognized this theory of harassment. *See, e.g., EEOC v. Boh Bros. Constr. Co., LLC,* 731 F.3d 444, 456 (5th Cir. 2013) (en banc) ("nothing in *Oncale* overturns or otherwise upsets the Court's holding in *Price Waterhouse*: a plaintiff may establish a sexual harassment claim with evidence of sex-stereotyping. Thus, the EEOC may rely on evidence that Wolfe viewed Woods as insufficiently masculine to prove its Title VII claim."); *Smith v. Salem,* 378 F.3d 566, 572 (6th Cir. 2004) (transsexual stated a Title VII claim by alleging that he was a victim of discrimination because his conduct and mannerisms "did not conform with his employers' and co-workers' sex stereotypes of how a man should look and behave"); *Nichols v. Azteca Rest. Enters., Inc.,* 256 F.3d 864 (9th Cir. 2001) (discrimination against male for acting too feminine is actionable under Title VII). In this regard, consider the relevance of the Court's recognition in *Price Waterhouse* (reproduced at page 597) that gender stereotyping is direct evidence of sex discrimination under Title VII.

This theory comes very close to finding discrimination on the basis of sexual orientation to be actionable. Although courts often go to great lengths to distinguish between sex discrimination and sexual orientation discrimination, *e.g., Vickers v. Fairfield Med. Ctr.,* 453 F.3d 757, 759 (6th Cir. 2006); *Dawson v. Bumble & Bumble,* 398 F.3d 211 (2d Cir. 2005), a number of commentators argue that such discrimination is properly viewed as sex discrimination within the meaning of Title VII. *See* Brian Soucek, *Perceived Homosexuals: Looking Gay Enough for Title VII,* 63 AM. U. L. REV. 715 (2014); Katherine M. Franke, *What's Wrong with Sexual Harassment?,* 49 STAN. L. REV. 691, 732 (1997); Zachary A. Kramer, *The Ultimate Gender Stereotype: Equalizing Gender-Conforming and Gender-Nonconforming Homosexuals Under Title VII,* 2004 U. ILL. L. REV. 465, 465 (2004); Camille Hébert, *Sexual Harassment as Discrimination "Because of . . . Sex": Have We Come Full Circle?* 27 OHIO N.U. L. REV. 439 (2001) (plaintiff harassed for failure to conform to gender stereotypes would meet the "because of . . . sex" requirement).

2. *Gender Harassment. Oncale*'s notion that sexual harassment is only a subset of sex discrimination is underscored by cases in which women complain not of unwelcome sexual advances but of environments that are hostile to women in other ways. For example, recall *Desert Palace,* reproduced at page 610. This was a discriminatory discharge case, not a contaminated work environment case, and thus, the Supreme Court apparently did not find it necessary to include some of the comments directed at and about plaintiff. But consider the facts as recounted in the Ninth Circuit's opinion from the hostile environment perspective:

> Costa also presented evidence that she was penalized for her failure to conform to sexual stereotypes. Although her fellow Teamsters frequently lost their tempers, swore at fellow employees, and sometimes had physical altercations, it was Costa, identified in one report as "the lady Teamster," who was called a "bitch," and told "you got more balls than the guys." Even at trial, and despite testimony that she "got along with most people" and had "few arguments," Caesars' managers continued to characterize her as "strong willed," "opinionated," and "confrontational," leading counsel to call her "bossy" in closing argument. Supervisor Karen Hallett, who later signed Costa's termination order, expressly declared her intent to "get rid of that bitch," referring to Costa.

Supervisors frequently used or tolerated verbal slurs that were sex-based or tinged with sexual overtones. Most memorably, one co-worker called her a "fucking cunt." When she wrote a letter to management expressing her concern with this epithet, which stood out from the ordinary rough-and-tumble banter, she received a three-day suspension in response. Although the other employee admitted using the epithet, Costa was faulted for "engaging in verbal confrontation with co-worker in the warehouse resulting in use of profane and vulgar language by other employee."

Costa v. Desert Palace, 299 F.3d 838, 845-46 (9th Cir. 2002) (en banc).

These epithets were not hurled at plaintiff because her co-workers desired to have sex with Costa — they wanted to drive her out of the workplace. One inference is that they did so because she was a woman — the only woman in that position. The courts have found that harassing conduct of a nonsexual nature can constitute sexual harassment. *See, e.g., Pucino v. Verizon Communs., Inc.*, 618 F.3d 112 (2d Cir. 2010) (proof that a female employee was subject to disparately harsh working conditions compared to men, including assignment to dangerous areas, refusal to provide assistance given to male co-workers, and access to restrooms, could establish a violation, especially when coupled with proof of ther supervisor's constant use of "bitch"); *EEOC v. Fairbrook Medical Clinic, P.A*, 609 F.3d 320, 327 (4th Cir. 2010) ("Although Kessel made offensive remarks in front of both male and female audiences, his use of 'sex-specific and derogatory terms' indicates that he intended to demean women."). *But see Smith v. Hy-Vee, Inc.*, 622 F.3d 904, 908 (8th Cir. 2010) (despite evidence that harasser touched plaintiff and made sexual references, there was no sufficient basis to infer that she was motivated by sexual desire because she subjected both men and women to the same behavior); *Love v. Motiva Enters. LLC*, 349 F. App'x 900, 903 (5th Cir. 2009) (although harassment was framed in sexual terms, there was no reason to believe that the harasser was either making implicit proposals for sexual activity or was lesbian given the context of her "rude and obnoxious persona, which was directed at all co-workers generally, and her overall insulting and intimidating attitude toward Love specifically.").

Vicki Schultz, in *Reconceptualizing Sexual Harassment*, 107 YALE L. J. 1683, 1686-87, 1689 (1998), argues against the "sexual desire-dominance paradigm" for sexual harassment because that paradigm "has served to exclude from legal understanding many of the most common and debilitating forms of harassment faced by women (and many men) at work each day." One of Schultz's solutions is for courts to employ a rebuttable presumption of illegal harassment when the harassment is directed at women who work in traditionally segregated job categories. *See also* Rebecca Hanner White, *There's Nothing Special About Sex: The Supreme Court Mainstreams Sexual Harassment*, 7 WM. & MARY BILL RTS. J. 725, 735-6 (1999) ("[Schultz's] approach makes sense intuitively, and is consistent with *Oncale*, provided that courts keep in mind that only an inference of sex-discrimination is created, not a conclusive method of proof. After all, a woman in a male-dominated workplace may be harassed because she is a woman, or she may be harassed because she is a jerk."). Given that Costa was the only woman in her workplace, how would the trier of fact decide the abuse aimed at her was because she was a woman doing "men's work" or because she was "a jerk"?

3. *Sex, Not Sexual Orientation.* If Oncale's employer can establish that his co-workers harassed him because he is a homosexual, can he nonetheless establish an actionable claim under Title VII? We will see that discrimination on the basis of sexual orientation is not generally actionable under Title VII. *See* page 711. The law thus requires courts to distinguish between harassment on the basis of sexual orientation (legal) and harassment on the basis of sex (illegal), and rejects the argument that harassment on the basis of sexual orientation is necessarily on the basis of sex.

Shepherd v. Slater Steel Corp., 168 F.3d 998 (7th Cir. 1999), read *Oncale* to establish two prongs by which same-sex harassment may be gender discrimination:

> (1) credible evidence that the harasser is gay or lesbian — in which case it is reasonable to assume that the harasser would not harass members of the other sex (or at least not with "explicit or implicit proposals of sexual activity"); and (2) proof that the plaintiff was harassed in "such sex-specific and derogatory terms" as to reveal an antipathy to persons of plaintiff's gender.

168 F.3d at 1009. The first prong obviously tracks heterosexual harassment where the harasser is interested in engaging in sexual conduct with the victim. The second prong suggests hostility to a gender, not to sexual orientation. But does it make sense to you? Since same-sex harassment is involved, the second prong posits that the harasser has "antipathy" to the gender he (or she) shares with the victim. When will this occur? When the antipathy is to the individual's orientation? *See generally* L. Camille Hébert, *Transforming Transsexual and Transgender Rights*, 15 WM. & MARY J. WOMEN & L. 535 (2009) (the term "sex" should be defined more broadly than courts have seen fit to do with respect to sexual minorities, to extend protection not only on biological status but gender-linked traits, including gender identity); *see also* Zachary A. Kramer, *Heterosexuality and Title VII*, 103 NW. U. L. REV. 205, 208-9 (2009) ("there is a double standard at work in employment discrimination cases. For lesbian and gay employees, sexual orientation is a burden because courts are primed to reject otherwise actionable discrimination claims on the theory that such claims are an attempt to bootstrap protection for sexual orientation into Title VII. However, rather than being burdened by their sexual orientation in employment discrimination cases, heterosexual employees are not affected by theirs.").

4. *The Equal-Opportunity Harasser.* To understand how the law can distinguish between sexual harassment and sexual orientation harassment, suppose a harasser targets both gays and lesbians, that is, he harasses anyone that he considers to be "deviant." Obviously, there is no sex discrimination here — he's an equal opportunity harasser. While the harassment is on the basis of orientation, that is not actionable under Title VII.

The equal opportunity harasser appears often in the literature and sometimes in the cases. In the heterosexual context, female plaintiffs have encountered the sometimes successful defense that the harasser directs his offensive conduct and remarks against both men and women and therefore does not violate Title VII. *See Reine v. Honeywell Int'l Inc.*, 362 F. App'x 395 (5th Cir. 2010) (recognizing equal opportunity harasser defense when both men and women were treated badly and only a few of the harassing comments related to sex). *But see Beckford v. Dep't of Corr.*, 605 F.3d 951, 960 (11th Cir. 2010) ("That the close management inmates are typically crude and even obscene does not mean that their harassment was indiscriminate. The employees presented evidence that the inmates called them cunts, whores, bitches, and sluts, and we have ruled that these gender-specific and highly offensive epithets evidence sex-based harassment under Title VII"); *Venezia v. Gottlieb Mem'l Hosp., Inc.*, 421 F.3d 468, 473 (7th Cir. 2005) (harassment of both husband and wife by different individuals did not necessarily mean that there was no sex discrimination). *See generally* Martin J. Katz, *Reconsidering Attraction in Sexual Harassment*, 79 IND. L.J. 101, 125-39 (2004); Ronald Turner, *Title VII and the Inequality-Enhancing Effects of the Bisexual and Equal Opportunity Harasser Defenses*, 7 U. PA. J. LAB. & EMP. L. 341, 342, 345 (2005).

    5. *Disparate Impact Theory.* If a court concludes that harassment was not because of sex in the intent sense but nevertheless had a greater effect on women than on men, perhaps because it occurred in a sex-segregated workplace, the disparate impact theory suggests a possible way to attack the mistreatment. *See* Camille Hébert, *The Disparate Impact of Sexual Harassment: Does Motive Matter?*, 53 KAN. L. REV. 341 (2004) (arguing that disparate impact should be applicable to sexual harassment cases because women as a group are disproportionately disadvantaged by sexually harassing conduct in the workplace); Kelly Cahill Timmons, *Sexual Harassment and Disparate Impact: Should Non-Targeted Workplace Sexual Conduct be Actionable Under Title VII?*, 81 NEB. L. REV. 1152, 1155 (2003) (concluding "that non-targeted sexual conduct in the workplace should be actionable only if the conduct's disproportionate impact on women is great").

EEOC v. Sunbelt Rentals, Inc.
521 F.3d 306 (4th Cir. 2008)

WILKINSON, Circuit Judge:

    This case arises from a Title VII action brought by the United States Equal Employment Opportunity Commission on behalf of Clinton Ingram, a Muslim American, against Sunbelt Rentals, Inc. The EEOC alleges that Ingram, while working at Sunbelt, was subjected to a religiously hostile work environment in violation of Title VII. The district court granted summary judgment for Sunbelt and dismissed the claim.

    Title VII extends the promise that no one should be subject to a discriminatorily hostile work environment. In the wake of September 11th, some Muslim Americans, completely innocent of any wrongdoing, became targets of gross misapprehensions and overbroad assumptions about their religious beliefs. But the event that shook the foundations of our buildings did not shake the premise of our founding — that here, in America, there is no heretical faith. Because the evidence, if proven, indicates that Ingram suffered severe and pervasive religious harassment in violation of Title VII, we reverse the district court's grant of summary judgment and remand with directions that this case proceed to trial.

I.

A.

    Sunbelt is a company that rents and sells construction equipment. In October 2001, a month after the September 11th attacks, it hired Ingram to work at its Gaithersburg, Maryland store. After initially working as a truck driver, Ingram was later promoted to the position of rental manager, a position he held until his termination in February 2003. As a rental manager, Ingram primarily worked at a rental counter located inside the store's showroom and was responsible for assisting customers with equipment rentals.

Ingram worked in close quarters with several other Sunbelt employees. In addition to Ingram, there were three other rental managers at the Gaithersburg location: David Gray, John "Hank" Parater, and Barry Fortna. Gray and Parater had work stations on either side of Ingram at the office's rental counter, and Fortna, the "lead rental manager," worked at a desk behind the counter.

In addition to his fellow rental managers, Ingram frequently interacted with Mike Warner, the store's shop foreman, and Steve Riddlemoser, the overall manager of the Gaithersburg office. When Riddlemoser was not in the office, Warner served as the "acting manager." If both Riddlemoser and Warner were absent, then Fortna was left in charge. The regional manager for the Gaithersburg location was Eddie Dempster.

Prior to joining Sunbelt, Ingram, who is an African American, converted to Islam while serving in the United States Army. It is undisputed that Sunbelt, as well as Ingram's coworkers, knew Ingram was a Muslim. In fact, Sunbelt permitted Ingram to use a private, upstairs room for short prayer sessions that were required by Ingram's faith. In addition, Sunbelt allowed Ingram to attend a weekly congregational prayer session that took place from 1:00-1:45 p.m. on Friday afternoons. Ingram also observed tenets of his faith at the workplace by keeping a beard and wearing a kufi, a traditional headgear worn by Muslim men. Notably, Ingram was the only Muslim employee at the Gaithersburg office.

During his time at Sunbelt, Ingram claims he was subjected to a hostile work environment on the basis of his religion. According to Ingram, the abusive environment was marked by a steady stream of demeaning comments and degrading actions directed against him by his coworkers — conduct that went unaddressed and unpunished by Sunbelt supervisors.

For instance, coworkers used religiously-charged epithets and often called Ingram names such as "Taliban" and "towel head." In addition, fellow employees frequently made fun of Ingram's appearance, challenged his allegiance to the United States, suggested he was a terrorist, and made comments associating all Muslims with senseless violence. Sometimes Ingram's supervisors personally participated in the harassment. Sunbelt responds, in turn, that Ingram also used profane and derogatory language in the workplace.

Additionally, Ingram was the victim of several religiously charged incidents. For instance, on one occasion, Gray held a metal detector to Ingram's head and, after the detector did not go off, called Ingram a "fake ass Muslim want-to-be turbine wearing ass." In a separate incident, Gray showed Ingram a stapler and said that "if anyone upsets you pretend this stapler is a model airplane [and] just toss it in the air, just repeatedly catch it, [and] don't say anything." Ingram understood this to be a reference to the September 11 attacks and another attempt by Gray to equate Ingram with terrorists. Finally, a cartoon was posted in the store's dispatch area depicting persons "dressed in Islamic or Muslim attire" as suicide bombers. [In the cartoon, an instructor with a bomb strapped to his body tells the others: "okay, pay attention" because "I'm only showing you . . . how this works once."] Taking offense, Ingram complained about the cartoon to the dispatcher and eventually tore it down.

In addition to these explicitly religious incidents, Ingram suffered from other forms of harassment. For example, his timecard, which was used to punch time in and out, was frequently hidden, especially on Fridays when he went to congregational prayer. Likewise, coworkers constantly unplugged his computer equipment and, on one occasion, defaced his business card by writing "dumb ass" over his name.

After nearly every incident of harassment, Ingram verbally complained to Riddlemoser, and sometimes Dempster and Warner. [These complaints did not resolve the matter and ultimately Ingram complained to Sunbelt's Human Resources Department. This, too, failed to stop the harassment. Although there was] a short period of relative improvement, the religious harassment and pranks "just basically started up again." For instance, Gray continued to harass Ingram about his appearance and his faith. After Ingram informed Dempster that the harassment was "starting to happen again," Dempster accused Ingram of "being paranoid," "seeing things," and "trying to build a case against" Sunbelt. The harassment allegedly continued until Ingram's termination in February 2003.

B.

[The district court granted summary judgment to Sunbelt, finding the harassment not sufficiently severe or pervasive to establish a prima facie case of a hostile work environment. The district court stated] "[t]here's a lot of coarse behavior that goes on in the workplace," and Sunbelt was "a little more rough and ready than, let us say, the Century Club of New York of which fine ladies are members." Second, the court stated that several of the incidents that Ingram complained about, such as the hiding of his timecard, lacked a direct "nexus with religion." Third, the court explained that if the explicitly religious incidents involving his coworkers were sufficiently severe or pervasive, Ingram would have included them in his written complaint to Human Resources. Because he did not, the district court presumed they must not have been sufficiently severe or pervasive. . . .

II . . .

In order to prove that Ingram suffered from a "discriminatorily hostile or abusive work environment," *Harris v. Forklift Systems, Inc.*, 510 U.S. 17 (1993), the EEOC must demonstrate that the harassment was (1) unwelcome, (2) because of religion, (3) sufficiently severe or pervasive to alter the conditions of employment and create an abusive atmosphere, and (4) imputable to the employer, *see Gilliam v. South Carolina Dep't of Juvenile Justice*, 474 F.3d 134, 142 (4th Cir. 2007).

[The court had no difficulty finding the conduct "unwelcome," given Ingram's response to his co-workers and his complaints to management. Nor did it have any difficulty with the religious nature of the comments, given that, for example, "Taliban" or "towel head" would not have been applied to a non-Muslim employee, and the co-workers "teased [him] about his appearance, particularly his kufi and beard."]

C.

The main area of contention here is whether the harassment alleged by Ingram was "sufficiently severe or pervasive to alter the conditions of [his] employment and create an abusive working environment." *Harris* (quoting *Meritor*). Viewed on summary judgment, the evidence establishes that Ingram persistently suffered from religious harassment of the most demeaning, degrading, and damaging sort. The district court erred when it held the EEOC had failed to satisfy this requirement.

1.

The "severe or pervasive" element of a hostile work environment claim "has both subjective and objective components." *Ocheltree v. Scollon Prods., Inc.*, 335 F.3d 325, 333 (4th Cir. 2003) (en banc) (citing *Harris*). First, the plaintiff must show that he "subjectively perceive[d] the environment to be abusive." *Harris*. Next, the plaintiff must demonstrate that the conduct was such that "a reasonable person in the plaintiff's position" would have found the environment objectively hostile or abusive. *Oncale v. Sundowner Offshore Servs., Inc.*. Because Sunbelt does not, and could not, challenge the EEOC's contention that the harassment seemed severe and pervasive to Ingram personally, we focus our attention on the element's objective component.

This objective inquiry "is not, and by its nature cannot be, a mathematically precise test." *Harris*. Rather, when determining whether the harassing conduct was objectively "severe or pervasive," we must look "at all the circumstances," including "the frequency of the discriminatory conduct; its severity; whether it is physically threatening or humiliating, or a mere offensive utterance; and whether it unreasonably interferes with an employee's work performance." *Id.*; *Ocheltree*. "[N]o single factor is" dispositive, *Harris*, as "[t]he real social impact of workplace behavior often depends on a constellation of surrounding circumstances, expectations, and relationships which are not fully captured by a simple recitation of the words used or the physical acts performed," *Oncale*.

While this standard surely prohibits an employment atmosphere that is "permeated with discriminatory intimidation, ridicule, and insult," *Harris*, it is equally clear that Title VII does not establish a "general civility code for the American workplace," *Oncale*. This is because, in order to be actionable, the harassing "conduct must be [so] extreme [as] to amount to a change in the terms and conditions of employment." *Faragher v. City of Boca Raton*, 524 U.S. 775, 788 (1998). Indeed, as the Court observed, "simple teasing, offhand comments, and isolated incidents (unless extremely serious) will not amount to discriminatory changes in the terms and conditions of employment." *Id.*; *see also Clark County Sch. Dist. v. Breeden*, 532 U.S. 268, 270-71 (2001).

Our circuit has likewise recognized that plaintiffs must clear a high bar in order to satisfy the severe or pervasive test. Workplaces are not always harmonious locales, and even incidents that would objectively give rise to bruised or wounded feelings will not on that account satisfy the severe or pervasive standard. Some rolling with the punches is a fact of workplace life. Thus, complaints premised on nothing more than "rude treatment by [coworkers]," *Baqir v. Principi*, 434 F.3d 733, 747 (4th Cir. 2006), "callous behavior by [one's] superiors," *Bass v. E.I. DuPont de Nemours & Co.*, 324 F.3d 761, 765 (4th Cir. 2003), or "a routine difference of opinion and personality conflict with [one's] supervisor," *Hawkins v. PepsiCo, Inc.*, 203 F.3d 274, 276 (4th Cir. 2000), are not actionable under Title VII.

The task then on summary judgment is to identify situations that a reasonable jury might find to be so out of the ordinary as to meet the severe or pervasive criterion. That is, instances where the environment was pervaded with discriminatory conduct "aimed to humiliate, ridicule, or intimidate," thereby creating an abusive atmosphere. *Jennings v. Univ. of North Carolina*, 482 F.3d 686, 695 (4th Cir. 2007) (en banc) (citing *Meritor*). With these principles in mind, we examine whether a reasonable person in Ingram's position would have found the environment to be sufficiently severe or hostile.

2.

The evidence indicates that Ingram suffered religious harassment that was "persistent, demeaning, unrelenting, and widespread." *Harris v. L & L Wings, Inc.*, 132 F.3d 978, 984 (4th Cir. 1997). It is impossible as an initial matter to ignore the context in which the harassment took place. In the time immediately following September 11th, religious tensions ran higher in much of the country, and Muslims were sometimes viewed through the prism of 9/11, rather than as the individuals they were. Sunbelt's Gaithersburg office was no exception. After the terrorist attacks took place, there was lots of talk amongst Sunbelt employees, especially by Gray, about how the "Muslim religion is bad." Likewise, after it was publicized that the D.C. snipers were Muslim, anti-Islam sentiment rose in the Sunbelt workplace. Ingram, the lone Muslim employee, was left to bear the verbal brunt of anti-Islamic sentiment.

Specifically, Ingram was subject to repeated comments that disparaged both him and his faith. Several coworkers, including one with supervisory authority, referred to Ingram in harshly derogatory terms. Mike Warner, the store's shop foreman, called Ingram "Taliban" "over and over again," as well as "towel head." Likewise, Sal Rindone, a Sunbelt mechanic, told Ingram that he thought Ingram was a member of the Taliban. This same coworker also challenged Ingram's allegiance to the United States, asking Ingram "are you on our side or are you on the Taliban's side," and telling him that if "you don't like America or where we stand, you can just leave." Ingram, a veteran of the United States Army, responded that he was not a member of the Taliban but rather "an American and a Muslim."

In addition, Ingram was persistently harassed about his appearance, particularly his kufi and beard. For example, Warner, when making fun of Ingram's appearance, "would make it known that" he thought Ingram actually "look[ed] like a Taliban." On at least one occasion, Gray called Ingram a "fake Muslim" because of his beard. As Gray later admitted, such "comments were made often." According to Ingram, the harassment by Gray was "an ongoing thing, daily."

Ingram was also harassed about his short, Sunbelt-sanctioned prayer sessions. Gray told Ingram "several times" that he had a "problem" with Ingram leaving his desk to pray. In addition, Ingram's timecard was often hidden on Fridays, the day he went to congregational prayer. Even more severe was a comment made by Warner to another coworker, which was later related to Ingram. Warner said that if he ever caught Ingram praying upstairs, that would be "the end of him."

In addition to the abusive comments made to and about Ingram personally, several coworkers made hostile remarks about Islam generally. For instance, rental manager Hank Parater told Ingram that the United States should go to Saudi Arabia and "kill them all," referring to Muslims in the Arab world. Parater also said that he wanted to be a Muslim so he could have eight wives. After it was announced on a television in the store's showroom that the D.C. snipers had been apprehended, another coworker stared at Ingram and shouted, "I should have known they were Muslims." Gray admitted that the treatment of Ingram likely stemmed from "the events of September 11th and the sniper attacks in our area."

Ingram was also the object of anti-Muslim crudities that associated Ingram, and the Muslim faith, with violence and terrorism. [The court repeated the metal detector, staple, and cartoon incidents. While focusing primarily on Ingram's "personal experience," the court also noted the affidavits of two Sunbelt customers who were Muslims, one of whom attested that Sunbelt employees called him a litany of derogatory names, including "Bin Laden," "Hezbullah," "Ayatollah," "Kadaffi," "Saddam Hussein," "terrorist," and "sun nigger."]

Ingram also was forced to endure harassment lacking a direct religious nexus. Coworkers frequently hid Ingram's timecard, unplugged his computer equipment, and defaced his business card with terms such as "dumb ass." Although similar pranks were played on other Sunbelt employees, there is evidence suggesting that Ingram suffered such harassment more often than others and more likely because of his religion. For instance, Ingram's timecard was hidden most frequently on Fridays, the day he went to congregational prayer. On the Friday before Ingram filed the written complaint, his timecard was hidden on at least five separate occasions. In light of the extensive, explicitly religious harassment by the same coworkers, a reasonable jury could infer that other harassing incidents were also motivated by a disdain for Ingram's faith.

Sunbelt makes much of the fact that those who participated in the harassment were merely Ingram's coworkers, and not anyone with supervisory authority over him. However, the evidence presented creates at least a triable issue in that regard. Warner, the store's shop foreman and a primary harasser of Ingram's, served as the acting manager whenever Riddlemoser was absent. At the very least, he was viewed as a "higher up" within the office. Similarly, Fortna, the lead rental manager, supervised Ingram's work and even signed the "supervisor" line on Ingram's disciplinary forms. As a result, a jury could infer that the harassment by Warner and Fortna had a greater impact given their supervisory status. *See Faragher.*

Likewise, Sunbelt insists the harassment could not have been sufficiently severe because, *inter alia*, it was never "physically threatening." While the presence of "physical threats undeniably strengthens a hostile work environment claim," we have not held that such evidence is required. *White v. BFI Waste Servs.*, 375 F.3d 288, 298 n.6 (4th Cir. 2004). Names can hurt as much as sticks and stones, and the Supreme Court has never indicated that the humiliation so frequently attached to hostile environments need be accompanied by physical threat or force.

While the district court suggested that the harassment might be discounted because the environment was inherently coarse, Title VII contains no such "crude environment" exception, and to read one into it might vitiate statutory safeguards for those who need them most. Of course, if Sunbelt's environment was somehow so universally crude that the treatment of Ingram was nothing out of the ordinary, the jury would be entitled to take that into account. However, the evidence here suggests that the jury could also take the opposite view — that the harassment of Ingram was unique.

Any of the above incidents, viewed in isolation, would not have been enough to have transformed the workplace into a hostile or abusive one. No employer can lightly be held liable for single or scattered incidents. We cannot ignore, however, the habitual use of epithets here or view the conduct without an eye for its cumulative effect.

Our precedent has made this point repeatedly. *See Amirmokri v. Baltimore Gas & Elec. Co.*, 60 F.3d 1126, 1131 (4th Cir. 1995) (finding the alleged harassment was sufficiently severe or pervasive because an Iranian plaintiff was called "names like 'the local terrorist,' a 'camel jockey' and 'the Emir of Waldorf'" on an almost daily basis).

Companies cannot, of course, be charged with cleansing their workplace of all offensive remarks. Such a task would be well-nigh impossible, and would encourage companies to adopt authoritarian traits. But we cannot regard as "merely offensive," and thus "beyond Title VII's purview," *Harris*, constant and repetitive abuse founded upon misperceptions that all Muslims possess hostile designs against the United States, that all Muslims support jihad, that all Muslims were sympathetic to the 9/11 attack, and that all Muslims are proponents of radical Islam.

If Americans were forced to practice their faith under the conditions to which Ingram was subject, the Free Exercise Clause and the embodiment of its values in the Title VII protections against workplace religious prejudice would ring quite hollow. Title VII makes plain that religious freedom in America entails more than the right to attend one's own synagogue, mosque, or church. Free religious exercise would mean little if restricted to places of worship or days of observance, only to disappear the next morning at work. In this regard, Title VII helps ensure the special nature of American unity, one not premised on homogeneity but upon the common allegiance to and customary practice of our constitutional ideals of mutual respect.

D.

[The court finally turned to the basis of the employer's liability for the actions of its workers and managers, finding that the standards for such liability were met.]

NOTES

1. *Other Bases of Discriminatory Harassment.* As *Sunbelt* illustrates, harassment claims under the antidiscrimination statutes have not been limited to sexual harassment. While sexual harassment predominates among the hostile environment cases under Title VII, the first case to recognize hostile environment as a basis for liability under Title VII, *Rogers v. EEOC*, 454 F.2d 234 (5th Cir. 1971), concerned an employer who "created an offensive work environment for employees by giving discriminatory service to its Hispanic clientele." Sexual harassment cases such as *Meritor* revived litigation over work environments contaminated by racial, national origin, or age discrimination. *See Ellis v. Houston*, 742 F.3d 307 (8th Cir. 2014) (even if particular acts experienced by individual officers were insufficiently severe or pervasive, the pattern of harassment suffered by five African American prison guards sufficed, especially in light of evidence that supervisors made or condoned racist comments in group settings on nearly a daily basis); *Lambert v. Peri Formworks Sys., Inc.*, 723 F.3d 863, 868-69 (7th Cir. 2013) (racial harassment could be found even though the most offensive statements — reference to workers as "donkeys" and a "gorilla" and the use of "nigger" — occurred over a period of several years, were not physically threatening, and did not affect Lambert's work performance; the statements were made on multiple occasions using terms that a trier of fact could view as racial slurs); *Rivera v. Rochester*

Genesee Reg'l Transp. Auth., 702 F.3d 685 (2d Cir. 2012) (Puerto Rican and African American plaintiffs established triable cases of national origin and racial harassment by each testifying to several instances where epithets like "spic," "Taco Bell," and "nigger" were used; there was also evidence about extensive bullying and physical harassment which could be found by a jury to be connected to the slurs).

Sunbelt was itself a religious harassment case under Title VII, *see also Griffin v. City of Portland*, 3:12-CV-01591-MO, 2013 WL 5785173 (D. Or. Oct. 25, 2013) (cursing, including the use of "Jesus Christ" as an expletive, could be harassment on the basis of religion). *See* posting of Charles A. Sullivan, *Stop Cursing, Damn It!* to Workplace Prof http://lawprofessors.typepad.com/laborprof_blog/2013/11/damn-it-stop-cursing.html. But there have also been successful claims under the ADA, *see Arrieta-Colon v. Wal-Mart P.R., Inc.*, 434 F.3d 75 (1st Cir. 2006) (upholding jury verdict of disability discrimination for plaintiff who was harassed because his penile implants left him in a constant state of semi-erection), and presumably age-based harassment would also be actionable.

2. *Harris.* The *Sunbelt* court repeatedly refers to *Harris v. Forklift Systems, Inc.*, 510 U.S. 17 (1993), where a unanimous Court, building on *Meritor*, established the standards for "severe or pervasive." Although the district court had recognized the severity of the harassment, it had dismissed because the comments were not "so severe as to be expected to seriously affect [Harris's] psychological well-being." Quoting *Meritor*, the Court wrote:

> When the workplace is permeated with "discriminatory intimidation, ridicule, and insult," that is "sufficiently severe or pervasive to alter the conditions of the victim's employment and create an abusive working environment," Title VII is violated.
>
> This standard, which we reaffirm today, takes a middle path between making actionable any conduct that is merely offensive and requiring the conduct to cause a tangible psychological injury. As we pointed out in *Meritor*, "mere utterance of an . . . epithet which engenders offensive feelings in an employee," does not sufficiently affect the conditions of employment to implicate Title VII. Conduct that is not severe or pervasive enough to create an objectively hostile or abusive work environment—an environment that a reasonable person would find hostile or abusive—is beyond Title VII's purview. Likewise, if the victim does not subjectively perceive the environment to be abusive, the conduct has not actually altered the conditions of the victim's employment, and there is no Title VII violation.
>
> But Title VII comes into play before the harassing conduct leads to a nervous breakdown. A discriminatorily abusive work environment, even one that does not seriously affect employees' psychological well-being, can and often will detract from employees' job performance, discourage employees from remaining on the job, or keep them from advancing in their careers. Moreover, even without regard to these tangible effects, the very fact that the discriminatory conduct was so severe or pervasive that it created a work environment abusive to employees because of their race, gender, religion, or national origin offends Title VII's broad rule of workplace equality. The appalling conduct alleged in *Meritor*, and the reference in that case to environments "'so heavily polluted with discrimination as to destroy completely the emotional and psychological stability of minority group workers,'" quoting *Rogers v. EEOC*, merely present some especially egregious examples of harassment. They do not mark the boundary of what is actionable.

530 U.S. at 21-22. Thus, while Title VII certainly "bars conduct that would seriously affect a reasonable person's psychological well-being, . . . the statute is not limited to such conduct. So long as the environment would reasonably be perceived, and is

perceived, as hostile or abusive, there is no need for it also to be psychologically injurious." *Id.* at 22.

The *Harris* Court stressed that "[t]his is not, and by its nature cannot be, a mathematically precise test," *id.* Rather, it requires "looking at all the circumstances. These may include the frequency of the discriminatory conduct; its severity; whether it is physically threatening or humiliating, or a mere offensive utterance; and whether it unreasonably interferes with an employee's work performance." *Id.* The employee's "psychological well-being" is relevant, but by no means the only factor. A recent article argues for a renewed focus on context in terms of the harasser's role in the employer's hierarchy. Susan Grover & Kimberley Piro, *Consider the Source: When the Harasser Is the Boss,* 79 FORDHAM L. REV. 499 (2010 *See also* commentaries by Kerri Stone, Mar. 17, 2011, and Henry Chambers, Feb. 24, 2001, http://worklaw.jotwell.com/.

3. *Applying* Harris. As *Sunbelt* well illustrates, *Harris* provides little in the way of answers even if it sets the governing analytic structure. The divergent views of the same conduct by the district court and the Fourth Circuit illustrate how indeterminate the "severe or pervasive" concepts are even after *Harris.* You might find a parallel in the tort of intentional infliction of emotional distress in Chapter 5, but courts in discriminatory harassment cases have tended to find claims stated far more often than under the common law. Is that because it's somehow more harmful to make an employee's life miserable for reasons related to her protected status than for other reasons?

In any event, many courts have applied the *Harris* standard, and the results are anything but consistent. *Compare Desardouin v. City of Rochester,* 708 F.3d 102 (2d Cir. 2013) (comments made on a weekly basis over several months, though not threatening, were more than merely offensive; for a male supervisor to repeatedly say to a female subordinate that her husband was "not taking care of [her] in bed" could readily be found to be a solicitation for sexual relations coupled with a claim of sexual prowess); *Gerald v. Univ. of P.R.,* 707 F.3d 7 (1st Cir. 2013) (testimony that her supervisor grabbed plaintiff's breasts, sexually propositioned her, and crassly asked in front of others why she would not have sex with him could be found sufficiently egregious to be actionable), *with Stevens v. Saint Elizabeth Med. Ctr., Inc.,* 533 F. App'x 634 (6th Cir. 2013) (conduct not such that a reasonable person would find objectively hostile when multiple text messages were neither offensive nor vulgar, and most were innocuous; the texts that inappropriately expressed continued affection and physical interactions in the office including kissing may have been unwanted or unsolicited but did not result "in a working environment permeated with discriminatory intimidation or ridicule, nor was it physically threatening such that it would have unreasonably interfered" with plaintiff's work performance).

4. *A Few Comments Not Enough?* Courts have sometimes resisted finding actionable harassment based only on a few offensive comments. In *Clark County School District v. Breeden,* reproduced at page 713, the Supreme Court held that no reasonable person could believe that telling a single joke with a sexual innuendo constituted actionable harassment. *See also Ladd v. Grand Trunk Western R.R.,* 552 F.3d 495, 501 (6th Cir. 2009) (where no actual touching took place and plaintiff testified to only one specific incident of a sex- or race-based epithet directed at her, a "total lack of specificity" as to other verbal abuse directed at her justified summary judgment for the employer despite evidence of other epithets — "lesbian," "dyke," and "gay" — that were not directed at her); *Sprague v. Thorn Americas, Inc.,* 129 F.3d 1355 (10th Cir. 1997) (sporadic comments over 16-month period, including joking request that plaintiff undo her top button, staring down her dress and joking about it, and referring to a jewelry item as "kinky," did not create a hostile environment). As in *Sunbelt*, courts have been more open to finding a hostile environment based on verbal harassment when the comments are alleged to be "commonplace," "ongoing," and "continuing" over a long period of time. *E.g., Mosby-Grant v. City of Hagerstown*, 630 F.3d 326 (4th Cir. 2010) (finding a triable claim of sexual harassment when police academy recruit produced evidence that she was targeted because of her sex, consistently made to feel like an outsider by her classmates and some instructors, sexist comments were frequently made to her or in her presence, and she was consistently subjected to taunting); *Vera v. McHugh*, 622 F.3d 17, 28 (1st Cir. 2010) (male supervisor's staring at plaintiff in a sexual way, repeatedly standing too close to her, and once calling her "babe," could support a reasonable jury finding of sexual harassment; although some lack of privacy and personal space was inherent in the situation, "Rodriguez went out of his way to violate Vera's privacy and the integrity of her personal space"); *Pucino v. Verizon Communs., Inc.*, 618 F.3d 112 (2d Cir. 2010) (constant use of "bitch" over several years). However, in *McCowan v. All Star Maintenance*, 273 F.3d 917 (10th Cir. 2001), the court found a jury question in a racially hostile work environment claim, even though the plaintiffs worked for only three weeks. Throughout their employment, they were subjected to vulgar and offensive speech, including such terms as "burrito-eating motherfuckers" and "stupid fucking Mexicans." The court overturned the lower court's grant of summary judgment, leaving it to the jury to determine whether the conduct was sufficiently severe or pervasive. And sometimes a claim can be stated with neither touching nor comments. *See Billings v. Town of Grafton*, 515 F.3d 39 (1st Cir. 2008) (even absent touching, sexual advances, or overtly sexual comments, a manager's repeatedly staring at his subordinate's breasts could constitute actionable harassment).

5. *Blue Collar Versus White Collar.* In discussing the requirement that conduct be severe or pervasive to be actionable, the *Oncale* court states, "in same-sex (as in all) harassment cases, that inquiry requires careful consideration of the social context in which particular behavior occurs and is experienced by its target." One possible meaning of this is that actions that may be severe in one context are mild in another. We saw a variation on this in *Sunbelt* where the employer argued that the religion-based comments were somehow less objectionable because of the general atmosphere of workers riding each other. In *Williams v. General Motors*, 187 F.3d 553 (6th Cir. 1999), the court held that the standard for establishing sexual harassment does not vary with the work environment. The same standard applies, therefore, whether the complaint is asserted in a coarse blue-collar environment or in a more refined professional environment. Is this holding consistent with *Oncale*?

6. *Is "Unwelcome" Still a Requirement? Harris* framed the core question for harassment cases as whether "the environment would reasonably be perceived, and is perceived, as hostile or abusive." This formulation conspicuously omitted any reference to whether particular conduct had to be "unwelcome" in order to be actionable, a requirement that *Meritor* had explicitly imposed. And many believe that *Harris* modified *sub silentio* that part of *Meritor*. If conduct is subjectively experienced by the subject as hostile or abusive, it can scarcely be "welcomed" by the subject. *See, e.g., Carr v. Allison Gas Turbine Div., Gen. Motors Corp.*, 32 F.3d 1007, 1008 (7th Cir. 1994) ("'Welcome sexual harassment' is an oxymoron"). Such a view of *Harris* also avoided one of the few aspects of *Meritor* that feminists found objectionable: the Court's statement that evidence of "a complainant's sexually provocative speech or dress" is "obviously relevant" to deciding "whether he or she found particular sexual

advances unwelcome." The Court did recognize the possibility that such evidence would be unduly prejudicial as compared to its probative value but stressed that "there is no per se rule against its admissibility." *Meritor*, 477 U.S. at 69. Assessing a plaintiff's sexual history or her personal style in order to resolve a case, whether it be a criminal prosecution for rape or a civil suit for sexual harassment, is profoundly disturbing and has resulted in amendments to the Rules of Evidence to restrict such inquiries. *See* Jane H. Aiken, *Protecting Plaintiffs' Sexual Pasts: Coping with Preconceptions Through Discretion*, 51 EMORY L. J. 559 (2002) (exploring the civil application of Rule 412).

But is unwelcomeness truly gone? Not according to the *Sunbelt* court, although it had no trouble in finding the religious comments to be unwelcome to Ingram. Some argue that this aspect of *Meritor* is alive and well, together with *Meritor*'s authorization of an inquiry into plaintiff's "dress and personal fantasies." Under this view, welcomeness is not a question of the victim's subjective reaction but, rather, what a reasonable person in the shoes of the alleged harasser would believe she wanted, welcomed, or would otherwise find unobjectionable. Even under such a view, some courts have been resolute in sharply restricting inquiries into the plaintiff's life. An extreme example is *Burns v. McGregor Electronic Industries*, 989 F.2d 959 (8th Cir. 1993), where the Eighth Circuit twice had to reverse the district court, which clearly disapproved of plaintiff's lifestyle. The Eighth Circuit held that a woman's *off-work* dress and activities were irrelevant to whether she welcomed advances at work. Similarly, the fact that she might welcome advances from some individuals does not mean that any man was free to make them:

> The plaintiff's choice to pose for a nude magazine outside work hours is not material to the issue of whether plaintiff found her employer's work-related conduct offensive. This is not a case where Burns posed in provocative and suggestive ways at work. Her private life, regardless how reprehensible the trier of fact might find it to be, did not provide lawful acquiescence to unwanted sexual advances at her work place by her employer. To hold otherwise would be contrary to Title VII's goal of ridding the work place of any kind of unwelcome sexual harassment. . . .

Burns, 989 F.2d at 963. The trial court made explicit findings that the conduct was not invited or solicited despite her posing naked for a nationally distributed magazine The court believed, however, that because of her outside conduct, including her "interest in having her nude pictures appear in a magazine containing much lewd and crude sexually explicit material," the uninvited sexual advances of her employer were not "in and of [themselves] offensive to her." *Id*. The trial court also explained that Burns "would not have been offended if someone she was attracted to did or said the same thing," but the appeals court rejected this approach: "This rationale would allow a complete stranger to pursue sexual behavior at work that a female worker would accept from her husband or boyfriend. This standard would allow a male employee to kiss or fondle a female worker at the workplace." *Id*. at 963.

But notice that even *Burns*, which essentially excludes off-work conduct, did not reject the welcomeness inquiry explicitly. Had plaintiff "posed in provocative and suggestive ways at work," it presumably would have admitted that evidence, although it may run afoul of Rule 412. *See Jaros v. LodgeNet Entm't Corp.*, 171 F. Supp. 2d 992 (D.S.D. 2001), *aff'd*, 294 F.3d 960 (8th Cir. 2002). While *Burns* was decided before *Harris*, post-*Harris* cases, like *Sunbelt*, continue to ask whether conduct was invited or welcomed. *E.g., EEOC v. Prospect Airport Servs.*, 621 F.3d 991, 997-98 (9th Cir. 2010) (the fact that most men might welcome sexual advances from a woman does not establish that the plaintiff did since "welcomeness is inherently subjective"; nevertheless, "for the conduct to be unwelcome for purposes of employer's liability for not stopping it, unwelcomeness has to be communicated"). Such cases put a burden on plaintiff to rebuff sexual advances or otherwise object to sexualized conduct before the harasser can be held responsible and therefore seem to provide harassers a free bite at the apple.

7. *When Is Severe or Pervasive Harassment OK?* Can harassment ever be justified? Establishments such as Hooters restaurants hire females as waitresses, dress them in outfits designed to be provocative, and advertise not just the food but also the sexually attractive personnel. If a Hooters waitress complains of sexual harassment by customers, can the employer justify it, perhaps as a BFOQ? The only decided case to raise this issue starkly is *Lyle v. Warner Brothers Television Productions*, 132 P.3d 211, 225-26 (Cal. 2006), where a writer for the "Friends" sitcom failed to recover under the state's fair employment law for the sexually oriented atmosphere in the studio:

> There is no dispute Friends was a situation comedy that featured young sexually active adults and sexual humor geared primarily toward adults. Aired episodes of the show often used sexual and anatomical language, innuendo, wordplay, and physical gestures to create humor concerning sex, including oral sex, anal sex, heterosexual sex, gay sex, "talking dirty" during sex, premature ejaculation, pornography, pedophiles, and "threesomes." The circumstance that this was a creative workplace focused on generating scripts for an adult-oriented comedy show featuring sexual themes is significant in assessing the existence of triable issues of facts regarding whether the writers' sexual antics and coarse sexual talk were aimed at plaintiff or at women in general, whether plaintiff and other women were singled out to see and hear what happened, and whether the conduct was otherwise motivated by plaintiff's gender.

Concluding that the record showed that the sexual discussions, including of the writers' own personal sexual experiences were "nondirected" conduct, the court found there was no harassment because of sex.

8. *Nontargeted Harassment.* As *Lyle* suggests, there has been some question as to whether harassment must be targeted at women in order to be actionable. *See Ocheltree v. Scollon Prods.*, 335 F.3d 325, 327 (4th Cir. 2003) (en banc). But the cases have generally not found the absence of targeting to be fatal to a claim. *See Hoyle v. Freightliner, LLC*, 650 F.3d 321 (4th Cir. 2011) (given the number of incidents and consistent describing of women in a sexually subservient and demeaning light, a reasonable jury could find an abusive work environment); *Patane v. Clark*, 508 F.3d 106 (2d Cir. 2007) (sexual harassment claim stated as to professor's watching of pornographic videotapes even though plaintiff, his secretary, did not see them when her complaint alleged she regularly observed the professor viewing pornographic videos and she had to handle such videos while opening and delivering his mail; the mere presence of pornography in the workplace can alter the status of women); *Gallagher v. C.H. Robinson Worldwide, Inc.*, 567 F.3d 263, 274 (6th Cir. 2009) ("Whether the offensive conduct was intentionally directed specifically at Gallagher or not, the fact remains that she had no means of escaping her co-workers' loud insulting language and degrading conversations; she was unavoidably exposed to it.").

Further, when harassment is targeted at the plaintiff, harassment of other women may be relevant to establishing that the conduct is actionable. After recognizing that its precedents permitted the factfinder to "consider similar acts of harassment of which a plaintiff becomes aware during the course of his or her employment, even if the harassing acts were directed at others or occurred outside of the plaintiff's presence," *Hawkins v. Anheuser-Busch, Inc.*, 517 F.3d 321, 336 (6th Cir. 2008), went on:

> [T]he appropriate weight to be given a prior act will be directly proportional to the act's proximity in time to the harassment at issue in the plaintiff's case. The further back in time the prior act occurred, in other words, the weaker the inference that the act bears a relationship to the current working environment. On the other hand, more weight should be given to acts committed by a serial harasser if the plaintiff knows that the same individual committed offending acts in the past. This is because a serial harasser left free to harass again leaves the impression that acts of harassment are tolerated at the workplace and supports a plaintiff's claim that the workplace is both objectively and subjectively hostile.

Id. at 336-37. *See also Ziskie v. Mineta*, 547 F.3d 220 (4th Cir. 2008) (district court erred in refusing to consider affidavits of plaintiff's female co-workers regarding harassment merely because it was not experienced firsthand by plaintiff; such evidence could lend credence to plaintiff's mistreatment claims, show the harassment was pervasive, or support a finding that she was treated poorly by co-workers because of her sex, and not some other reason).

9. *Harassment in Splitsville.* The recurring problem of consensual relationships gone bad has troubled harassment law. Even if welcomeness is, generally speaking, not a viable defense separate and apart from the *Harris* requirements, there is one situation where it might arise — where a consensual relationship ends. Although firing one's former lover seems analytically indistinguishable from discharging a person who will not have sex with the harasser in the first place, some courts have been more ambivalent about this scenario. *Compare Pipkins v. Temple Terrace*, 267 F.3d 1197, 1201 (11th Cir. 2001) (stating that, construing plaintiff's allegations in the light most favorable to her, "she merely portrays any action by Klein to have been taken because of his disappointment in their failed relationship. Again, such a motivation is not 'because of . . . sex.'") *with Green v. Adm'rs of the Tulane Educ. Fund*, 284 F.3d 642, 657 (5th Cir. 2002) ("[I]t was only after the relationship ended that Richardson began to harass her. This fact alone supports a jury's inference that he harassed her because she refused to continue to have a casual sexual relationship with him. As such, we conclude that there was sufficient evidence to support the jury's finding of sexual harassment."). *See also Forrest v. Brinker Int'l Payroll Co., LP*, 511 F.3d 225, 229 (1st Cir. 2007) ("In cases involving a prior failed relationship between an accused harasser and alleged victim, reasoning that the harassment could not have been motivated by the victim's sex because it was instead motivated by a romantic relationship gone sour establishes a false dichotomy. Presumably the prior relationship would never have occurred if the victim were not a member of the sex preferred by the harasser, and thus the victim's sex is inextricably linked to the harasser's decision to harass.").

Believe it or not, some management attorneys recommend a "love contract" for couples entering consensual relationships. Sharon Rabin-Margalioth, *Love at Work*, 13 Duke J. Gender L. & Pol'y 237, 253 n.98 (2006), writes that a typical love contract will be written something like this:

We hereby notify the Company that we wish to enter into a voluntary and mutual consensual social relationship. In entering into this relationship, we both understand and agree that we are both free to end the social relationship at any time. Should the social relationship end, we both agree that we shall not allow the breakup to negatively impact the performance of our duties. Prior to signing this Consensual Relationship Contract, we received and reviewed the Company Sexual Harassment Policy, a copy of which is attached hereto. By signing below, we acknowledge that the social relationship between us does not violate the Company's Sexual Harassment Policy, and that entering into the social relationship has not been made a condition or term of employment.

See also Vicki Schultz, *The Sanitized Workplace*, 112 YALE L.J. 2061, 2126-28 (2003). Do you think this would exonerate an employer of liability? Might it create other problems even if it did?

10. *Harassment Meets the First Amendment.* Hostile environment sexual harassment liability frequently is based on sexually offensive, obscene, or denigrating speech. Some harassment cases, however, have involved speech that is not sexually explicit and more clearly political in nature. An individual is free to get on a soap box and argue that women belong in the kitchen, not the workplace. Can that same individual bring his soapbox into the workplace and argue the same thing there? *See Lipsett v. University of Puerto Rico*, 864 F.2d 881, 903-4 (1st Cir. 1988) (female resident stated a Title VII claim by alleging that she was subjected to comments that women should not be surgeons). Is harassment law limited by the First Amendment? *See* David Bernstein, YOU CAN'T SAY THAT!: THE GROWING THREAT TO CIVIL LIBERTIES FROM ANTIDISCRIMINATION LAWS (2003); Miranda Oshige McGowan, *Certain Illusions About Speech: Why the Free-Speech Critique of Hostile Work Environment Harassment Is Wrong*, 19 CONST. COMMENT. 391 (2002); Helen L. Norton, *You Can't Ask (or Say) That: The First Amendment Implications of Civil Rights Restrictions on Decisionmaker Speech*, 11 WM. & MARY BILL RTS. J. 727, 729, 777 (2003); Eugene Volokh, *What Speech Does "Hostile Work Environment" Harassment Law Restrict?*, 85 GEO. L.J. 627 (1997); Kingsley R. Browne, *Zero Tolerance for the First Amendment: Title VII's Regulation of Employee Speech*, 27 OHIO N.U. L. REV. 563 (2001); Charles R. Calleros, *Title VII and the First Amendment: Content-Neutral Regulation, Disparate Impact, and the "Reasonable Person,"* 58 OHIO ST. L.J. 1217 (1997); Cynthia L. Estlund, *Freedom of Expression in the Workplace and the Problem of Discriminatory Harassment*, 75 TEX. L. REV. 687 (1997).

Despite the outpouring of scholarship on the subject, few cases have raised First Amendment problems with such suits, and the Supreme Court has, in dicta in *R.A.V. v. City of St. Paul, Minnesota*, 505 U.S. 377 (1992), suggested that there is no free speech concern:

[S]ince words can in some circumstances violate laws directed not against speech but against conduct (a law against treason, for example, is violated by telling the enemy the nation's defense secrets), a particular content-based subcategory of a proscribable class of speech can be swept up incidentally within the reach of a statute directed at conduct rather than speech. Thus, for example, sexually derogatory "fighting words," among other words, may produce a violation of Title VII's general prohibition against sexual discrimination in employment practices, 42 U.S.C. §2000e-2; 29 C.F.R. §1604.11 (1991). *See also* 18 U.S.C. §242; 42 U.S.C. §§1981, 1982. Where the government does not target conduct on the basis of its expressive content, acts are not shielded from regulation merely because they express a discriminatory idea or philosophy.

R.A.V., 505 U.S. at 389. Since *R.A.V.*, the Court decided *Harris* in which the sexually harassing behavior was primarily evidenced by offensive remarks. Although the constitutionality of imposing liability on the employer for those remarks was raised in briefs submitted in that case, the Court did not address the issue in its opinion. Does the dictum in *R.A.V.* explain why Hardy's statements in *Harris* are not protected?

11. *Constructive Discharge.* In many harassment cases, the plaintiff, unable to resolve the matter internally, quits. That was true, for example, in *Harris.* Assuming the sexual harassment was actionable, and the employer liable, can such a plaintiff recover for lost future earnings, or is she limited to the emotional distress caused by the harassment during the time she was employed? The question is one of "constructive discharge," that is, situations in which an employee's formal quitting is viewed as equivalent to being fired. The Supreme Court has held that the fact that harassment is sufficiently severe or pervasive to contaminate the work environment and thus be actionable is not necessarily sufficient to establish a constructive discharge. *Pennsylvania State Police v. Suders*, 542 U.S. 129 (2004), held that "A hostile-environment constructive discharge claim entails something more: A plaintiff who advances such a compound claim must show working conditions so intolerable that a reasonable person would have felt compelled to resign." Had Ingram quit, would he have been constructively discharged?

12. *Employer Liability.* Conduct by a supervisor, co-worker, or even customer may be harassment without making the employer liable for such conduct. In *Sunbelt* itself, the court, having found a triable claim of harassment, still had to go on to decide whether the employer was liable for such conduct. Because they are part and parcel of more general employer efforts to comply with the law and reduce legal exposure, issues of employer liability are treated in Chapter 13 on risk management.

Note on Grooming and Dress Codes

Perhaps the most blatant remaining form of gender discrimination in employment is employer dress and grooming codes, which frequently have disparate standards for males and females. How can such standards survive Title VII's prohibition of gender discrimination? In *Willingham v. Macon Telegraph Publ'g Co.*, 507 F.2d 1084, 1091-92 (5th Cir. 1975) (en banc), the Fifth Circuit denied a man's challenge to an employer's rule prohibiting male (but not female) employees from having hair longer than shoulder length:

> Equal employment *opportunity* may be secured only when employers are barred from discriminating against employees on the basis of immutable characteristics, such as race and national origin. Similarly, an employer cannot have one hiring policy for men and another for women *if* the distinction is based on some fundamental right. But a hiring policy that distinguishes on some other ground, such as grooming codes or length of hair, is related more closely to the employer's choice of how to run his business than to equality of employment opportunity. . . . [A] line must be drawn between distinctions grounded on such fundamental rights as the right to have children or to marry and those interfering with the manner in which an employer exercises his judgment as to the way to operate a business. Hair length is not immutable and in the situation of employer vis à vis employee enjoys no constitutional protection. If the employee objects to the grooming code he has

the right to reject it by looking elsewhere for employment, or alternatively he may choose to subordinate his preference by accepting the code along with the job. . . .

We adopt the view, therefore, that distinctions in employment practices between men and women on the basis of something other than immutable or protected characteristics do not inhibit employment *opportunity* in violation of Sec. 703(a). Congress sought only to give all persons equal access to the job market, not to limit an employer's right to exercise his informed judgment as to how best to run his shop.

We are in accord also with the alternative ground. . . . "From all that appears, equal job opportunities are available to both sexes. It does not appear that defendant fails to impose grooming standards for female employees; thus in this respect each sex is treated equally."

Willingham has received general acceptance: gender-specific differences in dress and grooming codes do not per se violate Title VII. *See, e.g., Harper v. Blockbuster Entm't Corp.*, 139 F.3d 1385 (11th Cir. 1998) (different hair length standards for men and women do not violate Title VII); *Tavora v. New York Mercantile Exch.*, 101 F.3d 907 (2d Cir. 1997) (same).

No one seems to doubt that permitting female, but not male, employees to have shoulder-length hair is sex discrimination in an analytic sense. As the Court said in another context, "[s]uch a practice does not pass the simple test of whether the evidence shows 'treatment of a person in a manner which but for that person's sex would be different.'" *City of L.A. Dep't of Water & Power v. Manhart*, 435 U.S. 702, 711 (1978). What, then, is the justification for permitting it? Does *Willingham* establish a de minimis test under which trivial sex distinctions do not warrant federal court intervention? That would explain the court's distinction between cases involving hair length and cases involving "fundamental rights." Remember, also, that some courts have required different treatment to have material adverse effects in order to constitute discrimination. Maybe hair length requirements are not material. Or is *Willingham* an example of a "volition" exception to Title VII: Employer requirements that can easily be met by an employee are not within the statutory proscription?

Declining protection because the different treatment is trivial is consistent with the courts' treatment of sexual harassment that is not sufficiently serious or pervasive to create a hostile environment. But even a minor incident of sexual harassment becomes actionable as a quid pro quo case when job benefits are contingent on acceptance of the discriminatory remarks or conduct. What if an employee is threatened with the loss of his job on the ground that his hair is too long? How can this be viewed as trivial?

Many commentators look on grooming cases as sui generis, that is, that they shouldn't be read to have much meaning beyond the context in which they arise, perhaps because the issues they address are perceived by many to be insignificant. But don't these cases reflect stereotypes so ingrained that they are not even recognized as such? *See* Karl E. Klare, *Power/Dressing: Regulation of Employee Appearance*, 26 NEW ENG. L. REV. 1395 (1992). Why is it that an employer can legally prohibit males from wearing dresses or eye shadow? Is it because there is something wrong with males assuming "female" roles? Is a man wrong to assume such roles in turn because females are inferior and a man demeans himself by aping them? Is it merely coincidence that society looks more favorably on women who appropriate "male" attire (e.g., the pants suit) than the other way around? Or perhaps the courts are simply applying what they perceive as legislative intent: Whatever Congress *said*, it did not *mean* to bar this kind of employer rule. Isn't it clear that the 1964 Congress did not intend Title VII to require a unisex dress code?

Several decisions have found Title VII violated when the employer's dress code did not treat women equally. In *Carroll v. Talman Federal Savings & Loan Ass'n*, 604 F.2d 1028 (7th Cir. 1979), the court considered a dress code allowing males to wear "customary business attire" but requiring women to wear uniforms. Although disclaiming any intent to pass on the reasonableness of general employer dress regulations, the court distinguished the case before it where the disparate treatment was demeaning to women: "While there is nothing offensive about uniforms per se, when some employees are uniformed and others not there is a natural tendency to assume that the uniformed women have a lesser professional status than their male colleagues attired in normal business clothes." *Id.* at 1033; *see also Frank v. United Air Lines*, 216 F.3d 845 (9th Cir. 2000) (an airline's differential weight standards for flight attendants were facially discriminatory because they imposed unequal burdens on men and women in how they were calculated). Expectations that there would be a sea change in this area were, however, dashed by *Jespersen v. Harrah's Operating Co.*, 444 F.3d 1104 (9th Cir. 2006) (7-4), which rejected a claim that sex-differentiated grooming policies were illegal because they placed an unequal burden on women due to the time and expense entailed in applying make-up.

The issue of appearance restrictions, whether framed as a discrimination issue or as a matter of personal autonomy has generated considerable attention in the law reviews. The *Duke Journal of Gender & Law* devoted an entire symposium issue to it in 2007. Similar articles also challenge grooming rules that affect African Americans. *See, e.g.,* Angela Onwuachi-Willig, *Another Hair Piece: Exploring New Strands of Analysis Under Title VII*, 98 Geo. L. J. 1079 (2010).

PROBLEM

9-4. You work as an employment lawyer. A young woman has come to see you seeking advice. She tells you that she works at a nearby mid-sized law firm. She is a relatively young associate, and this is her first job after her clerkship. She tells you she made a "big mistake" by getting "involved" with a partner at the firm. While she does not work in his practice group, she is sometimes assigned out to work with that group, which is how she got to know him. From her point of view, the relationship "didn't work out" and "wasn't that big a deal." However, she is beginning to be concerned that it's a much bigger deal for him.

She broke up with him two weeks ago, sending him an e-mail from her G-mail account, telling him the usual stuff. He responded with a series of three e-mails ranging from confused to hurt to angry. His last e-mail stated, "You'll be sorry about this. We had a very good thing going." He has not since communicated with her directly, but he snubs her when they meet in the halls, and she has heard from a senior associate that "Joe's badmouthing you with the partners big-time."

Your client will not be considered for partner for several years, but her annual review was last week, and she received a 7 (out of a scale of 10). In last year's annual review, she was rated an 8.5. The reviewing partner, who is in charge of her group, told her, "Don't worry about it, I'm sure you'll bounce back and there's no impact on salary or bonus." But she did not find her explanations for the slippage very satisfactory.

How would you advise her?

Note on Sexual Orientation Discrimination

Sexual orientation is not listed as a protected characteristic under Title VII, and discrimination on the basis of sexual orientation per se is not actionable under federal law. Although it is easy to frame sexual orientation discrimination as simple disparate treatment (a male, say, is discriminated against for engaging in conduct — sexual relations with males — that would not be a problem were he female), courts have not been willing to read Title VII to reach this result. *See, e.g., DeSantis v. Pac. Telephone & Telegraph Co.* 608 F.2d 327 (9th Cir. 1979).

It is possible, however, to frame discrimination on the basis of sexual orientation as a problem of gender stereotyping. Similar arguments can be made with respect to transgender or transsexual individuals. Early cases rejected such a theory. *See, e.g., Smith v. Liberty Mutual Ins. Co.*, 569 F.2d 325 (5th Cir. 1978) (finding discrimination against a male on the basis of his perceived "effeminacy" not within the statute); *DeSantis* (finding that male could be legally fired for being effeminate, even if he was not gay). However, the authority of such decisions was radically undercut by *Price Waterhouse v. Hopkins* (reproduced at page 597), which held it impermissible to discriminate against a woman because she is too masculine. It would seem that discrimination against a male for "effeminacy" or other failures to conform to male stereotypes would also be impermissible, and some courts have so held. In *Nichols v. Azteca Restaurant Enterprises, Inc.*, 256 F.3d 864 (9th Cir. 2001), the court found plaintiff had stated a claim under Title VII when he alleged he was discriminated against for acting "too feminine." It said *Price Waterhouse* prohibits discrimination based on sex stereotyping and thus to the extent *DeSantis* conflicts with *Price Waterhouse*, it is no longer good law. *See also Prowel v. Wise Bus. Forms, Inc.*, 579 F.3d 285 (3d Cir. 2009) (although the plaintiff might have been subjected to harassment because of his sexual orientation per se, there was enough basis to suspect that the harassment was because of his failure to conform to gender stereotypes to warrant a trial). *But see Hamm v. Weyauwega Milk Prods.*, 332 F.3d 1058, 1068 (7th Cir. 2003) (Posner, J., concurring) ("'sex stereotyping' should not be regarded as a form of sex discrimination, though it will sometimes, as in the *Hopkins* case, be evidence of sex discrimination."). Is it a very long step to prohibit discrimination on the basis of sexual orientation — the most extreme way in which members of one sex demonstrate a characteristic usually associated with the other sex? *See generally* Zachary A. Kramer, *Heterosexuality and Title VII*, 103 Nw. U. L. Rev. 205, 227-30 (2009); L. Camille Hébert, *Transforming Transsexual and Transgender Rights*, 15 Wm. & Mary J. Women & L. 535 (2009).

The absence of a federal statute prohibiting discrimination on the basis of sexual orientation has led to a number of other legal theories attacking such conduct. In public employment, sexual orientation discrimination has been challenged on the basis of the right of privacy, due process, free speech, and equal protection. Until recently, these constitutional attacks had very limited success, but developments such as *Lawrence v. Texas*, 539 U.S. 558 (2003) (striking down Texas same-sex sodomy law) and *Romer v. Evans*, 517 U.S. 620 (1996) (striking down Colorado law as discriminating against gays) augur more success for such claims, as does the Supreme Court's invalidation of the Defense of Marriage Act in *United States v. Windsor*, 133 S. Ct. 2675 (2013).

One significant setback for what Justice Scalia describes pejoratively as the "homosexual agenda," was *Boy Scouts of America v. Dale*, 530 U.S. 640 (2000), where the Court overturned a state court decision requiring the Boy Scouts to admit a gay scoutmaster under the state's law barring discrimination in public accommodations on the basis of sexual orientation. The Court held that so applying New Jersey's public accommodations law violated the Boy Scouts' "First Amendment right of expressive association." *Id.* at 644. Although *Dale* involved a state law relating to sexual orientation discrimination in public accommodations, some have warned that it might undercut antidiscrimination statutes like Title VII. *But see Rumsfeld v. Forum for Academic & Institutional Rights, Inc.*, 547 U.S. 47 (2006) (limiting the right of expressive association to situations where compliance with the at-issue law would indicate to the world that the association was endorsing a position).

Further, challenges based on state constitutions have also been successful. On the same day and in the same city where *DeSantis* was handed down, the Supreme Court of California decided *Gay Law Students Ass'n v. Pacific Telephone & Telegraph Co.*, 595 P.2d 592 (Cal. 1979), holding that gays could sue a public utility for employment discrimination under the equal protection clause of the California Constitution. *See also Goodridge v. Dep't of Pub. Health*, 798 N.E.2d 941 (Mass. 2003) (holding the state could not "deny the protections, benefits, and obligations conferred by civil marriage to two individuals of the same sex who wish to marry"); *Witt v. Dep't of the Air Force*, 527 F.3d 806, 819 (9th Cir. 2008) (2-1) (in assessing a challenge to the military's Don't Ask, Don't Tell policy "when the government attempts to intrude upon the personal and private lives of homosexuals, in a manner that implicates the rights identified in *Lawrence*, the government must advance an important governmental interest, the intrusion must significantly further that interest, and the intrusion must be necessary to further that interest. In other words, for the third factor, a less intrusive means must be unlikely to achieve substantially the government's interest.").

More broadly, a number of states have enacted their own civil rights legislation expressly covering sexual orientation. Such statutes typically protect against discrimination on the basis of sexual orientation, normally defined as including heterosexuality, bisexuality, and homosexuality. For a comprehensive listing, *see* http://www.lambdalegal.org. *See generally* Roberta Achtenberg & Karen Moulding, SEXUAL ORIENTATION AND THE LAW §§ 5.01-.07 (2008); While versions of an Employment Nondiscrimination Act ("ENDA") have been perennially introduced in Congress, it has yet to pass.

E. RETALIATION

In addition to prohibiting discrimination on the grounds of race, sex, religion, national origin, and age, Title VII, § 1981, and the ADEA create a remedy for certain retaliatory conduct. Retaliation is also prohibited by the ADA in somewhat different terms.

Section 704(a) of Title VII, 42 U.S.C. § 2000e-3(a), provides:

It shall be an unlawful employment practice for an employer to discriminate against any of his employees or applicants for employment . . . because he has opposed any practice made an unlawful employment practice by this title, or because he has made a charge, testified, assisted, or participated in any manner in an investigation, proceeding, or hearing under this title.

The ADEA prohibits retaliation in substantially identical language. 29 U.S.C. § 623(d). Even though § 1981 does not expressly prohibit retaliation, it has been held to do so through its prohibition of discrimination on account of race. *CBOCS West, Inc. v. Humphries*, 553 U.S. 442 (2008); *see also Jackson v. Birmingham Bd. of Educ.*, 544 U.S. 167 (2005) (retaliation for opposing sex discrimination was sex discrimination within the meaning of Title IX).

Clark County School District v. Breeden
532 U.S. 268 (2001)

Per Curiam.

[Plaintiff sued her employer, the Clark County School District, alleging that the District had taken two separate adverse employment actions against her in response to two different protected activities in which she had engaged.]

On October 21, 1994, [Ms. Breeden's] male supervisor met with [her] and another male employee to review the psychological evaluation reports of four job applicants. The report for one of the applicants disclosed that the applicant had once commented to a co-worker, "I hear making love to you is like making love to the Grand Canyon." At the meeting [Ms. Breeden's] supervisor read the comment aloud, looked at [her] and stated, "I don't know what that means." The other employee then said, "Well, I'll tell you later," and both men chuckled. [Ms. Breeden] later complained about the comment to the offending employee, to Assistant Superintendent George Ann Rice, the employee's supervisor, and to another assistant superintendent of petitioner. Her first claim of retaliation asserts that she was punished for these complaints.

The Court of Appeals for the Ninth Circuit has applied § 2000e-3(a) to protect employee "opposition" not just to practices that are actually "made . . . unlawful" by Title VII, but also to practices that the employee could reasonably believe were unlawful. We have no occasion to rule on the propriety of this interpretation, because even assuming it is correct, no one could reasonably believe that the incident recounted above violated Title VII.

Title VII forbids actions taken on the basis of sex that "discriminate against any individual with respect to his compensation, terms, conditions, or privileges of employment." 42 U.S.C. § 2000e-2(a)(1). Just three Terms ago, we reiterated, what was plain from our previous decisions, that sexual harassment is actionable under Title VII only if it is "so 'severe or pervasive' as to 'alter the conditions of [the victim's] employment and create an abusive working environment.'" (Only harassing conduct that is "severe or pervasive" can produce a "constructive alteration in the terms or conditions of employment"); *Faragher v. Boca Raton*, 524 U.S. 775 (1998), quoting *Meritor; Oncale v. Sundowner Offshore Services, Inc.*, [reproduced at page 687] (Title VII "forbids only behavior so objectively offensive as to alter the 'conditions' of the victim's employment"). Workplace conduct is not measured in isolation; instead, "whether an environment is sufficiently hostile or abusive" must be judged "by 'looking at all the circumstances,' including the 'frequency of the discriminatory conduct; its severity; whether it is physically threatening or humiliating, or a mere offensive utterance; and whether it unreasonably interferes with an employee's work performance.'" *Faragher v. Boca Raton* (quoting *Harris*). Hence, "[a] recurring point in [our] opinions is that simple teasing, offhand comments, and isolated incidents (unless extremely serious) will not amount to discriminatory changes in the 'terms and conditions of employment.'" *Faragher v. Boca Raton*.

No reasonable person could have believed that the single incident recounted above violated Title VII's standard. The ordinary terms and conditions of [Ms. Breeden's] job required her to review the sexually explicit statement in the course of screening job applicants. Her co-workers who participated in the hiring process were subject to the same requirement, and indeed, in the District Court [she] "conceded that it did not bother or upset her" to read the statement in the file. Her supervisor's comment, made at a meeting to review the application, that he did not know what the statement meant; her co-worker's responding comment; and the chuckling of both are at worst an "isolated incident" that cannot remotely be considered "extremely serious," as our cases require, *Faragher v. Boca Raton*. The holding of the Court of Appeals to the contrary must be reversed.

Besides claiming that she was punished for complaining to [the School District's] personnel about the alleged sexual harassment, [Ms. Breeden] also claimed that she was punished for filing charges against petitioner with the Nevada Equal Rights Commission and the Equal Employment Opportunity Commission (EEOC) and for filing the present suit. [She] filed her lawsuit on April 1, 1997; on April 10, 1997, [her] supervisor, Assistant Superintendent Rice, "mentioned to Allin Chandler, Executive Director of plaintiff's union, that she was contemplating transferring plaintiff to the position of Director of Professional Development Education"; and this transfer was "carried through" in May. In order to show, as her defense against summary judgment required, the existence of a causal connection between her protected activities and the transfer, [Ms. Breeden] "relied wholly on the temporal proximity of the filing of her complaint on April 1, 1997 and Rice's statement to plaintiff's union representative on April 10, 1997 that she was considering transferring plaintiff to the [new] position." The District Court, however, found that [Ms. Breeden] did not serve [the School District] with the summons and complaint until April 11, 1997, one day after Rice had made the statement, and Rice filed an affidavit stating that she did not become aware of the lawsuit until after April 11, a claim that [Ms. Breeden] did not challenge. Hence, the court concluded, [she] "had not shown that any causal connection exists between her protected activities and the adverse employment decision."

The Court of Appeals reversed, relying on two facts: The EEOC had issued a right-to-sue letter to [Ms. Breeden] three months before Rice announced she was contemplating the transfer, and the actual transfer occurred one month after Rice learned of [her] suit. The latter fact is immaterial in light of the fact that [the School District] concededly was contemplating the transfer before it learned of the suit. Employers need not suspend previously planned transfers upon discovering that a Title VII suit has been filed, and their proceeding along lines previously contemplated, though not yet definitively determined, is no evidence whatever of causality.

As for the right-to-sue letter: [Ms. Breeden] did not rely on that letter in the District Court and did not mention it in her opening brief on appeal. Her demonstration of causality all along had rested upon the connection between the transfer and the filing of her lawsuit—to which connection the letter was irrelevant. When, however, [the School District] answering brief in the Court of Appeals demonstrated conclusively the lack of causation between the filing of [Ms. Breeden's] lawsuit and Rice's decision, [she] mentioned the letter for the first time in her reply brief. The Ninth Circuit's opinion . . . suggests that the letter provided [the School District] with its first notice of [her] charge before the EEOC, and hence allowed the inference that the transfer proposal made three months later was [its] reaction to the charge. This will not do.

First, there is no indication that Rice even knew about the right-to-sue letter when she proposed transferring respondent. And second, if one presumes she knew about it, one must also presume that she (or her predecessor) knew *almost two years earlier* about the protected action (filing of the EEOC complaint) that the letter supposedly disclosed. . . . The cases that accept mere temporal proximity between an employer's knowledge of protected activity and an adverse employment action as sufficient evidence of causality to establish a prima facie case uniformly hold that the temporal proximity must be "very close," *Neal v. Ferguson Constr. Co.*, 237 F.3d 1248, 1253 (CA10 2001). *See, e.g., Richmond v. Oneok, Inc.*, 120 F.3d 205, 209 (CA10 1997) (3-month period insufficient); *Hughes v. Derwinski*, 967 F.2d 1168, 1174-1175 (CA7 1992) (4-month period insufficient). Action taken (as here) 20 months later suggests, by itself, no causality at all. . . .

NOTES

1. *Public Policy Tort.* Recall the public policy discussion in Chapter 4. Retaliation under the antidiscrimination statutes is simply a version of the rule that an employee cannot be discharged in violation of public policy. However, as will be explained in these Notes, the doctrine has developed under the antidiscrimination laws in more elaborate but not always intuitive ways.

2. *Prima Facie Case of Retaliation.* A standard formulation of the prima facie case for retaliation is found in *Kwan v. Andalex Grp., LLC*, 737 F.3d 834, 844 (2d Cir. 2013), which requires the plaintiff to show "(1) 'participation in a protected activity'; (2) the defendant's knowledge of the protected activity; (3) 'an adverse employment action'; and (4) 'a causal connection between the protected activity and the adverse employment action.'" (citation omitted). If plaintiff is able to establish such a case, the burden of production shifts to the employer to put into evidence a nonretaliatory reason for its action. At that point, the plaintiff may still prevail by proving that reason is a pretext for retaliation. *Jute v. Hamilton Sundstrand Corp.*, 420 F.3d 166, 179 (2d Cir. 2005). At issue in *Breeden* were the first and third prongs.

Proving causation is often the most difficult hurdle for plaintiffs since temporal proximity is typically not enough, even for a prima facie case, unless the protected conduct and the adverse action are very closely connected. *Tyler v. Univ. of Ark. Bd. of Trs.*, 628 F.3d 980, 986-87 (8th Cir. 2011) ("Generally, 'more than a temporal connection is required to present a genuine factual issue on retaliation,' and only in cases where the temporary proximity is very close can the plaintiff rest on it exclusively."). (citations omitted). Even assuming such proximity establishes a prima facie case, it may do little to prove that the defendant's nonretaliatory reason is a pretext. *El Sayed v. Hilton Hotels Corp.*, 627 F.3d 931, 933 (2d Cir. 2010). *See* Note 5, page 717.

3. *Opposition and Participation.* Shirley Breeden presented two distinct claims of protected conduct. One was for opposition conduct (her internal complaints), and the other was for participation conduct (her filing of charges to the state agency and the EEOC). Many courts and commentators perceive a sharp distinction between the protections of the "opposition" clause and the "participation" clause. While a plaintiff invoking the opposition clause must demonstrate a reasonable, good faith belief that the conduct complained of is unlawful, the participation clause may protect conduct without regard to its basis. One of the first "participation" cases, *Pettway v. American Cast Iron Pipe Co.*, 411 F.2d 998 (5th Cir. 1969), set the tone for these decisions by finding actionable retaliation when a worker was fired for filing an allegedly false and malicious charge with the EEOC—namely, that the employer had bought off an EEOC investigator. The court wrote: The purpose of §704(a) "is to protect the employee who utilizes the tools provided by Congress to protect his rights. The Act will be frustrated if the employer may unilaterally determine the truth or falsity of charges and take independent action." *Id.* at 1004-05; s*ee also Glover v. S. Carolina Law Enf.*, 170 F.3d 411 (4th Cir. 1999) (unreasonable deposition testimony protected by participation clause). *But see Benes v. A.B. Data, Ltd.*, 724 F.3d 752, 753 (7th Cir. 2013) (even participation in EEOC-sponsored mediation is not protected if the employee would have been fired for such conduct had it occurred in another context), discussed by Charles A. Sullivan, *Taking Civility Too Far* in http://law-professors.typepad.com/laborprof_blog/2013/08/taking-civility-too-far.html.

After the *Breeden* Court disposed of the plaintiff's "opposition clause" claim by deciding that no reasonable person could believe that she had been sexually harassed, it went on to consider the causation issue on her "participation" clause claim. It would have had no need to do so if filing of an "unreasonable" charge was unprotected. Does *Breeden* thus confirm the lower courts that have held that the participation clause prohibits retaliation even where the underlying discrimination claim lacks a reasonable basis? Would even a charge filed in bad faith be protected? *See* Lawrence D. Rosenthal, *Reading Too Much into What the Court Doesn't Write: How Some Federal Courts Have Limited Title VII's Participation Clause's Protections After* Clark County School District v. Breeden, 83 WASH. L. REV. 345 (2008) (arguing that some courts are incorrectly applying the reasonable belief standard to participating clause claims).

4. *Reasonable Belief.* While the reasonableness of a plaintiff's belief in the illegality of the challenged conduct may be irrelevant for participation, that does not seem to be true where opposition is at stake. *Breeden* assumed, but did not decide, that the opposition clause's protections attach if the challenged practice is not in fact unlawful. In other words, a reasonable, good faith belief that the employer has acted unlawfully may or may not suffice under the opposition clause. While the statutory language supports limiting the statute's protections only to opposition to conduct that is in fact unlawful, would such an interpretation be consistent with the policy objectives of §704? *See Robinson v. Shell Oil*, 519 U.S. 337 (1997) (the policy of §704 furthered by including former employees within the protections of the statute).

Assuming a reasonable, good faith belief is necessary, there are certain to be problems as to when an employee's perceptions are reasonable. *Compare Kelly v. Howard I. Shapiro & Assocs. Consulting Eng'rs, P.C.*, 716 F.3d 10 (2d Cir. 2013) ("paramour preferences" not actionable under Title VII, and plaintiff's complaints did not suggest that she was being discriminated against because of her sex despite the accusations of "sexual favoritism" and the continual repetition of the words "discrimination" and "harassment"), *with Battaglia v. United Parcel Service, Inc.*, 70 A.3d 602 (N.J. 2013) (plaintiff protected under state law for opposing continued use in management meetings of grossly sexist language even though no particular woman heard the remarks and therefore there was no actionable harassment). *See* Terry Smith, *Everyday Indignities: Race, Retaliation, and the Promise of Title VII*, 34 COLUM. HUM. RTS. L. REV. 529 (2003) (criticizing judicial reactions to opposition to "subtle discrimination"); *see also* B. Glenn George, *Revenge*, 83 TUL. L. REV. 439 (2008); Deborah L. Brake & Joanna L. Grossman, *The Failure of Title VII as a Rights Claiming System*, 86 N.C. L. REV. 859 (2008); Lawrence D. Rosenthal, *To Report or Not to Report: The Case for Eliminating the Objectively Reasonable Requirement for Opposition Activities Under Title VII's Anti-Retaliation Provision*, 39 ARIZ. ST. L.J. 1127 (2007).

   5. *Temporal Proximity.* Assuming protected conduct, the plaintiff must still show an adverse action and a causal link between the protected conduct and the adverse action. Does *Breeden* mean that the plaintiff always loses on summary judgment where the employer has denied retaliation and the only evidence of causation is that the adverse employment action occurred three months or more after the decision maker learned of the protected activity? Is it possible to assess the role of temporal proximity without looking at the other facts in the case? *See Twigg v. Hawker Beechcraft Corp.*, 659 F.3d 987, 1001-02, (10th Cir. 2011) ("[E]vidence of temporal proximity has minimal probative value in a retaliation case where intervening events between the employee's protected conduct and the challenged employment action provide a legitimate basis for the employer's action."); *Pinkerton v. Colorado Dept. of Transp.*, 563 F.3d 1052 (10th Cir. 2009) (termination within a few days of verification of the complaint plaintiff filed with employer, together with evidence that employer's reasons for firing plaintiff may not have been credible, held sufficient); *see also Fuhr v. Hazel Park Sch. Dist.*, 710 F.3d 668, 676 (6th Cir. 2013) ("while temporal proximity alone cannot establish a causal connection, a lack of temporal proximity alone can be fatal to an attempt to establish a causal connection under circumstances such as these" where there was a two-year gap between the latest act that might trigger retaliation and the claimed retaliation and no direct evidence).

   6. *Balancing Opposition and Employer Interests.* Opposition conduct may be less protected than participation conduct in another way. Where participation is concerned, the courts have not been sympathetic to countervailing employer interests. For example, courts have found employers guilty of unlawful retaliation when they treat differently an employee who files a discrimination charge, even if the employer's action seems justified from a business perspective. *See, e.g., EEOC v. Bd. of Governors of State Colls. and Univs.*, 957 F.2d 424 (7th Cir. 1992) (invalidating a collective bargaining agreement provision terminating grievance proceedings when a lawsuit is filed). *But see Richardson v. Comm'n on Human Rights & Opportunities*, 532 F.3d 114 (2d Cir. 2008) (election-of-remedies provision in a collective bargaining agreement, which provided that employee alleging discrimination may not arbitrate a dispute as a grievance if she filed a charge, did not violate Title VII). That the employer is invoking a neutral rule that would have been applied to employees engaging in other forms of litigation does not mean those rules may be applied to persons who have engaged in participation activities under employment discrimination statutes. In a sense, § 704's participation clause entitles plaintiffs to special treatment.

But what about the opposition clause? Can the form the employee's opposition takes remove her from the protections of the Act? As should be obvious from *McDonnell Douglas Corp. v. Green*, reproduced at page 573, the answer is yes. Recall that Green had engaged in a "stall in" to protest alleged discrimination by the company, and the company had asserted his participation in those activities as the explanation for why Green was not rehired. Although *McDonnell Douglas* did not directly rule on §704(a), as that claim was not before the Court, it wrote, in language broad enough to embrace §704(a): "Nothing in Title VII compels an employer to absolve and rehire one who has engaged in such deliberate, unlawful activity against it." *McDonnell Douglas*, 411 U.S. at 803. How far does *McDonnell Douglas* go in allowing an employer to discriminate because of the nature or form of an employee's "opposition"? Is it merely a "law and order" decision in that it permits retaliation where the opposition violates criminal statutes, or can it be read more broadly?

Rather than establishing a "disloyalty" bright line, the lower courts seem to be balancing employer and employee interests. *See, e.g, Hatmaker v. Mem'l Med. Ctr.*, 619 F.3d 741 (7th Cir. 2010) (holding that participation in an internal investigation is opposition, not participation, but, in any event, such conduct "doesn't insulate an employee from being discharged for conduct that, if it occurred outside an investigation, would warrant termination"); *Argyropoulos v. City of Alton*, 539 F.3d 724 (7th Cir. 2008) (employee who secretly recorded meeting with supervisors not protected). If so, what goes on the scales? *See Cruz v. Coach Stores, Inc.*, 202 F.3d 560 (2d Cir. 2000) (slapping co-worker in response to sexual harassment not a protected activity, certainly when other options were available to plaintiff); *Douglas v. DynMcDermott Petro. Oper. Co.*, 144 F.3d 364 (5th Cir. 1998) (unethical disclosure by attorney justified discharge even if that conduct was in opposition to discrimination). What if the employee is a high-level affirmative action official? *Johnson v. Univ. of Cincinnati*, 215 F.3d 561 (6th Cir. 2000) (Title VII protects VP for Human Resources advocating on behalf of women and minorities). Is the validity of the allegation or the employer's reaction a factor? What about the extent of any resulting disruption? *See Robbins v. Jefferson Cty. Sch. Dist.*, 186 F.3d 1253 (10th Cir. 1999). Could even substantial disruption be outweighed by employer provocation? Should the court consider whether the plaintiff was more disruptive than necessary or whether the plaintiff had ulterior motivations?

7. *Distinguishing Opposition from Participation.* Because the opposition and participation clauses offer different degrees of protection, it is important to distinguish between the two. In *Crawford v. Metro Gov't of Nashville & Davidson Counties*, 555 U.S. 271 (2008), the Supreme Court held that an employee's involvement in an employer's internal investigation into possible harassment was protected under the opposition clause:

"Oppose" goes beyond "active, consistent" behavior in ordinary discourse, where we would naturally use the word to speak of someone who has taken no action at all to advance a position beyond disclosing it. Countless people were known to "oppose" slavery before Emancipation, or are said to "oppose" capital punishment today, without writing public letters, taking to the streets, or resisting the government. And we would call it "opposition" if an employee took a stand against an employer's discriminatory practices not by "instigating" action, but by standing pat, say, by refusing to follow a supervisor's order to fire a junior worker for discriminatory reasons. There is, then, no reason to doubt that a person can "oppose" by responding to someone else's question just as surely as by provoking the discussion, and nothing in the statute requires a freakish rule protecting an employee who reports discrimination on her own initiative but not one who reports the same discrimination in the same words when her boss asks a question.

555 U.S. at 277-78 (citation omitted). *See also Sayger v. Riceland Foods, Inc.*, 735 F.3d 1025, 1032 (8th Cir. 2013) (employees who respond to internal efforts to address discrimination also protected).

The *Crawford* Court did not reach the question of whether it was also protected under the participation clause. The result was to assure a minimum level of protection but leave open whether the employee reasonably believed that the conduct she reported was harassment. Suppose she didn't. For example, suppose she just answered her employer's question without even thinking about whether the conduct was illegal. If that's not opposition, might it still be "participation," or does the statute require at least a formal charge or suit by somebody? *See generally* Deborah L. Brake, *Retaliation in an EEO World*, 89 IND. L.J. 115 (2014) (by deciding *Crawford* under the opposition clause the Court left witnesses still subject to the requirement that their answers reflect a reasonable belief in illegality).

8. *Third-party Retaliation*: The Supreme Court recently held that Title VII bars third-party retaliation, that is, situations where the individual alleging retaliation did not personally engage in any protected activity but suffers an adverse employment action because of another person's protected conduct. In *Thompson v. North Am. Stainless, LP*, 131 S. Ct. 863 (2011), the plaintiff was terminated after his fiancé, a co-worker, filed a sex discrimination claim with the EEOC. It was undisputed that the fiancé's filing was protected participation, and the Court had little trouble holding that retaliation against a third party — the plaintiff — was unlawful retaliation since a reasonable worker — the fiancé — might well be deterred from engaging in such conduct if she had known the consequences. We'll discuss that standard in the next principal case.

The Court viewed the more difficult question as being whether the plaintiff — as opposed to his fiancé — had standing to sue for the retaliation, but it ultimately so held. The Court rejected as "absurd" a standard that would allow anyone to sue when injured by a violation: "For example, a shareholder would be able to sue a company for firing a valuable employee for racially discriminatory reasons, so long as he could show that the value of his stock decreased as a consequence." 131 S. Ct. at 869. It also rejected the defendant's argument that only the person participating in the protected conduct could file suit, choosing instead to look to the "zone of interests" test from administrative law and holding that Title VII "incorporates this test, enabling suit by any plaintiff with an interest 'arguably [sought] to be protected by the statutes.'" *Id.* at 870. Under this test, the plaintiff had standing to challenge his discharge: He was an employee and "not an accidental victim of the retaliation — collateral damage, so to speak, of the employer's unlawful act. To the contrary, injuring him was the employer's intended means of harming Regalado. Hurting him was the unlawful act by which the employer punished her." *Id.*

9. *Expanding Protection Against Retaliation*. *Crawford* and *North American Stainless* both expanded protection against retaliation. But it is not the only case that has done so. In other recent decisions, the Court has held that the antidiscrimination provisions of 42 U.S.C. § 1981, *CBOS West, Inc. v Humphries*, 553 U.S. 442 (2008), and the federal employee sections of Title VII, *Gomez-Perez v. Potter*, 553 U.S. 474 (2008), implicitly bar retaliation. While the commentators generally viewed retaliation as the most plaintiff-friendly strand of Supreme Court employment discrimination jurisprudence, *e.g.*, Michael J. Zimmer, *A Pro-Employee Supreme Court?: The Retaliation Decisions*, 60 S.C. L. Rev. 917 (2009), the plaintiffs' winning streak came to an abrupt end in *University of Texas Southwestern Med. Center v. Nassar*, 133 S. Ct. 2517 (2013), where, as we have seen at page 609, the Court required but-for causation to prove a retaliation claim rather than the motivating factor standard applicable to "status discrimination." In its opinion, the majority offered a policy justification that suggests a majority of the Justices may be having second thoughts about the retaliation provisions:

> In addition lessening the causation standard could also contribute to the filing of frivolous claims, which would siphon resources from efforts by employer, administrative agencies, and courts to combat workplace harassment. Consider in this regard the case of an employee who knows that he or she is about to be fired for poor performance, given a lower pay grade, or even just transferred to a different assignment or location. To forestall that lawful action, he or she might be tempted to make an unfounded charge of racial, sexual, or religious discrimination; then, when the unrelated employment action comes, the employee could allege that it is retaliation. If respondent were to prevail in his argument here, that claim could be established by a lessened causation standard, all in order to prevent the undesired change in employment circumstances. Even if the employer could escape judgment after trial, the lessened causation standard would make it far more difficult to dismiss dubious claims at the summary judgment stage. It would be inconsistent with the structure and operation of Title VII to so raise the costs, both financial and reputational, on an employer whose actions were not in fact the result of any discriminatory or retaliatory intent. Yet there would be a significant risk of that consequence if respondent's position were adopted here.

Id. at 2531-32. What do you think of that argument? Even before *Nassar*, some commentators have argued for greater reliance on state antiretaliation provisions to correct holes in federal protection. Alex B. Long, *Viva State Employment Law! State Law Retaliation Claims in a Post-*Crawford/Burlington Northern *World*, 77 Tenn. L. Rev. 253, 257 (2010); Sandra F. Sperino, *Revitalizing State Employment Discrimination Law*, 20 Geo. Mason L. Rev. 545 (2013).

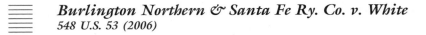

Burlington Northern & Santa Fe Ry. Co. v. White
548 U.S. 53 (2006)

Breyer, J.

Title VII of the Civil Rights Act of 1964 forbids employment discrimination against "any individual" based on that individual's "race, color, religion, sex, or national origin." A separate section of the Act—its anti-retaliation provision—forbids an employer from "discriminating against" an employee or job applicant because that individual "opposed any practice" made unlawful by Title VII or "made a charge, testified, assisted, or participated in" a Title VII proceeding or investigation. . . .

We conclude that the anti-retaliation provision does not confine the actions and harms it forbids to those that are related to employment or occur at the workplace. We also conclude that the provision covers those (and only those) employer actions that would have been materially adverse to a reasonable employee or job applicant. In the present context that means that the employer's actions must be harmful to the point that they could well dissuade a reasonable worker from making or supporting a charge of discrimination.

[Shortly after Sheila White, the only woman working in her department at the Railroad's Tennessee yard, complained of harassment by her supervisor, she was reassigned from her position operating a forklift to a track laborer job, a more physically demanding and dirtier job. The pay and benefits, however, were the same. After White filed a charge of discrimination with the EEOC, she was suspended without pay for 37 days, a suspension that would have become a termination had she not filed a grievance. The company contended White had been suspended because she was insubordinate. White did grieve her suspension, and the hearing officer found she had not been insubordinate and ordered her reinstated with backpay. White filed suit, alleging that the change in her job responsibilities and her suspension constituted actionable retaliation under Title VII. A jury agreed with White. The Sixth Circuit, en banc, affirmed the judgment in White's favor.]

II

Title VII's anti-retaliation provision forbids employer actions that "discriminate against" an employee (or job applicant) because he has "opposed" a practice that Title VII forbids or has "made a charge, testified, assisted, or participated in" a Title VII "investigation, proceeding, or hearing.". . . .

A

Petitioner and the Solicitor General both argue that the Sixth Circuit is correct to require a link between the challenged retaliatory action and the terms, conditions, or status of employment. They note that Title VII's substantive anti-discrimination provision protects an individual only from employment-related discrimination. They add that the anti-retaliation provision should be read *in pari materia* with the anti-discrimination provision. And they conclude that the employer actions prohibited by the anti-retaliation provision should similarly be limited to conduct that "affects the employee's 'compensation, terms, conditions, or privileges of employment.'"

We cannot agree. The language of the substantive provision differs from that of the anti-retaliation provision in important ways. Section 703(a) sets forth Title VII's core anti-discrimination provision in the following terms:

It shall be an unlawful employment practice for an employer—

(1) *to fail or refuse to hire or to discharge* any individual, or otherwise to discriminate against any individual *with respect to his compensation, terms, conditions, or privileges of employment*, because of such individual's race, color, religion, sex, or national origin; or

(2) to limit, segregate, or classify his employees or applicants for employment in any way *which would deprive or tend to deprive any individual of employment opportunities or otherwise adversely affect his status as an employee*, because of such individual's race, color, religion, sex, or national origin. (emphasis added).

Section 704(a) sets forth Title VII's anti-retaliation provision in the following terms:

> It shall be an unlawful employment practice for an employer *to discriminate against* any of his employees or applicants for employment . . . because he has opposed any practice made an unlawful employment practice by this subchapter, or because he has made a charge, testified, assisted, or participated in any manner in an investigation, proceeding, or hearing under this subchapter. (emphasis added).

The underscored words in the substantive provision — "hire," "discharge," "compensation, terms, conditions, or privileges of employment," "employment opportunities," and "status as an employee" — explicitly limit the scope of that provision to actions that affect employment or alter the conditions of the workplace. No such limiting words appear in the anti-retaliation provision. Given these linguistic differences, the question here is not whether identical or similar words should be read *in pari materia* to mean the same thing. Rather, the question is whether Congress intended its different words to make a legal difference. We normally presume that, where words differ as they differ here, "'Congress acts intentionally and purposely in the disparate inclusion or exclusion.'" *Russello v. United States*, 464 U.S. 16, 23 (1983).

There is strong reason to believe that Congress intended the differences that its language suggests, for the two provisions differ not only in language but in purpose as well. The anti-discrimination provision seeks a workplace where individuals are not discriminated against because of their racial, ethnic, religious, or gender-based status. *See McDonnell Douglas Corp. v. Green*, [reproduced at page 572]. The anti-retaliation provision seeks to secure that primary objective by preventing an employer from interfering (through retaliation) with an employee's efforts to secure or advance enforcement of the Act's basic guarantees. The substantive provision seeks to prevent injury to individuals based on who they are, *i.e.*, their status. The anti-retaliation provision seeks to prevent harm to individuals based on what they do, *i.e.*, their conduct.

To secure the first objective, Congress did not need to prohibit anything other than employment-related discrimination. The substantive provision's basic objective of "equality of employment opportunities" and the elimination of practices that tend to bring about "stratified job environments," would be achieved were all employment-related discrimination miraculously eliminated.

But one cannot secure the second objective by focusing only upon employer actions and harm that concern employment and the workplace. Were all such actions and harms eliminated, the anti-retaliation provision's objective would *not* be achieved. An employer can effectively retaliate against an employee by taking actions not directly related to his employment or by causing him harm *outside* the workplace. *See, e.g., Rochon v. Gonzales*, 438 F.3d [1211, 1213 (CADC 2006)] (FBI retaliation against employee "took the form of the FBI's refusal, contrary to policy, to investigate death threats a federal prisoner made against [the agent] and his wife"); *Berry v. Stevinson Chevrolet*, 74 F.3d 980, 984, 986 (CA10 1996) (finding actionable retaliation where employer filed false criminal charges against former employee who complained about discrimination). A provision limited to employment-related actions would not deter the many forms that effective retaliation can take. Hence, such a limited construction would fail to fully achieve the anti-retaliation provision's "primary purpose," namely, "maintaining unfettered access to statutory remedial mechanisms." *Robinson v. Shell Oil Co.*, 519 U.S. 337 (1997).

Thus, purpose reinforces what language already indicates, namely, that the anti-retaliation provision, unlike the substantive provision, is not limited to discriminatory actions that affect the terms and conditions of employment. . . .

For these reasons, we conclude that Title VII's substantive provision and its anti-retaliation provision are not coterminous. The scope of the anti-retaliation provision extends beyond workplace-related or employment-related retaliatory acts and harm. We therefore reject the standards applied in the Courts of Appeals that have treated the anti-retaliation provision as forbidding the same conduct prohibited by the anti-discrimination provision and that have limited actionable retaliation to so-called "ultimate employment decisions."

B

The anti-retaliation provision protects an individual not from all retaliation, but from retaliation that produces an injury or harm. As we have explained, the Courts of Appeals have used differing language to describe the level of seriousness to which this harm must rise before it becomes actionable retaliation. We agree with the formulation set forth by the Seventh and the District of Columbia Circuits. In our view, a plaintiff must show that a reasonable employee would have found the challenged action materially adverse, "which in this context means it well might have 'dissuaded a reasonable worker from making or supporting a charge of discrimination.'" *Rochon*. We speak of *material* adversity because we believe it is important to separate significant from trivial harms. Title VII, we have said, does not set forth "a general civility code for the American workplace." *Oncale v. Sundowner Offshore Services, Inc.*, [reproduced at page 687]; *see Faragher* (judicial standards for sexual harassment must "filter out complaints attacking 'the ordinary tribulations of the workplace, such as the sporadic use of abusive language, gender-related jokes, and occasional teasing'"). An employee's decision to report discriminatory behavior cannot immunize that employee from those petty slights or minor annoyances that often take place at work and that all employees experience. *See* 1 B. LINDEMANN & P. GROSSMAN, EMPLOYMENT DISCRIMINATION LAW 669 (3d ed. 1996) (noting that "courts have held that personality conflicts at work that generate antipathy" and "'snubbing' by supervisors and co-workers" are not actionable under §704(a)). The anti-retaliation provision seeks to prevent employer interference with "unfettered access" to Title VII's remedial mechanisms. *Robinson*. It does so by prohibiting employer actions that are likely "to deter victims of discrimination from complaining to the EEOC," the courts, and their employers. *Ibid*. And normally petty slights, minor annoyances, and simple lack of good manners will not create such deterrence. *See* 2 EEOC 1998 MANUAL §8, p. 8-13.

We refer to reactions of a *reasonable* employee because we believe that the provision's standard for judging harm must be objective. An objective standard is judicially administrable. It avoids the uncertainties and unfair discrepancies that can plague a judicial effort to determine a plaintiff's unusual subjective feelings. We have emphasized the need for objective standards in other Title VII contexts, and those same concerns animate our decision here. *See, e.g., Pennsylvania State Police v. Suders*, 542 U.S. 129 (2004) (constructive discharge doctrine); *Harris v. Forklift Systems, Inc.* (hostile work environment doctrine).

We phrase the standard in general terms because the significance of any given act of retaliation will often depend upon the particular circumstances. Context matters.

"The real social impact of workplace behavior often depends on a constellation of surrounding circumstances, expectations, and relationships which are not fully captured by a simple recitation of the words used or the physical acts performed." A schedule change in an employee's work schedule may make little difference to many workers, but may matter enormously to a young mother with school age children. *Cf., e.g., Washington* [*v. Ill. Dep't of Revenue*, 420 F.3d 658 (CA7 2005)] (finding flex-time schedule critical to employee with disabled child). A supervisor's refusal to invite an employee to lunch is normally trivial, a nonactionable petty slight. But to retaliate by excluding an employee from a weekly training lunch that contributes significantly to the employee's professional advancement might well deter a reasonable employee from complaining about discrimination. *See* 2 EEOC 1998 MANUAL § 8, p. 8-14. Hence, a legal standard that speaks in general terms rather than specific prohibited acts is preferable, for an "act that would be immaterial in some situations is material in others." *Washington*.

Finally, we note that contrary to the claim of the concurrence, this standard does *not* require a reviewing court or jury to consider "the nature of the discrimination that led to the filing of the charge." Rather, the standard is tied to the challenged retaliatory act, not the underlying conduct that forms the basis of the Title VII complaint. By focusing on the materiality of the challenged action and the perspective of a reasonable person in the plaintiff's position, we believe this standard will screen out trivial conduct while effectively capturing those acts that are likely to dissuade employees from complaining or assisting in complaints about discrimination.

III

Applying this standard to the facts of this case, we believe that there was a sufficient evidentiary basis to support the jury's verdict on White's retaliation claim. . . . Burlington does not question the jury's determination that the motivation for these acts was retaliatory. But it does question the statutory significance of the harm these acts caused. The District Court instructed the jury to determine whether respondent "suffered a materially adverse change in the terms or conditions of her employment," and the Sixth Circuit upheld the jury's finding based on that same stringent interpretation of the anti-retaliation provision (the interpretation that limits § 704 to the same employment-related conduct forbidden by § 703). Our holding today makes clear that the jury was not required to find that the challenged actions were related to the terms or conditions of employment. And insofar as the jury also found that the actions were "materially adverse," its findings are adequately supported.

First, Burlington argues that a reassignment of duties cannot constitute retaliatory discrimination where, as here, both the former and present duties fall within the same job description. We do not see why that is so. Almost every job category involves some responsibilities and duties that are less desirable than others. Common sense suggests that one good way to discourage an employee such as White from bringing discrimination charges would be to insist that she spend more time performing the more arduous duties and less time performing those that are easier or more agreeable. That is presumably why the EEOC has consistently found "retaliatory work assignments" to be a classic and "widely recognized" example of "forbidden retaliation." 2 EEOC 1991 MANUAL § 614.7, pp. 614-31 to 614-32. . . .

To be sure, reassignment of job duties is not automatically actionable. Whether a particular reassignment is materially adverse depends upon the circumstances of the particular case, and "should be judged from the perspective of a reasonable person in the plaintiff's position, considering 'all the circumstances.'" *Oncale.* But here, the jury had before it considerable evidence that the track labor duties were "by all accounts more arduous and dirtier"; that the "forklift operator position required more qualifications, which is an indication of prestige"; and that "the forklift operator position was objectively considered a better job and the male employees resented White for occupying it." Based on this record, a jury could reasonably conclude that the reassignment of responsibilities would have been materially adverse to a reasonable employee.

Second, Burlington argues that the 37-day suspension without pay lacked statutory significance because Burlington ultimately reinstated White with backpay.

. . . White did receive backpay. But White and her family had to live for 37 days without income. They did not know during that time whether or when White could return to work. Many reasonable employees would find a month without a paycheck to be a serious hardship. And White described to the jury the physical and emotional hardship that 37 days of having "no income, no money" in fact caused. ("That was the worst Christmas I had out of my life. No income, no money, and that made all of us feel bad. . . . I got very depressed"). Indeed, she obtained medical treatment for her emotional distress. A reasonable employee facing the choice between retaining her job (and paycheck) and filing a discrimination complaint might well choose the former. That is to say, an indefinite suspension without pay could well act as a deterrent, even if the suspended employee eventually received backpay. . . . Thus, the jury's conclusion that the 37-day suspension without pay was materially adverse was a reasonable one. . . .

[Justice Alito's concurring opinion omitted.]

NOTES

1. *Retaliation Outside the Workplace.* Prior to *Burlington*, the Court had held that former employees were protected from retaliation in terms of unfavorable references. *Robinson v. Shell Oil Co.*, 519 U.S. 337 (1997) (former employee given inaccurate references). In some sense, of course, that case involved retaliation outside the workplace. *Burlington* confirms that, holding that, while §703 reaches only actions that affect employment or that alter the conditions of the workplace, §704 is *not* limited to discriminatory acts that affect the terms and conditions of employment.

Occasionally a question has arisen as to whether an employer violates the retaliation provisions of the antidiscrimination statutes by bringing suit against the employee in retaliation for protected conduct. For example, would it be permissible for an employer to bring defamation charges against an employee who has alleged discrimination? The Supreme Court addressed a similar issue under the National Labor Relations Act. *BE&K Construction Co. v. NLRB*, 536 U.S. 516 (2002), held, in light of First Amendment concerns, that the NLRA did not prohibit reasonably based but unsuccessful lawsuits filed with a retaliatory purpose. A baseless suit would lack this justification and, after *Burlington*, would seem actionable.

2. *Adverse Employment Actions Under §703?* Given that the actions White complained of clearly affected her employment, why do you think the Court felt it necessary to decide whether §704 applied to actions that did not affect the terms and conditions of employment? Perhaps the Court reached out to resolve this question because it did not believe the actions, even though arising from the workplace, would have stated a claim under § 703? Obviously, this would have important implications for the concept of "adverse employment action" we discussed at page 580. In his concurring opinion in *Burlington*, Justice Alito disagreed with the majority's analysis, believing that the scope of §§ 703 and 704 are the same and both reach only materially adverse employment actions. But he found the actions White challenged to be materially adverse within the meaning of either section. As applied to § 703, this would be a more pro-plaintiff position in discrimination cases than many predicted of Justice Alito. *See generally* Lisa Durham Taylor, *Parsing Supreme Court Dicta and the Example of Non-Workplace Harms*, 57 DRAKE L. REV. 75 (2008); Lisa Durham Taylor, *Adding Subjective Fuel to the Vague-Standard Fire: A Proposal for Congressional Intervention After* Burlington Northern & Santa Fe Railway Co. v. White, 9 U. PA. J. LAB. & EMP. L. 533 (2007); Ernest F. Lidge III, *What Types of Employer Actions Are Cognizable Under Title VII?: The Ramifications of* Burlington Northern & Santa Fe Railroad Co. v. White, 59 RUTGERS L. REV. 497, 535 (2007).

3. *Third Party Retaliation and Material Adversity.* The *North American Stainless* Court thought it "obvious that a reasonable worker might be dissuaded from engaging in protected activity if she knew that her fiancé would be fired." 131 S. Ct. 868, but recognized that line-drawing problems would arise in deciding when the *Burlington Northern* standard would be satisfied when the retaliatory action was aimed at a third party:

> We must also decline to identify a fixed class of relationships for which third-party reprisals are unlawful. We expect that firing a close family member will almost always meet the *Burlington* standard, and inflicting a milder reprisal on a mere acquaintance will almost never do so, but beyond that we are reluctant to generalize. . . . Given the broad statutory text and the variety of workplace contexts in which retaliation may occur, Title VII's antiretaliation provision is simply not reducible to a comprehensive set of clear rules.

Id. at 868. The Court did, however, stress that the inquiry was to be "objective." *Id.* But, after *Burlington*, isn't the question whether the retaliatory action is likely to deter a reasonable employee from engaging in protected conduct? That would suggest that subjectivity enters the picture where the *employer's* motives are concerned. Isn't the correct test whether the actual employer (not a reasonable one) believed that acting against X would deter/punish protected conduct by Y, or at least by a reasonable employee in Y's position? For an excellent pre-*Thompson* discussion of the entire question of third-party retaliation, *see* Alex. B. Long, *The Troublemaker's Friend: Retaliation Against Third Parties and the Right of Association in the Workplace*, 59 FLA. L. REV. 931 (2007).

The *North American Stainless* Court's stress about context is playing out in the lower courts, which reflect a wide range of results as to when the *Burlington Northern* standard is satisfied. *E.g.*, *Rodríguez-Vives v. P.R. Firefighters Corps of P.R.*, 743 F.3d 278 (1st Cir. 2014) (at least the cumulative effect of a series of petty acts of retaliation, such as refusal to allow plaintiff to join other firefighters to travel on fire vehicles to lunch and being assigned to cook and clean, might dissuade a reasonable employee from opposing discrimination); *Colon v. Tracey*, 717 F.3d 43 (1st Cir. 2013) (summary judgment affirmed for employer when plaintiff claimed that she was demoted by being reassigned from human resources "generalist" to human resources "business partner," with no effect on her salary or job title, and was only temporary change).

4. *Threats Just Fine?* The Seventh Circuit seems to take the position that an unfulfilled threat cannot violate the antiretaliation provisions of the federal statutes or, at least, cannot support a claim for constructive discharge. *Chapin v. Fort-Rohr Motors, Inc.,* 621 F.3d 673 (7th Cir. 2010) (no constructive discharge in retaliation setting when employee quit work in response to threat to discharge him if he did not withdraw EEOC charge when there was no other basis to indicate imminent firing and employer asked him to return to work); *Goodman v. NSA, Inc.,* 621 F.3d 651, 656 (7th Cir. 2010) (unfulfilled threats to transfer plaintiff to positions she could not work were not actionable); *see also Ahern v. Shinseki,* 629 F.3d 49, 56 (1st Cir. 2010) ("Merely proposing a change in an employee's schedule does not, in and of itself, constitute a materially adverse action. To qualify, the proposal must be brought to fruition.") (citation omitted). Can't threats satisfy the *Burlington* standard? How about a threat of physical violence?

F. DISABILITY DISCRIMINATION

Protecting individuals with disabilities from discrimination in employment poses difficult problems. Legally, disability discrimination poses the threshold question of who is protected, that is, who is a "disabled" individual. Further, disabilities are sometimes relevant to an individual's ability to work. While many disabilities would not affect the performance of particular jobs at all, some disabilities deprive people of the physical and/or mental prerequisites to perform essential job functions. Prohibiting "discrimination" against such individuals would unduly interfere with employers' ability to select a qualified workforce. Other disabled individuals may be qualified to work but only if the employer accommodates their disability in some way. Such individuals, unlike most other statutorily protected groups, require some form of different treatment in order to enjoy equal access to employment opportunities and benefits. Merely guaranteeing equal treatment for similarly situated individuals in those situations does not adequately respond to the problem of promoting employment of the disabled.

The ADA seeks to deal with these problems in two separate ways. First, while generally barring disability discrimination, the statute broadens the defenses available to employers as compared with other antidiscrimination statutes. Employers are permitted to engage in disparate treatment on the basis of disability if the disabled employee is unable to perform the essential functions of the job. In addition, employers are free to use qualification standards that screen out disabled individuals if those qualifications are job-related and consistent with business necessity.

Counterbalancing this, disabled individuals have rights beyond those guaranteed to other groups protected by antidiscrimination legislation. The centerpiece of disability discrimination law is the employer's affirmative duty to provide reasonable accommodation to ensure that individuals with disabilities secure equal employment opportunities and benefits. The focus of the duty to accommodate is on equal employment opportunity, not merely equal treatment.

As a result, employers are legally obligated to treat covered employees equally or differently depending on the circumstances — employers must treat individuals with disabilities equally to nondisabled persons if they are qualified and their disabilities do not require accommodation; employers are permitted to treat such individuals differently, that is, to discriminate against them, if their disabilities cannot be accommodated; and employers are required to treat such individuals differently, and better than other workers, if reasonable accommodations are necessary to ensure equal employment opportunity and benefits.

Further, accommodation providing equal opportunity for individuals with disabilities can be costly for employers. The ADA, therefore, includes an "undue hardship" defense, which makes cost, usually irrelevant under the disparate treatment provisions of other antidiscrimination statutes, an express statutory defense to discrimination based on the duty to accommodate.

The focus of this section will be Title I of the ADA, which deals with employment, although other parts of the statute deal with important issues beyond employment. The ADA and associated regulations borrows extensively from the Rehabilitation Act of 1973, 29 U.S.C. §§ 701-95 (2014), which was a narrower federal statute covering only federal contractors and federal executive agencies. The Rehabilitation Act continues to operate in its original sphere, and its precedents influence ADA decisions, and the ADA regulations and Interpretive Guidance of the (EEOC) borrow from regulations under the earlier act.

The ADA was passed in 1990, but the first decade and a half of its life proved profoundly disappointing to disability advocates. The amorphous definition of disability permitted the courts to narrowly circumscribe the statute's reach. While we will examine the details of this development, the net result was that most cases under Title I of the ADA were dismissed because the plaintiffs were either not disabled within the meaning of the statute (as construed by the courts) or too disabled to perform the essential functions of the jobs they sought. The result of increasing dissatisfaction with a number of Supreme Court decisions was the Americans with Disabilities Act Amendment Act of 2008, Pub. L. 110-325, signed into law in on September 2008 and effective January 1, 2009. *See generally* Michelle A. Travis, *Impairment as Protected Status: A New Universality for Disability Rights*, 46 GA. L. REV. 937 (2012); Stacy A. Hickox, *The Underwhelming Impact of the Americans with Disabilities Act Amendments Act*, 40 U. BALT. L. REV. 419, 422-23 (2011); Alex B. Long, *Introducing the New and Improved Americans with Disabilities Act: Assessing the ADA Amendments Act of 2008*, 103 NW. U. L. REV. COLLOQUY 217 (2008); *see also* Jeffrey Douglas Jones, *Enfeebling the ADA: The ADA Amendments Act of 2008*, 62 OKLA. L. REV. 667, 669 (2010).

It seems clear that the ADAAA does not apply retroactively, *e.g., Parada v. Banco Indus. de Venez.*, 753 F.3d 62 (2d Cir. 2014), but it is having dramatic consequences for cases arising after 2008. This section focuses on the amended statute, although an understanding of the original ADA is critical to appreciating the potential of the current law.

1. The Meaning of "Disability"

In contrast to other statutes prohibiting discrimination in employment, establishing membership in the ADA's protected classification often requires extensive legal and factual analysis. Generally speaking, to claim protection under the ADA, a plaintiff must be "a qualified individual with a disability"; that is, the plaintiff must be an individual with a disability who can perform essential job functions with or without reasonable accommodation. Section 3(1) provides three definitions of "disability":

A. a physical or mental impairment that substantially limits one or more of the major life activities of . . . [an] individual;
B. a record of such an impairment; or
C. being regarded as having such an impairment.

This definition requires three inquiries. First, whether the individual has an impairment. The first part of the definition, § 3(2)(A), deals with an individual who has an actual impairment. It contains three elements, each of which is further defined in the EEOC's ADA regulations. Section 1630.2(h) of the regulations defines physical or mental *impairment* as:

1. Any physiological disorder or condition, cosmetic disfigurement, or anatomical loss affecting one or more of the following body systems: neurological, musculoskeletal, special sense organs, respiratory (including speech organs), cardiovascular, reproductive, digestive, genitor-urinary, hemic and lymphatic, skin, and endocrine; or
2. Any mental or psychological disorder, such as mental retardation, organic brain syndrome, emotional or mental illness, and specific learning disabilities.

The second inquiry is whether a "major life activity" is limited by the impairment. Originally, the definition of such activities was left to the EEOC's regulations, but the ADAAA added a statutory definition that both incorporated the EEOC's approach and broadened it. For purposes of determining whether an individual has an actual disability,

(A) major life activities include, but are not limited to, caring for oneself, performing manual tasks, seeing, hearing, eating, sleeping, walking, standing, lifting, bending, speaking, breathing, learning, reading, concentrating, thinking, communicating, and working.

(B) . . . a major life activity also includes the operation of a major bodily function, including but not limited to, functions of the immune system, normal cell growth, digestive, bowel, bladder, neurological, brain, respiratory, circulatory, endocrine, and reproductive functions.

42 U.S.C. § 12102 (2).

The third inquiry is whether the limitation is "substantial." As you might guess, this was a major point of debate both under the original ADA and in framing the Americans with Disabilities Act Amendments Act ("ADAAA"), and, as we will see, Congress's solution was less than elegant.

ADA coverage, however, does not depend on establishing an actual, present disability. As noted, § 3(2)(B) also reaches individuals with a "record" of an impairment, and § 3(2)(C) protects those that the employer "regards" as having an impairment. Once you have a better sense of what constitutes an actual disability, we will explore the "record" and "regarded as" prongs of the statutory prohibition.

a. *Actual Disability*

The Supreme Court first considered the meaning of disability in *School Board of Nassau County v. Arline*, 480 U.S. 273 (1987). *Arline* was a Rehabilitation Act case construing the definition of "handicapped individual," which is identical to the ADA's definition of individual with a disability. The school board fired Arline, an elementary school teacher, because it believed her active tuberculosis posed a threat to the health of others. When she sued, the board contended that a person with a contagious disease was not protected by the Rehabilitation Act if the adverse employment action was based on the employee's contagiousness and not on the condition itself. The Supreme Court disagreed. In finding Arline to be a handicapped individual, the Court refused to allow the school to disassociate the contagious effects of the teacher's impairment from the impairment itself. As the Court stated, "Arline's contagiousness and her physical impairment each resulted from the same underlying condition, tuberculosis. It would be unfair to allow an employer to seize upon the distinction between the effects of a disease on others and the effects of a disease on a patient and use that distinction to justify discriminatory intent." *Id.* at 282.

In light of *Arline*'s holding, is a person who tests positively for HIV, the virus that causes AIDS, an "individual with a disability"? Given that a contagious disease can be a "disability," a person who has developed AIDS is undoubtedly an "individual with a disability" under both the Rehabilitation Act and the ADA. That is, active AIDS clearly qualifies as a physical impairment and also substantially limits major life activities. But *Arline* left open the question whether an asymptomatic person can be considered "handicapped" solely on the basis of contagiousness.

In *Bragdon v. Abbott*, 524 U.S. 624 (1998), the plaintiff, infected with HIV, sued her dentist for disability discrimination when he required her cavity to be filled in a hospital instead of in his office. She sued under Title II of the statute, which prohibits discrimination in public accommodations; however, the definition of discrimination under the Title II is the same as that under Title I, thus rendering *Bragdon* relevant to employment. Applying the three-step analysis we have sketched, the Court first asked whether the condition at issue was a "physical impairment." *Id.* at 632. Given its effects on the immune system, the Court decided that HIV is a "physical impairment" from the moment of infection, regardless of the presence of symptoms. *Id.* Second, the Court asked whether the impairment affected a major life activity. *Id.* at 637. The plaintiff in this case relied successfully on the major life activities of reproduction and child bearing, but the Court noted that HIV affects many other major life activities. *Id.* at 638-39. Third, the Court examined whether the impairment's effect on reproduction was "substantial," *id.* at 639, concluding that HIV substantially limits the plaintiff's ability to bear children because of the risk of transmitting the disease. *Id.* The Court elaborated that, "the Act addresses substantial limitations on major life activities, not utter inabilities." *Id.* at 641. Accordingly, *Bragdon* upheld the plaintiff's claim under the ADA since HIV infection is a physical impairment that substantially limits the major life activity of reproduction. *Id.*

In a passage that has influenced numerous later cases, the Court stressed that "whether respondent has a disability covered by the ADA is an individualized inquiry." *Id.* at 657. Thus, what is a disability for one person may not be disabling for another. That meant the Court did not rule on whether HIV infection is a per se disability under the ADA, irrespective of its limiting effects on the activities of the particular plaintiff. *Id.* at 642.

Bragdon was not only the first case decided by the Court but it was also the high point of jurisprudence under the original ADA in terms of broadly reading the statute's coverage. Every other Court decision under Title I restricted the reach of the statute. One of the most significant retrenchments was in *Toyota Motor Mfg., Kentucky, Inc. v. Williams*, 534 U.S. 184 (2002). Plaintiff there was employed on a Toyota assembly line, where she worked with pneumatic tools. Ms. Williams developed carpal tunnel syndrome and related impairments that restricted her ability to perform manual tasks at her job. Toyota initially modified her job duties to accommodate her condition but ultimately refused to provide her the accommodation she sought; it then discharged her after her condition had worsened to the extent that she could not work at all. Williams sued under the ADA, claiming Toyota failed to reasonably accommodate her disability and terminated her employment.

The central issue before the Court was what major life activities counted. Williams claimed that the activity at stake was performing manual tasks, and the Court held that "to be substantially limited in performing manual tasks, an individual must have an impairment that prevents or severely restricts the individual from doing activities that are of central importance to most people's daily lives." 534 U.S. at 187. Thus, the opinion simultaneously broadened what counted as a major life activity and broadened what was necessary to be substantially limited. Do you see how that double play would dramatically narrow the ADA's reach? The narrower an activity may be defined and still count as major, the more likely it is that a plaintiff can prove she is substantially limited. Conversely, the broader the activity is defined, the less likely the plaintiff is substantially limited in performing it. For example, suppose a person is unable to walk long distances. If "walking" is a major life activity, the individual would be limited but perhaps not substantially limited; on the other hand, walking long distances is less likely to be viewed as a major life activity, but the person is more likely to be considered substantially limited.

In justifying its decision, the Court wrote that "substantially limited and major life activities" both "need to be interpreted strictly to create a demanding standard for qualifying as disabled" to implement Congress's goals in passing the ADA. 534 U.S. at 197. Congress didn't agree, and expressed that disagreement in a variety of ways in the ADAAA. Thus, it commanded that '[t]he definition of disability in this Act shall be construed in favor of broad coverage of individuals under this Act, to the maximum extent permitted by the terms of this Act," 42 U.S.C.A. § 12102(4)(A), in the process explicitly rejecting the *Williams* strict interpretation language. More specifically, as we have seen, the new statute defined major life activities very broadly.

As for "substantially limited," the ADAAA was more circuitous although very clear in its thrust. Thus, the amendments do not directly define the term. However, the ADAAA states that *Toyota* "has created an inappropriately high level of limitation necessary to necessary to obtain coverage under the ADA." Congress then went on to disapprove the then-effective EEOC regulations by expressing its "expectation" that the EEOC "will revise that portion of its current regulations that define the term 'substantially limits' as "significantly restricted' to be consistent with this Act" and its amendments. The ADAAA simultaneously answered a question the Supreme Court had raised by explicitly providing authority to the EEOC to issue regulations defining disability, and the agency has in fact issued regulations, 29 C.F.R.

Pt. 1630 (2014).[*] Finally, Congress commanded that "[t]he term "substantially limits" shall be interpreted consistently with the findings and purposes" of the ADAAA. § 12102(4)(B).

The success of the ADAAA in changing judicial attitudes remains to be seen. Since the ADAAA did not become effective until January 1, 2009, and is not retroactive, there are as yet few appellate cases interpreting it. However, the early returns indicate that the courts have gotten the message, at least as to who counts as "disabled." *See generally* Stephen F. Befort, *An Empirical Analysis of Case Outcomes Under the ADA Amendments Act*, 70 Wash & Lee L. Rev. 2027 (2013); Nicole B. Porter, *The New ADA Backlash*, Tenn. L. Rev., (2014).

Note on Impairments

The threshold requirement for a disability is an impairment, and with the ADAAA's broadening of "major life activities" and its watering down of "substantially limited," that threshold question is increasingly central to the determination of whether there is an actual disability. *Bragdon* found HIV to be an impairment from the moment of infection, and *Toyota* assumed that plaintiff's carpal tunnel condition constituted an impairment; rather the question was whether that impairment substantially limited a major life activity. But whether a condition is an impairment is not always easy. Foreseeing some problems, the ADAAA explicitly provided that "[a]n impairment that is episodic or in remission is a disability if it would substantially limit a major life activity when active." § 12102(4)(D). Does that mean, for instance, that multiple sclerosis is an impairment, even though, in its early stages, it can be relatively asymptomatic? The EEOC's proposed regulations list multiple sclerosis as an example of "Impairments that Will Consistently Meet the Definition of Disability." § 1630.2(j).

Despite this broad approach, the Act and its regulations specifically exclude certain conditions from the definition of impairment. ADA Sections 508 and 511 expressly exclude certain sex-related practices or conditions, such as homosexuality, bisexuality, transvestism, pedophilia, transexualism, and exhibitionism. Also excluded are compulsive gambling, kleptomania, pyromania, and disorders resulting from the current illegal use of psychoactive drugs. Further, the EEOC's Interpretive Guidance, 29 C.F.R. Part 1630 Appendix, provides that the term "physical or mental impairment" does not include physical characteristics, such as weight, height, and eye color,

---

[*] The extent to which courts should defer to EEOC regulations was more than a little confused before the ADAAA, and some uncertainty remains. Title I of the originally ADA conferred substantive rule-making authority on the EEOC, 42 U.S.C.A. § 12116, which would seem to require the courts to accord substantial deference under *Chevron U.S.A., Inc. v. Nat. Resources Defense Council, Inc.*, 467 U.S. 837 (1984), and its progeny. However, two problems arose. First, the EEOC carried out that mandate by issuing both regulations and an "Interpretive Guidance," and there has been question as to whether the Guidance is due the same deference as the regulations. Rebecca Hanner White, *Deference and Disability Discrimination*, 9 Mich. L. Rev. 532 (2000).

Secondly, *Sutton v. United Air Lines, Inc.*, refused to defer to the EEOC because the agency at that time had authority to interpret only Title I, and the interpretation at issue involved the prefatory umbrella provisions of the statute. This question has been resolved by the ADAAA, which expressly gives the EEOC (and other agencies charged with administering other Titles of the ADA) the authority to issue regulations relating to the definition of disability. 42 U.S.C.A. § 12205a. And deference to EEOC regulations now seems mandated by *Chevron U.S.A., Inc. v. Echazabal*, 536 U.S. 73 (2002) (deferring to EEOC interpretation of the "direct threat" defense even though it was broader than the statutory language).

that are in the "normal range" and are not the result of a physiological disorder. § 1630.2(h). The Interpretive Guidance also excludes common personality traits, illiteracy, economic disadvantages, and advanced age, although physical and mental impairments associated with aging may be covered. *See* 29 C.F.R. pt. 1630, app. § 1630.2(h), (j).

Although pregnancy shares many of the characteristics of a disability as defined by the ADA, the EEOC Interpretive Guidance states that pregnancy per se is not a disability covered by the statute because pregnancy is not an impairment. *See* 29 C.F.R. pt. 1630, app. § 1630.2(h); *see generally* Melissa Cole, *Beyond Sex Discrimination: Why Employers Discriminate Against Women with Disabilities When Their Employee Health Plans Exclude Contraceptives from Prescription Coverage*, 43 ARIZ. L. REV. 501, 521 (2001) ("For most women, pregnancy does not involve the sorts of substantial limitations that rise to the level of a disability. For those women who face grave health risks in pregnancy, however, the very potential of pregnancy constitutes a disability, a substantial limitation on the major life activity of reproduction.").

Interestingly, the proposed regulations are similar to the earlier regulations in suggesting that temporary conditions can be impairments, although it views them as unlikely to be disabilities: "Temporary, non-chronic impairments of short duration with little or no residual effects (such as the common cold, seasonal or common influenza, a sprained joint, minor and non-chronic gastrointestinal disorders, or a broken bone that is expected to heal completely) usually will not substantially limit a major life activity." § 1630.2(j). Is any physical characteristic outside what is considered the normal range an "impairment"? Consider unusual strength or high intelligence. Are these impairments (because they are out of the normal range), but not disabilities (because they do not substantially impair life activities)? Or are they not impairments at all because they are out of the normal range on the "positive," rather than the "negative," side? Is being left-handed an impairment?

What about individuals with genetic propensies but no actual disease at the moment? It seems unlikely that such individual are currently actually disabled within the meaning of the ADA. This is in part because such an individual will not ordinarily be substantially limited in a major life activity—although like *Bragdon*, some such conditions may limit reproduction for fear of passing on the condition to offspring. But genetic propensities will likely not be viewed as impairments because they are not certain to eventuate. A few diseases, like Huntington's, are inevitable for those with the allele, although they may not manifest the symptoms until late in life. Most "genetic diseases," however, simply make individuals more susceptible to the condition (although sometimes increasing the risk factor enormously). Is someone with the Huntington's allele but no symptoms impaired? If so, does this impairment substantially limit any major life activity? Even if the answer is yes, what about those genetic diseases whose appearance is not inevitable? *See generally* John V. Jacobi, *Genetic Discrimination in a Time of False Hopes*, 30 FLA. ST. U.L. REV. 363 (2003).

The Genetic Information Non-Discrimination Act of 2008 ("GINA"), 22 Stat. 881, codified at 42 U.S.C.A. § 2000ff, does not amend the ADA but does provide a separate source of protection against certain kinds of genetic discrimination. GINA prohibits discrimination by employers and health insurers based on genetic information. The EEOC is charged with enforcement of the employment provisions of the act and has promulgated final regulations to carry out Title II, the employment chapter. 29 C.F.R. Pt. 1635 (2014). In a nutshell, Title II of GINA prohibits the use of genetic information in employment, prohibits the intentional acquisition of genetic information about applicants and employees, and imposes strict confidentiality requirements. It applies to employers, public and private, with 15 or more employees. The EEOC's regulations regard the protections of GINA as absolute when it comes to an employer's *use* of genetic information; any use is strictly prohibited. Moreover, acquisition of genetic information by employers is restricted. *See generally* Jessica Roberts, *Preempting Discrimination: Lessons from the Genetic Information Nondiscrimination Act*, 63 VAND. L. REV. 439 (2010), (examining the justifications for passing preemptive genetic information discrimination legislation and concluding that Congress had twin objectives: a research justification and an antidiscrimination justification).

A final question about impairments relates to physical conditions caused at least in part by voluntary conduct. The First Circuit considered whether such conditions constitute impairments in *Cook v. Rhode Island Dept. of Mental Health*, 10 F.3d 17 (1st Cir. 1993). Bonnie Cook was morbidly obese, meaning that she weighed either more than twice her optimal weight or more than 100 pounds over her optimal weight. In response to her claim of discrimination under the Rehabilitation Act, the defendant argued that "'mutable' conditions are not the sort of impairments" covered by the Act because Cook could "simply lose weight and rid herself of any concomitant disability." *Id.* at 23. Although the court questioned whether "immutability is a prerequisite to the existence" of an "impairment," it found evidence in the record to support a finding that the dysfunctional metabolism underlying morbid obesity is permanent. The defendant also argued that morbid obesity cannot be an impairment because it is "caused, or at least exacerbated, by voluntary conduct." The court responded:

> The Rehabilitation Act contains no language suggesting that its protection is linked to how an individual became impaired, or whether an individual contributed to his or her impairment. On the contrary, the Act indisputably applies to numerous conditions that may be caused or exacerbated by voluntary conduct, such as alcoholism, AIDS, diabetes, cancer resulting from cigarette smoking, heart disease resulting from excesses of various types, and the like. Consequently, voluntariness, like mutability, is relevant only in determining whether a condition has a substantially limiting effect.

Id. at 24. *See generally* Jane Byeff Korn, *Fat*, 77 B.U. L. REV. 25 (1997). Does the ADAAA's command to broadly construe the definition of disability resolve this? *See* Jane Byeff Korn, *Too Fat*, 17 VA. J. SOC. POL'Y & L. 209, 211 (2010) ("While the ADAAA appears to provide more protection for most people with disabilities, this amendment will probably not protect people who are obese absent a significant change in our thinking about obesity.").

≡ *Summers v. Altarum Inst., Corp.,*
≡ *740 F.3d 325 (4th Cir. 2014)*

DIANA GRIBBON MOTZ, Circuit Judge:
Pursuant to recent amendments to the Americans with Disabilities Act, a sufficiently severe temporary impairment may constitute a disability. Because the district court held to the contrary, we reverse and remand.

I.

A.

Carl Summers appeals the dismissal of his complaint for failure to state a claim on which relief can be granted. Accordingly, we recount the facts as alleged by Summers.

In July 2011, Summers began work as a senior analyst for the Altarum Institute, a government contractor with an office in Alexandria, Virginia. Summers's job required him to travel to the Maryland offices of Altarum's client, the Defense Centers of Excellence for Psychological Health and Traumatic Brain Injury ("DCoE"). At DCoE, Summers conducted statistical research, wrote reports, and made presentations. Altarum policy authorized employees to work remotely if the client approved. The client, here DCoE, preferred contractors to work on-site during business hours, but permitted them to work remotely from home when "putting in extra time on [a] project."

On October 17, 2011, Summers fell and injured himself while exiting a commuter train on his way to DCoE. With a heavy bag slung over his shoulder, he lost his footing and struck both knees against the train platform. Paramedics took Summers to the hospital, where doctors determined that he had sustained serious injuries to both legs. Summers fractured his left leg and tore the meniscus tendon in his left knee. He also fractured his right ankle and ruptured the quadriceps-patellar tendon in his right leg. Repairing the left-leg fracture required surgery to fit a metal plate, screws, and bone into his tibia. Treating Summers's ruptured right quadriceps required another surgery to drill a hole in the patella and refasten his tendons to the knee.

Doctors forbade Summers from putting any weight on his left leg for six weeks and estimated that he would not be able to walk normally for seven months at the earliest. Without surgery, bed rest, pain medication, and physical therapy, Summers alleges that he would "likely" not have been able to walk for more than a year after the accident.

While hospitalized, Summers contacted an Altarum human-resources representative about obtaining short-term disability benefits and working from home as he recovered. The Altarum representative agreed to discuss "accommodations that would allow Summers to return to work," but suggested that Summers "take short-term disability and focus on getting well again." Summers sent emails to his supervisors at Altarum and DCoE seeking advice about how to return to work; he suggested "a plan in which he would take short-term disability for a few weeks, then start working remotely part-time, and then increase his hours gradually until he was full-time again."

Altarum's insurance provider granted Summers short-term disability benefits. But Altarum never followed up on Summers's request to discuss how he might successfully return to work. The company did not suggest any alternative reasonable accommodation or engage in any interactive process with Summers. Nor did Altarum tell Summers that there was "any problem with his plan for a graduated return to work." Instead, on November 30, Altarum simply informed Summers "that Altarum was terminating [him] effective December 1, 2011, in order to place another analyst in his role at DCoE."

B.

[Summers filed complaints in district court alleging, inter alia, that Altarum discriminated against him by wrongfully discharging him on account of his disability.

The lower court granted Altarum's Rule 12(b)(6) motion and dismissed both claims; it dismissed the termination claim] on the ground that Summers had failed to allege that he was disabled. The court reasoned that a "temporary condition, even up to a year, does not fall within the purview of the [A]ct" and so "the defendant's not disabled." The court further suggested that Summers was not disabled because he could have worked with the assistance of a wheelchair. . . .

II.

To survive a motion to dismiss, a complaint must state "a claim to relief that is plausible on its face." *Bell Atl. Corp. v. Twombly*, 550 U.S. 544, 570 (2007). We review de novo an appeal from a Rule 12(b)(6) dismissal, accepting the complaint as true and drawing reasonable inferences in the plaintiff's favor. . . .

A.

The ADA makes it unlawful for covered employers to "discriminate against a qualified individual on the basis of disability." The Act prohibits covered employers from discharging qualified employees because they are disabled. To establish a wrongful-discharge claim, a plaintiff must show, among other things, that he suffered from a "disability." *Young v. United Parcel Serv.*, 707 F.3d 437, 443 (4th Cir. 2013).

Under the ADA, a "disability" may take any of the following forms: (1) "a physical or mental impairment that substantially limits one or more major life activities" (the "actual-disability" prong); (2) "a record of such an impairment" (the "record-of" prong); or (3) "being regarded as having such an impairment" (the "regarded-as" prong). 42 U.S.C. § 12102(1). Summers alleges that he was disabled under the ADA's actual-disability prong. Specifically, he asserts that his impairment "substantially limit[ed]" his ability to walk — which the ADA recognizes as one of the "major life activities" whose substantial limitation qualifies as a disability. *Id.* § 12102(2)(A). Accordingly, if Summers's impairment substantially limited his ability to walk, he suffered a "disability" for purposes of the ADA.

B.

In September 2008, Congress broadened the definition of "disability" by enacting the ADA Amendments Act of 2008 ("ADAAA" or "amended Act"). In response to a series of Supreme Court decisions that Congress believed improperly restricted the scope of the ADA, it passed legislation with the stated purpose of "reinstating a broad scope of protection to be available under the ADA." § 2(b)(1). Particularly relevant to this case, Congress sought to override *Toyota Motor Manufacturing, Kentucky, Inc. v. Williams*, 534 U.S. 184, 199 (2002), in which the Supreme Court had adopted a strict construction of the term "disability" and suggested that a temporary impairment could not qualify as a disability under the Act. Congress believed that *Toyota* set an "inappropriately high level of limitation necessary to obtain coverage under the ADA." § 2(b)(5).

Abrogating *Toyota*, the amended Act provides that the definition of disability "shall be construed in favor of broad coverage of individuals under this chapter, to the maximum extent permitted by [its] terms." 42 U.S.C. § 12102(4)(A). Further, Congress instructed that the term "substantially limits" be interpreted consistently with the liberalized purposes of the ADAAA. § 12102(4)(B).[1] And Congress directed the Equal Employment Opportunity Commission ("EEOC") to revise its regulations defining the term "substantially limits" to render them consistent with the broadened scope of the statute. § 2(b)(6).

After notice and comment, the EEOC promulgated regulations clarifying that "[t]he term 'substantially limits' shall be construed broadly in favor of expansive coverage" and that the term is "not meant to be a demanding standard." 29 C.F.R. § 1630.2(j)(1)(i) (2013). The EEOC regulations also expressly provide that "effects of an impairment *lasting or expected to last fewer than six months* can be substantially limiting" for purposes of proving an actual disability. § 1630.2(j)(1)(ix) (emphasis added).

According to the appendix to the EEOC regulations, the "duration of an impairment is one factor that is relevant in determining whether the impairment substantially limits a major life activity." § 1630.2(j)(1)(ix)(app.). Although "[i]mpairments that last only for a short period of time are typically not covered," they may be covered "if sufficiently severe." *Id*. The EEOC appendix illustrates these principles: "[I]f an individual has a back impairment that results in a 20-pound lifting restriction that lasts for several months, he is substantially limited in the major life activity of lifting, and therefore covered under the first prong of the definition of disability." *Id*.

III.

In dismissing Summers's wrongful-discharge claim, the district court held that, even though Summers had "suffered a very serious injury," this injury did not constitute a disability because it was temporary and expected to heal within a year. That holding represented an entirely reasonable interpretation of *Toyota* and its progeny. But in 2008, Congress expressly abrogated *Toyota* by amending the ADA. We are the first appellate court to apply the amendment's expanded definition of "disability." Fortunately, the absence of appellate precedent presents no difficulty in this case: Summers has unquestionably alleged a "disability" under the ADAAA sufficiently plausible to survive a Rule 12(b)(6) motion.

A.

Summers alleges that his accident left him unable to walk for seven months and that without surgery, pain medication, and physical therapy, he "likely" would have been unable to walk for far longer.[3] The text and purpose of the ADAAA and its

---

1. The ADAAA provides, with respect to the "regarded-as" prong, that a plaintiff will not be disabled if his impairment is "transitory and minor," i.e. of "an actual or expected duration of 6 months or less." *Id*. § 12102(3)(B). It contains no similar durational requirement for the "actual-disability" prong.

3. In enacting the ADAAA, Congress clarified that courts must disregard so-called "mitigating measures" when determining whether an impairment constitutes a disability. The new statute and regulations require courts to evaluate a plaintiff's impairment as it would manifest without treatments such as medication, mobility devices, and physical therapy. 42 U.S.C. § 12102(4)(E)(i); 29 C.F.R. § 1630.2(j)(5). . . . Because Summers's impairment could constitute a disability with or without surgery, we need not address whether his surgeries constituted mitigating measures.

implementing regulations make clear that such an impairment can constitute a disability.

In the amended Act, after concluding that courts had construed the term "disability" too narrowly, Congress stated that it intended to liberalize the ADA "in favor of broad coverage." 42 U.S.C. § 12102(4)(A). Congress also mandated that the ADA, as amended, be interpreted as broadly as its text permits. *Id.* Furthermore, the EEOC, pursuant to its delegated authority to construe "disability" more generously, adopted new regulations providing that an impairment lasting less than six months can constitute a disability. 29 C.F.R. § 1630.2(j)(1)(ix). Although short-term impairments qualify as disabilities only if they are "sufficiently severe," *id.* § 1630.2(j)(1)(ix)(app.), it seems clear that the serious impairment alleged by Summers is severe enough to qualify. If, as the EEOC has concluded, a person who cannot lift more than twenty pounds for "several months" is sufficiently impaired to be disabled within the meaning of the amended Act, *id.*, then surely a person whose broken legs and injured tendons render him completely immobile for more than seven months is also disabled.

In holding that Summers's temporary injury could not constitute a disability as a matter of law, the district court erred not only in relying on pre-ADAAA cases but also in misapplying the ADA disability analysis. The court reasoned that, because Summers could have worked with a wheelchair, he must not have been disabled. This inverts the appropriate inquiry. A court must first establish whether a plaintiff is disabled by determining whether he suffers from a substantially limiting impairment. Only then may a court ask whether the plaintiff is capable of working with or without an accommodation. *See* 42 U.S.C. § 12102(4)(E)(i)(III) (the determination whether an impairment is substantially limiting "shall be made without regard to the ameliorative effects of . . . reasonable accommodations"). If the fact that a person could work with the help of a wheelchair meant he was not disabled under the Act, the ADA would be eviscerated.

B.

Despite the sweeping language of the amended Act and the clear regulations adopted by the EEOC, Altarum maintains that a temporary impairment cannot constitute a disability. In doing so, Altarum principally relies on pre-ADAAA cases that, as we have explained, the amended Act abrogated. Additionally, Altarum briefly advances two other arguments why Summers's leg injuries did not "substantially limit" his ability to walk.

1.

First, Altarum contends that the EEOC regulations defining a disability to include short-term impairments do not warrant deference under *Chevron, U.S.A., Inc. v. Natural Resources Defense Council, Inc.*, 467 U.S. 837 (1984). Altarum argues that Congress's intent "not to extend ADA coverage to those with temporary impairments expected to fully heal is evident," because such a "dramatic expansion of the ADA would have been accompanied by some pertinent statement of Congressional intent."

When a litigant challenges an agency's interpretation of a statute, we apply the familiar two-step *Chevron* analysis. First, we evaluate whether Congress has "directly spoken" to the precise question at issue. If traditional rules of statutory construction render the intent of Congress clear, "that is the end of the matter." *Chevron.* If the statute is "silent or ambiguous" with respect to the question at issue, we proceed to the second step — determining whether the agency's interpretation of the statute is reasonable. *Id.* An agency's reasonable interpretation will control, even if better interpretations are possible. *Id.*

Although Altarum contends that Congress's intent to withhold ADA coverage from temporarily impaired employees is "evident," no such intent seems evident to us. To be sure, the amended Act does preserve, without alteration, the requirement that an impairment be "substantial" to qualify as a disability. But Congress enacted the ADAAA to correct what it perceived as the Supreme Court's overly restrictive definition of this very term. And Congress expressly directed courts to construe the amended statute as broadly as possible. Moreover, while the ADAAA imposes a six-month requirement with respect to "regarded-as" disabilities, it imposes no such durational requirement for "actual" disabilities, thus suggesting that no such requirement was intended. *See Hamdan v. Rumsfeld,* 548 U.S. 557, 578 (2006) ("[A] negative inference may be drawn from the exclusion of language from one statutory provision that is included in other provisions of the same statute."). For these reasons, we must reject Altarum's contention that the amended Act clearly evinces Congress's intent to withhold ADA coverage for temporary impairments. At best, the statute is ambiguous with respect to whether temporary impairments may now qualify as disabilities.

Accordingly, we turn to step two of the *Chevron* analysis — determining whether the EEOC's interpretation is reasonable. We conclude that it is. The EEOC's decision to define disability to include severe temporary impairments entirely accords with the purpose of the amended Act. The stated goal of the ADAAA is to expand the scope of protection available under the Act as broadly as the text permits. The EEOC's interpretation — that the ADAAA may encompass temporary disabilities — advances this goal. Moreover, extending coverage to temporarily impaired employees produces consequences less "dramatic" than Altarum seems to envision. Prohibiting employers from discriminating against temporarily disabled employees will burden employers only as long as the disability endures. Temporary disabilities require only temporary accommodations.

2.

Alternatively, Altarum argues that, even deferring to the EEOC regulations, Summers's impairment does not qualify as a disability. Altarum maintains that the EEOC regulations do not apply to Summers's impairment because those regulations do not cover "temporary impairments due to injuries" even if they do cover "impairments due to permanent or long-term conditions that have only a short term impact."

But, in fact, the EEOC regulations provide no basis for distinguishing between temporary impairments caused by injuries, on one hand, and temporary impairments caused by permanent conditions, on the other. The regulations state only that the "effects of an impairment lasting or expected to last fewer than six months can be substantially limiting" — they say nothing about the cause of the impairment. 29 C.F.R. § 1630.2(j)(1)(ix).

Nor do the regulations suggest that an "injury" cannot be an "impairment." Rather, the EEOC defines an impairment broadly to include "[a]ny physiological disorder or condition, cosmetic disfigurement, or anatomical loss affecting one or more body systems," including the "musculoskeletal" system. *Id.* § 1630.2(h)(1). This expansive definition surely includes broken bones and torn tendons. And the EEOC elsewhere uses the terms "injury" and "impairment" interchangeably. *See id.* § 1630.2(j)(5) n.3 (app.); *id.* § 1630.15(f) (app.).

In sum, nothing about the ADAAA or its regulations suggests a distinction between impairments caused by temporary injuries and impairments caused by permanent conditions. Because Summers alleges a severe injury that prevented him from walking for at least seven months, he has stated a claim that this impairment "substantially limited" his ability to walk.

IV.

Under the ADAAA and its implementing regulations, an impairment is not categorically excluded from being a disability simply because it is temporary. The impairment alleged by Summers falls comfortably within the amended Act's expanded definition of disability. We therefore reverse the district court's dismissal of Summers's wrongful-discharge claim and remand the case for further proceedings consistent with this opinion.

NOTES

1. *The Analysis.* Mr. Summers won this round, but he will not necessarily win his claim. We now know that he is actually disabled, but we do not know whether he is "qualified": If his disability keeps him from performing the essential functions of his job (with or without reasonable accommodation), he will lose. As we will see, coming to work as usual might (or might not) be an essential function, and his limitation in that regard might (or might not) be reasonably accommodated (say, by some telecommuting). But once Summers established his actual disability and qualifications, Altarum (1) cannot discriminate against him on that basis, and (2) has to reasonably accommodate that disability — short of undue hardship.

Had the temporary nature of his condition meant he wasn't actually disabled, Summers might have claimed that Altarum "regarded" him as disabled. If the employer fired him because of his physical limitations, that might seem like a slam dunk. Proof of "regarded as" status would mean that Summers was (1) protected from discrimination but (2) not entitled to an accommodation. In this scenario, he need not be allowed to telecommute. But wait: Temporary conditions — those expected to last less than six months — are excluded from "regarded as" protection. So protection under this prong is not as obvious as it seems. If the impairment is neither an actual disability nor a "regarded as" disability, Altarum is free to fire Summers because of his injury.

2. *Temporary and Episodic Disabilities.* The *Summers* case is all about what "substantially limits" means, but it focuses on only one aspect of that inquiry: whether a temporary impairment is by definition not substantially limiting. The court holds no,

at least when the impairment is "sufficiently severe." This may seem like a no-brainer, at least in scenarios like the one confronted in the case—a serious injury coupled with long-term recovery. But note that the *Summers* opinion thinks the district court might have gotten it right under the original ADA—it was only the ADAAA that changed the analysis. This may give you some idea of why Congress reacted so strongly to judicial construction of the original statute.

But do you think the Fourth Circuit was correct under the amended law? Doesn't the statute allow employers to discriminate against short-term impairments under the "regarded as" prong? Isn't it odd that Congress seems to allow the very kind of discrimination under one prong that would be barred under another prong? Indeed, it's even odder since, as we've seen, an employer need not accommodate "regarded as" disabilities, only actual disabilities (and, according to the EEOC, "record of" disabilities). In short, the standard for coverage seems lower under the more demanding prong of the statute.

Maybe this is where the EEOC regulations and the "*Chevron* two-step" come in. Even assuming this result would be odd as a matter of statutory interpretation, the statute is at worse "ambiguous" because it leaves a "gap" by failing to expressly address the status of temporary impairments for the "actually disabled" prong. That's the first step of the *Chevron* analysis, and satisfaction of it essentially authorizes the EEOC to fill that gap. Since the Commission's regulations clearly include actual disabilities that are temporary conditions so long as they are sufficiently severe, we move to the second step, which asks whether the agency's interpretation is a reasonable (not necessarily preferable) one. Since the court isn't prepared to say the agency interpretation is unreasonable, the regulation stands.

Related to the notion of a temporary disability is the question of episodic ones—flair-ups of an underlying condition that are themselves temporary in nature even though the condition causing them is not. Unlike Summers, whose condition was expected to heal within a year, those who have the underlying impairment may expect such episodic manifestations to arise periodically in the future. But with respect to this question, there is no need to look to the regulations since the ADAAA speaks clearly, explicitly providing that "[a]n impairment that is episodic or in remission is a disability if it would substantially limit a major life activity when active." § 12102(4)(D). *See Gogos v. AMS Mech. Sys., Inc.*, 737 F.3d 1170, 1173 (7th Cir. 2013) (an episode of a blood-pressure spike and vision loss may be covered disabilities when both problems may be "episodic" manifestations of a longstanding blood-pressure condition; despite their short duration, they could be said to substantially impair two major life activities, circulatory function and eyesight. And, in any event, plaintiff's chronic blood-pressure condition could also qualify as a disability.).

3. *Major Life Activity*. There is no need to look to major life activities for the "regarded as" prong: It is enough that the employer discriminates on the basis of a nontemporary impairment. But to be protected from discrimination under the "actual disability" prong (and thus to be not only protected from discrimination but also entitled to reasonable accommodation), an employee must not only have an impairment but that impairment must substantially limit a major life activity.

Consider the ADAAA's effect on major life activities. This can be complicated. Recall that, in *Bragdon*, where the question was whether HIV affected a major life activity, the Court focused on the activity of reproduction since the plaintiff was a female who claimed to be substantially limited in her ability to bear a child because of the risk of passing on the disease to it. Where a male with HIV is concerned, however, there is no danger in fathering a child with HIV. Under the original ADA, such a plaintiff might have had to claim that his condition substantially limited him in having sex because of the aversion of potential sexual partners. But the ADAAA short circuits the whole question — major life activities now "include the operation of a major bodily function," and specifically lists the immune system. *Horgan v. Simmons,* 704 F. Supp. 2d 814 (N.D. Ill. 2010). And there is not much doubt that a plaintiff with HIV is substantially limited in terms of the functioning of his immune system.

Note on Major Life Activities

The ADAAA's amendment of the statute to include a definition of major life activities should significantly reduce the need to interpret that term. But it might be useful to survey some of the pre-ADAAA decisions to appreciate the confusion. Some of these decisions remain good law; many do not. For example, *Pack v. Kmart Corp.,* 166 F.3d 1300 (10th Cir. 1999), held that sleep is a major life activity, but concentration is not. The ADAAA lists both. *Head v. Glacier Northwest, Inc.,* 413 F.3d 1053, 1058 (9th Cir. 2005), viewed thinking, reading, interacting with others, and sleeping as major life activities. The ADAAA embraces all of these except "interacting with others," and it does include "communicating," which might or might not be the same thing. *Reeves v. Johnson Controls World Servs., Inc.,* 140 F.3d 144 (2d Cir. 1998), wrote that "everyday mobility" is not a major life activity where agoraphobia restricted plaintiff's ability to cross bridges and overpasses, enter tunnels, and board trains. The ADAAA doesn't list "everyday mobility" as a major life activity, but its list is not exhaustive.

Arline, Bragdon, and Williams all had physical disabilities, but as some of the cases we've just surveyed indicate, the ADA encompasses mental and emotional disabilities as well as physical ones. According to Ann Hubbard:

> There can be no doubt that Congress intended major life activities to reach beyond what makes life merely possible to what makes it enjoyable and meaningful. An activity's importance must be assessed in light of the full array of aspirations and opportunities our modern society offers. These include the everyday activities that allow an individual to participate in every aspect of our modern society: civic, social, educational, economic, vocational, professional, political, commercial, recreational and cultural. Activities in all of these public spheres, as well as in personal and family life, must therefore be included in the category of "major."

The Major Life Activity of Belonging, 39 WAKE FOREST L. REV. 217, 224-25 (2004); *see also* Ann Hubbard, *Meaningful Lives and Major Life Activities,* 55 ALA. L. REV. 997 (2004); Ann Hubbard, *The Major Life Activity of Caring,* 8 IOWA J. GENDER, RACE & JUST. 327 (2004); Ann Hubbard, *The Myth of Independence and the Major Life Activity of Caring,* 8 J. GENDER RACE & JUST. 327 (2004).

Prior to the ADAAA, there was also considerable confusion about whether working could be considered a major life activity. Both *Sutton* and *Toyota* explicitly reserved this question. The ADAAA resolves one bone of contention by explicitly including "working" in its list of major life activities. Nevertheless, *Sutton* looked to the then-existing EEOC regulations providing that, where the major life activity of working is alleged, plaintiffs are substantially limited only if they establish that they are excluded from "either a class of jobs or a broad range of jobs" as compared to persons with "comparable training, skills and abilities." 527 U.S. at 491 (quoting the applicable regulation). "The inability to perform a single, particular job does not constitute a substantial limitation in the major life activity of working." *Id.* The current regulations omit that language, but do not replace it with any meaningful definition. *See Allen v. SouthCrest Hosp.*, 455 F. App'x 827, 835 (10th Cir. 2011) (even after the ADAAA, plaintiff was required to show substantial limitation in performing a class of jobs or broad range of jobs).

Note on Substantially Limited

Once a major life activity is defined, the remaining question is whether the impairment substantially limits plaintiff's participation in it. The primary question before the *Toyota* court was whether Williams' impairment substantially limited her major life activity of performing manual tasks. The Court answered that question by stating that only if the impairment "prevents or severely restricts the individual from doing activities that are of central importance to most people's daily lives" will it be considered substantially limiting. Moreover, the Court required that the impairment's impact must also be permanent or long term. 534 U.S. at 198.

The ADAAA explicitly disapproved of *Toyota's* approach as setting "an inappropriately high level of limitation," and for good measure it also disapproved of the extant EEOC regulations: "Congress finds that the current Equal Employment Opportunity Commission ADA regulations defining the term 'substantially limits' as 'significantly restricted' are inconsistent with congressional intent, by expressing too high a standard." 42 U.S.C.A. § 12101.

Responding to this concern, § 1630.2(j)(1)(i) of the EEOC's regulations provides a number of "rules of construction," designed to expand statutory protection. The most sweeping sets the stage for the others:

> The term "substantially limits" shall be construed broadly in favor of expansive coverage, to the maximum extent permitted by the terms of the ADA. "Substantially limits" is not meant to be a demanding standard.

Subsequent rules provide more detail, but cut in favor of broad reach. Thus, [a]n impairment is a disability within the meaning of this section if it "substantially limits'" the ability of an individual to perform a major life activity as compared to most people in the general population," § 1630.2(j)(1)(iii), but it "need not prevent, or significantly or severely restrict, the individual from performing a major life activity in order to be considered a disability." *Id.* Further, "[i]n determining whether an individual has a disability, the focus is on how a major life activity is substantially limited, not on what an individual can do in spite of an impairment." § 1630.2(j)(1)(iv).

In short, if, as in *Summers*, the courts give deference to the EEOC regulations, much of the prior case law will be abrogated, and limitations will have to be much less "substantial" than before to meet the ADA's threshold.

Note on Mitigating Measures

One of the targets of the ADAAA was *Sutton v. United Airlines, Inc.* 527 U.S. 471 (1999), a case that held that individuals who used mitigating or ameliorative measures to deal with their impairment should be assessed in their mitigated state. While *Sutton* itself involved pilots rejected by an airline because they needed glasses for 20/20 vision, the opinion and two companion cases — *Murphy v. UPS*, 527 U.S. 516 (1999) (plaintiff's high blood pressure should be considered in his medicated state to assess substantial limitation), and *Albertson's, Inc. v. Kirkingburg*, 527 U.S. 555 (1999) (plaintiff's subconscious adjustments to his monocular vision should be considered in assessing substantial limitation) — threatened to radically cut back on the protected class. Indeed, Justice Stevens's dissent in *Sutton* argued that the majority's approach would permit an employer to discriminate against a veteran who lost a leg if his prosthesis was effective. 527 U.S. 497-98.

The ADAAA explicitly disapproved of *Sutton* and provides that "the determination of whether an impairment substantially limits a major life activity shall be made *without regard* to the ameliorative effects of mitigating measures," listing a number of mitigating measures such as medication, prosthetics, hearing aids, etc. However, the amended statute goes on to provide that "the ameliorative effects of the mitigating measures of ordinary eyeglasses or contact lenses shall be considered in determining whether an impairment substantially limits a major life activity." Accordingly, while Congress amended the statute in direct response to the result in *Sutton*, it essentially agreed that the *Sutton* plaintiffs were not to be considered persons with *actual* disabilities within the meaning of the ADA.

In the wake of the ADAAA, there remains a problem regarding those who do not use measures when they are available. Such individuals will be disabled (a matter that divided the courts prior to the ADAAA), but the failure to mitigate may sometimes make them unqualified. As we will see, a disabled person is otherwise qualified if she can perform the essential functions of the position with or without reasonable accommodation. The obvious question that will arise is the extent to which an employer must accommodate an individual who does not use mitigating measures to enable her to do the job at issue. *See generally* Jeannette Cox, *"Corrective" Surgery and the Americans with Disabilities Act*, 46 SAN DIEGO L. REV. 113 (2009). Finally, there is the question of whether the use of a mitigating measure might itself create a disability where none previously existed. *Sulima v. Tobyhanna Army Depot*, 602 F.3d 177, 187 (3d Cir. 2010), held that the side effects from medical treatment may themselves constitute an impairment under the ADA even if the condition treated is not itself disabling; however, since "'disability' connotes an involuntary condition," a plaintiff seeking protection on this theory must show both that the treatment was required in the "prudent judgment" of the medical profession and that there is not an equally efficacious available alternative that lacks similarly disabling side effects.

PROBLEMS

9-5. Sarah Smith is an assembly-line worker who is diabetic and dependent on insulin injections to maintain her glucose level. She must inject up to four times a day to maintain ideal glucose levels. If her glucose level drops too low, she will become hypoglycemic and go into a coma. If her glucose level is too high, it will cause long-term physical deterioration of numerous body systems. Since eating increases glucose levels, Sarah needs to inject one half hour before eating larger meals. Her doctor has recommended that she eat smaller and more frequent meals to help modulate variations in her glucose levels. Outside of work, Sarah leads an active life and exercises regularly. She must be careful to time her injections depending on her exercise and eating patterns. Exercise reduces glucose levels on a short-term basis and can upset the balance of insulin and glucose in the body, possibly resulting in a hypoglycemic reaction. Because Sarah is careful about her eating, exercise, and treatment regimen, her diabetes is reasonably well controlled. She does not yet exhibit any physical damage related to excess glucose levels. She carries small amounts of sugar with her to minimize the incidence of hypoglycemic reactions. Assembly-line workers operate on a very rigid schedule. Sarah wants to seek accommodations from her employer to make it easier for her to maintain her glucose levels while at work. Was Sarah an individual with a disability under the original ADA? What about under the ADA as amended?

9-6. Alpha-1 antitrypsin ("AAT") is a serum protein that protects the lungs from proteolytic enzymes. Approximately 80 percent of individuals who inherit an AAT deficiency from both parents develop chronic obstructive pulmonary disease ("COPD"). Individuals who inherit the deficiency from only one parent have an increased risk of developing COPD (one in ten), especially if they smoke or work in dusty environments. Tuan Lee, who inherited AAT deficiency from both of his parents, does not yet suffer from any symptoms of COPD. Is Tuan impaired? If so, is he substantially limited with respect to a major life activity and, therefore, protected under the ADA as amended?

b. Record of Such an Impairment

Section 3(2) of the ADA defines disability to include having a record of an impairment that substantially limits a major life activity. A variety of "records" contain such information, including employment records, medical records, and education records. However, "[t]he impairment indicated in the record must be an impairment that would substantially limit one or more of the individual's major life activities." 29 C.F.R. pt. 1630, app. § 1630.2(k). *See Colwell v. Suffolk County Police Dept.*, 158 F.3d 635, 645 (2d Cir. 1998) (hospitalization for cerebral hemorrhage was too vague and too short to be record of impairment); *Sherrod v. American Airlines, Inc.*, 132 F.3d 1112, 1120-21 (5th Cir. 1998) (hospitalization for back surgery was not a record of an impairment that would substantially limit a major life activity). *See generally* Alex B. Long, *(Whatever Happened to) The ADA's "Record of" Prong(?)*, 81 WASH. L. REV. 669 (2006).

PROBLEM

9-7. Reconsider Problems 9-5 and 9-6. Could you make a "record of impairment" argument on behalf of Sarah or Tuan?

c. Regarded as Having Such an Impairment

We saw earlier that individuals are protected by the ADA even if they are not actually impaired or if they are "regarded" by their employers as being impaired. *Sutton* read this provision of the statute as addressing two situations: "(1) a covered entity mistakenly believes that a person has a physical impairment that substantially limits one or more major life activities, or (2) a covered entity mistakenly believes that an actual, nonlimiting impairment substantially limits one or more major life activities." 527 U.S. at 489. The Court quoted EEOC regulations as indicating that such misperceptions often 'result from stereotypic assumptions not truly indicative of . . . individual ability.'"

The ADAAA changes this radically; it provides:

> (A) An individual meets the requirement of "being regarded as having such an impairment" if the individual establishes that he or she has been subjected to an action prohibited under this Act because of an actual or perceived physical or mental impairment whether or not the impairment limits or is perceived to limit a major life activity.

In other words, to be liable, the employer must still discriminate on the basis of an impairment, but there is no longer any requirement that the employer believe the impairment to be substantially limiting. Under the original statute, for example, *Brown v. Lester E. Cox Medical Center*, 286 F.3d 1040 (8th Cir. 2002), upheld a jury verdict for the plaintiff on her "regarded as" claim only when evidence showed that the employer regarded the plaintiff's multiple sclerosis as substantially limiting her ability to think because it believed her condition made her unfit for further employment in any capacity at the medical center. Under the ADAAA's approach, proving that the employer discriminated against the plaintiff because of her MS would suffice with no further inquiry (assuming the plaintiff to be otherwise qualified). Think about discrimination based on obesity. If that's an impairment, the inquiry is at an end under the "regarded as" prong.

"Regarded as" discrimination may be more common than might first appear. Professor Michelle Travis, in *Perceived Disabilities, Social Cognition, and "Innocent Mistakes,"* 55 Vand. L. Rev. 481 (2002), contends that "at least some perceived disabilities are likely to result not from consciously held, group-based prejudices or generalizations, but from nonmotivational cognitive processing errors," *id.* at 491, that is, errors that do not derive from conscious prejudices or even conscious group-based decision making. Of course, as we saw in *Summers*, the sweep of this prong is limited by the statutory provision that it "shall not apply to impairments that are transitory and minor. A transitory impairment is an impairment with an actual or expected duration of 6 months or less." Nevertheless, the "regarded as" prong now provides the broadest statutory protection.

Counterbalancing this dramatic expansion, however, the ADAAA effectively created a two-tiered structure for disability claims. For actual (and presumably "record of") disabilities, the statute continue to both forbid discrimination and mandate accommodation. But for "regarded as" claims, the ADAAA bars discrimination only; it does not mandate accommodation. *See generally* Stephen F. Befort, *Let's Try This Again: The ADA Amendments Act of 2008 Attempts to Reinvigorate the "Regarded As" Prong of the Statutory Definition of Disability*, 2010 Utah L. Rev. 993.

How would this apply to the *Sutton* plaintiffs? They presumably have no actual disability under the ADA, originally or as amended, since their corrective lenses may be taken into account in determining whether their visual impairments substantially limit one or more major life activities. But, corrected or not, they do have myopia, an impairment. And their prospective employer denied them employment because of their myopia. They thus would be considered individuals with a disability under the "regarded as" prong under the amended statute, although the "qualification standard" defense might avoid liability for United.

2. The Meaning of "Qualified Individual with a Disability"

Establishing the existence of a disability is necessary but not sufficient to bring an individual within Title I's protections since that statute prohibits discrimination only against "a *qualified* individual with a disability because of the disability of such individual." 42 U.S.C. § 12112(a) (2014) (emphasis added). In turn, Title I in § 12111(8) defines a "qualified individual with a disability" as:

> an individual with a disability who, with or without reasonable accommodation, can perform the essential functions of the employment position that such individual holds or desires. For the purposes of this title, consideration shall be given to the employer's judgment as to what functions of a job are essential, and if an employer has prepared a written description before advertising or interviewing applicants for the job, this description shall be considered evidence of the essential functions of the job.

This definition protects disabled individuals who can perform the essential tasks of their jobs and thus prevents employers from denying employment because a disability precludes the performance of nonessential or relatively unimportant aspects of the job. On the other hand, denying employment to someone who cannot perform the essential functions of the job with or without reasonable accommodation is perfectly legal. *See Majors v. GE Elec. Co.*, 714 F.3d 527 (7th Cir. 2013) (because plaintiff was permanently unable to lift more than twenty pounds, she could not perform an essential function of the auditor position without accommodation; further, the only accommodation she proposed was to have another worker lift heavy objects for her, and "[t]o have another employee perform a position's essential function, and to a certain extent perform the job for the employee, is not a reasonable accommodation"); *Olsen v. Capital Region Med. Ctr.*, 713 F.3d 1149, 1154 (8th Cir. 2013) (plaintiff's frequent epileptic seizures prevented her from being qualified for her position since an essential function of mammography technician was insuring patient safety, and she was unable to "adequately perform that function during the indefinite periods in which she was incapacitated"); *Hohn v. BNSF Ry. Co.*, 707 F.3d 995, 1003 (8th Cir. 2013) (upholding a jury verdict because sufficient evidence supported a finding that plaintiff's visual impairment prevented him from performing the essential functions of the locomotive machinist position safely or at all since the job entailed working "within, around, over and under locomotives" in a "a dynamic environment, with variable lighting, uneven surfaces, scaffolding, ladders, ramps, stairs, overhead objects, and large machinery and locomotives"). Accordingly, to determine whether an individual is qualified, it is necessary to distinguish the essential functions of the job from those that are not, an inquiry which tends to entail the question of whether a reasonable accommodation is available.

≡≡≡ ***EEOC v. Ford Motor Co.,***
752 F.3d 634 (6th Cir. 2014) *vacated and reh'g en banc granted,*
2014 U. S. App. LEXIS 17252 (6th Cir. 2014)

KAREN NELSON MOORE, Circuit Judge.

At issue in this case is whether a telecommuting arrangement could be a reasonable accommodation for an employee suffering from a debilitating disability. Charging party Jane Harris was terminated from her position as a resale steel buyer at Ford Motor Co. ("Ford") after she asked to telecommute several days per week in an attempt to control the symptoms of irritable bowel syndrome ("IBS"). . . . The district court granted summary judgment in favor of Ford. Because we find evidence in the record to create a genuine dispute as to whether Harris was qualified to work as a resale buyer . . . we REVERSE . . . .

I. Background

In 2003, Jane Harris was hired as a resale buyer at Ford. Resale steel buyers serve as intermediaries between steel suppliers and "stampers," the companies that use steel to produce parts for Ford. Their role is to respond to emergency supply issues to ensure that there is no gap in steel supply to the parts manufacturers. The position involved some individual tasks, such as updating spreadsheets and periodic site visits to observe the production process. However, "the essence of the job was group problem-solving, which required that a buyer be available to interact with members of the resale team, suppliers and others in the Ford system when problems arose." Ford managers made the business judgment that such meetings were most effectively handled face-to-face, and that email or teleconferencing was an insufficient substitute for in-person team problem-solving. Another resale buyer on Harris's team believed that she "could not work from home more than one day a week and be able to effectively perform the duties of the resale buyer position." Harris worked in this role until September 2009, when she was terminated.

Harris was a consistently competent, though not perfect, employee. . . .

Throughout her entire period of employment with Ford, Harris suffered from IBS, an illness that causes fecal incontinence. Over time, her symptoms worsened and, on particularly bad days, Harris would be unable even to drive to work or stand up from her desk without soiling herself. Harris began to take intermittent FMLA leave when she experienced severe IBS symptoms.

After she began taking leave, Harris's absences started to affect her job performance. In 2005, Dawn Gontko, Harris's supervisor at that time, responded to Harris's attendance problems by allowing her to work on a flex-time telecommuting schedule on a trial basis. Gontko deemed the trial unsuccessful because Harris "was unable to establish regular and consistent work hours." When Harris's absences continued,

Gontko placed her on Workplace Guidelines, a tool used by supervisors to assist employees in improving attendance. Jim Gordon, Gontko's successor, also found Harris's absences to be problematic. Although Ford did not approve remote work, Harris worked from home on an informal basis, including on evenings and weekends, to keep up with her work. However, Ford did not credit Harris with the time she spent working during non-"core" hours and marked the days that she stayed home because of her illness as absences. Ford took the position that "if [Harris] was too ill to come to work, she would be considered too ill to work." Time spent working after core business hours was considered "casual overtime" expected of salaried employees.

Ford also explained that work performed outside of core business hours is not a sufficient substitute for work during regular hours because employees cannot engage in team problem-solving or access suppliers to obtain information during off-hours. Indeed, when Harris worked nights and weekends, she made mistakes and missed deadlines because she lacked access to suppliers. For example, while working on Saturday, April 18, 2009, Harris submitted a purchase order containing incorrect pricing information because she could not immediately access the supplier on a weekend to obtain updated quotations. These mistakes added to the frustration of both suppliers and coworkers, who had to take time to correct them. Because Harris was not permitted to work remotely to mitigate the effect of her many unscheduled "absences," Gordon was forced to shift some of her work to himself or Harris's teammates. Under Ford's system of marking absences, in the first seven months of 2009 Harris was absent more often than she was present during core business hours.

In February 2009, Harris formally requested that she be permitted to telecommute on an as-needed basis as an accommodation for her disability. Ford utilized a telecommuting policy that authorized employees to work up to four days per week from a telecommuting site. The policy provides that all salaried employees are eligible to apply for a telecommuting arrangement, but specifically states that such arrangements are not appropriate for "all jobs, employees, work environments or even managers." Under this policy, several other buyers telecommuted on one scheduled day per week.

[Harris sought permission to telecommute and met with Ford managers to discuss the possibility, but Ford ultimately denied the request. Instead, Karen Jirik, a Ford personnel relations representative, suggested alternative accommodations, "including moving Harris's cubicle closer to the restroom or seeking another job within Ford more suitable for telecommuting." Harris rejected these options.]

[Harris filed a charge of discrimination with the EEOC, and there followed some Ford reactions that Harris claimed to be retaliation for filing that charge. Although the Sixth Circuit also found a triable ADA retaliation claim, those portions of the opinion are omitted. The EEOC filed a complaint on Harris's behalf, but the district court granted summary judgment in favor of Ford, reasoning that Harris was not a "qualified" individual on the basis of her excessive absenteeism. It declined "to second-guess an employer's business judgment regarding the essential functions of a job," and therefore held that Harris's request to telecommute up to four days per week was not a reasonable accommodation for her position.]

III.   Failure-To-Accommodate Claim

. . . When a plaintiff premises a discrimination claim upon an employer's failure to accommodate her disability, we analyze her claim under the following framework:

> (1) The plaintiff bears the burden of establishing that he or she is disabled. (2) The plaintiff bears the burden of establishing that he or she is "otherwise qualified" for the position despite his or her disability: (a) without accommodation from the employer; (b) with an alleged "essential" job requirement eliminated; or (c) with a proposed reasonable accommodation. (3) The employer will bear the burden of proving that a challenged job criterion is essential, and therefore a business necessity, or that a proposed accommodation will impose an undue hardship upon the employer.

Harris is indisputably disabled under the ADA: Her IBS is a physical impairment that substantially limits the operation of her bowel, a major bodily function. *See* 42 U.S.C. § 12102(1)(A), 12102(2)(B). The dispute in this case centers upon whether Harris was "otherwise qualified" for the resale steel buyer position. Harris has presented evidence to establish that she was qualified on two alternative bases: (a) she was qualified for the position after the elimination of the requirement that she be physically present at Ford facilities or (b) she was qualified for the position with a telecommuting accommodation. Because Harris has provided sufficient evidence to create a genuine dispute of material fact as to her qualification for the resale buyer position, the burden shifts to Ford to prove that either (a) the physical-presence requirement is an essential function of Harris's job or (b) the telecommuting arrangement would create an undue hardship.

A.   *Qualification with "Essential" Job Requirement Eliminated*

The EEOC offered evidence to demonstrate that, if the physical-presence requirement is eliminated, Harris is qualified for the resale-buyer position. Harris earned consistently positive performance reviews in the years leading up to her termination. Although she sometimes struggled with interpersonal relations, Harris's supervisors praised her for her knowledge of the steel industry and her ability to work diligently without close supervision. Ford's only serious criticism of Harris's job performance related to her frequent absences during severe IBS flare-ups. Thus, leaving attendance issues aside, no record evidence indicates that Harris lacked the qualifications necessary to fulfill her role as a resale steel buyer.

Because the EEOC can demonstrate that Harris was qualified for her position if physical attendance at the worksite is not considered, the burden shifts to Ford to prove that physical presence in the workplace is an "essential function" of the resale buyer position. Ford cannot indisputably carry its burden. For many positions, regular attendance at the work place is undoubtedly essential. *See Brenneman v. MedCentral Health Sys.*, 366 F.3d 412, 418 (6th Cir. 2004). Indeed, the dissent cites a litany of cases that extol the sanctity of the attendance requirement. *See, e.g., Samper v. Providence St. Vincent Med. Ctr.*, 675 F.3d 1233, 1235 (9th Cir. 2012); *Colón-Fontánez v. Municipality of San Juan*, 660 F.3d 17, 33 (1st Cir. 2011). What the dissent fails to recognize is that these cases focus on "predictable" and "regular" attendance in the workplace as an essential requirement of most jobs. The assumption implicit in the dissent's analysis and many of the early cases is that the "workplace" is the physical worksite provided by the employer. When we first developed the principle that attendance is an essential requirement of most jobs, technology was such that the workplace and an employer's brick-and-mortar location were synonymous. However, as technology has advanced in the intervening decades, and an ever-greater number of employers and employees utilize remote work arrangements, attendance at the workplace can no longer be assumed to mean attendance at the employer's physical location. Instead, the law must respond to the advance of technology in the employment context, as it has in other areas of modern life, and recognize that the "workplace" is anywhere that an employee can perform her job duties. Thus, the vital question in this case is not whether "attendance" was an essential job function for a resale buyer, but whether physical presence at the Ford facilities was truly essential. Determining whether physical presence is essential to a particular job is a "highly fact specific" question. Accordingly, we consider several factors to guide our inquiry, including written job descriptions, the business judgment of the employer, the amount of time spent performing the function, and the work experience of past and present employees in the same or similar positions. *See* 29 C.F.R. § 1630.2(n)(2).

Ford argues that physical attendance at the Ford workplace was critical to the group dynamic of the resale-buyer team. Our sister circuits have recognized that physical presence at an employer's facility may be an essential function for some positions specifically because they require extensive teamwork. *See Samper* ("Sometimes [attendance] is required simply because the employee must work as 'part of a team.' Other jobs require face-to-face interaction with clients and other employees." (internal citations omitted)); *Mason v. Avaya Commc'ns, Inc.*, 357 F.3d 1114, 1122 (10th Cir. 2004); *Vande Zande v. Wis. Dep't of Admin.*, 44 F.3d 538, 544 (7th Cir. 1995). Ford has provided evidence that teamwork was integral to the resale buyer position. One of Harris's coworkers believed, based on her experience in the same position, that she could not perform effectively as a resale buyer while telecommuting. In addition, several members of Ford's management team expressed their business judgment that physical attendance was essential for resale buyers because face-to-face interactions facilitate group problem-solving. However, as we have discussed, advancing technology has diminished the necessity of in-person contact to facilitate group conversations. The world has changed since the foundational opinions regarding physical presence in the workplace were issued: teleconferencing technologies that most people could not have conceived of in the 1990s are now commonplace. Indeed, Judge Posner presciently observed in *Vande Zande* that his conclusion that "team work under supervision generally cannot be performed at home without a substantial reduction in the quality of the employee's performance" would "no doubt change as communications technology advances." Therefore, we are not persuaded that positions that require a great deal of teamwork are inherently unsuitable to telecommuting arrangements.

Moreover, our inquiry does not end simply because Ford has expressed the business judgment that face-to-face interaction is desirable. Courts routinely defer to the business judgment of employers because courts are not equipped with the institutional knowledge to sit as "super personnel department[s]." However, we should not abdicate our responsibility as a court to company personnel boards: While we do not allow plaintiffs to redefine the essential functions of their jobs based on their personal beliefs about job requirements, neither should we allow employers to redefine the essential functions of an employee's position to serve their own interests. Rather, we should carefully consider all of the relevant factors, of which the employer's business judgment is only one.

While Ford has provided substantial evidence of its business judgment and the experience of other resale buyers, the EEOC has also offered evidence that casts doubt on the importance of face-to-face interactions at Ford. Harris's own experience over several years as a resale buyer indicates that in-person interaction may not be as important as Ford describes: Even when Harris was physically present at Ford facilities, "the vast majority of communications and interactions with both the internal and external stakeholders were done via conference call."[3] More fundamentally, Harris's position is not one that actually *requires* face-to-face interactions with clients. *Cf. Melange v. City of Ctr. Line, 482 F. App'x 81, 84 (6th Cir. 2012)* (concluding that a custodian must attend his physical workplace to complete the required manual labor); *Samper* (concluding that "on-site" attendance was an essential function of the job for a neo-natal nurse who provided direct patient care). Although Harris needed to conduct occasional site visits with steel suppliers, Ford has offered no evidence to prove that Harris would be less able to perform these site visits if she worked partially, or even primarily, from her home rather than Ford's facilities.[4] As additional evidence that physical presence at Ford was not an essential function of the job, the EEOC points to Ford's decision to extend telecommuting options to other resale buyers, albeit on a more limited basis than Harris's initial request. Although Ford has provided significant evidence that physical attendance was an essential function of the resale buyer position, the EEOC has offered at least enough evidence genuinely to dispute this conclusion.

B. Qualification with Reasonable Accommodation

Alternatively, the EEOC can demonstrate that Harris was qualified for the resale buyer position with a reasonable accommodation for her disability, namely a telecommuting arrangement. We have previously concluded that telecommuting is not a reasonable accommodation for most jobs, but that there may be "unusual case[s]" when telecommuting is reasonable because the "employee can effectively perform all

---

3. The dissent characterizes Harris's testimony on this point as "self-serving" and dismisses it out of hand, noting that any employee could provide testimony to show that her job was suitable to telecommuting. But the dissent fails to recognize that an employer can just as easily provide self-serving testimony that even marginal job functions are absolutely essential. It is not our role at the summary judgment stage to assess whether testimony is believable; such credibility contests are for the trier of fact to resolve. When reviewing a motion for summary judgment, we must accept all facts and draw all reasonable inferences in favor of the nonmovant. Thus, we accept as true Harris's testimony that she regularly attended meetings via teleconference even while at Ford facilities.

4. The EEOC argues that these occasional site visits do not disqualify Harris from employment as a resale buyer because she would be able to reschedule site visits if they fell on a day in which she experienced severe IBS symptoms. Ford counters that frequent rescheduling is not an acceptable solution because it would disrupt business and strain client relationships. Contrary to the dissent's characterization, there is no evidence in the record that Harris "was forced to routinely cancel [site visits] at the last minute"; rather, the record indicates that Harris anticipated rescheduling visits if they were ever to coincide with a day on which she was experiencing a flare-up. There is no evidence that such a problem would necessarily arise, much less that it would occur "routinely." The factual dispute regarding whether there is a reasonable solution to Harris's potential difficulty performing site visits should be resolved by a factfinder. Regardless, the requirement that resale buyers conduct site visits has no effect on whether physical attendance is an essential function of the position: A site visit requires the resale buyer to leave the location where she ordinarily works, whether it be a Ford facility or the employee's home.

work-related duties at home." *Smith v. Ameritech*, 129 F.3d 857, 867 (6th Cir. 1997) (internal quotation marks omitted). However, as we noted above, the class of cases in which an employee can fulfill all requirements of the job while working remotely has greatly expanded. The EEOC has presented sufficient evidence to create a genuine factual dispute as to whether Harris is one of those employees who can effectively work from home.

Ford argues that a telecommuting arrangement is generally not a reasonable accommodation for resale buyers because they must interact on a regular basis with other team members and access information that is unavailable during non-"core" business hours. This argument confuses remote work arrangements with flex-time arrangements. Requests for flex-time schedules may be unreasonable because businesses cannot "operate effectively when [their] employees are essentially permitted to set their own work hours." *EEOC v. Yellow Freight Sys., Inc.*, 253 F.3d 943, 951 (7th Cir. 2011) (en banc). Indeed, leave on a sporadic or unplanned basis may be an unreasonable accommodation. *See Samper; Buckles v. First Data Res., Inc.*, 176 F.3d 1098, 1101 (8th Cir. 1999) (finding the "[u]nfettered ability to leave work at any time" not to be a reasonable accommodation). However, telecommuting does not raise the same concerns as flex-time scheduling because an employer can still rely on an employee to be working during scheduled hours. Harris did not request to "simply miss work whenever she felt she needed to and apparently so long as she felt she needed to." *Samper*. Instead she requested that she be able to work from home when she felt she needed to *during normal business hours.* The arrangement Harris sought ensured that she would be available when needed to address an emergency or participate in an impromptu meeting. Ford's concern with scheduling meetings and knowing who could be relied upon to handle urgent matters did not depend on Harris's physical presence in the office, but rather on her consistent availability during "core" hours.

Ford's arguments based on specific performance problems that arose when Harris worked remotely also confuse telecommuting with flex-time arrangements. First, Ford asserts that Harris's repeated absences forced managers to shift a portion of her responsibilities to her coworkers, which both increased other employees' workloads and strained morale. A proposed accommodation that burdens other employees may be unreasonable, *Brenneman* (concluding that the medical leave a pharmacy technician requested as an accommodation for his disability was not reasonable because his absence "placed a great strain on the Pharmacy Department"), but the resale-buyer position is not one that requires most of an absent employee's work to be transferred to a coworker. For many jobs, an employee must be physically present at work to perform specific tasks; when the employee is not present, those duties must necessarily shift to the absent employee's coworkers. Harris's resale-buyer position differs because she does not need to interact in-person with equipment or people to perform the core functions of her job. Her coworkers were required to shoulder a portion of her work not because she was physically absent, but because Ford prohibited her from working remotely during the business day.

Second, Ford argues that Harris made pricing mistakes while working remotely because she could not immediately contact a supplier for accurate information. As with the first problem, however, this mistake arose because Ford prohibited Harris from working remotely during core business hours, when she could telephone suppliers to request accurate pricing information. Her physical presence at Ford was irrelevant: Whether working from Ford's facilities or from home, Harris would have called the supplier to obtain the necessary information. Ford has not provided any evidence that a telecommuting arrangement, as opposed to a flex-time arrangement, is inherently problematic.

Ford also argues that telecommuting is not a reasonable accommodation for Harris, compared to other resale buyers, because her request to telecommute for such a large portion of the work week was unreasonable and her previous attendance issues demonstrated she was not a suitable candidate for telecommuting. If Ford objected to Harris's request to telecommute for "up to four days per week," it was Ford's responsibility to engage in an interactive process to explore reasonable alternatives. 29 C.F.R. § 1630.2(o)(3). Harris was willing to discuss alternative accommodations, including a telecommuting arrangement for as few as one to two days per week. Ford's failure to engage in that discussion is not evidence that a telecommuting arrangement in any form was unreasonable.

Second, Ford cannot use Harris's past attendance issues as a basis to deny her accommodation because her absences were related to her disability. *Humphrey v. Mem'l Hosps. Ass'n*, 239 F.3d 1128, 1137 (9th Cir. 2001). In *Humphrey*, a medical transcriptionist with obsessive compulsive disorder was consistently tardy because of ritualistic grooming behaviors in the morning. The employer denied her request for accommodation with a work-from-home arrangement, relying on its policy of not allowing such arrangements for employees with a disciplinary record. In holding that the employer was not entitled to summary judgment, the court explained that "[i]t would be inconsistent with the purposes of the ADA to permit an employer to deny an otherwise reasonable accommodation because of past disciplinary action taken due to the disability sought to be accommodated." We find this reasoning persuasive. In the instant case, the EEOC has presented evidence that Harris's past attendance issues were related to her IBS flare-ups. Indeed, at times Harris would begin driving to work but be unable to complete her commute without losing control of her bowels. Thus, Ford cannot rely on Harris's past disability-related attendance issues to disqualify her from telecommuting.[6]

Finally, Ford argues that even if Harris's request for a telecommuting arrangement was reasonable, she is not "otherwise qualified" because she rejected alternative reasonable accommodations offered by Ford. When an employer "offers a reasonable counter accommodation, the employee cannot demand a different accommodation." *Jakubowski v. Christ Hosp., Inc.*, 627 F.3d 195, 203 (6th Cir. 2010). The alternative accommodation offered by an employer, however, must adequately address the employee's unique needs and reasonably accommodate her disability.

Ford offered two alternative accommodations to Harris: (1) moving her cubicle closer to the restroom or (2) finding an alternate position within Ford more suitable to telecommuting. The EEOC has provided evidence that casts doubt on whether these alternatives address the problems Harris experienced with her IBS. For example, Harris testified that she might soil herself merely by standing up from her desk. Clearly, moving Harris to a cubicle closer to the restroom does not address her needs if she has no control over her bowels for the time it would take to reach the restroom. Nor do we

---

6. Ford also claims that Harris is not a suitable candidate for telecommuting because she was "unable to establish regular and consistent work hours" during an earlier alternative work arrangement. However, the earlier trial was based on a "flex-time" arrangement, in which Harris was permitted to work during non-"core" business hours. As discussed above, the availability and consistency problems inherent in flex-time arrangements are not necessarily present in telecommuting arrangements because the employee can maintain a standard work schedule. Therefore, Harris's unsuccessful experiment with an alternative work arrangement in the past does not doom to failure the telecommuting arrangement she requested as an accommodation.

consider it reasonable, as the dissent suggests, to expect an employee to suffer the humiliation of soiling herself on a regular basis in front of her coworkers, merely because she could use Depends to contain the mess or bring a change of clothes to clean herself up after the fact. Likewise, Ford's offer to assist Harris in finding an alternative position within Ford was not a reasonable accommodation because there was no guarantee that such a position would be forthcoming. Furthermore, "reassignment of an employee is only considered when accommodation within the individual's current position would pose an undue hardship." *Cassidy v. Detroit Edison Co.*, 138 F.3d 629, 634 (6th Cir. 1998). Thus, although the employer ordinarily has the option of choosing an accommodation from among reasonable options, Ford was not entitled to force Harris to accept an alternative position in this case because the telecommuting arrangement proposed by Harris was a reasonable means of accommodating her disability.

Because the EEOC has provided evidence that Harris was qualified for the resale-buyer position with a reasonable telecommuting accommodation, the burden shifts to Ford to prove that such an accommodation would pose an undue burden. It is not sufficient that an employer shows that it will be inconvenienced in some way by the proposed accommodation: "We may assume that any accommodation would entail some hardship on the Company, but . . . undue hardship is something greater than hardship, and an employer does not sustain his burden of proof merely by showing that an accommodation would be bothersome to administer or disruptive of the operating routine." *Draper v. U.S. Pipe & Foundry Co.*, 527 F.2d 515, 520 (6th Cir. 1975) (internal quotation marks omitted). The ADA directs us to consider several factors when determining whether an accommodation imposes an undue hardship on an employer: (1) "the nature and cost of the accommodation," (2) the financial and personnel resources of the affected facility, (3) the resources of the employer as an entity, and (4) the structure and functions of the employer's workforce. 42 U.S.C. § 12111(10)(B). Although setting up a home workstation for Harris might entail some cost, considering Ford's financial resources and the size of its workforce, this cost is likely to be de minimis. Indeed, Ford has created a written policy in which it pledges to absorb these costs for all employees approved to telecommute. Therefore, Ford has not met its burden of proving that a telecommuting accommodation, even if reasonable, would create an undue hardship.

The EEOC has provided evidence that Harris is "otherwise qualified" for the resale-buyer position, either because her physical presence is not "essential" or because she requested a reasonable accommodation for her disability. It is important, at this juncture, to clarify that we are not rejecting the long line of precedent recognizing predictable attendance as an essential function of most jobs. Nor are we claiming that, because technology has advanced, most modern jobs are amenable to remote work arrangements. As we discussed above, many jobs continue to require physical presence because the employee must interact directly with people or objects at the worksite. We are merely recognizing that, given the state of modern technology, it is no longer the case that jobs suitable for telecommuting are "extraordinary" or "unusual." When we decided *Smith* [*v. Ameritech*, 129 F.3d 857, 867 (6th Cir. 1997)] in 1997, we responded to the world as it then existed; however, in the intervening years, communications technology has advanced to the point that it is no longer an "unusual case where an employee can effectively perform all work-related duties from home." In this case, we respond to the world as it exists now, and conclude that there is a genuine dispute of material fact regarding whether Harris can perform all of her job duties from a remote location. Accordingly, we reverse the district court's grant of summary judgment on the failure-to-accommodate claim. . . .

McKEAGUE, Circuit Judge, dissenting.

The majority holds that a telecommuting arrangement allowing an employee to telecommute four out of five days of the workweek on a spur-of-the-moment, unpredictable basis is a reasonable accommodation under the ADA for a position that involves routine face-to-face interactions. The stated law of this circuit, however, is that attending work on a regular, predictable schedule is an essential function of a job in all but the most unusual cases, namely, positions in which *all* job duties can be done remotely. The majority further holds that an employee's flat-out rejection of an employer's offer to help her find another position does not constitute an alternative reasonable accommodation, despite the fact that the reason talks could not evolve to a point of identifying a specific position was because of the employee's refusal to consider the possibility. . . .

I.

A.

The EEOC has simply failed to show that Harris could perform the essential functions of her job while telecommuting up to eighty percent of the workweek, or four out of five days, on an unpredictable schedule. The ADA protects qualified individuals "who, with or without reasonable accommodation, can perform the essential functions of the employment position[.]" 42 U.S.C. § 12111(8). The ADA requires courts to consider the employer's business judgment when determining the essential functions of a job. *Keith v. Cnty. of Oakland*, 703 F.3d 918, 925 (6th Cir. 2013). Moreover, this court has flatly held that "[a]n employee who cannot meet the attendance requirements of the job at issue cannot be considered a qualified individual protected by the ADA." *See Gantt v. Wilson Sporting Goods Co.*, 143 F.3d 1042, 1047 (6th Cir. 1998) (internal quotation marks omitted).

The majority states that Harris was a qualified individual based on two theories: either by eliminating the requirement of regular, predictable job attendance, or by permitting an unpredictable telecommuting arrangement that served as a work-around to regular job attendance. These "alternatives" are two sides of the same coin. Really, the EEOC's ADA discrimination claim turns on one question, summed up by one of our sister circuits as follows: "Just how essential is showing up for work on a predictable basis?" *Samper v. Providence Saint Vincent Med. Ctr.*, 675 F.3d 1233, 1235 (9th Cir. 2012).

This circuit has already addressed that question, and held that "excessive absenteeism" renders an individual unqualified under the ADA as a matter of law, *Brenneman v. MedCentral Health Sys.*, 366 F.3d 412, 419 (6th Cir. 2004), except in the "unusual case where an employee can effectively perform *all* work-related duties at home" without a substantial reduction in the quality of performance, *Smith v. Ameritech*, 129 F.3d 857, 867 (6th Cir. 1997) (emphasis added). The majority cannot contend that Harris's circumstances constitute such an "unusual case," and so the majority instead asserts that regular, predictable attendance is not an essential function of all jobs, states that Harris's position does not actually *require* showing up for work — despite the undisputed evidence in the record that many resale buyer duties could not be done at home — and notes that technology has advanced. I would instead follow this court's well-established precedent and affirm the district court's grant of summary judgment to Ford.

This court's precedent clearly states that an employee who cannot satisfy an employer's basic attendance requirements is unqualified under the ADA as a matter of law. *Brenneman*. We based our conclusion on evidence that the employee's being absent from the workplace created strain on his coworkers, and on testimony from the employee's supervisor that attendance was an essential function of the position. Of course, Ford has presented such evidence here: Ford's managers, as well as the other resale buyers, are in universal agreement that the resale buyer position requires face-to-face communications, and Harris's chronic, unpredictable absences — as well as the repeated errors she made while working from home — created considerable strain on the rest of the team. Yet the majority fails to credit this evidence, dismissing the commonsense conclusion that regular, predictable attendance is an essential function of almost every job, a move at odds with not only this circuit's precedent but also the case law of our sister circuits.

. . . I agree with the majority that teleconferencing is more commonplace today, and that the class of jobs in which all duties can be done at home has likely increased over the last few years. However, the fact that some *other* jobs may now fit these criteria does not help the EEOC's case, because such abstractions do not transform the resale buyer position into one of the jobs in which all duties may be done from home. Ford has offered overwhelming evidence to support its business judgment that impromptu meetings and problem-solving with the resale buyer team were most effectively handled face-to-face. The EEOC even concedes that the resale buyer position required in-person supplier-site visits, an important job duty that Harris by definition cannot perform from home. And yet the majority fails to credit this evidence and apply this circuit's well-established standard.

The evidence offered by the EEOC on which the majority rests its conclusion consists only of the fact that Ford provided other resale buyers with the option of telecommuting on a more limited basis, and Harris's self-serving testimony that the "vast majority" of her job could be completed pursuant to a telecommuting arrangement. First, the EEOC's mention of Ford's telecommuting policy, specifically Ford's flexibility in offering other resale buyers the option of telecommuting one to two days per week on a predictable schedule — provided that the telecommuting resale buyer would report to work should an emergency arise — does nothing to advance the EEOC's claim that unpredictable attendance, or that telecommuting up to four days per week, is reasonable for resale buyers. The difference between one or two days versus four days speaks for itself. Furthermore, in ignoring the difference between predictable and unpredictable attendance, the majority fails to recognize that an "employer is generally permitted to treat regular attendance as an essential job requirement and *need not accommodate erratic or unreliable attendance.*" *Basden v. Prof'l Transp., Inc.*, 714 F.3d 1034, 1037 (7th Cir. 2013) (emphasis added).

Second, Harris's personal opinion that her work could be done via telecommuting is also insufficient to raise a genuine issue of fact. There is a good reason courts "are reluctant to allow employees to define the essential functions of their positions based solely on their personal viewpoint and experience." This is because any employee could provide a court with "self-serving testimony" that her job was amenable to telecommuting. . . .

The majority, however, reasons that this case is different — not the "unusual case" described in our case law, but different — because Harris's position does not actually *require* face-to-face interactions. Except that it does: the record is clear that the position requires supplier-site visits, which by definition need to occur face-to-face.[4] It also bears mentioning that the position requires extensive teamwork with the resale buyer team, which includes impromptu meetings. I agree with our sister circuits that regularly attending work on a predictable schedule is an essential function of a job that requires such teamwork. Even the EEOC's own guidance recognizes that an employer is justified in refusing a telecommuting request when, among other things, it would be difficult for a telecommuting employee to participate in frequent "impromptu team meetings" to address ongoing developments. EEOC, Employer Best Practices for Workers with Caregiving Responsibilities, http://www.eeoc.gov/policy/docs/caregiver-best-practices.html (last visited Feb. 11, 2014). Instead of acknowledging this commonsense notion, or affording deference to Ford's business judgment, the majority does precisely what it claims not to do: it acts as a "super personnel department," deciding which positions actually *require* face-to-face inter-actions and which do not.

Similarly unconvincing is the majority's observation that "technology has advanced" or that the "world has changed." . . . I cannot identify anything in the record evidencing a change in the world, let alone anything in the majority opinion explaining how it is a new world in relation to this employee. In this case, the EEOC insists that most — again, not all — of Harris's work could be done using email or computers, and Harris claims that she could interact with stakeholders via conference call. While the majority dismisses our precedent in *Ameritech* and *Brenneman* on the basis that these are "early cases," it cannot be said that email, computers, or conference call capabilities were not available in 1997 or 2004, when these cases were decided. No new technologies are identified by the EEOC or the majority because none are impli-cated by the facts of this case. . . .

B.

Harris also is not a qualified individual under the ADA for the separate reason that she rejected reasonable accommodations offered by Ford. "It is well-settled that 'an employee cannot make his employer provide a specific accommodation if another reasonable accommodation is instead provided.'" *Keever v. City of Middletown*, 145 F.3d 809, 812 (6th Cir. 1998). And it is well-established that the "ultimate discretion to choose between effective accommodations" lies with the employer. . . . Because Harris refused all of Ford's offers to accommodate her, she cannot demand that Ford provide her with a wholly unpredictable telecommuting schedule.

4. Ford has in fact offered evidence to prove that Harris was unable to perform these site visits under her proposed arrangement. As the majority notes, Harris was absent from work more often than not. If Harris's condition is severe enough that she cannot reliably report to Ford's facilities, then she would also not be able to reliably report to the supplier sites for the scheduled visits. Clearly, the fact that Harris could not complete the site visits on schedule is why she was forced to routinely cancel them at the last minute, a practice that frustrated Ford's suppliers.

The first accommodation that Harris refused was Ford's offer to move Harris's cubicle closer to the restroom. The majority is correct to note Harris's testimony that she might soil herself merely by standing up, and so it is possible that this accommodation, when viewed in isolation, would not address the challenges caused by her medical condition. But Harris also refused to consider, either in conjunction with having her cubicle moved or separately, wearing Depends, a product designed for incontinence, which would have addressed that challenge. Harris also refused to consider, either in conjunction with having her cubicle moved or separately, bringing a change of clothes to the workplace, which would also have addressed that challenge.

The second accommodation that Harris refused was Ford's offer to assist her in finding within Ford another position with duties more amenable to the frequent, unpredictable telecommuting schedule that she wanted. This court has held that an employer who offers an employee another position has offered that employee a reasonable accommodation. *Keever* [*v. City of Middletown*, 145 F.3d 809, 813 (6th Cir. 1998)]. Harris rejected Ford's offer because she did not want to "start anew." Unlike the majority, I would find that Harris's refusal to even consider the possibility of another job does not raise an issue of material fact as to whether the offered accommodation was reasonable. Clearly, the reason talks between Ford and Harris never evolved to a place where a specific position was identified was because of Harris's unwillingness to entertain the idea. Under the majority's logic, had Harris not flat-out rejected Ford's offer but considered it in earnest, only to later refuse to transfer to a different position out of a fear of "starting anew," *this* would constitute a refusal of a reasonable accommodation. Apparently, an employee who is even less agreeable, who refuses the possibility of the idea at the onset, deserves a different outcome. I disagree. I would find that Harris's flat-out rejection of Ford's offer to transition her to a position more amenable to her scheduling needs did not render Ford's proposed accommodation unreasonable. I would therefore affirm the district court's grant of summary judgment to Ford on the ADA discrimination claim on this alternative basis. . . .

III.

My disagreement with the majority on the ADA discrimination and retaliation claims aside, it bears mentioning the unfortunate impact that this case will have on employees working for companies in this circuit. [T]he lesson for companies from this case is that, if you have a telecommuting policy, you have to let every employee use it to its full extent, even under unequal circumstances, even when it harms your business operations, because if you fail to do so, you could be in violation of the law. Of course, companies will respond to this case by tightening their telecommuting policies in order to avoid legal liability, and countless employees who benefit from generous telecommuting policies will be adversely affected by the limited flexibility. . . .

NOTES

1. *A Bleeding Edge Decision.* As we will see, the principal case was a dramatic departure from most of the circuit court authority on the issue of whether physical presence was an essential function of most jobs in the modern workplace. The panel

majority was, therefore, breaking new ground — although it stressed that its result was largely just a reflection of shifting practices in the workplace, often as a result of technological changes that meant that work no longer had to be rooted to a physical environment. Not only did the dissent disagree, but the Sixth Circuit voted to take the case en banc. That may or may not mean that the judges are skeptical of the majority's result, but it certainly means that the final decision is likely to make an even more important statement — one way or the other.

2. *Essential Functions.* What makes a job function "essential"? The EEOC's regulations define the term to mean the "fundamental job duties," as opposed to the "marginal functions" of the job. Factors to consider in making that distinction are whether the position exists to perform the function, the number of employees available to perform it, and/or whether the function is highly specialized, thus requiring special expertise. In addition to the employer's job description, other evidence to consider includes, although it is not limited to, the employer's judgment, the amount of time spent performing the function, the work experience of people previously or currently in the job or similar jobs, and the terms of any collective bargaining agreement. *See* 29 C.F.R. § 1630.2(n). Further, the fact that a function is performed rarely does not mean it is nonessential. *Hennagir v. Utah Dep't of Corr.*, 587 F.3d 1255 (10th Cir. 2009) (prison health care worker unable to complete emergency response training was not qualified to perform an essential job function no matter how rarely emergencies might arise). Numerous cases find a disability to disqualify individuals from particular jobs. *See EEOC v. Picture People, Inc.*, 684 F.3d 981 (10th Cir. 2012) (The employee, who was congenitally and profoundly deaf but communicated by writing notes, gesturing, pointing, and miming was found not qualified to do the essential functions of a photo studio job — with or without accommodation — in interacting with customers and selling photo packages.); *Shannon v. New York City Transit Auth.*, 332 F.3d 95 (2d Cir. 2003) (color-blind bus driver unable to perform essential functions of the job, which included recognizing traffic signals).

3. *Showing Up.* Woody Allen famously said, "Eighty percent of success is showing up." *Ford,* however, questions whether "showing up" is an essential function of at least this resale buyer job. Some would say that being present is often a way of doing a task, not the task itself. *See generally* Michelle A. Travis, *Recapturing the Transformative Potential of Employment Discrimination Law,* 62 WASH. & LEE L. REV. 3 (2005). But, as you might guess from the majority's efforts to distinguish prior cases, its emphasis on new technology, and the dissent's outrage, *Ford* is an outlier. Although short-term leaves with a fixed endpoint may be a reasonable accommodation for some disabilities, *cf. Murphy v. Samson Res. Co.*, 525 F. App'x 703 (10th Cir. 2013) ("a leave of absence is not a reasonable accommodation where, as here, an employee continues to seek leave and it is uncertain if or when she will be able to return to work"), most courts have drawn the line at requiring employers to accommodate employees by permitting them to work remotely or use flex-time to a greater extent than other workers. These issues are played out well in *Ford*'s majority and dissent. Who has the better of the argument?

By the way, note that the ADAAA does not bear directly on this issue since it did not amend the statute with respect to "qualified" or "reasonable accommodation." Of course, one could argue that the broad purpose of the ADAAA was to make the ADA more effective, which could support the majority. Or one could argue that Congress was presumably aware of the numerous cases holding that showing up was an essential function and chose not to alter that interpretation.

4. *Mixing Concepts.* A court approaching the qualifications questions often is confronted with two questions: Can the plaintiff perform the job without accommodation, and, if not, can he perform it with accommodation? Because accommodation can bear on the qualified question, the two concepts are often inextricably intertwined. Nevertheless, this reality can create confusion — as *Ford* illustrates. First, the majority has no trouble concluding plaintiff is qualified "if physical attendance is not considered," which means that there remains the question of whether such attendance is an essential function. Because Ford didn't establish that it was, there was a triable issue on that point. In other words, plaintiff might be qualified to do her job without any accommodation since showing up isn't "essential." Second, even if plaintiff were unable to do her job if Ford treated her as it treated other employees, she might be able to perform the work if Ford were to allow her to telecommute, that is to say, she would be qualified after a reasonable accommodation was provided. Dividing the world this way is pretty artificial, isn't it, at least in this case? After all, the only way plaintiff could do her job remotely is if she were to telecommute. Or is the point Professor Travis's: Presence is a *way* of performing, not the *task* that is being performed?

5. *Job Descriptions & Business Judgment.* The outcome in *Ford* may be explained less by a neutral evaluation of the facts than by the level of deference the respective opinions accord the employer's views of what's essential to perform the job. The ADA itself suggests some deference: § 12111(8) states that "consideration shall be given to the employer's judgment as to what functions of a job are essential" and that written job descriptions prepared prior to advertising or interviewing applicants "shall be considered evidence of the essential functions of the job." But such documentation is only "evidence." Doesn't that term suggest that the court can look behind what the employer says is essential?

To some extent this is certainly true. What is important is not necessarily what the employer claims to be an essential function but rather whether the employer treats a function as essential. *See Carmona v. Sw. Airlines Co.*, 604 F.3d 848 (5th Cir. 2010) (although plaintiff was not able to work regularly, he was able to perform the essential functions of his job as a flight attendant when he did work, and the employer's lenient policy regarding attendance allowed the jury to find that that was sufficient). On the other hand, there is little doubt that many courts seem to bend over backwards to defer to the employer's claims about essential job functions.

6. *Telecommuting vs. Flex-Time.* The Ford opinion draws a sharp distinction between these two forms of accommodation, and it's helpful to understand how each might accommodate different disabilities. *See McMillan v. City of New York*, 711 F.3d 120 (2d Cir. 2013) (arriving at any consistent time may not have been an essential requirement of the plaintiff's position given that his late arrivals were explicitly or implicitly approved for years and the employer's flex-time policy permitted some leeway; "banking" overtime hours, working through lunch, or working at home might allow plaintiff to fulfill his responsibilities). But these are only some of the possible accommodations to different disabilities in different workplaces. *See Rorrer v. City of Stow*, 743 F.3d 1025 (6th Cir. 2014) (plaintiff firefighter could be excused from driving rig given that others were available to perform that task).

7. *Who Proves What?* A plaintiff is not protected by the ADA unless she can perform the essential functions of the job. That would suggest that she has to establish what the essential functions are and her ability to perform them. Note, however, that the *Ford* majority put the burden on the employer to prove that attendance was essential, and other courts agree. *E.g., Supinski v. UPS,* 413 F. App'x 536, 540 (3d Cir. 2011); *Rehrs v. Iams Co.,* 486 F.3d 353, 356 (8th Cir. 2007).

With respect to reasonable accommodation, the plaintiff has the burden of showing that some accommodation is reasonable, while the defendant has the burden of establishing that a reasonable accommodation is an undue hardship. This may seem odd, and indeed it is: How can something both be reasonable and unduly burdensome? The Supreme Court's explanation is, essentially, that plaintiff's burden is "only [to] show that an 'accommodation' seems reasonable on its face, i.e., ordinarily or in the run of cases," at which point the employer "then must show special (typically case-specific) circumstances that demonstrate undue hardship in the particular circumstances." *US Airways, Inc. v. Barnett,* 535 U.S. 391, 401-02 (2002)

8. *Quality and Quantity of Work as Essential.* Suppose an individual can perform all the essential job tasks, but cannot meet the speed or quality standards set by the employer. The Interpretive Guidance provides:

> [T]he inquiry into essential functions is not intended to second guess an employer's business judgment with regard to production standards, whether qualitative or quantitative, nor to require employers to lower such standards. . . . If an employer requires its typists to be able to accurately type 75 words per minute, it will not be called upon to explain why an inaccurate work product, or a typing speed of 65 words per minute, would not be adequate. . . . However, if an employer does require accurate 75 word per minute typing . . . , it will have to show that it actually imposes such requirements on its employees in fact, and not simply on paper.

29 C.F.R. pt. 1630, app. § 1630.2(n); *see Milton v. Scrivner, Inc.,* 53 F.3d 1118 (10th Cir. 1995) (pace set by employer's new production standard constituted an essential function of grocery selector job). What arguments would you make on essential functions on behalf of a dyslexic lawyer who produces a good work product but is denied partnership on the basis of (relatively) low productivity? Is she a qualified individual with a disability? Note that the statute prohibits discriminatory qualification standards unless job-related for the position in question and consistent with business necessity and the duty of reasonable accommodation. *See* 42 U.S.C. § 12112(b)(6) (2014). Is the Interpretive Guidance consistent with this statutory provision?

9. *Associational Discrimination.* Even if an employee is not herself disabled under any of the three prongs, she may still not be discriminated against because of her relationship with a person who is disabled. 42 U.S.C. § 12112(b)(4) bars discrimination against "a qualified individual because of the known disability of an individual with whom the qualified individual is known to have a relationship or association." In this scenario, the protected person must be qualified, but the disabled person need not be.

For example, in *Dewitt v. Proctor Hosp.,* 517 F.3d 944 (7th Cir. 2008), a claim of discrimination on account of the plaintiff's association with her disabled husband was allowed to proceed where there was evidence that her discharge was an effort to avoid the high costs of her husband's cancer treatment; her supervisor's comments about "creative" cost-cutting and her suggestion that less expensive hospice care be considered, coupled with plaintiff's discharge shortly after review of medical claims, allowed inference that employer was concerned that husband might require treatment indefinitely. *See also Trujillo v. PacifiCorp,* 524 F.3d 1149 (10th Cir. 2008) (married employees raised factual issue as to whether the alleged reason for their discharges was a pretext for avoiding the high costs of their son's medical expenses). In *Dewitt*, Judge Posner concurred, suggesting, however, that, if the employer would have discriminated against anyone who ran up such high medical bills, there would have been no discrimination on the basis of disability. What do you think of that argument?

3. The Duty of Reasonable Accommodation

We have seen that a qualified individual with a disability is one who can perform the essential functions of the job she holds or desires — with or without reasonable accommodation. The concept of reasonable accommodation distinguishes the ADA from other antidiscrimination statutes. Under the ADA, it is not enough for an employer to treat its disabled employees the same — no better and no worse — than it treats its nondisabled employees. In appropriate circumstances, the employer must take affirmative steps that will allow disabled employees to perform their jobs — it must provide a "reasonable accommodation" where that will not result in "undue hardship." Failing to provide reasonable accommodations constitutes one form of discrimination under the statute.

While we have necessarily met the duty to reasonably accommodate as part of the "qualified" inquiry, we defer further consideration of it until Chapter 10, which discusses that question together with the Family and Medical Leave Act, the other major statute requiring employers to accommodate certain personal needs of their employees.

But it is important to remember that sometimes what might be viewed as a failure to accommodate could instead be analyzed as garden-variety discrimination. Thus, some courts have stressed that there is no ADA duty of accommodation (as opposed to the prohibition of discrimination) when the employer has a policy of excusing workers from all or some of their duties when they are temporarily incapacitated. In such cases, failure to treat a disabled worker equally is impermissible. *See Duello v. Buchanan County Bd. of Supervisors*, 628 F.3d 968, 974 (8th Cir. 2010) (employee failed to adduce evidence that the employer regularly excused workers from operating heavy machinery when they were temporarily unable to do so).

4. Discriminatory Qualification Standards

The ADA prohibits the use of discriminatory standards or selection criteria in hiring and classifying employees. Section 102(b) provides that "discriminate" includes

> 3. utilizing standards, criteria, or methods of administration . . . that have the effect of discrimination on the basis of disability, . . .
> 6. using qualification standards, employment tests, or other selection criteria that screen out or tend to screen out an individual with a disability or a class of individuals with disabilities unless the standard, test or other selection criteria, as used by the covered entity, is shown to be job-related for the position in question and is consistent with business necessity. . . .

Employers have at least three possible defenses to an allegation of discrimination under this definition. First, the language of the prohibition on discriminatory standards and selection criteria is reminiscent of disparate impact under Title VII; not surprisingly, ADA regulations indicate that both paragraphs are subject to a job-relatedness and business necessity defense similar to that permitted in disparate impact cases. *See* 29 C.F.R. §§ 1630.7, 1630.10. However, § 103(a), which sets forth defenses, provides that the use of criteria with a disparate impact on the basis of disability must also be consistent with the employer's duty to provide reasonable accommodation. *See* 29 C.F.R. § 1630.15(b)(1), (c). Second, standards or selection criterion may also be defended on the basis that they are permitted or required by another federal statute or regulation. *See* 29 C.F.R. § 1630.15(e). Third, ADA § 103(b) provides that "[t]he term 'qualification standards' may include a requirement that an individual shall not pose a direct threat to the health or safety of other individuals in the workplace."

In short, qualification standards that are either facially discriminatory or that have a disparate impact on disabled individuals can violate the ADA, but all discriminatory qualification standards may be defended as job-related and consistent with business necessity, permitted or required by another federal statute or regulation, or necessary to prevent a direct threat to health and safety.

Most challenges to qualification standards do not raise significant factual issues about whether the challenged standard or criteria actually screens out disabled individuals. Challenged standards frequently are facially discriminatory, such as vision requirements for drivers. Even standards or criteria that do not expressly implicate a disabling impairment are generally challenged on the ground that a disabled individual cannot meet the standard because of his or her disability. Thus, the fact that the standard or criteria screens out an individual with a disability is obvious. The primary issue in these cases, therefore, is whether the discriminatory standard or criteria can be defended.

This section first examines the direct threat defense. Second, it considers the job-relatedness and business necessity defense as applied to qualification standards that screen out disabled individuals, including those promulgated by the federal government. Finally, it addresses the disparate impact theory in disability discrimination cases.

a. Direct Threat

ADA § 103(b) provides that "[t]he term 'qualification standards' may include a requirement that an individual shall not pose a direct threat to the health or safety of other individuals in the workplace." Direct threat is defined by § 101(3) as a "significant risk to the health or safety of others" that cannot be eliminated by a reasonable accommodation. The EEOC requires the "direct threat" determination to be based on a reasonable medical judgment that considers such factors as the duration of the risk, the nature and severity of the potential harm, the likelihood of the potential harm, and the imminence of the potential harm. *See* 29 C.F.R. § 1630.2(r). Direct threat is simultaneously relevant to whether the individual with a disability is "qualified" to perform essential functions, whether the employer is justified in basing an employment decision on the individual's disability, and whether the employer has a duty to accommodate the individual's disability. It seems likely that the employer has the burden of proof on this issue. *EEOC v. Wal-Mart Stores, Inc.*, 477 F.3d 561 (8th Cir. 2007); *contra LaChance v. Duffy's Draft House, Inc.*, 146 F.3d 832, 835 (11th Cir. 1998) (plaintiff must prove absence of direct threat).

The ADA's "direct threat" provision is derived from the Supreme Court's decision in *School Board of Nassau County v. Arline*, 480 U.S. 273 (1987), which was decided under § 504 of the Rehabilitation Act. The Court held that an individual with tuberculosis was not otherwise qualified to be an elementary school teacher if she posed a significant risk of transmitting the disease to others and if that risk could not be eliminated through reasonable accommodation. In *Bragdon v. Abbott*, 524 U.S. 624 (1998), the defendant, a dentist, asserted that whether a risk is significant is to be assessed from the point of view of the person denying the service. The Court, however, stated that such assessments are to be made on the basis of medical or other objective evidence available at the time that the allegedly discriminatory action occurred. A good-faith belief that a significant risk exists is not enough, nor would any special deference be afforded a defendant who is himself a medical professional.

The EEOC's regulation interpreting "direct threat" defines the term to include "a significant risk of substantial harm to the health or safety *of the individual or others* that cannot be eliminated or reduced by reasonable accommodation." 29 C.F.R. § 1630.2(r) (emphasis added). The validity of that regulation was at issue in *Chevron U.S.A. Inc. v. Echazabal*, 536 U.S. 73 (2002). Echazabal suffered from Hepatitis C, which caused severe liver damage. Chevron had refused to hire him because the position in question involved exposure to toxins in Chevron's refinery that posed elevated risk of harm to his damaged liver. The trial court granted summary judgment for Chevron based on the EEOC's regulation, but the Ninth Circuit invalidated that regulation. Since the ADA specifically provided for a "threat to others" defense, but was silent on the issue of "threat to self," the Ninth Circuit reasoned that Congress intended to exclude "threat to self."

The Supreme Court disagreed, since the text of the statute suggests that an employer's qualification standards "may include," but not be limited to, harm to others. Second, the Court held that there is no evidence that Congress made a deliberate choice to omit "threat to self" from the affirmative defense's scope. Third, the Court noted the slippery slope of limiting the direct-threat defense to situations that would harm others in the workplace. Referring to the risk of injury to others *outside* the workplace, the Court posited, "If Typhoid Mary had come under the ADA, would a meat packer have been defenseless if Mary had sued after being turned away?" *See generally* Samuel R. Bagenstos, *The Supreme Court, The Americans with Disabilities Act, and Rational Discrimination*, 55 ALA. L. REV. 923 (2004).

While *Echazabal* involved one direct-threat issue, others often arise in the workplace. Thus, courts assessing the risk of hiring HIV-infected individuals have reached different results depending on the nature of the work involved. *Compare Chalk v. United States Dist. Court*, 840 F.2d 701 (9th Cir. 1988) (teacher with AIDS did not pose a "significant risk" in the workplace and his condition could be monitored to ensure that any secondary infections he contracted also would not pose a significant risk), *with Waddell v. Valley Forge Dental Assocs.*, 276 F.3d 1275 (11th Cir. 2001) (HIV-positive dental hygienist posed a direct threat to the health and safety of others).

The direct-threat defense is often raised in the context of employees with mental disabilities. In *The ADA, The Workplace, and the Myth of the "Dangerous Mentally Ill,"* 34 U.C. DAVIS L. REV. 849, 850-51 (2001), Professor Ann Hubbard notes that public fears concerning persons with mental disabilities are strikingly disproportionate to the risk of violence actually posed and cautioned that a direct-threat defense may not be based on erroneous risk assessments. *See also* Ann Hubbard, *Understanding and Implementing the ADA's Direct Threat Defense*, 95 NW. U. L. REV. 1279 (2001);

Jane Byeff Korn, *Crazy (Mental Illness Under the ADA)*, 36 U. Mich. J.L. Reform 585 (2003).

Another issue that arises in connection with a direct-threat situation is whether the risk can be reasonably accommodated. For instance, can an accommodation that would reduce health or safety risks be unreasonable because of the burden it would place on co-workers? Suppose co-workers could protect themselves against an individual's contagious disease by being vaccinated, wearing face masks and plastic gloves, or avoiding close contact with the person with a disability? *See Treadwell v. Alexander*, 707 F.2d 473 (11th Cir. 1983) (a proposed accommodation that would result in substantially increased workloads for co-workers was unreasonable); *cf.* 29 C.F.R. pt. 1630, app. § 1630.15(d) (describing accommodations that are an undue hardship).

b. Job-related and Consistent with Business Necessity

If a qualification standard excludes disabled individuals, it may still be permissible when it is "job-related and consistent with business necessity." In *Albertsons, Inc. v. Kirkingburg*, 527 U.S. 555 (1999), the employer fired the plaintiff from his job as a commercial truck driver because he failed to meet federal vision standards. Kirkingburg sued his employer under the ADA when it failed to rehire him after he attained a waiver from the Department of Transportation ("DOT") that would have licensed him despite his condition. Kirkingburg contended that the ADA forbids an employer from requiring as a job qualification that an employee meet a federal standard when that employee obtained a waiver of the applicable standard. The Supreme Court held that "it was error to read the regulations establishing the waiver program as modifying the content of the basic visual acuity standard in a way that disentitled an employer like Albertsons to insist on it." The Court added that the waiver program was an "experiment" without "empirical evidence," and it would not require an employer to participate. Justice Thomas concurred in the judgment on the grounds that Kirkingburg was not a "qualified individual with a disability" since he did not meet the minimum visual acuity level required by the government.

Kirkingburg thus holds that employers hiring drivers covered by DOT's regulations may adopt blanket rules excluding drivers who do not meet DOT's physical requirements. In other words, individualized assessments are not required in this context, and the employer need not present evidence of the job-relatedness or business necessity of the qualification. *Cf.* 29 C.F.R. § 1630.15(e) (1998) (providing that compliance with another federal law or regulation is a defense to liability under the ADA).

Bates v. UPS, 511 F.3d 974 (9th Cir. 2007) (en banc), approached the questions of justification more generally. It first rejected a BFOQ analysis (which the court had previously adopted). Instead:

> To show "job-relatedness," an employer must demonstrate that the qualification standard fairly and accurately measures the individual's actual ability to perform the essential functions of the job. When every person excluded by the qualification standard is a member of a protected class — that is, disabled persons — an employer must demonstrate a predictive or significant correlation between the qualification and performance of the job's essential functions.
>
> To show that the disputed qualification standard is "consistent with business necessity," the employer must show that it "substantially promote[s]" the business's needs.

"The 'business necessity' standard is quite high, and is not to be confused with mere expediency." For a safety-based qualification standard, "[i]n evaluating whether the risks addressed by . . . [the] qualification standard constitute a business necessity, the court should take into account the magnitude of possible harm as well as the probability of occurrence."

Finally, to show that "performance cannot be accomplished by reasonable accommodation," the employer must demonstrate either that no reasonable accommodation currently available would cure the performance deficiency or that such reasonable accommodation poses an "undue hardship" on the employer.

Id. at 996 (citations and footnotes omitted). The court then turned to the qualification standard allocation of burdens of proof, which it viewed as parallel to those for the direct-threat defense. It explained:

Because UPS has linked hearing with safe driving, UPS bears the burden to prove that nexus as part of its defense to use of the hearing qualification standard. The employees, however, bear the ultimate burden to show that they are qualified to perform the essential function of safely driving a package car. . . .

By requiring UPS to justify the hearing test under the business necessity defense, but also requiring plaintiffs to show that they can perform the essential functions of the job, we are not saying, nor does the ADA require, that employers must hire employees who cannot safely perform the job, particularly where safety itself is an essential function. Nor are we saying that an employer can never impose a safety standard that exceeds minimum requirements imposed by law. However, when an employer asserts a blanket safety-based qualification standard — beyond the essential job function — that is not mandated by law and that qualification standard screens out or tends to screen out an individual with a disability, the employer — not the employee — bears the burden of showing that the higher qualification standard is job-related and consistent with business necessity, and that performance cannot be achieved through reasonable accommodation.

Id. at 992. *See also Atkins v. Salazar,* 677 F.3d 667 (5th Cir. 2011) (upholding as business necessity certain physical requirements for park rangers).

c. Disparate Impact

Disparate impact discrimination is applicable under the ADA. For example, in *Raytheon Company v. Hernandez,* 540 U.S. 44 (2003), plaintiff was forced to resign from defendant's employ after testing positive for cocaine. Two years later, he reapplied for employment, but his application was denied. The company contended it had a policy of refusing to rehire anyone who had been terminated for violation of workplace conduct rules. The Supreme Court ruled the Ninth Circuit had mistakenly treated this as a disparate treatment claim when it was at most a disparate impact analysis. To the extent that a neutral policy (no rehiring of discharge workers) resulted in not rehiring addicts, it was not because of intentional discrimination against the disabled but because a neutral rule disproportionately affected them. While the Court recognized that disparate impact is viable under the ADA, its opinion left unexamined whether the defendant's "no rehire" policy would run afoul of the statute under disparate impact analysis because the plaintiff had not properly plead the disparate impact claim. *See* Elizabeth Roseman, Comment, *A Phoenix from the Ashes? Heightened Pleading*

Requirements in Disparate Impact Cases, 36 Seton Hall L. Rev. 1043 (2006). It also did not reach the question of whether the ADA requires an employer to bend neutral rehiring policies as a form of reasonable accommodation of a disabled worker. *See generally* Christine Neylon O'Brien, *Facially Neutral No-Rehire Rules and the Americans with Disabilities Act*, 22 Hofstra Lab. & Emp. L.J. 114 (2004).

Framing reasonable accommodation claims as disparate impact claims can in some cases raise difficult policy issues. Consider, for example, the request of a covered individual for extra sick leave to deal with medical problems. Restricting sick leave would not directly exclude the person from work, but it might make it more difficult for her to schedule doctor's appointments, or more expensive because she must take unpaid personal days to see the doctor. As a consequence this type of policy could result in fewer disabled persons being employed. This policy would "impact" individuals with disabilities because their needs differ from those of other individuals. Should disparate impact liability apply to claims like this?

The closest the Court has come to answering this is *Alexander v. Choate*, 469 U.S. 287 (1985), decided under the Rehabilitation Act. There, the Court rejected the claim that the Tennessee Medicaid Program's 14-day limitation on inpatient coverage would have an unlawful disparate impact on the disabled. How might *Choate* affect a claim by an individual with a disability for more sick leave than other individuals receive? Under the ADA, can such an employee attack a sick leave policy that restricts paid leave to 14 days on the ground that the policy has a disparate impact on employees with disabilities? The EEOC suggests that such a claim is not viable, but that an employee affected by such a policy may be entitled to leave as a reasonable accommodation:

> It should be noted, however, that some uniformly applied employment policies or practices, such as leave policies, are not subject to challenge under the adverse impact theory. "No-leave" policies (e.g., no leave during the first six months of employment) are likewise not subject to challenge under the adverse impact theory. However, an employer, in spite of its "no-leave" policy, may, in appropriate circumstances, have to consider the provision of leave to an employee with a disability as a reasonable accommodation, unless the provision of leave would impose an undue hardship.

29 C.F.R. pt. 1630, app. § 1630.15(c). Does this mean that the policy is legal but that accommodation is always required unless it is an undue hardship? Is there much difference between that view and declaring the policy illegal vis-à-vis the disabled except where undue hardship exists, which would then make the policy a business necessity?

Note on a Rock and a Hard Place

When a disabled worker is discharged, she often needs to seek disability benefits, typically Social Security disability. Eligibility for such benefits is generally contingent on inability to work. This creates a tension between the disabled worker's claim that she is sufficiently disabled to be eligible for those benefits and her possible ADA challenge to the discharge, which requires that she be a "qualified individual." In *Cleveland v. Policy Management Systems Corporation*, 526 U.S. 795 (1999), the plaintiff lost her job after suffering a stroke. She then filed a Social Security Disability Insurance ("SSDI") claim since she was "unable to work" because of her "condition."

Id. at 798. After receiving those benefits, the plaintiff filed an ADA claim against her employer for failing to provide her with "reasonable accommodations" so that she could have continued to perform her essential job functions. *Id.* Although the lower courts had held that a plaintiff cannot maintain two inconsistent positions for the purposes of SSDI and the ADA, the Supreme Court determined that a plaintiff's claim of total disability under the SSDI does not necessarily bar the plaintiff from filing an ADA claim for failure to make reasonable accommodations. *Id.* at 803. The Court stated that a plaintiff can be "unable to work" for purposes of the SSDI, and still may have been able to work if the employer had made "reasonable accommodations." *Id.* The Court noted that factual or legal inconsistencies must be explained by the plaintiff for the claim to survive summary judgment. *Id.* at 806.

After *Cleveland*, courts no longer presume that a claim for disability benefits is necessarily inconsistent with an ADA claim but instead closely examine the factual statements made in the benefits proceedings. *See, e.g., Smith v. Clark Cnty. Sch. Dist.*, 727 F.3d 950 (9th Cir. 2013) (While the *Cleveland's* standard applies not merely to a plaintiff's statements in applications for SSDI benefits but also in applications for state and private disability benefits and FMLA leave, there was no inherent conflict between plaintiff's representations in those settings and her ADA claim; first, impairments may change over time; and, second, since such schemes do not address whether an individual could perform the job with a reasonable accommodation, "it is possible that a person could claim he or she qualifies for disability benefits and still be able to work if accommodated."); *Kiely v. Heartland Rehabilitation Services Inc.*, 359 F.3d 386 (6th Cir. 2004) (legally blind former employee's application for Social Security disability benefits did not estop him from establishing claim under state disability law where he alleged that he applied for benefits on basis of his legal blindness, not inability to work). Suppose an employer requires employees who seek employer-provided disability benefits to sign a statement asserting, "I cannot perform the essential functions of any job with or without reasonable accommodation." Will signing such a statement bar a subsequent ADA claim?

If you were advising a discharged employee who you believe has a viable claim for disability discrimination, would you advise him to seek disability benefits? What factors would go into your advice?

G. PROCEDURES AND REMEDIES

Title VII creates an amalgam of methods—administrative and judicial—for enforcement of its substantive proscriptions, which both the ADA and ADEA follow with a few variations. The basic Title VII procedures for enforcement of the substantive rights it creates are found in 42 U.S.C. §2000e-5 (2014) and are very complicated, especially for unrepresented individuals. Many of the complications arise from two distinct periods of limitation, which together mean that it is relatively easy for a plaintiff to get to court after it's too late. *See generally* Charles A. Sullivan & Lauren Walter, EMPLOYMENT DISCRIMINATION LAW & PRACTICE (2008), ch. 12.

Title VII time limitations were forced onto the national stage by *Ledbetter v. Goodyear Tire & Rubber Co.*, 550 U.S. 618 (2007), which held that Title VII's charge filing period begins to run when the employee is notified of an adverse employment decision. In the case itself, the plaintiff, who had won a jury verdict, had learned about her raise (but not the raises of her male co-workers) years before she filed her charge. *Ledbetter's* rejection of her claim struck a nerve both on the Court and in Congress. Justice Ginsburg read a strong dissent from the bench in which she called on Congress to override the majority, and Congress responded with the Lilly Ledbetter Fair Pay Act of 2009 ("FPA"), Pub. L. No. 111-2, § 3, 123 Stat. 5, 5-6 (2009), However, the FPA, while both retroactive and applicable to other antidiscrimination laws, is limited to expanding the governing limitations period only for "a discriminatory compensation decision or other practice," thus leaving other acts of discrimination still subject to very complex and very rigorous limitations periods. *See generally* Charles A. Sullivan *Raising the Dead?: The Lilly Ledbetter Fair Pay Act*, 84 TUL. L. REV. 499 (2010) (examining the statutory scheme and arguing for a "causation-only" interpretation of the FPA).

Most suits under the antidiscrimination laws are individual disparate treatment claims brought by private persons. But the EEOC may also sue, and, as we saw in connection with the two systemic theories, class actions are often invoked to prosecute systemic claims. In such settings, the complications of discrimination law are magnified by the complications of class action law. All of this came to a head before the Supreme Court in *Wal-Mart Stores, Inc. v. Dukes*, 131 S. Ct. 2541 (2011), which both tightened the "commonality" requirements for class actions under Federal Rule of Civil Procedure 23(a) and required most such suits to be certified under Rule 23(b)(3), which requires notice to class members and an opportunity for them to opt out of the class. There is little doubt that this has been a major blow to private enforcement although class actions continue to be certified. *See generally* Joseph A. Seiner, *Weathering Wal-Mart*, 89 NOTRE DAME L. REV. 1343 (2014); Melissa Hart, *Civil Rights and Systemic Wrongs*, 32 BERKELEY J. EMP. & LAB. L. 455, 461 (2011). Title VII, § 1981, the ADEA, and Title I of the ADA have similar, but distinct, remedial schemes. *See generally* Sullivan & Walter, ch. 13. As a result, the availability of, and limitations on, different forms of relief varies from statute to statute. Generally speaking, however, the statutes offer a successful plaintiff the possibility of instatement or reinstatement (with appropriate seniority) as well as back pay and attorneys' fees. In appropriate cases, front pay (the same as back pay but measured from the time of judgment to the time the plaintiff resumes her rightful position) is also available. *See Pollard v. E. I. du Pont de Nemours & Co.*, 532 U.S. 843 (2001). However, back pay awards under all the statutes are to be reduced by amounts that were earned and could have been earned with reasonable diligence through alternative employment.

Title VII, the ADA, and § 1981 also offer compensatory and punitive damages, although both are capped under Title VII and the ADA. *See Pollard v. E. I. du Pont de Nemours & Co.*, 532 U.S. 843 (2001); Rebecca Hollander-Blumoff & Matthew T. Bodie, *The Effects of Jury Ignorance About Damage Caps: The Case of the 1991 Civil Rights Act*, 90 IOWA L. REV. 1365 (2005), but neither is available under the ADEA, which instead offers potential double recovery under the term "liquidated damages." Where available, compensatory damages include emotional injury.

Punitive damages may be awarded only upon a showing of "malice" or "reckless indifference" by an employer. *Kolstad v. American Dental Ass'n*, 527 U.S. 526 (1999). *See generally* Joseph Seiner, *The Failure of Punitive Damages in Employment Discrimination Cases: A Call for Change*, 50 WM. & MARY L. REV. 735 (2008); Stacy

A. Hickox, *In Reduction of Punitive Damages for Employment Discrimination: Are Courts Ignoring Our Juries?*, 54 MERCER L. REV. 1081, 1121 (2003).

A final remedial issue is whether the person who committed the discriminatory act has personal liability or whether liability is limited to the employer. *Miller v. Maxwell's Int'l, Inc.*, 991 F.2d 583 (9th Cir. 1993), held that neither Title VII nor the ADEA imposes personal liability. The court reasoned that these statutes are addressed to "employers," and even though this term is defined to include "agents" of the employer, this inclusion was intended to incorporate the doctrine of respondeat superior. Moreover, because both statutes exempt small employers from coverage, the court thought it "inconceivable" that Congress would have intended to impose liability on individual employees. Other appellate decisions have agreed that supervisory employees do not have personal liability to the discriminatee under Title VII, ADA Title I, and the ADEA. But employees do have personal liability to the discriminatee under § 1981 and may be reachable under state law analogs to the federal discrimination laws. *See generally* Rebecca Hanner White, *Vicarious and Personal Liability for Employment Discrimination*, 30 GA. L. REV. 509 (1996).

10

Accommodating Workers' Lives

This chapter addresses the obligations that arise when employees require some accommodation in order to meet the demands of the employer's workplace. Of course, many familiar employment practices can be viewed as accommodating the needs of some classes of workers while also meeting the needs of employers. For example, part-time work may allow some workers — for instance, parents of young children, and mothers in particular — more flexibility while enabling employers to tailor labor costs more closely to demand. "Seasonal" work also allows matching the needs of employees who cannot work all year (e.g., students or those employed in other seasonal jobs) to fill employer needs at times of peak demand. "Temporary" work (a word that reflects actual expectations rather than legal status given the ubiquity of the at-will rule) also allows a better matching of employer needs and employee availability than the more traditional full-time, full-year job. Finally, working from home, which has grown substantially with the advent of technology enabling telecommuting, reduces employer overhead and may maximize worker convenience especially for workers who are unable to commute to the traditional workplace due to physical problems or family commitments. Literally millions of individuals work in each of these statuses. *See generally* Katherine V.W. Stone, *Legal Protections for Atypical Employees: Employment Law for Workers Without Workplaces and Employees Without Employers*, 27 BERKELEY J. EMP. & LAB. L. 251, 255-56 (2006).

However, such employment structures are not without their problems. In Chapter 1, for example, we saw that "temp" help has morphed in some areas from its traditional form — rather than an agency providing truly short-term workers, the agency provides "leased" workers on a long-term basis. In such structures neither the employee nor the workplace at which she labors views the arrangement as temporary. Rather, the relationship is recast to shift costs and risks from the firm at which the contingent workers labor to the "employer" who leases them to that firm. And part-time employment has been criticized as frequently a device used to reduce labor costs not only by paying workers (usually female) lower rates than full-time workers but also by denying them fringe benefits such as health insurance. Similarly, seasonal work, while a useful mechanism for matching the needs of employers and employees in many sectors of the economy, also generates huge social problems as "migrant workers" crisscross the country as employment opportunities open and close. Finally, working from home has strong positives and strong negatives; we will see that telecommuting has tended to employ both very high-value employees and very low-value workers, such as telemarketers.

Beyond such structures, and the focus of this chapter, is the question of the extent to which the law does, or should, require employers to "accommodate" the differing needs of individuals who aspire to be as "normal" or "regular" as their circumstances permit. The two primary examples are workers with family caretaking responsibilities, in particular pregnant women and mothers, and disabled individuals, who may be able to perform effectively if the employer accommodates their disabilities. *See generally* Nicole Buonocore Porter, *Mutual Marginalization: Individuals with Disabilities and Workers with Caregiving Responsibilities*, available at http://papers.ssrn.com/sol3/papers.cfm?abstract_id=2215882 (exploring the similarities and differences regarding legal treatment of the disabled and caregivers). While a pregnant worker will usually be physically incapacitated for a relatively short time, the intermittent disruption caused by several pregnancies and the continuing demands of childcare create difficulties for many women far beyond any period of physical incapacity. Some of these difficulties may be traced to employer perceptions about the "commitment" of mothers or the "distractions" children place on mothers, but many women face significant challenges in managing their professional and personal lives beyond those addressed by the anti-discrimination mandates. Put simply, treating mothers equally with fathers will often not result in equality of outcomes.

As for the disabled, the courts narrowly construed the definition of "disability" under the original Americans with Disabilities Act ("ADA"), meaning that the duty of accommodation imposed by that Act reached relatively few individuals. With the 2008 passage of the ADAAA—the Americans with Disabilities Amendments Act—the protected class in terms of those with actual disabilities was greatly expanded, even though the new statute also made clear that there was no need to accommodate those who were merely "regarded as" disabled rather than actually disabled. *See* Chapter 9. The result is a renewed focus on accommodating individuals who have difficulty meeting the normal demands of a workplace but who could provide effective work if they were accommodated.

Similarly, feminists argue that Title VII's prohibition of pregnancy discrimination has had limited success because it is less the demands of pregnancy and the first few months of infant care that pose problems for the success of women than the continuing demands on women's time and attention from raising a family and, increasingly, taking care of elderly parents. *See also* Peggie R. Smith, *Elder Care, Gender, and Work: The Work-Family Issue of the 21st Century*, 25 BERKELEY J. EMP. & LAB. L. 351 (2004). While some men face similar challenges in reconciling the demands of home and the workplace, such responsibilities still fall disproportionately on women.

The law's response to this problem has been very limited but nevertheless highly controversial. The Family and Medical Leave Act ("FMLA") ensures 12 weeks of *unpaid* leave a year for a variety of purposes related to child-rearing and care for ill family members. The FMLA, however, covers larger employers only, applies to only relatively unusual life events (i.e., it does not permit leave for many garden-variety demands on worker time), and, in the end, provides only for unpaid leave, thus exacting a high price from the workers it protects.

Underlying this entire problem is the question of whether the traditional structure of most workplaces, which relies on permanent workers employed in a "full-time face-time" fashion, is necessary to productivity. *See* Michelle Travis, *Recapturing the Transformative Potential of Employment Discrimination Law*, 62 WASH. & LEE L. REV. 3, 6 (2005). The business world's resistance to the FMLA, and the courts' narrow construction of both Title VII's prohibition of pregnancy discrimination and the ADA's definition of disability are predicated to a large extent on the perception that the traditional model of employment is not only natural but also necessary for American businesses to continue to be competitive in a global economy.

This chapter attempts to grapple with the questions of accommodating various needs relating to workers' lives. While the focus will be on current legal regimes, the student should keep in mind two points. First, for their own business reasons firms may well take a more accommodationist stance than the law requires. To the extent that demands for good workers can be met by a more flexible approach to firm policies, such as the growth of "flextime," the law may prove ultimately to be far less important than economics; Michelle A. Travis, *What a Difference a Day Makes, or Does It? Work/Family Balance and the Four-Day Work Week*, 42 CONN. L. REV. 1223 (2010) (exploring the effects of flextime). Second, whatever the current state of the law, there is an increasing concern that it is not proactive enough in dealing with the legitimate life-cycle needs of the current workforce. Legal change may well be in the offing.

Section A deals with how the antidiscrimination laws bear on workers needing certain types of accommodations, briefly discussing the Title VII duty of reasonable accommodation of religion and then focusing on the more robust ADA duty of reasonable accommodation of disability. This sets the stage for section B, which considers the extent to which the general prohibition of sex discrimination under Title VII and the Pregnancy Discrimination Act may assist mothers in the workplace. It then turns to the FMLA, which protects both men and women whose health problems or family issues collide with the demands of the workplace.

A. ACCOMMODATION UNDER THE AMERICANS WITH DISABILITIES ACT

Title VII imposes very limited obligations on employers to address the needs of employees seeking accommodations. As we will see, the statute bars discrimination on the basis of pregnancy, but it merely requires equal treatment of pregnant workers — there is no requirement that pregnancy or childbirth, much less child-rearing, be accommodated.

One provision of Title VII does mandate that employers "reasonably accommodate" the religious practices and beliefs of their employees, but this command has been read so narrowly as to pose few demands on employers. Section 701(j) provides:

> The term "religion" includes all aspects of religious observance and practice, as well as belief, unless an employer demonstrates that he is unable to reasonably accommodate to an employee's or prospective employee's religious observance or practice without undue hardship on the conduct of the employer's business.

Despite the apparent sweep of this provision, the Supreme Court has interpreted this language to minimize its effect. Thus, *Trans World Airlines, Inc. v. Hardison*, 432

U.S. 63 (1977), upheld the discharge of an employee whose religion forbade him to work on his Sabbath. It rejected a variety of possible accommodations, including alterations in the seniority system established by a collective agreement. As for accommodations that would have left the seniority system intact, they, too, were not required since each involved some cost to the employer, and "[t]o require TWA to bear more than a de minimis cost in order to give Hardison Saturdays off is an undue hardship." *Id.* at 84. While the employee was free to seek shift-swaps from co-workers, honoring such voluntary swaps may often satisfy the employer's duty. *See also Ansonia Bd. of Educ. v. Philbrook*, 479 U.S. 60, 68 (1986) ("[W]here the employer has already reasonably accommodated the employee's religious needs, the statutory inquiry is at an end. The employer need not further show that each of the employee's alternative accommodations would result in undue hardship.").

The ADA, although using basically the same language as Title VII's religion clause, nevertheless imposes a more robust duty of accommodation. Thus, it declares as discriminatory

> not making reasonable accommodations to the known physical or mental limitations of an otherwise qualified individual with a disability who is an applicant or employee, unless such covered entity can demonstrate that the accommodation would impose an undue hardship on the operation of the business of such covered entity. . . .

§ 12112(b)(5)(A). While the ADA is treated in more detail in Chapter 9, our present concern is not with the protected class (qualified individuals with disabilities) but with the employer's duty of accommodation. Under the current statute, qualified persons with actual disabilities must be accommodated; those who are only "regarded as" disabled may not be discriminated against on the basis of their impairment but need not be accommodated

It is important to note, however, that the ADA's complicated structure makes reasonable accommodation relevant both to establishing and to defending against a discrimination claim based on the failure to accommodate. As we saw in Chapter 9, a person with a statutory "disability" is protected only if he or she is a "qualified individual," which is in turn defined as "an individual with a disability who, with or without reasonable accommodation, can perform the essential functions of the employment position that such individual holds or desires." § 12111(8). If a disabled individual can perform essential functions only with reasonable accommodation, the employer has a duty to provide those accommodations—short of an "undue hardship." While an employer need not accommodate the nonessential duties of a position other than excusing the employee from performing them, *Hoffman v. Caterpillar, Inc.*, 256 F.3d 568 (7th Cir. 2001), the ADA requires employers to make existing facilities readily accessible to individuals with disabilities. *See Feist v. Louisiana, Dep't of Justice, Office of the Atty. Gen.*, 730 F.3d 450 (5th Cir. 2013) (district court erred in requiring a nexus between the requested accommodation (a parking spot) and the essential functions of plaintiff's position).

But if the disabled individual cannot perform the job without accommodations that are not reasonable or that impose an undue hardship, she or he is not a "qualified individual," and therefore disparate treatment on the basis of disability is permitted and accommodating the disability is not required. *See Majors v. GE Elec. Co.*, 714 F.3d 527, 534 (7th Cir. 2013) (Because plaintiff was permanently unable to lift more than 20 pounds, she could not perform an essential function of the auditor position without accommodation; further, the only accommodation she proposed was to have another worker lift heavy objects for her, and "[t]o have another employee perform a position's essential function, and to a certain extent perform the job for the employee, is not a reasonable accommodation.").

What, then, is a "reasonable accommodation"? The statute provides that such accommodations include the following:

> (A) making existing facilities used by employees readily accessible to and usable by individuals with disabilities; and
> (B) job restructuring, part-time or modified work schedules, reassignment to a vacant position, acquisition or modification of equipment or devices, appropriate adjustment or modifications of examinations, training materials or policies, the provision of qualified readers or interpreters, and other similar accommodations for individuals with disabilities.

How far does "job restructuring" or "reassignment to a vacant position" go?

U.S. Airways, Inc. v. Barnett
535 U.S. 391 (2002)

Justice BREYER delivered the opinion of the Court.

The Americans with Disabilities Act of 1990 prohibits an employer from discriminating against an "individual with a disability" who, with "reasonable accommodation," can perform the essential functions of the job. This case, arising in the context of summary judgment, asks us how the Act resolves a potential conflict between: (1) the interests of a disabled worker who seeks assignment to a particular position as a "reasonable accommodation," and (2) the interests of other workers with superior rights to bid for the job under an employer's seniority system. In such a case, does the accommodation demand trump the seniority system?

In our view, the seniority system will prevail in the run of cases. As we interpret the statute, to show that a requested accommodation conflicts with the rules of a seniority system is ordinarily to show that the accommodation is not "reasonable." Hence such a showing will entitle an employer/defendant to summary judgment on the question — unless there is more. The plaintiff remains free to present evidence of special circumstances that make "reasonable" a seniority rule exception in the particular case. And such a showing will defeat the employer's demand for summary judgment.

I

In 1990, Robert Barnett, the plaintiff and respondent here, injured his back while working in a cargo-handling position at petitioner U.S. Airways, Inc. He invoked seniority rights and transferred to a less physically demanding mailroom position. Under U.S. Airways' seniority system, that position, like others, periodically became open to seniority-based employee bidding. In 1992, Barnett learned that at least two employees senior to him intended to bid for the mailroom job. He asked U.S. Airways to accommodate his disability-imposed limitations by making an exception that would allow him to remain in the mailroom. After permitting Barnett to continue his mailroom work for five months while it considered the matter, U.S. Airways eventually decided not to make an exception. And Barnett lost his job.

Barnett then brought this ADA suit claiming, among other things, that he was an "individual with a disability" capable of performing the essential functions of the mailroom job, that the mailroom job amounted to a "reasonable accommodation" of his disability, and that U.S. Airways, in refusing to assign him the job, unlawfully discriminated against him.

[The District Court granted summary judgment to U.S. Airways, stressing the decades-old use of a seniority system by USAir and that such seniority policies were common in the airline industry. In this context, "USAir employees were justified in relying upon the policy. As such, any significant alteration of that policy would result in undue hardship to both the company and its nondisabled employees." The Ninth Circuit reversed en banc, finding that a seniority system was merely a factor in a fact-intensive undue hardship analysis.]

II

In answering the question presented, we must consider the following statutory provisions. First, the ADA says that an employer may not "discriminate against a qualified individual with a disability." 42 U.S.C. §12112(a). Second, the ADA says that a "qualified" individual includes "an individual with a disability who, *with* or without *reasonable accommodation*, can perform the essential functions of" the relevant "employment position." §12111(8) (emphasis added). Third, the ADA says that "discrimination" includes an employer's "*not making reasonable accommodations* to the known physical or mental limitations of an otherwise qualified . . . employee, *unless* [the employer] can demonstrate that the accommodation would impose an *undue hardship* on the operation of [its] business." §12112(b)(5)(A) (emphasis added). Fourth, the ADA says that the term "'reasonable accommodation' may include . . . reassignment to a vacant position." §12111(9)(B).

The parties interpret this statutory language as applied to seniority systems in radically different ways. In US Airways' view, the fact that an accommodation would violate the rules of a seniority system always shows that the accommodation is not a "reasonable" one. In Barnett's polar opposite view, a seniority system violation never shows that an accommodation sought is not a "reasonable" one. Barnett concedes that a violation of seniority rules might help to show that the accommodation will work "undue" employer "hardship," but that is a matter for an employer to demonstrate case by case. . . .

A

U.S. Airways' claim that a seniority system virtually always trumps a conflicting accommodation demand rests primarily upon its view of how the Act treats workplace "preferences." Insofar as a requested accommodation violates a disability-neutral workplace rule, such as a seniority rule, it grants the employee with a disability treatment that other workers could not receive. Yet the Act, U.S. Airways says, seeks only "equal" treatment for those with disabilities. *See, e.g.*, 42 U.S.C. § 12101(a)(9). It does not, it contends, require an employer to grant preferential treatment. *Cf.* H. R. Rep. No. 101-485, pt. 2, p. 66 (1990); S. Rep. No. 101-116, pp. 26-27 (1989) (employer has no "obligation to prefer *applicants* with disabilities over other *applicants*" (emphasis added)). Hence it does not require the employer to grant a request that, in violating a disability-neutral rule, would provide a preference. . . .

While linguistically logical, this argument fails to recognize what the Act specifies, namely, that preferences will sometimes prove necessary to achieve the Act's basic equal opportunity goal. The Act requires preferences in the form of "reasonable accommodations" that are needed for those with disabilities to obtain the same work-place opportunities than those without disabilities automatically enjoy. By definition any special "accommodation" requires the employer to treat an employee with a disability differently, i.e., preferentially. And the fact that the difference in treatment violates an employer's disability-neutral rule cannot by itself place the accommodation beyond the Act's potential reach.

Were that not so, the "reasonable accommodation" provision could not accomplish its intended objective. Neutral office assignment rules would automatically prevent the accommodation of an employee whose disability-imposed limitations require him to work on the ground floor. Neutral "break-from-work" rules would automatically prevent the accommodation of an individual who needs additional breaks from work, perhaps to permit medical visits. Neutral furniture budget rules would automatically prevent the accommodation of an individual who needs a different kind of chair or desk. Many employers will have neutral rules governing the kinds of actions most needed to reasonably accommodate a worker with a disability. *See* 42 U.S.C. § 12111(9)(b) (setting forth examples such as "job restructuring," "part-time or modified work schedules," "acquisition or modification of equipment or devices," "and other similar accommodations"). Yet Congress, while providing such examples, said nothing suggesting that the presence of such neutral rules would create an automatic exemption. Nor have the lower courts made any such suggestion. *Cf. Garcia-Ayala v. Lederle Parenterals, Inc.*, 212 F.3d 638, 648 (CA1 2000) (requiring leave beyond that allowed under the company's own leave policy); *Hendricks-Robinson v. Excel Corp.*, 154 F.3d 685, 699 (CA7 1998) (requiring exception to employer's neutral "physical fitness" job requirement).

In sum, the nature of the "reasonable accommodation" requirement, the statutory examples, and the Act's silence about the exempting effect of neutral rules together convince us that the Act does not create any such automatic exemption. The simple fact that an accommodation would provide a "preference"—in the sense that it would permit the worker with a disability to violate a rule that others must obey—cannot, in and of itself, automatically show that the accommodation is not "reasonable." As a result, we reject the position taken by U.S. Airways and Justice Scalia to the contrary. . . .

B

Barnett argues that the statutory words "reasonable accommodation" mean only "effective accommodation," authorizing a court to consider the requested accommodation's ability to meet an individual's disability-related needs, and nothing more. On this view, a seniority rule violation, having nothing to do with the accommodation's effectiveness, has nothing to do with its "reasonableness." It might, at most, help to prove an "undue hardship on the operation of the business." . . . Barnett adds that any other view would make the words "reasonable accommodation" and "undue hardship" virtual mirror images — creating redundancy in the statute. And he says that any such other view would create a practical burden of proof dilemma.

The practical burden of proof dilemma arises, Barnett argues, because the statute imposes the burden of demonstrating an "undue hardship" upon the employer, while the burden of proving "reasonable accommodation" remains with the plaintiff, here the employee. This allocation seems sensible in that an employer can more frequently and easily prove the presence of business hardship than an employee can prove its absence. But suppose that an employee must counter a claim of "seniority rule violation" in order to prove that an "accommodation" request is "reasonable." Would that not force the employee to prove what is in effect an absence, i.e., an absence of hardship, despite the statute's insistence that the employer "demonstrate" hardship's presence?

These arguments do not persuade us that Barnett's legal interpretation of "reasonable" is correct. For one thing, in ordinary English the word "reasonable" does not mean "effective." It is the word "accommodation," not the word "reasonable," that conveys the need for effectiveness. An ineffective "modification" or "adjustment" will not accommodate a disabled individual's limitations. Nor does an ordinary English meaning of the term "reasonable accommodation" make of it a simple, redundant mirror image of the term "undue hardship." The statute refers to an "undue hardship on the operation of the business." 42 U.S.C. § 12112(b)(5)(A). Yet a demand for an effective accommodation could prove unreasonable because of its impact, not on business operations, but on fellow employees — say because it will lead to dismissals, relocations, or modification of employee benefits to which an employer, looking at the matter from the perspective of the business itself, may be relatively indifferent.

Neither does the statute's primary purpose require Barnett's special reading. The statute seeks to diminish or to eliminate the stereotypical thought processes, the thoughtless actions, and the hostile reactions that far too often bar those with disabilities from participating fully in the Nation's life, including the workplace. *See* generally §§ 12101(a) and (b). These objectives demand unprejudiced thought and reasonable responsive reaction on the part of employers and fellow workers alike. They will sometimes require affirmative conduct to promote entry of disabled people into the workforce. They do not, however, demand action beyond the realm of the reasonable. . . .

Finally, an ordinary language interpretation of the word "reasonable" does not create the "burden of proof" dilemma to which Barnett points. Many of the lower courts, while rejecting both U.S. Airways' and Barnett's more absolute views, have reconciled the phrases "reasonable accommodation" and "undue hardship" in a practical way.

They have held that a plaintiff/employee (to defeat a defendant/employer's motion for summary judgment) need only show that an "accommodation" seems reasonable on its face, i.e., ordinarily or in the run of cases. *See, e.g., Reed v. Lepage Bakeries, Inc.,* 244 F.3d 254, 259 (CA1 2001) (plaintiff meets burden on reasonableness by showing that, "at least on the face of things," the accommodation will be feasible for the employer).

Once the plaintiff has made this showing, the defendant/employer then must show special (typically case-specific) circumstances that demonstrate undue hardship in the particular circumstances. *See Reed* ("'undue hardship inquiry focuses on the hardships imposed . . . in the context of the particular [employer's] operations'").

Not every court has used the same language, but their results are functionally similar. In our opinion, that practical view of the statute, applied consistently with ordinary summary judgment principles, *see* FED. RULE CIV. PROC. 56, avoids Barnett's burden of proof dilemma, while reconciling the two statutory phrases ("reasonable accommodation" and "undue hardship").

III

The question in the present case focuses on the relationship between seniority systems and the plaintiff's need to show that an "accommodation" seems reasonable on its face, i.e., ordinarily or in the run of cases. We must assume that the plaintiff, an employee, is an "individual with a disability." He has requested assignment to a mailroom position as a "reasonable accommodation." We also assume that normally such a request would be reasonable within the meaning of the statute, were it not for one circumstance, namely, that the assignment would violate the rules of a seniority system. *See* § 12111(9) ("reasonable accommodation" may include "reassignment to a vacant position"). Does that circumstance mean that the proposed accommodation is not a "reasonable" one?

In our view, the answer to this question ordinarily is "yes." The statute does not require proof on a case-by-case basis that a seniority system should prevail. That is because it would not be reasonable in the run of cases that the assignment in question trump the rules of a seniority system. To the contrary, it will ordinarily be unreasonable for the assignment to prevail.

A

Several factors support our conclusion that a proposed accommodation will not be reasonable in the run of cases. Analogous case law supports this conclusion, for it has recognized the importance of seniority to employee-management relations. [The Court cited its Title VII *Hardison* opinion and numerous lower court decisions under the Rehabilitation Act, and the ADA holding that seniority systems found in collective bargaining agreements trump requested accommodations. The Court then noted that the advantages and disadvantages posed by violating seniority systems did not belong to collectively bargained systems alone.]

For one thing, the typical seniority system provides important employee benefits by creating, and fulfilling, employee expectations of fair, uniform treatment. These benefits include "job security and an opportunity for steady and predictable advancement based on objective standards." They include "an element of due process," limiting "unfairness in personnel decisions." And they consequently encourage employees to invest in the employing company, accepting "less than their value to the firm early in their careers" in return for greater benefits in later years.

Most important for present purposes, to require the typical employer to show more than the existence of a seniority system might well undermine the employees' expectations of consistent, uniform treatment—expectations upon which the senior-ity system's benefits depend. That is because such a rule would substitute a complex case-specific "accommodation" decision made by management for the more uniform, impersonal operation of seniority rules. Such management decision making, with its inevitable discretionary elements, would involve a matter of the greatest importance to employees, namely, layoffs; it would take place outside, as well as inside, the confines of a court case; and it might well take place fairly often. *Cf.* ADA, 42 U.S.C. § 12101(a)(1) (estimating that some 43 million Americans suffer from physical or mental disabilities). We can find nothing in the statute that suggests Congress intended to undermine seniority systems in this way. And we consequently conclude that the employer's showing of violation of the rules of a seniority system is by itself ordinarily sufficient.

B

The plaintiff (here the employee) nonetheless remains free to show that special circumstances warrant a finding that, despite the presence of a seniority system (which the ADA may not trump in the run of cases), the requested "accommodation" is "reasonable" on the particular facts. That is because special circumstances might alter the important expectations described above. The plaintiff might show, for example, that the employer, having retained the right to change the seniority system unilaterally, exercises that right fairly frequently, reducing employee expectations that the system will be followed—to the point where one more departure, needed to accommodate an individual with a disability, will not likely make a difference. The plaintiff might show that the system already contains exceptions such that, in the circumstances, one further exception is unlikely to matter. We do not mean these examples to exhaust the kinds of showings that a plaintiff might make. But we do mean to say that the plaintiff must bear the burden of showing special circumstances that make an exception from the seniority system reasonable in the particular case. And to do so, the plaintiff must explain why, in the particular case, an exception to the employer's seniority policy can constitute a "reasonable accommodation" even though in the ordinary case it cannot.

IV

[We conclude that "ordinarily" the ADA does not require] an employer to assign a disabled employee to a particular position even though another employee is entitled to that position under the employer's "established seniority system." . . . Hence, a showing that the assignment would violate the rules of a seniority system warrants summary judgment for the employer—unless there is more. The plaintiff must pre-sent evidence of that "more," namely, special circumstances surrounding the particular case that demonstrate the assignment is nonetheless reasonable. . . .

Justice O'CONNOR, concurring.
. . . Although a seniority system plays an important role in the workplace, . . . I would prefer to say that the effect of a seniority system on the

reasonableness of a reassignment as an accommodation for purposes of the ADA depends on whether the seniority system is legally enforceable. . . .

Justice SCALIA, with whom Justice THOMAS joins, dissenting. . . .

I

The Court begins its analysis by describing the ADA as declaring that an employer may not "discriminate against a qualified individual with a disability." In fact the Act says more: an employer may not "discriminate against a qualified individual with a disability *because of the disability* of such individual." 42 U.S.C. § 12112(a) (emphasis added). It further provides that discrimination includes "not making reasonable accommodations *to the known physical or mental limitations* of an otherwise qualified individual with a disability." § 12112(b)(5)(A) (emphasis added).

Read together, these provisions order employers to modify or remove (within reason) policies and practices that burden a disabled person "because of [his] disability." In other words, the ADA eliminates workplace barriers only if a disability prevents an employee from overcoming them—those barriers that would not be barriers but for the employee's disability. These include, for example, work stations that cannot accept the employee's wheelchair, or an assembly-line practice that requires long periods of standing. But they do not include rules and practices that bear no more heavily upon the disabled employee than upon others—even though an exemption from such a rule or practice might in a sense "make up for" the employee's disability. It is not a required accommodation, for example, to pay a disabled employee more than others at his grade level—even if that increment is earmarked for massage or physical therapy that would enable the employee to work with as little physical discomfort as his co-workers. That would be "accommodating" the disabled employee, but it would not be "making . . . accommodation to the known physical or mental limitations" of the employee, § 12112(b)(5)(A), because it would not eliminate any workplace practice that constitutes an obstacle because of his disability.

So also with exemption from a seniority system, which burdens the disabled and nondisabled alike. In particular cases, seniority rules may have a harsher effect upon the disabled employee than upon his co-workers. If the disabled employee is physically capable of performing only one task in the workplace, seniority rules may be, for him, the difference between employment and unemployment. But that does not make the seniority system a disability-related obstacle, any more than harsher impact upon the more needy disabled employee renders the salary system a disability-related obstacle. When one departs from this understanding, the ADA's accommodation provision becomes a standardless grab bag—leaving it to the courts to decide which workplace preferences (higher salary, longer vacations, reassignment to positions to which others are entitled) can be deemed "reasonable" to "make up for" the particular employee's disability. . . .

[These dissenters would have affirmed summary judgment for the defendant without providing the plaintiffs an opportunity to show that creating an exception to the seniority system was reasonable in the circumstances.]

[Justice SOUTER, with whom Justice GINSBURG joined, dissented.]

NOTES

1. *Collectively Bargained versus Unilaterally Created Seniority Systems.* The *Barnett* decision is reminiscent of the Supreme Court's refusal in *Hardison* to read Title VII's duty of religious accommodation to require modifications in the employer's seniority system. However, in at least two ways, *Barnett* is more dramatic. First, the ADA lacks Title VII's language privileging seniority systems. *See* 42 U.S.C. § 2000e-2(h) ("[I]t shall not be an unlawful employment practice for an employer to apply . . . different terms, conditions, or privileges of employment pursuant to a bona fide seniority . . . system"). Second, unlike TWA, the employer in *Barnett* was not caught between a rock and a hard place by virtue of a contractually enforceable collective bargaining agreement. Was the Supreme Court correct in its assumption that such a system generally confers the same advantages on workers as do those that result from collective bargaining? Justice O'Connor believed that a system could grant such advantages if it were legally enforceable; thus, she would have preferred to limit the presumption in favor of seniority systems to those the employer was contractually obligated to follow. She joined the Court's opinion, however, observing that the majority's rule and her preferred one will generally reach the same result. *See generally* Seth D. Harris, *Re-thinking the Economics of Discrimination:* U.S. Airways v. Barnett, *the ADA, and the Application of Internal Labor Market Theory,* 89 Iowa L. Rev. 123, 126 (2003) ("Justice Breyer's *Barnett* opinion can be best explained with reference to the view that an employer's seniority system can play an important role in shaping and protecting the employer's sunk investments/delayed dividends contract with its employees.").

2. *Accommodation as Preference.* The *Barnett* Court expressly acknowledged that the ADA will sometimes require that the disabled worker receive a preference. The notion that the ADA requires employers to favor disabled individuals in at least some circumstances, and therefore to incur greater costs for such persons than for their nondisabled co-workers, has generated considerable debate about the normative and economic justifications for this mandate. In short, why has Congress defined unlawful "discrimination" to include failing to accommodate?

The Equal Employment Opportunity Commission's ("EEOC") Interpretive Guidance describes reasonable accommodation in terms of according individuals with a disability "equal employment opportunity," which means "an opportunity to attain the same level of performance, or to enjoy the same level of benefits and privileges of employment as are available to the average similarly situated employee without a disability." 29 C.F.R. pt. 1630, app. § 1630.9. As you will see, this is the same argument made for pregnant women: Formal equality, in the sense of treating such individuals the same as other workers, will not allow them to participate equally in the workplace given the special demands placed on them by their family responsibilities. Is the argument stronger for the disabled? Why?

Failure to accommodate is discrimination by definition under the ADA, but there is an obvious difference between discrimination per se and a failure to accommodate. This has led to a lively literature on whether the duty to accommodate is consistent with the antidiscrimination commands of other statutes we have studied. Some of this literature views the disparate impact theory under Title VII as providing a rough analog to the ADA's duty to accommodate and therefore finds little difference between accommodation and antidiscrimination. *See, e.g.,* Mary Crossley, *Reasonable Accommodation as Part and Parcel of the Antidiscrimination Project,* 35 Rutgers L.J.

861 (2004); Michael Ashley Stein, *Same Struggle, Different Difference: ADA Accommodations as Antidiscrimination*, 153 U. PA. L. REV. 579 (2004); J. H. Verkerke, *Disaggregating Antidiscrimination and Accommodation*, 44 WM. & MARY L. REV. 1385 (2003); Stewart J. Schwab & Steven L. Willborn, *Reasonable Accommodation of Workplace Disabilities*, 44 WM. & MARY L. REV. 1197 (2003); Samuel R. Bagenstos, *"Rational Discrimination," Accommodation, and the Politics of (Disability) Civil Rights*, 89 VA. L. REV. 825 (2003); Samuel R. Bagenstos, *Subordination, Stigma, and "Disability,"* 86 VA. L. REV. 397 (2000); Christine Jolls, *Antidiscrimination and Accommodation*, 115 HARV. L. REV. 642 (2001);

3. *Accommodation Beyond Seniority Systems.* Although *Barnett* was decided in the context of a dispute over a seniority system, the issue raised by the case is much broader. Roughly speaking, accommodations can impose costs on the employer, fellow workers, both, or neither. *Barnett* expanded the notion of unreasonableness beyond the effect on business operations to the impact on co-employees. The Court held that, where a seniority system exists, such costs "ordinarily" need not be imposed. But suppose there's no seniority system?

When, if ever, will a disabled employee's request for reassignment to a vacant position entitle him to the job over other equally qualified (or better qualified) applicants? Recall that the Court "assumed" that plaintiff's request for reassignment to a vacant position would "normally . . . be reasonable within the meaning of the statute" but for the seniority system, which specified that seniority-based bidding would fill such vacancies. The lower courts had sharply disagreed on their answer to this question. *Compare Huber v. Wal-Mart Stores, Inc.*, 486 F.3d 480, 483 (8th Cir. 2007), *cert. dismissed*, 552 U.S. 1136 (2008) ("[T]he ADA is not an affirmative action statute and does not require an employer to reassign a qualified disabled employee to a vacant position when such a reassignment would violate a legitimate nondiscriminatory policy of the employer to hire the most qualified candidate."), *with Smith v. Midland Brake, Inc.*, 180 F.3d 1154, 1164-65 (10th Cir. 1999) (en banc) *Huber* has since been somewhat undercut by the Seventh Circuit's overruling of a decision on which *Huber* had relied. *EEOC v. United Airlines, Inc.*, 693 F.3d 760 (7th Cir. 2012), found that the *Barnett* majority's analysis required a different result. Do you agree?

Where the disabled worker is qualified but less qualified than a nondisabled worker, requiring reassignment to a vacant position will presumably impose costs on both co-workers and the employer. *See generally* Stacy M. Hickox, *Transfer as an Accommodation: Standards from Discrimination Cases and Theory*, 62 ARK. L. REV. 195 (2009); Nicole B. Porter, *Reasonable Burdens: Resolving the Conflict Between Disabled Employees and Their Coworkers*, 34 FLA. ST. U. L. REV. 313 (2007); Alex B. Long, *The ADA's Reasonable Accommodation Requirement and "Innocent Third Parties,"* 68 MO. L. REV. 863, 905 (2003); Cheryl L. Anderson, *"Neutral" Employer Policies and the ADA: The Implications of U.S. Airways Inc. v. Barnett Beyond Seniority Systems*, 51 DRAKE L. REV. 1 (2002). But surely the question of whether an accommodation is reasonable (or an undue hardship) can't turn solely on whether it involves costs. Or can it? We'll explore the cost question below. Reconsider this question after you read the next case.

Whatever the parameters of reasonable accommodation when an employer has a "vacant" position, any such obligation depends on the position in fact being available since, whatever the reassignment obligations of an employer might be to a disabled employee, they do not require creating a new job. *See Toronka v. Cont'l Airlines, Inc.*, 411 F. App'x 719, 726 (5th Cir. 2011) ("For reassignment to be a reasonable accommodation, a position 'must first exist and be vacant.' Therefore, if [plaintiff] was not qualified for any of the existing, vacant positions at Continental, then Continental did all it could. . . ."). Further, the courts have tended to view positions as not vacant for the purposes of the accommodation if any other worker might have a claim on them. *E.g., Turner v. City of Paris, Ky.*, 534 F. App'x 299 (6th Cir. 2013) (a position is not vacant if it is not currently so or will not be vacant within "a short period of time," perhaps a week); *Duvall v. Georgia-Pacific Consumer Prods., L.P.*, 607 F.3d 1255, 1262 (10th Cir. 2010) ("[A] position is 'vacant' with respect to a disabled employee for the purposes of the ADA if it would be available for a similarly-situated non-disabled employee"; thus, positions currently filled by "temporary" workers were not vacant within the meaning of the ADA where other employees could not seek them.).

4. *Knowing About the Need for Accommodation.* The employer's duty of accommodation is normally triggered by an employee's request. "In general . . . it is the responsibility of the individual with a disability to inform the employer that an accommodation is needed." 29 C.F.R. pt. 1630, app. § 1630.9. As we will see, the regulations envision an "interactive process" in which possible accommodations are considered. But the accommodation duty is in tension with the notion that an employer normally should not inquire into the existence of a disability. Obviously, when the employee raises her disability in a request for accommodation, the employer can ask for further information as part of the "interactive process," which we will explore shortly. But is it ever appropriate for the employer to raise the accommodation question on its own initiative? The regulations provide that "[i]f an employee with a known disability is having difficulty performing his or her job, an employer may inquire whether the employee is in need of a reasonable accommodation." 29 C.F.R. pt. 1630, app. § 1630.9. Suppose you represent an employer who suspects, but does not know, that an employee's deteriorating job performance is related to a disability. Do you advise your client to inquire about it? Wouldn't that elevate the risk of a disability discrimination claim if an adverse employment action was later taken against the individual? On the other hand, isn't there some risk in not initiating a conversation?

* * *

Although the ADA is now two decades old, there have been relatively few cases developing the duty of reasonable accommodation. That is largely because, as explored in Chapter 9, most of the action in the courts was devoted to the threshold question of whether the plaintiff was protected by the statute in the first place, with the courts taking such a strict view of disability that plaintiffs were usually found either not to be disabled or to be so disabled as to be unqualified to do the essential functions of the job. The 2008 passage of the ADAAA has changed that, bringing reasonable accommodation back to center stage.

In that endeavor, two aspects of the ADA duty intersect. One is procedural, the "interactive process" that the governing regulations require when an accommodation is requested. The second is substantive: What makes an accommodation "reasonable"? And when is hardship on the employer "undue"? This latter question is complicated by the fact that, although one could view hardship as merely one factor in the question of whether an accommodation was reasonable, *Barnett* divides them into two separate inquiries, with the burden of persuasion varying depending on what inquiry is the focus of concern. Thus, the *Barnett* Court endorsed the lower courts that "have held that a plaintiff/employee (to defeat a defendant/employer's motion for summary judgment) need only show that an 'accommodation' seems reasonable on its face, i.e., ordinarily or in the run of cases. . . . Once the plaintiff has made this showing, the defendant/employer then must show special (typically case-specific) circumstances that demonstrate undue hardship in the particular circumstances."

Let's see how these questions play out in a garden-variety accommodation case.

Lowe v. Independent School District No. 1 of Logan County, Oklahoma
363 F. App'x 548 (10th Cir. 2010)

[Plaintiff Terianne Lowe filed suit against her former employer, Independent School District No. 1 of Logan County, Oklahoma, for failure to reasonably accommodate her post-polio condition in violation of the ADA. The district court granted summary judgment in favor of the District, but the Tenth Circuit reversed.]

Ms. Lowe had polio as a child and, as a result, has worn leg braces for most of her life and has had several knee replacements. She has been advised by her physician that she will have to be in a wheelchair at some point and that walking and standing for long periods will accelerate the deterioration of her leg muscles.

Ms. Lowe was certified to teach a variety of science courses for grades seven through twelve and had experience as a classroom teacher. Since the 1988-89 school year, Ms. Lowe had been employed by the District as a high school counselor. Because a counselor is a "teacher" under state law, Ms. Lowe was employed under a standard teacher's contract with counseling duties added pursuant to a separate "extra duty" contract. Ms. Lowe's counselor position was sedentary and required no accommodation for her disability.

In the fall of 2005, as a result of complaints from parents and staff about Ms. Lowe's performance as a counselor at Guthrie High School, Terry Simpson, the District Superintendent, determined that Ms. Lowe's extra-duty contract as a counselor would not be renewed for the 2006-07 school year and that Ms. Lowe would, instead, be reassigned as a classroom teacher. Ms. Lowe was informed of this decision in March 2006 by Jan Chadwick, the principal of Guthrie High School. Ms. Lowe understood that her base salary as a teacher would not be affected by the reassignment but that she would lose the approximately $5700.00 in additional income she earned under the extra-duty contract as a counselor.

In May 2006, the temporary teaching contract of Mary Rhinehart expired and was not renewed by the District. Ms. Rhinehart had taught physical science at the high school in one of the smallest and most crowded classrooms that, as then configured, would not accommodate a walker or a wheelchair in the aisles between the lab tables. The physical science class, and all other science classes at the high school, were laboratory classes. The physical science class was the only opening for a science teacher at the high school for the 2006-07 school year.

Ms. Lowe, for reasons explained below, eventually came to understand that she would be reassigned to teach physical science in Ms. Rhinehart's small, crowded classroom. In order to plan for that contingency, Ms. Lowe met with Lori Allen, head of the Guthrie High School science department, to share with Ms. Allen her concerns about the reassignment in light of her disability. Ms. Allen did not question the need for such a meeting because she had learned from a school board member that Ms. Rhinehart was not retained in order to open up a teaching slot for Ms. Lowe in Ms. Rhinehart's former classroom. Together, Ms. Lowe and Ms. Allen compiled a list of accommodations they believed necessary in order for Ms. Lowe to teach physical science in the laboratory science classroom formerly used by Ms. Rhinehart. Before the end of the 2005-06 school year, Ms. Lowe presented the list of accommodations and a letter from her physician to principal Chadwick, her immediate supervisor, to Don Bowman, the District's human resources director, and to Superintendent Simpson. Shortly thereafter, Ms. Chadwick was told by Don Bowman that no accommodation would be made and that Ms. Lowe should be assigned to a non-laboratory science class.[2] Ms. Chadwick passed this information along to Ms. Lowe.

By August 2006, Ms. Lowe had heard nothing from the District regarding her request for accommodation, other than the message from Mr. Bowman, relayed by Ms. Chadwick, that no accommodation would be made. Two weeks before school was to begin, Mary Pratz, an advocacy specialist and representative with the Oklahoma Education Association, set up a meeting attended by Superintendent Simpson, Ms. Lowe, Michelle Redus, president of the Guthrie Association of Classroom Teachers, and herself. The purpose of the meeting was to discuss the accommodations Ms. Lowe believed she would need in order to teach physical science in Ms. Rhinehart's former classroom. It is clear that, at the time of the August meeting, Ms. Lowe believed that such would be her assignment come the start of the new school year.

As we will discuss below, there is significant disagreement among those present at the August meeting as to what actually was said. One thing is clear: Ms. Lowe was dissatisfied with the result of the meeting and submitted her resignation two days later. . . .

III. Discussion . . .

In order "[t]o establish her claim under the ADA, [Ms. Lowe] must show: (1) she is a disabled person within the meaning of the ADA; (2) she is able to perform the essential job functions with or without reasonable accommodation; and (3) [defendant] discriminated against her because of her disability." *Albert v. Smith's Food & Drug Ctrs., Inc.*, 356 F.3d 1242, 1249 (10th Cir. 2004).

There is no dispute as to the first two requirements. The issue is whether the District discriminated against Ms. Lowe because of her disability. "The ADA defines the term 'discriminate' to include 'not making *reasonable accommodations* to the known physical or mental limitations of an otherwise qualified individual with a disability who is an applicant or employee, unless such covered entity can demonstrate that the accommodation would impose an undue hardship on the operation of the business of such covered entity. . . .'"

[In *Smith v. Midland Brake, Inc.*, 180 F.3d 1154 (10th Cir. 1999) (en banc)] "[w]e noted that the employer and employee must engage in an interactive process to determine what [accommodation] would be appropriate." "The obligation to engage in an interactive process is inherent in the statutory obligation to offer a reasonable accommodation to an otherwise qualified disabled employee."

Once the District was in receipt of Ms. Lowe's list of possible accommodations and the letter from her doctor regarding the reassignment, it was required to proceed "in a reasonably interactive manner" with Ms. Lowe to determine what reasonable

---

2. Apparently at this point, Mr. Bowman, like Superintendent Simpson, did not know that all high-school science classes were laboratory classes.

accommodation might be made to the physical-science-teaching job in order for her to perform it successfully. *Id.* "The interactive process is typically an essential component of the process by which a reasonable accommodation can be determined," and "includes good-faith communications between the employer and employee." *Id.* "Neither party may create or destroy liability by causing a breakdown of the interactive process." *Albert.* A question of fact as to whether an employer has failed to interact in good faith and thus failed to reasonably accommodate will preclude summary judgment for the employer.

Defendant argues that "the interactive process is merely a means to achieve a reasonable accommodation rather than an independent substantive requirement." While that is true, *see Rehling v. City of Chicago,* 207 F.3d 1009, 1015-16 (7th Cir. 2000) (recognizing that the interactive process the ADA contemplates is not an end in itself), a plaintiff can prevail if she can "show that the result of the inadequate interactive process was the failure of the [employer] to fulfill its role in determining what specific actions must be taken . . . in order to provide the qualified individual a reasonable accommodation." In other words, a plaintiff must show "that the employer's failure to engage in an interactive process resulted in a failure to identify an appropriate accommodation for the qualified individual."

The first step in analyzing Ms. Lowe's failure-to-accommodate claim is to determine whether her ultimate resignation was, as the district court concluded, based merely on her speculation as to where she would be reassigned. Contrary to the district court, we think that, given the information available to Ms. Lowe, she could have reasonably concluded that she would be assigned to teach a physical science class in a small and crowded classroom.

Given all the evidence available to Ms. Lowe, much of it coming from defendant's agents, we think the district court erred in concluding that Ms. Lowe's view of the situation was based merely on her personal speculation. The fact that, even after the August meeting, Superintendent Simpson never informed Ms. Lowe that she would not have to teach in Ms. Rhinehart's classroom justified Ms. Lowe in her belief that she would not be able to resume duties as a classroom science teacher at Guthrie High School. Further, the District's late-advanced theory that it could have placed Ms. Lowe in a junior high science class was never conveyed to her.

We turn now to the facts relative to the interactive process. Early on, as mentioned above, Ms. Lowe learned from Principal Chadwick that no accommodation would be made. Ms. Chadwick had been told this by the District's human resources director, Don Bowman, shortly after the District received the letter from Ms. Lowe's doctor outlining necessary accommodations. After this indirect contact by Mr. Bowman, the District failed for at least four months to respond directly to Ms. Lowe's suggestions for accommodation and only did so when prodded to act by Mary Pratz, an official from the Oklahoma Education Association.

When a meeting was finally convened at Ms. Pratz's behest, even Superintendent Simpson admitted that he did not prepare for it, had not reviewed Ms. Lowe's list of suggested accommodations, and did not know coming into the meeting that all science classes at the high school were lab classes. There is no dispute that Ms. Redus stated that the master schedule for the upcoming year at the high school indicated that Ms. Lowe would be teaching physical science, although there is also evidence that master schedules are sometimes changed at the last minute.

The pivotal issue is whether Ms. Lowe was told, at any time, that she would either be accommodated to teach the physical science class or that she would not have to teach a lab science class at all. The evidence on this point is contradictory [and thus raises a genuine issue of material fact. Most of those present thought that Lowe was told no accommodation would be made although Superintendent Simpson testified, "I believe I indicated that there was a possibility she would not be in a lab science."]

In addition to concluding that Ms. Lowe's failure-to-accommodate claim was too speculative, the district court held that "[b]ecause plaintiff resigned before classes started, she cannot show that the defendant failed to accommodate her disability." We think this is wrong for two reasons.

First, Ms. Lowe's resignation did not preclude her failure-to-accommodate claim. In *Albert v. Smith's Food & Drug Ctrs., Inc.*, the plaintiff's severe asthma prevented her from continuing her job as a cashier. She applied unsuccessfully for other jobs with the defendant and worked for three weeks in customer service. The defendant then told her there were no more hours for her in customer service, but she could have her old cashier job back if her physician would approve. When he would not, the plaintiff stopped working and filed for unemployment. The fact that plaintiff had stopped working for the defendant did not preclude her from pursuing her failure-to-accommodate claim. Indeed, this court held that because the material facts about the interactive process were in dispute, it was error to grant summary judgment to the defendant.

To the extent the District implies that, had Ms. Lowe not resigned, it would have continued to work with her toward a reasonable accommodation, we note that the existence of a dispute concerning the status of the interactive process raises a genuine issue of material fact as to whether the District failed in its duty to reasonably accommodate Ms. Lowe.

Second, Ms. Lowe has raised a genuine issue of material fact on her constructive discharge claim. "Constructive discharge occurs when an employer unlawfully creates working conditions so intolerable that a reasonable person in the employee's position would feel forced to resign." *Strickland v. United Parcel Serv., Inc.*, 555 F.3d 1224, 1228 (10th Cir. 2009) (quotation omitted). "The standard is objective: the employer's subjective intent and the employee's subjective views on the situation are irrelevant. Whether a constructive discharge occurred is a question of fact." We conclude that a genuine issue of material fact exists as to whether a reasonable person, faced with a teaching assignment that will require much standing and moving about, and knowing that such activity will hasten her muscular degeneration and the need for a wheelchair, would have no other choice but to resign. *See Sanchez v. Denver Pub. Schs.*, 164 F.3d 527, 534 (10th Cir. 1998) (holding that the conditions of the job must be objectively intolerable and that the plaintiff must show that she had no other choice but to quit). . . .

IV. Conclusion

The evidence produced by Ms. Lowe raises a genuine issue of material fact as to whether, by failing to engage in the interactive process in good faith, the District failed to identify an appropriate accommodation and thus violated the ADA. It also raises a genuine issue of material fact as to whether a reasonable person, under the circumstances, would have felt compelled to resign. . . .

O'BRIEN, J., concurring.

[Although joining in the Order and Judgment, the concurrence stressed that Lowe was not happy to hear that she would be reassigned from her counselor position to that of a classroom teacher because she preferred being a counselor and did not want to return to the classroom. In April she applied for a position with Guthrie Job Corps, citing the reason for wanting to leave her position with the school district as "retirement." She was offered full-time employment by the Job Corps, which she accepted on June 12, 2006. While Lowe's assumptions about where and what she would teach may have been reasonable, she also knew that teachers were often reassigned at the last minute before school started. Further, Simpson may have simply wanted to keep his options open.]

On August 4, two days after the meeting and without requesting a definitive answer from Simpson as to what he would do in response to her concerns, Lowe sent her resignation letter, saying only, "Consider this my resignation. I am retiring." The letter gave no notice she was resigning due to the School District's failure to make reasonable accommodations, nor did she condition her resignation on such a failure. An employer is not liable for failing to assure an employee reasonable accommodations will be made. The statute imposes liability for "*not making* reasonable accommodations to the known physical or mental limitations of an otherwise qualified individual with a disability who is an applicant or employee. . . ." 42 U.S.C. § 12112(b)(5)(A) (emphasis added). Lowe's resignation may have short-circuited the process by not giving the School District an adequate time to respond. We cannot know whether a reasonable accommodation would or would not have been forthcoming. . . .

The School District argues, correctly, I think, that the interactive process is merely a method of facilitating statutory goals. It is a recommendation, not a statutory requirement. *White v. York Int'l Corp.*, 45 F.3d 357, 363 (10th Cir. 1995). "The federal regulations implementing the ADA 'envision an interactive process that requires *participation by both parties*.'" *Templeton v. Neodata Servs., Inc.*, 162 F.3d 617, 619 (10th Cir. 1998) (quoting *Beck v. Univ. of Wis. Bd. of Regents*, 75 F.3d 1130, 1135 (7th Cir. 1996)) (emphasis added). While it may be an essential component to understand the employee's needs, "a plaintiff cannot base a reasonable accommodation claim solely on the allegation that the employer failed to engage in an interactive process." *Rehling v. City of Chicago*, 207 F.3d 1009, 1016 (7th Cir. 2000) ("[T]he interactive process is a means and not an end in itself."). Clearly an employer could, with impunity, ignore the interactive process so long as it reasonably accommodated employee needs.

This case comes down to whether the School District would have accommodated Lowe's needs by reassignment to a non-laboratory classroom (as it could have done) had she not resigned in a huff.[7] Since the record does not supply an answer to that question with reasonable certainty this case must be tried.

---

7. The School District's behavior is not a model for interactive engagement. However, the interactive process creates a duty on both parties to act in good faith. *Smith v. Midland Brake, Inc.* Lowe's good faith in the process is equally as questionable as the School District's. It was no secret Lowe resented her removal from the counseling position and did not want to return to the classroom. Lowe testified "[t]here were some places that they could have put me and that were discussed with Mary Pratz and with Lori Allen [head of high school science department] and with Michelle Redus. There were places that they could have put me." But Lowe never presented these alternatives to Simpson. Lowe also testified there were some science classrooms at the high school where she could teach which would only require the lowering of the blackboard. The record does not indicate Lowe suggested she be assigned to these classrooms. Under these circumstances, it seems rather arbitrary to mention only the School District's shortcomings in the process.

NOTES

1. *Not Getting to the Merits.* Are you surprised that the court never determined whether the proposed accommodations were reasonable/not an undue hardship? Or did it? *Lowe* does say that the mere failure to pursue the interactive process is not a violation of the ADA. In this regard, the Tenth Circuit agrees with most other circuits that have been unwilling to impose liability on an employer solely for failure to engage in the interactive process. There must also be a showing that a reasonable accommodation could have been found had the process been pursued. *See Basden v. Prof'l Transp., Inc.,* 714 F.3d 1034, 1039 (7th Cir. 2013) (employer's failure to engage in the interactive process "is not an independent basis for liability under the statute, and that failure is actionable only if it prevents identification of an appropriate accommodation for a qualified individual."). However, failure to engage in the process may lead a court to give the benefit of any doubt to plaintiff. *See Spurling v. C & M Fine Pack, Inc.,* 739 F.3d 1055, 1061-62 (7th Cir. 2014) (claim stated when further medical testing and prescription medication to control plaintiff's narcolepsy were obvious possibilities that should have been explored in the interactive process). In any event, does this rule mean that the *Lowe* court necessarily found at least a genuine issue of material fact that plaintiff could have been reasonably accommodated without undue hardship? How could that be when it never discussed either the accommodations or the hardship?

2. *A Two-Way Street?* By definition, an "interactive process" involves both sides working together toward an accommodation. The *Lowe* concurrence suggests that plaintiff might have failed to do her part, which implies a downside to the interactive process requirement for employees: An employee who fails to participate in discussions about accommodation may forfeit protection against failure-to-accommodate discrimination. *E.g., Beck v. Univ. of Wis. Bd. of Regents,* 75 F.3d 1130 (7th Cir. 1996). In *Reed v. LePage Bakeries, Inc.,* 244 F.3d 254 (1st Cir. 2001), the court ruled that LePage had no obligation to accommodate Reed's disability because Reed had failed to provide LePage with the information necessary to create a suitable means to accommodate her bipolar disorder. *See also Goos v. Shell Oil Co.,* 451 F. App'x 700 (9th Cir. 2011) (employee's failure to accommodate claim dismissed when she failed to engage in the interactive process in good faith). Is that the point of the concurrence — especially footnote 7 — that at trial, plaintiff may have somehow waived her rights by not participating in the process? But the majority says, "[n]either party may create or destroy liability by causing a breakdown of the interactive process." In any event, if the employer's failure to interact is not a violation of the ADA unless there was a reasonable accommodation possible, perhaps the employee's failure is not a bar to suit if such participation would have been futile.

3. *The Effect of Plaintiff's Resignation.* The *Lowe* court had to dispose of three threshold issues to get to the merits. The first was whether plaintiff's resignation was based on mere speculation or rather her reasonable belief that she would not be accommodated. The second was whether, even if her belief were reasonable, her resignation somehow mooted her failure to accommodate claim. And the third issue was whether the failure to accommodate resulted in a constructive discharge. Plaintiff survived all three challenges, but suppose Ms. Lowe had consulted you after the August meeting. Given the duty to cooperate in the interactive process and the risks posed by resignation, would you have counseled her that she could resign and still sue? Wouldn't it be better advice to her to continue working, at least until the school year started? The denial of an accommodation will frequently make it difficult, but not impossible, for a disabled employee to continue to work, which means that some hard choices may have to be made. Given the demanding standard for constructive discharge, it is certainly possible that an employee who quits when she is not accommodated will have forfeited any ADA claim.

4. *What Accommodations?* In ADA accommodation cases, the devil is often in the details. Ms. Lowe's treating doctor wrote that his patient "has a functional limitation which requires sedentary work only. She is unable to repetitively climb stairs; is unable to kneel, squat, or crawl." Appendix. Given those limitations, these were Ms. Lowe's proposed "Laboratory Safety Modifications for Physical Disabilities":

Classroom will need to be modified so teacher can be accessible to each table. (Wider aisles to allow wheel chair/walker access)
- Lab stations will need to be lowered.
- Chalkboards/whiteboards will need to be lowered so are accessible from a sitting position.
- Overhead cart and screen will need to be modified to accommodate a sitting position.
- Eyewash station will need to be added that is accessible.
- Fume hood will need to be added that is accessible.
- Safety Shower will need to be added that is accessible.
- Fire extinguisher and fire blanket need to be lowered.
- Chemical and flammable storage will need to be modified so it is accessible.
- General lab equipment storage will need to be modified so it is accessible.
- Teacher aide will be needed to gather lab equipment, transport chemicals, and monitor safety issues during labs.

5. *Costs of Accommodation.* It's pretty clear that making all of these changes to the classroom would have entailed some direct costs, and there is also the possibility of indirect costs — such as potential lost student space. Of course, maybe some changes could have been eliminated had there been an interactive process. And it seems clear that plaintiffs are not entitled to their preferred accommodations: As long as the employer offers an accommodation that reasonably meets their needs, the statutory duty is satisfied. *Bunn v. Khoury Enters.*, 753 F.3d 676 (7th Cir. 2014) (once an employer provided a reasonable accommodation, it had discharged its obligations under the law, whether or not it engaged in the interactive process to explore other possible accommodations); *Hill v. Walker*, 737 F.3d 1209, 1217 (8th Cir. 2013) (Arkansas Department of Family Services not required to remove plaintiff family service worker from one particularly stressful case to accommodate her depression and anxiety when she rejected its proposed accommodation of having a supervisor attend visits with her); *Yovtcheva v. City of Phila. Water Dep't*, 518 F. App'x 116 (3d Cir. 2013) (city did not need to transfer asthmatic city chemist or use a solvent to which she was not sensitive when it offered her a reasonable accommodation by a partial-face respirator which she refused to attempt to use due to a panic attack she had suffered while using a full-face device). Could Ms. Lowe safely teach in the lab without all of the proposed changes?

Suppose Bowman and Sampson called you for advice before the meeting, and suppose that they told you that their physical plant staff had estimated the costs of the accommodation at $10,000. Is this reasonable? An undue hardship? The language of the statute suggests that real costs may have to be incurred in order to accommodate. Thus, §101(9) provides that qualified readers or interpreters may be a reasonable accommodation. Further, the Interpretive Guidance suggests that reasonable accommodations include providing personal assistants such as a page turner for an employee with no hands or a travel attendant for an employee who is blind. 29 C.F.R. pt. 1630, app. § 1630.2(o). *See generally* Mark C. Weber, *Unreasonable Accommodation and Due Hardship*, 62 FLA. L. REV. 1119 (2010) ("The duty to accommodate is a substantial obligation, one that may be expensive to satisfy, and one that is not subject to a cost-benefits balance, but rather a cost-resources balance; it is also subject to increase over time.").

The cases have not yet gone so far. *Vande Zande v. Wis. Dep't of Admin.*, 44 F.3d 538 (7th Cir. 1995), is the seminal reasonable accommodation case, and it involves a paraplegic plaintiff, who was employed by the state for three years. In order to enable her to perform her job duties, the State Department "made numerous accommodations" but refused her request for an at-home computer when pressure ulcers forced her to stay home. Despite this refusal, the plaintiff was able to complete all but 16.5 hours of work during her eight-week home confinement. The remaining time was covered by her paid sick leave reserves. She filed suit under the ADA alleging that her employer failed to reasonably accommodate her disability.

The Seventh Circuit, in an opinion written by Judge Posner, held that "[t]he employee must show that the accommodation is reasonable in the sense both of efficacious and proportionate to costs," 44 F.3d at 543, the approach later approved by *Barnett*. The court elaborated that an employer is not required to accommodate a disability by allowing the disabled worker to work, unsupervised, from home, since productivity would inevitably be reduced. *Id.* at 544-45. Accordingly, the employer's action was deemed reasonable as a matter of law. *Id.* at 545. The court also rejected the plaintiff's claim that the State Department was required to lower the communal kitchen sink by two inches so that she could use it instead of the bathroom sink. *Id.* at 546. "The duty of reasonable accommodation is satisfied when the employer does what is necessary to enable the disabled worker to work in *reasonable comfort*." *Id.* (emphasis added).

If we assume that Lowe could show that her proposals were "efficacious," can she also show that the hypothetical $10,000 is proportionate? Professor Sunstein critiques Posner's opinion for not providing any real content to the concept of "proportionate." Cass R. Sunstein, *Cost-Benefit Analysis Without Analyzing Costs or Benefits: Reasonable Accommodation, Balancing, and Stigmatic Harms*, 74 U. CHI. L. REV. 1895, 1904-05 (2007). With respect to Posner's statement that employees can't be accommodated by working from home because of concerns about supervision, he writes:

> Talk about casual empiricism! If the question is whether the costs of the accommodation are disproportionate to the benefits, we might want to make some kind of serious inquiry into both costs and benefits. What is the evidence that if workers telecommute, "their productivity will inevitably be greatly reduced"? In assessing benefits, do we ask how much disabled people are willing to pay to telecommute? Or do we ask how much they would have to be paid to be denied the right to telecommute? More particularly, what is the evidence that Vande Zande's own productivity was reduced? Did her productivity fall during the eight-week period in which she worked at home? What, in fact, is the nature of her job, such that "team work under supervisors" is required? It would seem important to ask and answer that question to assess her request to telecommute. But Judge Posner does not inquire.

Indeed, Sunstein suggests that *Vande Zande's* analysis boils down to nothing more than a judge's intuitions. Given the risk of a judge's reaction being negative, would you err on the side of granting the accommodation if you were advising the school district in *Lowe*? A recent decision from the Sixth Circuit revived the possibility that employers would be required to allow at least some workers to telecommute. *EEOC v. Ford Motor Co.*, 752 F.3d 634 (6th Cir. 2014) (2-1) (finding that a genuine issue of material fact existed as to whether employee's physical presence at the Ford facilities was an essential function of her job when much of her job involved teleconferences, despite Ford's business judgment that "face-time" was essential to the position), *vacated, reh'g en banc granted*, 2014 U.S. App. LEXIS 17252 (Aug. 29, 2014).

Finally, to the extent that costs have to be "proportionate" to benefits, some scholars have argued that benefits for nondisabled workers ought to be factored in. *See* Michelle A. Travis, *Lashing Back at the ADA Backlash: How the Americans with Disabilities Act Benefits Americans Without Disabilities*, 76 TENN. L. REV. 311 (2009); Elizabeth F. Emens, *Integrating Accommodation*, 156 U. PA. L. REV. 839 (2008). That doesn't seem applicable in *Lowe*, but suppose installation of a ramp or elevator benefits not only the disabled worker but also other workers and improves their productivity?

6. *Looking at Undue Hardship.* Suppose that, as the district's counsel, you conclude that the accommodation Lowe seeks may well be reasonable. *Barnett* nevertheless allows an employer to prevail if such an accommodation would be an undue hardship, a question that is analyzed separately. Section 101(10) of the ADA provides that "undue hardship" means "an action requiring significant difficulty or expense, when considered in light of" the following factors:

(i)   the nature and cost of the accommodation needed under this Act;

(ii) the overall financial resources of the facility or facilities involved in the provision of the reasonable accommodation; the number of persons employed at such facility; the effect on expenses and resources, or the impact otherwise of such accommodation upon the operation of the facility;

(iii) the overall financial resources of the covered entity; the overall size of the business of a covered entity with respect to the number of its employees; the number, type, and location of its facilities; and

(iv) the type of operation or operations of the covered entity, including the composition, structure, and functions of the workforce of such entity; the geographic separateness, administrative, or fiscal relationship of the facility or facilities in question to the covered entity.

42 U.S.C. § 12111(10) (2014).

In *Borkowski v. Valley Cent. Sch. Dist.*, 63 F.3d 131 (2d Cir. 1995), the court discussed these criteria, concluding that the issue of "undue hardship" is one of degree: "[E]ven this list of factors says little about how great a hardship an employer must bear before the hardship becomes undue." The court held that employers are not required to show that they would be driven to the brink of insolvency. It relied on ADA legislative history rejecting a provision that would have defined an undue hardship as one that threatened the continued existence of the employer. *Id.* at 139. "Where the employer is a government entity, Congress could not have intended the only limit on the employer's duty to make reasonable accommodation to be the full extent of the tax base on which the government entity could draw." *Id.; see generally* Steven B. Epstein, *In Search of a Bright Line: Determining When an Employer's Financial Hardship Becomes "Undue" Under the Americans with Disabilities Act*, 48 VAND. L. REV. 391 (1995) (proposing a mathematical model for determining undue hardship). *See also Vande Zande*, 44 F.3d at 543 (an accommodation is an undue hardship when it is unduly costly "in relation to the benefits of the accommodation to the disabled worker as well as to the employer's resources."). Do you understand how undue hardship might help the district in *Lowe*?

7. *Putting the Two Terms Together.* As a practical matter, one would expect that a plaintiff would typically be able to prove that a proposed accommodation was efficacious. The more serious question is likely to be whether its costs are proportionate to its benefits (although you should note that employees have incentives to propose less costly accommodations whose costs are, therefore, more likely to be proportionate). Costs, then, will tend to be the determinative factor as to the reasonableness of an accommodation. And they will, at least in extreme cases, be relevant to the undue hardship question. Despite the different burdens, aren't these the same question? Judge Posner's grand synthesis in *Vande Zande* was as follows:

> [C]osts enter at two points in the analysis of claims to an accommodation to a disability. The employee must show that the accommodation is reasonable in the sense both of efficacious and of proportional to costs. Even if this prima facie showing is made, the employer has an opportunity to prove that upon more careful consideration the costs are excessive in relation either to the benefits of the accommodation or to the employer's financial survival or health. . . . One interpretation of "undue hardship" is that it permits an employer to escape liability if he can carry the burden of proving that a disability accommodation reasonable for a normal employer would break him.

And *Barnett* seems to endorse this approach of looking to costs twice.

8. *Back to* Lowe. Now that you know what reasonable accommodation and undue hardship mean as a matter of law, was there a reasonable accommodation available in *Lowe*? It might have been costly to modify the classroom in question, especially if the result was space for fewer students. But why could the school not just assign Lowe to another, less cramped classroom? It might require bumping another teacher into Ms. Rheinhart's cramped space, but is that a problem? Does your answer depend on whether there's a seniority system in place regarding classrooms? And what about assigning Lowe to junior high classes?

9. *Full-time Face-time.* As *Vande Zande* suggests, a frequent question is whether an employer need accommodate by allowing an employee to work at home. Most circuits, in agreement with Posner, have found regularly and timely attendance at work to be an essential job function for most positions, thus foreclosing any need to accommodate individuals whose disabilities prevent them from working more or less normal schedules. If such individuals are unable to come to work regularly, they are not "otherwise qualified." If they are able to come to work but request an accommodation, that accommodation will not be reasonable if it deviates substantially from regular and timely attendance. *See, e.g., Basden v. Prof'l Transp., Inc.,* 714 F.3d 1034 (7th Cir. 2013) ("An employer is generally permitted to treat regular attendance as an essential job requirement and need not accommodate erratic or unreliable attendance," and plaintiff could not establish that a combination of leave and medication would have enabled her to return to work on a regular basis). Employers, therefore, generally are not required to accommodate disabled individuals by allowing numerous absences or by granting leaves of absence of indefinite duration. *See, e.g., Murphy v. Samson Res. Co.,* 525 F. App'x 703 (10th Cir. 2013) ("a leave of absence is not a reasonable accommodation where, as here, an employee continues to seek leave and it is uncertain if or when she will be able to return to work"); *Wilson v. Dollar Gen. Corp.,* 717 F.3d

337 (4th Cir. 2013) (plaintiff neither identified an accommodation other than inter-mittent leave nor "produced evidence that had he been granted such leave, he could have performed the essential functions of his position on his requested return date"). Despite the "full-time face-time" norm, a short-term leave of absence often will be viewed as a reasonable accommodation, *Robert v. Bd. of County Comm'rs of Brown County*, 691 F.3d 1211, 1218 (10th Cir. 2012) (a leave may be reasonable when the employee provides an estimated date of return and some assurance that she will be able to perform her essential duties in the "near future."), particularly when the employer's own policies provide for paid or unpaid leave as great as that requested by the disabled employee. *See, e.g., Nunes v. Wal-Mart Stores, Inc.*, 164 F.3d 1243 (9th Cir. 1999) (jury question on reasonableness when plaintiff was terminated before leave period under employer's policy expired); *see generally* Stacy A. Hickox and Joseph M. Guz-man, *Leave as an Accommodation: When Is Enough, Enough?* 62 Clev. St. L. Rev. 437 (2014); Stephen F. Befort, *The Most Difficult Reasonable Accommodation Issues: Reas-signment and Leave of Absence*, 37 Wake Forest L. Rev. 439 (2002). Do you think that the continued judicial skepticism about the reasonableness of working from home is justified in light of changes in American work patterns and the increased availability of technology enabling individuals to work remotely?

10. *"Voluntary" Accommodations.* Wisconsin provided Vande Zande with a number of accommodations. For example, it had bathrooms modified, had a step ramped, and bought adjustable furniture for plaintiff. *Vande Zande*, 44 F.3d at 544. These may or may not have been required in light of the court's opinion. The ADA Interpretive Guidance indicates that an employer is permitted to provide accom-modations beyond those required. *See* 29 C.F.R. pt. 1630, app. § 1630.9 ("nothing in this part [relating to reasonable accommodation] prohibits employers or other covered entities from providing accommodations beyond those required by this part"). If an employer provides a noncompulsory accommodation, can the employer withdraw the accommodation or refuse to extend it to other similarly situated disabled individuals? This might seem like a rhetorical question since providing the accommodation would seem to establish both that it is reasonable and not an undue hardship. But some courts suggest the answer may be yes! *See Phelps v. Optima Health, Inc.*, 251 F.3d 21, 26 (1st Cir. 2001) (employers providing employees an accommodation does not obligate them to continue providing it); *Holbrook v. City of Alpharetta, Ga.*, 112 F.3d 1522, 1528 (11th Cir. 1997) (police department did not violate ADA when it ceased to make noncompulsory accommodations for employee). However, the fact that an employer provides nonmandated accommodations to a disabled male employee may have implications for its duty to provide accommodations to pregnant women under the nondiscrimination commands of Title VII.

11. *Norms Trumping Law.* Many employers, often counseled by attorneys, have taken the initiative in developing protocols for engaging proactively with disabled employees about their need for accommodation. Such internal procedures often apply whenever an individual suffers a physical or mental limitation, whether or not that condition constitutes a recognized disability. This means that other workers may reap a benefit from the reasonable-accommodation requirement and that, in at least some instances, voluntary accommodations are achieved without the need for a pro-tracted legal dispute. According to Professor Stephen Befort:

> The ADA's interactive process [for accommodating claimed disabilities] has launched a quiet revolution that gets little coverage in the case reporter system. All over the United

States, disabled employees and human resources managers are joining together to invent mutually acceptable workplace solutions in the form of reasonable accommodations. The alternative dispute resolution format of the interactive process facilitates a creative and cooperative search for win-win outcomes. The prospect of litigation in the absence of a voluntary resolution provides a powerful incentive for both parties to conduct this search in good faith. The interactive process, in short, has significantly transformed procedural structures and norms impacting the disabled.

Accommodation at Work: Lessons from the Americans with Disabilities Act and Possibilities for Alleviating the American Worker Time Crunch, 13 CORNELL J. L. & PUB. POL'Y 615, 628 (2004); *see also* Rachel Arnow-Richman, *Public Law and Private Process: Toward an Incentivized Organizational Justice Model of Equal Employment Quality for Caregivers,* 2007 UTAH L. REV. 25 (2007). With the ADAAA's expansion of the actual "disability" category, employers are likely to have a renewed concern for accommodation.

PROBLEMS

10-1. Sam is hearing impaired. He has applied and has been turned down for a secretarial job that included answering phones. He comes to you for advice, informing you that he told the interviewer that he could perform all aspects of the job, except for answering the phone, without any accommodation. With respect to answering the phone, he proposed two alternatives at the interview: (1) eliminating the phone responsibilities or (2) providing a telecommunications device (TDD) that would allow him to answer the phone. The interviewer rejected Sam because neither alternative was "feasible."

In advising Sam, first focus on whether he is qualified for this job. What arguments can he make? What arguments can the employer make? If you conclude that Sam is qualified, which, if either, of the two alternatives is reasonable and not an undue hardship? What further information would you need to answer this question?

10-2. About five years ago, Jan developed a violent, and potentially fatal, food allergy to paprika. She is so sensitive that aromas from co-workers' food can trigger an attack, and an attack can, unless treated immediately, kill her. To avoid exposure, Jan uses a service dog named Penny, who has been trained at a cost of $10,000 to Jan to sniff paprika and warn Jan of its presence. Jan takes Penny everywhere, including to work. There was never a problem until recently, when a co-worker claimed that he was allergic to Penny and asked that she be removed from the workplace. You are advising the employer. What advice do you give? *See* Steven Greenhouse, *When Treating One Worker's Allergy Sets Off Another's,* N.Y. TIMES, May 11, 2010, Section A-10. *See generally* Jeannette Cox, *Disability Stigma and Intraclass Discrimination,* 62 FLA. L. REV. 429, 432-33 (2010); Kelly Cahill Timmons, *Accommodating Misconduct Under the American with Disabilities Act,* 57 FLA. L. REV. 187 (2005).

B. ANTIDISCRIMINATION, ACCOMMODATION, AND THE PROBLEM OF WORK-FAMILY BALANCE

In addition to needs that arise as a result of disability, many employees have family responsibilities that impact their ability to work. Perhaps the most common problem is the conflict faced by many workers, particularly women, in attempting to balance the demands of work and the responsibilities of caring for young children. But workers face a variety of life demands that can have such effects, ranging from obligations to aging parents, to family emergencies and sudden illnesses, to personal needs relating to their own health and well-being.

The legal obligations of employers in responding to such life needs are modest. Unlike disability, there is no general duty to accommodate workers' family and personal responsibilities. However, because most workers can expect to face such demands at some point in their lives, the limited rights that they have in such situations are profoundly important. For the same reason, employers can expect to face difficult questions about whether and when to accommodate the life needs of its workforce, both as a legal compliance problem and as a business strategy. This section considers two laws that apply to workers facing a subset of life events that can affect work: Title VII, as amended by the Pregnancy Discrimination Act, which prohibits discrimination on the basis of pregnancy; and the FMLA, which provides up to 12 weeks of unpaid leave to workers who need such leave for the birth or care of a new child or for their own illness or that of a family member. It goes on to consider perspectives on whether the law can and should be expanded in this area to require greater accommodation of workers' lives in light of the diversified needs of the modern workforce.

1. Pregnancy Under Title VII: The Limits of Formal Equality

In one of its first decisions under Title VII, the Supreme Court determined that discrimination against women on account of parentage, a quality they share with males, was illegal. In *Phillips v. Martin Marietta Corp.*, 400 U.S. 542 (1971), the employer barred the employment of women who were parents of preschool age children while similarly situated men were hired. The Supreme Court held such conduct illegal. While *Phillips* did recognize that such discrimination might be permissible if the employer could prove that not having preschool children was within the narrow "bona fide occupational qualification" ("BFOQ") exception for sex discrimination, *see* Chapter 9, the case has come to stand for the bedrock employment discrimination proposition that individuals must be treated as such and cannot be stereotyped as members of the sex or race to which they belong. Even if it were true, as Martin Marietta claimed, that, as a group, mothers of small children had worse attendance records than fathers, Title VII would render it illegal to treat individual mothers adversely on the basis of their gender.

Phillips was an easy case — it prohibited discrimination on account of a woman's status as a parent, a condition mothers shared with fathers. But the question of whether employers could treat women differently on account of pregnancy — a female physical condition that has no analog for males — proved more difficult for the Court. The Supreme Court's initial encounter with this problem was in *General Electric Co. v. Gilbert*, 429 U.S. 125 (1976), which held that discrimination on account of pregnancy was not per se sex discrimination within the meaning of Title VII. The case involved a fringe benefit plan for employees who could not work as a result of disabilities, but it excluded pregnancy-related disabilities. The Court rejected the plaintiff's claims, relying on its prior decision in *Geduldig v. Aiello*, 417 U.S. 484 (1974), which had upheld a similar state disability insurance plan against an equal protection challenge. In deciding *Gilbert*, the Court held that a pregnancy classification is not per se disparate treatment because of sex:

> The lack of identity between the excluded disability and gender as such under this insurance program becomes clear upon the most cursory analysis. The program divides potential recipients into two groups — pregnant women and nonpregnant persons. While the first group is exclusively female, the second includes members of both sexes.

429 U.S. at 135 (quoting *Geduldig*, 417 U.S. at 496-97 n.20). Thus, under *Gilbert* employers not only had no duty to accommodate pregnancy or motherhood but could also freely discriminate against "pregnant people."

In 1978, Congress responded by enacting the Pregnancy Discrimination Act ("PDA"), which added § 701(k) to Title VII. That section begins: "The terms 'because of sex' or 'on the basis of sex' include, but are not limited to, because of or on the basis of pregnancy, childbirth or related medical conditions. . . ." This sentence overruled *Gilbert* and promised more restrictions on how employers could treat women, at least during their pregnancies. It appears to proscribe all explicit pregnancy classifications that cannot be justified under the BFOQ defense, *see* Chapter 9, which allows sex discrimination only in highly exceptional circumstances. *See Harriss v. Pan Am. World Airways*, 649 F.2d 670 (9th Cir. 1980) (at a certain point in pregnancy, an employer's policy restricting employment of flight attendants may be justified by BFOQ concerns for passenger safety).

While some hoped that that the PDA would not only proscribe discrimination but also trigger a broader duty to accommodate pregnancy, those hopes were frustrated. After defining "sex" to include pregnancy and related conditions, the PDA goes on to impose the following standard for the treatment of pregnant women by employers: "Women affected by pregnancy, childbirth, or related medical conditions shall be treated the same for all employment-related purposes, including receipt of benefits under fringe benefit programs, as other persons not so affected but similar in their ability or inability to work." The circuit courts have cut back on the breadth of the proscription of pregnancy discrimination in the first clause of § 701(k) by viewing this second clause as limiting the first. Under this reading, the key is whether a woman "affected by pregnancy" is "treated the same" as a similarly situated man would be, that is, a man facing similar physical restrictions and limitations due to a different medical condition. If so, there is no violation of the statute even if pregnancy actually disadvantages a woman. *See generally* Joanna L. Grossman, *Pregnancy, Work, and the Promise of Equal Citizenship*, 98 GEO. L.J. 567, 570 (2010) ("The PDA . . . is modeled on a basic formal equality framework, which provides no absolute right to accommodation necessitated by pregnancy."); Kimberly A. Yuracko, *Trait Discrimination as Sex Discrimination: An Argument Against Neutrality*, 83 TEX. L. REV. 167 (2004) (in the PDA, "Congress renamed the trait at issue from pregnancy per se to the more generalized trait of physical disability and then reframed the cross-sex comparison in terms of this non-sex-specific trait.").

An early case so holding was *Marafino v. St. Louis County Circuit Court*, 707 F.2d 1005 (8th Cir. 1983), which found that the failure to hire the plaintiff as a law clerk for a state judge because she was pregnant did not violate §701(k). The court reasoned that the employer would not have hired anyone requiring a leave of absence shortly after beginning a short-term position. Thus, the employer did not discriminate against pregnant women but rather against persons (including but not limited to pregnant women) who would have to take a leave in the foreseeable future. *Marafino* has come to be the law.

Troupe v. May Department Stores Co.
20 F.3d 734 (7th Cir. 1994)

POSNER, Chief Judge.

The plaintiff, Kimberly Hern Troupe, was employed by the Lord & Taylor department store in Chicago as a saleswoman in the women's accessories department. She had begun working there in 1987, initially working part time but from July 1990 full time. Until the end of 1990 her work was entirely satisfactory. In December of that year, in the first trimester of a pregnancy, she began experiencing morning sickness of unusual severity. The following month she requested and was granted a return to part-time status, working from noon to 5:00 p.m. Partly it seems because she slept later under the new schedule, so that noon was "morning" for her, she continued to experience severe morning sickness at work, causing what her lawyer describes with understatement as "slight" or "occasional" tardiness. In the month that ended with a warning from her immediate supervisor, Jennifer Rauch, on February 18, she reported late to work, or left early, on nine out of the 21 working days. The day after the warning she was late again and this time received a written warning. After she was tardy three days in a row late in March, the company on March 29 placed her on probation for 60 days. During the probationary period Troupe was late eleven more days; and she was fired on June 7, shortly after the end of the probationary period. She testified at her deposition that on the way to the meeting with the defendant's human resources manager at which she was fired, Rauch told her that "I [Troupe] was going to be terminated because she [Rauch] didn't think I was coming back to work after I had my baby." Troupe was due to begin her maternity leave the next day. We do not know whether it was to be a paid maternity leave but at argument Lord & Taylor's counsel said that employees of Lord & Taylor are entitled to maternity leave with half pay. We must assume that after Troupe was fired she received no medical benefits from Lord & Taylor in connection with her pregnancy and the birth of her child; for she testified without contradiction that she received no monetary benefits of any kind, other than unemployment benefits, after June 7, 1991. We do not know whether Lord & Taylor was less tolerant of Troupe's tardiness than it would have been had the cause not been a medical condition related to pregnancy. There is no evidence on this question, vital as it is.

. . . The great, the undeniable fact is the plaintiff's tardiness. Her lawyer argues with great vigor that she should not be blamed—that she was genuinely ill, had a doctor's excuse, etc. That would be pertinent if Troupe were arguing that the Pregnancy Discrimination Act requires an employer to treat an employee afflicted by morning sickness better than the employer would treat an employee who was equally tardy for some other health reason. This is rightly not argued. If an employee who (like Troupe) does not have an employment contract cannot work because of illness, nothing in Title VII requires the employer to keep the employee on the payroll.

Against the inference that Troupe was fired because she was chronically late to arrive at work and chronically early to leave, she has only two facts to offer. The first is the timing of her discharge: she was fired the day before her maternity leave was to begin. Her morning sickness could not interfere with her work when she was not working because she was on maternity leave, and it could not interfere with her work when she returned to work after her maternity leave because her morning sickness would end at the latest with the birth of her child. Thus her employer fired her one day before the problem that the employer says caused her to be fired was certain to end. If the discharge of an unsatisfactory worker were a purely remedial measure rather than also, or instead, a deterrent one, the inference that Troupe wasn't really fired because of her tardiness would therefore be a powerful one. But that is a big "if." We must remember that after two warnings Troupe had been placed on probation for sixty days and that she had violated the implicit terms of probation by being as tardy during the probationary period as she had been before. If the company did not fire her, its warnings and threats would seem empty. Employees would be encouraged to flout work rules knowing that the only sanction would be a toothless warning or a meaningless period of probation.

Yet this is only an interpretation; and it might appear to be an issue for trial whether it is superior to Troupe's interpretation. But what is Troupe's interpretation? Not (as we understand it) that Lord & Taylor wanted to get back at her for becoming pregnant or having morning sickness. The only significance she asks us to attach to the timing of her discharge is as reinforcement for the inference that she asks us to draw from Rauch's statement about the reason for her termination: that she was terminated because her employer did not expect her to return to work after her maternity leave was up. We must decide whether a termination so motivated is discrimination within the meaning of the pregnancy amendment to Title VII.

Standing alone, it is not. (It could be a breach of contract, but that is not alleged.) Suppose that Lord & Taylor had an employee named Jones, a black employee scheduled to take a three-month paid sick leave for a kidney transplant; and whether thinking that he would not return to work when his leave was up or not wanting to incur the expense of paying him while he was on sick leave, the company fired him. In doing so it might be breaking its employment contract with Jones, if it had one, or violating a state statute requiring the payment of earned wages. But the company could not be found guilty of racial discrimination unless (in the absence of any of the other types of evidence of discrimination that we have discussed) there was evidence that it failed to exhibit comparable rapacity toward similarly situated employees of the white race. We must imagine a hypothetical Mr. Troupe, who is as tardy as Ms. Troupe was, also because of health problems, and who is about to take a protracted sick leave growing out of those problems at an expense to Lord & Taylor equal to that of Ms. Troupe's maternity leave. If Lord & Taylor would have fired our hypothetical Mr. Troupe, this implies that it fired Ms. Troupe not because she was pregnant but because she cost the company more than she was worth to it.

The Pregnancy Discrimination Act does not, despite the urgings of feminist scholars, *e.g.,* Herma Hill Kay, *Equality and Difference: The Case of Pregnancy,*

1 BERKELEY WOMEN'S L. J. 1, 30-31 (1985), require employers to offer maternity leave or take other steps to make it easier for pregnant women to work, *cf. Cal. Fed. Savs. & Loan Ass'n v. Guerra*, 479 U.S. 272, 286-87 (1987); 29 C.F.R. § 1604.10(b) and App. to Pt. 604 (EEOC Guidelines on Discrimination Because of Sex: Questions and Answers on the Pregnancy Discrimination Act) — to make it as easy, say, as it is for their spouses to continue working during pregnancy. Employers can treat pregnant women as badly as they treat similarly affected but nonpregnant employees, even to the point of "conditioning the availability of an employment benefit on an employee's decision to return to work after the end of the medical disability that pregnancy causes." *Maganuco v. Leyden Cmty. High Sch. Dist. 212*, 939 F.2d 440, 445 (7th Cir. 1991). *Maganuco* and other cases hold that disparate impact is a permissible theory of liability under the Pregnancy Discrimination Act, as it is under other provisions of Title VII. But, properly understood, disparate impact as a theory of liability is a means of dealing with the residues of past discrimination, rather than a warrant for favoritism. *Finnegan v. Trans World Airlines, Inc.*, 967 F.2d 1161, 1164 (7th Cir. 1992).

The plaintiff has made no effort to show that if all the pertinent facts were as they are except for the fact of her pregnancy, she would not have been fired. So in the end she has no evidence from which a rational trier of fact could infer that she was a victim of pregnancy discrimination. . . . The Pregnancy Discrimination Act requires the employer to ignore an employee's pregnancy, but . . . not her absence from work, unless the employer overlooks the comparable absences of nonpregnant employees — in which event it would not be ignoring pregnancy after all. Of course there may be no comparable absences, but we do not understand Troupe to be arguing that the reason she did not present evidence that nonpregnant employees were treated more favorably than she is that . . . there is no comparison group of Lord & Taylor employees. What to do in such a case is an issue for a case in which the issue is raised. (We do not even know how long Troupe's maternity leave was supposed to be.) We doubt that finding a comparison group would be that difficult. Troupe would be halfway home if she could find one nonpregnant employee of Lord & Taylor who had not been fired when about to begin a leave similar in length to hers. She either did not look, or did not find. Given the absence of other evidence, her failure to present any comparison evidence doomed her case.

NOTES

1. *Firing a Woman for Being Pregnant Is Sometimes OK.* Like *Marafino*, *Troupe* interprets the PDA to prohibit only conduct that treats pregnant women differently than "similarly situated" nonpregnant people. That means that it is OK to fire a woman because she is pregnant — as long as a similarly situated male (or nonpregnant woman) would be fired. Does this make sense? In *Newport News Shipbuilding & Dry Dock Co. v. E.E.O.C.*, 462 U.S. 669 (1983), the Supreme Court held illegal an employer's policy restricting medical insurance for pregnancy to female employees, and therefore excluding the wives of male employees. The Court wrote that the PDA establishes the following:

[F]or all Title VII purposes, discrimination based on a woman's pregnancy is, on its face, discrimination because of her sex. . . . By making clear that an employer could not discriminate on the basis of an employee's pregnancy, Congress did not erase the original prohibition against discrimination on the basis of an employee's sex.

Id. at 684-85. Is *Troupe* consistent with this view?

Troupe further narrows the statute's protection by adopting restrictive rules about proving different treatment based on pregnancy. How exactly is a pregnant employee to prove what her employer would do for a hypothetical similarly situated male employee? In finding Troupe's evidence insufficient, does Posner overlook the significance of the employer's disability and maternity leave policy? By adopting a leave policy, hasn't the employer acknowledged that disabled employees will receive leave if they meet the stated requirements? If so, is depriving Troupe of her leave inconsistent with the written policy, leaving no explanation for her termination other than her pregnancy?

2. *A Throwback? Troupe* seems to accept as nondiscriminatory the employer's concern that Troupe might not come back after her leave. Scholars have argued that "Kimberly Troupe appears to have fallen victim to sex stereotyping" because Lord & Taylor would probably not have concluded that a similarly situated employee, about to take disability leave, would fail to return to work after the leave. *See* Ann C. McGinley & Jeffrey W. Stempel, *Condescending Contradictions: Richard Posner's Pragmatism and Pregnancy Discrimination*, 46 Fla. L. Rev. 193, 221 (1994). Permitting the defendant to act on the assumption that Troupe would not return to work after her baby was born validates exactly the type of stereotype about women, especially pregnant women, that the PDA was intended to overcome. *Id.*

In *Maldonado v. U.S. Bank*, 186 F.3d 759 (7th Cir. 1999), a bank fired an employee upon learning she was pregnant, reasoning that her due date would render her unable to work during the summer, a particularly busy time of the year. The Seventh Circuit reversed summary judgment in the bank's favor, holding that an "employer cannot take anticipatory action unless it has a good faith basis, supported by sufficiently strong evidence, that the normal inconveniences of an employee's pregnancy will require special treatment." *Id.* at 767. Does this decision at least cut back on the more troubling aspects of the Seventh Circuit's decision in *Troupe*? One commentator describes the case as standing only for "the right of pregnant workers not to be *presumed* incapable." Joanna L. Grossman, *Pregnancy, Work, and the Promise of Equal Citizenship*, 98 Geo. L. J. 567, 607 (2010) (emphasis in original).

3. *No Accommodation Required.* Posner reads the statute as adopting a strict equal treatment rule and consequently imposing no duty to accommodate pregnant employees in any respect. The employer can discriminate against pregnancy to the extent that pregnancy has characteristics shared by other conditions (such as a temporary disability). That Ms. Troupe's morning sickness caused her absences is simply irrelevant if the employer would have discharged someone who was late for other reasons. As Posner explains, "The Pregnancy Discrimination Act does not, despite the urgings of feminist scholars, require employers to offer maternity leave or take other steps to make it easier for pregnant women to work."

Nevertheless, Posner is firm that the PDA at least guarantees Ms. Troupe equal treatment with the hypothetical Mr. Troupe. Or does it? Several circuits have refused to view pregnant women as alike in their ability or inability to work as compared to those injured on the job or those entitled to ADA accommodation. Thus, employer policies providing for light duty assignments for such injured workers have been found not to require light duty for women whose pregnancy prevents them from performing their normal jobs. This issue should be decided soon since the Supreme Court has granted certiorari in *Young v. UPS*, 707 F.3d 437 (4th Cir. 2013), *cert. granted*, 134 S. Ct. 2898 (2014), which had held that an employer policy limiting light duty accommodations to employees injured on the job or disabled under the ADA did not violate the PDA's command to treat pregnant workers the same as those similarly limited in their ability to work. *See generally* Deborah A. Widiss, Gilbert *Redux: The Interaction of the Pregnancy Discrimination Act and the Amended Americans with Disabilities Act*, 46 U.C. Davis 961 (2013) (the PDA's second sentence mandates equal accommodations for pregnant women with any accommodations offered other employees for any reason; thus, accommodations offered for worker limitations pursuant to the ADAAA must be offered to similarly situated pregnant women).

The *Troupe* reading, from the critics' perspective, is precisely the problem with the statute. Because of pregnancy, and motherhood more generally, many women find it harder than men, including fathers, to maintain consistent work performance and workforce attachment. This is due at least in part to the way American society is presently constructed, with women still assuming the bulk of child-rearing responsibilities. The Family and Medical Leave Act, which we will explore shortly, attempts to address some of these issues with varying degrees of success.

4. *Equal Treatment in Benefits.* While *Marafino* and *Troupe* use the second clause of the PDA to narrow the rights that might be granted by the first clause, the second clause of § 701(k) also plays an important role in ensuring that pregnant women are treated fairly by employers. If the statute consisted of the first clause only, employers would be required, at most, not to discriminate against women because of their pregnancies, leaving unresolved whether insurance coverage and leaves of absence could exclude pregnancy from coverage. Congress was unwilling to require employers to provide such benefits to pregnant women but did mandate, through the second clause, that employers who do provide such benefits to nonpregnant workers must extend them to women similarly situated "in their ability or inability to work."

Questions sometimes arise, however, about the extent to which employers can exclude fertility treatments and birth control from coverage, which could be viewed as pertaining to pregnancy-related conditions. *See In re Union Pac. R.R. Emp't Practices Litig.*, 479 F.3d 936, 938 (8th Cir. 2007) (the PDA did not require an employer to cover contraception for women when it did not do so for men); *Saks v. Franklin Covey Co.*, 316 F.3d 337 (2d Cir. 2003) (rejecting a claim that denial of fertility treatments violated Title VII). *But see Hall v. Nalco Co.*, 534 F.3d 644 (7th Cir. 2008) (finding denial of in vitro fertilization to be sex discrimination against women); *see generally* Stephen F. Befort & Elizabeth C. Borer, *Equitable Prescription Drug Coverage: Preventing Sex Discrimination in Employer-Provided Health Plans*, 70 La. L. Rev. 205 (2009).

5. *Disparate Impact.* Judge Posner in *Troupe* states that disparate impact is a viable theory under the PDA, a doctrine we encountered in Chapter 9. Some think that the command of the PDA that pregnant workers be treated the same as similarly situated, nonpregnant workers limits the PDA to only disparate treatment although the codification of the disparate impact theory in the Civil Rights Act of 1991 arguably would alter that conclusion. In any event Joanna L. Grossman, in *Pregnancy, Work, and the Promise of Equal Citizenship*, 98 Geo. L.J. 567, 616 (2010), correctly notes that disparate impact "has proved decidedly ineffectual thus far. The reality is that plaintiffs almost never prevail on such claims in the pregnancy context."

6. *The Bottom Line.* Suppose an employer has no leave policy for anyone. Does Title VII require that employer to provide leave to pregnant women? *Troupe* would say no from a disparate treatment perspective — since there are no nonpregnant people being given leave, there can be no sex discrimination. The case would also seem to bar disparate impact for such a policy. *See Stout v. Baxter Healthcare Corp.*, 282 F.3d 856, 861 (5th Cir. 2002) ("To hold otherwise would be to transform the PDA into a guarantee of medical leave for pregnant employees, something we have specifically held that the PDA does not do"). The bottom line, then, is that Title VII imposes no duty to accommodate pregnancy. Accordingly, most scholars believe that Title VII's protections do not address the fundamental problem posed by women's family caretaking responsibilities. However, others have argued that Title VII can often be deployed to address at least some of these problems.

═══ ### *Walsh v. National Computer Systems*
═══ *332 F.3d 1150 (8th Cir. 2003)*

National Computer Systems, Inc. (NCS) appeals from a judgment of the district court awarding Shireen A. Walsh compensatory damages, punitive damages, prejudgment interest, attorneys' fees, and costs totaling $625,526. . . .

We review the facts in the light most favorable to the jury's verdict. Walsh worked as an account representative in the customer service division of NCS from May 1993 through October 30, 1998. She was a salaried ("exempt") employee whose duties included selling and renewing service contracts on scanners sold to NCS customers. She was considered a "top performer." Walsh received multiple promotions, regular raises, and consistently favorable performance evaluations throughout her employment at NCS.

In March 1997, Barbara Mickelson became Walsh's supervisor. Walsh was pregnant at the time and experienced medical complications related to her pregnancy, requiring frequent medical attention. NCS maintained a policy that entitled exempt employees to take unlimited sick leave for doctor appointments for themselves or their children, but Mickelson repeatedly asked Walsh for advance notification and documentation of Walsh's doctor appointments. Other account representatives were not required to provide the same information about their appointments.

Walsh took full-time medical leave from April 7, 1997 until the birth of her son on May 9, 1997. She returned to work on August 4, 1997 after her maternity leave, and immediately experienced hostility from Mickelson. When Walsh was showing coworkers pictures of her son on her first day back to work, Mickelson told her to stop disrupting the office and to get back to work. Mickelson gave Walsh's coworkers the afternoon off to go to a craft fair as a reward for having covered Walsh's workload while she was on leave, but Walsh was told to stay in the office and watch the phones. One morning when Walsh arrived at 7:37 a.m. instead of 7:30 because she was delayed by her son's illness, she found an email sent from Mickelson at 7:33 that suggested that Mickelson was scrutinizing Walsh's hours. When Walsh asked if she could change her schedule to leave work at 4:30 p.m. instead of 5:00 because her son's daycare closed at 5:00, Mickelson told Walsh that her territory needed coverage until 5:00 and that "maybe she should look for another job." Other account representatives left work at 3:45 on a regular basis, and Mickelson testified at trial that Walsh's territory did not need to be covered through 5:00. Walsh was required to submit a vacation form when other workers were not. Mickelson attached signs ("Out — Sick Child") to Walsh's cubicle when Walsh had to care for her son, yet notes typically were not placed on other absent employees' cubicles. Mickelson reprimanded Walsh for "chit-chatting" in the cubicle section, when she was actually discussing work with a co-worker. Mickelson referred to Walsh's son as "the sickling." Mickelson placed a note in Walsh's personnel file regarding a minor incident involving Walsh's retrieval of a personal fax intended for a co-worker, as requested by the co-worker. Mickelson informed Walsh that she must make up "every minute" that she spent away from the office for doctors [sic] appointments for herself or her son and time spent caring for her son. No other employee was required to make up work for time missed due to appointments and other personal matters. At one point, Mickelson threw a phone book on Walsh's desk and told her to find a pediatrician who was open after hours. When Walsh told Mickelson she needed to pick her son up from daycare because he was ill, Mickelson replied, "Is this an April Fool's joke? If so, it's not at all funny." Walsh fainted at work as a result of stress and was brought to the hospital. The next day, Mickelson stopped at Walsh's cubicle and told her, "you better not be pregnant again."

In October 1997, Walsh reported to NCS's human resources representative, Mike McRath, that she was being treated differently than other account representatives and was required to make up time spent taking her son to the doctor. In the same month, Walsh's workload was increased without an increase in salary. McRath told her that if she was "accusing management of doing something unethical, she better have proof." In June 1998, when Walsh confronted Mickelson about the way she treated account representatives at a meeting, Mickelson swore at Walsh and pounded on the table. The next day Walsh told Mickelson that she wanted to be treated fairly, and Mickelson responded that it was an issue of manager's discretion. When Walsh reported Mickelson's behavior to Bruce Haseley, human resources manager, he appeared disinterested and told Walsh he could not take sides in the matter. Soon, department changes increased Walsh's responsibilities, which required her to work overtime. Walsh protested and Mickelson yelled at her. They went to Haseley's office for mediation, and Haseley offered no assistance. No investigation occurred either before or after Walsh's departure.

[Walsh ultimately began looking for another job and accepted employment with West Group. She submitted a letter of resignation to NCS but then reconsidered. She called Haseley to see if the situation with Mickelson could be worked out, but Haseley said he did not think that was possible. He did say he would speak with Mickelson, but later called Walsh back to tell her that Mickelson wished to continue with her termination.

At trial, the jury found that Walsh had been subjected to a hostile work environment and had been constructively discharged on the basis of pregnancy or gender discrimination. It awarded Walsh $11,000 for wage and benefit loss, $45,000 for other damages, and $382,145 in punitive damages. A judgment for Walsh of $438,145.40 was reduced by the district court as a result of Title VII's cap on compensatory and punitive damages and the court also reduced the punitive award to $300,000. However, it added attorneys' fees, and the final judgment of $625,525.90 was entered for Walsh.]

2. The Merits of the Case: Gender Discrimination on the Basis of Pregnancy

Even if NCS had preserved its right to appeal the jury's verdict on the hostile work environment claim, the facts of the case support Walsh's claim that she was a member of a protected class and was discriminated against on the basis of her pregnancy. . . . NCS argues that Walsh is alleging parent or caretaker discrimination, which is not proscribed by Title VII. *See Piantanida v. Wyman Ctr., Inc.*, 116 F.3d 340, 342 (8th Cir. 1997) (holding that childcare is not gender specific in the way that pregnancy and childbearing are, and that any discrimination experienced on the basis of a parent's decision to care for a child is not actionable because parenthood is not a protected class). Walsh asserts that she was discriminated against not because she was a new parent, but because she is a woman who had been pregnant, had taken a maternity leave, and might become pregnant again. "Potential pregnancy . . . is a medical condition that is sex-related because only women can become pregnant." *Krauel v. Iowa Methodist Med. Ctr.*, 95 F.3d 674, 680 (8th Cir. 1996). Because Walsh presented evidence that it was her potential to become pregnant in the future that served as a catalyst for Mickelson's discriminatory behavior, we will not disturb the jury verdict.

Once Walsh returned to work from her maternity leave, Mickelson made several discriminatory remarks to her. During a discussion about Walsh's coworker's pregnancy, Mickelson sarcastically commented to Walsh, "I suppose you'll be next." On another day, Walsh took a half-day vacation to go on a boat trip with her husband. After she returned, Mickelson stated, "Well, I suppose now we'll have another little Garrett [the name of Walsh's son] running around." On April 23, 1998, Walsh fainted at work and had to go to the hospital. The following day Mickelson stopped by Walsh's cubicle and said, "You better not be pregnant again!" Furthermore, when Walsh was pregnant, Mickelson asked Walsh for advanced [sic] notification and documentation of her doctor appointments, while other account representatives were not required to provide the same information concerning their appointments. Mickelson's comments, combined with the conduct detailed above . . . , provide ample support for the jury's finding that Walsh was discriminated against on the basis of her pregnancy.

C. Punitive Damages

Title VII allows for an award of punitive damages if the defendant committed illegal discrimination "with malice or with reckless indifference to the federally protected rights of an aggrieved individual." 42 U.S.C. § 1981a(b)(1). "Reckless indifference" means that the defendant had "knowledge that it may be acting in violation of federal law." *Kolstad v. Am. Dental Ass'n*, 527 U.S. 526, 535 (1999). Reckless indifference may be imputed to the employer if an employee commits a discriminatory act while serving in a managerial capacity and acts within the scope of employment. We have upheld punitive damages awards in cases where the employer has deliberately turned a deaf ear to discriminatory conduct. *Beard v. Flying J, Inc.*, 266 F.3d 792, 804 (8th Cir. 2001) (punitive damages appropriate where specific complaints about sexual assault were made and the company failed to take action).

The record shows that NCS had knowledge that it may have been acting in violation of federal law by not investigating Walsh's complaints that she was being treated unfairly. [Although a variety of managers admitted to knowing about NCS's nondiscrimination and antiharassment corporate policies, and there were at least ten separate reports to human resources that Walsh was being treated unfairly, NCS did not investigate the reported complaints.] Walsh told Haseley she would consider staying with NCS if he could assure her that her working conditions under Mickelson would improve. Haseley refused. Although Walsh may not have specifically stated to management that Mickelson's conduct rose to the level of a federal violation, she need not have made such a specific complaint. Mickelson, Haseley, Sherck and McRath were aware that NCS's nondiscrimination policy, consistent with federal law, prohibited comments and conduct that disparaged pregnancy and potential pregnancy. In light of these facts, we hold there is sufficient evidence that NCS demonstrated reckless indifference to the numerous allegations of pregnancy discrimination reported by several women, including Walsh.

[The court affirmed the verdict that NCS acted with the requisite reckless indifference to justify punitive damages and rejected the defendant's contention that the amount awarded was excessive and unconstitutional.]

NOTES

1. *Proving Bias.* Walsh's case was obviously far stronger than many because of the statements of her supervisor. Like most harassment cases, the "because of" prong was relatively easily satisfied by the directness of many of the harassing statements although such proof was bolstered by evidence of more favorably treated workers. Absent those statements by the supervisor, would the disparate application of work policies to Walsh as a mother have given rise to liability? Are you surprised that the person who seemed most hostile to Walsh was herself a woman?

2. *Accommodation as an Equal Treatment Issue.* Although *Walsh* is framed as a pregnancy harassment case, it suggests a fine line that both employers and employees must walk regarding accommodation. An employee can be fired for allowing childcare responsibilities to intrude too much into work time, but the employer must treat mothers and fathers the same in this regard. Thus, the absence of a duty to accommodate may, to some extent, be counterbalanced by a heightened concern for treating pregnant workers (and perhaps those with caregiving responsibilities) differently than other workers. In short, a plaintiff may be successful in proving disparate treatment by showing that, while an employer's failure to accommodate is not itself illegal, the particular failure to accommodate her was discriminatory. Some such claims have been successful, particularly in the context of accommodations needed for the physical demands of pregnancy. *See, e.g., Orr v. City of Albuquerque,* 531 F.3d 1210 (10th Cir. 2008) (upholding jury verdict for plaintiffs in light of evidence that they were required to use sick leave for their maternity leave when the employer's regulations permitted the use of vacation time and other employees were routinely allowed to use vacation or compensatory time for leave for purposes unrelated to a pregnancy); *Back v. Hastings on Hudson Union Free Sch. Dist.,* 365 F.3d 107 (2d Cir. 2004) (denying an employer summary judgment based on evidence that the employer stereotyped the "qualities of mothers" when it presumed the young mother would not be devoted to her job and when it implied that she could not be a good mother if she continued to work); *see also EEOC v. Houston Funding II, Ltd.,* 717 F.3d 425 (5th Cir. 2013) (adverse employment action against a female employee because she was lactating or expressing milk constituted sex discrimination). *Cf. Ames v. Nationwide Mut. Ins. Co.,* 760 F.3d 763 (8th Cir. 2014) (no constructive discharge because of pregnancy when plaintiff, upon returning from maternity leave, was not assisted finding a place to lactate when she did not give employer a reasonable opportunity to ameliorate the situation).

Nevertheless, there is a significant difference in theory between a duty to accommodate pregnancy and childbirth and plain vanilla discrimination. An employer can avoid liability for failing to accommodate pregnant women and mothers with childcare responsibilities by having inflexible work rules and not accommodating anyone. For example, an employer that had no "light work" policy for nonpregnant workers would have no duty to provide any light work to a pregnant employee. And, needless to say, if an employer does not have to accommodate the pregnancy of its female workers, it certainly does not have to accommodate childcare responsibilities.

In addition, the success of claims of discriminatory failure to accommodate may depend on evidence of preferential treatment of workers with personal needs unrelated to caregiving or pregnancy. Such comparators may not exist in a particular workplace, and, even if they do, the employer can always defend by demonstrating the absence of pretext, in other words, that there is a nondiscriminatory business reason for treating the comparators differently. *See, e.g., Tysinger v. Police Dep't of City of Zanesville,* 463 F.3d 569, 574 (6th Cir. 2006) (while two male officers suffered temporary incapacity like plaintiff, neither sought an accommodation of any kind and continued working in their usual assigned capacities; thus, they were not similarly situated to plaintiff).

3. *Accommodation from a Planning Perspective.* The risk of liability tied to the differential treatment of workers needing accommodations requires that employers be conscientious in deciding how to respond to workers' requests for deviations from regular work practices. If you were an employer, what type of policy would you institute? Would you (1) accommodate everyone; (2) accommodate no one; (3) trust your supervisors to make "appropriate" accommodation decisions? With respect to the last option, what kind of considerations should influence whether a particular accommodation was appropriate? If you were the supervisor, wouldn't your decision depend on the kind of work involved? The cost of the requested accommodations? The value of the particular employee to your team or the business as a whole? The anticipated duration of the accommodation? The need for managerial consistency? Do these questions point up some of the difficulties an employer might have in devising a policy or set of protocols for dealing with workers' individual needs and requests?

4. *Meet FReD.* Professor Joan Williams has used the terms "Family Responsibilities Employment Discrimination (FReD)," Joan C. Williams & Stephanie Bornstein *The Evolution of "FReD": Family Responsibilities Discrimination and Developments in the Law of Stereotyping and Implicit Bias,* 59 HASTINGS L. J. 1311 (2008), and the "maternal wall," Joan C. Williams & Nancy Segal, *Beyond the Maternal Wall: Relief for Family Caregivers Who Are Discriminated Against on the Job,* 26 HARV. WOMEN'S L. J. 77 (2003), to describe situations like that in *Walsh* and, more generally, to refer to barriers that impede the workplace advancement of women with childcare responsibilities, including differential accommodation, hostility, and stereotyping. While Walsh's success is by no means typical of cases where mothers have claimed sex discrimination, Professor Williams argues that Title VII has been more effective in dealing with these kinds of cases than is often realized, and she details a number of other legal theories under existing law that may be brought to bear in workplaces that do not accommodate mothers. *Id.* at 124, 151-60; *see also* Joan C. Williams, *The Social Psychology of Stereotyping: Using Social Science to Litigate Gender Discrimination Cases and Defang the "Cluelessness" Defense,* 7 EMP. RTS. & EMP. POL'Y J. 401 (2003). *But see* Julie C. Suk, *Are Gender Stereotypes Bad for Women? Rethinking Antidiscrimination Law and Work-Family Conflict,* 110 COLUM. L. REV. 1, 57 (2010) (while the law protects women against stereotyped responses, "when employers make the same demands on women and men, without regard for their caregiving responsibilities, people who are primary caregivers (usually women) will find it more difficult to meet the employer's expectations than people who are not primary caregivers (usually men).").

5. *A Disparate Impact Transformation?* We have seen that disparate impact has had a limited role in the pregnancy arena. Some scholars, nevertheless, have argued for an expanded use of the theory to challenge the "full-time face-time" norm for most American workplaces, that is, "traditional methods of organizing the when, where, and how of work performance, including the default preferences for full-time positions, unlimited hours, rigid work schedules, an uninterrupted worklife, and performance of work at a central location." Michelle A. Travis, *Recapturing the Transformative Potential of Employment Discrimination Law*, 62 WASH. & LEE L. REV. 3, 6 (2005). The argument is, essentially, that judges should look to a job's actual required tasks, not the current organizational structure under which they are performed. Disparate impact theory might require the latter to be modified unless the employer could demonstrate a business necessity for it.

If Professor Travis's views were to find their way into the case law, at least some workplaces would become more flexible and attuned to the needs of women, not only pregnant women but women with childcare responsibilities that limit their ability to participate in workplaces as they are presently structured. Accommodation would be achieved under the banner of disparate impact. Do you think courts should adopt Professor Travis's theory? Do you think judges are prepared to read Title VII as broadly as she urges? When you consider the FMLA in the next section, ask yourself if the shortcomings of that statute reflect limited political will to intrude very far on traditional employer prerogatives.

6. *Title VII No Obstacle to Some Accommodation.* While employers are not required to accommodate pregnant workers, they are permitted to do so, at least to some extent. *California Federal Savings & Loan Ass'n v. Guerra*, 479 U.S. 272 (1987), held that employers could provide some preferential treatment to pregnant workers without violating Title VII's prohibition of sex discrimination. In that case, the Court found no conflict between Title VII's prohibition of sex discrimination and a California statute which, in effect, created a right to unpaid maternity leave by granting women a right to return to comparable employment after delivery. The PDA was "a floor beneath which pregnancy disability benefits may not drop—not a ceiling above which they may not rise." *Id.* at 280. But the limits to such preferences are not clear. *Schafer v. Bd. of Pub. Educ. of the Sch. Dist. of Pittsburgh, Pa.*, 903 F.2d 243 (3d Cir. 1990), struck down a policy giving women one year's maternity leave while denying comparable paternity leave for men. Since the leave far exceeded the normal period of disability related to child-*bearing*, it was really child-*rearing* leave. According to the court, *Guerra* did not justify preferring mothers over fathers for this purpose since either parent could care for the child. *Id. See also Johnson v. Univ. of Iowa*, 431 F.3d 325 (8th Cir. 2005) (allowing biological mothers, but not fathers, to use accrued paid sick leave for absences after birth of a child is not gender discrimination because additional paid leave is provided to women for pregnancy-related disability, not child-rearing purposes). Issues of "preferential" treatment of mothers sometimes arise in cases brought by fathers with caregiving responsibilities who are denied accommodations or face hostility at work owing to stereotypes about caregiving as "women's work." *See generally* Keith Cunningham-Parmeter, *Men at Work, Fathers at Home: Uncovering the Masculine Face of Caregiver Discrimination*, 24 COLUM. J. GENDER & L. 253 (2013) (arguing that masculine norms deter men from asserting their caregiving needs while undermining their ability to prosecute discrimination claims); Christen Linke Young, *Childbearing, Childrearing, and Title VII: Parental Leave Policies at Large American Law Firms*, 118 YALE L.J. 1182, 1185 (2009) ("[S]ome firms provide mothers with extremely extended maternity leave — well in excess of their pregnancy-related disability — while offering fathers little or no paid time off when their children are born.").

7. *Employer Initiatives to Accommodate Family Caretaking.* While courts have been slow to require employers to significantly restructure work under the mantle of Title VII, some employers have been proactive. Flex-time" is increasingly offered by larger employers and innovations like the four-day work week have received positive reviews. Symposium, *Redefining Work: Implications of the Four-Day Work Week*, 42 CONN. L. REV. 1031 *et seq.* (2010). *But see* Robert C. Bird, *The Promise and Peril of Flexible Working Time*, http://papers.ssrn.com/sol3/papers.cfm?abstract_id= 2413129 (reporting survey results indicating that two-third of employers do not let any employees work at home even occasionally and an equivalent number do not let most workers vary start and end times).

8. *The ADA and the PDA.* As we saw in the previous section, the ADA requires employers to accommodate the disabilities of their workers. While §701(k) does not impose an obligation to give special treatment or otherwise accommodate pregnant workers, leave policies have proliferated under the impetus of the ADA, which means there is an increased number of employees granted leave for reasons other than pregnancy that may serve as comparators for a potential disparate treatment claim. Might an employee like Walsh claim a right to equal treatment with a disabled worker? Or does the fact that the employer grants leave to the disabled worker in order to comply with the ADA provide a nondiscriminatory justification for treating that worker more favorably? As we have seen, the circuits thus far have taken the latter view. *See* Note 3 at page 804.

9. *Beyond Antidiscrimination.* Because the protection provided by Title VII is limited, commentators have suggested a variety of responses beyond proposals like those of Professors Travis and Williams for reinterpreting existing statutes. The closest the nation has come to developing new law requiring work-family accommodations is the FMLA, which is treated next.

2. The Family and Medical Leave Act

Partly in response to some of the limits of discrimination law discussed in the previous section, Congress enacted the Family and Medical Leave Act ("FMLA") of 1993, which, together with its state analogs, is the major thrust of accommodation law for those who do not count as "disabled."

The FMLA is administered by the Department of Labor, which has elaborate regulations implementing the statute. 29 C.F.R. §825 (2014). The FMLA differs from the PDA, Congress's previous effort to address work-family conflict, in several ways. The statute goes beyond issues of gender discrimination and the challenges posed by pregnancy in an attempt to target the problem of work-family balance more broadly. It seeks to do this by extending rights to workers both for family care and for self-care. Thus, leave is required not only in connection with the birth of a child and to deal with serious family illnesses (family care) but also to deal with the worker's own serious illness (self-care). It protects workers in gender-neutral terms, providing the same rights to men and women workers with family responsibilities.

At the same time, the FMLA raises many of the same issues associated with existing discrimination law, including concerns about the limits of equality and the problem of preferential treatment. In addition, it has been subject to significant criticism, both by employers, who believe it improperly intrudes on managerial prerogative, and by advocates and feminists, who find it insufficient in addressing workers' needs, particularly those of mothers.

29 U.S.C. § 2612. Leave Requirement

(a) In general.

(1) *Entitlement to leave.* Subject to section 103, an eligible employee shall be entitled to a total of 12 workweeks of leave during any 12-month period for one or more of the following:

(A) Because of the birth of a son or daughter of the employee and in order to care for such son or daughter.

(B) Because of the placement of a son or daughter with the employee for adoption or foster care.

(C) In order to care for the spouse, or a son, daughter, or parent, of the employee, if such spouse, son, daughter, or parent has a serious health condition.

(D) Because of a serious health condition that makes the employee unable to perform the functions of the position of such employee.

(E) Because of any qualifying exigency (as the Secretary shall, by regulation, determine) arising out of the fact that the spouse, or a son, daughter, or parent of the employee is on covered active duty (or has been notified of an impending call or order to covered active duty) in the Armed Forces . . . .

(c) *Unpaid leave permitted.* Except as provided in subsection (d) [pertaining to the ability of the employer require or employee to elect to substitute existing paid leave for FMLA leave], leave granted under subsection (a) may consist of unpaid leave. . . .

29 U.S.C. § 2614. Employment and Benefits Protection

(a) Restoration to position

Except as provided in subsection (b) of this section, any eligible employee who takes leave under section 2612 of this title for the intended purpose of the leave shall be entitled, on return from such leave —

(A) to be restored by the employer to the position of employment held by the employee when the leave commenced; or

(B) to be restored to an equivalent position with equivalent employment benefits, pay, and other terms and conditions of employment.

(2) Loss of benefits

The taking of leave under section 2612 of this title shall not result in the loss of any employment benefit accrued prior to the date on which the leave commenced.

(3) Limitations

Nothing in this section shall be construed to entitle any restored employee to —

(A) the accrual of any seniority or employment benefits during any period of leave; or

(B) any right, benefit, or position of employment other than any right, benefit, or position to which the employee would have been entitled had the employee not taken the leave.

NOTES

1. *FMLA Coverage.* The FMLA has far more limited coverage than most of the other statutory schemes we treat in this book. For example, Title VII and the ADA reach all employers with 15 or more employees. By contrast, the FMLA applies only to employers with 50 or more employees. Further, unlike the antidiscrimination statutes, not all employees of covered employers are protected. Part-time employees, first-year employees, and even employees who work for small offices of larger employers are not entitled to leave under the FMLA. This is because the statute requires "eligible" employees to have worked for the employer for at least 12 months, § 2611(2)(A)(1), and for at least 1,250 hours during the year preceding the start of the leave, § 2611(2)(A)(ii), and to be employed at a worksite where the employer employs at least 50 employees within a 75-mile radius. § 2611(2)(B)(ii). *See Babcock v. BellSouth Adver. & Publ'g Corp.*, 348 F.3d 73 (4th Cir. 2003) (employee was entitled to extension of leave after being employed for one year, even though the employer would not have violated the statute had it denied leave when she first applied before her first anniversary); *Staunch v. Cont'l Airlines, Inc.*, 511 F.3d 625 (6th Cir. 2008) (flight attendant not entitled to FMLA leave when she had worked fewer than 1,250 hours).

2. *FMLA Benefits.* The statute's basic command is *unpaid* leave, which is defined as reinstating the employee to the same or an equivalent job when the leave ends. Elsewhere, the statute permits the employee to elect, or the employer to require, the use of any paid leave the employee may have accrued under the employer's other policies (vacation, paid sick time, etc.) during FMLA leave. *See* 29 U.S.C. § 2612(d)(2). As a practical matter, most employers insist on this, in part for administrative convenience and in part to ensure that employees do not take 12 weeks of FMLA leave and existing paid leave consecutively, resulting in a longer absence from work. The other principal advantage conferred by the FMLA is the requirement that employers maintain preexisting benefits, including health insurance, while the employee is on FMLA leave. However, the employee is obligated to continue paying his or her portion of the premiums, which can be onerous during a time in which the employee is not receiving a salary.

The fact that FMLA leave is unpaid is the key limitation and source of criticism of the statute. Only a relatively privileged class of workers is likely to be able to take full advantage of its benefits. A number of commentators have called for the provision of paid family/medical leave, funded by either the employer or government sources. *See, e.g.*, Samuel Issacharoff & Elyse Rosenblum, *Women and the Workplace: Accommodating the Demands of Pregnancy*, 94 COLUM. L. REV. 2154 (1994); Gillian Lester, *A Defense of Paid Family Leave*, 28 HARV. J.L. & GENDER 1 (2005); Michael Selmi, *Family Leave and the Gender Wage Gap*, 78 N.C. L. REV. 707, 770-73 (2000). There have also been initiatives to require paid leave at the state level. Currently only three states have implemented such a program, in all cases funded through a temporary disability insurance program. *See* CAL. UNEMP. INS. CODE § 3301 (2014); N.J. STAT. ANN. §§ 43:21-25-31 (West 2014); R.I. Gen. Laws § 28-41-34 *et seq.* (2014). Washington has yet to implement such a proposal although it was approved by the legislature in 2008. WASH. REV. CODE ANN. § 49.86.030 (West 2010).

3. *Limitations on FMLA Rights.* Despite the FMLA's general authorization of leave, the statute does have some limitations. For example, the statute expressly provides that seniority need not accrue during any statutory-mandated leave. § 2614(a)(3). Further, § 2614(b) creates an exception to the reinstatement right for "highly compensated employees" (the top ten percent of all employees in a designated geographic area),

but only if reinstatement would cause "substantial and grievous economic injury." 29 C.F.R. §825.218; *see Kephart v. Cherokee County, N.C.*, 229 F.3d 1142 (4th Cir. 2002). Third, the statute itself limits the family members for whose care leave may be taken, although the courts have not been grudging in interpreting this provision. *Gienapp v. Harbor Crest*, 756 F.3d 527, 531 (7th Cir. 2014) ("To the extent Harbor Crest maintains that Gienapp was not entitled to leave because she was not [her daughter's] "primary" caregiver, the argument lacks support in the statute. Employees are entitled to leave to provide "care" for their children; the word "primary" is just not there, and we can't add it. . . . But to the extent Harbor Crest contends that Gienapp provided care exclusively for her grandchildren, the argument has a statutory basis. What it lacks is a basis in undisputed fact."); *Ballard v. Chi. Park Dist.*, 741 F.3d 838, 839 (7th Cir. 2014) (the FMLA at least requires leave to physically care for a terminally ill parent's medical, hygienic, or nutritional needs while that parent was traveling away from home even if the care was not part of ongoing treatment of the condition.).

Finally, an employee who takes leave for her own health condition may be asked to provide a doctor's certification of her ability to resume work. §2614(a)(4). *See Wallace v. FedEx Corp.*, 2014 U.S. App. LEXIS 16208(6th Cir. Aug. 22, 2014) (upholding 29 C.F.R. §825.305(a) which allows an employer to require a medical-certification form within 15 days but also requires that employer to advise the employee of the consequences of failure to provide such a certification). There is some flexibility about leave, *see Hansen v. Fincantieri Marine Group, LLC*, 763 F.3d 832 (7th Cir. 2014) (employer may not deny intermittent FMLA leave merely because requests exceed the estimated length in his medical certification form), but an employee who exhausts her permitted leave and is still unable to work is not entitled to keep her job. *Hatchett v. Philander Smith Coll.*, 251 F.3d 670, 677 (8th Cir. 2001).

4. *Resistance and Reaction to Enactment of the FMLA.* The relatively narrow coverage of the FMLA and its limited unpaid benefit reflect strong resistance to the statute on the part of corporate America. The first President Bush vetoed two earlier versions of the statute, but the bill gained momentum when it was framed as addressing a "family" issue rather than a feminist one. Opponents of the FMLA argued that it started down the slippery slope of government-mandated policies, reducing corporate control over employee benefit programs. Employers worried about the effectiveness of temporary replacements and/or morale problems resulting from redistribution of work to cover FMLA leaves. Small business owners, in particular, complained of administrative costs, especially the statute's record-keeping and notice provisions.

5. *Impact of the FMLA.* In the almost two decades since the FMLA has been in effect, many employees have taken advantage of the rights it provides. A 2008 Department of Labor report noted an employer survey that indicated that 6.1 million persons, or eight percent of employees, utilized FMLA leave in 2005. http://www.dol.gov/whd/FMLA2007Report/Chapter11.pdf. Of these, 1.5 million used intermittent leave. The Employment Policy Foundation estimated the direct costs of such leave to employers to be $21 billion in terms of lost productivity, health benefits, and net labor replacement costs. But a 2007 survey by Human Resource Management found that 71 percent of respondents reported no noticeable productivity harm. It is true that co-workers of the statute's beneficiaries have noted concomitant increased coverage responsibilities: Two-thirds of employers reassign the absent worker's tasks to a co-worker, and assigning work to co-workers occurred more frequently from 2000-2003. http://www.policyarchive.org/handle/10207/bitstreams/12252.pdf; http://www.protectfamilyleave.org/research/2003_SHRM_FMLA_Survey.pdf. Thus, the high costs that corporations believed would come from compliance with the FMLA have apparently not materialized. Is that because other workers have largely been required to pick up the slack? Indeed, there is reason to think that the statute has resulted in some benefits to employers in improved staff retention, morale, and productivity. *See* Jane Waldfogel, *Family-Friendly Policies for Families with Young Children*, 5 EMP. RTS. & EMP. POL'Y J. 273, 290-91 (2001). Of course, this success is perhaps attributable to the very limited protections afforded by the FMLA. A more aggressive statute, such as one requiring paid leave, might generate a very different response.

6. *FMLA Irony.* There has been no constitutional challenge to the statute as far as it reaches private employment, but the Supreme Court has considered a claim that the FMLA could not constitutionally apply to the states because of the Eleventh Amendment. In *Nevada Department of Human Resources v. Hibbs*, 538 U.S. 721 (2003), the Court rejected that argument in an opinion replete with irony. The plaintiff in that case, William Hibbs, worked for the Department's Welfare Division. He sought, and was granted, leave under the FMLA to care for his ailing wife, who was recovering from a car accident, but he and the Department disagreed about the amount of leave. He was terminated when he failed to report to work when the Department required him to do so. He sued, and the Department interposed a claim of Eleventh Amendment immunity.

While the Eleventh Amendment generally bars private suits against the state without their consent, *Board of Trustees of Univ. of Ala. v. Garrett*, 531 U.S. 356 (2001) (barring ADA suits); *Kimel v. Fla. Bd. of Regents*, 528 U.S. 62 (2000) (barring ADEA suits), Congress may "abrogate such immunity in federal court if it makes its intention to abrogate unmistakably clear in the language of the statute and acts pursuant to a valid exercise of its power under § 5 of the Fourteenth Amendment." 538 U.S. at 726. Title VII has been interpreted to validly abrogate such immunity. *Fitzpatrick v. Bitzer*, 427 U.S. 445 (1976). Since there was no doubt that Congress had intended to abrogate states' immunity, *Hibbs* turned on whether Congress acted within its § 5 power in either attacking equal protection violations or enacting "prophylactic legislation that proscribes facially constitutional conduct, in order to prevent and deter unconstitutional conduct." *Id.* at 721-22. The Court held yes.

In enacting the FMLA, Congress looked to evidence that states continued to rely on invalid gender stereotypes in the employment context, specifically in the administration of leave benefits. That evidence, however, was not of continued discrimination against women but rather of discrimination against male workers. For example, one survey stated that 37 percent of surveyed private-sector employees were covered by maternity leave policies, while only 18 percent were covered by paternity leave policies. *Id.* at 730. Further, there was also evidence of "differential leave policies [for men and women that] were not attributable to any differential physical needs of men and women, but rather to the pervasive sex-role stereotype that caring for family members is women's work." *Id.* at 731. Finally, "even where state laws and policies were not facially discriminatory, they were applied in discriminatory ways." *Id.* at 732. The Court concluded that "the States' record of unconstitutional participation in, and fostering of, gender-based discrimination in the administration of leave benefits is weighty enough to justify the enactment of prophylactic § 5 legislation." *Id.* at 735.

In a later case dealing with the "self-care" provisions of the FMLA, *Coleman v. Court of Appeals*, 132 S. Ct. 1327 (2012), the Court found an insufficient basis for concluding that states had discriminated on the basis of sex in this regard, thus rendering that aspect of the statue unenforceable against state employees by private suit for damages.

The irony of *Hibbs*, was that, although the gender-neutral statute was largely designed to address the work-life concerns of women, it was upheld because of evidence of Congress's concern about discrimination against men. In *Family Leave and the Gender Wage Gap* 78 N.C. L. REV. 707, 708 (2000), Professor Michael Selmi argues that not only are employers' attitudes toward men as caregivers part of the problem, but male attitudes themselves also must change if women are to play a more central role in the workplace: "[I]ncreasing workplace equality will require persuading men to behave more like women, rather than trying to induce women to behave more like men. Achieving this objective would create a new workplace norm where all employees would be expected to have and spend time with their children, and employers would adapt to that reality." Accordingly, he would create greater incentives for men to take leave for the birth or adoption of a child. Does this go too far in urging that men be pressured or incentivized into taking leave? Is he too optimistic about the ability of the law to assist societal change?

7. *Has It Worked?* While passage of the FMLA is often viewed as a major, if very limited, advance in requiring employers to become more "family friendly" in gender-neutral terms, many commentators remain sharply critical of the inadequate response of the law to the obstacles faced by pregnant women and working mothers. The FMLA's principal contribution is that it supplements Title VII's prohibition of pregnancy discrimination by requiring accommodation of at least some of the more exigent demands of pregnancy and motherhood. Today, Ms. Troupe could take FMLA leave rather than lose her job. The statute guarantees employees who could otherwise be legally discharged under Title VII the right to return to their jobs after taking time off to give birth or care for their children. But even viewed together, the FMLA and Title VII provide a very limited accommodation regime for mothers. Normal childcare responsibilities are not addressed by the FMLA, and even caring for an ill child is not protected if a "serious health condition" is not in play. What constitutes a "serious health condition" is sometimes complicated, but most routine aliments that keep children home from school, such as colds and earaches, are not FMLA leave–eligible.

As a result, there have been calls for expanded accommodation of what one commentator calls the "caregiver conundrum," defined as the obstacles generated by "a set of norms in the workplace that were shaped by and for men." Nicole Buonocore Porter, *Synergistic Solutions: An Integrated Approach to Solving the Caregiver Conundrum for "Real" Workers*, 39 STETSON L. REV. 777, 781 (2010). As she sees it,

> The caregiver conundrum affects caregivers in three primary ways. First, many (perhaps most) caregivers need and want more workplace flexibility to meet the demands of their families, yet most workplaces do not provide the flexibility needed. Second, caregivers who choose to work reduced hours or part-time in order to spend more time taking care of their families do so at the significant cost of marginalizing their careers and being underpaid for their efforts. Third, parents and other caregivers in the lower-income brackets might need flexibility or reduced hours to meet their caregiving obligations but are financially unable to take time off for caregiving needs. These caregivers may also have difficulty meeting their workplace requirements because of inadequate or unreliable daycare.

Id. She offers as one solution a "Part-Time Parity Act," which would mandate pay and benefits proportional to those of full-time workers. *Id.* at 828-33. Other proposals would require FMLA leave for more quotidian childrearing, mandated accommodation in the form of required workplace flexibility, and accommodation tailored to individual caregiving needs similar to that granted religion and disability under other laws. *See also* Debbie N. Kaminer, *The Work-Family Conflict: Developing a Model of Parental Accommodation in the Workplace*, 54 Am. U. L. Rev. 305 (2004); Laura T. Kessler, *The Attachment Gap: Employment Discrimination Law, Women's Cultural Caregiving, and the Limits of Economic and Liberal Legal Theory*, 34 U. Mich. J. L. Reform 371, 386-87 (2001); Peggie R. Smith, *Accommodating Routine Parental Obligations in an Era of Work-Family Conflict: Lessons from Religious Accommodations*, 2001 Wis. L. Rev. 1443 (2001). *Cf.* Rachel Arnow-Richman, *Incenting Flexibility: The Relationship Between Public Law and Voluntary Action in Enhancing Work-Life Balance*, 42 Conn. L. Rev. 1081, 1099 (2010) (arguing that reasons such as "lack of information, cognitive biases, transaction costs, and other impediments" lead to suboptimal decisions with respect to leave: "In the context of workplace accommodations, this may mean that employers are under-serving caregivers (and in some instances themselves) by failing to make cost-neutral and even mutually advantageous accommodations.")

There have been a few efforts to provide more accommodation than the FMLA. A very limited federal response is the Affordable Care Act's requirement that employers provide lactation support for their workers, 29 U.S.C. § 207(r) (2104). At the state level, a number of states have family and medical leave laws that are similar to the FMLA. Recently, however, two states have enacted statutes expressly requiring reasonable accommodations for pregnancy other than unpaid leave. N.J. Stat. Ann. 10:512(s) (2104); W. Va. Code § 5:11B-2 (2014).

Might further measures also, at some point, create problems of theoretic consistency? Does privileging pregnancy, childbirth, and the early months of childrearing reinforce the notion that women's primary role is childrearing? Would extending such rights in a gender-neutral fashion solve that problem if, as Professor Selmi argues, women will be the primary ones to invoke such benefits? And, to the extent that benefits are used exclusively or primarily by women and are costly for employers, would imposing such requirements lead employers to avoid hiring women in the first place? While such conduct would violate Title VII, it might frequently be impossible to detect.

In part as a result of such concerns, some commentators have urged moving the focus away from enabling caregiving to making work more accessible to people of all backgrounds and family situations, for instance by reducing the work week and eliminating mandatory overtime. *See, e.g.*, Marion Crain, *"Where Have All the Cowboys Gone?": Marriage and Breadwinning in Postindustrial Society*, 60 Ohio St. L. J. 1877 (1999); Vicki Schultz, *Life's Work*, 100 Colum. L. Rev. 1881 (2000). Might such proposals be more likely to garner public and political support? Are they likely to be as helpful to women with caregiving responsibilities? The Great Recession has led some employers, largely in terms of saving money, to institute different work arrangements, most notably, the 4/40 workweek (four days of ten hours each). But there is reason to doubt that such changes will contribute substantially to better work-family balance, especially for women. Michelle A. Travis, *What a Difference a Day Makes, or Does It? Work/Family Balance and the Four-Day Work Week*, 42 Conn. L. Rev. 1223 (2010); Rachel Arnow-Richman, *Incenting Flexibility: The Relationship Between Public Law and Voluntary Action in Enhancing Work-Life Balance*, 42 Conn. L. Rev. 1081, 1099 (2010).

8. *Substantive Benefits and Redistributive Concerns.* The FMLA contains an affirmative directive — eligible employees must receive a specific substantive benefit — making it more of an accommodation statute like the ADA than a nondiscrimination statute like Title VII. Any kind of accommodation requirement raises redistribution concerns, particularly where the laws in question impose the costs of redistribution not on society generally but on the employers who are required to accommodate the workers in question. *See* Samuel R. Bagenstos, *The Future of Disability Law*, 114 YALE L. J. 1 (2004) (arguing that, because the ADA may serve as an open-ended tool of redistribution to people with disabilities, courts have attempted to constrain the mandate through antidiscrimination principles, such as employer fault, resulting in the law's failure to undo deep-rooted structural barriers to employment for people with disabilities).

Professor Arnow-Richman argues that the history of the ADA, and in particular courts' narrow interpretation of its accommodation mandate, bode poorly for the future of work-family accommodation. This is particularly true, she suggests, in what she describes as the contemporary "Me, Inc." economy:

> The desirability of employer-supported accommodation rests on two assumptions: (i) basic features of the contemporary workplace represent choices about work structure that can and should be changed; and (ii) it is reasonable to expect employers to absorb the costs associated with making those changes or with providing necessary benefits to employee caregivers.
>
> These assumptions are . . . especially problematic when examined against the history of government intervention in the workplace and the nature of modern employment relationships. [V]oluntarily-provided employer benefits . . . have been the dominant mode of addressing employee lifecycle needs for the majority of the twentieth century. Such an allocation of rights and responsibilities at work was enabled by a particular "social contract" of employment, one in which employers and employees anticipated a long-term symbiotic relationship often governed by a collective bargaining agreement. In contrast, today's work relationships are defined by a "Me, Inc." work culture — an employment environment in which workers are increasingly independent, short-term employment relationships predominate, collective action is all but absent, and employer reliance on contingent labor has dramatically expanded. In an economy where employees' futures depend not on their current employer but on the value of their human capital within the external labor market, the incentives for voluntary accommodation of employees' lifecycle needs are generally absent.

See Rachel Arnow-Richman, *Accommodation Subverted: The Future of Work/Family Initiatives in a "Me, Inc." World*, 12 TEX. J. WOMEN & L. 345, 373-88 (2003). She concludes that responding to the problem of inadequate accommodation of caregiving through government mandates "shows inadequate consideration for contemporary expectations about the way people work," and therefore imposing "extensive employer-funded accommodation in this context may overreach and spawn backlash." *Id.* at 374. Are you convinced by these concerns, or is Arnow-Richman's account overly pessimistic? Rather than caving to the "Me, Inc." work culture, should the law make wider efforts to dismantle what might appear to some observers as a race to the bottom?

9. *Hurting the People We Are Trying to Help?* Separate from concerns about fairness for employers are concerns about the impact of accommodation mandates on the group intended to benefit from them. Some authorities have raised questions about the consequences of statutes such as the FMLA and ADA. Christine Jolls, *Accommodation Mandates*, 53 STAN. L. REV. 223, 225, 291 (2000), writes that newer accommodation mandates, such as the ADA and FMLA are directed to "discrete, identifiable groups of workers, such as the disabled" to accommodate their "unique needs." For the FMLA, she warns that, because of significant occupational segregation, such an accommodation mandate will tend "to lower the relative wages of disadvantaged workers and to increase or decrease their relative employment levels depending on whether the value of the mandated accommodation exceeds or falls short of its cost." She predicts that, because the cost of unpaid leave is hard to monetize, a mandate that imposes such costs "may be more likely to be reflected in reductions in the relative employment levels of disadvantaged workers and less likely to be reflected in reductions in their relative wages." *Id; see also* John J. Donohue III, *Understanding the Reasons for and Impact of Legislatively Mandated Benefits for Selected Workers*, 53 STAN. L. REV. 897 (2001); *cf.* Cass R. Sunstein, *Human Behavior and the Law of Work*, 87 VA. L. REV. 205, 206-8 (2001) (supporting mandates as a default rule but allowing them to be waived). If Professor Jolls is correct, more accommodation would mean less employment for women (mothers) but more accommodating employment for those who obtain jobs. Is that a worthwhile trade-off? Who should decide?

10. *A Procedural Approach?* Is there a middle road that can expand caregiver rights while avoiding the pitfalls of accommodation mandates? Professor Arnow-Richman offers a proposal that would require new legislation but not create a new substantive right. She proposes that employers should have a duty to discuss caregiving accommodations with their employees, somewhat along the lines of the ADA's interactive process. Unlike the ADA, however, there would be no substantive duty to accommodate. "A procedural requirement imposed on the employer upon the conclusion of FMLA leave recognizes, for instance, that an employee who gives birth or adopts a new child cannot be expected to seamlessly return to full-time work upon the conclusion of the child's third month." Rachel Arnow-Richman, *Public Law and Private Process: Toward an Incentivized Organizational Justice Model of Equal Employment Quality for Caregivers*, 2007 UTAH L. REV. 25, 57. This approach would also have the advantage of shifting "the blunt effect of a one-size-fits-all mandated benefit" to a more flexible response by the employer and employee. *Id.* Framing the new right as procedural only with no substantive component "is critical to the political viability of the proposal both in terms of congressional adoption and the reliability of judicial enforcement." She would, however, shift a burden of proof under the FMLA or PDA for those employers who failed to engage in the interactive process. *Id.* at 58. *See also* Rachel Arnow-Richman, *Incenting Flexibility: The Relationship Between Public Law and Voluntary Action in Enhancing Work-Life Balance*, 42 CONN. L. REV. 1081 (2010) (arguing that mandated "interactive process" regarding accommodation is more likely to yield better results than such general policies as the 4/40 workweek, adopted by some employers). To what extent do procedural protections assist employees in the absence of mandates? In other words, does an employer have any incentive to accommodate an employee if the law does not so require? If not, do the litigation incentives proposed by Professor Arnow-Richman help? Might they impose additional risks?

Goelzer v. Sheboygan County, Wisconsin
604 F.3d 987 (7th Cir. 2010)

WILLIAMS, Circuit Judge.

After two decades of employment with her county government, Dorothy Goelzer was fired from her job. Her supervisor informed her of the termination decision two weeks before she was scheduled to begin two months of leave under the Family and Medical Leave Act (FMLA). This leave did not mark the first time Goelzer was away from work on FMLA leave, as Goelzer had taken a significant amount of authorized FMLA leave during the four preceding years to deal with her own health issues and those of her mother and husband. After she lost her job, Goelzer brought this suit and alleged that her employer had interfered with her right to reinstatement under the FMLA and had retaliated against her for taking FMLA leave. The defendants contend that her supervisor simply decided to hire another person with a larger skill set. [The district court granted summary judgment against plaintiff, but the Seventh Circuit reversed.]

I. Background

[Sheboygan County hired Dorothy Goelzer in 1986 as Clerk Typist in its office of the Register of Deeds. By 1999, she was the administrative assistant to Adam Payne, the Board's Administrative Coordinator. Payne consistently gave Goelzer good performance reviews and merit increases. In some of his evaluations, he praised her for rarely being absent.]

Goelzer began to have significant health issues in 2002. She had eye surgery in July and took approximately a month of FMLA leave during her surgery and recovery. She also had multiple doctors' appointments in the months before and after her surgery. All in all, she used 312.50 hours of sick leave in 2002, the equivalent of nearly eight forty-hour weeks. Payne wrote in Goelzer's 2002 performance evaluation that, "[t]hough Dorothy has had an excellent record in the past, (36 hours of sick leave in 2001), she utilized 312 hours or 39 days of sick leave in 2002."

Goelzer continued to have health problems in 2003. She . . . took time off on thirty-two different days during 2003 for her health issues and used a total of 176.50 hours of leave. Payne commented on Goelzer's use of sick leave again in that year's performance evaluation, stating: "Dorothy utilized 176.50 hours or 22 days of sick leave in 2003." He gave her an overall rating of 3.36, with a 3.5 in the attendance category. He did not award her a merit pay increase. [When Goelzer disagreed with Payne about no merit increase, Payne responded with a February 5, 2004 memorandum that again referred to her leave: "In fact, the past two years, use of sick leave and vacation combined, you were out of the office 113 days. As the only support person in the office, this has presented challenges in the functionality and duties associated with the office."]

Goelzer used 94 hours of sick leave in 2004. She received a merit increase of 1.5% after her 2004 evaluation. The next year, Goelzer's health was stable, but her mother's health was not. Goelzer took FMLA leave on nine days in 2004 for appointments related to her mother or husband, and her 2005 FMLA applications included requests for intermittent leave to care for her mother. Goelzer received a 1.25% merit increase after 2005. Goelzer stated in an affidavit that when she asked why she did not receive a higher merit pay increase, Payne responded that she had missed a lot of time at work due to appointments with her mother.

Goelzer learned in 2006 that she would need foot surgery that year. On May 10, 2006, Goelzer submitted an FMLA leave request for time away from work from September 22, 2006 to November 20, 2006 for her foot surgery and recovery. At Payne's request, Goelzer provided a medical certification for the foot surgery to Human Resources Director Michael Collard on June 1, 2006. Collard wrote directly to Goelzer's doctor five days later and asked whether Goelzer could return to light duty office work before November 19, 2006, and if so, when. Goelzer's doctor responded that she would be totally disabled and unable to work during that time period. The County eventually approved Goelzer's FMLA leave request on August 8.

On August 15, 2006, the Sheboygan County Board passed an ordinance that converted the position of County Administrative Coordinator to that of County Administrator. The Board also appointed Payne to serve as County Administrator. With this change, Payne now had the power under Wisconsin Statute § 59.18(3) to discharge Goelzer on his own, a power he did not previously have. Within the next ten days, Payne told Collard that he wanted to meet to discuss options for terminating Goelzer's employment. In preparation for the August 25, 2006 meeting, Collard prepared notes related to options, with a list that included "term outright, just need to change," "eliminate position," "Change T/O — reshuffle — create new position not qualified for," "Raise expectations & evaluate," and "Retaliation for FMLA?".

On September 8, 2006, two weeks before Goelzer was to commence FMLA leave for her foot surgery, Payne discharged Goelzer with an effective date of November 30, 2006. (Payne placed Goelzer on paid leave until November 30, 2006 so that she would receive the FMLA leave that had been previously approved.) At the time, Goelzer had used 67 hours of leave in 2006 and was scheduled to take an additional 328 hours related to her foot surgery. . . .

Payne did not immediately replace Goelzer. Instead, he first utilized an unpaid college intern. On January 16, 2007, the County Board enacted an ordinance that eliminated Goelzer's former position and replaced it with the position of "Assistant to the Administrator." It also increased the pay grade for the role from Grade 6 to Grade 8. Payne hired Kay Lorenz as the Assistant to the Administrator on March 19, 2007. . . .

II.   Analysis . . .

The FMLA allows an eligible employee with a serious health condition that renders the employee unable to perform her position to take twelve workweeks of leave during each twelve-month period. 29 U.S.C. § 2612(a)(1)(D). An employee may also utilize this leave to care for certain immediate relatives, including a parent or spouse, with a serious health condition. *Id.* § 2612(a)(1)(C). Under the FMLA, an employee on leave is entitled to the right to be restored to the same or an equivalent position that she had before she took qualifying leave. *Id.* § 2614(a)(1)-(2). An employer may not "interfere with, restrain, or deny the exercise of or the attempt to exercise" any FMLA rights. *Id.* § 2615(a)(1).

In addition, the FMLA affords protection to employees who are retaliated against because they exercise rights protected by the Act. *Lewis v. Sch. Dist. #70*, 523 F.3d 730, 741 (7th Cir. 2008). Pursuant to 29 U.S.C. § 2615(a)(2), it is "unlawful for any employer to discharge or in any other manner discriminate against any individual for opposing any practice made unlawful by this subchapter." The Act also makes it unlawful to "discharge" or "discriminate" against a person for taking part in proceedings or inquiries under the FMLA. 29 U.S.C. § 2615(b). We have construed these provisions as stating a cause of action for retaliation.

[The court determined that Goelzer's complaint alleged both interference and retaliation. One paragraph cited 29 U.S.C. § 2614(a)(1), the FMLA provision barring interference, while a different used the language of § 2615(a)(2), prohibiting retaliation.]

A. FMLA Interference

We first address Goelzer's interference argument. The plaintiff carries the burden of proving an FMLA interference claim. *Darst v. Interstate Brands Corp.*, 512 F.3d 903, 908 (7th Cir. 2008). To establish such a claim, an employee must show that: (1) she was eligible for the FMLA's protections; (2) her employer was covered by the FMLA; (3) she was entitled to take leave under the FMLA; (4) she provided sufficient notice of her intent to take leave; and (5) her employer denied her FMLA benefits to which she was entitled. *Burnett v. LFW, Inc.*, 472 F.3d 471, 477 (7th Cir. 2006). There is no dispute regarding the first four requirements; it is clear that the FMLA allowed Goelzer to take the leave that she did. The only issue is whether the defendants fired her to prevent her from exercising her right to reinstatement to her position. *See Simpson v. Office of the Chief Judge of the Circuit Court of Will County*, 559 F.3d 706, 712 (7th Cir. 2009) ("Firing an employee to prevent her from exercising her right to return to her prior position can certainly interfere with that employee's FMLA rights.").

An employee's right to reinstatement is not absolute. The FMLA allows an employer to refuse to restore an employee to the "former position when restoration would confer a 'right, benefit, or position of employment' that the employee would not have been entitled to if the employee had never left the workplace." *Kohls v. Beverly Enters. Wis., Inc.*, 259 F.3d 799, 805 (7th Cir. 2001) (citing 29 U.S.C. § 2614(a)(3)(B)); *see also* 29 C.F.R. § 825.216(a) ("An employee has no greater right to reinstatement or to other benefits and conditions of employment than if the employee has been continuously employed during the FMLA leave period."). In other words, an employee is not entitled to return to her former position if she would have been fired regardless of whether she took the leave.

The question at this stage of the proceedings, then, is whether a jury could find that the defendants did not reinstate Goelzer because she exercised her right to take FMLA leave. Payne and the County maintain that the answer is "no," as their position is that Goelzer's employment would have been terminated regardless of whether she took FMLA leave. They maintain that after Payne received a promotion to County Administrator, he simply exercised his new authority to replace Goelzer on his own with a person of his choosing. They stress that before his promotion, Payne would have needed the approval of the County through its Executive Committee before he could terminate Goelzer's employment. With the promotion to County Administrator, however, Payne could now make the termination decision on his own. And three weeks after he assumed his new role, Payne notified Goelzer she was losing her job, a decision he says had nothing to do with Goelzer's use of FMLA leave.

Michael Collard, the County's Human Resources Director, supports Payne's account. Collard asserts that Payne had expressed frustration for some time that Goelzer was not performing the tasks Payne had envisioned for her, and Collard also says that Payne had expressed a desire for an assistant with a greater skill set. In addition, although Payne did not immediately replace Goelzer and instead first utilized a college intern, Payne maintains that in the longer term he wanted the position to be enhanced to allow him to assign more sophisticated tasks beyond those that he says Goelzer could handle.

The defendants' account provides one possible explanation for the termination decision, and a jury might well choose to believe it. But there is another possibility as well. Goelzer contends that she lost her job because Payne and the County were not happy that she had exercised her right to take FMLA leave. . . . Even though the leave was authorized, we conclude that the evidence Goelzer introduced in response to the defendants' motion for summary judgment could lead a jury to find that she was denied reinstatement not because Payne simply wanted a different assistant, but because she had exercised her right to take leave under the FMLA.

A jury might be swayed by comments Payne made that could suggest frustration with Goelzer's use of FMLA leave. In her 2002 performance evaluation, for instance, Payne explicitly contrasted Goelzer's use of FMLA leave with her past "excellent" attendance, saying, "[t]hough Dorothy has had an excellent attendance record in the past, (36 hours of sick leave in 2001), she utilized 312 hours or 39 days of sick leave in 2002." Payne gave her a 3.5 rating in the "attendance" category in 2002. He noted her use of sick leave in the following year's performance evaluation as well, stating "Dorothy utilized 176 hours of 22 days of sick leave in 2003," and he gave her an overall rating of 3.36 that year but did not award a merit increase. Notably too, when Goelzer asked Payne in 2006 why she did not receive a higher merit increase based on her 2005 performance, she says that Payne responded that she had missed too much time from work to attend to appointments with her mother.

A jury might also look to the memorandum Payne wrote in 2004 in response to Goelzer's view that she should have received a merit increase, where he said in part: "you were out of the office having eye surgery in 2002 and 2003. In fact, the past two years, use of sick leave and vacation combined, you were out of the office 113 days. As the only support person in the office, this has presented challenges in the functionality and duties associated with the office." A jury might view this memorandum as evidence that Goelzer lost her job because she exercised her right to take FMLA leave, as it might Payne's comments in an evaluation he wrote in January 2006: "On occasion, I have been concerned with office and phone coverage. Dorothy had numerous appointments the past year and needs to be more cognitive of the time she is away from her desk or corresponding with others on non-related work activities." The defendants do not dispute that the FMLA protected Goelzer's attendance at these appointments, and a jury could look to those comments as indication that Payne was not pleased Goelzer had been absent for many FMLA-covered appointments, even though she was permitted to take them by the Act and an employer is not to interfere with that right.

Moreover, although Payne now maintains he had concerns about Goelzer's skill set and performance, he consistently gave her favorable performance reviews. He says now that her satisfactory performance ratings reflect his "lowered expectations" of her abilities, but the performance ratings themselves do not speak of lowered expectations, and a jury would not be compelled to credit this explanation. In fact, just over seven months before Payne told Goelzer she was being terminated, he had conducted Goelzer's annual performance review and concluded that her performance met or exceeded expectations in all areas.

A factfinder might also consider that, if Payne had serious problems with Goelzer's performance, he could have asked the County Board to terminate Goelzer's employment before he received the promotion, yet he did not do so. In addition, although Payne asserts that he wanted an assistant with a larger skill set, there are no documents evidencing a plan to restructure the assistant position before Goelzer's termination. And, of course, Payne told Goelzer that she was losing her job two weeks before she was scheduled to take two months of FMLA leave. In short, we are left with two competing accounts, either of which a jury could believe. So summary judgment is not appropriate, and we reverse its grant.

B. FMLA Retaliation

Goelzer also contends her FMLA retaliation theory should proceed to trial. The FMLA provides that it is unlawful for an employer "to discharge or in any manner discriminate against" any employee for opposing any practice the FMLA makes unlawful. 29 U.S.C. §2615(a)(2). The difference between a retaliation and interference theory is that the first "requires proof of discriminatory or retaliatory intent while [an interference theory] requires only proof that the employer denied the employee his or her entitlements under the Act." *Kauffman* [*v. Fed. Express Corp.*, 426 F.3d 880, 884 (7th Cir. 2005)]. To succeed on a retaliation claim, the plaintiff does not need to prove that "retaliation was the *only* reason for her termination; she may establish an FMLA retaliation claim by 'showing that the protected conduct was a substantial or motivating factor in the employer's decision'" *Lewis*.

A plaintiff may proceed under the direct or indirect methods of proof when attempting to establish an FMLA retaliation claim. *Burnett*. Under the direct method, the only method Goelzer employs, a plaintiff must present evidence that her employer took a materially adverse action against her because of her protected activity. If the plaintiff's evidence is contradicted, the case must proceed to trial unless the employer presents unrebutted evidence that it would have taken the adverse action against the plaintiff even if it did not have a retaliatory motive. That is, the plaintiff survives summary judgment by "'creating a triable issue of whether the adverse employment action of which she complains had a discriminatory motivation.'" *Lewis*.

Payne and the County maintain that a jury could not conclude that they intentionally discriminated against Goelzer for using FMLA leave. In addition to the evidence to which she pointed in support of her interference claim, Goelzer also directs our attention to Human Resources Director Collard's inquiry to Goelzer's physician that asked "[w]hether Ms. Goelzer would be physically able to work light duty in an office environment prior to November 19, 2006, and if so, when would be an appropriate time that we would expect her to return." [This inquiry likely violated the regulations which, at the time, prohibited an employer contacting an employee's physician without his permission. 29 C.F.R. §825.307. As since amended, the regulation allows an employer to "contact the health care provider for purposes of clarification and authentication of the medical certification . . . after the employer has given the employee an opportunity to cure any deficiencies. . . ." While the FMLA does not appear to provide a right to relief unless a violation of this regulation results in interference with the employee's rights under the statute, plaintiff] asserts that Collard's inquiry to her doctor supports her claim that the defendants had retaliated against her for using her FMLA leave.

Even if Collard's inquiry is put to the side, there is enough evidence in the record for a jury to find that the defendants fired Goelzer because she had utilized FMLA leave and not because Payne wanted to hire a new person with more skills. For example, Goelzer had received positive performance reviews, and none suggest on their face that they were the result of any "lowered expectations" from Payne. Payne denies that he made any oral derogatory comments regarding Goelzer's FMLA use, but that is for the jury to decide, and in any event the jury might view his written comments on Goelzer's performance evaluations regarding her use of FMLA leave as evidence that her use of FMLA leave motivated the termination decision. Payne also communicated the termination decision after he knew Goelzer planned to be out for two months on FMLA leave, and she had utilized a significant amount of FMLA leave in the years preceding the decision. Although the defendants disclaim any causal connection between Goelzer's requests for and use of FMLA leave and her firing, we conclude that a jury could find otherwise. As is the case with her interference theory, then, summary judgment is not appropriate on her retaliation action, and we reverse its grant in the defendants' favor. . . .

NOTES

1. *Qualifying Conditions.* There was no dispute in *Goelzer* that plaintiff's various leaves were both authentic and qualifying. That is, the defendant did not challenge either the genuineness of plaintiff's reasons for seeking leave or that these reasons satisfied the FMLA's requirements. The genuineness of employee claims is obviously often a difficult question for human resource departments, and the problem is made more difficult by the FMLA's limitations on contacting the plaintiff's doctor. Do you see why an employer might be satisfied with a doctor's note, and not wish to inquire further?

As for whether a particular set of circumstances qualifies for FMLA leave, that is often a complicated question. Perhaps the most difficult arises with respect to whether the plaintiff (or a family member) has a "serious health condition."

2. *Serious Health Conditions.* As you might expect, "serious health condition" is a term of art under the statute, and one that is extensively addressed by Department of Labor regulations. To appreciate some of the complexities, consider *Russell v. N. Broward Hosp.*, 346 F.3d 1335 (11th Cir. 2003). There, the defendant did not deny that Russell was out for medical reasons, but it argued that her absences were nonetheless not protected leave under the FMLA. Although Russell was badly injured (she fell at work, and was diagnosed with a fractured right elbow and a sprained ankle and related problems), the court found that her injury did not constitute a "serious health condition" under the FMLA. That was because the statute defines a "serious health condition" as "an illness, injury, impairment, or physical or mental condition that involves — (A) inpatient care in a hospital, hospice, or residential medical care facility; or (B) continuing treatment by a health care provider." *Id.* § 2611(11). Russell was not admitted to a hospital, so eligibility turned on whether she had undergone continuing treatment. While the statute itself does not define that term, the Department of Labor provided a detailed definition:

> (2) *Continuing Treatment* by a health care provider. A serious health condition involving continuing treatment by a health care provider includes any one or more of the following:
>
> > (i) A period of incapacity (i.e., inability to work, attend school or perform other regular daily activities due to the serious health condition, treatment therefor, or recovery therefrom) of more than three consecutive calendar days, and any subsequent treatment or period of incapacity relating to the same condition, that also involves:
> >
> > > (A) Treatment two or more times by a health care provider, by a nurse or physician's assistant under direct supervision of a health care provider, or by a provider of health care services (e.g., physical therapist) under orders of, or on referral by, a health care provider; or
> > >
> > > (B) Treatment by a health care provider on at least one occasion which results in a regimen of continuing treatment under the supervision of the health care provider. . . .

29 C.F.R. §825.113(a)(2)(i). Because Ms. Russell was not incapacitated for "more than three consecutive days," she was not entitled to FMLA leave. Although she was partially incapacitated for a number of days over a ten-day period, she was not fully incapacitated for the requisite time. While the regulations also provide for other varieties of "continuing treatment," such as incapacity due to pregnancy or prenatal care or due to a chronic serious health condition such as asthma, diabetes, or epilepsy, §825.113, none of these alternatives was applicable to plaintiff's situation. *See generally* Leslie A. Barry, Note, *Determining the Proper Standard of Proof for Incapacity Under the Family and Medical Leave Act*, 97 Iowa L. Rev. 931 (2012).

3. *Denial of Merit Raises.* Plaintiff in the principal case seemed to challenge only her dismissal. What if she had challenged the denial of a merit raise? Payne's own statements would seem to establish that her leave was a factor in denying a raise. That would mean that she should win on such a claim, regardless of the reason for her ultimate termination. Or is there something odd about having to factor in as much as 12 weeks of absenteeism in making merit determinations?

4. *Interference.* Do you understand the difference between the "interference" and "retaliation" claims at issue in *Goelzer*? Section 2615(a)(1) of the Act sets out the interference claim, providing:

> Exercise of rights. It shall be unlawful for any employer to interfere with, restrain, or deny the exercise of or the attempt to exercise, any right provided under this subchapter.

The paradigm cases under this provision are an employer's denial of a leave in the first place or its refusal to reinstate the employee to a comparable position when the leave is over. These disputes, then, typically boil down to whether the employee is leave-eligible. Thus, while the plaintiff has the burden of persuasion, carrying it does not require any proof of employer intent. As *Goelzer* frames it, "an employee must show that: (1) she was eligible for the FMLA's protections; (2) her employer was covered by the FMLA; (3) she was entitled to take leave under the FMLA; (4) she provided sufficient notice of her intent to take leave; and (5) her employer denied her FMLA benefits to which she was entitled."

However, the statute expressly provides that a restored employee is *not* entitled to "any right, benefit, or position of employment other than any right, benefit, or position to which the employee would have been entitled had the employee not taken the leave." 29 U.S.C. 2614(a)(3)(B). Thus, as recognized in the regulations, an employer may deny reinstatement to an employee on FMLA leave if that employee would have been terminated or her job eliminated had she continued working. *See* 29 C.F.R. 825.216; *Batacan v. Reliant Pharms., Inc.*, 228 F. App'x 702, 704 (9th Cir. 2007) (since an employee on leave has no greater right to reinstatement than if she had been continuously employed, "an employee taking FMLA leave may be terminated pursuant to a legitimate reduction in force.").

As applied to Ms. Goelzer, the only question was whether she would have been discharged in any event, and the Seventh Circuit has placed the burden of persuasion under the interference clause on the employee. *Rice v. Sunrise Express, Inc.*, 209 F.3d 1008, 1018 (7th Cir. 2000) ("the employee always bears the ultimate burden of establishing the right to the benefit" under the interference clause).

It is true that *Goelzer* quotes the Department of Labor regulations that appear to place a burden on the employer when it claims that the employee would have been terminated in any event: "An employer must be able to show that an employee would not otherwise have been employed at the time reinstatement is requested in order to deny restoration to employment." 29 C.F.R. § 825.216(a)(1). But the Seventh Circuit does not view this as justifying burden shifting; rather, it reads it as simply stating the substantive law. The other circuits to have squarely addressed the question have concluded the contrary. *Phillips v. Matthews*, 547 F.3d 905, 911 (8th Cir. 2008) ("The burden is on the employer to prove the reason for termination was unrelated to FMLA."); *Smith v. Diffee Ford-Lincoln-Mercury, Inc.*, 298 F.3d 955, 963 (10th Cir. 2002) ("[T]he regulation validly shifts to the employer the burden of proving that an employee, laid off during FMLA leave, would have been dismissed regardless of the employee's request for, or taking of, FMLA leave."). At any rate, the court finds a jury question on the issue — although Payne had "skill set" reasons for replacing Goelzer, there was genuine issue of material fact as to whether her past use of leave and her currently being "on track to use nearly 400 hours" influenced his decision. *See generally* Rachel Arnow-Richman, *Accommodation Subverted: The Future of Work/Family Initiatives in a "Me, Inc." World*, 12 Tex. J. Women & L. 345, 371 (2003) (criticizing *Rice* as contradicting the FMLA's accommodation-oriented approach to caregiving). *See also* Martin H. Malin, *Interference with the Right to Leave Under the Family and Medical Leave Act*, 7 Emp. Rts. & Emp. Pol'y J. 329 (2003).

5. *Retaliation.* Section 2615(a)(2) provides that it is unlawful for an employer "to discharge or in any other manner discriminate against any individual for opposing any practice made unlawful by this subchapter." The paradigm case for this is the employer who grants leave and reinstates the employee but then later discharges her for taking such leave. The circuits have agreed that lesser adverse actions will also support an FMLA retaliation claim, adopting the Title VII approach of *Burlington Northern & Santa Fe Railway v. White*, 548 U.S. 53 (2006), *see* page 720, which looks to whether the action taken would deter a reasonable employee from exercising his statutory rights. *See Crawford v. JP Morgan Chase & Co.*, 531 F. App'x 622, 627 (6th Cir. 2013) ("We join our sister circuits in concluding that *Burlington* applies to retaliation claims under the FMLA.").

Unlike an interference claim, a plaintiff making a retaliation claim must demonstrate not only a right to leave but also that the employer had a discriminatory reason for denying reinstatement or taking other adverse action. The courts generally apply Title VII proof structures to determine whether the requisite intent exists. *See, e.g., Brungart v. BellSouth Telecomms., Inc.* 231 F.3d 791, 798 (11th Cir. 2000). And some circuits have carried over the "honest belief" rule from Title VII cases to the FMLA. *See* page 584. In other words, a retaliation claim will fail even though the employee suffered an adverse employment action for seeking or using FMLA leave if the employer honestly believed the employee was abusing such leave. *E.g., Tillman v. Ohio Bell Tel. Co.*, 545 F. App'x 340, (6th Cir. 2013; *Medley v. Polk Co.*, 260 F.3d 1202, (10th Cir. 2001).

You may have noticed that the *Goelzer* court applied the "motivating factor analysis" to the causation issue regarding plaintiff's retaliation claim. The origins of this rule under the FMLA precede the Supreme Court's interpretation of the ADEA, *Gross v. FBL Fin. Servs., Inc.*, 557 U.S. 167 (2009), and, more pointedly, the retaliation protection of Title VII, *Univ. of Tex. Sw. Med. Ctr. v. Nassar*, 133 S. Ct. 2517 (2013), both of which require plaintiff to prove "determinative factor" or but-for causation. *See* pages 607-08. *Goelzer's* application of "contributing factor" in an FMLA case, accordingly, is suspect, but some circuits have continued to use motivating factor analysis in the wake of one or both of the Supreme Court's decisions. *See, e.g., Ion v. Chevron USA, Inc.*, 731 F.3d 379 (5th Cir. 2013); *Hunter v. Valley View Local Sch.*, 579 F.3d 688 (6th Cir. 2009).

6. *Role of the Regulations.* Given the vagueness of the statute and the (comparative) specificity of the regulations, a frequent question under the FMLA will be the meaning and validity of the Department of Labor's regulations. *See Downey v. Strain*, 510 F.3d 534 (5th Cir. 2007) (upholding regulations requiring employers to provide workers with individual notice that leave would be viewed as FMLA leave). The FMLA delegated to the Secretary of Labor the authority to "prescribe such regulations as are necessary to carry out" the FMLA's general requirements for leave. 29 U.S.C. § 2654. Under familiar principles of administrative law, that means substantial deference to the agency's interpretation of the statute.

We have encountered the "*Chevron* question" of the validity of administrative agency regulations in the context of the ADA in Chapter 9 where we saw that the pattern of deference was pretty checkered; indeed, the ADAAA was passed in part to reinforce EEOC authority. *See Summers v. Altarum Inst., Corp.*, reproduced at page 734. Neither has the Department of Labor gotten a free pass from the Court. *Ragsdale v. Wolverine World Wide, Inc.*, 535 U.S. 81 (2002), rejected a Department of Labor regulation providing that leave may not count against an employee's FMLA entitlement unless the employer promptly notified the employee that the leave has been designated as FMLA leave. The Court viewed the regulation as inconsistent with the statutory requirement of only 12 weeks of leave a year. Importantly, Ragsdale could not show that she had been prejudiced or harmed by the employer's failure to give notice. The Court did not decide what would happen in a case when an employee could show harm flowing from the employer's failure to provide notice.

7. *Intermittent Leave.* Notice that in *Goelzer*, the plaintiff often took "intermittent leave," typically for doctors' appointments. While leave is frequently thought of in extended terms, FMLA leave may be taken intermittently in blocks as small as an hour at a time (and, as discussed in the next note, without prior notice if the need for leave is unforeseeable). Obviously, some triggers for FMLA leave do not raise the question of intermittent leave (for example, illness for three days), while others often will (continuing treatment by a health care provider). Intermittent leave is required only when it is medically necessary, *Haggard v. Levi Strauss & Co.*, 8 F. App'x 599 (8th Cir. 2001) (physician's note for employee working half-days did not trigger right to intermittent leave because it did not state the medical necessity for the leave), which distinguishes it from other kinds of leave under the statute.

Because of the scheduling difficulties and potential disruption of such leave (and, perhaps because there is less of a pay "hit" for employees availing themselves of intermittent leave), some employers assert that this one is of the most onerous requirements of the FMLA. *See* Eric Paltell, *Intermittent Leave Under the Family and Medical Leave Act of 1993: Job Security for the Chronically Absent Employee?*, 10 LAB. LAW. 1 (1994). Do you think such concerns are legitimate or are they likely overstated? Do the facts in *Goelzer* influence your opinion?

Responding to these kinds of concerns, the statute and its regulations allow an employer to transfer an employee who seeks intermittent leave from a job where attendance is vital to an equivalent position where the employee's periodic absences will be less burdensome. 29 U.S.C. § 2612(b)(2); 29 C.F.R. § 825.204; *see Spangler v. Fed. Home Loan Bank of Des Moines*, 278 F.3d 847, 853 (8th Cir. 2002); *see also Carmona v. Sw. Airlines Co.*, 604 F.3d 848, 860 n.3 (5th Cir. 2010) ("[W]hile the FMLA can excuse an employee from his employer's ordinary attendance requirements, it does not do so where the employee requests the right to take intermittent leave without notice indefinitely. The FMLA also does not prevent the employee from being transferred to a different job with equivalent pay and benefits where his periodic absences will do less damage to the business."). *See generally* S. Elizabeth Wilborn Malloy, *The Interaction of the ADA, the FMLA, and Workers' Compensation: Why Can't We Be Friends?*, 41 BRANDEIS L.J. 821, 837 (2003).

8. *Employee Notice Requirements.* Another compliance issue that frequently arises in FMLA litigation concerns the law's notice requirements. The statute provides that, when the need for leave is foreseeable, an employee must generally give her employer no less than 30 days' advance notice, although there is some flexibility built into the regulations when it is not possible to do so. *See* 29 U.S.C. § 2612(e)(1) & (2)(B); 29 C.F.R. § 825.302. Goelzer apparently met these requirements, but not all employees are so careful. *See Righi v. SMC Corp. of Am.*, 632 F.3d 404 (7th Cir. 2011) (plaintiff's nine-day absence during a period that included six work days required notice; his vague reference to needing "the next couple days" could not be considered adequate notice of a request for FMLA leave of that more substantial duration). *Cf. Gienapp v. Harbor Crest*, 756 F.3d 527, 531 (7th Cir. 2014) (when an employee took qualified leave to care for her daughter who was suffering from cancer, the length of that leave was unforeseeable; employees are not required to tell the employer how much leave they need when they do not yet know themselves).

While the statute does not address notice requirements when leave is unforeseeable, the regulations provide that notice be given to the employer "as soon as practicable," and that should generally be "within the time prescribed by the employer's usual and customary notice requirements applicable to such leave." 29 C.F.R. § 825.303(a). The regulations go on to detail to whom notice may be given, by whom notice may be given, and how it may be provided. 29 C.F.R. § 825.303(b). "The employee need not expressly assert rights under the FMLA or even mention the FMLA, but need state only that leave is needed. The employer will be expected to obtain any additional required information through informal means." *Id. See Clinkscale v. St. Therese of New Hope*, 701 F.3d 825 (8th Cir. 2012) (an employee's exhibiting signs of severe distress and anxiety, causing her to be instructed to go home followed by a doctor's note the next day created a jury question as to whether she had provided the requisite notice a potentially FMLA-qualifying condition).

This can create some compliance challenges for the employer who must determine when it is appropriate to seek such additional information. While the employer will want to know if the leave is FMLA-eligible, most routine illnesses and common injuries do not trigger statutory protection. The employer may wish to balance its desire for certainty against administrative convenience issues as well as the potential awkwardness (and other liability risks) that may result from probing into an employee's personal situation. Recall from *Goelzer* that the regulations do not give the employer a blank check in following up with a health care provider.

The notice provisions can also create pitfalls for employees. Although the regulations are very generous to employees, particularly with respect to unforeseen needs, employees will not be entitled to FMLA leave unless they provide their employer information "sufficient to reasonably apprise it of the employee's request to take time off for a serious health condition." The point is that, even if the employee has what constitutes a qualifying condition, there is a further obligation to adequately inform the employer. *Compare Carter v. Ford Motor Co.*, 121 F.3d 1146 (8th Cir. 1997) (notice insufficient when Carter informed Ford that he was sick and did not know when he could return to work but did not offer further information regarding his condition); *Collins v. NTN-Bower Corp.*, 272 F.3d 1006 (7th Cir. 2001) (telling employer that employee was "sick" not sufficient); *with Spangler v. Fed. Home Loan Bank*, 278 F.3d 847 (8th Cir. 2002) (requesting time off for "depression again" is possibly a valid request when employer knew employee suffered from depression); *Price v. City of Fort Wayne*, 117 F.3d 1022 (7th Cir. 1997) (notice sufficient when employee filled out employer-provided leave request form, indicated that cause was medical need, and attached doctor's note requiring her to take the time off).

9. *Perfect Attendance Programs.* The effect of the FMLA on incentive programs to reward attendance generated considerable controversy. A plain language reading of the statute would seem to make individuals on FMLA-leave eligible, but such incentive programs arguably substantially improve productivity. The amended regulations make clear that such programs are permissible, even when they exclude participation by those taking FMLA leave. 29 C.F.R. §215(c)(2).

10. *The FMLA and the ADA.* The ADA and the FMLA overlap to some extent. Individuals who are covered by both statutes have more than one option for dealing with an impairment that necessitates frequent absences. Even if leave would not be a reasonable accommodation given their employer's needs, leave without pay under the FMLA is a statutory right as long as the employer is provided with adequate notice. In addition, employees with attendance problems that are health related, but who are not disabled within the meaning of the ADA, will still be entitled to leave without pay if their health problem is a "serious health condition" under the FMLA. The overlap between the ADA and FMLA can create tricky compliance issues for the employer, as well. For example, while an employee with a serious health condition will max out her FMLA entitlement after 12 weeks, if the employee's condition qualifies as a disability and she requests additional leave, the employer must consider whether granting it would be a reasonable accommodation.

11. *Individual Liability.* Unlike the antidiscrimination statutes but similar to the Fair Labor Standards Act (FLSA), the FMLA has been held to provide for individual liability for individuals acting for the employer, at least where private employers are concerned and perhaps for public employers as well. *See* 29 C.F.R. §825.104(d);

Haybarger v. Lawrence Cnty. Adult Prob. & Parole, 667 F.3d 408 (3d Cir. 2012). For example, Goelzer sued Adam Payne personally. *See generally* Sandra F. Sperino, *Under Construction: Questioning Whether Statutory Construction Principles Justify Individual Liability Under the Family and Medical Leave Act*, 71 Mo. L. Rev. 71 (2006); Sandra F. Sperino, *Chaos Theory: The Unintended Consequences of Expanding Individual Liability Under the Family and Medical Leave Act*, 9 Emp. Rts. & Emp. Pol'y J. 175 (2005). Given what you know about the two statutes, does it make sense to hold individuals liable for FMLA and minimum wage violations and leave violations but not gender discrimination?

12. *Counseling the Employer.* Prior to her health problems, Goelzer was frequently praised by Payne for her good attendance. In hindsight, was that a mistake? It certainly helped plaintiff establish that her later attendance problems were likely to be viewed as very problematic by him. Or was the problem not the earlier praise but Payne's repeated references to her absences after she began using her leave? And what about "the problem employee," the one who frequently misses work for questionable reasons? In *Russell*, the plaintiff had had attendance problems well before the accident that led to her discharge. It's possible, even probable, that the hospital believed she was malingering, or at least making a mountain out of a molehill. Of course, the hospital might be right or wrong in this belief, but, in an at-will world, it would be free to discharge such workers without fear of liability. Does the FMLA unduly restrict employers' ability to deal with such problems? *See* Sara Schlaefer Muoz, *A Good Idea, But . . . : Some Businesses Complain That the Family and Medical Leave Act Should Be More Aptly Named the Slackers Protection Act*, Wall St. J., Jan. 24, 2005. To what extent do problems like this suggest attorney involvement in what seem like normal human resources processes?

* * *

While a casebook tends to focus on cases, employers tend to view statutes like the FMLA as requiring systemic changes in employment policies. Thus, almost all covered employers have overhauled their leave policies in response to the passage of the statute. Attorneys representing employers will, therefore, frequently be involved in the task of drafting such policies and occasionally in the task of interpreting them when particularly problematic situations arise. One skill of the employer's lawyer, when wearing her drafting hat, is to create policies that are both legal and administrable by the Human Resources Department. The next problem asks you to do just that.

PROBLEMS

10-3. You are U.S. counsel for Ocyllis, Inc., a Canadian firm that has just acquired an American corporation. The Canadian general counsel, your boss, has asked you to review the possible application of several of Ocyllis's personnel policies for possible application and/or modification in the United States. The first such policy is reproduced below:

1. *Intent.* This policy is designed to facilitate reasonably flexible arrangements at the time of birth or adoption of children. The policy will enable both parents to combine a productive career with family responsibilities with minimal impact on the corporation.

2. *Eligibility.* Full-time and part-time employees, who have at least 13 weeks' continuous employment at the Corporation prior to the birth or adoption of a child are eligible for pregnancy, paternity, and/or parental leave. To be eligible for financial benefits from the Corporation, employees must have 26 weeks of continuous service prior to birth or adoption.

3. *Pregnancy Leave.* Pregnancy leave is available only to natural mothers. An eligible employee is entitled to paid pregnancy leave for up to 19 weeks at 85 percent of full pay. In exceptional circumstances, a pregnancy leave may be extended beyond the 19-week period, at the discretion of the Ocyllis Board of Directors. An employee is normally expected to give four weeks' notice of the date of return to work, should this be different from the previously agreed date.

4. *Paternity Leave.* Paternity leave is available only to natural fathers. An eligible employee is entitled to two weeks' leave with full salary, pay and benefits. Leave must be taken within the first 26 weeks after the birth of the child.

5. *Parental Leave.* Parental leave is available to all parents, natural and adoptive. An eligible employee is entitled to unpaid leave for up to 35 weeks. For natural mothers and fathers, parental leave is in addition to pregnancy or paternity leave. For natural mothers, parental leave commences when pregnancy leave ends. For natural fathers and adoptive parents, parental leave must begin no later than 52 weeks after the birth of the child or the date the adopted child first comes into the custody, care, and control of the employee.

6. *Benefits During Leave.* Employees who take advantage of these provisions will incur no loss in salary level and will be entitled to pension, health disability, and other benefits provided the employee contributes the necessary amount of the cost of benefits. Vacation and sick leave shall continue to accrue during leave.

Advise Ocyllis to what extent U.S. law requires changes in this policy. Note also where the policy may be more generous than U.S. law requires and advise Ocyllis on whether extending those provisions to its American operations is desirable.

10-4. You have now learned some of the basic nuts and bolts of FMLA coverage and enforcement and have had the opportunity to try your hand at implementing the law through a workplace policy. In light of this knowledge, imagine that you are a legislative aide to a U.S. Senator who has a strong interest in work/family issues and has publicly committed to introducing legislation to redress some of the perceived shortcomings of current law. She has asked you to do preliminary research and advise her about possible approaches. What would you recommend? Would you amend existing legislation like the FMLA or the PDA? Or might you propose new legislation? Who would your proposal protect and what would it require? Would it apply to all businesses and all workers, and, if not, how would you limit it? To the extent your proposal would generate costs, how should they be allocated among employers, workers, and/or taxpayers? Are there ways of framing your proposal that might be responsive to potential political and social resistance?

11

Wages and Benefits

This chapter provides an introduction to direct regulation of employee compensation, which includes wages, in-kind wage substitutes, and "fringe benefits," most notably health coverage, retirement benefits, and profit-sharing plans. This contrasts with some of the mandates discussed in the previous chapters that can protect compensation, but less directly. *See generally* Nantiya Ryan & Nancy Reichman, *Hours Equity Is the New Pay Equity*, 59 VILL. L. REV. 35 (2014) (discussing the various statutory frameworks for wage and hour equity in the workplace). For example, because worker pay and benefits are "terms and conditions of employment," the discriminatory behavior we studied in Chapter 9 that adversely affects these conditions is prohibited. In addition, in Chapter 10 we learned that the Family and Medical Leave Act mandates that employers maintain health benefits for employees during periods of leave covered by the statute, and the Pregnancy Discrimination Act requires employers to treat pregnancy-related leave the same as other types of short-term disability-based leave. Moreover, there are other employer-funded benefits or protections, such as mandated workers' compensation for work-related injuries and unemployment insurance.

Despite these limitations and the laws treated below, most compensation received by most workers is the result of private ordering. The vast majority of workers in the United States earn in excess of the wages mandated by the Fair Labor Standards Act ("FLSA"), 29 U.S.C.A. § 201-19 (2014), and state labor laws. These wages, therefore, are a result of individual employee-employer negotiation, collective bargaining, or, more generally, labor market forces, rather than regulation. In addition, as discussed in Chapter 1, to the extent that workers and firms may structure their relationships to avoid "employment" (usually through firm-independent contractor relationships), most of the protections discussed in this chapter do not apply at all. And, as we will address below, many employees are exempt from the FLSA's wage requirements.

Similarly, with very few exceptions, employers historically have not been obligated to provide their workers with health or retirement benefits. It is only their decision to do so that triggers the mandates of the Employee Retirement Income Security Act ("ERISA"), 29 U.S.C. § 1001-1461 (2014). However, as part of the health care reform package Congress passed in 2010, large employers are subject to tax penalties if they fail to provide health insurance coverage or provide coverage that is unaffordable, and their full-time employees qualify for subsidized coverage elsewhere. *See* 26 U.S.C. §4980H (2014).

This chapter focuses primarily on wage and hour protections and, in particular, the scope and limitations of the FLSA. Along the way, it will also touch on state wage and hour mandates. The chapter will conclude with a brief introduction to benefits regulation, outlining the broad contours of ERISA and the employer provisions of the new health care reform package.

A. WAGE PROTECTIONS

Wage protections for workers have a mixed history in the United States. Long before federal labor statutes favoring collective bargaining, *see* National Labor Relations Act, codified as amended at 29 U.S.C. §151-69 (2014), there were attempts to regulate directly abuses by employers. Some of the earliest efforts were state laws restricting child labor. Although a number of jurisdictions also passed statutes controlling the hours of employment of adults, the most far-reaching were frequently struck down by the Supreme Court in the substantive due process period when the Supreme Court interpreted the Fourteenth Amendment to prohibit states from "interfering" with employment contracts. *See, e.g., Lochner v. New York*, 198 U.S. 45 (1905). One major exception to Supreme Court hostility to such regulation was with respect to women. The famous Brandeis Brief provided the Supreme Court in *Muller v. Oregon*, 208 U.S. 412 (1908), with a basis for upholding legislation "protecting" women by limiting their hours of employment, while similar statutes applied to men were being struck down.

With the demise of substantive due process, *see, e.g., Opp Cotton Mills Inc. v. Adm'r of Wage & Hour Div.*, 312 U.S. 126 (1941); *W. Coast Hotel Co. v. Parrish*, 300 U.S. 379 (1937), statutes directly regulating hours worked and wages paid became the norm in the United States. At the federal level, the FLSA is the primary mechanism for dealing with perceived employer abuses. However, a number of other federal, state, and local laws also directly regulate worker pay.

Of course, government control of wage levels has always had its critics. Some claim that establishing a minimum wage above market rates harms social welfare and has adverse effects on the working poor, including artificially reducing the demand for labor. David Neumark & William Wascher, *Minimum Wages and Low-Wage Workers: How Well Does Reality Match the Rhetoric?* 92 MINN. L. REV. 1296 (2008); Daniel Shaviro, *The Minimum Wage, the Earned Income Credit and Optimal Subsidy Policy*, 64 U. CHI. L. REV. 405 (1997); *see also* John Foley, *Questioning the Merits of Federal Minimum Wage Legislation*, 5 GEO. J. L. & PUB. POL'Y 679 (2007) (arguing that the minimum wage increases unemployment, leads to higher inflation, and produces other detrimental effects on the poor). Others support the minimum wage on traditional and not-so-traditional grounds. *See, e.g.*, Bruce E. Kaufman, *Institutional Economics and the Minimum Wage: Broadening the Theoretical and Policy Debate*, 63 IND. & LAB. REL. REV. 427 (2010) (offering a number of justifications for the minimum wage, including addressing unequal bargaining power, promoting economic stability and long-term economic efficiency, and reducing labor market externalities); Noah D. Zatz, *The*

Minimum Wage as a Civil Rights Protection: An Alternative to the Antipoverty Arguments?, 1 U. CHI. LEGAL F. 1 (2009) (arguing that the minimum wage is justified not only as a poverty reduction tool, but also as a civil rights protection). Although the debate continues, most recent studies—often made possible by state-to-state differences in minimum wage floors—support the view that (at least modest) increases to the minimum wage have few adverse effects on employment rates, and recent surveys of economists tend to support the view that the overall benefits of modest increases outweigh the costs. *See, e.g.*, Dale Belman & Paul Wolfson, *The New Minimum Wage Research*, 21 UPJOHN INST. EMPL. RESEARCH NEWSLETTER No. 2 (April 2014), available at http://research.upjohn.org/cgi/viewcontent.cgi?article=1220&context=empl_research (summarizing the research); Chicago Booth, *Minimum Wage*, IGM Forum (Feb. 13, 2013), available at http://www.igmchicago.org/igm-economic-experts-panel/poll-results?SurveyID=SV_br0IEq5a9E77NMV (showing economists' survey responses); FISCAL POLICY INSTITUTE, STATES WITH MINIMUM WAGES ABOVE THE FEDERAL LEVEL HAVE HAD FASTER SMALL BUSINESS AND RETAIL JOB GROWTH (March 30, 2006), *available at* http://www.fiscalpolicy.org/FPISmallBusinessMin-Wage.pdf (finding employment in the retail sector showed greater improvement in areas of the country with higher state and local minimum wage requirements, possibly due to the greater spending power of low-wage workers); Richard A. Ippolito, *The Impact of the Minimum Wage If Workers Can Adjust Effort*, 46 J. LAW & ECON. 207 (2003) (contending that the minimum wage has little effect on employment, output, and profits).

The issue of the government's role in regulating wages is debated cyclically in Congress when efforts are made to increase the FLSA minimum wage. *See* William P. Quigley, *Full-Time Workers Should Not Be Poor: The Living Wage Movement*, 70 MISS. L. J. 889, 909-19 (2001). And, as explored in Chapter 1, discussions of wage regulation and wages generally are tied to other hot-button issues, including immigration. Perhaps unsurprisingly, although the basic protections afforded by the FLSA have persisted, the opponents of government regulation of wages have gained the upper hand at times, at least at the national level. For example, after an increase in 1997, the minimum wage remained at $5.15 an hour for a decade—reflecting a sharp decline in real wages. Moreover, as discussed below, some believe that the practical effect of new Department of Labor ("DOL") regulations promulgated in 2004 is to exempt more workers from the FLSA's overtime protections. The last time Congress enacted legislation increasing the minimum wage was in 2007. The floor increased in three steps, culminating in 2009 at $7.25 an hour. *See* 29 U.S.C.A. § 206(a)(1)(C) (2010). This increase also has had an impact on state law, which may provide protection for classes of workers excluded from coverage under the FLSA. For example, the federal increase boosted minimum wage levels in those jurisdictions that tie their wage requirements to federal law. The federal mandate now exceeds the minimum wage in some states, although a sizable number of states and municipalities have enacted a wage floor above the federal level. *See, e.g.*, U.S. Department of Labor Employment Standards Administration Wage and Hour Division, Minimum Wage Laws in the States, September 1, 2014, *available at* http://www.dol.gov/esa/minwage/america.htm (listing state minimum wage requirements). In addition, states often enact other kinds of wage protections or requirements, including wage payment laws that provide for civil and criminal liability for failure to pay promised wages.

1. The FLSA

The original purposes of the FLSA were to prevent certain historic employer abuses of labor — including child labor — and to ensure that every covered employee received at least a basic minimum wage and a premium for work exceeding the standard number of hours per week. The statute was also designed — through its overtime pay provisions — to create incentives to spread employment over a greater number of workers. Thus, the FLSA requires covered employers to pay covered employees a minimum wage (again, currently $7.25 for most covered workers); it also requires employers to pay workers an overtime premium at one half their "regular rate of pay" for hours worked in excess of 40 hours per week. *See* 29 U.S.C.A. §206(a)-(b), 207(a)(1) (2014). It is worth noting, however, that the FLSA's overtime provisions do not limit the number of hours an employee may be required to work and thus the statute does not protect from discharge workers who refuse to work overtime.

The FLSA also contains the Equal Pay Act, a very limited ban on sex discrimination in pay, *see id.* at §206(d), and provisions designed to curtail oppressive child labor and protect children's safety and educational opportunities, particularly for children under 16 years of age, *see id.* at §212(c). Finally, it establishes certain wage-related record-keeping requirements for employers. *See id.* at §211. Most of the planning, litigation, and public policy issues, however, relate to the minimum wage and overtime requirements.

With some exceptions, the substantive requirements of the FLSA are straightforward; in other words, when they are applicable, the FLSA's wage and hour requirements are fairly simple to apply. They are also mandatory and, hence, for the most part, cannot be waived via contract. Thus, private ordering plays a relatively small role where the FLSA operates. Of course, this raises an interesting, overarching policy question: Should the requirements of the FLSA be mandatory, or should employees and employers be allowed to waive these requirements, at least in some circumstances?

Nevertheless, given the current statutory and regulatory framework, FLSA litigation usually focuses on the statute's coverage — that is, issues surrounding who constitutes an "employee," who constitutes a covered employer, and who is otherwise exempt from the FLSA's protections or mandates. A few application issues have led to significant litigation, including determining what constitutes hours "worked" and calculating "rate of pay" for purposes of overtime.

a. Scope of Coverage

i. Employee and Employer

Because the FLSA broadly governs "employees" engaged in interstate commerce, the first step in determining whether the act applies at all is to determine whether a worker is an "employee" rather than another kind of worker — in most circumstances, an independent contractor. This definition of "employee" was addressed at length in Chapter 1, and its application in the FLSA context in particular was addressed in *Ansoumana v. Gristede's Operating Corp.*, reproduced at page 34.

Ansoumana also discussed aspects of who qualifies as an "employer" for FLSA purposes. Recall that there may be more than one "employer": a separate entity may be liable under the FLSA as a "joint employer." Moreover, supervisory personnel with direct control over employees may qualify as "employers" and, hence, may be individually liable for violations along with the firm or entity they control. Such personal liability for statutory violations is not unique but is quite rare. As *Ansoumana* indicated, extending liability to individual officers or controlling persons ensures that responsible parties have strong incentives to comply with the statute's mandates.

The *Ansoumana* decision, however, did not address the FLSA's "commerce" and "enterprise" coverage provisions. Any *employee* "engaged in commerce or in the production of goods for commerce" is covered by the Act, whether or not the employer is an enterprise engaged in commerce as statutorily defined. 29 U.S.C. § 206(a), 207(a)(1) (2014); *see Brennan v. Arnheim & Neely, Inc.*, 410 U.S. 512, 516-17 (1973). To be engaged in commerce, individual employees must be "performing work involving or related to the movement of persons or things (whether tangibles or intangibles, and including information and intelligence)" between states. 29 C.F.R. § 779.103. In addition, an employee is engaged in commerce when regularly engaging in interstate communication (such a using the mails or telephone) or when regularly traveling across state lines while working. Substantial, rather than sporadic or de minimis, interstate activities are required. Whether an employee's interstate activities are sufficiently substantial is a fact-intensive inquiry. *See, e.g., Locke v. St. Augustine's Episcopal Church*, 690 F. Supp. 2d 77 (E.D.N.Y. 2010) (holding after a detailed factual analysis that a church janitor was not an employee engaged in commerce under the FLSA, nor was his employer an enterprise engaged in commerce); *Bowrin v. Catholic Guardian Society*, 417 F. Supp. 2d 449 (S.D.N.Y. 2006) (finding that employees of a charitable organization were not engaged in commerce in most tasks they performed, but some tasks involving interstate travel were covered activities).

On the other hand, even an employee who is not individually engaged in such commerce will be covered if he or she is "employed in an enterprise engaged in commerce or in the production of goods for commerce." 29 U.S.C. § 206(a), 207(a)(1). The most difficult and litigated aspect of this requirement is what constitutes an "enterprise." Indeed, the scope of the employing enterprise is important for several other reasons. First, the FLSA has a minimum dollar volume limitation; it currently does not apply to employing enterprises whose annual gross volume of sales is less than $500,000. 29 U.S.C. § 203(s)(1)(A)(ii). In addition, whether several operations or entities constitute a single enterprise may be dispositive of whether the statute's overtime mandates have been satisfied; for example, if an employee works for two separate entities that constitute a single enterprise, the sum of the hours the employee works for both entities during a week will determine whether the employee is entitled to an overtime premium. Finally, if liability under the FLSA is established, recovery may depend on the scope of the enterprise when one part of an entity within it is insolvent.

The FLSA defines "enterprise" as follows:

"Enterprise" means the related activities performed (either through unified operation or common control) by any person or persons for a common business purpose, and includes all such activities whether performed in one or more establishments or by one or more corporate or other organizational units including departments of an establishment operated through leasing arrangements, but shall not include the related activities performed for such enterprise by an independent contractor.

29 U.S.C. § 203(r). Certain relationships or arrangements are exempted from enterprise treatment, including exclusive-dealership arrangements and franchises. *See id.* In *Brennan v. Arnheim & Neely, Inc.*, 410 U.S. 512, 518 (1973), the Supreme Court stated that the three main elements of this statutory definition are "related activities, unified operation or common control, and common business purpose." *See also* 29 C.F.R. § 779.202 ("[T]he enterprise includes all such related activities which are performed through 'unified operation' or 'common control' . . . even if they are performed by more than one person, or in more than one establishment, or by more than one corporate or other organizational unit."). Obviously, these elements overlap, and various pieces of evidence may be relevant to more than one. "Activities are 'related' when they are the same or similar." *Arnheim & Neely, Inc.*, 410 U.S. at 518; *see also Chao v. A-One Med. Servs., Inc.*, 346 F.3d 908 (9th Cir. 2003) (holding two companies to be one enterprise because both provided home health care services even though they serviced different types of patients under different levels of care with differing eligibility requirements); *Pierce v. Coleman Trucking, Inc.*, 2005 WL 2338822 (N.D. Ohio Sept. 23, 2005) (finding related activities when two companies engaged in identical asbestos removal activities and differed only in their union relationships).

According to DOL regulations, "common control"

> includes the power to direct, restrict, regulate, govern, or administer the performance of the activities. "Common" control includes the sharing of control and it is not limited to sole control or complete control by one person or corporation. "Common" control therefore exists where the performance of the described activities are [sic] controlled by one person or by a number of persons, corporations, or other organizational units acting together.

29 C.F.R. § 779.221; *see also Arnheim & Neely, Inc.*, 410 U.S. at 518 (finding that operations controlled through a fully integrated central office constituted a unified operation subject to common control). Common ownership is one factor in determining common control, but it is not dispositive. *See, e.g., Dole v. Odd Fellows Home Endowment Bd.*, 912 F.2d 689 (4th Cir. 1990).

Another regulation broadly defines common business purpose:

> Generally, the term "common business purpose" will encompass activities whether performed by one person or by more than one person, or corporation, or other business organization, which are directed to the same business objective or to similar objectives in which the group has an interest. The scope of the term "enterprise" encompasses a single business entity as well as a unified business system which performs related activities for a common business purpose.

29 C.F.R. § 779.213. This definition is consistent with the Supreme Court's treatment in *Arnheim & Neely, Inc.*, 410 U.S. at 518, finding a real estate management company's operations at a number of different, separately owned buildings had a common business purpose because the "activities at the several locations are tied together by the common business purpose of managing commercial properties for profit."

Finally, in 1974, Congress extended the definition of "employer" under the FLSA to include virtually all public employers. *See* Pub. L. 93-259, § 6, 88 Stat. 58-62 (1974); 29 U.S.C. § 203(d) (2014). The Supreme Court ultimately found this extension to be a proper exercise of Congress's Commerce Clause power and not inconsistent with the strictures of the Tenth Amendment. *See Garcia v. San Antonio Metro. Transit Auth.*, 469 U.S. 528 (1985). However, the combined effect of two subsequent Supreme Court decisions, *Seminole Tribe v. Florida*, 517 U.S. 44 (1996), and *Alden v. Maine*, 527 U.S. 706 (1999), renders states immune from *private* suits for damages under the FLSA. The Department of Labor may still enforce the FLSA against the states, and municipalities and other political subdivisions do not enjoy such sovereign immunity, and are, thus, frequently the target of private FLSA suits, *see, e.g., Acton v. City of Columbia*, 436 F.3d 969 (8th Cir. 2006).

ii. Exemptions

Even if a worker is a covered employee employed by one or more covered employers, the employee may nevertheless be exempt from the FLSA's protections. The FLSA and implementing DOL regulations contain a significant number of exemptions excluding certain categories of employees from the minimum wage requirements, the overtime provisions, or both. Many of the exemptions apply to employees in specific industries or subsectors of specific industries, or those holding jobs in certain, defined job categories. For example, some workers under 20 years of age may receive wages as low as $4.25 for the first 90 days of employment. In addition, various categories of transportation and agricultural workers are exempt from the FLSA's overtime requirements, and the statute contains separate overtime requirements for firefighters and law enforcement officials. Some seasonal employees are exempt from both the minimum wage and overtime requirements as well. Moreover, domestic workers traditionally have been excluded as well under the exemption for "companion services." However, in light of a new Labor Department rule, as of January 1, 2015, home health care workers employed through an agency or other third-party provider have wage and hour protections. *See* 29 C.F.R. § 552; *see also* Steven Greenhouse, *U.S. to Include Home Care Aides in Wage and Overtime Law*, N.Y. TIMES, September 17, 2013, at B1 (describing the new rule and its implications). Workers hired directly by individuals or families will remain exempt.

Public employees are subject to a number of unique provisions. Most notably, section 7(o) of the statute, 29 U.S.C. § 207(o), allows public employers to compensate employees who work overtime with compensatory time—that is, one and one half hours off for every hour worked in excess of 40 hours per week—instead of overtime pay. A frequently debated policy question is whether that same option should be available to private sector employees. Currently, "comp time" in lieu of overtime is not permitted even if both parties would prefer it.

When you encounter FLSA in practice, the first place to begin is to ascertain whether the situation you are confronting falls within one of the many exceptions to the general coverage provisions we have sketched. This chapter does not attempt to cover all of the various exemptions in the statute, *see, e.g.*, 29 U.S.C. § 213, but it does convey the flavor of the analysis while treating some of the more important exemptions in terms of numbers of workers excluded from the FLSA's protections.

The "White Collar" Exemptions

The best-known exemptions tend to be labeled generically as the "white collar" exemptions. Section 13(a)(1) of the FLSA completely exempts "any employee employed in a bona fide executive, administrative, or professional capacity." *See* 29 U.S.C. §213(a)(1). In subsequent amendments to the FLSA, Congress also added a special exemption for certain "computer employees" and "highly compensated" employees. *See* 29 U.S.C. §213(a)(17).

The goal underlying the white-collar exemptions, at least historically, was to exclude from coverage those workers not engaged directly in production but rather involved in management, administration, and the learned or creative professions. The §13(a)(1) exemptions were "premised on the belief that the workers exempted typically earned salaries well above the minimum wage, and they were presumed to enjoy other compensatory privileges such as above average fringe benefits and better opportunities for advancement, setting them apart from the nonexempt workers entitled to overtime pay." *See* 69 Fed. Reg. 22,122, 22, 123-24 (April 23, 2004). In addition, Congress believed that the work such employees performed was "difficult to standardize to any time frame and could not be easily spread to other workers after 40 hours in a week, making compliance with the overtime provisions difficult and generally precluding the potential job expansion intended by the FLSA's time-and-a-half overtime premium." *Id.* at 22,123. Such distinctions may be less meaningful today, as the American economy shifts from manufacturing to the provision of services, technology and communications, and creative professions. Views differ on whether this is a reason to expand or contract the exemptions.

DOL regulations govern the exemptions. *See* 20 C.F.R. §541. These regulations—which were first promulgated in the 1940s and remained largely unchanged until 2004—contained requirements that had to be satisfied in order for an employee to be treated as exempt. To qualify, an employee's compensation had to exceed a defined salary floor ($155 per week, or $8,060 annually) and had to be in the form of a set "salary," rather than an hourly wage subject to reductions based on the quality or quantity of work performed. In addition, an employee qualified for such exempt status only if his or her "primary duties" were "administrative," "professional," or "executive" in nature. Each of these duty classifications, in addition to the term "primary duty," was defined, although inexactly and, hence, was subject to widespread litigation.

In 2004, the DOL altered portions of the white-collar exemption regime. *See* Defining and Delimiting the Exemptions for Executive, Administrative, Professional, Outside Sales and Computer Employees, 29 C.F.R. §541 (2014). These changes generated great controversy in the mainstream media and in political circles because of their anticipated net effect; according to many commentators, they would significantly increase the number of workers exempt from the FLSA's protections wage and overtime protections.

The ultimate effect of the revised regulations is complex. In one way, the new rules benefit employees: They raise the qualifying salary level for these exemptions to $455 a week or $23,660 per year, meaning more workers are now nonexempt based on their wages alone, irrespective of their responsibilities. On the other hand, other provisions clearly exempt more employees. For example, the new rules exempt from coverage an employee "who leads a team of other employees assigned to complete major projects for the employer," without regard to whether the employee has direct supervisory authority over other team members. *See* 29 C.F.R. §541.203(c). In addition, more workers with only *some* executive duties are now exempt because the new "primary duty" test does not limit the amount of nonexempt work an employee can perform and still be considered an "executive." *See id.* Finally, the new regulations contain an additional exemption for employees earning more than $100,000 a year ("highly compensated employees"), without regard to primary duties; such an employee must perform only a single exempt task "customarily and regularly" in order to be exempt. *See* 29 C.F.R. § 541.601. Since the $100,000 trigger is not inflation-indexed, more and more employees will reach this status over time.

A primary purpose of these rules was to reduce the uncertainty the prior regulations produced and the litigation that resulted. *See* 69 Fed. Reg. 22,122 (Apr. 23, 2004). Various aspects of the exemptions do provide greater clarity. For instance, "salary" and the effect of reductions in pay for various purposes are now defined more clearly. *See* 29 C.F.R. § 541.602. Similarly, some exemptions are now better defined, including the computer employee, outside salesperson, and education exemptions. And new provisions set out categorical exclusions from the exemptions, including those for emergency response personnel, "blue collar" and other workers engaged only in manual or repetitive labor, *see* 29 C.F.R. § 541.3(a), (b), and nurse practitioners, *see* 29 C.F.R. 541.301(e)(2). Moreover, the new regulations provide a single primary duty test, abandoning the prior approach, which contained two different tests — the "long" and "short" tests — based on salary level. *See id.* at § 541.700.

Nevertheless, much in the new regulations parrots or parallels the prior regulations. For example, the purposes of the exemptions remain the same, and the basic distinction between production and administrative work continues to be paramount. Moreover, the definitions and terms that govern applicability of the exceptions are generally quite similar to those under the prior regime.

Also, determining whether an employee is exempt as an executive, administrator, or professional remains a highly fact-sensitive inquiry. And how the general rules governing these exemptions and the somewhat altered "primary duty test" may apply in particular situations continues to pose planning difficulties. Indeed, whether an employee who was nonexempt before is now exempt as an executive, administrator, or professional may not be clear. Few courts have applied the new regulations, and developing a guiding body of case law will take years. Employers and employees, therefore, will need to rely not only on the new regulations and the examples they provide in assessing exempt/nonexempt status but also on older case law, at least where the operative standards have not changed significantly.

The best way to appreciate the challenges facing employers, employees, and courts is to see how the white-collar exemptions are applied in relatively close cases. Thus, as a starting point, read the following case involving employees classified as "assistant managers" by their employers.

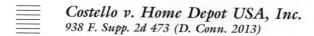

Costello v. Home Depot USA, Inc.
938 F. Supp. 2d 473 (D. Conn. 2013)

JANET C. HALL, District Judge.

Introduction

[Plaintiff James Costello brought this action against defendant Home Depot U.S.A., Inc. (Home Depot), alleging that he was not paid for overtime work in violation of the Fair Labor Standards Act (the "FLSA"), 29 U.S.C. § 207. Home Depot simultaneously filed this motion for summary judgment as to Costello arguing that there was no violation of the FLSA because he was properly categorized as an exempt executive employee in accordance with the FLSA's rules governing overtime payments. The motion was denied.]

III. Factual Background

[In 2004, two separate federal actions were filed alleging that Home Depot violated the FLSA with regard to merchandising assistant store managers ("MASMs"). The district court originally allowed the cases to proceed as a "collective" action (similar to a class action) but later reversed that decision. Separate multiple-plaintiff actions followed, including the present action. At this point, one of the remaining plaintiffs was James Costello.]

Home Depot operates large, warehouse-style retail stores that sell home improvement products and services. Home Depot stores are staffed by one Store Manager and up to seven Assistant Store Managers, a group that includes MASMs. MASMs are the second-highest-ranking employees in Home Depot stores, subordinate only to the Store Manager. The stores are divided into up to eleven core merchandising departments: Lumber, Building Materials, Flooring, Paint, Hardware, Plumbing, Electrical, Garden, Kitchen & Bath, Millwork, and Decor.

MASMs and Specialty ASMs [SASMs] oversee from one to eleven merchandising departments. Merchandising departments are staffed by sales associates and one department supervisor. MASMs supervise the department supervisors and associates assigned to their departments. Costello . . . dispute[s] whether all of the departments [he was] assigned to also had an assigned department supervisor, and [he] maintain[s] that the department supervisors are primarily responsible for supervision of associates in that department. The MASM job description states that, among other responsibilities, MASMs are responsible for "[m]aintaining department profitability," "provid[ing] leadership to Associates," and "[s]etting store objectives and ensuring [that] they are met." . . .

Costello was hired as a sales associate by Home Depot in March 1997. On July 29, 2002, Costello was promoted to the MASM position. Before his promotion, Costello went through a retail management assessment and training program. The parties dispute exactly what the training entailed or whether Costello received continuous training as an MASM, but agree the training included review of a Home Depot manual that covered various parts of store operations.

Costello began working as an MASM in Westerly, Rhode Island, in July 2002, and was transferred as an MASM to a store in Waterford, Connecticut, in September 2003, where he remained, with the exception of a temporary reassignment to a store in Lisbon, Connecticut, until his employment ended on January 1, 2006. At the Westerly store, Costello was assigned to the Lumber, Millwork, Building Materials, Hardware, Pro Desk, and Tool Rental Center departments, and for a short time, the Front Desk. The Pro Desk, Hardware, and Rental Center departments each had department supervisors, and there was a fourth department supervisor who managed the Lumber, Building Materials, and Millwork departments. These four department supervisors reported to Costello. When Costello was assigned to the Front Desk, an additional supervisor reported to him. A disputed number of other employees, including associates, also worked in the store.

[At the Waterford and Lisbon stores, Costello was likewise assigned to a number of departments, and the department supervisors reported to him.]

Costello resigned from Home Depot on either December 29, 2005, or January 1, 2006, and this resignation occurred around the time allegations by female employees were made against him. Home Depot claims that an investigation was performed relating to the complaints and that Costello was found to have violated the company's Code of Conduct and his employment was terminated.

The MASM job description states that the major tasks and responsibilities of the position include, "[r]ecruiting, interviewing applicants and making recommendations to the Store Manager about hiring for open positions." When assigned to the Westerly store, Costello assisted in preparing the store for its grand opening and was involved in hiring staff. Costello conducted 200 or 300 interviews and asked candidates about their product knowledge, departmental preferences, and previous experience. He made recommendations to the store manager or human resources manager about who should be hired based on his interviews, and at least some of these candidates were hired. Costello was then part of a group that was involved in deciding where the new employees would be placed and what salary they would be offered. Costello claims that the final hiring decisions were made by the store manager or human resources manager. Following the opening of the Westerly store, Costello conducted a few additional interviews and recommended that two employees be transferred in to the store from different Home Depot stores. Costello claims that he was not involved in the hiring process at the Waterford store.

Costello taught forklift training classes and, when he had a department supervisor who was training to be an ASM, he would involve him or her in performance review meetings with sales associates to observe how the process worked. The parties dispute whether Costello was responsible for ensuring that associates completed electronic training courses. Costello recommended that associates receive certain types of training for their development.

The MASM job description also states that the major tasks and responsibilities of MASMs includes, "[s]cheduling Associates' work and training time." As the stores where Costello worked, either the human resources manager or a store scheduler initially prepared the store schedule. Costello then had the opportunity to review the schedules, but the parties dispute whether Costello reviewed the schedules to ensure that the departments were adequately staffed. Costello would sometimes suggest changes to the store schedule when he determined there were not enough associates scheduled.

When Costello received a call that an employee would not be at work, Costello would attempt to get coverage for those positions for the departments he was responsible for, and would notify the department supervisors for the other affected departments. Costello did not need the store manager's approval to perform this task. Costello could approve or disapprove employee requests for the scheduling of vacation time, and requests for vacation time were first approved by department supervisors. Costello had the authority to sign off on edits to employee time records, but Costello asserts that this function was the principal responsibility of the operations manager.

Costello held meetings with department supervisors to communicate action items and set a timeline as to when the actions would get done. He also prepared task lists that needed to be done in a certain timeframe. When his store manager suggested areas for improvement, Costello developed plans to implement any necessary changes, and followed up to ensure the tasks he had assigned had been completed. The parties dispute how much of Costello's time was taken up with these activities.

The MASM job description also states that the major tasks and responsibilities of MASMs includes, "[c]oaching, training and developing Associates by providing both informal (e.g., on-floor coaching) and formal (e.g., written evaluation) job performance-based feedback." Costello was responsible for preparing performance evaluations for the hourly associates every six months, one for purposes of determining annual raises, and one interim review to track performance issues. Costello kept a file on each employee to track each employee's progress and updated these files on a monthly basis. Costello personally prepared performance reviews for department supervisors, but the parties dispute whether Costello delegated responsibility for the review process for sales associates. Costello met with department supervisors and sales associates to discuss the performance evaluations, and, at Waterford, the store managers would attend monetary reviews for department supervisors.

In the performance evaluations Costello completed, Costello was involved with the recommendation of leadership and potential codes for sales associates, which could impact pay raises. Costello estimates that his recommendations were accepted 90 percent of the time. Costello participated in meetings regarding annual raises of both sales associates and department supervisors and, made recommendations about the raises his employees should receive. Costello estimates those recommendations were followed 99 percent of the time. In addition to the semi-annual performance reviews, Costello could monitor and recognize associates' performance throughout the year. Costello was able to give merit badges to employees, the accumulation of which could lead to a $100 reward. Costello also recommended employees for various store awards.

Costello mentored employees to help them advance professionally and would discuss efficiency and profitability improvements with department supervisors. At the Westerly store, Costello would sometimes discuss with the store manager which associates were ready for a promotion; some of the individuals Costello identified were in fact promoted. At least one employee so identified was offered promotion but declined the offer.

The stores where Costello worked employed associates known as inventory management associates who put together initial merchandise orders and, in at least one performance evaluation, Costello was encouraged to have weekly meetings with those associates and department supervisors to ensure that departments were fully stocked. The parties dispute whether Costello was responsible for reviewing the orders. The parties dispute the degree to which Costello could determine what products to place along certain aisles and other parts of the store.

The MASM job description also states that the major tasks and responsibilities of MASMs includes, "[m]aintaining department profitability through report analysis, identifying trends, defining problems and developing appropriate responses in three or more departments." As part of his job as an MASM, Costello reviewed the Whole Store Report, which contained information related to profitability, "shrink," and labor hours, to see how his departments were doing. At meetings, Costello mentioned various actions he was taking to try to increase sales, including recommending increasing staff in critical time periods like weekends and holidays. Costello was responsible for ensuring the "shrink plan" was prepared and reviewing the shrink plan on a weekly basis. When shrink audits revealed that his departments were not performing well, Costello met with the department head and/or store manager to take corrective action.

Costello had the authority to discipline associates if he observed them acting contrary to Home Depot policies and procedures, including writing up the employee and determining corrective action. Costello disputes that the disciplinary action entailed involved more than filling out a form. Costello had the authority to send employees home if he determined they were behaving improperly, including if any employee disrespected a customer, was involved in a safety violation, brought weapons into the store, or was under the influence of alcohol or drugs. Costello exercised this authority when one of his employees climbed into a dumpster shoot. Costello stopped the employee, had him climb out of the shoot, punch out, and go home. Costello reported the incident to his store manager, and the employee was terminated. Costello attended the termination session.

Costello was responsible for coaching employees and memorializing verbal conversations about performance issues. Costello asserts this responsibility was shared by department supervisors. Consultation with human resources or the store manager was only required if the problem involved a safety or hazardous waste issue.

The MASM job description also states that the major tasks and responsibilities of MASMs includes, "[e]nsuring Safety of Customers and Associates." If there was a safety violation in the store when Costello was present, Costello was responsible for addressing it, and he would respond depending on the nature of the problem. Costello asserts this responsibility was shared with department supervisors. Costello walked his departments and inspected overhead material to make sure the items were properly situated, wrapped, and labeled. If there was a problem with the overhead items, Costello would find associates to fix the issue. Costello asserts that, if no associates were available, he was required by the store manager to fix the issue himself.

When Costello opened the store, he was responsible for walking the entire store to ensure there were no safety hazards; if he observed any safety issues, he would address it with the assistant manager for that department and have it corrected before the store was opened to the public. Costello ensured that anything outside the store was secured when he closed the store. The parties dispute whether Costello did this upon opening the store. Costello had the code for the store's alarms and was frequently called into work when the alarm went off. When called in to deal with the alarm, he had to shut off the alarm, deal with the police, walk the store, and reset the alarm.

Costello was responsible for helping to ensure customers were satisfied. Costello reviewed customer complaints, and had to devise a resolution within a day of receiving the complaint, which could include marking down the product, replacing the product, or calling the customer. Costello also reviewed secret shopper reports once a month to monitor the job performance of the sales associates. Costello addressed employee grievances, such as problems with other employees. In such a situation, Costello could coordinate the transfer of the employee to another department. Costello asserts such an action required approval of the store manager.

In the Westerly store, Costello sometimes served as the Manager on Duty ("MOD") for three to four hours for shifts when he either opened or closed the store. The parties dispute how often this occurred, and whether being MOD meant Costello was the only manager in the store at the time. . . .

Costello's starting salary as an MASM was $44,000 per year. In April 2003, this amount was increased to $45,800 per year. In April 2004, this amount was increased to $46,900 per year. In April 2005, this amount was increased to $50,000 per year. Costello understood that his salary was to cover all hours worked, and that he might have to work more than 55 hours per week.

In addition to his base salary, Costello was eligible for a bonus of up to 25 percent of his annual salary based on store sales and stock options based on his performance

848 ===== 11. Wages and Benefits

and the store's performance. Costello received a bonus for 2004 totaling $3,381.49. He received more than 1,300 stock options between 2003 and 2005. Hourly associates were not eligible to receive stock options or bonuses. From 2004 to 2005, the midrange hourly rates for sales associates and department supervisors in the market where Costello worked were $12.64 and $16.97, respectively. Costello asserts that this pay was supplemented by overtime pay, and that top pay for sales associates reached $17.57 per hour and for department supervisors reached $22.23 per hour.

Costello was held accountable for the profitability of his departments and making his sales plans, and he was evaluated in part on department sales performance . . . Costello spent up to three hours each week attending management meetings where he discussed sales plans, loss prevention, markdowns, new store programs, and shrink. Costello asserts that department supervisors also attended those meetings. Costello spent up to two hours each week walking the store by himself or with either his store manager or district manager. Costello spent an hour each week reviewing reports. Costello stated that keeping track of employees' performance issues was a "continuous operation."

Costello asserts that he spent the majority of his time on, and the majority of his duties concerned, customer service and manual labor. Costello also asserts that department supervisors were considered part of the management team and that they could serve as MOD. Costello asserts that department supervisors are directly responsible for supervising and counseling sales associates. Costello asserts that he did not make policy decisions for the stores in which he worked. . . .

IV. Discussion

The sole issue before the court is whether summary judgment is appropriate as to whether Costello [was] misclassified as exempt from the overtime requirements of the FLSA. Home Depot argues no issue of material fact exists as to this point and that [he was] properly classified as exempt under the "executive employee" provision of the FLSA.

The FLSA states that "no employer shall employ any of his employees . . . for a workweek longer than forty hours unless such employee receives compensation for his employment in excess of the hours above specified at a rate not less than one and one-half times the regular rate at which he is employed." 29 U.S.C. §207(a)(1). This overtime pay requirement does not apply to "any employee employed in a bona fide executive, administrative, or professional capacity." 29 U.S.C. §213(a)(1). . . . [T]here is no dispute that Costello . . . , in [his capacity as a MASM is] currently classified by Home Depot as exempt from the FLSA's overtime pay requirements or that Home Depot is an employer to which the FLSA applies.

"Since this exemption provides an affirmative defense to overtime claims, the employer has the burden of proving that a plaintiff is an exempt 'bona fide executive' by a preponderance of the evidence." *Scott v. SSP America, Inc.*, No. 09–CV–4339 (RRM) (VVP), 2011 WL 1204406, *6 (E.D.N.Y. Mar. 29, 2011). "Exemptions to the FLSA are 'narrowly construed against the employers seeking to assert them.'" *Bilyou* [v. *Dutchess Beer Distribs., Inc.*, 300 F.3d 217, 222 (2d Cir. 2002)] (quoting *Arnold v. Ben Kanowsky, Inc.*, 361 U.S. 388, 392 (1960)). "The determination of whether an employee is exempt from the overtime requirements of the FLSA is a 'highly fact intensive inquiry that must be made on a case-by-case basis in light of the totality of the circumstances.'" *Scott.* . . .

Under the "bona fide executive" exemption, as of 2004, federal regulations exempt an employee:

(1) Compensated on a salary basis at a rate of not less than $455 per week . . . ;
(2) Whose primary duty is management of the enterprise in which the employee is employed or of a customarily recognized department or subdivision thereof;
(3) Who customarily and regularly directs the work of two or more other employees; and
(4) Who has the authority to hire or fire other employees or whose suggestions and recommendations as to the hiring, firing, advancement, promotion or any other change of status of other employees are given particular weight.

29 C.F.R. § 541.100(a).

A. Costello

The court first turns to Costello. The court will consider the four factors governing application of the executive exemption.

1. First Factor

As to the first factor, concerning the rate of compensation, Costello does not dispute that this factor is satisfied as to him.

2. Third Factor

As to the third factor, concerning whether Costello customarily and regularly directed the work of two or more other employees, Costello does not appear to contest this fact. . . . Accordingly, the court deems this third factor satisfied for the purposes of this Motion for Summary Judgment.

3. Fourth Factor

The fourth factor concerns whether Costello had the authority to hire or fire other employees or whether his suggestions and recommendations as to the hiring, firing, advancement, promotion, or any other change of status of other employees were given particular weight. The regulations state:

To determine whether an employee's suggestions and recommendations are given "particular weight," factors to be considered include, but are not limited to, whether it is part of the employee's job duties to make such suggestions and recommendations; the frequency with which such suggestions and recommendations are made or requested; and the frequency with which the employee's suggestions and recommendations are relied upon. Generally, an executive's suggestions and recommendations must pertain to employees whom the executive customarily and regularly directs. It does not include an occasional suggestion with regard to the change in status of a co-worker. An employee's suggestions and recommendations may still be deemed to have "particular weight" even if a higher level manager's recommendation has more importance and even if the employee does not have authority to make the ultimate decision as to the employee's change in status.

29 C.F.R. § 541.105. Home Depot argues that the frequency of Costello's input into the interviewing process (over 200 interviews at the Westerly store), his input into the promotion and salary raise process for subordinates, and the relatively high frequency with which his suggestions were followed suggest that this factor is satisfied. Costello contends (briefly, and in a footnote) that because he did not have the ultimate authority to make these decisions (something Home Depot does not dispute), a material issue of fact remains as to whether his recommendations were given particular weight. The court notes that the regulations state that the frequency with which an employee's suggestions and recommendations are sought and relied upon are among the factors courts should consider when evaluating this factor. Here, Costello testified that 90 percent of his recommendations, which were relatively large in number, were ultimately agreed with. The court, however, notes the absence of affidavit testimony demonstrating that these recommendations actually had an impact on those receiving them. While such evidence is not absolutely necessary in order to grant a summary judgment motion, its absence fails to resolve the issue of material fact raised by Costello's testimony that his opinions were not accorded particular weight by his supervisors. Drawing all inferences in favor of Costello, as the court must on Home Depot's Motion for Summary Judgment, Home Depot has not established an absence of a material issue of fact as to this factor.

3. Second Factor

The court now turns to the second factor, concerning whether Costello's primary duty was management of the enterprise. As with the bulk of cases involving the executive exemption, it is this factor that is most hotly contested between the parties.

Federal regulations provide further instructions with respect to the definitions of both "management" and "primary duty." Before 2004, the regulations provided a list of duties that were generally understood to be managerial, including:

Interviewing, selecting, and training of employees; setting and adjusting their rates of pay and hours of work; directing their work; maintaining their production or sales records for use in supervision or control; appraising their productivity and efficiency for the purpose of recommending promotions or other changes in their status; handling their complaints and grievances and disciplining them when necessary; planning the work; determining the techniques to be used; apportioning the work among the workers; determining the type of materials, supplies, machinery or tools to be used or merchandise to be bought, stocked and sold; controlling the flow and distribution of materials or merchandise and supplies; providing for the safety of the men and the property.

29 C.F.R. § 541.102(b) (2003). The 2004 regulations added three additional duties to this list, including "providing for the . . . security of the employees or the property;

planning and controlling the budget; and monitoring or implementing legal compliance measures."

"'Primary duty' is defined by the regulations as 'the principal, main, major or most important duty that the employee performs.' To determine whether plaintiffs' performance of these exempt activities constitutes their 'primary duty,' a court must consider 'the character of an employee's job as a whole.'" *Mullins v. New York*, 653 F.3d 104, 106 (2d Cir. 2011) (quoting 29 C.F.R. § 541.700(a)). The pre–2004 explanation of primary duty included four factors a court should consider, in addition to "[t]he amount of time spent in the performance of the managerial duties," including:

> the relative importance of the managerial duties as compared with other types of duties, the frequency with which the employee exercises discretionary powers, his relative freedom from supervision, and the relationship between his salary and the wages paid other employees for the kind of nonexempt work performed by the supervisor.

29 C.F.R. § 541.103 (2003). The current [regulation] no longer mention "the frequency with which the employee exercises discretionary powers." *See* 29 C.F.R. § 541.700. However, courts understand this factor to be incorporated into an analysis of an employee's "relative freedom from supervision." *See, e.g., Morgan v. Family Dollar Stores*, 551 F.3d 1233, 1270 n. 57 (11th Cir. 2008). Additionally, the regulations outlining the meaning of "primary duty" explain:

> Assistant managers in a retail establishment who perform exempt executive work such as supervising and directing the work of other employees, ordering merchandise, managing the budget and authorizing payment of bills may have management as their primary duty even if the assistant managers spend more than 50 percent of the time performing nonexempt work such as running the cash register. However, if such assistant managers are closely supervised and earn little more than the nonexempt employees, the assistant managers generally would not satisfy the primary duty requirement.

29 C.F.R. § 541.700(c).

a. Relative Importance of Exempt Duties

The court turns first to the question of the relative importance of the managerial duties that Costello undertook.

Home Depot argues that Costello frequently performed managerial tasks as set out in 29 C.F.R. § 541.102, and that those tasks were Costello's principal value to the company. Home Depot argues:

> [Costello] (1) interviewed between 200 and 300 candidates and helped select candidates for hire; (2) trained employees; (3) adjusted employee schedules; (4) provided input concerning employees' rate of pay; (5) reviewed and analyzed various reports relevant to the management of his departments; (6) appraised productivity and efficiency and recommended several individuals for promotion; (7) handled both employee and customer complaints; (8) disciplined employees; (9) planned, assigned, and monitored work; (10) reviewed and approved product orders; (11) ensured the safety of the store; and (12) enforced Home Depot policy.

Home Depot further contends that these duties constituted Costello's principal value to Home Depot, which it claims is evident from the inherent import of the tasks performed (such as the periods during which Costello served as Manager on Duty), the rigor of the process of promotion and training that prepared Costello for his MASM duties, company performance evaluations that concentrated criticism on Costello's more managerial duties, and Costello's compensation arrangement, which involved the receipt of bonuses and stock options that were based on store sales.

Costello disputes this characterization, and argues:

> [T]he ultimate success or failure of the store did not hinge on Plaintiff performing his management duties, but the store would have failed if Plaintiff did not complete his non-managerial work. Indeed, it is clear from the testimony and other evidence on record that Plaintiff and other MASMs were expected to . . . make sure the store was clean, that it was in stock and customers were served no matter how many hours it took them to accomplish all of those tasks.

Unlike some of the other cases to consider the relative importance of an employee's more managerial duties, here the court does not have any direct testimony from Home Depot officials as to how the company viewed the importance of the various tasks assigned to and carried out by Costello. Instead, the court is left to attempt to divine such conclusions, in part, from what can only be described as a somewhat intuitive assessment of what duties are critical to a large-scale retail operation. The Second Circuit, however, clearly contemplates courts making such assessments. In *Donovan v. Burger King Corp.,* the court observed:

> [T]he record fully supports Judge Sifton's finding that the principal responsibilities of Assistant Managers, in the sense of being most important or critical to the success of the restaurant, are managerial. Many of the employees themselves so testified and it is clear that the restaurants could not operate successfully unless the managerial functions of Assistant Managers, such as determining amounts of food to be prepared, running cash checks, scheduling employees, keeping track of inventory, and assigning employees to particular jobs, were performed. For that reason, as well as the fact that much of the oversight of the operation can be carried out simultaneously with the performance of non-exempt work, we believe the principal or most important work of these employees is managerial.

Donovan v. Burger King Corp., 675 F.2d 516, 521 (2d Cir. 1982).

It is undisputed that Costello performed at least some of the tasks that track those outlined in *Donovan,* although the frequency with which Costello performed those tasks, and whether he was the only person performing them, is a matter of contention. Also unclear is how other employees regarded the importance of what Costello was doing. As stated above, unlike in *Donovan,* the defendants here provide no corroborating testimony or evidence as to whether Costello's ostensibly managerial tasks were "critical to the success" of the store. In *Clougher v. Home Depot,* the court considered a similar claim by an MASM in a Home Depot store. In that case, the employee conceded to performing some managerial tasks, but claimed, similarly to Costello, to performing those tasks infrequently, and only in a supporting role to his other, more important non-exempt work. The court found this dispute sufficient to preclude summary judgment because of outstanding factual issues. *See Clougher v. Home Depot,* 696 F. Supp. 2d 285, 291–92 (E.D.N.Y.2010). . . . Other courts have not found similar ambiguities sufficient to demonstrate a material issue of fact. . . .

Here, Costello certainly conducted a large number of interviews with potential hires over the course of his employment and had at least some input into the hiring process (although he did not make the ultimate determinations), participated in some training of lower-level employees, reviewed staffing schedules initially compiled by other employees (although Costello insists, and his deposition testimony seems to confirm, that Costello did not review those schedules for the purposes of ensuring adequate staffing), participated in worker performance evaluation, dealt with safety issues, and dealt with customer complaints. However, it also appears that many of these duties were sometimes shared by other employees, or, in the case of inventory orders, were sometimes carried out without any managerial supervision at all. The evidence in the record does not definitely answer these questions.

Perhaps the most potentially critical job function Costello performed related to his occasional duties as MOD, in which he would open or close the store, and was sometimes the only salaried manager in the store. Although sometimes accompanied by other managers, Costello would, during at least some of those periods, make sure the store had cashiers, open the vault, ensure department staffing, and run daily reports. Although a store manager held ultimate responsibility, Home Depot's argument that Costello's functions as MOD were indeed critical for store success are significantly more persuasive than its contentions regarding his other responsibilities. However, the amount of time actually spent on this activity is hotly disputed. . . . Here, given the absence of corroborating testimony from Home Depot officials or other employees regarding the importance of Costello's various tasks, divergent accounts of the amount of time actually spent on managerial tasks (including performance of MOD functions), the degree to which those functions were replicated by lower-level employees, Costello's testimony that he was informed by supervisors that customer service was his primary job function, and his somewhat uncertain degree of influence in hiring decisions, a material issue of fact remains as to the relative importance of Costello's managerial functions.

b. Time Spent Performing Non-Exempt Work

The court will also consider the amount of time Costello spent performing non-exempt work as part of its inquiry into whether managerial tasks constituted Costello's primary duty. The federal regulations state:

> The amount of time spent performing exempt work can be a useful guide in determining whether exempt work is the primary duty of an employee. This, employees who spend more than 50 percent of their time performing exempt work will generally satisfy the primary duty requirement. Time alone, however, is not the sole test, and nothing in this section requires that exempt employees spend more than 50 percent of their time performing exempt work. Employees who do not spend more than 50 percent of their time performing exempt duties may nonetheless meet the primary duty requirement if the other factors support such a conclusion.

29 C.F.R. § 541.700(b). Analysis of this section here is not particularly illuminating as Home Depot does not appear to argue that Costello crossed the 50 percent threshold in the performance of exempt managerial work. As is obvious from the regulation however, this fact is not dispositive one way or the other, as "Employees who do not spend more than 50 percent of their time performing exempt duties may

nonetheless meet the primary duty requirement if other factors support such a conclusion." Costello maintains that of a workweek that varied between 60 and 80 hours, around ten hours could be spent doing traditionally managerial tasks. Additionally (or possibly overlappingly), Costello engaged in MOD-related activities (either alone or with other managers) between nine and 40 hours per week.

In short, it is unclear which way this evidence cuts, or what the actual scope of Costello's duties, in terms of time spent, was. A variation between less than ten percent to nearly 50 percent of time spent, at least partially, doing managerial tasks is indeed a significant one for the purposes of this analysis. While perhaps less favorable to Costello's position than the issue of relative importance, the factual disputes here still create a material issue of fact as to Costello's primary duty that precludes determination as a matter of law. The court further notes that neither side has introduced evidence as to whether Costello was capable, given the tasks at hand, of simultaneously performing managerial and non-managerial tasks, something that courts which have found that employees were properly exempt have relied on when considering a situation in which the majority of an employee's time is spent on non-exempt tasks. . . . Given the fact-intensive nature of this inquiry, the court refrains from assuming the ease of such multitasking in the specific context of the Home Depot stores in which Costello worked. As such, a material issue of fact remains as to this factor which precludes determination as a matter of law.

c. Freedom from Direct Supervision . . .

Home Depot argues that Costello frequently exercised discretion, with a minimum of oversight, as a MASM. This discretion was primarily demonstrated through Costello's role in preparing performance reviews (a task Costello claims was often delegated to non-salaried employees), recommending annual raises and additional training, decisions related to dealing with employees who called out of work, dealing with customer complaints, and other such activities.

Further, Home Depot argues that, not only was Costello, when he was MOD, sometimes the only salaried manager in the store, even when the store manager was present Costello engaged in a great deal of discretionary activity as MASM as to the departments he was assigned to:

> [It] was Costello who: (1) ensured his departments were properly staffed; (2) planned the work to be done in each department; (3) delegated work to his subordinates and followed up to make sure it was done in a timely and correct manner; (4) ensured his subordinates were trained, both for their current position and so they would be ready to advance to the next level; (5) ensured proper merchandise was ordered; (6) inspected his departments for safety violations; (7) resolved employee and customer complaints; (8) made recommendations regarding annual raises for his employees; (9) counseled associates on disciplinary issues; (10) recognized his subordinates for exceptional performance; and (11) devised strategies to improved department sales.

Costello asserts that, while he performed many of these tasks, in many instances — particularly related to hiring, firing, and scheduling decisions — ultimate decision-making power and discretion lay elsewhere. Further he contends that he did so infrequently, and that when he did, he was in large part constrained by corporate policies.

The existence of corporate policies does not, categorically, limit such discretion. Further, Costello does not actually explain how, and in what sense, his discretionary powers were limited by specific corporate policies. More substantively, while Costello was always subject in the corporate chain of command to the store manager, he was also often accompanied by other managers while MOD, and while some tasks, such as ordering supplies and scheduling, were carried out in large part by others, it seems clear that Costello had a relatively free hand within his areas of influence. Taken together, these facts lay out a scope of activity that lends itself to a conclusion that Costello was relatively free from direct supervision. While this is not dispositive of the Motion for Summary Judgment, this factor appears to weigh in favor of Home Depot.

d. Salary

The court next considers how Costello's salary compares to wages paid non-exempt workers for performing similar tasks. Costello earned between $44,000 and $50,000 during the course of his employment, during which he was expected to work at least 55 hours per week, and sometimes worked between 60 and 80 hours per week. Additionally, Costello could receive performance bonuses and stock options, and received a bonus in 2004 for $3,381.49 and 1,300 stock options between 2003 and 2005. It is unclear what the total value of those stock options are, or when Costello received them.

The parties do not provide a breakdown of how many weeks per year Costello was expected to work. Assuming a 55 hour work week and a 52 week per year work schedule, Costello earned between $15.38 per hour ($846.15 per week) and $17.42 per hour ($961.54 per week). From 2004 to 2005, the mid-range hourly rate for sales associates was $12.64 per hour and for department supervisors was $16.97. . . .

The court does recognize that bonuses and stock options were unavailable to lower-level employees, something that suggests greater importance and a more central role for Costello. However, the dollar amounts in question, particularly when factoring in unresolved factual questions of which hourly rates it should compare and the availability of overtime for lower-level employees, do not appear to yield a significant disparity in compensation that suggest as a matter of law that Costello's primary duty was management. As such, it is not clear in which party's favor this factor weighs.

Taking all these factors together, it is clear that material issues of fact exist as to Costello's primary duty at Home Depot, precluding summary judgment. Accordingly, Home Depot's Motion for Summary Judgment as to Costello is denied.

NOTES

1. *Initial Impressions.* Costello had the title of manager, had some supervisory duties, and had some authority to exercise judgment in his work. Stepping back from legal doctrine, wouldn't you consider Costello to be white collar? Indeed, one of the lingering problems with these exemptions is that both employees and employers often fail to understand their scope. For example, many employees who view themselves as "white collar" — perhaps in part because they receive a "salary" rather than "hourly wages" — may simply assume that they are exempt and thus not demand overtime pay.

Such employees may instinctively prefer the exempt designation insofar as they associate that categorization with professional status, and may well view it as a proxy for the importance of their jobs and their value to the company. Employers, too, may be mistaken about the law or share similar perceptions about the relationship between exempt status and employee value. Consider as well that the FLSA places significant record-keeping responsibilities on employers with respect to the hours and compensation levels of nonexempt workers. This can create administrative burdens for the employer and negatively affect morale among employees who must keep track of and regularly report all of their work time.

2. *Certainty and the "Old" and "New" Regulations.* As discussed above, a major criticism of the "old" regulations governing the exemptions for executive, administrative, and professional employees was how little guidance they provided. In *Costello,* the court applies the post-2004 rules on the executive exemption but makes some reference to the pre-2004 rules, as well as draws some comparisons. Do you see much distinction between them in terms of certainty of outcomes or ease of application? Also, several of the precedents on which *Costello* relies applied the pre-2004 rules, further suggesting that the 2004 changes may not have altered the analysis significantly. Considering the purpose of the executive exemption inquiry — determining whether the workers at issue really do exercise significant authority — could it be any less fact-intensive? Greater certainty would be an upside, but what might be the downside of bright-line rules that seek to categorize workers *ex ante?*

In March 2014, President Obama directed the Secretary of Labor to reconsider the 2004 rules, contending that the existing white collar exemptions do not adequately protect worker wages and hours. *See* Executive Office of the President, *Memorandum for the Secretary of Labor,* Doc. No. 2014-06138, 79 Fed. Reg. 15209 (March 18, 2014). As this book went to press, the Department of Labor has not issued new regulations in response to this memorandum.

3. *Right Result?* Do you think the *Costello* court reached the right result? Are the distinctions the court draws between Costello and those that are exempt under the executive exemption meaningful? Are you satisfied with the tests the court articulated for making these determinations? Although the opinion is replete with detail, are there factors that should have been considered that were not?

4. *"Managers."* Costello is far from the only case in which employees identified as "managers" by their employers have successfully claimed that they are nonexempt. Indeed, Costello's claim was but one of 39 originally brought together by Home Depot assistant managers. Although the court severed the claims, each, including Costello's, could proceed separately. *See Costello v. Home Depot U.S.A., Inc.,* 888 F. Supp. 2d 258 (D. Conn. 2012) (severing 35 claims by assistant managers of stores in different states). And similar claims have been brought against Home Depot by assistant managers working elsewhere the country. Indeed, in recent years, misclassification of store and single-facility managers has been a particularly fertile area for litigation and large settlements. *See, e.g.,* http://www.lawyersandsettlements.com/settlements/employment-settlements/ (listing hundreds of large settlements in employment-related cases on an updated basis, including dozens of wage and hour settlements in claims brought by store and facility managers in the retail sector).

While much of this litigation has addressed assistant managers, other cases have involved the highest-ranking employees at their respective facilities. For example, in *McKinney v. United Store-All Centers LLC,* 656 F. Supp. 2d 114 (D.D.C. 2009), the court denied the employer's motion for summary judgment on the issue of whether employees hired as "primary managers" of its self-storage facilities — which leased storage units and rental trucks to customers — were exempt from the FLSA's overtime mandates under the administrative and executive employee exemptions. After engaging in a detailed analysis akin to that in *Costello*, the court concluded that, despite their rank at the firm's local facilities, there were genuine issues of material fact as to whether these employees' primary duties were executive (exercising significant authority) or administrative (exercising significant discretion) in nature.

5. *Administrative Employees.* Determining whether a worker is covered by the exemption for administrative employees, like the executive employee exemption, is often a highly fact-intensive inquiry. The DOL regulations provide that an "employee employed in a bona fide administrative capacity" means any employee:

(1) Compensated on a salary or fee basis at a rate of not less than $455 per week . . . exclusive of board, lodging or other facilities;

(2) Whose primary duty is the performance of office or non-manual work directly related to the management or general business operations of the employer or the employer's customers; and

(3) Whose primary duty includes the exercise of discretion and independent judgment with respect to matters of significance.

29 C.F.R. § 541.200. As the regulations recognize, this exemption overlaps with the one for executive employees. *See* 29 C.F.R. § 541.201. The key distinction is that administrative employees need not manage or supervise others — they need simply exercise discretion and independent judgment on important business matters. The exercise of discretion and independent judgment encompasses "the comparison and the evaluation of possible courses of conduct, and acting or making a decision after the various possibilities have been considered." 29 C.F.R. § 541.202. The employee must have the "authority to make an independent choice, free from immediate direction or supervision," although one can exercise discretion and independent judgment even if his or her decisions or recommendations are reviewed at a higher level. The regulations list a number of factors to consider in determining whether an employee exercises discretion and independent judgment. *See id.*

"Matters of significance" refers to the level of importance or consequence of the work performed. Areas in which work might qualify for the exemption include "tax; finance; accounting; budgeting; auditing; insurance; quality control; purchasing; procurement; advertising; marketing; research; safety and health; personnel management; human resources; employee benefits; labor relations; public relations, government relations; computer network, internet and database administration; legal and regulatory compliance; and similar activities." *See* 29 C.F.R. § 541.201. A number of specific examples of qualifying work are set forth in Note 7 below.

6. *Professional Employees.* Another exemption is for "professional employees," but the framework for determining which employees are exempt as "professionals" parallels, in many cases, the tests for determining executive or administrative employee status. The regulations provide that an "employee employed in a bona fide professional capacity" under the FLSA means an employee:

(1) Compensated on a salary or fee basis at a rate of not less than $455 per week . . . exclusive of board, lodging, or other facilities; and

(2) Whose primary duty is the performance of work:

(i) Requiring knowledge of an advanced type in a field of science or learning customarily acquired by a prolonged course of specialized intellectual instruction; or

(ii) Requiring invention, imagination, originality or talent in a recognized field of artistic or creative endeavor.

29 C.F.R. § 541.300. Note, however, that certain categories of licensed professionals are exempt regardless of their salary. *See, e.g.,* 29 C.F.R. § 541.304 (exempting employees who have "a valid license or certificate permitting the practice of law or medicine or any of their branches and is actually engaged in the practice thereof" as well as residents and interns pursuing such a profession). Yet courts tend to construe these categories narrowly. *See, e.g., Belt v. Emcee, Inc.* 444 F.3d 403 (5th Cir. 2006) (holding that nurse practitioners and physician assistants fell outside of the "practice of medicine" exception to the salary-basis test for determining professional exemption from overtime-pay requirements).

7. *The Outside Sales Exemption.* The FLSA and underlying regulations also provide an exemption for an "outside salesman," for whom the minimum salary requirements applicable to the previously discussed exemptions do not apply. *See* 29 U.S.C.A. § 213(a)(1); 29 C.F.R. § 541.500. The regulation defines outside salesman as any employee:

(1) Whose primary duty is:

(i) making sales within the meaning of section 3(k) of the Act, or

(ii) obtaining orders or contracts for services or for the use of facilities for which a consideration will be paid by the client or customer; and

(2) Who is customarily and regularly engaged away from the employer's place or places of business in performing such primary duty.

29 C.F.R. § 541.500(a).

This exemption, too, has been the subject of a fair amount of litigation. Indeed, in a recent decision of great significance to the pharmaceutical industry, the Supreme Court broadly construed the exemption, holding that pharmaceutical sales representatives whose primary duty was to obtain nonbinding commitments from physicians to prescribe their employer's prescription drugs in appropriate cases, qualified as "outside salesmen" exempt from FLSA's minimum wage and maximum hours requirements, contrary to the Department of Labor's view (of its own regulation) that a "sale" required more than such a nonbinding commitment. *See Christopher v. SmithKline Beecham Corp.*, 132 S. Ct. 2156 (2012).

8. *Guidance and Planning Implications.* Employment counsel are frequently called upon to make *ex ante* assessments of whether employees are exempt. Now that you are familiar with the tests for determining whether an employee is exempt under the executive and administrative exemptions, how comfortable would you be in making such assessments? Do the standards articulated facilitate category-wide treatment, or, as an attorney, would you feel it necessary to evaluate each person in each job? Further, to the extent that jobs often vary in reality from the corresponding job description, might you find it useful to visit each location to discuss the work with supervisors or even employees? Can you anticipate some problems in doing that?

There are some additional sources of guidance available beyond judicial decisions applying the regulations. Individual employers can seek feedback from the DOL on the exempt status of their employees. Upon such request, the DOL will issue a nonbinding opinion letter regarding the employees' status based on the facts the employer provided. In addition, the regulations themselves provide some particularized examples of workers who are or are not exempt. Consider, for instance, some of the examples provided in the regulations on the administrative exemption:

(a) Insurance claims adjusters generally meet the duties requirements for the administrative exemption, whether they work for an insurance company or other type of company, if their duties include activities such as interviewing insured's, witnesses and physicians; inspecting property damage; reviewing factual information to prepare damage estimates; evaluating and making recommendations regarding coverage of claims; determining liability and total value of a claim; negotiating settlements; and making recommendations regarding litigation. . . .

(c) An employee who leads a team of other employees assigned to complete major projects for the employer (such as purchasing, selling or closing all or part of the business, negotiating a real estate transaction or a collective bargaining agreement, or designing and implementing productivity improvements) generally meets the duties requirements for the administrative exemption, even if the employee does not have direct supervisory responsibility over the other employees on the team.

(d) An executive assistant or administrative assistant to a business owner or senior executive of a large business generally meets the duties requirements for the administrative exemption if such employee, without specific instructions or prescribed procedures, has been delegated authority regarding matters of significance.

(e) Human resources managers who formulate, interpret or implement employment policies and management consultants who study the operations of a business and propose changes in organization generally meet the duties requirements for the administrative exemption. However, personnel clerks who "screen" applicants to obtain data regarding their minimum qualifications and fitness for employment generally do not meet the duties requirements for the administrative exemption. . . .

(g) Ordinary inspection work generally does not meet the duties requirements for the administrative exemption. Inspectors normally perform specialized work along standardized lines involving well-established techniques and procedures which may have been catalogued and described in manuals or other sources. Such inspectors rely on techniques and skills acquired by special training or experience. They have some leeway in the performance of their work but only within closely prescribed limits.

29. C.F.R. § 541.203

Although employers' counsel ought to scrutinize carefully such examples, the guidance they provide may still be of limited assistance since they focus on relatively few of the thousands of positions in the American workplace. Moreover, as *Costello* and the qualifying language in each of the foregoing examples suggest, individual variations in the nature and scope of employees' duties can be dispositive even within an individual job category established by an employer. Seemingly "easy" determinations may not be so easy in light of such variations, and employers and their attorneys therefore must be careful not to rely too much on either category-based examples or earlier judicial decisions and opinion letters.

9. *Overtime Pay.* Given the higher social standing of white-collar workers, why would plaintiffs such as Costello want to *not* be exempt? While it may be too obvious to stress, they are not concerned with whether they were paid $7.25 an hour — undoubtedly, they receive more than that. These are not "minimum wage" cases at all, but illustrate that the FLSA can play an important role for higher-status employees who are asked to work overtime. Home Depot may have violated the law, but it may not have done so "willfully." Can you understand how easy it might be for an employer dealing with "white collar" or even "professional" workers not to focus on problems such as those raised in these cases? And what about the policy questions — assuming that the plaintiffs are being paid well above the $7.25 minimum wage after all their hours are counted, is it appropriate to require premium pay for "overtime"?

10. *Harms and Remedies.* Uncertainty is not the only reason that white-collar exemptions are frequently litigated: The amount of money potentially at stake provides an obvious incentive for these claims. This is particularly true for those cases brought as "collective" actions, a form of representative action (similar to a class action) expressly provided for in the FLSA, *see* 29 U.S.C. § 216(b), in which large numbers of employees may join together to seek relief. *Costello* is fairly typical — the litigation was pursued at least initially as a collective action involving many employees who were not paid overtime over long periods of time. In these kinds of cases, if the employer turns out to be wrong, liability for unpaid overtime compensation alone may climb into the millions of dollars. Indeed, if you do a little math in your head (time and a half for any hours over 40 during a week for a year or beyond), you will see how the damages for even one of these assistant managers will run deep into the tens of thousands of dollars. Then multiply that by the number of such assistant managers in the region who were originally joined the action. THEN multiply by the number of assistant managers who might be bringing similar actions around the country.

Note also that this case also illustrates that employers may be subject to "liquidated damages" — an additional amount equal to the amount of unpaid wages — for violations of the FLSA's overtime and minimum wage mandates. *See* 29 U.S.C. § 216(b). The court may, however, in its discretion award lesser or no liquidated damages if it finds that the employer's actions giving rise to FLSA liability were in good faith and that the employer had reasonable grounds for believing that his act or omission was not a violation. *See* 29 U.S.C. § 260; 29 C.F.R. § 790.22. Moreover, prevailing FLSA plaintiffs are also awarded their reasonable attorneys' fees. *See* 29 U.S.C. § 216(b). Finally, any person who willfully violates the provisions of the FLSA may be subject to criminal fines and imprisonment. *See* 29 U.S.C. § 216(a).

This potential liability accounts for the many high-profile cases, verdicts, and settlements in these cases in recent years. For example, like the "manager" cases discussed above, there has been a recent wave of overtime suits by employees in the financial industry. *See, e.g.,* Posting of Paul M. Secondo to WorkplaceProfBlog, http://lawprofessors.typepad.com/laborprof_blog/2006/05/smith_barney_ov.html (May 31, 2006) (discussing Citigroup's settlement with employees for $98 million). And there have been many suits brought by other kinds of workers resulting in large payouts. *See, e.g.,* http://www.lawyersandsettlements.com/settlements/employment-settlements/ (listing large wage and hour settlements).

As discussed in the notes following the *Ansoumana* case in Chapter 1, page 34, there have also been a number of successful and high-profile minimum-wage suits. However, as also mentioned, enforcement of wage and hour laws at the low end of the labor market is difficult and rare. *See id.* For this reason, wage and hour violations — sometimes referred to as "wage theft" — are widespread. *See, e.g.,* Brishen Rogers, *Toward Third-Party Liability for Wage Theft*, 11 BERKELEY J. EMPL. & LAB. L. 1, 10 n.33 (2010) (citing numerous recent studies showing that violations are common); *see also* ANNETTE BERNHARDT ET AL., THE GLOVES-OFF ECONOMY: WORKPLACE STANDARDS AT THE BOTTOM OF THE LABOR MARKET 7-8 (2008) (same). Indeed, while enforcement activities are on the rise, so too are underlying violations across the low-wage workforce. *See, e.g.,* Steven Greenhouse, *More Workers Are Claiming "Wage Theft,"* N.Y. TIMES, Sept. 1, 2014, at A1.

Chapter 1 discusses a number of phenomena that contribute to this underenforcement problem, including "employer" coverage questions, insolvency of fly-by-night labor contractors, and the socioeconomic vulnerability and immigrant status of workers. Insufficient remedies to incentivize private attorneys to bring these claims is another reason, since, in contrast to claims for overtime by higher-wage workers, the potential damages for lost wage claims for low-wage workers often are not substantial. Furthermore, due to a chronic lack of resources, the DOL and state agencies traditionally have been unable to fill the enforcement gap. *See* GLOVES OFF, *supra,* at 13. Still another factor is the array of procedural hurdles workers must overcome to obtain relief under the FLSA, including the statute's collective action mechanism for consolidating claims, 29 U.S.C. § 216(b), which, unlike ordinary class actions, require workers to opt into the suit. *See* Craig Becker & Paul Strauss, *Representing Low-Wage Workers in the Absence of a Class: The Peculiar Case of Section 16 of the Fair Labor Standards Act and the Underenforcement of Minimum Labor Standards*, 92 MINN. L. REV. 1317 (2006); Nantiya Ruan, *Facilitating Wage Theft: How Courts Use Procedural Rules to Undermine Substantive Rights of Low-Wage Workers*, 63 VAND. L. REV. 727 (2010); Scott A. Moss & Nantiya Ruan, *The Second-Class Class Action: How Courts Thwart Wage Rights by Misapplying Class Action Rules*, 61 AM. U. L. REV. 523 (2012); *see also Genesis Healthcare Corp. v. Symczyk,* 133 S. Ct. 1523 (2013) (holding that a collective action brought by single employee on behalf of herself and all similarly situated employees for employer's alleged violation of the FLSA was no longer justiciable when her individual claim became moot as result of offer of judgment by employer in an amount sufficient to make her whole). And, as discussed in detail in Chapter 13, collective enforcement of wage and hour laws also has been made more difficult by the Supreme Court's recent Federal Arbitration Act decisions. *Cf. Killion v. KeHE Dist., LLC.,* 761 F.3d 574 (6th Cir. 2014) (holding in an FLSA case that an employment agreement that contained a collective action waiver is invalid in the absence of an agreement to arbitrate). For a discussion of potential tax liability for wage theft and suggestions for improving enforcement, *see* Sachin S. Pandya, *Tax Liability for Wage Theft*, 3 COLUM. J. TAX L. 113 (2012).

11. *Erring on the Side of Safety?* Unlike mistakenly classifying an employee as exempt, mistakenly classifying an employee as nonexempt is unlikely to harm the employee. Since erroneously treating the employee as exempt poses great risks to the employer in terms of unpaid overtime plus interest, liquidated damages, and paying its own attorneys' fees and litigation costs and those of the plaintiff, it would seem that employers might choose to err on the side of classifying workers as nonexempt. But employers might discount the risks of liability by the (un)likelihood that the employee or the DOL will actually bring suit and prevail. Depending on the employer's view of the risks, the employer may be willing to accept the possibility of downstream liability to avoid paying overtime in the near term. And erring on the side of nonexempt status has its own obvious problem: the risk of substantial overtime payments. However, an employer who chooses this path could also limit such costs by avoiding overtime and hiring additional workers. Can you appreciate how complex a legal and business decision it is to decide whether positions are exempt or not? Realize too that over the course of time, even correct decisions may have to be reconsidered in light of changing workplace practices.

12. *Private Ordering Again.* We started our discussion of the FLSA by saying that there is relatively little role for private ordering. That's certainly true with respect to the substantive provisions — the workers could not prospectively waive their rights to overtime compensation in order to, say, get more overtime hours. But the exemptions analyzed in these cases can be viewed as opening a door to private ordering. An employer's structuring a job in certain ways will bring the employee within or without the exemption. Of course, there are real, if not legal, constraints on this type of planning. Hiring subordinates might result in exemption for the supervisor, but it also results in two more workers protected by the FLSA.

PROBLEM

11-1. Suppose you are an attorney at a large law firm. You have been asked by the firm's managing partner to give her advice on whether various "paralegals" are exempt employees. You are confident that the vast majority of paralegals are not exempt as "learned professionals," given that the new regulations explicitly provide that only paralegals possessing specialized degrees in other professional fields and applying that knowledge are exempt as such professionals. *See* 29 C.F.R. §541.301(e)(7). But might some paralegals be administrative employees?

You know that most paralegals in your firm — like the bulk of paralegals elsewhere — simply assist attorneys in completing various tasks, including drafting and filing legal documents and forms, preparing for trial, reviewing documents, communicating with clients, organizing documents and materials, performing basic compilations, and engaging in basic legal research. As to whether paralegals whose primary duties fit this description are exempt under the administrative exemption, your research reveals a recent Department of Labor Opinion Letter — providing a nonbinding legal opinion based on the facts provided by the employer — that offers a fairly definitive "no," indicating that such employees do not exercise the level of judgment and discretion necessary to satisfy the exemption's requirements:

> It continues to be our opinion that the duties of paralegal employees do not involve the exercise of discretion and independent judgment of the type required by section 541.200(a)(3) of the final regulations, thus an analysis of whether their work is related to management or general business operations is not necessary. The outline of the duties of the paralegal employees you provide describes the use of skills rather than discretion and independent judgment. The paralegals typically are drafting particular documents to assist attorneys on a particular case or matter. The paralegals are not themselves formulating or implementing management policies, utilizing authority to waive or deviate from established policies, providing expert advice, or planning business objectives in accordance with the dictates of 29 C.F.R. §541.202(b). Thus, . . . the paralegal employees appear to fit more

appropriately into that category of employees who apply particular skills and knowledge in preparing assignments. Employees who apply such skills and knowledge generally are not exercising independent judgment, even if they have some leeway in reaching a conclusion. In addition, most jurisdictions have strict prohibitions against the unauthorized practice of law by laypersons. Under the American Bar Association's Code of Professional Responsibility, a delegation of legal tasks to a lay person is proper only if the lawyer maintains a direct relationship with the client, supervises the delegated work, and has complete professional responsibility for the work produced. The implication of such strictures is that the paralegal employees you describe would not have the amount of authority to exercise independent judgments with regard to legal matters necessary to bring them within the administrative exemption.

Wage and Hour Division, U.S. Department of Labor, Opinion Letter FLSA 2005-54, 2005 WL 3638473 (December 16, 2005).

Despite the Opinion Letter, you know that paralegal duties vary enormously in your firm, and there is no formal job description for any of them. Indeed, some of the more experienced and successful paralegals in your firm have responsibilities requiring a significant amount of judgment. Accordingly, you inquire further and learn some pertinent information with regard to four such paralegals. In addition to performing the basic duties described above:

- Adrianne works in the Family Law group and is largely responsible for initial client screening and intake decisions;
- Boris, who has worked in the firm's Corporate Group for 15 years, has authority to update and edit the department's library of standard forms;
- Carlos is the person primarily responsible for pretrial document management in several multimillion-dollar cases for the Commercial Litigation group; and
- Devon, who works in your firm's human resources department, exercises fairly broad de facto authority to make various types of regulatory compliance decisions.

Under any of these circumstances, would the paralegal be exempt as an administrative employee? Do the examples from the regulations discussed in Note 7 above help? Does the Department's Opinion letter determine the outcome for any of them, or does its discussion of the discretion and independent judgment factor suggest rather that the outcome is far from clear? What other information, if any, might be helpful in making your assessment?

---

b. FLSA Application Problems

When an employee is entitled to the FLSA's minimum wage protections, overtime protections, or both, application of the requirements is often straightforward. Nevertheless, a few application issues have produced litigation. One set of these issues involves the calculation of hours or compensable time, and another involves rate-of-pay determinations.

i. Compensable Time

In applying the FLSA's minimum wage and overtime mandates, one must determine the number of hours an employee has worked. The original statute contained no definition of "work," "compensable time," or any other term addressing what counts as work or working hours. In a series of early cases, the Supreme Court held that the statute's definition of "employ" — "to suffer or permit to work" — means that employers must pay employees for productive activities they control or require and are for the employer's primary benefit. *See Tennessee Coal, Iron, & R.R. Co. v. Muscoda Local No. 123*, 321 U.S. 590 (1944); *Armour & Co. v. Wantock*, 323 U.S. 126 (1944); *Skidmore v. Swift & Co.*, 323 U.S. 134 (1944). The Court also held, however, that time spent in "incidental" activities is also compensable. *See Skidmore, supra.* This lack of clarity led Congress to pass the Portal-to-Portal Act of 1947, *see* 29 U.S.C. § 254 (2006), which explicitly *excludes* from compensable time (1) travel to and from work and the work site prior to or after the workday or principal work activities and (2) activities that are "preliminary to or postliminary to said principal activity or activities," unless such travel or activities are included as compensable time pursuant to custom or contract.

What constitutes "preliminary or postliminary" activities, however, has been the subject of a fair amount of litigation. In general, an employee's activities preparing for work or after ending work, such as putting on or taking off work clothes, are noncompensable. However, where such activities are "an integral and indispensable part of the principal activities," they remain compensable. *Mitchell v. King Packing Co.*, 350 U.S. 260, 262-63 (1956). Thus, while donning work clothes is normally noncompensable, putting on and taking off uniforms at work pursuant to employer requirements or industry custom, or for safety reasons, is compensable. *See, e.g., IBP, Inc. v. Alvarez*, 546 U.S. 21 (2005) (finding that where putting on and taking off required work gear and uniforms are integral and indispensable activities, time spent moving to and from changing areas to work areas constitutes compensable time as does time waiting to doff gear). *But see Sandifer v. U.S. Steel Corp.*, 134 S. Ct. 870 (2014) (finding that donning and doffing of clothes and safety gear is subject to collective bargaining and hence, not compensable pursuant to section 203(o) of the FLSA, when the safety gear was relatively de minimis compared to the clothing) It is also worth noting that preparing necessary tools or equipment is also compensable. *Mitchell*, 350 U.S. at 262-63 (finding knife-sharpening in a meat-packing plant is integral and indispensable to employee's principal activity of butchering); *see also* 29 C.F.R. § 790.8(c) (protective clothing for workers in a chemical plant).

Nevertheless, interpretation and application issues with regard to preliminary and postliminary activities continue to arise. For example, as this book was going to press, the Supreme Court finally resolved the much disputed question of whether time employees spend waiting for and undergoing security screenings before leaving work constitutes compensable activity, concluding that it does not. *See* Integrity Staffing Solutions, Inc. v. Busk, — S. Ct. —, 2014 WL 6885951 (Dec. 9, 2014).

Various other questions with regard to compensable time are addressed by detailed Department of Labor regulations. These include rules that distinguish compensable break times, sleep time, lunch and other meal times, and other "down" times from nonproductive portions of the day that are not compensable. In recent years, lawsuits over uncompensated break, meal, and other time have received significant attention. Perhaps most noteworthy is the recent wave of FLSA and state wage-and-hour lawsuits against Wal-Mart Stores, Inc., alleging various compensable time-related violations. Wal-Mart's total exposure in judgments and settlements was in the hundreds of millions of dollars. *See, e.g.*, Wage and Hour Lawsuits against Wal-Mart Settled for over $350 Million, December 30, 2008, *available at* http://www.aboutlawsuits.com/wage-and-hour-lawsuits-against-wal-mart-settled-2211/ (discussing Wal-Mart's agreement to pay between $352 million and $640 million to settle 63 wage and hour lawsuits filed in 42 states). *See generally* Michael Orey, *Wage Wars*, BUSINESSWEEK, October 1, 2007, *available at* http://www.businessweek.com/magazine/content/07_40/b4052001.htm.

The status of "on-call" time is another area in which there is much controversy and litigation. This issue has produced many disputes in certain job categories — for example, emergency response personnel, automated equipment and information systems maintenance personnel, and nonexempt medical workers. This is unsurprising considering the number of hours at issue and, hence, the enormous economic stakes for both employees and employers.

Pabst v. Oklahoma Gas & Electric Co.
228 F.3d 1128 (10th Cir. 2000)

LUCERO, Circuit Judge.

[W]e conclude that plaintiffs' on-call duties requiring them to continually monitor automated alarms by pager and computer were compensable under the FLSA. In so holding, we reject the argument that on-call monitoring time is not compensable unless contemporaneously reported to the employer as overtime. Further, we uphold the district court's determination that the employer's FLSA violation was not willful, and affirm both the award of prejudgment interest and the denial of liquidated damages. . . .

I

Plaintiffs are Electronic Technicians in Oklahoma Gas & Electric's ("OG&E") Facility Operations Department. Plaintiffs Pabst and Gilley were Electronic Technician I's ("Tech 1s") and plaintiff Barton was an Electronic Technician II ("Tech 2"). The three plaintiffs, along with two other employees, monitored automated heat, fire, and security systems in several OG&E buildings. Prior to an August 1994 reduction in force, these duties required twelve on-site employees working three eight-hour shifts.

Plaintiffs were on call to monitor OG&E building alarms weekdays from 4:30 p.m. to 7:30 a.m. and twenty-four hours a day on weekends. During these hours, alarms went to computers at Pabst's and Gilley's homes, as well as to pagers for all plaintiffs. After October 1994, Barton began to receive alarms at home via lap-top computer. Plaintiffs were required to respond to the alarms initially within ten minutes, then, after October 1996, within fifteen minutes. Failure to respond within the time limit was grounds for discipline. Each plaintiff was assigned, and required always to carry, an alpha-numeric pager. These pagers were only 70% reliable. The short response time, coupled with unreliable pagers, forced plaintiffs to remain at or near their homes while on call.

The district court found that plaintiffs received an average of three to five alarms per night, not including pages for security issues. Although not all alarms required plaintiffs to report to the office—it appears many could be fixed by remote computer—the district court found it took an average of forty-five minutes to respond to each alarm. Neither party disputes those findings on appeal.

[The district court also found that the employer did not utilize a rotational on-call schedule. A rotation "would not have been feasible because of the frequency of alarms and plaintiffs' differing areas of expertise."]

According to plaintiffs, their supervisor instructed them to report only on-call time spent responding to an alarm. OG&E paid plaintiffs for at least one hour for each alarm to which they responded, and two hours if they had to return to OG&E facilities. Plaintiffs apparently reported some, but not all, of the alarms they answered, but did not claim as overtime the remainder of their time spent on call.

Considerable testimony was presented regarding the extent to which monitoring interfered with plaintiffs' personal activities. Most significantly, an average of three to five alarms per night, each requiring on average forty-five minutes of work, severely disrupted plaintiffs' sleep habits; indeed, they testified to rarely experiencing more than five hours of uninterrupted sleep per night. In addition, even during waking hours, plaintiffs were unable to pursue many personal activities while on call because of the need to come into their homes to check their computers every fifteen minutes.

The district court found plaintiffs' on-call time compensable under the FLSA and awarded them compensation for fifteen hours per weekday and twenty-four hours per Saturday and Sunday, less any hours already paid for responding to alarms. . . .

II . . .

"Employ" is defined as including "to suffer or permit to work." §203(g). The pertinent question, and one with which courts have struggled, is whether on-call time is "work" for purposes of the statute. The FLSA does not explicitly address the issue of on-call time.[1] Courts, however, have developed a jurisprudence of on-call time, based on the Supreme Court cases of *Armour & Co. v. Wantock*, 323 U.S. 126 (1944), and *Skidmore v. Swift & Co.*, 323 U.S. 134 (1944). Those cases determine the relevant inquiry to be whether an employee is "engaged to wait" or "waiting to be engaged," *Skidmore*, or, alternatively, whether on-call time is spent predominantly for the benefit of the employer or the employee, *see Armour*. Necessarily, the inquiry is highly individualized and fact-based, and "requires consideration of the agreement between the parties, the nature and extent of the restrictions, the relationship between the services rendered and the on-call time, and all surrounding circumstances," *Boehm v. Kansas City Power & Light Co.*, 868 F.2d 1182, 1185 (10th Cir. 1989) (citing *Skidmore*). We also focus on the degree to which the burden on the employee interferes with his or her personal pursuits. *See Armitage v. City of Emporia*, 982 F.2d 430, 432 (10th Cir. 1992). Several facts are relevant in assessing that burden: number of calls, required

1. Although regulations promulgated by the Department of Labor address that issue, they are unhelpful to our analysis because they fail to anticipate a scenario, like that in the present case, in which an on-call employee is able to perform his or her duties from a location away from the employer's premises. *See* 29 C.F.R. §785.17 (stating that an "on call" employee is working if "required to remain on call on the employer's premises or so close thereto that he cannot use the time effectively for his own purposes"). More helpful are those regulations applicable to fire protection and law enforcement employees. *See* 29 C.F.R. §553.221(d) (stating that time spent on call is compensable if "the conditions placed on the employee's activities are so restrictive that the employee cannot use the time effectively for personal pursuits").

response time, and ability to engage in personal pursuits while on call. *See id.; Renfro v. City of Emporia*, 948 F.2d 1529, 1537-38 (10th Cir. 1991).

A

OG&E argues that it did not know plaintiffs were working the entire time they were on call and thus did not "suffer or permit" them to work. 29 U.S.C. § 203(g). Its theory goes as follows: Plaintiffs were responsible for reporting their own overtime;[2] because they reported only time spent responding to calls (and apparently not even all of that), rather than *all* of their on-call time, OG&E lacked knowledge that they were working and therefore did not suffer or permit them to work. This argument misinterprets the nature of the on-call time inquiry and borders on the disingenuous.

As a factual matter, OG&E's purported lack of actual knowledge is dubious. Plaintiffs cite record testimony detailing a reprimand Pabst received for attempting to report the entire time spent monitoring systems as overtime. . . . More significantly, OG&E's policy informed plaintiffs they would be compensated only for on-call time spent responding to an alarm. The only logical inference was that they would not be compensated for time spent monitoring their computers and pagers, unless they took some specific action responding to an alarm. To claim, then, that OG&E did not know plaintiffs were working because they did not report every hour of their evenings and weekends as overtime is misleading. While OG&E arguably may have lacked knowledge of the legal proposition that the FLSA required compensating plaintiffs for their on-call time under the system at issue, OG&E certainly knew that plaintiffs were performing the duties they had been assigned.

OG&E relies heavily on *Davis v. Food Lion*, 792 F.2d 1274, 1276 (4th Cir. 1986) for its knowledge theory. In *Davis*, the court found that "Food Lion has an established policy which prohibits employees from working unrecorded, so-called 'off-the-clock', hours." Davis argued that Food Lion's "Effective Scheduling" system required him to work such off-the-clock hours in order to perform his required duties and avoid reprimand. The Fourth Circuit held the FLSA "required Davis to prove Food Lion's actual or constructive knowledge of his overtime work," and found no clear error in the district court's "factual finding that Food Lion has no actual or constructive knowledge of Davis's off-the-clock work."

Davis is not applicable to the case before us. First, there is no evidence of anything like an explicit prohibition on plaintiffs' performing after-hours monitoring duties; on the contrary, such was the very essence of their responsibilities. Moreover, *Davis* was not, as plaintiffs correctly note, an on-call time case. In the on-call context, an employer who creates an on-call system obviously has constructive, if not actual, knowledge of employees' on-call duties. An employer must evaluate whether those duties are compensable under the FLSA, and if the employer concludes they are not, the employees do not bear the burden of submitting overtime requests for hours that fall outside the definition of what the employer classifies as compensable. Plaintiffs reported (apparently with some omissions) the hours to which they were entitled under OG&E's policy. That they did not report the entirety of their remaining on-

---

2. Plaintiffs worked a forty-hour week in addition to their time on call. Thus, to the extent on-call time was working time, it was compensable at the overtime rate. *See* 29 U.S.C. § 207.

call hours does not preclude the obvious conclusion that OG&E had knowledge of their on-call status.

[OG&E argued that its rotating on-call schedule meant that it had neither actual nor constructive knowledge of the full extent of plaintiffs' on-call hours. The argument was that OG&E believed only one plaintiff to be on call during a given week, and thus it did not know of the other two. But the district court noted that there was strong evidence against any such rotational schedule and that even OG&E conceded that there were weeks when two employees recorded time despite the supposed rotation. There was no clear error in the district court's findings.]

B

Whether a particular set of facts constitutes compensable "work" under the FLSA is a legal question we review de novo. *See Berry v. County of Sonoma*, 30 F.3d 1174, 1180 (9th Cir. 1994). In *Renfro*, we granted FLSA compensation to firefighters for their on-call time. *Renfro*'s facts include the following:

> the firefighter must be able to report to the stationhouse within twenty minutes of being paged or be subject to discipline; that the on-call periods are 24-hours in length; and primarily that the calls are frequent-a firefighter may receive as many as 13 calls during an on-call period, with a stated average frequency of 3-5 calls per on-call period.

OG&E emphasizes that all but one published Tenth Circuit case addressing on-call time have found it non-compensable. Counting published cases, however, is meaningless in resolving a fact-intensive question such as the compensability of on-call time. Rather, the proper question is which case is most analogous. . . . In sum, this case is far more analogous to *Renfro* than to the more numerous precedents cited by OG&E.

Although OG&E complains bitterly against having to compensate plaintiffs for working twenty-four hours a day, seven days a week, the cost to an employer of an "always on call" arrangement does not mean that such a system is not cognizable under the FLSA, so long as the on-call time qualifies as work under the relevant FLSA precedents. While one circuit has held that always being on call, while extremely burdensome, does not in and of itself make the on-call time compensable for FLSA purposes, *see Bright v. Houston Northwest Med. Ctr. Survivor, Inc.*, 934 F.2d 671, 678-79 (5th Cir. 1991) (en banc), another circuit found that requiring employees to monitor and respond all day, every day is a factor weighing in favor of compensability, *see Cross v. Arkansas Forestry Comm'n*, 938 F.2d 912, 916-17 (8th Cir. 1991) (holding that on-call time is compensable under the FLSA because employees were required to continuously monitor transmissions and respond within thirty minutes, and because they were subject to on-call status twenty-four hours per day for every day of a work period). We agree with both *Bright* and *Cross*. Although always being on call is not dispositive, such an added burden is relevant in assessing the extent to which all-the-time on-call duty deprives employees of the ability to engage in personal activities.

The only significant difference between the burden on the plaintiffs in *Renfro* and the burden on Pabst, Gilley, and Barton is that plaintiffs here often did not have to report to the employer's workplace in order to respond to calls. This lighter burden, however, is offset by the fact that plaintiffs, unlike the firefighters in *Renfro*, were not on call for "six shifts of twenty-four hours each in a 19-day cycle," but rather during *all* of their off-premises time. The frequency of calls here actually is greater than in *Renfro* because plaintiffs' calls during weekdays occurred during a fifteen hour, rather than a twenty-four hour, period. Additionally, in *Renfro*, we found on-call time compensable despite the fact that the firefighters "had participated in sports activities, socialized with friends and relatives, attended business meetings, gone shopping, gone out to eat, babysitted, and performed maintenance or other activities around their home." *Renfro* controls the application of the FLSA to the facts before us, and leads us to hold that the district court was correct in finding plaintiffs' on-call time compensable.

III

We next consider OG&E's claims that the award of overtime compensation should be reduced by subtracting out several time periods.

We reject, as a matter of law, OG&E's argument that time spent in personal pursuits should be subtracted. The relevant inquiry in on-call cases is not whether plaintiffs' duties prevented them from engaging in any and all personal activities during on-call time; rather it is "whether 'the time is spent predominantly for the employer's benefit or the employee's.'" *Boehm* (quoting *Armour*). This is a yes-no inquiry — whose benefit predominated? OG&E cites no authority for the proposition that a court must determine whose benefit predominated during each on-call hour. *Cf. Renfro* (holding firefighters' on-call time compensable even though they engaged in some personal pursuits during that time). OG&E's other arguments for reductions in the damages award, which pertain to individual plaintiffs, are factual issues subject to clear error review.

OG&E argues that Barton should not have been awarded overtime compensation from October 1994 through October 1, 1996 because during that time he was monitoring alarms only by pager and not by computer. OG&E primarily focuses on the comparatively small amount of remote overtime Barton charged during that period, as compared to Gilley and Pabst. However, we are persuaded the district court did not clearly err in determining that Barton, like Gilley and Pabst, received between three and five pages per night during this period, despite the comparatively smaller amount of overtime Barton recorded. . . .

[The court affirmed the district court's denial of liquidated damages, finding that the court did not abuse its discretion in concluding that OG&E's actions were reasonable and in good faith, despite its mistaken belief that the on-call time was noncompensable.]

NOTES

1. *A Costly Mistake.* Although this case was brought by only three employees, and the court ultimately rejected their bid for liquidated damages, OG&E's liability was still significant, given that these employees consistently worked a 24/7 schedule. Had OG&E known that the FLSA required overtime compensation for this time, how might it have structured its on-call regime to limit the amount it would have to pay out to its technicians? It might have instituted a real rotation system. Might it have

been cheaper to hire a fourth tech for a night shift than to pay overtime? Might knowledge of potential liability also have influenced how OG&E ran its operations—for example, what equipment it uses, what times of day this equipment should be running, how many resources it puts into daytime maintenance? The possibility of more reliable pagers jumps off the page.

2. *Disparate Outcomes and Planning Implications.* The *Pabst* court recognizes the differing views of the various circuit courts on when on-call time is compensable. Indeed, these differences are even more profound when one digs a little deeper. For example, *Bright v. Houston Northwest Medical Center Survivor, Inc.*, 934 F.2d 671 (5th Cir. 1991) (en banc), did not simply hold, as *Pabst* suggests, that always being on-call "does not in and of itself make the on-call time compensable for FLSA purposes." Rather, the *Bright* court held as a matter of law that a biomedical equipment repair technician on-call around the clock was not entitled to compensation for on-call periods except those in which he actually worked because (1) he was not required to remain at or very near the hospital where he worked, (2) he was free to be at his home or at any place he chose without advising his employer, and (3) he was "subject only to the restrictions that he be reachable by beeper, not be intoxicated, and be able to arrive at the hospital in 'approximately' twenty minutes." *Id.* at 676; *see also Adair v. Charter Cty. of Wayne*, 452 F.3d 482 (6th Cir. 2006) (finding officers employed by county airport were not entitled to overtime pay for off-duty time during which they were required to carry pagers and remain relatively near to work because they could engage in regular activities).

In light of these differing approaches and outcomes, the issue of on-call time provides a nice example of the planning difficulties for employers with operations in more than one part of the country. Should such an employer treat similarly situated employees differently based on local circuit law? Are there other reasons or constraints that might lead an employer not to make such distinctions?

3. *From Pagers to PDAs.* Pabst involved a pager, technology that is so last-millennium. In an era of smart phones, employees are increasingly expected to respond during what are, in theory, nonworking hours. Even when such responses are not expected, employees often do answer e-mails or calls off hours. *See, e.g.*, Cheryl Corley, *Using Your BlackBerry Off-Hours Could Be Overtime*, NPR.org, August 14, 2010, http://www.npr.org/templates/story/story.php?storyId= 129184907 (discussing a suit brought by a Chicago police officer for unpaid overtime because he felt obligated to log in to the Blackberry his department provided often after his shift was over). The employer might or might not know of the activity, or, at least, the extent of it. But, as we saw in Chapter 6, employers typically have the legal freedom and technological ability to track employee use of employer equipment 24/7. How should the law deal with this reality? *See generally* Sean L. McLaughlin, Comment, *Controlling Smart-Phone Abuse: The Fair Labor Standards Act's Definition of "Work" in Non-exempt Employee Claims for Overtime*, 58 U. KAN. L. REV. 737 (2010). If you were an employer's attorney, would you consider advising employees not to use company e-mail, phone, or other electronic devices during nonwork hours? That seems extreme, but the risks of liability might be pretty high. The alternative of monitoring such use and reacting on a more individual basis also seems problematic.

4. *Line Drawing.* Compensation for on-call time provides yet another example of the difficultly of drawing lines under the FLSA and the corresponding costs and risks for employers and employees trying to determine *ex ante* what the terms of their relationship will be. Congress may be institutionally incapable of drawing finer distinctions to avoid such problems. But, why doesn't the DOL attempt to make things clearer? In answering this question, consider the potential costs and risks of clarity. For example, are unforeseen loopholes and other unintended consequences more likely? Also, does greater specificity increase the need for more frequent regulatory amendments?

5. *Computer Personnel.* One obvious growth area in the "on-call" context in recent years involves information technology ("IT") and computer personnel. Given that virtually all public and private employers use such technology, and many, if not most, need their systems to operate 24 hours a day, employees are needed who can respond when there are software, hardware, and other problems. However, these employees pose an additional wrinkle to the "on-call" question. As mentioned above, some computer personnel are exempt under the special exemption for computer employees. *See* 29 U.S.C.A. § 213(a)(17). The new governing regulation, which closely tracks the statutory language, provides as follows:

29 C.F.R. § 541.400 General Rule for Computer Employees. . . .

(b) The section 13(a)(1) exemption applies to any computer employee compensated on a salary or fee basis at a rate of not less than $455 per week . . . , exclusive of board, lodging or other facilities, and the section 13(a)(17) exemption applies to any computer employee compensated on an hourly basis at a rate not less than $27.63 an hour. In addition, under either section 13(a)(1) or section 13(a)(17) of the Act, the exemptions apply only to computer employees whose primary duty consists of:

(1) The application of systems analysis techniques and procedures, including consulting with users, to determine hardware, software or system functional specifications;

(2) The design, development, documentation, analysis, creation, testing or modification of computer systems or programs, including prototypes, based on and related to user or system design specifications;

(3) The design, documentation, testing, creation or modification of computer programs related to machine operating systems; or

(4) A combination of the aforementioned duties, the performance of which requires the same level of skills.

The exemption does not include employees primarily engaged in the manufacture or repair of computer hardware and related equipment or those who merely use computers in their work. *See* 29 C.F.R. § 541.401.

In light of this exemption, think about the various kinds of computer or information employees with whom you have worked at school or while employed. Are any or all of your school's or your employer's IT employees exempt? Recall, of course, that some may already be exempt under the administrative or executive exemptions. Is this easy to determine or would you require more detail regarding duties to make an assessment? *Cf.* Wage and Hour Division, U.S. Department of Labor, Opinion Letter FLSA FLSA2006-42, 2006 WL 3406603 (October 26, 2006) (opining that an IT Support Specialist position in which the employee is primarily responsible for "installing, configuring, testing, and troubleshooting computer applications, networks, and hardware" does not involve the exercise of sufficient discretion to qualify for the administrative exemption and does not involve the "application of systems analysis techniques and procedures, including consulting with users, to determine hardware, software or system functional specifications" necessary to qualify for the computer employee exemption).

Among computer employees, how many are "on-call," at least some of the time? What about the *Pabst* plaintiffs? The employer never argued that these employees were exempt, only that their on-call time was not compensable. Do you see why?

In terms of policy, does it make sense to exempt these computer employees from the FLSA's strictures, including the overtime provisions that might mandate premium compensation for when they are on-call (assuming such time would otherwise satisfy the test articulated in *Pabst*)? In other words, are these computer employees more like learned and creative professionals or more like the technicians in *Pabst*? In answering this question consider not only what such computer employees do, but also their relative ability to protect themselves in the market. Is your answer today different than it might have been in 2000, at the height of the Internet and technology boom?

6. *New Frontiers in On-Call Work: "Just-In-Time" Employment.* Another emergent issue in this context is so-called just-in-time scheduling, in which employers in the service sector use software to track customer demand and then adjust workers' schedules as needed. This is highly efficient from the employer perspective since an employer can maintain a fairly exacting labor-hours-to-demand ratio. However, this technique leaves employees with little certainty about their schedule or the number of hours they will work, and results in fluctuating hours that preclude employees from working elsewhere or engaging in other activities. Currently, such idle time is not compensable under the FLSA. Moreover, although some states have sought to regulate work scheduling, scholars argue these protections are also inadequate. *See* Charlotte Alexander, Anna Haley-Lock, & Nantiya Ruan, *Stabilizing Low-Wage Work: Legal Remedies for Unpredictable Work Hours and Income Instability*, HARV. CR-CL L. REV. (forthcoming 2014), available at http://papers.ssrn.com/sol3/papers.cfm?abstract_id=2327903; *see also* Steven Greenhouse, *Part-Time Schedules, Full-Time Headaches*, N.Y. TIMES, July 18, 2014 at B1 (discussing the phenomenon and fledgling efforts at regulation at the state and local level).

PROBLEM

11-2. Oops, I Did It [Violated the FLSA?] Again. . . . This item appeared in Yahoo! News on March 30, 2006:

Former Spears Bodyguards Sue for Overtime

Three men hired to guard pop star Britney Spears have filed a lawsuit claiming they worked long hours and were not paid overtime.

The lawsuit, filed Tuesday in Superior Court, names three companies — Britney Brands Inc., Britney Touring Inc. and Team Tours Inc. — as responsible for not properly compensating former bodyguards Lonnie Jones, Randy Jones and Silas Dukes.

Together, the three men are seeking damages exceeding $25,000 for unpaid wages and benefits, their attorney Daniel Emilio said Wednesday. Messages left at the office of Spears' publicist Leslie Sloane Zelnick were not immediately returned.

Randy Jones and Dukes worked 12- to 16-hour shifts and were required to be on call 24 hours a day during trips with Spears, according to the lawsuit. Lonnie Jones worked 12-hour shifts, the suit said.

The trio claimed they were only paid a "straight salary," missed meals and didn't receive overtime pay.

Hired in 2004, the men claim they were laid off on Nov. 30, 2005 without receiving a final paycheck.

http://news.yahoo.com/s/ap/20060330/ap_on_en_mu/people_spears.

Suppose you were contacted by Ms. Spears' legal team and asked to assist in determining the risk of liability under the FLSA and preparing a possible defense. They send you the complaint, which, under California's liberal pleading regime, provides little detail in addition to what is set forth above. Their two questions for you are (1) whether these bodyguards might be exempt under the white-collar exemptions and (2) if not, whether their "on-call" time might constitute compensable hours. As to the first question, what additional information would you need to make this determination? Given what you know at this point, how likely is it that these bodyguards are exempt? As to the second question, what information would you need to determine whether the on-call time is compensable? Again, given what you know at this point, how likely is it that this time is compensable? Additionally, based on the facts provided so far, is there a possible further line of defense here? Hint: Take a look back at *Ansoumana. But see Schultz v. Capital Intern. Security, Inc.*, 460 F.3d 595 (4th Cir. 2006) (holding workers hired to provide security for Saudi prince were "employees" covered by FLSA because, among other things, prince and security company exercised nearly complete control over their jobs, they were paid a set rate per shift, some worked for the prince for several years, and he preferred workers who would stay over the long term).

Finally, switch gears and consider the plaintiffs' perspective. Although the complaint appears not to have done so at this point, could and should the plaintiffs have named Ms. Spears as a defendant in her personal capacity? After all, she's "not that innocent." Wouldn't that up the settlement value of the case?

---

ii. Calculating "Regular Rate of Pay"

As we have seen, the FLSA's overtime provisions require employers to pay covered workers "time and a half," that is, one and one-half times their "regular rate of pay" for hours in excess of 40 hours in any given week. *See* 29 U.S.C. § 207 (2014). What constitutes an employee's "regular rate of pay" is a fairly easy calculation when an employee receives only hourly wages or receives a salary and has a work week with standard hours. Thus, for example, an employee who receives a weekly salary of $1,000 for 40 hours of work has a regular rate of pay of $25 per hour. If the employee works 50 hours in a given week, the employer will have to pay the employee $1,375 for that week — $1,000 weekly salary for the first 40 hours plus $375 for the additional 10 hours ($25 multiplied by the 10 additional hours multiplied by the one-and-one-half overtime premium rate).

If the employee's salary compensates for fewer than 40 hours a week, then the employee is entitled to his or her regular rate for additional hours up to 40 hours, and the premium rate thereafter. Thus, for example, an employee who receives a weekly salary of $750 for 30 hours of work a week has a regular rate of $25 dollars per hour. If the employee works 50 hours in a given week, the employer will have to pay the employee $1,375 for that week—$750 weekly salary for 30 hours, plus $250 for 10 additional hours ($25 multiplied by 10), plus $375 for the remaining 10 hours ($25 multiplied by the 10 additional hours plus one-half that amount, representing the overtime premium).

The regular rate of pay calculation becomes more difficult, however, when the employee receives a salary for hours that are contemplated to fluctuate week-to-week or receives forms of compensation in addition to his or her hourly wage or salary. If the employee is so employed, a DOL regulation allows the employer to use a fluctuating workweek computation method to determine the regular rate and overtime pay. *See* 29 C.F.R. §778.114. This method still guarantees an overtime premium for each overtime hour worked, but, by allowing a recomputation of the regular rate each week based on the total hours worked, it in effect allows the employer to pay less of a premium per hour the more hours the employee works in any given week.

However, this calculation method is available only when (1) there is "a clear mutual understanding of the parties" that the salary is compensation for "the hours worked each workweek, whatever their number, rather than for working 40 hours or some other fixed weekly work period"; (2) the salary is sufficient to ensure a rate not less than the applicable minimum wage rate for every hour worked in any week (regardless of the number of hours worked); and (3) the employee actually receives the extra compensation, in addition to the base salary, for all overtime hours worked at a rate not less than one-half the employee's regular rate of pay. Thus, this is one context in which private ordering can alter an employee's rights under the FLSA, although the statute limits the potential impact of such ordering and its requirements provide baseline protections against employer abuse.

In terms of determining the employee's regular rate of pay when the employee receives compensation in addition to a regular wage or salary, the FLSA provides that this rate shall include "all remuneration for employment paid to, or on behalf of, the employee," unless the type of additional compensation falls within one of eight exclusions such as Christmas or birthday gifts, vacation pay, bonuses, and fringe benefits. *See* 29 U.S.C. §207(e). Determining the meaning of "remuneration for employment" and interpreting and applying the exclusions have proven difficult in some circumstances.

Acton v. City of Columbia
436 F.3d 969 (8th Cir. 2006)

Lay, Circuit Judge.

Chris N. Acton and ninety-nine current and former firefighters (the "firefighters") employed by the City of Columbia, Missouri (the "City") brought suit against the City for failing to include a series of payments in the firefighters' regular rate of pay, in violation of 29 U.S.C. §207(e) (the Fair Labor Standards Act or "FLSA").

[The district court granted the firefighters' summary judgment] motion in part, ruling that sick leave buy-back monies should be included in the firefighters' regular rate of pay. However, the district court also denied the firefighters' motion in part, ruling that monies received under the City's meal allowance program were excluded from the regular rate. Finally, the district court found no evidence that the City willfully violated the FLSA. . . .

IV. Sick Leave Buy-Back

Under the City's sick leave buy-back program, firefighters who work twenty-four hour work shifts during the course of one year accumulate ten days of sick leave. Firefighters who fail to use their sick leave are entitled to "sell back" any of the ten unused sick days to the City in exchange for a lump sum payment equal to 75% their regular hourly pay, provided the firefighter has amassed at least six months sick leave. The firefighters contend that all monies received from the sale of sick leave should be included in their regular rate of pay. The regular rate of pay calculation is critical because it provides the base point from which the firefighters' overtime compensation is calculated.

A. The Fair Labor Standards Act

Section 207(e) of the FLSA provides, in relevant part, that "all remuneration for employment paid to, or on behalf of, the employee" must be included in the employee's regular rate of pay, provided such remuneration is not prohibited by one of eight statutory exclusions listed under § 207(e)(1)-(8). 29 U.S.C. § 207(e). There is a statutory presumption "that remuneration in any form is included in the regular rate calculation. The burden is on the employer to establish that the remuneration in question falls under an exception." *Madison v. Res. for Human Dev. Inc.*, 233 F.3d 175, 187 (3d Cir. 2000).

Before beginning our analysis, we must clarify a preliminary matter of statutory construction under the FLSA that has been a point of confusion between the parties. First, the City argues sick leave buy-back monies do not constitute remuneration for employment. Next, the City contends sick leave buy-back monies are also excluded under § 207(e)(2) because they "are not made as compensation for [the employee's] hours of employment." *Id.* However, the language "not made as compensation for [the employee's] hours of employment" posited in § 207(e)(2) is but a mere rearticulation of the "remuneration for employment" requirement set forth in the preambulary language of § 207(e). Section 207(e)(2), properly understood, operates not as a separate basis for exclusion, but instead clarifies the types of payments that do not constitute remuneration for employment for purposes of § 207. Therefore, we treat the City's "remuneration for employment" and § 207(e)(2) arguments under the same mode of analysis. Finally, because both provisions modify one other, we must necessarily consider the express requirements of § 207(e)(2) and the federal regulations interpreting it when determining if sick leave buy-back monies constitute remuneration for employment.

1. Remuneration for Employment

Regulation 29 C.F.R. § 778.223 provides the touchstone for our inquiry because it addresses the scope of § 207(e)(2). Specifically, regulation § 778.223 addresses whether monies paid to employees for remaining on call are excluded from the regular rate under § 207(e)(2). The regulation concludes that monies paid to employees to remain on call, while not related to "any specific hours of work," are nevertheless awarded as "compensation for performing a duty involved in the employee's job" — namely, the employee's willingness and commitment to work unscheduled hours if requested. *See* 29 C.F.R. § 778.223. The plain language of the regulation makes clear that all monies paid as compensation for either a general or specific work-related duty should be included in the regular rate. The critical question before this court is whether sick leave buy-back monies compensate the firefighters for some specific or general duty of employment.

In order to qualify for sick leave buy-back payments, firefighters must come to work regularly for a period of several years in order to amass the requisite six month sick leave reserve. Then, the firefighters must also accrue additional sick leave in the present year in order to be eligible for buy-back. Thus, the primary effect of the buy-back program is to encourage firefighters to come to work regularly over a significant period of their employment tenure. We recognize consistent workplace attendance to be a general duty of employment and, therefore, rule that sick leave buy-back monies constitute remuneration for employment.[10]

The City sets forth three primary arguments to support its conclusion that sick leave buy-back payments are not remuneration for employment. First, the City argues its buy-back program was intended to promote two objectives unrelated to employee compensation. On the one hand, the sick leave buy-back program was intended to provide firefighters with a form of short-term disability insurance because the City does not have a disability policy covering employee illness or disability lasting six months or less. The sick leave buy-back program, with its six-month accrued sick leave requirement, was devised as a mechanism for employees to self-insure against personal illness or disability. Alternatively, the City argues its sick leave buy-back program discourages employees from treating sick leave as another form of vacation or personal leave because the program creates a money incentive for employees to accrue, but not use, their sick leave.

These arguments are not compelling. Even if the sick leave buy-back program was intended to provide employees with a form of short-term disability insurance and to discourage misuse of sick leave, one plain effect of the program is to reward regular workplace attendance through a non-discretionary, year-end, lump sum payment. The City's proffered justifications do not change the undisputed fact that the firefighters are plainly rewarded for regularly showing up for work over a period of years.

Second, the City also cites 29 C.F.R. § 825.125, a Department of Labor opinion letter, and a decision from a federal district court in the Northern District of Illinois to support its claim that bonuses awarded for perfect attendance do not require performance by the employee, but rather contemplate the absence of occurrences. 29 C.F.R. § 825.215 ("Bonuses for perfect attendance and safety do not require performance by the employee but rather contemplate the absence of occurrences."); Opinion Letter from Maria Echaveste, Administrator, U.S. Department of Labor (Mar. 21, 1994) ("Bonuses premised on 'perfect attendance' or 'perfect safety' are rewards not for work

---

10. We also note that sick leave buy-back monies do not resemble any of the payments expressly excluded under § 207(e)(2). *See* 29 C.F.R. § 778.224(a) (noting that payments excluded from the regular rate under § 207(e)(2) must "be 'similar' in character to the payments specifically described" in (e)(2)). Sick leave buy-back monies, in contrast to § 207(e)(2) payments, are awarded to employees for coming to work consistently, not for work that was never performed.

or production, but for compliance with rules."); *Dierlam v. Wesley Jessen Corp.*, 222 F. Supp. 2d 1052, 1057 (N.D. Ill. 2002) (noting that a bonus that does not require its recipient to meet production goals or quality standards "simply contemplates the non-occurrence of an event — [the recipient's] absence from work").

However, none of these three authorities address the applicability of § 207. Instead, each confronts the issue of whether an employee is entitled to a bonus for good attendance upon returning to work under the Family Medical Leave Act. The City's attempt to cite language taken out of context from authorities interpreting another federal statute in no way binds us in this case. To the extent the City uses these authorities to argue that consistent workplace attendance does not "require performance by the employee," we flatly disagree. We believe consistent workplace attendance *does* require performance. In the modern workplace, regular and prompt workplace attendance is a valued commodity, one for which the City appropriately rewards its employees.

Finally, the City cites the Sixth Circuit's decision in *Featsent v. City of Youngstown*, 70 F.3d 900 (6th Cir. 1995), to support its argument that sick leave buy-back monies do not constitute remuneration for employment. In *Featsent*, the Sixth Circuit ruled that monies paid to employees who did not submit medical claims and failed to use accrued sick leave were excluded from the regular rate of pay under § 207(e)(2) because such payments are "unrelated to the [employee's] compensation for services and hours of service."

We decline to follow the Sixth Circuit's decision in *Featsent*. The *Featsent* court failed to articulate any basis for its reasoning. The court did not distinguish regulation § 778.223 in reaching its conclusion, nor did it recognize and explain how payments awarded to an employee for not using accrued sick leave, which necessarily requires employees to work more days than they are required, is not tantamount to payment for services rendered. Because we are unpersuaded by the Sixth Circuit's analysis, we reject its conclusion.

2. Statutory Exceptions. . . .

Section 207(e)(5) provides:

[E]xtra compensation provided by a premium rate paid for certain hours worked by the employee in any day or workweek because such hours are hours worked in excess of eight in a day or in excess of the maximum workweek applicable to such employee under subsection (a) or in excess of the employee's normal working hours or regular working hours, as the case may be[.]

The dissent argues sick leave monies should be excluded under § 207(e)(5) because they constitute premium payments for specific hours worked. This analysis fails for several reasons. First, sick leave monies are not paid for specific hours worked. Instead, these payments compensate employees for a record of consistent attendance over the course of several years, not simply for working days during a given year they are otherwise entitled to take off.

Second, in order for payments to be excluded under § 207(e)(5), they must be "paid for certain hours worked by the employee in any day or workweek because such hours are hours worked in excess of eight in a day or in excess of the maximum [required in a] workweek." *Id*. Even assuming, as the dissent does, that sick leave buy-back payments are paid in sole recognition for the specific days a firefighter chooses to work instead of calling in sick, there is still no basis to exclude such payments under § 207(e)(5). Section 207(e)(5), by its own terms, limits its applicability to payments made for certain hours worked in excess of the employee's normal daily or weekly schedule. Under the dissent's approach, buy-back payments are, at best, premium payments for working normally scheduled hours.

Finally, § 207(e)(5) plainly excludes only "premium" payments — that is, payments no less than one and one-third the employee's regular rate. *See* 29 C.F.R. § 778.308(b). The dissent creatively "compounds" sick leave buy-back payments, which are awarded at the sub-premium rate of 75% the firefighters' hourly wage, with the firefighters' base hourly wage. This ignores the fact that the premium payments themselves must be at least one and one-third the employee's hourly rate. *See id*. Be this as it may, the dissent's approach, taken to its logical conclusion, yields unsettling results. Under the dissent's theory, all extra monies paid to employees for specific hours worked may be "compounded" with the employee's regular hourly rate and excluded under § 207(e)(5), in contravention of the express requirements of 29 C.F.R. § 778.207(b). *See* 29 C.F.R. § 778.207(b) (stating that non-overtime premiums for specific hours worked, such as nightshift differentials and hazard pay, must be included in the regular rate). Therefore, we rule that § 207(e)(5) does not exclude sick leave buy-back payments from the regular rate of pay. . . .

LOKEN, Chief Judge, dissenting. . . .

Sick leave buy-back payments admittedly do not fit comfortably within the exclusion in 29 U.S.C. § 207(e)(2) for "payments made for occasional periods when no work is performed." But the court is wrong to suggest that such payments "are not related to specific duties or hours worked." In my view, sick leave buy-back payments are functionally equivalent to premium overtime pay that is expressly excluded from an employee's regular rate. Like overtime, and unlike true attendance bonuses, these payments relate to specific hours *worked* — the days that the employee chose to work rather than to use paid sick leave.

As the Supreme Court said in the FLSA's formative years, "[t]o permit overtime premium to enter into the computation of the regular rate would be to allow overtime premium on overtime premium — a pyramiding that Congress could not have intended." *Bay Ridge Operating Co. v. Aaron*, 334 U.S. 446, 464 (1948). This principle was codified in 1949. *See* 29 U.S.C. § 207(e)(5)-(e)(7). If sick leave buy-back payments fit awkwardly under § 207(e)(2) because they relate to hours worked, rather than to hours not worked, these payments are squarely within the purview of the three exclusions found in subsections (e)(5)-(e)(7) that apply to "extra compensation provided by a premium rate paid for certain hours worked."[14]

Section 207(e)(5) excludes "extra compensation provided by a premium rate paid for certain hours worked . . . because such hours are hours worked . . . in excess of the employee's . . . regular working hours." A firefighter who works one or more paid sick leave days has worked in excess of his "regular working hours." If otherwise eligible under the City's program, he may sell unused sick leave to bring his total pay for sick

---

14. Unlike the exclusion in § 207(e)(2) for payments for hours not worked, compensation excluded from the employee's regular rate under subsections (e)(5)-(e)(7) "shall be creditable toward overtime compensation payable pursuant to this section." § 207(h). . . .

leave hours worked up to 175% of his regular rate. The related exclusion in §207(e)(6) applies to "extra compensation provided by a premium rate paid for work by the employee on . . . regular days of rest" if the premium rate is not less than one and one-half times the regular rate. These exclusions were intended to prevent the pyramiding of "overtime on overtime." They have been applied to a variety of overtime compensation programs.

In response, the court asserts that sick leave buy-back payments are not compensation at a premium rate. This ignores economic reality. The City agreed to pay the plaintiff firefighters for ten days of sick leave each year. If sick leave is used, the City must pay another employee to do the work, presumably at a rate at least equal to the regular rate of the firefighter on sick leave. If the firefighter instead works, leaving his sick leave unused, the City through the buy-back program pays, on top of the regular rate already paid, a premium equal to 75% of the firefighter's regular rate. Thus, for those days worked, the firefighter is paid 175% of his regular rate. This premium is greater than and functionally no different than the premium the FLSA requires employers to pay for overtime work—not less than one and one-half times (150%) the employee's regular rate. *See* 29 U.S.C. §207(a). And like overtime, extra compensation paid for unused sick leave is offset by the employer not incurring the expense of hiring additional workers or paying other employees to fill in.

It may make little difference whether the City's sick leave buy-back payments are excluded from a firefighter's regular rate under §207(e)(2) because they are "similar to payments made when no work is performed due to illness," *Featsent*, or under §207(e)(5) or (6) as overtime compensation paid at a premium rate. But the contrary decision of the district court and this court to include those payments in the regular rate both distorts FLSA principles and discourages use of a creative overtime payment device that benefits both employers and employees. I respectfully dissent from this decision.

NOTES

1. *Remuneration and Exclusions.* The majority engaged in a two-step inquiry. First, it had to decide whether the sick leave buy-back payments are "remuneration." That seems pretty clear, doesn't it? Why the fuss? Second, the court had to determine whether the payments, although remuneration, fell within one of the exclusions in the statute. The majority's explanation makes sense, doesn't it? But so does the dissent's! They come at the question using different paradigms. Who has the better approach? Why?

2. *Seeing the Forest.* Although the interpretation of the language of the statute and underlying regulations dominates the discussion, what are the real stakes in this case? In other words, now that the firefighters have prevailed, what effect will it have on their compensation? Who, in the buy-back program circumstance, may be benefiting under the surface? If you were the employer's counsel, would you recommend eliminating this or adjusting the employees' base rate of pay? Think about whether, going forward, this result is likely to be good, bad, or neutral for employees and employers.

3. *Planning Problems Continued.* Far more important than the particulars of the analysis in this case are the broader lessons for employment law counselors and human resources personnel. This case and the others in this chapter suggest that there are a number of traps for the unwary, and that each compensation decision must be analyzed from a number of perspectives to ensure the FLSA is not violated. Given the complexity and how costly mistakes may be, personnel and compensation decisions with potential FLSA implications ought to be undertaken with great care.

2. Other Wage Protections

At the federal level, the FLSA is the primary mechanism for dealing with perceived wage and hour abuses. However, federal law provides a number of other more narrowly drawn protections in certain contexts. For example, prevailing wage laws require various firms contracting with the federal government to compensate their workers at the prevailing minimum wage for like workers in the local labor market. *See, e.g.*, 40 U.S.C. §§ 3141-44, 3146, 3147 (Davis-Bacon Act); 41 U.S.C. §§ 35-43, 43a, 43b, 44, 45 (Walsh-Healey Act). Moreover, as mentioned previously, the Equal Pay Act mandates that male and female employees doing equal work in a workplace receive the same pay, absent some justification unrelated to sex.

But, as *Ansoumana* illustrates, there are also state and local wage and hour protections. This is because, unlike ERISA, discussed below, the FLSA does not preempt the field; that is, its protections are not exclusive. Thus, state and local governments may provide for wage and hour protections that exceed those in the FLSA. For example, many states have enacted their own prevailing wage laws for government contractors. Most states also have wage payment laws (including so-called "theft of service" statutes) that provide for civil and criminal liability for failure to pay promised wages. *See, e.g.*, Rita J. Verga, *An Advocate's Toolkit: Using Criminal "Theft of Service" Laws to Enforce Workers' Right to Be Paid*, 8 N.Y. City L. Rev. 283 (2005). Indeed, to ensure wages are paid, New York and Wisconsin have taken the extraordinary step of imposing pro rata liability on certain shareholders for unpaid wages (if and when the corporation does not meet its wage obligations). *See* N.Y. Bus. Corp. § 630; Wis. Stat. § 180.0622. States also impose what might be deemed "procedural" wage and hour protections; for instance, a California statute requires that commission agreements with certain sales representatives be in writing, and that the writing contain various information, including how the commission is computed. The statute also requires documentation of how payment is calculated when an employee's commissions are paid. *See* Cal. Civ. Code §§ 1738.10-.16 (2014); *Baker v. American Horticulture Supply, Inc.* 111 Cal. Rptr.3d 695 (Cal. Ct. App. 2010) (discussing the statute).

In addition, many states have their own minimum wage and overtime protections, which may increase the wage floor, further regulate hours or documentation, and/or extend protections to employees exempted by the FLSA (e.g., agricultural workers, seasonal workers, uncovered domestic workers, and workers employed by uncovered employers). Unsurprisingly, these laws vary greatly. *See* U.S. Department of Labor Employment Standards Administration Wage and Hour Division, Minimum Wage Laws in the States, *available at* http://www.dol.gov/esa/minwage/america.htm (listing state minimum wage and overtime protections). According to the DOL, as of September 1, 2014, five states have no minimum wage and three states have minimum wage requirements that are lower than the federal minimum. *See id.* Of course, the FLSA minimum wage governs most workers in these jurisdictions, and, thus, lower minimum wage standards will provide the floor only for those not within the FLSA. Nineteen states track the federal mandate, although their coverage may be broader. At that time, twenty-three states—mostly in the Northeast, the Upper

Midwest, and the West—and the District of Columbia had passed higher minimum wage requirements. However, on November 4, 2014, three more states (Arkansas, Nebraska, and South Dakota) passed higher minimum wage laws by ballot, which, once these provisions take effect, will bring the total number of states with higher wage floors to twenty-six. *See* Josh Barro, *The Upshot: Four States Vote to Raise Minimum Wage*, NY Times, November 4, 2014, p. 3. Currently, the District of Columbia has the highest basic minimum wage, $9.50 per hour (although it is set to rise to over $11.00 in 2016), followed by the State of Washington at $9.32 and Oregon at $9.10. *See id*. These significantly higher wage floors and their periodic increases indicate that, although minimum wage increases happen only sporadically at the federal level, proponents continue to enjoy success in particular regions of the country.

Several states also have their own overtime regulations. California, for example, requires that firms pay workers double-time (twice the regular rate) for hours worked in excess of 12 hours per day or 48 hours per week. *See id*. It is worth noting that such a double-overtime regime could have profound effects on litigation awards and, hence, employer incentives and planning. Consider, for example, how the bodyguards' potential recovery in the Spears case—*see* Problem 11-2—might differ under the California statute.

When possible under state law, municipalities may also regulate wages of employees within their borders. For example, as of September 2014, Seattle has the highest minimum wage in the country, at $15.00 per hour. Catherine Dunn, *Six Major Cities with Highest Minimum Wage*, Int'l Bus. Times, August 28, 2014, available at http://www.ibtimes.com/six-major-cities-highest-minimum-wage-1672802. Another effort in this direction is the movement to have cities enact "living wage" laws governing municipal contractors. *See generally* Scott L. Cummings & Steven A. Boutcher, *Mobilizing Local Government Law for Low-Wage Workers*, 1 Chi. Legal F. 187, 195 (2009) (discussing the broad reach of the Los Angeles Living Wage Ordinance, which imposes wage obligations above the federal and state minimums on employers that receive financial benefits from the municipality); Clayton P. Gillette, *Local Redistribution, Living Wage Ordinances, and Judicial Intervention*, 101 Nw. U. L. Rev. 1057 (2007) (discussing the growing number of local living wage ordinances and legal challenges to them); William Quigley, *Full-Time Workers Should Not Be Poor: The Living Wage Movement*, 70 Miss. L. J. 889 (2001); Jon Gertner, *What Is a Living Wage?*, N.Y. Times, Jan. 15, 2006, *available at* http://www.nytimes.com/2006/01/15/magazine/15wage.html (discussing the history of the living wage moment). For a more critical view of the effects of living wage ordinances, *see* David Neumark, *Living Wages: Protection for or Protection from Low-Wage Workers?*, 58 Indus. & Lab. Rel. Rev. 27 (2004) (suggesting that living wage laws may protect unionized workers from low-wage workers, rather than benefitting low-wage workers generally).

B.   FRINGE BENEFIT PROTECTIONS

An increasingly important aspect of employment compensation is fringe benefits, a term that includes everything from pensions and medical insurance to tuition reimbursement programs to free parking spaces. Unlike other industrialized nations, which tend to provide substantial government retirement, health, and insurance benefits through social legislation, the American approach to fringe benefits begins with a legally mandated but limited safety net or base of protection. As discussed in Chapter 12, federal law mandates that the states provide a scheme of workers' compensation for injuries on the job, and it also mandates an unemployment insurance regime. Social security law provides for limited retirement and disability benefits; Medicare finances health insurance for the elderly; and Medicaid provides health coverage for some of those not able to pay. 42 U.S.C. § 1396 *et seq.* (2014) ("Medicaid Act"); 42 U.S.C. § 426 *et seq.* (2014) ("Medicare Act"); 42 U.S.C. § 301 *et seq.* (2014) ("Social Security Act"). Some states supplement that "safety net" with additional programs.

Above this floor, the law leaves the decision to provide fringe benefits to employers' discretion. Employers may do so unilaterally, by individual contract, or as a result of collective negotiations with representatives of the workers. Not only do the federal and state governments directly provide to all citizens only minimal retirement, disability, and health benefits, but federal law historically has not mandated that employers provide such benefits, beyond their contributions to unemployment insurance and workers' compensation; with a few exceptions, neither has state law. However, as part of the health care reform package Congress passed in 2010, *see generally* Patient Protection and Affordable Care Act, Pub. L. No. 111-148, 124 Stat. 119 (2010) (as modified by the Health Care and Education Reconciliation Act of 2010 (Pub. L. 111-152, 124 Stat. 1029 (2010)) (hereinafter the Affordable Care Act or "ACA") (codified principally in various sections of 26, 29, and 42 U.S.C.A.), a large employer will face tax penalties beginning in 2014 if it does not offer health care coverage or offers coverage that is not "affordable," *see* 26 U.S.C.A. § 4980H (2014).

Nevertheless, at present, many employers provide no fringe benefits. Minimum-wage employers, for example, rarely provide health insurance benefits. Even paid "sick days" and vacation days are often unavailable, or are offered to employees only after a long probationary period. Thus, the decision to leave these terms of employment almost entirely to private ordering means that many workers lack basic benefits.

Rather than requiring fringe benefits, the federal government's approach traditionally has been to utilize various tax incentives to encourage employers to provide some fringe benefits. The Internal Revenue Code excludes specified employee benefits from what would otherwise be taxable income to the employee. Employees (and hence their employers) generally prefer such benefits to standard wages because they are not taxable to the employee at all or are at least tax-deferred. For example, a parking space may not be taxable at all; pension benefits will normally be taxable only at retirement.

Of course, the exclusion of certain compensation from employee income by casting it as a fringe benefit makes sense for the employer only if it gets to deduct the cost of the benefit as a business expense, as it could deduct wages. The Tax Code permits employers to do so, but in order to qualify, employers must observe certain principles, including those involving "nondiscrimination," a term of art in benefits law that will be discussed below. With regard to pension plans, the employer may deduct contributions to tax-qualified retirement plans, but the employees need not recognize any income based on that contribution until receipt of the benefit. Further, the investment income from accumulated contributions is tax-free at the time it is earned. As a result, compensation in fringe benefits is more valuable to employees who have a greater than zero effective tax rate than base rate compensation, which is fully taxable when received.

Once an employer provides certain fringe benefits, federal law regulates their operation through the requirements for exclusion set forth in the Tax Code and, for some schemes, through the Employee Retirement Income Security Act ("ERISA"), 29 U.S.C. §§ 1001-1461 (2014). These laws do not, however, determine the level or kind of benefits; that is left to the employer setting up the benefit plan.

The legal treatment of fringe benefits is so complex that it is a world unto its own. Indeed, "Employee Benefits" is both a specialty area of practice and a specialized law school course. Thus, this chapter will not provide comprehensive coverage of this subject. It will, however, give, a brief overview of ERISA's basic structure, some other benefits regulations, and the employer mandates of the ACA.

1. ERISA

Prior to the enactment of ERISA in 1974, "regulation" of fringe benefit plans in the United States was almost an accidental by-product of tax treatment and thus was tied to the Tax Code and the regulations and rulings of the Internal Revenue Service. This system was viewed by many as inadequate: "Horror" stories were told of older employees fired shortly before becoming eligible for benefits and of employers unable to pay employees and retirees the benefits promised, and neither the Tax Code nor the common law provided adequate remedies. Thus, ERISA's primary purpose was to protect employees' justified expectations with regard to certain benefits their employers promised them. In enacting ERISA, Congress maintained the parallel provisions of the Internal Revenue Code but created an entirely separate structure to regulate employee benefit plans. Accordingly, as amended, ERISA is codified at 29 U.S.C. §§ 1001-1461 (2014), and in scattered sections of the Internal Revenue Code.

ERISA does not mandate that employers establish employee benefit plans, nor does it dictate what kinds of benefits they may ultimately provide. It regulates such plans and benefits only once the employer has chosen to provide them. However, once the employer "opts in" to ERISA, the statute's mandates may affect the scope and the nature of the benefits offered. Despite the absence of legal compulsion to do so, many employers offer various kinds of benefit plans covered by ERISA. For example, according to the Bureau of Labor Statistics, in March 2010, retirement benefits were available to 74 percent of full-time workers in private industry, while access to medical care and paid sick leave was available to 86 percent and 74 percent of such workers, respectively. *See* Bureau of Labor Statistics, *Economic News Release* (July 27, 2010), *available at* http://www.bls.gov/news.release/ebs2.nr0.htm. However, part-time workers receive far fewer benefits: Only 39 percent of part-time workers had retirement benefits, and medical care and paid sick leave were provided to 24 and 26 percent, respectively. *See id.* Note also that participation numbers have declined from prior years, and the types of medical and retirement benefits employers are now offering may be less favorable to employees than in the past.

ERISA contains a complex statutory regime that is supplemented by agency regulations and a tremendous amount of case law on a number of issues of great import — including the statute's preemptive scope and the scope of judicial review of plan administrators' decisions. Although we must leave the bulk of these matters to an Employee Benefits course, what follows is a cursory glance at ERISA's key features.

a. Coverage

ERISA covers a broad array of employer fringe benefit plans. An "employee benefit plan" is within the statute if the plan is established or maintained by an "employer" or "union," although plans maintained by government employers, churches, and certain private plans are excluded. *See* 29 U.S.C. § 1003(a) and (b)(1)-(5). In addition to the threshold question of which individuals are "employees" (*see Yates v. Hendon*, reproduced at page 58 and *Vizcaino v. Microsoft Corporation*, discussed on page 20), there are issues about what qualifies as a "benefit plan" and who qualifies as a "participant."

Among employee benefit plans, the central distinction in the statute is between employee "welfare" benefit plans and employee "pension" benefit plans. The basic difference is the nature of the benefit: An employee pension benefit plan provides retirement income and an employee welfare benefit plan provides fringe benefits for nonretirement purposes such as medical insurance. To say it another way, a pension plan's benefits are payable only after the termination of covered employment, while a welfare plan is everything that is not a pension plan. This distinction is critically important: Consistent with its original purposes, ERISA mandates far more controls on pension plans than on welfare plans, and, as discussed below, because ERISA broadly preempts state regulation of employee benefit plans, this often results in a regulatory "void" — that is, an absence of legal protections — for welfare benefits.

ERISA contemplates two basic types of employee pension benefit plans: defined benefit and defined contribution plans. A defined benefit plan is what most people used to think of as a "pension": a promise by the employer to provide employees a guaranteed monthly retirement benefit defined by some formula based on the amount of the employee's compensation and her length of service. The alternative is the increasingly common defined contribution plan, which provides for an individual account for each participant and for benefits based solely upon the amount contributed to the participant's account, and any investment gains or losses in such account. A popular type of defined contribution plan is the "401(k)." The basic difference between the two types of plans is risk: In defined benefit plans, the employer bears the risks of investment since it guarantees a certain level of payment when employees retire; in defined contribution plans, the employee bears these risks since she makes the investment decisions and, upon retirement, gets only what has accumulated. Obviously, employees generally prefer the guaranteed benefit that a defined benefit plan affords, and employee advocates have emphasized their social benefits. But defined contribution plans are the choice of pragmatic employers wanting to avoid the risks of defined benefit plans, and the regulatory constraints ERISA and tax regulations place on such plans. *See Tibble v. Edison Int'l*, 729 F.3d 1110 (9th Cir. 2013), *cert. granted*, 13-550, 2014 WL 4916188 (U.S. Oct. 2, 2014) (review granted on question of "whether a claim that ERISA plan fiduciaries breached their duty of prudence by offering higher-cost retail-class mutual funds to plan participants, even though identical lower-cost institution-class mutual funds were available, is barred by 29 U.S.C. § 1113(1) when fiduciaries initially chose the higher-cost mutual funds as plan investments more than six years before the claim was filed"). Indeed, for these reasons and others, defined benefit plans are a dying breed: Private employers have rarely chosen to establish defined benefit plans in the last two decades, and many have recently "frozen" their defined benefit plans (i.e., barred new entrants or ceased accruals) or converted them to defined contribution plans.

b. Statutory Structure

The differences between the two types of pension plans providing retirement income, and between pension and welfare plans covering other fringe benefits, have profound effects on employer obligations under ERISA. These obligations can best be understood by describing the statutory structure. ERISA is divided into four subchapters: Title I provides protection for employee benefit rights by imposing reporting and disclosure requirements as well as fiduciary responsibilities on all benefits plans, establishing participation and vesting standards for pension plans, setting forth funding requirements for defined benefit plans, and providing an administrative and enforcement scheme. *See generally* 29 U.S.C. §§ 1002, 1102-06. Title I also contains newer provisions that address welfare benefit plans specifically, including requirements regarding worker loss of health insurance benefits upon termination, insurance portability, long-term care insurance, and health information privacy. Consolidated Omnibus Budget Reconciliation Act of 1985, 29 U.S.C. § 1181 *et seq.* (2014); Health Insurance Portability and Accountability Act of 1996, 29 U.S.C. § 1181-82 (2014); the Newborns' and Mothers' Health Protection Act of 1996, 29 U.S.C. § 1185 (2014); the Mental Health Parity Act of 1996, 29 U.S.C. § 1185a (2014); Women's Health and Cancer Rights Act of 1998, 29 U.S.C. § 185b (2014).

Title II amended the Tax Code to accommodate ERISA. Title III deals primarily with the relationship between ERISA and the Internal Revenue Code and their enforcement agencies, the DOL and the IRS. In order for employers and employees to be entitled to the tax advantages accorded to many fringe benefits under the Tax Code, the tax provisions must be satisfied. The requirements of ERISA must also be satisfied for those employee benefit plans that fall within its coverage. While retirement plans were first regulated through the Tax Code, many of those tax qualification standards were incorporated into ERISA, resulting in mirror-image rules applying under ERISA and the Tax Code.

There are, however, some important provisions dealing with tax-qualified pension plans found only in the Tax Code. The most important are the rules against "discrimination" in favor of highly compensated employees. Many of the Code sections providing tax preferences for different fringe benefits allow some, but not too much, discrimination in favor of the high and mighty. 26 U.S.C. §§ 401 and 414. The goal of the nondiscrimination provisions is to ensure that the tax subsidy does not benefit only or mostly higher-paid employees or business owners. The decision makers of employers want these benefits for themselves, for their families, and for those employees with the ability to demand such benefits from their employers. Pressure to protect the bottom-line profitability, however, gives these decision makers an incentive to withhold such benefits from most employees. Congress tried to encourage extension of benefits but rejected a flat rule prohibiting all discrimination, ostensibly because it would have caused too many employers to not provide certain fringe benefits at all.

Title IV regulates plan termination and establishes an insurance scheme for defined benefit plans, guaranteeing that participants in those plans are provided their benefits should their plan terminate. It creates the Pension Benefit Guaranty Corporation ("PBGC") to administer this insurance program. As suggested above, the fees for the PBGC insurance, the prerequisites to terminate a plan, and the potential residual liability established in Title IV create substantial disincentives to employers to create defined benefit retirement plans. In recent years, the preponderance of underfunded plans and the significant payouts the PBGC has made upon plan defaults have received significant public attention and led to calls for legal reform. The stricter funding requirements included in the Pension Protection Act of 2006, Pub. L. No. 190-280, 120 Stat. 780 (codified in various sections of 26 & 29 U.S.C.) were designed in part to address this concern, although whether these requirements are adequate remains the subject of controversy.

c. Preemption

There are few areas of the law more bedeviled by abstruse legal reasoning and inconsistent judicial decisions than ERISA preemption. The decisions on the subject — including those issued by the Supreme Court — are legion, as is the legal commentary, and even ERISA experts have difficulty navigating the resulting uncertain and peculiar framework. At the most general level, ERISA preemption involves both "field" and "conflict" preemption under ERISA's regulatory scheme. In terms of the former, ERISA preempts any state law that "relates to" an "employee benefit" plan; thus, ERISA's enforcement regime and substantive obligations are exclusive, even where ERISA does not mandate or otherwise regulate benefits. 29 U.S.C. § 1144; *see, e.g., New York State Conference of Blue Cross & Blue Shield Plans v. Travelers Ins., Inc.,* 514 U.S. 645 (1995) (discussing the breadth and history of ERISA preemption although ultimately finding a state law imposing surcharges on commercial insurers not preempted); *Egelhoff v. Egelhoff ex rel. Breiner,* 532 U.S. 141 (2001) (striking down a state statute that upon divorce revoked automatically the designation of a spouse as a beneficiary to the extent the law applied to ERISA benefit plans). The only exceptions are those matters — insurance, banking, or securities — that are expressly saved from ERISA's preemptive scope, unless such regulation is swept back into ERISA's coverage under the statute's "deemer" clause, which essentially preempts those state laws that affect self-funded (noninsured) welfare benefit plans. 29 U.S.C. § 1144 (b)(2); *see, e.g., Metropolitan Life Ins. Co. v. Massachusetts,* 471 U.S. 724 (1985) (upholding a state law mandating mental health care benefits in group health insurance policies under the savings clause and finding it not swept back into ERISA's scope under the deemer clause).

Leaving the considerable details aside, field preemption is of greatest import in the welfare benefit context because, although ERISA's welfare benefit provisions are relatively weak, preemption may preclude employer-related health care and other reforms at the state level. For example, in 2006, a federal court struck down as preempted under ERISA a 2006 Maryland law, popularly known as the "Walmart Bill," requiring that employers with more than 10,000 workers in Maryland pay a penalty to the state's health insurance program if they fail to devote at least 8 percent of their state payroll to health insurance for their employees. *See Retail Indus. Leaders Ass'n v. Fielder,* 435 F. Supp. 2d 481 (D. Md. 2006), *aff'd,* 475 F.3d 180 (4th Cir. 2007); *see generally* Edward A. Zelinsky, *Maryland's Wal-Mart Act: Policy and Preemption,* 28 Cardozo L. Rev. 847 (2007) (agreeing with the preemption decision and finding the statute ill-conceived as a matter of policy).

Conflict preemption centers on the exclusiveness of ERISA's enforcement scheme under 29 U.S.C. § 1132. As the Supreme Court has repeated a number of times, ERISA preempts any state law cause of action that duplicates, supplements, or supplants the ERISA civil enforcement remedies. *See, e.g., Aetna Health, Inc. v.*

Davila, 542 U.S. 200 (2004) (finding preempted plaintiffs' state law causes of action against their health maintenance organizations for failure to exercise ordinary care in coverage decisions). As discussed below, because the remedies provided by ERISA are limited, this kind of preemption sometimes precludes participants and beneficiaries harmed by plan administrators' or fiduciaries' breaches of duty from obtaining adequate relief. ERISA preemption therefore is highly controversial because it creates a kind of regulatory vacuum: State attempts to provide greater employee benefits protections are often preempted even though ERISA provides no substantive protection at all, and state law remedies necessary to make harmed parties whole are unavailable because of the exclusivity of ERISA's remedial regime.

d. Enforcement and Remedies

ERISA's primary enforcement provision, 29 U.S.C. §1132, authorizes civil actions by participants, beneficiaries, fiduciaries, employee benefit plans, and the Secretary of Labor. This section provides for a wide range of claims against plan administrators and other fiduciaries, but the remedies available are limited to the recovery of benefits, certain statutory penalties for nondisclosure, and equitable relief on behalf of the plan. *See CIGNA Corp v. Amara*, 131 S. Ct. 1866 (2011) (holding that a court may, as an equitable remedy, reform the terms of an employee benefits plan). Most types of compensatory damages (emotional distress, mental anguish, and other consequential damages) are unavailable, as are punitive damages. The remedies ERISA affords, therefore, may be inadequate to make the aggrieved party whole. For example, a participant in an employer-sponsored health care plan has no state law tort claim against the plan or plan administrator for an erroneous coverage decision that results in the failure to treat a medical condition, and equitable relief and the recovery of benefits ERISA affords fall far short of compensating the harm caused. *See, e.g., Corcoran v. United Health Care, Inc.*, 965 F.2d 1321 (5th Cir. 1992) (finding preempted state law claims against a plan administrator for failure to exercise due care in denying certification of hospitalization to a woman, which resulted in the death of her fetus, in spite of the fact that damages for emotional injuries are not available under ERISA); *US Airways, Inc. v. McCutchen*, 133 S. Ct. 1537 (2013) (holding that an ERISA plan's terms can require that a beneficiary reimburse the insurer for funds paid to the beneficiary upon the receipt of a monetary award for damages but that gaps in the contract (such as a failure to allow for allocation of attorney's fees paid) can be construed with equitable principles in mind). Thus, although §1132's coverage is broad, its remedies are narrow, which has led to significant criticism of the regime and calls for reform. *See Heimeshoff v. Hartford Life & Accident Ins. Co.*, 134 S. Ct. 604 (2014) (finding that an employee benefit plan covered by ERISA that requires any suit to recover benefits to be filed within three years is enforceable under §1132(a)(1)(b)); *see also* Paul Secunda, *Much ERISA Fun at the Supreme Court Today: Heimeshoff and Benefit SOL Accrual Issues*, WORKPLACE PROF BLOG (Oct. 15, 2013), http://law professors.typepad.com/laborprof_blog/2013/10/much-erisa-fun-at-the-supreme-court-today-heimeshoff-and-benefit-sol-accrual-issues.html. On a positive note for plaintiffs, ERISA does provide for recovery of attorneys' fees for prevailing parties, *see* §1132(e), which are typically not available for state common-law causes of action.

Denial-of-benefits claims are the most common claims against administrators of welfare benefit plans. A key and often-litigated issue in many such cases is the standard of review the court should apply to the administrator's decision to deny benefits. Where the employee benefit plan has granted the administrator discretion to make benefits decisions, courts normally will afford these decisions substantial deference, although an administrator conflict of interest is a factor to consider in determining whether the administrator abused its discretion. *See, e.g. Metropolitan Life Ins. Co. v. Glenn*, 554 U.S. 105 (2008); *see also Conkright v. Frommert*, 559 U.S. 506 (2010) (holding that deference ought to be accorded to an ERISA plan administrator despite the administrator's prior mistake in construing provisions of the plan).

Finally, ERISA contains an antidiscrimination and antiretaliation provision that makes it unlawful for any person to "discharge, fine, suspend, expel, discipline, or discriminate against a participant or beneficiary for exercising any right to which he is entitled under the provisions of an employee benefit plan . . . or for the purpose of interfering with the attainment of any right to which such participant may become entitled under the plan. . . ." 29 U.S.C. §1140. This protection is integral to ERISA because the statute was in large part a response to employers terminating employees just prior to their becoming vested under retirement plans. Again, although the scope of this section is broad, the remedies are limited to those set forth in §1132.

2. Employment-Related Benefits Not Governed by ERISA

Some employment-related benefits are not governed by ERISA. As discussed above, benefits that do not require the establishment of a "plan" — an administrative or processing scheme — or are not accumulated over time and payable upon a contingency beyond the employer's control are not governed by ERISA. In addition, some types of benefit plans are expressly excluded from ERISA's reach. One example we have already seen is an Employee Stock Purchase Plan ("ESPP"), one of two benefit plans at issue in *Vizcaino v. Microsoft Corp.*, discussed in Chapter 1, page 20. The ESPP is a supplemental benefit plan that, if qualified, is afforded favorable tax treatment but is excluded from ERISA coverage and therefore governed by state benefits law. *See* 26 U.S.C. §423.

Moreover, other types of benefits are governed by separate legal regimes. Two examples are workers' compensation and state-sponsored unemployment compensation. The former, which each state has established, is addressed in Chapter 12. Each state has also enacted a scheme of unemployment compensation. These programs originated in the 1930s when, through the Social Security Act, Congress provided incentives for states to adopt compulsory programs. They operate under federal standards, are federally funded, and are financed by a payroll tax on covered employers. As a result, the basic parameters of unemployment compensation regimes are similar in all states, although the details may vary widely.

To be eligible for such compensation, workers typically must have had a prior employment relationship (as opposed to some other type of relationship), must meet minimum earnings or working time standards, and must have been terminated involuntarily without fault. Obviously, whether a termination is involuntary and without fault is sometimes in controversy. An employee who is fired for work-related misconduct is ineligible, as is an employee who voluntarily quits without good cause. The concept is that employees need to be protected by insurance from economic dislocations over which they have no control. The "moral hazard" implicit in unemployment insurance is limited by excluding those employees who are fired for good reason or who quit without justification. Because employer payroll taxes are linked to claims experience, employers frequently contest employee claims of involuntary or no-fault termination. However, and consistent with the moral hazard approach, an employee who quits may still be entitled to coverage if he or she can demonstrate some kind of "good cause" for doing so. *See* Deborah Maranville, *Workplace Mythologies and Unemployment Insurance: Exit, Voice and Exhausting All Reasonable Alternatives to Quitting*, 31 HOFSTRA L. REV. 459 (2002). These include medical conditions and physical limitations. The question of whether a particular condition should be treated as the employee's choice or covered by insurance is reflected in the differing state approaches to when and whether pregnancy-related termination of employment should be covered. *See* Martin H. Malin, *Unemployment Compensation in a Time of Increasing Work-Family Conflicts*, 29 U. MICH. J.L. REFORM 131, 142 n.48 (1996). Of course, while former employees who are unable to work are ineligible for unemployment insurance, they may be eligible for other types of benefits (e.g., workers' compensation, private disability insurance, or state or federal disability benefits).

Unemployment compensation benefits tend to be based on the recipient's former wages but top out at a predetermined level, which is relatively low. They are also payable for only a fixed period of time (typically no longer than six months), although Congress has extended the period after certain dramatic occurrences, including Hurricane Katrina in 2005. *See* U.S. Department of Labor, Hurricane Recovery Assistance, *available at* http://www.dol.gov/opa/hurricane-recovery.htm; Press Release, Office of the House Democratic Leader Nancy Pelosi, Tens of Thousands of Katrina Survivors Are Still Suffering and the Future of Gulf Coast Remains Unclear (Feb. 28, 2006) (discussing a Senate bill extending unemployment benefits for 150,000 survivors of Hurricane Katrina). Congress has also extended benefits during recessions, including several extensions during the Great Recession that began in 2007, although they have proven to be politically controversial. *See, e.g.*, Carl Hulse, *Jobless Benefit Extension Clears Senate Hurdle*, N.Y. TIMES, at A16 (July 20, 2010) (discussing the heated debate over the further extension of benefits for those out of work six months or more).

Other limitations are imposed to encourage workers to find new employment, including requirements that recipients look for and accept suitable work. State unemployment compensation schemes are administered by state commissions, although these administrative regimes and their procedures must satisfy certain criteria in order to be entitled to federal reimbursements for their expenses. Some have urged that unemployment compensation schemes be reimagined to serve broader goals than the traditional short-term alleviation of economic dislocation. *See* Gillian Lester, *Unemployment Insurance and Wealth Redistribution*, 49 UCLA L. REV. 335 (2001).

3. Health Care Reform: Employee Benefits–Related Provisions of the ACA

Enacted in 2010, the ACA imposes a complex array of additional mandates and limitations on health insurance plans. These include tighter restrictions on eligibility requirements for health insurance plans; standards regarding administrative costs, pricing, and services offered; additional disclosures in tax returns and to employees;

and new provisions regarding employer "cafeteria" plans. The ACA also imposes a number of new taxes relating to the provision of health insurance and provides for new subsidies and tax credits for employers.

Perhaps the most significant change involving employee benefits are the provisions governing large employers and health care coverage. The ACA does not mandate that employers offer employees health insurance. However, beginning in 2014, an employer with at least 50 full-time employees (or equivalents) will face tax penalties if one or more of its full-time employees obtains subsidized coverage — that is, a premium credit or cost-sharing reduction for coverage — through a "qualified health insurance plan" (a nonemployer health plan established pursuant to the terms of the ACA). Put another way, the law's penalty provisions will apply if at least one full-time employee opts into a qualified health insurance plan and receives subsidized coverage because his or her qualifying employer (1) does not provide health insurance coverage, or (2) provides coverage that is not affordable. Some of the key provisions regarding large employers and their employees are as follows:

- An "applicable large employer" is defined as having "at least fifty full-time employees during the preceding calendar year." Full-time employees are those working 30 or more hours per week, excluding full-time seasonal employees who work for less than 120 days during the year. The hours worked by part-time employees are included in the calculation for determining whether the employer is covered. *See* 26 U.S.C.A. § 4980H.

- Regardless of whether an applicable large employer offers coverage, it will be liable for a tax penalty only if one or more of its full-time employees obtains coverage through a "qualified health insurance plan" (established elsewhere by the ACA) and the coverage is subsidized through a premium credit or cost-sharing reduction. Part-time workers are not included in penalty calculations, and an employer will not pay a penalty for any part-time employees, even if one or more receives subsidized coverage. *See* 26 U.S.C.A. § 4980H.

- As a general matter, an employee who is not offered employer-sponsored minimal essential health care coverage (as defined in 26 U.S.C.A. § 5000A) and who is not eligible for Medicaid or other programs may be eligible for premium credits for coverage through a qualified health plan when the employee's family income is between 133 percent and 400 percent of the federal poverty level. Employees who are offered employer-sponsored coverage can obtain such premium credits only if, in addition to the criteria above, they also are not enrolled in their employer's coverage because it is unaffordable — that is, either the employee's required contribution toward the plan premium would exceed 9.5 percent of their household income or the plan pays for less than 60 percent, on average, of covered health care expenses. *See* 26 U.S.C.A. § 36B.

- An applicable large employer that does not offer health insurance coverage will be subject to a penalty if one or more of its full-time employees receives subsidized coverage in a qualified health insurance plan. The monthly penalty assessed to employers who do not offer coverage will be equal to the number of full-time employees minus 30 multiplied by one-twelfth of $2,000. *See* 26 U.S.C.A. § 4980H.

- Employers that do offer health coverage will not be treated as meeting the employer requirements if at least one full-time employee obtains subsidized coverage in a qualified health insurance plan because, in addition to meeting the other eligibility criteria, the coverage is unaffordable. The monthly penalty assessed to the employer for each full-time employee who receives subsidized coverage will be one-twelfth of $3,000 for any applicable month. However, the total monthly penalty for an employer will not exceed the total number of the firm's full-time employees minus 30 multiplied by one-twelfth of $2,000. *See* 26 U.S.C.A. §4980H.

- Employers with more than 200 full-time employees that offer coverage must automatically enroll new full-time employees in a plan (and continue enrollment of current employees). Automatic enrollment programs will be required to include adequate notice and the opportunity for an employee to opt out. *See* 29 U.S.C.A. §218a.

Recent United States Supreme Court decisions, however, have affected the way that the provisions in ACA are applied to certain individuals and employers. In *National Federation of Independent Business v. Sebelius*, the Court held that the federal government had the power to impose an individual mandate that every eligible individual be insured only through Congress's taxing power and not through its power under either the Spending Clause or Commerce Clause. *See* 132 S. Ct. 2566 (2012). The Court therefore affirmed Congress's power to mandate that individuals purchase health insurance, which in turn enforces the provisions in the ACA that require (1) individuals to purchase health insurance or be subject to a tax penalty and (2) employers to make affordable health insurance available to their employees, or they too must pay a tax penalty. The Court later found that the Religious Freedom Restoration Act (RFRA) protects the religious interests of individuals controlling closely held corporations and that those individuals' right to religious freedom was infringed upon by being forced by ACA to provide health insurance coverage that includes contraception and abortion-inducing drugs against their religious beliefs. *See Burwell v. Hobby Lobby Stores, Inc.*, 134 S. Ct. 2751 (2014); *see also* Charles A. Sullivan, *RFRA Trumps ACA*, Workplace Prof Blog (June 30, 2014), http://law-professors.typepad.com/laborprof_blog/2014/06/rfra-trumps-aca.html.

12

Worker Safety and Health

From industrial accidents to occupational diseases, safety and health are pervasive problems in the workplace. The causes range from debatable dangers to evident perils, and emanate from physical surroundings, machinery, vehicles, chemicals, and, of course, other humans. Some risks are inherent in certain occupations (at least given present technology), but others can be reduced or even eliminated. For a host of reasons, the American workplace, as a whole, appears to be getting safer. For example, workplace fatalities declined from about 6,600 in 1994 to approximately 4,400 in 2013. U.S. DEPARTMENT OF LABOR, BUREAU OF LABOR STATISTICS (hereinafter "DOL, BLS"), 2013 CENSUS OF FATAL OCCUPATIONAL INJURIES CHARTS, 1992-2013 (preliminary data), *available at* http://www.bls.gov/iif/oshcfoi1.htm#charts. Similarly, the rate of occupational injury and illness cases in private industry declined from 5.0 per 100 full-time equivalent workers in 2003 to 3.5 in 2010 (the most recent year with reliable data). DOL, BLS, OCCUPATIONAL INJURIES AND ILLNESSES: INDUSTRY DATA, *available at* http://www.bls.gov/news.release/archives/osh_10202011.pdf; http://www.bls.gov/iif/oshwc/osh/os/ostb1355.pdf.

Nevertheless, there remain industries and sectors—for example, construction, farming, trucking, mining, and commercial fishing—that are relatively dangerous. And general improvements in safety do not assure that any particular worker or workplace will be injury-free. For example, in 2010, 3.1 million workers suffered some kind of job-related injury or illness (about 2.9 million from injuries). DOL, BLS, NEWS RELEASE, WORKPLACE INJURIES AND ILLNESSES, *available at* http://www.bls.gov/news.release/archives/osh_10202011.pdf. Moreover, work-related sickness and illness continue to raise significant public policy concerns: According to the National Institute for Occupational Safety and Health ("NIOSH"), 49,000 annual deaths are attributed to work-related diseases (about 134 per day), and workplace deaths and injuries cost the nation about $192 billion annually. NIOSH, WORKPLACE SAFETY AND HEALTH TOPICS, TRAUMATIC OCCUPATIONAL INJURIES, *available at* http://www.cdc.gov/niosh/injury/. In addition, occasionally high-profile incidents produce many injuries or deaths. In 2010, for example, the explosion of BP's Deepwater Horizon platform in the Gulf of Mexico killed 11 workers and injured 17, and the disaster at Massey Energy's Upper Big Branch Mine in West Virginia resulted in the death of 29 miners. The reported numbers also may significantly understate the incidence of workplace injury, disease, and death. *See, e.g.*, Steven Greenhouse, *Work-Related Injuries Underreported*, N.Y. TIMES, November 16, 2009, A18; Orly Lobel, *Interlocking Regulatory and Industrial Relations: The Governance of Workplace Safety*, 57 ADMIN. L. REV. 1071, 1079 n.31 (2005).

The problems of worker safety and health can be addressed in various ways. One is through private ordering. Health and safety issues are a frequent subject of collective bargaining agreements, and most such agreements, in addition to providing for health insurance, deal with at least some workplace safety issues, including safety standards and leave policies for injuries and illnesses. But collective bargaining is an imperfect means of improving worker safety and health, not only because such bargaining does not guarantee employer concessions or significant improvements, but also because the vast majority of workers are nonunionized. In theory, employees could bargain for health and safety protections individually, but, with the exception of health and disability insurance, terms addressing these issues directly are rarely part of individual employment agreements even where such agreements exist.

The statutory and other mandates discussed throughout this casebook address aspects of the problem in a variety of ways, albeit neither directly nor comprehensively. For example, as discussed in Chapter 4, whistleblower statutes and the public policy tort protect employees who have reported suspected safety hazards, refused to engage in dangerous activities, or otherwise assisted government officials in addressing safety concerns. We also saw in Chapter 7 that the National Labor Relations Act ensures even nonunionized workers the right to engage in "concerted activity" for a variety of ends, one of which is workplace health and safety. *See NLRB v. Washington Aluminum Co.*, 370 U.S. 9 (1962) (holding that a group of workers leaving their employment because of extreme cold was protected activity). Moreover, as covered in Chapters 9 and 10, fostering workplace safety and health plays an important role under the Americans with Disabilities Act, as either a by-product of the employer's obligation to reasonably accommodate disabled workers or, conversely, as a reason for refusing to provide certain accommodations. Likewise, other antidiscrimination provisions and the Family and Medical Leave Act implicate safety and health in various ways, including health- or injury-related leave policies and real or perceived gender-related health or safety risks, as addressed in a number of bona fide occupational qualification cases. Finally, as considered in Chapter 11, the Fair Labor Standards Act's ("FLSA") child labor provisions are premised on protecting the health and safety of this particularly vulnerable group. And ERISA's regulation of welfare benefit plans was originally designed to protect worker benefits, including health insurance, although that law does not require the provision of such benefits. In fact, its preemption doctrine defeats many state attempts to enhance health-related benefits.

Despite the pervasiveness of concerns over the safety and health of workers, the law has developed only two major regimes that deal directly and primarily with the question. One is state workers' compensation systems; the other is the federal Occupational Safety and Health Act ("OSHA"), 29 U.S.C. §§ 651 *et seq.* (2014). Much like pension law, workers' compensation has become its own discipline: Most law schools offer a separate course on it and many attorneys practice primarily or exclusively in this area. Nevertheless, because it is important that you have at least some acquaintance with workers' compensation and OSHA, both regimes are addressed briefly below.

The two systems have proven to be both important and, unsurprisingly, controversial. As mentioned in Chapter 5, in the early twentieth century, the workers' compensation system replaced the common-law tort of negligence with an administrative regime of strict liability for work-related injuries and diseases. This system provides more certain recovery for employees for physical injuries in accidents arising out of their employment, but subject to a trade-off: Workers' compensation restricts the amount of recovery and preempts others claims through workers' compensation exclusivity. There is some question as to whether the costs of this system create adequate incentives for employers to reduce safety hazards. Limitations on employer liability might reduce incentives to eliminate workplace hazards below the point a tort system would set and perhaps below what is acceptable from a societal perspective. *See generally* Emily A. Spieler, *Perpetuating Risk? Workers' Compensation and the Persistence of Occupational Injuries*, 31 HOUS. L. REV. 119 (1994). On the other hand, despite exclusivity, employers face substantial costs under workers' compensation, either directly as self-insurers or more commonly in terms of their compensation insurance premiums, which will reflect, at least to some extent, a company's claim history. *See* Michael J. Moore & W. Kip Viscusi, COMPENSATION MECHANISMS FOR JOB RISKS: WAGES, WORKERS' COMPENSATION, AND PRODUCT LIABILITY 151-78 (1990). The cost of the workers' compensation system has increased to the point where there has been recurrent talk of a compensation crisis. *See generally* Martha T. McCluskey, *Insurer Moral Hazard in the Workers' Compensation Crisis: Reforming Cost Inflation, Not Rate Suppression*, 5 EMP. RTS. & EMPLOY. POL'Y J. 55 (2001); Martha T. McCluskey, *The Illusion of Efficiency in Workers' Compensation "Reform,"* 50 RUTGERS L. REV. 657 (1998).

The other major legal regime addressing workplace safety is OSHA, which was enacted by Congress in 1970 and remains the most direct attack on the problem. Together with state counterparts and a few other federal safety regimes covering specific industries (such as the Mine Safety and Health Administration), OSHA seeks to prevent (instead of merely compensate) workplace injuries. *See generally* Mark Rothstein, OCCUPATIONAL SAFETY AND HEALTH LAW (2011 ed.). However, while the workplace has grown somewhat safer, it is not clear that OSHA gets much of the credit. Over time, many have questioned whether that regime, which consists largely of a regulatory scheme enforced by periodic agency inspection of worksites, rather than lawsuits brought by affected workers, is an effective means of ensuring safety and compliance. *See generally* Thomas O. McGarity & Sidney A. Shapiro, WORKERS AT RISK: THE FAILED PROMISE OF THE OCCUPATIONAL SAFETY AND HEALTH ADMINISTRATION (1993); Lobel, *supra*, at 1079-81, 1097-99. And there has been a wave of highly critical assessments of OSHA's performance in the last decade. *See* CTR. FOR PUB. INTEGRITY, BROKEN GOVERNMENT: AN EXAMINATION OF EXECUTIVE BRANCH FAILURES SINCE 2000 10-11 (2008); Susan Bisom-Rapp, *What We Learn in Troubled Times: Deregulation and Safe Work in the New Economy*, 55 WAYNE L. REV. 1097, 1231-39 (2009); Lynn Rhinehart, *Workers at Risk: The Unfulfilled Promise of the Occupational Safety and Health Act*, 111 W. VA. L. REV. 117, 121-23 (2008); *see also* David C. Vladeck, *The Failed Promise of Workplace Health Regulation*, 111 W. VA. L. REV. 15 (2008) (discussing the of recent coal mine disasters and the failure of federal workplace health and safety regimes to protect workers).

This chapter offers a brief overview of workers' compensation regimes and OSHA. It is not designed to be comprehensive. Rather, its aim is to introduce the history and structure of these two regimes; key elements, limitations, and litigated issues; and current controversies. The coverage of OSHA in particular is truncated, due in large part to the fact that a deeper dive would require detailed study of the regulations and the particulars with regard to individual regulations and enforcement actions.

A. WORKERS' COMPENSATION

1. The History of Workers' Compensation

In the late nineteenth and early twentieth centuries, workers often could not recover compensation for workplace injuries because of the "unholy trinity" of common law defenses: the fellow servant rule (which provided that the employer was not vicariously liable for worker injuries caused by negligent co-workers), assumption of risk, and contributory negligence. As courts gradually began removing these barriers, employers' fears of liability for workplace injuries grew. On the other side of the debate, those interested in protecting employees were concerned about the pace and completeness of common law change. These competing perspectives ultimately led to the "grand bargain," the universal adoption of workers' compensation schemes. In summarizing the origins of workers' compensation, Price Fishback and Shawn Kantor write:

> . . . The first decade of the twentieth century saw dramatic changes in the economic and legal environment surrounding workplace accident compensation, and these changes facilitated the formation of a political coalition in favor of workers' compensation. . . .
>
> The American movement for compensation legislation began in 1898, when the New York Social Reform Club presented the New York legislature with a compensation bill emulating the 1897 British law. The bill was killed in committee and deemed "too radical to pass" by the bill's legislative sponsor. As the economic and political environment changed over the next decade, the legislation obtained increasing support in response to an increase in employment in dangerous industries, an increased public awareness of workplace accident problems, and employers' worries about an increasingly unfavorable liability climate.
>
> Public awareness of workplace accidents during the period increased as shifts in employment across industries led to an increase in the share of workers in more dangerous jobs in manufacturing and mining and as the reporting of accident risk increased sharply. . . . [T]here was increased public awareness of workplace accidents because state labor departments, with their increasing budgets, improved their reporting of workplace injuries; therefore, the reported level of accident risk was rising. Reformers used these statistics to publicize the dangers and consequent financial hardships associated with workplace accidents.
>
> The greater attention paid to accident risk added to the consternation of employers because it occurred within an increasingly unfavorable liability climate. . . . [T]he number of states with employers' liability laws that restricted one or more of the employers' [common law tort] defenses for nonrailroad accidents rose from 7 in 1900 to 25 by 1913. The courts also modified the common-law defenses, which further exacerbated employers' uncertainty about the negligence liability system. Greater uncertainty about the law led employers and injured workers to accept the relatively high costs of litigation and test the bounds of the law more often, which in turn led to an increase in court cases at every level. In fact, the increased uncertainty was associated with a more than threefold rise in the number of state supreme court cases related to nonrailroad workplace accident litigation from 154 in 1900 to 490 in 1911. [Expanded liability combined with legal uncertainty] contributed to an increase in the liability insurance premiums that employers paid. . . . This was not merely an artifact of an ever-increasing insurance industry because liability insurance out-paced other forms of insurance. . . . While part of the increase in liability insurance premiums may have been caused by increases in coverage, anecdotal

evidence from several states suggests that increases in insurance rates also played a significant role.

Employers' worsening accident liability status in the early 1900s encouraged employer-supported lobbying groups to explore the possibility of a switch to a no-fault compensation system. Between 1908 and 1910 the National Civic Federation, which was composed of leaders from major corporations and conservative unions, devoted substantial time in their meetings to developing and promoting a workers' compensation bill. Meanwhile, the National Association of Manufacturers in 1910 called on its members to provide voluntary accident insurance, but then in 1911 the National Association of Manufacturers fully endorsed workers' compensation as a solution to the accident compensation problem. After forming in 1907 the American Association of Labor Legislation became one of the leading advocates for workers' compensation. The federal government, which often preceded most employers in offering relatively generous workplace benefits, established workers' compensation for federal workers in 1908 as a result of Theodore Roosevelt's strong support.

Employers' shift in interest toward workers' compensation coincided with changing sentiments among organized labor, whose ranks expanded from 868,000 in 1900 to 2.14 million in 1910, growing nearly three times faster than the labor force. The attitudes of major labor organizations went through a substantial change as they gained more experience with the results of employers' liability laws. Around the turn of the century, the American Federation of Labor believed that better accident compensation could be achieved by stripping employers of their three [tort] defenses. Organized labor's reluctance to embrace workers' compensation was part of a more general opposition to government regulation of the workplace on the theory that business interests controlled politics, and, thus, better benefits for workers could be achieved only through the voluntary organization of workers. But organized labor harshly criticized the fact that large numbers of injured workers were left uncompensated by the negligence system and that a large percentage of the insurance premiums that employers paid for liability never reached injured workers. In 1909, therefore, the American Federation of Labor switched its position and passed four resolutions supporting workers' compensation legislation, and the organization, at the federal level and through its state affiliates, became a vocal proponent of no-fault accident compensation.

The support from major employers' groups and organized labor led to the widespread adoption of workers' compensation. . . . In the second decade of the century . . . 43 states adopted workers' compensation. By 1930 all the states except Arkansas, Florida, Mississippi, and South Carolina had enacted the legislation. As Harry Weiss noted, "No other kind of labor legislation gained such general acceptance in so brief a period in this country."

The Adoption of Workers' Compensation in the United States, 1900-30, 41 J. L. & ECON. 305, 315-19 (1998); *see also* Lex K. Larson, LARSON'S WORKERS' COMPENSATION LAW §§ 2.07-.08 (Matthew Bender and Co., Inc., Rev. Ed. 2014). Fishback and Kantor go on to explain that the basic trade-offs between employer and employee interests continue to define workers' compensation regimes today:

Instead of being imposed by one interest group at the expense of other groups, workers' compensation was enacted because a broad-based coalition of divergent interests saw gains from reforming the negligence liability system. Employers anticipated a reduction in labor friction, a reduction in the uncertainty of their accident and court costs, and a reduction in the gap between what they paid for insurance and what injured workers received. In addition, they were able to pass at least some of the additional costs of workers' compensation benefits on to their workers in the form of lower real wages. Workers, on average, anticipated higher post-accident benefits from the new legislation. Even if they "bought" the better benefits through lower wages, they anticipated better "insurance" coverage against workplace accident risk. Further, insurers believed that the shift to workers' compensation would reduce problems with adverse selection, and thus they could expand their coverage of workplace accidents.

2. The Basic Structure of Workers' Compensation Statutes

Today, all states have workers' compensation regimes. Since their enactment in the early part of the last century, the basic structure of these statutes has remained the same. Because workers' compensation is a creature of state law, there are important variations; however, these regimes contain the same core components:

1. Insurance. A WC [workers' compensation] statute requires employers to secure and provide insurance for their employees against the losses suffered by reason of workplace injuries. Such insurance must come either from approved carriers or from the employer's own resources for self-insurance, as certified by a state agency.

2. Entitlement. Unlike the tort system, in which recovery against the employer (and its liability insurer) depends upon proof of both the employer's fault (and also the absence of worker fault), the injured employee may draw upon WC insurance if the injury was in any way caused by the job—i.e., if it "arose out of and in the course of employment."

3. Benefits. While a WC regime expands the basis of employer responsibility to encompass all job-related injuries, it reduces correspondingly the extent of the employer's legal responsibility for any particular injury. Rather than award full tort compensation for all economic and noneconomic losses suffered by each victim, the typical WC benefit scheme reimburses the victim [for medical costs and some portion of net wages lost due to temporary and permanent disabilities].

4. Administration. Primary responsibility for administering a WC scheme is conferred upon an administrative tribunal: the expectation is that this process will give workers quicker, easier, and less expensive access to the above benefit structure. Ideally, such ready access is also facilitated by substituting "cause" for "fault" as the precondition for recovery, and by replacing at-large damages tailored to each victim with the schedule formula designed for the average worker.

5. Exclusivity. The tacit assumption of the no-fault model is that victims as a group are better protected, ex ante, by such a guarantee of more limited redress for crucial financial losses from workplace injuries, even granting that in particular cases, viewed ex post, the individual worker who can establish fault would likely be able to collect more substantial tort compensation for all the economic and noneconomic consequences of the injury. Having made such an assumption and required the employer to provide and pay for this preferred WC system, the legislature then grants employers the *quid pro quo* of statutory immunity from any liability for these workplace injuries under the background tort system. . . .

Paul C. Weiler, *Workers' Compensation and Product Liability: The Interaction of a Tort and Non-Tort Regime*, 50 OHIO ST. L.J. 825, 826-30 (1989). While the core elements persist despite local variations, these laws have not been static over time; for example, benefits were liberalized in the 1970s, and, as a result of rising insurance costs many states retrenched in the late 1990s, enacting reforms limiting workers' compensation benefits and recoveries. *See generally* McCluskey, *The Illusion of Efficiency in Workers' Compensation "Reform," supra*, at 683-98.

Assuming a worker's injury is a compensable one to begin with, a topic that is addressed in the next section, workers' compensation laws provide benefits for physical injuries and illnesses—that is, medical benefits and wage-loss benefits for disabling conditions—and limited death benefits. Although medical expenses are normally completely covered, lost wages are subject to a statutory cap. Critically, workers' compensation also excludes pain and suffering damages and some emotional distress damages. Most states finance such benefits by requiring employers to self-insure (and satisfy the state that they are solvent enough to do so), purchase private workers' compensation insurance, or participate in a state-provided insurance plan.

The standard set of benefits generally includes:

- *Medical Expenses.* Workers' compensation regimes usually require complete coverage of all medical expenses reasonably required to cure or relieve the effects of workplace injuries and covered occupational diseases. These ordinarily include not only direct medical services, but also necessary incidental services such as transportation and medical equipment.

- *Temporary Disability Benefits.* All states' regimes provide for temporary disability benefits for a period of recovery after a worker has been injured. These benefits, which cover both total and partial disabilities, normally run from the time of the injury plus a waiting period (three to seven days) until the conclusion of the healing period. The healing period ends when the worker is able to return to work or has reached maximum medical improvement and must seek permanent disability benefits. Temporary benefits tend to be calculated based on a percentage (normally two-thirds, but sometimes only half) of the employee's lost wages, which in turn is based on the worker's average weekly wage for a preceding period—often 3, 6, or 12 months. However, such benefits are capped at a particular level per week, and the cap varies by jurisdiction.

- *Permanent Disability Benefits.* Permanent disabilities normally are broken into two categories: unscheduled and scheduled. *Scheduled disabilities* refers to permanent disabilities listed in a statutorily adopted schedule of possible injuries to designated parts of the body. These are compensated according to predetermined statutory amounts for the loss of particular body parts—that is, the actual loss of the limb or part or, in many cases, the loss of the use of that limb or part. The statute mandates a fixed rate that is paid for a specific number of weeks. These scheduled benefits are supposed to reflect roughly the standard amount of earning capacity lost from the injury. *Unscheduled disabilities* refer to those injuries not listed in the existing schedule. They are compensated based on the loss of earning capacity, normally determined after fact-finding by a vocational expert and capped at a statutory maximum. The amount awarded may be calculated based on a variety of factors, including prior average earnings, the loss of physical functions to the injured body part, the education and employment history of the worker, and the worker's ability to continue employment. If the worker can return to work, only functional impairment will be taken into account, and there is a cap (varying by state) on the amount that can be received. Although the method differs by state, a standard calculation provides the worker with his/her average salary for the time period he/she was completely incapacitated up to a maximum amount, and, thereafter, a percentage of the maximum amount allowed tied to the percentage of earning capacity lost (i.e., if the worker lost 40 percent of earning capacity, he/she would receive 40 percent of the maximum benefits). Given the calculation method, unscheduled benefits are specific to the worker and the injury suffered. States have allowed separate recovery for scheduled and unscheduled injuries if the employee can demonstrate that the loss of earning capacity is separate for the two injuries.

- *Vocational Rehabilitation Services.* Vocational services are aimed at getting the injured worker back to work in some capacity.
- *Death Benefits.* All states provide death benefits for spouses and dependents of employees who suffer fatal work-related injuries, although the benefits vary widely in both amount and duration. These benefits tend to be based on a percentage of the employee's average weekly wage, tied to the number of dependents, capped at a statutory maximum amount, and limited to a specified statutory period. Many states also provide limited benefits for funeral expenses. Some states have separate statutory provisions that increase the amount of death benefits for the dependents of certain types of workers, including police officers, firefighters, and paramedics.

Obviously, disputes may arise over what medical expenses are necessary and reasonable, whether and to what the extent an employee is disabled, the average weekly wages the employee earned prior to injury or death, who is a "dependent," and a host of other issues. Given their standardized structure, however, the amount of benefits owed in a particular case is far more predictable and certain than tort damages, facilitating efficient resolution of many potential disputes.

3. Coverage and Compensable Injuries

Given the structure of workers' compensation regimes, and in particular the fact that workers' compensation is no-fault and its benefits structure standardized, disputes that do arise as a result of workplace injuries and illnesses typically involve coverage and compensability — that is, whether the worker, employer, and particular injury fall within the scope of the regime. For example, take a moment to look back at *Fitzgerald v. Mobil Oil Corp.* in Chapter 1, page 10. In that case, Fitzgerald was hurt while working, and the disputed issue was whether he was an "employee" of Mobil Oil at the time: If so, his remedies against Mobil were limited to workers' compensation; if not, he could bring claims against Mobil in tort. In light of the benefits described above, why did Mobil Oil argue vigorously for employee status and Fitzgerald argue against it? Recall, however, that whether being an "employee" is in fact beneficial to a worker depends on the circumstances. Employment status (and hence, workers' compensation coverage) is beneficial where the worker might have difficulties recovering against the firm in tort — for instance, difficulty in establishing negligence or causation. What does this tell you about the circumstances surrounding the accident in *Fitzgerald*?

When worker and firm are found to be employee and employer, participation in the state's workers' compensation scheme is mandatory for the employer in all states except Texas and, in light of recent statutory amendments, Oklahoma, although very small employers are sometimes exempted, and many states exempt or limit coverage for certain agriculture and domestic workers. Nevertheless, the vast majority of employees are covered.

Where these threshold issues of employment and statutory coverage are satisfied, the next issue is whether the injury or illness is compensable. Compensable injuries are accidental injuries that occur in the course of employment and arise out of employment. The concept of "accident," the notion of "course of employment," and the requirement that an injury "arise out" of employment have each raised questions as to the reach of workers' compensation coverage. Further, some workplace illnesses, including occupational diseases, are subject to separate statutory treatment since they may not be accidental in the sense that they were not sudden or unexpected. This section considers each of these concepts.

a. Injuries Sustained "in the Course of" Employment

In most cases, determining whether a worker sustains an injury in the course of employment or outside of employment is easy. However, sometimes this issue is far from clear-cut because the worker's conduct or actions are outside of or inconsistent with the worker's job duties and are not for the benefit of the employer. Most cases falling into this gray area involve situations in which worker injuries occurred while the worker was traveling to or from work, on a "frolic or detour," engaging in "horseplay" or unauthorized conduct at work, participating in extracurricular activities somehow related to work, or acting in pursuit of personal interest. As you read, keep in mind that, while the "in the course of" employment inquiry is similar to the one courts use to determine whether an employer is liable for an employee's tort under the doctrine of respondeat superior (something you may have studied in your torts class and this book touched on in Chapter 1), the law governing this issue in the workers' compensation context is somewhat different, embodying its own set of considerations.

Kindel v. Ferco Rental, Inc.
899 P.2d 1058 (Kan. 1995)

LOCKETT, Judge.

A worker was killed on his return trip home from work. The worker's surviving spouse and minor children claimed death benefits. The Administrative Law Judge (ALJ) denied their claim, finding that the worker had abandoned his employment and therefore the accident did not arise out of and in the course of his employment. On review, the Workers Compensation Board (the Board) reversed the ALJ, finding that the worker's death arose out of and in the course of his employment. The employer appealed . . .

Donald L. Kindel was employed by Ferco Rental, Inc. (Ferco). On October 11, 1991, Kindel was transported in a company pickup truck from his home in Salina, Kansas, to a construction job site in Sabetha, Kansas. James Graham, Kindel's supervisor, was the driver of the truck. The company truck had been checked out to Graham to transport Kindel and other employees to and from the job site.

On the way to Sabetha, Graham and Kindel passed a former employee of Ferco. Kindel held up a note inviting the former co-worker to join them at the Outer Limits, a "striptease" bar adjacent to Interstate 70 on the west side of Topeka. At approximately 3:30 p.m., after completing the day's work at the job site in Sabetha, Graham and Kindel proceeded back toward Salina. On the way, the two men stopped at the Outer Limits for approximately four hours, where they became inebriated.

Graham suffers from amnesia and cannot recall any of the events occurring after they stopped at the Outer Limits. Graham testified, however, that it was Kindel's idea to stop at the Outer Limits; that Kindel made the arrangements to meet the former co-worker at the Outer Limits after work that day; and that if Kindel would have wanted to proceed straight home, Graham would have done so.

At approximately 8:50 p.m., the Kansas Highway Patrol received a call of a motor vehicle accident on Interstate 70. . . . When Trooper McCool arrived at the accident scene, he observed the Ferco truck overturned and lying in the south ditch of the westbound lane near an entrance to a rest area. Graham, who was driving, and Kindel had been partially ejected out of the truck's windshield. Kindel was deceased. Subsequent tests determined that Graham and Kindel had blood alcohol levels of .225 and .26, respectively.

Prior to the accident, Graham and Kindel were aware that Ferco had a policy that, except to obtain food or fuel, company vehicles were to be used only to go directly from the shop to the job site. Company vehicles were not to be used for personal pleasure or business. Ferco had a comprehensive drug and alcohol policy in place at the time of the accident which, among other things, prohibited workers from using the company equipment while under the influence of alcohol. Employees were not authorized to use a company vehicle to stop at a bar to consume alcohol. Kindel signed off on this policy on December 8, 1990. The employer asserted that when the employees stopped at the bar, authorization to use the company vehicle ceased and any further use of the company vehicle was not part of their employment.

At the time of the accident on October 11, 1991, Graham possessed a valid Kansas driver's license. Ferco was aware of Graham's propensity for drinking and driving. Graham had been charged with DUI some six days prior to this incident and had a previous conviction for which he had had his driver's license suspended. Graham understood that he was prohibited from drinking while using company equipment. Graham testified that the reason for stopping at the Outer Limits was to pursue pleasure and to have a good time. He said it was his understanding that when he pulled up at the Outer Limits, his work was over for the day.

Kindel's surviving spouse and minor children filed a workers compensation claim, seeking death benefits pursuant to K.S.A. 1991 Supp. 44-510b. The ALJ found "that the deviation was so substantial and there is not a causal connection between the deviation and the purpose of employment, nor a causal nexus between the resulting accident and death as to say that the claimant had ever returned to the scope of his employment. . . . The subsequent death, therefore, did not arise out of and in the course of his employment."

The ALJ made no findings as to whether Kindel's death resulted substantially from his intoxication. The claimants appealed.

After reviewing the record, the Board reached the opposite conclusion, finding that Kindel's death arose out of and in the course of his employment. The Board acknowledged case law from other jurisdictions supporting the ALJ's decision, but found case law supporting a finding of compensability to be more persuasive. The Board first noted that Kindel's trip to and from Sabetha, absent the detour, would have been considered a part of his employment. The Board stated that even if it assumed that the deviation from employment increased the risk of injury, the injury and resulting death resulted from the combined personal and work-related risks. The Board concluded that, under Kansas law, the increased risk attributable to the deviation did not, by itself, bar recovery. . . .

[The Board went on to conclude that "this case is not materially different from any other where a claimant deviates from his employment but has returned at the time of the accident. The Appeals Board therefore finds that claimant's death arose out of and in the course of his employment."]

The Board reversed the decision of the ALJ and remanded the case for a determination of the appropriate benefits. The employer appealed. . . .

Arising out of and in the Course of Employment

Although K.S.A.1991 Supp. 44-508(f), a codification of the longstanding "going and coming" rule, provides that injuries occurring while traveling to and from employment are generally not compensable, there is an exception which applies when travel upon the public roadways is an integral or necessary part of the employment. *See Blair v. Shaw*, 233 P.2d 731 (Kan. 1951); *Messenger v. Sage Drilling Co.*, 680 P.2d 556 (Kan. App. 1984). Because Kindel and other Ferco employees were expected to live out of town during the work weeks, and transportation to and from the remote site was in a company vehicle driven by a supervisor, this case falls within the exception to the general rule.

In any employment to which workers compensation laws apply, an employer is liable to pay compensation to an employee where the employee incurs personal injury by accident arising out of and in the course of employment. Whether an accident arises out of and in the course of the worker's employment depends upon the facts peculiar to the particular case.

The two phrases arising "out of" and "in the course of" employment, as used in our Workers Compensation Act, K.S.A. 44-501 *et seq.*, have separate and distinct meanings; they are conjunctive, and each condition must exist before compensation is allowable. The phrase "out of" employment points to the cause or origin of the accident and requires some causal connection between the accidental injury and the employment. An injury arises "out of" employment when there is apparent to the rational mind, upon consideration of all the circumstances, a causal connection between the conditions under which the work is required to be performed and the resulting injury. Thus, an injury arises "out of" employment if it arises out of the nature, conditions, obligations, and incidents of the employment. The phrase "in the course of" employment relates to the time, place, and circumstances under which the accident occurred and means the injury happened while the worker was at work in the employer's service.

Both the ALJ and the Board acknowledge the separate considerations inherent in the determination whether the death arose "out of" and "in the course of" employment. The ALJ concluded that the length of time Kindel spent at the Outer Limits and his substantial consumption of alcohol removed his subsequent activity from arising "in the course of" his employment, notwithstanding the fact he was on his homeward route at the time of the accident. The Board, on the other hand, determined that Kindel's injury and death resulted from combined risks attributable to his personal deviation *and* his employment, and held that the increased risk factor attributable to the deviation should not bar recovery. The point of disagreement between the ALJ and Board is whether the deviation was so substantial as to permanently remove the worker from the course of his employment, even though he later continued his homeward route. The parties cite various cases for support of their respective positions.

Two Kansas cases address a somewhat similar situation and determined whether the worker had abandoned his employer's business. They are *Angleton v. Starkan, Inc.*, 828 P.2d 933 (Kan. 1992), and *Woodring v. United Sash & Door Co.*, 103 P.2d 837 (Kan. 1940). . . . Angleton, who was employed as a truck driver for Starkan, was hauling a load of cattle when a pair of hijackers began following him in another truck. By conversation over the citizens band radio, one of the hijackers persuaded Angleton to pull off the highway to smoke marijuana. Angleton stopped his truck and got into the hijackers' truck. While Angleton was smoking a marijuana cigarette, one of the hijackers shot and killed him. . . .

The *Angleton* court first determined that absent the alleged marijuana episode, the accident occurred in the course of Angleton's employment. The court noted that at the time of his death, Angleton was en route to deliver his load of cattle to a feedlot on the route designated by his employer and that at the time Angleton pulled off the highway, he was driving his load in fulfillment of his employment obligations. The court further observed that Angleton was killed because he was responsible for the Starkan truck and cattle and his employment for Starkan transporting valuable cargo exposed him to an increased risk of injury of being robbed while on the highway.

The *Angleton* court then examined whether the alleged use of marijuana changed the district court's conclusion that the accident resulting in Angleton's death arose out of and in the course of his employment. The district court had noted that the only testimony that Angleton pulled off the highway to smoke marijuana was the testimony by one of the hijackers and found that testimony to be inherently unreliable. . . . The *Angleton* court determined that the record supported the district court's finding that the hijacker's testimony was unreliable and held that the testimony was not sufficient or reliable to support a finding that the worker's conduct constituted a deviation from his employment. The court found that Angleton's death arose in the course of and out of his employment.

In *Woodring* . . . , the claimant was a traveling salesman who lived in Salina. Woodring was sent by his employer to meet a client in Enterprise, Kansas, to further the employer's business. Prior to arriving at Enterprise, the claimant went to Minneapolis, Kansas, and picked up three friends who made the journey to Enterprise with him. When the worker arrived at Enterprise, he discovered the man he was supposed to meet was in Abilene. The claimant made no further attempts to contact the client, and instead proceeded to a local drinking establishment with his friends for "an hour or so" where he imbibed intoxicating liquor. Thereafter, while driving recklessly on his return journey to Salina, claimant was injured when his car overturned. . . .

The *Woodring* court then observed that where a business errand is the purpose of a worker's journey, the social incident of taking a few guests along for the pleasure of their company would not affect the worker's right to compensation for an injury sustained in the performance of that errand. The *Woodring* court noted that an intruding question was whether a worker, engaged in the employer's service, could be permitted to recover compensation for an injury sustained while operating an automobile on the public highway under the influence of intoxicating liquor in violation of a Kansas statute which made such an act a criminal offense punishable by fine or imprisonment or both. It found that because the district court had determined the business errand was finished or abandoned and that the worker had set about the pursuit of his own pleasure or indulgence, there was no theory of law or of justice which would impose on the employer the obligation to pay compensation for any injury sustained by the worker under such circumstances.

The claimants rely heavily on *Angleton* . . . for support of a finding of compensability in this case. The claimants seek to distinguish *Woodring*, noting that Kindel was a passenger being driven home by his supervisor in a company vehicle and that the supervisor was required to return his employer's vehicle. The employer fails to address the *Angleton* precedent, but contends that the rationale of *Woodring* should be applied to this case. It is important to note that in *Angleton* and *Woodring* there were allegations that the worker was violating the law. Here, although Kindel was intoxicated, the fact he drank was not a violation of the law nor was he violating a law, at the time he was killed.

In support of their arguments, both parties cite numerous cases from outside of Kansas. The most favorable case for the employer is *Calloway v. Workmen's Comp.*, 268 S.E.2d 132 (W. Va. 1980). In *Calloway*, the West Virginia Supreme Court found the claimant salesman's activity of drinking and tavern-hopping from midafternoon until 11 p.m. amounted to an abandonment of any business purpose such that the injuries he received in an accident shortly thereafter while being transported home were not compensable. The *Calloway* court acknowledged that workers compensation laws generally recognize that an employee is entitled to compensation for an injury received while travelling on behalf of his employer's business.

The court noted that where an employee deviates from the employer's business, the employee may be denied compensation if the injury occurs during the deviation and that once the employee ceases the deviation and returns to the employer's business, a subsequent injury is ordinarily compensable. The court then observed:

> In the case of a major deviation from the business purpose, most courts will bar compensation recovery on the theory that the deviation is so substantial that the employee must be deemed to have abandoned any business purpose and consequently cannot recover for injuries received, even though he has ceased the deviation and is returning to the business route or purpose. [Citations omitted.]
>   . . . A deviation generally consists of a personal or nonbusiness-related activity. The longer the deviation exists in time or the greater it varies from the normal business route or in purpose from the normal business objectives, the more likely that it will be characterized as major.

The *Calloway* court then reviewed a number of cases in which various courts have characterized an employee's deviations to be sufficiently major to deny compensation. The *Calloway* court concluded:

> In the present case, there is no dispute that the claimant was initially traveling on behalf of his employer in an attempt to solicit new business in the Logan County area. However, even under the facts liberally construed in his behalf, he had completed any company business in the midafternoon when he and his fellow employee began to frequent taverns. The continuation of this activity until 11:00 p.m. was a major deviation, not only in time but also in its nature. It can only be viewed as an abandonment of any business purpose.

The most favorable case for the claimants is *Rainear v. C.J. Rainear & Co.*, 307 A.2d 72 (N.J. 1973). In *Rainear*, the New Jersey Supreme Court held that where an automobile accident had occurred while the decedent was on his way home from work along a proper and permissible route, decedent's 10-hour stop at a restaurant and bar to eat and drink did not amount to such a departure from the decedent's reasonable sphere of employment as to bar a compensation award. In that case, the decedent's travel expenses were being paid by his employer. There was nothing in the record to confirm that drinking caused the accident. The *Rainear* court reviewed a number of cases awarding compensation to employees injured following a deviation. The court stated:

> There is nothing in the compensation law which fixes an arbitrary limit to the number of hours of deviation which may be terminated with travel coverage resumed. Thus if the decedent ate dinner at [the restaurant and bar] en route home and stayed there simply watching television for hours before continuing on his intended travel home, there clearly would be no rational basis for failing to apply the broad remedial principles embraced in [other New Jersey workers compensation cases]. While the fact that he also did some drinking there may have influenced the Appellate Division's negative result, the drinking really has no legal bearing here since there was no proof that the accident or death resulted from intoxication.

A deviation from the employer's work generally consists of a personal or nonbusiness-related activity. The longer the deviation exists in time or the greater it varies from the normal business route or in purpose from the normal business objectives, the more likely that the deviation will be characterized as major. In the case of a major deviation from the business purpose, most courts will bar compensation recovery on the theory that the deviation is so substantial that the employee must be deemed to have abandoned any business purpose and consequently cannot recover for injuries received, even though he or she has ceased the deviation and is returning to the business route or purpose.

Is there substantial evidence to support the Board's finding of compensability, *i.e.*, that Kindel's death arose in the course of his employment? The employer provided transportation. Kindel was a passenger and not the driver. He was being transported home after completion of his duties. Despite approximately four hours at the Outer Limits, the distance of the deviation was less than one quarter of a mile. Kindel was killed after resuming the route home. Under the facts, even though the worker was intoxicated, as a passenger in his employer's vehicle, he was not committing a violation of Kansas law. Kindel was killed while engaging in an activity contemplated by his employer while traveling on a public interstate highway. The fact he had been drinking has no legal bearing on the present compensation determination since there was no proof that the accident or Kindel's death resulted from Kindel's intoxication.

The workers compensation statutes are to be liberally construed to effect legislative intent and award compensation where it is reasonably possible to do so. We note that the workers compensation law does not fix an arbitrary limit on the number of hours of deviation, which may be terminated with travel coverage resumed. Whether there was a deviation, and if that deviation had terminated, is a question of fact to be determined by the administrative law judge or the Workers Compensation Board. Under our standard of review, we find that the Board did not act unreasonably, arbitrarily, or capriciously and there is substantial evidence to support the Board's conclusion that the fatal injury occurred in the course of Kindel's employment.

Did Death Result Substantially from Intoxication?

K.S.A. 1991 Supp. 44-501(d) provides:

If it is proved that the injury to the employee results . . . substantially from the employee's intoxication, any compensation in respect to that injury shall be disallowed. . . .

Employer contends that Kindel's intoxication was a substantially causative factor in bringing about his death. . . .

To defeat a workers compensation claim based on the worker's intoxication, an employer must prove not only that the worker was intoxicated, but also that such intoxication was the substantial cause of the injury. The presumption of intoxication provided for under the Kansas criminal statute is inapplicable in workers compensation cases. Evidence of the blood alcohol concentration of a workers compensation claimant is relevant to the issue of the cause of the accident in which the claimant is injured but does not give rise to a presumption of intoxication. . . .

To this court, the employer asserts that Kansas courts have recognized that a passenger owes a duty to exercise that care which a reasonably careful person would use for his or her own protection under the existing circumstances. . . .

Common-law defenses to tort theories of negligence do not apply to workers compensation claims. . . .

Because Kindel was covered by workers compensation, these defenses are not available to the employer; therefore, Kindel had no common-law duty as a passenger.

In addition, the employer failed to prove that Kindel's intoxication was a substantial cause of the injury. The testimony of Trooper McCool was that the alcohol level of the driver was a substantial cause of the accident. Neither the ALJ nor the Board concluded that the accident substantially resulted from Kindel's intoxication. The fact that Kindel was a passenger, and not the driver, defeats the employer's claim. . . .

≡ ## *Clodgo v. Rentavision, Inc.*
≡ *701 A.2d 1044 (Vt. 1997)*

GIBSON, Justice.

Defendant Rentavision, Inc. appeals a decision of the Commissioner of the Vermont Department of Labor and Industry awarding workers' compensation benefits to claimant Brian Clodgo. Rentavision argues the Commissioner erred in awarding compensation for an injury sustained while claimant and another employee were engaged in horseplay. We reverse.

On July 22, 1995, claimant was working as manager of Rentavision's store in Brattleboro. During a lull between customers, claimant began firing staples with a staple gun at a co-worker, who was sitting on a couch watching television. The co-worker first protested, but then, after claimant had fired twenty or thirty staples at him, fired three staples back at claimant. As claimant ducked, the third staple hit him in the eye. Claimant eventually reported the injury and filed a claim for workers' compensation benefits. Rentavision contested the award, arguing that claimant was engaged in noncompensable horseplay at the time of the injury. Following a hearing in March

1996, the Commissioner awarded permanent partial disability and vocational rehabilitation benefits, medical expenses, and attorney's fees and costs. This appeal followed. . . .

Compensable injuries under Vermont's Workers' Compensation Act are those received "by accident arising out of and in the course of . . . employment." 21 V.S.A. §618. Although only work-related injuries are compensable, we recognize that "even [employees] of maturer years [will] indulge in a moment's diversion from work to joke with or play a prank upon a fellow [employee]." *Leonbruno v. Champlain Silk Mills*, 128 N.E. 711, 711 (N.Y. 1920). For such a horseplay-related injury to be compensated, however, claimant must show that it both (1) arose out of the employment, and (2) occurred in the course of the employment. A nonparticipant injured by the horseplay of others will nearly always be able to meet this test, *see* 2 A. Larson & L. Larson, Workers' Compensation Law §23.61, at 5-199 (1997), while a participant may or may not recover. *See* 2 Larson & Larson, *supra*, §23.20, at 5-182 to 5-183.

In setting forth the applicable standard, the Commissioner stated that nothing short of specific intent to injure falls outside the scope of the Act. This overly broad statement was borrowed, however, from a case analyzing the exclusive-remedy aspects of workers' compensation law, made in the context where an employee attempts to prove specific intent by the employer to injure the employee. *See Kittell v. Vermont Weatherboard, Inc.*, 417 A.2d 926, 927 (Vt. 1980). Whether a horseplay participant is entitled to recover usually hinges on whether the injury occurred in the course of employment, which, in turn, depends on the extent of the employee's deviation from work duties. . . .

The question certified for review is whether claimant's horseplay bars him from recovery for the resulting injury under Vermont's Workers' Compensation Act. Rentavision contends the Commissioner misapplied the law in concluding that claimant's horseplay-related injury was compensable. We agree. An injury arises out of employment if it would not have occurred but for the fact that the conditions and obligations of the employment placed claimant in the position where he or she was injured. Thus, claimant must show that "but for" the employment and his position at work, the injury would not have happened.

Although the accident here would not have happened but for claimant's participation in the horseplay and therefore was not exclusively linked to his employment, it also was not a purely personal risk that would have occurred regardless of his location and activity on that day. He was injured during work hours with a staple gun provided for use on the job, and thus the findings support a causal connection between claimant's work conditions and the injury adequate to conclude that the accident arose out of his employment.

Nonetheless, claimant must also show that the injury occurred in the course of the employment. An accident occurs in the course of employment when it was within the period of time the employee was on duty at a place where the employee was reasonably expected to be *while fulfilling the duties of the employment contract*. Thus, while some horseplay among employees during work hours can be expected and is not an automatic bar to compensation, the key inquiry is whether the employee deviated too far from his or her duties.

The Commissioner must therefore consider (1) the extent and seriousness of the deviation; (2) the completeness of the deviation (i.e., whether the activity was commingled with performance of a work duty or was a complete abandonment of duty); (3) the extent to which the activity had become an accepted part of the employment;

and (4) the extent to which the nature of the employment may be expected to include some horseplay. The Commissioner found that although shooting staples was common among employees, such activity was not considered acceptable behavior by Rentavision. She made no finding concerning whether Rentavision knew that staple-shooting occurred at work, but did find that claimant made material misrepresentations of fact designed to avoid an inference of horseplay or inappropriate behavior in order that he might obtain workers' compensation benefits. Claimant makes no showing that shooting staples at fellow employees was an accepted part of claimant's employment or furthered Rentavision's interests.

The facts show that the accident was unrelated to any legitimate use of the staplers at the time, indicating there was no commingling of the horseplay with work duties. The Commissioner focused on the slack time inherent in claimant's job, but this factor alone is not dispositive. Although some horseplay was reasonably to be expected during idle periods between customers, the obvious dangerousness of shooting staples at fellow employees and the absence of connection between duties as a salesperson and the horseplay events indicates the accident occurred during a substantial deviation from work duties. Therefore, we reverse the Commissioner's award.

Reversed.

MORSE, Justice, dissenting.

I respectfully dissent. The Court reverses a decision of the Commissioner of the Vermont Department of Labor and Industry awarding workers' compensation benefits for an injury sustained while claimant was engaged in "horseplay" with another employee. The basic criteria of analysis utilized by the Commissioner are not disputed by the Court. Rather, the Court disagrees with the Commissioner's application of the law to the facts, holding that the horseplay constituted a substantial deviation from the course of employment and therefore was not compensable.

Under settled standards of review, the Court has stepped out of its proper role. The Court is not to second-guess the Commissioner's conclusions. . . .

With respect to the extent and seriousness of the deviation, as well as its completeness, the Commissioner found that claimant and his fellow employee had completed virtually all the work that needed to be done in the absence of customers and that business was very slow that day. When the injury occurred, claimant and his fellow employee were in a period of enforced idleness while they waited for customers. They were not actively pursuing any specific tasks and were passing the time as required by their jobs. As Larson points out, when there is a lull in work, there are no duties to abandon. During such periods, the deviation can be more substantial than at other times when an employee may be actively pursuing a task directly related to employment. *Id.* §23.65, at 5-219, 5-226 to 5-227. The Commissioner could thus reasonably conclude that the horseplay in this case did not constitute an abandonment of duties or even a serious deviation from the demands of work at that time of day.

Regarding the extent to which such horseplay had become an accepted activity, the Commissioner found that it had been a commonplace occurrence at the store. Although the executive assistant to defendant's president testified that claimant's horseplay was not considered acceptable behavior, he acknowledged that an employee would not be fired for engaging in such activity. The Commissioner thus reasonably concluded that the horseplay as engaged in by claimant, while not condoned by the employer, was a tacit part of employment.

Finally, the Commissioner could reasonably conclude that work in a retail establishment might be expected to include such horseplay. The Commissioner characterized the claimant and his fellow employee as "suffering through a very slow day in a retail establishment," having quoted Larson as noting that "idleness breeds mischief, so that if idleness is a fixture of the employment, its handmaiden mischief is also." (Quoting 2 Larson & Larson, *supra*, § 23.65, at 5-219.) Retail work necessitates passing time if there are no customers demanding attention. . . . The Commissioner's determination that the nature of the business lent itself to the horseplay in question was fairly and reasonably supported by the facts.

In sum, the Commissioner applied the proper legal standard to the facts, and the evidence fairly and reasonably supports the Commissioner's conclusion, a conclusion that, I might add, is a reasonable one given the policy of the law to help alleviate the consequences of injury in the workplace. . . .

NOTES

1. *A Sufficient Connection with Employment?* Ultimately, the "in the course of" and "arises out of" requirements seek to ensure that the injury was sufficiently connected with work or the workplace to justify shifting the risk of loss to the employer and the workers' compensation system. Based on your reading of *Kindel* and *Clodgo*, what is the legal standard for determining if an injury occurs "in the course of" employment? Why do the courts reach opposite conclusions on whether the injuries in question satisfied this standard? One could strongly argue that the horseplay at issue in *Clodgo* was not as significant a deviation from the workers' duties as conduct at issue in *Kindel*, which involved spending several hours at an off-site location. How can the cases be reconciled, if at all?

As discussed above, there is an ongoing debate about the efficiency and efficacy of workers' compensation — a system that costs billions of dollars a year. If rising costs and cost containment are legitimate concerns, why should the employer be responsible for injuries sustained outside the workplace and outside an employee's specified work duties and tasks? Why might such broad coverage be socially beneficial (i.e., worth the costs)? Even if you conclude that the employer's responsibility ought to extend beyond the scope of workplace duties in some circumstances, can the result in *Kindel* be justified?

2. *The Journey to and from Work.* Under the "going and coming rule," an injury occurring during a worker's journey to and from work — before and after work, or during the lunch break — is not compensable, unless it occurs on the work premises or in the employer's vehicle. *See* Larson, *supra*, at §§ 13.01, 15.01. However, there are a number of exceptions to this principle. Most importantly, travel to and from work is compensable if the journey itself is a substantial part of the worker's service or if, based on the employer's needs or requests, the journey is made with a special degree of inconvenience or urgency. Thus, for example, where travel to different locations is part of the job, the employee travels on a "special errand" for the employer, or the employee must travel to remote sites, such travel is often considered in the course of employment. *See id.* at §§ 13.01, 14.01-.06. Of increasing importance in the era of telecommuting, travel between home and work may be in the course of employment if home is a regular "second office." Why did the court find that the commute from work at issue in *Kindel* was in the course of employment?

3. *Worker Intoxication and Misconduct.* Injuries resulting from or relating to the use or abuse of alcohol or drugs are common subjects of controversy in the workers' compensation context. As we saw in *Kindel*, many states now limit recovery for injuries sustained as a result of intoxication, although the extent to which alcohol must have "caused" the injuries varies by statute and is a frequently litigated issue. *See, e.g., Cyr v. McDermott's, Inc.* 996 A.2d 709 (Vt. 2010) (reversing and remanding the labor commissioner's denial of workers' compensation benefits after finding that, although the worker was intoxicated when he ingested chemicals from a soda bottle that had been given to him while at work, there remained an issue whether the intoxication caused his resulting injuries) *see generally* Larson, *supra*, at §§ 36.01, 36.03. Why were Kindel's wife and children still able to recover benefits despite the intoxication provision in the Kansas statute? Were Graham's injuries compensable?

Some states also provide a statutory defense for "willful misconduct." Although this kind of defense could be interpreted broadly, courts generally have limited its application to deliberate or intentional violations of regulations designed to prevent serious injury or intentional and knowing violations of statutes designed to prevent the type of injury that occurred. *See* Larson, *supra*, at §§ 34.01-.03, 37.03. Thus, mere horseplay like that at issue in *Clogdo* would not constitute willful misconduct, although, as that case makes clear, such conduct may still fall outside the course of employment. Does the narrow reading of willful misconduct make sense in light of what you know about the purpose of the workers' compensation system and the "trade-offs" that it embodies?

Finally, note that the *Kindel* court rejects the employer's attempt to use common-law tort defenses, including the defense that a passenger is obliged to take reasonable care to ensure his or her own safety under the circumstances. Here again we see the trade-off underlying workers' compensation: Just as injured employees cannot bring common-law tort claims, employers cannot escape workers' compensation liability by presenting common-law defenses.

4. *Work-related Recreational or "Extracurricular" Activities.* A recurrent issue involving the connection between the injury and employment is whether recreational and social activities—for example, sports, exercising, games, social gatherings—are within the course of employment. As a general matter, they are—if they occur on the employers' premises during normal work breaks or otherwise incident to employment. In addition, such activities are within the course of employment when required by the employer or when the employer derives some direct benefit from the activity beyond mere enhancement of employee health or morale. *See generally* Larson, *supra*, at §§ 22.01-.05. The more tenuous the nexus between the activity and the workplace, work terms and hours, and direct employer sponsorship or support, the less likely it is that it will be found to be "in the course of" employment. *Compare Bender v. Dakota Resorts Mgmt., Inc.*, 700 N.W.2d 739 (S.D. 2005) (finding compensable injury sustained by employee of ski resort injured while skiing at the resort during his break, which he and other employees did on a regular basis); *E.C. Styberg Engineering Co., Inc. v. Lab. and Indus. Rev. Comm'n*, 692 N.W.2d 322 (Wis. Ct. App. 2004) (same for softball injury sustained during paid break) *with Montgomery County v. Smith*, 799 A.2d 406 (Md. Ct. App. 2002) (denying workers' compensation benefits to a worker injured while playing basketball after his workday in gym at detention center where he worked where employer did not require or sponsor activity). Courts remain deeply split over whether injuries occurring during employer-sponsored parties, picnics, and other events are within the course of employment, although distinctions sometimes hinge on the degree of employer pressure to attend or participate. *See* Larson, *supra*, at § 22.04; *see, e.g., Young v. Taylor-White, LLC*, 181 S.W.3d 324 (Tenn. 2005) (rejecting claim for benefits where injury occurred in a voluntary "three-legged race" at an employer-sponsored picnic); *State v. Dalton*, 878 A.2d 451 (Del. 2005) (awarding benefits where worker was hurt in charity softball game where evidence suggested that participation by police officers like claimant was expected). Some states have statutorily barred workers' compensation benefits for injuries sustained during recreational activities absent employer compulsion to participate. *See* Larson, *supra*, at § 22.02.

5. *"Personal Comfort" Doctrine.* Another issue that arises often in "in the course of" employment cases is the extent to which injuries that occur during employee deviations from work tasks to seek "personal comfort"—for example, eating, using the restroom, washing, resting, getting warm, and so forth—are compensable. The so-called "personal comfort" doctrine provides that such deviations are in the course of employment unless the departure is sufficiently great that it constitutes an intent to abandon the job temporarily or unless the method chosen is unusual or unreasonable, such that it cannot be considered incidental to employment. *See generally* Larson, *supra*, at §§ 21.01-.08. Although the inquiry is fact-specific, injuries are usually compensable in run-of-the-mill cases involving breaks for personal comforts at work during work hours. *See, e.g., Illinois Consol. Tel. Co. v. Indus. Comm'n*, 732 N.E.2d 49 (Ill. Ct. App. 2000) (awarding benefits to worker who was injured in a fall while returning to work from the restroom). Greater deviations, however, often are not compensable. *See, e.g., Galaida v. Autozone, Inc.*, 882 So.2d 1111 (Fla. Ct. App. 2004) (finding that, although an authorized cigarette break might qualify under the doctrine, a gunshot wound an employee received during such a break was not compensable because the employee's conduct—dropping a firearm while reaching for a cigarette—and resulting injury were not a foreseeable consequence of the break); *In re Estate of Fry*, 620 N.W.2d 449 (Wis. Ct. App. 2000) (estate of worker killed in traffic accident while en route to a medical appointment with employer's permission not entitled to recovery under personal comfort doctrine). Indeed, the doctrine applies only to injuries occurring on work premises or other areas where workers are authorized to be during work hours.

b. *"Arises out of" Employment*

≡ *Odyssey/Americare of Oklahoma v. Worden*
≡ *948 P.2d 309 (Okla. 1997)*

HODGES, Justice.

Odyssey/Americare of Oklahoma (Employer) and its insurer seek vacation of a Court of Civil Appeals opinion in this matter which sustained an order of the Workers' Compensation Court awarding benefits to Cheryl Worden (Claimant). The trial tribunal found that Claimant's injury arose out of her employment. This Court finds that there was not competent evidence to support that determination.

Claimant was a field nurse for Employer. She lived approximately twenty miles away from Employer's office. She went to Employer's office about once a week. Otherwise, she worked out of her home scheduling appointments with patients and traveling to visit them. At trial, the parties submitted a stipulation that Claimant was

Employer's employee covered under the Workers' Compensation Act. Claimant testified that as she was walking to her car to go to a patient appointment, she slipped on wet grass in her yard and fell injuring her foot and ankle. The grass was wet from rain. But for the patient appointment, she would not have left the house.

The trial tribunal originally denied the claim, finding that her injury did not arise out of and in the course of her employment. According to the court, "the claimant's injuries were as a result of a risk which was purely personal to the claimant and not as a result of a hazardous risk associated with the claimant's employment." . . .

Oklahoma law requires that an employer pay compensation only for "accidental personal injury sustained by the employee arising out of and in the course of his employment, without regard to fault. . . ." OKLA. STAT. tit. 85, §11 (1991). The term "in the course of employment" relates to the time, place, or circumstances under which the injury is sustained. The term "arise out of employment" contemplates the causal connection between the injury and the risks incident to employment. The two requirements are distinct and are not synonymous. *Id.* Only the "arise out of" requirement is at issue in this matter. The parties agree that Claimant was in the course of her employment at the time of injury.

There are three categories of injury-causing risk an employee may encounter while in the course of employment: risks solely connected with employment, which are compensable; personal risks, which are not compensable; and neutral risks, such as weather risks, which are neither distinctly connected with employment nor purely personal. *See* 1 LARSON'S WORKERS' COMPENSATION LAW §7.30 (1997). Whether a neutral risk that causes an injury is employment-related or personal is a question of fact to be decided in each case.

Nationwide, there have been five lines of interpretation of the "arising out of" requirement. 1 LARSON *supra* at §6. The "peculiar risk" doctrine required the claimant "to show that the source of the harm was in its nature peculiar to his occupation." *Id.* at §6.20. At one time the peculiar risk doctrine was the dominant test in American Workers' Compensation jurisprudence but it was gradually replaced by the "increased risk" doctrine.

The "increased risk" test "differs from the peculiar-risk test in that the distinctiveness of the employment risk can be contributed by the increased *quantity* of a risk that is *qualitatively* not peculiar to the employment." *Id.* The rule is often stated as a determination of whether the claimant's employment exposed the worker to more risk than that to which the general public was exposed.

An easier test for a claimant to meet is that of "actual risk." "Under this doctrine, a substantial number of courts are saying, in effect, 'We do not care whether the risk was also common to the public, if in fact it was a risk of *this* employment.'" *Id.* at §6.40.

A number of courts now apply the "positional risk" doctrine. It states that "[a]n injury arises out of employment if it would not have occurred *but for* the fact that the conditions on the employment placed claimant in the position where he was injured." *Id.* at §6.50.

A rarely used line of interpretation is that of "proximate cause." This test demands "that the harms be foreseeable as a hazard of this kind of employment, and that the chain of causation be not broken by any independent intervening cause, such as an act of God." *Id.* at §6.60. This line of authority is "encountered occasionally in opinions and old texts." *Id.*

Prior to the 1986 amendments to Oklahoma's Workers' Compensation Act, Oklahoma cases relied primarily on the increased risk doctrine to determine whether a risk arose out of a worker's employment. However, the peculiar risk and positional risk tests had also been applied. *See, e.g., Halliburton Services v. Alexander*, 547 P.2d 958, 961 (Okla. 1976) ("where accidental injury results from risk factor peculiar to task performed, it arises out of employment. . . ."); *Fox v. Nat'l Carrier*, 709 P.2d 1050, 1053 (Okla. 1985) (but for claimant's employment as truck driver he would not have been exposed to risk of choking on food at restaurant). But in 1986, the Oklahoma Legislature amended section 3(7) of title 85 to require that "only injuries having as their source a risk not purely personal but one that is reasonably connected with the conditions of employment shall be deemed to arise out of employment." The Legislature also repealed the provision which required an employer to produce "substantial evidence" to overcome a presumption that an injury was compensable under the Workers' Compensation Act. *See* OKLA. STAT. tit. 85, §27 (1981) (repealed). The presumption and its corresponding burdens of production and persuasion were abolished.

These statutory changes to the analysis of the "arise out of" requirement were explained in *Am. Mgmt. Sys., Inc. v. Burns*, 903 P.2d 288 (Okla. 1995). In *Burns*, a worker visiting Oklahoma City on a business trip for his employer was murdered in his hotel room by an unknown assailant with unknown motive. This Court explained that a claimant now has the burden of establishing the causal connection between injury and employment. "To establish injury or death as attributable to an employment-related risk, the operative force of a hazard, other than that which affects the public in general, must be identified." This Court specifically held that the positional risk test is now "unavailable for proving an injury's causal nexus to employment." Burn[s'] widow failed to establish that her husband's death arose out of his employment rather than from the ever-present risk of crime faced by the general public.

Despite the holding in *Burns*, the Court of Civil Appeals in this matter held that "because the risk responsible was clearly presented by the requirements of her employment, it does not matter whether the risk of injury to her was no greater than the risk to the general public." Thus, it applied essentially the positional risk test rejected in the 1986 amendments to the Workers' Compensation Act as explained in *Burns*.

The Court of Civil Appeals read two post-*Burns* cases as controlling this controversy, *Darco Transp. v. Dulen*, 922 P.2d [591 (Okla. 1996)] and *Stroud Mun. Hosp. v. Mooney*, 933 P.2d 872 (Okla. 1996). It noted that in each case compensation was allowed for traffic collision injuries even though the employee was exposed to the same street risk faced by the general motoring public. That is true, but for reasons that are not present in the instant claim.

In *Darco*, a cross-country truck driver was injured when the tractor-trailer rig he was driving was struck by a train at a crossing where the warning equipment had malfunctioned. The test this Court applied was the same increased risk test that had been applied in *Burns*. However, the accident risk the truck driver encountered in *Darco* arose out of his employment "because the perils of this servant's travel for his master [were] co-extensive with the risks of employment." *Darco*. Thus, for that truck driver the risk of traffic accident arose from the very nature of his employment.

The Court of Civil Appeals also read *Stroud Mun. Hosp. v. Mooney*, as modifying the rule in *Burns*. *Mooney* involved an exception to the "general rule that an injury sustained while going to or from an employer's premises is not one arising out of and in the course of employment." There, the special mission exception applied because the employee was instructed to return immediately from his lunch break at home to the emergency room of his employer's hospital in order for him to perform emergency blood work. The employee was injured in an automobile accident while he was attempting to comply with his employer's instruction. . . .

In this matter, there are no facts to indicate that Claimant was on a special mission outside regular working hours for her employer. In fact, the record demonstrated that she was within her regular working hours performing her usual tasks. *Mooney*'s special mission exception was not asserted by Claimant nor does it apply to these facts.

Neither *Darco* nor *Mooney* abrogate or modify the increased risk test required by the Workers' Compensation Act and described in *Burns*. . . .

This case is controlled by the increased risk test for the arising out of element of coverage provided in the Workers' Compensation Act. . . . The question is whether Claimant's employment subjected her to a risk that exceeded the ordinary hazards to which the general public is exposed. It did not.

Claimant encountered the neutral risk of wet and therefore slippery grass due to rain. Her employment exposed her to no more risk of injury from wet grass than that encountered by any member of the general public. No evidence was presented linking the risk to her employment. Although Claimant was undeniably in the course of her employment at the time of her injury, the injury did not arise from her employment. The trial tribunal's initial order denying coverage was correct. The order allowing compensation was error.

≡≡≡ *City of Brighton v. Rodriguez*
≡≡≡ *318 P.3d 496 (Colo. 2013)*

CHIEF JUSTICE RICE delivered the Opinion of the Court.

We granted certiorari to consider whether an "unexplained" fall—i.e., a fall with a truly unknown cause or mechanism—satisfies the "arising out of" employment requirement of Colorado's Workers' Compensation Act, section 8-41-301(1)(c), C.R.S. (2013), and is thus compensable as a work-related injury. . . .

Respondent Helen Rodriguez injured herself after falling down a flight of stairs at work. While we agree with the court of appeals' holding that Rodriguez's unexplained fall was compensable, we disagree with its reasoning. The court of appeals erred when it endorsed Rodriguez's view that her injuries arose out of employment because "uncertainty about the cause of an injury cannot properly bar a workers' compensation claim if every one of the potential causes satisfie[d] the conditions of recovery." . . . We hold that an unexplained fall necessarily stems from a "neutral" risk, *i.e.*, a risk that is attributable neither to the employment itself nor to the employee him- or herself. Under our longstanding "but-for" test, such an unexplained fall "arises out of" employment if the fall would not have occurred but for the fact that the conditions and obligations of employment placed the employee in the position where he or she was injured. Rodriguez's unexplained fall arose out of employment under this test. . . .

I. Facts and Procedural History

Rodriguez worked as a special events coordinator for the City of Brighton. On January 8, 2009, Rodriguez was walking to her office, which was located in the basement of the Brighton City Hall building ("City Hall"). She paused at the top of a flight of concrete stairs running along the outside of City Hall to greet two of her co-workers, Scott Miller and Dennis Williams, who were standing toward the bottom of the stairs. After a brief chat with Miller and Williams, she began to walk down the stairs, which were dry and unobstructed. All of a sudden, she tumbled forward. Rodriguez hit her head, lost consciousness, and did not remember precisely how she fell — for example, she did not know whether she tripped, slipped, lost her balance, or something else entirely. Prior to falling, Rodriguez was not experiencing a headache, neck pain, dizziness, or vision problems.

After her fall, Rodriguez was taken by ambulance to a nearby emergency room. She underwent Computed Tomography ("CT") and Magnetic Resonance Angiogram ("MRA") scans, which revealed four unruptured aneurysms on the right side of her brain. A few weeks later, she underwent surgery for these aneurysms.

As a result of her fall, Rodriguez experienced head, neck, and back injuries. . . . [The City argued] that the injuries resulting from Rodriguez's fall were not compensable because they did not "arise out of" her employment. Specifically, the City argued that either (1) her fall was caused by her brain aneurysms, or (2) her fall was "unexplained." A hearing on this matter was held before Administrative Law Judge Ted A. Krumreich ("the ALJ") in December of 2010.

Miller and Williams, the only witnesses to Rodriguez's fall, testified at this hearing. Both were located toward the bottom of the stairs when they paused to chat with Rodriguez. Neither knew why Rodriguez fell as she did. For example, neither saw her trip, slip, or lose her balance. Both testified that the stairs appeared to be dry and unobstructed. Specifically, Miller stated that Rodriguez took two to four steps, and then "all of a sudden just went forward." Williams testified that he observed Rodriguez descend a few steps prior to pitching forward, and that it appeared as if someone "just literally yanked a rug out from underneath her." Miller and Williams also testified that Rodriguez had been speaking and acting normally immediately prior to her fall.

At the hearing, the ALJ also heard testimony from Dr. Jeffrey Wunder, who had performed an independent medical examination of Rodriguez at the City's request. Dr. Wunder opined that the "most likely" cause of Rodriguez's fall was a fainting or dizziness episode caused by Rodriguez's brain aneurysms, although he could not state this conclusion with a "reasonable degree of medical probability." The ALJ also reviewed two opposing reports from Dr. Lynn Parry and Dr. Alexander Feldman. Both Dr. Parry and Dr. Feldman opined that Rodriguez's brain aneurysms were not the cause of her fall, as the aneurysms were asymptomatic prior to the fall.

In his Order, the ALJ specifically discredited Dr. Wunder's testimony and credited the testimony of the two other doctors. The ALJ found that Rodriguez's fall was not precipitated by her brain aneurysms, nor was it caused by her tripping or missing a step or by any dangerous condition on the stairs. The ALJ noted that the witnesses to the fall were unable to state precisely why it occurred and that Rodriguez herself could not remember. Thus, he concluded that Rodriguez's fall was "unexplained." As a result, he concluded that her injuries were noncompensable, because in failing to describe her fall's precise causal mechanism, Rodriguez also failed to show that her injury "arose out of" her employment as required by section 8-41-301(1)(c) . . .

[The Industrial Claims Appeals Office affirmed the ALJ's decision, and Rodriguez appealed. The court of appeals set aside the ICAO's order on procedural grounds, in the process endorsing Rodriguez's argument that uncertainty about the cause of an injury alone cannot bar a workers' compensation claim.]

III. Analysis

First, we review the well-established analytical categories that we have used to evaluate the three types of risks that cause injuries to employees in the workplace. We hold that an "unexplained" fall — *i.e.*, a fall with a truly unknown cause or mechanism — falls into the "neutral risk" category. Consistent with our longstanding precedent regarding neutral risks, we also hold that the "but-for" test applies to determine whether unexplained falls "arise out of" employment. Next, we apply this test to the facts of Rodriguez's case and hold that her injury "arose out of" employment under section 8-41-301(1)(c) and is accordingly compensable under the Act. . . .

A. *Rodriguez's Unexplained Fall Arose Out of Employment and Was Compensable Under the "But–For" Test*

To recover benefits under the Act, an employee's injury must both occur "in the course of" employment and "aris[e] out of" employment. § 8-41-301(1)(c). The employee must meet this standard by a preponderance of the evidence. § 8-43-201(1). The parties in this case agree that Rodriguez's injury occurred "in the course of" her employment; thus, our analysis focuses on determining whether her unexplained fall "arose out of" her employment.

The term "arising out of" refers to the origin or cause of an employee's injury. *Horodyskyj v. Karanian*, 32 P.3d 470, 475 (Colo. 2001). Specifically, the term calls for examination of the causal connection or nexus between the conditions and obligations of employment and the employee's injury. *Id.* An injury "arises out of" employment when it has its "origin in" an employee's work-related functions and is "sufficiently related to" those functions so as to be considered part of employment. *Id.* It is not essential, however, that an employee be engaged in an obligatory job function or in an activity resulting in a specific benefit to the employer at the time of the injury. *City of Boulder v. Streeb*, 706 P.2d 786, 791 (Colo. 1985). . . .

Here, the City concedes that the activity causing Rodriguez's injury — walking down the stairs to her basement office — was sufficiently work-related to be considered part of Rodriguez's employment. It argues, however, that Rodriguez necessarily could not provide a sufficient causal connection between her work activities and her injuries because she could not provide evidence regarding the precise *mechanism* for her fall down the stairs (e.g., tripping, slipping, or losing her balance). We disagree.

All risks that cause injury to employees can be placed within three well-established, overarching categories: (1) *employment risks,* which are directly tied to the work itself; (2) *personal risks,* which are inherently personal or private to the employee him- or herself; and (3) *neutral risks,* which are neither employment related nor personal. 1 ARTHUR LARSON & LEX K. LARSON, LARSON'S WORKERS' COMPENSATION LAW §§ 4.01-4.03, at 4-1 to 3 (2013) (hereinafter LARSON); *see also Horodyskyj*, 32 P.3d at 475–77 (dividing assaults by co-employees into these three categories for the purpose of determining whether an assault "arose out of" employment).

The first category, employment risks, encompasses risks inherent to the work environment itself. Employment risks include, for example, a gas explosion at work that burns an employee's body, *Rio Grande Motor Way v. De Merschman,* 68 P.2d 446,

447 (Colo. 1937), or the breakdown of an industrial machine that partially amputated an employee's finger, *Leffler v. ICAO*, 252 P.3d 50, 50 (Colo. App. 2010). The causal connection between such prototypical industrial risks and employment is intuitive and obvious, and the resulting injuries are universally considered to "arise out of" employment under the Act. *See id.; see also* LARSON, §4.01, at 4-2. Rodriguez's injury does not fit into this first risk category because the stairs were dry and free of obstructions, and the ALJ specifically found that nothing about the condition of the stairs contributed to Rodriguez's fall. *See In re Margeson*, 27 A.3d 663, 667 (N.H. 2011) ("Typically, a slip and fall is only attributable to an employment-related risk if it results from tripping on a defect or falling on an uneven or slippery surface on an employer's premises.").

In contrast, the second category contains risks that are entirely personal or private to the employee him- or herself. *See Horodyskyj*, 32 P.3d at 475–77; LARSON, §4.02, at 4-2. These risks include, for example, an employee's preexisting idiopathic illness or medical condition that is completely unrelated to his or her employment, such as fainting spells, heart disease, or epilepsy. *See, e.g., Irwin v. Indus. Comm'n*, 695 P.2d 763, 765–66 (Colo. App.1985) (holding that an employee who had a medical history of blacking out and who did so at work did not suffer an injury "arising out of" employment); *Gates Rubber Co. v. Indus. Comm'n*, 705 P.2d 6, 7 (Colo. App. 1985) (holding same, regarding an employee who had an epileptic seizure and struck his head on a level, nonslippery concrete floor). Such "personal risks" also include an assault at work arising solely from an employee's private, and not professional, life. *See, e.g., Velasquez v. Indus. Comm'n*, 581 P.2d 748, 749 (Colo. App. 1978) (holding that employees who were shot by a co-worker at work did not suffer injuries "arising out of" employment because the assailant had purely personal, and not employment-related, motivations for the attack). . . .

These types of *purely* idiopathic or personal injuries are generally not compensable under the Act, unless an exception applies.[3] *See Velasquez*, 581 P.2d at 749; *see also Irwin*, 695 P.2d at 765. Here, however, the ALJ specifically found that Rodriguez's fall was not attributable to her preexisting brain aneurysms and that there was no other evidence to indicate that her fall was caused by an idiopathic condition. We are bound by that factual finding. *See Metro Moving & Storage Co. v. Gussert*, 914 P.2d 411, 415 (Colo. App. 1995) (stating that a reviewing court should defer to the ALJ's resolution of conflicts in the evidence, including the medical evidence). Thus, Rodriguez's fall was not caused by a personal risk.

The third category includes injuries caused by so-called "neutral risks." *Horodyskyj*, 32 P.3d at 477. Such risks are considered neutral because they are not associated with either the employment itself nor with the employee him- or herself. *Id.* For example, a neutral risk was implicated when: (1) an employee was killed by car thieves on the way back from an employment errand, *Indus. Comm'n of Colo. v. Hunter*, 214 P. 393, 394 (Colo. 1923); (2) a farm hand was killed by a lightning strike while tending to his employer's horses, *Aetna Life Ins. Co. v. Indus. Comm'n*, 254 P. 995, 995 (Colo. 1927); (3) an employee was murdered by a random, insane man while on the job, *London Guarantee & Accident Co. v. McCoy*, 45 P.2d 900, 901–02 (Colo. 1935); and (4) an employee was injured after a co-employee accidentally discharged a hunting rifle in the employer's parking lot, *Kitchens v. Dep't of Labor & Emp't*, 486 P.2d 474, 475–77 (Colo. App. 1971).

We hold that an unexplained fall necessarily constitutes a neutral risk. It is clear that Rodriguez's fall was not the result of an occupational hazard or a personal risk.

Because the precise mechanism of her unexplained fall was neither occupational nor personal, by definition, such a fall is fundamentally similar to other neutral risks — like car thieves, lightning, murderous lunatics, and stray bullets — because none of these risks has a connection with the employee's work or with the employee him- or herself. *See* LARSON, § 7.04[1][c], at 7-31 ("[W]here the neutral-risk concept has been accepted for other purposes, a lot of confusion, circumlocutions, and fictions could be avoided in the unexplained-fall cases by merely accepting the proposition that what is unexplained is neutral.").

Importantly, however, injuries stemming from neutral risks, whether such risks be an employer's dry and unobstructed stairs or stray bullets, "arise out of" employment because they would not have occurred *but for* employment. That is, the employment causally contributed to the injury because it obligated the employee to engage in employment-related functions, errands, or duties at the time of injury. *See Horodyskyj,* 32 P.3d at 477 ("[A]n injury is compensable under the Act as long as it is triggered by a neutral source that is not specifically targeted at a particular employee and would have occurred to any person who happened to be in the position of the injured employee at the time and place in question."); *Circle K Store No. 1131 v. Indus. Comm'n,* 796 P.2d 893, 898 (Ariz. 1990) ("In a pure unexplained-fall case, there is no way in which an award can be justified as a matter of causation theory except by a recognition that . . . but-for reasoning satisfie[s] the 'arising [out of]' requirement." (internal quotation marks omitted)).

For over eighty years, this Court has consistently applied the "but-for" test (otherwise known as the "positional-risk" test) to injuries caused by neutral risks. *See Aetna,* 254 P. at 995 (holding that a lightning accident "arose out of" employment because the "employment required [the employee] to be in a position where the lightning struck him). . . . We reaffirm *Aetna*'s holding that injuries from neutral risks "arise out of" employment. We therefore hold that the "but-for" test applies to unexplained falls because an unexplained fall stems from a neutral risk. The "but-for" test provides that an injury from a neutral risk "arises out of" employment "if it would not have occurred *but for* the fact that the conditions and obligations of the employment placed [the] claimant in the position where he [or she] was injured." *Horodyskyj,* 32 P.3d at 477 (emphasis added) (quoting LARSON, § 3.05, at 3-5 to -6).

By applying the "but-for" test to unexplained falls, we reverse the court of appeals to the extent it held that an unexplained fall is compensable when "every one of the potential causes [of the fall] satisfies the conditions of recovery." Such a holding misses the mark because it introduces a kind of speculative fiction about all of the possible causes of a fall; such speculation is unhelpful when the evidence indicates that the cause of a fall is unknown. *See* LARSON, § 7.04[1][c], at 7-31. This fiction is also entirely avoidable if a fall is properly categorized as arising from *either* an employment-related risk or a personal/idiopathic risk or a neutral risk. If a fall is the result of an employment-related risk, it very likely "arose out of" employment; if it is the result of a preexisting, idiopathic condition, it did not (unless an exception applies). If the cause of a fall is truly unknown, however, and the fall thus stems from a neutral risk, the "but-for" test is applied to determine whether the fall "arose out of" employment. Specifically, the resulting injury "arises out of" employment if it would not have occurred *but for* the fact that the conditions and obligations of the employment placed the employee in the position where he or she was injured.

Moreover, some form of the "but-for" test appears to be the approach taken by the majority of states that have addressed unexplained falls. *See* LARSON, 7.04[1][a], at

7-24 ("In appraising the extent to which courts are willing to accept this general but-for theory . . . it is significant to note that most courts confronted with the unexplained-fall problem have seen fit to award compensation."). We are simply more persuaded by this approach than other possible alternatives.

Significantly, the "but-for" test does not relieve the employee of the burden of proving causation, nor does it suggest that all injuries that occur at work are compensated under workers' compensation law.[8] Rather, it acknowledges that an employee meets his or her burden to prove that an injury "arose out of" employment when the employee proves that an injury (1) had its "origin in" his or her work-related functions and is "sufficiently related to" those functions so as to be considered part of employment, and (2) arose from a neutral risk, whether that neutral risk is an unexplained fall down an employer's staircase or "an arrow out of nowhere." *See* LARSON, § 7.04[1][b], at 7-28.

Demanding more precision about the exact mechanism of a fall is inconsistent with the spirit of a statute that is designed to compensate workers for workplace accidents regardless of fault. *Sigala v. Atencio's Mkt.*, 184 P.3d 40, 43 (Colo. 2008); *see also Frohlick Crane Serv., Inc. v. Mack*, 510 P.2d 891, 893 (Colo. 1973) ("The statutory scheme grants the employee compensation . . . even though the employee may be negligent and even if the employer is not negligent."). Such an approach would also be antithetical to the clear remedial purposes of the Act. . . .

Additionally, a more demanding causation approach with regard to unexplained falls is inconsistent with our longstanding precedent regarding the compensability of injuries caused by neutral risks. For over eighty years, we have awarded benefits in cases involving neutral risks, which — by definition — are not connected to the employment itself. *See, e.g., Hunter*, 214 P. at 394 (murder by car thieves); *Aetna*, 254 P. at 995 (lightning strike); *McCoy*, 45 P.2d at 901–02 (murder by random insane man); *Kitchens*, 29 486 P.2d at 475–77 (co-employee accidentally shooting another co-employee with hunting rifle). Indeed, employees must only demonstrate that there were specific connections to employment in cases *not* involving neutral risks. For example, if an employee has epilepsy and is injured after having a seizure at work, the employee must show that he or she was exposed to an additional "special hazard" of employment. *See, e.g., Ramsdell v. Horn*, 781 P.2d 150, 152 (Colo. App. 1989) (holding that a carpenter's injuries from a fall were compensable because even though he fell as a result of an epileptic seizure, he did so while located on a twenty-five-foot-high scaffold, a "special hazard" of employment).

The City relies on *Finn v. Industrial Commission*, 437 P.2d 542 (Colo.1968), for the proposition that an unexplained fall can never "arise out of" employment. Specifically, the City points to the following language:

> We do not agree that a presumption exists that an employee found injured on his employer's premises is presumably injured from something arising out of his work, *i.e.*, that the doctrine of [r]es ipsa loquitur or some variation of it applies here. On the contrary, the burden of proof in these cases is on the claimant who must show a direct causal relationship between his employment and his injury

Id. at 544. A close examination of *Finn*'s facts reveals, however, that this Court upheld the denial of benefits in that case because the employee's injury was idiopathic. . . .

Thus, while *Finn*'s rationale is not a model of clarity, its central holding — that an injury due to a "mysterious innerbody malfunction" does not "arise out of" employment merely because that injury occurs at work—is entirely consistent with this Court's precedent regarding the non-compensability of idiopathic injuries. . . . We clarify here, however, that our statement in *Finn* that an employee must show a "direct causal relationship between his employment and his injury," applies only to cases involving idiopathic—and thus not unexplained—falls.

In sum, it is clear that Rodriguez's fall "arose out of" her employment. The ALJ specifically found that her fall was not caused by an employment-related risk (e.g., slippery, obstructed, or otherwise dangerous stairs), nor by a personal, idiopathic risk (e.g., her aneurysms). Rather, the cause was unknown, and thus her fall was unexplained. We hold that such an unexplained fall is necessarily caused by a neutral risk. Because Rodriguez's fall would not have occurred but for the fact that the conditions and obligations of her employment—namely, walking to her office during her work day—placed her on the stairs where she fell, her injury "arose out of" employment and is compensable. . . .

Justice Eid, dissenting.

To the majority, an unexplained injury that occurs at work is equivalent to being attacked by car thieves, struck by lightning, or hit by a stray bullet. I disagree. The cause of such "neutral risks" in those cases is perfectly clear—that is, the car thieves, the lightning bolt, or the stray bullets. Such injuries are covered by workers compensation because work put the claimant in the position to be injured by the causal force—that is, the thief, bolt, or bullet. Here, by contrast, the ALJ determined that the cause of Rodriguez's injury was unexplained, and therefore found the injury (correctly in my view) non-compensable. To put it differently, Rodriguez failed to prove that her injury "arose out of" her employment. By deeming such unexplained injuries compensable, the majority significantly expands the scope of workers' compensation coverage in Colorado. Because such decisions are, in my view, better left to the legislature, I respectfully dissent. . . .

In this case, as the majority observes, the ALJ did eliminate some potential causes of Rodriguez's injuries, finding that neither the condition of the stairs nor her pre-existing brain aneurysms caused the fall. But eliminating these two potential causes only shows two factors which did not cause the fall, and none that did. Without sufficient evidence to determine why Rodriguez fell, the ALJ ultimately concluded that the cause of the fall was "unexplained."

Because the cause of the fall was unexplained, Rodriguez could not, and did not, establish causation, and thus she did not carry her burden to show by a preponderance of the evidence that her injuries arose out of employment. In my view, we should simply affirm the ALJ's determination in all respects.

The majority nevertheless breathes new life into Rodriguez's claim by placing her unexplained fall on equal footing with "neutral risks" like car thieves, lightning bolts, or stray bullets. These risks are not merely neutral, however; they are also known. If an injury were to arise from any of these causes, the claimant could demonstrate to the ALJ not only how she was injured, but more importantly, that the injury "would not have occurred but for the fact that the conditions and obligations of employment placed the employee in the position" where she was exposed to the risk of being injured.

The majority's error, however, is to expand the concept of "neutral risks" to include injuries that occur at work *where the cause is not known*. Such an unexplained injury is not categorically "neutral," as the majority would have it. Rather, an unexplained injury defies categorization. It could have been caused by a neutral risk, but it could also be the result of an entirely personal risk of harm, or of an occupational hazard. In other words, "but for" the claimant's presence at work, the injury could have occurred anyway. Unlike an injury resulting from a known, neutral threat, an unexplained fall by definition does not establish causation, and therefore cannot satisfy the claimant's obligation to demonstrate that an injury arose out of employment.

Significantly, the majority does not question the ALJ's conclusion that the cause of Rodriguez's injury could not be determined, or offer a cause of its own. Yet somehow, the majority finds it "clear" that "Rodriguez's fall was not the result of an occupational hazard, nor a personal risk." In doing so, the majority extends the ALJ's ruling well beyond its purview. Far from ruling out all occupational hazards or personal risks as potential causes of the injury, the ALJ held only that the fall was not precipitated by Rodriguez's brain aneurysms, or by her tripping or missing a step or by any dangerous condition on the stairs. After eliminating these potential causes — and only these potential causes — the ALJ then concluded that the fall was "unexplained." Rather than extrapolating from this modest holding the broad conclusion that no occupational hazard or personal risk could have caused the injury, the majority should take the ALJ's determination for what it is: a testament to Rodriguez's failure to establish that her injuries arose out of her employment.

Compounding this error, the majority next implies that the ALJ required Rodriguez to prove the "precise mechanism" of her fall, and thus applied too strict of a causal test. That simply is not the case. The ALJ applied the well-established "preponderance of the evidence" standard. By finding that the cause of the fall was unexplained, however, the ALJ correctly determined that Rodriguez could not meet the burden of proof required to establishing the cause of her injury. Thus, the ALJ's determination was not the result of Rodriguez being required to bear an excessive burden. The burden which the ALJ placed upon Rodriguez was correct; she simply failed to carry that burden.

More significantly, the majority's position extends the ability to receive worker's compensation well beyond the scope prescribed by statute. The majority denies that its holding suggests "that all injuries that occur at work are compensated under workers' compensation law." But by placing unexplained injuries on equal ground with injuries with neutral (and known) causes, the majority makes it possible to receive compensation after merely demonstrating that an injury was sustained on the job. This has never been enough, at least until today, to establish entitlement to workers' compensation — a causal connection must be shown. Otherwise, it would have been unnecessary for the legislature to have included the "arising out of" requirement. *See Fetzer v. N.D. Workforce Safety and Ins.,* 815 N.W.2d 539, 543–44 (N.D. 2012) (holding, in a case involving an unexplained fall, that the "but-for reasoning of the positional risk doctrine is inconsistent with our statute that requires claimants to prove a causal connection between their employment and injury"). Thus, by holding that unexplained injuries are compensable, the majority significantly expands the scope of workers' compensation coverage in Colorado. Because I believe this expansion is an issue best left to the legislature, I respectfully dissent from the majority's opinion.

NOTES

1. *Comparing the Cases and the "Arising Out of" Tests.* The "arising out of" employment test is concerned with the causal connection between employment and the injury. Work your way through the *Worden* and *Rodriguez* analyses. First, consider

how similar the analyses are in terms of the focus of the inquiry and categorization of risks. What types of risks are universally compensable and what types clearly are not? Then turn to the differences in the tests the courts articulate for assessing the causal connection to employment with regard to neutral risks. Did these differences matter in these two cases? In other words, were the outcomes different because of the tests the courts articulated or because of distinguishable facts?

2. *The Five Approaches. Worden* lists the five traditional approaches to assessing a causal connection in cases involving neutral or mixed risks of injury. As the court indicates, the most stringent of the five, the proximate-cause test (requiring foreseeability and no intervening cause), is now largely obsolete. *See* LARSON, *supra*, at §§ 3.01, 3.06. The peculiar-risk doctrine, also fairly stringent, has largely been abandoned as well. *See id.* at §§ 3.01-.02. A sizable number of jurisdictions have adopted the most permissive of the approaches, the positional-risk test, including Colorado, as reaffirmed in *Rodriguez. See* LARSON, *supra*, at §§ 3.05, 8.04. However, in recent years, other jurisdictions, including North Dakota (in the *Fetzger* case cited in the dissent in *Rodriguez*), have eschewed the positional-risk test, opting instead for one of the stricter approaches. *See, e.g., Fetzer*, 815 N.W.2d at 543–44; *Dykhoff v. Xcel Energy*, 840 N.W.2d 821 (Minn. 2013) (holding employee injured from a slip and fall at work could not recover because the employer had not exposed her to a condition that placed her at an increased risk of injury beyond what she would experience in her nonwork life); *Mitchell v. Clark Cnty. Sch. Dist.*, 111 P.3d 1104, 1106 (Nev. 2005) (refusing to adopt the positional-risk test in the context of an unexplained injury at work).

Nevertheless, with the facts of *Worden* and *Rodriguez* as a backdrop, consider how the three viable approaches — actual risk, increased risk, and positional risk — might affect the outcome in close cases. In light of this, and the purposes of the workers' compensation regime, which of the three is the most appropriate? To test your understanding, what would have happened had Worden slipped on wet grass on arriving at a patient's home rather than on leaving her own home?

Now look back at *Kindel* and *Clodgo*. In both cases, the courts found that the employee's injuries arose out of employment. Why? Would it matter which of the three approaches the court had adopted?

3. *Proving Causation for Downstream Harm.* The *Rodriguez* court never reached the question of whether further "downstream" disabilities potentially traced to the original fall were causally connected to her employment and, hence, compensable. Obviously, an employee like Rodriguez will have won the battle but lost the war if on remand she is denied compensation for consequences such as worsening injuries, complications, and aggravation caused by intervening medical malpractice. Fortunately for such injured workers, most of the time when the primary injury has arisen from employment, all such consequences, are also compensable, absent an intervening cause attributable to the worker's own conduct. *See* LARSON, *supra*, at §§ 10.01-.12. Why do you suppose workers' compensation regimes take this liberal approach? In other words, what is to be gained by making the employer — via greater insurance premiums — bear the risk for all such downstream consequences, including even tortious medical treatment? Do these social benefits justify "charging" the employer for the injurious consequences of others?

4. *Workplace Assaults.* Whether an assault in the course of employment — by a co-worker or other third-party — "arises out of" employment has been the subject of much litigation and legislation. Assaults normally arise out of employment if, at a minimum, the risk of an assault is increased by the nature of the job or the work setting or if it was precipitated by a work-related dispute (e.g., an assault upon a supervisor). This means that, generally, assaults by co-workers or other third parties that are motivated by personal or private reasons do not arise out of employment, unless employment facilitates an assault that would not otherwise be made — for example, where the dangerous nature of the job increases the risk of an assault or, at least sometimes, where work friction and proximity are a contributing factor. *See, e.g., Sanderson Farms, Inc. v. Jackson*, 911 So. 2d 985 (Miss. Ct. App. 2005) (holding that employee's injuries from assault by co-employee following argument over personal loan did not arise out of employment); *see generally* LARSON, *supra*, at §§ 8.01-.03. However, some courts have held that an assault in the workplace (or during work hours) by a co-worker or third party is enough to establish that it arose out of employment. *See, e.g., Wal-Mart Stores, Inc. v. Reinholtz*, 955 P.2d 223 (Okla. 1998) (finding compensable injuries an employee sustained by rape by her supervisor because employment itself put claimant at greater risk of injury than the general public); *Redman Indus., Inc. v. Lang*, 943 P.2d 208 (Or. 1997) (same); *K-Mart Corp. v. Herring*, 188 P.3d 140 (Ok. 2008) (affirming the lower court's finding that a worker's injuries arose during the course of employment when, during a continuous seven-hour shift as night watchman with no scheduled breaks, he left the employer's premises to use the bathroom, decided to go to a fast food restaurant, and was shot outside the restaurant). The "assault exception" to workers' compensation coverage is sometimes separately codified rather than simply a variation of the "arising out of" employment analysis. *See, e.g.,* MINN. STAT. § 176.011, subd. 16 ("Personal injury does not include an injury caused by the act of a third person or fellow employee intended to injure the employee because of personal reasons, and not directed against the employee as an employee, or because of the employment.").

5. *In the Course of and Arising out of Employment.* Now that we have seen four cases addressing either the "in the course of" "arising out of" employment requirements, take a moment to consider what each element addresses. What type of connections with employment, specifically, is each requirement designed to test? For instance, why is it that, while the "arising out of" issue was hotly contested in both *Worden* and *Rodriguez*, the "in the course of" issue was not? Although these tests are distinct, keep in mind that, in many circumstances, the facts and analyses underlying the resolution of each are not so easily separated. For example, consider how a finding that an injury occurred in the course of employment is likely to affect the "arising out of" analysis under the positional risk doctrine. Similarly, in most jurisdictions, the "street-risk doctrine" provides that street- or highway-related injuries for employees — for example, delivery and sales people — whose duties increase their exposure to the hazards of "the street" arise out of employment. *See* LARSON, *supra*, at §§ 6.01-.06. Thus, if an employee is consistently on the road in the course of his or her employment, any injuries he or she might sustain during such travels are likely to also "arise out of" employment.

The leading treatise on workers' compensation suggests that there is interplay between the two inquiries: Where there is a weak "in the course of" connection, courts may require a stronger "arising out of" connection to support a finding of compensability, and vice versa. *See* LARSON, *supra*, at § 29.01. Might this sliding scale or "balancing out" process account for the varying results in the four cases we have read in this section?

c. *"Accidental" or "By Accident"*

In addition to the requirements that an injury arise in the course of employment and out of employment to be compensable, most state statutes also require that it normally be "accidental" or "by accident." The touchstone for whether the injury is "accidental" is unexpectedness: "an unlooked for mishap or an untoward event which is not expected or designed." *See* LARSON, *supra*, at § 42.02 (quoting the seminal English case of *Fenton v. Thorley & Co.*, [1903] A.C. 443). A further element of "accidental" recognized in many jurisdictions — although a highly criticized one — is that the injury must be traceable to a definite time, place, and occasion or cause, at least within reasonable limits. In other words, courts read "accident" or "by accident" to require that "an accident" be shown to have given rise to the injury. *See id.*

The main fault line running through the cases analyzing this element involves whether the notion of unexpectedness inherent in "accidental" requires an accidental cause or merely an accidental result. *Id.* at §§ 42.02, 43.01. The leading treatise provides the classic example of a situation in which the work-related cause is expected but the result is not: "A worker who, for years, has lifted hundred-pound sacks many times a day suffers a heart attack while lifting one in the usual way, and medical testimony confirms that the heavy lift did in fact cause the attack." *Id.* at § 42.02. Whether unexpected injuries resulting from such "usual" exertion or exposure are compensable varies by jurisdiction and the nature and definiteness of the injury. The vast majority of courts have found that sudden mechanical or structural changes in the body, such as something breaking, rupturing, or herniating, are accidental — even where the exertion causing the change is usual. Similarly, courts almost always find usual exposure causing freezing or sunstroke to be accidental. A less sizable majority find "generalized conditions" — for example, heart attacks, back injuries, muscle strains, and other similar problems — resulting from usual exertion to be accidental. The other jurisdictions require the injured worker to demonstrate that some kind of unusual or abnormal exertion or exposure (including, for example, excessive strain or work, or sudden shocks or falls) caused the injury. *See generally id.* at §§ 43.01-03. Of course, determining what constitutes a sufficiently unusual or abnormal exertion often poses difficult issues.

It is worth noting that workplace assaults may be "accidental." A workplace assault or battery by a co-worker or third-party, although intentional on the part of the perpetrator, may be sudden and unexpected by the employee and unexpected and unintended by the employer. Obviously, if the assault or other injurious action is intended by or attributable to the employer, then the injury is not accidental, and the employee may sue the employer in tort. In addition, as we have seen, even if deemed accidental, a co-worker or third-party assault resulting from a personal or private motive may nevertheless be excluded from workers' compensation coverage because it does not arise out of employment or is otherwise subject to a statutory "assault exception."

Relatedly, as discussed at the end of Chapter 5, a frequent subject of litigation is whether sexual harassment and other forms of discrimination are covered under workers' compensation or excluded as intentional or quasi-intentional conduct. The question typically arises not when the plaintiff files a compensation claim but rather when a harassed worker sues in tort or under a state antidiscrimination statute because the remedies that are available under such regimes — in particular those addressing mental and emotional distress — are unavailable under workers' compensation.

Normally, if there is no physical injury associated with such conduct, the victim will not be covered under the workers' compensation regime, and hence there will be no exclusivity. Where, however, the harassing or discriminatory behavior caused some type of physical injury—for example, a sexually-motivated assault or battery—the question is much closer, and, as discussed in Chapter 5, courts have not agreed on the answer. Of course, workers' compensation law does not preempt federal discrimination law, and thus, if the conduct rises to the level of actionable discrimination against the employer under Title VII or another federal antidiscrimination statute (*see* Chapter 9), the employee may bring such claims.

Another particularly troublesome category of "accident" cases involves diseases, including infectious diseases acquired through exposure at work, diseases aggravated by work exertion, diseases brought on or made worse by the work environment or temperature, and "occupational diseases" caused by exposure—sometimes over long periods—to harmful conditions tied to particular types of employment. There are circumstances in which diseases are clearly compensable, such as when the disease follows as a natural consequence of a work-related injury that is accidental or when it is a direct result of a particular workplace mishap, malfunction, or other unusual event. *See* LARSON, *supra*, at §42.03.

In many other contexts, however, the disease inquiry has proven difficult. One problem is the cause-result issue discussed above, and courts have been divided over whether routine exposure to conditions causing or aggravating diseases is compensable. Beyond this, some diseases, including occupational ones, are not unexpected at all—think of, for example, "black lung" disease, a condition not only expected but in fact anticipated when one works for extended periods in coal mines. Another concern involves indefiniteness, given the frequent difficulty of tracing diseases to particular occasions and causes or showing that they developed suddenly and unexpectedly. With diseases that are common in the general population, simply establishing a connection to work can be difficult. The employee may need to show that the disease was caused by work conditions rather than by routine or normal exposure to germs, toxins, or the actions of the worker herself. Consider, for instance, a worker whose job exposes him to toxins associated with lung cancer but who is also a smoker. Finally, the time element—that is, the delay in manifestation of the disease—also raises a host of potential proof and other problems, most notably in the occupational disease context.

All states have addressed aspects of these problems statutorily, and there are some federal regimes addressing particular diseases or industries. All state statutes include specific sections covering occupational diseases, and many are general in scope, covering all employment-related diseases. Others contain lists of covered conditions, but typically these statutes also include catchall provisions that extend to nonspecified diseases. Such statutes do *not* require evidence of unexpected or sudden triggering events. Rather, occupational disease coverage depends on whether there is a sufficiently recognizable link between the disease and the particular type of work at issue—work that at least increases the risk of such disease.

Note on Compensability of "Mental Injuries"

Whether work-related injuries that may be characterized as "mental," "stress-related," or "psychological" in nature are compensable under workers' compensation has produced an enormous amount of litigation and controversy. Early on, only "physical injuries" were contemplated under workers' compensation regimes, and thus, emotional distress and mental injuries were not compensable absent some corresponding physical injury or disorder. Over time, however, greater recognition has developed not only of the seriousness of various "mental injuries" but also of the need to compensate at least some such ailments. In addressing the physical-mental divide, courts and commentators have separated claims into four general categories: (1) physical stimuli causing physical injuries, (2) mental stimuli causing physical injuries (so-called "mental-physical"), (3) physical stimuli causing mental injuries ("physical-mental"), and (4) mental or nervous injuries caused by mental stimulus ("mental-mental"). *See generally* LARSON, *supra*, at §§ 56.01-.04.

Provided the injury is sufficiently connected to work and is accidental, category 1 claims have always been compensable. There is now general agreement that claims in categories 2 and 3 (mental-physical and physical-mental) are compensable as well, although states and courts may impose various proof requirements and limit recovery for mental injuries in a number of ways. A common example of a category 2 claim is a stress-induced heart attack; category 3 includes claims for psychological conditions that result from or are exacerbated by a physical injury.

Thus, currently, the controversy focuses largely on the final category — mental-mental claims. This group of workers' compensation claims raises the same types of concerns as emotional distress claims in tort, including floodgates issues, causation and diagnostic problems, and questions of proof. They also raise concerns about the cost of the workers' compensation system. Although most states now provide workers' compensation coverage for mental-mental claims, some do not. *See id.* at § 56.06[3]-[4]. Of the states that accept such claims, some require no greater showing than that required for claims for physical injuries; others require a showing that a sudden stimulus caused the psychological or mental injury; and still others require a showing that the mental stress was unusual in the given context. *See id. at* § 56.06[2]-[7]. Some state legislatures have amended their statutes to limit such claims in various ways, including requiring a heightened level or particular type of stress or mental impairment, increasing the burden of proof, imposing specific diagnostic guidelines, altering causation standards, limiting the amount of benefits, or excluding benefits altogether. *See id.* at § 56.06. Of course, compensability for such claims would benefit many employees, but those who prefer to sue in tort or some other state-law theory would be barred from doing so due to workers' compensation exclusivity.

Note on Exclusivity

Exclusivity is a core component of all workers' compensation regimes, and, as we have seen, the scope of the bar is frequently litigated in contexts in which tort or other remedies would otherwise be available and would be superior for the worker (e.g., offering greater damages for lost wages, damages for emotional and mental stress, and the potential for punitive damages). Whether workers' compensation provides the exclusive remedy normally depends on resolution of the various scope questions addressed above — that is, whether the worker is a covered "employee," whether the injury or illness arose in the course of and out of employment, whether the injury was accidental or the illness was an otherwise covered occupational disease, and whether the type of injury — for example, mental-mental — is compensable. In a few cases, however, courts have found that exclusivity extends beyond the scope of covered injuries, although these holdings are highly controversial. *See, e.g., Bias v. E. Associated Coal Corp.*, 640 S.E.2d 540 (W. Va. 2006) (holding that a common-law negligence claim for stress-related injuries employee sustained at work is preempted by workers' compensation exclusivity even though a statute precluding benefits for mental-mental injuries bars recovery under the state's workers' compensation regime).

It is worth noting that as states have narrowed the scope of compensable conditions and reduced benefits under their workers' compensation regimes, exclusivity has come under scrutiny. For example, a Florida trial court judge recently held that the state's exclusivity provision violates due process under both the U.S. and Florida constitutions because the state has so eroded workers compensation benefits over time that the system no longer constitutes a reasonable alternative to civil litigation for injured workers. *See Padgett v. Florida*, No. 11-13661 CA 25 (Fla. Cir. Ct. Aug. 13, 2014). Whether this decision survives on appeal or not, it sheds light on some of the cracks that are beginning to appear in the "grand bargain" struck a century ago.

Note, however, that even if workers' compensation is the exclusive remedy vis-à-vis the employer or employers, *see* Chapter 1, the worker may have a viable tort claim against third-parties whose conduct contributed to the injury. Furthermore, in many contexts in which an employee is injured or becomes ill, counsel will pursue additional remedies against third-party tortfeasors with resources, including manufacturers of defective products used by the employee, landowners, and other firms whose actions may affect the safety of the employee or workplace. Co-employees, customers, or other individuals whose negligent or intentional conduct causes the harm also may be liable, but often such tortfeasors lack sufficiently deep pockets to be worth suing. Finally, a few courts have recognized that employers are in some cases effectively "third parties" and subject to tort suit under the "dual capacity" doctrine, which provides that an employee may recover in tort against an employer if the employer caused or aggravated the injury while acting in a non-employer capacity. For example, an employer may be subject to a tort suit for providing negligent medical care for the employee that aggravated the employee's condition or for manufacturing a defective product that harms the employee at work.

B. OSHA

Workers' compensation regimes are supposed to create incentives for employers to improve workplace safety by mandating compensation for occupational injuries and diseases. In contrast, OSHA, the Occupational Safety and Health Act of 1970, 29 U.S.C. §§ 651-78 (2014), is designed to address safety directly by setting and enforcing standards to prevent workplace injuries and diseases. It does so through a top-down regulatory structure rather than through private enforcement or injury claims. OSHA is therefore an entirely different type of legal regime than workers' compensation. As a result, it produces a different kind of litigation — mostly addressing the setting of standards — and its own unique set of problems and controversies.

One issue that is rarely discussed is whether OSHA and workers' compensation ought to be viewed as interdependent rather than as entirely separate and distinct regimes. For example, might the social utility of the trade-off underlying workers' compensation depend to some extent on the quality of the OSHA regime? For an detailed treatment of the shortcomings under current law with regard to regulating workplace chemicals and a proposed reform designed to alter incentives under the workers compensation regime and push chemical manufacturers employers to cooperate in developing new OSHA exposure limits, *see* Jason R. Bent, *An Incentive-Based Approach to Regulating Workplace Chemicals,* 73 OHIO ST. L.J. 1389 (2012).

1. A Glance at OSHA's History and Structure

Prior to adoption of OSHA, state legislation had long regulated some workplace health and safety matters and federal legislation had addressed particular industries with a notorious history of safety problems, such as coal mines. Yet OSHA marked the first comprehensive national effort to deal with workplace safety. It is sweeping in its coverage, excluding only state and local government employers, employers covered by other safety regimes, and workplaces in states with approved safety plans. State occupational safety laws are preempted by OSHA unless the state adopts a plan approved by the Occupational Safety and Health Administration, in which case the state plan precludes federal activity. Nevertheless, more general state and local laws, such as those relating to fire safety, continue unaffected by OSHA, and workers' compensation regimes are expressly saved from preemption, despite their obvious relationship to workplace safety.

The statute created an elaborate administrative mechanism for its enforcement. The acronym OSHA is often used both to mean the Act itself and the agency within the Labor Department — the Occupational Safety and Health Administration — charged with implementing the statute. The administrative structure created by the statute is more complicated than those governing many other federal agencies, but the Secretary of Labor, acting through OSHA, is charged with promulgating and enforcing safety standards.

a. Safety Standards

Under § 5(a) of the Act, 29 U.S.C. § 654, safety standards come in two basic forms: the statute's "general duty clause" and specific standards promulgated by OSHA. The general duty clause is a catchall provision requiring a safe workplace even in the absence of more specific standards. However, it is residual in that it governs a potential workplace hazard only if no specific promulgated standard addresses the hazard.

The general duty provision states that an employer "shall furnish to each of his employees employment and a place of employment which are free from recognized hazards that are causing or are likely to cause death or serious physical harm to his employees." To prove a violation of the clause, the Secretary of Labor must establish that the employer failed to keep the workplace free of a hazard to which employees were exposed, that the hazard was "recognized" based on standard knowledge in the industry, that the hazard was likely to cause death or serious physical harm, and that there are feasible methods or measures for addressing the hazard. An employer, therefore, may violate the clause even though no employee has yet been harmed. The various elements of a violation of this clause have been the subject of occasional controversy, as has its application to particular hazards arguably addressed by specific standards.

Most of the debate, however, has focused on OSHA's promulgation of specific standards. The Act requires that employers "comply with occupational safety and health standards" promulgated by OSHA. There are three kinds of specific standards contemplated under the Act: interim standards, new or permanent standards, and temporary standards. In deriving specific standards, OSHA is assisted by a research agency, the National Institute for Occupational Safety and Health ("NIOSH"), located in the Department of Health and Human Services. NIOSH has no power to adopt standards; it simply advises OSHA.

Temporary standards are, in essence, emergency standards that OSHA may adopt with minimal procedures if it finds that a particular substance or new hazard poses a grave danger to employees and that an emergency measure is necessary to protect employees from such danger. *See* 29 U.S.C. §655(c). Given the high bar, OSHA has rarely adopted such emergency standards.

OSHA was also authorized to adopt so-called interim standards, which were intended to be placeholders for more considered efforts. These provisions were largely based on federal standards existing prior to OSHA or "consensus" (lowest common denominator) standards of various standards-producing institutions. OSHA adopted thousands of such standards shortly after the statute was enacted, creating a storm of controversy, in part because they imposed an immediate and complex array of new safety requirements on many employers. Many of these provisions were later abolished by statute, but, 35 years later, "interim" standards continue to make up the bulk of specific standards under OSHA.

After the initial period in which interim standards were to be adopted, OSHA was authorized to promulgate new or permanent standards (which may be completely new, or modify or revoke interim standards). Enactment of such standards, however, is subject to more rigorous administrative procedures and greater substantive limits than apply to interim standards. The substantive limits in particular have been the subject of legal challenges to proposed standards and the basis for criticism of the OSHA workplace safety regime.

Part of the difficulty stems from the generality of the statutory delegation. For example, §6(b)(5) of the statute states that the Secretary, in dealing with toxic or harmful physical agents, "shall set the standard which most adequately assures, to the extent feasible, on the basis of the best available evidence, that no employee will suffer material impairment of health or functional capacity." It also states that that "other considerations shall be the latest available scientific data in the field, the feasibility of the standards, and the experience gained under this and other health and safety laws." Section 3(8) of the statute defines a health and safety standard as one that is "reasonably necessary and appropriate to safe or healthful employment."

Through judicial refinement, some clearer requirements now have emerged. For example, to promulgate any permanent standard, OSHA must demonstrate that the regulation will reduce or eliminate a "significant risk" to worker health or safety. *Indus. Union Dep't v. Am. Petroleum Inst.*, 448 U.S. 607, 641 (1980). This risk must be sufficiently quantified to enable OSHA to characterize it as significant. *See id.* at 656. In addition, OSHA must demonstrate that the risk to health or safety is "material," *AFL-CIO v. OSHA*, 965 F.2d 962, 973 (11th Cir. 1992), and that the proposed standard is feasible — that is, "capable of being done, executed, or effected" by the regulated industry, both technologically and economically. *Am. Textile Mfrs. Inst. v. Donovan* ("*ATMI*"), 452 U.S. 490, 508-09 (1981). However, OSHA usually need not engage in a cost-benefit analysis — a determination of whether the costs of compliance with the proposed standard are reasonable when compared to its benefits. *See ATMI*, 452 U.S. at 506-22.

The agency's determinations with regard to risk, materiality, and feasibility are conclusive if they are "supported by substantial evidence in the record considered as a whole," 29 U.S.C. § 655(f), a standard that is not as deferential as "arbitrary and capricious" review but still falls far short of requiring scientific certainty or allowing de novo judicial inquiry. Nevertheless, these requirements do mandate that OSHA demonstrate that its standards are premised on available scientific evidence of probable benefits to worker health or safety—a significant hurdle in certain occupational disease and chemical exposure contexts.

Although not insurmountable, this need for substantial scientific support in a world of scientific uncertainty, combined with challenges by industry, other procedural hurdles, and resistance or delays within OSHA itself has resulted in few permanent standards actually being promulgated. *See generally* David Michaels & Celeste Monforton, *Scientific Evidence in the Regulatory System: Manufacturing Uncertainty and the Demise of the Formal Regulatory System*, 13 J. L. & POL'Y 17 (2005). For example, since its inception, OSHA has promulgated comprehensive standards for only about 30 chemical toxins, *see id.* at 28, sometimes only after being compelled to do so following judicial challenges by labor or workplace safety advocates. Consider how all of these factors combined to delay promulgation of standards at issue in the next case, which involves exposure to a particular toxin (hexavalent chromium) that clearly threatens worker health.

Public Citizen Research Health Group v. Chao
314 F.3d 143 (3d Cir. 2002)

BECKER, Chief Judge.

This opinion addresses a Petition by Public Citizen Health Research Group ("Public Citizen") to review the inaction of [OSHA], and to require OSHA to commence a rulemaking that would lower the permissible exposure limit for hexavalent chromium. It is not disputed that hexavalent chromium, which is widely used in various industries and which has been classified as a carcinogen, can have a deleterious effect on worker health. [NIOSH] has for several decades recommended that OSHA adopt a far more stringent permissible exposure limit ("PEL") for hexavalent chromium than the consensus [interim] standard it promulgated in 1971. In response to a 1993 petition for rulemaking, OSHA agreed that there was clear evidence that exposure to hexavalent chromium at the consensus level can result in excess risk of lung cancer and other chromium-related illnesses, and announced that it was initiating a rulemaking that it expected would conclude in 1995. However, nearly a decade after this announcement, nothing has happened, evincing a clear pattern of delay.

This matter was before us once before. . . . In that [1998] case, we declined Public Citizen's request to compel agency action. . . . At that time, OSHA represented that it intended to issue a proposed rule by September 1999, and we found such a deadline permissible in light of alleged competing policy priorities. . . . Yet, at the time of oral argument in this case, which was nine years after OSHA initially announced its intention to begin the rulemaking process, no rulemaking had yet been initiated, and it appeared that none would be in the foreseeable future. Indeed, at oral argument, OSHA's counsel admitted the possibility that OSHA might not promulgate a rule for another ten or twenty years, if at all.

We concluded that the delay had become unreasonable, and that while competing policy priorities might explain slow progress, they could not justify indefinite delay and recalcitrance in the face of an admittedly grave risk to public health. We therefore determined to grant the petition and to direct OSHA to proceed expeditiously with its hexavalent chromium rulemaking process. This opinion was drafted on an expedited basis . . . when we received OSHA's announcement that it had instituted the long-sought rulemaking process, stating that: "The health risks associated with occupational exposure to hexavalent chromium are serious and demand serious attention. . . . We are committed to developing a rule that ensures proper protection to safeguard workers who deal with hexavalent chromium."

This notice appears to have been prompted by the displeasure clearly evidenced by the panel during oral argument, especially the question posed to counsel whether they would be receptive to mediation regarding the timeframe for a judicially-ordered rulemaking. [In any event, the notice does not render the case moot because] the agency's action does not resolve an important facet of the case, namely Public Citizen's request that we order OSHA to issue a proposed rule within 90 days and supervise OSHA's progress.

Accordingly, we will publish the opinion that had been prepared to resolve the remedy issue, and will direct that Public Citizen and OSHA submit to a course of mediation for sixty days before The Honorable Walter K. Stapleton. If the parties cannot agree to a workable timetable during that period, the panel will issue and enforce a schedule of its own device. . . .

I. Facts and Procedural Posture

Hexavalent chromium is a compound found only rarely in nature but used widely in industry — for chrome plating, stainless steel welding, alloy production, and wood preservation. The dangers of exposure to it have long been recognized, and include ulceration of the stomach and skin, necrosis, perforation of the nasal septum, asthma, and dermatitis. More significantly, there is strong evidence that inhaled hexavalent chromium is carcinogenic. Since 1980, the Department of Health and Human Service's National Toxicology Program has designated various hexavalent chromium compounds as human carcinogens. The Environmental Protection Agency has been in accord since 1984. . . . Disturbingly, the primary evidence of hexavalent chromium's carcinogenicity comes not from animal studies, but from epidemiological studies of workers exposed to it; in short, as Public Citizen states, "the principal evidence is actual human body counts."

Soon after [OSHA] took effect in 1970, OSHA established a 100 $\mu g/m^3$ [a weight-to-volume ratio that can be converted to "parts per billion" by multiplying by the chemical weight of the compound] permissible exposure limit ("PEL") for inhalation exposure to hexavalent chromium. That level did not reflect OSHA's independent judgment about the appropriate standard, but rather constituted a "lowest common denominator" consensus standard to provide workers some measure of protection pending OSHA's consideration of the optimal long-term standard. The 1971 standard remains in effect. However, although today's foremost health concern regarding hexavalent chromium is its carcinogenicity, OSHA did not take that into account when promulgating the standard. . . .

Shortly after OSHA promulgated the consensus standard, NIOSH . . . urged OSHA to adopt a PEL of 1.9 $\mu g/m^3$, a level 1/52 of the existing standard. At that time, NIOSH concluded that the evidence of the carcinogenicity of a few specified hexavalent chromium compounds was lacking, but that all other forms were carcinogenic. Subsequently, however, NIOSH concluded that all forms of hexavalent chromium should be considered carcinogenic, and it recommended that the 1.9 $\mu g/m^3$ standard be applied to all such compounds.

In 1993, Public Citizen petitioned OSHA to issue an emergency temporary standard that would set a PEL of 0.5 $\mu g/m^3$ as an 8-hour weighted average. The Occupational Safety and Health Act requires OSHA to issue an emergency temporary standard without the usual notice-and-comment procedures if it finds that such action is needed to protect employees against grave danger. 29 U.S.C. §655(c). OSHA denied the petition because it contended that "the extremely stringent judicial and statutory criteria for issuing" an emergency standard were not met. It did, however, acknowledge that its existing standard was inadequate. . . . It therefore announced that [it would begin rulemaking on the matter and anticipated notice would be published in March 1995].

This timetable was short-lived. Only a month after its response to Public Citizen's rulemaking petition, OSHA reported that the date for issuance of a proposed standard had slipped from March to May 1995, and by May 1995 the anticipated issuance date had been pushed back again to December 1995. Thus began a pattern of delay. . . .

Amidst this ongoing delay, OSHA commissioned a comprehensive risk assessment of hexavalent chromium. This assessment, which became known as the "Crump Report," concluded that exposure at the current PEL (100 $\mu g/m^3$) over a 45-year working lifetime could be expected to result in between 88 and 342 excess cancer deaths per thousand workers. Moreover, the Crump Report concluded that significant numbers of excess cancer deaths could be expected even at much lower levels of exposure. . . .

OSHA's November 1996 semiannual regulatory agenda endorsed the Crump analysis, and OSHA explicitly acknowledged that "[t]here appears to be no dispute that the current PEL is too high" and "must be greatly reduced." Accordingly, OSHA stated that it was considering a new standard 10 to 100 times lower than the existing one. . . . Even at that level, it noted, there would be significant risk of excess cancer deaths.

Addressing these events in its present brief, OSHA contends that it was then concerned with methodological imperfections in the available data. For example, the Crump Report did not control for the effects of smoking or asbestos, factors obviously related to lung cancer incidence; if the studied populations of chromium-exposed workers smoked more than the general population, smoking could have accounted for some of the excess deaths. Industry groups therefore pressured OSHA to wait for the results of the then-forthcoming Johns Hopkins study, which, in the industry's view, was "expected to be the most accurate and complete database on chromium exposure and mortality available." OSHA also represents that budget cuts, government shutdowns, and new responsibilities under the Small Business Regulatory Enforcement Fairness Act of 1996 limited the resources available for hexavalent chromium rulemaking. In August 1997, OSHA explained to Public Citizen that work on the rule was continuing, but that these considerations had delayed progress and prevented it from expediting the rulemaking.

Public Citizen, discouraged by what it viewed as a pattern of inaction, urged OSHA in March 1997 to commit to a timetable for rulemaking. [OSHA did not so commit and, in 1997, Public Citizen sought review of OSHA's allegedly unreasonable delay before this Court.]

We declined Public Citizen's request to compel agency action, for we concluded that the facts did not yet "demonstrate that inaction is . . . unduly transgressive of the agency's own tentative deadlines." Key to our decision [were] our observation[s] that the Secretary of Labor has "quintessential discretion . . . to allocate OSHA's resources and set its priorities," [that the delays might be reasonable, and that the intervenors raised serious questions about the data underlying Public Citizen's calculations]. Given these scientific questions, OSHA's superior technical expertise, and its professed plan to issue a deadline for proposed rulemaking in September 1999, we concluded that OSHA's delay was not yet unreasonable.

Following our ruling, OSHA adhered to its September 1999 pledge in each of its regulatory agendas published through April 1999. But it in fact issued no proposed rule in September 1999, and in its November 1999 agenda it announced that its new target date was June 2001. . . .

Meanwhile, August 2000 saw the release of the long-awaited Johns Hopkins study on hexavalent chromium.[3] . . . [The Hopkins Study confirmed the elevated lung cancer risk from hexavalent chromium exposure observed in other studies.]

Although the Hopkins Study explicitly sought to address the shortcomings in previous empirical research, namely the lack of controls for smoking, asbestos, and other environmental factors, its release did not spur OSHA into action. The study was released in August 2000, but OSHA's November 2000 agenda pushed the date for a proposed rule back to September 2001. OSHA's second-most-recent agenda, issued December 3, 2001, reflected another, more radical departure from previous plans: for the first time since 1994, the hexavalent chromium rulemaking was denominated a "long-term action," and the timetable for action stated that the date for a proposed rule was "to be determined."

OSHA offers a number of explanations for the delay that has now become indefinite. It notes that "[t]he day the [Bush] Administration took office, it instructed the agencies that any new regulatory actions must be reviewed and approved by a department or agency head appointed after January 20, 2001." As it was not headed by a presidential appointee until August 3, 2001, OSHA contends that it could not begin to set its new regulatory priorities until that time. Even then, it asserts, two extraordinary unforeseen events—the attacks on the World Trade Center and Pentagon and the anthrax mailings—required it immediately to divert significant resources to safety efforts.

Even amidst these distractions, OSHA represents, it has continued to evaluate the need for a new hexavalent chromium rule. . . .

In OSHA's submission, the problem is that it "believes that the information now available is inconclusive on important issues, such as whether the epidemiological studies . . . apply to all Cr VI compounds and the utility of the data to establish a dose-response relationship." Although the Hopkins Study was a step forward, OSHA points out that its authors acknowledged certain limitations, particularly in estimating the cumulative exposure for the different individuals in the cohort. The

---

3. Public Citizen alleges that many of the Hopkins study's results, if not its actual data, had been available to OSHA since 1995.

study also did not resolve the dispute over whether all hexavalent chromium compounds present the same degree of risk. Because OSHA has decided that it would benefit from public input and expert criticism on these issues, it has published a request for information (RFI) in its August 2002 regulatory agenda. After the time for response, OSHA states, it will evaluate all of the information available and decide how to proceed.

Public Citizen brought the present petition for review alleging that "[d]eference to an agency's priorities and timetables only goes so far," and arguing that, "at some point, a court must tell an agency that enough is enough." The Administrative Procedure Act, 5 U.S.C. § 706(1), creates a right of action by an aggrieved party to compel unreasonably delayed agency action. When the action sought is the promulgation of an occupational exposure standard under 29 U.S.C. § 655, the federal courts of appeals have exclusive jurisdiction under 29 U.S.C. § 655(f), which we have interpreted to provide "jurisdiction to conduct judicial review over the health and safety standards issued by the Secretary of Labor, as well as over claims in which the Secretary has not yet acted but where her delay is allegedly unreasonable." [*Oil, Chem. & Atomic Workers Union v. OSHA*, 145 F.3d 120, 122 (3d Cir. 1998).]

II.   Discussion

. . . Our polestar is reasonableness, and while in 1997 we found reasonable OSHA's delay in the face of scientific uncertainty and competing regulatory priorities, we now find ourselves further from a new rule than we were then. We examine each of OSHA's justifications in turn.

A.   Has OSHA's Delay Been Excessive?

In 1993, OSHA acknowledged that the existing hexavalent chromium standard is inadequate and "that there is clear evidence that exposure to Cr VI at the current PEL of 100 μg/m3 can result in an excess risk of lung cancer and other Cr VI-related illnesses." That was fully nine years ago, and its first target date for a proposed rule — March 1995 — is now more than seven years past. OSHA has missed all ten of its self-imposed deadlines, including the September 1999 target it offered to this Court in *Oil Workers*. Far from drawing closer to a rulemaking, all evidence suggests that ground is being lost. OSHA's December 2001 regulatory agenda demoted the rulemaking from a "high priority" to a "long term action" with a timetable "to be determined." In fact, at oral argument, OSHA's counsel admitted the possibility that another ten or even twenty years might pass before it issues a rule, if it ever does.

OSHA responds that Public Citizen's concerns about the missed deadlines and recent reclassification are misconceived. It explains that under the Regulatory Flexibility Act, 5 U.S.C. § 602, agencies must publish regulatory agendas that include all rules the agency intends to propose or promulgate that are "likely to have a significant economic impact on a substantial number of small entities." A rule's inclusion in an agency's agenda does not, however, require the agency to consider or act on that item. *See* 5 U.S.C. § 602(d). . . .

Regarding hexavalent chromium's recent downgrade to a "long-term project," OSHA clarifies that this is a reflection of whether the rulemaking will be completed in a short period of time and represents that the designation carries no implication about a rulemaking's relative importance to other matters OSHA is considering. The items listed as "high priority" in the December 2001 agenda, it says, were simply those on which OSHA intended to take action in fiscal 2002. It therefore contends that the priority downgrade was more a clarification than a change in the agency's priorities.

We find neither of these explanations satisfactory. We agree with OSHA insofar as its failure strictly to follow its published agenda is not actionable, but this defense misses the point: OSHA's persistent failure to meet deadlines is not the disease itself, but rather a symptom of its dilatory approach to the hexavalent chromium rulemaking process. Similarly, even if OSHA's decision to downgrade the project's priority truly represents a clarification rather than a change, it still gives clear evidence that at least another year will pass before OSHA takes even the first formal step toward promulgating a rule. . . .

Section 6(b) of the Occupational Safety and Health Act requires the Secretary of Labor to "set the standard which most adequately assures, to the extent feasible, on the basis of the best available evidence, that no employee will suffer material impairment of health or functional capacity even if such employee has regular exposure to the hazard dealt with by such standard for the period of his working life." 29 U.S.C. §655(b). The Supreme Court has found that this language compels action: "Both the language and structure of the Act, as well as its legislative history, indicate that it was intended to require the elimination, as far as feasible, of significant risks of harm." *Indus. Union Dep't, AFL-CIO v. Am. Petroleum Inst.*, 448 U.S. 607, 641 (1980). As such, the agency's priorities are judicially reviewable, and this Court and others have compelled OSHA to take action to address significant risks. . . .

We find extreme OSHA's nine-year (and counting) delay since announcing its intention to begin the rulemaking process, even relative to delays other courts have condemned in comparable cases. Indeed, in no reported case has a court reviewed a delay this long without compelling action. . . .

OSHA contends that [among the various reported cases, in only one] did a court compel the agency to issue a *proposed* rule; the others dealt with situations where the agency had issued a proposed rule but was allegedly dilatory in issuing a final regulation. It further notes that [that one case was later characterized as exceptional and the project at issue was conceded to be urgent].

While we acknowledge that . . . the other cases are in some ways distinguishable from this one, we nonetheless regard them as valuable precedent. . . . At all events, we think it "exceptionally rare" that an agency would for years classify an action as a "high priority," only to demote it to a "long term project" upon the release of a study that provides more convincing evidence of the danger than had previously existed.

We are satisfied that OSHA's delay in this case is objectively extreme, and we find its regression alarming in the face of its own 1996 statement that "there appears to be no dispute that the current PEL is too high." We therefore conclude that, absent a scientific or policy-based justification for its delay, we must compel it to act.

B. Does Scientific Uncertainty Justify OSHA's Delay?

In . . . the first installment of this case, Public Citizen relied upon the Crump Report's finding that between 88 and 342 out of every 1,000 workers exposed to hexavalent chromium will die from cancer attributable to that exposure. We recognized, however, that there were "serious questions about the validity of the data and assumptions underlying Petitioner's calculations." For example, . . . it was "wrong to assume that all workers in industries dealing with chromium in some way or another are exposed to 100 $\mu g/m^3$ hexavalent chromium, every working day for 45 years." We likewise observed that some workers breathe through respirators that protect them from exposure to chromium, and that Public Citizen's calculations failed to distinguish between lead chromate and other hexavalent chromium compounds with potentially different carcinogenicities. Finally, and most importantly, we were troubled by the Crump Report's failure to control for smoking and asbestos inhalation, two factors likely related to lung cancer incidence.

Based on this imperfect science and our recognition that "OSHA . . . possesses enormous technical expertise we lack," we concluded that we were "not in a position to tell the Secretary how to do her job." OSHA offers several reasons for us to continue that deferential posture. First, OSHA allegedly "has not yet completed its evaluation of the Hopkins study." It points out that the study's authors acknowledged certain limitations of their data, particularly in estimating the cumulative exposure for different individuals in the cohort, and also that the study did not address the previous dispute over whether all hexavalent chromium compounds present the same degree of risk. OSHA summarizes that, "even assuming the Hopkins study is the most useful single study available, it does not answer all of the technically complex questions about carcinogenicity and other health effects that OSHA would need to resolve in developing a Cr VI rule."

Second, OSHA alleges that "Public Citizen virtually ignores the other critical components of a Cr VI rulemaking." One of OSHA's requirements is that a standard must be technologically feasible, and given that one governing hexavalent chromium would apply to numerous industries, the feasibility analysis is quite complex. While it admits that it has successfully addressed issues of comparable complexity in the past, it notes that "these efforts have not been successful where courts have found insufficient rigor in the agency's analysis of scientific and economic issues." *See, e.g.*, *Indus. Union Dep't; AFL-CIO v. OSHA*, 965 F.2d 962 (11th Cir. 1992). The bottom line, OSHA states, is that "[t]he belief that a chemical may be carcinogenic does not lead easily to the appropriate PEL for that chemical," and forcing it to issue a rule prematurely will likely result in that rule being overturned in court.

We agree with OSHA that the evidence may be imperfect, that the feasibility inquiry is formidable, and that premature rulemaking is undesirable. But given the history chronicled above, we find these concerns insufficient to justify further delay in regulating hexavalent chromium. First, while it is true that the Hopkins study's authors recognized certain limitations of their data, the epidemiological data as of the mid-1990s were sufficient for EPA, ATSDR, NIOSH, the National Toxicology Program, and the International Agency for Research on Cancer to find hexavalent chromium carcinogenic; for OSHA to commence a rulemaking proceeding; and for OSHA's contractor to estimate that exposures at a fraction of the current PEL would result in significant excess cancer deaths.

Moreover, OSHA based its delay on its professed desire to consider that study because of its superior data and ability to control for smoking. It was released in August 2000, more than two years ago, but it has hardly facilitated the rulemaking process.[5] OSHA now offers it as a justification for further inaction, claiming that it has not completed

---

5. Indeed, the Hopkins study's results were first presented publicly in 1995.

its evaluation of the study's findings and that the study's conclusions "can be much better assessed when experts in the field have had the opportunity to review and criticize it."

We are unconvinced. Public Citizen points out that, as the study was published in a peer-reviewed journal, experts in the field have already had the opportunity to criticize it. Notably, in the two years since its publication, "no response or letter criticizing it has been published." Especially since many of the study's findings have been available since 1995, the time for examining it has passed; we also note that, if further professional criticism is absolutely necessary, the notice-and-comment process will provide an ample opportunity.

Nor do we find persuasive OSHA's broad assertion that the Hopkins study "does not answer *all* of the technically complex questions . . . that OSHA would need to resolve in developing a Cr VI rule." This is obviously true, but without more it is irrelevant, for the Occupational Safety and Health Act does not *require* scientific certainty in the rulemaking process. Indeed, read fairly, the Act virtually forbids delay in pursuit of certainty—it requires regulation "on the basis of the best *available* evidence," 29 U.S.C. §655(b)(5) (emphasis added), and courts have warned that "OSHA cannot let workers suffer while it awaits the Godot of scientific certainty." *United Steelworkers of Am. v. Marshall*, 647 F.2d 1189, 1266 (D.C. Cir. 1980).

OSHA points to one specific shortcoming of the Hopkins study—that it "did not address the previous dispute over whether all hexavalent chromium compounds present the same degree of risk." That is indeed a question it did not resolve, and this uncertainty is the principal topic of [the brief filed by the intervenor, an industry advocate], which argues that the lead chromate used in pigments is not as carcinogenic as other hexavalent chromium compounds. The Hopkins study casts no light on this issue because its test population did not work in the pigment industry, but even without better data than that which existed in *Oil Workers* in 1997, we find this uncertainty insufficient to delay rulemaking further. Even if the chromate in pigments is not carcinogenic, an argument that, tellingly, OSHA itself does not offer, requiring concrete findings on this distinction would effectively hold hostage the thousands of workers who are exposed to non-pigment hexavalent chromium. We will not sanction that result when [OSHA flagged this issue in the prior litigation four years ago].

Finally, while we are sympathetic to OSHA's claim that a thorough feasibility analysis is both highly important and quite difficult, we cannot allow an imperfect analysis to justify indefinite delay. OSHA first announced a rulemaking nine years ago, and by its own account it has been examining the issue through NIOSH for at least four years. OSHA does not explain why this particular feasibility determination requires an extreme length of time, and it does not offer even a projection of how much time it might ultimately require. In such a situation, our traditional agency deference begins to resemble judicial abdication, and we conclude that scientific uncertainties and technical complexities, while no doubt considerable, can no longer justify delay. Judges on this court are not paid to decide the easy cases, and neither is OSHA. Difficult challenges go with the territory, and courts and agencies regularly surmount them. The notice-and-comment process should itself provide a fertile forum for gathering information on feasibility.

C. Do Competing Priorities Justify OSHA's Delay?

[OSHA argues that it exercised its discretion to concentrate its resources elsewhere. For example, in 1999 and 2000, OSHA "focused most of its rulemaking resources on issuing an ergonomics standard before the end of the former Administration's term." Because the Clinton Administration placed such great emphasis on quickly finalizing those standards, the process was remarkably compressed; OSHA issued a proposed rule on November 23, 1999, and a final rule less than a year later, on November 14, 2000, "a timetable that required tremendous agency resources."]

OSHA represents that the delays became worse when the Bush administration took office, [given the administration's directive not to approve new standards without approval of the new agency head, the delay in the appointment of an agency head, and the September 11 attacks and anthrax mailings].

We do not lightly discount these admittedly significant competing priorities . . . [but] we reach the ineluctable conclusion that hexavalent chromium has progressively fallen by the wayside. This is unacceptable. . . .

D. What Is the Proper Remedy?

Public Citizen requests that we direct OSHA to issue a proposed rule within 90 days, and to submit a schedule for finalizing the rule within 12 months thereafter. Neither OSHA's brief nor its recent announcement contains a proposed timetable, but it insists that Public Citizen's proposed pace of rulemaking "is unrealistic in light of the procedural, consultative, and analytical duties that constrain OSHA rulemaking and the historical time frames required for OSHA to develop a toxic chemical standard." For example, the Regulatory Flexibility Act, 5 U.S.C. §§ 601-12, requires it to prepare a regulatory flexibility analysis if the rule will have a "significant economic impact upon a substantial number of small entities," a mandate this rulemaking is sure to trigger. Also, the Small Business Regulatory Enforcement Fairness Act, 5 U.S.C. § 609(b), requires it to convene a review panel to address the rule's potential impacts on small entities. Finally, Executive Order 12866 requires that OSHA submit its proposal, including a detailed economic analysis, to the Office of Management and Budget, which is to review it within 90 days.

While we are certain that the time for action has arrived, we are cognizant of our lack of expertise in setting permissible exposure limits, and we recognize the damage that an ill-considered limit might cause. At oral argument, we presented the parties with a somewhat novel possibility: that they would submit to a course of mediation, conducted by a senior judge of this Court, in which they might work together toward a realistic timetable that we would then enforce. Both sides stated their willingness to engage in this process, and we think it the most promising way to develop a reasonable and workable schedule. We are, however, highly aware that this presents yet another opportunity for potentially indefinite bargaining and delay. We will therefore submit the matter to mediation for a period not to exceed sixty days, after which time, if the parties have not reached an accord, the panel will promulgate a schedule it deems appropriate. . . .

NOTES

1. *Even More Delays.* The Third Circuit's decision by no means ended the matter. When the parties could not agree, the Court adopted the mediator's recommendation and directed OSHA to publish a proposed rule no later than October 4, 2004, and to

publish a final standard no later than January 18, 2006. The Court subsequently granted OSHA an extension to February 28, 2006. *See* National Metal Finishing Resource Center, *OSHA Hexavalent Chromium PEL Page, available at* http://www.nmfrc.org/compliance/pel2.cfm. OSHA published its final rule that day, *see* 71 Fed. Reg. 10099-10385 (Feb. 28, 2006), some 13 years after OSHA agreed that there was evidence that the level of exposure to hexavalent chromium allowed by the 1971 interim standard posed an excessive risk to worker health. The final standard provides for a PEL of 5.0 $\mu g/m^3$, as opposed to the 0.5 $\mu g/m^3$ for which Public Citizen had petitioned. Thereafter, both Public Citizen and industry representatives filed suit challenging the final standard. OSHA issued corrections to the rule on June 23, 2006, and an amendment on October 30, 2006, reflecting a settlement agreement with various parties. *See* 71 Fed. Reg. 36,008 (June 23, 2006); 71 Fed. Reg. 63,238 (Oct. 30, 2006). Nevertheless, litigation continued on both the standard and OSHA's decision to alter certain employee notification requirements. Ultimately, the Third Circuit upheld the promulgated rules, except for the change in the notification requirements, which it remanded back to OSHA for further consideration. *See Public Citizen Health Research Group v. U.S. Dept. of Labor*, 557 F.3d 165 (3d Cir. 2009). There were yet further delays in implementing inspection and compliance programs; for example, the National Emphasis Program targeting hexavalent chromium did not go into effect until February 2010. *See* OSHA, *National Emphasis Program — Hexavalent Chromium*, Directive No. CPL 02-02-076 (Feb. 23, 2010), *available at* http://www.osha.gov/OshDoc/Directive_pdf/CPL_02-02-076.pdf.

2. *A Rare, Hard-Fought Victory.* As the history of this case and the tone of the court's opinion suggests, federal courts are loath to order agencies, including OSHA, to promulgate rules. *See* Sidney A. Shapiro & Richard W. Murphy, *Eight Things Americans Can't Figure Out About Controlling Administrative Power*, 61 ADMIN. L. REV. 5, 27 (2009) ("An agency's assertion that it has not had time to respond becomes less persuasive after a significant amount of time. Nevertheless, the courts normally do not force a response before the expiration of at least several years."); Alan B. Morrison, *Administrative Agencies Are Just Like Legislatures and Courts — Except When They're Not*, 59 ADMIN. L. REV. 79, 96 (2007) (stating that, although courts recognize they have the power to require agencies to reach a final decision on a request for rulemaking, they have been reluctant to do so except in extreme cases). Indeed, courts view themselves as far better equipped to review and reject agency actions, although, even in that context, they must be deferential to the agency's determinations. And inaction by OSHA is common.

So why, ultimately, did the Third Circuit take such an exceptional step in this case and order OSHA to act? Do you think the court overstepped? Certainly, some question whether a court should ever interfere when an agency chooses not to regulate, absent a clear congressional directive to act. What reasons, if any, justify court interference with an agency's discretion to determine whether to engage in the rulemaking process? In thinking about this question, recall the discussion of deference to administrative agencies in *Summers v. Altarum Inst., Corp.*, Chapter 9, page 734.

3. *The Role of Scientific and Technological Uncertainty.* Assuming OSHA's concerns about scientific and technological uncertainty were not simply a *post hoc* justification for dragging its feet, this case demonstrates how uncertainty arguments from regulated industries have deterred OSHA from acting, particularly with regard to allegedly harmful chemicals and substances. Consider how the substantial evidence requirement, combined with scientific and technological uncertainty regarding health risks and feasibility, may affect OSHA's decision making. First, developing the science to determine risk and feasibility takes time and resources. Given the nature of the inquiry, OSHA itself may have good-faith doubts about the science even after accumulating greater knowledge. For example, it may question the causal connection between exposure and disease, the levels of exposure that pose a danger, whether all forms of the substance pose equal problems, and so forth. Beyond this, OSHA officials know what to expect downstream — if the agency forges ahead with the rule-making process where any doubt exists, industry groups will challenge the scientific and technological bases for the proposed standards during the notice and comment period. *See generally* Michaels & Monforton, *supra*. If these challenges fail, these groups can seek relief from Congress and, if that fails, they may bring suit challenging the final version of the rule.

That said, what is the alternative? Should the requirements for OSHA to promulgate specific standards be more lenient? There are alternative approaches to rule making or judicial review that might strike the balance in favor of greater regulation to the benefit of workers. For example, Congress could amend the statute to provide for more deferential "arbitrary and capricious" review or to streamline procedures by reducing opportunities for public comment and participation. On the other hand, given the substantial costs on regulated employers, might it be good policy to require OSHA both to engage in a full notice and comment process and to make the rigorous showing of significant risk and feasibility that the law currently requires?

4. *Other Factors Contributing to Agency Inaction.* Uncertainty clearly was not the only reason for OSHA's inaction on hexavalent chromium. The various other reasons — limited resources, unforeseen events, other priorities, new procedural hurdles, changing agency leadership, and ideological preferences — played critical roles. Won't at least one of these factors always be present as OSHA attempts to regulate workplace hazards? If so, is this simply a story of a lack of political will or, alternatively, "capture" of the agency or Congress by powerful interest groups? Is it naive to think that OSHA can ever overcome industry attempts to delay or prevent standards promulgation? In other words, perhaps OSHA's approach to promulgating standards cannot be fixed. If it can be, how and by whom?

b. Enforcement

OSHA enforcement historically has been largely of the "command and control" variety. That is, OSHA inspectors issue citations for violations of specific standards or of the general duty clause. These citations, may range from "de minimis" ones with no penalty to "serious," and "willful" violations whose penalties can range up to $70,000. For a failure to abate violations, a $7,000 a day penalty is possible. Citations are not initially enforced in court. Rather, if contested, they are adjudicated administratively by the Occupational Safety and Health Review Commission ("OSHRC"), composed of three commissioners appointed by the president. Only after the OSHRC decision can an employer seek review in the appropriate court of appeals. Criminal sanctions are also available, but only when an employer makes false statements to an inspector, intentionally interferes with an inspection, or has actual knowledge of a dangerous condition that leads to a fatality. OSHA also provides some ancillary protections, including antiretaliation and disclosure provisions.

OSHA engages in regular inspections and will also inspect employers in response to employee complaints. Generally, inspections are conducted without advance notice, but, absent OSHA obtaining a warrant, an employer can refuse to allow access to its establishment. OSHA need not demonstrate probable cause of a criminal violation to obtain an administrative search warrant, but rather must have specific evidence of a violation or show satisfaction of reasonable standards for conducting the particular inspection. *See Marshall v. Barlow's, Inc.*, 436 U.S. 307 (1978). In many instances, however, employers waive the warrant requirement. Why do you think that is? *See generally* Note, *The Permissible Scope of OSHA Complaint Inspections*, 49 U. CHI. L. REV. 203 (1982).

Data from recent years provides some sense of the scope of OSHA's enforcement activity. In 2009, OSHA conducted 39,004 inspections and found 87,663 violations of OSHA's standards and regulations. About three quarters were "serious," but only a small percentage resulted in criminal charges. In 2013, the agency conducted nearly the same number of inspections (39,228), but violations decreased substantially, to 78,196. The percentage of violations deemed serious was close to the same, and criminal violations remained rare, dropping to just a handful. *See* OSHA, OCCUPATIONAL SAFETY AND HEALTH ENFORCEMENT (2013) [hereinafter "OSHA OSHE"], *available at* https://www.osha.gov/dep/2013_enforcement_summary.html. Note that these inspections are supplemented by those conducted by cooperating state agencies; in 2013, the number of such inspections was 50,436. OSHA, COMMONLY USED STATISTICS (2013) [hereinafter "OSHA CUS"], *available at* https://www.osha.gov/oshstats/commonstats.html. Although the number of inspections and cited violations have increased over historic lows in the mid-1990s, both total inspections and found violations are down dramatically from earlier years. *See* Public Citizen Health Research Group, *Report Detailing Occupational Safety and Health Administration Enforcement Actions from 1972 through 1998* (HRG Publication #1494), *available at* http://www.citizen.org/publications/release.cfm?ID=6693. Moreover, since OSHA was enacted in 1970, workplace deaths have fallen 65 percent and occupational injury and illness rates have fallen 67 percent. *See* OSHA OSHE, *supra*.

Still, OSHA's resources and capacity remain severely limited. Along with those working with state partners, OSHA can muster only about 2,200 inspectors. To put this in perspective, because OSHA is responsible for the health and safety of 130 million workers (employed at more than 8 million worksites), this translates into about one inspector for every 59,000 workers. *See* OSHA CUS, *supra*.

A very important aspect of OSHA's structure is what it does not permit: Unlike statutes such as Title VII and the FLSA, OSHA does not authorize private enforcement. As *Public Citizen* suggests, private parties may be able in extreme cases to compel OSHA to promulgate standards, but they cannot compel it to enforce those standards against particular violators. Occasionally, OSHA standards have been used to establish a standard of care in suits based on other theories, such as negligence. *See generally* Rothstein, *supra*, §§ 501, 502, and 513. Nevertheless, given the general absence of private enforcement, the significance of administrative enforcement (or the lack thereof) cannot be overstated.

2. OSHA's Troubled Past and Present, and Its Uncertain Future

The implementation and enforcement of OSHA have been much criticized from all sides. Employers have complained about the burdensomeness of the regulations, the "nitpickiness" of inspectors and excessiveness of citations, and the lack of recognition for good-faith efforts to comply. These types of criticisms and related advocacy efforts have had an impact, including the repeal of some of the interim regulations, the limited promulgation of new and permanent standards, successful challenges to certain OSHA initiatives, and reductions in OSHA's enforcement resources. In addition, as discussed in the *Public Citizen* case above, various changes in the law — including the Regulatory Flexibility Act and the Small Business Regulatory Enforcement Fairness Act — have imposed constraints on OSHA's ability to promulgate and enforce new standards.

On the other hand, labor and workplace safety advocates have long bemoaned OSHA's ineffectiveness in purging the workplace of preventable safety hazards, despite the overall decline in reported workplace fatalities, injuries, and violations. Many have expressed concern about the various substantive and procedural barriers to OSHA's promulgation of new specific regulations. But most critics have focused on enforcement, arguing that OSHA's efforts and the penalties resulting from violations are woefully inadequate. They argue, for example, that there are far too few inspections and resulting sanctions to create sufficient incentives for employers to comply with OSHA's mandates, particularly given the relatively weak penalties for most violations. *See, e.g.*, Cynthia Estlund, *Rebuilding the Law of the Workplace in an Era of Self-Regulation*, 105 COLUM. L. REV. 319, 360 (2005) (discussing OSHA's chronic underfunding and weak penalties); Susan Bisom Rapp, *What We Learn in Troubled Times: Deregulation and Safe Work in the New Economy*, 55 WAYNE L. REV. 1197, 1211, (2009) ("AFL-CIO Associate General Counsel Lynn Rhinehart recently noted that given its current level of resources, OSHA can conduct inspections of 'each workplace under its jurisdiction on average once every 133 years.'"). In addition, the effectiveness of OSHA's antiretaliation regime has been the subject of much criticism. *See, e.g.*, GAO, WHISTLEBLOWER PROTECTION: SUSTAINED MANAGEMENT ATTENTION NEEDED TO ADDRESS LONG-STANDING PROGRAM WEAKNESSES (August 2010), *available at* http://www.gao.gov/new.items/d10722.pdf; *see also* Jarod S. Gonzalez, *A Pot of Gold at the End of the Rainbow: An Economic Incentives-Based Approach to OSHA Whistleblowing*, 14 EMPL. RTS & EMPLOY. POL'Y J. 325 (2010) (discussing the weaknesses and limitations of OSHA's existing antiretaliation regime). In the eyes of these critics, the long-term trend toward reduced enforcement in the OSHA context and deregulation more generally have simply made things worse.

The vexing questions, then, are the extent to which the critiques of OSHA, from either side, are valid, and if so, whether realistic reforms might make the regime more effective. While scholarly commentaries on OSHA's history and problems are legion, we have seen some shifts in the prevailing winds in recent years.

For example, partially in response to industry pressure, during the George W. Bush administration in particular, OSHA shifted its focus towards greater self-regulation — that is, allowing employers to avoid an ordinary inspection schedule if they demonstrate their ability to comply with health and safety standards and improve their safety records. Currently all of these programs are voluntary. Industry groups were able to defeat the one compelled self-regulation program — the Cooperative Compliance Program — that they viewed as imposing obligations that were too onerous. *See* Orly Lobel, *Interlocking Regulatory and Industrial Relations: The Governance of Workplace Safety*, 57 ADMIN. L. REV. 1071, 1124-28 (2005).

In her article discussing the trends at the time, Professor Lobel discussed how efforts to improve OSHA and, more generally, workplace safety and health, had shifted away from the traditional bilateral debate between more or less regulation. For example, she discussed recent OSHA reforms that focus on neither top-down enforcement nor further deregulation but rather on promoting safety and health compliance or "self-regulation" efforts within regulated firms. Examples of this "third way" include OSHA's longstanding but then recently expanded Voluntary Protection Program ("VPP") and its Safety and Health Achievement Recognition Program ("SHARP"), both of which were designed to reward firms with certain levels of safety achievement and self-regulatory structures. The reward included exemption from general, scheduled inspections. *Id.* at 1105-07 (footnotes and citations omitted).

Early studies — including one conducted by the Government Accounting Office, ("GAO") showed these programs to be successful. *See id.* at 1108 (noting that the GAO study "found that participation in the programs has considerably reduced injury and illness rates, improved relationships with OSHA, improved productivity, and decreased worker compensation costs"). Looking ahead, Professor Lobel noted the potential of compliance-centered regimes, although she cautioned that, to prevent such public/private cooperation from becoming merely deregulation in disguise, steps must be taken to ensure that OSHA will indeed return to direct enforcement where firms fail to comply or improve safety through self-governance and that workers — the stakeholders OSHA is supposed to protect — have a voice in the governance. *See id.* at 1112-15.

In a contemporaneous article, Professor Cynthia Estlund also critiqued the new self-governance approach under OSHA. *See generally* Cynthia Estlund, *Rebuilding the Law of the Workplace in an Era of Self-Regulation*, 105 COLUM. L. REV. 319 (2005). Like Lobel, she discussed both the potential promise in self-regulation and the dangers of insufficient corresponding government oversight and the lack of worker involvement. Professor Estlund asserted that, for the governance approach to be effective in achieving statutory goals, it must be "monitored self-regulation":

> The basic template for effective self-regulation would be based on an explicit code of conduct encompassing at least employers' substantive legal obligations and employees' right, free from retaliation, to communicate with each other and with monitors and regulators regarding code compliance; code compliance would be the responsibility of specified managerial officials and would be monitored by independent outside monitors accountable in part to workers. Entry into the system would be encouraged by public and private enforcement mechanisms — targeted public enforcement and the threat of potent sanctions against the worst lawbreakers, and private rights of action on behalf of aggrieved employees, including whistleblowers — the full force of which would be mitigated or held in abeyance for employers engaged in a system of effective self-regulation.

See id. at 379. In other words, Professor Estlund suggested self-regulation under OSHA and elsewhere would be truly effective only if it embodies tripartite involvement of workers, employers, and government regulators. In addition, appropriate incentives must be sustained through ongoing monitoring by independent outsiders, the threat of sanctions and civil lawsuits for noncompliance with safety standards, and meaningful antiretaliation protection for whistleblowers. *See id.*

Unfortunately, agency leaders appear not to have heeded fully these kinds of suggestions and warnings. A 2009 GAO report found that, while VPP programs expanded significantly during the last years of the Bush administration, OSHA failed to develop adequate internal controls and mechanisms for assessing the programs' performance. The agency therefore was unable to ensure that only qualified worksites were allowed to participate in the program and that participants remained compliant with health and safety standards. The GAO also found significant rates of noncompliance among certain types of participating firms. *See generally* GAO, OSHA's VOLUNTARY PROTECTIONS PROGRAM: IMPROVED OVERSIGHT AND CONTROLS WOULD BETTER ENSURE PROGRAM QUALITY (May 2009), *available at* http://www.gao.gov/new.items/d09395.pdf.

In light of these findings and other enforcement priorities, the Obama Administration shifted resources away from voluntary compliance to other OSHA programs. *See* Steve Tuckey, *OSHA's Deeper Bite: The Obama Administration Injects New Power into the Occupational Safety Agency as Employers Find Themselves on the Defensive*, CBS Money Watch.com, April 1, 2010, *available at* http://findarticles.com/p/articles/mi_m0BJK/is_3_21/ai_n53519363/. Although it chose to scale back and tighten the VPP program rather than abandon it, the Obama administration's efforts, too, have come under scrutiny. *See* DOL OIG, VOLUNTARY PROTECTION PROGRAM: CONTROLS ARE NOT SUFFICIENT TO ENSURE ONLY WORKSITES WITH EXEMPLARY SAFETY AND HEALTH SYSTEMS REMAIN IN PROGRAM (December 16, 2013), *available at* http://www.oig.dol.gov/public/reports/oa/2014/02-14-201-10-105.pdf.

Whether this kind of approach could further OSHA's purposes more efficiently and effectively is uncertain, although reforms in the direction Professor Estlund envisions might very well promote far greater buy-in — and, hence, efforts that promote compliance — by both workers and firms. Still, regardless of its merits, are there reasons to doubt whether policy makers would ever be willing and able to craft, fund, and maintain such a regime?

Moving beyond self-regulatory approaches, the Obama Administration has turned its emphasis to greater agency and state enforcement efforts, including implementing a number of new regulatory initiatives, targeting enforcement in particular sectors, modestly increasing OSHA's budget, and hiring additional inspectors. *See, e.g.*, Laura Walter, *DOL 2011 Budget Request Includes OSHA Increase, Focus on Enforcement*, EHS Today, Feb. 1, 2010, *available at* http://ehstoday.com/standards/osha/dol-budget-request-osha-increase-focus-enforcement-2414/. As discussed above, these initiatives may have had some impact, as the number of violations dropped from 2009 to 2013. *See* OSHA OSHE, *supra*. Nevertheless, few doubt that, given OSHA's limited resources, there are many violations that the agency never uncovers.

PROBLEM

12-1. Suppose you work for the Workplace Safety and Health Institute, a nonpartisan "think tank" devoted to developing and advocating innovative and efficient ways to improve workplace safety and reduce work-related injuries and diseases. Given what you have seen in this chapter, what kinds of legal reforms might you advocate? In thinking about solutions, consider all possibilities, including, *inter alia*, greater direct regulation and enforcement of the "command and control" variety (more regulations and inspections, and greater sanctions); alternative regulatory arrangements that seek to promote "third way" self-regulation; greater protection against retaliation for whistleblowers or injured workers; reintroduction of tort liability for employer negligence; enhanced civil and criminal liability for responsible supervisors or officers; and employee empowerment, including greater protections for collective bargaining and bargaining units. At a general level, what are the costs and benefits of these various approaches? In light of the nature of the modern workplace, what are the practical impediments to implementation? Which methods might work in combination, and which would not?

Part Seven

RISK MANAGEMENT

13

Managing the Risks and Costs of Liability in Employment Disputes

To a considerable extent, this entire book has been about "risk management." Private ordering allows parties to structure their relationship as they see fit, creating certain legal obligations and limiting others. Chapters 1 through 3 dealt with the initial choice to create an employment relationship and on what terms. We saw that contracting parties can sometimes avoid "employment" altogether, a strategy often pursued by firms seeking to avoid the legal liabilities associated with that status. Even where an employment relationship exists, the ability to set terms contractually — coupled with the at-will presumption — often permits employers to limit their obligations to employees, for instance, by disclaiming contractual right to job security. Alternatively, in situations where the employer is willing to provide security, it can offset such provisions against other terms of the relationship.

Such risk management is largely in the hands of employers. Most workers face a take-it-or-leave-it choice as to whether a particular job carries employment status and the terms of any relationship that may be offered. Chapter 3 dealt primarily with the rather exceptional, highly valued worker, who may be able to trade salary and other benefits for enhanced job security or other favorable employment terms. More often, however, freedom of contract merely affords workers an ability to take or reject what the employer offers; they must then work with the tools that the public law regime provides to "employees," assuming they can establish that status, to maximize their position.

This does not mean, however, that the employer has free rein in structuring work relationships. Any decision it makes involves trade-offs. We saw in Chapters 1, 5, and 12 that the employer that avoids tort liability to workers by structuring its relationships as "employment" thereby assumes tort liability to third parties for its workers' actions and subjects itself to the workers' compensation regime. It also undertakes a host of other statutory risks and duties to its employees, including the antidiscrimination laws and the Family and Medical Leave Act, treated in Chapters 9 and 10, and the wage and benefits laws discussed in Chapter 11.

Moreover, employers cannot always be confident that their election of a particular status or set of terms will actually determine their legal obligations. We saw in Chapter 1 that the test for employment status is multi-factored and dependent on circumstances beyond the intent of the parties. Similarly, although employers may designate a particular relationship at will, alterations in at-will status may occur due to the promises and assurances of supervisors, written employment manuals, or implicit company policies and practices. Thus, despite the availability of contract law, and regardless of the ultimate structure chosen, both employers and employees often find their legal relationship ambiguous.

Perhaps most importantly, there are significant limits on the extent to which the law permits private ordering in workplace relationships. For instance, we saw in Chapter 8 that employers can use noncompetition agreements and related contract mechanisms to safeguard their trade secret rights and to reduce the risk of employee defection in an at-will world. However, the enforceability of such agreements is constrained by public policy, and employers are often unable to predict whether such contracts will provide the protection they seek. In addition, employers have very limited ability to structure or restructure terms of employment mandated by statutory law. An employer may not, for instance, limit its liability under state workers' compensation law in exchange for larger payments, nor may it substitute time off for overtime pay under federal wage and hour law, even if both parties would prefer that arrangement. And, of course, employers have no — or very limited — ability to "waive" substantive obligations arising under constitutional, tort, and antidiscrimination laws discussed in Chapters 4, 5, 7, 9, and 10.

In sum, the patchwork of laws governing workplace relationships — a combination of contract law principles operating against a backdrop of tort rules and general and employment-specific statutes and regulations — presents serious challenges to the cost-conscious, compliance-oriented employer. Thus, an important question to think about as you complete your study of employment law is the interaction between firms and workers in what might be described as "second level" efforts at risk management. These techniques are "second" level because they attempt to reduce employers' risks entailed by the initial policy choice as to whether to offer employment at all and in what form. They include efforts to ensure compliance with the law, prevent disputes, and reduce the costs associated with legal disputes when they inevitably arise. Larger employers frequently consult with attorneys and human resource experts before implementing policies or making personnel decisions to avoid running afoul of the law or even appearing to do so for fear of drawing a costly (even if ultimately unsuccessful) lawsuit. Similarly, where an employee contests a decision, employers frequently seek cost-effective ways of dealing with the dispute short of litigation, such as private resolution or settlement.

This chapter explores several ways in which employers respond to the risk of litigation and legal liability and employee responses to such efforts. It begins in Section A with employer efforts to prevent and resolve disputes in-house, with particular emphasis on sexual harassment. As a result of two seminal Supreme Court decisions on vicarious liability for hostile work environment claims, employers have strong incentives to take precautions against harassment and respond aggressively if it occurs.

The chapter then turns in Section B to employer termination practices and the use of severance and release agreements to avoid possible litigation. Particularly in large layoff situations, employers typically promise post-termination pay, and perhaps other benefits, in exchange for the employee's promise not to sue the employer.

Section C then considers several mechanisms that employers have used to reduce risks in litigation. The first is the increasingly common practice of requiring employees to sign pre-dispute arbitration agreements. Under such agreements, parties do not waive or settle the merits of claims but rather agree that, should a dispute arise, they will resolve it through a private arbitration process rather than through traditional litigation. The second is the use of stipulated damages clauses to safeguard employer interests by ensuring a monetary remedy is available in the event that an employee breaches its obligations to the employer.

Section D turns to yet another kind of risk management—passing the risk to others. It addresses the use of insurance as a means of managing the costs of liability to employees. Finally, Section E very briefly considers bankruptcy, which might be viewed, at least in some contexts, as the ultimate risk-management technique of employers.

As you read, you will understand that the study of risk management begins with techniques employers implement, but, as in the rest of this book, the focus quickly shifts to the responses of employees and the policy choices implicated in deciding how far the law should permit private ordering in this setting. From the employer's perspective, consider whether these risk management tools are effective in achieving employer goals and, if not, how they might be made more effective. Equally important, consider the effects of such measures on employees' ability to vindicate their rights. How should courts respond to second-level private ordering designed to avoid liability and public disputes? Is there a way to balance the employer's concerns about liability and costs of compliance with the employee's substantive and procedural rights? Are there places where private ordering has gone too far?

A. PREVENTIVE MEASURES AND CORRECTIVE ACTION

1. Anticipating and Responding to Hostile Work Environment Harassment

The best way to avoid litigation expenses is to resolve disputes internally, and employers use a variety of methods to do this. A very common technique is to develop internal procedures through which employees can air or report concerns before they develop into a legal problem. For instance, many companies have written complaint procedures under which employees are directed to report their concerns to particular personnel and follow up with reports to successively higher levels of management if the employee remains dissatisfied. A less formal approach is to establish an "open door" policy which invites employees to speak to any manager, or particular management personnel, on an as-needed basis. Depending on the employer, these approaches may be adopted in tandem and may have a greater or lesser degree of formality and structure.

For example, a Publix Supermarket Policy provides:

> It is just a fact of life that occasionally there will be problems and misunderstandings among people. If something bothers you, or if you need clarification of a Publix policy or procedure, please talk to a manager about it. Always remember, as a Publix associate you

can talk to anyone in management. Experience has shown, however, that many problems can best be worked out by the following steps:

1. Discuss your problem or raise your question directly with your immediate Supervisor/Manager/Department Head.
2. If the matter is not resolved or you still have a question or concern, go to the next highest level of management (for example, Store Manager, District Manager, Regional Director of Retail Operations, or a Vice-President).
3. Just remember — you can discuss your problem with anyone in management all the way to the top level. Also, your Divisional Human Resources Department is available to assist you with any matter at any time, and you may contact the Employee Assistance Department in Lakeland for confidential counseling.

Madray v. Publix Supermarkets, Inc., 208 F.3d 1290, 1295 (11th Cir. 2000).

Although such policies are common, they are not without some risk to employers. Employees have sometimes attempted to use open door policies as the basis of a contract claim when they are discharged. They might allege, for instance, that the employer failed to follow or participate in all steps of its process or that they were retaliated against for invoking the policy. While the Publix policy does not explicitly promise nonretaliation, it may impliedly do so, and some grievance policies are more explicit in immunizing employees who invoke company procedures. Thus, an occasional court has recognized a cause of action where the employee can show that she was retaliated against for pursuing open door avenues. *See, e.g., Holt v. Home Depot, U.S.A., Inc.*, 2004 U.S. Dist. LEXIS 824, 3-4 (D. Conn. 2004) ("[T]he jury could reasonably find that Home Depot's promise not to retaliate against employees for using the open-door procedure was so clear, emphatic, highly touted, and widely proclaimed that plaintiff could reasonably believe it was inviolable and thus not covered by general disclaimers in the handbook and application."); *Vida v. El Paso Employees' Fed. Credit Union*, 885 S.W.2d 177 (Tex. App. 1994) (cause of action if employer retaliated against plaintiff for use of its grievance procedure when the employee manual explicitly assured that no retaliation would occur). However, most courts have rejected such claims, in some cases because of language disclaiming the binding nature of the policy and in other instances because the policy did not constitute a sufficiently definite promise. *See, e.g., Haynes v. Level 3 Communs., LLC*, 167 F. App'x 712 (10th Cir. 2006) (employer's open-door policy too vague to constitute a contract or support a claim of promissory estoppel); *Stefano v. Micron Tech., Inc.*, 65 F. App'x 139, 142 (9th Cir. 2003) (existence of open-door policy did not bring plaintiff within any exception to at-will employment).

As a result, there is relatively little legal downside in adopting such policies, and they have significant advantages. In addition to limiting costly litigation, they may result in more favorable outcomes for both employees and employers. While litigation often entails a permanent severing of the employment relationship, successful internal resolution can enable the aggrieved employee to continue working. If the attempted resolution is not successful and the dispute winds up in litigation (whether court or arbitration), the employer's internal response can be a critical aid in its defense.

This is most true with respect to employment discrimination. In the Title VII context, the Supreme Court decided two cases in 1998 dealing with a sexual hostile work environment created by a supervisor in which employer efforts to prevent and respond to harassment figured prominently. In *Burlington Industries, Inc. v.*

Ellerth, 524 U.S. 742 (1998), the harassment took place while the supervisor and victim were away from the office on a business trip. In the other, *Faragher v. Boca Raton*, 524 U.S. 775 (1998), the victims were lifeguards who were harassed at a beach remote from the city employer. In both cases, the employees failed to complain about the harassment until after leaving their jobs. It was assumed for the purposes of the case that the conduct in question, if attributable to the employers, would have constituted actionable hostile environment harassment under Title VII, an issue you considered in Chapter 9. The employers essentially defended by arguing that they were not liable for the harassing conduct of the supervisors because the harassment did not result in any tangible employment action by the supervisor, such as a termination or demotion, and because the employees had not complained before leaving the company. Thus, the question before the Court was when an employer should be liable for harassing conduct, given lack of knowledge of the behavior by upper level management. This question is critical under Title VII since personal liability does not attach to an individual actor under the federal discrimination laws. *See* Rebecca Hanner White, *Vicarious and Personal Liability for Employment Discrimination*, 30 GA. L. REV. 509, 545-61 (1996). While some state antidiscrimination statutes provide for individual liability, and state courts sometimes find in favor of claims against harassers in their personal capacity, *see, e.g., Elezovic v. Ford Motor Co.*, 697 N.W.2d 851, 861 (Mich. 2005), it can be difficult for plaintiffs to collect on those judgments. As a result, an employee typically has no recovery — despite having proven harassment in the workplace — if the employer is not liable for the actions of the harasser.

Drawing on agency principles, the *Ellerth* and *Faragher* opinions laid out the structure for employer liability for supervisory harassment. First, there is automatic employer liability when a "supervisor" subjects plaintiff to "a tangible employment action, such as discharge, demotion, or undesirable reassignment." *Faragher* at 808. In such cases, the employer's liability is absolute and not subject to any defense. Second, when such a supervisor subjects plaintiff to conduct that is *not* a tangible employment action, such as a contaminated work environment, the employer is liable but subject to an affirmative defense. The Court explained:

> When a supervisor makes a tangible employment decision, there is assurance the injury could not have been inflicted absent the [supervisor's] agency relation [with the employer]. A tangible employment action in most cases inflicts direct economic harm. As a general proposition, only a supervisor, or other person acting with the authority of the company, can cause this sort of injury. A co-worker can break a co-worker's arm as easily as a supervisor, and anyone who has regular contact with an employee can inflict psychological injuries by his or her offensive conduct. But one co-worker (absent some elaborate scheme) cannot dock another's pay, nor can one co-worker demote another. . . .
>
> Tangible employment actions are the means by which the supervisor brings the official power of the enterprise to bear on subordinates. A tangible employment decision requires an official act of the enterprise, a company act. . . . The supervisor often must obtain the imprimatur of the enterprise and use its internal processes.
>
> For these reasons, a tangible employment action taken by the supervisor becomes for Title VII purposes the act of the employer. Whatever the exact contours of the aided in the agency relation standard, its requirements will always be met when a supervisor takes a tangible employment action against a subordinate. . . .
>
> Whether the agency relation aids in commission of supervisor harassment which does not culminate in a tangible employment action is less obvious. . . . On the one hand, a supervisor's power and authority invests his or her harassing conduct with a particular

threatening character, and in this sense, a supervisor always is aided by the agency relation. On the other hand, there are acts of harassment a supervisor might commit which might be the same acts a co-employee would commit, and there may be some circumstances where the supervisor's status makes little difference. . . .

In order to accommodate the agency principles of vicarious liability for harm caused by misuse of supervisory authority, as well as Title VII's equally basic policies of encouraging forethought by employers and saving action by objecting employees, we adopt the following holding. . . . An employer is subject to vicarious liability to a victimized employee for an actionable hostile environment created by a supervisor with immediate (or successively higher) authority over the employee. When no tangible employment action is taken, a defending employer may raise an affirmative defense to liability or damages. . . . The defense comprises two necessary elements: (a) that the employer exercised reasonable care to prevent and correct promptly any sexually harassing behavior, and (b) that the plaintiff employee unreasonably failed to take advantage of any preventive or corrective opportunities provided by the employer or to avoid harm otherwise. While proof that an employer had promulgated an antiharassment policy with complaint procedure is not necessary in every instance as a matter of law, the need for a stated policy suitable to the employment circumstances may appropriately be addressed in any case when litigating the first element of the defense. And while proof that an employee failed to fulfill the corresponding obligation of reasonable care to avoid harm is not limited to showing any unreasonable failure to use any complaint procedure provided by the employer, a demonstration of such failure will normally suffice to satisfy the employer's burden under the second element of the defense. No affirmative defense is available, however, when the supervisor's harassment culminates in a tangible employment action, such as discharge, demotion, or undesirable reassignment.

Ellerth, at 761-65.

Notice that the Court also alluded to a third scenario where employer liability for hostile work environment may be implicated — sexual harassment by a nonsupervisor, such as a co-worker (or even a customer). While *Ellerth* and *Faragher* did not address that situation directly, it is now clear that an employer is liable for nonsupervisory harassment only if it is negligent. *Vance v. Ball State University* 133 S. Ct. 2434, 2441 (2013) ("[A]n employer is directly liable for an employee's unlawful harassment if the employer was negligent with respect to the offensive behavior."). Thus, a hostile environment resulting from the activities of, say, co-workers will not result in any liability unless the employer knew or should have known of the problem and did not reasonably address it. This is viewed as a form of direct liability for the employer's own negligence as opposed to vicarious liability for the conduct of the harasser. However, the employer's policies and practices are still relevant to this assessment, insofar as negligence may occur where the employer fails to have processes in place to discover and reasonably respond to harassing behavior. As a practical matter, then, the employer's mechanisms to prevent and correct harassment apply both in the supervisor harassment and co-worker harassment cases, although the burdens of proof are reversed in the two situations.

This structure obviously makes the question of whether an individual is or is not a "supervisor" critical for either automatic or presumptive liability since harassment by a nonsupervisor subjects the employer to liability only if it is negligent. After considerable disagreement in the lower courts about the definition of supervisor, a majority of the Supreme Court defined it very narrowly in *Vance v. Ball State University* 133 S. Ct. 2434 (2013). Rejecting the argument that the term should include anyone with the ability "to exercise significant direction over another's daily work," *id*. at 2443, Justice Alito's opinion held that "an employer may be vicariously liable for an employee's unlawful harassment only when the employer has empowered that employee to take tangible employment actions against the victim, i.e., to effect a 'significant change in employment status, such as hiring, firing, failing to promote.'" *Id*. at 2443. The dissent by Justice Ginsburg, joined by Justices Breyer, Kagan, and Sotomayor would have taken a more functional approach, including "employees who control the day-to-day schedules and assignments of others." *Id*. at 2455.

The majority stressed the workability of such a definition in contrast to the "nebulous" definition of the EEOC and some lower courts: "[T]he *Ellerth/Faragher* framework is one under which supervisory status can usually be readily determined, generally by written documentation." *Id*. As for the suggestion that this approach leaves "employees unprotected against harassment by co-workers who possess the authority to inflict psychological injury by assigning unpleasant tasks or by altering the work environment in objectionable ways," the majority was unpersuaded:

> [T]he victims will be able to prevail simply by showing that the employer was negligent in permitting this harassment to occur, and the jury should be instructed that the nature and degree of authority wielded by the harasser is an important factor to be considered in determining whether the employer was negligent. The nature and degree of authority possessed by harassing employees varies greatly [but this] variety presents no problem for the negligence standard, which is thought to provide adequate protection for tort plaintiffs in many other situations. There is no reason why this standard, if accompanied by proper instructions, cannot provide the same service in the context at issue here.

Id. at 2451-52.

Despite the supposed clarity of the rule, there will certainly be gray areas given the Court's indication that a person may be a supervisor even if he or she lacks hiring or firing authority but can effect "reassignment with significantly different responsibilities, or a decision causing a significant change in benefits." *Id*. at 2442 (quoting *Ellerth*). Further, the majority cautioned that:

> [E]ven if an employer concentrates all decisionmaking authority in a few individuals, it likely will not isolate itself from heightened liability under *Faragher* and *Ellerth*. If an employer does attempt to confine decisionmaking power to a small number of individuals, those individuals will have a limited ability to exercise independent discretion when making decisions and will likely rely on other workers who actually interact with the affected employee. Under those circumstances, the employer may be held to have effectively delegated the power to take tangible employment actions to the employees on whose recommendations it relies. *See Ellerth*.

Id. at 2452. This obviously requires a focus on the realities of workplace decision making rather than the formalities and may implicate the cat's paw possibility we encountered in Chapter 9 at page 620.

In any event, post-*Vance*, most harassment cases will proceed as negligence claims, which means that the employee has the burden of proving the employer knew (or should have known) of the harassment and failed to respond reasonably. Effectively, that eliminates strict liability and shifts the burden of proof from the employer to establish an affirmative defense to the employee to establish both elements of her claim.

While allocating burdens might be very important in the litigation context, employers need to be concerned not with who proves what but whether they are acting appropriately in preventing and correcting illegality. An employer who reacts reasonably to harassment in situations where there is no supervisor involved will avoid direct liability, no matter how extreme the co-worker or customer harassment. And, absent a tangible employment action, an employer who takes appropriate steps to "prevent and correct" violations by supervisors will have satisfied the first prong of the affirmative defense and be halfway to avoiding vicarious liability.

Thus, *Ellerth* and *Faragher* understandably generated a cottage industry among lawyers and employment relation specialists about appropriate prevention and correction strategies. In the cases that follow, consider which employer actions are effective and which are not. Does the result in each case correspond to the effectiveness of the employer's response? In other words, does the existence of the affirmative defense encourage good employer practices, or does it encourage superficial efforts that simply make the employer look good in court, what has been dubbed "paper compliance" with the law? How could the employer have been more successful in avoiding and/or responding in each case?

Watson v. Home Depot USA, Inc.
2003 U.S. Dist. LEXIS 13406 (N.D. Ill. Aug. 1, 2003)

LEINENWEBER, J.

I. Background . . .

1. *Watson's Employment and Orientation*

In August 1999, Home Depot hired Watson as a sales associate for its North Avenue store in Chicago, Illinois. Shortly after being hired, Watson participated in Home Depot's orientation program, which lasted for about two weeks. Like all Home Depot employees, Watson received Copies of Home Depot's Respect, Harassment/Discrimination, Equal Employment Opportunity, and Open Door Policies as well as training on those polices. The Harassment/Discrimination Policy prohibits harassment or discrimination and states that "anyone who condones or fails to take appropriate action to address a violation of Home Depot's harassment/discrimination policy will be subject to disciplinary action up to and including termination." It further "prohibits retaliation against any associate who comes forward to report harassment and/or discrimination." The policy emphasizes the importance of reporting any harassing or disrespectful behavior and sets forth resources that an employee may use if they feel that the policy has been violated. These resources include contacting a member of management, the Store Manager, District Manager, Human Resource Manager, or Division Vice President of Human Resources, or using the Alert Line, a phone line that enables employees to report harassment anonymously. Watson also participated in a Respect for All People training program, which further addressed workplace harassment and discrimination issues and which again informed employees about procedures available at Home Depot for resolving harassment or discrimination concerns. A few months after hiring Watson, Home Depot transferred her to the Pro Sales Department, where her responsibilities included building relationships with and selling products to industrial, commercial, and other business customers. She appears to have performed her job satisfactorily and received a raise on July 3, 2000.

2. The Performance Notice

In the afternoon of July 13, 2000, however, Watson received an Associate Performance Notice for allegedly violating company policies or procedures. According to the Performance Notice, Watson's supervisors Victor Terrell, who served as Assistant Store Manager, and Ford Neubert, the Department Supervisor, found Watson in a friend's car in the Home Depot parking lot while she was supposed to be at her desk. Terrell and Neubert prepared the Performance Notice, which warned Watson to stay at her desk in the future and Terrell asked Watson to "clock out and go home." The Performance Notice was placed in Watson's file, but Home Depot took no further disciplinary action for this incident. Indeed, despite the fact that Watson had only worked for part of that day, Home Depot paid her for a full shift.

3. Events After July 13, 2000

Watson's relationship with Home Depot changed swiftly in the wake of the parking lot incident. Before leaving the store on July 13, she complained to Co-Store Manager, Al Stermer, about the confrontation and about being sent home for the day. Watson also contacted Home Depot's Midwest Region Human Resources Manager, James Owens ("Owens"), that day to complain that Terrell had belittled her and disciplined her unfairly.

[O]n July 14, Watson learned that her work schedule had been changed. Instead of working Monday to Friday from 8:00 a.m. to 5:00 p.m., she was now expected to work on the weekends with two weekdays off. As a single mother, Watson found this change burdensome and also complained about it to Owens.

On July 20, 2000, Owens called Jay Tippieconnic the Store Manager, to tell him that Watson had complained about a write-up she received. The next day, after a week of confusion about Watson's new schedule, Tippieconnic met with Watson to discuss the entire situation. During their conversation, Watson broke down and explained that the situation went beyond the write-up. She described how on April 6, 2000, Terrell had followed her home during lunch, had asked to come into her apartment, and had then forced her into having sex with him. In Watson's statement, she alleges that she also described Terrell's poor treatment of her, but it is unclear what poor treatment she described. After hearing Watson's story, Tippieconnic sent Watson home, telling her he would pay her for the rest of that day and for the weekend and assuring Watson that he would have Michelle Williams, a Loss Prevention Specialist with whom Watson appeared to be comfortable, contact her over the weekend. Tippieconnic next called Owens and District Manager Ron Johnston to set up a meeting with Watson for the following Monday. Over the weekend, he spoke with Watson twice, reassuring her that Home Depot would not abandon her.

The following Monday, Owens, Williams, and Tippieconnic waited to meet with Watson. Watson arrived several hours late, and handed them the sworn statement in which she detailed her interactions with Terrell prior to, including, and after the alleged April 6 sexual encounter. Watson stated that Terrell had kissed her on January 27, 2000, while they were having lunch together, and that he continued to flirt with her throughout February and March 2000. She also contended that during those months, Terrell failed to support her professionally, yelled at her at work, and was physical with her, at times grabbing her arm to move her from one spot to another. Watson stated that she complained to Terrell about his behavior and that he promised to improve. On April 6, however, Watson alleged that during her lunch hour, Terrell followed her home and, despite being told not to come into her apartment, entered Watson's home and raped her repeatedly. After the alleged rape, Watson stated that Terrell had become increasingly hostile toward her. Watson conceded that she was in a friend's car when Terrell and Neubert issued the Performance Notice. She claimed, however, that the friend was also her customer and had asked Watson to walk with her to explain Home Depot's credit and sales programs. She asserted that Terrell had punished her for the parking lot incident and changed her schedule in retaliation for Watson's refusal to engage in a sexual relationship with him.

After reading Watson's statement, Owens attempted to ask Watson questions about what she had written. Watson refused to provide additional information or to answer his questions and replied that everything she had to say was in the statement itself. Watson did express concern that she would be terminated and that Terrell would harm her, however, Owens assured Watson that Home Depot would immediately begin a complete investigation of her allegations and that she would not lose her job. He also asked Watson to think about whether she wished to continue to work at the North Avenue store, or whether she would prefer to be transferred elsewhere. During the investigation, Home Depot placed Watson on paid administrative leave and suspended Terrell.

4. The Investigation

At the end of July, Watson contacted the Chicago Police Department to report the April 6 incident. Meanwhile, as promised, Owens began the investigation of Watson's claim. Together with EEO Specialist Doris Stephenson and Associate Relations Manager Chris Nichols, Owens interviewed twenty-one people, including Terrell, Home Depot managers, supervisors, and employees, and non-Home Depot personnel whom Watson had identified as witnesses. None of the relevant witnesses corroborated Watson's allegations that Terrell had acted inappropriately toward her or had mistreated her. Owens, Stephenson, and Nichols interviewed Terrell twice, once on July 27 and again on August 9. Terrell denied all of Watson's allegations regarding inappropriate behavior. He denied ever having visited Watson's home and contended that he was at his apartment on April 6 at the time of the alleged assault. Although Watson had described Terrell as leaving her apartment at 5:15 p.m. on April 6, Terrell's landlady told Home Depot that she had spoken with Terrell between 4:30 p.m. and 5:00 p.m. that day. Watson's landlord also contested Watson's allegation that he had met Terrell when Terrell was entering Watson's apartment on April 6. The landlord showed Owens, Nichols, and Stephenson a copy of his own calendar that indicated that he was not at Watson's apartment building that afternoon.

With regard to the parking lot incident, the investigation team spoke with Deborah Crawford, who confirmed that she was with Watson in the parking lot on July 13 when Watson was reprimanded. They also spoke with Neubert, who told the investigators that Watson had become angry, yelled and threw the Performance Notice at Terrell when Terrell reprimanded her.

Owens also investigated Watson's allegations that Terrell had changed her schedule to punish her for not engaging in a sexual relationship with him. Ivan Justiano, an associate in the North Avenue store, told the investigation team that *he* was in charge of writing Watson's schedule and that he had previously scheduled her to work weekends. Owens reviewed all of Watson's time and payroll records and found no support for Watson's claim that she worked a set weekday schedule and never worked weekends.

Finally, Tippieconnic told the investigators that prior to July 21, 2000, Watson had never complained about Terrell and stated that he had been unaware of any of the events described in Watson's statement. Throughout the investigation, Watson repeatedly refused to discuss her statement with Owens or with any other members of the investigation team.

5. *After the Investigation*

On August 18, 2000, Home Depot concluded its investigation and determined that Watson's allegations of sexual harassment could not be substantiated. Despite its findings, Home Depot offered Watson the option of transferring to a different store in the same position and at the same pay. Home Depot also transferred Terrell to another store on July 31, 2000, so that Watson could remain at the North Avenue location if she wished. Instead of returning to Home Depot, however, Watson requested an unpaid medical leave of absence due to depression and temporary psychological distress, which Home Depot granted. Home Depot provided Watson with its medical leave policy, which explained that her employment would be terminated if she did not return to work after a one-year absence. After Watson failed to return to work upon expiration of her medical leave . . . she was terminated from active employment. . . .

II. Discussion . . .

[In *Burlington Industries, Inc. v. Ellerth* and *Faragher v. City of Boca Raton,*] the Supreme Court created a distinction between "cases in which the supervisor takes a tangible employment action against the subordinate and those in which he does not." *Molnar v. Booth,* 229 F.3d 593, 600 (7th Cir. 2000). The Supreme Court explained that an employer was vicariously liable "to a victimized employee for an actionable hostile environment created by a supervisor with immediate (or successively higher) authority over the employee" where "the supervisor's harassment culminates in a tangible employment action, such as discharge, demotion, or undesirable reassignment." In cases where the supervisor took no tangible employment action, however, the Supreme Court permitted the defending employer to raise an affirmative defense to liability or damages. . . .

[Watson does not contest] that Home Depot terminated Watson for failing to return from medical leave pursuant to company policy and that Terrell had been transferred to another Home Depot at the time Watson was terminated. Watson has failed to [establish] that there is a genuine issue for trial as to whether Terrell took tangible employment action against her [and therefore Home Depot may raise the affirmative defense to liability.] To defend itself successfully, Home Depot must establish: (a) that it exercised reasonable care to prevent and correct promptly any sexually harassing behavior, and (b) that Watson unreasonably failed to take advantage of any preventive or corrective opportunities provided by Home Depot or to avoid harm otherwise.

a. Home Depot's Exercise of Reasonable Care

To avoid liability, Home Depot must first demonstrate that it exercised "reasonable care to prevent and correct promptly any sexually harassing behavior." The existence of "an appropriate anti-harassment policy will often satisfy this first prong, because Title VII is designed to encourage the creation of anti-harassment policies and effective grievance mechanisms." *Shaw v. AutoZone, Inc.*, 180 F.3d 806, 811 (7th Cir. 1999). In this case, it is undisputed that Home Depot had numerous written policies in place throughout Watson's employment prohibiting sexual harassment. These policies included a Harassment/Discrimination Policy, a Respect Policy, and an Equal Employment Opportunity Policy. While the Harassment/Discrimination Policy could have been more tailored to address sexual harassment specifically, it stated clearly that "Home Depot does not tolerate harassment or discrimination" based on sex and directed employees to complain about conduct they found offensive, harassing or disrespectful.

These policies also established multiple procedures for employees to follow in the event that they experienced any harassment, thereby permitting employees to bypass the harassing supervisor in the complaint process. These procedures included contacting various managers, human resources personnel, or using the Alert Line, a phone line that enabled employees to report harassment anonymously. Home Depot also maintained an Open Door Policy, which emphasized that supervisors' doors were "always open" and that if a Department Supervisor or Assistant Manager could not help an employee, the problem "should be taken" up the chain of command. The Open Door Policy also reminded employees that the Human Resource Manager "is always available to help you with concerns and issues." Watson acknowledges that she received copies of these policies and underwent extensive training on the policies and procedures during her orientation.

Home Depot also acted swiftly and decisively to correct the harassment once it learned of Watson's allegations. After his initial meeting with Watson, Tippieconnic, the Store Manager, immediately gave her the weekend off with pay. He also set up a meeting the following Monday to discuss Watson's allegations. At that meeting, Owens assured Watson that Home Depot would investigate her allegations and offered Watson the choice of continuing to work at the North Avenue store, or of being transferred elsewhere with the same pay and position. Home Depot also immediately placed Watson on paid administrative leave and suspended Terrell. It then proceeded to do a thorough and extensive investigation of Watson's claims. Even though the investigation failed to substantiate Watson's allegations of sexual harassment, Home Depot transferred Terrell to another store so that Watson could remain at the North Avenue store if she wished. It also granted Watson's request for a one-year unpaid medical leave of absence.

In spite of these actions, Watson still contends that Home Depot did not take reasonable care to prevent and correct the harassment "until after the fact." The undisputed evidence establishes, however, that Home Depot had promulgated its policies and procedures regarding harassment before Watson began at Home Depot and before any alleged harassment occurred. Watson also appears to argue that Home Depot failed to correct the harassment by reneging on alleged promises to relocate her to another apartment and to assist her in dealing with the rape. Yet she places this argument in a paragraph dealing with her negligent retention claim, which the Court has dismissed. Moreover, she fails to adduce any evidence to support her contention that Home Depot made these promises. There is certainly nothing in the company policies to suggest that such actions are part of Home Depot standard procedures as Watson appears to suggest.

Regardless, the facts establish that Home Depot took reasonable steps to prevent sexual harassment and that, when faced with allegations of harassment, also took extensive steps to correct the violation. As a matter of law, Home Depot has satisfied the first prong of the *Ellerth/Faragher* affirmative defense.

b. Watson's Unreasonable Failure to Report Harassment

Home Depot must also establish that Watson "unreasonably failed to take advantage of any preventive or corrective opportunities provided by the employer or to avoid harm otherwise." According to Watson, the harassment began when Terrell kissed her on January 27, 2000. It continued through February and March 2000 when Terrell flirted with her, failed to give her professional support, yelled at her, and was physically aggressive with her. On April 6, Terrell allegedly raped her repeatedly. Despite her escalating problems with Terrell, Watson did not complain to anyone until she spoke to Owens on July 21, 2000. Home Depot argues that given Watson's knowledge of the harassment policies and procedures, that her delay in complaining about Terrell's behavior was unreasonable.

In her Response, Watson argues that she failed to complain about the harassment because she feared Terrell. It is, of course, asking a great deal to require a victim of sexual harassment to come forward and reveal what they have endured to their employer. But as the Supreme Court explained, "a victim has a duty to use such means as are reasonable under the circumstances to avoid or minimize[ ] damages." *Faragher.* This duty exists even if the employee fears confrontation, unpleasantness or retaliation in return for speaking out. In this case, Home Depot had established a variety of reasonable mechanisms for employees to report harassment, including the anonymous tip line and open-door policy that permitted employees to bypass the offending supervisor in reporting the harassment. Moreover, even if the alleged rape made Watson's fears of Terrell reasonable, she endured several months of harassment prior to the rape without alerting Home Depot. During this time, Watson complained directly to Terrell about his behavior and he promised to improve. When those promises proved hollow, Watson still chose not to use Home Depot's mechanisms for reporting the harassment.

"While proof that an employee failed to fulfill the corresponding obligation of reasonable care to avoid harm is not limited to showing an unreasonable failure to use any complaint procedure provided by the employer, a demonstration of such failure will normally suffice to satisfy the employer's burden under the second element of the defense." *Faragher*. Watson's failure to use Home Depot's procedures to report *any* of the harassment she allegedly suffered, despite her knowledge of those procedures, was unreasonable. Home Depot has satisfied the second element of the affirmative defense and, as a result, the Court grants summary judgment. . . .

NOTES

1. *Prong 1: Employer Preventive and Corrective Action.* Pay close attention to the risk management choices Home Depot made both before and after Watson's harassment complaint. According to *Ellerth* and *Faragher*, in order to satisfy the first prong of the affirmative defense the employer must exercise reasonable care both to prevent and to correct harassing behavior. What did Home Depot do to *prevent* harassment? Is the sexual harassment policy the only evidence of its prevention, or did it take other measures as well? What aspects of the policy itself convince the court that it is an effective preventive tool? Can you come up with a checklist of features, based on the court's opinion, that you would advise a future client to include in drafting its own harassment policy?

With respect to *correction*, the reasonableness of the employer's response depends on its likely ability to end the harassing behavior. Although the employer is not required to ensure that no harassment continues, it must take reasonable steps toward that end. A recurring factual question is whether the employer's response was adequate under the circumstances. Here Home Depot was not able to corroborate that harassment had occurred, which may make its position more difficult. If the employer does nothing in that situation and the harassment recurs, it may appear that it did not take the victim's complaint seriously, and it will probably have a hard time establishing the affirmative defense. *See also Sutherland v. Wal–Mart Stores, Inc.,* 632 F.3d 990 (7th Cir. 2011) (finding affirmative defense established despite questionable conclusion after an internal investigation that the plaintiff's claims could not be corroborated). However, if the employer takes action against the alleged harasser, it risks penalizing an innocent employee, which can itself have legal consequences. How did Home Depot handle this sensitive situation?

2. *Prong 2: The Victim's Unreasonable Failure to Report.* The second prong of the affirmative defense focuses not on the employer's actions but on the victim's. Is this an appropriate consideration? On the one hand, an employer arguably should not be responsible for behavior for which it genuinely could not have known. On the other, victims often — understandably — do not complain at the outset of harassment, hoping they can "handle" it themselves. *See* Linda Hamilton Krieger, *Employer Liability for Sexual Harassment — Normative, Descriptive, and Doctrinal Interactions: A Reply to Professors Beiner and Bisom-Rapp,* 24 U. ARK. LITTLE ROCK L. REV. 169, 180-83 (2001) (demonstrating that women rarely report harassment initially through formal channels and more frequently respond by ignoring the behavior, re-attributing it to benign motives, or attempting to confront or appease the harasser). Indeed, because a hostile-work-environment claim requires severe or pervasive conduct, victims are probably correct in thinking that a few minor incidents do not constitute illegal behavior. *See Clark County Sch. Dist. v. Breeden,* reproduced at page 799. Does the requirement that the victim not unreasonably delay in reporting suffice to handle this problem? How much time is unreasonable? In *Watson*, the victim waited approximately three months after the alleged assault (which was itself two months after the first inappropriate incident) before reporting. Courts have reached widely different results on this question. *Compare Mota v. Univ. of Tex. Houston Health Sci. Ctr.*, 261 F.3d 512 (5th Cir. 2001) (nine-month delay was reasonable) *with Pinkerton v. Colorado DOT*, 563 F.3d 1052 (10th Cir. 2009) (two-month delay was unreasonable); *Conatzer v. Medical Prof. Bldg. Serv.*, 95 F. App'x 276 (10th Cir. 2004) (17-day delay was unreasonable).

3. *Prompt Complaint Followed by Effective Remedial Action.* What would have happened had Watson reported her supervisor immediately and all other facts were identical? Would Home Depot still have prevailed? Because the two prongs of the affirmative defense are conjunctive, an employer should be held vicariously liable in that situation under a literal reading of the Court's language: It can establish the first prong (the employer took reasonable preventive and corrective action), but not the second required element (the victim unreasonably failed to complain). *See, e.g., Chapman v. Carmike Cinemas*, 307 F. App'x 164 (10th Cir. 2009) (summary judgment for employer improper where plaintiff immediately reported sexual assault despite the fact that employer terminated perpetrator because employer cannot establish unreasonable failure to report). Yet some courts have resisted that result, finding *Ellerth* and *Faragher*—cases involving inadequate policies and victims who did not report—factually distinguishable from cases involving prompt reporting and responsive action. *See, e.g., McCurdy v. Ark. State Police*, 375 F.3d 762 (8th Cir. 2004). What *should* the result be? Some commentators argue that, for policy reasons, the affirmative defense should remain available to employers who respond effectively, whether or not the employee unreasonably delays reporting. *See generally* Zev J. Eigen, Nicholas Menillo & David Sherwyn, *When Rules Are Made to be Broken*, http://papers.ssrn.com/sol3/papers.cfm?abstract_id=2225978 (arguing that lower courts are applying the affirmative defense to allow employers who appropriately "prevent and correct" harassment to avoid liability regardless of whether the employee acts reasonably to avail herself of employer mechanisms); David Sherwyn et al., *Don't Train Your Employees and Cancel Your "1-800" Harassment Hotline: An Empirical Examination and Correction of the Flaws in the Affirmative Defense to Sexual Harassment Charges*, 69 FORDHAM L. REV. 1265, 1280-84 (2000-01) (arguing that affirmative defense requirement that victim unreasonably fail to report creates incentive for employers to discourage reporting and recommending elimination of second prong of defense). On the other hand, is there a competing rationale for finding liability despite the employer's admirable response? *See* Joanna L. Grossman, *The First Bite Is Free: Employer Liability for Sexual Harassment*, 61 U. PITT. L. REV. 671, 711-15 (2000) (arguing that decisions focusing solely on employer corrective action impermissibly substitute a negligence standard for the Supreme Court's vicarious liability rule); Krieger, *supra*, at 169, 196-97 (suggesting that harassment is a reasonably foreseeable harm flowing from the operation of a business whose costs should be internalized).

4. *Victim Requests for Confidentiality.* What if the victim promptly reports but insists that the matter be kept confidential? Several courts have found in favor of employers in those situations, treating the victim's complaint as ineffective. *See, e.g., Hardage v. CBS Broad., Inc.*, 427 F.3d 1177, 1185-88 (9th Cir. 2005) (affirmative defense established where employee made "vague" complaints and insisted on confidentiality, saying he would handle the situation himself); *Olson v. Lowe's Home Ctrs. Inc.*, 130 F. App'x 380, 390 (11th Cir. 2005) (suggesting that, if plaintiff had stated she "did not want [the harasser]'s comments reported or acted upon, then [the employer] would not have been placed on proper notice of harassment). However, there is also contrary authority. *Malik v. Carrier Corp.*, 202 F.3d 97, 105-06 (2d Cir. 2000) ("Prudent employers will compel harassing employees to cease all such conduct and will not, even at a victim's request, tolerate inappropriate conduct that may, if not halted immediately, create a hostile environment."); *see also* Equal Employment Opportunity Commission ("EEOC") Enforcement Guidance: Vicarious Employer Liability for Unlawful Harassment by Supervisors, §V.C.1.d, No. 915.002 (June 18, 1999) (inaction by supervisor in response to confidential report could result in liability).

Suppose you are an employer who wishes to provide harassment training to its workforce. How should you advise your supervisors to handle a "confidential" complaint of harassment? One of the underlying concerns for employers is that, while the particular employee demanding confidentiality may thereby be precluded from suit, future employees who are harassed will be able to show the employer knew that there was a problem and failed to deal with it; in other words, as to potential victims, the employer will not be able to show reasonable steps to prevent the harassment.

5. *Complaints Outside the Chain of Command.* Another question pertaining to the second prong of the affirmative defense is whether the employer will be deemed to be on notice of the harassing behavior despite the failure to make a "formal" complaint through an established sexual harassment reporting procedure. "Open door" policies have sometimes backfired on employers in this regard. Several courts have held that an employer's open door policy justified an employee in concluding that she had satisfied her responsibility to complain about harassment by reporting the problem to any person authorized to hear general problems under such a policy. In one case the court rejected the defendant's argument that plaintiff had failed to utilize its complaint process:

> We recognize that Lowe's provided several means to report sexual harassment, such as calling a toll-free number or writing to Lowe's Internal Audit Department. However, these are alternative means by which Olson could have put Lowe's on notice of the harassment. The fact remains that Hall was a manager and Lowe's Open Door Program clearly allows employees to complain to "any member of management." Consequently, the district court erred in concluding that Olson did not complain to an appropriate person under Lowe's policies.

Olson v. Lowe's Home Ctrs. Inc., 130 F. App'x 380, 390 (11th Cir. 2005).

A related issue is whether an employee reasonably reports where she or he complains to the harassing supervisor but does not go further up the chain of command. Some courts have held that victims satisfy their reporting obligations in such situations, at least where the offending supervisor is designated as a proper recipient for complaints under the policy. *See, e.g., Gorzynski v. JetBlue Airways Corp.*, 596 F.3d 93 (2d Cir. 2010) ("We do not believe that the Supreme Court . . . intended that victims of sexual harassment . . . must go from manager to manager until they find someone who will address their complaints."). Others hold that employees who do not escalate their complaint up the chain of command or bypass the offending manager by using other channels designated in the employer's harassment policy failed to satisfy their reporting obligations. *See, e.g., Chapman, supra* (employee did not adequately avail herself of employer's remedial measures where she complained about hostile comments only to offending managers and failed to use company hotline or contact off-site managers designated in employer policy); *Madray v. Publix*, 208 F.3d 1290, 1301-02 (11th Cir. 2000) (finding unreasonable failure to report by employee harassed by store manager where policy required employee to report either to store manager, district manager, or division manager, and employee reported only to assistant managers within her store).

6. *Strategic Employer Reporting Restrictions.* Might rulings that find employees to have failed to pursue proper employer reporting policies encourage employers to narrow their reporting procedures to foreclose suits? One possibility is for an employer to designate only one or two individuals to whom complaints can be made. *See* Anne Lawton, *Operating in an Empirical Vacuum: The* Ellerth *and* Faragher *Affirmative Defense*, 13 COLUM. J. GENDER & L. 197 (2005) (critiquing judicial deference to employer's designation of appropriate persons to handle complaints). Another possibility is that employers will discourage complaints or at least place the employee in a bad light by requiring complaints to be made within a very short time of the harassment. *See Rennard v. Woodworker's Supply, Inc.*, 101 F. App'x 296, 300 (10th Cir. 2004) (plaintiff disciplined for failing to report sexual harassment within one week as required by employer policy); Anne Lawton, *The Bad Apple Theory in Sexual Harassment*, 13 GEO. MASON L. REV. 817, 850-55 (2005) (criticizing this practice for creating a private statute of limitations that trumps victims' federal rights). On the other hand, does the first prong of the defense limit the extent to which employers can use such strategies successfully? In other words, can a policy that significantly limits the manner and time frame in which a victim is required to report harassment still satisfy the preventive action component of the defense?

7. *Tangible Employment Actions.* The *Ellerth/Faragher* defense applies only to hostile work environment claims. The Supreme Court made clear in both cases that, where the supervisor engages in a tangible employment action that adversely affects the victim, vicarious liability is automatic. And *Vance v. Ball State University* makes clear that whether a harasser is a supervisor turns on whether he or she is able to inflict a tangible employment action. As a result, the concept is critical to the liability scheme the Court created, and will cause plaintiffs to often argue that the harassment they endured culminated in some more tangible adverse action. Could that argument have been made in *Watson*? The implication from Watson's complaint is that both the reprimand she received and the undesirable change in schedule were tied to the harassing behavior. If she could establish that causal connection, would the acts she complained of constitute tangible employment actions sufficient to impose vicarious liability?

Courts disagree as to the definition of tangible employment act. Some hold that a tangible employment act means an "ultimate" employment decision, such as a discharge. *See, e.g., Lutkewitte v. Gonzales*, 436 F.3d 248, 252 (D.C. Cir. 2006) (finding no tangible employment action in supervisor requiring subordinate to attend off-site conference or in victim's general fear that she would lose her job if she did not attend). Others take the view that any act that substantially affects a term or condition of employment suffices. *See, e.g., Green v. Administrators of Tulane Educational Fund*, 284 F.3d 642, 654-55 (5th Cir. 2002) (finding that "demotion, together with the substantial diminishment of her job responsibilities, was sufficient to constitute a tangible employment action" despite absence of any economic loss). A parallel debate in the retaliation context was resolved by the Supreme Court, which rejected lower court holdings making retaliation actionable only when it resulted in an "ultimate employment action." *See Burlington Northern & Santa Fe Ry. v. White*, 548 U.S.

53 (2006) (the anti-retaliation provision "covers those (and only those) employer actions that would have been materially adverse to a reasonable employee or job applicant."). Does this holding suggest a relaxed standard for tangible employment actions is appropriate in the sexual harassment context, or are these two different doctrines?

What is clear is that the act in question must be an official exercise of managerial judgment. In *Pennsylvania State Police v. Suders*, 542 U.S. 129 (2004), the Supreme Court addressed the question whether the *Ellerth/Faragher* defense was available to employers in situations where harassment culminated in a constructive discharge. The Third Circuit had held a constructive discharge, as the equivalent of a termination, constituted a tangible employment action, rendering the employer strictly liable for the victim's harassment. The Supreme Court reversed, explaining:

> Like the harassment considered in our pathmarking decisions [*Ellerth* and *Faragher*], harassment so intolerable as to cause a resignation may be effected through co-worker conduct, unofficial supervisory conduct, or official company acts. Unlike an actual termination, which is *always* effected through an official act of the company, a constructive discharge need not be. A constructive discharge involves both an employee's decision to leave and precipitating conduct: The former involves no official action; the latter, like a harassment claim without any constructive discharge assertion, may or may not involve official action.
>
> To be sure, a constructive discharge is functionally the same as an actual termination in damages-enhancing respects. . . . But when an official act does not underlie the constructive discharge, the *Ellerth* and *Faragher* analysis, we here hold, calls for extension of the affirmative defense to the employer. As those leading decisions indicate, official directions and declarations are the acts most likely to be brought home to the employer, the measures over which the employer can exercise greatest control. Absent "an official act of the enterprise," as the last straw, the employer ordinarily would have no particular reason to suspect that a resignation is not the typical kind daily occurring in the work force. And as *Ellerth* and *Faragher* further point out, an official act reflected in company records — a demotion or a reduction in compensation, for example — shows "beyond question" that the supervisor has used his managerial or controlling position to the employee's disadvantage. Absent such an official act, the extent to which the supervisor's misconduct has been aided by the agency relation, as we earlier recounted, is less certain. That uncertainty, our precedent establishes, justifies affording the employer the chance to establish, through the *Ellerth/Faragher* affirmative defense, that it should not be held vicariously liable.

Id. at 147-48. Do you agree with the Court's analysis? Does its resolution of the constructive discharge question shed any light on how it might resolve the outstanding question whether a tangible employment action requires an "ultimate" employment decision?

8. *Liability to the Putative Harasser?* The structure of the affirmative defense clearly encourages employers to discipline, even discharge, harassers. In *Watson*, Home Depot suspended Terrell during the investigation and later, despite concluding that Watson's allegations "could not be substantiated," transferred him to another store "so that Watson could remain at the North Avenue location if she wished." Did Home Depot risk liability to Terrell?

Since he was likely an at-will employee, contractual liability seems foreclosed, and the public policy tort is inapposite. In contrast, had there been a governing collective bargaining agreement, there would typically have been constraints on the employer's action, including limitations on the discipline that may be meted out: Even a person properly found to have been guilty of harassment can be disciplined only proportionate to the offense. *See Westvaco Corp. v. United Paperworkers Int'l Union*, 171 F.3d 971, 977 (4th Cir. 1999) ("the general public policy against sexual harassment is not sufficient to supplant labor arbitration of employee disciplinary sanctions"). Similarly, civil service laws and academic tenure protections might limit employer responses to harassment and other wrongful conduct by supervisors or co-workers in government and university settings.

What about privacy concerns and defamation? Suppose Terrell were in fact innocent of any wrongful conduct but word of the charges against him went around the workplace? Might the employer be responsible if its conduct caused rumors? Might it be liable for defamation? Would the mere fact of transferring Terrell have carried a defamatory message that he was guilty? Revisit Chapter 5 for these issues. Finally, what about sex discrimination? Might an employer's response to a charge of harassment be viewed as a violation of Title VII? *See Sassaman v. Gamache*, 566 F.3d 307 (2d Cir. 2009) (discharge of male on the basis that men had a propensity to harass, subjecting employer to potential liability by female claiming harassment, was actionable). *See also Russell v. City of Kansas City*, 414 F.3d 863, 868 (8th Cir. 2005) (white female supervisor demoted for allegedly fostering racially harassing workplace may have been the victim of discrimination when black and white males were given only a "slap on the wrist").

Williams v. Spartan Communications
No. 99-1566, 2000 U.S. App. LEXIS 5776 (4th Cir. March 30, 2000)

Motz, C.J.

Veneal Williams sold advertising from 1989 to 1995 for Spartan Communications, Incorporated, which runs a television station in Spartanburg, South Carolina. Her immediate supervisor was Local Sales Manager Mitchell Maund, who was promoted to that position in 1992. Williams alleges that between 1992 and 1995 Maund sexually assaulted her three times during business trips that the two took together. The second assault assertedly occurred in Williams' van, while the two were watching an R-rated movie rented on Maund's instructions.

On May 24, 1995, Williams reported Maund's assaults to Spartan General Sales Manager Greg Rose and Spartan Personnel Manager Donna Groothedde. Maund was out of town that day, but Rose, Groothedde and Spartan Vice President and General Manager Jack West met with him the following day, May 25. At that time, Maund admitted to renting and watching the movie in Williams' van. That afternoon, Maund, Rose, Groothedde, and West met again; as a result of Maund's admitted rental of the movie, he resigned. Maund received five months severance pay in return for releasing Spartan from liability for his dismissal. Due to the distress of continued sexual harassment, Williams left her job with Spartan and is now unemployed and in counseling.

[A magistrate judge granted summary judgment to Spartan. On appeal, the issue] is whether Spartan has established, as a matter of law, its entitlement to an affirmative defense to Williams' hostile environment claim. The Supreme Court has explained that "when no tangible employment action is taken, a defending employer may raise an affirmative defense" to a claim of "vicarious liability . . . for an actionable hostile environment created by a supervisor with immediate . . . authority over the employee." *Faragher v. Boca Raton*, 524 U.S. 775, 807 (1998); *Burlington Indus. v. Ellerth*, 524 U.S. 742, 765 (1998). To do so an employer must demonstrate by the "preponderance of the evidence" that (1) it "exercised reasonable care to prevent and correct promptly any sexually harassing behavior" and (2) "the plaintiff employee unreasonably failed to take advantage of any preventative [sic] or corrective opportunities provided by the employer or to avoid harm otherwise." The magistrate judge held that Spartan had satisfied both elements of the affirmative defense as a matter of law and so granted the company summary judgment.

We believe that this ruling was error. We need only discuss the first prong of the defense—whether Spartan has established, as a matter of law, that it "exercised reasonable care to prevent and correct promptly" the sexually harassing behavior.

The magistrate judge found that the following evidence demonstrated that Spartan had indisputably satisfied this prong: (1) Williams admitted that she knew of Spartan's anti-harassment policy, had attended a meeting at which it was discussed, and saw a posted notice of it, which identified persons to whom she could report improper conduct, and (2) Spartan forced Maund to resign as soon as it learned of Williams' allegations.

This rationale fails to recognize that while the existence of an antiharassment policy and prompt corrective action pursuant to it provides important evidence that an employer has acted to meet the first prong of the affirmative defense, such evidence does not compel this conclusion. Rather, any anti-harassment policy offered to satisfy the first prong of the *Faragher-Ellerth* defense must be "both reasonably designed and reasonably effectual." *Brown v. Perry*, 184 F.3d 388, 396 (4th Cir. 1999). Moreover, a prompt response to complaints of harassment made pursuant to a policy banning harassment does not necessarily establish the first prong of the affirmative defense.

The magistrate judge also entirely ignored substantial relevant evidence submitted by Williams that could lead a factfinder to conclude that Spartan's anti-harassment policy was not an effective preventive program. This evidence included: (1) Maund's deposition testimony that he received no training on sexual harassment and did not even recall any specific discussion of the anti-harassment policy; (2) senior Spartan management's toleration of and participation in lewd conversations and publication of sexually explicit jokes and cartoons in the workplace; (3) evidence that an employee's complaint to a Spartan manager about foul language and sexist jokes in the workplace produced no corrective action; (4) General Sales Manager Rose's comment that a secretary had been fired because "she didn't give him a blow job"; (5) Vice President and General Manager West's remark to male managers looking at female participants in a management training function, "Boys, I've stepped over better than that just to jack off"; (6) General Sales Manager West's comment after a sexual harassment training meeting, "does this mean we can't fuck the help any more"; (7) the close relationship between Maund (the alleged harasser) and West, Rose, and other senior managers at Spartan; and (8) the anti-harassment policy's failure, in contravention of EEOC guidelines, to assure those reporting harassment that they would not be subject to retaliation, particularly when the policy provided that "an employee who in bad faith falsely accuses another employee of harassment will be subject to disciplinary action up to and including termination."

In *Faragher*, the Supreme Court found a city was vicariously liable for harassment by lifeguard supervisors, despite the existence of a sexual harassment policy, when the plaintiff beach employees were "completely isolated from the City's higher management" and the city "failed to disseminate its policy against sexual harassment among the beach employees." In *Smith v. First Union National Bank*, 202 F.3d 234, 245 (4th Cir. 2000), we held that even though the employer's anti-harassment policy had been disseminated to employees it did not demonstrate, as a matter of law, that the employer had satisfied the first prong of the *Faragher* defense because the policy referred only to sexual conduct and was read by the plaintiff not to include nonsexual, gender-based harassment. We also emphasized that "employers cannot satisfy the first element of the *Faragher-Ellerth* affirmative defense if its management-level employees are discouraging the use of the complaint process."

Here Spartan disseminated an anti-harassment policy which failed to provide that complainants would be free from retaliation, and yet warned that false reports of harassment would subject a complainant to disciplinary action, "including termination." Although these features do not, in themselves, render the policy ineffective, when considered in conjunction with the conduct of most senior Spartan management, a policy with such features could be found to be ineffective. The outrageous comments by Vice President and General Manager West ("does this mean we cannot fuck the help anymore") and General Sales Manager Rose (a secretary was terminated because "she didn't give him a blow job") suggest not only that a complaint made pursuant to this anti-harassment policy might fall on deaf ears, but also that such a complaint might cause the complainant's termination. Indeed, Williams produced evidence that a Spartan employee decided not to complain of harassment because of fear of being fired. The long and close personal relationships between those managers who made the denigrating comments, West and Rose, and the alleged harasser, Maund, were so well known that several of the witnesses described them as members of the "Augusta Boys Club." Given these relationships, a factfinder could conclude that a complaint about Maund would receive a particularly skeptical response from Spartan management.

We note that Spartan's policy states that "any employee who feels they are being subjected to any form of harassment in violation of this policy should bring their complaint to the attention" of one of four members of management: "[1] the[] immediate supervisor, [2] the General Manager, [3] the appointed liaison, or [4] the Manager of Corporate Human Resources." Providing an employee recourse to multiple members of management is commendable. But Williams produced evidence that could lead a factfinder to determine that the extra protection seemingly afforded by this provision was illusory in her case. This is so because one of the four suggested recipients of harassment complaints was the harasser himself, Maund; another was his good friend, Vice President and General Manager West (the source of the "does this mean we can't fuck the help any more" and the "I've stepped over better than that just to jack off" remarks); and the remaining two managers reported to West, the General Manager of the station and Vice President of the entire company. Thus, the conduct of Spartan's senior management could be found to have isolated Williams from effective channels of complaint. A factfinder could conclude that the language in the anti-harassment policy together with the conduct of Spartan's most senior management "discouraged complaining about a supervisor's harassing behavior." *Smith*.

This is not to say that Williams has demonstrated that Spartan cannot establish the first prong of *Faragher's* affirmative defense. A factfinder may well ultimately conclude that Spartan's anti-harassment policy and prompt corrective action do establish this prong. However, we believe that when Williams' evidence is considered in the light most favorable to her, Spartan has not established the first prong as a matter of law. For these reasons, we reverse the district court's grant of summary judgment to Spartan.

REVERSED.

WILKINSON, C.J., dissenting.

I agree with the district court that Spartan Communications has established both prongs of the affirmative defense under *Faragher* and *Ellerth*. I would therefore uphold the grant of summary judgment. . . .

As to the first prong of the defense, Spartan exercised reasonable care to prevent and correct the sexually harassing behavior that Williams reported. Spartan put in place a strong anti-harassment policy that states the "working environment should be free of intimidation and harassment." The policy defines and prohibits sexual harassment and encourages employees to come forward with complaints. A complaint may be reported to any one of at least four different people, including the department head, general manager, appointed EEO liaison, and the manager of corporate human resources. Williams admits that she was aware of this policy. She attended a meeting at which the policy was discussed by the corporate personnel director and saw a posted notice prohibiting sexual harassment and identifying various persons to whom she could report any improper conduct. Spartan also took swift action to correct the alleged harassment. When Williams finally reported Maund's inappropriate behavior, Spartan immediately conducted an investigation and asked Maund to resign only two days after receiving Williams' complaint.

Though the existence of an anti-harassment policy is not sufficient to satisfy the first part of the affirmative defense, the policy here is "both reasonably designed and reasonably effectual." *Brown v. Perry*, 184 F.3d 388, 396 (4th Cir. 1999). The majority attempts to discredit the effectiveness of the policy by referring to lewd statements by management and to the fact that Spartan's policy did not contain an explicit anti-retaliation provision. Yet the majority does not assert that the policy was ineffective when complaints were reported or that Spartan had retaliated against any employee who made a complaint. There is simply "no evidence that [the] employer adopted or administered an anti-harassment policy in bad faith or that the policy was otherwise defective or dysfunctional." There is only the evidence that Spartan immediately terminated Maund when it learned of his misconduct. Because it had an effective policy, Spartan has satisfied the first part of the affirmative defense.

The majority's litany of crude remarks attributed to management does not undermine Spartan's affirmative defense. It is a rare case when some remarks could not be dredged up or alleged in order to challenge management's reasonableness. The affirmative defense focuses not on remarks, however, but on the conduct of employers and employees in preventing and addressing sexual harassment complaints. A collection of off-hand remarks unrelated to the harassment simply does not preclude Spartan from establishing the first prong of the affirmative defense on summary judgment. Indeed, the remarks related by the majority were not directed toward Williams. She was not even present when most of them were made. While no one would approve of the comments, Title VII is not intended to allow courts to act as censors of workplace speech or impose a general workplace civility code.

As to the second prong of the defense, Williams failed to take advantage of the opportunities provided by Spartan to avoid the sexual harassment. "[A] demonstration of such failure will normally suffice to satisfy the employer's burden under the second element of the defense." *Faragher*. In *Montero v. Agco Corp.*, the Ninth Circuit held that where the plaintiff knew about the company's policy, knew whom to contact with harassment complaints, and yet waited almost two years to report the harassment, the company "successfully established the second prong of the *Faragher* defense" and was entitled to judgment as a matter of law. 192 F.3d 856, 863 (9th Cir. 1999). Similarly, Williams knew about Spartan's policy, knew whom to contact with grievances, and yet waited three years to report the harassment. During this time, plaintiff was allegedly assaulted twice more, once while watching an R-rated movie in her van with Maund and again while with Maund in her hotel room. *Faragher* and *Ellerth* encourage employees to report such conduct precisely to avoid continued harassment. Spartan has established that Williams unreasonably failed to take advantage of the company's preventive and corrective measures. Williams "should not recover damages that could have been avoided if she had done so." *Faragher.*

By denying summary judgment in a case where the affirmative defense has been clearly established, the majority simply indicates an aversion to the Supreme Court's mandate in *Faragher* and *Ellerth*. In doing so, the majority creates the worst of all possible worlds. Despite the existence of a reasonable and effective complaint procedure, the employee continues to be harassed for nearly three years because no misconduct was reported. The company in turn has no opportunity to rectify unacceptable behavior. Such an outcome is the antithesis of Title VII's primary objective, which is "not to provide redress but to avoid harm." *Faragher.* The Supreme Court has explained that employer liability is limited to encourage the creation of effective anti-harassment policies and also to "encourage employees to report harassing conduct before it becomes severe or pervasive." *Ellerth.* Spartan attempted to prevent and acted to correct sexually harassing behavior. It should not be held liable when an employee fails to use the available channels for reporting harassment. As this court stated in Brown, "The law requires an employer to be reasonable, not clairvoyant or omnipotent."

I would affirm the judgment.

NOTES

1. *"Paper Compliance?"* *Williams* raises an important question—does a sexual harassment policy actually prevent harassment? More importantly, should the existence of such a policy absolve an employer of liability for harassment that occurs nevertheless? Many commentators have criticized the Supreme Court's decisions in *Ellerth* and *Faragher* for granting too much deference to employer policies and practices. *See, e.g.,* Susan Bisom-Rapp, *An Ounce of Prevention Is a Poor Substitute for a Pound of Cure: Confronting the Developing Jurisprudence of Education and Prevention in Employment Discrimination Law,* 22 BERKELEY J. EMP. & LAB. L. 1 (2001); Susan D. Carle, *Acknowledging Informal Power Dynamics in the Workplace: A Proposal for Further Development of the Vicarious Liability Doctrine in Hostile Environment Sexual Harassment Cases,* 13 DUKE J. GENDER L. & POL'Y 85 (2006); Joanna L. Grossman, *The Culture of Compliance: The Final Triumph of Form Over Substance in Sexual Harassment Law,* 26 HARV. WOMEN'S L.J. 3 (2003); Anne Lawton, *Operating in an Empirical Vacuum: The* Ellerth *and* Faragher *Affirmative Defense,* 13 COLUM. J. GENDER & L. 197 (2005). These commentators argue that the affirmative defense creates incentives for employers to go through the motions of being tough on harassment, establishing strongly worded policies and implementing training programs, but

that such practices do not get at the root cause of harassing behavior. Indeed, some have suggested that those practices come at the expense of more aggressive efforts to equalize the workplace and to respond to acts of discrimination. Consider Professor Lawton's take:

> [T]he courts are asking employers the wrong questions. Why are employers not required to show evidence of their efforts to evaluate and assess the impact of their organization's culture on the incidence of workplace harassment? If role models, such as supervisors, set the tone in the workplace . . . then should the employer not evaluate its supervisors, in part, on their efforts to enforce and comply with the employer's anti-harassment policy? . . .
>
> Finally, if employers depend on their anti-harassment policies and procedures to deter workplace harassment, should they not be required to evaluate those policies and procedures? Why do federal courts not require an employer to ask its own employees about their perceptions of the employer's procedure? If employees believe the employer does not punish harassers and penalizes victims who come forward with complaints of sexual harassment, why would an employer be allowed to prevail on the affirmative defense for simply drafting a policy and procedure that workers are reluctant to use?

13 COLUM. J. GENDER & L. at 233-35 (2005). She concludes that courts' equating policies with prevention essentially shifts the burden of proof to the employee on the reasonableness of the employer's prevention efforts. *Id.* at 235; *see also* Vicki Schultz, *The Sanitized Workplace*, 112 YALE L.J. 2061, 2174-77 (2003) (suggesting that liability for hostile work environment sexual harassment should turn on the extent of sex segregation in the particular workplace rather than employer's aggressiveness in policing sexual conduct).

Williams certainly demonstrates that it is possible for an employer to have a policy on the books and at the same time tolerate a work culture in which objectionable behavior endures. The question is whether courts will hold such employers accountable. *Williams* and other decisions find that an employer must do more than institute a policy or a training program to prevent and correct harassment. *See, e.g., Herndon v. City Manchester*, 284 S.W.3d. 682 (Mo. App. 2009) (concluding under state law version of affirmative defense that police department failed to take preventative measures despite its harassment policy where department failed to adequately examine offending officer's disciplinary record in past position and was aware that officer had previously engaged in harassment of nonemployee); *cf. Hawkins v. Anheuser-Busch, Inc.* 517 F.3d 321 (6th Cir. 2008) (concluding for purposes of co-worker harassment claim that "an employer's responsibility to prevent future harassment is heightened where it is dealing with a known serial harasser and is therefore on clear notice that the same employee has engaged in inappropriate behavior in the past"). However, the *Williams* decision provoked a strong dissent, and other courts have adopted the dissenting judge's more deferential view of employer practices. *See, e.g., Barrett v. Applied Radiant Energy Corp.*, 240 F.3d 262 (4th Cir. 2001) ("Distribution of an anti-harassment policy provides 'compelling proof' that the company exercised reasonable care in preventing and promptly correcting sexual harassment. The only way to rebut this proof is to show that the 'employer adopted or administered an anti-harassment policy in bad faith or that the policy was otherwise defective or dysfunctional.'"); David Sherwyn et al., *Don't Train Your Employees and Cancel Your "1-800" Harassment Hotline: An Empirical Examination and Correction of the Flaws in the Affirmative Defense to Sexual Harassment Charges*, 69 FORDHAM L. REV. 1265,

1285-86 (2000-01) (finding that among reported sexual harassment decisions between 1998 and 2000, all but one held that the employer satisfied the reasonable care requirement by maintaining a sexual harassment policy that allowed the victim the opportunity to report to someone other than a harassing supervisor).

2. *Conjunctive Elements.* The *Williams* court deals only with the first prong of the defense, and only with its first element — whether the employer engaged in preventive action. Since a reasonable jury could find that the employer failed to reasonably prevent harassment, the other aspects of the defense were irrelevant; if the jury so finds, the employer will be liable. Assume, however, that the court went on to complete the analysis. How would the employer fare? Prompt and effective *corrective* action was taken: immediately after Williams reported Maund's behavior, he resigned. As for the second prong, the harassment perpetrated against Williams continued for three years before she reported, which strongly suggests she was unreasonable in failing to report. Given these facts, the court's willingness to look beyond the employer's policy on harassment in assessing prevention was critical to the plaintiff's success.

3. *Reasonable Failures to Report.* Alternatively, could Williams successfully argue that her significant delay in reporting Maund's harassing behavior (as measured from his first act) was reasonable? Note the employer's sexual harassment policy did not offer assurances of nonretaliation, and as the court makes clear, the past comments of senior managers could give an employee good reason to fear that her complaint of harassment would not be taken seriously. Courts often are reluctant to find a failure to report reasonable where the victim cites only general fear and embarrassment. *See, e.g., Matvia v. Bald Head Isle Mgmt.,* 259 F.3d 261, 270 (4th Cir. 2001) (finding that general fear of negative reactions from co-workers, which ultimately came to fruition, did not justify failure to report; a retaliation claim is the proper avenue for dealing with retaliatory behavior should it occur). Other courts, however, have found that a victim's failure to report promptly could be reasonable in similar circumstances, as where the employer's work culture discouraged reporting or the victim had a specific basis for fearing retaliation. *See, e.g., Reed v. MBNA Mktg. Sys.,* 333 F.3d 27, 36-37 (1st Cir. 2003) (finding 17-year-old victim's failure to report reasonable where harasser told her his family had significant influence in the company and she would be fired for reporting); *Mota v. Univ. of Tex. Houston Health Sci. Ctr.,* 261 F.3d 512 (5th Cir. 2001) (finding untenured professor's delay in reporting harassment by prominent department head reasonable where harasser stated that people working in his department had to "get along" with him and that victim's immigration status could be jeopardized if he no longer worked as university employee).

4. *Supervisor versus Co-worker.* In both the *Watson* and *Williams* cases, the courts treated the harassment as being cause by a "supervisor." After *Vance v. Ball State University,* 133 S. Ct. 3424 (2103), that may or may not be correct. Terrell, for example, was only an Assistant Store Manager, and while he apparently had authority to issue the Performance Notice that did not seem to result in any further disciplinary action. If Terrell wasn't her supervisor, Wal-Mart would still be liable for his harassment but only on a negligence theory. Under that approach Watson would have to show that the employer knew or should have known that the harassment was taking place and failed to take remedial action. As this test suggests, courts will look at many of the same factors that are relevant under the affirmative defense in determining negligence. Reports to a "supervisor" are among the ways an employer might know or be deemed to know about co-worker harassment, while complaints to "co-workers" might not count, and the extent to which the employer exercises reasonable care in response to the co-worker's behavior largely replicates the inquiry under the corrective action prong of *Ellerth/Faragher*. Thus the critical distinction between the two tests is primarily the burden of proof.

In theory, an employee who is harassed by a supervisor ought to have an easier time obtaining relief than one harassed by a co-worker, since in the former case liability is automatic subject to the employer's defense. Ironically, in jurisdictions that defer significantly to the employer's policies, that is not always the case. Suppose that a visibly upset employee asks her supervisor for a shift change in order to avoid another employee who has "been giving [her] problems." If the employee declines to elaborate, a court that strictly reads the second prong of *Ellerth/Faragher* might conclude that the employee unreasonably failed to report the harasser's behavior. Yet depending on the facts, a jury might reasonably conclude that the supervisor should have known about the harassing behavior, the standard applicable to co-worker claims. *See Duch v. Jakubek*, 588 F.3d 757 (2d Cir. 2009) (jury could conclude that supervisor had constructive knowledge of co-worker harassment where employee requested shift change, employer observed employee "teary and red" when asked about the harasser, and supervisor knew harasser had engaged in past misconduct toward female employees).

5. *Beyond Sexual Harassment.* Although the Supreme Court's decisions in *Ellerth* and *Faragher* involved sexual harassment in particular, most courts have assumed that the affirmative defense applies to hostile work environment claims based on other protected characteristics and arising under sources of law other than Title VII's prohibition on sex discrimination. Might the concept of employer prevention and corrective action have bearing on employer liability for other forms of discrimination as well?. Proactive employer behavior can also limit the employee's damage award upon a successful showing of discrimination. *See Kolstad v. American Dental Ass'n*, 527 U.S. 526, 545 (1999) ("[I]n the punitive damages context, an employer may not be vicariously liable for the discriminatory employment decisions of managerial agents where these decisions are contrary to the employer's 'good-faith efforts to comply with Title VII.'").

6. *Treatment of the Harasser.* The *Williams* court noted that "as a result of Maund's admitted rental of the movie, he resigned. Maund received five months severance pay in return for releasing Spartan from liability for his dismissal." The majority does not further explore this, and the dissent seems to think that the employer did as much as could be expected when it "fired" Maund. Thus, the terms of the alleged harasser's termination apparently do not affect the adequacy of the employer's "correct" response. But why pay an admitted harasser severance? Is it because the admitted conduct was not necessarily harassment? Even so, what claims do you think Maund waived in return for his severance pay? If you were the employer's counsel, would you have recommended paying him five months' salary? Reconsider your answer when you have finished Section B.

PROBLEMS

13-1. Spectrum Stores, a regional convenience store chain, asks you to review its policy on sexual harassment. Spectrum owns approximately 25 stores and 2 warehouses across two states and employs over 300 employees. Approximately 20 of those employees, including its officers and human resources personnel, work in Spectrum's corporate headquarters. Orientation for all store personnel is conducted at the headquarters, and the following policy is distributed to all employees at that time:

> Spectrum Stores does not and will not tolerate harassment of our employees, applicants or customers. The term "harassment" includes but is not limited to: slurs, jokes and other verbal, graphic or physical conduct relating to an individual's race, color, sex, sexual orientation, or religion. "Harassment" also includes sexual advances, requests for sexual favors, unwelcome touching and other verbal, graphic or physical conduct of a sexual nature.

> VIOLATION OF THIS POLICY WILL SUBJECT THE EMPLOYEE TO DISCIPLINARY ACTION.

> If you feel that you are being harassed in any way you should notify your immediate supervisor. If you believe that a supervisor or a member of management has acted inconsistently with this policy and you are not comfortable bringing a complaint regarding harassment to your immediate supervisor or if you believe that your complaint concerning a co-worker, a customer, or a vendor has not been handled to your satisfaction, please immediately contact either the Vice President of Human Resources or the Executive Vice President.
> Please do not assume Spectrum is aware of your problem. Please bring your complaints and concerns to our attention so that we can resolve them.

Is there anything you would recommend adding to or changing in this policy? Are there any other practices or procedures you would recommend that Spectrum adopt? If you need further information to answer, what questions would you ask Spectrum's management before offering advice?

13-2. Terri Munroe was a shipping and receiving clerk in one of Spectrum Stores' warehouses and the only female employee at her worksite. Reed Gilbelt, a co-worker, frequently subjected Terri to sexual comments and lewd behavior. Among other things, he referred to her as "luscious" and "sweet cheeks," and on two occasions he suggested that Terri accompany him to the Red Roof Inn during a break. He frequently sent suggestive e-mails to her.

After enduring this behavior for six months, Terri reported Reed's conduct to her supervisor, Vincent Sing. Vincent laughed when he read the e-mails Terri showed him and told Terri that she should "resolve the problem on her own." Over the next three months, Sing engaged in suggestive behavior as well. He told Terri that he "had a job for her under his desk," remarked that Terri should wear shorter shorts on one occasion when he saw her standing on high equipment, and invited Terri out with him on three occasions. Once when Terri asked to be permitted to clock out early due to illness, Vincent told her she could only leave if she came home with him. When Terri refused, Vincent forced her to work until the end of her regular shift.

Three months after first reporting Reed's behavior to Vincent, Terri reported the behavior of both employees to Diane O'Connor, Spectrum's Human Resources Vice President. O'Connor placed Terri on paid leave and launched an immediate investigation, during which she interviewed over a dozen employees during the course of two weeks. As a result of the investigation,

Spectrum terminated Reed, and Vincent resigned. O'Connor informed Terri of this outcome and Terri returned to work. She did not experience any further harassment upon her return; however, she resigned from employment one month later citing her distress at the behavior she had endured prior to the investigation and being "shunned" upon her return to work by some co-workers who were upset about the departures of Reed and Vincent.

Assume that Spectrum maintains the sexual harassment policy laid out in problem 13-1 above and that the company provides sexual harassment training to all its employees. Suppose you represent Terri. Enumerate all of the discrimination claims and theories of liability that you can pursue against Spectrum. If Terri's experience amounts to severe and pervasive hostile behavior based on sex, can she establish that Spectrum should be vicariously liable for Reed's conduct? What about for Vincent's conduct? Think about how you would go about establishing this element of her claim(s), anticipate what arguments Spectrum is likely to make, and explain how you would respond to them.

2. Employer Investigations of Workplace Misconduct

Internal investigations of sexual harassment complaints are now standard practice among sophisticated employers, and they are used not only in dealing with allegations of discrimination, but in ensuring compliance with regulatory and criminal laws and dealing with civil liability on many fronts. Some internal investigations receive a great deal of media attention, such as the after-the-fact inquiry into the Penn State scandal by former FBI Director Louis Freer, *The Paterno Legacy, Changed Forever*, NY TIMES, July 13, 2012, at B11, and the New Jersey governor's office's internal investigation which exonerated Governor Chris Christie of personal involvement in the "Bridgegate" scandal. Michael Barbaro, *Report Details Claims by Ally: Christie Knew of Bridge Lane Closings*, N.Y. TIMES, Mar. 27, 2014, at A-1. They may be conducted by line managers, compliance officers, corporate counsel, or, as in the Penn State and New Jersey cases, outside counsel.

A firm might wish to have an attorney, often an outside attorney, conduct its internal investigation for a number of reasons. Foremost is the fact that investigations do not normally trigger privilege protections when conducted by nonlawyers. *See* Kathryn W. Munson, Comment, *Why Don't You Do Right? Corporate Fiduciary Law and the Self-Critical Analysis Privilege*, 88 TUL. L. REV. 651 (2014). There is the additional advantage of the perception of impartiality when an investigation is conducted by someone without a direct stake in the outcome. *See* Joanna L. Grossman, *The Culture of Compliance: The Final Triumph of Form over Substance in Sexual Harassment Law*, 26 HARV. WOMEN'S L. J. 3, 57-63 (2003) (discussing institutional and other biases in internal investigations). For the latter reason, there is also a tendency to have special counsel retained to investigate serious cases, especially when a higher-level official is the subject of a complaint. Using special counsel also avoids disqualification that may result from the same law firm both conducting the investigation and litigating any suit that ensues if the investigating attorney becomes a necessary witness. *See* Jeffrey A. Van Detta, *Lawyers as Investigators: How* Ellerth *and* Faragher *Reveal a Crisis of Ethics and Professionalism Through Trial Counsel*

Disqualification and Waivers of Privilege in Workplace Harassment Cases, 24 J. LEGAL PROF. 261 (1999/2000).

At the same time, investigations have generated difficult ethical questions for lawyers, who may be faced with conflicts of interest or even risk criminal liability should their work help hide client wrongdoing or obstruct investigations by outside authorities. *See* Peter J. Henning, *Targeting Legal Advice*, 54 AM. U. L. REV. 669, 694 (2005) (quoting the SEC's Director of Enforcement, Stephen Cutler, "One area of particular focus for us is the role of lawyers in internal investigations of their clients or companies. We are concerned that, in some instances, lawyers may have conducted investigations in such a manner as to help hide ongoing fraud, or may have taken actions to actively obstruct such investigations.").

a. Representing the Employer in an Investigation

From the employer's perspective, the purpose of an internal investigation is to ascertain the facts in order to determine the optimal course of action — while trying to avoid making matters worse. The resulting choices might include making no changes after finding no wrongdoing, improving procedures to avoid even the perception of future problems despite a finding of no wrongdoing, self-reporting violations to enforcement authorities or regulators, taking steps to remedy the situation by disciplining or discharging those responsible for illegal or unwise conduct, and making settlement offers to aggrieved persons. Of course, the employer's response will usually itself be constrained by various legal doctrines. For example, the antidiscrimination laws prohibit retaliation against those who participate in legal proceedings and even those who oppose discrimination. The Supreme Court recently reaffirmed this in *Crawford v. Metropolitan Gov't of Nashville & Davidson County*, 555 U.S. 271 (2009) (holding that an employee's response to questions during a harassment investigation constituted protected "opposition" conduct under Title VII's antiretaliation principle).

Whatever the ultimate action taken, the first step is to ascertain the facts. Practitioners have developed a number of strategies for maximizing the efficacy of fact seeking in these investigations while minimizing the risks the investigations themselves may create. For example, it is both common sense and standard practice to identify and safeguard electronic files and relevant documents since employees may well wish to hide or destroy them to protect themselves and/or the corporation. It is also important to have a set of protocols for conducting witness interviews. One set of commentators recommends two rounds of interviews, the first and more informal is "designed to stake out the field of inquiry," and the second round is more focused:

> The purposes of the preliminary round of interviews is to: (a) introduce the investigating attorney, explain what is happening, and secure the witness's cooperation and understanding of the need for confidentiality; (b) learn the witness's background and connection to the matter under investigation; (c) give each witness an idea of what is going to happen in the investigation; and (d) attempt to identify the universe of witnesses and pertinent documents.
>
> In the initial interview, every effort should be made to put the witness at ease and convey the notion that the investigating attorney views the witness as a collaborator in a joint effort to find out exactly what happened. The initial interview should be a

conversation — *not* an examination. The less the investigating attorney professes to know about the client and the client's industry during the initial interview, the better. Ideally, the investigating attorney assumes the role of student and asks the witness to assume the role of teacher. The investigating attorney should ask who *the witness* thinks the investigating attorney should interview and what documents *the witness* thinks the investigating attorney should review in order to find out what happened. The witness will probably end up telling the investigator the witness's version of what happened without much additional prompting. If the witness is not forthcoming, the investigating attorney will have to proceed to a second, more adversarial interview, as described below. The initial interview should end with the investigating attorney explaining that the investigation is ongoing and it is possible that the witness will have to be interviewed again. If the witness asks what is going to happen at the conclusion of the investigation, the only truthful answer is that the investigating attorney is simply gathering the facts, and that until those facts are unearthed, there is no way to predict the results of the investigation. . . .

[I]f there is some material disagreement between witnesses, or between witnesses and available documents, the investigating attorney will need to conduct a second round of interviews with those witnesses whose stories seem to conflict with those of other witnesses or with available documents. In contrast to the preliminary interview, the second interview should be more in the nature of an examination than a conversation. . . .

[T]he investigating attorney may want to employ a professional court reporter for this purpose. A verbatim transcript will remove any doubt as to what the witness actually said during the interview. An employee witness in fear of losing his or her job, or perhaps even of prosecution, may later deny having made crucial disclosures. . . . Another reason a court reporter may be beneficial in taking statements of crucial witnesses is that, in the event the government is notified of the facts discovered in the investigation, it will be in the company's best interest for the government to be satisfied that the company has engaged in a serious and professional effort to discover and document the facts. . . .

However, creating a verbatim transcript of witness interviews is contrary to the conventional wisdom of many practitioners. This conventional wisdom counsels against creating a verbatim transcript to protect against disclosure of such materials in the event a decision is made to voluntarily disclose the results of an internal investigation to the government. Instead, investigating attorneys often prepare post-interview memoranda that include the attorney's mental impressions and opinions so the memoranda will be protected by the work product doctrine. . . . [P]reserving applicable privileges is vitally important in conducting witness interviews. However, the government is requesting waiver of privileged materials with increasing frequency as a condition for the disclosing entity to receive credit for full cooperation. Therefore, preservation of privileges is ultimately uncertain, and may be less important than ensuring the accuracy of the testimony of critical witnesses. . . .

Ames Davis & Jennifer L. Weaver, *A Litigator's Approach to Interviewing Witnesses in Internal Investigations*, 17 HEALTH LAWYER 8, 9 (2005).

This passage suggests a number of the problems with internal investigations, including the very controversial practice of the Department of Justice and other state and federal regulatory authorities to demand (they might say "request") waivers of attorney-client privilege and work product protection as a condition of settlement discussions. Although the Department of Justice has retreated from a harsh position articulated in the so-called Thompson Memorandum, the current "McNulty Memorandum," Memorandum from Deputy Att'y Gen. Paul J. McNulty for Heads of Dep't Components and U.S. Attorneys (Dec. 12, 2006), *available at* http://www.usdoj .gov/dag/speeches/2006/mcnulty_memo.pdf, leaves the privilege still very much at risk. *See* American College of Trial Lawyers, *Recommended Practices for Companies and*

Their Counsel in Conducting Internal Investigations, 46 AM. CRIM. L. REV. 73 (2009). As Davis and Weaver suggest, the attorney investigator should make every effort to preserve these protections. Other commentators recommend a series of steps to maximize the probability of protecting privileges, including:

- Early lawyer involvement
- Explicit corporate request for legal (as opposed to business) advice
- Documenting the confidentiality of communications
- Restricting the internal flow of information
- Obtaining information from highest possible sources
- Labeling documents judiciously to avoid diluting protection for sensitive material
- Interposing legal conclusions, mental impressions, and strategies in all notes
- Treating former employee contacts as confidential for work product protection
- Deciding whether to release the report to a governmental agency, underwriter's counsel, accountants, or the press in light of the effect on privileges
- Express legal conclusions, opinions, and recommendations in the report to the board of directors

Thomas R. Mulroy & Eric J. Munoz, *The Internal Corporate Investigation*, 1 DEPAUL BUS. & COMM. L. J. 49, 82-84 (2002).

While the careful attorney will do her best to ensure that the privilege applies, she will also be aware that the protections may well be waived should a prosecutor threaten criminal charges or a regulator threaten a civil enforcement action. *See Angelone v. Xerox Corp.*, 2011 WL 4473534 (W.D.N.Y., September 26, 2011) (waiver of privilege and work-product protection by relying on attorney's report in defending a harassment complaint); *Reitz v. City of Mt. Juliet*, 680 F. Supp. 2d 888 (M.D. Tenn. 2010) (same); *see generally* David M. Zornow & Keith D. Krakaur, *On the Brink of a Brave New World: The Death of Privilege in Corporate Criminal Investigations*, 37 AM. CRIM. L. REV. 147 (2000). Further, the corporation may well choose to waive its privilege even if not pressed by a government agency. For example, while the EEOC does not demand privilege waivers as part of its investigations, an employer seeking to allay Commission doubts about the effectiveness of its sexual harassment or antidiscrimination policies might want to provide such reports.

One of the central problems of the internal investigation is the relationship of the investigator to the employee being questioned. That individual may not understand that the investigator is in no sense that person's attorney—especially if the investigation begins with a version of informal "conversation" described by Davis and Weaver. The potential for misunderstanding of the role of the attorney is especially great if (as is often the case) the attorney investigating the matter on behalf of the employer has previously represented the individual being questioned in matters in which the interests of the employer and employee were aligned.

New Jersey saw this play out in a high-profile case, *Speeney v. Rutgers*, 369 F. App'x 357 (3d Cir. 2010), which started with sexual harassment complaints by several students against a Rutgers University professor. Rutgers retained what was then the firm of Carpenter, Bennett & Morrissey both to represent it in the university's internal de-tenuring proceeding against the harasser and to defend it against a suit by him. Ultimately, both proceedings were resolved before any conclusion, with the professor leaving Rutgers. The students were apparently unhappy with the settlement and/or with any compensation to be paid to them on their own claims.

They were also unhappy with the law firm. In its representation of Rutgers, the firm interviewed the students who later became key witnesses in the internal proceedings and, presumably, would have been key to Rutgers's defense of the professor's suit. When the students brought suit, they not only pursued claims against Rutgers for the harassment, but also sued Carpenter for malpractice, asserting that they were not mere witnesses but rather clients of the firm. And, for good measure, they sought to have the firm disqualified from representing Rutgers in their suit against it.

The Third Circuit's decision was scarcely definitive. Since the plaintiffs ultimately settled their claims against Rutgers, the disqualification motion was moot when the matter reached the Third Circuit. But there was still the plaintiffs' malpractice claim against "their" lawyers, the Carpenter firm. While the district court had found that there was no attorney-client relationship, the Third Circuit remanded for another determination in light of new evidence the plaintiffs claim to have had. *See also Morin v. Me. Educ. Ass'n*, 993 A.2d 1097 (Me. 2010) (trial court exceeded its discretion in disqualifying employer's law firm in employee's discrimination suit; while attorney may have misrepresented his role in investigation by calling it "independent" and saying he did not represent employer, plaintiff was unable to show actual prejudice from employer being represented by attorneys from the same firm); *U.S. v. Ruehle*, 583 F.3d 600 (9th Cir. 2009) (upholding a finding that, despite a dual attorney-client relationship with both the firm and its CFO, certain of the CFO's statements were not privileged because he could not have believed they would be kept confidential).

As *Speeney* suggests, the safest course of action is for the investigating attorney to inform the employee explicitly that the investigator is not representing him and get a signed acknowledgment of that notification. Again, this is in tension with the informal initial approach to investigation some urge, but such an explanation also avoids the risk that the employee will later attempt to claim that the conversation was privileged because the employee reasonably (if wrongly) believed the attorney to be representing him. *See generally* Sarah Helene Duggin, *Internal Corporate Investigations: Legal Ethics, Professionalism and the Employee Interview*, 2003 COLUM. BUS. L. REV. 859. Professor Duggin reproduces Judge Frederick Lacey's suggested warning for use at the outset of all employee interviews conducted as part of internal corporate investigations:

> I am not your lawyer[;] I represent the corporation. It is the corporation's interests I have been retained to serve. You are entitled to have your own lawyer. If you cannot afford a lawyer, the corporation may or may not pay his fee. You may wish to consult with him before you confer with me. Among other things, you may wish to claim the privilege against self-incrimination. You may wish not to talk to me at all.
>
> What you tell me, if it relates to the performance of your duties, and is confidential, will be privileged. The privilege, however, requires explanation. It is not your privilege to claim. It is the corporation's privilege. Thus, not only can I tell, I must tell, others in the corporation what you have told me, if it is necessary to enable me to provide the legal services to the corporation that has retained it has retained me to provide.
>
> Moreover, the corporation can waive its privilege and thus, the president, or I, or someone else, can disclose to the authorities what you tell me if the corporation decides to waive its privilege.
>
> Also, if I find wrongdoing, I am under certain obligations to report it to the Board of Directors and perhaps the stockholders.
>
> Finally, the fact that our conversation is privileged does not mean that what you did or said is protected from disclosure just because you tell me about it. You may be

subpoenaed, for example, and required to tell what you did, or said or observed, even though you told me about it.

Do you understand?

Id. at 945-46. Judge Lacey dubbed this an "Adnarim" warning — "Miranda" spelled backward. While it is not constitutionally required (certainly not outside the public sector), it is ethically required in some circumstances and will usually be good practice. Those who resist any standard warning agree that it dispels any possible confusion about the relationship of the investigator to the witness but stress the risk is that it will discourage frank disclosure by the employee. Do you think that Davis and Weaver would favor providing such a warning? Wouldn't the warning tend to raise witness defenses, especially in the first, putting-the-witness-at-ease stage they recommend? Which approach would you use?

b. The Employee as Witness or Target

In the typical internal investigation, the individuals interviewed will be current employees, although former employees and "outsiders" such as suppliers or independent contractors may sometimes be asked to provide information. With out-siders, the biggest problem for the investigator is obtaining cooperation when she has neither legal process nor a command-and-control relationship. With current employ-ees, the attorney likely has the necessary leverage to obtain cooperation, simply because the employer can require the witness' participation. That leverage, however, creates its own risks, most notably the possibility that the employee participating under compul-sion will not be truthful.

Some employees, of course, have incentives to cooperate or, at least, few disin-centives. The person alleging sexual harassment, for example, will need to cooperate because of her responsibility to take advantage of her employer's mechanisms for correcting problems. True "innocent bystanders" in the firm may see no reason not to cooperate simply because they have little stake in the dispute and cooperation will clearly be expected as part of the job. But the person accused of wrongdoing or anyone who fears that he or she will be accused or blamed by the target, has more to worry about; and coworkers, subordinates, or supervisors of targets may be concerned about the consequences for them — whichever way the investigation proceeds.

Suppose an employee has been given Judge Lacey's Adnarim warning and has concerns about either being (or becoming) a target or risking the ire of the target or of those close to him. Can the warned worker refuse to cooperate, or at least demand that an attorney be present? In the union setting, federal labor law often accords members the right to have a union representative present. *See* Michael D. Moberly & Andrea G. Lisenbee, *Honing Our* Kraft?: *Reconciling Variations in the Remedial Treatment of* Weingarten *Violations*, 21 HOFSTRA LAB. & EMP. L. J. 523 (2004). It is possible some such rights exist outside the union context, but the National Labor Relations Board has vacillated on this issue and currently does not recognize such a right. *See* Ann C. Hodges, *The Limits of Multiple Rights and Remedies: A Call for Revisiting the Law of the Workplace*, 22 HOFSTRA LAB. & EMP. L. J. 601 (2005); Christine Neylon O'Brien, *The NLRB Waffling on* Weingarten *Rights*, 37 LOY. U. CHI. L. J. 111 (2005). As a result, it is not uncommon for employers to prohibit witnesses from bringing their own representative to an investigation.

There is, of course, no legal compulsion for the employee to answer questions, and the employee could refuse to appear without her attorney. Further, at least in circumstances where criminal liability is possible (rare in sexual harassment investigation, but common in a wide range of other investigations such as investigations into embezzlement), the employee's statements—particularly untruthful or misleading ones—can be used against her in subsequent criminal proceedings. Thus, a refusal to cooperate is sometimes the employee's wisest course of conduct. *See Hopp & Flesch, LLC v. Backstreet*, 123 P.3d 1176 (Colo. 2005) (attorney did not commit malpractice by advising employee not to participate in internal investigation because her statements could be used in subsequent criminal proceedings).

On the other hand, employees who do not cooperate risk discipline or termination and likely have little legal recourse against their employer. Generally speaking, there is no exception to the at-will rule that would prevent an employer from discharging an employee who refuses to cooperate. *Merkel v. Scovill, Inc.*, 787 F.2d 174 (6th Cir. 1986); *Costello v. St. Francis Hosp.*, 258 F. Supp. 2d 144 (E.D.N.Y. 2003). Indeed, it might even be good cause sufficient to justify firing even where an employee has some preexisting right to job security. *Lybarger v. City of Los Angeles*, 206 Cal. Rptr. 727 (Ct. App. 1984).

Privacy claims are also likely unavailing since the employer's need to ascertain whether there was a violation of law or company policy will almost always trump any privacy concerns, provided the inquiry is not overly broad. These issues will be front and center in many sexual harassment investigations. Of course, limitations on how information is gathered during an investigation still apply, such as the general prohibition on polygraph tests and any constraints imposed by tort law. *See Vasarhelyi v. New School for Social Research*, 646 N.Y.S.2d 795 (App. Div. 1996) (upholding a claim for intentional infliction of emotional distress arising out of outside attorneys' investigation); *see generally* Chapters 5 and 6. Thus, an employer could be subject to claims of false imprisonment or intentional infliction of emotional distress in the case of egregious employer misconduct. *But see Jones v. Dep't of Pub. Safety & Corr.*, 923 S. 2d 699 (La. Ct. App. 2005) (upholding discharge based in part on refusal of corrections officer to take a polygraph examination as part of a sexual harassment investigation).

The one situation where an employee could have greater legal protection is in a public employment setting. While a demand for cooperation on threat of dismissal seems permissible in the private sector, there is a split in authority as to whether a public entity's threat to discharge an employee who does not cooperate means any resulting statements were inadmissible as coerced self-incrimination. *See People v. Sapp*, 934 P.2d 1367, 1374 (Colo. 1997) (if the state created a belief that employees might be discharged for asserting the privilege against self-incrimination other than by stating that a witness was expected to testify truthfully, the resulting statement cannot be used against him). *But see Debnam v. North Carolina Dep't of Correction*, 432 S.E.2d 324 (N.C. 1993) (employer did not violate employee's right against self-incrimination by terminating him for refusing to answer questions; employer was not required to affirmatively inform employee of the law of use immunity before discharging him for refusing to answer questions that could have incriminated him).

c. Employee Right to Indemnification or a Defense?

Another issue raised by Judge Lacey's suggested warning is who will pay for the attorneys' fees of an employee who does seek the advice of counsel. The Adnarim warning assures the employee of the right to counsel, but goes on, "If you cannot afford a lawyer, the corporation may or may not pay his fee." This vagueness was probably intentional since prosecutors sometimes frown on advances of legal fees and even indemnification of employees, Duggin, *supra*, at 914-15, and internal investigators therefore tend to avoid committing on this issue prior to the conclusion of the investigation. For employees who cannot afford their own counsel, corporate punting on reimbursement may be the equivalent of saying no.

At any rate, problems can arise when the employer considers whether to provide for representation. First, assume the employer decides to do so, whether or not it feels obligated to take that step. Court Rule 1.8(f) controls cases in which an attorney "accept[s] compensation for representing a client from one other than the client,"[1] and, as indicated by the recent New Jersey Supreme Court case *In re State Grand Jury Investigation*, 983 A.2d 1097 (N.J. 2009), arranging for such representation can be problematic. In that case, the state sought to disqualify attorneys representing employees of a target firm because of how the firm had arranged for representation.

After reviewing Rule 1.8(f) and other ethical rules, the court ultimately rejected disqualification on the facts before it. However, it set forth six principles to govern such situations: (1) informed consent of the client, (2) barring the payer from "directing, regulating or interfering with the lawyer's professional judgment in representing his client," (3) no current attorney-client relationship between the lawyer and the payer, (4) prohibiting the lawyer from communicating with the payer "concerning the substance of the representation of his client," (5) processing payment of all attorney invoices as the payer would for its own counsel, and (6) barring the payer from ceasing to pay "without leave of court brought on prior written notice to the lawyer and the client." *Id.* at 495-97.

Although *In re State Grand Jury Investigation* arose in the criminal context, Rule 1.8(f) presumably applies to all situations where an employer pays the litigation expenses of its workers. Thus, attorneys would be well advised to take the Court's six factors into account when entering into any such relationship.

Assuming the employer is not willing to pay for counsel, the question is whether it has an obligation to do so. Whether any employee who does retain counsel, either for the investigation itself or any subsequent proceedings against him, has a right to indemnification is a complicated question, and may depend on whether the employer is in the public or private sector. In the public sector, state statutes often set the ground rules. *See, e.g., Prado v. State*, 895 A.2d 1154 (N. J. 2006) (state statute required Attorney General to defend employees unless the Attorney General determined that challenged conduct was "not within the scope of employment," was due to "actual fraud, willful misconduct or actual malice," or would "create a conflict of interest between the State and the employee").

In the private sector, many state corporate statutes require mandatory indemnification, but they are usually limited to corporate "officers." Some statutes, however,

---

1. The rule provides:
    (f) A lawyer shall not accept compensation for representing a client from one other than the client unless:
        (1) the client gives informed consent;
        (2) there is no interference with the lawyer's independence of professional judgment or with the lawyer-client relationship; and
        (3) information relating to representation of a client is protected as required by RPC 1.6.

are broad enough to reach ordinary employees. For example, an Illinois statute provides:

> To the extent that a present or former director, officer or *employee* of a corporation has been successful, on the merits or otherwise, in the defense of any action, suit or proceeding . . . such person shall be indemnified against expenses (including attorneys' fees) actually and reasonably incurred by such person in connection therewith, if the person acted in good faith and in a manner he or she reasonably believed to be in, or not opposed to, the best interests of the corporation.

805 ILCS 5/8.75(c) (emphasis added). Other states reach similar results under common-law principles. The RESTATEMENT (SECOND) OF AGENCY, for example, would impose on a principal a duty to indemnify the agent if there is an agreement to do so. RESTATEMENT (SECOND) OF AGENCY § 438; *see also Harris v. Howard Univ., Inc.,* 28 F. Supp. 2d 1, 14 (D.D.C. 1998) (finding pursuant to university by-laws that employer was required to indemnify plaintiff vice president for acts committed in good faith but not for those attributable to gross negligence). *Cf. City of Bell v. Superior Court,* 163 Cal. Rptr. 3d 90 (Cal. App. 2013) (indemnity clause in employment agreement with city regarding civil claims was "simply a third-party indemnification agreement, which does not apply to civil actions, by or on behalf of, the City itself," and, even if the city had contracted to provide the plaintiff a defense to criminal prosecutions, such an agreement would be unenforceable, as the city has no statutory power to make such an agreement.).

But a formal agreement is not necessary. The Restatement goes on:

> (2) In the absence of terms to the contrary in the agreement of employment, the principal has a duty to indemnify the agent where the agent

Section 439 of the Restatement is even more specific, providing that a

> principal is subject to a duty to exonerate an agent who is not barred by the illegality of his conduct to indemnify him for . . . (c) payments of damages to third persons which he is required to make on account of the authorized performance of an act which constitutes a tort or a breach of contract; (d) expenses of defending actions by third persons brought because of the agent's authorized conduct, such actions being unfounded but not brought in bad faith.

The underlying notion is akin to unjust enrichment. That is, to the extent that an employee is sued for pursuing the interests of his employer, the costs of defense are ones that are expended on behalf of that employer, and the employer has been unjustly enriched to the extent the employee, not the employer, has incurred them.

Notice, however, that the Restatement's requirement to repay the costs of a defense is subject to the limitation that the agent not be "barred by the illegality of his conduct." *Id.; see also* § 440 (no duty to indemnify agent for negligent behavior, conduct known by agent to violate law, or losses resulting in no benefit to principal). Other sections of the Illinois statute *permit,* but do not *require* indemnification even if the employer is found to have committed wrong. Thus, under both state statutory and common-law indemnification, it may be critical to indemnification that the employee prevails in defending himself on the underlying claim. *See, e.g., Farmers Ins. Group v. County of Santa Clara,* 906 P.2d 440, 450-51 (Cal. 1995) (indemnification of harasser not required under state statute requiring indemnification by public employers when harassment not within employee's scope of employment and does not serve employer's interests). *See also Delay v. Rosenthal Collins Group, Inc.*, 585 F.3d 1003 (6th Cir. 2009) (state law indemnification claims not preempted when plaintiff prevailed in suit against him by the CFTC under the Commodities Exchange Act).

A further problem is whether the employer is required to *advance* attorneys' fees, as opposed to repaying such fees when they have been incurred. As a practical matter, an employer refusing to pay fees until the conclusion of the litigation will put enormous pressure on most employees, and, in complex cases, it may well result in the employee being unable to retain an attorney. Thus, where the employer and employee's interests align, it is in the employer's interest to advance fees, as in the New Jersey *Grand Jury* case, although there is little legal compulsion on employers to do so. The exception is where the obligation to indemnify stems from a contractual commitment or a provision of the company's by-laws, as is sometimes the case with officers and high-level employees. *Aleynikov v. Goldman Sachs Grp., Inc.*, CIV. 12-5994 KM, 2013 WL 5739137 (D.N.J. Oct. 22, 2013) (plaintiff entitled to advancement of legal fees and expenses for his ongoing defense of a pending state criminal case but not necessarily to indemnification for legal fees and expenses already incurred regarding the dismissal of federal criminal charges, in large part because the indemnification claim — "an ordinary claim for damages based on events already concluded — is not marked by the same urgency that infuses the advancement claim."); *see also Homestore, Inc. v. Tafeen*, 888 A.2d 204, 211-14 (Del. 2005) (upholding advancement of litigation expenses to former officer required by corporate by-laws and rejecting argument that company need not advance litigation expenses because employee personally profited by alleged wrongdoing and had taken steps that made it harder for the corporation to collect on his undertaking); *International Airport Ctrs., L.L.C. v. Citrin*, 455 F.3d 749 (7th Cir. 2006) (rejecting an employer's effort to enjoin an employee's action seeking advancement under Delaware law). Since in most cases advancement of fees is voluntary, employers may condition their commitment on an undertaking of the employee to repay the moneys advanced if he is ultimately determined to have committed wrongdoing.

Finally, it is doubtful that any of these principles would apply when an employee who seeks recovery of costs of the counsel in the course of an internal investigation. The indemnification issue is cast in terms of shifting the costs from the agent to the principal when a third party sues. While the rule might apply even in the absence of formal proceedings, such as a settlement for "nuisance value," the internal investigation pits the employee-witness against the employer, not against any third party. This is particularly true where the investigation is in response to a harassment complaint. In such instances, the employer conducts the investigation with hopes of taking corrective action that will enable it to avoid vicarious liability in a subsequent lawsuit by the complaining party.

Should the internal investigation result in the discharge of the employee, who is then sued by the third party whose complaint may have triggered the investigation, a statutory or common law right of indemnification may well apply but may be dependent upon the employee being exonerated in the course of the proceedings. Further, to the extent the former employer refuses to advance attorneys' fees and costs, the former employee will be in a very difficult situation — regardless of the theoretic right to indemnification.

The bottom line, of course, is that the employee who is interviewed during, or is even the target of, an internal investigation is often faced with a number of unpalatable alternatives. The employee can refuse to cooperate and risk discipline or dismissal; the employee can cooperate and risk discipline, dismissal, and even the use of statements she makes in later criminal proceedings against her. *See* Saul Elbeinmarch, *When Employees Confess, Sometimes Falsely*, N.Y. TIMES, Mar. 9, 2014, at BU1 (reporting an assessment of numerous suits by ex-employees of Autozone that suggest that internal investigations by investigators trained in the same high-pressure techniques as the police, can result in false confessions as employees see the alternative of discharge as more attractive than potential arrest by the police). The employee can insist on an attorney to help her decide on her course of action, and will probably (but not certainly) have the request accommodated, but she may well be responsible for the attorneys' fees involved. Should the investigation result in her discharge, she will probably have no right against her former employee, except perhaps a right to indemnification should she prevail in any suit brought against her.

PROBLEMS

13-3. You have been consulted by an individual you know slightly from the local gym. He tells you that he is a midlevel manager at the local branch of Pal-Mart, a chain of superstores. He has had some recent disagreements with a female subordinate. Yesterday, he was told by a Human Resource specialist that he was being suspended temporarily with pay pending Pal-Mart's investigation of a complaint of sexual harassment. He was told to expect a call from an attorney with a large firm in the nearby city, who would be handling the investigation.

He has not been provided any further information, but he is sure that the complaint was made by his subordinate. He wants to know how to proceed. What further questions do you have for him?

13-4. You have been retained by Pal-Mart as special counsel to investigate the matter raised in Problem 13-3. You have received a "demand letter." Sketch out your strategy for investigating the matter.

B. CONDUCTING LAYOFFS AND OBTAINING RELEASE AGREEMENTS

One important risk management technique for employers is to obtain contractual releases of liability from terminated employees. It is generally understood that employees cannot prospectively waive substantive claims under any of the federal employment statutes; such legislation would be rendered wholly inoperative if employees could be required to waive or release rights as a condition of employment. *See Alexander v. Gardner-Denver Co.*, 415 U.S. 36, 51 (1974) ("[W]e think it clear that there can be no prospective waiver of an employee's rights under Title VII."). However, once a cause of action arises, the employee may release any claims he or she may have subject to certain conditions. Effective release agreements are typically obtained by providing terminated employees with severance pay contingent upon signing a waiver of rights.

We saw a variation on this in *Watson*, where Home Depot obtained the alleged harasser's "resignation" by providing him five months of severance pay.

Such "buy outs" often occur in cases of individual terminations, and they can be notorious when high-level executives leave major companies with "golden handshakes." *See In re the Walt Disney Co. Deriv. Litig.*, 906 A.2d 27 (Del. 2006) (rejecting breach of duty claims against board of directors for decisions to hire and shortly thereafter, fire the CEO with multimillion-dollar buy-out). However, much more modest packages are particularly common in the context of large-scale reductions in force ("RIFs"). RIFs pose many legal and practical challenges for employers. Companies must ensure they do not select employees for layoff based on an impermissible criterion, such as age. In addition, they must comply with certain statutory requirements, such as providing advance notice of layoffs. For example, the federal Workers Adjustment and Retraining Act, 29 U.S.C. § 2101 et seq. (2014) ("WARN"), requires covered employers engaging in "plant closings" or "mass layoffs" to usually provide 60 days' notice to affected workers. Perhaps most importantly, employers must be cognizant that the financial, social, and emotional effects of layoffs can be devastating to the affected employees and in the case of a closing, may have repercussions throughout the community where the company is located. Even smaller-scale layoffs may negatively affect the morale and productivity of those workers who remain employed. For all of these reasons, careful advance planning can be critical in maintaining a successful working environment post-layoff as well as avoiding liability to those who are "let go."

Williams v. Phillips Petroleum Co.
23 F.3d 930 (5th Cir. 1994)

WILLIAMS, J.

[In 1992, Phillips Petroleum Company, Phillips Gas Holding Company, Inc. ("PGHC"), and Phillips 66 Company, a division of Phillips Petroleum Company, reduced their work forces at their Houston Chemical Complex ("HCC") and laid off over 500 employees at their Bartlesville, Oklahoma, location. PGHC provided the Bartlesville workers 60 days' notice prior to the reduction in force. The defendants also laid off 27 workers at several locations in Houston to whom they did not provide notice. Six of the laid off Houston workers (the "original plaintiffs") brought suit alleging that defendants had violated WARN by failing to provide 60 days' notice. Subsequently, four of the workers laid off from the Bartlesville location (the "Bartlesville plaintiffs") sought to join the suit. All of the original and Bartlesville plaintiffs signed releases in connection with their terminations in exchange for what the employer described as enhanced layoff benefits. The district court refused to permit joinder of the Bartlesville plaintiffs and awarded summary judgment to the employer on the original plaintiffs' claims.]

III

A

The district court rendered summary judgment because no mass layoff occurred at the single sites of employment where the original plaintiffs worked. . . .

WARN requires covered employers to provide "affected employees" notice of a mass layoff. "Affected employees" include "employees who may reasonably be expected to experience an employment loss as a consequence of a proposed plant closing or mass layoff by their employer." 29 U.S.C. § 2101(a)(5). A "mass layoff" is defined as any employment loss at a single site of employment that involves one-third of the employees at that site and at least fifty employees, or at least 500 employees. 29 U.S.C. § 2101(a)(3); 20 C.F.R. § 639.3(c). If a "mass layoff" occurs, the employer must provide written notice to each affected employee at least sixty days prior to the layoff and inform various state and local officials of the mass layoff. 29 U.S.C. § 2102. An employer who violates WARN is liable for back pay, lost benefits, civil penalties, and attorneys' fees. 29 U.S.C. § 2104.

The statute does not define a "single site of employment." The rules promulgated by the Secretary of Labor provide that "[n]on-contiguous sites in the same geographic area which do not share the same staff or operational purpose should not be considered a single site." 20 C.F.R. § 639.3(i)(4). . . .

The Houston and Bartlesville layoffs cannot be aggregated to bootstrap the Houston plaintiffs over the WARN minimum required for a mass layoff. . . . It is not plausible, under any reasonable or good-faith reading of the regulations, that the Houston and Bartlesville plants — located in different states and hundreds of miles apart — could be considered a "single site" for purposes of WARN.

Employees were not rotated between the different sites, and the locations did not share staff and equipment. *See* 20 C.F.R. § 639.3(i)(3). No other "unusual circumstances" have been alleged that would support classifying the two plants as a "single site." *See* 20 C.F.R. § 639.3(i)(8); *Carpenters Dist. Counsel of New Orleans v. Dillard*, 15 F.3d 1275, 1290 (5th 1994). . . . The Bartlesville layoffs, accordingly, are irrelevant to the issue of whether the Houston employees were entitled to notice under WARN.

No mass layoff occurred at the single sites of employment where the original plaintiffs worked. Five of the plaintiffs worked at HCC's operations in three different locations in and around Houston. HCC laid off twenty-seven employees over a ten-month period. One of the named plaintiffs worked for PGHC in Houston; PGHC laid off eight employees who worked at that site. The layoffs at HCC and PGHC were not mass layoffs as defined by the Act, as the number of employees laid off did not meet the fifty-employee minimum. Thus, the Houston employees were not entitled to WARN notification. . . .

B

The district court also rendered summary judgment for Phillips because the plaintiffs had signed releases covering the allegations made in their complaint. . . . [2] Normally the release of federal claims is governed by federal law. *See, e.g., O'Hare v. Global Natural Resources, Inc.*, 898 F.2d 1015, 1017 (5th Cir. 1990) (Age Discrimination in Employment Act ("ADEA")); *Rogers v. General Elec. Co.*, 781 F.2d 452, 454 (5th Cir. 1986) (title VII of the Civil Rights Act of 1964). Public policy favors voluntary settlement of claims and enforcement of releases, *Rogers*, but a release of an employment

---

2. Although this discussion is unnecessary to the issue of whether WARN was violated, given our holding in part III.A., *supra*, we include it as a further indication that this action is frivolous.

or employment discrimination claim is valid only if it is "knowing" and "voluntary," *Alexander v. Gardner-Denver Co.*, 415 U.S. 36, 52 n.15 (1974). Once a party establishes that his opponent signed a release that addresses the claims at issue, received adequate consideration, and breached the release, the opponent has the burden of demonstrating that the release was invalid because of fraud, duress, material mistake, or some other defense. We examine the totality of circumstances to determine whether the releasor has established an appropriate defense. *O'Hare.*

1.

Each original plaintiff signed a release shortly after his or her termination of employment. The releases stated that signing the release was a condition to participation in the company's enhanced supplemental layoff pay plan, advised the employee to consult an attorney, gave ample time to consider the release, and specifically covered all claims relating to the individual's employment or layoff. The Bartlesville plaintiffs signed similar releases.

The requirements of WARN pertain to an individual's employment and termination, issues addressed in the releases. Phillips provided enhanced benefits for those employees who signed the releases. These benefits were in addition to the basic severance plan benefits that the employees would have received regardless of whether they had signed the releases. The original plaintiffs are making claims on matters addressed in their release, and the Bartlesville plaintiffs attempted to join the lawsuit that involved claims on matters addressed in their release. Thus, all elements of a valid release are present.

Williams has provided no credible evidence that the releases were obtained by fraud or duress. There is no genuine issue of material fact that the releases were valid.

Williams contends that the releases were invalid because they did not mention WARN. This argument is meritless. There is no obligation under WARN or the common law for the defendants to mention WARN for the releases to be valid. The releases stated that they included all claims relating to the "time of my employment or to my layoff. . . ." WARN applies to layoffs and the releases addressed all claims related to the plaintiffs' layoffs; thus, the releases barred WARN claims. *See Fair v. International Flavors & Fragrances, Inc.*, 905 F.2d 1114, 1117 (7th Cir. 1990) (holding that a release of claims relating to employment barred claim under Employee Retirement and Income Security Act of 1974 ("ERISA")).

Plaintiffs also argue that the waivers did not comply with the Older Workers Benefit Protection Act ("OWBPA"), 29 U.S.C. § 626(f). Plaintiffs have asserted no age discrimination claim, and their proffered analogy between WARN and the ADEA does not survive scrutiny. The OWBPA places specific requirements on waivers of age discrimination claims in order for them to be considered knowing and voluntary. This statute is a change from the common law, and there is no similar obligation imposed on employers under WARN.

Williams contends that the waivers are invalid under a totality of the circumstances test. She claims that the combination of five factors makes the waivers invalid, but she identifies no precedent suggesting that these factors are dispositive. Williams carried the burden to demonstrate that there was a genuine issue of material fact on a defense to the validity of the releases. She was obligated to produce some evidence of fraud, duress, or other basis for holding the release invalid. She has not done so, thus summary judgment was appropriate.

Even if we accept Williams's statement of the totality of circumstances test, she cannot prevail. She identifies several elements to consider: (1) a plaintiff's education and business experience; (2) the role of each plaintiff and class member in deciding the terms of the release; (3) the clarity of the agreement and all related documents referred to in the releases; (4) whether each plaintiff and class member was represented by or consulted with an attorney; and (5) the amount of time each plaintiff and class member had possession of or access to the release before signing it.

Concerning the plaintiffs' education and business experience, there [is] no evidence suggesting that they could not read or understand the releases. The cases relied upon by the plaintiffs are distinguishable by whether the individual who signed the release understood the claims released. There is nothing in the record establishing a genuine issue of material fact that the plaintiffs did not know what they were doing.

Plaintiffs argue that none of them negotiated the terms of the releases. There is no evidence that plaintiffs were denied an opportunity to negotiate, nor that they were given a "take it or leave it" offer. The releases informed each employee that he should consult a lawyer and allowed a reasonable period, in most instances up to forty-five days, to consider the releases. The plaintiffs signed the releases and never asserted in their declarations that Phillips had precluded them from negotiating. There is no evidence sufficient to create a genuine issue of material fact.

The releases were clear, simple, and easily understood. The release precluded all claims related to the plaintiffs' "employment" or "layoff." This is not technical jargon, and it covers the plaintiffs' WARN claims. The plaintiffs do not indicate what provisions could have been incomprehensible to them, as they were written in plain English. There is also no evidence of duress that could have forced them to sign involuntarily.

The plaintiffs also claim that the releases should be invalidated because the defendants presented no evidence that each plaintiff and class member actually consulted with an attorney. The releases signed by the plaintiffs stated:

> You should thoroughly review and understand the effect of the release before signing it. To the extent that you have any claims covered by this release, you will be waiving potentially valuable rights by signing. You are also advised to discuss this release with your lawyer.

Thus, defendants advised the plaintiffs to consult a lawyer. Plaintiffs suggest that Phillips should have offered to supply a lawyer, but they offer no authority imposing this duty. Even without signing the releases, plaintiffs were entitled to substantial layoff benefits that could have been used to finance a lawyer, either individually or jointly. It is not Phillips's fault that the plaintiffs chose not to consult a lawyer after being advised to do so. Plaintiffs do not contest the final element of the test, as they were given as much as forty-five days to consider the releases.

2.

Even if a release is tainted by misrepresentation or duress, it is ratified if the releasor retains the consideration after learning that the release is voidable. A person who signs a release, then sues his or her employer for matters covered under the release, is obligated to return the consideration. Offering to tender back the consideration after obtaining relief in the lawsuit would be insufficient to avoid a finding of ratification. *Grillet v. Sears, Roebuck & Co.*, 927 F.2d 217, 220-21 (5th Cir. 1991).

For signing the releases, the original plaintiffs as a group received $ 210,853.65 in consideration in an enhanced plan benefits and $56,632.38 in basic plan benefits. The original plaintiffs did not return the consideration to the defendants, even after making claims that the releases were voidable. Thus, the plaintiffs ratified the releases even if, *arguendo*, they were not knowingly and voluntarily signed. *Grillet.* . . .

NOTES

1. *A Tale of Several Regimes.* Understanding when a release agreement is effective depends on the applicable legal standard, which varies depending on the substantive claim being released. *Williams* deals with the standard for the validity of releases under WARN, a federal statute that does not deal explicitly with requirements for releasing claims. In upholding the plaintiffs' releases, the court applies a general "knowing and voluntary standard," which it drew from a Title VII case, *Alexander v. Gardner-Denver Co.*, 415 U.S. 36, 52, n.15 (1974). This test, elaborated in a variety of ways by the lower courts, applies to WARN, Title VII, the Americans with Disabilities Act ("ADA"), the Family and Medical Leave Act ("FMLA"), and ERISA.

In contrast, some statutes — most notably the ADEA — contain provisions directly governing release agreements or have been interpreted to impose special requirements. *Williams* alludes to, but declines to apply, the more demanding regime that exists under the Older Workers Benefit Protection Act. OWBPA is a 1991 amendment to the ADEA, which requires that a release be "knowing and voluntary" and that, "at a minimum," the employer comply with a variety of procedural requirements including:

(A) the waiver is part of an agreement between the individual and the employer that is written in a manner calculated to be understood by such individual, or by the average individual eligible to participate;

(B) the waiver specifically refers to rights or claims arising under this chapter;

(C) the individual does not waive rights or claims that may arise after the date the waiver is executed;

(D) the individual waives rights or claims only in exchange for consideration in addition to anything of value to which the individual already is entitled;

(E) the individual is advised in writing to consult with an attorney prior to executing the agreement;

(F) (i) the individual is given a period of at least 21 days within which to consider the agreement; or

(ii) if a waiver is requested in connection with an exit incentive or other employment termination program offered to a group or class of employees, the individual is given a period of at least 45 days within which to consider the agreement;

(G) the agreement provides that for a period of at least 7 days following the execution of such agreement, the individual may revoke the agreement, and the agreement shall not become effective or enforceable until the revocation period has expired. . . .

29 U.S.C. §626(f)(1). More specific disclosures are also required "if a waiver is requested in connection with an exit incentive or other employment termination program offered to a group or class of employees," *id.* at (H), and the statute has particular provisions governing settlement once an EEOC charge or suit has been filed. *Id.* at §626(f)(2). Even more protective of employees is the Fair Labor Standards Act, which generally deems waivers and settlement of claims unenforceable without Department of Labor supervision. *See* Evan Hudson-Plush, Note, *WARN's Place in the FLSA/Employment Discrimination Dichotomy: Why a Warning Cannot Be Waived*, 27 CARDOZO L. REV. 2929, 2945-48 (2006).

Finally, where the underlying claims involve only state law, a release is likely to be subjected to an even lower level of scrutiny than would be true under the general "knowing and voluntary" standard applied in *Williams* under WARN. Most likely, the validity of such releases would be determined as a matter of ordinary contract law, although state-to-state variations are possible depending in part on the right at issue.

2. *Comparing Standards: "Knowing and Voluntary" versus Common Law.* Invalidating a release agreement under basic contract principles can be quite difficult. The requisite consideration and assent are generally present and easy to establish: The employer provides severance or other benefits in exchange for the release, and both parties typically sign a written agreement. The only way for an employee to void the contract is to demonstrate a defense like fraud or duress. And, as the "tender back" discussion in *Williams* indicates, exercising a right to void a contract may require the return of the consideration received.

While a few federal courts treat the enforceability of releases as a matter of normal contract principles, the vast majority apply some version of a "totality of the circumstances" test to all non-OWBPA claims to determine whether a waiver is knowing and voluntary where federal statutory rights are at stake. That test looks to a number of factors, as one commentator explains:

> To determine whether a person's consent is knowing and voluntary under the totality of the circumstances, courts apply a list of factors: the person's education and business experience, the person's role in determining the release's provisions, the release's clarity and specificity, the time the person had to review and consider the release, whether the person read the release and considered its terms before signing it, whether the person knew or should have known his or her rights upon executing the release, whether the person was represented by an attorney or had other independent advice, whether there was consideration for the release, and whether the person's consent was induced by improper conduct by the employer, including whether the employer encouraged or discouraged the person from consulting with an attorney. This list is not exhaustive, and the absence of any one factor is not dispositive. The factors are not to be treated as a checklist, and courts do not insist on rigid adherence to them.

Daniel P. O'Gorman, *A State of Disarray: The "Knowing and Voluntary" Standard for Releasing Claims Under Title VII of the Civil Rights Act of 1964*, 8 U. PA. J. LAB. & EMP. L. 73, 85-88 (2005). *See also* Daniel P. O'Gorman, *Show Me the Money: The Applicability of Contract Law's Ratification and Tender-Back Doctrines to Title VII Releases*, 84 TUL. L. REV. 675, 728 (2010); Craig Robert Senn, *Knowing and Voluntary Waivers of Federal Employment Claims: Replacing the Totality of Circumstances Test with a "Waiver Certainty" Test*, 58 FLA. L. REV. 305 (2006). Which standard does *Williams* apply? Contract? Totality of the circumstances? Something in between?

3. *Comparing Standards: "Knowing and Voluntary" versus OWBPA.* There is obviously a large overlap between the factors used in the knowing and voluntary standard and the requirements OWBPA prescribes, but OWBPA is harder-edged. For example, while one factor under the knowing and voluntary test is the time the employee had to consider the release, OWBPA requires a minimum of 21/45 days and also prescribes a week's "cooling off" period for revocation. Courts have tended to require strict compliance with OWBPA. *See Am. Airlines, Inc. v. Cardoza-Rodriguez,* 133 F.3d 111 (1st Cir. 1998) (invalidating release for failure to explicitly advise employees to consult an attorney).

From a positivist perspective, it is easy to explain why ADEA claims are subject to more stringent requirements than claims under most other federal statutes — Congress so provided. But what justifies OWBPA's imposition of these highly specialized criteria? In other words, what is so special about releases of age discrimination claims in general and releases of such claims following an RIF in particular? Should comparable requirements be placed on other types of waivers, such as those in *Williams,* or ordinary severance agreements? What about waivers of procedural rights, like the right to a jury trial or agreements to shorten applicable statutes of limitations? We will revisit this last question when we look at pre-dispute arbitration agreements in the next section.

4. *Back to the Common Law.* Despite the development of specialized standards, the common law is not entirely irrelevant to assessing a release either under the knowing and voluntary standard or under OWBPA. For example, both incorporate the requirement of "consideration," and all releases are subject to contractual defenses. Note that *Williams* considers and rejects the applicability of the defenses of fraud and duress. The presence of undue influence, *see Odorizzi v. Bloomfield School Dist.,* 54 Cal. Rptr. 533 (Ct. App. 1966), unconscionability, *see* discussion on page 1015, or mistake could negate a release as well. These defenses may be relevant even in the ADEA context since OWBPA provides a floor, not a ceiling, and it is possible that an employer could comply with the letter of the statutory obligations but still mislead or over-persuade the employee in a way that triggers a common law contract defense. But, as the *Williams* court stresses, the common law places the burden of persuasion on the party challenging the release. Once the employer shows offer and acceptance and consideration, the contract is established, albeit subject to the employee proving some invalidating factor. In contrast, under the OWBPA, the burden is on the employer to demonstrate its compliance with the statutory requirements.

Contract is also an appropriate source of law for interpreting and applying a release agreement. Assuming the agreement is valid pursuant to the appropriate standard, contract principles will determine whether the release covers a particular claim, the terms of the employer's payment commitment, and other issues about scope and application of the agreement. *See, e.g., Riley v. American Family Mutual Ins.,* 881 F.2d 368, 373 (7th Cir. 1989) (finding it "unnecessary to create a distinct federal body of law" to interpret release agreement where "plain reading" indicated plaintiff had persevered only state administrative discrimination charge and waived right to *de novo* review by federal court). In cases of high-level employees, some of whom sign written agreements that cover issues of severance and layoff at the outset of employment, a release can raise contract interpretation questions similar to those explored in Chapter 3, such as whether termination was for cause or whether other contractual contingencies have been triggered. *See, e.g., Dell Computer Corp. v. Rodriguez,* 390 F.3d 377 (5th Cir. 2004) (parol evidence should be admitted to determine whether prior wrongdoing of CEO permitted employer to withhold stock under separation agreement).

5. *What About Bargaining Power?* In *Williams*, the plaintiffs, unable to prove fraud or duress, urged that their releases should be void in light of their lack of sophistication, limited education, and inability to negotiate vis-à-vis the employer. Why do you think the Fifth Circuit rejects this line of argument? Is the court rejecting the contention that the "totality of the circumstances" test applies to waivers of WARN rights? Or is it concluding that the plaintiffs failed to make their case under that standard? At one point, the court disparages the contention that the release agreement was a "take it or leave it offer," finding no evidence to support this claim. Is the court suggesting that the employees had more power to bargain than they realized? It seems unlikely that Phillips would have negotiated different terms with different employees, but that is not impossible. Is the court implicitly stating that the ability to dicker over terms is important to the validity of a contract? Or is the court simply unsympathetic to the plaintiffs given that they stood to gain $2 million in additional compensation and benefits under the release? Could an argument like the one advanced by the plaintiffs work in the OWBPA context, assuming the technical requirements of the statute have been satisfied?

6. *The Two-way Release.* While the main benefit for workers of signing a release is severance pay, there are sometimes other advantages, as where the release is reciprocal (waiving claims by the employer against the employee) or where it supersedes past agreements imposing duties on the employee. In *Avery Dennison Corp., v. Naimo*, 25 IER Cases 690 (N.D. Ill. 2006), the parties entered into an agreement terminating their employment relationship; the writing contained a merger clause stating that it superseded all prior agreements, including the employee's written employment agreement, which contained a 12-month noncompete. On the basis of that clause, a court dismissed the employer's subsequent attempt to enforce the noncompete against the employee, who began contacting former customers post-termination. The lesson for employers, as always, is to carefully read all the relevant documents. The employer in *Avery* most likely sought to merge the prior employment contract into the separation agreement in order to avoid any future employee claims to salary or benefits it owed during employment; in the process it failed to consider the prior contract's noncompetition clause. *Avery* also offers a reminder to employees. Getting laid off is difficult enough without a noncompete hampering one's prospects of re-employment. The presentation of a termination agreement is a good time to try to secure other benefits besides severance, such as a release from such commitments.

7. *"Good" Releases Crowding out "Bad" Ones.* Although *Williams* holds that OWBPA does not control outside the ADEA, risk-averse employers are well advised to satisfy the more demanding standards of OWBPA whenever they seek releases. Most releases, therefore, are structured along OWBPA lines. As a practical matter, this allows the employer to develop a single standardized release agreement and set of procedures that human resources personnel can use in all cases, without having to make individual judgments about whether a particular termination might implicate the ADEA. In addition, abiding by the OWBPA requirements provides enhanced certainty that the release will hold up if challenged since any release that satisfies OWBPA is almost certain to satisfy other tests. For employees, this means that those offered a release will have the opportunity to review, consider, and even revoke their agreement, effectively reaping the benefits of the OWBPA irrespective of whether they raise ADEA claims or are even protected by the statute. *See, e.g., Neely v. Good Samaritan Hosp.*, 345 F. App'x 39 (6th Cir. 2009) (release that granted worker time to consider the agreement consistent with OWBPA was properly revoked by race discrimination plaintiff notwithstanding fact that she never raised age discrimination claim).

8. *Ratification and Tendering Back. Williams* states that even if a release is subject to a valid contract defense, the employee will "ratify" the agreement if she retains the benefits of the agreement (the severance pay) despite learning the release is voidable. In short, a plaintiff who seeks to challenge a release must tender back the consideration received where only the knowing and voluntary standard governs. In contrast, ratification is not possible under OWBPA if the release is inadequate; there is therefore no need to tender back the consideration received in order to file an ADEA suit. *See Oubre v. Entergy Operations*, 522 U.S. 422, 427 (1998) (rejecting any requirement of ratification or requiring return of consideration: any such rule "would frustrate the statute's practical operation as well as its formal command" since discharged employees will often have spent the money received and therefore be unable to tender back).

9. *Waivers of Administrative Rights.* Although employees can release their rights to sue under the federal discrimination laws, including the ADEA where the OWBPA waiver requirements are met, employees may not release their rights to file administrative charges with the EEOC. *See* 29 U.S.C. § 629(f)(4); *EEOC v. Cosmair, Inc.*, 821 F.2d 1085 (5th 1987) (waiver of right to file administrative charges, if covered by employee's release, would be void against public policy). Why are releases of administrative claims so objectionable, particularly if the waiver complies with the stringent requirements of the OWBPA? What public policies are at stake with such releases that are not implicated by the employee's promise not to sue?

For employers, the distinction between waivers of legal and administrative rights is an important one. To the extent a release provision purports to waive administrative rights, that clause is generally considered void, and the employer may not treat the filing of an administrative charge as a breach of the agreement. The effect of such a provision on the rest of the release, however, is unclear. *Compare Wastak v. Lehigh Valley Health Network*, 342 F.3d 281, 292 (3d Cir. 2003) (finding administrative rights waiver severable and employee's promise not to sue enforceable notwithstanding the invalid clause) *with Bogacz v. MTP Prods., Inc.*, 694 F. Supp. 2d 400, 406 (W.D. Pa. 2010) (suggesting that release containing such a waiver of administrative rights could be misleading and therefore not knowing and voluntary under OWBPA regulations). Employers are increasingly dealing with this possibility by explicitly providing in their releases that signatories continue to have a right to file charges with relevant agencies.

10. *Will Uncle Sam Foot Part of the Bill?* From an employee's perspective, a question that often arises is whether a settlement can be structured to reduce the tax consequences, especially where large amounts are paid out in a given year. Other than stretching payouts over several years to avoid pushing the employee into a higher income bracket, the answer is usually no. Severance pay, like the wages it replaces, is taxable. Indeed, the Internal Revenue Code, 26 U.S.C § 104(a)(2) (2014), generally excludes from gross income only "the amount of any damages received (whether by suit or agreement) on account of personal injuries or sickness. As a result, not only severance but most employment-related recoveries — back pay, front pay, recoveries for emotional harm, etc. — became taxable. Only in a few instances, for example, physical assault or physical sexual harassment, may it be possible to characterize some or all of the settlement in such a way as to exclude it from taxable income. Further, the employee's attorney should alert her client that if proceeds of a settlement are taxable, the employer may legally withhold taxes on any payment made. *Rivera v. Baker West, Inc.*, 430 F.3d 1253 (9th Cir. 2005).

Taxation issues also loom large where attorney's fees are involved. Until recently, these were taxable to the employee as income, *Comm'r of Internal Revenue v. Banks*, 543 U.S. 426 (2005); although such fees were usually deductible, limitations on deductions and the Alternative Minimum Tax often meant that employees paid taxes on the fees they recovered after litigation or upon settlement and on the fees paid to their attorney. Adam Liptak, *Tax Bill Exceeds Award to Officer in Sex Bias Suit*, N.Y. TIMES, Aug. 11, 2002, §1, p. 18. Congress responded to this problem in the American Jobs Creation Act of 2004, which amended 26 U.S.C. §62 (19) to allow deduction of fees and costs, whether received in litigation or settlement, free of the restrictions that earlier applied.

PROBLEM

13-5. Harold Brown was a 59-year-old district sales manager for AMF Bowling Products Group. After 26 years of service, he was offered early retirement. Harold requested and was given the opportunity to take the offer to an attorney. After consultation, he accepted the offer by executing the following "Severance Agreement":

I. Resignation

I, HAROLD BROWN do voluntarily submit my resignation from AMF Bowling Products effective August 1.

II. Severance Payout

Based on 1.5 weeks of pay per completed year of service, severance pay will total $30,581. (37.5 weeks). . . .

III. Waiver

I, HAROLD BROWN, accept the severance entitlement outlined above and understand that this represents the entire severance entitlement and no other provisions are express or implied. I accept the terms and conditions of this entitlement and release AMF from any outstanding obligations or litigation in this matter.

Harold has come to believe that he was pushed to resign because of his age and would like to pursue litigation. How would you advise him on the question whether the above agreement precludes suit? Besides possible procedural defects under the OWBPA, do you see any contract-based arguments for challenging the agreement?

Note on Employer Obligations and Exceptions Under WARN

As *Williams* makes clear, an employer contemplating a RIF must take a number of specific procedural steps in planning and executing a layoff. While an effective release will cover a multitude of legal mistakes, employers must first attempt to comply with the governing statutory requirements. With respect to WARN, the first question is whether a proposed action requires notice. Determining whether WARN's notice provisions are triggered often turns on a number of technical questions. Generally speaking, WARN requires employers with 100 or more employees to provide 60 days' notice to affected employees in the event of a mass layoff or plant closing. As *Williams* demonstrates, whether an RIF constitutes a "mass layoff" at "a single site" may result in litigation. This can generate difficult problems of who counts as laid off. *Compare Collins v. Gee W. Seattle LLC*, 631 F.3d 1001 (9th Cir. 2011) (a business shutdown qualified under WARN even though fewer than 30 employees remained when the company closed when some 120 employees had left after an announcement that the plant would likely be closing; such employees had not "voluntarily departed" within the meaning of the statute), *with Ellis v. DHL Express Inc. (USA)*, 633 F.3d 522 (7th Cir. 2011) (employees who accepted a union-negotiated severance agreement were "voluntary departures" not to be counted towards WARN's triggering requirement). While Phillips Petroleum engaged in a "mass layoff" at its Oklahoma location, its layoffs in Houston did not meet the statutory minimum. *Cf. Davis v. Signal Int'l Texas GP, LLC*, 728 F.3d 482 (5th Cir. 2013) (two facilities constituted a "single site" of employment because they were one of the "truly unusual organizational situations" within the Labor Department regulation due to regular sharing of staff and similar organizational purposes).

Another common area of WARN litigation is the various exceptions to its notice requirement, two of which tend to recur often. First, in the case of a plant closing, an employer is excused from the 60-day requirement where providing notice would impede its ability to obtain capital or business that would enable the employer to avoid the closing. Second, in the case of both plant closings and layoffs, an employer is excused from the 60-day requirement where the closing or layoff is due to business circumstances that were not reasonably foreseeable; the employer, however, must still provide whatever notice is reasonable in the circumstances. A high-profile example of a layoff implicating the latter exception is *Roquet v. Arthur Andersen*, 398 F.3d 585 (7th Cir 2005). Workers who lost their jobs following the Department of Justice's indictment of Arthur Andersen in connection with the 2001 collapse of Enron brought suit against the accounting firm alleging violations of WARN in failing to provide them with advance notice of their layoffs. Arthur Andersen defended by arguing that the DOJ indictment and subsequent demise of the firm were not reasonably foreseeable. The plaintiffs countered that, once the DOJ began investigating Arthur Andersen in the wake of the Enron scandal, the firm should have known that it would lose business and need to massively reduce staff. In a divided decision, the Seventh Circuit found for the defendant:

> [T]he Department of Labor has provided some guidance regarding when the "unforeseen business circumstances" exception applies. . . . A business circumstance may be reasonably unforeseeable if it was caused by some sudden, dramatic, and unexpected action, or by conditions outside the employer's control. 20 C.F.R. § 639.9(b)(1).

When determining whether a mass layoff was caused by unforeseeable business circumstances, courts evaluate whether a similarly situated employer exercising reasonable judgment could have foreseen the circumstances that caused the layoff. *Id.* § 639.9(b)(2). Thus, a company will not be liable if, when confronted with potentially devastating occurrences, it reacts the same way that other reasonable employers within its own market would react.

The parties dispute whether Andersen established either element of the exception — causation and foreseeability. The district court concluded that the need for mass layoffs was caused by the public announcement of the indictment on March 14. We agree. Up until then, Andersen suffered no marked loss of business despite a spate of negative publicity. It is clear that economic hemorrhaging really did not begin until word of the indictment got out. The plaintiffs contend that Andersen's felonious misconduct caused the layoffs, not the indictment. But, while it is true that the illegal acts of some Andersen employees were the root cause of the firm's ultimate downfall, not until the indictment became public did it feel the pain. . . .

In determining whether a crippling business circumstance is foreseeable, we must bear in mind that "it is the 'probability of occurrence that makes a business circumstance "reasonably foreseeable,"' rather than the 'mere possibility of such a circumstance.'" The layoffs began on April 23, which means that Andersen was required to notify employees 60 days earlier, or February 22. The plaintiffs argue that the indictment was reasonably foreseeable on that date because "the DOJ disclosed to Andersen that an indictment was highly probable." But the record does not support this position. . . . Indeed, as of February 22 it was not a foregone conclusion that Andersen would be indicted as a company — in the past, the government typically went after culpable individuals, not companies as a whole. By all accounts, this was an unusual move by the DOJ. There is evidence in the record suggesting that Andersen could have reasonably foreseen the indictment by March 1 — the date it was told by the DOJ that it was being indicted. But hope still remained that the dreaded act could be stalled if not avoided.

Id. at 588-89. The court also noted that requiring notice under such circumstances could lead fragile companies to lay off workers prematurely rather than fighting to stay afloat. *Id.* at 589-90.

The dissent disagreed on the court's view of the facts and the law. It concluded that, while the firm could not have foreseen layoffs on February 22, it should have known that an RIF was coming when the DOJ informed it on March 1 of the likelihood of an indictment. The dissent found that Arthur Andersen should have at least been obligated to give notice as of that date and accused the majority of "tak[ing] an all-or-nothing approach — if 60 days' notice is impossible, then no notice at all is required," inconsistent with the statute. *Id.* at 591; *see also Pearce v. Faurecia Exhaust Sys., Inc.*, 29 F. App'x 454 (6th Cir. 2013) (when layoffs were caused by the bankruptcy of the employer's primary customer, defense of "unforeseeable business circumstances" applied); *In re Flexible Flyer Liquidating Trust*, 511 F. App'x 369 (5th Cir. 2013) (the sudden termination of all funding by lenders "presents a convincing example of an event that meets the unforeseeable business circumstance exception"); *USW Local 2660 v. U.S. Steel Corp.*, 683 F.3d 882 (8th Cir. 2012) (unforeseeable business circumstances exception applied when a mass layoff resulted from an unanticipated and dramatic major economic downturn, and the employer exercised commercially reasonable business judgment to continue operations for a period before concluding that "idling" an iron ore plant was necessary). *But see Sides v. Macon Cnty. Greyhound Park, Inc.*, 725 F.3d 1276, 1283-84 (11th Cir. 2013) (employer not within the unforeseeable business circumstance defense when it did not provide any notice to affected employees; media coverage of closures and company's use of Internet and billboards to publicize closure did not constitute adequate notice).

Arthur Andersen is not the only high-profile WARN case. *See* Sara Randazzo, *Dewey Settles Layoff Claims for $4.5 Million*, WSJ Law Blog, June 12, 2014, available at http://blogs.wsj.com/law/2014/06/12/dewey-settles-layoff-claims-for-4-5-million/ (reporting proposed settlement of claims against the former Dewey & LeBoeuf law firm stemming from its 2012 collapse).

Remedies under WARN are limited. The goal of the statute is not job protection as such; it seeks merely to provide employees with a window of time to plan for the disruption of a layoff, begin searching for new employment, and if necessary, obtain new skills. Consequently, an employee can receive only the wages and benefits to which he or she would otherwise have been entitled for each day of the violation (up to 60 days). *See Bledsoe v. Emery Worldwide Airlines, Inc.*, 635 F.3d 836 (6th Cir. 2011) (WARN remedy of back pay is equitable inasmuch as it is intended to restore wages and benefits employees were entitled to receive in lieu of 60-day notice of layoff, and therefore plaintiffs had no right to a jury trial). For the employer who might have to pay this amount to each worker in a mass layoff, the stakes are high. In addition, employers who violate WARN may, in some instances, be assessed a daily statutory penalty. 29 U.S.C. § 2104.

Note on Managing the Risk of Systemic Discrimination Claims in Planning a RIF

One of the most significant concerns of employers conducting a reduction in force is the risk of liability under discrimination laws. Particularly in large-scale layoffs, systemic claims may potentially be brought by class action. For these reasons, employers are well advised to carefully review the criteria they use in selecting employees for layoff. The employer must ensure not only that its managers do not intentionally base layoff decisions on protected status, but also that neutral criteria do not disparately impact workers with protected status, or, if they do, that the disparity can be legitimately explained by other business considerations. One group of practitioners offers the following checklist:

. . . II. Create and Document the Layoff Plan

A. Articulate and document economic and other business justifications for the layoff. If an employee files a wrongful layoff case, this documentation will lay the foundation for the employer's case. . . .

C. Articulate and document the basis for determining the number of positions the employer will cut in each work unit.

1. Determine the positions and skills within each work unit which the employer must retain to achieve its articulated business goals. This assessment should precede, and should not take into account, an assessment of the skills of the individual incumbents.

2. Establish criteria for determining which positions an employer will eliminate within a work unit to achieve articulated business goals.

D. Standardize the methodology and criteria for selecting individuals for layoff.

1. Use objective criteria to the extent possible. . . .

3. Define the method by which the employer will determine the relative ranking of employees for layoff purposes. [I]t is inadvisable to rely solely on past performance evaluations because these are likely to be written in highly complementary terms and are not designed for comparing employees on the skills, knowledge and abilities required for post-RIF jobs. Rather, it is more sensible to prepare special assessment ratings in connection with layoff selection which assess relative skills, knowledge, abilities and other qualifications. . . .

5. Accurately document the legitimate business factors that justify the particular layoff decision, e.g., comparative seniority, experience, performance evaluations and elimination of tasks performed by incumbent. . . .

V. Review the Tentative Layoff

A. Conduct an adverse impact analysis of the tentative layoff list by race, sex and appropriate age bands under the attorney-client privilege. . . .

C. Review the impending layoff in light of the following questions:

1. Are WARN Act notices necessary?

2. Will the layoff breach employment contracts (express contracts or promises implied from oral assurances, length of service, commendations or salary increases), the covenant of good faith and fair dealing, employee handbooks, labor contracts, layoff policies or past practices?

3. Will the layoff impact whistleblowers, complainers or persons about to vest in pension or retiree health benefits or violate other public policies?

4. Will the reduction in force affect workers on pregnancy leave, family leave or medical leave?

5. Is collective bargaining necessary?

Ethan Lipsig et al., *Planning and Implementing Reductions in Force*, C922 ALI-ABA 1165, 1231-36 (1994). As a practical matter, an employer that plans to obtain OWBPA releases will necessarily have to take some of these steps in order to provide the requisite disclosures to employees. In addition to its procedural requirements, OWBPA provides that where "an exit incentive or other employment termination program [is] offered to a group or class of employees," the employer must provide each employee with information about all employees eligible for the incentive or program, including their ages and job titles. The purpose of this provision is to give employees adequate information on which to determine whether it is in their interest to waive potential substantive claims. In effect, OWBPA thus ensures a kind of pre-suit discovery to would-be plaintiffs. Although employers may dislike the provision for this reason, compliance can be useful from a risk management perspective. As the excerpt suggests, culling this information may alert the employer in advance to possible liability risks raised by the statistical composition of its selected class of workers.

Employers who run into trouble in conducting a layoff tend to be those who fail to employ objective criteria, fail to apply such criteria consistently, or fail to document their layoff procedure. Consider the court's description of the RIF selection process in

Oberg v. Allied Van Lines, Inc., 1996 U.S. Dist. LEXIS 4717 (N.D. Ill. April 11, 1996):

> In advance [of the RIF Allied's parent company] sent two of its top ranking personnel managers to interview every manager at Allied. After doing so, these two officials developed a blueprint for the reductions which was carried out by Allied management.
>
> Allied thereafter launched a selection procedure in connection with its reduction which was unclear, undocumented and ripe for problems, including claims for discrimination. No written guidelines for termination were prepared. No documents were prepared to explain why certain employees were terminated compared to others and it appears that in some instances employees' evaluations were ignored.
>
> Naturally, different supervisors interpreted the criteria in different ways and applied them based upon the circumstances attendant to their own business units rather than in some rigid, mathematical manner. As Allied's senior management considered the changes, the names of individuals whose employment status would be affected by the changes were forwarded on to Allied's RIF committee. The committee consisted of Allied Human Resources and Legal Department personnel.

Among the evidence plaintiffs sought to rely on was the following statement from a report authored by executives of Allied's parent company to assist in the RIF:

> Despite the recent incidence of high turnover there are still many managers in the organization with very long service. No doubt this has encouraged the atmosphere of insular bureaucracy that still pervades part of the business.

Id. Do you see how the way the RIF was conducted could have encouraged, or at least enabled, age discrimination? As the lawyer for Allied, what would you have recommended the company do differently in planning major layoffs? Incidentally, the employer in *Oberg* had obtained releases from the terminated employees; however they were found invalid for failure to comply with all of the OWBPA disclosure requirements. *See Oberg v. Allied Van Lines, Inc.*, 11 F.3d 679 (7th Cir. 1993).

PROBLEM

13-6. Union Mortgage & Lending ("UML"), located in Boston, has acquired Connecticut Family Credit ("CFC"), located in Hartford, and plans to consolidate operations in Boston. CFC employed three accountants, of which UML must select two for layoff. Herk is a 61-year-old white male with 12 years of seniority. He currently earns $75,000 per year. His performance evaluations are consistently good but not outstanding. Joeline is a 42-year-old white woman with six years of seniority. She currently earns $68,000 per year. Her performance evaluations are similar to Herk's. She has strong ties to her previous employer of eight years, a large Connecticut-based bank with whom CFC did significant business. Miguel is a 29-year-old Hispanic male who arrived at CFC eight months ago from a big New York accounting firm. He earns $62,000 per year. His paper credentials exceed those of Herk and Joeline, and he has excellent interpersonal skills. Miguel's performance has not yet been formally evaluated;

however, the general manager at CFC believes he is a "rising star." UML consults you about which accountant to retain. How would you advise your client to go about this decision? What risks are associated with laying off each of these three employees? What additional information might you seek from CFC before deciding? Are there any special precautions UML should take once it makes its decision? Once you have made your selections, draft a separation letter which UML will send to the affected employees apprising them of the decision.

C. MANAGING UNFAVORABLE FORA AND ADVERSE LAW

The previous sections of this chapter explored methods employers may use for preventing employment disputes or at least resolving them internally. Inevitably, some disputes escalate to the point that an aggrieved worker wishes to pursue legal action. The traditional step in such situations is for the employee to file a complaint in court provided he or she has taken the requisite administrative steps in the case of claims arising under federal discrimination law. Such suits could often be brought as class collective actions, and, although the FEDERAL RULES OF CIVIL PROCEDURE have been interpreted to restrict the extent to which some claims may be pursued in this fashion, *see, e.g., Wal-Mart Stores, Inc. v. Dukes*, 131 S. Ct. 2541 (2011) (finding insufficient "commonality" among members of a million-plus employee class action to permit certification of a Title VII suit), such suits still posed the risk of substantial employer liability. One way that employers seeks to reduce the risks associated with this possibility is to alter contractually the default principle that disputes are litigated in the court the plaintiff chooses, complete with that forum's choice-of-law principles. Perhaps the most common method of doing this is to require all workers, as a condition of initial or continued employment, to arbitrate any dispute that may arise during the course of the employment relationship. Some employers go further and try to structure the arbitration terms, either procedurally or substantively, to minimize the risk of the employee prevailing or, at least, to reduce the amount of exposure in such situations. Perhaps the most dramatic way they do this is to foreclose not only any class action in court by requiring arbitration but also by framing such agreements to bar class arbitration. The result is that such mandatory arbitration agreements force employees to pursue dispute resolution individually, a choice that will often make it financially impossible for any claim to be pursued in any forum.

The issues regarding the validity of arbitration agreements are taken up in the first subsection. In addition, where law is uncertain or harm is difficult to prove, employers sometimes attempt to contractually define the financial consequences of a dispute, often through the use of a stipulated damages clause. This is covered in subsection 2.

1. Pre-dispute Arbitration Agreements

Arbitration is an alternative to traditional court litigation through which parties employ a third-party, nonjudicial decision maker to adjudicate their dispute in a private proceeding. From the perspective of the employer, the purpose of a pre-dispute arbitration agreement is to avoid protracted and expensive litigation and steer potential disputes to fora that the employer considers more cost-efficient, predictable, and, perhaps, friendlier to its interests. Because it is private, the arbitration process varies depending on the particular forum and rules the parties select. In many instances, parties opt for an established arbitration service, such as the American Arbitration Association, which has an extensive set of rules and procedures for resolving employment disputes and a cadre of trained arbitrators. *See AAA National Rules for the Resolution of Employment Disputes* (2005), *available at* http://www.adr.org/sp.asp?id=22075. But parties might also choose a less formal venue or develop their own set of rules and procedures. For these reasons, arbitrations vary significantly in terms of the expertise and background of the arbitrators; whether lawyers or other advocates participate; the formality with which testimony is presented; and the degree of attention to evidentiary and other procedural rules.

In theory, opting for arbitration does not reduce the risk of being on the losing end of a dispute but merely reduces the costs of resolving it by substituting a cheaper and speedier alternative mechanism. Such features could make arbitration a more accessible, and hence more effective, form of dispute resolution for employees who lack the time, financial resources, and access to counsel necessary to pursue litigation in court. *See* Samuel Estreicher, *Saturns for Rickshaws: The Stakes in the Debate over Predispute Employment Arbitration Agreements*, 16 OHIO ST. J. ON DISP. RESOL. 559 (2001). Indeed, arbitration is the typical means of resolving disputes in the collective bargaining context, although there the continued presence of the union as a "repeat player" may bulwark employee prospects for success.

However, arbitration is quicker and less costly precisely because certain procedures and safeguards associated with court litigation are abandoned. Further, since employers generally select the particular forum and its procedures, it is possible that arbitration will favor employers in both substantive outcomes and extent of remedies. Even in an objectively neutral forum and outside the collective bargaining context, the "repeat player" effect may lead arbitrators to favor those who are most likely to want to use their services in the future — employers. *See* Cynthia Estlund, *Rebuilding the Law of the Workplace in an Era of Self-Regulation*, 105 COLUM. L. REV. 319, 397-98 (2005).

Such concerns are heightened by the common employer practice of requiring employees to sign contracts to arbitrate upon applying for or commencing a job and well before a dispute actually arises. In contrast to the decision to arbitrate an existing dispute, an employee faced with a pre-dispute arbitration agreement is less likely to either appreciate the importance of choice of forum or consult counsel. *See* Matthew T. Bodie, *Questions About the Efficiency of Employment Arbitration Agreements*, 39 GA. L. REV. 1, 41 (2004) (pre-dispute arbitration agreements "are more likely to be based on primitive guesswork, or less, on the part of the employee" compared to post-dispute agreements and employers are likely to have significant informational advantages that they may use to the employees' disadvantage). Moreover, such agreements are generally boilerplate documents that individual employees are rarely in a position to refuse. If employees are not able to negotiate the terms or arbitration agreements, or even rationally weigh the trade-offs involved in agreeing to the employer's chosen forum and procedures, such agreements could effectively serve as waivers of substantive employment rights. *See* David S. Schwartz, *Mandatory Arbitration and Fairness*. 84 NOTRE DAME L. REV. 1247 (2009); Katherine V.W.

Stone, *Mandatory Arbitration of Individual Employment Rights: The Yellow Dog Contract of the 1990s*, 73 DENV. U. L. REV. 1017 (1996).

Yet another set of objections to arbitration stems from the fact that, as a private dispute resolution mechanism, arbitration may not serve the wider goals of the law, particularly the antidiscrimination statutes, even if it achieves justice in individual cases. Chief among the concerns are the confidentiality of the process, which arguably inhibits public education about discrimination and limits the development of the law by removing a large source of potential precedent cases. *See* Geraldine Szott Moohr, *Arbitration and the Goals of Employment Discrimination Law*, 56 WASH. & LEE L. REV. 395, 426-39 (1999).

Debates about the relative merits and limitations of arbitration as an alternative dispute resolution mechanism underlie an evolving body of doctrine on the legal enforceability of pre-dispute employment arbitration agreements. The starting point for that analysis is the 1925 Federal Arbitration Act ("FAA"), which provides that a written arbitration clause in any "contract evidencing a transaction involving commerce . . . shall be valid, irrevocable, and enforceable, save upon such grounds as exist at law or in equity for the revocation of any contract." 9 U.S.C. §2 (2014). If a party who has signed an arbitration agreement files suit in court, the FAA commands the judge to stay the proceedings on motion of the opposing party; this remits the plaintiff only to the designated arbitral forum for relief. While there are several limitations on the statute's scope, the Supreme Court has applied it sweepingly. *Circuit City Stores, Inc. v. Adams*, 532 U.S. 105 (2001) (holding most employment contracts within the FAA).

For our purposes, the most important set of issues concerns the relationship between private arbitration and employee statutory rights. Employment arbitration agreements typically apply to any workplace dispute, but they are typically invoked by employers defending against federal statutory claims, such as discrimination claims. The employee's right to be free from discrimination includes the statutory right to have her claims heard in a court of law before a jury. One of the foundational questions of private ordering in employment law is whether an employer can change that by private contract.

The question of enforceability of an arbitration agreement in the individual employment setting of a statutory employment claim was first addressed by the Supreme Court in *Gilmer v. Interstate/Johnson Lane Corp.*, 500 U.S. 20 (1995), an age discrimination suit. The plaintiff had signed an arbitration agreement in order to register as a securities representative with the New York Stock Exchange; that agreement, although not entered into with his employer, required Gilmer to arbitrate any dispute arising with other registered members of the exchange, including his employer. The Supreme Court held the agreement enforceable. It found nothing in the text or underlying policy of the ADEA that precluded the submission of age discrimination claims to private arbitration. *See generally* Charles A. Sullivan, *The Story of* Gilmer v. Interstate/Johnson Lane Corp: *Gilmering Antidiscrimination Law*, EMPLOYMENT DISCRIMINATION STORIES (Friedman ed., 2006).

In subsequent cases, the Court held that an arbitration agreement would be binding even if entered into directly between an employer and employee despite some arguable limiting language in the FAA, *Circuit City v. Adams*, 532 U.S. 105 (2001), and that a union could waive an individual's statutory right to a judicial forum in a collective bargaining agreement. *14 Penn Plaza, LLC v. Pyett*, 556 U.S. 247 (2009). *See generally* Alan Hyde, *Labor Arbitration of Discrimination Claims After*

14 Penn Plaza v. Pyett: *Letting Discrimination Defendants Decide Whether Plaintiffs May Sue Them,* 25 Ohio St. J. Disp. Resol. 975, 976 (2010); Margaret L. Moses, *The Pretext of Textualism: Disregarding Stare Decisis in* 14 Penn Plaza v. Pyett, 14 Lewis & Clark L. Rev. 825 (2010).

The Court has also held that the courts may not invalidate a contractual waiver of class arbitration even if the a plaintiff's cost of individually arbitrating a federal statutory claim exceeds potential recovery, *Am. Express Co. v. Italian Colors Rest.,* 133 S. Ct. 2304 (2013), and that the FAA preempts state law to the extent that it would treat arbitration agreements differently than other contracts. *See Doctor's Assocs. v. Casarotto,* 517 U.S. 681 (1996) (striking down state law prescribing special procedural requirements for arbitration agreements). *See, e.g.,* David S. Schwartz, *Correcting Federalism Mistakes in Statutory Interpretation: The Supreme Court and the Federal Arbitration Act,* 67 L. & Contemp. Probs. 5 (2004) (arguing that FAA preemption is inconsistent with congressional intent and contrary to Court's conservative majority's purported support for federalism).

Nevertheless, these decisions still left open the possibility that either "general" state law — such as unconscionability principles — or other federal protections might limit employers' ability to preclude class or collective claims, either in court or in the arbitral forum. The Supreme Court largely closed the door on such a possibility in the next principal case, and the possibility that such arbitration agreements violate the federal labor laws has not met with a favorable reception in the courts.

AT&T Mobility LLC v. Concepcion
131 S. Ct. 1740 (2011)

Justice Scalia delivered the opinion of the Court.

Section 2 of the Federal Arbitration Act (FAA) makes agreements to arbitrate "valid, irrevocable, and enforceable, save upon such grounds as exist at law or in equity for the revocation of any contract." 9 U.S.C. §2. We consider whether the FAA prohibits States from conditioning the enforceability of certain arbitration agreements on the availability of classwide arbitration procedures.

I

In February 2002, Vincent and Liza Concepcion entered into an agreement for the sale and servicing of cellular telephones with AT&T Mobility LCC (AT&T). The contract provided for arbitration of all disputes between the parties, but required that claims be brought in the parties' "individual capacity, and not as a plaintiff or class member in any purported class or representative proceeding." The agreement authorized AT&T to make unilateral amendments, which it did to the arbitration provision on several occasions. The version at issue in this case reflects revisions made in December 2006, which the parties agree are controlling.

The revised agreement provides that customers may initiate dispute proceedings by completing a one-page Notice of Dispute form available on AT&T's Web site. AT&T may then offer to settle the claim; if it does not, or if the dispute is not resolved within 30 days, the customer may invoke arbitration by filing a separate Demand for

Arbitration, also available on AT&T's Web site. In the event the parties proceed to arbitration, the agreement specifies that AT&T must pay all costs for nonfrivolous claims; that arbitration must take place in the county in which the customer is billed; that, for claims of $10,000 or less, the customer may choose whether the arbitration proceeds in person, by telephone, or based only on submissions; that either party may bring a claim in small claims court in lieu of arbitration; and that the arbitrator may award any form of individual relief, including injunctions and presumably punitive damages. The agreement, moreover, denies AT&T any ability to seek reimbursement of its attorney's fees, and, in the event that a customer receives an arbitration award greater than AT&T's last written settlement offer, requires AT&T to pay a $7,500 minimum recovery and twice the amount of the claimant's attorney's fees.

The Concepcions purchased AT&T service, which was advertised as including the provision of free phones; they were not charged for the phones, but they were charged $30.22 in sales tax based on the phones' retail value. [They later filed a complaint against AT&T, which was later consolidated with a putative class action alleging false advertising and fraud by AT&T's charging sales tax on phones it advertised as free. AT&T moved to compel arbitration under the terms of its contract with the Concepcions, and they opposed the motion on the ground that the arbitration agreement was unconscionable because it disallowed classwide procedures. Relying on the California Supreme Court's decision in *Discover Bank* v. *Superior Court*, 113 P.3d 1100 (2005), the district court found that the arbitration provision was unconscionable because AT&T had not shown that bilateral arbitration adequately substituted for the deterrent effects of class actions. The Ninth Circuit affirmed.]

II

The FAA was enacted in 1925 in response to widespread judicial hostility to arbitration agreements. *See Hall Street Associates, LLC v. Mattel, Inc.*, 552 U.S. 576, 581 (2008). Section 2, the "primary substantive provision of the Act," *Moses H. Cone Memorial Hospital v. Mercury Constr. Corp.*, 460 U.S. 1, 24 (1983), provides, in relevant part, as follows:

> A written provision in any maritime transaction or a contract evidencing a transaction involving commerce to settle by arbitration a controversy thereafter arising out of such contract or transaction . . . shall be valid, irrevocable, and enforceable, save upon such grounds as exist at law or in equity for the revocation of any contract.

9 U.S.C. §2.

We have described this provision as reflecting both a "liberal federal policy favoring arbitration," *Moses H. Cone*, and the "fundamental principle that arbitration is a matter of contract," *Rent-A-Center, West, Inc. v. Jackson*, 561 U.S. 63, 67 (2010). In line with these principles, courts must place arbitration agreements on an equal footing with other contracts, *Buckeye Check Cashing, Inc.* v. *Cardegna*, 546 U.S. 440, 443 (2006), and enforce them according to their terms, *Volt Information Sciences, Inc. v. Board of Trustees of Leland Stanford Junior Univ.*, 489 U.S. 468, 478 (1989).

The final phrase of §2, however, permits arbitration agreements to be declared unenforceable "upon such grounds as exist at law or in equity for the revocation of any contract." This saving clause permits agreements to arbitrate to be invalidated by "generally applicable contract defenses, such as fraud, duress, or unconscionability," but not by defenses that apply only to arbitration or that derive their meaning from the fact that an agreement to arbitrate is at issue. *Doctor's Associates, Inc. v. Casarotto,* 517 U.S. 681, 687 (1996); *see also Perry v. Thomas,* 482 U.S. 483, 492-93, n.9 (1987). The question in this case is whether §2 preempts California's rule classifying most collective-arbitration waivers in consumer contracts as unconscionable. We refer to this rule as the *Discover Bank* rule.

Under California law, courts may refuse to enforce any contract found "to have been unconscionable at the time it was made," or may "limit the application of any unconscionable clause." Cal. Civ. Code Ann. §1670.5(a) (West 1985). A finding of unconscionability requires "a 'procedural' and a 'substantive' element, the former focusing on 'oppression' or 'surprise' due to unequal bargaining power, the latter on 'overly harsh' or 'one-sided' results." *Armendariz v. Foundation Health Psychcare Servs.,* 6 P.3d 669, 690 (2000); accord, *Discover Bank.*

In *Discover Bank,* the California Supreme Court applied this framework to class-action waivers in arbitration agreements and held as follows:

> [W]hen the waiver is found in a consumer contract of adhesion in a setting in which disputes between the contracting parties predictably involve small amounts of damages, and when it is alleged that the party with the superior bargaining power has carried out a scheme to deliberately cheat large numbers of consumers out of individually small sums of money, then . . . the waiver becomes in practice the exemption of the party 'from responsibility for [its] own fraud, or willful injury to the person or property of another.' Under these circumstances, such waivers are unconscionable under California law and should not be enforced.

California courts have frequently applied this rule to find arbitration agreements unconscionable.

III

A

The Concepcions argue that the *Discover Bank* rule, given its origins in California's unconscionability doctrine and California's policy against exculpation, is a ground that "exist[s] at law or in equity for the revocation of any contract" under FAA §2. Moreover, they argue that even if we construe the *Discover Bank* rule as a prohibition on collective-action waivers rather than simply an application of unconscionability, the rule would still be applicable to all dispute-resolution contracts, since California prohibits waivers of class litigation as well.

When state law prohibits outright the arbitration of a particular type of claim, the analysis is straightforward: The conflicting rule is displaced by the FAA. *Preston v. Ferrer,* 552 U.S. 346, 353 (2008). But the inquiry becomes more complex when a doctrine normally thought to be generally applicable, such as duress or, as relevant here, unconscionability, is alleged to have been applied in a fashion that disfavors arbitration. In *Perry v. Thomas,* for example, we noted that the FAA's preemptive effect might extend even to grounds traditionally thought to exist "'at law or in equity for the revocation of any contract.' *Id.* (emphasis deleted). We said that a court may not "rely on the uniqueness of an agreement to arbitrate as a basis for a state-law holding that enforcement would be unconscionable, for this would enable the court to effect what . . . the state legislature cannot." *Id.*

An obvious illustration of this point would be a case finding unconscionable or unenforceable as against public policy consumer arbitration agreements that fail to provide for judicially monitored discovery. The rationalizations for such a holding are neither difficult to imagine nor different in kind from those articulated in *Discover Bank.* A court might reason that no consumer would knowingly waive his right to full discovery, as this would enable companies to hide their wrongdoing. Or the court might simply say that such agreements are exculpatory—restricting discovery would be of greater benefit to the company than the consumer, since the former is more likely to be sued than to sue. *See Discover Bank* (arguing that class waivers are similarly one-sided). And, the reasoning would continue, because such a rule applies the general principle of unconscionability or public-policy disapproval of exculpatory agreements, it is applicable to "any" contract and thus preserved by § 2 of the FAA. In practice, of course, the rule would have a disproportionate impact on arbitration agreements; but it would presumably apply to contracts purporting to restrict discovery in litigation as well.

Other examples are easy to imagine. The same argument might apply to a rule classifying as unconscionable arbitration agreements that fail to abide by the Federal Rules of Evidence, or that disallow an ultimate disposition by a jury (perhaps termed "a panel of twelve lay arbitrators" to help avoid preemption). Such examples are not fanciful, since the judicial hostility towards arbitration that prompted the FAA had manifested itself in "a great variety" of "devices and formulas" declaring arbitration against public policy. *Robert Lawrence Co. v. Devonshire Fabrics, Inc.,* 271 F.2d 402, 406 (CA2 1959). And although these statistics are not definitive, it is worth noting that California's courts have been more likely to hold contracts to arbitrate unconscionable than other contracts. Broome, *An Unconscionable Applicable of the Unconscionability Doctrine: How the California Courts are Circumventing the Federal Arbitration Act*, 3 HASTINGS BUS. L.J. 39, 54, 66 (2006); Randall, *Judicial Attitudes Toward Arbitration and the Resurgence of Unconscionability*, 52 BUFF. L. REV. 185, 186-87 (2004).

The Concepcions suggest that all this is just a parade of horribles, and no genuine worry. "Rules aimed at destroying arbitration" or "demanding procedures incompatible with arbitration," they concede, "would be preempted by the FAA because they cannot sensibly be reconciled with Section 2." The "grounds" available under § 2's saving clause, they admit, "should not be construed to include a State's mere preference for procedures that are incompatible with arbitration and 'would wholly eviscerate arbitration agreements.'"

We largely agree. Although § 2's saving clause preserves generally applicable contract defenses, nothing in it suggests an intent to preserve state-law rules that stand as an obstacle to the accomplishment of the FAA's objectives. As we have said, a federal statute's saving clause "'cannot in reason be construed as [allowing] a common law right, the continued existence of which would be absolutely inconsistent with the provisions of the act. In other words, the act cannot be held to destroy itself.'" *American Telephone & Telegraph Co. v. Central Office Telephone, Inc.,* 524 U.S. 214, 227-228 (1998).

We differ with the Concepcions only in the application of this analysis to the matter before us. We do not agree that rules requiring judicially monitored discovery or adherence to the Federal Rules of Evidence are "a far cry from this case." The overarching purpose of the FAA, evident in the text of §§ 2, 3, and 4, is to ensure the enforcement of arbitration agreements according to their terms so as to facilitate streamlined proceedings. Requiring the availability of classwide arbitration interferes with fundamental attributes of arbitration and thus creates a scheme inconsistent with the FAA.

B

The "principal purpose" of the FAA is to "ensur[e] that private arbitration agreements are enforced according to their terms." *Volt*; *see also Stolt-Nielsen S. A. v. AnimalFeeds Int'l Corp.*, 559 U.S. 662 (2010). This purpose is readily apparent from the FAA's text. Section 2 makes arbitration agreements "valid, irrevocable, and enforceable" as written (subject, of course, to the saving clause); § 3 requires courts to stay litigation of arbitral claims pending arbitration of those claims "in accordance with the terms of the agreement"; and § 4 requires courts to compel arbitration "in accordance with the terms of the agreement" upon the motion of either party to the agreement (assuming that the "making of the arbitration agreement or the failure . . . to perform the same" is not at issue). In light of these provisions, we have held that parties may agree to limit the issues subject to arbitration, *Mitsubishi Motors Corp. v. Soler Chrysler-Plymouth, Inc.*, 473 U.S. 614, 628 (1985), to arbitrate according to specific rules, *Volt*, and to limit *with whom* a party will arbitrate its disputes, *Stolt-Nielsen*.

The point of affording parties discretion in designing arbitration processes is to allow for efficient, streamlined procedures tailored to the type of dispute. It can be specified, for example, that the decision maker be a specialist in the relevant field, or that proceedings be kept confidential to protect trade secrets. And the informality of arbitral proceedings is itself desirable, reducing the cost and increasing the speed of dispute resolution. *14 Penn Plaza LLC v. Pyett*, 556 U.S. 247, 269 (2009); *Mitsubishi Motors Corp.*

The dissent quotes *Dean Witter Reynolds Inc. v. Byrd*, 470 U.S. 213, 219 (1985), as "'reject[ing] the suggestion that the overriding goal of the Arbitration Act was to promote the expeditious resolution of claims.'" That is greatly misleading. After saying (accurately enough) that "the overriding goal of the Arbitration Act was [not] to promote the expeditious resolution of claims," but to "ensure judicial enforcement of privately made agreements to arbitrate," *Dean Witter* went on to explain: "This is not to say that Congress was blind to the potential benefit of the legislation for expedited resolution of disputes. Far from it. . . ." It then quotes a House Report saying that "the costliness and delays of litigation . . . can be largely eliminated by agreements for arbitration." (Quoting H. R. Rep. No. 96, 68th Cong., 1st Sess., 2 (1924)). The concluding paragraph of this part of its discussion begins as follows:

> We therefore are not persuaded by the argument that the conflict between two goals of the Arbitration Act — enforcement of private agreements and encouragement of efficient and speedy dispute resolution — must be resolved in favor of the latter in order to realize the intent of the drafters.

In the present case, of course, those "two goals" do not conflict — and it is the dissent's view that would frustrate *both* of them.

Contrary to the dissent's view, our cases place it beyond dispute that the FAA was designed to promote arbitration. They have repeatedly described the Act as "embod[ying] [a] national policy favoring arbitration," *Buckeye Check Cashing*, and "a liberal federal policy favoring arbitration agreements, notwithstanding any state substantive or procedural policies to the contrary," *Moses H. Cone; see also Hall Street Assocs.* Thus, in *Preston v. Ferrer*, holding preempted a state-law rule requiring exhaustion of administrative remedies before arbitration, we said: "A prime objective of an agreement to arbitrate is to achieve 'streamlined proceedings and expeditious results,'" which objective would be "frustrated" by requiring a dispute to be heard by an agency first. That rule, we said, would "at the least, hinder speedy resolution of the controversy."[5]

California's *Discover Bank* rule similarly interferes with arbitration. Although the rule does not *require* classwide arbitration, it allows any party to a consumer contract to demand it *ex post*. The rule is limited to adhesion contracts, *Discover Bank*, but the times in which consumer contracts were anything other than adhesive are long past. The rule also requires that damages be predictably small, and that the consumer allege a scheme to cheat consumers. *Discover Bank*. The former requirement, however, is toothless and malleable . . . and the latter has no limiting effect, as all that is required is an allegation. Consumers remain free to bring and resolve their disputes on a bilateral basis under *Discover Bank*, and some may well do so; but there is little incentive for lawyers to arbitrate on behalf of individuals when they may do so for a class and reap far higher fees in the process. And faced with inevitable class arbitration, companies would have less incentive to continue resolving potentially duplicative claims on an individual basis.

Although we have had little occasion to examine classwide arbitration, our decision in *Stolt-Nielsen* is instructive. In that case we held that an arbitration panel exceeded its power under § 10(a)(4) of the FAA by imposing class procedures based on policy judgments rather than the arbitration agreement itself or some background principle of contract law that would affect its interpretation. We then held that the agreement at issue, which was silent on the question of class procedures, could not be interpreted to allow them because the "changes brought about by the shift from bilateral arbitration to class-action arbitration" are "fundamental." This is obvious as a structural matter: Classwide arbitration includes absent parties, necessitating additional and different procedures and involving higher stakes. Confidentiality becomes more difficult. And while it is theoretically possible to select an arbitrator with some expertise relevant to the class-certification question, arbitrators are not generally knowledgeable in the often-dominant procedural aspects of certification, such as the protection of absent parties. The conclusion follows that class arbitration, to the extent it is manufactured by *Discover Bank* rather than consensual, is inconsistent with the FAA.

---

5. Relying upon nothing more indicative of congressional understanding than statements of witnesses in committee hearings and a press release of Secretary of Commerce Herbert Hoover, the dissent suggests that Congress "thought that arbitration would be used primarily where merchants sought to resolve disputes of fact . . . [and] possessed roughly equivalent bargaining power." Such a limitation appears nowhere in the text of the FAA and has been explicitly rejected by our cases. "Relationships between securities dealers and investors, for example, may involve unequal bargaining power, but we [have] nevertheless held . . . that agreements to arbitrate in that context are enforceable." *Gilmer v. Interstate/Johnson Lane Corp.*,

First, the switch from bilateral to class arbitration sacrifices the principal advantage of arbitration — its informality — and makes the process slower, more costly, and more likely to generate procedural morass than final judgment. "In bilateral arbitration, parties forgo the procedural rigor and appellate review of the courts in order to realize the benefits of private dispute resolution: lower costs, greater efficiency and speed, and the ability to choose expert adjudicators to resolve specialized disputes." [*Stolt-Nielsen*]. But before an arbitrator may decide the merits of a claim in classwide procedures, he must first decide, for example, whether the class itself may be certified, whether the named parties are sufficiently representative and typical, and how discovery for the class should be conducted. [The majority cited data indicating that class consumer arbitration took far longer than individual arbitration.]

Second, class arbitration *requires* procedural formality. The AAA's rules governing class arbitrations mimic the Federal Rules of Civil Procedure for class litigation. Compare AAA, Supplementary Rules for Class Arbitrations (effective Oct. 8, 2003), online at http://www.adr.org/sp.asp?id=21936, with FED. RULE CIV. PROC. *23*. And while parties can alter those procedures by contract, an alternative is not obvious. If procedures are too informal, absent class members would not be bound by the arbitration. For a class-action money judgment to bind absentees in litigation, class representatives must at all times adequately represent absent class members, and absent members must be afforded notice, an opportunity to be heard, and a right to opt out of the class. *Phillips Petroleum Co. v. Shutts*, 472 U.S. 797, 811-12 (1985). At least this amount of process would presumably be required for absent parties to be bound by the results of arbitration.

We find it unlikely that in passing the FAA Congress meant to leave the disposition of these procedural requirements to an arbitrator. Indeed, class arbitration was not even envisioned by Congress when it passed the FAA in 1925; as the California Supreme Court admitted in *Discover Bank*, class arbitration is a "relatively recent development." And it is at the very least odd to think that an arbitrator would be entrusted with ensuring that third parties' due process rights are satisfied.

Third, class arbitration greatly increases risks to defendants. Informal procedures do of course have a cost: The absence of multilayered review makes it more likely that errors will go uncorrected. Defendants are willing to accept the costs of these errors in arbitration, since their impact is limited to the size of individual disputes, and presumably outweighed by savings from avoiding the courts. But when damages allegedly owed to tens of thousands of potential claimants are aggregated and decided at once, the risk of an error will often become unacceptable. Faced with even a small chance of a devastating loss, defendants will be pressured into settling questionable claims. Other courts have noted the risk of "in terrorem" settlements that class actions entail, see, *e.g.*, *Kohen v. Pac. Inv. Mgmt. Co. LLC & PIMCO Funds*, 571 F.3d 672, 677-78 (CA7 2009), and class arbitration would be no different.

Arbitration is poorly suited to the higher stakes of class litigation. In litigation, a defendant may appeal a certification decision on an interlocutory basis and, if unsuccessful, may appeal from a final judgment as well. Questions of law are reviewed *de novo* and questions of fact for clear error. In contrast, 9 U.S.C. § 10 allows a court to vacate an arbitral award *only* where the award "was procured by corruption, fraud, or undue means"; "there was evident partiality or corruption in the arbitrators"; "the arbitrators were guilty of misconduct in refusing to postpone the hearing . . . or in refusing to hear evidence pertinent and material to the controversy[,] or of any other misbehavior by which the rights of any party have been prejudiced"; or if the "arbitrators exceeded their powers, or so imperfectly executed them that a mutual, final, and definite award . . . was not made." . . . And parties may not contractually expand the grounds or nature of judicial review. *Hall Street Assocs.* We find it hard to believe that defendants would bet the company with no effective means of review, and even harder to believe that Congress would have intended to allow state courts to force such a decision.

The Concepcions contend that because parties may and sometimes do agree to aggregation, class procedures are not necessarily incompatible with arbitration. But the same could be said about procedures that the Concepcions admit States may not superimpose on arbitration. . . .

The dissent claims that class proceedings are necessary to prosecute small-dollar claims that might otherwise slip through the legal system. But States cannot require a procedure that is inconsistent with the FAA, even if it is desirable for unrelated reasons. Moreover, the claim here was most unlikely to go unresolved. As noted earlier, the arbitration agreement provides that AT&T will pay claimants a minimum of $7,500 and twice their attorney's fees if they obtain an arbitration award greater than AT&T's last settlement offer. The District Court found this scheme sufficient to provide incentive for the individual prosecution of meritorious claims that are not immediately settled, and the Ninth Circuit admitted that aggrieved customers who filed claims would be "essentially guarantee[d]" to be made whole. Indeed, the District Court concluded that the Concepcions were *better off* under their arbitration agreement with AT&T than they would have been as participants in a class action, which "could take months, if not years, and which may merely yield an opportunity to submit a claim for recovery of a small percentage of a few dollars."

* * *

Because it "stands as an obstacle to the accomplishment and execution of the full purposes and objectives of Congress," *Hines v. Davidowitz*, 312 U.S. 52, 67 (1941), California's *Discover Bank* rule is preempted by the FAA. . . .

[Justice Thomas concurred. Although he "reluctantly" joined the Court's opinion, he wrote separately to argue that "[a]s I would read it, the FAA requires that an agreement to arbitrate be enforced unless a party successfully challenges the formation of the arbitration agreement, such as by proving fraud or duress." That reading would require reversal because the *Discover Bank* rule "does not relate to defects in the making of an agreement."]

Justice BREYER, with whom Justice GINSBURG, Justice SOTOMAYOR, and Justice KAGAN join, dissenting.

The Federal Arbitration Act says that an arbitration agreement "shall be valid, irrevocable, and enforceable, *save upon such grounds as exist at law or in equity for the revocation of any contract.*" 9 U.S.C. § 2 (emphasis added). California law sets forth certain circumstances in which "class action waivers" in *any* contract are unenforceable. In my view, this rule of state law is consistent with the federal Act's language and primary objective. It does not "stan[d] as an obstacle" to the Act's "accomplishment and execution." *Hines v. Davidowitz*, 312 U.S. 52, 67 (1941). And the Court is wrong to hold that the federal Act pre-empts the rule of state law.

I

[The dissent reviewed the *Discover Bank* rule, concluding that it does not establish a "blanket policy" against class action waivers in the consumer context, but rather that "it represents the 'application of a more general [unconscionability] principle,'" citing *Gentry v. Superior Ct.*, 165 P. 3d 556, 564 (2007).]

II

A

The *Discover Bank* rule is consistent with the federal Act's language. It "applies equally to class action litigation waivers in contracts without arbitration agreements as it does to class arbitration waivers in contracts with such agreements." Linguistically speaking, it falls directly within the scope of the Act's exception permitting courts to refuse to enforce arbitration agreements on grounds that exist "for the revocation of *any* contract." 9 U.S.C. § 2 (emphasis added). The majority agrees.

B

The *Discover Bank* rule is also consistent with the basic "purpose behind" the Act. *Dean Witter Reynolds Inc. v. Byrd*, 470 U.S. 213, 219 (1985). We have described that purpose as one of "ensur[ing] judicial enforcement" of arbitration agreements; *see also Marine Transit Corp. v. Dreyfus*, 284 U.S. 263, 274, n.2 (1932) ("'The purpose of this bill is to make *valid and enforcible* agreements for arbitration'" (quoting H. R. Rep. No. 96, 68th Cong., 1st Sess., 1 (1924); emphasis added)); 65 Cong. Rec. 1931 (1924) ("It creates no new legislation, grants no new rights, except a remedy to enforce an agreement in commercial contracts and in admiralty contracts"). As is well known, prior to the federal Act, many courts expressed hostility to arbitration, for example by refusing to order specific performance of agreements to arbitrate. *See* S. Rep. No. 536, 68th Cong., 1st Sess., 2 (1924). The Act sought to eliminate that hostility by placing agreements to arbitrate "'*upon the same footing as other contracts*.' *Scherk v. Alberto-Culver Co.*, 417 U.S. 506, 511(1974) (quoting H. R. Rep. No. 96, at 2; emphasis added).

Congress was fully aware that arbitration could provide procedural and cost advantages. The House Report emphasized the "appropriate[ness]" of making arbitration agreements enforceable "at this time when there is so much agitation against the costliness and delays of litigation." And this Court has acknowledged that parties may enter into arbitration agreements in order to expedite the resolution of disputes. *See Preston v. Ferrer*, 552 U.S. 346, 357 (2008) (discussing "prime objective of an agreement to arbitrate"). *See also Mitsubishi Motors Corp. v. Soler Chrysler-Plymouth, Inc.*, 473 U.S. 614, 628 (1985).

But we have also cautioned against thinking that Congress' primary objective was to guarantee these particular procedural advantages. Rather, that primary objective was to secure the "enforcement" of agreements to arbitrate. . . .

Thus, insofar as we seek to implement Congress' intent, we should think more than twice before invalidating a state law that does just what § 2 requires, namely, puts agreements to arbitrate and agreements to litigate "upon the same footing."

III

The majority's contrary view (that *Discover Bank* stands as an "obstacle" to the accomplishment of the federal law's objective), rests primarily upon its claims that the *Discover Bank* rule increases the complexity of arbitration procedures, thereby discouraging parties from entering into arbitration agreements, and to that extent discriminating in practice against arbitration. These claims are not well founded.

For one thing, a state rule of law that would sometimes set aside as unconscionable a contract term that forbids class arbitration is not (as the majority claims) like a rule that would require "ultimate disposition by a jury" or "judicially monitored discovery" or use of "the Federal Rules of Evidence." Unlike the majority's examples, class arbitration is consistent with the use of arbitration. It is a form of arbitration that is well known in California and followed elsewhere. . . . And unlike the majority's examples, the *Discover Bank* rule imposes equivalent limitations on litigation; hence it cannot fairly be characterized as a targeted attack on arbitration.

[The dissent challenged the majority's view that that individual, rather than class, arbitration is a fundamental attribute of arbitration. When the FAA was passed, arbitration was not yet well developed and Congress "may well have thought that arbitration would be used primarily where merchants sought to resolve disputes of fact, not law, under the customs of their industries, where the parties possessed roughly equivalent bargaining power." This would suggest "if anything, that California's statute is consistent with, and indeed may help to further, the objectives that Congress had in mind."]

For another thing, the majority's argument that the *Discover Bank* rule will discourage arbitration rests critically upon the wrong comparison. The majority compares the complexity of class arbitration with that of bilateral arbitration. And it finds the former more complex. But, if incentives are at issue, the *relevant* comparison is not "arbitration with arbitration" but a comparison between class arbitration and judicial class actions. After all, in respect to the relevant set of contracts, the *Discover Bank* rule similarly and equally sets aside clauses that forbid class procedures — whether arbitration procedures or ordinary judicial procedures are at issue. . . .

The majority's related claim that the *Discover Bank* rule will discourage the use of arbitration because "[a]rbitration is poorly suited to . . . higher stakes" lacks empirical support. . . .

Further, even though contract defenses, *e.g.*, duress and unconscionability, slow down the dispute resolution process, federal arbitration law normally leaves such matters to the States. . . . The *Discover Bank* rule amounts to a variation on this theme. California is free to define unconscionability as it sees fit, and its common law is of no federal concern so long as the State does not adopt a special rule that disfavors arbitration.

Because California applies the same legal principles to address the unconscionability of class arbitration waivers as it does to address the unconscionability of any other contractual provision, the merits of class proceedings should not factor into our decision. If California had applied its law of duress to void an arbitration agreement, would it matter if the procedures in the coerced agreement were efficient?

Regardless, the majority highlights the disadvantages of class arbitrations, as it sees them. But class proceedings have countervailing advantages. In general agreements that forbid the consolidation of claims can lead small-dollar claimants to abandon their claims rather than to litigate. I suspect that it is true even here, for as the Court of Appeals recognized, AT&T can avoid the $7,500 payout (the payout that supposedly makes the Concepcions' arbitration worthwhile) simply by paying the claim's face value, such that "the maximum gain to a customer for the hassle of arbitrating a $30.22 dispute is still just $30.22."

What rational lawyer would have signed on to represent the Concepcions in litigation for the possibility of fees stemming from a $30.22 claim? . . .

NOTES

1. *A Consumer-Friendly Arbitration Agreement?* The AT&T arbitration agreement at issue was very consumer friendly, perhaps in an effort to make it more judicially palatable. A cynic might say that it was drafted to ensure that no class action or class arbitration proceeding would ever hold the corporation liable for millions of dollars while giving the seller the ability to refund the $30.22 to the relatively few consumers who actually filed a claim. That seems to be the dissent's assessment. Regardless of whether that's a correct view of the seller's motives, the Court's holding does not seem to be limited to "reasonable" arbitration provisions and, indeed, the Court soon held that the fact that individual arbitration would cost a plaintiff more than could be recovered from it was not a basis for invalidating an agreement to arbitrate. *Am. Express Co. v. Italian Colors Rest.*, 133 S. Ct. 2304 (2013).

2. *Unconscionability.* Although *Concepcion* arose in the consumer context, it is applicable to employment and, prior to the decision, there were a surprising number of decisions striking arbitration clauses in the employment area as unconscionable. Indeed, arbitration may have been the only area of American law where unconscionability doctrine seemed alive and well. *See generally* Jeffrey W. Stempel, *Arbitration, Unconscionability, and Equilibrium: The Return of Unconscionability Analysis as a Counterweight to Arbitration Formalism*, 19 OHIO ST. J. DISP. RESOL. 757, 766-67 (2004).

However, despite the Court's ruling in *Concepcion*, it did not hold that arbitration agreements could never be unconscionable. Thus, the prior case law may still be relevant to attacks on arbitration agreements, but obviously after *Concepcion* neither the fact that an agreement was entered into as a condition of employment nor the fact that the agreement bars class arbitration is enough for unconscionability. This is illustrated by subsequent developments in California. *See Iskanian v. CLS Transportation Los Angeles, LLC*, 327 P.3d 129 (Cal. 2014) (holding that *Concepcion* had overruled an earlier California Supreme Court decision, *Gentry v. Superior Court*, 165 P.3d 556, 568 (Cal. 2007), invalidating a class action waiver in a case alleging violation of FLSA overtime requirements).

In short, in order to find an agreement invalid on this ground, there must be proof of a more focused defect. *See, e.g., Hall v. Treasure Bay Virgin Isle. Corp.*, 371 F. App'x 311 (3d Cir. 2010) (arbitration agreement imposing 30-day statute of limitations and requiring nonprevailing party to pay costs was substantively unconscionable); *Murray v. United Food & Commercial Workers Intl. Union*, 289 F.3d 297, 302-04 (4th Cir. 2002) (arbitration agreement giving employer discretion in naming possible arbitrators and constraining arbitrators' ability to rule on authority of employer's president was unconscionable and unenforceable).

3. *"Not Arbitration" or "Waiving Substantive Rights"?* Would it be better to view cases such as *Hall* and *Murray* not as "unconscionability" decisions but rather as holding that the dispute resolution system was too one-sided to be considered arbitration (*Hall*) or as agreements purporting to waive nonwaivable rights (*Murray*)? After all, merely calling something an arbitration agreement doesn't make it one and adding remedial limitations to an agreement calling for arbitration doesn't convert those clauses into arbitration provisions.

However, the existence of unenforceable provisions does not necessarily invalidate a contract. Courts sometimes "sever" bad clauses, striking down only the objectionable provisions while still enforcing the agreement to arbitrate. *See, e.g., Morrison v. Circuit City Stores, Inc.*, 317 F.3d 646, 675 (6th Cir. 2003) (limitation on Title VII remedies unenforceable). *See also Ragone v. Atl. Video*, 595 F.3d 115 (2d Cir. 2010) (when employer agrees to waive potentially unconscionable provisions regarding a shortened statute of limitations and attorneys' fees, the court should enforce the arbitration agreement after severing such terms; the court cautioned that it might have reached a different result if the employer tried to enforce the objectionable clauses). Is this a good response to unconscionable arbitration agreements? Note that the practice is similar to the "blue pencil" approach some courts have applied in enforcing overbroad noncompete agreements, as discussed in Chapter 8, and it raises similar questions of encouraging employer overreaching. Some courts have responded to this concern by refusing to sever agreements that they view as such. *See, e.g., Parilla v. IAP Worldwide Services, VI, Inc.*, 368 F.3d 269, 289 (3d Cir. 2004) ("[A] multitude of unconscionable provisions in an agreement to arbitrate will preclude severance and enforcement of arbitration if they evidence a deliberate attempt by an employer to impose an arbitration scheme designed to discourage an employee's resort to arbitration or to produce results biased in the employer's favor."). What are the ethics of attorney participation in such drafting? *See* Martin H. Malin, *Ethical Concerns in Drafting Employment Arbitration Agreements After* Circuit City *and* Green Tree, 41 BRANDEIS L.J. 779 (2003).

4. *Understanding the Legal Significance of* Concepcion. A number of California decisions had struck down arbitration agreements as unconscionable, but *Discover Bank v. Superior Court*, 113 P.3d 1100 (Cal. 2005), was seminal. As the Supreme Court indicates, it found the arbitration provision unconscionable because it disallowed class-wide proceedings, and it was followed by *Gentry v. Superior Court*, 165 P.3d 556, 568 (Cal. 2007), which invalidated a class action waiver in a case alleging violation of FLSA overtime requirements. Thus, California put a major crimp in the use of arbitration agreements to foreclose class or collective dispute resolution.

It was common ground to the majority and dissent that state law could not discriminate against arbitration agreements, but California did not do so: It found waivers of the right to bring class actions in court to be equally objectionable to waiving the right to bring class arbitrations. What makes *Concepcion* groundbreaking from a legal standpoint was the majority's invalidation of a state rule that did not discriminate against arbitration because that law "stands as an obstacle to the accomplishment and execution of the full purposes and objectives of Congress." While the

FAA's language — "save upon such grounds that exist at law or in equity for the revocation of any contract" — might seem to authorize nondiscriminatory state laws, the Court viewed the statute as not suggesting any legislative intent to preserve state law rules that stand as an obstacle to the accomplishment of the FAA's objectives.

Concepcion, then, turned on whether a rule invalidating a waiver of the right to proceed as a class would impede the FAA's overarching purpose — which was is to ensure the enforcement of arbitration agreements according to their terms in order to facilitate informal, streamlined proceedings. Thus, parties may agree to limit the issues subject to arbitration, to arbitrate according to specific rules, and to limit with whom they will arbitrate. Class arbitration, unless agreed to by the parties, violated that principle because it would necessarily sacrifice arbitration's informality and make the process slower and more costly. Further, because it increased the risks to employers, the *Discover Bank* rule would discourage them from entering into arbitration agreements in the first place. The dissent, of course, disagreed, leaning heavily on what it saw as the nondiscriminatory thrust of the language.

5. *Understanding the Practical Significance of Concepcion.* It is hard to overstate the significance of the Court's decision. Class actions have been a battleground between employers and employees for years, but *Concepcion* provides an avenue for employers to avoid any such risk. A valid arbitration agreement will necessarily preclude any class court suit and a clause barring class arbitration will necessarily force employees into vindicating their rights, if at all, individually.

Given *Concepcion*, among the few potential remaining barriers to contractual bars to class claims in employment cases are the protections afforded by the National Labor Relations Act. Although the NLRA is often viewed as solely concerned with unionization and collective bargaining, it is framed in broader terms and protects the rights of covered workers to bring unfair labor practices charges before the NLRB and to engage in collective action. The next principal case reflects the Board's effort to rein in employee waivers of the right to proceed in a class or collective manner.

D.R. Horton, Inc. v. NLRB
737 F.3d 344 (5th Cir. 2013)

Leslie H. Southwick, Circuit Judge:

The National Labor Relations Board held that D.R. Horton, Inc. had violated the National Labor Relations Act by requiring its employees to sign an arbitration agreement that, among other things, prohibited an employee from pursuing claims in a collective or class action. On petition for review, we disagree and conclude that the Board's decision did not give proper weight to the Federal Arbitration Act. We uphold the Board, though, on requiring Horton to clarify with its employees that the arbitration agreement did not eliminate their rights to pursue claims of unfair labor practices with the Board.

Facts and Procedural History

Horton is a home builder with operations in over twenty states. In 2006, Horton began requiring all new and existing employees to sign, as a condition of employment, what it called a Mutual Arbitration Agreement. Three of its provisions are at issue in this appeal. First, the agreement provides that Horton and its employees "voluntarily waive all rights to trial in court before a judge or jury on all claims between them." Second, having waived their rights to a judicial proceeding, Horton and its employees agreed that "all disputes and claims" would "be determined exclusively by final and binding arbitration," including claims for "wages, benefits, or other compensation." Third, Horton and its employees agreed that "the arbitrator [would] not have the authority to consolidate the claims of other employees" and would "not have the authority to fashion a proceeding as a class or collective action or to award relief to a group or class of employees in one arbitration proceeding."

These provisions meant that employees could not pursue class or collective claims in an arbitral or judicial forum. Instead, all employment-related disputes were to be resolved through individual arbitration.

Michael Cuda worked for Horton as a superintendent from July 2005 to April 2006; he signed a Mutual Arbitration Agreement. In 2008, Cuda and a nationwide class of similarly situated superintendents sought to initiate arbitration of their claims that Horton had misclassified them as exempt from statutory overtime protections in violation of the Fair Labor Standards Act ("FLSA"). Horton responded that the arbitration agreement barred pursuit of collective claims, but invited Cuda and the other claimants to initiate individual arbitration proceedings. Cuda then filed an unfair labor practice charge, alleging that the class-action waiver violated the National Labor Relations Act ("NLRA").

[The Board found that the Mutual Arbitration Agreement violated Section 8(a)(1) because employees would reasonably interpret its language as precluding or restricting their right to file charges with the Board. It also found that the agreement violated Section 8(a)(1) because it required employees to waive their right to maintain joint, class, or collective employment-related actions in any forum. Horton filed a timely petition for review of the panel's decision, and the Board cross-applied for enforcement of its order.]

Discussion . . .

III. NLRA Sections 7 & 8(a)(1) and the Federal Arbitration Act

The Board concluded that Horton violated Sections 7 and 8(a)(1) of the NLRA by requiring its employees to sign the Mutual Arbitration Agreement, which "precludes them from filing joint, class, or collective claims addressing their wages, hours or other working conditions against the employer in any forum, arbitral or judicial." In reaching this conclusion, the Board first determined that the agreement interfered with the exercise of employees' substantive rights under Section 7 of the NLRA, which allows employees to act in concert with each other:

> Employees shall have the right to self-organization, to form, join, or assist labor organizations, to bargain collectively through representatives of their own choosing, *and to engage in other concerted activities for the purpose of collective bargaining or other mutual aid or protection*, and shall also have the right to refrain from any or all of such activities except to the extent that such right may be affected by an agreement requiring membership in a labor organization as a condition of employment as authorized in section 158(a)(3) of this title.

29 U.S.C. § 157 (emphasis added). The Board deemed it well-settled that the NLRA protects the right of employees to improve their working conditions through administrative and judicial forums.

Taking this view of Section 7, the Board held that the NLRA protects the right of employees to "join together to pursue workplace grievances, including through litigation" and arbitration. The Board concluded that an "individual who files a class or collective action regarding wages, hours or working conditions, whether in court or before an arbitrator, seeks to initiate or induce group action and is engaged in conduct protected by Section 7 . . . central to the [NLRA's] purposes." In the Board's opinion, by requiring employees to refrain from collective or class claims, the Mutual Arbitration Agreement infringed on the substantive rights protected by Section 7.

The other statutory component of the Board's analysis is Section 8(a)(1) of the NLRA. It defines unfair labor practices by an employer: "It shall be an unfair labor practice for an employer—(1) to interfere with, restrain, or coerce employees in the exercise of the rights guaranteed in section 157 of this title. . . ." 29 U.S.C. § 158(a). In light of the Board's interpretation of Section 7, it held that Horton had committed an unfair labor practice under Section 8 by requiring employees to agree not to act in concert in administrative and judicial proceedings.

Horton and several amici disagree with this interpretation of Section 7. According to Horton, the NLRA does not grant employees the substantive right to adjudicate claims collectively. Additionally, Horton argues that the Board's interpretation of Sections 7 and 8(a)(1) impermissibly conflicts with the FAA by prohibiting the enforcement of an arbitration agreement.

[Although a court must defer to the Board when it interprets an ambiguous provision of the NLRA, it need not do so when the Board's decisions implicate federal statutes and policies unrelated to the NLRA, such as the FAA.]

Section 7 effectuated Congress's intent to equalize bargaining power between employees and employers "by allowing employees to band together in confronting an employer regarding the terms and conditions of their employment," and that "[t]here is no indication that Congress intended to limit this protection to situations in which an employee's activity and that of his fellow employees combine with one another in any particular way." [*NLRB v. City Disposal*, 465 U.S. 822, 835 (1985).] On the other hand, no court decision prior to the Board's ruling under review today had held that the Section 7 right to engage in "concerted activities for the purpose of . . . other mutual aid or protection" prohibited class action waivers in arbitration agreements.

[Board precedent and some circuit court] cases under the NLRA give some support to the Board's analysis that collective and class claims, whether in lawsuits or in arbitration, are protected by Section 7. To stop here, though, is to make the NLRA the only relevant authority. The Federal Arbitration Act ("FAA") has equal importance in our review. Caselaw under the FAA points us in a different direction than the course taken by the Board. As an initial matter, arbitration has been deemed not to deny a party any statutory right. *See Mitsubishi Motors Corp. v. Soler Chrysler–Plymouth, Inc.*, 473 U.S. 614, 627 (1985). Courts repeatedly have rejected litigants' attempts to assert a statutory right that cannot be effectively vindicated through arbitration. To be clear, the Board did not say otherwise. It said the NLRA invalidates any bar to *class* arbitrations.

Although the Board is correct that none of those cases considered a Section 7 right to pursue legal claims concertedly, they nevertheless emphasize the barrier any statute faces before it will displace the FAA. The Board presents no cases that have overcome that barrier, and our research reveals very limited exceptions. . . .

The use of class action procedures, though, is not a substantive right. *See Amchem Prods., Inc. v. Windsor,* 521 U.S. 591, 612-13 (1997); *Deposit Guar. Nat'l Bank v. Roper,* 445 U.S. 326, 332 (1980) ("[T]he right of a litigant to employ Rule 23 is a procedural right only, ancillary to the litigation of substantive claims."). . . . The Board distinguished such caselaw on the basis that the NLRA is essentially *sui generis.* That act's fundamental precept is the right for employees to act collectively. Thus, Rule 23 is not the source of the right to the relevant collective actions. The NLRA is.

Even so, there are numerous decisions holding that there is no right to use class procedures under various employment-related statutory frameworks. For example, the Supreme Court has determined that there is no substantive right to class procedures under the Age Discrimination in Employment Act, 29 U.S.C. § 621 *et seq.* ("ADEA"), despite the statute providing for class procedures. *Gilmer v. Interstate/Johnson Lane Corp.,* 500 U.S. 20 (1991). Similarly, numerous courts have held that there is no substantive right to proceed collectively under the FLSA, the statute under which Cuda originally brought suit. *Carter v. Countrywide Credit Indus., Inc.,* 362 F.3d 294, 298 (5th Cir. 2004).

The Board determined that invalidating restrictions on class or collective actions would not conflict with the FAA. The Board reached this conclusion by first observing that when private contracts interfere with the functions of the NLRA, the NLRA prevails. The Board then noted that the FAA was intended to prevent courts from treating arbitration agreements less favorably than other private contracts, but the FAA allows for the non-enforcement of arbitration agreements on any "grounds as exist at law or in equity for the revocation of any contract." 9 U.S.C. § 2. It then reasoned that "[t]o find that an arbitration agreement must yield to the NLRA is to treat it no worse than any other private contract that conflicts with Federal labor law." The Board argues that any employee-employer contract prohibiting collective action fails under Section 7, and arbitration agreements are treated no worse and no better.

In so finding, the Board relied in part on its view that the policy behind the NLRA trumped the different policy considerations in the FAA that supported enforcement of arbitration agreements. The Board considered its holding to be a limited one, remarking that the only agreements affected by its decision were those between employers and employees. The Board recognized that "a party may not be compelled under the FAA to submit to class arbitration unless there is a contractual basis for concluding that the party *agreed* to do so." *Stolt–Nielsen S.A. v. AnimalFeeds Int'l Corp.,* 559 U.S. 662, 684 (2010). Even so, the Board concluded that it was not requiring parties to engage in class arbitration: "So long as the employer leaves open a judicial forum for class and collective claims, employees' NLRA rights are preserved without requiring the availability of class-wide arbitration," and "[e]mployers remain[ed] free to insist that *arbitral* proceedings be conducted on an individual basis."

The Board explained its interpretation of the NLRA as appropriately weighing the public policy interests involved and, to the extent the NLRA and FAA might conflict, suitably accommodating those statutes' interests. Had it found the two enactments to conflict, the Board believed the FAA would have to yield for also being in conflict with the Norris–LaGuardia Act of 1932, which prohibits agreements that prevent aiding by lawful means a person participating in a lawsuit arising out of a labor dispute, and which was passed seven years after the FAA.

We now evaluate the Board's reasoning. We start with the requirement under the FAA that arbitration agreements must be enforced according to their terms. Two

n.18 (1971); *see also Lockhart v. United States,* 546 U.S. 142, 148 (2005) (Scalia, J., concurring). The Board determined that the NLRA was the later statute. The FAA was enacted in 1925, then reenacted on July 30, 1947. The NLRA was enacted on July 5, 1935, and reenacted on June 23, 1947. The reenactments were part of a recodification of federal statutes that apparently made no substantive changes. An Act to codify and enact into positive law, Title 9 of the United States Code, entitled "Arbitration", Pub. L. No. 80–282, 61 Stat. 669 (1947). The relevance of the date of enactment is whether a repeal by implication arises. *Southern Scrap Material Co., LLC. v. ABC Ins. Co. (In re Southern Scrap Materials Co., LLC.),* 541 F.3d 584, 593 n.14 (5th Cir. 2008). The implication is based on the assumption that Congress is fully aware of prior enactments as it adopts new laws. *Id.* It is unclear whether that assumption has the same force for a recodification.

Of some importance is that the NLRA was enacted and reenacted prior to the advent in 1966 of modern class action practice. *See Ortiz v. Fibreboard Corp.,* 527 U.S. 815, 832–33 (1999). We find limited force to the argument that there is an inherent conflict between the FAA and NLRA when the NLRA would have to be protecting a right of access to a procedure that did not exist when the NLRA was (re)enacted.[10] The dates of enactment have no impact on our decision.

The NLRA should not be understood to contain a congressional command overriding application of the FAA. The burden is with the party opposing arbitration, *Gilmer,* 500 U.S. at 26, and here the Board has not shown that the NLRA's language, legislative history, or purpose support finding the necessary congressional command. Because the Board's interpretation does not fall within the FAA's "saving clause," and because the NLRA does not contain a congressional command exempting the statute from application of the FAA, the Mutual Arbitration Agreement must be enforced according to its terms.

We do not deny the force of the Board's efforts to distinguish the NLRA from all other statutes that have been found to give way to requirements of arbitration. The issue here is narrow: do the rights of collective action embodied in this labor statute make it distinguishable from cases which hold that arbitration must be individual arbitration? *See Concepcion.* We have explained the general reasoning that indicates the answer is "no." We add that we are loath to create a circuit split. Every one of our sister circuits to consider the issue has either suggested or expressly stated that they would not defer to the NLRB's rationale, and held arbitration agreements containing class waivers enforceable. *See Richards v. Ernst & Young, LLP,* 734 F.3d 871, 873-74 (9th Cir. 2013); *Sutherland v. Ernst & Young LLP,* 726 F.3d 290, 297-98 n.8 (2d Cir. 2013); *Owen v. Bristol Care, Inc.,* 702 F.3d 1050, 1055 (8th Cir. 2013).[11]

---

10. The Board also relied on the Norris–LaGuardia Act ("NLGA") to support its view that the FAA must give way to the NLRA. It is undisputed that the NLGA is outside the Board's interpretive ambit. *See Lechmere, Inc. [v. NLRB,* 502 U.S. 527, 536 (1992).] We also conclude that the Board's reasoning drawn from the NLGA is unpersuasive.

11. A thorough explanation of the strongest arguments in favor of the Board's decision, which embraces the Board's distinctions from earlier Supreme Court pronouncements on arbitrations and adding some of its own, appears in a recent law review article. Charles A. Sullivan & Timothy P. Glynn, *Horton Hatches the Egg: Concerted Action Includes Concerted Dispute Resolution,* 64 ALA. L. REV. 1013 (2013). We do not adopt its reasoning but note our consideration of its advocacy.

IV. *Mutual Arbitration Agreement's Violation of NLRA Section 8(a)(1)*

[The court upheld the Board's finding that the Mutual Arbitration Agreement violated Section 8(a)(1) and (4) "for including language that would lead employees to a reasonable belief that they were prohibited from filing unfair labor practice charges."] . . .

GRAVES, Judge, concurring in part and dissenting in part.

Because I would deny the petition for review, thus affirming the Board's decision in toto, I respectfully concur in part and dissent in part. Specifically, I disagree with the majority's finding that the Board's interpretation of sections 7 & 8(a)(1) of the National Labor Relations Act (NLRA) conflict with the Federal Arbitration Act (FAA).

The Mutual Arbitration Agreement (MAA) precludes employees from filing joint, class or collective claims in any forum. I agree with the Board that the MAA interferes with the exercise of employees' substantive rights under Section 7 of the NLRA, which provides, in relevant part, that employees have the right "to engage in other concerted activities for the purpose of collective bargaining or other mutual aid or protection. . . ." 29 U.S.C. § 157.

Further, as the Board specifically found, holding that the MAA violates the NLRA does not conflict with the FAA for several reasons: (1) "the purpose of the FAA was to prevent courts from treating arbitration agreements less favorably than other private contracts." *In re D.R. Horton, Inc.* "To find that an arbitration agreement must yield to the NLRA is to treat it no worse than any other private contract that conflicts with Federal labor law." *Id.*; (2) "the Supreme Court's jurisprudence under the FAA, permitting enforcement of agreements to arbitrate federal statutory claims, including employment claims, makes clear that the agreement may not require a party to 'forgo the substantive rights afforded by the statute.'" *Id.* "The right to engage in collective action — including collective *legal* action — is the core substantive right protected by the NLRA and is the foundation on which the Act and Federal labor policy rest." *Id.* (emphasis original); (3) "nothing in the text of the FAA suggests that an arbitration agreement that is inconsistent with the NLRA is nevertheless enforceable." *Id.* "To the contrary, Section 2 of the FAA . . . provides that arbitration agreements may be invalidated in whole or in part upon any 'grounds as exist at law or in equity for the revocation of any contract.'" *Id.*; and (4) "even if there were a direct conflict between the NLRA and the FAA, there are strong indications that the FAA would have to yield under the terms of the Norris–LaGuardia Act." *Id.*

I also agree with the Board's holding that Horton "violated Section 8(a)(1) by requiring employees to waive their right to collectively pursue employment-related claims in all forums, arbitral and judicial." *Id.* The Board made it clear that it was not mandating class arbitration in order to protect employees' rights under the NLRA, but rather was holding that employers may not compel employees to waive their NLRA right to collectively pursue litigation of employment claims in all forums, judicial and arbitral.

As acknowledged by the majority, we give the Board judicial deference in interpreting an ambiguous provision of a statute that it administers. *Lechmere, Inc. v. NLRB*, 502 U.S. 527, 536 (1992). Further, as acknowledged by the majority, there is authority to support the Board's analysis. . . .

NOTES

1. *Partial Victory.* The NLRB actually won the case since the Fifth Circuit upheld the Board's decision that, as drafted the "Mutual Arbitration Agreement" violated the NLRA because a reasonable employee might understand it to require giving up her right to file unfair labor practice charges with the Board. While not insignificant, the major effect of this ruling is likely to be employers amending their arbitration agreements to make clearer that worker rights to file with government agencies remain unaffected. The NLRB did, however, lose on the second and more sweeping holding: that by cutting off the right of employees to pursue both class (or joint) actions and class (or joint) arbitration, it infringed employee rights to act concertedly for mutual aid and protection. While not all employees are covered by the NLRA, the Board's ruling would have largely negated the effects of *Concepcion* — by having another federal statute trump the apparent command of the FAA. The panel decision is not necessarily the last word on the subject — indeed, in disputes arising in other circuits, neither the Board nor other courts are bound to follow it. To that end, the Board strongly reaffirmed *Horton* in *Murphy Oil USA, Inc.*, 361 N.L.R.B. 72 (2014). Nevertheless, this decision and the other circuit authority it cites it does call into serious doubt this potential limitation on bars to class treatment in arbitration agreements. *See also Iskanian v. CLS Transportation Los Angeles, LLC*, 327 P.2d 129 (Cal. 2014) ("We agree with the Fifth Circuit that, in light of *Concepcion*, the Board's rule is not covered by the FAA's savings clause."); *Johnmohammadi v. Bloomingdale's, Inc.*, 755 F.3d 1072 (9th Cir. 2014) (rejecting the *Horton* argument when the employer gave plaintiff the option of accepting or rejecting a class-action waiver).

2. *Is There a Conflict Between the NLRA and the FAA?* Although the National Labor Relations Act is often thought to apply to unions and collective bargaining agreements, its core provision — the right to concerted action, free of employer retaliation, for mutual aid and protection — applies to all covered workers, not merely those in unionized workplaces. Further, the Fifth Circuit seemed to accept that fact that, the FAA aside, the NLRA would protect the right of employees to band together to seek relief in the courts. As the Court said in *Eastex, Inc. v. NLRB*, 437 U.S. 556, 565-66 (1978), Section 7 "protects employees from retaliation by their employers when they seek to improve [their] working conditions through resort to administrative and judicial forums."

If this right is to give way, it must be because the FAA so commands, and that is the thrust of the Fifth Circuit's majority opinion. But the FAA was passed before the NLRA. Why would the earlier statute trump the later one? In the event of a conflict, wouldn't you expect exactly the opposite? Is the Fifth Circuit essentially treating the FAA as what has been called a "super-statute"? *See* William N. Eskridge, Jr. & John Ferejohn, *Super-Statutes*, 50 Duke L.J. 1215, 1215-16 (2001). What would be the basis for doing so? It is true that the Court has emphasized the importance of a national policy favoring arbitration over a series of decisions, but it has similarly emphasized the importance of our national labor policy over dozens of cases. Further, the Court recently explicitly denied any "preference for arbitration." *See 14 Penn Plaza LLC v. Pyett*, 556 U.S. 247, 267 n.9 (2009); *see generally* Charles A. Sullivan & Timothy P. Glynn, Horton *Hatches the Egg: Concerted Action Includes Concerted Dispute Resolution*, 64 Ala. L. Rev. 1013 (2013). *See also* Charles A. Sullivan & Timothy P. Glynn, *A Modest Opinion*, Empl. Rts & Emp. Pol'y J. — (forthcoming 2015).

3. *The Norris LaGuardia Act.* The Fifth Circuit gives short shrift to the claim that D.R. Horton's MAA violated the Norris LaGuardia Act, 29 U.S.C.A. §§ 102-103 (2014). That statute, which preceded the passage of the NLRA by several years, was passed in large part to invalidate "yellow dog" contracts, the paradigmatic form of which barred employees from joining unions. It declares that workers "shall be free from the interference, restraint, or coercion of employers of labor, or their agents, in the designation of such representatives or in self-organization or in other concerted activities for the purpose of collective bargaining or other mutual aid or protection." § 102. To achieve that end, it provides: "any . . . undertaking or promise in conflict with the public policy declared in [§ 102] is hereby declared to be contrary to the public policy of the United States, shall not be enforceable in any court of the United States." Do you understand why this is not explicit language that would reach Horton's MAA once it was determined that that agreement interfered with employee "concerted action for . . . mutual aid or protection"?

4. *Arbitration and Unions.* As the Fifth Circuit majority suggests, arbitration is a central feature of American labor relations, with almost every collective bargaining agreement incorporating an elaborate grievance mechanism, culminating in arbitration. But labor arbitration is the result of agreement between employers and the union as representative of the employees in the bargaining unit. Further, the union typically represents workers in any arbitration. Does it follow that, because arbitration is viewed as pro-employee in this context that it is necessarily pro-employee outside the unionized workplace?

5. *Comparing Costs, Comparing Access.* At the level at which the principal cases operate, there is little sense of how arbitration works in practice. Perhaps the first question is how arbitration will be financed. Unlike judges, arbitrators are private individuals rather than civil servants; the parties must pay for their services, which can easily cost more than a thousand dollars per day for each arbitrator. In contrast, a party need only pay a one-time filing fee to initiate a suit in federal court, and this may be waived on a demonstration of indigency.

Before you conclude that courts are more financially accessible than arbitration, however, consider the time and money that attorneys invest in preparing cases for trial. Many plaintiffs in employment cases do not pay out-of-pocket for legal representation, but as a consequence lawyers are extremely cautious about the cases they will pursue on contingency. It has been suggested that lawyers in private practice will not take on cases without a minimum of $75,000 in provable economic damages. Think about what types of employees are likely to have claims with this much money at stake. Would it surprise you to learn that an estimated 95 percent of employees who seek legal help are turned away? Does this change how you feel about arbitration? Of course, if arbitration is such a good idea, the employer and employee can always agree to arbitrate after a dispute has arisen — there is no need for an arbitration agreement as a condition of employment.

Even if aspects of arbitration are beneficial to some employees, that doesn't answer the question about who pays for it. If shifting part of the cost to the employee is prohibited, that must mean that the employer pays the full freight. Is that such a good idea? Won't arbitrators tend to be influenced by who is paying their fees?

6. *Government Suits.* Although the Supreme Court has supported private arbitration, it has drawn an important limit on the reach of its holdings as concerns public agencies. In *EEOC v. Waffle House,* 534 U.S. 279 (2002), the Court held that government agencies are not bound by a private agreement to arbitrate between an employer and employee. As a result of this decision, the EEOC or Department or Labor (and presumably analog state agencies) can take up a victim's cause by pursuing its own claim against the offending employer in court on behalf of the victim, even where that individual would be precluded from doing so on his or her own behalf. Indeed, the Court held that in so doing the EEOC could seek victim-specific relief including full monetary damages. *Id.* at 295-96 ("The agency may be seeking to vindicate a public interest, not simply provide make-whole relief for the employee, even when it pursues entirely victim-specific relief."). But before you conclude that this is a gaping loophole in the protection arbitration agreements afford employers, note that the EEOC prosecutes only a tiny fraction of discrimination charges lodged with it, and the Department of Labor can pursue only a similar tiny percentage of wage complaints. From an employer's risk management perspective, enforceable arbitration agreements still make good sense. And, of course, antidiscrimination claims are only a subset of potential employee suits.

7. *A Statutory Solution?* If one concludes that as a policy matter pre-dispute arbitration agreements of the kind at issue in *Concepcion* and *Horton* are not desirable, the simplest (if at the moment politically infeasible) way to eliminate the problem is statutory amendment. Congress could amend the FAA to more broadly and explicitly exempt employment agreements. Alternatively, Congress could amend the various federal antidiscrimination and minimum labor standards laws to preclude mandatory predispute arbitration of claims arising under those statutes. Congress took this approach in the Dodd-Frank financial reform bill, which amended whistleblower protections under Sarbanes-Oxley. *See* 18 U.S.C.A. § 1514A(e) (2014). Dodd-Frank also barred mandatory pre-dispute arbitration for the new whistleblower protections it created. *See* Chapter 5, pages 261-67. Pre-dispute agreements would also seem to be invalid under the federal Employee Polygraph Protection Act. *See* 29 U.S.C.A. § 2005(d) ("The rights and *procedures* provided by this chapter may not be waived by contract or otherwise.") (emphasis added). More recently, President Obama issued an executive order barring mandatory predispute arbitration provisions in employment contracts of federal contractors where the claim at stake arises under Title VII or state tort law related to sexual harassment. § 6 Executive Order: Fair Play and Safe Workplaces, July 31, 2014.

8. *Limiting Issues Arbitrated.* Although arbitration increasingly seems to be generally favored by employers, it should be clear that it is unsuitable for some of the situations we have encountered. For example, a breach of a noncompetition agreement might result in truly irreparable injury if injunctive relief had to be postponed until the enforcement of an arbitration award. Accordingly, even contracts that provide for arbitration of disputes sometimes carve out certain issues. *See generally* Erin O'Hara O'Connor, Kenneth J. Martin, & Randall S. Thomas, *Customizing Employment Arbitration*, 98 Iowa L. Rev. 133 (2012) (empirical study of CEO employment contracts finding that, while half of the agreements provide for arbitration, almost half of those carve out disputes pertaining to the confidentiality, noncompetition, nonsolicitation, and nondisparagement clauses).

* * *

If there are few legal obstacles to employers obtaining worker consent to arbitration agreements, the remaining issues will largely be those of normal contract analysis: When will an employee be said to have agreed to arbitrate her disputes?

≡≡ ### *Davis v. Nordstrom, Inc.*
≡≡ *755 F.3d 1089 (9th Cir. 2014)*

SMITH, Chief District Judge:

Following the United States Supreme Court's decision in *AT&T Mobility LLC v. Concepcion*, 131 S. Ct. 1740 (2011), Appellant Nordstrom, Inc. ("Nordstrom") made revisions to the employee arbitration policy contained in its employee handbook. These changes precluded employees from bringing most class action lawsuits. Despite these changes, weeks later, Nordstrom employee Faine Davis filed a class action lawsuit on behalf of herself and other similarly situated employees, alleging that Nordstrom violated various state and federal employment laws.

In time, Nordstrom, relying on the revised arbitration policy in its employee handbook sought to compel Davis to submit to individual arbitration of her claims. The district court held that Davis and Nordstrom did not enter into a valid arbitration agreement with respect to the revision, and therefore denied Nordstrom's motion to compel arbitration. Nordstrom appeals the district court's decision. Because we find that Nordstrom and Davis did indeed enter into a valid agreement to arbitrate disputes on an individual basis, we REVERSE the district court and REMAND for further proceedings consistent with this order. . . .

II.   Background

The basic facts are straightforward and not in dispute. On August 11, 2011, Davis filed a purported class action lawsuit against Nordstrom seeking redress for nonpayment of wages, failure to provide meal periods and rest breaks, and unfair competition. Relying on the company's employee handbook, Nordstrom moved to compel Davis to submit to individual arbitration of her claims. Davis acknowledges that she received a copy of the handbook when she first took her position at Nordstrom, and during her employment the company revised the handbook several times, always notifying Davis of the changes.

Two provisions of this handbook matter for this appeal. The first explained the circumstances under which Nordstrom employees were required to arbitrate their disputes with the company (the "arbitration provision"); the second required Nordstrom to provide employees with 30 days written notice of any substantive changes to the arbitration provision (the "notice provision"). The handbook provided that the notice provision was included to "allow employees time to consider the changes and decide whether or not to continue employment subject to the changes."

Prior to July 2011, the arbitration provision required employees to arbitrate individual disputes, but permitted employees to bring class action lawsuits against the company. In July 2011 and again in August 2011, Nordstrom revised the arbitration provision; both revisions required employees to arbitrate nearly all claims individually, and precluded employees from filing most class action lawsuits. To comply with the notice provision, Nordstrom sent letters to employees, including Davis, in June 2011 informing them of the change in the arbitration policy.[3] In this June letter, Nordstrom informed employees that "the Nordstrom Dispute Resolution Program

---

3. In the July 2011 revision to the arbitration provision, Nordstrom also completely removed the notice provision.

has been in place for several years. We've recently made updates to the program and want to ensure you have the current version." Along with this letter, Nordstrom included a copy of the entire Dispute Resolution Program, including the arbitration provision.

III. Discussion

The Federal Arbitration Act ("FAA"), 9 U.S.C. §§ 1, *et seq.*, reflects a "liberal federal policy" in favor of arbitration. *Concepcion.* Under the FAA, the role of the district court is to determine if a valid arbitration agreement exists, and if so, whether the agreement encompasses the dispute at issue.

A. Contract Formation

The district court determined that no revised agreement was ever reached—holding that Nordstrom had failed to provide employees with the required 30 days notice of the change in the arbitration provision, and to inform employees that their continued employment constituted acceptance of the new arbitration provision. Because we hold that Nordstrom complied with the notice requirement, and that California law imposes no duty upon Nordstrom specifically to inform employees that their continued employment constituted acceptance of new terms of employment, we reverse.

Arbitration is a product of contract. Parties are not required to arbitrate their disagreements unless they have agreed to do so. *Pinnacle Museum Tower Ass'n v. Pinnacle Mktg. Dev. (U.S.), LLC*, 282 P.3d 1217 (Cal. 2012) A contract to arbitrate will not be inferred absent a "clear agreement." *Avery v. Integrated Healthcare Holdings, Inc.*, 159 Cal. Rptr. 3d 444 (Cal. Ct. App. 2013). When determining whether a valid contract to arbitrate exists, we apply ordinary state law principles that govern contract formation. In California, a "clear agreement" to arbitrate may be either express or implied in fact. *Pinnacle Mktg. Dev.* The handbook Davis received when she began work established the ground rules of her employment, including that Davis and Nordstrom would arbitrate certain disputes. She accepted employment on this basis, so there was a binding agreement to arbitrate. Under California law, Nordstrom was permitted to unilaterally change the terms of Davis's employment, including those terms included in its employee handbook. *Craig v. Brown & Root, Inc.*, 100 Cal. Rptr. 2d 818 (Cal. Ct. App. 2000). Nordstrom was also entitled to enforce the terms of employment identified in this handbook, and any modifications made to it, as it could any other contract. *See id.* Indeed, "[i]t is settled that an employer may unilaterally alter the terms of an employment agreement,4 provided such alteration does not run afoul of the [California] Labor Code." *Schachter v. Citigroup, Inc.*, 218 P.3d 262 (Cal. 2009). Where an employee continues in his or her employment after being given notice of the changed terms or conditions, he or she has accepted those new terms or conditions. *Id.*

The parties have not provided, and we have not found, a case dictating that under California law Nordstrom was required to provide notice of the change in any particular way. Instead, "an employer may terminate or modify a contract with no fixed duration period after a reasonable time period, if it provides employees with reasonable notice, and the modification does not interfere with vested employee benefits." *Asmus v. Pac. Bell*, 999 P.2d 71 (Cal. 2000). Of course, if an employer has prescribed methods of policy modification and employee notice, it is incumbent upon the employer to abide by those methods. *Ferguson*. Here, the terms of the arbitration provision in Davis's initial handbook stated that Davis would be provided "30 days written notice of substantive changes . . . to allow [her] time to consider the changes and decide whether or not to continue employment subject to the changes."

The first question is whether Nordstrom complied with the notice requirement. The district court determined that Nordstrom made the revised arbitration provisions immediately applicable to its employees without providing 30 days written notice as required by the employee handbook. In reaching this conclusion the district court found three factors determinative: first, Nordstrom failed to submit evidence that the company told employees the policy change only went into effect after 30 days; second, the cover letter Nordstrom sent to employees accompanying the revised arbitration provision informed employees that the "current version" of the arbitration provision was enclosed implying it was immediately effective and; third, a Nordstrom human resources document set forth internal measures for implementing the changed policy. Davis relies on the same factors in this appeal.

Nordstrom argues that it sent the revised arbitration provision to all employees, including Davis, and that it did not enforce the provision against Davis, or anyone else, within 30 days of her receiving it. Additionally, Nordstrom asserts that during this 30 day time period, Davis never objected to the revised provision and she did not quit her job.

While the communications with its employees were not the model of clarity, we find that Nordstrom satisfied the minimal requirements under California law for providing employees with reasonable notice of a change to its employee handbook by sending a letter to Davis and other employees informing them of the modification, and not seeking to enforce the arbitration provision during the 30 day notice period.

The next question is whether Nordstrom was bound to inform Davis that her continued employment after receiving the letter constituted acceptance of new terms of employment. The district court found it was, but we disagree. . . . [However, in *Asmus* the California Supreme Court] held that an employer seeking to terminate a unilateral contract must provide reasonable notice of the termination and refrain from interfering with vested rights. This requirement also applies to unilateral contract modifications. Nowhere in *Asmus* did the California Supreme Court require that employees must be expressly told that continued employment constitutes acceptance, nor have any California state appellate court decisions imposed such a requirement.

NOTES

1. *Just Plain Contracts.* Having mastered the various tests for releases of substantive rights, were you surprised by the absence of a heightened "knowing and voluntary" standard for agreements to arbitrate in *Nordstrom*? Nor have any courts required such agreements to comply with OWBPA where ADEA claims are concerned.

See, e.g., Rosenberg v. Merrill Lynch, Pierce, Fenner & Smith, Inc., 170 F.3d 1 (1st Cir. 1999). Since the federal discrimination laws afford plaintiffs the right to a jury, one could argue that a waiver or release of that right should be subject to the same tests that apply to the release of substantive claims. Although a few courts appear to scrutinize closely employee assent to arbitration agreements, *see, e.g., Alonso v. Huron Valley Ambulance,* 357 F. App'x 487 (6th Cir. 2010) (finding agreement unenforceable where employees were given only general information about employer's alternative dispute process which was provided one month after they began employment), most simply apply normal contract analysis. Indeed, arguably that follows ineluctably from the language of § 2 of the FAA.

2. *Contract Formation.* If "plain vanilla" contract law applies to arbitration, employers seeking to enforce an arbitration agreement must establish offer, acceptance, and consideration. Like Nordstroms, a number of employers have attempted to impose arbitration on existing workers merely by unilaterally amending an employee handbook or providing an e-mail notification. Despite the principal case, the results in these situations have been mixed. *Compare Nordstroms* and *May v. Higbee Co.,* 372 F.3d 757, 764 (5th Cir. 2004) (assent to arbitration manifested by conduct where employee signed acknowledgment that she received copy of rules and unambiguously notified employees that they were deemed to have agreed to arbitration by continuing their employment), *with Campbell v. Gen. Dynamics Gov't Sys. Corp.,* 407 F.3d 546, 556-58 (1st Cir. 2005) (no enforceable arbitration agreement where policy distributed via hyperlink in e-mail notification and employee did not reply to message) and *Salazar v. Citadel Communs. Corp.,* 90 P.3d 466, 469-70 (N.M. 2004) (no enforceable arbitration agreement where policy was annexed to employee manual permitting employer to modify manual at will). Should the manner in which the employer establishes and communicates its arbitration policy matter in assessing contract enforceability? If most employees simply sign whatever documents the employer places before them in the application process, why is it any more objectionable to bind them to a handbook or e-mail arbitration policy?

3. *Consideration.* Normal contract analysis would not find any consideration problem in the usual mandatory agreement to arbitrate: After all, both sides are giving up something (the right to litigate in court) and gaining something (a different dispute resolution process), and, of course, the law "doesn't inquire into the adequacy of consideration." Plus, of course, the employee can be viewed as getting another benefit entirely for giving up her right to litigate: getting or continuing employment. Whether this analysis is too formalistic is another question. *See* Rachel Arnow-Richman, *Cube-wrap Contracts: The Rise of Delayed Term, Standard Form Employment Agreements,* 49 Ariz. L. Rev. 637, 655 (2007) (arguing that employers who insist on post-hire arbitration "capitalize on preexisting [power] imbalances" between the parties by delaying "deal-breaking terms" of employment until the point where the worker already has a sunk investment in his or her new job and is unable to refuse).

However, a few courts have held that an arbitration agreement is "illusory" and consequently lacking consideration where the agreement does not treat employer and employee claims equally or where the employer retains significant discretion over the arbitration policy. *See, e.g., Gibson v. Neighborhood Health Clinics,* 121 F.3d 1126 (7th Cir. 1997) (no consideration where only the employee agreed to arbitrate); *Cheek v. United Healthcare of Mid-Atlantic, Inc.,* 835 A.2d 656, 661 (Md. 2003) (refusing to enforce arbitration clause in employment manual which reserved to employer permission to alter agreement "at its sole and absolute discretion . . . with or without notice"); *see also Saylor v. Ryan's Family Steak Houses*, 613 S.E.2d 914, 924 (W. Va. 2005) ("meager" promise to review employment application insufficient consideration to support applicant's promise to submit all disputes to arbitration).

Most courts, however, have rejected this argument, pointing out that contract law does not require equivalency of obligation with respect to specific terms but merely that "the contract as a whole is otherwise supported by consideration on both sides." *Walters v. AAA Waterproofing*, 85 P.3d 389, 392 (Wash. Ct. App. 2004); *see also Oblix v. Winiecki*, 374 F.3d 488, 491 (7th Cir. 2004) (that the employer "did not promise to arbitrate all of its potential claims is neither here nor there. [Plaintiff] does not deny that the arbitration clause is supported by consideration — her salary."). As we saw in Note 8 on page 1027, not committing to arbitration, or at least carving out some matters for the court, might be very important to some employers.

4. *Invalidating Doctrines.* If assent and consideration are established, an employee's only means of defeating an arbitration agreement is to invoke one of the traditional defenses to contract explored in Section B, such as fraud, duress, or mistake, or unconscionability (although notice that Justice Thomas would not have read the FAA to permit any unconscionability attack, limiting the grounds for doing so to formation issues).

5. *Who Decides?* To this point, we have ignored one obvious question: who decides issues of unconscionability and other contractual defenses to arbitration clauses — a court or the arbitrator? As the cases you have read so far would suggest, issues of the validity of the arbitration agreement, including unconscionability, are generally decided by a court, under the theory that parties may not be compelled to use the arbitral forum absent an enforceable agreement. The Supreme Court recently reaffirmed that this is the general rule. *Granite Rock Co. v. International Brotherhood of Teamsters*, 561 U.S. 287 (2010). On the other hand, issues as to the scope of the arbitration clause, such as whether a particular type of dispute falls within the jurisdiction of the arbitrator, are generally decided by the arbitrator. The Supreme Court has made clear that this includes disputes over whether the agreement permits parties to bring class-based arbitration proceedings. *See Green Tree Financial Corp. v. Bazzle*, 539 U.S. 444 (2003). *Compare Stolt-Nielsen S. A. v. AnimalFeeds Int'l Corp.*, 559 U.S. 662 (2010) (overturning arbitral decision ordering class arbitration because it had no basis in the arbitration agreement) *with Oxford Health Plans LLC v. Sutter*, 133 S. Ct. 2064 (2013) (upholding arbitrator's order for class arbitration because the order was based on the agreement to arbitrate, whether or not it was a correct interpretation).

However, one Supreme Court arbitration case involving arbitration of an age discrimination claim blurs the distinction. In *Rent-A-Center West, Inc. v. Jackson*, 561 U.S. 63, 66 (2010), the employer's arbitration contract provided not only for arbitration of all employment disputes, but also that "[t]he Arbitrator, and not any federal, state, or local court or agency, shall have exclusive authority to resolve any dispute relating to . . . enforceability or formation of this Agreement, including . . . any claim that any part of this Agreement is void or voidable." The majority held that this committed any question as to unconscionability of the contract to the arbitrator. In light of *Rent-A-Center*, one would expect such delegation clauses to become increasingly common in employer-drafted contracts.

PROBLEM

13-7. You are in-house employment counsel for Cobalt Light Fixtures, a national company with employees all over the United States. The CEO would like to consider adopting an arbitration program as a means of reducing liability for employment disputes. She has asked you to make a recommendation and draft a sample contract. What would you counsel her about relative advantages and disadvantages to using arbitration? What features should your arbitration program have? Can you draft an agreement that would be enforceable in all states, including California? How would you recommend introducing it to the workforce?

2. Liquidated Damages Clauses

Smelkinson SYSCO v. Harrell
875 A.2d 188 (Md. 2002)

THIEME, J.

Appellant Smelkinson SYSCO, Inc. (SYSCO), asks us to enforce the stipulated damages provision of a Settlement Agreement and General Release that the company entered into with former employee James E. Harrell, appellee. The parties agreed, *inter alia*, that, if Harrell breached the agreement, SYSCO's damages would include the $185,000 the company paid to settle pending and future disputes with Harrell. [The trial court ruled that the clause was an unenforceable as a penalty.]

Harrell, a SYSCO truck driver for 13 years, filed race discrimination, labor complaints, and workers' compensation claims against the company. After consulting with counsel, Harrell and SYSCO settled those claims in a confidential "global" settlement covering all pending and potential claims involving Harrell and SYSCO. The parties executed a Settlement Agreement and General Release (the Settlement Agreement) dated July 2, 2001, and submitted it to the Workers' Compensation Commission for approval. The terms of that agreement became effective upon the Commission's August 31, 2001 approval of it as an "Agreement of Final Compromise and Settlement."

Under the Settlement Agreement, Harrell resigned his employment and promised never to seek re-employment with SYSCO. In addition, he covenanted that he would not "disparage" SYSCO and that he would "neither voluntarily aid nor voluntarily assist in any way third party claims made or pursued against the Company." SYSCO, in turn, agreed not to challenge Harrell's unemployment compensation appeal and to pay Harrell a total of $185,000.[3]

---

3. Of that payment, $149,999 was allocated to the workers' compensation claims and the remaining $35,001 was allocated to Harrell's federal labor and discrimination claims.

At issue in this appeal is the parties' agreement regarding damages. With independent counsel advising him, Harrell agreed to the following stipulated damages provision in Paragraph 7 of the Settlement Agreement:

> Mr. Harrell agrees not to disparage the Company and the Company agrees not to disparage Mr. Harrell. . . . It is expressly understood that this paragraph is a *substantial and material provision* of the Agreement and *a breach of this paragraph will support a cause of action* for breach of contract and will entitle the aggrieved parties *to recover damages flowing from such breach specifically, including, but not limited to, the recovery of any payments made pursuant to paragraph numbers 1 and 2 above as well as payments made pursuant to the Agreement of Final Compromise and Settlement pending before the Maryland Workers' Compensation Commission.* It is expressly agreed that *the non-exclusive damages set forth in this paragraph in the event of a breach are not a penalty but are fair and reasonable in light of the difficulty of proving prejudice to the Company in the event of such a breach.* . . .

(Emphasis added.)

Shortly after executing the Settlement Agreement and accepting full payment under it, Harrell breached his promises not to disparage SYSCO and not to assist third-party claimants. In a letter dated December 11, 2001, Harrell wrote to Mike Cutchember, a SYSCO shop steward, on behalf of John Womack, a SYSCO employee with whom Harrell worked. In its entirety, the letter states:

> John Womack called me on 12/14/01, about a problem with [J.B.] a white female supervisor at Sysco. He had said to me weeks before I left Sysco: she tried to get him fired, by blaming him for an accident, that happened two months earlier by someone else. We've talked off and on and he often said, that she has been harassing him at work. John Womack is one of the drivers I daily talked with for years while working at Sysco. I would make several drivers know what was going on in my affairs for my protection, and witness. I had also told him about [J.B.] hugging me and I didn't know if it was a plan they had against me.
>
> [J.B.] hugged me twice while in the warehouse at the docks; after she and [A.A.] came to a stop trying to get something on me. I told [P.M.] a shopsteward about [J.B.] hugging me; he said, that is sexual harassment. And I should file a complaint on her about that, but I didn't. This was a time when Sysco was doing everything they could to frame me for anything so they could fire me; but [there] was no legal reason, but the charges I filed against them concerning racial discrimination.
>
> A District Sales Manager rode with me on a route one day, and he was harassing the customers about me, and asking them "do I do my work". He also watched everything I did, how fast I drove, and came into the back room when I was talking to a customer and wrote notes as we talked. One salesperson tried to get a customer to write a bad letter against me to get me fired, but they refused. Three of the employees at that stop told me about this, this is the same place where [J.B.] and [A.A.] came harassing me and the customer for over an hour. If I can be of any more help let me know.

The next day, on December 12, 2002, Womack initiated race discrimination charges against SYSCO at the Maryland Commission on Human Relations. Like Harrell, Womack complained that he was the victim of racial discrimination by J.B., a white female safety supervisor.

[This letter came to SYSCO's attention as part of Womack's suit. SYSCO then filed suit against Harrell for breach of contract and ultimately moved for summary judgment. The trial court found Harrell in breach of the nondisparagement clause and of another prohibiting him for "aiding and assisting third-party claims" against SYSCO. He was prospectively ordered to "perform each and every obligation" imposed upon him by the Settlement Agreement, but the court held the liquidated damages clause applied only to disparagement, and held it unenforceable because it "smacks directly of a penalty." The court found it "hard to see how a simple disparagement . . . could in any reasonable way be equated to a damage amount of $185,000." The case proceeded to trial, after which the court entered judgment for SYSCO, granting nominal damages only.]

I. Stipulated Damages

SYSCO challenges the trial court's decision not to enforce the parties' agreement that SYSCO could recover the $185,000 it paid to Harrell if Harrell breached his non-disparagement covenant. We find merit in SYSCO's challenge, even though for the reasons set forth below, we do not view the clause in question as a liquidated damages agreement.

A. Liquidated Damages[4]

The term "liquidated damages" means a "specific sum of money . . . expressly stipulated by the parties to a . . . contract as the amount of damages to be recovered by either party for a breach of the agreement by the other." *Traylor v. Grafton*, 332 A.2d 651 (Md. 1975). As a general rule, "a liquidated damage clause is within the substantive law of contracts, and — if not a 'penalty' — is an enforceable provision as a sum agreed upon by the parties to be paid in the event of a breach, enforceable as any other provision or valid promise in the contract."

. . . The burden of proving that a particular damage stipulation is not enforceable is "on the party seeking to invalidate" it. Maryland courts generally consider the following three factors as the defining characteristics of an enforceable liquidated damages clause:

(1) clear and unambiguous language providing for "a certain sum";
(2) stipulated damages that represent reasonable compensation for the damages anticipated from the breach, measured prospectively at the time of the contract rather than in hindsight at the time of the breach; and

---

4. The Law of Liquidated Damages is one of the most ancient concepts in the law. For example, one of the relics of Hammurabi's reign (1795-1750 BC) is the code, which provides: "If a man has knocked out the eye of a patrician, his eye shall be knocked out." Jewish law provided some interesting remedies with societal as well as private law consequences. *Exodus* 22:1 provides: "If a man shall steal an ox, or a sheep, and kill it, or sell it; he shall restore five oxen for an ox, and four sheep for a sheep."

After quite literally centuries of veneration of these concepts, like the camel's nose under the tent, once the concept of "penalty" crept into this area, the law of liquidated damages became *sui generis* within the law of contracts by overtly insulting the freedom of parties to structure their own agreement which is universally acknowledged to be at the heart of the law of contracts. Why should such clauses be treated differently than other contract provisions that may be equally unfair or one-sided?

(3) a "mandatory binding agreement[ ] before the fact which may not be altered to correspond to actual damages determined after the fact."

See Holloway v. Faw, Casson & Co., 572 A.2d 510 (Md. 1990). . . .

By including an agreed damages provision in the contract, contracting parties reduce the cost of contract breakdown by eliminating the expense of calculating damages and by reducing the likelihood of litigation. Either or both parties to a contract, therefore, commonly enjoy the right to terminate at some cost. . . .

The trial court, Harrell, and SYSCO premised their debate over the enforcement of Paragraph 7 on the conclusion that this is a liquidated damages provision. As a threshold matter, we point out that this characterization is not dictated by the parties' use of the label "liquidated damages." Although courts certainly consider "the nomenclature used by the parties," we are not bound by it when other language and circumstances support a different conclusion. For example, the parties' description of their damage agreement as liquidated damages "is not determinative in passing upon whether or not the payment of the designated sum is in fact a penalty." Instead, "the decisive element is the intention of the parties," which "is to be gleaned from the subject matter, the language of the contract and the circumstances surrounding its execution[,]" taken as a whole. We follow the same approach in determining whether a stipulated damages remedy is a liquidated damages clause.

Although the trial court focused on the second feature of a valid liquidated damage agreement, we shall set aside, for the moment, the question of whether the amount of stipulated damages in Paragraph 7 is reasonable. This is because we conclude that the agreement lacks both the first and third characteristics of a liquidated damages clause, in that it does not clearly identify a "certain sum" and does not create a "binding agreement before the fact that may not be altered to correspond to actual damages." By agreeing that the non-breaching party is "entitled . . . to recover *damages flowing from* such breach" (emphasis added), Harrell and SYSCO selected the same type of *post hoc* yardstick that traditionally has been used to measure actual or "unliquidated" damages. Instead of agreeing to either a pre-determined amount of damages, or to a formula for damage, in the event of a breach, the parties more broadly agreed that the recoverable damages "flowing from such breach" would include the settlement payments. Significantly, they also agreed that SYSCO's damages would . . . be "not limited to" that amount if the company also could show other actual damages from Harrell's breach. The parties' understanding that this agreement was not a mandatory and binding stipulation fixing the amount of damages at the $185,000 paid to Harrell is underscored by their explicit agreement that the stipulated "damages set forth in this paragraph in the event of a breach" are "*non-exclusive.*" (Emphasis added.) Because Paragraph 7 does not contain a pre-determined "ceiling" on the amount of "damages flowing from" Harrell's breach of the *non-disparagement* covenant, we conclude that it is an unliquidated damage stipulation rather than a liquidated damages clause. . . .

B. Enforcement of Paragraph 7 Damages

It is debatable whether a stipulated damages clause such as the one before us is subject to the "reasonableness" or "penalty" standard that applies to a liquidated damages clause, or, instead, whether it is measured against a more deferent standard, such as unconscionability, that applies to other contractual terms. That question need not be answered to resolve this appeal, however. Assuming *arguendo* that this provision may not be enforced unless it is reasonable, we nevertheless conclude that it satisfies that test.

Determining whether a stipulated remedy is unreasonable "can be hard for the same reason the parties [find] it hard to calculate actual damages in the first place: what's the benchmark against which the stipulated damages will be compared to determine whether they are" reasonable? *Scavenger Sale Investors v. Bryant*, 288 F.3d 309, 311 (7th Cir. 2002). Moreover, as Judge Easterbrook observed in upholding the damages clause of a settlement agreement, "everything depends on which end of the telescope one looks through." *Id.*

Here, the language and circumstances surrounding the Settlement Agreement conclusively establish that both Harrell and SYSCO considered this stipulated damage remedy to be reasonable. They reasonably conceded that SYSCO would suffer harm to its reputation and/or additional labor and litigation expenses if Harrell continued to disparage the company for allegedly creating a hostile work environment in which long-term African-American union employees such as his co-worker Womack and himself were harassed, unfairly disciplined, not compensated for injuries, and retaliated against. In addition, Harrell reasonably acknowledged the difficulty SYSCO would have in proving a specific dollar figure for the "prejudice" "flowing from" his breach of the *non-disparagement* covenant. Thus, the record shows that Harrell understood that this settlement rested squarely on his assurances to SYSCO that this proof problem would not leave SYSCO out-of-pocket $185,000 with only a toothless remedy in the event he continued to disparage the company.

What SYSCO bought through the negotiated settlement, then, was immediate and long-term "peace" with Harrell, with the attendant right to expect that it would no longer have to expend money, effort, or goodwill in responding to his disparaging allegations. Indeed, the language in Paragraph 7 and the circumstances surrounding the execution of the Settlement Agreement leave no doubt that SYSCO and Harrell struck a bargain that was designed to prevent precisely what happened here—that SYSCO would pay Harrell $185,000 to drop all his allegations, claims, and agitations against the company, only to have Harrell later resume them. Without Harrell's assurance that he would not do so, SYSCO would not have agreed to pay Harrell $185,000 to settle his claims. Thus, Harrell's agreement that it is "fair and reasonable" for the "damages flowing from such breach" to include that settlement money was a negotiated cornerstone of this Settlement Agreement.

In this respect, Paragraph 7 fairly may be viewed as both a disincentive to Harrell *and* an assurance of performance to SYSCO. To the extent that it might arguably be characterized as exacting a "penalty for breach," we see nothing unreasonable about such a clearly understood and expressed *quid pro quo*. To the contrary, there are important reasons to enforce this remedy. . . .

In refusing to enforce Harrell's agreement regarding damages, the trial court effectively immunized Harrell from the consequences of deliberately breaching his obligations under the Settlement Agreement. We agree with SYSCO that, as a matter of policy and practice, if an employee is permitted to disregard the covenants upon which he settled, and then avoid the damage remedy that he agreed to, then "no employer should consider a settlement in these types of cases because it will likely be left without adequate redress in the event of a breach." . . .

As alternative grounds for this appeal, SYSCO complains that the trial court erred in refusing to let the jury decide the amount of its actual damages. . . . At trial and before this Court, however, SYSCO conceded that it did not offer any evidence that its pecuniary loss exceeded the $185,000 it paid in "peace money." To the contrary, counsel for SYSCO acknowledged the company's inability to prove such damages, observing that "this type of harm, which is reputational in nature, is hard, if not impossible, to quantify in dollar terms." Given this record, SYSCO is not entitled to a new jury trial on actual damages. . . .

NOTES

1. *Settlement versus Initial Contract. SYSCO* involves a nondisparagement clause and a stipulated damages clause in a settlement agreement. But both clauses, particularly stipulated damages clauses, can be used in basic employment contracts. As we saw in Chapter 3, contracts for fixed-term or other secure employment arrangements, particularly with high-level employees, are often structured to allow parties to "breach" upon payment, either by providing severance to an employee terminated without cause or requiring forfeiture of deferred compensation to the employee who voluntarily terminates prematurely. Nondisparagement contracts entered into upon hire have generally not been as common, but in an era of Internet-enhanced communications and proliferating blogs, there may be reason for employers to consider adopting them more frequently. As you consider the questions below, ask whether and when you might use either kind of clause in drafting the initial employment contract or in settling a matter after an employment dispute has arisen, or in both contexts.

2. *Nondisparagement versus Defamation.* One way of thinking about nondisparagement clauses is as a form of private ordering responding to the limits of tort law. Where an employee makes statements adverse to an employer's interests, an employer could pursue a defamation claim irrespective of whether the parties agreed to a nondisparagement clause. But, as we saw in the discussion of employee defamation claims in Chapter 5, the key to liability in this tort is the falsehood of the statement. Nondisparagement by virtue of a contract provision prevents the employee from saying or writing damaging things about the employer, even if they are true. Further, a valid nondisparagement clause will also avoid complicated questions such as whether a statement is privileged or represents an opinion rather than a fact that would likely arise if the same statement were to be challenged in tort. *See Eichelkraut v. Camp*, 513 S.E.2d 267 (Ga. Ct. App. 1999) (defamation law not relevant to contract claim for disparagement). And then there's the ethical issue. The N.Y. TIMES "Ethicist" column, June 30, 2013, p. 13, Magazine section, responded to a question about the ethics of not responding to a request by a friend or acquaintance about a former "genuinely bad boss," when a settlement agreement prohibited his discussing the case or making "disparaging" remarks to anyone. The Ethicist, via writer Chuck Klosterman, responded by critiquing contractual efforts to prevent individuals from speaking about their personal experience, but noted that when there was a contract

> I can't advise you to explicitly break a contract you signed. But I can advise you to do what you believe to be just, within the limitations of the contractual language. I would call the professional acquaintance and say the following: "I am aware that you're considering taking a job with [ ]. I'd love to talk to you about this, but I'm contractually unable to

discuss my departure from that company or the circumstances surrounding it. Legally, I also can't say anything about the company that could be construed as disparaging. So I'm just calling to tell you I can't talk about any of this." Unless your acquaintance has a brain made of concrete, this content-free conversation should achieve your intent. If the settlement is so watertight that you can't even disclose that the agreement exists, meet the acquaintance in person and say, "I used to work for the company you're considering joining." When he asks about the employment experience, silently stare at him with an expression of existential despair.

If you are a lawyer advising a client in these circumstances, would you give that advice?

3. *Nondisparagement of Employees.* Employers are not the only ones who seek nondisparagement protection, and it is common for settlement agreements to have mutual covenants providing that neither side will disparage the other. This provides employees with the same advantages as employers in avoiding the proof hurdles associated with a defamation claim. A similar way of protecting the interests of the employee is for parties to agree to the content of any reference the employer will supply if contacted by prospective employers. They may decide that an employer can supply only a "neutral" reference — dates of employment, titles held, and the like — or they may draft an actual reference letter and include it as part of the settlement agreement. *See, e.g., Giannecchini v. Hospital of St. Raphael*, 780 A.2d 1006, 1008 (Conn. Super. Ct. 2002). While obviously useful for employees, this practice can also be beneficial to the employer. As you saw in Chapter 5, references are a common source of defamation claims by employees. By obtaining the employee's approval of the reference in conjunction with a settlement of all claims, the employer can avoid the risk that future tort claims will arise.

4. *The Public's Right to Know?* Since nondisparagement clauses prevent individuals from speaking the truth, there is an obvious tension between such clauses and the public's general interest in learning more about individuals and entities with whom they might deal. Such agreements have been criticized as private gag orders through with parties can hide criminal or other misconduct from the public eye. At the same time, they can result in backlash where such behavior ultimately comes to light. The Catholic Church priest pedophilia scandals demonstrate that concealing serious wrongdoing can have devastating public relations effects as well as provide more ammunition to those injured by the employee wrongdoers.

Nondisparagement law is still in its infancy, but as of yet, courts have not been inclined to strike down nondisparagement clauses on public policy grounds, even in situations where such an argument was especially plausible. For example, *Patlovich v. Rudd*, 949 F. Supp. 585 (N. D. Ill. 1996), rejected such an argument in enforcing a nondisparagement clause against a former employee physician who alleged that another doctor in the employer's practice had made a medical error and tried to conceal it from the patient. The court recognized a policy in favor of open communication between doctor and patients, but it held that it did not reach the former employee's alleged disclosure of the error and cover-up via hundreds of anonymous letters. Perhaps more pointedly, the court in *Giannecchini v. Hospital of St. Raphael*, 780 A.2d 1006 (Conn. Super. Ct. 2002), held a hospital in breach of the terms of a settlement agreement that promised a neutral reference to a former nurse who had been discharged for making serious medication errors. It did so despite recognizing that the settlement agreement, while benefiting both contracting parties, was "affirmatively disadvantageous" to future patients. *Id.* at 1010; *see also Cooper Tire &*

Rubber Co. v. Farese, Farese & Farese Prof. Ass'n, 423 F.3d 446, 457 (5th Cir. 2005) (finding nondisclosure agreement not violative of public policy, despite fact that it could be used to hide illegal activity, where employer sought to enforce agreement against former employee who supplied affidavit and testimony concerning employer's alleged spoliation of evidence); *Katz v. S. Burlington Sch. Dist.*, 970 A.2d 1226, 1229 (Vt. 2009) ("Plaintiff's claim here is premised upon a vague allegation that the non-disparagement clause may prevent Durckel from 'blow[ing] the whistle on the district's corruption.' This is plainly insufficient to void the clause on public policy grounds."); *cf. Henley v. Cuyahoga County Bd. of Mental Retardation & Developmental Disabilities*, 141 F. App'x 437 (6th Cir. 2005) (rejecting First Amendment challenge to nondisparagement clause in agreement with public agency).

5. *Limiting Nondisparagement Clauses to Comply with Public Policy.* Most non-disparagement clauses are framed in terms of prohibiting employees from "voluntarily" disparaging the employer. The notion here is that employees are free to speak when they are subpoenaed or otherwise under legal compulsion. Further, employees may have a nonwaivable right to report what they believe to be law violations to the authorities. Some nondisparagement clauses make this distinction clear, perhaps to avoid criticism that they are overbroad and therefore invalid. In some cases, there is a more concrete public policy than a generalized public right to know. We saw in Chapter 9 that the antidiscrimination laws protect employees from retaliation for, inter alia, participating in proceedings raising discrimination claims, and the Supreme Court has made clear recently that retaliation against employees but outside the employment context is also barred. *See Burlington Northern & Santa Fe Ry. v. White*, reproduced at page 720. Might a nondisparagement clause violate this provision by barring an employee from reporting a violation to the EEOC? *See EEOC v. Severn Trent Servs.*, 358 F.3d 438 (7th Cir. 2004) (finding "inadequately reasoned" a district court opinion enjoining the employer from enforcing a nondisparagement clause to prevent a witness from participating in an EEOC investigation). Should an employer's suit for breach of a nondisparagement clause be barred by the antiretaliation provisions (or more generally, the public policy tort) where the employee voluntarily discloses discrimination or other violations of public policy to an enforcement agency? In *SYSCO* itself, could the suit be viewed as unlawful retaliation for opposing discrimination? *See generally* Richard Moberly, Jordan A. Thomas & Jason Zuckerman, *De Facto Gag Clauses: The Legality of Employment Agreements that Undermine Dodd-Frank's Whistleblower Provisions*, 30 ABA J. LAB. & EMP. L. — (forthcoming 2014) (discussing the enforceability of these increasingly prevalent contractual restrictions on whistleblowing, which variously (1) require an employee to notify the employer internally before disclosing to the SEC; (2) require the employee to waive any whistleblower bounty; and (3) condition the receipt of severance on compliance with confidentiality provisions).

6. *Enforcing Unenforceable Clauses.* The pairing of a stipulated damages clause with a nondisparagement clause in the *SYSCO* settlement agreement likely reflects some careful planning on the employer's part. While many firms want a nondisparagement commitment and such clauses are increasingly standard in settling employment (and other disputes), they are very difficult to enforce by way of damages. This is because harm is often hard to prove and even harder to quantify. In *SYSCO* itself, the agreement allowed the employer to obtain damages in addition to the amount it paid Harrell, but the employer essentially conceded its inability to prove any pecuniary loss suffered as a result of disparagement. Could SYSCO have claimed the costs of defending Womack's suit as damages? Maybe not, because Womack might have gone forward without Harrell's supporting letter, or because Harrell could have been subpoenaed by Womack in any event.

In this regard, nondisparagement clauses are similar to noncompetition clauses, which also pose proof of loss problems. It can be difficult for an employer to show, for instance, that a loss of business or profits resulted from the competitive behavior of a particular employee. Also, in both contexts, the cat is typically out of the bag once the disparagement or competition takes place. For this reason, both clauses are typically enforced by injunctions, often sought in advance of a breach. Once a breach occurs, however, a stipulated damages clause might be the only way for an employer to obtain any monetary relief in such cases.

On the other hand, stipulated damages clauses create their own enforceability problems — the employee is frequently judgment proof. While the employer prevails in *SYSCO*, it is by no means clear that it will be able to enforce any judgment it gets against Harrell. But if enforcement is even a possibility, it may influence employee conduct. This may be true even if the clause is invalid as a penalty. Some employers think the *in terrorem* effect of a possible large judgment hanging over the head of the employee is the best insurance of compliance, even if the validity of the clause is dubious. Is it appropriate for a lawyer to draft a clause she knows to be unenforceable?

7. *Liquidated Damages Versus Penalties.* This is the second time you have encountered a case in which an employee defends against an employer's claim on grounds that the contract provision in question was an unenforceable liquidated damages clause. In *American Consulting Environmental Safety Services, Inc. v. Schuck,* reproduced at page 551 in Chapter 8, the court held that the defendant-employee was not required to reimburse her employer for training costs, concluding that the repayment amount stipulated in the parties' contract was disproportionate to the employer's actual loss. The rule limiting the enforceability of stipulated damages clause to those that are reasonable has been subject to criticism. Footnote 4 of *SYSCO* argues that freedom of contract is antithetical with court-imposed limitations on stipulated damages and seems to suggest that freedom of contract should prevail. The footnote is inartful, however, in its reference to the Code of Hammurabi, which is comparable to a statute that prescribes penalties for particular forms of misconduct. A closer analogy is *The Merchant of Venice*, where the parties agreed that damages for failure to repay a loan will be, literally, a pound of flesh. Is Judge Thieme really arguing that parties should be able to set whatever they wish (perhaps short of dismemberment) as stipulated damages? Perhaps it depends on who the parties are and the nature of the contract. Note that stipulated damages clauses are especially common in heavily law-yered commercial agreements between sophisticated parties. But in the employment context, they have most often been used in connection with noncompetition clauses, where the employees may or may not be high-level. *See, e.g. Burzee v. Park Ave. Ins. Agency, Inc.,* 946 So. 2d 1200 (Fla. Dist. Ct. App. 2006) (refusing to enforce a $10,000 liquidated damages clause because it was not calibrated to the extent of the breach); *Junkin v. Northeast Ark. Internal Med. Clinic, P.A.,* 42 S.W.3d 432 (Ark. 2001). There is a lively academic literature on the merits of judicial policing of such clauses, focusing in particular on the economic case for and against intervention. *See, e.g., Lake River Corp. v. Carborundum Co.,* 769 F.2d 1284, 1288-89 (7th Cir. 1985); Alan Schwartz, *The Myth That Promisees Prefer Supracompensatory Remedies: An Analysis of Contracting for Damage Measures,* 100 YALE L. J. 369 (1990).

8. *Judge Thieme's Fancy Footwork.* Whatever the commentators contend, the law has historically viewed liquidated damages clauses, unlike most other contractual

terms, as subject to judicial policing. The RESTATEMENT (SECOND) OF CONTRACTS sets forth the conventional view in § 356(1):

> Damages for breach by either party may be liquidated in the agreement but only at an amount that is reasonable in the light of the anticipated or actual loss caused by the breach and the difficulties of proof of loss. A term fixing unreasonably large liquidated damages is unenforceable on grounds of public policy as a penalty.

Is the law in Maryland significantly different? Are you persuaded by the court's analysis that the clause in question is *not* a liquidated damages clause? The court seems to view it as a minimum damages clause, but isn't that a variety of liquidated damages? Since Judge Thieme goes on to conclude that the clause is not a penalty, the issue is not important in this case — but note that he has cleverly set up the possibility that such clauses in the future are not reviewable for "reasonableness" but only for unconscionability, a much more difficult basis for challenge.

Judge Thieme's discussion of reasonableness is itself a paragon of confusion. He focuses heavily on what Harrell understood and agreed to, but why should consent matter if the whole point of the reasonableness doctrine is that parties are not permitted to agree to penalties? He speaks of SYSCO losing the benefit of its bargain, but the company might have had used more reasonable means of protecting itself, for instance by drafting the agreement to permit it to rescind upon a breach the nondisparagement clause. Of course, true rescission would mean that, while the employer would recover the compensation paid, the employee would similarly regain the rights to assert the claims the settlement agreement was designed to extinguish. Perhaps that is precisely why the clause ought to be deemed unreasonable — it allows the employer to have its cake and eat it too. Finally, Judge Thieme appears concerned that, if the clause is not enforced, SYSCO will receive no damages from Harrell's breach. But that is simply a consequence of the fact that SYSCO cannot prove any loss; contract law does not permit damages unless actual harm is suffered.

The year after *SYSCO* was decided, the same court, without Judge Thieme sitting, handed down *Willard Packaging Co. v. Javier*, 899 A.2d 940, 955 (Md. Ct. Spec. App. 2006), which refused to enforce a $50,000 stipulated damages clause for a former employee's breach of a covenant not to compete, finding that "[n]o reasonable method was employed whatsoever in affixing the amount of stipulated damages in the case sub judice." The defendant had not been provided with any confidential information the employer had a legitimate interest in protecting and the clause "was merely meant to penalize and punish Javier for taking a job with a competitor of Willard, rather than to compensate Willard for any loss, especially in light of the concession by Willard's officer that appellee was not possessed of any particular skill or talent, which, if practiced for a competitor, would likely result in damage to Willard."

9. *Private Ordering in Response to Judicial Limits on Private Ordering.* Notice that the stipulated damages clause in *SYSCO* not only provides for a minimum recovery but affirmatively asserts that the amount is "fair and reasonable" and not a "penalty." What is going on here? May parties really "agree" *ex ante* on how a principle of public law will apply to their contract? In other words, may they stipulate as to a conclusion of law? Whether or not they may, they often try. In the noncompete context, for instance, it is increasingly common for agreements to contain language attesting to the reasonableness of the scope of the restraint or the right of the court to reduce the agreement if overbroad. To his credit, Judge Thieme does not rely on the "fair and reasonableness" language in assessing whether the stipulated amount runs afoul of the liquidated damages rule. Might it have been appropriate, however, to rely on it as evidence that the clause was in fact a liquidated damages clause? After all, it is quite certainly an invocation of the legal standard applicable to those types of clauses.

10. *Representing Harrell.* Nondisparagement clauses are so routine that attorneys sometimes treat them as simply more boilerplate. *SYSCO* makes clear that attorneys representing employees must at least drive home to their clients the seriousness of the clause and the resultant consequences of breach, particularly when the agreement includes a damages stipulation. In hindsight, maybe Harrell should have been advised not to sign the settlement in the first place. Or perhaps his lawyer should have made more of an effort to strike or limit the nondisparagement clause. If you were that lawyer, how would you have proceeded? Would you have tried to renegotiate, or would you have been concerned that doing so would jeopardize the deal? In other words, do you think the employer, if otherwise satisfied with the terms of settlement, would have been willing to go forward without the nondisparagement clause?

11. *Alternative Methods of Enforcing Settlement.* If the employer is worried about the possibility of breach and the dubious validity of a liquidated damage clause (or perhaps the uncollectability of any resultant judgment), are there any other planning techniques available? Another possibility for an employer worried about disparagement is to structure the payout not as a lump sum but as a stream of payments whose continuance depends on the employee not breaching the nondisparagement clause (or other clause in the contract).

PROBLEM

13-8. You are representing management in negotiating a settlement with the attorney for a former employee, an individual who is well liked by current employees and still socializes with them. He was employed in the Human Resources department for many years before his termination and had access to all relevant policies and their application by the corporation over that period of time. His lawyer indicated early in the negotiations that "there was a lot of dirty laundry" that would be relevant to the employee's age discrimination and state whistleblower claims. You are comfortable with all the terms of the proposed settlement, but are very concerned about the ex-employee stirring up trouble and/or leaking sensitive information. Try drafting language to include in the final agreement that will address these concerns. Do you think your draft will be acceptable to the employee's attorney?

D. EMPLOYMENT PRACTICES LIABILITY INSURANCE

Individuals and businesses often transfer risk for financial losses they may incur by paying premiums to insurance carriers. In the employment context, employers have been required for about a century to carry workers' compensation insurance, but until relatively recently there was little market (and therefore little availability) for insurance for other employment-related liabilities. This was largely because the law posed few risks for employers, other than contractual claims by very highly placed employees, which were not the kind of loss normally contemplated by insurance in any event.

As statutory and decisional employment law began providing more meaningful remedies, some employers sought to recover both the costs of defending suits by workers and liabilities incurred when such suits were successful by making claims under traditional business coverage, General Liability ("GL") policies, or Director and Officer ("D&O") policies. These efforts were often a stretch. For example, the typical GL policy obligates the insurer to pay damages arising from property damage or personal injury caused by a covered occurrence. *See* Francis J. Mootz III, *Insurance Coverage of Employment Discrimination Claims*, 52 U. MIAMI L. REV. 1, 10-11 (1997). In most cases, the policy would seem not to cover an employee's suit, and GL polices often reinforced this with an explicit "employee exclusion" typically providing that the policy does not cover "bodily injury" to any "employee of the insured arising out of and in the course of employment by the insured." *See Am. Motorists Ins. Co. v. L-C-A Sales Co.*, 713 A.2d 1007 (N.J. 1998) (policy exclusion precluded coverage for employee's age discrimination claim). *But cf. Griffin v. Cameron Coll.*, No. 96-0951 1997 U.S. Dist. LEXIS 14218, *5 (E.D. La. 1997) (mental anguish suffered by student as a result of alleged ADA violations by university constituted "bodily injury" under general liability policy). While GL policies have been found to reach a few employment-related claims, such as defamation, *see Meadowbrook v. Tower Insurance Co.*, 559 N.W.2d 411, 413 n.1 (Minn. 1997), they provided, at best, very spotty coverage for employment-related risks.

As the threat of substantial liability increased, insurance carriers had two responses. The first was to strengthen the exclusions to lessen the risk of being held liable under traditional policies; and the second was to develop a new product — Employment Practices Liability Insurance ("EPLI") policies, which are specifically geared to employment-related practices. These policies typically cover liability arising out of the insured's employment-related offenses against its employees, including the costs of defending claims. They may also cover liability by agents of the employer (personal liability is a risk for some aspects of employment law but not for others). A typical website offering such policies states that the following risks are covered:

- Sexual Harassment
- Discrimination
- Statute Violation
- Negligent Hiring
- Negligent Supervision
- Negligent Promotion
- Negligent Retention
- Disabilities
- Breach of Contract
- Wrongful Termination
- Loss of Consortium
- Emotional Distress
- Invasion of Privacy
- Drug Testing
- Mental Anguish
- Libel

- Slander
- Wage and Hour Disputes

See http://www.epli.com/ (last visited July 11, 2014). This range of coverage, however, may be somewhat deceptive. Insurance companies are in the business of managing their own risks, and some policies are subject to significant exclusions. For example, EPLI policies usually exclude punitive damages from coverage. Further, policies may have significant deductibles to reduce the "moral hazard" that insurance creates.

There is an ongoing debate as to whether coverage of risks such as punitive damages and, indeed, insurance for any intentional employer conduct is against public policy. The argument to this effect is that shifting the loss to insurers blunts the employer incentives to comply with the law. *See generally* Richard A. Bales & Julie McGhghy, *Insuring Title VII Violations*, 27 S. ILL. U. L. J. 71 (2002). The contrary argument is that insurance actually increases compliance. Insurance companies seek to limit their risk not only through exclusions from coverage, but also by taking steps to require that the firms they cover are well positioned from a liability perspective. Thus, they deny coverage, or at least charge higher premiums, to higher risks, that is, firms that do not have policies and procedures in place to reduce potential liability. As Professor Mootz puts it, "the regular and rational adjustment of premiums in response to proactive measures designed jointly by the insurer and the employer has the potential to have a profound impact in the workplace." Mootz, *supra*, at 78.

There is an evolving literature on how insurers attempt to reduce risk for their insureds. *See, e.g.,* Brian T. McMillan, *Managing the Risk of Employment-Related Practices Liabilities by Influencing the Behavior of Employee Claimants*, 21 W. NEW ENG. L. REV. 427 (1999); Jack S. McCalmon, *Effective Loss Control Techniques for Employment Practices Liabilities: An Assessment of How EPLI Carriers Should Seek to Transform the American Workplace*, 21 W. NEW ENG. L. REV. 447 (1999). Needless to say, a prime focus of such efforts is creation of "bullet-proof" prevent-and-correct policies in order to trigger the affirmative defense for sexual harassment claims. But procedures for dealing with employee complaints can also address other potential risks, and either avoid them or reduce the employer's exposure by creating the opportunity to resolve difficulties early. Even more basic management tools may be part of an insurer's checklist for a good risk. For example, such things as whether the potential insured has an employee handbook, requires employees to execute an acknowledge-ment of at-will status, or uses a formal employee evaluation policy may all be part of the insurer's decision to sell coverage and at what price. Similarly, the increasing require-ment of arbitration of employment disputes may stem in part from demands by insurers in an effort to reduce both potential adverse judgments and the cost of defending claims.

PROBLEM

13-9. You are outside counsel for new law firm, High Tech, which expects to open its doors within the next week. The firm is comprised largely of former attorneys of a much larger firm, Hanover & Windsor. It has three partners, all of whom were partners at Hanover, and five associates, most of whom were

Hanover associates. It also has about eight support staff, mostly paralegals and assistants. While the attorneys are all highly specialized in their field of expertise — patent law — they rely very heavily on you for advice on the business-oriented aspects of setting up a new business. And, because the firm's client base is still somewhat uncertain, it is determined to keep its expenses as low as possible for the first year.

You just received a phone call from Hi High, managing partner. He was meeting with an insurance agent about liability and malpractice insurance, and the agent pitched something called "EPLI," insurance against employment-related suits. The premium would be about $10,000 a year. High feels confident about his ability to assess risks for what he calls "normal" insurance, but is "out of my league" with this stuff.

He wants to know whether this is a good idea and what questions he should ask the agent before going forward. Advise him.

E. BANKRUPTCY AS RISK MANAGEMENT

While bankruptcy is a specialized field of study that can be, at most, mentioned here, it is a last-gasp risk management technique that some firms, particularly those in the airline industry, have successfully used to deal with financial problems caused in large part by collective bargaining agreements that impose higher costs on them than on their competitors. Another example is the automobile bankruptcies of GM and Chrysler. *See generally* Ralph Brubaker & Charles Jordan Tabb, *Bankruptcy Reorganizations and the Troubling Legacy of Chrysler and GM*, 2010 U. ILL. L. REV. 1375. Recently, the bankruptcy of the city of Detroit has generated considerable concern about how public employee pensions will be treated. Monica Davey & Steven Yaccinojuly, *Campaign Atmosphere Amid Detroit Vote on Debt Plan*, N.Y. TIMES, July 10, 2014, at A-1.

Outside the unionized setting, bankruptcy is less likely to be a tactic used by employers but it nevertheless poses a threat to individual employment contracts. This reality means that the attorney representing employees negotiating such arrangements needs to worry not only about paper rights but also about the solvency of the company. This is an increasing concern as the length of the contract stretches into the future. Similarly, bankruptcy can also jeopardize pending employment claims. *See generally* Joanne Gelfand, *The Treatment of Employment Discrimination Claims in Bankruptcy: Priority Status, Stay Relief, Dischargeability, and Exemptions*, 56 MIAMI L. REV. 601 (2002). Finally, the financial health of the company can influence an employee's preference for lump-sum payments over more structured arrangements.

Table of Cases

Principal cases are indicated by italics.

Table of Secondary Authorities

Kathryn Abrams, *Title VII and the Complex Female Subject*, 92 Mich. L. Rev. 2479 (1994), 658

Roger I. Abrams & Dennis R. Nolan, *Toward a Theory of "Just Cause" in Employee Discipline Cases*, 1985 Duke L.J. 594, 177

Roberta Achtenberg & Karen Moulding, Sexual Orientation and the Law (2008), 712

Jane H. Aiken, *Protecting Plaintiffs' Sexual Pasts: Coping with Preconceptions Through Discretion*, 51 Emory L.J. 559 (2002), 704

Charlotte Alexander, Anna Haley-Lock, and Nantiya Ruan, *Stabilizing Low-Wage Work: Legal Remedies for Unpredictable Work Hours and Income Instability*, Harv. CR-CL L. Rev. _____ (forthcoming 2014), 872

American College of Trial Lawyers, *Recommended Practices For Companies and Their Counsel in Conducting Internal Investigations*, 46 Am. Crim. L. Rev. 73 (2009), 978

On Amir & Orly Lobel, *Driving Performance: A Growth Theory of Noncompete Law*, 16 Stan. Tech. L. Rev. 833 (2013), 496

Cheryl L. Anderson, *"Neutral" Employer Policies and the ADA: The Implications of* U.S. Airways Inc. v. Barnett *Beyond Seniority Systems*, 51 Drake L. Rev. 1 (2002), 785

Bradley A. Areheart, *GINA, Privacy, and Antisubordination*, 46 Ga. L. Rev. 705 (2012), 359

Rachel Arnow-Richman, *Accommodation Subverted: The Future of Work/Family Initiatives in a "Me, Inc." World*, 12 Tex. J. Women & L. 345 (2003), 819, 828

_____, *Bargaining for Loyalty in the Information Age: A Reconsideration of the Role of Substantive Fairness in Enforcing Employee Noncompetes*, 80 Or. L. Rev. 1163 (2001), 495, 508

_____, *Cubewrap Contracts: The Rise of Delayed Term, Standard Form Employment Agreements*, 49 Ariz. L. Rev. 637 (2007), 1031

_____, *Cubewrap Contracts and Worker Mobility: The Dilution of Employee Bargaining Power via Standard Form Noncompetes*, 2006 Mich. St. L. Rev. 963, 494, 538

_____, *Employment as Transaction*, 39 Seton Hall L. Rev. 447 (2009), 82, 124

_____, *Incenting Flexibility: The Relationship Between Public Law and Voluntary Action in Enhancing Work-Life Balance*, 42 Conn. L. Rev. 1081 (2010), 818, 820

_____, *Just Notice: Re-Reforming Employment At-Will*, 58 UCLA L. Rev. 1 (2010), 113

_____, *Mainstreaming Employment Contract Law: The Common Law Case for Reasonable Notice of Termination*, 66 Fla. L. Rev. _____ (forthcoming), 79, 81

_____, *Noncompetes, Human Capital, and Contract Formation: What Employment Law Can Learn from Family Law*, 10 Tex. Wesleyan L. Rev. 155 (2003), 501

_____, *Public Law and Private Process: Toward an Incentivized Organizational Justice Model of Equal Employment Quality for Caregivers*, 2007 Utah L. Rev. 25 (2007), 798, 820

Regina Austin, *Employer Abuse, Worker Resistance, and the Tort of Intentional Infliction of Emotional Distress*, 41 Stan. L. Rev. 1 (1988), 308

Samuel R. Bagenstos, *The Future of Disability Law*, 114 Yale L.J. 1 (2004), 819

_____, *"Rational Discrimination," Accommodation, and the Politics of (Disability) Civil Rights*, 89 Va. L. Rev. 825 (2003), 785

_____, *Subordination, Stigma, and "Disability,"* 86 Va. L. Rev. 397 (2000), 785

_____, *The Supreme Court, The Americans with Disabilities Act, and Rational Discrimination*, 55 Ala. L. Rev. 923 (2004), 765

Stephen M. Bainbridge, *Abolishing Veil Piercing*, 43 Corp. Prac. Commentator 517 (2001), 62

Richard A. Bales, *The Discord Between Collective Bargaining and Individual Employment Rights: Theoretical Origins and a Proposed Reconciliation*, 77 B.U. L. Rev. 687 (1997), 320

Richard A. Bales & Julie McGhghy, *Insuring Title VII Violations*, 27 S. Ill. U.L.J. 71 (2002), 1045

J.M. Balkin, *Free Speech and Hostile Environments*, 99 Colum. L. Rev. 2295 (1999), 419

Ralph Richard Banks & Richard Thompson Ford, *(How) Does Unconscious Bias Matter?: Law, Politics, and Racial Inequality*, 58 Emory L.J. 1053 (2009), 571

Bruce Barry, *Speechless: The Erosion of Free Expression in the American Workplace* (2007), 475

Leslie A. Barry, Note, *Determining the Proper Standard of Proof for Incapacity Under the Family and Medical Leave Act*, 97 Iowa L. Rev. 931 (2012), 827

Katharine T. Bartlett, *Only Girls Wear Barrettes: Dress and Appearance Standards, Community Norms and Workplace Equality*, 92 Mich. L. Rev. 2541 (1994), 390

Scott R. Bauries, *Individual Academic Freedom: An Ordinary Concern of the First Amendment*, 83 Miss. L.J. 677 (2014), 444

Lucian Arye Bebchuk and Jesse Fried, *Pay Without Performance: Overview of the Issues*, 30 J. Corp. L. 647 (2005), 181

Lucian Arye Bebchuk et al., *Managerial Power and Rent Extraction in the Design of Executive Compensation*, 69 U. Chi. L. Rev. 751 (2002), 181

Craig Becker & Paul Strauss, *Representing Low-Wage Workers in the Absence of a Class: The Peculiar Case of Section 16 of the Fair Labor Standards Act and the Underenforcement of Minimum Labor Standards*, 92 Minn. L. Rev. 1317 (2006), 45, 861

Gary S. Becker, Human Capital: A Theoretical and Empirical Analysis (2d ed. 1975), 500

Mary Becker, *The Law and Economics of Racial Discrimination in Employment: Needed in the Nineties: Improved Individual and Structural Remedies for Racial and Sexual Disadvantages in Employment*, 79 Geo. L.J. 1659 (1991), 564, 571

Stephen F. Befort, *Accommodation at Work: Lessons from the Americans with Disabilities Act and Possibilities for Alleviating the American Worker Time Crunch*, 13 Cornell J. L. & Pub. Pol'y 615 (2004), 797

_____, *An Empirical Analysis of Case Outcomes Under the ADA Amendments Act*, 70 Wash. & Lee L. Rev. 2027 (2013), 732

_____, *Employee Handbooks and the Legal Effect of Disclaimers*, 13 Indus. Rel. L.J. 326 (1991/1992), 119

_____, *Labor and Employment Law at the Millennium: A Historical Review and Critical Assessment*, 43 B.C. L. Rev. 351 (2002), 42

_____, *Let's Try This Again: The ADA Amendments Act of 2008 Attempts to Reinvigorate the "Regarded As" Prong of the Statutory Definition of Disability*, 2010 Utah L. Rev. 993, 746

Richard E. Moberly, *Sarbanes-Oxley's Structural Model to Encourage Corporate Whistleblowers*, 2006 BYU L. Rev. 1107, 261

_____, *Sarbanes-Oxley's Whistleblower Provisions: Ten Years Later*, 64 S.C. L. Rev. 1 (2012), 261

_____, *Unfulfilled Expectations: An Empirical Analysis of Why Sarbanes-Oxley Whistleblowers Rarely Win*, 49 Wm. & Mary L. Rev. 65 (2007), 62, 260

Nancy M. Modesitt, *The Garcetti Virus*, 80 U. Cin. L. Rev. 137 (2011), 238

_____, *Why Whistleblowers Lose: An Empirical and Qualitative Analysis of State Court Cases*, 62 U. Kan. L. Rev. 165 (2013), 261

_____, *Wrongful Discharge: The Use of Federal Law as a Source of Public Policy*, 8 U. Pa. J. Lab. & Emp. L. 623 (2006), 228

Viva R. Moffat, *The Wrong Tool for the Job: The IP Problem with Non-Competition Agreements*, 52 Wm. & Mary L. Rev. 873 (2010), 495, 510

Geraldine Szott Moohr, *Arbitration and the Goals of Employment Discrimination Law*, 56 Wash. & Lee L. Rev. 395 (1999), 1004

Michael J. Moore & W. Kip Viscusi, Compensation Mechanisms for Job Risks: Wages, Workers' Compensation, and Product Liability (1990), 895

Francis J. Mootz III, *Insurance Coverage of Employment Discrimination Claims*, 52 U. Miami L. Rev. 1 (1997), 1044, 1045

Alan B. Morrison, *Administrative Agencies Are Just Like Legislatures and Courts—Except When They're Not*, 59 Admin. L. Rev. 79 (2007), 940

Margaret L. Moses, *The Pretext of Textualism: Disregarding Stare Decisis in* 14 Penn Plaza v. Pyett, 14 Lewis & Clark L. Rev. 825 (2010), 1005

Deanne M. Mosley & William C. Walter, *The Significance of the Classification of Employment Relationships in Determining Exposure to Liability*, 67 Miss. L.J. 613 (1998), 14

Scott A. Moss, *Students and Workers and Prisoners—Oh, My! A Cautionary Note about Excessive Institutional Tailoring of First Amendment Doctrine*, 54 UCLA L. Rev. 1635 (2007), 433

_____, *Women Choosing Diverse Workplaces: A Rational Preference with Disturbing Implications for Both Occupational Segregation and Economic Analysis of Law*, 27 Harv. Women's L.J. 1 (2004), 564

Scott A. Moss & Nantiya Ruan, *The Second-Class Class Action: How Courts Thwart Wage Rights by Misapplying Class Action Rules*, 61 Am. U. L. Rev. 523 (2012), 861

Thomas R. Mulroy & Eric J. Munoz, *The Internal Corporate Investigation*, 1 DePaul Bus. & Comm. L.J. 49 (2002), 979

Kathryn W. Munson, Comment, *Why Don't You Do Right? Corporate Fiduciary Law and the Self-Critical Analysis Privilege*, 88 Tul. L. Rev. 651 (2014), 976

Sheldon H. Nahmod, *Public Employee Speech, Categorical Balancing and § 1983: A Critique of Garcetti v. Ceballos*, 42 U. Rich. L. Rev. 561 (2008), 442

Niloofar Nejat-Bina, Comment, *Employers as Vigilant Chaperones Armed with Dating Waivers: The Intersection of Unwelcomeness and Employer Liability in Hostile Work Environment Sexual Harassment Law*, 20 Berk. J. Emp. & Lab. L. 325 (1999), 379

Lori A. Nessel, *Undocumented Immigrants in the Workplace: The Fallacy of Labor Protection and the Need for Reform*, 36 Harv. C.R.-C.L. L. Rev. 345 (2001), 48

David Neumark, *Living Wages: Protection for or Protection from Low-Wage Workers?*, 58 Indus. & Lab. Rel. Rev. 27 (2004), 881

David Neumark & William Wascher, *Minimum Wages and Low-Wage Workers: How Well Does Reality Match the Rhetoric?*, 92 Minn. L. Rev. 1296 (2008), 836

Adele Nicholas, *GCs Reveal Their Litigation Fears and Headaches*, Corp. Legal Times 72 (October 2004), xxx

Dennis R. Nolan et al., *Working Group on Chapter 1 of the Proposed Restatement of Employment Law: Existence of Employment Relationship*, 13 Emp. Rts. & Emp. Pol'y 43 (2009), 25

Helen L. Norton, *Constraining Public Employee Speech: Government's Control of Its Workers' Speech to Protect Its Own Expression*, 59 Duke L.J. 1 (2009), 388, 433

Index

"MEET ME ON BUNKER'S HILL!"

A Revealing and Personal Look at the Hull City Story

DAVID BOND

Published By
Tykesport Publications,
2 Conifer Close,
Maplewood Avenue, Hull,
East Yorkshire, HU5 5YU.

£15.00

"MEET ME ON BUNKER'S HILL!"

CONTENTS

ACKNOWLEDGEMENTS

The author views this book as a way of showing his gratitude to his parents, but he also acknowledges that he owes a considerable debt of thanks to many other people, particularly those who have helped with their personal thoughts, contributions and support. It has also been helpful to refer to background information provided by leading football historians such as Chris Elton, Leigh Edwards and the late Douglas Lamming and to have had the co-operation of the staff of the local-history department at Hull Central Library. The publishers are grateful to the Dorset Evening Echo in Bournemouth for permission to use one of their photographs. There has been no deliberate attempt to infringe copyright with any of the others.

Typesetting, layout and cover design by D. J. Simmons
Printed by V. Richardson & Sons Ltd., Hull
ISBN No. 0-9544015-1-4

Dedicated to the memory of my wonderful parents, Mary and Jim

FOREWORD BY ANDY DAVIDSON

I came to Hull City on trial after my brother David, who was a better footballer than I was, had asked for one on my behalf when he stopped over in the city with a consignment for Hull Docks because he was a long-distance lorrydriver. But at the start I was a lad who had just left school and I was very homesick because I'd left a small mining village in Scotland to come to a city that had been bombed to hell during the 1939-45 War. In 1947 Anlaby Road was rubble and there were stories about people who had spent every night for six weeks in air-raid shelters at the bottom of their gardens. It had been a rough time for the Hull people, but I came from a mining village in Scotland, where there was no such thing as a war. Douglas Water had only about 500 or 600 people and was very sheltered. I never went out of the village, so it was a big change to come to such a big place and the size of Hull was a shock when I first came. I ran home three times and wouldn't have stayed in Hull if my brother hadn't brought me back, but then I loved the place once I'd settled and I have never wanted to leave again.

I made a lot of friends and I took Hull City as my club. I broke my leg three times early in my career and was written about as some kind of "miracle" man when I recovered from them, but I didn't see it that way. Football was my life and I couldn't see myself turning to anything else, so I set out with one purpose after each accident - to get fit to play again. There were times when I had to fight a lone battle to get fit and watch the rest of the lads kicking a ball around. I daren't join in, but I had to show that those who said that I was finished were wrong. I had a couple of offers when I came out of the Forces because Newcastle United and Sheffield Wednesday were after me, but I had no inclination to go to either of them because City became very personal to me. I don't remember shaking hands with with people if we lost. But, if we'd won, then I'd shake hands with everybody - even the referees! At times the club grew stronger and stronger and my ambition has always been to see them play in the top flight of the League, but they never quite made it. There was a time during Raich Carter's era when it looked as if it would happen and then again when we had an exciting side under Cliff Britton. Terry Neill also had a good side when he first became manager, but again it collapsed.

Hull City have been a big part of my life and I know that the same applies to David Bond. I have known him for a long time and believe that he always had a good understanding of football of all the journalists who wrote about the club for the Hull Daily Mail under what years ago used to be the Three Crowns tag. While I am originally from Scotland, City became my club after serving them for more than 30 years as a player and in backroom roles. As a result, I have developed a long-standing interest in them and I know that the same applies to David.

Left - One of Hull City's first directors, builder Jack Bielby, who became the club's president and an FA shareholder, boasting that he never missed one of their council meetings.

Right - Dr. Clifford Durham-Pullan, who was Hull City's chairman when they reached the FA Cup semi-finals in 1930 for the only time in their history.

Right - The long-serving Jimmy Lodge, who stayed with Hull City in a variety of backroom jobs after initially joining them as a player.

Left - Sam Weaver, one of Hull City's long-throw experts.

Right - Ernie Bell, who played for Hull City both before and after the 1939-45 War and was captured at Dunkirk during it.

Left - One of Hull City's all-time greats, former England international Raich Carter.

Above - The autographs of Hull City's triumphant 1948-49 side from a menu before the first game of their record-breaking season at Tranmere. The names comprise Willie Buchan, Raich Carter, Jimmy Greenhalgh, Denis Durham, Norman Moore, Tom Berry, Harold Meens, Norman Fowler, Ken White, Ken Harrison, Eddie Burbanks, Billy Bly and George Lax.

Below Left - Hull City's popular winger Eddie Burbanks.

Below Right - Hull City's 1948-49 hero Jimmy Greenhalgh.

Above - Hull City's longest-serving player Billy Bly in dramatic goalkeeping action.
(Dorset Evening Echo)

Above Right - Andy Davidson, whose 520 League appearances for Hull City are a club record. He also served the club as a coach and assistant manager.

Above - Regular Hull City cartoonist Ern Shaw celebrates Hull City's promising start to the 1966-67 season in typical style.

Left - Colourful character Bill Bradbury, who holds Hull City's post-war record of 30 League goals in a season set in 1958-59.

Top Left - Hull City's goalscoring hero Ken Wagstaff, who was briefly the club's record signing for £40,000 in 1964.

Centre Left - Hull City's successful chairman of the 1980s, Don Robinson.

Bottom Left - The long-serving Garreth Roberts, who led Hull City to promotion in 1983 and 1985.

Below - Hull City's popular goalkeeper Tony Norman relaxes at the end of his coast-to-coast charity walk in 2005.

1
Boothferry Baptism

Ah, yes, I remember it well...At least I think I do. It was November 17, 1956, and I went to Boothferry Park to see Hull City play for the first time. I suppose that, because it is now 50 years ago, I might like people to believe that I tucked into a rusk at halftime, but I have to own up to being a touch older than that. My dad Jim took me to the game and my mum Mary made sure that we were wrapped up well before starting out. It was an FA Cup first-round tie against Gateshead, who were then a League club, so that dates me even more, and I can remember that we went to pick up the tickets for the game in midweek. My dad was a schoolteacher, so maybe it had been half-term for us both. I certainly did not play truant from Bellfield County Primary School in East Hull for the privilege of going to Boothferry Park just to see what it looked like and to pick up our tickets. It is probably hard to imagine that a cuptie between two sides in the old Third Division North should attract a gate of more than 12,000, but we found that it was impossible to buy two tickets for the West Stand seats next to each other. We were on the same row, but I can definitely recall that one of our seats was numbered 46 and the other 50. At my tender age I even felt a touch unnerved about being separated from my dad - albeit by a few feet. But, as we went home from picking up the tickets, my dad assured me that someone might kindly move on the day so that we could sit next to each other, which is what happened. I had seen newspaper pictures of some of the City players and on the way home I was sure that we recognised one of the goalkeepers, Bernard Fisher, standing at a bus-stop. But I might have been wrong because he spent a large part of that autumn on Army duty after being called up following the Suez crisis. More recently Bernard, though, admitted that there were times when he stood at bus-stops because he pointed out: "The players didn't all have cars in those days." Sadly, it dates us both!

Life, of course, was so different in those days and indeed not everyone had a car. My dad did not drive, so we would get to Boothferry Park from our home in East Hull by public transport. There was a bus ride into the city centre and then either a trip to the ground by train from Paragon Station to the Boothferry Park halt adjacent to the East Stand or a ride on the No. 69 trolley-bus down Anlaby Road from Paragon Street. The No. 69 turned round at the roundabout just before the ground at the junction of Anlaby Road, Anlaby High Road and Boothferry Road, so we had to walk the final few yards to the ground. And in those formative years there would often be a busy, buzzing crowd milling around outside a shop near the junction: after all, it belonged to City's popular, longest-serving player Billy Bly. His shop seemed to attract nearly as many fans as the Tigers - or probably they were always just the same people anyway! Later on I became more adventurous in my journeys to and from Boothferry Park because I began to cycle to games. We had family friends - Syd and Josie Holtby - who lived in Calvert Lane, so I would leave my bicycle at their house for safe keeping and then walk the short distance to Boothferry Park and back. It was going to be a long while before my dad and I were to go to Boothferry Park in the comparative luxury of a car. But there again a maximum wage was in force for players in those days and they were much more on a par with the fans who watched them. In fact, I have been told a number of stories by players who lived relatively close to the ground and how they themselves would walk to matches during the early postwar years.

I had been well-prepared for my first visit to a football match, though. For example, my parents had already bought me my first football annuals, so it was little wonder that I failed to shine in many other subjects at school. I still have a copy of the 1955-56 News Chronicle Football Annual by the noted Charles Buchan: it remains tatty and well-thumbed. I had also watched the FA Cup final on television - the 1955 one when Jackie Milburn scored in the first minute for Newcastle United against Manchester City - and I knew the names of the 92 League clubs because I can recall having spent

Saturday afternoons watching the football results come up in black and white on the BBC. We did not have a choice of colour or ITV or any other channel - terrestrial or satellite - in those days.

As far as Hull City were concerned, I had a vague recollection of the drama when they won a friendly against crack Hungarian side Vasas. I know that I had also watched the results on the television the previous season when I was amazed to note a 5-5 draw between Hull City and Blackpool in a friendly that amazingly attracted more than 22,000 fans. One of them was a youngster called Malcolm Lord: we had started together at Bellfield County Primary School when it first opened in May 1954 and he was visiting Boothferry Park for the first time that afternoon before becoming a hero on the pitch.

But watching the results on the television probably should have put me off going to watch City because they had always seemed to lose. There again they had been relegated at the end of the 1955-56 season, so what else should I have expected? I can recall reading newspaper cuttings of Leeds United's John Charles-inspired 4-1 win at Boothferry Park in April 1956. It was made all the ironic because Leeds, managed by Raich Carter, won promotion that day and condemned City at the same time. The same Bernard Fisher was in City's goal that day and it is intriguing that he travelled from his home in Dorset to watch the two clubs in action at Elland Road in a League game at the same level on the last day of 2005.

My big day eventually arrived and City beat Gateshead 4-0, but I confess that I can recall little about the game itself other than the fact that I was mightily impressed. Skipper Stan Mortensen scored the first goal after 28 minutes, he added a second on the hour and then Brian Cripsey and Bill Bradbury - with a penalty - scored two in two minutes. I can remember Morty's first goal vaguely and that it became misty as the game wore on, but, being November, it had been agreed that the tie would finish under floodlights, which were still in their relative infancy. In fact, it was a sense of the occasion and the joy of attending a football match in person that provided the clearer memories. But I have always wondered how I would have felt if City had lost. Would I have been so disappointed that I never went back to Boothferry Park again? Our lives as supporters have often governed by such trifles as winning and losing, after all.

It was not only a big day for me because wing-half Les Collinson also made his City debut as a replacement for the injured Andy Davidson - on the pitch. Les recalled: "I was 20 and still in the RAF. I can't really remember much about the game except that I enjoyed it and it wasn't as hard as I'd thought it might be. I was generally fit and it was no physical effort for me to cope with it. I went back to training on a night-time with still being in the RAF and I can remember thinking how easy it was. I also remember meeting Syd Gerrie before the game and he told me: 'Enjoy it, but you won't be in the side any more because Andy'll be back.' I've always thought that it was an odd thing to say - especially when I went on to be a regular in the side for nearly 10 years after that!" I gradually began to watch City more often and Les remains 17th in the club's all-time appearances list with 297 of them in the League! At least Syd Gerrie got part of his claim right because Andy did, of course, get back into the side on a regular basis.

I was obviously not deemed old enough to go to a League game just yet because my second visit to Boothferry Park was for the second round of the FA Cup three weeks later against York City. I can remember a little more of the game because Brian Bulless, who gave me my first glimpses of an educated left foot, scored twice in a 2-1 win in front of a 24,000-plus crowd. I can also recall my disappointment as City even had the audacity to concede a goal and had to hang on to go through. The prolific Arthur Bottom, at one time a target for the Tigers, ruined my day! York also included Hull-born winger Clive Colbridge, who had been on City's books as an amateur, and two other ex-Tigers, Tommy Forgan and Norman Wilkinson.

I did see my first League game before 1956 was out - and City managed only a draw. It finished

2-2 and was Scunthorpe United's first visit to Hull for a League game. Their side included ex-Tiger Jackie Brownsword and Jack Haigh, whose daughter Vicky became a racehorse trainer, scored one of their goals. Significantly, I stood at a game with my dad for the first time - in the Well in the West Stand. In fact, I doubt that I sat down at another game at Boothferry Park until I joined the Press corps in 1975.

In early 1957 I saw three more games in three months - two wins and a draw. There was a League game against York when the programme strangely devoted its pre-budget front page to an explanation as to how Entertainment Tax affected City. There was a win against a Chesterfield side including Dave Blakey, who was still scouting in 2006. And there was a victory over an Accrington Stanley side crammed with Scots. The fact that it was a League game also dates me! And there was a new Prime Minister called Harold Macmillan who kept trying to convince us that we had never had it so good: I normally distrust politicians, but, when it came to watching the Tigers, I probably believed him on this occasion!

Things changed for me and my dad in the 1957-58 season because we started to watch games from behind a goal on Bunker's Hill. The first one was against Halifax Town, City won 5-2 and Doug "Nobby" Clarke scored four of them. Doug said: "I always played at inside-forward at that time, so it was easier to score goals regularly then because I got more chances. It was only later on when I was played as a right-winger that I didn't score so much." City's giant centre-half Norman Nielson put through his own goal as my dad and I watched from a great height towards the corner of the Bunker's Hill terracing. I also seem to recall that we had just returned from a summer holiday at Hornsea and I had a poisoned leg as a result of a potent mixture of sand and eczema. And I had not yet mastered the art of using a fountain pen properly because even now there is ink all over the front of the programme, from where it had seeped through from filling in the halftime scores on the second page. In those days there were two sets of large capital letters around the railings next to the track on the East and West stands at Boothferry Park. At the interval stewards would fill in the latest scores. And there were bigger gaps between Y and Z than there were between A to X. That was because Y and Z needed more space because they provided the bigger scores in the rugby-league matches involving Hull FC and Hull Kingston Rovers, which were normally played on Saturdays during the winter in those days! Anyway none of it contrived to stop Doug, a player with a thunderous shot, from becoming one of my first heroes. There again there were 11 of them in every match in those days. After all, City never seemed to lose when my dad and I watched them. Supporting City was becoming a habit.

I soon had an amber-and-black scarf, which, I believe, my mum knitted specially for me, an amber-and-black bobble-cap and an amber-and-black rattle. I seem to recall that I was also allowed to buy my first amber-and-black rosette when I attended an FA Cup tie against Barnsley in early 1958. My dad, who was a dab hand at woodwork and even better at marquetry for that matter, made me the rattle and it survives in a rather battered state even today. It was not as big and noisy as the conventional rattle, but it served its purpose. The rattles at football matches were relics of two world wars. Rattles had been issued to the Air-Raid Precautions during the 1939-45 War as gas alarms. But the gas rattles had first been used in the 1914-18 War at battles such as the Somme and then at the wardens' posts during the Blitz in the 1939-45 War. They then found themselves on the soccer terraces, but rattles were a feature of football that died out as the 1960s progressed - probably because they were offensive weapons. In fact, I can remember standing on Bunker's Hill with my rattle for a game against Southend United and inadvertently stubbing out the cigarette - and probably the odd finger or two - of a fan who was near me. There was also a notable incident, which had nothing to do with me, when a fan was led away at City's replay with Chelsea in March 1966 with blood streaming down his face after accidentally being hit by a stray rattle.

We watched nearly every home game in 1957-58 and the Easter Saturday visit of Oldham Athletic was a magical occasion. I recall that normally few team changes needed to be announced over the PA system on match days, but this time Oldham made six. Maybe it had unsettled them because they lost 9-0 and every member of City's forward-line - Doug Clarke, Bill Bradbury, Colin Smith, Brian Bulless and Brian Cripsey - scored. For good measure there were hat-tricks for Bradbury - with the aid of a penalty - and Smith. It was the Tigers' biggest win at Boothferry Park and naturally I am still waiting to see City do any better in a League game anywhere! But Clarke said: "I can remember that we spent the last few minutes desperately trying to get a 10th." And Bulless, a true gentleman of football, added: "Bill Bradbury and Colin Smith got hat-tricks and the rest of the forward-line - Doug Clarke, Brian Cripsey and I - all scored once. I remember that David Teece, who had played for City, was in goal for Oldham and that we seemed to score every time we attacked. It was a day when everything went right." David Teece, meanwhile, was apparently left to rue his horoscope, which he had read on the way to the game: "An adventurous day which does not turn out as well as you might suppose..."

The sequel to that game, though, gave me an early demonstration of the vagaries of footballers' performances. Two days later the Tigers met promotion-chasing Bradford City at home and lost 3-1. City had not been beaten at home since the opening day of the season - a game against York that I had missed. Accordingly, the Easter Monday game was the first one that I had seen City, who finished fifth in the Third Division North and comfortably clinched their place in the new Third Division, lose. I really was temporarily depressed, grossly offended and almost heartbroken. In the course of one Easter weekend it had taught me a lesson about watching City that has stayed with me ever since: Always be prepared for the highs and the lows and a bumpy roller-coaster ride along the way.

A little more than a year later, though, I was watching the Tigers clinch promotion for the first time. It was achieved in a 2-0 win against Bury - their last home game of the season. City won 19 of their 23 home League games that season, so it was a marvellous time for someone who was not yet old enough to be allowed to travel away. In those days City always seemed to kick towards Bunker's Hill in the first half, but for a few extra old pence you could get a transfer to one of the other three covered stands, so it normally enabled you to be close to the goal that they were attacking in the second. Curiously, for some reason I can remember that my dad and I watched the game against Newport County - the only home defeat in the League that season - from the North Stand terracing. As a matter of superstition, I suspect that we made sure that we returned regularly to Bunker's Hill after that. That was where I remember watching a 3-3 Easter draw against Norwich City, who had just reached the FA Cup semi-finals as a Third Division club. Oddly enough, the gate of 24,156 was the biggest by one that I had been in, beating that cuptie against York in December 1956.

I, therefore, prepared myself to watch Second Division football for the first time - and there was a curious symmetry to it. City had been promoted as runners-up to Plymouth Argyle and they opened successive seasons at home to them. The first occasion in the Third Division heralded the debut of former England international left-winger Vic Metcalfe for City. But he was injured and did not reappear until the start of the following season in the Second Division when he promptly scored twice. The roller-coaster ride with the Tigers was pertinent again, though. Having just experienced promotion, I became immediately accustomed to watching a relegation season and plenty of home defeats in 1959-60. There was the worst of all - 5-0 against Lincoln City on former England international Jackie Sewell's debut. That seemed to suggest the worst for City even though it was still early in the season. A fortnight later it was Ralph Gubbins' debut in a 1-1 draw against Huddersfield Town and the rain poured down relentlessly. Chairman Harold Needler later said that he had built the South Stand to replace the vast open terracing of Bunker's Hill after feeling sorry for fans standing on it in bad weather. The downpour that afternoon probably should have been the catalyst for his thinking although it was still to take a while before anything was done.

At the end of September 1964 I was allowed to watch the Tigers in an away game for the first time. It was a 1-1 draw against Barnsley at Oakwell. I travelled by train with some friends to the game after school and I can recall standing behind the goal into which Doug Clarke scored. I went to away games only spasmodically during the 1964-65 season, but one of them brought immense disappointment. It was on Easter Saturday in 1965 at Mansfield, who won 2-1 and virtually ended City's promotion hopes. I somehow borrowed a hunting-horn for the game, but the rain got into it as I stood on one corner of Field Mill and it was as ineffective as the team turned out to be. Ken Wagstaff scored with a rare header on his return to Mansfield and City created chance after chance, but Town's goalkeeper Colin Treharne used up a season's luck as he made save after save with arms and legs and any part of his body that he could get in the way. It was the second time that season that a goalkeeper had denied City in an orthodox manner because Malcolm Heath had ridden his luck with some extravagant and eccentric saves for Lincoln City at Boothferry Park in the FA Cup before the Tigers lost the replay 3-1. But I was gradually learning some stark reality - that luck always seemed to desert City when it mattered most - and naturally I assumed that nobody else suffered in the same drastic way.

But the 1964-65 season represented a turning-point in the aspirations of City's fans. The club finally started to act big rather than just think big in the aftermath of chairman Harold Needler's gift to the club of £200,000 worth of shares in his Hoveringham Gravel business in January 1963. I recall making my way into the city centre from school one autumn evening in November 1964 and looking at the billboards for the Hull Daily Mail. They heralded a major new signing, so I asked one of my schoolfriends, Paddy Forde, if he I could peep at his copy of the paper after we had boarded the bus for home. It was all about the arrival of Ken Wagstaff from Mansfield Town and we were both amazed by the club-record £40,000 fee that had been spent on him by manager Cliff Britton. Waggy had to wait for his debut because he was ineligible for the FA Cup tie at Kidderminster Harriers, but the following week he made it in the League at home to Exeter City. He obliged with a goal in a 3-1 win in which Les Collinson was outstanding and also scored, but, above all, the whole concept of the club's ambitions had changed for the better. Waggy scored in his first six home League games and in all but one of his first 11 League outings. One of his 14 goals in that run against Watford was the result of a rebound to him after the referee had been knocked out by a clearance, so maybe the force was sometimes with City, after all. We celebrated the advent of 1965 with another £40,000 signing - left-winger Ian Butler - and a few days later another forward, Ken Houghton, arrived for another £40,000. Both came from Rotherham United and it was something of a surprise because it had always been assumed that another of their forwards, Albert Bennett, had been City's main target. I should own up that I went on a long trainspotting trip from school early in 1965 and entered into some banter about football with a railway guard when we stopped at Rotherham station close to Millmoor. He was a Millers fan and did not really welcome a posse of passengers from Hull that night!

And it was fittingly in the spring of 1965 that Bob Dylan was in the hit parade with his anthem The Times They are A-Changing. They seemed to be on the pitch, whose high-class reputation was then said to originate from the application of fish manure to produce a lush grass, and they certainly were off it. My beloved Bunker's Hill, for one thing, was technically to be no more because Harold Needler decided to cover it with a new £75,000 cantilever stand. The fans were no longer going to be drenched in wet weather and they could actually sit down to watch games from behind that goal. But the character had disappeared - the immense height of Bunker's Hill at one corner and the railings at the back on which you perched yourself with due care and attention in case you suddenly disappeared down the other side while celebrating a goal. It was no longer Bunker's Hill: it was supposed to be the more prosaic South Stand.

The club explained the historic change to the fans: "Bunker's Hill denoted the popular end of the ground and often the particular section which lacks cover and many facilities. It often afforded an excellent vantage point from which to observe the match although an oxygen mask is often called for - so rare must the atmosphere be at such heights. The south-west corner of Bunker's Hill fitted these descriptions. Indeed, so deep was the drop on the other side that a high barrier had to be put up to stop spectators from falling over the edge and disappearing into what were then allotments. In 1946 armies of eager supporters gave of their spare time to weed the ground, tidy up, paint and do anything to get it ship-shape. And when Boothferry Park was being built, Harold Needler promised to cover Bunker's Hill. But building permits were difficult to obtain then and, when they were available, the crowds did not come and money was short. It was during a game in 1964 that Mr. Needler again had his thoughts centred on Bunker's Hill when it suddenly rained heavily enough to send the crowd scampering for cover and huddling under the East Stand. This was save for one solitary brave soul bedecked in heavy-weather gear who stood his ground and never budged as the rain came down in torrents. Mr. Needler then insisted that something had to be done. Bunker's Hill was replaced by a £120,000-plus stand as bulldozers went into action when the 1964-65 season ended, dozens of deep piles were sunk and an army of workers got down to building a dream. The new semi-cantilever stand with 3,000 tip-up seats is now where Bunker's Hill used to be. A much smaller terrace now has an elegant canopy and the fans no longer have to dash for shelter when it rains. The stand is served by 21 turnstiles, boasts impeccable toilets, gracious staircases and an unparalleled view of the game, while the fans can lean against one of the 67 crush barriers."

But could I survive without my Bunker's Hill in the face of such estate-agency marketing patter? I naturally insisted on calling the southern end of the ground by the same name even when the new stand appeared. When its redevelopment was completed for the opening of the 1965-66 season, the official line from the club was that Bunker's Hill should henceforth be known as the South Stand because it was "a name more in keeping with the imposing appearance." At least it may have brought us good luck because the Tigers were duly promoted in style in 1965-66 and we younger fans now believed that we really had never had it so good. Only those older fans who recalled the Raich Carter era were able to put us firmly in our place.

The spirit of the 1965-66 season meant that I was keen to go to more away games, which I attended mainly with schoolfriends initially. But as I moved further afield, I started to travel on supporters' coaches and I got to know devoted fans such as Peter Lincoln and Craig Boba well. Peter has always a been a solid supporter through thick and thin and in those days he earned himself as a reputation for prolonging the annual shareholders' meetings with his keen questioning. But he cared passionately and typified a lot of what is good about the genuine fan when he was still stirring things up in the mid-1990s and became a dedicated chairman of the pressure group Tigers 2000.

Somewhere along the line I was given the chance to join City's elite band of fans known as the Happy Wanderers, who travelled away by minibus and hardly ever missed a game home and away. I am not sure just how I happened to be offered a seat on their prestigious minibus, but I had got to know them simply because they were dedicated regulars and there must have been a gap that I was allowed to fill. It was a joy to be in their midst because they were loyal fans to the core and great company with natural comedians such as Brian Hague and Terry Wilson among their number. The dull moments were supplied only by the team on the pitch as supporting them became a frustrating process at times. I travelled with the Happy Wanderers until the chance to cover City as a journalist cropped up in 1975.

When I left Hull's Hymers College in 1968, I went to Highbury Technical College in the Cosham area of Portsmouth to study journalism for a year. I had mysteriously convinced myself that I wanted to be an actor, but, when asked what I intended doing when I left school, I thought better of it and said instead that I fancied being a journalist. It was a whim rather than a distinct career plan, but my headmaster, Harry Roach, spoke to the school's head of mathematics, Geoff Underwood, about me because his father Ernest, who was known affectionately as "Tim," was the chief reporter at the Hull Daily Mail and indeed had also covered City's affairs for the newspaper at one stage during the early postwar years. As a result, I was advised to try to enrol on one of the evolving year-long journalism courses to do some basic training. There were only three centres providing them in the country - at Darlington, Harlow and Portsmouth. I found out that, if accepted, I would have to go to Portsmouth because I was a late applicant. There were about 70 places available on the three courses nationally and I had to go to London for a day-long examination for one of them. It all entailed written papers in the morning and going before an interview panel in the afternoon. I was not too confident that I would be accepted because so few places were available that I did not prepare to attend the day with the air of gravity that might have been expected. I decided, in fact, to put my whole potential career in jeopardy by telling the National Council for the Training of Journalists, who organised the courses, that I was prepared to attend the examination, but I had an important appointment back in Hull on the evening and would have to leave early in the afternoon to get a train home. They responded by saying that they understood my predicament and that I would be the first candidate to be interviewed in the afternoon so that I could make a quick getaway. What I did not tell them was exactly what the "important appointment" was - it was to see a pre-season friendly between City and Liverpool at Boothferry Park!

I can recall racing up and down steps and corridors at tube stations to reach King's Cross just in time to catch the train home for the match. I just managed to get back in time and was among the crowd of more than 12,000 who saw City lose 5-3. I was even accepted on to the journalism course, but rushing back just to see the Tigers in a friendly to the possible detriment of a career was somewhere between dedication and stupidity! Maybe I was luckier than City often seem to have been.

Going away to college meant that I would see less of City. I never missed home games and I remember listening to my transistor radio in my digs for news of the 1-1 draw with Sheffield United that ended my Boothferry Park run in September 1968. I still supported the club when I could, but probably saw them at away games in the south as often as I saw them at home that season. But my dad, who probably thought that I badly needed some kind of journalistic instruction in view of my modest record in English at school, would gallantly send me detailed reports of all the games that I missed. And I would sometimes spend weekends with my Auntie Amy, who lived at New Malden in Surrey, whenever City were playing in London. I can recall venturing to Millwall, whose fans were already a bit notorious, soon after going away to college and actually believing that it might help my personal safety when City went 2-0 down. But the Tigers hit back to win 3-2 thanks to a hat-trick from Ken Houghton and one of the locals turned to me after the late winner had gone in to ask me how long was left. "Only a few minutes, mate," I replied in my best Cockney accent. Maybe my one-time ambition to have been an actor had stood me in good stead, after all, when I was struck by a severe bout of cowardice that afternoon!

I was also there when City's visit to Portsmouth in February 1969 was one of only four League games to be played throughout the country, but I was sent to Brigg in Lincolnshire, where tbe Hull Daily Mail then had a branch office, when I got an apprenticeship on completion of my course and the restrictions as a supporter still applied because I was unable to attend midweek games home and away on a regular basis for the next three years. I then moved to Hull to work on weekly papers - they were probably "weakly" by the time that I had worked on them - but in 1975 everything changed dramatically for me. I had worked solely on weekly newspapers for six years when I was given the opportunity to cover City for the Mail.

As a result of what happened during the summer of 1975 I was effectively a City fan no longer. I was technically independent and had crossed over to being a sports writer for the Hull Daily Mail, who kindly gave me the chance to be their Tigers correspondent. Their sports editor, Jack Fluck, was due to retire during the autumn and Brian Taylor, who had done the City job for 20 years as Three Crowns and then under his own name, was destined to replace him. Brian, a much-underrated writer, had first hinted fairly casually that I might be considered as his successor the previous Christmas when we happened to discuss City's 3-1 home defeat by Nottingham Forest in a spare moment in an empty corridor at work. My immediate reaction was that naturally it would be a great job, but I doubted that I was up to it. I took a little persuasion, but I took up Brian's invitation to visit the Boothferry Park Press-box during the spring of 1975 to sample the working conditions. But I put everything to the back of my mind, did not build up my hopes unduly, got on with my life and wondered how many other candidates there were for the job anyway even though Brian seemed to want me to take it on. In mid-summer the editor of the Mail, Jack Whitfield, called me into his office and officially offered me the chance to succeed Brian, reminding me quite rightly that he hoped that I had a good working knowledge of other sports in addition to City and football.

I accepted the chance because I knew that I would never have forgiven myself if I had turned it down. My fellow City fans doubtless thought that I had been offered my ideal job for life. I saw things differently. I was very grateful and pleased to be given the chance to mix business with pleasure, which is not something that comes to a lot of people in life. Covering City for the Mail represented progress, but I never saw it as the be-all-and-end-all of what I might very loosely describe as a career. What put it all into context was the fact that my dad, who had done so much to encourage my early interest in the Tigers, had passed away in 1972 and had not lived to see me take up the chance. There was a tinge of regret about everything although my mum was pleased for me and reminded me that my dad would also have been happy for me. In addition, my mum was mapping out a new life for herself because she had just remarried. In April 1975 I gave her away - I did wonder if I should have asked for a record transfer fee for her because she was so dear and valuable to me - at her wedding to my stepfather Leslie in the morning, attended the reception in Beverley during lunchtime and then left early to watch City beat Blackpool 1-0 at home in the afternoon!

In previous times the City correspondent of the Hull Daily Mail had operated under a nom de plume. There had been Saturn, Mac, Athleo, Veritas - he had been Harry Comley, from Cottingham, who missed few games in the first 40 years of the club's history - and Three Crowns, but reporters had come out of the closet when I took over. It was agreed that it would be sensible for me to be in place from the start of 1975-76, so Brian Taylor helped me on my way while he waited for Jack Fluck's retirement during the autumn. Brian mentioned a touch ruefully that in 20 years he had been away with the club on a pre-season tour just once - a year earlier when they had gone to Scotland. It was ironically amusing, therefore, that I started off my stint with a pre-season tour to Scotland in 1975. It did not begin quietly, either. I had a day off on July 24 and went over to Sheffield to watch my beloved Yorkshire play county cricket against Nottinghamshire. It was agreed with the Mail that I would call in at their branch office at Goole on the way to check the final arrangements for the tour, so I telephoned secretary Malcolm "Mac" Stone, whom I knew reasonably well anyway because he had been a City fan before working for the club, and was told that the chairman Harold Needler had died. I rung the sports desk to tell them, left them to their devices with what was clearly a major story and relaxed at Sheffield. The next day we set off to Lanarkshire. I travelled on the team coach, but a spare car was taken along so that manager John Kaye, his assistant Andy Davidson, Mac and Ken Wagstaff, who had always been one of the chairman's favourites, could return to attend the funeral.

In the meantime, I covered my first two matches - at Ayr and Clyde - on tour and got to know the players and the management bit by bit. I probably tried to be a bit too clever by describing "Ayr raids" and suggesting that there was little that was "bonny about the game at Clyde" when tempers became frayed at one stage, but, above all, I did what I have always done in such circumstances - I never believed that I knew it all, I realised how lucky I was to be given the chance to cover City and I treated everything as a wonderful learning process. After all, I was just a football fan who was now privileged enough to be writing about the club he had supported for 19 years.

It did mean that I had a good grounding in how City fans thought and reacted and what they expected. I had to accept criticism from supporters as a journalist and every one of them is always entitled to his or her views, but sometimes the criticism tended to suggest that I had descended from another planet without a sixth sense or any kind of instinct about the club and their hopes. Were they unaware that they were having a go at someone who had been one of them and shared their emotions as fans? I still look at cuttings about some of the comments about me in letters to the Hull Daily Mail and I still believe even now that the fans totally missed the point. In the late 1970s, after all, there was often a lot of criticism of the players from the terraces as the fans became impatient and mid-table season followed mid-table season in the old Second Division. Familiarity had bred contempt and I backed the players publicly against the critical fans at one point. But it was something that you were not supposed to do in the public's eyes.

It seemed that some fans used to think that I was in the pay of the club when all I was trying to do was to be objective at any given time. The 1970s turned into a period of frustration for the fans after the heady ambitions and progress of the 1960s, but I could always see a certain amount of hope. The fans became impatient, but my view was that at least City were holding their own in the Second Division. I often wonder what they thought as everything deteriorated drastically - initially during the early 1980s and then again during the 1990s. They would surely have settled then for the pattern-less seasons in the old Second Division. At the same time I like to think that I have never lost sight of the fans' feelings and aspirations. After all, all that you are ever doing as a journalist is to be the middle person between the club and their public. You always try to interpret everything objectively and fairly and retain a valid perspective of everyone's views and interests, but it does not mean that you always get things right. You are arrogant if you believe that you always have. All you can do is to try to be as industrious and as honest as possible.

The nice aspect of it all is that my lucky break in 1975 has hopefully given me 31 years of fond friendships and few foes. They include many players, management teams and backroom staff and I have been lucky enough to have kept in touch with a lot of them because of my involvement with the Ex-Tigers' Association. But the fans are always important. They may not always grasp the inner workings of football and football clubs and they may not always want to steep themselves in their background, history and tradition, but they are not fools, they must be respected, they do pay their hard-earned money to attend games and they must never be underestimated. As a journalist, I have never felt that I should have to endure outright abuse from them, but it happens. When people are unreasonable, then I see no point in continuing the conversation. But if people have approached me sensibly, then I will normally talk about the club until the cows - or probably the Tigers - come home.

One supporter, Peter Wood, simply wandered up to me in a public-house one night in September 1976 after I had been soaked by relentless rain driven by a prevailing wind into the Press-box under a covered stand at Bolton Wanderers' old Burnden Park. I suppose that he was curious as to why someone was drying out in a pub! He was just concerned as to how City had lost 5-1, we evaluated everything as constructively as possible and we have remained good friends ever since. More recently, I was at a football dinner in Goole and was sitting near ex-Tiger Steve Richards, who introduced me to the other people at our table. They included brothers Bob and Ronnie Crossley, who were keen City fans. Both are publicans, but Bob and I nearly fell out before we had a chance to become friends because it was the autumn of 2002 and Jan Molby had just been sacked as City's manager. We had differing views, we started to express them strongly and we reached a compromise only slowly. At first Steve, who was there in his capacity as Goole AFC's manager and not in his role as a policeman, probably thought that he would have to dial 999 to keep us in order! But by the end of the evening Bob, who is a tremendous guy, and I had become firm friends, we realised that we had other common interests and we never seem to disagree any more! And by chance I started to chat regularly with a keen City fan called Jonathan Brock when he worked at the Willerby Manor Hotel. I was always tempted to stay late as he began his night shifts because he cared deeply about the club and the conversations with him were always thought-provoking. I was privileged to attend a memorial day for him in August 2006 after he had died suddenly at the age of 36.

Then there are the fans who are by and large my contemporaries and have shared the Tiger dreams for so long. Peter Lincoln is as whole-hearted and committed as ever although it is slightly annoying that he is a bit younger than I am and yet he has been watching City a bit longer than I have! I still regularly see loyal fans of the highest order such as Beryl Grassby, Ray Tupling and Graham Jackson who were among my travelling companions with the Happy Wanderers. There are many others and I have a high regard for their devotion.

I suspect that the most formative years in anyone's life are often the teenage ones, so there remains a romantic notion about my time on Bunker's Hill. In fact, the notions must be so romantic that I have conveniently forgotten that the team were never consistently successful in those days! As the 1950s turned into the 1960s, I nearly always watched City from Bunker's Hill with my dad and two schoolfriends who usually joined us - Rob Metcalfe and John Eyley. Rob's father Bob had been a City director, but he had severed his links with the club in the wake of relegation in 1960 and eventually the family allegiance was switched to Sheffield Wednesday. John eventually moved to Scotland in the late 1960s because of family reasons, but I caught up with him when I started my coverage of City as a journalist in 1975 with that pre-season tour. John became the company secretary for Barr Construction, who were the guiding light of Ayr United, and he became both a director and the secretary of the club.

When the demise of Bunker's Hill was decreed, I continued to watch the Tigers from what was left of it with other schoolfriends such as Chris Wells, Ian White, Paul Bainbridge, David Bennison, Ian Ireland, Rob Culpin and David Taylor. There were plenty of big crowds and a fair bit of success, but it was never the same as the South Stand and I suppose that I had inherited what I often think is a typical Hullensian trait - a reluctance to accept change. For example, I never wanted to leave Boothferry Park in 2002 for the KC Stadium in the first place. I am not opposed to the concept of a so-called state-of-the-art stadium, but I would have been happier if it had had a more appropriate name involving the traditions of the Circle and ideally I would have preferred it if Boothferry Park had been redeveloped as the "new" venue. There again the most important factor was to have a winning team on the pitch wherever it was. And we all had to accept that we had been on the merry-go-round of high hopes countered by false dawns at Boothferry Park for so long. Maybe it was time to accept change on this occasion and try to make the most of a fresh start.

Anyway life is never easy when City are involved and logic often seems to go out of the window. Was Bunker's Hill really Bunker's Hill, after all? I was always brought up to believe that it dovetailed nicely with the Spion Kop at Liverpool. But there are references throughout the club's history to fans effectively being known as Koppites at Hull - both at Anlaby Road and Boothferry Park. Indeed new chairman Harold Needler actually referred to Spion Kop rather than Bunker's Hill in his programme notes for the first game at Boothferry Park at the end of August 1946: "The difficulties we have had to face in connection with preparing the ground have been overcome only by the magnificent efforts of our architect, George Williams, who has been untiring with the plans, the applications for licences, the construction of the two stands, for which licences have been obtained, and the reconstruction of Spion Kop."

And how did any reference to Bunker's Hill occur in the first place? City themselves once offered an explanation: "The origins of Bunker's Hill are from the American War of Independence. A major battle took place on a 110ft. hill on the Charleston peninsula outside Boston in June 1775 involving a general called Bunker. British soldiers, numbering about 5,000, were short of ammunition and were told to shout and make a din to scare off the Yankees. The tale was brought home and eventually likened to noise created at football matches where the biggest crowds congregated in the cheapest enclosures at one end of grounds." There may, therefore, well be a direct link in City's case with the famed Boothferry Roar. But even though history has never been my strong point - I failed my O-level in it four times - it really was a long time from the American War of Independence to the evolution of League football in England and the ultimate creation of Boothferry Park.

Then there is the vexed question of whether we are discussing Bunker's Hill or just Bunker Hill because there are historical references to both. The Encyclopaedia Britannica refers regularly to "Bunker Hill," for example. At the same time everyone connected with City, to the best of my knowledge, always referred to Bunker's Hill at one end of Boothferry Park when it was in its pomp. But the American hostilities of 1775 involved two neighbouring hills - one possibly called Bunker's Hill and the smaller Breed's Hill. And there is a reference that suggests that Breed's Hill eventually became commonly called Bunker's Hill! So where exactly did we all stand in all weathers to watch City at Boothferry Park? Maybe my dad and I should have stayed in the seats because, as I say, life is never easy when City are involved...

I also have a confession to make. It may now be 50 years since I first went to watch City play, but I have not watched City play for 50 years. There is a subtle difference because there was a time when I was banned from Boothferry Park as a Pressman. It lasted from 1995 to 1997 and I did not see the Tigers play at all during the calendar year of 1996 because of the ban. Technically I could have paid to watch as a fan, but I was certainly not going to do so because of my objections to the way in which City were being run and the poor quality of the football that they were serving up. I, therefore, gave myself a year off for what I thought was good behaviour and what the regime of the time thought was bad behaviour. As I say, life is never easy when Hull City are involved...

2
The Times They Were A-Changing

One name governed most of the conversations about Hull City when I first started supported them during the autumn of 1956. And the irony of it all was that he had not even been with the club for more than four years. He was Raich Carter, who had dominated the postwar scene as City were watched by the the biggest attendances in their history. Everybody talked reverently about the Carter era, epitomised by the 1948-49 season when the Tigers clinched the Third Division North championship after winning their first nine League games of the season and reached the quarter-finals of the FA Cup in which they lost 1-0 at home to Manchester United in front of their record crowd of 55,019. Stories about him and his achievements were still fresh in many supporters' memories and they would not fade away. Such had been his impact that everything was compared unfavourably with his time at Boothferry Park, so it made life difficult for those who followed in his footsteps. The point had been underlined when City had been relegated from the Second Division in 1956 and the impetus of his era had been lost. Andy Davidson mused: "When Raich Carter left, City had an older side and some of the players were starting to wane. And how do you replace players of the calibre of Raich and Eddie Burbanks?"

The arrival of inside-forward Carter at Boothferry Park in April 1948 was sensational. It must have been because I was born nine months later! I never saw Raich play, but I was fortunate enough to get to know him well and he had that presence and belief that seemed to come naturally from being born into the North-East's hotbed of soccer. It may also be significant in the great pantheon of City's history that too often Raich's self-assurance seems to have been lacking in youngsters from East Yorkshire in comparison. Dennis Booth, later a City player and the club's assistant manager, used to say intriguingly: "In football you've got to have more front than Woolworth's window!" Raich had it in abundance and his powerful personality simply exuded the confidence to be successful.

Raich was extra special and some of the observations about him underline the point. Andy Davidson said of him: "Raich Carter had wonderful ability and was one of the all-time greats. He hardly used the right foot and he hardly ever headed the ball, but he still ran the games. In fact, he refereed them!" Perhaps the secret was also in a comment by Yorkshireman Willie Watson, who played for England at football and cricket, when he said: "Raich carried empty space around with him like an umbrella!" And the renowned playwright and City fan Alan Plater, who was born in the North-East himself, beautifully summed up the essential Raich: "He was the greatest of his kind and he knew it. He reinvented the game as he went along. He didn't just play it: he presided over it."

Ex-Tigers Ken Wagstaff and David Coates, who played for Raich when he managed Mansfield Town, also respected his influence to the hilt. Waggy, whose own magical career as a goalscorer was nurtured by Raich at Mansfield, said of him: "That man really was a legend. Raich Carter was the real genius. He not only taught me how to play football, but also how to be a man. I never saw him play during his own illustrious career, but you could see his immense skill in his training sessions. I've spoken to a lot of older Hull City fans and they tell me that he was absolutely brilliant at Boothferry Park and I can believe them because Raich certainly knew the game inside out." David, who came from Silksworth in the North-East, reflected: "Raich was easily the most outstanding personality I have met in the game. He was outstanding to look at because, even though he was not all that tall, he gave the impression of being a big man. He had an aura about him and he knew it. Raich had a wicked sense of humour and the ability to make a point firmly, but also humorously. He always coated his criticism with a touch of humour and he was always very generous with the people he played with."

Raich had played for England and made an impact with his home-town club Sunderland and then

Derby County before he transformed the Tigers' postwar skyline. He duly made his City debut in a 1-1 draw at home to York City on April 3, 1948. The gate was 32,466, then a Boothferry Park record: the attendance at the previous home game against Tranmere Rovers had been just 13,588. But Raich told in his autobiography about the importance of his colleagues not feeling in awe of him: "There was a lunch for the players at the Station Hotel in Hull to give me the chance of meeting them. From the start I made a point of trying to be friendly with the boys and make things easy. Football teams always welcome new members, but I was a bit concerned about all the publicity that had accompanied my transfer. I wondered whether it might have made the boys feel a bit antagonistic towards me. I did not want them to feel that I was putting them in the shade nor did I want there to be any suggestion that I had a superiority complex and was looking down my nose at them." His warm-up included signing autographs in the dressing-room until just before kick-off. He received goodwill messages from Derby and Luton Town's Sid Ottewell, whose wedding he had attended as the best man. The crowd included Arthur Drewery, a member of the FA's management committee and the chairman of their selection committee who was viewing Boothferry Park as a possible venue for representative games, and Willie Buchan's daughters, Moira and Sheena, who had never previously seen their father play. Oddly enough, the occasion was lost on York's regular centre-forward Alf Patrick because he missed the game to get married!

Raich soon became the Tigers' player-manager to mastermind the success of 1948-49 and leave an indelible mark on the city. He is, of course, remembered in football as a whole as an all-time great and even featured on a postage stamp for the Republic of Equatorial Guinea in strange circumstances when a set of eight top players were pictured on them to commemorate the 1974 World Cup. Philatelists indicate that there has been a trend for Eastern European countries in particular to use poorer colonies for money-making ventures with stamps. In fact, it is unlikely that the Republic of Equatorial Guinea, a Spanish colony, knew much about them. The stamps were rarely used and remain rare. A more enduring tribute has stood closer to home since the opening of the Raich Carter Sports Centre in his native Hendon in October 2001.

His formative years had been spent in the family public-house, the Ocean Queen, in Sunderland's dockland area, but his wife Pat said: "He didn't like pubs because he could see the sawdust and spittoons from his bedroom. Pubs represented a life when you didn't work. He was a great family man, but he wouldn't let his family get in the way of his job. He had that willpower and didn't drink, gamble or smoke. He never smoked and had only the occasional drink because he was dedicated. There was a public figure and a private one. The telephone was always ringing with people asking him for his opinions. They often asked him if he could remember such-and-such a goal and they were always amazed that he knew in detail how he scored them all. But at home he was the opposite of what he had to be as a footballer. He was quiet, witty and very easy to live with." His daughter Jane further illustrated the point: "He was very sensitive. He was a kind, soft man who would give away his money to tramps and helped other footballers. Football was all a stage act for him because he was performing once he got on to the field. Everybody liked to talk about football with him and I think he missed it when he wasn't directly involved in it." His son Raich junior, who became a keen City fan, had to live up his name, of course, but he said: "My dad gave me plenty of coaching, but I just did not have his talent. I finished up playing for a Hull Sunday League team called Titanic, but they kept going down!"

Raich had almost unbelievably known the darker side of soccer in his early years when Leicester City's manager Willie Orr, a former Scottish international, had told him: "You're too small to play football. You should go home and build yourself up physically. Get some brawn and weight on you and gain some experience of the game!" As a result, Raich served his apprenticeship as an electrician and yet insisted: "I knew that I did not want to go back to any form of electrical engineering or indeed take up any job outside football." But maybe the memories of the electrical training never quite left him because his family tell of a wonderful occasion when he was invited to switch on the seaside lights at Withernsea. They found it a touch ironic because Raich would always go round switching lights off when he was at home!

Raich eventually made his footballing mark with Sunderland, especially when they beat Preston North End in 3-1 in the 1937 FA Cup final at Wembley. The goalscorers were Raich, Bobby Gurney and Eddie Burbanks and it is strange to record that they all still have close family members in East Yorkshire even though none of the three was originally from the area. Raich passed away in October 1994 - just six months after Gurney, who has family in the Brough area. But they had graced a Football League ground for one last time when City met Sunderland at Boothferry Park in October 1988. The highlight of the pre-match entertainment came when Raich and Bobby kicked off from the centre-spot, passed the ball from one to the other and planted it into the South Stand net. It may have been eerily significant that the ensuing game was then a goalless draw!

Winger Eddie Burbanks also left lots of lasting memories of his time at Boothferry Park. Raich brought him to City from Sunderland, but later on they were also together at Leeds United. Eddie, who was naturally right-footed despite being a left-winger, was a miner's son from Bentley, near Doncaster. He had been an RAF physical training instructor during the 1939-45 War and played for Blackpool against Sheffield Wednesday in the 1943 Wartime Cup final. In 1946 he toured Denmark, Sweden and Norway with an FA XI who also included future City players Neil Franklin and Stan Mortensen. Eddie's rapport with Raich on the field stemmed from his League debut for Sunderland when he scored against Portsmouth because he said: "In the dressing-room before the game Raich came over to me and said: 'Don't worry, Eddie! Run into an open space and I'll do my best to put the ball in front of you!' Open spaces were made for me so often that afternoon that I might have had the playing-field to myself. I became quite confident and I began to hold on to the ball a bit longer." Eddie emerged from an era when wingers were encouraged to exhibit their natural talents and later said: "If I were a scout, I'd look for certain strengths in a player and then recommend him to the club. But although he may have instinctive skills, he gets them knocked out of him when he goes to a club because they tell him how to play. That annoys me. I like players with instincts and they should be allowed to express themselves instead of getting involved in the blackboards business."

In 1948-49 centre-forward Norman Moore finished as City's top League marksman with 22 goals in 31 games and was on the mark another six times in six FA Cup appearances that season. He was known for his aerial prowess, but placed it all in its context when he said: "I put it down to the wingers. We had Eddie Burbanks, for example, and he could cross the ball beautifully, he knew exactly where I was going to be and he would always try to put the ball just in front of me. But I could always get up higher than anybody else. It was a gift, but I did work on it as well. I also believe that it was hereditary. I'd always been told that my father Thomas could jump across two sets of lines from one platform to the other at Great Coates station near Grimsby although I even had a look at it and it isn't possible in my opinion! But he certainly was good at leaping from one point to the other and I do believe that my ability to jump high in the air was a gift from him."

Eddie lived little more than a corner-kick from Boothferry Park, but also ran a sweet and tobacco shop at 257 Holderness Road in East Hull for 23 years. And his wife Joyce said: "Eddie never sought to be the centre of attention. He was very kind, caring and easy-going. He could tear a strip off some-body, but not loudly. He was helpful and a soft touch. I saw him lose his temper only once, which was with a youth in the shop and he threw him through the door, but he was slow to anger." In other words he may have been quietly-spoken, but he held firm views and once said: "A lot of fans would talk to me for the sake of having someone to chat to and not through a love of football. I think they got a bit of reflected glory out of it. But I have never liked to be spoken to as a footballer - I'd rather it was as one citizen to another."

Eddie was also popular with his teammates for one good reason because Andy Davidson said: "Raich opened a hostel in Louis Street in Hull, where players could stay. Eddie Burbanks was just about the only player with a car, so there was some kind of rota by which people would queue up for lifts into training with him. The alternative was to walk over Argyle Street bridge and get a trolley bus down Anlaby Road to the ground, so you learned to be nice to Eddie!"

Another influential player to have left a lasting legacy from the Carter era was the versatile Viggo Jensen, a former Denmark international full-back who made a scoring debut for City against New Brighton in October 1948, playing as an inside-forward for the first time since he had appeared for Jutland against Copenhagen back home. He needed an interpreter to explain his intended role for the Tigers to him, but they won 4-1 and Jensen scored in his first three League games for the club. Viggo was a gentleman and, when I was in contact with him, he always insisted that he could speak English better than write it. As a result, he dictated correspondence intended for me to his son Per, who would then write it down for him. But he also apparently made the most of his linguistic abilities as his career blossomed with City because Andy Davidson said: "He didn't speak any English when he arrived, but it didn't take him long to learn it. But it didn't stop him from taking the mickey out of referees. If he'd done something wrong in a game, he would just say: 'Ja?' back to them and then they'd reply: 'Never mind then!' In fact, he spoke better English than a lot of people, but the referees didn't know it!"

Jensen's footballing ability was never in doubt, though, and it was once written of him: "He is certainly one of the greatest bargains ever to step on to an English football ground. The fans on the terraces admire his superb mastery and the magnificent physical fitness that carries him full speed throughout 90 minutes of the hardest game. He is fearless, but fair and he can play anywhere with equal facility - the hallmark of a great footballer." Andy Davidson added: "I believe that Viggo Jensen twice faced Stan Matthews and played him out of the games. He was a proper athlete who could do somersaults without touching the floor. He was a terrific player because he could play anywhere. He was a natural." Teammate Bob Dennison took up the point: "Viggo was just a brainy, intelligent footballer. He was a touch player who could play just as well at inside-forward as he could at full-back." And wing-half Jimmy Greenhalgh, who oddly played in 48 out of City's 49 games during the triumphant 1948-49 season, said: "Viggo Jensen opened the door to skills we'd never heard of and I have abiding memories of the range of his ability. For example, he was the first bloke to pull a ball down on his instep. We hadn't seen that kind of technical ability before."

Viggo made his mark on and off the pitch. For example, he received a benefit cheque of £750 from City in February 1954 and it came after he had increased the club's coffers by about £8,000 when he scored a last-minute penalty - which he himself had won against Alf Ramsey - to earn them a replay after a 1-1 draw against Tottenham Hotspur at Boothferry Park in front of a 46,839 crowd in the FA Cup fifth round. He recalled: "It had been decided before the game that I should take any penalty-kicks. I remember running round with the ball and all the Tottenham players flocking around the referee in a wild sort of protest. At last the ball was placed on the spot, but then it was kicked away. I placed the ball on the spot again and a Tottenham player came up and whispered to me: 'You'll never score.' But luckily I did." And the following October Viggo was granted permission by Hull Watch and Licensing Committee to sell hot dogs from a mobile canteen at an authorised street trader's stand at the junction of the city's Hessle Road and Rosamund Street. But on home match days he took the canteen to Boothferry Park where he sold Danish hot dogs on the forecourt at the entrance to the ground. The chief constable told the committee that it was a continental idea: no-one wanted to refuse him because of his hero status in the city.

There was a dance at Hull City Hall when Viggo left to return to Denmark in 1956 and teammate

David Coates recalled: "They did a do for him and had a massive whipround because he was so highly popular." Viggo was bought a mini-piano with the proceeeds of his testimonial fund, while the long-serving Billy Bly presented him with a clock at another function at City Supporters' Club's headquarters. And Viggo reflected: "I had so many wonderful adventures, but one of the things which I shall always remember and which impressed me so much during the first few years at Boothferry Park were the 30,000, 40,000 or 45,000 crowds. I cannot say more than I would do it all over again if I could go back to 1948. I would have liked to have played First Division football, but that was not to be. Eight years are a long time, but they passed too quickly." During the autumn of 1956 Jensen played his last game for City against Chester before returning to Denmark 10 days later. It was a matter of much personal regret, though, that I never saw Viggo play because his last game for City as a player was their last before my first game as a fan.

It is probably pertinent that my own Boothferry Park baptism followed the kind of controversy that always seemed to follow the Tigers around. They always appeared to be on the losing side in disputes, though, and that had been the case in Jensen's last game when City beat Chester 2-0. Referee Frank Collinge disallowed a goal in mysterious circumstances in the sixth minute and it led to a minor disturbance near the players' tunnel when the officials left the field at halftime. Bill Bradbury, who scored during the game, was eventually robbed him of a chance to be the Tigers' top League goalscorer that season - instead of sharing the honour with Doug Clarke on 18. Winger Brian Cripsey took a throw-in and one of the linesmen at once put up his flag. The referee waved play on, Cripsey cut in and passed to Bradbury, who put the ball in the back of the net, and everyone moved towards the centre for the restart. The referee had signalled a goal, but Chester's players queried the decision, so he consulted the linesman and awarded them a free-kick instead. The linesman indicated that City's skipper Stan Mortensen was in an offside position and had called for the ball without using a player's name. Mr. Collinge claimed that he had waved play on so that City benefited from the advantage law, but then opted to consult his assistant. But Mortensen said that the only time that he called for the ball was when he received it from the throw by Cripsey, who pointed out that it was impossible to be offside from it. And there was no suggestion that the ball was returned to the offside Mortensen after he had pushed it back to Cripsey from the throw-in.

A week later I stepped into the real world of the Tigers and their dramas myself for the first time. The hopes of the Raich Carter days had disappeared with relegation earlier in the year, but at least I was still lucky enough to see another City hero in action, goalkeeper Billy Bly. In 1964 Newcastle band the Animals released a track called "Gonna Send You Back to Walker," but I already knew where it was. I knew that Walker was in Newcastle because it was Billy's birthplace and I am glad that City never sent him back there!

Nowadays goalkeepers are bigger and are a protected species. In those days they were smaller, less muscular and more athletic. Billy's elastic athleticism meant that he was known as "the India Rubber Man," he was unbelievably agile and brave and he collected serious injuries time and time again, but he once said:"They say that all goalkeepers are daft, but it's not much use standing on the goal-line hoping for the best when you see a forward charging through." In view of his many injuries there was a touch more irony in another of his comments: "I love the game. Nobody twisted my arm to make me play." But Andy Davidson said: "Billy Bly was the best goalkeeper I played with or against. He was the best I've ever seen and could bounce about like a rubber ball." And Bly was even mentioned in a supporters' song from the 1940s, which was performed to the tune of "Sioux City Sue" with the words:

"I took my wife to a football match to see Hull City play,
We waited for a trolley bus for nearly half a day,
And when we got to Boothferry Park, the crowds were rolling in,

16

The bus conductor said to me: 'Do you think that they will win?'
Shoot, City, shoot! Shoot, City, shoot!
The grass is green, the ball is brown,
And we got in for half-a-crown,
Shoot, City, shoot! Shoot, City, shoot!
There ain't a guy as spry
As our goalie Billy Bly."

Known as Billy, he always signed his autograph Bill and is always named as another of the club's all-time greats. His son Roy recalled: "I remember sometimes waving to dad in the mornings when he would walk to Boothferry Park with neighbours such as Ken Harrison, Harold Meens, Denis Durham and Andy Conway. There were few cars on the roads in those days, but eventually dad bought a black Morris with handles facing the wrong way on the doors and foot platforms at the bottom of them on the outside. But my earliest memory of understanding what his job was came in 1958 when I was asked if I wanted to go to football to see him play. But my only thought was about going to Saturday pictures at the Carlton or Priory cinemas and that meant that my mum couldn't go to see dad play for City! I was still not interested in football until I went to a new school and we were told that there would be a practice at the end of the day. I rushed home and told my dad, who had just arrived home from training, so he went straight out that lunchtime and bought me a pair of boots. That was the kind of man he was. Then he taught me how to break them in by standing them in a bucket of water to stretch the leather and mould them to the shape of the feet because he had learned the trade of cobbling when he'd been in the Army. I was soon aware of how he used to suffer a lot of injuries, but he never complained and he never talked about pain. He said that they were just a part of his job and would just give us a wink and a smile."

His fellow City goalkeeper Bernard Fisher summed it up when he said: "It was claimed that Tony Norman was the club's best goalkeeper based on clean sheets and playing in a club-record 226 consecutive League game, but he never had the battering that Billy had when forwards were quite happy to put the man and the ball into the back of the net. Billy was also the best goalkeeper we'd ever seen when going down at a forward's feet in a one-to-one situation. And he never double-fisted a ball when he went to punch it. His argument was that you should catch it if you could get two fists to it."

Billy's life and times with City often reflected the club's own bumpy ride of hope and disappointment. He was City's longest-serving player and is fifth in the club's all-time list of League appearances on 403, but how many would there have been if it had not been for the 1939-45 War and his many injuries? And during the War he played in the same team as goalkeepers Bert Williams and Ted Ditchburn, but he took precedence over them and yet they both became England internationals. Roy Bly has a theory about Billy's misfortune in that respect: "During the War the servicemen received passes to go on home leave for so many hours and would return for short visits. But Stanley Rous, from the FA, had mentioned to my father that he was in the forefront of English goalkeepers and it would be only a matter of time before he would be selected for the national side. On one occasion my dad was granted a home-leave pass for 48 hours and he was asked to guest for a football club, which professional players often did at that time. He had guested himself for Lincoln City, Dumbarton and Hamilton Academicals, but this time he refused because he wanted to go to Newcastle to see my mum Dorothy. As a result, he felt very strongly that Rous put the boot into his England chances."

Denis Durham, a long-serving full-back or wing-half, had also had his fair share of injury and illness setbacks, but remains 25th in the club's list of most League appearances on 267. Born in the village of East Halton on the south side of the Humber bank, he recalled: "I had a trial in October 1946, but then went down with appendicitis and didn't play for the first team until the following May.

Fortunately it was a bad winter and there was an extended season into June and I was still able to get in a few games. I missed quite a few games because of injuries during the years, but they just happened. It was just one of those niggling things, but I stayed with the club until I was nearly 37, which wasn't bad."

Bly and Durham, though, stayed to play in two of the Tigers' promotion teams 10 years apart - in 1949 and 1959. My first experience of watching one came during the 1958-59 season - the first one in the de-regionalised Third Division. It began with one win in the first seven League games and ended in promotion to the Second Division as runners-up to Plymouth Argyle. The signs may have initially been pessimistic, especially when the Tigers lost their seventh League game 6-1 at Southampton, but bit by bit it turned out nice again and Bill Bradbury set a postwar club goalscoring record of 30 in the League in a season. Bill was a genuine character and was always entertaining whenever I had contact with him. He was also a ginger-haired rebel, so at one point we had something in common! His nature, though, meant that he probably never fulfilled his potential and Andy Davidson said: "Bill Bradbury had terrific ability and should have played far higher."

Bill had made an initial impact with the Tigers by scoring a hat-trick on his debut in a friendly against Vasas in October 1955, but the main legacy of his varied career were his goals in the 1958-59 promotion season. His wife Marjorie underlined the point: "Bill was on top of the world after scoring a hat-trick against Vasas in his first match. Then we got our house and Doug Clarke, Frank Harrison and Brian Cripsey were close by. We weren't at Coventry and Birmingham all that long and the longest that we stayed anywhere was at Hull. Bill loved it and I liked it, too. I didn't go down to the club, but Bill was confident and he used to enjoy his football and his training." Bill may not have scored so regularly at any other time, but his son Colin, who has contacted me regularly from both Canada and Australia to keep in touch with the Tigers' fortunes, felt that his father took his football more seriously than some people thought and pointed to the fact that he studied for his FA coaching badge on the same course as Jimmy Hill. It stood him in good stead when he coached Wigan Athletic as a non-League club and Colin said: "My dad was more of a character who liked a good social life as part of his sporting background. Maybe his temperament wasn't always suitable for football because he called a spade a spade and always had a opinion. But he always wanted to be in the game and he was a brainy player who didn't always get stuck in. But his goalscoring record speaks for itself and it was always a case of putting on a show for people."

Colin Smith was not far behind Bill in the goalscoring stakes in 1958-59 with 26 in the League. One of the leading lights in the formation of the Ex-Tigers' Association, he, too, took his coaching seriously at the end of his playing days and has been regularly been involved in it both locally and abroad. He was born in Doncaster, but his family came from Hedon and moved to Hull during the 1939-45 War: "I learnt my body swerve dodging the bullets! But I went to Chapman Street School and then Malet Lambert School, where I had the same teacher who was a soccer fanatic and that made a big difference." Colin is one of several members of that promotion squad who talk about the team spirit and camaraderie as the season took shape. He tells how the players used to supplement their pay by working together on local farms during the summers in those days before the abolition of the maximum wage and said: "I really enjoyed my time with City as a player. One of the differences in those days was that everybody lived in the area and we were with each other most of the time. The club had about 40 professionals and socially we moved around with each other more."

Brian Bulless, who played at left-back, left-half, inside-left and outside-left during that promotion campaign and is 11th in City's all-time appearances list with 326 in the League, took up the point: "We weren't a great side football-wise, but there was a hell of a team spirit. It was unbelievable, but everybody went everywhere together as a gang whenever we went out and I think that it gave us an extra ingredient. We got hammered at Southampton, but it might have geed us up and we pulled our fingers out because we then went on a hell of a run, especially at home. We maybe surprised ourselves, but there were some characters such as Andy Davidson and Bill Bradbury in that side. Andy was a 100 per cent player in every game and he set an example for everybody in the team. There was once a game at Chesterfield, who had a rough-looking character in their side. He was calling people names and riling them, so Andy ran right across the pitch to the other side of it to sort him out! Bill was a great fellow, but he was probably too outspoken and wasn't frightened to open his mouth when he thought he was right. Sometimes he was right and sometimes he was wrong, but it didn't bother him. He was also a hell of a good player and his goals speak for themselves."

Brian's contribution to the club is often underrated because he is one of the nicest, most self-effacing people you could hope to meet. In April 1965, in fact, he even said of his own testimonial game which finished 9-8 when City met a team of All-Stars: "The spectators don't want to see me. They want to see the players I am getting together." He also lived in the same area as his teammates of the late 1950s, but there was a slight difference in his case because he is still just down the road from Boothferry Park: "I eventually moved into what had been Bill Bradbury's club house. A lot of the players lived near each other in them in those days, but I was the only one to buy mine."

The theme of camaraderie was always said to be the catalyst for promotion in 1958-59 because a lot of the players stayed with the club for a long time. Doug Clarke is joint ninth in the club's all-time League appearances list with 369, but claims to be still awaiting his testimonial although he received a loyalty cheque after five years. He had a ferocious shot and recalled: "My son once introduced himself to someone in London and, when the fellow found out about the Hull link and that I was his dad, he complained that I'd injured him on Bunker's Hill with one of my shots! And I can remember taking a penalty against Norwich City during our promotion season and hitting the ball so hard and straight at the goalkeeper Sandy Kennon that it nearly took him into the net before I followed it up." And Doug added: "About half that team were just taken out of local soccer, but we all got on together. There were no cliques and everybody mixed in. That's what you should do, but that team weren't all that brilliant as individuals. It was just that that season we pulled together to work for each other. I really enjoyed my time in Hull and it's not the dead-end place that a lot of people say it is. I probably gave City my best years."

Defender Brian Garvey, whose father Bob had been a rugby-league winger with Hull FC, played rugby union at Endsleigh College, Hull, but there was no chance for him to play rugby-league, so he turned to soccer and played 232 League games for the Tigers. He also mentioned the spirit of 1958-59: "I made my debut in a 1-1 draw away to Bury in early 1958, but that was the only game I played that season. But I got into the team almost straightaway the following season when we got promotion even though I wasn't a full-time professional. I was an amateur and then a part-time professional when I came out of the Army and did my apprenticeship as a motor mechanic. I was just doing part-time training on Tuesdays and Thursday at Bootherry Park. We would train on the car-park if it were light or underneath one of the stands. I played a lot at left-back and left-half even though I was right-footed. My assets were tackling, heading and running. I didn't have a lot to do with Bob Brocklebank because I was one of the younger players. He would just seem to organise the training and pick the side. I was just glad to get into the first team. There were a lot of local players at the club at the time and I think that teamwork and comradeship came into it. Bill Bradbury and Colin Smith were scoring goals and that made a big difference, while the young players used their enthusiasm and effort for better results, which gave us confidence because it had looked early doors as if we might get relegated."

Paul Feasey, the side's captain when they were known as the Brocklebank Toddlers in response to the Busby Babes at Manchester United, felt that the training aided the cause because he said: "We were third from bottom after a few games, but then things clicked for some unknown reason. We won a few matches on the trot and then we seemed to put a few more wins together again every time we lost. It was just one of those things although we were lucky that we always had 11 players playing for one another, but all of a sudden we found ourselves up at the top by Christmas. But we always used to maintain that it helped us a lot when we trained on the club car-park. It made such a big difference to train on the ash because it was lighter going all the time and it was never any effort for us to get through games as far as fitness was concerned. It was before Cliff Britton took over and they opened up the back pitch, so we'd normally start off by training at Anlaby Road on the Circle, which was a heavy playing area. And it was noticeable that the team never seemed to do very well early in a season until we got on to the car-park. And it used to be blood-and-thunder training. We'd split up into five-a-side teams and have a bit of a league with the losers having to buy the Mars Bars for the winners at Billy Bly's sweet shop near the ground!"

Feasey himself was a leading figure at centre-half in those days, but he was not the biggest for the position, relying instead on impeccable timing in the air. "I reached only 5ft. 8½in., but you do daft things as a youngster and I can remember that, when I was between nine and 11, one of my hobbies on my way home from the pictures in York was to jump at the trees that overhung the pathways to see which branches I could touch. I wasn't thinking about being a professional footballer then, but that's the way it started in terms of being able to jump high and give myself leverage. I kept it up and would practise trying to 'climb' for hours and hours. And I was lucky that City signed Neil Franklin after I'd joined them. They were unfortunate that they didn't see the best of him because he had knee trouble that meant that he was never really fit. But he'd played for England and had been a hell of a player. And he was a toff - a fine fellow who would always be willing to help even though I was only a kid then. He wasn't all that tall himself - about 5ft. 10½in. - but he could get up to a fair height and was very powerful in the air, so I learned a lot from him."

Inside-forward David Coates also recalled how City put a bad start behind them in 1958-59: "We lost 6-1 at Southampton and I think that left us second from the bottom after only seven games, but then we came back to win three home games on the trot - Monday, Saturday and Monday again - and I remember meeting up with Brian Bulless at the Anlaby Park Hotel after the third one. I said to him: 'I think we're going to get promotion.' Brian told me that I was off my rocker, but I had that feeling about things because I thought we'd started to get such a good style about us. And twice that season we won six games on the trot. Doug Clarke had been moved out to the right regularly, we knew what Bill Bradbury and Colin Smith could do and I'd struck up a partnership on the left with Mike Bowering, so those five forwards had become a settled unit. I was an energy fanatic. My game was getting up and down the pitch and they called me the Gordon Pirie of football at City in those days! Bill Bradbury was at his best during that season and Colin Smith was a top-class finisher who would just drive the ball into the net even though he could never really run well. Colin scored more goals that season than Chris Chilton did when the club got promotion later on in 1966 and Bill scored more than Waggy did then. Brian Garvey came in and did well because of an injury to Brian Bulless, who was desperate to get back into the side when he got fit again. Andy Davidson was also injured and he wanted to play as soon as he could. I never felt that I got to know Andy well, but I admired him. He had a huge influence on things because he had a great desire to get stuck in and get people going. He was also a prodigious trainer and would train on his own when it was necessary."

Centre Stand passes for the 1958-59 season cost a mere £5 5s. and the success was masterminded by manager Bob Brocklebank and his assistant trainers, the Gillingham-born Johnny Mahon and the evergreen Jimmy Lodge. Brocklebank had played League football for Aston Villa and Burnley and managed Chesterfield and Birmingham City. He had been with Villa when they were relegated from the First Division for the first time in 1935-36 and the worst moment was surely their 7-1 defeat to Arsenal at Villa Park when Brocklebank had to provide his autograph in awkward circumstances.

Arsenal's England international Ted Drake, wearing what became his trademark bandage on his left knee for the first time, scored all seven of his side's goals, so Villa gave him the match ball, but also cleaned and washed it first and made sure that all their defeated players signed it for him! It might have helped when he faced relegation with City soon after his arrival in 1956 although Andy Davidson said: "Bob Brocklebank was far too soft to be a manager: he was just too nice a man." And Brian Bulless recalled: "I got on well with most of the managers. Raich Carter signed me on although I didn't have much to do with him, but Bob Jackson had become manager when I got into the team. He had a bow-tie and a pipe and he was all right. Bob Brocklebank was a gentleman and a good manager, but he was a quiet sort of bloke. Jimmy Lodge was a great fellow who gave us all a lot of encouragement." The fair-haired Mahon had been in the same successful Doncaster Grammar School team as Eddie Burbanks in 1928-29 and had then played for Doncaster Rovers, Leeds United and West Bromwich Albion before joining Huddersfield Town, breaking his leg eight minutes into his debut against Sunderland. He attempted a comeback with York City and then coached Elfsborg and Gothenburg in Sweden. Andy said of him: "He had his own ideas about the game and wasn't a bad coach. He was a nice fellow who took the game very seriously."

For once Brocklebank had been firm in his outlook after the bad start to 1958-59 because he said: "When the players don the Tigers' jerseys, I expect each one to go out on to the field and give everything for the club for the full 90 minutes. Mistakes will be forgiven, but I shall not countenance lack of effort." Equally, it would not have been City if everything had gone totally smoothly, of course, and there had been early-season transfer requests from Brian Bulless, Bill Bradbury and Brian Cripsey. And even after the results had improved and the team spirit had started to take effect, there was a transfer request from long-serving full-back Frank Harrison.

It happened in ironic circumstances, too. In August 1954 Gateshead-born Harrison, who had moved to Hull at the age of four and captained England during two of his four appearances as a youth international, had been the youngest City player since their re-formation to earn a benefit cheque, which was handed over at a ceremony in the club's boardroom attended by president Ken Percival, chairman Harold Needler, manager Bob Jackson and directors Stan Kershaw and Ron Buttery. Harrison, who was to break his leg the following December, said: "I have been very happy for the past five years and I just hope that I am with the club for another five years to get another one." But he ended up asking for a transfer in October 1958 because of barracking from the fans, one of whom had cruelly suggested that he should break his leg again. His stylish play did not always appeal to the public, but the outcome was that Graham Wilkinson replaced him for two games before everything settled down and he went on to play in the other 44 League games of the promotion season.

There was also a problem as the season approached its ultimate triumph. Promotion was clinched with a 2-0 home win over Bury and then it was a question of going for victory at Wrexham in the final League game to ensure the title ahead of Plymouth Argyle. But Wrexham won 5-1, City finished as runners-up and the sequel to the game had its own controversy. Brian Bulless explained: "All I know about my promotion-winning goal against Bury was that I was only a few yards out, but the ball went in and that was the main thing. But then we went to Wrexham and were beaten 5-1 when we needed just one point to be champions. After the game words were said when Stan Kershaw, one of the directors, came into the dressing-room. He said that the directors weren't too pleased even though we'd got promotion, but what was said didn't please the lads. We were singing in the bath afterwards because we'd done our job and got promotion, but then it all upset us."

There has always been a feeling that the incident left a sour taste for 1959-60 in the Second Division when the Tigers were relegated with only Bristol City below them. But Andy Davidson reasoned: "I think that in 1958-59 we had more luck than anyone else did. We were a fighting side, but we didn't have the skill to keep it going. We went up in 1959 on a prayer when everything went for us. But we were on our way to being relegated by the next Christmas because the side weren't good enough." And Brian Garvey added: "In 1959-60 we can't have been good enough. We needed better players with more experience and lost games simply because we were not up to standard. I was still young as a professional and was just training and playing and getting on with it, but under Cliff Britton I did feel that I went on to better things. Cliff Britton thought that I'd make a player because I could challenge for balls in the air and tackle."

City soon conceded 21 goals in five successive League games, so Bob Brocklebank came up with two main solutions during the autumn of 1959 - an influx of experienced forwards and a change of coach. Former England international Jackie Sewell, Ralph Gubbins and Roy Shiner made their debuts in three consecutive home games and Johnny Mahon, who had been with City since July 1953, was ousted from his coaching post. But there was little hope even though youngster Dave King scored twice on his League debut in a 3-1 win at Sunderland and finished with seven goals in nine League games to reflect the kind of scoring form that his good friend Dave Fraser had also found as a teenager in 1956 when he, too, tried to stave off relegation from the Second Division.

King, in fact, has always insisted that he was in awe of Jackie Sewell, who said: "Bob Brocklebank was a nice bloke and he was the reason why I moved to Hull. He knew all about me from when he was Birmingham City's manager and one day he was watching us train at Aston Villa. I enjoyed my time at Hull despite everything. I liked the place and the lads in the dressing-room were super blokes, especially 'Jock' Davidson, Brian Bulless and Doug Clarke. Dave King was another likeable lad and I sold him my golf clubs when I was getting rid of them." Oddly enough, Jackie had a City reunion at a golf tournament many years later when Bill Bradbury crept up on him unexpectedly!

The decision to replace Mahon was announced by vice-chairman Ron Buttery, who said: "We have decided that we would like to improve our training and coaching and we are advertising for a new trainer-coach. We do not know what Mr. Mahon's plans will be. We shall help him in any way if we can." Mahon, in fact, moved to Hull High School for Nautical Training to teach games, geography, mathematics and English. On the day of Gubbins' debut, meanwhile, City's board interviewed the former Blackburn Rovers and Newcastle United defender Jesse Carver, who had coached Holland, England B and Tottenham Hotspur, managed Coventry City and worked in Italian football with Juventus, Torino and Roma: accordingly, he chose Genoa instead!

City settled for a former Bevin Boy known as Angus McLean to his wife only and as Gus McLean to everyone else. He came from Queensferry in Flintshire, for whom he played as a defender even though he was a right-winger, but his family were mainly Scottish. It was ironic then that in 1949 he was a reserve for Wales against Scotland! Initially Gus became a grocer's errand boy, but was spotted by Wolverhampton Wanderers, had a trial and became a full-time professional on his 17th birthday, making his debut in a wartime game against Walsall. It brought him into contact with future City manager Major Frank Buckley and he recalled: "It was there that I got my first telling-off in soccer. Buckley, who frightened me to death at the time, took me to one side and said that, if I wanted to kick anyone, it should be someone on the other side! All out to make a good show, I had kicked Dennis Wilshaw in my enthusiasm!" Gus, who was noted for his powerful shot and had broken a goalkeeper's wrist with a penalty, spent 10 seasons at Molineux and played more than 300 games for Wolves in nine different positions. In 1952 he joined non-League Aberystwyth, but broke his leg on his debut. He then joined Bromsgrove before returning to the League with Bury and Crewe Alexandra. And in his second season with Wigan Athletic, then in the Lancashire Combination, he succeeded Ronnie Suart as player-manager, but had to retire from playing because of injury, so he concentrated on coaching. He stressed the importance of planning, once saying: "We had only five tactical talks in the 10 years I was at Wolves. We would have been an even better team if we had been drilled tactically."

City still went down and achieved it with the kind of big squad who were customary in those days before the abolition of the maximum wage in 1961. Defender Mick Brown, whose father Len had been on City's books, proved it because he did not play a senior game for the club between October 1959 and April 1964. Mick, who has had an illustrious career in management and coaching, including spells as Manchester United's assistant manager and chief scout, was born in Walsall and brought up in the Gloucester area, but he had relatives in the Hull area and had visited it on holiday. He had a trial with City when he was 15, worked for the Needler family as an apprentice joiner and signed as an amateur when he was 18, but he explained: "It was a bit different from nowadays. City were my club and I never entertained ideas of wanting to play for anyone else. But I was always the understudy to Andy Davidson, which was a thankless task because he played a record number of games for the club, so my chances were limited. If you look at it as a cold, hard professional, the best decision would have been to get a move, but you put down your roots as a schoolboy and I loved the area and the club. I played in the reserves a lot and I was happy to do so. We had the first team, the reserves and the A team and at one stage they had 47 professionals, but you couldn't take anything for granted. It is always a special occasion when I come back to Hull and I always get a buzz from it."

City, though, looked less favourably on long-serving players Billy Bly and Denis Durham, both of whom had shown resilience against repeated injury setbacks. There was a public outcry when Billy, who had been nicknamed "the brittle-boned hero," was released at the end of 1959-60 and not even allowed to make a farewell appearance in the final game of the season at home to Ipswich Town. It was a meaningless game, but Billy was told to play in the reserves instead. In July 1959 Denis, who had fought back from illness during 1953-54, a cartilage operation during 1955-56 and spinal damage at the end of 1957-58, had become a part-timer and reflected: "I was on my way out when we went up, but it would have been nice to play in the Second Division again because it gave you the chance to play at better grounds." He had taken a job with a paper-making firm in Grimsby, which may even have helped him when he became a newsagent after his career had finished, but he did not play in the first team during 1959-60.

Billy Bly did not have much luck with his testimonial match, either. The board had reluctantly allowed it only after the outcry about his sacking and even then City did not provide one of the sides for it, so it was between an Ex-Tigers' team and an All-Stars' XI. It was arranged for Boothferry Park, but even the timing of it caused problems. It coincided with a polio epidemic in Hull and then had to be switched because of a clash that restricted the players who would be available for it. Originally it was scheduled to take place on October 16, 1961, but then it was found that it clashed with a testimonial match for former England hero Nat Lofthouse, who had retired as a player earlier that year, at Bolton. But the game had been put back a week from October 9, so it clashed with Bly's match in Hull. Most of the players had already committed themselves to the Lofthouse game, so that had to take precedence and Bly's match had to be put back three days to October 19. Yet they still wanted to be part of the game in Hull, so Bly, accompanied by fellow goalkeeper Bernard Fisher, had to go to Bolton to negotiate for some top players for it. And fans were promised that any tickets that they had bought for the original date would still be valid.

Roy Shiner was another senior player to vanish during the summer of 1960 and even Jackie Sewell's departure a year later was coated in controversy because he said: "I had the chance to go to Northern Rhodesia and asked to go for three months, but I was rather shattered by Hull City's attitude. When I went abroad for the summer, one of the Needler brothers turned round and said that they wouldn't pay my summer wages and I could have a free transfer. I nearly dropped to my knees when I heard what he said because I was quite happy and things weren't too bad."

City were going nowhere quickly even though some new faces had appeared on the scene. Left-winger Charlie Crickmore, who had modelled himself on Eddie Burbanks as a schoolboy in Hull, had been given his first-team chance during 1959-60, for example. He had first joined the ground staff, recalling: "It was not that glamorous. We had to sweep the terraces, clean boots and even paint the roofs of the stands. I'd love to know what the Health and Safety people would make of that nowadays." Then he had turned professional as 17-year-old: "Bob Brocklebank asked me how I thought I was doing as a footballer. I've never been short of confidence and I proceeded to tell him exactly how well I was doing. Brocklebank replied: 'Oh, I'm pleased that you said that because you are now a professional at Hull City.' I was shaking so much that I could hardly write my name on the contract. I was now going to get £7 a week, it was 1959 and that was a lot of money. To be honest, I loved football so much that I would have played for nothing. They were wonderful years and I learned such a lot even though we were relegated in my first season."

Chris Chilton and new signings Eric McMillan and Dudley Price established themselves during the 1960-61 season, but there were more quirks and curios to note than any noticeable momentum that would satisfy the fans' appetite for success. Ralph Gubbins scored City's first goal in the new Football League Cup against his old club Bolton Wanderers and there was an FA Cup marathon that stretched to 510 minutes' play. And it all centred around the last minute of the first meeting between City and Darlington at Feethams, which was ruled to have ended at 1-1. But referee Jim Parkinson insisted that Darlington's equaliser by Bobby Baxter had gone through a hole in the net rather than over the bar when it finished up lodged behind the goal. City's goalkeeper Bernard Fisher said: "Many things were said, including talk about a hole in the net, but Baxter came in after the game and said that it was never a goal in the first place." And defender Brian Garvey added: "It was amazing. We were yelling and appealing, but you can't do anything about it. We went to see the referee and told him that it had gone outside the post and not into the net. The strange thing was that he said that it had gone through a hole, but the nets had already been checked. It took five games before we won through in the end." Even then it all ended in another Cup exit against Bolton...

By the summer of 1961 it was time for change and manager Bob Brocklebank was replaced by former England half-back Cliff Britton. It had been said of him as a player: "He was cool and elegant in his placing of the ball, especially with his long, swinging crosses into the opponents' goalmouth. Britton was the cultured ball artist - his accurate long passing and precise use of the ball a delight to watch. Long and lean and his fair hair gleaming, he was indeed a polished craftsman." He helped Everton to promotion as the Second Division champions, the First Division title and the FA Cup in successive seasons between 1931 and 1933. In 1945 he toured Italy with a British Army team and decided to retire to concentrate on management. He had been stationed in Yorkshire when he went into management, guiding Burnley to the 1947 FA Cup final. He returned to Everton to take charge, but resigned in 1956 and went to Preston, saying: "I have always believed that a manager should manage." At one stage of his career he had claimed that he was finished with management for good: luckily for the Tigers he had changed his mind.

He brought in the versatile Ray Henderson, goalscoring winger John McSeveney and the diminutive Alan Shaw for his first season and suggested that he knew his own mind in terms of planning because he used just 17 players throughout. But Shaw's arrival underlined a sign of the times as clubs reduced their squads. Having started on Bolton Wanderers' books, Shaw was one of those to feel the pinch at Preston North End, where he had worked with Britton. He explained: "It meant a lot to come to Hull City because there wasn't much else for me at the time. It was 1961 and the maximum wage was being abolished. Clubs had had between 40 and 45 members of staff and had been able to afford them because of the wage limits, but then it all changed. The established first-teamers wanted good money and rightly so, so the clubs wanted to keep their star players, but it meant that their staffing went down to about 20 to 25 players and the other 20 went on their ways. I was at Preston, but I was kicked out, so I went to Canada for six months and played for Hamilton Steelers. There were only four clubs in the league - two teams from Toronto and one from Montreal as well as ourselves - so we played each other about 12 times during the summer. But I got the chance to play against people such as Stan Matthews, Danny Blanchflower, Roy Gratrix and Tommy Younger. But then I heard that Hull were interested in me and I came straight back because I knew Cliff. He said that he'd give me a month, see how things went and then we'd talk. And it was brilliant while I was with City."

But there was not much to inspire us on Bunker's Hill because City's gates were down and in 1962-63 the quirks were up again. They lost one of the most dramatic games at Boothferry Park when they came back from 4-1 down to beat non-League Crook Town 5-4 in the FA Cup in November 1962. The Tigers had not gone out of the competition to non-League opposition since Tottenham Hotspur disposed of them in January 1907, but matchwinner Ray Henderson said: "To have lost to an amateur side would have been the end of the world for Cliff Britton because he got wound up like everyone else with every game being like life or death. I think that a certain amount of panic had crept in by halftime. Cliff was ashen-faced and I've always said that I would have given a fiver to have seen his face when we went 4-1 down soon after we'd kicked off for the second half. But once we realised that Crook were running out of steam, there was nothing in it. They suddenly caved in after we'd got our second goal." And two-goal John McSeveney said: "I've often quoted the Crook match to people as an example of what can happen if you get too cocky and confident. Crook got that way and I remember making it 4-2 after someone had tried to be too clever with a backpass and I nipped in. But they also began to get very tired as we fought back." And Brian Garvey added: "Crook seemed to catch us unawares and were 4-1 up. It looked as if it might have been a disaster, but it was a remarkable comeback to win 5-4. But they were a non-League side and we just put in some extra effort."

Then in January 1963 City's home game against Swindon Town was called off because of a frozen pitch at halftime with the score 0-0 - the first to be abandoned at Boothferry Park. It was replayed the following May and ended 1-1, John McSeveney scoring for City, but controversy surrounded Ernie Hunt's shot for Swindon's "goal," which was said to have lodged on the inside of the side-netting, according to referee Dick Windle. But City's goalkeeper Mike Williams' reaction was to run round the outside of his goal to retrieve the ball from the outside of the side-netting. There were scuffles among the crowd as City insisted that the ball never entered the goal and Andy Davidson said: "The groundsman Stan Coombs nearly got the sack because of what happened. The ball never went near the front of the net because the shot would have had to go in at an impossible angle for it to happen. But it lodged below the stanchion where some loose netting had been gathered up. The referee gave a goal, so we turned to a linesman and asked him how the ball could have gone into the goal, but he wouldn't answer us." All in all, I was already well aware that it was dangerous for me, my dad and my friends to have too many high hopes from high on Bunker's Hill.

Football clubs' fortunes are are often governed by the degree of expectancy among the fans. As we leaned lazily on the barriers on Bunker's Hill in the early 1960s, we really did not expect too much from Hull City. Going up in 1959 and coming down in 1960 had destroyed any illusions of lasting or grandiose success. It was back to the bread-and-butter of topsy-turvy times. But an announcement in the early part of 1963 changed all that because chairman Harold Needler gave the club £200,000 worth of shares in his Hoveringham gravel business and their value doubled not long afterwards. It was the platform for change for the better. There was scope to invest in players and the green, green grass of home at Boothferry Park was surrounded by new developments that meant that technically my beloved Bunker's Hill disappeared.

But nothing much happened for a while in terms of additions to the playing staff as manager Cliff Britton fastidiously looked after the family fortune at his disposal. One of the new arrivals, winger Alan Shaw, pointed out: "Cliff never spent money. He had built up a brilliant youth system when he'd been at Burnley and he'd done the same at Everton even though he'd had an open cheque-book." He had signed useful, underrated players such as Len Sharpe, Ray Henderson and John McSeveney and youngsters such as Chris Simpkin and Chris Chilton had started to mature. Britton's predecessor Bob Brocklebank, who retired to Paignton, where he ran a sweet shop after a spell in charge of Bradford City, later reflected: "They were my best discoveries. Chilton was one of about 80 lads we had down for a trial at Anlaby Road. There were four games going and I told our secretary John Adamson to sign him up after only 10 minutes of watching him. I signed Simpkin after watching him in a school-boys' match." John McSeveney, a goalscoring winger who was on the mark 22 times in the League in 1962-63, was underrated and he said: "Cliff said: 'I know I can rely on you.' I was never a pure winger, but I could always score goals. Yet I became the man the fans loved to hate even though I later scored 17 goals in a season after moving to the right-wing when Ian Butler arrived. I was 34 by then, so I was happy with that."

In 1963 Charlie Leyfield, who had played for Everton and Sheffield United and coached at Wrexham, was appointed as City's chief scout. Leyfield, who managed a hotel in Chester, had played alongside Britton at Goodison Park and had been in charge of Wales when City's trainer Gus McLean was their 12th man against Scotland. But the signings of Dennis Butler and Ron Rafferty proved to be the quiet before the transfer storm. In February 1964 Britton came under fire from fans following a 2-0 home defeat against his home-city club Bristol Rovers. City were in the middle of a seven-match League run without a win and Britton, under pressure to spend Harold Needler's investment heavily after the club's promotion hopes had disappeared, insisted: "I want the younger players who are able to bring success and make it last, so I am prepared to pay that little bit more for that type. The trouble is that that kind of player is difficult to buy. I know the players I want and have made approaches for them, but we cannot buy them until their clubs are ready to sell. I understand how the public feel, waiting all the time week after week for something to happen. It is hard to know what to say to supporters because a section of them pick on whatever you say, but I can only repeat that my object is to try to build a successful team." Within a year he had signed Ken Wagstaff from Mansfield Town and Ian Butler and Ken Houghton from Rotherham United - all for £40,000 - and the only way was up.

What was probably not so obvious was that Cliff Britton had quietly, but ruthlessly been going through the club from top to bottom. Some stalwarts left, for example. Brian Bulless reflected: "In 1963 I had to finish because I was struggling with a knee injury and I'd had an operation. It wasn't standing up to football, so I played my last game at home to Wrexham and we won 4-2. Chris Chilton got four goals in that match and I'll always remember it, but there again I'm sure he will, too!" And Brian Garvey mused: "In my last year I wasn't a regular. Harold Needler had spent a lot of money, so it was a matter of moving on. You don't realise what's going on, but people go in and out - and I was out."

Others would come and go quickly as Alan Shaw found out: "I'd had a good run of games in the first team, but then they left Len Sharpe and me out for two cupties against Everton. They brought in John McSeveney at outside-left, but then they left him out for a game and put George Cummins, who'd been a Republic of Ireland international midfield player, out there on a Friday night at Barnsley, so I realised that I was suddenly way out of the picture. I was playing for the reserves the next day and the coaches Gus McLean and John Simpson told me: 'We want you back in the first team.' We beat Darlington's reserves 2-1 and I scored, so John Simpson told me after the game that it was the best I'd ever played in his view and Gus leaned over and winked knowingly at me. But I never played another first-team game, so I said to myself: 'I want to be away.' It was important to me because you had only yearly contracts then. It would have been different if someone had said: 'Look, Alan, you're doing okay, so don't worry about the first team.' It might also have helped if I'd had a father figure to tell me to keep my 'trap' shut!"

Others had their moments of glory without becoming established first-teamers. Norman Corner, for example, scored twice on his debut at Brentford in a 3-1 win in the final game of 1963-64, but there was a quirky sideline to it because Billy Wilkinson believed that he had been stuck on 13 League goals for the season for nearly two months. It is thought that he also claimed one of the own goals accredited to the Tigers that season, but most record-books insist that he went into that final game on only 12. Billy apparently was so desperate to move off the 13 mark in what was his first full season in the first team that Corner felt sorry for him and set up a goal for him and forsook the chance to score a hat-trick on his debut. Norman said: "We played in a white strip and I scored two goals with headers from corners. But Billy said that he was fed up of being stuck on 13 League goals for the season, I had the choice of getting my hat-trick or setting one up for him, which I did. It was out of the world for me to score on my debut anyway and I thought that Cliff Britton was going to writhe my arm off in the dressing-room afterwards because he was shaking my hand so hard in congratulating me!"

By early 1965 Britton had installed a formidable forward-line for the Third Division although the Chillo and Waggy double act might never have come to fruition. As soon as Waggy was signed, there was speculation that he might have arrived as a replacement for Chillo, who at once attracted interest from Fulham and Crystal Palace. Similarly, City had been linked with Burnley's Gordon Harris and Blackburn Rovers' Mike Harrison before signing Ian Butler. But he and Ken Houghton, who had played for Silverwood Colliery - the club who had also spawned City centre-forward Simon Raleigh before the 1939-45 War - before signing for Rotherham, were signed within a week of each other. In fact, the Millers' manager Danny Williams was told by his seven-year-old son, Danny junior, who joined him on a trip to Boothferry Park to complete the Houghton deal: "Why do you bring them in ones, dad? Why don't you bring a bus?"

John McSeveney was switched to the right-wing to complete the new forward-line and summed it all up: "Cliff Britton went about rebuilding the club. If you scored more than the opposition, then he thought you were a good side because the most important thing to him was to attack. He did work on defence, but he was such a positive man that he always concentrated on attack." City went on a 15-match unbeaten run during 1964-65, but they capitulated during Easter and finished only fourth. McSeveney retired and Billy Wilkinson and Terry Heath were tried out in the No. 7 shirt the following season before Ray Henderson made the role his own. Maurice Swan became the first-choice goalkeeper again and Alan Jarvis stepped in after Gerry Summers had moved to Walsall

City were now promotion material, but the transition did not go entirely smoothly. Ray Henderson had been an inside-forward when he moved from Middlesbrough, for whom he had signed in Newcastle United's boardroom after helping Ashington to win the Northumberland Senior Cup final. But he had had to adjust to a new role and recalled: "We had an exceptional couple of years when we won so many games, but Cliff Britton and I had an ongoing battle because I didn't want to be a right-winger and I wasn't in a sense. The plan wasn't for me to play as an orthodox right-winger, but for me to play in a way that would let Waggy run free. I didn't want to play there, but I wanted to be in the team. We did well, but it wasn't my choice and I didn't really want to do it. I tried it for the first couple of games, but Bill Harris was coming to see me play against Oldham Athletic. I'd played with him at Middlesbrough and he was then manager of Bradford City, but I had no chance of leaving. You couldn't get a free transfer in those days unless you'd committed murder! I went in to see Cliff and came out after two hours, at the end of which he said: 'You'll be playing there.' Cliff being Cliff, he put me on the teamsheet, but I was okay once I was settled and I picked up a few goals, which was a bit of a bonus. He liked everyone to fit into a pattern, he was very methodical and he thought my role would improve the pattern of the team. He was also very determined, but he couldn't relax and let himself go."

City won the Third Division title and reached the FA Cup quarter-finals with some stylish, attacking football and Ray observed: "We used to play two-touch football in training - not for half an hour, but all the time. Cliff never missed a minute of training, he was always out there and he would see it all. Angus McLean suggested that I should talk to him instead of fighting with him. He knew that I could run with the ball, I started to come back in the afternoons and in the end it all became second nature. In the end I came away with a lot of good memories because we could all play a bit of football." Andy Davidson added: "Cliff had a photographic memory and would go through every player individually from one to 11 to assess their performances. I used to listen to him and think: 'You've got me right, but surely you couldn't do the same for the other 10.' But he did. If I'd made one mistake, he'd nail me for it on a Tuesday morning when he went through everybody's performances. He never forgot anything from the 90 minutes of a match and was a great tactician."

And Britton frowned on any kind of drinking culture at the club. Len Sharpe recalled: "Cliff used to stand there and watch all the training - right through the mornings and afternoons. I'd already been at Scunthorpe United for a long time, but if I'd have come across Cliff Britton as a young lad, then I know that I would have been a better player. He'd read through everybody in the team after a match and he never missed a thing. His reading of the game was excellent. He aimed for perfection and at times he got pretty near it. He always told you that you had to be able to pass the ball and his motto was: 'It's the final pass that counts.' Cliff was a connoisseur and had such a knowledge of the game. Harold Needler was a gentleman and, when I first met Cliff Britton, a few of us were having a drink and I said: 'Lager, please.' Then somebody told me that you didn't drink alcohol when Cliff was around." Dennis Butler added: "You couldn't help but look up to Cliff Britton. I couldn't kick with my left foot when I first went to Hull, but I was fairly good with both feet by the time I went to Reading because he'd worked on me. Cliff went into every detail about things and he was also a gentleman and a teetotaller. I can remember my first game at Watford when the other players were drinking ginger beer or milk or orange squash and I had a cider. Gus McLean, the coach, told me: 'Make that your first and last because this is a teetotal outfit' and he meant it. They were good years because we just missed out on promotion one year and then went up the next. They had good crowds of between 26,000 and 30,000 in the Third Division and there were more than 45,000 at the FA Cup replay against my old club Chelsea. They were good days when I was at Hull and we never really had any bad times even though we were stuck in mid-table in the Second Division for a few seasons. I played regularly - even up to leaving - so it was a big wrench when I was transferred from City to

Reading and I had to pull her-indoors away!"

The glorious Third Division title-winning season of 1965-66 when City scored 109 League goals will forever be associated with the twin spearhead of Chris Chilton and Ken Wagstaff. It was, though, a team effort because, for example, the other three regular forwards - Ray Henderson, Ken Houghton and Ian Butler - all reached double figures in terms of League goals, Andy Davidson and Mick Milner were enjoying promotion the second time around because they had been members of City's 1958-59 squad and Chris Simpkin was also an ever-present in the Third Division campaign. At the same time the Waggy - Chillo double act provided the icing on the cake and they had to settle for FA representative honours when more might have come to them if the Tigers had reached the top flight.

Waggy, who came through the ranks of the same Mansfield Youth League who had produced England's 1966 World Cup winner Ray Wilson, was a great player who never had the chance to ply his trade in the top flight, but he said: "It's no good being disappointed. Cliff Britton always said that he wouldn't sell Chris Chilton or me because our goals would keep him in a job for 10 years! And when Joe Harvey wanted to take us to Newcastle United, Harold Needler told him that he had a better chance of buying the town-hall clock. Chris was also a good player and we hit it off, both on the pitch and off it. We were different types on the pitch, but the friendship carried on off it. But all the players got on well in that promotion side and they were all good players."

Waggy believed that goalscorers were born rather than manufactured although he paid tribute to Raich Carter when they were together at Mansfield Town and Cliff Britton with City for helping him to develop a positional sense: "It is a gift. When you're in the penalty area, you mustn't panic, but you should take your time. You must be good positionally and you don't need to belt the ball into the net when you can side-foot it. I don't think that goalscoring can be taught because it's an instinct." Andy Davidson, his promotion-winning captain, always made the point that most strikers become edgy in tight penalty-box situations, but Waggy reacted the other way and had the innate knack of keeping cool, calm and collected and transferring the pressure to the defenders trying to stop him. Waggy also delighted in scoring for the Tigers against the top England internationals of the day - Gordon Banks with Stoke City, Peter Bonetti with Chelsea and Peter Shilton with Leicester City. He recalled: "I sat Gordon Banks down on his backside to score one in the FA Cup against Stoke City and put one to his other side when we met them again the following season. And it's nice to think that we put six past Peter Shilton in two matches against Leicester in one season. We always said that we'd score against him if we shot low because we reckoned that he didn't get down too well. But I never feared any goalkeeper and you can't afford to do so. You miss some chances, but then you'll always score your fair share if you keep trying to take them. And that's why you must keep going when things aren't going well because you start scoring again if you do. At the same time I always thought that I could play a bit and I was always helping to make goals for others if I weren't scoring them."

Chillo was the local lad who got better and better and briefly tasted First Division football when he left to join Coventry City, but he remains the club's leading goalscorer of all time with 193 in the League and will always be inextricably linked with the Tigers' goalscoring exploits of the 1960s. He recalled: "I think that Cliff Britton always knew that he had strikers who would score goals, but there was tremendous loyalty among those players to the club and to each other. We also had respect for the manager and everything was governed by that. I also brought those principles into the coaching side of football with me. I think they were possibly glory days. Certainly everybody knew all the players and we were never put on a pedestal on the financial side. We were just ordinary working blokes. And the majority of us were on the same kind of wage level as the people who were watching us when we played, so that always quashed any thoughts of resentment. When we were playing, we never felt sure that that we would always be in the side from one week to the next. It was always a case of still waiting for the teamsheet to go up on a Friday and nothing was taken for granted. We played in those years when it was so enjoyable to be involved in the game. I got one medal - for the Third Division championship - and the recognition of playing for my country at a certain level. In any walk of life you always have to have a target and it is very important to have pride whether you are at club or international level."

Regrettably, my friendship with Chris has been tested in recent years since I was asked to help him to write his life story in 2001. I made numerous 50-mile round trips to his house in Thorngumbald, where I was always made to feel welcome by Chris and his wife Margaret. Jeff Barmby, the chairman of the Ex-Tigers' Association, had brought us together for the project and helped him with arrangements to try to keep printing and paper costs to a minimum. Throughout the summer we assiduously went through Chillo's life and times, recording hours of it on cassettes. It was then my task to turn the stories into book form with his approval. We ploughed through everything, which I found very enjoyable, and finally got round to discussing the financial implications for us both towards the end of the summer. My view was that I was doing more of the work, but its success depended on Chillo's good name and reputation. I felt, therefore, that we should split any profits on a 50-50 basis, but Chris wanted the balance in his favour. There was a bit of a stand-off, but no major fall-out as far as I was concerned. Chris contacted me and asked if I would visit him again. We still had some interviewing to complete, so I readily agreed. He came up with a compromise and I accepted it in principle even though I still felt at heart that it was unfair on me in view of my time and input into the project. After all, I visited him every time: he never visited me although we did meet once at the Crooked Billet in East Hull. But we sat in Chillo's kitchen when we met up again and he insisted that all along I had been the only person with whom he wanted to produce the book, which was fair enough. But he also talked about the book as being his "pension" and that made me a little suspicious about his monetary approach. I viewed the book as a means to an end for both of us: Chris, it seemed, saw it as the end. I believed that our respective reputations might be enhanced if the book turned out to be a well-written, good read and it might open doors for both of us, but it seemed that Chris was staking everything on it.

Anyway we had a verbal understanding and not long afterwards I sent him two copies of a written contract between us - one each - for him to sign and an initial rough draft of the first two-thirds of the book because time was pressing for the intended Christmas market. Previous experience meant I had a reasonable idea as to what a book contract should include for the protection of all parties and I thought that the document was typical rather than controversial. But I would happily have discussed any potentially-contentious points with him in the hope that we could sort it all out amicably. I heard nothing, but I knew that Chris was due in hospital for a minor operation. I tried to contact him and leave messages, but there was no response. We missed the intended Christmas publication, so I wrote to Chris, but there was still no response. My view was that I did not want to waste months of work completely. The manuscript, including those chapters that I had sent to him, needed proper, incisive editing and it was probably far too long and rambling in places, but that could have been sorted out relatively quickly. But by 2002 I was unhappy that a deadline had been missed, Chris had not contacted me and the whole project seemed to be falling apart. Maybe I had upset him, but I still do not know why because he has telephoned me only once since and that was to ask for the return of some material that he had lent me to help with the manuscript. I duly posted the items to him.

I kept asking myself what had gone wrong. Was it the financial aspect? Was it a concern about part of the contract? Was it even because I had informed him out of courtesy that any profits that I made would have to be declared in tax returns because writing was my way of earning a living? Was it the way that the first two-thirds of the book had been written? I still do not know and I do not want to know, but I do know that the book eventually came out in whatever form in 2004, Steve McClaren chose to endorse it and I never received any recompense at all for my efforts. Neither have I ever bothered to read any of the book to find out if the first two-thirds were based in any way on what I had assembled. I am not sure how the final third - to use a football phrase - appeared although I was told that he had received some help from Mike Peterson, who has set himself up as a writer and historian on City matters in recent years. I had been suspicious about him when he criticised me about an error in one of my previous books, which would have been perfectly fair comment if he had not produced one which referred to City's benefactor as Harold Needham! A phrase about glass houses and stones springs to mind, but I am simply not interested in the whys and wherefores of the Chilton book any more. I had tried to remain loyal to the project: after all, I had a manuscript that I could easily have turned into an unauthorised biography for my own ends if I had so desired. I did think of taking legal action - not out of malice, but simply to protect my interests - but one way or another I just opted to move on and regret that it all ever had to happen in the way that it did.

It seemed that a lot had happened behind my back, but my fellow freelance journalist Mike Ackroyd kept me informed of developments during 2002. He told me that Chris had approached him about help with his life story and that there had been a meeting of possible interested parties at the Four-in-Hand in East Hull. I told Mike what had happened and, because he is a person of the highest moral character, he backed off. He said that he did not have the time to write it and I knew that he would be uncomfortable in taking up the cudgels after I - or anyone else for that matter - had already put a lot of time and effort into the project. Instead another local journalist Christine Jarvis, who was working for Mike's freelance agency at the time, was going to help out. Christine is also a keen City fan, but I pointed out to Mike that anyone helping with Chillo's project was obviously acting in direct opposition to my interests. Mike pointed out that it had been agreed that Christine would help out only in her spare time and not as someone employed by his agency, but he said that he would put her in the picture about my thoughts. Anyway they had never really made any progress with the idea and my respect for her remains intact. It was an unfortunate episode and I did at least have the compensation of knowing that some of Chillo's teammates felt that I might have been treated better about it.

But there was also an aspect of it all that gives an intriguing indication of the Waggy - Chillo double act that blossomed on the pitch for the Tigers. Outwardly they have always claimed to be the best of friends, but I believe that there has also been a strong rivalry between them. While we were discussing the book, Chillo was obssessed with the idea of Waggy doing a book about his life story before he did. I did not see any problem as long as the publication dates did not clash, but it was agreed that those of us who knew about Chillo's book plans should keep them to ourselves as much as possible. I stuck by the bargain and was happy enough because it is a way in which I often prefer to work. But there was a twist in the saga during 2002 when I was helping Waggy to organise a function for his 60th birthday. Waggy told me that he was doing a book about his life story and had heard that Chillo was doing one about his with me. I did not know how he had found out and replied that everything had been up in air for a while. He wished that Chillo had not tried to do the book behind his back because there would have been room for both life stories if he had been open with him about it. But he was going to carry on with his, which was perfectly reasonable. At the same time I wondered if Chris thought that I had spilled the beans to Waggy about his book. I have no idea who did, but I am certainly not guilty.

But if there is an implicit rivalry between the two, it was never noticeable on the pitch. They worked as a team, dovetailing immaculately and scoring and making goals for each other with great regularity. And while I may have been disappointed by Chillo's attitude about the book, I would never criticise him in any way as a player. He and Waggy formed a formidable partnership that provided me and many other fans with plenty of pleasure during a period of genuine optimism about City. And perhaps any thoughts of rivalry between Chris and Ken are never helped by those who always seem to have nothing better to do than indulge in polls as to City's greatest players. But it is not a question of who was the better player of the two: we should just be grateful that they both served the Tigers so well for so long. In the end they needed each other and the supply lines from their talented colleagues. John McSeveney reflected: "Cliff built the team round Chillo. He was unselfish and he was scoring goals on his own before Waggy came, but you always need different types of players in teams." And Len Sharpe added: "Waggy wouldn't have a shot for goal unless he felt he could score from where he was. He was also strong and hard to knock off the ball - just like Wayne Rooney. But we always had to look for Chris Chilton with the ball and he'd have played for England if he'd moved from Hull when he was 21. I remember when we beat Wrexham 4-2 and Chris got all four. We knew that Wrexham liked to play offside just inside their own half, so our sole object was to use the space behind them and Chris was the only one allowed to go for it because he had the pace."

Skipper Andy Davidson also referred to the team ethic that was important to the success of 1965-66: "Alan Jarvis and Chris Simpkin had terrific engines and towards the end of games they'd still be going along like express trains. Chris was a far better player than a lot of people gave him credit for being. They were both good tacklers and both of them could use the ball. Ray Henderson was the workhorse of the front-line and, when you add the rest of the forwards to the mix, they had to be the best side we had in my time." But no-one should underrate Andy's own contribution because he undoubtedly represented the heartbeat of the side. He played more League games than anybody else for City - 520 - a record which is likely to last a while longer because of their turnover of players in recent seasons. He is a character with a fund of fine stories, he is one of the most generous people I know and he is someone who should genuinely be described as having been Hull City through and through. And he still lives in East Yorkshire even though he was homesick when he first arrived in Hull from Scotland. He followed his brother Craig to City from the Lanarkshire mining village of Douglas Water, which had already produced their cousin James, who won eight Scotland caps as a centre-half while with Partick Thistle. Andy is also a relative of the legendary Bill Shankly: "He was the cousin of my father. We all grew up together and he made his name with a side called Glenbuck Cherrypickers. Eventually Bill was capped by Scotland, but he was never picked as often as he should have been."

The year of 1965 reached a fitting climax when City faced their closest rivals Millwall in the last two League games. The Tigers took over at the top when they won the Boxing Day bonanza at Boothferry Park 1-0 in front of what was then a record crowd for the non-regionalised Third Division of 40,231, but then they lost 3-0 at the Den the following evening. Another Scot, Tom Wilson, who played in 55 of the 59 games in which Millwall set an unbeaten home League record from August 1964 to January 1967, later joined City. But he recalled the Boxing Day clash from Millwall's perspective: "Chris Chilton crossed the ball from the right for the goal and Waggy and our defender John Gilchrist went up together for the ball. I think that John was trying to get the ball back to Alex Stepney, but it crept just inside the post." Tom was marking Waggy, who claimed it, but it was officially given to Gilchrist as an own goal. And he added: "Waggy always said that he didn't like me to mark him because I would hold off before tackling him. He preferred defenders to be tight on his back so that he could turn them. At the same time Waggy was a difficult player to mark because he always had something up his sleeve."

Tom remembered the impact of the big crowd as Millwall's party arrived: "We'd had a bad journey to Hull by train, but it was a tremendous sight when the bus taking us to the ground got near Boothferry Park. There were about 10 or 12 queues at the front of the ground, stretching right across the car-park. The fans were standing side by side laughing and joking and it was a big lift to us after our journey. The match itself was spoilt by the pitch because it was bone-hard. It was very grassy, but had a shiny look about it and, as the game wore on, it became more like a skating-rink. After the match the two teams travelled to London together for the return fixture. We both went by train from Hessle, but had to have police escorts to the station because of the size of the crowd." Millwall were eventually promoted, too, and Tom reflected: "I'd loved to have been at Millwall with City's forward-line because that would have made a team who would have taken some beating at any level at that time." The holiday promotion battles also meant a lot to Len Sharpe, who was recalled to City's side on the Boxing Day after an absence of almost four months, and he said: "It was a very important game and I was surprised to get called into the team, but it was lovely to run out and face such a big crowd. But it was hard because you had to adapt to the pace of the game. We travelled back with the Millwall team on the same train afterwards, but they brought in a fast lad called Barry Rowan and we lost 3-0."

The League success was backed up by an FA Cup run to the quarter-finals that gained momentum with the giantkilling of Southampton early in 1966. There was also a win over Fourth Division Southport, but the most epic ties were against two top-flight sides, Nottingham Forest in the fourth round and Chelsea in the sixth. The home tie against Forest proved what we had definitely started to believe on the terraces - that City could beat the best when the chance arose. And they were not at full strength because Mick Brown and Terry Heath were drafted into the line-up. Mick recalled: "I was told early in the week that I would be playing against Nottingham Forest, who had two useful wingers in Chris Crowe and Alan Hinton. Terry Heath also came in and scored the goals and yet we were both only regular reserve players. I played in a few games in place of Dennis Butler in the run-in for promotion and it was a good part of the season in which to play because we clinched promotion. It was when the pressure was on and I really enjoyed it." But Terry, previously a teammate of future City manager Colin Appleton at Leicester City, admitted: "I didn't think that I had a particularly good game. I scored the goals and that was it. I was the third-choice replacement for Chris Simpkin and all I did was to score the two goals. I appreciated every goal that I scored in my career, but at the same time I would always rather have a good game than score goals. And I can't remember much about the Forest game. For the first goal I got on to a backpass and the second was a shot from the edge of the box. I do remember that Ken Houghton moved into a more defensive role because of the last-minute change and that he had his best game of the season. But I was dropped the next week against QPR. That was the most disappointing part of it because it was a bitter pill at the end of it all. I knew it was going to be tough for me once Cliff Britton had spent £120,000 on Ken Wagstaff, Ken Houghton and Ian Butler. I was an inside-forward, but I was played out of position as a right-winger in the first team and in the end I probably enjoyed playing in the reserves more."

Ken Houghton was outstanding as he adjusted to a new role and then realised how demanding Cliff Britton was: "It was one of the easiest games in which I ever played. I played what was to become known as the sweeper's role and I was able to read the game. I was given plenty of room and I was allowed time to use the ball well. I wouldn't say that it was my best game for the club and I do get a bit annoyed at times when people come up to me and say that that's how they remember it. I had a lot of magic moments with City. I hardly made a mistake against Forest, but I always felt that I did well against First Division opposition. We did a great job tactically against Forest and that was because Cliff Britton's knowledge showed through. I admired Cliff so much as a manager, but I can remember that after that match he slated us and knocked me off my pedestal. I'd hit one bad pass during the game and Cliff brought me down to earth when we met to discuss it the following Tuesday because he kept harping on about it. I've never known such a perfectionist."

The ties with Chelsea were viewed as the pinnacle of City's season even though they drew the first and lost the other. It was the statement of intent that they were confident and capable of competing with the best in the land that spoke volumes for their adoring public. Chelsea's manager Tommy

Docherty said before the first tie: "Hull have not impressed me. I said before the draw was made that Hull would be the best one for us and I still think so. They are scoring plenty of goals, but they seem shaky in defence and I don't think they will live with us. They believe that defenders should defend and attackers attack: they seem old-fashioned in their team method." Docherty was being disrespectful to Cliff Britton, who had been his manager when he was at player at Preston. Britton replied quietly: "I don't think it is going to be such an easy match as Tommy thinks. We are going to Chelsea with a fair amount of hope of being in the hat on Monday." He was right because City earned a 2-2 draw at Stamford Bridge and Boothferry Park resounded to chants of "Big-mouth Docherty!" when Chelsea arrived to win the replay 3-1.

Ken Wagstaff scored twice late on at Chelsea after City had been 2-0 down and denied two penalties by referee Jack Taylor, who was to award one in the first minute of a World Cup final eight years later. Andy Davidson insisted: "I still think we should have won - and we would have if we'd got the breaks. We had two distinct penalties turned down and all these years later I still feel the same way. John Boyle handled on the line and Eddie McCreadie tapped Ken Wagstaff's legs and sent him flying. Cliff Britton was immaculate in everything he did and had worked everything out with a fine toothcomb. Everything went for them and against us, but we still had the pluck to fight back and get a draw. At the same time I don't think we should have been in that position. But we showed how good a side we were because we gave them a two-goal start - and neither of their goals was a good one. And the games have got to be highspots because Chelsea were one of the best sides in the country at the time." And City were reluctant to forgive Jack Taylor because Andy added: "He refereed us at Oxford soon after the first Chelsea game because he wasn't in charge of the replay and Ron Atkinson, who was their captain, couldn't understand why all the decisions seemed to go against them that day! But Taylor still insisted that they weren't penalties at Chelsea. We said to him: 'Didn't you watch the match on TV?' He tried to claim that it hadn't been on and we thought he was a bit shocked when we told him that we'd seen it on Anglia. On another occasion he was on tour with us when we played in Israel in a five-a-side tournament. He said to us: 'You don't like me' and I don't think that we denied it!"

There was an attendance of 45,328 for the replay at Boothferry Park on General Election Day in 1966, but City were left to concentrate on the League and savour a stunning long-range goal from Chris Simpkin, who said: "Everybody talks about my goal against Chelsea, but I can't remember anything about it. I'm told that I took the ball forward and scored from 30 yards. It was the funniest thing that the car-park was empty and the ground was full when Alan Jarvis and I got to that match. I always wanted to play for City and I was born 200 yards from Boothferry Park, but the two games against Chelsea are like a dream."

The statistics say it all about that wonderful season. A total of 525,440 fans - an average of 22,845 - watched City's home games in the Third Division. A total of 150,345 - averaging 37,586 - saw their four home FA Cup ties. And the heroes were entertained to a civic dinner by the Lord Mayor, Annie Major, at the Guildhall when she was presented with a basket of 69 amber roses by Harold Needler - representing their title-winning points total There was every sign that the success would continue in the early part of the following season when City briefly topped the Second Division table. There was belief around the club and among the fans, but injuries set in as 1966-67 unravelled and Cliff Britton turned to his youngsters in preference to going out and signing experienced players. Nowadays managers tend to waste money if they are given it to spend in vast amounts, but Britton was the opposite. He remained frugal - apart from the mid-season spell in 1964-65 when he signed Ken Wagstaff, Ian Butler and Ken Houghton in rapid succession. And it tallies with Alan Shaw's claim that he was always reluctant so spend money.

Andy Davidson suggested: "Cliff Britton had one weakness - he was too loyal. We lost 5-4 at

Ipswich when we looked as if it we'd carry on where we'd left off after promotion and do well in the Second Division. But Cliff brought in kids who had had no experience in the first team. He didn't seem to want to bring experienced players to the club and it was probably because he was too loyal to everyone - the first team, the reserves and the juniors." Alan Jarvis, who made his debut for Wales on the day of the Ipswich defeat, added: "That time was the most pleasant of them all for me in football. Hull City won the title and we had a hell of a run the season after, but then hard times set in. I always thought that Cliff Britton should have bought at least two new players when we won the Third Division. If I have a criticism of him, it was that he kept some people in the side when he really should have signed someone to go with the forward-line. I may not be quite at enthusiastic about him as some people such as Andy Davidson and Malcolm Lord, but he did a good job and I may never have got my chance without him. And he was a strong man - and all football clubs need one of them."

Any theories as to why City did not capitalise fully on Cliff Britton's era - as had also been the case after Raich Carter's success - might be confounded to a degree, though, because he had put a strong infrastructure in place. City's juniors had won the Northern Intermediate League in style in 1964-65, there were plenty of youngsters in the pipeline and it was probably only a matter of time and a question of balance.

Defenders Paddy Greenwood, Don Beardsley and Ray Pettit all became first-team regulars after starring in that successful junior side and forward Malcolm Lord went on to become 16th in the list of City's all-time League appearance holders on 298. He said: "I was most impressed with Cliff's thoroughness. He taught you the game, so you felt that you really were serving an apprenticeship. It was hard to get to know him well as a man, but he taught you a lot of discipline and gave you the best grounding possible in the game. He knew it so well and it was great to talk football with him in such depth. He also used to encourage skills such as passing and ball control. And the younger lads were always involved with the first team to give us an insight into what made good players. But we never used to train with them during Cup weeks. We were pushed out of the way so that everyone could concentrate on the first team for the cupties. And we were never allowed to mix with the senior players. During the week they used the home-team dressing-room and we were in the away-team room. We were not supposed to walk through the senior dressing-room and had to go out and down the back of the stand. If we did go into the senior dressing-room, we were usually asked: 'What reason do you have to be here?' At one point the club had 38 professionals and ran three teams, so it meant that five players didn't play if everybody was available. You could have two years as an apprentice and not play regularly for the club, so we spent our time wishing that we could move into the senior dressing-room because we then felt that we were near to making it as first-teamers."

Centre-half Geoff Barker added: "I joined the club just after they had signed Ken Wagstaff, Ken Houghton and Ian Butler when things were just starting to take off a bit. I left school and signed on the same day as Howard Baker for £4 a week. But I had a nine-shilling stamp to pay, so it ended up being £3 11s. We were all given jobs to do such as looking after the turnstiles or toilets, but I was given the bootroom. We had three teams and everyone had two pairs each - studs and rubbers. It was just before the introduction of substitutes, so every week I was in charge of 33 pairs of boots of two types, making a total of 132! Cliff Britton was the manager with Gus McLean and John Simpson helping him and then later on John McSeveney. Cliff was a disciplinarian and he would not let the ground staff go until he had been round to check that everything was spot on. Sometimes it would be quite late before he let you go home on Friday nights. Cliff was the main man and organised the training while Gus McLean and John Simpson looked after it for him. They were very much from the old school and every Wednesday they would have you doing so many laps of the track at Boothferry Park. Cliff was a perfectionist and they would also have you clipping balls into a circle in the gymnasium. It was just like learning any other trade. It was boring, but it stood you in good stead."

Full-back Roger de Vries later progressed through the system to become 12th in the club's all-time League appearances list on 318: "I first watched City as a fan when they had one season in the Second Division and brought in players such as Jackie Sewell, Roy Shiner and Ralph Gubbins. The player who really impressed me was Brian Bulless because he was so quick and such a natural runner. But then when the club built the gymnasium behind Boothferry Park in Cliff Britton's time, youngsters were allowed to go down to train in it on Tuesdays and Thursdays, so I wrote to the club to say that I was a keen footballer and a City fan. I then started training and that was when I first came across Gus McLean and John Simpson. And one night I was one of the lucky few who were held back afterwards and asked to sign schoolboy forms for the club. John McSeveney and Ray Henderson later took up the coaching, but my headteacher wanted me to stay on and go to college. I had no burning desire to be a teacher then and John told me that Cliff was going to ask me to sign part-time professional forms. He warned me: "Don't sign them! Become a full-time professional instead!" I took his advice and signed my first professional contract for £9 a week during the season and £10 a week during the summer! But there was a bonus for appearances so that in theory I had the chance to earn more for playing! I would go down to help to paint the ground with the apprentices and used to use the away-team dressing-room with them, but then I left players such as Howard Baker and Barry McCunnell behind when I turned professional at 18. I was then allowed to use the home-team dressing-room with the big names and personalities. I was never the most gregarious type, so I found it a bit daunting at first."

Some youngsters battled valiantly for first-team recognition and centre-forward David "Jack" Lill, from the East Riding seaside village of Aldbrough, had an incentive to emulate his hero Chris Chilton, who was from nearby Sproatley. But he recalled: "I was marked by Paul Madeley in my first game for the juniors against Leeds United and I think I got two kicks thoughout, but I look back on Hull City as my main club because of the way we were looked after. I was with some of the best players I've ever been with. Chris Chilton was my idol and I was a little bit in awe of him, but he looked after me very well. Cliff Britton was without doubt the most knowledgeable manager I've ever come across. He wrote me a super letter when I went to Rotherham United, wishing me all the best and saying that he was pleased I was doing well and had got my confidence back. I still have it. But maybe I was a better cricketer than footballer although the wicket at Aldbrough made me look even quicker than I was!" Lill, who later played for Cambridge United and King's Lynn, also ran the London Marathon, did some fell-running and had a spell as player-manager of Somersham Town when he played in the same team as his son Richard - just as he himself had been alongside his father Arthur for Aldbrough. And in December 1968 he also had the satisfaction of scoring for City in a 3-0 win at Huddersfield Town on a frozen pitch when Chillo grabbed the other two.

Things did not work out as well as might have been expected for some senior players either. City went out of the FA Cup 3-1 at Coventry in a second replay against Portsmouth in 1967 and Norman Corner played at centre-half in the first team for the first time in his first senior appearance for 2½ years: "My brother John lived 200 yards from the Highfield Road ground, so he came to the match and we had a good chat, but there was a bad report about me in one of the papers that blamed me for the defeat. The following day Cliff put it out that I was not to blame. I thought he was a gentleman and this proved it. He always had a few words with me, but I eventually left because sometimes I was playing well in the reserves and never seemed to get a bad review and yet I couldn't force my way into the first team regularly. I loved Hull, but I had the choice of going to Hartlepools United or Lincoln City and I decided that I didn't want to go back home to the North-East yet, so I chose Lincoln." Equally, half-back Tom Wilson joined the Tigers from Millwall in November 1967, but admitted: "I wasn't entirely happy with my form with City. They asked me to play a different type of game and maybe I didn't adapt to it as well as I'd hoped. At the same time the club should have reached the First Division then and I still wonder why it never materialised. It was a mystery to the players, but, although some people said that they never wanted to go up, that was certainly not the case."

Another disconcerting factor in the 1960s was the way in which the Boothferry Park boo boys often targeted certain players as the objects of their collective wrath. Malcolm Lord, Chris Simpkin and Les Collinson were among the victims, but they are all high up in City's all-time appearances lists with a combined total of 880 League games to their names. Malcolm recalled: "Les Collinson would say: 'As long as they're shouting at me, that's not so bad because it means that they're not shouting at one of the young players. The biggest thing for me was that people I rated as good managers kept picking me, so I tried to believe in myself and their judgment. The players and staff were also very good and encouraged me, but you don't play with the same confidence when people are criticising you. I thought that a lot of the criticism was unfair, but I'd seen how Chris Simpkin had beaten it and my attitude hardened. It was easier said than done, but it helped that other people appreciated what I was doing. Yet I couldn't understand it because City were my club and I wanted success as much as the fans. Maybe it was because I often wore the No. 7 shirt. John McSeveney, Terry Heath, Ray Henderson and Billy Wilkinson had suffered when they wore it during Cliff's time and it had happened before that. We would play with the right-winger withdrawn into deeper positions and the crowd probably wanted to see two wingers flying up the wings." Jack Lill added: "I had the best days of my football career with City and I just wish that they'd been a bit more successful for me, but I think that it was always difficult for the local guys. I remember watching a game with my pal Trevor Jackson and a fan nearby kept shouting: 'You're useless, Lill!' He didn't even realise that I was standing near him and that he was shouting at Mally Lord!"

There were also changes to City's backroom staff. Gus McLean fulfilled his wish to be a League manager when he joined Hartlepools United in 1967 as Brian Clough's successor. He then took backroom jobs at Rochdale and Southport and was working as a security officer for British Aerospace in Lancashire when he died at the age of 53 while on holiday in Guernsey. Ken Houghton said of him: "He was someone you automatically liked and helped me a great deal. He was a big, honest fellow and I had nothing but admiration for him." Gus also took Hull-born left-back John Simpson, who died at the age of 81 at Market Weighton in June 2000, with him to the Victoria Ground. He had been on City's books as an amateur before playing in the League with Huddersfield Town and York City and then returning to the Tigers as a physiotherapist and trainer. McLean's replacement was former Arsenal and Southampton player George Curtis, who had managed Brighton and Hove Albion and Stevenage Borough and coached England's youngsters and Sunderland. His motto was: "Players with character will do something for you out on the field when the chips are down." But it was not long before he left City to coach in America and it was clear that the momentum of 1966 was being lost for various reasons.

City were still capable of scoring goals regularly and yet they were still some way short of achieving their ultimate prize of the First Division. The attendances soon summed it all up. City had an average gate of 22,828 for promotion in 1965-66 and one of 24,275 for 1966-67, but they had the biggest drop in 1967-68 of 7,817. Harold Needler's generosity also seemed to be on the wane because money problems set in and in August 1968 manager Cliff Britton admitted: "The financial position is such that we would have to think about it if there were an offer for anyone on the staff." Oddly enough, Coventry City were linked with a move for Chris Chilton at the time. Equally oddly, Harold Needler's Repton-educated son Christopher, who was due to attend Trinity College, Cambridge, to study law and economics, joined the board at the age of 23, replacing George Rignall, who had died earlier in the year. Christopher had just qualified as an accountant...

The most significant change finally came in 1970 when Cliff Britton was made general manager and a new, young replacement was sought. The Needler choice as player-manager fell on Terry Neill, of Northern Ireland, Arsenal, PFA and TV's Quizball fame. He had worked as a schools' coach in North London, organised residential coaching courses for the Irish FA and coached Cambridge University for two years and said of Hull: "I knew that the time had come for me to have more of a say in my own destiny. I imagined a glorified fishing village, but then I drove through it. The sun was shining, the shopping centre looked good and there were wide roads and plenty of trees. It really set me burning when I came over the brow of a hill and saw the floodlights."

But Neill's blarney had an immediate effect and he said after a month in charge: "One of the reasons I accepted the job was because Cliff Britton was general manager. Not only will he take a load off me in the office, but he will be there to give advice. No matter how good your ideas are, you can lose out because of a lack of experience. I shall obviously be leaning on Cliff from time to time. After all, he has had a lifetime of experience in the game. I am still playing and I hope to be for a long time yet, but I have no illusions about the magnitude of the task. It won't be easy, but it never was and it never will be. I like it that way. But to look for difficulties is negative and I like to think of myself as a positive thinker. Football is full of heartaches. You have to accept the ups and downs, but, being Irish, I don't like to be down-hearted. The potential at Hull is so great - team-wise, facility-wise and attendance-wise. I know it sounds like a cliche, but I believe that they are equipped to be a First Division club. Public relations is a vital part of my job. I'm not interested in gimmicks, but I want a good relationship with local people as well as success on the field. Football is a branch of the entertainment industry and the people who watch us are part of the club. My aim is to entertain and that means playing attacking football."

But Terry Neill's arrival signalled a setback for Geoff Barker, who had just started to establish himself in his centre-half position. Geoff had been on holiday with Stuart "Pancho" Pearson and recalled the irony of it all: "During the summer we went camping to Torquay by car - just the two of us. We were lying on the beach sunbathing when we heard on the radio that Terry Neill had been appointed as City's new manager. Pancho turned to me said: 'That's you goosed!' I did play in one more first-team game at Cardiff the next season. Ian Butler wasn't well on the morning of the match, so I wore his No. 11 shirt. Terry Neill said that there was no point in changing all the numbers from the programme. We lost 5-1 and John Toshack got a hat-trick, but I scored with a header from a free-kick. It was on TV, but I've never seen it because we were still travelling back when it was on."

Neill's reign began with the Watney Cup - for the leading goalscorers in the four divisions not to have been promoted the previous season - and his first home game was a semi-final against a Manchester United side containing Bobby Charlton, Denis Law and George Best. The latest new dawn for City fans meant that it attracted a gate of 34,007 and I remember travelling to and from the tie on the old Humber ferry because I was working in Lincolnshire then. It ended with the Tigers losing after extra time and the first domestic penalty shoot-out and the final ferry's departure being held back for fans because of the late finish. Roger de Vries also made his home debut in the tie: "I don't have clear memories of it although I thought I had a good match and I remember that I came up against Willie Morgan a lot, but it was only later that I fully comprehended what a big match it was. It was quite incredible. You just had to go through the names on the teamsheets. Terry Neill looked at me at the end when it came to penalties and I said: 'I don't fancy it.' Ever since I've always wished that I'd taken one, but I probably needed a bit more confidence at the time."

All the same the fans' hopes had been rekindled. I recall watching the first away win in the League under Neill at Watford, hitch-hiking further south to reinvent myself as a hippy at the Isle of Wight music festival and then travelling straight up to Carlisle by train for the next fixture. But that was nothing out of the ordinary now that City had started to show their ambition again. They were soon among the pacesetters during the autumn and there was an odd sequel to a 1-0 win at Orient when Chris Chilton scored the winner. Orient's teenage centre-half Tommy Taylor expected a ticking-off for his error in the goal when he was called into manager Jimmy Bloomfield's office afterwards, but he found instead that he was moving to West Ham United in an £80,000 deal!

City's old flair was there and Neill said of Ian Butler: "He does so much with that left 'peg' of his that I'm thinking of buying him a glove for it at Christmas!" They were also mean at the back and conceded only one goal in one run of seven League games that brought six wins. And the character shone through on Boxing Day when City were trailing 4-1 at home to Sheffield Wednesday and hit back to draw 4-4. Malcolm Lord recalled: "Wednesday had three shots at goal and a penalty and found themselves 4-1 up, but then we scored three times in seven minutes near the end. The pity was that most of our fans had gone home by then!" The inspirational Chris Chilton added: "It was the first time that I ever lost my temper with my own players in the dressing-room afterwards because some of them had given up. I believe we might have won. About 10,000 fans had left, but they started to come back. Then the passing shoppers heard the excitement and came in. I always contended that there were more spectators at the end than the beginning."

In early 1971 another FA Cup run to the quarter-finals ensued and Terry Neill strengthened his squad by signing Bill Baxter from Ipswich Town and Ken Knighton from Blackburn Rovers. City fans, though, were used to anti-climax and the seeds were sown in a memorable, but frustrating week in early March when there were three games. The first game was an FA Cup sixth-round tie at home to Stoke City when the Tigers lost 3-2 after leading 2-0 and Ken Wagstaff recalled: "We thought we were on our way to the semi-finals of the FA Cup. There were more than 41,000 at Boothferry Park and they were going barmy as we led Stoke 2-0 just before halftime. They had Gordon Banks in goal and they were two of the sweetest moments in my life when I beat the great man in the first half. The first followed a cross from Chris Simpkin, Ian Butler headed it back and and I went to head it home. But I changed my mind, chested it down and fired past Banks and a couple of defenders. The second time Frankie Banks played the ball up to Chris Chilton, who passed to me. As I prepared to shoot, Banks dived to his right and I simply slotted the ball inside the near post. I had another chance just after my second goal, but hit the post and then a minute before the interval Terry Conroy pulled one back for Stoke. We still thought we were on our way, but John Ritchie equalised and then hit the winner. Even then we had not given up hope and Terry Neill sent in a header that Banks kept out with another of his world-class saves." As with so many of City's FA Cup highspots, though, it ended in a wrangle and Roger de Vries said: "It was controversial because they took a throw-in which should have been given to us. I gave the ball to them and they took a quick throw, which led to their third goal. I suppose I should have thrown the ball away and hoped that it landed in the third row of the stand. It was disappointing in the end and I suppose that it just goes to show that games change because of crucial moments."

Three days later City visited promotion rivals Sheffield United in what became known as the Battle of Bramall Lane. The Tigers, who gave debuts to Knighton and Baxter, won 2-1 with goals by Chris Simpkin and Ken Wagstaff in front of a 40,227 crowd in a game that threatened to boil over as referee Danny Lyden battled to keep it under control. Malcolm Lord recalled: "We did well to win because we came back from being a goal down. I can remember having a hand in one of our goals, but it was a rough game and in the first half the referee called the players together in the centre of the pitch to warn them. I could have imagined him sending everyone off!"

Barnsley-born Ken Knighton became an instant hero with the fans that night, though. His pedigree was interesting enough for a start. He had attended Mexborough Secondary Modern School, where he played in the same team as Ian Butler, he had gone to work down the pit at Denby Grange as a 15-year-old, he had toured New Zealand and the Far East with an FA XI managed by Jimmy Armfield during the summer of '69, he had joined Oldham Athletic when Ken Bates was their chairman, he had been a partner in a garage business in Preston and he cost City £60,000 from Blackburn. He said of the Battle of Bramall Lane: "I was a Sheffield Wednesday supporter as a schoolboy, so the Blades were the enemy when I played against them. But this was the first game I'd played in when the referee called the two teams together on the halfway line and told them to cool it! It was silly really, but it all started with Tony Currie going over the top of the ball to Roger de Vries. It was a disgraceful tackle and went unpunished. Tony Currie was an outstanding player, but you can't pull that kind of stroke. He should have been sent off, but I didn't think that the game was ever going to calm down after that because there was so much at stake. I was incensed and our coach John McSeveney said after that game that he would make sure that he was always in the same five-a-side team in training as I was! And the Sheffield United manager John Harris, who was never known to swear, used some foul language just before my name that night! Funnily enough, we then worked together at Sheffield Wednesday when I was appointed as their youth coach. I think he forgave me..."

Bill Baxter, who was a Scot who played for two English knights - Sir Alf Ramsey and Sir Bobby Robson - came from a school of hard knocks, too. He had helped Ipswich to the First Division title under Ramsey in 1962 and had fallen out with Robson when City signed him. Robson had once said of Baxter: "You couldn't find anyone who would be more distressed by defeat. Billy feels really sick about it and it is all tied up with his fighting ability and never-say-die attitude to every game. He's a very tough Scot and a really determined player." But future City coach Cyril Lea had to intervene in a dispute between them that led to Baxter's departure from Portman Road. Even so, he was keen to help City and said: "It's the type of game you play that counts and I'm not conscious of losing any speed. As a defender, I am always facing the play, so it is easier for me to read situations quickly. It's not that forwards lose their speed sooner - they need it more than we do."

I have spoken to City fans who genuinely felt that they saw the Promised Land of First Division football on the horizon after the Battle of Bramall Lane, but disappointment was round the corner again when City 1-0 at home to Oxford United four days after beating the Blades. The Tigers were going to finish fifth in the Second Division and Ken Knighton added: "There had been 40,000 at Sheffield and we thought we were on our way to promotion. It was a really crucial game for us and I thought we'd get promotion after winning it. But then came Oxford United, who had Ron Atkinson in their side. It was unbelievable because there were more than 25,000 at Boothferry Park for my home debut, but it was a dreadful game. I don't know why we lost, but quite often you get a special atmosphere when you're playing under lights in a midweek game and then you can't get going after it on a normal Saturday afternoon. What a great opportunity we had! I was with a great club with great supporters and I had a great time, but it all ended in abject disappointment. We had such a good team with Chris Chilton and Ken Wagstaff and they were high on my list to go up when I joined them. But then Chillo left us at the start of the next season and the team broke up. He and Waggy were two of the best players upfront together in any division at that time. Waggy was such a clinical finisher - in fact, it was too easy for him - and he was good enough to have played for England."

Harold Needler had said after Chilton's hat-trick against Sunderland in January 1971: "I'd want two George Bests and a cash adjustment before I'd even think of letting him go." He had a crowd of 28,350 for his testimonial game with Leeds United the following May, but then claimed that he had had too much of soccer and was in dispute about terms, so he missed the club's pre-season tour to Sweden. Ian Butler had also asked for a move because of the terms that he had been offered, but Chilton was fined two weeks' pay and banned for 14 days. Terry Neill said: "I have heard all kinds of rumours, but I do not know why he did not join us in Sweden until he comes and sees me. I want to be fair and hear the reason from him personally. We cannot allow one ripple to upset the whole boat. This job is not about one particular player, but about the whole club." But they cleared the air and Neill lifted the suspension. Chillo played in the opening two League games of 1971-72, but then joined Coventry for £92,000 in preference to Leicester City, Huddersfield Town and Chelsea. His explanation was: "I have been asked why I wanted to leave Hull, who are an ambitious club with good facilities and their eyes on the First Division. They kept telling me: 'If you want First Division football, why not come into it with us?' But they kept missing it and, because I was 28, I felt I had to make the break if I were to get into the First Division and make an impact."

It was the start of a period of general change and there was a new assistant manager - Tommy Docherty, whose arrival was not exactly a good public-relations exercise considering his outspoken comments about City when he had been in charge at Chelsea. It did not help when he soon claimed: "We are not going to miss Chris Chilton. We expect Stuart Pearson to be better." It probably did not help Pancho at the time although he was signed by Docherty after he had taken charge at Manchester United and went on to play for England! Another change involved John McSeveney, who was put in charge of youth development following Docherty's arrival, but then sacked a month later and replaced by Tommy Cavanagh, who took over as reserve trainer with Andy Davidson becoming youth coach. John said: "I'd helped to form the East Riding Coaches' Association and left the legacy of a youth policy that produced Stuart Pearson, Vince Grimes, John Hawley, Peter Daniel and Roy Greenwood among others. Pancho was a natural and John was a lovely, unassuming lad who came from Beverley on his bike to play. But I was ambitious and I was interviewed for the manager's job at Halifax Town. City gave me two weeks' notice because of it, but there was only one man who'd wanted me out." Ironically Ray Henderson took over at the Shay instead.

Neill took over as Northern Ireland's youngest-ever manager and Docherty was put in charge of Scotland on a two-match caretaker basis, leaving City to take over on a long-term basis in November 1971. The following month 50-year-old Wilf Dixon, who had coached Blackpool, West Bromwich Albion, Southend United and Aldershot, was appointed assistant manager with Tommy Cavanagh first-team coach, Andy Davidson reserve coach and Peter Sissons and Arthur Perry working with the juniors. More significantly, Cliff Britton had left and the players had presented him with an automatic teamaker.

It was hardly all quiet on the playing front, either. Ian Butler was unsettled, Ken Wagstaff verbally asked for a move, Chris Simpkin, who had attracted interest from Aston Villa, joined Blackpool for £30,000, Bill Baxter was loaned to Watford and John McSeveney, who had become Barnsley's manager, signed Paddy Greenwood. Jimmy McGill, a former Arsenal colleague of Neill, and John Kaye arrived and Ken Knighton was appointed skipper. On the pitch City lost to a Burnley side including Docherty's son Mick and at Queen's Park Rangers when Neill scored, was booked and was then sent off. City won three League games in a run of 21 to face relegation trouble, but they mounted a revival in the latter part of the season to finish 12th and won at Chillo's Coventry in the FA Cup for good measure. It was not what was expected, though, and it was the catalyst for regular mid-table finishes in the Second Division.

The fans had to be content with two Cup giantkillings. Ken Houghton scored the only goal of the FA Cup fourth-round tie in February 1973 when City beat West Ham at home and Roger de Vries scored the only goal of his career at Boothferry Park when Leicester were beaten 3-2 in a Football League Cup second-round replay in October 1973. He said: "I do still have a few jokes about it with friends because people always want to know whether it was a cross or a shot. The truth is that it was a bit of both! I lashed the ball goalwards so that anything might happen - and it did! But somebody - possibly Waggy - made a run across the face of the goalmouth to create a diversion, then I like to think that it left Peter Shilton in two minds and I beat him with tremendous velocity!"

But three more popular players - Ken Houghton, Ian Butler and Ken Knighton - moved on. And Ken Knighton summed up his departure to Sheffield Wednesday, the club he had supported as a youngster: "I do regret leaving when I did, but Terry Neill, the manager who signed me and then made me club captain, suddenly went the other way towards me. I don't know why, but there was a clash of personalities." And another highly-talented local product, Stuart Pearson, was sold to Manchester United in May 1974 although he said: "I owed a lot to my first manager, Cliff Britton. He was a strict disciplinarian and that probably stood me in good stead for the rest of my career. I enjoyed my times with some great players at City, especially Ken Wagstaff and Chris Chilton, but also with Ken Knighton, Ian McKechnie, Roy Greenwood, Geoff Barker and Mally Lord. I also learned a lot from manager Terry Neill, but it was such a shame that we couldn't make that final step into the top flight. We went very close in the early 1970s, but it was just not to be and they sold me to Manchester United. It was sad to leave City because they set me on the way to football success." City had signed Pancho, who scored four in a 5-1 home win over Portsmouth in October 1972, after his father Jim had told trainer John Simpson while he was painting the Boothferry Park stands: "I'll give you a gallon of paint if you give my son a trial." Pancho was sent along without the paint and the rest is history. In September 1974 Neill left to become Tottenham Hotspur's manager and City fans were left to wonder what all the fuss had been about. It was another example of history repeating itself as they felt let down yet again.

"Here's To You, Mr Robinson!"

Hull City were going nowhere when I first started watching them in the mid-1950s. The aura of the Raich Carter had worn off and they were in a state of suspended animation in the Third Division North. It should have come as no surprise then that they were going nowhere when I first started writing about them as a journalist in the mid-1970s. The aura of the Cliff Britton era had worn off and they were in a state of suspended animation in the Second Division. The only palpable difference, therefore, was that at least they were a division higher. The lack of a sense of direction was the same, though.

Chairman Harold Needler had just died and his son Christopher had been encouraged to replace him. Soon there were new directors, but the wave of enthusiam and purpose created by Harold's generosity 12 years earlier had long dissipated. I got to know the directors and they were basically decent people who were steady, but uninspiring in their outlook. The First Division was still a long way off because they lacked the panache and maybe even the latent ambition to take the club any further forward, but at least I could work with them comfortably. And it was a joy to work with the main backroom team of manager John "Yorky" Kaye, his assistant Andy Davidson, secretary Malcolm "Mac" Stone and physiotherapist Jeff Radcliffe. John would often not say a lot, but he was totally honest and hard-working and it was easy to have the utmost respect for him. He seemed to be more forthcoming person to person than on the telephone, but he was helpful and straight-talking. I was very lucky that he was the first manager with whom I had to deal on a day-to-day basis as a journalist. He deserved to do well and he deserved better backing to do well. He was bringing some youngsters through, but he was no long allowed to spend £40,000 regularly on players - as Cliff Britton had done 10 years earlier - and prices had, of course, gone up.

Dave "Sammy" Stewart, a mercurial Irish left-winger who had become the youngest League player in the club's history when he was given his debut as a 16-year-old by John, became a full international and had a spell with Chelsea, but probably should have done better on a long-term basis. But he soon underlined his potential when he formed an unlikely midfield partnership in an emergency with Ken Wagstaff, who was coming towards the end of his marvellous career, in a 2-0 home win over Sheffield United in the Football League Cup as they both played starring roles.

One of the other youngsters, defender Paul Haigh, who had been given his League debut a fortnight after Sammy just before his 17th birthday, said: "It was brilliant to get into the first team when I was so young because it was probably beyond my expectations at the time. I shall be eternally grateful to the two managers, Terry Neill and John Kaye. Terry Neill involved me in training with the first team and John Kaye gave me my big chance. There were other youngsters such as Dave Stewart and Dave Gibson whose potential they must also have seen, so they were exciting times. To say that I was nervous on my first-team debut is an understatement. It was against Sheffield Wednesday, who thought of themselves as one of the bigger teams in the Second Division at that time and I was playing against people I'd only just heard of about six months earlier. John Kaye gave me my first opportunity, but I don't think that he was ever quite given full rein at City to develop into a manager. He followed a big name in Terry Neill, but I don't think that he was given the chance to do things his way. But he was my type of person because he called a spade a spade and you knew where you stood with him. He came from the old school and gave the impression of being hewn out of granite!"

John had been able to spend a little more money initially when he signed Welsh international defender Dave Roberts and striker Alf Wood. But he had needed to be at his most persuasive to lure Roberts to Boothferry Park from Oxford United, whose management team were ex-Tigers Gerry Summers and Mick Brown. Dave explained: "If I'm being honest, it was a bit frustrating because there had been so much talk about big clubs such as Everton and Liverpool being interested in me and then I heard that I might get a £150,000 move to Norwich City, which I quite fancied because I knew a few of their players. Then all of a sudden Oxford told me: 'You've got to go and Hull City are the only club who've shown an interest in you.' It was completely out of the equation and came as quite a shock, but apparently they were one of the few clubs who could stump up some money to Oxford because they'd sold Stuart Pearson to Manchester United some months earlier and still had a bit in the bank. Oxford needed the money and Gerry Summers, who was a nice fellow, had problems because they'd got to the stage at which they'd had to pull the plug on all outgoing calls from the club and were taking only the incoming ones. I'd played against Hull when they were going for promotion and Oxford won 1-0 at Boothferry Park. Mick Brown told me that I'd be playing against two strikers who should be internationals. He meant Chillo and Waggy, of course, and he said that, if I did well against them, then that would be as good as it would get for me. In the end Hull kept banging balls up to them and I kept heading them out, but I remembered what crowds they were capable of getting. I'd just got married, I had 24 hours to think about the move and in the end I said: 'I'll go and give it a crack.' I'd just played for Oxford against Manchester United and my first game for Hull was against them. I won one and lost the other! But I wasn't dragged kicking and screaming to Hull and we met some nice people when we moved, so there were no regrets at all. I didn't know the manager John Kaye then, but I have so much admiration for him. He was such a man's man and a nice bloke."

But John then had to settle for snapping up players such as George Lyall, Jimmy McIntosh, Dave Sunley and the consistent Gordon Nisbet at bargain prices while convincing a still-expectant public that the club were progressing towards another tilt at promotion from the Second Division. Quite simply, he never stood a chance. There was a brief statement of intent when he signed Billy Bremner from Leeds United as the club pursued their well-worn policy of signing former international players towards the end of their careers. Billy's arrival came as something of a shock because a player of the similar pedigree, Alan Ball, had been his initial target. But the background to it all was slightly more sinister. One of the newer directors, Bob Chapman, who was outwardly a lovely, friendly man with a ready handshake, had developed a penchant for eyeing up transfer targets by looking through Rothman's Football Yearbook and working out their goals-per-games ratios as the benchmark in the search for established strikers. He would regularly quote these figures to me and it soon became clear that he was doing the same to the management team. It reached an unedifying low when John went to watch Ball play for Arsenal in a reserve game against Orient and a young teenage striker caught his eye instead. He was Frank Stapleton, he was untried and yet he was then available for a bargain £45,000. But he did not feature in the yearbook and he did not join the Tigers: he did have a highly-successful career at club and international level, though. Yorky eventually snapped up experienced strikers Alan Warboys and Bruce Bannister, who had been known as "Smash and Grab" when they had previously partnered each other, for smaller fees in his quest for progress.

John was expected to work miracles and made changes to his backroom staff, sacrificing likeable coach and former player Phil Holme and bringing the popular and highly-respected Ken Houghton back to the club to oversee youth development. Andy Davidson changed his role in order to step up the search for new players and another Leeds United hero Bobby Collins became first-team coach. But John was ritually sacked eight League games into the 1977-78 season after a 2-0 defeat at home to Mansfield Town even though City were just not far below halfway in the Second Division. He had slammed the telephone down after a heated exchange with a director on the morning of the match and Christopher Needler fired him a few minutes after it - before hastening away on holiday! A few of us stayed behind in the boardroom well into the evening to try to come to terms with what we thought was a disgusting move. Andy Davidson put it into another context: "The directors panicked when they sacked John Kaye and made a stupid decision. They'd been poking their noses in, but they would never have done that under Cliff Britton. When he was in charge, one of the directors, Stan Kershaw, came into the dressing-room after a game and told me: 'I'd pay Les Collinson your wages after the way you've just played.' I told him what I thought of him and Cliff fined me a week's wages for swearing at a director! He asked me: 'Do you think I'm deaf?' But he made sure that a director was never allowed in the dressing-room again to talk to his players."

Bobby Collins became caretaker manager, three days later City beat Tottenham Hotspur 2-0 at home and a lot of us met John Kaye socially at what was then the Crest Hotel at North Ferriby afterwards. I chatted to Alan Warboys, the scorer of City's two goals, but he was downbeat and merely mused as to how they had come a game too late to save Yorky's job. It was a good start for Bobby, though, and it soon became clear that he and his great friend Billy Bremner were on the shortlist to succeed John. Bobby was philosophical about his chances, while Billy sounded me out about everything on a coach trip south to an away game at Millwall and it was clear that he desperately wanted it. When Christopher Needler returned refreshed from his holiday, he apparently interviewed Bobby and Billy on the same Sunday afternoon at his home because Bobby later told me that he passed Billy going in the opposite direction on the A63 as they journeyed to and from their Leeds homes!

In the end Bobby was given the job. He told me that his approach had been low-key: he said that he had simply said that he was keen on it and would do his best. Billy, he understood, he had been more demanding and it had made Christopher wary. It was also clear that Bobby would have been prepared to be No. 2 to Billy, but that Billy would not have been prepared to be No. 2 to Bobby if a dream team involving them both had been feasible. Bobby understood Billy's disappointment, but he hoped that he would be content and backed off instead of continuing to treat him as just another player among his teammates. But Billy was unhappy and his friendship with Bobby had been compromised.

It may not have helped matters that I got on really well with Bobby, who would confide in me and tell me at great length about his plans during the coach trips to away games. The rapport had started early in the season after a 1-0 defeat at Southampton. We had scarcely reached the outskirts of the city when Bobby came to sit next to me. The players were playing cards and laughing and joking, while I was staring out of the window in pensive mood. Bobby said: "I'll talk to you because you look fed up. This lot are too happy too quickly after losing a football match. They should be thinking seriously about the game and working out what went wrong."

But Billy probably became a problem to Bobby, who, it became clear, hardly stood a chance once he had beaten him to the manager's post. Bobby toyed with the idea of promoting Ken Houghton to be his assistant, but plumped for Syd Owen, who had been part of ex-Tiger Don Revie's backroom team at Elland Road. Syd was a lovely man who was passionately steeped in his football. I remember an away trip to Cardiff when we were waiting in the hotel dining-room for our evening meals to arrive and Syd, who had a booming Birmingham accent, got on to the subject of tactics. He had arranged the condiments and cutlery into all kinds of systems to prove his points so that we had to retrieve them from all over the table before we could start to eat! I could not fault his enthusiasm and knowledge, but he was one of the old school and he was very serious and avuncular in his outlook. It meant that he was on a different wavelength from the players because of the generation gap and it was never going to work for him and Bobby. They lasted four months until Bob Chapman, who had taken over as chairman, sacked him.

Players rarely enjoy too many quick changes of management even if they feel that something is amiss because they are unhappy about having to prove themselves to different people over and over again. There is no sense of continuity and the Tigers were in free fall as Ken Houghton became the caretaker manager. A 2-1 defeat at Orient sent them down to the Third Division that they had left so gloriously in 1966 and I chatted to a disconsolate Roger de Vries as soon as I got on to the team coach. I thought that, as a local lad, he would be hurt by relegation more than most and he later explained: "It was a source of pride to me that I played nearly all my football in what was then the Second Division, so relegation meant a little extra to me and it was so sad for us to go down." Houghy was given the the manager's job on a long-term basis and another all-time City hero, Chris Chilton, joined the backroom staff as his youth coach soon after his return from South Africa. Houghy and Chillo piloted the juniors to the Northern Intermediate League title between them, so there was some hope lurking in the background.

Houghy signed Micky Horswill, John Farley and Keith Edwards and City finished eighth in their first season back in the Third Division. Keith, signed from Sheffield United for £60,000, scored 24 League goals and linked well with Bruce Bannister, but there were always comparisons between his workrate and his goalscoring. Quite simply, Keith was not the hardest worker outside the penalty box in those days, but he came alive and produced the goods inside it in situations that lesser players could never emulate. There were conflicting views in the City management because one argument was that Keith was doing his job exceptionally well and the other was that the all-round industry of the other 10 players had to be considered. Andy Davidson called him a predator and he was a deadly finisher who insisted that he did not mind missing chances, but he did mind missing the target. Keith once said: "I can recall just about all the goals from my career and my favourite at Boothferry Park was against Walsall when I ran nearly the full length of the pitch after picking the ball up from the edge of our penalty area - although I don't know what I was doing there in the first place!" It was a stunning solo effort in a 4-1 win and teammate Paul Haigh said: "Keith Edwards was the best goalscorer I played with or against in my era."

But Ken Houghton, Wilf McGuinness and Andy Davidson were sacked in December 1979 when they went on what turned out to be a run of 13 League games without a win. Chairman Bob Chapman and his personnel director Ian Blakey brought in a new regime on high wages for those days - Mike Smith as manager, Cyril Lea as his assistant and Bobby Brown as youth development officer. They all had Welsh connections and they struggled to turn things round despite bringing in a lot of new faces and getting rid of many of the old guard. Only a winner by Keith Edwards against Southend United in the penultimate game of the season - on the same day that Hull FC and Hull Kingston Rovers met at Wembley in the Rugby League Challenge Cup final - prevented the Tigers from tasting Fourth Division football for the first time.

Roger de Vries summed up the situation: "I enjoyed the early years more than the later ones because we'd got into the hiring and firing stages towards the end. But I've always regretted that I didn't play longer for the club. When Mike Smith came in at the start of January 1980, everybody was trying like hell, as is the case when there is a new manager. He told me: 'I like what I see and want to offer you a two-year contract.' I replied: 'That'll suit me fine.' But he said that there was a board meeting first and nothing came of it after that, so there was obviously somebody up there who didn't want me. All you want is the courtesy of a call and someone to explain the situation, but I was left-back, left midfield and left out!"

There was a triumphal aspect of the Southend game which I did not like. It came from relief, but City had not been successful: they had avoided failure and there was a subtle difference between the two. It did not solve the club's problems, either, because the 1980-81 season was even more disastrous. The Tigers won only one of their first 17 League games and it was soon obvious that there would be no escape this time. Fourth Division football was now becoming a harsh reality and the few, remaining fans had to brace themselves as their loyalty was tested to the hilt..

There were more controversial departures and the supporters were unhappy when the dependable Gordon Nisbet was sold to Plymouth Argyle. He recalled: "I didn't leave Hull City because I didn't like Hull City any more, but because it was beneficial for my career. The fans were always very appreciative and made it easier for me at Hull. I was sorry that I felt I had to go if any were disappointed that I left. I didn't want to leave the area because I'd made a lot of friends, but I didn't feel that I was wanted at City in the end. One reason for my transfer request was financial. I didn't want to be paid more than other players, but I felt that I should have been given as much as anyone else. I didn't feel that I was because players who had been inherited were rumoured to be getting less than those being brought into the club. The other reason why I asked for a move was to improve my game. I felt that my career had come to a bit of a stalemate. My biggest disappointment at Hull was John Kaye getting the sack because the club were in a good position in the Second Division when he left. Hull struggled to come to terms with things after John had left although I personally thought that Ken Houghton did a good job. It was a pity that he and John weren't given more financial support to have taken the club to a higher status."

Paul Haigh also left: "The catalyst for my departure was Mike Smith, who came in as manager with some grandiose ideas and started relying on some of his Welsh connections. I don't blame Mike Smith at all for coming to the club because that was the direction in which the board wanted things to move. But a lot of the younger players felt that we had reasonable potential and got fed up because we thought that we were putting in 100 per cent for about 30 per cent of the wages of some of those he'd brought in. I felt that it was time to move because the bridges had been burned. But money wasn't the reason why I went to Carlisle because in the end they offered me the same wages at Hull as I was going to get if I moved. But a lot of players such as John Hawley, Pete Daniel, Gordon Staniforth and Eddie Blackburn had gone and I thought that I was also among the young hopefuls who would never the chance to fulfil their potential because of circumstances. It seemed that a move was in my best interest and at least the transfer fee cleared one of the club's tax debts, but it was never in my remit to move on so early in my career."

The Tigers finished at the bottom of the Third Division and the following season it became clear that Chapman and Blakey, who had stepped down after relegation in 1980-81, overstepped the mark in financial terms. The management team were being well-paid, it seemed that most of their new signings were being well-paid in comparison with players who had already been at the club and the gates had dwindled when the gamble had not paid off. Something had to give - and it did towards the end of February 1982. Christopher Needler had realised too late what had been going on after resuming control as chairman and he tried to wrest back the initiative by placing the club into receivership. It baffled a lot of us because it was a practice that was common in business and rare in football at that time. Mike Smith and Cyril Lea were sacked, Chris Chilton and Bobby Brown were joint caretaker managers and the players feared for their futures. The club, it seemed, would not have one either unless someone came to the rescue.

Nearly three years earlier the perceptive and long-serving Malcolm Lord had played his last competitive game for the club. He knew that he had irked me a little when he went out of football and into business instead because it meant that someone who, in my view, had the qualities to be a top-class manager, coach or administrator had been lost to the game. He had been a member of the PFA's executive and had obtained the FA's full coaching badge, but he turned his back on football and his words of wisdom rang true: "I'd seen managers such as John Kaye and Ken Houghton get the sack as managers at Hull City and I thought that, if it could happen to blokes such as they were, then I wanted more security in my life. And I didn't want to put my future in the hands of people who knew less about football than I did."

I had not always seen eye to eye with Mike Smith, but he was intelligent enough to examine the significance of receivership and he made life difficult for Needler because none of us was entirely certain as to what his master plan for the club was - if indeed he had one. He certainly did know what he was doing, but he did not make it all that clear to all and sundry. He created doubts, especially in those of us who were not experts in business practice, and it was almost a case of: "Trust me, I'm a football club director!" I had just joined the Yorkshire Post - on a free transfer, I think - but Mike once even left me a message at their company sports ground, where I was playing in an in-house football match, as we tried to discover the full implications of receivership. He also invited me round to his house in Hessle to discuss everything as we tried to put pieces in the jigsaw. And amid all the uncertainty the players pulled together in their hour of need and Les "Tucker" Mutrie set a club record by scoring in nine successive League games. The Tigers finished eighth in their first season in the Fourth Division

Equally, I was not enamoured with the way in which the Chapman - Blakey partnership had brought the club to their knees. But Ian Blakey was extremely helpful to me as 1981-82 limped to its finish with everything in limbo. He tipped me off about a consortium who were interested in taking over the club and arranged for their members to be available on the car-park at Boothferry Park for a photo-call so that I could have the story first. The group included prominent businessmen such as Ian Glenton and Paul Dixon, but they could make no headway with Adrian Rapazzini, the receiver, and the whole scenario ended hilariously when assistant secretary Paul King politely asked us all to get off the club's land! Not long afterwards Ian Blakey gave me another tip-off when I met him by accident in Hull's Waterfront Nightclub, where I had gone on with some of the players on the Friday night after the final game of the season at Halifax. This time he told me that Scarborough entertainments entrepreneur Don Robinson had emerged as the favourite party to take City out of receivership. The Yorkshire Post did not normally indulge in gossip, but I persuaded them to let me write a speculative story. It was immediately played down elsewhere, but it was true.

In July 1972 City had drawn 2-2 in a pre-season friendly at Scarborough, whose director Don Robinson had needed four stitches in a hand wound after trying to break up some fighting on the terraces. If that were an indication that you did not mess about with him, then a look at his background underlined the point. Born at Green Hammerton, near York, he had followed in the footsteps of his father Joe by playing rugby league. He had had a short spell with Hull Kingston Rovers, but he had also been a boxer and a wrestler. Colin Appleton, whom Don immediately installed as the Tigers' new manager, had known him since their schooldays together in Scarborough and said: "I think that I first got to know him as a result of inter-school boxing matches. I don't think I ever fought him, but he'd have probably knocked me out if he did because he was very strong!"

In addition, Don, who had started in business by putting trampolines on Scarborough's beach, had wrestled as the mysterious, masked "Dr. Death." In January 1974, in fact, he suffered his first defeat in England when he was disqualified in a bout at Hull's Madeley Street baths against Rikki Starr, an American known as the "ballet-dancing wrestler." Dr. Death concentrated on hanging on to the nerve points round Starr's neck and received a warning in the second round when he refused to break from the hold. In the third round Dr. Death left Starr, who had taken the lead with a body press, in a daze after scraping his elbow bandage across his eyes. Dr. Death took advantage to equalise with a body press, but he was given a second warning and pelted with orange peel by the crowd! An angry Starr was given a warning for punching in the fifth round, but then Dr. Death again used his bandage across his eyes and was promptly disqualified. Dr. Death ran straight to the dressing-rooms amid cries from the crowd that he should be unmasked in defeat, but the promoter George de Relwyskow insisted that it was not in his contract that it should happen. Life at Boothferry Park would never be the same again...

Life was also enjoyable again after receivership and Garreth Roberts said: "Don was the best chairman I worked under. He was great for the club at the time because he was just who was needed. I thought he was brilliant - a top man. Some of his quotes about City being the first side to play on the moon were just plain daft and you wouldn't say that kind of thing nowadays. It was dead easy for people to take the mickey out of us after that, but it was Don's way of letting them know what a good team we were. He used to take us abroad for trips and up to Scarborough for a few days to keep us all together and he'd get us involved in all kinds of stunts. I can remember when he got me to feed some dolphins on one occasion. He told muggins to stand there with a fish in my teeth and this dolphin with its mouth wide open suddenly jumped up and took it!"

Popular goalkeeper Tony Norman added: "When you're in the bottom division and the receiver is called in, you can't get much lower. In fact, it was rock-bottom. It was just like falling to the bottom of the well and then slowly clambering up again. It was gradual, but at least it proved that there was bit of bounce left in the club. I didn't know many chairmen at that stage, but Don Robinson brought in his own ideas. And in those days there was still room for a bit of romance in some departments of football, whereas it is just an out-and-out business today. Don had his own style, but he was an entrepreneur and a businessman who did things his own way and still gave the club a lift. His ways were fairly successful, he was approachable and at least he was in the right place then. And if we were beaten, then he'd feel it just as much as the players and the supporters. On other occasions he might come into the players' lounge, put £20 behind the bar to buy the lads a drink and it was appreciated. He wasn't scared of going to the players and putting on a show. And at the end of nearly every season he would take us away on a tour. In fact, one November he just walked in after a game and said that in a couple of weeks or so we'd be going away to play a few games because we had a spare weekend. Then he explained that we were going to Bermuda for 10 days and leaving the Christmas shopping behind!"

To their credit Mike Smith and Cyril Lea, whom I still see regularly at games and respect immensely, left behind some useful players to form the basis of a squad to turn City's fortunes round. Colin Appleton had the experience and knowledge to do it. He had played for Scarborough in the Midland League as a 15-year-old and then managed them to FA Trophy glory at Wembley in partnership with Don in the 1970s. In-between he had made his name as a wing-half with Leicester City after their former player Reg Halton had recommended him to them when they had been at Scarborough together. Also at Scarborough at that time was jockey's son Terry Dyson, a winger who was spotted by Tottenham Hotspur while on Army service in London. He and Colin joined their clubs in 1954 and seven years later opposed each other in the FA Cup final. Colin, who had also played for Charlton Athletic, often seemed to talk in riddles, but then you would realise that it was all based on deep-rooted common-sense and that he had opened your eyes to another footballing gem. Colin is a thoroughly decent man and football conversations with him are worth treasuring.

On his arrival at Boothferry Park Colin unearthed a gem when he signed Billy Askew on a free transfer from Middlesbrough, he brought back the redoubtable Peter Skipper, whom Mike Smith had regretted releasing more than than any other player, with some financial aid from supporters and brought youngsters such as Garreth Roberts, Brian Marwood, Steve McClaren and Bobby McNeil to the fore to blend with the experienced players. A lot of players simply improved and matured under Colin's stewardship and the Tigers were promoted in 1982-83. Garreth said of Colin: "He would organise a whole series of meetings and sometimes you'd wonder what points he was trying to make, but then about two days later you'd realise what he'd meant. He was a very deep thinker on the game and the answer was always there if you listened to everything he said. In 1982-83 we kept virtually the same side for most of the season and it was Colin's way of getting us all together. We went up with a 0-0 draw at Chester in a game which wasn't a classic, but there were plenty of highlights such as a 7-0 home win over Stockport County when I scored and Andy Flounders got a hat-trick. The way we were playing at the time typified the togetherness and camaraderie between all the lads." And Tony Norman added: "Colin Appleton had his own eccentricities, but he did the job his way and he was similar to Don Robinson in that respect. But he made sure that he got the respect of the players and, even though he was never your best mate, he would still look after you. And, above all, he wanted to win things."

Garreth Roberts, Brian Marwood and Steve McClaren all had to show resilience to make the grade in League football. Garreth overcame his lack of height by sheer determination to become a "pocket battleship" of a player, Brian at one time looked as if he might not be strong enough to utilise his pace and skill to the full and Steve's slight build might initially have held him back. In fact, City paid for Steve to go on a regular diet of steaks so that he was less lightweight and Andy Davidson tells a story that he would come round his house to be fed on them - on condition that he stayed away from his daughters! Brian had been a central midfield player, a right-winger and then a versatile marksman who finished as the leading goalscorer in 1982-83 with 19 goals. His teammate Dennis Booth helped his development to such an extent that Brian gave him his England shirt after he had made a brief appearance as a substitute against Saudi Arabia in 1989. Brian has stayed in sport to work for the PFA and Nike as well as being a TV summariser, but he might also have been management material. Steve McClaren went down that road instead, but he seems to have changed a lot while working towards his accession to the England job because his sense of humour and personality have never come truly to the fore during interviews. He seems to be more serious nowadays, but then his jobs in management have hardly been light-hearted ones. Equally, he is very busy, but a local non-League club twice asked me if there were a possibility that Middlesbrough might send some kind of team to them for pre-season friendlies. On the first occasion I wrote to him and on the second occasion he told me to write to him, but I never had the courtesy of a reply one way or another to either letter.

All clubs have had skilful players who have irritatingly wasted their talents, but then there are others who give everything to maximise their chances. Peter Skipper and Billy Whitehurst came into the latter category to the extent that they arrived from the relatively-obscure reaches of non-League football, but worked hard at their games to adjust to life in the League. They got better and better and proved what can be achieved with desire and determination. They were tough and resilient and gave the side plenty of backbone. Pete formed an effective centre-back pairing with Dale Roberts and Billy, who showed that he had a big heart to match his frame when I was going through my divorce and he was living in the next village to me, worked well upfront with Les Mutrie. Garreth Roberts said of them: "Les was a prolific goalscorer who who did very well for us during the first season that we went up. He was great to play with because he was so good at bringing other players into the game. You always picked Billy first even when you were choosing sides in training. It never entered your head to do otherwise because he was so wide and tall and strong. It was the same in matches - we were always grateful that he was on our side rather than against us."

Andy Flounders, who became City's youngest first-teamer when he made his debut as a 16-year-old in October 1980, also began to chip in with goals regularly. He said: "It was a bit daunting at first under Mike Smith and Cyril Lea. There were some players such as Micky Horswill I'd seen on TV when I was young. But I had an enjoyable debut and then in my fourth game we played Charlton Athletic, whose side included Paul Walsh, who went on to play for England, in midfield. My first goal was a great feeling. I think that Brian Marwood played the ball in and I just got there before a defender to score. I played a bit more after the club had gone into receivership, but the following season I got my first senior hat-trick. We beat Stockport County 7-0 at home and we scored most of the goals early, so the game petered out in the second half. But I think Brian Marwood again made the goal for my hat-trick, which was a header from a few yards out. One of my relatives got the ball! I always felt that, being a local lad, I had to go out and try that bit harder because the club always seemed to go out and buy another forward if the team were firing blanks or not playing well. If you look at my record at Hull, I never seemed to start the season in the side and I ended up waiting to get my place. And in those days a team had only one substitute, so you didn't always get a chance. I was a midfield player as a schoolboy, so I don't know what turned me into a goalscorer, but it was a kind of progression. They moved me forward and you get used to situations. You've been in there before in the penalty box and after a time it all comes from memory so that you just sniff the goals out."

Colin Appleton was apparently given a pay rise for promotion - of £10 a week! But the Tigers were back - to quote the title of a song that they released at the time - and they were on a roll. They were undefeated in their opening 11 League games of 1983-84 and a second successive promotion began to look a possibility, but there was an inconsistent spell from Easter onwards and it all came down to the final game of the season at Burnley to try to pip Sheffield United. In those days the last round of fixtures in a division did not take place simultaneously, so City knew what they had to do - win by three goals. They won 2-0, so that they missed out on promotion by a goal or a point depending on how you wanted to analyse it. Brian Marwood scored both goals, but City would have gone up if he had not missed a penalty at home to promotion rivals Oxford United at the end of February. That was one example of how close it had been. Brian, who then left to join Sheffield Wednesday, reflected: "That night at Burnley will stand out in my mind for the rest of my life. You could not have stage-managed a better situation. There was a tremendous following from Hull, some fans from Sheffield United and a little bit of needle from when the match had been postponed. It was an ideal situation for a cliffhanger. We scored in the first half and then hit the post and missed a couple of good chances. But we kept battling away and scored a second. Strangely enough we didn't play very well after that and the last 15 minutes were total anti-climax. At the end I remember crying on the pitch, as did some of the other lads. Emotionally it had taken everything out of me."

Skipper Garreth Roberts added: "This was probably the most emotional game I ever played in. The build-up to it was intense because the situation gripped the whole city. The support we had at the game was unbelievable and to say that we were disappointed by the outcome was the biggest under-statement imaginable. Brian Marwood gave us a good start with a goal from the edge of the box and after 21 minutes he and Steve McClaren began a move on the right. The ball came across and I struck what I thought was a certain goal, but a wandering Vince Overson knocked it over the bar with a flailing knee. That just about summed up our luck. Brian scored another great goal after halftime and there were still 25 minutes left, so we still had a chance, but it just wasn't to be. The feeling in the dressing-room after the match was awful. Everyone was so quiet and hardly anyone spoke for a long time. Some players just wandered off to find their own little space, collect their thoughts and try to put it all into perspective. It was so hard to believe that we'd lost our promotion chance by one goal after 46 games."

The drama was not over, though. Colin Appleton resigned immediately after the game to take over as Swansea City's manager and Brian Marwood said: "I remember thinking afterwards that the whole thing was strange. We were so numb and down after the match and everybody was upset when they heard about Colin. Everybody just went quiet although a few of the lads then tried to talk him out of it. Unfortunately Colin never got the recognition he deserved. It looked bad that night - almost as if he were leaving a sinking ship - but he was a man of high principles." Garreth Roberts added: "About 15 minutes after the game another bombshell hit us when Colin Appleton said he was resigning. He said he had had enough and I think he would have resigned in any case - even if we'd gone up - for whatever reasons. There were repeated attempts by players to make him change his mind, but he was adamant about his decision. I think he was a big loss to the club because he had done such a good job in two seasons." Tony Norman reflected: "That's just football. You are just starting to think about how you've just missed out on promotion and you've just lost the manager, so it was a case of: 'Hello, what's round the corner again?'"

The manner of Colin's departure annoyed Don Robinson, but a lot has been exaggerated about their working relationship. In fact, Colin once told me that Don had even let him borrow his car to go for job interviews when they had been at Scarborough together so that he could maximise the situation because it would be good publicity for the club! And Colin said recently: "I've heard that he talks about me round Scarborough as if I were a god!"

It seems that Colin had also sown the seeds in Don's mind for Brian "Nobby" Horton to be his successor as City's player-manager because he had wanted to bring him to the club as a player. Brian was a midfield general, a leader and a winner. He was driven and demanding as a manager and always expected high standards. Apart from guiding the Tigers to promotion in his first season in charge, he built an infrastructure at Boothferry Park by nurturing a youth policy that had had to be put on the back burner because of financial constraints and he showed acute business acumen in the transfer market. He constantly picked up players for City at bargain prices and there are those who think that he did exceptionally well to get £150,000 for Macclesfield Town from them for Jon Parkin earlier this year! Nobby soon gained the respect of everyone who got to know him at Boothferry Park and it is just odd that his promotion with City in his first season as a manager remains the only one on his curriculum vitae. But the fact that he has still been in regular employment in the managerial rat race since is a testimony to his expertise. I know of some managers who have had a lazy approach towards talent-spotting, but Brian is an honest, hard-working individual who has always remained willing to scour the country in the quest to find players.

Tony Norman said: "Brian Horton was completely different from Colin Appleton and he was fairly young because he was a player-manager at the start. But he'd been there and done it as a player, so he had a bit of pedigree and you couldn't help but respect the fellow. He demanded effort, he'd built a solid foundation and we'd got something out of it simply because of his pure intensity." Garreth Roberts added: "We first met Brian when he came out to Florida, where we'd gone at the end of the season. He took us for training and it was a great way for him to to get to know the lads because we needed picking up after just missing out on promotion. Brian basically took up the slack and I think he knew we were still a good-enough team to do well. He made a few changes here and there, but he made sure that we went out on to the park feeling that nobody could beat us, especially at home. Everybody was working for each other and I think that Brian may compare that team favourably with any he's managed since. From a personal point of view it helped that he was also a midfield player and he never surrendered to anyone - even in training sessions, which got a bit lively and tasty at times!"

In 1984-85 Nobby took City on a 13-match unbeaten run and then a sequence of 15 games comprising 12 wins and only one defeat that culminated in promotion to the Second Division. It was clinched with a 1-0 win at Walsall and Pete Skipper said of his winner that day: "I'll never forget that goal. It came from a free-kick by Billy Askew on the edge of the penalty area and I headed it into the corner of the net, not giving their goalkeeper Ron Green a chance because he seemed to dive in instalments. It was an important goal because it came in a first half in which we were not playing well at all. In fact, we were getting a battering. It was a strange game because we didn't know that we had been promoted until well after we had left the field because there were other results to come in. I have nothing but respect for what Brian Horton did."

Garreth Roberts added: "There is no better feeling than clinching promotion at the end of the season, but this particular occasion was especially rewarding. It meant a lot because this win finally took us back into the Second Division only a year after we had missed out by just one goal in unfortunate circumstances. All the players and staff had shown a lot of character to bounce back immediately and do the job properly after such a big disappointment at the end of the previous season. It would have been a lot easier to have struggled in the middle of the table after the dramatic finish a year earlier, but the fact that we carried on and made sure the next season was very important and made up for the previous disappointment. Pete Skipper scored the all-important winner with a header from a corner, but it was also a great result because Walsall had been on the fringe of the promotion race themselves for most of the season. We could have had a far easier game in which we had to try to clinch promotion, but the fact that everyone worked hard to achieve victory made it all the more worthwhile. The second half was a continuous battle for us, but we were thoroughly competent and I shall always remember the celebrations on the pitch after we'd won. I think it was about half-an-hour before we finally went back into the dressing-room, but the champagne still flowed a lot longer than that."

Brian Horton had completed the transformation that Colin Appleton had started under Don Robinson, whose drive and personality had spread confidence and publicity that had never been the case before. Brian maintained the momentum when City finished sixth in their first season back in the Second Division in 1985-86, but Don was torn between his desire to take the club even further and still ensure that he balanced the books so that there would be no repeat of the financial chaos that had brought receivership. Garreth Roberts said: "We had a great team between 1982 and 1987 and, although we had a strong backbone, it needed an extra push then and we might have gone even further." In the early part of 1988 City went 13 League games with a win and Brian Horton was sacked immediately after the last of them - a 4-1 home defeat against Swindon Town. It it ironic that Brian had thrown in some of the promising youngsters in what had by then become a fairly-meaningless, end-of-season game for City and that the original fixture had been postponed. If it had been played on the scheduled date of January 23 instead of April 12, might things have turned out very differently? A deputation of Tony Norman, Peter Skipper and Garreth Roberts tried to persuade Don to change his mind and he was reported to have had second thoughts, but the decision stuck. Tony recalled: "In the end I think Brian just got frustrated. But we got into a bit of a rut and started losing. Confidence drops and, instead of going into a game thinking: 'We can win this,' you say to yourself: 'I hope I don't do anything wrong today.'"

Dennis Booth and Tom Wilson became joint caretaker managers and it looked as if they were going to take over on a long-term basis when Don allowed them to sign defender Steve Terry in the early part of the summer. Boothy was optimistic about his chances, but he was told that it was not to be as he returned from spending a weekend with his close friend Brian Marwood. Former Scotland international Eddie Gray was Don Robinson's choice as manager to succeed Brian Horton. We had something in common - the same birthday although Eddie is a year older than I am. Boothy nobly put his disappointment behind him, but it still hurt him after he had seemingly been so close to getting the job. It was, though, a season of utter enjoyment for me as a journalist. Eddie was decency personified. He set high moral standards, but he always relished bits of banter. He had been brought up in football with a strong set of characters at Leeds United and his honesty and general good humour belied a steely desire for success. He may have been misunderstood because he was not outwardly demonstrative, but there was no doubt that he cared. The repartee between us always took one geographical slant. He used to delight in trying to claim that Hull City were based in Humberside rather than Yorkshire because he knew it annoyed me. I responded by claiming that his beloved home-city club, Glasgow Celtic, played at Parkhead when he always insisted that their home ground was Celtic Park!

Defender Wayne Jacobs, one of Brian Horton's last signings, also sensed the excellent atmosphere during Eddie Gray's managerial reign because he said: "I enjoyed my time at Hull because on the playing front it was where I made my breakthrough as a first-team regular and plied my trade even though I'd had a few chances with Sheffield Wednesday. Eddie Gray was particularly good for me because he was a players' manager. If your form was fluctuating, he would always stick by you and that meant a lot. But the people of Hull received me well and I made some good friends, such as Neil

Buckley and his family and Ken and Ivy Norrie when I was in digs with them. I shall also remember the warmth of the people for the welcome that they gave me. We had a good team with players such as Billy Askew and Garreth Roberts, it was where I first made my name as a footballer and I enjoyed things on and off the park."

It was typical of the good atmosphere at Boothferry Park that season. And early in 1989 things were beginning to take off after Eddie had changed things round a bit, making a brave decision to sell the popular Tony Norman to Sunderland. Tony said: "I wasn't surprised because I knew that something was going on and everything had changed. Brian Horton would call me in and say they'd had a bid for me from such-and-such a club and that they'd been told that I wasn't for sale. And at least it was honest of him to put me in the picture. But Eddie Gray had told me that I could go if the club ever received the right kind of offer for me. What stunned me was how quickly it could happen when a bid did come in for me." Eddie was unhappy with my coverage of Tony's transfer in exchange for Iain Hesford and Billy Whitehurst. But Eddie simply made his point and there was never any semblance of a rift. I suspected that Don Robinson had been behind the comments because he was worried as to how the fans would react to Normo's departure because he was so popular. I think that it was also the reasoning behind Don's extreme attempts to maximise the anticipated popularity of Big Billy's homecoming.

Keith Edwards, brought back to City from Aberdeen by Brian Horton shortly before his sacking, scored even more regularly at the start of 1989 and Billy Whitehurst also made an impact. Keith had once thrown his shirt at Mike Smith in disgust when he had been substituted during his first spell at Boothferry Park, but there was no such reaction when Eddie did it. He seemed to respect him and Eddie once said: "I always made a point of explaining to Keith why I'd done it." Whitehurst and Edwards were on target in the FA Cup fourth round when City won 2-1 at Bradford City, who sacked their backroom team of future City managers Terry Dolan and Stan Ternent after the tie. They were also on the mark in the first half of the fifth round when there were a little more than 20,000 in Boothferry Park for the visit of Liverpool, who eventually won 3-2. Wayne Jacobs recalled: "It was a great time to face them and it was brilliant to be 2-1 up at halftime. I always tried to be positive and my thought at halftime was for us to keep going and just see where we ended up, but John Aldridge scored twice early in the second half and we lost 3-2."

I think that the exertions of the FA Cup tie with Liverpool and its accompanying build-up had left a lot of people mentally drained. City were never in danger of relegation, but they slipped down the table and all the impetus had gone. It should not have happened, but sometimes it does. The Tigers lost six League games in a row after the Liverpool defeat, beat Plymouth Argyle comfortably on Easter Saturday and then failed to win any of their remaining 11 matches. Eddie again tried to change things round by selling Andy Saville and bringing in Ian McParland and Peter Swan for a club record £200,000 and taking Malcolm Murray, who eventually moved on a long-term basis, and Duggie Bell on loan, but it was to no avail as far as results were concerned. I sensed in my private conversations with Don that he was thinking of changing the managerial team after just one season and urged him not to do anything in haste. City were essentially a happy club despite the poor run of results and Eddie and Boothy were getting to know how best to work with each other. I had spoken to both of them and Boothy was particularly receptive. He had felt an obligation to live in Eddie's shadow to a degree because of his respect for his achievements in the game, but a few things needed tightening up. I remember sitting in Boothy's house, he took everything in and said: "I've got to be go back to being the old Dennis Booth." I had reasoned, too, that I thought that in some ways he and Brian Horton had been similar - not just as midfield players, but also in their approach to management. But I thought that Eddie and Booth offered a better blend. Boothy promised to take my thoughts on board for what they were worth and realised that I was just trying to be constructive.

But it was all too late because it would now take a lot to deter Don from making changes. The crunch came with the East Riding Senior Cup final, which was not City's most important game of the season. I recall going out on to the pitch with Eddie while the two teams were warming up and mentioning my fears that Don was about to take drastic action even though I had tried to defuse the situation. Eddie shrugged and was typically phlegmatic. But City lost the final to Bridlington Town, managed by Colin Appleton. Former City junior Gary Brattan, who married singer David Whitfield's daughter Mandy, scored the only goal of the game and I heard later that Don had remarked about Colin being a master tactician. It was all too ominous. Eddie had said that he would catch up with me at the supporters' Player of the Year function at the 147 Club in Hull the following Friday night, but he was not there. He was so unlike him to fail to turn up because he took such responsibilities seriously, so I feared the worst. The following day I was due to go to Grimsby to cover some athletics, but I thought that I would check everything out first, so I telephoned Eddie at home and he confirmed that he had been sacked the previous afternoon. I then telephoned Boothy at home and the same had happened to him. I then telephoned Don and eventually he admitted everything somewhat reluctantly. He indicated that Eddie's successor would be appointed immediately and Colin's name came to the fore.

I decided to call in on Billy Whitehurst on my way to the athletics. He was sitting in front of his television with "teletext" fixed on the news of Eddie's sacking. He had an air of disbelief about it all and said that he had heard that Colin Appleton was about to return as manager. He indicated that he would ask for a transfer. I saw groundsman John Cooper and his family at the athletics. Again there was disbelief that Eddie had been sacked. Eddie had the respect of nearly everyone at the club, but Don had made up his mind and two days later he confirmed that Colin would return. I went down to Boothferry Park and Don insisted that I interviewed Big Billy about Colin's return. Billy had had a lot of time for Eddie and had mixed feelings about it. He said that he would do some kind of interview, but I said that I would not put him in an untenable position. It did not go down well with Don and I soon found myself almost ostracised. I was not allowed to travel on the team coach and it seemed that Colin had been instructed to help me as little as possible. It was awkward because Colin and I had always got on well, but I was stuck in the middle and he was stuck in the middle. We soldiered on, but it was a difficult situation that was aggravated by the poor start to Colin's second spell in charge. I think that some of the senior players were not behind him and he hardly stood a chance.

Don was determined to convince evrybody that he had made the right decision to bring Colin back. There was even a staged photograph of him doing some renovations around the club. Colin, in fact, had once gone into partnership with his former Leicester City teammate Ken Mellor when they opened a hardware and do-it-yourself shop because both were joiners before going into full-time football and could tackle any kind of carpentry. Colin once told me that he had never heard of the adage that people should be wary of going back into a job for a second spell. But it did not work out for him this time and the story of his two spells in charge intriguingly remains in an alcove off the living-room in his house. It is where he keeps all his records and memorabilia and it includes a big, black file about his times at Boothferry Park.

It was the Tigers' worst start to a season and they could not win to save their lives. Confidence ebbed away and it was summed up by a draw at Portsmouth in the fourth game when poor defensive work yielded an equaliser in a 2-2 draw. If City had held on for victory, then the tide might have turned and things might have been very different. It is often amazing how football fortune can be changed drastically by small, seemingly-isolated incidents. Colin had brought in only one major signing - midfield player Steve Doyle, who had been a City target for John Kaye when he was a youngster at Preston North End, from Sunderland - and he had let Tom Wilson go. His idea was to bring back Chris Chilton as his assistant. I spoke at length with Chillo at a social function at the

National public-house in Hull and he was certainly keen if the price were right. But everything reached a head before Colin could put his plan into practice. The turning-point was the 14th League game of the season - a 2-0 home defeat by Brighton and Hove Albion. City had still to win in the League and Don Robinson called me into the inner sanctum of the boardroom a few minutes after the game to announce his resignation as chairman. The two of us were left together and Don was in conciliatory mood. He was subdued by his own standards, he accepted that we had not been on the same wavelength at times in recent months and he was apologetic. Even though we had not been on the best of terms compared with our previous working relationship, I was disappointed to see him step down. He had achieved a lot for the club, some of his long-term ambitions had not received the backing that he had expected and maybe he had finally run of ideas. He had always had plenty of them - maybe some were a touch outrageous as he marketed the club to the hilt - and maybe he was concerned about his own popularity with the fans.

There was hardly ever a dull moment when Robbo was around and he had resurrected the club after the dark days of receivership. He would be a hard act to follow because of his vibrant personality. He may have got some decisions wrong, particularly towards the end of his reign, but the pluses far outweighed the minuses. After informing me of his decision to step down as chairman, he told me that Richard Chetham was to succeed him. Chetham had married into the Needler family and Don's theory was that he might have something to prove to them. Don reasoned that Richard's motivation for turning round the club's fortunes and trying to lead them into the top flight was to achieve something that Harold Needler had failed to do. It was sound enough thinking, but Don was a special chairman and few people could emulate him. But it dawned on me that maybe he thought that the decision to bring back Colin had backfired and he did not want to sack him, especially because he had appointed him only a few months earlier. Anyway Chetham did the job straightaway and reinstated Tom Wilson as the caretaker manager. Colin's second spell in charge had not generated a League win, but he was unlucky. Sadly the second spell had seemed to depreciate the success of the first in the public gaze. He was a first-class manager, a perceptive thinker on the game and a top human being who did not deserve to be in the least bit derided.

The favourite to take over from Colin was initially Ian Porterfield, but Chetham's choice of long-term replacement was Stan Ternent, a highly-respected coach who had had one brief spell as a manager at Blackpool. As a player, he had been involved in the incident that virtually ended Phil Holme's career when City won 1-0 at Carlisle in April 1973. I liked Stan a lot, but he could have varying moods. Even Tom Wilson, who became his assistant, later admitted it. Sometimes I did not know which way to take him because he could be terse one day and talkative the next. But I still felt that I could work with him even though he once refused to speak to me on a Sunday because he said that it was his day off! His coaching sessions were excellent whenever I popped along to see them and he transformed a side who had not won any of their opening 16 League games. He made a lot of signings and insisted that three of them - Malcolm Shotton, Gwyn Thomas and Dave Bamber - were there as the experienced heads to try to stave off relegation as the going remained tough. Stan contended that they had served their main purpose for the club if they helped them to stay up and anything further from them was a bonus. Other signings, such as the talented Leigh Palin, arrived with more of an eye to the future. City were 24th when Stan took over, but he had done the job supremely well because they were 14th by the end of the season.

Stan brought in a host of new players during the summer of 1990, but some of his signings misfired as City struggled again. They scored goals, but they conceded plenty, too, and in January 1991 he was sacked, wreaking revenge on Chetham in his book "Stan the Man" when he described him as "a bouffanted relic from Brideshead Revisited." He also referred pointedly to "unfulfilled promises" about money. Much later Danny Fullbrook wrote in tbe Hull Daily Mail: "Stan Ternent left the Tigers in all sorts of trouble after using the club's limited cheque-book recklessly. And City were all but doomed to relegation when Terry Dolan arrived from Rochdale." I beg to differ. It is true that some of Stan's signings did not work out, but had Danny ever discussed the circumstances with him? I did - long after he had left. One simple fact should always be remembered - Stan did not spend a penny without Chetham's sanction and he kept a diary of it all for good measure. Dolan was also left with almost half a season to turn the tide. City were leaking goals by the bucketful when Stan was sacked, but they were far from doomed. Significantly, I have spoken to players from 1990-91 and the general consensus of opinion is that, even though things were far from ideal, City would not have been relegated if Stan had stayed in charge. But it was time for change yet again and I duly turned up at a junior game at Saltend one Saturday morning to inform everyone that I had heard that Terry Dolan was to be the new manager with Jeff Lee as his assistant. Dolan, in fact, cost City £40,000 from Rochdale because of Chetham's means of making an approach to bring him to the club. And he transformed a side who scored and conceded plenty of goals into one who hardly scored or conceded any goals - and the result was relegation. He was the fifth longest-serving manager in the Football League when he left in 1997 and, more significantly, things were going to go from bad to worse for City - and also for me...

I had a sixth sense about the letter with a Tiger crest on the envelope that dropped through my letter-box in July 1995. It came from Hull City's chairman Martin Fish and read: "Dear David, I have felt for some time that you have not reported and portrayed the club's image in the Press to very good effect. As you know, you are given hospitality and free access to the Press-box at Boothferry Park and yet there is no real reciprocation to give the club a good Press. I doubt whether I shall be able to alter in any way the way you report the club's affairs and obviously you are entitled to your views in this regard. Equally so, however, the club are not prepared to offer the facilities previously given to you and have the right to invite or refuse access to the Press-box to anyone they wish. Accordingly, I wish to inform you that there will be no Press pass available to you for the forthcoming season and, while you may be disappointed about this, I trust you will understand my reasons for implementing it."

The letter was dated July 17, it was oddly signed "Yours sincerely," it raised certain fundamental points about the freedom of speech and it certainly came as no surprise to me. Quite simply it was the culmination of an underlying battle as the 1990s wore on and there was a major slump in the Tigers' fortunes. I knew that I had been on a collision course even though I was not really much of a threat to them because my work was relatively limited. But, as a freelance, I was an easy target. There would probably have been more of an uproar if the club had banned someone from, say, the Hull Daily Mail or BBC Radio Humberside. The club needed their goodwill on a daily basis, but I was self-employed and only on the fringe of everything, so they could easily make an example of me, maybe even as a deterrent to others. People repeatedly asked me what I had written that was so horrific that it brought a ban, but I have always believed that it was nothing drastic or specific at all. My view is that the club had embarked on a propaganda exercise and my "crime" was that I would not go along with it. I believed that it was not so much what I wrote, but more a case of what I exemplified - a rebel who would not play the game that the club wanted me to play.

The circumstances were dictated by City's inability to get out of the lowest tier of League football or convince the fans that solid progress was being made. The goalscoring duo of Andy Payton and Peter Swan had gone, while the club cashed in on players such as Leigh Jenkinson and fell out with others such as Russ Wilcox, who is one of the nicest, most decent guys in the game. They deserved credit for plucking goalkeeper Alan Fettis out of obscurity and turning him into a Northern Ireland international, but the conveyor-belt of young players coming through the system seemed to be grinding to a halt. Above all, there were few highlights or heroes. Linton Brown produced one bright moment in October 1994 with a quickfire hat-trick in a 7-1 home win over Crewe Alexandra and then there was Dean Windass.

Both Linton and Deano had played for Northwood, the Hull Sunday League team I had helped the highly-respected Peter Whinham to run. John Spinks and I took Dean to Northwood after he had been released by City as an 18-year-old and then spent a few days in France with Montpellier. I told Peter: "He will do things on the ball that will have you purring and wondering why he is not playing League football. Then there will be other days when he will probably be a liability and drive you mad." As it is, Dean became the only Northwood player to score an own goal with an overhead kick! Ex-Tiger Geoff Barker was North Ferriby United's manager and playing occasionally for Northwood, so he took Dean to Church Road when he was unbelievably playing in Bridlington Town's second team at times. Another ex-Tiger, Peter Daniel, continued the good work when he succeeded Geoff at North Ferriby and Peter Whinham decided to offer Dean a trial at Sunderland, for whom he was chief scout. The Tigers then stepped in. I believe that Brian Horton had been right to release Dean at 18 because his attitude was not always the best and City had a buoyant youth policy that was producing a steady stream of players. But, to be fair to Deano, he grabbed his second chance with both hands and deserves praise for having done so. He owes a lot to the two Peters and Geoff and he has worked hard on his fitness to stay in the game even if there are still the occasional extreme moments of behaviour that might be typical of someone who was born on April 1!

Dean turned his adversity to advantage when so many young footballers seem to believe that the game owes them a living when they fail to make the grade and he said: "My ability was never in question: it was just my size. I was a bit of a late developer and City let me go. At that time Brian Horton didn't think I was strong enough. I can remember the meeting with him when he said: 'Sorry. We're not giving you a contract, but we do think you've got the ability.' He said I was too small, had to grow and mature and that I would prove him wrong. You think your chance has gone, but I was working on a building site and I used to come home and go on a run every night to build myself up. Brian Horton did me a big favour. It made me realise that you can achieve what you want if you put your mind to it."

But there were plenty of dark clouds without silver linings at Boothferry Park in the early 1990s and it was unfair to gloss over things because, as a reporter, you are supposed to be objective. You may want to put the club in a good light whenever possible, but you still reserve the right to be critical if you feel that something radical is wrong. Fish's phrase about "not portraying the club's image to good effect" was risible. It was never my job. If I had been employed by the club as some kind of public-relations officer, then I deserved to be taken to task if the board felt that I had been in any way too critical or negative. But I was independent. I had the right to express my views as I saw fit and then take the consequences. As a sacked manager once said: "I stood up - and was counted!"

It was not the first time in City's history that they had fallen out with the Press. When chairman Alwyn Smith, vice-chairman Ken Wilson and secretary John Haller resigned in February 1913, for example, it was stressed that their decisions had nothing to do with "the dispute with the local Press and the Grimsby Town incident." Then there were some notorious incidents in the mid-1950s when the relationship between the club and the Press often seemed to take centre stage at the annual shareholders' meetings. In 1955 a shareholder accused club president Kenneth Percival of making "childish statements about the Press being to blame for the club's position." He replied: "I want to make it perfectly clear that I did not aspire to journalism, but at the same time no remarks of the Hull Daily Mail or anyone else will prevent me from saying what I think is right if I have the courage of my convictions that Hull City are getting a raw deal." The following year Percival blamed the Press for City's poor attendances and the Hull Daily Mail responded in a lengthy editorial: "He knows well enough that honest newspaper criticism keeps no-one away from football matches. If the customers stay away, it is simply and solely because they are not satisfied with the fare offered to them. As for our 'disgusting reports' of Hull City matches, Mr. Percival should see some of the letters we receive every other day from disgruntled supporters, who hold that, far from being harshly critical, the Hull Daily Mail are far too lenient and restrained in their criticisms. We shall make Mr. Percival a fair offer. He can try his own hand at the reporting job and turn in a match report and critique to the Hull Daily Mail. The model of perfection which would no doubt result might then be taken as a permanent pattern for the future."

It was all good, knockabout stuff - and there was more of it in 1958. A shareholder said at the annual meeting: "One of the things we most deplored was not losing matches, but the feud between the management and the Press. This mean, pettifogging war against the Press is not the way." Manager Bob Brocklebank replied: "There is an amicable understanding between the Hull Daily Mail and the football club now. We did not stop Three Crowns from reporting. It was only for the last three away matches that we withdrew the option of travelling with us." Pressed for the reason for the ban,

Brocklebank claimed: "It was done at the express wish of the players." It is not an ideal world and both Brian Taylor, my predecessor at the Hull Daily Mail, and I had our occasional skirmishes with the club, but they were always trivial tiffs that were solved quickly because you always felt that you were still dealing with honourable people. More recently, there have also been disagreements between City's chairman Adam Pearson and the Hull Daily Mail, too, and it is always a pity that it ever comes to talk of bans. But even though I would never condone everything about the way in which the media behave, I would always defend their right to freedom of speech.

In 1995 I soon sensed that there was no way of reaching a reasonable compromise, so naturally I decided to let as many people as possible know of my ban and it included doing an interview with Jeremy Butler for the Hull Daily Mail, which duly appeared on July 28. I was quoted as saying: "I knew what the letter would say when it dropped on my mat and I saw the club crest, so it wasn't much of a surprise. I don't want to get embroiled in a battle, but something that infringes a journalist's freedom of speech has to be fought. I would imagine that any journalist worth his salt would stand his corner on this one. The only allegation thrown up against me is that I've not written enough good things about the club, but that is not my job. My job is to be as fair and objective as possible in anything I write about Hull City." Fish replied: "We have the right to choose whom we want to allow in the ground. I am not against criticism, but there have been a number of things he has written during the last few years which have caused me, the management and players some upset. The main problem is the continual criticism no matter how well the team are playing. We've never had a favourable report. We must get away from the image of the 1960s. I respect that it was a successful period, but it doesn't make it easy for the present-day players and management to work with it being continually thrown at them. Let's think positively and go forward with the on-going success and not live in the past."

I was described in the article as being as "disappointed," which was probably the understatement of the year. And I believe that Fish had libelled me by stating: "We've never had a favourable report." I made some cursory inquiries as to the possibility of suing him about the remark because I have kept numerous clippings of my relevant articles during the 1990s and to me they show that his statement was untrue. It is true that I had little, if any respect for the regime, but I can honestly say that I did my utmost to try to be as fair to them as possible. What upset Fish and Dolan, I believe, was simply that they realised that in no circumstances would I slavishly toe their party line. I felt that the comment also cast a slur on my journalistic character and was told that I probably had a good case, but it would turn everything into a more drawn-out process, so I did not go down that avenue even though I was sorely attempted. Anyway libel cases tend to be preserve of the rich and famous rather than the ordinary man in - or out of - the Press-box!

But any sympathy for Fish's regime evaporated and I became determined to make life as awkward as possible for them. I was never going to overturn the decision because matters had gone far beyond compromise by then, but I was not going to go away quietly. The decision had certainly not hurt me in the least - apart from making a slight dent in my wallet - and I was mightily relieved that everything was out in the open. I was going to remain a thorn in their sides, it was time for fun and games and my attitude was that, if Fish and Dolan thought that I had already been unreasonable, then they would quickly find out just how bloody-minded and troublesome I could be once I forsook any semblance of objectivity. I had seen many managers, coaches and players come and go, so I was always confident of being a survivor and outlasting Fish and Dolan in City circles. It might take time and at that stage I was unsure as to what plans of actions to pursue, but I was determined that I would win the war even though they probably thought that they had won the initial battle.

I was not going to let up and there had been already been notable support from other quarters. Alan Plater, who is best-known as one of the country's leading playwrights, a devoted City fan and a wonderful person, had written to Fish on August 5: "I was stunned to read the news of your banning from Boothferry Park of my friend - and Hull City's friend - David Bond. There are two things involved here - one a matter of principle and one strictly personal. The matter of principle is simple enough. You are apparently saying: 'We want only journalists in the Press-box who will write good copy about the club.' Whichever way you add it up, it is a ham-fisted attempt at news management or, to use the nasty word, censorship. It's the same game played by our major political parties and many other institutions and it always gives off a bad stench. We are both in the entertainment business. A critic on a national broadsheet newspaper recently suggested that I should have my fingers broken. I won't be sending him a Christmas card, but at the same time it wouldn't occur to me to suggest that he should be banned from watching and reviewing my work. The personal angle is that David has been a passionate supporter of the club all his adult life, both publicly and privately. He has worked tirelessly for the Ex-Tigers' Association, most recently helping to organise a wonderful tribute to the great Andy Davidson, which I was privileged to attend. Living in London, I see the Tigers less often than I would wish although I have timed family visits to coincide with home matches and have had many a good adventure following them - from the 5-4 triumph at Orient to the 7-1 annihilation by West Ham United, plus many a battling 0-0 draw. But you'll have to manage without me as well - home or away - as long as David is banned. This probably doesn't matter a damn in the great scheme of things, but is an honest reaction to a dismal situation."

The ban, in fact, was the culmination of four years' pressure from Fish and Dolan, but I had refused to be intimidated. Twice I had been verbally threatened with a ban - near the end of 1991 by Fish because he objected to the publication of something that I had accurately reported and in early 1992 by Fish and Dolan because of remarks that they had heard that I had made in the Press-box regarding the state of the club. The first instance concerned a throwaway line in a national newspaper about City's finances. Fish claimed that its publication had had an adverse effect on the club's status, but at no point did he question its accuracy. He could hardly do so anyway because my reliable source was...Don Robinson! He was understandably concerned about the club's apparent deterioration and the public surely had a right to know anyway. It was ironic, though, that a journalist should be in trouble for being accurate: usually the inaccuracies cause the problems. The second incident was trivial, true and amounted to typical Press-box tittle-tattle, but it served to show how much the regime seemed to be worried by me.

Then about three weeks before the start of 1992-93 I had made my usual written application for a Press pass for the season. I heard nothing until the opening day of the season when I received a letter from secretary Tom Wilson, saying that spaces in the Press-box were at a premium and that I would have to apply for individual passes on a match-by-match basis in writing or by fax. Curiously, no other regular member of the Press corps at Boothferry Park seemed to receive the same kind of letter or had any trouble getting a pass for the season as usual. In fact, one non-journalist was allocated a Press pass for the season! At a later date Tom admitted that Fish had wanted to ban me then and he had warned him against it. The theme continued two seasons later when I was told that there would be no parking space for me at Boothferry Park: again other members of the Press were still allowed on to the car-park at the ground. I have always suspected that the regime believed that I would tamely give in and go along with what they wanted because I had been a City fan and then close to the club in my journalistic capacity.

I eventually reflected that the ban might be interpreted as the first tribute to my journalistic integrity that I had ever had! But on a practical basis it was annoying. I had operated as a freelance at Boothferry Park since 1990, so the ban quite simply cost me money. No access to the Press-box meant no work at City and that, in turn, meant that I was forced to pass it on to a fellow freelance and forfeit the accompanying earnings. Staff journalists or broadcasters suffer inconvenience if they are banned and nothing more: they do not have their earning power eroded. I never felt remotely sorry for myself: if anything there was a sense of relief that everything was finally out in the open after the minor irritations of the pressures that had previously been put on me. Quite simply, though, I had feared the worst because I was not the only victim of the regime. Former players Tom Wilson and Malcolm Shotton had joined the backroom staff, but they were unceremoniously ousted and I could also cite the treatment meted out to two popular players.

Garreth Roberts is second in the club's all-time League appearances list on 461 - a run that ended in December 1990 - and he recalled: "I knew my knee was bad because I'd been injured in a game at Charlton. But nearly two months later Terry Dolan became manager and he let me go even though he hadn't seen me play. I think that it was all to do with finance. They they asked me on the Friday if I wanted to coach the youth team, but then they changed their minds on the Monday. I felt very disappointed because I felt that I had a lot to offer on the coaching side." Wayne Jacobs had suffered a serious knee injury in a home game against Stoke City in January 1992 and then had his contract cancelled the following December. He recalled: "The club had an office in a house next to the ground and they called me in to tell me that they couldn't afford to keep me so they were letting me go. I was still injured, so I wasn't able to find another club, which made it worse. I walked into the ground and went round the pitch with tears rolling down my face. It was really, really disappointing. What then humbled me was that the other players said that they would pay my wages between them so that I could stay, which was phenomenal. The club wouldn't change their decision, but I shall always be grateful to that group of players for what they tried to do for me."

I did, though, feel a deep sense of injustice about the ban. If, as a journalist, I lost work because I was incompetent or unreliable, then it was entirely my fault. If I were legitimately sacked or replaced because of an editorial decision, it was merely a harsh fact of life. But to lose earnings because of an external force who really should have no jurisdiction over them was a bitter pill to swallow. There was also the little matter of the principle of freedom of speech in a so-called democratic society. The fans had a right to know all shades of opinion and then reach their own conclusions as to what they should believe. The fact that some fans - including some I had known for a long time - blindly believed the club's powerbrokers was disappointing. Surely, I told myself, they could read between the lines because the ban was a deprivation of freedom. I had to battle on, but I knew that it would not be easy.

Legally, there was little that I could do. As with individual homeowners, for example, a football club have the right to decide whom they do or do not wish to allow on to their premises. I merely mused that I was being treated in the same way as a common-or-garden football hooligan - except that my offensive weapons were my notebook and pen! There was a hint that I might be the victim of some form of restraint of trade, but all in all the legal processes seemed to offer little cause for optimism. I was barred only from the Press facilities: I was not actually banned from the ground. I could have paid to go in, but why on earth should I? I firmly believed that I had done nothing wrong, I had been doing my job as honestly and as objectively as possible and I had fallen foul of people who thought otherwise: it was as simple as that. And if I had paid to go in, I could still not gain access to managers and players for interviews and quotes that were an integral part of the demands of the work. Besides, I was not going to pay to go into the ground on principle because it meant swelling the coffers of a regime whose methods I deplored and whose football was not, in my opinion, worth the money to watch in the first place! If I had still been a Tigers fan, then I think I would have just about have given up and either taken up flower-arranging or joined the local aquarists' society instead!

I briefly toyed with the ludicrous notion of turning up on the terraces wearing an Elvis Presley mask that I had then! It seemed to be a light-hearted way of drawing attention to a serious situation because

I was convinced that the best way to fight the ban was by publicising my plight. But there were, as far as I knew, few precedents to guide me. The risk of upsetting a club goes with a football writer's territory. Day-to-day relationships between journalists and managers or directors often teeter on the brink, but tiffs had tended to be temporary because of the need for everyone to work together somehow on a long-term basis. In 20 years' reporting I had could vaguely recall being told of two other instances of bans although there may have been more. Such disputes had essentially been transient, but clubs were now beginning to expect reporters to be their unpaid public-relations agents and not much more. But I soon found about other spots of bother during the course of my ban. There had also been trouble at Derby County, Brighton and Hove Albion and Birmingham City and everything seemed to assume a new level at Plymouth Argyle in September 1997 when their chairman Dan McCauley banned the local Press, who promptly hired a crane to overlook Home Park so that they could still cover a match!

Oddly enough, I soon found out that some local sports journalists seemed to be almost willing to become little more than fawning mouth-pieces for City. Maybe they had seen what had happened to me and opted to take the easy way out in case the same thing happened to them, but I can never respect that attitude if it existed. But the times had changed because I believe that, when I started out in sports journalism in the mid-1970s, everyone in the fraternity would have rallied round, put communal pressure on the club and everything would have been sorted relatively quickly as if it had all been a storm in the proverbial teacup.

But only minimal backing seemed to come from own folk - my fellow journalists - although the highly-respected Mike Ackroyd, a fellow freelance who is from the old school of journalism, repeatedly helped me. Mike might have been banned himself, so I shall always be grateful for his stance because he was willing to put his head above the parapet when so many others seemed to lack the inclination to do so. I had told Mike that I thought that City would finally ban me, but he had insisted that it would never happen. I was almost triumphant in telling him that it had finally happened and that I had been right all along! Anyway Mike helped to publicise my plight while many other journalists seemed to forget one simple aspect of it all - my cause was their cause - and arranged to publicise my problem in the trade Press, notably the UK Press Gazette. I was also grateful to Roy Woodcock, the editor of the Advertiser series of free papers for which I assembled the sports coverage in those days, because he vigorously remonstrated with Fish in an exchange of correspondence and a subsequent article. Amy Lawrence, David Ginola's biographer, mentioned my situation in an article about the club in the national football magazine 4-4-2 and, as the autumn rolled on, the Sunday Times exposed the increasing number of disputes between clubs and the media and the writer Simon Reeve later sent me a letter of support, ending it "Yours in solidarity..."

Another long-standing friend and colleague Peter Moore, again an old-school journalist of high standards, also gave me splendid support. We had worked together at the Hull Daily Mail when he was the chief sub-editor and then the deputy editor, but by this time he had become the editor of the Grimsby Evening Telegraph. When Peter heard about my plight, he offered his unequivocal support by contacting Lancaster Gate, then still the headquarters of the FA, about it. On October 4 he wrote to the FA's chief executive Graham Kelly: "As the editor of a regional evening newspaper, the Grimsby Evening Telegraph, I am writing to express my concern about the action of one of your member clubs, Hull City, through their chairman Martin Fish in banning a sports writer from working at their ground. I enclose a copy of the letter from the club to the journalist concerned, David Bond, whom I have known for a number of years. That point is irrelevant: what is more worrying is that Mr. Fish's action negates the freedom of speech and expression that we all hold dear and sets a dangerous precedent for any club who wish to oppose the right to fair and objective reporting. I realise that this is a sensitive matter, but I feel you ought to know about it. Perhaps you could suggest a way by which it could be resolved. The individual concerned is suffering a serious financial loss and is not able to call on any trade-union support. I know that the Mail on Sunday sports desk share my concerns about the situation and the stance of Hull City AFC. The Rugby League themselves issue Press passes to individual writers and photographers instead of the clubs. Should the FA now take on that onus in soccer, too?"

I was, of course, prepared to allow Peter a touch of journalistic licence by referring to "a serious financial loss." It was never that drastic, but the principle involved was, of course, the same if I had lost one penny or many pounds. I did, though, have to forfeit fairly lucrative work covering City's home games for the Mail on Sunday, as Peter pointed out. They also gave me good support, but their then sports-desk secretary Patsy John eventually told me that their efforts to reason with Fish had fallen on stony ground. She said amusingly that they had found Fish to be a typically stubborn Yorkshireman! I might normally have respected him for that kind of stance, but I was more bothered about proving to him that I was an even more obstinate Tyke! The Mail on Sunday, though, were looking for someone to cover Grimsby Town's home games, so they offered me that role as compensation for my Tigers troubles and I was grateful for their backing in this respect.

I also sensed that I had backing from some grass-roots fans, who naturally suspected that information was being suppressed when they heard about my ban. They encouraged me to take action so that they were kept informed of developments and the outcome was that I began to produce monthly bulletins for them. It was to be typed on A4 paper, it was to be about 900 words in length, it was to be issued free and a small group of fans, ably marshalled by Peter Wood, would look after its distribution. The idea was that they would run off a few copies and hand them out at matches or at any other venues that they deemed to be relevant. The first one duly appeared in November 1995.

I reckoned that I would never be reinstated by the City regime, so the only viable alternative was to try to embarrass them from afar and remind them that I was not quietly fading into the sunset. They had seemed to cast me as Public Enemy No. 1, so I decided that in that case I might as well live up to the reputation. It was soon clear that the regime were seeing the bulletins themselves, but that did not worry me in the least. In fact, I preferred it that way. And I wanted to remind them that they had drawn up the battle-lines, I was merely responding and that all the fair-minded objectivity that I always tried to maintain in my coverage of City matters had flown out of the window. If they thought that I was bad enough to be banned, they would now discover that I could be far, far worse by adopting an unashamedly one-sided approach towards them. I was now a rebel with a cause.

I knew that I still had the sources to find out what was going on at the club, so the bulletins became a humble means of reinforcing my right to freedom of speech and keeping the public informed. In fact, I was relishing the chance to face the City regime head-on, but it did mean that my only hope of reinstatement was to do my utmost to remove them from office first. I certainly was not going to set a time limit on it, but one big factor started to work in my favour as the 1995-96 season took shape. The team were doing badly in the Second Division, in which they had performed respectably during the previous two seasons, and the natives on the terraces were becoming restless. By the first Saturday in October they were at the bottom of the table, where they were to remain for the rest of the season, and I had to capitalise on it. It was all supremely ironic, of course: as a supporter, I had always wanted the team to do well, but now I desperately wanted them to lose. I am very open about my opinion in this respect although I can understand that some fans might not like the attitude. I was fighting a personal battle, so failure on the pitch benefited my cause. I also believed that short-term failure would work towards the club's long-term benefit and that it was a case of one step back to go two steps forward, but I have often wondered what the fans who believed the same way as I did must have felt. It must have been so difficult for them to reconcile themselves with their thinking because they were actually paying money to support the club, but did they perversely have to feel that a lack of success on the pitch was the only way forward? Did they cheer when City won or did they reflect that every defeat was a step towards changes that might bring better times?

Producing the bulletins would never bring down the regime. They were a minute means to an end and an ethical reminder that I had no right to be silenced. And the fact that I had been banned in the first place made me realise that I could offend the regime very easily, so it was a case of just chipping away. I knew that I was never going to weaken or waver, I was never remotely depressed about the ban by the club whom I had once supported fervently and I remained upbeat throughout that I could play a small role in getting rid of the regime in the end. Some good chances came my way, such as the occasion in early 1996 when a newspaper cutting from Scotland was passed on to me. The article included comments by former City hero Dean Windass that compared the training at City unfavourably with those at his new club Aberdeen. I took the opportunity to leak the contents of the article to the Hull Daily Mail and it caused a stink. Not long afterwards City's players were banned from speaking to sections of the media, so maybe the regime were becoming rattled. As relegation to the fourth level of English League football beckoned for only the second time in the club's history, I believed that it was the beginning of the end.

Relegation was confirmed with a 2-1 home defeat against Crewe Alexandra in April 1996 as City lost their last five League games in what was one of the worst seasons ever. That was bad enough in itself, but then Fish committed what I regarded as tactical errors that would take the level of public opposition to him on to a higher plain. He announced that the management team of Terry Dolan and Jeff Lee would have their contracts extended. They still a year left to run on their present deals, so it was unnecessary to lengthen them at that stage anyway. In terms of football logic, if Fish still had faith in them, then he could just give them a chance to redeem themselves by producing a promotion campaign during the remaining year of their deals. But he gave them both two further years at the club in addition to what was already there. Dolan had taken City to relegation twice, emulating Bob Brocklebank, but those of us who opposed the regime expected the news. He and Fish had tried to buy themselves time in the public domain by reminding everybody regularly about the club's poor finances, but sometimes management regimes have to work all the harder on shoestring budgets by developing team spirit and extra commitment from the players and striving to evolve a durable youth policy. No-one should blame Dolan and Lee for accepting the contracts if they were offered them, but the decision was a major turning-point and was surely a faux pas by Fish. Fans realised that Dolan would never be held accountable for the club's struggles. In fact, I have never known a chairman and a manager to be as close as Fish and Dolan were. I have never advocated sackings - too many are carried out by directors who panic in the face of fans' fury - but this time City had an unbelievably-lenient chairman and perhaps people were questioning it.

Fish then compounded his indiscretion for the Tigers' final home game of the season against Bradford City. He agreed with the police that regular City fans should move from their customary standing and sitting areas to accommodate the high number of fans from Bradford, whose side were pushing for a place in the play-offs. I never knew who was the more responsible for the decision - Fish or the police commander concerned, Bryan Calam, who would reinvent himself as a club official in a forthcoming regime under former English tennis star David Lloyd. But the game attracted a crowd of 8,900, the biggest of the season, and the enforced movement of the fans ensured that the club would generate a lot of extra money on a one-off basis. But there were pitch invasions amid the discontent and a section of City fans, long-suffering and not surprisingly inflamed by the invasion of their territory, organised a protest petition against the regime under the guise of a pressure group called Tigers 2000. Their long-term mission was to bring about change for the better by the end of the millennium and their short-term aim was the removal of the board and the management team. Circumstances dictated that they had something in common with me.

Tigers 2000 produced a statement of intent about the club's future as they saw it, they canvassed for members and they began to hold well-supported public meetings for those who had become disillusioned with the state of affairs at Boothferry Park. They encouraged me to take a direct involvement, but I preferred to remain on the fringes even though they obviously had my backing because their cause was my cause even though we had different agenda for requiring change. For the record, I was never a member of Tigers 2000 even though it seemed to be suggested in some quarters. But there again a lot of untrue allegations were made against me both before and after the ban. A City fanzine, for example, apparently carried some scurrilous articles by a correspondent called Dave Bore. They might well have been a parody of me, my name and my style for all that I know, but I certainly did not write them or have anything whatever to do with them. But I did agree to meet Tigers 2000's hastily-assembled committee and found that I knew most of them anyway because they were long-established fans.

I had always believed that I should be independent as a journalist - after all, this was at the crux of Fish's errant argument that I should always be on the club's side - in terms of making up my own mind instead of having it made up for me. My main aim was my reinstatement as a journalist at Boothferry Park, but, even though I opted against adhering to requests from Tigers 2000 to attend or address their meetings or sign any of their documents, I respected the genuine fans' aspirations. I settled instead for meeting some of their committee members at Ken Wagstaff's Marlborough Club in Hessle. Normally I met four fans - Peter Lincoln, Angie Rowe, Dave Dewberry and Geoff Bradley - and was impressed by their determination and courage. I had often travelled to away games as a fan with the dedicated Peter, who was Tigers 2000's chairman and had never shied away from letting the club know his feelings if he believed in a cause. Angie, who became Tigers 2000's secretary, emerged as a forceful influence and assumed the mantle of getting under the skin of everyone who opposed the group by doing some dogged detective work. Dave, who had often been one of my sternest critics when I was writing about the club, was the daddy of all City protesters. There were times when he had probably gone over the top, but his heart had always been in the right place and we were now thinking very much on the same lines. Geoff was probably quieter amd more methodical, but always had a perceptive sense of what was going on. Above all, they were good, honest and decent City fans who felt betrayed.

I preferred to stay in the background a lot, but I advised them when and where I could, I acted as a kind of unofficial consultant and supplied them with a bit of ammunition and a few jottings here and there to try to maintain the impetus of their campaign. Freddie Cowell, who had been unceremoniously sacked at the end of the season after working for the club's youth set-up on a part-time basis for 18 years, joined the fray in the same kind of way. Waggy, meanwhile, was elected as the president of Tigers 2000 and also chipped in helpfully. I warned him that he would get himself trouble with the regime, but he insisted that they would never ban him. They did!

A summer of discontent unfolded. Tigers 2000 established strong links with the fanzine Tiger Rag and began disseminating plenty of literature to back their cause. I stopped producing my bulletins during the close season, but I had developed a penchant for mind games with Fish and wrote to the club to seek a Press ticket for the 1996-97 season. After all, the original letter banning me had indicated that it applied to 1995-96. Naturally I am still awaiting a reply to my application for 1996-97!

I also opted to continue to be my own man and keep myself at a discreet distance from Tigers 2000 if I felt it necessary. One summer Saturday afternoon, for example, they hired an open-topped bus to ride round the city to promote their aims: curiously, their itinerary included a visit to Fish's house. Tigers 2000 always insisted that they would keep their protest action within the law and nothing too sinister happened, but I thought that they were carrying things a bit too far in this instance. Fish understandably tried to discredit them and he was helped with a sympathy vote by other excessive action from outraged fans, who were not connected with Tigers 2000 to my knowledge. I would never condone protest trips to people's homes, unsavoury items pushed through letter-boxes and cars being damaged. At the same time I was ready in other ways if it had to be a dirty fight for my livelihood. For example, I managed just in case to obtain a copy of Terry Dolan's contract and to dig out a cutting of a court case in which Richard Chetham had once been involved.

Fish soldiered on to the start of 1996-97 season and I sensed a growing sense of despair among the Tigers 2000 committee that they had still not ousted him. Maybe they were concerned that everything would just blow over if the team started the new season well in the Third Division. As it was, City remained undefeated in their first 10 League games, but Fish did not help his cause amid it all when they entertained Barnet on August 31, 1996, which was the 50th anniversary of the opening of Boothferry Park. It is in no way disrespectful to Barnet and their achievements, but a club of City's potential should never have been in the same division as they were in the first place, so the occasion put a lot about the previous 50 years neatly and sadly into perspective. At the same time it was a great chance for City to repair their tarnished public-relations image, but apparently it turned out to be a damp squib. There was a token attempt to invite some past players to the occasion: strangely, Fish did not ask me for help because I - more than most - knew where a lot of them were because of my involvement with the Ex-Tigers' Association! But two of the all-time heroes, Waggy and Chris Chilton, were deliberately snubbed because they had shown their opposition to the regime.

In that same week I decided to leave the closet and agreed to address one of the regular open meetings organised by Tigers 2000. I changed my mind and ventured again into the public domain because I had had no reply to my polite application for a Press pass for the new season: nothing had changed although I had naturally not expected it to have done. I turned up, therefore, for a meeting at the venue I have always known as the Royal Station Hotel in Hull although its name had probably changed by then and has probably changed again a few times since. It was all very civil and dignified as I outlined the background to my ban and then answered questions from the floor. In fact, the overall mood was low-key and hinted that morale was sagging because the new season had started with the status quo intact at Boothferry Park.

But I had planned to have something in reserve for the meeting. For many years the nameplate from the steam engine that had been called Hull City had stood imperiously over the players' tunnel at Boothferry Park. It was a legacy of the golden age of steam locomotives and, as its B17 class had slowly been scrapped, many of the nameplates had been passed on to the clubs concerned. I advised the audience to take a closer look over the tunnel when they next visited Boothferry Park because the nameplate from the locomotive was no longer there: in its place was a plastic replica. I assured everyone that Fish had secretly sold the original to a dealer in Chesterfield some time ago for £10,000 minus the cheap replacement so that he could raise some badly-needed money when they could not afford to pay the players' wages.

I have never disclosed the source of my information, but I had heard about the sale during the summer, I had kept it up my sleeve and my announcement seemed to breathe new life into Tigers 2000. I sensed the sound of serious scribbling around me as the group realised that they had the chance of something new to investigate. They were always willing to delve and discovered that the original nameplate had been sold on to a railway museum in the Lincolnshire town of Louth. They also obtained a photo-copy of the sale document to the Chesterfield dealer and found out that the then secretary, Tom Wilson, had returned from the excursion with the money in notes in a carrier-bag. In addition, a dislliusioned vice-president of the club, Neil Howe, who was threatening litigation against them concerning another matter, said that he had been told that no VAT had allegedly been paid on the sale. More significantly, the sale of the nameplate attracted wider publicity in the local media and further incensed the public: I received telephone calls from trainspotting buffs as well as keen football followers on the subject. In their eyes it was a case of selling off a significant sample of the club's heritage and the fact that it had all been done furtively fuelled the fury even more. The nameplate, funnily enough, never scored a goal for City, but it symbolised a lot to the public and its sale symbolised strongly what was really going on behind the scenes.

The timing of my announcement about the nameplate might have been helpful, but where did it fit into the overall scheme of things in its own right? If the team had been doing well, would the sale have been all that significant? But it served to show that Tigers 2000 were not going to fade away and they were able to keep up their momentum. I resumed my monthly bulletins because I had been asked at the open meeting to do so, the editors of Tiger Rag became more acidic in their Saturday articles in the Hull Daily Mail and Freddie Cowell and his wife Elaine provided further perceptive background information to help Tigers 2000's strategy, so Fish's escape routes were slowly being eroded.

I also let it be known that that club were allegedly operating in breach of their articles of association, which stated: "The number of directors will not be less than four." When businessman Martin St. Quinton resigned from the board during the autumn of 1993, it had left the complement at just three - Fish and two previous chairmen, Christopher Needler and Richard Chetham. Midway through the 1996-97 season Chetham announced that he was standing down and it was only then that Fish and Needler sought to introduce a change to the articles at the annual shareholders' meeting so that only a minimum of two directors was required. Maybe I had embarrassed them into submission: more significantly, that annual meeting had to be suspended and then reconvened because of the constant criticism of the regime. Another previous chairman, Don Robinson, had been treated with apparent disdain by Needler when he launched a takeover bid for the club during the autumn of 1996 and it had furthered annoyed a lot of fans and shareholders. The level of disgust was underlined in November 1996 when only 1,775 people turned up for a home game against Torquay United, the lowest home League attendance in the club's history.

In December 1996 there were joint protests from both sets of fans during a 3-0 defeat at Brighton. Another major protest took place during the home game against Exeter City two months later. There was also a winding-up order from the Inland Revenue in respect of a £200,000 bill, which Needler believed he could deflect by selling Boothferry Park. East Yorkshire Motor Services then refused to supply any more vehicles because they were owed £3,000 for 15 trips. Fish attacked their attitude, saying: "They have probably taken the view that they have got to get in first, which is a typical attitude for them. We owe them £3,000, but there again we owe everybody money." In my opinion it was an astonishing admission from an accountant. Another protest occurred at the final game at home to Scarborough, who won 2-0, as City finished 17th: at that point it was the worst season in their history.

In the meantime, I had had the chance to reinvent myself partially in football terms. Chris Pitson, the financial director of the Hull Daily Mail, was a good, knowledgeable football man who scouted for his favourite club Swansea City in his spare time. He needed back-up in 1996 and asked me if I fancied scouting for Swansea with him while the ban was in force. It was clear that it was likely to be awkward if I had to do a scouting job at Boothferry Park, so an understanding was reached which meant that I never went there to compromise myself or Swansea, but the whole process revitalised me during the ban. Swansea's management team were Jan Molby and Billy Ayre and I scouted for them for 15 months until they left in October 1997. Billy, who sadly passed away in 2002, promised to contact me when he returned to the game and four months later he kept his word when he became Frank Burrows' assistant manager at Cardiff City. I had nearly eight years with Cardiff until I was asked if I would like to join Bolton Wanderers in October of last year and the experience has enhanced my football education and enabled me overall to get to know some wonderful people at all three clubs. Billy, in particular, was a special football man and a human being of the highest calibre and I owed him a lot for his support and approach. The scouting opened up new doors for me and I have thoroughly enjoyed it. It has not been work because I have only ever been reimbursed by clubs for my travelling expenses and have never reached the heady heights of being a scout who earns a wage from his club with a contract or a retainer.

Not surprisingly, there have been odd occasions when City fans seem to have thought that I have betrayed them by scouting elsewhere, but it would never have happened if Fish had not banned me. But you cannot choose the club for whom you scout and it is simply the nature of the game that City have never asked me to scout for them and I would never expect them to do so. Scouting has been an unexpected extra enjoyable experience linked with football for me. I have been lucky to have been involved in it for 10 years, but I am not exactly going to thank Fish for inadvertently giving me that opportunity!

And it did not then mean that I lost sight of my personal battle for journalistic acceptance. When Plymouth Argyle's chairman Dan McCauley threatened to charge journalists £10 per match to cover games from the Press-box at Home Park, the Football League's assistant secretary Andy Williamson responded by saying: "Obviously we want to see all clubs try to generate harmonious relationships with the local Press and the media in general. Any thought of charging the media to cover matches and ostracising them is completely contrary to the spirit of the guidelines we have issued." It sounded as if they might be supportive of my situation, so I wrote to Williamson and detailed the background to my ban. I have always had a lengthy suspicion of the people running football, so I was not surprised that I never even had the courtesy of a reply. Was my case too hot to handle? Or might it have been an example of a football authority fudging an issue when the pressure mounted? I shall never know.

But I made headway elsewhere. Sue Mott, who had been a colleague of mine at the Hull Daily Mail, publicised my cause with a piece in her "Heroes and Villains" column in the Daily Telegraph. And towards the end of the season I was quoted in an article about banned soccer writers in the national magazine Goal. It was no longer a question of whether or not the City regime would fold, but when. They finished 17th in the Third Division, nine places lower than the previous worst in their history, and had to stave off another winding-up order in the High Court. The only doubt concerned who was in line to replace Fish and his cronies.

Tim Wilby had played rugby league in Hull when the code experienced a golden era in the city. The local highspot was surely the 1980 Rugby League Challenge Cup final when the city's big two, Hull FC and Hull Kingston Rovers, met at Wembley. Hull had lost 10-5, but Wilby had scored their only try. He then went on his rugby-league travels and based himself in London, but returned to Hull to become the chairman of Hull FC, renaming them Hull Sharks and quickly building a squad capable of achieving Super League status during the summer of 1997. Amid the uproar at City during 1996-97 he also dropped hints that he was involved in a business enterprise who might be keen on taking over the club and began to liaise behind the scenes with Tigers 2000's secretary Angie Rowe. But there was talk of a rival interest from a southern businessman called Michael Cambridge, so Christopher Needler, now City's major shareholder and Fish's only fellow director, hesitated. Wilby called his bluff by threatening to drop his interest, Cambridge soon disappeared from the scene and Needler was forced into a rethink. Wilby was back in the driving seat and it quickly became clear that he had substantial backing from Great Britain's Davis Cup tennis captain David Lloyd, who had done well for himself with a string of leisure centres that bore his name.

A summer of protracted negotiations dragged on until it became official towards the end of June 1997 that Needler had agreed to sell City to Wilby and Lloyd. They bought out the Needler family's 64 per cent shareholding in the club for £2.4m. and there was immediate speculation that the Tigers might ground-share with Hull Sharks at their Boulevard home - a suggestion that did not please many fans - while a new stadium was built for them both in the city. It was also clear that City's management team of Terry Dolan and Jeff Lee were on their way out although Fish, defiant to the end, refused to admit it, but big names such as Peter Beardsley, Chris Waddle and Ray Wilkins were already being linked with a managerial vacancy that did not officially exist. Everything was caught up in a kind of suspended animation while a series of snags and technical hitches were resolved, but gradually there was an air of optimism that a new era was dawning for City fans.

I remain grateful to the people who supported me during my ban, but there is little doubt that a lot of people will always tend to believe that there was no smoke without fire and it is an unwarranted stigma with which I have had to live. I am always willing to own up to my mistakes, but fighting my corner in the way that I did was certainly not one of them in my mind. In this instance I shall always staunchly believe that I was always in the right.

There were people closely involved in the club during the Fish and Dolan regime - especially physiotherapist Jeff Radcliffe, Football in the Community officer John Davies and stadium manager John Cooper - whom I respected and regarded as friends and I did not want to fall out with them just because we might have held differing views about what was going on. But I do believe that there were others who may have never forgiven me and seen me fairly contemptuously as nothing more than a disruptive influence. All I would say is that I felt that I had every right to be disruptive when I was fighting for my livelihood and freedom of speech in the same breath. What would they have done in the same situation?

As far as Martin Fish and Terry Dolan are concerned, I feel nothing towards them. I basically do not want to have anything to do with them because of the difficulties that they caused me. I do not want to be rude to them or argumentative with them: I just do not want to speak to them because it is now in the past and everybody has moved on. There have been people who have told me that Fish apparently regretted banning me, but it leaves me cold if there is any truth in it and I have no interest in knowing if it were ever so. The simple fact is that I was banned. Their commercial manager Simon Cawkill, whom I have known since our schooldays together, once told me that he felt that Fish listened too much to Dolan, but again I am not interested in such whys and wherefores and who was really to blame. It happened, you deal with it while trying outwardly to maintain as much dignity as possible when inside you are seething and you move on.

As far as assistant manager Jeff Lee was concerned, I absolve him of any blame even though he was obviously an integral part of the regime. I had differences of opinion with Jeff long before the ban, but he is a straight-talking Northerner with strong beliefs and I certainly see no harm in that. We have met up from time to time on scouting engagements, chatted amicably about the game and I find him good company. In fact, I even telephoned him to commiserate with him when he lost a backroom job at Huddersfield Town.

At the same time I have scant respect for Richard Chetham and his time with the club. I discovered that, unknown to me, he had been lobbied on my behalf and replied that my ban was nothing to do with him even though there was a point when he was the major shareholder and might have held sway in trying to diffuse the situation. Does that mean that he, too, supported my ban? I have to assume that he did. Apparently he once asked a journalist colleague why I never spoke too much to him afterwards: I would have thought that it was obvious. Ironically, Chetham and Angie Rowe ended up living in the same road as I do, so it seemed surreal one Saturday lunchtime when I saw them both driving off in the opposite direction as I set off to a home game.

Christopher Needler, meanwhile, ended up being a major disappointment to me. He was often very capable, but I honestly believe that he did not share the family passion for the game. He once told me that he had disliked being City's chairman and he was, of course, always faced with the problem of living in his father Harold's shadow. At one stage he was memorably quoted as saying that he preferred his garden in France to watching City play. If that were the case, why did he hang on for so long? It was probably to try to preserve the Needler's family name with the club, to do right by them and to enact some kind of filial duty. Ironically, his mother Hilary and sister Vanessa are members of the Needler dynasty who have more keenly retained their interests in the club. But I believe that the Needler name would have been respected far more if Christopher had acted differently in the best interests of City long before he finally pulled out. In the end I think that sadly he merely made matters worse for himself and the family.

I was reinstated as a journalist at Boothferry Park in time for 1997-98 after a two-year absence, but I decided that I would remain as detached and dispassionate as possible about everything and just get on with my job. It has stayed that way ever since. I shall always believe that I did nothing wrong, but I am equally aware that the mud sticks and that it is natural for people to assume that there was no smoke without fire. I had enjoyed the battle to stick up for my rights and never became dismayed or hurt emotionally by the situation.

I became fed up, though, when people used to say how lucky I was to be banned, considering the state that the club were in. It was a shallow attitude from folk who could not accept the fact that freedom of expression and the right to earn my living had been at stake. As a sports journalist, you are the humble link between the club and their public. If that link is removed, then people should seriously wonder what the regime at a club have to hide and why they want to hide it. And if there is nothing to hide, then logically there is no need to impose a ban in the first place. I value the support that I received during those two years, but if I lost favour with some observers for standing up for my rights, then they are the ones with the problem, not me. In a business sense the directors and owners are always in charge of football clubs, but in all other senses they belong to their fans. And, as paying customers, they should always have the right to evaluate all the relevant views expressed about their clubs. I rest my case.

In the end the fans had spoken. It cannot have been easy at times for the players, but they were professionals and had to get on with their jobs as best they could. Perhaps some of them disliked me without bothering to analyse my situation, but those whom I got to know were largely decent, honest people even though they were with the Tigers during the worst spell in their history. Maybe they were just in the wrong place at the wrong time. But I have a lot of time for Neil Mann, who is a great guy: in fact, I was supposed to be the chairman of his testimonial committee until the club stepped in and seemed to organise it instead. And I also respect the whole-hearted Gregor Rioch, who said: "It was probably the most difficult period in the club's history. I was just a young lad trying to get the chance to become a first-team regular with a club. I'd been at Peterborough and both clubs were struggling, but in the end Peterborough survived in what was then the Second Division and Hull went down. I thought about the decision to come to Hull and I just felt that it was a great opportunity. It seemed that Hull might become a big club again and it was just that their potential wasn't being used to the full. They should have been a big club and everybody could see and feel it, but I spent three years with them in the bottom division of the League and I get fed up with that tag. But maybe I came to the club too early."

And the players, it seemed, could recognise the fans' fervour even though the club were at a low ebb because Greg added: "I remember winning against Darlington on my debut when Duane Darby got a hat-trick and everything looked all right, but then it filtered off. The following season David Lloyd and Mark Hateley came in and there was talk about a new stadium and new players, but obviously all the promises weren't kept. But I was made captain at 22 and it's the kind of opportunity you can't turn down. The passion of the people and the supporters matched my passion. I made some good friends because my wife Jane is from Cottingham and some of my best pals are from the village of Brough, which was where I lived. The people treated me well, it's always a pleasure to go back and it was nice to be part of it, but we weren't good enough as a team and struggled to match the expectation of the locals. Being an outsider, it was still a big disappointment, but you have to respect the fans and I don't think that the lads worried too much when there were all the protests. When we played Scarborough at Easter in 1999 and we were both trying to stay in the League, there was a crowd of nearly 14,000 at Boothferry Park and we could see what the club could do if things went right. We had some good games in the League Cup at Crystal Palace and Newcastle when we had a great following and John Barnes was their captain. But then there were games such as the FA Cup tie against Hednesford Town when we went out to a lower-league team. We had so many chances and I was involved in two penalty decisions that didn't go our way. That game just summed up what the club were going through and it hurt." And Dai d'Auria said on his goalscoring League debut in a 3-1 defeat at Rotherham in August 1998: "Our supporters were magnificent. I got goose-pimples playing away in front of such fanatical support."

I soon met some members of the new regime at Boothferry Park - at the Boulevard! Jeff Barmby and I were summoned there on a wet Thursday in June 1997 to discuss how the Ex-Tigers' Association might help and to exchange general views about the club. The new people seemed to be pleasant enough, but I was unsure as to just how much they were football people. But Peter Tunks, the chief executive of Hull Sharks, promised that my ban had ended and the opinion was reinforced when Tim Wilby addressed a public meeting at Hull City Hall organised in conjunction with Tigers 2000. Their secretary Angie Rowe, who briefly worked for the club under the new regime although I had advised her against it, had kindly sent me an invitation and I ended up sitting on the front row with luminaries such as Freddie and Elaine Cowell, Chris Chilton and Frank McGorrighan, then one of two known survivors from the first City team to play a League game at Boothferry Park in 1946. I was introduced as "an encyclopaedia on Hull City" even though I was not wearing an anorak and could have done without it all, but I had a duty to support the people who had helped me even though all I wanted to do was simply to get on with my job.

Wilby was hailed as Hull's new soccer Messiah and everything was a bit triumphal and almost evangelical about the evening. But it guaranteed nothing and the proof of the pudding would be in the action and not the words. In another political context, I could not help but recall Neil Kinnock's pre-General Election rally for the Labour party earlier in the decade and how that had badly misfired. I believed that the club were being left in a poor condition and it would need a considerable amount of experience and expertise to put everything right. Did the new regime have enough of it to transform matters and provide success for the fans? It gradually became clear that they did not.

Former England international Mark Hateley became the new manager with Billy Kirkwood as his assistant, Tim Wilby became the chairman of a new three-man board with David Lloyd and their financial adviser Albert Harrison and Ian McMahon, a former Oldham Athletic and Rochdale player, was appointed as managing director. Martin Fish and Christopher Needler resigned from the board on August 15. I had already returned to the Press-box at Boothferry Park for a pre-season friendly against Hearts on July 18, having been issued with a one-off pass signed by M. W. Fish, secretary! On August 25 Jackie Bell, announcing herself as the new secretary, telephoned me at home to confirm that my first season-long Press pass since 1992 would be awaiting me at that night's Coca-Cola Cup tie against Macclesfield Town.

The old place looked the same - old! But I was glad to be back after battling to stick by my principles and serving what was then thought to be the longest ban ever imposed by a club on a journalist although Neil Hallam, who had first suggested to me that I had set such an infamous record, later overtook me because of his problems at Derby County. It meant that, though, that I had not seen the Tigers play during the calendar year of 1996. It was my first break for 40 years, but it had been an enforced one. And I did sneak quietly, but defiantly into Boothferry Park on one occasion during my ban - when the East Riding Referees' Association invited me to be the guest speaker at their monthly meeting held in the club's sponsors' suite in September 1995. I always wondered if Fish ever found out that I was in the entirely strange situation of being popular with referees while having received a red card from the chairman!

The next four years were among the worst in City's history, though. The renewed hopes inspired by the public meeting at Hull City Hall were dashed as the club stumbled through more and more crises. City's brave, new world did not evolve: instead things went from very bad to even worse. But I simply kept everything and everyone discreetly at arm's length after my ban because my passion for the club had been eroded a little. Hateley could not produce any managerial magic, Wilby resigned in September 1997 after a brief reign, Michael Appleton became the chief executive of the holding company who controlled both City and Hull Sharks and in April 1998 City became the last side to lose a League game to Doncaster Rovers until August 2003! Lloyd's approach to public relations made him unpopular after a number of scathing outbursts and I thought that some of the people surrounding him were lightweight in terms of football expertise. But I am less critical of Lloyd, who also had a wrangle about the lease that supermarket Kwik Save had on the north end of Boothferry Park, than many because he did invest in the club and attempt to change things for the better. But in 1997-98 City were 22nd in the Third Division at the end of their worst season ever. The Tigers were bad, Brighton and Hove Albion were worse and luckily Doncaster were much worse as they went out of the League.

But City won only four of their first 24 League games in 1998-99 and it looked as if the city of Hull would end the 20th century in the same way as it had begun it - without a Football League club! And it was advantage to the fans when they threw tennis balls on to the pitch before a Worthington Cup tie at Bolton as a protest against David Lloyd's suggestion that he might move the Tigers to the Boulevard. He also hinted at putting City up for sale and at the start of October 1998 he announced his intention to leave the club. City were bottom of the Third Division and on the market at £1.8m. He claimed that the wage bill was the biggest in the division with Hateley, who had seldom been fit enough to carry out his dual role as player and manager, taking up the bulk of it. Lloyd gave a scathing radio broadcast that was probably the final alienation from the fans. As in 1982, the public rallied round in response to a financial crisis. There was a crowd of 8,594 - compared with 3,882 six days earlier - as they lost 2-1 at home to Cardiff City. But was there a buyer out there anywhere?

There was talk that Don Robinson, who had once ridden a horse round Boothferry Park as one of his publicity stunts, might return on a white charger, but his interest appeared to be dismissed fairly shabbily from what I could discern. I firmly believed that one local consortium - involving Ian Glenton, Malcolm Lord, John Page, Stefano Lucatello and Peter Whinham - would have been ideal with their collective football and business knowledge, but they found that negotiating with Lloyd was difficult and that Hateley's wages were a drawback because they wanted to get rid of him. I know that they had even spoken to John Barnwell, the chief executive of the League Managers' Association, and were ready to line up John Ward, who had just left Bristol City as manager, as Hateley's replacement. But, as with Don, they were foiled and the name of former Scunthorpe United chairman Tom Belton began to emerge.

I tipped off Matt Barlow at the Hull Daily Mail about Belton and he was more than grateful. He found it ironic because Belton had been at Scunthorpe when his father Frank, who became the Tigers' assistant manager this year, was in charge at Glanford Park during the mid-1980s. I was more suspicious of Tom because I had been told that Martin Fish had made some kind of approach to him to come to City when things had gone pear-shaped under his regime. I was very much in the background, but I managed to get a message about it to Tom, whose public-relations skills were excellent, through a third party and he always played down the link. The Belton link allied to a Sheffield-based consortium led by Nick Buchanan was confirmed by November and Hateley was on his way. Belton became chairman and Warren Joyce became caretaker player-manager.

Neil Warnock, whom Don Robinson had thought about bringing to Boothferry Park as Brian Horton's successor, was linked with the job, but Joyce, who had riled protesting fans when he scored twice in a 3-0 home win over Brighton in March 1997 and opted to celebrate in front of the empty East Stand, was given it on a longer-term basis. It might have been a risk because of his lack of managerial experience, especially in such a fraught situation, but Belton had obviously seen a spark and got it right. Joycey brought in John McGovern as his assistant and they eventually engineered safety. I recalled speaking to McGovern at a game at Grimsby when he was doing some media work and explaining to him about my ban at Hull, but he appalled me by showing no sympathy whatever. How would he have felt in the same situation, I asked myself? I also remember a notable ex-Tiger telling me that he had been contacted by a former Boothferry Park teammate, who had recommended a promising youngster to him. The lad had links with Australia and Holland and the local ex-Tiger had been asked to find out if the club might be interested in him. But he had ended up speaking to McGovern, who had apparently been sarcastic to him. Anyway there can be no doubt that the management team of Joyce and McGovern were City's saviours and deserve the highest praise for the way in which they improved City's fortunes with what became known as the "Great Escape" squad in 1999. By early February the Tigers were finally off the bottom of the table and they finished five points clear of the relegation place as Scarborough went down after goalkeeper Jimmy Glass's goalscoring glory at Carlisle.

Above all, Joycey had an aptitude for spotting the type of players to dig City out of their hole. Defender Justin Whittle, a top-class professional, was one of the first to arrive and said: "When I signed for Hull, everyone was telling me that I was mad. We looked as if we were in an impossible position, but Warren Joyce turned it around even though he didn't have any experience as a manager. We just went out and battled in every game. The results started to pick up and so did the confidence." And no-one was at the hub of the fighting spirit more than midfield player Gary Brabin, who said: "It really did look bleak when I first joined. It looked like certain relegation. I remember going into the changing-room before my debut against Rotherham United and thinking to myself: 'Have I done the right thing?' Everybody was low and there was no atmosphere. But Warren Joyce realised what was needed and brought in a few characters such as me, Jon Whitney and Mark Bonner. I didn't really know anyone apart from Michael Quigley. I hadn't heard of most of the players and there seemed to be a lot of local lads. But from that first match I knew that they had fight and determination. There were good players such as Mark Greaves and David Brown, they all obviously wanted it and I was full of optimism after that. The only time that I had any doubt was when I first went into the dressing-room. I knew it was going to be hard work, but I went in with an open mind and the good thing was that I didn't know what it had been like when it was really low. I don't know if some players had been ready to throw in the towel, so maybe they did need some new faces and characters. But I didn't sign for the club to be relegated and I really didn't believe that we would be, so I never felt any pressure. All of a sudden we were on a roll and I found myself enjoying it. It seems that people were not taking the club seriously in those days because they had a few seasons near the bottom. But staying up with Hull that season was the high point of my career and I'm proud of it. It would have ruined the club if we'd gone down and it was one of the saddest moments of my career when I left because Hull City remain in my heart."

There was only one problem with the so-called Great Escape team, of course - they were not successful: they avoided failure. It is true that without them City might never have had the platform from which they were eventually going to build in the early part of the 21st century, but they were unable to maintain what had actually been promotion form in the second half of 1998-99. There was also more boardroom unrest. David Bennett, one of the Sheffield consortium, had been ousted from the board in the spring of 1999 and Belton was replaced as chairman the following autumn. It happened against a backcloth of concern about the involvement of businessman Stephen Hinchliffe, who had been disqualified from acting as a company director for seven years, and inquiries being made about the club's running by Humberside Fraud Squad and the FA's compliance unit. And it coincided with City having to borrow £50,000 from the PFA to pay players' wages. Buchanan became chairman and insisted: "Every decision which we make is in the best interests of Hull City. I'm one of life's fighters and the harder people hit me, the harder I'll hit back." Joyce, meanwhile, had brought in a host of new players for 1999-2000, but the Tigers were in the bottom half of the Third Division throughout and he and McGovern were sacked towards the end of the season.

The experienced Brian Little was brought in with two assistants, David Moore, whose uncle Norman had been City's top goalscorer in 1948-49, and Kevan Smith. But there were two runs of seven League games without a win in 2000-01 and more trouble was on the horizon. During the summer of 2000 City had been locked out of Boothferry Park in a dispute about unpaid rent with David Lloyd, who was still the club's landlord, but they agreed to pay the arrears of £108,000. The undaunted Buchanan claimed that the board had a five-year plan to take City into the First Division: in fact, he had gone by the following spring. In February 2001 Lloyd instructed bailiffs to change the locks at Boothferry Park because of another dispute about a bill for unpaid rent. The figure was £45,000 this time, but Lloyd said: "It's the only way to bring the parties to the table. They can't play football unless I allow them in. I am insignificant. The only thing I own is the pitch. I want all the parties - owners, council and Inland Revenue - to come to a deal to allow football to be played at Hull for a long time." In addition, a High Court judge in Leeds put the club in administration after a tax debt of £230,000 had been revealed. Buchanan and directors Phillip Webster and Andy Daykin quit after talks with Kroll Buchler Phillips, the administrators, and only David Capper as the director of football administration and solicitor Richard Ibbotson as the company secretary survived the cull. The administrators also negotiated with Lloyd to reopen the gates as a buyer was sought. Five bids were received and a new fans' pressure group called the Tigers' Co-operative, who were totally well-meaning and yet unrealistic, bravely launched one of them. Surrey-based businessman Mel Griffin's interest enabled him to purchase Boothferry Park, which he still owns, there was a bid from a New York consortium and Belton re-emerged as a possible buyer.

The administrators held a creditors' meeting in Willerby and it transpired that Customs and Excise and the Inland Revenue accounted for almost two-thirds of the club's £1.6m. debt. The Ex-Tigers' Association were among the creditors as chairman Jeff Barmby and I represented them. It was going to be interesting - and perhaps the only taxing aspect of it was that I found myself on the same side as the Inland Revenue! The Ex-Tigers were owed £320: Jeff was owed a lot more himself as an individual! Other creditors included David Capper, Nick Buchanan, Steven Hinchliffe, Andy Daykin, Phillip Webster, John Cooper, Jeff Radcliffe, Brian Little, Kevan Smith, the players, the FA, the Football League and the PFA. Lloyd's company, Bridgestate Developments of Godalming in Surrey, were owed £44,201.72 and then there were hotels, printers, agents, the police and other football clubs. Maybe it was all summed up by the fact that arrears of £335.25 were owed to the Mad Hatter, from Chacombe in Oxfordshire!

But a new buyer emerged after a creditors' agreement had been accepted. The administrators made no specific announcement at the meeting about the club's salvation, but it soon became clear that Leeds United's commercial director Adam Pearson had come to the rescue. Amid it all Brian Little deserved credit for conducting himself impeccably and skilfully, using his experience to keep the playing side ticking over to such an extent that the team won five games out of five to earn him the divisional manager-of-the-month award for February. Justin Whittle reflected: "We went for weeks without being paid and a few lads wondered whether or not the situation would change. It was worrying, especially with families to feed and mortgages to pay. It would have been easy to walk away, but I couldn't because I knew that I would be letting everyone down. The fans were great and Brian Little did a great job as manager because he was going through the same as we were." Amazingly City were undefeated in their final 11 League games and reached the play-offs for the only time in their history, losing to Leyton Orient in the semi-finals.

Little ensured an influx of new players during the summer of 2001 and City were among the Third Division leaders in 2001-02 after losing only one of their first 16 League games, but then the old inconsistency set in. And Adam Pearson gave a hint of how demanding and ambitious he was when he sacked Little towards the end of February 2002 even though the Tigers were still in contention for the play-offs. A trend had developed with City managers, in fact, although it went largely unnoticed. Stan Ternent, Warren Joyce and Brian Little had all worked wonders in their first seasons in charge, they had then gone out and signed plenty of fresh faces who failed to maintain the momentum and they had finally lost their jobs after less than two years in the City hot seat. I can never understand, though, why Stan was never popular with the fans even though he came into the same category as the others.

If Adam Pearson's attitude towards Little had been ruthless, then it was even more so towards his successor, former Denmark, Ajax and Liverpool hero Jan Molby. I knew Jan well because I had scouted for him for 15 months at Swansea during my journalistic ban and thought that it was a good appointment. Pearson seemed to think so, too, because he said: "I know we've got the right man." But only 12 matches into 2002-03 he was the wrong man because he, too, was sacked. Jan is a larger-than-life character who lives on the edge at times, but I thought that he had plenty of managerial assets. One was certainly his judgment and knowledge of players and his legacy to the club included Ian Ashbee, Stuart Green and Stuart Elliott, all of whom were to play key roles in the imminent re-emergence from the shadows. There were stories of dressing-room unrest, but Jan's sides had normally made slow starts. It happened at Swansea when he guided them into the play-offs and it happened at Kidderminster Harriers when he led them into the Football League. But he was not going to be given the time for it to happen with City.

I still believe that he left behind a decent squad for his successor, who turned out to be former England winger Peter Taylor. City immediately had two convincing wins - 3-0 at home to Rochdale and 4-1 at Torquay - so perhaps there was hope of turning things round with the minimum of fuss, but there was yet another batch of new players. Forty of them were used throughout the season, in fact, so it looked as if it were the first signs of "Tinker" Taylor. Adam Pearson had said that he had had to fire Molby because he needed impetus as the club prepared to leave Boothferry Park to move into a new stadium next to their old Anlaby Road home, but he did not get it for the entry of the gladiators. City were 18th when Molby left and were just 13th by the end of the season. Based on the treatment meted out to Molby, Taylor was perhaps lucky to have survived.

Attendances shot up, though, with more than 22,000 packed into the Kingston Communications Stadium for City's first League game there against Hartlepool United on Boxing Day 2002. And in one sense the wheel had pleasantly turned full circle. Ian Bell became a match-day steward for the Tigers in 2000, so it meant that he was on duty for the last game at Boothferry Park and the first one at the KC Stadium. His father Ernie, meanwhile, had played in the first game at Boothferry Park when he rejoined City after the 1939-45 War. But he was also one of the few players to have seen prewar action at the old Anlaby Road ground on the KC Stadium site, too.

The new stadium's name was unimaginative and unwieldy and was a sop to marketing values. I know that it could hardly be called Pearson Park because there already is one in Hull, but I wish, say, that the word "Circle" had been incorporated into the new name. But the change of venue modernised the club in effect, putting things on to a new financial plain although the genuine fans must never be treated mercenarily because of it. The Bells, in fact, knew all about the old ways in terms of money, too, because Ian said: "My dad became one of the top inspectors in the Inland Revenue, but he also had a part-time clerical job with City and used to count the money and receipts at home matches. The secretary Cyril Lee lived in the first house next to the car-park at Boothferry Park, but John Adamson didn't want to live there when he took over from him. But Cyril also had his own office at Boothferry Park, which was where they eventually put the players' lounge. As soon as the second half started, we'd go in there and count the money. I'd help out, but there might have been only between £2,000 and £3,000 in those days. They would bring it in in paper bags and we'd put the notes, silver and copper into a big blanket, but it still took counting. But my dad would help for about the first 20 minutes of the second half and then he'd sneak off to watch the game!" It serves as a reminder that it is not always progress in the money-orientated world of football if it veers away from its grass roots.

But new stadia invariably signal new outlooks and progress and City were finally to achieve it in football terms with successive promotions in 2003-04 and 2004-05. And plenty of financial backing was needed because the Tigers went up with 27 players in 2003-04 and 29 in 2004-05: the figures compare with 22 in 1948-49, 21 in 1958-59, 19 in 1965-66, 20 in 1982-83 and 21 in 1984-85 in the club's other postwar promotion seasons. They are odd statistics because successful teams generally use fewer players because there is less need for changes, but maybe they are just representative of the way in which the game has gone.

The first promotion was achieved at Yeovil on May 1, 2004 - on a nostalgic day for me because it turned out to be my mum's last birthday - after Taylor had brought in a strike partnership of Ben Burgess and Danny Allsopp, who produced the goods in the Third Division with some handy back-up from Stuart Elliott. The following season Elliott had a purple patch in mid-season with 14 goals in 11 League games before being injured and that probably more than anything tipped the promotion scales City's way. It is still 40 years since the Tigers won a title, though, because they finished up runners-up on both occasions in their back-to-back promotions.

Peter Taylor will rightly go down in the annals as one of City's most successful managers ever, but the football was effective rather than inspiring. But Taylor always seemed to be honest in his appraisal of performances and no-one can deny that he did the job that was required of him. But I found some aspects of his stewardship enigmatic: for example, there seemed to be a regular revolving-door of senior players, some of whom did not even last for a season with City, so why were they signed in the first place? For every excellent signing such as Damien Delaney, who has lasted the course admirably, there seemed to be plenty of others who did not. Neither could I understand the attitude to young players. If, for example, Scott Wiseman and Russell Fry were good enough to be selected by Taylor alongside Premiership players for England Under-20s, why could they not hold down regular spots in a Championship side? Paul Anderson was sold to Liverpool before he had the chance to show what he could achieve with the Tigers, so it must have been frustrating for youth coaches Billy Russell and Neil Mann at times. But there is always the premise that only the first team really matter because their results dictate the standing of the club and the management team.

During the summer of 2006, though, Taylor seemed hell-bent on leaving and initially he seemed to be close to joining Charlton Athletic. It led to a rift with Pearson, who was said to have toyed briefly with the idea of sacking him and it might have been understandable if he had. Soon afterwards Taylor went to Crystal Palace instead and finally sailed off into his southern sunset - which I always expected him to do anyway because I am afraid that I am cynical about southerners when they work up north. His assistant Colin Murphy survived, his coach Steve Butler left and a new management team of Phil Parkinson and Frank Barlow arrived. That hardly went smoothly because of negotiations with

Colchester United, whom Parkinson wanted to leave after guiding them into the Championship for the first time ever. Curiously, Barlow, who is a top-class football man, arrived as assistant manager - after City had reached an agreement with Nottingham Forest, where had finished the 2005-06 season as joint caretaker manager with ex-Tiger Ian "Charlie" McParland - before Parkinson arrived as No. 1. Parkinson had a local link to the extent that, as an apprentice at Southampton, he had been responsible for looking after ex-Tiger Steve Moran's boots. Frank, meanwhile, had once scored four second-half goals for top-of-the-table Sheffield United against City in a Northern Intermediate League game that they won 10-0 although he insisted: "I can't remember scoring four goals in any match!" But ex-Tiger Geoff Barker remembered him from his spell as manager of North Ferriby United because he said: "Frank used to run courses with coaching advice for non-League managers on Sunday mornings on Barnsley's training ground adjacent to Oakwell. I went over a few times when I was manager at Ferriby. They were very good sessions and extremely helpful." The signs were optimistic - Parkinson as the young, up-and-coming manager who had had success in a soccer backwater while learning his trade and Barlow as the older hand who had seen and done everything in the game and might be a perfect foil for him while he continued to gain experience in management.

There was a fair bit for them to sort out, though, and this is Hull City, so towards the end of October Frank was sacked as some kind of scapegoat and replaced by Phil Brown as the side slumped to the bottom of the Championship table, so maybe the roller-coaster ride is continuing. But Adam Pearson has at least produced the goods so far and seems single-minded in his desire to take the Tigers to the top. In fact, he has been a breath of fresh air after all the shenanigans of the 1990s and the ensuing false dawns. He has brought in good football people such as secretary Phil Hough, he is courteous enough to reply to correspondence and he has shown that he has a feel for City's soul because the relationship between the club and the Ex-Tigers' Association has improved out of all recognition since the days when we were viewed as a threat because we were involved in a past that at that stage compared a bit too favourably with the present. I might even get to like the KC Stadium as much as Boothferry Park! But I probably got off on the wrong foot at the new ground after the friendly against Sunderland that opened it in December 2002 when unbelievably I was haunted by the sight of a certain Martin Fish toddling out of the directors' room at the end of it. It was not his ghost - it was the real thing!

I have been following Hull City's fortunes for almost half their existence. They started with friendlies and FA Cup ties in 1904, I started in 1956 and we are all still searching for the Holy Grail of topflight English football in 2006. There is a temptation, though, to think that you are just watching new history in the making as you embark on your interest in a professional football club. I was no different from anyone else in that respect. What I did not realise initially, of course, was that everything that I have experienced in the past 50 years is basically an action replay of all the twists and turns of their roller-coaster ride. There was evidence fronm the early days of many of the hallmarks and characteristics of the club that I have encountered. It is a bit like Christmas TV - nothing is new and everything is a repeat! In 1999, in fact, City even had their own great escape!

There was controversy from the outset, for example. The grey-bearded figure of the Lord Mayor of Hull, Alderman William Jarman, a Liberal who had been born in Market Harborough in 1842, was technically the first person to kick a ball in a City match as they began with a friendly against Notts County at the Boulevard on September 1, 1904. It was five o'clock on a Thursday afternoon and Jarman went on to the pitch in his official chain of office to set the ball in motion. City led 1-0 at halftime thanks to a goal by George Rushton, who made it 2-0 before Arthur Green beat goalkeeper Jimmy Whitehouse from the penalty spot and Harry Mainman equalised for County near the end to leave it 2-2. But who exactly figured in the Tigers' line-up? The team were aged between 20 - Peter Howe and Fred Wolfe - and 30 - Fred Leiper. Whitehouse was the tallest at 5ft. 11½in., Harry Wilkinson was the smallest at 5ft. 7in., Leiper was the heaviest at 13st. 10lb. and William Martin was the lightest at 11st. 4lb., but there is a doubt about the identity of one of the wingers. Some sources say that Wilkinson played at outside-left with someone called McKiernan, who had had links with the then non-League Brighton and Hove Albion, on the right-wing. But there are official club histories which insist that Wilkinson wore No. 7 and that the left-winger was a mysterious player called Burke, who was aged 23, 5ft. 8in. and 13st. 2lb. and never featured again for the club. Neither for that matter did anyone called McKiernan.

Football in general was in a state of controversy by the time that City ventured into the League after being admitted to the Second Division for 1905-06 because a rift had developed between amateurs and professionals. The Corinthians' amateur attitude had shone through as far back as 1891, for example, when they objected to the introduction of the penalty kick on the grounds that no sportsman would incur such a punishment and that it was a slur on the good names of footballers in general! But the 1905-06 season was accepted as signifying the parting of the ways because the source of English football culture had been in the public schools and universities and yet it had started to shift towards the working masses. The professionals were gaining a stranglehold and creating a closed shop, leaving the amateurs to rebel resentfully against it. And the international between England and Wales in Cardiff in March 1906 was significant in terms of the transition because of its mixture of amateurs and professionals. And what did City do? The following month they decided to try to integrate left-winger Gordon Wright, one of the English amateurs from that game, with their professionals. It was contentious in theory, but luckily it worked well in practice.

City have always had heroes and Wright was arguably their first one after he had scored directly from a corner on his debut in a 4-0 win over West Bromwich Albion. He returned to become a regular from 1906-07, became captain and was eventually regarded as the Tigers' most influential player before the 1914-18 War. Wright had been born in Surrey in 1884, he had been educated at Ramsgate's St. Laurence School and Queen's College, Cambridge, where he was awarded Blues from 1904 to 1906, and he came to Hull to teach at Hymers College, where his specialist subjects were mathematics and football. City snapped him up because of a local link - his father William, who had attended Dublin's Trinity College, was then the vicar of North Ferriby. Club chairman Alwyn Smith had established the contact to pave the way for the arrival of Wright, who had signed a form a while before his League debut, but it was said: "City will be fortunate if they get him to assist them more often during the vacations next season, but this stylish forward has plenty of engagements to fulfil either for his college or the Corinthians." Wright had captained the Corinthians and happily adjusted to his professional teammates when he skippered City, saying: "They are good fellows and they play very hard." He was occasionally limited with City, though, because he had to teach on Saturday mornings. Ironically, one of his colleagues on Hymers' staff was an England rugby-union international Bill Cobby, whose father was also an East Riding vicar.

Hymers' official greeting went accordingly: "We welcome this term Mr. E. G. D. Wright, of Queen's College, Cambridge, as form-master of the Lower First. Mr. Wright, who is a Corinthian, an international and a Cambridge Blue, will have charge of school football." His methods seemed to pay off, too, because winger Thomas Allen, the school's football captain, said of him during his first season: "Although only a few matches have been played, the result of Mr. Wright's coaching is evident. Each member of the team seems to know his exact place on the field, so that but little bunching is seen and the game is played in a more scientific way. On the whole the style of football is a great improvement on that of last year and the best thanks of all are due to Mr. Wright, who has taken such a great interest and given everybody the benefit of his knowledge." And in 1907 James Soutter, the next football captain, continued: "Many thanks are due to Mr. Wright for the trouble and interest he has taken in improving school football. This season has been more successful than was at first anticipated: this is largely because of the keenness shown by the team and Mr. Wright's coaching." And when he left Hymers in 1909, it was reported: "Mr. E. G. D. Wright, form-master of 1B, did so much in the short time that he was with us to raise the standard of school football. He was an untiring and energetic coach and it was with regret that we took leave of him. A small presentation was made to him by the football teams and, in bidding us farewell and wishing us good luck, he begged us to remember what he had taught us and said that he was well-rewarded if he had done only a little good."

The significance of Wright's contribution to Hymers seems to have reflected the beneficial effect that he had on the Tigers during his stay with them as a player until 1913. When he left to take up a post as a mining engineer in South Africa, it was said of him: "His undoubted abilities and his excellent sportsmanship have made him one of the most popular players in the Second Division. He was a bona fide amateur and one of the type who refuse to make profit out of the game. He has always kept his expenses down to a low level and has absolutely refused to receive one cent more than the actual figure. The international has played purely for the love of the game and to assist the club." Wright had won only that one full cap for England, but he played in a further 20 games that were classified as amateur internationals. It means that he technically set the trend for a long line of players, including Raich Carter, Neil Franklin, Wilf Mannion, Jackie Sewell, Emlyn Hughes, Peter Barnes, Nicky Barmby and Danny Mills, to have played for City after their England careers had been over.

Those who became City's all-time revered heroes, though, found that the demands on them became great. Raich Carter, probably the greatest of them, found himself reading the lesson for Canon Thomas Tardrew in St. Mary's Church in Beverley the day after a record 55,019 fans had packed into Boothferry Park to see the Tigers lose 1-0 to Manchester United in the FA Cup quarter-finals in February 1949. And Raich later reflected: "I soon found that my role in Hull was not confined to that of a footballer and manager. I was a public figure asked to tour factories in order to give an added fillip to the production drive. Presenting prizes, opening fetes, attending charity and social functions, giving lectures, making speeches - all these became part of my daily routine. Hull was indeed a soccer-conscious city. I had never known anything like it anywhere."

And if there were early heroes such as Wright, City also had their big characters during the formative years, too. Perhaps the most outstanding one was the controversial Bill McCracken, who had joined Newcastle United from Belfast Distillery in 1904 as an international full-back with Northern Ireland, leaving behind an apprenticeship in the building trade. But he had gone on a 13-year one-man international strike in 1907 when he found that England's players had been paid 10 guineas a man for international duty and the Irish players had been awarded only £2 in comparison. McCracken became City's manager towards the end of 1922-23 and a lot of negotiations had to take place for the move to come to fruition. He won his final international cap after his 40th birthday against Scotland in March 1923 after having agreed to join City, but he also insisted that Newcastle should retain his playing registration to the end of the season so that he qualified for a third benefit. McCracken then persisted in using offside tactics with full-back George Goldsmith taking on the role of organising the trap on the pitch. He became known as "the Offside King," confusing opposing forwards by manoeuvring them into static positions and forcing a change in the laws by 1925 when it was decided that an attacker needed to have only two opponents between himself and the goal instead of three. His tactics meant that he was regularly barracked, but he insisted: "As I saw it, it meant that I was doing my job right. I'd have worried if the air hadn't been blue with four-letter words bandied about my name! I know we were criticised in some quarters for persisting with the offside game. But in my opinion it was justified with the playing strength we had. The trouble was that, under the amended laws, it was a less reliable tactic than in my playing days." And it was reported: "McCracken became one of the most heartily-detested players in soccer. But he argued that he was playing within the laws and that, if opposing forwards gave as much thought to their game as he did, they would not find themselves offside so often."

McCracken, who went on to guide the club to the FA Cup semi-finals and relegation in the same season in 1929-30, also won a power game with City's board, seizing control of team affairs from them because they had previously had their own selection committee. It further proved that he was a steely character, but at the end of 1930-31 he left after lengthy discussions with chairman John Barraclough. The players, though, presented him with an English crystal electric table lamp and skipper Matt Bell publicly said that he regretted his departure. McCracken's typical parting shot was: "The players have not always seen eye to eye with me in connection with some of the advice I endeavoured to give them, but it was always tendered with the best of motives and in the kindest of spirit. Doubtless they will realise the value of it more fully in the future." McCracken eventually lived in the Catford area of London and was 94 when he retired from scouting with Watford. He was still playing golf at the age of 92 and his grandson Bill said: "He could find the greens in regulation fashion, but unfortunately his eyesight was so bad that he needed seven or eight putts. But what a tremendous man he was - so full of energy!"

A lot of the time the directors must take the responsibility for City's ultimate failure to reach the top flight because they have always held reins of power with the exception of the occasions when the worst financial crises have left the solvency experts doing overtime instead. And some of the directors have been compelling characters from a range of backgrounds in their desire to be the harbingers of good times for the fans. There has been no greater entrepreneur than Don Robinson, who brought both flamboyancy and success, but some of the earlier directors also had their idiosyncracies.

Marcus Andrews, one of the club's founding fathers, was remarkable, for example, because he began his teaching career in Hull at the age of just 13! While still a schoolboy, he took a class at the city's Lambert Street School under supervision, but then he qualified at St. John's College in York for the profession that he was to follow for more than 50 years. He became assistant master at Hull's Northumberland Avenue School and then headmaster of two others in the city - St. Mark's-in-the-Groves and Clifton Street - until his retirement in 1943. Andrews, who lived latterly in Anlaby and died at the age of 69 in April 1948, was the president of both Hull Headmasters' Association and Hull Boys' Football Association and his intriguing hobby was marine modelling.

And if football is swamped with marketing people nowadays, then City can lay claim to having had one of them, Ernest Morison, on the board from the outset. He was born in Hull in 1868, privately educated and worked as an apprentice in the reporting department of the Hull News after a brief spell with the Post Office. In 1889 he published and edited the Hull and East Riding Athlete and four years later he founded Morison's Advertising Agency and produced Amusements, the recognised medium for entertainment information and only the second publication of its kind in the United Kingdom. From 1898 to 1902 Morison published and edited Publicity, then the second advertising magazine marketed in the United Kingdom. He also published the first Hull Corporation Telephone Directory and was a freeman of Hull. Morison, who also enjoyed swimming, hockey and cycling, was a City director for 15 years until his retirement as their vice-chairman in 1919 and was given the credit for concocting the nickname of the Tigers because of the team's colours of amber and black. Awarded an OBE, he later moved to London, where he was a member of the Constitutional Club. In 1923 he compiled the first bibliography of British advertising and was a lecturer from 1923 to 1930, during which he visited America. Morison also edited the club's programmes from their formation until 1914 when Harry Comley took over and later reflected: "I presented the bound volumes to City when they held a bazaar to raise funds, so I suppose that someone in Hull may have kept them. They had all the records of the club's trials and tribulations from the earliest years."

It also helped to be a doctor in City's early years. George Lilley, their first vice-chairman, had been born in Hull in May 1855 and studied to become a doctor at Middlesex Hospital in London. He lived and practised at Beaumont House in Hull's Williamson Street and was a prominent Conservative politician, becoming a member of Hull City Council for Drypool Ward in November 1900. Lilley was also interested in Poor Law work, he was a member of Sculcoates Board of Guardians from 1894 and he was a member of Hull and Goole Port Sanitary Authority. He was also a Druid, a Forester and a member of the Minerva Lodge of Freemasons and the Humber Chapter, so it is surreal to contemplate how he might have dressed for City's board meetings! Lilley, who also presented cups locally for football and cricket, died in July 1926 at the age of 71 after failing to recover from an appendix operation, but it is curious that his death coincided with the elevation of another doctor, Clifford Durham-Pullan, to the Tigers' chairmanship. Dr. Durham-Pullan was born at Farsley in West Yorkshire and died at his home in Hull's Anlaby Road in March 1937. He was a successful captain of Durham University's cricket team and also a keen athlete, but took his degrees at Edinburgh and Glasgow in 1917. He is believed to have come to Hull for the first time in 1921 and became City's surgeon, taking over as chairman in 1925. He stayed until the end of 1929-30 and was then elected vice-president.

And if the doctors failed, then Arthur Shepherd, who was a City director for 24 years and their chairman until reorganisation after the 1939-45 War, was always on hand because he was an undertaker who also provided wedding cars. It mean that advertisements to promote his work included the memorable line that he had "hearses and limousines" at his disposal! Shepherd, who was born in 1883 and died at his home in Hull's Bricknell Avenue at the age of 78 in August 1961, was also Lord Mayor in 1933 and a Rotarian. But he inadvertently picked up a bit of business in October 1936 when City's manager died! The Tigers were unbeaten in their first eight League games in 1936-37, but manager David Menzies missed the ninth - a 3-2 home win over Gateshead - because of a severe chill and the following day he died from a heart attack while sitting in a chair at his home, Driffield House, in Hull's Anlaby Road. A widower, he was with his only daughter Kathleen, a businesswoman in Leeds, at the time. It was still a shock because Menzies had indicated that he hoped to watch the reserves at Denaby during the week, but his immediate legacy was that City were by then the only unbeaten side in all four divisions. Menzies' funeral took place in Hull at Anlaby Road Presbyterian Church, where he had been a member, although his interment took place in Bradford, the other city with which he had a strong allegiance - at Shipley's Nab Wood cemetery. And Shepherd's family business, who were based in Hull's Brunswick Avenue, found that they were designated to look after the funeral arrangements.

On a brighter note in the 1930s Arnold Hibbert, who had a spell as City's vice-chairman, was the principal of Richards, Hibbert and Company from 1919 and became the chairman of the Yorkshire and North-East Division of the Corporation of Insurance Brokers. But he was also the chairman of Hull Amateur Operatic Society, a director of Hull's New Theatre and a founder director of the Little Theatre in the city. He had an actor son called Geoffrey, so presumably they were well-placed to recognise any play-acting on the pitch!

Another director, Alwyn Smith, proved early on that there was also an irony surrounding the many financial crises to colour the Tigers' history. Smith, who had soon taken over as City's chairman from William Gilyott as the club sought to establish themselves, came from a family who had been bankers in Nottingham dating back almost to medieval times. They were later first known in East Yorkshire as Russian merchants who operated under the name of Wilberforce and Smith, of High Street, Hull. In fact, the Wilberforce fortune from business was eventually inherited by one called William, the famed abolitionist of slavery, while his partner Abel Smith joined Thomas Thompson, from Ganstead, to form a major private bank at Wilberforce House in High Street. On Thompson's death in 1828 the company moved to Whitefriargate in Hull and became known as Samuel Smith Brothers and Company. At one stage Alwyn Smith was their manager and then joint manager of what became the Union of London and Smith's Bank Limited after a series of amalgamations. It might have been assumed that Smith's banking background would have helped to put the club on a firm financial footing, but a crisis ensued in February 1913 when he, vice-chairman Kenneth Wilson and secretary John Haller resigned after a board meeting.

They were duly praised for their efforts on behalf of the club, but all was not what it seemed and the situation became clearer the following month after the Tigers had beaten Grimsby Town 5-0 at home because they immediately sold centre-forward Stan Fazackerley to Sheffield United for £1,000. City obviously needed the money from the transfer because it was stated: "The club have not received the support that they should have done when it was most needed, so the deal will further help to improve the financial position at the end of the season. It is for financial reasons that Fazackerley has been allowed to depart. The club are likely to be £500 down on the season and there is also a summer wages bill of £1,000 to consider. The amount received for Fazackerley will clear off the adverse balance and help towards the summer wages." In fact, director and programme editor Ernest Morison later reflected: "I happened to be one of the original City directors when the popular custom from time to time was to have to make a whipround to pay the week's expenses." Curiously enough, Morison was promoting his advertising business in the programme with the slogan: "Morison's modern methods make money." Manager Ambrose Langley left soon afterwards and was replaced by the legendary Herbert Chapman's brother Harry, who was one of City's players and a student of anatomy, so presumably he could understand the board's body language!

Fazackerley's departure was also an early instance of City selling one of their better players - a trend that was to irk the fans periodically throughout the club's history. A more controversial example had occurred a little earlier in December 1911 with the £1,550 sale of popular centre-forward Tom "Boy" Browell to Everton. It brought an angry reaction from the supporters, who enraged the directors so much that the club issued a statement the following month: "Tom Browell's transfer fee was more than three times as large as any the club have ever received or given for a player. It was also £300 higher than any ever previously given by Everton. In explanation of the club directors' actions, they were in this instance actuated by the best motives and results to date have fully justified the parting with Tom Browell, one of the cleverest players the club have yet possessed. If other clubs come along with similarly-huge cheques, Hull City shall be tempted to part with other players whose places they may have confidence in being able to fill either from the reserves or from other quarters. Up to now no-one can say that the management have been bad judges of the right sort of material, so there is no reason why there should be any fears on this score in the future. The greatest fear is that section of the newspaper letter-writing public who rush into print on the slightest provocation and so completely lose their heads in farcical fashion because the team do not win every match they play. These 'ink-spillers' are not shareholders of the club, so their threats against the directors are absolutely worthless and they can have no voice whatever in the club's doings until they make the huge sacrifice of obtaining one or more 10-shilling shares." There was also a fascinating clause in the deal to sell Browell because it was agreed that "Everton should pay Hull City a visit next Hull Fair Day additional to the transfer fee." Sure enough, they turned up for a friendly in October 1912, drew a 10,000 crowd to Anlaby Road and won 7-4 even though Fazackerley hit a hat-trick for City.

It was still an early indication that City's fans might be volatile at times. There have been numerous examples of players being barracked throughout the club's history and one of the first to suffer was inside-forward Ronnie Starling, who had been called a football genius at the age of 16 when he was scoring goals for Washington Colliery. Manager Bill McCracken offered him a trial and was so impressed that he caught the first train back to the pit village in Durham to snap Starling up as an office boy at the club. The precocious Starling, who had been in his school team at the age of eight, then played as an amateur until turning professional on his 17th birthday in 1926. But his style of play did not always please the fans and he asked for a transfer, moving to Newcastle United for £4,000 - then City's second-best sale behind the £5,250 paid by Sunderland for Mick "Rubberneck" Gilhooley. Starling then led Sheffield Wednesday to success in the 1935 FA Cup final and was capped by England twice - once after he had moved on to Aston Villa. Even though he sought a move away from Anlaby Road, Starling enjoyed life at Anlaby Road and said: "I had some very happy years with Hull City. Bill McCracken signed me and he was a very good manager. He was a very honest man, very fair to everybody and he knew the game inside out." But full-back John "Jock" Gibson also spoke of the criticism received by Starling from the crowd, saying: "We used to tell him at halftime: 'Don't let them worry you! Forget them and just play your normal game!'"

Jimmy Lodge described Starling as "a good-living boy and yet a mixer and he was a grand player with ideas of his own." He was also one of the City's early hard men because he once played with a boil on his face and it burst when he took a knock. His teammates apparently reassured him that it was better than having it lanced! And Gibson, for his part, became another of City's regulars to be sold to balance the books in the early years when he also joined Sheffield United. He later recalled: "I was always happy at Hull. I did not want to leave, but they were short of cash and the £5,000 they got for me helped to keep them going." But he moved on condition that he could still live and train in Hull and the promise was kept until United's manager John Nicholson was killed while getting off a tramcar in Sheffield on his way to a game against Aston Villa. The Blades then wanted him to move from his home in Hull's Anlaby Park and he did do - only to Luton Town instead. And Gibson reflected: "Going to Sheffield United was one of the biggest mistakes of my life. If I had my time again, I would have come to Hull and stayed in Hull."

There were also early examples of trouble involving City's fans that underlined their mischievous natures. In January 1907 one fan at the FA Cup tie against Tottenham Hotspur was asked the time and took out his gold watch. Ten minutes later he looked at its chain to find that it was minus the watch! And there was bother at the end of City's 1-0 home defeat to Preston North End in April 1934 when fans pelted the referee with a mixture of orange peel and cushions. It resulted in the closure of Anlaby Road by the FA for 14 days although the Football League helped the club by allowing them to start 1934-35 with two away games.

There were also moments of controversy on the pitch in the early years. One of them occurred in 1928-29 when Ken McDonald had a purple patch with 22 goals in the first 22 League games, including all five at home to Bristol City. One of his goals was in a 1-1 draw at Middlesbrough in September 1928 when it was poetically written that "it was not a game to look back upon with fragrant memory." This time City's centre-half Arthur Childs, who was later a publican in Darlington and a steward at Whitley Bay Golf Club, was in trouble in the North-East when he was sent off in strange circumstances. There were 10 minutes left when Childs, who would also be dismissed in the Tigers' FA Cup semi-final against Arsenal the following season, tackled 'Boro's winger Willie Millar, who hugged his arm as he got up, noticed that it was bleeding profusely and found that he had suffered a nasty gash. The referee, whose name ironically was Hull, asked to see Childs' boots and sent him to the dressing-room to have a nail removed. But he would not let Childs back on to the pitch when he reappeared wearing a new pair of boots, so battling City finished the game with only nine fit men because Arthur Prince had been a limping passenger during the second half. City's manager Bill McCracken agreed that the referee was right, but pointed out: "Nails work through because of the present hard state of the ground. If the boots of all the players in both teams had been examined, it is quite likely that many nails would have been found to be protruding."

A lot of the controversy on the field, though, seemed to coincide with City's most enthralling FA Cup runs. Those of us who saw City's cupties against Chelsea in 1966 and Stoke City in 1971 can bear testimony to it, but they were only following a trend that had started with their first excursion into the competition in 1904-05. In the preliminary round they were drawn at home to Stockton, but the Boulevard was needed for rugby, so the Tigers ceded ground advantage. They, therefore, set off for Stockton by train at 8.35am for a 4pm kick-off and were soon 2-0 ahead. But Stockton led 3-2 by halftime and City's defensive approach annoyed the home fans even though the tie finished 3-3. The result was that the Tigers' party left the ground amid booing and jeering and had stones thrown at the open wagonette that they also used. It naturally meant another away tie for the replay, which City lost 4-1, and goalkeeper Jimmy Whitehouse had seemingly threatened to take a gun to it. Then there was a controversial exit in 1910-11 when it was claimed that one of Newcastle United's goals in their 3-2 win in a third-round tie should have been disallowed for offside and that was followed in 1914-15 by a 4-2 defeat at Bolton, who were said to have been awarded two dubious penalties to rob City of a possible chance of reaching the semi-finals for the first time.

In 1929-30 the Tigers were eight minutes from Wembley on a sunny afternoon at Elland Road, Leeds, when they were 2-1 up in their semi-final against one of Arsenal's greatest sides, including Alex James, David Jack, Eddie Hapgood and Cliff "Boy" Bastin. But the Gunners, whose forward-line were known as "the £30,000 attack," had been 2-0 down at halftime and needed a late equaliser by Bastin, who went on to become the youngest FA Cup finalist, to force a replay at Villa Park. David Jack, who had been the first goalscorer at Wembley while with Bolton Wanderers, scored the only goal of the replay, but it was claimed that the ball had gone out of play in the build-up to it and City's Bert "Paddy" Mills said: "As we were running off the field, the referee said: 'Never mind, Paddy, there are two good teams in the final!' I'd never heard anything like it, so I reported it to the manager Bill McCracken when we got back to the dressing-room. He asked if I were sure about what the referee had said and, if so, whether I would repeat it in front of the directors and the FA. I said I'd tell it to anybody and in the end they suspended the referee for life." There was another controversy, too, as Ronnie Starling mentioned: "There was a lot of excitement when we beat Newcastle United in the sixth round and then met Arsenal. But in the replay Arthur Childs was ordered off, so we finished with 10 men and lost to a late goal."

It was the same kind of story in 1948-49 when City played in seven FA Cup ties - as was the case in 1929-30 and 1965-66. The Tigers were full of confidence for their quarter-final at home to holders Manchester United after beating First Division opposition Stoke City 2-0 at the Victoria Ground with goals by Norman Moore and Jimmy Greenhalgh. That fifth-round triumph became viewed as the highlight of the run because City then lost 1-0 to United when it was claimed that the ball had again gone out of play in the move leading up to the goal. Defender Tom Berry recalled the two ties: "A lot of people from my Air Force days came from the Stoke area, so they were at the match. I can remember that it was a very, very good game and it wasn't a fluke result. I think we played very well that day and weren't lucky at all. We deserved to win and, in fact, I think it was our best win of the season. Norman was one of the best headers of a ball I've known and I can still remember Jimmy's goal because he bundled the ball into the net and then fell over. He was a good player and one of the funniest blokes I ever met. We didn't think we had a cat in hell's chance, but we won and the feeling was marvellous. But then we lost to Manchester United and I thought that we were a shade unlucky." Centre-half Harold Meens added: "We used to play for one another and, if a player was having an off-day, then we would do our best to keep the ball away from him. Our defensive record was the best that City ever had because we had only 28 goals scored against us in a full League season. I was really proud to be a member of that particular side. I think that the most thrilling game of my career was at Stoke when they had a few internationals in their side, including Neil Franklin. The Manchester United cuptie was most disappointing because we were beaten by a debatable goal. A lot of people said that the ball was over the line when Jimmy Delaney crossed it for Stan Pearson to put it in. I couldn't see, but Allan Mellor, who was tackling Delaney, said that it was definitely over." And Andy Davidson said: "Jimmy Delaney was one of my heroes, but they said that four of our players were turning away because the ball had gone out. Then they found that a goal had been given."

There has, therefore, always been a suggestion lurking in the background that City's hopes of reaching the top have been stifled by nothing more than plain and simple bad luck. Their previous ground at Anlaby Road, for example, suffered from its own roller-coaster ride, which may have been predictable simply because it was so close to the site of Hull Fair! The roof of a stand blew off in a 3-0 defeat against Leeds City in January 1916 and bomb damage destroyed part of it during the 1939-45 War so that it was reckoned that it would take £1,000 to repair it, forcing City to end their lease in 1943. But the omens had been there in more spectacular fashion with the club's own form of uprising during Easter 1914 because things took a turn for the worse after they had lost three games - one against Wolverhampton Wanderers and two against Bury - during the holiday period to dash their promotion push from the Second Division.

They lost 1-0 at home to Bury on Easter Monday and then lost a 3,000-capacity stand because it was reported: "After three consecutive defeats at Easter Hull City's cup of sorrow was filled to the brim by the destruction of the grandstand by fire. Sympathy must be expressed with the hard-working club officials who have had such a heart-breaking termination to the season's working. Incendiarism is suspected, but the loss is covered by insurance. Some people believe that the suffragettes were responsible, but there are no apparent indications that they have been at work. In less than half an hour the stand was a mass of flames, giving out a heat which it was impossible to approach within 40 yards. Everything seemed safe after the crowd had departed and the groundsman had locked up the place following the usual look-round. It was just on midnight when the sky was suddenly illuminated by the flames, which shot up in the darkness and could be seen for several miles. The entrance to the City ground is a rather tenuous one, but the fire brigade took a short cut, playing havoc with cricket pitches that will bring tears to the eyes of their owners."

At 11.55pm a policeman noticed the fire and four vehicles - three steamers and a chemical engine - were sent to the scene. One of the directors thought that the workhouse was on fire and it was stated: "At the north end of the ground there was stabling for a couple of horses used in keeping it in order, but they were got out safely before the flames reached the end of the stand. The safe was reduced to fragments, which were later discovered amid the charred wood and iron. A number of people ran over the county-cricket pitch in their hurry to get to the fire and a good deal of damage was done because it was on the soft side. Hundreds of holidaymakers were provided with something better than a firework display as a wind-up to the day's enjoyment." It was impossible to save the west stand, which extended from the cricket-ground entrance to the north-stand end, a portion of which was also involved. Iron stanchions were melted and twisted and then fell, causing the corrugated roof to come down in sections with a series of crashes. The flames also charred a section of the railings surrounding the cricket circle.

One first-team game, one reserve game and several charity matches still had to be played and chairman James Spring said: "Our collection included the first sixpence taken at the turnstiles and we had a fine series of framed photographs of the team from the commencement. Several mascots sent along to the club, including one presented by the Hull Forge, were also devoured. We are covered by insurance and the re-erecting of a new stand will be considered at an early meeting of the directors. The oil stove in the directors' room had nothing to do with it because it was out hours before the fire. We shall have to manage without the best stand. We shall be able to clear the debris off the ground and erect some railings. It's a difficult job, but we shall get over it. We have lost absolutely all our books and records, which had been removed to the offices, and this will make it very awkward for us. We thought our important documents would be safe in the safe." It probably served as a severe warning to the club, though, because the amazing postscript to it all was that in the corresponding game between the two clubs in 1921 City's goalscorer was called Flood. If Martin Peters was supposed to have been 10 years ahead of his time, then Charlie Flood must have been seven years behind it in City parlance!

Misfortunes also hindered the backroom staff at times, too. Ernest Morison moved to Finchley in North London after leaving City as a director, but he was back in attendance for the club's first FA Cup semi-final against Arsenal at Elland Road, Leeds, in March 1930. But he recalled: "On that thrilling day I never saw one of the four goals scored, which were all at the same end, from my seat in the stand because of the heavy pillars where I was unlucky enough to be!" And then there was the case of Archibald Dixon, who had been born in East Hull in 1900, joined City as their part-time financial secretary and served them for 22 years until 1944. In local politics he became the vice-president of East Hull Conservative Association at the age of 25 and joined Hull City Council in 1950, representing Sutton Ward and becoming the leader of the Tory group. Dixon, who died in February 1983, became an alderman in 1968 and an honorary alderman six years later, but perhaps his political career mirrored City's perennial fortunes in terms of being so near and yet so far. In 1971 he was nominated for Lord Mayor, but then missed out when the balance of power switched from the Tories to Labour!

Then there was the sequel to the departure of Haydn Green, the first manager to guide City to promotion, in March 1934. Green, who resigned at a board meeting, had brought in a lot of good players, such as Jack Hill, Tom Gardner, Russell Wainscoat, Bill McNaughton, Stan Denby, Cliff Hubbard, Charlie Sargeant and John Quantick. In fact, McNaughton still holds the club record of scoring 41 League goals in a season in the side who won the Third Division North title under Green in 1932-33. The club announced that they would advertise for Green's successor, the directors duly met the candidates at their offices in Hull's Lowgate and then made an appointment from within the ranks by choosing the club's captain Jack Hill, who had been one of the applicants. Chairman John Barraclough said: "The directors have gone into the appointment of a new team manager very carefully and earnestly. There were many applicants for the position and their merits received every consideration, but the selection of the popular captain of the team was the unanimous decision of the board. We felt that he was not only qualified for the post by the length and nature of his wide experience in the game, but also because he has been in close touch with the club's present players. This knowledge will be very helpful to him in the attempt to carry the club into the First Division." But Hill might have been forgiven for wondering if Lady Luck was really going to smile on him because he was given the job in April - on Friday the 13th!

The proof of it all then came in 1935-36 when City changed their colours from the traditional amber and black. The new colours were kept back to the opening League game of the season at home to Fulham when it was reported: "City turned out in the club's new colours of ultra-marine shirts with white collars and cuffs. They wore white knickers and blue-and-white striped hose. On the breast of the shirt was the coat of arms of Hull - three crowns - and the whole attire presented a smart appearance." But Hill resigned in January 1936 after the colours had led to one of the worst seasons in the club's history as City finished bottom of the Second Division with only five wins to their name.

And there was an example of misfortune for Hull-born forward Ernie Bell during the summer of 1938 when the moral climate of the day meant that he had to leave the Tigers to join Mansfield Town. His son Ian explained: "My dad was picked up as a 17-year-old schoolboy by the club because he had played for Blundell Street Boys, who won everything in the city for years, and one of his teammates was Solly Waxman, who went on to play for Hull Kingston Rovers. But my dad had to leave City to join Mansfield because of his father, Ernie senior. He was a professional trumpeter, but he was a bit naughty and my dad was told that they couldn't afford any kind of scandal associated with the club. Apparently they'd turned down a bid for him from Tottenham Hotspur, but he ended up at Mansfield." Ernie senior played with Cyril Stapleton's band, the Mudlarks and Lonnie Donegan, but Ian added: "My dad was the eldest of four with Joe, Winnie and Norah and in the end he had to bring up the whole family on his football wages, so he never spoke about his father. Winnie, who was a dancer in pantomimes, married Dai Davies, who was also a City player."

It may also be counted as bad luck when a club reserve one of their most prestigious performances for an occasion when it did not really matter. But Andy Davidson feels that that was just what the Tigers did in October 1955 when they met Hungarian side Vasas, who were touring England, at Boothferry Park in a friendly. Andy said: "We were right down on our luck and yet we had one of our greatest victories. Vasas had played Sheffield Wednesday and whipped them 7-1. Wolves should also have played them, but they had to back out and there was an uproar when we were given the game because we were at the foot of the Second Division. We had taken only three points from 12 games while Wednesday were at the top. The Press slammed the match on the grounds that we had no chance and that British football would be a laughing-stock after the certain slaughter. The powers-that-be were implored to call the game off and to find better opposition for Vasas. Even many of our own fans were against the match, but the lads, stung by all the criticism, played like heroes, beat Vasas 3-1 and Bill Bradbury, who had just joined us from Birmingham City, got a hat-trick. To be fair, we outplayed them and the win was no fluke. And it tasted all the sweeter because we upheld British soccer prestige."

There has never been a shortage of good human-interest stories surrounding City and in the early years the most touching of them arguably concerned those who served during two world wars. Some of the directors were even heavily involved in the 1914-18 War. In September 1914, for example, Ernest Morison obtained a commission in the 12th Battalion of the East Yorkshire Regiment, serving in Egypt and France until 1918, reaching the rank of captain and twice being mentioned in dispatches. And Arthur Shepherd, a guardsman, fought at the Battle of Loos during the autumn of 1915, but was then invalided out of the Army in 1917. As a result, he became a champion for the welfare of ex-servicemen and was the secretary of the local branch of the National Federation of Discharged Soldiers and Sailors, who nominated him for Beverley Ward on Hull City Council in a four-cornered by-election in 1918. It was the only time when he had to fight an election in 30 years on the council and in 1930 he became an alderman for Marfleet Ward. In 1932 he became an honorary life member of the British Legion and he was also a member of Sculcoates Board of Guardians for nine years.

City even had a major as a manager - Franklin Buckley, who was said to have been a offered a contract worth a then astronomical £5,000 a year when he took over in May 1946. Buckley, who was born in the Urmston area of Manchester in November 1982, played for Aston Villa, Brighton and Hove Albion, Manchester United, Manchester City, Birmingham City, Derby County and Bradford City before injuries during the 1914-18 War ended his career. As an officer of field rank, he commanded the noted Footballers' Battalion of the Middlesex Regiment, but was severely wounded at the Battle of the Somme in 1916 and some of the shrapnel remained lodged in his lungs for the rest of his life. The long-serving Jimmy Lodge, who joined the Tigers as a full-back in 1919, served as a lance-corporal with the 50th Division (Signals) of the Royal Engineers. He was also wounded at the Somme and awarded the Military Medal for bravery in action. He recovered from his wounds and returned to active service during which he was awarded a Bar to his medal for further bravery at Ypres, also serving at Arras, Passchendale, Langemarck and High Wood. Jimmy then received two further awards for action "beyond the call of duty." He was awarded the Distinguished Conduct Medal at Le Cateau and received a Bar for further gallantry in the Mormal Forest. For his troubles he received a bullet in the shoulder and a piece of shrapnel in the elbow.

Augustus Smith, who scored 17 goals in 34 games as an inside-forward in City's first season of 1904-05, actually managed to turn the 1914-18 War to his advantage. He did not stay to play League football with the Tigers, but moved instead to Goole Town and played for them against the visiting 18th Hussars, who persuaded him to enlist and become an Army footballer. But he was captured during the 1914-18 War and remained a prisoner for four years, spending part of the time in Holland. He then obtained his Army discharge and was awarded a pension, but chose to stay in Holland, became involved in football again in the Hague and then received "a good inducement" to coach a team in Rotterdam, who were then regarded as one of the best in the country.

City players faced the same kind of situations during the 1939-45 War and at least three of them - Denis Durham, Joe Robinson and Ernie Bell - were known to have been among the troops at Dunkirk. Robinson had been a dispatch rider with the Northumberland Fusiliers when he was captured at Dunkirk. He was a prisoner of war for 5½ years had weighed 13st 4lb. when he joined up. But he was 9st. 6lb. when he left the Army. Private Ernie Bell was listed as missing in June 1940 and became an orderly in a hospital ward. His son Ian said: "My dad was in the Royal Army Medical Corps, so he didn't have a gun and was captured at Dunkirk and marched through Germany for two weeks. Some of the prisoners were given poisoned water and apparently my dad was not much more than skin and bone for a while. He was in a prisoner-of-war camp near the Polish border for about 4½ years. After about two years he was called into the commandant's office and he thought he was going to be taken out and shot. Instead they were rounding up all the professional footballers to get them fit. Then they played in international games with countries such as England, Wales, Scotland, Ireland, Poland and Russia and it provided the idea for the film 'Escape to Victory' even though they glamorised it by bringing in people such as Sylvester Stallone and Michael Caine. But the gist of the story is what happened to my dad - except that there was no escape plan in real life! But I think that my dad was just about the only non-international in the England team because people such as 'Dixie' Dean, Cliff Britton, Joe Mercer and Stanley Matthews were with him. My dad and 'Dixie' Dean became good drinking friends, while Cliff Britton never had a drink and never swore and yet everybody had the absolute respect for him because he was such a lovely bloke."

Ernie Bell and centre-half Harold Meens, two of the few City players to be with the club both before and after the 1939-45 War, had both been in the Royal Army Medical Corps. Curiously, Ernie Blackburn, their manager when the war broke out, had served in the Royal Army Medical Corps in France for four years during the 1914-18 War. Born in Rawtenstall, he at one time lived only a few doors away from the chairman of the Football League and FA vice-president Charles Sutcliffe, but he was never given a chance of his own when the club were restructured at the end of the conflict. The two world wars, in fact, destroyed football careers when players in particular might have been at their peaks. Ernie Bell's son Ian said: "My dad didn't really speak about the War years for a long time, but he wasn't a bitter man even though he lost some of his best playing years to it." Ernie's brother-in-law Dai Davies took it a stage further when he reflected: "I think I would have been capped by Wales if it hadn't been for the War." And many playing careers were put on hold after the 1939-45 War because of National Service and goalkeeper Bernard Fisher was probably able to sum up best the futility created by a mixture of politics and sport when he was suddenly called up because of the Suez crisis: "I was recalled to the regiment during the autumn of 1956, playing a few games before sailing to Port Said in Egypt, where out troopship ran aground with 3,000 of us on board. It took two days to move the ship and get the troops off it, so what a target we would have been if Egypt had had an air force! The whole Suez conflict was a fiasco."

The toughness of the times in comparison with the glamorous lifestyles of many 21st-century footballers was epitomised by George Lax, City's trainer after the end of the 1939-45 War. He said: "A professional footballer must make a whole-time job of keeping fit. There's no way out of it if you want to stay in the game and make a success of it. But I can recommend it. I was a miner's son and football gave me my chance to see the world outside the pithead. I enjoyed football after the War when the population were hungry for football and there were not even sufficient shirts for the players."

Dai Davies, a record-breaker for City because he scored the final goal when they beat Carlisle United 11-1 at home in January 1939 for their biggest-ever League win, came from the pits of the Rhondda Valley as an 18-year-old who was playing junior soccer for Aberaman. But he was soon grateful for the escape route that moving to Anlaby Road and then Boothferry Park had given him: "I signed for City just before my 19th birthday. I thought I'd got to Land's End when I first came to Hull because I'd never been out of Wales before. It broke my heart when I first came, but my major problem was that people couldn't understand me! But there were many scouts after me when I played and I wouldn't go because the people in Hull were always good to me. I always got a cheer from Bunker's Hill and in the end I never regretted coming to Hull."

Harold Meens had served in Iraq and Germany as a nursing orderly during the 1939-45 War, so he told City that he was interested in becoming a masseur as injury threatened to end his playing career. Meens had done some coaching and scouting for the club, but was told that he would be given a backroom job if he gained his qualifications for a place on the backroom staff. Accordingly, he took a correspondence course, paid for it out of his own pocket, brushed up on it at Leatherhead and qualified. He was then told that he was not being retained and later admitted: "It was a big disappointment to me then." Meens then qualified as a physiotherapist and went into business with George Lax, a trained chiropodist. But the venture lasted only six weeks before Lax moved back to Ireland and Meens' only means of moving back to City was to become a steward in the North Stand at Boothferry Park during the 1980s.

And if anything clearly demonstrated the roller-coaster ride of the fortunes that followed City folk, then it was probably the transition from 1938 to 1939 on the field. The Tigers finished 1938 with two heavy away defeats - 6-1 at New Brighton and 6-2 at Bradford City. But their response was to start 1939 with that 11-1 win over Carlisle United and they had six goalscorers - Bill Dickinson with a hat-trick, Arthur Cunliffe, Cliff Hubbard and Dai Davies with two apiece, Charlie Robinson and George Richardson. But the feelings of anti-climax and disappointment for City fans are rooted in the events of April 1910 when they needed only a draw to clinch promotion to the First Division in their final game at Oldham Athletic. But there was a sloping quagmire of a pitch, some rough skirmishes and a 3-0 defeat for the Tigers that left him in third place in the Second Division table. Oldham went up with Manchester City instead and, to make matters worse, one of their goals was scored by Alf Toward, who had left City only the previous December. It is of little consolation nearly a century later that it remains City's best season because it has left a painful legacy for generations of players, officials and fans ever since. There was even a chance that the Tigers might still have gone up by default because Woolwich Arsenal were threatened with closure because of financial problems, but they survived after a crisis meeting at London's Imperial Hotel the following month. City, in fact, were regularly among the Second Division's elite in those days because they had finished fourth a year earlier when a local supporter of both rugby and soccer was recorded as saying: "If they are not careful, they will find themselves in the First Division." We are still waiting.

There is an art in the way in which criticism is expressed. If it is constructive and not personally abusive, then most players will accept it. They might not like it, of course, but they acknowledge that it is part and parcel of the game and I believe that the crux of the matter is not so much what you say or write but how you do it But some aspects of the media are now very destructive and I have always tended to keep the way in which views are put forward in many so-called fanzines at a discreet distance. I have read fanzines in which some of the criticism is so barbed that it borders on the libellous and is irresponsible rather than clever. At all levels of the game, though, there is a dark humour that may be amusing or irritating depending on the circumstances.

I suppose, for example, that players have been derogatively termed as comedians at times. But in one case it could have been legitimately applied to a Hull City player because one of the top music-hall comedians of all time, George Robey, once wore their colours. Known as the Prime Minister of Mirth, his real name was George Wade and he was born in London in September 1869. He studied in Dresden, he once took a clerical post with a tramway construction company in Birmingham, he also lived in Birkenhead for a while and he attended Cambridge University. But it was stated: "Boredom with office routine led him to take up football - a game at which he excelled - and to sing comic songs with fellow amateurs at smoking concerts and charity shows. He changed his name and sported a soutane, bowler hat, bald wig, red nose and blacked eyebrows. As a young man, Robey was a considerable footballer and he even turned out for professional sides." In fact, he had spells on the books of Millwall, Chelsea and Fulham in the early 1900s and played his last game alongside the noted Charles Buchan at the age of 52. He was also a sprinter, played tennis and practised cricket at Lord's, becoming a close friend of luminaries such as Pelham Warner, Charles Fry, Archie MacLaren and Kumar Ranjitsinhji.

It seems that Robey would try to involve himself in some kind of sport - often for charity events - in many of the towns and cities in which he appeared on tour. On one such occasion he was appearing in Hull although many of the details are sketchy. One report, for example, said that he played in goal in a game for the Tigers, but it seems more likely he appeared at inside-forward. The time is also unclear, but it seems to have been close to the club's formation in early September 1904. Apparently Robey's original plan was to support the former Gloucestershire wicketkeeper Harry Wrathall's benefit match. Wrathall was then Hull Cricket Club's coach, so Robey turned up at the Circle to help him out, but it rained and the game never got under way. But it was the time of the year when the football and cricket seasons were overlapping, so Robey was met by a deputation of officials from City at the pavilion. They asked him to sign an amateur form for the club and the story goes that he duly turned out in a reserve game for them against Nottingham Forest that same afternoon.

There are other genuine City links with comedy talent, too. Venn Tracey is an excellent Oldham-based comedian on the after-dinner circuit and has appeared at Ex-Tigers' functions, but he has an even closer connection with the club because his brother is popular forward Doug Clarke, a member of the 1958-59 promotion team. And then there was the time when someone called Bob Davis technically wore City's amber and black when he was a director of Birmingham City and better-known as comedian and musician Jasper Carrott.

I had known Jasper well for about 10 years from his folk-club days when his act included nearly as much music as humour and in the early 1980s he was appearing at Hull's New Theatre for two nights during one weekend. Two days before his arrival on the Saturday I received a telephone call at the Hull Daily Mail offices from his tour manager, Les Ward, who said: "Jasper's staying at the Grange Park Hotel in Willerby while he's appearing in Hull and he's asked me to ring you to find out if there's a football match he can play in while he's in the area." It would have been difficult to register him for, say, a Hull Sunday League game and I suspected that he wanted something a touch less rigorous and more light-hearted anyway. I spoke, therefore, to my colleague Malcolm Richardson, who in turn contacted Jeff Barmby, the chairman of the Ex-Tigers' Association. Jeff then spoke to ex-Tiger Dave Fraser, who was a warder at Everthorpe Borstal at that time and between them they superbly managed to conjure up a game for Jasper.

It was a question of what was the most expedient at such short notice, so plans for a game between the Ex-Tigers and an Everthorpe XI with players from the surrounding villages were hastily put in motion. I then had to tell Jasper what was happening and I caught up with him while he was having a salad in the New Theatre's bar. I said: "I don't know how to put this, Jasper, but we do have a match for you to play in on Sunday morning. That's the good news, but the bad news is that it's taking place at a borstal!" He looked up from his meal, stopped eating and gave me his knife. "Take this, Bondy, go over there in the corner and cut your throat, will you?" he indicated. I offered him a fuller explanation, he readily accepted it, he started eating again and my life was duly spared! I met him on the Sunday morning at the Grange Park and we went off to Everthorpe, where a good time was had by all - except perhaps Jasper, who missed a penalty for the Ex-Tigers! He did, though, wear City's colours and also provided a hilarious, off-the-cuff lunchtime cabaret afterwards when he was asked to draw the raffle in the clubhouse for some fund-raising.

All in all, a sense of humour is paramount for a journalist and for anyone working closely with a professional football club. As a sports journalist, it is essential to laugh now and then in order to retain some kind of basic sanity when the pressure of deadlines creep closer. It is particularly scary during games when you have to communicate your words to your office. When I started out with the Hull Daily Mail, there were no mobile telephones or lap-tops. It was a time of land-line telephones and typewriters - and not much more. It meant that your reports and the means of conveying them left everything in the humble hands of fate at times. When doing match reports for the Sports Mail, you used to spend 90 minutes trying to do three things at the same time - watching events on the pitch, making notes about them and dictating them by telephone to a copy-taker back at the office. The outcome was that time passed incredibly quickly and even the drabbest of goalless draws never seemed to drag.

But it was always essential to make sure that I had a telephone link with the office that suited my needs. I would have to ring my reports for the Sports Mail through in various stages with introductions before the kick-offs, running copy on the major incidents as they happened during play and quickly-assembled, analytical summaries on the final whistle. It did not help much, therefore, when there were the inevitable gremlins and they inevitably arose on the away trips.

I could never understand, for example, why the telephone lines seemed clearer from Plymouth - the furthest that City could travel for an away League game - than they were from just across the Pennines in Lancashire. Maybe it helped that City always seemed to do well at Home Park and badly in Lancashire. City lost 5-1 at Bolton Wanderers' old Burnden Park ground in September 1976 when it poured with rain incessantly and the prevailing wind was driving it relentlessly towards the open Press-box. The line was bad enough, but I kept having to duck down at regular intervals to avoid the next sweep of wind and rain that soaked everything, including my suit and the telephone. I think it must have been a year later when I was telephoning my end-of-match summary through after City had battled to a draw at Burnley. An irate Burnley fan approached the open Press-box and kept rocking backwards and forwards on the bench at which I was sitting before starting to bang on the desk. The gist of his loud and garbled message was: "We want the truth. This is the worst Burnley side I've seen for years. What are you going to do about it?" The reply went: "Nothing, pal, because I'm from Hull and I'd be grateful you'd shut up, go away and let me get on with the last bit of my report because I'm right on edition time!" He left slightly more quietly, but in a slightly worse mood.

And even though everything was reasonably satisfactory at Plymouth, it was far from the case just down the road at Exeter. I have visited St. James' Park only once and that was just about enough. They had a Press-box that seated three people and an alternative of sitting at a table further down the stand and filing reports by the light of candles. And the candles seemed to go out whenever a train roared past at the back of the ground.

I rarely relished trips to London, where my telephone experiences were sometimes far from capital. I was once waiting in the Press-room at Leyton Orient for a representative from an agency providing a telephone for me to arrive. Time was pressing because I needed to telephone the teams and my introduction before the kick-off and there was no sign of anyone. The agency representative finally arrived and said that he would search for the telephone immediately. "Don't you know where it is?" I asked. He replied: "Yes, it's locked in a box, but there's a problem. I don't know the combination number to unlock the box. Hang on while I see if I can remember it..." He eventually unlocked it after a period of trial and error that left me rushing to ring through my preview just as the game started. On a trip to Charlton Athletic it proved to be equally as frustrating in the same kind of circumstances. It was the same agency, a different representative and another telephone problem. Time was again of the essence as the kick-off drew ever closer and I was mortified to be told that the telephone I was to use did not appear to be working. "But don't worry!" said the agency representative as he proceeded to try gain entry to the mechanics of the instrument by prising open the bottom with a pair of scissors. His obvious lack of technical know-how meant that arrangements had to be made hastily for me to use another telephone and again the game was under way as I started to preview it. A trip to Brentford also proved to be difficult. It was the same agency, a different representative and another dodgy telephone. "We have a problem," he told me. I told myself that I had a problem with London in general. He continued: "The telephone appears to be working perfectly well from its connection in the Press-room, but not at all from its connection in the Press-box. I suppose that doesn't help you." I pointed out that I could hardly cover the game from the Press-room under the stand just because that seemed to be only place from which my telephone worked properly. His solution was to ask me to share a telephone with someone else who also needed to use it much of the time that the game was in progress. Somehow we both survived with difficulty.

I do prefer the north to the south as a matter of Yorkshire principle, but one afternoon at Sheffield United in 1989 left me frustrated. I was just about to sum up City's brave display quickly at the end of the game when I could hear the distant ringing sound of a bell. I soon realised that it was at the other end of my telephone line and my worst fears were confirmed when my copytaker informed me: "The fire alarm's gone off here at the Mail. We're all being evacuated as a matter of procedure. There's no point in hanging on. Bye for now!" The report on the match was later than any of the tackles in it that evening!

I may be heathily wary of modern technology, but I do not doubt its value after such escapades. I look back and wonder how the reports ever arrived at their destination remotely intact. In fact, I have to smile about it or it would be time for the men in white coats to come and take me away. Fortunately, the system, was basically acceptable half the time - because those were the home games at Boothferry Park, whose Press-box was spacious, enclosed, central and placed at a good vantage point. You had to endure the folk who masked your view of the game as they clambered around in the directors' box below you after arriving back late for the start of a second half. They objected if you politely tapped on the Press-box window to them in the hope that they would sit down quickly, but my hardline view was: "If you've come to a football match, then watch it! If you want to socialise on a Saturday afternoon, go elsewhere! And if you don't like my attitude, then I'll willingly come round to where you work and prevent you from getting on with the job properly!"

On another ocassion the respected cartoonist Ern Shaw, who was responsible for many memorable drawings of City interest in their early history, slipped and fell as he entered the Press-box at Boothferry Park from the back of it. He split his head open, there was blood everywhere - most of it seemed to drop on to my colleague Mike Ackroyd's best sports jacket - and he could not be moved, so we called for an ambulance. There was then the unedifying spectacle of paramedics trying to fit a stretcher into the Press-box so that poor Ern could be taken away for treatment. The whole exercise had the hallmarks of an Eric Sykes silent comedy and somehow I was constantly dictating my report on the telephone amid the din and disquiet.

The only other problem that I encountered at Boothferry Park caused much merriment among my colleagues. It happened more than once in the build-up to my journalistic ban from the ground in 1995. The hospitality for the media at the KC Stadium nowadays is top-notch, but in those days you might get just a set of plastic cups and an urn with tea in it. It was well-known that I was the only regular inhabitant of the Press-box who could not survive without having plenty of sugar in his tea to sustain him. The sugar was supplied in a separate plastic cup and there were occasions when I put my two spoonfuls in my tea, stirred them in vigorously and took a sip to find that we had been given salt instead of sugar. I have often wondered whether the regime were trying to poison me instead of ban me!

While submitting my reports in often difficult circumstances, I was lucky to have some excellent copytakers at the other end, including freelance journalist Tony Fairhurst and deputy editor Peter Moore's sister-in-law Geraldine. Telephone lines were normally crackly and a catchphrase emerged between Tony and me. One of us would bawl down the line: "Can you hear me because I can hear you?" And the other would probably shout the same thing back. It is a miracle of old technology that we always seemed to survive the madness of it all and the reports reached their destination.

In fact, there were always plenty of laughs with my colleagues at the Hull Daily Mail. In my first spell of covering the Tigers for them, I worked with a brilliant sub-editor called Dave Carsberg, whose job was to edit my Saturday-afternoon reports amid the mayhem of the immediacy of it all. To give us a realistic chance of assembling everything in time we would invariably go through the two squads on Fridays and come up with potentially dreadful puns for Dave's main headline on the City reports for the front pages of the Sports Mail. My input was minimal, but Dave inevitably came up with up wonderfully witty headlines with deceptive ease. It was a joy to work with such a journalistic genius.

But it was our close friend and colleague Peter Moore who nearly caused me to miss the team coach to an away game for the only time. I had done my piece for the first edition when I was provided with an update on City's squad for later editions after fitness tests during Friday-morning training. Time was tight because we were embarking on the longest trip possible to Plymouth and the coach was due to set off at lunchtime. I had no alternative but to catch up with the sports editor Brian Taylor in the composing-room to give him the rundown of the changes to the squad because I did not have enough time to rewrite my story. I was happy to leave everything in his capable hands because of the rush to get down to Boothferry Park to meet the coach. I was taking a small suitcase with me, but it was hardly full because I was travelling light, bearing mind that it was, after all, only a one-night stay. It probably contained football reference books, a sponge-bag and a pair of pyjamas that looked like Rupert Bear on a bad day! I chased back to the sports desk, shouted my farewells and picked up what I thought was my lightweight suitcase in readiness for my hasty exit. In fact, I nearly wrenched my arm off as I dropped the suitcase on to the floor with a resounding clang. Everything fell out to reveal that during my absence in the composing-room Peter had placed a number of heavy metal blocks that were relics from the old, traditional printing method at strategic intervals in the suitcase, so that it was hard to lift it at all. I ran out to the sound of much laughter and my own cursing and reached the coach just before it set off.

And what you write or broadcast can get you into trouble in more ways than one, of course. In August 1976 City lost 1-0 at Orient in the Football League Cup and part of my match report in the Hull Daily Mail appeared as follows: "Heppolette supplied Cunningham with a chance from which Wealands had to make a point-blank save and then shot himself." I was not indicating an apparent suicide attempt by City's goalkeeper Jeff Wealands, but something had been lost in the translation over the telephone and it should have read: "Heppolette supplied Cunningham with a chance from which Wealands had to make a point-blank save and then tried a shot himself." But the offending item duly appeared in Punch as a clanger and at the time was I was not amused! And in 1981 City's Nick Deacy and Crewe Alexandra's Alan Ricketts were both injured when they challenged each other in a game at Boothferry Park. It prompted a local-radio journalist to tell his listeners: "There was a clash of heads and Deacy went off with Ricketts..." Someone else in the Press-box obliged by observing: "That's strange. I thought it was a disease that only kids could get!" And there may even be a chance of an action replay now that the Tigers have signed Welsh international Sam Ricketts!

There was also a bleak humour when I sometimes had to do things that surely exceeded my humble call of duty. For example, I once received a telephone call at eight o'clock on a Sunday morning from an ex-Tiger's wife to ask if her husband, who, it seemed, had gone temporarily AWOL, had stayed overnight at my house. He had not, but I was not certain that she believed me. On another occasion I was asked by an ex-Tiger's girlfriend if I would lend her some badly-needed support by accompanying her to a hospital in Hull to find out the results of her pregnancy test. She was - and I did! It is odd that you appear to go into it as a soccer writer and come out of it as a social worker!

Nothing at times is sacred. I once received a telephone call from Japan from ex-Tiger Craig Norrie, who had been playing for Hiroshima. He said: "Hello, Bondy, I'm thinking of coming home and I just wondered if you could do anything to try to find me a club back in England." I explained: "Not at this time of day, Nogger! It's five o'clock in the morning!" Back came his reply: "I'm ever so sorry, Bondy. I think I've got the time difference wrong. I thought it was five o'clock in the afternoon in England!" There was a pause before he added: "How are you?" "Tired!" I told him with unwarranted politeness. And when City visited Bermuda in 1988, I was allowed to sit on the bench with the management and the substitutes while I reported on the games. The idea of writing down the details of substitutions and submitting them to an official had already been introduced over there, so it was useful to have me on hand to do the relevant paperwork. But it poured with rain during one game and I suddenly looked round to find that I was virtually alone on the bench. I was soaked as I carried out my dual role and everybody else was sheltering!

And you can get into scrapes when you least expect it. I still laugh with ex-Tigers John "Gunner" Davies and Steve Richards about an incident at an international cricket tournament at the old Melton Sporting Club. It was a fund-raising event involving former Test players partnering local businesses in a small-sided competition. It was not the most serious of cricketing occasions, but justice had to be done to it by at least recording the events of the day accurately. Accordingly the three of us were asked if we would take charge of the scorebox, but on our way across to it John and Steve confessed that they had not a clue about the technicalities of cricket scoring. They told me, therefore, I would have to do the scoring and they would merely work the numbers in the box and acknowledge the umpires. But I have never seen myself as a cricket scorer and certainly lack the concentration to do it remotely competently for long periods, so I was hardly in my element with tbe situation for starters. But I was then subjected to relentless, merciless mickey-taking from the other two.

I was struggling to keep up-to-date with events on the pitch and becoming more and more irritated, which naturally meant that they were winding me up more and more. All of a sudden I had had enough, rose from my seat in the scorebox, turned round to leave and told them: "Right, that's it. I'm off. You can do the scoring yourselves." Neither I nor they have probably ever known just how serious my threat was or not. But it was absolutely hilarious to see the look of sheer panic in the other two's eyes. They insisted spontaneously: "No. Don't go, Bondy! We were only joking. We haven't a clue as to how to do the scoring. We need you." I sat back down again amid fits of laughter and then it became very serious. I was allowed to get on with the job in relative peace and vowed that I would never step into another cricket scorebox to act as a scorer ever again. I have kept my promise and they have had the satisfaction of knowing that they ended a not-very-promising career for good that day...

It is essential to remember always that the very nature of football insists that it breeds character and characters. Fun and laughter are rarely absent from the football fraternity whenever they get together and sometimes it also spills over into the boardroom. Don Robinson was an amazing character when he was City's chairman and there was an amusing occasion when he tangled with one of football's funny folks. In May 1988 the Tigers went to Marbella for an end-of-season trip that included a game against Real Balompedica Linense near the Spanish border with Gibraltar. It was all a bit surreal, though, because Don had sacked Brian Horton as manager the previous month, so Dennis Booth and Tom Wilson were in charge of the party as joint caretaker managers and not surprisingly speculation was readily rife about the managerial vacancy. To cap it all, Don was not too well at one stage and was on medication. During our stay the City party spent a day at the Sotogrande golf complex and at the end of it Robbo was walking awkwardly back to the team coach because he was "running in" some new shoes. Boothy, a renowned joker, suggested to him that he should have been taking his tablets orally instead of putting them in his shoes. The outcome was Robinson's revenge - a crushing headlock that was a relic of his days in the wrestling ring!

Later in the trip Don arranged for City's staff and me to spend an evening at vice-president Toni Dalli's restaurant-cum-club near Torremolinos. Toni, a well-known singer who had been based in Yorkshire at one stage, was connected with the Tigers between 1985 and 1990 and looked after us regally. We had an idyllic view of the clear-blue Mediterranean from our table, Toni sang for his guests and went from table to table to socialise and we were further intrigued by the occupants of the tables next to ours. Toni told us that at one table there was a family birthday celebration involving some English folk who were taking full advantage of the fact that Spain did not have an extradition treaty with Great Britain, while at the other was the actor, Sean Connery, with a business friend. Don at once insisted that Connery should be given an official City tie as a memento, but he could not decide who should go over and present him with it. I told him that I would have been perfectly prepared to do it were not for the fact that Connery might be a touch suspicious if I went over and introduced myself by saying: "My name's Bond..." I seem to recall that the outcome was that Toni agreed to present the tie and I duly received my headlock from Don!

When it comes to comedians and characters, City's 1970s midfield trio of Chris Galvin, Vince Grimes and George Lyall took some beating. I was once having a lunchtime drink in the centre of Hull with some of the players when Chris Galvin button-holed me about something that I had written about him. I was naturally on the defensive when Chris said: "Right, I've read your report about Saturday's game and I want to take issue about something you wrote. I quote: 'Galvin made little impact...'" There was a pause, I was about to try to defend myself when Chris continued with a straight face: "I know exactly how I played, so why didn't you just put that I was crap?" It ended up in laughter all round. Chris, who would apparently instigate serious political arguments involving Steve Deere and Jeff Wealands after training and then leave them to it, was a natural comedian. He once took to the stage at a nightclub in Hull, to which we had been invited as guests, and told the house band that he was going to sing the old folk anthem "Early One Morning" in G. He then proceeded to sing it as badly as possible - perhaps even in the key of H instead - in an attempt to ruin the band's reputation as he tried to blame them for the cacophony. Vince always looked innocent with his deadpan expression, but was the opposite. He could keep a straight face while winding up people relentlessly. A group of us went to a nightclub in Hull just before Christmas one year and soon discovered that Vinny had developed a new chat-up line with the ladies. He told them that he was a local priest and had ventured into the nightclub to try to save their souls. It almost worked in some instances even though he introduced himself to them under the curiously-familiar name of Father Francis Banks!

Dennis Booth and Peter Taylor, who were teammates at Southend United before climbing on to the City bandwagon in different capacities, had a reputation as impressionists with Norman Wisdom as one of their favourite targets. George Lyall was also a handy mimic, but his speciality would cause havoc during meals in hotels on away trips. He could capture the sound of the new-fangled telephones of the time with unerring ease, so he would impersonate them in the hotel restaurants. Waiter after waiter would hear the telephone ring, drop what they were doing to answer it and then find that there was nobody on the other end of the line. There would be mystified shrugs of shoulders and the bewildered waiters would return to their chores. But George would catch them out time after time and we tried not to choke on our food amid our mirth.

Sometimes you just hit it off with someone and that was certainly the case for me with Boothy because we soon found out that we had the same sense of humour. At one point, in fact, the two of us might, for example, have formed a Tommy Cooper Appreciation Society with Billy Whitehurst. Boothy and I used to set each other off so that laughter was always in the air. We socialised together a lot and, being teetotal, I normally ended up being his unofficial driver. The outcome was that he did nothing but complain about my driving. In December 1988 we arrived back in Hull from Bermuda after a long journey in difficult circumstances and decided that the first thing that we would do when we arrived at Boothferry Park would be to go to the Hop Pole in Willerby to acclimatise ourselves to England again. My car had been left outside the ground and I initially struggled to find reverse gear as I readjusted to driving again. My difficulty led to a prolonged tirade from Boothy about the poor quality of my driving. I told him: "Boothy, since I last drove a car 10 days ago, I've been on three coaches, three aircraft, four boat trips from one part of Bermuda to another, a succession of taxis on the island and a pal's motorcycle, which I nearly fell off on a mini-roundabout." He merely suggested that I must be a liability with all forms of transport and duly bought me a drink in the Hop Pole on account of the fact that he was just mightily relieved to have arrived there in one piece.

In fact, Boothy and I often used to meet at the Hop Pole, especially to unwind early on Saturday evenings after home games. Sometimes a few of the players might join us, but on one occasion early in 1989 it was the scene of our greatest triumph when we ventured in there on our own. We were on good form because I am sure that City had won and we had both changed into dinner-jackets because we were due to attend a function for Garreth Roberts' testimonial during the evening. We started wise-cracking and winding each other up and the jokes and one-liners were flowing fast. Our attire attracted some attention from some of the regulars and we explained that we were due at a major function in Willerby. We heard a few days later that a barmaid had overheard us, listened to our quickfire patter and assumed that we were simply rehearsing our act because we must have been the star comedy cabaret at the event. We did, I think, own up to the truth and there is solace in recording that the double act of Boothy and Bondy never appeared in public or thought of re-forming for one of the TV talent shows that are far too frequent nowadays.

There was also an occasion when Boothy and I found that we were staying in the same hotel as a party of anaesthetists before an away trip to Southampton. While we were having our breakfast on the Saturday, an announcement was made over the hotel tannoy, asking the anaesthetists to report to reception as soon as possible because their coach was awaiting them. As we passed through the hotel lobby after breakfast, Boothy could not resist going up to the receptionist and informing her: "There seems to be a problem with the anaesthetists because no-one can wake them up!" He kept a straight face, she kept an equally-straight face and we waited around while she innocently started to ring round all their rooms in an attempt to stir them!

But Boothy was so naturally funny and quick-witted that I think that he was often misunderstood. He could play the clown, but there is much more to him than that because he was also very serious about the game and wanting to win. It was even suggested that Don Robinson had thought about him as managerial material at one stage, but then wondered if he could be serious enough to do the job. If it were at all true, it grossly underestimated his capabilities. When he was sacked as assistant manager by Don, he was soon snapped up by Graham Taylor, with whom he had previously worked at Lincoln City and Watford, to join the coaching staff at Aston Villa. One of Boothy's roles in addition to general coaching duties with the first team was to liaise regularly with the players and keep them united in a happy frame of mind because of his tremendous personality. Characters of Boothy's type are always needed in dressing-rooms to lighten the mood at significant times of tension, but it should be underlined that he always knew when to adopt a sense of humour and when to adopt a tone of gravity.

It seems, though, that the Tigers enticed characters into their midst from the early days and George "Geordie" Maddison, who is third in the club's all-time League appearances list on 430, proved the theory that goalkeepers are usually a bit mad because he was eccentric and extrovert at times. He used to attract hordes of supporters behind his goal and maintain running commentaries on games for their benefit! "Geordie" also used to throw sweets to children behind his goal and toss them coins that might have been left behind during collections. And he disliked staying on his line, so he would occasionally leave his penalty area and beat an opponent before kicking upfield. On one occasion Maddison had little to do on a cold day while playing for the reserves, so the fans provided him with a brazier in his goalmouth to keep him warm. It is unclear as to whether "Geordie" himself might originally have left it nearby, but the referee stepped in quickly and decided that he could keep it provided that he moved it out of the field of play! And Maddison was also superstitious because he would always put on his left boot first and insist that he was the last player to leave the dressing-room to go out for games.

Immediately after the 1939-45 War manager Major Frank Buckley's renowned steely approach did not deter inside-forward Frank McGorrigan and Andy Davidson recalled: "Frank was a lovely man and a natural comedian. When Major Buckley came into the dressing-room, it would go quiet apart from Frank who was never worried about him and would carry on yattering away as if nothing had happened. Frank's favourite trick was to try to 'nutmeg' opposition players. Sometimes he would run round the other side of them after doing it and sometimes he just wouldn't bother. I told him that I wanted to start doing it, but he said that I was too young to try it and needed to grow a bit!" Frank was sold to Blackburn Rovers for £6,000 in February 1947 in the first postwar transfer of note involving City and it created an uproar among the fans who complained about it vigorously in letters to the Hull Daily Mail. But perhaps he had left because Buckley had found him too hot to handle!

Former England centre-forward Stan Mortensen was a character who commuted from Blackpool, where he was a town councillor at one time, after joining City in November 1955. Full-back Bob Dennison recalled how he would arrive for training: "The door would burst open and a voice would shout: 'Have no fear, Morty's here!' And he would turn up with all kinds of things such as Blackpool rock for all the players' children as presents." Morty had starred in what was known as the Stanley Matthews final when Blackpool beat Bolton Wanderers 4-3 to win the FA Cup at Wembley in 1953. And he would say: "I'm the only person to have scored a hat-trick in an FA Cup final and have it named after someone else!" He managed Blackpool, had a shop in the town and also worked as a hosiery salesman, gleefully telling people at the time: "I travel in ladies' underwear!" And in 1956 Morty toured East Yorkshire with his popular "Spotlight on Soccer," which was described as "an intimate and racy talk!"

One of his playing colleagues at City was inside-forward Bill Bradbury and Andy Davidson said of him: "He really was a clown at times and probably should have been a comedian rather than a footballer." In 1995 Eric Cantona was sent off after a tussle with ex-Tiger Richard Shaw while playing for Manchester United against Crystal Palace and then caused a rumpus when he went into the crowd to attack a fan, but Bill Bradbury arguably set the precedent for it. His close friend and teammate Brian Bulless recalled: "I remember one game when Bill was taking a corner at the old Bunker's Hill end and someone in the crowd shouted at him as he was going to take it. Bill just bounced the ball on the fan's head, caught the rebound and took the corner!" Goalkeeper Bernard Fisher tells another classic story about Bill: "One very foggy day Angus McLean shouted to us while we were running round the track at Boothferry Park in training: 'Where the hell's Bill Bradbury?' or words to that effect. Suddenly the groundsman Stan Coombs' grass-cutting machine stopped near us and we all thought that he would be driving it. But it was Bill, who was wrapped up in Stan's coat and hood." The story also goes that manager Bob Brocklebank then came out to watch training and said: "Good morning, Stan!" when the grass-cutter rolled past him. Apparently Bill just carried on mowing and replied: "Good morning, boss!"

Another contemporary of theirs, Jack Bennion, joined City in 1957 after manager Bob Brocklebank was said to have beaten off competition from 15 other clubs to sign him. Jack worked locally in four bookmakers' offices after retiring from football, but teammate Mike Bowering recalled: "Jack was forever betting and we would often to go to watch the greyhounds. Jack would spend a lot of money and encourage us. One night I saw Neil Cubie leaning on the rails looking depressed and I think that that might have been the occasion when we left him asleep on a billiards table in a club!" Another teammate Mick Brown said of him: "Jack promised my father that he would look after me, so he suggested that after training we should spend our lunchtimes in Hull at Hammond's perfume counter. I thought that this was a bit odd, so I asked Jack why and he explained: 'A lot of beautiful ladies work on the perfume counter at Hammond's and all the beautiful ladies who don't work on it spend their lunchtimes buying something from the perfume counter at Hammond's!'"

Goalkeeper Ian McKechnie had been conscious of his weight when he was with Southend United, so he used to do extra training that included a job digging trenches on a building site in the Pitsea district of Essex. It still meant that he was a larger-than-life character who made an immediate impact when he joined City in 1966 because of his powerful kicking, his resemblance to singer Frankie Vaughan and his declared liking for oranges which meant his goalmouth would be bombarded with them by fans during the warm-up for games at Boothferry Park. And it was apparently on a trip to Plymouth in October 1966 that he caused quite a stir. Midfield player Malcolm Lord recalled: "We stayed at Torquay and on the morning of the match we were all walking along the front past some kind of floral hall. All the ladies looked at us as we went by and mistook Ian for Frankie Vaughan! We could see them nudge each other right along the line, so Kechers waved to them and did an impression by high-kicking his way round the corner much to their amazement!" But players can expect laughter rather than sympathy from colleagues in times of distress and Kechers suffered for his art at Oxford in November 1970 even though City won 3-0. It was so cold that he asked trainer John McSeveney to rub in some warming oil at halftime. But early in the second half Ian's face became splattered with mud and he removed his gloves to wipe it away. Unfortunately some of the oil then got into his eyes.and he could not stop them from streaming!

Striker Billy Whitehurst was a throwback to the old days of characters and you always had to be on your guard because he was strong and he liked a laugh. And City's youth officer Freddie Cowell could vouch for it all after an incident before a reserve game against Darlington at Feethams in March 1989. He explained: "I playfully tapped Billy on the shoulder in the dressing-room and his response was to lift me above his head and give me what was known as an airplane spin. All I can remember is clipping the strip light as I went round and round and then he let me down and put me in the kit basket!"

And where there are characters, there tend to be pratical jokes. When Danish hero Viggo Jensen joined the Tigers in 1948, he could not speak any English, but his teammates in the club's hostel were apparently not too helpful. They claimed that they were telling him how to be polite when, in fact, the opposite was true because, for example, they encouraged him to put a seven-letter expletive in front of the words: "Thank you!" Accordingly, the story goes that his landlady served up one of his first meals since arriving in England and Viggo promptly and unwittingly shocked her - to the wicked delight of his teammates - when he tried to show his gratitude by exclaiming: "——— thank you!"

Don Beardsley apparently caused a problem on one occasion at Boothferry Park because fellow defender Geoff Barker recalled: "There were a gang of Irish workers who were doing something to the floodlights and Don shouted to the top that there was a telephone call for them. One of them came down and it took him about a quarter-of-an-hour because of all the safety procedures. When he got down, we told him that there was no 'phone call. Don had long gone, but if they could have found him, then I reckon that we'd have been looking for a new full-back!"

In those days anti-social rock bands developed a craze for "trashing" hotel rooms, but footballers had their fun in a more sedate manner. Ken Houghton used to be the master of manoeuvres when it came to moving things around and it was well-known that beds would disappear and then reappear in strange places, sometimes going up and down in lifts unattended! On one occasion Ken and his removal men comprising his teammates offered an apprenticeship in their ways to young goalkeeper Peter Walters. Ken explained: "We put him on look-out and, when he was looking the other way, we moved his bed from his room and left it up a tree nearby!" Ken also joined the club on their close-season tour to the West Indies in 1973 when the players stayed in a hotel where there were little chalets for rooms. He apparently found a way into player-manager Terry Neill's chalet, took everything out and then put it back exactly as he had found it on the lawn behind it. "By that time I knew that I was leaving the club anyway!" he said.

And it was hardly a case of hotel happiness for some of us during City's final preparations for 1976-77, which included a stay at a training camp at Bewdley Hill near Kidderminster for the best part of a week before the opening League game at Hereford. Secretary Malcolm "Mac" Stone and I, though, did not join the party until the day before the game. Mac, who was originally from the area, drove down and I travelled by train, so we shared a hotel room because we were the late arrivals. After the early-evening meal Mac and manager John Kaye drove off to visit old friends in the West Midlands and I went up to our room, where I suddenly received a telephone call from Roger de Vries. He said that the players were out of touch with events in Hull during the week and suggested that I joined them in the bar, where they were allowed to be briefly, to update them. Roger was more level-headed than many and had always seemed to be totally trustworthy, so it all sounded perfectly plausible. It might have been a touch suspicious that the players wanted to be friendly towards me, but I succumbed to duty and went down to meet them. I did not know that somehow they had gained access to a master key for all the bedrooms and the interest in Hullensian matters was merely a ploy to get me out of the way. Vinny Grimes had a single room opposite the one occupied by Mac and me and in it he had found a cot. The idea was that some of the players would switch the cot for a bed in our room while I was downstairs in the bar with the rest of them.

After the players had adjourned to their rooms for an early night, there was not much Friday-night socialising left with John and Mac being absent, so I went back up to my own room relatively soon. Naturally I found one bed and one cot and it was inappropriate that I should disturb any of the players to seek the straight swap back of the other bed, which was in Vinny's room, and the cot. I then determined that I should claim squatter's rights and make sure that I occupied the one remaining bed before Mac returned, which I did. When he finally arrived back, I pretended to be asleep and tried desperately to keep a straight face. Mac naturally muttered a few oaths and tried to wake me up, but I just played possum as best I could. He grumbled for a while and then turned out the light after taking a small mattress and a bit of bedding from the cot before making up a bed of a kind and lying down on the floor. There were inquiries, explanations and much laughter the following morning and I seem to recall that Mac had a spot of back trouble not long afterwards, so I naturally assumed that one thing had led to another.

The sorry tale did not end there, though. While the players had had access to our room, they had rigged it in certain ways and I probably suffered more than Mac in this respect. The bristles on my toothbrush had been burned down, presumably with a cigarette lighter, so that it was rendered useless. My tube of toothpaste had had the bottom of it cut off so that everything came out in positive torrents at both ends when I squeezed it. Black shoe polish had been smeared round the toilet seat in the adjoining bathroom so that you hardly had a ring of confidence if you needed to sit on the "throne." And a stinging ointment, possibly provided by physiotherapist Jeff Radcliffe, had been daubed round the ear-piece of the telephone in the room. John Kaye had said beforehand: "The players have a chance to get to know each other even better, they learn a few home truths about each other and they find that they are talking about football all the time." It might have been wonderful for team spirit, but I am not too sure whether I agree with his theories in their entirety! And I suspect that Mac had even greater doubts about them!

There was another incident before a game at Colchester in April 1979 when I found that Derek Hood and Rob McDonald had got a spare key to my bedroom. I had managed to avoid a bucket of water that had been strategically placed over the door, but realised that they were planning to do far worse as soon I left the room, so I had to play a waiting-game with them and stay inside it until they eventually went away. A far more congenial incident of that kind had occurred in February 1959 when Jimmy Lodge was presented with a television set to mark the 40th anniversary of his arrival at the club. According to vice-chairman Ron Buttery, there had been contributions from different sources such as manager Bob Brocklebank, directors, players, ground staff, office staff, the supporters' club and the auxiliary group, but they had had to make sure that Jimmy was attending to duties at Boothferry Park with trainer Johnny Mahon on the previous Sunday morning so that a television aerial could be put up at his house in his absence to maintain the surprise element!

There was plenty of camaraderie around the club in the late 1970s and Mac recalled: "The players shaved off half of physiotherapist Jeff Radcliffe's beard and he had to finish the job himself! And Wilf McGuinness and Andy Davidson were great characters when they were on the coaching staff. One night Andy had a party, but we were under strict orders not to mention that England had beaten Scotland at Hampden Park earlier in the day because he was so upset by the result. Wilf, who is one of the funniest people I've ever met, turned up in an old raincoat and, when he took it off, he had his old England blazer and tie on underneath. He was persuaded to take then off for fear of upsetting Andy, but underneath them he was wearing his old England No. 6 shirt!"

Wilf was also at his best one Christmas Eve. He disguised himself in possibly the same old raincoat and put on a wig and hat as he went round the club. He told one young player that he was a City fan who was home for Christmas and would be grateful for the players' autographs. They were duly collected and presented to him, but then he unveiled himself as their coach! The disguise went back on and he said that he was Irish journalist from a national tabloid newspaper and would like an interview with the manager Ken Houghton. He was granted one and utterly baffled Ken by asking him if were true that he might be interested in signing various players. Naturally Wilf got all the possible targets right and Houghy was perplexed and concerned that the news of his potential signings had seemed to leak out to the Press. It was apparently a matter of great relief to Ken when Wilf unveiled himself again! The disguise went back on again as a few of us crossed the road from Boothferry Park to the Three Tuns for a festive lunchtime drink. The assistant groundsman Frank Mobbs was already in there with his wife and the disguised Wilf playfully began chatting her up. Frank hesitated at first, but was becoming increasingly niggled as it went on. The rest of us desperately tried to maintain straight faces as the tension mounted and it was again relief all-round when Wilf again unveiled himself just as Frank was beginning to get really annoyed by the undue care and attention that his wife was receiving!

Those of us who were not players were always susceptible to pranks from those who were and Mac was on the receiving end from defender Dave Roberts one morning. Dave explained: "One day I was sitting at home at North Ferriby with nothing to do before I went into training, so I decided to ring up Mac Stone at the ground. I put on an accent, told him that I was from a club in the area and said that I had an outstanding bill for some champagne to be paid, which was in his name. He had signed it and I asked him if he'd settle it immediately because it had got to the end of March and it would soon be the new financial year. He denied any knowledge of it, of course, and said that he would get back to me, so I told him that I'd be back in touch instead. I said that I didn't want it to go to court and he said that he would get the police involved! I set off for training and found that all hell had kicked off when I got there. John Kaye wanted a word with me beforehand and explained that there had been a tab for some champagne at the club, which had been signed in Mac's name. He thought that some of the lads might have signed it, but I didn't let on, so we were all called into the dressing-room and Mac came in to address us. He repeated that it was a matter for the police, so we should own up if we knew anything about it and I just asked him what the date was. He thought for a few seconds and then said: "It's April the First, isn't it?" In the end he took it well and he got his own back by putting something in the programme when I told him that I'd been to Hornsea and all I could find was some pottery place and no beach!"

And Houghy was again at his best in 1979 when Arthur Anderson left City's backroom team to join Hull Kingston Rovers' commercial operation. Ken still decided to invite him to a party at his house, which had been arranged for a Saturday night after the Tigers had lost 2-1 at Chester earlier in the day. But Houghy had gone to great lengths to make sure that Arthur wrongly believed that it was a fancy-dress affair. Ken even persuaded me to ring him up in the week before the party to find out what he would be wearing and what fancy-dress advice he could give me. Accordingly, all the other guests turned up in perfectly normal states of dress and were primed that Arthur might arrive in fancy dress. During the evening there was a knock at the back door and there was Arthur, replete in a red-and-black court jester's outfit with pointed feet and bells where most people would not dream of having them. His wife was a resplendent Queen of Spain. I gave them both a lift home to save them from trying to explain everything to a taxi-driver..:

But in January 1989 I was a victim myself when I went along to Boothferry Park for a chat with manager Eddie Gray. I seem to recall that I was wearing a tracksuit because it was my day off, but Eddie and I were celebrating our birthdays. There had already been much merriment because one of the apprentices, Mark Hutchinson, had his birthday the same day. There was a ritual recognition of the feat among the club's youngsters and I was soon informed that Mark had been tied up in a near-by supermarket trolley, had his clothes removed and been dumped ceremoniously on the Boothferry Park centre-spot! Eddie and I had a chat about club matters and then went out on to the edge of the pitch for a general conversation when I realised that there was some activity among the apprentices in the players' tunnel. They then pointed out that it was a good time for birthdays and were going to help me to celebrate mine! They hoisted me aloft and carried me towards the away dressing-room, which was their lair during the week. I tried to thank them for their interest in my birthday, but emphasised the point that it was Eddie's, too. I asked why he was not being subjected to the same treatment as I was. I was ignored and, as I was carried along, I suddenly realised that Eddie was, in fact, egging them on, so there was obviously not much loyalty among Capricorns! Once in the dressing-room I was tossed fully-clothed into the fully-filled bath. As I splattered to my feet amid the communal glee I discovered that assistant groundsman Ken Norrie had followed the procession and had taken great delight in my plight. As Eddie and Ken made the most of the moment, the youngsters decided that it was time for more fun. They turned to Ken and rebuked him for laughing at my discomfort, picking him up and throwing him in after me. I staggered out as he was thrown in, so it was clearly a straight swap! Thankfully the lads took my wet clothes to be dried out and left me clad in towels in the match officials' room. It was literally good, clean fun!

On another occasion I had a brush with the law during the festive period in 1992 as I was proceeding in an easterly direction, so to speak, along Holderness Road into East Hull one Sunday evening. I was on my way to a party and had just driven over North Bridge when I noticed a police patrol car behind me, so I immediately made sure that I continued at 29½ mph. The traffic lights on Witham were at red when I reached them, so I duly stopped as the patrol car pulled up on my inside. I just stared ahead in the rather forlorn hope that I would not draw any attention to myself and set off when the lights turned to green. I had gone about 200 yards further on when I noticed that the police car's blue light was flashing and its occupant was signalling me to stop. I pulled in as I convinced myself that I was surely not committing any road traffic offence, but I was still filled with a sense of foreboding and trepidation as I got out to meet the officer as he emerged from his vehicle. "I just thought I'd wish you a happy Christmas, sir," he said benignly. All of a sudden I realised that the laughing policeman was former City defender Bobby McNeil! I playfully pretended to assault him in the execution of his duty and he, equally playfully, sent me on my relieved way after a quick chat.

Then there are those humorous happenings that would never be considered for a television "sitcom" or comedy drama because they are too unbelievable or offbeat, but they still bear the hallmark of reality. Wally Chapman and Eddie Edwards, who played for the Tigers at different levels, were good pals and yet once travelled separately to the same game as rival scouts. Wally was representing City and Eddie was, as usual, working for former England international Allan Clarke. But City's youth officer and their mutual friend Freddie Cowell said: "Wally wanted to remain anonymous, so he immediately went to hide behind a convenient tree when he arrived at the game and found Eddie already hiding behind it!"

An incident in February 1968 gives hope to anyone who has ever cherished an ambition to play for the Tigers. Midfield player Malcolm Lord, who admittedly had had a little first-team experience already, went along to watch City beat Motherwell 4-0 in a friendly at Boothferry Park. He was not scheduled to be involved in the game, so he simply joined the crowd of 6,799 on the terraces, but a funny thing happened while he was standing among the fans. He explained: "The game was in aid of the trawler-disaster fund and I went along with my wife Margaret, whom I had not yet married then, and my dad. We were in the South Stand when just before halftime Ray Henderson, who was on the coaching staff, walked round the track and beckoned to me. He told me to get changed at once and I came out in the second half in place of Ian Davidson!" He might have been able to learn a lesson from Arthur Shepherd, who was a City director for 22 years until the club's re-formation after the 1939-45 War. In 1902 Arthur had signed for Hull Kingston Rovers and one of his first games was a derby against Hull FC. Two days later he duly went to watch his teammate Jim Barry play for Wales against England at the Boulevard. But suddenly there was a call from England's dressing-room for a scrum-half when it was found that Halifax's Archie Wrigg had missed his train connection, so 19-year-old Shepherd, who had played just four senior games of rugby league, made himself available and went on to score two tries in a 14-6 win. "I think I got 10 shillings for playing!" he said. But his competitive rugby-league career never reached such a dizzy height again and it was finished by a knee injury while he was playing for Holderness Falcons.

A similar kind of scenario enveloped goalkeeper Bernard Fisher in March 1956 after he had made arrangements for his wedding in his home city of York at 10 o'clock on Easter Saturday morning and to play for City's reserves at Bootham Crescent in the Midland League in the afternoon. But his best-laid plan did not work out because Bernard explained: "My last first-team game had been at Bristol City the previous November, but we lost 5-2 and I was dropped - and rightly so because I was a bit out of my depth in a struggling team. My next first-team game was when we drew 2-2 at home to Fulham and Johnny Haynes scored their goals. I played in it because Billy Bly broke his ankle in a 2-0 defeat at Blackburn the day before, which was Good Friday. On the Saturday I had arranged to marry in York and play for City away to York's reserves in the afternoon. As a result, I married and then had to catch a train to Hull and a taxi to Boothferry Park with my wife. We arrived half-an-hour before the kick-off! I also remember playing in the return game against Blackburn on the Easter Monday and losing 3-0. A voice from the crowd shouted to me: 'That's what married life does for you!'"

Andy Davidson now loves East Yorkshire despite having been homesick when he first joined City, but he has retained his distinct Scottish accent - something which caused him a spot of bother during the build-up to a match at Plymouth in the 1970s. The City party were ordering their preferences for their light pre-match meals in their hotel when Andy was approached by a waiter, who looked and sounded just like the character Manuel in Fawlty Towers, which was at the height of its first wave of popularity at the time. Andy told him in his rich Scottish accent that he would like a Spanish omelette and the waiter duly disappeared with the order. When the waiter returned a few minutes later with an omelette, Andy took one look at it and was immediately put off eating anything because it looked on first inspection as if there might be some greeny, black bits of mould on it. A perplexed Andy asked what exactly the meal was supposed to be and the waiter replied: "It's your spinach omelette, sir!" Andy also told another tale of life on the road with Chris Chilton and Ken Wagstaff during the 1960s: "When we stayed in hotels on Friday nights for the long away trips, Cliff Britton always used to arrange for us to go to either the cinema or theatre locally. As soon as the lights went down, Chillo and Waggy would sneak out and find somewhere to have a drink while the film or play was on. And they always seemed to know when they were due to finish because they would creep back in just before the end so that they were never missed!"

Defender Ray Pettit also had travel troubles. He wanted to return to his home city of Hull when his playing career ended. It seemed natural enough, therefore, that he should look for a job in the advertisement columns of the Hull Daily Mail, but he finished up working in the south as a result of it! He explained: "I saw an advertisement for a job with the Customs and Excise. I applied for it because I thought it would be a good chance to get back to Hull, but, typical of the civil service, they posted me down to Southend! I was given an office job at the VAT headquarters in Southend and did it for three years. I then joined the investigations division in London which is involved in drugs, VAT, fraud, customs and smuggling." It was specialised work that took Ray all round the country and landed him in a spot of bother when he returned north on one occasion. Ken Houghton, his teammate with City and his manager at Scarborough, was then working for Davis Freight at Immingham and was walking round the docks one day when he was sure that he saw Ray. The chance meeting was totally unexpected, but Houghy was certain of the sighting, so he naturally called to Ray. The story goes that Ray walked hurriedly on and ignored him. Houghy kept calling to him on the lines of: "Ray, is that you? Ray Pettit? How are you? It's your old pal Houghy." It seems that Houghy's tone changed somewhat, though, as Ray kept his head down and continually ignored him, so the calls seemingly turned to: "Have I done something to offend you, Ray? Don't you want a word? There's no need to be rude." It was only much later on that Ray, who still lives in Essex, was able to explain his apparently-unfriendly manner when he told Houghy that he had actually been on a top-secret, under-cover investigation at the time!

Youth development officer Bobby Brown accidentally struck a blow for equality of the sexes when he went to watch City's reserves play at Grimsby in October 1980 and took his wife Joy with him. Brown and manager Mike Smith were offered drinks and Bobby saw to it that Joy duly had a cup of tea and joined the gathering. It was only a while later that they discovered that Joy had unwittingly invaded the Mariners' boardroom, becoming the first woman to do so in the club's 101-year existence!

Silly situations also confronted players after they had left City. In 1963 Billy Bly was playing for Hull Brunswick against Bridlington Trinity, who scored against him - after just 15 seconds of their game in the East Riding County League. No Brunswick player had touched the ball by the time that David Crawford scored for Trinity and Bly, then in his 40s, not surprisingly admitted: "That's the quickest goal I've ever had scored against me." Half-back John Hart had a spell with Bridlington Town when ex-Tiger Dave King was their player-manager. And Dave admitted: "John was once booked for a foul I'd done at Mexborough because of mistaken identity. I never owned up at the time, but I think it was just about the only booking that he ever got because he was always such a gentleman!" Wing-half Joe Stocks, who was a rat-catcher at one time, revisited his old club Goole Town one afternoon after going whippet racing, bringing his prize dog with him and tethering it in the home dressing-room. But Jeff Barmby explained: "It scoffed all the sandwiches and started growling and whining. Unfortunately they'd left the PA system on and the dog caused quite a stir because it could be heard all over the ground during the match and no-one knew what was going on!"

At times the humour in football is distinctly dark and often inspired by comments from managers and players. It is generally a world of uninspiring cliches, but there are the more enlightened moments. Postwar City manager Major Frank Buckley, for example, was noted for his sharp tongue and some of his sayings in soccer were legendary. He is said to have told one young insde-forward: "If you had petrol for brains, son, you would never get out of the garage." And he supposedly subdued a confident winger by telling him: "You remind me more and more of Matthews every time I see you. But I'm talking of Jessie - not Stanley!" But the humour may also have served to shroud another side of Buckley's nature if some of his deeds are to be believed. After all, he would also set up a ball on two bricks for a player who was not striking it cleanly and tell him to run up and hit it. When the player naturally asked what would happen if he accidentally kicked the bricks, Buckley would reply: "You'll break your ankle and it'll serve you right."

Buckley's bleak humour meant that the opinions of him were diverse. Centre-half Harold Meens described him as "one of the finest managers I have ever known" and trainer George Lax said: "He was one of the greatest of football managers and I learned from him how to get the best out of players and how to make everyone happy." But Andy Davidson said: "Buckley was very ruthless. His career had been in the Army and I'm not sure that he knew all that much about football. He would have about 300 trialists down on Tuesdays and they would all get no more than 15 to 30 minutes in which to prove themselves. He was a good talker, but he would teach you how to go over the ball. They would take the old sleepers from the railway, put a ball against them and you had to tackle them. Sometimes you'd finish off running with blood." And Martin Reagan added: "Major Buckley didn't have many bosom friends and I could never get too close to him. He was a nice enough fellow, but very demanding and expected everyone to have the same attitude. But when I went to

Middlesbrough, the manager was David Jack and he was a great disappointment because he never had any contact with the players. At least Major Buckley spoke to you."

Full-back Jackie Brownsword knew what it was like to get on the wrong side of Buckley, who always had his dog Bryn Jones, named after the Welsh international he had nurtured as Wolverhampton Wanderers' manager, with him. Jackie played his two final games for the Tigers on the left-wing in November 1946 and explained: "Major Buckley started experimenting and he thought I'd make a good winger because I also did athletics and could do 100 yards in 10.3 seconds. But you need talent upfront and, although I could stop people, I couldn't take them on." But there may have been another odd reason why Jackie's career at Boothferry Park did not last long: "Doncaster was the main picking-up point for our away games in the Third Division North in those days, I was still living at Bentley and we had a goalkeeper called Cyril Hannaby, who was from Balby and also got on the bus with me. The directors often travelled with the team and on one occasion I had to look for a vacant seat. I found one and went to sit on it, but then realised that Major Buckley's dog was wrapped up in a blanket on it. I picked the dog up and threw it on the floor, so perhaps that's why I didn't play too many games for the club after that!"

Andy Davidson himself, though, was not entirely bereft of the dark humour of the soccer hard man. And he admitted: "I hated playing at right-back because I didn't think that I was getting into the game enough, so I used to say to opposition wingers from the start that they had one of two choices - the cottage hospital or the infirmary. I would then point out that the food was better at the cottage hospital, but that the surgeons were better at the infirmary! Funnily enough they nearly always seemed to settle for playing at left-back instead of on the left wing after that! I was sent off only twice in my career and one occasion was the first game of the season at Coventry after we'd been promoted in 1966 when Bobby Gould made a personal remark to me, so I retaliated. When it came to the return game at Boothferry Park, Bobby came up to me before the start and apologised for what he'd said. I still told him about his choice of hospitals and he went as white as a shroud!"

Andy's teammates were also quick to praise his uncompromising outlook. Winger Mike Bowering recalled: "Andy once told me when we were playing Chesterfield that they had a full-back who could be easily wound up if I said a few things to him, so I started to make some personal comments about his family as a joke. All of a sudden it was as if he had steam coming out of his ears and I suddenly thought that I might be in mortal danger. Fortunately Andy realised what was happening and ran 40 yards across the pitch from where he'd been playing to outside-left where I was and sorted the full-back out for me!" Dennis Butler formed a formidable full-back partnership with Andy and recalled: "I can remember one game at Plymouth when Nicky Jennings started on the left-wing for them. And it was an occasion when Andy tried to talk a player out of the game by telling him early on: 'You can make up your mind, but you and the ball won't both be going past me!'"

City's Scottish wing-half Tommy Martin had a reputation for being a skilful player who tended to opt out if matters ever turned a bit nasty, but on one occasion he apparently disproved the theory. He acquired himself a pair of special boots with a soft lining to help him on an icy pitch and one of the opposition players bated him about how ineffective they looked. The story goes that Martin then trod all over his opponent with his studs when no-one else was looking to prove otherwise! And Mike Bowering's League baptism in 1958 soon made him realise what might be in store for him: "My first game was a goalless draw at home to Swindon Town, who had former City player John Neal at right-back, so I was up against him. But John was an absolute gentleman and I couldn't have asked to be up against a nicer person on my debut. He said: 'You've nothing to worry about. I won't kick you.' I thought that that was really nice of him, but he paused and then added: 'But watch out for our right-half because he will!'"

Physiotherapists also see the darker side of football humour at times. The long-serving Jimmy

Lodge was generally popular with everyone and Len Sharpe said: "He was a lovely bloke and so laid back about everything." The goodwill seemingly evaporated in the treatment room on occasions, though, because Andy Davidson recalled: "Jimmy looked after people and was dedicated to the club. He was a great character, but he used to make up a potion with a paste and some linen and tell you: 'This won't hurt, you son.' All of a sudden it would burn you and you'd jump up off the treatment table. He would let out a little giggle and they'd be just about sweeping you off the ceiling!" Jeff "Muff" Radcliffe, cruelly dismissed by the Tigers in 1998 when he was two weeks of completing 25 years' service with the club, tells a story about an apprentice who came in for treatment for an injury after he had been bitten by a dog. Jeff told him to stretch out on his couch, surveyed his damaged leg and innocently asked for a medical clue: "Where did the dog bite you then?" The reply came back: "Just round the corner from the digs..."

There is also a dark humour surrounding footballing superstitions. One instance concerned City's visit to Oldham Athletic in the first round of the FA Cup in January 1912. The Tigers were 13th out of the draw, 13 players sat down to dinner in the build-up for the tie, the team won a whist match by 13 during the preparations, the match was played on the 13th and Charles Best, their goalscorer in a 1-1 draw, had slept in No. 13 bedroom in the team's hotel. Hopes were high for the replay because City had drawn at Oldham, then a struggling First Division club, and it was noted that the club programme for the replay was No. 13 of the season. But it became clear that 13 really was not the Tigers' lucky number because Oldham won it 1-0. Goalkeeper Bernard Fisher also told of a training tale of superstition: "One day Billy Bly went out just after the rest of us to train round the Boothferry Park track. We were opposite the players' entrance when Billy came out and trainer Angus McLean shouted to him: 'Run the other way!' That meant him going left to right, but Billy replied: 'I've run round the other way round the track for 20 years, so I'm not changing now.' A right argument took place and Billy trained by himself for a few weeks until it all settled down."

Humorous moments can work in someone's favour, too. City apparently sent a deputation of seven directors to try to sign Raich Carter from Derby County in 1948. Eventually Derby rested him for an evening game at home to Liverpool to enable him to sort out his future and the deputation were in action again. Raich reckoned a joke then confirmed the deal because he said: "As soon as I arrived, I was surrounded by the seven Hull City directors and rushed off to the Derby boardroom. I said: 'What again? The Seven Dwarfs after Snow White?' That gag clinched it. There and then I signed the forms for Hull City." Jackie Brownsword also experienced amusing moments of good fortune. He played in City's 5-1 win at New Brighton in October 1946 and a 1-0 home defeat against Rochdale a week later and recalled: "The club looked after me well because I was a smoker and I can remember the directors giving me a carton of cigarettes, which were then rationed, after we'd won at New Brighton. My other big memory of those days concerns the game against Rochdale when I was on the line to defend a corner. Our goalkeeper Cyril Hannaby punched it out to the edge of the penalty area and one of their forwards hit it straight back with great force. I was daft enough to stick my head in the way of it and ended up in the back of the net, but the ball didn't. I didn't even know what happened in the second half after that, but the following week there was a letter from a fan for me which said how plucky I'd been and contained £1 as a thank-you for saving a goal."

Wing-half Alan Jarvis became the final piece in City's playing jigsaw when he got into the first team in October 1965. But his League debut in a 3-0 defeat on a Friday night at Workington had a touch of irony about it. His teammate Malcolm Lord recalled: "We'd been winning a reserve game at Boothferry Park quite easily, so at halftime Billy Wilkinson and Ron Rafferty bet Alan £2 that we wouldn't sit on the ball during play in the second half. He did do and won the bet, but the club fined him £5! But the next week Gerry Summers was transferred, so Alan went into the first team for his debut and never looked back." Alan himself observed: "I'd got pig-sick of playing in the reserves at the time!" And he then made his full international debut for Wales exactly a year after his League baptism.

There again some humorous incidents can work against you. In 2004 I was caught up in an unseemly adventure with BBC-TV's Look North! after I had written an article for the East Riding of Yorkshire Council's monthly newspaper about the high incidence of obesity in the area. I tried to use some humour to increase awareness of the problem, but there might have been a hidden agenda somewhere because the TV presenters Peter Levy and Christa Ackroyd either did not understand it or did not want to understand it. Incredibly they proceeded to lambast me for promoting fitness through sport and even someone called Paul Hudson, who seems to have become a weatherman after failing his examinations in fashion design, chipped in to insult me. They should seriously look at the remarkable lead set by ex-Tiger Bob Dennison, who was always respected as a fitness fanatic and has still been out running regularly during the autumn of 2006 at the age of 74.

Bob's insistence on proper preparation, for example, shone through when he coached the East Riding Seniors: "I used to get the players off the coach a mile or so from the ground and tell them to run the rest of the way as a warm-up. They didn't half create about having to do it!" But it backfired when he was coaching Wolfreton Youth Club and once took them on a midweek run from Willerby during training. They ran about 10 miles and the players started complaining that it was far too long, bearing in mind that they had an important match the following Saturday. But Bob had not told them when they started out that the game had been cancelled and he wanted them to have a long run so that they could maintain their fitness for the following week. It was only when they were getting close to home near Swanland that Bob let it be known to the grumbling squad that there was no game that weekend. As a result, the players picked him up and promptly threw him into the village pond on their way past!

Bob is a lovely guy, but he also got into some scrapes during his playing career. In February 1955 City won 2-1 at Middlesbrough and Bob recalled: "It was Wilf Mannion's first game back at Ayresome Park and there were more people outside the ground than in it." He also believed that he had his best game in the Tigers' colours that day and it was written of him: "Young Dennison's work caught the eye of many shrewd observers in the North-East and they think that City have an England back in the making." The highlight, though, came afterwards when he was praised by Middlesbrough's manager - Bob Dennison! City's Bob Dennison recalled: "He just said: 'Congratulations on the way you played - from one Bob Dennison to another!'" Bob was less lucky on another occasion, though: "I once entered 'Find the Ball' in the Hull Daily Mail when I realised that I was in the photograph - but I still didn't win! To make it worse, I then found that I'd also got a copy of the original photograph with the ball on it!"

Dressing-room humour does not often lend itself to noticeably witty nicknames. But in September 1931 John "Jack" Diamond, who was from Middlesbrough and later played for clubs in Ireland and Wales, played in a 3-0 home win over Barrow. It was his only League appearance for the club, but he stayed long enough to acquire the nickname of "Legs" - apparently after an American gangster of the day. It is well-known that England's manager Steve McClaren no longer enjoys his nicknames of "Sid" and "BB" from his time with the Tigers even though no-one seems to know their original derivations for certain. Don Robinson's choice of "BB," though, is understood to have stemmed from two out of the following three - birds, booze and burgers - to reflect Steve's lifestyle of the day! But surely the most ingenious nickname for a City player was given to inside-forward "Dai" Davies, whose full name was David Daniel Davies. He was one of the few players who continued where he had left off with the Tigers after the 1939-45 War and in the currency of the time his initials of D.D.D. earned him the nickname of "3d." - or "Threepence" - from his teammates!

Some amusing anecdotes have stood the test of time in City's annals, but did they really happen?

Sometimes stories survive because of their quality rather than their veracity. One yarn concerns Doug Clarke, who was supposed to have encouraged his teammates to back a dog at long odds at a greyhound meeting at Hull's Craven Park after receiving a hot tip from the kennels, but it dropped dead during the race concerned. But Doug insisted: "I probably wished it had, but it didn't!" There was also supposed to be a wonderful story that utility player Stuart Blampey became annoyed with his teammates during a game of Travel Scrabble on the team coach when they insisted that a particularly valuable word of his did not exist. Apparently he then opened the coach's sun-roof, picked up the Scrabble kit and threw it out. In theory, there might then have been a poor motorist who had broken down and added to his woe when he picked up a Q on the hard shoulder, but Blamps said cryptically: "I can't remember the incident, but I'm not saying that it didn't happen because it might have done!" Then there is the oft-quoted tale about an occasion when manager Mike Smith was apparently asked about the state of the Boothferry Park after a match had been postponed on it and told a local-radio reporter: "Two-thirds of the pitch were frozen, but the other half was playable!" They are decent tales, but I can merely apologise if the incidents did not quite happen in the way that they have been handed down. And I can always quote the journalistic maxim: "Never let the facts get in the way of a good story!"

8

Travellers' Tales

It is actually very surprising that I have watched Hull City as frequently as I have during the past 50 years because I failed my geography O-level four times out of four when I was at school! I tend to tell people that the first three failures resulted from my inability to find the examination room, but it was a subject to which I did readily adjust. I may have been hit by a travelling blight, but it seems that I am not the only one if certain stories about City players are to be believed. They have been told regularly, but I have no reason to doubt the truth of them. For example, there was supposed to one player, who was apparently concerned that his proposed move to Scotland might hit a snag because he did not have a passport! On another occasion an international player apparently claimed that he was leaving City to join Middlesbrough because he had to move south for the benefit of his wife's health! And manager Mike Smith was only slightly more geographically blessed in 1980 when he took the players to see the placing of the final section of roadway on the Humber Bridge and said: "What a difference in time-saving it will be when we travel to Norwich and Ipswich!"

Curious stories linking Hull City with travel, in fact, have been in evidence from the early days when manager Ambrose Langley and director Fred Stringer used a novel way of signing a player. They had already snapped up two of the Browell brothers Anthony and George, when they paid homage to Hull's maritime image as they moved in to sign a third, Tommy, in 1910. Such was the determination of Langley and Stringer that they apparently rowed across the River Tyne to get to the Browells' home territory of Walbottle on the outskirts of Newcastle. They were successful in their mission, but it is open to conjecture as to whether it affected Tommy "Boy" Browell in any kind of peculiar way because he ended up working as a tram-driver in Blackpool!

Signing players, in fact, has not always been easy, especially when there have been deadlines to meet. The invention of the fax machine helped clubs immeasurably and some of the extreme escapades have now been averted. For example, when the Tigers signed former England defender Neil Franklin from Stoke City in February 1951, the transfer forms were sent by train from Hull to the Potteries. Malcolm "Mac" Stone, though, almost seemed to turn such occasions into an art form when he was City's secretary and a typical example occurred when they signed defender Dave Roberts from Oxford United in February 1975. City wanted to sign him in enough time to allow him to make his debut against Manchester United at Old Trafford that weekend, so Mac had to dash to London to complete the forms with Oxford, but there was a railway signalmen's strike that hampered his progress. Mac's train went to Goole and was then brought back to Staddlethorpe to go to Doncaster via Selby. But there was a delay at Doncaster and a journey that normally lasted four hours took nearly twice as long, so Mac arrived in London at 4pm with an hour to spare to the signing deadline. He finally sent the relevant forms from the Football League's London office to their headquarters at Lytham St. Anne's by telex in time, but at one stage City had even thought of telling him to get off the train and proceed by road - either by taxi or by sending a car to pick him up!

Enabling the players to travel to matches in time, though, has been equally as hazardous on occasions and one startling example of that occurred during City's early years. Towards the end of September 1919 the club faced travel difficulties when they had to go to Bury, then managed by ex-Tiger Billy Cameron, for a Second Division game because of what was described as "the paralysis of the iron road!" It was stated: "The team might not even get to Bury if the threatened strike on the railway matures." In the end alternative arrangements were made for the City party to travel overnight to Lancashire when the national strike did go ahead.

And it was reported: "The Hull City team and officials who made the journey to Bury on Friday afternoon will have anything but pleasant remarks to make regarding the men who called the strike and prevented them from travelling by the accustomed medium. Very early on Friday the officials of the club had no faith in the avoidance of the railway strike and got to work with the arrangements for doing the long journey by motor charabanc. It was estimated that the journey to Bury would occupy about six hours and that was the idea when the Tigers' party left the ground at three o'clock on Friday afternoon. The route taken was not the shortest one in the estimation of several of the party and the poor players were in an awful condition when the charabanc was still miles away from its destination nearing midnight and the rain was falling fast. Only a canvas cover kept them from being wet through and the cold and driving rain were hard to endure. Bury was reached just before two o'clock in the morning - nearly 12 hours of bowling over hills and dales. The party, almost numb with cold and cramped with sitting, got out of the vehicle with a fervent: 'Thank goodness!' that was qualified with the knowledge that the whole journey had to be gone over again in a few hours' time. The party were not long in being refreshed with hot drinks and good suppers and were in bed before three o'clock. Bury's supporters appreciated the efforts of the Tigers' directorate to see that the strike should not interfere with the game, but the effects of the journey had not worn off when the players were called upon to take the field. The return journey was started at eight o'clock in the evening and was by way of Burnley, Leeds, York and Beverley, being completed shortly after five o'clock on Sunday morning. Hull City have had many disconcerting experiences, but none to equal the Bury journey."

The Tigers lost 2-0, but in those days the return fixtures went ahead the following week for the most part, so the Bury party faced a similarly-taxing journey and set off at three o'clock on the Friday afternoon in the hope of arriving in Hull five hours later. But it was a lot easier for the referee for the return game at Anlaby Road - he was E. A. Wilkinson and almost unbelievably he had to travel all the way to the game from...Hull! The Tigers won 4-2 this time, so it might be curious to consider the reasons behind their sudden change of fortune against the same opposition! The strike was over by the following Saturday, though, and City duly made their plans to travel to Nottingham Forest by train, starting out at 9.10am. It was still an early start in comparison with modern-day travelling prospects, but City could be forgiven for not taking any kind of chance.

Travelling was still far from easy in the immediate postwar years and City's visit to Tranmere in October 1946 proved the point. City set off from Hull at 7.30am and arrived at Prenton Park at 2pm in those pre-motorway days. But it certainly did not deter centre-forward Benny Lester, who hit a hat-trick as the Tigers triumphed 3-1 for their first League victory both under Major Frank Buckley's management and since the 1939-45 War. And there were various means of travel for City's three-match summer tour to Denmark and Sweden in 1948 soon after Raich Carter had been appointed as their player-manager. First of all, a party of players and officials left Hull's Paragon Station by train on the Yorkshire Pullman to travel to London's Heathrow Airport, from where they flew to Copenhagen on a Dutch aircraft. There they met up with a group led by chairman Harold Needler, who had set off earlier by sea. Wing-half Jimmy Greenhalgh, meanwhile, was more concerned about his personal means of mobility because a pair of shoes, which he had sent for repair, were returned to him just before departure. And they were wrapped in a box with an amber-and-black ribbon, a lucky horseshoe and a goodwill message! In October 1948 City did not even stay together overnight before their 2-0 win away to Hartlepools United. The City party were based at Saltburn with one exception - Billy Bly, who was allowed to stay in Hartlepool itself as a guest of Jimmy Keen. Bly and Keen had both played for Walker Celtic in their home city of Newcastle although Keen, who had been a top-class sprinter, was much the elder of the two. It also became complicated when City were drawn away to Grimsby Town in the FA Cup fourth round in January 1949. About 5,000 fans defied the fog to travel to the tie by ferry across the River Humber, but club president Kenneth Percival was less lucky. He chartered an Auster aircraft from Brough with the North Sea Air Transport Company once they had been able to find a field in which they could land near Grimsby. But the fog caused the flight to be called off with visibility down to less than 100 yards, so Percival had to go by road instead.

In October 1962 City were supposed to visit Queen's Park Rangers, but Chris Chilton recalled: "We were due to meet them in their first match at London's White City. We left for the game in plenty of time and were then stuck in the traffic, which was a frustrating experience. We just sat and waited in the coach and the minutes ticked away. But we worried for nothing because the game was called off following very heavy rain." There was a similar kind of incident in London in the 1970s when City's coach was held up in heavy traffic on the way to Fulham and it looked as if they were facing a disciplinary reprimand for arriving at Craven Cottage too late to hand in the teamsheet. Their solution was to fill in the teamsheet while stuck in the traffic jam and then sent a messenger ahead with it - full-back Roger de Vries! He said: "I was always pretty fit in those days and could run and run, so, when we we were about a mile away from the ground, I was told to run ahead of the traffic to get the teamsheet in on time!"

City twice toured Scandinavia in 1971 and 1972, taking part in the July Cup in Sweden as part of their pre-season build-ups during Terry Neill's management. One of them began with crossing the Humber by ferry and then sailing from Immingham to Gothenburg and Neill said: "Most of us were feeling queasy after the bad crossing although we all recovered. The weather was terrible with heavy rain, so perhaps it was rather fortunate that our opening match was postponed with the boys feeling ill."

In February 1973 City lost 3-0 at Coventry in the FA Cup and their coach broke down at their overnight headquarters on the outskirts of the city. Hotel staff lent the players their minibus to take the team to Highfield Road with Terry Neill, his assistant Wilf Dixon and physiotherapist Jeff Radcliffe travelling by taxi. City were two goals down after 25 minutes and Neill observed afterwards: "I knew that it was going to be one of those days when we couldn't get morning newspapers or cigarettes at the hotel and the bus broke down on the way to the ground."

It was, therefore, brave of them to try to travel abroad in the Anglo-Italian Cup the following month when they faced Fiorentina. First of all their coach broke down near Boothferry Park and they had to rush to Leeds-Bradford Airport at Yeadon to fly to London. They had just boarded their next aircraft when they were asked to disembark because of a technical fault. They were then about to take off from Heathrow Airport when they were told that there would be a two-hour delay because of a problem with air control over France. As a result, they were late arriving in Milan and missed their connecting flight to Pisa. They managed to get seats on a later flight, but they did not arrive at their destination until nearly midnight after 15 hours' travelling. They went ahead with plans to train the following morning, but then lost 1-0. They then had to fly back to fulfil a League game at Oxford and lost it 5-2.

In November 1974 City, who had just appointed John Kaye as their manager, were scheduled to visit Notts County, but their coach developed engine trouble and broke down at their hotel at Barnby Moor, near Retford, en route. While the City party had lunch, a replacement coach was ordered, but it was delayed in a traffic jam at roadworks near Goole and then held up at two closed level crossings. Eventually it arrived just as the resourceful City party set off to cover the remaining 30 miles or so in a fleet of five taxis. They finally reached Meadow Lane just in time for the game, but promptly lost it 5-0. John said afterwards: "It is by no means an excuse for getting whacked 5-0, but I felt that having to mess about with taxis prevented us from getting the right atmosphere in the dressing-room before we went out. We never got into the right frame of mind or sorted out what we were trying to do, so we were disorganised." Yet what made the occasion even more superbly ironic was the headline about the club in an inside page of the Sports Mail on that Saturday night: "Hull City boss

John Kaye can take his L-plates down."

In October 1978 City were away to Gillingham and we stayed overnight a few miles away in the Maidstone area near Leeds Castle. City officials spoke to the hotel's manager after the pre-match meals to seek advice as to the best way to the Priestfield Stadium and he responded willingly and assiduously in as much detail as possible, so it seemed unlikely that we could go wrong. The City party gave themselves enough time for the journey in accordance with his directions and followed his instructions precisely only to realise that he had not been much of a football fan because he has sent us to the wrong ground in Gillingham - a military establishment near Chatham, where a services game was due to take place that afternoon! Unfortunately it was foggy by then, so there was little hope of following any kind of military precision because the one guarantee for anyone wanting to find any League ground in times of distress was no longer easily visible - the floodlights. In the end we did just get to the Priestfield Stadium in time, but City lost 2-0.

But travelling troubles surrounding City reached a peak in January 1984 when it was more a case of what did not happen than what did. Quite simply the Tigers failed to fulfil a fixture at Burnley because of the excessive travel conditions on the M62 and a fearful furore followed. City did not play a home game during that month: they completed just two away fixtures. But it was the one that got away that caused all the trouble. The club had basically done away with having pre-match meals at hotels near their destinations for Saturday-morning away trips. They had meant early starts because the meals were traditionally served more than three hours before kick-off time to help the players' digestion. There would then be periods of relaxation, normally involving watching lunchtime football programmes in television rooms, followed by short trips to the away grounds. But the abolition of stops for pre-match meals resulted in starting off much later and going straight to the grounds. At the time it was probably an economy measure, but on this occasion it cost City a lot more.

They set off for Turf Moor with the coach only about half-full and that was believed to have made it more difficult to handle once we experienced blizzard conditions on the M62. It felt as if the coach were swaying from side to side and driver Glen Holt did wonderfully well to keep it under control in the snow and wind. The road itself was a touch icy and we were starting to wonder if we were ever going to reach Burnley once we encountered the hills of the West Riding. Steve "Sid" McClaren had dropped out of the party because of injury on the morning of the match and Garreth Roberts, who was sitting behind me, memorably mentioned:"You hear about these disasters when someone escapes because of a twist of fate. Sid might be the only one left by Monday and may have to take over as manager..." I also recall that the club's chaplain, Allen Bagshawe, was also on the coach, so memories of the lyrics of the Everly Brothers' disaster classic "Ebony Eyes" came to me! I doubt that anyone was at all frightened, but there was possibly a feeling of apprehension.

At one stage two lanes of the M62 were blocked by an overturned vehicle and the speed limit was down to 40 mph. Glen said: "The conditions were appalling. They were the worst I've known in eight years of driving Hull City and it was difficult to keep the bus under control. It was the worst wind I've driven in for a very long time and at one point I felt that for the first time in my life that a bus I was driving might be going to go over." City set off just after their intended 11.30am start, having agreed with Burnley the previous day not to set off before a pitch inspection at 10.30am. We slowly and warily made our way to Hartshead Moor services on the M62, which was about 25 miles from Turf Moor, and stopped for manager Colin Appleton to telephone Burnley to tell them that we were late and it was by no means certain that we would be able to get through. He said: "I asked Burnley for a police escort, but I was waiting about 20 minutes for them to 'phone me back about it." In the end it was agreed that we would turn back and wend our way carefully home, but unfortunately a lot of travelling City fans had reached Burnley and the Turf Moor pitch was perfectly playable. Referee Ken Baker technically called the game off because of doubts about the Tigers' time of arrival, but the outcome was that they had clearly failed to fulfil a fixture and there was a danger that they might either have to concede the game or face a points deduction, which would have been disastrous when they were challenging for promotion. But there was also an extreme suggestion that City might be thrown out of the Football League.

I was asked to submit my view of the journey and the circumstances, as were others, and I did send a 900-word statement to the League. But I opted not to attend the first inquiry into the controversy in Manchester, which was somewhere between instinct and wisdom because none of the intended witnesses was called and no decision was finalised. And I do seem to remember that those who did travel at the club's expense had a difficult journey home because of a long railway delay! A full commission of inquiry did eventually proceed at Manchester's Midland Hotel, where City were represented by chairman Don Robinson, Colin Appleton, secretary Ivor White and Glen Holt. Referee Baker and Burnley's secretary Bob Bradshaw also attended the hearing and the Tigers got off remarkable lightly with a £2,500 fine. They also agreed to pay £4,000 to cover Burnley's match-day expenses on the day concerned.

Robbo commented: "We got a very fair hearing. They decided that there were extenuating circumstances, namely the arduous weather conditions. It was one of those things that won't happen again in 100 years. There has been a lot of pressure because of what happened and we are relieved by the outcome, but it is now part of the club's history. We like to think positively at Hull City and we can look forward again and concentrate on becoming Third Division champions." History shows, though, that the game was played on its own in midweek at the end of the season - which would not be permitted nowadays - when City knew that they needed to win by three or more goals to go up at all. They missed out, of course, by winning only 2-0. But who knows what the result and overall outcome would have been if the Tigers had actually completed their journey to Burnley on that freezing Saturday in January?

Steve McClaren may have missed out on that tortuous trip, but he has had his own travel trouble on the road to becoming England's manager. He gave Colin Appleton the nickname of "Tractor Man" after one juicy journey, but his career might have changed direction when he left City to join Derby County because Steve Richards said: "We'd shared a flat and then a house together and Steve asked me if I'd go with him when he went to have talks with Derby. He'd just got a new Scirocco and we went in it, but it broke down on the M1. Fortunately Derby were good enough to send a recovery vehicle to pick us up and I told Steve to ask them to throw in another new car as part of the deal!" It was not an isolated escapade, though, because Garreth Roberts said: "Steve had just got an MG sports car when steam suddenly started to come from it, so he took the radiator cap off and it blew up all over his chest. I think he got something like second-degree burns and the players didn't give him much sympathy for a few months even though we were glad that it didn't end up being too serious." And Stan McEwan added: "We used to go to Garforth College in Leeds to look for something to do after football. It was a business course because we were too engrossed in our playing careers and in those days you were hardly ever encouraged to take a job in football. Every Thursday we'd head off down the motorway. He had an MG sports car, but I could see the white lines on the road from the bottom of it! After that I insisted that it was safer if I drove in my car."

For my own part, I was quite brave when travelling with City took on a new dimension for me during 1986-87 as the fixtures began to pile up towards the end of the season. Manager Brian Horton had allowed me to travel on the team coach to cover away games involving the reserves and the juniors. But I broke new ground in May 1987 when the two teams played away on the same day. Covering both games, though, was feasible because they were both in the North-East. It just took a little imagination. The itinerary involved watching the juniors against Hartlepool United at the Victoria Ground in the morning and the reserves against Newcastle United at St. James' Park in the evening. I was able to do so because of the club's help and the fact that they needed winger Leigh Jenkinson to be involved in both games. Oddly enough, City's youth coach Dave King was unable to travel to Hartlepool because of his teaching commitments, so it was decided that midfield player Bobby Doyle would take charge of the juniors. Bob had been badly injured in a controversial challenge by Doncaster Rovers' player-manager David Cusack in what was supposed to have been a pre-season friendly. He had spent the season trying to battle back and had eventually fitted in four more League appearances, but had had to concede defeat and was preparing to retire from League football. At the same time he was a highly-respected senior player, so he was sensibly given the chance to be a coach for the day in Kingy's absence. The outcome was that the juniors won 1-0 at Hartlepool with Matt Sharpe's first goal in Northern Intermediate League football and Bob, accordingly, became the most successful youth coach in City's history!

It had been agreed with reserve coach Tom Wilson that Jenks and I would be taken to an agreed meeting-point before the junior party continued their journey home. I seem to think that we were jettisoned at the junction of the A179 and the A19 to wait for the reserves' coach. Fortunately it was a sunny day, but we must have looked like a couple of errant hitch-hikers from a seedy road movie as we waited for what seemed to be an eternity on the grass verge. We hoped that the arrangements would be synchronised satisfactorily, but I am sure that we talked about what we would do if we ended up being stuck "in the middle of nowhere" with not much more than a pair of football boots, a notebook and a bit of loose change between us if everything went wrong. Would we, for example, thumb a lift north to Newcastle or south en route to Hull if the reserves' coach missed us for whatever reason? Eventually it turned up, we were grilled about the juniors' performance and we arrived safely at St. James' Park. Assistant manager Dennis Booth made a playing comeback at the age of 38, the reserves drew 0-0 and Jenks started the game after having been used only as a substitute for the juniors earlier on.

I suspect that I may have set up a personal-best of seeing two away games involving City teams in the same day without a goal being conceded by either of them. It also meant that I was able to set up a 100 per cent record of being the only person to see every minute of every game - home and away - played by the juniors that season because no-one else - either players or backroom staff - had been present at them all. It was a season when, as a freelance journalist, I scored a century in one sense. I saw more than 100 different competitive games involving City teams at different levels during 1986-87 with the final tally closing on 106 a few days later from what I can remember. It spoke volumes, too, for the spirit of co-operation with the club in those days in the 1980s: after all, 10 years later I could not even get into Boothferry Park to cover games! And all it needed was a touch of geographical common-sense for everything to work out well. It also provided much-needed "match practice" for Bobby Doyle, a great guy who might have become a great coach because of his knowledge and approach to the game, in his future career because he left the club and the area at the end of the season - to become a long-distance lorrydriver! Even now, his annual Christmas cards still arrive safely to my home, too.

In theory, it should be a lot easier for players to find their way to their various home bases, but it did not always happen. Defender Richard Jobson, a recent recruit from Watford, went AWOL before a game against Bristol Rovers in March 1985 when he was seen setting off for Boothferry Park, but apparently turned away from the ground with it in his sights and journeyed south to sort out some pressing problem. There was a second occasion soon afterwards when he went missing before a reserve game, but he became one of the club's best defenders in recent years when he turned up regularly thereafter. Even more recently, there was a spell when so many of the players lived away from Hull that one of midfield player Michael Quigley's tasks was to pick them up in a minibus to transport them to East Yorkshire for their various commitments.

Earlier in City's history that had been occasional hiccups when players lived in their native North Lincolnshire before the advent of the Humber Bridge. Grimsby-born Norman Moore, one of the 1948-49 title-winning heroes, was one. He explained: "I used to travel on the ferry every day, so I got to know the captain and used to go up on the bridge with him, too. I used to pick up Denis Durham and we used to travel through together. And I used to be on the ferry with the fans from New Holland on match days. I couldn't get on a bus from the ferry because there were too many people on it, so I used to walk to Boothferry Park all along Anlaby Road and jump on a bus if I thought I saw one that was empty. But on one occasion we were due to play a Saturday game in London and the bus was supposed to leave Hull at nine o'clock on the Friday. Denis and I caught the eight o'clock ferry and we should have been in Hull in time to catch the coach, but the ferry got stuck on a sand-bank and we didn't get to Boothferry Park until lunchtime. The bus was still waiting for us when we arrived late, so we were in trouble that day!"

In the 1960s Scunthorpe-born utility player Len Sharpe was another. He said: "I was still living in Scunthorpe when I joined City and it was agreed that I would come over to Hull for training just two days a week. So I would drive to the ferry at New Holland, come across on it and then catch a bus to Boothferry Park. Then I'd go back by the same means. There were times when they would put me in digs and at one point they put Gerry Summers and me up in a new hotel on the outskirts of Hull because he'd just joined the club. Even in those days Gerry was very much into diet and having the proper food for a professional footballer, so we'd regularly have things such as T-bone steaks while we were staying in the hotel. But Cliff Britton called us into his office when he received the hotel bill and asked why it had cost so much for our food. We explained everything to him and his reply was: 'It would have been cheaper for me to have bought Jimmy Greaves than you two put together!'"

Then there are the problems when the players arrive safely and yet their kit does not. Terry Neill's reign as City's player-manager began in August 1970 with a 4-0 victory at Peterborough in the Watney Cup. Coach John McSeveney found before the tie, though, that the kit included two No. 9 shirts, but no No. 6. But to the best of my knowledge left-half Chris Simpkin did not have to rectify matters by wearing one of them upside down! Then the following August Chris Chilton was in trou-ble for missing the pre-season trip to Sweden, but his boots travelled even more badly than he did. They had not been packed for the opening League game of the season at Charlton and he had to play in a borrowed pair. And by the end of the month his boots had been made for walking - to Coventry City!

A precedent had probably been set when City visited Southport on Christmas Day 1947 and their preparations were thrown into disarray. They stayed overnight in Liverpool before the game and woke on Christmas morning to find that the team coach and their kit had been stolen, so Southport had to lend them their old colours of black-and-white shirts. The Tigers won 2-1 and a replacement coach was sent to Southport, but then Liverpool police telephoned afterwards to say that they had found the missing one in a Merseyside suburb. Unfortunately some of the players' gear was still missing. But there was another worrying tale of travel on City's coach concerning more Merseyside mayhem for a reserve game at Liverpool in 1986 because there was a shot on target before it had even started! The coach was on its way through the West Derby suburb of Liverpool en route to Anfield when a sniper shattered its back window with what was later thought be an air-gun pellet. One suggestion was that it was merely a brick that was responsible for the damage, but an examina-tion of the window made it less likely. Assistant manager Dennis Booth recalled: "No-one was in any danger. The lads just heard a crack as something struck the back window and shattered the glass." We had to stop to check the damage and ended up using a fleet of taxis and a car provided by a Liverpool director to take us on the final stretch to the ground. As a journalist, I was deemed to be one of the least important members of the coach party, of course, so travelling reserve Neil Story and

I had to wait to transport the kit in the final taxi. After the match we travelled home safely on a replacement coach while the original one was taken to Blackpool for repairs.

Travel troubles have also been known to haunt City's management. In 1971 Tommy Docherty, who had been manager of Porto, arrived late in Hull to become the club's assistant manager because his car had broken down. One of the most-travelled coaches in professional football history, he then announced: "I have finished flitting around. I am here to stay." So should we have been surprised when he was on his travels yet again a few months later to become Scotland's manager? Then in April 2003 City lost 2-1 at Rochdale after being two goals down in the opening 18 minutes to goals by Lee McEvilly and Darren Hockenhull. On the day of the match a headline over an article by defender Justin Whittle in the Hull Daily Mail read with wonderful irony: "Rochdale is not an easy place to go." And it was certainly true in manager Peter Taylor's case because he did not arrive until halftime after being stuck for three hours in a traffic jam on the M62 near Eccles. Taylor, who had been trying to sign new players, explained: "It was a very frustrating time, especially when you hear that your team are losing 2-0. That didn't help. I don't think that my absence was a factor although I'm sure that it was a bit different for the players. All of a sudden they must have been thinking: 'Where is he?' Hopefully they are thinking that I must have been looking at players all over the place."

Even though I started out as a journalist covering City with a pre-season trip to Scotland during the summer of 1975, I have never travelled abroad a lot, largely because I still think that there are wonderful areas of England worth exploring. But I did travel by ferry to Holland for a long weekend in April 1981 to stay with Rob McDonald, the ex-Tiger who made far more of an impact on the Continent than he ever did at home even though he briefly wore the coveted No. 9 shirt with Newcastle United. He explained: "The different style of play suited me in Holland because I'd got quicker-thinking players around me. I was stagnant at Hull and would never have improved if I'd stayed. Playing in Holland gave me an opportunity to see how I could do against good players. I played in a pre-season match for Hull City at Bridlington Trinity and within a month I was scoring two goals against Ajax in Amsterdam." My trip was an education in learning at first-hand quarters how the Dutch, then one of the world's leading football nations with their panache for the so-called "total football," built up their soccer system. But the weekend was hardly educational in terms of seeing how Rob was coping with League football in Holland. I went with one of his friends, Willem Straatman, to watch him play for FC Wageningen at third-placed Utrecht, who won 5-0, but he pulled his hamstring after 28 minutes, went off seven minutes later and that was it! Even though I class myself as a Yorkshireman rather than an Englishman, I even became just a touch patriotic when the United Kingdom for once won the Eurovision Song Contest with Bucks Fizz singing "Making Your Minds Up" during the stay. I think that we went to an English-style public-house in the area and managed not to get too jingoistic.

City's own club trips abroad began with a trip to the Continent in May 1908, but I had never been anywhere by aeroplane until chairman Don Robinson took control of my life by inviting me to join them on their foreign tours. The first one took place at the end of the the 1987-88 season while Robbo was searching for a replacement for the recently-sacked Brian Horton, so all kinds of "red herrings" as to the possible identity of his successor were put my way. But I found that I was on the receiving end of numerous wind-ups for the whole of the trip to Marbella in Spain - possibly because I was an "outsider" as a journalist and, therefore, ripe as being cannon fodder. Nothing is ever simple in life, of course, and I should have been suspicious from the start when I discovered that my first-ever trip by aeroplane was to take place on Friday the 13th. Director Richard Chetham was so superstitious that he decided not take any risks and flew out prematurely on Thursday the 12th instead! I was daft enough to let everyone know that I had not flown before and joint caretaker manager Tom Wilson led the flurry of wind-ups as we took off.

Don was then kind enough to take a carload of us on a day trip to Gibraltar, but we had been given a warning beforehand about his driving. It seemed to be another wind-up because he drove perfectly all the way there and nearly perfectly all the way back on what was, after all, one of Spain's more manic highways. He did, though, blot his copybook slightly when he drove his hired car up the approach to the Atalaya Park Hotel in San Pedro, where we were staying, and struck the foot of a concrete wall as he went to park it!

In November 1988 there was a suggestion that it should be never on Sunday for City's games because they lost 4-0 at Stoke. But as we boarded the coach home, chairman Don Robinson confirmed that I was to be invited to join the club on a mid-season break - to Bermuda! The Tigers had a gap in their fixtures before Christmas after visiting West Bromwich Albion and Don had decided to take the club away for 10 days. Manager Eddie Gray, though, was to stay behind to look after club matters with a brief to concentrate on means of team strengthening. It meant that the City party would travel to London after the game at the Hawthorns, stay overnight near Heathrow Airport and then fly to Bermuda via New York the following day. Three fixtures had been lined up during the trip, so it was more of a change of environment than a break for the players. But there was a problem soon after we had arrived because it would not stop raining. On the Monday afternoon I telephoned the sports desk of the Hull Daily Mail to report in and inform them that the first game had been put back because of a waterlogged pitch at the Pembroke Hamilton Club, which was not far from our hotel. They could not believe that I had flown halfway round the world to what was supposed to be a touch of paradise for a postponement. My colleague Richard Tingle told me: "It's a nice sunny day in Hull for December!"

One of the first jobs for us was to indulge in a spot of public relations on the island, so Richard Jobson and I were chosen - or possibly instructed - to visit one of the local television stations to do an interview about the trip. We were picked up and brought back by taxi and thought that our treatment was quite special. It was only after we had been on the island for a few days that we discovered that nearly everybody travelled by taxi because the Bermudians very rarely used private cars! The most remarkable aspect of the television interview was the way in which we were addressed. The interviewer introduced us as Jobson and Bond, which probably sounded like a firm of undertakers, and never once used our first names. We did not expect to be called by the more formal Mr. Jobson and Mr. Bond, but it sounds as if we were back in a strict regime at school when we were asked questions on the lines of: "What are your plans for the trip then, Jobson?" and "How do you like the island, Bond?" Anyway the people at the television station were otherwise pleasant and there were no hints that we would be kept behind in detention at the end of the interview!

There was another form of transport that was popular in Bermuda - the motorcycle. Three young officers from Humberside Police were doing a spell of duty on the island and I had been designated by their families to take their Christmas presents out to them. The lads, in turn, would look after me well. One of them, Phil North, whose father Bill had briefly been a cricket colleague of mine, offered to take me "for a spin" on his motorcycle as part of my introduction to the island and I was a pretty poor pillion passenger! At one point we approached a mini-roundabout and I was so certain that we were going to fall off that I decided to throw my weight to the opposite side from Phil. I did not know that you were supposed to throw your weight to the inside when going round corners or roundabouts, so it was something of a miracle that we stayed on. Phil, who informed me what I should have been doing unnecessarily politely, worked wonders to keep us both on board and I opted not to go anywhere by motorcycle for the rest of the trip. The players, in fact, were banned from travelling by motorcycle during the visit and I can understand why!

Physiotherapist Jeff Radcliffe and I did take a short boat trip from the bottom of the hotel garden to the capital St. John's and back, but I resolved to either walk or run if taxis were not needed. One walk was with Don Robinson and lasted about five miles. It was refreshing because Don outlined his plans for the club off the record. He knew what he wanted to do to try to take City on to the next stage - the First Division - and it all sounded positive and optimistic, but he was unhappy that the Needler family had not seemed to willing to back his ideas financially and they never came to fruition. I had just started to do some regular running and I was sharing a room with Billy Askew on the trip. Billy had had an injury problem and was a member of the party in order that he could improve his fitness. There was a golf course attached to our hotel, so Billy and I would run round it and often goalkeeper Tony Norman would join us. And while the other players were training, Billy, Jeff and I would go off to the other side of the island to an idyllic spot called Horse Shoe Bay. I would run there and back and, while we were there, we did a series of repetition runs up and down its plentiful sand dunes so that Billy could build up his strength and I could diminish mine.

The most disturbing aspect of the trip, though, came on the night that we were preparing to return home in time for Christmas. Most of the television on Bermuda was from American stations and Ken de Mange and I were watching a broadcast in the hotel lobby before teatime when there was a newsflash about a Pan-Am aircraft that had gone off the radar between London and New York - the journey that we ourselves had taken only a few days earlier. The next newsflash indicated that the American aircraft may have been lost somewhere near Carlisle. Some of the other players had joined us and, as the news unfolded, we realised that we were being told about the Lockerbie Disaster. All of a sudden England and Christmas seemed a lot further away. The mood of the party became sombre and the evening meal before our departure - from St. John's to Heathrow - seemed to be more akin to the Last Supper. When we arrived at the airport to leave, passengers were being turned away because they had had too much to drink in an attempt to forget about the imminent flight. The deflated City party, who had flown by Pan-Am from New York to St. John's on the outward journey, just went ahead with it in a subdued manner that was naturally bereft of the usual high spirits and good humour. We were all grateful to land at Heathrow safe and sound the following morning.

My third and final experience of flying and going on a trip abroad with City came during the build-up to the 1990-91 season. It was to Bulgaria and it was again masterminded by Don Robinson, who had suggested it because he was involved in some business ventures, especially a golfing complex, out there. Manager Stan Ternent had agreed to let a Yorkshire TV crew, led by the admirable John Helm, do a documentary memorably called "A Kick in the Balkans" of the trip, so we all had to be on our guard. But there was some time for sight-seeing in the Vitosha Mountains just outside our base in Sofia and I travelled up them with members of the City party on yet another mode of transport - a cable car. Meanwhile, Dave Bamber and Garreth Roberts were rooming near me in our hotel and Dave had a "ghetto-blaster" with him so that he could regularly listen to the BBC's foreign broadcasts to keep in touch with the news back home. One day one bulletin stopped us in our tracks because it informed us that Iraq had invaded Kuwait and a Gulf war might be impending. I remember asking an English businessman in the hotel how close we were to the possible conflict. He replied: "The good news is that we've got Turkey between us and Iraq and the bad news is that Turkey have yet to be on the winning side in three world wars." Two of my worst subjects at school - history and geography - were suddenly haunting me and I realised that I really did not mix well with flying on Tigers' tours. I have been grounded ever since.

It seemed that away days were fraught from City's early days, in fact. Travelling was obviously less sophisticated, but they got about a bit in their desperate attempt to clinch First Division status at the end of 1909-10, for example. They trained at Cleethorpes before a visit to Gainsborough Trinity and a home game against West Bromwich Albion, both of which they won. Accordingly, they returned to Cleethorpes and then moved on to Blackpool before the final game at Oldham, which would decide their fate. But they lost 3-0 and have never been so close to the top flight since. And in February 1915 City prepared for an FA Cup tie at Southampton by staying at Worthing's Central Hotel. But three days before the game the players saw Worthing lifeboat called out to a schooner-rigged boat. The lifeboat twice capsized and a member of the crew, Jack Burgess, was washed away. Then there was the saga of the summer tour to Turkey in 1950 and the story of a match that is not in the record-books because it failed to last the distance. Some of City's players were apparently on £7 a week during the season and £5 a week during the close season, so they had the chance to make up the shortfall because they were on a bonus of £1 per goal in Turkey and they duly went 3-0 up in the first few minutes. At that point the home fans rioted, the police and Army were called in, the rest of the tour was cancelled and the players never got their £1 bonuses for the three goals that they had managed to score so quickly!

Perfect preparations for a game might, therefore, go awry and amiss despite all the good intentions. When City were drawn at Sunderland in the FA Cup fourth round in 1975-76, it was decided that the players would go away to Scarborough in the week building up to the tie. It was not a new formula because it was the kind of idea that had gained momentum during the 1960s even when City were drawn at home. It was felt that it would work wonders for team bonding although I doubt that it was called that in those days. It seemed, though, that George Lyall had eroded it somewhat because the players competed against each other in all kinds of different sports during the stay and he seemed to win on every occasion! On the Friday night secretary Mac Stone and I travelled on an empty team coach from Hull to Scarborough with driver Jack Horner, a lovely man who was respected by the players even though he had more sedate musical tastes for journeys than they did. Jack had dropped off the City party at the start of the week and then returned to base, so it must have looked as if it were a badly-supported coach trip to the coast as we went to pick everyone up! Oddly enough, it was on that trip that we discussed the fact that Jack's employers, Boddy's, were soon to be no longer in charge of City's travel. The Tigers party, supposedly in good humour after their few days from it all together, moved up to a hotel near the seafront at Seaham for an overnight stop before the cuptie. The problem then was that towards the end of the evening it began to snow heavily and manager John Kaye, Jeff Radcliffe, Mac Stone and I took an evil delight in watching from the hotel lounge as various vehicles tried to negotiate a roundabout outside with an icy stretch on its approach. I think that we gave the drivers marks for artistic content as they slithered all over the place. Needless to say, the cuptie was called off early the following morning and the extra spirit of togetherness was probably lost on the journey home because City lost 1-0 when the tie finally went ahead nine days later.

As I approached 40, I tried to keep myself reasonably fit and humbly took up running after covering athletics for the Hull Daily Mail in addition to being responsible writing about the Tigers. During 1988-89, though, I met my match because I ended up with my own fitness trainer at times when assistant manager Dennis Booth would either encourage, cajole or compel me to do some testing runs round Boothferry Park. They were based on what the players might do, especially in pre-season training - 12-minute runs and "doing the steps." In the first instance it was a question of running round the track at Boothferry Park for 12 minutes and trying to complete at least eight laps in the time, but I never quite managed it. Boothy also put me through some shuttle runs up and round the South Stand, taking in the front and back steps without missing any out. I soon discovered that they were designed for me to try to keep up with manager Eddie Gray on the longer away trips. Eddie was always keen to utilise the fitness centres in the hotels in which we stayed, but he was also a good runner and would dare me to try to keep up with him on the roads. I seem to recall a dummy run of some kind when City visited Bournemouth in the early part of the season and we ended up on the seafront on a rainy afternoon - or it might just have been that I ran like a dummy! When we visited Ipswich towards the end of the season, Eddie insisted on a run as soon as we arrived at a hotel on the outskirts of the town. We ran as far as Portman Road to look at the stadium and it was only on the way back that I realised that it was uphill most of the way. Eddie, whose wife Linda had been a top runner, left me behind before kindly slowing down to give me a chance of catching him up! And I can remember that a couple of away games later he insisted upon on a run along Brighton's promenade before breakfast on the morning of the match. I usually have enough trouble getting up for breakfast, so running before it was alien to me. Away trips were becoming hard work, Eddie showed me up again and my respect for him genuinely increased.

The 1988-89 season was also notable for the advent of inflatable products among supporters of football clubs. It started with Manchester City's fans with their inflatable bananas and a madcap craze soon took a stranglehold. They were in evidence when the Tigers lost 4-1 at Maine Road in January 1989 and soon afterwards I somehow managed to get hold of a copy of a brochure for a range of the products. To my delight I found that the list included inflatable tigers, so I decided to market them on behalf of Garreth Roberts' testimonial appeal, of which I was his chairman. It would have been ideal to have had a supply of them available in readiness for the FA Cup tie at home to Liverpool the following month when interest in the club was high again and Boothferry Park was filled to its limited capacity. But the inflatable products could be bought only at an address in London and I had to wait until City visited Chelsea 10 days after the cuptie. Everything worked out well for that midweek trip because the City party travelled down to London on the morning of the match and then rested in a hotel during the afternoon. I had time to kill and I realised that the hotel was only about two miles from the address marketing the inflatables, so I set off to walk to it. It was a private address, but it contained a lock-up warehouse, of which Arthur Daley, I am sure, would have been proud in "Minder." I walked round the warehouse, which naturally captured the imagination with its amazing array of inflatable products, and did a deal for a batch of tigers on behalf of Garreth. I then trudged back to the hotel through the streets of London with my somewhat bulky purchase and found that most members of the City party greeted my efforts with a mixture of disbelief and maybe even disdain.

Garreth thought that I was mad although he eventually agreed to have his photograph taken with one for publicity purposes a few days later. But I suspect that I caused something of a stir as the team coach pulled into Stamford Bridge when I tried to blow up one of the tigers, which were about three feet long when fully extended. But I discovered that the small tube for inflating it was situated midway between its hind legs, so the whole process took on a decidedly-dubious tone! Anyway City lost 2-1 that night although Garreth responded positively by scoring their first goal at Chelsea since 1905 - in what was only the third League game in the club's history. I seem to recall that the tigers did make a small profit for his funds, but they were never quite the "nice little earner" that they were supposed to be, probably because City became embroiled in a poor sequence of form after their FA Cup run and the season ended on a low note. The outcome of a different way of passing a spare afternoon on a City away trip was that I was, in fact, left with a few spare tigers at one time, so I blew one up at home and stuck it conspicuously on the ledge of my sitting-room window as a very humble form of deterrent to any would-be burglars!

Hotels loom large in football clubs' travel arrangements, but can they affect results, performances and even people's livelihoods? City's visit to Brentford in December 1979 hinted that they can. Several players involved in that trip told me that the club booked them into an inferior hotel in London as a cost-cutting exercise and the poor facilities even affected their sleep patterns. One member of the party described the accommodation as "a doss-house to save the club a few quid." The outcome was that the Tigers were thrashed 7-2 at Griffin Park and soon afterwards the management team of Ken Houghton, Andy Davidson and Wilf McGuinness were sacked by chairman Bob Chapman and personnel director Ian Blakey. It ended Andy's link with the club lasting more than 30 years in different roles and he admitted: "Hull City were the biggest part of my working life, so I took it hard. I was only scouting for them at the time, but they made their decision and I had to go."

Trips to Plymouth were the longest possible that City had to make in the League, but they were nearly always enjoyable because there was a spell when they had a good record at Home Park. But the trips never seemed to pass without incident and there was one involving Andy when he was assistant manager in the 1970s. We normally stayed at good hotels, but in those days they did not have the fitness centres that are nearly always part and parcel of them nowadays. We always thought that we had done well if we stayed in a hotel with a just a mere sauna and Andy, physiotherapist Jeff Radcliffe and I were usually the first to want to make the most of them. One Saturday morning we were chatting and passing the time away in a sauna at a hotel in Plymouth when a lady came in to join us. Andy was always one for devilishly stoking up the coals in saunas to get them as hot as possible in the belief that we might be taking maximum advantage of them, but this time it proved too much for this poor lady, so she politely turned round to us and said: "It's a bit hot in here. I hope you don't mind if I open the door." She did do and, as the cooler air blew inside, it was one of the few times that I have seen rendered Andy speechless, which was just as well because I dread to think what he would have said if the shock of her action had not temporarily flummoxed him! There was no chance of any hot air from any of us!

In fact, we often stayed in the Holiday Inn in Plymouth and there was another odd incident during a pre-match meal when we stayed there in April 1979. While we were waiting for our meals to arrive, Micky Horswill, who had been signed from the Pilgrims, regaled us in a very matter-of-fact way with a story about his stay in the hotel soon after moving to Home Park. I seem to think that his brief statement went roughly as follows: "Funnily enough we're sitting now where I was having a meal soon after coming to Plymouth and a bloke committed suicide by jumping out of one of the top-floor windows. In fact, he landed on the ground outside there..." He pointed out of a nearby window, there was a stunned silence and few of us really had much of a stomach for our pre-match meals after that! It was the Micky's first game back at Home Park since joining City, who won it 4-3. But manager Ken Houghton made a point of telling him not to approach the game in any kind of head-strong manner just because he was playing against his old club. The kick-off to Plymouth went ahead and the referee blew up for it to be retaken because Micky had encroached from it. The game restarted, Micky charged forward at Gary Megson and basically put him out of the game. It was all over after about eight seconds of the start and I think that it probably remains the quickest booking by any City player ever...

There was hotel hassle of a different kind when City were scheduled to visit Blackpool on New Year's Day in 1977, so. A trip to Blackpool would not normally have needed an overnight stop, but it was natural to keep the players together under supervision on the night before, so the City party were booked into a hotel in Preston for New Year's Eve. The backroom staff adjourned to the bar and the players went to their rooms after the evening meals and pools manager Joe Witherington joined us during the evening. The players had been told that they could come down to see in 1977 and we all assembled in an ante-room just before midnight. We all sung "Auld Lang Syne," we wished one another well and shook hands with each other and Joe said a few fitting words. The players then returned to their rooms and the staff returned to the bar. It was then that the fun began. It might have been the season of goodwill to all men, but a family fight broke out at the table of drinkers next to us in the bar, so manager John Kaye had to intervene and sort it out. Then the night porter ventured in a bad state to state that someone had cracked him on the head with a bottle while he was delivering drinks to some guests, so physiotherapist Jeff Radcliffe had to go to his room to collect his medical gear and returned to give him first aid. City drew 0-0 at Bloomfield Road later in the day and youngster Dave Gibson suffered a broken bone in his leg as the result of a controversial tackle by former

England star Mike Summerbee and the team coach was delayed after the game, so Radders really did not experience much peace or goodwill at all on the first day of the year.

There was a slightly-carefree approach to City's final game of 1975-76 for various reasons. The Tigers were in a comfortable mid-table placing in the Second Division as they ventured to Southampton after a thoroughly-inconsistent campaign. The Tigers had lost only once in 11 League games before being thumped 4-1 by promotion-chasing Sunderland on Easter Saturday and there had been some strong exchanges in the wake of it between manager John Kaye and some of his players en route to Carlisle two days later. It was nothing more than one of the many differences of opinion that may be run-of-the-mill during the course of a season at any football club as passions often run high, but all was not sweetness and light and matters nearly boiled over during the pre-match meal. Anyway City worked hard for a goalless draw at Brunton Park and John sensibly lightened the mood as much as possible on the journey home. It was also pertinent to keep everything ticking over smoothly at Southampton, who had other things on their minds because they were due to meet Manchester United in the FA Cup final at Wembley the following week. The Tigers were playing for pride and the Saints were probably playing to avoid injury. City were to lose 1-0, but there was an excellent atmosphere on the evening before the game. City had established a good link with HMS Tiger, whose representatives, normally led by a top man called Charlie Stirling, always tried to organise a social occasion of some kind when the club visited the south coast and the ship was in dock somewhere in the vicinity.

The socialising did not involve the players - just the backroom staff and me. Accordingly, we were told by the HMS Tiger crowd that we had been invited to a party in Gosport on the night before the game at the Dell. The immediate difficulty was how to get there and back with a minimum of fuss, but the coachdriver Glen Holt came up trumps. He agreed to transport us on the team coach, but there was a slight problem. No-one really wanted to draw undue attention to a Second Division club's team coach travelling up and down the south coach late at night or in the early hours before a League fixture. Again the intrepid Holty provided a wonderful solution. First of all he took down the sign indicating "Hull City team coach" that was always displayed behind the front window. And he replaced it by going through the many destination possibilities on the blind above the front window and stopped at "Brighton." It was felt that it might adequately preserve a certain amount of anonymity for the team coach and its occupants, but it turned out to be only a temporary reprieve. The coach duly arrived at a hotel in Gosport, where we had agreed to meet before moving on to the party. It was near the seafront, we had just got the drinks in and we were looking out on a pleasant early-evening vista when John Kaye was spotted. A middle-aged couple, who were on a few days' holiday, politely approached us and said: "Excuse us, but aren't you John Kaye, the Hull City manager?" Yorky owned up and the couple said: "We thought you were, but we weren't sure. It's just that we live just round the corner from you in Kirkella..." The cover of anonymity had been well and truly blown. I think that John perhaps muttered something about "a small world," but his reaction was typically rather more blunt after they had left our company.

Later on we moved on in the team coach to the party and the sight of it parked across at least two entrances on a modern housing estate with music blaring out from one of the addresses must have been a touch incongruous by the early hours. We eventually set off back to the hotel and I think that we may have offered a lift towards home to some of the partygoers, but the return journey to Southampton did not go entirely smoothly. One male partygoer and one female partygoer decided that it would be nice to spent a few minutes in close proximity to one another on the way, so they comfortably cuddled up on one of the long seats towards the back of the coach. Any romantic notions were soon dispelled, though, because Holty contrived to ensure that the coach was subject to an unnerving amount of "kangaroo" fuel on the way - a technique that he later developed to epic proportions when I tried to have a pee in the mobile toilet on the coach before a game at Port Vale. Anyway the happy couple soon became unhappy and a stream of oaths followed every "bump" in the road. To make matters worse, the coach was forced to stop at a set of traffic-lights at one stage and, while we were waiting for the green light, a drunk tried in vain to clamber on to the coach while shouting that he wanted to go to Brighton! None of it affected the game the next day, of course, but for the record City ended up with the same result as Manchester United against Southampton a week later - a 1-0 defeat.

A jolting coach caused a more pressing kind of problem on the way to a game at Southampton in November 1986 - an injury to a player. City were travelling to a Full Members' Cup tie when goalkeeper Tony Norman was unexpectedly ruled out of it en route. He explained: "We travelled down to Southampton on the day of the match and on the coach we got changed from our tracksuits into our suits just before we stopped for something to eat. But all of a sudden the bus rolled on the motorway. That was all it was, but I was on one leg trying to put the other one into my trousers and my back clicked. From then it was dead simple: my back began to tighten up and soon became solid and we couldn't do anything to loosen it up." Central defender Peter Skipper had to take over from him in goal because the competition was considered to be relatively unimportant by most clubs and they did not burden themselves unduly with large squads for away ties. But I had played against Skip in a Hull Sunday League game in which he had performed creditably in goal and City escaped with only a 2-1 defeat.

There was also something of a standing joke about Normo's back and artificial playing surfaces. He will openly admit to hating them, as will many goalkeepers, and he always seemed to require fitness tests before travelling to play on Oldham Athletic's old "plastic" pitch. He holds the record for the longest unbroken run of League appearances in the club's history - 226 - and it duly came to an end in September 1988 at Boundary Park. And I should have known better when I joined him on various stages of a charity walk during the spring of 2005. Normo was raising funds for the Children's Heart Federation by doing Wainwright's traditional coast-to-coast walk from St. Bees, near Whitehaven, to Robin Hood's Bay in North Yorkshire. The first stage on which I joined him was between Thwaite and Reeth in remote North Yorkshire. It soon took on a surreal aspect because we went through Gunnerside - his former City goalkeeping partner John Davies is nicknamed "Gunner" and only occasionally got into the "side" because of him - and then saw a sign to Crackpot! And I had naturally thought that I would be perfectly safe to walk with him, but he needed to rely on his mental toughness to complete the stretch - because he was consistently hampered by severe back trouble!

Footballers, in fact, are notoriously fickle about travelling as pen portraits of them in match programmes often prove. So often their pet dislike is recorded as "travelling to and from away matches," but midfield player Malcolm Lord had every reason for not enjoying the experience in one instance at Plymouth in October 1966 when he was name as the 13th man in the party in the days when a side were allowed to use only one substitute. He explained: "We got £4 appearance money with the first team, but I didn't get it because I was only 13th man. I would have been richer in the reserves, so I complained to Cliff Britton. He put £2 extra in my wage packet instead - the win bonus with the reserves!"

And there were times when the travelling journalist's job also comprised driving the cars belonging to people who were going on the coach if the insurance allowed it. I think I did it for George Lyall, Stan Ternent and John Kaye when they needed their cars with them on away trips. But my former colleague Simon Redfern told a magnificent tale of when he was asked to drive striker Alan Taylor's car to Lincoln in February 1984. He asked me to go along with him for company and, when I got in, he insisted that the cassette that had been playing was a recording of the 1975 FA Cup final

- when Taylor scored twice for West Ham United! I later heard that Alan had become a milkman in East Anglia, so perhaps he then drove around to the sound of "Ernie" by Benny Hill instead!

I often used to like to catch up on a bit of sleep on away trips, but stood little chance of it in reality, especially when the players would wile away the journey by playing Travel Scrabble. I became an unofficial consultant about the validity of certain words, so I would be ritually awoken from my slumbers to adjudicate on disputes. I never checked whether I was asked because they thought that I might have an idea about words as a journalist or because it was a convenient excuse to disturb my sleep pattern.

Playing cards and Scrabble were once the most popular pastimes for passing the time on away trips if dubious magazines were unavailable for close scrutiny. At one stage manager John Kaye and I became regular partners in a card school when we took on secretary Mac Stone and physiotherapist Jeff Radcliffe at whist - although no money ever changed hands, of course. But it all backfired on me in January 1977 after the Tigers had been giantkilled in the FA Cup by Port Vale. I thought that John might be under a bit of pressure at the time, so I thought that I would try to relieve it and clear the air by getting him a public vote of confidence from the chairman Christopher Needler. I duly did so, but John was not best pleased because he felt that it was a bit unnecessary. As a result of the article, he duly dropped me from the card school as a punishment and promoted first-team coach Phil Holme to be his partner in my place! I was relegated to playing Travel Scrabble with some of the players at the back of the coach and got into further controversy when I refused to let one of the lads, who shall remain nameless, use up all his final letters with the word L-O-A-B when he claimed it was part of the ear! Eventually, though, the club sacked Phil as coach three months later - and that meant that John had to give me back my first-team place in the whist school as his partner. The partnership lasted until John, who was one of City's most underrated managers in my view, was sacked himself the following October. I then reverted to sleeping on the bus - if the lads would let me.

There would also be disputes about the choice of blockbuster films and music tapes to enliven coach journeys. Veteran coachdriver Jack Horner was deliberately driven to distraction by players in the 1970s when they chose loud, modern music on away trips. Poor Jack's party piece was to threaten to throw the offending tapes off the coach when the players repeatedly asked for them to be turned up. They would then ask him what music he preferred and he would name singers from more sedate and serene bygone eras. The replies would then be: "Sorry, we haven't got anything by him, Jack" or "Never heard of him, Jack." Even in Bulgaria there was a dispute about the choice of music on a hired coach between manager Stan Ternent and his new signing Tony Finnigan. Stan had got fed up of listening to Finn's modern soul sounds and demanded the sobriety of country-and-western ditties. I cannot remember how it was resolved, but Stan got my vote on the Bulgarian jury! Another problem on coach journeys would be created if a television set was provided because it was near impossible to get a good picture that was remotely in focus. It was irritating when there was a football programme on because there was always interference even though some players gallantly offered to produce delicate balancing acts with the controls while trying to tune the television in properly with the coach hurtling down a motorway.

Coach travel might generally lead to anxious moments for journalists. You had to adopt a sixth sense as to what you could or could not report if you overheard something that was supposed to be off the record, but even then you were not always safe. Radio Humberside journalist Peter Ward was once on the receiving end after a goalless draw at Chelsea in February 1976. My view was that City deserved some praise after battling for a point during a poor run of form. But the game had been dire as a spectacle and Peter had apparently said that "City had played as if rigor mortis had set in." The comment was passed on to players from their families when they rang home after the match because we were staying overnight in London before travelling back the next day. When Peter got on to the bus the following morning, he was greeted with a bit of flak and loud comments among the players such as: "My rigor mortis feels bad this morning. How's yours?" For my own part, there was an occasion in April 1978 after a 1-0 win at Charlton when Billy Bremner came to sit next to me near the front of the coach and told me that I had been out of order in something that I had written about the disappointment about relegation. I had written that City might have been expected to have done better in 1977-78 because they had a number of players in their ranks with international experience at different levels. As a former Scottish international, Billy took exception to the comment and proceeded to tear into me. We both had ginger hair in those days and I can recall almost spitting out my response to him. It was never a loud slanging-match, but I am sure that everybody knew what had been going on. In the end he moved down the bus, but it is a situation that you want to avoid even though you know that the potential for it is always lurking in the shadows. To be fair to Billy, he had made his point and he was always amicable after he had left the club a few days later. And one of the other internationals, Dave Roberts, had the good grace to come up to me later and tell me to take no notice of Billy...

Coach trips can throw up all kinds of strange occurrences - literally. According to his teammates, forward Doug Clarke had a reputation for feeling queasy or fainting if the City party ever passed serious road accidents. And there might have been blood on the seats on a trip to Rochdale in the early 1980s. No-one was entirely certain where Spotland was once we had left the M62, but Billy Whitehurst assumed the role of navigator and started to provide directions that probably had to be obeyed. It prompted Dennis Booth to take his life in his hands at the back of the coach by courageously stating: "He might be able to find the ground, but I bet he can't find the back of the net when he reaches it!"

Occasionally directors would travel on the team coach to away games and the players by and large did not relish their company. They would often move around the bus to avoid sitting near them in case they had to indulge in polite conversation with them. Often I used to end up talking to the directors because everyone connected with the club seemed to be making up excuses for not being sociable with them! There is a grand story about one occasion when Micky Horswill was cornered and ended up with a director sitting next to him. Micky kept looking out of the window to try to keep the conversation to a minmum, but the director concerned persistently tried to be chatty. Eventually the director turned the topic of conversation to Manchester City to remind Micky that they were one of his old clubs. Micky said little, but the director gallantly carried on, saying: "They had some very good players when you were with them, didn't they, Micky?" Micky gave a curt acknowledgement of the statement, but was unable to keep a straight face any longer when the director then said: "Yes, I always thought that Asa Channon was a great player!"

Arriving at games in time was always essential, of course, but it has never deterred City from having some other adventures when they have been homeward-bound. In February 1913 City lost 3-1 away to Birmingham City in what was Alwyn Smith's last game as their chairman and their travel plans left little margin for error because it was reported: "The Tigers made very hurried journeys. They left Cannon Street Station in Hull at 9.40 and they had only 20 minutes after the match to catch their train home. Taxis were engaged to take the players from the ground to the station." And in March 1954 City did not arrive back home from a Saturday game at Plymouth until 4pm on the Sunday "after almost 16 hours of continuous travel." They then met Falkirk in a friendly on the Monday evening.

In my early days of covering City we even stopped for evening meals on the way home from the longer away trips. I can recall times when we stopped at Nottingham on the way back from Luton and Newbury on the way back from Portsmouth. The club's great generosity soon stopped, though, and I suspect that many of the players welcomed the change simply because it meant that they had a better chance of getting back to Hull in time to make the most of the local nightspots! But in May 1988 there was a detour with a difference on the way home from an away game after City had ended the season with a goalless draw at Reading. Caretaker manager Dennis Booth decided to show everyone round the high spots of his heritage. Boothy came from Stanley Common in Derbyshire, we had all heard how marvellous it was supposed to be from him and now we were about to find out. The coach pulled off the M1, we had a conducted tour of the local sights, we were taken for a drink in one of the local hostelries that he used whenever he went back home and he even met his dad in it. But what did Boothy's local street credibility little good was the moment when he directed the coach on to a housing estate and got us temporarily lost!

In the early part of 1988 I had been at the centre of another detour when City suffered two heavy away defeats and there was a notable travelling link between them. I was not travelling on the team coach regularly at that time. I seem to recall that I made my way separately for the shorter trips, but could travel with the team for the overnight stops. On New Year's Day the Tigers lost 5-0 at Aston Villa and I journeyed with a photographer by company car provided by the Hull Daily Mail. I found out later that one reason given for the heavy defeat was the team's hurried arrival at Villa Park after a delay en route. It appeared that the coach went to one motorway service station to pick up some players and one of them, Tim Hotte, went to another by mistake. The party were held up quite simply because one faction went to Woodall on the M1, the other went to Hartshead Moor on the M62 and never the twain did meet until Tim turned up at Villa Park by car after realising that something has gone drastically wrong! The situation irked manager Brian Horton so much that he then decreed that only players and the important backroom staff could travel on the team coach. I have a feeling that he even told director Richard Chetham to make his own way to away games although an exception was made in my case for the FA Cup when City visited Watford in the third round. But a clampdown without any exceptions eventually ensued, which was unfortunate for me when the Tigers visited Bournemouth on February 6. It was agreed that I should travel to and from the game at Dean Court by train, but I deliberately booked into the same hotel as the team for the overnight stop. The City party arrived before me and I remember waving to the management through a window as they talked in the hotel's restaurant after their evening meals. I eventually had my meal and everything was sociable and friendly for the trip. I made my point by walking to Dean Court from the hotel rather than accepting a short lift on the coach. But I did ask if I could leave my overnight bag on the coach during the game, which was allowed without hesitation.

But City were embarking on a phase of heavy defeats at Bournemouth. This time they lost 6-2, the following season they lost 5-1 and in 1989-90 they lost 5-4. After the game I duly went to collect my bag, find my way to the railway station and hoped that I negotiated all the necessary train connections to get me back home sometime on Saturday night without undue problems. Brian had been as honest as ever about the defeat in his after-match Press conference and was just getting back on to the coach himself as I went to collect my bag from it. "You might as well travel back with us," he told me. I accepted the lift because it would save time and possible train complications and everything went smoothly until we got towards the end of the M62 when Brian asked me where I wanted dropping off. I said that I had left my car at Brough railway station on the Friday afternoon. He replied that that was no problem and immediately directed the coachdriver to make a detour to the station so that I could pick up my car after we had reached the A63. The players were naturally a bit fed up with the long journey after being thrashed, so they started to complain quite strongly when they realised that we were making a detour through Brough and questioned the reasoning for it. Brian told them in no uncertain terms: "We're dropping off Bondy at his car at the railway station because we need all the help we can get from him after that kind of result!" At the same time I always wondered what time I might have reached home if City had won...

But it had been less comfortable in September 1975 when City lost 1-0 at Charlton on a Friday night, stayed in London overnight and then travelled home on the Saturday. It was one of the bleakest coach journeys that we ever encountered and I have a feeling that manager John Kaye conveniently missed it because he went on a scouting mission, but Roger de Vries recalled: "The windscreen was shattered, so the driver wrapped himself up, which included putting a rug round himself, and drove us home without it. The rest of us curled up at the back of the coach, but the weather was miserable and it was a horrible journey for everyone."

And comfort was also absent after one of City's best displays of the 1975-76 season at Plymouth when they won 4-1 in an FA Cup third-round replay. We stayed overnight after the game and most of the lads were duly shown round the city until the early hours by representatives of HMS Tiger. The trouble started, though, on the long journey back because Jeff Wealands, George Lyall and I suddenly started to struggle with a stomach bug. Luckily there was a toilet on the team coach, so the three of us basically took it in regular turns to take full advantage of it. But technically it was just our luck that we should suffer from "the runs" on the longest away run possible. In fact, I was still making frequent toilet trips later in the week when I was back at work at the Hull Daily Mail. And I returned from one such sojourn to be told that my emergency visit had forced me to miss an important telephone call from manager John Kaye. It was only to tell me that he had just sold winger Roy Greenwood to Sunderland for £140,000, so I did pause briefly to wonder if I had really got my priorities right that morning...

At least I got home, which is more than City's commercial manager Arthur Anderson did on one occasion. Arthur would travel on the team coach for the shorter away trips and disaster struck for him after a 1-1 draw at Bury in October 1978 when he nipped briefly into the social club at Gigg Lane just before the City party were due to leave on the journey home. Manager Ken Houghton explained: "I'd told everyone to be back on the coach by an appointed time, but Arthur nipped into the social club for some cigarettes and we set off without him." As the coach eventually made its way along the M62, Houghy innocently asked where Arthur was. Someone, therefore, shouted to the players: "Is Arthur at the back of the bus with you lot?" The reply came: "No, he's at the front with you." The response from the front came back: "Oh, no, he's not." It might have come from a classic pantomime script. By this time Arthur had made his way to Bury's railway station to find a way home because he had, of course, missed the bus. Apparently the train journey from Bury to Hull on a Saturday night was tortuous and lengthy and he finally arrived home very late in the evening.

In April 1989 I probably took my life into my hands on our way back from a 1-1 draw at Ipswich. The Grand National had been won by Little Polveir earlier in the afternoon and Billy Whitehurst, who had scored City's goal, had organised a sweepstake on the race for all the passengers. It is not the kind of sporting participation that interests me in the least, so I had politely told him that I would give it a miss. Big Billy was distinctly unhappy about my refusal to take part, so he tried to get the coach stopped. He told manager Eddie Gray that he wanted me thrown off it for what he memorably described as a breach of "the spirit of the bus." In a way I suppose that I could see his point to the extent that we were all part of the coach party together and naturally I did not fancy trying to find an alternative means of getting home from deepest, darkest Suffolk to East Yorkshire on a spring Saturday evening. Fortunately Eddie held sway and Billy, who had meant what he had said as far as I was concerned, benevolently respected his decision to allow me to stay on, but not without some muttering for the rest of the journey. He was still a touch displeased with me when he got off the coach just off the A63 near South Cave. I stayed on the coach because assistant manager Dennis Booth and I had agreed to go for a drink in Willerby, as was often our custom in those days. Being teetotal, I tended to be Boothy's driver and I dropped him off at home midway through the evening. I began to drive home and thought that I would call in briefly at the Bear Inn in South Cave on my way, which I did. And who should be propping up a corner of the bar but Big Billy? I was not going to avoid him, so I went up to him and he greeted me with open arms. He was in a great mood and had forgotten the disagreement. In fact, I think that we led a brief sing-song at the end of the evening. It was an excellent sociable night all-round and I could not help but thinking how lucky I was to enjoy it because I might still have been making my way back from Suffolk - by thumb and feet!

Travel has often been a source of frustration for fans, too. In September 1970 I was a victim myself as a supporter when journeying to a Football League Cup tie at West Ham and the coach company concerned managed to get us to Upton Park just in time for halftime! A parallel situation occurred in the same competition in November 1975 when City lost 2-1 at Doncaster Rovers and some visiting fans did not get into the ground until nearly halftime because there were only three turnstiles to serve more than 1,000 of them. Some City fans had arrived an hour before the kick-off even though they had already been held up by an accident near Brough and roadworks on the M62, but the police then told them at the Belle Vue Ground: "Don't blame us! The club have not got enough turnstiles."

It is a fierce fact of life that away travel sometimes causes anxiety to supporters and it is often necessary to be clever and creative to ensure that destinations are reached safely and satisfactorily. In March 1948, for example, the extreme travelling behaviour of City fans came to the fore during the three-game Easter period. City were scheduled to be away at New Brighton on Good Friday and away at Oldham on Easter Saturday, so most supporters decided to stay overnight between the matches to reduce the travelling. But one party of them actually arrived back in Hull after the New Brighton match at 7.40am and soon departed by train for Oldham at 8.55am! And none of the supporters saw the Tigers score a goal because they lost 1-0 at New Brighton and drew 0-0 at Oldham. And at the height of the Tigers' popularity in February 1949 a total of 27 supporters flew from Brough to Meir for the big FA Cup tie at Stoke, while some fans from Bridlington hired taxis for the day! There was an almost parallel curiosity in August 1974 when Ray Tupling and I hired a car to take us to a game at Southampton. But the players, who drew 3-3, flew to the Dell and yet hardly did so in style because they travelled from the comparative obscurity of Paull Airfield east of Hull in two aircraft belonging to Humber Airways.

At one point Ray and I were both privileged to be members of the Happy Wanderers, an intrepid group of City fans who, not surprisingly, got into plenty of scrapes on their frequent travels. Their trips began during the 1956-57 season when Bernard "Ben" Feldhun, Dorothy Kirby and John Urwin started to travel on a minibus called "The Happy Wanderer." "Pop" Sanderson was the organiser and his son Jim, Jill Kirby, Kathleen Constable, June Gelder, David Whitworth, Ian Myers, Harold Lister, Zena Wilson, Fred Francis, Alan Swales and Harold Tarbottom regularly accompanied them. Sheila Bowes, Edith Pullen, Gwynneth Pullen, Brian Hague, Ron Barlow, Stan Edwards, Terry Wilson, Beryl Grassby, Janice Rawling, Frank Noble, Gina Galloway, Graham Jackson, Jenny Clark, Doug Saunders, Ken Woodward, Terry "Duke" Ellington and Ray Tupling followed at various stages. The "Happy Wanderer," in fact, was eventually replaced by the "Happy Rover" and the fans twice changed bus firms, but they could still recount tales of arriving late for games at Millwall, Reading and West Ham.

Dorothy Kirby told a tale of an away fixture at Sheffield Wednesday when they could not find Hillsborough. They stopped to ask the way and were told to follow the tramlines. "We did and ended up in the tramshed!" she said. And even if there were not enough of them to fill a minibus, they would try all possible means to make sure that they would see the Tigers. Terry quoted an occasion when six of them found that the coach was full and they had missed a train, so they went by taxi to Barnsley. It cost them 28 shillings per head and their taxi-driver told them that they were mad, but Terry added: "He was a City fan really, so he watched the game!" Terry told of another trip when they stopped at Gloucester after a game at Bristol Rovers and were walking down the street when a large board on some scaffolding for Christmas decorations crashed down near them. He said: "In another couple of seconds we'd have been killed stone-dead!" But festivities were never allowed to derail their dedication to travelling away to watch City because they spent the first moments of 1972 in the minibus on a garage forecourt in Goole to let in the New Year soon after setting off for an overnight trip to Portsmouth.

Other hazards included a trip to Exeter in April 1965 when they stopped for lunch at Bristol on the Sunday after the game. Ben Feldhun explained: "Jack Bolton, the driver, was just getting out of the bus when he dropped its keys down a drain." They removed the grating, borrowed a brush from the nearest public toilet and tied it to an empy beer can, but still could not reach it. In the end the bus was restarted with the aid of a hairgrip borrowed from one of the lady fans! The following April there was further consternation on a trip to Oxford because Ben said: "We were watching the match when they asked over the PA system if our driver would go to the car-park and move the bus urgently so that a midwife could get out to go and deliver a baby!"

Brian Hague, a quick-witted character who had played music locally, was determined not to be beaten when there were not sufficient folk to fill the minibus for a Friday-night game at Watford in March 1970. He was forced to hitch-hike back from the game and was rescued by a lorrydriver who had to stop at Northampton en route. It meant that they had to unload cabbages in a market in pouring rain at three o'clock in the morning before resuming their journey! It had been a natural sequel to an occasion in November 1964 when 17-year-old City fans Mike French and Ken Houghton hitch-hiked from Hull to the Tigers' FA Cup tie at Kidderminster Harriers overnight after setting off at 3pm on the Friday. They reached Kidderminster at 4am on the Saturday, made their way to the Aggborough ground and unfurled their sleeping-bags in the directors' box, which was where club secretary Ted Gamson found them when he arrived to finalise the preparations for the tie!

There is also a yarn involving a group of City fans on a trip to Millwall because one of them, Ian White, explained: "In those days in the 1960s we would give ourselves plenty of time to see the sights of London before going off to the matches. On this occasion we visited Regent's Park and hired some boats to take out on to the lake. But two of the fans, Dick Mars and Arthur Dearing, had trouble with their boat, which capsized in the middle of the lake and they ended up swimming back to the shore fully-clothed. Then Arthur saw his City scarf at the side of the boat, so he went in again to fetch it! Fortunately they found a dry-cleaners' shop nearby, so they sat in their toilet while their clothes were dried!"

But there can be serious drawbacks for those fans who like to be able to claim that they never miss a match home or away. For example, a total of 34 of them missed the Football League Cup tie at Orient in September 1976 when their coach broke down just south of Leicester. The coach had developed an oil fault and alternator trouble and, although a replacement was sent, it arrived too late to get them to London. As a result, Graham Jackson missed his first City game home and away on mainland in Britain since August 1969 when they had lost 2-1 at Blackburn. He said: "I decided to go by bus because my car has not been going too well, but, to my great displeasure, we never got to the match. We were left absolutely stranded." In another instance, though, the club themselves came to the rescue when a supporters' coach broke down after City had lost 2-0 at Swansea in January 1998. This time fans were not left stranded because player-manager Mark Hateley offered them a trip home on the team coach. And in April 2006 some City fans missed the start of the last game of the season at Watford because they were late setting off from Hull when they suddenly found that one of their coaches did not have a driver, so they had to wait for a "substitute" to be brought in.

I reckon that at one point I had seen the Tigers play at 89 of the 92 League grounds although the concept leads to irregularities. The occasional advent of ground-sharing begs the question as to whether you are allowed to count the ground or the club among your tally. Then there may be a case of having seen City play at a club's old ground but not a newer stadium. Again, do you count the club or the ground? And I have seen the Tigers play reserve games and an FA Youth Cup tie at Everton, but not a first-team fixture at Goodison Park, so am I allowed to include it in my tally? At least I once had something in common with benefactor Harold Needler, who had not only driven his car 8888H behind the Iron Curtain to support England, but had also at one stage seen City play on 89 League grounds. Above all, the travel trails should never be underrated and devoted fan Trevor Pearce, from Hornsea, began 2006-07 with a record of having seen City in every League game, FA Cup tie, Football League Cup tie and Associate Members' Cup tie in their different guises since April 1985 when he missed the club's 2-0 defeat at Bristol City on Easter Monday. Quite simply, he deserves a medal the size of a spare wheel not only for his loyalty, but also for his ability to have defied the travel demons to achieve it.

City and their followers then have been embroiled in plenty of escapades while travelling to and from matches - and at times they seem fated by ironic occurrences and strange scrapes. And it is probably fair to suggest that it was all summed up in manager Terry Dolan's programme notes for the club's home game against Port Vale in January 1994. Dolan had been to assess Vale at home in an FA Cup replay against Southampton in midweek and most of his notes were taken up with the tortuous tale of his travel problems in getting to Vale Park. He had had trouble getting on to the M6 and insisted in his programme summary: "We are now in an era when travelling by road is becoming increasingly difficult and in my opinion Thomas Beecham has got a lot to answer for in running down the rail system." Sir Thomas Beecham, of course, had little to do with far-reaching transport decisions and was a noted conductor - but of orchestras rather than on the buses or railways! Dr. Richard Beeching, though, certainly did ruin the railways in the 1960s and would probably have been pleased to escape the blame in this instance. At the same time I was twice in the same sports quiz teams as Dolan, who was a more-than-useful contributor, so I do not believe for one minute that he actually got the names wrong intentionally. It was more likely that something was lost in the translation, but it did provide another amusing quirk in the Tigers' travellers' tales.

9
Here Today, Gone Tomorrow

There was an ironic touch to the timing of the inaugural meeting of the Ex-Tigers' Association for former Hull City players - because it took place three days after record goalscorer Chris Chilton had played his last match for the club. Chilton moved on to Coventry City in a £90,000 deal after scoring 193 goals in 415 League appearances for the Tigers - and it coincided with the official birth of the Ex-Tigers' Association at a meeting in the social club at Boothferry Park on August 24, 1971. The meeting was the culmination of an idea nurtured by another successful City centre-forward, Colin Smith, since April of that year when a team of ex-Tigers, oddly enough, met North Ferriby United in a game to raise funds for Chilton's testimonial. The match attracted a crowd of almost 500 and Colin said: "It proved that people would turn out to watch former Hull City men in action again and I thought that a team such as this might raise no end of funds for the needy. It also gave the players the chance to get together again besides making money for charity. They all said how much they enjoyed it and that more fixtures should be arranged."

In addition, David Coates, who had played in the same promotion-winning forward-line with Colin in 1958-59, had started to organise annual reunions in Hull in local public-houses for his former teammates. The basics, therefore, were in place and it just needed Colin's drive to make things happen. In the end, he was voted in as the new association's first chairman and the story goes that it was done in his absence because he was away on business with the now-defunct Hull Brunswick, where he was player-manager, for the early part of the evening when the meeting was held!

The meeting elected Fred Ramsden as secretary and Bob Larter as treasurer with a further three committeemen, comprising ex-players Brian Bulless, Denis Durham and Paul Feasey, who were all at the meeting. Bill McCracken, Jimmy Lodge and Charlie Flood were made life members and four vice-presidents - Don Revie, Alan Plater, Tom Courtenay and Malcolm Richardson - were elected. The meeting attracted an attendance of 23 and the other former first-team players present were Billy Bly, Frank Harrison, Wilf Hassall, John McSeveney, Andy Davidson, Dave Fraser, Eric McMillan, Bob Dennison, Mike Bowering, Joe Stocks, Dave King, Alan Shaw, Benny Bridges and Ken Smales.

The number of charity games duly increased and several still take place every season. Most take place to raise funds for good causes in Hull and the surrounding villages, but there have also been fixtures against showbiz, TV, radio and media sides and three fund-raising games against ex-Grimsby Town sides in 1999, 2000 and 2006. There have been several notable guest players in Ex-Tigers' line-ups. For example, local rugby-league hero Johnny Whiteley filled in as a goalkeeper in the early years and full-back Wayne Jacobs played in one Easter Sunday game at North Ferriby to help his fitness after City had controversially freed him following a serious knee injury. Not long afterwards Jacobs joined Rotherham United and went on to give long service to Bradford City.

There have been other guests who have represented the Ex-Tigers and yet they have not technically been ex-Tigers. I did actually represent Hull City in a cricket match when they played in a friendly at Sewerby during the football pre-season build-up in 1977. Chris Galvin, who was a useful player who had appeared in the Huddersfield League, organised it, there was a shortage of cricketing Tigers wanting to take part and I was graciously allowed to turn out. The cliff-top at Sewerby is a wonderful location in which to play cricket, but it has to be recorded that I had bowled fairly badly - even by my modest standards - and I fared little better when I was given the chance to open the batting. I have always suspected that it was a ploy by the lads to make sure that I got a duck because I opened with Vinny Grimes, who spent the whole of our partnership trying to run me out. What had been miscalculated was that I was perfectly capable of getting myself out cheaply in any case and I duly perished for one - having hit the ball to all four corners of the crease - because of one of the

133

flaws in my batting technique!

Even though it was an enjoyable occasion, it is hardly enough to qualify me as a Tiger. I might have had better luck if I had been allowed to join City on their pre-season tour to Holland two years later. There were some intriguing substitutes in one of the games - a 5-0 win at Bergum - because they included coach Wilf McGuinness, coachdriver Glen Holt and physiotherapist Jeff Radcliffe. Manager Ken Houghton was another substitute although he had, of course, qualified as a genuine ex-Tiger long before. I wonder if they ever had international clearance - either beforehand or afterwards! I have always believed that maybe I, too, might have been awarded a run-out at some stage of that match if I had been sent to cover the tour It does underline the point that people have not always had to do too much to qualify as an authentic ex-Tiger. All the genuine contenders really need to have done is to have worn the amber and black - or an accepted alternative strip - as a player at any level or as a full-time member of the backroom staff.

The possibilities, therefore, are amazing and seemingly endless and the Ex-Tigers are lucky to be able to continue playing games for good causes with the help of regulars such as Peter Skipper, Steve Brentano, Rob Smith, Neil Sellers, Mike Smith, Lee Warren, Kenny Baker, Andy Saville, Tim Hotte, Russ Wilcox, Malcolm Shotton, Gregor Rioch, Gary Brabin, Neil Mann, Matty Edeson, Kenny Harrison, Carl Heath, Mark Carroll and Colin Moody, some of whom who travel from out of town to play whenever they can. Andy, in fact, scored four goals in a game as a grandfather in October 2006, but I challenge anyone to provide a definitive list of every qualified ex-Tiger. It is surely an impossible task because the documents may not be available to list everyone who has turned out for the club - however briefly at whatever level. After all, the early club records were destroyed in the Anlaby Road fire of 1914.

And it is better to include everyone who is known to have represented the club because it is also difficult to define what constitutes a "game." The Ex-Tigers, for example, still have to go through the procedure of obtaining permits to sanction their friendlies from the East Riding County Football Association, the parent organisation of whom they have to be members. Presumably, therefore, it is possible to qualify as an ex-Tiger simply by being involved in any game which is officially autho-rised. Even that can be misleading if, say, abandoned games are thrown into the melting-pot. After all, goals do not count in abandonments, but bookings and sending-offs do, so what about counting appearances in them? But the appearances are also erased with the goals and the goalscorers.

City played in the FA Cup in their first season, but they did not play League fixtures until their sec-ond. Hull-born Alan Hardaker did not mastermind the Football League Cup until 1960. They have been the major competitions, but there have been numerous others in which the club have featured, including the East Riding Senior Cup, the West Riding Cup, the Billy Bly Memorial Trophy, the Terry Gibbon Memorial Trophy, the East Riding Invitation Trophy, the July Cup, the Newland Orphanage Cup, the Football League Group Cup, the Football League Trophy, the Associate Members' Cup, the Full Members' Cup, the Anglo-Scottish Cup, the Anglo-Italian Cup, the Watney Cup and the Third Division North Cup. Then there are reserve games, A-team games, minors' games and junior games. Then there are friendlies, testimonial matches and wartime games. Some of the players to appear at these and other levels may been here today and gone tomorrow, but so have some of the competitions in which they turned out!

Those players who have represented City include many whose opportunities to wear the amber and black have been limited. Their appearances have been forever fleeting and frequently forgotten and yet it has not always been their fault because tricks of fickle fate have often lent a hand. In the early days centre-forward John Christmass, who had been playing for Atkins Limited, scored four goals in the first quarter of his debut for City Reserves against Mexborough in February 1915. He was described as "a young player with some brawn about him" and hailed as the new Tommy Browell.

But the 1914-18 War prevented him from playing in the League for the Tigers although he scored four goals in his first three games for them in what was known in wartime football in September 1915. Then there were those who appeared only in City's opening two League games of the aborted 1939-40 season - at home to Lincoln City and away at Southport - which were technically expunged from the records because of the 1939-45 War. Jack Curnow, Richard Lowe, Dennis Quigley and Thomas Smith played in both of them, while Patrick Gilmore appeared only at Southport.

All kinds of circumstances may have led to players' short stays with City and trialists provide one category that caused more of them than most. It is virtually impossible to list everybody who had a trial at various levels, particularly because there have been so many of them and partly because some of the earlier records are comparatively vague. Some of the stories about trialists, however, have thrown up some weird and wonderful circumstances and again fate often tended to lend a hand in deciding the players' destinies.

In a lot of instances, too, they tell the tales of the ones who got away. They may not have been in the right place at the right time with City, but they bounced back to become international players. In the early years after the 1914-18 War, for example, right-back Doug Gray had a trial with the Tigers, but was allowed to leave. Gray instead went on play for Glasgow Rangers from 1925 to 1947, winning a host of trophies with them, and also represent Scotland 10 times between 1928 and 1932 before having a spell on Clyde's coaching staff. Goalkeeper Ted Sagar had a trial with City in November 1928 while playing for Thorne Colliery in the Doncaster Senior League. He was 18, came from nearly Moorends and went on to play for England four times. But if he had stayed with the Tigers, he might have become their longest-serving goalkeeper instead of Billy Bly because four months later he joined Everton and amazingly remained with them until May 1953. He made 465 League appearances for the Toffees and one of his teammates was future City manager Cliff Britton.

Striker Kevin Hector had a trial with City after being sent to the club by John Kavanagh, their scout in the Leeds area, and played for the juniors at Anlaby Road. Leeds-born Hector said: "I was 16 at the time and played on either the left or the right wing, but obviously Hull City couldn't have thought very much of me. I then had a trial with Bradford Park Avenue and they signed me. Apart from Bradford, Hull were the only club with whom I had a trial." City Juniors' coach Wally Chapman gave him a glowing report and later recalled: "My biggest regret is that we didn't sign Kevin Hector when we had him on trial, but the manager Bob Brocklebank said that we couldn't afford to take any more players that season." Brocklebank later claimed: "It must have been before my time!" Oddly enough, though, he later tried to sign Hector from Bradford PA when he was in charge of Bradford City. Hector, meanwhile, twice played for England in 1974 during his long spell with Derby County.

Full-back Stuart Pearce, as with Hector, worked under Brian Clough's management for a significant part of his career, which included winning 78 caps for England, whom he also captained. But it might have been a very different story because he had a trial with the Tigers. He trained as an electrician and spent his early days, to use his own words, "wiring houses." He added: "I had four years in goal on a Sunday morning supplementing my semi-professional career with my mates." But Pearce played at left-back for City's reserves in a 1-1 draw at Grimsby in October 1980 when he came on trial from Wealdstone with England non-League international John Watson. A wet night in Grimsby may not be the perception of paradise for an 18-year-old from Shepherd's Bush and Pearce admitted in his autobiography "Psycho": "I was average." It seems that he was never likely to sign for City because he had a pact with Watson that he would do whatever he did. The older Watson was initially less keen to make the transition into League football because of his family and business commitments, so Pearce followed his lead. But Watson changed his mind at one stage of the negotiations and yet it still ended with neither of them staying. Defender Steve Richards played alongside Pearce that night and joked: "I made him look good and I headed a few his way! I can remember the game vaguely, but nobody really knew Stuart Pearce at the time although he did show that he was as tough as old boots. He was good and could boot the ball a mile! The management were fussing around him at the end of the game to try to get him to sign, but I think that the money wasn't good enough for him to go full-time then." And it was never officially recorded as to whether the torrential rain at Blundell Park ever had any significance on Pearce's thinking, but Grimsby's reserves did include Mike Brolly!

During the autumn of 1971 City's player-manager Terry Neill had planned to return to his native Northern Ireland to snap up a promising young player from Distillery called Martin O'Neill. But the plans were put on hold and O'Neill signed for Nottingham Forest instead before becoming a Northern Ireland international and highly-respected manager. In November 1987 City were keeping tabs on a young forward with Crewe Alexandra called David Platt and youth coach Dave King was sent to watch him at Halifax one Friday night. He scored in Crewe's 2-1 win, but two months later he joined Aston Villa instead on his way to becoming an England international. In October 1999 three Jamaican World Cup players Ian Goodison, Theodore Whitmore, who had scored twice in their 2-1 win over Japan in France in 1998, and Steve Malcolm all played on trial for City in the reserves' 3-3 draw at home to Chesterfield. Goodison and Whitmore were soon offered deals, but defender Malcolm was not taken on even though he won 76 international caps.

Inside-forward Peter Martin was an England amateur international youth trialist, but was not signed by a League club until May 1969 when Middlesbrough offered him on a one-year contract after he had scored five goals in four junior games for them. Previously, though, he had had trials with City and Hartlepool United. More recently Yorkshire-born striker Cameron Jerome briefly had a trial with the Tigers when he was looking for a club, but there was a lot of competition for his services and Cardiff City snapped him up. It seems that Jerome had trials with several clubs, including Grimsby Town, whose former striker Paul Wilkinson, Cardiff's reserve-team coach, pounced. City were one of those clubs who missed out, Jerome made his name with Cardiff, represented England under-21s earlier this year and cost Birmingham City an initial £3m. when he moved on earlier this year.

Then there have been the examples of internationals who had trials with City in the reserves in the twilight of their careers and did not feature in the first team despite their pedigrees. Colin Appleton gave former England defender Brian Greenhoff a trial during his first spell in charge of the club in November 1983 and former Liverpool hero and Scotland international Steve Nicol had a trial in the early part of 1998-99 while Mark Hateley was in charge, but he went on to play for Doncaster Rovers in the Football Conference instead.

One of the most amazing tales involving an international player - especially in view of the global nature of today's football - concerned 25-year-old Jens-Peter Hansen, who came to City in November 1952 with a big reputation in his native Denmark, but red tape prevented him from playing for the club. The Tigers initially had approval for him to play and he travelled with them to their Southsea base in readiness for their visit to Southampton at the end of the month. Hansen had spent a day with his new colleagues, but on the day of the match the Football League notified City that they has rescinded their original permission for him to play and were referring the matter to their management committee instead. The Football League's secretary Fred Howarth said that the full committee had to vet him because he was a foreign player. But on December 5 the League told City that Hansen would not be allowed to play for them because his registration was deemed to be "only temporary." It was not their wish for Continental players to play in the League, according to their president Arthur Drewery in a telephone call to City's chairman Harold Needler.

Manager Bob Jackson could not understand the objection because FIFA and the English and Danish national associations had sanctioned Hansen's move and the League already included some foreign players. He said: "We signed Hansen in all good faith as an amateur in accordance with the laws of the FA and the Football League. We then sent the form off to the League and were told that the registration would be acknowledged and returned by post. We were assured that the position was in order, but were surprised when the League rang through to say that we could not play Hansen because the registration was of a temporary nature. I spoke personally with Fred Howarth, the League's secretary, who told me that the matter would be considered by their management committee and that I should have the necessary permission after they had met. We never received a letter from the League, however, so we decided to contact them again to know how we stood. We were informed that Mr. Howarth was not in the office, but we also contacted the FA again and we were once more told that this registration was all in order as far as they and FIFA were concerned. The refusal, therefore, is in direct opposition to the highest authorities of the game and provides strong food for thought. Harold Needler then tried to contact Arthur Drewry and eventually succeeded. Mr. Needler explained that the club had received no word whatsoever from the League as to whether Hansen could play. Mr. Drewry refused to give us permission, stating that the management committee had decided that they could not give approval because Hansen's appearances for the Tigers would be a temporary measure. We dispute this most strongly on the grounds that Hansen is an amateur and entitled to play anywhere at any time, having been given the permission of his home association. This is necessary to meet FIFA's requirements and, if the international authority give their sanction, we are unable to appreciate why the League should not. We do not know what we have to do in future to register players. We have kept to every rule laid down by the FA and the Football League, so it makes me wonder what is behind this refusal." Hansen had arrived with a glowing reference from the Tigers' Viggo Jensen, a former teammate, that he was Denmark's top player. As with Jensen, he had won 15 international caps for Denmark and played for them in the Olympic Games at Helsinki in 1952. He had also scored four goals for Esbjerg against Alborg while playing alongside Jensen, but his ambition to play League football in England was never fulfilled.

Another foreign player who never progressed into City's first team was South African right-winger Danny van Vuuren, who was signed from Clyde in May 1950. In fact, it seemed in those days that City signed a player from Clyde every two months because right-back Alec Gibson had made the move in the March and inside-forward Alf Ackerman arrived in the July. Van Vuuren was from Cape Town, he had served as a pilot in the South African air force during the 1939-45 War and he had joined Clyde from Bulawayo in what was then Southern Rhodesia. He played in three first-team games for them during the 1949-50 season before having a trial in City's reserves against Grantham. He impressed the City hierarchy, but that was as far as it went.

The same applied to Bishop Auckland's Corbett Cresswell, whose father Warneford was an England international full-back. Corbett was an England amateur international who had a trial with the Tigers as an 18-year-old when Bob Brocklebank was in charge, but City faced competition from Wolverhampton Wanderers, Everton, Leeds United and Liverpool when he hinted that he fancied turning professional on completion of his National Service. But Corbett, who was said to have "much of the calm confidence of his dad," did make his mark in the Bishop Auckland side who dominated the FA Amateur Cup in the 1950s and become an England amateur international. Brocklebank also snapped up Finland international goalkeeper Mauno Rintanen, who played four League games for City in the early part of the 1956-57 season, which is more than his compatriot Olavi Leskinen did. Rintanen recommended Leskinen, who was also a Finnish international, to the Tigers when he came to England on a three-year business appointment and he signed amateur forms for the club in February 1961. But he did not play because he suffered a knee injury and his work then also took him out of the area. City then lost contact with Leskinen after Brocklebank left the following summer. By that time Leskinen had apparently lost interest in playing for them anyway.

Two other trialists from the North-East were goalkeepers Derek Forster and Dave Clarke.

Newcastle-born Forster, who became the youngest player to appear in the First Division when he made his League debut for Sunderland against Leicester City at the age of 15 years and 185 days in August 1964. But he had a trial lasting several days with City during the previous season before deciding to join Sunderland. Clarke, who was with Newcastle United when they won the Inter-Cities' Fairs Cup in 1968-69 and briefly played League football for Doncaster Rovers, found that his fate was literally in his own hands when he had a trial with the Tigers. Clarke, who played in Blyth Spartans' three FA Cup ties against City in December 1980 and is still involved in goalkeeping coaching in the North-East, had a trial at Boothferry Park as a 14-year-old, but recalled: "Ken Wagstaff hurt my wrist so badly during a kick-in on the first day that I spent the rest of the time on the treatment table!" Curiously, Blyth's side also included former City full-back Paul Walker, who never made it into the first team, and Clarke's fellow England non-League international Les Mutrie, who did after moving to Boothferry Park in a £30,000 deal after the cupties.

Fate also took an ironic hand in August 1966 when Frank Banks went on to become joint 18th in City's list of all-time League appearances on 288 after joining the club on a two-month trial following his release by Southend United. But another 19-year-old, goalkeeper Bill Jones, who was an apprentice joiner playing semi-professionally for South Liverpool, joined City at the same time for a second trial with the club - and still failed to make the grade at Boothferry Park. And a trick of fate haunted City when they lost 1-0 at non-League Chester City in the LDV Vans Trophy in December 2000. The Tigers had given midfield player Paul Carden a two-week trial during the 1999-2000 season, but he was offered only a short-term deal, moved on and then came back to score Chester's winner.

Then there were the days when City gave trials to players in the first team and in some cases they did not earn second League appearances. James Marshall, who had been with Newcastle side St. Peter's Albion and later played for Preston Colliery in his native Durham, made his only League appearance for City as a trialist at outside-left in a 1-1 draw at home to Stoke in February 1921. And during the 1946-47 campaign there was a positive spate of them. Alan Smith appeared in the sixth game of the season - and the fourth at Boothferry Park - as a left-winger in a 2-1 defeat against Gateshead in September 1946. In May 1947 there were three others - James Jones at inside-left in a 1-0 home defeat against Oldham Athletic and centre-forward Ted Alberry and left-winger Tom Teasdale in a 1-0 home win over Barrow. Their chances came during a period when manager Major Frank Buckley introduced numerous trialists, but their arrivals were hardly heralded and their departures were equally as anonymous amid the many players who came and went quickly at different levels that season. Curiously, some of City's other first-team debutants for City during the same month - Denis Durham, Ken Harrison and Norman Moore - stayed on to make much more important impacts in the club's colours.

There are many other players to have made only one League appearance for City, but some of them are the subject of intriguing tales. Most clubs will have given youngsters one outing at the end of a meaningless season and then discarded them, but City had players who were briefly ever-presents for their only League appearances because they played in the opening games of seasons.

Centre-forward Peter Nicholson played his only League game at the start of 1960-61 when they found themselves back in the Third Division - a 4-0 defeat at Colchester United - but was then left out. Eric McMillan also made his City debut that day after moving for Chelsea, but something more significant harmed Nicholson's prospects. The Tigers' third debutant at Colchester was 17-year-old Chris Chilton, who wore the No. 8 shirt. But two days later Nicholson was omitted and Chilton played the first of his numerous games at centre-forward when City beat Newport County 5-1. The previous season Nicholson had scored 12 goals in 12 games for the A team and made one other first-team appearance before he had played for the reserves. It was a friendly against Leeds United at

Boothferry Park when City, wearing their proposed new strip of amber-and-black striped shirts with white shorts and white socks for the first time, lost 1-0. Leeds' line-up included ex-Tiger Don Revie and another 17-year-old right-winger who was to end up at Boothferry Park - Billy Bremner. Defender Kim Wassell was similarly briefly an ever-present during 1983-84 because his only senior appearance for City was in a 4-1 home win over Burnley on the opening day. He then lost his place at left-back to another newcomer, Mick Hollifield, as City were unbeaten in their first 11 League games, but at least he was in good full-back company against Burnley because they included a young Lee Dixon, who went on to play for England.

A lot of City's one-game wonders in the League were chosen as temporary deputies for regulars and one of them, left-back Cecil Robson, made his sole appearance on a Christmas Day - in a goal-less draw at Clapton Orient in 1924. Alex Thom, though, was back for the return fixture the next day. Robson, from County Durham, had been Bill McCracken's first signing as a manager and was known for his powerful shooting. He later played for Reading, Derby County, Southend United, Rochdale and Oldham Athletic before returning to East Yorkshire to become a publican, working for Hull Brewery for 15 years and taking charge at the Paragon Hotel in Hull and the Duke of Cumberland in North Ferriby. He then became a licensee in the Derby area and had retired because of ill-health only a month before his death in Ashbourne in October 1966. Centre-half John Wright was another player whose only League game for City was on Christmas Day - in a 3-1 win at Southport in 1947. He did, though, make one other senior appearance for the club - 51 weeks later in an FA Cup replay at Reading, which the Tigers won 2-1 when he deputised for Harold Meens, who had suffered a head injury in the first meeting. As a result, Wright, who played in the same school side as ex-Tiger Stan Mortensen even though he was 18 months younger, became the forgotten hero of City's FA Cup exploits that season.

Equally, wing-half Ken White, from Selby, made his only League appearance for the Tigers in the same successful season, deputising for Jimmy Greenhalgh in a 4-2 defeat at Bradford City in February 1949 that was sandwiched between the big FA Cup ties against Stoke City and Manchester United. It was similar to the situations faced by Emlyn Williams and Tom Surrey when they made their only League appearances for City in successive games in March 1930. Both wore the No. 9 shirt with Williams playing before the FA Cup semi-final ties with Arsenal, in which "Paddy" Mills was at centre-forward instead, and Surrey playing after them. Their respective League appearances ended in heavy defeats as City tumbled towards relegation and it was harder on Surrey, who had scored a hat-trick on his debut for the reserves earlier in the season.

Probably the first deputy for a regular who played in one League game for City was an amateur James Cleland, who was at inside-right in a 4-0 home defeat by Huddersfield Town in April 1915 in place of Billy Cameron. A schoolteacher, he played for Beverley Barracks against City's reserves the following year before representing the club again in wartime football. In December 1924 James Iremonger made his only League appearance for City as the deputy for George Maddison, who had just taken over as the first-choice goalkeeper from Billy Mercer. Iremonger played in a 4-2 home win over Sheffield Wednesday and came from Wilford to the south of Nottingham, having joined the Tigers from nearby Clifton Colliery. But he came from a notable family because his father, James senior, who came from Norton in East Yorkshire, played twice for England as a full-back and was a successful opening batsman with Nottinghamshire as a cricketer. In addition, James junior played for City at the same time as his uncle Albert, a 6ft. 5in. giant, was coming to the end of his lengthy spell as a goalkeeper with Notts County. Albert, in fact, had played against the Tigers in their inaugural game in September 1904 - a friendly that ended 2-2.

Left-back Bernard Bradford made his only League appearance as a deputy for the popular Matt Bell in a 2-1 home defeat against Nottingham Forest in November 1929. Ironically, he came from the Walker area of Newcastle, as did a much longer-serving Tiger, goalkeeper Billy Bly. Another left-back, Edward Lloyd, played his only League game in a 3-1 defeat at Bradford Park Avenue in April 1934 as Cliff Woodhead's deputy. It was the only game that Woodhead missed in 1933-34, but Lloyd was a regular fixture elsewhere - notably at Stockport County and Carlisle United.

Goalkeeper Ron Capewell kept a clean sheet in a 1-0 home win over Bury in April 1955, but then had to make way for Billy Bly's return. In September 1956 Ken Smales played his only League game at left-back in a 4-1 defeat at Bradford Park Avenue before Viggo Jensen returned five days later. Two months later Jensen went back home to Denmark, but Smales was never given a second chance. In September 1962 winger Archie Taylor made his only League appearance in a 2-0 defeat at Swindon, but Doug Clarke was back in the side five days later. Centre-forward Eric Holah, who later became a schoolteacher in Bridlington before moving south, was the deputy for Chris Chilton at home to Watford in April 1961 and even scored in a 3-2 win. Chilton himself had scored twice in a 2-1 win at Chesterfield the previous day - on Good Friday - but it did Holah's cause little good. Chilton was back on the Easter Monday for the return game with Chesterfield and Holah, whose sister Audrey married ex-Tiger Dave Fraser, had the scant consolation of knowing that his only goal-scoring League appearance had taken place on April 1! In April 1977 full-back Grahame "Josh" McGifford, who was a millowner's son from Wallington in Surrey and yet had been brought up in Cheshire, deputised for Peter Daniel in a 3-0 defeat at Oldham. It was his only League appearance for the Tigers and he was booked in it! And he received it at the end of the game when referee Colin Seel cautioned three City players for sarcastically applauding him off the pitch because of a remark that he had made to Billy Bremner.

Inevitably, some of the one-day wonders were involved in odd situations. Right-back Walter Goodin played for Beverley Barracks against the old amateur Hull City club in the semi-final of the Beverley Hospital Cup in March 1903. He then helped the new City to a 2-1 home win over Lincoln City in the final game of their first League campaign in 1905-06. In February 1923 Scotsman Allan Livingstone played his one League game for the Tigers at inside-left in a 2-0 defeat at Clapton Orient, for whom he later signed. He had joined City from Dumbarton Harp and went on his travels to clubs in Scotland, Wales and England after that. His elder brother Duggie was better-known as a defender with Glasgow Celtic and Everton and the manager of Newcastle United, Fulham and Chesterfield, for whom he signed winger Mike Bowering from City during the summer of 1960.

Central defender Ian Bennyworth made his only League appearance in a 1-0 home defeat against Bury in May 1980 after City had just avoided relegation to the Fourth Division for the first time. There was another young debutant in the Tigers' line-up the same day - Steve McClaren! Bennyworth's consolation might have been that at least he lasted the full 90 minutes, while McClaren was replaced by Paul Moss. Bennyworth later made more of a name for himself when he helped Scarborough to become the first club to gain automatic promotion to the Football League in 1987 when one of his teammates was Neil Sellers, who had been on the Tigers' books without getting into the first team. Sellers did not then stay on to experience League football with Scarborough either, but he had become an England non-League international and still plays for the ex-Tigers regularly at the age of 51.

Midfield player Mark Bonner scored the only goal at home to Rotherham United in the first League game of 1999, never played for the club again because of injury and returned to Cardiff City as his loan spell was cut short. But his winner helped the Tigers to start to turn the corner in their fight to stay in the League and teammate Gary Brabin said: "Mark didn't stay long, but he got the winner against Rotherham and I'd like to think that those of us who were newcomers gave the place a lift." Utility player Manuel Rui Marques played only one League game after joining City on loan - a 1-1 draw at Ipswich in March 2006. He was unable to retain his place in the side because the

Tigers entertained his parent club Leeds United the following week, so he was ineligible. Remarkably, though, he did pop up in the World Cup later in the year when he played for Angola as a substitute for the final 17 minutes of their 1-1 draw with Iran in Leipzig.

There are those whose sole competitive senior appearances for the Tigers were in the major cup competitions. Goalkeeper George Cook and defenders Matthew Carney and George Brooks played only in the FA Cup second qualifying round in October 1905 when City won 2-0 at Denaby United. But there is always a doubt as to whether it strictly counted as a first-team game because the Tigers had been forced to play the tie on the same day as they also faced Manchester United in the Second Division at the Boulevard after they had failed to get one of the fixtures postponed. And a sequel was that clubs were "precluded from playing reserve teams in cupties." In November 1995 midfield player Lee Pridmore started his only game when he appeared in the goalless draw at home to Wrexham in the FA Cup Cup first round. Two others made their only senior appearances in the Football League Cup first round. Striker Matty Hopkin came on as a substitute in a 3-1 home win over Notts County in August 1993 and goalkeeper Sergio Leite, who had previously agreed to join City the previous season and then changed his mind, appeared in the 2-1 defeat at Blackpool in August 2005.

Then there are those whose brief moments of glory for City occurred mainly in the so-called lesser cups. Utility player Paul Olsson played in friendlies for City, but also made one competitive appearance in the Associate Members' Cup when they were the beaten finalists in 1983-84. In May 1984 Olly went for quality rather than quantity when he faced Sheffield United in a quarter-final tie, which City won 1-0 at Boothferry Park and he scored the winner. Defender Neil Cockin played in the same game and had managed his only other senior appearance in the Football League Cup at home to Lincoln City in 1983. In October 2002 Jamie Heard, Scott Kerr, who later gained England non-League international representative honours, and Liam Chapman started in a 3-1 defeat at Port Vale in the LDV Vans Trophy. Further down the competitive line came Paul Blackburn, a highly-respected goalkeeper in non-League and local football, who played for City in what was dubbed the Anglo-American Cup in April 1984 when they beat Tampa Bay Rowdies 3-0 at Boothferry Park, but he also helped out the club on other occasions, notably a reserve game against Manchester United at Old Trafford. And in September 1994 the Tigers had a goalkeeping crisis for the Yorkshire Electricity Cup final at Huddersfield Town. Alan Fettis was on Northern Ireland international duty, Steve Wilson was injured and Richard White had just left the club. The spot went to Chris Hill, from Brandesburton, who was then North Ferriby United's reserve goalkeeper, backed up by the veteran Ged Stead, who also became a local referee and even had a spell in rugby union with Hornsea.

In 1965 the advent of substitutes, initially for injured players only, increased the possibilities. And there have been players whose only League action for City was as substitutes, such as Barry McCunnell in December 1969, Mark Kilgallon in August 1980, Keith Parkinson in November 1981, Dean Stowe against his home-town club Burnley in March 1993, Richard Fidler in December 1995 and Caleb Folan while on loan from Leeds United in December 2001.

Then there are those who have been substitutes for City and not made it on to the pitch. It happened to Rob Smith in the days of one substitute per team, but the game in October 1968 attracted a crowd of 24,307 when the Tigers beat Derby County 1-0. Smith, who later played League soccer for Grimsby Town and Hartlepool United, reflected: "Derby won the Second Division championship that season, but eventually I had to go because I couldn't see myself becoming a first-team regular at Hull. I was disappointed because I always thought I was good enough, but the competition was tough in those days. There were other youngsters such as Ray Pettit, Paddy Greenwood, Mally Lord, Geoff Barker and Roger de Vries, who signed for the club on the same day as I did. I stayed at Hull until Terry Neill became manager and Tommy Docherty joined him as his assistant. And it was the Doc who fixed me up at Grimsby. He said that they were trying to build a First Division team at City and

I probably wouldn't get into it, but I'd always do a good job in the Third Division or Fourth Division. At least he was honest with me." Such are the vagaries of footballing fortune, though, that de Vries in contrast is 12th in City's all-time League appearances list. Smith's consolation back in his home city is that he remains the oldest regular playing member of the Ex-Tigers. He added: "I think it's wonderful really. I still suffer from a lot of wear and tear in my knees and other strains and stresses I've picked up during the years. But I get by now because of my experience and the fact that there are some quality players alongside me!"

Equally, midfield player Mark Robinson, who had spells with Guisborough Town and Middlesbrough, did well on trial with the Tigers during the 1982-83 season, but was released because they could not afford to take him on to the payroll. But he was an unused substitute in City's 1-1 home draw with Halifax Town on Boxing Day, 1982. Middlesbrough-born Robinson then moved on to Hartlepool United, for whom he did at least make 35 League appearances. In December 1998 the injury-hit Tigers pulled off a giantkilling act when they won 2-1 at Luton Town to knock them out of the FA Cup. It meant that goalkeeper Phil Poole, who was from the North-East, and defender Danny Brown, who later played for Gainsborough Trinity and Ossett Town when ex-Tiger Steve Richards was their manager, were close to the upset without joining in it after being called up as substitutes in the emergency.

In addition, the formal introduction of a loan system in 1970 added another string to the "occasional" bow. There had been occasional examples of loans previously, in fact, because City included left-winger Horace Cumner, who was later capped three times by Wales, in their last 12 League games of 1937-38 after taking him on loan from Arsenal's nursery club Margate. And defender Harold Kirman was endearingly presented wth a pen-and-pencil set by Gillingham in recognition for his services after it had been ruled that City had merely loaned him to them for a long time - between July 1952 and January 1955! Later in the year he did actually play twice in the League for the Tigers. But the club's first loan signing during 1970-71 was Newcastle-born defender Jack Carmichael, who joined them from Arsenal. He did not appear in City's League team, though, and later moved to Peterborough United and Swindon Town to play his League soccer before becoming a publican. And the same kind of scenario was still occurring in October 2002 when goalkeeper Saul Deeney was brought in on loan from Notts County and yet never played for the first team. But another loan signing, midfield player Gary Gill from Middlesbrough, might have cost City dearly - perhaps even a points deduction - if he had been brought off the substitutes' bench at Bristol Rovers in December 1983. He was not properly registered at first because of an administrative error, but luckily everything had been sorted out properly by the time that he did make his one League appearance for City as a substitute in a 1-0 win at Rotherham later in the month.

Then there are examples of varied family fortunes. The trend began in 1904-05 when Oscar and Henry Mackrill, who were the sons of a yeast merchant and attended Hull's Hymers College, became the first brothers to play for the new Hull City club. The family home had been in Woodville Terrace off the Boulevard in Hull, but they later moved to the Thwaite in Cottingham. Henry was the 191st pupil to be registered at Hymers, where he studied between 1894 and 1896, but he played just one match for City - on the right-wing in a 2-2 draw against Middlesbrough Reserves in October 1904. But his brother Oscar, a Hymers pupil from 1896 to 1902, had already played in a run of four friendlies from September 1904 and the two FA Cup ties against Stockton the same month, scoring City's first goal in the competition in the first of them. Oscar, in fact, joined City from Old Hymerians after having being awarded a Blue for the long jump at Cambridge University, while Henry had played rugby union for Hull and East Riding before his only appearance for the Tigers.

Winger Jimmy Keen made 17 League appearances for City during 1924-25 and was more successful with the club than his younger relative Errington, who was also known as either Ike or Eric. As with Billy Bly, they came from the Walker area of Newcastle, but Errington played four times for England while with Derby County and yet failed to make City's first team when he tried his luck during Major Frank Buckley's spell in charge. And in March 1939 left-back Archer Stokes, from Kirkella, made his only League appearance for the Tigers in a 2-0 home defeat against Rotherham United. Oddly enough his brother Ernest fared slightly better, making two appearances for City at left-back during wartime football in 1944.

Stan Alexander was a regular goalscorer for City and later helped out on the coaching staff, but it did not work out for his brother Jack when he had a spell on the club's books. Another prolific marksman Norman Moore's son David was an apprentice with City during Cliff Britton's time as manager without progressing into the first team and later became a director of his father's Grimsby-based paper firm Humberside Wrappings instead. Curiously, Norman's nephew David had a spell with the Tigers as their physiotherapist when Brian Little managed the club.

In 1956 City forward Doug Clarke's brother Alan signed for City. He had just been called up for Army service at the time of the Suez crisis and joined the club when he visited Doug while on leave. In addition, Doug's son Stuart had a trial with City and stayed with all-time hero Billy Bly at the same time as future England international Brian Marwood. Eric McMillan played in 150 League games for City, but his brother Trevor and nephew Andre, later a York City regular, were briefly on the club's books without reaching the first team. Maybe the most poignant family tale, though, involved the Tigers' goalscoring winger and then coach John McSeveney. His brother Bobby had a spell with City, but John explained: "Cliff Britton offered him a deal, but he wouldn't take it. It was during the time of the polio epidemic in Hull in 1961, but Bobby said that he wanted to go back to his girlfriend in Shotts because they were thinking of getting married. But when he got back, she'd gone off with someone else, so he lost out on the possibility of two contracts in only a matter of a few days!"

Nicky Barmby joined City in 2004 - 22 years after being an eight-year-old mascot for the club against Scunthorpe United at Boothferry Park - with 23 England international appearances to his credit, but his father Jeff did not play for the first team. Jeff said: "I joined the club at 17 when Bob Brocklebank was the manager. I'd got into the reserves, but then I ended up going back into the A team after Cliff Britton had taken over. I was probably a bit big-headed in those days because I believed that some of the lads who were playing for the reserves weren't as good as I was and yet I was only in the A team. I discussed it with Wilf English, who was always round City in various capacities at the time, and he suggested that I should sort it out with Cliff Britton. Cliff told me that he would give me a run of 12 trial games in the reserves to prove my point. In those days the coaching staff used to mark performances out of five and one of them, John Simpson, told me that he'd given me only one out of five in all 12 games, so I told them what they could do with the club!" Jeff briefly played League football with York City, had a trial with Bournemouth and then followed his father's instructions to find himself a trade. The outcome is that he has been the match-day electrician at City games at both Boothferry Park and the KC Stadium, he was a Wembley winner with Scarborough in the FA Trophy in an illustrious goal-laden non-League career and has been a mainstay of the Ex-Tigers' Association for most of their existence.

Then there are the players who might logically have been expected to play first-team football for City, but it did not materialise for one reason or another. For example, a number of City's England youth internationals failed to reach the first team, including Salford-born Roy Saunders, who had a trial during Major Frank Buckley's managership and joined them as an amateur as a 15-year-old and spent three seasons in the reserves and juniors before moving to Liverpool in 1948. But he played for England at youth level and captained the East Riding County FA's representative team, eventually joining Swansea Town in 1959 and enabling his son Dean to play for Wales. Andy Davidson said:

"Roy Saunders was a hard man, but he was also a great laugh. He was always scruffy and would come down to Boothferry Park with his collars frayed, but he was some footballer who captained the England youth team. The trouble was that Buckley didn't have any time for him." Contrastingly, defender Paul Mudd represented England Schoolboys, but at least played in one League game for City - a 1-0 defeat at Birmingham City in May 1989.

Half-back Tom Neal joined City from Leeds United, but never played a League game for them after reaching an agreement about his future when David Menzies had a second spell as manager in 1936. Neal had had five years with Leeds, but spent six weeks in hospital in Newcastle with severe head pains after signing for City. He was advised to retire from football on medical grounds and had a further examination in Hull following talks with Menzies. The outcome was that he retired and returned to his home in New Washington in County Durham. Scottish centre-forward Alex Merrie was transferred from five non-English clubs to English clubs during his career - St. Mirren to Portsmouth in 1925, Ayr United to the Tigers in November 1933, Clyde to Crewe Alexandra in August 1934, Brechin City to Aldershot in November 1935 and Cork City to Gloucester City in February 1937. But he, too, failed to reach City's first team with the Tigers. William Wood, a 23-year-old Barnsley-born full-back, cost £5,000 from Sunderland in July 1951, but made no first-team appearances for the Tigers. He had made only one League appearance for Sunderland, but then moved to Sheffield United in the summer of 1952.

Winger Clive Colbridge came through the ranks of Hull City Police Boys' Club as a young player and was on City's books during Raich Carter's time as manager. He sought his release and joined Hull Brunswick, but then teamed up with former City manager Major Frank Buckley at Leeds United after recording a hat-trick in a trial game. He was transferred to York City after returning to Leeds at the end of his National Service. Manager Bob Brocklebank tipped Bolton-born full-back Harold Mather, who had been with Burnley for 18 years, as a possible City captain when he signed him in the mid-1950s. In fact, Mather, who became involved in a court case in Rochdale, had eight football jobs in different capacities in seven years - with Nelson, Kettering Town, Colwyn Bay, Grimsby Town, Accrington Stanley and in South Africa and Iraq. He also had a spell with Limerick, but never played a first-team game for the Tigers and Brocklebank acknowledged at the club's annual shareholders' meeting in December 1956: "Mistakes can be made and I don't mind admitting that I made one." But it did not deter him from returning to his old club Birmingham City to sign another full-back Bill Kennea in 1960 and he, too, never played in the Tigers' first team.

When City's juniors won the Northern Intermediate League title in 1964-65, Gerry Ingram was their regular goalscoring left-winger, but, unlike many of his teammates, he was rejected and drifted into local non-League football with Hull Brunswick, with whom he became an out-and-out striker. Brunswick's president Dick Smith knew Blackpool's manager Stan Mortensen because he had been a City director when the former England international moved to Boothferry Park in 1955. Ingram had a successful trial with the Seasiders, progressed into the first team, scoring against City in their 1-0 win at Boothferry Park in September 1967, and then sampled further League football with Preston North End and Bradford City. He said: "I'll never forget that goal because it was probably the best one I ever scored and it gave me great pleasure, considering that I'd never really forgiven City for not signing me." Wing-half John Hart, who became a farmer at East Newton in Holderness, captained England Schoolboys and City's juniors in 1964-65, but never reached the first team after being linked with Manchester United and Sheffield United. He recalled: "City's coach Gus McLean came to see me and I changed my mind about going to Sheffield. It all went quite well with City for four years because we had a good youth team and the development of the players was good. But then it started to go wrong and I think I was just one of a number of players from a good, young team who didn't really get the proper opportunities. We heard that the manager Cliff Britton wanted to stick with the experienced players and that Gus McLean wanted to bring in some of the younger ones. In the end it all petered out and came to a standstill, but that's just the way it goes and at least I tried." More recently, goalkeeper Nicky Baxter was on City's books and had a spell with Manchester United between 2000 and 2002, but did not play League football and returned instead to his home-town club Bridlington Town.

But it is hard to beat one of the most remarkable transfer stories in City's history from August 1961 when manager Cliff Britton was hopeful of completing his third close-season signing after snapping up Ray Henderson and John McSeveney. And he seeemed to have found someone when he acquired 26-year-old Bill Wright from Plymouth Argyle. Wright had previously played for his home-town club Blackpool, Leicester City and Newcastle United and had posed problems for City while playing against them for Argyle at Home Park in December 1959. Significantly, he was described as a utility forward, but he insisted that he wanted to play for the Tigers only on the left-wing. But he did not play there in a trial game and was provisionally named at centre-forward for the reserves as City prepared for the new season. Wright then sought a showdown with Britton, who remained adamant that he could not guarantee him a spot at outside-left because of the size of the club's playing staff. Wright then decided that he wanted to leave City, who had not yet paid the agreed transfer fee to Plymouth and were still trying to fix up accommodation for him, so they released him from his contract at his own request. The Tigers, meanwhile, gave a month's trial to 5ft. 2in. left-winger Alan Shaw, whom Britton knew from their time together at Preston North End, and he became the smallest first-teamer in the club's history!

Then there are the quirky examples of some of City's lesser-known signings. In 1957 they snapped up 20-year-old full-back Brian Taylor from the Wigan area. He had been on Liverpool's books as an amateur and joined the Tigers as a part-time professional while he was serving an apprenticeship as an engineer. He never made the grade in the first team, but his arrival at Boothferry Park was reported in the Hull Daily Mail by Three Crowns, which was then, of course, a pseudonym for Brian Taylor! Brian Taylor the journalist covered the club's affairs for 20 years: Brian Taylor the player did not last very long at all. Full-back Alan Hetherington was an amateur with Chelsea and turned professional just before being called up for his National Service, during which he played on the bone-hard pitches of Malaya alongside City's reserve inside-forward John Bickenson. He then returned to Stamford Bridge, but Chelsea eventually gave him a free transfer and in September 1957 he joined City on a month's trial as a 20-year-old after a spell as a lumberjack at a camp in Sweden! He stayed a bit longer, but Hetherington oddly did not pull up many trees at Boothferry Park and his only first-team appearance was at right-back in a friendly at Lincoln City in February 1958 when they won 5-2 with a rare hat-trick by David Coates.

Then there are other players who played briefly for City's reserves on trial and became Football League managers in addition to Stuart Pearce. Midfield player Steve Beaglehole appeared as a promising youngster and later managed Doncaster Rovers, while defender Graham Rodger, who took charge of Grimsby Town in 2006, was nearing the end of his career, when he was given a chance. A lot was expected of Scottish duo Alec Martin and Billy Brown when coach John McSeveney brought them to Boothferry Park in the late 1960s, but neither reached the first team. Martin, whom McSeveney eventually recommended him to Motherwell, where his brother Willie was the trainer, admitted: "My trouble at Hull was a lack of confidence in myself." But Brown has had a long career in management, working regularly as the No. 2 to Jim Jefferies, including a spell together at Bradford City.

There have been City players who have had strong links locally with rugby league. Winger Terry Murray, who was capped once by the Republic of Ireland, became the brother-in-law of rugby-league half-back Rowley Moat, who had spells with both Hull FC and Hull Kingston Rovers. And Rowley once recalled: "We were all together for a 25th wedding anniversary celebration when Terry saw Raich Carter in the same hotel and said that he would introduce me to him. The funny thing then was all Raich wanted to talk about was rugby!" Bobby Colgrave was a regular goalscorer for City's A team alongside Peter Nicholson and had four years on the club's books as a centre-forward. But, having failed to reach the first team, he then became a successful player in local rugby league, winning BARLA's player-of-the-year award in 1975-76. At first he stayed in local soccer with Kingburn Athletic after leaving the Tigers, but then switched to rugby league as a full-back with Fenner's. Having been a centre-forward in one code, he became a centre and a forward in the other, representing England at amateur level. Bobby was also a light-heavyweight boxer and once lost to Hull's Roger Tighe, who won a gold medal at the Commonwealth Games in Jamaica in 1966.

Nobody, though, has played in the first teams of the Hull's three professional teams, but burly Sam Evans arguably was the closest. He came from a soccer background because he was born in Sunderland and moved to Hull at the age of four. He was once on City's books, but he did not reach first-team status. But he said: "I'd always been a soccer man and my ambition was to play it professionally, but I wasn't good enough. I'd played basketball, cricket and rugby union in the Army, but I saw myself as a bit of a centre-forward. I signed amateur forms for City and played a couple of times for their old A team while I was in the Army. Raich Carter was the manager then, but nothing came of it." And at the age of 22 he joined Rovers after their coach Jackie Feetham had invited him to Craven Park for a trial, reflecting: "I think that nearly all the lads were dockers, but they did a lot for me and I found that rugby league was my sort of game." A goal-kicking forward, Evans won Yorkshire representative honours and then moved to Wakefield Trinity in a player-exchange deal involving Bob Coverdale. Then he broke his leg in his second game for Trinity against Hull at the Boulevard - and joined them in September 1959 after he had recovered from the injury. He then played for the Airlie Birds at Wembley in the 1960 Rugby League Challenge Cup final when they lost 38-5 to Wakefield! Sam also served in the Household Cavalry for six years, took up wrestling and became a well-known doorman at local clubs. The wrestling also brought him another link with the Tigers because he once fought future chairman Don Robinson. Sam explained: "When I was with Hull FC, we used to train at Madeley Street baths, where the wrestling was held and we got to know some of the lads well. They suggested that I had a little go at it. I thought it would be fair enough and one thing led to another. Don promoted a lot of the wrestling in the north and it was always a laugh with him. There were a lot of characters around in those days."

Similarly, Bill Riches, once known as one of rugby-league's gentlemen, represented Hull Schoolboys at soccer and played for City's reserves when he was 17. In May 1938 he was one of five players to be retained by the Tigers even though they had not yet appeared in first-team football. Riches never did play in League football for City, but one of the other five was Billy Bly, who became their longest-serving player! Born in Hull in 1920, Riches did play in three wartime games for City - two at left-half and one at left-back - while serving in the RAF as well as guesting for Bournemouth. But while he was in the services, he was persuaded to turn his attention to rugby league after meeting someone called John Terry! The circumstances were ironic because Riches turned out for Batley, who were Terry's team, when they were a man short for a game against Hull FC at the Boulevard. He scored a try, Batley signed him during the halftime interval and Hull, who had originally invited him along, then found out that they had missed out on his services when they made him a full-time offer at the end of the game! Riches, who played in the centre, stayed with Batley until he finally moved to Hull in a player-exchange deal in 1953, beating off competition from Hull Kingston Rovers. Riches then captained Yorkshire before eventually returning to Batley in December 1955 and finally retiring at the age of 36.

Then there are the examples of those who appeared briefly for City and then made a name for themselves in different soccer contexts. Frank Coultas represented Hull Schoolboys and joined City as an amateur, but an ankle injury ended his playing career as a centre-half and in 1934 he took up refereeing instead. He continued to officiate locally and twice recovered from bouts of rheumatic fever to pursue his career until he was promoted to the Football League's supplementary list in 1947. Four years later he was promoted to the League's full list after being a linesman at the FA Amateur Cup final between Bishop Auckland and Pegasus. The Football League had a ruling that referees should come off their active list at the age of 47 and things looked bleak for Coultas five years later. His 47th birthday fell three days before the start of 1956-57, so he was told that he would have to retire, but then the League relented when they met during the summer and let Coultas, Jack Topliss and Mervyn Griffiths continue for another season. The outcome was that Coultas was given charge of the 1957 FA Cup final when Aston Villa beat Manchester United 2-1 at Wembley. Coultas, though, had bounced back from adversity on three occasions and the story goes that his toughness was illustrated when he refereed one of City's reserve games. During the match he apparently borrowed a pair of pliers from the bench to pull out one of his teeth before continuing as if nothing had happened! Coultas eventually moved to Willerby, where he became a neighbour of Arnold Josephs, who had refereed the 1929 FA Cup final between Portsmouth and Bolton Wanderers. Not long after Coultas had refereed the FA Cup final, John Hodson's promising career with the Tigers was ended prematurely by injury, but he, too, went on to have a noteworthy career as a referee.

Then there was Hull-born Alan Hardaker, whose brother Ernest was once the chairman of rugby-league neighbours Hull FC. Alan attended Constable Street School and Riley High School in his home city before starting work in the town clerk's department of Hull City Council in 1929. He was the Lord Mayor of Hull's secretary from 1936 to 1939 before serving in the Royal Navy during the 1939-45 War, reaching the rank of lieutenant-commander. Alan returned to local government in 1946, spending five years as the Lord Mayor of Portsmouth's secretary. He then joined the Football League as their assistant secretary in 1951 and became their secretary for 22 years from the start of 1957 before being appointed as their director-general. Hardaker described himself as a tenacious half-back as a player with Municipal Sports, Beverley White Star and the East Riding seniors' representative side who won the Northern Counties' Amateur Championship in 1935. But he was also on City's books for a two-year period and played for the reserves, opting to stay as an amateur. Manager Jack Hill asked him to turn professional, but Hardaker's response was that he preferred working in the Lord Mayor's office in Hull. He was awarded an OBE and died in March 1980 at the age of 67.

Conversely, City have also benefited well from players who were "here today and gone tomorrow" elsewhere. Midfield player David Livermore was surplus to requirements at Leeds United after they had signed Kevin Nicholls from Luton Town during the summer of 2006. He was allowed to leave less than a fortnight after joining Leeds from Millwall and moved to City instead. He admitted: "It's been a bit of a whirlwind and I'm feeling a bit shell-shocked." But he did move from Leeds to Hull on Yorkshire Day! Equally, Ken Wagstaff was one of City's all-time greats, but when he joined Goole Town during the 1978-78, he managed to play in only one game for them - at Northwich Victoria.

And amid it all is the vexed question of what actually constitutes being "here today and gone tomorrow" in City terms. As a goalkeeper, Wally Chapman never progressed to the first team. He signed amateur forms for the club on his 19th birthday in December 1927, but remained as an understudy to George Maddison and Fred Gibson. Yet Wally, who died in 1982, hardly disappeared quickly and quietly from the City scene because he was still serving them on an amateur basis 50 years later! Wally, a sales representative for 30 years before qualifying as a schoolteacher at the age of 50, remained as an amateur during his playing years simply because reserve goalkeepers did not usually turn professional even though they were regularly on stand-by. His amateur status did permit him to have spells with York City and Yorkshire Amateurs, but he always enjoyed his playing career at

Anlaby Road because he said: "You still felt part of the scene because it was considered as something to be a Hull City player. It was as simple as that." Wally later served City mainly as a scout after manager Jack Hill had initially used him as one during the 1935-36 season. But then he made an unexpected comeback as an outfield player in a wartime game: "City were playing Halifax Town, who turned up with only 10 players. I'd just paid my admission money when Ernie Blackburn, who was then City's manager, asked if I would turn out. I played at outside-right for Halifax and nearly scored, so I think it's fair to say that I gave myself value for money!" Wally also played for one of City's teams as a 45-year-old when Bob Jackson was in charge and he kept a clean sheet for the Ex-Tigers when he had a 10-minute outing at the age of 64. And he was still active in a different role as a 67-year-old in April 1976 when City played Scunthorpe United in a reserve game at Boothferry Park: "A linesman failed to turn up and I turned out when no-one answered the call for a qualified official. The weather was terrible and at halftime my trousers were so wet that we had to wring them out. In the end I had to wear tracksuit bottoms to go home. But it made my night as the teams came off at the end when one of the Scunthorpe players put his arm round my neck and said: 'Well done, old man!'"

Recording City players who might come under any general clasification of being here today and gone tomorrow, therefore, will never be an easy exercise. One particular example sums it up because Ernie Bell's place in City's history is well-documented, but the part played by his brother Joe is less well-known. Apparently Joe Bell did make a first-team appearance for the Tigers, but it has never previously been recognised. There is a doubt as to just when it was, but the odds are that it was in one of two wartime games at York City in 1944 because it would surely have been discovered and caused a problem if it had happened in a League game. One instance was a 1-0 defeat in what was known as the Football League North at the end of September and the other was in a Football League War Cup tie on Christmas Day. And Ernie's son Ian explained: "My dad always told me that there was an occasion when they were playing York away and one of the City players couldn't get to Anlaby Road to travel to the game, so they were a man short. His brother Joe lived nearby in Granville Street, so they picked him up as they set off and got him to play under the other bloke's name. Dad said that they got Joe out of bed because he'd just come home from sea and had been out the night before! I was told that Joe claimed that he was the best player on the pitch, but my dad just said that he didn't let them down!"

10
Extra Time

Loyal Hull City supporter Beryl Marshall, with whom I had travelled on the Happy Wanderers' minibus when she was Beryl Grassby, was visiting Goathland in North Yorkshire during the summer of 2006 when she decided that quite by chance she had found the ideal present for me. It may all sound very touching, but, it was, in fact, a mug inscribed: "Grumpy, old man!" I had better own up that there might have been an appropriate aspect of her choice. I do not feel old, but I suppose that I must admit to becoming increasingly grumpy...

In fact, I might get into the the England team for grumpy grumbling. When ex-Tiger Gerry Bowler died earlier this year, for example, I was contacted by a journalist called Sian Harrison. I tried to help and took the trouble to telephone her back twice, but what happened? She just quoted me inaccurately as saying things that anyone with a basic knowledge of City and their heritage would never have said - and I certainly did not. It reminded me of an incident when I was chatting to Mick Docherty in the Boothferry Park boardroom just after he had joined City's coaching staff in 1990. A local radio journalist was standing by and the Doc began to regale us with a tale about his father. The Doc and I giggled, but the radio journalist interrupted with a question. "Who is your father?" he asked Mick. "Tommy Docherty," came his wonderfully-deadpan reply. "Oh," said the radio journalist in a matter-of-fact way as he nodded innocently. I had turned away in an attempt to suppress a guffaw because I dare not look at Mick's face in case we both cracked up.

My good friend Chris Pitson, whom I got to respect as a person and football aficionado when he was the financial director of the Hull Daily Mail, once hinted that there were too many people involved in the soccer media who were fans first and journalists second when it should be the other way round. They think that they are ideal for the media because they have been supporters and do not need any formal training or experience. Chris was perceptively right. I trained as a journalist, it has been my trade in various guises and I have tried to follow it to the best of my ability even if people do not like me or agree with me. I did gain some journalistic qualifications, which is in stark contrast with some of the so-called reporters who have inhabited Press-boxes around the country - the schoolteachers, bus drivers, lawyers and greengrocers to name but a few. Were they trained journalists? Were they just fans who were trying something out even if they had no recognised qualifications for it? And how would they have liked it if I had tried to earn some extra pocket money by embarking on their day jobs without any proper training?

There are lots of people muscling in on the media scene nowadays and I could wax lyrical about certain aspects of it - poor dress codes, the deplorable use of English, the obsession with cliche-ridden quotes, TV commentators who shout and bawl and pundits who lack the depth to do anything but state the obvious. Curiously, they tend to be ex-players who spent their careers complaining about the media. But then all of a sudden they have become media-friendly if some earnings are available in what is a now a personality-obsessed society.

Then there was the so-called journalist who overheard a conversation I had in the Press-box at Boothferry Park in 1997, approached me after the game and incredibly asked if I would let him have all the details of my contacts book. Last year a fan from West Yorkshire wrote to me about a book that he was writing and asked if I would let him have some of the dressing-room secrets of my experience. Then a complete stranger came up to me in the Press room at the KC Stadium in 2006 and asked if I would disclose to him the whereabouts of some ex-Tigers because he was planning to organise a dinner for a reason that he never gave. I was then told that he was criticising me behind my back because I had not been more helpful.

Being the Ex-Tigers' Association's secretary has increased the potential problems. Jeff Barmby is an admirable, long-serving chairman who has kept the organisation vibrant almost single-handedly at times. But Jeff has just one slight weakness - he tends to lose telephone numbers fairly often, so I became secretary simply because I am better at collecting them and then hanging on to them in a reasonably-efficient manner in comparison. Technically I was already a member of the ex-Tigers' committee anyway because I once turned up to cover their annual meeting at North Ferriby United's clubhouse. I was immediately voted on to the committee and it was nothing to do with any specialist skills that I might offer them: it was merely the outcome of being there!

But being their secretary involves trust. Ex-players give us their details because, for example, they are confident that we shall not pass on their home telephone numbers, most of which are ex-directory, to outsiders with ritual abandon. It is worth mentioning one particular case. Billy Whitehurst once gave me his home telephone number on condition that I did not pass it on to anyone else. Not long afterwards Steve McClaren, who was then Derby County's assistant manager, rung me at home to ask if I had Billy's number. I gave him the number of his public-house in Sheffield rather than disclosing the home number. I do not doubt for one moment that Big Billy would have minded Steve having his home telephone number, but that was not the point: it was still imperative to me that I should honour Billy's request. I refuse to betray such confidences, so I suspect that I am viewed as either grumpy or awkward - or both - when I refuse to hand over information to all and sundry at the drop of a hat. But what do people seriously expect me to do? I wish that they would just leave me alone and not put me in such a position in the first place.

I appreciate that I have been fortunate enough to have been in an environment in which I have been able to build up a lot of data about former City players, but I have also had to work hard to do my own research, extend my own education about the club and maintain my own contacts. And many of the queries come from people whose jobs are to know a lot about the Tigers and their heritage if they are really passionate about the club. Unfortunately I am not a charity at the disposal of those who are not and I believe that I can soon spot those whose approach almost borders on the parasitic. At the same time I try to be reasonable, I treat situations and people on their merits and sometimes it is possible to work out compromises.

For example, it has been enjoyable to help out the Senior Tigers in a small way. They are over-60s who meet on a monthly basis during the season and are genuine, long-serving fans who have followed City's fortunes longer than I have and have a vast reservoir of knowledge about their favourite club. I respect them immensely and their loyalty to City means far more to me than a lot of recent arrivals on the scene with more audacity than substance. But that, to me, has been the problem with the KC Stadium. It is a wonderful emporium, but its novelty value has attracted people who seldom came to Boothferry Park. And do the members of the corporate bandwagon - otherwise now known nationally as "the prawn-cocktail brigade" - really care about the club? Where were they when times were bad? Are they really interested in the club's tradition or have they suddenly appeared on a whim? When City have had attendances of about 18,000 at home games in recent years, I would suggest that there are 6,000 genuine supporters and about 12,000 KC Stadium fans who have suddenly emerged from the anonymity of the nearest woodwork. I am intelligent enough to realise that the corporate backing has helped the club's progress and put them on a higher financial plain, but the diehards' contribution must never be undervalued because there would probably have been no Hull City without them during the lean years and no bandwagon on to which the casual crusaders could clamber.

I remember Alan Plater, the playwright and genuine City supporter, telling me at a game at Rochdale in 1983 that he would miss some of the smaller away grounds with character and characters spilling out of every nook and cranny now that the club had been promoted from the Fourth Division. As usual, he was right. In idealistic terms it is more important that whenever possible football should remain the preserve of the working people in preference to being the plaything of the rich and famous. Those of us who love the game welcome its high profile provided that it does not sell its soul to the smooth men in smoother suits.

But football has become ever more global and the Tigers have understandably embraced the trend, recruiting players from further and further afield. At one time it might have sufficed just to have Roy Shiner, Charlie Flood and Gareth Williams from the Isle of Wight, George Spence from the Isle of Bute and George Lyall from John o' Groats in addition to players from many other parts of the United Kingdom. But in terms of birthplaces, there have been some from further afield in Europe, including Viggo Jensen and Julian Johnsson from Denmark, Mauno Rintanen from Finland, Sergio Leite from Portugal, Antonio Doncel from Spain, Richard Sneekes from Holland and Hamilton McNeill from Malta. From even further-flung outposts there have been Americans John "Jock" Gibson and Glyn "Boaz" Myhill, Australians Jason van Blerk and Danny Allsopp, New Zealander Heremaia Ngata, South Africans Neil Cubie, Roland Tulloch, George Wienand, Norman Nielson and Alf Ackerman, Iain Hesford from Zambia and Manuel Rui Marques from Angola, Jamaicans Theodore Whitmore and Ian Goodison, Bermudian Kyle Lightbourne, Adrian Caceres from Argentina and Bert "Paddy" Mills from India. And in 2002 City also appointed a Danish manager - Jan Molby, who was the first non-Englishman to be in charge of the club since Terry Neill's departure in 1974.

A lot of them have intriguing international stories about their backgrounds. Full-back Jock Gibson was born in Philadelphia, but came to England as a two-year-old when his family settled in Sheffield, where his father worked as a colliery engineer. When he was 13, they moved to Hamilton in Scotland and "Jock" played for Netherburn and Blantyre Celtic. He was signed by Sunderland and joined City in 1922 in preference to nine other clubs on the advice of Mick Gilhooley, who had moved in the opposite direction. At one stage he was tipped to gain Scottish international honours - until he owned up to being an American! Promotion-winning goalkeeper Glyn Myhill, whose mother is Welsh, was born in Modesto in California six weeks prematurely while his parents were on holiday in the Grand Canyon and they had to pay a £50,000 fee for him - oddly enough the same as he cost the Tigers - in hospital costs. And the story goes that Myhill, who joined City from Aston Villa in December 2003, picked up the nickname Boaz because his family travelled a lot in general.

Midfield player Julian Johnsson was born in Denmark, played for Sogndal in Norway before joining City in 2001 and IA Akranes in Iceland after leaving them and played internationally for the Faroe Islands, where he was later the player-coach of B68 Toftir. But he regretted leaving the Tigers because he said: "I loved the atmosphere around every game on Boothferry Park. I remember that there were great expectations for the team, but we did not quite fulfil them. It was the biggest mistake in my career ever to leave Hull City and England. But you make some bad and good choices in your career." Equally as cosmopolitan, midfield player Richard Sneekes was an Amsterdam-born Dutch under-21 international who played and worked in Denmark, where he was involved in banking, and returned to England to help out with an Italian restaurant called Angelos in the Wylde Green area of Birmingham. He said: "There are four brothers, two of whom are partners and two of whom have come over from Sardinia to help out. I pay the bills and do the book-keeping. It's very small and very nice, but I enjoy it and it's a good life."

And just as Glyn Myhill had becomer known as Boaz, so was inside-forward Bertram Mills known as Paddy. His Army father John was from Liverpool and his mother Annie was from Skegness. Paddy was the youngest of seven children and first came to England as a five-year-old, moving with the family to Barton-upon-Humber two years later. He had been born at Multan in India and said: "I didn't know any English when I first came over. When I first went to school, I often used to break into Hindustani!" In 1920 he first joined City from Barton Town on a wage of £2 a week and later had the distinction of being the oldest-surviving player to have been with Notts County, who are the oldest-surviving League club in England. And Mills can claim an odd parallel with striker Stephen McPhee, who cost City a club record £400,000 from Beira Mar during the summer of 2005. He was born in Scotland, brought up in Holland, where he joined Vitesse Arnhem as a youngster, and signed from Portugal: "I went out to Holland with my parents, but they left after two years and I moved in with a foster family, who couldn't speak English, so I had to learn how to speak fluent Dutch."

Names, in fact, have caused increasing fascination in the Tigers' annals. Full-back Roger de Vries claimed that his Dutch surname was as common in Holland and South Africa as Smith is in Britain. His foreign ancestry was so far back, though, that he could not lay claim to international recognition elsewhere. Ironically, winger Graeme Atkinson might have played for Holland, though, because of a family connection on his mother Mary's side. Another winger, Tim Hotte, can boast a surname which is French-Canadian in origin and should strictly be pronounced as "Hot."

Andy Davidson followed his elder brother, who was a winger with the club in 1946 and 1947 to City, but there was a query about his first name because Andy explained: "He was known as Craig back home, but he was called David in Hull. He was a better player than I was and was naturally two-footed, but he got injured, needed six operations and never played again. And Newcastle United had offered £15,000 for him two weeks before it first happened." In 2001 striker Gary Fletcher briefly played for the Tigers, but his surname developed into Taylor-Fletcher when he was Lincoln City - apparently because his wife wanted to retain the "Taylor" part of it because she was the last in the lineage. Then there was the utility player known as "Junior" Lewis who helped City to successive promotions in 2004 and 2005. But "Junior" was only his nickname and his real name was even more athletic - Karl Lewis!

Maybe some of the name games are to be expected, though. After all, City had Mick Tait and George Lyall on their books in the 1970s, they won promotions in 1983 and 1985 with Andy Flounders and Gary Swann and they "raced" to safety in the Football League in 1998-99 with Andy Oakes and Duane Darby. There may have had to be a bit of licence with some of the spellings, but there again are City the only club to sign two players whose names are in the titles of novelty songs by Val Doonican - Brian McGinty in 1997 and Damien Delaney in 2002?

City also had a few players who became dab hands at earning themselves international recognition in more unconventional ways. Winger Martin Reagan's curriculum vitae includes a 12-year stint as England's football coach that included two World Cup triumphs. The opportunity arose when the FA asked him to take charge of the national side - for women! He said: "They were looking for someone to take the job and I was delighted to do it. They asked me to be the England women's manager and coach although it was separately run through the Women's Football Association at the time. There weren't the same links that there are today and the women had very little support, which was a tragedy in itself, and they were very independent. They were always short of cash and that was reflected in the organisation and the way that things were done. Even then we had only about half the amount of players they had in Germany and a small fraction of the numbers that the Americans had. There were about 6,000 registered players in England in those days, but the women's game has been spreading like wildfire and now there are about 50,000. But I did the job from 1979 to 1991 and we went to places such as Italy and Japan. In fact, we went to Italy four times and twice won their Little World Cup tournament." Jackie Sewell, meanwhile, left City during the summer of 1961 to take up an offer in Africa and ended up representing the same country under two different names because he played twice for Northern Rhodesia as captain and then once for them after they had become Zambia! Jackie also coached Zambia, but it was all a bit odd anyway because he had already played six times for England during his Sheffield Wednesday days.

Another City winger Dave Fraser, a Scot from Newtongrange, gained football representative honours for England when their prison-service team played against Holland and Scotland! And technically it made him a double international because he had gained schoolboy honours with Scotland, too. Yet another City winger Charlie Crickmore retired from professional football at the age of 30 in 1972 after serving six League clubs and said: "I knew straightaway that I had made the right decision to quit football and become a fireman." He spent 24 years as a fireman before retiring at the compulsory age of 55 and becoming a heavy-goods driving instructor, but made the most of one of the fringe benefits of it because he added: "I started to play for the local fire-brigade football team and became the first Hull man to play for the England Fire Brigade side. I was on the mark twice in a 5-2 win in Scotland, once in a 4-0 win over the British Army and once in a 2-1 win over Holland, so I played three games and scored four goals for England." Equally, defender Ray Pettit also gained international honours for England late in his football career as a result of his work. In 1979 he played for England against France in an international game between the two countries' Customs and Excise departments that took place every two years. He explained: "I ended up having three days in Paris and getting something free from the Customs!"

Crickmore also had yet another career in football because he eventually qualified as a local referee. He said: "I'd be pretty hard on players because of my background in professional soccer. I'd tell them exactly what I wanted and warn them to behave before we'd even kicked off. I'd try to nip anything in the bud before we started." But his was not the first case of City players becoming match officials because there was a notable occasion when two of them did so in conjunction with one of the club directors. In February 1914 a challenge match for charity took place at Anlaby Road between 11 Coverdale brothers from Hull and Holderness, who won 3-0, and 11 Charlesworth brothers from the Scunthorpe area. The referee was City director Jack Bielby and players Billy Halligan and Patsy O'Connell were his linesmen.

Family ties, in fact, have also played a part in the Tigers' heritage. Inside-forward Jack Needham, who played for City in 1920 after spells with Mansfield Town, Birmingham City and Wolverhampton Wanderers, had a curious family connection. Jack Shelton, who played for Walsall for 13 years, was the son of Jack, senior, an FA Cup winner with Wolves in 1908, but when his father died, his mother married Needham - so Jack, junior, became both the son and stepson of two noted League players.

City's hero George Maddison had a son called George and he, too, was a goalkeeper. And they both signed for the same manager - Bill McCracken. George, senior, joined City a year after McCracken had become City's manager in 1923 and George, junior, signed for him after he had taken charge of Aldershot. Then there was the battle between brothers Brian and Alan Little. Alan had been chief scout when Brian was City's manager as they prepared for 2001-02. But in October 2001 Alan succeeded Paul Bracewell as Halifax Town's manager, so that the brothers opposed each other when City went to the Shay in early February 2002. The Tigers won 1-0, but the season ended badly for both. City sacked Brian before the end of it and Halifax finished bottom of the Third Division to tumble out of the League for a second time. In February 2006 City's defender Leon Cort opposed his elder brother Carl when Wolverhampton Wanderers visited the KC Stadium to win 3-2. Defender Leon scored the Tigers' equaliser to make it 1-1, but striker Carl had the last word by snatching Wolves' 89th-minute winner.

Then there were family ties between City players and music and drama. I once obtained the autograph of Tony Mercer, who was one of the three lead soloists in the Black and White Minstrel Show on TV with Dai Francis and John Boulter, at Scarborough Cricket Festival when they were appearing in a summer season at the town's Futurist Theatre. Tony, in fact, had been a promising footballer until his career was ended by knee trouble and he concentrated instead on music. But the injury prevented him from following in the family footsteps because his father David, a right-winger, had started his League career with the Tigers in 1914 after spells with Prescot Cables and Skelmersdale near his native St. Helen's. David "Magical" Mercer was later sold to Sheffield United for a then record £4,500 fee in 1920 and went on to win two England caps. But the family dynasty did not end with David, who took a public-house at Swinton, near Rotherham, when he left the game. Tony also had a Sheffield-born uncle called Frank Barson, a centre-half who played once for England while he was with Aston Villa. In addition, David Mercer's brother Arthur was one of his teammates at Bramall Lane and his son Arthur played for Torquay United, one of his father's other clubs. William Clark was hardly the most successful left-winger in the Tigers' history because he played in only one League game - a 1-0 home defeat against Blackpool in March 1920. But he was the step-grandfather of Tim Healy, who has become one of the country's leading television actors with starring roles in numerous dramas including "'Auf Wiedersehen, Pet,'" "Boys from the Bush" and "Heartburn Hotel."

City, in fact, have also been lucky to rely on the support of several genuine celebrity fans, such as film director Mark Herman, playwright Alan Plater, actors Sir Tom Courtenay, Roy North and Barrie Rutter and Sade's bass guitarist Paul Denman. They have been repeatedly been generously support-ive of both the club and a host of accompanying good causes, always underpinning their thoughts with a lovely, gentle humour. They have added to City folklore in delightful style and it is worth recording that Ken Wagstaff once had a racehorse called Waggy, which was co-owned by Hull busi-nessmen Cyril Wheeler and Wally Palmer, named after him. It actually won regularly at Redcar dur-ing 1968 and completed its third victory at the course on the day before City opened their League programme at Blackpool. Tom Courtenay, though, was similarly animal crackers because he once owned a Dalmatian dog called Wagstaff, which he brought to Boothferry Park on one occasion. Wagstaff the dog was then introduced to Wagstaff the player and Ian McKechnie is said to have remarked: "The dog's better looking, but Ken's got more spots!"

Some of City's players, in fact, have shown different artistic leanings. Scottish inside-forward George Martin, who nearly put a spoke in Joe Payne's record of 10 goals in a Football League game for Luton Town in their 12-0 win over Bristol Rovers in April 1936 by following up to make sure that the ball was over the line for one of them, was an operatic tenor and a prize-wnning sculptor. Reserve goalkeeper Wally Chapman was a dab hand at playing the harmonica, having been tutored by the virtuoso Tommy Reilly, who famously played the theme tune to TV programme "Dixon of Dock Green." Utility player Dennis Burnett once had to describe himself as a professional musician to get into Norwegian soccer where there were no professionals. The description was a way of fit-ting in with Norway's requirements when he became the full-time player-manager of FC Haugar in 1980 and he admitted: "I do play the organ, but I don't give concerts. But I just had to work every-thing within the framework of the system." Defender Geoff Barker and striker Nick Deacy are use-ful guitarists, defender Dave Roberts helps to run a project called Major Music in South Wales that helped the career of Automatic, a band who have reached the charts in 2006, and winger Gordon Staniforth played the saxophone.

Utility player Paddy Greenwood once wanted to be an architect, but painted in oils and did sketch-es, defender Frank Banks was a notable cartoonist and forward Terry Heath has done well for him-self as a painter, once bringing one of his pictures to an ex-Tigers function for fund-raising. Defender Ian Bennyworth was a junior ballroom dancing champion and, more remarkably and probably obscurely, utility player Norman Corner won a prize for his tropical fish, which he would watch for half-an-hour for match-day relaxation. He explained: "One of my relatives had a tank in his house and he got one for me. At one point I had four tanks of tropical fish and even won a medal for them at a tournament in Hull. I was not that good at recognising the different fish, but I got a lot of relax-ation from watching them before games and I found that they would also calm you down when you came home after playing. We kept them until I moved back to the North-East and couldn't find a spot in the house for them."

City players have had success after turning their attention to other sports, too. Intriguingly, Keith Edwards and Billy Whitehurst were not just twin strikers who had two spells with the club - they have both owned racing greyhounds as well at different times. Johnny Linaker was a talented swimmer, Ken Wagstaff was a first-class rifle shot, Mick Milner has done well since he became one of the many footballers, including centre-forward Jack Acquroff who was noted for turning up for training wearing plus-fours, to turn to golf. Then there have been the table-tennis stars - Welshman Dai Davies represented Yorkshire, Syd Gerrie represented the North of Scotland and Ken Harrison represented a Hull side who visited Rotterdam. Alex Gibson, Jimmy Keen, Tommy "Tich" Mason, Charlie Nicklas, Ernie Shepherd, Bob Dennison and Stuart Blampey all became involved in different aspects of athletics. Mason was also a noted boxer - as was fellow winger William Johnson - and became an Army welterweight champion, while Curtis Woodhouse won his first professional fight at the same weight in September 2006 when he beat Dean Marcantonio at London's Grosvenor House Hotel.

Goalkeepers Billy Bly and Bernard Fisher played Continental handball in Hull, Ernie Phillips and Ray Smith used to play bowls regularly and Gordon Staniforth, not one of City's biggest players, combines basketball and football coaching with his duties at York College. Forward Vinny Townend was one of the fastest players on City's books before the 1914-18 War, but played in only 12 League games. But he put his pace to good use after his retirement. He played for Olympia Cricket Club after footballing spells with Selby Town and Goole Town and then became an athletics coach. Townend, who was living in Denison Road in his home town of Selby when he died at the age of 68 in February 1958, helped the career of sprinter Stanley Engelhart from nearby Barlby. And Engelhart, who was born in 1905, had Townend as his mentor when he won a 220 yards race in Hamilton in Canada and then when he went to the 1932 Olympic Games in Los Angeles to take part in the equivalent of the 200 metres and the 4 x 400 metres relay.

Other City players have also excelled at cricket, including those who played in the county game such as Sam Weaver with Somerset in 1936, Raich Carter with Derbyshire in 1946, Jim Melville with Warwickshire in 1936 and Stan Montgomery with Glamorgan from 1949 to 1953. Carter also played for Durham, while Joe Kitchen represented Lincolnshire and Mick Brown, Phil Holme and Brian Marwood were also close to breaking into the county game. But Rotherham-born centre-half Charles Lee did particularly well after being one of six City players, none of whom had played in the first team, to be released after the triumphant 1948-49 season. He concentrated on his cricket and played for Yorkshire in 1952 before joining Derbyshire, for whom he was an opening batsman from 1954 to 1964 when he was 40. He hit more than 1,000 runs in a season eight times and captained the county towards the end of his career.

Those who played in different standards of league cricket have included Tommy Bleakley, Arthur Charlesworth, Albert Turner, James Iremonger, Charlie Flood, Eddie Edwards, Eddie Burbanks, Ken Harrison, Colin Smith, David King, Gerry Summers, Ken Houghton, Ken Wagstaff, Chris Chilton, Paddy Greenwood, David Lill, Ray Pettit, Jeff Wealands, Gordon Nisbet, Jeff Hemmerman, Vince Grimes, Chris Galvin, John Kaye, Craig Norrie, Peter Skipper, Paul Olsson, Rob Dewhurst and John Eyre. In fact, Ernie Bell once held the postwar record for the highest score in the East Riding Amateur League when, as captain, he scored 123 with 22 boundaries for the Inland Revenue against Reckitt's III, while Frank Harrison played for Hull Savings Bank in the 1966 Circle Cup, helping them to the semi-finals in which he was out for 16 for the first time in the competition, so it left him with an average of 190 from four innings!

Chris Simpkin, Alan Jarvis and Steve Deere have played squash regularly, but dabbling in other sports often brought concern about non-football injuries. Chris, who was also a finalist in the Yorkshire under-15 tennis championships, was told by Cliff Britton to stop playing squash, so he had to continue playing for Welton under the assumed name of Robinson! He explained: "I split my eye playing squash just before City were due to play a match against Swindon. Cliff wouldn't allow me to play after that, so I then had to go under an alias!" Bob Dennison had had the same kind of problem when he played hockey: "Bob Brocklebank saw me with a hockey stick on the crossbar of my bicycle and told me not to play in case I was injured. But I continued playing and my wife Pam had to have two hockey sticks on her crossbar!" Alan Jarvis, meanwhile, once damaged his left eye when hit by a friend's squash racket - and that was after he had severely injured his right eye while playing for Mansfield Town against his home-town club Wrexham in May 1972.

Garreth Roberts and Roger de Vries have also done well in local tennis circles in recent years. Roger actually played in the national veterans' finals, but it presented him with a poser that dated back to his football days. He explained: "I was always quite good with both feet. I was quite strong on my left, but I carried the ball with my right. When I was at Blackburn, the coach Mick Heaton once asked me: 'Are you sure you're not right-footed?' Probably I was naturally! But I played tennis left-handed and yet I'm now obsessed with golf, for which I use my right hand, as I did when I was batting at cricket!"

Relatively speaking, Republic of Ireland international Terry Murray became the brother-in-law of Rowley Moat, who played rugby league for both Hull FC and Hull Kingston Rovers, Tom Wilson became the father-in-law of jockey Graham Bradley and Billy Wilkinson became the son-in-law of Melbourne-born jockey Jack Brace, who raced in Australia, India and England. Brace piloted home the first of nearly 2,000 winners in 1921 as he built his reputation in Australia, he was four times the top jockey in India, where he rode for Sir Victor Sassoon's string, he survived a 'plane crash in Iraq and then he came to England in 1948 because his wife Muriel was from Hull, where they opened a sweet shop after he had retired following a controversy at Newmarket in 1956! David Brightwell came from international sporting stock because his mother won gold in the 800 metres and silver in the 400 metres at the 1964 Olympic Games in Tokyo as 24-year-old schoolteacher Ann Packer from Berkshire. Robbie Brightwell, then her fiance, missed out in the 400 metres, but was in the 4 x 400 metres relay team who set three records in reaching the final.

But City players' footballing feats have normally taken the most prominence. For example, some have started and ended their League careers with the club with a flourish. Left-winger Ernie Shepherd scored for City with his first kick for the club - at Darlington in a 1-0 win on March 12, 1949 - after joining them from West Bromwich Albion and right-winger Ron Young laid on a goal for Chris Chilton 20 seconds into his League debut in a 7-0 win over Barnsley under the new Boothferry Park floodlights in October 1964. He said: "I can remember the entire evening as if it were yesterday because I was quite ill with nerves. But the lights were good, the crowd were good and the night was good." Conversely, midfield player George Lyall finished his League career by scoring a goal because he broke his left leg in doing so after 64 minutes of a 2-2 draw at home to Bolton Wanderers in February 1977. He said: "There was a crack as I went down and I knew straightaway that my leg was broken, but I didn't find out that I'd scored as well until I got into the dressing-room. But I suppose that, if you have to leave a game through injury, then the best time to do it is when you've scored." Lyall stretched to score as Bolton's defender Sam Allardyce tried to block his path, but insisted: "His right leg missed me altogether and he just seemed to catch me with his left as he came across me. But a reporter from a national newspaper asked me if there were any feeling about the tackle and I said that the main thing I wanted to make clear was that it was a complete accident." The match had been featured on Yorkshire TV and Lyall admitted when he watched it: "I broke out in a cold sweat as it got nearer the incident." Lyall joked that some of his teammates had taken him books to read so that he would know some new words for playing Scrabble on the team coach, but he did not manage a comeback. He did, though, briefly maintain a passing interest in the written word - because he became a newsagent in Elloughton!

Forwards Billy Halligan and Les Thompson took everything a stage further because they both scored in their first and last League games for City. Halligan, an Irishman from Athlone, joined City from Wolverhampton Wanderers during the summer of 1913 and duly made his debut at Blackpool in the first League game of the season, scoring in a 2-2 draw. In 1914-15 Halligan played in 37 out of the 38 League games, scoring 17 times. It included a goal in the final League game of the season - a 4-1 home win over Grimsby Town in April 1915. Halligan guested for Manchester United and Rochdale in wartime football, but never reappeared for the Tigers at the end of the 1914-18 War because he moved to Preston North End. Thompson, a left-sided utility player who was booked for a foul on Bryan Robson on his senior debut against Manchester United, was given his first League start for the Tigers in October 1987 when he scored the only goal of the game when they beat Ipswich Town at home. He was also on the mark in City's first-ever League win away to Newcastle United in May 1991. The Tigers won 2-1 in their last League game of the season, but they were already relegated from the Second Division and Thompson's reward was to be given a free transfer by manager Terry Dolan.

Meanwhile, left-winger Dave Fraser, who carried a little red duck as a lucky mascot at the start of his League career, is in City's record-books for scoring their first home League goal under floodlights and their last goal on Christmas Day and both came in 1-1 draws. The floodlit goal came in April 1956 in a rearranged game with Doncaster Rovers and he said. "I can remember that Charlie Williams, the comedian who died this year, played for Doncaster and the goal was a header from a cross by Johnny Stephens on the right. I'd scored twice on my League debut in the previous game at Rotherham and I was only 18, so life was great for me at the time." The last Christmas Day goal was at home to Gateshead in 1957 and he recalled: "I can remember that it was a right-footer and I didn't score many of them. I scored from some distance, but my right foot was usually a 'swinger' that I just used for standing on."

City have naturally been involved in some odd own-goal mishaps and technically one of them was scored for them by England's 1966 World Cup winner George Cohen. In October 1965 the Football League beat the League of Ireland 5-1 in an inter-league match at Boothferry Park. But there was a 60-minute practice match the previous day in which the Tigers' promotion side beat the Football League 2-0. Chris Chilton scored one and Cohen put through his own goal for the other. In August 1970 Tom Wilson scored a hat-trick for City's reserves at Sunderland. But they won 3-1 and Wilson was also accredited with an own goal for Sunderland! And in September 2000 City beat Cardiff City 2-0 at home with the aid of two own goals - by Danny Gabbidon and David Greene.

Arthur Grimsdell, Tottenham Hotspur's England wing-half of the 1920s, was accredited as being one of the first long-throw experts, but the Tigers have had their fair share of them at different stages from the prewar Sam Weaver and Tommy Gardner to the postwar Raich Carter and Jack Bennion and the recent Andy Holt, Sam Collins and Sam Ricketts. Wing-half Gardner, who made 67 League appearances for City between 1932 and 1934 before winning two England caps after moving on to Aston Villa and was a member of their 1933 Third Division North title-winning squad, was up there with the best because in 1932 he won a special competition when his throw was measured at 32 yards 2 inches. It was said that Weaver started his long throws because he was not too impressed with Grimsdell's efforts. He said: "I just took them up myself with medicine balls in training. In the end it was almost possible to do it without trying. I could throw from the halfway line and put the ball into the penalty box. I didn't have to train for long throws any more although on one occasion I pulled an abdominal muscle, which kept me out for six weeks! And in the old days a ball seemed as if it were a ton weight when it got wet." And Jack Bennion recalled: "We used to have competitions for long throw-ins at Burnley. We'd stand on the touchline and throw as far as we could. Gradually I got quite good at it. It was all a question of the stomach muscles and the timing of the throw."

George Rushton was one of City's first centre-forwards, playing in their inaugural season in 1904-05 and then spending two seasons in the League with them. Rushton, who was born in a house overlooking Stoke's Victoria Ground and was a close friend of Stanley Matthews' father, scored twice in City's first fixture against Notts County in September 1904 and then recorded the club's first hat-trick later in the month. But controversy occurred in November 1905 when the Tigers won 2-1 at Leeds City in an FA Cup third qualifying-round replay at Holbeck on a pitch on which "the glutinous mud was thinly disguised by sawdust and corn ears." Rushton, who lived in Bean Street off Hull's Anlaby Road, was injured and went to the side of the pitch to receive attention. Suddenly the ball came his way and he dashed straight back on to the pitch with it to score. It was reported: "Rushton rehabilitated himself and his reappearance after a short absence for injury was as dramatic as a climax of a tragedy. He and George Spence made play and pretty and sure finessing culminated in the opening score." Apparently an inquiry was held and a rule was introduced, stating that a player had to report to the referee before returning to the pitch after leaving it for treatment for an injury or any other reason. Whether Rushton's spontaneous ingenuity brought about a change in one of football's laws is open to debate because another story tells of Barnsley's defender Dicky Downs, who was having treatment behind the goal when, wearing only one boot, he suddenly rushed on and cleared an attack in the replayed 1912 FA Cup final against West Bromwich Albion. But City's cuptie was being watched by the Football League president J. J. Bentley, who would, therefore, have been in an ideal situation to appreciate the problem caused when a loophole had been exploited. The rules were also exploited a little when City beat Southport 5-1 at home in November 1948 in the only game in which all four of their heroes - Raich Carter, Eddie Burbanks, Norman Moore and Viggo Jensen - scored. It was misty, so the game, watched by former Yorkshire cricket captain Brian Sellers, kicked off three minutes early and halftime was cancelled because of fears about the light.

Andy Conway scored five goals in six League appearances for City during 1948, but his brief goalscoring stint with City reached a peak in odd circumstances on the club's three-match summer tour to Scandinavia. It took place in May 1948 and comprised two games in Denmark and one in Sweden. Conway scored four times and goalkeeper Alec Corbett saved a penalty in the second game against a Kolding XI "selected from stars of various areas covered by the Jutland League," which City won 5-1. Perhaps their achievements might have been helped by a special factor - the size of the footballs used. It was reported: "The ball used in the Danish games is slightly smaller than those on English soccer fields." It was not the only local custom in evidence because City skipper Jack Taylor was presented with a bunch of tulips from Kolding officials before the game. And the size of footballs also preoccupied the thinking of coach George Curtis, who had a brief spell with City when Angus McLean and John Simpson left to take charge of Hartlepools United in 1967. At one stage in his career Curtis had players training with small plastic balls, which, he believed, would help them to cope better with full-sized footballs when they needed to do so.

There was a different kind of problem when City won 3-0 at Halifax Town in the Football League Cup in August 1968 because the tie coincided with the speedway season. Town had tried to increase their income by having speedway at the Shay, but they literally had to cut corners when the seasons overlapped. The corners of the football pitch were cut away to make the curves for the speedway track and the Tigers discovered that board platforms were fitted at them with loose turfing laid on them to accommodate football. And there was also a drop of four inches along the lengths of the pitch to the speedway straights, which were only a foot from the touchlines. And City's luck was perhaps typified in September 1973 when referee Bob Matthewson accidentally headed clear a goalbound shot by Stuart Blampey in a goalless draw at home to West Bromwich Albion!

Football's quirks have also involved City's managers, who include two to have managed them twice - David Menzies and Colin Appleton - one who has taken them up twice - Peter Taylor - and two who have taken them down twice - Bob Brocklebank and Terry Dolan. Others can claim different notoriety. Mike Smith wrote a book curiously entitled "Success in Football," which was first published in 1973 and reprinted in 1978. But by 1981 he had guided Hull City into the Fourth Division for the first time. In 1977 Terry Neill was named as one of the Top 10 Tiemen of the Year. And those nominated with him included newscasters Kenneth Kendall, Richard Baker, Leonard Parkin and Gordon Honeycombe, comedian Bruce Forsyth, actor Gerald Harper, Tory MP Nicholas Fairburn, disc-jockey David Jacobs and comedy scriptwriter Jimmy Perry. Others have had footballing distinctions. John Kaye was voted the Midlands' Footballer of the Year for the 1965-66 season and Eddie Gray won the "Football Monthly" Trophy as the best player in the 1970 FA Cup final first meeting at Wembley while playing for Leeds United against Chelsea. Brian Horton completed 1,000 games as a manager when he was at Macclesfield Town in early November 2004 and one-time assistant manager John McGovern achieved the rare feat of playing in all four divisions of the Football League while still a teenager with Hartlepool United and Derby County,

And not surprisingly a lot of the best City anecdotes affect two subjects - goalkeepers, who seem to be known the world over for their innate eccentricities, and penalties, the bane of English football whenever it comes to shoot-outs. Maybe more note should have been taken of the Tigers' background because they played their part in a bit of football history in August 1970 when they faced Manchester United in a Watney Cup semi-final at Boothferry Park in front of 34,007 fans. It was the first competitive domestic game to feature a penalty shoot-out following a 1-1 draw after extra time and it took place in front of what had been the Bunker's Hill end of the ground. George Best, Brian Kidd and Bobby Charlton scored for United with Terry Neill, Ken Houghton and Ian Butler on the mark for City. Ian McKechnie then saved from Denis Law, but Ken Wagstaff shot wide. Willie Morgan then scored for United, but McKechnie missed City's fifth spot-kick and they lost the tie.

Ian said: "I used to take the penalties for the reserves when I was at Southend. I knew Alex Stepney, who was in the Manchester United goal, from when he was at Millwall and I was with Arsenal and Southend and there was some talk about goalkeepers always being the heroes and never the villains in such circumstances. I never quite figured out why I took the vital penalty. We'd practised taking penalties in every training session for the previous two weeks, but I wasn't supposed to take one. The trouble was that everyone else bottled it once there was a match situation. I told John McSeveney, who was then the coach, and he said: 'Don't be stupid!' But no-one else would take it when it came to it. Alex asked: 'What are you doing?' when I started walking back with him towards the goal where the penalties were being taken. I said I was taking one against him and he said: 'You're joking.' It might have worked or I might have hit the corner-flag. As it was, I hit the bar! None of the City players talked to me afterwards because I'd lost them their win bonuses. They blamed me even though I was the only one who'd take it. And the daft thing was that we'd had a blatant penalty turned down in the first 90 minutes..."

Ironically McKechnie and Ian Butler had previously reached the final of knockout competition in Birmingham in which both of them had to take and try to save penalties! And an odd sequel to it all that it was not the end of City link's with big footballing names and penalties that week because because they quickly arranged a friendly at Bradford City to fill the gap by their failure to reach the Watney Cup final. Bradford's side included Michael Owen's father Terry, their new signing from Everton, and the Tigers' stand-in goalkeeper Peter Walters saved a penalty from Bruce Bannister, who later moved to Boothferry Park.

Maybe that week proved that there was a need for penalty coaches because they now seem to have them for just about everything else and City once had the ideal person for the job in their ranks. In March 1964 Jack Brownsword became the first full-back to score 50 goals in his career even though he did not score for City in his brief postwar spell with them. He said: "I think I was actually in the Guinness Book of Records as the full-back who'd scored the most goals in League soccer. It's all kidology with a penalty because the goalkeeper's trying to read your mind and you're trying to read his. But I always used to pop them just inside the post because the goalkeepers were at full stretch to reach them there. And I heard that Graham Taylor often used to take some penalties after training and would tell people: 'I'm going to try to do a Jackie Brownsword!'" And it seems that City were still worried about penalties when Stuart Pearson had his saved by goalkeeper Jim Allan in a 1-1 draw at Swindon in January 1974. Pearson explained: "On Friday night Jimmy McGill dreamt that we got a penalty, that I hit it where I usually hit them and the goalkeeper saved it. When I put the ball down, I thought: 'Should I hit it to the other side?,' but I decided that to be worried about a dream was just a load of honey. But I neither hit it nor placed it in the end."

There have, in fact, been occasions when there have been penalty doubles in City's games as if the action replays were serving timely reminders on them. One occurred in January 1948 when Scottish inside-forward Willie Buchan made his debut for City after being signed from Blackpool for £5,000 the previous day. The Tigers beat Rotherham United 5-3 at home and Buchan soon underlined his reputation as a penalty-taker of note. Buchan was renowned for leaving goalkeepers marooned without shooting with any notable power from the spot, but there was a quirk to his first goal for the club. Martin Reagan first took a 61st-minute penalty, but it was ruled that the goalkeeper had moved too soon, so it was retaken by Buchan, who made no mistake. And 13 minutes later Buchan scored with a second penalty. There were also two other doubles that day because Welshman George Murphy, who later became a publican in Leeds, scored two of the Tigers' other goals, while defender Allan Mellor added a quirk of his own by scoring for both sides - one being an own goal for the Millers.

In August 1960 Chris Chilton made his first-team debut at inside-right at Colchester United, who won 4-0. And the Tigers, whose forward-line had an average age of 19, gave away two penalties for handling offences in the first half of their first League match of the season. Eric McMillan, who was making his City debut after leaving Chelsea, and Les Collinson conceded the spot-kicks and United's left-half Cyril Hammond registered a double of his own by converting them both after 37 and 45 minutes. Colchester then added a further double after halftime when Martin King scored two of his own in the 48th and 56th minutes. In an action replay City also gave away two penalties for handball - by Matt Hocking and Mark Greaves - in a 2-2 draw at Chester in August 1998. David Flitcroft scored one and missed one. But the Tigers were also given two penalties in the game: David d'Auria had one saved and Mark Hateley scored one. It was one of those days because there were also two sendings-off - after two of the penalties had been awarded - and nine bookings.

In February 1964 the Tigers lost 4-3 at home to Bournemouth and were on the wrong end of a penalty double. City had been 3-1 down, but fought back to 3-3 before going behind again when they were awarded two penalties in quick succession - both for handling offences. In the 80th minute former Northern Ireland international Dick Keith handled a shot from Ron Rafferty, but Chris Chilton missed from the spot when he fired high on to Bunker's Hill. Two minutes later Tommy Standley handled a header by Ray Henderson and this time John McSeveney took the penalty, but he shot wide. City, in fact, had a third penalty appeal for handball rejected three minutes later because another infringement had occurred elsewhere: maybe it was just as well! And Rafferty, who had been a teammate of Bournemouth's manager Reg Flewin at Portsmouth, was back in the side after a five-month lay-off with a broken foot to add a double of his own - his first two goals for the club. But it might, of course, have been a hat-trick if Keith had not stopped his shot for the first penalty. It was also City's first home defeat of the season, while Charlie Crickmore scored one of the Cherries' goals against his home-city club.

Goalkeeper Jeff "Lurch" Wealands saved two penalties in a 2-1 win at Nottingham Forest in

September 1975. After 13 minutes he denied John Robertson, who, however, followed up to scramble home the rebound after Roger de Vries was ruled to have fouled Terry Curran, who later had a spell on loan to City. In the 73rd minute Forest were awarded a second penalty when Ian Bowyer tangled with Stuart Croft and this time Wealands pushed Robertson's spot-kick round the post for a corner. And in January 2006 Glyn Myhill also saved two penalties in a game when the Tigers won 3-0 at Stoke. After 50 minutes Sam Collins fouled Paul Gallagher, who took the spot-kick himself, but Myhill saved comfortably to his right. In the 65th minute Stoke were awarded a second penalty after a challenge by John Welsh on Peter Sweeney, but Luke Chadwick struck it straight at Myhill, who clutched it at waist height.

Wealands and Myhill, though, feature in another City goalkeeping category in less heroic circumstances. Wealands was beaten by probably the longest shot that ever produced a goal against City when his opposite number, Ray Cashley, punted the ball downfield and it bounced over him in a 3-1 defeat on a wet and windy night at Bristol City in September 1973. And in March 2006 City lost 3-2 at Leicester City, who took a 2-1 lead in ther 64th minute when their midfield player Joey Gudjonnsson beat Myhill with a shot from just inside his own half. Then there are two City goalkeepers who scored with kicks down the middle after they had left the club - Iain Hesford for Maidstone United against Hereford United in a 3-2 win in November 1991 and Matt Glennon for St. Johnstone in a 2-2 draw against Ross County in March 2006.

Curiously Ian McKechnie did score two goals for City - one in a 7-6 win over Leeds United at Boothferry Park in May 1971 and one during a 12-0 win over a Berbice FA XI in New Amsterdam in June 1973. He said: "The only goals I got for City were in friendlies. There was one during the tour of the West Indies and another when I came on in place of Ian Butler on the left-wing in Chris Chilton's testimonial match against Leeds and stroked one past David Harvey from 20 yards with great aplomb! But my only other goal was as a goalkeeper in Arsenal's third team when I booted one right down the pitch and it flew in. I was a left-winger when I was 18, but I never played a first-team game for Arsenal as an outfield player. But, as with a lot of goalkeepers, I always enjoyed playing out of goal in five-a-sides."

But in April 1926 City included their own George Martin in a benefit match for Norwich City's captain George Martin at the Nest and won 5-2 and there was another odd penalty double. City's goalkeeper George Maddison scored from the penalty spot midway through the first-half after a shot by George Whitworth had been handled. But near the end Norwich were also awarded a penalty after a handling offence and their goalkeeper Charlie Dennington stepped up to take it, but Maddison turned his drive round the post. In May 1988 Welsh international Tony Norman became an outfield player in a 10-0 win at Rudston and Kilham in a friendly after Peter Skipper had replaced him in goal and he duly scored just before the game was cut short because of bad light. But pride of place surely goes to Northern Ireland international goalkeeper Alan Fettis, who scored two League goals for City in the first of his two spells with the club. In December 1994 he came off the substitutes' bench to score in a 3-1 home win over Oxford United and in May 1995 he actually started the last game of the season at Blackpool in the No. 8 shirt while his rival Steve Wilson was recalled in goal in his place, scoring in a 2-1 win.

In November 1954, though, City were on the receiving end when they beat EfB Esbjerg 7-2 in a friendly at Boothferry Park in which Viggo Jensen captained them against his old club. It was 4-0 to the Tigers at halftime and the remaining five goals came in an 11-minute spell early in the second half, one of them a penalty to Esbjerg. Their regular penalty-taker was their 20-year-old goalkeeper Egil Petersen, who had scored more than 50 times previously from the spot and duly obliged again. Oddly enough, City's manager Bob Jackson has just returned from a scouting mission to Scotland, where one of his targets was East Fife's Scottish international Charlie "Legs" Fleming. Neither signed, but Fleming, who had scored twice on his only appearance for Scotland a year earlier, was nearly as well-known for his goalkeeping capabilities as his "cannonball" shooting.

In August 1979 Eddie "Noddy" Blackburn started a friendly at Bergum in Holland in goal, but was then replaced by Paul Frankish and played as an outfield substitute for Peter Skipper in a 5-0 win although he failed to score. Skipper also took over from Tony Norman in goal in different circumstances in a 2-1 defeat at Southampton in the Full Members' Cup in November 1986: he actually started the tie after Normo had injured his back on the journey to the south. But a predecent had been set by wing-half Joe Edelston when he played in goal in a friendly that ended 1-1 at Lincoln City in December 1915.

But there was a far more spectacular example of City using an emergency goalkeeper in the FA Cup first round against Wolverhanpton Wanderers in January 1925. In the first meeting, which ended in a 1-1 draw at Anlaby Road, George Maddison, who had only just established himself as the first-choice goalkeeper, received "a maimed hand." It was reported: "Maddison went down to meet the ball and sustained the injury that may keep him out of the game for a few weeks. Maddison is not having the best of luck since his promotion to the first team. Even if he betrays a somewhat excitable disposition, he is a great custodian and two of his clearances, including the one in which he injured himself, were worthy of his predecessors in Hull City's goal." But there was a surprise when full-back Matt Bell stepped in to take his place.

City stayed at the Regent Hotel in Leamington Spa as they prepared for the replay five days later and Thomas Dyke, the reserve goalkeeper, travelled with them, but there was a doubt about his eligibility for the tie. It was, though, reported: "Bell has given satisfactory examples of custodianship at Leamington and, not being without experience, it is felt that he will capably discharge his new duties." In the end he kept a clean sheet and City won 1-0 with a goal by "Paddy" Mills, who converted a cross by George Richardson after 104 minutes. It was said of Bell: "The City 'keeper evoked an encouraging cheer from the few Hull supporters present. Bell made a brave show in the circumstances, but his strangeness to the position was obvious. He acquitted himself with wonderful security and throughout the whole match only once perhaps gave the least suspicion that the job was comparatively strange to him. His display was most encouraging in the circumstances he found himself in. His colleagues never hesitated to kick the ball back to him when the occasion warranted it and he disposed of high shots and low shots with coolness and promptitude." In the end, though, it was a stopgap measure because it was stated: "The search for an effective understudy to Maddison is being made in earnest." Herbert Bown, who had retired the previous summer, was recruited and played in five games while Maddison remained on the sidelines. Aged 31, he had been a goalscorer during his time with Halifax Town.

The introduction of five substitutes meant that there is nearly always an experienced goalkeeper on the bench nowadays, but there had previously been plenty of instances of outfield players having to take over in goal in injury emergencies. One of the oddest concerned Welsh international wing-half Bill Harris, who had to deputise for Middlesbrough in goal - against his old club City at Boothferry Park! City won 3-0 in a second replay in the Football League Cup second round in October 1962 and 'Boro' goalkeeper Arthur Lightening, who had already saved a penalty from Andy Davidson, went off with back trouble in the 57th minute. Harris replaced him and remained defiant until extra time and at least he had previous experience of the position - for the Tigers! It happened in April 1952 when he took over in goal after Billy Bly had been hurt in a 4-0 defeat at Nottingham Forest.

City, in fact, have featured in a League game in which they fielded three different goalkeepers. In January 1931 they visited Lincoln City and started out with Fred Gibson in goal because George Maddison was already out of action with a wrist injury. But Gibson, who had been in the side for the previous two months, was carried off on a stretcher with a badly-bruised back after half-an-hour, so

Matt Bell again stepped up in the emergency. But this time he had to be led off injured early in the second half, reducing City to nine men in those pre-substitute days. Arthur Childs then became City's third goalkeeper of the day, but they went down 3-0 as it was noted: "Vigour came before science in Lincoln's game."

There was an action replay in March 1954 when Billy Bly was injured in a friendly against Falkirk and Trevor Porteous replaced him in goal until halftime. Although substitutes were not an accepted feature of games in those days, Tommy Forgan got changed and came on to play in goal for the second half as City won 7-1. It was particularly harsh on Bly because he had just been called up for the England B squad and his son Roy explained: "City's manager Bob Jackson made my dad play even though it was just a friendly. Dad refused to play at first and argued that, if he were injured, he would lose more than the £3 fee which players were given for friendlies at that time. Not long before halftime he went up towards the crossbar to make a save and the force of the ball snapped his wrist against it. He said that he wanted to see chairman Harold Needler and he did after Jackson had given him only 30 shillings as his fee because he had played in less than half the game! And it was the only time that dad was given a sniff of playing for his country." And in July 2006 City again ended up using three goalkeepers in their 4-0 win at North Ferriby United during the pre-season build-up. Matt Duke began in goal, but broke his nose in a collision and youngster Curtis Aspden, who was preparing for a loan move to Scarborough, replaced him until halftime. Glyn "Boaz" Myhill then played for the second half and the irony of it all was that the game was the annual one between City and Ferriby for the Billy Bly Memorial Trophy...

The boot was on the other foot, though, in December 2004, when Tranmere Rovers visited the KC Stadium. This time the Tigers won 6-1 and their cause was helped because Rovers fielded three goalkeepers on this occasion. John Achterberg began in goal, but limped off after 20 minutes after a collision with City's striker Delroy Facey. Substitute goalkeeper Russell Howarth replaced him, but suffered a head injury in a clash with City's forward Stuart Elliott just before halftime. It was 1-0 to the Tigers at the interval, but Howarth did not emerge for the second half, so it became one-way traffic after that. Rovers' third goalkeeper, oddly enough, was ex-Tiger Theodore Whitmore, who also came on as a substitute, but did not adjust to the role and really made only token efforts to stem the tide. Whitmore was by now in the same defence as fellow ex-Tiger Ian Goodison and Elliott finished up with a hat-trick, including a penalty, and a booking. But it marred former City manager Brian Little's return to Hull in charge of Tranmere and he said: "By halftime I sensed it wasn't going to be our day. Challenges on goalkeepers are normally frowned upon, but we've had two of them hurt and absolutely nothing has been done about it."

Two ex-Tigers have claimed special trebles with other clubs. David Coates is said to have scored a first-half hat-trick for Mansfield Town that included a goal with his right foot, a goal with his left foot and a goal with his head. He is then supposed to have telephoned home at halftime to let everyone know that it was definitely true if they heard about it elsewhere before he got back! Dennis Booth, who is neither tall nor a striker, tells of a hat-trick of headers that he scored in one game for Lincoln City. Taking it a stage further, maybe the oddest foursome comprised the bookings that Chris Galvin earned in his first four games for City after joining them from Leeds United during the summer of 1973.

Drama, therefore, has been a frequent feature of City's escapades, but there have also been examples of genuine tragedy and sadness involving the club as they have reflected all the facts of everyday life better than any TV soap opera. It it never more explicit than in the cases of those players who were killed in action during two world wars. They include John "Jackie" Smith, one of the club's great goalscorers in the early years, left-back Doug Morgan and winger Patrick Lavery during the 1914-18 War. Hull-born right-winger George Salvidge died during the 1939-45 War when there was

163

also the poignant story of Leeds United's English international inside-forward Eric Stephenson. Born at Bexleyheath in Kent, he played for City against Huddersfield Town in a wartime game in November 1939 while he was stationed at Hull's Londesborough Barracks. He agreed to play for 30 shillings, but it turned out to be one of his last games because he was killed in action in Burma in September 1944 while serving as a major with the Gurkha Rifles.

Inside-forward David "Soldier" Wilson scored four times in 10 League games for City in 1905-06 after joining them from Heart of Midlothian. He scored in their first League outing when they beat Barnsley 4-1 at home and played in the next eight games, but joined Leeds City in a £120 deal soon after his 10th game. But in October 1906 he collapsed and died in the dressing-room after playing for Leeds against Burnley. Belfast-born Sammy Hamilton was an Irish schoolboy international who joined City from Ebbw Vale and scored seven times in 27 games during the 1924-25 season. It was said of him: "He possessed a mastery of the ball, which, with development, promised to earn him high honours in the game." He then played in two friendlies against Grimsby Town in April 1925 when the offside law was being revised, scoring twice in the second one when City won 4-2 as an experiment of having no offsides in the central third of the pitch was given a trial. It was his last goal for the club, though, because he developed "a nasal complaint that seriously impaired his health" the followng August. He had an operation in a Hull nursing home, but failed to recover and died. Centre-forward Simon Raleigh left City for Gillingham during the summer of 1932, but on December 1, 1934, he died when he was concussed while playing for them against Brighton and Hove Albion in a Third Division South game at the Priestfield Stadium. One report said that he was in collision with an opponent, but another insisted that he took the full force of a free-kick to Brighton on his head on a wet, muddy day when the ball was very heavy. Raleigh died in hospital the same night and a verdict of "accidental death" was recorded on him at his inquest. In September 1998 16-year-old apprentice midfield player Mike Artymiuk, from Hedon, left Boothferry Park feeling unwell and died from meningitis overnight. Player-manager Mark Hateley brought former England international David "Rocky" Rocastle to City on loan from Chelsea during the autumn of 1997. They knew each other well and Rocky said: "Mark lived next door to me when he was at Queen's Park Rangers and we'd chat over the garden fence about the game. He knew my situation better than anyone: I was sick of fixing the guttering on a Saturday instead of playing first-team football." But he died at the age of 33 in March 2001. I met him briefly just once and he was a delightful man.

When injury ended his playing career with City, centre-half Harry Brown moved into coaching after going on a course at Birmingham University. He then ran sessions in Hull and Driffield, coached for the East Riding County FA and in 1959 took over at Bridlington Central United when they became the first local non-League side to have a coach. In April 1963 Brown watched Bridlington Town beat Farsley Celtic with a goal by ex-Tiger Mike Head and then embarked on a family trip to Cambridge with his wife Thelma and nephew Andrew when he stopped on the A1 at South Witham, south of Grantham, for petrol. As he was walking from his car to a garage on the other side of the road, he was hit by three vehicles, including a fast-moving Jaguar that failed to stop and may have been the one that killed him. He was 45 and lived at Hedon. Full-back Steve Malcolm, a City trialist with his Jamaican international teammates Ian Goodison and Theodore Whitmore, died in a car accident in January 2001. It happened near Montego Bay after he had played for Jamaica against Bulgaria in Kingston.

Equally public were the deaths of prewar City heroes and George Maddison, Stan Alexander and Ernie Blenkinsop. The outgoing Maddison was 58 when he died in May 1959. He lived on Wold Road in Hull - in an area where many City players were based at the time - and had made the short journey to Manor Club. "Geordie," who had been working for a local marine engineering firm, was a noted singer and had gone on stage in response to requests. He had just performed two songs when he suddenly put the hands that had defied so many forwards to his head and collapsed. An ambulance was called, but he had passed away by the time that it arrived at Hull Royal Infirmary. Alexander, who lived in Hull Road, Anlaby, died at the age of 55 while loading a trailer at the Kingston Street warehouse of British Railways in June 1961. He had joined the Royal Navy in 1940, serving on minesweepers and the supply run to the Normandy beaches. City signed Blenkinsop from Cudworth United Methodists in his home mining village for £75. They were promised a further £25 when he played in the first team and received a belated Christmas present in December 1921 when he made his debut just down the road in a 2-0 defeat at Rotherham County. He left the Tigers to join Sheffield Wednesday and went on to play 26 times for England. But he collapsed while serving one of his customers at the Sportsman public-house in Sheffield in April 1969 at the age of 67.

But everybody with an interest in the Tigers on and off the pitch has lived for the day that the club will play top-flight English League football. Certainly we all retained the utmost hope that the dream would be fulfilled when we first started out as supporters. As we grow older, though, we become reflectively phlegmatic. In September 2006 some fans showed me some photographs of an overgrown Boothferry Park. The field of our dreams was in some disarray even though its six floodlight pylons remain on the landscape as a testimony to my contemporaries who have been forever amber and black. Brian Garvey summed it up for me when he said: "I know we have the KC Stadium and all its attributes. The club have had big plans and had to do it, but I come from a different era as an ex-Tiger and it is nice to have some memories of Boothferry Park." At the same time the Hull attitude must be positive and outward-looking if the top-flight dream is ever to be realised. The city's geographical isolation "40 miles down a railway siding" must not continue to breed some people who are too content to be introspective big fish in a small sea - to echo Hull's maritime heritage. As Mick Brown said: "The trouble with Hull is that it's not on most people's maps."

Perhaps, though, there is still hope for some of us with age although I was sitting next to Damien Delaney at a function earlier in 2006 when we got on to the subject of Irish music and I mentioned a band called Horslips. I said that I enjoyed their electric-folk sound and that I had got to know them quite well after interviewing them. "Ah, yes, my dad told me about them!" he replied with no flicker of emotion. Even so I am claiming a Boothferry Park record as the oldest debutant on the ground - at the age of 53! It happened at the club's open day during the pre-season build-up in 2002 when a combination of City employees, media folk and ex-Tigers turned out in a friendly for the occasion. I do believe that everybody else was either young than I was or had trod the Boothferry turf previously, but I was one of those who failed to distinguish himself, so, if anyone can eclipse me, I am very willing to hand over my claim to the record! But such notions might pale into insignificance if you believe everything you might have read about the oldest player to appear in City's first team. I believe that Eddie Burbanks may hold the record when he played just after his 40th birthday in April 1953, but, according to the 1987-88 Rothman's Football Yearbook, Andy Payton is the answer. A misprint put Andy's date of birth as October 23, 1906, which means that he was 80 when he made his League debut as a substitute at Stoke in April 1987! In subsequent editions the publication put his date of birth as October 23, 1966, and it was not until later that they produced his correct date of birth - October 23, 1967.

We learn with age to try to enjoy our passion for football in a positive context. City hero Jimmy Greenhalgh said: "I was a working-class player - a bread-and-butter player who would never be classed as a great player. But I was a reasonably good professional and my memories of football are golden. The only kickback I get from my playing days is a feeling of satisfaction." And Syd Gerrie added: "The goals were something I never counted because I just thought that playing soccer was a marvellous way of making a living. People talked about soccer slavery, but I was doing something I really enjoyed."

And at one time the Tigers technically were simply the best because they beat the world club champions Nacional Internazionale from Montevideo 4-2 at Boothferry Park in April 1972. Nacional had played in Turkey and Iran, but their planned trip to Yugoslavia had been called off because of a smallpox outbreak, so City stepped in and they had had to make the venture worthwhile because it cost them £7,000 to stage the game. But if we want to dream in a different way, then it is essential to quote from the 1971 book called "They Used to Play on Grass" about a side called the Commoners. Co-written by England's assistant manager Terry Venables and Gordon Williams, it included the immortal sentence: "Hull City, who were riding high at the top of the First Division, had comfortably beaten the Commoners."

And while I may be grumpy at times, I am also very grateful because I have been very lucky and privileged. Ken Knighton once said: "My dad made sure that there was always a football in the house. That way I could never forget football." Thankfully I came from the same kind of Yorkshire environment. Hull City's fortunes on the pitch have comprised highs and lows in similar amounts and they still have not reached their Holy Grail, but my humble involvement off the pitch has comprised far more highs than lows. There have been setbacks, but I have been fortunate to meet some wonderful people along the way and hopefully make plenty of friends from all facets of the football fraternity. As Mike Bowering said in September 2006: "I would say that 99.99 per cent of those I met during my time in football were great people and it was a pleasure to be among them." There are certainly a lot of people for whom I have grown to have immense respect. But we may grow grumpy as we grow older and there is nothing wrong with challenging things and standing up for your causes if you believe that there is ever an injustice to be fought. Above all, though, I am so grateful for the upbringing that I was given by my parents, the opportunities that they gave me and the time that they devoted to me. And one of the most special opportunities that they gave me during my idyllic, formative years with them was to watch Hull City and to be able to say to people: "Meet me on Bunker's Hill..."